HALSBURY'S

Laws of England

FOURTH EDITION
REISSUE

Volume 49(1)

HALSBURY'S

Laws of England

FOURTH EDITION
REISSUE

LORD HAILSHAM OF ST. MARYLEBONE

Lord High Chancellor of Great Britain
1970–74 and 1979–87

Volume 49 (1)

BUTTERWORTHS

LONDON   1996

UNITED KINGDOM	Butterworths, a Division of Reed Elsevier (UK) Ltd Halsbury House, 35 Chancery Lane, **London** WC2A 1EL and 4 Hill Street, **Edinburgh** EH2 3JZ
AUSTRALIA	Butterworths, **Sydney, Melbourne, Brisbane, Adelaide, Perth, Canberra** and **Hobart**
CANADA	Butterworths Canada Ltd, **Toronto** and **Vancouver**
HONG KONG	Butterworths Asia, **Hong Kong**
IRELAND	Butterworth (Ireland) Ltd, **Dublin**
MALAYSIA	Malayan Law Journal Sdn Bhd, **Kuala Lumpur**
NEW ZEALAND	Butterworths of New Zealand Ltd, **Wellington** and **Auckland**
SINGAPORE	Butterworths Asia, **Singapore**
SOUTH AFRICA	Butterworth Publishers (Pty) Ltd, **Durban**
USA	Michie, **Charlottesville**, Virginia

FIRST EDITION

Published in 31 volumes between 1907 and 1917 under the Editorship of the Rt. Hon. the Earl of Halsbury, Lord High Chancellor of Great Britain, 1885–86, 1886–92 and 1895–1905

SECOND EDITION

Published in 37 volumes between 1931 and 1942 under the Editorship of the Rt. Hon. the Viscount Hailsham, Lord High Chancellor of Great Britain, 1928–29 and 1935–38

THIRD EDITION

Published in 43 volumes between 1952 and 1964 under the Editorship of the Rt. Hon. the Viscount Simonds, Lord High Chancellor of Great Britain, 1951–54

FOURTH EDITION

Published in 56 volumes between 1973 and 1987 under the Editorship of the Rt. Hon. Lord Hailsham of St. Marylebone, Lord High Chancellor of Great Britain, 1970–74 and 1979–87

ISBN (complete set, standard binding) 0 406 03400 1
(this volume, standard binding) 0 406 06568 3

Printed and bound in Great Britain by Clays Ltd, St Ives plc.

Editor in Chief

THE RIGHT HONOURABLE

LORD HAILSHAM OF ST. MARYLEBONE

LORD HIGH CHANCELLOR OF GREAT BRITAIN

1970–74 and 1979–87

Editor of this Volume

CAROL MARSH, M.A., LL.B.

Managing Editor (Commissioning)

DEBORAH SAUNDERS, B.A.,
OF GRAY'S INN, BARRISTER

Senior Sub-editor

CLAIRE MASSON, M.A.,
A SOLICITOR OF THE SUPREME COURT

Sub-editors

HELEN HALVEY, LL.B.

HEON STEVENSON, B.A.,
OF GRAY'S INN, BARRISTER

Administrative Manager

SARAH L. HORNSBY, DIP. PUB.

Indexer

B. BURKE, B.Sc.

Publisher

JAMES BOWMAN, LL.B.,
A SOLICITOR OF THE SUPREME COURT

The Titles in Volume 49(1) have been contributed by:

VALUE ADDED TAX   ROGER THOMAS, M.A., B.C.L.,
                               of Lincoln's Inn, Barrister

VALUERS AND SURVEYORS   JOHN MURDOCH, LL.B., A.C.I.Arb.,
                               Senior Lecturer in Law, The University of
                               Reading

WAR AND ARMED CONFLICT   PETER ROWE, LL.B., LL.M., PhD.,
                               of Lincoln's Inn, Barrister; Professor of Law,
                               University of Lancaster

The law stated in this volume is in general that in force on 31 October 1996,
although subsequent changes have been included wherever possible.

TABLE OF CONTENTS

REFERENCES AND ABBREVIATIONS

ACT	Australian Capital Territory
AJIL	American Journal of International Law (1907 to date)
A-G	Attorney General
Adv-Gen	Advocate General
affd	affirmed
Alta	Alberta
affg	affirming
App	Appendix
art	article
Aust	Australia
B	Baron
BC	British Columbia
BYIL	British Yearbook of International Law
C	Command Paper (of a series published before 1900)
c	chapter number of an Act
CA	Court of Appeal
CAC	Central Arbitration Committee
CA in Ch	Court of Appeal in Chancery
CB	Chief Baron
CCA	Court of Criminal Appeal
CC Fees Order 1982	County Court Fees Order 1982 (SI 1982/1706) as subsequently amended (see the current County Court Practice)
CCR	County Court Rules 1981 (SI 1981/1687) as subsequently amended (see the current County Court Practice)
CCR	Court for Crown Cases Reserved
C-MAC	Courts-Martial Appeal Court
CO	Crown Office
COD	Crown Office Digest
Can	Canada
Cd	Command Paper (of the series published 1900–18)
Cf	compare
ch	chapter
cl	clause
Cm	Command Paper (of the series published 1986 to date)
Cmd	Command Paper (of the series published 1919–56)

Cmnd	Command Paper (of the series published 1956–86)
Comr	Commissioner
Court Forms (2nd Edn)	Atkin's Encyclopaedia of Court Forms in Civil Proceedings, 2nd Edn. See note 2, p *16* post
Court Funds Rules 1987	Court Funds Rules 1987 (SI 1987/821) as subsequently amended (see the current Supreme Court Practice and County Court Practice)
DC	Divisional Court
DPP	Director of Public Prosecutions
EAT	Employment Appeal Tribunal
EC	European Community
ECJ	Court of Justice of the European Community
EComHR	European Commission of Human Rights
ECSC	European Coal and Steel Community
EEC	European Economic Community
EFTA	European Free Trade Association
Edn	Edition
Euratom	European Atomic Energy Community
Ex Ch	Court of Exchequer Chamber
ex p	ex parte
Fed	Federal
Forms & Precedents (5th Edn)	Encyclopaedia of Forms and Precedents other than Court Forms, 5th Edn. See note 2, p *16* post
GLC	Greater London Council
HC	High Court
HC	House of Commons
HL	House of Lords
ILPr	International Litigation Procedure
IRC	Inland Revenue Commissioners
Ind	India
Int Rels	International Relations
Ir	Ireland
J	Justice
JA	Judge of Appeal
JC	Justiciary Cases
Kan	Kansas
LA	Lord Advocate
LC	Lord Chancellor
LCC	London County Council
LCJ	Lord Chief Justice
LJ	Lord Justice of Appeal
LoN	League of Nations
LRC	Law Reports of the Commonwealth (1985–date)
MR	Master of the Rolls
Man	Manitoba
n	note

NB..	New Brunswick
NI...	Northern Ireland
NIJB	Northern Ireland Judgment Bulletin
NS	Nova Scotia
NSW	New South Wales
NZ	New Zealand
OJ..	The Official Journal of the European Community published by the Office for Official Publications of the European Community
Ont...	Ontario
P	President
PC	Judicial Committee of the Privy Council
PEI	Prince Edward Island
q	question
QBD...	Queen's Bench Division of the High Court
Qld	Queensland
Que	Quebec
r...	rule
RDC	Rural District Council
RPC..	Restrictive Practices Court
RSC	Rules of the Supreme Court 1965 (SI 1965/1776) as subsequently amended (see the current Supreme Court Practice)
reg	regulation
Res	Resolution
revsd	reversed
Rly	Railway
s...	section
SA..	South Africa
S Aust	South Australia
SC	Supreme Court
SC Fees Order 1980......................	Supreme Court Fees Order 1980 (SI 1980/821) as subsequently amended (see the current Supreme Court Practice)
SI	Statutory Instruments published by authority
SR & O	Statutory Rules and Orders published by authority
SR & O Rev 1904.......................	Revised Edition comprising all Public and General Statutory Rules and Orders in force on 31 December 1903
SR & O Rev 1948.......................	Revised Edition comprising all Public and General Statutory Rules and Orders and Statutory Instruments in force on 31 December 1948
SRNI...	Statutory Rules of Northern Ireland
Sask..	Saskatchewan
Sch...	Schedule

Sess	Session
Sing	Singapore
TS	Treaty Series
Tanz	Tanzania
Tas	Tasmania
UDC	Urban District Council
UN	United Nations
V–C	Vice-Chancellor
Vict	Victoria
W Aust	Western Australia
Zimb	Zimbabwe

NOTE 1. A general list of the abbreviations of law reports and other sources used in this work can be found in vol 54 (Reissue) Consolidated Table of Cases at p *v* et seq.

NOTE 2. Where references are made to other publications, the volume number precedes and the page number follows the name of the publication; eg the reference '12 Forms & Precedents (5th Edn) 44' refers to volume 12 of the Encyclopaedia of Forms and Precedents, page 44.

NOTE 3. An English statute is cited by short title or, where there is no short title, by regnal year and chapter number together with the name by which it is commonly known or a description of its subject matter and date. In the case of a foreign statute, the mode of citation generally follows the style of citation in use in the country concerned with the addition, where necessary, of the name of the country in parentheses.

NOTE 4. A statutory instrument is cited by short title, if any, followed by the year and number, or, if unnumbered, the date.

TABLE OF STATUTES

TABLE OF STATUTORY
INSTRUMENTS

Reference should be made to the Supreme Court Practice for the
Rules of the Supreme Court.

TABLE OF EUROPEAN COMMUNITY LEGISLATION

DECISIONS

TABLE OF TREATIES
AND CONVENTIONS

TABLE OF CASES

A

PARA

C

PARA

F

H

PARA

I

J

PARA

PARA

PARA

Q

R

VALUE ADDED TAX

1. INTRODUCTION

1. The legislation relating to value added tax. Value added tax ('VAT') was introduced in 1972[1] and first became chargeable on 1 April 1973[2]. The principal provisions relating to the tax have been consolidated in the Value Added Tax Act 1994 which came into force on 1 September 1994[3]. There is also a considerable body of subordinate legislation which regulates the operation of the tax[4].

1 Ie by the Finance Act 1972, which implemented the First and Second Council Directives of the European Community on the harmonisation of legislation of member states concerning turnover taxes (EC Council Directive 67/227 (OJ 71, 14.4.67, p 1301) (subsequently amended); and EC Council Directive 67/228 (OJ 71, 14.4.67, p 1303) (repealed)) ('the First and Second Directives'). See also the Green Paper on Value Added Tax (Cmnd 4621) issued at the time of the budget statement in 1971 and the White Paper on Value Added Tax (Cmnd 4929) which was issued concurrently with the budget statement in 1972 and contained the provisions of the tax to be included in the Finance Bill 1972 in advance of publication of the entire bill. The tax was substantially altered with effect from 1 January 1978 by the restatement of value added tax effected by the Finance Act 1977 s 14, Sch 6 (repealed), which implemented the Sixth Council Directive on the harmonisation of legislation of member states concerning turnover taxes (EC Council Directive 77/388) (OJ L145, 13.6.77, p 1) ('the Sixth Directive'), relating to the scope of VAT. The tax underwent a further substantial revision on 1 January 1993, with the implementation by the Finance (No 2) Act 1992 s 14, Sch 3 (as amended) and related subordinate legislation of the transitional arrangements for the abolition of fiscal frontiers within the European Community following the amendment of the Sixth Directive by EC Council Directive 91/680 (OJ L376, 31.12.91, p 1). Further changes were made on 1 June 1996 by the Finance Act 1996 ss 25–29, Sch 3, which introduced a fiscal warehousing regime and other simplification measures in order to give effect to EC Council Directive 95/7 (OJ L102, 5.5.95, p 18) ('the Second VAT Simplification Directive'): see para 132 et seq post.

2 See the Finance Act 1972 s 47(1) (repealed).

3 Value Added Tax Act 1994 s 101(1).

4 See in particular the Value Added Tax Regulations 1995, SI 1995/2518 (amended by SI 1995/3043; SI 1995/3147; SI 1996/210; SI 1996/1198; SI 1996/1250; and SI 1996/2098); and the Value Added Tax Tribunals Rules 1986, SI 1986/590 (amended by SI 1991/186; SI 1994/2617); and paras 10 et seq, 293 et seq post.

2. The European legislative basis of value added tax. Although the statutory basis of value added tax in United Kingdom law is the Value Added Tax Act 1994, the Act itself is derived from the Sixth Directive. As an adherent to the Treaty establishing the European Community, the United Kingdom is required to take all appropriate measures to ensure fulfilment of the obligations arising out of the Treaty or which result from action taken by Community institutions[1]. Although the United Kingdom has a discretion as to the form and method by which it implements the Sixth Directive, it is obliged to ensure that the results intended by that directive are in fact achieved by its domestic legislation[2]. In practice there is a need to have constant reference to the Sixth Directive and to the various decisions of the European Court of Justice in relation to VAT and allied topics in order properly to interpret and apply the domestic legislation[3].

1 See the EC Treaty (Treaty Establishing the European Community (Rome, 25 March 1957; TS 1 (1973); Cmnd 5179)) art 5; the European Communities Act 1972 s 2 (as amended); and EUROPEAN COMMUNITIES. The implementing provisions in domestic law are presently to be found in the Value Added Tax Act 1994 and regulations made thereunder: see para 5 et seq post.

 EC Council Directive 77/388 (OJ L145, 13.6.77, p 1) does not prevent a member state from maintaining or introducing taxes on insurance contracts, taxes on betting and gambling, excise duties, stamp duties and, more generally, any taxes, duties or charges which cannot be characterised as turnover taxes, provided that those taxes, duties or charges do not, in trade between member states, give rise to formalities connected with the crossing of frontiers: see art 33 (substituted by EC Council Directive 91/680 (OJ L376, 31.12.91, p 1)). In Case C-109/90 *Giant NV v Gemeente Overijse* [1991] ECR I-1385, [1993] STC 651, ECJ, it was held that a tax was a turnover tax for this purpose if it had the effect of compromising the functioning of the common system of VAT by levying a charge on the movement of goods and services and on commercial transactions in the same way as VAT, following Case 295/84 *Rousseau Wilmot SA v Caisse de Compensation de l'Organisation Autonome Nationale de l'Industrie et du Commerce (Organic)* [1985] ECR 3759, [1986] 3 CMLR 677, ECJ; and Case 252/86 *Bergandi v Directeur Général des Impôts* [1988] ECR 1343, [1991] STC 529, ECJ; followed in Case C-208/91 *Beaulande v Directeur des Services Fiscaux de Nantes* [1992] ECR I-6709, [1996] STC 1111, ECJ; therefore an 'entertainment tax', levied on entrance fees and cloakroom charges, was not such a tax because it was not a general tax, being applicable only to a limited class of goods or services, it was not charged at each stage of production and distribution, and it was charged not on value added at each stage but on the gross amount charged at one stage. An 'employment market levy' which was charged at each stage of the production and distribution process as a percentage of the undertaking's sales, with a deduction of purchases on which the levy had been imposed at an earlier stage, was, however, precluded by EC Council Directive 77/388 art 33 (as substituted): Case C-200/90 *Dansk Denkavit ApS and P Poulsen Trading ApS supported by Monsanto-Searle A/S v Skatteministeriet* [1992] ECR I-2217, [1994] STC 482, ECJ (which also deals with the issue whether the effect of a decision of the European Court of Justice that national law was incompatible with the Sixth Directive should be limited ratione temporis: held, it was inappropriate to limit the effect of the judgment since the prohibition was quite apparent from the terms of the Sixth Directive and the European Commission had drawn the Danish Government's attention to the issue a few weeks after the introduction of the levy). In Case C-62/93 *BP Supergas Anonimos Etairia Geniki Emporiki-Viomichaniki kai Antiprossopeion v Greece* [1995] ECR I-1883, [1995] STC 805, ECJ, it was held that a system of collecting VAT on the full consumer price of petroleum products at the beginning of the marketing process, with intermediate companies being neither obliged to account for VAT nor entitled to deduct input tax, was contrary to the fundamental principle of VAT by which VAT was applied at each stage of the production or distribution process after deduction of the VAT which had been levied directly on transactions relating to outputs.

2   See the EC Treaty art 189 (substituted by the Maastricht Treaty (Treaty on European Union (Maastricht, 7 February 1992; Cm 1934)) Title II art G(60)); and Case 6/64 *Costa v ENEL* [1964] ECR 585, [1964] CMLR 425, ECJ. See also EUROPEAN COMMUNITIES vol 51 para 3.01 et seq for a full explanation of the interaction between Community law and United Kingdom domestic law. For a recent example of this see Case C-96/91 *EC Commission v Spain* [1992] ECR I-3789, [1996] STC 672, ECJ, where it was held that Spain was in breach of its obligation to enable travellers exporting goods in their personal luggage to obtain remission of VAT, by requiring them to present to Customs a 'special invoice', which had to be purchased from the Spanish tax authorities; by imposing this requirement, Spain went beyond what was necessary to ensure the correct levying of VAT and had rendered the exercise of the right of remission practically impossible, or excessively difficult. See also Joined Cases 123/87, 30/87 *Jorion, née Jeunehomme, et Société Anonyme d'étude et de gestion immobilière 'EGI' v Belgium* [1988] ECR 4517, ECJ. The principle of equal treatment expressed in EC Council Directive 77/388 art 22(8) was intended only to regulate trade transactions between member states and not transactions which took place within a single member state: Case C217-94 *Eismann Alto Adige Srl v Ufficio IVA di Bolzano* [1996] STC 1374, ECJ.

3   As to the Sixth Directive see para 1 note 1 ante; and EUROPEAN COMMUNITIES.

3. The status of Community law. In consequence of the European Communities Act 1972[1], the courts are empowered to consider whether United Kingdom legislation complies with the Community legislation to which it purports to give effect. A court which is required to construe domestic legislation must proceed from the assumption that the terms of the United Kingdom statute are consonant with the terms of directives in the same field[2]. The courts are not, however, obliged to distort the meaning of a British statute to conform with Community law if that law is not directly applicable[3]. In an action against the state, in a case where the statute does not conform with Community law, an individual may rely on the Community provision in preference to the domestic legislation provided that the relevant Community provision is of direct effect[4]. In the context of a directive, a provision is of direct effect if, so far as its subject-matter is concerned, it is unconditional and sufficiently precise[5]. In matters relating to value added tax, where actions will generally involve disputes with the Commissioners of Customs and Excise ('the commissioners'), the taxpayer is therefore entitled to rely on the direct effect of appropriate provisions of the Sixth Directive; whilst the commissioners are obliged to have regard only to domestic legislation[6]. In addition, the United Kingdom courts are obliged to take judicial notice not only of decisions of the European Court of Justice or any court attached to it but also of any expression of opinion by such a court on any question of the meaning or effect of any Community instrument[7]. Where such a question is raised before a court or tribunal, the court or tribunal may request the European Court of Justice to give a preliminary ruling on the matter, if it considers that the question is necessary to enable it to give judgment[8].

It is contrary to Community law to apply a domestic procedural rule which precludes a national court acting within the scope of its jurisdiction from considering of its own motion the compatibility of a measure of domestic law with Community law[9].

1   Ie the European Communities Act 1972 s 2 (as amended): see para 2 ante; and EUROPEAN COMMUNITIES.

2   This rule of construction obtains whether the directive precedes or postdates the statute in question: Case 14/83 *Von Colson and Kamann v Land Nordrhein-Westfalen* [1984] ECR 1891, [1986] 2 CMLR 430, ECJ; Case C-106/89 *Marleasing SA v La Comercial Internacional de Alimentación SA* [1990] ECR I-4135, [1992] 1 CMLR 305, ECJ; Case C-32/93 *Webb v EMO Air Cargo (UK) Ltd* [1994] QB 718, [1994] 4 All ER 115, ECJ. Where necessary, the court will imply words into the statute to ensure that the United Kingdom complies with its treaty obligations: *Litster v Forth Dry Dock and Engineering Co Ltd* [1990] 1 AC 546, [1989] 1 All ER 1134, HL. However, cf the decision in *Robert Gordon's College v Customs and Excise Comrs* [1996] 1 WLR 201, [1995] STC 1093, HL (where, on a strict literal reading of a statutory provision, the domestic legislation appears to be inconsistent with the relevant EC Directive, then, in the case of a dispute between an individual and the state (in the form of the commissioners), the court is entitled to disregard the domestic legislation and apply the directive without more).

3   *Duke v GEC Reliance Ltd* [1988] AC 618 at 640–642, [1988] 1 All ER 626 at 636–637, HL, per Lord Templeman. 'Directly applicable' in this context probably means 'directly effective'. Not all provisions of EC Council Directive 77/388 (OJ L145, 13.6.77, p 1) are directly effective; thus some articles expressly permit a member state to derogate from their application in whole or in part: see eg arts 6(2), 10(2), 11(A)(4), 11(C)(1). Others leave a margin of discretion in their application: eg art 20(4). In addition, art 27(1) enables member states to apply for authorisation from the EC Commission and Council to introduce measures intended to simplify the procedure for charging VAT; and art 27(5) enabled member states which applied such simplification measures on 1 January 1977 to retain such measures, provided that they notified the Commission of them before 1 January 1978. In reliance on these derogating provisions, the United Kingdom introduced a number of simplification measures, such as the system of retail schemes (see paras 185–187 post). The EC Council has also given the United Kingdom permission to effect the following simplification measures: (1) a tax accounting scheme for gold, to prevent fraud or tax evasion (EC Council Decision 84/469 (OJ L264, 05.10.84, p 27); (2) a flat-rate system for determining the amount of fuel used for private purposes in company cars (EC Council Decision 86/356 (OJ L212, 02.08.86, p 35)); (3) a simplified calculation of the VAT chargeable on long stays in hotels; (4) a system requiring taxable traders selling by retail though unregistered traders to account for VAT on the open market retail price (EC Council Decision 89/534 (OJ L280, 29.09.89, p 54)); (5) a system of substituting market value where supplies or intra-Community acquisitions of goods take place between closely-connected persons who are not both fully taxable (EC Council Decision 92/546 (OJ L351, 02.12.92, p 34)); (6) a cash accounting system for traders whose turnover does not exceed £350,000 per annum (EC Council Decision 93/111 (OJ L43, 20.02.93, p 46)); (7) a provision designed to prevent tax avoidance by transactions with and within VAT groups (EC Council Decision 93/204 (OJ L88, 08.04.93, p 43)); (8) to exempt certain supplies of services (relating to work on temporarily imported goods or to the transport of goods) to persons who would have been entitled to claim a refund of the VAT which would otherwise have been charged on those services (EC Council Decision 93/563 (OJ L273, 5.11.93, p 49)); (9) a flat-rate restriction of recovery of input tax on the purchase or leasing of passenger cars intended for partial private use (EC Council Decision 95/252 (OJ L159, 11.07.95, p 19)). In Case 5/84 *Direct Cosmetics Ltd v Customs and Excise Comrs* [1985] ECR 617, [1985] STC 479, ECJ, it was held that the subsequent legislative amendment of national legislation which had been notified to the Commission under EC Council Directive 77/388 art 27 itself required to be notified and approved; and, in the absence of such approval, could not be relied on against an individual before the national courts.

4 The phrase 'individual' has a broad meaning in the context of the Sixth Directive: it has been held to encompass any person who or which is subject qua taxpayer to the domestic provisions implementing the Directive, for example, local authorities: Joined Cases 231/87, 129/88 *Ufficio Distrettuale delle Imposte Dirette di Fiorenzuola d'Arda v Commune di Carpaneto Piacentino and Ufficio Provinciale Imposta sul Valore Aggiunto di Piacenza* [1989] ECR 3233, [1991] STC 205, ECJ. As to the Sixth Directive see para 1 note 1 ante; and EUROPEAN COMMUNITIES. Member states are obliged to make good damage caused to individuals by breaches of Community law attributable to the state, even where the national legislature is responsible for the breach; the rule of Community law breached must, however, be intended to confer rights on the individuals, the breach must be sufficiently serious and there must be a direct causal link between the breach and the damage sustained by them: see Joined Cases C-46/93, C-48/93 *Brasserie du Pêcheur SA v Germany, R v Secretary of State for Transport, ex p Factortame Ltd* [1996] QB 404, [1996] All ER (EC) 301, ECJ.

5 See Case 8/81 *Becker v Finanzamt Münster-Innenstadt* [1982] ECR 53 at 71, [1982] 1 CMLR 499 at 512–513, ECJ.

6 But the commissioners will be entitled to ask the court if possible to construe the United Kingdom statute as conforming with the directive.

7 See the European Communities Act 1972 s 3(1), (2) (amended by the European Communities (Amendment) Act 1986 s 2; extended to decisions and expressions of opinion by the EFTA Court by the European Economic Area Act 1993 s 4(a)); and STATUTES vol 44(1) (Reissue) para 1352; EUROPEAN COMMUNITIES vol 51 para 3.06.

8 EC Treaty art 177 (substituted by the Maastricht Treaty Title II art G(56)). The domestic court or tribunal must bring the matter before the European Court if it is a court or tribunal against whose decision there is no judicial remedy under national law: EC Treaty art 177 (as so substituted). The Court of Appeal has identified certain matters which a judge should bear in mind in deciding whether to make a reference: (1) whether the point is conclusive; (2) whether there has been a previous ruling which decides or substantially decides the point; (3) whether the point is reasonably clear and free from doubt ('acte claire'): if it is, it is simply necessary to apply, rather than to interpret, Community law; (4) that it is necessary for the facts to have been decided before a reference can be made: *HP Bulmer Ltd v J Bollinger SA* [1974] Ch 401 at 422–425, [1974] 2 All ER 1226 at 1234–1235, CA, per Lord Denning MR; *BLP Group plc v Customs and Excise Comrs, Swallowfield plc v Customs and Excise Comrs* [1994] STC 41, CA. See also Case 283/81 *CILFIT Srl and Lanificio di Gavardo SpA v Ministry of Health* [1982] ECR 3415 at 3430–3431, [1983] 1 CMLR 472 at 490–491, ECJ; *Customs and Excise Comrs v ApS Samex (Hanil Synthetic Fiber Industrial Co Ltd, third party)* [1983] 1 All ER 1042, [1983] 3 CMLR 194; *Lord Bethell v SociSABENA)* [1983] 3 CMLR 1; *R v Pharmaceutical Society of Great Britain, ex p Association of Pharmaceutical Importers* [1987] 3 CMLR 951, CA; *R v International Stock Exchange of the United Kingdom and the Republic of Ireland Ltd, ex p Else* [1993] QB 534 at 545, [1993] 1 All ER 420 at 426, CA, per Bingham MR; and *Conoco Ltd v Customs and Excise Comrs* [1995] STC 1022.

9 See Case C-312/93 *Peterbroeck, Van Campenhout & Cie SCS v Belgium* [1995] ECR I-4599, [1996] 1 CMLR 793, ECJ.

4. The scope and nature of value added tax. Value added tax ('VAT'[1]) is charged on the supply[2] of goods or services in the United Kingdom[3], on the acquisition in the United Kingdom of any goods from other member states of the European Community[4] and on the importation of goods from places outside the member states[5]. The tax is a tax on the final consumer, in as much as the final consumer is unable to recover or claim credit for the VAT included in the cost of supplies made to him. Its administration involves a credit mechanism system whereby a taxable person who is charged tax on the supplies which he receives is entitled, subject to certain exceptions, to set off that tax against the tax charged by him on the supplies which he makes to other persons. He is thus accountable only for the excess of the tax on the supplies made by him over the tax on the supplies made to him[6]. Where the tax on the supplies to him for which he is entitled to credit exceeds the tax on the supplies made by him, he is entitled to claim payment of the excess from the Commissioners of Customs and Excise[7].

The VAT on the supply to a taxable person of any goods or services for the purpose of a business[8] carried on or to be carried on by him[9], the VAT on the acquisition by a taxable person of any goods from another member state[10] and the VAT paid or payable by a taxable person on the importation of any goods used or to be used for the purpose of a business carried on or to be carried on by him[11] are known as his 'input tax'[12] and form the basis of the taxable person's entitlement to credit in computing his liability to VAT[13].

The VAT on the supplies made by the taxable person, or on the acquisition of goods by him from another member state[14] is known as his 'output tax'[15]. It is these amounts for which, subject to his entitlement to credit for input tax incurred, the taxable person must account to the commissioners[16].

Value added tax is chargeable on a supply of goods or services only where (1) the supply is a taxable supply[17]; (2) the goods or services are supplied by a taxable person in the course of a business carried on by him; and (3) the supply is made in the United Kingdom[18]. It is a liability of the person making the supply[19]; and VAT on any acquisition of goods from another member state is a liability of the person who acquires the goods[20]. Value added tax on the importation of goods from places outside the member states is chargeable and payable as if it were a duty of customs[21].

The Provisional Collection of Taxes Act 1968, which allows for the collection of taxes during the period from the expiration of an annual tax until the coming into force of the new Finance Act[22], applies in relation to VAT[23]. Where, by virtue of a resolution having effect thereunder, VAT has been paid at a rate specified in the resolution on the supply of any goods or services, or on the acquisition of goods from another member state, by reference to a value determined[24] in accordance with statute, then:

(1) if any of that VAT is subsequently repayable[25] in consequence of the restoration in relation to that supply or acquisition of a lower rate, the amount repayable is the difference between the VAT paid by reference to that value at the rate specified in the resolution and the VAT that would have been payable by reference to that value at the lower rate[26];

(2) if before the VAT is paid it ceases to be chargeable at that rate in consequence of the restoration in relation to that supply or acquisition of a lower rate, the VAT chargeable at the lower rate is charged by reference to the same value as that by reference to which VAT would have been chargeable at the rate specified in the resolution[27].

The VAT that may be credited as input tax[28] or refunded[29] does not, however, include VAT that has been repaid by virtue of head (1) above[30] or that would be so repayable if it had been paid[31].

1 References in the Value Added Tax Act 1994 to VAT are references to value added tax: s 1(1).
2 Ie including anything treated as such a supply: ibid s 1(1)(a). For the meaning of 'supply' see para 21 post; and as to deemed supplies see para 24 post.
3 Ibid s 1(1)(a). 'United Kingdom' means Great Britain and Northern Ireland: Interpretation Act 1978 s 5, Sch 1. 'Great Britain' means England, Scotland and Wales: Union with Scotland Act 1706, preamble art I; Interpretation Act 1978 s 22(1), Sch 2 para 5(a). Neither the Channel Islands nor the Isle of Man are within the United Kingdom. For these purposes, references to the United Kingdom include the territorial sea of the United Kingdom: Value Added Tax Act 1994 s 96(11). See also the Value Added Tax (Isle of Man) Order 1982, SI 1982/1067; and para 9 post; and see generally CONSTITUTIONAL LAW AND HUMAN RIGHTS vol 8(2) (Reissue) para 3.
4 Value Added Tax Act 1994 ss 1(1)(b), 96(1). As to the territories treated for the purposes of VAT as excluded from, or included in, the European Community see para 10 post.
5 Ibid s 1(1)(c). Prior to 1 January 1993, VAT was levied on the importation of goods from other countries, whether within or outside the European Community. VAT was abolished on the importation of goods from other member states with effect from 1 January 1993; thenceforward VAT is imposed on the acquisition from other member states of (1) goods by a taxable person; and (2) new means of transport (whether or not by a taxable person): see s 10(1); and para 13 post. For the meaning of 'taxable person' see paras 12 note 4, 55 post.
6 See ibid s 25(2); and para 202 post. For the exceptions to the right to deduct input tax see para 204 et seq post.
7 See ibid s 25(3); and para 202 post.
8 For the meaning of 'business' see para 17 post.

9   Value Added Tax Act 1994 s 24(1)(a).
10 Ibid s 24(1)(b).
11 Ibid s 24(1)(c).
12 See ibid s 24(1).
13 See para 201 post.
14 Subject to the Value Added Tax Act 1994 s 93(1) (see para 10 post), 'another member state' means any member state of the European Community other than the United Kingdom; and 'other member states' is to be construed accordingly: s 96(1).
15 See ibid s 24(2).
16 See para 202 post.
17 For the meaning of 'taxable supply' see para 12 note 1 post.
18 See the Value Added Tax Act 1994 s 4(1); and para 12 post. In many instances the place of supply will vary, according to whether the supply is determined to be one of goods or services: see eg Case C-231/94 *Faaborg-Gelting Linien A/S v Finanzamt Flensburg* [1996] All ER (EC) 656, [1996] STC 774, ECJ (a supply of a meal in a restaurant on a ferry operating between Denmark and Germany was a supply of services, and thus supplied where the ferry operator had established his business (Denmark) and not where the supply was made (German territorial waters), as would have been the case had the supply been one of goods). See EC Council Directive 77/388 (OJ L145, 13.6.77, p 1) art 9(1); the Value Added Tax Act 1994 s 7 (as amended); and para 39 et seq post.
19 See ibid s 1(2).
20 Ibid s 1(3).
21 Ibid s 1(4). As such it is payable by the importer, ordinarily on making an entry of the goods for customs clearance purposes: see the Customs and Excise Management Act 1979 s 37A (as added and amended), s 43(1) (as amended); the Customs Controls on Importation of Goods Regulations 1991, SI 1991/2724, reg 5 (as amended); and CUSTOMS AND EXCISE. As to deferment of tax see the Customs Duties (Deferred Payment) Regulations 1976, SI 1976/1223 (amended by SI 1978/1725); and CUSTOMS AND EXCISE.
22 See INCOME TAXATION vol 23 (Reissue) para 19; and PARLIAMENT.
23 See the Provisional Collection of Taxes Act 1968 s 1(1) (amended by, inter alia, the Value Added Tax Act 1983 s 50(1), Sch 9 para 1).
24 Ie a value determined under the Value Added Tax Act 1994 s 19(2) (see para 85 post) or s 20(3) (see para 98 post): s 90(1)(a).
25 Ie by virtue of the Provisional Collection of Taxes Act 1968 s 1(6) or (7) or s 5(3) (failure of resolution): see INCOME TAXATION vol 23 (Reissue) paras 19, 23.
26 Value Added Tax Act 1994 s 90(1).
27 Ibid s 90(2).
28 Ie under ibid s 25: see para 202 post.
29 Ie under ibid ss 33, 35 or 40: see paras 258–259, 263 post.
30 Ie repaid by virtue of the provisions mentioned therein: see note 25 supra.
31 Value Added Tax Act 1994 s 90(3).

5. Rate of value added tax; in general. The standard rate of value added tax is 17.5 per cent[1]. The tax is charged:

(1) on a supply[2] of goods or services, by reference to the value of the supply;

(2) on an acquisition of goods from another member state[3], by reference to the value of the acquisition; and

(3) on an importation of goods from a place outside the member states[4], by reference to the value of the goods,

the relevant value in each case being determined in accordance with the Value Added Tax Act 1994[5].

The Treasury may by order increase or decrease the rate of VAT for the time being in force[6] by such percentage (not exceeding 25 per cent of the rate in force) as may be specified in the order[7]. Any such order ceases to have effect at the expiration of the period of one year unless continued in force by a further order[8].

In addition to the standard rate there are two other rates of VAT in force. The zero rate is given to certain supplies of goods and services specified in Schedule 8 to the Value Added Tax Act 1994 as well as to supplies of goods where the goods are exported to a place outside the European Community[9]. The effect of a supply being zero-rated is that, whilst no VAT is actually levied on the supply itself, a registered person who makes such supplies is able to recover as input tax[10] any tax charged on supplies made to him for the purpose of the onward zero-rated supply[11]. A reduced rate of 8 per cent is levied on supplies, acquisitions and importation of fuel (other than road fuels) and power for domestic use or for use by a charity otherwise than in the course or furtherance of a business[12].

1   Value Added Tax Act 1994 s 2(1) (amended by the Finance Act 1995 s 21(2), (6)). Originally, the rate of VAT was 10%. This was reduced to 8% on 27 July 1974 by the Value Added Tax (Change of Rate) Order 1974, SI 1974/1224 (revoked), except in relation to certain hydrocarbon oils, in respect of which the rate was increased to 25% on 18 November 1974. This rate ('the higher rate') was extended to a range of 'luxury' items on 1 May 1975 by the Finance Act 1975 s 17, Sch 17 (repealed); was reduced to 12.5% on 12 April 1976 by the Finance Act 1976 s 17 (repealed); and was abolished with effect from 18 June 1979 when the standard rate of VAT was increased to 15% by the Finance (No 2) Act 1979 s 1(1) (repealed). The rate of VAT was further increased to 17.5% with effect from 1 April 1991 by the Finance Act 1991 s 13 (repealed). As to zero-rated supplies see para 158 et seq post.

2   For the meaning of 'supply' see para 21 post.

3   For the meaning of 'another member state' see para 4 note 14 ante.

5   Value Added Tax Act 1994 s 1(1)(a)–(c). As to the manner of determining the relevant values see s 19, Sch 6 (as amended); and para 85 et seq post.

6   In relation to an order to continue, vary or replace a previous such order, this reference to the rate for the time being in force is a reference to the rate which would be in force if no order had been made under ibid s 2(2): s 2(3). The effect is that it is not open to the Treasury, by incremental adjustments, to increase or decrease the rate of VAT by more than 25% of the rate last fixed by statute.

7   Ibid s 2(2). For an example of such an order see the Value Added Tax (Change of Rate) Order 1974, SI 1974/1224 (revoked). An order increasing the rate of tax must be laid before the House of Commons and requires an affirmative resolution: see the Value Added Tax Act 1994 s 97(4)(c)(i); and para 8 post. As to affirmative resolutions see STATUTES vol 44(1) (Reissue) para 1518; and PARLIAMENT.

8   Ibid s 2(2).

9   See para 158 et seq post.

10 For the meaning of 'input tax' see paras 4 ante, 201 post.

11 See para 203 et seq post. As to registration see para 56 et seq post.

12 See the Value Added Tax Act 1994 s 2(1A), Sch A1 (added by the Finance Act 1995 s 21); and para 6 post. Such domestic use or use by a charity is a 'qualifying use' for those purposes: see the Value Added Tax Act 1994 Sch A1 para 1(2) (as so added). As to the meaning of 'in the course or furtherance of a business' see paras 12 note 5, 17 note 2 post.

6. The reduced rate charge. Value added tax charged on any supply[1] of a specified fuel[2] for a qualifying use[3] or any equivalent acquisition or importation[4] is charged at the rate of 8 per cent[5]. Where there is a supply of goods partly for qualifying use and partly not, if at least 60 per cent of the goods are supplied for qualifying use, the whole supply is treated as a supply for qualifying use, and in any other case an apportionment must be made to determine the extent to which the supply is a supply for qualifying use[6].

Supplies of certain fuel in small quantities are deemed always to be for domestic (and thus qualifying) use[7]. Supplies in larger quantities[8] are for domestic use if, and only if, the goods supplied are for use in:

(1)   a building, or part of a building, which consists of a dwelling or a number of dwellings;

(2)   a building, or part of a building, used for a relevant residential purpose;

(3)   self-catering holiday accommodation[9];

(4)   a caravan; or

(5)   a houseboat[10].

'Use for a relevant residential purpose' means use as:

(a)   a home or other institution providing residential accommodation for children;

(b)   a home or other institution providing residential accommodation with personal care for persons in need of such care by reason of old age, disablement, past or present dependence on alcohol or drugs or past or present mental disorder;

(c)   a hospice;

(d)   residential accommodation for students or school pupils;

(e)   residential accommodation for members of any of the armed forces;

(f)   a monastery, nunnery or similar establishment; or

(g)   an institution which is the sole or main residence of at least 90 per cent of its residents,

in each case excepting use as a hospital, a prison or similar institution or an hotel or inn or similar establishment[11].

The Treasury may by order vary the above provisions by adding to or deleting from them any description of supply for the time being specified, or by varying any other provision for the time being contained, therein[12].

---

1   For the meaning of 'supply' see para 21 post.

2   The specified fuels are: (1) coal, coke or other solid substances held out for sale solely as fuel (including combustible materials put up for sale for kindling fires but not including matches); (2) coal gas, water gas, producer gases or similar gases (but neither this head nor head (3) infra includes any road fuel gas within the meaning of the Hydrocarbon Oil Duties Act 1979 on which a duty of excise has been charged or is chargeable); (3) petroleum gases, or other gaseous hydrocarbons, whether in a gaseous or liquid state (but see head (2) supra); (4) fuel oil, gas oil or kerosene (not including hydrocarbon oil on which a duty of excise has been or is to be charged without relief from, or rebate of, such duty by virtue of the provisions of the 1979 Act); or (5) electricity, heat or air-conditioning: Value Added Tax Act 1994 s 2(1A), Sch A1 paras 1(1), 4(1)–(3) (s 2(1A)–(1C), Sch A1 added by the Finance Act 1995 s 21(1)–(3)). For these purposes, 'fuel oil' means heavy oil which contains in solution an amount of asphaltenes of not less than 0.5% or which contains less than 0.5% but not less than 0.1% of asphaltenes and has a closed flash point not exceeding 150°C: Value Added Tax Act 1994 Sch A1 para 4(4) (as so added). 'Gas oil' means heavy oil of which not more than 50% by volume distils at a temperature not exceeding 240°C and of which more than 50% by volume distils at a temperature not exceeding 340°C; and 'kerosene' means heavy oil of which more than 50% by volume distils at a temperature not exceeding 240°C: Sch A1 para 4(5), (6) (as so added). 'Heavy oil' means hydrocarbon oil other than light oil; 'hydrocarbon oil' means petroleum oil, coal tar and oil produced from coal, shale, peat or any other bituminous substance, and all liquid hydrocarbons, but does not include such hydrocarbons or bituminous or asphaltic substances as are (a) solid or semi-solid at a temperature of 15°C; or (b) gaseous at a temperature of 15°C and under a pressure of 1013.25 millibars; and 'light oil' means hydrocarbon oil of which not less than 90% by volume distils at a temperature not exceeding 210°C, or which gives off an inflammable vapour at a temperature of less than 23°C when tested in the manner prescribed by the Acts relating to petroleum: Hydrocarbon Oil Duties Act 1979 s 1(1)–(4) (applied by the Value Added Tax Act 1994 Sch A1 para 4(7) (as so added)).

3   Ie for domestic use or non-commercial use by a charity: see para 5 note 12 ante.

4   This reference to an equivalent acquisition or importation, in relation to any supply for the time being falling within the Value Added Tax Act 1994 Sch A1 para 1 (as added: see note 2 supra), is a reference to any acquisition from another member state of goods the supply of which would be such a supply, or any importation from a place outside the member states of any such goods: s 2(1B) (as so added). For the meaning of 'another member state' see para 4 note 14 ante; and as to when goods are imported from a place outside the member states see para 103 note 2 post.

5   Ibid s 2(1A) (as added: see note 2 supra). The reduced rate charge applies in relation to any supply made on or after 1 April 1995 and any acquisition or importation taking place on or after that date: Finance Act 1995 s 21(6).

6   Value Added Tax Act 1994 Sch A1 para 1(3) (as added: see note 2 supra). The supply of any form of power, heat, refrigeration or ventilation is a supply of goods: see s 5(1), Sch 4 para 3; and para 24 note 1 post.

7   The following supplies are always for domestic use (ibid Sch A1 para 2 (as added: see note 2 supra)), ie a supply:

(1)   of not more than one tonne of coal or coke held out for sale as domestic fuel (Sch A1 para 2(a) (as so added));

(2)   of wood, peat or charcoal not intended for sale by the recipient (Sch A1 para 2(b) (as so added));

(3)   to a person at any premises of piped gas (ie gas within ibid Sch A1 para 1(1)(b) (as so added), or petroleum gas in a gaseous state, provided through pipes) where the gas, together with any other

piped gas provided to him at the premises by the same supplier, was not provided at a rate exceeding 150 therms (or, if the supplier charges for the gas by reference to the number of kilowatt hours supplied, 4,397 kilowatt hours) a month (Sch A1 para 2(c) (as so added));

(4) of petroleum gas in a liquid state where the gas is supplied in cylinders the net weight of each of which is less than 50 kg and either the number of cylinders supplied is 20 or fewer or the gas is not intended for sale by the recipient (Sch A1 para 2(d) (as so added));

(5) a supply of petroleum gas in a liquid state, otherwise than in cylinders, to a person at any premises at which he is not able to store more than two tonnes of such gas (Sch A1 para 2(e) (as so added));

(6) a supply of not more than 2,300 litres of fuel oil, gas oil or kerosene (Sch A1 para 2(f) (as so added));

(7) a supply of electricity to a person at any premises where the electricity (together with any other electricity provided to him at the premises, by the same supplier, was not provided at a rate exceeding 1,000 kilowatt hours a month (Sch A1 para 2(g) (as so added)).

8 Ie supplies not within ibid Sch A1 para 2 (as added: see note 2 supra): see note 7 supra.

9 For these purposes, self-catering holiday accommodation includes any accommodation advertised or held out as such: ibid Sch A1 para 3(3) (as added: see note 2 supra).

10 Ibid Sch A1 para 3(1) (as added: see note 2 supra). For these purposes, 'houseboat' means a boat or other floating decked structure designed or adapted for use solely as a place of permanent habitation and not having means of, or capable of being readily adapted for, self-propulsion: Sch A1 para 3(4) (as added: see note 2 supra).

11 Ibid Sch A1 para 3(2) (as added: see note 2 supra).

12 Ibid s 2(1C) (as added: see note 2 supra). Any such order must be laid before the House of Commons and requires an affirmative resolution: see the Value Added Tax Act 1994 s 97(4)(aa) (added by the Finance Act 1995 s 21(4)); and para 8 post. As to affirmative resolutions see STATUTES vol 44(1) (Reissue) para 1518; and PARLIAMENT. At the date at which this volume states the law, no such order had been made.

7. Administration. Value added tax is under the care and management of the Commissioners of Customs and Excise[1] and is an assigned matter, being a matter in relation to which the commissioners are for the time being required in pursuance of an enactment to perform duties[2]. All money and securities for money collected or received in Great Britain[3] for or on account of the tax must be placed to the general account of the commissioners kept[4] at the Bank of England[5]. Under their general powers of management the commissioners from time to time issue notices for the information of traders upon whose activities VAT impinges and notices to the public generally[6]. The commissioners have also made agreements with various trade bodies which permit members of those bodies to use procedures to meet their obligations under VAT law which take into account their individual circumstances[7].

1 Value Added Tax Act 1994 s 58, Sch 11 para 1(1).

2 See the Customs and Excise Management Act 1979 s 1(1); and CUSTOMS AND EXCISE.

3 For the meaning of 'Great Britain' see para 4 note 3 ante.

4 Ie under the Customs and Excise Management Act 1979 s 17 (as amended): see customs and excise.

5 Value Added Tax Act 1994 Sch 11 para 1(2)(a). As to money and securities collected and received in Northern Ireland see Sch 11 para 1(2)(b). 'Money' includes currencies other than sterling: s 96(1).

6 Copies of these notices may be obtained upon application to any local VAT office. These notices are subject to revision and cancellation without notice.

7 See eg Customs and Excise Business Brief 18/93 [1993] STI 987, announcing details of an agreement with representatives of racecourses and other trade bodies about recovery of input tax. For the meaning of 'input tax' see paras 4 ante, 201 post.

8. Subordinate legislation. Any order made by the Treasury[1] or the Lord Chancellor[2] under the Value Added Tax Act 1994 and any regulations made by the Commissioners of Customs and Excise[3] or any rules made thereunder must be made by statutory instrument[4]. Regulations made by the commissioners and certain Treasury orders[5] are subject to annulment in pursuance of a resolution of the House of Commons[6]. Under this negative resolution procedure the instrument must be laid[7] before the House of

Commons as soon as may be after it has been made, and if that House within 40 days[8] from the date on which it was laid resolves that it be annulled it thereupon ceases to have effect[9].

Other Treasury orders[10] are subject to a procedure which may be described as the affirmative resolution procedure[11]. Such an order must be laid before the House of Commons; and it ceases to have effect on the expiration of a period of 28 days[12] from the date on which it was made unless before the end of that period it has been approved by a resolution of the House of Commons; but this is without prejudice to anything previously done under it or to the making of a new order[13]. An order:

(1) which makes provision for securing that services which are specified in the order should be treated as supplied in the course or furtherance of a business[14]; or

(2) which provides that payments should be made on account of VAT[15]; or

(3) substituting a lesser sum for the sum for the time being specified as the value of a gift which does not constitute a supply[16]; or

(4) varying the provisions for the reduced charge on supplies of fuel for a qualifying use[17]; or

(5) making provision for increasing the rate of tax in force at the time of the making of the order[18], or for excepting any input tax from credit in computing a taxable person's liability to account for VAT[19], or for varying the schedules in relation to zero–rating or exemptions[20]; or

(6) which amends the rules relating to the application of VAT to land or buildings[21]; or

(7) relating to the flat rate scheme for farmers[22],

requires an affirmative resolution[23].

Directions and notices which are issued by the commissioners under their general powers of management[24] are not required to be made by statutory instrument. Notwithstanding the absence of a system of Parliamentary scrutiny for such notices, some notices have the effect of delegated legislation[25].

A statutory instrument containing an order prescribing classes of appeals in which there is a right of appeal to the Court of Appeal[26] or rules of procedure in relation to VAT and duties tribunals[27] is, however, subject to annulment in pursuance of a resolution of either House of Parliament[28].

1   For an example of such powers see para 141 post.
2   For an example of such powers see para 299 post.
3   See the Value Added Tax Act 1994 s 96(1).
4   Ibid s 97(1). See further the Statutory Instruments Act 1946 s 1(2); and STATUTES vol 44(1) (Reissue) paras 1502–1503.
5   Ie a statutory instrument made under any provision of the Value Added Tax Act 1994 except (1) an order made under s 79 (see para 266 post); (2) an instrument as respects which any other parliamentary procedure is expressly provided; or (3) an instrument containing an order appointing a day for the purposes of any provision of the 1994 Act, being a day as from which the provision will have effect, with or without amendments, or will cease to have effect: s 97(5)(a)–(c).
6   Ibid s 97(5).
7   As to the laying of documents before Parliament see the Statutory Instruments Act 1946 s 4; and STATUTES vol 44(1) (Reissue) para 1515.
8   The reckoning of this period is governed by ibid ss 4(3), 5(1), 7(1): see STATUTES vol 44(1) (Reissue) paras 1515–1517.
9   Ibid ss 5, 7(2); Value Added Tax Act 1994 s 97(5).
10 Ie an order to which ibid s 97(3) applies: see heads (1)–(7) in the text.
11 As to affirmative resolutions see STATUTES vol 44(1) (Reissue) para 1518; and PARLIAMENT.
12 In reckoning this period no account is to be taken of any time during which Parliament is dissolved or prorogued or during which the House of Commons is adjourned for more than four days: Value Added Tax Act 1994 s 97(3).
13 Ibid s 97(3).

14   Ie an order under ibid s 5(4): see para 24 note 25 post. As to the meaning of 'in the course or furtherance of a business' see paras 12 note 5, 17 note 2 post.

15   Ie an order under ibid s 28 (as amended): see para 229 post.

16   Ie an order under s 5(1), Sch 4 para 5(7) (as added): see para 24 post.

17   Ie an order under ibid s 2(1C) (as added): see para 6 ante.

18   As to the rate of VAT see para 5 ante.

19   Ie under the Value Added Tax Act 1994 s 25: see para 202 et seq post.

20   Ie orders for varying ibid s 30(2), Sch 8 (as amended) (see para 158 et seq post) or s 31(1), Sch 9 (as amended) (see para 141 et seq post) so as to abolish the zero-rating of a supply or to abolish the exemption of a supply without zero-rating it. For the meaning of 'supply' see para 21 post.

21   Ie an order under ibid s 51 (see paras 28, 143 post), and affecting Sch 10, except one making only such amendments to Sch 10 which are consequential on an order which itself varies Sch 8 (as amended) or Sch 9 (as amended) otherwise than in a manner falling within s 97(4)(c)(iii) (see the text to note 20 supra): see s 97(4)(d). 'Land' includes buildings and other structures, land covered with water, and any estate, interest, easement, servitude or right in or over land: Interpretation Act 1978 s 5, Sch 2 para 4(1)(a).

22   Ie an order under the Value Added Tax Act 1994 s 54(4) or (8): see para 79 post.

23   Ibid s 97(4) (amended by the Finance Act 1995 s 21(4), (6); and by the Finance Act 1996 ss 33(3), 205(1), Sch 4 Pt IV).

24   See para 7 ante.

25   For an example of this see Customs and Excise Notice 727 *VAT: Retail Schemes* (1 April 1993); and para 185 post. The legislative basis for delegated legislation in the case of retail schemes is the Value Added Tax Act 1994 s 58, Sch 11 para 2(6), which provides that regulations may make special provision for taxable supplies by retailers and in particular for permitting the value of supplies to be determined 'by such method or methods as may have been described in any notice published by the commissioners ...': see para 225 post.

26   Ie an order under the Value Added Tax Act 1994 s 86: see para 321 post.

27   Ie rules under ibid s 82(1), Sch 12 para 9: see para 299 post.

28   Ibid s 97(2).

9. Territorial extent; Northern Ireland and the Isle of Man. Value added tax is chargeable in Northern Ireland as part of the United Kingdom[1]. For the purposes of the constitution of Northern Ireland, VAT is an excepted matter, control of which cannot be transferred to Northern Ireland[2]. All money collected or received on account of the tax in Northern Ireland is paid into the Consolidated Fund of the United Kingdom in such manner as the Treasury may direct[3].

The Isle of Man, which is not for these purposes a part of the United Kingdom, introduced VAT into the island by an Act of Tynwald[4]. For the purpose of giving effect to any agreement between the government of the United Kingdom and the government of the Isle of Man whereby both countries are to be treated as a single area for the purposes of VAT[5], Her Majesty may by Order in Council[6] make provision for securing that tax is charged under the Value Added Tax Act 1994 as if all or any of the references therein to the United Kingdom included both the United Kingdom and the Isle of Man, but so that tax is not charged under both Acts in respect of the same transaction[7]. Such an order may make provision, inter alia:

(1)   for determining, or enabling the Commissioners of Customs and Excise to determine, under which Act a person is to be registered and for transferring a person registered under one Act to the register kept under the other[8]; and

(2)   for treating a person who is a taxable person for the purposes of the Act of Tynwald as a taxable person for all or any of the purposes of the 1994 Act[9].

The order may also make such modifications of any provision contained in or having effect under any Act of Parliament relating to value added tax as appears necessary or expedient for the purposes of the order[10].

1   Value Added Tax Act 1994 s 101(3). For the meaning of 'United Kingdom' see para 4 note 3 ante.

2   Northern Ireland Constitution Act 1973 s 2(2), Sch 2 para 8: see CONSTITUTIONAL LAW AND HUMAN RIGHTS vol 8(2) (Reissue) para 70.

3   Value Added Tax Act 1994 s 58, Sch 11 para 1(2)(b). For the meaning of 'United Kingdom' see para 4 note 3 ante; and for the meaning of 'money' see para 7 note 5 ante. As to the Consolidated Fund see CONSTITUTIONAL LAW AND HUMAN RIGHTS vol 8(2) (Reissue) para 711.

4   See the Finance (Isle of Man) Act 1972 (an Act of Tynwald).

5   Ie for the purposes of VAT charged under the Value Added Tax Act 1994 and VAT charged under the corresponding Act of Tynwald: Isle of Man Act 1979 s 6(1) (s 6 amended by the Value Added Tax Act 1983 Sch 9 para 3; and by the Value Added Tax Act 1994 s 100(1), Sch 14 para 7(2)).

6   The Order in Council currently in force is the Value Added Tax (Isle of Man) Order 1982, SI 1982/1067, which continues to have effect by virtue of the Interpretation Act 1978 s 17(2)(b); and the Value Added Tax Act 1994 ss 100(1), 101(4), Sch 13 para 23. See also the Value Added Tax (Isle of Man) (No 2) Order 1982, SI 1982/1068.

7   Isle of Man Act 1979 s 6(1) (as amended: see note 5 supra).

8   Ibid s 6(2)(a). A person otherwise liable to be registered under both Acts may be registered under either but not both Acts: see the Value Added Tax (Isle of Man) Order 1982 art 11. As to registration under the Value Added Tax Act 1994 see para 56 et seq post.

9   Isle of Man Act 1979 s 6(2)(b) (as amended: see note 5 supra). For the other provision that may be made see s 6(2)(c)–(h) (as so amended).

10   Ibid s 6(3).

10. Territories to be treated as excluded from or included in the territory of the Community and of the member states. The Commissioners of Customs and Excise may by regulations make provision for the territory of the Community, or for the member states, to be treated for any purposes of the Value Added Tax Act 1994 as including or excluding such territories as may be prescribed[1]. The Channel Islands, Andorra, San Marino and the Aland Islands are treated as excluded from the territory of the European Community for those purposes[2]. The Canary Islands, the overseas departments of the French Republic[3] and Mount Athos are treated as excluded both from the territory of the Community and from the territory of Spain, the French Republic and the Hellenic Republic respectively[4].

The territory of the Community is treated for those purposes as excluding Austria, Finland and Sweden ('the acceding states') in relation to goods:

(1)   which are the subject of a supply[5] made in an acceding state before 1 January 1995 and which in pursuance of that supply are removed to the United Kingdom[6] on or after 20 October 1995 if they are goods in the case of which provisions of the law of the acceding state in question[7] have prevented VAT from being charged on that supply[8]; and

(2)   which were subject to a suspension regime[9] before 1 January 1995 and which by virtue of any Community legislation were to remain, for VAT purposes only, subject to that regime for a period beginning with that date and which cease to be subject to that regime on or after 20 October 1995[10];

but this does not apply to:

(a)   goods which are exported on or after 20 October 1995 to a place outside the member states[11];

(b)   goods which are not means of transport and are removed on or after 20 October 1995 from a temporary admission procedure[12] in order to be returned to the person in an acceding state who had exported them from that state[13];

(c)   means of transport which are removed on or after 20 October 1995 from a temporary admission procedure[14] and which were first brought into service before 1 January 1987, or have a value not exceeding £4,000, or have been charged in an acceding state with VAT which has not been remitted or refunded by reason of their exportation and to such other tax, if any, to which means of transport of that class or description are normally chargeable[15].

The Principality of Monaco is treated as included in the territory of the French Republic for the purposes of the Value Added Tax Act 1994, the Isle of Man is treated as included in the territory of the United Kingdom, and both of them are treated as included in the territory of the Community[16].

1   Value Added Tax Act 1994 s 93(1). Without prejudice to the generality of this power, and of the power conferred by s 16 (application of customs enactments: see para 105 post), the commissioners may, for any purposes of the Value Added Tax Act 1994, by regulations provide for prescribed provisions of any customs and excise legislation to apply in relation to cases where any territory is treated under s 93(1) as excluded from the territory of the Community, with such exceptions and adaptations as may be prescribed: s 93(2). The reference to customs and excise legislation is a reference to any enactment or subordinate legislation or Community legislation, whenever passed, made or adopted, which has effect in relation to, or to any assigned matter connected with, the importation or exportation of goods; and 'assigned matter' has the same meaning as in the Customs and Excise Management Act 1979 (ie any matter in relation to which the commissioners are for the time being required in pursuance of any enactment to perform any duties: see s 1(1)): Value Added Tax Act 1994 s 93(3), (4). See further para 105 post.

2   Value Added Tax Regulations 1995, SI 1995/2518, reg 136.

3   Ie Guadeloupe, Martinique, Réunion, St Pierre and Miquelon and French Guiana: ibid reg 137(b).

4   Ibid reg 137.

5   For the meaning of 'supply' see para 21 post.

6   For the meaning of 'United Kingdom' see para 4 note 3 ante.

7   Ie the provisions having effect for purposes corresponding to the Value Added Tax Act 1994 s 30(6)(a) or, so far as it applies to exportations, s 30(8): see para 177 post.

8   Value Added Tax Regulations 1995 reg 138(1), (2)(a).

9   For these purposes, goods are treated as having become subject to a suspension regime if (1) on their entry into the territory of the Community (a) they were placed under a temporary admission procedure with full exemption from import duties, in temporary storage, in a free zone, or under customs warehousing arrangements or inward processing arrangements; or (b) they were admitted into the territorial waters of the United Kingdom for the purpose of being incorporated into drilling or production platforms, for the purposes of the construction, repair, maintenance, alteration or fitting-out of such platforms, for the purpose of linking such platforms to the mainland of the United Kingdom, or for the purpose of fuelling or provisioning such platforms; or (2) they were placed under any customs transit procedure in pursuance of a supply made in the course of a business, and, in the case in question, the time that any Community customs debt in relation to the goods would be incurred in the United Kingdom if the accession to the European Union of the acceding states were disregarded would fall to be determined by reference to the matters mentioned in head (1)(a) or (b) supra: ibid reg 138(3). As to Community customs debts see further para 103 note 5 post.

10   Ibid reg 138(1), (2)(b).

11   Ibid reg 138(4)(a).

12   Ie such as is referred to in ibid reg 138(3)(a)(i): see note 9 head (1)(a) supra.

13   Ibid reg 138(4)(b).

14   See note 12 supra.

15   Value Added Tax Regulations 1995 reg 138(4)(c).

16   Ibid reg 138(5). See further para 104 post.

11. Power to make regulations relating to taxation under the laws of other member states. The Commissioners of Customs and Excise may make provision by regulations for the manner in which any of the following are to be or may be proved for any of the purposes of the Value Added Tax Act 1994:

(1)   the effect of any provisions of the law of any other member state[1];

(2)   that provisions of any such law correspond or have a purpose corresponding, in relation to any member state, to or to the purpose of any provision of the 1994 Act[2].

They may also provide by regulations:

(a) for a person to be treated for prescribed[3] purposes as taxable in another member state[4] only where he has given such notification, and furnished such other information, to the commissioners as may be prescribed[5];

(b) for the form and manner in which any notification or information is to be given or furnished under the regulations and the particulars which it is to contain[6];

(c) for the proportion of any consideration[7] for any transaction which is to be taken for VAT purposes as representing a liability for VAT under the law of another member state to be conclusively determined by reference to such invoices[8] or in such other manner as may be prescribed[9].

In any proceedings, whether civil or criminal, a certificate of the commissioners that a person was or was not, at any date, taxable in another member state, or that any VAT payable under the law of another member state has or has not been paid, is sufficient evidence of that fact until the contrary is proved, and any document purporting to be such a certificate is deemed to be such a certificate until the contrary is proved[10].

The powers of the commissioners under the relevant information provisions[11] are exercisable, for the purpose of facilitating compliance with any Community obligations, with respect to matters that are relevant to a charge to VAT under the law of another member state as they are exercisable with respect to matters that are relevant for any of the purposes of the 1994 Act[12].

---

1 Value Added Tax Act 1994 s 92(3)(a). References, in relation to another member state, to the law of that member state are to be construed for the purposes of VAT as confined to so much of that law of that member state as for the time being has effect for the purposes of any Community instrument relating to VAT: s 92(1). For the meaning of 'another member state' see para 4 note 14 ante.

2 Ibid s 92(3)(b).

3 'Prescribed' means prescribed by regulations made by the commissioners under the Value Added Tax Act 1994: s 96(1).

4 References for the purposes of VAT to a person being taxable in another member state are references to that person being taxable under so much of the law of that member state as makes provision for purposes corresponding, in relation to that member state, to the purposes of so much of the Value Added Tax Act 1994 as makes provision as to whether a person is a taxable person: s 92(2)(a). For the meaning of 'taxable person' see paras 12 note 4, 55 post.

5 Ibid s 92(4)(a).

6 Ibid s 92(4)(b).

7 For the meaning of 'consideration' generally see para 86 post.

8 'Invoice' includes any document similar to an invoice: ibid s 96(1). Subject to s 58, Sch 11 para 3(2) (see para 240 post), in any provision contained in or having effect under the Value Added Tax Act 1994 'document' includes, in addition to a document in writing, (1) any map, plan, graph or drawing; (2) any photograph; (3) any disc, tape, sound track or other device in which sounds or other data (not being visual images) are embodied so as to be capable, with or without the aid of some other equipment, of being reproduced therefrom; and (4) any film, including a microfilm, and any negative, tape or other device in which one or more visual images are embodied so as to be capable, with or without the aid of some other equipment, of being reproduced therefrom: Civil Evidence Act 1968 s 10(1) (applied by the Value Added Tax Act 1994 s 96(6)).

9 Ibid s 92(4)(c).

10 Ibid s 92(5).

11 This reference to the relevant information provisions is a reference to the provisions of ibid s 73(7) (see para 247 post) and s 58, Sch 11 (as amended) (see para 225 et seq post) relating to (1) the keeping of accounts; (2) the making of returns and the submission of other documents to the commissioners; (3) the production, use and contents of invoices; (4) the keeping and preservation of records; and (5) the furnishing of information and the production of documents: s 92(7).

12 Ibid s 92(6). This provision is without prejudice to the generality of any of the powers of the commissioners under the relevant information provisions: s 92(6).

2. THE CHARGE TO VALUE ADDED TAX

(1) SUPPLY OF GOODS AND SERVICES

(i) In general

12. Charge to tax. Value added tax is charged on any supply[1] of goods and services made in the United Kingdom[2] in circumstances where the supply is a taxable supply[3] made by a taxable person[4] in the course or furtherance of any business[5] carried on by him[6]. The tax is a liability of the person making the supply[7].

1   For the meaning of 'supply' see para 21 post.
2   For the meaning of 'United Kingdom' see para 4 note 3 ante.
3   A 'taxable supply' is a supply of goods and services made in the United Kingdom other than an exempt supply: Value Added Tax Act 1994 s 4(2). As to exempt supplies see para 141 et seq post. Taxable supplies may be made by persons other than taxable persons (see note 4 infra); and taxable supplies may also be made by taxable persons otherwise than in the course or furtherance of their business (see note 5 infra); but VAT may only be charged on taxable supplies made by taxable persons in the course or furtherance of a business: *Schemepanel Trading Ltd v Customs and Excise Comrs* (1995) VAT Decision 13647; affd [1996] STC 871.
4   A person is a 'taxable person' while he is, or is required to be, registered under the Value Added Tax Act 1994: s 3(1). Any reference in the Value Added Tax Act 1994 to being registered is to be construed in accordance with s 3(3) (see para 56 note 2 post): s 96(2). For the rules relating to registration see para 56 et seq post.
5   For the meaning of 'business' see para 17 post. If a limited company has been formed for the purpose of carrying on business and supplies goods or services for reward, it will be difficult to resist the conclusion that the supply is in the course or furtherance of the company's business, even if the supply is not of a kind ordinarily made by the company and even if it is the first or only supply of its kind: *Fusetron Ltd v Customs and Excise Comrs* [1993] 2 CMLR 613. The existence of a term in a lease prohibiting the use of premises for business purposes is not conclusive that they are not so used: *Rootes (t/a The Shutford Stud) v Customs and Excise Comrs* (1992) VAT Decision 6808, [1992] STI 215. Giving a long-service award to an employee involves a supply in the course of business: *RHM Bakeries (Northern) Ltd v Customs and Excise Comrs* [1979] STC 72 (but as to gifts costing less than £15 see the Value Added Tax Act 1994 s 5(1), Sch 4 para 5(2) (as amended); and para 24 note 10 post).
        There is an apparent inconsistency in the authorities as to whether sales which are made to finance a VAT-registered business are to be treated as 'in the furtherance of the business'. In *Ridley v Customs and Excise Comrs* [1983] VATTR 81, it was held that the sale of sporting rights over farmland on which the taxpayer carried on his trade was liable to VAT, notwithstanding that the rights themselves had never been used for the purposes of the business, on the ground that the sums raised were to be used to reduce the business overdraft; but in *Stirling v Customs and Excise Comrs* [1986] 2 CMLR 117, [1985] VATTR 232 the sale of personal assets to meet liabilities incurred by the taxpayer in the course of his business was considered to be outside the scope of VAT, having regard to EC Council Directive 77/388 (OJ L145, 13.6.77, p 1) art 2(1); in disposing of such assets, the trader was not a taxable person 'acting as such'. Cf *Trustees of the Mellerstain Trust v Customs and Excise Comrs* [1989] VATTR 223, where the tribunal sought to reconcile *Ridley v Customs and Excise Comrs* supra with *Stirling v Customs and Excise Comrs* supra, explaining that the land in *Ridley v Customs and Excise Comrs* supra was already a business asset which the trader had simply exploited in an alternative way. As to whether VAT charged on supplies made to a trader can be recovered as input tax see para 201 et seq post. As to the meaning of 'in the course or furtherance of a business' see also para 17 note 2 post.
6   Value Added Tax Act 1994 s 4(1).
7   Ibid s 1(2). VAT becomes due at the time of supply (s 1(2)); but this rule is modified by the provisions relating to accounting for and paying VAT (see para 225 et seq post). As to determining the time of supply see para 29 et seq post.

13. Taxable acquisitions of goods from other member states. The member states of the European Community have been working towards the creation of a Single European Market in which the same consequences with respect to value added tax will follow whenever goods or services are supplied within the Community, wherever the vendor and purchaser may be located. To that end VAT and customs duties were abolished on importations of goods and supplies of services between different member states with effect from 1 January 1993[1]. However, in order to prevent distortion of competition during an interim period prior to the harmonisation of VAT rates in different states, provision is made for a 'reverse charge' to be levied on the importer of certain goods or services from other member states[2]. In the case of goods this is achieved by the imposition of VAT on specified 'acquisitions of goods from other member states', that is to say acquisitions of goods in pursuance of a transaction which is (or is treated[3] as) a supply[4] of goods and which involves the removal[5] of the goods from another member state[6]. There are three classes of case in which a liability to VAT on acquisition arises:

(1)   any acquisition by any person[7] from another member state of a new means of transport[8] is liable to VAT[9] if it takes place in the United Kingdom[10] otherwise than in pursuance of a taxable supply[11] and it is not an exempt acquisition[12];

(2)   any acquisition by any person[13] of goods subject to a duty of excise from another member state is liable to VAT[14] if:

  (a)   it takes place in the United Kingdom, otherwise than in pursuance of a taxable supply[15];

  (b)   it is not an exempt acquisition[16];

  (c)   the supplier is taxable in another member state at the time of the transaction in pursuance of which the goods are acquired and acts in the course or furtherance of a business[17] carried on by him in participating in that transaction[18];

  (d)   the goods are acquired either in the course or furtherance of a business carried on by any person or in the course or furtherance of any activities carried on otherwise than by way of business by any body corporate or by any club, association, organisation or other unincorporated body[19]; and

  (e)   it is the person who carries on that business or those activities who acquires the goods[20];

(3)   any acquisition of goods from another member state by a taxable person[21] which takes place in the United Kingdom otherwise than in pursuance of a taxable supply is liable to VAT[22] if it is not an exempt acquisition[23] and it takes place in the circumstances set out in heads (2)(c) to (2)(e) above[24].

Where a taxable acquisition is made by a taxable person who is fully taxable[25], he will in general[26] bring into his VAT account the amount of the taxable acquisition both as a taxable output and as a corresponding deductible input[27].

The removal of goods to the United Kingdom in pursuance of a supply to a taxable person, made by a person in another member state, where VAT on that supply is to be accounted for and paid in another member state by reference to the profit margin on the supply[28] is not, however, treated as the acquisition of goods from another member state[29].

1   See EC Council Directive 91/680 (OJ L376, 31.12.91, p 1) art 3; EC Council Directive 92/111 (OJ L384, 30.12.92, p 47) art 4.

2   As to the reverse charge on services see the Value Added Tax Act 1994 s 8; and para 27 post; and as to the value of taxable acquisitions see s 20; and para 98 post.

3   Ie for the purposes of the Value Added Tax Act 1994: see paras 12 ante, 14 et seq post. As to deemed supplies see para 24 post.

4   For the meaning of 'supply' see para 21 post. Where the person with the property in any goods does not change in consequence of anything which is treated for VAT purposes as a supply of goods, that supply is treated for those purposes as a transaction in pursuance of which there is an acquisition of goods by the person making it: ibid s 11(3).

5   There is no statutory definition of 'removal' for these purposes, which must therefore be given its ordinary meaning of a physical taking from one place to another. It is immaterial for these purposes

whether the removal of the goods from the other member state is by or under the directions of the supplier or by or under the directions of the person who acquires them or any other person: ibid s 11(2).

6   Ibid s 11(1). In relation to such an acquisition, references to the supplier are to be construed accordingly: s 11(1). References to goods being acquired by a person in another member state are references to goods being treated as so acquired in accordance with provisions of the law of that member state corresponding, in relation to that member state, to so much of the Value Added Tax Act 1994 as makes provision for treating goods as acquired in the United Kingdom from another member state: s 92(2). For the meaning of 'another member state' see para 4 note 14 ante; and for the meaning of 'United Kingdom' see para 4 note 3 ante. As to the meaning of 'the law of that member state' see para 11 note 1 ante.

The Treasury may by order provide with respect to any description of transaction that the acquisition of goods in pursuance of a transaction of that description is not to be treated for VAT purposes as the acquisition of goods from another member state: s 11(4). In exercise of the power so conferred, the Treasury has made the Value Added Tax (Special Provisions) Order 1995, SI 1995/1268, art 7: see the text and notes 28–29 infra. In addition, by virtue of the Interpretation Act 1978 s 17(2)(b), the Value Added Tax (Treatment of Transactions) (No 2) Order 1992, SI 1992/3132 (treatment of certain supplies of gold to central banks in member states: see para 169 post) has effect as if so made.

7   Ie whether or not that person is a taxable person: see the Value Added Tax Act 1994 s 10(1)(c). For the meaning of 'taxable person' see paras 12 note 4 ante, 55 post.

8   'Means of transport', in the expression 'new means of transport', means any of (1) any ship exceeding 7.5 m in length; (2) any aircraft the take-off weight of which exceeds 1,550 kg; (3) any motorised land vehicle which (a) has an engine with a displacement or cylinder capacity exceeding 48 cubic cm; or (b) is constructed or adapted to be electrically propelled using more than 7.2 kW; but a ship, aircraft or motorised land vehicle does not fall within heads (1)–(3) supra unless it is intended for the transport of persons or goods: ibid s 95(1), (2). 'Ship' includes hovercraft: s 96(1). A crane is not a means of transport: *BPH Equipment Ltd v Customs and Excise Comrs* (1996) VAT Decision 13914, [1996] STI 779.

A means of transport is to be treated as new, in relation to any supply or any acquisition from another member state, at any time unless at that time (i) the period that has elapsed since its first entry into service is more than three months, in the case of a ship or aircraft, and more than six months, in the case of a land vehicle; and (ii) it has, since its first entry into service, travelled under its own power for more than 100 hours, in the case of a ship, for more than 40 hours in the case of an aircraft, and for more than 6,000 km, in the case of a land vehicle: Value Added Tax Act 1994 s 95(3) (amended by the Value Added Tax (Means of Transport) Order 1994, SI 1994/3128). The Treasury may by order vary the Value Added Tax Act 1994 s 95 (as amended) by adding or deleting any ship, aircraft or vehicle of a description specified in the order to or from those which are for the time being specified in heads (1)–(3) supra and by altering, omitting or adding to the provisions of s 95(3) (as so amended) for determining whether a means of transport is new: s 95(4). As to the making of orders generally see para 8 ante. In exercise of the power so conferred, the Treasury has made the Value Added Tax (Means of Transport) Order 1994 cited supra. The Commissioners of Customs and Excise may by regulations make provision specifying the circumstances in which a means of transport is to be treated for these purposes as having first entered into service: Value Added Tax Act 1994 s 95(5). A new means of transport is to be treated as having first entered into service, in the case of a ship or aircraft, when it is delivered from its manufacturer to its first purchaser or owner, or on its first being made available to its first purchaser or owner, whichever is the earlier; or, if its manufacturer takes it into use for demonstration purposes, on its being first taken into such use: Value Added Tax Regulations 1995, SI 1995/2518, reg 147(1)(a). In the case of a motorised land vehicle, it is to be treated as having first entered into service: (A) on its first registration for road use by the competent authority in the member state of its manufacture or when a liability to register for road use is first incurred in the member state of its manufacture, whichever is the earlier; (B) if it is not liable to be registered for road use in the member state of its manufacture, on its removal by its first purchaser or owner, or on its first delivery or on its being made available to its first purchaser, whichever is the earliest; or (C) if its manufacturer takes it into use for demonstration purposes, on its first being taken into such use: reg 147(1)(b). Where the times specified in reg 147(1) cannot be established to the commissioners' satisfaction, a means of transport is to be treated as having first entered into service on the issue of an invoice relating to the first supply of the means of transport: reg 147(2).

Member states must, however, exempt certain supplies of new means of transport dispatched or transported to the purchaser by or on behalf of the vendor or the purchaser out of the territory referred to in EC Council Directive 77/388 (OJ L145, 13.6.77, p 1) art 3 (substituted by EC Council Directive 91/680; amended by EC Council Directive 92/111) but within the Community: see EC Council Directive 77/388 art 28c(A)(b) (added by EC Council Directive 91/680). See further the Value Added Tax Regulations 1995, SI 1995/2518, regs 149–155; and paras 183, 263 post. See also Customs and Excise Notice 728 *VAT: Motor Vehicles, Boats, Aircraft; Intra-EC Movements by Private Persons* (1 August 1995).

9   Value Added Tax Act 1994 s 10(1), (2)(a).

10   Goods are treated (subject to ibid s 18 (as amended) (see paras 130–131 post) and s 18B (as added) (see para 134 post)) as acquired in the United Kingdom if they are acquired pursuant to a transaction which involves their removal to the United Kingdom and does not involve their removal from the United Kingdom, and are otherwise treated as acquired outside the United Kingdom: s 13(1), (2) (s 13(1) amended by the Finance Act 1996 s 26(1), Sch 3 para 4). Goods are also treated as acquired in the United Kingdom if they are acquired by a person who, for the purpose of their acquisition, makes use of a number assigned to him for the purposes of VAT in the United Kingdom (ie his VAT registration number): Value Added Tax Act 1994 s 13(3). This does not, however, require any goods to be treated as acquired in the United Kingdom where it is established, in accordance with regulations made by the Commissioners of Customs and Excise for these purposes, that VAT (1) has been paid in another member state on the acquisition of those goods; and (2) fell to be paid by virtue of the provisions of the law of that member state corresponding, in relation to that member state, to the provision made by s 13(2): s 13(4). The commissioners may by regulations make provision, for these purposes, (a) for the circumstances in which a person is to be treated as having been assigned a number for the purposes of VAT in the United Kingdom; (b) for the circumstances in which a person is to be treated as having made use of such a number for the purposes of the acquisition of any goods; and (c) for the refund, in prescribed circumstances, of VAT paid in the United Kingdom on acquisitions of goods in relation to which the conditions specified in heads (1) and (2) supra are satisfied: s 13(5).

     As to the place of supply see ibid s 7 (as amended); and para 39 et seq post. By EC Council Directive 77/388 art 28c(A)(a) (as added and amended), incorporated in United Kingdom law by the Value Added Tax Act 1994 s 30(8) and the Value Added Tax Regulations 1995, SI 1995/2518, reg 134, a supply of goods dispatched or transported by a vendor of goods to another member state can be zero-rated if the supply is made to a person taxable in that other member state: see para 181 post. For this purpose the trader is required to obtain the customer's overseas VAT registration number: Customs and Excise Notice 725 *VAT: The Single Market* (1 February 1994) para 2.2.

11   Value Added Tax Act 1994 s 10(1)(b). For the meaning of 'taxable supply' see para 12 note 3 ante.

12   Ibid s 10(2)(b). An acquisition of goods from another member state is an exempt acquisition if the goods are acquired in pursuance of an exempt supply: s 31(1). As to exempt supplies see s 31(1), Sch 9 (as amended): and para 141 et seq post.

13   See note 7 supra.

14   Value Added Tax Act 1994 s 10(1)(c).

15   Ibid s 10(1)(a), (b).

16   Ibid s 10(2)(b).

17   As to the meaning of 'in the course or furtherance of a business' see para 12 note 5 ante.

18   Value Added Tax Act 1994 s 10(3)(c). For the meaning of 'taxable in another member state' see para 11 note 4 ante.

19   Ibid s 10(3)(a).

20   Ibid s 10(3)(b).

21   Ibid s 10(1)(c). A person is required to register for VAT when, during a calendar year, he has made 'relevant acquisitions' whose value exceeds £47,000, or when there are reasonable grounds for believing that the value of his relevant acquisitions in the next 30 days will exceed £47,000: see para 63 post. Accordingly, any person, other than a private individual, which makes substantial purchases from other member states in order to avoid United Kingdom VAT is likely to become registrable as a result of its acquisitions.

22   Ibid s 10(1)(a), (b).

23   Ibid s 10(2)(b).

24   Ibid s 10(2)(a), (3).

25   As to partial exemption see para 209 et seq post.

26   The recovery of input tax on certain acquisitions of motor cars is wholly or partially blocked, even for fully-taxable traders: see para 208 post. For the meaning of 'input tax' see paras 4 ante, 201 post.

27   As to accounting for VAT see para 225 et seq post.

28   Ie by virtue of the law of that member state corresponding to the Value Added Tax Act 1994 s 50A (as added) (margin schemes: see para 188 post) and any orders made thereunder: Value Added Tax (Special Provisions) Order 1995, SI 1995/1268, art 7.

29   Ibid art 7.

14. Taxable supply on removal of goods to another member state. The counterpart to the charge on acquisition of goods from another member state[1] is the taxable supply[2] which (subject to certain exceptions for temporarily removed goods) is imposed on the removal of goods to another member state[3]. Where[4] goods forming part of the assets of any business[5]: (1) are removed from any member state by or under the directions of the person carrying on the business; and (2) are so removed in the course or furtherance of that business for the purpose of being taken to a place in a member state other than that from which they are removed, then, whether or not the removal is or is connected with a transaction for a consideration, that is a supply of goods by that person[6]. This rule will apply whether the trader removes the goods in order to sell them, or in order to use them in the course of his trade, or otherwise. However, if the removal takes place as part of a process whereby the trader is to transfer or dispose of the goods so that they no longer form part of the assets of his business, whether or not for a consideration, the removal is treated as falling within the general rule by which such transactions are treated as supplies of goods (with a consequential charge to value added tax[7]) and not under the specific rule for removals to another member state[8].

If, therefore, the removal is made by a taxable person[9], it will be treated as a supply liable to VAT. Where, however, the Commissioners of Customs and Excise are satisfied that the supply in question involves both the removal of the goods from the United Kingdom[10] and their acquisition in another member state by a person who is liable for VAT on the acquisition[11] and that there has been compliance with such other conditions as are specified by regulations[12] or have been imposed by the commissioners, the deemed supply will be zero-rated[13].

The goods will, on removal to the other member state, be liable to VAT in that state in accordance with that country's rules on acquisitions of goods from other member states, and it may be necessary, for that reason, for the trader to register for VAT in that state.

1   See para 13 ante.
2   For the meaning of 'taxable supply' see para 12 note 3 ante.
3   See the Value Added Tax Act 1994 s 5(1), Sch 4 para 6; and the text and notes 4–13 infra. For the exceptions to this charge to VAT see para 15 post.
4   Ie save where the transaction falls within ibid Sch 4 para 5(1): see para 24 post.
5   As to the meaning of 'business' see para 17 post.
6   Value Added Tax Act 1994 Sch 4 para 6(1). As to the meaning of 'in the course or furtherance of a business' see paras 12 note 5 ante, 17 note 2 post.
7   Ie under ibid Sch 4 para 5 (as amended): see para 24 post.
8   See ibid Sch 4 para 6(1).
9   For the meaning of 'taxable person' see paras 12 note 4 ante, 55 post.
10 For the meaning of 'United Kingdom' see para 4 note 3 ante.
11 Ie in accordance with provisions of the law of that member state corresponding, in relation to that member state, to the provisions of the Value Added Tax Act 1994 s 10: see para 13 ante. As to the interpretation of references to the law of another member state see para 11 ante.
12 Where the commissioners are satisfied that: (1) a supply of goods by a taxable person involves their removal from the United Kingdom, (2) the supply is to a person taxable in another member state, (3) the goods have been removed to another member state, and (4) the goods are not goods in relation to whose supply the taxable person has opted, pursuant to the Value Added Tax Act 1994 s 50A (as added) (see para 188 post), for VAT to be charged by reference to the profit margin on the supply, the supply is to be zero-rated, subject to such conditions as the commissioners may impose: Value Added Tax Regulations 1995, SI 1995/2518, reg 134. For supplies to customers in other member states the commissioners require that: (a) the supplier obtains and shows on his VAT sales invoice his customer's VAT registration number (with a two-digit country code prefix); (b) the goods are sent or transported out of the United Kingdom to a destination in another member state; and (c) the supplier holds commercial documentary evidence that the goods have been removed from the United Kingdom (guidance on proof of removal of goods is given in Customs and Excise Notice 703 *VAT: Exports and Removals of Goods from the United Kingdom* (January 1993)): see Customs and Excise Notice 725 *VAT: The Single Market* (1 February 1994) para 2.2(a). If these conditions are not satisfied, the commissioners require the trader to charge and account for tax on the goods in the United Kingdom (unless the supply of the goods is normally zero-rated in the United Kingdom). The commissioners impose similar requirements where a trader removes goods to another member state for the purposes of his trade. However, they additionally expect the trader to be registered for VAT in the other member state (since the trader will be liable for VAT there on the acquisition of the goods), and to use his overseas VAT registration number

to support zero-rating of the deemed supply: Customs and Excise Notice 725 para 2.4. For the record-keeping and accounting requirements relating to removals see the Value Added Tax Regulations 1995 regs 21, 22 (as amended); and para 244 post; reg 33; and para 221 post.

13   See the Value Added Tax Act 1994 s 30(8); and para 177 post.

15.   Where removal of goods to another member state is not a taxable supply.

The removal of goods to another member state[1] is not treated as effecting a supply[2] for the purposes of value added tax where: (1) the goods are removed from any member state in the course of their removal from one part of that member state to another part of the same member state[3]; or (2) the goods have been removed from a place outside the member states for entry into the territory of the Community and are removed from a member state before the time when any Community customs debt[4] in respect of any Community customs duty on their entry into that territory would be incurred[5]. Additionally, it is provided[6] that the rule that the removal of goods involves a supply of those goods for VAT is not to apply:

(a)   where the supply of the goods would be treated as having been made in a member state other than the member state of dispatch by virtue of the distance selling rules[7]; or

(b)   where the supply of the goods would be treated as having been made in the member state of dispatch[8]; or

(c)   where the goods are removed[9] for the purpose of the owner either delivering them to a person to whom he is supplying those goods, or taking possession of them from a person who is supplying those goods to him, where (in either case) the supply is or will be[10] zero-rated[11].

There is no supply by removal for the purposes of VAT:

(i)   either where goods are temporarily removed for treatment or processing[12]; or where the goods are returned to the member state of dispatch after the completion of the treatment or processing[13];

(ii)   either where the goods have been removed for the purpose of delivering them to another person in order that he can value or carry out any work on them and the supply which is thus to be made will be a supply of services treated as having been made in the member state of arrival[14]; or where the goods are returned to the member state of dispatch on the completion of the valuation or work[15];

(iii)   either where goods are temporarily removed for the purposes of making a supply of services[16]; or where the goods are returned after the owner has ceased to use them in making the supply of services[17];

(iv)   either where temporary importation relief[18] would have been afforded had the goods been imported from a place outside the member states and the owner intends, within two years from the date of removal, to export the goods to a place outside the member states or remove them to a member state other than the member state of arrival[19]; or where the goods are subsequently removed to a member state other than that of arrival in accordance with the owner's previously expressed intention[20].

Where goods have been removed from a member state to a place in any other member state, that removal falls within head (i), head (v) or head (vii) above, and the owner's relevant intention is fulfilled[21], the owner need not make any entry in the VAT payable portion of that part of his VAT account which relates to the prescribed accounting period[22] in which he would be liable to account for any VAT chargeable in respect of the removal[23].

1   For the meaning of 'another member state' see para 4 note 14 ante.

2   Ie the Value Added Tax Act 1994 s 5(1), Sch 4 para 6(1) (see para 14 ante) does not apply: Sch 4 para 6(2). For the meaning of 'supply' see para 21 post.

3   Ibid Sch 4 para 6(2)(a). Thus VAT is not charged on the removal of goods where eg goods are shipped from one part of France to another via Dover, or from Liverpool to Grimsby via Calais.

4   As to the charge of VAT on the importation of goods see para 103 et seq post.

5   Value Added Tax Act 1994 Sch 4 para 6(2)(b). As to the places treated as excluded from, or included in, the territory of the Community for VAT purposes see para 10 ante.

6   Ie by the Value Added Tax (Removal of Goods) Order 1992, SI 1992/3111, art 4.

7   See para 42 post.

8   Ie by virtue of the Value Added Tax (Place of Supply of Goods) Order 1992, SI 1992/3283: see para 43 post.

9   The removal must be by or under the directions of the owner: Value Added Tax (Removal of Goods) Order 1992 art 4(c).

10   Ie by virtue of Value Added Tax Act 1994 s 30(6) or (8) (see para 177 post): Value Added Tax (Removal of Goods) Order 1992 art 4; Interpretation Act 1978 s 17(2)(b).

11   Value Added Tax (Removal of Goods) Order 1992 art 4.

12   The following conditions must be satisfied: (1) the owner is registered in the member state of dispatch and is not registered in the member state of arrival; (2) the goods have been removed for the purpose of delivering them to another person who is to produce goods by applying a treatment or process to the goods removed; and (3) the owner intends that the goods produced will be returned to him by their removal to the member state of dispatch upon completion of the treatment or process: ibid art 4(d). The relevant intention of the owner must be fulfilled: art 5.

13   Ibid art 4(h).

14   Ibid art 4(e).

15   Ibid art 4(i).

16   The following conditions must be satisfied: (1) the owner is established in the member state of dispatch and is not established in the member state of arrival; (2) the goods are removed for the sole purpose of their being used by the owner in the course of a supply of services to be made by him; (3) at the time of their removal there exists a legally binding obligation to make that supply of services; and (4) the owner intends to remove them to the member state of dispatch upon his ceasing to use them in the course of making the supply: ibid art 4(f). The relevant intention of the owner must be fulfilled: art 5.

17   Ibid art 4(h).

18   As to relief from VAT on importation see para 109 et seq post.

19   Value Added Tax (Removal of Goods) Order 1992 art 4(g). The relevant intention of the owner must be fulfilled: art 5.

20   Ibid art 4(h).

21   Ie the condition described in ibid art 5 (see notes 12, 16, 19 supra) has been fulfilled: Value Added Tax Regulations 1995, SI 1995/2518, regs 24, 42(2), (3).

22   For the meaning of 'prescribed accounting period' see para 105 note 16 post.

23   Value Added Tax Regulations 1995 reg 42(1), (2). Where, however, the condition mentioned in note 21 supra has not been complied with and an amount of VAT has become payable, the owner must make a positive entry for the relevant amount of VAT in the VAT payable portion of that part of his VAT account which relates to the prescribed accounting period in which the condition was not complied with: reg 42(3). 'Positive entry' means an amount entered into the VAT account as a positive amount: reg 24. As to the VAT account; and the VAT payable portion thereof, see para 237 post.

16. Triangulation. In order to simplify the treatment for value added tax purposes of supplies of goods passing from one member state to another by a chain of transactions involving an intermediate supplier (generally known as 'triangulation'), the option is given to the intermediate supplier to elect to treat the supply as made directly from the original owner of the goods[1] to the ultimate purchaser ('the customer')[2]. If the intermediate supplier elects to do this, the customer is obliged to account for VAT as on a taxable acquisition[3] of the goods from another member state[4]. This simplification is available in two cases, the first of which arises where the customer is registered for VAT in the United Kingdom and the second where the intermediate supplier is so registered. In the first such case, where:

(1)   a person ('the original supplier') makes a supply[5] of goods to a person who belongs in another member state[6] ('the intermediate supplier');

(2)   that supply involves the removal of the goods from another member state and their removal to the United Kingdom but does not involve the removal of the goods from the United Kingdom;

(3)   both the original supply and the removal of the goods to the United Kingdom are for the purposes of the making of a supply by the intermediate supplier to another person ('the customer') who is registered for the purposes of VAT;

(4)   neither of those supplies involves the removal of the goods from a member state in which the intermediate supplier is taxable[7] at the time of the removal without also involving the previous removal of the goods to that member state; and

(5)   there would be a taxable acquisition by the customer if the supply to him involved the removal of goods from another member state to the United Kingdom,

the supply by the original supplier to the intermediate supplier is disregarded for the purposes of VAT and the supply by the intermediate supplier to the customer is then treated for those purposes[8] as if it did involve the removal of the goods from another member state to the United Kingdom[9]. An intermediate supplier who has made or intends to make a supply to which he wishes the above provisions to apply must notify the Commissioners of Customs and Excise and the customer in writing of his intention to do so[10]. The notification must be made no later than the provision of the first invoice[11] in relation to the supply to which it relates, and sent both to the office designated by the commissioners for the receipt of such notifications, and to the customer[12]. Where an intermediate supplier has complied with these notification requirements in relation to the first supply to a customer, they are deemed to have been satisfied in relation to all subsequent supplies to that customer while the intermediate supplier continues to belong in another member state[13].

In the second such case, where:

(a)   any goods are acquired from another member state in a case which corresponds, in relation to another member state, to the first case described in heads (1) to (5) above in relation to the United Kingdom; and

(b)   the person who acquires the goods is registered for VAT in the United Kingdom and would be the intermediate supplier in relation to that corresponding case,

the supply to him of those goods and the supply by him of those goods to the person who would be the customer in that corresponding case are both disregarded[14] for the purposes of VAT[15].

Special rules apply for the tax treatment of installed or assembled goods[16].

The simplified procedure[17] does not apply in relation to any supply unless the intermediate supplier complies with such requirements as to the furnishing, both to the commissioners and to the customer, of invoices and other documents[18], and of information, as the commissioners may by regulations prescribe[19].

1   The simplification rules (ie the provisions of the Value Added Tax Act 1994 s 14) do not apply to any transaction by which the goods were supplied to the intermediate supplier before 1 January 1993: see s 14(8).
2   See ibid s 14; and the text and notes 6–19 infra.
3   As to the charge on taxable acquisitions see para 13 ante.
4   See the Value Added Tax 1994 s 14(1), (6); and the text and notes 6–19 infra.
5   For the meaning of 'supply' see para 21 post.
6   A person belongs in another member state for these purposes if: (1) he does not have any business establishment or other fixed establishment in the United Kingdom and does not have his usual place of residence in the United Kingdom (see para 46 post); (2) he is neither registered for the purposes of VAT nor required to be so registered (see para 56 et seq post); (3) he does not have a VAT representative and is not for the time being required to appoint one (see para 62 post); and (4) he is taxable in another member state: Value Added Tax Act 1994 s 14(5)(a)–(d). In determining for the purposes of head (2) supra whether a person is required to be registered for VAT, any supplies which would fall to be

disregarded by virtue of s 14 if he did belong in another member state and complied with the requirements prescribed under s 14(3) (see the text and notes 10–13, 17–19 infra; and paras 41, 243 post) must be disregarded: s 14(5). For the meaning of 'another member state' see para 14 ante; for the meaning of 'United Kingdom' see para 4 note 3 ante; and for the meaning of 'registered' see paras 12 note 4 ante, 56 note 2 post. For the meaning of 'taxable in another member state' see note 7 infra.

7   For these purposes, references to a person being taxable in another member state do not include references to a person who is so taxable by virtue only of provisions of the law of another member state corresponding to the provisions of the Value Added Tax Act 1994 by virtue of which a person who is not registered under that Act is a taxable person if he is required to be so registered: s 14(7). For the meaning of references to the law of another member state see para 11 note 1 ante; and for the meaning of 'taxable in another member state' generally see para 11 note 4 ante.

8   Ie other than for the purposes of registration under ibid s 3(2), Sch 3 (as amended) in respect of acquisitions from another member state: see para 63 post.

9   Ibid s 14(1). The result will be that the customer will be liable to account for VAT on his purchase of goods as if he had made a taxable acquisition of the goods. Where s 14 has the effect of deeming a taxable acquisition to have been made, the time of supply is taken to be the day of the issue of the prescribed invoice: see s 14(4) (applying s 12(1) (as amended) (see para 38 post) with the omission of the words from 'whichever' to 'acquisition; and' at the end of s 12(1)(a)).

10   Value Added Tax Regulations 1995, SI 1995/2518, reg 11(1). The notification must contain the following particulars: (1) the name and address of the intermediate supplier; (2) the number including the alphabetical code by which the intermediate supplier is identified for VAT purposes, which was used or is to be used for the purpose of the supply to him by the original supplier; (3) the date upon which the goods were first delivered or are intended to be first delivered; and (4) the name, address and registration number of the customer to whom the goods have been supplied or are to be supplied: reg 11(2). 'Alphabetical code' means the prescribed alphabetical prefix which is used to identify the member state: see reg 2(1). 'Registration number' means the number allocated by the commissioners to a taxable person in the certificate of registration issued to him: reg 2(1). For the meaning of 'taxable person' see paras 12 note 4 ante, 55 post.

11   Ie in accordance with ibid reg 18: see para 243 post.

12   Ibid reg 11(3). Notifications must be made separately in relation to each customer to whom it is intended to make supplies to which the intermediate supplier wishes the Value Added Tax Act 1994 s 14(1) to apply: Value Added Tax Regulations 1995 reg 11(4).

13   Ibid reg 11(5).

14   Ie other than for the purposes of the information provisions referred to in the Value Added Tax Act 1994 s 92(7) (see para 11 ante): s 14(6).

15   Ibid s 14(6). This provision is without prejudice to s 13(4) (place of acquisition: see para 13 note 10 ante): s 14(6). In this case, the intermediate supplier must comply with the requirements of the Value Added Tax Regulations 1995 regs 17, 20: see para 243 post.

16   See the Value Added Tax Act 1994 s 14(2); and para 41 post.

17   Ie ibid s 14(1): see heads (1)–(5) in the text.

18   For the meaning of 'invoice' and 'document' see para 11 note 8 ante.

19   Ibid s 14(3). Such regulations may provide for the times at which, and the form and manner in which, any document or information is to be furnished and the particulars which it is to contain: s 14(3). In exercise of the power so conferred, the commissioners have made the Value Added Tax Regulations 1995 reg 11 (see the text and notes 10–13 supra) and regs 18, 20 (see para 243 post). The regulations are so framed that the intermediate supplier is given a choice whether or not to operate the simplified procedure: if he wishes the procedure to operate, he must correspondingly comply with the relevant regulations.

17. Meaning of 'business'.

17. Meaning of 'business'. Supplies which are not made in the course or furtherance of a business are outside the scope of value added tax. There is no exhaustive statutory definition of 'business'[1] for the purposes of the tax[2], but it includes any trade, profession or vocation[3]. Leaving aside activities which are required by statute to be treated as constituting the carrying on of a business, the word 'business' is to be given its natural meaning and does not require that what is done must be done commercially, in the popular sense, or with the object of profit[4]. The activity must, however, involve the making of supplies over an appreciable tract of time and with such frequency as to amount to a recognisable and identifiable activity of the person on whom the liability to tax is to fall[5].

There are special provisions governing the taxation of business carried on by the Crown, local authorities, groups of companies or partnerships, and of businesses carried on in divisions by companies or by unincorporated bodies, personal representatives and agents[6].

1   The use of the word 'business' is peculiar to the United Kingdom and does not appear in EC Council Directive 77/388 (OJ L145, 13.6.77, p 1) under which VAT is charged on supplies of goods or services effected for consideration by a taxable person acting as such: art 2(1). A 'taxable person' is defined for those purposes as any person who independently carries out any economic activity, whatever the purpose or results of that activity (art 4(1)); and 'economic activity' comprises all activities of producers, traders and persons supplying services including mining and agricultural activities and activities of the professions (art 4(2)). The exploitation of tangible or intangible property for the purpose of obtaining an income therefrom on a continuing basis is also to be considered an economic activity: art 4(2). The concept of 'business' in the United Kingdom legislation appears to be intended to correspond to this definition of 'economic activity'. Member states may also treat as a taxable person anyone who carries out on an occasional basis a transaction relating to any of the activities specified in art 4(2); and in particular, the supply before first occupation of buildings or parts of buildings, as well as the land on which they stand, and the supply of building land: see art 4(3). The United Kingdom has not specifically availed itself of the permission.

2   For judicial consideration of the meaning of 'business' see *Customs and Excise Comrs v Apple and Pear Development Council* [1987] 2 CMLR 634, [1986] STC 192, HL; Case 102/86 *Apple and Pear Development Council v Customs and Excise Comrs* [1988] ECR 1443, [1988] 2 All ER 922, ECJ (council's activities did not amount to a supply effected for consideration where charges imposed on growers by statute without regard to the benefits provided to each grower); *Customs and Excise Comrs v Morrison's Academy Boarding Houses Association* [1978] STC 1, Ct of Sess (activities carried on without the intention of making a profit nevertheless to be considered a business); *National Water Council v Customs and Excise Comrs* [1979] STC 157 (services supplied in the performance of a statutory duty could nevertheless be treated as supplied in the course of a business); *Church of Scientology of California v Customs and Excise Comrs* [1980] CMLR 114, [1979] STC 297 (affd [1981] 1 All ER 1035, [1981] STC 65, CA) (a body which propagates a religion or religious philosophy may nonetheless as a matter of law be regarded as carrying on a business for VAT purposes); *Customs and Excise Comrs v Royal Exchange Theatre Trust* [1979] 3 All ER 797, [1979] STC 728 per Neill J (business-like activities carried on otherwise than for the purpose of making supplies for a consideration could not amount to a business for VAT); *Customs and Excise Comrs v Lord Fisher* [1981] 2 All ER 147, [1981] STC 238 per Gibson J ('business' for VAT purposes does not include any activity which is carried on only for pleasure and social enjoyment, even though the organiser may require contributions towards the cost of the activity from other participants); *Cumbrae Properties (1963) Ltd v Customs and Excise Comrs* [1981] STC 799 (secondment of staff to another company within the same ownership made in the course of the company's business); *Three H Aircraft Hire (a firm) v Customs and Excise Comrs* [1982] STC 653 (a finding that a partnership existed was not conclusive that a business existed for VAT purposes); *Greater London Red Cross Blood Transfusion Service v Customs and Excise Comrs* [1983] VATTR 241 (provision of a voluntary service to the community does not amount to a business); *Whitechapel Art Gallery v Customs and Excise Comrs* [1986] STC 156 (the free admission of members of the public to art exhibitions was not a business activity, and could not be regarded as predominantly concerned with, or incidental to, the gallery's business activities); *Institute of Chartered Accountants in England and Wales v Customs and Excise Comrs* [1996] STC 799 (the regulatory function of the institute in issuing licences (for a fee) to persons carrying on investment business did not constitute either a business or an economic activity). Where a trader assigned her business to another in return for a weekly payment, the fact that she continued to be registered for VAT and to make the VAT returns was no evidence that it was she who carried on the business: *Nasim (t/a Yasmine Restaurant) v Customs and Excise Comrs* [1987] STC 387. For other judicial consideration by the European Court of Justice of 'economic activity' 'taxable person' and allied phrases see: Case 89/81 *Staatssecretaris van Financiën v Hong Kong Trade Development Council* [1982] ECR 1277, [1983] 1 CMLR 73, ECJ (a person who habitually provides services free of charge cannot be considered to be a taxable person entitled to recover VAT); Case 235/85 *EC Commission v Netherlands* [1987] ECR 1471, [1988] 2 CMLR 921, ECJ (private persons exercising the powers of a public authority in return for a fee are engaged in an economic activity for VAT purposes; similarly Case C-202/90 *Ayuntamiento de Sevilla v Recaudadores de Tributos de las Zonas Primera y Segunda* [1991] ECR I-4247, [1993] STC 659, ECJ; Case 269/86 *Mol v Inspecteur der Invoerrechten en Accijnzen* [1988] ECR 3627, [1989] 3 CMLR 729, ECJ; Case 289/86 *Vereniging Happy Family Rustenburgerstraat v Inspecteur der Omzetbelasting* [1988] ECR 3655, [1989] 3 CMLR 743, ECJ (the illegal sale of drugs not an economic activity); Joined Cases 231/87, 129/88 *Ufficio Distrettuale delle Imposte Dirette di Fiorenzuola*

d'Arda v Commune di Carpaneto Piacentino and Ufficio Provinciale Imposta sul Valore Aggiunto di Piacenza [1989] ECR 3233, [1991] STC 205, ECJ (activities carried on by a local authority under the same legal conditions as private traders should be considered taxable economic activities despite EC Council Directive 77/388 art 4(5)); Case C-186/89 *WM van Tiem v Staatssecretaris van Financiën* [1990] ECR I-4363, [1993] STC 91, ECJ ('exploitation of property' extends to all forms of transactions by which it is sought to obtain income from goods on a continuing basis, whatever legal form they might take; accordingly, a grant of building rights for a consideration is to be considered an economic activity and thus taxable); Case C-60/90 *Polysar Investments Netherlands BV v Inspecteur der Invoerrechten en Accijnzen, Arnhem* [1991] ECR I-3111, [1993] STC 222, ECJ (a holding company whose functions are restricted to the mere holding of shares and the receipt of dividends therefrom does not carry on an economic activity); Case C-333/91 *Satam SA v Minister for the Budget* [1993] ECR I-3513, [1993] STI 1077, ECJ; cf Case C-306/94 *Régie Dauphinoise–Cabinet A Forest SARL v Ministre du Budget* [1996] CMLR 193, [1996] STC 1176, ECJ (the investment of security deposits by an estate manager for its own benefit constituted a supply made by a taxable person acting as such and therefore falling within the scope of VAT); Case C-20/91 *De Jong v Staatssecretaris van Financiën* [1992] ECR I-2847, [1995] STC 727, ECJ; Case C-291/92 *Finanzamt Uelzen v Armbrecht* [1995] ECR I-2775, [1995] STC 997, ECJ (a taxable person performing a transaction in a private capacity was not a 'taxable person acting as such' within EC Council Directive 77/388 art 2(1); eg where he sold property which he had chosen to reserve for his private use); Case C-155/94 *Wellcome Trust Ltd v Customs and Excise Comrs* [1996] All ER (EC) 589, [1996] STC 945, ECJ (the sale of shares held as part of an investment portfolio was nothing more than an exercise of the investor's rights of ownership and, even if regularly carried out on a large scale, did not amount to an economic activity within EC Council Directive 77/388 art 4). The concept of economic activity referred to in both the first and second sentences of art 4(2) does not include activities carried out on an occasional basis only; but the hiring out of tangible property must be regarded as 'exploitation' of such property, within the second sentence thereof, if it is done for the purpose of obtaining income from it on a continuing basis. Whether or not this is so must be determined by the national court, evaluating all the circumstances of the particular case: Case C-230/94 *Enkler v Finanzamt Homburg* [1996] STC 1316, ECJ. See also para 12 note 5 ante.

3   Value Added Tax Act 1994 s 94(1).

4   *Customs and Excise Comrs v Morrison's Academy Boarding Houses Association* [1978] STC 1 at 5 per Lord Emslie.

5   *Customs and Excise Comrs v Morrison's Academy Boarding Houses Association* [1978] STC 1 at 8 per Lord Cameron. However, contrast Case C-155/94 *Wellcome Trust Ltd v Customs and Excise Comrs* [1996] All ER (EC) 589 at 598–599, [1996] STC 945 at 954 per Advocate-General Lenz (if an activity is treated as an economic activity, within the meaning of the Sixth Directive, it will remain so even if completed in a single day).

6   See the Value Added Tax Act 1994 ss 41–48 (as amended); and paras 65–66, 191 et seq post.

18. The activities of clubs and associations.

The following are deemed to be the carrying on of a business for the purposes of value added tax: (1) the provision by a club, association or organisation[1] for a subscription or other consideration[2] of the facilities[3] or advantages available to its members[4]; and (2) the admission, for a consideration, of persons to any premises[5]. Where, however, a body has objects which are in the public domain and are of a political, religious, philanthropic, philosophical or patriotic nature, it is not to be treated as carrying on a business only because its members subscribe to it, if the subscription obtains no facility or advantage for the subscriber other than the right to participate in its management or receive reports on its activities[6].

1   Exemption from VAT is granted in respect of supplies of certain goods and services made by trades unions and certain professional associations by the Value Added Tax Act 1994 s 31(1), Sch 9 Pt II Group 9: see para 153 post. For the meaning of 'business' generally see para 17 ante.

2   Various attempts have been made by clubs to obtain sums from members without incurring a liability to account for VAT on the whole, or part, of the sums obtained. Thus, in *Trewby v Customs & Excise Comrs* [1976] 2 All ER 199, [1976] 1 WLR 932, DC, it was contended that since the members were beneficial owners of the land on which the club stood, the subscriptions were paid to obtain an interest in the land (which would have been the receipt of an exempt supply within the Value Added Tax Act 1994 Sch 9 Pt II Group 1 (as amended), rather than for the facilities available on the land); held that members merely obtained a licence to enter the premises rather than a licence to occupy; and that this did not obtain exemption. See also *Exeter Golf and Country Club Ltd v Customs and Excise Comrs* [1981] STC 211, CA (where members were obliged to make an interest-free loan to the club in lieu of an entrance fee, the

supply fell within the Finance Act 1972 s 10(3) (now repealed; replaced by the Value Added Tax Act 1994 s 19(1)) as a supply for a consideration not consisting wholly of money); *Lord Advocate v Largs Golf Club* [1985] STC 226, Ct of Sess (members were obliged to purchase a unit in a trust which had purchased the freehold of the golf course; held that the purchase of the unit was part of the consideration for membership, notwithstanding that it was paid to a third party). Cf *Arsenal Football Club plc v Customs and Excise Comrs* (1996) VAT Decision 14011, [1996] STI 965 (not of course a members' club case), where the link between the giving of a loan and the obtaining of a season ticket were held to be insufficiently direct to treat the making of the former as part of the consideration for the latter.

3   'Facilities' is to be construed as the means or opportunity to do something more easily: *Club Cricket Conference v Customs and Excise Comrs* [1973] VATTR 53. An unincorporated non-profit-making body established by universities to promote and co-ordinate inter-university sport with no commercial element in its activities is not an association providing facilities for its members, but such services as are supplied are more in the nature of advantages of membership: *Universities Athletic Union v Customs and Excise Comrs* [1974] VATTR 118. Where a non-profit-making club serves liquor to its members it carries on the business of providing drinking facilities for its members: *Carlton Lodge Club v Customs and Excise Comrs* [1974] 3 All ER 798, [1975] 1 WLR 66, DC. See also *Eastbourne Town Radio Cars Association v Customs and Excise Comrs* [1996] STC 1469 (where a non-profit-making association acted as agent for its members in paying each member's share of the joint expenses they incurred in the provision of office premises and a communications network, to enable them to provide a car hire service, the contribution made by each member in the discharge of his share of the expenses was not consideration for a supply by the association).

4   Value Added Tax Act 1994 s 94(2)(a).

5   Ibid s 94(2)(b).

6   Ibid s 94(3). On the meaning of 'philanthropic' see *Rotary International v Customs and Excise Comrs* [1991] VATTR 177, where it was also contended that the Value Added Tax Act 1994 s 94(3) does not correctly implement EC Council Directive 77/388 (OJ L145, 13.6.77, p 1) art 13(A)(1)(l) (exemption for supply of services, and goods closely linked thereto, for the benefit of their members in return for a subscription fixed in accordance with their rules by non-profit making organisations with aims of a political, trade union, religious, patriotic, philosophical, philanthropic or civic nature, provided that this exemption is not likely to cause distortion of competition). As to this question cf *English Speaking Union of the Commonwealth v Customs and Excise Comrs* [1981] 1 CMLR 581, [1980] VATTR 184 with Case 8/81 *Becker v Finanzamt Münster-Innenstadt* [1982] I ECR 53, [1982] 1 CMLR 499, ECJ.

19. Offices held by professionals etc.

Where a person, in the course or furtherance of a trade, profession or vocation, accepts any office, services supplied by him as the holder of that office are treated, for the purposes of value added tax, as supplied in the course or furtherance of the trade, profession or vocation[1]. This may be contrasted with the usual position of employees and office-holders, who are outside the scope of VAT[2].

1   Value Added Tax Act 1994 s 94(4). Thus eg the services of an accountant appointed as auditor of a company are subject to VAT. In *Gardner v Customs and Excise Comrs* [1989] VATTR 132, the appellant accepted office as Chairman of the Prince of Wales Trust before he set up on his own account, and registered for VAT, as a business consultant; it was held that he had not accepted office 'in the course of' his profession and was not liable to account for VAT on the reimbursement of expenses made to him by the Trust.

2   Such persons are assumed not to be carrying on a business: see eg *Rickarby v Customs and Excise Comrs* [1973] VATTR 186. The matter is clearer in EC Council Directive 77/388 (OJ L145, 13.6.77, p 1) art 4(1), which defines a 'taxable person' as 'any person who independently carries out in any place any economic activity': see para 17 note 1 ante.

20. The termination and transfer of businesses.

Anything which is done in connection with the termination or intended termination of a business[1] is treated, for the purposes of value added tax, as being done in the course or furtherance of that business[2]. Likewise, the disposition of a business as a going concern[3], or of its assets or liabilities (whether or not in connection with its reorganisation or winding up), is treated as a supply[4] made in the course or furtherance of the business[5]. The following supplies by a person of assets of his business are, however, treated as neither a supply of goods nor a supply of services for the purposes of VAT:

(1)   their supply to a person to whom he transfers his business as a going concern where the assets are to be used by the transferee in carrying on the same kind of business, whether or not as part of any existing business, that is carried on by the transferor, and, in a case where the transferor is a taxable person[6], the transferee is already a taxable person or a person defined as such in Manx law[7], or becomes a taxable person immediately as a result of the transfer[8];

(2)   their supply to a person to whom he transfers part of his business as a going concern where that part is capable of separate operation, the assets are to be used by the transferee in carrying on the same kind of business[9] as that carried on by the transferor in relation to that part, and, in a case where the transferor is a taxable person, the transferee is already a taxable person or a person defined as such in Manx law, or becomes a taxable person immediately as a result of the transfer[10].

A supply of assets consisting of a grant which would fall within certain exemptions relating to land[11] but for an election[12] made by the transferor[13], or a grant of a fee simple[14], is not treated as neither a supply of goods nor a supply of services by virtue of heads (1) and (2) above unless the transferee has made an election in relation to the land concerned which has effect on the relevant date[15] and has given any written notification of the election required[16] no later than the relevant date[17].

1   For the meaning of 'business' see para 17 ante.
2   Value Added Tax Act 1994 s 94(5). As to the meaning of 'in the course or furtherance of a business' see paras 12 note 5, 17 note 2 ante.
3   Special rules, however, apply to prevent VAT liabilities arising on the transfer of a business, or a part of a business, as a going concern: see the Value Added Tax (Special Provisions) Order 1995, SI 1995/1268, art 5; and the text and notes 6–17 infra.
4   For the meaning of 'supply' see para 21 post.
5   Value Added Tax Act 1994 s 94(6).
6   For the meaning of 'taxable person' see paras 12 note 4 ante, 55 post.
7   Ie defined in the Value Added Tax and other Taxes Act 1973 (an Act of Tynwald) s 2(2): Value Added Tax (Special Provisions) Order 1995 arts 2, 5(1)(a)(ii).
8   Ibid art 5(1)(a). The sale of industrial units to unregistered pension fund trustees is outside the scope of art 5 by reason of this provision: *Gould and Cullen v Customs and Excise Comrs* [1994] 1 CMLR 347, [1993] VATTR 209. By concession, Customs permit a transfer of a property letting business to be treated as a going concern (and so as outside the scope of VAT) even where the legal title to the land is transferred, not to the person who will carry on the business but to a nominee, provided that the name of the beneficial owner is disclosed to the transferor: see Customs and Excise Business Brief 10/96 (5 June 1996) [1996] STI 984.
9   Ie whether or not as part of any existing business: ibid art 5(1)(b).
10   Ibid art 5(1)(b). As to transfers of going concerns see further para 196 post. Although the effect of art 5 is to treat the transfer as not involving a supply for VAT purposes, this does not also mean that the goods supplied are not treated as acquired as trading stock for the purpose of the operation of retail scheme B: *Customs and Excise Comrs v Co-operative Wholesale Society Ltd* [1995] STC 983. As to retail schemes see paras 185–187 et seq post.
11   Ie which would fall within the Value Added Tax Act 1994 s 31(1), Sch 9 Pt II Group 1 (as amended): see para 142 post.
12   'Election' for these purposes means an election having effect under ibid s 51(1), Sch 10 para 2 (as amended) (election to waive exemption: see para 143 post): Value Added Tax (Special Provisions) Order 1995 art 5(3).
13   For these purposes, 'transferor' and 'transferee' include a relevant associate of either respectively as defined in the Value Added Tax Act 1994 Sch 10 para 3(7) (see para 143 post): Value Added Tax (Special Provisions) Order 1995 art 5(3).
14   Ie a grant which falls within the Value Added Tax Act 1994 Sch 9 Pt II Group 1 item 1(a): see para 142 post.
15   'Relevant date' means the date upon which the grant would have been treated as having been made or, if there is more than one such date, the earliest of them: Value Added Tax (Special Provisions) Order 1995 art 5(3).

16 Ie required by the Value Added Tax Act 1994 Sch 10 para 3(6) (as substituted): see para 144 post.
17 Value Added Tax (Special Provisions) Order 1995 art 5(2).

21. Meaning of 'supply'. 'Supply' includes all forms of supply but does not include anything done otherwise than for a consideration[1]. The legislation relating to value added tax distinguishes supplies of goods from supplies of services[2]; in particular, there are different rules relating to the place and time of supply.[3] Anything which is not a supply of goods but is done for a consideration (including, if so done, the granting, assignment or surrender of any right) is treated as a supply of services[4]. The Treasury may by order provide with respect to any description of transaction (1) that it is to be treated as a supply of goods and not as a supply of services[5]; or (2) that it is to be treated as a supply of services and not as a supply of goods[6]; or (3) that it is to be treated as neither a supply of goods nor a supply of services[7].

1   Value Added Tax Act 1994 s 5(2)(a). This is subject to any provision made by s 5(1), Sch 4 (as amended) (see paras 15 ante, 24 post) and to Treasury orders under s 5(3)–(6) (see the text and notes 5–7 infra; and paras 24, 26 post): s 5(2). For the meaning of 'consideration' generally see para 86 post. The question as to when foreign currency dealings amount to a supply has been referred to the European Court of Justice in Case C-172/96 *Customs and Excise Comrs v First National Bank of Chicago* [1996] STI 1231. A sale by a receiver of stolen goods is still a sale for VAT purposes, obliging the receiver to account for VAT: *Customs and Excise Comrs v Oliver* [1980] 1 All ER 353, [1980] STC 73. 'Supply' is the passing of possession in goods pursuant to an arrangement whereunder the supplier agrees to part with possession and the recipient agrees to take possession; and by 'possession' is meant in this context control over the goods, in the sense of having the immediate facility for their use: *Customs and Excise Comrs v Oliver* supra, followed in *Tas-Stage Ltd v Customs and Excise Comrs* [1988] STC 436. Where an employer provided premises and equipment for a canteen, together with the services of an employee to cook the meals, there was a supply of the food in the canteen, even though the meals were provided at cost out of money collected by the canteen manager from the employees and never passed through the firm's accounts: *Barker (Mr and Mrs) v Customs and Excise Comrs* (1990) VAT Decision 4589, [1990] STI 394. A supply of goods may take place notwithstanding that the supplier never takes possession of the goods himself: *Customs and Excise Comrs v John Willmott Housing Ltd* [1987] STC 692. If a purchaser obtains property from a trader by fraud and the trader subsequently avoids the contract, there is no supply for VAT: *Harry B Litherland & Co Ltd v Customs and Excise Comrs* [1978] VATTR 226. VAT may not be levied on (1) the illegal importation of drugs into the European Community (Case 294/82 *Senta Einberger v Hauptzollamt Freiburg (No 2)* [1984] ECR 1177, [1985] 1 CMLR 765, ECJ); or (2) the illegal sale of narcotics within a member state (Case 269/86 *Mol v Inspecteur der Invoerrechten en Accijnzen* [1988] ECR 3627, [1989] 3 CMLR 729, ECJ; Case 289/86 *Vereniging Happy Family Rustenburgerstraat v Inspecteur der Omzetbelasting* [1988] ECR 3655, [1989] 3 CMLR 743, ECJ). This restriction does not, however, apply to goods which may lawfully be traded on the market, but which are illegally exported: Case C-111/92 *Lange v Finanzamt Fürstenfeldbruck* [1994] 1 CMLR 573, ECJ. The supply of goods and services by a charity in connection with a fund-raising event is treated as made in the course or furtherance of its business if made against payment; but such supplies are exempt supplies, in accordance with the Value Added Tax Act 1994 s 31(1), Sch 9 Pt II Group 12: see para 156 post. Where, though, the supply is not in connection with a fund-raising event (as defined in Sch 9 Pt II Group 12), it is taxable in the ordinary way: *Customs and Excise Comrs v Tron Theatre Ltd* [1994] STC 177. As to the meaning of 'in the course or furtherance of a business' see paras 12 note 5, 17 note 2 ante.

2   The rules are contained in Value Added Tax Act 1994 Sch 4 (as amended): see para 24 post. Occasionally it can be difficult to determine whether a transaction involves a supply of goods or a supply of services; it has been said that regard must be had to all the circumstances in which the transaction takes place in order to identify its characteristic features: Case C-231/94 *Faaborg-Gelting Linien A/S v Finanzamt Flensburg* [1996] All ER (EC) 656, [1996] STC 774, ECJ. Thus, the supply of prepared food and drink for immediate consumption in a restaurant on board a ferry was 'characterised by a cluster of features and acts, of which the provision of food was only one component, and in which services largely predominate'. It was, therefore, held to be a supply of services, in contrast to the position which would have obtained had the transaction related to 'take-away food'. Another substantially more difficult case is that where a customer provides his own materials to a supplier to make up into an item of goods, eg where a customer takes an old gold bracelet to a jeweller to be melted down and used (perhaps with other gold) to make a new item of jewellery: see *Customs and Excise Comrs v Sai Jewellers, Sai Jewellers v Customs and Excise Comrs* [1996] STC 269; in some instances it will be found that there are two sales, one by the customer to the

jeweller, and the other vice versa; and in other instances, that the jeweller is simply providing a service of 'refashioning' the customer's bracelet.

3   See para 29 et seq post.

4   Value Added Tax Act 1994 s 5(2)(b). If a credit card company buys at a discount from a retailer a debt owed to the retailer by one of its cardholders, the company is to be treated as making a supply of services (ie the service of clearing the debt) for a consideration (ie the discount): *Customs and Excise Comrs v Diners Club Ltd* [1989] 2 All ER 385, [1989] STC 407, CA; *Customs and Excise Comrs v High Street Vouchers Ltd* [1990] STC 575; Case C-18/92 *Chaussures Bally SA v Ministry of Finance, Belgium* [1993] ECR I-2871, [1993] STI 944, ECJ. A distinction is drawn between compensation (which is not within the scope of VAT) and consideration, though it may be difficult to distinguish the one from the other. See Customs and Excise Press Notice 82/87 (payments under out of court settlements which are essentially compensatory and do not directly relate to supplies of goods and services are outside the scope of VAT); and [1992] 32 LS Gaz p 32 (9 September 1992) (report of meeting between the Law Society and the commissioners in relation to that notice). See also *Cooper Chasney Ltd v Customs and Excise Comrs* [1990] 3 CMLR 509, (1990) VAT Decision 4898 (taxpayer, C, was held to have made a taxable supply when, having sued another company for an alleged infringement of its name, it received £30,000 in settlement under an agreement whereby C gave up its right to use the name); *Customs and Excise Comrs v Bass plc* [1993] STC 42 (charge made by a hotelier when a customer fails to arrive, having made a guaranteed reservation, is a supply of services, ie making available a room); *Reich v Customs and Excise Comrs* (1993) VAT Decision 9548, [1993] STI 358, (a payment of £35,000 under a Tomlin order in settlement of a claim for alleged commission was held to be partly compensatory and outside the scope of VAT, in the absence of proof of any supplies; cf *JE Greves & Son v Customs and Excise Comrs* [1993] VATTR 127, where the tribunal held that a payment of £450,000 under a Tomlin order was consideration for an exempt supply of the taxpayer's possessory interest in land); *Holiday Inns (UK) Ltd v Customs and Excise Comrs* [1993] VATTR 321 (compensation of £2m on the termination of an hotel management agreement, representing loss of future fees, was held to be outside the scope of VAT (for other proceedings in this matter see *Customs and Excise Comrs v Croydon Hotel and Leisure Co Ltd* [1995] STC 855; revsd [1996] STC 1105, CA)); cf *Lloyds Bank plc v Customs and Excise Comrs* (1996) VAT Decision 14181, [1996] STI 1358, where the parties amended a lease (where the landlord had opted to tax) to make provision for termination and for compensation on termination in order that the lessee might immediately exercise the right to terminate; it was held that the entire transaction was, in substance and reality, one by which consideration was paid by the lessee in return for the grant by the landlord of an option to surrender the lease.

A farmer's undertaking to cease milk production is not a supply of services and the compensation paid to him is not subject to VAT: Case C-215/94 *Mohr v Finanzamt Bad Segeberg* [1996] ECR I-959, [1996] STC 328, ECJ.

5   Ibid s 5(3)(a). In the exercise of this power, the Treasury has made the Value Added Tax (Fiscal Warehousing) (Treatment of Transactions) Order 1996, SI 1996/1255, which came into force on 1 June 1996: art 1. A transaction fulfilling the prescribed description is to be treated as a supply of goods and not as a supply of services: art 3(1). The prescribed description is that there is a supply which is not a retail transaction involving the transfer of any undivided share of property in eligible goods and either (1) that supply takes place while the goods in question are subject to a fiscal warehousing regime; or (2) the transferee causes the goods in question to be placed in a fiscal warehousing regime after receiving that supply but before the supply, if any, which next occurs involving the transfer of any property in those goods: art 3(2). In construing art 3(2), any supply referred to therein must be treated as taking place at the material time for that supply: art 2(2). For these purposes, 'supply' means a supply for the purposes of the Value Added Tax Act 1994 s 5(2)(a); 'eligible goods' has the meaning given by s 18B(6) (as added) (see para 134 note 1 post); and 'material time' has the meaning given by s 18F(1) (as added) (see para 134 note 3 post): Value Added Tax (Fiscal Warehousing) (Treatment of Transactions) Order 1996 art 2(1). As to goods subject to a fiscal warehousing regime see para 132 et seq post.

By virtue of the Interpretation Act 1978 s 17(2)(b), the Value Added Tax Act (Water) Order 1989, SI 1989/1114 (which treats the supply of water as a supply of goods and not of services, in so far as it would not otherwise be a supply of goods: see art 2), also has effect as if made under the Value Added Tax Act 1994 s 5(3)(a).

6   Ibid s 5(3)(b). At the date at which this volume states the law, no such order had been made, but, by virtue of the Interpretation Act 1978 s 17(2)(b), the Value Added Tax Act (Tour Operators) Order 1987, SI 1987/1806 (amended by SI 1992/3125; SI 1995/1495) (which treats combinations of supplies of goods or services made by a tour operator for the benefit of travellers as a single supply of services: see art 3(2)) has effect as if so made.

7   Value Added Tax Act 1994 s 5(3)(c). In exercise of the power so conferred, the Treasury has made (1) the Value Added Tax (Treatment of Transactions) Order 1995, SI 1995/958, which excludes from the scope of VAT the transfer of ownership in certain second-hand goods and works of art imported from

outside the EC with a view to possible sale (see para 22 post); (2) the Value Added Tax (Special Provisions) Order 1995, SI 1995/1268 (amended by SI 1995/1385) (see paras 20 ante, 22 post); and (3) the Value Added Tax (Cars) (Amendment) Order 1995, SI 1995/1269; and the Value Added Tax (Cars) (Amendment) (No 2) Order 1995, SI 1995/1667 (see para 23 post).

By virtue of the Interpretation Act 1978 s 17(2)(b), the following orders also have effect as if so made: (a) the Value Added Tax (Treatment of Transactions) Order 1992, SI 1992/630 (which excludes from the scope of VAT the provision of a motor car by an employer to his employee in circumstances where the employee has a choice between a higher salary and a lower salary together with the use of the car (save to the extent that the employer charges the employee an amount in excess of the differential for the provision of the benefit): see art 2); (b) the Value Added Tax (Removal of Goods) Order 1992, SI 1992/3111 (which precludes certain removals of goods from one member state to another being treated as supplies of goods by the Value Added Tax Act 1994 Sch 4 para 6: see para 15 ante); (c) the Value Added Tax (Supply of Temporarily Imported Goods) Order 1992, SI 1992/3130 (which excludes from the scope of VAT supplies of goods held under temporary importation arrangements with total relief from customs duty within the meaning of EC Council Regulation 3599/82 (OJ L376, 31.12.82, p 1) (repealed: see now EC Council Regulation 2913/92 (OJ L302, 19.10.92, p 1), provided that the goods remain eligible for those importation arrangements and the supply is to a person established outside the member states: see the Value Added Tax (Supply of Temporarily Imported Goods) Order 1992 art 2); (d) the Value Added Tax (Cars) Order 1992, SI 1992/3122 (amended by SI 1995/1269; SI 1995/1667) (which excludes from the scope of the tax the disposal of used cars which have been repossessed under a finance agreement or in settlement of a claim under an insurance policy, certain disposals of cars for no consideration and certain hirings and non-business use of motor cars free of charge or for less than full consideration: see art 4 (as so amended); and para 23 post).

22. Transactions for which special provision is made. The transfer of ownership in second-hand goods imported from a place outside the member states[1] with a view to their sale by auction, or in works of art[2] imported from such a place for the purposes of exhibition, with a view to possible sale, at a time when those goods or works of art are still subject to arrangements for temporary importation with total exemption from export duty[3], is treated as neither a supply[4] of goods nor a supply of services[5]. The provision of any services relating to such a transfer of ownership is similarly so treated[6].

Each of the following descriptions of transaction is treated as neither a supply of goods nor a supply of services:

(1)   the disposal of any works of art[7], antiques[8] and collectors' items[9] or second-hand goods[10] which have been repossessed under the terms of a finance agreement[11];

(2)   the disposal of any such items or goods by an insurer[12] who has taken possession of them in settlement of a claim under a policy of insurance[13];

(3)   the disposal of a boat or an aircraft by a mortgagee after he has taken possession of it under the terms of a marine mortgage[14] or an aircraft mortgage[15];

(4)   the assignment by the owner of goods comprised in a hire purchase or conditional sale agreement of his rights and interests under that agreement, and the goods comprised in it, to a bank or other financial institution[16];

(5)   services provided in connection with a supply of goods by an agent acting in his own name to the purchaser of the goods the consideration[17] for which is taken into account under the margin scheme[18] in calculating the price at which the agent obtained the goods[19];

(6)   services in connection with the sale of goods provided by an auctioneer[20] acting in his own name to the vendor or the purchaser of the goods the consideration for which is taken into account under the margin scheme[21] in calculating the price at which the auctioneer obtained or sold the goods[22];

(7)   the removal of goods to the United Kingdom[23] in pursuance of a supply to a person made by a person in another member state[24] where value added tax on that supply is to be accounted for and paid in another member state by reference to the profit margin[25] on that supply[26].

Such treatment is afforded to transactions falling within one of heads (1) to (3) above only if (a) the goods disposed of are in the same condition at the time of disposal as they were when they were repossessed or taken into possession; and (b) a supply of the goods in the United Kingdom made by the person from whom, in each case, they were obtained would not be chargeable with VAT, or would have been chargeable with VAT on less than the full value of the supply[27]. Those heads do not apply to reimported goods which were previously exported from the United Kingdom or the Isle of Man free of VAT[28] or to imported goods which have not borne VAT chargeable[29] in the United Kingdom or the Isle of Man[30].

The exchange of a reconditioned article for an unserviceable article of a similar kind by a person who regularly offers in the course of his business[31] to provide a reconditioning facility by that means is treated as a supply of services and not as a supply of goods[32].

1   As to goods imported from a place outside the member states see para 103 note 2 post; and as to the territories treated as included in, or excluded from, the territories of the member states for VAT purposes see para 10 ante.
2   For these purposes, 'works of art' means (1) paintings, drawings and pastels executed by hand but not comprised in manufactured articles that have been hand-painted or hand-decorated; collages and similar decorative plaques; (2) original engravings, lithographs and other prints; (3) original sculptures and statuary, in any material: Value Added Tax (Treatment of Transactions) Order 1995, SI 1995/958, art 2.
3   Ie in accordance with EC Council Regulation 2913/92 (OJ L302, 19.10.92, p 1) arts 137–141, 144(1); and EC Commission Regulation 2454/93 (OJ L253, 11.11.93, p1) art 682(1)(a) or (c): see CUSTOMS AND EXCISE; EUROPEAN COMMUNITIES.
4   For the meaning of 'supply' see para 21 ante.
5   Value Added Tax (Treatment of Transactions) Order 1995 art 3(1). Article 3(1), (2) does not apply in relation to any transfer of ownership in second-hand goods which is effected otherwise than by sale by auction: art 3(3).
6   Ibid art 3(2).
7   For these purposes, 'works of art' means the following goods:
    (1) pictures, collages and similar decorative plaques, paintings and drawings, executed entirely by hand by the artist, other than plans and drawings for architectural, engineering, industrial, commercial, topographical or similar purposes, hand-decorated manufactured articles, theatrical scenery, studio back-cloths or the like of painted canvas (Value Added Tax (Special Provisions) Order 1995, SI 1995/1268, art 2);
    (2) original engravings, prints and lithographs, being impressions produced in limited numbers directly in black and white or in colour of one or of several plates executed entirely by hand by the artist irrespective of the process or of the material employed by him, but not including any mechanical or photomechanical process (art 2);
    (3) original sculptures and statuary in any material provided that they are executed entirely by the artist, sculpture casts the production of which is limited to eight copies (or if the casts were produced before 1 January 1989, such greater number of copies as the Commissioners of Customs and Excise may in any particular case allow) and supervised by the artist or his successors in title (art 2);
    (4) tapestries and wall textiles made by hand from original designs provided by artists, provided that there are not more than eight copies of each (art 2);
    (5) individual pieces of ceramics executed entirely by the artist and signed by him, enamels on copper, executed entirely by hand, limited to eight numbered copies bearing the signature of the artist or the studio, excluding articles of jewellery and goldsmiths' and silversmiths' wares (art 2);
    (6) photographs taken by the artist, printed by him or under his supervision, signed and numbered and limited to 30 copies, all sizes and mounts included (art 2).
8   'Antiques' means objects, other than works of art or collectors' items, which are more than 100 years old: ibid art 2. For the meaning of 'collectors' items see note 9 infra.
9   'Collectors' items' means the following goods: (1) postage or revenue stamps, postmarks, first-day covers, pre-stamped stationery and the like, franked, or if unfranked not being of legal tender and not being for use as legal tender; (2) collections and collectors' pieces of zoological, botanical, mineralogical, anatomical, historical, archaeological, palaeontological, ethnographic or numismatic interest: ibid art 2.
10 'Second-hand goods' means tangible movable property that is suitable for further use as it is or after repair, other than motor cars, works of art, collectors' items or antiques and other than precious metals and precious stones: ibid art 2. Second-hand goods in this context include second-hand horses and ponies: see

Customs and Excise Notice 718 *Margin Schemes for Second-hand Goods, Works of Art, Antiques and Collectors' Items* (1 June 1995) Pt VIII.

'Motor car' means any motor vehicle of a kind normally used on public roads which has three or more wheels and either (1) is constructed or adapted solely or mainly for the carriage of passengers; or (2) has to the rear of the driver's seat roofed accommodation which is fitted with side windows or which is constructed or adapted for the fitting of side windows; but does not include (a) vehicles capable of accommodating only one person or suitable for carrying 12 or more persons; (b) vehicles of not less than three tonnes unladen weight; (c) caravans, ambulances and prison vans; (d) vehicles of a type approved by the Assistant Commissioner of Police of the Metropolis as conforming to the condition of fitness for the time being laid down by him for the purposes of the London Cab Order 1934, SR & O 1934/1346 (as amended); (e) vehicles constructed for a special purpose other than the carriage of persons and having no other accommodation for carrying persons than such as is incidental to that purpose: Value Added Tax (Special Provisions) Order 1995 art 2.

11 Ibid art 4(1)(a), (3). 'Finance agreement' means an agreement for the sale of goods whereby the property in those goods is not to be transferred until the whole of the price has been paid and the seller retains the right to repossess the goods: art 2.

12 'Insurer' means a person permitted, in accordance with the Insurance Companies Act 1982 s 2 (as amended) to effect and carry out contracts of insurance against risks of loss of, or damage to, goods: Value Added Tax (Special Provisions) Order 1995 art 2. See INSURANCE vol 25 (Reissue) para 19.

13 Ibid art 4(1)(b), (3).

14 'Marine mortgage' means a mortgage which is registered in accordance with the Merchant Shipping Act 1995 and by virtue of which a boat, but not any share of it, is made a security for a loan: Value Added Tax (Special Provisions) Order 1995 art 2; Interpretation Act 1978 s 17(2)(a).

15 Value Added Tax (Special Provisions) Order 1995 art 4(1)(c), (d). 'Aircraft mortgage' means a mortgage which is registered in accordance with the Mortgaging of Aircraft Order 1972, SI 1972/1268 (as amended): Value Added Tax (Special Provisions) Order 1995 art 2. See AVIATION vol 2 (Reissue) para 1334.

16 Ibid art 5(4).

17 For the meaning of 'consideration' generally see para 86 post.

18 Ie by virtue of the Value Added Tax (Special Provisions) Order 1995 art 12(6): see para 189 post.

19 Ibid art 9.

20 'Auctioneer' means a person who sells or offers for sale goods at any public sale where persons become purchasers by competition, being the highest bidders: ibid art 2.

21 Ie by virtue of ibid art 12(7): see para 189 post.

22 Ibid art 10.

23 For the meaning of 'United Kingdom' see para 4 note 3 ante.

24 For the meaning of 'another member state' see para 4 note 14 ante.

25 Ie by virtue of the law of that member state corresponding to the Value Added Tax Act 1994 s 50A (as added) (see para 188 post) and any orders made thereunder (see paras 189–190 post): Value Added Tax (Special Provisions) Order 1995 art 7. As to the construction of references to the corresponding law of another member state see para 11 ante.

26 Ibid art 8. That a sale of trading stock in the course of a transfer of a business as a going concern is to be treated as neither a supply of goods nor a supply of services (by reason of the Value Added Tax (Special Provisions) Order 1995: see art 5(1)–(3); and para 20 ante) is no justification for treating the goods as if they had not been received by the purchaser, and therefore requiring them to be omitted from the computation of 'goods received' under Retail Scheme B: *Customs and Excise Comrs v Co-operative Wholesale Society Ltd* [1995] STC 983, disapproving *Kelly and Kelly v Customs and Excise Comrs* (1989) VAT Decision 4139 (unreported). As to retail schemes see paras 185–187 post.

27 Value Added Tax (Special Provisions) Order 1995 art 4(1). Artcile 4(1) thus envisages that the person from whom the goods were repossessed would either not be a taxable person or would have operated the margin scheme in relation to those goods.

28 Ie free of VAT chargeable under the Value Added Tax Act 1994 or the Value Added Tax and other Taxes Act 1973 (an Act of Tynwald) by reason of the zero-rating provisions of either Act, or regulations made under either Act: Value Added Tax (Special Provisions) Order 1995 arts 2, 4(2) (amended by SI 1995/1385).

29 Ie chargeable under either of the Acts mentioned in note 28 supra: Value Added Tax (Special Provisions) Order 1995 art 4(2).

30 Ibid art 4(2) (as amended: see note 28 supra).

31 For the meaning of 'business' see para 17 ante.

32 Value Added Tax (Special Provisions) Order 1995 art 6.

23. Special provisions relating to motor cars. Each of the following descriptions of transaction is treated as neither a supply[1] of goods nor a supply of services:

(1) the disposal of a used motor car[2] by a person who repossessed it under the terms of a finance agreement[3], where the motor car is in the same condition as it was in when it was repossessed[4];

(2) the disposal of a used motor car by an insurer[5] who has taken it in the settlement of a claim under a policy of insurance, where the motor car is disposed of in the same condition as it was in when it was so taken[6];

(3) the disposal of a motor car for no consideration[7];

(4) services in connection with a supply of a used motor car provided by an agent acting in his own name to the purchaser of the motor car the consideration for which is taken into account under the margin scheme[8] in calculating the price at which the agent sold the motor car[9];

(5) services in connection with the sale of a used motor car provided by an auctioneer[11] acting in his own name to the vendor or the purchaser of the motor car the consideration for which is taken into account under the margin scheme in calculating the price at which the auctioneer obtained or sold the motor car[12];

(6) a relevant supply of services[13] by a taxable person to whom a motor car has been let on hire or supplied or by whom a motor car has been acquired from another member state[14] or imported[15].

Nothing in heads (1) and (2) above, however, is to be construed as meaning that a transaction is not a supply for the purposes of the statutory provisions[16] relating to the acquisition of goods from another member state[17]. Additionally, the above provisions do not apply:

(a) in relation to a case falling within heads (1) to (3) above, unless the tax on any previous supply, acquisition or importation was wholly excluded from credit[18] as input tax[19];

(b) in relation to a case falling within head (6) above, unless the tax on any previous letting on hire, supply, acquisition or importation was wholly or partly excluded from such credit[20].

1   For the meaning of 'supply' see para 21 ante.
2   For these purposes, 'motor car' means any motor vehicle of a kind normally used on public roads which has three or more wheels and either (1) is constructed or adapted solely or mainly for the carriage of passengers; or (2) has to the rear of the driver's seat roofed accommodation which is fitted with side windows or which is constructed or adapted for the fitting of side windows; but does not include (a) vehicles capable of accommodating only one person or suitable for carrying 12 or more persons; (b) vehicles of not less than three tonnes unladen weight; (c) caravans, ambulances and prison vans; (d) vehicles of a type approved by the Assistant Commissioner of Police of the Metropolis as conforming to the condition of fitness for the time being laid down by him for the purposes of the London Cab Order 1934, SR & O 1934/1346 (as amended); (e) vehicles constructed for a special purpose other than the carriage of persons and having no other accommodation for carrying persons than such as is incidental to that purpose: Value Added Tax (Cars) Order 1992, SI 1992/3122, art 2. See also Customs and Excise Notice 718 *Margin Schemes for Second-hand Goods, Works of Art, Antiques and Collectors' Items* (1 June 1995) Pt VII.
3   For these purposes, 'finance agreement' means an agreement for the sale of goods whereby the property in those goods is not to be transferred until the whole of the price has been paid and the seller retains the right to repossess the goods: Value Added Tax (Cars) Order 1992 art 2.
4   Ibid art 4(1)(a).
5   For these purposes, 'insurer' means a person permitted, in accordance with the Insurance Companies Act 1982 s 2 (as amended), to effect and carry out contracts of insurance against risks of loss of, or damage to, goods; Value Added Tax (Cars) Order 1992 art 2. See INSURANCE vol 25 (Reissue) para 19.
6   Ibid art 4(1)(b).
7   Ibid art 4(1)(c) (amended by SI 1995/1667). For the meaning of 'consideration' generally see para 86 post.

8   Ie by virtue of ibid art 8(6) (as substituted): see para 190 post. The provision set out in head (4) in the text
    in fact refers to art 8(8) but it is thought that this must be a drafting error, as art 8 (as originally made)
    consisted of art 8(1)–(5), and art 8 (as substituted) consists of art 8(1)–(7).
9   Ibid art 4(1)(d) (added by SI 1995/1269).
11 For these purposes, 'auctioneer' means a person who sells, or offers for sale, goods at any public sale where persons
    become purchasers by competition, being the highest bidders: ibid art 2 (definition added by SI 1995/1269).
12 Ibid art 4(1)(e) (added by SI 1995/1269). The provision set out in head (5) in the text refers to the
    consideration being taken into account by virtue of art 8(9), but it is thought that this is a drafting error:
    see note 8 supra. The correct reference would appear to be to art 8(7) (as substituted): see para 190 post.
13 For these purposes, a relevant supply of services is (1) the letting on hire of a motor car to any person for
    no consideration or for a consideration which is less than that which would be payable in money if it
    were a commercial transaction conducted at arm's length; or (2) the making available of a motor car,
    otherwise than by letting it on hire, to any person (including, where the taxable person is an individual,
    himself, and where the taxable person is a partnership, a partner) for private use, whether or not for a
    consideration: ibid art 4(1C) (added by SI 1995/1667). For the meaning of 'taxable person' see paras 12
    note 4 ante, 55 post.
14 For the meaning of 'another member state' see para 4 note 14 ante.
15 Value Added Tax (Cars) Order 1992 art 4(1)(f) (added by SI 1995/1667).
16 Ie for the purposes of the Value Added Tax Act 1994 s 11(1)(a): see para 13 ante.
17 Value Added Tax (Cars) Order 1992 art 4(2) (amended by SI 1995/1269).
18 Ie excluded from credit under the Value Added Tax Act 1994 s 25: see para 202 post.
19 Value Added Tax (Cars) Order 1992 art 4(1C) (added by SI 1995/1667). For the meaning of 'input tax'
    see paras 4 ante, 201 post.
20 Ibid art 4(1D) (added by SI 1995/1667).

24. Deemed supplies. The Value Added Tax Act 1994 makes specific provision for
certain supplies of services to be treated as supplies of goods[1] and vice versa. In addition,
it treats some activities which would not otherwise involve any supply for VAT purposes
(for example because not made for a consideration) as a supply of goods or, in some
instances, as a supply of services[2].

Any transfer of the whole property in goods[3] is a supply of goods[4], but the transfer of
an undivided share of the property in goods or of the possession of goods (for example
the letting of goods on hire, or the lending of goods) is treated as a supply of services[5]. If,
however, the possession of goods is transferred under an agreement for their sale or under
an agreement which expressly contemplates that property in the goods will also pass at
some time in the future (determined by, or ascertainable from, the agreement but in any
case no later than the time when the goods are fully paid for) then this is a supply of
goods[6]. The grant, assignment or surrender of a major interest in land is treated as a supply
of goods[7].

Where goods forming part of the assets of a business are transferred or disposed of by
or under the directions of the person carrying on the business so as no longer to form part
of those assets, and whether or not for a consideration, that is a supply of goods by that
person[8] in the course or furtherance of his business[9]. Exceptions are made: (1) for small
business gifts[10]; and (2) for gifts of samples[11]. Where goods held or used for the purposes
of a business are, by or under the direction of the person carrying on the business, put to
any private use or used, or made available to any person for use, for any purpose other
than a purpose of the business, that is a supply of services in the course or furtherance of
the business[12]. These rules do not require anything which a person carrying on a business
does otherwise than for a consideration in relation to any goods to be treated as a supply
except in a case where that person is entitled[13] to credit for the whole or any part of the
VAT charged on the supply, acquisition or importation of those goods or of anything
comprised in them[14].

The removal of goods forming part of the assets of a business from one member state
to another member state, by or under the directions of the trader, is treated as a supply of
goods if it would not otherwise have so been treated[15].

Where goods forming part of the assets of a business carried on by a taxable person[16] are sold by another under a power exercisable by him, in or towards satisfaction of a debt owed by the taxable person, they are deemed to be supplied by the taxable person in the course or furtherance of that business[17].

Where a person ceases to be a taxable person, any goods then forming part of the assets of a business carried on by him are deemed to be supplied by him in the course of that business immediately before he ceases to be a taxable person unless (a) the business is transferred as a going concern to another taxable person[18]; (b) the business is carried on by another person who is treated under regulations made by the Commissioners of Customs and Excise as a taxable person[19]; or (c) the VAT on the deemed supply would be no more than £250[20]. The charge is not, however, so imposed on any goods in the case of which the taxable person can show to the commissioners' satisfaction that no credit for input tax[21] has been allowed to him[22], that the goods did not become his as part of the assets of a business which was transferred to him as a going concern by another taxable person and that he has not obtained transitional relief[23] in respect of the goods[24].

The Treasury may make provision by order for securing, with respect to services of any description specified in the order, that where a person carrying on a business does anything which is not a supply of services but would, if done for a consideration, be a supply of services of a description specified in the order, and such other conditions as may be specified in the order are satisfied, those services are treated as being supplied by him in the course or furtherance of the business[25]. Where a person carrying on a business puts services which have been supplied to him to any private use, or uses or makes them available to any person for use, for a purpose other than a purpose of his business, he is treated as supplying the services in the course or furtherance of his business[26]. No supply is, however, deemed to be so made in respect of any services:

(i)   which are used or made available for a consideration[27];

(ii)   except those in respect of which the person carrying on the business was entitled to credit[28] for the whole or any part of the input tax on their supply to him[29];

(iii) in respect of which any part of the tax on their supply to the person carrying on the business was not counted, by virtue of an apportionment[30], as being input tax[31]; or

(iv)   which are catering or accommodation services supplied by an employer[32] to his employees[33].

Nor do these deeming provisions apply to any supply of services consisting of the letting on hire of a motor car[34] where one half of the input tax on that letting on hire was excluded[35] from credit[36].

---

1   Thus the supply of any form of power, heat, refrigeration or ventilation is treated as a supply of goods: Value Added Tax Act 1994 s 5(1), Sch 4 para 3. See also Case C-393/92 *Municipality of Almelo v NV Energiebedrijf IJsselmij* [1994] ECR I–1477 at 1516, ECJ (electricity goods, not a service); and as to the taxation of domestic fuel supplies see para 6 ante. For the meaning of 'supply' see para 21 ante.

2   See eg the Value Added Tax Act 1994 Sch 4 para 5(1); and the text and note 8 infra.

3   There is no statutory definition of 'goods' for these purposes; but they are assumed to be restricted to tangible movable property. Supplies of intangible property and of choses in action, such as shares, copyright, patents and trademarks, will be supplies of services: see s 8(2), Sch 5 para 1, which assumes that transfers and assignments of such rights are supplies of services. See also EC Council Directive 77/388 (OJ L145, 13.6.77, p 1) art 6(1), which provides that assignments of intangible property are supplies of services. Supplies of land are separately dealt with by the Value Added Tax Act 1994 Sch 4 para 4: see the text to note 7 infra. The issue of, or dealing in, commercial paper is treated by the Commissioners of Customs and Excise as a supply of services: Customs and Excise Business Brief 11/91 [1991] STI 757. The provision of a telephone card enabling the purchaser to make telephone calls is a supply of services; even if the purchaser is only interested in collecting the card and not in using the units contained in the card, there is still a supply of services, not goods: what is important is the nature of the transaction and not the state of mind of the parties to the transaction: *Farrow v Customs and Excise*

Comrs (1993) VAT Decision 10612, [1993] STI 1188. If A is paid by B to supply goods to C, there is no supply of goods by A to B unless B (at least briefly) obtains a proprietary right in the goods supplied: *Customs and Excise Comrs v Sooner Foods Ltd* [1983] STC 376 at 380–381, ECJ; *British Airways plc v Customs and Excise Comrs* [1996] STC 1127. As to whether the supply of restaurant meals (in contrast to the supply of take-away food) is a supply of goods or services see Case C-231/94 *Faaborg-Gelting Linien A/S v Finanzamt Flensburg* [1996] All ER (EC) 656, [1996] STC 774, ECJ. Accordingly, B cannot claim an input tax deduction for the VAT charged on the supply. Cf the position with supplies of services: *P & O European Ferries (Dover) Ltd v Customs and Excise Comrs* [1992] VATTR 221; *Ibstock Building Products Ltd v Customs and Excise Comrs* [1987] VATTR 1. Consider also *Philips Exports Ltd v Customs and Excise Comrs* [1990] STC 508n (there can be a supply of goods by A to B where property is transferred from A to B and instantaneously is sold on to C by A as B's agent). There is no need for the legal title to property to pass for there to be a supply of goods: it is sufficient if the purchaser obtains the power to dispose of the goods as if he were owner: Case C-320/88 *Staatssecretaris van Financiën v Shipping and Forwarding Enterprise Safe BV* [1990] ECR I-285, [1991] STC 627, ECJ.

4   Value Added Tax Act 1994 Sch 4 para 1(1).

5   Ibid Sch 4 para 1(1)(a), (b).

6   Ibid Sch 4 para 1(2). See *Tas-Stage Ltd v Customs and Excise Comrs* [1988] STC 436.

7   Value Added Tax Act 1994 Sch 4 para 4. A 'major interest' in land means the fee simple or a tenancy for a term certain exceeding 21 years: s 96(1). This does not mean that land is treated as goods for the purposes of VAT but only that supplies of land are treated as supplies of goods: it is for this reason necessary in Sch 4 para 9 to make specific provision for the application of Sch 4 paras 5–8 (as amended) (see the text and notes 13–23 infra) to land. Schedule 4 paras 5–8 (as amended) have effect in relation to land forming part of the assets of, or held or used for the purposes of, a business as if it were goods forming part of those assets, or held or used for those purposes (Sch 4 para 9(1)); and in their application by virtue of this provision, references to transfer, disposition or sale have effect as references to the grant or assignment of any interest in, right over or licence to occupy the land concerned (Sch 4 para 9(2)). See also Sch 4 para 9(3); cited in note 8 infra. A 'time-share' grant of the right to occupy a holiday cottage for one specific week each year for 80 years did not amount to the grant of a major interest in land: *Cottage Holiday Associates Ltd v Customs and Excise Comrs* [1983] QB 735, [1983] STC 278.

8   Value Added Tax Act 1994 Sch 4 para 5(1). For an interesting case where the taxpayer was arguing for the application of Sch 4 para 5(1) (because the goods were magazines, whose supply would be zero-rated, enabling the partially exempt trader a greater input tax recovery rate) see *Post Office v Customs and Excise Comrs* (1996) VAT Decision 14075, [1996] STI 1215. In the case of a business carried on by an individual, the Value Added Tax Act 1994 Sch 4 para 5(1) applies to any transfer or disposition of goods in favour of himself personally: Sch 4 para 5(6)(a). Since a disposal which falls within Sch 4 para 5(1) must be at the direction of the trader, goods which are stolen are not the subject of a supply for VAT purposes. The value of the supply is determined by s 19(1), Sch 6 para 6 (see para 91 post); but if the parties are 'connected' and the recipient would be unable to recover all the VAT on the supply, the commissioners are entitled to direct that the supply be treated as having taken place at the open market value of the goods (see Sch 6 para 1; and para 87 post). Special rules apply to interests in land; in cases where Sch 4 para 5(1) applies to land forming part of the assets of a business, the supply is treated as one of services and not of goods unless the transaction involves either the grant or assignment of a major interest in land or a grant or assignment otherwise than for a consideration: Sch 4 para 9(3). It is the practice of the commissioners to treat agreements by developers and local authorities under the Town and Country Planning Act 1990 s 106 (as substituted) (see TOWN AND COUNTRY PLANNING vol 46 (Reissue) para 172) and with statutory undertakers to confer planning gain on the local authority, or to vest roads or sewers etc in the statutory undertaker, as outside the scope of VAT: see Customs and Excise Notice 742 *Land and Property* (1 December 1995) para 7.12. A similar approach is taken where a developer of a private housing estate vests the common areas in a management company for nominal monetary consideration: Customs and Excise Notice 742 para 7.14.

9   Value Added Tax Act 1994 Sch 4 para 5(6). As to the meaning of 'in the course or furtherance of a business' see paras 12 note 5, 17 note 2 ante.

10   Ie a gift of goods made in the course or furtherance of the business (otherwise than as one forming part of a series or succession of gifts made to the same person from time to time) where the cost to the donor is not more than £15: see ibid Sch 4 para 5(2)(a) (amended by the Finance Act 1996 s 33(1), (4) in relation to gifts made after 28 November 1995). The Treasury may by order substitute for the sum for the time being so specified such sum, not being less than £10, as it thinks fit: Value Added Tax Act 1994 Sch 5 para 5(7) (added by the Finance Act 1996 s 33(2)). As to the meaning of 'gift' in these circumstances see *GUS Merchandise Corpn Ltd v Customs and Excise Comrs* [1981] 1 WLR 1309, [1981] STC 569, CA (articles of low value, supplied by a mail order company as inducements to persons to become 'agents', otherwise than in circumstances demonstrating an absence of intention to create legal relations, were not gifts within what is now the Value Added Tax Act 1994 Sch 4 para 5(2)(a)) (as so

amended); Case C-33/93 *Empire Stores Ltd v Customs and Excise Comrs* [1994] 3 All ER 90, [1994] STC 623, ECJ (where inducements of low value were provided by a mail order company in return for persons introducing themselves or their friends to the company, the supplies were taxable transactions within EC Council Directive 77/388 art 5(6), the taxable amount of which was the price paid by the company for the articles given). As to the meaning of, and the determination of the value of, consideration for VAT purposes see para 86 et seq post. An exception is made for certain supplies of goods (and services: see the text to note 12 infra) made by an employer in favour of his employees, where the supplies consist in the provision (1) in the course of catering, of food or beverages; or (2) of accommodation in a hotel, inn, boarding house or similar establishment: see the Value Added Tax Act 1994 Sch 6 para 10; and para 93 post. See also *Goodfellow v Customs and Excise Comrs* [1986] VATTR 119 (hotel employees were engaged at the minimum rates of pay then permissible in the hotel sector, as determined by reference to a former Wages Council Order which specified a rate varied according to whether the employee was provided with board and lodgings; there was no agreement to provide the board and lodgings for a monetary consideration, so that the value of the supply was nil, in accordance with the Value Added Tax Act 1994 Sch 6 para 10).

11   Ibid Sch 4 para 5(2)(b). Where, however, a person is given a number of samples by the same person, whether all on one occasion or on different occasions, and those samples are identical or do not differ in any material respect from each other, the exception is available for one only or, as the case may be, the first to be given only: see Sch 4 para 5(3).

12   Ibid Sch 4 para 5(4), (6). This applies whether or not consideration is given: Sch 4 para 5(4) (amended by the Finance Act 1995 s 33(1), (3)(a)). The Value Added Tax Act 1994 Sch 4 para 5(4) (as so amended) applies to goods used, or made available for use, by himself personally: Sch 4 para 5(6)(b) (as so amended)). If the supply takes place otherwise than for consideration, it is treated as having a value equal to the full cost to the taxable person of providing the services: Sch 6 para 7(b) (amended by the Finance Act 1995 s 33(3)(b)). Where consideration is given, that consideration is used as the value of the supply unless the supply is between connected persons, when the Value Added Tax Act 1994 Sch 6 para 1 may apply: see note 8 supra. There is an exception for the provision of certain supplies of services by an employer to his employee: see note 10 supra. See also the Value Added Tax (Treatment of Transactions) Order 1992, SI 1992/630; and para 21 note 7 ante. There is substantial difficulty as to the interaction of the Value Added Tax Act 1994 Sch 4 para 5(4) and s 24(5): see para 201 note 13 post.

13   Ie under the Value Added Tax Act 1994 s 25 or s 26: see paras 202–203 post.

14   Ibid Sch 4 para 5(5). This accords with EC Council Directive 77/388 arts 5(7) (supplies of goods) and 6(2)(a) (supplies of services), which require non-business transactions in, and use of, goods to be treated as supplies for the purposes of VAT in cases where the VAT on the goods was wholly or partly recoverable by the taxable person. Accordingly, where a trader bought a second-hand car from a private individual (which was considered to carry with it residual VAT from its initial purchase in the second-hand sale price) and was, in accordance with the German turnover tax law, unable to recover the residual VAT, art 6(2)(a) precluded an output tax charge on the private use made by him of the car: Case 50/88 *Kühne v Finanzamt München III* [1989] ECR 1925, [1990] STC 749, ECJ.

15   See the Value Added Tax Act 1994 Sch 4 para 6; and para 15 ante. This provision has to be read in conjunction with the provisions relating to the place of supply of goods (s 7 (as amended): see paras 39–42 post) and those dealing with the acquisition of goods from another member state (ss 10, 11: see para 13 ante) and is concerned with the case where a trader, having claimed credit for input tax on the purchase of goods, subsequently takes them outside the scope of United Kingdom VAT law, by exporting the goods from the United Kingdom before their sale. A trader is only liable for United Kingdom VAT on supplies of goods or services made in the United Kingdom (see s 4; and para 12 ante); and would only pay tax on goods sold elsewhere in the EC if he were liable to VAT in the member state to which the goods were taken. This principle offers a potential method of avoiding VAT which is obviated by the provisions of Sch 4 para 6, which ensures that a taxable supply is made on removal. The value of the supply is determined by Sch 6 para 6: see para 91 post. Certain exceptions to the notional supply are made by the Value Added Tax (Removal of Goods) Order 1992, SI 1992/3111: see para 15 ante. By virtue of the Value Added Tax Act 1994.s 30(8) (see para 177 post), a removal of goods to another member state will be zero-rated provided that the commissioners are satisfied both that the goods have been removed from the United Kingdom and that they will have been the subject of a taxable acquisition in another member state by the exporter or another; the consequence is that no charge to VAT will be imposed on the trader removing goods to another part of the Community provided that corresponding VAT provisions will operate on him in the member state which is the destination of the goods. It should also be noted that the Value Added Tax Act 1994 does not provide for a notional supply where goods are removed to a place outside the EC because sales of goods which are to be exported from the Community are zero-rated: see further para 177 et seq post.

16   For the meaning of 'taxable person' see paras 12 note 4 ante, 55 post.

17 Value Added Tax Act 1994 Sch 4 para 7. The sale under a forced sale by a sheriff's officer or county court bailiff is thus deemed to be a supply made by the taxable person in the course or furtherance of his business. The provisions made by regulations under s 58, Sch 11 para 2 (see para 225 post) for cases where goods are treated as supplied by a taxable person by virtue of Sch 4 para 7 may require VAT chargeable on the supply to be accounted for and paid, and particulars of it to be provided, by such other person and in such manner as may be specified in the regulations: Sch 11 para 2(12). As to the information required by the commissioners from the person effecting the sale see the Value Added Tax Regulations 1995, SI 1995/2518, reg 27; and para 240 note 20 post.

18 Value Added Tax Act 1994 Sch 4 para 8(1)(a). The notional supply is treated as made not only when a person ceases trading but also when he deregisters. As to registration see para 56 et seq post. However, there is no notional supply of goods on a person deregistering on obtaining certification within the flat-rate scheme for farmers (see para 79 et seq post): see Sch 4 para 8(3). Sch 6 para 6 applies to determine the value of the notional supply under Sch 4 para 8: see note 8 supra. As to transfers of businesses as going concerns see para 196 post; and as to the termination and transfer of businesses see para 20 ante.

19 Value Added Tax Act 1994 Sch 4 para 8(1)(b). The regulations in question are made under s 46(4) which relates to persons who carry on a business of a taxable person who has died or become bankrupt or incapacitated: see para 70 post.

20 Ibid Sch 4 para 8(1)(c). The Treasury may by order increase or further increase the sum specified in Sch 4 para 8(1)(c): Sch 4 para 8(4). As to the making of orders generally see para 8 ante. At the date at which this volume states the law, no such order had been made.

21 For the meaning of 'input tax' see paras 4 ante, 201 post.

22 Ie in respect of the supply of the goods, their acquisition from another member state or their importation from a place outside a member state: Value Added Tax Act 1994 Sch 4 para 8(2)(a). As to credits for input tax see para 236 post.

23 Ie under the Finance Act 1973 s 4 (repealed) (relief for tax- or duty-paid stock at the commencement of VAT).

24 Value Added Tax Act 1994 Sch 4 para 8(2).

25 Ibid s 5(4). Such an order may provide for the method by which the value of any supply of services which is treated as taking place by virtue of the order is to be calculated: s 5(8). At the date at which this volume states the law, no such order had been made; but by virtue of the Interpretation Act 1978 s 17(2)(b), the Value Added Tax (Supply of Services) Order 1993, SI 1993/1507 (amended by SI 1995/1668), has effect as if so made. See the text and notes 26–36 infra.

26 Ibid art 3 (amended by SI 1995/1668). In the case of a business carried on by an individual, these provisions apply to services used, or made available for use, by himself personally: art 4. The value of the supply which a person is so treated as making is taken to be such part of the value of the supply of the services to him as fairly and reasonably represents the cost to him of providing the services: art 5. Where there is only minor or occasional non-business use of the services, the 1993 Order can be ignored; and in other cases the value of the supply can be calculated, if the taxpayer so wishes, by using his normal accounting convention for depreciating assets: see Customs and Excise Business Brief 17/94 [1994] STI 1156 at 1157. Nothing in the Value Added Tax (Supply of Services) Order 1993 is to be construed as making any person liable for any tax which, taken together with any tax for which he was liable as a result of a previous supply of the same services which he was treated as making by virtue thereof, would exceed the amount of input tax for which he was entitled to credit in respect of the services used, or made available for use, by him; and, where the tax chargeable would otherwise exceed the amount of that credit: (1) he is not to be treated as making a supply of the services where the amount of that credit has already been equalled or exceeded; and (2) in any other case, the value of the supply is to be reduced accordingly: art 7.

27 Ibid art 6(a).

28 Ie under the Value Added Tax Act 1994 ss 25, 26: see paras 202–203 post.

29 Value Added Tax (Supply of Services) Order 1993 art 6(b) (amended by SI 1995/1668).

30 Ie under the Value Added Tax Act 1994 s 24(5): see para 201 note 13 post.

31 Value Added Tax (Supply of Services) Order 1993 art 6(c) (amended by SI 1995/1688).

32 Ie the services fall within the Value Added Tax Act 1994 s 19(1), Sch 6 para 10: see note 10 supra; and para 93 post.

33 Value Added Tax Act (Supply of Services) Order 1993 art 6(d).

34 For these purposes, 'motor car' has the same meaning as in the Value Added Tax (Input Tax) Order 1992, SI 1992/3222, art 2 (see para 208 post): Value Added Tax (Supply of Services) Order 1993 art 6A(2) (added by SI 1995/1668).

35 Ie excluded from credit under the Value Added Tax Act 1994 s 5 by virtue of the Value Added Tax (Input Tax) Order 1992 art 7 (as amended): see para 208 post.

36 Value Added Tax (Supply of Services) Order 1993 art 6A(1) (added by SI 1995/1668).

25. Composite and separate supplies. When the goods or services provided under a contract consist of a number of different elements, it is a question of law[1], to be determined objectively[2], whether the supplier has made a single supply or a number of separate supplies. The distinction is only of significance where the different elements would, if separately supplied, be subject to value added tax at different rates[3]; where the transaction is treated as involving a composite supply the court is obliged to determine the liability of that supply to VAT[4]. The question to be asked in determining whether there has been a single suppply or several supplies has been identified as: 'was the supply of [the one item] incidental to, or an integral part of, the supply of the other?'[5].

1   British Railways Board v Customs and Excise Comrs [1977] 2 All ER 873 at 875–876, [1977] 1 WLR 588 at 591, CA, per Lord Denning MR and at 879 and 595 per Browne LJ (provision, against payment, of rail card, entitling holder to reduced price travel, was part of a single zero-rated supply of transport services); on a similar issue in relation to the purchase of discount cards to buy children's clothing at a reduced price see Mothercare (UK) Ltd v Customs and Excise Comrs [1993] VATTR 391. Nevertheless, it has also been admitted to be 'a matter of impression on which different minds might reach different conclusions': Card Protection Plan Ltd v Customs and Excise Comrs [1994] 1 CMLR 756, [1994] STC 199, CA.

2   See British Airways plc v Customs and Excise Comrs [1990] STC 643, CA (decision as to whether in-flight catering an integral part of zero-rated supply of transport to be made objectively).

3   Inevitably, one or other party will be seeking to establish that the whole, or part, of the supply is within the scope of zero-rating or an exemption. The general principle for VAT is that supplies of goods or services effected for consideration are to be subject to VAT and that any exemption given by EC Council Directive 77/388 (OJ L145, 13.6.77, p 1) art 13 is to be interpreted strictly: Case 348/87 Stichting Uitvoering Financiële Acties v Staatssecretaris van Financiën [1989] ECR 1737, [1991] 2 CMLR 429, ECJ. It would seem to follow, therefore, that general principles favour separation of supplies, at least in cases where the composite supply would otherwise be exempt or zero-rated (since that which would be standard-rated if supplied alone is thereby subsumed in a larger exempt transaction). For this reason, in Case 416/85 EC Commission v United Kingdom [1990] 2 QB 130, [1988] ECR 3127, ECJ, it was held that EC Council Directive 77/388 art 13(A)(1)(c) covered only the provision of medical care in the exercise of the medical and paramedical professions and that it excluded the supply of goods, as defined in art 5, without prejudice to minor provisions of goods which were indissociable from the service provided (so that the dispensing of spectacles in the course of the provision of the services of an ophthalmic optician could not be treated as exempt: see also Customs and Excise Comrs v Leightons Ltd, Customs and Excise Comrs v Eye-Tech Opticians (No 1) and Eye-Tech Opticians (No 2) [1995] STC 458 (the supply of the dispensing services of an optician was not integral to the standard-rated supply of spectacles)). The (otherwise taxable) letting of premises and sites for parking is not to be excepted from the exemption for the letting of immovable property in EC Council Directive 77/388 art 13(B)(b) where such lettings are 'closely linked to the letting of immovable property to be used for another purposes, such as residential or commercial property, which are themselves exempt from VAT': Case 173/88 Skatteministeriet v Henriksen [1989] ECR 2763, [1990] STC 768, ECJ. See also Customs and Excise Comrs v Wellington Private Hospital [1995] STC 628 (the supply of drugs and prostheses in connection with the treatment in hospital of a patient formed part of an exempt single composite supply of medical care within the Value Added Tax Act 1994 s 31(1), Sch 9 Pt II Group 7 item 4 (see para 151 post) and EC Council Directive 77/388 art 13(A)(1)(b)); and see Customs and Excise Business Brief 13/96 (July 1996) [1996] STI 1200 on composite supplies by hairdressing salons to individual stylists.

4   The issue of single or multiple supplies has been further considered in: Customs and Excise Comrs v Automobile Association [1974] 1 All ER 1257, [1974] 1 WLR 1447, DC (subscriptions to clubs entitling members to separate supplies of (1) benefit of membership (standard-rated); and (2) books and magazines (zero-rated)); Trewby v Customs and Excise Comrs [1976] 2 All ER 199, [1976] 1 WLR 932, DC (standard-rated membership of Hurlingham Club did not involve any separate exempt supply of an undivided share in land); Customs and Excise Comrs v Guy Butler (International) Ltd [1977] QB 377, [1976] 2 All ER 700, CA (supply of services by money broker of making arrangements for a loan against the issue of a certificate of deposit was a single supply notwithstanding that the broker received payment for its services from both parties); British Airports Authority v Customs and Excise Comrs [1977] 1 All ER 497, [1977] 1 WLR 302, CA (an agreement to permit a retailer to occupy a site at an airport did not also involve a separate supply of the right to sell from the site); Customs and Excise Comrs v Scott [1978] STC 191 (no separate zero-rated supply of feed (grass) when transaction was 'the entire transaction of keeping a horse'); Customs and Excise Comrs v Bushby [1979] STC 8 (no separate zero-rated supply of feed where taxpayers supplied stud

services to clients, notwithstanding an itemised bill); *Spigot Lodge Ltd v Customs and Excise Comrs* [1985] STC 255 (where S supplied service of training racehorses to R, who provided S with the feed for his own horse and others trained by S, and only charged for the feed supplied by S to others, there was no composite supply by S in respect of the training and feeding of R's horses).

5   *Customs and Excise Comrs v United Biscuits (UK) Ltd (t/a Simmers)* [1992] STC 325 (a decorative tin costing more than the biscuits it contained was an integral part of a zero-rated supply of biscuits); approved in *Card Protection Plan Ltd v Customs and Excise Comrs* [1994] 1 CMLR 756, [1994] STC 199, CA (a supply of insurance was an incidental part of a standard-rated supply of card registration services). By way of guidance it has been explained that a distinction will generally be drawn between a simple, single, transaction consisting of two or more elements (which will be treated as single composite transaction) and a big commercial contract involving the provision of goods and services of various kinds, where the contract is more likely to be treated as involving distinct supplies: *Bophuthatswana National Commercial Corpn Ltd v Customs and Excise Comrs* [1993] STC 702, CA; *Rayner & Keeler Ltd v Customs and Excise Comrs* [1994] STC 724. In addition, where it is impracticable to apportion the consideration between the various alleged separate supplies, this points against a finding of separate supplies: *British Airways plc v Customs and Excise Comrs* [1990] STC 643 at 648, CA, per Parker LJ; *Card Protection Plan Ltd v Customs and Excise Comrs* supra; *Virgin Atlantic Airways Ltd v Customs and Excise Comrs, Canadian Airlines International Ltd v Customs and Excise Comrs* [1995] STC 341 (the provision of a limousine service between the passenger's home in the United Kingdom and the airport was an integral part of a single zero-rated supply of international transport); *Customs and Excise Comrs v Leightons Ltd, Customs and Excise Comrs v Eye-Tech Opticians (No 1) and Eye-Tech Opticians (No 2)* [1995] STC 458 at 463.

26. Self-supply. The Treasury may make provision, by order[1], for securing[2] that where in such circumstances as may be specified in the order goods of a description so specified are taken possession of or produced by a person in the course or furtherance of a business[3] carried on by him and (1) are neither supplied to another person nor incorporated[4] in other goods produced in the course or furtherance of that business; but (2) are used by him for the purpose of a business carried on by him, the goods are treated for the purposes of the Value Added Tax Act 1994 as being both supplied to him for the purpose of that business and supplied by him in the course or furtherance of it[5].

Where a person in the course or furtherance of any business carried on by him produces printed matter[6] and that matter is not supplied to another person or incorporated in other goods produced in the course or furtherance of that business, but is used by him for the purpose of a business carried on by him, then the printed matter is treated for VAT purposes as both supplied to him for the purpose of that business and supplied by him in the course or furtherance of that business[7]. This rule does not, however, apply if:

(a)   the person is a fully taxable person[8];

(b)   the value of the supplies[9] falling to be treated as made by and to that person would not, if those were the only supplies made or to be made by that person, make him liable to be registered for VAT[10]; or

(c)   the Commissioners of Customs and Excise are satisfied that the VAT, if any, which would be attributable to the supplies after allowing for any credit for input tax[11] would be negligible and have given, and not withdrawn, a direction that the rule is not to apply[12].

The Treasury may also make provision, by order, for securing, with respect to services of any description specified in the order, that where (i) a person in the course or furtherance of a business carried on by him does anything for the purpose of that business which is not a supply of services but would, if done for a consideration[13], be a supply of services of a description specified in the order; and (ii) such other conditions as may be specified in the order are satisfied, the services are treated for the purposes of VAT as being both supplied to him for the purpose of that business and supplied by him in the course or furtherance of it[14].

The self-supply rules are designed to restrict the loss of VAT which would occur if a trader who would have been unable to recover (in whole or in part) the input tax on supplies made to him were able to produce the goods or supply the services from his own resources[15]. The effect of goods or services being treated as self-supplied is that the trader has to account to the Commissioners of Customs and Excise for the output tax[16] which is deemed to be incorporated in the notional consideration on the supply which he is treated as making. He is then treated as having incurred input tax on the same supply, which is also notionally received by him; and he may recover that input tax to the extent permitted by the rules generally applicable to him[17].

In order to prevent the fraudulent evasion of VAT, self-supply rules have been introduced in relation to supplies of gold. Where a taxable person makes a supply of gold[18] to a person who is himself a taxable person at the time when the supply is made and who is supplied in connection with the carrying on by him of any business, it is for the person supplied, on the supplier's behalf, to account for and pay tax on the supply, and not for the supplier[19].

Any motor car[20] which:

(A)   has been produced by a taxable person otherwise than by the conversion of a vehicle obtained by him;

(B)   has been produced by the taxable person by the conversion of another vehicle, whether a motor car or not, and in relation to which the statutory condition[21] is satisfied; or

(C)   was supplied to, or acquired from another member state[22] or imported by, a taxable person and in relation to which that condition is satisfied,

is treated as both supplied to the taxable person for the purposes of a business carried on by him and supplied by him for the purposes of that business, if that motor car has not been supplied by him in the course or furtherance of a business carried on by him and is not used by him exclusively for the purposes of such a business[23]. This provision does not, however, apply to any motor car which has been supplied to, or acquired from another member state or imported by, a taxable person primarily for the purpose of being provided by him for hire with the services of a driver for the purpose of carrying passengers, or for self-drive hire[24]. Nor does it apply to any motor car which has been supplied, acquired or imported by a taxable person primarily for the purpose of being used as a vehicle in which instruction in the driving of a motor car is to be given by him[25]. In such cases, where the motor car is neither supplied nor converted into another vehicle (whether a motor car or not) by the taxable person in the course or furtherance of any business carried on by him, and is used by him primarily for a purpose other than the purposes referred to above[26], but is not used exclusively for the purposes of a business carried on by him, it is treated as both supplied to him for the purposes of that business and supplied by him in the course or furtherance of that business[27].

1   As to the making of orders generally see para 8 ante.

2   Ie subject to any exceptions provided for by or under the order: Value Added Tax Act 1994 s 5(5).

3   As to the meaning of 'in the course or furtherance of a business' see paras 12 note 5, 17 note 2 ante.

4   Where goods are manufactured or produced from any other goods, those other goods are treated as incorporated in the first-mentioned goods for these purposes: Value Added Tax Act 1994 s 5(7).

5   Ibid s 5(5). In exercise of the power so conferred, the Treasury has made (1) the Value Added Tax (Special Provisions) Order 1995, SI 1995/1268, art 11 (see the text and notes 6–12 infra); (2) the Value Added Tax (Cars) (Amendment) Order 1995, SI 1995/1269; and the Value Added Tax (Cars) (Amendment) (No 2) Order 1995, SI 1995/1667 (see notes 21–26 infra). In addition, by virtue of the Interpretation Act 1978 s 17(2)(b), the Value Added Tax (Cars) Order 1992, SI 1992/3122 (amended by SI 1995/1269; SI 1995/1667) has effect as if so made: see the text and notes 20–27 infra).

6   For these purposes, 'printed matter' includes printed stationery but does not include anything produced by duplicating or photocopying: Value Added Tax (Special Provisions) Order 1995 art 2.

7   Ibid art 11(1). Where printed matter is destroyed before being used for the purposes of the business there is no self-supply: *Nationwide Building Society v Customs and Excise Comrs* [1993] VATTR 205. The deemed self-supply need not take place at the standard rate; so that a self-supply of advertising stationery by a

charity may be zero-rated by the Value Added Tax Act 1994 s 30(2), Sch 8 Pt II Group 15 item 8 (see para 173 post): *Royal Society for the Encouragement of Arts, Manufacture and Commerce v Customs and Excise Comrs* (1996) VAT Decision 14007, [1996] STI 964.

8 A person is a fully taxable person for these purposes if the only input tax of his to which he is not entitled to credit at the end of any prescribed accounting period or longer period is input tax which is excluded from credit under the Value Added Tax Act 1994 s 25 (see para 202 post) by virtue of any order made under s 25(7): Value Added Tax (Special Provisions) Order 1995 art 11(3). For the meaning of 'input tax' see paras 4 ante, 201 post; for the meaning of 'prescribed accounting period' see para 202 note 4 post; and for the meaning of 'taxable person' generally see paras 12 note 4, 55 ante.

9 For the meaning of 'supply' see para 21 ante.

10 Ie pursuant to the provisions of the Value Added Tax Act 1994 s 3(2), Sch 1 (as amended): see para 56 et seq post.

11 Ie under ibid s 25 or s 26: see paras 202–203 post.

12 Value Added Tax (Special Provisions) Order 1995 art 11(2). Article 11 applies in relation to any bodies corporate which are treated for the purposes of the Value Added Tax Act 1994 s 43 (as amended) as members of a group as if those bodies were one person, but any printed matter which would fall to be treated as supplied to and by that person are to be treated as supplied to and by the representative member: art 11(4).

13 For the meaning of 'consideration' generally see para 86 post. The value of the self-supply of goods is determined by the Value Added Tax Act 1994 s 19(1), Sch 6 para 6: see paras 24 note 8 ante, 91 post.

14 Ibid s 5(6). An order made under s 5(6) may provide for the method by which the value of any supply of services which is treated as taking place by virtue of the order is to be calculated: s 5(8). At the date at which this volume states the law, no such order had been made, but, by virtue of the Interpretation Act 1978 s 17(2)(b), the Value Added Tax (Self-supply of Construction Services) Order 1989, SI 1989/472 (which brings within the tax certain self-supplies of construction services by builders, made in the course or furtherance of the business and for the purposes of that business, where the value of the services is not less than £100,000), has effect as if so made. The value of the self-supply is to be taken as the open market value of the services: art 4(1).

15 As to the rules determining the right to claim credit for input tax see para 203 et seq post. In essence, a trader who makes exempt supplies is unable to recover the input tax on supplies made to him for the purpose of those supplies. In addition, special rules exist which disentitle, in whole or in part, the majority of traders from recovering input tax on the purchase or leasing of cars: see para 208 post.

16 For the meaning of 'output tax' see paras 4 ante, 201 post.

17 See para 203 et seq post.

18 For these purposes, references to a supply of gold are references to (1) any supply of goods consisting in fine gold, in gold grain of any purity or in gold coins of any purity; or (2) any supply of goods containing gold where the consideration for the supply (apart from any VAT) is, or is equivalent to, an amount which does not exceed, or exceeds by no more than a negligible amount, the open market value of the gold contained in the goods; or (3) any supply of services consisting in the application to another person's goods of a treatment or process which produces goods a supply of which would fall within head (1) supra: Value Added Tax Act 1994 s 55(5) (amended by the Finance Act 1996 ss 29(3), 32(1), (2), 205(1), Sch 41 Pt IV). The Treasury may by order provide for the Value Added Tax Act 1994 s 55 (as so amended) to apply, as it applies to the supplies so specified, to such other supplies of goods consisting in or containing any precious or semi-precious metal or stones, or services relating to, or to anything containing, any precious or semi-precious metal or stones, as may be specified in the order: s 55(6). At the date at which this volume states the law, no such order had been made.

19 Ibid s 55(2). So much of the Value Added Tax Act 1994 and of any other enactment or any subordinate legislation as has effect for the purposes of, or in connection with, the enforcement of any obligation to account for and pay VAT applies for these purposes in relation to any person who is required under s 55(2) to account for and pay any VAT as if that VAT were VAT on a supply made by him: s 55(3).

20 For the meaning of 'motor car' see para 23 note 2 ante.

21 Ie the condition set out in the Value Added Tax (Cars) Order 1992 art 5(2) (substituted by SI 1995/1667). That condition is that the tax on the supply to, or acquisition or importation by, the taxable person of the motor car or the vehicle from which it was converted, was not wholly excluded from credit under the Value Added Tax Act 1994 s 25 (see para 202 post): Value Added Tax (Cars) Order 1992 art 5(2) (as so substituted).

22 For the meaning of 'another member state' see para 4 note 14 ante.

23 Value Added Tax (Cars) Order 1992 art 5(1), (3) (substituted by SI 1995/1667). In determining for these purpose whether a car is used exclusively for the purposes of a business, the Value Added Tax (Input Tax) Order 1992, SI 1992/3222, art 7 (as amended) (see para 208 post) applies as it would apply for the purpose of determining whether he so intended to use it: Value Added Tax (Cars) Order 1992 art 6A (added by SI 1995/1667). Articles 5, 6 (as so substituted) apply in relation to any bodies corporate which are treated

for the purposes of the Value Added Tax Act 1994 s 43 (as amended) (see paras 66, 191 post) as members of a group as if those bodies were one person, but any motor car which would fall to be treated as supplied to and by that person is treated as supplied to and by the representative member: Value Added Tax (Cars) Order 1992 art 7 (amended by SI 1995/1269). The Value Added Tax Act 1994 s 5(1), Sch 4 para 5(4) (see para 24 ante) does not apply in relation to a motor car to which either the Value Added Tax (Cars) Order 1992 art 5 (as substituted) or art 6 (as substituted) applies which is used or made available in circumstances where it would otherwise be treated as supplied to and by a taxable person: art 4A (added by SI 1995/1667). For the meaning of 'the representative member' see para 66 post.

24   Ibid arts 5(1), 6(1)(a), (b) (substituted by SI 1995/1667). For these purposes, 'self-drive hire' means hire where the hirer is the person normally expected to drive the motor car and the period of hire to each hirer, together with the period of hire of any other motor car expected to be hired to him by the taxable person, will normally be less than 30 consecutive days, and less than 90 days in any period of 12 months: art 6(2).
25   Ibid arts 5(1), 6(1)(c) (as substituted: see note 24 supra).
26   Ie the purposes described in ibid art 6(1)(a)–(c) (as substituted: see note 24 supra): art 6(1A)(b) (added by SI 1995/1667).
27   Ibid art 6(1A) (as added: see note 26 supra).

27. The reverse charge. Where relevant services[1] are supplied by a person who belongs in a country other than the United Kingdom[2] and received by a person ('the recipient') who belongs in the United Kingdom[3] for the purposes of any business[4] carried on by him, then all the same consequences for value added tax[5] are to follow as if the recipient had himself supplied the services in the United Kingdom in the course or furtherance of his business[6] and that supply were a taxable supply[7]. Supplies which are so treated as made by the recipient are not, however, to be taken into account as supplies made by him when determining any allowance of input tax[8] in his case[9].

1   'Relevant services' means services of a description specified in the Value Added Tax Act 1994 s 8(2), Sch 5, not being services within any of the descriptions specified in s 31(1), Sch 9 (as amended) (exemptions: see para 141 et seq post): s 8(2). The list of relevant services is as follows: (1) transfers and assignments of copyright, patents, licences, trademarks and similar rights; (2) advertising services; (3) services of consultants, engineers, consultancy bureaux, lawyers, accountants and other similar services; data processing and provision of information (but excluding from this head any services relating to land); (4) acceptance of any obligation to refrain from pursuing or exercising, in whole or part, any business activity or any such rights as are referred to in head (1) supra; (5) banking, financial and insurance services (including reinsurance, but not including the provision of safe deposit facilities); (6) the supply of staff; (7) the letting on hire of goods other than means of transport; and (8) the services rendered by one person to another in procuring for the other any of the services mentioned in heads (1)–(7) supra: Sch 5 paras 1–8. Any services not of such a specified description are also included, when supplied to a recipient registered under the Value Added Tax Act 1994: Sch 5 para 9. See also note 3 infra. The Treasury may by order add to, or vary, Sch 5; and this power includes power, where any services whose place of supply is determined by an order under s 7(11) (see para 39 post) are added thereto, to provide that s 8(1) is to have effect in relation to those services as if a person belongs in the United Kingdom for the purposes of s 8(1)(b) if, and only if, he is a taxable person: s 8(5), (6). For the meaning of 'registered' see para 12 note 4 ante; and for the meaning of 'taxable person' see paras 12 note 4 ante, 55 post.
2   For the meaning of 'United Kingdom' see para 4 note 3 ante.
3   The rules determining where the supplier or recipient of services belongs are to be found in the Value Added Tax Act 1994 s 9: see paras 46–54 post. Section 8(1) has effect in relation to any services which are of a description specified in Sch 5 para 9 (see note 1 supra) and whose place of supply is determined by an order under s 7(11) (see para 39 post) to be in the United Kingdom, as if the recipient belonged in the United Kingdom for the purposes of s 8(1)(b): Sch 5 para 10.
4   For the meaning of 'business' see para 17 ante.
5   Ie and in particular, so much as charges VAT on a supply and entitles a taxable person to credit for input tax: Value Added Tax Act 1994 s 8(1). For the meaning of 'supply' see para 21 ante; and for the meaning of 'input tax' see paras 4 ante, 201 post.
6   For the meaning of 'in the course or furtherance of a business' see paras 12 note 5, 17 note 2 ante.
7   Value Added Tax Act 1994 s 8(1). Section 8 is designed to prevent partially-exempt traders (see para 203 et seq post) circumventing the limitation on their recovery of input tax by buying in VAT-free services from abroad. The particular concern with relevant services is that such services are treated as supplied where they are received (see EC Council Directive 77/388 (OJ L145, 13.6.77, p 1) art 9(2)(e)) and will

therefore not be charged to tax in the member state where the supplier of the service belongs. Article 21(1)(b) enables member states to recover the VAT on a reverse charge not only from the recipient of the supply but also from the supplier. The United Kingdom has not availed itself of this right.

In applying the Value Added Tax Act 1994 s 8(1), the supply of services treated as made by the recipient is assumed to have been made at a time to be determined in accordance with regulations prescribing rules for attributing a time of supply in cases within that provision: s 8(4). Services which are treated as made by a taxable person under s 8(1) are treated as being supplied when the supplies are paid for or, if the consideration is not in money, on the last day of the prescribed accounting period in which the services are performed: Value Added Tax Regulations 1995, SI 1995/2518, reg 82. They must therefore be included in the trader's VAT return for that period. For the meaning of 'prescribed accounting period' see para 105 note 16 post.

Where the services are supplied for a consideration in money, the value of the supply is taken to be such amount as is equal to that consideration; where the consideration does not consist wholly in money, the value of the supply is treated as such amount in money as is equal to that consideration: Sch 6 para 8. The consequence is that the price actually paid by the trader for the performance of the services is deemed to be exclusive of VAT. Thus, if the trader pays £1,000 for foreign legal advice, he must bring £175 into his next VAT return as output tax (though he may, correspondingly, be entitled to credit for a like amount in the same return as input tax). This may be contrasted with the general rule, in s 19(2), that the value of a supply is to be taken be such amount as, with the addition of the VAT chargeable, is equal to the consideration: see para 85 post. For the meaning of 'money' see para 7 note 5 ante.

8   Ie under ibid s 26(1): see para 203 post.
9   Ibid s 8(2).

28. The developer's self-supply charge. Until 1 March 1995, complex rules existed to ensure that persons who constructed or enlarged certain buildings or civil engineering works, which were to be used otherwise than for the purposes of a fully-taxable business, were able to recover the input tax incurred in the course of construction but were obliged to account for value added tax on using or going into occupation of the building or work or on making an exempt grant of an interest in the building or work[1]. These rules were abolished with effect from that date[2]; but transitional provisions exist in relation to buildings and works where construction commenced prior to that date. Those transitional provisions are set out below; in each case, it is predicated that a person (a 'developer'[3]) has procured the construction[4] of a building or civil engineering work of a description to which the provisions apply[5].

On the first occasion during the period beginning with the day when the construction of such a building or work is first planned and ending ten years after its completion on which the developer grants an interest in, right over or licence to occupy the building or work (or any part of it) which is an exempt supply[6], or is in occupation of the building or uses the work (or any part of it) when not a fully-taxable person[7], that interest, right or licence held by the developer is treated[8] as supplied to the developer for the purpose of a business carried on by him and supplied by him in the course or furtherance of the business[9] on the last day of the prescribed accounting period during which it applies or, if later, of the prescribed accounting period during which the building or work becomes substantially ready for occupation or use[10]. The supply so treated as made is taken to be a taxable supply[11]; but no charge occurs if the relevant grant is made before construction is planned[12]. In order to secure the final abolition of the developer's self-supply charge, it is provided that where a building or civil engineering work is within the scope of the provisions but there has been no relevant grant by 1 March 1997 and the ten-year period has not then expired, the occurrence of that date will itself be a triggering event for the purposes of that charge[13].

Where a developer is a tenant, lessee or licensee and becomes liable to a charge to VAT under these provisions[14] in respect of his tenancy, lease or licence he must forthwith notify his landlord, lessor or licensor of the date from which the tenancy, lease or licence becomes a developmental tenancy, developmental lease or developmental licence[15] for the purposes of the provisions relating to exempt supplies of land[16].

1   See the Value Added Tax Act 1994 s 51, Sch 10 paras 5, 6 (as originally enacted).

2   See the Value Added Tax (Buildings and Land) Order 1995, SI 1995/279, arts 2, 6, 7.

3   For these purposes 'developer', in relation to a building or work, means a person who (1) constructs it; (2) orders it to be constructed; or (3) finances its construction, with a view to granting an interest in, right over or licence to occupy it, or any part of it, or to occupying or using it, or any part of it, for his own purposes: Value Added Tax Act 1994 Sch 10 para 5(5). On a strict construction of Sch 10 (as amended), therefore, a person does not cease to be a developer simply because he grants a lease which is a taxable supply. However, the validity of these provisions has been called into question by the decision in *Robert Gordon's College v Customs and Excise Comrs* [1996] 1 WLR 201, [1995] STC 1093, HL, in which it was held that the domestic legislation relating to the developer's self-supply charge failed properly to implement the relevant provisions of EC Council Directive 77/388 (OJ L145, 13.6.77, p 1) (ie arts 5(7)(a), 6(3)), in making provision for a self-supply charge in circumstances where the developer had granted a lease to another and then occupied the property under the terms of a licence from that person. Where a body corporate treated under the Value Added Tax Act 1994 s 43 (as amended) (see paras 66, 191 post) as a member of a group is a developer in relation to a building or work, and it grants an interest in, right over or licence to occupy the building or work, or any part of it, to another body corporate which is so treated as a member of the group, then for these purposes, the following are treated, as from the time of the grant, as also being a developer in relation to the building or work, ie any body corporate which (a) was treated as a member of the same group as the body corporate making the grant at the time of the grant; or (b) has been so treated at any later time when the body corporate by which the grant was made had an interest in, right over or licence to occupy the building or work, or any part of it; or (c) has been treated as a member of the same group as a body corporate within head (a) or (b) supra, or this head, at a time when that body corporate has an interest in, right over or licence to occupy the building or work, or any part of it: Sch 10 para 5(6), (7). This provision prevents the avoidance of the rules by the simple device of granting an interest by means not involving a supply for VAT purposes: see para 191 post.

    For the meaning of 'grant' see para 142 note 2 post (definition applied by Sch 10 para 9 (amended by the Value Added Tax (Buildings and Land) Order 1995 arts 2, 9). Where the benefit of the consideration for the grant of an interest in, right over or licence to occupy land accrues to a person but that person is not the person making the grant, the person to whom the benefit accrues is treated for the purposes of the Value Added Tax Act 1994 as the person making the grant, and to the extent that any input tax of the person actually making the grant is attributable to the grant it is treated as input tax of the person to whom the benefit accrues: Sch 10 para 8(1) (prospectively renumbered by the Finance Act 1995 s 26(2) as from a day to be appointed under s 26(3)). Where the consideration for the grant of an interest in, right over or licence to occupy land is such that its provision is enforceable primarily by the person who, as owner of an interest in or right in or over that land, actually made the grant, or by another person in his capacity as the owner for the time being of that interest or right or of any other interest or right in or over that land, that person, and not any person (other than that person) to whom a benefit accrues by virtue of his being a beneficiary under a trust relating to the land, or the proceeds of sale of any land, is taken for these purposes to be the person to whom the benefit of the consideration accrues: Value Added Tax Act 1994 Sch 10 para 8(2) (prospectively added by the Finance Act 1995 s 26(2)). This provision does not, however, apply to the extent that the Commissioners of Customs and Excise, on an application made in the prescribed manner jointly by (i) the person who would otherwise be taken thereunder to be the person to whom the benefit of the consideration accrues; and (ii) all the persons for the time being in existence who, as beneficiaries under such a trust as is mentioned therein, are persons who have or may become entitled to, or to a share of, the consideration, or for whose benefit any of it is to be or may be applied, may direct that the benefit of the consideration is to be treated for these purposes as a benefit accruing to the persons falling within head (ii) supra and not, unless he also falls within that head, to the person falling within head (i) supra: Value Added Tax Act 1994 Sch 10 para 8(3) (as so added).

4   The developer's self-supply charge (ie ibid Sch 10 para 5(1), (2), (3A)–(7) (as amended)) also applies in relation to any of the following reconstructions, enlargements or extensions:

    (1) a reconstruction, enlargement or extension of an existing building which is commenced on or after 1 January 1992 and before 1 March 1995 and (a) which is carried out wholly or partly on land ('new land') adjoining the curtilage of the existing building; or (b) as a result of which the gross external floor area of the reconstructed, enlarged or extended building, excluding any floor area on new building land, exceeds the gross external floor area of the existing building by not less than 20% of the gross external floor area of the existing building;

    (2) a reconstruction of an existing building which is commenced within that period and in the course of which at least 80% of the area of the floor structures of the existing building is removed;

    (3) a reconstruction, enlargement or extension of a civil engineering work which is commenced within that period and which is carried out wholly or partly on land ('new land') adjoining the land on or in which the existing work is situated,

as if references to the building or work were references to the reconstructed, enlarged or extended building or work and as if references to construction were references to reconstruction, enlargement or extension: Sch 10 para 5(8) (amended by the Value Added Tax (Buildings and Land) Order 1995 arts 2, 6). For the purposes of head (1) supra, extensions to an existing building include the provision of any annex having internal access to the existing building: Sch 10 para 5(9). The developer's self-supply charge does not, however, apply to a reconstruction, enlargement or extension falling within heads (1) or (3) supra where the developer has held an interest in at least 75% of all the land on which the reconstructed, enlarged or extended building or work stands, or is constructed, throughout the period of ten years ending with the last day of the prescribed accounting period during which that building or work becomes substantially ready for occupation or use: Sch 10 para 5(10)(a) (as so amended). Nor does it apply to a reconstruction, enlargement or extension (i) to the extent that it results in such an enlargement of the gross external floor area as is mentioned in head (1) supra; or (ii) falling within head (2) supra, where (in either case) the interest in, right over or licence to occupy the building concerned, or any part of it, has already been treated as supplied to and by the developer under Sch 10 para 6(1) (see the text and notes 8–10 infra): Sch 10 para 5(10)(b) (as so amended).

5 The provisions apply to: (1) any building neither designed as a dwelling or number of dwellings nor intended for use solely for a relevant residential or a relevant charitable purpose; (2) any civil engineering work other than a work necessary for the development of a permanent park for residential caravans, provided in each case that construction of it was commenced after 1 August 1989 and before 1 March 1995 and that no grant of the fee simple in it falling within s 31(1), Sch 9 Pt II Group 1 item 1(a)(ii) or (iv) (see para 142 post) has been made before the occasion concerned: see Sch 10 para 5(2), (3) (amended by the Value Added Tax (Buildings and Land) Order 1995 arts 2, 6). A building or work to which these provisions would otherwise apply does not, however, fall within them if (i) construction of it was commenced before 1 March 1995 but had not been completed by that date; and (ii) the developer makes no claim after that date to credit due for input tax, entitlement to which is dependent upon his being treated in due course as having made a supply by virtue of the Value Added Tax Act 1994 Sch 10 para 6 (as amended), and either he has made no such claim prior to that date or he accounts to the commissioners for a sum equal to any such credit that has previously been claimed: Sch 10 para 5(3A) (added by the Value Added Tax (Buildings and Land) Order 1995 arts 2, 6). For the meaning of 'designed as a dwelling', 'relevant residential purpose' and 'relevant charitable purpose' see para 163 notes 8–10 post (definitions applied by Sch 10 para 9 (as amended: see note 3 supra)); for the meaning of 'construction' see para 163 note 6 post (definition as so applied); and for the meaning of 'input tax' see paras 4 ante, 201 post. As to when a building or work is completed see para 142 note 6 post (definition as so applied).

6 For the meaning of 'exempt supply' see para 141 post.

7 Value Added Tax Act 1994 Sch 10 para 5(1)(a) (substituted by the Value Added Tax (Buildings and Land) Order 1995 arts 2, 6). For these purposes, a taxable person is treated as a fully-taxable person in any prescribed accounting period if either (1) at the end of that period he is entitled to credit for input tax on all supplies to, and acquisitions and importations by, him in the period (apart from any on which input tax is excluded from credit by virtue of the Value Added Tax Act 1994 s 25(7) (see paras 204–208 post); or (2) he does not use the building or work at any time during the period in, or in connection with, making any exempt supplies of goods or services: Sch 10 para 5(4) (amended by the Value Added Tax (Buildings and Land) Order 1995 arts 2, 6). For the meaning of 'taxable person' see paras 12 note 4 ante, 55 post; and for the meaning of 'prescribed accounting period' see para 202 note 4 post.

8 Ie for the purposes of the Value Added Tax Act 1994: Sch 10 para 6(1).

9 As to the meaning of 'in the course or furtherance of a business' see paras 12 note 5, 17 note 2 ante.

10 Value Added Tax Act 1994 Sch 10 para 6(1).

11 Ibid Sch 10 para 6(2). However, if the value of the self-supply proves to be less than £100,000, there is deemed to have been no such supply: see Sch 10 para 6(5). The value of the supply is the aggregate of (1) the value of grants relating to the land on which the building or work is constructed made, or to be made, to the developer, but excluding, in a case where construction commenced before 1 January 1992, the value of any grants to be made for consideration in the form of rent the amount of which cannot be ascertained by the developer when the supply is treated as made, and in any other case excluding the value of any grants made before the relevant day (a) to the extent that consideration for such grants was in the form of rent, and to the extent that such rent was properly attributable to a building which has been demolished; (b) in respect of a building which has been reconstructed, enlarged or extended so that the reconstruction, enlargement or extension falls within Sch 10 para 5(8)(a)(ii) (see note 4 head (1)(b) supra), and does not fall also within Sch 10 para 5(8)(b) (as amended) (see note 4 head (2) supra), to the extent that consideration for such grants was in the form of rent, and to the extent that such rent was properly attributable to the building as it existed before the commencement of the reconstruction, enlargement or extension; (c) in respect of a building which has been so reconstructed that the reconstruction falls within Sch 10 para 5(8)(b) (as amended) , to the extent that consideration for such grants was in the form of rent, and to the extent that such rent was properly attributable to the building before the reconstruction

commenced; and also excluding the value of any grants falling within Sch 9 Pt II Group 1 item 1(b) (see para 142 post); (2) the value of all the taxable supplies of goods and services, other than any that are zero-rated, made or to be made for or in connection with the construction of the building or work: Sch 10 para 6(2). For the purposes of head (1)(a) supra, 'the relevant day' is the day on which the demolition of the building in question commenced; and for the purposes of heads (1)(b), (c) supra, 'the relevant day' is the day on which the reconstruction, enlargement or extension in question commenced: Sch 10 para 6(6). For the commissioners' explanation of the valuation rules see Customs and Excise Notice 742 *Land and Property* (1 December 1995) Appendix B. As to self-supplies of construction services see para 26 note 14 ante. For the meaning of 'taxable supply' see para 12 note 3 ante.

Where the rate of VAT ('the lower rate') chargeable on a supply ('the construction supply') falling within head (2) supra, the value of which is included in the value of a supply ('the self-supply') treated as made by Sch 10 para 6(1) is lower than the rate of VAT ('the current rate') chargeable on that self-supply, then VAT on the self-supply is charged at the lower rate on so much of its value as is comprised of the relevant part of the value of the construction supply and at the current rate on the remainder of its value: Sch 10 para 6(3). 'The relevant part of the value of the construction supply' means (i) where the construction supply is a supply of goods, the value of such of those goods as have actually been delivered by the supplier; (ii) where the construction supply is a supply of services, the value of such of those services as have actually been performed by the supplier, on or before the last day upon which the lower rate is in force: Sch 10 para 6(4).

In the application of Sch 10 para 6(1)–(6) (as amended) to a reconstruction, enlargement or extension to which Sch 10 para 5(1), (2), (3A)–(7) (as amended) applies by virtue of Sch 10 para 5(8) (as amended) (see note 4 supra), references to the building or work are to be construed as references to the reconstructed, enlarged or extended building or work and references to construction are to be construed as references to reconstruction, enlargement or extension: Sch 10 para 6(7)(a) (amended by the Value Added Tax (Buildings and Land) Order 1995 arts 2, 7(a)). Furthermore, the reference in head (1)(a) supra to the value of grants relating to the land on which the building or work is constructed is to be construed as a reference, in relation to a reconstruction, enlargement or extension (A) of an existing building to the extent that it falls within the Value Added Tax Act 1994 Sch 10 para 5(8)(a)(i) (see note 4 head (1)(a) supra) and does not fall also within Sch 10 para 5(8)(b) (as amended) (see note 4 head (2) supra), to the value of grants relating to the new building land; (B) of an existing building to the extent that it falls within Sch 10 para 5(8)(a)(ii) (see note 4 head (1)(b) supra) and does not fall also Sch 10 para 5(8)(b) (as amended), to the value of grants relating to the land on which the existing building stands multiplied by the appropriate fraction; (C) to a work falling within Sch 10 para 5(8)(c) (as amended) (see note 4 head (3) supra), to the value of grants relating to new land: Sch 10 para 6(7)(b). The 'appropriate fraction' is calculated by dividing the additional gross external floor area resulting from the reconstruction, enlargement or extension, excluding any floor area on new building land, by the gross external floor area of the reconstructed, enlarged or extended building, excluding any floor area on new building land: Sch 10 para 6(8). As to what is an existing building see para 163 note 6 post (applied by virtue of Sch 10 para 9 (as amended: see note 3 supra)).

12   See ibid Sch 10 para 5(1) (as substituted); and the text and notes 6–7 supra.

13   See ibid Sch 10 para 5(1)(b) (as substituted: see note 7 supra). Where Sch 10 para 6 (as amended) applied by virtue of Sch 10 para 5(1)(b) (as so substituted), it has effect as if (1) in Sch 10 para 6(1) the words '(or any part of it)' were omitted and for the words 'the last day' to 'ready for occupation or use' there were substituted '1 March 1997'; (2) in Sch 10 para 6(2)(a) the words 'or to be made' and the words 'to be made' were omitted; (3) in Sch 10 para 6(2)(b) the words 'or to be made' were omitted; and (4) Sch 10 para 6(5) were omitted: Sch 10 para 6(9) (added by the Value Added Tax (Buildings and Land) Order 1995 arts 2, 7(b)).

14   Ie under the Value Added Tax Act 1994 Sch 10 para 6(1), except where that provision applies by virtue of Sch 10 para 5(1)(b) (as substituted: see note 7 supra): Sch 10 para 7(1) (amended by the Value Added Tax (Buildings and Land) Order 1995 art 8).

15   Ie for the purposes of the Value Added Tax Act 1994 s 31(1), Sch 9 Pt II Group 1 item 1(b): see para 142 post.

16   Ibid Sch 10 para 7(1)(a). In a case falling within Sch 10 para 5(8)(a)(ii) (see note 4 head (1)(b) supra), he must also give such notification of the appropriate fraction determined in accordance with Sch 10 para 6(8) (see note 11 supra): Sch 10 para 7(1)(b). Where the appropriate fraction has been so notified, any supply made pursuant to the tenancy, lease or licence in question is treated as made pursuant to a developmental tenancy, developmental lease or developmental licence (a 'developmental supply') as if, and only to the extent that, the consideration for the developmental supply is for an amount equal to the whole of the consideration for the supply made pursuant to the tenancy, lease or licence, multiplied by the appropriate fraction: Sch 10 para 7(2).

(ii) Time of Supply or Acquisition

A. IN GENERAL

29. The general rules. In relation to goods the general rule is that a supply[1] is treated as taking place for the purposes of the charge to value added tax[2] (1) if the goods are to be removed, at the time of the removal[3]; (2) if the goods are not to be removed, at the time when they are made available to the person to whom they are supplied[4]; and (3) if the goods (having been sent or taken on approval or sale or return or similar terms) are removed before it is known whether a supply will take place, at the time when it becomes certain that the supply has taken place, or, if sooner, 12 months after the removal[5].

In the case of services, the general rule is that a supply is treated as taking place at the time when the services are performed[6].

If, before the time applicable under the general rules[7], the person making the supply issues a VAT invoice[8] in respect of it or if, before the time applicable under head (1) or head (2) above or the time applicable under the general rule in relation to services, he receives a payment in respect of it, the supply is, to the extent covered by the invoice or payment, treated as taking place at the time the invoice is issued or the payment is received[9]. Furthermore if, within 14 days[10] after the time applicable under the general rules, the person making the supply issues a VAT invoice in respect of it, then unless he has notified the Commissioners of Customs and Excise in writing that he elects otherwise, the supply is (to the extent that it is not treated as taking place at an earlier date by virtue of the issue of a VAT invoice prior to, or by virtue of payment before, the time applicable under the general rule[11]) treated as taking place at the time the invoice is issued[12].

The commissioners may, at the request of a taxable person, by direction alter the time at which supplies made by him, or such supplies made by him as may be specified in the direction, are to be treated as taking place[13].

1　For the meaning of 'supply' see para 21 ante.

2　As to the charge to tax see para 12 et seq ante; and as to the rate of charge see paras 5–6 ante.

3　Value Added Tax Act 1994 s 6(1), (2)(a). The Commissioners of Customs and Excise generally refer to the time of supply as the 'tax point'. By concession, the commissioners permit operators of coin-operated machines to delay accounting for VAT until the coins are removed from the machines, notwithstanding that the tax point is, technically, the moment when the machine is used: Customs and Excise Notice 748 *Extra-statutory Concessions* (1 August 1995) concession 12.

4　Value Added Tax Act 1994 s 6(1), (2)(b).

5　Ibid s 6(1), (2)(c). The provisions of s 6 (as amended) apply subject to s 18 (as amended) (see paras 130–132 post), ss 18B, 18C (as added) (see paras 134, 140 post): s 6(1) (amended by the Finance Act 1996 s 26(1), Sch 3 para 1).

6　Ibid s 6(1), (3). See also note 5 supra. See *Trustees for the Greater World Association Trust v Customs and Excise Comrs* [1989] VATTR 91 (in the usual case, an estate agent's services are supplied on completion and not on exchange of contracts); *Mercantile Contracts Ltd v Customs and Excise Comrs* (1990) VAT Decisions 4357, 5266, [1990] STI 90, 918 (where a builder who converted flats was, by the contract, to be paid five years later, and was obliged to maintain the flats in the meantime, his services could be divided into two and VAT was due on completion of the performance of the works of conversion).

7　Ie under the Value Added Tax Act 1994 s 6(1)–(3) (as amended): see the text and notes 1–6 supra.

8　'VAT invoice' means such an invoice as is required under ibid s 58, Sch 11 para 2(1) (see para 225 post), or would be so required if the person to whom the supply is made were a person to whom such an invoice should be issued: s 6(15). For the meaning of 'invoice' see para 11 note 8 ante. The commissioners have stated that the rules relating to the time of supply which depend on the issue of a VAT invoice do not apply to zero-rated supplies: Customs and Excise Notice 700 *The VAT Guide* (March 1996) para 47. The consequence is that the tax point for a zero-rated supply cannot be advanced or delayed by the issue of a document purporting to be a VAT invoice, although the tax point could be altered by a payment in advance. This appears to be based on the Value Added Tax Regulations 1995, SI 1995/2518, reg 20(a) (see para 243 post) which provides that reg 13 (which imposes an obligation to provide a VAT invoice) does not apply to any zero-rated supply other than a supply for the purposes of acquisition. However, in *Customs and Excise Comrs v Faith Construction Ltd* [1990] 1 QB 905 at 916, [1989] STC 539 at 543, CA (see note 9 infra), Parker LJ stated that the assertion was 'questionable'. A VAT invoice is not 'issued' for the purposes of VAT unless it had been delivered into the purchaser's possession: *Customs and Excise Comrs v Woolfold Motor Co Ltd* [1983] STC 715. A tax point is not created on the issue of a VAT invoice where the supply does not subsequently take place: *Broadwell Land plc v Customs and Excise Comrs* [1993] VATTR 346. See also Case C-342/87 *Genius Holding BV v Staatssecretaris van Financiën* [1989] ECR 4227, [1991] STC 239, ECJ.

9   Value Added Tax Act 1994 s 6(4). Thus, where a deposit is received prior to the supply of goods, the supply takes place partly at the time when the deposit is paid and partly when the goods are supplied, or the remainder of the consideration is paid: *Purshotam M Pattni & Sons v Customs and Excise Comrs* [1987] STC 1 (but consider also the effect of the Value Added Tax Act 1994 s 88 (supplies spanning a change in VAT rates: see para 30 post) on the facts of that case). Section 6(4)–(10) (see the text and notes 10–13 infra; and para 38 post) does not apply for determining when any supply of gold is to be treated as taking place: s 55(4). For the meaning of 'supply of gold' for these purposes see para 26 note 18 ante. Section 6(4) cannot apply to a case where the effect of its operation would be to treat an otherwise taxable supply as taking place at a time and in circumstances when the supply would fall to be disregarded for VAT purposes (eg because the parties were, at that time, members of the same VAT group); s 6(4) only applies where the person making the supply is a taxable person making a taxable supply, being someone who is in a position to issue a VAT invoice, and does not apply to a person from whom no VAT would be due: *Thorn Materials Supply Ltd v Customs and Excise Comrs* (4 November 1996, unreported), CA.

     In *Customs and Excise Comrs v Faith Construction Ltd* [1990] 1 QB 905, [1989] STC 539, CA, schemes were devised to effect payment of consideration for building services prior to such services ceasing to be zero-rated on a change in the law. In each case the court held that payment was received when money was paid into the builder's account, notwithstanding that he immediately lent the money back, or that he could only draw the money out of his account against architects' certificates. It was sufficient that the client had in each case discharged his contractual obligation to make payment. A payment is made for VAT purposes, even if the customer retains an equitable interest in the money pending performance: *Customs and Excise Comrs v Richmond Theatre Management Ltd* [1995] STC 257. See also *Old Chigwellians' Club v Customs and Excise Comrs* [1987] VATTR 66 (payments made towards future life membership of club; no supply for VAT until pupil had been elected to the club); cf *Customs and Excise Comrs v Moonrakers Guest House Ltd* [1992] STC 544 (deposits for holiday accommodation, which would be returned on cancellation if the room was relet, constituted payment for the purpose of the Value Added Tax Act 1994 s 6(4)); *Bruce Banks Sails Ltd v Customs and Excise Comrs* [1990] VATTR 175 (the mere fact that a contract might be rescinded and the deposit returned did not prevent a tax point arising on the receipt of the deposit); *Nigel Mansell Sports Car Ltd v Customs and Excise Comrs* [1991] VATTR 491 (in the absence of a contract for a supply, the payment of a returnable 'good faith' deposit was outside the scope of VAT). There is no tax point by reason of the Value Added Tax Act 1994 s 6(4) where payment is made for non-existent goods, at least where the goods never come into existence: *Theotrue Holdings Ltd v Customs and Excise Comrs* [1983] VATTR 88; *Northern Counties Co-operative Enterprises Ltd v Customs and Excise Comrs* [1986] VATTR 250; *Munn v Customs and Excise Comrs* [1989] VATTR 11. The Value Added Tax Act 1994 s 6(4) involves a permitted derogation from the general rules relating to the time of supply laid down by EC Council Directive 77/388 (OJ L145, 13.6.77, p 1) art 10(1). As to the extent of the right to derogate under art 10(2) see Case C-144/94 *Ufficio IVA di Trapani v Italittica SpA* [1995] ECR I-3653, [1995] STC 1059, ECJ.

10   The commissioners may, at the request of a taxable person, direct that this provision is to apply in relation to supplies made by him, or such supplies made by him as may be specified in the direction, as if for the period of 14 days there were substituted such longer period as may be specified in the direction: Value Added Tax Act 1994 s 6(6). See also note 12 infra. For the meaning of 'taxable person' see paras 12 note 4 ante, 55 post.

11   Ie the time mentioned in ibid s 6(4): see the text to note 9 supra.

12   Ibid s 6(5). Where a taxable person provides a document to himself which (1) purports to be a VAT invoice in respect of a supply of goods or services to him by another taxable person; and (2) is, in accordance with regulations under Sch 11 para 2 (as amended) (see para 225 post), treated as the VAT invoice required by the regulations to be provided by the supplier, then s 6(5), (6) has effect in relation to that supply as if (a) the provision of the document to himself by the first-mentioned taxable person were the issue by the supplier of a VAT invoice in respect of the supply; and (b) any notice of election given or request made by the first-mentioned taxable person for the purposes of those provisions had been given or made by the supplier: s 6(9).

13   Ibid s 6(10). This may be done either (1) by directing those supplies to be treated as taking place (a) at times or on dates determined by or by reference to the occurrence of some event described in the

direction; or (b) at times or on dates determined by or by reference to the time when some event so described would in the ordinary course of events occur, the resulting times or dates being in every case earlier than would otherwise apply; or (2) by directing that, notwithstanding s 6(5), (6), those supplies are to be treated, to the extent that they are not treated as taking place at the time mentioned in s 6(4), as taking place (a) at the beginning of the relevant working period, as defined in his case in and for the purposes of the direction; or (b) at the end of the relevant working period, as so defined: s 6(10).

30. Supplies spanning change of rate etc. The general rules relating to the time of supply for the purposes of value added tax[1] are overridden by numerous specific provisions[2] which substitute for the basic tax points[3] dates determined by reference to payment or the issue of a VAT invoice[4] or by agreement between the supplier and the Commissioners of Customs and Excise. Where, however, there is a change in the rate of VAT in force[5] or in the descriptions of exempt or zero-rated supplies or acquisitions[6], the supplier is free to determine that the tax point should be taken as the basic tax point rather than that which would be established by the specific provisions[7].

Where:

(1) any acquisition of goods from another member state which is affected by the change would not have been affected, in whole or in part, if it had been treated as taking place at the time of the event which, in relation to that acquisition, is the first relevant event for the purposes of taxing the acquisition; or

(2) any acquisition of goods from another member state which is not so affected would have been affected, in whole or in part, if it had been treated as taking place at the time of that event,

the rate at which VAT is chargeable on the acquisition, or any question whether it is zero-rated or exempt must, if the person making the acquisition so elects, be determined as at the time of that event[8].

1 See para 29 ante.
2 See in particular the Value Added Tax Act 1994 s 6(4), (5), (6), (10); and paras 29 ante, 31 et seq post. Specific arrangements have also been approved for establishing the time of supply in the case of corporate purchasing cards: see VAT Information Sheet 13/95 (1 September 1995).
3 These tax points are those established by the Value Added Tax Act 1994 s 6(1)–(3) (see para 29 ante) and are generally referred to as 'the basic tax points': see Customs and Excise Notice 700 *The VAT Guide* (March 1966) Pt 5 para 44.
4 For the meaning of 'VAT invoice' see para 29 note 8 ante.
5 Ie the rate in force under the Value Added Tax Act 1994 s 2 (as amended): see paras 5–6 ante.
6 References for these purposes to an acquisition being zero-rated are references to an acquisition from another member state being one in relation to which ibid s 30(3) (see para 175 post) provides for no VAT to be chargeable: s 88(7). As to exempt supplies or acquisitions see para 141 et seq post; and as to zero-rated supplies or acquisitions see para 158 et seq post. For the meaning of 'another member state' see para 4 note 14 ante; and as to goods acquired in another member state see para 13 ante.
7 See the Value Added Tax Act 1994 s 88(1), (2). Where (1) a supply affected by the change would, apart from s 6(4), (5), (6) or (10), be treated under s 6(2) or (3) as made wholly or partly at a time when it would not have been affected by the change; or (2) a supply not so affected by the change would, apart from those provisions, be treated under s 6(2) or (3) as made wholly or partly at a time when it would have been so affected, the rate at which VAT is chargeable on the supply, or any question whether it is zero-rated or exempt, may, at the election of the supplier, be determined without regard to s 6(4), (5), (6) or (10): s 88(2). Any power to make regulations under the Value Added Tax Act 1994 with respect to the time when a supply is to be treated as taking place includes power to provide for s 88 to apply as if the references in s 88(2) to s 6(4), (5), (6) or (10) includes references to specified provisions of the regulations: s 88(3). Section 88 applies as if those references included references to the Value Added Tax Regulations 1995, SI 1995/2518, regs 81, 82, 84, 85, 86(1)–(4), 88–93 (see paras 27 ante, 31 et seq post): reg 95. Regulations under the Value Added Tax Act 1994 s 58, Sch 11 para 2 (as amended) (see para 225 post) may make provision for the replacement or correction of any VAT invoice which relates to a supply in respect of which an election is made under s 88 but which was issued before the election was made: s 88(5). If a VAT invoice has previously been raised for a supply in respect of which an election is made under s 88, the supplier is, within 14 days of the change, obliged to provide his customer with a credit note headed: 'Credit note – change of VAT rate' and containing specified particulars: see the Value Added Tax Regulations 1995 reg 15; and para 242 post.

No election may be made under the Value Added Tax Act 1994 s 88 in respect of a supply to which s 6(9) (see para 31 post) or s 5(1), Sch 4 para 7 (see para 24 ante) applies: s 88(6).

8   Ibid s 88(4).

B. IN PARTICULAR CASES

31. Power to make specific rules. The Commissioners of Customs and Excise may make provision by regulations with respect to the time at which, notwithstanding the general rules[1], a supply[2] is to be treated as taking place for the purposes of value added tax[3] in cases where:

(1)   it is a supply of goods or services for a consideration the whole or part of which is determined or payable periodically, or from time to time, or at the end of any period[4]; or

(2)   it is a supply of goods for a consideration the whole or part of which is determined at the time when the goods are appropriated for any purpose[5]; or

(3)   there is a supply to which the provisions relating to gold[6] apply[7]; or

(4)   there is a deemed supply[8] of services[9].

For any such case the regulations may provide for goods or services to be treated as separately and successively supplied at prescribed times or intervals[10].

Where goods are treated as the subject of a self-supply[11], the supply is treated as taking place when they are appropriated to use by the trader for the purpose of his business[12].

When goods are transferred or disposed of, otherwise than for consideration, in circumstances such that they cease to form part of the assets of a business and are thereby deemed to be supplied by the trader[13], the supply is treated as taking place when the goods are so transferred or disposed of[14].

Where a person ceases to be a taxable person[15], any goods then forming part of the assets of a business carried on by him are generally deemed to be supplied immediately before he ceases to be a taxable person[16].

The commissioners may approve arrangements whereby registered traders operate what are known as self-billing arrangements, by which the recipient provides himself with a document which purports to be a VAT invoice[17]. In such a case, the usual rules apply, with the issue of the self-billed invoice being treated as the issue of the VAT invoice in determining the tax point, and with any election, request or notice required for the purposes of those rules being made by the recipient rather than the supplier[18].

The ordinary tax point rules are excluded in the case of supplies of designated travel services[19] by tour operators[20]. Instead, at the election of the tour operator making them, all supplies comprising (in whole or in part) a designated travel service are treated as taking place either (a) when the traveller commences a journey, or occupies any accommodation supplied, whichever is the earlier; or (b) when any payment is received by the tour operator in respect of that supply which, when aggregated with any earlier such payments, exceeds 20 per cent of the total consideration, to the extent covered by that and any earlier such payment, except in so far as any earlier such payment has already been treated as determining the time of part of that supply[21]. Except as the commissioners may otherwise allow, all supplies comprising in whole or in part a designated travel service made by the same tour operator are treated as taking place at the time determined under one only of these methods[22].

The time of supply of fuel appropriated to private use is the time when the fuel is put into the fuel tank of the individual[23].

1   Ie notwithstanding the Value Added Tax Act 1994 s 6(2)–(8), (11), (13) or s 55(4): see para 29 ante; the text and notes 11–14 infra; and para 38 post.

2   For the meaning of 'supply' see para 21 ante.

3   Value Added Tax Act 1994 s 6(14).
4   Ibid s 6(14)(a). See the Value Added Tax Regulations 1995, SI 1995/2518, reg 90(1); and para 32 post. For the meaning of 'consideration' generally see para 86 post.
5   Value Added Tax Act 1994 s 6(14)(b). This caters, eg, for cases where goods are stored on the buyer's premises but the supplier retains the property in them until the buyer appropriates the goods for use. Except in relation to (1) a supply mentioned in s 6(2)(c) (see para 29 head (2) ante); or (2) a supply to which s 6(7), (8) (see para 38 post) applies, where goods are supplied under an agreement whereby the supplier retains the property therein until the goods or part of them are appropriated under the agreement by the buyer and in circumstances where the whole or part of the consideration is determined at that time, a supply of any of the goods is treated as taking place at the earliest of the following dates: (a) the date of appropriation by the buyer; (b) the date when a VAT invoice is issued by the supplier; or (c) the date when a payment is received by the supplier: Value Added Tax Regulations 1995 reg 88(1). If, however, the supplier issues a VAT invoice within 14 days of the appropriation of the goods or part of them by the buyer, the provisions of the Value Added Tax Act 1994 s 6(5) (see para 29 text to notes 11–12 ante) apply to that supply (ie the usual tax point applies): Value Added Tax Regulations 1995 reg 88(2).
6   Ie the Value Added Tax Act 1994 s 55 (as amended): see paras 26 ante, 56 post.
7   Ibid s 6(14)(c).
8   Ie by virtue of ibid s 5(1), Sch 4 para 5(4) (see para 24 ante) or an order under s 5(4): see the Value Added Tax (Supply of Services) Order 1993, SI 1993/1507 (as amended); and para 24 text and notes 26–33 ante. See also the Value Added Tax Act 1994 s 6(13); and note 12 infra.
9   Ibid s 6(14)(d). Where such services are supplied for any period, they are treated as being supplied on the last day of the supplier's prescribed accounting period (or periods) in which the services are performed, or the goods made available or used, as the case may be: Value Added Tax Regulations 1995 reg 81(1), (2). For the meaning of 'prescribed accounting period' see para 105 note 16 post.
10 Value Added Tax Act 1994 s 6(14). See eg the Value Added Tax Regulations 1995 reg 90; and para 37 post.
11 Ie by Treasury order made under the Value Added Tax Act 1994 s 5(5): see para 26 ante.
12 See ibid s 6(11). Goods are not so appropriated until set aside out of a larger bulk: *A & B Motors (Newton-le-Willows) v Customs and Excise Comrs* [1981] VATTR 29. A similar tax point is found where there is a supply of services by virtue only of the Value Added Tax Act 1994 Sch 4 para 5(4) (see para 24 note 25 ante); the supply is then treated as taking place when the goods are appropriated to the relevant use: s 6(13).
13 Ie where there is a supply of goods by virtue only of ibid Sch 4 para 5(1): see para 24 ante.
14 Ibid s 6(12).
15 For the meaning of 'taxable person' see paras 12 note 4 ante, 55 post.
16 See the Value Added Tax Act 1994 Sch 4 para 8; and para 24 text and notes 18–24 ante.
17 See the Value Added Tax Regulations 1995 reg 13(3); but cf *UDL Construction plc (in administrative receivership and compulsory liquidation) v Customs and Excise Comrs* (1995) VAT Decision 13714, [1995] STI 2034 on the tax point which applies when a trader issues a VAT invoice in disregard of existing self-billing arrangements. As to self-billing schemes see para 240 post.
18 See the Value Added Tax Act 1994 s 6(9); and para 29 ante.
19 A 'designated travel service' is a supply of goods or services acquired for the purposes of his business, and supplies for the benefit of a traveller without material alteration or further processing, by a tour operator in a member state in which he has established his business or has a fixed establishment: Value Added Tax (Tour Operators) Order 1987, SI 1987/1806, art 3(1).
20 Ie as a result of the Value Added Tax Act 1994 s 53(2)(e) (see para 200 post); and the Value Added Tax (Tour Operators) Order 1987 (as amended) (see para 200 post). As to the tour operators' margin scheme see para 200 post.
21 Ibid art 4(2).
22 Ibid art 4(3). If, however, a tour operator elects to use the payment method of determining the time of supply, but payment is not received in respect of all or part of the supply, the time of any part of the supply which has not been determined by that method is treated as occurring at the earlier of the traveller beginning his journey or first occupying any accommodation supplied to him: art 4(4). In other words, a supply is then treated as taking place for a consideration equal to the residue of the cost of the designated travel service.
23 See the Value Added Tax Act 1994 s 56(6); and para 95 post.

32. Continuous supplies of services and certain goods. Where services are supplied for a period for a consideration[1] the whole or part of which is determined or payable periodically or from time to time, they are treated as separately and successively supplied at the earlier of the following times:

(1)   each time that a payment in respect of the supplies is received by the supplier; or

(2)   each time that the supplier issues a VAT invoice[2] relating to the supplies[3].

Where separate and successive supplies of such services are made under an agreement which provides for successive payments, and at or about the beginning of any period not exceeding one year the supplier issues a VAT invoice containing specified additional[4] particulars, the services are treated as separately and successively supplied each time that a payment in respect of them becomes due or is received by the supplier, whichever is the earlier[5]. Where, however, there is a change in the value added tax chargeable on supplies of the description to which such an invoice relates on or before any of the dates that a payment is due as stated on it, that invoice ceases to be treated as a VAT invoice in respect of any such supplies for which payments are due after the change and not received before the change[6].

Similar rules apply in relation to:

(a)   successive payments made in consequence of the grant of a long lease or tenancy which is treated[7] as a supply of goods[8]; and

(b)   most supplies[9] of water[10], gas[11] or any form of power, heat, refrigeration and ventilation[12].

In the case of supplies falling within head (a) above, the rules for the time of supply are identical to those for the continuous supply of services[13]. In the case of supplies falling within head (b) above, a supply is treated as taking place each time that a payment in respect of the supply is received by the supplier, or a VAT invoice relating to the supply is issued by the supplier, whichever is the earlier[14]. Where the whole or part of the consideration for a supply of water or gas, or of power in the form of electricity, is determined or payable periodically or from time to time, goods are treated as separately and successively supplied either each time that a part of the consideration is received by the supplier, or each time that the supplier issues a VAT invoice relating to the supply, whichever is the earlier[15]; and where such separate and successive supplies are made under an agreement which provides for successive payments, and at or about the beginning of any period not exceeding one year the supplier issues a VAT invoice containing specified additional[16] particulars, the goods are treated as separately and successively supplied each time that a payment in respect of them becomes due or is received by the supplier, whichever is the earlier[17]. Where, however, there is a change in the value added tax chargeable on supplies of the description to which such an invoice relates on or before any of the dates that a payment is due as stated on it, that invoice ceases to be treated as a VAT invoice in respect of any such supplies for which payments are due after the change and not received before the change[18].

A supply of water[19], gas or any form of power, heat, refrigeration or ventilation which is excluded from the above provisions[20] is treated as taking place on the day of the issue of a VAT invoice in respect of the supply[21].

Where the regulations[22] provide for a supply to be treated as taking place each time that a payment (however expressed) is received, or an invoice is issued, the supply is to be treated as taking place only to the extent covered by the payment or invoice[23].

1   For the meaning of 'consideration' see para 86 post. There is no payment for the purposes of the Value Added Tax Regulations 1995, SI 1995/2518, reg 90 (see the text and notes 2–6 infra) unless the sum in question constitutes consideration for value added tax purposes. Accordingly, overpayments made erroneously by customers receiving continuous services did not fall to be charged to VAT until the following quarter's invoice was issued, crediting the sum overpaid against the customer's then liability: *Customs and Excise Comrs v British Telecommunications plc* [1996] STC 818, CA. Substantial difficulties are encountered in practice in determining whether there is a liability to, and accounting for, VAT on management services, ie supplies of staff etc between connected companies, eg where one company claims to be offering a (possibly free) payroll service to another company rather than providing staff in return for a reimbursement of salary. Such reimbursements are treated as continuous supplies of services: *Customs and Excise Comrs v Tarmac Roadstone Holdings Ltd* [1987] STC 610, CA. In such cases, the time of supply is likely to be the date of payment, which may occur on the date on

which a journal transfer is made between purchase and sales ledger accounts or an entry is made in an inter-company account having a debit balance: *Pentex Oil Ltd v Customs and Excise Comrs* (1992) VAT Decision 7989, [1992] STI 927; *Legal & Contractual Services Ltd v Customs and Excise Comrs* [1984] VATTR 85. In *Missionfine Ltd (t/a GT Air Services) v Customs and Excise Comrs* (1993) VAT Decision 10331 (unreported), the tribunal upheld an assessment to VAT which assumed that the time of supply of management services was the date on which the directors of the supplier signed annual accounts which contained an entry in respect of the services. In *Waverley Housing Management Ltd v Customs and Excise Comrs* (1994) VAT Decision 11765, [1994] STI 573, it was held that the temporary retention of rents in lieu of invoicing management services, pending group registration for VAT, did not constitute payment for the purposes of the Value Added Tax Regulations 1995 reg 90. As to VAT on groups of companies see para 191 post.

2   For the meaning of 'VAT invoice' see para 29 note 8 ante.

3   Value Added Tax Regulations 1995 reg 90(1), partially implementing the Value Added Tax Act 1994 s 6(14)(a), which empowers the commissioners to make provision with respect to the time at which a supply is to be treated as taking place, inter alia, where it is a supply of goods or services for a consideration the whole or part of which is determined or payable periodically, or from time to time, or at the end of any period: see para 31 ante. See *Rice v Customs and Excise Comrs* [1996] STC 581, CA (a trader had made continuous supplies of services to a customer at a time when he was not registered for VAT. Although an invoice had been sent to the customer, payment was not received until after the trader had registered; held that the rules for determining the time of the supply (which was taken to be the time of payment because the earlier invoice could not be a VAT invoice) did not also determine whether the supply was made by a taxable person, so that the trader was not liable to account for VAT on the supply). It was also noted in *Rice v Customs and Excise Comrs* supra that the Value Added Tax Regulations 1995 reg 90(1) fails to make specific provision for the case where the consideration for the supply is determined at the end of any period.

4   Ie in addition to the particulars specified in ibid reg 14 (as amended): see para 241 post. The specified additional particulars are: (1) the dates on which payments under the agreement are to become due in the period; (2) the amount payable, excluding value added tax, on each such date; and (3) the rate of VAT in force at the time of issue of the VAT invoice and the amount of VAT chargeable in accordance with that rate on each of such payments: reg 90(2)(a)–(c). See *Simkins Partnership v Customs and Excise Comrs* (1993) VAT Decision 9705 (unreported) (treatment of invoice for 1991–92 contributions to Solicitors Indemnity Fund).

5   Value Added Tax Regulations 1995 reg 90(2).

6   Ibid reg 90(3).

7   Ie by virtue of the Value Added Tax Act 1994 s 5(1), Sch 4 para 4: see para 24 text and note 7 ante.

8   See the Value Added Tax Regulations 1995 reg 85.

9   Ie except a supply to which the Value Added Tax Act 1994 s 6(7), (8) (certain intra-Community removals of goods: see paras 29 ante, 38 post) applies: Value Added Tax Regulations 1995 86(1).

10   Ie other than (1) distilled water, deionised water and water of similar purity; and (2) water comprised in any of the excepted items set out in the Value Added Tax Act 1994 s 30(2), Sch 8 Pt II Group 1 (see para 159 post): Value Added Tax Regulations 1995 reg 86(1)(a).

11   Ie either (1) coal gas, water gas, producer gases or similar gases; or (2) petroleum gases or other gaseous hydrocarbons in a gaseous state: ibid reg 86(1)(b), (c).

12   Ibid reg 86(1)(d).

13   See ibid reg 85(1)–(3).

14   Ibid reg 86(1).

15   Ibid reg 86(2).

16   S e note 4 supra.

17   Value Added Tax Regulations 1995 reg 86(3).

18   Ibid reg 86(4).

19   Ie other than (1) distilled water, deionised water and water of similar purity; and (2) water comprised in any of the excepted items set out in the Value Added Tax Act 1994 Sch 8 Pt II Group 1: see the Value Added Tax Regulations 1995 reg 86(1)(a).

20   Ie a supply to which the Value Added Tax Act 1994 s 6(7), (8) applies: Value Added Tax Regulations 1995 reg 86(5).

21   Ibid reg 86(5).

22   Ie ibid Pt XI (regs 81–95): see paras 27, 30–31 ante; the text and notes 1–21 supra; and para 33 et seq post.

23   Ibid reg 94.

33. Supplies in the construction industry. Where services, or services together with goods, are supplied in the course of the construction, alteration, demolition, repair or maintenance of a building or of any civil engineering work under a contract which provides for payments for such supplies[1] to be made periodically or from time to time, a supply is treated as taking place at the earlier of the following times:

(1)   each time that a payment is received by the supplier where the consideration[2] for the contract is wholly in money[3]; or

(2)   each time that the supplier issues a VAT invoice[4].

1   For the meaning of 'supply' see para 21 ante.
2   For the meaning of 'consideration' see para 86 post.
3   Value Added Tax Regulations 1995, SI 1995/2518, reg 93(1)(a). For the meaning of 'money' see para 7 note 5 ante.
4   Ibid reg 93(1)(b). The supply takes place only to the extent covered by the payment or invoice: see reg 94; and para 32 text to notes 21–22 ante. For the meaning of 'VAT invoice' see para 29 note 8 ante. Regulation 93 is only concerned with actual supplies of services under a contract and cannot determine the time of a deemed supply made under the Value Added Tax Act 1994 s 47(3) (as amended) (see para 195 post): *Wirral Metropolitan Borough v Customs and Excise Comrs* [1995] STC 597. It is common practice in the construction industry to adopt special arrangements for the provision of documents corresponding to VAT invoices; in some cases the supplier will operate a self-billing system; in others, the parties will proceed by way of 'authenticated receipts': see para 240 post. Where such documents are provided, they may, subject to certain specified conditions, be treated as VAT invoices: see the Value Added Tax Regulations 1995 reg 13(3), (4); and para 240 post.

34. Retention payments. Where any contract for the supply[1] of goods[2] or services provides for the retention of any part of the consideration[3] by a person pending full and satisfactory performance of the contract, or any part of it, by the supplier, goods or services are treated as separately and successively supplied at the following times:

(1)   the time determined[4] in accordance with the statutory requirements[5]; and

(2)   the earlier of either the time that a payment in respect of any part of the consideration which has been retained pursuant to the contract is received by the supplier or the time that the supplier issues a VAT invoice[6] relating to any such part[7].

1   For the meaning of 'supply' see para 21 ante.
2   Ie other than a supply to which the Value Added Tax Act 1994 s 6(7), (8) (see paras 29 ante, 38 post) applies: Value Added Tax Regulations 1995, SI 1995/2518, reg 89.
3   For the meaning of 'consideration' see para 86 ante.
4   Ie determined in accordance with the Value Added Tax Act 1994 s 6(2)–(6), (9), (10) or (13), as the case may require: see paras 29, 31 ante.
5   Value Added Tax Regulations 1995 reg 89(1).
6   For the meaning of 'VAT invoice' see para 29 note 8 ante.
7   Value Added Tax Regulations 1995 reg 86(2). The supply takes place only to the extent covered by the payment or invoice: see reg 94; and para 32 text to notes 21–22 ante.

35. Special cases relating to land. Where an interest in, or right over, land is compulsorily purchased[1], and at the time determined in accordance with the normal rules[2] the person from whom it is purchased does not know the amount of payment that he is to receive in respect of the purchase, then goods or services, as the case may be, are treated as supplied each time that person receives any payment for the purchase[3].

Where a person ('the grantor') grants or assigns the fee simple in any land and at the time of the grant or assignment the total consideration for it is not determinable[4], then goods are treated as separately and successively supplied at the following times:

(1)   the time determined[5] in accordance with the usual rules[6]; and

(2)   the earlier of either each time that any part of the consideration which was not determinable at the usual time is received by the grantor or each time that he issues a VAT invoice[7] in respect of such a part[8].

1   Ie by or under any enactment: Value Added Tax Regulations 1995, SI 1995/2518, reg 84(1). As to the compulsory purchase of land see generally COMPULSORY ACQUISITION.
2   Ie in accordance with the Value Added Tax Act 1994 s 6(2) or (3): see para 29 ante.
3   Value Added Tax Regulations 1995 reg 84(1).
4   Eg if the price is dependent on the obtaining of planning permission.
5   Ie determined in accordance with the Value Added Tax Act 1994 s 6(2)–(6), (9) or (10) as the case may require: see paras 29, 31 ante.
6   Value Added Tax Regulations 1995 reg 84(2)(a).
7   For the meaning of 'VAT invoice' see para 29 note 8 ante.
8   Value Added Tax Regulations 1995 reg 84(2)(b). The supply takes place only to the extent covered by the payment or invoice: see reg 94; and para 32 text to notes 21–22 ante.

36. Barristers' services. Services supplied by a barrister (acting in that capacity) are treated as taking place at whichever is the earliest of the following times:

(1)   when the fee in respect of those services is received by the barrister[1];

(2)   when the barrister issues a VAT invoice[2] in respect of them[3]; or

(3)   the day when the barrister ceases to practise as such[4].

1   Value Added Tax Regulations 1995, SI 1995/2518, reg 92(a).
2   For the meaning of 'VAT invoice' see para 29 note 8 ante.
3   Value Added Tax Regulations 1995 reg 92(b).
4   Ibid reg 92(c).

37. Royalties etc. Where the whole amount of the consideration[1] for a supply[2] of services was not ascertainable at the time when the services were performed and subsequently the use of the benefit of those services by a person other than the supplier gives rise to any payment of consideration for that supply which is:

(1)   in whole or in part determined or payable periodically or from time to time or at the end of any period;

(2)   additional to the amount, if any, already payable for the supply; and

(3)   not a payment to which the rules relating to continuous supplies of services[3] apply,

a further supply is treated as taking place each time that a payment in respect of the use of the benefit of those services is received by the supplier or a VAT invoice[4] is issued by the supplier, whichever is the earlier[5].

1   For the meaning of 'consideration' see para 86 post.
2   For the meaning of 'supply' see para 21 ante.
3   Ie the Value Added Tax Regulations 1995, SI 1995/2518, reg 90: see para 32 ante.
4   For the meaning of 'VAT invoice' see para 29 note 8 ante.
5   Value Added Tax Regulations 1995 reg 91.

38. Movement of goods between United Kingdom and other member states. Particular rules exist to determine the tax point[1] for supplies[2] connected with the movement of goods from or to the United Kingdom[3]. Where any supply of goods involves both the removal of the goods from the United Kingdom and their acquisition in another member state[4] by a person who is liable for value added tax on the acquisition in accordance with provisions of the law of that member state[5] corresponding to the United Kingdom rules on acquisitions[6], the general rules[7] do not apply and the supply is treated as taking place on whichever is the earlier of (1) the fifteenth day of the month following that in which the removal in question takes place; and (2) the day of issue of a VAT invoice[8] (or other invoice prescribed by the Commissioners of Customs and Excise[9]) in respect of the supply[10]. A corresponding rule applies where goods are acquired from another member state; in such a case the acquisition is treated as taking place on whichever is the earlier of (a) the fifteenth day of the month following that in which the event occurs which is the first relevant event, in relation to that acquisition, for the purposes of taxing the acquisition[11]; and (b) the day of the issue, in respect of the transaction in pursuance of which the goods are acquired, of an invoice of such a description as the commissioners may prescribe by regulations[12]. The commissioners may also make provision by regulations with respect to the time at which an acquisition is to be treated as taking place in prescribed cases where the whole or part of any consideration[13] comprised in the transaction in pursuance of which the goods are acquired is determined or payable periodically, or from time to time, or at the end of a period[14].

Where goods consisting of certain supplies of water[15], gas[16] or any form of power, heat, refrigeration or ventilation[17] are acquired from another member state and the whole or part of any consideration comprised in the transaction in pursuance of which the goods are acquired is payable periodically, or from time to time, goods are treated as separately and successively acquired on each occasion that the supplier issues an invoice[18] in respect of the transaction[19].

Where there is a reverse charge on relevant services[20], the time of supply is either the date of payment or, if consideration was otherwise than in money, the last day of the prescribed accounting period[21] in which the services were performed[22].

1   For the meaning of 'tax point' see para 29 note 3 ante.
2   For the meaning of 'supply' see para 21 ante.
3   See the text and notes 4–22 infra. For the meaning of 'United Kingdom' see para 4 note 3 ante.
4   For the meaning of 'another member state' see para 4 note 14 ante; and as to when goods are acquired in another member state see para 13 note 6 ante.
5   For the meaning of 'law of another member state' see para 11 note 1 ante.
6   Ie the Value Added Tax Act 1994 s 10: see para 13 ante.
7   Ie ibid s 6(2), (4)–(6), (10)–(12): see paras 29, 31 ante.
8   For the meaning of 'VAT invoice' see para 29 note 8 ante.
9   Ie prescribed by regulations: Value Added Tax Act 1994 s 6(8)(b). At the date at which this volume states the law, no such regulations had been made. At present, a registered taxable person is obliged by the Value Added Tax Regulations 1995, SI 1995/2518, reg 13(1)(b) to provide a VAT invoice when making a supply of goods or services, other than an exempt supply, to a person in another member state. However, the prescribed contents of such an invoice are somewhat different from those required of a tax invoice provided to a registered person in the United Kingdom: see reg 14(2).
10   Value Added Tax Act 1994 s 6(7), (8). These provisions do not apply for determining when any supply of gold is to be treated as taking place: see s 55(4); and para 29 note 9 ante. For the meaning of 'supply of gold' see para 26 note 18 ante.
11   The event which, in relation to any acquisition of goods from another member state, is the first relevant event for the purposes of taxing the acquisition is the first removal of the goods which is involved in the transaction in pursuance of which they are acquired: ibid s 12(2).
12   Ibid s 12(1). Heads (a)–(b) in the text are subject to s 18 (as amended) (see paras 130–131 post) and s 18B (as added) (see para 134 post) and to any regulations made under s 12(3) (see the text and notes 13–14 infra): s 12(1) (amended by the Finance Act 1996 s 26(1), Sch 3 para 3). Where the time that goods are acquired from another member state falls to be so determined by reference to the day of the issue, in respect of the transaction in pursuance of which the goods are acquired, of an invoice of such description as the commissioners may by regulations prescribe, the invoice must be one which is issued by the supplier under the provisions of the law of the member state where the goods were supplied, corresponding in relation to that member state to the provisions of the Value Added Tax Regulations 1995 regs 13, 14 (as amended) (see paras 240–241 post): reg 83. Where the time of the acquisition of any goods from another member state is determined by reference to the issue of such an invoice, VAT must be accounted for and paid in respect of the acquisition only on so much of its value as is shown on that invoice: reg 26. As to accounting for VAT generally see para 225 et seq post.
13   For the meaning of 'consideration' see para 86 post.
14   Value Added Tax Act 1994 s 12(3).
15   Ie such water as is described in the Value Added Tax Regulations 1995 reg 86(1)(a): see para 32 ante.
16   Ie gas as described in ibid reg 86(1)(b) or (c): see para 32 ante.
17   Ie as described in ibid reg 86(1)(d): see para 32 ante.
18   Ie an invoice such as is described in ibid reg 83: see note 12 supra.

19 Ibid reg 87. The supply takes place only to the extent covered by the invoice: see reg 94; and para 32 text to notes 21–22 ante.
20 See para 27 ante.
21 For the meaning of 'prescribed accounting period' see para 105 note 16 post.
22 See the Value Added Tax Regulations 1995 reg 82; and para 27 ante.

(iii) Place of Supply

A. IN GENERAL

39. Place of supply; introduction. Value added tax is charged on certain supplies of goods and services made in the United Kingdom[1], on taxable acquisitions of goods from other member states of the European Community[2], on the receipt of certain supplies of services from abroad[3], and on the importation of goods into the United Kingdom from places outside the European Community[4]. In consequence of the creation of the Single European Market[5] there may be said to be two sets of rules determining the place of supply: those which may apply where a transaction involves a Community element; and those which apply when it does not.

The Treasury may provide by order for varying the rules for determining where a supply[6] of goods or services is made, either in relation to goods or services generally or to particular goods or services specified in the order[7].

1 See para 4 ante. For the meaning of 'United Kingdom' see para 4 note 3 ante.
2 As to taxable acquisitions see para 13 ante.
3 As to the reverse charge see para 27 ante.
4 As to VAT on importation see para 103 et seq post.
5 See EC Council Directive 91/680 (OJ L376, 31.12.91, p 1); and para 1 note 1 ante.
6 For the meaning of 'supply' see para 21 ante.
7 Value Added Tax Act 1994 s 7(11). At the date at which this volume states the law, no such orders had been made, but, by virtue of the Interpretation Act 1978 s 17(2)(b), the following orders have effect as if so made: (1) the Value Added Tax (Tour Operators) Order 1987, SI 1987/1806 (amended by SI 1992/3125; SI 1995/1495) (see para 54 post); (2) the Value Added Tax (Place of Supply of Services) Order 1992, SI 1992/3121 (amended by SI 1995/3038) (see para 47 et seq post); and (3) the Value Added Tax (Place of Supply of Goods) Order 1992, SI 1992/3283 (see para 43 post). See also Customs and Excise Notice 741 *VAT: Place of Supply of Services* (1 October 1994).

B. SUPPLY OF GOODS

40. The general rule. If the supply[1] of any goods does not involve their removal[2] from or to the United Kingdom[3] they are to be treated as supplied in the United Kingdom if they are in the United Kingdom; and they are otherwise[4] to be treated as supplied outside the United Kingdom[5]. This general rule gives way, in particular cases, to more specific rules[6].

1 For the meaning of 'supply' see para 21 ante.
2 Where goods leave and re-enter the United Kingdom in the course of their removal from a place in the United Kingdom to another place in the United Kingdom, the removal is not to be treated as a removal from or to the United Kingdom: Value Added Tax Act 1994 s 7(8).
3 For the meaning of 'United Kingdom' see para 4 note 3 ante. See also the Value Added Tax (Isle of Man) Order 1982, SI 1982/1067, which makes specific provision for the operation of VAT in relation to transactions involving the Isle of Man; and para 9 ante.
4 Presumably 'otherwise' means 'if they are not in the United Kingdom'. The general rule intends to deal with cases where the goods do not cross the borders of the United Kingdom in the course of the supply.
5 Value Added Tax Act 1994 s 7(1), (2). These provisions apply subject to s 14 (see para 16 ante), s 18 (as amended) (see paras 130–131 post) and s 18B (as added) (see para 134 post): s 7(1) (amended by the Finance Act 1996 s 26(1), Sch 3 para 2).
6 See para 41 et seq post.

41. Installed or assembled goods. Goods are treated as supplied in the United Kingdom[1] where their supply[2] involves their installation or assembly at a place in the United Kingdom to which they are removed; and as supplied outside the United Kingdom where their supply involves their installation or assembly at a place outside the United Kingdom to which they are removed[3].

Where:

(1) a person belonging in another member state[4] makes a supply of goods to a person who is registered[5] for value added tax, which involves their installation or assembly at a place in the United Kingdom to which they are removed[6]; and

(2) there would be a taxable acquisition[7] by the registered person if that supply were treated as not being a taxable supply[8] but as involving the removal of the goods from another member state to the United Kingdom[9],

that supply is to be so treated except for the purposes of the provisions[10] relating to registration[11]. The person making the supply must, however, comply with such requirements as to the furnishing[12] of invoices[13] and other documents[14] and of information to the Commissioners of Customs and Excise and to the person supplied as the commissioners may prescribe by regulations[15].

A person belonging in another member state who has made or who intends to make a supply to which he wishes heads (1) and (2) above to apply must notify[16] the commissioners and the registered person in writing of his intention to do so[16]. The notification must be made no later than the provision of the first invoice[17] in relation to the supply to which it relates, and must be sent to the office designated by the commissioners for the receipt of such notifications and to the registered person to whom the goods are to be supplied[18]. Where a person belonging in another member state has complied with these notification requirements in relation to the first such supply to a registered person, they are deemed to have been satisfied in relation to all subsequent supplies to that registered person while the person making the supply continues to belong in another member state[19].

1 For the meaning of 'United Kingdom' see para 4 note 3 ante.
2 For the meaning of 'supply' see para 21 ante.
3 Value Added Tax Act 1994 s 7(3). It will be understood that this rule only applies where the supplier of the goods is also obliged, as part of his supply, to perform, or procure another to perform, the installation or assembly. It is not sufficient if the goods are supplied to the customer in circumstances which require the customer to carry out the installation etc. For an example of a dispute as to the nature of a supply involving the installation of machinery see *AZO-Maschinenfabrik Adolf Zimmerman GmbH v Customs and Excise Comrs* [1987] VATTR 25; cf *George Kuikka Ltd v Customs and Excise Comrs* [1990] VATTR 185 (which appears to have proceeded on the incorrect assumption that it is unnecessary to construe a pre-existing domestic statute in order to comply with a directive subsequent in time, where the United Kingdom has not implemented it; cf Case 14/83 *Von Colson and Kamann v Land Nordrhein-Westfalen* [1984] ECR 1891, [1986] 2 CMLR 430, ECJ; and Case C-106/89 *Marleasing SA v La Commercial Internacional de Alimentación SA* [1990] ECR I-4135, [1993] BCC 421, ECJ; followed in *Webb v EMO Air Cargo (UK) Ltd* [1992] 4 All ER 929, [1993] 1 WLR 49, HL).
4 As to when a person belongs in another member state for these purposes see para 16 note 6 ante; and for the meaning of 'another member state' see para 4 note 14 ante.
5 Ie under the Value Added Tax Act 1994: see para 56 et seq post.
6 Ibid s 14(2)(a). As to the general rules relating to the simplified procedure for triangulation see para 16 ante.
7 For the meaning of 'taxable acquisition' see para 13 ante.
8 For the meaning of 'taxable supply' see para 12 note 3 ante.
9 Value Added Tax Act 1994 s 14(2)(b).
10 Ie for the purposes of ibid s 3(2), Sch 3 (as amended): see para 63 et seq post.
11 Ibid s 14(2).
12 Ie whether before or after the supply is made: ibid s 14(3).
13 For the meaning of 'invoice' see para 11 note 8 ante.
14 For the meaning of 'document' see para 11 note 8 ante.

15 Value Added Tax Act 1994 s 14(3). The regulations may provide for the times at which, and the form and manner in which, any document or information is to be furnished and for the particulars which it is to contain: s 14(3). In exercise of the power so conferred, the commissioners have made the Value Added Tax Regulations 1995, SI 1995/2518, reg 12 (see the text and notes 16–19 infra) and regs 19, 20 (see para 243 post).

16 Ibid reg 12(1). The notification must contain the following particulars: (1) the name and address of the person belonging in another member state; (2) the number, including the alphabetical code, by which the person belonging in another member state is identified for VAT purposes in the member state in which he belongs; (3) the date upon which the installation or assembly of the goods was commenced or is intended to commence; and (4) the name, address and registration number of the registered person to whom the goods have been, or are to be, supplied: reg 12(2). For the meaning of 'alphabetical code' and 'registration number' see para 16 note 10 ante.

17 Ie in accordance with ibid reg 19: see para 243 post. For the meaning of 'invoice' see para 11 note 8 ante.

18 Ibid reg 12(3). Notifications must be made separately in relation to each registered person to whom it is intended to make supplies to which the person belonging in another member state wishes the Value Added Tax Act 1994 s 14(2) (see heads (1)–(2) in the text) to apply: Value Added Tax Regulations 1995 reg 12(4).

19 Ibid reg 12(5).

42. Distance selling. If the supply[1] of goods involves their removal from another member state[2] to the United Kingdom[3], otherwise than in circumstances where the supplier must arrange for their installation or assembly[4], the goods are to be treated as supplied in the United Kingdom where:

(1) the supply involves the removal of the goods to the United Kingdom by or under the directions of the person who supplies them[5];

(2) the supply is a transaction in pursuance of which the goods are acquired in the United Kingdom from another member state by a person who is not a taxable person[6];

(3) the supplier is either registered[7] or is liable[8] to be registered for value added tax[9]; and

(4) the supply is neither a supply of goods consisting in a new means of transport[10] nor anything which is treated[11] as a supply by virtue only of certain statutory provisions[12] relating to the transfer or removal of goods so as no longer to form part of the assets of a business[13].

A corresponding rule[14] ensures that goods which do not consist in a new means of transport are treated as supplied outside the United Kingdom where:

(a) the supply involves the removal of the goods, by or under the direction of the person who supplies them, to another member state[15];

(b) the person who makes the supply is taxable in another member state[16]; and

(c) the provisions of the law of that member state[17] corresponding to the provisions made by heads (1) to (3) above make that person liable to VAT on the supply[18].

1 For the meaning of 'supply' see para 21 ante.

2 For the meaning of 'another member state' see para 4 note 14 ante.

3 As to when goods are treated as removed to the United Kingdom for these purposes see the Value Added Tax Act 1994 s 7(8); and para 40 ante. For the meaning of 'United Kingdom' see para 4 note 3 ante.

4 Ie where the place of supply is not determined under ibid s 7(2) or (3): see paras 40–41 ante.

5 Ibid s 7(4)(a).

6 Ibid s 7(4)(b). For the meaning of 'taxable person' see paras 12 note 4 ante, 55 post.

7 Ie under the Value Added Tax Act 1994: see para 56 et seq post.

8 Ie is liable to be registered under ibid s 3(2), Sch 2 (see para 60 et seq post) or would be so liable if he were not already registered or liable to be registered under s 3(2), Sch 1 (as amended) (see para 56 et seq post): s 7(4)(c)(ii).

9 Ibid s 7(4)(c). In the case of distance selling, special registration rules exist. In addition to the usual rules in Sch 1 (as amended) (see para 56 post), Sch 2 provides that persons making distance sales to United Kingdom consumers whose value exceeds £70,000 during the course of a calendar year must register thereunder: see para 60 post.

10 For the meaning of 'new means of transport' see para 13 note 8 ante.

11 Ie for the purposes of the Value Added Tax Act 1994: s 7(4)(d).

12 Ie by virtue only of ibid s 5(1), Sch 4 para 5(1) (see para 24 ante) or Sch 4 para 6 (see paras 14–15 ante): s 7(4)(d).

13 Ibid s 7(4)(d). This rule is intended to prevent distortion of competition in the Single Market during the transitional period by traders selling by mail order from a member state which happens to impose a lower rate of VAT on the goods sold than that where the customers belong, eg, book clubs selling zero-rated books out of the United Kingdom to consumers in other member states, most of which set a lower, but not a zero, rate for supplies of printed matter. The rules introduced by EC Council Directive 91/680 (OJ L376, 31.12.91, p 1) and incorporated in United Kingdom law with effect from 1 January 1993 are intended to be of transitional effect only, pending the complete harmonisation of VAT and VAT rates throughout the Community. No date has yet been set for the completion of the transitional period. See also para 1 ante.

14 Ie the Value Added Tax Act 1994 s 7(5): see the text and notes 15–17 infra. Section 7(5) applies to goods whose place of supply is not determined under any of s 7(2), (3) or (4): s 7(5).

15 Ibid s 7(5)(a).

16 Ibid s 7(5)(b). For the meaning of 'taxable in another member state' see para 11 note 4 ante.

17 For the meaning of references to the law of another member state see para 11 note 1 ante.

18 Value Added Tax Act 1994 s 7(5)(c). Section 7(5) does not, however, apply in relation to any supply in a case where the liability mentioned in head (c) in the text depends on the exercise by any person of an option in the United Kingdom corresponding to such an option as is mentioned in Sch 2 para 1(2) (see para 60 post) unless that person has given, and has not withdrawn, a notification to the Commissioners of Customs and Excise that he wishes his supplies to be treated as taking place outside the United Kingdom where they are supplies in relation to which the other requirements of s 7(5) are satisfied: s 7(5). The rule will not, therefore, apply to treat the supply as made outside the United Kingdom unless, in a case where the supplier has an option whether or not to register as taxable in another member state (because he has yet to reach the relevant threshold for registration for distance selling in that state: see note 9 supra for the United Kingdom's limit), he has exercised the option to be taxed in that state. The commissioners may by regulations provide that a notification for these purposes is not to be given or withdrawn except in such circumstances, and in such form and manner, as may be prescribed: s 7(9). At the date at which this volume states the law, no such regulations had been made. As to the making of regulations generally see para 8 ante.

43. Goods in the course of a Community transport.

Where goods are supplied on board a ship, aircraft or train in the course of a Community transport[1], they are treated as supplied at the point of departure[2]. Goods supplied for consumption on board a ship or an aircraft in the course of a Community transport are, however, treated as supplied outside the member states[3]. For these purposes (1) part of transportation where it is expected that a different means of transport will be used; and (2) the homeward stage of a return trip[4], are each treated as separate transportation[5].

These provisions to not apply to any goods supplied as part of a pleasure cruise, including a cruise wholly or partly for the purposes of education and training[6].

1 'Community transport' means the transportation of passengers between the point of departure and the point of arrival in the course of which (1) there is a stop in a member state other than that in which lies the point of departure; and (2) there is no stop in a country which is not a member state: Value Added Tax (Place of Supply of Goods) Order 1992, SI 1992/3283, art 3. 'Point of departure' means the first place in the member states where it is expected that passengers will commence their journey or, where there has been a leg which involved a stop in a place outside the member states, the first such place after such a leg has been completed; and 'point of arrival' means the last place in the member states where it is expected that passengers who have commenced their journey at a place in a member state will terminate their journey or, where there is to follow a leg which will involve a stop in a place outside the member states, the last such place before that leg is undertaken: art 3. See also Case C-331/94 *EC Commission v Greece* [1996] STC 1168, ECJ (failure of member state to comply with EC Council Directive 77/388 (OJ L145, 13.6.77, p 1) arts 2, 9(2)(b) by exempting transport services supplied in territorial waters from VAT).

2 Ibid art 4. This provision, taken together with the definition of 'Community transport', effectively ring-fences each part of a journey which takes place within the Community from any part which takes place outside.

3   Ibid art 5. Presumably goods supplied for consumption on board Eurostar trains and similar trains operating between different member states are treated as supplied in the member state from which the train departed.
4   'Return trip' means any journey involving two or more countries where it is expected that the means of transport will stop in the country from which it originally departed: ibid art 3.
5   Ibid art 6.
6   Ibid arts 3, 7.

44. Importation of goods into the United Kingdom. Goods whose place of supply is not determined under any of the rules previously described[1] are treated as supplied in the United Kingdom[2] where their supply[3] involves their being imported from a place outside the member states[4] and the person who supplies them is the person by whom, or under whose directions, they are so imported[5].

1   Ie under the Value Added Tax Act 1994 s 7(2)–(5): see paras 40–42 ante.
2   For the meaning of 'United Kingdom' see para 4 note 3 ante.
3   For the meaning of 'supply' see para 21 ante.
4   As to places treated as outside the member states for VAT purposes see para 10 ante.
5   Value Added Tax Act 1994 s 7(6). As to imported goods see further para 103 et seq post.

45. Removal of goods to or from the United Kingdom. Goods whose place of supply is not determined under any of the rules previously described[1], but whose supply[2] involves their removal to or from the United Kingdom[3], are treated as supplied in the United Kingdom where their supply involves their removal from the United Kingdom without also involving their previous removal to the United Kingdom[4]; and as supplied outside the United Kingdom in any other case[5].

1   Ie under the Value Added Tax Act 1994 s 7(2)–(6): see paras 40–44 ante.
2   For the meaning of 'supply' see para 21 ante.
3   As to when goods are treated as removed to the United Kingdom for these purposes see the Value Added Tax Act 1994 s 7(8); and para 40 ante. For the meaning of 'United Kingdom' see para 4 note 3 ante.
4   Ibid s 7(7)(a).
5   Ibid s 7(7)(b).

C. SUPPLY OF SERVICES

46. The general rule. A supply[1] of services is treated as made in the United Kingdom[2] if the supplier belongs in the United Kingdom; and as made in another country (and not in the United Kingdom) if the supplier belongs in that other country[3]. A supplier of services is treated as belonging in a country if: (1) he has a business establishment[4], or some other fixed establishment[5], there and no such establishment elsewhere[6]; or (2) he has no such establishment (there or elsewhere) but his usual place of residence[7] is there[8]; or (3) he has such establishments both there and elsewhere but the establishment of his which is most directly concerned with the supply is there[9].

This general rule gives way to a number of specific rules whereby, in particular cases, the place of supply is deemed to be elsewhere than the country where the supplier belongs[10].

1   For the meaning of 'supply' see para 21 ante.
2   For the meaning of 'United Kingdom' see para 4 note 3 ante.
3   Value Added Tax Act 1994 s 7(10). The question whether, in relation to any supply of services, the supplier or the recipient of the supply belongs in one country or another is to be determined, subject to any provision made under s 8(6) (see para 27 ante) in accordance with s 9: see the text and notes 4–9 infra; and para 49 post. As to the views of the Commissioners of Customs and Excise on the rules determining the place of supply of services see Customs and Excise Notice 741 *VAT: Place of Supply of Services* (1 October 1994). See also Customs and Excise Business Brief 8/93 [1993] STI 540–541 on

supplies of services to businesses in other EC member states and accounting for VAT; outside the scope and reverse charge services. The commissioners have announced that, in accordance with EC Council Directive 77/388 (OJ L145, 13.6.77, p 1) art 27, the United Kingdom has requested the EC Commission to consider a proposal for a derogation from art 9, which established the EC place of supply rules, in order to negate a distortion in competition caused by non-EC supplies of telecommunication services being able to supply such services to EC customers without charging VAT: see Customs and Excise Business Brief 21/96 [1996] STI 1662. See also written answer of the European Commission to European Parliamentary Written Question E-0787/96 (OJ C297, 8.10.96, p 27), reported in [1996] STI 1719. As to derogation under EC Council Directive 77/388 art 27 see para 3 ante.

4 For these purposes, but not for any other purpose, a person carrying on a business through a branch or agency in any country is treated as having a business establishment there: Value Added Tax Act 1994 s 9(5)(a). In the Sixth Directive, the wording is: 'the place where the supplier has established his business or has a fixed establishment': see EC Council Directive 77/388 art 9(1). As to the meaning of 'agency' see *Customs and Excise Comrs v Johnson* [1980] STC 624; and see para 195 post. For a case where the Value Added Tax Act 1994 s 9(5) was impliedly held inapplicable see *DFDS A/S v Customs and Excise Comrs* (1994) VAT Decision 12588, [1994] STI 1305; on appeal [1995] STI 1190, cited in para 54 note 2 post; and see *WH Payne & Co v Customs and Excise Comrs* (1995) VAT Decision 13668, [1995] STI 2024, where the tribunal held that the extension of the meaning of 'business establishment' by the Value Added Tax Act 1994 s 9(5)(a) was not consistent with EC Council Directive 77/388 art 9, since it treated the branch or agency as the business establishment of the trader, rather than as an alternative to be used where treating the supply as having been made at the place where the trader had established his business would lead to an irrational result, or would create a conflict with another member state. See also *Chinese Channel Ltd (Hong Kong) v Customs and Excise Comrs* (1996) VAT Decision 14003, [1996] STI 961.

5 See *Binder Hamlyn v Customs and Excise Comrs* [1983] VATTR 171 (company which carried on business only in Jamaica held to belong in the United Kingdom because it had a 'fixed establishment', albeit not a business establishment in the United Kingdom, since it maintained a registered office for company law purposes at its accountants' premises). Cf Case 168/84 *Berkholz v Finanzamt Hamburg-Mitte-Altstadt* [1985] ECR 2251, [1985] 3 CMLR 667, ECJ (taxpayer installed and operated gaming machines, inter alia, on sea-going vessels, without maintaining a permanent staff on board; services could not be deemed to be supplied at an establishment other than the place where the supplier had established his business (ie, a place could not be considered to be a fixed establishment) unless the place in question had a certain minimum size and both the human and technical resources necessary for the provision of the services were permanently present. The installation of the machines on board such vessels did not meet these minimum criteria. Furthermore, the place where the supplier had established his business was the primary point of reference for the purposes of EC Council Directive 77/388 art 9, and regard was only to be had to another establishment from which the services were supplied if the reference to the place where the supplier had established his business did not lead to a rational result for tax purposes, or created a conflict with another member state). See also Case C-231/94 *Faaborg-Gelting Linien A/S v Finanzamt Flensburg* [1996] All ER (EC) 656, [1996] STC 774, ECJ. In *Vincent Consultants Ltd v Customs and Excise Comrs* [1989] CMLR 374, [1988] VATTR 152, the tribunal considered both *Binder Hamlyn v Customs and Excise Comrs* supra and *Berkholz v Finanzamt Hamburg-Mitte-Altstadt* supra and concluded that a distinction was to be drawn between cases dependent on the place where the supplier belonged (*Berkholz v Finanzamt Hamburg-Mitte-Altstadt* supra) and cases dependent on where the recipient belonged (*Binder Hamlyn v Customs and Excise Comrs* supra; *Vincent Consultants Ltd v Customs and Excise Comrs* supra); in the latter case, the test was whether the establishment had a sufficient minimum strength to enable it to receive and use the specified services in question. See also *Chantrey Vellacott v Customs and Excise Comrs* [1992] VATTR 138 (held that not every registered office could be a 'fixed establishment'; and that the test in *Vincent Consultants Ltd v Customs and Excise Comrs* supra was one of fact). In *WH Payne & Co v Customs and Excise Comrs* (1995) VAT Decision 13668, [1995] STI 2024, the tribunal held that for the purpose of EC Council Directive 77/388 art 9(2)(e), the supplier or customer would have only one business establishment, notwithstanding that there could be any number of fixed establishments from or to which services are supplied or received; and that the phrase 'the place where a person has established his business' referred to the place of its head office, headquarters or principal place of business, if that was the main seat of economic activity, rather than to the registered office, if no economic activity took place there. It followed that a British Virgin Islands company which owned investment properties in the United Kingdom which it employed letting agents to run had no such establishment in the United Kingdom. See also *Chinese Channel Ltd (Hong Kong) v Customs and Excise Comrs* (1996) VAT Decision 14003, [1996] STI 961.

6 Value Added Tax Act 1994 s 9(1), (2)(a).

7 'Usual place of residence', in the case of a body corporate, means the place where it is legally constituted: ibid s 9(5)(b). In EC Council Directive 77/388 art 9(1), the test is significantly different, ie 'the place where he has his permanent address or usually resides'.

8   Value Added Tax Act 1994 s 9(1), (2)(b).
9   Ibid s 9(1), (2)(c).
10 See paras 39 note 7 ante, 47 et seq post; and see Case C-327/94 *Dudda v Finanzamt Bergisch Gladbach* [1996] STC 1290, ECJ (EC Council Directive 77/388 art 9(1), while laying down the general rule as to where services were to be treated as having taken place, did not take precedence over art 9(2), which set out a number of specific instances when particular services were deemed to be supplied elsewhere).

47. Place of supply of services relating to land. Where a supply[1] of services consists of:
(1)   the grant, assignment or surrender of:
     (a)   any interest in or right over land;
     (b)   a personal right to call for or be granted any interest in or right over land; or
     (c)   a licence to occupy land or any other contractual right exercisable over or in relation to land;
(2)   any works of construction, demolition, conversion, reconstruction, alteration, enlargement, repair or maintenance of a building or civil engineering work; or
(3)   services such as are supplied by estate agents, auctioneers, architects, surveyors, engineers and others involved in matters relating to land,
the supply is treated as made where the land in connection with which the supply is made is situated[2].

1   For the meaning of 'supply' see para 21 ante.
2   Value Added Tax (Place of Supply of Services) Order 1992, SI 1992/3121, arts 4, 5.

48. Services supplied where performed. Where a supply[1] of services consists of:
(1)   cultural, artistic, sporting, scientific, educational or entertainment services[2];
(2)   services relating to exhibitions, conferences or meetings[3];
(3)   services ancillary to any supply of a description within head (1) or head (2) above, including services of organising any such supply[4];
(4)   the valuation of, or work carried out on, any goods[5],
the supply is treated as made where the services are physically carried out[6].

1   For the meaning of 'supply' see para 21 ante.
2   See the Value Added Tax (Place of Supply of Services) Order 1992, SI 1992/3121, arts 4, 15(a). In *British Sky Broadcasting Ltd v Customs and Excise Comrs* (1994) VAT Decision 12394, [1994] STI 1188, satellite broadcasting was held to be the supply of entertainment; but not of a kind within EC Council Directive 77/388 (OJ L145, 13.6.77, p 1) art 9(2)(c), and thus not within the Value Added Tax (Place of Supply of Services) Order 1992 art 15(a), since that was concerned with performance before a live audience. See also *Hutchvision Hong Kong Ltd v Customs and Excise Comrs* (1993) VAT Decision 10509, [1993] STI 1124. In Case C-327/94 *Dudda v Finanzamt Bergisch Gladbach* [1996] STC 1290, ECJ, it was held that the supply of sound engineering for artistic or entertainment events was of a kind within E . Council Directive 77/388 art 9(2) and was thus deemed to take place where the services were physically performed.
3   See the Value Added Tax (Place of Supply of Services) Order 1992 art 15(b).
4   See ibid art 15(c).
5   Ie save as provided by ibid art 14 (as amended) (see para 53 post): art 15(d) (amended by SI 1995/3038).
6   Ibid art 15 (amended by SI 1995/3038).

49. Services supplied where received. Where a supply[1] consists of any of the services described below, and the recipient of that supply either (1) belongs[2] in a country (other than the Isle of Man) which is not a member state; or (2) is a person who belongs in a member state, but in a country other than that in which the supplier belongs, and in either case he receives the supply for the purpose of a business carried on by him and is not treated[3] as having himself supplied the services, that supply is treated as made where the recipient belongs[4]. The relevant services are:

(a)   transfers and assignments of copyright, patents, licences, trademarks and similar rights[5];

(b)   advertising services[6];

(c)   services of consultants, engineers, consultancy bureaux, lawyers, accountants and other similar services; data processing and provision of information (excluding any services relating to land)[7];

(d)   acceptance of any obligation to refrain from pursuing or exercising, in whole or in part, any business activity or any such rights as are referred to in head (1) above[8];

(e)   banking, financial[9] and insurance services (including reinsurance but excluding the provision of safe deposit facilities)[10];

(f)   the supply of staff[11];

(g)   the letting on hire of goods other than means of transport[12]; and

(h)   the services rendered by one person to another in procuring for the other any of the services mentioned in heads (a) to (g) above[13].

If the supply of services is made to an individual and received by him otherwise than for the purposes of any business carried on by him, he is treated as belonging in whatever country he has his usual place of residence[14]. In other cases, the person to whom the supply is made is treated as belonging in a country if:

(i)   either he has a business establishment[15], or some other fixed establishment, there and no such establishment elsewhere, or he has no such establishment (there or elsewhere) but his usual place of residence is there[16]; or

(ii)   he has such establishments both in that country and elsewhere and the establishment of his at which, or for the purposes of which, the services are most directly used or to be used is in that country[17].

1   For the meaning of 'supply' see para 21 ante.
2   See notes 14–17 infra.
3   Ie by virtue of the Value Added Tax Act 1994 s 8 (the reverse charge): see para 27 ante.
4   Value Added Tax (Place of Supply of Services) Order 1992, SI 1992/3121, art 16 (amended by SI 1995/3038). In *Omnicom UK plc v Customs and Excise Comrs* (1994) VAT Decision 12605, [1994] STI 1307 (affd on appeal sub nom *Diversified Agency Services Ltd v Customs and Excise Comrs* [1996] STC 398) the issue arose as to whether the Value Added Tax (Place of Supply of Services) Order 1992 art 16(b)(i) (as originally made) was incompatible with EC Council Directive 77/388 (OJ L145, 13.6.77, p 1) art 9(2)(e) (which identified the place where the customer belonged as that in which he had established his business), in specifically requiring the supply to be received by the customer for the purpose of a business carried on by him; both the tribunal and, subsequently, the court held that art 9(2)(e), in requiring that the supply be performed 'for' a taxable person, imposed a like requirement. It was, therefore, insufficient for the supplier to be able to treat the supply as outside the scope of VAT that he held evidence of the recipient's taxable status in the country to which he belonged.
5   Value Added Tax Act 1994 s 8(2), Sch 5 para 1 (Sch 5 paras 1–8 applied by the Value Added Tax (Place of Supply of Services) Order 1992 art 16 (as amended: see note 4 supra)). The commissioners appear to accept that the provision extends to the granting of such rights as well as to their transfer or assignment: see Customs and Excise Notice 741 *VAT: Place of Supply of Services* (1 October 1994) para 9.10.
6   Value Added Tax Act 1994 Sch 5 para 2 (as applied: see note 5 supra). See Joined Cases C-68/92, C-73/92 *EC Commission v France, EC Commission v Luxembourg, EC Commission v Spain* [1995] 2 CMLR 1, ECJ ('advertising services' included the supply of free goods in the course of an advertising campaign, as well as the organisation of public relations events and other promotional activities involving the conveyance of a message intended to inform consumers of the existence and qualities of a particular product or service, with a view to increasing sales); *LS & A International Ltd v Customs and Excise Comrs* (1989) VAT Decision 3717 (unreported) (purchase of paper pulp for a client's brochures held to be a supply of advertising services).
7   Value Added Tax Act 1994 Sch 5 para 3 (as applied: see note 5 supra).
8   Ibid Sch 5 para 4 (as applied: see note 5 supra).
9   The grant of a metal option is not a financial service for these purposes, since head (e) in the text connotes, and is confined to, services in connection with money and credit (*Gardner Lohmann Ltd v Customs and Excise Comrs* [1981] VATTR 76); nor are the services of rent collection and property management financial services (*Culverpalm Ltd v Customs and Excise Comrs* [1984] VATTR 199).

10 Value Added Tax Act 1994 Sch 5 para 5 (as applied: see note 5 supra).

11 Ibid Sch 5 para 6 (as applied: see note 5 supra). In *Strollmoor v Customs and Excise Comrs* (1991) VAT Decision 5454, [1991] STI 64, the supply of accounting and administrative staff to non-resident (but United Kingdom incorporated and registered) investment companies owning buildings in the United Kingdom was held to be outside the scope of this provision both because the recipient belonged in the United Kingdom for the purposes of the supply and because the supply was not of staff but of management services.

12 Value Added Tax Act 1994 Sch 5 para 7 (as applied: see note 5 supra). As to the hire of means of transport see para 52 post.

13 Ibid Sch 5 para 8 (as applied: see note 5 supra).

14 Ibid s 9(1), (3). For the meaning of 'usual place of residence' for these purposes see para 46 note 7 ante. Foreign military personnel serving in the United Kingdom for an average of three years were held to belong here in *USAA Ltd v Customs and Excise Comrs* (1993) VAT Decision 10369 (unreported).

15 For the meaning of 'business establishment' for these purposes see para 46 note 4 ante.

16 Value Added Tax Act 1994 s 9(1), (4)(a) (applying s 9(2)(a), (b)).

17 Ibid s 9(1), (4)(b).

50. The transport of passengers and goods. Services which consist of the transportation of passengers[1] or goods are treated as supplied in the country in which the transportation takes place to the extent, and only to the extent, that it takes place in that country[2]. Any transportation which takes place partly outside the territorial jurisdiction of a country is, however, treated as taking place wholly within that country where it takes place in the course of a journey between two points in that country[3] and the means of transport used does not put in or land in another country in the course of the journey between those two points[4]. Where a supply consists of ancillary transport services[5] it is treated as made where those services are physically performed[6], unless the services are provided in connection with the intra-Community transport of goods[7] and the recipient makes use of a registration number[8] for the purposes of the supply, in which case the supply is treated as made in the member state which issued the registration number if, and only if, the supply would otherwise be treated as taking place in a different member state[9].

Any goods or services provided as part of a pleasure cruise[10], or services consisting of the transportation of any luggage, or motor vehicle, accompanying a passenger, are treated as supplied in the same place as the transportation of the passenger[11] is treated as supplied, whether or not they would otherwise be treated as supplied separately[12].

1 The transportation of passengers includes, it appears, the supply of a pleasure cruise by the owner of the vessel: *Customs and Excise Comrs v Peninsular and Oriental Steam Navigation Co Ltd* [1996] STC 698; and see Customs and Excise Business Brief 14/96 [1996] STI 1247 (VAT treatment of holiday and other cruises); and Customs and Excise Notice 741 *VAT: Place of Supply of Services* (1 October 1994) para 5.3. Although such services are not specifically mentioned in the Value Added Tax (Place of Supply of Services) Order 1992, SI 1992/3121, art 6 (see the text and note 2 infra), art 8 extends transportation of passengers to include such a cruise for the ancillary purposes of that provision: see note 10 infra. If, however, a pleasure cruise or other passenger transport is part of a supply of designated travel services, the rules for tour operators will apply: see para 54 post.

2 Value Added Tax (Place of Supply of Services) Order 1992, SI 1992/3121, art 6.

3 Ie whether or not as part of a longer journey involving travel to or from another country: ibid art 7(a).

4 Ibid art 7. Thus if a ferry transports passengers from Liverpool to Dublin via the Isle of Man, the leg from Liverpool to the Isle of Man is treated as made in the United Kingdom, with the remainder being outside the scope of United Kingdom value added tax: Customs and Excise Notice 741 *VAT: Place of Supply of Services* (1 October 1994) para 5.2. In Case 283/84 *Trans Tirreno Express SpA v Ufficio Provinciale IVA, Sassari* [1986] ECR 231, [1986] 2 CMLR 100, ECJ, it was held that a member state could impose VAT on a transport operation effected between two points in the same state, but in the course of which the vessel left the national territory and passed through international waters, provided that it did not thereby encroach on the tax jurisdiction of another member state. See also Case C-331/94 *EC Commission v Greece* [1996] STC 1168, ECJ. As to the place of supply of goods in the course of a Community transport

(ie a journey which involves making a stop in a member state other than that of departure but does not involve a stop in a country which is not a member state) see the Value Added Tax (Place of Supply of Goods) Order 1992, SI 1992/3283; and para 43 ante.

5   'Ancillary transport services' means loading, unloading, handling and similar activities: Value Added Tax (Place of Supply of Services) Order 1992 art 2.

6   Ibid art 9.

7   'Intra-Community transport of goods' means the transportation of goods which begins in one member state and ends in a different member state: ibid art 2.

8   'Registration number' means an identifying number assigned to a person by a member state for the purposes of VAT in that member state: ibid art 2.

9   Ibid art 9, applying art 14(b).

10 'Pleasure cruise' includes a cruise wholly or partly for the purposes of education or training; ibid art 2.

11 For these purposes, a pleasure cruise is treated as the transportation of passengers: ibid art 8.

12 Ibid art 8.

51. The intra-Community transport of goods. Where a supply[1] of services consists of the intra-Community transport of goods[2], it is treated as made in the member state in which the transportation of the goods begins[3], unless the recipient makes use of a registration number[4] for the purposes of the supply, in which case the supply is treated as made in the member state which issued the registration number if, and only if, the supply would otherwise be treated as taking place in a different member state[5].

1   For the meaning of 'supply' see para 21 ante.

2   For the meaning of 'intra-Community transport of goods' see para 50 note 7 ante.

3   Value Added Tax (Place of Supply of Services) Order 1992, SI 1992/3121, art 10.

4   For the meaning of 'registration number' see para 50 note 8 ante.

5   Value Added Tax (Place of Supply of Services) Order 1992 art 10, applying art 14(a).

52. The hire of means of transport. Where a supply[1] of services consists of the letting on hire of a means of transport[2] and those services would otherwise be treated as supplied in the United Kingdom[3], they are not treated as supplied there if the effective use and enjoyment of the means of transport during the period of hire takes place outside the member states[4]. Correspondingly, where a supply of services consists of the letting on hire of any means of transport and those services would otherwise be treated as supplied in a place outside the member states, they are treated as supplied in the United Kingdom if the effective use and enjoyment of the means of transport during the period of hire takes place within the United Kingdom[5].

1   For the meaning of 'supply' see para 21 ante.

2   In Case 51/88 *Hamann v Finanzamt Hamburg-Eimbüttel* [1989] ECR 767, [1991] STC 193, ECJ, it was held that the term 'means of transport' should be interpreted widely and included anything which might be used to go from one place to another, including ocean-going sailing yachts, even if used by hirers for sporting purposes rather than for the transportation of goods or passengers. However, in *BPH Equipment Ltd v Customs and Excise Comrs* (1996) VAT Decision 13914, [1996] STI 779, the hire of a 'crawler' crane for the purposes of excavations by a United Kingdom company to a company registered in the Netherlands was held to be a supply of services made where the hirer belonged and not a supply of a means of transport made where the owner belonged.

3   For the meaning of 'United Kingdom' see para 4 note 3 ante.

4   Value Added Tax (Place of Supply of Services) Order 1992, SI 1992/3121, art 17. In *IDS Aircraft Ltd v Customs and Excise Comrs* (1994) VAT Decision 12452, [1994] STI 1229, it was held (in a case concerned with the position prior to the introduction of the Value Added Tax (Place of Supply of Services) Order 1992 (as amended)) that an aircraft was 'used' in a country when it simply overflew that country without landing in it. Quaere whether this is 'effective' use.

5   Value Added Tax (Place of Supply of Services) Order 1992 art 18.

53. Services of intermediaries. Where services consist of the making of arrangements:

(1)　for the intra–Community transport of goods[1] or of any other activity intended to facilitate the making of such a supply[2], they are treated as supplied in the member state where the transportation of the goods begins[3];

(2)　for the supply by or to another person of ancillary transport services[4] in connection with the intra-Community transport of goods or of any activity intended to facilitate the making of such a supply, they are treated as supplied in the member state where the ancillary transport services are physically performed[5];

(3)　for a supply by or to another person, or consist of any other activity intended to facilitate the making of such a supply[6], those services are treated as supplied in the same place as the supply by or to that other person is treated as made[7].

Where, however, a supply of services:

(a)　falls within heads (1) to (3) above;

(b)　consists of the valuation of, or work carried out on, any goods, provided the goods do not thereafter remain in the United Kingdom[8]; or

(c)　consists of ancillary transport services provided in connection with the intra-Community transport of goods,

and the recipient of those services makes use of a registration number[9] for the purposes of the supply, the supply is treated as made in the member state which issued the registration number if, and only if, the supply would otherwise be treated as taking place in a different member state[10].

1　For the meaning of 'intra–Community transport of goods' see para 50 note 7 ante.
2　For the meaning of 'supply' see para 21 ante.
3　Value Added Tax (Place of Supply of Services) Order 1992, SI 1992/3121, art 11.
4　For the meaning of 'ancillary transport services' see para 50 note 5 ante.
5　Value Added Tax (Place of Supply of Services) Order 1992 art 12.
6　Ie being supply which is not of a description within ibid art 9 (see para 50 ante), art 10 (see para 51 ante) or art 16 (as amended) (see para 49 ante): art 13.
7　Ibid art 13.
8　For the meaning of 'United Kingdom' see para 4 note 3 ante.
9　For the meaning of 'registration number' see para 50 note 8 ante.
10　Value Added Tax (Place of Supply of Services) Order 1992 art 14 (amended by SI 1995/3038).

54. Tour operators. A designated travel service[1] is treated as supplied in the member state in which the tour operator has established his business[2]. If, however, the supply[3] was made from a fixed establishment, it is treated as made in the member state in which the fixed establishment is situated[4].

1　For the meaning of 'designated travel service' see para 31 note 19 ante. As to the tour operators' margin scheme see para 200 post.
2　Value Added Tax (Tour Operators) Order 1987, SI 1987/1806, art 5(1), (2) (substituted by SI 1992/3125). There is no need for this provision to consider supplies made from establishments outside the Community, since these will not be designated travel services: see para 31 note 19 ante. In *DFDS A/S v Customs and Excise Comrs* (1994) VAT Decision 12588, [1994] STI 1305; on appeal [1995] STI 1190, the tribunal held that the phrase 'established his business' indicated the headquarters of the taxpayer, or his principal place of business, having regard to EC Council Directive 77/388 (OJ L145, 13.6.77, p 1) arts 9(2)(e), 26(2); but that the alternative place of supply (applicable 'if the supply was made from a fixed place of business') had exclusive effect whenever it was capable of applying. However, the fixed place of business of an English agent was not a fixed establishment of the Danish parent for the purposes of the margin scheme, because the Value Added Tax Act 1994 s 9(5) (which treats a person carrying on business in a country through a branch or agency as having a business establishment in that country: see para 46 note 4 ante) expressly applies only for the purposes of s 9. On appeal by the commissioners to the High Court, the question of the establishment of a place of business was referred to the European Court of Justice. See also *Gulliver's Travel Agency Ltd v Customs and Excise Comrs* (1994) VAT Decision 12494, [1994] STI 1258.

3   For the meaning of 'supply' see para 21 ante.

4   Value Added Tax (Tour Operators) Order 1987 art 5(2) (as substituted: see note 2 supra).

(2) TAXABLE PERSONS

(i) In general

55. Taxable persons. In order to be taxable a supply must be made by a taxable person in the course or furtherance of a business[1] carried on by him[2]. A person is a taxable person[3] while he is, or is required to be, registered[4] under the Value Added Tax Act 1994[5]. Each person is entitled only to a single registration for VAT purposes[6]. It follows that, if a person registers for VAT (even voluntarily) in respect of one activity, he is a taxable person for the purposes of all his business activities and must charge and account for VAT accordingly, notwithstanding that the value of the supplies in a particular business is minimal; and even though the value of all his business supplies taken together is below the threshold for registration[7]. However, the question whether any particular activity carried on by that taxable person is within the scope of VAT will still depend on whether that activity amounts to a business for VAT purposes[8].

There are special provisions which apply to the Crown[9], local authorities[10], groups of companies[11], partnerships[12], businesses carried on in divisions or by unincorporated bodies[13], personal representatives[14], agents[15], non-residents[16], co-owners of land[17], tour operators[18], persons who buy gold[19] and farmers[20]. In certain circumstances the Commissioners of Customs and Excise have power[21] to make a direction treating separate persons (whether legal or natural) as a single taxable person carrying on the activities of a business described in the direction and as liable to be registered for VAT[22].

1   For the meaning of 'business' see the Value Added Tax Act 1994 s 94; and para 17 ante. See also EC Council Directive 77/388 (OJ L145, 13.6.77, p 1) art 4(1) (a 'taxable person' is any person who independently carries out in any place any economic activity specified in art 4(2), whatever the purpose or results of that activity). It is because employees do not independently carry out any economic activity that they are not taxable persons for value added tax: see *Rickarby v Customs and Excise Comrs* [1973] VATTR 186; and Case C-202/90 *Ayuntamiento de Sevilla v Recaudadores de Tributos de las Zonas Primera y Segunda* [1991] ECR I-4247, [1993] STC 659, ECJ. Where a person's activity consisted exclusively in providing services for no direct consideration, there was no basis of assessment and the person was not a taxable person: Case 89/81 *Staatssecretaris van Financiën v Hong Kong Trade Development Council* [1982] ECR 1277, [1983] 1 CMLR 73, ECJ. See also Case C-60/90 *Polysar Investments Netherlands BV v Inspecteur der Invoerrechten en Accijnzen, Arnhem* [1991] ECR I-3111, [1993] STC 222, ECJ (a holding company whose sole purpose was to acquire holdings in other undertakings, without involving itself directly or indirectly in the management of those undertakings, did not, without prejudice to its rights as a shareholder, have the status of a taxable person). By EC Council Directive 77/388 art 4(5), states, regional and local government authorities and other bodies governed by public law are not to be considered taxable persons in respect of the activities or transactions in which they engage as public authorities, even where they collect dues, fees, contributions or payments in connection with such activities or transactions. In Case 235/85 *EC Commission v Netherlands* [1987] ECR 1471, [1988] 2 CMLR 921, ECJ, it was held that notaries and bailiffs, when performing their official services, thereby carry out independent economic activities consisting in the supply of services to third parties, in return for fees for their own account and are thus taxable persons for VAT purposes within the Sixth Directive, notwithstanding that they exercise the powers of a public authority. See Joined Cases 231/87, 129/88 *Ufficio Distrettuale delle Imposte Dirette di Fiorenzuola d'Arda v Commune di Carpaneto Piacentino and Ufficio Provinciale Imposta sul Valore Aggiunto di Piacenza* [1989] ECR 3233, [1991] STC 205, ECJ, where the court drew a distinction between the activities of bodies governed by public law acting 'as public authorities', in accordance with the EC Council Directive 77/388 art 4(5), if they acted under the special legal regime applicable to them; and activities of such bodies when acting under the same legal conditions as applicable to private traders, when they could not be regarded as acting 'as public authorities' and were prima facie outside the scope of art 4(5). See also Case C-202/90 *Ayuntamiento de Sevilla v Recaudadores de Tributos de las Zonas Primera y Segunda* supra (EC Council Directive 77/388 art 4(5) did not apply to

the collection of taxes by private individuals, who were entitled to retain a percentage of taxes collected by way of remuneration). On the implementation of art 4(5) in United Kingdom VAT law see *Arts Council of Great Britain v Customs and Excise Comrs* (1994) VAT Decision 11991, [1994] STI 713; cf *Haringey London Borough Council v Customs and Excise Comrs* (1992) VAT Decision 8820, [1994] VATTR 70, [1992] STI 1036 (on appeal [1995] STC 830); and as to the meaning of 'in the course or furtherance of a business' see paras 12 note 5, 17 note 2 ante.

2   See the Value Added Tax Act 1994 s 4(1); and para 12 ante.

3   In Case 268/83 *DA Rompelman and EA Rompelman-van Deelen v Minister van Financiën* [1985] ECR 655, [1985] 3 CMLR 202, ECJ, it was held that a person who carries out acts of investment closely linked with, and necessary for, the future exploitation of an immovable asset must thenceforward be considered a taxable person for the purposes of EC Council Directive 77/388 art 4. In Case C-110/94 *Intercommunale voor Zeewaterontzilting (INZO) (in liquidation) v Belgium* [1996] ECR I-857, [1996] STC 569, ECJ, it was held that where a tax authority accepts that a company, which has declared its intention to begin an economic activity giving rise to taxable transactions, has the status of a taxable person for the purposes of VAT, the carrying out of a study to investigate the financial viability of the activity itself is part of the economic activity in respect of which input tax may be recovered; and, except in cases of fraud or abuse, the status of a taxable person may not retrospectively be withdrawn if, as a result of the study, taxable transactions do not take place.

4   As to registration see para 56 et seq post.

5   Value Added Tax Act 1994 ss 3(1), 96(1).

6   *Customs and Excise Comrs v Glassborow* [1975] QB 465, [1974] 1 All ER 1041, DC. See para 68 post.

7   Though he may be entitled to seek to have his registration cancelled, in accordance with the Value Added Tax Act 1994 s 3(2), Sch 1 para 13: see para 73 post.

8   See para 17 et seq ante.

9   See para 194 post.

10   See para 65 post.

11   See paras 66, 191 post.

12   See para 68 post.

13   See para 67 post.

14   See para 70 post.

15   See para 195 post.

16   See para 62 post.

17   See para 68 post.

18   See para 200 post.

19   See paras 123, 169 post.

20   See para 79 post.

21   Ie under the Value Added Tax Act 1994 Sch 1 para 2: see para 59 post.

22   As to the registration of the single taxable person see para 59 post.

(ii) Liability to be Registered

A. IN GENERAL

56. Registration of persons; the general rules. A person is a taxable person[1] while he is, or is required to be, registered under the Value Added Tax Act 1994[2]. A trader may register and thus become a taxable person either voluntarily or by compulsion[3].

There are two basic tests as to the liability to be registered, the first of which is historic and the second prospective. On the historic basis, a person who makes taxable supplies[4] but is not registered becomes liable to be registered at the end of any month[5] if the value of his taxable supplies in the period of one year then ending has exceeded £47,000[6]; but a person is not liable to be registered on this ground if the Commissioners of Customs and Excise are satisfied that the value of his taxable supplies in the period of one year beginning at the time at which he would otherwise have become liable to be registered will not exceed £45,000[7]. On the prospective basis, a person who makes taxable supplies is liable to be registered at any time, if there are reasonable grounds for believing that the value of his taxable supplies in the period of 30 days then beginning will exceed £47,000[8].

The value of a supply of goods or services is determined for these purposes on the basis that no VAT is chargeable on the supply[9]. In addition, supplies of goods or services that are capital assets of the business in the course or furtherance of which they are supplied are to be disregarded[10], as well any taxable supplies which would not be treated as such apart from the statutory provisions with regard to distance selling to consumers in the United Kingdom[11] by a trader belonging in another member state[12]. Supplies made at a time when a person was previously registered for VAT are disregarded for the purposes of the historic basis of liability[13] if his registration was cancelled by the commissioners[14] and they are satisfied that before that cancellation he had given them all the information they needed in order to determine whether to cancel the registration[15].

Where a business carried on by a taxable person is transferred to another person as a going concern[16], the transferee is treated, for the purpose of determining whether he is liable to be registered for VAT, as having carried on the business before as well as after the transfer and supplies by him are treated accordingly[17]. Where the transferee is not registered at the time of the transfer, he becomes liable to be registered at that time if the value of his taxable supplies[18] in the period of one year ending at the time of the transfer has exceeded £47,000[19], or if there are reasonable grounds for believing that the value of his taxable supplies in the period of 30 days beginning at the time of the transfer will exceed £47,000[20].

A local authority[21] which makes taxable supplies[22] is liable to be registered for VAT whatever the value of its supplies[23].

A person is treated as having become liable to be registered under these provisions[24] at any time when he would have become so liable thereunder but for any registration which is subsequently cancelled[25] either because he was not registrable or because he did not have the intention by reference to which he was registered[26].

An appeal lies to a VAT and duties tribunal against any decision of the commissioners as to registration[27].

1   For the meaning of 'taxable person' see paras 12 note 4, 55 ante.
2   Value Added Tax Act 1994 s 3(1). References to registration are references to being registered under any of Schs 1–3 (as amended) (see the text and notes 4–19 infra; and para 57 et seq post); and persons registered thereunder must be registered in a single register kept by the Commissioners of Customs and Excise for the purposes of the 1994 Act: s 3(3). The commissioners may make provision as to the inclusion and correction of information in that register with respect to the Schedule under which any person is registered: s 3(4). See the Value Added Tax Regulations 1995, SI 1995/2518, regs 5–7; note 5 infra; and para 58 et seq post. As to the making of regulations generally see para 8 ante. There is no reference in EC Council Directive 77/388 (OJ L145, 13.6.77, p 1) to registration, but all member states have a system by which taxable persons are assigned unique identification numbers, in order to prevent fraud, as permitted by art 22(8).
       The Commissioners of Customs and Excise may by regulations make provision for requiring taxable persons to notify to them such particulars of changes in circumstances relating to those persons or any business carried on by them as appear to the commissioners to be required for the purpose of keeping the register up to date: Value Added Tax Act 1994 s 58, Sch 11 para 7(1). Every registered person, except one to whom Sch 1 para 11 (see para 71 post), Sch 1 para 12 (see para 72 post) or Sch 1 para 13(1), (2) or (3) (see para 73 post), Sch 2 para 5 (see para 75 post) or Sch 3 para 5 (see para 77 post) applies must, within 30 days of any changes being made in the name, constitution or ownership of his business, or of any other event which may necessitate the variation of the register or cancellation of his registration, notify the commissioners in writing of such a change or event and furnish them with full particulars of it: Value Added Tax Regulations 1995 reg 5(2).
3   As to voluntary registration see para 58 post.
4   For the meaning of 'taxable supply' see para 12 note 3 ante. References in the Value Added Tax Act 1994 Sch 1 (as amended) to supplies are references to supplies made in the course or furtherance of a business: Sch 1 para 19. By virtue of this statutory definition, in determining liability to register one leaves out of account the value of exempt supplies but takes into account not only standard-rated supplies but also zero-rated supplies. However, a person who makes zero-rated supplies may request the commissioners to exempt him from registration: see the Value Added Tax Act 1994 Sch 1 para 14(1); and para 57 post. As

to the standard rate of VAT see para 5 ante; and as to zero-rating see para 158 et seq post. For the meaning of 'supply' see para 21 ante; and for the meaning of 'in the course or furtherance of a business' see paras 12 note 5, 17 note 2 ante.

5   He must notify the commissioners of that liability within 30 days of the end of the relevant month: ibid Sch 1 para 5(1). The commissioners must register any person to whom this provision applies, whether or not he so notifies them, with effect from the end of month following the relevant month or from such earlier date as may be agreed between them and him: Sch 1 para 5(2). The 'relevant month', in relation to a person who so becomes liable to be registered, means the month at the end of which he becomes liable to be registered by virtue of Sch 1 para 1(1)(a) (as amended: see note 6 infra): Sch 1 para 5(3). See *Arthurs v Customs and Excise Comrs* (1995) VAT Decision 13650, [1995] STI 1977. Where, however, a person becomes liable to be registered by virtue of the Value Added Tax Act 1994 Sch 1 para 1(1)(a) (as amended) and by virtue of Sch 1 para 1(1)(b) (as amended) or Sch 1 para 1(2) (as amended) at the same time, the commissioners must register him in accordance with Sch 1 para 6(2) (see note 8 infra) or Sch 1 para 7(2) (see note 21 infra), as the case may be, rather than Sch 1 para 5(2): Sch 1 para 8.

   Any notification required under Sch 1 (as amended) must be made in such form and contain such particulars as the commissioners may prescribe by regulations: Sch 1 para 17. Where any person is required under Sch 1 para 5(1) or Sch 1 para 6(1) (see note 8 infra) to notify the commissioners of his liability to be registered, the notification must contain the particulars, including the declaration, set out in the Value Added Tax Regulations 1995 reg 5(1), Sch 1, Form 1 and must be made in that form; but where the notification is made by a partnership, it must also contain the particulars set out in Sch 1, Form 2: reg 5(1).

6   Value Added Tax Act 1994 Sch 1 para 1(1)(a) (amended by the Value Added Tax (Increase of Registration Limits) Order 1995, SI 1995/3037, art 2(a)). The Treasury may by order substitute for any of the sums for the time being specified in the Value Added Tax Act 1994 Sch 1 (as amended) such greater sums as it thinks fit: Sch 1 para 15. In exercise of this power, the Treasury has made the Value Added Tax (Increase of Registration Limits) Order 1995 cited supra. However, the United Kingdom's authority to set its VAT registration threshold is given by EC Council Directive 77/388 art 24(2)(c). It would therefore appear that the Treasury's power is restricted to adjustments which maintain the value of the threshold in real terms. As to the making of orders generally see para 8 ante.

   In determining the value of a person's supplies for the purposes of the Value Added Tax Act 1994 Sch 1 para 1(1) or (2) (as amended), supplies to which s 18B(4) (as added) (last acquisition or supply of goods before removal from fiscal warehousing: see para 134 post) applies and supplies treated as made by him under s 18C(3) (as added) (self-supply of services on removal of goods from warehousing: see para 140 post) are to be disregarded: Sch 1 para 1(9) (added by the Finance Act 1996 s 26(1), Sch 3 para 13).

7   Value Added Tax Act 1994 Sch 1 para 1(3) (amended by the Value Added Tax (Increase of Registration Limits) Order 1995 art 2(b)). As to the Treasury's power to substitute a greater sum see note 6 supra.

8   Value Added Tax Act 1994 Sch 1 para 1(1)(b) (as amended: see note 6 supra). As to valuation of a person's supplies, and as to the Treasury's power to substitute a greater sum, see note 6 supra. A person who so becomes liable to be registered must notify the commissioners of his liability before the end of the period by reference to which the liability arises (Sch 1 para 6(1)); and the commissioners must register any such person (whether or not he so notifies them) with effect from the beginning of that period (Sch 1 para 6(2)). See also note 5 supra.

9   Ibid Sch 1 para 16. This must be understood in the context of the usual rules governing the value of supplies made for a cash consideration that the value of a supply is such amount as, with the addition of the VAT chargeable, is equal to the consideration: see s 19(2); and para 85 post. The effect of Sch 1 para 16 is that the value of supplies for registration (and more importantly for the purposes of cancellation of registration: see para 73 post) is taken to be the gross and not the net consideration. Thus if a trader sells an asset for £117.50, for the purposes of determining whether or not his registration should be cancelled, the value of the supply is taken to be £117.50 and not £100, even though he will be obliged to account to Customs for £17.50 VAT on the sale. Quaere whether the same would be true if the trader were to sell the asset for '£100 plus VAT'.

   Where any person makes a supply of gold to another person and that supply is a taxable supply but not a zero-rated supply, the supply is treated for the purposes of Sch 1 (as amended) (1) as a taxable supply of that other person, as well as a taxable supply of the person who makes it; and (2) in so far as that other person is supplied in connection with the carrying on by him of any business, as a supply made by him in the course or furtherance of that business; but nothing in head (2) supra requires any supply to be disregarded for the purposes of Sch 1 (as amended) on the grounds that it is a supply of capital assets of that other person's business (see further the text and note 10 infra): s 55(1). For the meaning of 'supply of gold' see para 26 note 18 ante.

10 Ibid Sch 1 para 1(7). Cf the distinction drawn by s 5(1), Sch 4 para 1 (see para 24 ante) between the transfer of the whole property in goods, which is a supply of goods, and the transfer of an undivided share of the property, or of the possession of goods, which is a supply of services. Schedule 1 para 1(7) is

designed to leave out of account supplies of minor interests in capital goods as well as the transfer of the whole property in such goods. Where, however, an interest in, right over, or licence to occupy any land would be so disregarded for the purposes of Sch 1 para 1(1) or (2) (as amended), it is not disregarded if it is supplied on a taxable supply which is not zero-rated: Sch 1 para 1(8). As to the charge to VAT on the supply of an interest see para 142 post. As to the meaning of 'capital goods' see Case 51/76 *Verbond van Nederlandse Ondernemingen v Inspecteur der Invoerrechten en Accijnzen* [1977] ECR 113, [1977] 1 CMLR 413, ECJ, in the context of EC Council Directive 67/227 (OJ 71, 14.4.47, p 1301) art 17; *Trustees of the Mellerstain Trust v Customs and Excise Comrs* [1989] VATTR 223 at 235 et seq (a sale of paintings by trustees to create a maintenance fund for an historic house which it was intended subsequently to open to the public was a supply of capital goods, which fell to be disregarded in accordance with the Value Added Tax Act 1994 Sch 1 para 1(7) when determining whether the trustees were liable to be registered (and thus whether they were obliged to account for VAT on the sale of the paintings)).

11 Ie apart from ibid s 7(4): see para 26 ante. For the meaning of 'United Kingdom' see para 4 note 3 ante.

12 Ibid Sch 1 para 1(7). For the meaning of 'another member state' see para 4 note 14 ante.

13 Ie for the purposes of ibid Sch 1 para 1(1)(a) (as amended): see the text and notes 3–6 supra. This provision also applies in a case falling within Sch 1 para 1(2)(a) (as amended) (transfer of a business as a going concern: see the text and notes 18–19 infra): Sch 1 para 1(4).

14 Ie cancelled otherwise than under ibid Sch 1 para 13(3) (see para 73 post), Sch 2 para 6(2) (see para 76 post) or Sch 3 para 6(3) (see para 78 post): Sch 1 para 1(4)(a).

15 Ibid Sch 1 para 1(4).

16 As to the VAT treatment of transfers of businesses as going concerns see para 196 post.

17 Value Added Tax Act 1994 s 49(1)(a). The Value Added Tax Regulations 1995, SI 1995/2518, reg 6(1) makes provision for the transferor and transferee jointly to apply for the registration number of the transferor to be assigned to the transferee: see para 74 post. Consequentially, the transferee becomes liable for any outstanding output tax for which the transferor has failed to account to Customs and Excise and entitled to credit for or repayment of any input tax to which the transferor was entitled: see reg 6(3); and para 74 post.

18 Ie the supplies which are treated as his by virtue of the Value Added Tax Act 1994 s 49(1)(a): see the text and note 17 supra.

19 Ibid Sch 1 para 1(2)(a) (amended by the Value Added Tax (Increase of Registration Limits) Order 1995 art 2(a)). As to valuation of a person's supplies, and as to the Treasury's power to substitute a greater sum, see note 6 supra.

20 Value Added Tax Act 1994 Sch 1 para 1(2)(b) (as amended: see note 19 supra). As to valuation of a persons' supplies, and as to the Treasury's power to substitute a greater sum, see note 6 supra. A person who becomes liable to be registered by virtue of Sch 1 para 1(2) (as so amended) must notify the commissioners of the liability within 30 days of the time when the business is transferred (Sch 1 para 7(1)); and the commissioners must register any such person, whether or not he so notifies them, with effect from the time when the business is transferred (Sch 1 para 7(2)).

Where the transferee of a business has been registered in substitution for the transferor, and with the transferor's registration number, any liability of the transferor existing at the date of the transfer to make a return or to account for or pay VAT under the Value Added Tax Regulations 1995 becomes the liability of the transferee: see para 74 post.

21 'Local authority' means the council of a county, county borough, district, London borough, parish or group of parishes (or, in Wales, community or group of communities), the Common Council of the City of London, the Council of the Isles of Scilly, and any joint committee or joint board established by two or more of the above: ibid s 96(1), (4) (amended by the Local Government Reorganisation (Wales) (Consequential Amendments No 2) Order 1995, SI 1995/1510).

22 As to the business activities of local authorities and similar public bodies see para 65 post.

23 See the Value Added Tax Act 1994 s 42; and para 65 post.

24 Ie under ibid Sch 1 (as amended): see the text and notes 1–20 supra.

25 Ie cancelled under ibid Sch 1 para 13(3) (see para 73 post), Sch 2 para 6(2) (see para 76 post) or Sch 3 para 6(3) (see para 78 post): Sch 1 para 1(5).

26 Ibid Sch 1 para 1(5).

27 Ibid s 83(a). As to appeals see generally para 293 et seq post.

57. Exemption from registration. Where a person who makes or intends to make taxable supplies[1] satisfies the Commissioners of Customs and Excise that any such supply is zero-rated[2] or would be zero-rated if he were a taxable person[3], they may, if he so requests and they think fit, exempt him from registration[4] until it appears to them that the request should no longer be acted upon or is withdrawn[5].

Where there is a material change in the nature of the supplies made by a person so exempted from registration, he must notify the commissioners of the change within 30 days of the date on which it occurred or, if no particular day is identifiable as the day on which it occurred, within 30 days of the end of the quarter in which it occurred[6]. Where there is a material alteration in any quarter in the proportion of taxable supplies of such a person that are zero-rated, he must notify the commissioners of the alteration within 30 days of the end of the quarter[7].

1   For the meaning of 'taxable supplies' see para 12 note 3 ante. See also para 56 note 4 ante.
2   For the meaning of 'zero-rated' see para 158 post.
3   For the meaning of 'taxable person' see paras 12 note 4, 55 ante.
4   Ie under the Value Added Tax Act 1994 s 3(2), Sch 1 (as amended): see paras 56 ante, 58 et seq post.
5   Ibid Sch 1 para 14(1). The trader is thus relieved from the administrative burdens attendant upon registration, at the expense of losing the right to repayment of the input tax which he incurs on the purchase of supplies for the purposes of his business. See *Fong v Customs and Excise Comrs* [1978] VATTR 75 (repayment trader (in the sense that her input tax generally exceeded her output tax) applied for exemption from registration under the Value Added Tax Act 1994 Sch 1 para 14(1); the commissioners claimed that their power to exempt businesses from registration was restricted to those which made only zero-rated supplies; held that, on a correct interpretation of Sch 1 para 14(1), the commissioners had a discretion to exempt any trader who made, inter alia, zero-rated supplies and, further, that their decision was appealable under s 83(a) (see para 296 post)).
6   Ibid Sch 1 para 14(2).
7   Ibid Sch 1 para 14(3). As to the penalty for failure to comply with these requirements see para 279 post.

58. Voluntary registration. Where a person who is not liable to be registered for value added tax[1] and is not already so registered satisfies the Commissioners of Customs and Excise that he makes taxable supplies[2] or that he is carrying on a business and intends to make taxable supplies in the course or furtherance of that business[3], the commissioners must, if he so requests, register him with effect from the day on which the request is made or from such earlier date as may be agreed between them and him[4].

Where a person who:

(1)   has a business establishment[5] in the United Kingdom[6] or his usual place of residence[7] in the United Kingdom[8];

(2)   does not make and does not intend to make taxable supplies[9]; and

(3)   is not liable to be registered for VAT and is not already so registered[10],

satisfies the commissioners either that he makes supplies outside the United Kingdom which would be taxable supplies if made in the United Kingdom[11] or that he is carrying on a business and intends to make such supplies in the course or furtherance of that business, they must, if he so requests, register him with effect from the day on which the request is made, or from such earlier date as may be agreed between them and him[12]. A person who has been voluntarily registered under this provision and who makes or forms the intention of making taxable supplies must notify the commissioners of that fact within 30 days of the day on which he does so[13].

1   Ie under the Value Added Tax Act 1994: see para 56 ante. For the meaning of 'registered' see paras 12 note 4, 56 note 2 ante. A person may not be liable to registration eg because the value of his supplies or intended supplies fall below the registration threshold.
2   For the meaning of 'taxable supplies' see para 12 note 3 ante. See also para 56 note 4 ante.
3   As to the meaning of 'in the course or furtherance of a business' see paras 12 note 5, 17 note 2 ante.
4   Value Added Tax Act 1994 s 3(2), Sch 1 para 9. The advantage of registration is that it enables the trader to recover the VAT on supplies made to him for the purposes of his business as input tax: see para 201 et seq post.
    In Case 268/83 *DA Rompelman and EA Rompelman-van Deelen v Minister van Financiën* [1985] ECR 655, [1985] 3 CMLR 202, ECJ, it was held that a taxable activity began as soon as the first investment expenditure was incurred for the purposes of and with a view to carrying on an undertaking, so that an intending trader was immediately entitled to recover tax on supplies made to him for the purposes of that

activity under EC Council Directive 77/388 (OJ L145, 13.6.77, p 1) art 17 (as amended); but that the Revenue authorities were permitted to require a declared intention of trading to be supported by objective evidence. See also Case C-110/94 *Intercommunale voor Zeewaterontzilting (INZO) (in liquidation) v Belgium* [1996] ECR I-857, [1996] STC 569, ECJ. In *Merseyside Cablevision Ltd v Customs and Excise Comrs* [1987] VATTR 134 it was held that the United Kingdom system as it then existed did not conform with the Sixth Directive, because it left the discretion as to whether an intending trader might register for VAT with the commissioners and not with the trader. As a result, the provision which is now the Value Added Tax Act 1994 Sch 1 para 9 was introduced; and the commissioners are now obliged to register an intending trader provided that he produces the necessary objective evidence of his declared intention to trade. If the commissioners are not satisfied by the evidence produced by the applicant, he may appeal to the VAT tribunal, which has supervisory jurisdiction: *Golden Pyramid Ltd v Customs and Excise Comrs* [1993] 2 CMLR 321.

5   For these purposes, a person carrying on a business through a branch or agency in the United Kingdom is treated as having a business establishment in the United Kingdom: Value Added Tax Act 1994 Sch 1 para 10(4)(a). As to the meaning of 'business establishment' and related phrases see also para 46 ante.

6   For the meaning of 'United Kingdom' see para 4 note 3 ante.

7   For these purposes, 'usual place of residence', in relation to a body corporate, means the place where it is legally constituted: Value Added Tax Act 1994 Sch 1 para 10(4)(b).

8   Ibid Sch 1 para 10(3)(a).

9   Ibid Sch 1 para 10(3)(b).

10   Ibid Sch 1 para 10(1).

11   Ibid Sch 1 para 10(2).

12   Ibid Sch 1 para 10(1)–(3).

13   Ibid Sch 1 para 12(b). The notification must be made in writing to the commissioners and must state the date on which he made, or formed the intention of making, taxable supplies: Value Added Tax Regulations 1995, SI 1995/2518, reg 5(3)(c).

59. Registration of two or more persons as a single taxable person.

If the Commissioners of Customs and Excise make a direction to that effect[1], the persons named in the direction are treated as a single taxable person[2] carrying on the activities of a business described in the direction and that taxable person is liable to be registered[3] for value added tax with effect from the date of the direction or from such later date as the direction may specify[4]. The commissioners may not make such a direction naming any person unless they are satisfied that:

(1)   he is making (or has made) taxable supplies[5];

(2)   the activities in the course of which he makes or made those taxable supplies form only part of certain activities being carried on either concurrently or previously (or both) by one or more other persons which should properly be regarded as those of the business described in the commissioners' direction[6];

(3)   if all the taxable supplies of that business were taken into account, a person carrying it on would at the time of the direction be liable to be registered[7] for VAT by virtue of the value of the supplies[8]; and

(4)   the main reason, or one of the main reasons, for the person concerned carrying on the activities in the way that he does is the avoidance of a liability[9] to be registered[10].

Such a direction must be served on each of the persons named in it[11].

Where, after a direction has been so given specifying a description of business, it appears to the commissioners that a person who was not named in it is making taxable supplies in the course of activities which should properly be regarded as part of the activities of that business, the commissioners may make and serve on him a supplementary direction referring to the earlier direction and the description of business specified in it and adding that person's name to those of the persons named in the earlier direction with effect from the date on which he began to make those taxable supplies or, if it was later, the date with effect from which the single taxable person referred to in the earlier direction became liable to be registered[12].

If, immediately before a direction or supplementary direction is made, any person named in it is registered in respect of the taxable supplies made by him which are the subject of the direction[13], he ceases to be liable to be registered with effect from the date on which the single taxable person concerned became liable to be registered or the date of the direction, whichever is the later[14].

Where a direction is made, then:

(a) the taxable person carrying on the business specified in the direction is registrable in such name as the persons named in the direction may jointly nominate by notice in writing given to the commissioners not later than 14 days after the date of the direction or, in default of such a nomination, in such name as may be specified in the direction[15];

(b) any supply of goods or services by or to one of the constituent members[16] in the course of the activities of the taxable person is treated as a supply by or to that person[17];

(c) any acquisition of goods from another member state[18] by one of the constituent members in the course of the activities of the taxable person is treated as an acquisition by that person[19];

(d) each of the constituent members is jointly and severally liable for any VAT due from the taxable person[20];

(e) any failure by the taxable person to comply with any statutory requirement[21] is treated as a failure by each of the constituent members severally[22]; and

(f) the constituent members are treated[23] as a partnership carrying on the business of the taxable person and any question as to the scope of the activities of that business at any time is to be determined accordingly[24].

If it appears to the commissioners that any person who is one of the constituent members should no longer be regarded as such for the purposes of heads (d) and (e) above and they give notice to that effect, he is not to have any liability[25] for anything done after the date specified in that notice and, accordingly, on that date he is treated as having ceased to be a member of the partnership referred to in head (f) above[26].

1   Ie a direction under the Value Added Tax Act 1994 s 3(2), Sch 1 para 2: see the text and notes 2–26 infra.

2   For the meaning of 'taxable person' see paras 12 note 4, 55 ante.

3   Ie under the Value Added Tax Act 1994 Sch 1 (as amended): see paras 56–58 ante, 71–74 post.

4   Ibid Sch 1 para 2(1).

5   Ibid Sch 1 para 2(2)(a). For the meaning of 'taxable supplies' see para 12 note 3 ante. See also para 56 note 4 ante.

6   Ibid Sch 1 para 2(2)(b).

7   Ie by virtue of ibid Sch 1 para 1 (as amended): see para 56 ante.

8   Ibid Sch 1 para 2(2)(c).

9   Ie whether that liability would be his, another person's, or that of two or more persons jointly: ibid Sch 1 para 2(2)(d).

10   Ibid Sch 1 para 2(2). See *Osman v Customs and Excise Comrs* [1989] STC 596 (where it was contended that the Value Added Tax Act 1994 Sch 1 para 2 was inconsistent with EC Council Directive 77/388 (OJ L145, 13.6.77, p 1) art 4(4) (which permits a member state (after consultation) to treat as a single taxable person persons who, while legally independent, are closely bound to one another by financial, economic and organisational links); held that the words 'properly so regarded' in the Value Added Tax Act 1994 Sch 1 para 2(2)(b) (see head (2) in the text) require the commissioners to determine that the conditions of EC Council Directive 77/388 art 4(4) have been satisfied); *Chamberlain v Customs and Excise Comrs* [1989] STC 505 (supervisory jurisdiction of a tribunal when considering an appeal from a direction under the Value Added Tax Act 1994 Sch 1 para 2). See also Joined Cases 181/78, 229/78 *Ketelhandel P van Paassen BV v Staatssecretaris van Financiën, Minister van Financiën v Denkavit Dienstbetoon BV* [1979] ECR 2063, [1980] 2 CMLR 47, ECJ, on the predecessor to EC Council Directive 77/388 art 4(4) (ie EC Council Directive 67/228 (OJ 71, 14.4.67, p 1303) art 16 (repealed)). In *Thompson, Thompson & Giblin v Customs and Excise Comrs* (1990) VAT Decision 4196, [1990] STI 65 it was held that the commissioners could not impute the motivation of one person to another, where that other

had neither been interviewed by Customs nor given any opportunity of explaining his reasons for keeping his business activities separate from the other.

11 Value Added Tax Act 1994 Sch 1 para 2(3).
12 Ibid Sch 1 para 2(4).
13 Ie the taxable supplies made by him as mentioned in ibid Sch 1 para 2(2) or (4): see the text to notes 10, 12 supra.
14 Ibid Sch 1 para 2(5). He may, of course, wish, or indeed be obliged, to remain registered in respect of other business activities; but he will in any event cease to include the supplies attributable to the single taxable person in his own VAT return.
15 Ibid Sch 1 para 2(7)(a).
16 In relation to a business specified in a direction under ibid Sch 1 para 2, the persons named in the direction, together with any person named in a supplementary direction relating to that business, being the persons who together are to be treated as the taxable person, are referred to as 'the constituent members': Sch 1 para 2(6).
17 Ibid Sch 1 para 2(7)(b).
18 For the meaning of 'another member state' see para 4 note 14 ante; and as to acquisitions from another member state see para 13 ante.
19 Ibid Sch 1 para 2(7)(c).
20 Ibid Sch 1 para 2(7)(d).
21 Ie any requirement imposed by or under the Value Added Tax Act 1994: Sch 1 para 2(7)(e).
22 Ibid Sch 1 para 2(7)(e). This provision is without prejudice to Sch 1 para 2(7)(d) (see head (d) in the text): Sch 1 para 2(7)(e).
23 Ie subject to ibid Sch 1 para 2(7)(a)–(e): see heads (a)–(e) in the text.
24 Ibid Sch 1 para 2(7)(f). As to the registration and VAT obligations of partnerships see para 68 post.
25 Ie by virtue of ibid Sch 1 para 2(7)(d), (e): see heads (d)–(e) in the text.
26 Ibid Sch 1 para 2(8).

B. SUPPLIES FROM OTHER MEMBER STATES

60. Registration in the single market; distance sales. A person who is not registered for value added tax[1] and is not liable to be registered under the general rules relating to taxable supplies[2] becomes liable to be registered[3] on any day if, in the period beginning with 1 January of the year in which that day falls, that person has made relevant supplies whose value exceeds £70,000[4]. A supply of goods is a 'relevant supply' for these purposes where the supply:

(1) involves the removal of the goods to the United Kingdom[5] by or under the directions of the person making the supply[6];

(2) does not involve the installation or assembly of the goods at a place in the United Kingdom[7];

(3) is a transaction in pursuance of which goods are acquired in the United Kingdom from another member state[8] by a person who is not a taxable person[9];

(4) is made on or after 1 January 1993 and in the course or furtherance of a business[10] carried on by the supplier[11];

(5) is neither an exempt supply nor a supply of goods which are subject to a duty of excise or consist in a new means of transport[12] and is not anything which is treated as having been supplied by reason of certain[13] deeming provisions[14].

Once a trader becomes so registrable, his relevant supplies will be treated as made in the United Kingdom and he will be obliged to account for VAT on those sales accordingly[15].

A person who is not registered or liable to be registered for VAT[16] becomes liable to be registered where:

(a) that person has exercised any option[17], in accordance with the law of any member state where he is taxable, for treating relevant supplies made by him as taking place outside that member state[18];

(b) the supplies to which the option relates involve the removal of goods from that member state and, apart from the exercise of the option, would be treated as taking place in that member state in accordance with its law[19]; and

(c) that person makes a relevant supply at a time when the option is in force in relation to him[20].

A person who is not registered or liable to be registered for VAT also becomes liable to be registered if he makes a supply of goods subject to a duty of excise[21] which involves the removal of the goods to the United Kingdom by or under his directions[22] and which fulfils certain other statutory requirements[23].

A person is treated as having become liable to be registered under these provisions at any time when he would have become so liable thereunder but for any registration which is subsequently cancelled[24] either because he was not registrable or because he did not have the intention by reference to which he was registered[25].

1   Ie under the Value Added Tax Act 1994: see paras 56 et seq ante, 61 et seq post.
2   Ie under ibid s 3(2), Sch 1 (as amended): see paras 56–59 ante.
3   Ie under ibid s 3(2), Sch 3: see the text and notes 4–23 infra; and para 61 et seq post.
4   Ibid Sch 2 para 1(1). The Treasury may by order substitute for any of the sums for the time being specified in Sch 2 such greater sums as it thinks fit: Sch 2 para 8. At the date at which this volume states the law, no such order had been made. Cf Sch 1 para 15; and para 56 note 6 ante. In determining the value of any relevant supplies for these purposes, so much of the consideration for any supply as represents any liability of the supplier, under the law of another member state, for VAT on that supply is to be disregarded: Sch 2 para 1(6). Supplies to which s 18B(4) (as added) (last acquisition or supply of goods before removal from fiscal warehousing: see para 134 post) applies are also to be disregarded for these purposes: Sch 2 para 1(7) (added by the Finance Act 1996 s 26(1), Sch 3 para 14). For the meaning of 'another member state' see para 4 note 14 ante; for the meaning of 'supply' see para 21 ante; and as to the meaning of references to the law of another member state see para 11 note 1 ante.
        A person who becomes liable to be registered under the Value Added Tax Act 1994 Sch 2 must notify the Commissioners of Customs and Excise of his liability within the period of 30 days after the date on which the liability arises: Value Added Tax Act 1994 Sch 2 para 3(1). The commissioners must register any such person, whether or not he so notifies them, with effect from the day on which the liability arose or from such earlier date as may be agreed between them and him: Sch 1 para 3(2). Any notification required under Sch 2 must be made in such form and must contain such particulars as the commissioners may prescribe by regulations: Sch 2 para 9. Where any person is so required to notify the commissioners of his liability to be registered, the notification must contain the particulars, including the declaration, set out in the Value Added Tax Regulations 1995, SI 1995/2518, reg 5(1), Sch 1, Form 6 and must be made in that form; but where the notification is made by a partnership, it must also contain the particulars set out in Sch 1, Form 2: reg 5(1).
5   For the meaning of 'United Kingdom' see para 4 note 3 ante.
6   Value Added Tax Act 1994 Sch 2 para 10(a).
7   Ibid Sch 2 para 10(b).
8   As to acquisition from another member state see para 13 ante.
9   Value Added Tax Act 1994 Sch 2 para 10(c). For the meaning of 'taxable person' see paras 12 note 4, 55 ante.
10   As to the meaning of 'in the course or furtherance of a business' see paras 12 note 5, 17 note 2 ante.
11   Value Added Tax Act 1994 Sch 2 para 10(d).
12   For the meaning of 'new means of transport' see para 13 note 8 ante.
13   Ie by reason only of ibid s 5(2), Sch 4 para 5(1) (see para 24 ante) or Sch 4 para 6 (see paras 14–15 ante): Sch 2 para 10(e).
14   Ibid Sch 2 para 10(e).
15   Ordinarily, goods which are supplied from abroad and which must be removed to the United Kingdom would be treated as supplied outside the United Kingdom and thus would not be taxable: see ibid ss 4(2), 7(7); and paras 12–13, 45 ante. Where, however, goods are sold in circumstances falling within s 7(4) (see para 42 ante), they are treated as supplied in the United Kingdom and the supplier must accordingly account for VAT on the sale. One condition of s 7(4) is that the supplier is liable to be registered under Sch 2 or would be so liable were he not already registered or liable to be registered under Sch 1 (as amended). Thus, once a distance seller has exceeded the £47,000 limit in the course of a calendar year, he becomes liable to registration under Sch 2 and his subsequent distance sales (though not his prior sales) are treated as made in the United Kingdom.
16   Ie as mentioned in ibid Sch 2 para 1(1)(a), (b): see the text to notes 1–4 supra.
17   Where a person has exercised an option in the United Kingdom corresponding to such an option, in respect of supplies involving the removal of goods to another member state, he must notify the commissioners in writing of the exercise of that option not less than 30 days before the date on which

the first supply to which the option relates is made; and the notification must contain the name of the member state to which the goods have been, or are to be, removed under the direction or control of the person making the supply: Value Added Tax Regulations 1995 reg 98(1), (2). Within 30 days of the first such supply he must furnish to the commissioners documentary evidence that he has notified the member state of the exercise of his option: reg 98(3). Where a person notified the commissioners in accordance with reg 98(1), he may withdraw his notification by giving a further written notification, but it must specify the date on which the first notification is to be withdrawn and that date must not be earlier than (1) the 1 January which is, or next follows, the second anniversary of the date of the making of the first supply to which the option relates; and (2) the day 30 days after the receipt by the commissioners of the further notification, and not later than 30 days before the date of the first supply which he intends to make after the withdrawal: reg 98(4).

EC Council Directive 77/388 (OJ L145, 13.6.77, p 1) art 28b(B)(3) (added by EC Council Directive 91/680 (OJ L376, 31.12.91, p 1) provides that each member state is to grant an option to a trader who would be treated as making supplies of goods in the country from which the goods are dispatched (because the value of his supplies into the member state of receipt do not exceed the threshold, eg in the United Kingdom of £70,000), entitling him to elect that his supplies should be treated as made in the member state to which the goods are dispatched. It is difficult to find a provision in the United Kingdom legislation which effectively implements art 28b(B)(3) (as so added). It is apprehended that the proviso to the Value Added Tax Act 1994 s 7(5) (see para 42 ante) is intended to do so; but it appears to proceed on the basis that the option itself will have been conferred by another provision of the Act, of which there appears to be none. In practice, the commissioners permit a trader to exercise an option of the kind mentioned in EC Council Directive 77/388 art 28b(B)(3) (as so added): see Customs and Excise Notice 725 *VAT: The Single Market* (1 February 1994) para 4.3; and the Value Added Tax Regulations 1995 reg 98 cited supra.

18   Value Added Tax Act 1994 Sch 2 para 2(1), (2)(a).
19   Ibid Sch 2 para 1(2)(b).
20   Ibid Sch 2 para 1(2)(c).
21   Ibid Sch 2 para 1(3)(a). In this case there is no minimum registration limit.
22   Ibid Sch 2 para 1(3)(b).
23   Ibid Sch 2 para 1(3). Those conditions are that (1) it is a transaction in pursuance of which the goods are acquired in the United Kingdom from another member state by a person who is not a taxable person; (2) it is made on or after 1 January 1993 and in the course or furtherance of a business carried on by the supplier; and (3) it is not anything which is treated as a supply for the purposes of the Value Added Tax Act 1994 by virtue only of Sch 4 para 5(1) or Sch 4 para 6: Sch 2 para 1(3)(c)–(e).
24   Ie cancelled under ibid Sch 1 para 13(3) (see para 73 post), Sch 2 para 6(2) (see para 76 post) or Sch 3 para 6(3) (see para 78 post): Sch 2 para 1(4).
25   Ibid Sch 2 para 1(4).

61. Voluntary registration. Where a person who is not liable to be registered for value added tax[1], and is not already registered, satisfies the Commissioners of Customs and Excise that he intends:

    (1)   to exercise an option in another member state to treat his distance sales to the United Kingdom as supplied in the United Kingdom[2] and to make relevant supplies[3] to which that option will relate[4];

    (2)   from a specified date to make relevant supplies to which any such option that he has exercised will relate[5]; or

    (3)   from a specified date to make supplies in relation to which the statutory conditions relating to goods subject to a duty of excise[6] will be satisfied[7],

and requests to be registered[8], the commissioners may register him with effect from such date as may be agreed between them and him[9]. The registration may be subject to such conditions as the commissioners think fit to impose[10].

1   Ie under the Value Added Tax Act 1994: see paras 56 et seq ante, 62 et seq post.
2   Ie such an option as is mentioned in ibid s 3(2), Sch 2 para 1(2): see para 60 ante. For the meaning of 'another member state' see para 4 note 14 ante; and for the meaning of 'United Kingdom' see para 4 note 3 ante.
3   For the meaning of 'relevant supplies' see para 60 ante.
4   Value Added Tax Act 1994 Sch 2 para 4(1)(a)(i).
5   Ibid Sch 2 para 4(1)(a)(ii).

6   Ie the conditions mentioned in ibid Sch 2 para 1(3); see para 60 ante.
7   Ibid Sch 2 para 4(1)(a)(iii).
8   Ibid Sch 2 para 4(1)(b). The request must be for registration under Sch 2: Sch 2 para 4(1)(b).
9   Ibid Sch 2 para 4(1). Where, however, a person who is entitled to be registered under s 3(2), Sch 1 para 9
     or 10 (see para 58 ante) requests registration under this provision, he must be registered under Sch 1 (as
     amended) and not under Sch 2: Sch 2 para 4(3).
10   Ibid Sch 2 para 4(1). Conditions may be so imposed wholly or partly by reference to, or without reference
     to, any conditions prescribed for these purposes, and may, whenever imposed, be subsequently varied by
     the commissioners: Sch 2 para 4(2).

62. Value added tax representatives. The Commissioners of Customs and Excise
may direct any person who:

(1)   is a taxable person[1] for the purposes of value added tax or who, without being a
       taxable person, makes taxable supplies[2] or acquires goods in the United
       Kingdom[3] from one or more other member states[4]; and

(2)   does not have any business establishment or other fixed establishment in the
       United Kingdom, or, being an individual, does not have his usual place of
       residence in the United Kingdom[5],

to appoint another person (a 'VAT representative') to act on his behalf in relation to
VAT[6]. Any such person may also, with the agreement of the commissioners, appoint
a VAT representative without having been required[7] to do so[8].

Where any person is appointed by virtue of these provisions to be a VAT
representative of another ('his principal'), then that representative is entitled to act on his
principal's behalf for any statutory purpose relating to VAT[9] and must secure his
principal's compliance with and discharge of the obligations and liabilities to which is
principal is subject[10] in relation to VAT[11]. He is not, however, thereby himself liable to
be registered for VAT[12]. Nevertheless, the commissioners may make regulations
requiring the registration of the names of VAT representatives against the names of their
principals in any register kept for the purposes of the Value Added Tax Act 1994 and
making it the duty of a VAT representative, for the purposes of registration, to notify the
commissioners within a prescribed period that his appointment has taken effect or has
ceased to have effect[13].

1   For the meaning of 'taxable person' see paras 12 note 4, 55 ante.
2   For the meaning of 'taxable supply' see para 12 note 3 ante.
3   For the meaning of 'United Kingdom' see para 4 note 3 ante.
4   Value Added Tax Act 1994 s 48(1)(a).
5   Ibid s 48(1)(b), (c).
6   Ibid s 48(1). Where a person fails to appoint a VAT representative in accordance with any direction under
     s 48(1), the commissioners may require him to provide such security, or further security, as they may
     think appropriate for the payment of any VAT which is or may become due from him: s 48(7). An appeal
     to a VAT and duties tribunal lies against such a direction: s 83(l). As to VAT and duties tribunals see para
     293 et seq post. A person is not, however, to be treated as having been directed to appoint a VAT
     representative, or as having been required to provide such security, unless the commissioners have either
     served notice of the direction or requirement on him, or taken all such other steps as appear to them to
     be reasonable for bringing the direction or requirement to his attention: s 48(8).
         The commissioners may make provision by regulations as to the manner and circumstances in which a
     person is to be appointed, or is to be treated as having ceased to be, another's VAT representative: s 48(6).
     In exercise of the power so conferred, the commissioners have made the Value Added Tax Regulations
     1995, SI 1995/2518, reg 10. The VAT representative must notify the commissioners of his appointment in
     accordance with reg 10(1), Sch 1, Form 8, within 30 days of the date on which his appointment became
     effective and the notification must contain the particulars, including the declaration, set out in that form,
     and must be accompanied by evidence of his appointment: reg 10(1), (2).
7   Ie under the Value Added Tax Act 1994 s 48(1): see the text and notes 1–6 supra.
8   Ibid s 48(2).

9   Ie for any of the purposes of the Value Added Tax Act 1994, of any other enactment, whenever passed, relating to VAT, or of any subordinate legislation made under the 1994 Act or any such enactment: ibid s 48(3)(a). As to subordinate legislation see para 7 ante.

10   Ie by virtue of the Value Added Tax Act 1994 or any other enactment, or any subordinate legislation such as is mentioned in note 9 supra: s 48(3)(b).

11   Ibid s 48(3)(a), (b). The VAT representative is personally liable in respect of any failure to secure his principal's compliance with or discharge of any such obligation or liability, and anything done for purposes connected with acting on his principal's behalf, as if the obligations and liabilities imposed on his principal were imposed jointly and severally on the VAT representative and his principal: s 48(3)(c). The VAT representative is not, however, thereby guilty of any offence except in so far as (1) he has consented to, or connived in, the commission of the offence by his principal; (2) the commission of the offence by his principal is attributable to any neglect on the part of the VAT representative; or (3) the offence consists in a contravention by the VAT representative of an obligation which, by virtue of s 48(3), is imposed both on the VAT representative and on his principal: s 48(5). As to offences see further para 267 et seq post.

12   Ibid s 48(4).

13   Ibid s 48(4). Regulations under s 48(6) may include such provision as the commissioners think fit for these purposes with respect to the making or deletion of entries in the register: s 48(6).

     Where a person is appointed by virtue of s 48 to be a VAT representative, the commissioners must register the name of that representative against the name of his principal in the register kept for the purposes of the Value Added Tax Act 1994: Value Added Tax Regulations 1995 reg 10(3). Every VAT representative who is registered in accordance with reg 10 must, within 30 days of any changes being made in the name, constitution or ownership of his business or of his ceasing to be a person's VAT representative, or of any other event occurring which may necessitate the variation of the register, notify the commissioners in writing of such change, cessation or event and furnish them with full particulars thereof: reg 10(4).

     The date upon which the appointment of a VAT representative ('the first VAT representative') is regarded as having ceased for these purposes is treated as being whichever is the earliest of the following times: (1) when the commissioners receive any notification in accordance with reg 5(2) (see para 56 ante); or (2) when the commissioners receive a notification of appointment in accordance with reg 10(1) of a person other than the first VAT representative; or (3) when the commissioners receive a notification of cessation in accordance with reg 5(2); or (4) when the commissioners receive a notification of cessation in accordance with reg 10(4); or (5) when a VAT representative dies, becomes insolvent or becomes incapacitated: reg 10(5)(a)–(e). However, if the commissioners have not received a notification such as is mentioned in all or any of heads (1), (3) or (4) supra and another person has been appointed as a VAT representative by virtue of the Value Added Tax Act 1994 s 48, they may treat the date of cessation as the date of appointment of that other person: Value Added Tax Regulations 1995 reg 10(5). In relation to a company which is a VAT representative, the references in head (5) supra to the VAT representative becoming insolvent or incapacitated are to be construed as references to its going into liquidation or receivership or to an administration order being made in relation to it: reg 10(6).

C. ACQUISITIONS FROM OTHER MEMBER STATES

63. Registration in the single market; taxable acquisitions of goods. A person who is not registered for value added tax and is not otherwise liable to be registered[1] becomes liable to be registered[2]: (1) at the end of any month, if, in the period beginning with 1 January of the year in which that month falls, that person had made relevant acquisitions whose value exceeds £47,000[3]; or (2) at any time, if there are reasonable grounds for believing that the value of his relevant acquisitions in the period of 30 days then beginning will exceed £47,000[4]. An acquisition of goods from another member state is a 'relevant acquisition' where: (a) it is a taxable acquisition[5] of goods other than goods which are subject to a duty of excise or consist in a new means of transport[6]; and (b) it is an acquisition otherwise than in pursuance of a taxable supply[7] and is treated for VAT purposes as taking place in the United Kingdom[8].

A person is treated as having become liable to be registered under these provisions at any time when he would have become so liable but for any registration which is subsequently cancelled[9] either because he was not registrable or because he did not have the intention by reference to which he was registered[10].

Where, however, a person who makes or intends to make relevant acquisitions satisfies the Commissioners of Customs and Excise that any such acquisition would be in pursuance of a transaction which would be zero-rated[11] if it were a taxable supply by a taxable person[12], the commissioners may exempt him from registration at his request, and if he thinks fit, until it appears to them that the request should no longer be acted upon or is withdrawn[13].

1   Ie under the Value Added Tax Act 1994 s 3(2), Sch 1 (as amended) or Sch 2: see para 56 et seq ante.
2   Ie under ibid Sch 3 (as amended): see the text and notes 3–12 infra; and para 64 post.
3   Ibid Sch 3 para 1(1) (Sch 3 para 1 amended by the Value Added Tax (Increase of Registration Limits) Order 1995, SI 1995/3037, art 3). In determining the value of any person's relevant acquisitions for these purposes, so much of the consideration for any acquisition as represents any liability of the supplier, under the law of another member state, for VAT on the transaction in pursuance of which the acquisition is made, is to be disregarded: Value Added Tax Act 1994 Sch 3 para 1(5). Acquisitions to which s 18B(4) (as added) (last acquisition or supply of goods before removal from fiscal warehousing: see para 134 post) applies are also to be disregarded: Sch 3 para 1(6) (added by the Finance Act 1996 s 26(1), Sch 3 para 15). The Treasury may by order substitute for any of the sums for the time being specified in the Value Added Tax Act 1994 Sch 3 (as amended) such greater sums as it thinks fit: Sch 3 para 9. In exercise of this power, the Treasury has made the Value Added Tax (Increase of Registration Limits) Order 1995 cited supra. Cf para 56 note 6 ante. For the meaning of 'another member state' see para 4 note 14 ante; and as to the meaning of references to the law of another member state see para 11 note 1 ante.
     A person who becomes liable to be registered under this provision must notify the Commissioners of Customs and Excise of the liability within 30 days of the end of the month when he becomes so liable (Value Added Tax Act 1994 Sch 3 para 3(1)(a)); and the commissioners must register any such person, whether or not he so notifies them, with effect from the end of the month following the month at the end of which the liability arose, or from such earlier time as may be agreed between them and him (Sch 3 para 3(2), (3)(a)). Any notification required under Sch 3 (as amended) must be made in such form and must contain such particulars as the commissioners may prescribe by regulations: Sch 3 para 10. The notification must contain the particulars, including the declaration, set out in the Value Added Tax Regulations 1995, SI 1995/2518, reg 5(1), Sch 1, Form 7, and must be set out in that form; but where the notification is made by a partnership, it must also contain the particulars set out in Sch 1, Form 2: reg 5(1).
4   Value Added Tax Act 1994 Sch 3 para 1(2) (as amended: see note 3 supra). As to determining the value of the acquisitions see note 3 supra. A person who becomes liable to be registered under this provision must notify the commissioners of the liability before the end of the period by reference to which the liability arises (Sch 3 para 3(1)(b)); and the commissioners must register any such person, whether or not he so notifies them, with effect from the beginning of the period by reference to which the liability arose or from such earlier time as may be agreed between them and him (Sch 3 para 3(2), (3)(b)). As to the form of notification see note 3 supra.
5   For the meaning of 'taxable acquisition' see para 13 ante.
6   For the meaning of 'new means of transport' see para 13 note 8 ante.
7   For the meaning of 'taxable supply' see para 12 note 3 ante.
8   Value Added Tax Act 1994 Sch 3 para 11(a), (b). The event which, in relation to that acquisition, is the first relevant event for the purposes of taxing that acquisition must have occurred on or after 1 January 1993: Sch 3 para 11(c).
9   Ie under ibid Sch 3 para 6(3) (see para 73 post) or under Sch 1 para 13(3) (see para 76 post) or Sch 2 para 6(2) (see para 78 post): Sch 3 para 1(3).
10   Ibid Sch 3 para 1(3).
11   For the meaning of 'zero-rated' see para 158 post.
12   For the meaning of 'taxable person' see paras 12 note 4, 55 ante.
13   Value Added Tax Act 1994 Sch 3 para 8(1). Where a person who is so exempted from registration makes any relevant acquisition in pursuance of any transaction which would, if it were a taxable supply by a taxable person, be chargeable to VAT otherwise than as a zero-rated supply, he must notify the commissioners of the change within 30 days of the date on which he made the acquisition: Sch 3 para 8(2). For a similar provision exempting a person from an obligation to register when making zero-rated supplies see Sch 1 para 14; para 57 ante; and *Fong v Customs and Excise Comrs* [1978] VATTR 75.

64. Voluntary registration. Where a person who is not liable to be registered for value added tax and is not already registered[1] satisfies the Commissioners of Customs and Excise:

     (1)   that he makes relevant acquisitions[2]; or

(2)   that he intends to make relevant acquisitions from a specified date[3], and requests to be registered[4], they must register him[5]. In a case falling within head (1) above, the registration takes effect from the day on which the request is made or from such earlier date as may be agreed between them and him[6], while in a case falling within head (2) above the registration may be subject to such conditions as the commissioners think fit to impose[7] and takes effect from such date as may be agreed between them and him[8].

1   For the meaning of 'registered' see paras 12 note 4, 56 note 2 ante.
2   Value Added Tax Act 1994 s 3(2), Sch 3 para 4(1). For the meaning of 'relevant acquisitions' see para 63 ante.
3   Ibid Sch 3 para 4(2)(a).
4   In a case falling within head (2) in the text, the request must be for registration under ibid Sch 3 (as amended) (see para 63 ante): Sch 3 para 4(2)(b).
5   Ibid Sch 3 para 4(1), (2). Where, however, a person who is entitled to be registered under s 3(2), Sch 1 para 9 or 10 (see para 58 ante) requests registration, he must be registered under Sch 1 (as amended) (see para 56 et seq ante) and not under Sch 3 (as amended): Sch 3 para 4(4).
6   Ibid Sch 3 para 4(1).
7   The conditions may be imposed wholly or partly by, or without, reference to any conditions prescribed for these purposes and may, whenever imposed, subsequently be varied by the commissioners: ibid Sch 3 para 4(3). For the meaning of 'prescribed' see para 11 note 3 ante.
8   Ibid Sch 3 para 4(2).

D.   REGISTRATION IN SPECIAL CASES

65.   Local authorities. A local authority[1] which makes taxable supplies[2] is liable to be registered[3] whatever the value of its supplies, and accordingly the registration provisions[4] apply in a case where the value of taxable supplies made by a local authority in any period of one year does not exceed the sum specified for the time being as the threshold for compulsory registration[5] as if that value exceeded that sum[6].

1   For the meaning of 'local authority' see para 56 note 21 ante.
2   For the meaning of 'taxable supply' see para 12 note 3 ante.
3   For the meaning of 'registered' see paras 12 note 4, 56 note 2 ante.
4   Ie the Value Added Tax Act 1994 s 3(2), Sch 1 (as amended): see para 56 et seq ante.
5   Ie the sum for the time being specified in ibid Sch 1 para 1(1)(a) (as amended): see para 56 ante.
6   Ibid s 42.

66.   Groups of companies. Two or more bodies corporate are eligible to be treated as members of a group[1] for the purposes of value added tax if each is resident, or has an established place of business, in the United Kingdom[2] and (1) one of them controls[3] each of the others; or (2) one person (whether a body corporate or an individual) controls all of them; or (3) two or more individuals carrying on a business in partnership control all of them[4]. Where an application to that effect is made to the Commissioners of Customs and Excise with respect to two or more bodies corporate eligible to be treated as members of a group, then from the beginning of a prescribed accounting period[5] they are to be so treated, and one of them is to be the representative member, unless the commissioners refuse the application[6]. The application must be made by one of the bodies concerned, or by the person controlling them; and must be made not less than 90 days before the date from which it is to take effect, or at such later time as the commissioners may allow[7]. The commissioners may not refuse the application unless it appears to them necessary to do so for the protection of the revenue[8]. To ensure, however, that these provisions are not used for the avoidance of tax, the commissioners may in certain circumstances[9] give a direction requiring it to be assumed, in relation to a body corporate, that it did not fall to be treated, or is not to be treated, as a member of a group, or of a particular group described in the direction, for a specified period[10].

Where any bodies corporate are treated as members of a group and an application is made to the commissioners then, from the beginning of a prescribed accounting period:

(a) a further body eligible to be so treated may be included among the bodies so treated; or

(b) a body corporate may be excluded from the bodies so treated; or

(c) another member of the group may be substituted as the representative member, or

(d) the bodies corporate may cease to be treated as members of a group,

unless the commissioners refuse the application[11].

Where a body corporate is treated as a member of a group by reason of being controlled by any person and it appears to the commissioners that it has ceased to be so controlled, they must terminate that treatment, by notice given to that person, from such date as may be specified in the notice[12].

A tour operator[13] is not eligible to be treated as a member of a group for VAT if any other member of the group (i) has an overseas establishment; (ii) makes supplies outside the United Kingdom which would be taxable supplies if made in the United Kingdom; and (iii) supplies goods or services which will become, or are intended to become, a designated travel service[14].

1 As to the effect of treatment as a group see further paras 191–193 post.
2 For the meaning of 'United Kingdom' see para 4 note 3 ante.
3 For these purposes, a body corporate is taken to control another body corporate if it is empowered by statute to control that body's activities or if it is that body's holding company within the meaning of the Companies Act 1985 s 736 (as substituted) (see COMPANIES); and an individual or individuals is or are taken to control a body corporate if he or they, were he or they a company, would be that body's holding company within the meaning of that Act: Value Added Tax Act 1994 s 43(8). The commissioners have no discretion to treat two or more companies as a group unless one of the conditions specified in s 43(3) is fulfilled (*Du Vergier & Co Ltd v Customs and Excise Comrs* [1973] VATTR 11); but in certain circumstances they may give a direction that a body corporate was, or is, to be treated as a member of any group of which it was, or is, eligible to be a member for a specified period (see the Value Added Tax Act 1994 s 43(9), Sch 9A para 3(3)(b) (added by the Finance Act 1996 s 29(1), (2)); and para 193 post).
4 Value Added Tax Act 1994 s 43(3).
5 For the meaning of 'prescribed accounting period' see para 202 note 4 post.
6 Value Added Tax Act 1994 s 43(4). Any business carried on by a member of the group is treated as carried on by the representative member: see s 43(1) (as amended); and para 191 post.
7 Ibid s 43(7). The commissioners' discretion extends to allowing retrospective group registration: *Customs and Excise Comrs v Save and Prosper Group* [1979] STC 205.
8 Value Added Tax Act 1994 s 43(4). Appeal against a refusal by the commissioners to allow a group registration lies to a VAT and duties tribunal: see s 83(g); and para 296 post.
9 Ie in the circumstances set out in ibid s 43(9), Sch 9A (as added: see note 3 supra): see para 193 post.
10 Ibid Sch 9A para 3(3)(a) (as added: see note 3 supra). See further para 193 post.
11 Ibid s 43(5) (amended by the Finance Act 1995 s 25(1), (3)). If it appears to the commissioners necessary to do so for the protection of the revenue, they may refuse any application made to the effect mentioned (1) in the Value Added Tax Act 1994 s 43(5)(a) or (c) (see heads (a), (c) in the text); or (2) in s 43(5)(b) or (d) (see heads (b), (d) in the text) in a case that does not appear to them to fall within s 43(6) (see the text to note 10 infra): s 43(5A) (added by the Finance Act 1995 s 25(4)).
12 Value Added Tax Act 1994 s 43(6). As to the service of notices generally see para 291 post
13 As to the rules relating to the tour operators' margin scheme see para 200 post; and as to the place of supply of designated travel services see para 54 ante.
14 Value Added Tax (Tour Operators) Order 1987, SI 1987/1806, reg 13.

67. Registration where business is carried on in divisions. The registration[1] of a body corporate carrying on a business[2] in several divisions may, if it so requests, and the Commissioners of Customs and Excise see fit, be in the names of those divisions[3].

1   For the meaning of 'registration' see para 56 note 2 ante.
2   For these purposes, references to a business include references to any other activities in the course or furtherance of which any body corporate acquires goods from another member state: Value Added Tax Act 1994 s 46(6). As to the meaning of 'in the course or furtherance of a business' see paras 12 note 5, 17 note 2 ante; and for the meaning of 'another member state' see para 4 note 14 ante. As to acquisitions from another member state see para 13 ante.
3   Ibid s 46(1). Thus a company carrying on business in divisions may, if it so requests, have more than one registration number.

68. Registration of partnerships and co-owners.

The registration[1] for value added tax of persons carrying on (1) a business[2] in partnership; or (2) any other activities in partnership in the course or furtherance[3] of which they acquire goods from other member states, may be in the name of the firm[4]. No account is taken, in determining whether goods or services are supplied to or by such persons, or are acquired by such persons from another member state[5], of any change in the partnership[6]. If the same persons carry on in partnership together more than one business, they may only have a single registration for VAT, even if each business is carried on under different names[7].

A person who has ceased to be a member of a partnership is regarded[8] as continuing to be a member for the purposes of VAT (and, in particular, for the purpose of any liability for VAT on the supply of goods or services by the partnership, or on the acquisition of goods by the partnership from another member state) until the date on which a change in the partnership is notified to the Commissioners of Customs and Excise[9].

Where two or more persons together make, or are treated as making, a supply consisting in the grant, assignment or surrender of any interest in or right over land[10], those persons ('the grantors') are to be treated, both in relation to that supply and in relation to any other supply with respect to which the grantors are the same, as a single person ('the property-owner') who is distinct from each of the grantors individually[11]. Registration of the property-owner for VAT is made in the names of the grantors acting together as a property-owner[12]. The grantors are jointly and severally liable in respect of the obligations treated as falling on the property-owner[13]. Where there is a change in some (but not all) of the persons who are for the time being to be treated as the grantors in relation to any such supply, the change is disregarded for VAT purposes in relation to any prescribed accounting period beginning before the change is notified to the commissioners in the prescribed manner[14].

1   For the meaning of 'registration' see para 36 note 2 ante.
2   For the meaning of 'business' see para 17 ante.
3   As to the meaning of 'in the course or furtherance' of a business see paras 12 note 5, 17 note 2 ante.
4   Value Added Tax Act 1994 s 45(1). The predecessor of this provision did not affect the obligation of the commissioners to raise separate assessments, and to serve separate notices of assessment, on each partner, since for VAT purposes a partnership was not a person but a group of taxable persons: *Customs and Excise Comrs v Evans (t/a the Grape Escape Wine Bar)* [1982] STC 342. The law was changed as a result of *Customs and Excise Comrs v Evans* supra with the result that it is now necessary, where a partnership takes over a business previously carried on by one member, or a partner continues a business previously carried on by the partnership, to treat the change as requiring the cancellation of the previous registration and the registration of the continuing trader. In addition, it is no longer necessary to serve an assessment on each partner: see note 9 infra.
5   For the meaning of 'another member state' see para 4 note 14 ante; and as to acquisitions from another member state see para 13 ante.
6   Value Added Tax Act 1994 s 45(1). Section 45(1), (3) (see note 9 infra) does not affect the extent to which, under the Partnership Act 1890 s 9 (see PARTNERSHIP vol 35 (Reissue) para 65), a partner is liable for VAT owed by the firm; but where a person is a partner in a firm during part only of a prescribed accounting period, his liability for VAT on the supply by the firm of goods or services during that accounting period or on the acquisition during that period by the firm of any goods from another member state is such proportion of the firm's liability as may be just: Value Added Tax Act 1994 s 45(5). For the

meaning of 'supply' see para 21 ante; for the meaning of 'prescribed accounting period' see para 202 note 4 post; and as to acquisitions from other member states see para 13 ante.

7   *Customs and Excise Comrs v Glassborow* [1975] QB 465, [1974] 1 All ER 1041, DC; *J & E Harris v Customs and Excise Comrs* (1977) VAT Decision 373 (unreported). Cf *H Saunders and TG Sorrell v Customs and Excise Comrs* [1980] VATTR 53 (where A and B form two limited partnerships, in one of which A is the general partner and B the limited partner and in the other of which the position is reversed, each partnership is entitled to separate registration).

8   Ie without prejudice to the Partnership Act 1890 s 36 (rights of persons dealing with firm against apparent members of firm): see PARTNERSHIP vol 35 (Reissue) para 183.

9   Value Added Tax Act 1994 s 45(2). The commissioners may make provision by regulations under the 1994 Act for determining by what persons anything required by or under that Act to be done by a person carrying on a business is to be done where the business is carried on in partnership: s 46(2). Where any notice is required to be given for the purposes of VAT by a partnership, it is the joint and several liability of all the partners to give such notice, provided that a notice given by one partner is a sufficient compliance with any such requirement: Value Added Tax Regulations 1995, SI 1995/2518, reg 7(1).

Where a person ceases to be a member of a partnership during a prescribed accounting period, or is treated as so doing by virtue of the Value Added Tax Act 1994 s 45(2), any notice, whether of assessment or otherwise, which is served on the partnership and relates to, or to any matter arising in, that period or any earlier period during the whole or part of which he was a member of the partnership is to be treated as served also on him: s 45(3). See also note 6 supra. Thus service of a notice of assessment on the partnership will operate as service on all the partners (including any ex-partner who has failed to notify the commissioners in writing that he has ceased to be a member of the firm: see *Bengal Brasserie v Customs and Excise Comrs* [1991] VATTR 210, doubting *Ahmed v Customs and Excise Comrs* [1988] VATTR 1).

Without prejudice to the Partnership Act 1890 s 16 (notice to acting partner to be notice to the firm) (see PARTNERSHIP vol 35 (Reissue) para 44), any notice, whether of assessment or otherwise, which is addressed to a partnership by the name in which it is registered by virtue of the Value Added Tax Act 1994 s 45(1) and is served in accordance with the 1994 Act is treated for the purposes of that Act as served on the partnership and accordingly, where s 45(3) applies, as served also on the former partner: s 45(4).

10 For this purpose, a licence to occupy land is to be taken to be a right over land: ibid s 51A(1) (s 51A added by the Finance Act 1995 s 26(1), (4), as from a day to be appointed under s 26(3)).

11 Value Added Tax Act 1994 s 51A(1), (2) (as added: see note 10 supra).

12 Ibid s 51A(3) (as added: see note 10 supra).

13 Ibid s 51A(4) (as added: see note 10 supra).

14 Ibid s 51A(6)(a) (as added: see note 10 supra). Any notice (whether of assessment or otherwise) which is addressed to the property-owner by the name in which the property-owner is registered and is served on any of the grantors is treated as served on the property-owner (s 51A(5)) (as so added); and any notice, whether of assessment or otherwise, which is served, at any time after a notification of change in some but not all of the persons who are the grantors, and which relates to a prescribed accounting period beginning before the change, is treated as served on the persons who were the property-owner in the earlier period (s 51A(6)(b)) (as so added). As to the similar provisions in relation to partnerships see note 9 supra.

69. Registration of clubs, associations and organisations.

The Commissioners of Customs and Excise may make provision by regulations[1] for determining by what persons anything required to be done for the purposes of value added tax[2] by a person carrying on a business[3] is to be done where the business is carried on by a club, association or organisation the affairs of which are managed by its members or a committee or committees of its members[4].

The registration[5] of any such club, association or organisation may be in the name of the club, association or organisation[6]. In determining whether goods or services are supplied[7] to or by such a club, association or organisation, or whether goods are acquired by it from another member state[8], no account is taken of any change in its members[9].

1   Ie under the Value Added Tax Act 1994: s 96(1). As to the making of regulations generally see para 8 ante.
2   Ie required by or under the Value Added Tax Act 1994: s 46(2).
3   For these purposes, references to a business include references to any other activities in the course or furtherance of which any club, association, organisation or other unincorporated body acquires goods from another member state: ibid s 46(6). As to the meaning of 'in the course or furtherance of a business' see paras 12 note 5, 17 note 2 ante; and for the meaning of 'another member state' see para 4 note 14 ante. As to acquisitions from another member state see para 13 ante.

4   Ibid s 46(2). In exercise of this power, the commissioners have made the Value Added Tax Regulations 1995, SI 1995/2518, reg 8. Anything required to be done by or under the Value Added Tax Act 1994, the 1995 Regulations or otherwise, by or on behalf of such a club, association or organisation, is the joint and several responsibility of: (1) every member holding office as president, chairman, treasurer, secretary or any similar office; or in default of any of these (2) every member holding office as a member of a committee; or in default of any of these (3) every member, provided that if it is done by any official, committee member or member referred to in heads (1)–(3) supra, that is sufficient compliance with any such requirement: reg 8.

5   For the meaning of 'registration' see para 56 note 2 ante.

6   Value Added Tax Act 1994 s 46(3).

7   The provision of the facilities or advantages of membership for a subscription or other consideration is deemed to be the carrying on of a business: see ibid s 94(2)(a); and para 18 ante.

8   As to registration in respect of taxable acquisitions from other member states see para 63 ante; and for the meaning of 'another member state' see para 4 note 14 ante.

9   Value Added Tax Act 1994 s 46(3).

70. Effect on registration of persons dying, becoming bankrupt or otherwise incapacitated. The Commissioners of Customs and Excise may make provision by regulations[1] for persons who carry on a business[2] of a taxable person[3] who has died or become bankrupt or has become incapacitated[4] to be treated for a limited time as taxable persons, and for securing continuity in the application of the Value Added Tax Act 1994 in cases where persons are so treated[5].

If a taxable person dies or becomes bankrupt or incapacitated the commissioners may, from the date on which he died or became bankrupt or incapacitated[6] until some other person is registered in respect of the taxable supplies[7] made or intended to be made by that taxable person in the course or furtherance of his business[8], or until the incapacity ceases, treat as a taxable person any person carrying on that business[9]. In consequence, the provisions of the Value Added Tax Act 1994 and of any regulations made thereunder[10] apply to the person who is so treated as though he were a registered person[11]. Any person carrying on the business of a person who has died or become bankrupt or incapacitated must, within 21 days of commencing to do so, inform the commissioners, in writing, of the fact that he has begun to do so and also of the date of the death or of the bankruptcy order, or of the nature of the incapacity and the date on which it began[12].

1   Ie regulations under the Value Added Tax Act 1994: s 96(1).

2   For the meaning of 'business' for these purposes see paras 67 note 2, 69 note 3 ante.

3   For the meaning of 'taxable person' see paras 12 note 4, 55 ante.

4   In relation to a company which is a taxable person, this reference to the taxable person having become bankrupt or having become incapacitated is to be construed as a reference to its being in liquidation or receivership or to an administration order being in force in relation to it: Value Added Tax Act 1994 s 46(5); and see the Value Added Tax Regulations 1995, SI 1995/2518, reg 9(3).

5   Ibid s 46(4). In the exercise of this power, the commissioners have made the Value Added Tax Regulations 1995 reg 9: see the text and notes 6–12 infra.

6   As to the construction of this provision in relation to a company see note 4 supra. 'Going into receivership' contemplates the general incapacity which results from administrative receivership and not the partial incapacity which results from the appointment of a receiver of specific properties under the Law of Property Act 1925 or an equivalent power: *Sargent v Customs and Excise Comrs* [1995] 1 WLR 821, [1995] STC 398, CA. A receiver with such specific powers only could not, therefore, be treated by the commissioners as a taxable person; but was nevertheless obliged to account to the commissioners for the VAT on rents he collected under the Law of Property Act 1925 s 109(8): *Sargent v Customs and Excise Comrs* supra. See also *Re John Willment (Ashford) Ltd* [1979] 2 All ER 615, [1980] 1 WLR 73.

7   For the meaning of 'taxable supply' see para 12 note 3 ante.

8   As to the meaning of 'in the course or furtherance of a business' see paras 12 note 5, 17 note 2 ante.

9   Value Added Tax Regulations 1995 reg 9(1). As to the priority of VAT in bankruptcy or winding up see the Insolvency Act 1986 ss 175, 328, s 386 (as amended), s 387, Sch 3; and BANKRUPTCY; COMPANIES. However, where a trader incurs a liability to pay the commissioners VAT, penalties, interest or surcharge and an insolvency procedure is commenced in relation to him, any credit for VAT which subsequently

arises is to be paid to the insolvency practitioner without any set-off for the pre-insolvency liability: see the Value Added Tax Act 1994 s 81(4A) (as added); and para 254 post.

10 As to subordinate legislation generally see para 8 ante.

11 Value Added Tax Regulations 1995 reg 9(1).

12 Ibid reg 9(2) (amended by SI 1996/1250).

(iii) Termination and Cancellation of Registration

A. TERMINATION ETC RELATING TO TAXABLE SUPPLIES

71. Termination of liability to registration. A person who has become liable to be registered for value added tax[1] ceases to be so liable at any time if the Commissioners of Customs and Excise are satisfied in relation to that time that he has ceased to make taxable supplies[2] or that he is not at that time a person in relation to whom any of the statutory conditions[3] is satisfied[4].

A person who has become liable to be, and has been, registered for VAT[5] ceases to be so at any time after being registered if the commissioners are satisfied that the value of his taxable supplies in the period of one year then beginning will not exceed £45,000[6]. He does not, however, so cease to be liable if the commissioners are satisfied that the reason the value of his taxable supplies will not exceed that sum is that in the period in question he will cease making taxable supplies or will suspend making them for a period of 30 days or more[7].

A registered person[8] who ceases to make, or have the intention of making, taxable supplies must notify the commissioners of the day on which he does so unless he would, when he so ceases, be otherwise liable or entitled to be registered if his registration and any enactment preventing a person from being liable to be registered under different provisions at the same time were disregarded[9]. Every such notification must be made in writing to the commissioners and must state the date on which he ceased to make, or have the intention of making, taxable supplies[10].

1 Ie under the Value Added Tax Act 1994 s 3(2), Sch 1 (as amended): see para 56 et seq ante.

2 For the meaning of 'taxable supply' see para 12 note 3 ante. See also para 56 note 4 ante.

3 Ie the conditions specified in the Value Added Tax Act 1994 Sch 1 para 1(1)(a), (b), (2)(a), (b) (as amended): see paras 56, 59 ante.

4 Ibid Sch 1 para 3. He does not, however, cease to be liable to be so registered except in accordance with Sch 1 para 2(5) (see para 59 ante), Sch 1 para 3 or Sch 1 para 4 (as amended) (see the text and notes 5–7 infra): Sch 1 para 1(6).

5 See note 1 supra.

6 Value Added Tax Act 1994 Sch 1 para 4(1) (Sch 1 para 4(1), (2) amended by the Value Added Tax (Increase of Registration Limits) Order 1995, SI 1995/3037, art 2(b)). In determining the value of a person's supplies for the these purposes, supplies of goods or services that are capital assets of the business in the course or furtherance of which they are supplied, and any taxable supplies which would not be taxable supplies apart from the Value Added Tax Act 1994 s 7(4) (distance selling: see para 42 ante) are to be disregarded: Sch 1 para 4(3). Where, however, an interest in, right over or licence to occupy any land would thereby be disregarded, it is not to be so if it is supplied on a taxable supply which is not zero-rated: Sch 1 para 4(4). As to the meaning of 'in the course or furtherance of a business' see paras 12 note 5, 17 note 2 ante; and as to zero-rating see para 158 et seq post.

7 Ibid Sch 1 para 4(2) (as amended: see note 6 supra).

8 Ie a person registered under ibid Sch 1 para 5 or 6 (see para 56 ante) or Sch 1 para 9 (see para 58 ante): Sch 1 para 11.

9 Ibid Sch 1 para 11.

10 Value Added Tax Regulations 1995, SI 1995/2518, reg 5(3)(a).

72. Cessation of entitlement to voluntary registration. A person who has been voluntarily registered[1] and who ceases to make, or have the intention of making, supplies outside the United Kingdom[2] which would be taxable supplies[3] if made in the United Kingdom[4] must notify the Commissioners of Customs and Excise of that fact within 30 days of the day on which he does so unless he would, when he so ceases, be otherwise liable or entitled to be registered if his registration and any enactment preventing a person from being liable to be registered under different provisions at the same time were disregarded[5]. The notification must be made in writing and must state the date on which he ceased to make, or have the intention of making, the supplies[6]. Similar provisions apply if he makes, or forms the intention of making, taxable supplies[7].

1   Ie under the Value Added Tax Act 1994 s 3(2), Sch 1 para 10: see para 58 ante.
2   For the meaning of 'United Kingdom' see para 4 note 3 ante.
3   For the meaning of 'taxable supplies' see para 12 note 3 ante. See also para 56 note 4 ante.
4   Ie supplies within the Value Added Tax Act 1994 Sch 1 para 10(2): see para 58 ante.
5   Ibid Sch 1 para 12.
6   Value Added Tax Regulations 1995, SI 1995/2518, reg 5(3)(b).
7   See the Value Added Tax Act 1994 Sch 1 para 12(b); and para 58 ante.

73. Cancellation of registration. Where a registered person[1] satisfies the Commissioners of Customs and Excise that he is not liable to be registered in respect of taxable supplies[2], and if he so requests, they must cancel his registration with effect from the day on which the request is made or from such later date as may be agreed between them and him[3]. They may not, however, so cancel a person's registration with effect from any time unless they are satisfied that it is not a time when that person would be subject to a requirement[4] to be registered for value added tax[5].

Where the commissioners are satisfied that a registered person has ceased to be registrable, they may cancel his registration with effect from the day on which he so ceased or from such later date as may be agreed between them and him[6] but they may not so cancel a person's registration with effect from any time unless they are satisfied that it is not a time when that person would be subject to a requirement, or entitled[7], to be registered for VAT[8].

Where the commissioners are satisfied that on the day on which a registered person was registered he was not registrable, they may cancel his registration with effect from that day[9].

Appeal lies to a VAT and duties tribunal against any decision of the commissioners as to the cancellation of registration[10].

1   For these purposes, any reference to a registered person is a reference to a person who is registered under the Value Added Tax Act 1994 s 3(2), Sch 1 (as amended) (see para 56 et seq ante): Sch 1 para 13(7).
2   Ie registered under ibid Sch 1 (as amended): Sch 1 para 13(1).
3   Ibid Sch 1 para 13(1). It appears that the power to cancel a person's VAT registration is discretionary but subject to the supervision of the VAT and duties tribunal : *Brookes v Customs and Excise Comrs* [1994] VATTR 35. However, this area of the law is currently in some confusion: see para 296 post and *John Dee Ltd v Customs and Excise Comrs* [1995] STC 941, CA (function of tribunal is appellate, not supervisory).
4   In determining whether a person would be subject to a requirement to be registered at any time, so much of any provision of the Value Added Tax Act 1994 as prevents a person from becoming liable or entitled to be registered when he is already registered or when he is so liable under any other provision is to be disregarded: Sch 1 para 13(6).
5   Ibid Sch 1 para 13(4).
6   Ibid Sch 1 para 13(2).
7   In determining whether a person would be entitled to be registered at any time, so much of any provision of the Value Added Tax Act 1994 as prevents a person from becoming liable or entitled to be registered when he is already registered or when he is so liable under any other provision is to be disregarded: Sch 1 para 13(6).
8   Ibid Sch 1 para 13(5).
9   Ibid Sch 1 para 13(3).
10 See ibid s 83(a); and para 296 post.

74. Cancellation and transfer of registration on transfer of a going concern.

Where a business is transferred as a going concern[1] and:

(1) the registration[2] of the transferor has not already been cancelled;

(2) on the transfer of the business, the registration of the transferor is to be cancelled and either the transferee becomes liable to be registered or the Commissioners of Customs and Excise agree to register him voluntarily[3]; and

(3) an application is made in the prescribed form[4] by or on behalf of both the transferor and the transferee of that business,

the commissioners may cancel the registration of the transferor as from the date of the transfer and register the transferee with the registration number previously allocated to the transferor[5].

Where the transferee of a business has been so registered in substitution for the transferor of that business, and with the transferor's registration number:

(a) any liability of the transferor existing at the date of the transfer to make a return or to account for or pay value added tax[6] becomes the liability of the transferee;

(b) any right of the transferor, whether or not existing at the date of the transfer, to credit for, or to repayment of, input tax[7] becomes the right of the transferee; and

(c) any right of either the transferor, whether or not existing at the date of the transfer, or the transferee to payment by the commissioners[8] is satisfied by payment to either of them[9].

---

1 See para 56 text and notes 16–20 ante. For the meaning of 'business' see para 17 ante.

2 Ie under the Value Added Tax Act 1994 s 3(2), Sch 1 (as amended): see para 56 et seq ante.

3 Ie under ibid Sch 1 para 9: see para 58 ante.

4 Ie in the form set out in the Value Added Tax Regulations 1995, SI 1995/2518, reg 6(1)(d), Sch 1, Form 3: reg 6(1)(d).

5 Ibid reg 6(1). An application under reg 6(1) constitutes notification for the purposes of the Value Added Tax Act 1994 Sch 1 para 11 (see para 71 ante): Value Added Tax Regulations 1995 reg 6(2). For the meaning of 'registration number' see para 16 note 10 ante.

   An application under reg 6(1) can prove exceedingly expensive for the transferee: see eg *Ponsonby and Ponsonby v Customs and Excise Comrs* [1988] STC 28. In *Bjellica (t/a Eddy's Domestic Appliances) v Customs and Excise Comrs* [1994] 1 CMLR 437, [1993] STC 730 (affd on other grounds [1995] STC 329, CA) Leonard J rejected the contention for the trader that the Value Added Tax Regulations 1995 reg 6(1) is inconsistent with the Sixth Directive, since it only imposes the obligation to pay VAT on 'taxable persons who carry out taxable transactions' and not on the successors to such a person. The relevant assessment had been raised, inter alia, on the original trader; and his successors had given a contractual undertaking, in their application form for the transfer of the VAT number, to the commissioners to discharge the predecessor's outstanding VAT liability if called upon to do so. As to the Sixth Directive see para 1 note 1 ante.

6 Ie under the Value Added Tax Regulations 1995 reg 25 or reg 41 (as amended): see paras 130, 191, 226 et seq post.

7 For the meaning of 'input tax' see para 201 post.

8 Ie under the Value Added Tax Act 1994 s 25(3): see para 202 post.

9 Value Added Tax Regulations 1995 reg 6(3). Additionally, where the transferee of a business has been registered in substitution for, and with the registration number of, the transferor during a prescribed accounting period subsequent to that in which the transfer of the business took place but with effect from the date of the transfer of the business, and any return has been made, VAT accounted for and paid, or right to credit for input tax claimed, either by or in the name of the transferee or the transferor, it is treated as having been done by the transferee: reg 6(4). For the meaning of 'prescribed accounting period' see reg 25; and para 105 note 16 post.

B. TERMINATION ETC RELATING TO DISTANCE SALES

75. Matters affecting continuance of registration. A person who has become liable to be registered for value added tax by reason of his distance sales into the United Kingdom[1] ceases to be so liable if at any time:

(1) the relevant supplies[2] made by him in the year ending with 31 December last before that time did not have a value exceeding £70,000 and did not include any supply[3] in relation to which the statutory conditions[4] were satisfied[5]; and

(2) the Commissioners of Customs and Excise are satisfied that the value of his relevant supplies in the year immediately following that year will not exceed £70,000 and that those supplies will not include a supply in relation to which those conditions are satisfied[6].

A person does not, however, cease to be liable to be so registered (a) except in accordance with the above provisions[7]; nor (b) at any time when an option for treating relevant supplies made by him as taking place outside a member state where he is taxable[8] is in force in relation to him[9].

Any person registered by reason of his distance sales into the United Kingdom who ceases to be so registrable[10] must notify the Commissioners of Customs and Excise of that fact within 30 days of the day on which he does so[11]. A person who has been voluntarily registered[12] by reference to any intention of his to exercise any option or to make supplies of any description must notify the commissioners within 30 days of exercising that option or, as the case may be, of the first occasion after his registration when he makes such a supply, that he has exercised the option or made such a supply[13].

Where a person has exercised an option in accordance with the law of any member state[14] where he is taxable for treating relevant supplies made by him as taking place outside that member state[15] and that option ceases to have effect in relation to any relevant supplies by him, whether as a consequence of its revocation or otherwise, he must notify the commissioners, within 30 days of the option's ceasing to have effect, that it has done so[16].

1   Ie any person registered under the Value Added Tax Act 1994 s 3(2), Sch 2: see para 60 et seq ante. For the meaning of 'United Kingdom' see para 4 note 3 ante.
2   For the meaning of 'relevant supplies' see para 60 ante.
3   For the meaning of 'supply' see para 21 ante.
4   Ie the conditions mentioned in the Value Added Tax Act 1994 Sch 2 para 1(3): see para 60 ante.
5   Ibid Sch 2 para 2(1)(a).
6   Ibid Sch 2 para 2(1)(b).
7   Ibid Sch 2 para 1(5).
8   Ie such an option as is mentioned in ibid Sch 2 para 1(2): see para 60 ante.
9   Ibid Sch 2 para 2(2).
10 For these purposes, a person ceases to be registrable under the Value Added Tax Act 1994 where (1) he ceases to be a person who would be liable or entitled to be registered if his registration and any enactment preventing a person from being liable to be registered under different provisions at the same time were disregarded; or (2) in the case of a person who, having been registered under Sch 2 para 4 (voluntary registration: see para 61 ante), has not been such a person during the period of his registration, he ceases to have any such intention as is mentioned in Sch 2 para 4(1)(a): Sch 2 para 5(4).
11 Ibid Sch 2 para 5(1). The notification must be made in writing to the commissioners and must state the date on which he ceased to make, or have the intention of making, supplies: Value Added Tax Regulations 1995, SI 1995/2158, reg 5(3)(d).
12 Ie under the Value Added Tax Act 1994 Sch 2 para 4: see para 61 ante.
13 Ibid Sch 2 para 5(2).
14 As to the meaning of references to the law of another member state see para 11 note 1 ante.

15 Ie such an option as is mentioned in the Value Added Tax Act 1994 Sch 2 para 1(2): see para 60 ante.
16 Ibid Sch 2 para 5(3).

76. Cancellation of registration. Where a person registered in respect of his distance sales[1] satisfies the Commissioners of Customs and Excise that he is not liable to be so registered, and if he so requests, they must cancel his registration with effect from the day on which the request is made or from such later date as may be agreed between them and him[2]. They may not, however, so cancel a person's registration with effect from any time unless they are satisfied that it is not a time when he would be subject to a requirement[3] to be registered for value added tax[4].

Where the commissioners are satisfied that, on the day on which a person was registered in respect of his distance sales, he was not liable to be so registered and he did not, in the case of a person voluntarily registered[5], have the intention by reference to which he was registered, they may cancel his registration with effect from that day[6].

Where the commissioners are satisfied that a person who has been voluntarily registered, and is not for the time being liable to be registered, in respect of his distance sales (1) has not, by the date specified in his request to be registered, begun to make relevant supplies[7], exercised the option in question or, as the case may be, begun to make supplies in relation to which the statutory conditions[8] are satisfied; or (2) has contravened any condition[9] of his registration, they may cancel his registration with effect from the date so specified or, as the case may be, the date of the contravention, or from such later date as may be agreed between them and him[10]. They may not, however, so cancel a person's registration with effect from any time unless they are satisfied that it is not a time when that person would be subject to a requirement, or entitled[11], to be registered for VAT[12].

The registration of a person who has exercised an option in accordance with the law of any member state[13] where he is taxable for treating relevant supplies made by him as taking place outside that member state[14] may not be cancelled with effect from any time before the 1 January which is, or next follows, the second anniversary of the date on which his registration took effect[15].

Appeal lies to a VAT and duties tribunal against any decision of the commissioners as to the cancellation of registration[16].

1 Ie registered under the Value Added Tax Act 1994 s 3(2), Sch 2: see para 60 et seq ante.
2 Ibid Sch 2 para 6(1).
3 In determining whether a person would be subject to a requirement to be registered at any time, so much of any provision of the Value Added Tax Act 1994 as prevents a person from becoming liable or entitled to be registered when he is already registered or when he is so liable under any other provision is to be disregarded: Sch 2 para 7(4).
4 Ibid Sch 2 para 7(1).
5 Ie registered under ibid Sch 2 para 4: see para 61 ante.
6 Ibid Sch 2 para 6(2).
7 For the meaning of 'relevant supplies' see para 60 ante.
8 Ie the conditions mentioned in the Value Added Tax Act 1994 Sch 2 para 1(3): see para 60 ante.
9 As to the imposition of conditions see para 61 ante.
10 Value Added Tax Act 1994 Sch 2 para 6(3).
11 In determining whether a person would be entitled to be registered at any time, so much of any provision of the Value Added Tax Act 1994 as prevents a person from becoming liable or entitled to be registered when he is already registered or when he is so liable under any other provision is to be disregarded: Sch 2 para 7(4).
12 Ibid Sch 2 para 7(2).
13 As to the meaning of references to the law of another member state see para 11 note 1 ante.
14 Ie such an option as is mentioned in the Value Added Tax Act 1994 Sch 2 para 1(2): see para 60 ante.

15 Ibid Sch 2 para 7(3).
16 See ibid s 83(a); and para 296 post.

C. TERMINATION ETC IN RESPECT OF TAXABLE ACQUISITIONS

77. Matters affecting continuance of registration. A person who has become liable to be registered in respect of his taxable acquisitions from other member states[1] ceases to be so liable if at any time:

(1) his relevant acquisitions[2] in the year ending with 31 December last before that time did not have a value exceeding £47,000[3]; and

(2) the Commissioners of Customs and Excise are satisfied that the value of his relevant acquisitions in the year immediately following that year will not exceed £47,000[4].

A person does not, however, cease to be liable to be so registered (a) except in accordance with the above provisions[5]; nor (b) if at any time there are reasonable grounds for believing that the value of his relevant acquisitions in the period of 30 days then beginning will exceed £47,000[6].

Any person so registered in respect of his taxable acquisitions from other member states who ceases to be registrable for value added tax[7] must notify the commissioners of that fact within 30 days of the day on which he does so[8]. The notification must be made in writing to the commissioners and must state the date on which he ceased to make, or have the intention of making, a relevant acquisition[9].

A person who has been voluntarily registered[10] must notify the commissioners in writing, within 30 days of the first occasion after his registration when he makes a relevant acquisition, that he has done so[11].

1 Ie registered under the Value Added Tax Act 1994 s 3(2), Sch 3 (as amended): see para 63 et seq ante.
2 For the meaning of 'relevant acquisition' see para 63 ante.
3 Value Added Tax Act 1994 Sch 3 para 2(1)(a) (Sch 3 para 2 amended by the Value Added Tax (Increase of Registration Limits) Order 1995, SI 1995/3037, art 3). As to the Treasury's power to substitute a greater sum see para 63 note 3 ante.
4 Value Added Tax Act 1994 Sch 3 para 2(1)(b) (as amended: see note 3 supra).
5 Ibid Sch 3 para 1(4).
6 Ibid Sch 3 para 2(2) (as amended: see note 3 supra).
7 For these purposes, a person ceases to be registrable under the Value Added Tax Act 1994 where (1) he ceases to be a person who would be liable or entitled to be registered if his registration and any enactment preventing a person from being liable to be registered under different provisions at the same time were disregarded; or (2) in the case of a person who, having been registered under Sch 3 para 4(2) (voluntary registration: see para 64 ante), has not been such a person during his period of registration, he ceases to have any intention of making relevant acquisitions: Sch 3 para 5(3).
8 Ibid Sch 3 para 5(1).
9 Value Added Tax Regulations 1995, SI 1995/2518, reg 5(3)(e).
10 Ie under the Value Added Tax Act 1994 Sch 3 para 4(2): see para 64 ante.
11 Ibid Sch 3 para 5(2); Value Added Tax Regulations 1995 reg 5(3).

78. Cancellation of registration. Where a person who has been registered in respect of his taxable acquisitions[1] satisfies the Commissioners of Customs and Excise that he is not liable to be so registered, and if he so requests, they must cancel his registration with effect from the day on which the request is made or from such later date as may be agreed between them and him[2]. They may not, however, so cancel a person's registration with effect from any time unless they are satisfied that it is not a time when that person would be subject to a requirement[3] to be registered for value added tax[4].

Where the commissioners are satisfied that a person registered in respect of his taxable acquisitions has ceased, since his registration, to be so registrable[5], they may cancel his registration with effect from the day on which he so ceased or from such later date as may be agreed between them and him[6]. They may not, however, so cancel his registration with effect from any time unless they are satisfied that it is not a time when that person would be subject to a requirement, or entitled[7], to be registered for VAT[8].

Where the commissioners are satisfied that:

(1) on the day on which a person was registered in respect of his taxable acquisitions he was not so registrable, and, in the case of a person who was voluntarily registered[9], that he did not have the intention by reference to which he was registered, they may cancel his registration with effect from that day[10];

(2) a person who has been voluntarily registered[11] and is not for the time being liable to be registered has not begun, by the date specified in his request to be registered, to make relevant acquisitions, or has contravened any condition[12] of his registration, they may cancel his registration with effect from the date so specified or, as the case may be, the date of the contravention, or from such later date as may be agreed between them and him[13].

The registration of a person who is voluntarily registered[14] or who would not, if he were not registered, be liable or entitled to be registered under any provision of the Value Added Tax Act 1994 except the provisions relating to voluntary registration in respect of taxable acquisitions[15], must not be cancelled with effect from any time before the 1 January which is, or next follows, the second anniversary of the date on which his registration took effect[16]; but this does not apply to cancellation under head (1) or head (2) above[17].

---

1   Ie registered under the Value Added Tax Act 1994 s 3(2), Sch 3 (as amended): see para 63 et seq ante.
2   Ibid Sch 3 para 6(1).
3   In determining for these purposes whether a person would be subject to a requirement to be registered at any time, so much of any provision of the Value Added Tax Act 1994 as prevents a person from becoming liable or entitled to be registered when he is already registered or when he is so liable under any other provision is to be disregarded: Sch 3 para 7(5).
4   Ibid Sch 3 para 7(1).
5   For these purposes, a person is registrable under ibid Sch 3 (as amended) at any time when he is liable to be so registered or is a person who makes relevant acquisitions: Sch 3 para 6(5). For the meaning of 'relevant acquisition' see para 63 ante.
6   Ibid Sch 3 para 6(2).
7   In determining for these purposes whether a person would be entitled to be registered at any time, so much of any provision of the Value Added Tax Act 1994 as prevents a person from becoming liable or entitled to be registered when he is already registered or when he is so liable under any other provision is to be disregarded: Sch 3 para 7(5).
8   Ibid Sch 3 para 7(2).
9   Ie under ibid Sch 3 para 4(2): see para 64 ante.
10 Ibid Sch 3 para 6(3).
11 See note 9 supra.
12 As to the imposition of conditions see para 64 ante.
13 Value Added Tax Act 1994 Sch 3 para 6(4). They may not, however, so cancel a person's registration with effect from any time unless they are satisfied that it is not a time when that person would be subject to a requirement, or entitled, to be registered under the Value Added Tax Act 1994: Sch 3 para 7(2).
14 Ie under ibid Sch 3 para 4(1)–(4): see para 64 ante.
15 Ie ibid Sch 3 para 4: see para 64 ante.
16 Ibid Sch 3 para 7(3).
17 Ibid Sch 3 para 7(4).

(iv) Certification of Farmers etc

79. Power to certify farmers etc for value added tax purposes. A farmer who would otherwise be obliged to be registered for VAT, or who would be eligible for voluntary registration, may instead apply to the Commissioners of Customs and Excise for certification under the flat-rate scheme for farmers[1]. The commissioners may certify[2] any person who satisfies them:

(1) that he is carrying on a business involving one or more designated activities[3];

(2) that he is of such a description and has complied with such requirements as may be prescribed[4]; and

(3) where an earlier certification of that person has been cancelled, that more than the prescribed period has elapsed since the cancellation or that such other conditions as may be prescribed are satisfied[5].

Where a person is for the time being so certified then, whether or not he is a taxable person[6], so much of any supply[7] to him or any goods or services as is allocated to the relevant part of his business[8] in accordance with provision contained in regulations is disregarded for the purposes of determining whether he is, has become or has ceased to be liable or entitled to be registered[9] for VAT with respect to his taxable supplies[10]. Where he makes supplies of goods or services in the course or furtherance of the relevant part of his business to a taxable person, he must include a flat-rate amount in the consideration which may be treated as VAT incurred by the recipient for the purposes of input tax credit[11]. This amount ('the flat-rate addition') is retained by the farmer and may be recovered by the recipient of the supply as if it were input tax[12]. The flat-rate addition may be included in all supplies, even those that would be zero-rated if made by a taxable person, since it is not a rate of VAT but merely a method of compensating farmers for the input tax they have foregone by electing not to register. If a flat-rate farmer sells goods by auction, the flat-rate addition may be added to the price at which the goods are sold, if purchased by a taxable person, except where the auctioneer acts as principal, rather than as the farmer's agent[13].

Regulations made for these purposes may provide:

(a) for the form and manner in which an application for certification, or for the cancellation of any such certification, is to be made[14];

(b) for the cases and manner in which the commissioners may cancel a person's certification[15];

(c) for entitlement to a credit in respect of input tax[16] to depend on the issue of an invoice[17] containing such particulars as may be prescribed, or as may be notified by the commissioners in accordance with provision contained in regulations[18]; and

(d) for the imposition on certified persons of obligations with respect to the keeping, preservation and production of such records as may be prescribed and of obligations to comply with such requirements with respect to any of those matters as may be so notified[19].

---

1   See the text and notes 2–16 infra; and para 80 et seq post.

2   Ie in accordance with such provision as may be contained in regulations made by them under the Value Added Tax Act 1994: ss 54(1), 96(1). See the Value Added Tax Regulations 1995, SI 1995/2518, Pt XXIV (regs 202–211); and para 80 et seq post.

3   Value Added Tax Act 1994 s 54(1)(a). 'Designated activities' means such activities, being activities carried on by a person who, by virtue of carrying them on, falls to be treated as a farmer for the purposes of EC Council Directive 77/388 (OJ L145, 13.6.77, p 1) art 25 (common flat-rate scheme for farmers), as the Treasury may by order designate: Value Added Tax Act 1994 s 54(8). At the date at which this volume states the law, no such order had been made, but, by virtue of the

Interpretation Act 1978 s 17(2)(b), the Value Added Tax (Flat-rate Scheme for Farmers) (Designated Activities) Order 1992, SI 1992/3220, has effect as if so made. As to the activities so designated see para 80 post. For the meaning of 'business' see para 17 ante.

4   Ibid s 54(1)(b). For the meaning of 'prescribed' see para 11 note 3 ante.

5   Ibid s 54(1)(c).

6   For the meaning of 'taxable person' see paras 12 note 4, 55 ante.

7   For the meaning of 'supply' see para 21 ante.

8   For these purposes, references in relation to any person to the relevant part of his business are references (1) where the whole of his business relates to the carrying on of one or more designated activities, to that business; and (2) in any other case, to so much of his business as does so relate: Value Added Tax Act 1994 s 54(7).

9   Ie under ibid s 3(2), Sch 1 (as amended): see para 56 et seq ante.

10 Ibid s 54(2).

11 The commissioners may by regulations provide for an amount included in the consideration for any taxable supply which is made (1) in the course or furtherance of the relevant part of his business by a person who is for the time being certified under ibid s 54; (2) at a time when that person is not a taxable person; and (3) to a taxable person, to be treated, for the purpose of determining the entitlement of the person supplied to credit under ss 25, 26 (see paras 202–203 post), as VAT on a supply to that person: s 54(3); and see the Value Added Tax Regulations 1995, SI 1995/2518, reg 209(1). The amount which, for the purposes of any provision so made, may be included in the consideration for any supply is to be an amount equal to such percentage as the Treasury may by order specify of the sum which, with the addition of that amount, is equal to the consideration for the supply: Value Added Tax Act 1994 s 54(4). At the date at which this volume states the law, no such order had been made but, by virtue of the Interpretation Act 1978 s 17(2)(b), the Value Added Tax (Flat-rate Scheme for Farmers) (Percentage Addition) Order 1992, SI 1992/3221, has effect as if so made. The percentage referred to is 4%: art 2. As to the meaning of 'in the course or furtherance of a business' see paras 12 note 5, 17 note 2 ante.

12 Save as the commissioners may otherwise allow or direct generally or specially, a taxable person claiming entitlement to a credit of such an amount must do so on the return made by him for the prescribed accounting period in which the invoice specified in the Value Added Tax Regulations 1995 reg 209(3) is issued by a certified person: reg 209(2). A taxable person is not so entitled to credit unless there has been issued an invoice containing the following particulars: (a) an identifying number; (b) the name, address and certificate number of the certified person by whom the invoice is issued; (c) the name and address of the person to whom the goods or services are supplied; (d) the time of the supply; (e) a description of the goods or services supplied; (f) the consideration for the supply or, in the case of any increase or decrease in the consideration, the amount of that increase or decrease excluding the amount as is mentioned in reg 209(1); and (g) the amount as so mentioned, which is entitled 'Flat-rate Addition' or 'FRA': reg 209(3). For the meaning of 'prescribed accounting period' see para 105 note 16 post.

13 Customs and Excise Business Brief 10/92 [1992] STI 726 at 728.

14 Ibid s 54(6)(a): see para 81 post.

15 Ibid s 54(6)(b): see para 84 post.

16 Ie such a credit as is mentioned in ibid s 54(3): s 54(6)(c).

17 For the meaning of 'invoice' see para 11 note 8 ante.

18 Value Added Tax Act 1994 s 54(6)(c).

19 Ib 1 s 54(6)(d): see para 82 post.

80. Designated activities. The following are designated activities[1] for the purposes of the flat-rate scheme for farmers[2]:

(1) crop production consisting of:
  (a) general agriculture, including viticulture;
  (b) the growing of fruit and vegetables, flowers and ornamental plants, whether in the open or under glass;
  (c) the production of mushrooms, spices, seeds and propagating materials; and
  (d) nurseries[3];

(2) general stock farming, poultry farming, rabbit farming, bee-keeping, silkworm farming and snail farming[4];

(3)   forestry consisting of the growing, felling and general husbandry of trees in a forest, wood or copse[5];

(4)   fresh-water fishing, fish farming, the breeding of mussels, oysters and other molluscs and crustaceans and frog farming[6]; and

(5)   the processing by a person of products derived from his activities falling within the above descriptions, provided that he uses only such means as are normally employed in the course of such activities[7].

Certain services[8] are also designated activities provided that:

(i)   the person performing them also carries out activities falling within one or more of heads (1) to (5) above;

(ii)   he performs them himself or they are performed by his employees, or both; and

(iii) any equipment he uses in carrying them out, or hires to another for agricultural purposes, is equipment which he also uses for carrying out his other designated activities[9].

1   For the meaning of 'designated activities' see para 79 note 3 ante.
2   Value Added Tax (Flat-rate Scheme for Farmers) (Designated Activities) Order 1992, SI 1992/3220, art 2(1). As to the flat-rate scheme for farmers see para 79 ante.
3   Ibid art 2(1), Schedule Pt I.
4   Ibid Schedule Pt II.
5   Ibid Schedule Pt III.
6   Ibid Schedule Pt IV.
7   Ibid Schedule Pt V.
8   Those services are: (1) field work, reaping and mowing, threshing, bailing, collecting, harvesting, sowing and planting; (2) packing and preparing for market (including drying, cleaning, grinding, disinfecting and ensilaging) of agricultural products for market; (3) storage of agricultural products; (4) stock minding, rearing and fattening; (5) hiring out of equipment for use in any designated activities; (6) technical assistance in relation to any designated activities; (7) destruction of weeds and pests, dusting and spaying of crops and land; (8) operation of irrigation and drainage equipment; and (9) lopping, tree felling and other forestry services: ibid Schedule Pt VI. The Commissioners of Customs and Excise do not consider the following, inter alia, to be designated activities: dealing in, and the training of, animals; dairy co-operatives that do not produce their own milk; sawmills; and other activities once removed from farming: Customs and Excise Business Brief 10/92 [1992] STI 726 at 727.
9   Value Added Tax (Flat-rate Scheme for Farmers) (Designated Activities) Order 1992 art 2(2).

81. Admission to the scheme and certification. If the prescribed conditions[1] are satisfied, the Commissioners of Customs and Excise must certify that a person is a flat-rate farmer for the purposes of the flat-rate scheme[2]. Where a person is for the time being so certified, then whether or not that person is a taxable person[3], any supply[4] of goods or services made by him in the course or furtherance of the relevant part of his business[5] is to be disregarded for the purpose of determining whether he is, has become or has ceased to be liable or entitled to be registered[6] for value added tax[7].

Where the commissioners certify that a person is a flat-rate farmer for the purposes of the scheme, the certificate issued by them is effective from the date on which the application for certification is received by them or, if the person so requests, a later date which is no more than 30 days after that date[8]. An earlier date may, however, be agreed[9], but no certificate is to be effective from a date before the date when the person's registration[10] is cancelled[11].

Where a person who has been certified and is no longer so certified makes a further application, that person may not be certified for a period of three years from the date of the cancellation[12] of his previous certificate except in certain specified circumstances[13].

If a farmer deregisters solely in order to become a flat-rate farmer he will not have to account for output tax on his stocks and other physical assets on hand, even if he claimed input tax when purchasing them[14].

1   The prescribed conditions are that (1) the person satisfies the Commissioners of Customs and Excise that he is carrying on a business involving one or more designated activities; (2) he has not in the three years preceding the date of his application for certification been convicted of any offence in relation to value added tax, made any payment to compound proceedings in respect of VAT under the Customs and Excise Management Act 1979 s 152 (as applied by the Value Added Tax Act 1994 s 72(12)) (see para 267 post) or been assessed to a penalty under s 60 (see para 272 post); (3) he makes an application for certification on the form set out in the Value Added Tax Regulations 1995, SI 1995/2518, reg 204(c), Sch 1, Form 14; and (4) he satisfies the commissioners that he is a person in respect of whom the total of the amounts mentioned in reg 209 (see para 79 ante) relating to supplies made in the year following the date of his certification will not exceed by £3,000 or more the amount of input tax to which he would otherwise be entitled to credit in that year: reg 204(a)–(d). For the meaning of 'designated activities' see para 80 ante.
2   Ibid reg 203(1). As to the flat-rate scheme see para 79 ante.
3   For the meaning of 'taxable person' see paras 12 note 4, 55 ante.
4   For the meaning of 'supply' see para 21 ante.
5   For the meaning of 'the relevant part of his business' see para 79 note 8 ante; and as to the meaning of 'in the course or furtherance of a business' see paras 12 note 5, 17 note 2 ante.
6   Ie under the Value Added Tax Act 1994 s 3(2), Sch 1 (as amended): see para 56 et seq ante.
7   Value Added Tax Regulations 1995 reg 203(2).
8   Ibid reg 205(a), (c).
9   Ibid reg 205(b).
10 Ie under the Value Added Tax Act 1994 Sch 1 (as amended) or Sch 3 (as amended): see para 56 et seq ante.
11 Value Added Tax Regulations 1995 reg 205. No certificate is effective from a date earlier than 1 January 1993: reg 205. As to the cancellation of registration see para 71 et seq ante.
12 As to the cancellation of certificates see para 84 post.
13 Value Added Tax Regulations 1995 reg 208. The commissioners may certify from the date of his further application a person who has not been registered under the Value Added Tax Act 1994 Sch 1 (as amended) or Sch 3 (as amended) at any time since the cancellation of the previous certificate; and where the circumstances as are mentioned in s 5(1), Sch 4 para 8(1)(c) (see para 24 ante) apply, the commissioners may certify the person mentioned in Sch 4 para 8(1)(c) on a date after the expiry of one year from the date of the cancellation of his previous certificate: Value Added Tax Regulations 1995 reg 208(a), (b).
14 See Customs and Excise Business Brief 10/92 [1992] STI 726 at 727.

82. Duty to keep and produce records. For the purposes of the flat-rate scheme for farmers[1] every certified person[2] must keep and preserve his business and accounting records and copies of all specified invoices[3] issued by him or on his behalf[4]. Upon demand made by an authorised person, every certified person must produce any such documents, or cause them to be produced, for inspection at his principal place of business or such other place as the authorised person may reasonably require, and at such time as he may so require[5]. He must permit an authorised person to take copies of, or make extracts from, any such document, or to remove it at a reasonable time and for a reasonable period[6]. Where any documents so removed are lost or damaged, the Commissioners of Customs and Excise are liable to compensate their owner for any expenses reasonably incurred by him in replacing or repairing the documents[7].

1   As to the flat-rate scheme for farmers see para 79 ante.
2   'Certified person' means a person certified as a flat-rate farmer for the purposes of the flat-rate scheme under the Value Added Tax Regulations 1995, SI 1995/2518, reg 203: see para 81 ante.
3   Ie all invoices specified in ibid reg 209(3): see para 79 ante.
4   Ibid reg 210(1). Every certified person must comply with such requirements with respect to the keeping, preservation and production of records as the Commissioners of Customs and Excise may notify to him:

reg 210(2). He must keep and preserve such records as are required by reg 210(1) or by notification for a period of six years or such lesser period as the commissioners may allow: reg 210(3).

5   Ibid reg 211(1)(a). 'Authorised person' means any person acting under the authority of the commissioners: Value Added Tax Act 1994 s 96(1); Interpretation Act 1978 s 11.

6   Value Added Tax Regulations 1995 reg 211(1)(b). Where a document removed by an authorised person is reasonably required for the proper conduct of a business, he must, as soon as practicable, provide a copy of that document, free of charge, to the person by whom it was produced or caused to be produced: reg 211(2).

7   Ibid reg 211(3).

83. Death, bankruptcy or incapacity of certified person. If a certified person[1] dies or becomes bankrupt or incapacitated[2], the Commissioners of Customs and Excise may treat any person carrying on his designated activities[3] as a certified person from the date on which the first person died or became bankrupt or incapacitated, until either some other person is certified in respect of those activities, or the incapacity ceases[4].

1   For the meaning of 'certified person' see para 82 note 2 ante.

2   In relation to a company which is a certified person, references to that person becoming bankrupt or incapacitated are to be construed as references to its going into liquidation or receivership or to an administration order being made in relation to it: Value Added Tax Regulations 1995, SI 1995/2518, reg 207(3).

3   A person carrying on such designated activities must, within 30 days of commencing to do so, inform the commissioners in writing of that fact and of the date of the death, or of the nature of the incapacity and the date on which it began: ibid reg 207(2). For the meaning of 'designated activities' see paras 79 note 3, 80 ante.

4   Ibid reg 207(1). The provisions of the Value Added Tax Act 1994 and of any regulations made thereunder apply to any person so treated as if he were a certified person: reg 207(1).

84. Cancellation of certificates. The Commissioners of Customs and Excise may cancel a person's certificate under the flat-rate scheme for farmers[1] in any case where:

(1)   a statement false in a material particular was made by him or on his behalf in relation to his application for certification[2];

(2)   he has been convicted of an offence in connection with value added tax or has made a payment[3] to compound such proceedings[4];

(3)   he has been assessed[5] to a penalty[6];

(4)   he ceases to be involved in designated activities[7];

(5)   he dies, becomes bankrupt or incapacitated[8];

(6)   he is liable to be registered[9] for VAT[10];

(7)   he makes an application in writing for cancellation[11];

(8)   he makes an application in writing[12] for registration[13];

(9)   they consider it necessary to do so for the protection of the revenue[14]; or

(10)   they are not satisfied that any of the grounds for cancellation of a certificate mentioned in heads (1) to (8) above do not apply[15].

1   As to the flat-rate scheme for farmers see para 79 ante.

2   Value Added Tax Regulations 1995, SI 1995/2518, reg 206(1)(a). The effective date of the cancellation is the date when the commissioners discover that such a statement has been made: reg 206(2)(a).

3   Ie under the Customs and Excise Management Act 1979 s 152 as applied by the Value Added Tax Act 1994 s 72(12): see para 267 post.

4   Value Added Tax Regulations 1995 reg 206(1)(b). The effective date of the cancellation is the date of his conviction or the date on which a sum is paid to compound proceedings: reg 206(2)(b).

5   Ie under the Value Added Tax Act 1994 s 60: see para 272 post.

6   Value Added Tax Regulations 1995 reg 206(1)(c). The effective date of the cancellation is 30 days after the date when the assessment is notified: reg 206(2)(c).

7   Ibid reg 206(1)(d). The effective date of the cancellation is the date of the cessation of designated activities:
     reg 206(2)(d). For the meaning of 'designated activities' see paras 79 note 3, 80 ante.
8   Ibid reg 206(1)(e). The effective date of the cancellation is the date on which he died, became bankrupt
     or incapacitated: reg 206(2)(e). In relation to a company which is a certified person, the references to the
     certified person becoming bankrupt or incapacitated are to be construed as references to its going into
     liquidation or receivership or to an administration order being made in relation to it: reg 207(3).
9   Ie under the Value Added Tax Act 1994 s 3(2), Sch 1 (as amended) (see para 56 et seq ante) or Sch 3 (as
     amended) (see para 63 et seq ante): Value Added Tax Regulations 1995 reg 206(1)(f).
10   Ibid reg 206(1)(f). The effective date of the cancellation is the effective date of registration: reg 206(2)(f).
11   Ibid reg 206(1)(g). The effective date of the cancellation is not less than one year after the effective date
     of his certificate, or such earlier date as the commissioners may agree: reg 206(2)(g).
12   Ie an application for registration under the Value Added Tax Act 1994 Sch 1 (as amended) or Sch 3 (as
     amended), which is deemed to be an application for cancellation of his certificate; Value Added Tax
     Regulations 1995 reg 206(1)(h).
13   Ibid reg 206(1)(h). The effective date of the cancellation is not less than one year after the effective date
     of his certificate or such earlier date as the commissioners may agree: reg 206(2)(h).
14   Ibid reg 206(1)(i). The effective date of the cancellation is the date on which the commissioners consider
     a risk to the revenue arises: reg 206(2)(i).
15   Ibid reg 206(1)(j). The effective date of the cancellation is the date mentioned in reg 206(2)(a)–(h) as
     appropriate: reg 206(2)(j).

(3) VALUE OF GOODS OR SERVICES

(i) In general

85. The valuation of supplies of goods or services. The manner of determining
the value of a supply of goods or services for the purposes of value added tax depends
on the form of consideration given for the supply[1]. If the supply is for a consideration[2]
in money its value is taken to be such amount as, with the addition of the VAT
chargeable, is equal to the consideration[3]. If the supply is for a consideration not
consisting, or not wholly consisting, of money, its value is taken to be such amount in
money as, with the addition of the VAT chargeable, is equivalent to the consideration[4].
Where a supply of any goods or services is not the only matter to which a consideration
in money relates, the supply is deemed to be for such part of the consideration as is
properly attributable to it[5].

1   See the text and notes 2–5 infra; and para 86 et seq post. For the meaning of 'supply' see para 21 ante.
2   For the meaning of 'consideration' see para 86 post.
3   Value Added Tax Act 1994 s 19(1), (2). Thus if goods whose supply attracts VAT at the standard rate of
     17.5% (see para 5 ante) are sold for cash consideration of £117.50, the value of the supply is £100, on
     which VAT of £17.50 is chargeable. Where goods are purchased with vouchers which the customers
     have acquired from a third party, the value of the supply for VAT is the face value of the voucher and
     not the lesser amount eventually received by the trader from the third party: *Davies v Customs and Excise
     Comrs* [1975] 1 All ER 309, [1975] 1 WLR 204, DC. Correspondingly, where the issuer of the voucher
     redeems the voucher for less than its face value, the issuer provides the service of redemption for a
     consideration equal to the amount foregone by the retailer: *Customs and Excise Comrs v High Street Vouchers
     Ltd* [1990] STC 575, following *Customs and Excise Comrs v Diners Club Ltd* [1989] 2 All ER 385, [1989]
     STC 407, CA. The commission which is deducted by a credit card company in paying the retailer under
     a credit card transaction may not be deducted in arriving at the consideration for the supply by the retailer
     to his customer: Case C-18/92 *Chaussures Bally SA v Belgian Ministry of Finance* [1993] ECR I-2871,
     [1993] STI 944, ECJ. Cf *Primback Ltd v Customs and Excise Comrs* [1996] STC 757, CA (where goods are
     sold on terms allowing interest-free credit, financed by a third party, the amount on which the retailer is
     to account for VAT (as part of his daily gross takings under his retail scheme: see para 185 post) is the net
     amount he receives from the finance company and not the shelf price of the goods). The general
     provisions of the Value Added Tax Act 1994 s 19(2)–(4) are subject to the specific provisions of s 19(1),
     Sch 6 (as amended) (see para 86 et seq post): s 19(1). In determining the value of a supply under s 19, one

is not concerned with the motives of either the supplier or the recipient, so that, where the consideration is in money, the measure of the value of the supply is the money consideration, notwithstanding that the recipient understood that the payment was made out of a sense of public duty or included a large element of donation: *Customs and Excise Comrs v Battersea Leisure Ltd* [1992] STC 213; *Customs and Excise Comrs v Tron Theatre Ltd* [1994] STC 177 (Ct of Sess); *High Peak Theatre Trust Ltd v Customs and Excise Comrs* (1995) VAT Decision 13678, [1995] STI 2029. As to the exemption for supplies made by charities in the course of fund-raising events see para 156 post; and as to the valuation of acquisitions of goods from other member states see para 98 post.

Regulations made by the commissioners under the Value Added Tax Act 1994 may require that in prescribed circumstances there is to be taken into account, as constituting part of the consideration for the purpose of s 19(2) (where it would not otherwise be so taken into account), money paid in respect of the supply by persons other than those to whom the supply is made: Sch 6 para 12. For the meaning of 'money' see para 7 note 5 ante.

4   Value Added Tax Act 1994 s 19(3).
5   Ibid s 19(4).

86. Meaning of 'consideration'. For the purposes of value added tax, 'consideration' does not bear the technical meaning given to that word by the English law of contract[1]; for something which is given to a supplier to constitute consideration for VAT purposes, it must be capable of being expressed in monetary terms and there must be a direct link between the service provided and the consideration received[2]. In determining the value of a supply for which consideration is given otherwise than in money, a subjective valuation must be ascribed to that which is received, and not a value estimated according to objective criteria[3]. The value of a supply paid for in foreign currency is taken as the sterling equivalent at the time of supply[4].

The taxable amount (on which VAT is to be charged) includes everything[5] which constitutes the consideration which is obtained by the supplier from the purchaser, the customer or a third party[6] for such supplies including subsidies directly linked to the price of such supplies[7]. However, one must exclude from the taxable amount: (1) price reductions by way of discount for early payment[8]; (2) price discounts and rebates allowed to the customer and accounted for at the time of supply[9]; and (3) the amounts received by a taxable person from his purchaser or customer as repayment for expenses paid out in the name and for the account of the latter and which are entered in a suspense account[10]. In the case of cancellation, refusal or total or partial non-payment, or where the price is reduced after the supply takes place, the taxable amount is reduced[11].

1   As to that meaning see CONTRACT vol 9 para 309 et seq.
2   See Case 154/80 *Staatssecretaris van Financiën v Cooperatïeve Aardappelenbewaarplaats GA* [1981] ECR 445, [1981] 3 CMLR 337, ECJ (a case under EC Council Directive 67/228 (OJ 71, 14.4.67) art 8(a) (repealed)) (where a potato growers' co-operative which ran a warehouse for the storage of its members' goods did not impose a storage charge for the service provided, as no charge was made, the service was not supplied against payment, so that there was no consideration for VAT purposes; a reduction in the value of the members' shares as a result of the failure to charge for storage involved no direct link between the so-called consideration and the service provided); Case 102/86 *Apple and Pear Development Council v Customs and Excise Comrs* [1988] ECR 1443, [1988] 2 All ER 922, ECJ (compulsory contributions imposed under power conferred by subordinate legislation did not constitute consideration because there was no relationship between the contribution made and the level of service received); *Institute of Leisure and Amenity Management v Customs and Excise Comrs* [1988] STC 602 (the Institute was liable to account for VAT on voluntary contributions obtained from its members in return for which each member received various services). Where a trade development organisation was funded by contributions from its government and a percentage levy on imports and exports of goods, there was no direct link between the sums received and the services provided so that that organisation was not a taxable person making supplies for a consideration: Case 89/81 *Staatssecretaris van Financiën v Hong Kong Trade Development Council* [1982] ECR 1277, [1983] 1 CMLR 73, ECJ. Similarly, a local authority grant to fund a legal advice centre was not consideration for a supply for VAT purposes (*Hillingdon Legal Resources Centre Ltd v Customs and Excise Comrs* [1991]

VATTR 39); nor a local authority grant to a charity proving work experience (*Trustees of the Bowthorpe Community Trust v Customs and Excise Comrs* (1995) VAT Decision 12978, [1995] STI 649); cf *Netherlands Board of Tourism v Customs and Excise Comrs* (1995) VAT Decision 12935, [1995] STI 502 (the taxpayer made a taxable supply of services against consideration when it agreed to promote Dutch tourism in return for the Dutch Government agreeing to fund the cost of the services of promotion). The Arts Council does not make supplies for a consideration when it receives or distributes the yearly Parliamentary grant in aid: *Arts Council of Great Britain v Customs and Excise Comrs* (1994) VAT Decision 11991, [1994] STI 713; see also *Institute of Chartered Accountants in England and Wales v Customs and Excise Comrs* [1996] STC 799 (where the institute licensed persons wishing to carry on investment business, or to acts as auditors or insolvency practitioners, that activity was essentially regulatory in nature and was therefore not an economic activity, notwithstanding that fees were charged for the provision of the licence); *British Field Sports Society v Customs and Excise Comrs* (1996) VAT Decision 14189, [1996] STI 1377 (political lobbying against legislation relating to field sports constituted a business activity, the consideration for which was the members' subscription to the society). Interest awarded by a court in proceedings to recover a debt for services supplied was not consideration for VAT purposes: Case 222/81 *BAZ Bausystem AG v Finanzamt München für Körperschaften* [1982] ECR 2527, [1982] 3 CMLR 688, ECJ. Where the appellant was a barrel-organ player who solicited voluntary donations from passers-by, there was no direct link between the provision of the music and the receipt of a donation, because the fact and size of each donation was determined by the passer-by and not by agreement between the parties: Case C-16/93 *Tolsma v Inspecteur der Omzetbelasting Leeuwarden* [1994] I-ECR 743, [1994] STC 509, ECJ. As to whether cash paid by competitors in a 'spot the ball' competition constituted consideration, where the contract between the parties was legally unenforceable, and as to the amount, if any, of such consideration, see *Town and Country Factors Ltd v Customs and Excise Comrs* (1996) VAT Decision 14405, [1996] STI 1644, where the tribunal proposed to refer the matter to the European Court of Justice. See also *Arsenal Football Club plc v Customs and Excise Comrs* (1996) VAT Decision 14011, [1996] STI 965; cf *Telewest Communications Group Ltd v Customs and Excise Comrs* (1996) VAT Decision 14383, [1996] STI 1639 (where a customer obtained cable TV services from an operator both by entering into an agreement and by giving an undertaking to permit the operator to remove the customer's satellite dish, the latter undertaking was an ingredient in the taxable consideration provided by the customer). Where a company provided management services to its employees' pension fund under a contract which provided that the contributions it was obliged to make should be calculated on a basis which took account of the expenditure it incurred in the supply of the services, there was no supply by the company for consideration, liable to VAT: *National Coal Board v Customs and Excise Comrs* [1982] STC 863; and see *Eastbourne Town Radio Cars Association v Customs and Excise Comrs* [1996] STC 1469. In Case C-215/94 *Mohr v Finanzamt Bad Segeberg* [1996] ECR I-959, [1996] STC 328, ECJ, it was held that an undertaking given by a farmer to discontinue milk production in consequence of which he obtained compensation was not a supply of services for consideration, liable to VAT, since there was an absence of 'consumption'; the Community, by compensating the farmer, was not obtaining a supply of goods or services, but acting in the common interest of promoting the proper functioning of the Community milk market. Quaere whether this principle applies to all forms of statutory compensation. See also *Goodfellow v Customs and Excise Comrs* [1986] VATTR 119; and *Co-operative Insurance Society Ltd v Customs and Excise Comrs* [1992] 3 CMLR 10, [1992] VATTR 44; cf *Customs and Excise Comrs v High Street Vouchers Ltd* [1990] STC 575 (see para 85 note 3 ante).

3   Case 154/80 *Staatssecretaris van Financiën v Cooperatieve Aardappelenbewaarplaats GA* [1981] ECR 445, [1981] 3 CMLR 337, ECJ (see note 2 supra); Case 230/87 *Naturally Yours Cosmetics Ltd v Customs and Excise Comrs* [1988] ECR 6365, [1988] STC 879, ECJ (the taxpayer was a cosmetics supplier which sold products wholesale to 'consultants' who persuaded 'hostesses' to hold parties at which the products would be sold retail. The consultants gave each hostess a 'gift' of a pot of cream as a reward for holding the party and were able to purchase items to be used as gifts for £1.50 instead of the usual wholesale price of £10.14. The consideration for the pot of cream was held to be not merely the cash consideration but in addition the service provided by the consultant of procuring a hostess to arrange a sales party; and the value of that service was the subjective value of the service to the taxpayer, which could be identified as the reduction in the usual wholesale price to the consultant). See also Case C-33/93 *Empire Stores Ltd v Customs and Excise Comrs* [1994] 3 All ER 90, [1994] STC 623, ECJ; *Customs and Excise Comrs v Pippa-Dee Parties Ltd* [1981] STC 495 (where Ralph Gibson J did not consider the application of EC Council Directive 77/388 (OJ L145, 13.6.77, p 1) and applied an English law definition of 'consideration'); cf Case 102/86 *Apple and Pear Development Council v Customs and Excise Comrs* [1988] ECR 1443, [1988] STC 221, ECJ; and *Rosgill Group Ltd v Customs and Excise Comrs* (1995) VAT Decision 13265, [1995] STI 1113.

4   See the Value Added Tax Act 1994 s 19(1), Sch 6 para 11; and para 102 post. Where an invoice is expressed in alternative currencies, of which sterling is one, the value of the supply is taken to be the value

expressed in sterling: *Advansys plc v Customs and Excise Comrs* (1990) VAT Decision 4427, [1990] STI 161; and see Customs and Excise Notice 700 *The VAT Guide* (March 1996) para 3.1(f).

5   Where a supplier incurs expenditure in rendering a service to a customer, and a separate item is included in the bill for the 'disbursement', the disbursement forms part of the taxable amount on which VAT must be charged to the client. Thus where a solicitor incurred zero-rated expenditure on air and rail fares in rendering services to a client, VAT at the standard rate had to be accounted for when the item was charged as a disbursement in the client's bill: *Rowe & Maw (a firm) v Customs and Excise Comrs* [1975] 2 All ER 444, [1975] STC 340, DC. Cf disbursements made by a solicitor acting as agent for a client, eg stamp duty or Land Registry fees, where the supply is received by the client as principal, on which VAT need not be charged: see the text to note 10 infra. Similarly, where one company pays the salaries of employees of another company seconded to it, those payments are treated as consideration for the standard-rated supply of staff: *Customs and Excise Comrs v Tarmac Roadstone Holdings Ltd* [1987] STC 610, CA; cf *Durham Aged Mineworkers' Homes Association v Customs and Excise Comrs* [1994] STC 553. If maintenance contributions are paid to trustees for the purpose of being expended on the upkeep of a block of flats, the contributions are not consideration for a supply of services by the trustees, since the trustees have no right to deal with those moneys as their own: *Nell Gwynn House Maintenance Fund Trustees v Customs and Excise Comrs* [1996] STC 310, CA, following Case C-38/93 *HJ Glawe Spiel-und Unterhaltungsgeräte Aufstellungsgesellschaft GmbH & Co KG v Finanzamt Hamburg-Barmbeck-Uhlenhhorst* [1994] ECR I-1679, [1994] STC 543, ECJ (VAT is chargeable only on the amount which in accordance with local law is removable by the owner from a gaming machine and not on the amount which the players insert). Cf *Customs and Excise Comrs v Richmond Theatre Management Ltd* [1995] STC 257. Where a landlord agreed to permit a tenant to occupy a building rent-free in return for carrying out works of repair, the benefit of rent-free occupation was consideration for the supply of building services: *Ridgeon's Bulk Ltd v Customs and Excise Comrs* [1992] VATTR 169; affd [1994] STC 427. A 'fine' imposed under the terms of a contract between a video store and the customer for the late return of the video is consideration and not compensation: *Leigh (t/a Moor Lane Video) v Customs and Excise Comrs* [1990] VATTR 59. Under EC Council Directive 77/388 art 11(A)(2), the taxable amount is to include: (1) taxes, duties, levies and charges, excluding the VAT itself; and (2) incidental expenses, such as commission, packing, transport and insurance costs charged by the supplier to the purchaser or customer; and it is open to a member state to treat expenses covered by a separate agreement as incidental expenses. However, this provision has not been implemented by the United Kingdom, with the result that, in *British Telecommunications plc v Customs and Excise Comrs* (1996) VAT Decision 14072, [1996] STI 1214, it was held that the separate delivery charge imposed by manufacturers on the sale of cars to the taxpayer was consideration for a distinct supply, not caught by the Value Added Tax (Input Tax) Order 1992, SI 1992/3222, art 7 (as amended) (see para 208 post).

6   Where a company held an annual dinner at which trophies were awarded to various categories of 'players of the year', and sold tickets for the event, it was held that payment for tickets to the event was directly linked to the presentation of the trophies; so that there was no supply of the trophies otherwise than for a consideration, within the Value Added Tax Act 1994 s 5(1), Sch 4 para 5 (as amended) (see para 24 ante), Sch 6 para 6 (see para 91 post): *Customs and Excise Comrs v Professional Footballers' Association (Enterprises) Ltd* [1993] 1 WLR 153, [1993] STC 86, HL. Similarly, video tapes distributed free of charge to doctors containing advertisements, in accordance with the supplier's contracts with its advertisers, were not within the Value Added Tax Act 1994 Sch 4 para 5 (as amended): *Customs and Excise Comrs v Telemed Ltd* [1992] STC 89. Where B acquires title to vehicles by discharging A's outstanding debts under a hire-purchase agreement, A is to be taken to have supplied the vehicles to B for a consideration equal to the debt thus discharged: *Phillip Drakard Trading Ltd v Customs and Excise Comrs* [1992] STC 568.

7   EC Council Directive 77/388 (OJ L145, 13.6.77, p 1) art 11(A)(1)(a); and see *Trafalgar Tours Ltd v Customs and Excise Comrs* [1990] 3 CMLR 68, [1990] STC 127, CA (parent company which belonged outside the member states arranged for subsidiary companies in member states to organise tours for overseas customers; the relevant subsidiary would then receive a percentage of the price paid by the customers, the remainder being retained by the parent company; parent company held to be acting only as an agent for the subsidiary; and the consideration for the supply made by the subsidiary (on which VAT was chargeable) was the whole price paid by the customer, rather than the reduced amount received by the subsidiary). An optional service charge does not form part of the consideration: *NDP Co Ltd v Customs and Excise Comrs* [1988] VATTR 40.

8   EC Council Directive 77/388 art 11(A)(3)(a); and see also the Value Added Tax Act 1994 Sch 6 para 4(1) (where goods or services are supplied for a consideration in money and on terms allowing for prompt payment, the consideration is to be taken for the purposes of s 19 as reduced by the discount whether or not payment is made in accordance with those terms). Schedule 6 para 4(1) does not, however, apply where the terms include any provision for payment by instalment: Sch 6 para 4(2). For the meaning of 'money' see para 7 note 5 ante. It is difficult to see that Sch 6 para 4 is an accurate implementation of EC Council Directive 77/388 art 11(A)(3)(a).

If the Commissioners of Customs and Excise serve a notice under the Value Added Tax Act 1994 Sch 6 para 3 on a taxable person, requiring him to account for VAT on the open market value of goods supplied to unregistered intermediaries (see para 89 post) it is unnecessary to consider whether any discount given to the intermediaries falls within Sch 6 para 4, since it must be ignored for VAT purposes: *Gold Star Publications Ltd v Customs and Excise Comrs* [1992] 3 CMLR 1, [1992] STC 365.

9   EC Council Directive 77/388 art 11(A)(3)(b). This has no statutory equivalent in the United Kingdom legislation; but the provision has direct effect. As to the principle of direct effect see para 3 ante. In *Co-operative Retail Services Ltd v Customs and Excise Comrs* [1992] 3 CMLR 541, [1992] VATTR 60, the 'dividends' provided by the society and credited to members' share accounts on the purchase of goods were held to be a discount within EC Council Directive 77/388 art 11(A)(3)(b). In Case C-126/88 *Boots Co plc v Customs and Excise Comrs* [1990] ECR I-1235, [1990] STC 387, ECJ, it was held that, having regard to the juxtaposition of 'price discount' and 'price rebate', a restrictive meaning should not be given to either of them; and that they covered both the case in which part of the price indicated is not paid and that in which part of the price paid is returned to the customer at the time of purchase. So, where a customer who bought one item was given a voucher entitling him to a discount on a later purchase, the taxable amount of the latter supply was the sum in fact paid: the voucher itself was not part of the consideration for the second supply. As to reductions occurring after the supply takes place see EC Council Directive 77/388 art 11(C)(1); and note 11 infra. See also Case C-33/93 *Empire Stores Ltd v Customs and Excise Comrs* [1994] 3 All ER 90, [1994] STC 623, ECJ.

10   EC Council Directive 77/388 art 11(A)(3)(c). Again, there is no statutory equivalent in the United Kingdom; but the provision has direct effect: see *Scally v Customs and Excise Comrs* [1989] VATTR 245.

11   EC Council Directive 77/388 art 11(C)(1). The reduction is to be made under conditions to be determined by the member states; and in the case of total or partial non-payment, member states may derogate from the rule. The commissioners have admitted that art 11(C)(1) has direct effect: cf *Mannesmann Demag Hamilton Ltd v Customs and Excise Comrs* [1983] VATTR 156. Nevertheless, they have claimed, in argument before the VAT tribunal in *Goldsmiths (Jewellers) Ltd v Customs and Excise Comrs* (1994) VAT Decision 12694, [1994] STI 1374 (a case involving a barter agreement), that the United Kingdom has derogated from EC Council Directive 77/388 art 11(C)(1) by implementing what is now the Value Added Tax Act 1994 s 36 (bad debts: see para 260 post), which only permits a refund of VAT in a case where the consideration for the supply was a price in money. The VAT tribunal has sought a preliminary ruling from the European Court whether the United Kingdom was empowered so to derogate from the Directive. However, there are other indications that the United Kingdom may not have derogated in the manner suggested by the commissioners; the Value Added Tax Regulations 1995, SI 1995/2518, reg 38 (see para 239 post) provides for an adjustment in a person's VAT account where there has been an increase or decrease in the consideration for a supply in a prescribed accounting period after that in which the original supply took place; and in *AEG (UK) Ltd v Customs and Excise Comrs* (1993) VAT Decision 10944, [1993] STI 1301, the tribunal held that where a washing machine repairer refunds the cost of the service if the customer subsequently purchases a new machine (from a third party), the refund falls to be treated as a discount from the cost of the service under EC Council Directive 77/388 art 11(C)(1) and VAT is to be recoverable accordingly. It would appear that the credit note procedure offered by the commissioners is based on art 11(C)(1): see the VAT Regulations 1995 reg 38; and Customs and Excise Notice 700 *The VAT Guide* (March 1996) para 7.1.

(ii) Valuation in Special Cases

87. Consideration less than open market value. Where (1) the value of a supply[1] made by a taxable person[2] for a consideration[3] in money[4] is less than its open market value; (2) the person making the supply and the person to whom it is made are connected[5]; and (3) if the supply is a taxable supply[6], the person to whom the supply is made is not entitled[7] to credit for all the value added tax on the supply, the Commissioners of Customs and Excise may direct[8] that the value of the supply is to be taken to be its open market value[9]. For the purposes of VAT, the 'open market value' of a supply of goods or services is taken to be the amount that would fall to be taken to be its value for VAT[10] if the supply were made for such consideration in money as would be payable by a person not standing in a relationship with any person which would affect that consideration[11].

1   For the meaning of 'supply' see para 21 ante.
2   For the meaning of 'taxable person' see paras 12 note 4, 55 ante.
3   For the meaning of 'consideration' see para 86 ante.
4   For the meaning of 'money' see para 7 note 5 ante.
5   Any question whether one person is connected with another for these purposes is to be determined in accordance with the Income and Corporation Taxes Act 1988 s 839 (as amended) (see INCOME TAXATION vol 23 (Reissue) para 1250): Value Added Tax Act 1994 s 19(1), Sch 6 para 1(4).
6   For the meaning of 'taxable supply' see para 12 note 3 ante.
7   Ie under the Value Added Tax Act 1994 ss 25, 26: see paras 202–203 post.
8   Any such direction must be given by notice in writing to the person making the supply; but no direction may be given more than three years after the time of the supply: ibid Sch 6 para 1(2). A direction may be varied or withdrawn by a further direction given in writing: Sch 6 para 13. An appeal lies to a VAT and duties tribunal against the making of such a direction: see s 83(v); and para 296 post.
9   Ibid Sch 6 para 1(1). This provision involves an authorised derogation from EC Council Directive 77/388 arts 11(A)(1)(a), 28e(1) (as added): see EC Council Decision 92/546 (OJ L351, 2.12.92, p 34). The Value Added Tax Act 1994 Sch 6 para 1(1) does not apply to a supply to which Sch 6 para 10 (see para 93 post) applies: Sch 6 para 1(5).
      A direction so given to a person in respect of a supply made by him may include a direction that the value of any supply (1) which is made by him after the giving of the notice, or after such later date as may be specified in the notice; and (2) as to which the conditions in heads (1)–(3) in the text are satisfied, is to be taken to be its open market value: Sch 1 para 1(3).
10   Ie under ibid s 19(2): see para 85 ante.
11   Ibid s 19(5). In other words, if a registered trader sells to his son for £50 goods which ordinarily he would have sold for £117.50, the commissioners may direct that the trader treat the value of the supply for VAT purposes as being £100 (provided that the son is not a fully-taxable trader buying for the purposes of his own VAT-registered business).

88. Supply to non-taxable persons of goods to be sold retail.

Where the whole or part of a business[1] carried on by a taxable person[2] consists in supplying to a number of persons goods to be sold[3], whether by them or by others, by retail, and those persons are not taxable persons, the Commissioners of Customs and Excise may direct[4] that the value of any such supply by him is to be taken to be its open market value[5] on a sale by retail[6].

1   For the meaning of 'business' see para 17 ante.
2   For the meaning of 'taxable person' see paras 12 note 4, 55 ante.
3   Where a registered trader sold goods to unregistered persons in circumstances where there was no condition for resale attached, but with the intention that some of the goods would be sold on, it would be unrealistic to hold that no part of the trader's business could be said to consist in supplying goods to be sold by retail: *Fine Art Developments plc v Customs and Excise Comrs* [1996] 1 All ER 888, [1996] STC 246, HL. The Value Added Tax Act 1994 s 19(1), Sch 6 para 2 involves an authorised derogation from the provisions of EC Council Directive 77/388 (OJ L145, 13.6.77, p 1) art 11(A)(1)(a): EC Council Decision 89/534 (OJ L280, 29.9.89, p 54). The decision as to what is the open market value is thus a matter for the national authorities and ultimately for the national court: *Fine Art Developments plc v Customs and Excise Comrs* supra. It is irrelevant that the trader carries on business as he does for commercial, rather than for tax-avoidance, reasons: Joined Cases 138/86, 139/86 *Direct Cosmetics Ltd v Customs and Excise Comrs, Laughtons Photographs Ltd v Customs and Excise Comrs* [1988] ECR 3937, [1988] STC 540, ECJ. Where the available evidence would not enable the taxable person to ascertain the open market value, the Commissioners of Customs and Excise may serve a notice under the Value Added Tax Act 1994 Sch 6 para 2: *Beckbell Ltd v Customs and Excise Comrs* [1993] VATTR 212.
4   The direction must be made by notice in writing to the taxable person and can only apply to supplies made by him after the giving of such notice or after such later date as may be specified in the notice: Value Added Tax Act 1994 Sch 6 para 2. A direction may be varied or withdrawn by a further direction: Sch 6 para 13. An appeal lies to a VAT and duties tribunal against the making of such a direction under s 83(v): see para 296 post.
5   For the meaning of 'open market value' see para 87 text to notes 10–11 ante. In Joined Cases 138/86, 139/86 *Direct Cosmetics Ltd and Laughtons Photographs Ltd v Customs and Excise Comrs* [1988] ECR 3937, [1988] STC 540, ECJ, it was held that 'the open market value' must be understood as meaning the value that is closest to the commercial value on a sale by retail, ie the actual price paid by the final consumer; cf *Fine Art Developments plc v Customs and Excise Comrs* [1996] 1 All ER 888 at 899, [1996] STC 246 at

256, HL, per Lord Keith (the actual price referred to must be the actual price paid by the final consumer of similar goods, not of the particular goods in question, since if that were known there would be no question of taking the market value unless the parties were not at arm's length).

6   Value Added Tax Act 1994 Sch 6 para 2.

89. Goods removed to the United Kingdom. Where any goods whose supply[1] involves their removal to the United Kingdom[2] are charged, in connection with that removal, with a duty of excise[3] or are subject[4] to any Community customs duty or agricultural levy, the value of the supply for the purposes of value added tax is taken to be the sum of its value on ordinary VAT principles[5] and the amount of the duty or agricultural levy which has been or is to be paid in respect of the goods[6]. Where the time of supply of any dutiable goods[7], or of any goods which comprise a mixture of dutiable goods and other goods, is determined[8] to be the duty point[9], the value of the supply is similarly determined[10].

1   For the meaning of 'supply' see para 21 ante.
2   Eg where there has been an acquisition of goods from another member state: see the Value Added Tax Act 1994 ss 1(1)(a), 11; and paras 4, 13 ante. For the meaning of 'United Kingdom' see para 4 note 3 ante.
3   Ibid s 19(1), Sch 6 para 3(1)(a).
4   Ie in accordance with any provision for the time being having effect for transitional purposes in connection with the accession of any state to the European Community: ibid Sch 6 para 3(1)(b).
5   Ie apart from ibid Sch 6 para 3: Sch 6 para 3(1). As to the general principles of valuation see para 85 ante.
6   Ibid Sch 6 para 3(1). Any reference to the amount of any duty of excise on any goods is to be taken to be a reference to the amount of duty charged on those goods with any addition or deduction falling to be made under the Excise Duties (Surcharges or Rebates) Act 1979 s 1 (as amended) (see CUSTOMS AND EXCISE): Value Added Tax Act 1994 s 96(5).
7   For these purposes, 'dutiable goods' means any goods which are subject (1) to a duty of excise; or (2) in accordance with any provision for the time being having effect for transitional purposes in connection with the accession of any state to the European Community, to any Community customs duty or agricultural levy: ibid s 18(6) (definition applied by Sch 6 para 3(2)).
8   Ie under ibid s 18 (as amended): see para 130 post.
9   For these purposes, 'the duty point', in relation to any goods, means (1) in the case of goods which are subject to a duty of excise, the time when the requirement to pay the duty on those goods takes effect; and (2) in the case of goods which are not so subject, the time when any Community customs debt in respect of duty on the entry of the goods into the territory of the Community would be incurred or, as the case may be, the corresponding time in relation to any such duty or levy as is mentioned in note 7 head (2) supra: ibid s 18(6) (definition applied by Sch 6 para 3(2)).
10   Ibid Sch 6 para 3(1).

90. Right to receive goods or services granted for consideration. Where a right to receive goods or services for an amount on any token, stamp or voucher is granted for a consideration[1], the consideration is disregarded for the purposes of value added tax except to the extent, if any, that it exceeds that amount[2].

1   For the meaning of 'consideration' see para 86 ante.
2   Value Added Tax Act 1994 s 19(1), Sch 6 para 5. It is by this provision that postage stamps are excluded from a charge to VAT; but this exclusion causes difficulty when, rather than having a face value, the stamp merely indicates that it entitles the letter to be delivered 'First Class' or 'Second Class'. Where a taxable person sold cards entitling the holder to a discount on the cost of a meal at certain restaurants, the cards were not within the scope of this provision and VAT was chargeable on the net price of the card; but the retailer supplying meals at a discounted price in accordance with the terms of the card would only be liable to account for VAT on the discounted price: *Customs and Excise Comrs v Granton Marketing Ltd, Customs and Excise Comrs v Wentwalk Ltd* [1996] STC 1049, CA. Where vouchers were sold to retailers to be provided to customers and it was a term of the contract that the vouchers could only be redeemed by the customer and not by the retailer, the sale of the voucher did not fall within the Value Added Tax Act 1994 Sch 6 para 5: *Customs and Excise Comrs v Showmarch Marketing Ltd* [1994] STC 19. The operation

of the Value Added Tax Act 1994 Sch 6 para 5 was referred for the consideration of the European Court of Justice in *Argos Distributors Ltd v Customs and Excise Comrs* (1994) VAT Decision 12708, [1994] STI 1378; however, the court's decision on another point (see Case C-288/94 *Argos Distributors Ltd v Customs and Excise Comrs* [1996] STC 1359, ECJ) made the decision of that question unnecessary.

91. Deemed supplies of goods or services. Specific provision is made for the value of certain deemed supplies of goods and services[1]. Where there is a deemed supply of goods by virtue of:

   (1)   a Treasury order relating to self-supply[2]; or

   (2)   the statutory provisions relating to the transfer or disposal of assets[3] or the removal of goods to another member state[4] (but otherwise than for a consideration); or

   (3)   the statutory provisions relating to supplies by persons ceasing to be taxable persons[5],

the value of the supply[6] is taken to be:

   (a)   such consideration in money as would be payable[7] by the person making the supply if he were, at the time of the supply, to purchase goods identical in every respect (including age and condition) to the goods concerned[8]; or

   (b)   where the value cannot be ascertained under head (a) above, such consideration in money as would be payable[9] by that person if he were at that time to purchase goods similar to, and of the same age and condition as, the goods concerned[10]; or

   (c)   if the value cannot be ascertained under either head (a) or head (b) above, the cost of producing the goods concerned if they were produced at that time[11].

Similarly, where there is a deemed supply of services by virtue of a Treasury order[12] or the statutory provisions relating to private use[13] (but otherwise than for a consideration), the value of the supply[14] is taken to be the full cost to the taxable person of providing the services[15]. Where any supply of services is treated[16] as made by the person by whom they are received, the value of the supply is taken to be:

   (i)   in a case where the consideration for which the services were in fact supplied to him was a consideration in money, such amount as is equal to that consideration; and

   (ii)   in a case where that consideration did not consist, or did not wholly consist, of money, such amount in money as is equivalent to that consideration[17].

1   As to deemed supplies generally see para 24 ante.
2   Ie an order under the Value Added Tax Act 1994 s 5(5): see para 26 ante.
3   Ie ibid s 5(1), Sch 4 para 5(1): see para 24 ante.
4   Ie ibid Sch 4 para 6: see para 14 ante. For the meaning of 'another member state' see para 4 note 14 ante.
5   Ie ibid Sch 4 para 8: see para 24 ante. For the meaning of 'taxable person' see paras 12 note 4, 55 ante.
6   Ie except a supply to which ibid Sch 6 para 10 applies: see para 93 post. For the meaning of 'supply' see para 21 ante. See Customs and Excise Notice 252 *Valuation of Imported Goods for Customs Purposes, VAT and Trade Statistics* for an explanation of the views of the Commissioners of Customs and Excise on the application of these valuation principles.
7   For these purposes, the amount of consideration in money that would be payable by any person if he were to purchase any goods is to be taken to be the amount that would be so payable after the deduction of any amount included in the purchase price in respect of VAT on the supply of the goods to that person: ibid Sch 6 para 6(3). For the meaning of 'consideration' generally see para 86 ante; and for the meaning of 'money' see para 7 note 5 ante.
8   Ibid Sch 6 para 6(1), (2)(a).
9   See note 7 supra.
10   Value Added Tax Act 1994 Sch 6 para 6(1), (2)(b).
11   Ibid Sch 6 para 6(1), (2)(c).
12   Ie under ibid s 5(4): see para 24 ante.
13   Ie ibid Sch 4 para 5(4): see para 24 ante.
14   See note 6 supra.

15 Value Added Tax Act 1994 Sch 6 para 7 (amended by the Finance Act 1995 s 33(1), (3)(b)). This provision does not apply to a supply to which the Value Added Tax Act 1994 Sch 6 para 10 applies: Sch 6 para 7 (as so amended). As to what constitutes the full cost of such a supply see *Customs and Excise Comrs v Teknequip Ltd* [1987] STC 664. The charge on the private use of goods is derived from EC Council Directive 77/388 (OJ L145, 13.6.77, p 1) art 6(1), and arises only exceptionally, so that art 6(1) must be interpreted strictly. Accordingly, the charge is limited to the use of the goods themselves and does not extend to services supplied by third parties for the purposes of maintaining or using the goods, where the taxable person is unable to deduct the input tax paid: Case C-193/91 *Finanzamt München III v Möhsche* [1993] ECR I-2615, ECJ. When determining the taxable amount under EC Council Directive 77/388 art 6(1), the periods in which goods are at a taxable person's disposal in a way that he can actually use them at any time for private purposes must be taken into account: Case C-230/94 *Enkler v Finanzamt Homburg* [1996] STI 1316, ECJ.

16 Ie by virtue of the Value Added Tax Act 1994 s 8: see para 27 ante.

17 Ibid Sch 6 para 8.

92. Supply of services consisting of provision of accommodation. Where a supply[1] of services consists in the provision to an individual of accommodation[2] in a hotel, inn or boarding house or other similar establishment[3] for a period exceeding four weeks[4], and throughout that period the accommodation is provided for the use of the individual either alone or together with one or more other persons who occupy the accommodation with him otherwise than at their own expense, whether incurred directly or indirectly, the value of so much of the supply as is in excess of four weeks is reduced to such part of it as is attributable to facilities other than the right to occupy the accommodation[5]. The part so attributable is not, however, to be taken to be less than 20 per cent[6].

1 For the meaning of 'supply' see para 21 ante.

2 Ie sleeping accommodation, or accommodation in rooms which are provided in conjunction with sleeping accommodation or for the purpose of a supply of catering: see the Value Added Tax Act 1994 s 31(1), Sch 9 Pt II Group 1 item 1(d) (applied by s 19(1), Sch 6 para 9(1)).

3 'Similar establishment' includes premises in which there is provided furnished sleeping accommodation, whether with or without the provision of board or facilities for the preparation of food, and which are used by or held out as being suitable for use by visitors or travellers: ibid Sch 9 Pt II Group 1 note 9.

4 See *Elga and Askar Co Ltd v Customs and Excise Comrs* [1983] STC 628 (decided under the previous, more generous, rules) (reduction does not apply unless the room is supplied to the individual for continual occupation throughout the period in excess of four weeks). The Value Added Tax Act 1994 Sch 6 para 9 constitutes a derogation corresponding to an exemption for the letting of immovable property under EC Council Directive 77/388 (OJ L145, 13.6.77, p 1) art 13(B)(b)(1) and is permitted by an authorisation deemed to have been adopted on 10 December 1986.

5 Value Added Tax Act 1994 Sch 6 para 9(1), (2)(a).

6 Ibid Sch 6 para 9(2)(b).

93. Supply of certain goods or services by employer. The value of a supply[1] of goods or services, whether or not for a consideration[2], which is made by an employer and consists of (1) the provision of food or beverages to his employees; or (2) the provision of accommodation for his employees in a hotel, inn, boarding house or similar establishment[3], is taken to be nil unless the supply is for a consideration consisting wholly or partly of money[4], in which case its value is determined without regard to any consideration other than money[5].

1 For the meaning of 'supply' see para 21 ante.

2 For the meaning of 'consideration' see para 86 ante.

3 Cf para 92 note 3 ante.

4 For the meaning of 'money' see para 7 note 5 ante.

5 Value Added Tax Act 1994 s 19(1), Sch 6 para 10(1), (2). See *Goodfellow v Customs and Excise Comrs* [1986] VATTR 119.

94. Supply of goods or services whose value is not determined in sterling.
Where there is a supply[1] or goods or services and any sum relevant for determining the value of the supply is expressed in a currency other than sterling, then, for the purpose of valuing the supply, that sum is to be converted into sterling at the market rate which would apply in the United Kingdom[2] on the relevant day[3] to a purchase with sterling by the person to whom they are supplied of that sum in the currency in question[4]. Where, however, the Commissioners of Customs and Excise have published a notice[5] which specifies rates of exchange for these purposes, or methods of determining rates of exchange, a rate specified in or determined in accordance with the notice applies[6] in the case of any supply by a person who opts, in such manner as may be allowed by the commissioners, for the use of that rate in relation to that supply[7]. Such an option for the use of a particular rate or method of determining a rate may not be exercised by any person except in relation to all such supplies by him as are of a particular description or after a particular date, and may not be withdrawn or varied except with the consent of the commissioners and in such manner as they may require[8].

1   For the meaning of 'supply' see para 21 ante.
2   For the meaning of 'United Kingdom' see para 4 note 3 ante.
3   The time by reference to which the appropriate rate of exchange is to be determined for the purpose of valuing any supply is the time when the supply takes place; and accordingly the day on which it takes place is the relevant day for these purposes: Value Added Tax Act 1994 s 19(1), Sch 6 para 11(7).
4   Ibid Sch 6 para 11(1). Where an invoice is expressed in alternative currencies, of which sterling is one, the value of the supply is taken to be the value expressed in sterling: *Advansys plc v Customs and Excise Comrs* (1990) VAT Decision 4427, [1990] STI 161; and see Customs and Excise Notice 700 *The VAT Guide* (March 1996) para 3.1(f).
5   A notice published by the commissioners for these purposes may be withdrawn or varied by a subsequent notice published by them: Value Added Tax Act 1994 Sch 6 para 11(6).
6   Ie instead of the rate for which ibid Sch 6 para 11(1) provides (see the text and notes 1–4 supra): Sch 6 para 11(2).
7   Ibid Sch 6 para 11(2). In specifying a method of determining a rate of exchange, a notice so published may allow a person to apply to the commissioners for the use, for the purpose of valuing some or all of his supplies, of a rate of exchange which is different from any which would otherwise apply: Sch 6 para 11(4). On an application made in accordance with provision contained in such a notice, the commissioners may authorise the use with respect to the applicant of such a rate of exchange, in such circumstances, in relation to such supplies and subject to such conditions as they think fit: Sch 6 para 11(5).
8   Ibid Sch 6 para 11(3).

95. Fuel for private use. The special rules described below permit a trader to treat all fuel which he purchases as acquired for the purposes of his taxable business, while imposing a scale charge on the trader in respect of each employee, or each car, which is supplied with fuel for private use during the course of a prescribed accounting period[1]. 'Fuel for private use' means fuel which, having been supplied to or imported by a taxable person[2], or manufactured by such a person, in the course of his business[3]:

(1)   is provided, or to be provided, by the taxable person to an individual[4] for private use in his own vehicle[5] or a vehicle allocated to him[6] and is so provided by reason of that individual's employment[7]; or

(2)   is appropriated, or to be appropriated, by an individual who is the taxable person for private use in his own vehicle[8]; or

(3)   is provided, or to be provided, to any of the individual partners in a partnership which is the taxable person for private use in the partner's own vehicle[9].

Fuel is not to be regarded as provided to any person for his private use if it is supplied at a price which (a) in the case of fuel supplied to or imported by the taxable person, is not less than the price at which it was so supplied or imported; and (b) in the case of fuel manufactured by the taxable person, is not less than the aggregate of the cost of the raw material and of manufacturing together with any excise duty thereon[10].

At the time at which fuel for private use is put into the fuel tank of an individual's own vehicle or that of a vehicle allocated to him, the fuel is deemed for the purposes of value added tax to have been supplied to him by the taxable person in the course or furtherance of his business for a consideration[11]. Where the fuel is appropriated by the taxable person to his own private use, he is treated as supplying it to himself in his private capacity[12]. In any prescribed accounting period in which the taxable person is treated by virtue of these provisions as supplying fuel for private use to an individual, the consideration for all the supplies made to that individual in that period in respect of any one vehicle[13] is taken to be the appropriate amount[14] for a vehicle of that description and to be inclusive of VAT[15]. The appropriate amount is set out in the statutory table[16] which prescribes different scale fees according to the cubic capacity[17] of the vehicle's engine and the length of the prescribed accounting period[18]. The Treasury may by order substitute a different statutory table with effect from the beginning of any prescribed accounting period[19].

By concession, where a registered person makes no claim for input tax[20] on purchases of road fuel, whether for business or private journeys, the VAT scale charge is not applied[21].

1   See the text and notes 2–21 infra. These rules obviate the difficulties which would arise if a trader or the Commissioners of Customs and Excise were obliged to value the amount of fuel which a trader or his employees may use for private purposes.

2   For these purposes, any reference to (1) fuel supplied to a taxable person includes a reference to fuel acquired by a taxable person from another member state; and (2) fuel imported by a taxable person is confined to a reference to fuel imported by that person from a place outside the member states: Value Added Tax Act 1994 s 56(3)(b). For the meaning of 'taxable person' see paras 12 note 4, 55 ante; and for the meaning of 'another member state' see para 4 note 14 ante. As to the territories deemed to be included in, or excluded from, the member states for VAT purposes see para 10 ante.

3   For the meaning of 'business' see para 17 ante.

4   Where under the Value Added Tax Act 1994 s 43 (as amended) any bodies corporate are treated as members of a group (see paras 66 ante, 191 post), any provision of fuel by a member of the group to an individual is treated for these purposes as provision by the representative member: s 56(4). For the meaning of 'the representative member' see para 66 ante.

5   For these purposes, any reference to an individual's own vehicle is to be construed as including any vehicle of which for the time being he has the use (other than a vehicle allocated to him, which falls under ibid s 56(3)(d): see note 6 infra): s 56(3)(c). 'Vehicle' means a mechanically propelled road vehicle other than a motor cycle or an invalid carriage as defined in the Road Traffic Act 1988 s 185(1): Value Added Tax Act 1994 s 56(10).

6   A vehicle is treated as allocated to an individual at any time if at that time it is made available (without any transfer of the property in it) either to the individual himself or to any other person, and is so made available by reason of the individual's employment and for private use: ibid s 56(3)(d). A vehicle (ie a pool car) is not regarded as so allocated to an individual in any prescribed accounting period if: (1) in that period it was made available to, and actually used by, more than one of the employees of one or more employers and, in the case of each of them, was made available to him by reason of his employment but was not in that period ordinarily used by any one of them to the exclusion of the others; (2) in the case of each of the employees, any private use of the vehicle made by him in that period was merely incidental to his other use of it in that period; and (3) it was in that period not normally kept overnight on or in the vicinity of any residential premises where any of the employees was residing, except while being kept overnight on premises occupied by the person making the vehicle available to them: s 56(9). 'Employment' includes any office; and related expressions are to be construed accordingly: s 56(10). For the meaning of 'prescribed accounting period' see para 202 note 4 post .

7   Ibid s 56(1)(a), (3)(a). Fuel provided by an employer to an employee and fuel which is provided to any person for private use in a vehicle which, by virtue of s 56(3)(d) (see note 6 supra) is for the time being taken as allocated to the employee is taken to be provided to the employee by reason of his employment: s 56(3)(e).

8   Ibid s 56(1)(b), (3)(a).

9   Ibid s 56(1)(c), (3)(a).
10 Ibid s 56(2).
11 Ibid s 56(6). For the meaning of 'consideration' generally see para 86 ante. The consideration is determined in accordance with s 56(7): see the text and notes 13–15 ante. As to the meaning of 'in the course or furtherance of a business' see paras 12 note 5, 17 note 2 ante.
12 Ibid s 56(6).
13 In any case where (1) in any prescribed accounting period, fuel for private use is, by virtue of ibid s 56(6), treated as supplied to an individual in respect of one vehicle for a part of the period and in respect of another vehicle for another part of the period; and (2) at the end of that period one of those vehicles neither belongs to him nor is allocated to him, this provision has effect as if the supplies made to the individual during those parts of the period were in respect of only one vehicle: s 56(8).
14 Ie the amount which is appropriate by virtue of ibid s 57 (as amended): see the text and notes 16–19 infra.
15 Ibid s 56(7).
16 Ie ibid s 57(3), Table A (substituted, at the date which this volume states the law, by the Finance Act 1995 s 30; and amended by the Value Added Tax (Increase of Consideration for Fuel) Order 1995, SI 1995/3040, art 2). The current Table A is as follows:

TABLE A			
DESCRIPTION OF VEHICLE (engine type, cylinder capacity)	12 month period	3 month period	1 month period
Diesel engine			
2,000 cc or less	£640	£160	£53
more than 2,000 cc	£820	£205	£68
Any other type of engine			
1400 cc or less	£710	£177	£59
1400–2,000 cc	£890	£222	£74
more than 2,000 cc	£1,320	£330	£110

17 In the case of a vehicle having an internal combustion engine with one or more reciprocating pistons, its cubic capacity for the purposes of ibid s 57(3), Table A (as substituted and amended: see note 16 supra) is the capacity of its engine as calculated for the purposes of the Vehicle Excise and Registration Act 1994: Value Added Tax Act 1994 s 57(7). In the case of a vehicle not falling within s 57(7), its cubic capacity is such as may be determined for these purposes by order by the Treasury: s 57(8). As to the making of orders generally see para 8 ante.
18 Ibid s 57(1). 'The prescribed accounting period' for these purposes means that in respect of supplies in which the consideration is to be determined: s 57(1). Where the prescribed accounting period is a period of 12 months, the consideration appropriate to any vehicle is that specified in relation to a vehicle of the appropriate description in the second column of s 57(3), Table A (as substituted and amended: see note 16 supra); where it is a period of three months, the consideration appropriate to any vehicle is that specified in relation to a vehicle of the appropriate description in the third column thereof; and where it is a period of one month, the consideration appropriate to any vehicle is that specified in relation to a vehicle of the appropriate description in the fourth column thereof: s 57(1A), (2), (3) (respectively added and amended by the Finance Act 1995 s 30).
    Where by virtue of the Value Added Tax Act 1994 s 56(8) (see note 13 supra) s 56(7) has effect as if, in the prescribed accounting period, supplies of fuel for private use made in respect of two or more vehicles were made in respect of only one vehicle, the consideration appropriate is determined as follows: (1) if each of the two or more vehicles falls within the same description of vehicle specified in s 57(3), Table A (as so substituted and amended), that Table applies as if only one of the vehicles were to be considered throughout the whole period; and (2) if one of those vehicles falls within a description of vehicle specified in that Table which is different from the other or others, the consideration is the aggregate of the relevant fractions of the consideration appropriate for each description of vehicle under that Table: s 57(5). For the purposes of head (2) supra, the relevant fraction in relation to any vehicle is

that which the part of the prescribed accounting period in which fuel for private use was supplied in respect of that vehicle bears to the whole of that period: s 57(6).

19 Ibid s 57(4). In exercise of the power so conferred, the Treasury has made the Value Added Tax (Increase of Consideration for Fuel) Order 1995 (see note 16 supra), which came into force in relation to a taxable person from the beginning of the first of his prescribed accounting periods which began after 5 April 1996: art 1.

20 As to the credit for input tax incurred on the purchase of fuel for private use see the Value Added Tax Act 1994 s 56(5); and para 201 post. For the meaning of 'input tax' see paras 4 ante, 201 post.

21 See Customs and Excise Notice 748 *Extra-statutory Concessions* (1 August 1995) concession 7.

96. Gaming machines. Where a person plays a game of chance[1] by means of a gaming machine[2], then for the purposes of value added tax the amount paid by him to play[3] is treated as the consideration[4] for a supply[5] of services to him[6]. The value to be taken as the value of the supplies so made in any period[7] is determined[8] as if the consideration for the supplies were reduced by an amount equal to the amount (if any) received in that period by persons[9] playing successfully[10].

1 For these purposes, 'game of chance' has the same meaning as in the Gaming Act 1968 (see BETTING, GAMING AND LOTTERIES vol 4(1) (Reissue) para 123): Value Added Tax Act 1994 s 23(4).

2 For these purposes, 'gaming machine' means a machine in respect of which the following conditions are satisfied: (1) it is constructed or adapted for playing a game of chance by means of it; (2) a player pays to play the machine (except where he may play payment-free as the result of having previously played successfully) either by inserting a coin or a token into the machine or in some other way; and (3) the element of chance in the machine is provided by means of the machine: ibid s 23(4). As to the general exemption from VAT for betting, gaming and lotteries see s 31(1), Sch 9 Pt II Group 4; and para 148 post. The exemption does not extend to the provision of a gaming machine: Sch 9 Pt II Group 4 note 1(d). The exclusion from exemption for gaming machines is not inconsistent with EC Council Directive 77/388 (OJ L145, 13.6.77, p 1) art 13(B)(f); and the phrase 'the provision of gaming machines' means the provision to players: *Feehan v Customs and Excise Comrs* [1995] STC 75.

3 The insertion of a token into a machine is treated for these purposes as the payment of an amount equal to that for which the token can be obtained: Value Added Tax Act 1994 s 23(3).

4 For the meaning of 'consideration' generally see para 86 ante.

5 For the meaning of 'supply' see para 21 ante.

6 Value Added Tax Act 1994 s 23(1). Section 23(1) is without prejudice to s 23(2) (see the text and notes 7–10 infra): s 23(1).

7 It is apprehended that 'period' refers to the machine owner's prescribed accounting period. For the meaning of 'prescribed accounting period' see para 202 note 4 post.

8 An authorised person may at any reasonable time require a person making a supply under the Value Added Tax Act 1994 s 23(1) or any person acting on his behalf: (1) to open any gaming machine; and (2) to carry out any other operation to enable the authorised person to ascertain the amount which is to be taken as the value of supplies made in the circumstances mentioned in s 23(1): s 58, Sch 11 para 9. For the meaning of 'authorised person' see para 82 note 5 ante.

9 Ie other than the person making the supply or persons acting on his behalf: ibid s 23(2).

10 Ibid s 23(2). For these purposes, the receipt of a token by a person playing successfully is treated: (1) if the token is of a kind used to play the machine, as the receipt of an amount equal to that for which such a token can be exchanged; and (2) if it is not of such a kind but can be exchanged for money, as the receipt of an amount equal to that for which it can be exchanged: s 23(3). For the meaning of 'money' see para 7 note 5 ante.

97. Adjustments to contracts on changes in value added tax. Where, after the making of a contract for the supply[1] of goods or services and before the goods or services are supplied, there is a change in the value added tax charged on the supply[2], then, unless the contract otherwise provided, there is added to or deducted from the consideration[3] for the supply an amount equal to the change[4]. This provision applies in relation to a tenancy or lease as it applies in relation to a contract, except that a term of a tenancy or lease is not to be taken to provide that the rule set out above is not to apply in the case of the tenancy or lease if the term does not specifically refer to VAT or to the statutory provision containing that rule[5].

1   For the meaning of 'supply' see para 21 ante.
2   For these purposes, references, references to a change in the VAT charged on a supply include references to a change to or from no VAT being charged on the supply (including a change attributable to the making of an election to waive exemption under the Value Added Tax Act 1994 s 51(1), Sch 10 para 2 (as amended) (see para 143 post): s 89(3). In *Jaymarke Development Ltd v Elinacre Ltd (in liquidation)* [1992] STC 575, the parties had contracted to sell and buy a parcel of land for a price which, the contract stated, was 'deemed to be inclusive of VAT'. The vendors did not elect to waive exemption, in consequence of which the sale was an exempt supply of land; it was held that the purchasers were not entitled to claim to recover an amount of the price equal to the VAT which would have been charged, had the election to waive exemption been made. Under the Value Added Tax Act 1994 s 88, the supplier may elect that in specified circumstances the rate of VAT on supplies which span a change in the rate of VAT in force or in the description of exempt or zero-rated goods or acquisitions is to be determined without regard to those provisions of s 6 (as amended) (see paras 29, 31, 38 ante) which would affect the time at which the supply would otherwise be treated as taking place: see para 30 ante. In *Rice v Customs and Excise Comrs* [1996] STC 581, CA, Staughton LJ indicated that it was open to question whether the Value Added Tax Act 1994 s 89 was applicable in a case where, between the time of contract and the time of supply, the supplier became registered for VAT.
3   For the meaning of 'consideration' generally see para 86 ante.
4   Value Added Tax Act 1994 s 89(1).
5   Ibid s 89(2). If, therefore, a lease is granted at a rent of £10,000 per annum, and the landlord subsequently elects to waive exemption, the tenant will subsequently be obliged to pay rent of £10,000 plus VAT of £1,750 unless he can rely on a term of the lease which provides that the rent is inclusive of VAT (if any) or which specifically precludes an adjustment of consideration under s 89, whether on the landlord electing to waive exemption or otherwise.

(iii) Valuation of Acquisitions from Other Member States

98. In general. A reverse charge arises where there is a taxable acquisition of goods from another member state[1]. The value of any acquisition of goods from another member state is taken to be the value of the transaction in pursuance of which the goods are acquired[2]. If the goods are acquired from another member state otherwise than in pursuance of a taxable supply[3], the usual rules which apply for determining the value of a supply of goods or services[4] do not apply in relation to the transaction[5] and its value is determined in accordance with provisions[6] directed specifically to the valuation of acquisitions[7]. As a general rule, if the transaction is for a consideration in money[8], its value is taken to be such amount as is equal to the consideration[9]. If it is for a consideration not consisting, or not wholly consisting, of money, its value is taken to be such amount in money as is equivalent to the consideration[10]. Where the transaction in pursuance of which goods are acquired from another member state is not the only matter to which a consideration in money relates, the transaction is deemed to be for such part of the consideration as is properly attributable to it[11].

1   See para 13 ante. For the meaning of 'taxable acquisition' see para 13 ante; and for the meaning of 'another member state' see para 4 note 14 ante.
2   Value Added Tax Act 1994 s 20(1). This provision is subject to s 18C (as added: see para 140 post): s 20(1) (amended by the Finance Act 1996 s 26(1), Sch 3 para 6). As to acquisitions from another member state see para 13 ante.
3   Ie in which case the acquisition may be a taxable acquisition: see para 13 ante. For the meaning of 'taxable supply' see para 12 note 3 ante.
4   Ie the Value Added Tax Act 1994 s 19, Sch 6: see para 86 et seq ante.

5   Ibid s 20(2)(b).

6   Ie ibid s 20, Sch 7: see the text and notes 7–11 ante; and para 99 et seq post. It is fair to say that these rules are the mirror image of the ordinary rules of valuation of supplies, taking into account the expectation that VAT will not have been charged on the supply by the member state from which the goods were acquired.

7   See ibid s 20(2)(a).

8   For the meaning of 'consideration' generally see para 86 ante; and for the meaning of 'money' see para 7 note 5 ante.

9   Value Added Tax Act 1994 s 20(3). As to the procedure for determining the sterling equivalent of consideration in foreign currency see Sch 7 para 4; and para 102 post.

10   Ibid s 20(4).

11   Ibid s 20(5).

99. Consideration in money less than market value. Where, in the case of the acquisition of any goods from another member state[1]:

(1)   the relevant transaction[2] is for a consideration in money[3];

(2)   the value of the relevant transaction is otherwise less than the transaction's open market value[4];

(3)   the supplier and the person who acquires the goods are connected[5]; and

(4)   that person is not entitled[6] to credit for all the value added tax on the acquisition,

the Commissioners of Customs and Excise may direct that the value of the relevant transaction is to be taken to be its open market value[7]. The direction must be given by notice in writing to the person by whom the acquisition is made; but no such direction may be given more than three years after the relevant time[8].

A direction so given may be varied or withdrawn by the commissioners by a further direction given by notice in writing[9].

1   For the meaning of 'another member state' see para 4 note 14 ante; and as to acquisitions from other member states see para 13 ante.

2   For these purposes, 'relevant transaction', in relation to any acquisition of goods from another member state, means the transaction in pursuance of which the goods are acquired: Value Added Tax Act 1994 s 20(2), Sch 7 para 5.

3   For the meaning of 'consideration' generally see para 86 ante; and for the meaning of 'money' see para 7 note 5 ante.

4   For these purposes, the open market value of a transaction in pursuance of which goods are acquired from another member state is taken to be the amount which would fall to be taken as its value under the Value Added Tax Act 1994 s 20(3) (see para 98 ante) if it were for such consideration in money as would be payable by a person standing in no such relationship with any person as would affect that consideration: Sch 7 para 1(4). For the meaning of 'open market value' generally see para 87 ante.

5   Any question whether a person is connected with another is to be determined, for these purposes, in accordance with the Income and Corporation Taxes Act 1988 s 839 (as amended) (see INCOME TAXATION vol 23 (Reissue) para 1250): Value Added Tax Act 1994 Sch 7 para 1(5).

6   Ie under ibid ss 25, 26: see paras 202–203 post.

7   Ibid Sch 7 para 1(1). A direction so given to a person in respect of a transaction may include a direction that the value of any transaction (1) in pursuance of which goods are acquired by him from another member state after the giving of the notice, or after such later date as may be specified in the notice; and (2) as to which the conditions in heads (1)–(4) in the text are satisfied, is to be taken to be its open market value: Sch 7 para 1(3). An appeal lies to the VAT and duties tribunal against a direction under Sch 7 para 1: see s 83(w); and para 296 post.

8   Ibid Sch 7 para 1(2). 'The relevant time', in relation to any acquisition of goods from another member state, means (1) if the person by whom the goods are acquired is not a taxable person and the time of acquisition does not fall to be determined in accordance with regulations made under s 12(3) (see para 38 ante), the time of the event which, in relation to that acquisition, is the first relevant event for the purposes of taxing the acquisition; and (2) in any other case, the time of acquisition: Sch 7 para 5.

9   Ibid Sch 7 para 1(6).

100. Goods charged with excise or customs duty or agricultural levy. Where, in such cases as the Commissioners of Customs and Excise may prescribe by regulations[1], goods acquired in the United Kingdom[2] from another member state[3] are charged in connection with their removal to the United Kingdom with a duty of excise, or are subject[4] on that removal to any Community customs duty or agricultural levy, then the value of the relevant transaction[5] must be taken to be the sum of its value as otherwise determined[6] and the amount, so far as not already included in that value, of the duty or agricultural levy which has been or is to be paid in respect of those goods[7]. This provision does not, however, require the inclusion of any amount of duty or agricultural levy in the value of a transaction in pursuance of which there in an acquisition of goods which is treated[8] as taking place before the time which is the duty point[9].

1   Ie under the Value Added Tax Act 1994: s 96(1). As to the making of regulations generally see para 8 ante. In exercise of the power so conferred, the commissioners have made the Value Added Tax Regulations 1995, SI 1995/2518, regs 96, 97: see notes 2–9 infra.
2   For the meaning of 'United Kingdom' see para 4 note 3 ante.
3   For the meaning of 'another member state' see para 4 note 14 ante.
4   Ie in accordance with any provision for the time being having effect for transitional purposes in connection with the accession of any state to the European Community: Value Added Tax Act 1994 s 20(2), Sch 7 para 2(1)(b).
5   For the meaning of 'relevant transaction' see para 99 note 2 ante. This definition is also applied by the Value Added Tax Regulations 1995 reg 96.
6   Ie as determined apart from the Value Added Tax Act 1994 Sch 7 para 2: Sch 7 para 2; Value Added Tax Regulations 1995 reg 97(1).
7   Value Added Tax Act 1994 Sch 7 para 2(1); Value Added Tax Regulations 1995 reg 97(1). As to the amount of any duty of excise see para 89 note 6 ante.
8   Ie under the Value Added Tax Act 1994 s 18(4): see para 130 post.
9   Ibid Sch 7 para 2(2); Value Added Tax Regulations 1995 reg 97(2). The duty point referred to is the duty point within the meaning of the Value Added Tax Act 1994 s 18 (see paras 89 note 9 ante, 130 post): Value Added Tax Act 1994 Sch 7 para 2(2); Value Added Tax Regulations 1995 reg 97(2).

101. Goods acquired otherwise than for a consideration. Where goods are acquired from another member state[1] in pursuance of anything which is treated as a supply for value added tax purposes[2], then in a case where there is no consideration[3] the value of the relevant transaction[4] is taken to be:

(1)   such consideration in money[5] as would be payable by the supplier if he were, at the time of the acquisition, to purchase goods identical in every respect, including age and condition, as the goods concerned; or

(2)   where the value cannot be ascertained in accordance with head (1) above, such consideration in money as would be payable by the supplier if he were, at that time, to purchase goods similar to, and of the same age and condition as, the goods concerned; or

(3)   where the value cannot be ascertained in accordance with head (1) or head (2) above, the cost of producing the goods concerned if they were produced at that time[6].

1   For the meaning of 'another member state' see para 4 note 14 ante.
2   Ie by virtue of the Value Added Tax Act 1994 s 5(1), Sch 4 para 5(1) (where goods forming part of the assets of a business are transferred or disposed of so as no longer to form part of those assets: see para 24 ante) or Sch 4 para 6 (where goods forming part of the assets of a business are removed from any member state by or under the directions of the person carrying on the business, in the course or furtherance of the business, for the purpose of being taken to a place in a member state other than that from which they are removed: see para 14 ante): s 20(2), Sch 7 para 3(1). For the meaning of 'supply' see para 21 ante; and as to the meaning of 'in the course or furtherance of a business' see paras 12 note 5, 17 note 2 ante.

3　For the meaning of 'consideration' generally see para 86 ante.

4　For the meaning of 'relevant transaction' see para 99 note 2 ante.

5　For these purposes, the amount of consideration in money that would be payable by any person if he were to purchase any goods is taken to be the amount that would be so payable after the deduction of any amount included in the purchase price in respect of VAT on the supply of goods to that person: Value Added Tax Act 1994 Sch 7 para 3(3). For the meaning of 'money' see para 7 note 5 ante.

6　Ibid Sch 7 para 3(1), (2). For an explanation of the views of the Commissioners of Customs and Excise on the application of these valuation principles see Customs and Excise Notice 252 *Valuation of Imported Goods for Customs Purposes, VAT and Trade Statistics*.

102. Value of goods expressed in foreign currency. Where goods are acquired from another member state[1] and any sum relevant for determining the value of the relevant transaction[2] is expressed in a currency other than sterling, then, for the purpose of valuing that transaction, that sum is to be converted into sterling at the market rate which would apply in the United Kingdom[3] on the relevant day[4] to a purchase with sterling, by the person making the acquisition, of that sum in the currency in question[5]. Where, however, the Commissioners of Customs and Excise have published a notice which specifies rates of exchange, or methods of determining rates of exchange, for these purposes, a rate specified in or determined in accordance with the notice as for the time being in force applies instead[6] in the case of any transaction in pursuance of which goods are acquired by a person who opts, in such manner as may be allowed by the commissioners, for the use of that rate in relation to that transaction[7]. Such an option for the use of a particular rate or method of determining a rate may not be exercised by any person except in relation to all such transactions in pursuance of which goods are acquired by him from another member state as are of a particular description or after a particular date, and may not be withdrawn or varied except with the consent of the commissioners and in such manner as they may require[8].

1　For the meaning of 'another member state' see para 4 note 14 ante.

2　For the meaning of 'relevant transaction' see para 99 note 2 ante.

3　For the meaning of 'United Kingdom' see para 4 note 3 ante.

4　Where goods are acquired from another member state, the appropriate rate of exchange is to be determined for the purpose of valuing the relevant transaction by reference to the relevant time; and, accordingly, the day on which that time falls is the relevant day for these purposes: Value Added Tax Act 1994 s 20(2), Sch 7 para 4(7). For the meaning of 'the relevant time' see para 99 note 8 ante.

5　Ibid Sch 7 para 4(1).

6　Ie instead of the rate for which ibid Sch 7 para 4(1) provides: Sch 7 para 4(2).

7　Ibid Sch 7 para 4(2). A notice published by the commissioners for these purposes may be withdrawn or varied by a subsequent notice so published: Sch 7 para 4(6).

　In specifying a method of determining a rate of exchange, a notice so published by the commissioners may allow a person to apply to them for the use, for the purpose of valuing some or all of the transactions in pursuance of which goods are acquired by him from another member state, of a rate of exchange which is different from any which would otherwise apply: Sch 7 para 4(4). On an application made in accordance with provision contained in such a notice, the commissioners may authorise the use with respect to the applicant of such a rate of exchange, in such circumstances, in relation to such transactions and subject to such conditions as they think fit: Sch 7 para 4(5).

8　Ibid Sch 7 para 4(3).

(4) VALUE ADDED TAX ON THE IMPORTATION OF GOODS

(i) In general

103. Charge on importation; in general. In addition to being charged on the supply of goods and services in the United Kingdom[1] and on the acquisition of goods in the United Kingdom from other member states[2], value added tax is charged on the importation of goods from places outside the member states[3]. Value added tax on the importation of goods from places outside the member states is charged and payable as if it were a duty of customs[4]. Goods are treated for the purposes of VAT as imported no earlier than the time at which a Community customs debt in respect of duty on their entry into the Community would be incurred[5]; and the person who is treated as importing any goods from outside the member states is the person who would be liable to discharge any such Community customs debt[6].

The question whether or not goods have entered the territory of the Community, the time when any Community customs debt in respect of duty on the entry of any goods into the territory would be incurred, and the person by whom any such debt would fall to be discharged, are to be determined[7] according to the Community legislation applicable to goods which are in fact subject to such duties, whether or not the goods in question are themselves so subject[8].

---

1   For the meaning of 'United Kingdom' see para 4 note 3 ante.

2   The Commissioners of Customs and Excise have power to make provision for the territory of the Community, or for the member states, to be treated for any value added tax purposes as including or excluding prescribed territories: see s 93(1); and para 10 ante. As to the prescribed territories see para 10 ante. In accordance with the policy on fiscal frontiers in the European Community, VAT ceased to be charged on importation of goods into the United Kingdom from other member states on 31 December 1992 (see para 1 note 1 ante); instead, it is charged on taxable acquisitions in the United Kingdom from other member states (see para 13 ante). Goods are imported from a place outside the member states where: (1) having been removed from a place outside the member states, they enter the territory of the Community; (2) they enter that territory by being removed to the United Kingdom or are removed to the United Kingdom after entering that territory; or (3) the circumstances are such that it is on their removal to the United Kingdom or subsequently while they are in the United Kingdom that any Community customs debt in respect of duty on their entry into the territory of the Community would be incurred: s 15(1). Section 15(1), (2) (see the text to notes 5–6 infra) does not, however, apply, except in so far as the context otherwise requires or provision to the contrary is contained in regulations under s 16(1) (see para 105 post), for construing any references to importation or to an importer in any enactment or subordinate legislation applied for the purposes of the Value Added Tax Act 1994 by s 16(1): s 15(3).

3   Ibid s 1(1). An importer is liable to pay tax on importation whether or not he is a taxable person. If he is a taxable person he will be entitled to claim tax paid on an importation of goods as deductible input tax provided the goods are used or are to be used for the purpose of a business carried on or to be carried on by him: see s 24(1)(c); and para 201 post. Where goods are imported by a taxable person from a place outside the member states and supplied by him as agent for a person who is not a taxable person, they may be treated as imported and supplied by the taxable person as principal: see s 47(1)(b); and para 195 post. For exceptions to the right to deduct as input tax the tax charged on importation see paras 204–208 post.

VAT is not chargeable on the importation of goods in respect of which there is an absolute prohibition on importation or circulation within the Community: see Case 50/80 *Horvath v Hauptzollamt Hamburg-Jonas* [1981] ECR 385, [1982] 2 CMLR 522, ECJ; Case 221/81 *Wolf v Hauptzollamt Düsseldorf* [1982] ECR 3681, [1983] 2 CMLR 170, ECJ; Case 240/81 *Einberger v Hauptzollamt Freiburg* [1982] ECR 3699, [1983] 2 CMLR 170, ECJ; Case 294/82 *Einberger v Hauptzollamt Freiburg (No 2)* [1984] ECR 1177, [1985] 1 CMLR 765, ECJ (narcotics imported otherwise than through strictly controlled economic channels); Case C-343/89 *Witzemann v Hauptzollamt München-Mitte* [1990] ECR 4477, [1993] STC 108, ECJ (counterfeit currency); see also Case 269/86 *Mol v Inspecteur der Invoerrechten en Accijnzen* [1988] ECR

3627, [1989] 3 CMLR 729, ECJ; Case 289/86 *Vereniging Happy Family Rustenburgerstraat v Inspecteur der Omzetbelasting* [1988] ECR 3655, [1989] 3 CMLR 743, ECJ.

4   Value Added Tax Act 1994 s 1(4).

5   See ibid s 15(2)(a). See also note 2 supra. The time at which a customs debt is incurred is determined in accordance with EC Council Regulation 2913/92 (OJ L302, 19.10.92, p 1) (the Community Customs Code) Title VII Ch 2 (arts 201–242). The general rule is that a customs debt on importation is incurred through: (1) the release for free circulation of goods liable to import duties; or (2) the placing of such goods under the temporary importation procedure with partial relief from import duties: art 201(1). A customs debt is incurred at the time of acceptance of the customs declaration in question (art 201(2)) and is the liability of the declarant (see art 201(3)). The Code came into effect on 1 January 1993, replacing the domestic provisions of each member state which previously had governed the procedure for customs declarations and the payment of duties (in the United Kingdom implemented by the Customs and Excise Management Act 1979). See Case C-166/94 *Pezzullo Molini Pastifici Mangimifici SpA v Ministero delle Finanze* [1996] ECR I-331, [1996] STC 1236, ECJ (default interest on VAT chargeable on importation cannot begin to run before the tax becomes chargeable, ie on the goods ceasing to be covered by arrangements for transit or temporary importation). See further CUSTOMS AND EXCISE; EUROPEAN COMMUNITIES.

6   Value Added Tax Act 1994 s 15(2)(b). See also note 2 supra.

7   Ie subject to ibid s 93: see para 10 ante.

8   Ibid s 96(3).

104. Goods entering the United Kingdom from prescribed territories.

Where goods enter the United Kingdom[1] from the prescribed territories which are treated as excluded from the territory of the European Community[2], or are exported from the United Kingdom to those territories, the formalities relating to the entry of goods into the customs territory of the Community[3] or the export of goods to a place outside that customs territory[4] must be completed[5].

Where goods enter the United Kingdom from the prescribed territories[6] and those goods are intended for another member state[7], or other destination outside the United Kingdom transport of the goods to which destination involves their passage through another member state, the internal Community transit procedure[8] applies[9].

1   For the meaning of 'United Kingdom' see para 4 note 3 ante.

2   Ie the territories prescribed in the Value Added Tax Regulations 1995, SI 1995/2518, regs 136 or 137: see para 10 text and notes 2–4 ante.

3   Ie the formalities contained in EC Council Regulation 2913/92 (OJ L302, 19.10.92, p 1); EC Commission Regulation 2454/93 (OJ L 253, 11.10.93, p 1) (as amended); and the Customs Controls on Importation of Goods Regulations 1991, SI 1991/2724 (amended by SI 1993/3014): see CUSTOMS AND EXCISE; EUROPEAN COMMUNITIES.

4   Ie the formalities contained in EC Council Regulation 2913/92; and EC Commission Regulation 2454/93 (as amended): see CUSTOMS AND EXCISE; EUROPEAN COMMUNITIES.

5   V 'ue Added Tax Regulations 1995 reg 140(1), (2).

6   See note 1 supra.

7   For the meaning of 'another member state' see para 4 note 14 ante.

8   Ie the procedure described in EC Council Regulation 2913/92; and EC Commission Regulation 2454/93 (as amended): see CUSTOMS AND EXCISE; EUROPEAN COMMUNITIES.

9   Value Added Tax Regulations 1995 reg 141.

105. Application of customs enactments.

As a general rule[1] the provision made by or under the Customs and Excise Acts 1979[2] and the other enactments and subordinate legislation for the time being having effect generally in relation to duties of customs and excise charged on the importation of goods into the United Kingdom[3], together with the Community legislation[4] for the time being having effect in relation to Community customs duties charged on goods entering the territory of the Community, apply, so far as relevant, in relation to any value added tax chargeable on the importation of goods from places outside the member states as they apply in relation to any such duty of customs or excise or Community customs duties[5].

Goods imported by post from places outside the member states, other than by datapost packet[6], not exceeding £2,000 in value, or such greater sum as is determined for the time being by the Commissioners of Customs and Excise, by a registered person[7] in the course of a business[8] carried on by him may[9] be delivered without payment of VAT if he has given such security as the commissioners may require and his registration number[10] is shown on the customs declaration attached to or accompanying the package[11]. The registered person must account for VAT chargeable on the goods on their importation, together with any VAT chargeable on the supply[12] of goods or services by him or on the acquisition of goods by him from another member state[13] in a return[14] furnished by him[15] for the prescribed accounting period[16] during which the goods were imported[17].

Regulations under the Post Office Act 1953[18] may make special provision in relation to VAT[19].

1   Ie subject to such exceptions and adaptations as the Commissioners of Customs and Excise may by regulations prescribe and except where the contrary intention appears: Value Added Tax Act 1994 s 16(1). As to the exceptions and adaptations so prescribed see note 2 infra.

2   'The Customs and Excise Acts 1979' means (1) the Customs and Excise Management Act 1979; (2) the Customs and Excise Duties (General Reliefs) Act 1979; (3) the Alcoholic Liquor Duties Act 1979; (4) the Hydrocarbon Oil Duties Act 1979; and (5) the Tobacco Products Duty Act 1979: see the Customs and Excise Management Act 1979 s 1(1) (definition amended by the Finance (No 2) Act 1992 s 1, Sch 1 para 1); and CUSTOMS AND EXCISE.

The following provisions of those Acts do not, however, so apply:

(a)   the Customs and Excise Management Act 1979 s 43(5) (provisions as to duty on reimported goods); s 125(1), (2) (valuation of goods for the purpose of ad valorem duties); s 126 (charge of excise duty on manufactured or composite imported articles); and s 127(1)(b) (determination of disputes as to duties on imported goods) (Value Added Tax Regulations 1995, SI 1995/2518, reg 118(c));

(b)   the Customs and Excise Duties (General Reliefs) Act 1979 other than ss 8, 9(b) (Value Added Tax Regulations 1995 reg 118(d); but see the Customs and Excise (Personal Relief for Goods Permanently Imported) Order 1992, SI 1992/3193, made under the Customs and Excise Duties (General Reliefs) Act 1979 ss 7, 13; and CUSTOMS AND EXCISE);

(c)   the Alcoholic Liquor Duties Act 1979 s 7 (exemption from duty on spirits in articles used for medical purposes); s 8 (repayment of duty on spirits for medical or scientific purposes); s 9 (remission of duty on spirits for methylation); s 10 (remission of duty on spirits for use in art or manufacture); s 22(4) (drawback on exportation of tinctures or spirits of wine); and ss 42, 43 (drawback on exportation and warehousing of beer) (Value Added Tax Regulations 1995 reg 118(a));

(d)   the Hydrocarbon Oil Duties Act 1979 s 9 (relief for certain industrial uses); s 15 (drawback of duty on exportation etc of certain goods); s 16 (drawback of duty on exportation etc of power methylated spirits); s 17 (repayment of duty on heavy oil used by horticultural producers); s 18 (repayment of duty on fuel for ships in home waters); s 19 (repayment of duty on fuel used in fishing boats etc); s 20 (relief from duty on oil contaminated or accidentally mixed in warehouse); and s 20AA (as added) (power to allow reliefs) (Value Added Tax Regulations 1995 reg 118(b)); and

(e)   the Tobacco Products Duty Act 1979 s 2(2) (remission or repayment of duty on tobacco products) (Value Added Tax Regulations 1995 reg 118(f)).

Nor do the Isle of Man Act 1979 ss 8, 9 (removal of goods from Isle of Man to United Kingdom) so apply: Value Added Tax Regulations 1995 118(e).

The Customs and Excise Management Act 1979 s 125(3) has effect in its application, by virtue of the Value Added Tax Act 1994 s 16(1), as if the reference to the preceding subsections of the Customs and Excise Management Act 1979 s 125 included a reference to the Value Added Tax Act 1994 s 21 (as amended) (see paras 106–107 post): Value Added Tax Regulations 1995 reg 121.

Where goods are imported into the United Kingdom from the territories prescribed in reg 136 or 137 (see para 10 ante), customs and excise legislation applies, so far as relevant, in relation to any VAT chargeable upon such importation with the same exceptions and adaptations as are prescribed in regs 118–121 in relation to the application of the Value Added Tax Act 1994 s 16(1): Value Added Tax

Regulations 1995 reg 142. Where goods are imported into the United Kingdom from the territories prescribed in reg 137, the Finance (No 2) Act 1992 (enforcement powers: see CUSTOMS AND EXCISE) applies in relation to any VAT chargeable upon such importation as if references therein to 'member states' excluded the territories so prescribed: Value Added Tax Regulations 1995 reg 143. For the meaning of 'United Kingdom' see para 4 note 3 ante.

3   The Excise Warehousing (Etc) Regulations 1988, SI 1988/809, regs 16(4), (5), 19(1)(b), are excepted from the subordinate legislation which is to apply as so mentioned: Value Added Tax Regulations 1995 reg 119.

4   See EC Council Regulation 2913/92 (OJ L302, 19.10.92, p 1); and EC Commission Regulation 2454/93 (OJ L253, 11.10.93, p 211) (amended by EC Commission Regulation 3665/93 (OJ L335, 31.12.93, p 13)). The following Community legislation, however, is excepted:

   (1)   EC Council Regulation 918/83 (OJ L105, 23,4.83, p 1) on conditional reliefs from duty on the final importation of goods, and any implementing regulations made thereunder (Value Added Tax Regulations 1995 reg 120(1));

   (2)   EC Council Regulation 2913/92 arts 126–128 (drawback system of inward processing relief); arts 130–136 (processing for free circulation); art 137 so far as it relates to partial relief on temporary importation, and art 142; arts 145–160 (outward processing); arts 185–187 (returned goods); and art 229(b) (interest payable on a customs debt) (Value Added Tax Regulations 1995 reg 120(2)(a));

   (3)   EC Commission Regulation 2454/93 arts 624–647 (drawback system of inward processing relief); arts 650–669 (processing for free circulation); art 690 (partial relief on temporary importation); arts 748–787 (outward processing); and arts 844–856, 882 (returned goods) (Value Added Tax Regulations 1995 reg 120(2)(b));

   (4)   EC Council Regulation 2658/87 (OJ L256, 7.9.87, p 1) on the tariff and statistical nomenclature and on the Common Customs Tariff and implementing regulations made thereunder (end use relief), save and in so far as those regulations apply to goods admitted into territorial waters (a) in order to be incorporated into drilling or production platforms, for purposes of the construction, repair, maintenance, alteration or fitting-out of such platforms, or to link such drilling or production platforms to the mainland of the United Kingdom; or (b) for the fuelling and provisioning of drilling or production platforms) (Value Added Tax Regulations 1995 reg 120(3)).

5   Value Added Tax Act 1994 s 16(1).

6   'Datapost packet' means a postal packet containing goods which is posted in the United Kingdom as a datapost packet for transmission to a place outside the United Kingdom in accordance with the terms of a contract entered into between the Post Office and the sender of the packet, or which is received at a post office in the United Kingdom from a place outside the United Kingdom for transmission and delivery in the United Kingdom as if it were a datapost packet: Value Added Tax Regulations 1995 reg 2(1).

7   'Registered person' means a person registered by the commissioners under the Value Added Tax Act 1994 s 3(2), Sch 1 (as amended), Sch 2 or Sch 3 (as amended) (see para 56 et seq ante): Value Added Tax Regulations 1995 reg 2(1).

8   For the meaning of 'business' see para 17 ante.

9   Ie with the authority of the proper officer: Value Added Tax Regulations 1995 reg 122. 'Proper officer' means the person appointed or authorised by the commissioners to act in respect of any matter in the course of his duties: reg 2(1).

10   For the meaning of 'registration number' see para 16 note 10 ante.

11   Value Added Tax Regulations 1995 reg 122.

12   For the meaning of 'supply' see para 21 ante.

13   For the meaning of 'acquisition from another member state' see para 13 ante.

14   'Return' means a return which is required to be made in accordance with the Value Added Tax Regulations 1995 reg 25 (see para 226 et seq post): reg 2(1).

15   Ie in accordance with the Value Added Tax Regulations 1995 (see para 226 et seq post): reg 122.

16   'Prescribed accounting period' means, subject to ibid reg 99(1) (see para 209 post), a period such as is referred to in reg 25: reg 2(1).

17   Ibid reg 122.

18   Ie under the Post Office Act 1953 s 16 (application of customs enactments to postal packets): see POST OFFICE vol 36 para 780 et seq.

19   Value Added Tax Act 1994 s 16(2). See the Postal Packets (Customs and Excise) Regulations, SI 1986/260 (as amended); and POST OFFICE. The expressions 'duty' and 'duty of customs and excise' used therein include VAT: see reg 2(1).

106. Value of imported goods. The value of goods imported from a place outside the member states[1] is determined[2] for the purposes of value added tax according to the rules applicable in the case of Community customs duties, whether or not the goods are subject to any such duties[3]. This value is, however, taken to include[4]:

(1) all taxes, duties and other charges levied either outside or, by reason of importation, within the United Kingdom[5] (other than VAT)[6];

(2) all incidental expenses, such as commission, packing, transport and insurance costs up to the goods' first destination[7] in the United Kingdom[8]; and

(3) if at the time of the importation of the goods from a place outside the member states a further destination for the goods is known, and that destination is within the United Kingdom or another member state[9], all such incidental expenses in so far as they result from the transport of the goods to that other destination[10].

Subject to these provisions:

(a) where goods are imported from a place outside the member states for a consideration[11] which is or includes a price in money[12] payable as on the transfer of property;

(b) the terms on which the goods are so imported allow a discount for prompt payment of that price but do not include provision for payment of that price by instalments; and

(c) payment of that price is made in accordance with those terms, so that the discount falls to be allowed,

the value of the goods is taken to be reduced by the amount of the discount[13].

1　For the meaning of 'goods imported from a place outside the member states' see para 103 note 2 ante. As to the territories included in, or excluded from, the member states for VAT purposes see para 10 ante.

2　Ie subject to the Value Added Tax Act 1994 s 21(2)–(4) (as amended): see the text and notes 4–12 infra; and para 107 post.

3　Ibid s 21(1) (amended by the Finance Act 1995 s 22). As to Community valuation rules see EC Council Regulation 2913/92 (OJ L302, 19.10.92, p 1) arts 28–36; and EC Commission Regulation 2454/93 (OJ L253, 11.10.93, p 211) arts 141–162, Annexes 23, 24 (amended by EC Commission Regulation 1762/95 (OJ L171, 21.7.95, p 8); and by the Act of Accession 1994 art 29 Annex I (OJ L1, 1.1.95, p 213)).

4　Ie in so far as they are not already included in that value in accordance with the rules mentioned in the Value Added Tax Act 1994 s 21(1): see the text and notes 1–3 supra.

5　For the meaning of 'United Kingdom' see para 4 note 3 ante.

6　Value Added Tax Act 1994 s 21(2)(a) (amended by the Finance Act 1996 ss 27(1), (3), 205(1), Sch 41 Pt IV).

7　For these purposes, 'the goods' first destination' means the place mentioned on the consignment note or any other document by means of which the goods are imported into the United Kingdom, or in the absence of such documentation it means the place of the first transfer of cargo in the United Kingdom: Value Added Tax Act 1994 s 21(2) (as amended: see note 6 supra). For the meaning of 'document' see para 11 note 8 ante.

8　Ibid s 21(2)(b) (substituted by the Finance Act 1996 s 27(3)).

9　For the meaning of 'another member state' see para 4 note 14 ante.

10　Value Added Tax Act 1994 s 21(2)(c) (added by the Finance Act 1996 s 27(3)).

11　For the meaning of 'consideration' generally see para 86 ante.

12　For the meaning of 'money' see para 7 note 5 ante.

13　Value Added Tax Act 1994 s 21(3).

107. Valuation of certain imported works of art. The value of any goods which are imported from a place outside the member states[1] and which fall within certain specified descriptions[2] of works of art[3], antiques[4] or collectors' pieces[5] is taken, for the purposes of value added tax, to be an amount equal to 14.29 per cent[6] of the amount which otherwise would be taken to be their value[7].

1   For the meaning of 'goods imported from a place outside the member states' see para 103 note 2 ante.

2   Ie a description specified in the Value Added Tax Act 1994 s 21(5) (as amended): see the text and notes 3–5 infra.

3   'Work of art' means goods falling within any of the following descriptions: (1) paintings, drawing and pastels executed by hand but not comprised in manufactured articles that have been hand-painted or hand-decorated; (2) original engravings, lithographs and other prints; (3) original sculptures and statuary, in any material: ibid s 21(6) (s 21(4)–(7) added by the Finance Act 1995 s 22). For the views of the Commissioners of Customs and Excise on the application of this and other definitions for the purpose of the relief see Customs and Excise Notice 718 *Margin Schemes for Second-hand Goods, Works of Art, Antiques and Collectors' Items* (1 June 1995) Annex 1. The works of art falling within the specified description are (a) any work of art which was obtained by any person before 1 April 1973 (otherwise than by his producing it or by succession on the death of the person who produced it); (b) any work of art which was (i) exported from the United Kingdom before 1 April 1973; or (ii) exported from the United Kingdom on or after that date and before 1 January 1993 by a person who, had he supplied it in the United Kingdom at the date when it was exported, would not have had to account for VAT on the full value of the supply; or (iii) exported from the United Kingdom on or after 1 January 1993 by such a person to a place which, at the time, was outside the member states: Value Added Tax Act 1994 s 21(5)(a), (b) (as so added). It is a further requirement that, whether the work of art falls within head (a) or head (b) supra, it must not have been imported between the time it was exported and the importation in question: s 21(5) (as so added).

4   Ie any antique more than 100 years old, being neither a work of art nor pearls or loose gem stones: ibid s 21(5)(c) (as added: see note 3 supra).

5   Ie collectors' pieces of zoological, botanical, mineralogical, anatomical, historical, archaeological, paleontological or ethnographic interest: ibid s 21(5)(d) (as added: see note 3 supra).

6   An order under ibid s 2(2) (increase or decrease in rate of VAT: see para 5 ante) may contain provision making such alteration of the percentage specified as the Treasury considers appropriate in consequence of any increase or decrease by that order of the rate of VAT: s 21(7) (as added: see note 3 supra).

7   Ibid s 21(4) (as added: see note 3 supra). This gives an effective rate for VAT on such items of 2.5% of what would otherwise be their value for VAT purposes.

108. Goods imported for private purposes; avoidance of double charge.
Where goods are imported by a taxable person[1] from a place outside the member states[2] and (1) at the time of importation they belong wholly or partly to another person; and (2) the purposes for which they are to be used include private purposes[3] either of himself or of the other, value added tax paid or payable by the taxable person on the importation of the goods is not regarded as input tax[4] to be deducted or credited[5] but he may make a separate claim to the Commissioners of Customs and Excise for it to be repaid[6]. The commissioners must allow the claim if they are satisfied that to disallow it would result, in effect, in a double charge to VAT; and where they do allow it they may do so only to the extent necessary to avoid the double charge[7].

Any amount allowed by the commissioners on the claim must be paid by them to the taxable person[8]. An appeal lies to the VAT and duties tribunal against any decision of the commissioners relating to such a claim[9].

1   For the meaning of 'taxable person' see paras 12 note 4, 55 ante.

2   As to goods imported from a place outside the member states see para 103 note 2 ante; and as to the territories included in, or excluded from, the member states for VAT purposes see para 10 ante.

3   This reference to a person's private purposes is to purposes which are not those of any business carried on by him: Value Added Tax Act 1994 s 27(5). For the meaning of 'business' see para 17 ante.

4   For the meaning of 'input tax' see paras 4 ante, 201 post.

5   Ie under the Value Added Tax Act 1994 s 25: see para 202 post.

6   Ibid s 27(1).

7   Ibid s 27(2). In considering such a claim, the commissioners must have regard to the circumstances of the importation and, so far as appearing to them to be relevant, things done with, or occurring in relation to, the goods at any subsequent time: s 27(3).

8   Ibid s 27(4).

9   See ibid s 83(f); and para 296 post.

(ii) Relief from Value Added Tax on Importation

109. In general. The Treasury may by order make provision for giving relief from the whole or part of the value added tax chargeable on the importation of goods from places outside the member states[1] subject to such conditions (including the conditions prohibiting or restricting the disposal of, or dealing with, the goods) as may be imposed by or under the order, if and so far as the relief appears to the Treasury to be necessary or expedient having regard to any international agreements or arrangements[2].

The Commissioners of Customs and Excise may by regulations make provision for remitting or repaying, if they think fit, the whole or part of the VAT chargeable on the importation of any goods from places outside the member states which are shown to their satisfaction to have been previously exported from the United Kingdom[3] or removed from any member state[4].

The VAT chargeable on the importation of goods from a place outside the member states which have been previously exported from the member states is thus not payable[5] if the commissioners are satisfied that:

(1) the importer is not a taxable person[6], or, if he is, the goods are imported otherwise than in the course of his business[7];

(2) the goods were last exported from the member states by him or on his behalf[8];

(3) either the goods were supplied, acquired in or imported into a member state before their export, and any VAT or other tax due on that supply[9], acquisition or importation was paid and neither has been, nor will be, refunded, or the goods are imported by the person who made them[10];

(4) the goods were not exported free of VAT by reason of the zero-rating provisions[11] or under any regulations made thereunder or free of purchase tax[12], or by reason of the provisions of the law of another member state[13] corresponding, in relation to that state, to those provisions[14];

(5) the goods have not been subject to process or repair outside the member states other than necessary running repairs which did not result in any increase in their value[15]; and

(6) the goods:

    (a) were at the time of exportation intended to be reimported; or

    (b) have been returned for repair or replacement or after rejection by a customer outside the member states, or because it was not possible to deliver them to such a customer; or

    (c) were prior to the time of exportation in private use and possession in the member states[16].

The commissioners may also make provision by regulations for enabling goods imported from a place outside the member states by a taxable person in the course or furtherance[17] of any business carried on by him to be delivered or removed, subject to such conditions or restrictions as the commissioners may impose for the protection of the revenue, without payment of the VAT chargeable on the importation, and for that VAT to be accounted for together with the VAT chargeable on the supply of goods or services by him or on the acquisition of goods by him from other member states[18]. The VAT chargeable on the importation of goods from a place outside the member states which have previously been exported from the member states is thus not payable[19] if the commissioners are satisfied that:

(i) the importer is a taxable person importing the goods in the course of his business[20];

(ii)   the goods were last exported from the member states by him or on his behalf[21];

(iii)   the goods have not been subject to process or repair outside the member states other than necessary running repairs which did not increase their value[22];

(iv)   the goods:

    (A)   were owned by him at the time of exportation and have remained his property, or

    (B)   were owned by him at the time of exportation and have been returned after rejection by a customer outside the member states or because it was not possible to deliver them to such a customer; or

    (C)   have been returned from the continental shelf[23]; and

(v)   if the goods were supplied in, acquired in or imported into a member state before their export, any VAT or other tax chargeable on that supply, acquisition or importation was accounted for or paid and neither has been, nor will be, refunded[24].

Where goods which have been temporarily exported from the member states are reimported after having undergone repair, process or adaptation, or after having been made up or reworked, outside the member states, the VAT chargeable on the importation of goods from a place outside the member states is payable as if the treatment or process had been carried out in the United Kingdom, provided the commissioners are satisfied that at the time of exportation the goods were intended to be reimported after completion of the treatment or process outside the member states and that the ownership in the goods was not transferred to any other person at exportation or during the time they were abroad[25].

1   As to importation of goods from other member states see para 103 note 2 ante.

2   Value Added Tax Act 1994 s 37(1). In any case where (1) it is proposed that goods which have been imported from a place outside the member states by any person ('the original importer') with the benefit of such relief are to be transferred to another person ('the transferee'); and (2) on an application made by the transferee, the Commissioners of Customs and Excise so direct, the Value Added Tax Act 1994 has effect as if, on the date of the transfer of the goods (and in place of the transfer), the goods were exported by the original importer and imported by the transferee, and, accordingly, where appropriate, provision made under s 37(1) has effect in relation to the VAT chargeable on the importation of the goods by the transferee: s 37(2).

    In exercise of the power conferred by s 37(1), the Treasury has made the Value Added Tax (Imported Goods) Relief (Amendment) Order 1995, SI 1995/3222, which came into force on 1 January 1996: art 1. In addition, by virtue of the Interpretation Act 1978 s 17(2)(b), the Value Added Tax (Imported Goods) Relief Order 1984, SI 1984/746 (amended by SI 1987/155; SI 1987/2108; SI 1988/1193; SI 1988/2212; SI 1990/2548; SI 1992/3120; and SI 1995/3222) has effect as if made thereunder. See further para 111 et seq post. The 1984 Order applies without prejudice to relief from tax on the importation of goods afforded under or by virtue of any other enactment (art 3(1)); and nothing therein is to be construed as authorising a person to import anything from a place outside or within the member states in contravention of any prohibition or restriction for the time being in force with respect thereto under or by virtue of any enactment (art 3(2) (substituted by SI 1992/3120). As to goods imported from outside the member states see para 103 note 2 ante.

3   For the meaning of 'United Kingdom' see para 4 note 3 ante.

4   Value Added Tax Act 1994 s 37(3). In exercise of the power so conferred, the commissioners have made the Value Added Tax Regulations 1995, SI 1995/2518, regs 124–126: see the text and notes 5–25 infra.

5   Ie subject to such conditions as the Commissioners may impose: ibid reg 124.

6   For the meaning of 'taxable person' see paras 12 note 4, 55 ante.

7   Value Added Tax Regulations 1995 reg 124(a). For the meaning of 'business' see para 17 ante.

8   Ibid reg 124(b).

9   For the meaning of 'supply' see para 21 ante.

10   Value Added Tax Regulations 1995 reg 124(c).

11   Ie under the Value Added Tax Act 1994 s 30(6) or (8): see para 177 post.

12   Purchase tax ceased to be chargeable when it would have been due after 31 March 1973: Finance Act 1972 s 54(1).

13 As to the meaning of references to the law of another member state see para 11 note 1 ante; and for the meaning of 'another member state' see para 4 note 14 ante.
14 Value Added Tax Regulations 1995 reg 124(d).
15 Ibid reg 124(e).
16 Ibid reg 124(f).
17 As to the meaning of 'in the course or furtherance' of a business see paras 12 note 5, 17 note 2 ante.
18 Value Added Tax Act 1994 s 38.
19 Ie subject to such conditions as the commissioners may impose: Value Added Tax Regulations 1995 reg 125.
20 Ibid reg 125(a).
21 Ibid reg 125(b).
22 Ibid reg 125(c).
23 Ibid reg 125(d). As to the continental shelf see FOREIGN RELATIONS LAW vol 18 para 1488.
24 Ibid reg 125(e).
25 Ibid reg 126. It seems that the effect of this provision is to restrict the charge to VAT to the value of the work done, together with ancillary costs.

110. Temporary importations. The Commissioners of Customs and Excise may make provision by regulations for remitting or repaying the whole or part of the value added tax chargeable on the importation of any goods from places outside the member states[1] if they are satisfied that the goods have been or are to be re-exported or otherwise removed from the United Kingdom[2] and they think fit to do so in all the circumstances and having regard to the tax chargeable on the supply[3] of like goods in the United Kingdom and to any VAT which may have become chargeable in another member state[4] in respect of the goods[5]. The VAT chargeable on the importation of goods from a place outside the member states is thus not payable[6] where:

(1)   a taxable person[7] makes a supply of goods which is to be zero-rated[8];
(2)   the goods so imported are the subject of that supply; and
(3)   the commissioners are satisfied that the importer:
   (a)   intends to remove the goods to another member state; and
   (b)   is importing the goods in the course of a supply by him of those goods in accordance with the relevant[9] statutory provisions[10].

The commissioners may require the deposit of security[11] as a condition of granting the relief afforded by these provisions[12]. The relief continues to apply provided that the importer removes the goods to another member state within one month of the date of importation, or within such longer period as the commissioners may allow, and provided that he supplies the goods in accordance with the relevant[13] statutory provisions[14].

1   For the meaning of 'goods imported from a place outside the member states' see para 103 note 2 ante.
2   For the meaning of 'United Kingdom' see para 4 note 3 ante.
3   For the meaning of 'supply' see para 21 ante.
4   For the meaning of 'another member state' see para 4 note 14 ante.
5   Value Added Tax Act 1994 s 37(4). In exercise of the power so conferred, the commissioners have made the Value Added Tax Regulations 1995, SI 1995/2518, reg 123: see the text and notes 6–14 infra.
6   Ie subject to such conditions as the commissioners may impose: ibid reg 123(1).
7   For the meaning of 'taxable person' see paras 12 note 4, 55 ante.
8   Ie in accordance with the Value Added Tax Act 1994 s 30(8)(a)(i), (ii), (b): see para 177 post.
9   Ie the provisions of ibid s 30(8)(a)(i), (ii), (b); and of any regulations made thereunder: see para 177 post.
10 Value Added Tax Regulations 1995 reg 123(1).
11 The amount of the security must not exceed the amount of VAT chargeable on the importation: ibid reg 123(2).
12 Ibid reg 123(2).
13 See note 9 supra.
14 Value Added Tax Regulations 1995 reg 123(3).

111. Relief for United Nations goods. No value added tax is payable on the importation[1], for whatever purpose, of goods produced by the United Nations or by a United Nations organisation which are:

(1) holograms for laser projection, multi-media kits or materials for programmed instruction, including materials in kit form, with the corresponding printed materials[2]; or

(2) goods classified under any specified heading or sub-heading[3] and within the limits of relief specified[4] in relation to that heading or sub-heading[5].

1 For these purposes, except where it appears in the Value Added Tax (Imported Goods) Relief Order 1984, SI 1984/746, art 3(2) (as substituted) (see para 109 note 2 ante), 'import' means import from a place outside the member states and 'importation' and 'imported' are to be construed accordingly: art 2(4) (added by SI 1992/3120).

2 Ibid art 4(a), Sch 1 Pt I.

3 Ie any heading or sub-heading specified in ibid art 4(b), Sch 1 Pt II col 1 (substituted by SI 1987/2108): see note 5 infra. For these purposes, references to a heading or sub-heading are references to a heading or sub-heading of the Combined Nomenclature of the European Community: art 2(2) (amended by SI 1987/2108).

4 Ie specified in ibid Sch 1 Pt II col 2 (as substituted: see note 3 supra).

5 Ibid art 4(b). The goods so classified include (1) certain films of an educational, scientific or cultural character; (2) certain newsreels, with or without soundtrack, depicting events of current news value at the time of importation and, in the case of each importer, not exceeding two copies of each subject for copying; (3) certain archival film material; (4) certain recreational film particularly suited for children and young people; (5) certain microcards or other information storage media required in computerised information and documentation services of an educational, scientific or cultural character and wall charts designed solely for demonstration and education; (6) certain patterns, models and wall charts of an educational, scientific or cultural character, designed solely for demonstration and education; and (7) certain mock-ups or visualisations of abstract concepts such as molecular structures or mathematical formulae: see Sch 1 Pt II (as substituted: see note 3 supra).

112. Relief for capital goods and equipment on transfer of activities. No value added tax is payable on the importation[1] of capital goods and equipment[2] (including livestock, other than livestock in the possession of dealers) imported by a person for the purposes of a business[3] he has ceased to carry on abroad[4] and which he has notified the Commissioners of Customs and Excise is to be (1) carried on by him in the member states[5]; and (2) concerned exclusively with making taxable supplies[6]. This relief applies only where the goods:

(a) have been used in the course of the business for at least 12 months before it ceased to be carried on abroad;

(b) are imported within 12 months of the date on which that business ceased to be carried on abroad, or within such longer period as the commissioners allow; and

(c) are appropriate both to the nature and size of the business to be carried on in the member states[7].

It is a condition of the relief that the goods are put to the contemplated use in the member states[8].

1 For the meaning of 'importation' and related expressions see para 111 note 1 ante.

2 For these purposes, 'capital goods and equipment' does not include (1) food of a kind used for human consumption or animal feeding stuffs; (2) fuel; (3) stocks of raw materials and finished or semi-finished products; or (4) any motor vehicle in respect of which deduction of input tax was disallowed by the Value Added Tax (Cars) Order 1980, SI 1980/442, art 4 (revoked): Value Added Tax (Imported Goods) Relief Order 1984, SI 1984/746, art 5(2), Sch 2 Group 1 note (1).

3 For the meaning of 'business' see para 17 ante.

4 'Abroad' means a place outside the member states: Value Added Tax (Imported Goods) Relief Order 1984 art 2(1) (definition substituted by SI 1992/3120). As to the territories deemed to be included in, or excluded from, the member states for VAT purposes see para 10 ante.

5   For these purposes, a person is not treated as intending to carry on a business in the member states if that business is to be merged with, or absorbed by, another business already carried on there: ibid Sch 2 Group 1 note (2) (amended by virtue of art 2(5) (added by SI 1992/3120)).
6   Ibid art 5(1), Sch 2 Group 1 item 1 (as amended: see note 5 supra). For the meaning of 'taxable supplies' see para 12 note 3 ante.
7   Ibid Sch 2 Group 1 note (3) (as amended: see note 5 supra).
8   See ibid art 6(1) (as amended: see note 5 supra).

113. Relief for the promotion of trade. No value added tax is payable on:
   (1)   articles of no intrinsic commercial value sent[1] free of charge by suppliers of goods and services for the sole purpose of advertising[2];
   (2)   samples of negligible value of a kind and in quantities capable of being used solely for soliciting orders for goods of the same kind[3];
   (3)   printed advertising matter, including catalogues, price lists, directions for use or brochures, which relates to goods for sale or hire by a person established outside the member states[4], or to transport, commercial or banking services offered by a person established in a third country[5], and which clearly displays the name of the person by whom such goods or services are offered[6];
   (4)   goods to be distributed free of charge at an event[7], as small representative samples[8], for use or consumption by the public[9];
   (5)   goods imported solely for the purpose of being demonstrated at an event[10];
   (6)   goods imported solely for the purpose of being used in the demonstration of any machine or apparatus displayed at an event[11];
   (7)   paints, varnishes, wallpaper and other materials of low value to be used in the building, fitting-out and decoration of a temporary stand at an event[12];
   (8)   catalogues, prospectuses, price lists, advertising posters, calendars (whether or not illustrated), unframed photographs and other printed matter or articles advertising goods displayed at an event, supplied without charge for the purpose of distribution free of charge to the public at that event[13].

Heads (4), (5) and (6) above do not apply to fuels, alcoholic beverages or tobacco products[14]; and heads (4) to (8) above apply only where the aggregate value and quantity of the goods is appropriate to the nature of the event, the number of visitors and the extent of the exhibitor's participation in it[15].

It is a condition of this relief that the goods are put to the use by reference to which it is afforded, or that the purpose by reference to which it is afforded is fulfilled, in the member states[16]. Where relief has been afforded by virtue of head (5), head (6) or head (7) above in respect of goods for demonstration or use, it is a condition of the relief that in the course of, or as a result of, that demonstration or use, the goods are consumed or destroyed or rendered incapable of being used again for the same purpose[17].

1   'Sent' means sent from a place outside the member states: Value Added Tax (Imported Goods) Relief Order 1984, SI 1984/746, art 2(1) (definition added by SI 1992/3120).
2   Ibid art 5(1), Sch 2 Group 3 item 1.
3   Ibid Sch 2 Group 3 item 2. Where the Commissioners of Customs and Excise so require, Sch 2 Group 3 item 2 applies only to goods which are rendered permanently unusable, except as samples, by being torn, perforated, clearly and indelibly marked, or by any other process: art 5(2), Sch 2 Group 3 note (1).
4   As to where a person is established for VAT purposes cf para 54 note 2 ante; and as to the territories deemed to be included in, or excluded from, the member states for VAT purposes see para 10 ante.
5   'Third country' means a place outside the member states: Value Added Tax (Imported Goods) Relief Order 1984 art 2(1) (definition added by SI 1992/3120).
6   Ibid Sch 2 Group 3 item 3 (substituted by SI 1988/2212; amended by SI 1992/3120). Save in the case of imported printed matter intended for distribution free of charge and relating to either goods for sale or hire, Sch 2 Group 3 item 3 does not apply to (1) any consignment containing two or more copies of

different documents; (2) any consignment containing two or more copies of the same document, unless the total gross weight of that consignment does not exceed 1 kg; or (3) any goods which are the subject of grouped consignments from the same consignor to the same consignee: Sch 2 Group 3 note (2) (as so amended).

7 'Event' means any of the following: (1) any trade, industrial, agricultural or craft exhibition, fair or similar show or display, not being an exhibition, fair, show or display organised for private purposes in a shop or on business premises with a view to the sale of the goods displayed; (2) any exhibition or meeting which is primarily organised (a) for a charitable purpose; or (b) to promote any branch of learning, art, craft, sport or scientific, technical, educational, cultural or trade union activity, or tourism; or (c) to promote friendship between peoples; or (d) to promote religious knowledge or worship; (3) any meeting of representatives of any international organisation or international group of organisations; and (4) any representative meeting or ceremony of an official or commemorative character: ibid Sch 2 Group 3 note (3).

8 For these purposes, 'representative samples' means goods which are (1) imported free of charge or obtained at such event from goods imported in bulk; (2) identifiable as advertising samples of low value; (3) not easily marketable and, where appropriate, packaged in quantities which are less than the lowest quantity of the same goods as marketed; and (4) intended to be consumed at such event, where the goods comprise foodstuffs or beverages not packaged as described in head (3) supra: ibid Sch 2 Group 3 note (4).

9 Ibid Sch 3 Group 3 item 4.

10 Ibid Sch 2 Group 3 item 5.

11 Ibid Sch 2 Group 3 item 6.

12 Ibid Sch 2 Group 3 item 7.

13 Ibid Sch 2 Group 3 item 8.

14 Ibid Sch 2 Group 3 note (5). 'Alcoholic beverages' means beverages falling within the Combined Nomenclature of the European Community headings 22.03–22.08: Value Added Tax (Imported Goods) Relief Order 1984 art 2(1), (2) (definition amended by SI 1988/1193; and by virtue of SI 1987/2108). 'Tobacco products' means cigarettes, cigars, hand-rolling and other smoking tobacco, and chewing tobacco, in each case manufactured wholly or partly from tobacco or any substance used as a substitute for tobacco, but does not include herbal smoking products: Tobacco Products Duty Act 1979 s 1(1) (applied by the Value Added Tax (Imported Goods) Relief Order 1984 art 2(1)). See further CUSTOMS AND EXCISE.

15 Ibid Sch 2 Group 3 note (6).

16 See ibid art 6(1) (amended by virtue of art 2(5) (added by SI 1992/3120)).

17 Ibid art 6(2).

114. Goods for testing. Value added tax is not charged on goods imported[1] for the purpose of examination, analysis or testing to determine their composition, quality or other technical characteristics, to provide information or for industrial or commercial research[2]. This relief does not apply to goods exceeding the quantities necessary for these purposes or where the examination, analysis or testing itself constitutes a sales promotion[3]. It is a condition of the relief that the purpose by reference to which it is afforded is fulfilled in the member states[4]. Where the relief has been afforded in respect of goods for examination, analysis or testing, the relief is also subject to the following conditions:

(1) the examination, analysis or testing must be completed within such time as the Commissioners of Customs and Excise may require; and

(2) any goods not completely used up or destroyed in the course of, or as a result of, such examination, analysis or testing, and any products resulting therefrom, must forthwith be destroyed or rendered commercially worthless, or exported[5].

1 For the meaning of 'imported' see para 111 note 1 ante.

2 Value Added Tax (Imported Goods) Relief Order 1984, SI 1984/786, art 5(1), Sch 2 Group 4 item 1.

3 Ibid art 5(2), Sch 2 Group 4 note.

4 See ibid art 6(1) (amended by virtue of art 2(5) (added by SI 1992/3120)).

5 Ibid art 6(3).

115. Goods relating to health. Value added tax is not charged on the following goods imported[1] for health-related purposes:

(1) animals specially prepared for laboratory use and sent free of charge to a relevant establishment[2];

(2) biological or chemical substances sent to a relevant establishment from a place outside the member states[3];

(3) human blood[4];

(4) products for therapeutic purposes, derived from human blood[5];

(5) human (including foetal) organs or tissue for diagnostic or therapeutic purposes or medical research[6];

(6) reagents[7] for use in blood type grouping, or for the detection of blood grouping incompatibilities, by approved institutions or laboratories, exclusively for non-commercial medical or scientific purposes[8];

(7) reagents for use in the determination of human tissue types by approved institutions or laboratories, exclusively for non-commercial medical or scientific purposes[9];

(8) pharmaceutical products imported by or on behalf of persons or animals for their use while visiting the member states to participate in an international sporting event[10];

(9) samples of reference substances approved by the World Health Organisation for the quality control of materials used in the manufacture of medicinal products[11].

Heads (3) to (7) above include special packaging essential for transport of the goods and any solvents or accessories necessary for their use[12].

It is a condition of this relief that the goods are put to the use by reference to which it is afforded, or that the purpose by reference to which it is afforded is fulfilled, in the member states[13].

1 For the meaning of 'imported' see para 111 note 1 ante.
2 Value Added Tax (Imported Goods) Relief Order 1984, SI 1984/746, art 5(1), Sch 2 Group 5 item 1. 'Relevant establishment' means (1) a public establishment, or a department of such establishment, principally engaged in education or scientific research; or (2) a private establishment so engaged, which is approved by the Secretary of State: arts 2(1), 5(2), Sch 2 Group 5 note (1) (amended by SI 1992/3120).
3 Ibid Sch 2 Group 5 item 3 (amended by SI 1992/3120). The relief applies only where the goods fulfil the conditions laid down under or by virtue of EC Council Regulation 918/83 (OJ L105, 23.4.83, p 1) art 60: Value Added Tax (Imported Goods) Relief Order 1984 Sch 2 Group 5 note (2) (amended by SI 1988/2212).
4 Ibid Sch 2 Group 5 item 4. See also the text to note 12 infra.
5 Ibid Sch 2 Group 5 item 5. See also the text to note 12 infra.
6 Ibid Sch 2 Group 5 item 6. See also the text to note 12 infra.
7 'Reagents' means all reagents, whether of human, animal, plant, or other, origin: ibid Sch 2 Group 5 note (4).
8 Ibid Sch 2 Group 5 item 7. See also the text to note 12 infra.
9 Ibid Sch 2 Group 5 item 8. See also the text to note 12 infra.
10 Ibid Sch 2 Group 5 item 9 (amended by virtue of art 2(5) (added by SI 1992/3120)).
11 Ibid Sch 2 Group 5 item 10 (added by SI 1988/2212). This relief applies only to samples addressed to consignees authorised to receive them free of tax: Sch 2 Group 5 note (5) (as so added).
12 Ibid Sch 2 Group 5 note (3).
13 See ibid art 6(1).

116. Charitable goods. Value added tax is not charged on the importation[1] of:

(1) basic necessities[2] obtained without charge for distribution free of charge to the needy by a state organisation or other charitable or philanthropic organisation approved by the Secretary of State ('a relevant organisation')[3];

(2)   goods donated by a person established abroad[4] to a relevant organisation for use to raise funds at occasional charity events for the benefit of the needy[5];

(3)   equipment and office materials donated by a person established abroad to a relevant organisation for meeting its operating needs or carrying out its charitable aims[6];

(4)   goods imported by a relevant organisation for distribution or loan, free of charge, to victims of a disaster affecting the territory of one or more member states[7];

(5)   goods imported by a relevant organisation for meeting its operating needs in the relief of a disaster affecting the territory of one or more member states[8];

(6)   articles donated to, and imported by, an organisation approved by the Secretary of State which is principally engaged in the education of, or the provision of assistance to, blind or other physically or mentally handicapped persons and which are for supply[9] to such persons and specially designed for the education, employment or social advancement of such persons[10];

(7)   spare parts, components or accessories for any article of a kind mentioned in head (6) above, including tools for its maintenance, checking, calibration or repair[11].

Heads (1) to (3) above do not include alcoholic beverages or tobacco products[12], coffee, tea, or motor vehicles other than ambulances[13]; heads (2), (3) and (6) above do not apply where there is any commercial intent on the part of the donor[14]; and heads (4) and (5) above apply only where the EC Commission has made a decision authorising importation of the goods[15].

It is a condition of this relief that the goods are put to the use by reference to which it is afforded, or that the purpose by reference to which it is afforded is fulfilled, in the member states[16]. Where relief is afforded in respect of any such goods, it is a condition of the relief that the goods are not lent, hired out or transferred, except in accordance with the provisions of heads (1) to (7) above relating to those goods[17]. Where any goods in respect of which such relief has been afforded (a) are to be lent, hired out, transferred or used except in accordance with the above provisions; or (b) remain in the possession of an organisation which has ceased to fulfil any condition subject to which it is approved by the Secretary of State, and written notification of this is given to the Commissioners of Customs and Excise, the VAT payable on the goods is to be determined as if the goods had been imported on the date when it becomes due, provided that where the amount of the VAT first relieved is less, that lesser amount becomes payable[18].

1   For the meaning of 'importation' and related expressions see para 111 note 1 ante.
2   'Basic necessities' means food, medicines, clothing, blankets, orthopaedic equipment and crutches, required to meet a person's immediate needs: Value Added Tax (Imported Goods) Relief Order 1984, SI 1984/746, art 5(2), Sch 2 Group 6 note (2). See, however, the text to notes 12–13 infra.
3   Ibid arts 2(1), 5(1), Sch 2 Group 6 item 1, note (1).
4   For the meaning of 'abroad' see para 112 note 4 ante.
5   Value Added Tax (Imported Goods) Relief Order 1984 Sch 2 Group 6 item 2. See also the text to notes 12–14 infra.
6   Ibid Sch 2 Group 6 item 3. See also the text to notes 12–14 infra.
7   Ibid Sch 2 Group 6 item 4. See also the text to note 15 infra.
8   Ibid Sch 2 Group 6 item 5. See also the text to note 15 infra.
9   For these purposes, 'supply' means any loan, hiring out or transfer, for consideration or free of charge, other than on a profit-making basis: ibid Sch 2 Group 6 note (7).
10   Ibid art 2(1), Sch 2 Group 6 note (6). See also the text to note 14 infra.
11   Ibid Sch 2 Group 6 item 7. This relief applies only where the goods are imported with an article of a kind mentioned in head (6) in the text to which they relate, or, if imported subsequently, are identifiable as being intended for that article, where relief from VAT on that article has been afforded by virtue of that head or would have been so afforded if such article were imported with the goods which relate to it: Sch 2 Group 6 note (8).
12   For the meaning of 'alcoholic beverages' and 'tobacco products' see para 113 note 14 ante.

13 Value Added Tax (Imported Goods) Relief Order 1984 Sch 2 Group 6 note (3).
14 Ibid Sch 2 Group 6 note (4).
15 Ibid Sch 2 Group 6 note (5).
16 See ibid art 6(1) (amended by virtue of art 2(5) (added by SI 1992/3120)).
17 Ibid art 7(1). This does not, however, apply, and relief continues to be afforded, where goods are lent, hired out or transferred to an organisation which would be entitled to relief by virtue of Sch 2 Group 6 if importing the goods on that date, on condition that (1) prior notification in writing is received by the Commissioners of Customs and Excise; and (2) the goods are used solely in accordance with the provisions of Sch 2 Group 6 relating to them: art 7(2).
18 Ibid art 8.

117. Printed matter etc. Value added tax is not charged on the importation[1] of:

(1) documents[2] sent[3] free of charge to public services in the member states[4];

(2) foreign[5] government publications and publications of official international bodies intended for free distribution[6];

(3) ballot papers for elections organised by bodies abroad[7];

(4) specimen signatures and printed circulars concerning signatures, forming part of exchanges of information between bankers or public services[8];

(5) official printed matter sent to a central bank in the member states[9];

(6) documents sent by companies incorporated abroad to bearers of, or subscribers to, securities issued by such companies[10];

(7) files, archives and other documents for use at international meetings, conferences or congresses and reports of such gatherings[11];

(8) plans, technical drawings, traced designs and other documents sent by any person for the purpose of participating in a competition in the member states or to obtain or fulfil an order executed abroad[12];

(9) documents to be used in examinations held in the member states on behalf of institutions established abroad[13];

(10) printed forms to be used as official documents in the international movement of vehicles or goods pursuant to international conventions[14];

(11) printed forms, labels, tickets and similar documents sent to travel agents[15] in the member states by transport and tourist undertakings abroad[16];

(12) used commercial documents[17];

(13) official printed forms from national or international authorities[18];

(14) printed matter conforming to international standards, for distribution by an association in the member states and sent by a corresponding association abroad[19];

(15) documents sent for the purpose of free distribution to encourage persons to visit foreign countries, in particular to attend cultural, tourist, sporting, religious, trade or professional meetings or events[20];

(16) foreign hotel lists and yearbooks published by or on behalf of official tourist agencies and timetables for foreign transport services, for free distribution[21];

(17) yearbooks, lists of telephone and telex numbers, hotel lists, catalogues for fairs, specimens of craft goods of negligible value and literature on museums, universities, spas or other similar establishments, supplied as reference material to accredited representatives or correspondents appointed by official national tourist agencies and not intended for distribution[22];

(18) official publications issued under the authority of the country of exportation, international institutions, regional or local authorities and bodies governed by public law established in the country of exportation[23];

(19) printed matter distributed by foreign political organisations[24] on the occasion of elections to the European Parliament or national elections in the country in which the printed matter originates[25].

Heads (15) and (16) above do not apply where the goods contain more than 25 per cent of private commercial advertising[26]; and heads (18) and (19) above apply only to publications or printed matter on which VAT or any other tax has been paid in the third country[27] from which they have been exported and which have not benefited, by virtue of their exportation, from any relief from payment thereof[28].

It is a condition of this relief that the goods are put to the use by reference to which it is afforded, or that the purpose by reference to which it is afforded is fulfilled, in the member states[29].

1   For the meaning of 'importation' and related expressions see para 111 note 1 ante.
2   The Value Added Tax Act 1994 s 96(6) (meaning of 'document' etc: see para 11 note 8 ante) does not apply for these purposes: Value Added Tax (Imported Goods) Relief Order 1984, SI 1984/746, art 2(3); Interpretation Act 1978 s 17(2)(a), (b).
3   For the meaning of 'sent' see para 113 note 1 ante.
4   Value Added Tax (Imported Goods) Relief Order 1984 art 5(1), Sch 2 Group 7 item 1 (amended by virtue of art 2(5) (added by SI 1992/3120)).
5   'Foreign' means a country other than the member states: ibid art 5(2), Sch 2 Group 7 note (5) (as amended: see note 4 supra).
6   Ibid Sch 2 Group 7 item 2.
7   Ibid Sch 2 Group 7 item 3.
8   Ibid Sch 2 Group 7 item 4.
9   Ibid Sch 2 Group 7 item 5 (as amended: see note 4 supra).
10 Ibid Sch 2 Group 7 item 6.
11 Ibid Sch 2 Group 7 item 7.
12 Ibid Sch 2 Group 7 item 8.
13 Ibid Sch 2 Group 7 item 9.
14 Ibid Sch 2 Group 7 item 10.
15 'Travel agent' includes airlines, national railway undertakings, ferry operators and similar organisations: ibid Sch 2 Group 7 note (4) (added by SI 1992/3120).
16 Ibid Sch 2 Group 7 item 11.
17 Ibid Sch 2 Group 7 item 12.
18 Ibid Sch 2 Group 7 item 13.
19 Ibid Sch 2 Group 7 item 14.
20 Ibid Sch 2 Group 7 item 15. See also the text to note 26 infra.
21 Ibid Sch 2 Group 7 item 16. See also the text to note 26 infra.
22 Ibid Sch 2 Group 7 item 17.
23 Ibid Sch 2 Group 7 item 18 (added by SI 1988/2212). See also the text to notes 27–28 infra.
24 'Foreign political organisations' means those which are officially recognised as such in the United Kingdom: ibid Sch 2 Group 7 note (3) (substituted by SI 1988/2212). For the meaning of 'United Kingdom' see para 4 note 3 ante.
25 Ibid Sch 2 Group 7 item 19 (added by SI 1988/2212). See also the text to notes 27–28 infra.
26 Ibid Sch 2 Group 7 note (1) (substituted by SI 1988/2212).
27 For the meaning of 'third country' see para 113 note 5 ante.
28 Value Added Tax (Imported Goods) Relief Order 1984 Sch 2 Group 7 note (2) (substituted by SI 1992/3120).
29 See ibid art 6(1) (amended by virtue of art 2(5) (added by SI 1992/3120)).

118. Articles sent for miscellaneous purposes. Value added tax is not charged on the importation[1] of:

(1) material relating to trademarks, patterns or designs and supporting documents and applications for patents, imported for the purpose of being submitted to bodies competent to deal with protection of copyright or industrial or commercial patent rights[2];

(2) objects imported for the purpose of being submitted as evidence, or for a like purpose, to a court or other official body in the member states[3];

(3) photographs, slides and stereotype mats for photographs, whether or not captioned, sent[4] to press agencies and publishers of newspapers and magazines[4];

(4)   recorded media, including punched cards, sound recordings and microfilm, sent free of charge for the transmission of information[5];

(5)   any honorary decoration conferred by a government or head of state abroad[6] on a person resident in the member states and imported on his behalf[7];

(6)   any cup, medal or similar article of an essentially symbolic nature, intended as a tribute to activities in the arts, sciences, sport, or the public service, or in recognition of merit at a particular event, which is either donated by an authority established abroad for the purpose of being presented in the member states or awarded abroad to a person resident in the member states and imported on his behalf[8];

(7)   goods (other than alcoholic beverages or tobacco products[9]) sent on an occasional basis as gifts in token of friendship or goodwill between bodies, public authorities or groups carrying on an activity in the public interest[10];

(8)   any consignment of goods, other than alcoholic beverages, tobacco products, perfumes or toilet waters, not exceeding £18 in value[11];

(9)   awards, trophies and souvenirs of a symbolic nature and of limited value intended for distribution free of charge at business conferences or similar events to persons normally resident in a country other than the member states[12].

Heads (5) to (7) and (9) above do not apply to any importation of a commercial character[13].

It is a condition of this relief that the goods are put to the use by reference to which it is afforded, or that the purpose by reference to which it is afforded is fulfilled, in the member states[14].

1   For the meaning of 'importation' and related expressions see para 111 note 1 ante.
2   Value Added Tax (Imported Goods) Relief Order 1984, SI 1984/786, art 5(1), Sch 2 Group 8 item 1. As to the meaning of 'document' see para 117 note 2 ante.
3   Ibid Sch 2 Group 8 item 2 (amended by virtue of art 2(5) (added by SI 1992/3120)).
4   Ibid Sch 2 Group 8 item 3.
5   Ibid Sch 2 Group 8 item 4.
6   For the meaning of 'abroad' see para 112 note 4 ante.
7   Value Added Tax (Imported Goods) Relief Order 1984 Sch 2 Group 8 item 5. See also the text to note 13 infra.
8   Ibid Sch 2 Group 8 item 6. See also the text to note 13 infra.
9   For the meaning of 'alcoholic beverages' and 'tobacco products' see para 113 note 14 ante.
10   Value Added Tax (Imported Goods) Relief Order 1984 Sch 2 Group 8 item 7. See also the text to note 13 infra.
11   Ibid Sch 2 Group 8 item 8 (amended by SI 1988/2212; SI 1995/3222).
12   Ibid Sch 2 Group 8 item 9 (added by SI 1988/2212; amended by virtue of art 2(5) (added by SI 1992/3120)).
13   Ibid Sch 2 Group 8 note (substituted by SI 1988/2212).
14   See ibid art 6(1) (amended by virtue of art 2(5) (added by SI 1992/3120)).

119. Works of arts and collectors' pieces. Value added tax is not charged on the importation[1] of works of art and collectors' pieces imported for a purpose other than sale by museums, galleries or other institutions approved by the Secretary of State[2]. This relief applies only where the goods are (1) of an educational, scientific or cultural character; and (2) imported free of charge or, if for a consideration, are not supplied to the importer in the course or furtherance[3] of any business[4].

It is a condition of this relief that the goods are put to the use by reference to which it is afforded, or that the purpose by reference to which it is afforded is fulfilled, in the member states[5].

1 For the meaning of 'importation' and related expressions see para 111 note 1 ante.
2 Value Added Tax (Imported Goods) Relief Order 1984, SI 1984/746, arts 2(1), 5(1), Sch 2 Group 9 item 1.
3 As to the meaning of 'in the course or furtherance of a business' see paras 12 note 5, 17 note 2 ante.
4 Value Added Tax (Imported Goods) Relief Order 1984 Sch 2 Group 9 note.
5 See ibid art 6(1) (amended by virtue of art 2(5) (added by SI 1992/3120)).

120. Transport. Value added tax is not charged on the importation[1] of:

(1) fuel contained in the standard tanks[2] of a vehicle[3] or of a special container[4] for use exclusively by that vehicle or container[5];

(2) fuel, not exceeding 10 litres for each vehicle, contained in portable tanks carried by a vehicle for use exclusively by that vehicle[6];

(3) lubricants contained in a vehicle for use exclusively by that vehicle[7];

(4) litter, fodder and feeding stuffs contained in any means of transport carrying animals for the use of such animals during their journey[8];

(5) disposable packings for the stowage and protection of goods during their transportation to the member states[9].

It is a condition of this relief that the goods are put to the use by reference to which it is afforded, or that the purpose by reference to which it is afforded is fulfilled, in the member states[10].

1 For the meaning of 'importation' and related expressions see para 111 note 1 ante.
2 'Standard tanks' means any of the following: (1) tanks permanently fitted to a vehicle and which are fitted to all vehicles of that type by the manufacturer, to supply directly fuel for the purpose of propulsion and, where appropriate, for the operation, during transport, of refrigeration systems and other systems; (2) gas tanks fitted to vehicles designed for the direct use of gas as a fuel; (3) tanks fitted to ancillary systems with which a vehicle is equipped; and (4) tanks permanently fitted to a special container and which are fitted to all special containers of that type by the manufacturer, to supply directly fuel for the operation, during transport, of refrigeration systems and other systems with which special containers are equipped: Value Added Tax (Imported Goods) Relief Order 1984, SI 1984/746, art 5(2), Sch 2 Group 10 note (1) (Sch 2 Group 10 substituted by SI 1988/2212). For the meaning of 'vehicle' and 'special container' see notes 3–4 infra.
3 'Vehicle' means any motor road vehicle: ibid Sch 2 Group 10 note (2) (as substituted: see note 2 supra).
4 'Special container' means any container fitted with specially designed apparatus for refrigeration systems, oxygenation systems, thermal insulation systems and other systems: ibid Sch 2 Group 10 note (3) (as substituted: see note 2 supra).
5 Ibid art 5(1), Sch 2 Group 10 item 1 (as substituted: see note 2 supra).
6 Ibid Sch 2 Group 10 item 2 (as substituted: see note 2 supra). This relief does not apply in the case of any special purpose vehicle or a vehicle which, by its type of construction and equipment, is designed for and capable of transporting goods or more than nine persons including the driver: Sch 2 Group 10 note (4) (as so substituted).
7 Ibid Sch 2 Group 10 item 3 (as substituted: see note 2 supra). This relief applies only to lubricants necessary for the normal operation of the vehicle during its journey: Sch 2 Group 10 note (5) (as so substituted).
8 Ibid Sch 2 Group 10 item 4 (as substituted: see note 2 supra).
9 Ibid Sch 2 Group 10 item 5 (as substituted: see note 2 supra; amended by virtue of art 2(5) (added by SI 1992/3120)). This relief applies only where the cost of the packings is included in the consideration for the goods transported: Sch 2 Group 10 note (6) (as so substituted).
10 See ibid art 6(1) (amended by virtue of art 2(5) (added by SI 1992/3120)).

121. Goods relating to war graves, funerals etc. Value added tax is not charged on the importation[1] of:

(1) goods imported by an organisation approved by the Secretary of State for use in the construction, upkeep or ornamentation of cemeteries, tombs and memorials in the member states which commemorate war victims of other countries[2];

(2)   coffins containing human remains[3];

(3)   urns containing human ashes[4];

(4)   flowers, wreaths and other ornamental objects accompanying such coffins or urns[5];

(5)   flowers, wreaths and other ornamental objects imported without any commercial intent by a person resident abroad[6] for use at a funeral or to decorate a grave[7].

It is a condition of this relief that the goods are put to the use by reference to which it is afforded, or that the purpose by reference to which it is afforded is fulfilled, in the member states[8].

1   For the meaning of 'importation' and related expressions see para 111 note 1 ante.
2   Value Added Tax (Imported Goods) Relief Order 1984, SI 1984/746, art 5(1), Sch 2 Group 11 item 1 (amended by virtue of art 2(5) (added by SI 1992/3120)).
3   Ibid Sch 2 Group 11 item 2.
4   Ibid Sch 2 Group 11 item 3.
5   Ibid Sch 2 Group 11 item 4.
6   For the meaning of 'abroad' see para 112 note 4 ante.
7   Value Added Tax (Imported Goods) Relief Order 1984 Sch 2 Group 11 item 5.
8   See ibid art 6(1) (amended by virtue of art 2(5) (added by SI 1992/3120)).

122. Small non-commercial consignments of goods. No value added tax is payable on the importation from a place outside the member states[1] of goods forming part of a small consignment[2] of a non-commercial character[3]. A consignment is of a non-commercial character for these purposes only if:

(1)   it is consigned by one individual to another;

(2)   it is not imported for any consideration[4] in money[5] or money's worth; and

(3)   it is intended for the personal use of the consignee or that of his family and not for any commercial purpose[6].

No relief may be given under these provisions unless the consignment is of an occasional nature[7]. Nor may relief be given in respect of any tobacco products[8], alcohol and alcoholic beverages[9], tafia and saké, or perfumes or toilet waters, where a small consignment of a non-commercial character contains such goods in excess of the specified[10] quantity[11].

This relief does not apply to goods contained in the baggage of a person entering the United Kingdom or carried with such a person[12].

1   As to when goods are imported from a place outside the member states see para 103 note 2 ante.
2   For these purposes, 'small consignment' means a consignment, not forming part of a larger consignment, containing goods with a value for customs purposes not exceeding £36: Value Added Tax (Small Non-commercial Consignments) Relief Order 1986, SI 1986/939, art 3(2) (amended by SI 1992/3118).
3   Ibid art 3(1) (amended by SI 1992/3118).
4   For the meaning of 'consideration' see para 86 ante.
5   For the meaning of 'money' see para 7 note 5 ante.
6   Value Added Tax (Small Non-commercial Consignments) Relief Order 1986 art 3(3).
7   Ibid art 4 (substituted by SI 1992/3118).
8   Ie being cigarettes, cigars or smoking tobacco: ibid art 5(a).
9   Ie being spirits or wine: ibid art 5(b).
10   For the specified quantities see ibid art 5, Schedule.
11   Ibid art 5.
12   Ibid art 6. For the meaning of 'United Kingdom' see para 4 note 3 ante.

123. Gold imported by a central bank. The value added tax chargeable upon the importation of gold, including gold coins, from a place outside the member states[1] is not payable where the importation is by a central bank[2].

1 As to when goods are imported from a place outside the member states see para 103 note 2 ante.
2 Value Added Tax (Imported Gold) Relief Order 1992, SI 1992/3124, art 2.

(iii) Free Zones

124. In general. The Treasury may by order designate any area in the United Kingdom as a special area for customs purposes (a 'free zone')[1]. Goods which are chargeable with value added tax may (subject to any contrary provision made by any directly applicable Community provision[2]) be moved into a free zone and remain as free zone goods[3] without payment of VAT[4].

The Commissioners of Customs and Excise may make provision by regulations ('free zone regulations') with respect to the movement of goods into, and the removal of goods from, any free zone and with respect to the keeping, securing and treatment of goods which are within a free zone[5]. Without prejudice to the generality of this power, free zone regulations may make provision:

(1) for enabling the commissioners to allow goods to be removed from a free zone without payment of VAT in such circumstances and subject to such conditions as they may determine[6];

(2) for determining, where any VAT becomes payable in respect of goods which cease to be free zone goods, the rates of any VAT applicable and the time at which those goods cease to be free zone goods[7];

(3) for determining for the purpose of enabling VAT to be charged in respect of free zone goods in a case where a person wishes to pay that VAT notwithstanding that the goods will continue to be free zone goods, the rate of VAT to be applied[8]; and

(4) permitting free zone goods to be destroyed without payment of VAT in such circumstances and subject to such conditions as the commissioners may determine[9].

With respect to free zone goods or the movement of goods into any free zone, the commissioners may make provision by regulations:

(a) for relief from the whole or part of any VAT chargeable on the importation of goods into the United Kingdom in such circumstances as they may determine[10];

(b) in place of, or in addition to, any provision made[11] for determining the time when a supply[12] of goods which are or have been free zone goods is to be treated as taking place for the purposes of the charge to VAT[13]; and

(c) as to the treatment, for the purposes of VAT, of goods which are manufactured or produced within a free zone from other goods or which have other goods incorporated in them while they are free zone goods[14].

1 Customs and Excise Management Act 1979 s 100A(1), (2) (added by the Finance Act 1984 s 8, Sch 4 Pt I). The order must be made by statutory instrument and is known as a 'designation order': see s 110A(5), (6) (as so added). An order so made (1) has effect for such period as may be specified in it; (2) may be made so as to take effect, in relation to the area or any part of the area designated by a previous such order, on the expiry of the period specified in the previous order; (3) must appoint one or more person as the responsible authority or authorities for the free zone; (4) may impose on any such authority such conditions or restrictions as may be specified; and (5) may be revoked if the Commissioners of Customs and Excise are satisfied that there has been a failure to comply with any condition or restriction: s 100A(3) (as so added).

The Treasury may by order (a) from time to time vary the conditions or restrictions imposed by a designation order or, with the agreement of the responsible authority, the area designated; or (b) appoint one or more persons as the responsible authority or authorities either in addition to or in substitution for any person appointed as such by a designation order: s 100A(4) (as so added). For the meaning of 'United Kingdom' see para 4 note 3 ante.

In exercise of the power so conferred, the Treasury has made the following free zone designation orders: the Free Zone (Birmingham Airport) Designation Order 1991, SI 1991/1737; the Free Zone (Liverpool) Designation Order 1991, SI 1991/1738; the Free Zone (Prestwick Airport) Designation Order 1991, SI 1991/1739; the Free Zone (Southampton) Designation Order 1991, SI 1991/1740 (varied by SI 1994/1410; SI 1996/2615); the Free Zone (Port of Tilbury) Designation Order 1992, SI 1992/1282; the Free Zone (Humberside) Designation Order 1994, SI 1994/144; and the Free Zone (Port of Sheerness) Designation Order 1994, SI 1994/2898.

2   As to the meaning of 'directly applicable Community provision' see para 3 ante.
3   Subject to the provisions of the free zone regulations (see the text and notes 5–9 infra), 'free zone goods' means goods which are within a free zone: Value Added Tax Act 1994 s 17(3).
4   Ibid s 17(2). Section 17 applies in relation to VAT chargeable on the importation of goods from outside the member states; and 'free zone' has the meaning given by the Customs and Excise Management Act 1979 s 100A(2) (as added) (see note 1 supra): Value Added Tax Act 1994 s 17(1).
5   Ibid s 17(3). At the date at which this volume states the law, no such regulations had been made, but, by virtue of the Interpretation Act 1978 s 17(2)(b), the Free Zone Regulations 1984, SI 1984/1177 (amended by SI 1988/710) have effect as if so made. See para 125 et seq post. As to the making of regulations generally see para 8 ante.

The general administration of free zones is now governed by EC Council Regulation 2913/92 (OJ L302, 19.10.92, p 1) and EC Commission Regulation 2454/93 (OJ L253, 11.10.93, p 1) (as amended); and the 1984 regulations cited supra have therefore lapsed except in relation to VAT. See further the Free Zone Regulations 1991, SI 1991/2727 (amended by SI 1993/3014), made under the European Communities Act 1972 s 2(2), repealing the Customs and Excise Management Act 1979 ss 100B–100E (as added), but continuing ss 100B, 100C(1), (3) in force in relation to their application to VAT: Free Zone Regulations 1991 reg 3. Those provisions were repealed by the Value Added Tax Act 1994 s 100(2), Sch 15; and replaced by s 17(2)–(4): see the text to notes 2–4 supra, 6–9 infra.

6   Ibid s 17(4)(a).
7   Ibid s 17(4)(b).
8   Ibid s 17(4)(c).
9   Ibid s 17(4)(d).
10   Ibid s 17(5)(a).
11   Ie by ibid s 6 (as amended) (see paras 29, 31, 38 ante) or any other enactment: s 17(5)(b).
12   For the meaning of 'supply' see para 21 ante.
13   Value Added Tax Act 1994 s 17(5)(c).
14   Ibid s 17(5)(d).

125. Security and controls. The Commissioners of Customs and Excise may by direction impose obligations on the responsible authority for a free zone[1] to ensure the security of that free zone; and where that authority fails to comply with the direction and the commissioners thereby incur any expenditure, that expenditure is recoverable on demand by the commissioners as a civil debt from that responsible authority[2].

The responsible authority must not permit any person to take up residence within a free zone[3].

Any person entering or leaving a free zone must answer such questions as any officer[4] may put to him with respect to any goods and must, if required by the officer, produce those goods for examination at such place as the commissioners may direct[5]. Any officer may board a vehicle at a time while it is entering or leaving a free zone and search any part of it[6].

Any officer may at any time enter upon and inspect a free zone and all buildings and goods within the zone[7].

Goods in a free zone must be produced to the proper officer[8] for examination on request[9]. He may require any such goods to be segregated and marked or otherwise identified[10].

The occupier of any premises upon which free zone goods are kept or, where the commissioners so direct, the responsible authority on his behalf, must keep such records relating to the goods as the commissioners may direct[11].

1   For the meaning of 'free zone' see para 124 ante.
2   Free Zone Regulations 1984, SI 1984/1177, reg 3.
3   Ibid reg 4.
4   'Officer' means a person commissioned by the commissioners: Customs and Excise Management Act 1979 s 1(1).
5   Ibid s 100F(1) (s 100F added by the Finance Act 1984 s 8, Sch 4 Pt I).
6   Customs and Excise Management Act 1979 s 100F(2) (as added: see note 4 supra).
7   Ibid s 100F(3) (as added: see note 4 supra).
8   For the meaning of 'proper officer' see para 105 note 9 ante.
9   Free Zone Regulations 1984 reg 22.
10   Ibid reg 23.
11   Ibid reg 24(1). The records must be kept in the free zone or such other place as the commissioners may allow and must be in such form, and be preserved for such term not exceeding three years from the date the goods are removed from the free zone, as they may direct: reg 24(2). As to production of the records see reg 24(3).

126. Excise goods which may become free zone goods without payment of duty. Goods chargeable with excise duty may be moved into a free zone[1] in accordance with the free zone regulations[2] without payment of that duty and remain as free zone goods[3], provided that they are goods which, by or under the Customs and Excise Acts[4], the Commissioners of Customs and Excise may allow to be removed or delivered without payment of excise duty and which have been allowed to be so removed or delivered[5].

1   For the meaning of 'free zone' see para 124 ante.
2   Ie the Free Zone Regulations 1984, SI 1984/1177; see paras 125 ante, 127 et seq post.
3   For the meaning of 'free zone goods' see para 124 ante.
4   For the meaning of 'the Customs and Excise Acts' see para 105 note 2 ante.
5   Free Zone Regulations 1984 reg 5.

127. Movement of goods into free zone. Goods moved into a free zone[1] are not free zone goods[2] unless, within such time as the Commissioners of Customs and Excise may direct, such particulars as they may direct have been entered into a record to be kept by the occupier of the premises at which the goods are received or, if the commissioners so direct, by the responsible authority[3]. Where the proprietor of free zone goods wishes to obtain an acknowledgment that the goods are Community goods[4] he must deliver to the proper officer[5], within the relevant period[6], a document in such form and containing such particulars as the commissioners may direct, together with such supporting evidence as will enable the officer to establish to his satisfaction that they are Community goods[7]. If so satisfied, the proper officer must provide a written acknowledgment[8] of such Community status[9].

Goods moved into a free zone which are subject to another customs procedure are not free zone goods until the proprietor of the goods has presented them to the proper officer and that procedure has been discharged[10].

1   For the meaning of 'free zone' see para 124 ante.
2   For the meaning of 'free zone goods' see para 124 ante.
3   Free Zone Regulations 1984, SI 1984/1177, reg 6(1) (amended by SI 1988/710).
4   'Community goods' means goods which fulfil the conditions of the EC Treaty art 9(2) and goods covered by the ECSC Treaty (Treaty establishing the European Coal and Steel Community (Paris, 18 April 1951;

TS 16 (1979); Cmnd 7461) which are in free circulation in the Community in accordance therewith: Free Zone Regulations 1984 reg 2.

5   For the meaning of 'proper officer' see para 105 note 9 ante.
6   'The relevant period' means a period not exceeding seven days from the time the goods become free zone goods or from the time an entry for free circulation under the Free Zone Regulations 1984 reg 17(2) (see para 128 post) is accepted: reg 7(3).
7   Ibid reg 7(1).
8   The written acknowledgment must consist of a copy of the document containing particulars of the goods indorsed by the proper officer: ibid reg 7(2).
9   Ibid reg 7(1).
10 Ibid reg 8.

128. Entry and removal of free zone goods. Before any free zone goods[1] are removed from a free zone[2] for home use or transfer to another customs procedure providing for suspension of, or relief from customs duty or agricultural levy, the goods must be entered[3] for that purpose[4]. The Commissioners of Customs and Excise may, however, allow the goods to be removed from the free zone for such a purpose, on the application of their proprietor, without the goods being entered if such particulars as the commissioners may direct are entered in a record to be kept by the proprietor of the goods[5]. Where goods are allowed to be removed from the free zone in this way, the proprietor of the goods must comply with any conditions that the commissioners may impose[6].

Free zone goods which have been entered[7], or in respect of which the required particulars[8] have been entered in the record, must be removed forthwith from the free zone[9]. No goods may, however, be removed from a free zone except with the authority of, and in accordance with any requirement made by, the proper officer[10].

Where the proprietor of free zone goods wishes to pay any customs duty or agricultural levy chargeable on the goods and for the goods to remain as free zone goods, the goods must be entered for free circulation[11]. Where the goods are so entered, value added tax on importation is not to be paid at the time customs duty is paid[12].

Where free zone goods have been supplied whilst in the free zone to a person who is neither registered or liable to be registered for VAT[13] and he enters the goods for home use, the amount of VAT payable is reduced by the amount of tax paid on the supply[14].

1   For the meaning of 'free zone goods' see para 124 ante.
2   For the meaning of 'free zone' see para 124 ante.
3   The goods are entered by the proprietor of the goods delivering to the proper officer an entry of them in such form and manner, containing such particulars and accompanied by such documents as the Commissioners of Customs and Excise may direct: Free Zone Regulations 1984, SI 1984/1177, reg 10(1). Acceptance of an entry by the proper officer must be signified in such manner as the commissioners may direct: reg 10(2). Where free zone goods are required to be entered under reg 17, the commissioners may direct that if the proprietor of the goods (1) enters such particulars as they may direct in a record to be kept by him; and (2) furnishes a schedule to the proper officer at such place and at such intervals as they may direct, an entry of the goods is to be taken to have been delivered and accepted when the particulars are entered in the record: reg 10(3). For the meaning of 'proper officer' see para 105 note 9 ante.
4   Ibid reg 11.
5   Ibid reg 12(1).
6   Ibid reg 12(2).
7   Ie under ibid reg 11: see the text to note 4 supra.
8   Ie under ibid reg 12: see the text to notes 5–6 supra.
9   Ibid reg 13.
10 Ibid reg 15.
11 Ibid reg 17(2).
12 Ibid reg 18(2).
13 As to registration see para 56 et seq ante.
14 Free Zone Regulations 1984 reg 27.

129. Offences, penalties and forfeiture. In the event of any contravention or failure to comply with (1) any relevant Community provision[1] or any requirement or condition imposed by or under, or any undertaking given pursuant to, any such provision; or (2) any free zone regulation[2], the person responsible for the contravention or failure is liable on summary conviction to a penalty of level 3 on the standard scale[3], together with a penalty of £40 for each day on which the contravention or failure continues, and any goods in respect of which the offence was committed are liable to forfeiture[4].

1   The relevant Community provisions are: (1) EC Council Regulation 2913/92 (OJ L302, 19.10.92, p 1) arts 59, 101(a)–(c), 105, 110 and 111; (2) EC Commission Regulation 2454/93 (OJ L253, 11.10.93, p 1) arts 223, 269, 513, 517, 522, 523, 527, 528–534, 536, 864: Free Zone Regulations 1991, SI 1991/2727, reg 2, Schedule (substituted by SI 1993/3014).

2   Ie any regulation made under the Value Added Tax Act 1994 s 17(3), (5): see para 124 ante.

3   The 'standard scale' means the standard scale of maximum fines for summary offences as set out in the Criminal Justice Act 1982 s 37(2) (as substituted): Interpretation Act 1978 s 5, Sch 1 (amended by the Criminal Justice Act 1988 s 170(1), Sch 15 para 58(a)). See CRIMINAL LAW vol 11(2) (Reissue) para 808; and MAGISTRATES. At the date at which this volume states the law, the standard scale is as follows: level 1, £200; level 2, £500; level 3, £1,000; level 4, £2,500; level 5, £5,000: Criminal Justice Act 1982 s 37(2) (substituted by the Criminal Justice Act 1991 s 17(1)). As to the determination of the amount of the fine actually imposed, as distinct from the level on the standard scale which it may not exceed, see the Criminal Justice Act 1991 s 18 (substituted by the Criminal Justice Act 1993 s 65); and MAGISTRATES.

4   Free Zone Regulations 1991 reg 6; Interpretation Act 1978 s 17(2)(b). The Customs and Excise Management Act 1979 s 139, Sch 3 (as amended) (detention, seizure and condemnation of goods), ss 144–148, 150–155 (as amended) (proceedings for offences, mitigation of penalties, proof and other matters) apply for these purposes: see the Free Zone Regulations 1991 reg 7. See further CUSTOMS AND EXCISE.

(iv) Warehousing Regimes

A.   GOODS SUBJECT TO WAREHOUSING REGIMES; IN GENERAL

130. Goods subject to a warehousing regime. The acquisition of goods from another member state[1], or the supply[2] of those goods, is treated for the purposes of value added tax as taking place outside the United Kingdom[3] where:

(1)   they have been removed from a place outside the member states and have entered the territory of the Community[4];

(2)   the material time[5] for any acquisition of those goods from another member state or for any supply of those goods is while they are subject to a warehousing regime[6] and before the duty point[7]; and

(3)   those goods are not mixed with any dutiable goods[8] which were produced or manufactured in the United Kingdom or acquired from another member state[9].

Similarly, where any dutiable goods are acquired from another member state[10] or any person makes a supply of:

(a)   any dutiable goods which were produced or manufactured in the United Kingdom or acquired from another member state; or

(b)   any goods comprising a mixture of such goods and other goods[11],

and the material time for the acquisition or supply is while the goods in question are subject to a warehousing regime and before the duty point, that acquisition or supply is treated as taking place outside the United Kingdom if the material time for any subsequent supply of those goods is also while the goods are subject to the warehousing regime and before the duty point[12]. Where the material time for any acquisition or supply of goods in relation to which this provision applies is while the goods are subject to a warehousing regime and before the duty point, but the acquisition or supply nevertheless falls to be treated for VAT purposes as taking place in the United Kingdom[13], then:

(i)   that acquisition or supply is treated as taking place at the earlier of the time when the goods are removed from the warehousing regime and the duty point[14]; and

(ii)   in the case of a supply, any VAT payable on the supply must be paid[15] at the time when the supply is so treated as taking place and either by the person by whom the goods are so removed, or by the person who is required to pay the duty or agricultural levy and together with that duty or levy[16].

Where in respect of any supply by a taxable person of dutiable goods, or an acquisition by any person from another member state of dutiable goods, the time of supply or acquisition precedes the duty point in relation to those goods, the VAT in respect of that supply or acquisition must be accounted for and paid, and any question as to the inclusion of any duty in the value of the supply or acquisition must be determined, by reference to the duty point or by reference to such later time as the Commissioners of Customs and Excise may determine[17].

1   For the meaning of 'acquisition of goods from another member state' see para 13 ante.
2   For the meaning of 'supply' see para 21 ante.
3   Ie and thus as outside the scope of United Kingdom VAT. For the meaning of 'United Kingdom' see para 4 note 3 ante.
4   Value Added Tax Act 1994 s 18(1)(a). As to the territory of the Community for the purposes of VAT see para 10 ante.
5   For these purposes, 'material time' means (1) in relation to any acquisition or supply the time of which is determined in accordance with regulations under ibid s 6(14) (see para 31 ante) or s 12(3) (see para 38 ante), such time as may be prescribed for these purposes by those regulations; (2) in relation to any other acquisition, the time of the event which, in relation to the acquisition, is the first relevant event for the purpose of taxing it; and (3) in relation to any other supply, the time when the supply would be treated as taking place in accordance with s 6(2) if s 6(2)(c) (see para 29 ante) were omitted: s 18(6).
6   For these purposes, references to goods being subject to a warehousing regime are references to goods being kept in a warehouse or being transported between warehouses, whether in the same or different member states, without the payment in a member state of any duty, levy or VAT, and references to the removal of goods from a warehousing regime are to be construed accordingly: ibid s 18(7). 'Warehouse' means any warehouse where goods may be stored in any member state without payment of any one or more of the following: (1) Community customs duty; (2) any agricultural levy of the European Community; (3) VAT on the importation of the goods into any member state; (4) any duty of excise or any duty which is equivalent in another member state to a duty of excise: s 18(6).
7   Ibid s 18(1)(b). For the meaning of 'the duty point' see para 89 note 9 ante.
8   For the meaning of 'dutiable goods' see para 89 note 7 ante.
9   Value Added Tax Act 1994 s 18(1)(c).
10   Ibid s 18(2)(a).
11   Ibid s 18(2)(b).
12   Ibid s 18(2), (3). The effect of this is that VAT is only leviable on the last supply or acquisition of goods occurring whilst they are subject to the warehousing regime and before the duty point. The last such supply or acquisition is therefore treated as taking place in the United Kingdom: see the text and notes 13–16 infra.
13   Ie by virtue of ibid s 18(2), (3): see note 12 supra.
14   Ibid s 18(4)(a).
15   Ie subject to any regulations made under s 18(5) (as substituted): see para 131 post.
16   Ibid s 18(4)(b).
17   Value Added Tax Regulations 1995, SI 1995/2518, reg 41(1). As to accounting for VAT generally see para 225 et seq post.

131. Deferred payment of value added tax. The Commissioners of Customs and Excise may make provision by regulations for enabling a taxable person[1] to pay any value added tax he is required to pay on the last supply of goods which have been subject to a warehousing regime[2] at a later time than that provided for by statute[3]. Such regulations may in particular make provision for either or both of the following:

(1) for the taxable person to pay the VAT together with the VAT chargeable on other supplies by him of goods and services[4];

(2) for the taxable person to pay the VAT together with any duty of excise deferment of which has been granted[5] to him[6],

and they may make different provision for different descriptions of taxable person and for different descriptions of goods[7].

A person registered for VAT[8] who is an approved person for the purposes of deferred payment of excise duties[9] in respect of goods which are at a specified warehouse and who is liable (a) to pay VAT[10] on a supply of goods while the goods are subject to a warehousing regime; or (b) to pay VAT[11] on a supply of specified services[12], may pay that VAT at or before the relevant time[13] instead of at the time provided for[14] by statute[15]. Where any goods of a kind chargeable to a duty of excise qualify for any relief of that duty, that relief is disregarded for the purposes of determining the relevant time[16].

1 For the meaning of 'taxable person' see paras 12 note 4, 55 ante.
2 Ie any VAT he is required to pay by virtue of the Value Added Tax Act 1994 s 18(4)(b): see para 130 ante. For the meaning of 'supply' see para 21 ante; and for the meaning of 'subject to a warehousing regime' see para 130 note 6 ante.
3 Ibid s 18(5) (substituted by the Finance Act 1995 s 29).
4 Value Added Tax Act 1994 s 18(5A)(a) (added by the Finance Act 1995 s 29).
5 Ie under the Customs and Excise Management Act 1979 s 127A (as added): see CUSTOMS AND EXCISE.
6 Value Added Tax Act 1994 s 18(5A)(b) (as added: see note 4 supra).
7 Ibid s 18(5A) (as added: see note 4 supra).
8 For the meaning of 'registered person' see para 105 note 7 ante.
9 Ie an approved person within the meaning of the Excise Duties (Deferred Payment) Regulations 1992, SI 1992/3152 (which allow for deferred payment of excise duty in certain circumstances on (1) wine, made-wine, cider, spirits, hydrocarbon oils; and (2) beer imported by a registered excise dealer and shipper: see CUSTOMS AND EXCISE): Value Added Tax Regulations 1995, SI 1995/2518, reg 43(1).
10 Ie liable under the Value Added Tax Act 1994 s 18(4)(b): see para 130 ante.
11 Ie liable under ibid s 18D(2) (as added): see para 136 post.
12 Ie a supply of services to which ibid s 18C(3) (as added) applies (specified services performed on or in relation to goods which are subject to a warehousing regime): see para 140 post.
13 The relevant time means (1) in relation to hydrocarbon oils, the 15th day of the month immediately following the month on which those oils were removed from the warehousing regime; and (2) in relation to any other goods subject to a duty of excise, the day ('payment day') on which the registered person is required to pay the excise duty on the goods in accordance with the Excise Duties (Deferred Payment) Regulations 1992 reg 5: Value Added Tax Regulations 1995 reg 43(3). See also the text to note 14 infra.
14 Ie provided for by the Value Added Tax Act 1994 s 18(4)(b) (see para 130 ante) or s 18D(2)(a) (as added) (see para 136 post): Value Added Tax Regulations 1995 reg 43(2) (substituted by SI 1996/1250).
15 Ibid reg 43(1), (2) (reg 43(2) as substituted: see note 14 supra).
16 Ibid reg 43(4).

B. FISCAL WAREHOUSING

132. In general. In order to give effect to the Second Value Added Tax Simplification Directive[1], a system of fiscal warehousing was introduced with effect from 1 June 1996[2], enabling various commodities ('eligible goods')[3], to be traded free from VAT within the regime of the warehouse[4]. Since the fiscal warehousing regime is designed to form part of a Community VAT simplification process, the value of supplies and acquisitions[5] made within a fiscal warehouse are disregarded in determining whether the supplier is obliged to register for VAT[6]; but the supplier, or acquirer, as the case may be, is nevertheless liable to account for the VAT on standard-rated supplies or acquisitions if he would have been liable to register but for the simplification[7].

Certain transactions involving a supply of eligible goods are treated as supplies of goods and not supplies of services for the purposes of VAT[8].

1   Ie EC Council Directive 95/7 (OJ L102, 5.5.95, p 18): see EUROPEAN COMMUNITIES.
2   See the Finance Act 1996 ss 25–29, Sch 3; and para 133 et seq post. See also Customs and Excise Notice 702/8 *Fiscal Warehousing* (June 1996).
3   The commodities which are capable of being eligible goods are: tin, copper, zinc, nickel, aluminium, lead, indium, silver, platinum, palladium and rhodium, cereals (including unprocessed rice), oil seeds and oleaginous fruits, nuts, olives, grains and seeds (including soya beans), potatoes, unroasted coffee, tea, cocoa beans (whether whole or broken, raw or roasted), raw sugar, rubber (in primary forms or in plates, sheets or strip), wool, chemicals in bulk, mineral oils (including propane and butane and crude petroleum oils) and vegetable oils and fats and their fractions (whether or not refined but not chemically modified): see the Value Added Tax Act 1994 s 18B(6), Sch 5A (added by the Finance Act 1996 s 26(1), Sch 3 para 18). The Treasury may by order vary the Value Added Tax Act 1994 Sch 5A (as so added) by adding to or deleting from it any goods or varying any description of goods: s 18B(8) (added by the Finance Act 1996 Sch 3 para 5). At the date at which this volume states the law, no such order had been made.
4   See the Value Added Tax Act 1994 ss 18B, 18C (added by the Finance Act 1996 Sch 3 para 5); and paras 134, 140 post.
5   Ie supplies or acquisitions which are deemed to take place in accordance with the Value Added Tax Act 1994 s 18B(4) (as added: see note 4 supra) (last acquisition or supply of goods before their removal from the fiscal warehouse): see para 134 post.
6   See ibid s 3(2), Sch 1 para 1(9), Sch 2 para 1(7), Sch 3 para 1(6) (added by the Finance Act 1996 Sch 3 paras 13, 14, 15 respectively); and paras 56, 60, 63 ante.
7   See the Value Added Tax Act 1994 s 18B(5) (as added: see note 4 supra); and para 134 post.
8   See the Value Added Tax (Fiscal Warehousing) (Treatment of Transactions) Order 1996, SI 1996/1255; and para 21 note 5 ante.

133. Approval of fiscal warehousekeeper. If it appears to them to be proper, the Commissioners of Customs and Excise may upon application[1] approve any registered person[2] as a fiscal warehousekeeper[3]. In considering an application by a person to be a fiscal warehousekeeper, the commissioners may take into account any matter which they consider relevant, and in particular[4] all or any one or more of the following[5]:

(1)   his record of compliance and ability to comply with the statutory requirements[6] relating to value added tax[7];

(2)   his record of compliance and ability to comply with the requirements of the Customs and Excise Acts[8] and regulations made thereunder[9];

(3)   his record of compliance and ability to comply with Community customs provisions[10];

(4)   his record of compliance and ability to comply with the requirements of other member states relating to VAT and duties equivalent to duties of excise[11];

(5)   if the applicant is a company, the records of compliance and ability to comply with the matters set out in heads (1) to (4) above of its directors, persons connected[12] with its directors, its managing officers[13], any shadow directors[14] or any of those persons and, if it is a close company[15], the records of compliance and ability to comply with those matters of the beneficial owners of the shares of the company or any of them[16]; and

(6)   if the applicant is an individual, the records of compliance and ability to comply with the matters set out in heads (1) to (4) above of any company of which he is or has been a director, managing officer or shadow director or, in the case of a close company, a shareholder or the beneficial owner of shares[17].

An approval may be subject to such conditions as the commissioners may impose[18]. Subject to those conditions, and to any relevant regulations[19], such a person is entitled to keep a fiscal warehouse[20]. The approval must be notified in writing and takes effect on its being made, or on any later date specified for the purpose in the notification[21]. A person approved under these provisions remains a fiscal warehousekeeper until he ceases to be a registered person or until he notifies the commissioners in writing that he is to cease to be a fiscal warehousekeeper[22]. If, however, the commissioners consider it appropriate they may from time to time:

(a)   impose conditions on a fiscal warehousekeeper in addition to those conditions, if any, which they imposed on approval, and vary or revoke any conditions previously imposed[23];

(b)   withdraw approval of any person as a fiscal warehousekeeper[24]; and

(c)   withdraw fiscal warehouse status from any premises[25].

Any such withdrawal of approval or other act must be notified by the commissioners to the fiscal warehousekeeper in writing, and takes effect on the notification being made, or on any later date specified for the purpose in the notification[26].

An appeal lies to a VAT and duties tribunal against any decision of the commissioners:

(i)   as to whether or not a person is to be approved as a fiscal warehousekeeper or the conditions from time to time subject to which he is so approved;

(ii)   for the withdrawal of any such approval; or

(iii)   for the withdrawal of fiscal warehouse status from any premises[27].

1   The application must be in writing in such form as the commissioners may direct and must be accompanied by such information as they may require: Value Added Tax Act 1994 s 18A(7) (s 18A added by the Finance Act 1996 s 26(1), Sch 3 para 5).

2   Without prejudice to the provisions of the Value Added Tax Act 1994 s 43 (as amended) concerning liability for VAT (see paras 66 ante, 191 post), in s 18A(1), (2) (as added: see note 1 supra) 'registered person' includes any body corporate which under s 43 (as amended) is for the time being treated as a member of a group: s 18A(9) (as so added).

3   Ibid s 18A(1) (as added: see note 1 supra). 'Fiscal warehousekeeper' means a person so approved: s 18F(1) (as so added). 'Fiscal warehouse' means such place in the United Kingdom in the occupation or under the control of the fiscal warehousekeeper, not being retail premises, as he notifies to the commissioners in writing and from which that status has not been withdrawn; and such a place becomes a fiscal warehouse on receipt by the commissioners of that notification or on the date stated in it as the date from which it is to have effect, whichever is the later, and, subject to s 18A(6) (as so added) (see heads (a)–(c) in the text), remains a fiscal warehouse so long as it is in the occupation or under the control of the fiscal warehousekeeper or until he notifies the commissioners in writing that it is to cease to be a fiscal warehouse: ss 18A(3), 18F(1) (as so added). For the meaning of 'United Kingdom' see para 4 note 3 ante.

4   Ie without prejudice to the generality of this provision: ibid s 18A(4) (as added: see note 1 supra).

5   Ibid s 18A(4) (as added: see note 1 supra).

6   Ie the requirements of the Value Added Tax Act 1994 and regulations made thereunder: see paras 5 ante, 134 et seq post.

7   Ibid s 18A(4)(a) (as added: see note 1 supra).

8   For the meaning of 'the Customs and Excise Acts' see para 105 note 2 ante.

9   Value Added Tax Act 1994 s 18A(4)(b) (as added: see note 1 supra).

10   Ibid s 18A(4)(c) (as added: see note 1 supra).

11   Ibid s 18A(4)(d) (as added: see note 1 supra).

12   A person is 'connected' with a director for these purposes if that person is the director's wife or husband, or is a relative, or the wife or husband of a relative, of the director or of the director's wife or husband: ibid s 24(7) (applied by s 18A(4) (as added: see note 1 supra)).

13   A 'managing officer', in relation to a body corporate, means any manager, secretary or other similar officer of the body corporate or any person purporting to act in any such capacity or as a director: ibid s 61(6) (applied by s 18A(4) (as added: see note 1 supra)).

14   In relation to a company, 'shadow director' means a person in accordance with whose directions or instructions the directors of the company are accustomed to act; but a person is not deemed a shadow director by reason only that the directors act on advice given by him in a professional capacity: Companies Act 1985 s 741(2) (applied by the Value Added Tax Act 1994 s 18A(4) (as added: see note 1 supra)).

15   For these purposes, 'close company' has the meaning given by the Income and Corporation Taxes Act 1988 (see INCOME TAXATION vol 23 (Reissue) para 1292): Value Added Tax Act 1994 s 18A(4) (as added: see note 1 supra).

16   Ibid s 18A(4)(e) (as added: see note 1 supra).

17   Ibid s 18A(4)(f) (as added: see note 1 supra).

18 Ibid s 18A(1) (as added: see note 1 supra).
19 Ie regulations made under ibid s 18F (as added): see para 139 post.
20 Ibid s 18A(2) (as added: see note 1 supra).
21 Ibid s 18A(8) (as added: see note 1 supra).
22 Ibid s 18A(5) (as added: see note 1 supra).
23 Ibid s 18A(6)(a) (as added: see note 1 supra).
24 Ibid s 18A(6)(b) (as added: see note 1 supra).
25 Ibid s 18A(6)(c) (as added: see note 1 supra).
26 Ibid s 18A(8) (as added: see note 1 supra).
27 See ibid s 83(da) (added by the Finance Act 1996 Sch 3 para 12); and para 296 post.

134. Acquisitions and supplies treated as taking place outside the United Kingdom. Where there is an acquisition of eligible goods[1] from another member state[2] and either:

(1) the acquisition takes place while the goods are subject to a fiscal warehousing regime[3]; or

(2) the acquirer causes the goods to be placed in such a regime after the acquisition but before the supply[4], if any, of those goods which next occurs[5],

then, provided that the acquirer, not later than the time of the acquisition, prepares and keeps a certificate[6] that the goods are subject to a fiscal warehousing regime or, as the case may be, that he will cause head (2) above to be satisfied[7], the acquisition is treated, for the purposes of value added tax, as taking place outside the United Kingdom[8] if any subsequent supply of those goods is while they are subject to the fiscal warehousing regime[9]. If, however, the subsequent supply is not made while the goods are so subject, and the acquisition thus falls to be treated as taking place in the United Kingdom, it is treated as taking place when the goods are removed from the fiscal warehousing regime[10].

Similarly, where there is a supply of eligible goods and either:

(a) the supply takes place while the goods are subject to a fiscal warehousing regime[11]; or

(b) after that supply, but before the supply, if any, of those goods which next occurs, the person to whom the former supply is made causes the goods to be placed in a fiscal warehousing regime[12],

then, provided that the supply is not a retail transaction[13] and that, in a case falling within head (b) above, the person to whom the supply is made gives the supplier a certificate that he will cause head (b) above to be satisfied[14], the supply is treated as taking place outside the United Kingdom if any subsequent supply of those goods is made while they are subject to the fiscal warehousing regime[15]. If, however, there is no subsequent supply which is made while the goods are so subject, so that the certified supply falls to be treated as taking place in the United Kingdom, it is treated as taking place when the goods are removed from the fiscal warehousing regime[16].

Where:

(i) an acquisition or supply is treated by virtue of these provisions as taking place when the goods are removed from the fiscal warehousing regime[17];

(ii) the acquisition or supply is taxable[18] and not zero-rated[19]; and

(iii) the acquirer or supplier is not a taxable person[20] but would be if the value of that acquisition or supply were taken into account in establishing liability to registration[21],

VAT is chargeable on that acquisition or supply notwithstanding that the acquirer or supplier is not a taxable person[22].

Any value added tax payable on a supply treated as taking place on removal[23] or an acquisition treated as taking place on removal where the acquirer is not a taxable person[24]

must be paid at the time when the supply or acquisition is treated[25] as taking place and by the person by whom the goods are removed or, as the case may be, by the person who is required to pay the excise duty and together with that duty[26]. The Commissioners of Customs and Excise may, however, make provision by regulations for enabling a taxable person to pay the VAT he is so required to pay at a later time[27]; and they may make different provisions for different descriptions of taxable persons and for different descriptions of goods and services[28].

1   For these purposes, 'eligible goods' means goods (1) of a description falling within the Value Added Tax Act 1994 s 18B(6), Sch 5A (added by the Finance Act 1996 s 26(1), Sch 3 paras 5, 18) (see para 132 note 3 ante); (2) upon which any import duties, as defined in EC Council Regulation 2913/92 (OJ L302, 19.10.92, p 1) art 4(10) have been either paid or deferred under art 224 or regulations made under the Customs and Excise Management Act 1979 s 45 (deferred payment of customs duty: see CUSTOMS AND EXCISE); (3) upon which, in the case of goods imported from a place outside the member states, any VAT chargeable under the Value Added Tax Act 1994 s 1(1)(c) (see paras 4, 103 ante) has been either paid or deferred in accordance with Community customs provisions; and (4) upon which, in the case of goods subject to a duty of excise, that duty has been either paid or deferred under the Customs and Excise Management Act 1979 s 127A (as added) (see CUSTOMS AND EXCISE): Value Added Tax Act 1994 ss 18B(6), 18F(1) (ss 18B–18F added by the Finance Act 1996 Sch 3 para 5).

2   Value Added Tax Act 1994 s 18B(1)(a), (b) (as added: see note 1 supra). For the meaning of 'another member state' see para 4 note 14 ante.

3   Ibid s 18B(1)(c)(i) (as added: see note 1 supra). For these purposes, any reference to goods being subject to a fiscal warehousing regime is, subject to any regulations made under the Value Added Tax Act 1994 s 18F(8)(e) (as so added) (see para 139 post), a reference to eligible goods being kept in a fiscal warehouse or being transferred between fiscal warehouses in accordance with such regulations; and any reference to the removal of goods from a fiscal warehousing regime is to be construed accordingly: s 18F(2) (as so added). Except for the purposes of s 18B(4) (as so added) (see the text to notes 10, 16 infra), an acquisition or supply is treated as taking place at the material time for the acquisition or supply: s 18B(7) (as so added). 'Material time' means (1) in relation to any acquisition or supply the time of which is determined in accordance with regulations under s 6(14) (see para 31 ante) or s 12(3) (see para 38 ante), such time as may be prescribed for these purposes by those regulations; (2) in relation to any other acquisition, the time when the goods reach the destination to which they are dispatched from the member state in question; (3) in relation to any other supply of goods, the time when the supply would be treated as taking place in accordance with s 6(2) if s 6(2)(c) were omitted (see para 29 ante); and (4) in relation to any other supply of services, the time when the services are performed: s 18F(1) (as so added).

    Upon any eligible goods entering a fiscal warehouse, the relevant fiscal warehousekeeper must record their entry in his relevant fiscal warehousing record; and eligible goods are only subject to or in a fiscal warehousing regime at any time while they are allocated to that regime in the relevant fiscal warehousing record, while they are not identified in that record as having been transferred, or prior to their removal from that regime: Value Added Tax Regulations 1995, SI 1995/2518, reg 145E(1), (2) (added by SI 1996/1250). For these purposes, where a fiscal warehousekeeper keeps one or more fiscal warehouses there is a single fiscal warehousing regime associated with him, and 'relevant fiscal warehousekeeper', 'relevant fiscal warehouse', 'relevant fiscal warehousing regime', 'his fiscal warehouse', 'his fiscal warehousing regime' and related expressions are to be construed accordingly: reg 145A(2) (as so added). As to fiscal warehousing records see para 222 post.

4   For the meaning of 'supply' see para 21 ante.

5   Value Added Tax Act 1994 s 18B(1)(c)(ii) (as added: see note 1 supra).

6   The certificate must be in such form, and kept for such period, as the Commissioners of Customs and Excise may specify by regulations: ibid s 18B(1)(d) (as added: see note 1 supra). The certificate must contain the information indicated in the Value Added Tax Regulations 1995, SI 1995/2518, reg 145B(1), Sch 1, Form 17 (added by SI 1996/1250): reg 145B(1) (as so added). Such a certificate prepared by an acquirer who is not a taxable person must be kept by him for a period of six years commencing on the day the certificate is prepared; and he must produce it to a proper officer when that officer requests him to do so: reg 145B(2) (as so added). For the meaning of 'proper officer' see para 105 note 9 ante.

7   Value Added Tax Act 1994 s 18B(1)(d) (as added: see note 1 supra).

8   For the meaning of 'United Kingdom' see para 4 note 3 ante.

9   Value Added Tax Act 1994 s 18B(3) (as added: see note 1 supra).

10 Ibid s 18B(4) (as added: see note 1 supra).

11 Ibid s 18B(2)(a), (b), (c)(i) (as added: see note 1 supra).
12 Ibid s 18B(2)(c)(ii) (as added: see note 1 supra).
13 Ibid s 18B(2)(e) (as added: see note 1 supra).
14 Ibid s 18B(2)(d) (as added: see note 1 supra). The certificate must be in such form as the commissioners may specify by regulations: s 18B(2)(d) (as so added). It must contain the information indicated in the Value Added Tax Regulations 1995 Sch 1, Form 17 (added by SI 1996/1250): reg 145B(1) (as so added).
15 Value Added Tax Act 1994 s 18B(3) (as added: see note 1 supra).
16 Ibid s 18B(4) (as added: see note 1 supra).
17 Ie where ibid s 18B(4) (as added: see note 1 supra) applies: see the text to notes 10, 16 supra.
18 For the meaning of 'taxable acquisition' and 'taxable supply' see paras 13, 12 note 3 respectively ante.
19 For the meaning of 'zero-rated' see para 158 post.
20 For the meaning of 'taxable person' see paras 12 note 4, 55 ante.
21 Ie would be a taxable person were it not for the Value Added Tax Act 1994 s 3(2), Sch 1 para 1(9) (as added), Sch 2 para 1(7) (as added) or Sch 3 para 1(6) (as added): see paras 45, 60, 63 ante.
22 Ibid s 18B(5) (as added: see note 1 supra).
23 Ie a supply to which the Value Added Tax Act 1994 s 18B(4) (as added) applies and which is treated as taking place on the removal of the goods from the fiscal warehouse: see the text and note 16 supra.
24 Ie an acquisition to which ibid s 18B(5) (as added) applies and which is treated as taking place on the removal of the goods from the fiscal warehouse: see heads (i)–(iii) in the text.
25 Ie under ibid s 18B (as added): see the text and notes 1–22 supra.
26 Ibid s 18D(1), (2) (s 18D added by the Finance Act 1996 s 26(1), Sch 3 para 5).
27 Ibid s 18D(3) (as added: see note 5 supra). See the Value Added Tax Regulations 1995, SI 1995/2518, reg 43(2) (substituted by SI 1996/1250); and para 131 ante.
28 Value Added Tax Act 1994 s 18D(3) (as added: see note 5 supra).

135. Fiscal warehousing transfers taking place in the United Kingdom.

A fiscal warehousekeeper[1] ('the original fiscal warehousekeeper') may permit eligible goods[2] which are subject to his fiscal warehousing regime[3] ('the original regime') to be transferred to another fiscal warehousing regime ('the other regime') without those goods being treated as removed from the original regime[4]. The original fiscal warehousekeeper must not, however, allow eligible goods to exit from his fiscal warehousing regime in pursuance of this provision before he receives a written undertaking from the fiscal warehousekeeper in relation to that other fiscal warehousing regime ('the other fiscal warehousekeeper') that, in respect of those eligible goods, the other fiscal warehousekeeper will comply with the following requirements[5]:

(1) that upon the entry of the goods to his fiscal warehouse, he will record that entry in his fiscal warehousing record[6] and allocate those goods to his fiscal warehousing regime[7]; and

(2) that within 30 days commencing with the day on which those goods left the original fiscal warehouse, he will deliver, or cause to be delivered, to the original fiscal warehousekeeper a certificate in a form acceptable to the Commissioners of Customs and Excise confirming that he has recorded the entry of those goods to his fiscal warehouse and allocated them to his fiscal warehousing regime and that he will retain a copy of that certificate as part of his fiscal warehousing record[8].

1 For the meaning of 'fiscal warehousekeeper' see para 133 note 3 ante.
2 For the meaning of 'eligible goods' see para 134 note 1 ante (definition applied by the Value Added Tax Regulations 1995, SI 1995/2518, reg 145A(1) (added by SI 1996/1250)).
3 As to the meaning of 'his fiscal warehousing regime' see para 134 note 3 ante.
4 Value Added Tax Regulations 1995 reg 145G(1) (reg 145G added by SI 1996/1250).
5 Ibid reg 145G(2) (as added: see note 4 supra).
6 As to the fiscal warehousing record see para 222 post.
7 Value Added Tax Regulations 1995 reg 145G(3)(a), (b) (as added: see note 4 supra).
8 Ibid reg 145G(3)(c), (d) (as added: see note 4 supra).

136. Removal from warehousing and transfers overseas. Without prejudice to the provisions relating to change of status[1], eligible goods[2] which are allocated to a fiscal warehousing regime[3] may only be removed from that regime at the following times and in any of the following circumstances:

(1) when an entry in respect of those eligible goods is made in the relevant fiscal warehousing record[4] which indicates the time and date of their removal from that regime[5];

(2) when the eligible goods are moved outside the fiscal warehouse in respect of which they are allocated to a fiscal warehousing regime, except in the case of movements between fiscal warehouses kept by the same fiscal warehousekeeper[6]; or

(3) at the time immediately preceding a retail sale of those eligible goods[7].

Eligible goods which are subject to a fiscal warehousing regime are not treated as removed from that regime, but as transferred or as being in the process of transfer, as the case requires, in any of the following circumstances:

(a) where the goods in question are transferred, or are in the process of transfer, to another fiscal warehousing regime[8];

(b) where the goods in question are transferred, or are in the process of transfer, to arrangements which correspond in effect, under the law of another member state[9], to the statutory provisions relating to fiscal warehousing[10];

(c) where the goods in question are exported, or are in the process of being exported, to a place outside the member states[11]; or

(d) where the goods in question are moved temporarily to a place other than the relevant fiscal warehouse for repair, processing, treatment or other operations, subject to the prior agreement of, and to conditions to be imposed by, the commissioners[12].

A fiscal warehousekeeper must not remove, or allow the removal of, any eligible goods from his fiscal warehousing regime at any time before either he has inspected and placed on his fiscal warehousing record a copy of the relevant removal document issued by the Commissioners of Customs and Excise[13] or he has been provided with the registration number of a person registered for VAT and a written undertaking from that person that any VAT payable by that person as the result of any removal of eligible goods from that fiscal warehousing regime will be accounted for[14] on that person's VAT return[15]. Where a fiscal warehousekeeper allows the removal of any eligible goods to take place from his fiscal warehousing regime otherwise than in accordance with these requirements, he is jointly and severally liable with the person who removes the goods for the payment of the VAT payable[16] to the commissioners[17].

1 Ie ibid s 18F(5), (6) (as added): see para 138 post.
2 For the meaning of 'eligible goods' see para 134 note 1 ante (definition applied by the Value Added Tax Regulations 1995, SI 1995/2518, reg 145A(1) (added by SI 1996/1250)).
3 For the meaning of 'fiscal warehousing regime' see para 134 note 3 ante.
4 As to the fiscal warehousing record see para 222 post.
5 Value Added Tax Regulations 1995 reg 145H(1)(a) (regs 145H–145J added by SI 1996/1250).
6 Ibid reg 145H(1)(b) (as added: see note 5 supra).
7 Ibid reg 145H(1)(c) (as added: see note 5 supra). The person who is treated as the person who removes, or causes the removal of, the relevant goods from the relevant fiscal warehousing regime in any of the circumstances described in heads (1)–(3) in the text is either the person who causes any of those circumstances to occur or, in the case of head (3) in the text, the person who makes the retail sale there referred to: reg 145H(1) (as so added).
8 Ie in pursuance of ibid reg 145G(1) (as added): see para 135 ante. In such a case, the certificate referred to in reg 145G(3)(c) (as added) confirming the completion of a transfer of eligible goods from the relevant fiscal warehousing regime to another fiscal warehousing regime should be

received within 30 days commencing on the day on which the goods leave the fiscal warehouse: reg 145H(3), (4)(a) (as added: see note 5 supra). If it is not, or if the documents referred to in reg 145H(4)(b), (c) (as so added) (see notes 10–11 infra) are not received in time, the relevant fiscal warehousekeeper must (1) make an entry by way of adjustment to his fiscal warehousing record to show the relevant goods as having been removed from his fiscal warehousing regime at the time and on the day when they left; (2) identify in his fiscal warehousing record the person on whose instructions he allowed the goods to leave his fiscal warehouse as the person removing those goods and that person's address and registration number, if any; and (3) notify the person on whose instructions he allowed the goods to leave his fiscal warehouse that the relevant document has not been received by him in time: reg 145H(3) (as so added). For the meaning of 'registration number' see para 16 note 10 ante.

9   As to the construction of references to the law of another member state see para 11 note 1 ante.

10   Ie arrangements which correspond to the Value Added Tax Act 1994 s 18B(3) (as added) (see para 134 ante), whether or not those arrangements also correspond in effect to s 18C(1) (as added) (zero-rating of certain specified services performed in a fiscal or other warehousing regime: see para 140 post): Value Added Tax Regulations 1995 reg 145H(2)(b) (as added: see note 5 supra). A document evidencing completion of the transfer should be received within 60 days of the goods leaving the fiscal warehouse: reg 145H(3), (4)(b) (as so added). As to the action to be taken by the fiscal warehousekeeper if it is not see note 8 supra.

11   A document evidencing the export of the goods to that place should be received within 60 days of the goods leaving the fiscal warehouse: reg 145H(3), (4)(c) (as added: see note 5 supra). As to the action to be taken by the fiscal warehousekeeper if it is not see note 8 supra. As to the territories included in, or excluded from, the member states for VAT purposes see para 10 ante.

12   Ibid reg 145H(2) (as added: see note 5 supra).

13   Ie the document issued under ibid reg 145J(1) (as added: see note 5 supra): reg 145I(1)(a) (as so added). In respect of a person who is seeking to remove, or cause the removal of, eligible goods from a fiscal warehousing regime, the commissioners may accept from, or on his behalf, payment of the VAT payable (if any) as a result of that removal and issue to that person a document bearing a reference or identification number: reg 145J(1) (as so added). The commissioners need not act in accordance with this provision unless they are satisfied as to (1) the value and material time of any supply of the relevant goods in the fiscal warehousing regime which is treated as taking place in the United Kingdom under the Value Added Tax Act 1994 s 18B(4) (as added) (see para 134 ante) and the status of the person who made that supply; (2) the nature and quantity of the relevant eligible goods; (3) the value of any relevant self-supplies of specified services treated as made under s 18C(3) (as added) (see para 140 post) in the course or furtherance of his business by the person who is to remove the relevant goods, or by the person on whose behalf the goods are to be removed, at the time they are removed from the fiscal warehousing regime; and (4) the nature and material time of any relevant supplies of specified services in respect of which the self-supplies referred to in head (3) supra are treated as being identical (certain supplies of services on or in relation to goods while those goods are subject to the fiscal warehousing regime): Value Added Tax Regulations 1995 reg 145J(2) (as so added). In head (1) supra, 'status' is a reference to whether the person in question is, or is required to be, registered under the Value Added Tax Act 1994 (see para 56 et seq ante) or would be required to be so registered were it not for s 3(2), Sch 1 para 1(9) (as added) (see para 56 ante), Sch 2 para 1(7) (as added) (see para 60 ante), Sch 3 para 1(6) (as added) (see para 63 ante) or any of those provisions: Value Added Tax Regulations 1995 reg 145J(3) (as so added).

14   Ie in accordance with ibid reg 40(1)(c) (as substituted): see para 227 post.

15   Ibid reg 145I(1) (as added: see note 5 supra).

16   Ie under the Value Added Tax Act 1994 s 18D(2) (as added): see para 134 ante.

17   Value Added Tax Regulations 1995 reg 145I(2) (as added: see note 5 supra). This provision is without prejudice to the Value Added Tax Act 1994 s 18E (as added) (deficiency in fiscally warehoused goods: see para 137 post): Value Added Tax Regulations 1995 reg 145I(2) (as so added).

137. Deficiency in fiscally warehoused goods. Where goods have been subject to a fiscal warehousing regime[1] and, before being lawfully removed from the fiscal warehouse, they are found to be missing or deficient, the Commissioners of Customs and Excise may require the fiscal warehousekeeper[2] to pay immediately in respect of the missing goods, or of the whole or any part of the deficiency, as they see fit, the value added tax that would have been chargeable[3]. This provision does not, however, apply if it is shown to the satisfaction of the commissioners that the absence of, or deficiency in, the goods can be accounted for by natural waste or other legitimate cause[4].

1   As to goods subject to a fiscal warehousing regime see para 133 note 3 ante.
2   For the meaning of 'fiscal warehousekeeper' see para 133 note 3 ante.
3   Value Added Tax Act 1994 s 18E(1), (2) (s 18E added by the Finance Act 1996 s 26(1), Sch 3 para 5). 'VAT that would have been chargeable' means VAT that would have been chargeable on a supply of the missing goods, or the amount of goods by which the goods are deficient, taking place at the time immediately before the absence arose or the deficiency occurred, if the value of that supply were the open market value; but where that time cannot be ascertained to the commissioners' satisfaction, the VAT that would have been chargeable is the greater of the amounts of VAT which would have been chargeable on a supply of those goods (1) if the value of that supply were the highest open market value during the period ('the relevant period') commencing when the goods were placed in the fiscal warehousing regime and ending when the absence or deficiency came to the notice of the commissioners; or (2) if the rate of VAT chargeable on that supply were the highest rate chargeable on a supply of such goods during the relevant period and the value of that supply were the highest open market value while that rate prevailed: s 18E(3) (as so added). This provision has effect without prejudice to any penalty incurred under any other provision of the Value Added Tax Act 1994 or regulations made under it: s 18E(4) (as so added). As to penalties see para 272 et seq post. For the meaning of 'open market value' see para 87 ante.
4   Ibid s 18E(2) (as added: see note 3 supra).

138. Changes in eligible goods or in status of fiscal warehousekeeper or fiscal warehouse. Where, as a result of an operation on eligible goods[1] subject to a fiscal warehousing regime[2], they change their nature but the resulting goods are also eligible goods, the provisions relating to warehousing and fiscal warehousing[3] apply as if the resulting goods were the original goods[4]. Where, however, as a result of an operation on such goods they cease to be eligible goods, those provisions apply on their ceasing to be so as if they had at that time been removed[5] from the fiscal warehousing regime and the proprietor of the goods is treated for that purpose as if he were the person removing them[6].

Where any person ceases to be a fiscal warehousekeeper[7] or any premises cease to have fiscal warehouse[8] status, the provisions relating to warehousing and fiscal warehousing[9] apply as if the goods of which he is the fiscal warehousekeeper, or the goods in the fiscal warehouse, had at that time been removed from the fiscal warehousing regime and the proprietor of the goods is treated for that purpose as if he were the person removing them[10].

1   For the meaning of 'eligible goods' see para 134 note 1 ante.
2   As to goods subject to a fiscal warehousing regime see para 134 note 3 ante.
3   Ie the Value Added Tax Act 1994 ss 18B–18F (added by the Finance Act 1996 s 26(1), Sch 3 para 5): see paras 133 et seq ante, 139–140 post.
4   Ibid s 18F(4) (as added: see note 3 supra).
5   As to the removal of goods from a fiscal warehousing regime see para 134 note 3 ante.
6   Value Added Tax Act 1994 s 18F(5) (as added: see note 3 supra).
7   For the meaning of 'fiscal warehousekeeper' see para 133 note 3 ante.
8   For the meaning of 'fiscal warehouse' see para 133 note 3 ante.
9   See note 3 supra.
10 Value Added Tax Act 1994 s 18F(6) (as added: see note 3 supra).

139. Power to make regulations. The Commissioners of Customs and Excise may make regulations governing the deposit, keeping, securing and treatment of goods in a fiscal warehouse[1] and the removal[2] of goods from such a warehouse[3]. Without prejudice to the generality of this power, the regulations may include provisions:

(1) as to the keeping, preservation and production of records and the furnishing of returns and information by fiscal warehousekeepers and any other persons in relation to:

   (a) goods which are, have been or are to be subject to a fiscal warehousing regime[4] and other goods which are, have been or are to be kept in fiscal warehouses[5];

   (b) fiscal warehouse premises and fiscal warehousekeepers[6] and their businesses[7];

(2) requiring goods deposited in a fiscal warehouse to be produced to or made available for inspection by an authorised person on request by him[8];

(3) prohibiting the carrying out on fiscally warehoused goods of such operations as they may prescribe[9];

(4) regulating the transfer of goods from one fiscal warehouse to another[10];

(5) concerning goods which, though kept in a fiscal warehouse, are not eligible goods[11] or are not intended by a relevant person to be goods in respect of which reliefs[12] are to be enjoyed[13];

(6) prohibiting the fiscal warehousekeeper from allowing goods to be removed from the fiscal warehousing regime without payment of any value added tax payable[14] on or by reference to that removal and, if in breach of that prohibition he allows goods to be so removed, making him liable for the VAT jointly and severally with the remover[15],

and may contain such incidental or supplementary provisions as the commissioners think necessary or expedient[16]. The regulations may make different provision for different cases[17].

1   For the meaning of 'fiscal warehouse' see para 133 note 3 ante.
2   As to the removal of goods from a fiscal warehouse see para 134 note 3 ante.
3   Value Added Tax Act 1994 s 18F(7) (s 18F added by the Finance Act 1996 s 26(1), Sch 3 para 5). In the exercise of this power, the commissioners have made the Value Added Tax Regulations 1995, SI 1995/2518, Pt XVI(A) (regs 145A–145J, Sch 1A) (added by SI 1996/1250), which came into force on 1 June 1996: see the Value Added Tax (Amendment) (No 3) Regulations 1996, SI 1996/1250, reg 1(1). See also the Value Added Tax Regulations 1995 reg 40 (substituted by SI 1996/1250).
4   As to goods subject to a fiscal warehousing regime see para 134 note 3 ante.
5   Value Added Tax Act 1994 s 18F(8)(a)(i), (ii) (as added: see note 3 supra). See the Value Added Tax Regulations 1995 reg 40 (as substituted); and para 227 post; reg 145B (as added); and para 134 ante; regs 145C, 145D (as added); and para 140 post; reg 145E (as added); and para 134 ante; and reg 145F, Sch 1A (as added); and para 222 post.
6   For the meaning of 'fiscal warehousekeeper' see para 133 note 3 ante.
7   Value Added Tax Act 1994 s 18F(8)(a)(iii), (iv) (as added: see note 3 supra).
8   Ibid s 18F(8)(b) (as added: see note 3 supra). See the Value Added Tax Regulations 1995 reg 145F(5)(b) (as added); and para 222 post.
9   Value Added Tax Act 1994 s 18F(8)(c) (as added: see note 3 supra).
10   Ibid s 18F(8)(d) (as added: see note 3 supra). See the Value Added Tax Regulations 1995 reg 145G (as added); and para 135 ante.
11   For the meaning of 'eligible goods' see para 134 note 1 ante.
12   Ie under the Value Added Tax Act 1994 ss 18A–18F (as added): see paras 133 et seq ante, 140 post.
13   Ibid s 18F(8)(e) (as added: see note 3 supra).
14   Ie under ibid s 18D (as added): see paras 136, ante, 140 post.
15   Ibid s 18F(8)(f) (as added: see note 3 supra). See the Value Added Tax Regulations 1995 regs 145H–145J (as added); and para 136 ante.
16   Value Added Tax Act 1994 s 18F(8) (as added: see note 3 supra).

17 Ibid s 18F(9) (as added: see note 3 supra). This may include different provision for different fiscal warehousekeepers or descriptions of fiscal warehousekeeper, for fiscal warehousekeepers of different descriptions or for goods of different classes or descriptions or of the same class or description in different circumstances: s 18F(9) (as so added).

C. SERVICES PERFORMED WITHIN A FISCAL OR OTHER WAREHOUSING REGIME

140. Services performed within a warehousing or fiscal warehousing regime. Where a taxable person[1] makes a supply[2] of specified services[3] which are wholly performed on or in relation to goods while those goods are subject to a warehousing or fiscal warehousing regime[4], his supply is zero-rated[5] if:

(1) except where the services are the supply by an occupier of a warehouse or a fiscal warehousekeeper of warehousing or fiscally warehousing the goods, the person to whom the supply is made gives the supplier a certificate[6] that the services are performed as described above[7];

(2) the supply of services would otherwise be taxable[8] and not zero-rated[9]; and

(3) the supplier issues to the person to whom the supply is made an invoice[10] of the prescribed[11] description[12].

The advantage of zero-rating is, however, lost[13] unless there is a supply of the goods in question the material time[14] for which is (a) while the goods are subject to a warehousing or fiscal warehousing regime; and (b) after the material time for the zero-rated supply of services[15]. If there is no such supply of the goods, the following provisions apply:

(i) a supply of services identical to the zero-rated supply of services is treated for the purposes of value added tax as being both made, for the purposes of his business, to the person by whom the zero-rated supply of services was actually made and as made by him in the course or furtherance[17] of his business at the time the goods are removed from the warehousing or fiscal warehousing regime or, if earlier, at the duty point[18];

(ii) that supply has the same value as the zero-rated supply of services[19];

(iii) that supply is a taxable and not a zero-rated supply[20]; and

(iv) VAT is charged on that supply even if the person treated as making it is not a taxable person[21].

Any value added tax payable on a supply so treated as taking place on removal or on the duty point[22] must be paid at the time when the supply is so treated as taking place and by the person by whom the goods are removed or, as the case may be, by the person who is required to pay the excise duty and together with that duty[23]. The Commissioners of Customs and Excise may, however, make provision by regulations for enabling a taxable person to pay the VAT he is so required to pay at a later time[24]; and they may make different provisions for different descriptions of taxable persons and for different descriptions of goods and services[25].

1   For the meaning of 'taxable person' see paras 12 note 4, 55 ante.
2   For the meaning of 'supply' see para 21 ante.
3   For these purposes, 'specified services' means: (1) services of an occupier of a warehouse or of a fiscal warehousekeeper of keeping the goods in question in a warehousing or fiscal warehousing regime; (2) in relation to goods subject to a warehousing regime, services of carrying out on the goods operations which are permitted to be carried out under Community customs provisions or warehousing regulations; and (3) in relation to goods subject to a fiscal warehousing regime, services of carrying out on the goods any physical operations (other than any operations

prohibited by regulations made under the Value Added Tax Act 1994 s 18F (as added) (see para 139 ante) (eg preservation and repacking operations): s 18C(4) (ss 18C, 18F added by the Finance Act 1996 s 26(1), Sch 3 para 5). For these purposes 'warehouse', except in the expression 'fiscal warehouse', has the same meaning as in the Value Added Tax Act 1994 s 18(6) (see para 130 note 6 ante): Value Added Tax Act 1994 s 18F(1) (as so added). 'Warehousing regulations' means regulations made under the Customs and Excise Management Act 1979 s 93 (as amended) (see CUSTOMS AND EXCISE): Customs and Excise Management Act 1979 s 1(1) (definition applied by the Value Added Tax Act 1994 s 18F(1) (as so added)). For the meaning of 'fiscal warehouse' and 'fiscal warehousekeeper' see para 133 note 3 ante; and as to goods subject to a fiscal warehousing regime see para 134 note 3 ante. For these purposes, any reference to goods being subject to a warehousing regime (as opposed to a fiscal warehousing regime) or to the removal of goods from such a regime has the same meaning as in s 18(7) (see para 130 note 6 ante): see s 18F(3) (as so added).

4   Ibid s 18C(1)(a), (b) (as added: see note 3 supra).

5   Ibid s 18C(1) (as added: see note 3 supra). For the meaning of 'zero-rated' see para 158 post.

6   The certificate must be in such form as the Commissioners of Customs and Excise may specify by regulations: ibid s 18(1)(c) (as added: see note 3 supra). The certificate must contain the information indicated in the Value Added Tax Regulations 1995, SI 1995/2518, reg 145C, Sch 1, Form 18 (added by SI 1996/1250): reg 145C (as so added).

7   Value Added Tax Act 1994 s 18(1)(c) (as added: see note 3 supra).

8   For the meaning of 'taxable supplies' see para 12 note 3 ante.

9   Value Added Tax Act 1994 s 18C(1)(d) (as added: see note 3 supra).

10   For the meaning of 'invoice' see para 11 note 8 ante.

11   Ie of such a description as the commissioners may by regulations prescribe: Value Added Tax Act 1994 s 18C(1)(e) (as added: see note 3 supra). The invoice is to be known as a VAT invoice and must state the following particulars, unless the commissioners allow any of these requirements to be relaxed or dispensed with: (1) an identifying number; (2) the material time of the supply of the services in question; (3) the date of the issue of the invoice; (4) the name, an address and the registration number of the supplier; (5) the name and an address of the person to whom the services are supplied; (6) a description sufficient to identify the nature of the services supplied; (7) the extent of the services and the amount payable, excluding VAT, expressed in sterling; (8) the rate of any cash discount offered; (9) the rate of VAT as zero%; and (10) a declaration that in respect of the supply of services in question, the requirements of s 18C(1) (as so added) will be, or have been, satisfied: Value Added Tax Regulations 1995 reg 145D(1), (2) (added by SI 1996/1250). The supplier of the services in question must issue the invoice to the person to whom the supply is made within 30 days of the material time of that supply of services, or within such longer period as the commissioners may allow in general or special directions: reg 145D(3) (as so added). 'Material time' has the meaning given by the Value Added Tax Act 1994 s 18F(1) (as added) in the case of a fiscal warehousing regime (see para 134 note 3 ante) and the meaning given by s 18(6) (see para 130 note 5 ante) in relation to a warehousing regime: Value Added Tax Regulations 1995 reg 145A(1) (as so added).

12   Value Added Tax Act 1994 s 18C(1)(e) (as added: see note 3 supra).

13   Ie ibid s 18C(3) (as added: see note 3 supra) applies: see heads (i)–(iv) in the text.

14   For the meaning of 'material time' see para 134 note 3 ante.

15   See the Value Added Tax Act 1994 s 18C(2) (as added: see note 3 supra).

16   For the meaning of 'business' see para 17 ante.

17   As to the meaning of 'in the course or furtherance' of a business see paras 12 note 5, 17 note 2 ante.

18   Value Added Tax Act 1994 s 18C(3)(a) (as added: see note 3 supra). In other words, there is a deemed taxable self-supply. As to self-supplies see para 26 ante. For these purposes, 'duty point' has the same meaning as in s 18(6) (see para 89 note 9 ante): s 18F(1) (as so added).

19   Ibid s 18C(3)(b) (as added: see note 3 supra).

20   Ibid s 18C(3)(c) (as added: see note 3 supra).

21   Ibid s 18C(3)(d) (as added: see note 3 supra).

22   Ie a supply to which ibid s 18C(3) (as added: see note 3 supra) applies: see heads (i)–(iv) in the text.

23   Ibid s 18D(1), (2) (s 18D added by the Finance Act 1996 Sch 3 para 5).

24   Value Added Tax Act 1994 s 18D(3) (as added: see note 23 supra). See the Value Added Tax Regulations 1995, SI 1995/2518, reg 43(2) (as substituted): and para 131 ante.

25   Value Added Tax Act 1994 s 18D(3) (as added: see note 23 supra).

3. EXEMPTIONS AND RELIEFS

(1) EXEMPT SUPPLIES AND ACQUISITIONS

(i) In general

141. Meaning of 'exempt supply' and 'exempt acquisition'. A supply[1] of goods or services is an exempt supply if it is of a description for the time being specified in Schedule 9 to the Value Added Tax Act 1994 and an acquisition of goods from another member state[2] is an exempt acquisition if the goods are acquired in pursuance of an exempt supply[3]. The Treasury may by order vary the relevant provisions[4] by adding to or deleting from them any description of supply or by varying any description of supply for the time being specified in them[5]. The supplies specified are divided into the following groups[6], which are described in detail in subsequent paragraphs: (1) land[7]; (2) insurance[8]; (3) postal services[9]; (4) betting, gaming and lotteries[10]; (5) finance[11]; (6) education[12]; (7) health and welfare[13]; (8) burial and cremation[14]; (9) trades unions and professional bodies[15]; (10) sport, sports competitions and physical education[16]; (11) works of art etc[17]; (12) fund-raising events by charities and other qualifying bodies[18]; and (13) cultural services[19].

VAT is not chargeable on exempt supplies[20]. A supplier is not, therefore, entitled to credit for the input tax[21] which he incurs on supplies made to him for the purposes of his exempt activities[22]. Certain anti-avoidance measures ensure that partially exempt traders suffer an appropriate amount of irrecoverable input tax on supplies made to them for the purposes of their business[23].

Certain exemptions which are directed towards activities which are socially beneficial are available only to legal, and not to natural persons[24]. This distinction, which exists in the Sixth Directive[25], has not always been clearly made in United Kingdom law; but it is clear that an individual whose supplies would otherwise be exempted under one of the relevant exemptions may rely on the direct effect of the Sixth Directive in order to treat his supplies as standard-rated[26].

1   For the meaning of 'supply' see para 21 ante.
2   As to acquisitions of goods from other member states see para 13 ante; and for the meaning of 'another member state' see para 4 note 14 ante.
3   Value Added Tax Act 1994 s 31(1). Section 31(1), Sch 9 (as amended) is to be interpreted in accordance with the notes contained in it: s 96(9).
4   Ie ibid Sch 9 Pts I, II (as amended): see para 142 et seq post. The powers conferred by the Value Added Tax Act 1994 to vary Sch 9 (as amended) include a power to add to, vary or delete the notes thereto: s 96(9).
5   Ibid s 31(2). In exercise of the power so conferred, the Treasury has made the Value Added Tax (Education) (No 2) Order 1994, SI 1994/2969 (amending the Value Added Tax Act 1994 Sch 9 Pt II Group 6: see para 150 post); the Value Added Tax (Land) Order 1995, SI 1995/282 (amending the Value Added Tax Act 1994 Sch 9 Pt II Group 1: see para 142 post); and the Value Added Tax (Cultural Services) Order 1996, SI 1996/1256 (substituting the Value Added Tax Act 1994 Sch 9 Pt II Group 12 note 3 (see para 156 note 5 post) and adding Sch 9 Pt II Group 13 (see para 157 post). As to the making of orders generally see para 8 ante. Schedule 9 (as amended) may be varied so as to describe a supply of goods by reference to the use which has been made of them or to other matters unrelated to the characteristics of the goods themselves: s 31(2). However, the description of supplies which is contained in Sch 9 (as amended) is derived from EC Council Directive 77/388 (OJ L145 13.6.77, p 1) and, subject to limited opportunities for derogation, must reflect the exemptions which are permitted thereby: see para

3 ante; and Case 235/85 *EC Commission v Netherlands* [1987] ECR 1471, [1988] 2 CMLR 921, ECJ (exemptions from VAT must be expressly provided for and precisely defined); Case 348/87 *Stichting Uitvoering Financiële Acties v Staatssecretaris van Financiën* [1989] ECR 1737, [1991] 2 CMLR 429, ECJ (supplies of goods or services effected for consideration are, generally, to be subject to VAT and any exemption given by EC Council Directive 77/388 art 13 is to be interpreted strictly); Case C-453/93 *Bulthuis-Griffioen v Inspecteur der Omzetbelasting* [1995] ECR I-2341, [1995] STC 954, ECJ. For a fuller consideration of this topic and as to composite and separate supplies generally see para 25 text and notes 3–4 ante.

6   The descriptions of groups in the Value Added Tax Act 1994 Sch 9 (as amended) are for ease of reference only and do not affect the interpretation of the descriptions of items in them: s 96(10).

7   See para 142 post.

8   See para 146 post.

9   See para 147 post.

10   See para 148 post.

11   See para 149 post.

12   See para 150 post.

13   See para 151 post.

14   See para 152 post.

15   See para 153 post.

16   See para 154 post.

17   See para 155 post.

18   See para 156 post.

19   See para 157 post.

20   See the Value Added Tax Act 1994 s 4(1), (2); and para 12 ante.

21   For the meaning of 'input tax' see paras 4 ante, 201 post.

22   As to allowable input tax generally see the Value Added Tax Act 1994 ss 25, 26; and paras 202–203 post. As to the methods of calculating input tax where a taxable person has both taxable and exempt supplies see s 26(3); the Value Added Tax Regulations 1995, SI 1995/2518, Pt XIV (regs 99–111); and para 209 et seq post.

23   As to goods supplied to a trader for the purpose of his business see the Value Added Tax Act 1994 s 5(5); and para 26 ante (self-supply). As to the reverse charge on supplies received from abroad see s 8; and para 27 ante. These provisions only apply to traders whose business activities are exempt or partially exempt, and do not apply to final consumers who take similar steps to avoid incurring irrecoverable VAT: see paras 26–27 ante.

24   See EC Council Directive 77/388 art 13(A)(1)(b), (g), (h), (i), (l), (m), (n), (o). The corresponding provisions in the Value Added Tax Act 1994 are Sch 9 Pt II Group 7 items 4, 9 (medical treatment and welfare services: see para 151 post); Sch 9 Pt II Group 6 item 1 (education etc: see para 150 post); Sch 9 Pt II Group 7 item 10 (religious communities: see para 151 post); Sch 9 Pt II Group 9 (trade unions and professional bodies: see para 153 post); Sch 9 Pt II Group 10 (sport etc: see para 154 post); and Sch 9 Pt II Group 13 (as added) (cultural services: see para 157 post).

25   See Case C-453/93 *Bulthuis-Griffioen v Inspecteur der Omzetbelasting* [1995] ECR I-2341, [1995] STC 954, ECJ.

26   *Kaul (t/a Alpha Case Services) v Customs and Excise Comrs* (1996) VAT Decision 14028, [1996] STI 996. Regrettably, the tribunal did not explain whether its view was that EC Council Directive 77/388 art 13(A)(1)(b) had direct effect, or that the Value Added Tax Act 1994 Sch 9 Pt II Group 7 item 4 was, on a proper construction, only to be considered to extend to legal persons.

(ii) Exempt Supplies of Land

142. In general. Subject to certain exceptions[1], the grant[2] of any interest in or right over land[3] or of any licence to occupy[4] land is an exempt supply[5]. The exceptions are:

(1)   the grant of the fee simple in:

     (a)   a building which has not been completed[6] and which is neither designed as a dwelling or number of dwellings[7] nor intended for use solely for a relevant residential purpose[8] or relevant charitable purpose[9];

(b)   a new[10] building which is neither designed as a dwelling or a number of dwellings nor intended for use solely for a relevant residential purpose or a relevant charitable purpose after the grant[11];

(c)   a civil engineering work which has not been completed[12]; or

(d)   a new civil engineering work[13];

(2)   a supply made pursuant to a developmental tenancy, developmental lease, or developmental licence[14];

(3)   the grant of any interest, right or licence consisting or a right to take game or fish unless at the time of the grant the grantor grants to the grantee the fee simple of the land over which the right to take game or fish is exercisable[15];

(4)   the provision in a hotel, inn, boarding house or similar establishment[16] of sleeping accommodation or of accommodation in rooms which are provided in conjunction with sleeping accommodation or for the purpose of a supply of catering[17];

(5)   the grant of any interest in, right over, or licence to occupy holiday accommodation[18];

(6)   the provision of seasonal pitches for caravans[19], and the grant of facilities at caravan parks to persons for whom such pitches are provided[20];

(7)   the provision of pitches for tents or of camping facilities[21];

(8)   the grant of facilities for parking a vehicle[22];

(9)   the grant of any right to fell and remove standing timber[23];

(10)   the grant of facilities for housing, or storage of, an aircraft or for mooring[24], or storage of, a ship, boat or other vessel[25];

(11)   the grant of any right to occupy a box, seat or other accommodation at a sports ground, theatre, concert hall or other place of entertainment[26];

(12)   the grant of facilities for playing any sport or participating in physical recreation[27];

(13)   the grant of any right, including an equitable right or right under an option or right of pre-emption, to call for or be granted any interest or right which would fall within any of the above heads other than head (2)[28].

---

1   See heads (1)–(13) in the text.

2   'Grant' includes an assignment or surrender and the supply made by the person to whom an interest is surrendered when there is a reverse surrender: Value Added Tax Act 1994 s 31(1), Sch 9 Pt II Group 1 note 1 (substituted by the Value Added Tax (Land) Order 1995, SI 1995/282, arts 2, 3). A 'reverse surrender' is one in which the person to whom the interest is surrendered is paid by the person by whom the interest is being surrendered to accept the surrender: Value Added Tax Act 1994 Sch 9 Pt II Group 1 note 1A (added by the Value Added Tax (Land) Order 1995 arts 2, 4). A variation of a lease may take effect in law as a surrender or regrant: see generally LANDLORD AND TENANT vol 27(1) (Reissue) para 122 et seq.

    The Commissioners of Customs and Excise have had considerable difficulty in properly analysing the liability to VAT of the various supplies which may be made by a tenant or a landlord in relation to the grant, variation or surrender of a lease. Originally, they adopted the position that only the grant of the lease and the surrender of the lease could be treated as exempt from VAT; and any ancillary payments which were made (eg a reverse premium paid by the landlord to the tenant to persuade him to accept the lease, or a payment made by the tenant to the landlord to persuade him to accept the surrender or variation in the terms of a lease) were standard-rated. However, following the decision in Case C-63/92 *Lubbock Fine & Co v Customs and Excise Comrs* [1994] QB 571, [1994] STC 101, ECJ (payment received by a tenant from a landlord for surrendering the residue of a lease to the landlord is itself consideration for an exempt supply of land under EC Council Directive 77/388 (OJ L145, 13.6.77, p 1) art 13(B)(b), on the ground that where a given transaction, such as the letting of a building which would be taxed on the basis of the rents paid, falls within the scope of an exemption, a change in the contractual relationship must also be regarded as falling within the scope of the exemption), the commissioners have accepted (1) that a payment for a variation of a lease is consideration for an exempt supply unless the landlord has elected to waive exemption under the Value Added Tax Act 1994 s 51(1), Sch 10 para 2 (as amended) (see para 143 post) (Customs and Excise Business Brief 16/94 [1994] STI 1011); (2) that, in cases where the landlord has not elected to waive exemption, a payment for the lifting of a restrictive covenant is consideration for an exempt supply (Customs and Excise Business Brief 17/94 [1994] STI 1158); and (3) that, following the decision in *Central Capital Corpn Ltd v Customs and Excise Comrs* (1995) VAT Decision 13319, [1995] STI 1151 (any payment made by a landlord to a tenant or by a tenant to a landlord should be treated as potentially within the scope of the exemption in EC Council Directive 77/388 art 13(B)(b)), the supply made by a landlord in accepting the surrender of his tenant's lease in return for a payment made by the tenant is also exempt in the ordinary case (Customs and Excise Business Brief 18/95 [1995] STI 1380); and see *Lloyds Bank plc v Customs and Excise Comrs* (1996) VAT Decision 14181, [1996] STI 1358. It would appear that the decision in *Central Capital Corpn Ltd v Customs and Excise Comrs* supra may cover the case of a reverse premium paid to a tenant to induce him to accept the grant of a lease, but it is not clear that the commissioners are of this view: see Customs and Excise Notice 742 *Land and Property* (1 December 1995) para 5.2; cf *Neville Russell v Customs and Excise Comrs* [1987] VATTR 194.

An apportionment of rent between vendor and purchaser on sale of freehold reversion is outside the scope of VAT: see [1991] STI 485. It is also the long-standing policy of the commissioners that rent-free periods are outside the scope of VAT unless, in return, the tenant performs services for the landlord, eg where the tenant is obliged to fit out the building to a particular standard during the period: 20 HC Official Report (6th series) written answers col 119 (17 December 1991); but see *Ridgeon's Bulk Ltd v Customs and Excise Comrs* [1992] VATTR 169; affd [1994] STC 427. If maintenance contributions are paid to trustees for the purpose of being expended on the upkeep of a block of flats, the contributions are not consideration for a supply of services by the trustees, since the trustees have no right to deal with those moneys as their own: *Nell Gwynn House Maintenance Fund Trustees v Customs and Excise Comrs* [1996] STC 310, CA, following Case C-38/93 *HJ Glawe Spiel-und Unterhaltungsgeräte Aufstellungsgesellschaft GmbH & Co KG v Finanzamt Hamburg-Barmbeck-Uhlenhorst* [1994] ECR I-1679, [1994] STC 543, ECJ.

3   For the meaning of 'land' see para 8 note 21 ante.

4   A distinction must be drawn between the grant or assignment of a licence to occupy land (which may be exempt) and the grant or assignment of a licence to go upon land (which is not). In the view of the commissioners, a licence to occupy land is created when the following criteria are satisfied: (1) land is let, whether orally or in writing, under terms that fall short of a formal tenancy; and (2) the occupier has a clearly defined area or site to the exclusion of other people; and (3) the grant amounts to the occupation of the land rather than the right to use the facilities it may offer: Customs and Excise Notice 742 *Land and Property* (1 December 1995) para 2.7. A licence to enter the grounds of a club and enjoy its facilities is therefore standard-rated: *Trewby v Customs and Excise Comrs* [1976] 2 All ER 199, [1976] 1 WLR 932, DC; *King v Customs and Excise Comrs* [1980] VATTR 60 (the grant of a non-exclusive grazing licence was not a licence to occupy land); *Wolverhampton and Dudley Breweries plc v Customs and Excise Comrs* [1990] VATTR 131 (agreements for the installation of amusement machines did not confer a licence to occupy land). Cf *British Airports Authority v Customs and Excise Comrs* [1977] 1 All ER 497, [1977] 1 WLR 302, CA (the right to display and sell merchandise from shop in airport was an exempt licence to occupy land and did not involve a separate standard-rated supply); *Swindon Masonic Association Ltd v Customs and Excise Comrs* [1978] VATTR 200 (permission to use buildings for meeting was a licence to occupy land); *Tameside Metropolitan Borough Council v Customs and Excise Comrs* [1979] VATTR 93 (the hire for one business day of a site on which to place a market stall was an exempt licence to occupy land); *Business Enterprises (UK) Ltd v Customs and Excise Comrs* [1988] VATTR 160 (the grant of an exclusive right to occupy a serviced office suite, subject to retention of key for cleaning purposes, was an exempt composite supply of licence to occupy land); and see para 25 ante. Cf *Greater London Council v Customs and Excise Comrs* [1982] VATTR 94 (grant of a licence to use a concert hall; provision of stewards and ticket-issuing facilities by licensor were separate standard-rated supplies of services). An exempt supply of letting might lose its identity as such in a case where sufficient non-exempt supplies were added to the exempt supply to create a new composite supply: *Haringey London Borough Council v Customs and Excise Comrs* (1994) VAT Decision 12050, [1994] STI 1027 (revsd on other grounds [1995] STC 830); *Swiss National Tourist Office v Customs and Excise Comrs* (1995) VAT Decision 13192, [1995] STI 990 (payment for sharing a stand at an exhibition not consideration for an exempt supply).

5   Value Added Tax Act 1994 Sch 9 Pt II Group 1 item 1. For the meaning of 'exempt supply' see para 141 ante.

6   A building is taken to be completed when an architect issues a certificate of practical completion in relation to it or it is first fully occupied, whichever happens first; and a civil engineering work is taken to be completed when an engineer issues a certificate of completion in relation to it or it is first fully used, whichever happens first: Value Added Tax Act 1994 Sch 9 Pt II Group 1 note 2. The exemption under Sch 9 Pt II Group 1 (as amended) for the supply of land other than certain supplies relating to new or partially completed buildings and civil engineering works is intended, it seems, to reflect EC Council Directive 77/388 art 13(B)(h) which requires member states to exempt the supply of land which has not

been built on other than building land as described in art 4(3)(b), which describes building land as 'any unimproved or improved land defined as such by the member state'. In Case C-468/93 *Gemeente Emmen v Belastingdienst Grote Ondernemingen, Haren* [1996] All ER (EC) 372, [1996] STC 496, ECJ, the court held that it was for each member state, and not for the court, to define the concept of 'building land' for those purposes.

7 For the meaning of 'designed as a dwelling or a number of dwellings' see the Value Added Tax Act 1994 s 30(2), Sch 8 Pt II Group 5 note 2 (as substituted); and para 163 note 8 post (applied by Sch 9 Pt II Group 1 note 3 (amended by the Value Added Tax (Land) Order 1995 arts 2, 5)).

8 For the meaning of 'use for a relevant residential purpose' see the Value Added Tax Act 1994 Sch 8 Pt II Group 5 notes 4–5, 12 (as substituted); and para 163 note 9 post (applied by Sch 9 Pt II Group 1 note 3 (as amended: see note 7 supra)).

9 Value Added Tax Act 1994 Sch 9 Pt II Group 1 item 1(a)(i). For the meaning of 'use for a relevant charitable purpose' see Sch 8 Pt II Group 5 notes 6, 12; and para 163 note 10 post (applied by Sch 9 Pt II Group 1 note 3 (as amended: see note 7 supra)).

10 A building or civil engineering work is new if it was completed less than three years before the grant: ibid Sch 9 Pt II Group 1 note 4.

11 Ibid Sch 9 Pt II Group 1 item 1(a)(ii). The grant of the fee simple in a building completed before 1 April 1989 is not thereby excluded unless the grant is the first grant of the fee simple made on or after that date and the building was not fully occupied before that date: Sch 9 Pt II Group 1 notes 5, 6.

12 Ibid Sch 9 Pt II Group 1 item 1(a)(iii). See also note 6 supra.

13 Ibid Sch 9 Pt II Group 1 item 1(a)(iv). See also note 10 supra. The grant of the fee simple in a work completed before 1 April 1989 is not thereby excluded unless the grant is the first grant of the fee simple made on or after that date and the work was not fully used before that date: Sch 9 Pt II Group 1 notes 5, 6.

14 Ibid Sch 9 Pt II Group 1 item 1(b). A tenancy of, lease of or licence to occupy a building or work is treated as becoming a developmental tenancy, lease or licence (as the case may be) when a tenancy of, lease of or licence to occupy a building or work, whose construction, reconstruction, enlargement or extension commenced on or after 1 January 1992 is treated as being supplied to and by the developer under s 51(1), Sch 10 para 6(1) (see para 28 ante), except where Sch 10 para 6(1) applies by virtue of Sch 10 para 5(1)(b) (as substituted) (see para 28 ante): Sch 9 Pt II Group 1 note 7 (amended by the Value Added Tax (Land) Order 1995 arts 2, 6). The effect of the rule is that rent and other consideration payable under the tenancy or lease etc after 1 January 1992 becomes subject to VAT at the standard rate.

15 Value Added Tax Act 1994 Sch 9 Pt II Group 1 item 1(c). Where a grant of an interest in, right over or licence to occupy land (ie other than of the fee simple of the relevant land) includes a valuable right to take game or fish, an apportionment must be made to determine the supply so falling outside the exemption granted by Sch 9 Pt II Group 1 (as amended): Sch 9 Pt II Group 1 note 8. This operates as an exception to the general rule that a composite supply takes its status (as a standard-rated, exempt or zero-rated supply) from its principal element: see para 25 ante.

16 'Similar establishment' includes premises in which there is provided furnished sleeping accommodation, whether with or without the provision of board or facilities for the preparation of food, which are used by or held out as being suitable for use by visitors or travellers: Value Added Tax Act 1994 Sch 9 Pt II Group 1 note 9. See *Namecourt Ltd v Customs and Excise Comrs* [1984] VATTR 22; *Westminster City Council v Customs and Excise Comrs* [1989] VATTR 71. It is irrelevant that the majority of occupants may be permanently resident if the premises also offer lodging to the casual visitor: *McGrath v Customs and Excise Comrs* [1992] STC 371n. As to special rules for valuing long-stay accommodation of this kind see s 19(1), Sch 6 para 9; and para 92 ante. A student hall of residence licensed as such by a university has been held not to be carrying on business as a hotel, inn or boarding house, or to be an establishment similar thereto: *McMurray (a Governor of Allen Hall) v Customs and Excise Comrs* [1973] VATTR 161; and see also *International Students House v Customs and Excise Comrs* (1996) VAT Decision 14420, [1996] STI 1722.

17 Value Added Tax Act 1994 Sch 9 Pt II Group 1 item 1(d).

18 Ibid Sch 9 Pt II Group 1 item 1(e). 'Holiday accommodation' includes any accommodation in a building, hut (including a beach hut or chalet), caravan, houseboat or tent which is advertised or held out as holiday accommodation or as suitable for holiday or leisure use, but excludes any accommodation within head (4) in the text: Sch 9 Pt II Group 1 note 13. Schedule 9 Group 1 item 1(e) includes (1) any grant excluded from Sch 8 Pt II Group 5 item 1 (as substituted) (see para 163 post) by Sch 8 Pt II Group 5 note 13 (as substituted) (ie the grant of an interest in a building, or in part of a building, designed as a dwelling or a number of dwellings, or the site of such a building, if the interest granted is such that the grantee is not entitled to reside in the building throughout the year, or residence there throughout the year, or the use of the building or part as the grantee's principal private residence, is prevented by the terms of a covenant, statutory planning consent, or similar permission); (2) any supply made pursuant to a tenancy, lease or licence under which the grantee is or has been

permitted to erect and occupy holiday accommodation: Sch 9 Pt II Group 1 note 11 (amended by the Value Added Tax (Land) Order 1995 arts 2, 7); revsg *Haven Leisure Ltd v Customs and Excise Comrs* [1990] VATTR 77 (where it had been decided that the grant of a 40-year lease of a chalet which had previously been let as holiday accommodation was an exempt supply of the chalet and not a standard-rated supply of holiday accommodation). The Value Added Tax Act 1994 Sch 8 Pt II Group 5 note 13(a) (as substituted) (which exempts a grant of an interest in, or in any part of, a building designed as a dwelling or number of dwellings) has been criticised as being discriminatory and as exceeding the limitation on the exemption for land imposed by EC Council Directive 77/388 art 13(B)(b)(1): see *Ashworth v Customs and Excise Comrs* (1995) VAT Decision 12924, [1995] STI 478; and para 163 post. 'Houseboat' includes a houseboat within the meaning of the Value Added Tax Act 1994 Sch 8 Pt II Group 9 (ie a boat or other floating structure designed or adapted for use solely as a place of permanent habitation and not having means of, or capable of being readily adapted for, self-propulsion: see para 168 post): Sch 9 Pt II Group 1 note 10.

The exclusion from exemption under Sch 9 Pt II Group 1 item 1(e) does not extend to a grant, in respect of a building or part of a building which is not a new building (see note 7 supra), of (a) the fee simple; or (b) a tenancy, lease or licence to the extent that the grant is made for a consideration in the form of a premium: Sch 9 Pt II Group 1 note 12.

There was no taxable supply of holiday accommodation (enabling the owner to recover input tax on his expenditure) where flats had been advertised as holiday accommodation but had not been let to holidaymakers: *Cooper & Chapman (Builders) Ltd v Customs and Excise Comrs* [1993] STC 1, distinguishing *Sheppard v Customs and Excise Comrs* [1977] VATTR 272. The issue of a certificate evidencing a right to occupy a house for one or more weeks per annum in perpetuity (a time-share agreement) (*American Real Estate (Scotland) Ltd v Customs and Excise Comrs* [1980] VATTR 88), and an arrangement whereby each customer had the right to occupy for one or more weeks per annum for a period of 28 years, followed by a right to participate in the proceeds of sale of the freehold (*Cretney v Customs and Excise Comrs* [1983] VATTR 271) have both been held to be supplies of holiday accommodation. The grant of an annual licence to use a beach hut has been held to be a supply of holiday accommodation, notwithstanding that the hut might not be used as a dwelling: *Poole Borough Council v Customs and Excise Comrs* [1992] VATTR 88.

19 A seasonal pitch is a pitch which is provided for a period of less than a year or which is provided for a period longer than a year but which the person to whom it is provided is prevented by the terms of any covenant, statutory planning consent or similar permission from occupying by living in a caravan at all times throughout the period for which the pitch is provided: Value Added Tax Act 1994 Sch 9 Pt II Group 1 note 14. The supply of a residential caravan may be zero-rated under Sch 8 Pt II Group 9: Customs and Excise Leaflet 701/20/89 *Caravans and Houseboats*; and see para 168 post. The supply of services in the course of the construction of any civil engineering work necessary for the development of a permanent park for residential caravans is also zero-rated: see the Value Added Tax Act 1994 Sch 8 Pt II Group 5 item 2(b) (as substituted); and para 163 post.

20 Ibid Sch 9 Pt II Group 1 item 1(f).

21 Ibid Sch 9 Pt II Group 1 item 1(g). No distinction is made for these purposes between seasonal and permanent pitches: cf the provision made in relation to caravans (see head (6) in the text).

22 Ibid Sch 9 Pt II Group 1 item 1(h). Where a lock-up garage is let, the plain implication is that facilities have been granted for parking a vehicle unless use for that purpose is expressly precluded by the terms of the lease: *Customs and Excise Comrs v Trinity Factoring Services Ltd* [1994] STC 504. It has been held, however, that the letting of premises and sites for parking vehicles cannot be excluded from the exemption where the letting thereof is closely linked to the letting of immovable property to be used for another purpose, such as residential or commercial property, which is itself exempt, so that the two lettings constitute a single economic transaction: Case 173/88 *Skatteministeriet v Henriksen* [1989] ECR 2763, [1990] STC 768, ECJ. As to the commissioners' views see Customs and Excise Leaflet 701/24/92 *Parking Facilities* (1 September 1992).

23 Value Added Tax Act 1994 Sch 9 Pt II Group 1 item 1(j).

24 'Mooring' includes anchoring or berthing: ibid Sch 9 Pt II Group 1 note 15.

25 Ibid Sch 9 Pt II Group 1 item 1(k). Some supplies of these facilities qualify for zero-rating as 'handling services' under Sch 8 Pt II Group 8 item 6(a) when supplied in a port or Customs airport: see Customs and Excise Notice 744 *VAT: Passenger Transport, International Freight, Ships and Aircraft* (November 1984) Ch VII; and para 167 post. The supply of mooring for a houseboat is exempt: Customs and Excise Leaflet 701/20/89 *Caravans and Houseboats* para 19. See *Roberts v Customs and Excise Comrs* [1992] VATTR 30 (a temporarily unseaworthy yacht falls within the Value Added Tax Act 1994 Sch 9 Pt II Group 1 item 1(k), which does not require the vessel to be capable of navigation; and is not within Sch 8 Pt II Group 9 (see para 168 post) if not designed or adapted solely for use as a place of permanent habitation).

26 Ibid Sch 9 Pt II Group 1 item 1(l). This provision is designed to reverse both the decision in *Customs and Excise Comrs v Zinn* [1988] STC 57 (where the transfer of the residue of a 999-year lease in a specified seat in the Royal Albert Hall was held to be exempt from VAT because the ability to enjoy performances was merely consequential on, and not the subject of, the assignment of the right to the seat itself) and the decision in *Customs and Excise Comrs v Parkinson* [1989] STC 51 (see note 15 supra).

27 Value Added Tax Act 1994 Sch 9 Pt II Group 1 item 1(m). This exclusion from exemption does not apply where the grant of the facilities is for (1) a continuous period of use exceeding 24 hours; or (2) a series of ten or more periods, whether or not exceeding 24 hours in total, where the following conditions are satisfied: (a) each period is in respect of the same activity carried on at the same place; (b) the interval between each period is not less than one day and not more than 14 days; (c) consideration is payable by reference to the whole series and is evidenced by written agreement; (d) the grantee has exclusive use of the facilities; and (e) the grantee is a school, a club, an association, or an organisation representing affiliated clubs or constituent associations: Sch 9 Pt II Group 1 note 16. As to applicable commissioners' views see Customs and Excise Leaflet 742/1/90 *Letting Facilities for Sport and Physical Recreation*. Certain grants and supplies relating to sports, sports competitions and physical education may be exempted by the Value Added Tax Act 1994 Sch 9 Pt II Group 10: see para 154 post.

28 Ibid Sch 9 Pt II Group 1 item 1(n).

143. Election to waive exemption. A grant[1] made in relation to any land[2] in which a person has an interest does not fall within the exemption from value added tax[3] if and to the extent that it is made at a time when an election to waive that exemption[4] has effect in relation to the land and is made either by the person who made the election or, where that person is a body corporate, by that person or a relevant associate[5]. The owner of an interest in land who makes such an election can recover the VAT which he may suffer on, for example, construction services for the purpose of developing the land and he can avoid, in some instances, the developer's self-supply charge[6]. No input tax[7] on any supply[8] or importation which would otherwise be allowable by virtue of the operation of these provisions is, however, allowed if the supply or importation took place before the first day for which the election in question has effect[9]; but this restriction does not apply where the person by whom the election was made has not made any grant falling within the exemption provisions[10] before the first day for which it has effect[11]. In cases where input tax is allowable on a supply or importation which took place before the first day for which the election in question has effect[12], the input tax is recoverable only at the end of the prescribed accounting period in which the election is notified to the Commissioners of Customs and Excise[13]. An election may be made by conduct, as, for example by charging a tenant VAT on the rent payable under a lease[14].

The owner of an interest in land cannot, however, make such an election in relation to a grant if the grant is made:

(1) in relation to a building or part of a building intended for use as a dwelling or number of dwellings[15] or solely for a relevant residential purpose[16]; or

(2) in relation to a building or part of a building intended for use solely for a relevant charitable purpose[17] other than as an office[18]; or

(3) in relation to a pitch for a residential caravan[19]; or

(4) in relation to facilities for the mooring of a residential houseboat[20]; or

(5) to a registered housing association[21] and the association has given to the grantor a certificate stating that the land is to be used (after any necessary demolition work) for the construction of a building or buildings intended for use as a dwelling or number of dwellings or solely for a relevant residential purpose; or

(6) to an individual and the land is to be used for the construction, otherwise than in the course or furtherance of a business[23] carried on by him, of a building intended for use by him as a dwelling[24]; or

(7)   on or after 30 November 1994, if the person making the grant and the person to whom the grant is made are connected persons[25], and either of them is not a fully taxable person[26].

1   For the meaning of 'grant' see para 142 note 2 ante (definition applied by the Value Added Tax Act 1994 s 51(1), Sch 10 para 9 (amended by the Value Added Tax (Buildings and Land) Order 1995, SI 1995/279, art 9)).

2   For the meaning of 'land' see para 8 note 21 ante.

3   Ie the Value Added Tax Act 1994 s 31(1), Sch 9 Pt II Group 1 (as amended): see para 142 ante. As to when a contract for the sale of land specifies the purchase price 'deemed to be inclusive of VAT' where the vendor has not elected to waive exemption see *Jaymarke Development Ltd v Elinacre Ltd (in liquidation)* [1992] STC 575, Ct of Sess.

4   Ie an election under the Value Added Tax Act 1994 Sch 10 para 2 (as amended): see the text and notes 5–14 infra; and paras 144–145 post.

5   Ibid Sch 10 para 2(1) (amended by the Value Added Tax (Buildings and Land) Order 1994, SI 1994/3013, arts 1, 2). A 'relevant associate', in relation to a body corporate by which such an election has been made in relation to any building or land, means a body corporate which under the Value Added Tax Act 1994 s 43 (as amended) (see paras 66 ante, 191 post) (1) was treated as a member of the same group as the body corporate by which the election was made at the time when the election first had effect; (2) has been so treated at any later time when the body corporate by which the election was made had an interest in, right over or licence to occupy the building or land, or any part of it; or (3) has been treated as a member of the same group as a body corporate within head (1) or (2) supra at a time when that body corporate had an interest in, right over or licence to occupy the building or land, or any part of it: Sch 10 para 3(7).

6   As to the self-supply charge see ibid Sch 10 paras 5, 6 (as amended); and para 28 ante. Under EC Council Directive 77/388 (OJ L145, 13.6.77, p 1) art 13(C) (which permits member states to grant an option for taxation in certain cases of supply relating to land) a taxpayer may, by the exercise of such an option, convert an exempt supply into a taxable supply, although a supply which falls outside the scope of tax cannot thereby be converted into a taxable supply: Case C-291/92 *Finanzamt Uelzen v Armbrecht* [1995] ECR I-2775, [1995] STC 997, ECJ.

7   For the meaning of 'input tax' see paras 4 ante, 201 post.

8   For the meaning of 'supply' see para 21 ante.

9   Value Added Tax Act 1994 Sch 10 para 2(4). This restriction has been held not to be inconsistent with EC Council Directive 77/388 art 17: *Newcourt Property Fund v Customs and Excise Comrs* (1991) VAT Decision 5825 (unreported); *Bradshaw (Taylor Dyne Ltd Pension Fund Trustees) v Customs and Excise Comrs* [1992] VATTR 315; *Acre Friendly Society v Customs and Excise Comrs* [1992] VATTR 308.

10   Ie falling within the Value Added Tax Act 1994 Sch 9 Pt II Group 1 (as amended): see para 142 ante.

11   Ibid Sch 10 para 2(5)(a). Nor does Sch 10 para 2(4) apply (1) in relation to any election having effect from any day on or after 1 January 1992, except in relation to input tax on a supply or importation which took place before 1 August 1989 (Sch 10 para 2(8)); or (2) in relation to input tax on grants or other supplies made in the period beginning with 1 April 1989 and ending with 31 July 1989 if (a) they would have been zero-rated by virtue of Sch 8 Pt II Group 5 items 1, 2 (see para 163 post) or exempt by virtue of Sch 9 Pt II Group 1 item 1 (as amended) (see para 142 ante) but for the amendments made by the Finance Act 1989 s 18, Sch 3; and (b) the election has effect from 1 August 1989 (Value Added Tax Act 1994 Sch 10 para 2(7) (amended by the Value Added Tax (Buildings and Land) Order 1995, SI 1995/279, arts 2, 3)); or (3) where the person by whom the election was made has, before the first day for which the election has effect, made in relation to that land a grant or grants falling within the Value Added Tax Act 1994 Sch 9 Pt II Group 1 (as amended), but the grant, or all the grants, were made in the period beginning with 1 April 1989 and ending with 31 July 1989, and would have been taxable supplies but for the amendments made by the Finance Act 1989 Sch 3 (Value Added Tax Act 1994 Sch 10 para 2(5)(b)). Schedule 10 para 2(5) does not make allowable any input tax on supplies or importations taking place before 1 August 1989 unless (i) it is attributable by or under regulations to grants made by the person on or after 1 April 1989 which would have been taxable supplies but for the amendments made by the Finance Act 1989 Sch 3; and (ii) the election has effect from 1 August 1989: Value Added Tax Act 1994 Sch 10 para 2(6).

13   *Lawson Mardon Group Pension Scheme v Customs and Excise Comrs* (1993) VAT Decision 10231, [1993] STI 948.

14   *Fencing Supplies Ltd v Customs and Excise Comrs* [1993] VATTR 302.

15   As to the meaning of 'intended for use as a dwelling or a number of dwellings' see the Value Added Tax Act 1994 s 30(2), Sch 8 Pt II Group 5 note 2 (as substituted); and para 163 note 8 post (applied by Sch 10 para 9 (amended by the Value Added Tax (Buildings and Land) Order 1995 arts 2, 9)).

16　Value Added Tax Act 1994 Sch 10 para 2(2)(a). For the meaning of 'use for a relevant residential purpose' see Sch 8 Pt II Group 5 notes 4–5, 12 (as substituted); and para 163 note 9 post (applied by Sch 10 para 9 (as amended: see note 15 supra)). By concession, with effect from 12 February 1996, Sch 10 para 2(2)(a) may be disregarded where a grant in relation to a building or part of a building is made to a person who intends to make a grant of that building, or part, which will be zero-rated by virtue of Sch 8 Pt II Group 5 item 1(b) (as substituted: see para 163 post): Customs and Excise Press Notice 9/96 (13 February 1996) [1996] STI 307. The effect of this is to enable the VAT incurred prior to the sale of commercial property which is to be converted into domestic dwellings to be recovered in full, rather than being passed on as part of the price for an exempt supply, as was previously the case.

17　For the meaning of 'use for a relevant charitable purpose' see the Value Added Tax Act 1994 Sch 8 Pt II Group 5 notes 6, 12; and para 163 note 10 post (applied by Sch 10 para 9 (as amended: see note 15 supra)).

18　Ibid Sch 10 para 2(2)(b).

19　Value Added Tax Act 1994 Sch 10 para 2(2)(c) (added by the Value Added Tax (Buildings and Land) Order 1995, SI 1995/279, arts 2, 3). A caravan is not a residential caravan if residence in it throughout the year is prevented by the terms of a covenant, statutory planning consent or similar permission: Value Added Tax Act 1994 Sch 8 Pt II Group 5 note 19 (as substituted) (applied by Sch 10 para 9 (as amended: see note 15 supra).

20　Ibid Sch 10 para 2(2)(d) (added by the Value Added Tax (Buildings and Land) Order 1995 arts 2, 3). For these purposes, 'houseboat' means a boat or other floating decked structure designed or adapted for use solely as a place of permanent habitation and not having means of, or capable of being readily adapted for, self-propulsion: Value Added Tax Act 1994 Sch 8 Pt II Group 9 item 2 (applied by Sch 10 para 3(7A)(a) (added by the Value Added Tax (Buildings and Land) Order 1995 arts 2, 4)). A houseboat is not a residential houseboat if residence in it throughout the year is prevented by the terms of a covenant, statutory planning consent or similar permission: Value Added Tax Act 1994 Sch 10 para 3(7A)(b) (as so added).

21　'Registered housing association' means a registered housing association within the meaning of the Housing Associations Act 1985 (see HOUSING): Value Added Tax Act 1994 Sch 10 para 3(8).

22　Ibid Sch 10 para 2(3)(a).

23　For the meaning of 'in the course or furtherance of a business' see paras 12 note 5, 17 note 2 ante.

24　Value Added Tax Act 1994 Sch 10 para 2(3)(b).

25　For these purposes, any question whether a person is connected with another is to be determined in accordance with the Income and Corporation Taxes Act 1988 s 839 (as amended) (see INCOME TAXATION vol 23 (Reissue) para 1250): Value Added Tax Act 1994 s 96(1), Sch 10 para 3(8A)(a) (added by the Value Added Tax (Buildings and Land) Order 1994, SI 1994/3013, arts 1, 2(b)).

26　Value Added Tax Act 1994 Sch 10 para 2(3A) (added by the Value Added Tax (Buildings and Land) Order 1994 arts 1, 2(a)). A person is a fully taxable person for these purposes if at the end of the prescribed accounting period of his in which the grant is made he is entitled to credit for input tax on all supplies to, and acquisitions and importations by, him in that period, apart from any on which the input tax is excluded from credit by virtue of the Value Added Tax Act 1994 s 25(7) (see para 108 post): Sch 10 para 3(8A)(b) (as added: see note 25 supra). For the meaning of 'prescribed accounting period' see para 202 note 4 post.

144. Effect of election to waive exemption. An election to waive exemption[1] has effect in relation to any land[2] specified, or of a description specified, in the election[3], although where it is made in relation to a building, or part of a building (or planned building), it has effect in relation to the whole of the building and all the land within its curtilage. The election has effect, subject to the provisions set out below[5], either from the beginning of the day on which it is made or of any later day specified in it or, where the election was made before 1 November 1989, from the beginning of 1 August 1989 or of any later day so specified[6]. In addition, in the case of a body corporate, an election binds not only that body but also any relevant associate[7] of that body[8].

An election made before 1 March 1995 has effect after that date only if it also had effect before that date or if written notification of the election is given to the Commissioners of Customs and Excise not later than the end of the period of 30 days beginning with the day on which the election was made, or not later than the end of such longer period beginning with that day as the commissioners may in any particular case allow, together with such information as they may require[9].

An election made on or after 1 March 1995 has effect after that date only if (1) written notification of the election is given to the commissioners not later than the end of the period of 30 days beginning with the day on which the election is made, or not later than the end of such longer period beginning with that day as the commissioners may in any particular case allow, together with such information as they may require; and (2) in a case in which the prior written permission of the commissioners must be obtained[10], that permission has been given[11]. Such prior written permission is required where a person who wishes to make an election in relation to any land ('the relevant land') to have effect on or after 1 January 1992 has made, makes or intends to make an exempt grant[12] in relation to the relevant land at any time between 1 August 1989 and before the beginning of the day from which he wishes an election in relation to the relevant land to have effect[13]. In such a case he may not make an election in relation to the relevant land unless the conditions for automatic permission specified in a notice published by the commissioners[14] are met or he obtains the prior written permission of the commissioners[15]. The commissioners must give such permission only if they are satisfied, having regard to all the circumstances of the case and in particular to (a) the total value of exempt grants in relation to the relevant land made or to be made before the day from which the person wishes his election to have effect; (b) the expected total value of grants relating to the relevant land that would be taxable if the election were to have effect; and (c) the total amount of input tax which has been incurred on or after 1 August 1989 or is likely to be incurred in relation to the relevant land, that there would be secured a fair and reasonable attribution of the input tax mentioned in head (c) above to grants in relation to the relevant land which, if the election were to have effect, would be taxable[16]. An owner of an interest in land who wishes to obtain such permission to waive exemption is expected to write to his local value added tax office setting out proposals for the attribution of previously incurred input tax[17].

1   Ie an election under the Value Added Tax Act 1994 s 51(1), Sch 10 para 2 (as amended): see para 143 ante.
2   For the meaning of 'land' see para 8 note 21 ante.
3   Value Added Tax Act 1994 Sch 10 para 3(2).
4   Ibid Sch 10 para 3(3). For these purposes, buildings which are linked internally or by a covered walkway, and complexes consisting of a number of units grouped around a fully inclosed concourse, are taken to be a single building (if they would otherwise not be): Sch 10 para 3(3) (amended by the Value Added Tax (Buildings and Land) Order 1995, SI 1995/279, arts 2, 4).
5   Ie the Value Added Tax Act 1994 Sch 10 para 3(6)–(9) (as amended): see the text and notes 6–18 infra; and para 145 post.
6   Ibid Sch 10 para 3(1).
7   For the meaning of 'relevant associate' see para 143 note 5 ante.
8   See the Value Added Tax Act 1994 Sch 10 para 2(1) (as amended); and para 143 ante. The election is given such a wide scope to prevent the landowner obtaining the benefits of the recovery of input tax whilst avoiding the corresponding output VAT charge on sale by transferring the land within its VAT group. As to VAT groups see para 191 post; and as to the effect of the existence of the option to waive exemption on stamp duty see Inland Revenue Statement of Practice SP 11/91 (12 September 1991) [1991] STI 818; and Institute of Chartered Accountants of England and Wales Guidance Note 19/92 *Inland Revenue Statement of Practice SP 11/91 – Stamp Duty and VAT; Interaction* (14 December 1992) [1992] STI 1109. For the meaning of 'input tax' and 'output tax' see paras 4 ante, 201 post.
9   Value Added Tax Act 1994 Sch 10 para 3(6)(a) (substituted by the Value Added Tax (Buildings and Land) Order 1995 arts 2, 4).
10 See the text and notes 12–15 infra.
11 Value Added Tax Act 1994 Sch 10 para 3(6)(b) (as substituted: see note 9 supra).
12 For the meaning of 'grant' see para 142 note 2 ante (definition applied by ibid Sch 10 para 9 (amended by the Value Added Tax (Buildings and Land) Order 1995, SI 1995/279, art 9)).
13 Value Added Tax Act 1994 Sch 10 para 3(9).
14 At the date at which this volume states the law, no such notice had been published.
15 Value Added Tax Act 1994 Sch 10 para 3(9) (amended by the Value Added Tax (Buildings and Land) Order 1995 arts 2, 4). Where, after such an election has been made, the building in question would fall

within the scope of the capital goods scheme (see para 216 post), it is not open to the commissioners to accept a method of attribution and recovery of input tax other than that laid down by the capital goods scheme itself: *Customs and Excise Comrs v R & R Pension Fund Trustees* [1996] STC 889. Quaere whether there is a right of appeal to the VAT and duties tribunal if the appellant's complaint is as to the conditions imposed by the commissioners under the Value Added Tax Act 1994 Sch 10 para 3(9) (as so amended): see *Customs and Excise Comrs v R & R Pension Fund Trustees* supra at 896 per Buxton J, referring to *Kohanzad v Customs and Excise Comrs* [1994] STC 967, *John Dee Ltd v Customs and Excise Comrs* [1995] STC 941, CA and *Customs and Excise Comrs v JH Corbitt (Numismatists) Ltd* [1981] AC 22, [1980] 2 All ER 72, HL; *Island Trading Co Ltd v Customs and Excise Comrs* (1996) VAT Decision 13838, [1996] STI 572. As to the decisions against which an appeal lies see para 296 post.

16   Value Added Tax Act 1994 Sch 10 para 3(9).
17   Customs and Excise Notice 742 *Land and Property* (1 December 1995) para 9.8.

145. Revocability of election to waive exemption. Subject to certain exceptions[1], an election to waive exemption[2] is irrevocable[3]. Where, however, less than three months have elapsed since the day on which the election had effect and:

    (1)   no tax has become chargeable and no credit for input tax[4] has been claimed by virtue of the election; and

    (2)   no grant[5] in relation to the land[6] which is the subject of the election has been made which, by virtue of being a supply[7] of the assets of a business[8] to a person to whom the business (or part of it) is being transferred as a going concern, has been treated as neither a supply of goods nor a supply of services; and

    (3)   the person making the election obtains the written consent of the Commissioners of Customs and Excise,

the election may be revoked from the date on which it was made[9].

Where more than 20 years have elapsed since the day on which the election had effect and the person making the election obtains the written consent of the commissioners, the election may be revoked from the date on which that consent is given or such later date as they may specify in that consent[10].

1   See the text and notes 3–10 infra.
2   Ie an election under the Value Added Tax Act 1994 s 51(1), Sch 10 para 2 (as amended): see para 143 ante.
3   Ibid Sch 10 para 3(4) (substituted by the Value Added Tax (Buildings and Land) Order 1995, SI 1995/279, arts 2, 4).
4   As to credits for input tax see paras 202–203 post. For the meaning of 'input tax' see paras 4 ante, 201 post.
5   For the meaning of 'grant' see para 142 note 2 ante (definition applied by the Value Added Tax Act 1994 Sch 10 para 9 (amended by the Value Added Tax (Buildings and Land) Order 1995 arts 2, 9)).
6   For the meaning of 'land' see para 8 note 21 ante.
7   For the meaning of 'supply' see para 21 ante.
8   For the meaning of 'business' see para 17 ante.
9   Value Added Tax Act Sch 10 para 3(5) (substituted by the Value Added Tax (Buildings and Land) Order 1995 arts 2, 4).
10   Value Added Tax Act Sch 10 para 3(5) (as substituted: see note 9 supra).

(iii) Other Exempt Supplies

146. Insurance. Supplies of the following descriptions are exempt supplies[1]:

    (1)   the provision of insurance and reinsurance by (a) a person permitted in accordance with the Insurance Companies Act 1982[2] to carry on insurance business; or (b) an insurer who belongs outside the United Kingdom[3] against any risks or other things described in certain provisions[4] of that Act[5];

    (2)   the provision of insurance and reinsurance by the Export Credits Guarantee Department[6];

(3)   the making of arrangements for the provision of any such insurance or reinsurance as is mentioned above[7]; and

(4)   the handling of insurance claims by insurance brokers, insurance agents and persons permitted to carry on insurance business as described in head (1) above[8].

1   See the Value Added Tax Act 1994 s 31(1), Sch 9 Pt II Group 2; and heads (1)–(4) in the text. For the meaning of 'exempt supply' see para 141 ante. As to the views of the Commissioners of Customs and Excise on this Group see Customs and Excise Leaflet 701/36/92 *Insurance* (1 February 1992). A reverse charge may arise under the Value Added Tax Act 1994 s 8 (see para 27 ante), eg where insurance services (including reinsurance, but not including the provision of safe deposit facilities) are supplied by a person belonging in a country other than the United Kingdom and are received by a person who belongs in the United Kingdom for the purposes of any business carried on by him, unless the services fall within the exemptions provided in the Value Added Tax Act 1994 Sch 9 (as amended). See further para 27 ante.

2   Ie in accordance with the Insurance Companies Act 1982 s 2 (as amended): see INSURANCE vol 25 (Reissue) para 19.

3   For the meaning of 'United Kingdom' see para 4 note 3 ante.

4   Ie described in the Insurance Companies Act 1982 ss 1, 3, Schs 1, 2 (as amended): see INSURANCE vol 25 (Reissue) para 18.

5   Value Added Tax Act 1994 Sch 9 Pt II Group 2 item 1. It was held, eg, that when a consumer hired a television set and, at the same time and by the same agreement, applied to enter into an insurance policy with an insurance company, and each appellant was the holding company of a group of companies of which one hired television sets and another was an insurance company, there were separate supplies of the hire of the television (standard-rated) and of insurance (exempt), rather than a single composite supply of a television: *Thorn EMI plc and Granada plc v Customs and Excise Comrs* [1993] VATTR 94. But a company which provided card registration services and in addition engaged an insurance broker to provide a policy of insurance indemnifying the cardholder against fraudulent misuse of his credit cards for a fee of £16 was held simply to be making a standard-rated supply of convenience, to which the provision of insurance was merely incidental: *Card Protection Plan Ltd v Customs and Excise Comrs* [1994] 1 CMLR 756, [1994] STC 199, CA. The handling for a fee of a claim on behalf of a committee set up to negotiate policies on behalf of a number of insurance companies is a supply of services for a consideration and is not exempt as part of the provision of insurance: *National Transit Insurance Co Ltd v Customs and Excise Comrs* [1974] VATTR 158. As to composite and separate supplies see para 25 ante.

6   Value Added Tax Act 1994 Sch 9 Pt II Group 2 item 2. As to the Export Credits Guarantee Department see TRADE, INDUSTRY AND INDUSTRIAL RELATIONS vol 47 (Reissue) para 801 et seq.

7   Ibid Sch 9 Pt II Group 2 item 3. The provision of a credit card protection scheme containing a very small element of insurance was a single supply of a card registration service; but, that apart, would have qualified in part as making arrangements for the provision of insurance, notwithstanding that the insurance contract was made between the insurance company and the trader: *Card Protection Plan Ltd v Customs and Excise Comrs* [1994] 1 CMLR 756, [1994] STC 199, CA; cf *Company Moves v Customs and Excise Comrs* [1990] VATTR 50 (where a removal firm agrees to indemnify a customer against breakages and takes out insurance to meet that liability, the firm provides insurance to that customer of a kind falling within the Value Added Tax Act 1994 Sch 9 Pt II Group 2 item 1 (but not exempt because it is not permitted to carry on insurance business as required) and is not making arrangements within Sch 9 Pt II Group 2 item 3, since the customer has no rights against the insurance company).

    It has been held that Sch 9 Pt II Group 2 item 3 does not restrict exemption to cases where the trader had negotiated a specific insurance policy with an insurance company on behalf of a customer, but extends to (1) the carrying out of a direct mail campaign on behalf of the insurance company to customers of members of the Barclays group of companies (*Barclays Bank plc v Customs and Excise Comrs* [1991] VATTR 466); (2) supplies made to insurance brokers in the form of the creation of new insurance products and the negotiation with insurers for the underwriting of such products (*Countrywide Insurance Marketing Ltd v Customs and Excise Comrs* [1994] 3 CMLR 125, [1993] VATTR 277); and (3) arranging travel insurance with insurers on behalf of and for ferry operators to provide to their passengers (*Curtis Edington and Say Ltd v Customs and Excise Comrs* (1994) VAT Decision 11699, [1994] STI 451); cf *Company Moves v Customs and Excise Comrs supra; Dogbreeders Associates v Customs and Excise Comrs* [1989] VATTR 317. Following these decisions the commissioners announced their intention of carrying out a review of the scope of certain exemptions described in the Value Added Tax Act 1994 Sch 9 Pt II Group 2: see Customs and Excise News Release 52/94 [1994] STI 1643.

8   Value Added Tax Act 1994 Sch 9 Pt II Group 2 item 4. Schedule 9 Pt II Group 2 item 4 does not include supplies by loss adjusters, average adjusters, motor assessors, surveyors or other experts, or legal services in connection with the assessment of any claim: Sch 9 Pt II Group 2 item 4 proviso. The separate fee charged by an insurance broker for arranging the valuation of a car for the purposes of a policy of

insurance was exempt as an integral part of the provision of that policy: *Lancaster Insurance Services Ltd v Customs and Excise Comrs* (1991) VAT Decision 5455, [1991] STI 76. It has been held that where the appellant carried on business, inter alia, as trustee of various pension funds, and in the course of that business various policies of insurance to secure the payment of annuities were effected, the appellant's services were neither arrangements made for the provision of insurance within the Value Added Tax Act 1994 Sch 9 Pt II Group 2 item 3 (since the business, qua trustee, was the insured) nor handling of insurance claims within Sch 9 Pt II Group 2 item 4: *Federated Pensions Services Ltd v Customs and Excise Comrs* [1992] VATTR 358.

147. Postal services. The conveyance of postal packets[1] by the Post Office[2] and the supply by the Post Office of any services in connection with the conveyance of postal packets are exempt supplies[4]. Where a retailer sells goods by mail order and adds postage as a separate item on the bill, the separate charge is nevertheless, as a general rule, subject to value added tax at the standard rate because the charge is for the service of delivering goods through the Post Office and not a disbursement[5]. In certain cases direct mailing services may be treated as an exempt disbursement[6]. International freight transport and ancillary transport services may be zero-rated or outside the scope of VAT in certain circumstances, such as where goods are transported to or from a place outside the European Community[7].

1   'Postal packet' means a letter, postcard, reply postcard, newspaper, printed packet, sample packet or parcel, and every packet or article transmissible by post other than a telegram: Post Office Act 1953 s 87(1) (applied with modifications by the Value Added Tax Act 1994 s 31(1), Sch 9 Pt II Group 3 note 1).
2   Value Added Tax Act 1994 Sch 9 Pt II Group 3 item 1.
3   Ibid Sch 9 Pt II Group 3 item 2. Schedule 9 Pt II Group 3 item 2 does not include the letting on hire of goods: Sch 9 Pt II Group 3 note 2. The sale of unused United Kingdom or Isle of Man postage stamps which are valid for postage (ie stamps denominated in decimal currency or in multiples of £1, being of the present monarch's reign) are not subject to VAT if sold at or below face value; but VAT is charged on the amount by which the price paid exceeds the face value of the stamp: see Customs and Excise Leaflet 701/8/85 *Postage Stamps and Philatelic Supplies*. Stamps over 100 years old may fall within the margin scheme for antique dealers: see para 188 post.
4   Value Added Tax Act 1994 Sch 9 Pt II Group 3. For the meaning of 'exempt supply' see para 141 ante.
5   *BSN (Import and Export) Ltd v Customs and Excise Comrs* [1980] VATTR 177.
6   See Customs and Excise Leaflet 700/24/94 *Postage and Delivery Charges* (1 June 1994).
7   See para 50 ante.

148. Betting, gaming and lotteries. The provision of any facilities[1] for the placing of bets or the playing of any game of chance[2] is an exempt supply[3]. This exemption does not, however, extend to or include:

(1)   admission to any premises[4]; or

(2)   the granting of a right to take part in a game in respect of which a charge may be made by virtue of certain regulations under the Gaming Act 1968[5]; or

(3)   the provision by a club of such facilities to its members as are available to them on payment of their subscription but without further charge; or

(4)   the provision of a gaming machine[6].

The granting of a right to take part in a lottery is also an exempt supply[7].

1   Although the meaning of 'the provision of any facilities for the placing of bets or the playing of a game of chance', is inherently unclear, when construed in the light of the wording and purpose of EC Council Directive 77/388 (OJ L145, 13.6.77, p 1) art 13(B)(f) it excludes gambling from the scope of VAT. It does not, however, exclude the physical supply of gambling equipment to a casino from charge: *Customs and Excise Comrs v Annabel's Casino* [1995] STC 225.
2   'Game of chance' has the meaning given in the Gaming Act 1968 (see s 52 (as amended); and BETTING, GAMING AND LOTTERIES vol 4(1) (Reissue) para 123): Value Added Tax Act 1994 s 31(1), Sch 9 Pt II Group 4 note 2.
3   Ibid Sch 9 Pt II Group 4 item 1. For the meaning of 'exempt supply' see para 141 ante.

4   Where a charge is made on entry to a club on nights when bingo is to be played, it must be asked whether payment is made in order to play the game or in order to gain admission to the premises: *Tynewydd Labour Working Men's Club and Institute v Customs and Excise Comrs* [1979] STC 570.

5   Ie regulations made by virtue of the Gaming Act 1968 s 14: see CLUBS vol 6 (Reissue) para 339.

6   Value Added Tax Act 1994 Sch 9 Pt II Group 4 item 1 note 1. 'Gaming machine' means a machine in respect of which the following conditions are satisfied: (1) it is constructed or adapted for playing a game of chance by means of it; and (2) a player pays to play the machine (except where he has an opportunity to play payment free as the result of having previously played successfully) either by inserting a coin or token into the machine or in some other way; and (3) the element of chance in the game is provided by means of the machine: Value Added Tax Act 1994 Sch 9 Pt II Group 4 item 1 note 3. As to the valuation of the consideration provided in the case of a supply of services by way of a gaming machine see para 96 ante. The imposition of VAT on the proceeds from gaming machines is not incompatible with EC Council Directive 77/388 art 13(B)(f): *R v Ryan* [1994] 2 CMLR 399, [1994] STC 446; *Feehan v Customs and Excise Comrs* [1995] 1 CMLR 193, [1995] STC 75; see also Case C-38/93 *HJ Glawe Spiel-und Unterhaltungsgeräte Aufstellungsgesellschaft GmbH & Co v Finanzamt Hamburg-Barmbeck-Uhlenhorst* [1994] ECR I-1679, [1994] STC 543, ECJ.

7   Value Added Tax Act 1994 Sch 9 Pt II Group 4 item 2.

149.   Finance. Supplies of the following descriptions are exempt supplies[1]:

(1)   the issue, transfer or receipt of, or any dealing with, money[2], any security for money or any note or order for the payment of money[3];

(2)   the making of any advance or the granting of any credit[4];

(3)   the provision of the facility of instalment credit finance in a hire-purchase, conditional sale or credit sale agreement for which facility a separate charge is made and disclosed to the recipient of the supply of goods[5];

(4)   the provision of administrative arrangements and documentation and the transfer of title to goods in connection with the supply described in head (3) above if the total consideration therefor is specified in the agreement and does not exceed £10[6];

(5)   the making of arrangements for any transaction comprised in head (1), (2), (3) or (4) above or the underwriting of an issue within head (1) above[7];

(6)   the issue, transfer or receipt of, or any dealing with, certain securities or secondary securities which are:

(a)   shares, stocks, bonds, notes (other than promissory notes), debentures, debenture stock or shares in an oil royalty; or

(b)   any document[8] relating to money, in any currency, which has been deposited with the issuer or some other person, being a document which recognises an obligation to pay a stated amount to bearer or to order, with or without interest, and being a document by the delivery of which, with or without indorsement, the right to receive that stated amount is transferable; or

(c)   any bill, note or other obligation of the Treasury or of a government in any part of the world, being a document by the delivery of which, with or without indorsement, title is transferable, and not being an obligation which is or has been legal tender in any part of the world; or

(d)   any letter of allotment or rights, any warrant conferring an option to acquire a security included in this head or in heads (a) to (c) above or head (e) below, any renounceable or scrip certificates, rights coupons, coupons representing dividends or interest on such a security, bonds mandates or other documents conferring or containing evidence of title to or rights in respect of such a security; or

(e) units or other documents conferring rights under any trust established for the purpose, or having the effect of providing, for persons having funds available for investment, facilities for the participation by them as beneficiaries under the trust, in any profits or income arising from the acquisition, holding, management or disposal of any property whatsoever[9];

(7) the making of arrangements for, or the underwriting of, any transaction within head (6) above[10];

(8) the operation of any current, deposit or savings account[11]; and

(9) the management of an authorised unit trust scheme or of a trust-based scheme by the operator of the scheme[12].

These provisions include within their scope any supply by a person carrying on a credit card, charge card or similar payment card operation made in connection with that operation to a person who accepts the card used in the operation when presented to him in payment for goods or services[13]. Accordingly, where a credit card company pays a discounted amount to a retailer consequent upon the cardholder purchasing goods with the assistance of the card, the credit card company makes a supply of finance[14] to the retailer[15]. Whether the issuer of 'fuel cards' supplies finance or petrol depends on a combination of the precise terms of the contract between the parties and of the determination of when property in the fuel passed to the cardholder[16].

1 See the Value Added Tax Act 1994 s 31(1), Sch 9 Pt II Group 5; and heads (1)–(9) in the text. Schedule 9 Pt II Group 5 does not include the supply of a coin or a banknote as a collector's piece or as an investment article: Sch 9 Pt II Group 5 note 2. For the meaning of 'exempt supply' see para 141 ante.

2 'Dealing with money' does not include the service of transporting cash between bank branches (*Williams & Glyn's Bank v Customs and Excise Comrs* [1974] VATTR 262) or the restocking of cash machines (*Nationwide Anglia Building Society v Customs and Excise Comrs* (1994) VAT Decision 11826, [1994] STI 607); but cf a credit-checking service provided by a security firm, involving the collecting, opening and counting of sealed cash containers from a bank's customers (*Barclays Bank plc v Customs and Excise Comrs* [1988] 2 CMLR 263, [1988] VATTR 23). For the meaning of 'money' see para 7 note 5 ante.

3 Value Added Tax Act 1994 Sch 9 Pt II Group 5 item 1. Transactions falling within Sch 9 Pt II Group 5 item 6 (see head (6) in the text) are excluded from Sch 9 Pt II Group 5 item 1: Sch 9 Pt II Group 5 note 1.

4 Ibid Sch 9 Pt II Group 5 item 2. This provision includes the supply of credit by a person, in connection with a supply of goods or services by him, for which a separate charge is made and disclosed to the recipient of the supply of goods or services: Sch 9 Pt II Group 5 note 3. As to the requirement of a stated specified separate charge see the text and note 5 infra. For the meaning of 'supply' see para 21 ante.

5 Ibid Sch 9 Pt II Group 5 item 3. A separate charge is made (so that the supply is exempt), even if not expressly stated, if the charge can be determined by a simple calculation from the information made available to the customer: *Freight Transport Leasing Ltd v Customs and Excise Comrs* [1991] VATTR 142.

6 Value Added Tax Act 1994 Sch 9 Pt II Group 5 item 4.

7 Ibid Sch 9 Pt II Group 5 item 5. Where a solicitor's firm retains the interest on its client general deposit account, that retention is consideration for an exempt supply: *Hedges and Mercer v Customs and Excise Comrs* [1976] VATTR 146. Neither the service provided by an investigator in checking the status of debts for a bank prior to its making a loan against the debts (*Minster Associates v Customs and Excise Comrs* (1990) VAT Decision 4580, [1990] STI 353) nor the provision of facilities, against a fee, by an estate agent to financial consultants to enable them to interview possible clients (*Wright Manley Ltd v Customs and Excise Comrs* (1993) VAT Decision 10295, [1993] STI 980) is exempt under the Value Added Tax Act 1994 Sch 9 Pt II Group 5 item 5. As to what constitutes the making of arrangements for the granting of credit see *Barclays Bank plc v Customs and Excise Comrs* [1991] VATTR 466; *Countrywide Insurance Marketing Ltd v Customs and Excise Comrs* [1994] 3 CMLR 125, [1993] VATTR 277; and *Curtis Edington and Say Ltd v Customs and Excise Comrs* (1994) VAT Decision 11699, [1994] STI 451 (all of which were concerned with the making of arrangements for the provision of insurance); and para 146 note 4 ante. Whilst there has to be a clear nexus between the arrangements and the granting of credit, the arrangements do not need to lead to a specific exempt transaction: *Civil Service Motoring Association v Customs and Excise Comrs* (1996) VAT Decision 14022, [1996] STI 993.

8 For the meaning of 'document' see para 11 note 8 ante.

9 Value Added Tax Act 1994 Sch 9 Pt II Group 5 item 6.

10 Ibid Sch 9 Pt II Group 5 item 7. The service of acting as an intermediary between a lender and a bank borrowing against the issue of a certificate of deposit has been held to be making arrangements for a

transaction within head (6) in the text (for which there was no exemption under the legislation then applicable): *Customs and Excise Comrs v Guy Butler (International) Ltd* [1977] QB 377, [1976] 2 All ER 700, CA. The Value Added Tax Act 1994 Sch 9 Pt II Group 5 item 7 includes the introduction to a person effecting transactions in securities or secondary securities within Sch 9 Pt II Group 5 item 6 (see head (6) in the text) of a person seeking to acquire or dispose of such securities: Sch 9 Pt II Group 5 note 5.

11 Ibid Sch 9 Pt II Group 5 item 8.

12 Ibid Sch 9 Pt II Group 5 item 9. 'Authorised unit trust scheme' and 'operator' have the same meanings as in the Financial Services Act 1986 s 207(1); and 'trust based scheme' has the same meaning as in the Financial Services Act 1986 (Single Property Schemes) (Exemption) Regulations 1989, SI 1989/28, reg 2(1)(b): Value Added Tax Act 1994 Sch 9 Pt II Group 5 note 6.

13 Ibid Sch 9 Pt II Group 5 note 4.

14 Ie within ibid Sch 9 Pt II Group 5 item 1: see head (1) in the text.

15 *Customs and Excise Comrs v Diners Club Ltd* [1989] 2 All ER 385, [1989] STC 407, CA.

16 See *Harpur Group Ltd v Customs and Excise Comrs* (1994) VAT Decision 12001, [1994] STI 716. The commissioners subsequently commenced a review of the terms of all such cards: Customs and Excise Business Brief 25/94 [1994] STI 1645.

150. Education. Supplies of the following descriptions are exempt supplies[1]:

(1)   the provision by an eligible body[2] of education, research (where supplied to an eligible body) or vocational training[3];

(2)   the supply of private tuition, in a subject ordinarily taught in a school or university, by an individual teacher acting independently of an employer[4];

(3)   the provision of examination services[5] by or to an eligible body, or to a person receiving education or vocational training which is either exempt by virtue of head (1) or (2) above or head (5) below or is provided otherwise than in the course or furtherance of a business[6];

(4)   the supply of any goods or services (other than examination services) which are closely related to a supply of a description falling within head (1) above ('the principal supply') by or to the eligible body making the principal supply provided both that the goods or services are for the direct use of the pupil, student or trainee (as the case may be) receiving the principal supply and that, where the supply is to the eligible body making the principal supply, it is made by another eligible body[7];

(5)   the provision of vocational training, and the supply of any goods or services essential thereto by the person providing the vocational training[8], to the extent that the consideration payable is ultimately a charge to funds provided pursuant to arrangements[9] made under certain statutes[10];

(6)   the provision of facilities by a youth club[11] or an association of youth clubs to its members or by an association of youth clubs to members of a youth club which is a member of that association[12].

1 See the Value Added Tax Act 1994 s 31(1), Sch 9 Pt II Group 6; and heads (1)–(6) in the text. For the meaning of 'exempt supply' see para 141 ante.

2 An 'eligible body' for these purposes is:

(1)   a school within the meaning of the Education Acts 1944 to 1993 which is (a) provisionally or finally registered or deemed to be registered as a school within the meaning of that legislation in a register of independent schools; or (b) a school in respect of which grants are made by the Secretary of State to the proprietor or managers; or (c) a maintained school within the meaning of the Education Act 1993; or (d) a grant-maintained school within the meaning of the Education Act 1993 s 22; or (e) a grant-maintained special school within the meaning of the Education Act 1993 s 182(3) (Value Added Tax Act 1994 Sch 9 Pt II Group 6 note 1(a));

(2)   a United Kingdom University, and any college, institution, school or hall of such a university (Sch 9 Pt II Group 6 note 1(b));

(3)   an institution falling within the Further and Higher Education Act 1992 s 91(3)(a), (b) or s 91(5)(b), (c) (Value Added Tax Act 1994 Sch 9 Pt II Group 6 note 1(c));

(4)   a public body of a description in Sch 9 Pt II Group 7 note 5 (see para 151 note 2 post) (Sch 9 Pt II Group 6 note 1(d));

(5)   a body which is precluded from distributing and does not distribute any profit it makes and which applies any profits made from supplies of a description within Sch 9 Pt II Group 6 (as amended) to the continuance or improvement of such supplies (Sch 9 Pt II Group 6 note 1(e) (substituted by the Value Added Tax (Education) (No 2) Order 1994, SI 1994/2969, arts 2, 3));

(6)   a body not falling within heads (1) to (5) supra which provides the teaching of English as a foreign language (Value Added Tax Act 1994 Sch 9 Pt II Group 6 note 1(f) (substituted by the Value Added Tax (Education) (No 2) Order 1994 arts 2, 4)).

As to the Education Acts 1944 to 1993 (and those which may now be cited by the collective title Education Acts 1944 to 1994) see the Education Act 1994 s 27(2); and EDUCATION. For the meaning of 'school' in those Acts see the Further and Higher Education Act 1992 s 14(5); and EDUCATION. For the meaning of 'United Kingdom' see para 4 note 3 ante.

A supply by a body which is an eligible body only by virtue of falling within head (6) supra does not fall within the Value Added Tax Act 1994 Sch 9 Pt II Group 6 (as amended) in so far as it consists of the provision of anything other than the teaching of English as a foreign language: Sch 9 Pt II Group 6 note 2 (amended by the Value Added Tax (Education) (No 2) Order 1994 arts 2, 5). As to the earlier test, ie whether the body was providing education otherwise than for profit, see *Customs and Excise Comrs v Bell Concord Educational Trust Ltd* [1990] 1 QB 1040, [1989] 2 All ER 217, CA. There is a systematic intention to make a profit (in the terms of EC Council Directive 77/388 (OJ L145, 13.6.77, p 1) art 13(A)(2)(a)) where an individual carries on activities in a manner which seeks to achieve a positive revenue not exceeding the amount which she would have had to pay another as an employed person: Case C-453/93 *Bulthuis-Griffioen v Inspecteur der Omzetbelasting* [1995] ECR I-2341 at 2349–2350, [1995] STC 954 at 959, ECJ (opinion of the Advocate-General); and see *Manuel (t/a Stage Coach Centre for the Performing Arts) v Customs and Excise Comrs* (1992) VAT Decision 6623, [1992] STI 47; and cf *North London College of Accountancy Ltd v Customs and Excise Comrs* (1996) VAT Decision 14054, [1996] STI 1101. In any event an eligible 'body' can only be a legal person and not a school carried on by an individual (or, presumably, a partnership): *Bulthuis-Griffioen v Inspecteur der Omzetbelasting* supra; *Kaul (t/a Alpha Care Services) v Customs and Excise Comrs* (1996) VAT Decision 14028, [1996] STI 996.

3   Value Added Tax Act 1994 Sch 9 Pt II Group 6 item 1. 'Vocational training' means training, retraining or the provision of work experience for any trade, profession or employment, or any voluntary work connected with (1) education, health, safety, or welfare; or (2) the carrying out of activities of a charitable nature: Value Added Tax Act 1994 Sch 9 Pt II Group 6 note 3 (substituted by the Value Added Tax (Education) (No 2) Order 1994 arts 2, 6). The supply to a sponsor of the services of a youth trainee in accordance with the Youth Training Scheme is taxable at the standard rate, even though the consideration received from the sponsor is applied in the provision of vocational training: *North West Leicestershire Youth Training Scheme Ltd v Customs and Excise Comrs* [1989] VATTR 321.

4   Value Added Tax Act 1994 Sch 9 Pt II Group 6 item 2.

5   Examination services' include the setting and marking of examinations, the setting of educational or training standards, the making of assessments and other services provided with a view to ensuring educational and training standards are maintained: ibid Sch 9 Pt II Group 6 note 4.

6   Ibid Sch 9 Pt II Group 6 item 3.

7   Ibid Sch 9 Pt II Group 6 item 4. The provision of car parking facilities in a university for the use of staff is incidental to (and presumably, therefore, closely related to) the provision of education: see *RA Archer v Customs and Excise Comrs (No 2)* [1975] VATTR 1.

8   For these purposes, a supply of goods or services is not to be taken to be essential to the provision of vocational training unless the goods or services are provided directly to the trainee: Value Added Tax Act 1994 Sch 9 Pt II Group 6 note 5.

9   Ie arrangements made under the Employment and Training Act 1973 s 2 (as substituted and amended): see EMPLOYMENT vol 16 (Reissue) para 436. As to VAT exemption for supplies of government-funded vocational training see Customs and Excise Business Brief 13/96 (July 1996) [1996] STI 1201.

10   Value Added Tax Act 1994 Sch 9 Pt II Group 6 item 5. The provision of master-classes for a fee by the members of a quartet in connection with the teaching services of two universities has been held to be the exempt supply of the provision of education by each university to the students and not the provision of services by the quartet to the universities: *Alberni String Quartet v Customs and Excise Comrs* [1990] VATTR 166; sed quaere. For a similar decision in another context see *Clark v Customs and Excise Comrs* [1996] STC 263.

11   A club is a 'youth club' if (1) it is established to promote the social, physical, educational or spiritual development of its members; (2) its members are mainly under 21 years of age; and (3) it is precluded from distributing and does not distribute any profit it makes, and applies any profits made from supplies of a description within the Value Added Tax Act 1994 Sch 9 Pt II Group 6 (as amended) to the continuance or improvement of such supplies: Sch 9 Pt II Group 6 note 6 (applying Sch 9 Pt II Group

6 note 1(e) (i), (ii) (as substituted: see note 2 head (5) supra)). Schedule 9 Pt II Group 6 note 6 in fact refers to satisfying the requirements of Sch 9 Pt II Group 6 note 1(f)(i), (ii) but it is apprehended that this should have been amended to refer to Sch 9 Pt II Group 6 note 1(e)(i), (ii) when note 1 was amended by the Value Added Tax (Education) (No 2) Order 1994.

12   Value Added Tax Act 1994 Sch 9 Pt II Group 6 item 6. The World Association of Girl Guides and Girl Scouts is not a youth club or association of youth clubs within the meaning of Sch 9 Pt II Group 6 item 6 (*World Association of Girl Guides and Girl Scouts v Customs and Excise Comrs* [1984] VATTR 28); and the Value Added Tax Act 1994 Sch 9 Pt II Group 6 item 6 does not extend to a club part of which has a youth section (*Haggs Castle Golf Club v Customs and Excise Comrs* (1995) VAT Decision 13653, [1995] STI 1979). See also Customs and Excise Notice 701/35/95 *Youth Clubs* (1 July 1992) para 2.

151. Health and welfare. Supplies of the following descriptions are exempt supplies[1]:

(1)   the supply of services by a person registered or enrolled in certain specified registers of health practitioners[2];

(2)   the supply of any services or dental prostheses by persons registered or enrolled in certain registers of dental practitioners or by a dental technician[3];

(3)   the supply of any services by a person registered in the register of pharmaceutical chemists[4];

(4)   the provision of care[5] or medical or surgical treatment and, in connection with it, the supply of any goods, in any hospital or other institution approved, licensed, registered or exempted from registration by any minister or other authority pursuant to a provision of a public general Act of Parliament, not being a provision which is capable of being brought into effect at different times in relation to different local authority areas[6];

(5)   the provision of a deputy for a person registered in the register of medical practitioners or the register of medical practitioners with limited registration[7];

(6)   human blood[8];

(7)   products for therapeutic purposes, derived from human blood[9];

(8)   human (including foetal) organs or tissue for diagnostic or therapeutic purposes or medical research[10];

(9)   the supply, otherwise than for profit[11], by a charity or public body[12] of welfare services[13] and of goods supplied in connection therewith[14];

(10)   the supply, otherwise than for profit, of goods and services incidental to the provision of spiritual welfare by a religious community to a resident member of that community in return for a subscription or other consideration paid as a condition of membership[15]; and

(11)   the supply of transport services for sick or injured persons in vehicles specially designed for that purpose[16].

1   See the Value Added Tax Act 1994 s 31(1), Sch 9 Pt II Group 7; and heads (1)–(11) in the text. For the meaning of 'exempt supply' see para 141 ante.

2   Ibid Sch 9 Pt II Group 7 item 1. The relevant registers are as follows: (1) the register of medical practitioners and the register of medical practitioners with limited registration; (2) either of the registers of ophthalmic opticians or the register of dispensing opticians kept under the Opticians Act 1989 or either of the lists kept under s 9 of bodies corporate carrying on business as ophthalmic opticians or as dispensing opticians; (3) any register kept under the Professions Supplementary to Medicine Act 1960; (4) the register of qualified nurses, midwives and health visitors kept under the Nurses, Midwives and Health Visitors Act 1979 s 10; (5) the register of dispensers of hearing aids or the register of persons employing such dispensers maintained under the Hearing Aid Council Act 1968 s 2: Value Added Tax Act 1994 Sch 9 Pt II Group 7 item 1(a)–(e) . As to these registers and rolls see MEDICINE.

    The United Kingdom has a discretion as to whether or not to extend the exemption to particular paramedical organisations: *Barkworth v Customs and Excise Comrs* [1988] 3 CMLR 759, [1988] STC 771. For the purposes of the Value Added Tax Act 1994 Sch 9 Pt II Group 7, a person who is not registered in the visiting EC practitioners list in the register of medical practitioners at the time he performs services in an urgent case of the kind mentioned in the Medical Act 1983 s 18(3) (see MEDICINE) is to be treated as being registered in that list where he is entitled to be registered in accordance with s 18: Value Added Tax Act 1994 Sch 9 Pt II Group 7 note 4.

Exemption is not granted under Sch 9 Pt II Group 7 item 1 to the letting on hire of goods except where the letting is in connection with a supply of other services comprised in the item: Sch 9 Pt II Group 7 note 1; and see *Aslan Imaging Ltd v Customs and Excise Comrs* [1989] VATTR 54; cf *Cleary & Cleary (t/a Mobile X-Rays) v Customs and Excise Comrs* (1992) VAT Decision 7305, [1992] STI 532. Exemption is extended to include supplies of services made by a person who is not registered or enrolled in any of the registers or rolls specified in the Value Added Tax Act 1994 Sch 9 Pt II Group 7 item 1(a)–(d) where the services are wholly performed or directly supervised by a person who is so registered or enrolled: Sch 9 Pt II Group 7 note 2. The supply of medical facilities by a company employing doctors and nurses is standard-rated: *Harlow Industrial Health Service Ltd v Customs and Excise Comrs* [1974] VATTR 30. Guidelines have been issued to the representative bodies of the healthcare professions as to what the commissioners will accept as 'direct supervision': see Customs and Excise News Release 23/96 (11 April 1996) [1996] STI 704. As to supplies made by hospitals see the text and note 5 infra. An agency providing self-employed temporary nurses to hospitals is providing nurses and not nursing services and its services are not therefore within the Value Added Tax Act 1994 Sch 9 Pt II Group 7 item 1: *Customs and Excise Comrs v Reed Personnel Services Ltd* [1995] STC 588. See also *British Nursing Co-operation Ltd v Customs and Excise Comrs* (1992) VAT Decision 8816, [1992] STI 1036; *Sheffield and Rotherham Nursing Agency v Customs and Excise Comrs* (1993) VAT Decision 11279, [1993] STI 1621; *South Hams Nursing Agency v Customs and Excise Comrs* (1995) VAT Decision 13027, [1995] STI 710. Cf *Allied Medicare Nursing Services Ltd v Customs and Excise Comrs* (1991) VAT Decision 5485, [1991] STI 79; *Elder Home Care Ltd v Customs and Excise Comrs* (1993) VAT Decision 11185, [1993] STI 1390.

Where spectacles are supplied by a company which employs a dispensing optician to advise and fit the customer with the spectacles, the company makes both a standard-rated supply of the spectacles and an exempt supply of the services of the optician: *Customs and Excise Comrs v Leightons Ltd, Customs and Excise Comrs v Eye-Tech Opticians (No 1) and Eye-Tech Opticians (No 2)* [1995] STC 458; and see Case 353/85 *EC Commission v United Kingdom* [1988] ECR 817, [1988] STC 251, ECJ. Where a supply of drugs or prostheses is integral to a supply of medical care in a hospital it is necessarily exempt as part of that larger composite supply of medical care and cannot be recharacterised as a zero-rated supply of drugs: *Customs and Excise Comrs v Wellington Private Hospital* [1995] STC 628. As to single and composite supplies see para 25 ante.

3 Value Added Tax Act 1994, Sch 9 Pt II Group 7 item 2. The specified registers etc are: (1) the dentists' register; and (2) any roll of dental auxiliaries having effect under the Dentists Act 1984 s 45: Value Added Tax Act 1994 Sch 9 Pt II Group 7 item 2(a), (b) . Exemption is extended to include supplies of services made by a person who is not so registered or enrolled where the services are wholly performed or directly supervised by a person who is so registered or enrolled: Sch 9 Pt II Group 7 note 2. For a useful statement of practice issued by the commissioners on VAT and supplies by dentists see VAT Information Sheet 5/96 *VAT: Supplies by Dentists* (May 1996) [1996] STI 1112.

4 Value Added Tax Act 1994 Sch 9 Pt II Group 7 item 3. The register is that kept under the Pharmacy Act 1954: see MEDICINE. The letting of goods on hire is not exempt under the Value Added Tax Act 1994 Sch 9 Pt II Group 7 item 3: Sch 9 Pt II Group 7 note 3.

5 The provision of care extends, but is limited, to services supplied for patients necessarily involving in their performance some personal contact with the patients; and the exemption covers not only the supply of employees to perform such services but also the supply of the services of persons supervising and controlling the performance of such services; and cleaning services provided by a contractor are therefore not exempt: *Crothall & Co Ltd v Customs and Excise Comrs* [1973] VATTR 20. The provision of telephones to patients is not exempt: *League of Friends of Poole General Hospital v Customs and Excise Comrs* (1993) VAT Decision 10621, [1993] STI 1189. However, the provision of accommodation and food to a child patient's parent is a necessary ingredient of the supply of care to the child and is thus exempt: *Nuffield Nursing Home Trust v Customs and Excise Comrs* [1989] VATTR 62.

6 Value Added Tax Act 1994, Sch 9 Pt II Group 7 item 4. This provision does not exempt the provision of care by individuals or other natural persons; but applies only to legal persons: *Kaul (t/a Alpha Care Services) v Customs and Excise Comrs* (1996) VAT Decision 14208, [1996] STI 996, following Case C-453/93 *Bulthuis-Griffioen v Inspecteur der Omzetbelasting* [1995] ECR I-2341, [1995] STC 954, ECJ. Like all exemptions, it must be read in the context of its European source, which exempts 'hospital and medical care and closely related activities undertaken by bodies governed by public law or, under social conditions comparable to those applicable to bodies governed by public law, by hospitals, centres for medical treatment or diagnosis and other duly recognised establishments of a similar nature': see EC Council Directive 77/388 (OJ L145, 13.6.77, p 1) art 13(A)(1)(b). Nevertheless, the European provision appears to be significantly narrower than the United Kingdom equivalent, which exempts 'care or medical or surgical treatment' and so

implies that the care itself need not be medical. As to care in this context see the text and note 5 supra. As to the interpretation of the Value Added Tax Act 1994 generally see para 3 ante. For the meaning of 'local authority' see para 56 note 21 ante.

7   Ibid Sch 9 Pt II Group 7 item 5.

8   Ibid Sch 9 Pt II Group 7 item 6.

9   Ibid Sch 9 Pt II Group 7 item 7.

10   Ibid Sch 9 Pt II Group 7 item 8.

11   The phrase 'otherwise than for profit' must be interpreted in the context of EC Council Directive 77/388 art 13(A)(2)(a): *Customs and Excise Comrs v Bell Concord Educational Trust Ltd* [1990] 1 QB 1040, [1989] 2 All ER 217, CA. There is a systematic intention to make a profit (in the terms of EC Council Directive 77/388 art 13(A)(2)(a)) where an individual carries on activities in a manner which seeks to achieve a positive revenue not exceeding the amount which she would have had to pay another as an employed person: Case C-453/93 *Bulthuis-Griffioen v Inspecteur der Omzetbelasting* [1995] ECR I-2341 at 2349–2350, [1995] STC 954 at 959, ECJ (opinion of the Advocate-General); and see *Manuel (t/a Stage Coach Centre for the Performing Arts) v Customs and Excise Comrs* (1992) VAT Decision 6623, [1992] STI 47; and cf *North London College of Accountancy Ltd v Customs and Excise Comrs* (1996) VAT Decision 14054, [1996] STI 1101.

12   'Public body' means: (1) a government department within the meaning of the Value Added Tax Act 1994 s 41(6) (see para 194 post); (2) a local authority; (3) a body which acts under any enactment or instrument for public purposes and not for its own profit and which performs functions similar to those of a government department or local authority: Sch 9 Pt II Group 7 note 5.

13   'Welfare services' means services which are directly connected with (1) the provision of care, treatment or instruction designed to promote the physical or mental welfare of elderly, sick, distressed or disabled persons; (2) the protection of children and young persons; or (3) the provision of spiritual welfare by a religious institution as part of a course of instruction or a retreat, not being a course or a retreat designed primarily to provide recreation or a holiday: ibid Sch 9 Pt II Group 7 note 6.

14   Ibid Sch 9 Pt II Group 7 item 9, which implements EC Council Directive 77/388 art 13(A)(1)(g): *Yoga for Health Foundation v Customs and Excise Comrs* [1985] 1 CMLR 340, [1984] STC 630. The Value Added Tax Act 1994 Sch 9 Pt II Group 7 item 9 does not include the supply of accommodation or catering except where it is ancillary to the provision of care, treatment or instruction: Sch 9 Pt II Group 7 note 7. Cf *International Bible Students Association v Customs and Excise Comrs* [1988] 1 CMLR 491, [1988] STC 412 and *Peterborough Diocesan Conference and Retreat House v Customs and Excise Comrs* (1996) VAT Decision 14081, [1996] STI 1236. The provision of 'extra sheltered housing' supplied to persons not capable of caring for themselves may involve the supply of welfare services within the Value Added Tax Act 1994 Sch 9 Pt II Group 7 item 9: *Viewpoint Housing Association Ltd v Customs and Excise Comrs* (1995) VAT Decision 13148, [1995] STI 831. This provision does not exempt the provision of care by individuals or other natural persons, but applies only to legal persons: Case C-453/93 *Bulthuis-Griffioen v Inspecteur der Omzetbelasting* [1995] ECR I-2341, [1995] STC 954, ECJ; and see *Kaul (t/a Alpha Care Services) v Customs and Excise Comrs* (1996) VAT Decision 14208, [1996] STI 996.

15   Value Added Tax Act 1994 Sch 9 Pt II Group 7 item 10.

16   Ibid Sch 9 Pt II Group 7 item 11.

152. Burial and cremation. Supplies of the following descriptions are exempt supplies[1]: (1) the disposal of the remains of the dead[2]; and (2) the making of arrangements for or in connection with such disposal[3].

1   See the Value Added Tax Act 1994 s 31(1), Sch 9 Pt II Group 8; and heads (1)–(2) in the text. For the meaning of 'exempt supply' see para 141 ante.

2   Ibid Sch 9 Pt II Group 8 item 1.

3   Ibid Sch 9 Pt II Group 8 item 2.

153. Trade unions and professional bodies. Supplies by any of the following non-profit-making organisations to its members of such services[1] and, in connection with those services, of such goods as are both referable only to the organisation's aims and are available without payment other than a membership subscription[2] are exempt supplies[3]:

(1)   a trade union[4] or other organisation of persons having as its main object the negotiation on behalf of its members of the terms and conditions of their employment[5];

(2) a professional association, membership of which is wholly or mainly restricted to individuals who have or are seeking a qualification appropriate to the practice of the profession concerned[6];

(3) an association whose primary purpose is the advancement of a particular branch of knowledge, or the fostering of professional expertise, connected with the past or present professions or employments of its members[7];

(4) an association whose primary purpose is to make representations to the government on legislation and other public matters which affect the business or professional interests of its members[8].

1   This exemption does not include any right of admission to any premises, event or performance to which non-members are admitted for a consideration: Value Added Tax Act 1994 s 31(1), Sch 9 Pt II Group 9 note 1.
2   Ibid Sch 9 Pt II Group 9 applies, inter alia, to organisations and associations whose membership consists wholly or mainly of constituent or affiliated associations which as individual associations would be comprised within Sch 9 Pt II Group 9; and 'member' is to be construed as including such an association and 'membership subscription' includes an affiliation fee or similar levy: Sch 9 Pt II Group 9 note 3.
3   See ibid Sch 9 Pt II Group 9; and heads (1)–(4) in the text. For the meaning of 'exempt supply' see para 141 ante. As to the meaning of 'otherwise than for profit' see para 151 note 11 ante.
4   'Trade union' has the meaning assigned to it by the Trade Union and Labour Relations (Consolidation) Act 1992 s 1 (see TRADE, INDUSTRY AND INDUSTRIAL RELATIONS vol 47 (Reissue) para 1001): Value Added Tax Act 1994 Sch 9 Pt II Group 9 note 2.
5   Ibid Sch 9 Pt II Group 9 item 1(a).
6   Ibid Sch 9 Pt II Group 9 item 1(b).
7   Ibid Sch 9 Pt II Group 9 item 1(c). This item does not apply unless the association restricts its membership wholly or mainly to individuals whose present or previous professions or employments are directly connected with the purposes of the association: Sch 9 Pt II Group 9 note 4. An association of managers of local authority recreation facilities is not a professional association: *Institute of Leisure and Amenity Management v Customs and Excise Comrs* [1988] STC 602. An association comprising the directors of every United Kingdom polytechnic is not an association of professional persons and does not have as its purpose the fostering of teaching as an art: *Committee of Directors of Polytechnics v Customs and Excise Comrs* [1993] 2 CMLR 490, [1992] STC 873. A voluntary association of employees in the retail motor trade, whose objects were to improve work standards and career structures with a view to enhancing the public image of the trade and those who worked in it, was not a professional organisation because the range of activities undertaken by its members was too diverse: *Institute of the Motor Industry v Customs and Excise Comrs* (1996) VAT Decision 14393, [1996] STI 1642.
    The Value Added Tax Act 1994 Sch 9 Pt II Group 9 item 1(c) does not apply unless membership is restricted wholly or mainly to individuals whose present or previous profession or employment is (or was) directly connected with the purposes of the association: *Royal Photographic Society v Customs and Excise Comrs* [1978] VATTR 191. An association whose primary purpose was to advance the education of the public in organic farming (a branch of the science of agriculture) was within the Value Added Tax Act 1994 Sch 9 Pt II Group 9 item 1(c) since the association was likely to improve its own members' ability to understand and make use of such science in connection with their own employment: *British Organic Farmers v Customs and Excise Comrs* [1988] VATTR 64. An association whose primary purpose was the advancement of a particular branch of knowledge connected with the past or present professions or employments of its members was within the Value Added Tax Act Sch 9 Pt II Group 9 item 1(c) notwithstanding that it was not a professional organisation: *British Association for Counselling v Customs and Excise Comrs* (1994) VAT Decision 11855, [1994] STI 638.
8   Value Added Tax Act 1994 Sch 9 Pt II Group 9 item 1(d). This item does not apply unless the association restricts its membership wholly or mainly to individuals or corporate bodies whose business or professional interests are directly connected with the purposes of the association: Sch 9 Pt II Group 9 note 5. For the meaning of 'business' see para 17 ante.

154. Sport, sports competitions and physical education. Supplies of the following descriptions are exempt supplies[1]:

(1) the grant of a right to enter a competition in sport or physical recreation where the consideration for the grant consists in money[2] which is to be allocated wholly towards the provision of a prize or prizes awarded in that competition[3];

(2)   the grant, by a non-profit making body established for the purposes of sport or physical recreation, of a right to enter a competition in such an activity[4];

(3)   the supply by a non-profit making body[5] to an individual, except, where the body operates a membership scheme, to an individual who is not a member[6], of services closely linked with, and essential to, sport or physical education in which the individual is taking part[7].

1   See the Value Added Tax Act 1994 s 31(1), Sch 9 Pt II Group 10; and heads (1)–(3) in the text. For the meaning of 'exempt supply' see para 141 ante.

2   For the meaning of 'money' see para 7 note 5 ante.

3   Value Added Tax Act 1994 Sch 9 Pt II Group 10 item 1. Match fees paid to meet expenses and not paid on to the competition organisers are not exempt: *Wimborne Rugby Football Club v Customs and Excise Comrs* (1990) VAT Decision 4547, [1990] STI 215.

4   Value Added Tax Act 1994 Sch 9 Pt II Group 10 item 2.

5   For the purposes of ibid Sch 9 Pt II Group 10 item 3 (but not, apparently, for the purposes of Sch 9 Pt II Group 10 item 2), a 'non-profit making body' does not include: (1) a local authority; (2) a government department within the meaning of ibid s 41(6) (see para 194 post); or (3) a non-departmental public body which is listed in *Public Bodies* (Office of Public Service and Science; 1993 Edn): Value Added Tax Act 1994 Sch 9 Pt II Group 10 note 3. The exemption under Sch 9 Pt II Group 10 item 3 extends beyond competition fees to fees charged for casual play by members: *Chard Bowling Club v Customs and Excise Comrs* (1995) VAT Decision 13575, [1995] STI 1732. See, however, *Royal Pigeon Racing Association v Customs and Excise Comrs* (1996) VAT Decision 14006, [1996] STI 963 (the exemption, which is derived from EC Council Directive 77/388 art 13(A)(1)(m), does not extend to sports where the individual to whom the services are supplied does not take part in the main sporting activity, which is carried out by an animal or bird); and see the written answer of the European Commission to European Parliamentary Written Question E-3320/95 (OJ C173, 17.06.96, p 5) (although the application of EC Council Directive 77/388 art 13(A)(1)(m) is mandatory in all member states, by the use of the phrase 'certain services' (in exempting 'certain services closely linked to sport or physical education ...'), the legal text gives some discretion to national authorities). As to the meaning of 'otherwise than for profit' see para 151 note 11 ante.

6   An individual is only considered to be a member of a non-profit making body for the purposes of the Value Added Tax Act 1994 Sch 9 Pt II Group 10 item 3 where he is granted membership for a period of three months or more: Sch 9 Pt II Group 10 note 2. Where a sports centre operated by a charitable trust or similar non-profit making body makes a supply of sporting or physical education services of a kind which would normally qualify for exemption from VAT but does not operate a full membership scheme (eg the members do not have voting rights) such services will, if provided to individuals or groups of individuals, be exempt from VAT irrespective of whether the users are called members. However, where there is a full membership scheme, which operates in relation to selected activities, exemption of qualifying services is restricted to supplies to members: Customs and Excise Business Brief 3/96 [1996] STI 309, following *Basingstoke and District Sports Trust Ltd v Customs and Excise Comrs* (1995) VAT Decision 13347, [1995] STI 1273.

7   Value Added Tax Act 1994 Sch 9 Pt II Group 10 item 3. There is no need for the recipient of the supply to be engaged physically in the sport when the supply was made, so that berthing and hard-standing fees charged by a yacht club to its members were exempt within Sch 9 Pt II Group 10 item 3: *Swansea Yacht and Sub-Aqua Club v Customs and Excise Comrs* (1996) VAT Decision 13938, [1996] STI 829. As to the need to apportion where dissociable supplies of sporting and other services are provided see *Royal Thames Yacht Club v Customs and Excise Comrs* (1996) VAT Decision 14046, [1996] STI 1020. The Value Added Tax Act 1994 Sch 9 Pt II Group 10 item 3 does not include the supply of any services by a non-profit making body of residential accommodation, catering or transport: Sch 9 Pt II Group 10 note 1.

155. Works of art. Supplies of the following descriptions are exempt supplies[1]:

(1)   the disposal of an object with respect to which estate duty is not chargeable[2];

(2)   the disposal of an object with respect to which inheritance tax is not chargeable[3] by virtue of the conditional exemption relating to deaths before 7 April 1976[4];

(3)   the disposal of property with respect to which inheritance tax is not chargeable[5] by virtue of the statutory provisions relating to gifts for national purposes or disposals in satisfaction of tax[6];

(4)   the disposal of an asset in a case in which any gain accruing on that disposal is not a chargeable gain[7] by virtue of the statutory provisions relating to works of art[8].

Exemption is thus given on the disposal of items on which conditional exemption for estate duty or inheritance tax purposes has been conferred; on the disposal of items of substantial public interest which are sold by private treaty to a national museum at a reduced price in order to exclude them from a charge to inheritance tax; and to works of art which are accepted by the Treasury in satisfaction of a liability to inheritance tax[9].

1   See the Value Added Tax 1994 s 31(1), Sch 9 Pt II Group 11; and heads (1)–(4) in the text. For the meaning of 'exempt supply' see para 141 ante.

2   Ibid Sch 9 Pt II Group 11 item 1. The reference to estate duty which is not chargeable is to estate duty not chargeable by virtue of the Finance Act 1953 s 30(3), the Finance Act 1956 s 34(1) or the Finance Act 1930 s 40(2)(proviso) (all repealed): Value Added Tax Act 1994 Sch 9 Pt II Group 11 item 1. As to the transition from estate duty (now abolished) see the Inheritance Tax Act 1984 s 273, Sch 6 (as amended); and INHERITANCE TAXATION.

3   Ie by virtue of the Inheritance Tax Act 1984 s 35(1), Sch 5 paras 1(3)(a), 1(4), 3(4)(a) or by virtue of the words following Sch 5 para 3(4): see INHERITANCE TAXATION vol 24 (Reissue) paras 543–544.

4   Value Added Tax Act 1994 Sch 9 Pt II Group 11 item 2.

5   Ie by virtue of the Inheritance Tax Act 1984 s 32(4) or s 32A(5) or (7) (as added): see INHERITANCE TAXATION vol 24 (Reissue) para 539.

6   Value Added Tax Act 1994 Sch 9 Pt II Group 11 item 3.

7   Ie by virtue of the Taxation of Chargeable Gains Act 1992 s 258(2): see CAPITAL GAINS TAXATION vol 5(1) (Reissue) para 229.

8   Value Added Tax Act 1994 Sch 9 Pt II Group 11 item 4.

9   See the text and notes 1–8 supra.

156. Fund-raising events by charities and other qualifying bodies.

The following supplies of goods and services are exempt supplies[1]:

(1)   the supply of goods and services by a charity in connection with a fund-raising event[2] organised for charitable purposes by a charity[3] or jointly by more than one charity[4];

(2)   the supply of goods and services by a qualifying body[5] in connection with a fund-raising event organised exclusively for its own benefit[6].

1   See the Value Added Tax Act 1994 s 31(1), Sch 9 Pt II Group 12; and heads (1)–(2) in the text. For the meaning of 'exempt supply' see para 141 ante.

2   A 'fund-raising event' means a fête, ball, bazaar, gala show, performance or similar event, which is separate from and which does not form any part of a series or regular run of like or similar events: ibid Sch 9 Pt II Group 12 note 1. Seven performances of a play during the course of a 'Renaissance in Belfast Week' constituted a series of like events outside the scope of the exemption; and the United Kingdom was entitled to restrict the scope of Sch 9 Pt II Group 12 to single events, having regard to the terms of EC Council Directive 77/388 (OJ L145, 13.6.77, p 1) art 13(A)(1)(o): *Northern Ireland Council for Voluntary Action v Customs and Excise Comrs* [1991] VATTR 32. A three-day real ale and jazz festival can, however, constitute a single fund-raising event: *Reading Cricket and Hockey Club v Customs and Excise Comrs* (1995) VAT Decision 13656, [1995] STI 1979. A fund-raising event need not have as its purpose the raising of capital; but the raising of funds must be the main purpose of the event: *Blaydon Rugby Football Club v Customs and Excise Comrs* (1996) VAT Decision 13901, [1996] STI 750.

3   For these purposes, 'charity' includes a body corporate which is wholly owned by a charity and whose profits (from whatever source) are payable to a charity by virtue of a deed of covenant or trust or otherwise: Value Added Tax Act 1994 Sch 9 Pt II Group 12 note 2.

4   Ibid Sch 9 Pt II Group 12 item 1.

5   For these purposes, 'qualifying body' means (1) any non-profit making body whose objects are of any description mentioned in ibid s 94(3) (see para 18 ante); (2) any non-profit making organisation mentioned in Sch 9 Pt II Group 9 item 1 (see para 153 ante); (3) any non-profit making body whose principal purpose is the provision of facilities for persons to take part in sport or physical education; or (4) any body which is an eligible body for the purposes of Sch 9 Pt II Group 13 item 2 (as added) (see para

157 post): Sch 9 Pt II Group 12 note 3 (substituted by the Value Added Tax (Cultural Services) Order 1996, SI 1996/1256). As to the meaning of 'otherwise than for profit' see para 151 note 11 ante.
6   Value Added Tax Act 1994 Sch 9 Pt II Group 12 item 2.

157. Cultural services etc. The supply[1] by a public body[2] or by an eligible body[3] of a right of admission to (1) a museum, gallery, art exhibition or zoo[4]; or (2) a theatrical, musical or choreographic performance of a cultural nature[5], is an exempt supply[6]. In the case of a supply by a public body, however, the exemption does not include any supply the exemption of which would be likely to create distortions of competition such as to place a commercial enterprise carried on by a taxable person[7] at a disadvantage[8].

1   For the meaning of 'supply' see para 21 ante.
2   For these purposes, 'public body' means (1) a local authority; (2) a government department within the meaning of the Value Added Tax Act 1994 s 41(6) (see para 194 note 4 post); or (3) a non-departmental public body which is listed in *Public Bodies* (Office of Public Service; 1995 Edn): Value Added Tax Act 1994 s 31(1), Sch 9 Pt II Group 13 note 1 (Sch 9 Pt II Group 13 added by the Value Added Tax (Cultural Services) Order 1996, SI 1996/1256, with effect from 1 June 1996: see arts 1, 2). For the meaning of 'local authority' see para 56 note 21 ante.
3   For these purposes, 'eligible body' means any body, other than a public body, which (1) is precluded from distributing, and does not distribute, any profit it makes; (2) applies any profits made from supplies of a description falling within the exemption to the continuance or improvement of the facilities made available by means of the supplies; and (3) is managed and administered on a voluntary basis by persons who have no direct or indirect financial interest in its activities: Value Added Tax Act 1994 Sch 9 Pt II Group 13 note 2 (as added: see note 2 supra).
3   Ibid Sch 9 Pt II Group 13 item 1(a) (in relation to public bodies); Sch 9 Pt II Group 13 item 2(a) (in relation to eligible bodies) (both as added: see note 2 supra).
4   Ibid Sch 9 Pt II Group 13 item 1(b) (in relation to public bodies); Sch 9 Pt II Group 13 item 2(b) (in relation to eligible bodies) (both as added: see note 2 supra). Schedule 9 Group 13 item 1(b) (as so added) includes the supply of a right of admission to a performance only if the performance is provided exclusively by one or more public bodies, one or more eligible bodies or any combination of public bodies and eligible bodies: Sch 9 Pt II Group 13 note 4 (as so added).
6   Ibid Sch 9 Pt II Group 13 (as added: see note 2 supra). For the meaning of 'exempt supply' see para 141 ante.
7   For the meaning of 'taxable person' see paras 12 note 4, 55 ante.
8   Value Added Tax Act 1994 Sch 9 Pt II Group 13 note 3 (as added: see note 2 supra).

(2) ZERO-RATED SUPPLIES

(i) In general

158. Meaning of 'zero-rated supply'; zero-rated groups of supplies. Where a taxable person[1] supplies goods or services and the supply[2] is zero-rated, then, whether or not value added tax would otherwise be chargeable on the supply, no VAT is charged on the supply, but it is in all other respects treated as a taxable supply[3], and accordingly the rate at which VAT is treated as charged on the supply is nil[4]. A supply of goods or services is zero-rated if the goods or services are of a description for the time being specified in Schedule 8 to the Value Added Tax Act 1994[5] or the supply is of a description for the time being so specified[6]. A supply by a person of services which consist of applying a treatment or process to another person's goods is also zero-rated if by doing so if produces goods and either those goods are of a specified description[7] or a supply by him of those goods to the person to whom he supplies the services would be of such a description[8].

The following 16 groups of supplies are zero-rated: (1) food[9]; (2) sewerage services and water[10]; (3) books etc[11]; (4) talking books for the blind and handicapped and wireless sets for the blind[12]; (5) construction of buildings etc[13]; (6) protected buildings[14]; (7) international services[15]; (8) transport[16]; (9) caravans and houseboats[17]; (10) gold and (11) bank notes[18]; (12) drugs, medicines, aids for the handicapped, etc[19]; (13) imports, exports etc[20]; (14) tax-free shops[21]; (15) charities, etc[22]; and (16) clothing[23] and footwear[24]. Certain supplies, acquisitions and importations not specified within these groups are also zero-rated[25].

1 For the meaning of 'taxable person' see paras 12 note 4, 55 ante.
2 For the meaning of 'supply' see para 21 ante.
3 For the meaning of 'taxable supply' see para 12 note 3 ante.
4 Value Added Tax Act 1994 s 30(1). As zero-rated supplies are still taxable supplies, the taxable person may claim to deduct or recover input tax attributable to them in accordance with s 26 (see para 203 post); and unless the supplier is exempted from registration he must be registered for VAT in the ordinary way: see s 3(2), Sch 1 para 14; and para 57 ante. For the meaning of 'input tax' see paras 4 ante, 201 post.
5 See ibid s 30(2), Sch 8 Pts I, II (as amended); heads (1)–(16) in the text; and para 159 et seq post. The Treasury may by order vary Sch 8 (as amended) by adding to or deleting from it any description for the time being specified in it: s 30(4). In exercise of the power so conferred, the Treasury has made the following orders: (1) the Value Added Tax (Transport) Order 1994, SI 1994/3014 (see para 167 post); (2) the Value Added Tax (Construction of Buildings) Order 1995, SI 1995/280 (see para 163 post); (3) the Value Added Tax (Protected Buildings) Order 1995, SI 1995/283 (see para 165 post); (4) the Value Added Tax (Supply of Pharmaceutical Goods) Order 1995, SI 1995/652 (see para 170 post); (5) the Value Added Tax (Transport) Order 1995, SI 1995/653 (see para 167 post); (6) the Value Added Tax (Ships and Aircraft) Order 1995, SI 1995/3039 (see para 167 post); and (7) the Value Added Tax (Anti-avoidance (Heating)) Order 1996, SI 1996/1661 (see para 160 post). As to the power to make such orders see para 8 ante. The Treasury's power by order under the Value Added Tax Act 1994 s 30 (as amended) to vary Sch 8 (as amended) includes power to apply any variation made by the order for the purposes of s 35 (as amended) (see para 259 post) and power to make such consequential modifications of s 35 (as amended) as it may think fit: s 35(5) (added by the Finance Act 1996 s 30(3).
6 Value Added Tax Act 1994 s 30(2).
7 Ie a description for the time being specified in ibid Sch 8 (as amended): see heads (1)–(16) in the text; and para 159 et seq post.
8 Ibid s 30(2A) (added by the Finance Act 1996 s 29(1), (2), (5) in relation to supplies made on or after 1 January 1996).
9 See para 159 post.
10 See para 160 post.
11 See para 161 post.
12 See para 162 post.
13 See para 163 post.
14 See para 165 post.
15 See para 166 post.
16 See para 167 post.
17 See para 168 post.
18 See para 169 post.
19 See para 170 post.
20 See para 171 post.
21 See para 172 post.
22 See para 173 post. As to exports by charities see para 176 post.
23 See para 174 post.
24 These descriptions of groups are for ease of reference only, and do not affect the interpretation of the descriptions of items in those groups: Value Added Tax Act 1994 s 96(10). Schedule 8 (as amended) is to be interpreted in accordance with the notes contained in it; and accordingly the powers conferred by the Value Added Tax Act 1994 to vary Sch 8 (as amended) (see note 5 supra) include a power to add to, delete or vary those notes: s 96(9).
25 See para 175 et seq post.

(ii) Specified Supplies

159. Food. Supplies[1] of the majority of foodstuffs, and the animals and plants from which they are made ('general items'[2]), are zero-rated[3] unless they constitute a supply in the course of catering[4]. Certain categories of foodstuffs ('excepted items') are not zero-rated[5] but may contain within them particular foodstuffs ('items overriding the exceptions') which are zero-rated[6].

Under this scheme the following are zero-rated:

(1) food[7] of a kind used for human consumption[8];

(2) animal[9] feeding stuffs[10];

(3) seeds or other means of propagation of plants comprised in heads (1) and (2) above[11];

(4) live animals of a kind generally used as, or yielding or producing, food for human consumption[12].

Additionally, preparations and extracts of meat, yeast or egg are items overriding the exceptions and thus zero-rated[13].

The following are excepted items:

(a) ice cream, ice lollies, frozen yoghurt, water ices and similar frozen products, and prepared mixes and powders for making such products[14], but not yoghurt unsuitable for immediate consumption when frozen[15];

(b) confectionery[16], not including cakes or biscuits (other than biscuits wholly or partly covered with chocolate or some product similar in taste and appearance)[17] or drained cherries or candied peels[18];

(c) beverages chargeable with any duty of excise specifically charged on spirits, beer, wine or made-wine and preparations thereof[19];

(d) other beverages (including fruit juices and bottled waters) and syrups, concentrates, essences, powders, crystals or other products for the preparation of beverages[20], but not including tea, maté, herbal teas and similar products and preparations and extracts thereof[21], cocoa, coffee and chicory and other roasted coffee substitutes, and preparations and extracts thereof[22] or milk and preparations and extracts thereof[23];

(e) any of the following when packaged for human consumption without further preparation: potato crisps, potato sticks, potato puffs, and similar products made from the potato, or from potato flour, or from potato starch, and savoury food products obtained by the swelling of cereals or cereal products, and salted or roasted nuts other than nuts in shell[24];

(f) pet foods (canned, packaged or prepared), packaged foods (not being pet foods) for birds other than poultry or game, and biscuits and meal for cats and dogs[25];

(g) goods described in heads (1), (2) and (3) above which are canned, bottled, packaged or prepared for use in the domestic brewing of any beer, the domestic making of any cider or perry or the domestic production of any wine or made-wine[26].

Supplies in the course of catering are not zero-rated[27]. Such supplies include (i) a supply of anything for consumption on the premises on which it is supplied; and (ii) any supply of hot food[28] for consumption off those premises[29].

1   Any supply described in the Value Added Tax Act 1994 s 30(2), Sch 8 Pt II Group 1 also includes a supply of services described in s 5(1), Sch 4 para 1(1) (ie any supply of services consisting in the transfer of the undivided share of the property in goods, or the transfer of possession of goods: see para 14 ante): Sch 8 Pt II Group 1 note 7. For the meaning of 'supply' see para 21 ante. The United Kingdom has decided to exercise the option given by EC Council Directive 95/7 (OJ L102, 5.5.95, p 18) to retain the zero-rating

of process work on materials which results in zero-rated goods: see Customs and Excise Business Brief 23/95 [1995] STI 1662.

2   See the Value Added Tax Act 1994 s 30(2), Sch 8 Pt II Group 1 general items, items 1–4; and heads (1)–(4) in the text.

3   For the meaning of 'zero-rated supply' see para 158 ante.

4   Value Added Tax Act 1994 Sch 8 Pt II Group 1.

5   Ibid Sch 8 Pt II Group 1: see Sch 8 Pt II Group 1 excepted items, items 1–7; and heads (a)–(g) in the text.

6   Ibid Sch 8 Pt II Group 1: see Sch 8 Pt II Group 1 items overriding the exceptions, items 1–7; the text to note 13 infra; and heads (a)–(g) in the text.

7   'Food' includes drink: ibid Sch 8 Pt II Group 1 note 1. In order to be food a product need not be supplied in edible form nor fit for immediate use, provided that it consists substantially of items of nutritional value and is used in manufacturing other food: *Customs and Excise Comrs v Macphie & Co (Glenbervie) Ltd* [1992] STC 886 (supply of ingredient for the in-store baking of bread rolls); *Soni v Customs and Excise Comrs* [1980] VATTR 9 (chewing preparation called paan zero-rated as it had a measurable nutritive effect). Cf *Marfleet Refining Co Ltd v Customs and Excise Comrs* [1974] VATTR 289 (cod liver oil tablets not food). A sale of a tin of biscuits, where the cost of the packing exceeded the cost of the contents, was nevertheless a composite zero-rated supply of food: *Customs and Excise Comrs v United Biscuits (United Kingdom) Ltd (t/a Simmers)* [1992] STC 325. As to composite and separate supplies generally see para 25 ante.

8   Value Added Tax Act 1994 Sch 8 Pt II Group 1 general items, item 1.

9   'Animal' includes bird, fish, crustacean and mollusc: ibid Sch 8 Pt II Group 1 note 2.

10 Ibid Sch 8 Pt II Group 1 general items, item 2. As to the treatment of a 'grass livery' service offered to owners of horses see *Fidler (t/a Holt Manor Farm Partners)* (1995) VAT Decision 12892, [1995] STI 420.

11 Value Added Tax Act 1994 Sch 8 Pt II Group 1 general items, item 3. A supply of a kit for growing mushrooms, consisting of a bucket containing a mushroom spore-infused growing medium in a mixture of lime and peat, a label and an instruction leaflet was zero-rated as a supply within Sch 8 Pt II Group 1 general items, item 3, save as to the bucket, which was standard-rated: *Cheshire Mushroom Farm v Customs and Excise Comrs* [1974] VATTR 87. Cf *Customs and Excise Comrs v United Biscuits (United Kingdom) Ltd (t/a Simmers)* [1992] STC 325; and note 7 supra.

12 Value Added Tax Act 1994 Sch 8 Pt II Group 1 general items, item 4. For a case where the issue arose whether the animals in question were of a kind generally used as food for human consumption see *Customs and Excise Comrs v Lawson-Tancred* [1988] STC 326n (Dinkesbuhl and Scaly carp).

13 Value Added Tax Act 1994 Sch 8 Pt II Group 1 items overriding the exceptions, item 7.

14 Ibid Sch 8 Pt II Group 1 excepted items, item 1. The words 'similar frozen products' refer to similarity to any of the items previously mentioned and not merely to similarity to water ices, as contended by the appellant in *Ross Young Holdings Ltd v Customs and Excise Comrs* (1996) VAT Decision 13972, [1996] STI 941.

15 Value Added Tax Act 1994 Sch 8 Pt II Group 1 items overriding the exceptions, item 1; Sch 8 Pt II Group 1 note 4.

16 'Confectionery' includes chocolates, sweets and biscuits; drained, glacé or crystallised fruits; and any item of sweetened prepared food which is normally eaten with the fingers: ibid Sch 8 Pt II Group 1 note 5. This provision reverses *Customs and Excise Comrs v Quaker Oats Ltd* [1987] STC 683.

17 Value Added Tax Act 1994 Sch 8 Pt II Group 1 excepted items, item 2.

18 Ibid Sch 8 Pt II Group 1 items overriding the exceptions, items 2, 3; Sch 8 Pt II Group 1 note 5.

19 Ibid Sch 8 Pt II Group 1 excepted items, item 3. A 'beverage' is a liquid characteristically taken to increase bodily liquid levels, to slake the thirst, to fortify or to give pleasure; and it does not therefore encompass a 'health drink' sold as a food supplement with (in the words of the VAT and duties tribunal) 'an unpleasant taste' which 'would not have been consumed for pleasure': *Bioconcepts Ltd v Customs and Excise Comrs* (1993) VAT Decision 11287, [1993] STI 1621; cf *Smith Kline Beecham plc v Customs and Excise Comrs* (1995) VAT Decision 13674, [1995] STI 2028.

20 Value Added Tax Act 1994 Sch 8 Pt II Group 1 excepted items, item 4.

21 Ibid Sch 8 Pt II Group 1 items overriding the exceptions, item 4; Sch 8 Pt II Group 1 note 6. An iced tea product marketed as tea but not made or flavoured in a traditional way was held not to be 'tea' for these purposes in *Snapple Beverage Corpn (now Quaker Oats Ltd)* (1995) VAT Decision 13690, [1995] STI 2031.

22 Value Added Tax Act 1994 Sch 8 Pt II Group 1 items overriding the exceptions, item 5; Sch 8 Pt II Group 1 note 6.

23 Ibid Sch 8 Pt II Group 1 items overriding the exceptions, item 6; Sch 8 Pt II Group 1 note 6.

24 Ibid Sch 8 Pt II Group 1 excepted items, item 5.

25 Ibid Sch 8 Pt II Group 1 excepted items, item 6. Pet foods are foodstuffs offered by the supplier as being food primarily intended for pets (ie animals kept primarily for affection or ornament), irrespective of the recipient's intention: *Pope Lane Pet Food Supplies Ltd v Customs and Excise Comrs* [1986] VATTR 221; cf

Peters and Riddles (t/a Mill Lane Farm Shop) v Customs and Excise Comrs (1995) VAT Decision 12937, [1995] STI 533. Similarly the sale of minced chicken for working dogs was properly zero-rated: *Norman Riding Poultry Farm Ltd v Customs and Excise Comrs* [1989] VATTR 124. An additive solely serving to aid digestion is not a 'feeding stuff' since it is not a nutrient: *Chapman & Frearson Ltd v Customs and Excise Comrs* (1990) VAT Decision 4428, [1990] STI 161.

26 Value Added Tax Act 1994 Sch 8 Pt II Group 1 excepted items, item 7.

27 Ibid Sch 8 Pt II Group 1(a). Such supplies therefore attract VAT at the standard rate: see para 5 ante. A 'supply in the course of catering' can be a supply of food for consumption off the premises if the supply is incidental to another activity, eg of a sporting, business, entertainment or social character: *Customs and Excise Comrs v Cope* [1981] STC 532 at 538 (sale of seafood from stalls at a race-ground). Where a sandwich bar prepared sandwich platters in varying sizes, and sold them under the rubric 'for meetings' it did not necessarily follow that the sales were supplies in the course of catering, since the bar was not concerned whether the food was consumed at a function or not: *Out to Lunch (a firm) v Customs and Excise Comrs* (1995) VAT Decision 13031, [1995] STI 711. The sale of food from buffets around a football ground is a sale of food for consumption on the premises (ie the football ground) and is therefore a supply in the course of catering: *Bristol City Football Supporters Club v Customs and Excise Comrs* [1975] VATTR 93; but cf *Travellers Fare Ltd v Customs and Excise Comrs* (1995) VAT Decision 13482, [1995] STI 1586 (sales of cold food on railway station premises not supplies in the course of catering). When drinks are sold from vending machines, the premises are the premises in which the machine is situated: *Macklin Services (Vending) West Ltd v Customs and Excise Comrs* [1979] VATTR 31. The sale of food from a kiosk in a shopping centre is not a sale of food for consumption on the premises unless there is a delineated area capable of constituting the premises: *Armstrong v Customs and Excise Comrs* [1984] VATTR 53; cf *Crownlion (Seafood) Ltd v Customs and Excise Comrs* [1985] VATTR 188 (where a specific area was set aside in the shopping centre for tables at which food purchased from a number of kiosks could be consumed). Where a trader sold doughnuts from a van at agricultural shows or horse-race meetings, the sales were of food for consumption on the premises of the show-ground or the racecourse, as the case might be; but when the same trader sold similar food from his van in Battersea Park, the supplies were not in the course of catering, since the park could not constitute premises: *Skilton and Gregory v Customs and Excise Comrs* (1994) VAT Decision 11723, [1994] STI 511; *Fresh Sea Foods Barry Ltd v Customs and Excise Comrs* [1991] VATTR 388. Sales of sandwiches from a snack bar operating out of one room in a office block did not constitute supplies of food to be consumed on the premises, notwithstanding that the majority of the food was consumed in offices within the building, since the relevant premises were simply the room from which the sandwiches were sold: *R v Customs and Excise Comrs, ex p Sims (t/a Supersonic Snacks)* [1988] STC 210.

The word 'for' in 'for consumption on the premises' is purposive: *R v Customs and Excise Comrs, ex p Sims (t/a Supersonic Snacks)* supra (obiter), following *John Pimblett & Sons Ltd v Customs and Excise Comrs* [1987] STC 202; and followed on this point in *Zeldaline Ltd v Customs and Excise Comrs* [1989] VATTR 191 (sales of sandwiches from baskets in hallways of office blocks were not made 'for consumption on the premises' when the vendor had no intention as to whether the food would be so consumed). A person cannot be said so to supply food unless he has some right or licence to be on the premises in question: *Zeldaline Ltd v Customs and Excise Comrs* supra. Sales of 'party trays' by a supermarket, in a form convenient for entertaining, were held not to be a supply in the course of catering in *Safeway Stores plc v Customs and Excise Comrs* (1996) VAT Decision 14067, [1996] STI 1213, disapproving the earlier tribunal decision in *Chasney Ltd v Customs and Excise Comrs* [1989] VATTR 152, having regard, inter alia, to the fact that the food was not delivered, the trays were non-returnable and the advertising did not mention catering as such; a supply in the course of catering usually involved something more in the nature of a personal relationship than that involved on the facts before the tribunal.

28 'Hot food' means food which (1) has been heated for the purposes of enabling it to be consumed at a temperature above the ambient air temperature; and (2) is at the time of the supply above that temperature: Value Added Tax Act 1994 Sch 8 Pt II Group 1 note 3(i), (ii). The purposes in head (1) supra are those of the supplier and not those of the customer. A bakery that heated pies in order to attract customers with their smell was held not to have heated them for the purpose of enabling them to be consumed at a temperature above the ambient air temperature simply because it was aware that some of them would be so eaten: *John Pimblett & Sons Ltd v Customs and Excise Comrs* [1988] STC 358, CA; *Stewarts Supermarket Ltd v Customs and Excise Comrs* (1995) VAT Decision 13338, [1995] STI 1253; *Three Cooks Ltd v Customs and Excise Comrs* (1995) VAT Decision 13352, [1995] STI 1273.

29 Value Added Tax Act 1994 Sch 8 Pt II Group 1 note 3(a), (b).

160. Sewerage services and water. The following are zero-rated supplies[1]:

    (1)   services of (a) reception, disposal or treatment of foul water or sewage in bulk[2]; and (b) emptying of cesspools, septic tanks or similar receptacles which are used otherwise than in connection with the carrying on, in the course of a business[3], of a relevant industrial activity[4]; and

    (2)   the supply, for use otherwise than in connection with the carrying on, in the course of a business, of a relevant industrial activity, of water[5] other than (a) distilled water, deionised water and water of similar purity; (b) water comprised in any of the categories of foodstuffs which are excepted items[6] for the purposes of exemption from value added tax; and (c) water which has been heated so that it is supplied at a temperature higher than that at which it was before it was heated[7].

1   See the Value Added Tax Act 1994 s 30(2), Sch 8 Pt II Group 2 (as amended); and heads (1)–(2) in the text. For the meaning of 'zero-rated supply' see para 158 ante; and for the meaning of 'supply' see para 21 ante.

2   Ibid Sch 8 Pt II Group 2 item 1(a).

3   For the meaning of 'business' see para 17 ante.

4   Value Added Tax Act 1994 Sch 8 Pt II Group 2 item 1(b). A 'relevant industrial activity' is any activity described in the Central Statistical Office Standard Industrial Classification (1980 Edn) Divisions 1–5: Value Added Tax Act 1994 Sch 8 Pt II Group 2 note.

5   Ibid Sch 8 Pt II Group 2 item 2. Where water is supplied as an integral part of the provision of launderette facilities there is no supply of goods but a supply of services which is taxable at the standard rate: *Mander Laundries v Customs and Excise Comrs* [1973] VATTR 136. As to composite and separate supplies generally see para 25 ante; and as to the standard rate of VAT see para 5 ante.

6   Ie the excepted items set out in the Value Added Tax Act 1994 Sch 8 Pt II Group 1 excepted items, items 1–7: see para 159 heads (a)–(g) ante.

7   Ibid Sch 8 Pt II Group 2 items 2(a)–(c) (item 2(c) added by the Value Added Tax (Anti-avoidance (Heating)) Order 1996, SI 1996/1661, with effect from 27 June 1996: see art 1).

161. Books etc. Supplies[1] of the following descriptions which are not drawings for industrial, architectural engineering, commercial or similar purposes[2] are zero-rated[3]:

    (1)   books[4], booklets[5], brochures, pamphlets and leaflets[6];

    (2)   newspapers, journals and periodicals[7];

    (3)   children's picture books and painting books[8];

    (4)   music (printed, duplicated or manuscript)[9];

    (5)   maps, charts[10] and topographical plans[11];

    (6)   covers, cases and other articles supplied with items within the above heads and not separately accounted for[12];

    (7)   supplies of services[13] by way of the transfer of any undivided share of the property in, or of the possession of, goods comprised in the above heads[14].

1   For the meaning of 'supply' see para 21 ante.

2   Value Added Tax Act 1994 s 30(2), Sch 8 Pt II Group 3 note (a).

3   See ibid Sch 8 Pt II Group 3; and heads (1)–(7) in the text. For the meaning of 'zero-rated supply' see para 158 ante. The provision of camera-ready copy to a publisher in return for a share of the profits from the publication has been held to be a standard-rated sale of rights: *International Institute for Strategic Studies v Customs and Excise Comrs* (1995) VAT Decision 13551, [1995] STI 1685. As to the standard rate of VAT see para 5 ante.

4   'Books' do not include an article intended in due course to form part of a book unless the article when supplied can be said, without anything further being done to it, to form a part of an existing or specific book: *Butler & Tanner Ltd v Customs and Excise Comrs* [1974] VATTR 72. Binders for weekly parts of a work are not component parts of a book: *Fabbri & Partners Ltd v Customs and Excise Comrs* [1973] VATTR 49; *Marshall Cavendish Ltd v Customs and Excise Comrs* [1973] VATTR 65; *International Master Publishers Ltd v Customs and Excise Comrs* (1992) VAT Decision 8807, [1992] STI 984. Diaries and address books whose main purpose is to be written in are neither books nor booklets for the purposes of the Value

Added Tax Act 1994 Sch 8 Pt II Group 3, since the minimum characteristic of a book is that it is to be read or looked at: *Customs and Excise Comrs v Colour Offset Ltd* [1995] STC 85. The supply of an album of wedding photographs was not zero-rated as the supply of a book: *Draper v Customs and Excise Comrs* (1981) VAT Decision 1107 (unreported).

A children's book of 16 pages containing four pages of text and 12 pages designed to be cut to make toys was a book: *WF Graham (Northampton) Ltd v Customs and Excise Comrs* (1980) VAT Decision 908 (unreported). Where a college supplied both books (which are zero-rated) and tuition (which in this instance was standard-rated) as parts of a correspondence course for which a single fee was charged, the supplies were found to be separate and severable and the consideration apportionable: *Rapid Results College Ltd v Customs and Excise Comrs* [1973] VATTR 197; *LSA (Full Time Courses) Ltd v Customs and Excise Comrs* [1983] VATTR 256; but cf *EW (Computer Training) Ltd v Customs and Excise Comrs* (1991) VAT Decision 5453, [1991] STI 63; and *International News Syndicate Ltd v Customs and Excise Comrs* (1996) VAT Decision 14425, [1996] STI 1724.

5   A booklet containing vouchers entitling the holder to discounted admission to various facilities is not zero-rated as a booklet when it is merely a convenient means by which the vendor makes a supply of services: *Graham Leisure Ltd v Customs and Excise Comrs* [1983] VATTR 12; *Interleisure Club Ltd v Customs and Excise Comrs* (1992) VAT Decision 7458, [1992] STI 608.

6   Value Added Tax Act 1994 Sch 8 Pt II Group 3 item 1. A 'leaflet' is to be given its dictionary meaning, ie a small-sized leaf of paper which may be folded into leaves but not stitched, containing printed matter. A poster is so large as to be outside the concept of a leaflet: *Cronsvale Ltd v Customs and Excise Comrs* [1983] VATTR 313. Packs of unfolded pre-school teaching 'dictionary cards' were neither books nor booklets; and A2 story sheets were not leaflets because (inter alia) they were not for general distribution: *Odhams Leisure Group Ltd v Customs and Excise Comrs* [1992] STC 332. Laminated recipe cards were not leaflets (*International Master Publishers Ltd v Customs and Excise Comrs* (1992) VAT Decision 8807, [1992] STI 984); and tax cards (glossy cards containing various items of information relating to tax rates) were not leaflets, since they were printed on stiff card and thus could not readily be folded whereas a leaflet is normally limp (*Tax Briefs Ltd v Customs and Excise Comrs* (1992) VAT Decision 9258 (unreported)); following *Panini Publishing Ltd v Customs and Excise Comrs, Mirror Group Newspapers Ltd v Customs and Excise Comrs* (1989) VAT Decision 3876, [1989] STI 762).

7   Value Added Tax Act 1994 Sch 8 Pt II Group 3 item 2. A monthly 'property guide' in newspaper form distributed free by estate agents which consisted mainly of advertising was not a newspaper since it contained no news, and it was not a periodical since it was not published for distribution and sale to the general public; it was therefore standard-rated: *Snushall v Customs and Excise Comrs* [1982] STC 537.

'Periodical' has its ordinary meaning. Theatre programmes in which advertising space is sold are not 'periodicals' within the ordinary meaning of the word: *Stilwell Darby & Co Ltd v Customs and Excise Comrs* [1973] VATTR 145. A racing information paper which was published on each day during the year on which a greyhound meeting was held was neither a newspaper (it contained no news), nor a journal (for the same reason and because it was not published on a daily basis) nor a periodical (because the frequency with which it appeared was determined by an event and not by time): *Evans & Marland Ltd v Customs and Excise Comrs* [1988] VATTR 125. A poster magazine which also contains text and special photographs may, however, be a periodical: *Emap Consumer Magazines Ltd v Customs and Excise Comrs* (1995) VAT Decision 13322, [1995] STI 1173; *European Publishing Consultants Ltd v Customs and Excise Comrs* (1996) VAT Decision 13841, [1996] STI 643.

8   Value Added Tax Act 1994 Sch 8 Pt II Group 3 item 3.

9   Ibid Sch 8 Pt II Group 3 item 4.

10   'Charts' is to be read as limited to articles of the same genus as maps and topographical plans and does not extend to genealogical charts of the kings and queens of England: *Brooks Histographic Ltd v Customs and Excise Comrs* [1984] VATTR 46.

11   Value Added Tax Act 1994 Sch 8 Pt II Group 3 item 5.

12   Ibid Sch 8 Pt II Group 3 item 6.

13   Ie supplies of the services described in ibid s 5(1), Sch 4 para 1(1): see para 24 ante.

14   Ibid Sch 8 Pt II Group 3 note (b).

162. Talking books for the blind and handicapped; wireless sets for the blind.

The following are zero-rated supplies[1]:

(1)   the supply, including the letting on hire[2], to the Royal National Institute for the Blind, the National Listening Library or other similar charities of:

     (a)   magnetic tape specially adapted for the recording and reproduction of speech for the blind or severely handicapped;

(b)   apparatus designed or specially adapted for the making on a magnetic tape, by way of the transfer of recorded speech from another magnetic tape, of a recording described in head (f) below;

(c)   apparatus designed or specially adapted for transfer to magnetic tapes of a recording made by apparatus described in head (b) above;

(d)   apparatus for rewinding magnetic tape described in head (f) below;

(e)   apparatus designed or specially adapted for the reproduction from recorded magnetic tape of speech for the blind or severely handicapped which is not available for use otherwise than by the blind or severely handicapped;

(f)   magnetic tape upon which has been recorded speech for the blind or severely handicapped, such recording being suitable for reproduction only in the apparatus mentioned in head (e) above;

(g)   apparatus solely for the making on a magnetic tape of a sound recording which is for use by the blind or severely handicapped;

(h)   parts and accessories (other than a magnetic tape for use with apparatus described in head (g) above) for goods comprised in heads (a) to (g) above;

(i)   the supply of a service of repair or maintenance of any goods comprised in heads (a) to (h) above[3];

(2) the supply, including the letting on hire[4], to a charity of wireless receiving sets or apparatus solely for the making and reproduction of a sound recording on a magnetic tape permanently contained in a cassette, being goods solely for gratuitous loan to the blind[5].

1   See the Value Added Tax Act 1994 s 30(2), Sch 8 Pt II Group 4; and heads (1)–(2) in the text. For the meaning of 'zero-rated supply' see para 158 ante; and for the meaning of 'supply' see para 21 ante.
2   Ibid Sch 8 Pt II Group 4 note.
3   Ibid Sch 8 Pt II Group 4 item 1.
4   Ibid Sch 8 Pt II Group 4 note.
5   Ibid Sch 8 Pt II Group 4 item 2.

163. Construction of buildings etc. The following are zero-rated supplies[1]:

(1) the first[2] grant[3] of a major interest[4] in, or in any part of, the relevant building, dwelling or its site[5], by a person:

(a)   constructing[6] a building[7] which is designed as a dwelling or number of dwellings[8] or intended for use solely for a relevant residential purpose[9] or a relevant charitable[10] purpose[11]; or

(b)   converting a non-residential building or a non-residential part of a building[12] into a building designed as a dwelling or number of dwellings or a building intended solely for a relevant residential purpose[13];

(2) the supply of any services related to the relevant construction (other than the services of an architect, surveyor or any person acting as consultant or in a supervisory capacity) in the course of the construction[14] of:

(a)   a building designed as a dwelling or number of dwellings or intended[15] for use solely for a relevant residential purpose or a relevant charitable purpose[16]; or

(b)   any civil engineering work[17] necessary for the development of a permanent park for residential caravans[18];

(3) the supply to a registered housing association[19] of any services related to the relevant conversion (other than the services of an architect, surveyor or any person acting as consultant or in a supervisory capacity) in the course of

conversion of a non-residential building or a non-residential part of a building[20] into:

(a) a building or part of a building designed as a dwelling or a number of dwellings[21]; or

(b) a building or part of a building intended for use solely for a relevant residential purpose[22]; and

(4) the supply of building materials[23] to a person to whom the supplier is supplying services within head (2) or head (3) above which include the incorporation of the materials into the building (or its site) in question[24].

The grant of an interest in, or in any part of, either a building designed as a dwelling or number of dwellings, or the site of such a building, is not within head (1) above if the interest granted is such that the grantee is not entitled to reside in the building, or part, throughout the year[25]. Nor is it within that head if residence there throughout the year, or the use of the building or part as the grantee's principal private residence, is prevented by the terms of a covenant, statutory planning consent or similar permission[26].

Where part of a building that is constructed is designed as a dwelling or number of dwellings or is intended for use solely for a relevant residential purpose or relevant charitable purpose and part is not, or part of a building that is converted is designed as a dwelling or number of dwellings or is used solely for a relevant residential purpose and part is not, then a grant or other supply relating only to the part so designed or intended for that use (or its site) is treated as relating to a building so designed or intended for such use[27]. A grant or other supply relating only to the part neither so designed nor intended for such use (or its site) is not so treated[28]. In the case of any other grant or other supply relating to, or to any part of, the building (or its site), an apportionment is made to determine the extent to which it is to be so treated[29].

1   See the Value Added Tax Act 1994 s 30(2), Sch 8 Pt II Group 5 (substituted by the Value Added Tax (Construction of Buildings) Order 1995, SI 1995/280); and the text and notes 2–29 infra. As to the interpretation of the Value Added Tax Act 1994 Sch 8 Pt II Group 5 (as so substituted) by the Commissioners of Customs and Excise see Customs and Excise Notice 708 *Buildings and Construction* (1 March 1995). The Value Added Tax Act 1994 s 30(3) (see paras 158 ante, 175 post) does not apply to goods forming part of a description of supply in Sch 8 Pt II Group 5 (as so substituted): Sch 8 Pt II Group 5 note 24 (as so substituted). For the meaning of 'zero-rated supply' see para 158 ante; and for the meaning of 'supply' see para 21 ante.

2   The inclusion in ibid Sch 8 Pt II Group 5 item 1 (as substituted: see note 1 supra) of the word 'first' reverses earlier authority to the effect that zero-rating was available when a building was sold after having been first let.

3   'Grant' includes an assignment or surrender: ibid Sch 8 Pt II Group 5 note 1 (as substituted: see note 1 supra).

4   For the meaning of 'major interest' see para 24 note 7 ante. Where the major interest granted is a tenancy or lease, then (1) if a premium is payable, the grant falls within head (1) in the text only to the extent that it is made for consideration in the form of the premium; and (2) if a premium is not payable, the grant falls within that head only to the extent that it is made for consideration in the form of the first payment of rent due under the tenancy or lease: ibid Sch 8 Pt II Group 5 note 14 (as substituted: see note 1 supra). The grant of a 'time share' entitling the holder to occupy property during specified weeks of each year for a period of 80 years in England is not the grant of a major interest in land: *Cottage Holiday Associates Ltd v Customs and Excise Comrs* [1983] QB 735, [1983] STC 278; and as to Scotland see *American Real Estate (Scotland) Ltd v Customs and Excise Comrs* [1980] VATTR 88. As to the exclusion of such grants from exemption under the Value Added Tax Act 1994 s 31(1), Sch 9 Pt II Group 1 (as amended) see para 142 note 18 ante. For the meaning of 'consideration' generally see para 86 ante.

5   Ibid Sch 8 Pt II Group 5 item 1 (as substituted: see note 1 supra). A 'site' does not refer to the whole acreage of a development site in relation to a single building constructed thereon but only to a reasonable

plot of land surrounding the building: *Stapenhill Developments Ltd v Customs and Excise Comrs* [1984] VATTR 1 at 10.

6   The construction of a building does not include (1) the conversion, reconstruction, or alteration of an existing building; or (2) any enlargement of, or extension to, an existing building except to the extent that the enlargement or extension creates an additional dwelling or dwellings; or (3) the construction of an annex to an existing building unless (a) the annex is intended for use solely for a relevant charitable purpose and is capable of functioning independently from the existing building; and (b) the only access or, where there is more than one means of access, the main access to the annex is not via the existing building and the main access to the existing building is not via the annex: Value Added Tax Act 1994 Sch 8 Pt II Group 5 notes 16, 17 (as substituted: see note 1 supra).

A building only ceases to be an existing building when: (i) demolished completely to ground level; or (ii) the part remaining above ground level consists of no more than a single facade (or, where a corner site, a double facade), the retention of which is a condition or requirement of statutory planning consent or similar permission: Sch 8 Pt II Group 5 note 18 (as so substituted).

Although there has been considerable litigation since the introduction of VAT as to the meanings of 'construction', 'reconstruction', 'alteration', 'enlargement' and related phrases and as to what is an 'existing building', most of the authorities relate to equivalent predecessor provisions to Sch 8 Pt II Group 5 (as substituted), which have taken substantially different forms since 1973. Many such authorities may, therefore, be of little relevance in interpreting the meaning of the same words in the context of the present Sch 8 Pt II Group 5 (as substituted): *Customs and Excise Comrs v London Diocesan Fund, Customs and Excise Comrs v Elliot, Customs and Excise Comrs v Penwith Property Co Ltd* [1993] STC 369. As to the earlier authorities which remain relevant see notes 7–22 infra.

7   As to the meaning of 'person constructing a building' see *Monsell Youell Developments Ltd v Customs and Excise Comrs* [1978] VATTR 1 (a speculative land dealer which sold plots of land having laid out the surrounding infrastructure was not a 'person constructing a building' for the purposes of the equivalent predecessor provisions of the Value Added Tax Act 1995 Sch 8 Pt II Group 5 (as substituted: see note 1 supra)); *Hulme Educational Foundation v Customs and Excise Comrs* [1978] VATTR 179 at 189 (the words should be given their everyday meaning and encompass both the person who constructs the building itself, in the sense of putting brick upon brick, and the person who, by himself or through an agent, enters into a contract or arrangement with another under which that other puts brick upon brick for him); *David Wickens Properties Ltd v Customs and Excise Comrs* [1982] VATTR 143 (a person converting a house into offices is not a 'person constructing a building'); *Customs and Excise Comrs v Link Housing Association Ltd* [1992] STC 718 (the phrase included a person who had constructed a completed building).

In determining whether there has been a 'conversion, reconstruction, or alteration of an existing building' within the meaning of the Value Added Tax Act 1994 Sch 8 Pt II Group 5 note 16(a) (as substituted) (see note 6 head (1) supra), the building as it presently stands is compared with the building as it stood before any work, whether of demolition or construction, began in order to ask whether the work amounted to the conversion, reconstruction, or alteration of the original building in the sense in which those words are commonly used or whether the end result is, in fact, a new building. If a number of buildings existed before the work began, the test is to ask whether the work amounted to the conversion, reconstruction or alteration of one or more of them: see *Customs and Excise Comrs v London Diocesan Fund, Customs and Excise Comrs v Elliot, Customs and Excise Comrs v Penwith Property Co Ltd* [1993] STC 369 at 380 per McCullough J; *Customs and Excise Comrs v Lewis* [1994] STC 739.

'Reconstruction' connotes replication of what was once, but is no longer, there (*Wimpey Group Services Ltd v Customs and Excise Comrs* [1988] STC 625, CA); but the 'new building' test in *Customs and Excise Comrs v London Diocesan Fund, Customs and Excise Comrs v Elliot, Customs and Excise Comrs v Penwith Property Co Ltd* supra is not satisfied (so that zero-rating will not be granted) if it could reasonably be said that the original building still exists although it has been transformed into a new building (see *Customs and Excise Comrs v Marchday Holdings Ltd* [1995] STC 898 per Laws J). Where a new building is constructed which is wholly independent in every way from an adjoining building, apart from the fact that there is a party wall, the new building cannot properly be described as an enlargement of the existing building; but the position might well be different where the two buildings were connected by a door and the planning permission required the new building to be an extension of the original: *Customs and Excise Comrs v Perry* [1983] STC 383. Where, however, the new building had an entirely different function from the existing building there was no enlargement: *Customs and Excise Comrs v Great Shelford Free Church (Baptist)* [1987] STC 249; cf *Charles Gray (Builders) Ltd v Customs and Excise Comrs* [1990] STC 650, where an entirely separate and independent house, which was so constructed as to appear to be an enlargement of an existing house, was held to be an enlargement, having regard to the terms of the planning permission. It may be, however, that the decisions in *Customs and Excise Comrs v Perry* supra and *Customs and Excise*

Comrs v Great Shelford Free Church (Baptist) supra have been overtaken by the subsequent amendments to the legislation, in particular by the introduction of the Value Added Tax Act 1994 Sch 8 Pt II Group 5 note 16(b) (as substituted); and that *Customs and Excise Comrs v London Diocesan Fund, Customs and Excise Comrs v Elliot, Customs and Excise Comrs v Penwith Property Co Ltd* supra and the subsequent authorities must now be read in the context of Value Added Tax Act 1994 Sch 8 Pt II Group 5 note 18 (as substituted): see note 6 supra.

8   A building is designed as a dwelling or a number of dwellings where, in relation to each dwelling, the following conditions are satisfied: (1) the dwelling consists of self-contained living accommodation; (2) there is no provision for direct internal access from the dwelling to any other dwelling or part of a dwelling; (3) the separate use or disposal of the dwelling is not prohibited by the term of any covenant, statutory planning consent or similar provision; and (4) statutory planning consent has been granted in respect of the dwelling and its construction or conversion has been carried out in accordance with that consent: ibid Sch 8 Pt II Group 5 note 2 (as substituted: see note 1 supra). These provisions are intended to ensure that 'granny flats' and similar extensions to existing houses should not qualify for zero-rating: Customs and Excise Notice 708 *Buildings and Construction* (1 March 1995) para 2.5. The question whether a refurbished building was designed as a dwelling or number of dwellings was to be considered in relation to the building as it was when originally constructed: *University of Bath v Customs and Excise Comrs* (1996) VAT Decision 14235, [1996] STI 1492.
   The construction of, or conversion of a non-residential building to, a building designed as a dwelling or a number of dwellings includes the construction of, or conversion of a non-residential building to, a garage provided that the dwelling and the garage are constructed or converted at the same time and that the garage is intended to be occupied with the dwelling or one of the dwellings: Value Added Tax Act 1994 Sch 8 Pt II Group 5 note 3 (as so substituted). References to a non-residential building or a non-residential part of a building do not include a reference to a garage occupied together with a dwelling: Sch 8 Pt II Group 5 note 8 (as so substituted). As to non-residential buildings see note 12 infra.

9   'Use for a relevant residential purpose' means use as (1) a home or other institution providing residential accommodation for children; (2) a home or other institution providing residential accommodation with personal care for persons in need of personal care by reason of old age, disablement, past or present dependence on alcohol or drugs or past or present mental disorder; (3) a hospice; (4) residential accommodation for students or school pupils; (5) residential accommodation for members of any of the armed forces; (6) a monastery, nunnery or similar establishment; or (7) an institution which is the sole or main residence of at least 90% of its residents, except use as a hospital, a prison or similar institution or a hotel, inn or similar establishment: ibid Sch 8 Pt II Group 5 note 4 (as substituted: see note 1 supra).
   Where a number of buildings are constructed at the same time and on the same site, and they are intended to be used together as a unit solely for a relevant residential purpose, then each of those buildings, to the extent that it would not otherwise be so regarded, is to be treated as intended for use solely for a relevant residential purpose: Sch 8 Pt II Group 5 note 5 (as so substituted). This avoids the difficulty which otherwise would arise in relation to ancillary buildings which themselves do not satisfy the strict conditions required in Sch 8 Pt II Group 5 note 4 (as so substituted).

10 'Use for a relevant charitable purpose' means use by a charity in either or both of the following ways, ie (1) otherwise than in the course or furtherance of a business; (2) as a village hall or similarly in providing social or recreational facilities for a local community: ibid Sch 8 Pt II Group 5 note 6 (as substituted: see note 1 supra). The construction of a classroom for a fee-paying school was not for a relevant charitable purpose, since the provision of education in such circumstances amounts to a business: *Leighton Park School v Customs and Excise Comrs* (1993) VAT Decision 9392, [1993] STI 313. The construction, at the expense of a charity, of a building to house a scanner in a hospital was not for a relevant charitable purpose since the hospital itself was not a charity: *League of Friends of Kingston Hospital v Customs and Excise Comrs* (1995) VAT Decision 12764, [1995] STI 68; and see *Royal Academy of Music v Customs and Excise Comrs* (1994) VAT Decision 11871, [1994] STI 655. For the meaning of 'in the course or furtherance of a business' see paras 12 note 5, 17 note 2 ante; and *Newtownbutler Playgroup Ltd v Customs and Excise Comrs* (1995) VAT Decision 13741, [1996] STI 254.

11 Value Added Tax Act 1994 Sch 8 Pt II Group 5 item 1(a) (as substituted: see note 1 supra).

12 'Non-residential', in relation to a building or part of a building, means (1) neither designed nor adapted for use as a dwelling or a number of dwellings, nor for a relevant residential purpose; or (2) if so designed or adapted, constructed before, and not used as a dwelling since, 1 April 1973: ibid Sch 8 Pt II Group 5 note 7 (as substituted: see note 1 supra). The conversion, other than to a building designed for a relevant residential purpose, of a non-residential part of a building which already contains a residential part is not included within heads (1)(b) or (3) in the text unless the result of that conversion is to create an additional dwelling or dwellings: Sch 8 Pt II Group 5 note 9 (as so substituted). A garage occupied with a building

is not a non-residential building or part of a building (see note 8 supra); its conversion or subsequent sale will not, therefore, qualify for zero-rating.

13 Ibid Sch 8 Pt II Group 5 item 1(b) (as substituted: see note 1 supra).

14 Ibid Sch 8 Pt II Group 5 item 2 (as substituted: see note 1 supra). Where a service falling within the description in heads (2) or (3) in the text is supplied in part in relation to the construction or conversion of a building and in part for other purposes, an apportionment may be made to determine the extent to which the supply is to be treated as falling within that head: Sch 8 Pt II Group 5 note 11 (as so substituted). Services are supplied 'in the course of the construction of a building' where the services are supplied contemporaneously or consecutively in relation to a new building and they have a substantial connection with the new building, as when, for example, off-site civil engineering works are carried out for the benefit of the new building as well as for existing buildings: *Customs and Excise Comrs v Rannoch School Ltd* [1993] STC 389, Ct of Sess.

Heads (2)–(3) in the text do not include the supply of services described in the Value Added Tax Act 1994 s 5(1), Sch 4 para 1(1) (transfer of an undivided share in land, or of the possession of land: see para 24 ante) or Sch 4 para 5(4) (deemed supply which occurs when a person puts land forming part of a business to private use, or makes the land available to any person for use for any purpose other than a purpose of the business: see para 24 ante): Sch 8 Pt II Group 5 note 20 (as so substituted). In *Customs and Excise Comrs v St Mary's Roman Catholic High School* [1996] STC 1091, it was held that the words 'in the course of construction' gave a wider scope to the services included in the Value Added Tax Act 1994 Sch 8 Pt II Group 5 item 2 (as substituted) than those relating to the construction of the building itself; but that there must still be a relation between them and the construction of the building; either the services must facilitate the construction of the building or they must produce in their finished result one whole with the building; and this connection must be both functional (which test the school playground in issue satisfied) and temporal; a playground constructed 13 years after the building it was to service failed the latter test.

15 Where all or part of a building is intended for use solely for a relevant residential purpose or a relevant charitable purpose (1) a supply relating to the building (or any part of it) is not taken for these purposes or the purposes of head (4) in the text as relating to a building intended for such use unless it is made to a person who intends to use the building (or part) for such a purpose (see *League of Friends of Kingston Hospital v Customs and Excise Comrs* (1995) VAT Decision 12764, [1995] STI 68); and (2) a grant or other supply relating to the building (or part of it) is not taken as relating to a building intended for such use unless, before it is made, the person to whom it is made has given to the person making it a certificate in such form as may be specified in a notice published by the commissioners stating that the grant or other supply (or a specified part of it) so relates: Value Added Tax Act 1994 Sch 8 Pt II Group 5 note 12 (as substituted: see note 1 supra). The relevant form is set out as Customs and Excise Notice 708 *Buildings and Construction* (1 March 1995) Annex A. The commissioners, by concession, permit a certain amount of 'non-qualifying use' of a building otherwise intended for relevant residential or relevant charitable purposes to the extent that, if the customer certifies that the building will be used for a qualifying purpose for at least 90% of the total time the building is available for use, the supplier can ignore the non-qualifying use and zero-rate his supplies; but if the non-qualifying use of the building (or part) exceeds this amount, the supplies must be wholly standard-rated: see Customs and Excise Notice 708 para 3.2.

There may be a claw-back from the recipient of the VAT which would have been charged on the supplies relating to the building if there is a change of use, or disposal, of the building within ten years: see para 164 post.

16 Value Added Tax Act 1994 Sch 8 Pt II Group 5 item 2(a) (as substituted: see note 1 supra).

17 This reference to the construction of a civil engineering work does not include a reference to the conversion, reconstruction, alteration or enlargement of a work: ibid Sch 8 Pt II Group 5 note 15 (as substituted: see note 1 supra). As to the ambit of these words see note 7 supra.

18 Ibid Sch 8 Pt II Group 5 item 2(b) (as substituted: see note 1 supra). A caravan is not a residential caravan if residence in it throughout the year is prevented by the terms of a covenant, statutory planning consent or similar permission: Sch 8 Pt II Group 5 note 19 (as so substituted); and see *Customs and Excise Comrs v Barratt* [1995] STC 661n.

19 'Registered housing association' means a registered housing association within the meaning of the Housing Associations Act 1985 (see HOUSING): Value Added Tax Act 1994 Sch 8 Pt II Group 5 note 21 (as substituted: see note 1 supra).

20 Ibid Sch 8 Pt II Group 5 item 3 (as substituted: see note 1 supra). The conversion, other than to a building designed for a relevant residential purpose, of a non-residential part of a building which already contains a residential part is not included unless the result of that conversion is to create an additional dwelling or dwellings: see Sch 8 Pt II Group 5 note 9 (as so substituted); and note 12 supra. See also note 7 supra.

21 Ibid Sch 8 Pt II Group 5 item 3(a) (as substituted: see note 1 supra).

22 Ibid Sch 8 Pt II Group 5 item 3(b) (as substituted: see note 1 supra).

23   'Building materials', in relation to any description of a building, means goods of a description ordinarily incorporated by builders in a building of that description or its site (see *Customs and Excise Comrs v Smitmit Design Centre Ltd, Customs and Excise Comrs v Sharp's Bedroom Design Ltd* [1982] STC 525), but does not include:

    (1)   finished or prefabricated furniture, other than furniture designed to be fitted in kitchens;

    (2)   materials for the construction of fitted furniture, other than kitchen furniture;

    (3)   electrical or gas appliances, unless the appliance is an appliance which is (a) designed to heat space or water (or both) or to provide ventilation, air cooling, air purification or dust extraction; or (b) intended for use in a building designed as a number of dwellings and is a door entry system, a waste disposal unit or a machine for compacting waste; or (c) a burglar alarm, fire alarm, or fire safety equipment or designed solely for the purpose of enabling aid to be summoned in an emergency; or (d) a lift or hoist;

    (4)   carpets or carpeting material,

and for these purposes the 'incorporation' of goods in a building includes their installation as fittings: Value Added Tax Act 1994 Sch 8 Pt II Group 5 notes 22, 23 (as substituted: see note 1 supra).

The undertaking of joinery work off-site, to be delivered to the site where it would be installed by a third party builder, did not constitute the supply of building materials within the equivalent predecessor provision to Sch 8 Pt II Group 5 item 4 (as so substituted) merely because the joiner was obliged to rectify the work on-site if it proved to be defective: *Customs and Excise Comrs v Jeffs (t/a J & J Joinery)* [1995] STC 759. The expression 'fitted furniture' should be given its ordinary popular meaning: *Customs and Excise Comrs v McLean Homes Midland Ltd* [1993] STC 335. The requirement that the building materials be supplied to the person to whom the supplier is also supplying services reverses the decision in *Customs and Excise Comrs v John Willmott Housing Ltd* [1987] STC 692 at 696.

24   Value Added Tax Act 1994 Sch 8 Pt II Group 5 item 4 (as substituted: see note 1 supra). For the meaning of 'intended for use' as applied to head (2) in the text see Sch 8 Pt II Group 5 note 12 (as so substituted); and note 15 supra.

25   Ibid Sch 8 Pt II Group 5 note 13(a), (b), (i) (as substituted: see note 1 supra). This provision has been criticised as being discriminatory and as exceeding the limitation on the exemption for land imposed by EC Council Directive 77/388 (OJ L145, 13.6.77, p 1) art 13(B)(b)(1); and the VAT and duties tribunal refused to apply it where the taxpayer was prohibited from occupying property which was not accommodation in the 'hotel sector or in a sector with a similar function': *Ashworth v Customs and Excise Comrs* (1995) VAT Decision 12924, [1995] STI 478.

26   Value Added Tax Act 1994 Sch 8 Pt II Group 5 note 13(a), (b), (ii) (as substituted: see note 1 supra).

27   Ibid Sch 8 Pt II Group 5 note 10(a), (b), (i) (as substituted: see note 1 supra).

28   Ibid Sch 8 Pt II Group 5 note 10(a), (b), (ii) (as substituted: see note 1 supra).

29   Ibid Sch 8 Pt II Group 5 note 10(a), (b), (iii) (as substituted: see note 1 supra).

164. Residential and charitable buildings; change of use etc. Where a person receives a supply which is wholly or partly zero-rated[1] because it relates to a building (or a part of a building) which is intended for use solely for a relevant residential purpose[2] or a relevant charitable purpose[3], the scope of zero-rating may be reduced if one of a number of events occurs within 10 years of the completion[4] of the building[5]. Thus, where:

    (1)   one or more relevant zero-rated supplies[6] relating to a building (or part of a building) have been made to any person[7];

    (2)   within the period of 10 years beginning with the day on which the building is completed, the person grants an interest in, right over or licence to occupy the building or any part of it (or the building or any part of it including, consisting of or forming part of the part to which the relevant zero-rated supply or supplies related); and

    (3)   after the grant the whole or any part of the building, or the part to which the grant relates (or the whole of the building or of the part to which the grant relates, or any part of it including, consisting of or forming part of the part to which the relevant zero-rated supply or supplies related) is not intended for use solely for a relevant residential purpose or a relevant charitable purpose[8],

then to the extent that the grant relates to so much of the building as (a) by reason of its intended use gave rise to the relevant zero-rated supply or supplies; and (b) is not intended for use solely for a relevant residential purpose or a relevant charitable purpose after the grant, it is taken to be a taxable supply[9] in the course or furtherance of a business[10] which is not zero-rated[11], if it would not otherwise be such a supply[12]. Where:

(i)   one or more relevant zero-rated supplies relating to a building (or part of a building) have been made to any person; and

(ii)   within the period of 10 years beginning with the day on which the building is completed, the person uses the building or any part of it (or the building or any part of it including, consisting of or forming part of the part to which the relevant zero-rated supply or supplies related) for a purpose which is neither a relevant residential purpose nor a relevant charitable purpose[13],

his interest in, right over or licence to occupy so much of the building as (A) by reason of its intended use gave rise to the relevant zero-rated supply or supplies, and (B) is used otherwise than for a relevant residential purpose or a relevant charitable purpose, is treated for the purposes of the Value Added Tax Act 1994 as supplied to him for the purpose of a business carried on by him and supplied by him in the course or furtherance of the business when he first uses it for a purpose which is neither a relevant residential purpose nor a relevant charitable purpose[14].

Where heads (A) and (B) above apply, the supply is taken to be a taxable supply which is not zero-rated[15], if it would not otherwise be such a supply; and the value of the supply is such that the amount of VAT chargeable on it is equal to the amount of VAT which would have been chargeable on the relevant zero-rated supply (or, where there was more than one such supply, the aggregate amount which would have been chargeable on them) had so much of the building as is mentioned in those heads not been intended for use solely for a relevant residential purpose or a relevant charitable purpose[16].

1   For the meaning of 'zero-rated supply' generally see para 158 ante; and for the meaning of 'supply' see para 21 ante. See also note 6 infra.

2   For the meaning of 'use for a relevant residential purpose' see the Value Added Tax Act 1994 s 30(2), Sch 8 Pt II Group 5 notes 4, 5 (as substituted); and para 163 note 9 ante (applied by s 51(1), Sch 10 para 9 (amended by the Value Added Tax (Buildings and Land) Order 1995, SI 1995/279, arts 2, 9)).

3   For the meaning of 'use for a relevant charitable purpose' see the Value Added Tax Act 1994 Sch 8 Pt II Group 5 note 6 (as substituted); and para 163 note 10 ante (applied by Sch 10 para 9 (as amended: see note 2 supra)).

4   As to when a building is complete see ibid s 31(1), Sch 9 Pt II Group 1 note 2; and see para 142 note 6 ante (applied by Sch 10 para 9 (as amended: see note 2 supra)).

5   See ibid Sch 10 para 1; and the text and notes 6–16 infra.

6   For these purposes, 'relevant zero-rated supply' means a grant or other supply taking place on or after 1 April 1989 which (1) relates to a building intended for use solely for a relevant residential purpose or a relevant charitable purpose or part of such a building; and (2) is zero-rated, in whole or in part, by virtue of ibid Sch 8 Pt II Group 5 (as substituted) (see para 163 ante): Sch 10 para 1(1). For the meaning of 'grant' see Sch 9 Pt II Group 1 notes 1, 1A (as substituted and added); and para 142 note 2 ante (applied by Sch 10 para 9 (as amended: see note 2 supra)).

7   It would seem that, if an event within ibid Sch 10 para 1 occurs, it is only the recipient of the zero-rated supply (the 'any person' to whom the zero-rated supply has been made) who suffers 'claw-back' of VAT; and that if, therefore, that person assigns his interest in the land to another person who intends to use the building for a relevant residential or relevant charitable purpose, and an event within Sch 10 para 1 occurs, that assignee will not suffer 'claw-back' of VAT.

8   Ibid Sch 10 para 1(2).

9   For the meaning of 'taxable supply' see para 12 note 3 ante.

10   For the meaning of 'in the course or furtherance of a business' see paras 12 note 5, 17 note 2 ante.

11   Ie by virtue the Value Added Tax Act 1994 Sch 8 Pt II Group 5 (as substituted): see para 163 ante.

12   Ibid Sch 10 para 1(3).

13   Ibid Sch 10 para 1(4).

14   Ibid Sch 10 para 1(5).

15   See note 11 supra.

16   Value Added Tax Act 1994 Sch 10 para 1(6).

165. Protected buildings. The following are zero-rated supplies[1]:

(1) the first[2] grant[3] by a person substantially reconstructing[4] a protected building[5], of a major interest[6] in, or in any part of, the building or its site[7];

(2) the supply, in the course of an approved[8] alteration[9] of a protected building, of any services[10] other than the services of an architect, surveyor or any person acting as consultant or in a supervisory capacity[11];

(3) the supply of building materials[12] to a person to whom the supplier is supplying services within head (2) above which include the incorporation[13] of the materials into the building or its site[14].

A protected building means a building which is designed to remain as or become a dwelling or number of dwellings[15] or is intended for use solely for a relevant residential purpose[16] or a relevant charitable purpose[17] after the reconstruction or alteration and which in either case is a listed building[18] or a scheduled[19] monument[20].

When part of a protected building that is substantially reconstructed is designed to remain as or become a dwelling or a number of dwellings, or is intended for use solely for a relevant residential or relevant charitable purpose, and part is not:

(a) a grant or other supply relating only to the part so designed or intended for such use, or its site, is treated as relating to a building so designed or intended for such use;

(b) a grant or other supply relating only to the part neither so designed nor intended for such use, or its site, is not so treated; and

(c) in the case of any other grant or other supply relating to, or to any part of, the building, or its site, an apportionment is made to determine the extent to which it is to be so treated[21].

1   See the Value Added Tax Act 1994 s 30(2), Sch 8 Pt II Group 6 (substituted by the Value Added Tax (Protected Buildings) Order 1995, SI 1995/283); and the text and notes 2–21 infra. The Value Added Tax Act 1994 s 30(3) (see paras 158 ante, 175 post) does not apply to goods forming part of a description of supply in Sch 8 Pt II Group 6 (as so substituted): see Sch 8 Pt II Group 5 note 24 (as substituted); and para 163 note 1 ante (applied by Sch 8 Pt II Group 6 note 3 (as so substituted)). For the meaning of 'zero-rated supply' see para 158 ante; and for the meaning of 'supply' see para 21 ante. As to the interpretation by the Commissioners of Customs and Excise of Sch 8 Pt II Group 6 (as so substituted) see Customs and Excise Notice 708 *Buildings and Construction* (1 March 1995) Pt 8.

2   The inclusion of the word 'first' modifies earlier authority to the effect that zero-rating was available when a building was sold after having been first let; as to that earlier authority see *Customs and Excise Comrs v Link Housing Association Ltd* [1992] STC 718.

3   'Grant' includes an assignment or surrender: see the Value Added Tax Act 1994 Sch 8 Pt II Group 5 note 1 (as substituted); and para 163 note 3 ante (applied by Sch 8 Pt II Group 6 note 3 (as substituted: see note 1 supra)).

4   The present participle 'reconstructing' does not exclude from this provision a grant which takes place after the reconstruction has been completed: *Customs and Excise Comrs v Link Housing Association Ltd* [1992] STC 718; but see note 2 supra.

     For the purposes of the Value Added Tax Act 1994 Sch 8 Pt II Group 6 item 1 (as substituted: see note 1 supra) a protected building is not regarded as substantially reconstructed unless the reconstruction is such that at least one of the following conditions is fulfilled when the reconstruction is completed: (1) that, of the works carried out to effect the reconstruction, at least three-fifths, measured by reference to cost, are of such a nature that the supply of services, other than excluded services (ie the services of an architect, surveyor or other person acting as consultant or in a supervisory capacity), materials and other items to carry out the works, would, if supplied by a taxable person, be within either Sch 8 Pt II Group 6 item 2 (as so substituted) or Sch 8 Pt II Group 6 item 3 (as so substituted) (see heads (2)–(3) in the text); and (2) that the reconstructed building incorporates no more of the original building (ie, the building as it was before the reconstruction began) than the external walls, together with other external features of architectural or historic interest: Sch 8 Pt II Group 6 note 4 (as so substituted). For the meaning of 'protected building' see the text and notes 15–20 infra.

5   See the text and notes 15-20 post.

6   For the meaning of 'major interest' see para 24 note 7 ante.

7   Value Added Tax Act 1994 Sch 8 Pt II Group 6 item 1 (as substituted: see note 1 supra). As to the meaning of 'site' see *Stapenhill Developments Ltd v Customs and Excise Comrs* [1984] VATTR 1 at 10; and para 163 note 5 ante.

8   'Approved alteration' means: (1) in the case of a protected building which is an ecclesiastical building to which the Planning (Listed Buildings and Conservation Areas) Act 1990 s 60 applies (see TOWN AND COUNTRY PLANNING vol 46 (Reissue) para 903), any works of alteration; and (2) in any other case, works of alteration which may not, or but for the existence of a Crown interest or Duchy interest could not, be carried out unless authorised under, or under any provision of (a) Pt I (ss 1–68) (as amended) (see TOWN AND COUNTRY PLANNING vol 46 (Reissue) para 903 et seq); or (b) the Ancient Monuments and Archaeological Areas Act 1979 Pt I (ss 1–32) (as amended) (see OPEN SPACES AND HISTORIC BUILDINGS vol 34 para 595 et seq), and for which, except in the case of a Crown interest or Duchy interest, consent has been obtained under any provision of that Part of the relevant Act; but 'approved alteration' does not include any works of repair or maintenance, or any incidental alteration to the fabric of a building which results from the carrying out of works of repairs or maintenance work: Value Added Tax Act 1994 Sch 8 Pt II Group 6 note 6 (as substituted: see note 1 supra). 'Crown interest' means an interest belonging to Her Majesty in right of the Crown, or belonging to a government department, and includes any estate or interest held in right of the Prince and Steward of Scotland; and 'Duchy interest' means an interest belonging to Her Majesty in right of the Duchy of Lancaster, or belonging to the Duchy of Cornwall: Ancient Monuments and Archaeological Areas Act 1979 s 50(4) (applied by the Value Added Tax Act 1994 Sch 8 Pt II Group 6 note 8 (as so substituted)). It does not follow from the fact that listed building consent was obtained for works carried out that those works necessarily constitute 'alterations' for the purpose of Sch 8 Pt II Group 6 item 2 (as substituted): *Mann v Customs and Excise Comrs* (1996) VAT Decision 14004, [1996] STI 962.

     A building which is used or which is available for use by a minister of religion wholly or mainly as a residence from which to perform the duties of his office is not an ecclesiastical building for the purposes of head (1) supra: Value Added Tax Act 1994 Sch 8 Pt II Group 6 note 7 (as so substituted). The word 'mainly' probably means 'more than half', though there is nothing here to indicate by reference to what this is calculated; cf *Fawcett Properties Ltd v Buckingham County Council* [1961] AC 636 at 669, [1960] 3 All ER 503 at 512, HL, per Lord Morton of Henryton; and see also *Re Hatschek's Patents, ex p Zerenner* [1909] 2 Ch 68; *Miller v Ottilie (Owners)* [1944] KB 188, [1944] 1 All ER 277; *Franklin v Gramophone Co Ltd* [1948] 1 KB 542 at 555, [1948] 1 All ER 353 at 358, CA, per Somervell LJ; and *Berthelemey v Neale* [1952] 1 All ER 437, 96 Sol Jo 165, CA.

9   As to the meaning of 'alteration' see para 163 notes 6–7 ante. The construction of a building separate from, but in the curtilage of, a protected building does not constitute an alteration of the protected building for these purposes: Value Added Tax Act 1994 Sch 8 Pt II Group 6 note 10 (as substituted: see note 1 supra). A barn connected to a protected building by a covered walkway was not separate from the protected building within the meaning of Sch 8 Pt II Group 6 note 10 (as so substituted), so that alterations to the barn qualified for zero-rating: *Customs and Excise Comrs v Arbib* [1995] STC 490. In *ACT Construction Ltd v Customs and Excise Comrs* [1982] 1 All ER 84, [1982] STC 25, HL (relating to previous legislation, now repealed) works of underpinning were held to be new work, converting short-life buildings into buildings with a long life and, as such, incapable of falling within the classification of 'repair or maintenance', which was a single, composite phrase, in which the words used were not antithetical (and which might, in some cases, overlap with 'structural alteration'); see also *Customs and Excise Comrs v Windflower Housing Association* [1995] STC 860.

10   These services do not include the services described in the Value Added Tax Act 1994 s 5(1) Sch 4 paras 1(1), 5(4) (see para 24 ante): Sch 8 Pt II Group 6 note 11 (as substituted: see note 1 supra).

11   Ibid Sch 8 Pt II Group 6 item 2 (as substituted: see note 1 supra). Where a service is supplied in part in relation to an approved alteration of a building, and in part for other purposes, an apportionment may be made to determine the extent to which the supply is to be treated as falling within Sch 8 Pt II Group 6 item 2 (as so substituted): Sch 8 Pt II Group 6 note 9 (as so substituted).

12   For the meaning of 'building materials' see ibid Sch 8 Pt II Group 5 note 22 (as substituted); and para 163 note 23 ante (applied by Sch 8 Pt II Group 6 note 3 (as substituted: see note 1 supra)).

13   'Incorporation' includes the installation of the goods as fittings: see ibid Sch 8 Pt II Group 5 note 23 (as substituted) and para 163 note 23 ante (applied by Sch 8 Pt II Group 6 note 3 (as substituted: see note 1 supra)).

14   Ibid Sch 8 Pt II Group 6 item 3 (as substituted: see note 1 supra). The undertaking of joinery work off-site, to be delivered to the site where it would be installed by a third party builder, did not constitute the supply of building materials within the equivalent predecessor provisions to Sch 8 Pt II Group 6 item 3 (as so substituted) merely because the joiner was obliged to rectify the work on-site if it proved to be defective: *Customs and Excise Comrs v Jeffs (t/a J & J Joinery)* [1995] STC 759.

15   For these purposes, a building is designed to remain as or become a dwelling or number of dwellings where in relation to each dwelling the following conditions are satisfied: (1) the dwelling consists of

self-contained living accommodation; (2) there is no provision for direct internal access from the dwelling to any other dwelling or part of a dwelling; and (3) the separate use or disposal of the dwelling is not prohibited by the terms of any covenant, statutory planning consent or similar provision; and includes a garage (occupied together with a dwelling) either constructed at the same time as the building or, where the building has been substantially reconstructed, at the same time as that reconstruction: Value Added Tax Act 1994 Sch 8 Pt II Group 6 note 2 (as substituted: see note 1 supra). See also Sch 8 Pt II Group 5 notes 13, 14 (as substituted); and para 163 notes 4, 25 ante (applied with the necessary modifications by Sch 8 Pt II Group 6 note 3 (as so substituted)). The limitation that a building must be designed to remain as a dwelling refers to its purpose and not to its use: *Mann v Customs and Excise Comrs* (1996) VAT Decision 14004, [1996] STI 962. By concession, developers of buildings which were granted a certificate of immunity from listing as a protected building issued by the Secretary of State for National Heritage prior to 16 April 1996, and which, on the grant of a major interest following substantial reconstruction, are to be used solely for a non-business charitable purpose, are given a status equivalent to that for protected buildings, with the result that the works carried out will be zero-rated if (but for the certificate) they would have fallen within the Value Added Tax Act 1994 Sch 8 Pt II Group 6 (as substituted): Customs and Excise News Release 25/96 (16 April 1996) [1996] STI 761. However, the exemption is not available in respect of certificates granted after that date; and developers will be expected to decide on the relative merits of immunity from listing and the zero-rating of their works. In *Morfee v Customs and Excise Comrs* (1996) VAT Decision 13816, [1996] STI 469, it was held that the zero-rating afforded to a dwelling which was a protected building could extend to other buildings (such as a barn) which formed part of the dwelling.

16   For the meaning of 'relevant residential purpose' see the Value Added Tax Act 1994 Sch 8 Pt II Group 5 note 4 (as substituted); and para 163 note 9 ante (applied by Sch 8 Pt II Group 6 note 3 (as substituted: see note 1 supra)). See also Sch 8 Pt II Group 5 note 12 (as substituted); and para 163 note 15 ante (as so applied, with the necessary modifications).

17   For the meaning of 'relevant charitable purpose' see ibid Sch 8 Pt II Group 5 note 6 (as substituted); and para 163 note 10 ante (applied by Sch 8 Pt II Group 6 note 3 (as substituted: see note 1 supra)). See also Sch 8 Pt II Group 5 note 12 (as substituted) and para 163 note 15 ante (as so applied, with the necessary modifications).

18   Ie a listed building within the meaning of the Planning (Listed Buildings and Conservation Areas) Act 1990: see TOWN AND COUNTRY PLANNING vol 46 (Reissue) para 891.

19   Ie a scheduled monument within the meaning of the Ancient Monuments and Archaeological Areas Act 1979: see OPEN SPACES vol 34 para 595 et seq.

20   Value Added Tax Act 1994 Sch 8 Pt II Group 6 note 1 (as substituted: see note 1 supra). The intention is that 'granny flats' and similar extensions to existing houses should not qualify for zero-rating: Customs and Excise Notice 708 *Buildings and Construction* (1 March 1995) para 8.10.

21   Value Added Tax Act 1994 Sch 8 Pt II Group 5 note 5 (as substituted: see note 1 supra).

166. International services. The following are zero-rated supplies[1]:

(1)   the supply of services of work carried out on goods which, for that purpose, have been obtained or acquired in, or imported into, any of the member states and which are intended to be, and in fact are, subsequently exported to a place outside the member states[2] (a) by or on behalf of the supplier[3]; or (b) where the recipient of the services belongs in a place outside the member states, by or on behalf of the recipient[4];

(2)   the supply of services consisting of the making of arrangements for (a) the export of any goods to a place outside the member states[5]; (b) a supply of services of the description specified in head (1) above[6]; or (c) any supply of services which is made outside the member states[7].

Exempt supplies of services of insurance[8] and finance[9] are excluded from zero-rating under heads (1) and (2) above[10].

1   See the Value Added Tax Act 1994 s 30(2), Sch 8 Pt II Group 7; and heads (1)–(2) in the text. By class concession, the United Kingdom zero-rates supplies of services of valuation of goods or work on goods performed in the United Kingdom for customers who belong in other member states: see Customs and Excise Business Brief 26/93 [1993] STI 1217; and as to supplies of work on goods to businesses in other member states see Customs and Excise Business Brief 11/93 [1993] STI 680. Training services supplied

to overseas governments are zero-rated by concession: Customs and Excise Business Brief 32/93 [1993] STI 1332.

2   As to the territories included in, or excluded from, the member states for the purposes of VAT see para 10 ante.

3   Value Added Tax Act 1994 Sch 8 Pt II Group 7 item 1(a).

4   Ibid Sch 8 Pt II Group 7 item 1(b).

5   Ibid Sch 8 Pt II Group 7 item 2(a).

6   Ibid Sch 8 Pt II Group 7 item 2(b).

7   Ibid Sch 8 Pt II Group 7 item 2(c).

8   Ie supplies of services of insurance falling within ibid s 31(1), Sch 9 Pt II Group 2: see para 146 ante.

9   Ie supplies of services of finance falling within ibid s 31(1), Sch 9 Pt II Group 5: see para 149 ante.

10   Ibid Sch 8 Pt II Group 7 note.

167. Transport. The following are zero-rated supplies[1]:

(1)   the supply, repair or maintenance of a qualifying ship[2] or the modification or conversion of any such ship, provided that when so modified or converted it will remain a qualifying ship[3], including the letting on hire of such goods as this head includes[4];

(2)   the supply, repair or maintenance of a qualifying aircraft[5] or the modification or conversion of any such aircraft, provided that when so modified or converted it will remain a qualifying aircraft[6], including the letting on hire of such goods as this head includes[7];

(3)   the supply of parts and equipment, of a kind ordinarily installed or incorporated in, and to be installed or incorporated in, the propulsion, navigation or communication systems or the general structure of a qualifying ship or qualifying aircraft[8], including the letting on hire of such goods as this head includes[9] but not including the supply of parts and equipment to a government department unless certain conditions are fulfilled[10];

(4)   the supply of life jackets, life rafts, smoke hoods and similar safety equipment for use in a qualifying ship or qualifying aircraft[11], including the letting on hire of such goods as this head includes[12] but not including the supply of parts and equipment to a government department unless certain conditions are fulfilled[13];

(5)   the supply to, and repair or maintenance for, a charity providing rescue or assistance at sea of (a) any lifeboat[14]; (b) carriage equipment designed solely for the launching and recovery of lifeboats; (c) tractors for the sole use of the launching and recovery of lifeboats; (d) winches and hauling equipment for the sole use of the recovery of lifeboats[15], including the letting on hire of such goods as this head includes[16];

(6)   the construction, modification, repair or maintenance for a charity providing rescue or assistance at sea of slipways used solely for the launching and recovery of lifeboats[17], including the letting on hire of such goods as this head includes[18];

(7)   the supply of spare parts or accessories to a charity providing rescue or assistance at sea for use in, or with goods comprised in, head (5) above or slipways comprised in head (6) above[19], including the letting on hire of such goods as this head includes[20];

(8)   transport of passengers[21] (a) in any vehicle, ship or aircraft designed or adapted to carry not less than 12 passengers; (b) by the Post Office; (c) on any scheduled flight; or (d) from a place within to a place outside the United Kingdom, or vice versa, to the extent that those services are supplied in the United Kingdom[22];

(9)   the transport of goods from a place within to a place outside the member states, or vice versa, to the extent that those services are supplied within the United Kingdom[23];

(10) any services provided for (a) the handling of ships or aircraft in a port, customs and excise airport[24] or outside the United Kingdom; or (b) the handling or storage, in a port or customs and excise airport or on land adjacent to a port, of goods carried in a ship or aircraft[25]; but not including the letting on hire of goods[26];

(11) air navigation services[27];

(12) pilotage services[28];

(13) salvage or towage services[29];

(14) any services supplied for, or in connection with, the surveying of any ship or aircraft or the classification of any ship or aircraft for the purposes of any register[30];

(15) the making of arrangements for (a) the supply of, or of space in, any ship or aircraft[31]; (b) the supply of any service included in heads (1) and (2), (5) to (14) above and (16) and (17) below[32]; or the supply of any goods of a description falling within head (3) or head (4) above[33];

(16) the supply of services consisting of (a) the handling or storage of goods at, or their transport to or from, a place at which they are to be exported to, or have been imported from, a place outside the member states; or (b) the handling or storage of such goods in connection with such transport[34];

(17) the supply, to a person who receives the supply for the purpose of a business carried on by him and who belongs outside the United Kingdom, of services of a description specified in heads (10)(a), (11), (14) or (15)(a) above[35];

(18) the supply of a designated travel service[36] to be enjoyed outside the European Community, to the extent to which the supply is so enjoyed[37]; and

(19) intra-Community transport services[38] supplied in connection with the transport of goods to or from the Azores or Madeira or between those places, to the extent that the services are treated as supplied in the United Kingdom[39].

1   See the Value Added Tax Act 1994 s 30(2), Sch 8 Pt II Group 8 (as amended); and heads (1)–(19) in the text. For the meaning of 'zero-rated supply' see para 158 ante; and for the meaning of 'supply' see para 21 ante.

2   A 'qualifying ship' is any ship of a gross tonnage of not less than 15 tons which is neither designed nor adapted for use for recreation or pleasure: ibid Sch 8 Pt II Group 8 note A1(a) (added by the Value Added Tax (Ships and Aircraft) Order 1995, SI 1995/3039, art 2(e)). For these purposes the supply of a qualifying ship or, as the case may be, aircraft (see head (2) in the text) includes the supply of services under a charter of that ship or aircraft except where the services supplied under such a charter consist wholly of one or more of the following: (1) transport of passengers; (2) accommodation; (3) entertainment; (4) education, and are services wholly performed in the United Kingdom: Value Added Tax Act 1994 Sch 8 Pt II Group 8 note 1 (amended by the Value Added Tax (Ships and Aircraft) Order 1995 art 2(f)). For the meaning of 'ship' see para 13 note 8 ante; and for the meaning of 'United Kingdom' see para 4 note 3 ante.

3   Value Added Tax Act 1994 Sch 8 Pt II Group 8 item 1 (substituted by the Value Added Tax (Ships and Aircraft) Order 1995 art 2(a)). As to the meaning of repair and maintenance in this context see *A & P Appledore (Falmouth) Ltd v Customs and Excise Comrs* [1992] VATTR 22.

4   Value Added Tax Act 1994 Sch 8 Pt II Group 8 note 2.

5   A 'qualifying aircraft' is any aircraft of a weight of not less than 8,000 kg which is neither designed nor adapted for use for recreation or pleasure: ibid Sch 8 Pt II Group 8 note A1(b) (as added: see note 2 supra).

6   Ibid Sch 8 Pt II Group 8 item 2 (substituted by the Value Added Tax (Ships and Aircraft) Order 1995 art 2(b)); and see note 3 supra.

7   Value Added Tax Act 1994 Sch 8 Pt II Group 8 note 2.

8   Ibid Sch 8 Pt II Group 8 item 2A (added by the Value Added Tax (Ships and Aircraft) Order 1995 art 2(c)).

9   Value Added Tax Act 1994 Sch 8 Pt II Group 8 note 2 (amended by Value Added Tax (Ships and Aircraft) Order 1995 art 2(g)).

10 Value Added Tax Act 1994 Sch 8 Pt II Group 8 note 2A (added by the Value Added Tax (Ships and Aircraft) Order 1995 art 2(h)). The conditions are that (1) the parts and equipment are installed or incorporated in the course of a supply which is treated as being made in the course or furtherance of a business carried on by the department; or (2) they are to be installed or incorporated in ships or aircraft used for the purpose of

providing rescue or assistance at sea: Value Added Tax Act 1994 Sch 8 Pt II Group 8 note 2A (as so added). For the meaning of 'in the course or furtherance of a business' see paras 12 note 5, 17 note 2 ante.

11 Ibid Sch 8 Pt II Group 8 item 2B (as added: see note 8 supra).

12 See note 9 supra.

13 See note 10 supra.

14 'Lifeboat' means any vessel used or to be used solely for rescue or assistance at sea: ibid Sch 8 Pt II Group 8 note 4.

15 Ibid Sch 8 Pt II Group 8 item 3(a). Heads (5)–(7) in the text do not apply unless, before the supply is made, the recipient of the supply gives to the person making the supply a certificate stating the name and address of the recipient and that the supply is of a description specified in those heads: Sch 8 Pt II Group 8 note 3.

16 Ibid Sch 8 Pt II Group 8 note 2.

17 Ibid Sch 8 Pt II Group 8 item 3(b); and see note 15 supra.

18 Ibid Sch 8 Pt II Group 8 note 2.

19 Ibid Sch 8 Pt II Group 8 item 3(c); and see note 15 supra.

20 Ibid Sch 8 Pt II Group 8 note 2.

21 The 'transport of passengers' signifies the carriage of passengers from one place to another and excludes travel on an amusement device, such as a 'big dipper', where movement is in effect confined to one spot: *Customs and Excise Comrs v Blackpool Pleasure Beach Co* [1974] 1 All ER 1011, [1974] STC 138. The supply of an identity card enabling the holder to obtain railway tickets at reduced price is a payment in advance for 'transport' within the Value Added Tax Act 1994 Sch 8 Pt II Group 8 item 4: *British Railways Board v Customs and Excise Comrs* [1977] 2 All ER 873, [1977] 1 WLR 588, CA.

22 Value Added Tax Act 1994 Sch 8 Pt II Group 8 item 4. This head does not include the transport of passengers (1) in any vehicle to, from or within a place of entertainment, recreation or amusement, or to, from or within a place of cultural, scientific, historical or similar interest, by the person, or a person connected with him, who supplies a right of admission to, or a right to use the facilities at, such a place; (2) in a motor vehicle (ie any mechanically propelled vehicle intended or adapted for use on the roads) between a car park, or land adjacent thereto, and an airport passenger terminal (or land adjacent thereto) by the person, or a person connected with him, who supplies facilities for the parking of vehicles in that car park; or (3) in an aircraft where the flight is advertised or held out to be for the purpose of providing entertainment, recreation or amusement or the experience of flying, or the experience of flying in that particular aircraft, and not primarily for the purpose of transporting passengers from one place to another: Sch 8 Pt II Group 8 notes 4A, 4C (added by the Value Added Tax (Transport) Order 1994, SI 1994/3014, arts 2, 3). For these purposes any question whether a person is connected with another is to be determined in accordance with the Income and Corporation Taxes Act s 839 (as amended) (see INCOME TAXATION vol 23 (Reissue) para 1250): Value Added Tax Act 1994 s 96(1), Sch 8 Pt II Group 8 note 4B (as so added).

The word 'recreation' does not include use as a home, so that the supply of a houseboat capable of self-propulsion is zero-rated under this head: *Everett and London Tideway Harbour Co Ltd v Customs and Excise Comrs* (1994) VAT Decision 11736, [1994] STI 539. The supply of a travel card conferring the right to reduced-price rail travel is zero-rated as a part-payment in advance for the travel: *British Railways Board v Customs and Excise Comrs* [1977] 2 All ER 873, [1977] 1 WLR 588, CA. The provision of in-flight catering is an integral part of the supply of transport: *British Airways plc v Customs and Excise Comrs* [1990] STC 643, CA. Membership fees paid to a travel club entitling members to discounted travel are zero-rated: *UK Travel Agent Ltd v Customs and Excise Comrs* (1995) VAT Decision 12861, [1995] STI 369. The provision of a limousine to take a passenger to and from the airport was part of the supply of the transport of passengers 'from a place within the United Kingdom...' etc within the Value Added Tax Act 1994 Sch 8 Pt II Group 8 item 4(d): *Virgin Atlantic Airways Ltd v Customs and Excise Comrs, Canadian Airlines International Ltd v Customs and Excise Comrs* [1995] STC 341. As to the commissioners' views on the tax treatment of airline passenger 'perks' see Customs and Excise Business Brief 4/96 [1996] STI 482. The supply for consideration of vouchers exchangeable for air travel is zero-rated as part of the arrangements for such travel: *Facthaven Incentive Marketing Ltd v Customs and Excise Comrs* (1991) VAT Decision 6443, [1991] STI 880. A pleasure cruise is (or is capable of being) a zero-rated supply of transport services, to which the hedonistic elements are merely incidental: *Customs and Excise Comrs v Peninsular and Oriental Steam Navigation Co Ltd* [1996] STC 698; *Virgin Atlantic Airways Ltd v Customs and Excise Comrs* (1996) VAT Decision 13480, [1996] STI 575); and see *Ashton (t/a Country Hotel Narrowboats) v Customs and Excise Comrs* (1996) VAT Decision 14197 [1996] STI 1381 (narrow boat cruises on canals may be zero-rated as supplies of passenger transport). See also Customs and Excise Business Brief 14/96 (July 1996) [1996] STI 1247, setting out the tests the commissioners will apply in determining whether or not a pleasure cruise constitutes a single zero-rated supply of transport.

23 Value Added Tax Act 1994 Sch 8 Pt II Group 8 item 5. As to the territories included in, or excluded from, the member states for VAT purposes see para 10 ante.

24 'Port' and 'customs and excise airport' have the same meanings as in the Customs and Excise Management Act 1979 (see CUSTOMS AND EXCISE): Value Added Tax Act 1994 s 96(1); Sch 8 Pt II Group 8 note 6.

25 Ibid Sch 8 Pt II Group 8 item 6. Except for the purposes of heads (16)–(17) in the text, head (10)(a) in the text only includes the supply of services where the ships or aircraft referred to in that head are qualifying ships or qualifying aircraft: Sch 8 Pt II Group 8 note 7 (amended by the Value Added Tax (Ships and Aircraft) Order 1995, SI 1995/3039, art 2(i)).

26 Value Added Tax Act 1994 Sch 8 Pt II Group 8 note 5.

27 Ibid Sch 8 Pt II Group 8 item 6A (added by the Value Added Tax (Transport) Order 1995, SI 1995/653, arts 2, 3). 'Air navigation services' has the same meaning as in the Civil Aviation Act 1982 (see AVIATION vol 2 (Reissue) para 1371 note 2): Value Added Tax Act 1994 Sch 8 Pt II Group 8 note 6A (added by the Value Added Tax (Transport) Order 1995 arts 2, 5). Except for the purposes of heads (16)–(17) in the text, head (11) in the text only includes the supply of any services where the ships or aircraft referred to in that head are qualifying ships or qualifying aircraft: Value Added Tax Act 1994 Sch 8 Pt II Group 8 note 7 (amended by the Value Added Tax (Transport) Order 1995 arts 2, 6; and by the Value Added Tax (Ships and Aircraft) Order 1995, SI 1995/3039, art 2(i)).

28 Value Added Tax Act 1994 Sch 8 Pt II Group 8 item 7.

29 Ibid Sch 8 Pt II Group 8 item 8.

30 Ibid Sch 8 Pt II Group 8 item 9. Except for the purposes of heads (16)–(17) in the text, head (14) in the text only includes the supply of any services where the ships or aircraft referred to in that head are qualifying ships or qualifying aircraft: Sch 8 Pt II Group 8 note 7 (as amended: see note 24 supra).

31 Ibid Sch 8 Pt II Group 8 item 10(a) (amended by the Value Added Tax (Ships and Aircraft) Order 1995, SI 1995/3039, art 2(d)). Except for the purposes of heads (16)–(17) in the text, head (15)(a) in the text only includes the supply of any services where the ships or aircraft referred to in that head are qualifying ships or qualifying aircraft: Value Added Tax Act 1994 Sch 8 Pt II Group 8 note 7 (as amended: see note 24 supra).

32 Ibid Sch 8 Pt II Group 8 item 10(b).

33 Ibid Sch 8 Pt II Group 8 item 10(c) (added by the Value Added Tax (Ships and Aircraft) Order 1995, SI 1995/3039, art 2(i)).

34 Value Added Tax Act 1994 Sch 8 Pt II Group 8 item 11(a).

35 Ibid Sch 8 Pt II Group 8 item 11(b) (amended by the Value Added Tax (Transport) Order 1995, SI 1995/653, arts 2, 4).

36 For these purposes, 'designated travel service' has the same meaning as in the Value Added Tax (Tour Operators) Order 1987, SI 1987/1806 (see para 31 note 19 ante): Value Added Tax Act 1994 Sch 8 Pt II Group 8 note 8. As to the tour operators' margin scheme see para 200 post.

37 Ibid Sch 8 Pt II Group 8 item 12. This provision affords zero-rating to goods and services bought in by a tour operator to be supplied on to a traveller which are enjoyed outside the European Community; but to the extent that the goods or services are enjoyed within the Community they are standard-rated. As to the standard rate of VAT see para 5 ante.

38 'Intra-Community transport services' means: (1) the intra-Community transport of goods within the meaning of the Value Added Tax (Place of Supply of Services) Order 1992, SI 1992/3121 (as amended) (see para 50 note 7 ante); (2) ancillary transport services within the meaning of that order (see para 50 note 5 ante) which are provided in connection with the intra-Community transport of goods; or (3) the making of arrangements for the supply by or to another person of a supply within heads (1) or (2) supra or any other activity which is intended to facilitate the making of such a supply, and, for this purpose only, the Azores and Madeira are each treated as a separate member state: Value Added Tax Act 1994 Sch 8 Pt II Group 8 note 9.

39 Ibid Sch 8 Pt II Group 8 item 13.

168. Caravans and houseboats. The following supplies are zero-rated[1]:

(1) caravans exceeding the limits of size for the time being permitted for the use on roads of a trailer drawn by a motor vehicle having an unladen weight of less than 2,030 kg[2];

(2) houseboats, being boats or other floating decked structures designed or adapted for use solely as places of permanent habitation and not having means of, or capable of being readily adapted for, self-propulsion[3]; and

(3) the supply of services consisting of the transfer of any undivided share of the property in, or of the possession of[4], such a caravan or houseboat or the supply of such a caravan or houseboat for private[5] use[6].

1 See the Value Added Tax Act 1994 s 30(2), Sch 8 Pt II Group 9; and heads (1)–(3) in the text. For the meaning of 'zero-rated supply' see para 158 ante; and for the meaning of 'supply' see para 21 ante. Schedule 8 Pt II Group 9 does not include (1) removable contents other than certain specified goods; or (2) the supply of accommodation in a caravan or houseboat: Sch 8 Pt II Group 9 note (a), (b). The goods specified for the purposes of head (1) supra are 'goods of a kind mentioned in Sch 8 Pt II Group 5 item 3'; but no such goods are mentioned in that item as substituted by the Value Added Tax (Construction of Buildings) Order 1995, SI 1995/280): see para 163 ante. The reference is presumably intended to be to either to the Value Added Tax Act 1994 Sch 8 Pt II Group 5 item 3 as originally enacted (builders' materials) or to Sch 8 Pt II Group 5 item 4 (as substituted) (building materials: see para 163 head (4) ante).

2 Value Added Tax Act 1994 Sch 8 Pt II Group 9 item 1.

3 Ibid Sch 8 Pt II Group 9 item 2. See *Roberts v Customs and Excise Comrs* [1992] VATTR 30 (a temporarily unseaworthy yacht falls within the Value Added Tax Act 1994 Sch 9 Pt II Group 1 item 1(k) (see para 142 ante), which does not require the vessel to be capable of navigation; and is not within Sch 8 Pt II Group 9 if not designed or adapted solely for use as a place of permanent habitation).

4 Ie services of the kind described in ibid s 5(1), Sch 4 para 1(1): see para 24 ante.

5 Ie services of the kind described in ibid Sch 4 para 5(4): see para 24 ante. The wording of Sch 8 Pt II Group 9 item 3 refers to Sch 4 para 5(3), but it is thought that this reference is intended to be to Sch 4 para 5(4), as the equivalent predecessor provision to Sch 8 Pt II Group 9 item 3 in the Value Added Tax Act 1983 referred to the equivalent predecessor provision in that Act of the Value Added Tax Act 1994 Sch 4 para 5(4); and Sch 4 para 5(3) refers to a supply of goods in the form of samples, and not to a supply of services. See also Sch 8 Pt II Group 6 note 11 (as substituted), referring to Sch 4 paras 1(1), 5(4); and para 165 note 10 ante.

6 Ibid Sch 8 Pt II Group 9 item 3.

169. Gold and bank notes.

169. Gold and bank notes. The following are zero-rated supplies[1]:

(1) the supply, by a central bank to another central bank or a member of the London Gold Market, of gold[2] held in the United Kingdom[3]; and

(2) the supply, by a member of the London Gold Market to a central bank, of gold held in the United Kingdom[4].

Supplies of gold in other circumstances are subject to VAT at the standard rate[5].

The issue by a bank of a note payable to bearer on demand is a zero-rated supply[6].

1 See the Value Added Tax Act 1994 s 30(2), Sch 8 Pt II Group 10; and heads (1)–(2) in the text. Schedule 8 Group 10 includes: (1) the granting of a right to acquire a quantity of gold; and (2) any supply described therein which, by virtue of s 5(1), Sch 4 para 1 is a supply of services (ie the transfer of any undivided share of gold or of the possession of gold: see para 24 ante): Sch 8 Pt II Group 10 note 3. Section 30(3) (see paras 158 ante, 175 post) does not apply to goods forming part of a description of supply in Sch 8 Pt II Group 10 (Sch 8 Pt II Group 10 note 2); but where gold (including, for this purpose, gold coins) is supplied to a central bank by a supplier in another member state, and the transaction involves the removal of the gold from that or some other member state to the United Kingdom, the taking possession of the gold by the central bank concerned is not treated as involving an acquisition of goods from another member state (and the transaction is therefore outside the scope of VAT): Value Added Tax (Treatment of Transactions) (No 2) Order 1992, SI 1992/3132, art 2; Interpretation Act 1978 s 17(2)(b). Similarly, the tax chargeable upon the importation of gold (including gold coins) from a place outside the member states is not payable where the importation is by a central bank: see the Value Added Tax (Imported Gold) Relief Order 1992, SI 1992/3124; and para 123 ante. For the meaning of 'United Kingdom' see para 4 note 3 ante; and for the meaning of 'another member state' see para 4 note 14 ante.

2 'Gold' includes gold coins: Value Added Tax Act 1994 Sch 8 Pt II Group 10 note 1.

3 Ibid Sch 8 Pt II Group 10 item 1.

4 Ibid Sch 8 Pt II Group 10 item 2.

5 See Customs and Excise Leaflet 701/21/93 (1 April 1993). Because of the opportunity for fraud, a compulsory special accounting and payment system exists for gold transactions. Where a taxable person makes a supply of gold to a person who (1) is himself a taxable person at the time when the supply is made; and (2) is supplied in connection with the carrying on by him of any business, it is for the person supplied, on the supplier's behalf, to account for and pay tax on the supply, and not for the supplier: see the Value Added Tax Act 1994 s 55(2); and para 26 ante.

6 Value Added Tax Act 1994 Sch 8 Pt II Group 11.

170. Drugs, medicines, aids for the handicapped etc. The following are zero-rated supplies[1]:

(1) the supply of any goods, or of services of letting on hire of any goods[2], dispensed, by a person registered in the register of pharmaceutical chemists[3], on the prescription of a person registered in the register of medical practitioners, the register of medical practitioners with limited registration[4] or the dentists'[5] register[6];

(2) the supply of any goods, or of services of letting on hire of any goods[7], in accordance with a requirement or authorisation under certain regulations[8] by a person registered in the register of medical practitioners or the register of medical practitioners with limited registration[9];

(3) the supply to a handicapped[10] person for domestic or his personal use, or to a charity for making available to handicapped persons, by sale or otherwise, for domestic or their personal use, of, or of services of letting on hire of[11]:

    (a) medical or surgical appliances designed solely for the relief of a severe abnormality or severe injury;

    (b) electrically or mechanically adjustable beds designed for invalids;

    (c) commode chairs, commode stools, devices incorporating a bidet jet and warm air drier and frames or other devices for sitting over or rising from a sanitary appliance;

    (d) chair lifts or stair lifts designed for use in connection with invalid wheelchairs;

    (e) hoists and lifters designed for use by invalids;

    (f) motor vehicles designed or substantially and permanently adapted for the carriage of a person in a wheelchair or on a stretcher and of no more than five other persons;

    (g) equipment and appliances not included in heads (a) to (f) above designed solely for use by a handicapped person;

    (h) parts and accessories designed solely for use in or with goods described in heads (a) to (g) above; and

    (i) boats designed or substantially and permanently adapted for use by handicapped persons[12];

(4) the supply to a handicapped person of services of adapting goods to suit his condition[13];

(5) the supply to a charity of services of adapting goods to suit the condition of a handicapped person to whom the goods are to be made available, by sale or otherwise, by the charity[14];

(6) the supply to a handicapped person or to a charity of a service of repair or maintenance of any goods specified in head (3) above or in head (7), head (19) or head (20) below and supplied as described in the relevant head[15];

(7) the supply of goods in connection with a supply described in head (4), head (5) or head (6) above[16];

(8) the supply to a handicapped person or to a charity of services necessarily performed in the installation of equipment or appliances (including parts and accessories therefor) specified in head (3) above and supplied as described in that head[17];

(9) the supply to a handicapped person of a service of constructing ramps or widening doorways or passages for the purpose of facilitating his entry to or movement within his private residence[18];

(10) the supply to a charity of a service described in head (9) above for the purpose of facilitating a handicapped person's entry to or movement within any building[19];

(11) the supply to a handicapped person of a service of providing, extending or adapting a bathroom, washroom or lavatory in his private residence where such provision, extension or adaptation is necessary by reason of his condition[20];

(12) the supply to a charity of a service of providing, extending or adapting a bathroom, washroom or lavatory for use by handicapped persons in a residential home where such provision, extension or adaptation is necessary by reason of the condition of the handicapped persons[21];

(13) the supply to a charity of a service of providing, extending or adapting a washroom or lavatory for use by handicapped persons in a building, or any part of a building, used principally by a charity for charitable purposes where such provision, extension or adaptation is necessary to facilitate the use of the washroom or lavatory by handicapped persons[22];

(14) the supply of goods in connection with a supply described in head (9), head (10), head (11) or head (12) above[23];

(15) the letting on hire of a motor vehicle for a period of not less than three years to a handicapped person in receipt of a disability living allowance[24] by virtue of entitlement to the mobility component or of mobility supplement[25] where the lessor's business[26] consists predominantly of the provision of motor vehicles to such persons[27];

(16) the sale of a motor vehicle which had been let on hire in the circumstances described in head (15) above where such sale constitutes the first supply of the vehicle after the end of the period of such letting[28];

(17) the supply to a handicapped person of services necessarily performed in the installation of a lift for the purpose of facilitating his movement between floors within his private residence[29];

(18) the supply to a charity providing a permanent or temporary residence or day-centre for handicapped persons of services necessarily performed in the installation of a lift for the purpose of facilitating the movement of handicapped persons between floors within that building[30];

(19) the supply of goods in connection with a supply described in head (17) or head (18) above[31];

(20) the supply to a handicapped person for domestic or his personal use, or to a charity for making available to handicapped persons by sale or otherwise for domestic or their personal use, of an alarm system designed to be capable of operation by a handicapped person, and to enable him to alert directly a specified person or a control centre[32]; and

(21) the supply of services necessarily performed by a control centre in receiving and responding to calls from an alarm system specified in head (20) above[33].

1 See the Value Added Tax Act 1994 s 30(2), Sch 8 Pt II Group 12 (as amended); and heads (1)–(21) in the text. For the meaning of 'zero-rated supply' see para 158 ante; and for the meaning of 'supply' see para 21 ante. Section 30(3) (see paras 158 ante, 175 post) does not apply to goods forming part of a description of supply in heads (1) or (2) in the text, nor to other goods forming part of a description of supply in Sch 8 Pt II Group 12 (as amended), except where those other goods are acquired from another member state or imported from a place outside the member states by a handicapped person for domestic or his personal use, or by a charity for making available to handicapped persons, by sale or otherwise, for domestic or their personal use: Sch 8 Pt II Group 12 note 1 (amended by the Value Added Tax (Supply of Pharmaceutical Goods) Order 1995, SI 1995/652, arts 2, 4). For the meaning of 'another member state' see para 4 note 14 ante; and as to the territories included in, or excluded from, the member states for VAT purposes see para 10 ante.

2 Value Added Tax Act 1994 Sch 8 Pt II Group 12 note 5.

3 Ie the register kept under the Pharmacy Act 1954: see MEDICINE vol 30 (Reissue) para 702 et seq.

4 As to these registers see MEDICINE vol 30 (Reissue) paras 71 et seq.

5 As to this register see MEDICINE vol 30 (Reissue) para 318 et seq.

6 Value Added Tax Act 1994, Sch 8 Pt II Group 12 item 1. For the purposes of this item a person who is not registered in the visiting EC practitioners list in the register of medical practitioners at the time he performs services in an urgent case as mentioned in the Medical Act 1983 s 18(3) (see MEDICINE vol 30 (Reissue) para 93) is to be treated as being registered in that list where he is entitled to be registered in accordance with s 18: Sch 8 Pt II Group 12 note 2. The provision to a patient of a stock drug kept on the ward of a private hospital is not zero-rated because: (1) the supply of the goods is an integral part of the composite supply of care under s 31(1), Sch 9 Pt II Group 7 item 4 (see para 151 ante); and (2) it is not supplied by a pharmacist on the prescription of a registered medical practitioner: *Customs and Excise Comrs v Wellington Private Hospital* [1995] STC 628 at 644.

7 Value Added Tax Act 1994 Sch 8 Pt II Group 12 note 5 (amended by the Value Added Tax (Supply of Pharmaceutical Goods) Order 1995 arts 2, 5).

8 Ie the National Health Service (Pharmaceutical Services) Regulations 1992, SI 1992/662, reg 20: see MEDICINE vol 30 (Reissue) para 7; NATIONAL HEALTH.

9 Value Added Tax Act 1994 Sch 8 Pt II Group 12 item 1A (added by the Value Added Tax (Supply of Pharmaceutical Goods) Order 1995 arts 2, 3).

10 'Handicapped' means chronically sick or disabled: Value Added Tax Act 1994 Sch 8 Pt II Group 12 note 3. This has been held to include persons suffering chronic pain (usually lasting three months or more): *Neen Design Ltd v Customs and Excise Comrs* (1994) VAT Decision 11782, [1994] STI 589 (devices designed for the relief of such chronic pain are zero-rated, notwithstanding that when they are supplied to other persons they are taxed at the standard rate).

11 Value Added Tax Act 1994 Sch 8 Pt II Group 12 note 5.

12 Ibid Sch 8 Pt II Group 12 item 2. Schedule 8 Group 12 item 2 does not include hearing aids (except hearing aids designed for the auditory training of deaf children), dentures, spectacles and contact lenses, but is deemed to include: (1) clothing, footwear and wigs; (2) invalid wheelchairs, and invalid carriages other than mechanically propelled vehicles intended or adapted for use on roads; and (3) renal haemodialysis units, oxygen concentrators, artificial respirators and other similar apparatus: Sch 8 Pt II Group 12 note 4. It does not, however, extend to the provision of surgically implanted prostheses (which, in any event, form part of a larger composite supply of hospital treatment within Sch 9 Pt II Group 7 item 4): *Customs and Excise Comrs v Wellington Private Hospital* [1995] STC 628 at 647. A person is an 'invalid' within head (3)(b) in the text if he is ill, unwell, weak or infirm, whether permanently or temporarily, as a result of some medical condition: *Niagara Holdings Ltd v Customs and Excise Comrs* (1994) VAT Decision 11400, [1994] STI 116. For an adapted vehicle to fall within head (3)(f) in the text, the person to whom it is supplied must be able to sit in it in a wheelchair: *Oliver v Customs and Excise Comrs* (1993) VAT Decision 10579, [1993] STI 1185. An appliance is 'designed solely for use by a handicapped person' within head (3)(g) in the text if it is specially designed for handicapped persons, even though it is also capable of being used by persons who are not handicapped: *Hobden v Customs and Excise Comrs* LON/85/52 (VAT Decision 1875); *Foxer Industries v Customs and Excise Comrs* (1996) VAT Decision 13817, [1996] STI 470; *Tempur Pedic (UK) Ltd v Customs and Excise Comrs* (1996) VAT Decision 13744, [1996] STI 255; cf *Princess Louise Scottish Hospital v Customs and Excise Comrs* [1983] VATTR 191. A fire escape made large enough to hold persons in wheelchairs was not designed solely for use by the handicapped, nor was it an adaptation of 'goods' (supposedly, in this case, the building to which the fire escape was attached) to suit the condition of a handicapped person, since land is not 'goods' for this purpose: *Arthritis Care v Customs and Excise Comrs* (1996) VAT Decision 13974, [1996] STI 941.

13 Value Added Tax Act 1994 Sch 8 Pt II Group 12 item 3. Where the goods are adapted in accordance with head (4) in the text prior to their supply to the handicapped person, an apportionment must be made to determine the supply of services which falls within that head: Sch 8 Pt II Group 12 note 8.

14 Ibid Sch 8 Pt II Group 12 item 4. Where the goods are adapted in accordance head (5) in the text prior to their supply to the charity, an apportionment must be made to determine the supply of services which falls within that head: Sch 8 Pt II Group 12 note 8.

15 Ibid Sch 8 Pt II Group 12 item 5.

16 Ibid Sch 8 Pt II Group 12 item 6.

17 Ibid Sch 8 Pt II Group 12 item 7.

18 Ibid Sch 8 Pt II Group 12 item 8.

19 Ibid Sch 8 Pt II Group 12 item 9.

20 Ibid Sch 8 Pt II Group 12 item 10.

21 Ibid Sch 8 Pt II Group 12 item 11. The installation of thermostatic valves on washbasins in bedrooms does not relate to a 'washroom': *Mid-Derbyshire Cheshire Home v Customs and Excise Comrs* (1990) VAT Decision 4512, [1990] STI 210.

22 Value Added Tax Act 1994 Sch 8 Pt II Group 12 item 12.

23 Ibid Sch 8 Pt II Group 12 item 13.

24 A 'disability living allowance' is a disability living allowance within the meaning of the Social Security Contributions and Benefits Act 1992 s 71: Value Added Tax Act 1994 Sch 8 Pt II Group 12 note 7(a).

25 A 'mobility supplement' is a mobility supplement within the meaning of the Naval, Military and Air Forces etc (Disablement and Death) Service Pensions Order 1983, SI 1983/883, art 26A (as added and amended); the Personal Injuries (Civilians) Scheme 1983, SI 1983/686, art 25A (as added and amended) or the Motor Vehicles (Exemption from Vehicles Excise Duty) Order 1985, SI 1985/722, art 3: Value Added Tax Act 1994 Sch 8 Pt II Group 12 note 7(b).

26 For the meaning of 'business' see para 17 ante.

27 Value Added Tax Act 1994 Sch 8 Pt II Group 12 item 14. Head (15) in the text applies only (1) where the vehicle is unused at the commencement of the period of letting; and (2) where the consideration for the letting consists wholly or partly of sums paid to the lessor by the Department of Social Security or the Ministry of Defence on behalf of the lessee in respect of the mobility component of the disability living allowance or mobility supplement to which he is entitled: Sch 8 Pt II Group 12 note 6.

28 Ibid Sch 8 Pt II Group 12 item 15.

29 Ibid Sch 8 Pt II Group 12 item 16.

30 Ibid Sch 8 Pt II Group 12 item 17. The phrase 'day-centre' emphasises provision of particular facilities for groups or for people who need them and does not merely indicate a place resorted to by handicapped persons during the day: *University of Warwick Students Union v Customs and Excise Comrs* (1996) VAT Decision 13821, [1996] STI 568.

31 Value Added Tax Act 1994 Sch 8 Pt II Group 12 item 18.

32 Ibid Sch 8 Pt II Group 12 item 19. For these purposes, and the purposes of head (21) in the text, a 'specified person or control centre' is a person or centre who or which (1) is appointed to receive directly calls activated by an alarm system described in the relevant head; and (2) retains information about the handicapped person to assist him in the event of illness, injury or similar emergency: Sch 8 Pt II Group 12 note 9.

33 Ibid Sch 8 Pt II Group 12 item 20.

171. Imports, exports etc. The following are zero-rated supplies[1]:

(1) the supply, before the delivery of an entry[2] under an agreement requiring the purchaser to make such entry, of goods imported from a place outside the member states[3];

(2) the supply to or by an overseas authority[4], overseas body[5] or overseas trader[6], charged with the management of any defence project which is the subject of an international collaboration arrangement[7] or under direct contract with any government or government sponsored international body participating in a defence project under such an arrangement, of goods or services in the course of giving effect to that arrangement[8]; and

(3) the supply to an overseas authority, overseas body or overseas trader of jigs, patterns, templates, dies, punches and similar machine tools used in the United Kingdom solely for the manufacture of goods for export to places outside the member states[9], except where that authority, body or trader is a taxable person[10], another member state[11], any part of or place in another member state, the government of any such member state, part or place, a body established in another member state or a person who carries on business, or has a place of business, in another member state[12].

The various other reliefs from value added tax on importation are discussed elsewhere in this title[13].

1 See the Value Added Tax Act 1994 s 30(2), Sch 8 Pt II Group 13; and heads (1)–(3) in the text. For the meaning of 'zero-rated supply' see para 158 ante; and for the meaning of 'supply' see para 21 ante.

2 Ie an 'entry' within the meaning of the Customs Controls on Importation of Goods Regulations 1991, SI 1991/2724, reg 5 (as amended): see CUSTOMS AND EXCISE.

3 Value Added Tax Act 1994 Sch 8 Pt II Group 13 item 1. As to the territories included in, or excluded from, the member states for VAT purposes see para 10 ante.

4 'Overseas authority' means any country other than the United Kingdom or any part of, or place in, such a country or the government of any such country, part or place: ibid Sch 8 Pt II Group 13 note 2. For the meaning of 'United Kingdom' see para 4 note 3 ante.

5 'Overseas body' means a body established outside the United Kingdom: ibid Sch 8 Pt II Group 13 note 3.

6   'Overseas trader' means a person who carries on a business and has his principal place of business outside
     the United Kingdom: ibid Sch 8 Pt II Group 13 note 4. For the meaning of 'business' see para 17 ante.
7   An 'international collaboration arrangement' means any arrangement which (1) is made between the
     United Kingdom government and the government of one or more other countries, or any government-
     sponsored international body for collaboration in a joint project of research, development or production;
     and (2) includes provision for participating governments to relieve the cost of the project from taxation:
     ibid Sch 8 Pt II Group 13 note 1.
8   Ibid Sch 8 Pt II Group 13 item 2.
9   Ibid Sch 8 Pt II Group 13 item 3.
10   For the meaning of 'taxable person' see paras 12 note 4, 55 ante.
11   For the meaning of 'another member state' see para 4 note 14 ante.
12   Value Added Tax Act 1994 Sch 8 Pt II Group 13 note 5.
13   See paras 109 et seq ante, 175 et seq post.

172. Tax-free shops. The supply[1], by a person in the course of carrying on business[2] in a tax-free shop[3], to a traveller[4] making a relevant journey[5], of goods of certain specified descriptions is zero-rated[6] if those goods are either (1) goods not listed below which do not exceed a value of £75 in aggregate and which are to be carried in the traveller's personal luggage[7]; or (2) goods listed below which do not exceed the specified quantities[8] and which are to be carried in the traveller's personal luggage[9]. The goods referred to, and the quantities specified, are:

(a)   alcoholic beverages with an alcoholic strength of more than 22 per cent by
       volume (1 litre) or alcoholic beverages with an alcoholic strength of not more
       than 22 per cent by volume, fortified wines and sparkling wines (including made-
       wines) (2 litres);
(b)   still wines (including made-wines) (2 litres);
(c)   perfume (60 millilitres);
(d)   toilet water (250 millilitres);
(e)   cigarettes (200) or cigarillos (100) or cigars (50) or smoking tobacco (250
       grammes)[10].

The supply of any such goods is also zero-rated when made to a traveller on board an aircraft or ship making a relevant journey by a person who supplies the traveller's air or sea transport or by any other person authorised by that person[11].

    The above provisions do not, however, apply where the supply is to a traveller under 17 years of age of goods falling within heads (a) to (e) above, other than perfumes and toilet waters[12].

1   For the meaning of 'supply' see para 21 ante.
2   For the meaning of 'business' see para 17 ante.
3   'Tax-free shop' means any shop which is situated within an airport, port or Channel Tunnel terminal and
     which is approved by the Commissioners of Customs and Excise for the supply of goods for these
     purposes: Value Added Tax Act 1994 s 30(2), Sch 8 Pt II Group 14 note 2. 'Channel Tunnel terminal'
     means the area situated in the vicinity of Cheriton, Folkestone referred to in the Channel Tunnel Act
     1987 s 1(7)(b) (see RAILWAYS): Value Added Tax Act 1994 Sch 8 Pt II Group 14 note 2.
4   'Traveller' means any passenger travelling under a transport document for air or sea travel stating that the
     immediate destination is a place in another member state, including such a transport document stating
     that the final destination is a place outside the member states, or for shuttle train travel: ibid Sch 8 Pt II
     Group 14 note 4. For these purposes, 'shuttle train' has the meaning given by the Channel Tunnel Act
     1987 s 1(9) (see RAILWAYS): Value Added Tax Act 1994 Sch 8 Pt II Group 14 note 6. For the meaning
     of 'another member state' see para 4 note 14 ante. As to travellers under the age of 17 years see, however,
     the text and note 12 infra.
5   'Relevant journey' means a journey by air or sea from the United Kingdom to a place in another member
     state where the traveller is to disembark and includes, for the purposes of ibid Sch 8 Pt II Group 14 item
     1 (see heads (1)–(2) in the text), a journey by a Channel Tunnel shuttle train: Sch 8 Pt II Group 14 note 3.
6   For the meaning of 'zero-rated supply' see para 158 ante.

7   Value Added Tax Act 1994 Sch 8 Pt II Group 14 item 1(a) (amended by the Value Added Tax (Tax Free Shops) Order 1995, SI 1995/3041, art 2). For the purpose of determining the aggregate value of any goods referred to in head (1) in the text, only the whole of the value of any item, or group of items which are normally sold as a set or collection, may be included in the aggregate value of £75: Value Added Tax Act 1994 Sch 8 Pt II Group 14 note 1 (as so amended).
8   Ie the quantities set out in ibid Sch 8 Pt II Group 14 item 1, Table col 2: see heads (a)–(e) in the text.
9   Ibid Sch 8 Pt II Group 14 item 1(b).
10 Ibid Sch 8 Pt II Group 14 item 1, Table.
11 Ibid Sch 8 Pt II Group 14 item 2. Zero-rating is not afforded under Sch 8 Pt II Group 14 item 2 to a journey by a Channel Tunnel shuttle train, since such a journey is not a relevant journey for the purposes of that item: see Sch 8 Pt II Group 14 note 3; and note 5 supra.
12 Ibid Sch 8 Pt II Group 14 note 5.

173. Charities. The following are zero-rated supplies[1]:

(1)   the supply by a charity[2] of any goods which have been donated for sale or the supply of such goods by a taxable person[3] who has covenanted by deed to give all the profits of that supply to a charity[4];

(2)   the donation of any goods for sale or export by a charity described in head (1) above or by a taxable person described in that head[5];

(3)   the export of any goods by a charity to a place outside the member states[6];

(4)   the supply of any relevant goods[7] for donation to a nominated eligible body[8] where the goods are purchased with funds provided by a charity or from voluntary contributions[9], and the letting on hire of such goods[10], unless the donee of the goods is not a charity and has contributed in whole or in part to the funds for the purchase of goods[11];

(5)   the supply of any relevant goods (including computer services by way of the provision of computer software solely for use in medical research, diagnosis or treatment[12]) to an eligible body which pays for them with funds provided by a charity or from voluntary contributions, or to an eligible body which is a charitable institution providing care or medical or surgical treatment for handicapped persons[13], and the letting on hire of such goods[14], unless the body to whom the goods are supplied is not a charity and has contributed in whole or in part to the funds for the purchase of the goods[15];

(6)   repair and maintenance of relevant goods owned by or let on hire to[16] an eligible body[17] where the supply is paid for with funds which have been provided by a charity or from voluntary contributions and, in a case where the owner of the goods repaired or maintained is not a charity, it has not contributed in whole or in part to those funds[18];

(7)   the supply of goods in connection with the supply described in head (6) above[19] where the supply is paid for as described in that head[20];

(8)   the supply to a charity, for the purpose of raising money for, or making known the objects or reasons for the objects of, the charity, of:

(a)   the broadcast on television or radio or screening in a cinema of an advertisement; or

(b)   the publication of an advertisement in any newspaper, journal, poster, programme, annual, leaflet, brochure, pamphlet, periodical or similar publication; or

(c)   any goods or services in connection with the preparation of an advertisement within head (b) above[21];

(9)   the supply to a charity providing care or medical or surgical treatment for human beings or animals[22], or engaging in medical or veterinary research, of a medicinal

product[23] where the supply is solely for use by the charity in such care, treatment or research[24];

(10) the supply to a charity of a substance directly used for synthesis or testing in the course of medical or veterinary research[25].

1   See the Value Added Tax Act 1994 s 30(2), Sch 8 Pt II Group 15 (as amended); and heads (1)–(10) in the text. For the meaning of 'zero-rated supply' see para 158 ante; and for the meaning of 'supply' see para 21 ante.

2   'Charity' is not defined for the purposes of VAT (except to include a body wholly owned by a charity in ibid s 31(1), Sch 9 Pt II Group 12 note 2 (see para 156 note 3 ante)), but EC Council Directive 77/388 (OJ L145, 13.6.77. p 1) art 13(A)(1)(g) affords exemption to 'the supply of services and of goods linked to welfare and social security work ... by ... other organisations recognised as charitable by the member state concerned'. As to the essentials of charitable purposes generally see CHARITIES.

3   For the meaning of 'taxable person' see paras 12 note 4, 55 ante.

4   Value Added Tax Act 1994 Sch 8 Pt II Group 15 item 1. Head (1) in the text applies only if the supply is a sale of goods donated to that charity or taxable person: Sch 8 Pt II Group 15 note 1.

5   Ibid Sch 8 Pt II Group 15 item 2.

6   Ibid Sch 8 Pt II Group 15 item 3. As to the territories included in, or excluded from, the member states for VAT purposes see para 10 ante.

7   'Relevant goods' means:
    (1)   medical, scientific, computer, video, sterilising, laboratory or refrigeration equipment for use in medical or veterinary research, training, diagnosis or treatment (ibid Sch 8 Pt II Group 14 note 3(a));
    (2)   ambulances (Sch 8 Pt II Group 14 note 3(b));
    (3)   parts or accessories for use in or with goods described in heads (1) or (2) supra (Sch 8 Pt II Group 14 note 3(c));
    (4)   goods of a kind described in Sch 8 Pt II Group 12 item 2 (ie aids for the handicapped: see para 170 ante) (Sch 8 Pt II Group 14 note 3(d));
    (5)   motor vehicles (other than vehicles with more than 50 seats) designed or substantially and permanently adapted for the safe carriage of a handicapped person in a wheelchair provided that (a) in the case of vehicles with more than 16 but fewer than 27 seats, such provision exists for at least two people; (b) in the case of vehicles with more than 26 but fewer than 37 seats, such provision exists for at least three people; (c) in the case of vehicles with more than 36 but fewer than 47 seats, such provision exists for at least four people; (d) in the case of vehicles with more than 46 seats, such provision exists for at least five people; (e) there is either a fitted electrically or hydraulically operated lift or, in the case of vehicles with fewer than 17 seats, a fitted ramp to provide access for a passenger in a wheelchair (Sch 8 Pt II Group 14 note 3(e));
    (6)   motor vehicles (with more than six but fewer than 51 seats) for use by an eligible body providing care for blind, deaf, mentally handicapped or terminally sick persons mainly to transport such persons (Sch 8 Pt II Group 14 note 3(f));
    (7)   telecommunication, aural, visual, light-enhancing or heat-detecting equipment (not being equipment ordinarily supplied for private or recreational use) solely for use for the purpose of rescue or first aid services undertaken by a charitable institution providing such services (Sch 8 Pt II Group 15 note 3(g)).
    In determining whether goods are 'relevant goods' it must be asked (i) whether the goods are medical; and (ii) whether they are supplied for use in medical diagnosis or treatment: *Customs and Excise Comrs v David Lewis Centre* [1995] STC 485 (where the installation of observation windows and the construction of a soft games area for the disabled were held not to involve supplies of relevant goods). As to the meaning of 'medical or scientific equipment' see *Clinical Computing Ltd v Customs and Excise Comrs* [1983] VATTR 121; and *Lancer UK Ltd v Customs and Excise Comrs* [1986] VATTR 112. 'Handicapped' means chronically sick or disabled: Value Added Tax Act 1994 Sch 8 Pt II Group 15 note 5; and see para 170 note 10 ante. It does not include persons suffering from dyslexia: *Dyslexia Institute Ltd v Customs and Excise Comrs* (1994) VAT Decision 12654, [1994] STI 1339. For the meaning of 'eligible body' see note 8 infra.

8   An 'eligible body' means (1) a Health Authority or Special Health Authority in England and Wales, a Health Board in Scotland or a Health and Social Services Board in Northern Ireland; (2) a hospital whose activities are not carried on for profit; (3) a research institution whose activities are not carried on for profit; (4) a charitable institution providing care or medical or surgical treatment for handicapped persons; (5) a charitable institution providing rescue or first-aid services; and (6) a National Health Service trust established under the National Health Service and Community Care Act 1990 Pt I (ss 1–26) (as amended): Value Added Tax Act 1994 Sch 8 Pt II Group 15 note 4 (amended by the Health Authorities Act 1995 s 2(1), Sch 1 Pt III para 127). 'Care' in head (4) supra involves a continuing role in supervising

or looking after a person and not simply the donation of equipment and an attitude of concern or eagerness to help: *Medical Care Foundation v Customs and Excise Comrs* [1991] VATTR 28. A medical centre comprising a pharmacy, waiting room and office, several consulting rooms, dental treatment rooms and facilities for carrying out minor operations was held not to be a 'hospital' for the purposes of head (2) supra: *Medicare Français v Customs and Excise Comrs* (1996) VAT Decision 13929, [1996] STI 781.

9 Value Added Tax Act 1994 Sch 8 Pt II Group 15 item 4.

10 Ibid Sch 8 Pt II Group 15 note 9. References to the purchase or ownership of goods must therefore be read as including references to their hiring or possession: Sch 8 Pt II Group 15 note 9.

11 Ibid Sch 8 Pt II Group 15 note 6.

12 Ibid Sch 8 Pt II Group 15 note 10.

13 Ibid Sch 8 Pt II Group 15 item 5.

14 Ibid Sch 8 Pt II Group 15 note 9; and see note 10 supra.

15 Ibid Sch 8 Pt II Group 15 note 7. 'Care' in this context connotes having charge or protection of someone or something and covers the provision of accommodation, providing for daily needs, safe transport and a secure daytime environment; however, care of the handicapped need not be a special function of the recipient body, nor need the care it provides be exclusively for handicapped persons: *Help the Aged v Customs and Excise Comrs* (1996) VAT Decision 14180, [1996] STI 1356; but see Customs and Excise Business Brief 18/96 [1996] STI 1439.

16 Value Added Tax Act 1994 Sch 8 Pt II Group 15 note 9; and see note 10 supra.

17 Ibid Sch 8 Pt II Group 15 item 6.

18 Ibid Sch 8 Pt II Group 15 note 8.

19 Ibid Sch 8 Pt II Group 15 item 7.

20 Ibid Sch 8 Pt II Group 15 note 8.

21 Ibid Sch 8 Pt II Group 15 item 8. For the commissioners' views on what kinds of supply of advertising provided to charities are zero-rated see Customs and Excise Notice 701/1/95 *Charities* (1 January 1995) para 16(c)–(e); but cf *Royal Society for the Encouragement of Arts, Manufacture and Commerce v Customs and Excise Comrs* (1996) VAT Decision 14007, [1996] STI 964 (the Value Added Tax Act 1994 Sch 8 Pt II Group 15 item 8 includes the self-supply by a charity of the goods and services used in connection with the production of an advertisement which conveys (however briefly and incidentally) the object of the charity). Following the decision in this case, the commissioners announced (Customs and Excise Business Brief 9/96) that they would, from 1 June 1996, no longer accept that recruitment advertisements for paid staff were eligible for zero-rating, even when they carried a 'qualifying message', so that, unless the advertisement's primary purpose is making known the objects of the charity, it does not fall within the scope of the relief. Advertisements for volunteers (including VSO workers) still attract relief: see [1996] STI 953. As to charity stationery see Customs and Excise Business Brief 18/96 [1996] STI 1439 at 1440.

An advertisement need not be both for the purpose of raising money for the charity and for the purpose of making known its objects: *Sussex County Association of Change Ringers v Customs and Excise Comrs* (1996) VAT Decision 14116, [1996] STI 1262.

22 'Animals' includes any species of the animal kingdom: ibid Value Added Tax Act 1994 Sch 8 Pt II Group 15 note 2.

23 For these purposes, a 'medicinal product' means any substance or article (not being an instrument, apparatus or appliance) which is for use wholly or mainly in either or both of the following ways: (1) by being administered (within the meaning of the Medicines Act 1968 s 130(9) (as amended): see MEDICINE vol 30 (Reissue) para 716 note 9) to one or more human beings or animals for a medicinal purpose (within the meaning of s 130(2): see MEDICINE vol 30 (Reissue) para 860); or (2) as an ingredient in the preparation of a substance or article which is to be administered to one or more human beings or animals for a medicinal purpose: Value Added Tax Act 1994 Sch 8 Pt II Group 15 note 11. For these purposes, 'substance' and 'ingredient' have the meanings assigned to them by the Medicines Act 1968 s 132 (see MEDICINE vol 30 (Reissue) paras 716, 859): Value Added Tax Act 1994, Sch 8 Pt II Group 15 note 12. As to the meaning of 'wholly or mainly' see para 165 note 8 ante.

24 Ibid Sch 8 Pt II Group 15 item 9.

25 Ibid Sch 8 Pt II Group 15 item 10.

174. Clothing and footwear. The following are zero-rated supplies[1]:

(1) the supply of articles designed as clothing, including hats and other headgear[2], or footwear for young children and not suitable for older persons[3], but excluding certain articles made wholly or partly of fur skin[4];

(2) the supply to a person for use otherwise than by employees of his of protective boots and helmets for industrial use[5], provided that those goods satisfy the required[6] standards[7];

(3)   the supply of protective helmets for wear by a person driving or riding a motor bicycle[8], provided that they satisfy the required standards[9]; and

(4)   the supply of certain services[10] in respect of the goods comprised in heads (1) to (3) above[11].

1   See the Value Added Tax Act 1994 s 30(2), Sch 8 Pt II Group 16; and heads (1)–(4) in the text. For the meaning of 'zero-rated supply' see para 158 ante; and for the meaning of 'supply' see para 21 ante.

2   Ibid Sch 8 Pt II Group 16 note 1; and see *Cassidy (t/a Balou) v Customs and Excise Comrs* (1991) VAT Decision 5670, [1991] STI 458.

3   Value Added Tax Act 1994 Sch 8 Pt II Group 16 item 1. The pleating of material for skirts for girls has been held to be within Sch 8 Pt II Group 16 item 1, even though further work would have to be carried out before the articles could be worn: *Customs and Excise Comrs v Ali Baba Tex Ltd* [1992] 3 CMLR 725, [1992] STC 590 (having regard to the Value Added Tax Act 1994 s 5(1), Sch 4 para 2 (repealed): see now s 30(2A) (as added), which enables a supply of services to be zero-rated if it consists in the application of a treatment or process to another's goods, if, inter alia, by doing so he produces goods of a description for the time being specified in Sch 8 (as amended); and para 158 ante); cf *Warley Denim Services v Customs and Excise Comrs* (1993) VAT Decision 10396, [1993] STI 1080. The mere fact that goods are intended for use by children does not exclude the possibility that they might be suitable for older persons, such as might be the case with one-size fashion knitwear: *Jeffery Green & Co Ltd v Customs and Excise Comrs* [1974] VATTR 94. Goods are not suitable for older persons if, eg, they carry designs which would expose an adult to ridicule or contempt: *Charles Owen & Co (Bow) Ltd v Customs and Excise Comrs* [1993] VATTR 514. For a schedule of maximum sizes see Customs and Excise News Release 14/94 (15 March 1994). On the commissioners' views as to what constitutes the maximum size for boys' footwear to be zero-rated see Customs and Excise Business Brief 8/96 [1996] STI 911. The sale of discount cards enabling holders to purchase children's clothing at a reduced price was zero-rated as falling within head (1) in the text: *Mothercare (UK) Ltd v Customs and Excise Comrs* [1993] VATTR 391, following *British Railways Board v Customs and Excise Comrs* [1977] 2 All ER 873, [1977] 1 WLR 588, CA. As to composite and separate supplies see para 25 ante.

4   The Value Added Tax Act 1994 Sch 8 Pt II Group 16 item 1 does not include articles of clothing made wholly or partly of fur skin other than (1) headgear; (2) gloves; (3) buttons, belts and buckles; and (4) any garment merely trimmed with fur skin, unless the trimming has an area greater than one-fifth of the area of the outside material or, in the case of a new garment, represents a cost to the manufacturer greater than the cost to him of the other components: Sch 8 Pt II Group 16 note 2. 'Fur skin' means any skin with fur, hair or wool attached except (a) rabbit skin; (b) wooled sheep or lamb skin; and (c) the skin, if neither tanned nor dressed, of bovine cattle (including buffalo), equine animals, goats or kids (other than Yemen, Mongolian and Tibetan goats or kids), swine (including peccary), chamois, gazelles, deer or dogs: Sch 8 Pt II Group 16 note 3.

5   Ibid Sch 8 Pt II Group 16 item 2.

6   Heads (2)–(3) in the text apply only where the goods to which they refer are (1) goods which are manufactured to standards approved by the British Standards Institution and bear a marking indicating compliance with the specification relating to such goods; or (2) goods which are manufactured to standards which satisfy requirements imposed (whether under the law of the United Kingdom or the law of any other member state) for giving effect to EC Council Directive 89/686 (OJ L399, 30.12.89, p 18) (as amended) and bear any mark of conformity provided for by virtue of that directive in relation to those goods: Value Added Tax Act 1994 Sch 8 Pt II Group 16 note 4. For the meaning of 'United Kingdom' see para 4 note 3 ante; for the meaning of 'another member state' see para 4 note 14 ante; and as to the construction of references to the law of another member state see para 11 ante.

7   Ibid Sch 8 Pt II Group 16 note 4.

8   Ibid Sch 8 Pt II Group 16 item 3.

9   Ibid Sch 8 Pt II Group 16 note 4; and see note 6 supra.

10   Ie the supply of the services described in ibid s 5(1), Sch 4 para 1(1) (transfer of an undivided share of, or of the possession of, the relevant goods: see para 24 ante); or Sch 4 para 5(4) (deemed supply where goods are used or made available for a non-business purpose; see para 24 ante); see Sch 8 Pt II Group 16 note 5. Schedule 8 Pt II Group 16 note 5 in fact refers to Sch 4 para 5(3) (supply of samples, which is a supply of goods not of services: see para 24 ante). As to the likely intention of the draftsman to apply Sch 4 para 5(4) rather than Sch 4 para 5(3) see para 168 note 5 ante.

11   Ibid Sch 8 Pt II Group 16 note 5; and see note 10 supra. In the case of goods comprised in head (2) in the text, Sch 8 Pt II Group 16 note 5 applies only if the goods are for use otherwise than by employees of the person to whom the services are supplied: Sch 8 Pt II Group 16 note 5.

(iii)   Zero–rated Imports and Exports

175. The zero–rated acquisition and importation of goods. Where goods of a description for the time being specified as being zero-rated[1], or of a description forming part of a description of supply[2] for the time being so specified, are acquired in the United Kingdom[3] from another member state[4], or are imported into the United Kingdom from a place outside the member states[5], no value added tax is chargeable on their acquisition or importation[6], except as otherwise[7] provided[8].

1   Ie under the Value Added Tax Act 1994 s 30(2), Sch 8 (as amended): see para 159 et seq ante. For the meaning of 'zero-rated supply' see para 158 ante.
2   For the meaning of 'supply' see para 21 ante.
3   For the meaning of 'United Kingdom' see para 4 note 3 ante.
4   As to the charge on acquisitions from other member states see para 13 ante; and for the meaning of 'another member state' see para 4 note 14 ante.
5   As to the territories included in, or excluded from, the member states for VAT purposes see para 10 ante.
6   Value Added Tax Act 1994 s 30(3).
7   Ie as otherwise provided by the Value Added Tax Act 1994 Sch 8 (as amended): see para 159 et seq ante. There are, eg, limitations on the quantity of goods offered for sale in tax-free shops which qualify for zero-rating as well as on the persons who, on importing such goods, may be entitled to the benefit of zero-rating: see para 172 ante. A zero-rated acquisition, although not subject to VAT, may nevertheless constitute a taxable acquisition within s 10(2), since it will not be an exempt acquisition: see para 13 note 12 ante. As to other exclusions from zero-rating of importations and taxable acquisitions see paras 163, 165, 169 ante.
8   Ibid s 30(3).

176. Exports by charities. The export of any goods by a charity[1] to a place outside the member states[2] is treated for the purposes of the Value Added Tax Act 1994 as a supply[3] made by the charity (1) in the United Kingdom[4]; and (2) in the course or furtherance of a business[5] carried on by the charity[6]. The effect of this rule is that charities may recover as input tax[7] VAT incurred on the supplies made to them for the purposes of the export even though the goods are exported otherwise than for consideration[8].

1   As to the meaning of 'charity' see para 173 note 2 ante.
2   As to the export of goods to a place outside the member states see para 13 ante; and as to the territories included in, or excluded from, the member states for value added tax purposes see para 10 ante.
3   For the meaning of 'supply' see para 21 ante.
4   For the meaning of 'United Kingdom' see para 4 note 3 ante.
5   For the meaning of 'in the course or furtherance of a business' see paras 12 note 5, 17 note 2 ante.
6   Value Added Tax Act 1994 s 30(5) (substituted by the Finance Act 1995 s 28).
7   For the meaning of 'input tax' see paras 4 ante, 201 post.
8   See Customs and Excise News Release 13/94 [1994] STI 1522.

177. The zero–rating of exported goods and services; in general. In addition to supplies[1] within the specified groups[2], the following are zero-rated supplies[3]:

(1)   a supply of goods if the Commissioners of Customs and Excise are satisfied that the person supplying the goods has exported them to a place outside the member states[4] and if such other conditions, if any, as may be specified in regulations[5] or as the commissioners may impose are fulfilled[6];

(2)   a supply of goods if the commissioners are satisfied that the person supplying the goods has shipped them for use as stores on a voyage or flight to an eventual destination outside the United Kingdom[7], or as merchandise for sale by retail to persons carried on such a voyage or flight in a ship[8] or aircraft and if such other conditions, if any, as may be specified in regulations or as the commissioners may

impose are fulfilled[9], except in the case of goods shipped for use as stores on a voyage or flight to be made by the person to whom the goods were supplied and to be made for a purpose which is private[10].

Regulations may also provide for the zero-rating of:

(a) supplies of goods, or of such goods as may be specified in them, in cases where the commissioners are satisfied that the goods have been, or are to be, exported to a place outside the member states, or that the supply in question involves both the removal of the goods from the United Kingdom and their acquisition in another member state[11] by a person who is liable for value added tax on the acquisition in accordance with certain provisions[12] of the law of that member state[13];

(b) supplies of goods, or of such goods as may be specified in regulations, in cases where the commissioners are satisfied that the supply in question involves both the removal of the goods from a fiscal warehousing regime[14] and their being placed in a warehousing regime in another member state[15], or in such member state or states as may be prescribed[16];

(c) a supply of services which is made where goods are let on hire and the commissioners are satisfied that the goods have been, or are to be, removed from the United Kingdom during the period of the letting[17],

and if, in each case, such other conditions, if any, as may be specified in the regulations or as the commissioners may impose are fulfilled[18].

Where the supply of any goods has been zero-rated by virtue of head (1) or head (2) above or in pursuance of regulations made under head (a), head (b) or head (c) above and either:

(i) the goods are found in the United Kingdom after the date on which they were alleged to have been or were to be exported or shipped or otherwise removed from the United Kingdom; or

(ii) any condition specified in the relevant regulations or imposed by the commissioners is not complied with,

and the presence of the goods in the United Kingdom after that date or the non-observance of the condition has not been authorised by the commissioners for these purposes, the goods are liable to forfeiture[19] and the VAT that would have been chargeable on the supply but for the zero-rating becomes payable forthwith by the person to whom the goods were supplied or by any person in whose possession the goods are found in the United Kingdom; but the commissioners may, if they think fit, waive payment of the whole or part of that VAT[20].

---

1 For the meaning of 'supply' see para 21 ante.

2 Ie within the Value Added Tax Act 1994 s 30(2), Sch 8 (as amended): see para 159 et seq ante.

3 For the meaning of 'zero-rated supply' see para 158 ante.

4 As to goods exported to a place outside the member states see para 13 ante; and as to the territories included in, or excluded from, the member states for VAT purposes see para 10 ante.

5 Ie in regulations made under the Value Added Tax Act 1994: s 96(1). See the Value Added Tax Regulations 1995, SI 1995/2518, regs 127–129; and paras 178–180 post. As to the making of regulations generally see para 8 ante.

6 Value Added Tax Act 1994 s 30(6)(a). See Customs and Excise Notice 703 *VAT: Exports and Removals of Goods from the United Kingdom* (January 1993). The commissioners are entitled to insist that very strict conditions are complied with before zero-rating is granted and that those conditions, and conditions specified in accordance with the Value Added Tax Act 1994 s 30(8)(b) (see the text and note 18 infra) have been satisfied: see *Henry Moss of London Ltd v Customs and Excise Comrs* [1981] 2 All ER 86, [1981] STC 139, CA. It is, however, irrelevant that it may be illegal to export the relevant goods to the country to which they are exported: zero-rating must still be conceded: Case C-111/92 *Lange v Finanzamt Fürstenfeldbruck* [1994] 1 CMLR 573, ECJ.

7 For the meaning of 'United Kingdom' see para 4 note 3 ante.

8   For the meaning of 'ship' see para 13 note 8 ante. Zero-rating is only available if the goods are supplied to the vessel operator which will itself use the goods for refuelling or provisioning and does not extend to supplies to an intermediary at a previous stage in the commercial chain; on the other hand, there is no requirement that the goods should actually be loaded on board the vessels at the time of their supply to the operator: Case C-185/89 *Staatssecretaris van Financiën v Velker International Oil Co Ltd NV* [1990] ECR I-2561, [1991] STC 640, ECJ, interpreting EC Council Directive 77/388 (OJ L145, 13.6.77, p 1) art 15(4).

9   Value Added Tax Act 1994 s 30(6)(b).

10   Ibid s 30(7).

11   For the meaning of 'another member state' see para 4 note 14 ante; and as to the acquisition of goods in another member state see para 13 note 6 ante.

12   Ie provisions of the law of that member state corresponding, in relation to that member state, to the provisions of the Value Added Tax Act 1994 s 10: see para 13 ante. As to the construction of references to the corresponding law of another member state see para 11 ante.

13   Ibid s 30(8)(a); and see para 180 post.

14   Ie within the meaning of ibid s 18F(2) (as added): see para 134 note 3 ante.

15   Ie where that regime is established by provisions of the law of that member state corresponding, in relation to that member state, to the provisions of ibid ss 18A, 18B (as added): see paras 133–134 ante. For the meaning of 'warehousing regime' see para 130 note 6 ante.

16   Ibid s 30(8A)(a) (added by the Finance Act 1996 s 26(1), Sch 3 para 7).

17   Value Added Tax Act 1994 s 30(9); and see para 179 post.

18   Ibid s 30(8)(b); s 30(8A)(b) (as added: see note 16 supra); s 30(9).

19   Ie the Customs and Excise Management Act 1979: Value Added Tax Act 1994 s 96(1). See CUSTOMS AND EXCISE.

20   Ibid s 30(10) (amended by the Finance Act 1996 Sch 3 para 7). While an Order in Council under the Isle of Man Act 1979 s 6 (as amended) is in force (see para 9 ante), the Value Added Tax Act 1994 s 30(10) (as so amended) has effect as if the reference to goods zero-rated under the regulations there mentioned included a reference to goods zero-rated under any corresponding regulations made under the Act of Tynwald: Isle of Man Act 1979 s 6(4)(a) (amended by the Value Added Tax Act 1983 s 50(1); and by the Value Added Tax Act 1994 s 100(1), Sch 14 para 7(2)).

178. Supplies to export houses. Where goods are supplied to an export house[1] but are not at any time delivered to the export house in the United Kingdom and:

    (1)   the goods are delivered by the supplier direct to a port, customs and excise airport or approved inland clearance depot[2] for immediate shipment or to an export packer for delivery direct to a port, customs and excise airport or approved inland clearance depot for immediate shipment to the order of the export house; and

    (2)   the goods are exported to a place outside the member states,

the supply is zero-rated[3], subject to such conditions as the Commissioners of Customs and Excise may impose[4].

1   For these purposes, 'export house' means any person registered in the United Kingdom who in the course of his business in the United Kingdom arranges or finances the export of goods from the United Kingdom to a place outside the member states: Value Added Tax Regulations 1995, SI 1995/2518, reg 117(3). For the meaning of 'registered' see para 56 note 2 ante; for the meaning of 'business' see para 17 ante; and for the meaning of 'United Kingdom' see para 4 note 3 ante. As to the territories included in, or excluded from, the member states for VAT purposes see para 10 ante.

2   'Approved inland clearance depot' means any inland premises approved by the Commissioners of Customs and Excise for the clearance of goods for customs and excise purposes: ibid reg 117(1).

3   Ibid reg 127. For the meaning of 'zero-rated supply' see para 158 ante; and for the meaning of 'supply' see para 21 ante.

4   Ibid reg 127. As to the imposition of conditions see para 177 note 6 ante.

179. Export of freight containers. Where the Commissioners of Customs and Excise are satisfied that a container[1] is to be exported to a place outside the member states[2], its supply[3] is zero-rated[4], subject to such conditions as they may impose[5].

1   For these purposes, 'container' means an article of transport equipment (lift-van, movable tank or other similar structure) which is (1) fully or partially inclosed to constitute a compartment intended for containing goods; (2) of a permanent character and accordingly strong enough to be suitable for repeated use; (3) specially designed to facilitate the carriage of goods, by one or more modes of transport, without intermediate reloading; (4) designed for ready handling, particularly when being transferred from one mode of transport to another; (5) designed to be easy to fill and to empty; and (6) having an internal volume of one cubic metre or more; and the term 'container' includes the accessories and equipment of the container, appropriate for the type concerned, provided that they are carried with the container, but does not include vehicles, accessories or spare parts of vehicles, or packaging: Value Added Tax Regulations 1995, SI 1995/2518, reg 117(2).

2   As to the territories treated as included in, or excluded from, the member states for VAT purposes see para 10 ante.

3   For the meaning of 'supply' see para 21 ante.

4   Value Added Tax Regulations 1995 reg 128. For the meaning of 'zero-rated supply' see para 158 ante.

5   Ibid reg 128. As to the imposition of conditions see para 177 note 6 ante. See also Customs and Excise Notice 703/1/95 *Supply of Freight Containers for Export or Removal from the United Kingdom* (1 March 1995).

180. Supplies to overseas persons. Except in the case of a supply[1] to any person who is a member of the crew of any ship or aircraft departing from the United Kingdom[2] or the Isle of Man, where the Commissioners of Customs and Excise are satisfied that:

    (1)   goods intended for export to a place outside the member states[3] have been supplied, otherwise than to a taxable person[4], to a person not resident in the United Kingdom, a trader who has no business[5] establishment in the United Kingdom from which taxable supplies[6] are made, or an overseas authority[7]; and

    (2)   the goods were exported to a place outside the member states,

the supply is zero-rated[8], subject to such conditions as the commissioners may impose[9].

1   For the meaning of 'supply' see para 21 ante.

2   For the meaning of 'United Kingdom' see para 4 note 3 ante.

3   As to the territories included in, or excluded from, the member states for VAT purposes see para 10 ante.

4   For the meaning of 'taxable person' see paras 12 note 4, 55 ante.

5   For the meaning of 'business' see para 17 ante.

6   For the meaning of 'taxable supply' see para 12 note 3 ante.

7   For these purposes, 'overseas authority' means any country other than the United Kingdom or any part of, or place in, such a country or the government of any such country, part or place: Value Added Tax Regulations 1995, SI 1995/2518, reg 117(7).

8   Ibid reg 129(1), (2). For the meaning of 'zero-rated supply' see para 158 ante.

9   Ibid reg 129(1). As to the imposition of conditions see para 177 note 6 ante.

181. Supplies to persons taxable in another member state. Where   the Commissioners of Customs and Excise are satisfied that:

    (1)   a supply[1] of goods by a taxable person[2] involves their removal from the United Kingdom[3];

    (2)   the supply is to a person taxable in another member state[4];

    (3)   the goods have been removed to another member state; and

    (4)   the goods are not goods in relation to whose supply the taxable person has opted[5] for value added tax be charged by reference to the profit margin on the supply,

the supply is zero-rated[6], subject to such conditions as the commissioners may impose[7].

1   For the meaning of 'supply' see para 21 ante.

2   For the meaning of 'taxable person' see paras 12 note 4, 55 ante.

3   For the meaning of 'United Kingdom' see para 4 note 3 ante.

4   For the meaning of 'another member state' see para 4 note 14 ante; and for the meaning of 'taxable in another member state' see para 11 note 4 ante.

5   Ie pursuant to the Value Added Tax Act 1994 s 50A (as added): see para 188 post.

6   Value Added Tax Regulations 1995, SI 1995/2518, reg 134. For the meaning of 'zero-rated supply' see para 158 ante.

7   Ibid reg 134. As to the imposition of conditions see generally para 177 note 6 ante. In relation to supplies
      to customers in other member states the commissioners require that: (1) the supplier obtains and shows
      on his VAT sales invoice his customer's VAT registration number (with a two-digit country code prefix);
      (2) the goods are sent or transported out of the United Kingdom to a destination in another member state;
      and (3) the supplier holds commercial documentary evidence that the goods have been removed from
      the United Kingdom (guidance on proof of removal of goods is given in Customs and Excise Notice 703
      VAT: Exports and Removals of Goods from the United Kingdom (January 1993)): Customs and Excise Notice
      725 *VAT: The Single Market* (1 February 1994) para 2.2(a). If these conditions are not satisfied, the
      commissioners require the trader to charge and account for tax on the goods in the United Kingdom
      unless the supply of the goods is normally zero-rated in the United Kingdom: Customs and Excise Notice
      725 para 2.2(a).

182. Supplies of goods subject to excise duty to persons who are not taxable in another member state. Where the Commissioners of Customs and Excise are satisfied that:

(1)   a supply[1] by a taxable person[2] of goods subject to excise duty[3] involves their removal from the United Kingdom[4] to another member state[5];

(2)   that supply is other than to a person taxable in another member state[6] and the place of supply is not treated[7] as outside the United Kingdom;

(3)   the goods have been removed to another member state in accordance with the provisions of the regulations relating to the holding, movement and warehousing of excise goods and registered excise dealers and shippers[8]; and

(4)   the goods are not goods in relation to whose supply the taxable person has opted[9] for value added tax to be charged by reference to the profit margin on the supply,

the supply is zero-rated[10], subject to such conditions as the commissioners may impose[11].

1   For the meaning of 'supply' see para 21 ante.
2   For the meaning of 'taxable person' see paras 12 note 4, 55 ante.
3   As to the amount of excise duty chargeable see para 89 note 6 ante.
4   For the meaning of 'United Kingdom' see para 4 note 3 ante.
5   For the meaning of 'another member state' see para 4 note 14 ante.
6   For the meaning of 'taxable in another member state' see para 11 note 4 ante.
7   Ie by virtue of the Value Added Tax Act 1994 s 7(5): see para 42 ante.
8   Ie in accordance with the provisions of the Excise Goods (Holding, Movement, Warehousing and
      REDS) Regulations 1992, SI 1992/3135 (as amended): see CUSTOMS AND EXCISE.
9   Ie pursuant to the Value Added Tax Act 1994 s 50A (as added): see para 188 post.
10   Value Added Tax Regulations 1995, SI 1995/2518, reg 135. For the meaning of 'zero-rated supply' see
      para 158 ante.
11   Ibid reg 135. As to the imposition of conditions see para 177 note 6 ante.

183. Supplies to persons departing from the member states etc. Subject to such conditions as the Commissioners of Customs and Excise may impose[1], the following supplies[2] are zero-rated[3]:

(1)   the supply of goods[4], where they are satisfied that:

       (a)   the goods have been supplied to, and delivered direct to, a ship[5] or aircraft on behalf of either a member of the crew, who is an overseas visitor[6], of any ship or aircraft departing from the United Kingdom[7] or the Isle of Man to an immediate destination outside the member states[8] or a person who is not an overseas visitor but who has been resident in the member states for at least 365 days in the last two years immediately preceding the date of supply of the goods and who at the time of supply intends to depart from the United Kingdom or the Isle of Man for an immediate destination outside the member states and remain outside the member states for a period of at least 12 months; and

(b)   the goods were produced to the proper officer[9] on exportation, except as the commissioners may allow; and

(c)   the goods were exported in that ship or aircraft, or in such other ship or aircraft as they may allow[10];

(2)   except in the case of a supply to any person who is a member of the crew of any ship or aircraft departing from the member states[11], the supply of goods[12], where the commissioners are satisfied that:

(a)   the goods have been supplied to a person who is an overseas visitor and who, at the time of supply, intended to depart from the member states before the end of the third month following that in which the supply is effected and that the goods should accompany him;

(b)   except as they may allow, the goods were produced to the competent authorities for the purposes of the common system of value added tax in the member state from which the goods were finally exported to a place outside the member states; and

(c)   the goods were exported to a place outside the member states[13].

On application by an overseas visitor who intends to depart from the member states within 15 months and to remain outside the member states for a period of at least six months, the commissioners may permit him within 12 months of his intended departure to acquire a new motor vehicle from a registered person[14], without payment of VAT, for subsequent export and its supply is zero-rated, subject to such conditions as they may impose[15]. Similarly, on application by any person who intends to depart from the member states within nine months and to remain outside the member states for a period of at least six months, the commissioners may permit him within six months of his intended departure to purchase a new motor vehicle from a registered person, without payment of VAT, for subsequent export and its supply is also zero-rated, subject to such conditions as they may impose[16].

On application by a person who is not taxable in another member state[17] and who intends to purchase a new means of transport[18] in the United Kingdom and to remove that new means of transport to another member state, the commissioners may permit that person to purchase a new means of transport without payment of VAT, for subsequent removal to another member state within two months of the date of supply, and its supply is zero-rated, subject to such conditions as they may impose[19].

1   Value Added Tax Regulations 1995, SI 1995/2518, regs 130, 131(1). As to the imposition of conditions generally see para 177 note 6 ante.

2   For the meaning of 'supply' see para 21 ante.

3   For the meaning of 'zero-rated supply' see para 158 ante.

4   For the purposes of heads (1)–(2) in the text, 'goods' not include a motor vehicle or a boat intended to be exported under its own power: Value Added Tax Regulations 1995 reg 117(4) (substituted by SI 1996/210).

5   For the purposes of heads (1)–(2) in the text, 'ship' includes a hovercraft within the meaning of the Hovercraft Act 1968: Value Added Tax Regulations 1995 reg 117(9).

6   For the purposes of ibid Pt XVI (regs 117–145) (as amended), 'overseas visitor' means a person who (1) during the two years immediately preceding the date of the supply mentioned in regs 130, 131 (see heads (1)–(2) in the text) or the date of the application mentioned in reg 132 (see the text and notes 14–15 infra), has not been in the member states for more than 365 days; or (2) for the purposes of reg 132, during the six years immediately preceding the date of the application has not been in the member states for more than 1,095 days: reg 117(8).

7   For the meaning of 'United Kingdom' see para 4 note 3 ante.

8   As to the territories included in, or excluded from, the member states for VAT purposes see para 10 ante.

9   For the meaning of 'proper officer' see para 105 note 9 ante.

10 Value Added Tax Regulations 1995 reg 130.

11 Ibid reg 131(2).

12 The conditions for the application of zero–rating under ibid reg 131 are set out in Customs and Excise Notice 704 *Retail Exports* (April 1993). Goods excluded from the operation of the retail export scheme include (1) motor vehicles and sailaway boats (see note 4 supra); (2) goods over £600 in value, intended for the customer's business purposes (see Customs and Excise Notice 703 *VAT: Exports and Removals of Goods from the United Kingdom* (January 1993)); (3) goods for consumption within the member states; goods requiring an export licence, other than antiques; unmounted gemstones; and bullion (see Customs and Excise Notice 704 para 1.7).

13 Value Added Tax Regulations 1995 reg 131(1) (amended by SI 1995/3147). For a case where letters from the recipients of supplies were accepted by the VAT and duties tribunal as evidence of exportation see *Kingdom Sportswear Ltd v Customs and Excise Comrs* [1991] VATTR 55.

14 For the meaning of 'registered person' see para 105 note 7 ante.

15 Value Added Tax Regulations 1995 reg 132.

16 Ibid reg 133.

17 For the meaning of 'taxable in another member state' see para 11 note 4 ante; and for the meaning of 'another member state' see para 4 note 14 ante.

18 For the meaning of 'new means of transport' see para 13 note 8 ante.

19 Value Added Tax Regulations 1995 reg 155.

184. Applications of customs and excise legislation. Where goods are exported from the United Kingdom[1] (1) to certain territories which are treated as excluded from the territory of the Community for the purposes of value added tax[2]; or (2) to certain other territories which are treated for those purposes as excluded both from the territory of the member states and from the territory of the Community[3], the provisions relating to the export of goods to a place outside the customs territory of the Community[4] apply for the purpose of ensuring the correct application of the zero rate of VAT to such goods[5]. The provisions made by or under the Customs and Excise Management Act 1979 in relation to the exportation of goods to places outside the member states also apply[6], so far as relevant, for the purpose of ensuring the correct application of the zero rate of VAT to the goods[7].

1 For the meaning of 'United Kingdom' see para 4 note 3 ante.

2 Ie the territories prescribed in the Value Added Tax Regulations 1995, SI 1995/2518, reg 136: see para 10 text and note 2 ante.

3 Ie the territories prescribed in ibid reg 137: see para 10 text and notes 3–4 ante.

4 Ie the provisions contained in EC Council Regulation 2913/92 (OJ L302, 19.10.92, p1) (establishing the Community Customs Code); and EC Commission Regulation 2454/93 (OJ L253, 11.11.93, p 1) (as amended) (implementation of that code): see further CUSTOMS AND EXCISE; EUROPEAN COMMUNITIES. For these purposes, 'customs territory of the Community' has the same meaning as it has for the purposes of EC Council Regulation 2913/92: Value Added Tax Regulations 1995 reg 117(10).

5 Ibid reg 144. Where goods are exported to those prescribed territories, the formalities relating to the export of goods to a place outside the customs territory of the Community contained in EC Council Regulation 2913/92 and EC Commission Regulation 2454/93 (as amended) must be completed: Value Added Tax Regulations 1995 reg 140(2).

6 Ie subject to ibid reg 145(2): reg 145(1). Where goods are being exported from the United Kingdom to the territories prescribed in the Value Added Tax Regulations 1995 reg 137, the Finance (No 2) Act 1992 s 4 (enforcement powers: see CUSTOMS AND EXCISE) applies to such goods as if references therein to 'member states' excluded the territories so prescribed: Value Added Tax Regulations 1995 reg 145(2).

7 Value Added Tax Act Regulations 1995 reg 145(1). See further CUSTOMS AND EXCISE.

(3) RETAIL SCHEMES

185. In general. The Commissioners of Customs and Excise may permit the value which is to be taken as the value, in any prescribed accounting period[1] or part of such a period, of supplies[2] by a retailer which are taxable at other than the zero rate[3] to be determined by a method agreed with that retailer or by any method described in a notice[4] published by the commissioners for that purpose (a 'scheme')[5]; and they may publish any notice accordingly[6]. The commissioners may vary the terms of any method by publishing a fresh notice or a notice which amends an existing notice, or by adapting any method by agreement with any retailer[7]. No retailer may at any time use more than one scheme except as provided for in any notice or as the commissioners may otherwise allow[8]. The commissioners may refuse to permit the value of taxable supplies[9] to be determined in accordance with a scheme if it appears to them that the use of any particular scheme does not produce a fair and reasonable valuation during any period, that it is necessary to do so for the protection of the revenue or that the retailer could reasonably be expected to account for value added tax in accordance with the regulations generally[10] applicable[11].

Save as the commissioners may otherwise allow, a retailer who accounts for value added tax on the basis of taxable supplies valued in accordance with any scheme must, so long as he remains a taxable person[12], continue to do so for a period of not less than one year from the adoption of that scheme by him, and any change by a retailer from one scheme to another must be made at the end of any complete year reckoned from the beginning of the prescribed accounting period in which he first adopted the scheme[13]. Any retailer using any scheme must notify the commissioners in writing on every return[14] made by him which scheme he is using[15].

Where a retailer agrees a particular method of calculating the value of his supplies with the commissioners, his agreement takes effect in contract; and he may be bound by terms which the commissioners impose as a condition of acceptance of the scheme[16].

Where, pursuant to any enactment, there is a change in the VAT charged on any supply, including a change to or from no VAT being charged on that supply, a retailer using any scheme must take such steps relating to it as are directed in any notice applicable to him, or as may be agreed between him and the commissioners[17].

A retailer must notify the commissioners before ceasing to account for VAT on the basis of taxable supplies valued in accordance with these provisions[18], and may be required to pay VAT on such proportion as the commissioners may consider fair and reasonable of any sums due to him at the end of the prescribed accounting period in which he last used a scheme[19].

1   For the meaning of 'prescribed accounting period' see para 105 note 16 ante.

2   For the meaning of 'supply' see para 21 ante.

3   As to zero-rated supplies see para 158 et seq ante.

4   For these purposes, 'notice' means any notice or leaflet published by the commissioners pursuant to the Value Added Tax Regulations 1995, SI 1995/2518, Pt IX (regs 66–75) (see the text and notes 5–19 infra; and para 186 post): reg 66.

5   Ibid regs 66, 67(1). See further Customs and Excise Notice 727 *Retail Schemes* (1 April 1993). As to the power to make retail schemes see the Value Added Tax Act 1994 s 58, Sch 11 para 2(6); and para 225 post. Retail schemes represent a derogation from the provisions of EC Council Directive 77/388 (OJ L145, 13.6.1977, p 1), and were preserved by the service of notification by the United Kingdom on the EC Commission in accordance with art 27(2). The commissioners are only entitled by regulation to make arrangements by which special provision may be made for the value of supplies rather than the time of supply, and it is doubtful whether the words of the Value Added Tax Act 1994 Sch 11 para 2(6) are adequate to justify any general derogation from the basic scheme by regulation. Customs and Excise Notice 727 could not, therefore, have the effect which the commissioners claimed that it had, namely of adjusting the time of supply when there was a change in the rate of VAT: *Customs and Excise Comrs v Next plc, Customs and Excise Comrs v Grattan plc* [1995] STC 651 per Judge J.

     Customs and Excise Notice 727 is to be read in the light of the Value Added Tax Act 1994 as a whole, so that, when interpreting the delegated legislation made thereby, it must be assumed that references to 'self-financed supplies of credit' include cases where one member of a VAT group provides credit to customers of other members of the group, since the members of the group must be treated as a single taxable person: *Customs and Excise Comrs v Kingfisher plc* [1994] STC 63 per Popplewell J. As to VAT groups see paras 66 ante, 191 et seq post. Where a retailer has an existing arrangement with a finance company that in order to facilitate interest free credit to customers the finance company will pay a lesser sum to the retailer than the advertised price of the goods, the retailer is only liable to account for output tax on the sums received from the finance company and not the sums charged to the customer: *Primback Ltd v Customs and Excise Comrs* [1996] STC 757, CA. Sales of retail items to customers registered for VAT must be accounted for outside the retail schemes: *Oxford, Swindon and Gloucester Co-operative Society v Customs and Excise Comrs* [1995] STC 583 (this case was, however, subsequently the subject of an appeal by the taxpayer, which was conceded by the commissioners before the matter was heard by the Court of Appeal).

6   Value Added Tax Regulations 1995 reg 67(1).
7   Ibid reg 67(2).
8   Ibid reg 69. As to changing from one scheme to another and the criteria for applying any such change retrospectively see eg *Vulgar v Customs and Excise Comrs* [1976] VATTR 197; *Lewis and Lewis v Customs and Excise Comrs* (1996) VAT Decision 14085, 370 Tax Journal (5 September 1996) p 24; *L & P Fryer (a firm) v Customs and Excise Comrs* (1996) VAT Decision 14265, [1996] STI 1539.
9   For the meaning of 'taxable supply' see para 12 note 3 ante.
10 Ie in accordance with regulations made under the Value Added Tax Act 1994 Sch 11 para 2(1): see para 225 post. As to accounting for VAT generally see para 225 et seq post.
11 Value Added Tax Regulations 1995 reg 68. An appeal lies to a VAT and duties tribunal against any decision of the commissioners refusing to permit the value of supplies to be determined by a method described in a notice published under the Value Added Tax Act 1994 Sch 11 para 2(6): see s 83(x); and para 296 post. See also *Customs and Excise Comrs v J Boardmans (1980) Ltd* [1986] STC 10.
12 For the meaning of 'taxable person' see paras 12 note 4, 55 ante.
13 Value Added Tax Regulations 1995 reg 71.
14 For the meaning of 'return' see para 105 note 14 ante.
15 Value Added Tax Regulations 1995 reg 70.
16 *GUS Merchandise v Customs and Excise Comrs (No 2)* [1993] STC 738. As to where the commissioners were taken to have permitted a special scheme by conduct (so that the trader could not subsequently change schemes until the end of a complete year) see *Wellington Private Hospital Ltd (No 2) v Customs and Excise Comrs* [1993] VATTR 86.
17 Value Added Tax Regulations 1995 reg 75. The commissioners cannot, however, rely on the retail scheme provisions to adjust the time of supply: *Customs and Excise Comrs v Next plc, Customs and Excise Comrs v Grattan plc* [1995] STC 651 per Judge J. As to the operation of retail scheme B in relation to stock acquired on a transfer of a business as a going concern see *Customs and Excise Comrs v Co-operative Wholesale Society Ltd* [1995] STC 983.
18 Value Added Tax Regulations 1995 reg 72(1).
19 Ibid reg 72(2).

186. Treatment of supplies of food.

Where the supplies[1] by any retailer include both supplies of food which are zero-rated[2] and supplies of food in the course of catering[3], he must either (1) keep such records as will enable the proportion of the value of such supplies which is to be attributed to zero-rated and all other supplies to be determined to the satisfaction of the Commissioners of Customs and Excise; or (2) where he can satisfy the commissioners that it is impracticable to keep such records, make an estimate of the proportion of the value of such supplies which is to be attributed to zero-rated and all other supplies[4].

Where any retailer makes an estimate in accordance with head (2) above, value added tax is to be accounted for on the basis of that estimate; but, if at any time he has evidence, or the commissioners are satisfied, that the estimate is no longer accurate, he must thereupon make a further such estimate and must inform the commissioners accordingly, and VAT must then accounted for on the basis of that further estimate from such date as the commissioners may direct[5]. Where the commissioners are not satisfied with any further estimate so made, they may determine the proportion of the value of supplies which is to be attributed to the various descriptions of supplies and VAT must be accounted for in accordance with that determination from such date as the commissioners direct[6].

1   For the meaning of 'supply' see para 21 ante.
2   Ie under the Value Added Tax Act 1994 s 30(2), Sch 8 Pt II Group 1: see para 159 ante. For the meaning of 'zero-rated supply' see para 158 ante.

3   For the meaning of 'in the course of catering' see para 159 note 27 ante. Such supplies are standard-rated: see para 159 text and notes 27–29 ante.
4   Value Added Tax Regulations 1995, SI 1995/2518, reg 73(1).
5   Ibid reg 73(2).
6   Ibid reg 73(3).

187. Treatment of supplies of drugs, medicines, aids for the handicapped etc. A retailer who makes supplies[1] of certain drugs, medicines, aids for the handicapped and related goods[2] must, in making calculations in order to use any retail scheme[3], make an adjustment to those calculations in the manner prescribed by a notice[4] published by the Commissioners of Customs and Excise for that purpose or in accordance with any agreement made by them with any such retailer[5]. The commissioners may vary the manner of adjustment of such calculations either by publishing a fresh notice or by agreement with any retailer[6].

1   For the meaning of 'supply' see para 21 ante.
2   Ie supplies of a description specified in the Value Added Tax Act 1994 s 30(2), Sch 8 Pt II Group 12 (as amended): see para 170 ante.
3   For the meaning of 'scheme' see para 185 ante.
4   For the meaning of 'notice' see para 185 note 4 ante. See Customs and Excise Notice 727 *Retail Schemes* (1 April 1993) Appendix B: Retail Chemists.
5   Value Added Tax Regulations 1995, SI 1995/2518, reg 74(1).
6   Ibid reg 74(2).

(4) MARGIN SCHEMES

188. In general. The Treasury may by order[1] provide for a taxable person[2] to be entitled to opt that, where he makes certain supplies[3], value added tax is to be charged by reference to the profit margin on the supplies instead of by reference to their value[4]. An option for the purposes of such an order is exercisable, and may be withdrawn, in such manner as may be required by the order[5].

An order under these provisions may be made in relation to:

(1)   supplies of works of art, antiques or collectors' items[6];
(2)   supplies of motor vehicles[7];
(3)   supplies of second-hand goods[8]; and
(4)   any supply of goods through a person who acts as an agent, but in his own name, in relation to the supply[9].

The profit margin on a supply to which these provisions apply is taken, for the purposes of an order made under them, to be equal to the amount, if any, by which the price at which the person making the supply obtained the goods in question is exceeded by the price at which he supplies them[10]; and the price at which a person has obtained any goods and the price at which he supplies them must each be calculated in accordance with the provisions contained in the relevant order[11]. Such an order may provide:

(a)   that the consideration[12] for any services supplied in connection with a supply of goods by a person who acts as an agent, but in his own name, in relation to the supply of the goods is to be treated for the purposes of any such order as an amount to be taken into account in computing the profit margin on the supply of the goods, instead of being separately chargeable to VAT as comprised in the value of the services supplied[13];
(b)   for the total profit margin on all the goods of a particular description supplied by a person in any prescribed accounting period[14] to be calculated in a specified manner[15].

1   Such an order may (1) make different provision for different cases; and (2) make provisions of the order subject to such general or special directions as may, in accordance with the order, be given by the Commissioners of Customs and Excise with respect to any matter to which the order relates: Value Added Tax Act 1994 s 50A(8) (s 50A added by the Finance Act 1995 s 24(1)).

2   For the meaning of 'taxable person' see paras 12 note 4, 55 ante.

3   Ie any such description of supplies to which the Value Added Tax Act 1994 s 50A (as added) applies as may be specified in the order: s 50A(1) (as added: see note 1 supra). As to those supplies see heads (1)–(4) in the text.

4   Ibid s 50A(1) (as added: see note 1 supra). In exercise of the power so conferred, and of other statutory powers, the Treasury has made the following orders: (1) the Value Added Tax (Special Provisions) Order 1995, SI 1995/1268 (amended by SI 1995/1385) (see para 189 post); (2) the Value Added Tax (Cars) (Amendment) Order 1995, SI 1995/1269 (see para 190 post); and (3) the Value Added Tax (Cars) (Amendment) (No 2) Order 1995, SI 1995/1667 (see para 190 post). In addition, by virtue of the Interpretation Act 1978 s 17(2)(b), the Value Added Tax (Cars) Order 1992, SI 1992/3122 (as amended) (see para 190 post) now partly has effect as if so made.

      The Value Added Tax Act 1994 s 50A (as added: see note 1 supra) implements EC Council Directive 94/5 (OJ L60, 3.3.94, p 16): see Customs and Excise News Release 20/95 [1995] STI 628. As to the commissioners' views on margin schemes see Customs and Excise Notice 718 *Margin Schemes for Second-hand Goods, Works of Art, Antiques and Collectors' Items* (1 June 1995).

5   Value Added Tax Act 1994 s 50A(3) (as added: see note 1 supra).

6   Ibid s 50A(2)(a) (as added: see note 1 supra). See the Value Added Tax (Special Provisions) Order 1995 art 12; and para 189 post.

7   Value Added Tax Act 1994 s 50A(2)(b) (as added: see note 1 supra). See the Value Added Tax (Cars) Order 1992 art 8 (as substituted and amended); and para 190 post.

8   Value Added Tax Act 1994 s 50A(2)(c) (as added: see note 1 supra). See the Value Added Tax (Special Provisions) Order 1995 art 12; and para 189 post. In Case C-131/91 *'K' Line Air Service Europe BV v Eulaerts NV and Belgium* [1992] ECR I-4513, [1996] STC 597, ECJ, it was held that EC Council Directive 77/388 (OJ L145, 13.6.77, p 1) art 32 (now replaced by art 26a) was intended to establish a special system to ensure that goods on which VAT had been definitively charged were not taxed a second time. It followed that it was not intended to apply to supplies of used goods where the supplier had, as a taxable person, been able to exercise a right of deduction under art 17. 'Second-hand goods' thus has a special meaning for VAT purposes.

9   Value Added Tax Act 1994 s 50A(2)(d) (as added: see note 1 supra). See the Value Added Tax (Special Provisions) Order 1995 art 12(6); and para 189 post.

10   Value Added Tax Act 1994 s 50A(4) (as added: see note 1 supra). Section 50A(4) (as so added) is subject to s 50A(7) (as so added): see head (b) in the text.

11   Ibid s 50A(5) (as added: see note 1 supra).

12   For the meaning of 'consideration' generally see para 86 ante.

13   Value Added Tax Act 1994 s 50A(6) (as added: see note 1 supra).

14   For the meaning of 'prescribed accounting period' see para 202 note 4 post.

15   Value Added Tax Act 1994 s 50A(7) (as added: see note 1 supra). The order may provide for the total profit margin to be calculated by: (1) aggregating all the prices at which that person obtained goods of that description in that period together with any amount carried forward to that period in pursuance of head (4) infra; (2) aggregating all the prices at which he supplies goods of that description in the period; (3) treating the total profit margin on goods supplied in that period as being equal to the amount, if any, by which, for that period, the aggregate calculated in pursuance of head (1) supra is exceeded by the aggregate calculated in pursuance of head (2) supra; and (4) treating any amount by which, for that period, the aggregate calculated in pursuance of head (2) supra is exceeded by the aggregate calculated in pursuance of head (1) supra as an amount to be carried forward to the following prescribed accounting period so as to be included, for the period to which it is carried forward, in any aggregate falling to be calculated in pursuance of head (1) supra: s 50A(7)(a)–(d) (as so added). In pursuance of this provision the Treasury has made the Value Added Tax (Special Provisions) Order 1995, SI 1995/1268, art 13, which makes provision for a simplified method of accounting known as 'global accounting': see para 189 text and notes 23–25 post.

189. Relief for eligible supplies. Where a person supplies goods which are either works of art[1], antiques[2] or collectors' items[3] or second-hand goods[4], of which he took possession in any of the specified circumstances[5], he may opt to account for the value added tax chargeable on the supply[6] on the profit margin on the supply instead of by reference to its value[7]. A taxable person may not, however, opt to account in this manner where:

(1)   the supply is a letting on hire;

(2)   an invoice or similar document[8] showing an amount as being VAT or as being attributable to VAT is issued in respect of the supply;

(3)   the supply is of an air gun, unless the taxable person is registered for the purposes of the Firearms Act 1968; or

(4)   the supply is of goods which are being disposed of in certain specified circumstances[9] but which is not disregarded by virtue of the provisions[10] relating to those circumstances[11].

A taxable person may only exercise the option to account under a margin scheme in relation to supplies of (a) works of art supplied to him by, or acquired from another member state by him from, their creator or his successor in title[12]; or (b) works of art, antiques or collectors' items which he imported himself[13], if at the same time he exercises that option in relation to supplies of goods within the other head as well[14].

With certain exceptions[15], for the purposes of determining the profit margin the price at which goods were obtained is calculated as follows:

(i)   where the taxable person took possession of the goods pursuant to a supply, the price is calculated in the same way as the consideration for the supply would be calculated for the purposes of the Value Added Tax Act 1994[16];

(ii)   where the taxable person is a sole proprietor and the goods were supplied to him in his private capacity, the price is calculated in the same way as the consideration for the supply to him as a private individual would be calculated for the purposes of the 1994 Act[17];

(iii)   where the goods are a work of art which was acquired from another member state by the taxable person pursuant to a supply to him by the creator of the item or his successor in title, the price is calculated in the same way as the value of the acquisition would be calculated for the purposes of the 1994 Act plus the VAT chargeable on the acquisition[18];

(iv)   where the goods are a work of art, an antique or a collectors' item which the taxable person has imported himself, the price is calculated in the same way as the value of the goods for the purpose of charging VAT on their importation would be calculated for the purposes of the 1994 Act plus any VAT chargeable on their importation[19],

and the price at which the goods are sold is calculated in the same way as the consideration for the supply would[20] be calculated[21].

A taxable person who has opted to account for VAT on the profit margin of a supply of eligible goods in accordance with the above provisions may account for VAT on the total profit margin on goods supplied by him during a prescribed accounting period[22], calculated in the prescribed manner[23], instead of the profit margin on each supply[24]. This method of global accounting is not, however, available in relation to supplies of motor vehicles, aircraft, boats and outboard motors, caravans and motor caravans, horses and ponies, or any other individual items whose value, calculated in accordance with heads (i) to (iv) above, exceeds £500[25].

1   For the meaning of 'works of art' see para 22 note 7 ante.

2   For the meaning of 'antiques' see para 22 note 8 ante.

3   For the meaning of 'collectors' items' see para 22 note 9 ante.

4   For the meaning of 'second-hand goods' see para 22 note 10 ante.

5   Ie the circumstances specified in the Value Added Tax (Special Provisions) Order 1995, SI 1995/1268, art 12(3): art 12(1). Those circumstances are that (1) the taxable person took possession of the goods pursuant to (a) a supply in respect of which no VAT was chargeable under the Value

Added Tax Act 1994 or the Value Added Tax and Other Taxes Act 1973 (an Act of Tynwald) ('the Manx Act': see art 2) (eg a sale by a private individual); (b) a supply on which VAT was chargeable on the profit margin in accordance with the Value Added Tax (Special Provisions) Order 1995 art 12(1) or a corresponding provision made under the Manx Act or a corresponding provision of the law of another member state (ie the margin scheme); (c) a transaction which was treated by virtue of any order made under the Value Added Tax Act 1994 s 5(3) (see para 21 ante) or under the corresponding provisions of the Manx Act as being neither a supply of goods nor a supply of services; or (d) if the goods are a work of art, a supply to the taxable person by or an acquisition from another member state by him from its creator or his successor in title (Value Added Tax (Special Provisions) Order 1995 art 12(3)(a)); and (2) if the goods are a work of art, an antique, or a collector's item, that they were imported by the taxable person himself (art 12(3)(b)). As to the construction of references to the corresponding law of another member state see para 11 ante; for the meaning of 'another member state' see para 4 note 14 ante; and for the meaning of 'taxable person' see paras 12 note 4, 55 ante.

Where a taxable person takes possession of goods in the circumstances set out in heads (1)(d), (2) supra, and opts to be taxed under a margin scheme in respect of those goods, the exercise of the option (i) must be notified by him to the Commissioners of Customs and Excise in writing; (ii) has effect from the date of that notification or such later date as may be specified therein; and (iii) unless the taxable person elects to account for the VAT which is chargeable on any particular supply of such goods by reference to the value of that supply, applies to all supplies of such goods made by the taxable person in the period ending two years after the date on which it first had effect or the date on which written notification of its revocation is given to the commissioners, whichever is the later: art 12(8), (9). As to the removal of goods to the United Kingdom pursuant to a supply of those goods under a margin scheme in another member state see arts 7, 8; and paras 13, 22 ante; and as to taxable acquisitions from another member state see para 13 ante.

7   Ibid art 12(1), (2). Article 12(1) is without prejudice to art 13 (global accounting: see the text and notes 22–25 infra) and subject to complying with such conditions as the commissioners of may direct, either in a notice published by them for these purposes or otherwise: art 12(1). See Customs and Excise Notice 718 *Margin Schemes for Second-hand Goods, Works of Art, Antiques and Collectors' Items* (1 June 1995).

8   For the meaning of 'invoice' and 'document' see para 11 note 8 ante.

9   Ie the circumstances mentioned in the Value Added Tax Act (Special Provisions) Order 1995 art 4(1)(a), (b), (c) or (d) (goods repossessed or taken possession of under the terms of a finance agreement or policy of insurance etc): see para 22 ante.

10 Ie by virtue of ibid art 4 (disposal of reimported goods previously exported from the United Kingdom or the Isle of Man free of VAT): see para 22 ante.

11 Ibid art 12(4)(a).

12 Ie works of art of which he took possession in the circumstances mentioned in ibid art 12(3)(a)(iv): see note 5 head (1)(d) supra.

13 Ie works of art etc of which he took possession in the circumstances mentioned in ibid art 12(3)(b): see note 5 head (2) supra.

14 Ibid art 12(4)(b).

15 Ie subject to ibid art 12(6): art 12(5). Where the taxable person is an agent acting in his own name, the price at which the goods were obtained is calculated in accordance with head (i) in the text, but the selling price calculated in accordance with head (ii) in the text is increased by the amount of any consideration payable to the taxable person in respect of services supplied by him to the purchaser in connection with the supply of the goods: art 12(6). Instead of calculating the price at which goods were obtained or supplied in accordance with art 12(6), an auctioneer acting in his own name may (1) calculate the price at which they were obtained by deducting from the successful bid the consideration for any services supplied by him to the vendor in connection with the sale of goods; (2) calculate the price at which they were supplied by adding to the successful bid the consideration for any supply of services by him to the purchaser in connection with the sale of the goods, in either or both cases excluding the consideration for supplies of services that are not chargeable to VAT: art 12(7). For the meaning of 'consideration' generally see para 86 ante.

16 Ibid art 12(5)(a)(i).

17 Ibid art 12(5)(a)(ii).

18 Ibid art 12(5)(a)(iii).

19 Ibid art 12(5)(a)(iv).

20 Ie would be calculated for the purposes of the Value Added Tax Act 1994: see para 85 et seq ante.

21 Value Added Tax Act (Special Provisions) Order 1995 art 12(5)(b).

22 For the meaning of 'prescribed accounting period' see para 202 note 4 post.

23 Ie in accordance with the Value Added Tax Act (Special Provisions) Order 1995 art 13(3): art 13(1). The total profit margin for a prescribed accounting period is the amount, if any, by which the total

selling price calculated in accordance with art 13(5) exceeds the total purchase price calculated in accordance with art 13(4): art 13(3). The total selling price is calculated by aggregating, for all goods sold during the period, the prices for which they were sold, calculated in accordance with art 12(5) or (6) as appropriate (art 13(4)); and the total purchase price is calculated by aggregating, for all goods obtained during the period, the prices at which they were obtained, calculated in accordance with art 12(5), and adding that total to the amount, if any, carried forward from the previous period in accordance with art 13(6) (art 13(5)). If in any prescribed accounting period the total purchase price calculated in accordance with art 13(5) exceeds the total selling price, the excess amount is carried forward to the following prescribed accounting period for inclusion in the calculation of the total purchase price for that period: art 13(6).

24 Ibid art 13(1). The taxable person must comply with such conditions as the commissioners may direct in a notice published by them for these purposes: art 13(1).
25 Ibid art 13(2).

190. Relief for second-hand motor cars. Where a person supplies a used motor car[1] which he took possession of in any of the specified circumstances[2], he may opt to account for the value added tax chargeable on the supply on the profit margin on the supply instead of by reference to its value[3]. This relief is not, however, available in relation to:

(1) a supply which is a letting on hire;

(2) the supply by any person of a motor car which was produced by him, if it was neither previously supplied by him in the course or furtherance of any business[4] carried on by him nor treated[5] as so supplied;

(3) any supply, if an invoice or similar document[6] showing an amount as being VAT or as being attributable to VAT is issued in respect of the supply[7].

Subject to one exception[8], for the purposes of determining the profit margin, the price at which the motor car was obtained is calculated as follows:

(a) where the taxable person took possession of the used motor car pursuant to a supply, in the same way as the consideration for the supply would be calculated for the purposes of the Value Added Tax Act 1994;

(b) where the taxable person is a sole proprietor and the used motor car was supplied to him in his private capacity, in the same way as the consideration for the supply to him as a private individual would be calculated for those purposes[9],

and the price at which the motor car is sold is calculated in the same way as the consideration for the supply would[10] be calculated[11].

1 For the meaning of 'motor car' see para 23 note 2 ante. As to the views of the Commissioners of Customs and Excise on the meaning of 'used motor car' see Customs and Excise Press Release (25 June 1982) [1982] STI 278; but see also Case C-131/91 *'K' Line Air Service Europe BV v Eulaerts NV and Belgium* [1992] ECR I-4513, [1996] STC 597, ECJ. As to when value added tax, having been wholly excluded from credit under regulations made under the Value Added Tax Act 1994 s 25(7) (see para 204 post), is charged on the subsequent sale of a car see the Value Added Tax (Input Tax) Order 1992, SI 1992/3222, art 7(4) (as amended); and para 208 post.

2 Ie the circumstances specified in the Value Added Tax (Cars) Order 1992, SI 1992/3122, art 8(2) (substituted by SI 1995/1269; amended by SI 1995/1667): art 8(1) (as so substituted). The specified circumstances are that the taxable person took possession of the motor car pursuant to (1) a supply in respect of which no VAT was chargeable under the Value Added Tax Act 1994 or under the Value Added Tax and Other Taxes Act 1973 (an Act of Tynwald) ('the Manx Act': see the Value Added Tax (Cars) Order 1992 art 2 (definition added by SI 1995/1269)) (eg on a sale by a private individual); (2) a supply on which VAT was chargeable on the profit margin in accordance with art 8(1) (as so substituted) or a corresponding provision made under the Manx Act or a corresponding provision of the law of another member state; (3) a supply to which the provisions of the Value Added Tax (Input Tax) Order 1992 art 7(4) (as amended) applied; (4) a transaction which was treated by virtue of any order made under the Value Added Tax Act 1994 s 5(3) (see para 21 ante) or under the corresponding provisions of the Manx Act as being neither a supply of goods nor a supply of services: Value Added Tax (Cars) Order 1992 art 8(2) (as so substituted and amended). For the meaning of 'taxable person' see paras 12 note 4, 55 ante; for the meaning of 'supply' see para 21 ante; and as to the construction of references to the corresponding law of another member state see para 11 ante.

3   Ibid art 8(1) (as substituted: see note 2 supra). The taxable person must comply with such conditions, including the keeping of such records and accounts, as the commissioners may direct, either in a notice published by them for these purposes or otherwise: art 8(1) (as so substituted).
4   For the meaning of 'in the course or furtherance of a business' see paras 12 note 5, 17 note 2 ante.
5   Ie by virtue of the Value Added Tax (Cars) Order 1992 art 5 (as substituted): see para 26 ante.
6   For the meaning of 'invoice' and 'document' see para 11 note 8 ante.
7   Value Added Tax (Cars) Order 1992 art 8(3) (as substituted and amended: see note 2 supra).
8   Ie subject to ibid art 8(6) (substituted by SI 1995/1269): art 8(5) (as so substituted). Where the taxable person is an agent acting in his own name, the price at which the motor car was obtained is calculated in accordance with heads (a)–(b) in the text but the selling price calculated in accordance with art 8(5) (as so substituted) (see the text and notes 10–11 infra) is increased by the amount of any consideration payable to the taxable person in respect of services supplied by him to the purchaser in connection with the supply of the motor car: art 8(6) (as so substituted). Instead of calculating the price at which the motor car was obtained or supplied in accordance with art 8(6) (as so substituted), an auctioneer acting in his own name may (1) calculate the price at which the motor car was obtained by deducting from the successful bid the consideration for any services supplied by him to the vendor in connection with the sale of the motor car; (2) calculate the price at which the motor car was supplied by adding to the successful bid the consideration for any supply of services by him to the purchaser in connection with the sale of the motor car, in either, or both, cases excluding the consideration for supplies of services that are not chargeable to VAT: art 8(7) (as so substituted). For the meaning of 'consideration' generally see para 86 ante; and for the meaning of 'auctioneer' see para 23 note 11 ante.
9   Ibid art 8(5)(a) (substituted by SI 1995/1269).
10 Ie for the purposes of the Value Added Tax Act 1994: see para 85 et seq ante.
11 Value Added Tax (Cars) Order 1992 art 8(5)(b) (as substituted: see note 9 supra).

4. SPECIAL CASES

(1) GROUPS OF COMPANIES

191. In general. Where any bodies corporate are treated as members of a group[1], any business[2] carried on by a member of the group is treated as carried on by the representative member[3], and

(1)   any supply[4] of goods or services by a member of the group to another member of the group is disregarded[5];

(2)   any supply to which head (1) above does not apply and which is a supply of goods or services by or to a member of the group is treated as a supply by or to the representative member[6]; and

(3)   any value added tax paid or payable by a member of the group on the acquisition of goods from another member state[7] or on the importation of goods from a place outside the member states[8] is treated as paid or payable by the representative member and the goods are treated as acquired[9] or imported[10] by the representative member for certain specified purposes[11].

All members of the group are jointly and severally liable for any VAT due from the representative member[12].

The Treasury may make provision by order[13] for securing that any goods or services which, if all the members of the group were one person, would fall to be treated as supplied to or by that person, are treated as supplied to and by the representative member[14]. Additional anti-avoidance provisions apply in relation to groups[15].

1   Ie under the Value Added Tax Act 1994 s 43 (as amended): see the text and notes 2–15 infra; and para 66 ante.

2   For the meaning of 'business' see para 17 ante.

3   Value Added Tax Act 1994 s 43(1). As to the representative member see para 66 ante.

4   For the meaning of 'supply' see para 21 ante.

5   Value Added Tax Act 1994 s 43(1)(a). The purpose of s 43 (as amended) is to treat a group of companies as a single entity, taxable through its representative member, so that in applying Customs and Excise Notice 727 *Retail Schemes* (1 April 1993) (which has effect as delegated legislation: see para 8 ante), credit provided to a customer by another member of the same VAT group as the retailer must be treated as self-financed credit provided by the representative member: *Customs and Excise Comrs v Kingfisher plc* [1994] STC 63; see also *BOC International Ltd v Customs and Excise Comrs* [1982] VATTR 84; *Midland Bank plc v Customs and Excise Comrs* [1991] VATTR 525.

    Where 28 April 1996 falls within the prescribed accounting period of a taxable person, and that prescribed accounting period ends on or after 1 June 1996, the following provisions apply until the day after the end of that prescribed accounting period: (1) any VAT chargeable on a supply of goods or services by one member of a group to another to which head (1) in the text does not apply because the person making the supply and the person supplied do not continue to be members of that group until the specified time is treated as chargeable, if it would otherwise be chargeable in an earlier period, in the first prescribed accounting period in which either the body making the supply or the body supplied, or both, no longer continues or continue to be members of that group (Value Added Tax Regulations 1995, SI 1995/2518, reg 41(2)); and (2) the specified time is (a) in the case of a supply of goods which are to be removed in pursuance of the supply, a time after the removal; (b) in the case of any other supply of goods, a time after the goods have been made available, in pursuance of the supply, to the body supplied; and (c) in the case of a supply of services, a time after the services have been performed (reg 41(3)). Regulation 41(2), (3) is revoked, subject to the transitional provision set out supra, by SI 1996/1250. For the meaning of 'prescribed accounting period' see para 202 note 4 post.

6   Value Added Tax Act 1994 s 43(1)(b) (amended by the Finance Act 1995 s 25(2)).

7   For the meaning of 'another member state' see para 4 note 14 ante.

8   As to the territories included in, or excluded from, the member states for VAT purposes see para 10 ante.

9   Ie for the purposes of the Value Added Tax Act 1994 s 73(7): see para 247 post.

10 Ie for the purposes of ibid s 38 (see para 109 ante) and s 73(7) (see para 247 post): s 43(1)(c).

11 Ibid s 43(1)(c).

12 Ibid s 43(1).

13 Ie under ibid s 5(5) or (6): see para 26 ante.

14 Ibid s 43(2). See eg the Value Added Tax Act (Special Provisions) Order 1995, SI 1995/1268, art 11(4); and para 26 ante.

15 See the Value Added Tax Act 1994 s 43(9), Sch 9A (added by the Finance Act 1996 s 31(1), (2), Sch 4); and para 193 post. As to the potential for abuse of the system of group registration for VAT see eg *Thorn Materials Supply Ltd v Customs and Excise Comrs, Thorn Resources Ltd v Customs and Excise Comrs* (1995) VAT Decision 12914, [1995] STI 477 (revsd on appeal: see *Thorn Materials Supply Ltd v Customs and Excise Comrs, Thorn Resources Ltd v Customs and Excise Comrs* (4 November 1996, unreported), CA).

192. Supplies to groups. With certain exceptions[1], where:

(1)   a business[2], or part of a business, carried on by a taxable person[3] is transferred as a going concern[4] to a body corporate treated as a member of a group[5] for value added tax purposes;

(2)   on the transfer of the business or part, chargeable assets[6] of the business are transferred to the body corporate; and

(3)   the transfer of the assets is treated[7] as neither a supply of goods nor a supply of services[8],

then the chargeable assets are treated for the purposes of the Value Added Tax Act 1994 as being, on the day on which they are transferred, both supplied to the representative member[9] of the group for the purpose of its business and supplied by that member in the course or furtherance of its business[10].

This provision does not apply:

(a)   if the representative member of the group is entitled to credit for the whole of the input tax[11] on supplies to it and acquisitions and importations by it during the prescribed accounting period[12] in which the assets are transferred and during any longer period to which certain regulations[13] relate and in which the assets are transferred[14];

(b)   if the Commissioners of Customs and Excise are satisfied that the assets were assets of the taxable person transferring them more than three years before the day on which they are transferred[15]; or

(c)   to the extent that the chargeable assets consist of capital items in respect of which certain regulations[16] in force when the assets are transferred provide for adjustment to the deduction of input tax[17].

The value of a supply treated as made to or by a representative member by virtue of the above provisions is taken to be the open market value[18] of the chargeable assets[19]; but the supply treated as so made is not taken into account as a supply made by the representative member when determining the allowance of input tax[20] in his case[21].

The commissioners may reduce the VAT chargeable[22] in a case where they are satisfied that the person by whom the chargeable assets are transferred has not received credit for the full amount of input tax arising on the supply to, or acquisition or importation by, him of the chargeable assets[23].

1   Ie subject to the Value Added Tax Act 1994 s 44(2)–(4): see heads (a)–(c) in the text.
2   For the meaning of 'business' see para 17 ante.
3   For the meaning of 'taxable person' see paras 12 note 4, 55 ante.
4   As to transfer as a going concern see ibid s 49; and paras 74 ante, 196, 220 post.
5   Ie under the Value Added Tax Act 1994 s 43 (as amended): see paras 66, 191 ante.
6   For these purposes, assets are chargeable assets if their supply in the United Kingdom by a taxable person in the course or furtherance of his business would be a taxable supply (and not a zero-rated supply): ibid s 44(10). For the meaning of 'United Kingdom' see para 4 note 3 ante; for the meaning of 'supply' see para 21 ante; for the meaning of 'taxable supply' see para 12 note 3 ante; and for the meaning of 'zero-rated supply' see para 158 ante.
7   Ie so treated by virtue of ibid s 5(3)(c): see para 21 ante.
8   See eg the Value Added Tax (Special Provisions) Order 1995, SI 1995/1268, art 5; and para 20 ante. As to the substantial avoidance of VAT by this device see *Friary Leasing Ltd v Customs and Excise Comrs* (1989) VAT Decision 3893, [1989] STI 772.
9   As to the representative member see para 66 ante.
10   Value Added Tax Act 1994 s 44(1), (5). A self-supply charge is thus imposed, which must be left out of account by the representative member when calculating the amount of input tax in can recover under its partial exemption method: see s 44(6); and the text to notes 20–21 infra. As to the partial exemption method see para 209 post.
11   For the meaning of 'input tax' see paras 4 ante, 201 post.
12   F. · the meaning of 'prescribed accounting period' see para 202 note 4 post.
13   Ie regulations under the Value Added Tax Act 1994 s 26(3)(b): see the Value Added Tax Regulations 1995, SI 1995/2518, regs 99–111; and para 209 et seq post.
14   Value Added Tax Act 1994 s 44(2).
15   Ibid s 44(3).
16   Ie regulations made under ibid s 26(3), (4) (the capital goods scheme): see para 209 et seq post.
17   Ibid s 44(4).
18   For these purposes, the open market value of any chargeable assets is taken to be the price that would be paid on a sale (on which no VAT is payable) between a buyer and a seller who are not in such a relationship as to affect the price: ibid s 44(8).
19   Ibid s 44(7).
20   Ie under ibid s 26: see para 203 post.
21   Ibid s 44(6).
22   Ie chargeable by virtue of ibid s 44(5): see the text to notes 9–10 supra.
23   Ibid s 44(9). As to goods which are subject to a capital goods scheme see para 198 post.

193. Power to give anti-avoidance directions. In order to prevent the avoidance of value added tax by the device of joining or leaving a group at an advantageous time, the Commissioners of Customs and Excise have wide powers to make directions counteracting the effect of a group relationship or of the termination of a group relationship. They may give a direction[1] if, in any case:

(1)   a relevant event has occurred, that is to say, a body corporate either begins to be, or ceases to be, treated as a member of a group[2] or enters into any transaction[3];

(2)   the statutory condition[4] is fulfilled[5];

(3)   that condition would not be fulfilled apart from the occurrence of that event[6]; and

(4)   in the case of an event which is the entering into of a transaction by a body corporate, the transaction in question is not a supply[7] which is the only supply by reference to which the case falls within heads (1) to (3) above[8].

The statutory condition which must be fulfilled is that:

(a)   there has been, or will or may be, a taxable supply[9] on which VAT has been, or will or may be, charged otherwise than by reference to the supply's full value[10];

(b)   there is at least a part of the supply which is not or, as the case may be, would not be zero-rated[11]; and

(c)   the charging of VAT on the supply otherwise than by reference to its full value gives rise or, as the case may be, would give rise to a tax advantage[12],

and the charging of VAT on a supply ('the undercharged supply') otherwise than by reference to its full value is taken to give rise to a tax advantage if, and only if, a person has become entitled either to credit for input tax[13] allowable as attributable to that supply or any part of it[14], or to any repayment[15] in respect of that supply or any part of it[16]. The commissioners may not give a direction by reference to a relevant event if they are satisfied that the change in the treatment of the body corporate, or the transaction in question, had as its main purpose or as each of its main purposes a genuine commercial purpose unconnected with the fulfilment of the statutory condition[17].

The directions that may be given under these provisions are either:

(i)   a direction relating to any supply of goods or services that has been made, in whole or in part, by one body corporate to another[18], which requires it to be assumed[19], if that would not otherwise be the case, that, to the extent described in the direction, the supply was not a supply falling to be disregarded[20] as being a supply by one member of a group to another[21]; or

(ii)   a direction relating to a particular body corporate[22] which requires it to be assumed, if that would not otherwise be the case, that for the period described in the direction[23] the body corporate either (A) did not fall to be, or should not be, treated as a member of a group or of a particular group described in the direction or (B) fell to be, or should be, treated as a member of any group so described of which it was or is eligible[24] to be a member for that period[25].

A direction so given may vary the effect of a previous direction[26]. It may not be given more than six years after the later of (A) the occurrence of the relevant event by reference to which it is given[27]; and (B) the time when the relevant entitlement arose[28].

The commissioners may at any time withdraw a direction by notice in writing to the person to whom it was given[29]. An appeal lies to the VAT and duties tribunal against any direction so given[30].

---

1   Ie a direction under the Value Added Tax Act 1994 s 43(9), Sch 9A (added by the Finance Act 1996 s 31(1), (2), Sch 4): see the text and notes 2–29 infra. The anti-avoidance provisions are

designed to counteract devices such as those used in *Thorn Materials Supply Ltd v Customs and Excise Comrs, Thorn Resources Ltd v Customs and Excise Comrs* (1995) VAT Decision 12914, [1995] STI 477, where a company made a supply of goods to another member of the group for a consideration which was substantially, but not completely, received whilst the parties were in the group relationship, left the group and subsequently acquired the assets which it had contracted to supply. It therefore claimed to be able to attribute the input tax it suffered on the purchase of the goods to the supply it made when outside the group relationship, whilst accounting for VAT only on the fraction of the consideration which remained to be paid. On appeal by the commissioners from the tribunal direct to the Court of Appeal, however, the decision was reversed: *Thorn Materials Supply Ltd v Customs and Excise Comrs* (4 November 1996, unreported), CA (held that the Value Added Tax Act 1994 s 6(4) (which advances the time of supply where a VAT invoice is issued before goods are physically supplied: see para 29 ante) cannot apply to treat a supply as taking place at a time when it would be disregarded for VAT purposes because at that time the parties were within the same VAT group). As to appeals direct to the Court of Appeal see para 321 post.

A direction so given to any person must be given to him by notice in writing: Value Added Tax Act 1994 Sch 9A para 5(3) (as so added). The giving of any notice or notification to any receiver, liquidator or person otherwise acting in a representative capacity in relation to another is treated for these purposes as the giving of a notice or notification to the person in relation to whom he so acts: Sch 9A para 7(2) (as so added). For the commissioners' statement of practice on their intended application of the powers conferred on them by Sch 9A (as so added) see [1996] STI 1116; and as to assessments consequential on a direction see para 250 post.

2   For these purposes, references to being treated as a member of a group are to be construed in accordance with the Value Added Tax Act 1994 s 43 (as amended) (see paras 66, 191 ante): Sch 9A para 7(1) (as added: see note 1 supra).

3   Ibid Sch 9A para 1(1)(a), (2) (as added: see note 1 supra). A direction must specify the relevant event by reference to which it is given: Sch 9A para 5(4) (as so added). It may not be given by reference to a relevant event occurring on or before 28 November 1995, but subject to that and to the six-year time limit (see the text to notes 27–28 infra), may be given by reference to a relevant event occurring before the coming into force of these provisions (ie 29 April 1996): Sch 9A para 4(2), (3)(a) (as so added).

4   Ie the condition specified in ibid Sch 9A para 1(3) (as added: see note 1 supra): see heads (a)–(c) in the text.

5   Ibid Sch 9A para 1(1)(b) (as added: see note 1 supra).

6   Ibid Sch 9A para 1(1)(c) (as added: see note 1 supra).

7   For the meaning of 'supply' see para 21 ante.

8   Value Added Tax Act 1994 Sch 9A para 1(1)(d) (as added: see note 1 supra).

9   For the meaning of 'taxable supply' see para 12 note 3 ante.

10 Value Added Tax Act 1994 Sch 9A para 1(3)(a) (as added: see note 1 supra). References to the full value of a supply are references to the amount which (having regard to any direction under s 19(1), Sch 6 para 1 (see para 87 ante)) would be the full value of that supply for the purposes of the charge to VAT if that supply were not a supply falling to be disregarded, to any extent, in pursuance of s 43(1)(a) (see para 191 ante): Sch 9A para 1(9) (as so added).

11 Ibid Sch 9A para 1(3)(b) (as added: see note 1 supra). For the meaning of 'zero-rated supply' see para 158 ante.

12 Ibid Sch 9A para 1(3)(c) (as added: see note 1 supra).

13 For the meaning of 'input tax' see paras 4 ante, 201 post.

14 Value Added Tax Act 1994 Sch 9A para 1(4)(a) (as added: see note 1 supra). The cases where a person is so taken to have become entitled to a credit for input tax allowable as attributable to the undercharged supply, or to a part of it, include any case where (1) a person has become entitled to a credit for any input tax on the supply to him, or the acquisition or importation by him, of any goods and services; and (2) whatever the supplies to which the credit was treated as attributable when the entitlement to it arose, those goods or services are used by him in making the undercharged supply, or a part of it: Sch 9A para 1(5) (as so added). Any question whether any credit for input tax to which a person has become entitled was, or is to be taken to have been, a credit allowable as attributable to the whole or any part of a supply is to be determined, in relation to a supply of a right to goods or services or to a supply of goods or services by virtue of such a right, as if the supply of the right and supplies made by virtue of the right were a single supply of which the supply of the right and each of those supplies constituted different parts: Sch 9A para 1(8)(a) (as so added). References to the supply of a right to goods or services include references to the supply of any right, option or priority with respect to the supply of goods and services, and to the supply of an interest deriving from any right to goods or services: Sch 9A para 1(10) (as so added).

For these purposes, where (a) there is a supply of any of the assets of a business of a person ('the transferor') to a person to whom the whole or any part of that business is transferred as a going concern ('the transferee'); and (b) that supply is treated, in accordance with an order under s 5(3) (see para 21 ante), as being neither a supply of goods nor a supply of services (see the Value Added Tax Act (Special Provisions) Order 1995, SI 1995/1268, art 5; and para 20 ante), the question, so far as it falls to be determined by reference to those assets, whether a credit for input tax to which any person has become entitled is one allowable as attributable to the whole or any part of a supply is to be determined as if the transferor and the transferee were the same person: Value Added Tax Act 1994 Sch 9A para 1(6) (as so added). Where, in such a case, the transferor himself acquired any of the assets in question by way of a supply falling within heads (a)–(b) supra, Sch 9A para 1(6) (as so added) has the effect, as respects the assets so acquired, of requiring the person from whom those assets were acquired to be treated for the purposes of Sch 9A para 1(4), (5) (as so added) as the same person as the transferor and the transferee, and so on in the case of any number of successive supplies falling within those heads: Sch 9A para 1(7) (as so added).

15 Ie in accordance with regulations under ibid s 39: see para 261 et seq post. Any question whether any repayment is a repayment in respect of the whole or any part of a supply is to be determined, in relation to a supply of a right to goods or services or to a supply of goods or services by virtue of such a right, as if the supply of the right and supplies made by virtue of the right were a single supply of which the supply of the right and each of those supplies constituted different parts: Sch 9A para 1(8)(b) (as so added).

16 Ibid Sch 9A para 1(4)(b) (as added: see note 1 supra).

17 Ibid Sch 9A para 2 (as added: see note 1 supra).

18 Ibid Sch 9A para 3(1)(a) (as added: see note 1 supra). A direction relating to a supply may be given to (1) the person who made the supply to which the direction relates; or (2) any body corporate which, at the time when the direction is given, is the representative member of a group of which that person was treated as being a member at the time of the supply: Sch 9A para 5(1) (as so added). As to the representative member see para 66 ante.

19 Where a direction requires any assumptions to be made, then (1) so far as the assumptions relate to times on or after the day on which the direction is given, the Value Added Tax Act 1994 has effect in relation to such times in accordance with those assumptions; and Sch 9A para 6 (as added) (see para 250 post) applies for giving effect to those assumptions in so far as they relate to earlier times: Sch 9A para 3(4) (as added: see note 1 supra). Subject to the six-year time limit (see the text to notes 27–28 infra), a direction may require assumptions to be made in relation to times, including times before 29 November 1995, falling before the occurrence of the relevant event by reference to which the direction is given, or before the relevant entitlement arose; and this reference to the relevant entitlement is a reference to the entitlement by reference to which the requirements of Sch 9A para 1(4) (as so added) are taken to be satisfied for the purposes of that direction: Sch 9A para 4(3)(b), (4) (as so added).

The refusal or non-refusal by the commissioners of an application under s 43 (as amended) (see paras 66, 191 ante) does not prejudice their power to give a direction under these provisions requiring any case to be assumed to be what it would have been had the application not been refused or, as the case may be, had it been refused: Sch 9A para 3(8) (as so added).

20 Ie in pursuance of ibid s 43(1)(a): see para 191 ante.

21 Ibid Sch 9A para 3(2) (as added: see note 1 supra).

22 Ibid Sch 9A para 3(1)(b) (as added: see note 1 supra). A direction relating to a body corporate ('the relevant body') may be given to that body or to any body corporate which at the time when the direction is given is, or in pursuance of the direction is to be treated as, the representative member of a group of which the relevant body (1) is treated as being a member; (2) was treated as being a member at a time to which the direction relates; or (3) is to be treated as being, or having been, a member at any such time: Sch 9A para 5(2) (as so added).

23 Ie a period comprising times before the giving of the direction or times afterwards, or both: ibid Sch 9A para 3(3) (as added: see note 1 supra).

24 For these purposes, references to being eligible to be treated as a member of a group are to be construed in accordance with ibid s 43 (as amended) (see paras 66, 191 ante): Sch 9A para 7(1) (as added: see note 1 supra).

25 Ibid Sch 9A para 3(3) (as added: see note 1 supra). A direction falling within head (B) in the text may identify in relation to any times or period the body corporate which is to be assumed to have been, or to be, the representative member of the group at those times or for that period: Sch 9A para 3(5) (as so added).

26 Ibid Sch 9A para 3(6) (as added: see note 1 supra).

27 Ibid Sch 9A para 4(1)(a) (as added: see note 1 supra); and see note 3 supra.

28 Ibid Sch 9A para 4(1)(b) (as added: see note 1 supra); and see note 19 supra.

29 Ibid Sch 9A para 3(7) (as added: see note 1 supra).

30 See ibid s 83(wa) (as added); and para 296 post.

(2) OTHER SPECIAL CASES

194. The Crown. The Value Added Tax Act 1994 applies in relation to supplies[1] by the Crown as it applies in relation to taxable supplies[2] by taxable persons[3].

Where the supply by a government department[4] of any goods or services does not amount to the carrying on of a business[5] but it appears to the Treasury that similar goods or services are or might be supplied by taxable persons in the course or furtherance of any business[6], then, if and to the extent that the Treasury so directs, the supply of those goods or services by that department is to be treated for the purposes of the Value Added Tax Act 1994 as a supply in the course or furtherance of any business carried on by it[7].

Where VAT is chargeable on the supply of goods or services to a government department, on the acquisition of any goods by a government department from another member state[8] or on the importation of any goods by a government department from a place outside the member states[9] and the supply, acquisition or importation is not for the purpose of (1) any business carried on by the department; or (2) a supply by the department which, by virtue of a direction by the Treasury[10], is treated as a supply in the course or furtherance of a business, then, if and to the extent that the Treasury so directs, the Commissioners of Customs and Excise must, on a claim made by the department at such time and in such form and manner as the commissioners may determine, refund to it the amount of the VAT so chargeable[11]. The commissioners may, however, make the refunding of any amount so due conditional upon compliance by the claimant with requirements with respect to the keeping, preservation and production of records relating to the supply, acquisition or importation in question[12].

1   For the meaning of 'supply' see para 21 ante.
2   For the meaning of 'taxable supply' see para 12 note 3 ante.
3   Value Added Tax Act 1994 s 41(1). For the meaning of 'taxable person' see paras 12 note 4, 55 ante.
4   For these purposes, 'government department' includes a Northern Ireland department, a Northern Ireland health and social services body, any body of persons exercising functions on behalf of a minister of the Crown (including a health service body as defined in the National Health Service and Community Care Act 1990 s 60(7) (ie a health authority within the meaning of the National Health Service Act 1977, a Family Health Services Authority, the Dental Practice Board and the Public Health Laboratory Service Board)), and any part of a government department designated for these purposes by a direction of the Treasury: Value Added Tax Act 1994 s 41(6). For the meaning of 'a Northern Ireland health and social services body' see s 41(8). For the purposes of s 41(6), a National Health Service trust established under the National Health Service and Community Care Act 1990 Pt I (ss 1–26) (as amended) or the National Health Service (Scotland) Act 1978 is to be regarded as a body of persons exercising functions on behalf of a minister of the Crown: Value Added Tax Act 1994 s 41(7).
    For the purposes of s 41, goods or services obtained by one government department from another government department are treated, if and to the extent that the Treasury so directs, as supplied by that other department, and similarly as regards goods or services obtained by or from the Crown Estate Commissioners: s 41(5).
5   For the meaning of 'business' see para 17 ante.
6   For the meaning of 'in the course or furtherance of a business' see paras 12 note 5, 17 note 2 ante.
7   Value Added Tax Act 1994 s 41(2). As to current Treasury directions see the London Gazette, 2 April 1993.
8   For the meaning of 'another member state' see para 4 note 14 ante.
9   As to the territories included in, or excluded from, the member states for VAT purposes see para 10 ante.
10 Ie under the Value Added Tax Act 1994 s 41(2): see the text and notes 4–7 supra.
11 Ibid s 41(3). As to the current Treasury direction see the London Gazette, 2 July 1996.
12 Value Added Tax Act 1994 s 41(4).

195. Agents. Where (1) goods are acquired from another member state[1] by a person who is not a taxable person[2] and a taxable person acts in relation to the acquisition and then supplies the goods as agent for the person by whom they are so acquired; or (2) goods are imported from a place outside the member states[3] by a taxable person who supplies them as agent for a person who is not a taxable person, then if the taxable person acts in relation to the supply[4] in his own name, the goods are treated for the purposes of value added tax as acquired and supplied or, as the case may be, as imported and supplied by the taxable person as principal[5].

Where, in the case of any supply of goods to which the above provision does not apply, goods are supplied through an agent who acts in his own name, the supply is treated both as a supply to the agent and as a supply by the agent[6].

Where services are supplied through an agent who acts in his own name, the Commissioners of Customs and Excise may, if they think fit, treat the supply both as a supply to the agent and as a supply by the agent[7].

1   As to the acquisition of goods from other member states see para 13 ante; and for the meaning of 'another member state' see para 4 note 14 ante.
2   For the meaning of 'taxable person' see paras 12 note 4, 55 ante. A person who is not resident in the United Kingdom and whose place, or principal place, of business is outside the United Kingdom may be treated for these purposes as not being a taxable person if, as a result, he will not be required to be registered under the Value Added Tax Act 1994: s 47(2). For the meaning of 'United Kingdom' see para 4 note 3 ante. As to registration for VAT see para 56 et seq ante.
3   As to the territories included in, or excluded from, the member states for VAT purposes see para 10 ante.
4   For the meaning of 'supply' see para 21 ante.
5   Value Added Tax Act 1994 s 47(1) (amended by the Finance Act 1995 s 23(1), (4)(a)). Thus the agent is responsible for the VAT on acquisition or importation and on the on-supply, notwithstanding that the goods might ordinarily not attract VAT because the principal is not a registered person.
6   Value Added Tax Act 1994 s 47(2A) (added by the Finance Act 1995 s 23(2), (4)(b)). This can have the effect of imposing a charge to VAT at the standard rate in a case where the supply to the principal would, if made directly, have been zero-rated: see eg Customs and Excise Business Brief 16/96 [1996] STI 1310. It also has the effect of imposing a charge to VAT on the retail selling price of goods, where the retailer is acting as agent for an unregistered principal, thereby reversing the effect of cases such as *Potter (t/a P & R Potter Wholesale) v Customs and Excise Comrs* [1985] STC 45, CA, *Hill (t/a K Hill & Co) v Customs and Excise Comrs* [1988] STC 424, *Customs and Excise Comrs v Paget* [1989] STC 773 and *Customs and Excise Comrs v Music & Video Exchange Ltd* [1992] STC 220. As to the standard rate of VAT see para 5 ante; and for the meaning of 'zero-rated supply' see para 158 ante.
7   Value Added Tax Act 1994 s 47(3) (amended by the Finance Act 1995 s 23(3), Sch 29 Pt VI). Thus the person to whom the services are supplied can receive a VAT invoice in the agent's name, without needing to disclose to him the principal's identity. As to the statutory provisions relating to VAT invoices see para 240 et seq post; and as to general provisions relating to undisclosed principals see AGENCY vol 1(2) (Reissue) para 62. As to the provision of nursing services through nursing agencies see *Customs and Excise Comrs v Reed Personnel Services Ltd* [1995] STC 588; *Allied Medicare Nursing Services Ltd v Customs and Excise Comrs* (1991) VAT Decision 5485, [1991] STI 79; *Parkinson v Customs and Excise Comrs* (1991) VAT Decision 6017, [1991] STI 696; *British Nursing Co-operation Ltd v Customs and Excise Comrs* (1992) VAT Decision 8816, [1992] STI 1036; *BUPA Nursing Services Ltd v Customs and Excise Comrs* (1993) VAT Decision 10010, [1993] STI 660; *Sheffield and Rotherham Nursing Agency v Customs and Excise Comrs* (1993) VAT Decision 11279, [1993] STI 1621; *South Hams Nursing Agency v Customs and Excise Comrs* (1995) VAT Decision 13027, [1995] STI 710.
    There is a body of authorities on whether supplies to third parties by independent contractors are being made by the contractor or by the person who has contracted to use the contractor's services. This issue arises frequently in connection with hairdressers, taxi drivers, driving schools and similar institutions, where the customer is more likely to believe that he is being provided with services by the institution than by the independent contractor. In such cases, it is not enough to know that the person supplying services is not an employee; it must also be established that he is providing his services to the customer and not to the company which has engaged him: *Cronin (t/a Cronin Driving School) v Customs and Excise Comrs* [1991] STC 333; *Hosmer v Customs and Excise Comrs* (1992) VAT Decision 7313, [1992] STI 559; *Customs and Excise Comrs v MacHenry's (Hairdressers) Ltd* [1993] STC 170; *Carless v Customs and Excise Comrs* [1993] STC 632; *Hamiltax v Customs and Excise Comrs* (1992) VAT Decision 8948, [1992] STI 1067; *Customs and Excise Comrs v Jane Montgomery (Hair Stylists) Ltd* [1994] STC 256; *Clark v Customs and Excise Comrs* [1996] STC 263. For a similar case in relation to supplies of goods see *Customs and Excise Comrs v Music and Video Exchange Ltd* [1992] STC 220. Where the commissioners decide to treat a supply

of services through an agent as a supply to, and a supply by, the agent, the two supplies are deemed to take place simultaneously and cannot be treated as taking place at different times, by reference to the payments made and received by the agent: *Wirral Metropolitan Borough v Customs and Excise Comrs* [1995] STC 597.

196. Transfers of going concerns. Where a business[1] carried on by a taxable person[2] is transferred to another person as a going concern[3], then, for the purpose of determining whether the transferee is liable to be registered under the Value Added Tax Act 1994, he is treated as having carried on the business before as well as after the transfer, and supplies[4] by the transferor are treated accordingly[5]. Any records relating to the business which are required to be preserved for any period after the transfer[6] are to be preserved by the transferee instead of by the transferor, unless the Commissioners of Customs and Excise, at the request of the transferor, otherwise direct[7].

Without prejudice to the above provision, the commissioners may by regulations make provision for securing continuity in the application of the Value Added Tax Act 1994 in cases where a business carried on by a taxable person is transferred to another person as a going concern and the transferee is registered under that Act in substitution for the transferor[8]. Such regulations may in particular provide (1) for certain statutory liabilities and duties[9] of the transferor to become, to such extent as may be provided by the regulations, liabilities and duties of the transferee[10]; and (2) for any right of either of them to repayment or credit in respect of VAT to be satisfied by making a repayment or allowing a credit to the other[11]. No such provision as is mentioned in head (1) or head (2) above is, however, to have effect in relation to any transferor and transferee unless an application in that behalf has been made by them under the regulations[12].

1   For the meaning of 'business' see para 17 ante.
2   For the meaning of 'taxable person' see paras 12 note 4, 55 ante.
3   There is no statutory definition of 'transfer of a business as a going concern'. Courts and tribunals have consistently adopted dicta in *Kenmir Ltd v Frizzell* [1968] 1 All ER 414 at 418, [1968] 1 WLR 329 at 335 per Widgery J: 'regard must be had to the substance of the transaction rather than its form; consideration being given to the whole of the circumstances ... the vital consideration is whether the effect of the transaction is to put the transferee in possession of a going concern the activities of which he could carry on without interruption'; see also Case 24/85 *Spijkers v Gebroeders Benedik Abattoir CV and Alfred Benedik en Zonen BV* [1986] ECR 1119, [1986] 2 CMLR 296 (Advocate-General). Thus it has been held sufficient that the transferee, having acquired the transferor's business assets, sold the old stock prior to commencing a new trade from the same premises: *Customs and Excise Comrs v Dearwood Ltd* [1986] STC 327. The Value Added Tax (Special Provisions) Order 1995, SI 1995/1268, art 5 (see para 20 ante) applies to any transfer of a business, notwithstanding that it may only be part of the business of the transferor: *Acrefirst Ltd v Customs and Excise Comrs* [1985] VATTR 133. There is no need to transfer the premises from which a business is carried on in order to transfer the business: *Baltic Leasing Ltd v Customs and Excise Comrs* [1986] VATTR 98. The grant of a franchise of a business does not constitute the transfer of a business as a going concern: *Delta Newsagents Ltd v Customs and Excise Comrs* [1986] VATTR 261. The sale of some business assets and the majority of the business's stock in trade does not constitute a transfer of a business as a going concern where the intention of the transferor is to realise funds to keep the business going (distinguishing *Customs and Excise Comrs v Dearwood Ltd* supra; and not following *Kenmir Ltd v Frizzel* supra): *Customs and Excise Comrs v Padglade Ltd* [1995] STC 602); and see *Farm Facilities (Fork Lift) Ltd v Customs and Excise Comrs* [1987] VATTR 80; *Morland & Co plc v Customs and Excise Comrs* [1992] VATTR 411; *Hartley Engineering Ltd v Customs and Excise Comrs* (1994) VAT Decision 12385, [1994] STI 1185. To constitute a transfer of a business as a going concern within the Value Added Tax (Special Provisions) Order 1995 art 5, the business must have been carried on by the transferor for a period; thus the transfer by a parent company to its subsidiaries of various food stores, which it had purchased from third parties, was outside the scope of what is now the Value Added Tax (Special Provisions) Order 1995 art 5 and VAT should have been charged on the transfer: *Kwik Save Group plc v Customs and Excise Comrs* (1995) VAT Decision 12749, [1995] STI 64.
3   For the meaning of 'supply' see para 21 ante.
5   Value Added Tax Act 1994 s 49(1)(a). There are particular rules for registration which apply where a person who is not registered for VAT acquires a business as a going concern from a taxable person: see the Value Added Tax Act 1994 s 3(2), Sch 1 para 1(2) (as amended); the Value Added Tax Regulations

1995, SI 1995/2518, reg 6(1); and paras 56, 74 ante. As to the keeping of records on the transfer of a going concern see para 220 post. As to the treatment of assets supplied by a trader which formed part of his business to another to whom he transfers his business as a going concern and related matters see the Value Added Tax (Special Provisions) Order 1995 art 5; and para 20 ante; as to the exempt supply of land see para 142 ante; and as to the election to waive exemption see para 143 ante.

6   Ie under the Value Added Tax Act 1994 s 58, Sch 11 para 6: see para 219 post.
7   Value Added Tax Act 1994 s 49(1)(b).
8   Ibid s 49(2). See the Value Added Tax Regulations 1995 reg 6; and para 74 ante.
9   Ie rights and duties under the Value Added Tax Act 1994, excluding ss 59–70 (as amended) (see para 272 et seq post): s 49(3)(a).
10   Ibid s 49(3)(a).
11   Ibid s 49(3)(b).
12   Ibid s 49(3).

197. Terminal markets. The Treasury may by order make provision for modifying the provisions of the Value Added Tax Act 1994 in their application to dealings on terminal markets[1] and to such persons ordinarily engaged in such dealings as may be specified in the order, subject to such conditions as may be so specified[2]. Such an order may include[3] provision for:

(1)   zero-rating[4] the supply[5] of any goods or services or for treating the supply of any goods or services as exempt[6];

(2)   the registration under the Value Added Tax Act 1994 of any body of persons representing persons ordinarily engaged in dealing on a terminal market and for disregarding such dealings (a) by persons so represented in determining liability to be registered under, and (b) between persons so represented for all the purposes of, that Act[7];

(3)   for refunding, to such persons as may be specified by or under the order, input tax[8] attributable to such dealings on a terminal market as may be so specified[9],

and may contain such incidental and supplementary provisions as appear to the Treasury to be necessary or expedient[10].

An order under this provision may make different provision with respect to different terminal markets and with respect to different commodities[11].

The following supplies of goods or services in the course of dealings on a terminal market[12] are zero-rated:

(i)   the sale by or to a member of the market[13] of any goods ordinarily dealt with on the market[14];

(ii)   the grant by or to a member of the market of a right to acquire such goods[15];

(iii)   where a sale of goods or the grant of a right zero-rated under head (i) or head (ii) above is made in dealings between members of the market acting as agents, the supply by those members to their principals of their services in so acting[16].

1   The expression 'terminal markets' is not defined in the Value Added Tax Act 1994, but the following explanation may be helpful. The commodity markets in London and elsewhere are organised associations of traders who buy and sell various commodities. In the terminal markets there is a significant degree of trading in 'futures', ie transactions where the contract provides for delivery at some specified date in the future as distinct from 'spot' transactions which provide for immediate delivery. See also note 12 infra.

2   Value Added Tax Act 1994 s 50(1). At the date at which this volume states the law, no such order had been made; but, by virtue of the Interpretation Act 1978 s 17(2)(b), the Value Added Tax (Terminal Markets) Order 1973, SI 1973/173, (amended by SI 1975/385; SI 1980/304; SI 1981/338; SI 1984/202; SI 1985/1046; and SI 1987/806) has effect as if so made. As to the making of orders generally see para 8 ante.

3   But without prejudice to the generality of the Value Added Tax Act 1994 s 50(1): s 50(2).

4   As to zero-rating see para 158 et seq ante.

5   For the meaning of 'supply' see para 21 ante.

6   Value Added Tax Act 1994 s 50(2)(a). For the meaning of 'exempt supply' see para 141 ante.

7   Ibid s 50(2)(b). As to registration see para 56 et seq ante.

8   For the meaning of 'input tax' see paras 4 ante, 201 post.
9   Value Added Tax Act 1994 s 50(2)(c).
10 Ibid s 50(2).
11 Ibid s 50(3).
12 Ie a terminal market to which the Value Added Tax (Terminal Markets) Order 1973 (as amended) applies: art 3(1). Those markets are: the London Metal Exchange, the London Rubber Market, the London Cocoa Terminal Market, the London Coffee Terminal Market, the London Sugar Terminal Market, the London Vegetable Oil Terminal Market, the London Wool Terminal Market, the London Gold Market, the London Silver Market, the London Meat Futures Market, the London Grain Futures Market, the London Soya Bean Meal Futures Market, the Liverpool Barley Futures Market, the International Petroleum Exchange of London, the London Potato Futures Market and the London Platinum and Palladium Market: art 2(2) (as amended: see note 2 supra).
13 References to a member of a market include any person ordinarily engaged in dealings on the market: ibid art 2(3).
14 Ibid art 3(1)(a). The zero-rating of a sale by virtue of this provision is subject to the condition that the sale is either (1) a sale which, as a result of other dealings on the market, does not lead to a delivery of the goods by the seller to the buyer; or (2) a sale by and to a member of the market which (a) if the market is the London Metal Exchange, is a sale between members entitled to deal in the ring; (b) if the market is the London Cocoa Terminal Market, the London Coffee Terminal Market, the London Meat Futures Market, the International Petroleum Exchange of London, the London Potato Futures Market, the London Soya Bean Meal Futures Market, the London Sugar Terminal Market, the London Vegetable Oil Terminal Market or the London Wool Terminal Market, is a sale registered with the International Commodities Clearing House Limited; (c) if the market is the London Grain Futures Market, is a sale registered in the Clearing House of the Grain and Feed Trade Association Limited; and (d) if the market is the Liverpool Barley Futures Market, is a sale registered at the Clearing House of the Liverpool Corn Trade Association Limited: Value Added Tax (Terminal Markets) Order 1973 art 3(2) (amended by SI 1975/385; SI 1981/338; and SI 1984/202).
15 Ibid art 3(1)(b). The zero-rating of the grant of a right by virtue of this provision is subject to the condition that either (1) the right is exercisable at a date later than that on which it is granted; or (2) any sale resulting from the exercise of the right would be a sale with respect to which the condition in ibid art 3(2) (as amended) (see note 14 supra) is satisfied: art 3(3).
16 Ibid art 3(1)(c).

198. Capital goods. The Treasury may by order[1] make provision for the giving of relief, in such cases, to such extent and subject to such exceptions as may be specified in the order, from value added tax paid on the supply[2], acquisition or importation for the purpose of a business[3] carried on by any person of machinery or plant, or any specified description of machinery or plant, where that VAT or part of that VAT cannot be credited as input tax[4] and such other conditions are satisfied as may be specified in the order[5].

1   As to the power to make orders generally see para 8 ante.
2   For the meaning of 'supply' see para 21 ante.
3   For the meaning of 'business' see para 17 ante.
4   Ie that VAT cannot be credited under the Value Added Tax Act 1994 s 25: see para 203 post. For the meaning of 'input tax' see paras 4 ante, 201 post; and as to the right to deduct it see s 24(1); and para 201 et seq post.
5   Ibid s 34(1). Without prejudice to the generality of this provision, an order so made may provide for relief to be given by deduction or refunding of VAT and for aggregating or excluding the aggregation of value where goods of the same description are supplied, acquired or imported together: s 34(2). At the date at which this volume states the law, no such order had been made.

199. Trading stamp schemes. The Commissioners of Customs and Excise may by regulations[1] modify certain statutory provisions relating to the valuation of supplies of goods and services and the valuation of acquisitions from other member states[2] for the purpose of providing, in place of those provisions, for the manner of determining for the purposes of VAT the value of a supply[3] of goods, or the value of a transaction in pursuance of which goods are acquired from another member state[4], in a case where the goods are supplied or acquired under a trading stamp scheme[5]. This power is, however, no longer intended to be exercised[6]; and trading stamps are now treated in the same way as other discount vouchers[7].

1   As to the power to make regulations generally see para 8 ante.
2   Ie the Value Added Tax Act 1994 ss 19, 20 (see paras 85, 87 et seq ante), Schs 6, 7 (see para 87 et seq ante): s 52.
3   For the meaning of 'supply' see para 21 ante.
4   As to the acquisition of goods from another member state see para 13 ante.
5   Value Added Tax Act 1994 s 52. 'Trading stamp scheme' has the meaning which it bears under the Trading Stamps Act 1964 or the Trading Stamps Act (Northern Ireland) 1965 or under any scheme of an equivalent description which is in operation in another member state: Value Added Tax Act 1994 s 52. As to trading stamps and trading stamp schemes see SALE OF GOODS vol 41 para 898 et seq.
6   The previous regulations, contained in the Value Added Tax (Treatment of Transactions) (No 1) Order 1973, SI 1973/325; and in the Value Added Tax Regulations 1995, SI 1995/2518, Part X (regs 76–80) have been revoked by, respectively, the Value Added Tax (Treatment of Transactions) (Trading Stamps) Order 1995, SI 1995/3042; and the Value Added Tax (Trading Stamps) Regulations 1995, SI 1995/3043, in each case with effect from 1 June 1996. See also Customs and Excise News Release B6/95 [1995] STI 1906.
7   As to the treatment of discount vouchers see para 86 ante. The determination of the correct VAT treatment of discount vouchers is exceptionally difficult. Apart from Case C-126/88 *Boots Co plc v Customs and Excise Comrs* [1990] ECR I-1235, [1990] STC 387, ECJ (see para 86 note 9 ante), two other cases relating to vouchers have been decided by the European Court of Justice on references from English courts or tribunals (see Case C-288/94 *Argos Distributors Ltd v Customs and Excise Comrs* [1996] STC 1359, ECJ; Case C-317/94 *Elida Gibbs Ltd v Customs and Excise Comrs* [1996] STC 1387, ECJ); and two are presently before that court on such a reference (see *Goldsmiths (Jewellers) Ltd v Customs and Excise Comrs* (1994) VAT Decision 12694, [1994] STI 1374; and *Conoco Ltd v Customs and Excise Comrs* [1995] STC 1022). A further reference is to be made in relation to co-operative dividend stamps by the Manchester tribunal in *Sheffield Co-Operative Society Ltd v Customs and Excise Comrs* MAN/94/1170, MAN/95/1670. In Case C-288/94 *Argos Distributors Ltd v Customs and Excise Comrs* supra the court held that where a supplier sells a voucher to a buyer at a discount, and promises subsequently to accept that voucher at its face value in full or part payment of the price of goods purchased by a customer other than the buyer of the voucher, but who is unaware of the price paid for the voucher, the consideration represented by the voucher is the sum actually received by the supplier on the sale of the voucher; the effect is that the supplier is liable to account for VAT only on the discounted amount. In Case C-317/94 *Elida Gibbs Ltd v Customs and Excise Comrs* supra the court held that (1) where a manufacturer issued a money-off coupon in the course of a promotional campaign to members of the public, which is redeemable, at the amount stated on the coupon, by the manufacturer in favour of a retailer who has accepted the coupon in part payment for a specified item of goods, the amount on which the manufacturer is obliged to account for VAT on goods sold by wholesale and purchased in the course of the campaign is the selling price charged by him less the amount refunded in respect of the voucher; and (2) where a manufacturer sells goods to a retailer, which carry on their packaging a cash-back coupon for a stated amount, and the customer presents the coupon to the manufacturer for redemption, the taxable amount on which the manufacturer must account for VAT is the selling price of the goods charged to the retailer less the amount indicated on the coupon and refunded. Particular difficulty has been experienced in relation to the Value Added Tax Act 1994 s 19(1), Sch 6 para 5: see para 90 ante. The commissioners have indicated in Customs and Excise Business Brief 10/96 [1996] STI 981 how they propose to deal with business promotion coupon schemes consequent upon the removal of the trading stamps rules: (a) where vouchers are sold by a promoter, the acquisition of goods in return for the vouchers (the 'redemption' of the vouchers) will not be treated as a business gift but as having been acquired for the consideration paid for the vouchers themselves, so that no further VAT is due on the redemption of the vouchers (cf the Value Added Tax Act 1994 s 5(1), Sch 4 para 5(2); and see para 24 ante); (b) where a manufacturer issues vouchers or stamps with the sale of trade goods, and the vouchers etc are redeemable against other goods, the redemption is not treated as a business gift but as if the consideration for the premium goods (those with which the vouchers were issued) included an element of consideration for the redemption goods (cf Sch 4 para 5(2)); but (c) where such redemption goods are put to a non-business use by the trade customer, a charge will be imposed under Sch 4 para 5(4) (see para 24 ante); (d) where a retailer or manufacturer issues vouchers or stamps to a member of the public purchasing goods, the provision of the redemption goods in return for the voucher will not be treated as a business gift (cf Sch 4 para 5(2)); (5) where a voucher is redeemed for goods or services provided by a third party to the customer, but paid for by the manufacturer or retailer, the latter may not claim credit for the input tax on the supply of the redemption benefit, because the supply has not been made to him but to the customer. The effect of this approach (which apparently is intended to be a simplification measure, rather than necessarily reflecting the strict legal position) is that,

in some cases it will be possible that standard-rated redemption goods will be acquired without a charge to VAT (where, eg, the premium goods were zero-rated).

200. Tour operators. The Treasury may by order[1] modify the application of the Value Added Tax Act 1994 in relation to supplies[2] of goods or services by tour operators[3] or in relation to such of those supplies as may be determined under the order[4]. Such an order may make particular provision for:

(1) two or more supplies of goods or services by a tour operator to be treated as a single supply of services[5];

(2) the value of that supply to be ascertained, in such manner as may be determined by or under the order, by reference to the difference between sums paid or payable to, and sums paid or payable by, the tour operator[6];

(3) account to be taken, in determining the VAT chargeable on that supply, of the different rates of VAT that would have been applicable apart from the rules relating to tour operators[7];

(4) excluding any body corporate from the application of the provisions relating to groups[8] of companies[9]; and

(5) as to the time when a supply by a tour operator is to be treated as taking place[10].

The value of a designated travel service[11] is determined by reference to the difference between sums paid or payable to, and sums paid or payable by, the tour operator in respect of that service, calculated in such manner as the Commissioners of Customs and Excise may specify[12]. Where (a) a supply of goods or services is acquired for a consideration in money for the purpose of supplying a designated travel service; (b) the value of the supply is greater than its open market value; and (c) the supplier and tour operator are connected[13], the commissioners may direct that the value of the supply is to be deemed to be its open market value for the purpose of calculating the value of the designated travel service[14]. A tour operator who makes no supplies of designated travel services consisting of accommodation or transport may, however, treat a supply of a designated travel service as not being a supply of such a service if there are reasonable grounds for believing that the value[15] of all such supplies made by him in the period of one year then beginning will not exceed one per cent of the value of all supplies made by him in that period[16].

Input tax on goods or services acquired by a tour operator for resupply as a designated travel service is excluded from credit[17] as such tax[18].

1 The Value Added Tax Act 1994 s 97(3) (see para 8 ante) does not apply to such an order, notwithstanding that it makes provision for excluding any VAT from credit under s 25 (see para 203 post): s 53(4). As to the making of orders generally see para 8 ante. The effect of the scheme is to require a tour operator to account only for output tax on his 'margin' in relation to supplies falling within the scope of the scheme ('designated travel services'); but, correspondingly, to prevent him claiming credit for input tax on any supplies which he uses in making scheme supplies. The tour operator's 'margin' is, in simple terms, the difference between the VAT–inclusive purchase price of the designated travel service and his selling price of that service: see the text to note 12 infra.

2 For the meaning of 'supply' see para 21 ante.

3 For these purposes, 'tour operator' includes a travel agent acting as principal and any other person providing for the benefit of travellers services of any kind commonly provided by tour operators or travel agents: Value Added Tax Act 1994 s 53(3). In *Madgett and Baldwin (t/a Howden Court Hotel) v Customs and Excise Comrs* [1996] STC 167, the High Court referred to the European Court of Justice the question whether hoteliers who made arrangements with a coach hire firm to collect and return hotel customers to specified pick-up points in another part of the country, and who provided a sight-seeing tour of Devon to those customers, were tour operators or travel agents within the meaning of EC Council Directive 77/388 (OJ L145, 13.6.77, p 1) art 26. Article 26 also applies to tour operators who provide accommodation but who do not provide transport: Case C–163/91 *Van Ginkel Waddinxveen BV and Reis-en Passagebureau Van Ginkel BV v Inspecteur der Omzetbelasting, Utrecht* [1992] ECR I–5723, [1996] STC 825, ECJ. In *Norman Allen Group Travel Ltd v Customs and Excise Comrs*

(1996) VAT Decision 14158) [1996] STI 1353, it was held that supplies of block bookings of ferry journeys and hotel accommodation sold on a wholesale basis to United Kingdom travel companies, although supplies of designated travel services, were outside the scope of the tour operators' margin scheme, which only applies to supplies to 'travellers', following *Independent Coach Travel (Wholesaling) Ltd v Customs and Excise Comrs* [1994] 2 CMLR 257, [1993] VATTR 357. See now VAT Information Sheet 2/96 *Tour Operators' Margin Scheme; Practical Implementation of the Trader to Trader (Wholesale) Option* (July 1996). Other schemes, also introduced with effect from 1 January 1996 and designed to alleviate the effect of the tour operators' margin scheme are the 'airline charter option' and the 'agency option'. Under the airline charter option, a tour operator who charters an entire aeroplane for one or more flight slots over an entire holiday season, and who obtains catering services and transfer services from other suppliers, may zero-rate the provision of the air transport element to his customers: see VAT Information Sheet 3/96 *Tour Operators' Margin Scheme; Practical Implementation of the Airline Charter Option* (July 1996). Under the agency option, a tour operator who genuinely acquires passenger transport as agent for his customers may treat the expenditure on the flight, etc, as a zero-rated disbursement on their behalf: see VAT Information Sheet 4/96 *Tour Operators' Margin Scheme; Practical Implementationof the Agency Option* (July 1996).

4   Value Added Tax Act 1994 s 53(1). In exercise of the power so conferred, the Treasury has made the Value Added Tax (Tour Operators) (Amendment) Order 1995, SI 1995/1495, which came into force on 1 January 1996; art 1. In addition, by virtue of the Interpretation Act 1978 s 17(2)(b), the Value Added Tax (Tour Operators) Order 1987, SI 1987/1806 (amended by SI 1992/3125; SI 1995/1495; and by the Value Added Tax Act 1994 s 100(2), Sch 15) has effect as if so made.

5   Ibid s 53(2)(a). See the Value Added Tax (Tour Operators) Order 1987 art 3(2); and para 21 note 6 ante.

6   Value Added Tax Act 1994 s 53(2)(b). See the Value Added Tax (Tour Operators) Order 1987 arts 7–9; and the text and notes 11–14 infra.

7   Ibid s 53(2)(c). At the date at which this volume states the law, no such provision has been made, and none has effect as if so made following the revocation of the Value Added Tax (Tour Operators) Order 1987 art 10 (relating to bought-in international passenger transport services) by the Value Added Tax (Tour Operators) (Amendment) Order 1995 art 2. From 1 January 1996 a tour operator's margin on the provision of transport within the European Community has been standard-rated. The effect of this provision has been mitigated, though, by the Commissioners of Customs and Excise having invited tour operators to revise contractual arrangements with suppliers of such transport services, or with customers, so that the operator acts as agent for one or other party and does not act in his own name. In this case, the supply of such transport falls outside the scope of the 1987 Order: see Customs and Excise News Release 50/95 [1995] STI 1663; and Customs and Excise Business Brief 2/96 [1996] STI 266. As to the mitigation of tax where there is a supply of transport (or other services) partly within and partly outside the European Community see EC Council Directive 77/388 (OJ L145, 13.6.77, p 1) art 26(3); and Case C-74/91 *EC Commission v Germany* [1992] ECR I-5437, [1996] STC 843, ECJ.

8   Ie the Value Added Tax Act 1994 s 43 (as amended): see paras 66, 191 ante.

9   Ibid s 53(2)(d). See the Value Added Tax (Tour Operators) Order 1987 art 13; and para 66 text and notes 13–14 ante.

10 Value Added Tax Act 1994 s 53(2)(e). See the Value Added Tax (Tour Operators) Order 1987 art 4; and para 31 text and notes 19–22 ante. As to the place of supply of such services see para 54 ante.

11 For the meaning of 'designated travel service' see para 31 note 19 ante.

12 Value Added Tax (Tour Operators) Order 1987 art 7. Where goods and services were acquired before 1 April 1988, however, and input tax credit was claimed in respect of them, but they were supplied as a designated travel service, or as part of such a service, after that date, art 7 does not apply: see art 9. For the meaning of 'input tax' see paras 4 ante, 201 post. As to the calculation of value under art 7 see *Madgett and Baldwin (t/a Howden Court Hotel) v Customs and Excise Comrs* [1996] STC 167 (where the court remitted to the VAT and duties tribunal for further consideration the question whether the basis of apportionment set out by the commissioners in Customs and Excise Leaflet 709/5/88 (now replaced by Customs and Excise Leaflet 709/5/96 *Tour Operators' Margin Schemes* (1 January 1996) which has, as did its predecessor, statutory force by virtue of the Value Added Tax (Tour Operators) Order 1987 art 7) was contrary to Community law, on the ground that it could not be regarded as a rational or suitable basis for valuing the consideration for different parts of the package.

13 Any question whether a person is connected with another is to be determined in accordance with the Income and Corporation Taxes Act 1988 s 839 (as amended) (see INCOME TAXATION vol 23 (Reissue) para 1250): Value Added Tax (Tour Operators) Order 1987 art 8(4).

14 Ibid art 8(1). A direction so given must be given by notice in writing to the tour operator acquiring the supply; but no direction may be given more than three years after the time of the supply: art 8(2). A direction so given to a tour operator in respect of a supply acquired by him may also include a direction that, for the purpose of calculating the value of the designated travel service, the value of any supply fulfilling the prescribed conditions which is acquired by him after the giving of the notice (or after such

later time as may be specified in the notice) is deemed to be its open market value: art 8(3). As to the specified conditions see the text to note 13 supra.

15 For these purposes, the value of any supplies is to be calculated in accordance with the Value Added Tax Act 1994 s 19 (see paras 85, 87 ante): Value Added Tax (Tour Operators) Order 1987 art 14(2); Interpretation Act 1978 s 17(2)(b).

16 Value Added Tax (Tour Operators) Order 1987 art 14(1).

17 Ie under the Value Added Tax Act 1994 ss 25, 26: see paras 202–204 post.

18 Value Added Tax (Tour Operators) Order 1987 art 12; Interpretation Act 1978 s 17(2)(b). See *Aer Lingus plc v Customs and Excise Comrs* [1992] VATTR 438 (the provision by an airline of a free hotel room or free car hire in connection with the purchase of a ticket is the provision of services of a kind commonly provided by tour operators or travel agents, in respect of which there is not entitlement to input tax credit); cf *Virgin Atlantic Airways Ltd v Customs and Excise Comrs* [1993] VATTR 136 (the tribunal came to the opposite conclusion in relation to similar services (the provision of a chauffeured limousine or free car hire in connection with the purchase of an airline ticket)).

5. ACCOUNTING AND ASSESSMENT

(1) INPUT TAX AND OUTPUT TAX

(i) In general

201. Meaning of 'input tax' and 'output tax'. In relation to a taxable person[1], 'input tax' consists of the following tax: (1) value added tax on the supply[2] to him of any goods or services[3]; (2) VAT on the acquisition by him from another member state of any goods[4]; and (3) VAT paid or payable by him on the importation of any goods from a place outside the member states[5], provided, in each case, that the goods or services are used, or to be used, for the purpose of any business[6] carried on, or to be carried on, by him[7].

In addition, VAT on the supply, acquisition, or importation of fuel for private use[8] is treated as input tax, notwithstanding that the fuel is neither used, nor to be used, for the purposes of a business carried on by the taxable person[9]. Where, however, goods and services are supplied to a company, or goods are acquired by a company from another member state or imported by a company from a place outside the member states, and those goods or services are used or to be used in connection with the provision of accommodation by the company, they are not to be treated as used, or to be used, for the purposes of any business carried on by the company to the extent that the accommodation is used or to be used for domestic purposes by a director[10] of the company or any person connected[11] with a director of the company[12].

Where goods or services which have been supplied to a taxable person, goods which have been acquired by a taxable person from another member state, or goods which have been imported by a taxable person from a place outside the member states, are used, or to be used, partly for the purposes of a business carried on or to be carried on by him and partly for other purposes, VAT on supplies, acquisitions and importations must be apportioned so that only so much as is referable to his business purposes is counted as his input tax[13].

The Treasury may, by order, provide that where goods or services of a description specified in the order are supplied to a person who is not a taxable person, they are to be treated[14], in such circumstances as may be specified in the order, as supplied to such other person as may be determined in accordance with the order[15]. The Commissioners of Customs and Excise may provide by regulations[16]:

(a)   for VAT on the supply of goods or services to a taxable person, VAT on the acquisition of goods by a taxable person from other member states and VAT paid or payable by a taxable person on the importation of goods from places outside the member states to be treated as input tax only if, and to the extent that, the charge to VAT is evidenced and quantified by reference to such documents as may be specified in the regulations or the commissioners may direct, either generally or in particular cases or classes of cases[17];

(b)   for a taxable person to count as his input tax[18] VAT on the supply to him of goods or services or on the acquisition of goods by him from another member state or paid by him on the importation of goods from places outside the member states notwithstanding that he was not a taxable person at the time of the supply, acquisition or payment[19];

(c)   for a taxable person that is a body corporate to count as its input tax[20] VAT on the supply, acquisition or importation of goods before the company's incorporation for appropriation to the company or its business or on the supply of services before that time for its benefit or in connection with its incorporation[21];

(d)   in the case of a person who has been, but is no longer, a taxable person, for him to be paid by the commissioners the amount of any VAT on a supply of services made to him for the purposes of the business carried on by him when he was a taxable person[22].

Subject to the above provisions, 'output tax', in relation to a taxable person, means the VAT on supplies which he makes or on the acquisition by him of goods from another member state, including VAT which is also to be counted as input tax by virtue of head (1) above[23]. Where the commissioners are satisfied that a person is not able to account for the exact amount of output tax chargeable in any period, he may estimate a part of his output tax for that period, provided that any such estimated amount is adjusted and exactly accounted for as VAT chargeable in the next prescribed accounting period[24] or, if the exact amount is still not known and the commissioners are satisfied that it could not with due diligence be ascertained, in the next but one prescribed accounting period[25].

1   For the meaning of 'taxable person' see paras 12 note 4, 55 ante.

2   For the meaning of 'supply' see para 21 ante.

3   Value Added Tax Act 1994 s 24(1)(a).

4   Ibid s 24(1)(b). As to the acquisition of goods from another member state see para 13 ante.

5   Ibid s 24(1)(c). As to the charge to VAT on importation from places outside the member states see para 103 ante; and as to the territories included in, and excluded from, the member states for VAT purposes see para 10 ante.

6   For the meaning of 'business' see para 17 ante. The question whether goods or services have been used, or are to be used, 'for the purpose' of a business carried on by the taxable person has been considered in myriad cases. Perhaps the most significant of these is *Ian Flockton Developments Ltd v Customs and Excise Comrs* [1987] STC 394 at 400 per Stuart-Smith J (the test is a subjective one; the fact-finding tribunal must look into the taxpayer's mind as it was at the relevant time to discover his object. Where the taxpayer is a company, the relevant mind or minds is or are that or those of the person or persons controlling the company, or entitled to act, and acting for the company). See also *Anholt v Customs and Excise Comrs* [1989] VATTR 297 (membership of a sports club may be for the purposes of an actor's profession, where he has a role requiring him to portray an athletic character); *Rock Lambert v Customs and Excise Comrs* (1992) VAT Decision 6637, [1992] STI 60 (VAT on solicitors' fees on the sale of a house to meet partnership business debts not incurred for the purpose of the business); *Turner (t/a Turner Agricultural) v Customs and Excise Comrs* [1992] STC 621 (VAT on defendant's costs incurred by unsuccessful plaintiff in action not incurred for the purposes of plaintiff's business). Parliament has sought to impose a partial curb on the recovery of input tax on luxuries, amusements and entertainment, not only by disallowing credit as input tax for tax on the supply, acquisition or importation of goods or services to be used for the purposes of business entertainment (see para 206 post) but also by limiting the rights of a taxpayer to appeal against a decision of the commissioners that VAT incurred by the trader does not, or does not fully, qualify as input tax which may be credited or allowed under the Value Added Tax Act 1994 s 26; the tribunal may not allow the appeal unless it considers that the commissioners' determination was one which it was unreasonable to make: see s 84(4); and paras 296 note 9, 297 post;

and see *John Price Business Courses Ltd v Customs and Excise Comrs* (1995) VAT Decision 13135, [1995] STI 829 (VAT paid on subscription for a tennis club by a tax consultant not for the purposes of business and in any event falling within the Value Added Tax Act 1994 s 84(4)). Where expenditure is incurred on a supply of goods or services to be used both for business entertainment and to a measurable extent for other business purposes, a trader is entitled to a partial credit in respect of the input tax, based on an apportionment between entertainment and non-entertainment business use: *Thorn EMI plc v Customs and Excise Comrs* [1995] STC 674, CA, over-ruling *Customs and Excise Comrs v Plant Repair and Services (South Wales) Ltd* [1994] STC 232. Where there is a genuine business purpose, however small, in making a purchase of an asset (a personalised number plate), the VAT on the supply is deductible in full: *Welbeck Video plc v Customs and Excise Comrs* [1994] 2 CMLR 717, following Case C-97/90 *Lennartz v Finanzamt München III* [1991] ECR I-3795, [1995] STC 514, ECJ; and *Ian Flockton Developments Ltd v Customs and Excise Comrs* supra.

7   Value Added Tax 1994 s 24(1). Strictly speaking, the VAT on each supply made to the taxable person will not have been his personal liability, but the liability of the person making the supply: see s 1(2); and para 12 ante. However, the VAT on that supply will have been determined on the basis that the consideration for the supply is inclusive of the VAT chargeable (see s 19; and para 85 et seq ante), so that it may be seen that the recipient effectively suffers the VAT on the supply. The right to deduct input tax (under EC Council Directive 77/388 (OJ L145, 13.6.77, p 1) art 17(2)) only arises if the tax was properly due from the supplier; and VAT is not recoverable simply because it is mentioned as such on an invoice: Case C-342/87 *Genius Holding BV v Staatssecretaris van Financiën* [1989] ECR 4227, [1991] STC 239, ECJ.

No credit is allowed for sums paid by a trader by way of input tax under a contract to supply goods which are either non-existent (because the supplier is a fraudster) or which never belong to the supplier or which never come into existence because the would-be supplier ceases trading, whether through insolvency or otherwise, before the goods are supplied: *Howard v Customs and Excise Comrs* (1981) VAT Decision 1106 (unreported); *Theotrue Holdings Ltd v Customs and Excise Comrs* [1983] VATTR 88; *Northern Counties Co-operative Enterprises Ltd v Customs and Excise Comrs* [1986] VATTR 250; *Munn v Customs and Excise Comrs* [1989] VATTR 11; *Broadwell Land plc v Customs and Excise Comrs* [1993] VATTR 346; *Customs and Excise Comrs v Pennystar Ltd* [1996] STC 163. Quaere whether the position may be different where the proposed supply is one of services rather than goods: see *IMO Precision Controls Ltd v Customs and Excise Comrs* (1992) VAT Decision 7948, [1992] STI 893; *Customs and Excise Comrs v Moonrakers Guest House Ltd* [1992] STC 544; *Customs and Excise Comrs v Bass plc* [1993] STC 42. It appears that input tax recovery will be permitted if, at the time of the claim, it is uncertain whether or not the supply will take place: *Bethway & Moss Ltd v Customs and Excise Comrs* MAN/86/331 (VAT Decision 2667, unreported); *Broadwell Land plc v Customs and Excise Comrs* supra; *Customs and Excise Comrs v Moonrakers Guest House Ltd* supra. Where a trader buys second-hand goods from a non-taxable vendor, then, notwithstanding that an amount of the VAT charged on the original sale will still be contained in the second-hand price, the purchaser is unable to claim credit for that tax as his input tax, unless there is specific domestic legislation which makes provision for him to do so: Case C-165/88 *ORO Amsterdam Beheer BV and Concerto BV v Inspecteur der Omzetbelasting* [1989] ECR 4081, [1991] STC 614, ECJ. No such provision is made by the Value Added Tax Act 1994.

8   For the meaning of 'fuel for private use' see para 95 ante.

9   Value Added Tax Act 1994 s 56(5). This is because the trader is liable for output tax in each prescribed accounting period in which he uses, or supplies to another, fuel for private use: see para 95 ante. By concession, where a registered person makes no claim for input tax on purchases of road fuel, whether for business or private journeys, the scale charge is not applied: see Customs and Excise Notice 748 *Extra-statutory Concessions* (1 August 1995) concession 7.

10   For these purposes, 'director' means (1) in relation to a company whose affairs are managed by a board of directors or similar body, a member of that board or similar body; (2) in relation to a company whose affairs are managed by a single director or similar person, that director or person; (3) in relation to a company whose affairs are managed by the members themselves, a member of the company: Value Added Tax Act 1994 s 24(7).

11   A person is connected with a director if that person is the director's wife or husband, or is a relative, or the wife or husband of a relative, of the director or of the director's wife or husband: ibid s 24(7).

12   Ibid s 24(3). As to the apportionment of expenditure on a farmhouse see *RS & EM Wright Ltd v Customs and Excise Comrs* (1995) VAT Decision 12984, [1995] STI 651; and Customs and Excise Business Brief 18/96 [1996] STI 1439 at 1441.

13   Value Added Tax Act 1994 s 24(5). This provision is the subject of much difficulty: even the Commissioners of Customs and Excise have admitted that it is probably in contravention of EC Council Directive 77/388 arts 5(6), 17: see Customs and Excise Leaflet 700/55/93 *VAT Input Tax Appeals: Luxuries, Amusements and Entertainment* Annex B, considering the decision in Case C-97/90 *Lennartz v Finanzamt München III* [1991] ECR I-3795, [1995] STC 514, ECJ, that a taxable person who uses goods

for the purposes of an economic activity has the right on their acquisition to deduct input tax however small the proportion of business use, which 'calls into question the provisions' of the Value Added Tax Act 1994 s 24(5). The commissioners therefore concluded that: 'If taxable persons choose to apply the *Lennartz* judgment and to take input tax deduction in full, they must account for output tax in each accounting period on the private or non-business use. This means they must keep records showing how the asset has been used.' Notwithstanding this admission, in *North East Media Development Trust Ltd v Customs and Excise Comrs* (1995) VAT Decision 13104, [1995] STI 743 the commissioners sought to defend a claim by the trader that Case C-97/90 *Lennartz v Finanzamt München III* supra was inconsistent with the predecessor of the Value Added Tax Act 1994 s 24(5) by referring to what is now s 5(1), Sch 4 para 5(4) (see para 24 ante), contending (as was accepted by the tribunal) that this provision effected the implementation by the United Kingdom of EC Council Directive 77/388 art 5(6) and that the United Kingdom had, therefore, simply given taxpayers a choice as to whether to reclaim input tax in full under art 17, on the basis that the onward non-business use would be treated as a supply in the course of business, or to apportion the deductible input tax and thereafter have no obligation to account for output tax on the non-business application of the goods. In *Mounty & Sons and Hurd v Customs and Excise Comrs* (1995) VAT Decision 12985, [1995] STI 651, the tribunal (which heard the two taxpayers' cases together) held that supplies of services (in the form of repairs to farmhouses used partly for private purposes) were outside the principle in Case C-97/90 *Lennartz v Finanzamt München III* supra and that the input tax on those services was only partly deductible, in accordance with the Value Added Tax Act 1994 s 24(5). Where the s 24(5) apportionment does apply this is a separate apportionment from that made because the business is partially exempt: see para 203 post. No apportionment of VAT falls to be made under s 24(5) by reference to fuel supplied for private use: s 56(5).

A taxpayer may treat an acquisition of goods or services as partly for business purposes and partly for non-business purposes and, by excluding part of the goods or services from his business, neither recover VAT as input tax on that part nor be obliged to account for output tax on that part on the eventual sale of the goods: see Case C-291/92 *Finanzamt Uelzen v Armbrecht* [1995] ECR I-2775, [1995] STC 997, ECJ. See also Case 50/88 *Kühne v Finanzamt München III* [1989] ECR 1925, [1990] STC 749, ECJ; Case C-193/91 *Finanzamt München III v Möhsche* [1993] ECR I-2615, [1993] STI 945, ECJ.

14 Ie for the purposes of the Value Added Tax Act 1994 s 24(1), (2): see the text and notes 1–7 supra, 23 infra.

15 Ibid s 24(4). As to the making of orders generally see para 8 ante. At the date at which this volume states the law, no such order had been made, but, by virtue of the Interpretation Act 1978 s 17(2)(b), the Value Added Tax (Person Supplied) Order 1991, SI 1991/2306, has effect as if so made. Where road fuel is supplied to a person who is not a taxable person and a taxable person pays to him (1) the actual cost to him of the fuel; or (2) an amount, the whole or part of which approximates to and is paid in order to reimburse him for the cost of the fuel (whether or not the taxable person makes any payment in order to reimburse him for any other cost), the fuel is to be treated as having been supplied to the taxable person for the purpose of a business carried on by him and for a consideration equal to the amount reimbursed (excluding any reimbursement of any cost other than the cost of the fuel): arts 2, 3. The amount mentioned in head (2) supra is to be determined by reference to (a) the total distances travelled by the vehicle in which the fuel is used, whether or not including distances travelled otherwise than for the purposes of the business of the taxable person; and (b) the cylinder capacity of the vehicle: art 2. This provision was introduced to reverse the decision in *McLean Homes Midland Ltd v Customs and Excise Comrs* (1990) VAT Decision 5010, [1990] STI 802 (employer could not obtain input tax credit for reimbursements he made in respect of fuel supplied to an employee which he used for the purposes of his employer's business). Cf Case 165/86 *Leesportefeuille 'Intiem' CV v Staatssecretaris van Financiën* [1988] ECR 1471, [1989] 2 CMLR 856, ECJ, where the opposite conclusion was reached (in a case where the employer had entered into a prior contract with the relevant garage).

16 Ie under the Value Added Tax Act 1994: see s 96(1). As to the making of regulations generally see para 8 ante.

17 Ibid s 24(6)(a).

18 Ie in such circumstances, to such extent and subject to such conditions as may be prescribed: ibid s 24(6)(b), (c). For the meaning of 'prescribed' see para 11 note 3 ante.

19 Ibid s 24(6)(b).

20 See note 18 supra.

21 Value Added Tax Act 1994 s 24(6)(c).

22 Ibid s 24(6)(d).

23 Ibid s 24(2). Since the VAT on acquisitions of goods from other member states is treated both as the taxable person's input tax and output tax it will be found that the taxable person only has to account for VAT on such acquisitions if he is either partially exempt (see para 209 et seq post) or if the goods in question are wholly or partly excluded from credit (see paras 204–208 post). VAT on importation of

goods from places outside the member states is not treated as the taxable person's output tax as the tax is accounted for on entry of the goods: see para 103 ante.

24 For the meaning of 'prescribed accounting period' see para 105 note 16 ante.

25 Value Added Tax Regulations 1995, SI 1995/2518, reg 28. As to accounting for VAT see para 225 et seq post.

202. The payment of tax. A taxable person[1] must account for and pay value added tax, both in respect of supplies[2] made by him, and the acquisition by him from another member state[3] of any goods, by reference to 'prescribed accounting periods'[4] at such time and in such manner as may be determined by or under regulations made by the Commissioners of Customs and Excise[5]. At the end of each prescribed accounting period, the taxable person is entitled[6] to credit for so much of his input tax[7] as is allowable[8] and then to deduct that amount from any output tax[9] that is due from him[10]. If, however, either no output tax is due at the end of the period, or the amount of the credit exceeds that of the output tax, then the amount of the credit or, as the case may be, the amount of the excess is paid[11] to the taxable person by the commissioners[12]. An amount so due is referred to as a 'VAT credit'[13].

The whole or any part of the credit may[14] be held over to be credited in and for a subsequent period, either on the taxable person's own application or in accordance with general or special directions given by the commissioners from time to time, if regulations[15] so allow[16]. In addition, where at the end of any period a VAT credit is due to a taxable person who has failed to submit returns for any earlier period[17], the commissioners may withhold payment of the credit until he has complied with that statutory requirement[18].

A deduction of input tax from output tax[19] may not be made, nor may a VAT credit be paid, except on a claim made in the prescribed[20] manner and time[21]. In the case of a person who has made no taxable supplies[22] in the period concerned or in any previous period, payment of a VAT credit is made subject to such conditions, if any, as the commissioners think fit to impose[23].

As a condition of allowing or repaying any input tax to any person, the commissioners may require the production of such documents[24] relating to VAT as may have been supplied to him; and they may, if they think it necessary for the protection of the revenue, require the giving of such security for the amount of the payment as appears to them appropriate as a condition of making any VAT credit[25].

Where, at the end of a prescribed accounting period, the amount of VAT due from any person or the amount of any VAT credit would be less than £1, that amount is treated as nil[26].

1 For the meaning of 'taxable person' see paras 12 note 4, 55 ante.

2 For the meaning of 'supply' see para 21 ante.

3 As to the acquisition of goods from another member state see para 13 ante.

4 For the purposes of value added tax, 'prescribed accounting period' has the meaning given by this provision: see the Value Added Tax Act 1994 s 96(1). See also the Value Added Tax Regulations 1995, SI 1995/2518 regs 2(1), 25; and paras 105 note 16 ante, 226 post.

5 Value Added Tax Act 1994 ss 25(1), 96(1). Regulations may make different provision for different circumstances: s 25(1). In exercise of the power so conferred, the commissioners have made the Value Added Tax Regulations 1995 Pt V (regs 24–43): see paras 15, 131 ante, 219 et seq post. As to the making of regulations generally see para 8 ante.

6 Ie subject to the provisions of the Value Added Tax Act 1994 s 25: see the text and notes 1–5 supra, 7–23 infra; and para 204 post.

7 For the meaning of 'input tax' see paras 4, 201 ante.

8 Ie under the Value Added Tax Act 1994 s 26: see para 203 post.

9 For the meaning of 'output tax' see paras 4, 201 ante.

10 Ibid s 25(2).

11 Ie subject to ibid s 25(4), (5): see the text to notes 15–21 infra.

12 Ibid s 25(3).
13 Ibid s 25(3). As to security for the payment of a VAT credit see the text and notes 24–25 infra. The commissioners are not automatically obliged to repay a sum claimed as a VAT credit if they have suspicions that a repayment may not be due; they must have a reasonable opportunity to investigate the claim: *R v Customs and Excise Comrs, ex p Strangewood Ltd* [1987] STC 502.
14 Ie subject to and in accordance with regulations made by the commissioners: ibid s 25(4).
15 Ie regulations made under ibid s 25(4): see note 14 supra. At the date at which this volume states the law, no such regulations had been made.
16 Ibid s 25(4).
17 Ie as required by the Value Added Tax Act 1994: s 25(5). As to VAT returns see para 226 et seq post.
18 Ibid s 25(5). The trader is then obliged to pay to the commissioners the net amount of VAT due from him, ie his output tax less his input tax for the period.
19 Ie a deduction under ibid s 25(2): see the text to notes 6–10 supra.
20 Ie in such manner and at such time as may be determined by or under regulations made by the commissioners: ibid s 25(6). Save as the commissioners may otherwise allow or direct either generally or specially, a person claiming deduction of input tax under s 25(2) must do so on a return made by him for the prescribed accounting period in which the VAT becomes chargeable: Value Added Tax Regulations 1995 reg 29(1). This is subject to reg 29(2) (see para 236 post): reg 29(1).
21 Value Added Tax Act 1994 s 25(6). No specific manner or time for making a claim for payment of a VAT credit (as opposed to claiming a deduction: see note 20 supra) has been prescribed (eg where the trader makes only zero-rated supplies). See, however, *Trustees of the Victoria and Albert Museum v Customs and Excise Comrs* (1995) VAT Decision 13552, [1995] STI 1686 ('a person claiming a deduction' includes 'a person claiming a deduction whether or not there is output tax from which a deduction can be made' (ie a person claiming a payment and not a deduction)) (this point not considered on appeal [1996] STC 1016).
22 For the meaning of 'taxable supplies' see para 12 note 3 ante.
23 Value Added Tax Act 1994 s 25(6). This provision enables the commissioners to recover payments of VAT credit made to 'intending traders', who claim to have incurred input tax for the purposes of business in which they will make taxable supplies; but subsequently fail to make any such supplies. Such persons are entitled to register for VAT and to recover input tax provided that they can satisfy the fiscal authorities by objective circumstances of their stated intention: Case 268/83 *DA Rompelman and EA Rompelman-van Deelen v Minister van Financiën* [1985] ECR 655, [1985] 3 CMLR 202, ECJ. See also Case C-110/94 *Intercommunale voor Zeewaterontzilting (INZO) (in liquidation) v Belgium* [1996] ECR I-857, [1996] STC 569, ECJ (where a tax authority accepts that a company, which has declared its intention to begin an economic activity giving rise to taxable transactions, has the status of a taxable person for the purposes of VAT, the carrying out of a study to investigate the financial viability of the activity itself is part of the economic activity in respect of which input tax may be recovered; and, except in cases of fraud or abuse, the status of a taxable person may not retrospectively be withdrawn if, as a result of the study, taxable transactions do not take place). It would seem that the Value Added Tax Act 1994 s 25(6) may only be exercised in such circumstances: see *Hordern v Customs and Excise Comrs* [1992] VATTR 382, where the tribunal held, having regard to Case 268/83 *DA Rompelman and EA Rompelman-van Deelen v Minister van Financiën* supra, that a condition imposed under what is now the Value Added Tax Act 1994 s 25(6) was contrary to the Sixth Directive, discriminatory and unenforceable.
24 For the meaning of 'document' see para 11 note 8 ante.
25 Value Added Tax Act 1994 s 58, Sch 11 para 4(1). For other provisions relating to security see s 48(7) (relating to the failure of an overseas trader to appoint a VAT representative: see para 62 ante); and see generally para 246 post.
26 Ibid Sch 11 para 2(13).

(ii) Deduction of Input Tax

203. Extent of right to deduct input tax. Subject to certain exceptions[1], the amount of input tax[2] for which a taxable person[3] is entitled to credit at the end of any period is so much of the input tax for the period[4] as is allowable by or under regulations as being attributable to certain supplies[5] made, or to be made, by him in the course or furtherance of his business[6]. Those supplies are: (1) taxable supplies[7]; (2) supplies made outside the United Kingdom[8] which would be taxable supplies if made in the United Kingdom[9]; and (3) such other supplies made outside the United Kingdom and such exempt supplies[10] as the Treasury may specify by order[11] for these purposes[12].

The Commissioners of Customs and Excise must make regulations for securing a fair and reasonable attribution of input tax to the supplies described above[13]. Such regulations may provide for:

(a) determining a proportion by reference to which input tax for any prescribed accounting period[14] is to be provisionally attributed to those supplies[15];

(b) adjusting, in accordance with a proportion determined in like manner for any longer period comprising two or more prescribed accounting periods (or parts of such periods), the provisional attribution for any of those periods[16];

(c) the making of payments in respect of input tax, by the commissioners to a taxable person (or a person who has been a taxable person) or by a taxable person (or a person who has been a taxable person) to the commissioners, in cases where events prove inaccurate an estimate on the basis of which an attribution was made[17]; and

(d) preventing input tax on a supply which a person makes to himself[18] from being allowable as attributable to that supply[19].

Such regulations may make different provision for different circumstances and, in particular may make different provision for different descriptions of goods or services, and may contain such incidental and supplementary provisions as appear to the commissioners necessary or expedient[20].

The amount of any input tax which may be deducted by any person is a matter on which an appeal lies to a VAT and duties tribunal[21].

1   See paras 204–208 post.
2   For the meaning of 'input tax' see paras 4, 201 ante.
3   For the meaning of 'taxable person' see paras 12 note 4, 55 ante.
4   Ie input tax on supplies, acquisitions and importations in the period: Value Added Tax Act 1994 s 26(1). For the meaning of 'supply' see para 21 ante.
5   Ie supplies within ibid s 26(2): see heads (1)–(3) in the text.
6   Ibid s 26(1), (2). For the meaning of 'in the course or furtherance of a business' see paras 12 note 5, 17 note 2 ante. The relevant regulations are the Value Added Tax Regulations 1995, SI 1995/2518, regs 99–110: see para 209 et seq post. Nothing in those regulations is to be construed as allowing a taxable person to deduct the whole or any part of VAT on the importation or acquisition by him of goods or the supply to him of goods or services where those goods or services are not used, or to be used, by him in making supplies in the course or furtherance of a business carried on by him: reg 100. Where a trader is not entitled to deduct the entirety of his input tax he is generally described as 'partially exempt' and the method of computing his deductible input tax is described as his 'partial exemption method.' The legislation and regulations reflect EC Council Directive 77/388 (OJ L145, 13.6.77, p 1) art 17(2), (5). Article 17(5) permits member states to select amongst various different methods of determining the deductible proportion of a trader's input tax. The United Kingdom has adopted different partial exemption methods at different periods. Between April 1987 and April 1992, the standard partial exemption method was based on art 17(5)(c) which enables a member state to authorise or compel a taxable person to make the deduction on the basis of the use of all or part of the goods and services in respect of which input tax credit is claimed. Since 1 April 1992, the United Kingdom has adopted the apportionment determined under art 19, which permits deduction of a proportion of the input tax, made up of a fraction of which the numerator is the total amount of turnover per year, exclusive of VAT, attributable to transactions in respect of which VAT is deductible under art 17(2), (3), and the denominator is the total amount of turnover per year attributable to transactions included in the numerator and to transactions in respect of which VAT is not deductible. Article 19(1) further permits member states to include in the denominator the amount of subsidies other than those specified in art 11(A)(1)(a) (ie subsidies directly linked to the price of the trader's supplies). The United Kingdom has not availed itself of this latter permission.

In order to qualify for deduction as input tax, there must be a clear nexus between the matter in relation to which the expenditure is incurred and the business itself; it is not sufficient that the business benefits generally from the expenditure: *Customs and Excise Comrs v Rosner* [1994] STC 228 (legal expenses defending trader from criminal charges and thereby enabling his business to continue not deductible); *Midland Bank plc v Customs and Excise Comrs* (1996) VAT Decision 14144, [1996] STI 1302 (VAT on legal fees incurred in unsuccessfully defending action for negligent misrepresentation made in the course of providing services to plaintiff, deductible); *Child (t/a Child & Co and Videoland) v Customs and Excise Comrs* (1992) VAT Decision 6827, [1992] STI 237; *Spillane v Customs and Excise Comrs* [1990] STC 212 (no deduction for VAT on legal fees incurred in committal proceedings relating to the trader's fraudulent business after the business had ceased). In a number of cases, the issue of deductibility of expenditure on benefits (in particular, hotel accommodation) enjoyed by a party other than the payer has been considered. Technically, there would appear to be a distinction between the question whether the supply has been made to the person claiming the credit and the issue of whether the expenditure was incurred for the purposes of that person's business; but the distinction has not always clearly been made by the courts. In either case, the issues are questions of fact for the tribunal which may only be disturbed in accordance with the principle of *Edwards (Inspector of Taxes) v Bairstow* [1956] AC 14, 36 TC 207, HL (if the facts found are such that no person acting judicially and properly instructed as to the law could have come to the determination under appeal). Generally it has been found that there is a supply to the company which pays for the room, for the purposes of its business; but there is a corresponding onwards supply on which output tax must be accounted: *Celtic Football and Athletic Co Ltd v Customs and Excise Comrs* [1983] STC 470 (where there was no argument that there was an onward supply); *Football Association v Customs and Excise Comrs* [1985] VATTR 106; *Ibstock Building Products v Customs and Excise Comrs* [1987] VATTR 1; *Stormseal (UPVC) Window Co Ltd v Customs and Excise Comrs* [1989] VATTR 303. See also *Customs and Excise Comrs v British Railways Board* [1975] 3 All ER 451, [1975] STC 498; *Manchester Ship Canal Co v Customs and Excise Comrs* [1982] STC 351 (input tax incurred in connection with the administration of a pension fund by an employer may be recovered as incurred for the purposes of its business); and *Customs and Excise Comrs v Redrow Group plc* [1996] STC 365 (developer able to deduct VAT on estate agents' fees incurred when selling the houses of potential purchasers (because supply made to the developer, it being admitted that expenditure was for the purposes of its business)). Cf *Customs and Excise Comrs v Sooner Foods Ltd* [1983] STC 376 (where the firm met the cost of gift goods being provided to its customers by a third party, in accordance with a promotion scheme it was running, it was not entitled to recover the input tax on the supply of the goods, since they were not supplied to it but to its customers (quaere whether the company was entitled to recover input tax on the cost as a supply of services, if not of goods)); and *British Airways plc v Customs and Excise Comrs* [1996] STC 1127 (refreshments provided by airport catering outlets to the appellant's passengers, when flights were delayed, and where the appellant met the whole or part of the expense, were not provided to the appellant and could not, therefore, form the subject of an input tax claim by it).

7   Value Added Tax Act 1994 s 26(2)(a). For the meaning of 'taxable supplies' see para 12 note 3 ante.

8   For the meaning of 'United Kingdom' see para 4 note 3 ante.

9   Value Added Tax Act 1994 s 26(2)(b). For the rules relating to the place of supply of goods and services see para 39 et seq ante.

10 For the meaning of 'exempt supplies' see para 141 ante.

11 As to the making of orders generally see para 8 ante.

12 Value Added Tax Act 1994 s 26(2)(c). At the date at which this volume states the law, no such order had been made, but, by virtue of the Interpretation Act 1978 s 17(2)(b), the Value Added Tax (Input Tax) (Specified Supplies) Order 1992, SI 1992/3123, has effect as if so made. The following supplies are specified for these purposes: (1) services which are supplied to a person who belongs outside the member states; (2) services which are directly linked to the export of goods to a place outside the member states; and (3) services which consist of the making of arrangements for a supply of services of a description specified in head (1) or head (2) supra, in each case provided that the supply is exempt, or would have been exempt if made in the United Kingdom, by virtue of any item of the Value Added Tax Act 1994 s 31(1), Sch 9 Pt II Group 2 (insurance) (see para 146 ante), or by virtue any one of Sch 9 Pt II Group 5 items 1–8 (finance) (see para 149 ante): see the Value Added Tax (Input Tax) (Specified Supplies) Order 1992 arts 2, 3. This corresponds with EC Council Directive 77/388 art 17(3). By extra-statutory concession, the commissioners allow businesses which make only such exempt supplies (and which are not, therefore, entitled to register under the usual rules: see para 56 et seq ante) to register. Furthermore, where such a business was making such supplies on 1 January 1993 (when such supplies ceased to be zero-rated and became exempt on a change in the place of supply rules) the commissioners permit retrospective registration to that date: see Customs and Excise Notice 748 *Extra-statutory Concessions* (1 August 1995) concession 25.

13 Value Added Tax Act 1994 s 26(3). See the Value Added Tax Regulations 1995 regs 99–110; and para 209 et seq post. These provisions have been said to be exhaustive, so that there is no basis for an argument that, where the apportionment provisions appear to give an unfair result, the trader may rely on the general provisions of the Value Added Tax Act 1994 s 26 to obtain greater recovery of input tax: *Customs and Excise Comrs v University of Wales College, Cardiff* [1995] STC 611. Cf *Dwyer Property Ltd v Customs and Excise Comrs* [1995] STC 1035; and *Customs and Excise Comrs v Dennis Rye Ltd* [1996] STC 27.

14 For the meaning of 'prescribed accounting period' see para 202 note 4 ante.

15 Value Added Tax Act 1994 s 26(3)(a). See the Value Added Tax Regulations 1995 regs 101–102; and paras 210–211 post. For the commissioner's views on the recovery of VAT charged by an investigating accountant in carrying out a viability study prior to a loan by a bank to a trader see Customs and Excise Business Brief 6/95 [1995] STI 568.

16 Value Added Tax Act 1994 s 26(3)(b). See the Value Added Tax Regulations 1995 reg 107; and para 214 post.

17 Value Added Tax Act 1994 s 26(3)(c). See the Value Added Tax Regulations 1995 regs 108–109; and para 214 post.

18 Ie under or by virtue of any provision of the Value Added Tax Act 1994: s 26(3)(d). As to self-supply see para 26 ante.

19 Ibid s 26(3)(d). See the Value Added Tax Regulations 1995 reg 104; and para 210 post.

20 Value Added Tax Act 1995 s 26(4). This provision is without prejudice to the generality of s 26(3): s 26(4).

21 See ibid s 83(e); and para 296 post.

204. Exceptions to the right to deduct input tax; in general.

The Treasury may by order provide, in relation to such supplies[1], acquisitions and importations as the order may specify, that value added tax charged on them is to be excluded from any credit[2] as input tax[3]. Any such provision may be framed by reference to the description of goods or services supplied or goods acquired or imported, the persons by whom they are supplied, acquired or imported or to whom they are supplied, the purpose for which they are supplied, acquired or imported, or any circumstances whatsoever[4]; and any such order may contain provision for consequential relief from output tax[5].

1 For the meaning of 'supply' see para 21 ante.

2 Ie any credit under the Value Added Tax Act 1994 s 25: see para 203 ante.

3 Ibid s 25(7). For the meaning of 'input tax' see paras 4, 201 ante. As to the making of orders generally see para 8 ante.

4 Ibid s 25(7)(a).

5 Ibid s 25(7)(b). In exercise of the power so conferred, the Treasury has made (1) the Value Added Tax (Input Tax) (Amendment) Order 1995, SI 1995/281; (2) the Value Added Tax (Input Tax) (Amendment) (No 2) Order 1995, SI 1995/1267; and (3) the Value Added Tax (Input Tax) (Amendment) (No 3) Order 1995, SI 1995/1666; these orders all amend the Value Added Tax (Input Tax) Order 1992, SI 1992/3222, which, by virtue of the Interpretation Act 1978 s 17(2)(b), has effect as if so made. See para 205 et seq post. See also the Value Added Tax (Tour Operators) Order 1987, SI 1987/1806, art 12; and para 200 ante.

205. Disallowance of input tax on works of art etc and second-hand goods.

Value added tax charged on the supply[1], acquisition from another member state[2] or importation of works of art[3], antiques[4] and collectors' items[5] and second-hand goods[6] which are supplied to, or acquired from another member state or imported by, a taxable person[7] in certain specified circumstances[8] is excluded from any credit[9] as input tax[10]. In gener l, this exclusion applies to a supply on which VAT was chargeable[11] on the profit margin[12] or to a supply which was treated for VAT purposes as if it were for a consideration calculated in accordance with certain provisions[13] relating to motor cars[14]. Where, however (1) the goods are a work of art, an antique or a collectors' item and the taxable person imported the goods himself[15]; or (2) the goods are a work of art which was supplied to the taxable person by, or acquired by him from another member state from, the creator or his successor in title[16], the tax on the supply or acquisition is excluded from credit as input tax[17] only if the taxable person has opted to account for VAT on his supplies of such goods on the profit margin and has not elected to account[18] for VAT on his supply of the goods by reference to its value[19].

1 For the meaning of 'supply' see para 21 ante.

2 As to the acquisition of goods from another member state see para 13 ante; and for the meaning of 'another member state' see para 4 note 14 ante.

3   For these purposes, 'works of art' means the following goods: (1) pictures, collages and similar decorative plaques, paintings and drawings, executed entirely by hand by the artist (other than plans and drawings for architectural, engineering, industrial, commercial, topographical or similar purposes), hand-decorated manufactured articles, theatrical scenery, studio back-cloths or the like of painted canvas; (2) original engravings, prints and lithographs, being impressions produced in limited numbers directly in black and white or in colour of one or of several plates executed entirely by hand by the artist irrespective of the process or of the material employed by him (but not including any mechanical or photomechanical process); (3) original sculptures and statuary, in any material, provided that they are executed entirely by the artist; (4) sculpture casts the production of which is limited to eight copies (or if the casts were produced before 1 January 1989, limited to such greater number of copies as the Commissioners of Customs and Excise may in any particular case allow) and supervised by the artist or his successors in title; (5) tapestries and wall textiles made by hand from original designs provided by artists (provided that there are not more than eight copies of each); (6) individual pieces of ceramics executed entirely by the artist and signed by him, enamels on copper, executed entirely by hand, limited to eight numbered copies bearing the signature of the artist or the studio (excluding articles of jewellery and goldsmiths' and silversmiths' wares); (7) photographs taken by the artist, printed by him or under his supervision, signed and numbered and limited to 30 copies (all sizes and mounts included): Value Added Tax (Input Tax) Order 1992, SI 1992/3222, art 3 (definition substituted by SI 1995/1267).

4   'Antiques' means objects other than works of art or collectors' items which are more than 100 years old: ibid art 3 (definition substituted by SI 1995/1267).

5   'Collectors' items' means the following goods: (1) postage or revenue stamps, postmarks, first-day covers, pre-stamped stationery and the like, which are either franked, or, if they are unfranked, are not of legal tender and not for use as legal tender; and (2) collections and collectors' pieces of zoological, botanical, mineralogical, anatomical, historical, archaeological, palaeontological, ethnographic or numismatic interest: ibid art 3 (definition substituted by SI 1995/1267).

6   'Second-hand goods' means tangible movable property, including motor cars, that is suitable for further use as it is or after repair, other than works of art, collectors' items or antiques and other than precious metals and precious stones: ibid art 3 (definition added by SI 1995/1267). For the meaning of 'motor car' see para 208 note 5 post.

7   For the meaning of 'taxable person' see paras 12 note 4, 55 ante.

8   Ie the circumstances described in the Value Added Tax (Input Tax) Order 1992 art 4(3) (as substituted and amended): see the text and notes 11–14 infra.

9   Ie any credit under the Value Added Tax Act 1994 s 25: see para 203 ante.

10   Value Added Tax (Input Tax) Order 1992 art 4(1), (2) (art 4 substituted by SI 1995/1267).

11   Ie by virtue of an order under the Value Added Tax Act 1994 s 50A (as added) (margin schemes: see para 188 ante) or a corresponding provision of the Value Added Tax and Other Taxes Act 1973 (an Act of Tynwald) or by virtue of a corresponding provision of the law of another member state: Value Added Tax (Input Tax) Order 1992 art 4(3)(a) (as substituted: see note 10 supra). As to the meaning of references to the law of another member state see para 11 note 1 ante.

12   Ibid art 4(3)(a) (as substituted: see note 10 supra).

13   Ie in accordance with ibid art 7(4) (as amended): see para 208 post.

14   Ibid art 4(3)(aa) (added by SI 1995/1666).

15   Ibid art 4(3)(b) (as substituted: see note 10 supra).

16   Ibid art 4(3)(c) (as substituted: see note 10 supra).

17   Ie ibid art 4(1) (as substituted) applies: see the text to notes 1–10 supra.

18   Ie in accordance with the provisions of an order made under the Value Added Tax Act 1994 s 50A (as added): see para 92 ante.

19   Value Added Tax (Input Tax) Order 1992 art 4(4) (as substituted: see note 10 supra).

206. Disallowance of input tax on business entertainment. Value added tax charged on any goods or services supplied to a taxable person[1], or on any goods acquired by a taxable person or on any goods imported by him, is excluded from any credit as input tax[2] where the goods or services are used, or to be used, by the taxable person for the purposes of business entertainment[3]. 'Business entertainment' means entertainment, including hospitality of any kind, provided by a taxable person in connection with a business[4] carried on by him, but does not include the provision of any such entertainment for either or both (1) employees of the taxable person[5]; or (2) if the taxable person is a body corporate, its directors or persons otherwise engaged in its management, unless the provision of entertainment for such persons is incidental to its provision for others[6]. Where a taxable person has claimed no input tax on a supply[7], acquisition or importation of any goods, or on a supply of any services, by reason of these provisions, VAT is charged on a supply by him of the goods in question, other than a letting on hire, or on a supply by him of the services in question, as if that supply were for a consideration equal to the excess of (a) the consideration for which the goods or services are supplied by him over (b) the relevant amount[8], and accordingly is not charged unless there is such an excess[9].

1   For the meaning of 'taxable person' see paras 12 note 4, 55 ante.
2   Ie excluded from any credit under the Value Added Tax Act 1994 s 25: see para 203 ante. For the meaning of 'input tax' see paras 4, 201 ante.
3   Value Added Tax (Input Tax) Order 1992, SI 1992/3222, art 5(1) (amended by SI 1995/281).
4   For the meaning of 'business' see para 17 ante.
5   Entertaining of guests at staff parties does, however, constitute 'business entertainment': see Customs and Excise Business Brief 21/95 [1995] STI 1599.
6   Value Added Tax (Input Tax) Order 1992 art 5(3). Hospitality in the form of free meals and accommodation provided to sales representatives at a training seminar is business entertainment within the scope of the 1992 Order: *Customs and Excise Comrs v Shaklee International* [1981] STC 776, CA. Where, however, such hospitality was provided in satisfaction of a reciprocal obligation incurred in participating in an international football tournament it was not 'business entertainment', because it was not free of charge to the recipient: *Celtic Football & Athletic Co Ltd v Customs and Excise Comrs* [1983] STC 470, Ct of Sess. A dinner dance provided as a reward to one's employees is not business entertainment: *KPMG Peat Marwick McLintock v Customs and Excise Comrs* (1993) VAT Decision 10135, [1993] STI 912. Cf *BMW (GB) Ltd v Customs and Excise Comrs* (1996) VAT Decision 14034, [1996] STI 997; and *Sundeck plc (formerly Appledore Finance plc) v Customs and Excise Comrs* (1996) VAT Decision 10451, [1996] STI 1023.
7   For the meaning of 'supply' see para 21 ante.
8   'The relevant amount' for these purposes is: (1) if the goods or services in question had been supplied to the taxable person, the consideration for the supply to him; (2) if the goods in question had been acquired by him from another member state, the value of their acquisition plus the tax chargeable thereon; (3) if the goods in question had been imported by him, the value of the goods for the purposes of charging tax on importation plus any tax chargeable on their importation: Value Added Tax (Input Tax) Order 1992 art 5(4).
9   Ibid art 5(2). Where expenditure is incurred on a supply of goods or services to be used both for business entertainment and to a measurable extent for other business purposes, a trader is entitled to a partial credit in respect of the input tax based on an apportionment between entertainment and non-entertainment business use: *Thorn EMI plc v Customs and Excise Comrs* [1995] STC 674, CA, over-ruling *Customs and Excise Comrs v Plant Repair and Services (South Wales) Ltd* [1994] STC 232. See also the Value Added Tax Act 1994 s 84(4) (limitation on right to appeal against decision of the commissioners disallowing credit for tax as input tax on the ground that the relevant supply was of something in the nature of a luxury, amusement or entertainment); and para 297 post.

207. Disallowance of input tax on certain building works. Where a taxable person[1] constructing, or effecting any works to, a building, in either case for the purpose of making a grant of a major interest[2] in it, or in any part of it or its site, incorporates goods other than building materials[3] in any part of the building or its site, input tax[4] on the supply[5], acquisition or importation of the goods is excluded from credit[6].

1   For the meaning of 'taxable person' see paras 12 note 4, 55 ante.
2   Ie a major interest which is of a description in the Value Added Tax Act 1994 s 30(2), Sch 8 (as amended): see para 158 et seq ante. For the meaning of 'major interest' see para 24 note 7 ante.
3   'Building materials' means any goods the supply of which would be zero-rated if supplied by a taxable person to a person to whom he is also making a supply of a description within the Value Added Tax Act 1994 s 30(2), Sch 8 Pt II Group 5 item 2 or item 3 (as substituted) (see para 163 ante) or Sch 8 Pt II Group 6 item 2 (as substituted) (see para 165 ante): Value Added Tax (Input Tax) Order 1992, SI 1992/3222, art 2 (definition added by SI 1995/281). As to the zero-rating of the supply of services in the course of the construction of certain buildings see para 163 ante; as to the zero-rating of supplies made in relation to protected buildings see para 165 ante; and for the meaning of 'zero-rated' see para 158 ante.
4   For the meaning of 'input tax' see paras 4, 201 ante.
5   For the meaning of 'supply' see para 21 ante.

6   Value Added Tax (Input Tax) Order 1992 art 6 (substituted: by SI 1995/281). The credit referred to is
     credit under the Value Added Tax Act 1994 s 25: see para 203 ante.

208. Input tax on motor cars. As a general rule[1], the value added tax charged on the supply[2] to, or the acquisition from another member state[3] or importation by, a taxable person[4] of a motor car[5] is excluded from any credit[6] as input tax[7]. Where the supply is a letting of a motor car on hire, one-half of the tax is excluded from credit[8]. That apart, the general rule does not apply[9] and VAT is not excluded from credit where:

(1)   a 'qualifying motor car'[10] is let on hire or supplied to, or acquired from another member state or imported by, a taxable person and the relevant condition[11] is satisfied[12];

(2)   the supply is a letting on hire of a motor car which is not a qualifying motor car[13];

(3)   the motor car is unused and is supplied to a taxable person whose only taxable supplies[14] are concerned with the letting of motor cars on hire to another taxable person whose business consists predominantly of the letting on hire of motor vehicles to handicapped persons[15] in receipt of a disability living allowance[16];

(4)   the motor car is unused and is supplied on a letting on hire to a taxable person whose business consists predominantly of the letting on hire of motor vehicles to handicapped persons in receipt of a disability living allowance by a taxable person whose only taxable supplies are concerned with the letting on hire of motor cars to such a taxable person[17].

On the supply by a taxable person of a motor car[18] in respect of which VAT has been wholly excluded from credit[19], VAT is chargeable as if the supply were for a consideration equal to the excess of the consideration for which the motor car is supplied by him over the relevant amount[20] and accordingly is not charged unless there is such an excess[21].

1   Ie subject to the Value Added Tax (Input Tax) Order 1992, SI 1992/3222, art 7(2)–(2H) (as substituted
     and added): see the text and notes 9–17 infra.
2   'Supply' for these purposes includes a letting on hire: ibid art 7(1)(a) (amended by SI 1995/1666). For the
     meaning of 'supply' generally see para 21 ante.
3   For the meaning of 'another member state' see para 4 note 14 ante; and as to acquisition from another
     member state see para 13 ante.
4   For the meaning of 'taxable person' see paras 12 note 4, 55 ante.
5   'Motor car' means any motor vehicle of a kind normally used on public roads which has three or more
     wheels and either (1) is constructed or adapted solely or mainly for the carriage of passengers; or (2) has
     to the rear of the driver's seat roofed accommodation which is fitted with side windows or which is
     constructed or adapted for the fitting of side windows; but does not include (a) vehicles capable of
     accommodating only one person or suitable for carrying 12 or more persons; (b) vehicles of not less than
     three tonnes unladen weight; (c) caravans, ambulances and prison vans; (d) vehicles of a type approved
     by the Assistant Commissioner of Police of the Metropolis as conforming to the condition of fitness for
     the time being laid down by him for the purposes of the London Cab Order 1934; or (e) vehicles
     constructed for a special purpose other than the carriage of persons and having no other accommodation
     for carrying persons than such as is incidental to that purpose: Value Added Tax (Input Tax) Order 1992
     art 2 (using the same definition as in the Value Added Tax (Cars) Order 1992, SI 1992/3122, art 2: see
     para 23 note 2 ante). See *Customs and Excise Comrs v Jeynes (t/a Midland International (Hire) Caterers* [1984]
     STC 30 (a Range Rover registered as a heavy goods vehicle was nevertheless a motor car, since one need
     have regard only to the physical characteristics of the vehicle). The issue is not whether the particular
     vehicle is normally used on the road etc, but whether it belongs to a category of vehicles which is
     generally so used, so that continental models of Ford Escorts were within what is now the Value Added
     Tax (Cars) Order 1992 (as amended): *Withers of Winsford Ltd v Customs and Excise Comrs* [1988] STC 431,
     following *Customs and Excise Comrs v Mechanical Services (Trailer Engineers) Ltd* [1979] 1 All ER 501, [1979]
     STC 79, CA.
6   Ie under the Value Added Tax Act 1994 s 25: see para 203 ante.
7   Value Added Tax (Input Tax) Order 1992 art 7(1) (amended by SI 1995/1666). In *Royscot Leasing Ltd
     and Royscot Industrial Leasing Ltd v Customs and Excise Comrs, Allied Domecq plc v Customs and Excise Comrs,
     TC Harrison Group Ltd v Customs and Excise Comrs* [1996] STC 898, the appellants unsuccessfully sought
     to argue that the United Kingdom's restrictions on the recovery of input tax on the acquisition of cars

for business purposes (as they had existed prior to the 1995 amendments) was incompatible with both the Second and the Sixth Directives. Input tax on the delivery charge made by vendors on the sale of motor cars is not restricted by the Value Added Tax (Input Tax) Order 1992 art 7 (as amended), being consideration for a separate supply: *British Telecommunications plc v Customs and Excise Comrs* (1996) VAT Decision 14072, [1996] STI 1214. As to the operation of the transitional provisions in the Value Added Tax (Input Tax) Order 1992 art 7 (as amended) see *BRS Automotive Ltd v Customs and Excise Comrs* (1996) VAT Decision 14112, [1996] STI 1260.

8   Value Added Tax (Input Tax) Order 1992 art 7(2H) (art 7(2A)–(2H) added by SI 1995/1666).

9   Ie ibid art 7(1) (as amended) does not apply: art 7(2) (substituted by SI 1995/1666).

10   A motor car is a qualifying motor car for these purposes if (1) it has never been supplied, acquired from another member state, or imported in circumstances in which the VAT on that supply, acquisition or importation was wholly excluded from credit as input tax by virtue of ibid art 7(1) (as amended: see note 7 supra); or (2) a taxable person has elected for it to be treated as such: art 7(2A) (as added: see note 8 supra). A taxable person may only elect for a motor car to be treated as a qualifying motor car if (a) it is first registered on or after 1 August 1995; (b) it was supplied to, or acquired from another member state or imported by, him prior to that date in circumstances in which the VAT on that supply, acquisition or importation was wholly excluded from credit as input tax by virtue of art 7(1) (as originally made); and (c) it had not been supplied on a letting on hire by him prior to 1 August 1995: art 7(2B) (as so added). A motor car that is supplied, acquired from another member state or imported on or after 1 August 1995 and which would otherwise be a qualifying motor car by virtue of head (1) supra is not such a car if it was supplied on a letting on hire prior to that date by the person to whom it is supplied or by whom it is acquired or imported (as the case may be): art 7(2C) (as so added). References to registration of a motor car mean registration in accordance with the Vehicle Excise and Registration Act 1994 s 21 (see CUSTOMS AND EXCISE; ROAD TRAFFIC): Value Added Tax (Input Tax) Order 1992 art 7(2D) (as added: see note 8 supra). The VAT on the supply of a car which is not a qualifying motor car may nevertheless be entitled to credit as input tax if it is a supply by letting on hire: see head (2) in the text.

    Where a registered person provides a VAT invoice relating, in whole or in part, to the supply of the letting on hire of a motor car other than for self-drive hire, he is obliged to state on the invoice whether or not the motor car is a qualifying motor car under art 7(2A) (as so added): see the Value Added Tax Regulations 1995, SI 1995/2518, reg 14(6) (as added); and para 241 head (b) post.

11   The relevant condition is that the letting on hire, supply, acquisition or importation (as the case may be) is to a taxable person who intends to use the motor car either exclusively for the purposes of a business carried on by him (subject to the Value Added Tax (Input Tax) Order 1992 art 7(2G) (as added: see note 8 supra) or primarily for a relevant purpose: art 7(2E) (as so added). A relevant purpose, in relation to a motor car which is let on hire or supplied to, or acquired or imported by, a taxable person (as the case may be), is any of the following purposes: (1) to provide it on hire with the services of a driver for the purpose of carrying passengers; (2) to provide it for self-drive hire; or (3) to use it as a vehicle in which instruction in the driving of a motor car is to be given by him: art 7(2F) (as so added). 'Self-drive hire' means hire where the hirer is the person normally expected to drive the motor car and the period of hire to each hirer, together with the period of hire of any other motor car expected to be hired to him by the taxable person, will normally be less than 30 consecutive days and will normally be less than 90 days in any period of 12 months: art 7(3)(b).

    A taxable person is not be taken to intend to use a motor car exclusively for the purposes of a business carried on by him if he intends (a) to let it on hire to any person either for no consideration or for a consideration which is less than that which would be payable in money if it were a commercial transaction conducted at arm's length; or (b) to make it available (otherwise than by letting it on hire) to any person (including, where the taxable person is an individual, himself, or where the taxable person is a partnership, a partner) for private use, whether or not for a consideration: art 7(2G) (as added: see note 8 supra). For the meaning of 'business' see para 17 ante. It is clear that the Commissioners of Customs and Excise accept that the intention of the taxable person must be tested at the time when the input tax is incurred, since they have stated that the business must genuinely have no intention to make the car available for private use at that time; and that they will closely examine any purported change of intention following input tax recovery: Customs and Excise Business Brief 15/95 [1995] STI 1263.

12   Value Added Tax (Input Tax) Order 1992 art 7(2)(a) (as substituted: see note 9 supra).

13   Ibid art 7(2)(b) (as substituted: see note 9 supra).

14   For the meaning of 'taxable supply' see para 12 note 3 ante.

15   Ie his business consists predominantly of making supplies of a description falling within the Value Added Tax Act 1994 s 30(2), Sch 8 Pt II Group 12 item 14: see para 170 ante.

16   Value Added Tax (Input Tax) Order 1992 art 7(2)(c) (as substituted: see note 9 supra). There is no statutory definition of an unused motor car, but the commissioners have expressed their views on its meaning by a Press Release dated 25 June 1982: see [1982] STI 278.

17   Value Added Tax (Input Tax) Order 1992 art 7(2)(d) (as substituted: see note 9 supra).

18　Ie other than one which is a qualifying motor car by virtue of ibid art 7(2A)(b) (as added: see note 8 supra): see note 10 head (2) supra.

19　Ie by virtue of ibid art 7(1) (as amended: see note 7 supra) or of any other provision made or having effect as if made under the Value Added Tax Act 1994 s 25(7) (see para 204 ante): Value Added Tax (Input Tax) Order 1992 art 7(4) (amended by SI 1995/281; SI 1995/1666).

20　For these purposes, the relevant amount is: (1) if the motor car had been obtained by the taxable person by way of a supply to him by another taxable person, the consideration for that supply; (2) if the motor car had been treated as supplied by the taxable person to himself by virtue of an order made under the Value Added Tax Act 1994 s 5(5) (see para 26 ante), the value of that supply plus the tax chargeable thereon; (3) if the motor car had been acquired by the taxable person from another member state, the value of that acquisition plus the tax chargeable thereon; (4) if the motor car had been imported by the taxable person, the value of the motor car for the purposes of charging tax on importation together with any tax chargeable on its importation: Value Added Tax (Input Tax) Order 1992 art 7(5) (amended by SI 1995/281).

21　Ibid art 7(4) (as amended: see note 19 supra).

209. Input tax and partial exemption; in general. The determination of a taxable person's entitlement to credit for input tax[1] is, in theory, carried out in two stages. At the first stage, which arises at the end of the prescribed accounting period in which the input tax is incurred, the taxable person is entitled provisionally to deduct the amount of input tax which, in accordance with regulations, is attributable to taxable supplies[2]. However, a taxable person[3] who incurs exempt input tax[4] has applied to him a longer period which in most cases will correspond with the tax year[5]. In such a case, the taxable person must generally recalculate the amount of his input tax which is attributable to his taxable supplies during the longer period[6]. Where, on carrying out that recalculation, it is ascertained that there was an over-deduction or under-deduction of input tax, the trader makes the appropriate adjustment in his next following return[7].

1　For the meaning of 'input tax' see paras 4, 201 ante.

2　See the Value Added Tax Regulations 1995, SI 1995/2518, reg 101(1); and para 210 post. For the meaning of 'taxable supply' see para 12 note 3 ante; and for the meaning of 'prescribed accounting period' generally see paras 105 note 16, 202 note 4 ante. See, however, note 5 infra.

3　For the meaning of 'taxable person' see paras 12 note 4, 55 ante.

4　'Exempt input tax' means: (1) input tax, or a proportion of input tax, which is attributable to exempt supplies in accordance with the method used under the Value Added Tax Regulations 1995 reg 101 (see para 210 post), or a method approved or directed to be used under reg 102 (see para 211 post) as the case may be; and (2) input tax, or a proportion of input tax, which is attributable to supplies outside the United Kingdom which would be exempt if made in the United Kingdom, not being supplies specified in an order under the Value Added Tax Act 1994 s 26(2)(c) (see para 203 ante), according to the extent to which the goods or services on which the input tax was incurred are used or to be used in making such supplies (or in accordance with a method approved or directed to be used under the Value Added Tax Regulations 1995 reg 102, as the case may be): reg 99(1)(a). For the meaning of 'United Kingdom' see para 4 note 3 ante. Essentially, exempt input tax is input tax which cannot be attributed, or be treated as attributable, to taxable supplies in accordance with the partial exemption rules.

5　See ibid reg 99(3), (4). The Commissioners of Customs and Excise may, however, approve in the case of a taxable person who incurs exempt input tax, or a class of such persons, that a longer period is to apply which need not correspond with a tax year: reg 99(3), (7). The 'tax year' of a taxable person means (1) the first period of 12 calendar months commencing on the first day of April, May or June, according to the prescribed accounting periods allocated to him, next following his effective date of registration (determined in accordance with the Value Added Tax Act 1994 s 3(2), Sch 1 (as amended): see para 56 et seq ante); or (2) any subsequent period of 12 calendar months commencing on the day following the end of his first, or any subsequent, tax year: Value Added Tax Regulations 1995 reg 99(1)(d). However, the commissioners may approve or direct that a tax year is to be a period of other than 12 calendar months or that it is to commence on another date than that determined in accordance with head (1) or head (2) supra: reg 99(1)(d). For the purposes of Pt XIV (regs 99–111) (see para 210 et seq post), 'prescribed accounting period' means (a) a prescribed accounting period such as is referred to in reg 25 (see para 226 post); or (b) a special accounting period, where the first prescribed accounting period would otherwise be six months or longer, save that this does not apply where the reference to the prescribed accounting period is used solely in order to identify a particular return: reg 99(1)(b). 'Special accounting period' means each of a succession of periods of the same length as the next prescribed accounting period which does not exceed three months; and (i) the last such period ends on the day before the commencement of that next prescribed accounting period; and (ii) the first such period commences on the effective date of registration determined in accordance with the Value Added Tax Act 1994 Sch 1 (as amended) and ends on the day before the commencement of the second such period: Value Added Tax Regulations 1995 reg 99(1)(c). For the meaning of 'return' see para 105 note 14 ante.

Where, however, a taxable person did not incur exempt input tax in his immediately preceding tax year or registration period, his longer period begins on the first day of the prescribed accounting period in which he incurs exempt input tax and ends on the last day of that tax year, except where he incurs exempt input tax only in the last prescribed accounting period of his tax year, in which case no longer period is to be applied to him in respect of that tax year: reg 99(4). A taxable person who incurs exempt input tax during his registration period has applied to him a longer period which begins on the first day on which he incurs exempt input tax and ends on the day before the commencement of his first tax year: reg 99(3), (5). In the case of a taxable person ceasing to be taxable (see para 55 ante) during a longer period applicable to him, that longer period ends on the day on which he ceases to be taxable: reg 99(3), (6). The 'registration period' of a taxable person means the period commencing on his effective date of registration determined in accordance with the Value Added Tax Act 1994 Sch 1 (as amended) and ending on the day before the commencement of his first tax year: Value Added Tax Regulations 1995 reg 99(2).

6   See ibid reg 107(1); and para 214 post.
7   See ibid reg 107(1)(c); and para 214 post.

210. Attribution of input tax to taxable supplies; the general method. The amount of input tax[1] which a taxable person[2] is entitled to deduct provisionally is the amount which is attributable to taxable supplies[3] in accordance with the following provisions[4]. In respect of each prescribed accounting period[5], goods imported or acquired by, and goods or services supplied to, the taxable person in the period must be identified[6]. There is attributed to taxable supplies the whole of the input tax on such of those goods or services as are used, or to be used, by the taxable person exclusively[7] in making taxable supplies[8]. No part of the input tax on such of those goods or services as are used, or to be used, by the taxable person exclusively in making exempt supplies[9], or in carrying on any activity other than the making of taxable supplies, is to be attributed to taxable supplies[10].

There is also attributed to taxable supplies such proportion of the input tax on such of those goods or services as are used, or to be used, by the taxable person in making both taxable and exempt supplies[11] as bears the same ratio to the total of such input tax as the value of taxable supplies made by him bears to the value of all supplies made by him in the period[12]. In calculating this proportion there is excluded:

(1)   any sum receivable by the taxable person in respect of any supply of capital goods[13] used by him for the purposes of his business[14];

(2)   any sum receivable by him in respect of any of certain descriptions of supplies[15] made by him which are incidental to one or more of his business activities[16];

(3)   that part of the value of any supply of goods on which output tax[17] is not chargeable by virtue of any Treasury order[18] unless the taxable person has imported, acquired or been supplied with the goods for the purposes of selling them[19]; and

(4)   the value of any supply which the taxable person makes[20] to himself[21].

1   For the meaning of 'input tax' see paras 4, 201 ante.
2   For the meaning of 'taxable person' see paras 12 note 4, 55 ante.
3   For the meaning of 'taxable supply' see para 12 note 3 ante.
4   Value Added Tax Regulations 1995, SI 1995/2518 reg 101.
5   For the meaning of 'prescribed accounting period' for these purposes see para 209 note 5 ante.
6   Value Added Tax Regulations 1995 reg 101(2)(a) (amended by SI 1996/1250). Supplies of goods and services to which reg 41(2) (former anti-avoidance provisions relating to groups of companies: revoked with savings) applies are treated as supplied in the period in which the value added tax on

those supplies is treated by virtue of reg 41 (as originally made) as being chargeable: see reg 101(5) (amended by SI 1995/3147; revoked, with a saving in respect of prescribed accounting periods ending on or after 1 June 1996 within which 28 April 1996 fell, by SI 1996/1250). As to the treatment of groups for VAT purposes see paras 66, 191 et seq ante.

7   For the distinction between 'used wholly in making taxable supplies' (which was the test applied by the relevant regulations until 1 April 1992) and 'used exclusively in making taxable supplies' see *Imperial War Museum v Customs and Excise Comrs* [1992] VATTR 346. Where a partially-exempt reinsurance company incurred VAT on legal fees in connection with disputes arising from treaties to provide taxable supplies of reinsurance services, the expenses were not merely a consequence of those taxable supplies but were an incident of the supply of reinsurance and were, having regard to the reality of the transaction, used both wholly and exclusively 'in making' the taxable supplies of reinsurance: *Customs and Excise Comrs v Deutsche Ruck UK Reinsurance Co Ltd* [1995] STC 495, following *Customs and Excise Comrs v Pippa-Dee Parties Ltd* [1981] STC 495 and *Customs and Excise Comrs v Diners Club Ltd* [1989] 2 All ER 385, [1989] STC 407, CA; and, similarly, *Midland Bank plc v Customs and Excise Comrs* (1996) VAT Decision 14144, [1996] STI 1302 (where the facts were the converse of those in *Customs and Excise Comrs v Deutsche Ruck UK Reinsurance Co Ltd* supra, being concerned with the deductibility of the VAT on legal fees incurred in the unsuccessful defence of an action for misrepresentation arising from a supply of services to the plaintiff).

8   Value Added Tax Regulations 1995 reg 101(2)(b). Where, however, a person is treated as making a supply to himself under or by virtue of any provision of the Value Added Tax Act 1994, the input tax on that supply is not to be allowed as attributable to that supply: reg 104. Instead, such input tax will fall to be allowed, if at all, as part of the taxable person's residual input tax: see the text and note 11 infra. As to self-supply see para 26 ante.

In order to be able to attribute an amount of input tax to the taxable supplies made by the trader, it must be shown that there is a direct and immediate link between the expenditure and the supplies; the ultimate aim of the trader in incurring the expense (his 'purpose') is irrelevant: Case C-4/94 *BLP Group plc v Customs and Excise Comrs* [1995] ECR I-983, [1995] STC 424, ECJ. The Community legislation, proceeding from an ideal image of a chain of transactions, intends to attach to each transaction only so much VAT liability as corresponds to the added value accruing in that transaction, so that there is deducted from the total amount of VAT the tax which has been occasioned by the preceding link in the chain. Accordingly, where a trader incurs professional fees in an issue of shares to fund its taxable trade, the VAT on the fees is not deductible because the expense is linked directly and immediately to the intervening exempt supply (of shares); but this does not mean that VAT on overheads is non-deductible: such VAT is, rather, to be apportioned between taxable and exempt supplies in accordance with the apportionment method adopted in the relevant member state: see Case C-4/94 *BLP Group plc v Customs and Excise Comrs* supra. See also *Schemepanel Trading Ltd v Customs and Excise Comrs* [1996] STC 871 (input tax can only be deducted to the extent that it is a cost component of a taxable supply; where, therefore, a builder, before registering for VAT, received certain stage payments for work done and, subsequent to registration, discharged bills for supplies made to him whilst he was unregistered (and which thus related both to work done on which he had not charged VAT and work done on which he had charged VAT), he could only recover tax charged on supplies mde to him as input tax to the extent that it was a cost component of his taxable supplies, notwithstanding the rules relating to the time of supply, following *Neuvale Ltd v Customs and Excise Comrs* [1989] STC 395, CA)); and see also *Customs and Excise Comrs v Harpcombe Ltd* [1996] STC 726. If a trader incurs expense in acquiring the shares in a company in order to extract the business assets from it to use in its own taxable trade, the VAT element of the expense is deductible since there is no intervening exempt supply by the trader to which the expenditure can more directly be linked: *Customs and Excise Comrs v UBAF Bank Ltd* [1996] STC 372, CA. Value added tax incurred by a trader in obtaining professional advice as to how to raise capital, before the trader decided to proceed by means of a share issue, was deductible as a general overhead of his business: *Banner Management Ltd v Customs and Excise Comrs* [1991] VATTR 254. The commissioners have announced that, following *Customs and Excise Comrs v UBAF Bank Ltd* supra, and with effect from 1 June 1996, where a business acquires assets by way of a transfer as a going concern and the assets are used exclusively to make taxable supplies, the VAT incurred on the cost of acquiring those assets may be attributed to those supplies and VAT recovered accordingly; an apportionment of such VAT must be made where the assets are to be used both for taxable and exempt supplies: see Customs and Excise Business Brief 7/96 [1996] STI 843.

9   For the meaning of 'exempt supplies' see para 141 ante.

10 Value Added Tax Regulations 1995 reg 101(2)(c).

11 This proportion is commonly known as 'residual input tax'.

12 Value Added Tax Regulations 1995 reg 101(2)(d). The result is that the recoverable residual input tax is determined by the following formula:

$$\frac{\text{residual input tax} \ \times \ \text{value of taxable supplies in period}}{\text{total input tax for period}}$$

The ratio so calculated is to be expressed as a percentage and, if that percentage is not a whole number, is rounded up to the next whole number: reg 101(4).

13 There is no statutory definition of 'capital goods' for these purposes. They were defined in Case 51/76 *Verbond van Nederlandse Ondernemingen v Inspecteur der Invoerrechten en Accijnzen* [1977] ECR 113, [1977] 1 CMLR 413, ECJ (for the purposes of the Second Directive (now repealed)) as: 'goods used for the purposes of some business activity and distinguishable by their durable nature and their value and such that the acquisition costs are not normally treated as current expenditure but written off over several years'. See also EC Council Directive 77/388 (OJ L145, 13.6.77, p 1) art 17(7).

14 Value Added Tax Regulations 1995 reg 101(3)(a).

15 The relevant descriptions of supply are as follows: (1) any supply which falls within the Value Added Tax Act 1994 s 30(2), Sch 8 Pt II Group 5 item 1 (grants, by a person constructing the building, of a major interest in a building designed as a dwelling or intended for a relevant residential or charitable purpose etc: see para 163 ante), or Sch 8 Pt II Group 6 item 1 (as substituted) (grant of a major interest in a protected building by a person substantially reconstructing it: see para 165 ante); (2) any grant which falls within s 31(1), Sch 9 Pt II Group 1 item 1 (grant of any interest in, or right over, land or of any licence to occupy land: see para 142 ante); (3) any grant which falls within Sch 9 Pt II Group 1 item 1(a) (grant of a fee simple in certain new buildings or civil engineering works: see para 142 ante); (4) any grant which would fall within Sch 9 Pt II Group 1 item 1 but for an election to waive exemption having effect under s 51(1), Sch 10 para 2 (as amended) (see para 143 ante); and (5) any supply which falls within Sch 9 Pt II Group 5 (finance: see para 149 ante): Value Added Tax Regulations 1995 reg 101(3)(b).

16 Ibid reg 101(3)(b).

17 For the meaning of 'output tax' see paras 4, 201 ante.

18 Ie any order under the Value Added Tax Act 1994 s 25(7): see para 204 ante.

19 Value Added Tax Regulations 1995 reg 101(3)(c). For cases where output tax is restricted on a supply of goods under the Value Added Tax Act 1994 s 25(7) see the Value Added Tax (Input Tax) Order 1992, SI 1992/3222, art 5(2) (re-supply of business entertainment); and para 206 ante; art 7(4) (as amended) (onward supply of motor car in respect of which input tax has been excluded from credit); and para 208 ante.

20 Ie under or by virtue of any provision of the Value Added Tax Act 1994: see para 26 ante.

21 Value Added Tax Regulations 1995 reg 101(3)(d).

211. Partial exemption calculation; special methods. The Commissioners of Customs and Excise may approve or direct[1] the use by a taxable person[2] of a method other than the general method of attributing input tax[3] to taxable supplies[4]. If, however, the use of a method was allowed prior to 1 August 1989 and that method would otherwise allow it, the value of any supply[5] which the taxable person makes to himself[6] and the input tax on such a supply must not be included in the calculation[7]. In addition, notwithstanding any provision of any method which has been so approved or directed to be used and which purports to have the contrary effect, the value of any specified supply[8] must be excluded in calculating the proportion of any residual input tax[9] which is to be treated as attributable to taxable supplies[10].

A taxable person using a method which has been approved or directed to be used by the commissioners must continue to use that method until the commissioners approve or direct the termination of its use[11].

1 Any direction under these provisions takes effect from the date upon which the commissioners give the direction, or from such later date as they may specify: Value Added Tax Regulations 1995, SI 1995/2518, reg 101(4).

2 For the meaning of 'taxable person' see paras 12 note 4, 55 ante.

3 Ie the method specified in the Value Added Tax Regulations 1995 reg 101: see para 210 ante. For the meaning of 'input tax' see paras 4, 201 ante.

4 Ibid reg 102(1). For the meaning of 'taxable supplies' see para 12 note 3 ante.

5 For the meaning of 'supply' see para 21 ante.

6 Ie under or by virtue of any provision of the Value Added Tax Act 1994: see para 26 ante.

7 Value Added Tax Regulations 1995 reg 102(1)(a), (b).

8 Ie any supply within the Value Added Tax Regulations 1995 reg 101(3): see para 210 ante.

9 Ie any input tax on goods or services which are used, or to be used, by the taxable person in making both taxable and exempt supplies: see para 210 note 11 ante. For the meaning of 'exempt supplies' see para 141 ante.

10 Ibid reg 102(2).

11 Ibid reg 102(3). The commissioners are entitled informally to give notice to a trader terminating the use of a special method, having regard to reg 4, which provides that any requirement, direction, demand or permission by the commissioners under or for the purposes of the regulations may be made or given by a notice in writing or otherwise: *S and U Stores plc v Customs and Excise Comrs* [1985] STC 506.

212. Attribution of input tax to foreign and specified supplies.

Input tax[1] incurred by a taxable person[2] in any prescribed accounting period[3] on goods imported or acquired by, or goods or services supplied to, him which are used or to be used by him (in whole or in part) in making (1) supplies[4] outside the United Kingdom[5] which would be taxable supplies[6] if made in the United Kingdom; or (2) certain specified supplies[7], may be treated as attributed to taxable supplies to the extent that the goods or services are so used, or to be used, expressed as a proportion of the whole use or intended use[8]. Where such input tax has been incurred on goods or services which are used or to be used in making both a supply of a prescribed description relating to financial dealings[9] and any other supply, and the first-mentioned supply is incidental to one or more of the taxable person's business activities[10], that input tax must be attributed to taxable supplies notwithstanding any provision of any method that the taxable person is required or allowed to use[11] purporting to have the contrary effect[12].

1 For the meaning of 'input tax' see paras 4, 201 ante.

2 For the meaning of 'taxable person' see paras 12 note 4, 55 ante.

3 For the meaning of 'prescribed accounting period' for these purposes see para 209 note 5 ante.

4 For the meaning of 'supply' see para 21 ante.

5 For the meaning of 'United Kingdom' see para 4 note 3 ante.

6 For the meaning of 'taxable supply' see para 12 note 3 ante.

7 Ie supplies specified in an order under the Value Added Tax Act 1994 s 26(2)(c): see para 203 ante. For a description of the supplies so specified see the Value Added Tax (Input Tax) (Specified Supplies) Order 1992, SI 1992/3123; and para 203 note 12 ante.

8 Value Added Tax Regulations 1995, SI 1995/2518 reg 103(1). Credit may thus be claimed for the tax.

9 Ie a supply within the Value Added Tax Act 1994 s 30(2), Sch 9 Pt II Group 5 item 1 (issue, transfer or receipt of, or any dealing with, money, any security for money or any note or order for the payment of money: see para 149 ante) or Sch 9 Pt II Group 5 item 6 (issue, transfer or receipt of, or any dealing with, any specified security or secondary security of money: see para 149 ante): Value Added Tax Regulations 1995 reg 103(2)(a).

10 As to the meaning of 'incidental' see *Customs and Excise Comrs v CH Beazer (Holdings) plc* [1989] STC 549; and for the meaning of 'business' see para 17 ante.

11 Ie under the Value Added Tax Regulations 1995 Pt XIV (regs 99–111): see paras 209 et seq ante, 213 et seq post.

12 Ibid reg 103(2). For the purpose of attributing to taxable supplies any input tax of the description in reg 103(2), it is deemed to be the only input tax incurred by the taxable person in the prescribed accounting period concerned: reg 103(3).

213. Treatment of input tax attributable to exempt supplies as being attributable to taxable supplies.

Subject to certain exceptions[1], any exempt input tax[2] which is attributable to supplies[3] of the following descriptions is treated as attributable to taxable supplies[4]:

(1) any deposit of money;

(2) the grant of any lease or tenancy of, or any licence to occupy, any land where in any longer period[5] the input tax[6] attributable to all such supplies by the grantor

is less than £1,000 and no exempt input tax is incurred by the grantor in respect of any exempt supply[7] other than a supply of a description so specified[8];

(3) any service of making arrangements for the provision of insurance or reinsurance[9];

(4) services of arranging any mortgage, or any hire purchase, credit sale or conditional sale transaction; and

(5) the assignment of any debt due to the assignor in respect of a supply of goods or services made by him[10].

These provisions do not, however, apply where the exempt input tax of the taxable person (excluding any such tax attributable to supplies of the above descriptions) cannot be treated as attributable to taxable supplies[11] because it exceeds the statutory de minimis limits[12].

Where in any prescribed accounting period[13] or in any longer period the exempt input tax of a taxable person does not amount to more than £625 per month on average, and does not exceed one half of all his input tax for the period concerned, all such input tax in that period is treated as attributable to taxable supplies[14].

1   This provision does not apply where the supply is made by the taxable person in the course of carrying on a business of, or a business similar to, any of the following: a bank, an accepting house, an insurance company, insurance agent or insurance broker, an investment trust or unit trust, an investment company, a Stock Exchange broker/dealer or share dealing company, a trustee of a pension fund, a unit trust management company, a building society, a discount house, a finance house, a friendly society, a money lender, a money broker, a mortgage broker, a pawnbroker, a debt factor, or a credit or charge card company: Value Added Tax Regulations 1995, SI 1995/2518 reg 105(2). However, a taxable person who carries on one or more of such specified businesses is not treated as having made the supply in the course of carrying on such a business if he made the supply exclusively in the course of carrying on a business which is not so specified: reg 105(3). For the meaning of 'taxable person' see paras 12 note 4, 55 ante; and for the meaning of 'business' see para 17 ante.

2   For the meaning of 'exempt input tax' see para 209 note 4 ante.

3   For these purposes, 'supplies', except in the expression 'taxable supplies', is to be construed as including supplies made outside the United Kingdom which would be exempt if made in the United Kingdom, (other than supplies specified in an order under the Value Added Tax Act 1994 s 26(2)(c): see para 203 note 12 ante); and 'supply' is to be construed accordingly: Value Added Tax Regulations 1995 reg 105(5). For the meaning of 'United Kingdom' see para 4 note 3 ante.

4   For the meaning of 'taxable supply' see para 12 note 3 ante.

5   For the meaning of 'longer period' see para 209 note 5 ante.

6   For the meaning of 'input tax' see paras 4, 201 ante.

7   For the meaning of 'exempt supply' see para 141 ante.

8   Ie of a description specified in the Value Added Tax Regulations 1995 reg 105: see heads (1)–(5) in the text.

9   Ie any services comprised in the Value Added Tax Act 1994 s 30(2), Sch 9 Pt II Group 2 item 3: see para 146 ante.

10   Value Added Tax Regulations 1995 reg 105(1).

11   Ie under ibid reg 106: see the text and notes 13–15 infra.

12   See ibid reg 105(4).

13   For the meaning of 'prescribed accounting period' for these purposes see para 209 note 5 ante.

14   Value Added Tax Regulations 1995 reg 106(1). In the application of reg 106(1) to a longer period, any treatment of exempt input tax as attributable to taxable supplies in any prescribed accounting period is to be disregarded, and no account is to be taken of any amount or amounts which may be deductible or payable under reg 115 (the capital goods scheme: see para 218 post): reg 106(2). The rules contained in reg 106 are generally known as 'the de minimis rules'.

214. Adjustment of attribution. Where a taxable person[1] to whom a longer period[2] is applicable has provisionally attributed an amount of input tax[3] to taxable supplies[4] in accordance with a method, and all his exempt input tax[5] in that longer period cannot be attributed to taxable supplies in accordance with the rules relating to incidental financial transactions or the de minimis rules[6], he must:

(1)   determine for the longer period the amount of input tax which is attributable to taxable supplies according to the method used in the prescribed accounting periods[7];

(2)   ascertain whether there has been, overall, an over-deduction or an under-deduction of input tax, having regard to the determination made under head (1) above and to the sum of the amounts of input tax, if any, which were deducted in the returns[8] for the prescribed accounting periods[9]; and

(3)   include any such amount of over-deduction or under-deduction in a return for the first prescribed accounting period next following the longer period, except where the Commissioners of Customs and Excise allow another return to be used for this purpose[10].

The commissioners may dispense with this requirement to adjust[11].

Where, however, a taxable person to whom a longer period is applicable has provisionally attributed an amount of input tax to taxable supplies in accordance with a method, and all his exempt input tax in that longer period can be treated as attributable to taxable supplies in accordance with the rules relating to incidental financial transactions or the de minimis rules, he must[12]:

(a)   calculate the difference between the total amount of his input tax for that longer period and the sum of the amounts of input tax deducted in the returns for the prescribed accounting periods; and

(b)   include any such amount of under-deduction in a return for the first prescribed accounting period next following the longer period, except where the commissioners allow another return to be used for this purpose[13].

In addition to the process of re-attribution of input tax which a taxable person with exempt input tax must carry out in his longer period, further adjustments may be required where a taxable person uses, or forms an intention to use, goods or services for a purpose other than that which he originally intended[14]. Such adjustments are only required, or possible, if the change of use or intention occurs before any use of the kind originally intended is made of the supplies in question[15]. Where:

(i)   a taxable person has deducted an amount of input tax which has been attributed to taxable supplies because he intended to use the goods or services in making either taxable supplies, or both taxable and exempt supplies[16]; and

(ii)   during a period of six years commencing on the first day of the prescribed accounting period in which the attribution was determined and before that intention is fulfilled, he uses or forms an intention to use the goods or services concerned in making exempt supplies or (if his original intention was to use the goods in making taxable supplies), in making both taxable and exempt supplies[17],

the taxable person must account, on the return for the prescribed accounting period in which the use occurs or the intention is formed, as the case may be, for an amount equal to the input tax which has ceased to be attributable to taxable supplies in accordance with the method which he was required to use when the input tax was first attributed, unless the commissioners otherwise allow[18]. He must repay that amount to the commissioners[19].

Where a taxable person has incurred an amount of input tax which has not been attributed to taxable supplies because he intended to use the goods or services in making either exempt supplies, or both taxable and exempt supplies, and during a period of six years commencing on the first day of the prescribed accounting period in which the attribution was determined and before that intention is fulfilled, he uses or forms an intention to use the goods or services concerned in making taxable supplies or (if his original intention was to use the goods in making exempt supplies), in making both taxable and exempt supplies[20], then the commissioners must[21] pay to the taxable person an amount equal to the input tax which has become attributable to taxable supplies in accordance with the method which he was required to use when the input tax was first attributed[22].

1 For the meaning of 'taxable person' see paras 12 note 4, 55 ante.
2 For the meaning of 'longer period' see para 209 note 5 ante.
3 For the meaning of 'input tax' see paras 4, 201 ante.
4 For the meaning of 'taxable supply' see para 12 note 3 ante.
5 Ie under the Value Added Tax Regulations 1995, SI 1995/2518, reg 105: see para 213 ante. 'Incidental financial transactions' is not a phrase used by the legislation in this context.
6 Ie the rules contained in ibid reg 106: see para 213 note 14 ante.
7 Ibid reg 107(1)(a). For the meaning of 'prescribed accounting period' for these purposes see para 209 note 5 ante.
8 For the meaning of 'return' see para 105 note 14 ante.
9 Value Added Tax Regulations 1995 reg 107(1)(b).
10 Ibid reg 107(1)(c).
11 Ibid reg 107(1).
12 Technically, it would appear that the taxable person has made an 'error' in accounting for VAT or in his returns, and he is obliged, therefore, to correct the error either in accordance with ibid reg 34 (see para 238 post) or in such manner and within such time as the commissioners may allow (see reg 35; and para 238 post). See *Customs and Excise Comrs v Fine Art Developments plc* [1989] STC 85 at 90, HL, per Lord Keith.
13 Value Added Tax Regulations 1995 reg 107(2).
14 See ibid regs 108–110; and the text and notes 16–22 infra.
15 See ibid regs 108(1), 109(1); and the text and notes 17, 20 infra.
16 For these purposes, 'exempt supplies' includes supplies outside the United Kingdom which would be exempt if made in the United Kingdom, other than taxable supplies; and 'taxable supplies' includes the supplies referred to in ibid reg 103 (see para 212 ante): reg 110(1). For the meaning of 'exempt supplies' generally see para 141 ante; and for the meaning of 'United Kingdom' see para 4 note 3 ante. Any question as to the nature of any supply is to be determined in accordance with the provisions of the Value Added Tax Act 1994 and any regulations or orders made thereunder in force at the time when the input tax was first attributed: regs 108(3), 109(3).
17 Ibid reg 108(1).
18 Ibid reg 108(2). The predecessor to reg 108, the Value Added Tax (General) Regulations 1985, SI 1985/886, reg 34 (revoked) led to the assertion by the commissioners of a method of attribution known as the 'first supply rule', generally relying on the decision in *Sheffield Co-operative Society Ltd v Customs and Excise Comrs* [1987] VATTR 216 that where that provision applied, there was no scope for an apportionment between taxable and exempt supplies because the whole of the input tax had been used in making the first exempt supply. The validity of this approach was examined in *Customs and Excise Comrs v Briararch Ltd, Customs and Excise Comrs v Curtis Henderson Ltd* [1992] STC 732 (buildings had been redeveloped with the intention of making taxable supplies from them, but before that intention could be realised, short exempt leases were granted of the whole building; held that it could not properly be said that the supplies for which input tax credit was claimed were wholly used in making exempt supplies, since the intention to make future taxable supplies continued to exist; and, in such cases, the Value Added Tax (General) Regulations 1985 reg 34 (revoked) envisaged an apportionment). The same principle continues to apply in relation to the Value Added Tax Regulations 1995 regs 108, 109. See also *Cooper & Chapman (Builders) Ltd v Customs and Excise Comrs* [1993] STC 1; cf *Customs and Excise Comrs v University of Wales College, Cardiff* [1995] STC 611. The decisions in Case C-4/94 *BLP Group plc v Customs and Excise Comrs* [1996] 1 WLR 174, [1995] STC 424, ECJ, and *Robert Gordon's College v Customs and Excise Comrs* [1996] 1 WLR 201, [1995] STC 1093, HL, may, however, affect the application of the principle in *Customs and Excise Comrs v Briararch Ltd, Customs and Excise Comrs v Curtis Henderson Ltd* supra. In *Svenska International plc v Customs and Excise Comrs* [1996] STC 1000, the commissioners sought to use the predecessor provision (ie the Value Added Tax (General) Regulations 1985, SI 1985/886, reg 34 (revoked)) to recover input tax deducted by one company on making supplies to another, where the companies subsequently became grouped for VAT and where payment for the supplies was only made after the group registration had been effected; it was held that that regulation only applied where a taxable person used a supply or appropriated it for use in making an exempt supply or in carrying out an activity other than making taxable supplies; and it could have no effect where supplies made by one taxable person to another ceased to be characterised as such by reason of group registration. As to supplies to and by members of a VAT group see para 192 ante; and as to the registration of companies as a group for VAT purposes see para 66 ante.

19 Value Added Tax Regulations 1995 reg 108(2). Where the use to which the goods or services concerned are put includes the making of supplies outside the United Kingdom, and at the time when the taxable person was first required to attribute the input tax he was not required to use a method approved or directed under reg 102 (see para 211 ante) or that method did not provide expressly for the attribution of input tax to supplies outside the United Kingdom, then the amount for which the taxable person is liable to account to the commissioners is calculated by reference to the extent to which the goods or services concerned are used or intended to be used in making taxable supplies, expressed as a proportion of the whole use or intended use: reg 110(2). However reg 103 (which is made applicable to reg 100 for this purpose by reg 110(1)(b)) provides that 'taxable supplies' includes supplies made outside the United Kingdom which would be taxable supplies if made in the United Kingdom and supplies specified in an order under the Value Added Tax Act 1994 s 26(2)(c) (see paras 203, 212 ante); use for such purposes will, therefore, form part of the numerator of the apportionment fraction.

20 Value Added Tax Regulations 1995 reg 109(1).

21 Ie on receipt of an application made by the taxable person in such form and manner and containing such particulars as they may direct: ibid reg 109(2).

22 Ibid reg 109(2). Where the use to which the goods or services concerned are put includes the making of supplies outside the United Kingdom, and at the time when the taxable person was first required to attribute the input tax he was not required to use a method approved or directed under reg 102 (see para 211 ante) or that method did not provide expressly for the attribution of input tax to supplies outside the United Kingdom, then the amount which the taxable person is entitled to be paid is calculated by reference to the extent to which the goods or services concerned are used or intended to be used in making taxable supplies, expressed as a proportion of the whole use or intended use: reg 110(2). See further note 19 supra.

215. Exceptional claims for value added tax relief. On a claim made in the prescribed manner[1], the Commissioners of Customs and Excise may authorise a taxable person to treat as if it were input tax[2]:

(1)   VAT on supplies[3] of goods or services made to him before the date with effect from which he was, or was required to be, registered[4], or which was paid by him on the importation or acquisition of goods before that date, for the purposes of a business[5] which either was, or was to be, carried on by him at the time of the supply or payment[6];

(2)   in the case of a body corporate, VAT on goods obtained for it before its incorporation, or on the supply of services before that time for its benefit or in connection with its incorporation, provided that the person to whom the supply was made or who paid VAT on the importation or acquisition:

  (a)   became a member, officer or employee of the body and was reimbursed, or has received an undertaking to be reimbursed, by the body for the whole amount of the price paid for the goods or services;

  (b)   was not at the time of the importation, acquisition or supply a taxable person; and

  (c)   imported, acquired or was supplied with the goods, or received the services, for the purpose of a business to be carried on by the body and has not used them for any purpose other than such a business[7].

No VAT may, however, be so treated as input tax in respect of goods or services which had been supplied or, in the case of goods, consumed[8], by the taxable person, or, in a case falling within head (2) above, by the person who imported, acquired or was supplied with the goods or services, before the date with effect from which the taxable person was registered or was required to be registered[9]. Nor may VAT be so treated as input tax in respect of services performed upon goods in respect of which a claim would be denied as mentioned above[10], or in respect of services which had been supplied to the taxable person or, in a case falling within head (2) above, to the person who received the services, more than six months before the date of the taxable person's registration[11].

Correspondingly, if a person who has been, but is no longer, a taxable person makes a claim in such manner and supported by such evidence as the commissioners may require, they may pay to him the amount of any VAT on the supply of services to him after the date with effect from which he ceased to be, or to be required to be, registered and which was attributable to any taxable supply[12] made by him in the course or furtherance[13] of any business which was carried on by him when he was, or was required to be, registered[14].

1   Ie in accordance with the Value Added Tax Regulations 1995, SI 1995/2518, reg 111(3): reg 111(1). Save as the Commissioners of Customs and Excise may otherwise allow, a claim must be made on the first return the taxable person makes and must be supported by invoices and other evidence as the commissioners may require: reg 111(3). It is necessary to make special provision for the evidence required to support the claim, since the claimant will not have received a VAT invoice (which is only required under reg 13(1)(a) where a registered person makes a taxable supply in the United Kingdom to another taxable person: see para 240 post). For the meaning of 'return' see para 105 note 14 ante; and for the meaning of 'invoice' see para 11 note 8 ante. For the meaning of 'taxable person' see paras 12 note 4, 55 ante.
2   For the meaning of 'input tax' see paras 4, 201 ante.
3   For the meaning of 'supply' see para 21 ante.
4   For the meaning of 'registered' see para 56 note 2 ante.
5   For the meaning of 'business' see para 17 ante.
6   Value Added Tax Regulations 1995 reg 111(1)(a). For a case in which the commissioners were held rightly to have refused a claim for relief see *Gulland Properties Ltd v Customs and Excise Comrs* (1996) VAT Decision 13955, [1996] STI 938.
7   Value Added Tax Regulations 1995 reg 111(1)(b).
8   Ie save as the commissioners may otherwise allow: ibid reg 111(2)(a).
9   Ibid reg 111(2)(a). A taxable person making a claim under reg 111(1) must thus compile and preserve, for such period as the commissioners may require, (1) in respect of goods, a stock account showing separately quantities purchased, quantities used in the making of other goods, date of purchase and date and manner of subsequent disposals of both such quantities; and (2) in respect of services, a list showing their description, date of purchase and date of disposal, if any: reg 111(4).
10 Ibid reg 111(2)(b).
11 Ibid reg 111(2)(c).
12 For the meaning of 'taxable supply' see para 12 note 3 ante.
13 For the meaning of 'in the course or furtherance of a business' see paras 12 note 5, 17 note 2 ante.
14 Value Added Tax Regulations 1995 reg 111(5).

216. The capital goods scheme. Provision is made for an adjustment to the attribution of input tax[1] to taxable and exempt supplies in the case of substantial amounts of input tax incurred on certain types of capital item[2]. This method of adjustment is usually referred to as 'the capital goods scheme'.

The capital items to which the scheme applies are items of any of the following descriptions:

(1)   a computer or an item of computer equipment of a value of not less than £50,000 supplied to, or imported or acquired by, the owner[3];

(2)   land or a building or part of a building where the value of the interest therein supplied to the owner (by way of a taxable supply[4] which is not a zero-rated supply[5]) is not less than £250,000, excluding so much of that value as may consist of rent[6];

(3)   a building or part of a building where:
   (a)   the owner's interest in, right over, or licence to occupy the building or part of the building is treated as supplied to him on a change of use from a relevant residential or relevant charitable purpose[7]; and
   (b)   the value of that supply[8] is not less than £250,000[9];

(4)   a building or part of a building where:
   (a)   the owner's interest in, right over, or licence to occupy the building or part of the building is treated as supplied to him under the developer's self-supply provisions[10]; and

(b)   the value of that supply[11] is not less than £250,000[12];

(5)   a building, other than one falling, or capable of falling, within head (3) or head (4) above, which has been constructed by the owner and which is first brought into use by him on or after 1 April 1990 where the aggregate of the value of taxable grants relating to the land on which the building is constructed which are made to the owner, on or after that date, and of the value of all the taxable supplies of goods and services (other than any that are zero-rated) made or to be made to the owner for or in connection with the construction of the building on or after that date, is not less than £250,000[13]; and

(6)   a building which the owner alters, or an extension or an annex which he constructs, where:

(a)   additional floor area is created in the altered building, extension or annex, of not less than 10 per cent of the floor area of the building before the alteration in question is carried out, or the extension or annex in question is constructed; and

(b)   the value of all the taxable supplies of goods and services (other than any that are zero-rated) made or to be made to the owner for or in connection with the alteration, extension or annex in question on or after 1 April 1990 is not less than £250,000[14].

1   For the meaning of 'input tax' see paras 4, 201 ante. The general rule is that input tax may not be re-attributed between taxable and exempt supplies after the expiry of a taxable person's longer period, save where there has been a change of use or intention before any other use is made of the supply: see para 214 ante.

2   See the Value Added Tax Regulations 1995, SI 1995/2518, Pt XV (regs 112–116); the text and notes 3–14 infra; and para 217 et seq post. Any reference therein to a capital item is to be construed as a capital item to which Pt XV applies by virtue of reg 113 (see the text and notes 3–14 infra), being an item which a person ('the owner') uses in the course or furtherance of a business carried on by him, and for the purpose of that business, otherwise than solely for the purpose of selling the item: reg 112(2). For the meaning of 'in the course or furtherance of a business' see paras 12 note 5, 17 note 2 ante.

3   Ibid reg 113(a).

4   For the meaning of 'taxable supply' see para 12 note 3 ante.

5   For the meaning of 'zero-rated' see para 158 ante.

6   Value Added Tax Regulations 1995 reg 113(b).

7   Ie is treated as supplied to him under the Value Added Tax Act 1994 s 51(1), Sch 10 para 1(5): see para 164 ante.

8   Ie determined in accordance with ibid Sch 10 para 1(6)(b): see para 164 ante.

9   Value Added Tax Regulations 1995 reg 113(c).

10   Ie is treated as supplied to him under the Value Added Tax Act 1994 Sch 10 para 6(1): see para 28 ante. As to the phasing out of these provisions see para 28 ante.

11   Ie determined in accordance with ibid Sch 10 para 6(2): see para 28 ante.

12   Value Added Tax Regulations 1995 reg 113(d).

13   Ibid reg 113(e).

14   Ibid reg 113(f).

217. Period of adjustment under the capital goods scheme. The proportion, if any, of the total input tax[1] on a capital item[2] which may be deducted under the partial exemption rules[3] is subject to adjustments in accordance with the provisions of the capital goods scheme[4]. The adjustments must be made over a period determined as follows[5]. In the case of a computer, or an item of computer equipment[6], the period of adjustment consists of five successive intervals[7], as it does in the case of an interest in land or a building or a part of a building[8] which is supplied to the owner[9] at a time when the interest has less than ten years to run[10]. In relation to a capital item of any other description, the period of adjustment consists of ten successive intervals[11].

The first interval applicable to a capital item is determined as follows:

(1)   where the owner is a registered person[12] when he imports, acquires or is supplied with the item as a capital item, the first interval commences on the day of the importation, acquisition or supply[13] and ends on the day before the commencement of his tax year[14] following that day[15];

(2)   where the owner is a registered person when he appropriates an item to use as a capital item[16], the first interval commences on the day he first so uses it and ends on the day before the commencement of his tax year following that day[17];

(3)   where the capital item is a building or part of a building and the owner's interest in, right over, or licence to occupy it is treated as supplied to him on a change of use from a relevant residential or relevant charitable purpose[18], the first interval commences on the day that interest, right or licence is so treated as supplied to him[19] and ends on the day before the commencement of his tax year following that day[20];

(4)   where the capital item is a building or part of a building, and the owner's interest in, right over, or licence to occupy it is treated as supplied to him under the developer's self-supply provisions[21], the first interval commences on the later of 1 April 1990 and the day the owner first uses the building or part, and ends on the day before the commencement of his tax year following the day of commencement of the first interval[22];

(5)   where the capital item is a building constructed by the owner and first brought into use by him on or after 1 April 1990[23], or where it is a building which the owner alters, or an extension or annex which he constructs[24], the first interval commences on the day on which the owner first uses it, or first uses the altered building or the extension or annex in question, and ends on the day before the commencement of his tax year following that day[25];

(6)   where the owner is not a registered person when he first uses an item as a capital item, and subsequently becomes a registered person, the first interval corresponds with his registration period[26];

(7)   where the owner is not a registered person when he first uses an item as a capital item, and subsequently is included among bodies treated as members of a group[27], the first interval corresponds with, or is that part still remaining of, the then current tax year of that group[28].

Thereafter, each subsequent interval applicable to a capital item corresponds with a longer period[29] applicable to the owner or, if no longer period applies to him, a tax year of his[30]. Where, however, the owner of a capital item:

(a)   is a registered person and subsequently becomes a member of a group[31] during the period of adjustment applicable to the capital item, the interval then applying to it ends on the day before the owner is first included in the group and each subsequent interval, if any, applicable to the capital item ends on the last day of a longer period applicable to that group or, if no longer period applies, ends on the last day of a tax year of that group[32];

(b)   ceases to be a member of such a group during the period of adjustment applicable to the capital item, the interval then applying to it ends on the day that the owner so ceases to be a member and the next interval, if any, applicable to the capital item corresponds with a longer period applying to the owner or, if no longer period applies, corresponds with a tax year of the owner[33].

Where the owner of a capital item transfers it during the period of adjustment applicable to it, in the course of the transfer of his business or of part of his business as a going concern, the interval then applying to the capital item ends on the day of the transfer, and each subsequent interval, if any, applicable to the capital item ends on the last day of a longer period applying to the new owner or, if no longer period applies, ends on the day before the commencement of a tax year of the new owner[34].

1   For the meaning of 'input tax' see paras 4, 201 ante.
2   For the meaning of 'capital item' see para 216 note 2 ante.
3   Ie under the Value Added Tax Regulations 1995, SI 1995/2518, Pt XIV (regs 99–111): see paras 209–215 ante.
4   Ibid reg 114(1). As to the capital goods scheme see para 216 ante.
5   Ibid reg 114(2).
6   Ie a capital item of a description falling within ibid reg 113(a): see para 216 head (1) ante.
7   Ibid reg 114(2)(a).
8   Ie a capital item of a description falling within ibid reg 113(b): see para 216 head (2) ante.
9   For the meaning of 'the owner' for these purposes see para 216 note 2 ante.
10 Value Added Tax Regulations 1995 reg 114(3)(b).
11 Ibid reg 114(3)(c).
12 For the meaning of 'registered person' see para 56 note 7 ante.
13 For the meaning of 'supply' see para 21 ante.
14 For the meaning of 'tax year' see para 209 note 5 ante (definition applied by the Value Added Tax Regulations 1995 reg 112(1)).
15 Ibid reg 114(4)(a).
16 Ie when he appropriates the item from trading stock.
17 Value Added Tax Regulations 1995 reg 114(4)(b).
18 Ie when the capital item is of a description falling within ibid reg 113(c): see para 216 head (3) ante.
19 Ie under the Value Added Tax Act 1994 s 51(1), Sch 10 para 1(5): see para 164 ante.
20 Value Added Tax Regulations 1995 reg 114(4)(c).
21 Ie when the capital item is of a description falling within ibid reg 113(d): see para 216 head (4) ante.
22 Value Added Tax Regulations 1995 reg 114(4)(d).
23 Ie when the capital item is of a description falling within ibid reg 113(e): see para 216 head (5) ante.
24 Ie when the capital item is of a description falling within ibid reg 113(f): see para 216 head (6) ante.
25 Ibid reg 114(4)(e).
26 Ibid reg 114(4)(f)(i). For the meaning of 'registration period' see para 209 note 5 ante (definition applied by reg 112(1)).
27 Ie under the Value Added Tax Act 1994 s 43 (as amended): see paras 66, 191 ante.
28 Value Added Tax Regulations 1995 reg 114(4)(f)(ii).
29 For the meaning of 'longer period' see para 209 note 5 ante (definition applied by ibid reg 112(1)).
30 Ibid reg 114(5).
31 See note 27 supra.
32 Value Added Tax Regulations 1995 reg 114(6)(a).
33 Ibid reg 114(6)(b). If, however, the owner of a capital item ceases to be a member of such a group ('the first group') during the period of adjustment applicable to the capital item, and is immediately thereafter included in another such group ('the second group'), the interval applying to the capital item immediately before the owner ceases to be a member of the first group ends on the day that the owner so ceases and each subsequent interval, if any, ends on the last day of a longer period applicable to the second group, or if no longer period applies, ends on the last day of a tax year of the second group: reg 114(6) proviso.
34 Ibid reg 114(7). Where, however, the new owner has, under reg 6(1) (see para 74 ante), been registered with the registration number of, and in substitution for, the transferor, the interval applying to the capital item at the time of the transfer does not end on the day of the transfer, and accordingly ends on the last day of the longer period applying to the new owner immediately after the transfer or, if no longer period then applies to him, ends on the last day of his tax year following the day of the transfer: reg 114(7) proviso. For the meaning of 'registration number' see para 16 note 10 ante.

218. Method of adjustment under the capital goods scheme. In the first interval in which a taxable person[1] incurs input tax[2] on a capital item[3], he will be entitled to attribute the input tax to his taxable supplies[4] in accordance with his partial exemption method[5] and, subject to the effect of that method, may be able in that period to recover the entirety of the input tax which he suffered on the supply to him of the capital item[6]. The capital goods scheme[7] begins to operate after the end of the first interval of adjustment[8]. Where in a subsequent interval[9] applicable to a capital item, the extent to which the item is used in making taxable supplies[10] increases (or decreases) from the extent to which it was so used in the first interval applicable to it, the owner may deduct (or is obliged to pay to the Commissioners of Customs and Excise) for that subsequent interval an amount calculated by dividing the total input tax on the capital item[11] by the total period of adjustment[12] and multiplying the result by the adjustment percentage[13].

Where the whole of the owner's interest in a capital item is supplied by him, or the owner is deemed or would have been deemed[14] to supply a capital item[15] during an interval other than the last interval applicable to the capital item, then if the supply or deemed supply is:

(1) a taxable supply, the owner is treated as using the capital item for each of the remaining complete intervals applicable to it wholly in making taxable supplies[16]; or

(2) an exempt supply, the owner is treated as not using the capital item for any of the remaining complete intervals applicable to it in making any taxable supplies[17],

and the owner must calculate for each of the remaining complete intervals applicable to it[18] such amount as he may deduct or such amount as he may be liable to pay to the commissioners[19]. The aggregate of the amounts that he may deduct in relation to a capital item in pursuance of this provision may not, however, exceed the output tax[20] chargeable by him on the supply of the capital item[21].

If a capital item is irretrievably lost or stolen or is totally destroyed, or if, being an interest in land[22], it expires, during the period of adjustment applicable to it, no further adjustment is made in any subsequent complete intervals applicable to it[23].

1   For the meaning of 'taxable person' see paras 12 note 4, 55 ante.
2   For the meaning of 'input tax' see paras 4, 201 ante.
3   For the meaning of 'capital item' see para 216 note 2 ante.
4   For the meaning of 'taxable supply' see para 12 note 3 ante.
5   As to partial exemption methods see para 209 et seq ante.
6   See para 209 et seq ante. It is no part of the purpose of the capital goods scheme to restrict the amount of input tax a trader may immediately recover; rather, it seeks more accurately to determine the proportion of taxable supplies to which the capital item is attributable over the whole or part of the period in which the trader uses it, subject to a maximum adjustment period of ten years.
7   As to the capital goods scheme see para 216 ante.
8   See the text and notes 9–23 infra.
9   As to subsequent intervals see para 217 ante.
10   For these purposes, an attribution of the total input tax on the capital item is determined for each subsequent interval applicable to it in accordance with the method used under the Value Added Tax Regulations 1995, SI 1995/2518, Pt XIV (regs 99–111) (see para 209 et seq ante) for that interval and the proportion of the input tax thereby determined to be attributable to taxable supplies is treated as being the extent to which the capital item is used in making taxable supplies in that subsequent interval: reg 116(1). In any particular case the Commissioners of Customs and Excise may allow another method by which, or may direct the manner in which, the extent to which a capital item is used in making taxable supplies in any subsequent interval applicable to it is to be ascertained: reg 116(2). Regulation 116(2) is of limited application and is directed towards the case where there is a change in the relevant proportion of the capital goods devoted to exempt and non-exempt uses (eg in the area of land so devoted); it is not directed towards the case where a belated election to waive exemption is made under the Value Added Tax Act 1994 s 51(1), Sch 10 para 3(9) (as amended) (see para 144 ante): *Customs and Excise Comrs v R & R Pension Fund Trustees* [1996] STC 889 at 896. Where the owner of a building which is a capital item of his grants or assigns a tenancy or lease in the whole or any part of that building and that grant or assignment is a zero-rated supply to the extent only as provided by (1) the Value Added Tax Act 1994 s 30(2), Sch 8 Pt II Group 5 note 14 (as substituted) (see para 163 ante), or by Sch 8 Pt II Group 5 note 14 (as substituted) as applied to Sch 8 Pt II Group 6 note 3 (as substituted) (see para 165 ante); or (2) s 100(1), Sch 13 para 8 (transitional provisions), any subsequent exempt supply of his arising directly from that grant or assignment is to be disregarded in determining the extent to which the capital item is used in making taxable supplies in any interval applicable to it: Value Added Tax Regulations 1995 reg 116(3) (amended by SI 1995/3147). For the meaning of 'owner' see para 216 note 2 ante.

11   'The total input tax on the capital item' means, in relation to a capital item falling within: (1) the Value Added Tax Regulations 1995 reg 113(a) or (b) (see para 216 heads (1)–(2) ante), the value added tax charged on the supply to, or on the importation or acquisition by, the owner of the capital item, other than VAT charged on rent (if any); (2) reg 113(c) or (d) (see para 216 heads (3)–(4) ante), the VAT charged on the supply which the owner is treated as making to himself under the Value Added Tax Act 1994 s 51(1), Sch 10 para 1(5) or 6(1) (see para 28 ante), as the case may require: (3) the Value Added Tax Regulations 1995 reg 113(e) or (f) (see para 216 heads (5)–(6) ante), the aggregate of the VAT charged on the supplies described therein, as the case may require, other than VAT charged on rent (if any); and includes, in relation to any capital item, any VAT charged as input tax under reg 111 (see para 215 ante) which relates to the capital item, other than such VAT charged on rent, if any; and for these purposes references to the owner are to be construed as references to the person who incurred the total input tax on the capital item: reg 115(5). For the meaning of 'supply' see para 21 ante; and as to zero-rated supplies see para 158 et seq ante.

12   Ie the total number of successive intervals: see para 217 ante. Where the capital item falls within ibid reg 114(3)(a) or (b) (see para 217 text and notes 7–10 ante), that number is five; and where the capital item falls within reg 114(3)(c) (ie in any other case) that number is ten: see reg 115(1)(a), (b).

13   Ibid reg 115(1), (2). 'The adjustment percentage' means the difference, if any, between the extent, expressed as a percentage, to which the capital item is used, or is regarded as being used, in making taxable supplies in the first interval applicable to it, and the extent to which it is so used or is treated under reg 115(3) (see heads (1)–(2) in the text) as being so used in the subsequent interval in question: reg 115(5).

    A taxable person claiming any amount pursuant to reg 115(1), or liable to pay any amount pursuant to reg 115(2), must include that amount in a return for the second prescribed accounting period next following the interval to which that amount relates, except where the commissioners allow another return to be used for this purpose: reg 115(6). Where, however, an interval has come to an end (1) under reg 114(6)(b) because the owner of the capital item has ceased to be a member of a group under the Value Added Tax Act 1994 s 43 (as amended) (see paras 66, 191 ante), any amount claimable from the commissioners or payable to them, as the case may be, in respect of that interval must be included in a return for that group for the second prescribed accounting period after the end of the tax year of the group in which the interval in question fell; or (2) under the Value Added Tax Regulations 1995 reg 114(7) because the owner has transferred part of his business as a going concern and he remains a registered person after the transfer, any amount claimable from the commissioners or payable to them, as the case may be, in respect of that interval must be included in a return by him for the second prescribed accounting period after the end of his tax year in which the interval in question fell, except (in either case) where the commissioners allow another return to be used for this purpose: reg 115(6). For the meaning of 'return' see para 105 note 14 ante; for the meaning of 'registered person' see para 105 note 7 ante; and for the meaning of 'prescribed accounting period' and 'tax year' see para 209 note 5 ante (the last two definitions applied by reg 112(1)).

14   Ie but for the fact that the VAT on the deemed supply, whether by virtue of its value or because it is zero-rated or exempt, would not have been more than £250: ibid reg 115(3). As to exempt supplies see para 141 et seq ante.

15   Ie pursuant to the Value Added Tax Act 1994 s 5(1), Sch 4 para 8(1): see para 24 ante.

16   Value Added Tax Regulations 1995 reg 115(3)(a).

17   Ibid reg 115(3)(b).

18   Ie in accordance with ibid reg 115(1) or (2), as the case may be.

19   Ibid reg 115(3). A taxable person claiming any amount or amounts, or liable to pay any amount or amounts, pursuant to reg 115(3), must include that amount or those amounts in a return for the second prescribed accounting period next following the interval in which the supply, or deemed supply, in question takes place except where the commissioners allow another return to be used for this purpose: reg 115(7).

20   For the meaning of 'output tax' see paras 4, 201 ante.

21   Value Added Tax Regulations 1995 reg 115(3) proviso.

22   Ie if it is of a kind falling within ibid reg 114(3)(b): see para 217 ante.

23   Ibid reg 114(4).

(2) RECORDS AND INFORMATION

219. Duty to keep records. Every taxable person[1] must keep such records as the Commissioners of Customs and Excise may by regulations require[2], and every person who, at a time when he is not a taxable person, acquires in the United Kingdom from another member state[3] any goods which are subject to a duty of excise or consist in a new means of transport[4] must keep such records with respect to the acquisition, if it is a taxable acquisition[5] and is not in pursuance of a taxable supply[6], as the commissioners may so require[6].

The commissioners may require any such records to be preserved for such period not exceeding six years as they may require[7]. The duty to preserve records may be discharged by the preservation of the information contained in them by such means as the commissioners may approve[8], and where that information is so preserved a copy of any document forming part of the records is, subject to certain limitations[9], admissible in evidence in any proceedings, whether civil or criminal, to the same extent as the records themselves[10]. As a condition of approving any means of preserving information contained in any records, the commissioners may impose such reasonable requirements as appear to them necessary for securing that the information will be as readily available to them as if the records themselves had been preserved[11].

1   For the meaning of 'taxable person' see paras 12 note 4, 55 ante.

2   The regulations may make different provision for different cases and may be framed by reference to such records as may be specified in any notice published by the commissioners in pursuance of the regulations and not withdrawn by a further notice: Value Added Tax Act 1994 s 58, Sch 11 para 6(2). The notice currently in force relating to record-keeping is Customs and Excise Notice 700 *The VAT Guide* (March 1996) Pt 8, which explains that the records must be kept up to date and be in sufficient detail to enable the trader correctly to calculate the amount of VAT that he is obliged to pay, or may claim from, the commissioners; but that the records need not be kept in any particular form. However, it is a requirement that the records be kept in a way which enables the commissioners to check easily the figures which the trader has used to complete his VAT return; and, if the records fail to satisfy this criterion, the commissioners will direct the trader to make the necessary changes: Customs and Excise Notice 700 para 8.1. In exercise of the power to make regulations conferred by the Value Added Tax Act 1994 Sch 11 para 6, the commissioners have made the Value Added Tax Regulations 1995, SI 1995/2518, reg 31 et seq. For the purpose of accounting for VAT, every taxable person must keep the following records: (1) his business and accounting records; (2) his VAT account; (3) copies of all VAT invoices issued by him; (4) all VAT invoices received by him; (5) all certificates prepared by him relating to acquisitions by him of goods from other member states or given to him relating to supplies by him of goods or services, provided that, owing to provisions in force which concern fiscal or other warehousing regimes (see para 130 et seq ante), those acquisitions or supplies are either zero-rated or treated for VAT purposes as taking place outside the United Kingdom; (6) documentation received by him relating to acquisitions by him of any goods from other member states; (7) copy documentation issued by him relating to the transfer, dispatch or transportation of goods by him to other member states; (8) documentation received by him relating to the transfer, dispatch or transportation of goods by him to other member states; (9) documentation relating to importations and exportations by him; and (10) all credit notes, debit notes, or other documents which evidence an increase or decrease in consideration that are received, and copies of all such documents that are issued, by him: reg 31(1) (amended by SI 1996/1250). In relation to a trade or business of a specified description, or for the purposes of any scheme established by, or under, regulations made under the Value Added Tax Act 1994, the commissioners may supplement the list of records so required by a notice published by them for that purpose: reg 31(2). As to the making of regulations generally see para 8 ante. For the meaning of 'document' see para 11 note 8 ante; for the meaning of 'United Kingdom' see para 4 note 3 ante; and for the meaning of 'another member state' see para 4 note 14 ante. As to zero-rated supplies see para 158 et seq ante.

3   As to acquisition from another member state see para 13 ante.

4   For the meaning of 'new means of transport' see para 13 note 8 ante.

5   For the meaning of 'taxable acquisition' see para 13 ante.

6   Value Added Tax Act 1994 Sch 11 para 6(1). Every person who, at a time when he is not a taxable person, acquires in the United Kingdom from another member state any goods which are subject to a duty of excise or consist of a new means of transport must, for the purposes of accounting for VAT, keep such records with respect to the acquisition as may be specified in any notice published by the commissioners in pursuance of reg 31: reg 31(3). See Customs and Excise Notice 728 *VAT: Motor Vehicles, Boats, Aircraft: Intra-EC Movements by Private Persons* (1 August 1995).

7   Value Added Tax Act 1994, Sch 11 para 6(3). Permission is sometimes given at local level to small traders to preserve some records for a shorter period where the usual requirement would involve the trader in

undue expense or cause him serious storage difficulties: Customs and Excise Leaflet 700/21/95 *Keeping Records and Accounts* (1 March 1995) para 14.

8   This provision is intended to enable records to be preserved on microfilms or on computer storage media.

9   A statement contained in a document produced by a computer is not to be admissible in evidence by virtue of the Value Added Tax Act 1994 Sch 11 para 6(4): (1) in civil proceedings in England and Wales, except in accordance with the Civil Evidence Act 1968 ss 5, 6 (see EVIDENCE vol 17 para 59); (2) in criminal proceedings in England and Wales, except in accordance with the Police and Criminal Evidence Act 1984 ss 69, 70; and the Criminal Justice Act 1988 Pt II (ss 23–28) (as amended) (see CRIMINAL LAW vol 11(2) (Reissue) para 1158): Value Added Tax Act 1994 Sch 11 para 6(6). As to the production of tax invoices by the use of a computer see Sch 11 para 3; and para 240 note 11 post.

10   Ibid Sch 11 para 6(4).

11   Ibid Sch 11 para 6(5).

220. Duty to preserve records on transfer of business. Where a business[1] carried on by a taxable person[2] is transferred to another person as a going concern, any records relating to the business which are required[3] to be preserved after the transfer must be preserved by the transferee instead of by the transferor unless the Commissioners of Customs and Excise at the request of the transferor otherwise direct[4].

1   For the meaning of 'business' see para 17 ante.
2   For the meaning of 'taxable person' see paras 12 note 4, 55 ante.
3   Ie by the Value Added Tax Act 1994 s 58, Sch 11 para 6(1): see para 219 ante.
4   Ibid s 49(1)(b).

221. Register of temporary movement of goods. Every taxable person[1] must keep and maintain a register to be known as the register of temporary movement of goods to and from other member states[2]. Where goods have been moved to or received from another member state[3] and they are to be returned within a period of two years of the date of their first removal or receipt, the register must contain the following information:

(1)   the date of removal of goods to another member state and the date of receipt of those goods when they are returned from that member state or another member state[4];

(2)   the date of receipt of goods from another member state and the date of removal of those goods when they are returned to that member state or another member state[5];

(3)   a description of the goods, sufficient to identify them[6];

(4)   a description of any process, work or other operation carried out on the goods either in the United Kingdom[7] or in another member state[8];

(5)   the consideration[9] for the supply[10] of the goods[11]; and

(6)   the consideration for the supply of any processing, work or other operation carried out on the goods either in the United Kingdom or another member state[12].

The Commissioners of Customs and Excise may, by a notice published by them for the purpose, supplement this list of information in relation to a trade or business[13] of a description specified by them[14].

1   For the meaning of 'taxable person' see paras 12 note 4, 55 ante.
2   Value Added Tax Regulations 1995, SI 1995/2518, reg 33(1).
3   For the meaning of 'another member state' see para 4 note 14 ante.
4   Value Added Tax Regulations 1995 reg 33(2)(a), (b).
5   Ibid reg 33(2)(c), (d).
6   Ibid reg 33(2)(e).
7   For the meaning of 'United Kingdom' see para 4 note 3 ante.
8   Value Added Tax Regulations 1995 reg 33(2)(f).
9   For the meaning of 'consideration' generally see para 86 ante.
10   For the meaning of 'supply' see para 21 ante.

11 Value Added Tax Regulations 1995 reg 33(2)(g).
12 Ibid reg 33(2)(h).
13 For the meaning of 'business' see para 17 ante.
14 Value Added Tax Regulations 1995 reg 33(3).

222. Fiscal warehousing record and stock control. A fiscal warehousekeeper[1] must maintain[2] a fiscal warehousekeeping record for any fiscal warehouse in respect of which he is the relevant fiscal warehousekeeper[3]. That record may be maintained in any manner acceptable to the Commissioners of Customs and Excise and must, in particular, be capable of ready use by any proper officer[4] in the course of his duties and of reproduction into a form suitable for any proper officer readily to use at a place other than the relevant fiscal warehouse[5].

The fiscal warehousing record must accurately identify:

(1) any eligible goods[6] which enter or exit the fiscal warehouse, their nature and quantity, and the time and date when they so enter or exit[7];

(2) any goods which are not eligible goods and which enter or exit the fiscal warehouse for storage[8], their nature and quantity, and the time and date when they so enter or exit[9];

(3) all eligible goods which are allocated to or removed from the fiscal warehousing regime associated with the relevant fiscal warehousekeeper, the time and date when the allocation or removal takes place, and the location of the eligible goods while they are allocated to the relevant regime[10];

(4) as 'transferred goods' all eligible goods which are transferred directly from the fiscal warehousing regime to another fiscal warehousing regime, the time and date when the transfer starts, and the address of the fiscal warehouse to which the goods in question are transferred[11];

(5) as 'transferred goods' all eligible goods which are transferred directly from the fiscal warehousing regime to corresponding arrangements in another member state[12], the date and time when the transfer starts, and the address of the place in the other member state to which the goods in question are transferred[13];

(6) as 'transferred goods (by reason of export)' all eligible goods which are directly exported from the fiscal warehousing regime to a place outside the member states[14], the date and time when the movement of the goods which is directly associated with the export starts, and the address of the place outside the member states to which the goods in question are consigned[15];

(7) the nature of any services which are performed on or in relation to eligible goods while those goods are allocated to the relevant fiscal warehousing regime, the date when the services are performed, the particular eligible goods on or in relation to which they are performed, and the name, address and registration number[16], if any, of the supplier of those services[17].

The fiscal warehousing record must include the prescribed documents[18] relating to transfers and specified services[19] and must identify the name and address of any person who at any time removes or causes the removal of any goods from the fiscal warehousing regime as well as that person's registration number if he is registered for value added tax[20]. It must incorporate any modifications to the above features or requirements which the commissioners may require in respect of the relevant fiscal warehousekeeper[21]. A fiscal warehousekeeper may, with the prior agreement of the commissioners, maintain a fiscal warehousing record in which any of those features or requirements are relaxed or dispensed with[22].

The relevant fiscal warehousing record is not required, in respect of any goods, to record events more than six years following (a) the transfer or removal of those goods from the relevant fiscal warehousing regime; or (b) the exit of those goods from the relevant fiscal warehouse in the case of goods which were not allocated to the relevant fiscal warehousing regime[23].

Upon receiving a request to do so from any proper officer, a fiscal warehousekeeper must facilitate and permit that officer to inspect any goods which are stored or deposited in his fiscal warehouse, whether or not those goods are allocated to the relevant fiscal warehousing regime[24].

1   For the meaning of 'fiscal warehousekeeper' see para 133 note 3 ante.
2   Ie in addition to the records referred to in the Value Added Tax Regulations 1995, SI 1995/2518, reg 31 (as amended): see para 219 ante.
3   Ibid reg 145F(1) (reg 145F, Sch 1A added by SI 1996/1250). As to the meaning of 'relevant fiscal warehousekeeper' and related expressions see para 134 note 3 ante.
4   For the meaning of 'proper officer' see para 105 note 9 ante.
5   Value Added Tax Regulations 1995 reg 145F(2) (as added: see note 3 supra).
6   For the meaning of 'eligible goods' see paras 132 note 3, 134 note 1 ante (definition applied by ibid reg 145A(1) (added by SI 1996/1250).
7   Ibid reg 145F(3), Sch 1A para 1(a) (as added: see note 3 supra).
8   Ie other than goods which enter for purposes wholly incidental to such storage: ibid Sch 1A para 1(b) (as added: see note 3 supra).
9   Ibid Sch 1A para 1(b) (as added: see note 3 supra).
10   Ibid Sch 1A para 1(c) (as added: see note 3 supra).
11   Ibid Sch 1A para 1(d) (as added: see note 3 supra). The record must be adjusted to show a removal, and not a transfer, where the certificate of transfer within the United Kingdom referred to in reg 145G(3)(c) (as added) (see para 135 ante) is not received in time from the other fiscal warehousekeeper: Sch 1A para 4(a) (as so added). The record must also evidence any notification made under reg 145H(3)(c) (as added) (see para 136 ante) to the person on whose instructions the goods were allowed to leave the fiscal warehouse: Sch 1A para 4(c) (as so added). For the meaning of 'United Kingdom' see para 4 note 3 ante.
12   Ie under ibid reg 145H(2)(b) (as added): see para 136J ante. For the meaning of 'another member state' see para 4 note 14 ante.
13   Ibid Sch 1A para 1(e) (as added: see note 3 supra). The record must be adjusted to show a removal, and not a transfer, whether the document referred to in reg 145H(4)(b) (as added) (see para 136 ante) is not received in time: Sch 1A para 4(b) (as so added). As to recording any notification under reg 145H(3)(c) (as added) to the person on whose instructions the goods were allowed to leave the fiscal warehouse see Sch 1A para 4(c) (as so added); and note 11 supra.
14   Ie under ibid reg 145H(2)(c) (as added): see para 136 ante. As to the territories included in, or excluded from, the member states for VAT purposes see para 10 ante.
15   Ibid Sch 1A para 1(f) (as added: see note 3 supra). The record must be adjusted to show a removal, and not a transfer, whether the document referred to in reg 145H(4)(c) (as added) (see para 136 ante) is not received in time: Sch 1A para 4(b) (as so added). As to recording any notification under reg 145H(3)(c) (as added) to the person on whose instructions the goods were allowed to leave the fiscal warehouse see Sch 1A para 4(c) (as so added); and note 11 supra.
16   For the meaning of 'registration number' see para 16 note 10 ante.
17   Value Added Tax Regulations 1995 Sch 1A para 2 (as added: see note 3 supra).
18   The record must include (1) the written undertaking from the other fiscal warehousekeeper relating to a transfer made within the United Kingdom referred to in ibid reg 145G(2) (as added) and the certificate from the other fiscal warehousekeeper confirming a transfer so made which is referred to in reg 145G(3)(c) (as added) (see para 135 ante) and must relate them to the relevant transfer; (2) the copy of the certificate relating to a transfer received by the relevant fiscal warehousekeeper from another fiscal warehousing regime [sic] within the United Kingdom referred to in reg 145G(3)(d) (as added) and must relate that copy to the relevant allocation to his relevant fiscal warehousing regime; (3) the document relating to the completion of a transfer to corresponding arrangements in another member state referred to in reg 145H(4)(b) (as added) (see para 136 ante) and must relate that document to the relevant transfer; and (4) the document relating to the completion of an export to a place outside the member states referred to in reg 145H(4)(c) (as added) (see para 136 ante) and must relate that document to the export in question: Sch 1A para 3(a)–(d) (as added: see note 3 supra).
19   Ibid Sch 1A para 3 (as added: see note 3 supra).
20   Ibid Sch 1A para 5(a) (as added: see note 3 supra). The record must also include a copy of the removal document issued by the commissioners under reg 145J(1) (as added) (see para 136 ante) and must relate it to the relevant removal: Sch 1A para 5(b) (as so added).
21   Ibid Sch 1A para 6(a) (as added: see note 3 supra).
22   Ibid Sch 1A para 6(b) (as added: see note 3 supra).

23 Ibid reg 145F(4) (as added: see note 3 supra).
24 Ibid reg 145F(5)(b) (as added: see note 3 supra). As to production and inspection of the fiscal warehousing record see para 224 text and notes 17–20 post.

223. Summary application for furnishing of information. The Commissioners of Customs and Excise may apply in a summary manner[1] to the High Court for the delivery of any accounts, the production of any books or the furnishing of any information, required to be delivered, produced or furnished under the enactments relating to value added tax[2].

1 For the procedure see RSC Ord 77 r 8; and CROWN PROCEEDINGS.
2 See the Crown Proceedings Act 1947 s 14(2)(d) (amended by the Finance Act 1972 s 55(1), (7)). The extent of the obligation to produce accounts where ordered on summary application to the High Court under the Crown Proceedings Act 1947 was considered in *Customs and Excise Comrs v Ingram* [1948] 1 All ER 927, CA (for further related proceedings see [1949] 2 KB 103, [1949] 1 All ER 896, CA). See also CROWN PROCEEDINGS.

224. Furnishing of information and production of documents. Every person who is concerned, in whatever capacity, in the supply[1] of goods or services in the course or furtherance of a business[2] or to whom such a supply is made, every person who is concerned, in whatever capacity, in the acquisition of goods from another member state[3] and every person who is concerned, in whatever capacity, in the importation of goods from a place outside the member states[4] in the course or furtherance of a business must:

(1) furnish to the Commissioners of Customs and Excise, within such time and in such form as they may reasonably require[5], such information relating to the goods[6] or services or to the supply, acquisition or importation as the commissioners may reasonably specify[7]; and

(2) upon demand made by an authorised person[8], produce or cause to be produced for inspection by that person, at the principal place of business of the person upon whom the demand is made or at such other place as the authorised person may reasonably require, and at such time as the authorised person may reasonably require, any documents[9] relating to the goods or services or to the supply, acquisition or importation[10].

The authorised person may take copies of, or make extracts from, any document so produced[11].

Where an authorised person has such power to require the production of any documents from any person, he has the same power to require the production of documents from any other person who appears to him to be in possession of them; but where that other person claims a lien on any document produced by him, the production is without prejudice to the lien[12].

If it appears to him to be necessary to do so, an authorised person may, at a reasonable time and for a reasonable period, remove any document produced to him under these provisions[13]. Where a lien is claimed on a document produced in response to the demand of the authorised person[14], his removal of the document (at a reasonable time and for a reasonable period) is not regarded as breaking the lien[15].

Where any documents removed under these powers are lost or damaged, the commissioners are liable to compensate their owner for any expenses reasonably incurred by him in replacing or repairing the documents[16].

A fiscal warehousekeeper[17], upon receiving a request to do so from any proper officer[18], must produce his fiscal warehousing record[19] to that officer and permit him to inspect and take copies of it or of any part of it, as that officer may require[20].

1   For the meaning of 'supply' see para 21 ante.

2   For the meaning of 'in the course or furtherance of a business' see paras 12 note 5, 17 note 2 ante.

3   As to when goods are acquired from another member state see para 13 ante.

4   As to the territories included in, or excluded from, the member states for VAT purposes see para 10 ante.

5   If a demand for information is made in the proper manner the trader is bound to answer the demand within the time and in the form required, whether or not the answer may tend to incriminate him: *Customs and Excise Comrs v Harz* [1967] 1 AC 760 at 816, [1967] 1 All ER 177 at 181, HL, per Lord Reid (a case relating to purchase tax); cf *Customs and Excise Comrs v Ingram* [1948] 1 All ER 927 at 929, CA, per Lord Goddard CJ (also relating to purchase tax) ('it is quite a commonplace of legislation designed to protect the revenue of the Crown, as it is realised that all the information must generally be within the knowledge of the taxpayer or the subject, to put an onus on him or to oblige him to do certain things which may have the effect of incriminating him'). See also *EMI Records Ltd v Spillane* [1986] 2 All ER 1016 at 1022, [1986] 1 WLR 967 at 974 per Browne Wilkinson V-C (there is no room in the Value Added Tax Act 1994 s 58, Sch 11 para 7(2) (see heads (1)–(2) in the text) for an implied exception for documents which might be self-incriminating). However, the power does appear to give the commissioners the right to require the person in question to give oral answers to questions asked without any prior warning: *Customs and Excise Comrs v Harz* supra at 816–817 and 181–182.

6   As a matter of ordinary English it is not easy to see why 'relating to the goods' should not mean and include information not only as to the character of the goods but also what has happened to them: *Customs and Excise Comrs v Ingram* [1949] 2 KB 103 at 108, [1949] 1 All ER 896 at 900, CA, per Evershed LJ.

7   Value Added Tax Act 1994 Sch 11 para 7(2)(a).

8   For the meaning of 'authorised person' see para 82 note 5 ante.

9   For the meaning of 'document' see para 11 note 8 ante.

10   Value Added Tax Act 1994 Sch 11 para 7(2)(b). For these purposes, 'documents relating to the supply of goods or services, to the acquisition of goods from another member state or to the importation of goods from a place outside the member states' includes any profit and loss account and balance sheet relating to the business in the course of which the goods or services are supplied or the goods are imported or (in the case of an acquisition from another member state) relating to any business or other activities of the person by whom the goods are acquired: Sch 11 para 7(4).

11   Ibid Sch 11 para 7(5).

12   Ibid Sch 11 para 7(3). The authorised person may take copies of, or make extracts from, any document so produced: Sch 11 para 7(5).

13   Ibid Sch 11 para 7(6). On request, the authorised person must provide a receipt for any document so removed: Sch 11 para 7(6). Where a document so removed is reasonably required for the proper conduct of a business, the authorised person must, as soon as practicable, provide a copy of the document, free of charge, to the person by whom it was produced or caused to be produced: Sch 11 para 7(7).

14   Ie produced under ibid Sch 11 para 7(3): see the text to note 12 supra.

15   Ibid Sch 11 para 7(6). However, where documents are held by solicitors under an Anton Piller order, they may only be inspected or copied with the leave of the court: *Customs and Excise Comrs v AE Hamlin & Co (a firm)* [1983] 3 All ER 654, [1984] 1 WLR 509; cf *EMI Records Ltd v Spillane* [1986] 2 All ER 1016 at 1022, [1986] 1 WLR 967 at 974 (a person falling within what is now the Value Added Tax Act 1994 Sch 11 para 7(2) can only be required to produce documents in the hands of his servants or agents if they hold those documents to his sole order). Accordingly, production of documents cannot be demanded under Sch 11 para 7(3) from any person who does not hold those documents to the sole order of a person within the description in Sch 11 para 7(2), with the result that, in the ordinary case of documents seized under an Anton Piller order, the solicitors holding the documents cannot validly be served with a notice to produce under Sch 11 para 7(3). As to Anton Piller orders see *Anton Piller KG v Manufacturing Processes Ltd* [1976] Ch 55, [1976] 1 All ER 779, CA; and INJUNCTIONS vol 24 (Reissue) para 872 et seq.

16   Value Added Tax Act 1994 Sch 11 para 7(8).

17   For the meaning of 'fiscal warehousekeeper' see para 133 note 3 ante.

18   For the meaning of 'proper officer' see para 105 note 9 ante.

19   As to the fiscal warehousing record see para 222 ante.

20   Value Added Tax Regulations 1995, SI 1995/2518, reg 145F(5)(a) (added by SI 1996/1250).

(3) ACCOUNTING FOR VALUE ADDED TAX

(i) In general

225. Provision which may be made by regulations. Regulations made by the Commissioners of Customs and Excise[1] may:

(1) require the keeping of accounts and the making of returns in such form and manner as may be specified in them[2];

(2) require taxable persons[3] supplying goods or services in such cases, or to persons of such descriptions, as may be so specified to provide the persons supplied with invoices[4] (to be known as 'value added tax invoices') containing statements of such particulars as may be so specified of the supply, and of the persons by and to whom the goods or services are supplied and containing such an indication as may be required by the regulations of whether VAT is chargeable on the supply[5] and such particulars of any VAT which is so chargeable as may be so specified[6];

(3) where they require a VAT invoice to be provided in connection with any description of supply, require it to be provided within a prescribed time after the supply is treated as taking place, or at such time before the supply is treated as taking place as may be required by the regulations, and may allow for an invoice to be issued later than required by the regulations where it is issued in accordance with general or special directions given by the commissioners[7];

(4) confer power on the commissioners to allow the requirements of any regulations as to the statements and other matters to be contained in a VAT invoice to be relaxed or dispensed with[8];

(5) require the submission to the commissioners by taxable persons, at such times and intervals, in such cases and in such form and manner as may be specified in the regulations, or determined by the commissioners in accordance with powers conferred by the regulations, of statements containing such particulars of transactions in which the taxable persons are concerned and which involve the movement of goods between member states, and of the persons concerned in those transactions, as may be prescribed[9];

(6) make provision in relation to cases where:

(a) any goods which are subject to a duty of excise or consist in a new means of transport[10] are acquired in the United Kingdom[11] from another member state[12] by any person;

(b) the acquisition of the goods is a taxable acquisition[13] and is not in pursuance of a taxable supply[14]; and

(c) that person is not a taxable person at the time of the acquisition,

for requiring the person who acquires the goods to give to the commissioners such notification of the acquisition, and for requiring any VAT on the acquisition to be paid, at such time and in such form or manner as may be specified in the regulations[15];

(7) provide for a notification required by virtue of head (6) above to contain such particulars relating to the notified acquisition and any VAT chargeable thereon as may be specified in the regulations and to be given, in prescribed cases, by the personal representative, trustee in bankruptcy, interim or permanent trustee, receiver, liquidator or person otherwise acting in a representative capacity in relation to the person who makes that acquisition[16];

   (8) make special provision for such taxable supplies by retailers of any goods, or of any description of goods, or of services, or any description of services, as may be determined by or under the regulations[17];

   (9) make provision whereby, in such cases and subject to such conditions as may be determined by or under the regulations, VAT in respect of a supply may be accounted for and paid by reference to the time when consideration[18] for the supply is received[19];

 (10) make provision whereby, in such cases and subject to such conditions as may be determined by or under the regulations, VAT in respect of any supply by a taxable person of dutiable goods[20] and VAT in respect of an acquisition by any person from another member state of dutiable goods may be accounted for and paid, and any question as to the inclusion of any duty or agricultural levy in the value of the supply or acquisition determined, by reference to the duty point[21] or to such later time as the commissioners may allow[22];

 (11) provide for the time when any invoice described in regulations made for the purposes of the time of supply[23] or time of acquisition[24] is to be treated as having been issued and provide for VAT accounted for and paid by reference to the date of issue of such an invoice to be confined to VAT on so much of the value of the supply or acquisition as is shown on the invoice[25];

 (12) make provision:

     (a) for treating VAT chargeable in one prescribed accounting period as chargeable in another such period[26]; and

     (b) with respect to the making of entries in accounts for the purpose of making adjustments, whether for the correction of errors or otherwise[27]; and

     (c) for the making of financial adjustments in connection with the making of entries in accounts for the purpose mentioned in head (b) above[28]; and

     (d) for a person, for purposes connected with the making of any such entry or financial adjustment, to be required to provide to any prescribed person, or to retain, a document[29] in the prescribed form containing prescribed particulars of the matters to which the entry or adjustment relates[30]; and

     (e) for enabling the commissioners, in such cases as they may think fit, to dispense with or relax a requirement imposed by regulations made by virtue of head (d) above[31];

 (13) make different provision for different circumstances and may provide for different dates as the commencement of prescribed accounting periods applicable to different persons[32].

1 Ie under the Value Added Tax Act 1994 s 58, Sch 11 para 2 (as amended): see the text and notes 2–32 infra.

2 Ibid Sch 11 para 2(1).

3 For the meaning of 'taxable person' see paras 12 note 4, 55 ante.

4 For the meaning of 'invoice' see para 11 note 8 ante.

5 Ie under the Value Added Tax Act 1994 or the law of another member state; Sch 11 para 2(1). For the meaning of references to the law of another member state see para 11 ante; and for the meaning of 'supply' see para 21 ante.

6 Ibid Sch 11 para 2(1).

7 Ibid Sch 11 para 2(2).

8 Ibid Sch 11 para 2(2A) (added by the Finance Act 1996 s 38(1), (2)).

9 Value Added Tax Act 1994 Sch 11 para 2(3).

10 For the meaning of 'new means of transport' see para 13 note 8 ante.

11 For the meaning of 'United Kingdom' see para 4 note 3 ante.

12 For the meaning of 'another member state' see para 4 note 14 ante. As to acquisitions from another member state see para 13 ante.
13 For the meaning of 'taxable acquisition' see para 13 ante.
14 For the meaning of 'taxable supply' see para 12 note 3 ante.
15 Value Added Tax Act 1994 Sch 11 para 2(4). See para 252 post.
16 Ibid Sch 11 para 2(5).
17 Ibid Sch 11 para 2(6). In particular, the regulations may make provision (1) for permitting the value which is to be taken as the value of the supplies in any prescribed accounting period or part of it to be determined, subject to any limitations or restrictions, by such method or one of such methods as may have been described in any notice published by the commissioners in pursuance of the regulations and not withdrawn by a further notice or as may be agreed with the commissioners; and (2) for determining the proportion of the value of the supplies which is to be attributed to any description of supplies; and (3) for adjusting that value and proportion for periods comprising two or more prescribed accounting periods or parts of them: Sch 11 para 2(6)(a)–(c). For the meaning of 'prescribed accounting period' see para 202 note 4 ante.
18 For the meaning of 'consideration' generally see para 86 ante.
19 Value Added Tax Act 1994 Sch 11 para 2(7). Any such regulations may make such modifications of the provisions of the Value Added Tax Act 1994, including in particular, but without prejudice to the generality of this power, the provisions as to the time when, and the circumstances in which, credit for input tax is to be allowed, as appear to the commissioners necessary or expedient: Sch 11 para 2(7). For the meaning of 'input tax' see paras 4, 201 ante.
20 For the meaning of 'dutiable goods' see para 89 note 7 ante (definition applied by ibid Sch 11 para 2(8)).
21 For the meaning of 'duty point' see para 89 note 9 ante (definition applied by ibid Sch 11 para 2(8)).
22 Ibid Sch 11 para 2(8).
23 Ie for the purposes of ibid s 6(8)(b): see para 38 ante.
24 Ie for the purposes of ibid s 12(1)(b): see para 38 ante.
25 Ibid Sch 11 para 2(9).
26 Ibid Sch 11 para 2(10)(a). See para 227 post.
27 Ibid Sch 11 para 2(10)(b).
28 Ibid Sch 11 para 2(10)(c).
29 For the meaning of 'document' see para 11 note 8 ante.
30 Value Added Tax Act 1994 Sch 11 para 2(10)(d) (added by the Finance Act 1996 s 38(1), (3)).
31 Value Added Tax Act 1994 Sch 11 para 2(10)(e) (as added: see note 30 supra).
32 Ibid Sch 11 para 2(11).

226. The value added tax return. The general rule is that a taxable person[1] must, for each prescribed accounting period[2], account for and pay VAT both in respect of supplies[3] made by him, and in respect of the acquisition by him of goods from other member states[4]. Every person who is registered[5], or who was or is required to be registered, must make a return[6] to the Controller, Customs and Excise Value Added Tax Central Unit ('the controller')[7], not later than the last day of the month next following the end of the period to which it relates[8]. The relevant period is a period of a quarter or, in the case of a person who is registered, a period of three months ending on the dates notified either in the certificate of registration[9] issued to him or otherwise[10]. The return must be made on the prescribed form[11] showing the amount of VAT payable by or to him and containing full information in respect of the other matters specified in the form and a declaration, signed by him, that the return is true and complete[12]. The first return must be for the period which includes the effective date[13] upon which the person was or should have been registered and that period begins on that date[14].

The Commissioners of Customs and Excise may allow or direct a person to make returns in respect of periods of one month and to make those returns within one month of the periods to which they relate[15]. Any person to whom the commissioners give such a direction must comply with it[16].

Any person who ceases to be liable to be registered[17], or to be entitled to be registered[18], must, unless another person has been registered with his registration number[19] in substitution for him[20], make a final return to the controller[21]. In the case of a person who was or is registered, that return must be made within one month of the effective date for cancellation of his registration, and in the case of any other person, within one month of the date upon which he ceases to be liable to be registered, and in either case must be in respect of the final period ending on that date and in substitution for the return for the period in which that date occurs[22]. The final return must contain full information in respect of the matters specified in the prescribed form[23] and a declaration, signed by the person making it, that the return is true and complete[24].

1   For the meaning of 'taxable person' see paras 12 note 4, 55 ante.
2   For the meaning of 'prescribed accounting period' see para 202 note 4 ante. Regulations made for the purposes of accounting for VAT, in relation to VAT invoices and for the payment of VAT may make different provision for different circumstances and may provide for different dates as the commencement of prescribed accounting periods applicable to different persons: see the Value Added Tax Act 1994 s 58, Sch 11 para 2(11); and para 225 head (13) ante.
3   For the meaning of 'supply' see para 21 ante.
4   See the Value Added Tax Act 1994 s 25(1); and para 203 ante. As to acquisitions from other member states see para 13 ante; and for the meaning of 'another member state' see para 4 note 14 ante.
5   For the meaning of 'registered' see para 56 note 2 ante.
6   For the meaning of 'return' see para 105 note 14 ante.
7   Where the Commissioners of Customs and Excise consider it necessary, in any particular case, they may allow or direct a person to make returns to a specified address; and any person to whom they give any such direction must comply with it: Value Added Tax Regulations 1995, SI 1995/2518, reg 25(1)(d), (2).
8   Ibid reg 25(1). Where the commissioners consider it necessary in any particular case to vary the date by which any return must be made, they may allow or direct any person to make returns accordingly, and any person to whom they give any such direction must comply with it: Value Added Tax Regulations 1995, SI 1995/2518, reg 25(1)(c), (2).
9   As to registration see para 56 et seq ante.
10   Value Added Tax Regulations 1995 reg 25(1). Where the commissioners consider it necessary in any particular case to vary the length of any period or the date on which any period begins or ends, they may allow or direct any person to make returns accordingly, whether or not the period so varied has ended: reg 25(1)(c). This can be convenient for traders (eg retailers) who wish to draw up their accounts by reference to cycles of weeks, rather than on a monthly basis. In *Bjellica (t/a Eddy's Domestic Appliances) v Customs and Excise Comrs* [1995] STC 329, CA, it was held that the commissioners could validly require a trader to make a return for a period of 12 Directive 77/388 (OJ L145, 13.6.77, p 1) art 22(4) (which permits member states to fix different intervals at which a trader must make a VAT return, provided that such intervals do not exceed a year).
11   For the prescribed form see ibid reg 25(1), Sch 1, Form 4. A copy of Form 4 is automatically sent to the registered person for each prescribed accounting period.
12   Ibid reg 25(1). Where a person is so required to make a return to the controller, the amounts to be entered on that return must be determined as follows: (1) in the box opposite the legend 'VAT due in this period on sales and other outputs' must be entered the aggregate of all the entries in the VAT payable portion of that part of the VAT account which relates to the prescribed accounting period for which the return is made, except that the total of the output tax due in that period on acquisitions from other member states must be entered instead in the box opposite the legend 'VAT due in this period on acquisitions from other EC member states'; (2) in the box opposite the legend 'VAT reclaimed in this period on purchases and other inputs' (including acquisitions from other member states' must be entered the aggregate of all the entries in the VAT allowable portion of that part of the VAT account which relates to the prescribed accounting period for which the return is made; and (3) where any correction has been made and a return calculated in accordance with the regulations, then any such return is regarded as correcting any earlier returns to which regs 34, 35 (see para 238 post) apply: reg 39(1)–(4). As to the VAT account see para 237 post; for the meaning of 'output tax' see paras 4, 201 ante; and as to goods acquired in another member state see para 13 ante.
     Any retailer who uses a retail scheme must notify the commissioners of the scheme which he is using in writing on every VAT return which he makes: reg 70. As to retail schemes see para 185 ante. Returns must be made as long as a person remains registered for VAT, notwithstanding that he has ceased trading: *Keogh v Gordon* [1979] 1 All ER 89, [1979] 1 All ER 89, [1978] STC 340. In *Aikman v White* [1986] STC 1 and *Hayman v Griffiths, Walker v Hanby* [1988] QB 97, [1987] STC 649 it was held that a return was 'furnished' (in the words of the regulation then applicable) to the controller when it was posted in the prepaid envelope provided by the commissioners for the purpose, since the commissioners thereby adopted the Post Office agent to receive the return. However, these decisions substantially turned on the wording of the statutory form, Form 4 as it then stood; and that form was

amended as a result of the two decisions. The decisions were not followed in *Customs and Excise Comrs v W Timms & Son (Builders) Ltd* [1992] STC 374, where MacPherson J held that, in the context of a claim for repayment supplement on a repayment of tax allegedly delayed by the commissioners (see para 266 post), a return was not 'received' until it was actually received, since only then could it be processed by Customs and Excise.

13 Ie determined in accordance with the Value Added Tax Act 1994 s 3(2), Schs 1–3 (as amended): see para 56 et seq ante.
14 Value Added Tax Regulations 1995 reg 25(1)(b).
15 Ibid reg 25(1)(a). Persons (commonly known as 'repayment traders') whose input tax regularly exceeds their output tax (eg because their supplies are zero-rated) will often request monthly accounting since they thereby recover their excess input tax more rapidly.
16 Ibid reg 25(2).
17 See para 71 et seq ante.
18 Ie under either one or both of the Value Added Tax Act 1994 Sch 1 paras 9, 10: see para 58 ante.
19 For the meaning of 'registration number' see para 16 note 10 ante.
20 Ie under the Value Added Tax Regulations 1995 reg 6: see para 74 ante.
21 Ibid reg 25(4).
22 Ibid reg 25(4).
23 For the prescribed form see ibid reg 25(4), Sch 1, Form 5.
24 Ibid reg 25(4).

227. Payment of value added tax; in general. Save as the Commissioners of Customs and Excise may otherwise allow or direct[1], any person making a return[2] must, in respect of the period to which the return relates, account in that return for:

(1)   all his output tax[3];

(2)   all value added tax for which he is accountable by virtue of the regulations relating to importations, exportations and removals[4];

(3)   all VAT which he is required to pay as a result of the removal of goods from a fiscal warehousing regime[5]; and

(4)   all VAT which he is required to pay as a result of a supply of specified services, performed on or in relation to goods at a time when they are subject to a warehousing regime[6], being zero-rated[7] where:

   (a)   that warehousing regime is one where goods are stored without payment of any duty of excise;

   (b)   those goods are subject to a duty of excise;

   (c)   those goods have been the subject to an acquisition from another member state[8] and the material time for that acquisition was while those goods were subject to that warehousing regime; and

   (d)   there was no supply[9] of those goods while they were subject to that warehousing regime[10].

The amount to be entered on that return must be determined in accordance with the relevant regulations[11].

   Any person required to make a return must pay to the Controller, Customs and Excise VAT Central Unit, not later than the last day on which he is required to make that return, such amount of VAT as is payable by him in respect of the period to which the return relates[12]. The commissioners may, however, allow VAT chargeable in any period to be treated as being chargeable in such later period as they may specify[13].

1   Value Added Tax Regulations 1995, SI 1995/2518, reg 40(3) (substituted by SI 1996/1250).
2   For the meaning of 'return' see para 105 note 14 ante.
3   For the meaning of 'output tax' see paras 4, 201 ante.
4   Ie by virtue of the Value Added Tax Regulations 1995 Pt XVI (regs 117–145): see paras 11, 104 et seq, 178 et seq ante.

5   For the meaning of 'fiscal warehousing regime' see para 134 note 3 ante.
6   For the meaning of 'subject to a warehousing regime' see para 130 note 6 ante.
7   For the meaning of 'zero-rated' see para 158 ante.
8   As to the acquisition of goods from another member state see para 13 ante; and for the meaning of 'another member state' see para 4 note 14 ante.
9   For the meaning of 'supply' see para 21 ante.
10 Value Added Tax Regulations 1995 reg 40(1)(a)–(d) (substituted by SI 1996/1250).
11 Ibid reg 40(1) (as substituted: see note 10 supra).
12 Ibid reg 40(2) (substituted by SI 1996/1250).
13 Ibid reg 25(5). As to the power to make such provision see the Value Added Tax Act 1994 s 58, Sch 11 para 2(10)(a); and para 225 head (12)(a) ante.

(ii) The Cash Accounting Scheme

228. The cash accounting scheme. The effect of the value added tax rules is that a trader is obliged to account and pay to the Commissioners of Customs and Excise VAT which he may not have received from his customers, since VAT is charged on supplies made during the prescribed accounting period[1] and the time of supply of goods and services is, as a general rule[2], when the goods are removed or made available and when the services are performed[3]. In order to relieve the small trader from the burden of accounting for VAT which he has not received, the cash accounting scheme was introduced[4]. A taxable person[5] may, subject to such conditions as are described in a notice published by the commissioners[6], account for VAT in accordance with a scheme ('the scheme') by which the operative dates for VAT accounting purposes are:

(1)   for output tax[7], the day on which payment or other consideration[8] is received or the date of any cheque, if later; and

(2)   for input tax[9], the date on which payment is made or other consideration is given, or the date of any cheque, if later[10].

A taxable person is eligible to begin to operate the scheme if:

(a)   he has reasonable grounds for believing that the value of taxable supplies[11] made, or to be made, by him in the period of one year then beginning will not exceed £350,000[12];

(b)   he has made all returns[13] which he is required to make and has satisfied certain other administrative requirements[14];

(c)   he has not in the period of one year preceding that time been convicted of any offence in relation to VAT[15], made any payment to compound proceedings in respect of VAT[16], been assessed to a penalty[17] or ceased to be entitled[18] to continue to operate the scheme[19].

The scheme does not apply to lease purchase agreements, hire purchase agreements, conditional sale agreements, credit sale agreements or supplies where a VAT invoice[20] is issued and full payment of the amount shown on the invoice is not due for a period in excess of 12 months from the date of the issue of the invoice[21].

A person may remain in the scheme unless at the end of one of his prescribed accounting periods the value of taxable supplies made by him in a period of one year then ending has exceeded £437,500 and the value of the taxable supplies made by him in the period of one year then beginning has exceeded £350,000, in which case he must cease to operate the scheme with effect from the end of the second mentioned period of one year[22]. He may withdraw from the scheme at the end of one of his prescribed accounting periods where he derives no benefit from remaining in it or he is unable, by reason of his accounting system, to comply with its requirements[23]. A person who ceases to operate the scheme, either of his own volition or because the value of taxable supplies made by him exceeds the level so provided for, may continue to use the scheme for supplies made and received while he operated the scheme but he may not otherwise account for and pay VAT thereunder[24]. He may be required to account for and pay, on a return made for the prescribed accounting period in which he ceased to operate the scheme, all VAT which he would have been required to pay to the commissioners during the time when he operated the scheme, if he had not then been operating it, less all VAT accounted for and paid to the commissioners in accordance with the scheme, subject to any adjustment for credit for input tax, notwithstanding that he has already withdrawn from the scheme of his own volition[25].

Where a person operating the scheme becomes insolvent and ceases to trade, other than for the purpose of disposing of stocks and assets, he must within two months account for VAT on supplies made and received in the previous six months which has not otherwise been accounted for, subject to any adjustment for credit for input tax[26]. Where a person operating the scheme ceases business[27] or ceases to be registered[28], or dies or becomes bankrupt or incapacitated, he or his representative must, within two months or such longer period as the commissioners may allow, make a return accounting for, and pay, VAT on supplies made and received during the previous six months which has not otherwise been accounted for, subject to any adjustment for credit for input tax; and VAT in respect of any payment or other consideration received for earlier supplies must be accounted for and paid when received[29]. Where a business or part of a business carried on by a person operating the scheme is transferred as a going concern, special arrangements apply[30].

A person is not entitled to continue to operate the scheme where:

(i)   he has, while operating it, been convicted of an offence in connection with VAT or has made a payment to compound such proceedings[31];

(ii) he has, while operating it, been assessed to a penalty[32] or to a surcharge[33];

(iii) he has failed to leave the scheme[34];

(iv) he has claimed input tax as though he had not been operating the scheme; or

(v)   the commissioners consider it necessary for the protection of the revenue that he is not to be so entitled[35].

A person who so ceases to be entitled to continue to operate the scheme must account for and pay, on a return made for the prescribed accounting period in which he ceased to be so entitled, all VAT which he would have been required to pay to the commissioners during the time when he operated the scheme, had he not then been operating it, less all VAT accounted for and paid to the commissioners in accordance with the scheme, and subject to any adjustment for credit for input tax[36].

Except in the specified circumstances[37], VAT must be accounted for and paid to the commissioners by the due date prescribed for the accounting period in which payment or other consideration for the supply is received[38]. Input tax may be credited either in the prescribed accounting period in which payment or consideration for a supply is given, or in such later period as may be agreed with the commissioners[39]. A person operating the scheme must obtain and keep for a period of six years, or such longer period as the commissioners may allow, a receipted and dated VAT invoice from any taxable person to whom he has made a payment in money[40] in respect of a taxable supply and in such circumstances a taxable person must on request provide such a receipted and dated VAT invoice[41].

1   For the meaning of 'prescribed accounting period' see para 202 note 4 ante.
2   As to the rules determining the time of supply for VAT purposes see paras 29–38 ante.
3   See para 29 ante.
4   As to the cash accounting scheme see the text and notes 5–41 infra.

5 For the meaning of 'taxable person' see paras 12 note 4, 55 ante.
6 For these purposes, 'notice' means any notice published pursuant to the Value Added Tax Regulations 1995, SI 1995/2518, Pt VIII (regs 56–65): reg 56. The relevant notice is Customs and Excise Notice 731 (1 May 1994) which imposes these conditions: a trader who is eligible to use the scheme and wishes to do so must (1) use it for the whole of his business; (2) stay in it for at least two years, unless the value of his taxable supplies goes over the limits for the scheme or the trader shows the commissioners that he is not gaining any benefit from being in the scheme; or that his accounting system cannot cope with its requirements (this corresponds with reg 60(3): see the text to note 23 infra); (3) meet the record-keeping requirements set out in Customs and Excise Notice 731 para 8; and (4) start to use it at the beginning of a tax period: see para 5. Without prejudice to the right of a person to withdraw from the scheme, the commissioners may vary its terms by publishing a fresh notice: Value Added Tax Regulations 1995 reg 59.
7 For the meaning of 'output tax' see paras 4, 201 ante.
8 For the meaning of 'consideration' generally see para 86 ante.
9 For the meaning of 'input tax' see paras 4, 201 ante.
10 Value Added Tax Regulations 1995 reg 57, implementing the Value Added Tax Act 1994 s 58, Sch 11 para 2(7): see para 225 ante.
11 For the meaning of 'taxable supply' see para 12 note 3 ante.
12 Value Added Tax Regulations 1995 reg 58(1)(a).
13 For the meaning of 'return' see para 105 note 14 ante.
14 See the Value Added Tax Regulations 1995 reg 58(1)(b). The other requirements are that he has (1) paid to the commissioners all such sums shown as due on those returns and on any assessments made either under the Value Added Tax Act 1994 s 76 (as amended) (see para 251 post) or Sch 11 (as amended) (see para 225 ante); or (2) agreed an arrangement with the commissioners for any outstanding amount of such sums as are referred to in head (1) supra to be paid in instalments over a specified period: Value Added Tax Regulations 1995 reg 58(1)(b)(i), (ii).
15 As to offences see para 267 et seq post.
16 Ie under the Customs and Excise Management Act 1979 s 152: see CUSTOMS AND EXCISE.
17 Ie under the Value Added Tax Act 1994 s 60: see para 272 post.
18 Ie by virtue of the Value Added Tax Regulations 1995 reg 64(1): see heads (i)–(v) in the text.
19 Ibid reg 58(1)(c). A person who becomes eligible to begin to operate the scheme may do so at the beginning of his next prescribed accounting period: reg 60(1).
20 For the meaning of 'VAT invoice' see para 29 note 8 ante.
21 Value Added Tax Regulations 1995 reg 58(2).
22 Ibid reg 60(2). This is subject to reg 64: see heads (i)–(v) in the text.
23 Ibid reg 60(3).
24 Ibid reg 61.
25 Ibid reg 64(3). These requirements are seldom imposed in practice.
26 Ibid reg 62. As to credit for input tax see 203 et seq ante.
27 For the meaning of 'business' see para 17 ante.
28 For the meaning of 'registered' see para 56 note 2 ante.
29 Value Added Tax Regulations 1995 reg 63(1).
30 See ibid reg 63(2), (3). Where a business or part of a business carried on by a person operating the scheme is transferred as a going concern and reg 6(1) (see para 74 ante) does not apply, the transferor must within two months make a return accounting for, and pay, VAT on supplies made and received during the previous six months which has not otherwise been accounted for, subject to any adjustment for credit for input tax, and VAT in respect of any payment or other consideration received for earlier supplies must be accounted for and paid when received: reg 63(2). Where a business carried on by a person operating the scheme is transferred in circumstances where reg 6(2) applies, the transferee must continue to account for and pay VAT as if he were a person operating the scheme on supplies made and received by the transferor prior to the date of transfer: reg 6(3).
31 See note 16 supra.
32 Ie under the Value Added Tax Act 1994 s 60 (see para 272 post), s 63 (see para 275 post), s 67 (as amended) (see para 279 post) or s 69 (see para 282 post): Value Added Tax Regulations 1995 reg 64(1)(b).
33 Ie under the Value Added Tax Act 1994 s 59 (as amended): see para 283 post.
34 Ie as required by the Value Added Tax Regulations 1995 reg 60(2): see the text to note 22 supra.
35 Ibid reg 64(1).
36 Ibid reg 64(2).
37 Ie the circumstances set out in ibid regs 61–63: see the text and notes 24, 27–30 supra.
38 Ibid reg 65(1).
39 Ibid reg 65(2).
40 For these purposes, 'money' means banknotes or coins: ibid reg 56.
41 Ibid reg 65(3). A person operating the scheme must keep for a period of six years, or such lesser period as the commissioners may allow, a copy of any receipt which he gives under reg 65(3): reg 65(4).

(iii) Payments on Account

229. Liability to make payments on account of value added tax. If the Treasury considers it desirable to do so in the interests of the national economy, it may make an order providing that a taxable person[1] of a description specified in the order is to be under a duty to pay, on account of any VAT he may become liable to pay in respect of a prescribed accounting period[2], amounts determined in accordance with the order, and to do so at such times as are so determined[3]. The Commissioners of Customs and Excise may give directions, to persons who are or may become liable by virtue of any such order to make payments on account of VAT, about the manner in which they are to make such payments; and where such a direction has been given to any person and has not subsequently been withdrawn, any duty of that person by virtue of such an order to make such a payment has effect as if it included a requirement for the payment to be made in the manner directed[4]. Where an order is so made, the commissioners may also make regulations containing such supplementary, incidental or consequential provisions as appear to them to be necessary or expedient[5].

A taxable person is liable to make payments on account[6] if:

(1) the total amount of tax which he was liable to pay in respect of the prescribed accounting periods, the ends of which fell within the period of one year[7] ending on the last day of his last prescribed accounting period ending before the previous 1 December, exceeded £2 million[8]; or

(2) he does not fall within head (1) above but the total amount of tax which he was liable to pay in respect of the prescribed accounting periods, the ends of which fell within any one period of one year[9] ending on the last day of a prescribed accounting period of his ending after 30 November of the previous year, exceeded £2 million[10].

The payments on account must be made in respect of any VAT the taxable person may become liable to pay in respect of each prescribed accounting period exceeding one month beginning on or after 1 April each year, but in the case of a taxable person falling within head (2) above there is no duty to pay such amounts in respect of a prescribed accounting period other than one beginning after the basic period[11]. Where the taxable person has a prescribed accounting period exceeding one month which begins on or after 2 March each year and ends on or before 30 June each year, he is under a like duty to make payments on account in respect of that prescribed accounting period[12]. If, however, the total amount of tax which a taxable person who is under a duty to make payments on account was liable to pay in respect of the prescribed accounting periods the ends of which fell within any one period of one year ending after the end of the basic period was less than £1,600,000, then, with effect from the date of the written approval by the commissioners of a written application by the taxable person to that effect, he ceases to be under a duty to make payments on account[13].

1   For the meaning of 'taxable person' see paras 12 note 4, 55 ante.
2   For the meaning of 'prescribed accounting period' see para 202 note 4 ante.
3   Value Added Tax Act 1994 s 28(1), (2). The power to demand payments on account arises from EC Council Directive 77/388 (OJ L145, 13.6.77, p 1) art 22(5) which enables member states to demand interim payments. For a case where national provisions supposedly implementing art 22(5) were held to be invalid see Case C-10/92 *Balocchi v Ministero delle Finanze dello Stato* [1993] STI 1348, ECJ.

    In exercise of the power so conferred, the Treasury has made the Value Added Tax (Payments on Account) (Amendment) Order 1995, SI 1995/291; and Value Added Tax (Payments on Account) (Amendment) Order 1996, SI 1996/1196; both amending the Value Added Tax (Payments on Account) Order 1993, SI 1993/2001, which has effect as if so made by virtue of the Interpretation Act 1978 s 17(2)(b).

See the text and notes 6–13 infra; and para 230 et seq post. As to the making of orders generally see para 8 ante.

4   Value Added Tax Act 1994 s 28(2A) (added by the Finance Act 1996 s 34).
5   Value Added Tax Act 1994 s 28(3). A provision of an order or regulations under s 28 (as amended) may be made in such way as the Treasury or, as the case may be, the commissioners, may think fit, whether by amending provisions of, or made under, the enactments relating to VAT or otherwise: s 28(4). Such an order or such regulations may make different provision for different circumstances: s 28(5). As to the making of regulations generally see para 8 ante. Where the commissioners, in exercise of their power under s 28(2A) (as added: see note 4 supra), have directed the manner in which payments on account are to be made, a person who is liable to make such payments must also pay any amount of VAT payable in respect of a return for any prescribed accounting period in the like manner: Value Added Tax Regulations 1995, SI 1995/2518, reg 40A (added by SI 1996/1198). For the meaning of 'return' see para 105 note 14 ante.
6   'Payments on account' means amounts determined in accordance with the Value Added Tax (Payments on Account) Order 1993 (as amended) at times so determined: art 4(1). As to the calculation of the payments and the time for payment see para 230 et seq post.
7   Where in any year ending 30 November a prescribed accounting period of the taxable person did not begin on the first day, or did not end on the last day, of a month, the period of one year is to be regarded as having comprised those prescribed accounting periods which related to the tax periods ending within the year ending 30 November of that year to which references are shown in the certificate of registration issued to him: ibid art 5(2) (substituted by SI 1995/291). As to the meaning of 'tax year' cf para 209 note 5 ante; and as to registration see para 56 et seq ante.
8   Ibid art 5(1) (substituted by SI 1995/291). This provision is subject to art 16 (as amended): see para 232 post.
9   Where, in the period of the year referred to in head (2) in the text, a prescribed accounting period of the taxable person did not begin on the first day or did not end on the last day of a month, that period of one year is to be regarded for these purposes as having comprised those prescribed accounting periods which related to the tax periods ending within that period of one year to which references are shown in the certificate of registration issued to him: ibid art 6(2).
10   Ibid art 6(1) (amended by SI 1995/291). This provision is subject to art 16 (as amended): see para 232 post.
11   Ibid art 4(1) (amended by SI 1995/291). 'The basic period' means, in relation to a taxable person falling within art 5 (as substituted) or art 6 (as amended), the period of one year in which there ended the prescribed accounting periods in respect of which his liability to pay a total amount of tax exceeding £2m caused him to become such a taxable person: art 2(1).
12   Ibid art 4(2) (substituted by SI 1995/291).
13   Ibid art 7.

230. Time for payment. A payment on account[1] must be made to the Controller, Customs and Excise Value Added Tax Central Unit in respect of each prescribed accounting period[2] not later than the last day of the month next following the end of the first complete month included in it and the last day of the month next following the end of the second complete month included in it[3]. Where, however, a prescribed accounting period does not begin on the first day or does not end on the last day of a month, the first payment on account must be made not later than the last day of the month next following the end of the first complete month included in it and the second payment on account must be made not later than the last day of the month next following the end of the second complete month included in it[4]. This rule is subject to exceptions where a prescribed accounting period:

   (1)   does not comprise more complete months than one, in which case the first payment on account must be made not later than the last day of that month and the second payment on account must be made not later than the end of the prescribed accounting period[5];

   (2)   comprises an incomplete month followed by two complete months, in which case the first payment must be made not later than the end of the first complete month and the second not later than the end of the second complete month[6]; or

   (3)   comprises an incomplete month followed by two complete months and an incomplete month, in which case the first payment must be made not later than

the end of the first complete month and the second not later than the end of the second complete month[7].

A payment on account and a payment in respect of a return[8] for a prescribed accounting period made by a person liable to make payments on account[9] are not treated as having been made by the last day on which they are required to be made[10] unless they are made in such a manner as secures that all transactions that need to be completed can be completed before the whole of the amount becomes available to the Commissioners of Customs and Excise[11]. Where a taxable person[12] fails to make a payment on account by the last day by which he is required to make it, that payment on account is recoverable as if it were VAT due from him[13].

1   For the meaning of 'payment on account' see para 229 note 6 ante.
2   For the meaning of 'prescribed accounting period' see para 202 note 4 ante.
3   Value Added Tax (Payments on Account) Order 1993, SI 1993/2001, art 8. Article 8 thus requires two payments to be made in respect of each prescribed accounting period. Article 8 is subject to art 9 (as amended) (see heads (1)–(3) in the text): art 8 (amended by SI 1996/1196).
4   Ibid art 9(a), (b) (amended by SI 1996/1196).
5   Ibid art 9(i).
6   Ibid art 9(ii).
7   Ibid art 9(iii).
8   For the meaning of 'return' see para 105 note 14 ante.
9   Ie a return to which the Value Added Tax Regulations 1995, SI 1995/2518, reg 40A (as added) applies: see para 229 ante.
10   For these purposes and the purposes of ibid reg 47 (see the text and notes 12–13 infra), references to a payment being made by any day include references to its being made on that day: reg 46A(2) (added by SI 1996/1198).
11   Ibid reg 46A(1) (added by SI 1996/1198).
12   For the meaning of 'taxable person' see paras 12 note 4, 55 ante.
13   Value Added Tax Regulations 1995 reg 47.

231. Calculation of payments on account. The amount of each payment on account[1] to be made by a taxable person[2] equals one twenty-fourth[3] of the total amount of value added tax, excluding the tax on goods imported from countries other than member states, which he was liable to pay in respect of the prescribed accounting periods[4] the ends of which fell either within a specified period ('the reference period')[5] or the basic period[6], depending on the head of liability[7] within which he falls[8]. If, however, the total amount of such tax which he was liable to pay in respect of the prescribed accounting periods the ends of which fell within any one period of one year ending after the end of either his reference period or the basic period, as applicable, was less than 80 per cent of the total amount of tax relevant in his case[9], then the total amount of tax by reference to which his payments on account fall to be calculated is reduced accordingly[10] with effect from the date of the written approval by the Commissioners of Customs and Excise of a written application by him to that effect[11]. That amount is also to be so reduced where such a period of one year has not ended but the commissioners are satisfied that the total amount of tax, excluding the tax on goods imported from countries other than member states, which the taxable person will be liable to pay in respect of the prescribed accounting periods the ends of which fall within that year will be less than 80 per cent of the total amount of tax relevant in his case[12].

If the total amount of tax, excluding the tax on goods imported from countries other than member states, which the taxable person was liable to pay in respect of the prescribed accounting periods the ends of which fell within any one period of one year ending after the end of either his reference period or the basic period, as applicable, exceeded by 20 per cent or more the total amount of tax by reference to which his payments on account are currently calculated, then, with effect from the end of that period of one year, the total amount of tax by reference to which his payments on account fall to be calculated is to be increased accordingly[13] and the amount of each payment on account beginning with the first payment on account which falls to be made after the end of that period of one year equals one twenty-fourth of the increased amount[14]. Where the payments on account payable by a taxable person have been so increased and:

(1)   the total amount of tax, excluding the tax on goods imported from countries other than member states, which he was liable to pay in respect of the prescribed accounting periods the ends of which fell within any one period of one year ending after that increase has taken effect was less than 80 per cent of the total amount of tax by reference to which his payments on account are currently calculated; or

(2)   where such a period of one year has not ended, the commissioners are satisfied that the total amount of tax, excluding the tax on goods imported from countries other than member states, which he will be liable to pay in respect of the prescribed accounting periods the ends of which fall within that year will be less than 80 per cent of the total amount of tax by reference to which his payments on account are currently calculated,

then, with effect from the date of the written approval by the commissioners of a written application by the taxable person to that effect, the total amount of tax by reference to which his payments on account fall to be calculated is reduced accordingly and the amount of each payment on account beginning with the first payment on account which falls to be made after the date of that approval equals one twenty-fourth of the reduced amount[15].

Instead of paying the amount calculated in accordance with these rules[16], a taxable person who is under a duty to make payment on account may elect to pay an amount equal to his liability to VAT, excluding the tax on goods imported from countries other than member states, for the preceding month[17]. A person making such an election must notify the commissioners in writing of the election and of the date, being a date not less than 30 days after the date of the notification, on which it is to take effect[18]. The election continues to have effect until a later date notified by the taxable person in writing to the commissioners, which may not be earlier than the first anniversary of the date on which the election took effect[19].

Where the commissioners are satisfied that an amount paid by a taxable person who has made such an election is less than the amount required to be paid[20], they may notify him in writing that his election is to cease to have effect from a date specified in the notification[21].

The commissioners must give to a taxable person who is under a duty to make payments on account notification in writing of the amounts that he is under a duty to pay, how those amounts have been calculated and the times for payment of those amounts[22]. If in respect of a prescribed accounting period the total amount of the payments on account made by the taxable person exceeds the amount of VAT due from him in respect of that period, the amount of excess must be paid to him by the commissioners if, and to the extent that, it is not required[23] to be set against any sum which he is liable to pay to them[24].

1   For the meaning of 'payment on account' see para 229 note 6 ante.
2   For the meaning of 'taxable person' see paras 12 note 4, 55 ante.
3   This figure has effect from 1 June 1996: see the Value Added Tax (Payments on Account) (Amendment) Order 1996, SI 1996/1196, art 1.
4   For the meaning of 'prescribed accounting period' see para 202 note 4 ante.
5   Ie in the case of a taxable person who falls within the Value Added Tax (Payments on Account) Order 1993, SI 1993/2001, art 5 (as substituted) (see para 229 head (1) ante); and subject to art 12A (as added)

(see the text and notes 16–21 infra), arts 13–15 (as amended): art 11(1) (amended by SI 1996/1196). The reference period is: (1) 1 October to 30 September in the basic period where he has a prescribed accounting period beginning in April in any year in which he is under a duty to make payments on account; (2) 1 November to 31 October in the basic period where he has a prescribed accounting period beginning in May in any such year; and (3) 1 December to 30 November in the basic period where he has a prescribed accounting period beginning in June in any such year: art 2(1); art 11(1)(a)–(c) (substituted by SI 1995/291). Where in the period of the year mentioned in heads (1)–(3) supra a prescribed accounting period of the taxable person did not begin on the first day or did not end on the last day of a month, the reference period is regarded for these purposes as having comprised those prescribed accounting periods which related to the tax periods ending within the period of the year mentioned in head (1), (2) or (3) supra as appropriate to which references are shown in the certificate of registration issued to him: art 11(2). For the meaning of 'basic period' see para 229 note 11 ante; and as to registration see para 56 et seq ante.

6   Ie in the case of a taxable person falling within ibid art 6 (as amended) (see para 229 head (2) ante): art 12.
7   Ie depending on whether the taxable person falls within ibid art 5 (as substituted), in which case his liability is calculated in respect of prescribed accounting periods the ends of which fell within the reference period, or within art 6 (as amended), in which case it is calculated in respect of prescribed accounting periods the ends of which fell within the basic period: see art 11 (as amended); arts 12–15 (as amended); and the text and notes 1–6 supra, 8–15 infra.
8   Ibid arts 11(1), 12 (amended by SI 1996/1196).
9   Ie the total amount relevant under ibid art 11 (as amended) or the total amount referred to in art 12 (as amended): art 13(a)(i), (ii).
10 Any reference in ibid arts 13–15 (as amended) to the total amount of tax by reference to which a taxable person's payments on account fall to be calculated being 'reduced accordingly' or 'increased accordingly' is in each case a reference to a reduction or increase of the same proportion as the difference between the total amount of tax by reference to which his payments on account are currently calculated and the total amount of tax, excluding the tax on goods imported from countries other than member states, which he was, or which the commissioners are satisfied that he will be, liable to pay in respect of the prescribed accounting periods the ends of which fall within the year referred to in the relevant provisions of the article in question: art 2(2).
11 Ibid art 13(a). The amount of each payment on account beginning with the first payment on account which falls to be made after the date of the commissioners' written approval equals one twenty-fourth of the reduced amount: art 13 (amended by SI 1996/1196).
12 See ibid art 13(b); and see also note 11 supra.
13 See note 10 supra.
14 Ibid art 14 (amended by SI 1996/1196).
15 Ibid art 15 (amended by SI 1996/1196).
16 Ie calculated in accordance with ibid arts 11, 12 (as amended): see the text and notes 1–8 supra.
17 Ibid art 12A(1) (added by SI 1996/1196). A person may not make such an election within 12 months of the date on which any previous election made by him ceased to have effect by virtue of art 12A(4) (as so added) (see the text to note 21 infra): art 12A(5) (as so added).
18 Ibid art 12A(2) (added by SI 1996/1196).
19 Ibid art 12A(3) (added by SI 1996/1196).
20 Ie by virtue of ibid art 12A(1) (as added: see note 17 supra).
21 Ibid art 12A(4) (added by SI 1996/1196).
22 Value Added Tax Regulations 1995, SI 1995/2518, reg 45. As to the time for payment see para 230 ante. Regulation 45 does not apply in a case to which reg 48 (see para 232 post) applies: reg 45.
23 Ie by the Value Added Tax Act 1994 s 81 (as amended): see para 254 post.
24 Value Added Tax Regulations 1995 reg 46. Regulation 46 does not apply in a case to which reg 48 (see para 232 post) applies: reg 46.

232. Special provisions relating to bodies corporate. Where the registration[1] of a body corporate is, and was throughout the relevant prescribed accounting periods[2], in the names of divisions[3] and those divisions are the same divisions, that body corporate is not under a duty to make payments on account[4] by virtue of falling within either of the heads of liability[5]. It is, however, under a duty to make payments on account by reference to the business[6] of any division if the total amount of tax which it was liable to pay in respect of the prescribed accounting periods of that division the ends of which fell within the period of one year[7] ending on the last day of (1) that division's last prescribed accounting period ending before 1 December of the previous year; or (2) a prescribed accounting period of that division ending after 30 November of the previous year, and which was referable to the business of that division, exceeded £2 million[8]. Where a relevant division[9] has a prescribed accounting period exceeding one month which begins on or after 2 March each year and ends on or before 30 June each year, the body corporate is under a like duty to make payments on account in respect of that prescribed accounting period[10].

Where payments on account so fall to be made, they must be calculated and made separately in the case of each relevant division as if it were a taxable person and must be remitted to the Controller, Customs and Excise Value Added Tax Central Unit through that division[11]. The Commissioners of Customs and Excise must notify a relevant division in writing of the amounts of the payments on account that the body corporate is under a duty to make by reference to the business of that division, how those amounts have been calculated and the times for payment of those amounts[12]. If, in respect of a prescribed accounting period, the total amount of the payments on account made by a body corporate by reference to the business of a particular relevant division exceeds the amount of VAT due from the body corporate in respect of that period by reference to that business, the amount of the excess must be paid to the body corporate by the commissioners if, and to the extent that, it is not required[13] to be set against any sum which the body corporate is liable to pay to them[14].

The provisions relating to payments on account apply to any bodies corporate which are treated as members of a group[15] as if those bodies were one taxable person; and where there is a duty to make a payment on account it is the responsibility of the representative member[16], except that in default of payment by the representative member it is the joint and several responsibility of each member of the group[17].

1   As to registration see para 56 et seq ante.
2   Ie the prescribed accounting periods mentioned in the Value Added Tax (Payments on Account) Order 1993, SI 1993/2001, art 5(1) (as substituted) or art 6(1) (as amended): see para 229 ante. For the meaning of 'prescribed accounting period' see para 202 note 4 ante.
3   Ie under the Value Added Tax Act 1994 s 46(1): see para 67 ante.
4   For the meaning of 'payment on account' see para 229 note 6 ante.
5   Value Added Tax (Payments on Account) Order 1993 art 16(1). The heads of liability referred to are arts 5, 6 (as substituted and amended respectively): see para 229 ante.
6   For the meaning of 'business' see para 17 ante.
7   The Value Added Tax (Payments on Account) Order 1993 arts 5(2) (as substituted), 6(2) (period of one year to be regarded as having comprised certain prescribed accounting periods: see para 229 ante) apply for these purposes as if for the references therein to the taxable person there were substituted references to a relevant division: art 16(3). For the meaning of 'taxable person' see paras 12 note 4, 55 ante; and for the meaning of 'relevant division' see note 9 infra.
8   Ibid art 16(1) (amended by SI 1995/291).
9   For these purposes, 'relevant division' means a division by reference to the business of which a body corporate is under a duty to make payments on account by virtue of ibid art 16(1) (as amended): art 16(6). See also the Value Added Tax Regulations 1995, SI 1995/2518, reg 44.
10 Value Added Tax (Payments on Account) Order 1993 art 16(2) (substituted by SI 1995/291).
11 Ibid art 16(4). In relation to a body corporate to which art 16 (as amended) applies, references in art 7 (see para 229 ante), arts 13–15 (see para 231 ante) to (1) the total amount of tax which a taxable person was or will be liable to pay are to be construed as references to the total amount of such tax referable to the business of a relevant division; and (2) an application by the taxable person are to be construed as references to an application by the division in respect of which the application is made: art 16(5).
12 Value Added Tax Regulations 1995 reg 48(1).
13 Ie by the Value Added Tax Act 1994 s 81 (as amended): see para 254 post. Section 81 (as amended) does not require any amount which is due to be so paid by the commissioners to a body corporate by reference to the business of a particular relevant division to be set against any sum due from the body corporate otherwise than by reference to that business or to the liabilities of the body corporate arising in connection with that division: Value Added Tax Regulations 1995 reg 48(3).
14 Ibid reg 48(2).
15 Ie under the Value Added Tax Act 1994 s 43 (as amended): see paras 66, 191 ante.

16 For the meaning of 'the representative member' see para 66 ante.
17 Value Added Tax (Payments on Account) Order 1993 art 17 (amended by SI 1996/1196).

(iv) The Annual Accounting Scheme

233. The scheme. The Commissioners of Customs and Excise may authorise a taxable person[1] to pay and account for value added tax by reference to any transitional accounting period[2] and any subsequent current accounting year[3] at such times, and for such amounts, as may be determined in accordance with the annual accounting scheme[4] ('the scheme')[5]. A taxable person authorised to pay and account for VAT in accordance with the scheme must, where the value of taxable supplies[6] made by him in the period of 12 months ending on the day before the first day of his current accounting year does not exceed £100,000 (or, where he was paying quarterly sums under the scheme in that period, £110,000), pay to the commissioners by credit transfer[7] the quarterly sum[8] or the agreed quarterly sum[9], no later than the last working day[10] of each of the fourth, seventh and tenth months of his current accounting year[11]. Where, however, that sum does not exceed £400, no quarterly payment need be made[12]. In all other cases, a taxable person so authorised must pay to the commissioners by credit transfer the monthly sum[13] or the agreed monthly sum[14] in nine equal monthly instalments commencing on the last day working day of the fourth month of his current accounting year[15]. In all cases, a taxable person so authorised must make a return[16] in respect of that year by the last working day of the second month following the end of that current accounting year, together with any outstanding payment due to the commissioners in respect of his liability for VAT declared on that return[17]. Similar provisions apply in relation to transitional accounting periods of four months or more[18]. Where the transitional accounting period is less than four months, the authorised person must make a return in respect of that period by the last working day of the first month following the end of the transitional accounting period, together with any outstanding payment due to the commissioners in respect of his liability for VAT declared on that return[19].

1 For the meaning of 'taxable person' see paras 12 note 4, 55 ante.
2 'Transitional accounting period' means the period commencing on the first day of a person's prescribed accounting period in which the commissioners authorise him to use the annual accounting scheme and ending on the day immediately preceding the first day of that person's first current accounting year, and is a prescribed accounting period within the meaning of the Value Added Tax Act 1994 s 25(1) (see para 202 ante): Value Added Tax Regulations 1995, SI 1995/2518, reg 49 (substituted by SI 1996/542). For the meaning of 'prescribed accounting period' see para 105 note 16 ante; and for the meaning of 'current accounting year' see note 3 infra.
3 'Current accounting year' means the period of 12 months commencing on a date indicated by the commissioners in their notification of authorisation of a person, or, while a person remains authorised, the most recent anniversary of it, and is a prescribed accounting period within the meaning of the Value Added Tax Act 1994 s 25(1): Value Added Tax Regulations 1995 reg 49 (as substituted: see note 2 supra).
4 Ie the annual accounting scheme established by ibid regs 50, 51 (as substituted): reg 49 (as substituted: see note 2 supra).
5 Ibid reg 50(1) (substituted by SI 1996/542).
6 For the meaning of 'taxable supply' see para 12 note 3 ante.
7 'Credit transfer' means the transfer of funds from one bank account to another under a mandate given by the payer to the bank making the transfer: Value Added Tax Regulations 1995 reg 49 (as substituted: see note 2 supra).
8 'The quarterly sum' means a sum equal to 20% of the total amount of VAT which a taxable person was liable to pay to the commissioners in the 12 months immediately preceding the first day of his current accounting year: ibid reg 49 (as substituted: see note 2 supra).
9 'The agreed quarterly sum' means a sum agreed with the commissioners, not being less than 20% of a taxable person's estimated liability for VAT in his current accounting year: ibid reg 49 (as substituted: see note 2 supra).

10 'Working day' means any day of the week other than Saturday, Sunday, a bank holiday or a public holiday: ibid reg 49 (as substituted: see note 2 supra).

11 Ibid reg 50(2)(a)(i), (3) (substituted by SI 1996/542).

12 Ibid reg 50(2)(a)(i) (as substituted: see note 11 ante).

13 'The monthly sum' means a sum equal to 10% of the total amount of VAT which a taxable person was liable to pay to the commissioners in the 12 months immediately preceding the first day of his current accounting year: ibid reg 49 (as substituted: see note 2 supra).

14 'The agreed monthly sum' means a sum agreed with the commissioners, not being less than 10% of a taxable person's estimated liability for VAT, in his current accounting year: ibid reg 49 (as substituted: see note 2 supra).

15 Ibid reg 50(2)(a)(ii) (as substituted: see note 11 supra).

16 For the meaning of 'return' see para 105 note 14 ante.

17 Value Added Tax Regulations 1995 reg 50(2)(b) (as substituted: see note 11 supra).

18 In such a case: (1) if the value of the authorised person's taxable supplies during the period of 12 months immediately preceding the first day of his transitional accounting period did not exceed £100,000, he must pay to the commissioners by credit transfer on each relevant quarterly date the quarterly sum, save that where that sum does not exceed £400 no quarterly payment need be made; (2) in all other cases, the authorised person must pay to the commissioners by credit transfer on each relevant monthly date the monthly sum; and (3) the authorised person must make a return in respect of the transitional accounting period by the last working day of the second month following the end of that period, together with any outstanding payment due to the commissioners in respect of his liability for VAT declared on that return ibid reg 51(a) (substituted by SI 1996/542). For these purposes, 'the quarterly sum' means a sum equal to 20% of the total amount of VAT which a taxable person was liable to pay to the commissioners in the 12 months immediately preceding the first day of his transitional accounting period; 'the monthly sum' means a sum equal to 10% of that amount; 'relevant quarterly date' means the last working day of the fourth and, where a period has such months, the seventh and the tenth months of a transitional accounting period; and 'relevant monthly date' means the last working day of the fourth and each successive month of a transitional accounting period: reg 49 (as substituted: see note 2 supra).

19 Ibid reg 51(b) (as substituted: see note 18 supra).

234. Admission to the scheme. A taxable person[1] is eligible to apply for authorisation under the annual accounting scheme[2] if:

(1) he has been registered[3] for at least one year at the date of his application for authorisation;

(2) he has reasonable grounds for believing that the value of taxable supplies[4] made, or to be made, by him in the period of 12 months beginning on the date of his application for authorisation will not exceed £300,000;

(3) his registration is not in the name of a group[5] or of a division[6]; and

(4) he has not in the 12 months preceding the date of his application for authorisation ceased to operate the scheme[7].

The commissioners may refuse to authorise a person where they consider it necessary to do so for the protection of the revenue[8].

An authorised person[9] must continue to account for VAT in accordance with the scheme unless he ceases to be authorised[10].

1 For the meaning of 'taxable person' see paras 12 note 4, 55 ante.

2 As to the annual accounting scheme see para 233 ante.

3 For the meaning of 'registered' see para 56 note 2 ante.

4 For the meaning of 'taxable supply' see para 12 note 3 ante.

5 Ie under the Value Added Tax Act 1994 s 43(1) (as amended): see paras 66, 191 ante.

6 Ie under ibid s 46(1): see para 67 ante.

7 Value Added Tax Regulations 1995, SI 1995/2518, reg 52(1) (substituted by SI 1996/542).

8 Ibid reg 52(2) (as substituted: see note 7 supra).

9 'Authorised person' means a person who has been authorised by the commissioners in accordance with ibid reg 50(1) (as substituted) (see para 233 ante): reg 49 (as so substituted).

10 Ibid reg 53(1) (substituted by SI 1996/542). As to cessation of authorisation see para 235 post.

235. Cessation and termination of authorisation. An authorised person[1] ceases to be authorised when:

(1)   at the end of any transitional accounting period[2] or current accounting year[3] the value of taxable supplies[4] made by him in that period or, as the case may be, that year, has exceeded £375,000[5]; or

(2)   his authorisation is terminated[6]; or

(3)   he becomes insolvent and ceases to trade, other than for the purpose of disposing of stocks and assets, or ceases business[7] or ceases to be registered[8] or dies, becomes bankrupt or incapacitated[9]; or

(4)   he ceases to operate the scheme of his own volition[10].

The Commissioners of Customs and Excise may terminate an authorisation in any case where:

(a)   a false statement has been made by or on behalf of an authorised person in relation to his application for authorisation[11]; or

(b)   an authorised person fails to make a return[12] by the due date[13]; or

(c)   such a person fails to make any prescribed[14] payment[15]; or

(d)   they receive a notification[16] that the authorised person has reason to believe that the value of taxable supplies made by him during a transitional accounting period or current accounting year will exceed £375,000[17]; or

(e)   at any time during an authorised person's transitional accounting period or current accounting year they have reason to believe that the value of taxable supplies he will make during the period or year will exceed that sum[18]; or

(f)   it is necessary to do so for the protection of the revenue[19]; or

(g)   an authorised person has not, in relation to a return made by him prior to authorisation, paid to the commissioners all such sums shown as due on it[20]; or

(h)   an authorised person has not, in relation to any assessment[21], paid to the commissioners all such sums shown as due on it[22].

Where an authorised person ceases to be authorised, he, or, as the case may be, his representative, must make a return together with any outstanding payment due to the commissioners in respect of his liability for value added tax[23] and account for and pay VAT from the day following the day on which he ceases to be authorised, as provided for otherwise than under the annual accounting scheme[24].

1   For the meaning of 'authorised person' see para 234 note 9 ante.
2   For the meaning of 'transitional accounting period' see para 233 note 2 ante.
3   For the meaning of 'current accounting year' see para 233 note 3 ante.
4   For the meaning of 'taxable supply' see para 12 note 3 ante.
5   Value Added Tax Regulations 1995, SI 1995/2518, reg 53(2)(a) (substituted by SI 1996/542). The authorised person then ceases to be authorised from the day following the last day of the relevant transitional accounting period or the current accounting year: see reg 55(1)(a) (as so substituted).
6   Ibid reg 53(2)(b) (as substituted: see note 5 supra). The authorised person then ceases to be authorised from the day on which the Commissioners of Customs and Excise terminated his authorisation in accordance with reg 54 (as so substituted): see reg 55(1)(b) (as so substituted).
7   For the meaning of 'business' see para 17 ante.
8   For the meaning of 'registered' see para 56 note 2 ante.
9   Value Added Tax Regulations 1995 reg 53(2)(c) (as substituted: see note 5 supra). The authorised person then ceases to be authorised from the day on which any of the events mentioned in head (3) in the text occurs: see reg 55(1)(c) (as so substituted).
10 Ibid reg 53(2)(d) (as substituted: see note 5 supra). The authorised person then ceases to be authorised from the date on which the commissioners are notified in writing of his decision to cease using the scheme: see reg 55(1)(d) (as so substituted).
11 Ibid reg 54(1)(a) (substituted by SI 1996/542).
12 Ie in accordance with ibid reg 50(2)(b) (as substituted) or reg 51(a)(iii) or (b) (as substituted): see para 233 ante. For the meaning of 'return' see para 105 note 14 ante.
13 Ibid reg 54(1)(b) (as substituted: see note 11 supra).

14 Ie any payment prescribed in ibid reg 50 (as substituted) or reg 51 (as substituted): see para 233 ante.
15 Ibid reg 54(1)(c) (as substituted: see note 11 supra).
16 Ie in accordance with ibid reg 54(2) (substituted by SI 1996/542): reg 54(1)(d) (as so substituted). An authorised person must notify the commissioners in writing where he has reason to believe as is mentioned in head (d) in the text: reg 54(2) (as so substituted).
17 Ibid reg 54(1)(d) (as substituted: see note 11 supra).
18 Ibid reg 54(1)(e) (as substituted: see note 11 supra).
19 Ibid reg 54(1)(f) (as substituted: see note 11 supra).
20 Ibid reg 54(1)(g) (as substituted: see note 11 supra).
21 Ie any assessment made under either the Value Added Tax Act 1994 s 73 (see paras 247, 252 post) or s 76 (as amended) (see para 251 post): Value Added Tax Regulations 1995 reg 54(1)(h) (as substituted: see note 11 supra).
22 Ibid reg 54(1)(h) (as substituted: see note 11 supra).
23 If his authorisation ceases before the end of his transitional accounting period or current accounting year, he must make a return within two months of the date specified in ibid reg 55(1)(b), (c) or (d) (as substituted) (see notes 6, 9–10 supra), together with any outstanding payment due to the commissioners in respect of his liability for VAT for that part of the period or year arising before the date he ceased to be authorised: reg 55(2)(a) (substituted by SI 1996/542). If his authorisation ceases at the end of his transitional accounting period or current accounting year, he must make a return together with any outstanding payment due to the commissioners in respect of his liability for VAT in accordance with reg 51 (as substituted) or reg 50 (as substituted) (see para 233 ante): reg 55(2)(b) (as so substituted).
24 Ibid reg 55(2) (as substituted: see note 23 supra).

(v) Claims for Input Tax

236. In general. A person claiming deduction of input tax[1] must do so on the return[2] made by him for the prescribed accounting period[3] in which the value added tax became chargeable[4]. At the time of so claiming the deduction, a person must hold the required document or invoice[5] or such other documentary evidence of the charge to VAT as the Commissioners of Customs and Excise may direct[6].

Where the commissioners are satisfied that a person is not able to claim the exact amount of input tax to be deducted by him in any period, he may estimate a part of his input tax for that period, provided that the estimated amount is adjusted and exactly accounted for as VAT deductible in the next prescribed accounting period or, if the exact amount is still not known and the commissioners are satisfied that it could not with due diligence be ascertained, in the next but one prescribed accounting period[7]. If a trader fails to claim deduction of input tax in his return for the correct prescribed accounting period, he will have made an error in accounting for VAT and in his return; he must correct the error in such manner and within such time as the commissioners may require[8].

1 Ie under the Value Added Tax Act 1994 s 25(2): see para 202 ante.
2 For the meaning of 'return' see para 105 note 14 ante.
3 For the meaning of 'prescribed accounting period' see para 105 note 16 ante.
4 Value Added Tax Regulations 1995, SI 1995/2518, reg 29(1). Regulation 29(1) applies save as the Commissioners of Customs and Excise otherwise allow or direct, either generally or specially: reg 29(1).
5 If the claim is in respect of: (1) a supply from another taxable person, he must hold the document which is required to be provided under the Value Added Tax Regulations 1995 reg 13 (see para 240 post); (2) a supply under the Value Added Tax Act 1994 s 8(1) (see para 27 ante), he must hold the relative invoice from the supplier; (3) an importation of goods, he must hold a document authenticated or issued by the proper officer, showing the claimant as importer, consignee or owner and showing the amount of VAT charged on the goods; (4) goods which have been removed from a warehouse, he must hold a document authenticated or issued by the proper officer showing the claimant's particulars and the amount of VAT charged on the goods; (5) an acquisition by him from another member state of any goods other than a new means of transport, he must hold a document required by the authority in that other member state to be issued showing his registration number including the prefix 'GB', the registration number of the supplier including the alphabetical code of the member state in which the supplier is registered, the

consideration for the supply exclusive of VAT, the date of issue of the document and description sufficient to identify the goods supplied; or (6) an acquisition by him from another member state of a new means of transport, he must hold a document required by the authority in that other member state to be issued showing his registration number including the prefix 'GB', the registration number of the supplier including the alphabetical code of the member state in which the supplier is registered, the consideration for the supply exclusive of VAT, the date of issue of the document and description sufficient to identify the acquisition as a new means of transport as specified in s 95 (as amended) (see para 13 note 8 ante): Value Added Tax Regulations 1995 reg 29(2). For the meaning of 'supply' see para 21 ante; for the meaning of 'taxable person' see paras 12 note 4, 55 ante; for the meaning of 'document' and 'invoice' see para 11 note 8 ante; for the meaning of 'proper officer' see para 105 note 9 ante; for the meaning of 'new means of transport' see para 13 note 8 ante; and for the meaning of 'registration number' and 'alphabetical code' see para 16 note 10 ante.

6   Ibid reg 29(2); and see *Kohanzad v Customs and Excise Comrs* [1994] STC 967; *Vaughan v Customs and Excise Comrs* (1996) VAT Decision 14050, [1996] STI 1022.
7   Ibid reg 29(3).
8   See ibid reg 35. Where the total amount of the error does not exceed £2,000, the error may be corrected under reg 34: see para 238 post.

(vi) Value Added Tax Accounts and Invoices

237. Duty to keep accounts. Every taxable person[1] must keep and maintain an account to be known as the value added tax account[2], divided into separate parts relating to the taxable person's prescribed accounting periods[3]. Each such part must be further divided into two portions to be known as 'the VAT payable portion' and 'the VAT allowable portion'[4].

The VAT payable portion for each prescribed accounting period comprises:

(1)   a total of the output tax[5] due from the taxable person for that period;
(2)   a total of the output tax due on acquisitions from other member states[6] by the taxable person for that period;
(3)   every correction or adjustment to the VAT payable portion which is required or allowed[7]; and
(4)   every adjustment to the amount of VAT payable by the taxable person for that period which is required or allowed by or under any relevant[8] regulations[9].

The VAT allowable portion for each prescribed accounting period comprises:

(a)   a total of the input tax[10] allowable to the taxable person for that period[11];
(b)   a total of the input tax allowable in respect of acquisitions from other member states by the taxable person for that period[12];
(c)   every correction or adjustment to the VAT allowable portion which is required or allowed[13]; and
(d)   every adjustment to the amount of input tax allowable to the taxable person for that period which is required or allowed by or under any relevant regulations[14].

1   For the meaning of 'taxable person' see paras 12 note 4, 55 ante.
2   Value Added Tax Regulations 1995, SI 1995/2518, reg 32(1).
3   Ibid reg 32(2). For the meaning of 'prescribed accounting period' see para 105 note 16 ante.
4 . Ibid reg 32(2).
5   For the meaning of 'output tax' see paras 4, 201 ante.
6   As to acquisitions from other member states see para 13 ante.
7   Ie by the Value Added Tax Regulations 1995 regs 34 or 35 (see para 238 post) or reg 38 (see para 239 post): reg 32(3)(c).
8   Ie by any regulations made under the Value Added Tax Act 1994: Value Added Tax Regulations 1995 reg 32(3)(d).
9   Ibid reg 32(3).
10   For the meaning of 'input tax' see paras 4, 201 ante.
11   Ie by virtue of the Value Added Tax Act 1994 s 26: see para 203 ante.

12 See note 11 supra.
13 Ie by the Value Added Tax Regulations 1995 regs 34, 35 or 38: reg 32(4)(c).
14 Ibid reg 32(4).

238. Correction of errors. Where a taxable person[1] has made a return[2], or returns, to the Controller, Customs and Excise Value Added Tax Central Unit, which overstated or understated his liability to VAT or his entitlement to a payment in respect of a credit for input tax[3], and in relation to all such overstatements or understatements discovered by that person during a prescribed accounting period[4] the difference between under-declarations of liability[5] and over-declarations of liability[6] does not exceed £2,000, the taxable person may correct his VAT account[7] in accordance with these provisions[8]. In the VAT payable portion[9], where the amount of any overstatements of output tax is greater than the amount of any understatements of output tax, a negative entry must be made for the amount of the excess, or, where the amount of any such understatements is greater than the amount of any such overstatements, a positive entry must be made for the amount of the excess[10]. In the VAT allowable portion[11], where the amount of any overstatements of credit for input tax is greater than the amount of any understatements of credit for input tax, a negative entry must be made for the amount of the excess, or, where the amount of any such understatements is greater than the amount of any such overstatements, a positive entry must be made for the amount of the excess[12]. Every entry so required must be made in that part of the VAT account which relates to the prescribed accounting period in which the overstatements or understatements in any earlier returns were discovered[13]. The entry must make reference to the returns to which it applies and to any documentation relating to the overstatements or understatements[14].

Where a taxable person has made an error in accounting for VAT, or in any return made by him, then unless he corrects it in accordance with the procedure described above, he must correct it in such manner and within such time as the Commissioners of Customs and Excise may require[15].

1 For the meaning of 'taxable person' see paras 12 note 4, 55 ante.
2 For the meaning of 'return' see para 105 note 14 ante.
3 Ie a payment under the Value Added Tax Act 1994 s 25(3): see para 202 ante. For the meaning of 'input tax' see paras 4, 201 ante.
4 For the meaning of 'prescribed accounting period' see para 105 note 16 ante.
5 'Under-declarations of liability' means the aggregate of (1) the amount (if any) by which credit for input tax was overstated in any return; and (2) the amount (if any) by which output tax was understated in any return: Value Added Tax Regulations 1995, SI 1995/2518, reg 34(2)(a). For the meaning of 'output tax' see paras 4, 201 ante.
6 'Over-declarations of liability' means the aggregate of (1) the amount (if any) by which credit for input tax was understated in any return; and (2) the amount (if any) by which output tax was overstated in any return: ibid reg 34(2)(b).
7 As to the VAT account see para 237 ante.
8 Value Added Tax Regulations 1995 regs 34(1), (3). Where the conditions as to the amount of the difference do not apply, the VAT account may not be corrected by virtue of reg 34: reg 34(7).
9 See para 237 heads (1)–(4) ante.
10 Value Added Tax Regulations 1995 reg 34(4).
11 See para 237 heads (a)–(d) ante.
12 Value Added Tax Regulations 1995 reg 34(5).
13 Ibid reg 34(6)(a).
14 Ibid reg 34(6)(b), (c).
15 Ibid reg 35. See also note 8 supra. The commissioners have given guidance as to what they require in Customs and Excise Notice 700 *The VAT Guide* (March 1996) para 8.10 and Customs and Excise Leaflet 700/45/93 *How to Correct Errors you Find on your VAT Returns* (the trader must notify his local VAT office of the error, either by making a 'voluntary disclosure' by letter, or on Form VAT 652). A 'voluntary disclosure' must be made not only of under-declarations of liability but also for erroneous over-declarations

of liability: *Customs and Excise Comrs v Fine Art Developments plc* [1989] STC 85 at 90, HL, per Lord Keith. As to recovery of overpaid VAT see para 264 post. As to the meaning of 'error' see *Trustees of the Victoria and Albert Museum v Customs and Excise Comrs* [1996] STC 1016.

239. Adjustments in the course of business. Where there is an increase or a decrease in consideration[1] for a supply[2] which includes an amount of value added tax, and the increase or decrease occurs after the end of the prescribed accounting period[3] in which the original supply took place, the taxable person must adjust his VAT account in accordance with the following provisions[4]. The maker of the supply must make a positive entry[5] for the relevant amount of VAT in the VAT payable portion of his VAT account[6], in the case of an increase in consideration, and a negative entry[7] in the case of a decrease in consideration[8]. The recipient of the supply, if he is a taxable person, must make a positive entry for the relevant amount of VAT in the VAT allowable portion of his VAT account, in the case of an increase in consideration, and a negative entry in the case of a decrease in consideration[9]. Every such entry must be made in that part of the VAT account which relates to the prescribed accounting period in which the increase or decrease is given effect in the business[10] accounts of the taxable person[11].

1   For these purposes, 'increase in consideration' means an increase in the consideration due on a supply made by a taxable person which is evidenced by a credit or debit note or any other document having the same effect; and 'decrease in consideration' is to be interpreted accordingly: Value Added Tax Regulations 1995, SI 1995/2518, reg 24. For the meaning of 'consideration' see para 86 ante; for the meaning of 'taxable person' see paras 12 note 4, 55 ante; and for the meaning of 'document' see para 11 note 8 ante.
2   For the meaning of 'supply' see para 21 ante.
3   For the meaning of 'prescribed accounting period' see para 105 note 16 ante.
4   Value Added Tax Regulations 1995 reg 38(1), (2).
5   For the meaning of 'positive entry' see para 15 note 23 ante.
6   As to the VAT account, and the VAT payable and VAT allowable portions thereof, see para 237 ante.
7   'Negative entry' means an amount entered into the VAT account as a negative amount: Value Added Tax Regulations 1995 reg 24.
8   Ibid reg 38(3).
9   Ibid reg 38(4).
10 For the meaning of 'business' see para 17 ante.
11 Value Added Tax Regulations 1995 reg 38(5). Any such entry required to be made in the VAT account of an insolvent person must, however, be made in that part of the VAT account which relates to the prescribed accounting period in which the supply was made or received: reg 38(6). For these purposes, 'insolvent person' means (1) an individual who has been adjudged bankrupt; (2) a company in relation to which (a) a voluntary arrangement under the Insolvency Act 1986 Pt I (ss 1–7) (see COMPANIES) has been approved; (b) an administration order has been made; (c) an administrative receiver has been appointed; (d) a resolution for voluntary winding up has been passed; or (e) an order for its winding up has been made by the court at a time when it had not already gone into liquidation by passing a resolution for voluntary winding up: Value Added Tax Regulations 1995 reg 24.
    None of the circumstances to which reg 38 applies is to be regarded as giving rise to any application of regs 34, 35 (correction of errors: see para 238 ante): reg 38(7).

240. Obligation to provide a value added tax invoice. Where a registered person[1] (1) makes a taxable supply[2] in the United Kingdom[3] to a taxable person[4]; or (2) makes a supply[5] of goods or services other than an exempt supply[6] to a person in another member state[7]; or (3) receives a payment on account in respect of a supply he has made or intends to make from a person in another member state, he must provide such persons as are mentioned above with a VAT invoice[8], unless, in the case of that supply, he is entitled to issue, and issues, a VAT invoice pursuant to the provisions[9] relating to certain supplies of services performed on goods while they are subject to a warehousing or fiscal warehousing regime[10]. The invoice must be provided within 30 days of the time when the supply is treated[11] as taking place, or within such longer period as the Commissioners of Customs and Excise may allow in general or special directions[12].

Since a VAT invoice is nothing more than a document[13] which contains the prescribed particulars[14], it is possible for a consignment or delivery note or similar document which is issued by the supplier before the time of supply and which contains the prescribed particulars to constitute a VAT invoice. The result is that a tax point[15] may inadvertently be created by the issue of such a document. However, in the case of goods sent or taken on approval or sale or return or similar terms[16] and in the case where, within a specified time, a person making a supply issues a VAT invoice and the supply is then treated as taking place at the time the invoice is issued[17], any consignment or delivery note or similar document, or any copy of it, issued by the supplier before the time of supply is not to be treated as a VAT invoice provided it is indorsed: 'This is not a VAT invoice'[18].

Where goods forming part of the assets of the business[19] of a taxable person are, under a power exercisable by another person, sold by the other in or towards satisfaction of a debt owed by the taxable person and are deemed to have been supplied by the taxable person in the course or furtherance of his business[20], the particulars of the VAT chargeable on such a supply of goods must be provided by the person selling them[21] on a document containing the prescribed particulars[22]. Where such a document is issued to the buyer it is treated[23] as a VAT invoice provided by the person by whom the goods are deemed[24] to be supplied[25].

Where a registered person[26] provides a document to himself which purports to be a VAT invoice in respect of a supply of goods or services to him by another taxable person registered in the United Kingdom, that document may, with the commissioners' approval, be treated as the VAT invoice required[27] to be provided by the supplier[28]. This procedure is known as 'self-billing'; and is often used where the recipient of the supply is in a better position than the supplier to issue the required invoices[29]. Similarly, where the person who makes a supply to which certain provisions relating to the construction industry[30] apply gives an authenticated receipt[31] containing the prescribed particulars, that document is treated as the VAT invoice required to be provided[32] on condition that no VAT invoice[33] is issued[34]. Where, however, a taxable person ('the recipient') provides a document to himself which purports to be an invoice in respect of a taxable supply of goods or services to him by another taxable person, and that document understates the VAT chargeable on the supply, the commissioners may, by notice served on the recipient and on the supplier, elect that the amount of VAT understated by the document is to be regarded for all purposes as VAT due from the recipient and not from the supplier[35].

A registered person who is a retailer is not required to provide a VAT invoice except at the request of a customer who is a taxable person in respect of any supply to him[36]. In the event that the retailer is requested to provide a VAT invoice to such a customer, that invoice need contain only limited particulars[37] if (but only if) the consideration[38] for the supply does not exceed £100[39].

The above provisions do not apply to certain specified supplies[40] made in the United Kingdom[41].

1   For the meaning of 'registered person' see para 105 note 7 ante.
2   For the meaning of 'taxable supply' see para 12 note 3 ante.
3   For the meaning of 'United Kingdom' see para 4 note 3 ante.
4   For the meaning of 'taxable person' see paras 12 note 4, 55 ante.
5   For the meaning of 'supply' see para 21 ante.
6   For the meaning of 'exempt supply' see para 141 ante.
7   For the meaning of 'another member state' see para 4 note 14 ante.
8   For the meaning of 'VAT invoice' see para 29 note 8 ante.

9   Ie pursuant to the Value Added Tax Act 1994 s 18C(1)(e) (as added) (see para 140 ante) and the Value Added Tax Regulations 1995, SI 1995/2518, reg 145D(1) (as added) (see para 140 ante): reg 13(1) (amended by SI 1996/1250).

10 Ibid reg 13(1) (as amended: see note 9 supra). For the meaning of 'subject to a warehousing regime' see para 130 note 6 ante; and for the meaning of 'subject to a fiscal warehousing regime' see para 134 note 3 ante.

11 Ie under the Value Added Tax Act 1994 s 6 (as amended): see para 29 et seq ante.

12 Value Added Tax Regulations 1995 reg 13(5). The 30-day requirement also applies to documents treated as VAT invoices by virtue of regs 13(2)–(4) (see the text and notes 17–32 infra): see reg 13(5). See also Customs and Excise Notice 700 *The VAT Guide* (March 1996) para 6.1(c).

13 For the meaning of 'document' see para 11 note 8 ante. For the purposes of any provision contained in or having effect under the Value Added Tax Act 1994 which relates to VAT invoices, a person is to be treated as issuing, or as providing another person with, a VAT invoice if the requisite particulars are recorded in a computer and transmitted by electronic means and without the delivery of any document: s 58, Sch 11 para 3(1). No provision relating to VAT invoices is, however, to be treated as complied with by the production by means of a computer of any material other than a document in writing, by delivering any such material so produced or by making any such transmission as is mentioned in Sch 11 para 3(1) unless the person producing or delivering the material or making the transmission (and, in the case of delivered material or a transmission, the person receiving it) (1) has given the commissioners at least one month's notice in writing that he proposes to produce or deliver such material or make such transmissions (or, as the case may be, to receive such material or transmissions); and (2) he complies with such requirements as may be specified in regulations or as the commissioners may from time to time impose in his case: Sch 11 para 3(2). Without prejudice to the generality of the powers conferred by Sch 11 para 2(9) (see para 225 ante), regulations made by virtue thereof may provide for the provisions of Sch 11 para 3(1), (2) to apply, subject to such exceptions and adaptations as may be prescribed, in relation to any invoice which is described in regulations made for the purposes of s 6(8)(b) (see para 38 ante) or s 12(1)(b) (see para 38 ante) as they apply in relation to VAT invoices: Sch 11 para 3(3).

14 For the prescribed particulars see para 241 post.

15 For the meaning of 'tax point' see para 29 note 3 ante.

16 Ie where a supply takes place as described in the Value Added Tax Act 1994 s 6(2)(c): see para 29 ante.

17 Ie where a supply takes place as described in ibid s 6(5): see para 29 ante.

18 Value Added Tax Regulations 1995 reg 14(3).

19 For the meaning of 'business' see para 17 ante.

20 Ie where goods are supplied as described in the Value Added Tax Act 1994 s 5(1), Sch 4 para 7: see para 24 ante.

21 On a sale by auction, the particulars are to be provided by the auctioneer: Value Added Tax Regulations 1995 reg 13(2).

22 Ibid reg 13(2). The prescribed particulars are those required in the case of a VAT invoice by reg 14(1): see para 241 post. In addition, the auctioneer (in the case of a sale by auction) or, where the sale is otherwise than by auction, the person selling the goods, must, whether or not registered under the Value Added Tax Act 1994, within 21 days of the sale: (1) furnish to the Controller, Customs and Excise Value Added Tax Central Unit, a statement showing (a) his name and address and, if registered, his registration number; (b) the name, address and registration number of the person whose goods were sold; (c) the date of the sale; (d) the description and quantity of goods sold at each rate of VAT; and (e) the amount for which they were sold and the amount of VAT charged at each rate; (2) pay the amount of VAT due; and (3) send to the person whose goods were sold a copy of the statement referred to in head (1) supra: Value Added Tax Regulations 1995 reg 27(a)–(c). Correspondingly, both the auctioneer (or other person selling the goods) and the person whose goods were sold must exclude the VAT chargeable on the supply of those goods from any return made under the Value Added Tax Regulations 1995: reg 27(c). For the meaning of 'registration number' see para 16 note 10 ante; and for the meaning of 'return' see para 105 note 14 ante.

23 Ie for the purposes of ibid reg 13(1)(a): see head (1) in the text.

24 Ie in accordance with the Value Added Tax Act 1994 Sch 4 para 7: see para 24 ante.

25 Value Added Tax Regulations 1995 reg 13(2).

26 For the meaning of 'registered person' see para 105 note 7 ante.

27 Ie under the Value Added Tax Regulations 1995 reg 13(1)(a): see head (1) in the text.

28 Ibid reg 13(3).

29 Eg, where bills are to be paid against architects' certificates. The self-billing system may only be used with the commissioners' approval; and for this purpose, the commissioners will require the recipient to enter into a contract with them, imposing, inter alia, conditions that the supplier agrees: (1) to the recipient operating the self-billing system; and (2) not to issue VAT invoices himself. However, if the supplier

does issue a VAT invoice before a self-billed invoice is raised, this is the VAT invoice required for the purposes of reg 13: *UDL Construction plc (in administrative receivership and compulsory liquidation) v Customs and Excise Comrs* (1995) VAT Decision 13714, [1995] STI 2034 (where the tribunal chairman stated that the self-billing procedure was a gross violation of the integrity of the VAT system which 'should be strictly controlled and policed'). If a person operating a self-billing system pays VAT to a supplier who has been deregistered, he may not recover the VAT on the self-billed invoice as input tax, notwithstanding that the commissioners have failed to notify him that the supplier is no longer registered for VAT: *Credit Ancillary Services Ltd v Customs and Excise Comrs* [1986] VATTR 204; *Shani Fashion Industries Ltd v Customs and Excise Comrs* (1993) VAT Decision 9789, [1993] STI 385.

30 Ie the Value Added Tax Regulations 1995 reg 93: see para 33 ante.

31 Such a receipt may be used to found the recipient's claim for input tax: see ibid reg 29(2)(a); and para 236 ante.

32 See note 27 supra.

33 Ie or similar document which was intended to be or could be construed as being a VAT invoice for the supply to which the receipt relates: Value Added Tax Regulations 1995 reg 13(4).

34 Ibid reg 13(4).

35 Value Added Tax Act 1994 s 29.

36 Value Added Tax Regulations 1995 reg 16(1). The exception does not apply if the customer is in another member state: reg 16(1).

37 A retailer's invoice need only contain the following particulars: (1) the name, address and registration number of the retailer; (2) the time of the supply; (3) a description sufficient to identify the goods or services supplied; (4) the total amount payable including VAT; and (5) for each rate of VAT chargeable, the gross amount payable including VAT, and the VAT rate applicable: ibid reg 16(1)(a)–(e). Such an invoice must not contain any reference to any exempt supply: reg 16(2). As to the rate of VAT see paras 5–6 ante. As to exempt supplies see para 141 et seq ante.

38 For the meaning of 'consideration' generally see para 86 ante.

39 Value Added Tax Regulations 1995 reg 16(1).

40 Ie (1) any zero-rated supply other than a supply for the purposes of an acquisition in another member state; (2) any supply to which an order under the Value Added Tax Act 1994 s 25(7) (see para 204 ante) applies; (3) any supply on which VAT is charged although it is not made for consideration (see para 24 ante); and (4) any supply to which an order made under s 32 (repealed) applies: Value Added Tax Regulations 1995 reg 20. The commissioners consider the effect of head (1) supra is that the time of a zero-rated supply cannot be advanced by the issue of a VAT invoice but only by the making of a payment: but see para 29 note 8 ante. Presumably head (4) supra should now be taken to refer to the Value Added Tax Act 1994 s 50A (as added) (margin schemes: see para 188 ante). For the meaning of 'zero-rated' see para 158 ante.

41 Value Added Tax Regulations 1995 reg 20.

241. Contents of value added tax invoice. A registered person[1] providing a VAT invoice[2] must[3] state on it the following particulars:

(1) an identifying number;

(2) the time of the supply[4];

(3) the date of the issue of the document[5];

(4) the name, address and registration number[6] of the supplier;

(5) the name and address of the person to whom the goods or services are supplied;

(6) the type of supply by reference to the specified categories[7];

(7) a description sufficient to identify the goods or services supplied;

(8) for each description, the quantity of the goods or the extent of the services, and the rate of VAT[8] and the amount payable, excluding VAT, expressed in sterling;

(9) the gross total amount payable, excluding VAT, expressed in sterling;

(10) the rate of any cash discount offered;

(11) each rate of VAT chargeable and the amount of VAT chargeable, expressed in sterling, at each such rate; and

(12) the total amount of VAT chargeable, expressed in sterling[9].

Where a registered person provides a VAT invoice to a person in another member state[10], except as the Commissioners of Customs and Excise may otherwise allow the invoice must contain all the particulars mentioned in heads (1) to (7) and (10) above and certain other additional[11] particulars[12].

Where a registered person provides an invoice containing the required particulars[13] and specifies on it any goods or services which are the subject of an exempt or zero-rated supply[14], he must distinguish on the invoice between the goods or services which are the subject of an exempt, zero-rated or other supply and state separately the gross total amount payable in respect of each supply and rate[15]. Where a registered person provides a VAT invoice:

(a) relating in whole or in part to a supply the VAT upon which is required to be accounted for and paid by the person supplied, on the supplier's behalf, the supplier must state that fact, and the amount of VAT so to be accounted for and paid, on the VAT invoice[16];

(b) relating in whole or in part to a supply of the letting on hire of a motor car other than for self-drive hire, he must state on the invoice whether that motor car is a qualifying[17] vehicle[18].

1 For the meaning of 'registered person' see para 105 note 7 ante.
2 For the meaning of 'VAT invoice' see para 29 note 8 ante; and as to the obligation to supply such an invoice see para 240 ante.
3 Ie subject to the Value Added Tax Regulations 1995, SI 1995/2518, reg 14(2) (see the text and notes 10–12 infra); and reg 16 (see para 240 ante) and save as the Commissioners of Customs and Excise may otherwise allow: reg 14(1) (amended by SI 1996/1250).
4 For the meaning of 'supply' see para 21 ante; and as to the time of supply see para 29 et seq ante.
5 For the meaning of 'document' see para 11 note 8 ante. As to the issuing of VAT invoices by the use of a computer see para 240 note 13 ante.
6 For the meaning of 'registration number' see para 16 note 10 ante.
7 Ie (1) a supply by sale; (2) a supply on hire purchase or any similar transaction; (3) a supply by loan; (4) a supply by way of exchange; (5) a supply on hire, lease or rental; (6) a supply of goods made from the customer's materials; (7) a supply by sale on commission; (8) a supply on sale or return or similar terms; or (9) any other type of supply which the Commissioners of Customs and Excise may at any time by notice specify: Value Added Tax Regulations 1995 reg 14(1)(f).
8 As to rates of VAT see paras 5–6 ante.
9 Value Added Tax Regulations 1995 reg 14(1). As to the correct amount to include in a VAT invoice where a discount was offered to a part-exchange customer but the supply of the new car was made, without reference to the discount, to a finance company see *First County Garages Ltd v Customs and Excise Comrs* (1996) VAT Decision 14417, [1996] STI 1721.
10 For the meaning of 'another member state' see para 4 note 14 ante.
11 Ie (1) the letters 'GB' as a prefix to his registration number; (2) the registration number, if any, of the recipient of the supply of goods or services (which registration number is also to contain the alphabetical code of the member state in which that recipient is registered); (3) the gross amount payable, excluding VAT; (4) where the supply is of a new means of transport as defined in the Value Added Tax Act 1994 s 95 (as amended) (see para 13 note 8 ante) a description sufficient to identify it as a new means of transport; (5) for each description, the quantity of the goods or the extent of the services, and (where a positive rate of VAT is chargeable) the rate of VAT and the amount payable, excluding VAT, expressed in sterling; and (6) (where the supply of goods is a taxable supply) the information as specified in heads (11)–(12) in the text: Value Added Tax Regulations 1995 reg 14(2).
12 Ibid reg 14(2) (amended by SI 1996/1250).
13 Ie the particulars specified in ibid reg 14(1) (see heads (1)–(12) in the text) and reg 14(3) (see para 240 ante): reg 14(4).
14 For the meaning of 'exempt supply' see para 141 ante; and for the meaning of 'zero-rated supply' see para 158 ante.
15 Value Added Tax Regulations 1995 reg 14(4).
16 Ibid reg 14(5). This would appear to apply, eg, to a supply consisting in part of gold falling within the Value Added Tax Act 1995 s 55 (as amended): see para 26 ante.
17 Ie under the Value Added Tax (Input Tax) Order 1992, SI 1992/3222, art 7(2A) (as added): see para 208 ante.
18 Value Added Tax Regulations 1995 reg 14(6) (added by SI 1995/3147).

242. Credit notes on a change in the rate of value added tax. Where there is a change in the rate of VAT in force[1], or in the descriptions of exempt or zero-rated supplies[2], and a VAT invoice[3] which relates to a supply[4] in respect of which an election as to the time of supply[5] has been made was issued before the election was made, the person making the supply must, within 14 days after any such change, provide the person to whom the supply was made with a credit note[6]. The credit note must bear the prescribed heading[7] and contain the prescribed particulars[8].

1 Ie under the Value Added Tax Act 1994 s 2 (as amended): see paras 5–6 ante.
2 As to exempt supplies see para 141 et seq ante; and as to zero-rated supplies see para 158 et seq ante.
3 For the meaning of 'VAT invoice' see para 29 note 8 ante; as to the obligation to supply such invoices see para 240 ante; and as to their contents see para 241 ante.
4 For the meaning of 'supply' see para 21 ante.
5 Ie an election under the Value Added Tax Act 1994 s 88: see para 30 ante.
6 Value Added Tax Regulations 1995, SI 1995/2518, reg 15.
7 Ie the heading 'Credit note – change of VAT rate': ibid reg 15.
8 Ibid reg 15. The prescribed particulars are: (1) the identifying number and date of issue of the credit note; (2) the name, address and registration number of the supplier; (3) the name and address of the person to whom the supply is made; (4) the identifying number and date of issue of the VAT invoice; (5) a description sufficient to identify the goods or services supplied; and (6) the amount being credited in respect of VAT: reg 15(a)–(f). For the meaning of 'registration number' see para 16 note 10 ante.

243. Accounting for the purposes of triangulation. An intermediate supplier may elect that the supply of goods which he makes to a customer registered in the United Kingdom[1] is to be treated instead as a taxable acquisition[2] by his customer, on which the customer alone is obliged to account for value added tax[3]. Where the intermediate supplier intends to use the simplified procedure[4], he is obliged to notify both the Commissioners of Customs and Excise and the customer in writing of his intention to do so[5]. On each occasion that an intermediate supplier makes or intends to make a supply[6] to which he wishes the simplified procedure to apply, he must provide the customer with an invoice in the prescribed form[7].

If the intermediate supplier is registered in the United Kingdom for the purposes of VAT, he may elect that the transaction is treated simply as a removal of goods from one member state to another, with a taxable acquisition by the customer in the member state of destination; and he is then treated as making neither a taxable acquisition of the goods nor a taxable supply[8] of them[9]. Where a registered person[10] makes a supply to which this provision applies he must nevertheless provide the person supplied with an invoice in respect of that supply[11].

Similar provisions apply where a person who belongs in another member state[12] wishes to operate the simplified procedure for goods installed or assembled in the United Kingdom[13]. That person must notify both the Commissioners of Customs and Excise and the customer in writing of his intention to rely on the procedure[14]; and on each occasion that he makes or intends to make a supply to which he wishes that procedure to apply he must provide the registered person to whom the supply is made with an invoice in the prescribed form[15].

The above requirements obliging suppliers to provide invoices in prescribed forms to their customers do not apply to certain specified supplies[16] made in the United Kingdom[17].

1 For the meaning of 'registered' see para 56 note 2 ante; and for the meaning of 'United Kingdom' see para 4 note 3 ante.
2 For the meaning of 'taxable acquisition' see para 13 ante.
3 See para 16 ante.
4 Ie the procedure permitted under the Value Added Tax Act 1994 s 14(1): see para 16 ante.
5 See the Value Added Tax Regulations 1995, SI 1995/2518, reg 11; and para 16 ante.
6 For the meaning of 'supply' see para 21 ante.

7   Value Added Tax Regulations 1995 reg 18(1). An invoice so provided must: (1) comply with the provisions of the law corresponding, in relation to the member state which provided the intermediate supplier with the identification number for VAT purposes used, or to be used, by him for the purpose of the supply to him by the original supplier of the goods which were subsequently removed to the United Kingdom, to reg 17 (see the text and notes 10–11 infra); (2) be provided no later than 15 days after the time at which the supply would have been treated as taking place by or under the Value Added Tax Act 1994 s 6 (as amended) (see para 29 et seq ante) but for s 14(1); (3) cover no less than the extent of the supply which would have been so treated as taking place but for s 14(1) at the time that such an invoice is provided; and (4) bear the legend: 'VAT: EC ARTICLE 28 SIMPLIFICATION INVOICE': Value Added Tax Regulations 1995 reg 18(2). Where, however, an intermediate supplier makes a supply such as is mentioned in reg 18(1) and he has already provided the customer with an invoice that complies with the requirements of heads (1), (3)–(4) supra, he is not required to provide the customer with a further invoice in relation to that supply: reg 18(3). Where he makes such a supply and he provides the customer with an invoice (a) such as is described in reg 18(2), (3), that invoice is treated as if it were an invoice for the purpose of reg 83 (see para 38 ante); (b) that complies only with the requirements of head (1) supra, that invoice is treated, for the purposes of reg 18 only, as a VAT invoice: reg 18(4), (5). For the meaning of 'invoice' see para 11 ante; for the meaning of 'VAT invoice' see para 29 note 8 ante; and as to the obligation to provide, and the contents of, VAT invoices see paras 240–241 ante. For the meaning of references to the law of another member state see para 11 ante.
8   For the meaning of 'taxable supply' see para 12 note 3 ante.
9   See the Value Added Tax Act 1994 s 14(6); and para 16 ante.
10   For the meaning of 'registered person' see para 105 note 7 ante.
11   Value Added Tax Regulations 1995 reg 17(1). The invoice must comply with the requirements of regs 13, 14 (see paras 240–241 ante) and must bear the legend: 'VAT: EC ARTICLE 28 SIMPLIFICATION INVOICE': reg 17(2).
12   For the meaning of 'another member state' see para 4 note 14 ante.
13   As to this procedure see the Value Added Tax Act 1994 s 14(2); and para 41 ante.
14   See the Value Added Tax Regulations 1995 reg 12; and para 41 ante.
15   Ibid reg 19(1). An invoice so provided by a person belonging in another member state must: (1) comply with the provisions of the law of the member state in which he belongs corresponding in relation to that member state to the provisions of reg 14 (see para 241 ante); (2) be provided no later than 15 days after the time that the supply of the goods would have been treated as having taken place by or under the Value Added Tax Act 1994 s 6 (as amended) but for s 14(2); (3) cover no less than the extent of the supply which would, but for s 14(2), have been treated as having taken place by or under s 6 (as amended) at the time that such an invoice is provided; and (4) bear the legend 'SECTION 14(2) VATA INVOICE': Value Added Tax Regulations 1995 reg 19(2). Where, however, a person belonging in another member state makes a supply such as is mentioned in reg 19(1) and he has already provided the registered person with an invoice that complies with the requirements of heads (1), (3)–(4) supra, he is not required to provide the registered person with a further invoice in relation to that supply: reg 19(3). Where a person belonging in a member state makes such a supply and he provides the registered person with an invoice (a) such as is described in regs 19(2), (3), that invoice is treated as if it were an invoice for the purpose of reg 83; (b) that complies only with the requirements of head (1) supra, that invoice is treated, for the purposes of reg 19 only, as if it were a VAT invoice: reg 19(4), (5).
16   Ie (1) any zero-rated supply other than a supply for the purposes of an acquisition in another member state; (2) any supply to which an order under the Value Added Tax Act 1994 s 25(7) (see para 204 ante) applies; (3) any supply on which VAT is charged although it is not made for consideration (see para 24 ante); and (4) any supply to which an order made under s 32 (repealed) applies: Value Added Tax Regulations 1995 reg 20. The commissioners consider the effect of head (1) supra is that the time of a zero-rated supply cannot be advanced by the issue of a VAT invoice but only by the making of a payment: but see para 29 note 8 ante. Presumably head (4) supra should now be taken to refer to the Value Added Tax Act 1994 s 50A (as added) (margin schemes: see para 188 ante). For the meaning of 'zero-rated' see para 158 ante.
17   Value Added Tax Regulations 1995 reg 20.

244. EC sales statements. Every taxable person[1] who in any period of a quarter has made a supply[2] of, or has dispatched, transported or transferred, goods[3] to a person who is or was registered in another member state[4] must submit a statement in relation to that period to the Commissioners of Customs and Excise[5]. The statement must be in the prescribed form[6] containing full information[7] as well as a declaration signed by him that it is true and complete and must be submitted no later than 42 days after the end of the quarter[8]. The commissioners may, however, allow a taxable person to submit such statements in respect of periods of one month[9]. Additionally, where a taxable person satisfies the commissioners either that, at the end of any month, the value of his taxable supplies[10] in the period of one year then ending is less than the relevant figure[11] or that, at any time, there are reasonable grounds for believing that the value of his taxable supplies in the period of one year beginning at that or any later time will not exceed the relevant figure, and the prescribed condition[12] is satisfied, the commissioners may allow that person to submit a statement which relates to the period of that year[13].

Where the commissioners have allowed a taxable person to make returns[14] in respect of periods longer than three months[15] and they are satisfied that the prescribed conditions[16] are fulfilled, they may allow that person to submit statements in respect of periods identical to those that have been allowed for the making of his returns[17].

Every taxable person who has made a supply of a new means of transport[18] in any period of a quarter to a person for the purpose of acquisition by him in another member state must submit a statement to the commissioners in relation to that period, no later than 42 days after its end[19].

Any taxable person who ceases to be registered[20] must submit a final statement to the commissioners[21] no later than 42 days after the date with effect from which his registration has been cancelled, unless another person has been registered[22] with his registration number and in substitution for him[23].

1   For the meaning of 'taxable person' see paras 12 note 4, 55 ante.
2   For the meaning of 'supply' see para 21 ante.
3   There is no corresponding provision relating to services.
4   'Registered in another member state' means registered in accordance with the measures adopted by the competent authority in another member state for the purposes of the common system of value added tax and 'registered' is to be construed accordingly for these purposes: Value Added Tax Regulations 1995, SI 1995/2518, reg 21.
5   Ibid reg 22(1). 'Statement' means the statement which a taxable person is required to submit in accordance with Pt IV (regs 21–23) (amended by SI 1996/210): reg 21. Where the commissioners consider it necessary in a particular case, they may allow or direct a taxable person to submit statements to a specified address: reg 22(1) proviso (d).
6   For the prescribed form see ibid reg 22(1), Sch 1, Form 12.
7   Ie the information specified in ibid reg 22(3) (as amended) or reg 22(5): reg 22(1) (amended by SI 1996/210). Save as the commissioners may otherwise allow or direct, a taxable person must in any such statement specify (1) his name, address and registration number, which number must include the prefix 'GB'; (2) the date of the submission of the statement; (3) the date of the last day of the period to which the statement refers; (4) the registration number of each person acquiring or deemed to have acquired goods in the period, including the alphabetical code of the member state in which each such person is registered; and (5) the total value of the goods supplied in the period to each person mentioned in head (4) supra: reg 22(3) (as so amended). Where a taxable person makes a supply such as is mentioned in reg 18(1) (see para 243 ante), he must specify in the statement the information mentioned in heads (1)–(5) supra and (a) the figure '2' in the box marked 'indicator' on Sch 1, Form 12; and (b) the total value of the goods supplied to him: reg 22(5). 'Total value' means the consideration for the supply including the costs of any freight transport services and services ancillary to the transport of goods charged by the supplier of the goods to the customer: reg 21. For the meaning of 'registration number' and 'alphabetical code' see para 16 note 10 ante.
8   Ibid reg 22(1) (as amended: see note 7 supra).
9   Ibid reg 22(1) proviso (a). The statement must be submitted no later than 42 days after the end of the quarter in which the month occurs: reg 22(2)(a).
10   For the meaning of 'taxable supply' see para 12 note 3 ante.
11   The 'relevant figure' means the sum of the amount mentioned in the Value Added Tax Act 1994 s 3(2), Sch 1 para 1(1)(a) (as amended) (ie the VAT registration limit (currently £47,000): see para 32 ante) and £25,500 (thus £72,500): Value Added Tax Regulations 1995 reg 21.
12   Ie either that (1) at the end of any month, the value of his supplies to persons registered in other member states in the period of one year then ending is less than £11,000; or (2) at any time, there are reasonable grounds for believing that the value of his supplies to such persons will not exceed that figure in the period of one year beginning at that or at any later time: reg 22(1) proviso (b)(iii), (iv).
13   Ibid reg 22(1) proviso (b)(i), (ii). The statement must contain full information as specified in reg 22(3)(a)–(d) (as amended) (see note 7 supra) and a declaration signed by him that it is true and complete: reg 22(1)

proviso (b). It must be submitted no later than 42 days after the end of the period of the year to which the statement relates: reg 22(2)(b).

14　For the meaning of 'return' see para 105 note 14 ante.

15　Ie under the Value Added Tax Regulations 1995 reg 25: see para 226 ante.

16　Ie either that (1) at the end of any month, the value of the taxable person's taxable supplies in the period of one year then ending is less than £145,000; or (2) at any time, there are reasonable grounds for believing that the value of those supplies in the period of one year beginning at that or any later time will not exceed that amount; and either that (a) at the end of any month, the value of his supplies to persons registered in other member states in the period of one year then ending is less than £11,000; or (b) at any time, there are reasonable grounds for believing that the value of such supplies in the period of one year beginning at that or any later time will not exceed £11,000: ibid reg 22(1) proviso (c)(i)–(iv).

17　Ibid reg 22(1) proviso (c). Each statement must contain full information as specified in reg 22(3), (5), as the case may require, and a declaration signed by him that the statement is true and complete: reg 22(1) proviso (c) (amended by SI 1996/210). The statement must be submitted no later than 42 days after the end of the period in respect of which the commissioners have allowed a return to be furnished: reg 22(2)(c).

18　For the meaning of 'new means of transport' see para 13 note 8 ante.

19　Value Added Tax Regulations 1995 reg 22(6). The statement must contain the particulars, including the declaration made by the taxable person, set out in Sch 1, Form 13: reg 22(6). Where the commissioners consider it necessary in a particular case, they may allow or direct a taxable person to submit the statement to a specified address: reg 22(6) proviso.

20　Ie under the Value Added Tax Act 1994 s 3(2), Sch 1 (as amended): see para 56 et seq ante.

21　The final statement must be on either the Value Added Tax Regulations 1995 Sch 1, Form 12 or Form 13, as the case may require, and must contain, unless the commissioners in any case otherwise allow or direct, (1) the information specified in reg 22(3) or (5), or the full information required by Sch 1, Form 13 or both, as the case may require; and (2) a declaration signed by the taxable person that the statement is true and complete: reg 23 (amended by SI 1996/210).

22　Ie under ibid reg 6(3): see para 74 ante.

23　Ibid reg 23.

245. Persons acting in a representative capacity. Where any person who is subject to any prescribed requirements relating to accounting, payment and record-keeping[1] dies or becomes incapacitated[2] and control of his assets passes to another person, who is a personal representative, trustee in bankruptcy, receiver, liquidator or person otherwise acting in a representative capacity, that other person must, if the Commissioners of Customs and Excise require it, and so long as he has control of those assets, comply with the relevant requirements[3]. Any requirement to pay value added tax, however, applies to that other person only to the extent of the assets of the deceased or incapacitated person over which he has control[4].

1　Ie the requirements under the Value Added Tax Regulations 1995, SI 1995/2518, Pt V (regs 24–43): see paras 131, 226 et seq ante, 264 post.

2　'Incapacitated' in this context, means 'incapable of carrying on one's business' and contemplates a general incapacity which, like death or bankruptcy, would make it impossible for any business to be carried on by the taxable person: *Sargent v Customs and Excise Comrs* [1995] 1 WLR 821 at 826, [1995] STC 398 at 401, CA, per Nourse LJ (decided in the context of the Value Added Tax Regulations 1995 reg 9 (see para 70 ante)).

3　Ibid reg 30. Part V applies to the representative person in the same way as it would have applied to the deceased or incapacitated person, had that person not been deceased or incapacitated, except in relation to the payment of value added tax (see the text to note 4 infra): reg 30. Where the commissioners have so required of any person, the period in respect of which taxable supplies were being made by the person who died or became incapacitated ends on the day previous to the date when death or incapacity took place: reg 25(3)(a). Subject to reg 25(1)(c) (see para 226 ante), a return made on behalf of that person must be made in respect of that period no later than the last day of the month next following the end of that period, and the next period starts on the day following that period and ends, and all subsequent periods begin and end, on the date previously determined under reg 25(1): reg 25(3)(b), (c).

4　Ibid reg 30 proviso.

246. Power to require security. Where it appears to the Commissioners of Customs and Excise requisite to do so for the protection of the revenue, they may require a taxable person[1], as a condition of his supplying goods or services under a taxable supply[2], to give security, or further security, of such amount and in such manner as they may determine, for the payment of any value added tax which is or may become due from him[3]. If, in contravention of such a requirement for security, any person supplies goods or services, he is liable on summary conviction to a penalty of level 5 on the standard scale[4].

An appeal lies to a VAT and duties tribunal against the requirement of security for this purpose[5].

1   For the meaning of 'taxable person' see paras 12 note 4, 55 ante.
2   For the meaning of 'taxable supply' see para 12 note 3 ante.
3   Value Added Tax Act 1994 s 58, Sch 11 para 4(2). This provision is without prejudice to the power of the commissioners under s 48(7) (see para 62 ante): Sch 11 para 4(2). As to the security for the making of VAT credits see para 202 ante.
4   Ibid s 72(11). As to the standard scale see para 129 note 3 ante.
5   Ibid s 83(l). The nature of the appeal has been the subject of some judicial debate: see *Customs and Excise Comrs v Peachtree Enterprises Ltd* [1994] STC 747 (jurisdiction of the VAT and duties tribunal supervisory only and, in accordance with the principle in *Associated Provincial Picture Houses Ltd v Wednesbury Corpn* [1948] 1 KB 223, [1947] 2 All ER 680, CA, the tribunal should not substitute its decision for that of the commissioners); cf *John Dee Ltd v Customs and Excise Comrs* [1995] STC 941, CA (tribunal's jurisdiction more strictly appellate in nature; nevertheless, in applying the statutory condition of whether it was requisite for the protection of the revenue that a person be required to give security for VAT, the tribunal should apply the test laid down in *Customs and Excise Comrs v JH Corbitt (Numismatists) Ltd* [1981] AC 22, [1980] 2 All ER 72, HL, in considering whether the commissioners had acted in a way in which no reasonable panel of commissioners could have acted, or had taken some irrelevant matter into account or had disregarded something to which they should have given weight, or had erred in point of law. Once this was decided, the tribunal had (if necessary) to remit the issue to the commissioners for further consideration and could not exercise the discretion itself; but where the tribunal concluded that the decision of the commissioners would inevitably have been the same, even if they had carried out their task properly, it was unnecessary to remit the matter to the commissioners, and their decision could stand). It is difficult to see how the latter approach differs from a supervisory jurisdiction. As to appeals generally see para 293 et seq post. The commissioners were held to have acted unreasonably in *Wold Construction Co Ltd v Customs and Excise Comrs* (1994) VAT Decision 11704, [1994] STI 452, when they sought security for VAT from an established repayment trader. For a case where costs on the indemnity basis were awarded against the commissioners for imposing a requirement of security for VAT for an improper purpose see *VSP Marketing Ltd v Customs and Excise Comrs (No 3)* (1995) VAT Decision 13587, [1995] STI 1756 (commissioners had sought to impose the requirement in order to persuade the trader to discharge its predecessor's VAT liability).

(4) ASSESSMENTS

247. Assessments for failure to make returns etc. Where a person has failed to make any returns required in relation to value added tax[1] or to keep any documents[2] and afford the facilities necessary to verify those returns, or where it appears to the Commissioners of Customs and Excise that those returns are incomplete or incorrect, they may assess the amount of VAT due from him[3] to the best of their judgment[4] and notify it to him[5].

In any case where, for any prescribed accounting period[6], there has been paid or credited to any person as being a repayment or refund of VAT, or as being due to him as a VAT credit[7], an amount which ought not to have been so paid or credited, or which would not have been so paid or credited had the facts been known or been as they later turn out to be, the commissioners may assess that amount as being VAT due from him for that period and notify it to him accordingly[8]. An amount which has been paid to any person as being due to him as a VAT credit, and which ought not to have been so paid by reason of the cancellation of his registration[9], may be so assessed notwithstanding that cancellation[10].

Where a taxable person, in the course or furtherance of a business[11] carried on by him, has (1) been supplied with any goods, acquired any goods from another member state[12] or otherwise obtained possession or control of any goods; or (2) imported any goods from a place outside the member states[13], the commissioners may require him from time to time to account for the goods[14]. If he fails to prove that the goods have been or are available to be supplied by him, or have been exported or otherwise removed from the United Kingdom[15] (without being exported or removed by way of supply[16]), or have been lost or destroyed, the commissioners may assess to the best of their judgment and notify to him the amount of VAT that would have been chargeable in respect of the supply of the goods if they had been supplied by him[17].

Where a fiscal warehousekeeper[18] has failed to pay VAT required by the commissioners[19], they may assess to the best of their judgment the amount of that VAT due from him and notify it to him[20]. Similarly, where it appears to the commissioners that goods have been removed from a warehouse[21] or fiscal warehouse[22] without payment of the VAT payable on that removal[23], they may assess to the best of their judgment the amount of VAT due from the person removing the goods or other person liable and notify it to him[24].

A special rule exists for cases where the commissioners make an assessment[25] as a result of a person's failure to make a return for a prescribed accounting period and the VAT assessed has been paid but no proper return has been made for the period to which the assessment related[26]. In any such case where the commissioners find it necessary to make another assessment[27] as a result of a failure by that person, or a person acting in a representative capacity in relation to him, to make a return for a later prescribed accounting period, they may, if they think fit having regard to the earlier failure, specify in the later assessment an amount of VAT greater than that which they would otherwise have considered to be appropriate[28].

Where an amount has been assessed and notified to any person under any of the above provisions, it is[29] deemed to be an amount of VAT due from him and may be recovered accordingly, unless, or except to the extent that, the assessment has subsequently been withdrawn or reduced[30].

1 Ie any returns required under the Value Added Tax Act 1994 or under any provision repealed by that Act: s 73(1). As to the requirement to make returns see para 226 ante. For the meaning of 'return' see para 105 note 14 ante.

2 For the meaning of 'document' see para 11 note 8 ante.

3 Where the person who failed to make a return, or who makes a return which appears to the commissioners to be incomplete or incorrect, was required to make the return as a personal representative, trustee in bankruptcy, interim or permanent trustee, receiver, liquidator or person otherwise acting in a representative capacity in relation to another person, the Value Added Tax Act 1994 s 73(1) applies as if the reference to VAT due from him included a reference to VAT due from that other person: s 73(5).

4 In order to make an assessment to the best of their judgment, the commissioners must exercise their powers in such a way that they make a value judgment on the material which is before them. They must exercise their function honestly and bona fide and it would be a misuse of their power if the commissioners were to decide on a figure which they knew was, or thought was, in excess of the amount which could possibly be payable, leaving it to the taxpayer to seek to reduce it on appeal (but see ibid s 73(8); and the text to notes 25–28 for an exception to this). There must be some material before the commissioners; if they have none at all, their judgment cannot be exercised. However, the primary obligation is on the taxpayer himself to make his return; and the commissioners cannot be required to do the work of the taxpayer. Therefore, the commissioners are not obliged to carry out exhaustive investigations; only fairly to consider all material placed before them; and, on that material, to come to a decision which is one which is reasonable and not arbitrary as to the amount of the tax which is due: *Van Boeckel v Customs and Excise Comrs* [1981] 2 All ER 505 at 508, [1981] STC 290 at

292 per Woolf J. See also *Schlumberger Inland Services Inc v Customs and Excise Comrs* [1987] STC 228; *Holder v Customs and Excise Comrs* [1989] STC 327; *Spillane v Customs and Excise Comrs* [1990] STC 212; *Barber v Customs and Excise Comrs* [1992] VATTR 144; *Farnocchia v Customs and Excise Comrs* [1994] STC 881; *Dwyer Property Ltd v Customs and Excise Comrs* [1995] STC 1035; *Georgiou (t/a Marios Chippery) v Customs and Excise Comrs* [1996] STC 463, CA. Whether the commissioners have assessed the amount of tax due to the best of their judgment is a question of fact for the tribunal: *Seto v Customs and Excise Comrs* [1981] STC 698, Ct of Sess. If it is decided that an assessment has not been made to the best of the commissioners' judgment, the assessment is a nullity and cannot be saved by the excision of the incorrect elements: *Barber v Customs and Excise Comrs* supra. The phrase 'best of judgment' connotes a deliberate choice between possible alternatives and a mere want of care does not make an assessment invalid: *Gauntlett v Customs and Excise Comrs* (1996) VAT Decision 13921, [1996] STI 780.

5   Value Added Tax Act 1994 s 73(1). For these purposes, notification to a personal representative, trustee in bankruptcy, interim or permanent trustee, receiver, liquidator or person otherwise so acting is treated as notification to the person in relation to whom he so acts: s 73(10). As to service of the notification see s 98; and para 291 post. See also *Din v Customs and Excise Comrs* [1984] VATTR 228 at 232 (nothing in the VAT legislation requires 'such a thing as an assessment which must itself be served upon a taxpayer, or, indeed, taken physically into his hand'); and *House (t/a P & J Autos) v Customs and Excise Comrs* [1996] STC 154, CA. In the case of a partnership it is sufficient to serve the notice of assessment on the partnership rather than on each partner: *Bengal Brasserie v Customs and Excise Comrs* [1991] VATTR 210.

6   For the meaning of 'prescribed accounting period' see para 202 note 4 ante. Although the Value Added Tax Act 1994 s 73 (as amended) is framed in terms of prescribed accounting periods, each assessment may be for more than one period. Difficulty has arisen where a single entry in a notice of assessment (the document which is sent to the trader) relates to more than one period, and in particular when the entry relates in part to a time falling outside the limitation period for making such an assessment. As to the limitation periods applicable to assessments and such 'global assessments' see para 252 post.

7   For the meaning of 'VAT credit' see ibid s 25(3); and para 202 ante.

8   Ibid s 73(2).

9   Ie under ibid s 3(2), Sch 1 para 13(2)–(6) (see para 73 ante), Sch 2 para 6(2) (see para 76 ante) or Sch 3 para 6(2) or Sch 3 para 6(3) (see para 78 ante): s 73(3)(b).

10   Ibid s 73(3). Where a person is assessed under s 73(1) and (2) in respect of the same prescribed accounting period the assessments may be combined and notified to him as one assessment: s 73(4). It is not, however, possible for the commissioners to treat an assessment for overclaimed input tax as an assessment for under-declared output tax: *Ridgeons Bulk Ltd v Customs and Excise Comrs* [1994] STC 427, distinguishing *Football Association Ltd v Customs and Excise Comrs* [1985] VATTR 106 and *Customs and Excise Comrs v Sooner Foods Ltd* [1983] STC 376; following, inter alia, *Silvermere Golf and Equestrian Centre Ltd v Customs and Excise Comrs* [1981] VATTR 106 and *Jeudwine v Customs and Excise Comrs* [1977] VATTR 115.

11   For the meaning of 'in the course or furtherance of a business' see paras 12 note 5, 17 note 2 ante.

12   As to acquisitions from other member states see para 13 ante. For the meaning of 'another member state' see para 4 note 14 ante.

13   For the meaning of 'imported from a place outside the member states' see para 103 note 2 ante.

14   Ibid s 73(7).

15   For the meaning of 'United Kingdom' see para 4 note 3 ante.

16   For the meaning of 'supply' see para 21 ante.

17   Value Added Tax Act 1994 s 73(7).

18   For the meaning of 'fiscal warehousekeeper' see para 133 note 3 ante.

19   Ie required under the Value Added Tax Act 1994 s 18E(2) (as added): see para 137 ante.

20   Ibid s 73(7A) (added by the Finance Act 1996 s 26(1), Sch 3 para 10).

21   For the meaning of 'warehouse' see para 130 note 6 ante.

22   For the meaning of 'fiscal warehouse' see para 133 note 3 ante.

23   Ie payable under the Value Added Tax Act 1994 s 18(4) (see para 130 ante) or s 18D (as added) (see para 134 ante): s 73(7B) (as added: see note 20 supra).

24   Ibid s 73(7B) (as added: see note 20 supra).

25   Ie under ibid s 73(1): see the text and notes 1–5 supra.

26   See ibid s 73(8)(a), (b).

27   See note 25 supra.

28   Value Added Tax Act 1994 s 73(8).

29   Ie subject to the provisions of the Value Added Tax Act 1994 as to appeals: see para 293 et seq post.

30   Ibid s 73(9) (amended by the Finance Act 1996 Sch 3 para 11). If, however, the assessment is a nullity, because the time limit for making it has expired, it seems that it is void ab initio and the person assessed may defend proceedings brought to recover the tax assessed, rather than by making an appeal to the VAT and duties tribunal: *Lord Advocate v Shanks (t/a Shanks & Co)* [1992] STC 928, Ct of Sess. Quaere whether the principle is applicable in England; cf *IRC v Pearlberg* [1953] 1 All ER 388, 34 TC 57, CA; *IRC v Soul*

(1976) 51 TC 86, CA; *IRC v Aken* [1990] 1 WLR 1374, [1990] STC 497, CA; and INCOME TAXATION vol 23 (Reissue) para 1658.

248. Assessments in cases of certain acquisitions by non-taxable persons.

Where (1) a taxable acquisition[1] of goods subject to excise duty or of a new means of transport[2] takes place in the United Kingdom[3]; (2) the acquisition is not in pursuance of a taxable supply[4]; and (3) the person acquiring the goods is not a taxable person[5] at the time of the acquisition, the person acquiring the goods must notify the Commissioners of Customs and Excise of the acquisition[6]. He must pay the value added tax due upon the acquisition at the time of notification[7] or, if he has acquired a new means of transport, within 30 days of the commissioners issuing a written demand to him detailing the VAT due and requesting payment[8].

Where, at a time when a person was not a taxable person, he acquires any such goods in the United Kingdom from another member state[9], and:

(a)   notification of that acquisition has not been given to the commissioners;

(b)   the commissioners are not satisfied that the particulars relating to the acquisition in any notification given to them are accurate and complete; or

(c)   there has been a failure to supply the commissioners with the information necessary to verify the particulars contained in any such notification,

the commissioners may assess the amount of VAT due on the acquisition to the best of their judgment[11] and notify[12] their assessment to that person[13]. Where an amount has been so assessed and notified to any person, it is deemed to be an amount of VAT due from him and may be recovered accordingly, unless, or except to the extent that, the assessment has subsequently been withdrawn or reduced[14].

1   For the meaning of 'taxable acquisition' see para 13 ante.
2   For the meaning of 'new means of transport' see para 13 note 8 ante.
3   For the meaning of 'United Kingdom' see para 4 note 3 ante.
4   For the meaning of 'taxable supply' see para 12 note 3 ante.
5   For the meaning of 'taxable person' see paras 12 note 4, 55 ante.
6   Value Added Tax Regulations 1995, SI 1995/2518, regs 36(1), 148(1). In the case of goods subject to excise duty, the notification must (1) be made at the time of the acquisition or the arrival of the goods in the United Kingdom, whichever is the later; (2) be in writing in the English language and contain (a) the name and current address of the person acquiring the goods; (b) the time of acquisition; (c) the date when the goods arrived in the United Kingdom; (d) the value of the goods including any excise duty payable; and (e) the VAT due upon the acquisition; and (3) include a declaration, signed by the person who is required to make the notification, that all the information entered in it is true and complete: reg 36(1)–(3). Where a person required to make such notification dies or becomes incapacitated and control of his assets passes to another person, being a personal representative, trustee in bankruptcy, receiver, liquidator or person otherwise acting in a representative capacity, that other person is required to make the notification so long as he has such control: reg 36(5).

In the case of a new means of transport, the notification must (i) be made within seven days of the time of the acquisition or the arrival of the goods in the United Kingdom, whichever is the later; (ii) be in writing in the English language and contain (A) the name and current address of the person acquiring the new means of transport; (B) the time of the acquisition; (C) the date when the new means of transport arrived in the United Kingdom; (D) a full description of the new means of transport, including any registration mark allocated to it by any competent authority in another member state prior to its arrival in the United Kingdom and any chassis, hull or airframe identification number and engine number; (E) the consideration for the transaction in pursuance of which the new means of transport was acquired; (F) the name and address of the supplier in the member state from which the transport was acquired; (G) the place where the new means of transport can be inspected; and (H) the date of notification; (iii) include a declaration, signed by the person who is required to make the notification or a person authorised in that behalf in writing, that all the information entered in it is true and complete; and (iv) be made at, or sent to, any office designated by the commissioners for the receipt of such notifications: reg 148(1)–(4).

7   Ibid regs 36(4), 148(5). In the case of goods subject to excise duty, the payment must be made in any event no later than the last day on which the person is required to make the notification: reg 36(4). This

requirement to pay VAT applies to a person acting in a representative capacity (see note 6 supra) only to the extent of the assets of the deceased or incapacitated person over which he has control; but reg 36 otherwise applies to a person so acting in the same way as it would have applied to the deceased or incapacitated person had that person not been deceased or incapacitated: reg 36(5).

8   Ibid reg 148(5).
9   For the meaning of 'another member state' see para 4 note 14 ante.
10   Ie by the person who is required to give one by regulations made under the Value Added Tax Act 1994 s 58, Sch 11 para 2(4): see para 225 ante. For the regulations so made see the text and notes 1–8 supra.
11   As to assessments to the best of the commissioners' judgment see para 247 note 4 ante.
12   For the purposes of assessment, notification to a personal representative, trustee in bankruptcy, interim or permanent trustee, receiver, liquidator or person otherwise acting in a representative capacity in relation to the person who made the acquisition in question is treated as notification to the person in relation to whom he so acts: Value Added Tax Act 1994 s 75(4). See also note 6 supra. As to the method of notification see s 98; and para 291 post.
13   Ibid s 75(1).
14   Ibid s 75(3).

249. Interest on value added tax recovered or recoverable by assessment.

Where an assessment is made because of a failure to make returns[1], and at least one of the following conditions is fulfilled:

(1)   the assessment relates to a prescribed accounting period[2] in respect of which either a return has previously been made, or an earlier assessment has already been notified to the person concerned[3];

(2)   the assessment relates to a prescribed accounting period which exceeds three months and begins on the date with effect from which the person concerned was, or was required to be, registered[4]; or

(3)   the assessment relates to a prescribed accounting period at the beginning of which the person concerned was, but should no longer have been, exempted[5] from registration[6],

the whole of the amount assessed carries interest at the applicable rate[7] from the reckonable date[8] until payment[9]. In the case of other assessments[10], the whole of the amount assessed carries such interest without the need to fulfil the conditions set out in heads (1) to (3) above[11]. Where the circumstances are such that an assessment carrying interest could have been made[12], but before the assessment is made the VAT due or other amount concerned was paid, so that no such assessment was necessary, the whole of the amount paid carries interest at the applicable rate from the reckonable date until the date on which it was paid[13].

Where, however, the period[14] for which any amount would otherwise carry interest under the above provisions would exceed three years, the part of that period for which that amount carries interest is confined to the last three years of that period[15].

If an unauthorised person[16] issues an invoice showing an amount as being VAT or as including an amount attributable to VAT, interest is charged on the amount which is so shown or is to be taken as representing VAT at the applicable rate from the date of the invoice until payment[17].

Interest under these provisions must be paid without any deduction of income tax[18].

1   Ie an assessment under the Value Added Tax Act 1994 s 73(1): see para 247 ante. For the meaning of 'return' see para 105 note 14 ante.
2   For the meaning of 'prescribed accounting period' see para 202 note 4 ante.
3   Value Added Tax Act 1994 s 74(1)(a).
4   Ibid s 74(1)(b). For the meaning of 'registered' see para 56 note 2 ante.
5   Ie under ibid s 3(2), Sch 1 para 14(1) (see para 57 ante) or Sch 3 para 8 (see para 63 ante): s 74(1)(c).
6   Ibid s 74(1)(c).
7   Ie the rate applicable under the Finance Act 1996 s 197: Value Added Tax Act 1994 s 74(1) (amended by the Finance Act 1996 s 197(2)(c), (6)(d)(i)). The rate of interest so applicable is the rate which is provided for by regulations made by the Treasury: s 197(1). This provision has effect for periods beginning on or after

such day as the Treasury may by order made by statutory instrument appoint and has effect in relation to interest running from before that day as well as in relation to interest running from, or from after, that day: see s 197(7). Regulations so made may (1) make different provision for different enactments or for different purposes of the same enactment; (2) either themselves specify a rate of interest for the purposes of an enactment or make provision for any such rate to be determined, and to change from time to time, by reference to such rate or the average of such rates as may be referred to in the regulations; (3) provide for rates to be reduced below, or increased above, what they otherwise would be by specified amounts or by reference to specified formulae; (4) provide for rates arrived at by reference to averages or formulae to be rounded up or down; (5) provide for circumstances in which changes of rates of interest are or are not to take place; and (6) provide that changes of rates are to have effect for periods beginning on or after a day determined in accordance with the regulations in relation to interest running from before that day, as well as in relation to interest running from, or from after, that day: s 197(3). The power to make such regulations is exercisable by statutory instrument subject to annulment in pursuance of a resolution of the House of Commons: s 197(4). Where (a) regulations so made provide, without specifying the rate determined in accordance with the regulations, for a new method of determining the rate applicable for the purposes of any enactment; or (b) the rate which, in accordance with regulations so made, is the rate applicable for the purposes of any enactment, changes otherwise than by virtue of the making of regulations specifying a new rate, the Commissioners of Customs and Excise must make an order specifying the new rate and the day from which, in accordance with the regulations, it has effect: s 197(5). With effect from 6 February 1996, the prescribed rate is 6.25% per annum: see the Value Added Tax Act 1994 (Interest on Tax) (Prescribed Rate) Order 1996, SI 1996/165, arts 1, 2.

8   For these purposes, the reckonable date is the latest date on which, accordance with regulations made under the Value Added Tax Act 1994, a return is required to be make for the prescribed accounting period to which the amount assessed or paid relates: see s 74(5)(b).

9   Ibid s 74(1). This is subject to s 76(8) (see para 251 post): s 74(1). Interest runs from the reckonable date even if that date is a non-business day within the meaning of the Bills of Exchange Act 1882 s 92 (as amended) (ie a Saturday, Sunday, Good Friday, Christmas Day, a bank holiday, a day appointed by royal proclamation as a public fast or thanksgiving day or a day declared by order to be a non-business day: see s 92 (amended by the Banking and Financial Dealings Act 1971 ss 3(1), 4(4)): Value Added Tax Act 1994 s 74(5). The assessment for interest is made under s 76(1)(c) (see para 251 post) and is discretionary; but the only remedy if the commissioners fail to exercise their discretion not to charge interest is by way of an application for judicial review: see *Dollar Land (Feltham) Ltd, Dollar Land (Cumbernauld) Ltd, Dollar Land (Calthorpe House) Ltd v Customs and Excise Comrs* [1995] STC 414.

10 Ie an assessment under any provision of the Value Added Tax Act 1994 s 73 (as amended) except s 73(1): s 74(1).

11 Ibid s 74(1). Where the amount assessed or paid is such an amount as is referred to in s 73(2)(a) or (b) (see para 247 ante), the reckonable date is the seventh day after the day on which a written instruction was issued by the commissioners directing the making of the payment of the amount which ought not to have been repaid or paid to the person concerned: s 74(5)(a). In all other cases, s 74(5)(b) (see note 8 supra) applies, but in the case of an amount assessed under s 73(7) (see para 247 ante), the sum assessed is taken for those purposes to relate to the period for which the assessment was made: s 74(5)(b), (c).

12 Ie an assessment falling within ibid s 74(1): see the text and notes 1–11 supra.

13 Ibid s 74(2) (amended by the Finance Act 1996 s 197(2)(c), (6)(d)(i)). See also note 7 supra.

14 Ie (1) the period before the assessment in question for which any amount would carry interest under the Value Added Tax Act 1994 s 74(1); or (2) the period for which any amount would carry interest under s 74(2) (as amended): s 74(3)(a), (b).

15 Ibid s 74(3).

16 'An unauthorised person' means anyone other than (1) a person registered under the Value Added Tax Act 1994 (see para 56 et seq ante); or (2) a body corporate treated for the purposes of s 43 (as amended) as a member of a group (see paras 66, 191 ante); or (3) a person treated as a taxable person under regulations made under s 46(4) (see para 70 ante); or (4) a person authorised to issue an invoice under regulations made under s 58, Sch 11 para 2(12) (see para 225 ante); or (5) a person acting on behalf of the Crown: s 67(2) (applied by s 74(4)). For the meaning of 'taxable person' see paras 12 note 4, 55 ante; and for the meaning of 'invoice' see para 11 note 8 ante.

17 Ibid s 74(4) (amended by the Finance Act 1996 s 197(2)(c), (6)(d)(i)). See also note 7 supra.

18 Value Added Tax Act 1994 s 74(7).

250. Assessment in consequence of group anti-avoidance direction. Where a direction is given under the anti-avoidance provisions relating to groups[1] and there is an amount of value added tax ('the unpaid tax') for which a relevant person[2] would have been liable before the giving of the direction[3] if the facts had accorded with the assumptions specified in the direction, the Commissioners of Customs and Excise may, to the best of their judgment, assess the amount of unpaid tax as tax due from the person to whom the direction was given or another relevant person and notify their assessment to that person[4]. Where any assessment falls to be made under these provisions in a case in which the commissioners are satisfied that the actual revenue loss[5] is less than the unpaid tax, the total amount to be assessed must not exceed what appears to them, to the best of their judgment, to be the amount of that loss[6].

An assessment may not be made under these provisions more than one year after the day on which the direction to which it relates was given, or in the case of any direction that has been withdrawn[7].

Where an amount has been assessed on any person under these provisions and notified to him:

(1)   that amount is deemed[8] to be an amount of VAT due from him[9];

(2)   that amount may be recovered accordingly, either from that person or, in the case of a body corporate that is for the time being treated as a member of a group, from the representative member of that group[10]; and

(3)   to the extent that more than one person is liable by virtue of any such assessment in respect of the same amount of unpaid tax, those persons are treated as jointly and severally liable for that amount[11],

but heads (1) to (3) above do not have effect if or to the extent that the assessment in question has been withdrawn or reduced[12].

The statutory provisions relating to interest[13] and supplementary assessments[14] apply in relation to such assessments with certain modifications[15]. An appeal lies to a VAT and duties tribunal against such an assessment[16].

---

1   Ie under the Value Added Tax Act 1994 s 43(9), Sch 9A (as added): see para 193 ante.

2   'A relevant person', in relation to a direction, means (1) the person to whom the direction is given; (2) the body corporate which was the representative member of any group of which that person was treated as being, or in pursuance of the direction is to be treated as having been, a member at a time to which the assumption specified in the direction relates; and (3) any body corporate which, in pursuance of the direction, is to be treated as having been the representative member of such a group: ibid Sch 9A para 6(11) (Sch 9A added by the Finance Act 1996 s 31(2), Sch 4). As to the construction for these purposes of references to being treated as a member of a group see para 193 note 2 ante; and for the meaning of 'representative member' see para 66 ante.

3   This reference to an amount of VAT for which a person would, on particular assumptions, have been liable before the giving of a direction under the Value Added Tax Act 1994 Sch 9A (as added: see note 2 supra) is a reference to the aggregate of the following: (1) any amount of output tax which, on those assumptions but not otherwise, would have been due from a relevant person at the end of a prescribed accounting period ending before the giving of the direction; (2) the amount of any credit for input tax to which a relevant person is treated as having been entitled at the end of such an accounting period but to which he would not have been entitled on those assumptions; and (3) the amount of any repayment of tax made to a relevant person in accordance with regulations under s 39 (see paras 261–262 post) but to which he would not have been entitled on those assumptions: Sch 9A para 6(2) (as so added). For the meaning of 'output tax' and 'input tax' see paras 4, 201 ante; and for the meaning of 'prescribed accounting period' see para 202 note 4 ante.

4   Ibid Sch 9A para 6(1) (as added: see note 2 supra). Such an assessment relating to a direction may be notified to the person to whom that direction is given by being incorporated in the same notice as that direction: Sch 9A para 6(5) (as so added). As to notification to receivers, liquidators or persons otherwise acting in a representative capacity see para 193 note 1 ante.

5   For the purposes of making an assessment under these provisions in relation to any direction, the actual revenue loss must be taken to be equal to the amount of the unpaid tax less the amount given by aggregating the amounts of every entitlement to credit for input tax or to a repayment in accordance with regulations made under ibid s 39, which, whether as an entitlement of the person in relation to whom the assessment is made or as an entitlement of any other person, would have arisen on the assumptions contained in the direction, but not otherwise: Sch 9A para 6(4) (as added: see note 2 supra).

6   Ibid Sch 9A para 6(3) (as added: see note 2 supra).

7   Ibid Sch 9A para 6(6) (as added: see note 2 supra).

8   Ie subject to the provisions of the Value Added Tax Act 1994 as to appeals: see para 293 et seq post.
9   Ibid Sch 9A para 6(7)(a) (as added: see note 2 supra).
10 Ibid Sch 9A para 6(7)(b) (as added: see note 2 supra).
11 Ibid Sch 9A para 6(7)(c) (as added: see note 2 supra).
12 Ibid Sch 9A para 6(8) (as added: see note 2 supra).
13 Ie ibid s 74 (as amended): see para 249 ante.
14 Ie ibid s 77(6): see para 252 post.
15 Ibid Sch 9A para 6(9) (as added: see note 2 supra). Section 74 (as amended) so applies as if the reference
    in s 74(1) to the reckonable date were a reference to the date on which the assessment is notified: Sch 9A
    para 6(9) (as so added). Where any person is so liable to interest under s 74, s 76 (as amended) (see para
    251 post) has effect in relation to that liability with the omission of s 76(2)–(6) (as amended); and s 77 (as
    amended) (see para 252 post), except s 77(6), does not apply to an assessment of the amount due by way
    of interest; and (without prejudice to the power to make assessments for interest for later periods)) the
    interest to which any assessment made under s 76 (as amended) by virtue of these provisions may relate
    is confined to interest for a period of no more than two years ending with the time when the assessment
    to interest is made: Sch 9A para 6(10) (as so added).
16 See ibid s 83(wa) (as added); and para 296 post.

251. Assessment of amounts due by way of penalty, interest or surcharge.
Where any person is liable to a default surcharge[1] or to a penalty[2] or for interest on value added tax recovered or recoverable by assessment[3], the Commissioners of Customs and Excise may[4] assess the amount due by way of penalty, interest or surcharge and notify it to him accordingly[5]. The fact that any conduct giving rise to a penalty may have ceased before an assessment is made does not affect the commissioners' power to make an assessment[6].

As a general rule, the commissioners are to make assessments of an amount due by way of penalties, interest and surcharge in respect of a prescribed accounting period[7]; but in any case where the amount of any penalty, interest or surcharge falls to be calculated by reference to VAT which was not paid when it should have been and that VAT, or the supply[8] which gives rise to it, cannot be readily attributed to any one or more prescribed accounting periods, it is treated as VAT due for such period or periods as the commissioners determine to the best of their judgment and which they notify to the person liable[9].

Where a person is assessed under this provision to an amount due by way of any penalty, interest or surcharge[10] and is also assessed to VAT[11] for the relevant prescribed accounting period, the assessments may be combined and notified to him as one assessment, but the amount of the penalty, interest or surcharge must be separately identified in the notice[12]. Similarly, where a person is assessed to a penalty for failing to give notification to the commissioners of the acquisition of specified goods from another member state[13], that assessment may be combined with an assessment for the amount of VAT due on the relevant acquisition[14] and the two assessments notified together, provided that the amount of the penalty is separately identified in the notice[15].

In the case of an amount due by way of penalty for a failure to submit an EC sales statement[16], or for breach of a regulatory requirement[17], or interest[18], the notice of assessment must specify a date, not later than the date of the notice, to which the aggregate amount of the penalty which is assessed or, as the case may be, the amount of interest is calculated[19]. If the penalty or interest continues to accrue after that date, a further assessment or assessments may be made in respect of amounts which so accrue[20].

If an amount is assessed and notified to any person under these provisions, then unless, or except to the extent that, the assessment is withdrawn or reduced, that amount is recoverable as if it were VAT due from him[21].

A person may appeal against any penalty, or surcharge, or the amount of any penalty, interest or surcharge specified in an assessment, to a VAT and duties tribunal[22].

1 Ie under the Value Added Tax Act 1994 s 59 (as amended) or s 59A (as added): see paras 283–284 post.

2 Ie under any of ibid ss 60–69 (as amended): see para 272 et seq post.

3 Ie interest under ibid s 74 (as amended): see para 249 ante.

4 The commissioners have a discretion whether or not to impose a surcharge or a penalty, or to charge interest, which they exercise by deciding whether or not to assess: see *Dollar Land (Feltham) Ltd, Dollar Land (Cumbernauld) Ltd, Dollar Land (Calthorpe House) Ltd v Customs and Excise Comrs* [1995] STC 414 (neither the right given to a taxpayer to appeal against the liability to default surcharge, nor the right of appeal against the amount of the surcharge, includes an express reference to a right of appeal against the decision of the commissioners to assess to surcharge, nor does the VAT and duties tribunal have an implied power to review the commissioners' decision to impose a surcharge; the only remedy against an improper exercise of the commissioners' discretion is by way of an application to the High Court for judicial review). Cf *Customs and Excise Comrs v John Dee Ltd* [1995] STC 941, CA (a decision relating to the commissioners' discretion to require security for VAT under the Value Added Tax Act 1994 s 58, Sch 11 para 4(2) (see para 246 ante)).

5 Ibid s 76(1) (amended by the Finance Act 1996 s 35(1), (7)). Notification to a personal representative, trustee in bankruptcy, interim or permanent trustee, receiver, liquidator or person otherwise acting in a representative capacity in relation to the person who made the acquisition in question is treated as notification to the person in relation to whom he so acts: Value Added Tax Act 1994 s 76(10). Under s 81(3), where an amount is due from the commissioners to any person, in accordance with the Value Added Tax Act 1994, and that person is liable to pay a sum by way of VAT, penalty, interest or surcharge, the amount due from the commissioners is set against the sum which the person is liable to pay to the commissioners; and, to the extent of the set-off, the obligations of the commissioners and the person concerned are discharged: see para 254 post. The effect of this would appear to be to enable the commissioners to effect a set-off even where there has been no assessment to the VAT or penalty, etc under the appropriate provision.

6 Ibid s 76(1). However, where a person is liable for a penalty under s 69 (breach of regulatory provisions: see para 282 post) for a failure to comply with a requirement of a kind described in s 69(1)(c)–(f), no assessment may be made of the amount due in respect of the penalty unless within the period of two years preceding the assessment the commissioners have issued him with a written warning of the consequences of a continuing failure to comply with the relevant requirement: s 76(2).

7 Ibid s 76(3). The prescribed accounting period is referred to as 'the relevant period': s 76(3). In the case of (1) a surcharge under s 59 (as amended) or s 59A (as added), the relevant period is the prescribed accounting period in respect of which the taxable person is in default and in respect of which the surcharge arises; (2) a penalty under s 60 relating to the evasion of VAT (see para 272 post), the relevant period is the prescribed accounting period for which the VAT evaded was due; (3) a penalty under s 60 relating to the obtaining of the payment of a VAT credit, the relevant period is the prescribed accounting period in respect of which the payment was obtained; (4) a penalty under s 63 (see para 275 post), the relevant period is the prescribed accounting period for which liability to VAT was understated or in respect of which entitlement to a VAT credit was overstated; and (5) interest under s 74 (see para 249 ante), the relevant period is the prescribed accounting period in respect of which the VAT (or the amount assessed as VAT) was due: s 76(3)(a)–(e) (amended by the Finance Act 1996 s 35(1), (7)). As to the ability to make a global assessment in all cases see para 252 post; and *Georgiou (t/a Mario's Chippery) v Customs and Excise Comrs* [1996] STC 463, CA.

8 For the meaning of 'supply' see para 21 ante.

9 Value Added Tax Act 1994 s 76(4).

10 Ie any penalty, interest or surcharge falling within ibid s 76(3) (as amended): see note 7 supra.

11 Ie under ibid s 73(1), (2) or (7) or s 73(7A) or (7B) (as added): see para 247 ante.

12 Ibid s 76(5) (amended by the Finance Act 1996 s 26(1), Sch 3 para 11).

13 Ie under the Value Added Tax Act 1994 s 67(1)(b): see para 279 post. For the meaning of 'another member state' see para 4 note 14 ante; and as to the required notification see the Value Added Tax Regulations 1995, SI 1995/2518, regs 36, 148; and para 248 ante.

14 Ie under the Value Added Tax Act 1994 s 75: see para 248 ante.

15 Ibid s 76(6).

16 Ie under ibid s 66: see para 278 post.

17 Ie under ibid s 69: see para 282 post.

18 Ie under ibid s 74 (as amended): see para 249 ante.

19 Ibid s 76(7)(a). If, within such period as may be notified by the commissioners to the person liable to a penalty under s 66 or s 69 or for interest under s 74 (as amended), a failure or default falling within s 66(1) or s 69(1) is remedied, or the VAT or other amount referred to in s 74(1) is paid, it is treated for the purposes of the provision in question as paid or remedied on the date so specified: s 76(8).

20 Ibid s 76(7)(b).

21 Ibid s 76(9). As to the recovery of VAT see para 253 et seq post.

22 See ibid s 83(n), (q); and para 296 post.

252. Time limits for making assessments. Subject to specific exceptions, an assessment[1] may not be made more than six years after the end of the prescribed accounting period[2] or importation or acquisition concerned[3]. If, however, value added tax has been lost as a result of conduct involving dishonesty[4], or for which a person has been convicted of fraud, or in circumstances giving rise to a penalty[5], an assessment may be made within 20 years of the prescribed accounting period or importation or acquisition concerned[6]. Where a person has died and, after his death, the Commissioners of Customs and Excise propose to assess a sum as due by reason of some conduct, however described, of the deceased (including a sum due by way of penalty, interest or surcharge[7]), the assessment may not be made more than three years after the death[8]. If the circumstances are such that, had the deceased still been living, the 20-year limitation period would have applied[9], that period is inapplicable; but the commissioners may make any assessment that could have been made immediately after the death at any time within three years after it[10].

Where the commissioners wish to make an assessment, on one of the grounds relating to failure to make returns[11], of an amount of VAT due for any prescribed accounting period[12], the assessment must be made within the time limits prescribed by the general rules set out above; but, in any event, may not be made after the later of (1) two years after the end of the prescribed accounting period; or (2) one year after evidence of facts, sufficient in the opinion of the commissioners[13] to justify the making of the assessment, comes to their knowledge[14].

Where the commissioners wish to make an assessment on someone who is not a taxable person in respect of an acquisition of certain goods from another member state[15], the assessment must be made within the time limits prescribed by the general rules set out above; but, in any event, may not be made after the later of (a) two years after the time when a notification of the acquisition of the goods in question is given to the commissioners by the person who is required to do so[16]; and (b) one year after evidence of the facts, sufficient in the opinion of the commissioners to justify the making of the assessment, comes to their knowledge[17].

The commissioners may make a single, or 'global', assessment covering more than one prescribed accounting period[18]. In practice this is done when it is impossible or impracticable for them to identify the specific accounting period or periods for which the tax claimed is due; but the power to make such an assessment is not confined to such cases[19]. Where such an assessment is made, the time limit for the assessment begins to run from the end of the first prescribed accounting period included in the assessment[20]. It is a question of fact whether, in any case, there has been a global assessment or a number of separate assessments notified to the taxpayer on the same form[21]. This question of fact is not resolved by the form of the notice of assessment sent to the taxpayer; but by the form of the assessment actually made by the commissioners[22]. To be valid, the notice of assessment (taken together, if necessary, with any accompanying documents) must specify the full period assessed, and not merely the date on which it ends[23].

Where, after the making of an assessment, further evidence of facts, sufficient in the opinion of the commissioners to justify the making of an assessment, comes to the commissioners' knowledge, they may make another assessment, in addition to any earlier assessment[24] provided that the further assessment falls within the limitation rules for making assessments[25].

1   Ie an assessment made under the Value Added Tax Act 1994 s 73, s 75 or s 76 (as amended): see paras 247–251 ante. An assessment is made when the decision to assess is recorded, together with the amount

of the assessment, and not when a notice of assessment is delivered to the trader: *Grunwick Processing Laboratories Ltd v Customs and Excise Comrs* [1986] STC 441 (affd [1987] STC 357, CA); *Babber (t/a Ram Parkash Sunderdass) v Customs and Excise Comrs* [1991] VATTR 268; *Customs and Excise Comrs v Post Office* [1995] STC 749; and see *British Teleflower Service Ltd v Customs and Excise Comrs* (1996) VAT Decision 13756, [1996] STI 290.

2   For the meaning of 'prescribed accounting period' see para 202 note 4 ante. In relation to an assessment under the Value Added Tax Act 1994 s 76 (as amended), any reference in s 77(1) or (2) to the prescribed accounting period concerned is a reference to that period which, in the case of the penalty, interest or surcharge concerned, is the relevant period referred to in s 76(3) (as amended) (see para 251 note 7 ante): s 77(3).

3   Ibid s 77(1)(a). In the case of an assessment under s 76 (as amended) of an amount due by way of a penalty which is not among those referred to in s 76(3) (as amended) (see para 251 note 7 ante), an assessment may not be made more than six years after the event giving rise to the penalty: s 77(1)(b). An assessment under s 76 (as amended) of an amount due by way of any penalty, interest or surcharge referred to in s 76(3) (as amended) may be made at any time before the expiry of the period of two years beginning (1) in the case of a penalty under s 65 (see para 277 post) or s 66 (see para 278 post), with the time when facts sufficient in the opinion of the Commissioners of Customs and Excise to indicate, as the case may be, (a) that the statement in question contained a material inaccuracy; or (b) that there had been a default within the meaning of s 66(1), came to the commissioners' knowledge; and (2) in any other case, with the time when the amount of VAT due for the prescribed accounting period concerned has been finally determined: s 77(2).

An assessment which is made out of time is a nullity ab initio, with the consequence, semble, that the person assessed may defend the collection proceedings, rather than appealing the assessment: *Lord Advocate v Shanks (t/a Shanks & Co)* [1992] STC 928, Ct of Sess; but see also *IRC v Pearlberg* [1953] 1 All ER 388, 34 TC 57, CA; *IRC v Soul* (1976) 51 TC 86, CA; and *IRC v Aken* [1990] 1 WLR 1374, [1990] STC 497, CA; and INCOME TAXATION vol 23 (Reissue) para 1658.

4   Ie conduct falling within the Value Added Tax Act 1994 s 60(1): see para 272 post.

5   Ie under ibid s 67 (as amended): see para 279 post.

6   Ibid s 77(4).

7   As to sums due by way of penalty, interest or surcharge see para 272 et seq post.

8   Value Added Tax Act 1994 s 77(5)(a).

9   Ie the circumstances are as set out in ibid s 77(4): see the text and notes 4–6 supra.

10 See ibid s 77(5)(b). The consequence of this is that the extended time limit under s 77(4) applies to determine whether the commissioners could have made an assessment immediately after the death; and, if they could (eg the death fell five years after the end of the prescribed accounting period in which the VAT was lost by reason of the deceased's fraud), they retain power to make an assessment within the three years following the death.

11 Ie under ibid s 73(1), (2) or (3): see para 247 ante.

12 In *Customs and Excise Comrs v Croydon Hotel & Leisure Co Ltd* [1996] STC 1105, CA, a taxpayer who did not possess a valid VAT invoice in consequence became entitled to claim credit for input tax not in the prescribed accounting period in which the supply was made, but at a later time when the commissioners allowed the deduction. The commissioners imposed a condition that the credit would be repaid if the payment in respect of which the tax credit was claimed proved to be compensation, rather than consideration (see *Holiday Inns (UK) Ltd v Customs and Excise Comrs* [1993] VATTR 321). The tribunal had held that the payment was indeed compensation (and thus outside the scope of VAT), whereupon an assessment was raised to recover the input tax overpaid; held, revsg *Customs and Excise Comrs v Croydon Hotel & Leisure Co Ltd* [1995] STC 855 per Popplewell J, that the essential commencement of the limitation period for assessment was not when the right to repayment arose, but when the right to claim repayment arose, ie when the trader received the commissioners' direction that he might make such a claim. The commissioners' assessment was, therefore, made in time.

13 See *Parekh v Customs and Excise Comrs* [1984] STC 284 (commissioners issued assessments under what is now the Value Added Tax Act 1994 s 73(1) because the traders had failed to render any VAT returns; traders responded by making nil returns and commissioners thereupon withdrew the original assessments and raised fresh assessments; held that the later assessments were out of time, because the nil returns did not amount to or contain evidence of facts relating to the liability to be assessed). This point is significant because, unless a trader has made all the returns which he is obliged to make, he cannot appeal; accordingly where an assessment is raised because of a failure to make returns, it would follow, but for *Parekh v Customs and Excise Comrs* supra, that a fresh limitation period would be started by the trader making returns to enable himself to bring an appeal against the original assessment. Although an assessment must be made within one year of evidence of facts coming to the knowledge of the commissioners, it does not have to be notified to the taxpayer within the year; but it is unenforceable until notification has been made: *Grunwick Processing Laboratories Ltd v Customs and Excise*

Comrs [1986] STC 441 (affd without discussion of this point [1987] STC 357, CA). See also *Schlumberger Inland Services Inc v Customs and Excise Comrs* [1987] STC 228; *Cutts v Customs and Excise Comrs* [1989] STC 201.

14 Value Added Tax Act 1994 s 73(6). Actual and not constructive knowledge of the commissioners is necessary before time starts running: *Spillane v Customs and Excise Comrs* [1990] STC 212; *Customs and Excise Comrs v Post Office* [1995] STC 749; *British Teleflower Service Ltd v Customs and Excise Comrs* (1996) VAT Decision 13756, [1996] STI 290. Whether the commissioners have evidence of facts sufficient to justify the making of the assessment is a mixed question of fact and law: *Customs and Excise Comrs v Post Office* supra. Accordingly, save where the commissioners have been perverse, the tribunal cannot substitute its own view of what facts justify the making of the assessment, but only decide when the last of those facts came to the knowledge of the commissioners: *Cumbrae Properties (1963) Ltd v Customs and Excise Comrs* [1981] STC 799; *GT Garages (Scarborough) Ltd v Customs and Excise Comrs* [1983] VATTR 214.

15 Ie an assessment under the Value Added Tax Act 1994 s 75: see para 248 ante. For the meaning of 'another member state' see para 4 note 14 ante.

16 Ie the person who is required to give a notification by regulations made under the Value Added Tax Act 1994 s 58, Sch 11 para 2(4) (see para 225 ante): see the Value Added Tax Regulations 1995, SI 1995/2518, regs 36, 148; and para 248 ante.

17 Value Added Tax Act 1994 s 75(2). For the meaning of 'knowledge' in this context see the authorities cited in note 14 supra.

18 *SJ Grange Ltd v Customs and Excise Comrs* [1979] 1 WLR 239 at 242, [1979] STC 183 at 193, CA; *Heyfordian Travel Ltd v Customs and Excise Comrs* [1979] VATTR 139; *International Language Centres Ltd v Customs and Excise Comrs* [1983] STC 394 at 396; *Customs and Excise Comrs v Le Rififi Ltd* [1995] STC 103, CA. In *International Language Centres Ltd v Customs and Excise Comrs* supra Woolf J held the assessments before him to be invalid as global assessments. In later proceedings in relation to the same tax, the commissioners brought writ proceedings to recover VAT on the basis that it had been included in the trader's VAT returns; and the court held that the trader had no defence to the action, notwithstanding that the assessments themselves were out of time: *Customs and Excise Comrs v International Language Centres Ltd* [1986] STC 279.

19 See *Customs and Excise Comrs v Le Rififi Ltd* [1995] STC 103 at 107, CA; *House (t/a P & J Autos) v Customs and Excise Comrs* [1996] STC 154, CA, not following *SJ Grange Ltd v Customs and Excise Comrs* [1979] 1 WLR 239, [1979] STC 183, CA, per Lord Denning MR; disapproving *International Language Centres Ltd v Customs and Excise Comrs* [1983] STC 394 at 396 per Woolf J on this point.

20 *SJ Grange Ltd v Customs and Excise Comrs* [1979] 1 WLR 239, [1979] STC 183, CA; *Heyfordian Travel Ltd v Customs and Excise Comrs* [1979] VATTR 139; *International Language Centres Ltd v Customs and Excise Comrs* [1983] STC 394; *Customs and Excise Comrs v Le Rififi Ltd* [1995] STC 103, CA.

21 *Customs and Excise Comrs v Le Rififi Ltd* [1995] STC 103, CA, not following *Don Pasquale (a firm) v Customs and Excise Comrs* [1990] STC 556, CA, on whether a notice of assessment in the form used in both cases constituted a global assessment.

22 However, in many cases, the only material available to the tribunal will be the notice of assessment itself which then stands as the best evidence: *Customs and Excise Comrs v Le Rififi Ltd* [1995] STC 103 at 107, CA.

23 *House (t/a P & J Autos) v Customs and Excise Comrs* [1996] STC 154 at 162, CA (the assessment of the tax considered due and the notification of the assessment to the taxpayer are separate operations and the form of notification is, for that reason, of little importance provided that the taxpayer is adequately notified), following *Grunwick Processing Laboratories Ltd v Customs and Excise Comrs* [1986] STC 441 at 442, *Don Pasquale (a firm) v Customs and Excise Comrs* [1990] STC 556 at 562, CA, and *Customs and Excise Comrs v Le Rififi Ltd* [1995] STC 103 at 106–107, CA; and disapproving *Bell v Customs and Excise Comrs* [1979] VATTR 115 and *SAS Fashions Ltd v Customs and Excise Comrs* (1993) VAT Decision 9426, [1993] STI 343.

24 Value Added Tax Act 1994 ss 73(6), 75(2). If, however, otherwise than in circumstances falling within s 73(6)(b) (see head (2) in the text) or s 75(2)(b) (see head (b) in the text), it appears to the commissioners that the amount which ought to have been assessed in an assessment under s 73, s 75 or s 76 (as amended) exceeds the amount which was so assessed, then the commissioners may make a supplementary assessment of the amount of the excess (under the like provision as that assessment was made) on or before the last day on which that assessment could have been made and may notify the person concerned accordingly: s 77(6).

25 See *Parekh v Customs and Excise Comrs* [1984] STC 284 per Woolf J (if the two year limitation period has expired, so that the commissioners are relying on the extension given to them of one year after further facts have come to their knowledge, they should only be able to make an assessment based on those additional facts). See also *Jeudwine v Customs and Excise Comrs* [1977] VATTR 115 (further assessment held to be invalid because no new facts had come to the commissioners' knowledge between making the

first assessment and the further assessment). Cf *Yuen Tung Restaurant Ltd v Customs and Excise Comrs, Far East Restaurant v Customs and Excise Comrs, Tsun Loi Cheung and Yuen Tung Restaurant Ltd v Customs and Excise Comrs* [1993] VATTR 226 (commissioners withdrew the original assessment (which they considered to be invalid for failing to specify the period of assessment) and issued a fresh assessment; held that the commissioners were entitled to treat the withdrawn assessment as never having been issued; and to make a fresh assessment within the time limit applicable to the original assessment).

(5) RECOVERY OF VALUE ADDED TAX

253. Recovery by civil action. Value added tax due from any person is recoverable as a debt due to the Crown[1]. In addition to the general right to bring the proceedings, the Commissioners of Customs and Excise may apply in a summary manner[2] to the High Court for payment of VAT[3].

1   Value Added Tax Act 1994 s 58, Sch 11 para 5(1). VAT is due if it has been collected by the trader from his customers, even if an assessment to recover has failed by reason of the statutory limitation rules (see para 252 ante); accordingly, the commissioners may bring a writ action to recover the VAT identified in the trader's returns in accordance with Sch 11 para 5(1): *Customs and Excise Comrs v International Language Centres Ltd* [1986] STC 279; cf *Barratt Construction Ltd v Customs and Excise Comrs* [1989] VATTR 204. Where an amount by way of surcharge, interest or penalty has been assessed under the Value Added Tax Act 1994 s 76 (as amended), it is recoverable as if it were VAT due from the person assessed, except to the extent that the assessment is withdrawn or reduced: see s 76(9); and para 251 ante.
2   For the procedure see RSC Ord 77 r 8; and CROWN PROCEEDINGS.
3   See the Crown Proceedings Act 1947 s 14(2)(c) (amended by the Finance Act 1972 s 55(1)); and CROWN PROCEEDINGS.

254. Set-off of credits. Where an amount is due from the Commissioners of Customs and Excise to any person under any provision relating to value added tax ('the credit'), and that person is liable to pay a sum by way of VAT, penalty, interest or surcharge, the amount which the commissioners are due to pay him is set against the amount he is liable to pay the commissioners ('the debit') and, to the extent of the set-off, the obligations of the commissioners and the person concerned are discharged[1]. This provision does not, however, require the credit to be set off against the debit in any case where an insolvency procedure has been applied[2] to the person entitled to the credit, if the credit became due after that procedure was applied to him[3] and the liability to pay the debit either arose before that procedure was so applied or, having arisen afterwards, relates to, or to matters occurring in the course of, the carrying on of any business[4] at times before the procedure was so applied[5].

1   Value Added Tax Act 1994 s 81(3). See *R v Customs and Excise Comrs, ex p Richmond, Re Potco Realisation Ltd* [1989] STC 429.
2   References, in relation to any person, to the application of an insolvency procedure to that person do not include: (1) the making of a bankruptcy order, winding-up order, administration order or an award of sequestration at a time when any such arrangement or deed as is mentioned in the Value Added Tax Act 1994 s 81(4B)(d)–(f) (as added) (see note 3 heads (4)–(6) infra) is in force in relation to that person; (2) the making of a winding-up order at any of the following times, ie (a) immediately upon the discharge of an administration order made in relation to that person; (b) when that person is being wound up voluntarily; or (c) when that person is in administrative receivership; or (3) the making of an administration order in relation to that person at any time when that person is in administrative receivership: s 81(4C) (s 81(4A)–(4D) added by the Finance Act 1995 s 27). For these purposes, a person is regarded as being in administrative receivership throughout any continuous period for which, disregarding any temporary vacancy in the office of receiver, there is an administrative receiver of that person, and the reference in s 81(4B) (as so added) (see note 3 infra) to a person being put into administrative receivership is to be construed accordingly: s 81(4D) (as so added). 'Administration order' means an administration order under the Insolvency Act 1986 Pt II (ss 8–27) (as amended); and 'administrative receiver' means an administrative receiver within the meaning of s 25: Value Added Tax Act 1994 s 81(5)(a), (b) (amended by the Finance Act 1995 s 27). See further COMPANIES.

3 An insolvency procedure is taken to be applied to any person: (1) when a bankruptcy order, winding-up order, administration order or an award of sequestration is made in relation to that person; (2) when that person is put into administrative receivership; (3) when that person, being a corporation, passes a resolution for voluntary winding up; (4) when any voluntary arrangement approved in accordance with the Insolvency Act 1986 Pt I (ss 1–7) or Pt VIII (ss 252–263) comes into force in relation to that person; (5) when a deed of arrangement registered in accordance with the Deeds of Arrangement Act 1914 takes effect in relation to that person; or (6) when that person's estate becomes vested in any other person as that person's trustee under a trust deed within the meaning of the Bankruptcy (Scotland) Act 1985: s 81(4B) (as added: see note 2 supra), s 81(5)(c). See further BANKRUPTCY; COMPANIES.

4 For the meaning of 'business' see para 17 ante.

5 Value Added Tax Act 1994 s 81(4A) (as added: see note 2 supra).

255. Recovery of amount shown on invoice as tax. Where an invoice[1] shows a supply[2] of goods or services as taking place with value added tax chargeable on it, an amount equal to that which is shown on the invoice as VAT or, if VAT is not separately shown, to so much of the total amount shown as payable as is to be taken as representing VAT on the supply, is recoverable from the person who issued the invoice[3]. The amount is recoverable whether or not:

(1) the invoice is a VAT invoice[4];

(2) the supply shown on the invoice actually takes or has taken place, or the amount shown as VAT, or any amount of VAT, is or was chargeable on the supply; or

(3) the person issuing the invoice is a taxable person[5].

Any sum which is recoverable from a person under this provision is recoverable as a debt due to the Crown[6].

1 For the meaning of 'invoice' see para 11 note 8 ante.

2 For the meaning of 'supply' see para 21 ante.

3 Value Added Tax Act 1994 s 58, Sch 11 para 5(2). See *Customs and Excise Comrs v Wells* [1981] STC 588 (a person is liable for VAT shown on invoices which he issues in the name of a company prior to its registration; but is not liable for invoices issued after the company is registered, even though the later invoices are issued in the wrong name).

4 Ie issued in pursuance of the Value Added Tax Act 1994 Sch 11 para 2(1): see para 225 ante. For the meaning of 'VAT invoice' see para 29 note 8 ante; as to the obligation to issue such an invoice see para 240 ante; and as to the contents of the invoice see para 241 ante.

5 Ibid Sch 11 para 5(3). For the meaning of 'taxable person' see paras 12 note 4, 55 ante.

6 Ibid Sch 11 para 5(3). If the sum so recoverable is VAT it is recoverable as such (and thus as a debt due to the Crown: see para 253 ante); and the sum is otherwise recoverable as a debt so due: Sch 11 para 5(3).

256. Recovery by distress. The Commissioners of Customs and Excise may by regulations make provision for authorising distress to be levied on the goods and chattels of any person refusing or neglecting to pay any value added tax due from him, or any amount recoverable as if it were VAT due from him[1], and for the disposal of any goods or chattels on which distress is levied in pursuance of the regulations[2]. They may also make provision for the imposition and recovery of costs, charges, expenses and fees in connection with anything done under the regulations[3].

If, upon written demand, a person neglects or refuses to pay VAT which he is required to pay[4], or to pay any amount which is recoverable as if it were VAT, a collector[5] may distrain on that person's goods and chattels and by warrant signed by him direct any authorised person[6] to levy such distress[7]. Where, however, an amount of tax is assessed and notified to a person[8] (other than an amount which has been assessed as due upon failure by a person to make a return[9]), no distress may be levied until 30 days after that amount became due[10]. A person in respect of whose goods and chattels a warrant has been signed is liable for all costs and charges in connection with anything done under these provisions[11].

If the person whose goods have been distrained does not pay the sum due, together with the costs and charges, within five days of a levy, the distress may be sold by the authorised person for payment of the sums due and all costs and charges. The costs and charges of taking, keeping and selling the distress may then be retained by the authorised person and any surplus remaining after the deduction of those amounts, and of the sum due, must be restored to the owner of the goods which were distrained[12].

1   This provision has effect as if any sum required by way of security under the Value Added Tax Act 1994 s 48(7) (see para 62 ante) were recoverable as if it were VAT due from the person who is required to provide it: s 58, Sch 11 para 5(10).
2   Ibid Sch 11 para 5(4). As to the making of regulations generally see para 8 ante.
3   Ibid Sch 11 para 5(4). In exercise of the power so conferred, the commissioners have made the Value Added Tax Regulations 1995, SI 1995/2518, reg 212 (as amended): see the text and notes 4–12 infra.
4   Ie under the Value Added Tax Act 1994 or any order or any regulations made thereunder: Value Added Tax Regulations 1995 reg 212(1).
5   'Collector' includes deputy collector and assistant collector (ibid reg 2(1)); and for this purpose extends to an officer not below the rank of job band 7 (reg 212(1) (amended by SI 1996/2098)). For these purposes, 'job band', followed by a number between 1 and 12, means the band for the purposes of pay and grading in which the job an officer performs is ranked in the system applicable to Customs and Excise: reg A212 (added by SI 1996/2098).
6   For the meaning of 'authorised person' see para 82 note 5 ante.
7   Value Added Tax Regulations 1995 reg 212(1). The levy must be executed by or under the direction of, and in the presence of, the authorised person: reg 212(2).
8   Ie under the Value Added Tax Act 1994 s 73(9): see para 247 ante.
9   Ie under ibid s 73(1): see para 247 ante. For the meaning of 'return' see para 105 note 14 ante.
10   Value Added Tax Regulations 1995 reg 212(1). The levying of distress does not, of itself, extinguish any right to appeal against the assessment under which distraint has been made: *Davies v Customs and Excise Comrs* [1979] VATTR 162.
11   Value Added Tax Regulations 1995 reg 212(3).
12   Ibid reg 212(4).

257. Evidence by certificate. A certificate[1] of the Commissioners of Customs and Excise that:

(1)   a person was, or was not, at any date registered for value added tax[2]; or

(2)   any return required[3] to be made has not been made or had not been made at any date; or

(3)   any statement or notification required to be submitted or given to the commissioners in accordance with any relevant regulations[4] has not been submitted or given or had not been submitted or given at any date; or

(4)   any VAT shown as due in any return or assessment[5] has not been paid,

is sufficient evidence of the fact until the contrary is proved[6]. A photograph of any document[7] furnished to the commissioners for the purpose of the provisions relating to VAT and certified by them to be such a photograph is admissible in any proceedings, whether civil or criminal, to the same extent as the document itself[8].

1   Any document purporting to be a certificate under the Value Added Tax Act 1994 s 58, Sch 11 para 14(1) or (2) (see the text and notes 2–8 infra) is deemed to be such a certificate until the contrary is proved: Sch 11 para 14(3).
2   Ie under the Value Added Tax Act 1994: see para 56 et seq ante. For the meaning of 'registered' see para 56 note 2 ante.
3   Ie by or under the Value Added Tax Act 1994: Sch 11 para 14(1)(b). For the meaning of 'return' see para 105 note 14 ante.
4   Ie regulations made under ibid Sch 11 para 2(3) or (4): see para 225 ante.
5   Ie made in pursuance of the Value Added Tax Act 1994: Sch 11 para 14(1)(d). As to assessments see paras 247–252 ante.
6   Ibid Sch 11 para 14(1).

7   For the meaning of 'document' see para 11 note 8 ante.
8   Value Added Tax Act 1994 Sch 11 para 14(2).

(6) REFUNDS OF VALUE ADDED TAX

258. Refund of tax to local authorities and other public bodies. Where   value added tax is chargeable on the supply[1] of goods or services to a local authority[2] or other specified public body[3] on the acquisition of any goods by that authority or body from another member state[4] or on the importation of any goods by that authority or body from a place outside the member states[5], and the supply, acquisition or importation is not for the purpose of any business[6] carried on by the authority or body, the Commissioners of Customs and Excise must refund to that authority or body the amount of the VAT so chargeable on a claim made by it at such time and in such manner as they may determine[7].

Where goods or services so supplied to, or acquired or imported by, the authority or body cannot conveniently be distinguished from goods or services supplied to, or acquired or imported by, it for the purpose of a business carried on by it, the amount to be refunded under these provisions is the amount which remains after deducting from the whole of the VAT chargeable on the supply, acquisition or importation such proportion as appears to the commissioners to be attributable to the carrying on of the business[8]. The commissioners may, however, include in the VAT so refunded any VAT attributable to exempt supplies[9] by the authority or body, where the VAT attributable to the carrying on of the business includes such VAT but it is, in the commissioners' opinion, an insignificant proportion of the VAT so chargeable[10].

No VAT may be refunded under these provisions to:

(1)   a general lighthouse authority if that VAT is, in the commissioners' opinion, attributable to activities other than those concerned with the provision, maintenance or management of lights or other navigational aids[11];

(2)   a nominated news provider if that VAT is, in the commissioner's opinion, attributable to activities other than the provision of news programmes for broadcasting by holders of regional Channel 3 licences[12].

The commissioners must also refund to the government of Northern Ireland the amount of the VAT charged on the supply of goods or services to that government, on the acquisition of any goods by that government from another member state or on the importation of any goods by that government from a place outside the member states, after deducting an agreed amount[13] attributable to supplies, acquisitions and importations for the purpose of a business carried on by the government of Northern Ireland[14].

1   For these purposes, references to VAT chargeable do not include any VAT which, by virtue of any order under the Value Added Tax Act 1994 s 25(7) (see para 204 ante), is excluded from credit under s 25 (see para 202 ante): s 33(6).

2   For the meaning of 'local authority' see para 56 note 21 ante.

3   The other bodies to which these provisions apply are: (1) an internal drainage board; (2) a passenger transport authority or executive within the meaning of the Transport Act 1968 Pt II (ss 9–23A) (as amended); (3) a port health authority within the meaning of the Public Health (Control of Disease) Act 1984; (4) a police authority and the Receiver for the Metropolitan Police District; (5) a development corporation within the meaning of the New Towns Act 1981 and the Commission for the New Towns; (6) a general lighthouse authority within the meaning of the Merchant Shipping Act 1995 Pt VIII (ss 193–223); (7) the British Broadcasting Corporation; (8) a nominated news provider as defined by the Broadcasting Act 1990 s 31(3); and (9) any body specified for these purposes by an order made by the Treasury: Value Added Tax Act 1994 s 33(3)(c)–(k) (amended by the Merchant Shipping Act 1995 s 314, Sch 13 para 95). In exercise of the power so conferred, the Treasury has made the Value Added Tax (Refund of Tax) Order 1995, SI 1995/1978, specifying the Environment Agency for these purposes (see

art 2); and the Value Added Tax (Refund of Tax) (No 2) Order 1995, SI 1995/2999, specifying a National Park authority within the meaning of the Environment Act 1995 s 63; and a fire authority constituted by a combination scheme made under the Fire Services Act 1947 s 6 (as amended) (see the Value Added Tax (Refund of Tax) (No 2) Order 1995 art 2). In addition, by virtue of the Interpretation Act 1978 s 17(2)(b), the following orders have effect as if so made: (a) the Value Added Tax (Refund of Tax) (No 2) Order 1973, SI 1973/2121 (specifying various water authorities; this order does not appear to have been revoked despite water privatisation; see further WATER); (b) the Value Added Tax (Refund of Tax) Order 1976, SI 1976/2028, specifying the Commissions for Local Administration in England and Wales; (c) the Value Added Tax (Refund of Tax) Order 1985, SI 1985/1101, specifying certain bodies established under the Local Government Act 1985; (d) the Value Added Tax (Refund of Tax) Order 1986, SI 1986/336, specifying a probation committee, constituted by the Powers of Criminal Courts Act 1973 s 47(a), Sch 3 para 2, a magistrates' courts committee and the charter trustees constituted by the Local Government Act 1972 s 246(4) or (5); (e) the Value Added Tax (Refund of Tax) (No 2) Order 1986, SI 1986/532, specifying authorities established under the Local Government Act 1985 s 10 (as amended); and (f) the Value Added Tax (Refund of Tax) Order 1989, SI 1989/1217 (amended by virtue of the Environment Act 1995 s 120(1), Sch 22 para 233(1)), now specifying the Environment Agency (but see also the Value Added Tax (Refund of Tax) Order 1995 listed supra). As to the agency see further WATER.

4 For the meaning of 'another member state' see para 4 note 14 ante; and as to acquisition from another member state see para 13 ante.

5 As to goods imported from a place outside the member states see para 103 note 2 ante.

6 For the meaning of 'business' see para 17 ante.

7 Value Added Tax Act 1994 s 33(1). For the commissioners' views on the operation of s 33 (as amended) see Customs and Excise Notice 749 *Local Authorities and Similar Bodies* (1 April 1995) (published prior to the decision of Dyson J in *Haringey London Borough Council v Customs and Excise Comrs* [1995] STC 830, and now to be read in the light of that case and Customs and Excise Business Brief 11/95 [1996] STI 964. It is a peculiarity of the Value Added Tax Act 1994 s 33 (as amended) that it does not appear to be authorised by any provision of the Sixth Directive: see *Haringey London Borough Council v Customs and Excise Comrs* (1992) VAT Decision 8820, [1994] VATTR 70 (on appeal [1995] STC 830). EC Council Directive 77/388 (OJ L145, 13.6.77, p 1) art 4(5), which it most closely resembles, is not designed to allow a refund of tax incurred by a local authority otherwise than for its business purposes, but only to define for what purposes such a body is to be treated as a taxable person for VAT. As to the application of art 4(5) see Case 235/85 *EC Commission v Netherlands* [1987] ECR 1471, [1988] 2 CMLR 921, ECJ; Case C-202/90 *Ayuntamiento de Sevilla v Recaudadores de Tributos de las Zonas Primera y Segunda* [1991] ECR I-4247, [1993] STC 659, ECJ; Cases 231/87, 129/88 *Ufficio Distrettuale delle Imposte Dirette di Fiorenzuola d'Arda v Commune di Carpaneto Piacentino and Ufficio Provinciale Imposta sul Valore Aggiunto di Piacenza* [1989] ECR 3233, [1991] STC 205, ECJ (activities carried on by a local authority under the same legal conditions as other private traders should be considered taxable economic activities despite EC Council Directive 77/388 art 4(5)).

8 Value Added Tax Act 1994 s 33(2). The commissioners have set out directions as to the manner in which local authorities should carry out this apportionment in Customs and Excise Notice 749 *Local Authorities and Similar Bodies* (1 April 1995). For a discussion of the status of the previous editions of Customs and Excise Notice 749 see *Haringey London Borough Council v Customs and Excise Comrs* [1995] STC 830.

9 Ie in accordance with regulations under the Value Added Tax Act 1994 s 26: see para 203 ante. For the relevant regulations see the Value Added Tax Regulations 1995, SI 1995/2518, regs 99–111; and para 203 et seq ante. For the meaning of 'exempt supplies' see para 141 ante.

10 Value Added Tax Act 1994 s 33(2)(a), (b). The commissioners have, in Customs and Excise Notice 749 *Local Authorities and Similar Bodies* (1 April 1995) paras 4.4–4.5, explained what they will consider to be an 'insignificant' proportion of the VAT so chargeable; but these guidelines are to be changed with effect from 1 April 1997: see Customs and Excise Business Brief 20/96 [1996] STI 1578. See also *Haringey London Borough Council v Customs and Excise Comrs* [1995] STC 830.

11 Ibid s 33(4).

12 Ibid s 33(5). For the meaning of 'regional Channel 3 licences' see the Broadcasting Act 1990 Pt I (ss 1–71); and TELECOMMUNICATIONS AND BROADCASTING.

13 Ie such amount as may be agreed between the commissioners and the Department of Finance and Personnel for Northern Ireland: Value Added Tax Act 1994 s 99.

14 Ibid s 99. As to the government of Northern Ireland see further CONSTITUTIONAL LAW AND HUMAN RIGHTS vol 8(2) (Reissue) para 67 et seq.

259. Refund of value added tax to persons constructing certain buildings.
Where a person carries out certain building works, his carrying out of those works is
lawful and otherwise than in the course or furtherance of any business[1], and VAT is
chargeable on the supply[2], acquisition or importation of any goods used by him for the
purposes of the works[3], the Commissioners of Customs and Excise must refund to that
person the amount of VAT so chargeable[4] if that person makes a claim[5] in that behalf[6].
The works to which this provision applies are:

(1) the construction of a building designed as a dwelling or number of dwellings[7];

(2) the construction of a building for use solely for a relevant residential purpose[8] or
     relevant charitable purpose[9]; and

(3) a residential conversion[10].

Where a person ('the relevant person') carries out a residential conversion by
arranging for any of the work of the conversion to be done by another ('a contractor')
who is not acting as an architect, surveyor or consultant or in a supervisory capacity, and
the relevant person's carrying out of the conversion is lawful and otherwise than in the
course or furtherance of any business, then if VAT is chargeable on services consisting in
the work done by the contractor the commissioners must refund its amount to the
relevant person on a claim made in that behalf[11].

The commissioners are not required to entertain a claim for a refund of VAT under
these provisions unless the claim:

(a) is made within such time and in such form and manner; and

(b) contains such information; and

(c) is accompanied by such documents[12], whether by way of evidence or otherwise,
as the commissioners prescribe[13] or determine[14].

The amount of any refund under these provisions is a matter on which appeal lies to
a VAT and duties tribunal[15].

1   For the meaning of 'in the course or furtherance of a business' see paras 12 note 5, 17 note 2 ante.
2   These provisions have effect as if this reference to the VAT chargeable on the supply of any goods
    included a reference to VAT chargeable on the supply in accordance with the law of another member
    state: Value Added Tax Act 1994 s 35(3)(a). The provisions of the Value Added Tax Act 1994 and of any
    other enactment or subordinate legislation, whenever passed or made, so far as they relate to a refund
    under s 35 (as amended) are to be construed accordingly: s 35(3). For the meaning of 'supply' see para 21
    ante; for the meaning of 'another member state' see para 4 note 14 ante; and as to the meaning of
    references to the law of another member state see para 11 ante.
3   Goods are treated as used for the purposes of works to which these provisions apply by the person carrying
    out the works in so far only as they are building materials which, in the course of the works, are
    incorporated in the building in question or its site: ibid s 35(1B) (s 35(1A)–(1D) added by the Finance
    Act 1996 s 30(1)).
4   In relation to VAT chargeable in accordance with the law of another member state, the Value Added Tax
    Act 1994 s 35 (as amended) has effect as if references to refunding VAT to any person were references to
    paying that person an amount equal to the VAT chargeable in accordance with the law of that member
    state: s 35(3)(b). The provisions of the Value Added Tax Act 1994 and of any other enactment or
    subordinate legislation, whenever passed or made, so far as they relate to a refund under s 35 (as amended)
    are to be construed accordingly: s 35(3).
5   A claimant must make his claim in respect of a relevant building by (1) furnishing to the commissioners,
    no later than three months after the completion of the building, the prescribed form containing the full
    particulars required therein; and (2) at the same time furnishing to them (a) a certificate of completion
    obtained from a local authority or such other documentary evidence of completion of the building as is
    satisfactory to the commissioners; (b) an invoice showing the registration number of the person supplying
    the goods, whether or not such an invoice is a VAT invoice, in respect of each supply of goods on which
    VAT has been paid which have been incorporated into the building or its site; (c) in respect of imported
    goods which have been incorporated into the building or its site, documentary evidence of their
    importation and of the VAT paid thereon; (d) documentary evidence that planning permission for the
    building had been granted; and (e) a certificate signed by a quantity surveyor or architect that the goods
    shown in the claim were or, in his judgment, were likely to have been, incorporated into the building or

its site: Value Added Tax Regulations 1995, SI 1995/2518, reg 201. 'Relevant building' means a building in respect of which a claimant makes a claim for a refund of VAT pursuant to the Value Added Tax Act 1994 s 35 (as amended): Value Added Tax Regulations 1995 reg 200.

6   Value Added Tax Act 1994 s 35(1) (substituted by the Finance Act 1996 s 30(1)). A penalty may be imposed for dishonestly claiming such a refund (see s 60(1), (2); and para 272 post); it is also an offence for a person knowingly to be concerned in, or in the taking of steps with a view to, the fraudulent obtaining, by himself or another, of a such refund (see s 72(1), (2); and para 268 post).

7   As to when a building is designed as a dwelling or a number of dwellings see ibid s 30(2), Sch 8 Pt II Group 5 note 2 (as substituted); and para 163 note 8 ante (applied by s 35(4) (added by the Finance Act 1996 s 30(3)). The Treasury's power by order under the Value Added Tax Act 1994 s 30 (as amended) to vary Sch 8 (as amended) (see s 30(4); and para 158 ante) includes power to apply any variation so made for the purposes of s 35 (as amended) and to make such consequential modifications of s 35 (as amended) as it thinks fit: s 35(5) (as so added).

8   For the meaning of 'use for a relevant residential purpose' see ibid Sch 8 Pt II Group 5 note 4 (as substituted); and para 163 note 9 ante (as applied: see note 7 supra).

9   For the meaning of 'use for a relevant charitable purpose' see ibid Sch 8 Pt II Group 5 note 6 (as substituted); and para 163 note 10 ante (as applied: see note 7 supra).

10   Ibid s 35(1A) (as added: see note 3 supra). For these purposes, works constitute a residential conversion to the extent that they consist in the conversion of a non-residential building, or a non-residential part of a building, into (1) a building designed as a dwelling or a number of dwellings; (2) a building intended for use solely for a relevant residential purpose; or (3) anything which would fall within head (1) or (2) supra if different parts of a building were treated as separate buildings: s 35(1D) (as so added). For the meaning of 'non-residential' see Sch 8 Pt II Group 5 note 7 (as substituted); and para 163 note 12 ante (as applied: see note 7 supra). A person effecting an enlargement of an existing residential building is not entitled to a refund of VAT under these provisions: see eg *Customs and Excise Comrs v Perry* [1983] STC 383.

11   Value Added Tax Act 1994 s 35(1C) (as added: see note 3 supra).

12   For the meaning of 'document' see para 11 note 8 ante.

13   Ie by regulations under the Value Added Tax Act 1994: see ss 35(2), 96(1).

14   Ibid s 35(2) (amended by the Finance Act 1996 s 30(2)). The commissioners may determine the documents to accompany the claim in accordance with the regulations: Value Added Tax Act 1994 s 35(2) (as so amended). In exercise of the power so conferred, the commissioners have made the Value Added Tax Regulations 1995 regs 200–201: see note 5 supra.

15   See the Value Added Tax Act 1994 s 83(g); and para 296 post.

260. Bad debt relief. Where a person has supplied goods or services for a consideration in money[1] and has accounted for and paid value added tax on the supply[2], then if the whole or any part of the consideration for the supply has been written off in his accounts as a bad debt and a period of six months, beginning with the date of the supply[3], has elapsed, the person is entitled[4], on making a claim to the Commissioners of Customs and Excise, to a refund of the amount of VAT chargeable by reference to the outstanding amount[5]. The 'outstanding amount' means:

(1)   if at the time of the claim the person has received no payment by way of the consideration written off in his accounts as a bad debt[6], an amount equal to the amount of the consideration so written off; or

(2)   if at that time he has received a payment or payments by way of the consideration so written off, an amount by which the payment, or the aggregate of the payments, is exceeded by the amount of the consideration so written off[7].

A person is not entitled to a refund under these provisions unless:

(a)   the value of the supply[8] is equal to or less than its open market value[9]; and

(b)   in the case of a supply of goods, the property in the goods has passed to the person to whom they were supplied or to a person deriving title from, through or under that person[10].

Regulations made by the commissioners for these purposes may:

(i)   require a claim to be made at such time and in such form and manner as may be specified by or under the regulations[11];

(ii) require a claim to be evidenced and quantified by reference to such records and other documents[12] as may be so specified[13];

(iii) require the claimant to keep, for such period and in such form and manner as may be so specified, those records and documents and a record of such information relating to the claim and to subsequent payments by way of consideration as may be so specified[14];

(iv) require the repayment of a refund allowed under these provisions where any requirement of the regulations is not complied with[15];

(v) require the repayment of the whole or, as the case may be, an appropriate part of a refund so allowed where the claimant subsequently receives any payment, or further payment, by way of the consideration written off in his accounts as a bad debt[16];

(vi) include such supplementary, incidental, consequential or transitional provisions as appear to the commissioners to be necessary or expedient for these purposes[17]; and

(vii) make different provision for different circumstances[18].

1   The origin of bad debt relief is EC Council Directive 77/388 (OJ L145, 13.6.77, p 1) art 11(C)(1), by which the 'taxable amount' for VAT purposes is reduced (under conditions which are to be determined by the member states) in the case of cancellation, refusal or total or partial non-payment, or where the price is reduced after the supply takes place. The Commissioners of Customs and Excise deny claims for bad debt relief where the consideration for the supply was to have been otherwise than in money. In *Goldsmiths (Jewellers) Ltd v Customs and Excise Comrs* (1994) VAT Decision 12694, [1994] STI 1374, the question whether the power of member states to derogate from the rule in EC Council Directive 77/388 art 11(C)(1) enables the United Kingdom to exclude barter transactions from bad debt relief has been referred to the European Court of Justice. For the meaning of 'money' see para 7 note 5 ante; and for the meaning of 'consideration' generally see para 86 ante.

2   For the meaning of 'supply' see para 21 ante.

3   The Value Added Tax Act 1994 s 6 (see para 29 et seq ante) applies for determining the time when a supply is to be treated as taking place for the purposes of construing these provisions: s 36(8).

4   Ie subject to the provisions of s 36 and to regulations under it: s 36(2). See the text and notes 5–18 infra.

5   Ibid s 36(1), (2). Save as the commissioners may otherwise allow or direct, the claimant must make a claim to them by including the correct amount of the refund in the box opposite the legend 'VAT reclaimed in this period on purchases and other inputs' on his return: Value Added Tax Regulations 1995, SI 1995/2518, reg 166(1). If at a time the claimant becomes entitled to a refund he is no longer required to make a return to the commissioners, he must make a claim to them in such form and manner as they may direct: reg 166(2). For the meaning of 'return' see para 105 note 14 ante.

6   The whole or any part of the consideration for a supply is taken to have been written off as a bad debt when an entry is made in relation to that supply in the refunds for bad debts account in accordance with ibid reg 168 (see note 14 infra); and this provision has effect regardless of whether a claim can be made in relation to that supply at that time: reg 172(1), (2). Where the claimant owes an amount of money to the purchaser which can be set off, the consideration written off in the accounts must be reduced by the amount so owed (reg 172(1), (3)); and where the claimant holds in relation to the purchaser an enforceable security, the consideration written off in the accounts of the claimant must be reduced by the value of that security (reg 172(1), (4)). 'Purchaser' means a person to whom the claimant made a relevant supply; 'relevant supply' means any taxable supply upon which a claim is based; and 'security' means any mortgage, charge, lien or other security: reg 165. For the meaning of 'taxable supply' see para 12 note 3 ante. The effect of these rules is that a trader is able to write off as a bad debt any debt which has been outstanding for more than six months, even though the debtor is good for the debt.

7   Value Added Tax Act 1994 s 36(3). Where, due to errors of the commissioners, the trader was obliged to issue 'VAT only' invoices, the outstanding amount was held to be equal to the value of the invoices: *Palmer (t/a R & K Engineering) v Customs and Excise Comrs* (1994) VAT Decision 11739, [1994] STI 540.

8   As to the value of a supply see para 85 et seq ante.

9   Value Added Tax Act 1994 s 36(4)(a). For the meaning of 'open market value' see para 87 text to notes 10–11 ante.

10   Ibid s 36(4)(b). Bad debt relief is not, therefore, available where the supplier can rely on an effective reservation of title clause (a 'Romalpa' clause). As to such clauses see *Aluminium Industrie Vaassen BV v Romalpa Aluminium Ltd* [1976] 2 All ER 552, [1976] 1 WLR 676, CA; and other authorities cited in EQUITY vol 16 (Reissue) para 911.

11 Value Added Tax Act 1994 s 36(5)(a). See the Value Added Tax Regulations 1995 reg 166; and note 5 supra.
12 For the meaning of 'document' see para 11 note 8 ante.
13 Value Added Tax Act 1994 s 36(5)(b). Save as the commissioners may otherwise allow, before he makes a claim the claimant must hold in respect of each relevant supply (1) either a copy of any VAT invoice which was provided in accordance with the Value Added Tax Regulations 1995 Pt III (regs 13–20) (see para 240 et seq ante) or, where there was no obligation to provide a VAT invoice, a document which shows the time, nature and purchaser of the relevant goods and services, and the consideration for them; (2) records or other documents showing that he has accounted for and paid the VAT on them; and (3) records or other documents showing that the consideration has been written off in his accounts as a bad debt: reg 167. For the meaning of 'VAT invoice' see para 29 note 8 ante.
14 Value Added Tax Act 1994 s 36(5)(c). Any person who makes a claim to the commissioners must keep a record of that claim: Value Added Tax Regulations 1995 reg 168(1). Save as the commissioners may otherwise allow, the record must consist of the following information in respect of each claim made: (1) in respect of each relevant supply for that claim (a) the amount of VAT chargeable; (b) the prescribed accounting period in which the VAT chargeable was accounted for and paid to the commissioners; (c) the date and number of any invoice issued in relation to the supply or, where there is no such invoice, such information as is necessary to identify the time, nature and purchaser of it; and (d) any payment received for it; (2) the outstanding amount to which the claim relates; (3) the amount of the claim; and (4) the prescribed accounting period in which the claim was made: reg 168(2). Any records created in pursuance of reg 168 must be kept in a single account to be known as the 'refunds for bad debts account': reg 168(3). 'Payment' means any payment or part-payment which is made by any person to the claimant by way of consideration for a supply regardless of whether such payment extinguishes the purchaser's debt to the claimant or not: reg 165. For the meaning of 'prescribed accounting period' see para 105 note 16 ante; and for the meaning of 'invoice' see para 11 note 8 ante.
    Save as the commissioners may otherwise allow, the claimant must preserve the documents, invoices and records which he holds in accordance with regs 167, 168 for a period of four years from the date of the making of the claim: reg 169(1). Upon demand made by an authorised person, he must produce or cause to be produced any such documents, invoices and records for inspection by the authorised person and permit him to remove them at a reasonable time and for a reasonable period: reg 169(2). For the meaning of 'authorised person' see para 82 note 5 ante.
15 Value Added Tax Act 1994 s 36(5)(d). Save as the commissioners may otherwise allow, where the claimant fails to comply with the requirements of the Value Added Tax Regulations 1995 reg 167 (see note 13 supra), regs 168, 169 (see note 14 supra) or reg 170 (see note 17 infra), he must repay to them the amount of the refund obtained by the claim to which the failure to comply relates; and he must repay the money by including that amount in the box opposite the legend 'VAT due in this period on sales and other outputs' on his return for the prescribed accounting period which the commissioners designate for that purpose: reg 171(3). If, at the time the claimant is required to repay any amount, he is no longer required to make returns to the commissioners, he must repay that amount to them at such time and in such form and manner as they may direct: reg 171(4).
16 Value Added Tax Act 1994 s 36(5)(e). Where a claimant has received a refund upon a claim, and either (1) a payment for the relevant supply is subsequently received; or (2) a payment is, by virtue of the Value Added Tax Regulations 1995 reg 170 (see note 17 infra), treated as attributed to the relevant supply, he must repay to the commissioners such an amount as equals the amount of the refund or the balance of it, multiplied by a fraction of which the numerator is the amount so received or attributed and the denominator is the amount of the outstanding consideration: reg 171(1). He must repay that amount to them by including it in the box opposite the legend 'VAT due in this period on sales and other outputs' on his return for the prescribed accounting period in which the payment is received: reg 171(2). As to the method of payment where he is no longer required to make returns see reg 171(4); and note 15 supra.
17 Value Added Tax Act 1994 s 36(5)(f). The provisions which may be so included in regulations may include rules (1) for ascertaining (a) whether, when and to what extent consideration is to be taken to have been written off in accounts as a bad debt; (b) whether a payment is to be taken as received by way of consideration for a particular supply; (c) whether, and to what extent, a payment is to be taken as received by way of consideration written off in accounts as a bad debt; (2) dealing with particular cases, such as those involving part payment or mutual debts; and in particular such rules may vary the way in which the following amounts are to be calculated: (a) the outstanding amount mentioned in s 36(2); and (b) the amount of any repayment where a refund has been allowed under s 36: s 36(6), (7).
    Where the claimant made more than one supply, whether taxable or otherwise, to the purchaser, and a payment is received in relation to those supplies, the payment must be attributed to each supply in accordance with the following rules: Value Added Tax Regulations 1995 reg 170(1). The payment must be attributed to the supply which is the earliest in time and, if not wholly attributed to that supply, thereafter to supplies in the order of the dates on which they were made, except that such attribution

must not be made to any supply if the payment was allocated to that supply by the purchaser at the time of payment and the consideration for that supply was paid in full: reg 170(2). Where (i) the earliest supply and other supplies to which the whole of the payment could be attributed under this rule occur on one day; or (ii) the supplies to which the balance of the payment could be attributed thereunder occur on one day, the payment must be attributed to those supplies by multiplying, for each supply, the payment received by a fraction of which the numerator is the outstanding consideration for that supply and the denominator is the total outstanding consideration for those supplies: reg 170(3).

18   Value Added Tax Act 1994 s 36(5)(g). For transitional provisions relating to bad debt relief under the Value Added Tax Act 1983 s 22 (repealed) see the Value Added Tax Regulations 1995 Pt XVIII (regs 156–164).

261. Repayment of value added tax to Community traders. The Commissioners of Customs and Excise may provide, by means of a scheme embodied in regulations[1], for the repayment to persons carrying on business[2] in another member state[3] of value added tax on supplies to them in the United Kingdom or on the importation of goods by them from places outside the member states[4] which would be input tax[5] of theirs if they were taxable persons[6] in the United Kingdom[7]. The relief is not available to persons carrying on business in the United Kingdom[8].

Repayment must be made in such cases only, and subject to such conditions[9], as the scheme may prescribe[10]. The scheme may provide:

(1)   for claims and repayments to be made only through agents in the United Kingdom[11];

(2)   either generally or for specified purposes for the agents to be treated as if they were taxable persons and for treating claims as if they were returns[12] and repayments as if they were repayments of input tax[13]; and

(3)   for generally regulating the methods by which the amount of any repayment is to be determined and the repayment is to be made[14].

A person to whom the scheme applies is entitled[15] to be repaid VAT charged on goods imported by him from a place outside the member states in respect of which no other relief is available or on supplies made to him in the United Kingdom if that VAT would be input tax of his were he a taxable person in the United Kingdom[16]. The scheme applies to any supply of goods or services made in the United Kingdom or to any importation of goods from a place outside the member states but does not apply to:

(a)   a supply or importation of goods or a supply of services which the claimant has used or intends to use for the purpose of any supply by him in the United Kingdom; or

(b)   a supply or importation of goods which the claimant has removed or intends to remove to another member state, or which he has exported or intends to export to a place outside the member states[17].

VAT charged on a supply which, if made to a taxable person, would be excluded from any credit for input tax[18] is not, however, to be repaid under the scheme[19]; nor is VAT charged on a supply to a travel agent[20] which is for the direct benefit of a traveller other than the travel agent or his employee[21]. No claim may be made for less than £16[22], nor for less than £130 in respect of VAT charged on supplies or on importations from a place outside the member states made during a period of less than one calendar year, except where that period represents the final part of a calendar year[23]. An appeal lies to a VAT and duties tribunal against a decision as to the amount of a repayment to which a person is entitled[24].

If any claimant furnishes or sends to the commissioners for the purposes of the scheme a document which is false, or which has been altered after issue to that person, the commissioners may refuse to repay any VAT claimed by that claimant for the period of two years from the date when the relevant claim was made[25]; and if a sum has been repaid to a claimant as a result of an incorrect claim, the amount of any subsequent repayment to that claimant may be reduced by that sum[26].

1   The scheme for Community traders is contained in the Value Added Tax Regulations 1995, SI 1995/2518, Pt XX (regs 173–184): see notes 3–26 infra. As to the power to make regulations generally see para 8 ante.

2   For the meaning of 'business' see para 17 ante.

3   For the meaning of 'another member state' see para 4 note 14 ante. The Value Added Tax Regulations 1995 Pt XX applies to a person carrying on a business in a member state other than the United Kingdom but does not apply to such a person in any period referred to in reg 179 (see note 10 and the text and notes 22–23 infra) if during that period (1) he was established in the United Kingdom; or (2) he made supplies in the United Kingdom of goods or services other than (a) transport of freight outside the United Kingdom or to or from a place outside the United Kingdom or services ancillary thereto; (b) services where the VAT on the supply is payable solely by the person to whom the services are supplied in accordance with the provisions of the Value Added Tax Act s 8 (the reverse charge: see para 27 ante); and (c) goods where the VAT on the supply is payable solely by the person to whom they are supplied as provided for in s 14 (acquisitions from other member states: see paras 16, 41 ante): Value Added Tax Regulations 1995 reg 175. A person is treated as being established in a country for these purposes if (i) he has there an establishment from which business transactions are effected; or (ii) he has no such establishment, there or elsewhere, but his usual place of residence is there: reg 173(2). A person carrying on business through a branch or agency in any country is treated as having there an establishment from which business transactions are effected (reg 173(3)(a)); and 'usual place of residence' in relation to a body corporate, means the place where it is legally constituted (reg 173(3)(b)). For the meaning of 'supply' see para 21 ante; and for the meaning of 'United Kingdom' see para 4 note 3 ante.

4   As to the importation of goods from a place outside the member states see para 103 note 2 ante.

5   For the meaning of 'input tax' see paras 4, 201 ante.

6   For the meaning of 'taxable person' see paras 12 note 4, 55 ante.

7   Value Added Tax Act 1994 s 39(1), (2)(a). This power to provide for the repayment to such persons of VAT which would be input tax of theirs if they were taxable persons in the United Kingdom includes power to provide for the payment to such persons of sums equal to amounts which, if they were taxable persons in the United Kingdom, would be input tax of their by virtue of regulations under s 54 (flat-rate scheme for farmers: see para 79 et seq ante); and references in s 39, or in any other enactment, to a repayment of VAT are to be construed accordingly: s 54(5).

8   Ibid s 39(2).

9   Ie being conditions specified in the regulations or imposed by the commissioners either generally or in particular cases: ibid s 39(3).

10   Ibid s 39(3). A person claiming a repayment of VAT under the Value Added Tax Regulations 1995 Pt XX must (1) complete in the English language and send to the commissioners either the prescribed form or a form designed for the purpose by any official authority, containing full information in respect of all the matters specified in the form and a declaration as set out in it; (2) at the same time furnish (a) a certificate of status issued by the official authority of the member state in which the claimant is established, either on the prescribed form or on the form designed by the official authority for the purpose; and (b) such documentary evidence of an entitlement to deduct VAT as may be required of a taxable person claiming a deduction of input tax in accordance with the provisions of reg 29 (see para 236 ante): reg 178(1). Where the commissioners are in possession of a certificate of status issued not more than 12 months before the date of the claim, the claimant is not required to furnish a further certificate: reg 178(2). The commissioners must refuse to accept any document referred to in head (2)(b) supra if it bears an official stamp indicating that it had been furnished in support of an earlier claim: reg 178(3). For the prescribed forms for the purposes of heads (1)–(2) supra see reg 178(1), Sch 1, Forms 15, 16 respectively. 'Official authority' means the authority in a member state designated to issue the certificate referred to in head (2)(a) supra; and 'claimant' means a person making a claim under Pt XX or a person on whose behalf such a claim is made: reg 173(1). For the meaning of 'document' see para 11 note 8 ante.

       The claim for repayment must be made not later than six months after the end of the calendar year in which the VAT was charged, and must be in respect of VAT charged on supplies or on importations from a place outside the member states made during a period of not less than three months and not more than one calendar year, provided that a claim may be in respect of VAT charged on supplies or on importations from a place outside the member states made during a period of less than three months where that period represents the final part of a calendar year: reg 179(1). 'Calendar year' means the period of 12 months beginning with the first day of January in any year: reg 173(1).

11   Value Added Tax Act 1994 s 39(3)(a).

12   For the meaning of 'return' see para 105 note 14 ante. For the purposes of ibid s 73 (as amended) (see paras 247, 252 ante), any claim made under the Value Added Tax Regulations 1995 Pt XX is treated as

a return required under the Value Added Tax Act 1994 s 58, Sch 11 para 2 (as amended) (see para 225 ante): Value Added Tax Regulations 1995 reg 181.

13 Value Added Tax Act 1994 s 39(3)(b). For the purposes of s 83(c) (appeals: see para 296 post), repayments claimed under the Value Added Tax Regulations 1995 Pt XX are treated as the amount of any input tax which may be credited to a person: reg 182.

14 Value Added Tax Act 1994 s 39(3)(c). Where any repayment is to be made to a claimant in the country in which he is established, the commissioners may reduce the amount of the repayment by the amount of any bank charges or costs incurred as a result of it: Value Added Tax Regulations 1995 reg 180.

15 Ie subject to the other provisions of ibid Pt XX: see notes 3, 10, 12–14 supra; and the text and notes 16–26 infra.

16 Ibid reg 174.

17 Ibid reg 176.

18 Ie under the Value Added Tax Act 1994 s 25: see para 202 ante.

19 Value Added Tax Regulations 1995 reg 177(1)(a).

20 'Travel agent' includes a tour operator and any person who purchases and supplies services of a kind enjoyed by travellers: ibid reg 177(2).

21 Ibid reg 177(1)(b).

22 Ibid reg 179(2).

23 Ibid reg 179(3).

24 See the Value Added Tax Act 1994 s 83(c); and para 296 post (applied by the Value Added Tax Regulations 1995 reg 182: see note 13 supra).

25 Ibid reg 183.

26 Ibid reg 184.

262. Repayment of value added tax to third country traders. The Commissioners of Customs and Excise may provide, by means of a scheme embodied in regulations[1], for the repayment to persons carrying on business[2] in countries other than the member states[3] of value added tax on supplies to them in the United Kingdom or on the importation of goods by them from places outside the member states[4] which would be input tax[5] of theirs if they were taxable persons in the United Kingdom[6]. The relief is not available to persons carrying on business in the United Kingdom[7].

Repayment must be made in such cases only, and subject to such conditions[8], as the scheme may prescribe[9].

A person to whom the scheme applies is entitled[10] to be repaid VAT charged on goods imported by him into the United Kingdom in respect of which no other relief is available or on supplies made to him in the United Kingdom if that VAT would be input tax of his were he a taxable person in the United Kingdom[11]. The scheme applies to any supply of goods or services made in the United Kingdom or to any importation of goods into the United Kingdom on or after 1 July 1994 but does not apply to any supply or importation which:

(1) the trader has used or intends to use for the purpose of any supply by him in the United Kingdom; or

(2) has been exported or is intended for exportation from the United Kingdom by or on behalf of the trader[12].

VAT charged on a supply which, if made to a taxable person, would be excluded from any credit for input tax[13] is not, however, to be repaid under the scheme[14]; nor is VAT charged on a supply to a travel agent[15] which is for the direct benefit of a traveller other than the travel agent or his employee to be repaid[16]. No claim may be made for less than £16[17], nor for less than £130 in respect of VAT charged on supplies or on importations made during a period of less than the prescribed year, except where that period represents the final part of the prescribed year[18]. An appeal lies to a VAT and duties tribunal against a decision as to the amount of a repayment to which a person is entitled[19].

If any claimant furnishes or sends to the commissioners for the purposes of the scheme a document which is false, or which has been altered after issue to that person, the commissioners may refuse to repay any VAT claimed by that claimant for the period of two years from the date when the relevant claim was made[20]; and if a sum has been repaid to a claimant as a result of an incorrect claim, the amount of any subsequent repayment to that claimant may be reduced by that sum[21].

1   The scheme for third country traders is contained in the Value Added Tax Regulations 1995, SI 1995/2518, Pt XXI (regs 185–197): see notes 3, 9–21 infra. As to the power to make regulations generally see para 8 ante.

2   For the meaning of 'business' see para 17 ante.

3   Ie if, pursuant to any EC Community directive, rules are adopted by the EC Council about refunds of VAT to persons established elsewhere than in the member states: Value Added Tax Act 1994 s 39(2)(b). For the meaning of 'another member state' see para 4 note 14 ante; and as to the territories treated as included in, or excluded from, the territory of the member states for VAT purposes see para 10 ante.

    The Value Added Tax Regulations 1995 Pt XXI applies to any trader, but not if during any period determined under reg 192 (see note 9 infra) (1) he was established in any of the member states; or (2) he made supplies in the United Kingdom of goods or services other than (a) transport of freight outside the United Kingdom or to or from a place outside the United Kingdom or services ancillary thereto; (b) services where the VAT on the supply is payable solely by the person to whom the services are supplied in accordance with the provisions of the Value Added Tax Act s 8 (the reverse charge: see para 27 ante); and (c) goods where the VAT on the supply is payable solely by the person to whom they are supplied: Value Added Tax Regulations 1995 reg 188(2). A person is treated as being established in a country for these purposes if (i) he has there a business establishment; or (ii) he has no such establishment, there or elsewhere, but his usual place of residence is there: reg 185(2). A person carrying on business through a branch or agency in any country is treated as being established there (reg 185(3)(a)); and where the person is a body corporate its usual place of residence is the place where it is legally constituted (reg 185(3)(b)). 'Trader' means a person carrying on a business who is established in a third country and who is not a taxable person in the United Kingdom; and 'third country' means a country other than those comprising the member states of the European Community: reg 185(1). For the meaning of 'supply' see para 21 ante; for the meaning of 'United Kingdom' see para 4 note 3 ante; and for the meaning of 'taxable person' see paras 12 note 4, 55 ante.

4   As to the importation of goods from a place outside the member states see para 103 note 2 ante.

5   For the meaning of 'input tax' see paras 4, 201 ante.

6   Value Added Tax Act 1994 s 39(1), (2)(b). See also s 54(5); and para 261 note 7 ante.

7   Ibid s 39(2).

8   Ie being conditions specified in the regulations or imposed by the commissioners either generally or in particular cases: ibid s 39(3).

9   Ibid s 39(3). As to the matters for which the scheme may provide see s 39(3)(a)–(c); and para 261 ante.

    A person claiming a repayment of VAT under the Value Added Tax Regulations 1995 Pt XXI must (1) complete in the English language and send to the commissioners either the prescribed form or a like form produced by any official authority, containing full information in respect of all the matters specified in the form and a declaration as set out in it; (2) at the same time furnish (a) a certificate of status issued by the official authority of the third country in which the trader is established, either on the prescribed form or on a like form produced by the official authority; and (b) such documentary evidence of an entitlement to deduct input tax as may be required of a taxable person claiming a deduction of input tax in accordance with the provisions of reg 29 (see para 225 ante): reg 191(1). Where the commissioners are in possession of a certificate of status issued not more than 12 months before the date of the claim, the claimant is not required to furnish a further certificate: reg 191(2). The commissioners must refuse to accept any document referred to in head (2)(b) supra if it bears an official stamp indicating that it had been furnished in support of an earlier claim: reg 191(3). For the prescribed forms for the purposes of heads (1)–(2) supra see reg 191(1), Sch 1, Forms 9, 10 respectively. 'Official authority' means any government body or agency in any country which is recognised by the commissioners as having authority to act for these purposes; and 'claimant' means a person making a claim under Pt XXI or a person on whose behalf a claim is made and any agent acting on his behalf as his VAT representative: reg 185(1). As a condition of allowing a repayment, the commissioners may require a trader to appoint a VAT representative to act on his behalf: reg 187. For these purposes, 'VAT representative' means any person established in the United Kingdom and registered for VAT purposes in accordance with the provisions of the Value Added Tax Act 1994 s 3(2), Sch 1 (as amended) (see para 56 et seq ante) who acts as agent on behalf of a claimant: Value Added Tax Regulations 1995 reg 185(1). For the meaning of 'document' see para 11 note 8 ante; and as to VAT representatives generally see para 62 ante.

    A claim must be made not later than six months after the end of the prescribed year in which the VAT was charged, and must be in respect of VAT charged on supplies or on importations made during a period of not less than three months and not more than 12 months, provided that a claim may be in respect of

VAT charged on supplies or on importations made during a period of less than three months where that period represents the final part of the prescribed year: reg 192(1). 'Prescribed year' means the period of 12 months beginning on the first day of July in any year: reg 185(1).

10   Ie subject to the other provisions of ibid Pt XXI: see notes 3, 9 supra; and the text and notes 11–21 infra.

11   Ibid reg 186. Save as the commissioners may otherwise allow, however, a trader to whom Pt XXI applies who is established in a third country having a comparable system of turnover taxes is not entitled to any refunds under Pt XXI unless that country provides reciprocal arrangements for refunds to be made to taxable persons who are established in the United Kingdom: reg 188(1).

12   Ibid reg 189.

13   Ie under the Value Added Tax Act 1994 s 25: see para 202 ante.

14   Value Added Tax Regulations 1995 reg 190(1)(a).

15   'Travel agent' includes a tour operator and any person who purchases and supplies services of a kind enjoyed by travellers: ibid reg 190(2).

16   Ibid reg 190(1)(b).

17   Ibid reg 192(2).

18   Ibid reg 192(3).

19   See the Value Added Tax Act 1994 s 83(c); and para 296 post (applied by the Value Added Tax Regulations 1995 reg 194, whereby repayments claimed under Pt XXI are to be treated for appeal purposes as the amount of any input tax which may be credited to a person). Where any repayment is to be made to a claimant in the country in which he is established, the commissioners may reduce the amount of the repayment by the amount of any bank charges or costs incurred as a result of it: reg 193. For the purposes of the Value Added Tax Act 1994 s 73 (as amended) (assessments: see paras 247, 252 ante), any claim made under the Value Added Tax Regulations 1995 Pt XXI is treated as a return required under the Value Added Tax Act 1994 s 58, Sch 11 para 2 (as amended) (see para 225 ante): Value Added Tax Regulations 1995 reg 194.

20   See ibid reg 196.

21   Ibid reg 197.

263. Refunds in relation to new means of transport supplied to other member states. Where a person who is not a taxable person[1] makes a supply[2] of goods, consisting in a new means of transport[3], which involves the removal of the goods to another member state[4], the Commissioners of Customs and Excise must refund to him, on a claim made in that behalf (1) the amount of any value added tax on the supply to him of that means of transport; or (2) the amount of any VAT paid by him on the acquisition of that means of transport from another member state, or on its importation from a place outside the member states[5]. The amount of VAT so refunded must not, however, exceed the amount that would have been payable on the supply involving the removal if it had been a taxable supply[6] by a taxable person and had not been a zero-rated supply[7].

The commissioners are not entitled to entertain a claim for refund of VAT under these provisions unless the claim is made within such time, and in such form and manner, contains such information and is accompanied by such documents[8], whether by way of evidence or otherwise, as they may prescribe by regulations[9]. A claimant must make his claim in writing no earlier than one month, and no later than 14 days, prior to making the supply of the new means of transport by virtue of which the claim arises[10]. The claim must be made at, or sent to, any office designated by the commissioners for the receipt of such claims[11]; it must contain the prescribed information[12] and must be accompanied by the prescribed documents[13]. The claim must include a declaration, signed by the claimant or a person authorised by him in that behalf in writing, that all the information entered in or accompanying it is true and complete[14]. It must be completed by the submission to the commissioners of the sales invoice or similar document identifying the new means of transport and showing the price paid by the claimant's customer and documentary evidence that the new means of transport has been removed to another member state[15].

1   For the meaning of 'taxable person' see paras 12 note 4, 55 ante.

2   For the meaning of 'supply' see para 21 ante.

3   For the meaning of 'new means of transport' see para 13 note 8 ante.

4   For the meaning of 'another member state' see para 4 note 14 ante.

5   Value Added Tax Act 1994 s 40(1). As to acquisition from another member state see para 13 note 6 ante; and as to importation from a place outside the member states see para 103 note 2 ante.

6   For the meaning of 'taxable supply' see para 12 note 3 ante.

7   Value Added Tax Act 1994 s 40(2). The effect of this is that the claimant cannot recover the full amount of the VAT which he paid on the acquisition of the means of transport if he subsequently sells it for a smaller sum. For the meaning of 'zero-rated' see para 158 ante.

8   For the meaning of 'document' see para 11 note 8 ante.

9   Value Added Tax Act 1994 s 40(3). In exercise of the power so conferred, the commissioners have made the Value Added Tax Regulations 1995, SI 1995/2518, regs 149–154: see the text and notes 10–15 infra.

10   Ibid reg 149.

11   Ibid reg 150.

12   Ibid reg 151. The prescribed information is (1) the name, current address and telephone number of the claimant; (2) the place where the new means of transport is kept and the times when it may be inspected; (3) the name and address of the person who supplied the new means of transport to the claimant; (4) the price paid by the claimant for the supply to him of the new means of transport excluding any VAT; (5) the amount of any VAT paid by the claimant on the supply to him of the new means of transport; (6) the amount of any VAT paid by the claimant on the acquisition of the new means of transport from another member state or on its importation from a place outside the member states; (7) the name and address of the proposed purchaser, the member state to which the new means of transport is to be removed, and the date of the proposed purchase; (8) the price to be paid by the proposed purchaser; (9) a full description of the new means of transport including, in the case of motorised land vehicles, its mileage since its first entry into service and, in the case of ships and aircraft, its hours of use since its first entry into service; (10) in the case of a ship, its length in metres; (11) in the case of an aircraft, its take-off weight in kilograms; (12) in the case of a motorised land vehicle powered by a combustion engine, its displacement or cylinder capacity in cubic centimetres, and in the case of an electrically propelled motorised land vehicle, its maximum power output in kilowatts, described to the nearest tenth of a kilowatt; and (13) the amount of the refund being claimed: reg 151(a)–(m).

13   Ibid reg 152. The prescribed documents are (1) the invoice issued by the person who supplied the new means of transport to the claimant or such other documentary evidence of purchase as is satisfactory to the commissioners; (2) in respect of a new means of transport imported from a place outside the member states by the claimant, documentary evidence of its importation and of the VAT paid on it; and (3) in respect of a new means of transport acquired by the claimant from another member state, documentary evidence of the VAT paid on it: reg 152(a)–(c). For the meaning of 'invoice' see para 11 note 8 ante.

14   Ibid reg 153.

15   Ibid reg 154.

264. Recovery of overpaid value added tax.

Where a person has paid an amount to the Commissioners of Customs and Excise by way of VAT which was not VAT due to them, they are liable, on a claim being made for the purpose[1], to repay the amount to him[2]. No amount may be claimed under this provision after the expiry of six years from the date on which it was paid[3], except that where an amount has been paid to the commissioners by reason of a mistake[4], a claim for the repayment of the amount may be made at any time before the expiry of six years from the date on which the claimant discovered the mistake or could with reasonable diligence have discovered it[5].

The commissioners are not liable to repay an amount paid to them by way of VAT by virtue of the fact that it was not VAT due to them, except in accordance with this provision[6]; and it is a defence to a claim for recovery of overpaid VAT that repayment of an amount would unjustly enrich[7] the claimant[8].

1   A claim must be made in such form and manner, and be supported by such documentary evidence, as the commissioners prescribe by regulations; and the regulations may make different provision for different cases: Value Added Tax Act 1994 s 80(6). A claim must be made in writing to the commissioners and must state, by reference to such documentary evidence as is in the possession of the claimant, the amount of the claim and the method by which that amount was calculated: Value Added Tax Regulations 1995, SI 1995/2518, reg 37.

2   Value Added Tax Act 1994 s 80(1), (2). The provisions now contained in s 80 were first introduced in the Finance Act 1989 s 24 (repealed) in substitution for the previous system under which a trader was able to correct errors by adjustment of his subsequent VAT returns: see *Betterware Products Ltd v Customs and*

    Excise Comrs (No 2) [1988] STC 6; and *Customs and Excise Comrs v Fine Art Developments plc* [1989] STC 85, HL; cf *Woodcock v Customs and Excise Comrs* [1989] AC 914, [1989] STC 237 (where the traders unsuccessfully sought to recover over-paid VAT by writ action rather than by adjusting their VAT returns: even now, such an action would fail, having regard to the Value Added Tax Act 1994 s 80(7): see the text to note 7 infra).

3   Ibid s 80(4).

4   As to the meaning of 'mistake' see the following cases on the meaning of 'error': *Customs and Excise Comrs v Fine Art Developments plc* [1989] AC 914, [1989] STC 85, HL; *Aer Lingus v Customs and Excise Comrs* [1992] VATTR 438; *University of Edinburgh v Customs and Excise Comrs* (1991) VAT Decision 6569 (unreported); *North East Media Development Trust Ltd v Customs and Excise Comrs* (1995) VAT Decision 13104, [1995] STI 743; *Trustees of the Victoria and Albert Museum v Customs and Excise Comrs* [1996] STC 1016.

5   Value Added Tax Act 1994 s 80(4), (5). It has been proposed that, with effect from 18 July 1996, the commissioners should not be liable to repay any amount paid to them more than three years before the making of the claim: see the exposed draft: Time limits on repayments of VAT, unjust enrichment and statutory interest; Consultation on draft Finance Bill clauses; and Customs and Excise News Release 42/96 [1996] STI 1249.

6   Value Added Tax Act 1994 s 80(7).

7   For the meaning of 'unjust enrichment' in this context see Case 68/79 *Hans Just I/S v Danish Ministry for Fiscal Affairs* [1980] ECR 501, [1981] 2 CMLR 714, ECJ; Case 199/82 *Amministrazione delle Finanze dello Stato v SpA San Giorgio* [1983] ECR 3595, [1985] 2 CMLR 658, ECJ; Joined Cases 331/85, 376/85, 378/85 *Les Fils de Jules Bianco SA and J Girard Fils SA v Directeur Général des Douanes et Droits Indirects* [1988] ECR 1099, [1989] 3 CMLR 36, ECJ; Case 104/86 *EC Commission v Italy* [1988] ECR 1799, [1989] 3 CMLR 25, ECJ; Case 207/87 *Weissgerber v Finanzamt Neustadt an der Weinstrasse* [1988] ECR 4433, [1991] STC 589, ECJ; *Customs and Excise Comrs v McMaster Stores (Scotland) Ltd (in receivership)* [1995] STC 846; *Lamdec Ltd v Customs and Excise Comrs* [1991] VATTR 296; *Creative Facility Ltd v Customs and Excise Comrs, Oblique Press v Customs and Excise Comrs* (1993) VAT Decision 10891, [1993] STI 1276; *Computeach International Ltd v Customs and Excise Comrs* [1994] VATTR 237; *National and Provincial Building Society v Customs and Excise Comrs* (1996) VAT Decision 14017, [1996] STI 967; and *Hardman v Customs and Excise Comrs* (1996) VAT Decision 14045, [1996] STI 998. See also *Woolwich Equitable Building Society v IRC* [1993] AC 70, [1992] 3 All ER 737, HL. Customs will not normally refuse to refund money where claimants indicate that they are willing to pass on the money to the customers who paid the tax, or where the claimants provide documentary evidence that due to economic circumstances (eg competition with other persons carrying on an identical business) none of the tax, or only some of it, was passed on to customers: Customs and Excise Business Brief 8/95 [1995] STI 762 (which deals with claims for repayment by dispensing opticians following the cases of *Customs and Excise Comrs v Leightons Ltd, Customs and Excise Comrs v Eye-Tech Opticians (No 1) and Eye-Tech Opticians (No 2)* [1995] STC 458). At the date at which this volume states the law, draft legislation had been published redefining the concept of 'unjust enrichment', but these proposals had not been enacted: see the exposed draft referred to in note 5 supra.

8   Value Added Tax Act 1994 s 80(3).

265. Interest in certain cases of official error. Where, due to an error on the part of the Commissioners of Customs and Excise[1], a person has:

    (1)   accounted to them for an amount by way of output tax[2] which was not output tax due from him and which they are in consequence liable to repay to him; or

    (2)   failed to claim credit for input tax[3] for an amount for which he was entitled so to claim credit and which they are in consequence liable to pay to him; or

    (3)   otherwise paid to them by way of VAT an amount that was not VAT due and which they are in consequence liable to repay to him; or

    (4)   suffered delay in receiving payment[4] of an amount due to him from them in connection with VAT[5],

then the commissioners must pay interest[6] to him on that amount[7] for the applicable period[8] if, and to the extent that, they would not otherwise be liable to do so[9]. They are, however, so liable to pay interest only on a claim made in writing for that purpose[10]; and no such claim may be made after the expiry of six years from the date on which the claimant discovered the error or could with reasonable diligence have discovered it[11].

Nothing in these provisions requires the commissioners to pay interest on any amount which falls to be increased by a repayment supplement[12] or, where an amount is so increased, on so much of the increased amount as represents the supplement[13].

Any interest payable by the commissioners[14] to a person on a sum due to him[15] is treated as an amount due[16] by way of credit[17].

1   As to the meaning of 'error' see para 264 note 4 ante. In *North East Media Development Trust Ltd v Customs and Excise Comrs* (1995) VAT Decision 13104, [1995] STI 743, the tribunal held that the failure of the United Kingdom properly to implement a provision of the Sixth Directive (see para 1 ante) having direct effect would not have been an 'error on the part of the commissioners' having regard to the constitutional doctrine of the separation of powers (but see CONSTITUTIONAL LAW AND HUMAN RIGHTS vol 8(2) (Reissue) para 8); but the commissioners had erred in giving incorrect guidance to the appellant in the course of correspondence. It is not sufficient for the operation of the Value Added Tax Act 1994 s 78 (see the text and notes 2–13 infra) that there has been an error on the part of the commissioners; it must have been relied upon by the claimant, since the over-payment etc by the claimant must have been due to the error of the commissioners: *North East Media Development Trust Ltd v Customs and Excise Comrs* supra. See also *American Express Bank Ltd v Customs and Excise Comrs* (1993) VAT Decision 9748 (unreported); *Wheeler (t/a Wheeler Motor Co) v Customs and Excise Comrs* (1995) VAT Decision 13617, [1995] STI 1971. The failure of an officer to identify an under-claim of credit during control visits does not constitute an error on the part of the commissioners: *Newton Newton v Customs and Excise Comrs* (1993) VAT Decision 11372 (unreported).

2   For the meaning of 'output tax' see paras 4, 201 ante.

3   Ie under the Value Added Tax Act 1994 s 25: see para 202 ante. For the meaning of 'input tax' see paras 4, 201 ante.

4   Any reference for these purposes to receiving a payment from the commissioners includes a reference to the discharge, by way of set-off, of their liability to make it: ibid s 78(12)(a).

5   Ibid s 78(1)(a)–(d).

6   The interest is payable at the rate applicable under the Finance Act 1996 s 197 (see para 249 ante): Value Added Tax Act 1994 s 78(3) (amended by the Finance Act 1996 s 197(6)(d)(ii)). This provision has effect for periods beginning on or after such day as the Treasury may by order made by statutory instrument appoint and has effect in relation to interest running from before that day as well as in relation to interest running from, or from after, that day: see s 197(7).
     The interest is simple interest only, but the interest itself may be a payment due, attracting interest from the date on which a written claim for interest is furnished to the commissioners: *National Council of YMCAs Inc v Customs and Excise Comrs* [1993] VATTR 299. See also *S & DE Jarman v Customs and Excise Comrs* (1993) VAT Decision 11637 (unreported). It has been proposed that this rule should be reversed by statute: see the draft Value Added Tax Act 1994 s 78(1A), intended to have effect from 18 July 1996; exposed draft: Time limits on repayments of VAT, unjust enrichment and statutory interest; Consultation on draft Finance Bill clauses; and Customs and Excise News Release 42/96 [1996] STI 1249.

7   In *North East Media Development Trust Ltd v Customs and Excise Comrs (No 2)* (1995) VAT Decision 13425, [1995] STI 1365, and *North East Media Development Trust Ltd v Customs and Excise Comrs* (1996) VAT Decision 14416, [1996] STI 1645, the tribunal held that, where the error of the commissioners had caused the claimant to fail not only to claim sufficient credit for input tax but also to account for an amount of output tax, interest was payable on the net amount of input tax under-claimed less output tax undeclared.

8   The 'applicable period' is: (1) in a case falling within head (1) or (2) in the text, the period beginning with the appropriate commencement date and ending with the date on which the commissioners authorise payment of the amount on which the interest is payable; (2) in a case falling within head (3) in the text, the period beginning with the date on which the payment is received by the commissioners and ending with the date on which they authorise payment of the amount on which the interest is payable; and (3) in a case falling within head (4) in the text, the period beginning with the date on which, apart from the error, the commissioners might reasonably have been expected to authorise payment of the amount on which the interest is payable and ending with the date on which they in fact authorise payment of that amount: Value Added Tax Act 1994 s 78(4), (6), (7). In s 78(4) (see head (1) supra), 'the appropriate commencement date': (a) in a case where an amount would have been due from the person by way of VAT in connection with the relevant return, had his input tax and output tax been as stated in that return, means the date on which the commissioners received payment of that amount; and (b) in a case where no such payment would have been due from him in connection with that return, means the date on which the commissioners would, apart from the error, have authorised payment of the amount on which the interest is payable; and 'the relevant return' means the return in which the person accounted for, or ought to have claimed credit for, the amount on which the interest is payable: s 78(5). For these purposes, any reference to a return is a reference to a return required to be made in accordance with s 58, Sch 11

para 2 (as amended) (see para 225 ante): s 78(12)(b). For the meaning of 'return' generally see para 105 note 14 ante.

In determining in accordance with heads (1)–(3) supra the applicable period for the purposes of s 78(1), there must be left out of account any period referable to the raising and answering of any reasonable inquiry relating to any matter giving rise to, or otherwise connected with, the person's entitlement to interest under these provisions (s 78(8)); and in determining whether any period is so referable, there must be taken to be so referable any period which (i) begins with the date on which the commissioners first consider it necessary to make such an inquiry; and (ii) ends with the date on which the commissioners satisfy themselves that they have received a complete answer to the inquiry or determine not to make the inquiry or, if they have made it, not to pursue it further, but excluding so much of that period as may be prescribed (s 78(9)). It is immaterial whether any inquiry is in fact made or whether it is or might have been made of the person referred to in s 78(1) or of an authorised person or of some other person: s 78(9). For the meaning of 'authorised person' see para 82 note 5 ante.

9   Ibid s 78(1).
10   Ibid s 78(10).
11   Ibid s 78(11). See *Bonanni v Customs and Excise Comrs* (1994) VAT Decision 11823, [1994] STI 605. It has been proposed that, with effect from 18 July 1996, the commissioners should not be liable to repay any amount paid to them more than three years before the making of the claim: see the exposed draft: Time limits on repayments of VAT, unjust enrichment and statutory interest; Consultation on draft Finance Bill clauses; and Customs and Excise News Release 42/96 [1996] STI 1249.
12   Ie under the Value Added Tax Act 1994 s 79: see para 266 post.
13   Ibid s 78(2).
14   Ie whether under an enactment or instrument or otherwise: ibid s 81(1).
15   Ie under or by virtue of any provision of the Value Added Tax Act 1994: s 81(1).
16   Ie under ibid s 25(3): see para 202 ante.
17   Ibid s 81(1). Section 81(1) is to be disregarded for the purpose of determining a person's entitlement to interest or the amount of interest to which he is entitled: s 81(2).

266. Repayment supplement in respect of certain delayed payments or refunds.

In certain circumstances, described below, where (1) a person is entitled to a value added tax credit[1]; or (2) a body which is registered[2] is entitled to a refund under the provisions relating to refunds to public bodies[3], the amount which would otherwise be due by way of that payment or refund is increased by the addition of a supplement equal to 5 per cent of that amount or £50, whichever is the greater[4]. A repayment supplement is due if:

(a)   the requisite return or claim[5] is received[6] by the Commissioners of Customs and Excise not later than the last day on which it is required to be furnished or made;

(b)   a written instruction directing the making of the payment or refund is not issued by the commissioners within the period of 30 days[7] beginning on the date of the receipt by the commissioners of that return or claim; and

(c)   the amount shown on that return or claim as due by way of payment or refund does not exceed the payment or refund which was in fact due by more than 5 per cent of that payment or refund or £250, (whichever is the greater)[8].

Except for the purpose of determining the amount of the supplement, a supplement paid to any person under head (1) above is treated as an amount due to him by way of a VAT credit[9] and a supplement paid to any body under head (2) above is treated as an amount due to it[10] by way of refund[11].

1   As to VAT credits see the Value Added Tax Act 1994 s 25(3); and para 202 ante.
2   For the meaning of 'registered' see para 56 note 2 ante.
3   Ie a body to which the Value Added Tax Act 1994 s 33 (as amended) applies: see para 258 ante.
4   Ibid s 79(1). A right to recover input tax which arises on the making of an election to waive exemption (see s 51(1), Sch 10 para 2 (as amended); and para 143 ante) which has retrospective effect does not per se also give rise to a right to repayment supplement: *Lawson Mardon Group Pension Scheme v Customs and Excise Comrs* (1993) VAT Decision 10231, [1993] STI 948. There is no right to a repayment supplement until either the Commissioners of Customs and Excise have completed

their inquiries into the matter (see note 7 infra), or the tribunal directs that a supplement be paid: *British Steel Exports Ltd v Customs and Excise Comrs* (1992) VAT Decision 7562, [1992] STI 689. The distinction between a repayment supplement and interest under the Value Added Tax Act 1994 s 78 (see para 265 ante) is that the repayment supplement is fixed as 5% of the credit due, and is payable in full if the commissioners exceed the permitted period for payment by as little as a day.

5   'Requisite return or claim' means (1) in relation to a payment, the return for the prescribed accounting period concerned which is required to be furnished in accordance with regulations under the Value Added Tax Act 1994; and (2) in relation to a refund, the claim which is required to be made in accordance with the commissioners' determination under s 33 (as amended) (see para 258 ante): s 79(6). For the meaning of 'return' see para 105 note 14 ante; for the meaning of 'prescribed accounting period' see para 202 note 4 ante; and as to the furnishing of returns see para 226 et seq ante.

6   No repayment supplement is payable unless the requisite return is not only posted by the claimant but actually received by the commissioners: *Customs and Excise Comrs v W Timms & Son (Builders) Ltd* [1992] STC 374.

7   If the Treasury by order so directs, any period specified in the order is to be disregarded for the purpose of calculating the period of 30 days: Value Added Tax Act 1994 s 79(7). At the date at which this volume states the law, no such order had been made. The burden of proving when a payment instruction has been 'issued' rests on the commissioners: *Aston v Customs and Excise Comrs* [1991] VATTR 170.

Regulations may provide that, in computing the period of 30 days, there are to be left out of account periods determined in accordance with the regulations and referable to (1) the raising and answering of any reasonable inquiry relating to the requisite return or claim; (2) the correction by the commissioners of any errors or omissions in that return or claim; and (3) in the case of a payment, (a) any such continuing failure to submit returns as is referred to in the Value Added Tax Act 1994 s 25(5) (see para 202 ante); and (b) compliance with any such condition as is referred to in s 58, Sch 11 para 4(1) (see para 202 ante): s 79(3); and see the Value Added Tax Regulations 1995, SI 1995/2518, reg 198. In determining for those purposes whether any period is referable to the raising and answering of such an inquiry, there is to be taken as so referable any period which begins with the date on which the commissioners first consider it necessary to make such an inquiry and ends with the date on which the commissioners satisfy themselves that they have received a complete answer to the inquiry or determine not to make the inquiry or, if they have made it, not to pursue it further, but excluding so much of that period as may be prescribed: s 79(4). It is immaterial whether any inquiry is in fact made or whether it is or might have been made of the person or body making the requisite return or claim or of an authorised person or of some other person: s 79(4) (revsg *Customs and Excise Comrs v L Rowland & Co (Retail) Ltd* [1992] STC 647 per Auld J, which followed *Five Oaks Properties Ltd v Customs and Excise Comrs* [1991] VATTR 318). As to inquiries by the commissioners see *Kitsfern Ltd v Customs and Excise Comrs* [1989] VATTR 312; *Olive Tree Press Ltd v Customs and Excise Comrs* (1990) VAT Decision 5349, [1990] STI 995. For the meaning of 'authorised person' see para 82 note 5 ante.

For the purpose of determining the duration of the periods referred to in heads (1)–(3) supra, the following rules apply: (i) in the case of the period mentioned in head (1) supra, it is taken to have begun on the date when the commissioners first raised the inquiry and to have ended on the date when they received a complete answer to their inquiry; (ii) in the case of the period mentioned in head (2) supra, it is taken to have begun on the date when the error or omission first came to the notice of the commissioners and to have ended on the date when the error or omission was corrected by them; (iii) in the case of the period mentioned in head (3)(a) supra, it is determined in accordance with a certificate of the commissioners under the Value Added Tax Act 1994 Sch 11 para 14(1)(b) (see para 257 ante); and (iv) in the case of the period mentioned in head (3)(b) supra, it is taken to have begun on the date of the service of the written notice of the commissioners which required the production of documents or the giving of security and to have ended on the day when they received the required documents or the required security: Value Added Tax Regulations 1995 reg 199.

8   Value Added Tax Act 1994 s 79(2).

9   Ibid s 79(5)(a). It would seem that an appeal to the VAT and duties tribunal may thus be made against a decision as to the making of the supplement under s 83(c): see para 296 post.

10   Ie under ibid s 33 (as amended): see para 258 ante.

11   Ibid s 79(5)(b). There is no specific right of appeal against a refusal of the commissioners to make payment of a refund under s 33 (as amended): it would seem, therefore, that there correspondingly is no specific right to appeal against a refusal to pay a supplement on such a refund.

6. OFFENCES AND PENALTIES

(1) CRIMINAL OFFENCES

267. Proceedings in respect of criminal offences. Certain provisions of the Customs and Excise Management Act 1979 relating to proceedings for offences, mitigation of penalties[1], and certain other matters apply in relation to offences[2] relating to value added tax[3] and penalties imposed for such offences as they apply in relation to offences and penalties under the Customs and Excise Acts[4]. No proceedings for such an offence may be instituted except by order of the Commissioners of Customs and Excise or by a law officer of the Crown[5]. Proceedings for an indictable offence[6] may not be commenced after the end of 20 years beginning with the day on which the offence was committed[7]; and proceedings for a summary offence[8] may not be commenced after the end of the period of three years beginning with the day on which the offence was committed but, subject to that, may be commenced at any time within six months from the date on which sufficient evidence to warrant the proceedings came to the knowledge of the prosecuting authority[9].

Although the maximum term of imprisonment which may be imposed for some offences relating to VAT is seven years, such a term can only be imposed upon conviction upon indictment, and on summary conviction the maximum term of imprisonment is six months[10]. If a magistrates' court orders a person to be imprisoned in addition to imposing a penalty for the same offence, and also orders him, whether at the same time or subsequently, to be imprisoned for a further term in respect of his failure to pay the penalty, the aggregate of those terms must not exceed 15 months[11].

Where in any proceedings for an offence relating to VAT any question arises whether or not VAT on any goods or services has become due or has been paid or secured, the burden of proof lies upon the accused person[12].

Statements made or documents[13] produced by or on behalf of a person are not inadmissible in any criminal proceedings against the person concerned in respect of any offence in connection with or in relation to VAT by reason only that it has been drawn to his attention that, in relation to VAT, the commissioners may assess an amount due by way of a civil penalty instead of instituting criminal proceedings and, though no undertaking can be given as to whether the commissioners will make such an assessment in the case of any person, it is their practice to be influenced by the fact that a person has made a full confession of any dishonest conduct to which he has been a party and has given full facilities for investigation, and that the commissioners or, on appeal, a tribunal have or has power[14] to reduce a civil penalty imposed[15] for the dishonest evasion of VAT, and he was or may have been induced thereby to make the statements or produce the documents[16].

1   Ie the Customs and Excise Management Act 1979 ss 145–155 (as amended): see CUSTOMS AND EXCISE.
2   Ie including any act or omission in respect of which a penalty is imposed: Value Added Tax Act 1994 s 72(12). For these purposes, references to penalties do not include references to penalties under ss 60–70 (as amended) (see para 272 et seq post): s 72(13).
3   As to such offences see para 268 et seq post.

4   Value Added Tax Act 1994 s 72(12). For the meaning of 'the Customs and Excise Acts' see para 105 note 2 ante.

5   See the Customs and Excise Management Act 1979 s 145(1), (5); and CUSTOMS AND EXCISE. Any proceedings under the Customs and Excise Acts instituted in a magistrates' court, and any such proceedings instituted in a court of summary jurisdiction in Northern Ireland, must be commenced in the name of an officer: s 145(2). Where, however, a person has been arrested for any offence for which he is liable to be arrested under the Customs and Excise Acts, any court before which he is brought may proceed to deal with the case although the proceedings have not been instituted by order of the commissioners or have not been commenced in the name of an officer: s 145(6) (amended by the Police and Criminal Evidence Act 1984 s 114(1)). As to the application of these provisions see the text and notes 1–4 supra.

6   For the meaning of 'indictable offence' see CRIMINAL LAW vol 11(2) (Reissue) para 803 note 1. Fraud cases should be tried summarily unless the fraud has been committed or disguised in a sophisticated manner and/or one of the features of the case is the high value of the unrecovered property: *Practice Note (Mode of Trial: Guidelines)* [1990] 1 WLR 1439, DC. In those circumstances, unless there are mitigating factors, case law suggests that the offence is a serious one for which a period of imprisonment exceeding six months can be expected: *R v Northampton Magistrates' Court, ex p Customs and Excise Comrs* (1994) 158 JP 1083, DC.

7   Customs and Excise Management Act 1979 s 146A(2) (s 146A added by the Finance Act 1989 s 16(1), (4) in relation to offences committed after 26 July 1989). As to the application of this provision see the text and notes 1–4 supra.

8   For the meaning of 'summary offence' see CRIMINAL LAW vol 11(2) (Reissue) para 803 note 3.

9   Customs and Excise Management Act 1979 s 146A(3) (as added: see note 7 supra). As to the application of this provision see the text and notes 1–4 supra.

10   See the Value Added Tax Act 1994 s 72(1)(a), (b), (3)(i), (ii), (8)(a), (b); and paras 268–269 post.

11   See the Customs and Excise Management Act 1979 s 149(1); and CUSTOMS AND EXCISE. As to the application of this provision see the text and notes 1–4 supra.

12   See ibid s 154(2); and CUSTOMS AND EXCISE. As to the application of this provision see the text and notes 1–4 supra.

13   For the meaning of 'document' see para 11 note 8 ante.

14   Ie under the Value Added Tax Act 1994 s 70: see para 280 post.

15   Ie under ibid s 60: see para 272 post.

16   Ibid s 60(4), (5)(a).

268. Fraudulent evasion of value added tax. If any person is knowingly concerned in, or in the taking of steps[1] with a view to, the fraudulent evasion of VAT[2] by him or any other person, he is liable (1) on summary conviction, to a penalty of the statutory maximum[3] or of three times the amount of the VAT[4], whichever is the greater, or to imprisonment for a term not exceeding six months, or to both[5]; or (2) on conviction on indictment, to a penalty of any amount or to imprisonment for a term not exceeding seven years, or to both[6].

Where a person's conduct during any specified period must have involved the commission of the offence of the fraudulent evasion of VAT then, whether or not the particulars of that offence are known, he is guilty of an offence and liable (a) on summary conviction, to a penalty of the statutory maximum or, if greater, three times the amount of the VAT that was or was intended to be evaded by his conduct, or to imprisonment for a term not exceeding six months, or to both[7]; or (b) on conviction on indictment, to a penalty of any amount or to imprisonment for a term not exceeding seven years, or to both[8].

Where an authorised person[9] has reasonable grounds for suspecting that such an offence has been committed, he may arrest anyone whom he has such grounds for suspecting to be guilty of the offence[10].

Apart from offences specific to VAT, such as that of the fraudulent evasion of VAT, prosecutions may also be brought under general criminal law for offences such as cheating the public revenue[11].

1   Necessary particulars of such steps must be given to provide reasonable information as to the nature of the offence: see *Robertson v Rosenberg* [1951] WN 97, [1951] 1 TLR 417, DC (a case decided on a similar provision of the former purchase tax law).

2   Any reference to the evasion of VAT includes a reference to the obtaining of: (1) the payment of a VAT credit (see para 202 ante); or (2) a refund under the Value Added Tax Act 1994 s 35 (as amended) (refund of VAT to persons constructing certain buildings: see para 259 ante), s 36 (bad debts: see para 260 ante) or s 40 (refunds in relation to new means of transport supplied to other member states: see para 263 ante) or under the Value Added Tax Act 1983 s 22 (repealed subject to transitional provisions) (the old system for the refund of VAT on bad debts); or (3) a refund under any regulations made by virtue of the Value Added Tax Act 1994 s 13(5) (refunds of VAT paid in the United Kingdom on goods on which VAT paid on acquisition in another member state: see para 13 ante); or (4) a repayment under s 39 (repayment of VAT to those in business overseas: see paras 261–262 ante): s 72(2)(a)–(d). See also *R v Dealy* [1995] 1 WLR 658, [1995] STC 217, CA.

3   The 'statutory maximum' is the prescribed sum within the meaning of the Magistrates' Courts Act 1980 s 32 (as amended) and, as from 1 October 1992, is £5,000: s 32(9) (amended by the Criminal Justice Act 1991 s 17(2)).

4   For these purposes, any reference to the amount of the VAT is to be construed: (1) in relation to VAT itself or a VAT credit, as a reference to the aggregate of the amount (if any) falsely claimed by way of credit for input tax and the amount (if any) by which output tax was falsely understated; and (2) in relation to a refund or repayment falling within the Value Added Tax Act 1994 s 72(2)(b), (c) or (d) (see note 2 heads (2)–(4) supra) the amount falsely claimed by way of refund or repayment: s 72(2)(i), (ii). For the meaning of 'input tax' and 'output tax' see paras 4, 201 ante.

5   Ibid s 72(1)(a).

6   Ibid s 72(1)(b). As to the form of the indictment see *R v Asif* (1985) 82 Cr App Rep 123, CA; *R v Ike* [1996] STC 391, CA. See also *R v Choudhoury, R v Uddin* [1996] STC 1163, CA.

7   Value Added Tax Act 1994 s 72(8)(a).

8   Ibid s 72(8)(b). While an Order in Council is in force under the Isle of Man Act 1979 s 6 (see para 8 ante), the Value Added Tax Act 1994 s 72(8) has effect as if the reference to offences under the provisions there mentioned included a reference to offences under the corresponding provisions of the Act of Tynwald: Isle of Man Act 1979 s 6(4)(c) (amended by the Value Added Tax Act 1983 s 50(1), Sch 9 para 3; and by the Value Added Tax Act 1994 s 100, Sch 14 para 7(2)).

9   For the meaning of 'authorised person' see para 82 note 5 ante.

10 Value Added Tax Act 1994 s 72(9).

11 See the Theft Act 1968 s 32(1)(a); and CRIMINAL LAW vol 11(1) (Reissue) para 578. There is no anomaly in the continuing existence of both common-law and statutory offences for the same behaviour: *R v Mavji* [1987] 2 All ER 758 at 761, [1986] STC 508 at 510, CA; *R v Ryan* [1994] 2 CMLR 399, [1994] STC 446, CA. The offence of cheating the revenue is satisfied by omission; there is no requirement of a positive act of deception, so that a failure to register for VAT, or to make returns and to pay VAT to the commissioners when tax was due sufficed to constitute the commission of the offence: *R v Redford* [1988] STC 845, 89 Cr App Rep 1, CA; and as to charging statutory conspiracy see *R v Mulligan* [1990] STC 220, CA.

269. Offences in connection with false documents and false statements. If any person with intent to deceive produces, furnishes or sends[1] for the purposes of the Value Added Tax Act 1994, or otherwise makes use for those purposes of, any document which is false in a material particular, or in furnishing any information for the purposes of that Act makes any statement which he knows to be false in a material particular or recklessly makes a statement which is false in a material particular, he is liable on summary conviction to a penalty of the statutory maximum[2] or to imprisonment for a term not exceeding six months, or to both; or, on conviction on indictment, to a penalty of any amount or to imprisonment for a term not exceeding seven years, or to both[3]. Where, however, the document which is false in a material particular is a VAT return[4] or the information which he so furnishes is contained in or otherwise relevant to such a return, he is liable on summary conviction to an alternative penalty equal to three times the aggregate of the amount (if any) falsely claimed by way of credit for input tax[5] and the amount (if any) by which output tax[6] was falsely understated, if that is greater than the statutory maximum (as well as being liable to the term of imprisonment stated above)[7]. Likewise, if the document which is false in a material particular is a claim for a refund[8] or repayment of VAT[9], or the information which he so furnishes is contained in or otherwise relevant to such a claim, he is liable on summary conviction to an alternative penalty equal to three times the amount falsely claimed, if that is greater than the statutory maximum (as well as being liable to the term of imprisonment stated above)[10].

Where a person's conduct during any specified period must have involved the commission of one or other of the above offences then, whether or not the particulars of that offence or those offences are known, he is guilty of an offence and liable on summary conviction to a penalty of the statutory maximum or, if greater, three times the amount of any VAT that was or was intended to be evaded by his conduct, or to imprisonment for a term not exceeding six months, or to both, or, on conviction on indictment, to a penalty of any amount or to imprisonment for a term not exceeding seven years, or to both[11].

Where an authorised person[12] has reasonable grounds for suspecting that any such offence as is described above has been committed, he may arrest anyone whom he has such grounds for suspecting to be guilty of the offence[13].

1   This reference to furnishing, sending or otherwise making use of a document which is false in a material particular, with intent to deceive, includes a reference to furnishing, sending or otherwise making use of such a document, with intent to secure that a machine will respond to the document as if it were a true document: Value Added Tax Act 1994 s 72(6). This obviates unmeritorious contentions in respect of machine-read VAT returns. 'Producing, furnishing or sending' a document includes causing a document to be produced, furnished or sent: see s 72(7). For the meaning of 'document' see para 11 note 8 ante.

2   As to the statutory maximum see para 268 note 3 ante.

3   Value Added Tax 1994 s 72(3). As to the form of the indictment see *R v Asif* (1985) 82 Cr App Rep 123, CA; *R v Ike* [1996] STC 391, CA. See also *R v Choudhoury, R v Uddin* [1996] STC 1163, CA.

4   For the meaning of 'return' see para 105 note 14 ante.

5   For the meaning of 'input tax' see paras 4, 201 ante. As to credit for input tax see para 202 ante.

6   For the meaning of 'output tax' see paras 4, 201 ante.

7   Value Added Tax Act 1994 s 72(3)(i), (4).

8   Ie under ibid s 35 (as amended) (refund of VAT to persons constructing certain buildings: see para 259 ante); s 36 (bad debts: see para 260 ante); or s 40 (refunds in relation to new means of transport supplied to other member states: see para 263 ante); or under the Value Added Tax Act 1983 s 22 (repealed subject to transitional provisions) (the old system for the refund of VAT on bad debts); or under any regulations made by virtue of the Value Added Tax Act 1994 s 13(5) (refunds of VAT paid in the United Kingdom on goods on which VAT paid on acquisition in another member state: see para 13 ante): s 72(5)(a).

9   Ie a repayment under ibid s 39 (repayment of VAT to those in business overseas: see paras 261–262 ante): s 72(5)(a).

10 Ibid s 72(3)(i), (5).

11 Ibid s 72(8). See also para 268 note 8 ante.

12 For the meaning of 'authorised person' see para 82 note 5 ante.

13 Value Added Tax Act 1994 s 72(9).

270.   Offences in connection with acquiring possession of or dealing with any goods or accepting supply of any services. If any person acquires possession of or deals with any goods, or accepts the supply[1] of any services, having reason to believe that value added tax on the supply of the goods or services, on the acquisition of the goods from another member state[2] or on the importation of the goods from a place outside the member states[3], has been or will be evaded, he is liable on summary conviction to a penalty of level 5 on the standard scale[4] or three times the amount of the VAT, whichever is the greater[5].

1 For the meaning of 'supply' see para 21 ante.
2 For the meaning of 'another member state' see para 4 note 14 ante. As to the acquisition of goods from another member state see para 13 ante.
3 As to the importation of goods from a place outside the member states see para 103 note 2 ante; and as to the territories included in, or excluded from, the territories of the member states see para 10 ante.
4 As to the standard scale see para 129 note 3 ante.
5 Value Added Tax Act 1994 s 72(10).

271. Offences in connection with the giving of security. If any person supplies goods or services in contravention of the provisions relating to the giving of security[1], he is liable on summary conviction to a penalty of level 5 on the standard scale[2].

1 Ie in contravention of the Value Added Tax Act 1994 s 58, Sch 11 para 4(2): see para 246 ante.
2 Ibid s 72(11). As to the standard scale see para 129 note 3 ante.

(2) CIVIL PENALTIES

272. Value added tax evasion; conduct involving dishonesty. In any case where, for the purpose of evading VAT[1], a person does any act or omits to take any action, and his conduct involves dishonesty[2], whether or not it is such as to give rise to criminal liability[3], he is liable to a penalty equal to the amount of VAT evaded or sought to be evaded[4] by his conduct[5]. If, however, the person has been convicted of an offence by reason of that conduct, whether under the Value Added Tax Act 1994 or otherwise, that conduct does not also give rise to such a penalty[6].

Statements made or documents[7] produced by or on behalf of a person are not inadmissible in any proceedings against him for the recovery of any sum due from him in connection with or in relation to VAT by reason only that it has been drawn to his attention that, in relation to VAT, the Commissioners of Customs and Excise may assess an amount due by way of a civil penalty instead of instituting criminal proceedings and, though no undertaking can be given as to whether the commissioners will make such an assessment in the case of any person, it is their practice to be influenced by the fact that a person has made a full confession of any dishonest conduct to which he has been a party and has given full facilities for investigation, and that the commissioners or, on appeal, a tribunal have or has power[8] to reduce the penalty for the dishonest evasion of VAT and that he was, or may have been, induced thereby to make the statements or produce the documents[9].

On an appeal against an assessment to a penalty for dishonest evasion of VAT, the burden of proof as to the allegations that for the purpose of evading VAT, a person has done any act or omitted to take any action, and that his conduct involved dishonesty, lies upon the commissioners[10].

1 This reference to evading VAT includes a reference to obtaining any of the following sums, in circumstances where the person is not entitled to that sum: (1) a refund under any regulations made by virtue of Value Added Tax Act 1994 s 13(5) (refunds of VAT paid in the United Kingdom on goods on which VAT was paid on acquisition in another member state: see para 13 ante); (2) a VAT credit (see para 202 ante); (3) a refund under s 35 (as amended) (refund of VAT to persons constructing certain buildings: see para 259 ante); s 36 (bad debts: see para 260 ante); or s 40 (refunds in relation to new means of transport supplied to other member states: see para 263 ante); or under the Value Added Tax Act 1983 s 22 (repealed subject to transitional provisions) (the old system for the refund of VAT on bad debts); and (4) a repayment under the Value Added Tax Act 1994 s 39 (repayment of VAT to those in business overseas: see paras 261–262 ante): s 60(2). An appeal lies against the imposition of a penalty under these provisions: see s 83(n); and para 296 post.

2   For the meaning of 'dishonesty' see *Gandhi Tandoori Restaurant v Customs and Excise Comrs* [1989] VATTR 39. If it is reasonably possible that the taxpayer had a genuine, albeit mistaken, belief that his conduct was not wrong, he is not guilty of dishonesty: *Nandera v Customs and Excise Comrs* (1992) VAT Decision 7880, [1992] STI 861.

3   As to criminal offences involving VAT see para 267 et seq ante.

4   This reference to the amount of the VAT evaded or sought to be evaded by a person's conduct is to be construed: (1) in relation to VAT itself or a VAT credit, as a reference to the aggregate of the amount (if any) falsely claimed by way of credit for input tax and the amount (if any) by which output tax was falsely understated; and (2) in relation to the refunds and repayments mentioned in note 1 supra, the amount falsely claimed by way of refund or repayment: Value Added Tax Act 1994 s 60(3). The phrase is not exhaustive of the kinds of tax which may be evaded, so that tax not included in a return (because none was made) can also be tax evaded: *Stevenson and Telford Building and Design Ltd v Customs and Excise Comrs* [1996] STC 1096, CA. The commissioners or, on appeal, a tribunal may reduce the penalty under the Value Added Tax Act 1994 s 60 to such amount (including nil) as they think proper: see s 70(1); and para 280 post. For the meaning of 'input tax' and 'output tax' see paras 4, 201 ante.

5   Ibid s 60(1). A failure to register or to make any returns for VAT may amount to dishonest acts of omission, for which a penalty may be imposed under s 60: *Stevenson and Telford Building and Design Ltd v Customs and Excise Comrs* [1996] STC 1096, CA.

6   Value Added Tax Act 1994 s 60(6).

7   For the meaning of 'document' see para 11 note 8 ante.

8   Ie under the Value Added Tax Act 1994 s 70: see para 280 post.

9   Ibid s 60(4), (5)(b).

10 Ibid s 60(7). See *Parker v Customs and Excise Comrs* [1989] VATTR 258 (the commissioners must prove deliberate dishonesty to a high degree of probability). As to appeals against penalties see para 296 et seq post.

273. Liability of directors. Where it appears to the Commissioners of Customs and Excise that a body corporate is liable to a penalty for the dishonest evasion of value added tax[1] and that the conduct giving rise to that penalty is, in whole or in part, attributable to the dishonesty of a person who is (or at the material time was) a director[2] or managing officer[3] of the body corporate (a 'named officer'), the commissioners may serve a notice on the body corporate and on the named officer[4]. Such a notice must state the amount of the penalty to which the company is liable (the 'basic penalty') and that the commissioners propose to recover a specified portion, which may be the whole, of the basic penalty from the named officer[5]. The specified portion of the basic penalty is then recoverable from the named officer as if he were personally liable to a penalty for dishonest evasion of VAT which corresponds to that portion and the amount of that penalty may be assessed[6] and notified to him accordingly[7]. Where such a notice is served, the amount which may be assessed as the amount due by way of penalty from the body corporate is only so much (if any) of the basic penalty as is not assessed on and notified to a named officer by virtue of these provisions[8] and the body corporate is treated as discharged from liability for so much of the basic penalty as is so assessed and notified[9].

There are only limited rights of appeal where such a notice is served. No appeal lies against the service of the notice as such[10]. Where, however, a body corporate is assessed as liable to any of the basic penalty, it may appeal against the commissioners' decision as to its liability to a penalty and against the amount of the basic penalty as if it were specified in the assessment[11]; and where an assessment is made on a named officer, he may appeal against the commissioners' decision that the conduct of the body corporate is, in whole or in part, attributable to his dishonesty and against their decision as to the portion of the penalty which the commissioners propose to recover from him[12].

1   Ie under the Value Added Tax Act 1994 s 60: see para 272 ante.
2   Where the affairs of a body corporate are managed by its members, these provisions apply in relation to the conduct of a member in connection with his functions of management as if he were a director of the body corporate: ibid s 61(6).
3   For these purposes, a 'managing officer', in relation to a body corporate, means any manager, secretary or other similar officer of the body corporate or any person purporting to act in any such capacity or as a director: ibid s 61(6).
4   Ibid s 61(1). No formality is required in serving a notice under s 61(1) (*Customs and Excise Comrs v Bassimeh* [1995] STC 910 at 915) so that there is no need to divide the notice into separate penalties for each prescribed accounting period in which the body corporate was guilty of dishonest evasion of VAT, nor indeed to provide more information to the director than that set out in the Value Added Tax Act 1994 s 61(2) (see the text and note 5 infra) (*Customs and Excise Comrs v Bassimeh* supra at 917).
5   Value Added Tax Act 1994 s 61(2). Before the commissioners can levy a penalty on a director equal to the whole amount for the company is liable, they must establish that he is wholly responsible for its dishonest conduct. The relative culpability of one of a number of named officers is a material consideration in the exercise of the powers of the commissioners under s 61; but where directors have collaborated in procuring the body corporate's dishonest conduct, each is, prima facie, responsible for the whole: *Customs and Excise Comrs v Bassimeh* [1995] STC 910 at 920.
6   Ie under the Value Added Tax Act 1994 s 76 (as amended): see para 251 ante.
7   Ibid s 61(3).
8   Ibid s 61(4)(a).
9   Ibid s 61(4)(b).
10 Ibid s 61(5).
11 Ibid s 61(5)(a).
12 Ibid s 61(5)(b).

274. Incorrect certificates as to zero-rating etc. Where a person by whom one or more acquisitions, or to whom one or more supplies[1], are, or are to be, made:

(1)   gives to the supplier a certificate that the supply or supplies fall, or will fall, wholly or partly within the reliefs relating to the construction of buildings[2] or protected buildings[3] or the exemption relating to land[4];

(2)   gave to the supplier a certificate that the supplies fell within certain previous statutory exemptions and reliefs[5];

(3)   prepares a certificate that the goods are subject to a fiscal warehousing regime[6] or gives a supplier a certificate stating that he will cause them to be placed in such a regime[7]; or

(4)   gives a supplier a certificate that services are wholly performed in or in relation to goods subject to a warehousing or fiscal warehousing regime[8],

and the certificate is incorrect, the person giving or preparing, or who gave, the certificate is liable to a penalty[9]. The amount of the penalty is equal to the difference between the amount of the value added tax which would have been chargeable on the supply or supplies if the certificate had been correct and the amount of VAT which was actually so chargeable[10].

If the person who gave or prepared a certificate satisfies the Commissioners of Customs and Excise or, on appeal, a VAT and duties tribunal that there is a reasonable excuse for his having given or prepared it, the giving or preparing of a certificate does not give rise to a penalty under these provisions[11]. Where a person is convicted of an offence (whether under the Value Added Tax Act 1994 or otherwise) by reason of giving or preparing a certificate, the giving or preparing of the certificate does not also give rise to a penalty under these provisions[12].

1   For the meaning of 'supply' see para 21 ante.
2   Ie within the Value Added Tax Act 1994 s 30(2), Sch 8 Pt II Group 5 (as substituted): see para 163 ante.
3   Ie within Sch 8 Pt II Group 6 (as substituted): see para 165 ante.
4   Ie within ibid s 31(1), Sch 9 Pt II Group 1 (as amended): see para 142 ante.

5 Ie within the Value Added Tax Act 1983 s 16, Sch 5 Group 7 (repealed) for the purposes of the Finance Act 1989 s 18, Sch 3 para 13(4)(f) (repealed). The Value Added Tax Act 1983 Sch 5 Group 7 (repealed) related to the former zero-rating of fuel and power. It is believed that the reference should be to Sch 5 Group 8 (repealed), since the Finance Act 1989 Sch 3 para 13(4)(f) (repealed) dealt with the need for a certificate in order that a building qualified for zero-rating under certain transitional provisions.

6 Ie a certificate in accordance with the Value Added Tax Act 1994 s 18B(1)(d) (as added): see para 134 ante.

7 Ie a certificate in accordance with ibid s 18B(2)(d) (as added): see para 134 ante.

8 Ie a certificate in accordance with ibid s 18C(1)(c) (as added): see para 140 ante.

9 Value Added Tax Act 1994 s 62(1) (amended by the Finance Act 1996 ss 26(1), 205(1), Sch 3 para 8(1), (2), Sch 41 Pt IV). An appeal lies against the imposition of such a penalty: see the Value Added Tax Act 1994 s 83(n); and para 296 post.

10 Value Added Tax Act 1994 s 62(2).

11 Ibid s 62(3) (amended by the Finance Act 1996 Sch 3 para 8(3), (4)).

12 Value Added Tax Act 1994 s 62(4) (amended by the Finance Act 1996 Sch 3 para 8(3)).

275. Penalty for misdeclaration or neglect resulting in value added tax loss.
In certain circumstances specified below a person is liable to a penalty where a return[1] is made for a prescribed accounting period[2] which understates his liability to VAT or overstates his entitlement to a VAT credit[3], or where an assessment is made for a prescribed accounting period which understates his liability to VAT and, at the end of the period of 30 days beginning on the date of the assessment, he has not taken all such steps as are reasonable to draw the understatement to the attention of the Commissioners for Customs and Excise[4]. The penalty is an amount equal to 15 per cent of the VAT which would have been lost[5] if the inaccuracy had not been discovered[6]. The circumstances are that the VAT for the period concerned which would have been lost had the inaccuracy not been discovered equals or exceeds whichever is the lesser of £1 million and 30 per cent of the relevant amount[7] for that period[8].

Conduct falling within the above provisions does not give rise to liability to a penalty if the person concerned satisfies the commissioners (or, on appeal, a VAT and duties tribunal) that there is a reasonable excuse for the conduct[9], or, at a time when he had no reason to believe that inquiries were being made by the commissioners into his affairs, so far as they relate to VAT, he furnished to the commissioners full information with respect to the inaccuracy concerned[10]. Where, by reason of conduct falling within this provision, a person is convicted of an offence, whether under the Value Added Tax Act 1994 or otherwise, or a person is assessed to a penalty for evasion of VAT[11], that conduct does not also give rise to liability to a penalty under the above provisions[12].

1 For the meaning of 'return' see para 105 note 14 ante.

2 For the meaning of 'prescribed accounting period' see para 202 note 4 ante.

3 For the meaning of 'VAT credit' see the Value Added Tax Act 1994 s 25(3); and para 202 ante.

4 Ibid s 63(1). An appeal lies against the imposition of a penalty: see s 83(n): and para 296 post. As to the powers of the commissioners and, on appeal, of the VAT and duties tribunal, to mitigate the penalty see para 280 post.

5 Any reference for these purposes to the VAT for a prescribed accounting period which would have been lost if an inaccuracy had not been discovered is a reference to the amount of the understatement of liability or, as the case may be, overstatement of entitlement referred to, in relation to that period, in ibid s 63(1): s 63(3). This reverses the decision in *Customs and Excise Comrs v Peninsular and Oriental Steam Navigation Co* [1994] STC 259, CA. Where, however, a return for any prescribed accounting period overstates or understates to any extent a person's liability to VAT or his entitlement to a VAT credit, and that return is corrected, in such circumstances and in accordance with such conditions as may be prescribed, by a return for a later such period which understates or overstates, to the corresponding extent, that liability or entitlement, it is assumed for these purposes that the statements made by each of those returns, so far as they are not inaccurate in any other respect, are correct statements for the accounting period to which it relates: Value

Added Tax Act 1994 s 63(8); and see Customs and Excise Press Release 26/91 [1991] STI 324 (a serious misdeclaration penalty (as this penalty is generally known) will not normally be imposed when a VAT return for a registered trader is misdeclared but this has been corrected by a compensating misdeclaration in respect of the same transactions for the following period with no overall loss of VAT). See also HC Official Report, SC A (Finance Bill), 24 March 1994, cols 819–821. The effect of the Value Added Tax Act 1994 s 63(8) is to avoid the prospect of the maker of the returns being liable to a penalty in respect of both returns (provided that the returns contain no other inaccuracy of a kind falling within the scope of s 63). As to the correction of errors see the Value Added Tax Regulations 1995, SI 1995/2518, regs 34, 35; and para 238 ante.

6   Value Added Tax Act 1994 s 63(1).

7   In relation to a prescribed accounting period, 'the relevant amount' means, where the inaccuracy is contained in the return, the gross amount of VAT for that period; and where the inaccuracy lies in an uncorrected assessment, the true amount of VAT for the period: ibid s 63(4). 'The gross amount of tax', in relation to a prescribed accounting period, means the aggregate of the amount of credit for input tax and the amount of output tax which should have been stated on the return for the period: s 63(5). 'The true amount of VAT', in relation to a prescribed accounting period, means the amount of VAT which was due from the person concerned for that period or, as the case may be, the amount of the VAT credit (if any) to which he was entitled for that period: s 63(7). In relation to a prescribed accounting period, any reference in ss 59–69 (as amended) to credit for input tax includes a references to any sum which, in a return for that period, is claimed as a deduction from VAT due: s 71(2).

    In relation to any return which, in accordance with prescribed requirements, includes a single amount as the aggregate for the prescribed accounting period to which the return relates of the amount representing credit for input tax and any other amounts representing refunds or repayments of VAT to which there is an entitlement, references to the amount of credit for input tax have effect, so far as they would not so have effect by virtue of s 63(9), as references to the amount of that aggregate: s 63(6). In the case of a public body which is registered and to which s 33 (as amended) (see para 258 ante) applies, s 63 has effect as if any reference (1) to a VAT credit included a reference to a refund under s 33 (as amended); and (2) to credit for input tax included a reference to VAT chargeable on supplies, acquisitions or importations which were not for the purposes of any business carried on by the body: s 63(9). (The tax refunded to a public body under s 33 (as amended) is not input tax within s 25, since it is not tax on supplies for the purposes of a business carried on by the body). For the meaning of 'registered' see para 56 note 2 ante; and for the meaning of 'business' see para 17 ante.

8   Ibid s 63(2). See *Customs and Excise Comrs v Nomura Property Management Services Ltd* [1994] STC 461 (the taxpayer unsuccessfully sought to avoid a penalty under the predecessor to the Value Added Tax Act 1994 s 63, by contending that the errors in the return were so incredible as to render the return a nullity (the figures for the various boxes were transposed); it was held that there was no class of error which would invalidate a return, disapproving *Gwent County Council v Customs and Excise Comrs* (1991) VAT Decision 6153, [1991] STI 811).

9   Value Added Tax Act 1994 s 63(10)(a). In the case of appeals against a serious misdeclaration penalty (though not in default surcharge cases: see para 283 post), where the taxpayer is unaware of the error, it has been said that if a reasonable, conscientious, business person who knew all the facts of the case, and who was alive to and accepted the need to comply with one's responsibilities in regard to the rendering of VAT returns, would consider that the taxpayer, in acting as it did in the circumstances in which it found itself, had acted with due care in the preparation of its return it would have a reasonable excuse: *Appropriate Technology Ltd v Customs and Excise Comrs* [1991] VATTR 226, approved in *Frank Galliers Ltd v Customs and Excise Comrs* [1993] STC 284 as a useful, though not a comprehensive, test. If a trader innocently errs in a one-off case, in accounting for VAT in a field other than that in which he generally operates, he may claim reasonable excuse even if the material statutory provision would have been perfectly clear to a layman who had identified and read it: *Nor-Clean Ltd v Customs and Excise Comrs* [1991] VATTR 239. Where the taxpayer's excuse for acting with what appears, prima facie, to be a want of care, is the existence of pressures and problems, the question must be whether the taxpayer has acted with proper care in the context of such evidence as there is as to pressures and problems: *Frank Galliers Ltd v Customs and Excise Comrs* supra at 293; see also *Clean Car Co Ltd v Customs and Excise Comrs* [1991] VATTR 234. An insufficiency of funds to pay any VAT due is not a reasonable excuse: Value Added Tax Act 1994 s 71(1)(a). Nor, where reliance is placed on any other person to perform any task, is either the fact of that reliance or any dilatoriness or inaccuracy on the part of the person relied upon a reasonable excuse: s 71(1)(b). See *Customs and Excise Comrs v Salevon Ltd, Customs and Excise Comrs v Harris* [1989] STC 907 (where a trader relies on a professional adviser to perform the tasks imposed on him by statute as well as to advise him about his obligations, but the adviser fails in those duties, the trader is deprived of a defence of reasonable excuse by what is now the Value Added Tax Act

1994 s 71(1)(b)). See also Institute of Chartered Accountants in England and Wales Memorandum TR 836 *VAT: Levy of a Serious Misdeclaration Penalty following Advice from a Professional Adviser* (where the law is ambiguous or there has been room for a genuine difference of opinion about its interpretation, which is subsequently clarified by statute, there may well be scope for a successful plea of reasonable excuse for a misdeclaration on a VAT return which was rendered before the law was clarified, on the basis that, at the time when the return was prepared, the relevant legislation was unclear or ambiguous; the fact that the trader was relying on the advice of an independent tax adviser is irrelevant, since the reasonable excuse lies in the ambiguity, or uncertainty of interpretation, of the relevant legal provision: see paras 8–9): [1991] STI 576. The Value Added Tax Act 1994 s 71(1)(b) does not impose more stringent requirements for the establishment of a reasonable excuse in cases where the taxpayer has relied on other persons than where no such reliance has been placed; it merely excludes the facts of delegation or culpable delay or inaccuracy of a third party from constituting a reasonable excuse: *Frank Galliers Ltd v Customs and Excise Comrs* supra. It is therefore open to the taxpayer to invite the court to go behind the inaccuracy etc of the adviser to investigate whether the reason why the adviser was inaccurate itself gives rise to a reasonable excuse. See, similarly, *Customs and Excise Comrs v Steptoe* [1992] STC 757, CA; *Nor-Clean Ltd v Customs and Excise Comrs* supra; *Walsh Bros (Tunnelling) Ltd v Customs and Excise Comrs* (1992) VAT Decision 7186, [1992] STI 486; and *DJ Trimming Ltd v Customs and Excise Comrs* (1992) VAT Decision 7733, [1992] STI 789.

10 Value Added Tax Act 1994 s 63(10)(b). A considerable number of cases have come before the tribunal on whether there has been truly 'voluntary' disclosure; and on whether the disclosure takes place before the trader has reason to believe that inquiries were being made into his affairs in relation to VAT, not all of which appear to be fully reconcilable. In *Taunton Deane Borough Council v Customs and Excise Comrs* (1990) VAT Decision 5545 (unreported), it was held that a disclosure made under the shadow of an official review (eg in the course of a control visit) is not a voluntary disclosure. In *Moor Lodge Developments Ltd v Customs and Excise Comrs* (1992) VAT Decision 7285, [1992] STI 514, a disclosure made in respect of a misdeclaration by a company to an officer carrying out a control visit on a connected partnership was held to afford protection from a penalty; cf *FR Jenks (Overseas) Ltd v Customs and Excise Comrs* (1992) VAT Decision 8858 (unreported), following *Taunton Deane Borough Council v Customs and Excise Comrs* supra. For a case where the tribunal held that the commissioners were estopped from imposing a misdeclaration penalty see *AB Gee of Ripley Ltd v Customs and Excise Comrs* [1991] VATTR 217.

11 Ie under the Value Added Tax Act 1994 s 60: see para 272 ante.

12 Ibid s 63(11).

276. Repeated misdeclarations. The Commissioners of Customs and Excise may serve notice (a 'penalty liability notice') on a person where there is a material inaccuracy[1] made in his value added tax return[2] in respect of any prescribed accounting period[3]. In any case where:

    (1)   there is such a material inaccuracy[4];

    (2)   such a notice specifying a penalty period is served on the person concerned before the end of five consecutive prescribed accounting periods beginning with the period in respect of which there was the material inaccuracy[5]; and

    (3)   the penalty period so specified is the period of eight consecutive prescribed accounting periods, beginning with that in which the date of the notice falls[6],

then if there is a material inaccuracy in respect of any of the prescribed accounting periods falling within the penalty period specified in the notice, the person concerned is liable, except in relation to the first of those periods in respect of which there is a material inaccuracy, to a penalty equal to 15 per cent of the VAT for the prescribed accounting period in question which would have been lost[7] if the inaccuracy had not been discovered[8].

In any case where:

    (a)   a return has been made for a prescribed accounting period which understates a person's liability to VAT or overstates his entitlement to a VAT credit[9]; and

(b) the VAT for that period which would have been lost had the inaccuracy not been discovered equals or exceeds the lesser of £500,000 and 10 per cent of the gross amount of tax for that period[10],

the inaccuracy is regarded, subject to certain exceptions[11], as material[12]. An inaccuracy is not, however, regarded as material if the person concerned satisfies the commissioners or, on appeal, a VAT and duties tribunal that there is a reasonable excuse for the inaccuracy[13]. Nor is it regarded as material if:

(i) he furnished the commissioners with full information with respect to the inaccuracy at a time when he had no reason to believe that inquiries were being made by the commissioners into his affairs, so far as they relate to VAT[14]; or

(ii) by reason of conduct falling within the scope of the provision, the person concerned is convicted of an offence (whether under the Value Added Tax Act 1994 or otherwise)[15] or is assessed to a penalty either for dishonest evasion of VAT[16] or for misdeclaration or neglect[17] resulting in VAT loss[18].

Where any of these exceptions requires any inaccuracy to be regarded as not material for the purposes of the serving of a penalty liability notice, any such notice served in respect of that inaccuracy is deemed not to have been served[19].

1　As to what constitutes a material inaccuracy see the Value Added Tax Act 1994 s 64(1); and heads (a)–(b) in the text.

2　For the meaning of 'return' see para 105 note 14 ante.

3　See the Value Added Tax Act 1994 s 64(2); and heads (1)–(3) in the text. For the meaning of 'prescribed accounting period' see para 202 note 4 ante.

4　Ibid s 64(2)(a).

5　Ibid s 64(2)(b), (c).

6　Ibid s 64(2)(d).

7　For the meaning of 'the VAT which would have been lost' see ibid s 63(3) (applied by s 64(4)); and para 275 note 5 ante.

8　Ibid s 64(3). An appeal lies against the imposition of such a penalty: see s 83(n); and para 296 post. As to the powers of the commissioners and, on appeal, of the VAT and duties tribunal, to mitigate the penalty see para 280 post.

9　Ibid s 64(1)(a). For the meaning of 'VAT credit' see s 25(3); and para 202 ante. In relation to a public body which is registered and to which s 33 (as amended) (see para 258 ante) applies, s 64 (as amended) applies as if any reference to a VAT credit included a reference to a refund under s 33 (as amended) and as if any reference to credit for input tax included a reference to the VAT chargeable on supplies, acquisitions and importations which were not for the purposes of any business carried on by the body: s 63(9) (applied by s 64(4)). The tax refunded to a public body under s 33 (as amended) is not input tax within s 25, since it is not tax on supplies for the purposes of a business carried on by the body: see para 258 ante. For the meaning of 'registered' see para 56 note 2 ante; for the meaning of 'input tax' see paras 4, 201 ante; for the meaning of 'supply' see para 21 ante; and for the meaning of 'business' see para 17 ante.

10　Ibid s 64(1)(b). For the meaning of 'the gross amount of tax' see s 63(5) (applied by s 64(4)); and para 275 note 7 ante.

11　See ibid s 64(5), s 64(6) (as substituted); and the text and notes 13–18 infra.

12　Ibid s 64(1). As to the correction of errors see, however, s 63(8) (applied by s 64(4)); and para 275 note 5 ante.

13　Ibid s 64(5)(a). As to what is a 'reasonable excuse' see para 275 note 9 ante.

14　Ibid s 64(5)(b).

15　Ibid s 64(6)(a) (substituted by the Finance Act 1996 s 36(1)). As to criminal offences in relation to VAT see para 267 et seq ante.

16　Ie under the Value Added Tax Act 1994 s 60: see para 272 ante.

17　Ie under ibid s 63: see para 275 ante. An inaccuracy by reason of which a person has been assessed to a penalty under s 63 is not, however, prevented from being regarded (1) as a material inaccuracy in respect of which the commissioners may serve a penalty liability notice under s 64(2); or (2) as a material inaccuracy for the purposes of s 64(3) by reference to which any prescribed accounting period falling within the penalty period is to be treated as the first prescribed accounting period so falling in respect of which there is a material inaccuracy: s 64(6A) (added by the Finance Act 1996 s 36(1)).

18   Value Added Tax Act 1994 s 64(6)(b) (as substituted: see note 15 supra).
19   Ibid s 64(7) (substituted by the Finance Act 1996 s 36(1)).

277. Inaccuracies in EC sales statements. A person is liable to a penalty of £100 in respect of an EC sales statement[1] where:

(1)   such a statement containing a material inaccuracy[2] has been submitted by him to the Commissioners of Customs and Excise[3];

(2)   within six months of discovering the inaccuracy, the commissioners have issued him with a written warning identifying that statement and stating that future inaccuracies might result in the service of a notice for the purposes of these provisions[4];

(3)   another EC sales statement containing a material inaccuracy ('the second inaccurate statement') has been submitted by that person to the commissioners[5];

(4)   its submission date[6] fell within the period of two years beginning with the day after the warning was issued[7];

(5)   within six months of discovering the inaccuracy in the second inaccurate statement, the commissioners have served that person with a notice identifying that statement and stating that future inaccuracies will attract a penalty under these provisions[8];

(6)   yet another EC sales statement containing a material inaccuracy is submitted by that person to the commissioners[9]; and

(7)   the submission date for that further statement is not more than two years after the service of the notice or the date on which any previous statement attracting a penalty was submitted by that person to the commissioners[10].

The penalty is incurred in respect of the statement falling within head (6) above[11].

Subject to certain exceptions[12], an EC sales statement is regarded as containing a material inaccuracy if, having regard to the matters required to be included in the statement, the inclusion or omission of any information from the statement is misleading in any material respect[13]. An inaccuracy contained in an EC sales statement is not, however, regarded as material if:

(a)   the person who submitted it satisfies the commissioners or, on appeal, a VAT and duties tribunal that there is a reasonable excuse[14] for the inaccuracy[15]; or

(b)   he furnished the commissioners with full information with respect to the inaccuracy at a time when he had no reason to believe that inquiries were being made by them into his affairs[16].

Furthermore where, by reason of the submission of a statement containing a material inaccuracy by any person, that person is convicted of an offence (whether under the Value Added Tax Act 1994 or otherwise)[17], the inaccuracy to which the conviction relates is regarded as not being material[18].

Where the only statement identified in a warning or notice served for the purposes of head (2) or head (5) above is one which is regarded[19] as containing no material inaccuracies, that warning or notice is deemed not to have been issued or served for those purposes[20].

1   'EC sales statement' means any statement which is required to be submitted to the Commissioners of Customs and Excise in accordance with regulations under the Value Added Tax Act 1994 s 58, Sch 11 para 2(3) (see para 225 ante): s 65(6). See the Value Added Tax Regulations 1995, SI 1995/2518, Pt IV (regs 21–23) (as amended); and para 244 ante.
2   As to when a statement contains a material inaccuracy see the text and notes 13–18 infra.
3   Value Added Tax Act 1994 s 65(1)(a).
4   Ibid s 65(1)(b).
5   Ibid s 65(1)(c).

6   'Submission date', in relation to an EC sales statement, means whichever is the earlier of the last day for
    the submission of the statement to the commissioners in accordance with the regulations (see note 1
    supra) and the day on which it was in fact submitted to them: ibid s 65(6).
7   Ibid s 65(1)(d).
8   Ibid s 65(1)(e).
9   Ibid s 65(1)(f).
10 Ibid s 65(1)(g).
11 Ibid s 65(1). An appeal lies against the imposition of such a penalty: see s 83(n); and para 296 post.
12 See the text and notes 14–18 infra.
13 Value Added Tax Act 1994 s 65(2).
14 As to what constitutes a reasonable excuse see para 275 note 9 ante.
15 Value Added Tax Act 1994 s 65(3)(a).
16 Ibid s 65(3)(b).
17 As to criminal offences in connection with VAT see para 267 et seq ante.
18 Value Added Tax Act 1994 s 65(4).
19 Ie whether by virtue of ibid s 65(3) or (4) or otherwise: s 65(5).
20 Ibid s 65(5).

278. Failure to submit an EC sales statement. If, by the last day on which a person is required[1] to submit an EC sales statement[2] for any prescribed period[3] to the Commissioners of Customs and Excise, they have not received it, that person is regarded as being in default in relation to that statement until it is submitted[4]. Where any person is thus in default, the commissioners may serve notice on him stating:

(1)   that he is in default in relation to the statement specified in the notice[5];
(2)   that, subject to the liability mentioned in head (4) below, no action will be taken if he remedies the default before the end of the period of 14 days beginning with the day after the service of the notice[6];
(3)   that if the default is not so remedied, he will become liable in respect of his default to penalties calculated on a daily basis from the end of that period[7]; and
(4)   that he will become liable, without any further notices being served under these provisions, to penalties if he commits any more defaults before a period of 12 months has elapsed without his being in default[8].

Where a person has been served with such a notice, he becomes liable:

(a)   to a penalty in respect of the statement to which the notice relates, if that statement is not submitted before the end of the period of 14 days beginning with the day after the service of the notice[9]; and
(b)   whether or not that statement is so submitted, to a penalty in respect of any EC sales statement the last day for the submission of which is after the service and before the expiry of the notice and in relation to which he is in default[10].

A notice so served on any person continues in effect until the end of the period of 12 months beginning with the day after the service of the notice[11]. Where, however, at any time in that period of 12 months that person is in default in relation to any EC sales statement other than one in relation to which he was in default when the notice was served, the notice continues in force until a period of 12 months has elapsed without that person becoming liable to a penalty in respect of any EC sales statement[12].

The amount of any penalty to which a person who has been served with such a notice is liable is whichever is the greater of £50 and a daily penalty of either £5 or the relevant amount[13] for every day the default continues, up to a maximum of 100 days[14]. In the case of a liability in respect of the statement to which the notice relates, the daily penalty of £5 applies for every day the default continued after the end of the period of 14 days beginning with the day after the service of the notice, up to that 100-day maximum[15]. In the case of a liability in respect of any other statement, the daily penalty of the relevant amount applies for every day for which the default continues up to that 100-day maximum[16].

If a person who would otherwise be liable to a penalty under these provisions satisfies the commissioners or, on appeal, the VAT and duties tribunal that an EC sales statement was submitted at such a time and in such a manner that it was reasonable to expect that it would be received by the commissioners within the appropriate time limit, or that there is a reasonable excuse[17] for such a statement not having been dispatched, he is treated[18] as not having been in default in relation to that statement and is not liable to any such penalty in respect of that statement[19]. Any notice served[20] exclusively in relation to the failure to submit that statement then has no effect for these purposes[21].

1 Ie in accordance with regulations under the Value Added Tax Act 1994: s 66(1). See the Value Added Tax Regulations 1995, SI 1995/2518, Pt IV (regs 21–23) (as amended); and para 244 ante.
2 An 'EC sales statement' means any statement which is required to be submitted to the Commissioners of Customs and Excise in accordance with regulations under the Value Added Tax Act 1994 s 58, Sch 11 para 2(3) (see para 225 ante): s 66(9). As to the relevant regulations see note 1 supra.
3 For the meaning of 'prescribed' see para 11 note 3 ante. Generally speaking, an EC sales statement must be submitted within 42 days after the end of each quarter: see the Value Added Tax Regulations 1995 reg 22(1) (as amended); and para 244 ante.
4 Value Added Tax Act 1994 s 66(1).
5 Ibid s 66(2)(a).
6 Ibid s 66(2)(b).
7 Ibid s 66(2)(c).
8 Ibid s 66(2)(d).
9 Ibid s 66(3)(a).
10 Ibid s 66(3)(b). An appeal lies against the imposition of any such penalty: see s 83(n); and para 296 post.
11 Ibid s 66(4)(a).
12 Ibid s 66(4)(b).
13 'The relevant amount', in relation to a person served with a notice under ibid s 66(2), means (1) £5 where, that person not having been liable to a penalty in respect of the statement to which the notice relates, the statement in question is the first statement in respect of which that person has become liable to a penalty while the notice has been in force; (2) £10 where the statement in question is the second statement in respect of which he has become so liable while the notice has been in force, counting the statement to which the notice relates where he has become liable in respect of that statement; and (3) £15 in any other case: s 66(6). If it appears to the Treasury that there has been a change in the value of money since 1 January 1993 or, as the case may be, the last occasion when the sums specified in relation to daily penalties were varied, the Treasury may by order substitute for the sums for the time being specified such other sums as appear to it to be justified by the change; but such an order is not to apply to any default in relation to a statement the last day for the submission of which was before the order comes into force: s 66(8). At the date at which this volume states the law, no such order had been made. As to the making of orders generally see para 8 ante.
14 See ibid s 66(5).
15 See ibid s 66(5)(a).
16 See ibid s 66(5)(b).
17 As to what constitutes a reasonable excuse see para 275 note 9 ante.
18 Ie for these purposes and for the purposes of the Value Added Tax Act 1994 ss 59–65 (as amended) (see paras 272 et seq ante, 283 post); ss 67–71 (as amended) (see para 279 et seq post); s 73 (see paras 247, 252 ante); s 75 (see paras 248, 252 ante); and s 76 (as amended) (see para 251 ante): s 66(7).
19 Ibid s 66(7).
20 Ie under ibid s 66(2): see heads (1)–(4) in the text.
21 Ibid s 66(7).

279. Failure to notify and unauthorised issue of invoices. In any case where a person fails to comply with any specified notification requirements relating to registration[1] or with a requirement of regulations relating to the acquisition of goods subject to a duty of excise or a new means of transport[2] from another member state[3], he is liable, subject to certain exceptions[4], to a penalty equal to the specified percentage[5] of the relevant value added tax[6] or, if greater (or if the circumstances are such that there is no relevant VAT), to a penalty of £50[7]. In addition, if an unauthorised person[8] issues one or more invoices[9] showing an amount as being VAT or as including an amount attributable to VAT, he too is liable, subject to the same exceptions, to such a penalty[10].

Conduct falling within this provision does not give rise to liability to a penalty if the person concerned satisfies the Commissioners of Customs and Excise or, on appeal, a VAT and duties tribunal that there is a reasonable excuse[11] for his conduct[12]. Nor does conduct give rise to such liability if, by reason of that conduct, a person is convicted of an offence (whether under the Value Added Tax Act 1994 or otherwise)[13] or is assessed to a penalty[14] for dishonest evasion of VAT[15].

1   Ie, with any of the Value Added Tax Act 1994 s 3(2), Sch 1 paras 5, 6, 7 (see para 56 ante); Sch 1 para 14(2), (3) (see para 57 ante); Sch 2 para 3 (see para 60 ante); Sch 3 paras 3, 8(2) (see para 63 ante): s 67(1)(a) (amended by the Finance Act 1996 s 37(1)). See *Customs and Excise Comrs v Shingleton* [1988] STC 190.

2   For the meaning of 'new means of transport' see para 13 note 8 ante.

3   Ie regulations under the Value Added Tax Act 1994 s 58, Sch 11 para 2(4) (see para 225 ante): s 67(1)(b). See the Value Added Tax Regulations 1995, SI 1995/2518, regs 36, 148; and para 248 ante. For the meaning of 'another member state' see para 4 note 14 ante; and as to the acquisition of goods from other member states see para 13 ante.

4   See the Value Added Tax Act 1994 s 67(8), (9); and the text and notes 11–15 infra.

5   The 'specified percentage' is: (1) where the relevant VAT is given by ibid s 67(3)(a) (as amended) or s 67(3)(b) (see note 6 heads (1)–(2) infra), 5% if the period referred to therein does not exceed nine months and 10% if that period exceeds nine months but does not exceed 18 months; (2) where the relevant VAT is given by s 67(3)(c) (see note 6 head (3) infra), 5% if the failure in question did not continue for more than three months and 10% if it continued for more than three months but did not continue for more than six months; and (3) 15% in any other case: s 67(4) (amended by the Finance Act 1995 s 32(1), (3), (4) with effect where a penalty is assessed after 31 December 1994, but not in the case of a supplementary assessment if the original assessment was made on or before that date, in which case the specified percentages are 10%, 20% and 30% respectively: see the Value Added Tax Act 1994 s 67(4) (as originally enacted)). The VAT and duties tribunal has no power to mitigate the penalty: *Rhodes v Customs and Excise Comrs* [1986] VATTR 72. For the meaning of 'relevant VAT' see note 6 infra.

6   'Relevant VAT' means, in relation to a person's failure to comply with (1) the Value Added Tax Act 1994 Sch 1 paras 5, 6 or 7, Sch 2 para 3 or Sch 3 para 3, the VAT, if any, for which he is liable for the period beginning on the date with effect from which he is required to be registered in accordance with the relevant provision and ending on the date on which the commissioners received notification of, or otherwise became fully aware of, his liability to be registered (s 67(3)(a)) (amended by the Finance Act 1996 s 37(1)(b)); (2) the Value Added Tax Act 1994 Sch 1 para 14(2) or (3) or Sch 3 para 8(2), the VAT, if any, for which, but for any exemption from registration, he would be liable for the period beginning on the date of the change or alteration referred to in that provision and ending on the date on which the commissioners received notification of, or otherwise became fully aware of, that change or alteration (s 67(3)(b)); and (3) a requirement of regulations under Sch 11 para 2(4), the VAT on the acquisition to which the failure relates (s 67(3)(c)). In relation to any person who became liable to be registered by virtue of Sch 1 para 1(2) (as amended) (see para 56 ante) before 1 January 1996 but who had not notified the commissioners of the liability before that date, s 67 (as amended) has effect as if in s 67(3)(a) (as so amended) for the words 'the date with effect from which he is, in accordance with that paragraph [ie 'the relevant provision: see head (1) supra], required to be registered' there were substituted '1 January 1996': Finance Act 1996 s 37(2)(b), (3). The 'VAT for which a person is liable' at the time when the commissioners become aware of his liability to register includes the VAT on supplies made before that time, but which the person would only have been obliged to account for and pay at a later time had he been registered: *Corthine v Customs and Excise Comrs* [1988] VATTR 90.

Where the amount of VAT which would otherwise be treated, for the purposes of the Value Added Tax Act 1994 s 67(1) (as amended) as the relevant VAT in relation to a failure mentioned in s 67(3)(a) (as so amended) includes VAT on the acquisition of goods from another member state, and the commissioners are satisfied that VAT has been paid under the law of another member state on the supply in pursuance of which those goods were acquired, then, in the determination of the amount of the relevant VAT in relation to that failure, an allowance is made for the VAT paid under the law of that member state: s 67(5). The amount of the allowance must not exceed the amount of the VAT due on the acquisition but is otherwise equal to the amount of VAT which the commissioners are satisfied has been paid on that supply under the law of that member state: s 67(5). Similarly, where the amount of VAT which would otherwise be treated for those purposes as the relevant amount in relation to such a failure includes VAT chargeable by virtue of s 7(4) (see para 42 ante) on any supply, and the commissioners are satisfied that VAT has been paid under the law of another member state on that supply, an allowance is made for the VAT paid under the law of the other member state: s 67(6). The amount of that allowance must not exceed the amount of VAT chargeable by virtue of s 7(4) on that supply but is otherwise equal to the amount of VAT which the commissioners are satisfied has been paid on that supply under the law of that other member state: s 67(6). For the meaning of 'another member state' see para 4 note 14 ante; and for the meaning of references to the law of another member state see para 11 ante.

7 Ibid s 67(1). An appeal lies against the imposition of such a penalty: see s 83(n); and para 296 post. As to the powers of the commissioners and, on appeal, of the VAT and duties tribunal to mitigate the penalty see para 280 post. If it appears to the Treasury that there has been a change in the value of money since 25 July 1985 or, as the case may be, the last occasion when the power conferred by this provision was exercised, the Treasury may by order substitute for the sum for the time being specified in s 67(1) such other sum as appears to it to be justified by the change: s 67(10). Such an order does not apply in relation to a failure to comply which ended on or before the date on which the order comes into force: s 67(11). At the date at which this volume states the law, no such order had been made. As to the making of orders generally see para 8 ante.

8 An 'unauthorised person' means anyone other than (1) a person who is registered for VAT (see para 56 et seq ante); or (2) a body corporate treated for the purposes of ibid s 43 (as amended) as a member of a group (see paras 66, 191 ante); or (3) a person treated as a taxable person under regulations made under s 46(4) (see para 70 ante); or (4) a person authorised to issue an invoice under regulations made under Sch 11 para 2(12) (see para 225 ante); or (5) a person acting on behalf of the Crown: s 67(2). For the meaning of 'invoice' see para 11 note 8 ante.

9 Ibid s 67 (as amended) has effect in relation to any invoice which (1) for the purposes of any provision made under s 54(3) (flat-rate scheme for farmers: see para 79 et seq ante) shows an amount as included in the consideration for any supply; and (2) either fails to comply with the requirements of any regulations made under s 54 or is issued by a person who is not for the time being authorised to do so for the purposes of s 54, as if the person issuing the invoice were an unauthorised person and that amount were shown on the invoice as an amount attributable to VAT: s 67(7).

10 See ibid s 67(1)(c). In this case, the specified percentage is 15% (s 67(4)(c) (as amended: see note 6 supra)); and the relevant VAT is the amount which is, or the aggregate of the amounts which are, shown on the invoice or invoices as VAT, or to be taken as representing VAT (s 67(3)(d)).

11 As to what constitutes a reasonable excuse see para 275 note 9 ante. See also *Neal v Customs and Excise Comrs* [1988] STC 131 (a distinction is to be drawn between basic ignorance of the primary law governing VAT, which cannot afford a reasonable excuse, and ignorance of aspects of law which less directly impinge on such liability, which might); *Customs and Excise Comrs v Salevon Ltd, Customs and Excise Comrs v Harris* [1989] STC 907; *Parkinson v Customs and Excise Comrs* [1986] VATTR 126; *Zaveri v Customs and Excise Comrs* [1986] VATTR 133; *Selwyn v Customs and Excise Comrs* [1986] VATTR 142 (cf *Tomkins (t/a Options) v Customs and Excise Comrs* (1994) VAT Decision 11738, [1994] STI 540); *Electric Tool Repair Ltd v Customs and Excise Comrs* [1986] VATTR 257; *Hutchings v Customs and Excise Comrs* [1987] VATTR 58; *Jenkinson v Customs and Excise Comrs* [1988] VATTR 45; *George v Customs and Excise Comrs* [1991] VATTR 313; *Chapman v Customs and Excise Comrs* [1992] VATTR 402.

12 Value Added Tax Act 1994 s 67(8).

13 As to criminal offences in relation to VAT see para 267 et seq ante.

14 Ie a penalty under the Value Added Tax Act 1994 s 60: see para 275 ante.

15 Ibid s 67(9).

280. Mitigation of penalties. Where a person is liable to a penalty in respect of dishonest evasion of value added tax[1], misdeclaration or neglect resulting in VAT loss[2], repeated misdeclarations[3], failure to notify[4] or unauthorised issue of invoices[5], the Commissioners of Customs and Excise may reduce the penalty to such amount, including nil, as they think proper[6]. A VAT and duties tribunal has the same power on an appeal[7] and may also, on an appeal relating to a penalty so reduced by the commissioners, cancel the whole or any part of the reduction made by the commissioners[8].

In exercising these powers, neither the commissioners nor any tribunal may take into account any of the following matters[9]:

(1) the insufficiency of the funds available to any person for paying any VAT due or for paying the amount of the penalty;

(2) the fact that there has, in the case in question or in that case taken with any other cases, been no, or no significant, loss of VAT; or

(3) the fact that the person liable to the penalty or a person acting on his behalf has acted in good faith[10].

1   Ie under the Value Added Tax Act 1994 s 60: see para 272 ante.
2   Ie under ibid s 63: see para 275 ante.
3   Ie under ibid s 64: see para 276 ante.
4   Ie under ibid s 67 (as amended): see s 67(1)(a), (b) (as amended); and para 279 ante.
5   Ie under ibid s 67 (as amended): see s 67(1)(c); and para 279 ante.
6   Ibid s 70(1). The power to mitigate only applies in respect of penalties assessed after 26 July 1993: see *Heron v Customs and Excise Comrs* (1996) VAT Decision 13529, [1996] STI 469. For the first case in which mitigation was assessed by a tribunal see *Jordan v Customs and Excise Comrs* (1995) VAT Decision 12616, 316 Tax Journal (13 July 1995) p 20.
7   Value Added Tax Act 1994 s 70(1).
8   Ibid s 70(2); and see *James Ashworth Waterfoot (Successors) Ltd v Customs and Excise Comrs* (1996) VAT Decision 13851, [1996] STI 646 (the tribunal's power to increase penalties under the Value Added Tax Act 1994 s 70(2) should be exercised sparingly).
9   Ibid s 70(3).
10 Ibid s 70(4).

281. Breaches of walking possession agreements. Where a distress is authorised to be levied[1] on the goods and chattels of a person (a 'person in default') who has refused or neglected to pay any value added tax due or any amount recoverable as if it were VAT due, the person levying the distress and the person in default may enter into a walking possession agreement[2]. A 'walking possession agreement' means an agreement under which, in consideration of the property distrained upon being allowed to remain in the custody of the person in default and of the delaying of its sale, the person in default acknowledges that the property specified in the agreement is under distraint and held in walking possession; and undertakes that, except with the consent of the Commissioners of Customs and Excise and subject to such conditions as they may impose, he will not remove or allow the removal of any of the specified property from the premises[3]. If the person in default is in breach of the undertaking contained in a walking possession agreement, he is liable to a penalty equal to half of the VAT or to half of the amount which was recoverable as if it were VAT[4]. He is not, however, liable to such a penalty if he satisfies the commissioners or, on appeal, a VAT and duties tribunal that there is a reasonable excuse[5] for the breach in question[6].

1   Ie in accordance with regulations under the Value Added Tax Act 1994 s 58, Sch 11 para 5(4): see para 256 ante.
2   See ibid s 68(1).
3   Ibid s 68(2).
4   Ibid s 68(3). An appeal lies against the imposition of a penalty under s 68: see s 83(n); and para 296 post.
5   For the meaning of 'reasonable excuse' see ibid s 71; and para 275 note 9 ante.
6   Ibid s 68(4). Section 68 does not extend to Scotland: s 68(5).

282. Breaches of regulatory provisions. If any person fails to comply with any one of a number of regulatory requirements[1], he is liable, subject to certain conditions set out below, to a penalty equal to the prescribed rate[2] multiplied by the number of days for which the failure continues (up to a maximum of 100) or, if greater, to a penalty of £50[3].

If any person fails to comply with a requirement to preserve records[4] he is liable, subject to certain conditions set out below, to a penalty of £500[5].

A failure by any person to comply with any regulatory requirement or to preserve records does not give rise to liability to a penalty under these provisions if the person concerned satisfies the Commissioners of Customs and Excise (or, on appeal, a VAT and duties tribunal) that there is a reasonable excuse for the failure[6]. Moreover if, by reason of a failure to comply with regulatory requirements or to preserve records, a person is convicted of an offence (whether under the Value Added Tax Act 1994 or otherwise), or is assessed to a default surcharge[7] or is assessed to a penalty for dishonest evasion of VAT[8] or for misdeclaration or neglect resulting in VAT loss[9], that conduct does not also give rise to liability to a penalty under these provisions[10].

1   Ie a requirement imposed under (1) the Value Added Tax Act 1994 s 3(2), Sch 1 para 11 (notification of end of liability or entitlement to be registered: see para 71 ante); or Sch 1 para 12 (notification that the registered person has ceased to make supplies outside the United Kingdom which would be taxable supplies if made in the United Kingdom, or has made or formed the intention of making taxable supplies: see paras 58, 72 ante); or Sch 2 para 5 or Sch 3 para 5 (notification of matters affecting continuance of registration: see paras 75, 77 ante); (2) any regulations made under s 48 (see para 62 ante) requiring a VAT representative, for the purposes of registration, to notify the Commissioners of Customs and Excise that his appointment has taken effect or has ceased to have effect (see the Value Added Tax Regulations 1995, SI 1995/2518, reg 10; and para 62 ante); (3) the Value Added Tax Act 1994 s 58, Sch 11 para 6(1) (duty to keep records: see para 219 ante) or Sch 11 para 7 (furnishing of information and production of documents: ibid s 69(2), Sch 12 para 9 (rules of procedure before VAT and duties tribunals: see para 299 post); (5) any order made by the Treasury under the Value Added Tax Act 1994; (6) any regulations made under the European Communities Act 1972 and relating to VAT; or (7) under the Value Added Tax Act 1994 s 18A (as added) in the form of a condition imposed by the commissioners under s 18A(1) or (6) (as added) (see para 133 ante): s 69(1) (amended by the Finance Act 1996 s 26(1), Sch 3 para 9). The Value Added Tax Act 1994 s 69 (as amended) applies in relation to failures occurring before as well as after 1 September 1994 (ie the commencement date of the Value Added Tax Act 1994), and for that purpose any reference to any provision of the 1994 Act includes a reference to the corresponding provision of the enactments repealed by that Act: s 69(10).

2   In relation to a failure to comply with any regulatory requirement, the 'prescribed rate' is determined by reference to the number of occasions in the period of two years preceding the beginning of the failure in question on which the person concerned has previously failed to comply with that requirement: ibid s 69(3). The rate is: (1) £5 if there has been no such previous occasion in that period (s 69(3)(a)); (2) £10 if there has been only one such occasion in that period (s 69(3)(b)); and (3) £15 in any other case (s 69(3)(c)). However, for the purposes of s 69(3): (a) a failure to comply with any regulatory requirement is disregarded if, as a result of the failure, the person concerned became liable for a surcharge under s 59 (as amended) (see para 283 post) or s 59A (as added) (see para 284 post); (b) a continuing failure to comply with any such requirement is regarded as one occasion of failure occurring on the date on which the failure began; (c) if the same omission gives rise to a failure to comply with more than one such requirement, it is regarded as the occasion of only one failure; and (d) in relation to a failure to comply with a requirement imposed by regulations as to the furnishing of a return or as to the payment of VAT, a previous failure to comply with such a requirement as to either of those matters is regarded as a previous failure to comply with the requirement in question: s 69(4) (amended by the Finance Act 1996 s 35(1), (6)). If it appears to the Treasury that there has been a change in the value of money since 25 July 1985, or since the last occasion when this power was exercised, it may by order substitute for the sums for the time being specified in the Value Added Tax Act 1994 s 69(2), (3)(a)–(c) such other sums as appear to it to be justified by the change: s 69(7). Such an order does not, however, apply to a failure which began before the date on which the order comes into force: s 69(7). At the date at which this volume states the law, no such order had been made.

3   Ibid s 69(1). In addition, where the failure referred to in s 69(1) consists in (1) not paying the VAT due in respect of any period within the time required by regulations under s 25(1) (see para 202 ante); or (2) not furnishing a return in respect of any period within the time required by regulations under Sch 11 para 2(1) (see para 225 ante), the prescribed rate is the greater of that which is appropriate under 69(3)(a), (b) or (c) (see note 2 supra) and an amount equal to one-sixth, one-third or one-half of 1% of the VAT due in respect of that period (the appropriate fraction being determined according to whether s 69(3)(a), (b) or (c) is applicable): s 69(5). For the purposes of s 69(5), the VAT due is (a) if the person has furnished a return, the VAT shown in the return as that for which he is accountable in respect of the period in question; or (b) in any other case, such VAT as has been assessed for that period and notified to him under s 73(1) (see para 247 ante): s 69(6). However, where a person is liable for a penalty under s 69 for a failure to comply with a requirement of a kind described in s 69(1)(c)–(f) (see note 1 heads (3)–(6) supra), no assessment may be made of the amount

due in respect of the penalty unless within the preceding two years the commissioners have issued him with a written warning of the consequences of a continuing failure to comply with the relevant requirement: see s 76(2); and para 251 ante.

4 Ie a requirement imposed under ibid Sch 11 para 6(3): see para 219 ante.
5 Ibid s 69(2).
6 Ibid s 69(8). A failure in respect of which the commissioners or tribunal have or has been so satisfied is disregarded for the purposes of s 69(3) (see note 2 supra): s 69(8). For the meaning of 'reasonable excuse' see s 71; and para 275 note 9 ante.
7 Ie under ibid s 59 (as amended) (see para 283 post) or s 59A (as added) (see para 284 post): s 69(9) (amended by the Finance Act 1996 s 35(1), (6)).
8 Ie under the Value Added Tax Act 1994 s 60: see para 272 ante.
9 Ie under ibid s 63: see para 275 ante.
10 Ibid s 69(9) (as amended: see note 7 supra).

283. The default surcharge. If, by the last day on which a taxable person[1] is required[2] to furnish a return[3] for a prescribed accounting period[4], the Commissioners of Customs and Excise have not received that return, or the commissioners have received that return but have not received the amount of value added tax shown on the return as payable by him in respect of that period, the taxable person is regarded as being in default in respect of that period for the purposes of the default surcharge provisions[5]. A person is not, however, to be regarded as being in default in respect of any prescribed accounting period for these purposes if that period is one in respect of which he is required by virtue of any order under the statutory provisions relating to payments on account[6] to make any payment on account of VAT[7].

Once a taxable person is in default in respect of a prescribed accounting period, the commissioners may serve notice on him (a 'surcharge liability notice'), specifying as a surcharge period a period ending on the first anniversary of the last day of the prescribed accounting period the default for which led to the service of the notice, and beginning, in general[8], on the date of the notice[9]. If a taxable person on whom a surcharge liability notice has been served is in default in respect of a prescribed accounting period ending within the surcharge period which is specified in (or extended by[10]) the notice, and he has outstanding VAT[11] for the prescribed accounting period in which he is in default, he is liable, subject to certain conditions set out below, to a surcharge equal to whichever is the greater of the specified percentage[12] of his outstanding VAT for that prescribed accounting period and £30[13].

A person is not liable to a surcharge, and is treated as not having been in default in respect of the prescribed accounting period in question, if he satisfies the commissioners (or, on appeal, a VAT and duties tribunal) that, in the case of a default which is material to the surcharge[14] the return or, as the case may be, the VAT shown on the return, was dispatched at such a time and in such a manner that it was reasonable to expect that it would be received by the commissioners within the appropriate time limit, or that there is a reasonable excuse[15] for the return or VAT not having been so dispatched[16]. In such a case, any surcharge liability notice the service of which depended on that default is deemed not to have been served[17]. In addition, in any case where the conduct by virtue of which a person is in default in respect of a prescribed accounting period is also conduct constituting a breach of a regulatory provision[18] and by reason of that conduct the person concerned is assessed to a penalty[19], the default is left out of account for the purposes of the default surcharge provisions[20] relating to the service of a default surcharge notice and to the computation and imposition of surcharges[21].

Where a prescribed accounting period which is not one ending on or after 29 April 1996 in respect of which a taxable person is liable[22] to make any payment on account of VAT (that is to say, not a 'section 28 accounting period')[23] ends within a surcharge period begun or extended by the service on a taxable person of a surcharge liability notice under the default surcharge provisions relating to payments on account[24], the above provisions have effect as if:

(1)   the prescribed accounting period that is not a section 28 accounting period were deemed to be a period ending within a surcharge period begun or extended by a notice served under them[25];

(2)   any question (a) whether a surcharge period was begun or extended by the notice or (b) whether the taxable person was in default in respect of any prescribed accounting period which was a section 28 accounting period but ended within the surcharge period begun or extended by that notice, were to be determined as it would be determined for the purposes of the default surcharge provisions relating to payments on account[26]; and

(3)   that person were to be treated as having had outstanding VAT for a section 28 accounting period in any case where the aggregate value of his defaults in respect of that period[27] was more than nil[28].

1   For the meaning of 'taxable person' see paras 12 note 4, 55 ante.

2   Ie in accordance with regulations under the Value Added Tax Act 1994: see the Value Added Tax Regulations 1995, SI 1995/2518, reg 25; and para 226 ante.

3   For the meaning of 'return' see para 105 note 14 ante.

4   For the meaning of 'prescribed accounting period' see para 202 note 4 ante.

5   Value Added Tax Act 1994 s 59(1). Section 59(1) is subject to s 59(1A) (as added: see note 7 infra): s 59(1) (amended by the Finance Act 1996 s 35(3)). The mere fact of being in default does not lead to the imposition of surcharge; the surcharge arises when, after a surcharge liability notice has been issued, the taxable person is similarly in default within the period specified. The liability to a surcharge is not a liability to VAT; and does not, therefore, pass to a successor to the trader's VAT registration, under the Value Added Tax Regulations 1995 reg 6 (see para 74 ante): *Greenline Transport (North Wales) Ltd v Customs and Excise Comrs* (1991) VAT Decision 5756, [1991] STI 429.

6   Ie under the Value Added Tax Act 1994 s 28 (as amended): see para 229 ante.

7   Ibid s 59(1A) (added by the Finance Act 1996 s 35(1), (3)).

8   If a surcharge liability notice is served by reason of a default in respect of a prescribed accounting period and that period ends at or before the expiry of an existing surcharge period already notified to the taxable person concerned, the surcharge period specified in that notice is to be expressed as a continuation of the existing surcharge period and accordingly that existing period and its extension are regarded as a single surcharge period for the purposes of the default surcharge provisions: Value Added Tax Act 1994 s 59(3). If a taxable person does not receive the original surcharge liability notice, any subsequent notice under s 59(3) which purports to extend the original surcharge liability period is invalid: *Dow Engineering v Customs and Excise Comrs* (1991) VAT Decision 5771, [1991] STI 459; *Eidographics Ltd v Customs and Excise Comrs* [1991] VATTR 449; *Dow Chemical Co Ltd v Customs and Excise Comrs* (1996) VAT Decision 13954, [1996] STI 894. This may no longer be true, since the commissioners have amended the wording on surcharge liability notices, so that 'extension' notices also specify a new surcharge period, in the event that the earlier notice was defective or did not reach the taxpayer: see *Goldfinch Transport Ltd v Customs and Excise Comrs* (1996) VAT Decision 14145, [1996] STI 1352.

9   See the Value Added Tax Act 1994 s 59(2).

10   As to the extension of the period see note 8 supra.

11   For these purposes, a person has outstanding VAT for a prescribed period if some or all of the VAT for which he is liable in respect of that period has not been paid by the last day on which he is required to make a return for that period; and this reference to a person's outstanding VAT for a prescribed accounting period is to so much of the VAT for which he is so liable as has not been paid by that day: Value Added Tax Act 1994 s 59(6). For these purposes, references to a thing's being done by any day include references to its being done on that day: s 59(11) (added by the Finance Act 1996 s 35(1), (4)).

12   The specified percentage is determined in relation to a prescribed accounting period by reference to the number of such periods in respect of which the taxable person is in default during the surcharge period and for which he has outstanding VAT, so that in relation to (1) the first such period, the specified percentage is 2%; (2) the second such period, the specified percentage is 5%; (3) the third such period, the specified percentage is 10%; and (4) each such period after the third, the specified percentage is 15%: Value Added Tax Act 1994 s 59(5). If there is no outstanding VAT for a period, and the commissioners decide to exercise their discretion not to assess in the minimum amount of £30,

this does not affect (ie reduce) the specified percentage for the next default: *GB Techniques Ltd v Customs and Excise Comrs* [1988] VATTR 95.

13   Value Added Tax Act 1994 s 59(4).

14   A default is material to a surcharge if (1) it is the default which, by virtue of ibid s 59(4), gives rise to the surcharge; or (2) it is a default which was taken into account in the service of the surcharge liability notice upon which the surcharge depends and the person concerned has not previously been liable to a surcharge in respect of a prescribed accounting period ending within the surcharge period specified in or extended by that notice: s 59(8). The effect of this is that a taxable person cannot complain about the service of a surcharge liability notice simpliciter; rather, he has to await the imposition of a surcharge, when he may raise the question of whether he is properly to be treated as in default, either in relation to the original alleged default or in relation to the default in respect of which he has been made liable to a surcharge. An appeal lies to a VAT and duties tribunal against any liability to a surcharge under s 59 (as amended): see s 83(n); and para 296 post.

15   For the meaning of 'reasonable excuse' see ibid s 71; and paras 275 note 9, 279 note 11 ante. The non-receipt of a surcharge liability notice in relation to an earlier default does not constitute a reasonable excuse for default in relation to a later return: *Customs and Excise Comrs v Medway Draughting and Technical Services Ltd, Customs and Excise Comrs v Adplates Offset Ltd* [1989] STC 346 at 353. In *Customs and Excise Comrs v Salevon Ltd, Customs and Excise Comrs v Harris* [1989] STC 907, a company suffered cash-flow problems through the dishonesty of its company secretary; its subsequent failure to pay its VAT on time constituted a reasonable excuse, notwithstanding the Value Added Tax Act 1994 s 71, since it was the dishonesty of the secretary rather than the shortage of funds which caused the company to fall into arrears in the payment of its tax. In *First Continental Ltd v Customs and Excise Comrs* (1996) VAT Decision 14057, [1996] STI 1101, a company which had taken reasonable precautions before buying a business to ensure it enjoyed a turnover sufficient to meet its obligations to the bank etc was held to have a reasonable excuse for defaulting in seven successive periods when it transpired that potential turnover had been misrepresented by the vendors. Cf *Alpha Numeric Ltd v Customs and Excise Comrs* (1991) VAT Decision 5519, [1991] STI 98 (company held not to have a reasonable excuse, where it failed to pay because the managing director had been assured by the finance director (who subsequently resigned) that payment had already been effected); and *Profile Security Services Ltd v Customs and Excise Comrs* [1996] STC 808 (the words 'any other person' in what is now the Value Added Tax Act 1994 s 71(1) bear their usual wide meaning, with the result that s 71(1) excludes reliance on a trusted employee as much as reliance on a third party). The mere loss of money by theft, in circumstances where the trader remained able to meet its VAT liabilities, did not amount to a reasonable excuse for non-payment: *Caddies-Wainwright Ltd v Customs and Excise Comrs* (1991) VAT Decision 5657, [1991] STI 228. Where a trader is owed money, wrongly assessed by the Inland Revenue which has not been repaid, the lack of funds can constitute a reasonable excuse (even where the trader is on the cash accounting scheme: see para 228 ante) (*Keogh v Customs and Excise Comrs* (1993) VAT Decision 10710, [1993] STI 1206); but it is no excuse that another company in the same ownership (but not the same VAT group) has not received a repayment from the Commissioners (*Artful Dodger (Kilmarnock) Ltd v Lord Advocate* [1993] STC 330). In *Customs and Excise Comrs v Steptoe* [1992] STC 757, CA, it was held that whilst the mere insufficiency of funds would not constitute a reasonable excuse, the underlying cause would, if even the exercise of reasonable foresight and due diligence and a proper regard to the fact that tax would become due on a particular date, would not have avoided the insufficiency of funds which led to the non-payment. The delivery to the commissioners of a cheque which was dishonoured on presentation was not payment for the purposes of VAT; and the fact that the cheque was presented unexpectedly early was not a reasonable excuse: *Customs and Excise Comrs v Palco Industry Co Ltd* [1990] STC 594. In *Barney & Freeman v Customs and Excise Comrs* [1990] VATTR 19, it was held that if the commissioners gave an unclear direction to a trader (relating to the use of credit transfers for the payment of VAT) and subsequently appeared to confirm a particular interpretation of the direction by not imposing a surcharge when the trader adopted a course of action based on that interpretation, they could not subsequently impose a surcharge for the trader's continuing application of that interpretation.

16   Value Added Tax Act 1994 s 59(7).

17   Ibid s 59(7). If the surcharge liability notice is to be disregarded, no surcharge may be imposed in relation to any default which falls within the period previously specified by the notice: *Montreux Fabrics v Customs and Excise Comrs* [1988] VATTR 71. The Interpretation Act 1978 s 7 (see STATUTES vol 44(1) (Reissue) para 1388) does not apply to deem surcharge liability notices to be served at the time when they would have been delivered in the ordinary course of the post, since the scheme of the 1994 Act is that taxpayers should be given notice of their liability to surcharge: *Customs and Excise Comrs v Medway Draughting and Technical Services Ltd, Customs and Excise Comrs v Adplates Offset Ltd* [1989] STC 346.

18   Ie conduct falling within the Value Added Tax Act 1994 s 69(1): see para 283 ante.

19   Ie under ibid s 69 (as amended): see para 283 ante.

20   Ie ibid s 59(2)–(5): see the text and notes 8–12 supra.

21   Ibid s 59(9). If the commissioners, after consultation with the Treasury, so direct, a default in respect of a prescribed accounting period specified in the direction is to be left out of account for the purposes of s 59(2)–(5): s 59(10).

22   Ie by virtue of an order under ibid s 28 (as amended): see para 229 ante.

23   See ibid s 59B(4) (s 59B added by the Finance Act 1996 s 35(1), (5)).

24   Ie under ibid s 59A (as added): see para 284 post.

25   Ibid s 59B(1)(b), (3)(a) (as added: see note 23 supra).

26   Ibid s 59B(1)(b), (3)(b) (as added: see note 23 supra).

27   Ie for the purposes of ibid s 59A (as added): see para 284 post.

28   Ibid s 59B(1)(b), (3)(c) (as added: see note 23 supra).

284. The default surcharge in respect of payments on account. A taxable person[1] is regarded as in default in respect of any prescribed accounting period[2] if the period is one in which he is required[3] to make any payment on account of value added tax and either (1) a payment which he is so required to make in respect of that period has not been received in full by the Commissioners of Customs and Excise by the day on which it became due[4]; or (2) he would, but for the statutory provision relating to payments on account[5], be in default in respect of that period for the purposes of the default surcharge provisions[6].

Where a taxable person is in default in respect of a prescribed accounting period, the commissioners may serve notice on him (a 'surcharge liability notice') specifying as a surcharge period for these purposes a period which begins, in general[7], on the date of the notice and ends on the first anniversary of the last day of the prescribed accounting period the default for which led to the service of the notice[8]. If a taxable person on whom a surcharge liability notice has been served is in default in respect of a prescribed accounting period ending within the surcharge period specified in, or extended by[9], that notice, and the aggregate value of his defaults[10] in respect of that prescribed accounting period is more than nil, that person is liable to a surcharge equal to whichever is the greater of £30 and the specified percentage[11] of the aggregate value of his defaults in respect of that prescribed accounting period[12].

If a person who would otherwise be liable to a surcharge under these provisions satisfies the commissioners or, on appeal, a VAT and duties tribunal:

(a)   in the case of a default that is material for the purposes of the surcharge[13] and falls within head (1) above, that the payment on account of VAT was dispatched at such a time and in such a manner that it was reasonable to expect that it would be received by the commissioners on the day on which it became due, or that there is a reasonable excuse[14] for the payment not having been so dispatched; or

(b)   in the case of a default that is material for the purposes of the surcharge and falls within head (2) above, that the specified condition[15] is satisfied as respects the default,

he is not liable to the surcharge and is treated[16] as not having been in default in respect of the prescribed accounting period in question and, accordingly, any surcharge liability notice the service of which depended upon that default is deemed not to have been served[17]. In addition, in any case where the conduct by virtue of which a person is in default in respect of a prescribed accounting period is also conduct constituting a breach of a regulatory provision[18] and by reason of that conduct the person concerned is assessed to a penalty[19], the default is left out of account for the purposes of the default surcharge provisions[20] relating to the service of a default surcharge notice in respect of payments on account and to the computation and imposition of surcharges[21].

Where a prescribed accounting period ending on or after 29 April 1996 in respect of which a taxable person is liable[22] to make any payment on account of VAT (a 'section 28 accounting period')[23] ends within a surcharge period begun or extended by the service on a taxable person[24] of a surcharge liability notice under the general default surcharge provisions[25], the above provisions have effect as if that accounting period were deemed to be a period ending within a surcharge period begun or extended by a notice served under them but as if any question (i) whether a surcharge period was begun or extended by the notice; or (ii) whether the taxable person was in default in respect of any prescribed accounting period which was not a section 28 accounting period but ended within the surcharge period begun or extended by that notice, were to be determined as it would be determined for the purposes of the general default surcharge provisions[26].

1 For the meaning of 'taxable person' see paras 12 note 4, 55 ante.
2 For the meaning of 'prescribed accounting period' see para 202 note 4 ante.
3 Ie by virtue of an order under the Value Added Tax Act 1994 s 28 (as amended): see para 229 ante.
4 For these purposes, the commissioners are taken not to receive a payment by the day on which it becomes due unless it is made in such a manner as secures, in a case where the payment is made otherwise than in cash, that, by the last day for the payment of that amount, all the transactions can be completed before the whole amount of the payment becomes available to the commissioners: ibid s 59A(12) (s 59A added by the Finance Act 1996 s 35(1), (2)). References to a thing's being done by any day include references to its being done on that day: Value Added Tax Act 1994 s 59A(14) (as so added).
5 Ie but for ibid s 59(1A) (as added): see para 283 ante.
6 Ibid s 59A(1) (as added: see note 4 supra). The default surcharge provisions referred to in the text are the provisions of s 59 (as amended): see para 283 ante. In determining for these purposes whether any person would, but for s 59(1A) (as added), be in default in respect of any period for the purposes of s 59 (as amended), s 59A(12) (as added: see note 4 supra) is deemed to apply for the purposes of s 59 (as amended) as it applies for the purposes of s 59A (as so added): s 59A(13) (as so added). The liability to a surcharge is not a liability to VAT; and does not, therefore, pass to a successor to the trader's VAT registration: see *Greenline Transport (North Wales) Ltd v Customs and Excise Comrs* (1991) VAT Decision 5756, [1991] STI 429.
7 If a surcharge liability notice is served by reason of a default in respect of a prescribed accounting period and that period ends at or before the expiry of an existing surcharge period already notified to the taxable person concerned, the surcharge period specified in that notice is to be expressed as a continuation of the existing surcharge period and, accordingly, the existing period and its extension are regarded as a single surcharge period: Value Added Tax Act 1994 s 59A(3) (as added: see note 4 supra).
8 See ibid s 59A(2) (as added: see note 4 supra).
9 See note 7 supra.
10 For these purposes, the aggregate value of a person's defaults in respect of a prescribed accounting period is calculated as follows: (1) where the whole or any part of a payment in respect of that period on account of VAT was not received by the commissioners by the day on which it became due, an amount equal to that payment or, as the case may be, to that part of it is taken to be the value of the default relating to that payment; (2) if there is more than one default with a value given by head (1) supra, those values are aggregated; (3) the total given by head (2) supra, or, where there is only one default, the value of the default under head (1) supra, is taken to be the value for that period of that person's defaults on payments on account; (4) the value of any default by that person which is a default falling within head (2) in the text is taken to be equal to the amount of any outstanding VAT less the amount of unpaid payments on account; and (5) the aggregate value of a person's defaults in respect of that period is taken to be the aggregate of (a) the value for that period of that person's defaults (if any) on payments on account; and (b) the value of any default of his in respect of that period that falls within head (2) in the text: Value Added Tax Act 1994 s 59A(6) (as added: see note 4 supra). In the application of s 59A(6) (as so added) for the calculation of the aggregate value of a person's defaults in respect of a prescribed accounting period: (i) the amount of outstanding VAT referred to in head (4) supra is the amount, if any, which would be the amount of that person's outstanding VAT for that period for the purposes of s 59(4) (see para 283 ante); and (ii) the amount of unpaid payments on account so referred to is the amount, if any, equal to so much of any payments on account of VAT (being payments in respect of that period) as has not been received by the commissioners by the last day on which that person is required, as mentioned in s 59(1) (as amended) (see para 283 ante) to make a return for that period: s 59A(7) (as so added).
11 The specified percentage is determined in relation to a prescribed accounting period by reference to the number of such periods during the surcharge period which are periods in respect of which the taxable

person is in default and in respect of which the value of his defaults is more than nil, so that the specified percentage is, in relation to: (1) the first such prescribed accounting period, 2%; (2) the second such period, 5%; (3) the third such period, 10%; and (4) each such period after the third, 15%: ibid s 59A(5) (as added: see note 4 supra). If there is no such amount and the commissioners decide to exercise their discretion not to assess in the minimum amount of £30 (see para 251 ante) this does not affect (ie reduce) the specified percentage for the next default: see *GB Techniques Ltd v Customs and Excise Comrs* [1988] VATTR 95.

12   Value Added Tax Act 1994 s 59A(4) (as added: see note 4 supra).

13   For these purposes, a default is material to a surcharge if (1) it is the default which, by virtue of ibid s 59A(4) (as added: see note 4 supra), gives rise to the surcharge; or (2) it is a default which was taken into account in the service of the surcharge liability notice upon which the surcharge depends and the person concerned has not previously been liable to a surcharge in respect of a prescribed accounting period ending within the surcharge period specified in or extended by that notice: s 59A(9) (as so added).

14   For the meaning of 'reasonable excuse' see ibid s 71; and para 275 note 9 ante.

15   Ie the condition specified in ibid s 59(7)(a) or (b): see para 283 ante.

16   Ie for the purposes of ibid s 59A(1)–(7) (as added): see the text and notes 1–12 supra.

17   Ibid s 59A(8) (as added: see note 4 supra). If the surcharge liability notice is to be disregarded, no surcharge may be imposed in relation to any default which falls within the period previously specified by the notice: *Montreux Fabrics v Customs and Excise Comrs* [1988] VATTR 71. The Interpretation Act 1978 s 7 (see STATUTES vol 44(1) (Reissue) para 1388) does not apply to deem surcharge liability notices to be served at the time when they would have been delivered in the ordinary course of the post, since the scheme of the Value Added Tax Act 1994 is that taxpayers should be given notice of their liability to surcharge: *Customs and Excise Comrs v Medway Draughting and Technical Services Limited, Customs and Excise Comrs v Adplates Offset Limited* [1989] STC 346.

18   Ie conduct falling within the Value Added Tax Act 1994 s 69(1): see para 282 ante.

19   Ie under ibid s 69 (as amended): see para 282 ante.

20   Ie ibid s 59A(2)–(5) (as added): see the text and notes 7–11 supra.

21   Ibid s 59A(10) (as added: see note 4 supra). If the commissioners, after consultation with the Treasury, so direct, a default in respect of a prescribed accounting period specified in the direction is to be left out of account for the purposes of s 59A(2)–(5) (as so added): s 59A(11) (as so added).

22   Ie by virtue of an order under ibid s 28 (as amended): see para 229 ante.

23   See ibid s 59B(4) (s 59B added by the Finance Act 1996 s 35(1), (5)).

24   Ie whether before or after the coming into force of the Value Added Tax Act 1994 s 59A (as added): s 59B(1)(a) (as added: see note 23 supra).

25   Ie under the Value Added Tax Act 1994 s 59 (as amended): see para 283 ante.

26   Ibid s 59B(1)(a), (2) (as added: see note 23 supra).

7. ENFORCEMENT AND ANCILLARY POWERS

285. Powers of entry. For the purpose of exercising any powers[1] under the Value Added Tax Act 1994, an authorised person[2] may at any reasonable time enter premises used in connection with the carrying on of a business[3].

1   Eg for the taking of samples: see para 287 post.

2   For the meaning of 'authorised person' see para 82 note 5 ante.

3   Value Added Tax Act 1994 s 58, Sch 11 para 10(1). For the meaning of 'business' see para 17 ante.

286. Power of inspection. Where an authorised person[1] has reasonable cause to believe that any premises are used in connection with the supply of goods under taxable supplies[2] or with the acquisition of goods under taxable acquisitions from other member states[3] and that goods to be so supplied or acquired are on those premises, or that any premises are used as a fiscal warehouse[4], he may at any reasonable time enter and inspect those premises and inspect any goods found on them[5].

1   For the meaning of 'authorised person' see para 82 note 5 ante.
2   For the meaning of 'taxable supply' see para 12 note 3 ante.
3   As to taxable acquisitions of goods from other member states see para 13 ante.
4   For the meaning of 'fiscal warehouse' see para 133 note 3 ante.
5   Value Added Tax Act 1994 s 58, Sch 11 para 10(2) (amended by the Finance Act 1996 s 26(1), Sch 3 para 17).

287. Power to take samples. If it appears to an authorised person[1] necessary for the protection of the revenue against mistake or fraud, he may at any time take, from the goods in the possession of any person who supplies goods, or acquires goods from another member state[2], or in the possession of a fiscal warehousekeeper[3], such samples as the authorised person may require with a view to determining how the goods or the materials of which they are made ought to be, or to have been, treated for the purposes of value added tax[4]. Any sample taken under this provision is to be disposed of and accounted for in such manner as the Commissioners of Customs and Excise may direct[5]. Where a sample is taken from the goods in any person's possession and is not returned to him within a reasonable time and in good condition, the commissioners must pay him by way of compensation a sum equal to the cost of the sample to him or such larger sum as they may determine[6].

1   For the meaning of 'authorised person' see para 82 note 5 ante.
2   As to taxable acquisitions of goods from other member states see para 13 ante; and for the meaning of 'another member state' see para 4 note 14 ante.
3   For the meaning of 'fiscal warehousekeeper' see para 133 note 3 ante.
4   Value Added Tax Act 1994 s 58, Sch 11 para 8(1) (amended by the Finance Act 1996 s 26(1), Sch 3 para 16).
5   Value Added Tax Act 1994 Sch 11 para 8(2).
6   Ibid Sch 11 para 8(3).

288. Power of search. If a justice of the peace is satisfied on information on oath that there is reasonable ground for suspecting that a fraud offence[1] which appears to be of a serious nature is being, has been or is about to be committed on any premises, or that evidence of the commission of such an offence is to be found there, he may issue a warrant in writing authorising (subject to certain conditions set out below) any authorised person[2] to enter those premises, if necessary by force, at any time within one month from the time of the issue of the warrant and to search them[3]. Any person who enters the premises under the authority of the warrant may:

(1)   take with him such other persons as appear to him to be necessary[4];

(2)   seize and remove any documents[5] or other things whatsoever found on the premises which he has reasonable cause to believe may be required as evidence for the purposes of proceedings in respect of such an offence[6]; and

(3)   search or cause to be searched any person found on the premises whom he has reasonable cause to believe to be in possession of any such documents or other things[7].

The powers conferred by such a warrant are not, however, exercisable:

(a)   by more than such number of authorised persons as may be specified in the warrant; nor

(b)   outside such times of day as may be so specified; nor

(c)   (if the warrant so provides) otherwise than in the presence of a constable in uniform[8].

1 A 'fraud offence' means an offence under any provision of the Value Added Tax Act 1994 s 72(1)–(8) (see paras 267–271 ante): s 58, Sch 11 para 10(4).

2 For the meaning of 'authorised person' see para 82 note 5 ante.

3 Value Added Tax Act 1994 Sch 11 para 10(3). An authorised person seeking to exercise the powers conferred by such a warrant or, if there is more than one such authorised person, that one of them who is in charge of the search, must provide a copy of the warrant indorsed with his name to the occupier of the premises concerned, if he is present at the time the search is to begin: Sch 11 para 10(6)(a). If at that time the occupier is not present but a person who appears to the authorised person to be in charge of the premises is present, the copy must be supplied to that person: Sch 11 para 10(6)(b). If neither Sch 11 para 10(6)(a) or (b) applies, the copy must be left in a prominent place on the premises: Sch 11 para 10(6)(c).

4 Ibid Sch 11 para 10(3)(a).

5 For the meaning of 'document' see para 11 note 8 ante.

6 Value Added Tax Act 1994 Sch 11 para 10(3)(b).

7 Ibid Sch 11 para 10(3)(c). No woman or girl may be searched except by a woman: Sch 11 para 10(3).
    While an Order in Council under the Isle of Man Act 1979 s 6 (as amended) is in force (see para 8 ante), the Value Added Tax Act 1994 Sch 11 para 10(3) has effect as if the references to an offence in connection with the tax included references to an offence in connection with the tax charged under the Act of Tynwald: Isle of Man Act 1979 s 6(4)(b) (amended by the Value Added Tax Act 1983 s 50(1), Sch 9 para 3; and by the Value Added Tax Act 1994 s 100, Sch 14 para 7(2)).

8 Ibid Sch 11 para 10(5).

289. Order for access to recorded information.

If a justice of the peace is satisfied, on an application by an authorised person[1], that there are reasonable grounds for believing that an offence in connection with value added tax is being, has been or is about to be committed, and that any recorded information[2] which may be required as evidence for the purpose of any proceedings in respect of such an offence is in the possession of any person, he may make an order[3] that the person who appears to the justice to be in possession of the recorded information to which the application relates must:

(1) give an authorised person access[4] to it; and

(2) permit an authorised person to remove and take away any of it which he reasonably considers necessary,

not later than the end of the period of seven days (beginning on the date of the order) or of such longer period as the order may specify[5].

1 For the meaning of 'authorised person' see para 82 note 5 ante.

2 Ie including any document of any nature whatsoever: Value Added Tax Act 1994 s 58, Sch 11 para 11(1)(b). For the meaning of 'document' see para 11 note 8 ante.

3 Ibid Sch 11 para 11(1). This provision is without prejudice to Sch 11 para 7 (furnishing of information and production of documents: see para 224 ante) and Sch 11 para 10 (entry and search of premises and persons: see paras 285–286, 288 ante): Sch 11 para 11(5). The test is whether there are reasonable grounds for belief that an offence has been, is being or is about to be committed; and mere suspicion is not enough. Furthermore, the magistrate must satisfy himself, before making the order, that there are reasonable grounds for that belief and may not simply accept the statement of belief made by the applicant: *R v Epsom Justices, ex p Bell* [1989] STC 169, DC. Applications should be made inter partes wherever possible and should ordinarily therefore be made on notice, not only to those from whom access is sought but also to those who are obviously likely to be affected by the order: *R v City of London Magistrates Court, ex p Asif* [1996] STC 611, DC.

4 If an order is made requiring a person to give an authorised person access to recorded information he must also permit the authorised person to take copies of it or to make extracts from it: Value Added Tax Act 1994 Sch 11 para 11(3). Where the recorded information consists of information contained in a computer, the order has effect as an order to produce the information in a form in which it is visible and legible and, if the authorised person wishes to remove it, in a form in which it can be removed: Sch 11 para 11(4).

5 Ibid Sch 11 para 11(2).

290. Procedure when documents are removed. An authorised person[1] who removes anything in the exercise of a power conferred[2] on him, must, if so requested by a person showing himself to be the occupier of premises from which it was removed, or to have had custody or control of it immediately before the removal, provide that person with a record of what he removed[3] within a reasonable time from the making of the request[4].

If a request for permission to be granted access to anything which has been removed by an authorised person, and is retained by the Commissioners of Customs and Excise for the purposes of investigating an offence, is made to the officer in overall charge of the investigation[5] by a person who had custody or control of the thing immediately before it was so removed or by someone acting on behalf of such a person, the officer must allow the person who made the request access to it under the supervision of an authorised person[6].

There is no duty to grant access to, or to supply a photograph or copy of, anything if the officer in overall charge of the investigation for the purposes of which it was removed has reasonable grounds for believing that to do so would prejudice that investigation, the investigation of an offence other than the offence for the purposes of the investigation of which the thing was removed or any criminal proceedings which may be brought as a result either of the investigation of which he is in charge or of any investigation of another offence[7].

If a magistrates' court[8] is satisfied, on an application[9] made way of complaint, that a person has failed to comply with a requirement imposed by the above provisions, the court may order that person to comply with the requirement within such time and in such manner as may be specified in the order[10].

1   For the meaning of 'authorised person' see para 82 note 5 ante.
2   Ie by or under the Value Added Tax Act 1994 s 58, Sch 11 para 10 (see paras 285–286, 288 ante) or Sch 11 para 11 (see para 289 ante): Sch 11 para 12(1).
3   Ibid Sch 11 para 12(1).
4   Ibid Sch 11 para 12(2).
5   For these purposes, any reference to the officer in overall charge of the investigation is a reference to the person whose name and address are indorsed on the warrant or order concerned as being the officer so in charge: ibid Sch 11 para 12(8).
6   Ibid Sch 11 para 12(3). Similarly, if a request for a photograph or copy of any such thing is made to the officer in overall charge of the investigation by such a person, the officer must allow the person who makes the request access to it under the supervision of an authorised person for the purpose of photographing it or copying it, or must photograph or copy it, or cause it to be photographed or copied; and that photograph or copy must be supplied to the person who made the request within a reasonable time from the making of the request: Sch 11 para 12(4), (5), (6).
7   Ibid Sch 11 para 12(7).
8   See ibid Sch 11 para 13(3)(a).
9   An application must be made, in the case of a failure to comply with any of the requirements imposed by ibid Sch 11 para 12(1), (2), by the occupier of the premises from which the thing in question was removed or by the person who had custody or control of it immediately before it was so removed, and, in any other case, by the person who had such custody or control: Sch 11 para 13(2).
10   Ibid Sch 11 para 13(1), (4).

291. Service of notices. Any notice, notification, requirement or demand to be served on, given to, or made of any person for any of the purposes of the Value Added Tax Act 1994 may be served, given, or made by sending it by post in a letter addressed to that person or his VAT representative[1] at his (or his representative's) last or usual residence or place of business[2].

1   As to VAT representatives see the Value Added Tax Act 1994 s 48; and para 62 ante.

2   Ibid s 98. By the Interpretation Act 1978 s 7, where an Act authorises or requires any document to be served by post, then, unless the contrary intention appears, the service is deemed to be effected by properly addressing, pre-paying and posting a letter containing the document and, unless the contrary is proved, to have been effected at the time at which the letter would be delivered in the ordinary course of the post: see STATUTES vol 44(1) (Reissue) para 1388. For a VAT case in which it was held that the statutory provision (the Value Added Tax Act 1994 s 59 (as amended (default surcharges: see para 283 ante)) did provide to the contrary, thereby excluding the application of the Interpretation Act 1978 s 7, see *Customs and Excise Comrs v Medway Draughting and Technical Services Ltd, Customs and Excise Comrs v Adplates Offset Ltd* [1989] STC 346.

292. Disclosure of information for statistical purposes. The Commissioners of Customs and Excise, or an authorised officer of the commissioners, may disclose certain particulars to an authorised officer of the Department of Trade and Industry or the Central Statistical Office of the Chancellor of the Exchequer for the purpose of the compilation or maintenance by that department or office of a central register of businesses[1] or for the purpose of any statistical survey conducted or to be conducted by that department or office[2]. The particulars which may be so disclosed are:

    (1)   numbers allocated by the commissioners on the registration of persons under the Value Added Tax Act 1994[3] and reference numbers for members of a group[4];

    (2)   names, trading styles and addresses of persons so registered or of members of groups and status and trade classifications of businesses; and

    (3)   actual or estimated value of supplies[5],

in each case obtained or recorded by the commissioners in pursuance of the Value Added Tax Act 1994[6].

No information so obtained by an officer of the department or office mentioned above may be disclosed except to an officer of a government department[7] for the purpose for which the information was obtained, or for a like purpose[8], although this does not prevent the disclosure:

    (a)   of any information in the form of a summary so framed as not to enable particulars to be identified as particulars relating to a particular person or to the business carried on by a particular person; or

    (b)   with the consent of any person, of any information enabling particulars to be identified as particulars relating only to him or to a business carried on by him[9].

If any person who has obtained any information by virtue of these provisions discloses it in contravention of the above prohibition, he is liable on summary conviction to a fine not exceeding the statutory maximum and on conviction on indictment to imprisonment for a term not exceeding two years, or to a fine of any amount, or to both[10].

1   For the meaning of 'business' see para 17 ante.

2   Value Added Tax Act 1994 s 91(1). For these purposes, references to the Department of Trade and Industry or the Central Statistical Office include references to any Northern Ireland department carrying out similar functions: s 91(5).

3   As to registration see para 56 et seq ante.

4   As to group registration of bodies corporate see para 66 ante.

5   For the meaning of 'supply' see para 21 ante.

6   Value Added Tax Act 1994 s 91(1).

7   Ie including a Northern Ireland department: ibid s 91(2).

8   Ibid s 91(2).

9   Ibid s 91(3).

10   Ibid s 91(4). As to the statutory maximum see para 268 note 3 ante.

8. APPEALS

(1) VAT AND DUTIES TRIBUNALS

293. Establishment of VAT and duties tribunals. For the purpose of hearing appeals in respect of a range of matters relating to value added tax, VAT and duties tribunals[1] have been established for England and Wales, Scotland and Northern Ireland[2]. The Lord Chancellor[3] determines the number of VAT and duties tribunals that should be established, which sit at such times and at such places as he may from time to time determine[4].

The tribunals are supervised by the Council on Tribunals[5]. The appropriate tribunal centre[6] for any appeal is the tribunal centre for the time being appointed by the president[7] for the area in which is situated the address to which the disputed decision[8] was sent by the Commissioners of Customs and Excise or the tribunal centre to which the appeal against the disputed decision may be transferred[9].

1   VAT tribunals were renamed VAT and duties tribunals by the Finance Act 1994 ss 7(1), (2) (repealed by the Value Added Tax Act 1994 s 100, Sch 15) and this change is preserved by the Value Added Tax Act 1994 s 82(1), Sch 12 para 1(2); thus for any reference in the Value Added Tax Act 1994 Sch 12 to VAT tribunals there is, as from the commencement of Sch 12, to be substituted a reference to VAT and duties tribunals: Sch 12 para 1(2). Any reference in the Value Added Tax Act 1994 to a tribunal is a reference to a tribunal constituted in accordance with s 82(1), Sch 12, and that Schedule has effect generally with respect to appointments to, and the procedure and administration of, the tribunals: s 82(1). The tribunals continue to have jurisdiction in relation to matters relating to VAT conferred on them by Pt V (ss 82–87) (as amended) (see para 296 et seq post) and jurisdiction in relation to matters relating to customs and excise conferred by the Finance Act 1994 Pt I Ch II (ss 7–18) (as amended): Value Added Tax Act 1994 s 82(2). Any reference in any enactment or any subordinate legislation to a value added tax tribunal (or to a VAT tribunal) is to be construed in accordance with Sch 12 para 1(1)–(3), and cognate expressions are to be construed accordingly: Sch 12 para 1(4).

     Officers and staff may be appointed under the Courts Act 1971 s 27 (as amended) for carrying out the administrative work of the tribunals in England and Wales: Value Added Tax Act 1994 s 82(3).

2   At the date at which this volume states the law, there are tribunal centres in London (at the London Tribunal Centre, 15–19 Bedford Avenue, London, WC1B 3AS), Edinburgh (at the Edinburgh Tribunal Centre, 44 Palmerston Place, Edinburgh EH12 5BJ) and Manchester (at the Manchester Tribunal Centre, Warwickgate House, Warwick Road, Manchester M16 0GP). Tribunals occasionally sit outside these centres. Information about the tribunals is contained in *VAT: Appeals and Applications to the Tribunals; Explanatory Leaflet* (revised as at April 1993) which is obtainable at any tribunal centre or from any Customs and Excise VAT office.

3   In relation to Scotland, the functions of the Lord Chancellor are carried out by the Secretary of State for Scotland: Value Added Tax Act 1994 Sch 12 para 4.

4   Ibid Sch 12 para 4.

5   Ie under the Tribunals and Inquiries Act 1992 s 1, Sch 1 para 44 (amended by the Finance Act 1994 s 7(6)). As to the Council on Tribunals generally see ADMINISTRATIVE LAW vol 1(1) (Reissue) paras 48–50.

6   'Tribunal centre' means an administrative office of the VAT and duties tribunals: Value Added Tax Tribunals Rules 1986, SI 1986/590, r 2 (definition amended by SI 1994/2617).

7   As to the president see para 294 post.

8   'Disputed decision' means the decision of the Commissioners of Customs and Excise against which an appellant or intending appellant appeals or desires to appeal to a tribunal: Value Added Tax Tribunals Rules 1986 r 2. 'Appellant' means a person who brings an appeal under the Value Added Tax Act 1994 s 83 (as amended) (see para 296 post) or under the Finance Act 1994 s 16 (see CUSTOMS AND EXCISE) or s 60 (see INSURANCE): Value Added Tax Tribunals Rules 1986 r 2 (definition substituted by SI 1994/2617).

9   Ibid r 2. As to the difficulties incurred by the commissioners in serving out of the jurisdiction see *Interbet Trading Ltd v Customs and Excise Comrs* [1977] VATTR 63; and for later proceedings when the commissioners re-served a notice requiring the company to register for VAT at the premises of an

intermediary company whose services it used see *Interbet Trading Ltd v Customs and Excise Comrs (No 2)* [1978] VATTR 235.

294. The president. There is a president of VAT and duties tribunals who performs the functions conferred on him[1] in any part of the United Kingdom[2], and who sits ex officio as chairman at a sitting of a tribunal[3]. The president is appointed by the Lord Chancellor after consultation with the Lord Advocate and must be a person who has a ten year general qualification[4] or who is an advocate or solicitor in Scotland of at least ten years' standing, or who is a member of the Bar of Northern Ireland or a solicitor of the Supreme Court of Northern Ireland of at least ten years' standing[5].

Subject to the conditions described below, the appointment of the president is for such term and subject to such conditions as may be determined by the Lord Chancellor, after consultation with the Lord Advocate, and a person who ceases to hold the office of president is eligible for re-appointment[6]. The president may resign his office at any time and must vacate his office on the day on which he attains the age of 70, but if the Lord Chancellor, after consultation with the Lord Advocate, considers it desirable in the public interest that the president should continue in office for a further period, he may authorise him to continue in office, either generally or for such purpose as he may notify to the president, for a period not exceeding one year and not extending beyond the day on which the president attains the age of 75[7]. Similarly if, on the expiry of the period for which a president is authorised to continue in office, the Lord Chancellor, after consultation with the Lord Advocate, considers it desirable in the public interest to retain the person in office for a further period, he may authorise him to continue in office, either generally or for such purpose as he may notify to the president, for a further period not exceeding one year and not extending beyond the day on which the president attains the age of 75[8].

The president is paid such salary or fees, and there may be paid to or in respect of a former president such pension, allowance or gratuity, as the Lord Chancellor may with the approval of the Treasury determine[9]. If a person ceases to be president of VAT and duties tribunals and it appears to the Lord Chancellor that there are special circumstances which make it right that he should receive compensation, there may be paid to that person a sum of such amount as the Lord Chancellor may with the approval of the Treasury determine[10].

The Lord Chancellor may, if he thinks fit and after consultation with the Lord Advocate, remove the president from office on the ground of incapacity or misbehaviour[11]. The functions of the president may, if he is for any reason unable to act or his office is vacant, be discharged by a person nominated for the purpose by the Lord Chancellor after consultation with the Lord Advocate[12]. The president is barred from legal practice[13].

1   Ie conferred on him by the Value Added Tax Act 1994 s 82(1), Sch 12: see the text and notes 2–14 infra; and para 295 et seq post.
2   Ibid Sch 12 para 2(1). For the meaning of 'United Kingdom' see para 4 note 3 ante.
3   See ibid Sch 12 para 6.
4   Ie within the meaning of the Courts and Legal Services Act 1990 s 71: see SOLICITORS vol 44(1) (Reissue) para 91.
5   Value Added Tax Act 1994 Sch 12 para 2(2).
6   Ibid Sch 12 para 2(3).
7   Ibid Sch 12 para 3(3); Judicial Pensions and Retirement Act 1993 ss 26(4), (5), 31.
8   Ibid s 26(6).
9   Value Added Tax Act 1994 Sch 12 para 3(6). This provision, so far as relating to pensions, allowances and gratuities, does not have effect in relation to a person to whom the Judicial Pensions and Retirement Act 1993 Pt I (ss 1–18) applies, except to the extent provided under or by that Act: Value Added Tax Act

1994 Sch 12 para 3(7). The Judicial Pensions and Retirement Act 1993 Pt I applies to the president: see s 1(6), Sch 1 Pt II; and COURTS.
10   Value Added Tax Act 1994 Sch 12 para 3(8).
11   Ibid Sch 12 para 3(4).
12   Ibid Sch 12 para 3(5).
13   See the Courts and Legal Services Act 1990 s 75, Sch 11.

295. Composition and membership of tribunals. A VAT and duties tribunal consists of a chairman[1] sitting either with two other members or with one other member or alone[2]. If the tribunal does not consist of the chairman sitting alone, its decisions may be taken by a majority of votes and the chairman, if sitting with one other member, has the casting vote[3]. For each sitting of a tribunal the chairman is either the president[4] or, if so authorised by the president, a member of the appropriate panel of chairmen[5]; and any other member of the tribunal must be a person selected from the appropriate panel of other members[6], the selection being made either by the president or by a member of the panel of chairmen authorised by the president to make it[7].

There is a panel of chairmen and a panel of other members of VAT and duties tribunals for England and Wales, Scotland and Northern Ireland respectively[8], and one member of each panel of chairmen is known as vice-president of VAT and duties tribunals[9]. Appointments to a panel of chairmen are made by the appropriate authority, that is to say, in England and Wales, the Lord Chancellor[10], and appointments to a panel of other members are made by the Treasury[11]. No person may be appointed to a panel of chairmen of tribunals for England and Wales or Northern Ireland unless he is a person who has a seven year general qualification[12] or is a member of the Bar of Northern Ireland or is a solicitor of the Supreme Court of Northern Ireland of at least seven years' standing[13].

Subject to the conditions described below, the appointment of a chairman of tribunals is for such term and subject to such conditions as may be determined by the Lord Chancellor, and a person who ceases to hold the office of chairman is eligible for re-appointment[14]. A chairman of tribunals may resign his office at any time and must vacate his office on the day on which he attains the age of 70 years, subject to the statutory power to authorise his continuance in office up to the age of 75[15] which also applies in respect of the president of tribunals[16].

There must be paid to a chairman of VAT and duties tribunals such salary or fees, and to other members such fees, as the Lord Chancellor, with the approval of the Treasury, may determine; and there may be paid to or in respect of a former chairman of tribunals such pension, allowance or gratuity as the Lord Chancellor may with the approval of the Treasury determine[17]. If a person ceases to be a chairman of VAT and duties tribunals and it appears to the Lord Chancellor that there are special circumstances which make it right that he should receive compensation, there may be paid to that person a sum of such amount as the Lord Chancellor may with the approval of the Treasury determine[18].

The Lord Chancellor may, if he thinks fit, remove a chairman of VAT and duties tribunals from office on the ground of incapacity or misbehaviour[19]. A person who holds the office of president, vice-president or full-time chairman of a tribunal is disqualified for membership of the House of Commons[20]. No member of a tribunal may be compelled to serve on a jury in Northern Ireland[21] and the president, vice-president and chairman are ineligible for jury service in England and Wales[22].

All or any of the following powers of a tribunal or chairman may be exercised by the registrar[23] of the VAT and duties tribunals:

(1) power to give or make any direction by consent of the parties to the appeal or application;

(2) power to give or make any direction on the application of one party which is not opposed by the other party to the application;

(3) power to issue a witness summons;

(4) power to postpone any hearing; and

(5) power to extend the time for the service of any notice of appeal, notice of application or other document at the appropriate tribunal centre[24] for a period not exceeding one month without prior notice or reference to any party or other person and without a hearing[25].

The registrar has power to sign a direction recording the outcome of an appeal and any award or direction given or made by the tribunal during or at the conclusion of the hearing of an appeal[26] and to sign any document recording any direction given or made by him under the above provisions[27].

---

1 'Chairman' includes the president and any vice-president: Value Added Tax Tribunals Rules 1986, SI 1986/590, r 2.

2 Value Added Tax Act 1994 s 82(1), Sch 12 para 5(1).

3 Ibid Sch 12 para 5(2).

4 As to the president see para 294 ante.

5 Ie the panel constituted in accordance with the Value Added Tax Act 1994 Sch 12 para 7: see the text and notes 8–13 infra.

6 See note 5 supra.

7 Value Added Tax Act 1994 Sch 12 para 6.

8 Ibid Sch 12 para 7(1).

9 Ibid Sch 12 para 7(2).

10 Ibid Sch 12 para 7(3)(a).

11 Ibid Sch 12 para 7(3).

12 Ie within the meaning of the Courts and Legal Services Act 1990 s 71: see SOLICITORS vol 44(1) (Reissue) para 91.

13 Value Added Tax Act 1994 Sch 12 para 7(4)(a), (b).

14 Ibid Sch 12 para 7(3)(a), (5).

15 Ie the Judicial Pensions and Retirement Act 1993 s 26(4)–(6): see para 294 text and notes 8–9 ante.

16 See the Value Added Tax Act 1994 Sch 12 para 7(6).

17 Ibid Sch 12 para 7(8). This provision, so far as relating to pensions, allowances and gratuities, does not have effect in relation to a person to whom the Judicial Pensions and Retirement Act 1993 Pt I (ss 1–18) applies, except to the extent provided under or by that Act: Value Added Tax Act 1994 Sch 12 para 7(9). The Judicial Pensions and Retirement Act 1993 Pt I applies to the chairman: see s 1(6), Sch 1 Pt II.

18 Value Added Tax Act 1994 Sch 12 para 7(10).

19 Ibid Sch 12 para 7(7).

20 House of Commons Disqualification Act 1975 s 1, Sch 1 Pt III; and see PARLIAMENT.

21 Value Added Tax Act 1994 Sch 12 para 8.

22 Juries Act 1974 s 1, Sch 1 Pt I Group A. The registrar is also ineligible: Sch 1 Pt I Group A.

23 'The registrar' means the registrar of the VAT and duties tribunals, or any member of the administrative staff of the VAT and duties tribunals authorised by the president to perform for the time being all or any of the duties of a registrar under the Value Added Tax Tribunals Rules 1986: r 2 (definition amended by SI 1994/2617).

24 As to the appropriate tribunal centre see para 293 ante.

25 Value Added Tax Tribunals Rules 1986 r 33(1).

26 Ie as provided by ibid r 30(1): see para 318 text and note 1 post.

27 Ibid r 33(2).

(2) APPEALS TO VAT AND DUTIES TRIBUNALS

296. Decisions against which an appeal lies. Subject to certain conditions[1], an appeal lies to a VAT and duties tribunal with respect to any of the following matters[2]:

(1) the registration or cancellation of registration[3] of any person for the purposes of VAT[4];

(2) the VAT chargeable on the supply of any goods or services, on the acquisition of goods from another member state[5] or, subject to certain exceptions[6], on the importation of goods[7] from a place outside the member states[8];

(3) the amount of any input tax[9] which may be credited to a person[10];

(4) any claim for a refund of VAT[11] where goods have been acquired from, and VAT paid in, another member state[12];

(5) a decision of the Commissioners of Customs and Excise[13] as to whether or not a person is to be approved as a fiscal warehousekeeper[14] or the conditions from time to time subject to which he is so approved, for the withdrawal of any such approval or for the withdrawal of fiscal warehouse status from any premises[15];

(6) the proportion of input tax which is allowable[16] as a credit[17];

(7) a claim by a taxable person[18] in respect of goods imported for private purposes[19];

(8) the amount of any refunds[20] to persons constructing certain buildings[21];

(9) a claim for a refund[22] under the provisions relating to bad debt relief[23];

(10) the amount of any refunds in relation to new means of transport[24] supplied to other member states[25];

(11) any refusal of an application[26] by bodies corporate for treatment as members of a group for VAT purposes[27];

(12) the requirement of any security where a taxable person has failed to appoint a VAT representative[28] or where it appears requisite[29] to the commissioners[30];

(13) any refusal or cancellation of certification for the purposes of the flat rate scheme for farmers[31], or any refusal to cancel such certification[32];

(14) any liability[33] to a penalty or surcharge[34];

(15) a decision by the commissioners[35] as to liability to a penalty for conduct attributable to the dishonesty of a named officer of a body corporate[36];

(16) an assessment in respect of failure to make VAT returns and certain other matters[37] or the amount of such an assessment[38];

(17) the amount of any penalty, interest or surcharge specified[39] in an assessment[40];

(18) the making of an assessment[41] under the extended time limit available in the cases of fraud or dishonesty[42];

(19) any liability of the commissioners to pay interest in consequence of official error[43], or the amount of interest so payable[44];

(20) a claim for the repayment[45] of an amount of overpaid VAT[46];

(21) any direction or supplementary direction[47] to treat persons as a single taxable person[48];

(22) any direction[49] that the value of a supply be taken to be its open market value[50];

(23) any direction[51] as to the value of a relevant acquisition of goods from another member state[52];

(24) any direction or assessment[53] under the anti-avoidance provisions relating to groups[54];

(25) any refusal to permit the value of supplies to be determined by a retail scheme method described in a published[55] notice[56];

(26) any refusal of authorisation or termination of authorisation in connection with the cash accounting scheme[57];

(27) any requirements imposed by the commissioners[58] in a particular case in respect of the production of VAT invoices by means of a computer[59].

Where an appeal is against a decision of the commissioners which depended upon a prior decision taken by them in relation to the appellant[60], the fact that the prior decision is not within the above categories does not prevent the tribunal from allowing the appeal on the ground that it would have allowed an appeal against the prior decision[61].

1 Ie subject to the Value Added Tax Act 1994 s 84 (as amended): see para 297 post.

2 Ibid s 83. The tribunal has no general supervisory jurisdiction over the administrative decisions of the commissioners: *Dollar Land (Feltham) Ltd, Dollar Land (Cumbernauld) Ltd, Dollar Land (Calthorpe House) Ltd v Customs and Excise Comrs* [1995] STC 414 (following *Customs and Excise Comrs v JH Corbitt (Numismatists) Ltd* [1981] AC 22, [1980] 2 All ER 72, HL; and disapproving *Food Engineering Ltd v Customs and Excise Comrs* [1992] VATTR 327). Thus no appeal lies to the tribunal except in relation to the matters listed in the Value Added Tax Act 1994 s 83 (as amended); eg there is no appeal against a refusal of the commissioners to make a refund under s 33 (as amended): see para 258 ante. The function of the tribunal is appellate, but the powers of the tribunal in any particular case depend upon an examination of the decision against which the appeal is brought.

As to where the tribunal has been held to have a supervisory jurisdiction under what is now s 83 (as amended) see *Customs and Excise Comrs v Save and Prosper Group Ltd* [1979] STC 205 (Value Added Tax Act 1994 s 83(k)); *Mr Wishmore Ltd v Customs and Excise Comrs* [1988] STC 723; *Customs and Excise Comrs v Peachtree Enterprises Ltd* [1994] STC 747 (Value Added Tax Act 1994 s 83(l)); *Food Engineering Ltd v Customs and Excise Comrs* supra (Value Added Tax Act 1994 s 83(n)); *Chamberlain v Customs and Excise Comrs* [1989] STC 505 (Value Added Tax Act 1994 s 83(u)); *Moore v Customs and Excise Comrs* [1989] VATTR 276 (Value Added Tax Act 1994 s 83(v)); *Pollitt v Customs and Excise Comrs* (1990) VAT Decision 4463, [1990] STI 177; *Low v Customs and Excise Comrs* (1991) VAT Decision 5536, [1991] STI 165; *Wadlewski v Customs and Excise Comrs* (1995) VAT Decision 13340, [1995] STI 1255 (Value Added Tax Act 1994 s 83(x)); *Mainline Fabrications v Customs and Excise Comrs* (1992) VAT Decision 7010 (unreported) (Value Added Tax Act 1994 s 83(y)). All these cases must, however, be read in the light of *Dollar Land (Feltham) Ltd, Dollar Land (Cumbernauld) Ltd, Dollar Land (Calthorpe House) Ltd v Customs and Excise Comrs* supra, in which *Food Engineering Ltd v Customs and Excise Comrs* supra and the tribunal cases which followed it were expressly disapproved.

If there is no right of appeal to a tribunal, it may be that an application may be made to the High Court for judicial review of the commissioners' decision; but see para 320 note 2 post. As to the role and function of VAT and duties tribunals generally see *Georgiou (t/a Marios Chippery) v Customs and Excise Comrs* [1995] STC 1101 at 1107 et seq; affd [1996] STC 463, CA. Under the previous legislation (ie the Value Added Tax Act 1983 s 40 (repealed)), an appeal only lay to the tribunal against a decision of the commissioners with respect to one of the matters specified in that section. The words 'a decision of the commissioners' have been omitted from the consolidated provision (ie the Value Added Tax Act 1994 s 83 (as amended)) and it is a matter of debate whether, in consequence, an appeal can be brought without awaiting a decision of the commissioners. In practice, it is difficult to see how an appeal could properly be constituted without some form of lis between the appellant and the commissioners.

3 As to registration and deregistration see the Value Added Tax Act 1994 s 3, Schs 1–3 (as amended); and para 56 et seq ante.

4 Ibid s 83(a). A decision by the commissioners as to the accounting periods to be adopted by the taxpayer and the method of paying VAT does not constitute a decision as to registration, even though the requirements in question are set out on the certificate of registration: *Punchwell Ltd v Customs and Excise Comrs* [1981] VATTR 93.

5 As to the charge to tax on such acquisitions see the Value Added Tax Act 1994 s 10; and para 13 ante. For the meaning of 'another member state' see para 4 note 14 ante.

6 No appeal lies with respect to the subject-matter of any decision which by virtue of ibid s 16 (application of customs enactments: see para 105 ante) is one to which the Finance Act 1994 s 14 applies (decisions subject to review: see CUSTOMS AND EXCISE), unless the decision (1) relates exclusively to one or both of the following: (a) whether or not the Value Added Tax Act 1994 s 30(3) (zero-rating of specified imported goods: see para 175 ante) applies in relation to the importation of the goods in question; and (b) if it does not, the rate of tax charged on those goods; and (2) is not one in respect of which notice has been given to the commissioners under the Finance Act 1994 s 14 requiring them to review it: Value Added Tax Act 1994 s 84(9).

7 As to general provisions relating to imported goods see ibid s 15; and para 103 ante.

8 Ibid s 83(b). Appeals under s 83(b) are subject to the requirements of s 84(3): see para 297 text and note 9 post. As to the territories included in, or excluded from, the member states for VAT purposes see para 10 ante. The tribunal does not have power to substitute its opinion for that of the commissioners as to

what facts are sufficient to justify the making of an assessment: *Cumbrae Properties (1963) Ltd v Customs and Excise Comrs* [1981] STC 799; *Customs and Excise Comrs v JH Corbitt (Numismatists) Ltd* [1981] AC 22, [1980] 2 All ER 72, HL. As to the periods within which the commissioners must make their assessment see para 252 ante. An appeal under the Value Added Tax Act 1994 s 83(b) lies not only on the amount of VAT charged following an assessment but also as to whether there was any supply at all: *R v London VAT Tribunal and Customs and Excise Comrs, ex p Theodorou* [1989] STC 292. For the meaning of 'supply' see para 21 ante.

No appeal lies under the Value Added Tax Act 1994 s 83(b) in respect of the correct VAT treatment of future supplies as an appeal must relate to a supply made, in respect of which the commissioners have determined the amount of VAT payable: *Odhams Leisure Group Ltd v Customs and Excise Comrs* [1992] STC 332; *Morgan (t/a Parochial Church Council of Emmanuel Church, Northwood, Middlesex) v Customs and Excise Comrs* [1973] VATTR 76; *Strangewood v Customs and Excise Comrs* [1988] VATTR 35 (where the commissioners deliberately avoided making any decision as to the appellant's claim for repayment of input tax whilst they continued investigations into his affairs); and see *Anglia Energy Conservation Ltd v Customs and Excise Comrs* (1996) VAT Decision 14216, [1996] STI 1428.

9   For the meaning of 'input tax' see paras 4, 201 ante. A person may only deduct VAT incurred by him on supplies of goods or services if those goods or services are used or are to be used by him in making taxable supplies. Expenditure on luxuries, amusements or entertainment will be particularly carefully scrutinised by the commissioners and if they decide that the expenditure was not strictly business expenditure, input tax treatment will be denied: see Customs and Excise Leaflet 700/55/93 *VAT Input Tax Appeals: Luxuries, Amusements and Entertainment*. The importance of this in the context of appeals is that there is only a limited right of appeal against a denial or restriction of input tax credit on the supply, acquisition or importation of something in the nature of a luxury, amusement or entertainment. As to such cases see the Value Added Tax Act 1994 s 84(4); and para 297 post.

10   Value Added Tax Act 1994 s 83(c). See *Customs and Excise Comrs v C & A Modes* [1979] STC 433. It appears that the tribunal has a supervisory jurisdiction under the Value Added Tax Act 1994 s 83(c) over a decision by the commissioners not to accept alternative evidence as sufficient to support an input tax claim: *Kohanzad v Customs and Excise Comrs* [1994] STC 967; *Richmond Resources Ltd (in liquidation) v Customs and Excise Comrs* (1995) VAT Decision 13435, [1995] STI 1374; cf *John Dee Ltd v Customs and Excise Comrs* [1995] STC 941, CA; *Customs and Excise Comrs v R & R Pension Fund Trustees* [1996] STC 889 at 896–897 per Buxton J; and see note 2 supra.

11   Ie under regulations made under the Value Added Tax Act 1994 s 13(5): see para 13 ante.

12   Ibid s 83(d).

13   Ie under ibid s 18A (as added): see para 133 ante.

14   For the meaning of 'fiscal warehousekeeper' see para 133 note 3 ante.

15   Value Added Tax Act 1994 s 83(da) (added by the Finance Act 1996 s 26(1), Sch 3 para 12).

16   Ie under the Value Added Tax Act 1994 s 26: see para 203 ante.

17   Ibid s 83(e).

18   Ie under ibid s 27: see para 108 ante. For the meaning of 'taxable person' see paras 12 note 4, 55 ante.

19   Ibid s 83(f).

20   Ie refunds allowable under ibid s 35 (as amended): see para 259 ante.

21   Ibid s 83(g).

22   Ie under ibid s 36 (see para 260 ante); or under the Value Added Tax Act 1983 s 22 (repealed): Value Added Tax Act 1994 s 83(h).

23   Ibid s 83(h).

24   Ie under ibid s 40: see para 263 ante. For the meaning of 'new means of transport' see para 13 note 8 ante.

25   Ibid s 83(j).

26   Ie under ibid s 43 (as amended): see paras 66, 191 ante.

27   Ibid s 83(k).

28   Ie a requirement of security under ibid s 48(7): see para 62 ante.

29   Ie under ibid s 58, Sch 11 para 4(2): see para 246 ante.

30   Ibid s 83(l). It has been said that the jurisdiction of the tribunal on an appeal against such a decision is supervisory in nature: see *Dollar Land (Feltham) Ltd, Dollar Land (Cumbernauld) Ltd, Dollar Land (Calthorpe House) Ltd v Customs and Excise Comrs* [1995] STC 414 at 418–419 per Judge J; and *John Dee Ltd v Customs and Excise Comrs* [1995] STC 941 at 952, CA. There is no right of appeal against a requirement of security on the repayment of input tax under the Value Added Tax Act 1994 Sch 11 para 4(1): *Strangewood Ltd v Customs and Excise Comrs* [1988] VATTR 35; and see para 202 ante.

31   Ie a refusal or cancellation of certification under the Value Added Tax Act 1994 s 54: see para 79 et seq ante.

32   Ibid s 83(m).

33   Ie by virtue of any of the provisions of ibid ss 59–69 (as amended): see paras 272–284 ante. An appeal made under s 83(n) may not be entertained by a tribunal unless the requirements of s 84(3) have been

satisfied: see para 297 post. As to the powers of a tribunal when an appeal is brought against a decision of a kind within s 83(n) see *John Dee Ltd v Customs and Excise Comrs* [1995] STC 941, CA; cf *Dollar Land (Feltham) Ltd, Dollar Land (Cumbernauld) Ltd, Dollar Land (Calthorpe House) Ltd v Customs and Excise Comrs* [1995] STC 414 at 418–419 per Judge J.

34 Value Added Tax Act 1994 s 83(n).

35 Ie a decision under ibid s 61 in accordance with s 61(5): see para 273 ante.

36 Ibid s 83(o).

37 Ie an assessment under (1) ibid s 73(1) or (2) in respect of a period for which the appellant has made a return (see para 247 ante); or (2) s 73(7), s 73(7A) (as added) or s 73(7B) (as added) (see para 247 ante); or (3) s 75 (see paras 248, 252 ante): s 83(p)(i)–(iii) (amended by the Finance Act 1996 Sch 3 para 12). Where the commissioners reduce the amount of an assessment in accordance with s 73(9) (as amended) after an appeal has been made, and issue a notice of the amended assessment, there is a single appeal covering both assessments rather than a separate right of appeal against the amended assessment. Accordingly, if a tribunal dismisses the appeal against the original assessment because the disputed tax has not been paid or deposited (see para 297 post), there is no residual right of appeal in relation to the amended assessment: *Sitar Tandoori Restaurants v Customs and Excise Comrs* [1993] STC 582.

38 Value Added Tax Act 1994 s 83(p) (as amended: see note 37 supra). As to the conditions with which the appellant must comply in order for an appeal made under s 83(p) (as so amended) to be entertained see s 84(3); and para 297 post. Where, on an appeal against a decision with respect to any of the matters mentioned in s 83(p) (as so amended), it is found that the amount specified in the assessment is less than it ought to have been, and the tribunal gives a direction specifying the correct amount, the assessment has effect as an assessment of the amount specified in the direction, and that amount is deemed to have been notified to the appellant: s 84(5).

39 Ie under ibid s 76 (as amended): see para 251 ante.

40 Ibid s 83(q). As to the conditions with which the appellant must comply in order for an appeal made under s 83(q) to be entertained see s 84(3); and para 297 post. As to mitigation of penalties see s 70 (as amended); and para 280 ante. Without prejudice to the power to mitigate, nothing in s 83(q) confers on a tribunal any power to vary an amount assessed by way of penalty or by way of interest or surcharge except to the extent necessary to reduce it to the amount which is appropriate under ss 59–70 (as amended); and 'penalty' includes an amount assessed by virtue of s 61(3) or s 61(4)(a) (see para 273 ante): s 84(6). As to the burden of proof on an appeal against an assessment under s 60 see s 60(7); and para 272 ante.

41 Ie on the basis set out in ibid s 77(4): see para 252 ante.

42 Ibid s 83(r).

43 Ie a liability to pay interest under ibid s 78 (as amended): see para 265 ante.

44 Ibid s 83(s).

45 Ie under ibid s 80: see para 264 ante.

46 Ibid s 83(t).

47 Ie made under ibid s 3, Sch 1 para 2: see para 59 ante.

48 Ibid s 83(u). The tribunal may not, however, allow an appeal against a direction falling within s 83(u) unless it considers that the commissioners could not reasonably have been satisfied as to the matters in Sch 1 para 2(2)(a)–(d) or, as the case may be, as to the matters in Sch 1 para 2(4): s 84(7). The test on an appeal is whether no reasonable body of commissioners could properly have formed the view that they did: see *Chamberlain v Customs and Excise Comrs* [1989] STC 505.

49 Ie a direction made the Value Added Tax Act 1994 s 19, Sch 6 paras 1 or 2: see paras 87–88 ante. An appeal may also lie under the Value Added Tax Act 1983 Sch 4 para 2 (repealed) as to the value of imported goods: see the Value Added Tax Act 1994 s 83(v).

50 Ibid s 83(v). See also *Moore v Customs and Excise Comrs* [1989] VATTR 276.

51 Ie under the Value Added Tax Act 1994 s 20, Sch 7 para 1: see para 99 ante.

52 Ibid s 83(w).

53 Ie under ibid s 43(9), Sch 9A (as added): see para 193 ante.

54 Ibid s 83(wa) (added by the Finance Act 1996 s 31(3)). Where there is an appeal against a decision to make such a direction, the cases in which the tribunal must allow the appeal include (in addition to the case where the conditions for the making of the direction were not fulfilled), the case where the tribunal is satisfied, in relation to the relevant event by reference to which the direction was given, that (1) the change in the treatment of the body corporate; or (2) the transaction in question, had as its main purpose or, as the case may be, as each of its main purposes a genuine commercial purpose unconnected with the fulfilment of the condition specified in Sch 9A para 1(3) (as added) (see para 193 ante): s 84(7A) (added by the Finance Act 1996 s 31(4)).

55 Ie a notice published under the Value Added Tax Act 1994 s 58, Sch 11 para 2(6): see para 225 ante.

56 Ibid s 83(x). As to retail schemes see para 185 et seq ante.

57　Ibid s 83(y). The cash accounting scheme is made under Sch 11 para 2(7): see para 225 ante. As to the cash accounting scheme see para 228 ante.

58　Ie requirements imposed under ibid Sch 11 para 3(2)(b): see para 256 note 11 ante.

59　Ibid s 83(z).

60　For the meaning of 'appellant' see para 293 note 8 ante.

61　Value Added Tax Act 1994 s 84(10). In this way the tribunal is given a power which its ostensible lack of a supervisory jurisdiction would otherwise preclude: see *Customs and Excise Comrs v JH Corbitt (Numismatists) Ltd* [1981] AC 22, [1980] 2 All ER 72, HL; *John Dee Ltd v Customs and Excise Comrs* [1995] STC 941 at 945, CA. Thus the tribunal may allow an appeal against the more recent, appealable, decision, but not against the earlier decision outside the scope of the Value Added Tax Act 1994 s 83 (as amended) upon which the more recent decision depended: see *'XL' (Stevenage) Ltd v Customs and Excise Comrs* [1981] VATTR 192 at 196; *Grimsby and District Sunday Football League v Customs and Excise Comrs* [1982] VATTR 210. In exercising this jurisdiction, the tribunal should only allow the appeal if it comes to the conclusion that there has been a wrongful exercise of discretion by the commissioners: *Pinetree Housing Association Ltd v Customs and Excise Comrs* [1983] VATTR 227, following *Charles Osenton & Co v Johnston* [1942] AC 130 at 138, [1941] 2 All ER 245 at 250, HL; *Blue Boar Property & Investment Co Ltd v Customs and Excise Comrs* [1984] VATTR 12; *Bardsley v Customs and Excise Comrs* [1984] VATTR 171; *Brookes v Customs and Excise Comrs* [1994] VATTR 35; and *Shepherd v Customs and Excise Comrs* [1994] VATTR 47. A decision of the commissioners as to the application of an extra-statutory concession is incapable of being a prior decision within the Value Added Tax Act 1994 s 84(10): *Customs and Excise Comrs v Arnold* [1996] STC 1271 per Hidden J, disapproving *British Teleflower Service Ltd v Customs and Excise Comrs* (1996) VAT Decision 13756, [1996] STI 290.

297. Pre-conditions to the entertainment of an appeal. Prima facie, an appeal[1] may not be entertained[2] unless the appellant[3] has made all the returns which he is required to make[4] and has paid the amounts of value added tax shown in those returns as payable by him[5]. This provision applies to all appeals brought under any of the prescribed heads[6] but the prohibition is not absolute, and the Commissioners of Customs and Excise can therefore waive it[7].

Where the appeal is against a decision with respect to certain specified matters[8], it may not be entertained unless (1) the amount which the commissioners have determined to be payable as VAT has been paid or deposited with them; or (2) on being satisfied that the appellant would otherwise suffer hardship the commissioners agree, or the tribunal decides, that the appeal should be entertained notwithstanding that that amount has not been paid or deposited[9]. Where on an appeal it is found that the whole or part of any amount so paid or deposited is not due, or that the whole or part of any VAT credit due to the appellant has not been paid, so much of that amount as is found not to be due or not to have been paid is to be repaid (or, as the case may be, paid) with interest at such rate as the tribunal may determine; and where the appeal has been entertained notwithstanding that an amount determined by the commissioners to be payable as VAT has not been paid or deposited and it is found on the appeal that that amount is due, the tribunal may, if it thinks fit, direct that the amount is to be paid with interest at such rate as may be specified in the direction[10].

A tribunal can hear an appeal brought by a person who is not a taxable person[11]; and, in particular, an appeal may be brought by the recipient of a supply if he can establish that any tax chargeable on it has been paid by him and that he has a sufficient interest in obtaining a decision thereon[12].

Except in the case of an appeal relating to the input tax that might be credited to any person at the end of a prescribed accounting period[13] beginning before 27 July 1993[14], where:

(a)　there is an appeal against a decision of the commissioners with respect to, or to so much of any assessment as concerns, the amount of input tax[15] that may be credited to any person or the proportion of input tax allowable[16]; and

(b)　that appeal relates, in whole or in part, to any determination by the commissioners either as to the purposes for which any goods or services were used, or were to be used, by any person or as to whether, or to what extent, the matters to which any input tax was attributable were or included matters other than the making of certain supplies made or to be made by the taxable person in the course or furtherance of his business[17]; and

(c)   VAT for which, in pursuance of that determination, there is no entitlement to a credit is VAT on the supply, acquisition or importation of something in the nature of a luxury, amusement or entertainment[18],

the tribunal may not allow the appeal or, as the case may be, so much of it as relates to that determination, unless it considers that the determination is one which it was unreasonable to make or which it would have been unreasonable to make if information brought to the attention of the tribunal that could not have been brought to the attention of the commissioners had been available to be taken into account when the determination was made[19].

1   Ie an appeal under the Value Added Tax Act 1994 s 83 (as amended): see para 296 ante.

2   A tribunal 'entertains' an appeal either where the commissioners raise the issue of competency under the Value Added Tax Tribunal Rules 1986, SI 1986/590, r 6 (see para 301 post), and that issue is decided in the taxpayer's favour or, where no issue of competency is raised, from the date of service of the notice of hearing in accordance with r 23 (see para 313 post): *Customs and Excise Comrs v Hubbard Foundation Scotland* [1981] STC 593, Ct of Sess. If the commissioners serve a notice under what is now the Value Added Tax Tribunals Rules 1986 r 6, a preliminary hearing will be arranged to consider the matter; if the appellant applies for a direction that his appeal be entertained without payment or deposit of the tax, the hearing of that application will be arranged, where possible, at the same time as the preliminary hearing; and if the appellant's application is dismissed, the tribunal may adjourn the consideration of the question of competency in order to allow the appellant time to pay or deposit the disputed tax: *Practice Note* [1981] VATTR 65.

3   For the meaning of 'appellant' see para 293 note 8 ante.

4   Ie is required to make under the Value Added Tax Act 1994 s 58, Sch 11 para 2(1): see para 225 ante. As to VAT returns see para 226 et seq ante.

5   Ibid s 84(2) (amended by the Finance Act 1995 ss 31, 162, Sch 29 Pt VI(4)). The requirement is that the taxpayer has paid all amounts which he acknowledges are due by his inclusion of them in his VAT returns. Unless, therefore, the commissioners exercise their discretion to waive the requirement, the tribunal may not entertain the appeal merely because the appellant would suffer hardship if he were obliged to make payment of the amount shown as due (eg because he is not permitted to operate the cash accounting scheme and has not received payment of the VAT shown as due in his return): *R v London VAT Tribunal and Customs and Excise Comrs, ex p Theodorou* [1989] STC 292 at 296–297, disapproving *R v VAT Tribunal, ex p Happer* [1982] 1 WLR 1261, [1982] STC 700, and *R v VAT Tribunal, ex p Minster Associates* [1988] STC 386. See also *R v VAT Tribunal, ex p Cohen* [1984] STC 361n (irregularity of proceeding by way of judicial review from decision of the tribunal not to entertain an appeal). However, it has been held that where the appellant is a person other than the supplier (eg the recipient of the supply) the Value Added Tax Act 1994 s 84(2) (as so amended) does not apply to the appeal: see *Processed Vegetable Growers Association Ltd v Customs and Excise Comrs* [1973] VATTR 87.

6   Ie all the heads within the Value Added Tax Act 1994 s 83 (as amended): see para 296 ante.

7   *Gittins v Customs and Excise Comrs* [1974] VATTR 109.

8   Ie a decision with respect to any of the matters specified in the Value Added Tax Act 1994 s 83(b) (see para 296 head (2) ante), s 83(n) (see para 296 head 14 ante), s 83(p) (as amended) (see para 296 head (16) ante) or s 83(q) (see para 296 head (17) ante): s 84(3). It has been held that where the commissioners issue an assessment to recover input tax allegedly wrongly deducted by the trader, the tribunal is entitled to entertain the appeal notwithstanding that the trader did not pay or deposit the tax, since the appeal was against the amount of the input tax to which the appellant was entitled to credit (under s 83(c)) and not an appeal against the assessment within the scope of s 83(p) (as amended)). This remains the case notwithstanding the amendment to the provisions for assessment by the introduction of what is now s 73(2) (see para 247 ante): see *Boltgate Ltd v Customs and Excise Comrs* [1982] VATTR 120; *Brian Gubby Ltd v Customs and Excise Comrs* [1985] VATTR 59; *Trust Securities Holdings Ltd v Customs and Excise Comrs* [1990] VATTR 1.

9   Value Added Tax Act 1994 s 84(3). Section 84 (as amended) is limited in its application to appeals by persons accountable for the tax in dispute (*Processed Vegetable Growers Association Ltd v Customs and Excise Comrs* [1973] VATTR 87 at 96–97); so that third parties may appeal without satisfying the conditions of the Value Added Tax Act 1994 s 84(3). The tribunal does not have power to require the appellant to

deposit part of the tax in dispute if it considers that he could pay that amount but no more without suffering hardship: *Don Pasquale (a firm) v Customs and Excise Comrs* [1990] STC 556, CA (not followed in *Customs and Excise Comrs v Le Rififi Ltd* [1995] STC 103, CA, so far as *Don Pasquale (a firm) v Customs and Excise Comrs* supra decided that the standard form of notice of assessment used to notify a number of assessments constituted a global assessment for the purposes of VAT). As to global assessments see para 252 ante.

10   Value Added Tax Act 1994 s 84(8).

11   A considerable number of the grounds of appeal (see ibid s 83 (as amended); and para 296 ante) relate to claims for refunds of tax by persons who will not be registered for VAT. For the meaning of 'taxable person' see paras 12 note 4, 55 ante; and as to registration for VAT see para 56 et seq ante.

12   An appellant has a sufficient interest if he can show that the tax chargeable on the supply under a contract was to be added to the money otherwise payable under it; or if he can show that there were future supplies of a like nature to be made between the parties: *Processed Vegetable Growers Association Ltd v Customs and Excise Comrs* [1973] VATTR 87. See also *Cameron v Customs and Excise Comrs* [1973] VATTR 177; *Gumbrell and Dodson Bros v Customs and Excise Comrs* [1973] VATTR 171. Where the recipient has no legal right to recover the disputed VAT from the supplier, she has no or insufficient interest to maintain an appeal (*Payton v Customs and Excise Comrs* [1974] VATTR 140); but it may be that if an appeal were successful the supplier would hold any repayment on constructive trust for the appellant (see *Williams & Glyn's Bank Ltd v Customs and Excise Comrs* [1974] VATTR 262; *JC Skeffington v Customs and Excise Comrs* LON/74/35 (VAT Decision 102A, unreported)). An appellant who is a recipient of a supply has sufficient interest to bring an appeal when he has deposited the VAT with the commissioners upon their promise to repay if he is successful: *Gilbourne v Customs and Excise Comrs* [1974] VATTR 209; *Williams & Glyn's Bank Ltd v Customs and Excise Comrs* supra. In a case where the commissioners decided that a property management company was supplying its services to the owner of the managed premises rather than to the tenants it was held the owner did not have sufficient interest to appeal against that decision: *Kingsley-Smith v Customs and Excise Comrs* (1996) VAT Decision 13787, [1996] STI 406.

13   For the meaning of 'prescribed accounting period' see para 202 note 4 ante.

14   Value Added Tax Act 1994 s 84(11).

15   For the meaning of 'input tax' see paras 4, 201 ante.

16   Ie allowable under the Value Added Tax Act 1994 s 26: see para 203 ante.

17   Ie those supplies specified in ibid s 26(2): see para 203 ante.

18   See para 296 note 9 ante.

19   Value Added Tax Act 1994 s 84(4). Section 84(4) is not to be construed as implying that the commissioners' decision as to whether something is a luxury, amusement or entertainment is conclusive, as such a construction would be incompatible with express mandatory provisions of EC Council Directive 77/388 (OJ L145, 13.6.77, p 1) arts 17(2), (6): see *Myatt and Leason v Customs and Excise Comrs* (1996) VAT Decision 13780, [1996] STI 404.

298. Settling appeals by agreement. Subject to certain conditions[1], where a person gives notice of appeal[2] and, before the appeal is determined by a VAT and duties tribunal[3], the Commissioners of Customs and Excise and the appellant[4] come to an agreement (whether in writing or otherwise) under the terms of which the decision under appeal is to be treated as upheld without variation, or as varied in a particular manner, or as discharged or cancelled, the same consequences ensue for all purposes as would have ensued if, at the time when the agreement was reached, a tribunal had determined the appeal in accordance with the terms of the agreement, including any terms as to costs[5]. This provision will not, however, apply if within 30 days of the date of the agreement the appellant gives notice in writing to the commissioners that he wishes to repudiate or resile from the agreement[6].

Where an agreement is not in writing, the above provisions do not apply unless the fact that an agreement was reached, and the terms agreed, are confirmed by notice in writing given by the commissioners to the appellant or by the appellant to the commissioners; and references in those provisions to the time when the agreement was come to are to be construed as references to the time of the giving of that notice of confirmation[7].

Where (1) a person who has given a notice of appeal notifies the commissioners, whether orally or in writing, that he desires not to proceed with the appeal; and (2) 30 days have elapsed since the giving of the notification without the commissioners giving to the appellant notice in writing indicating that they are unwilling for the appeal to be treated as withdrawn, the above provisions have effect as if, at the date of the appellant's notification, the appellant and the commissioners had reached an agreement, orally or in writing, that the decision under appeal should be upheld without variation[8].

1   Ie subject to the provisions of the Value Added Tax Act 1994 s 85: see the text and notes 2–8 infra.
2   Ie under ibid s 83 (as amended): see para 296 ante.
3   As to VAT and duties tribunals see para 293 et seq ante; and as to the procedure on an appeal see para 299 et seq post.
4   For these purposes, references to an agreement being come to with an appellant or the giving of notice or notification to or by an appellant extend to agreements which are come to with, and to the giving of a notice or notification to or by, a person acting on behalf of the appellant in relation to the appeal: Value Added Tax Act 1994 s 85(5). For the meaning of 'appellant' see para 293 note 8 ante.
5   Ibid s 85(1). 'Costs' include fees, charges, disbursements, expenses and remuneration: Value Added Tax Tribunals Rules 1986, SI 1986/590, r 2. As to costs generally see para 317 post.
6   See the Value Added Tax Act 1994 s 85(2). As to service of notice see para 291 ante. Thus the appellant, and the appellant alone, is allowed a 'cooling-off period'. The commissioners do not have any right to resile from or to repudiate the agreement: *Lamdec Ltd v Customs and Excise Comrs* [1991] VATTR 296. However, it may be that the ordinary law of contract applies to agreements under the Value Added Tax Act 1994 s 85 as it apparently applies to agreements made under the Taxes Management Act 1970 s 54, whereby rectification can be ordered of defective agreements; in which case an agreement under the Value Added Tax Act 1994 s 85 might also be declared to be void or voidable for fraud or mistake: see *R v Inspector of Taxes, ex p Bass Holdings Ltd, Richart (Inspector of Taxes) v Bass Holdings Ltd* [1993] STC 122. See further INCOME TAXATION vol 23 (Reissue) para 1681.
7   Value Added Tax Act 1994 s 85(3).
8   Ibid s 85(4). As to the application of s 85 to appeals in relation to landfill tax see the Finance Act 1996 s 56(8); and CUSTOMS AND EXCISE; PUBLIC HEALTH.

299. Rules of procedure before VAT and duties tribunals. The Lord Chancellor, after consultation with the Lord Advocate, may make rules[1] with respect to the procedure to be followed on appeals to, and in other proceedings before, VAT and duties tribunals[2], and such rules may include provisions:

(1)   for limiting the time within which appeals may be brought[3];
(2)   for enabling hearings to be held in private in such circumstances as may be determined by or under the rules[4];
(3)   for parties to proceedings to be represented by such persons as may be determined by or under the rules[5];
(4)   for requiring persons to attend to give evidence[6];
(5)   for discovery and for requiring persons to produce documents[7];
(6)   for the payment of expenses and allowances to persons attending as witnesses or producing documents[8];
(7)   for the award and recovery of costs[9];
(8)   for authorising the administration of oaths to witnesses[10]; and
(9)   with respect to the joinder of appeals brought by different persons where a notice of penalty is served[11] and the appeals relate to, or to different portions of, the basic penalty referred to in the notice[12].

A person who fails to comply with a direction or summons issued by a VAT tribunal[13] is liable to a penalty not exceeding £1,000[14]. This penalty may be awarded summarily by a tribunal notwithstanding that no proceedings for its recovery have been commenced[15]. An appeal from the award of a penalty under this provision lies to the High Court[16], and on such an appeal the court may either confirm or reverse the decision of the tribunal or reduce or increase the sum awarded[17]. A penalty awarded by virtue of these provisions is recoverable as if it were VAT due from the person liable to the penalty[18].

A tribunal may, however, of its own motion or on the application of any party to an appeal or application, waive any breach or non-observance of the procedural rules or of any decision or direction of a tribunal on such terms as it may think just[19].

Where the parties to an appeal or application have agreed upon the terms of any decision or direction to be given by a tribunal, a tribunal may give a decision or make a direction in accordance with those terms without a hearing[20].

1   In the exercise of the power so conferred, the Lord Chancellor has made the Value Added Tax Tribunals (Amendment) Rules 1994, SI 1994/2617, which came into force on 1 November 1994: r 1. In addition, by virtue of the Interpretation Act 1978 s 17(2)(b), the Value Added Tax Tribunals Rules 1986, SI 1986/590 (amended by SI 1991/186; SI 1994/2617), have effect as if so made. See further paras 293, 298 ante, 300 et seq post.

2   Value Added Tax Act 1994 s 82(1), Sch 12 para 9. As to VAT and duties tribunals see para 293 et seq ante.

3   Ibid Sch 12 para 9(a). See the Value Added Tax Tribunals Rules 1986 r 4; and para 300 post.

4   Value Added Tax Act 1994 Sch 12 para 9(b). See the Value Added Tax Tribunals Rules 1986 r 24; and para 313 post.

5   Value Added Tax Act 1994 Sch 12 para 9(c). See the Value Added Tax Tribunals Rules 1986 r 25; and para 313 post.

6   Value Added Tax Act 1994 Sch 12 para 9(d). See the Value Added Tax Tribunals Rules 1986 rr 22, 26 (as amended); and paras 311, 314 post.

7   Value Added Tax Act 1994 Sch 12 para 9(e). See the Value Added Tax Tribunals Rules 1986 rr 20, 21; and paras 308–309 post.

8   Value Added Tax Act 1994 Sch 12 para 9(f). See the Value Added Tax Tribunals Rules 1986 r 22; and para 311 post.

9   Value Added Tax Act 1994 Sch 12 para 9(g). See the Value Added Tax Tribunals Rules 1986 r 30; and para 318 post. For the meaning of 'costs' see para 298 note 5 ante.

10 Value Added Tax Act 1994 Sch 12 para 9(h). See the Value Added Tax Tribunals Rules 1986 r 28(2); and para 316 post.

11 Ie under the Value Added Tax Act 1994 s 61: see para 273 ante.

12 Ibid Sch 12 para 9(j). See also *VAT: Appeals and Applications to the Tribunals: Explanatory Leaflet* (revised as at April 1993), although this has no binding force; and see *Practice Notes* [1973] VATTR 215 on procedure on appeals and applications to tribunals, together with certain simple precedents. The Lord Chancellor's Department has also produced various forms which may be used to make an appeal (Trib 1); to comply with the requirement to serve a list of documents (Trib 2); to make a witness statement (Trib 3); or to make an application (Trib 5). It is not necessary to use the forms, provided that the appellant or other party complies with the requirements of the Value Added Tax Tribunal Rules 1986.

13 Ie issued under rules made under the Value Added Tax Act 1994 Sch 12 para 9; and see note 1 supra.

14 Ibid Sch 12 para 10(1). The Commissioners of Customs and Excise may also be made subject to a penalty under this provision: *Freight Transport Leasing Ltd v Customs and Excise Comrs* [1992] VATTR 176; *Wine Warehouses Europe Ltd v Customs and Excise Comrs* [1993] VATTR 307.

15 Value Added Tax Act 1994 Sch 12 para 10(2).

16 As to appeals to the High Court see para 320 post.

17 Value Added Tax Act 1994 Sch 12 para 10(3).

18 Ibid Sch 12 para 10(4).

19 Value Added Tax Tribunals Rules 1986 r 19(5).

20 Ibid r 17.

300. Serving notice of appeal. An appeal to a VAT and duties tribunal is brought by a notice of appeal[1] served[2] at the appropriate tribunal centre[3]. The notice of appeal must be signed by or on behalf of the appellant[4] and must:

(1)   state the appellant's name and address;

(2)   state the date (if any) with effect from which the appellant was registered for tax and the nature of his business;

(3)   state the address of the office of the Commissioners of Customs and Excise from which the disputed decision[5] was sent,

(4)   state the date of the document containing that decision and the address to which it was sent;

(5)   have attached to it a copy of the document containing the disputed decision; and

(6)   set out, or have attached to it a document containing, the grounds of appeal, including, in the case of a reasonable excuse appeal[6], particulars of the excuse relied on[7].

The notice of appeal must also have attached to it a copy of any letter from the commissioners extending the appellant's time to appeal against the disputed decision and a copy of any further letter from the commissioners notifying him of a date from which his time to appeal against the disputed decision is to run[8].

Subject to the tribunal's power[9], and to that of the commissioners[10], to extend the time within which the appellant must service his notice of appeal, that notice must be served at the appropriate tribunal centre before the expiration of 30 days after the date of the document containing the disputed decision of the commissioners[11].

A proper officer[12] must send an acknowledgment of the service of the notice of appeal at the appropriate tribunal centre to the appellant and a copy of the notice of appeal and any accompanying documents to the commissioners, and the acknowledgment and the copy of the notice of appeal must state the date of service and the date of notification of the notice of appeal[13].

Except in the case of a decision or direction of a tribunal[14], for the purposes of determining the issues in dispute or of correcting an error or defect in an appeal or application or intended appeal, a tribunal may at any time, either of its own motion or on the application of any party to the appeal or application or any other person interested, direct that a notice of appeal, notice of application, statement of case, reply, particulars or other document in the proceedings be amended in such manner as may be specified in that direction on such terms as it may think fit[15].

1   A notice of appeal does not have to be made on any particular form, but form Trib 1, provided by the Lord Chancellor's Department, may be used.

2   As to service see the Value Added Tax Tribunal Rules 1986, SI 1986/590, r 31 (as amended); and para 312 post.

3   Ibid r 3(1). For the meaning of 'appropriate tribunal centre' see para 293 ante. No appeal lies against a decision sent to an address at a place for which no tribunal centre has been appointed: *Interbet Trading Ltd v Customs and Excise Comrs* [1977] VATTR 63; *Interbet Trading Ltd v Customs and Excise Comrs (No 2)* [1978] VATTR 235.

    A tribunal, on the application of a party to an appeal, may direct that the appeal and all proceedings in it be transferred to the tribunal centre specified in that direction, whereupon, for the purposes of the Value Added Tax Tribunals Rules 1986 (as amended), the tribunal centre specified in the direction becomes the appropriate tribunal centre for the appeal and all proceedings in it, without prejudice to the power of a tribunal to give a further direction relating to the appeal under this provision: r 15. As to the parties to an appeal see para 306 post.

4   For the meaning of 'appellant' see para 293 note 8 ante.

5   For the meaning of 'disputed decision' see para 293 note 7 ante.

6   A 'reasonable excuse appeal' is an appeal which, according to the notice of appeal or other document received from the appellant at the appropriate tribunal centre, is against a decision of the commissioners with respect to the liability to, or the amount of, a penalty or surcharge on grounds confined to those set out in the Value Added Tax Act 1994 ss 59(7), 62(3), 63(10), 64(5), 65, 66, 67(8), 68(4) or 69(8) (see para 272 et seq ante); or in the Finance Act 1994 ss 9, 10, 11 (see CUSTOMS AND EXCISE) or s 64, Sch 7 paras 14–19 (see INSURANCE): Value Added Tax Tribunals Rules 1986 r 2 (definition substituted by SI 1994/2617).

7   Ibid r 3(2).

8   Ibid r 3(3).

9   See ibid r 19 (as amended); and para 307 post.

10   If, during the period of 30 days after the date of the document containing the disputed decision, the commissioners notify the appellant by letter that his time to appeal against the disputed decision is extended until the expiration of 21 days after a date set out in that letter, or to be set out in a further letter to him, a notice of appeal against that disputed decision may be served at the appropriate tribunal centre at any time before the expiration of the period of 21 days set out in the letter or further letter: ibid r 4(2).

11   Ibid r 4(1).

12 'Proper officer' means a member of the administrative staff of the VAT and duties tribunals appointed by a chairman to perform the duties of a proper officer under the Value Added Tax Tribunals Rules 1986 (as amended): r 2 (amended by SI 1994/2617).

13 Ibid r 5 (amended by SI 1991/186). 'Date of notification', in relation to any document, means the date on which a proper officer sends that document, or a copy of that document to any person under the Value Added Tax Tribunals Rules 1986 (as amended): r 2 (definition added by SI 1991/186).

14 Ibid r 14(2).

15 Ibid r 14(1).

301. Notice that an appeal does not lie or cannot be entertained. Where the Commissioners of Customs and Excise contend that an appeal does not lie to, or cannot be entertained by, a VAT and duties tribunal they must serve a notice to that effect at the appropriate tribunal centre[1] containing the grounds for that contention and applying for the appeal to be struck out or dismissed[2] as soon as practicable after the receipt by them of the notice of appeal[3]. Any such notice served by the commissioners must be accompanied by a copy of the disputed decision[4] unless a copy of it has been served previously at the appropriate tribunal centre by either party to the appeal[5]. In a reasonable excuse[6] or mitigation[7] appeal the hearing of any such application made by the commissioners may immediately precede the hearing of the substantive appeal[8]. A proper officer[9] must send a copy of any notice or certificate served and of any accompanying document or documents to the appellant[10].

1 As to the appropriate tribunal centre see para 293 ante; and as to the service of notices see para 312 post.

2 As to the dismissal of an appeal see the Value Added Tax Tribunals Rules 1986, SI 1986/590, r 18; and para 304 post.

3 Ibid r 6(1).

4 For the meaning of 'disputed decision' see para 293 note 7 ante.

5 Value Added Tax Tribunals Rules 1986 r 6(1). As to the parties to the appeal see para 306 post.

6 For the meaning of 'reasonable excuse appeal' see para 300 note 6 ante.

7 A 'mitigation appeal' is an appeal which, according to the notice of appeal or other document received from the appellant at the appropriate tribunal centre, is against a decision of the commissioners with respect to the amount of a penalty on the grounds set out in the Finance Act 1985 s 13(4) (repealed) (in respect of penalties imposed before 27 July 1993), the Value Added Tax Act 1994 s 70 (see para 280 ante); the Finance Act 1994 s 8 (see CUSTOMS AND EXCISE); or s 64, Sch 7 para 13 (see INSURANCE): Value Added Tax Tribunals Rules 1986 r 2 (definition amended by SI 1994/2617). For the meaning of 'appellant' see para 293 note 8 ante.

8 Ibid r 6(3).

9 For the meaning of 'proper officer' see para 300 note 12 ante.

10 Value Added Tax Tribunals Rules 1986 r 6(4).

302. Procedure after service of notice of appeal. Unless a VAT and duties tribunal otherwise directs, in appeals other than reasonable excuse[1], mitigation[2] and evasion penalty[3] appeals the Commissioners of Customs and Excise must, within the period of 30 days after (1) the date of notification[4] of the notice of appeal; or (2) the date of notification of the notice of withdrawal of an application to have the appeal struck out or dismissed[5]; or (3) the date on which a direction in the appeal is released dismissing any such application[6], whichever is the latest, serve at the appropriate tribunal centre[7] a statement of case in the appeal setting out the matters and facts on which they rely to support the disputed decision[8] and the statutory provision under which the tax or penalty is assessed or the decision is made[9].

Any statement of case served by the commissioners[10] must be accompanied by a copy of the disputed decision unless a copy of that decision has been served previously at the appropriate tribunal centre by either party to the appeal[11]. In a reasonable excuse or mitigation appeal the commissioners must serve a copy of the disputed decision at the appropriate tribunal centre as soon as practicable after they have received the copy of the notice of appeal unless a copy of that decision has been so served previously by the appellant[12]. A proper officer[13] must send (a) an acknowledgement of the service at the appropriate tribunal centre of any statement of case, defence, reply or particulars in any appeal to the party serving it or them; and (b) a copy of that document or particulars and any other accompanying document to the other party to the appeal[14].

Where, on an appeal against a decision with respect to an assessment or the amount of an assessment, the commissioners wish to contend that an amount specified in the assessment is less than it ought to have been, they must so state in their statement of case in that appeal, indicating the amount of the alleged deficiency and the manner in which it has been calculated[15].

A tribunal may at any time direct a party to an appeal to serve further particulars of his case at the appropriate tribunal centre for the appeal within such period from the date of that direction (not being less than 14 days) as it may specify in the direction[16].

1   For the meaning of 'reasonable excuse appeal' see para 300 note 6 ante.
2   For the meaning of 'mitigation appeal' see para 301 note 7 ante.
3   An 'evasion penalty appeal' is an appeal against an assessment to a penalty under the Value Added Tax Act 1994 s 60 (see para 272 ante) or s 61 (see para 273 ante), or under the Finance Act 1994 s 8 (see CUSTOMS AND EXCISE) or s 64, Sch 7 para 12 (see INSURANCE), which is not solely a mitigation appeal and any accompanying appeal by the appellant against an assessment for the amount of tax alleged to have been evaded by the same conduct as that in the appeal against the assessment to a penalty: Value Added Tax Tribunals Rules 1986 r 2 (definition added by SI 1994/2617). For the meaning of 'the appellant' see para 293 note 8 ante.
4   For the meaning of 'date of notification' see para 300 note 13 ante.
5   Ie an application under the Value Added Tax Tribunals Rules 1986 r 6: see para 301 ante.
6   Ie in accordance with ibid r 30 (as amended): see para 318 post.
7   As to the appropriate tribunal centre see para 293 ante.
8   For the meaning of 'disputed decision' see para 293 note 7 ante.
9   Value Added Tax Tribunals Rules 1986 r 8 (amended by SI 1991/186; SI 1994/2617). The purpose of the statement of case is to let the appellant know the way in which the commissioners wish to put their case: *GUS Merchandise Corpn Ltd v Customs and Excise Comrs, Customs and Excise Comrs v GUS Merchandise Corpn Ltd* [1992] STC 776 at 781. The commissioners may not always be allowed to amend a statement of case: see *Optimum Personnel Evaluation (Operations) Ltd v Customs and Excise Comrs* (1987) VAT Decision 2334 (unreported); *Vorngrove Ltd v Customs and Excise Comrs* (1984) VAT Decision 1733 (unreported). The commissioners can be put on terms: see *Dormers Builders (London) Ltd v Customs and Excise Comrs* [1986] VATTR 69.
10 Ie under the Value Added Tax Tribunals Rules 1986 r 7 (as amended) (see para 303 post) or r 8: r 10(1).
11 Ibid r 10(1). As to the parties to the appeal see para 306 post.
12 Ibid r 10(2).
13 For the meaning of 'proper officer' see para 300 note 12 ante.
14 Value Added Tax Tribunals Rules 1986 r 10(3).
15 Ibid r 9(2).
16 Ibid r 9(1).

303. Statement of case, defence and reply in an evasion penalty appeal.
Unless a VAT and duties tribunal otherwise directs, in an evasion penalty appeal[1]:

(1)   the Commissioners of Customs and Excise must, within 42 days of the date of notification[2] of the notice of appeal[3] or the withdrawal or dismissal of any application made by them[4], whichever is later, serve at the appropriate tribunal centre[5] a statement of case in the appeal setting out the matters and facts on which they rely for the making of the penalty assessment and (where it, too, is disputed) the making of the assessment for the tax alleged to have been evaded by the same conduct[6];

(2)   the statement of case must include full particulars of the alleged dishonesty and must state the statutory provision under which the penalty or tax is assessed or the decision is made[7];

(3)   the appellant[8] must, within 42 days of the date of notification of that statement of case, serve at the appropriate tribunal centre a defence to it setting out the matters and facts on which he relies for his defence[9]; and

(4)   the commissioners may, within 21 days of the date of notification of the defence, serve at the appropriate tribunal centre a reply to the defence and must do so if it is necessary thereby to set out specifically any matter or any fact showing illegality, or which (a) they allege makes the defence not maintainable; or (b) if not specifically set out, might take the appellant by surprise; or (c) raises any issue of fact not arising out of the statement of case[10].

At any hearing of an evasion penalty appeal the commissioners are not required to prove, or to bring evidence relating to, any matter or fact which is admitted by the appellant in his defence[11]. Every statement of case, defence and reply must be divided into paragraphs numbered consecutively, each allegation being, so far as is convenient, contained in a separate paragraph[12]. Each such document must contain in summary form a brief statement of the matters and facts on which the party relies but not the evidence by which those facts are to be proved[13]. A party may raise a point of law in such documents[14].

1   For the meaning of 'evasion penalty appeal' see para 302 note 3 ante.
2   For the meaning of 'date of notification' see para 300 note 13 ante.
3   As to the notice of appeal see para 300 ante.
4   As to the withdrawal or dismissal of an application see para 304 post.
5   As to the appropriate tribunal centre see para 293 ante.
6   Value Added Tax Tribunals Rules 1986, SI 1986/590, r 7(1)(a) (amended by SI 1991/186; SI 1994/2617). An extension of the time limit for serving a statement of case will not be granted as a matter of course, eg where Customs has lost some of the paperwork: see *Sonat Offshore (UK) Ltd v Customs and Excise Comrs* (1996) VAT Decision 14021 (unreported).
7   Value Added Tax Tribunals Rules 1986 r 7(1)(aa) (added by SI 1994/2617).
8   For the meaning of 'appellant' see para 293 note 8 ante.
9   Value Added Tax Rules 1986 r 7(1)(b) (amended by SI 1991/186).
10   Ibid r 7(1)(c) (amended by SI 1991/186).
11   Ibid r 7(2) (amended by SI 1994/2617).
12   Ibid r 7(3).
13   Ibid r 7(4).
14   Ibid r 7(5).

304. Power of tribunal to strike out or dismiss an appeal. A VAT and duties tribunal must strike out an appeal where no appeal against the disputed decision[1] lies to a tribunal, and must dismiss an appeal where it cannot be entertained by a tribunal[2]. A tribunal may dismiss an appeal for want of prosecution where the appellant[3] or the person to whom the interest or liability of the appellant has been assigned or transmitted, or upon whom that interest or liability has devolved, has been guilty of inordinate or inexcusable delay[4]. Except where an appeal or application is allowed by consent[5], no appeal may be struck out or dismissed without a hearing[6].

1   For the meaning of 'disputed decision' see para 293 note 8 ante.
2   Value Added Tax Tribunals Rules 1986, SI 1986/590, r 18(1). As to when a tribunal 'entertains' an appeal see para 297 note 2 ante.
3   For the meaning of 'appellant' see para 293 note 8 ante.
4   Value Added Tax Tribunals Rules 1986 r 18(2).
5   Ie in accordance with ibid r 17: see para 299 ante.
6   Ibid r 18(3); and see *Abedin v Customs and Excise Comrs* [1979] STC 426.

305. Withdrawal of an appeal or application. An appellant[1] or applicant may at any time withdraw his appeal or application by serving at the appropriate tribunal centre[2] a notice of withdrawal signed by him or on his behalf, and a proper officer[3] must send a copy of it to the other parties to the appeal[4]. The withdrawal of an appeal or application under this provision does not prevent a party to it from applying[5] for an award or direction as to his or their costs[6] or for a direction[7] for the payment or repayment of a sum of money with interest; nor does it prevent a tribunal from making such an award or direction if it thinks fit so to do[8].

1   For the meaning of 'appellant' see para 293 note 8 ante.
2   As to the appropriate tribunal centre see para 293 note 6 ante.
3   For the meaning of 'proper officer' see para 300 note 12 ante.
4   Value Added Tax Tribunals Rules 1986, SI 1986/590, r 16(1) (amended by SI 1994/2617). As to the parties to the appeal see para 306 post.
5   Ie under ibid r 29 (as amended): see para 316 post.
6   For the meaning of 'costs' see para 298 note 5 ante.
7   Ie under the Value Added Tax Act 1994 s 84(8): see para 297 ante.
8   Value Added Tax Tribunals Rules 1986 r 16(2) (amended by SI 1994/2617).

306. Parties to an appeal. Subject to any direction made where, in the course of proceedings, the liability or interest of the applicant passes to another person by reason of death, insolvency or otherwise[1], the parties to an appeal are the appellant[2] and the Commissioners of Customs and Excise[3]. In general only the addressee of a decision has a right of appeal[4], and appeals are brought by the taxable person who, if tax is chargeable, is accountable for the tax, although a VAT and duties tribunal will entertain an appeal from another person who has sufficient legal interest to maintain the appeal[5].

One or more partners in a firm which is not a legal person distinct from the partners of whom it is composed may appeal against a decision of the commissioners relating to the firm or its business, or apply to a tribunal in an appeal or intended appeal, in the name of the firm and, unless a tribunal otherwise directs, such proceedings are to be carried on in the name of the firm, but with the same consequences as would have ensued if the appeal or application had been brought in the names of the partners[6].

Where, in the course of proceedings, the liability or interest of the appellant or applicant passes to another person ('the successor') by reason of death, insolvency, or otherwise, the tribunal may direct, on the application of the commissioners or the successor, and with the written consent of the successor, that the successor be substituted for the applicant or appellant in the proceedings[7]. If the tribunal is satisfied that there is no person interested in the application or appeal, or the successor fails to give written consent for his substitution in the proceedings within a period of two months after being requested to do so by the tribunal, that tribunal may, of its own motion or on application by the commissioners and after giving prior written notice to the successor, dismiss the application or appeal[8].

Neither a bankrupt nor a discharged bankrupt has any locus standi in an appeal; but the trustee in bankruptcy may assign the right of appeal to the discharged bankrupt[9].

1   Ie any direction made under the Value Added Tax Tribunals Rules 1986, SI 1986/590, r 13 (as substituted): see the text and notes 7–8 infra.
2   For the meaning of 'appellant' see para 293 note 8 ante.
3   Value Added Tax Tribunals Rules 1986 r 3(4). In certain circumstances, however, a third party may intervene: see *Schwarcz v Aeresta Ltd and Customs and Excise Comrs* [1989] STC 230. Power is given to the tribunal under the Value Added Tax Tribunals Rules 1986 r 19(3) (as amended: see para 307 post) to join third parties to an appeal if it is necessary or expedient to ensure the speedy and just determination of that appeal; but it may be made a condition of the joinder of such a party that it should not at any stage (including on appeal) apply for its costs: *Barclays Bank plc v Customs and Excise Comrs and Visa International Service Association (third party)* [1992] VATTR 229 at 239.
4   *Davis Advertising Service Ltd v Customs and Excise Comrs* [1973] VATTR 16.

5　An appellant has a sufficient interest if he can show that the tax chargeable on the supply under a contract was to be added to the money otherwise payable under it; or if he can show that there were future supplies of a like nature to be made between the parties: *Processed Vegetable Growers Association Ltd v Customs and Excise Comrs* [1973] VATTR 87. See also *Cameron v Customs and Excise Comrs* [1973] VATTR 177; *Gumbrell and Dodson Bros v Customs and Excise Comrs* [1973] VATTR 171. Where the recipient has no legal right to recover the disputed VAT from the supplier, she has no or insufficient interest to maintain an appeal (*Payton v Customs and Excise Comrs* [1974] VATTR 140); but a supplier will hold any repayment on a successful appeal on constructive trust for the appellant (*Williams & Glyn's Bank Ltd v Customs and Excise Comrs* [1974] VATTR 262). See also *JC Skeffington v Customs and Excise Comrs* LON/74/35 (VAT Decision 102A, unreported). An appellant who is a recipient of a supply has sufficient interest to bring an appeal if he deposits the VAT with the commissioners upon their promise to repay if he is successful: *Gilbourne v Customs and Excise Comrs* [1974] VATTR 209; *Williams & Glyn's Bank Ltd v Customs and Excise Comrs* supra. Where the commissioners decided that a property management company was supplying its services to the owner of the managed premises rather than to the tenants it was held the owner did not have sufficient interest to appeal that decision: *Kingsley-Smith v Customs and Excise Comrs* (1996) VAT Decision 13787, [1996] STI 406.

6　Value Added Tax Tribunals Rules 1986 r 12 (amended by SI 1994/2617).

7　Ibid r 13(1), (2) (substituted by SI 1994/2617).

8　Ibid r 13(3) (substituted by SI 1994/2617). See *L'Arome International Ltd v Customs and Excise Comrs* (1996) VAT Decision 14419, [1996] STI 1722.

9　See *Hunt v Customs and Excise Comrs* [1992] VATTR 255.

307. Directions. An application to a VAT and duties tribunal, made otherwise than at a hearing, for the issue of a witness summons[1] or a direction (including a hardship direction[2] or a direction for the setting aside of a witness summons) must be made by notice[3] served[4] at the appropriate tribunal centre[5]. The notice must (1) state the name and address of the applicant; (2) state the direction sought or details of the witness summons sought to be issued or set aside; and (3) set out, or have attached to it a document containing, the grounds of the application[6].

Additionally, any notice of application by an intending appellant[7] must:

(a)　state the address of the office of the Commissioners of Customs and Excise from which the disputed decision[8] was sent;

(b)　state the date of the disputed decision and the address to which it was sent;

(c)　set out shortly the disputed decision or have attached to it a copy of the document containing the disputed decision; and

(d)　have attached to it a copy of any letter from the commissioners extending the applicant's time to appeal against the disputed decision together with a copy of any letter from the commissioners notifying him of a date from which his time of appeal against the disputed decision is to run[9].

A notice of application for a hardship direction must be served at the appropriate tribunal centre within the period for the service of the notice of appeal[10]. Except as provided in certain provisions relating to witness summonses and summonses to third parties[11], the parties to an application are the parties to the appeal or intended appeal[12], and, except as so provided, a proper officer[13] must send an acknowledgement of the service of a notice of application at the appropriate tribunal centre to the applicant and must also send a copy of that notice and of any accompanying documents to the other party, if any, to the application[14]. The acknowledgment and copy of the notice of application must state the date of service and the date of notification of the notice of application[15].

Within 14 days of the date of notification of a notice of application, the other party to the application, if any, must indicate whether or not he consents to it and, if he does not consent to it, the reason why he does not so consent[16].

A tribunal may of its own motion or on the application of any party to an appeal or application extend the time within which a party to the appeal or application, or any other person, is required or authorised[17] to do anything in relation to the appeal or application (including the time for service for a notice of application) upon such terms as it may think fit[18]. A tribunal may make a direction under this provision of its own motion without prior notice or reference to any party or other person and without a hearing[19]. Without prejudice to these provisions, a tribunal may of its own motion, or on the application of a party to an appeal or application or other person interested, give or make any direction as to the conduct of, or as to any matter or thing in connection with, the appeal or application which it may think necessary or expedient to ensure the speedy and just determination of the appeal, including the joining of other persons as parties to the appeal[20].

Where a notice is served in relation to the evasion of VAT[21] and appeals are brought by different persons which relate to, or to different portions of, the basic penalty referred to in the notice, the tribunal may, of its own motion or on the application of any party to any such appeal, give any direction it thinks fit as to the joinder of the appeals[22].

If any party to an appeal or application or any other person fails to comply with any direction of a tribunal, a tribunal may allow or dismiss the appeal or application[23].

1   For the meaning of 'witness summons' in this context see the Value Added Tax Tribunals Rules 1986, SI 1986/590, r 22(1); and para 311 post.

2   A 'hardship direction' is a direction that an appeal or an intended appeal should be entertained notwithstanding that the amount which the Commissioners of Customs and Excise have determined to be payable as tax has not been paid or deposited with them: ibid r 2 (definition added by SI 1991/186).

3   Although there is no prescribed form of notice, form Trib 5, available from the Lord Chancellor's Department, may be used for making such an application.

4   As to methods of service see para 312 post.

5   Value Added Tax Tribunals Rules 1986 r 11(1) (amended by SI 1991/186). As to the appropriate tribunal centre see para 293 ante.

6   Ibid r 11(2).

7   For the meaning of 'appellant' see para 293 note 8 ante.

8   For the meaning of 'disputed decision' see para 293 note 7 ante.

9   Value Added Tax Tribunals Rules 1986 r 11(3).

10   Ibid r 11(4) (amended by SI 1991/186).

11   Ie ibid r 22 (as amended): see para 311 post.

12   Ibid r 11(5). As to the parties to an appeal see para 306 ante.

13   For the meaning of 'proper officer' see para 300 note 12 ante.

14   Value Added Tax Tribunals Rules 1986 r 11(6)(a), (b).

15   Ibid r 11(6) (amended by SI 1991/186). For the meaning of 'date of notification' see para 300 note 13 ante.

16   Ibid r 11(7) (amended by SI 1991/186). As to where the parties to the application are agreed upon the terms of the direction to be given by the tribunal see para 299 text and note 20 ante.

17   Ie by the Value Added Tax Tribunals Rules 1986 (as amended); or by any decision or direction of a tribunal: r 19(1).

18   Ibid r 19(1). As to matters to be taken into account on an application under r 19(1) see *Price v Customs and Excise Comrs* [1978] VATTR 115; *Trippett v Customs and Excise Comrs* [1978] VATTR 260. The tribunal has no jurisdiction to entertain an appeal against an assessment where the commissioners have obtained judgment in the High Court for the sum assessed unless and until the judgment has been set aside: *Brough v Customs and Excise Comrs* MAN/77/317 (VAT Decision 562, unreported); *Ullah v Customs and Excise Comrs* (1978) VAT Decision 561 (unreported); *Digwa v Customs and Excise Comrs* [1978] VATTR 119. As to where a tribunal refused to exercise its power to extend the time within which the intending appellant could appeal because the tax in dispute had been paid to the commissioners voluntarily under a mistake of law see *Kyffin v Customs and Excise Comrs* [1978] VATTR 175 (*William Whiteley Ltd v R* (1909) 101 LT 741 considered). Quaere whether the same decision would now be reached, following *Woolwich Equitable Building Society v IRC* [1993] AC 70, [1992] 3 All ER 737, HL. See also *J Walter Thompson UK Holdings Ltd v Customs and Excise Comrs* (1996) VAT Decision 14058, [1996] STI 1102.

19   Value Added Tax Tribunals Rules 1986 r 19(2).

20   Ibid r 19(3) (amended by SI 1994/2617).

21   Ie under the Value Added Tax Act 1994 s 61: see para 273 ante.

22   Value Added Tax Tribunals Rules 1986 r 19(3A) (added by SI 1994/2617).

23 Ibid r 19(4) (amended by SI 1991/186). In Scotland a tribunal's decision to allow an appeal because the commissioners had failed to comply with an 'unless' order has been upheld by the court (see *Customs and Excise Comrs v Young* [1993] STC 394, Ct of Sess); but the English tribunals are reluctant to allow appeals in such circumstances as they can impose a penalty on the commissioners under the Value Added Tax Act 1994 s 82(1), Sch 12 para 10 (see para 299 ante).

    The tribunal may also refuse the commissioners the opportunity to amend their case, confining them to the grounds contained in their decision letter: see *Faccenda Chicken v Customs and Excise Comrs* [1992] VATTR 395 at 401 (although such a refusal was not in fact thought appropriate in that case) (followed in *Charles F Hunter Ltd v Customs and Excise Comrs* (1993) VAT Decision 11619 (unreported)). An appeal will not be allowed by reason of the failure of the commissioners to comply with the Value Added Tax Tribunals Rules 1986 (as amended) or a direction of a tribunal unless there is a likelihood of serious prejudice to the appellant, or contumelious disobedience by the defaulting party: *Wine Warehouses Europe Ltd v Customs and Excise Comrs* [1993] VATTR 307.

    As to penalties which the tribunal may award in the event of a party's failure to comply with a direction or summons see para 299 text and note 14 ante.

308. Disclosure, inspection and production of documents.

Each of the parties to an appeal[1] other than a reasonable excuse[2] or mitigation[3] appeal, and each of the parties to an application for a hardship direction[4] must, before the expiration of the prescribed time[5], serve at the appropriate tribunal centre[6] a list of the documents in his possession, custody or power which he proposes to produce at the hearing of the appeal or application[7].

Additionally, and without prejudice to the above provisions, a VAT and duties tribunal may, on the application of a party to an appeal and where it appears necessary for disposing fairly of the proceedings, direct the other party to the appeal to serve at the appropriate tribunal centre for the appeal, within such period as it may specify, a list of the documents, or any class of documents, which are or have been in his possession, custody or power relating to any question in issue in the appeal; and may at the same time or subsequently order him to make and serve an affidavit verifying that list[8]. If a party desires to claim that any document included in a list of documents served by him in pursuance of a such a direction is privileged from production in the appeal, that claim must be made in the list of documents with a sufficient statement of the grounds of privilege[9].

A proper officer[10] must send a copy of any list of documents and any affidavit served under these provisions to the other party to the appeal or application and that other party is entitled to inspect and take copies of the documents set out in the list which are in the possession, custody or power of the party who made the list and are not privileged from production in the appeal, at such time and place as he and the party who served the list of documents may agree or a tribunal may direct[11]. At the hearing of an appeal or application, a party must produce any document included in a list of documents so served by him in relation to that appeal or application which is in his possession, custody or power and is not privileged from production when called upon to do so by the other party to the appeal or application[12].

1   As to the parties to an appeal see para 306 ante.
2   For the meaning of 'reasonable excuse appeal' see para 300 note 6 ante.
3   For the meaning of 'mitigation appeal' see para 301 note 7 ante.
4   For the meaning of 'hardship direction' see para 307 note 2 ante.
5   A list of documents must be served: (1) in the case of an evasion penalty appeal, within a period of 15 days after the last day for the service by the Commissioners of Customs and Excise of any reply pursuant to the Value Added Tax Tribunals Rules 1986, SI 1986/590, r 7(1)(c) (as amended) (see para 303 ante); (2) in any other appeal except a reasonable excuse appeal or a mitigation appeal, within a period of 30 days after (a) the date of notification of the notice of appeal; or (b) the date of notification of the notice of withdrawal of any application under r 6 (see para 301 ante) in the appeal; or (c) the date on which a direction dismissing any application under r 6 is released in accordance with r 30 (as amended) (see para 318 post), whichever is the latest; (3) in an application for a hardship direction, within a period of 30 days

after the date of notification of the application: r 20(2) (amended by SI 1991/186; SI 1994/2617). For the meaning of 'evasion penalty appeal' see para 302 note 3 ante; and for the meaning of 'date of notification' see para 300 note 13 ante.

6   As to the appropriate tribunal centre see para 293 ante.

7   Value Added Tax Tribunals Rules 1986 r 20(1) (amended by SI 1991/186). The list of documents to be served by the commissioners in accordance with this provision must contain a reference to the documents relied upon in reaching a decision on a review under the Finance Act 1994 s 15 or s 59: Value Added Tax Tribunals Rules 1986 r 20(1A) (added by SI 1994/2617).

   Failure to include a document in a list does not preclude the document's admission before the tribunal. The High Court may remit a case to the tribunal for rehearing if it refuses to admit documents whose existence has only come to light shortly before the hearing. The tribunal has a discretion as to whether or not to admit documents not contained on a party's list, but must exercise this discretion rationally and in accordance with the principles of natural justice: see *GUS Merchandise Corpn Ltd v Customs and Excise Comrs, Customs and Excise Comrs v GUS Merchandise Corpn Ltd* [1992] STC 776. The commissioners are entitled to rely on documents before the tribunal which were not included in their list without making an application under the Value Added Tax Tribunals Rules 1986 r 19 (as amended) (see para 307 ante) if the documents in question only became relevant when the appellant advanced a fresh argument at the hearing: *Koca v Customs and Excise Comrs* [1996] STC 58.

8   Value Added Tax Tribunals Rules 1986 r 20(3).

9   Ibid r 20(4).

10 For the meaning of 'proper officer' see para 300 note 12 ante.

11 Value Added Tax Tribunals Rules 1986 r 20(5).

12 Ibid r 20(6).

309. Witness statements. A party to an appeal[1] may, within the prescribed time[2], serve at the appropriate tribunal centre[3] a statement in writing (a 'witness statement') containing evidence proposed to be given by any person at the hearing of the appeal[4]. A witness statement must contain the name, address and description of the person proposing to give the evidence contained in it and must be signed by him[5]. A proper officer[6] must send a copy of a witness statement served at the appropriate tribunal centre to the other party to the appeal, and that copy must state the date of service and the date of notification of the witness statement and must contain, or be accompanied by, a note to the effect that, unless a notice of objection to it is served, the witness statement may be read at the hearing of the appeal as evidence of the facts stated in it without the person who made it giving oral evidence at the hearing[7].

If a party objects to a witness statement being read at the hearing of the appeal as evidence of any fact stated in it, he must serve a notice of objection to the witness statement at the appropriate tribunal centre not later than 14 days after the date of notification of that witness statement there, whereupon a proper officer must send a copy of the notice of objection to the other party and the witness statement must not be read or admitted in evidence at the hearing although the person who signed it may give evidence orally at the hearing[8]. Subject to this provision and unless a tribunal otherwise directs, a witness statement signed by any person and duly served is admissible in evidence at the hearing of the appeal as evidence of any fact stated in it of which oral evidence by him at that hearing would be admissible[9].

1   As to parties to an appeal see para 306 ante.

2   A witness statement must be served (1) in the case of an evasion penalty appeal, before the expiration of 21 days after the last day for the service by the Commissioners of Customs and Excise of a reply pursuant to the Value Added Tax Tribunals Rules 1986, SI 1986/590, r 7(1)(c) (as amended) (see para 303 ante); (2) in the case of a mitigation appeal or a reasonable excuse appeal, before the expiration of 21 days after the date of notification of the notice of appeal; and (3) in the case of any other appeal, before the expiration of 21 days after the date of notification of the commissioners' statement of case: r 21(6) (amended by SI 1991/186; SI 1994/2617). For the meaning of 'evasion penalty appeal' see para 302 note 3 ante; for the meaning of 'mitigation appeal' see para 301 note 7 ante; for the meaning of 'reasonable excuse appeal' see para 300 note 6 ante; and for the meaning of 'date of notification' see para 300 note 13 ante.

3 As to the appropriate tribunal centre see para 293 ante.
4 Value Added Tax Tribunals Rules 1986 r 21(1).
5 Ibid r 21(2).
6 For the meaning of 'proper officer' see para 300 note 12 ante.
7 Value Added Tax Tribunals Rules 1986 r 21(3) (amended by SI 1991/186).
8 Ibid r 21(4) (amended by SI 1991/186).
9 Ibid r 21(5). Even if no witness statement is duly served, hearsay evidence may be adduced before the tribunal unless objection is raised or the tribunal decides of its own volition to exclude the evidence: *Wayne Farley Ltd v Customs and Excise Comrs* [1986] STC 487.

310. Affidavits and depositions made in other legal proceedings.

If (1) an affidavit or deposition made in other legal proceedings, whether civil or criminal, is specified as such in a list of documents served[1] by a party to an appeal[2] or application or in a notice[3] served by such a party at the appropriate tribunal centre[4]; and (2) it is stated in that list or notice that the party serving it proposes to give that affidavit or deposition in evidence at the hearing of the appeal or application and that the person who made that affidavit or deposition is dead or is outside the United Kingdom[5] or is unfit by reason of his bodily or mental condition to attend as a witness, or that, despite the exercise of reasonable diligence, it has not been possible to find him, then the affidavit or deposition is admissible[6] at the hearing of the appeal or application as evidence of any fact stated in it of which oral evidence by the person who made the affidavit or deposition would be admissible[7].

If a party objects to an affidavit or deposition being read and admitted as evidence under these provisions, he must serve a notice of application for directions with regard to that affidavit or deposition at the appropriate tribunal centre not later than 21 days after the date of notification of the list of documents or notice[8]. At the hearing of such an application, a VAT and duties tribunal may give directions as to whether, and if so how and on what conditions, the affidavit or deposition may be admitted as evidence and, where applicable, as to the manner in which the affidavit or deposition is to be proved, and the affidavit or deposition is admissible as evidence to the extent and on the conditions, if any, specified in the direction but not further or otherwise[9]. The members of the tribunal hearing such an application must not sit on the hearing of the appeal or application to which the above-mentioned application for directions relates[10].

1 Ie served under the Value Added Tax Tribunals Rules 1986, SI 1986/590, r 20(1) (as amended): see para 308 ante. Any such notice must be served before the expiration of 21 days after the date of notification of the notice of appeal or notice of application: r 21A(2) (r 21A added by SI 1991/186). For the meaning of 'date of notification' see para 300 note 13 ante.
2 As to the parties to an appeal see para 306 ante.
3 Ie in the case of an appeal or application to which the Value Added Tax Tribunals Rules 1986 r 20(1) (as amended) does not apply: r 21A(1)(a) (as added: see note 1 supra).
4 As to the appropriate tribunal centre see para 293 ante.
5 For the meaning of 'United Kingdom' see para 4 note 3 ante.
6 Ie subject to the Value Added Tax Tribunals Rules r 21A(2)–(6) (as added): see note 1 supra and the text and notes 7–10 infra.
7 Ibid r 21A(1) (as added: see note 1 supra). When a proper officer sends a copy of any such list or notice as is mentioned in r 21A(1) (as so added) to any person pursuant to r 11(6)(b) (see para 176 ante) or r 20(5) (see para 308 ante), he must also send to that person a copy of r 21A (as so added): r 21A(3) (as so added).
8 Ibid r 21A(4) (as added: see note 1 supra).
9 Ibid r 21A(5) (as added: see note 1 supra).
10 Ibid r 21A(6) (as added: see note 1 supra). As to breach of a similar requirement under the Taxes Management Act 1970 requiring the rehearing of the appeal see *Sutherland v Gustar (Inspector of Taxes)* [1994] Ch 304, [1994] STC 387, CA.

311. Witness summonses and summonses to third parties. Where a witness is required by a party to an appeal[1] or application to attend the hearing of an appeal or application to give oral evidence or to produce any document in his possession, custody or power necessary for the purpose of that hearing, a chairman[2] or the registrar[3] must, upon the application of that party, issue a summons requiring the attendance of the witness at the hearing or the production of the document, wherever the witness may be in the United Kingdom[4] or the Isle of Man[5].

Where a party to an appeal or application desires to inspect any document necessary for the purpose of the hearing of that appeal or application which is in the possession, custody or power of any other person in the United Kingdom or the Isle of Man (whether or not that other person is a party to the appeal or application) a chairman or registrar must, upon the application of that party, issue a summons requiring either (1) the attendance of the other person at such date, time and place as the chairman or the registrar may direct and then and there for that person to produce the document for inspection by the party or his representative and to allow the party or his representative then and there to peruse the document and to take a copy of it; or (2) the other person to post the document by ordinary post to an address in the United Kingdom or Isle of Man by first class mail in an envelope duly prepaid and properly addressed to the party requiring to inspect it[6].

A chairman or the registrar may issue a summons under this provision without prior notice or reference to the applicant or any other person and without a hearing, the only party to the application being the applicant[7]. A summons so issued must be signed by a chairman or the registrar and must be served (a) where the witness or third party is an individual, by leaving a copy of the summons with him and showing him the original of it; or (b) where the witness or third party is a body corporate, by sending a copy of the summons by post to, or leaving it at, the registered or principal office in the United Kingdom or the Isle of Man of the body to be served, not less than four days before the day on which the attendance of the witness or third party or the posting of the document is thereby required[8]. Such a summons must contain a statement, or be accompanied by a note, to the effect that the witness or third party may apply, by a notice served at the tribunal centre[9] from which the summons was issued, for a direction that the summons be set aside[10].

A witness summons so issued for the purpose of a hearing and duly served has effect until the conclusion of the hearing at which the attendance of the witness is thereby required[11]. No person is, however, to be required to attend to give evidence or to produce any document at any hearing or otherwise under these provisions[12] which he could not be required to give or produce on the trial of an action in a court of law[13]; and no person is bound to attend any hearing or to produce or post any document for the purpose of a hearing or for inspection and perusal in accordance with such a summons unless a reasonable and sufficient sum of money to defray the expenses of coming to, attending at and returning from the hearing or place of inspection and perusal was tendered to him at the time when the summons was served on him[14].

A tribunal may, upon the application of any person served at the appropriate tribunal centre, set aside a summons so served upon him[15].

1   As to the parties to an appeal see para 306 ante.
2   As to the chairman see para 295 ante.
3   As to the registrar see para 295 ante.
4   For the meaning of 'United Kingdom' see para 4 note 3 ante.
5   Value Added Tax Tribunals Rules 1986, SI 1986/590, r 22(1).
6   Ibid r 22(2).
7   Ibid r 22(3).

8 Ibid r 22(4) (amended by SI 1991/186; SI 1994/2617).
9 As to the appropriate tribunal centre see para 293 ante.
10 Value Added Tax Tribunals Rules 1986 r 22(4) (as amended: see note 8 supra).
11 Ibid r 22(5).
12 Ie under ibid r 22(2): see the text and note 6 supra.
13 Ibid r 22(6).
14 Ibid r 22(7).
15 Ibid r 22(8). The parties to an application to set aside a summons issued under this rule are the applicant and the party who obtained the issue of the summons: r 22(9).

312. Service of notices and documents. Service of a notice of appeal, notice of application or other document is effected by handing the document to a proper officer[1] at the appropriate tribunal centre[2] or by its being received there through the post or by a facsimile of it being received there through a facsimile transmission process[3].

Any notice of appeal, notice of application or other document[4] handed in or received at a tribunal centre other than the appropriate tribunal centre may be sent by post in a letter addressed to a proper officer at the appropriate tribunal centre or handed back to the person from whom it was received, or sent by post in a letter addressed to the person from whom it appears to have been received or by whom it appears to have been sent[5].

Any document authorised or required to be sent to the Commissioners of Customs and Excise may be sent to them by post[6] in a letter addressed to them at the address of the office of theirs from which the disputed decision[7] appears to have been sent, or handed or sent to them by post or in such manner and at such address as the commissioners may from time to time request by a general notice served at the appropriate tribunal centre[8].

Any document authorised or required to be sent to any party to an appeal or application other than the commissioners may be sent by post (1) in a letter addressed to him at his address stated in his notice of appeal or application; or (2) in a letter addressed to any person named in his notice of appeal or application as having been instructed to act for him in connection with that appeal or application at the address stated in it; or (3) in a letter addressed to such person and at such address as he may specify from time to time by notice served at the appropriate tribunal centre[9]. Where, however, partners appeal or apply to a tribunal in the name of their firm, any document sent by post (a) in a letter addressed to the firm at the address of the firm stated in the notice of appeal or notice of application; or (b) to any person named in that notice as having been instructed to act for the firm at the address given in it; or (c) to any other address the partners may from time to time specify by notice served at the appropriate tribunal centre, is deemed to have been duly sent to all those partners[10].

Subject to the above provisions, any document authorised or required to be sent to any party to an appeal or application, or to another person, may be sent by post in a letter addressed to him at his usual or last known address or addressed to him or to that other person at such address as he may from time to time specify by notice served at the appropriate tribunal centre[11].

1 For the meaning of 'proper officer' see para 300 note 12 ante.
2 As to the appropriate tribunal centre see para 293 ante.
3 Value Added Tax Tribunals Rules 1986, SI 1986/590, r 31(1) (amended by SI 1991/186).
4 Ie including a facsimile of a document: ibid r 31(2) (amended by SI 1991/186).
5 Ibid r 31(2) (as amended: see note 4 supra).
6 For these purposes, any reference to the sending of any document to any party to an appeal or application or to any other person by post is to be construed as including a reference to the transmission of a facsimile of that document by facsimile transmission process: ibid r 32(4) (added by SI 1991/186). As to the parties to an appeal see para 306 ante.
7 For the meaning of 'disputed decision' see para 293 note 7 ante.
8 Value Added Tax Tribunals Rules 1986, 1986/590, r 32(1).

9   Ibid r 32(2).
10   Ibid r 32(2) proviso.
11   Ibid r 32(3).

313. Notice of hearings. A proper officer[1] must send to the parties to the appeal[2] a notice stating the place where, and the date and time when, an appeal will be heard which, unless the parties otherwise agree, must be not earlier than 14 days after the date on which the notice is sent[3].

Unless a VAT and duties tribunal otherwise directs, an application made at a hearing must be heard forthwith, and no notice of the hearing need be sent to the parties to it[4]. Subject to this, a proper officer must send a notice stating the place where, and the date and time when, an application will be heard which, unless the parties otherwise agree, must not be earlier than 14 days after the date on which the notice is sent (1) in the case of an application for the issue of a witness summons[5], to the applicant; (2) in the case of an application to set aside the issue of a witness summons, to the applicant and the party who obtained the issue of the witness summons; and (3) in the case of any other application, to the parties to that application[6].

1   For the meaning of 'proper officer' see para 300 note 12 ante.
2   As to the parties to an appeal see para 306 ante.
3   Value Added Tax Tribunals Rules 1986, SI 1986/590, r 23(1). As to the service of notice see para 312 ante.
4   Ibid r 23(2).
5   As to witness summonses see para 311 ante.
6   Value Added Tax Tribunals Rules 1986 r 23(3).

314. Failure to appear at a hearing. If, when an appeal or application is called on for hearing, a party to it[1] does not appear in person or by his representative[2], the VAT and duties tribunal may proceed to consider the appeal or application in the absence of that party[3]. If at that time no party to the hearing appears in person or by his representative, a tribunal may dismiss or strike out the appeal or application but may, on the application of any such party or of any person interested which is served at the appropriate tribunal centre[4] within 14 days after the decision or direction of the tribunal was released[5], reinstate the appeal or application on such terms as it thinks just[6].

The tribunal may set aside any decision or direction given in the absence of a party on such terms as it thinks just, on the application of that party or of any other person interested which is served at the appropriate tribunal centre within 14 days after the date when the decision or direction of the tribunal was released[7]; but where a party makes such an application and does not attend the hearing of it, he is not entitled to apply to have a decision or direction of the tribunal on the hearing of that application set aside[8].

1   As to the parties to an appeal see para 306 ante.
2   As to representation at a hearing see para 315 post.
3   Value Added Tax Tribunals Rules 1986, SI 1986/590, r 26(2) (amended by SI 1994/2617). For an example of a decision to proceed in the absence of the taxpayer see *Sandley (t/a Bemba Sandley Management Co) v Customs and Excise Comrs* [1995] STC 230n.
4   As to the appropriate tribunal centre see para 293 ante; and as to service of applications see para 312 ante.
5   Ie released in accordance with the Value Added Tax Tribunals Rules 1986 r 30 (as amended): see para 318 post.
6   Ibid r 26(1) (amended by SI 1991/186).
7   Ibid r 26(3) (added by SI 1994/2617).
8   Ibid r 26(4) (added by SI 1994/2617).

315. Procedure at a hearing. The hearing of an appeal must be in public unless, on the application of a party to the appeal[1], a VAT and duties tribunal directs that the whole or any part of the hearing should take place in private[2]. The hearing of any application made otherwise than at or subsequent to the hearing of an appeal must, however, take place in private unless a tribunal otherwise directs[3]. Any member of the Council on Tribunals[4] or the Scottish Committee of the Council on Tribunals may (in that capacity) attend the hearing of any appeal or application notwithstanding that it takes place in private[5].

At the hearing of an appeal or application, any party to it other than the Commissioners of Customs and Excise may conduct his case himself or may be represented by any person whom he may appoint for the purpose[6]. The commissioners may be represented at any hearing at which they are entitled to attend by any person whom they may appoint for the purpose[7].

At the hearing of an appeal or application other than an evasion penalty appeal[8] the tribunal must allow:

(1) the appellant[9] or applicant or his representative to open his case;
(2) the appellant or applicant to give evidence in support of the appeal or application and to produce documentary evidence;
(3) the appellant or applicant or his representative to call other witnesses to give evidence in support of the appeal or application or to produce documentary evidence, and to re-examine any such witness following his cross-examination;
(4) the other party to the appeal or application or his representative to cross-examine any witness called to give evidence in support of the appeal or application (including the appellant or applicant if he gives evidence);
(5) the other party or his representative to open his case;
(6) the other party to give evidence in opposition to the appeal or application and to produce documentary evidence;
(7) the other party or his representative to call other witnesses to give evidence in opposition to the appeal or application or to produce documentary evidence and to re-examine any such witness following his cross-examination;
(8) the appellant or applicant or his representative to cross-examine any witness called to give evidence in opposition to the appeal or application (including the other party to it if he gives evidence);
(9) the other party or his representative to make a second address closing his case; and
(10) the appellant or applicant or his representative to make a final address closing his case[10].

At the hearing of an evasion penalty appeal the tribunal must follow the same procedure as is set out in heads (1) to (10) above with the prescribed modifications[11].

At the hearing of an appeal or application, the chairman[12] and any other member of the tribunal may put any question to any witness called to give evidence at it, including a party to the appeal or application if he gives evidence[13]. Subject to the above provisions, a tribunal may regulate its own procedure as it may think fit, and in particular may determine the order in which the matters mentioned in heads (1) to (10) above are to take place[14]. A chairman or the registrar[15] may postpone the hearing of any appeal or application[16], and a tribunal may adjourn the hearing of any appeal or application on such terms as it may think just[17].

1 As to the parties to an appeal see para 306 ante.
2 Value Added Tax Tribunals Rules 1986, SI 1986/590, r 24(1).
3 Ibid r 24(2). The tribunal may, however, publish its decision if it thinks fit: *RMSG v Customs and Excise Comrs* (1994) VAT Decision 11921, [1994] STI 686.
4 As to the Council on Tribunals see ADMINISTRATIVE LAW vol 1(1) (Reissue) paras 48–50.

5   Value Added Tax Tribunals Rules 1986 r 24(3). Hearings of appeals should, whenever possible, be in public: see *Guy Butler (International) Ltd v Customs and Excise Comrs* [1974] VATTR 199. A direction that the whole or part of a hearing should be in private will only be made in exceptional circumstances, such as where the disclosure of confidential information would harm an appellant in his business, or if the evidence to be given would involve such disclosure of a process as would prejudice the appellant's competitive position: *Consortium International Ltd v Customs and Excise Comrs, Consortium Communications International Club v Customs and Excise Comrs* (1979) VAT Decision 824 (unreported). Where a tribunal has directed that the hearing of the appeal be in private it would, nevertheless, be contrary to natural justice for the other party's expert witness to be excluded from the proceedings: *R v Manchester VAT Tribunal, ex p Customs and Excise Comrs* (February 1982, unreported, QB).

6   Value Added Tax Tribunals Rules 1986 r 25(a).
7   Ibid r 25(b).
8   For the meaning of 'evasion penalty appeal' see para 302 note 3 ante.
9   For the meaning of 'appellant' see para 293 note 8 ante.
10 Value Added Tax Tribunals Rules 1986 r 27(1) (amended by SI 1994/2617).
11 See ibid r 27(2) (substituted by SI 1994/2617). That procedure applies as if there were substituted (1) 'the Commissioners of Customs and Excise' for 'the appellant or applicant'; (2) 'their' for 'his' in heads (1), (3), (8) and (10) in the text; (3) 'in opposition to' for 'in support of' in heads (2), (3) and (4) in the text; and (4) 'in support of' for 'in opposition to' in heads (6), (7) and (8) in the text: r 27(2) (as so substituted). The procedure set out in heads (1)–(10) in the text applies with the same modifications at the hearing of an appeal against a penalty imposed under the Customs and Excise Management Act 1979 s 114(2) or the Hydrocarbon Oil Duties Act 1979 s 22 or s 23 (see CUSTOMS AND EXCISE): Value Added Tax Tribunals Rules 1986 r 27(2) (as so substituted).
12 As to the chairman see para 295 ante.
13 Value Added Tax Tribunals Rules 1986 r 27(3).
14 Ibid r 27(4) (amended by SI 1994/2617).
15 As to the registrar see para 295 ante.
16 Value Added Tax Tribunals Rules 1986 r 27(5).
17 Ibid r 27(6). A tribunal may refuse to adjourn a hearing and, having heard it, dismiss the appeal, if the appellant is absent and his representative is inadequately instructed or if there is a history of attempted delay by the appellant: *Whatton v Customs and Excise Comrs* [1996] STC 519.

316.   Evidence at a hearing. Subject to certain provisions as to witness statements[1] and as to the tendering of affidavits and depositions made in other legal proceedings[2], a VAT and duties tribunal may direct or allow evidence of any fact to be given in any manner it thinks fit and may not refuse evidence tendered to it on the grounds only that it would be inadmissible in a court of law[3].

A tribunal may require oral evidence of a witness, including a party to an appeal[4] or application, to be given on oath or affirmation and, for that purpose, a chairman[5] and any member of the administrative staff of the tribunals on the direction of a chairman has power to administer oaths or take affirmations[6].

At the hearing of an appeal or application, a tribunal must allow a party to produce any document set out in his list of documents[7] and unless a tribunal otherwise directs (1) any document contained in that list of documents which appears to be an original document is deemed to be an original document printed, written, signed or executed as it appears to have been; and (2) any document contained in the list of documents which appears to be a copy is deemed to be a true copy[8].

1   Ie the Value Added Tax Tribunals Rules 1986, SI 1986/590, r 21(4) (as amended), r 21(5): see para 309 ante. The tribunal may exercise its discretion to allow evidence in the form of a statement of a person who is overseas to be given, but should, as a rule, be slow to do so: *Presman (Bullion) Ltd v Customs and Excise Comrs* [1986] VATTR 136. The weight to be accorded such evidence is a matter for the tribunal: *Bord v Customs and Excise Comrs* (1992) VAT Decision 7946, [1992] STI 879. As to the admission of documents not contained on a party's list see *GUS Merchandise Corpn Ltd v Customs and Excise Comrs, Customs and Excise Comrs v GUS Merchandise Corpn Ltd* [1992] STC 776.
2   Ie the Value Added Tax Tribunals Rules 1986 r 21A (as added): see para 310 ante.

3   Ibid r 28(1) (amended by SI 1991/186). It has been held that evidence in the form of travaux préparatoires
     might be given as an aid to interpreting the Sixth Directive: Case 324/82 *EC Commission v Belgium* [1984]
     ECR 1861, [1985] 1 CMLR 364, ECJ. As to the admission of hearsay evidence when an appellant's
     representative fails to object see *Wayne Farley Ltd v Customs and Excise Comrs* [1986] STC 487; *Hanif v
     Customs and Excise Comrs* (1990) VAT Decision 6430 (unreported). As to the Sixth Directive see para 1
     note 1 ante.
4   As to the parties to an appeal see para 306 ante.
5   As to the chairman see para 295 ante.
6   Value Added Tax Tribunals Rules 1986 r 28(2).
7   Ie the list served under ibid r 20 (as amended): see para 308 ante.
8   Ibid r 28(3).

317. Awards and directions as to costs. A VAT and duties tribunal may direct that
a party to an appeal[1] or applicant must pay to the other party to the appeal or application
(1) within such period as it may specify, such sum as it may determine on account of the
costs[2] of that other party of, and incidental to and consequent upon, the appeal or
application; or (2) the costs of that other party of, and incidental to and consequent upon,
the appeal or application to be taxed by a taxing master of the Supreme Court or a district
judge of the High Court on such basis as it may specify[3].

Any costs awarded under these provisions are recoverable as a civil debt[4].

1   As to the parties to an appeal see para 306 ante.
2   For the meaning of 'costs' see para 298 note 5 ante. Where the appellant is a litigant in person, the tribunal
     is restricted to the common-law award of the litigant's out of pocket expenses in accordance with
     Buckland v Watts [1970] 1 QB 27, [1969] 2 All ER 985, CA. The tribunal may not award him costs for
     time spent preparing for the appeal, since the Litigants in Person (Costs and Expenses) Act 1975 does not
     extend to the VAT and duties tribunal: *Customs and Excise Comrs v Ross* [1990] 2 All ER 65, [1990] STC
     353; *Nader (t/a Try Us) v Customs and Excise Comrs* [1993] STC 806, CA. It has been held that a company
     is not a litigant in person when it is represented at the hearing by one of its directors, so that costs can be
     recovered for time spent by the director in preparation for the appeal (*GA Boyd Building Services Ltd v
     Customs and Excise Comrs* [1993] VATTR 26); but the opposite conclusion was reached in *Rupert Page
     Developments Ltd v Customs and Excise Comrs* [1993] VATTR 152 and impliedly in *Alpha International Coal
     Ltd v Customs and Excise Comrs* (1994) VAT Decision 11441, [1994] STI 162, where costs were recovered
     for the time spent by an accountant who happened also to be company secretary, on the ground that he
     was acting in his capacity as an independent agent of the company.
3   Value Added Tax Tribunals Rules 1986, SI 1986/590, r 29(1) (amended by SI 1991/186). Where a
     tribunal gives a direction under head (2) in the text in proceedings in England and Wales, the
     provisions of RSC Ord 62 apply, with the necessary modifications, to the taxation of the costs as if the
     proceedings in the tribunal were a cause or matter in the Supreme Court: Value Added Tax Tribunals
     Rules 1986 r 29(2). As to proceedings in Northern Ireland see r 29(4) (amended by SI 1994/2617).
     There are presently two bases of costs, costs on the standard basis and costs on an indemnity basis: see
     RSC Ord 62; and PRACTICE AND PROCEDURE. The latter are rarely awarded by the tribunal and it is
     likely that they are only available to an appellant if the commissioners have 'acted disgracefully' to such
     an extent as to make the case 'a wholly exceptional one': *H & B Motors (Dorchester) v Customs and Excise
     Comrs* (1993) VAT Decision 11209, [1993] STI 1428. Thus such costs were awarded where the
     commissioners had sought to exercise powers given to them by the Value Added Tax Act 1994 s 58,
     Sch 11 para 4(2) (see para 246 ante) for an improper purpose: *VSP Marketing Ltd v Customs and Excise
     Comrs* (1994) VAT Decision 12636, [1994] STI 1321. See also *KTS Fashions Ltd v Customs and Excise
     Comrs* (1992) VAT Decision 6782, [1992] STI 174.
         Cost should generally follow the event; it has been held that it is improper to deny a successful appellant
     his costs merely because his accountants have created a substantial degree of animosity prior to the appeal
     by the terms in which they have corresponded with the commissioners: *Zoungrou v Customs and Excise
     Comrs* [1989] STC 313. Costs may be awarded where one party concedes before the appeal is heard
     (*Surrey College Ltd v Customs and Excise Comrs* [1992] VATTR 181); but an appeal cannot be continued
     after a compromise has been reached in order to obtain an award of costs; the costs must form part of the
     compromise (*Cadogan Club Ltd v Customs and Excise Comrs* (1978) VAT Decision 548 (unreported)).
         The commissioners do not generally seek an award of costs; but (unless the appeal involves an
     important point of law requiring clarification) they do so in exceptional tribunal hearings of substantial
     and complex cases where large sums are involved and which are comparable with High Court cases. They

also consider seeking costs where the appellant has misused the tribunal procedure as, for instance, in frivolous or vexatious cases, or where he has failed to appear or to be represented at a mutually arranged hearing without sufficient explanation, or where he has first produced at a hearing relevant evidence which ought properly to have been disclosed at an earlier stage and which could have saved public funds had it been produced timeously. The commissioners normally seek an award of costs in unsuccessful evasion penalty appeals on the ground that such cases are comparable with High Court cases: 102 HC Official Report (6th series) written answers cols *459–460* (24 July 1986); Customs and Excise Press Notice 1132 [1986] STI 574. Costs are recoverable on an indemnity basis only, and are not recoverable where the appellant has agreed that he would only be obliged to pay his representative if and to the extent that an award of costs were made in his favour: *Customs and Excise Comrs v Vaz, Portcullis (VAT Consultancy) Ltd intervening* [1995] STC 14.

4   Value Added Tax Tribunals Rules 1986 r 29(5).

318. Decisions and directions.

318. Decisions and directions. At the conclusion of the hearing of an appeal the chairman[1] may give or announce the decision of the tribunal[2]. Where he does so at the conclusion of the hearing of a mitigation appeal[3] or a reasonable excuse appeal[4], he may ask the parties present at the hearing whether they require the decision to be recorded in a written document[5], and, if none of the parties present so requires, the appeal will be treated for the purposes of the following provisions as if it had been an application[6]. Subject to those exceptions, the decision of the tribunal must be recorded in a written document containing the findings of fact by the tribunal and its reasons for the decision, and that document must be signed by the chairman[7].

If, however, a party to the appeal so requests by notice in writing served at the appropriate tribunal centre[8] within one year of the date on which the decision is released in accordance with these provisions, the outcome of the appeal, together with any award and direction as to costs[9], or for the payment or repayment of any sum of money with or without interest, given or made by the tribunal during or at the conclusion of the hearing of the appeal must be recorded in a written direction which must be signed by a chairman or the registrar[10].

At the conclusion of the hearing of an application, whether or not the chairman gives or announces the decision of the tribunal, the outcome of the application, together with any award or direction given or made by the tribunal during or at the conclusion of the hearing, must be recorded in a written direction which must be signed by a chairman or the registrar[11]. If, however, a party to the application so requests by notice in writing served at the appropriate tribunal centre within 14 days of the date on which the direction is released in accordance with these provisions, the decision of the tribunal on the application must be recorded in a written document containing the findings of fact by the tribunal and its reasons for the decision which must be signed by a chairman[12].

A proper officer[13] must send a copy of the tribunal's decision and of any direction in an appeal to each party to the appeal and a duplicate of the direction and of any decision in an application to each party to the application[14]. Every decision in an appeal must bear the date when the copies of it are released to be sent to the parties and any direction, and all copies of any direction, recording the outcome of the appeal must state that date[15]. Every direction on an application must bear the date when the copies of it are released to be sent to the parties, and any decision on that application which is given or made[16] and all copies of it must state that date[17].

A chairman or the registrar may correct any clerical mistake or other error in expressing his manifest intention in a decision or direction signed by him, but if a chairman or the registrar corrects any such document after a copy of it has been sent to a party, a proper officer must as soon as practicable thereafter send a copy of the corrected document, or of the page or pages which have been corrected, to that party[18].

Where a copy of a decision or a direction dismissing an appeal or application or containing a decision or direction given or made in the absence of a party is sent to a party or other person entitled to apply[19] to have the appeal or application reinstated or the decision or direction set aside, the copy must contain or be accompanied by a note to that effect[20].

1 As to the chairman see para 295 ante.
2 Value Added Tax Tribunals Rules 1986, SI 1986/590, r 30(1) (amended by SI 1991/186).
3 For the meaning of 'mitigation appeal' see para 301 note 7 ante.
4 For the meaning of 'reasonable excuse appeal' see para 300 note 6 ante.
5 Ie in accordance with the Value Added Tax Tribunals Rules 1986 r 30(1) (as amended: see note 1 supra).
6 Ibid r 30(8) (added by SI 1991/186; substituted by SI 1994/2617).
7 Ibid r 30(1) proviso (as amended: see note 2 supra).
8 As to the appropriate tribunal centre see para 293 ante.
9 For the meaning of 'costs' see para 298 note 5 ante; and as to awards and directions as to costs see para 317 ante.
10 Value Added Tax Tribunals Rules 1986 r 30(1) (as amended: see note 2 supra). The registrar has power to sign a direction recording the outcome of an appeal and any award or direction given or made by the tribunal during or at the conclusion of the hearing of an appeal as provided by r 30(1) (as so amended): r 33(2). As to the registrar see para 295 ante.
11 Ibid r 30(2).
12 Ibid r 30(2) proviso (amended by SI 1991/186).
13 For the meaning of 'proper officer' see para 300 note 12 ante.
14 Value Added Tax Tribunals Rules 1986 r 30(3).
15 Ibid r 30(4).
16 Ie under ibid r 30(2) proviso (as amended): see the text and note 12 supra.
17 Ibid r 30(5).
18 Ibid r 30(6).
19 Ie under ibid r 26 (as amended): see para 314 ante.
20 Ibid r 30(7). The tribunal has no power to reinstate an appeal which has been settled by agreement under the Value Added Tax Act 1994 s 85: *Abbey Life Japan Trust v Customs and Excise Comrs* (1993) VAT Decision 11205, [1993] STI 1406.

319. Enforcement of tribunal decisions etc. Where on an appeal it is found that the whole or part of any amount paid or deposited[1] is not due, or that the whole or part of any value added tax credit[2] due to the appellant has not been paid, so much of that amount as is found not to be due or not to have been paid is to be repaid (or, as the case may be, paid) with interest at such rate as the VAT and duties tribunal may determine; and where the appeal has been entertained notwithstanding that an amount determined by the Commissioners of Customs and Excise to be payable as VAT has not been paid or deposited and it is found on the appeal that that amount is due, the tribunal may, if it thinks fit, direct that the amount is to be paid with interest at such rate as may be specified in the direction[3].

Where it is found on an appeal against an assessment[4] that the amount specified in the assessment is less than it ought to have been, and the tribunal gives a direction specifying the correct amount, the assessment has effect as an assessment of the amount specified in the direction, and that amount is deemed to have been notified to the appellant[5].

If the decision of a VAT and duties tribunal[6] in England and Wales on an appeal under the Value Added Tax Act 1994[7] is registered by the Commissioners of Customs and Excise in accordance with rules of court, payment of (1) any amount which, as a result of the decision, is, or is recoverable as, VAT due from any person; and (2) any costs[8] awarded to the commissioners by the decision, may be enforced by the High Court as if that amount or, as the case may be, the amount of those costs, were an amount due to the commissioners in pursuance of a judgment or order of the High Court[9].

The tribunal has no power to direct the commissioners to pay sums which they admit to be due to a taxpayer[10].

A tribunal has power to direct a stay of proceedings on its decision on such terms as it may consider just, but should only make such a direction in exceptional circumstances and should not do so merely because one party has appealed against that decision to the High Court[11].

1   Ie in accordance with the Value Added Tax Act 1994 s 84(3)(a): see para 297 ante.
2   As to VAT credits see para 202 ante.
3   Value Added Tax Act 1994 s 84(8). As to the entertainment of an appeal without payment or deposit of tax see para 297 ante.
4   Ie an appeal against a decision with respect to any of the matters mentioned in ibid s 83(p) (as amended): see para 296 ante.
5   Ibid s 84(5).
6   Including an order (however described) made by a tribunal for giving effect to a decision: ibid s 87(5).
7   Ie under ibid s 83 (as amended): see para 296 ante.
8   For the meaning of 'costs' see para 298 note 5 ante.
9   Value Added Tax Act 1994 s 87(1). As to the enforcement of a decision in Northern Ireland see s 87(3), (4). As to the application of s 87 to appeals in relation to landfill tax see the Finance Act 1996 s 56(8); and CUSTOMS AND EXCISE; PUBLIC HEALTH.
10 *Royal College of Obstetricians and Gynaecologists v Customs and Excise Comrs* (1996) VAT Decision 14558 (unreported).
11 *Thorn Electrical Industries Ltd v Customs and Excise Comrs, British Relay Ltd v Customs and Excise Comrs, Visionhire Ltd v Customs and Excise Comrs* [1974] VATTR 62.

(3) FURTHER APPEALS AND REFERENCES

320. Appeal from a VAT and duties tribunal to the High Court. If any party to proceedings before a VAT and duties tribunal is dissatisfied in point of law with a decision of the tribunal he may, according as rules of court provide[1], either appeal from the tribunal to the High Court or require the tribunal to state and sign a case for the opinion of the High Court[2]. The High Court may give any judgment or decision and make any order which ought to have been given or made by the tribunal and may make such further or other order as the case may require, or may remit the matter with the opinion of the court for rehearing and determination by the tribunal[3].

1   See RSC Ord 55, Ord 94 rr 8(1), 9(1); and ADMINISTRATIVE LAW. As to the procedure on such an appeal see PRACTICE AND PROCEDURE. Further points of law not taken below may be argued: see Ord 55 r 6; and *Pittalis v Grant* [1989] QB 605, [1989] 2 All ER 622, CA (an appeal from a county court, distinguished in *Lenihan v Customs and Excise Comrs* [1992] STC 478); and see *Customs and Excise Comrs v Ferrero UK Ltd* [1996] STC 866. However, the general rule of an appellate court is not to allow a new point to be raised except on a point of law which no evidence could alter: see *A-G v Aramayo* [1925] 1 KB 86, 9 TC 445, CA (affd sub nom *Aramayo Francke Mines Ltd v Eccott (Inspector of Taxes)* [1925] AC 634, HL); *Moriarty (Inspector of Taxes) v Evans Medical Supplies Ltd* [1957] 3 All ER 718, 37 TC 540, HL; *Girobank plc v Clarke (Inspector of Taxes)* [1996] STC 540.
2   Tribunals and Inquiries Act 1992 ss 1, 11(1), Sch 1 para 44 (amended by the Finance Act 1994 s 7(6)). The appellant has 56 days from the date on which the decision of the tribunal is released in which to file his appeal; see RSC Ord 91 r 6(3). In *Customs and Excise Comrs v Facthaven Incentive Marketing Ltd* [1992] STC 839n, the commissioners sought leave to extend the time for appealing some four months after time; their application was dismissed because the trader was in liquidation and the disputed sums were unlikely in any event to be recovered; the court was unwilling to allow the appeal procedure to be used simply to establish a principle. Generally speaking, the High Court is hostile to attempts to bring appeals against decisions or directions of VAT and duties tribunals by way of judicial review, indicating that the proper approach is by way of an appeal in accordance with the Tribunals and Inquiries Act 1992: see *R v VAT Tribunal, ex p Cohen* [1984] STC 361n; *R v London VAT Tribunal and Customs and Excise Comrs, ex p*

Theodorou [1989] STC 292; *R v Customs and Excise Comrs and London VAT Tribunal, ex p Menzies* [1990] STC 263, CA; *R v VAT Tribunal, ex p Jenny Braden Holidays Ltd* (10 March 1994, unreported, QB); *R v London VAT and Duties Tribunal, ex p Conoco Ltd* [1995] STC 468; cf *R v VAT Tribunal, ex p Happer* [1982] 1 WLR 1261, [1982] STC 700; *R v Customs and Excise Comrs, ex p Sims (t/a Supersonic Snacks)* [1988] STC 210; *R v VAT Tribunal, ex p Minster Associates* [1988] STC 386. Note, however, that in none of these latter cases does the issue of the correct form of appeal seem to have been raised.

3   RSC Ord 55 r 7(5); and see *Customs and Excise Comrs v Ferrero UK Ltd* [1996] STC 866 at 869 per Potts J.

321. Appeal from the tribunal to the Court of Appeal. The Lord Chancellor may by order provide that in such classes of appeal as may be prescribed by the order, and subject to the consent of the parties and to such other conditions as may be so prescribed, an appeal from a VAT and duties tribunal is to lie to the Court of Appeal[1].

If any party to proceedings before a VAT and duties tribunal is dissatisfied in point of law with a decision of the tribunal he may appeal from the tribunal direct to the Court of Appeal if (1) the parties consent[2]; (2) the tribunal indorses its decision with a certificate that the decision involves a point of law relating wholly or mainly to the construction of an enactment, or of a statutory instrument, or of any of the Community Treaties or of any Community instruments, which has been fully argued before it and fully considered by it[3]; and (3) the leave of a single judge of the Court of Appeal has been[4] obtained[5]. A party who wishes to appeal in this way must apply to the tribunal[6] for a certificate under head (2) above at the conclusion of the hearing or within 21 days after the date when the decision of the tribunal was released[7].

1   Value Added Tax Act 1994 s 86(1). Such an order may provide that the Tribunals and Inquiries Act 1992 s 11 (which provides for appeals to the High Court from a tribunal) is to have effect, in relation to any appeal to which the order applies, with such modifications as may be specified in the order: Value Added Tax Act 1994 s 86(2). At the date at which this volume states the law, no such order had been made, but, by virtue of the Interpretation Act 1978 s 17(2)(b), the Value Added Tax Tribunals Appeals Order 1986, SI 1986/2288 (as amended) partly has effect as if so made: see notes 2–7 infra. As to appeals to the High Court see para 320 ante.

2   Value Added Tax Tribunals Appeals Order 1986, SI 1986/2288, art 2(a).

3   Ibid art 2(b).

4   Ie pursuant to the Supreme Court Act 1981 s 54(6); and see RSC Ord 59 r 22; and PRACTICE AND PROCEDURE.

5   Value Added Tax Tribunals Appeals Order 1986 art 2(2)(c).

6   Ie in accordance with the Value Added Tax Tribunals Rules 1986, SI 1986/590, r 11 (as amended): see para 307 ante.

7   Ibid r 30A (added by SI 1986/2290; amended by SI 1994/2617). As to the release of the tribunal's decision see r 30 (as amended); and para 318 ante.

322–400. References to the European Court of Justice. Where a question as to the validity and interpretation of Community law[1] is raised before any court or tribunal[2] of a member state, that court or tribunal may, if it considers that a decision on the question is necessary to enable it to give judgment, request the European Court of Justice to give a ruling on it[3]. Where any such question is raised in a case pending before a court or tribunal of a member state against whose decisions there is no judicial remedy under national law, that court or tribunal must bring the matter before the Court of Justice[4].

These provisions are of particular significance in view of the European legislative basis of value added tax[5].

1   Ie a question as to (1) the interpretation of the EC Treaty; (2) the validity and interpretation of acts of the institutions of the Community and of the proposed European Central Bank; and (3) the interpretation of the statutes of bodies established by an act of the EC Council, where those statutes so provide: see the EC Treaty art 177(a)–(c) (substituted by the Maastricht Treaty Title II art G(56)).

2   As to VAT and duties tribunals see para 293 et seq ante.
3   See the EC Treaty art 177 (as substituted: see note 1 supra). For guidelines as to when such a reference
     should be made see *HP Bulmer Ltd v J Bollinger SA* [1974] Ch 401 at 422–425, [1974] 2 All ER 1226 at
     1234–1236, CA, per Lord Denning MR; and see further *Henn and Darby v DPP* [1981] AC 850 at 906,
     sub nom *R v Henn, R v Darby* [1980] 2 All ER 166 at 197–198, HL, per Lord Diplock; Case 283/81
     CILFIT Srl and Lanificio di Gavardo SpA v Ministry of Health [1982] ECR 3415, [1983] 1 CMLR 472, ECJ;
     Customs and Excise Comrs v ApS Samex [1983] 1 All ER 1042, [1983] 3 CMLR 194; *Lord Bethell v Société
     Anonyme Belge d'Exploitation de la Navigation Aerienne (SABENA)* [1983] 3 CMLR 1; *R v Pharmaceutical
     Society of Great Britain, ex p Association of Pharmaceutical Importers* [1987] 3 CMLR 951, CA; *R v International
     Stock Exchange of the United Kingdom and the Republic of Ireland, ex p Else* [1993] QB 534, [1993] 1 All ER
     420, CA; *BLP Group plc v Customs and Excise Comrs, Swallowfield plc v Customs and Excise Comrs* [1994]
     STC 41, CA; *Conoco Ltd v Customs and Excise Comrs* [1995] STC 1022; and para 3 note 8 ante.
4   See the EC Treaty art 177 (as substituted: see note 1 supra).
5   See para 2 ante. The determination of the correct VAT treatment of discount vouchers is exceptionally
     difficult and has occasioned a number of references to the European Court of Justice: see paras 86, 199
     note 7 ante.

VALUERS AND SURVEYORS

1. INTRODUCTION

401. Meaning of 'valuer', 'appraiser' and 'surveyor'. The terms 'valuer' and 'appraiser' have similar meanings[1]. An appraiser is a person appointed and sworn to estimate the value of property[2], while a valuer is a person who estimates or assesses values; that is, in the present context, a person who estimates or assesses the worth or value of, or who fixes a price for, property[3]. However, while definitions of 'valuer' and 'valuation' commonly place the main emphasis on value or worth in a material sense[4], an 'appraiser' may also be a person who estimates the amount, quality or excellence of property[5].

The term 'surveyor' usually describes a person whose business it is to inspect and examine land, houses or other property and to calculate and report upon its actual or prospective value or productiveness for certain purposes[6], although surveyors also perform other functions[7].

1 The term 'appraiser' was the more commonly used in statutes passed before the beginning of the twentieth century: see the Distress for Rent Act 1689 s 1 (as amended); the Appraisers Licences Act 1806 (repealed); and the Law of Distress Amendment Act 1888 s 5.
2 Compact Oxford English Dictionary (2nd Edn, 1991) p 65. An appraiser is not necessarily required to be sworn before he acts, notwithstanding that statute may require him to be sworn in particular cases: see eg the Distress for Rent Act 1689 s 1 (amended by the Parish Constables Act 1872 s 13).
3 Compact Oxford English Dictionary (2nd Edn, 1991) p 2212.
4 'The term 'valuer' (with a capital 'V' at any rate) is used nowadays to denote a member of a recognised profession comprised of persons possessed of skill and experience in assessing the market price of property, particularly real property': *Sudbrook Trading Estate Ltd v Eggleton* [1983] 1 AC 444 at 477, [1982] 3 All ER 1 at 5, HL, per Lord Diplock. The Compact Oxford English Dictionary (2nd Edn, 1991) p 2212 defines 'valuation', inter alia, as an 'estimated value: worth or price as determined by deliberate determination' and as 'value or worth, especially of a material nature'. As to valuations for statutory purposes see paras 404–408 post; and as to contractual valuations see paras 409–411 post.
5 See the text and note 2 supra. As to appraisement as opposed to valuation see *Pappa v Rose* (1872) LR 7 CP 525, Ex Ch (broker required to decide whether raisins delivered were of 'fair average quality' as specified in contract of sale). As to the appraisement of arrested ships see ADMIRALTY vol 1(1) (Reissue) paras 397, 443, 531.
6 Compact Oxford English Dictionary (2nd Edn, 1991) p 1974. 'Survey' is defined as meaning, inter alia, 'to examine the condition of a property on behalf of its prospective buyer': p 1974.
7 See the Compact Oxford English Dictionary (2nd Edn, 1991) p 1974. 'Surveyor' primarily means 'one who has the oversight or superintendence of a person or thing; an overseer, supervisor' but can also mean, inter alia, 'one who designs, and superintends the construction of, a building; a practical architect' or 'one whose business it is to survey land etc; one who makes surveys, or practices surveying': p 1974.

An idea of the range of functions carried out by surveyors may be gained from the seven divisions or specialisations of the Royal Institution of Chartered Surveyors (see para 402 post). These are: general practice (which includes valuation of land and buildings); quantity surveying; building surveying; land agency and agriculture; planning and development; land and hydrographic surveying; and minerals surveying. As to the functions of quantity surveyors see BUILDING CONTRACTS, ARCHITECTS, ENGINEERS and SURVEYORS vol 4(2) (Reissue) paras 499–500, 554–556. As to the appointment and functions of surveyors of ships see SHIPPING.

402. Professional bodies. There is no general statutory regulation of, or restriction upon qualification and practice as, a valuer or surveyor[1], but most valuers and surveyors are members of one or more of a number of professional organisations, in particular the Royal Institution of Chartered Surveyors[2] and the Incorporated Society of Valuers and Auctioneers[3]. Members of the Central Association of Agricultural Valuers[4] and of the Institute of Revenues, Rating and Valuation are frequently concerned with valuations of land for specific purposes[5].

1   Certain inspections or valuations must be carried out by members of either the Royal Institution of Chartered Surveyors (see note 2 infra) or the Incorporated Society of Valuers and Auctioneers (see note 3 infra), or persons satisfying other prescribed requirements: see eg the Charities Act 1993 s 36; and CHARITIES vol 5(2) (Reissue) para 329; the Leasehold Reform, Housing and Urban Development Act 1993 ss 13(6), 78; and LANDLORD AND TENANT vols 27(1), (2) (Reissue) paras 1424, 323 respectively. Certain instruments relating to farm business tenancies may be prepared by a member of either of those bodies or of the Central Association of Agricultural Valuers: see the Solicitors Act 1974 s 22 (amended by, inter alia, the Agricultural Tenancies Act 1995 s 35); and SOLICITORS vol 44(1) (Reissue) para 528.

2   The Royal Institution of Chartered Surveyors (RICS), which was founded in 1868 and incorporated by Royal Charter in 1881, adopted its present title in 1947. It was established to advance the profession of surveyor and the interest of its members. The address of the institution is 12 Great George Street, London SW1P 3AD. The society publishes the *RICS Appraisal and Valuation Manual* (1st Edn, 1995; revised June 1996) which has replaced, with effect from 1 January 1996, the former *Statements of Asset Valuation Practice and Guidance Notes* (known as 'the Red Book') and *Manual of Valuation Guidance Notes* (known as 'the White Book'). The manual lays down mandatory standards of professional practice which are also applicable to members of the other professional bodies mentioned in this paragraph.

3   The Incorporated Society of Valuers and Auctioneers (ISVA) was formed in 1968 by a merger between the Incorporated Society of Auctioneers and Landed Property Agents (founded in 1924) and the Valuers Institution (founded in 1928). Its objects include the protection and advancement of the professional standards of its members, and the promotion in the public interest of the professional competence of valuers, auctioneers, estate agents and surveyors. The address of the Society is 3 Cadogan Gate, London SW1X 0AS. Members of the ISVA must comply with the standards of professional practice set out in the *RICS Appraisal and Valuation Manual* (1st Edn, 1995): see p 2.

4   See note 1 supra.

5   The Institute of Revenues, Rating and Valuation (IRRV), like the RICS and the ISVA, requires its members to comply with the *RICS Appraisal and Valuation Manual* (1st Edn, 1995): see p 2.

403. The Valuation Office. The Valuation Office is an Executive Agency of the Inland Revenue, and was created in 1991 through the merger of the valuation office organisations for England and Wales and for Scotland[1]. The office exists to provide a range of estate surveying and valuation services to government departments and to other clients in the public sector.

Most of the work of the office consists in helping local authorities to administer the rating and council tax systems[2], and it undertakes valuations of land and buildings on behalf of the Inland Revenue[3]. The office also assesses and recovers contributions in lieu of rates[4], and provides valuation assistance to government departments and other public bodies which need it in order to exercise their statutory functions[5].

An officer of the Valuation Office has power to enter upon land in order to survey it or estimate its value in connection with claims for the compulsory acquisition of that land or any other land or with claims for compensation arising under various statutes[6].

1   These organisations had been established in 1910 as part of the Inland Revenue to undertake valuation work in connection with land value duties which were imposed by the Finance Act 1910 and have since been abolished. A 'next steps' review of the Valuation Office which was carried out in 1995 concluded that it should continue as an executive agency within the Inland Revenue; a second review is likely in the year 2000. As to executive agencies and the 'next steps' initative see CONSTUTIONAL LAW AND HUMAN RIGHTS vol 8(2) (Reissue) para 551.

2   Ie by compiling and keeping up to date lists of assessments on which liability to council tax or non-domestic rates is based: see para 405 post.

3   Such valuations are carried out mainly, though not exclusively, for the purposes of capital gains tax and inheritance tax: see generally CAPITAL GAINS TAXATION; INHERITANCE TAXATION.

4   Such contributions are made by government departments (which are exempt from rating) in respect of properties which they occupy, and are intended to correspond with the amount of rates which would be payable if there were no exemption. The task of assessing and collecting appropriate contributions is carried out by the Crown Property Unit of the Valuation Office.

5   Some of the work within this category is specifically allocated by statute to the Valuation Office: eg valuations of a dwelling house for the purpose of the tenant's 'right to buy' (see the Housing Act 1985 Pt V (ss 118–188) (as amended); and LANDLORD AND TENANT vol 27(2) (Reissue) para 1628 et seq, especially para 1661); and valuations of property occupied by secure tenants for the purpose of the

purchase of the freehold by an approved person from a public sector landlord (see the Housing Act 1988 Pt IV (ss 93–114) (as amended); and LANDLORD AND TENANT vol 27(2) (Reissue) para 1192 et seq, especially paras 1205–1211). In respect of work which is not so allocated (including valuations in respect of acquisition and compensation claims arising under road schemes, asset valuations for various public bodies, and valuations in connection with housing benefit claims), the Valuation Office tenders in competition with other organisations.

6   See generally TOWN AND COUNTRY PLANNING vol 46 (Reissue) paras 33–35.

2. STATUTORY AND CONTRACTUAL VALUATIONS

(1) VALUATION FOR STATUTORY PURPOSES

404. Compulsory acquisition. If a person served with a notice to treat[1] by an authority possessing powers of compulsory acquisition[2] does not agree with the authority as to the amount of compensation to be paid for his interest in the land or for any damage sustained by him by reason of the execution of the works, the question of the disputed compensation must be referred to the Lands Tribunal[3]. If a person claims compensation in respect of any land which has been taken for, or injuriously affected by, the execution of works, any dispute as to the compensation must likewise be referred to the Lands Tribunal[4].

If a person whose land is to be compulsorily acquired is prevented from treating by absence from the United Kingdom[5], or if he cannot be found after diligent inquiry has been made, the amount of compensation must normally be determined by an able practical surveyor selected from the members of the Lands Tribunal and must be paid into court[6]. If land is to be compulsorily acquired from a person under any disability or incapacity, compensation must not be less than an amount determined by the valuation of two able practical surveyors, one appointed by each party, except where compensation has been determined under compulsory powers[7].

Where an authority acquiring land under compulsory powers wishes to enter and use the land before the purchase price or compensation has been fixed, it may do so by paying into court the value of the land as determined by an able practical surveyor[8]. Such a surveyor must examine the premises properly to form a fair judgment of their value[9] but, if he does so in good faith and in pursuance of his duty, the fact that the sum is inadequate or that he valued without sufficient knowledge of the relevant facts does not entitle the owner to an injunction restraining the purchaser from taking possession of the land pending a proper valuation[10].

1   As to notice to treat see COMPULSORY ACQUISITION vol 8(1) (Reissue) para 100 et seq.
2   As to such authorities see generally COMPULSORY ACQUISITION vol 8(1) (Reissue) paras 3–5.
3   See COMPULSORY ACQUISITION vol 8(1) (Reissue) para 200. As to the Lands Tribunal generally, and as to the assessment of compensation, see COMPULSORY ACQUISITION vol 8(1) (Reissue) paras 202 et seq, 233 et seq.
4   See COMPULSORY ACQUISITION vol 8(1) (Reissue) paras 200 (reference of dispute), 353 et seq (assessment of compensation).
5   'United Kingdom' means Great Britain and Northern Ireland: Interpretation Act 1978 s 5, Sch 1. 'Great Britain' means England, Scotland and Wales: Union with Scotland Act 1706, preamble art I; Interpretation Act 1978 s 22(1), Sch 2 para 5(a). Neither the Channel Islands nor the Isle of Man are within the United Kingdom. See further CONSTITUTIONAL LAW AND HUMAN RIGHTS vol 8(2) (Reissue) para 3.
6   See COMPULSORY ACQUISITION vol 8(1) (Reissue) para 200.
7   See COMPULSORY ACQUISITION vol 8(1) (Reissue) para 97.
8   See COMPULSORY ACQUISITION vol 8 (1) (Reissue) para 123 et seq.

9   *Cotter v Metropolitan Rly Co* as reported in (1864) 10 LT 777, where it was held that it was insufficient for the valuer to conclude that all houses in a street were of the same value because their exteriors were identical.

10 *River Roden Co Ltd v Barking Town UDC* (1902) 18 TLR 542; affd 18 TLR 608, CA. Cf *Cotter v Metropolitan Rly Co* as reported in (1864) 10 LT 777, where an injunction was granted because the surveyor had never entered the buildings which he purported to have valued.

405. Rating and council tax. Valuation officers appointed by the Inland Revenue[1] are responsible for compiling and maintaining valuation lists of non-domestic property for the purposes of rating[2] and for dealing with proposals for alterations to such lists[3]. Listing officers appointed by the Inland Revenue[4] have similar responsibilities in relation to the valuation of dwellings for the purposes of council tax[5].

1   The Commissioners of Inland Revenue must appoint a valuation officer for each billing authority and the central valuation officer: Local Government Finance Act 1988 s 61(1) (amended by the Local Government Finance Act 1992 ss 117(1), 118(1), Sch 13 para 69). The remuneration of, and any expenses incurred by, valuation officers in carrying out their functions in relation to non-domestic rating (including the remuneration and expenses of persons, whether or not in the service of the Crown, exmployed to assist them) must be paid out of money provided by Parliament: Local Government Finance Act 1988 s 61(2).

2   See ibid s 41 (amended by the Local Government and Housing Act 1989 s 139, Sch 5 paras 1, 19, 79(3); and by the Local Government Finance Act 1992 ss 117(1), 118(1), Sch 13 para 59); and RATING vol 39 (Supp) paras 1–8, 14B, 134, 143A.

3   See the Local Government Finance Act 1988 s 55(2); the Non-Domestic Rating (Alteration of Lists and Appeals) Regulations 1993, SI 1993/291 (amended by SI 1994/1809; SI 1995/363; SI 1995/609; and SI 1995/623); and RATING vol 39 (Supp) paras 144–149.

4   The Commissioners of Inland Revenue must appoint a listing officer for each billing authority: Local Government Finance Act 1992 s 20(1). The remuneration of, and any expenses incurred by, listing officers in carrying out their functions in relation to council tax (including the remuneration and expenses of persons, whether or not in the service of the Crown, to assist them) must be paid out of money provided by Parliament: see s 20(2), (3).

5   See ibid Pt I Ch II (ss 20–29); the Council Tax (Alteration of Lists and Appeals) Regulations 1993, SI 1993/290 (amended by SI 1994/1746; SI 1995/363; and modified by virtue of SI 1995/624); and RATING VOL 39 (Supp) para 14A.

406. Companies and other corporate bodies. A public company must not allot shares as fully or partly paid up for a consideration other than cash unless the consideration has been independently valued and a report as to its value made to the company within the preceding six months[1]. Before a building society advances money on the security of land, a written report on the value of the land and any factors likely materially to affect its value must be obtained from a person who is competent to value and who is not disqualified from making such a report[2]. Periodic actuarial valuations are required as a means of investigating the financial condition of insurance companies[3], industrial assurance companies[4] and registered societies which are not friendly societies[5].

1   See the Companies Act 1985 s 103(1); and COMPANIES vol 7(1) (1996 Reissue) para 468 et seq.

2   See the Building Societies Act 1986 s 13(1); and BUILDING SOCIETIES vol 4(2) (Reissue) para 858.

3   See the Insurance Companies Act 1982 s 18(1); and INSURANCE vol 25 (Reissue) para 823.

4   See INDUSTRIAL ASSURANCE vol 24 (Reissue) para 293 et seq.

5   See the Friendly Societies Act 1974 s 41 (repealed in relation to friendly societies by the Friendly Societies Act 1992 s 95); and FRIENDLY SOCIETIES vol 19(1) (Reissue) paras 233–235.

407. Distress and execution. If, following a distress for rent, an appraisement of the chattels distrained is necessary before sale[1], the appraisers must be reasonably competent, although not necessarily professional appraisers[2], and they must be disinterested persons[3]. Two appraisers are necessary unless the tenant consents to one acting[4]. An appraisement may also be required following a distress for certain taxes[5] and other duties[6].

For the purpose of selling or valuing goods seized in execution under court process, the district judge in the county court may appoint such brokers and appraisers as appear to him to be necessary[7]. The judge in the county court may appoint in writing any court bailiff to act as a broker or appraiser for these purposes[8].

1   As to when an appraisement is necessary see DISTRESS vol 13 para 317.
2   *Roden v Eyton* (1848) 6 CB 427.
3   See the cases cited in DISTRESS vol 13 para 317 note 5.
4   See *Allen v Flicker* (1839) 10 Ad & El 640; and DISTRESS vol 13 para 317.
5   See eg the Taxes Management Act 1970 s 61(5) (amended by the Finance Act 1989 ss 152(1),(5), 187(1), Sch 17 Pt VII); the Value Added Tax Act 1994 s 58, Sch 11 para 5(4); VALUE ADDED TAX para 256 ante; and DISTRESS vol 13 para 434 et seq; INCOME TAXATION vol 23 (Reissue) para 1724.
6   See eg the Merchant Shipping Act 1995 s 208 (distress for general light dues); and SHIPPING.
7   See the County Courts Act 1984 s 95(1) (amended by virtue of the Courts and Legal Services Act 1990 s 74); and COUNTY COURTS vol 10 para 490.
8   See the County Courts Act 1984 s 96(1); and COUNTY COURTS vol 10 para 490. A bailiff so appointed may, without other licence in that behalf, perform all the duties which brokers or appraisers appointed under s 95 (as amended) may perform: s 96(2).

408. Executors and trustees. If a personal representative proposes to exercise his statutory power of appropriation, he must fix the value of the respective parts of the assets and liabilities of the deceased, and for that purpose must employ a duly qualified valuer when necessary[1]. An appropriation of a mortgage at par without such an ascertainment of the value of the mortgage as a security may be a breach of trust if the mortgaged property is in fact in bad condition[2].

Trustees may employ duly qualified agents to ascertain the value of trust property, and any valuation so made in good faith is binding on all persons interested under the trust[3]. A trustee lending money on the security of any property on which he can properly lend is not chargeable with breach of trust by reason only of the proportion of the loan to the value of the property, if the loan was made under advice contained in a report as to the property's value made by a person reasonably believed to be an able practical surveyor or valuer and employed independently of any owner of the property, and if the loan does not exceed two-thirds of the value stated in the report[4].

1   See the Administration of Estates Act 1925 s 41(3); and EXECUTORS vol 17 para 1363.
2   See *Re Brookes, Brookes v Taylor* [1914] 1 Ch 558, where the mortgaged premises were derelict and practically worthless and the trustee had appropriated the mortgage at par without either inspecting the mortgaged premises or making any inquiry as to their actual value as a security.
3   See the Trustee Act 1925 s 22(3); and TRUSTS vol 48 (Reissue) para 914.
4   See ibid s 8(1); and TRUSTS vol 48 (Reissue) para 881. As a general rule, a trustee who proposes to lend on the security of any property should obtain a report as to its value from an independent surveyor or valuer before making the loan, and should not advance more than two-thirds of the value as stated in the report: *Shaw v Cates* [1909] 1 Ch 389. If a valuer properly appointed makes his valuation on a wrong principle, the trustee, having employed a skilled agent, is not liable (*Re Pearson, Oxley v Scarth* (1884) 51 LT 692); but a mortgagee exercising a power to sell the mortgaged property will be liable to the mortgagor if the negligence of his duly appointed agent leads to a sale at an undervalue (*Cuckmere Brick Co Ltd v Mutual Finance Ltd* [1971] Ch 949 at 973, [1971] 2 All ER 633 at 649, CA, per Cross LJ).

(2) VALUATION FOR CONTRACTUAL PURPOSES

409. Effect of contractual provision for valuation. An agreement under which property is to be transferred at a 'fair price' or at a 'reasonable valuation' is not void for uncertainty, and the court may decree specific performance of such an agreement and order such inquiries as may be necessary to ascertain the fair price[1].

Where parties have agreed to transfer property at a price to be fixed by a valuer or valuers appointed by the parties and the valuation machinery breaks down[2], a fundamental question of construction is whether the prescribed mode of ascertaining the price is an essential term of the contract or whether the mode of ascertainment, though indicated in the contract, is subsidiary and non-essential[3]. It the valuation machinery which has broken down is held to be subsidiary and not an essential term of the contract (or testamentary option)[4], the court may intervene and substitute other machinery to ascertain the price in order that the agreement may be carried out[5]. Even where, on a true construction, the use of the valuation machinery which has broken down is to be regarded as an essential term of the agreement[6], the court may intervene and provide substitute machinery if the agreement has already been partly performed[7], or if the valuation provision relates to a subsidiary part of a wider contract which is itself valid and enforceable[8].

1   *Gaskarth v Lord Lowther* (1805) 12 Ves 107; *Milnes v Gery* (1807) 14 Ves 400 at 407 per Grant MR; *Morgan v Milman* (1853) 3 De GM & G 24 at 34 per Lord Cranworth LC; *Talbot v Talbot* [1968] Ch 1, [1967] 2 All ER 920, CA; and see SPECIFIC PERFORMANCE vol 44(1) (Reissue) paras 851–853.

2   Such a breakdown may result from the act of one of the parties (eg where he refuses to appoint a valuer or denies an appointed valuer access to the property), from failure of the duly appointed valuers to agree on the price or on the identity of a required umpire, or from causes beyond the control of the parties or their valuers, such as the death of an umpire or his failure to complete the valuation by the prescribed date. But such distinctions, being tangential to the question of whether a prescription as to the mode of valuation is an essential term, are rarely to be relied on: see *Sudbrook Trading Estate Ltd v Eggleton* [1983] 1 AC 444 at 484, [1982] 3 All ER 1 at 10, HL, per Lord Fraser of Tullybelton.

3   Under modern conditions, contractual terms providing for a particular method of assessing price will normally be regarded as subsidiary to the main purpose of the agreement, which is for sale and purchase of the property at a fair or reasonable value: *Sudbrook Trading Estate Ltd v Eggleton* [1983] 1 AC 444 at 484, [1982] 3 All ER 1 at 10, HL, per Lord Fraser of Tullybelton.

4   'A testamentary option is something which potentially can become a contract on its exercise at any time by the person holding the option ... because the person getting a property under a testamentary option gets it by exercising that option and entering into a contract in that behalf with the executors': *Talbot v Talbot* [1968] Ch 1 at 9–10, [1967] 2 All ER 920 at 921–922, CA, per Scarman LJ (testator provided for two of his children to have option of purchasing two farms at a 'reasonable valuation', but prescribed no valuation machinery and none was agreed by the beneficiaries).

5   *Sudbrook Trading Estate Ltd v Eggleton* [1983] 1 AC 444, [1982] 3 All ER 1, HL (lease gave the lessee an option to purchase the freehold at a price to be agreed by valuers appointed by the parties and the landlord refused to appoint a valuer); *Re Malpass* [1985] Ch 42, [1984] 2 All ER 313 (an option was given by will to purchase a farm at a value to be determined by the district valuer, but the district valuer declined to value the property). The alternative remedy of a mandatory injunction compelling the vendor to appoint a valuer has been held to be unsuitable because the only sanction for non-compliance would be imprisonment for contempt of court: see *Sudbrook Trading Estate Ltd v Eggleton* supra. However, the court probably may, in an appropriate case, order a party to do what is necessary to make the contractual machinery work, eg by appointing a valuer or seeking such an appointment from the designated professional body (*Royal Bank of Scotland plc v Jennings* [1995] 2 EGLR 87; disapproving *Harben Style Ltd v Rhodes Trust* [1995] 1 EGLR 118) or by allowing a duly appointed valuer to enter and carry out his valuation (*Morse v Merest* (1821) 6 Madd 26; *Smith v Peters* (1875) LR 20 Eq 511).

6   In most present-day cases a prescription as to the mode of valuation is unlikely to be construed as an essential term of the contract unless it seeks to harness special knowledge which is needed to determine the value of the property in question, such as an auditor's knowledge of a company whose shares are to be valued: see *Sudbrook Trading Estate Ltd v Eggleton* [1983] 1 AC 444 at 484, [1982] 3 All ER 1 at 10, HL, per Lord Fraser of Tullybelton.

7   *Sudbrook Trading Estate Ltd v Eggleton* [1983] 1 AC 444 at 484, [1982] 3 All ER 1 at 11, HL, per Lord Fraser of Tullybelton; *Gregory v Mighell* (1811) 18 Ves 328; *Dinham v Bradford* (1869) 5 Ch App 519; *Beer v Bowden* [1981] 1 All ER 1070, [1981] 1 WLR 522n, CA.

8   *Sudbrook Trading Estate Ltd v Eggleton* [1983] 1 AC 444 at 485, [1982] 3 All ER 1 at 11, HL, per Lord Fraser of Tullybelton; *Dinham v Bradford* (1869) 5 Ch App 519; *Richardson v Smith* (1870) 5 Ch App 648; *Smith v Peters* (1875) LR 20 Eq 511.

410. Valuer as arbitrator or independent expert. Where a valuer[1] is appointed to settle a dispute between two parties, or to decide a matter on which they have opposing interests[2], the valuer may or may not act as an arbitrator in reaching his decision[3]. Whether or not he is so acting affects his potential liability for negligence[4] and also determines the extent to which his decision is binding upon the parties[5]. As from the date on which the Arbitration Act 1996 comes into force[6], an arbitrator (unlike a ordinary valuer)[7] is not to be liable for anything done or omitted in the discharge or purported discharge of his functions as arbitrator, unless the act or omission is shown to have been in bad faith[8], and will thus not be liable for negligence[9]. The extent to which this statutory provision changes the existing law is doubtful, since many authorities have decided that an arbitrator already enjoys such immunity[10]. An arbitrator's decision is, however, subject to certain rights of appeal[11]. Neither a 'mutual valuer'[12] nor a 'quasi-arbitrator' is likely to enjoy an arbitrator's immunity[13], and if the primary process intended is one of valuation rather than arbitration, calling the valuer an 'umpire' will not give him immunity[14].

The question whether a given valuer has been appointed as an arbitrator[15] is determined not only by the way he is described in the agreement which appoints him[16], but by the agreement construed as a whole[17]. Thus the parties' original intent may be inferred from the appointing clause interpreted in the light of other clauses in the document[18]. Where the agreement is ambiguous or allows for different options, subsequent events may indicate which option was taken up, and, therefore, whether in the event the valuer appointed was an arbitrator[19].

A valuer who is not appointed as an arbitrator but who nevertheless claims immunity from liability for negligence must show that, in all the circumstances of the case, his functions are judicial in character[20]. That is not simply a matter of acting fairly as between the parties[21], or being required to determine a question as between opposed interests[22], and has been said to depend on the existence of a formulated dispute between two parties[23]. Where the valuer's functions are not judicial in character, a valuer by whose decision two parties agree to be bound owes a duty of care to both parties and, if negligent in reaching his decision, will be liable to the party who is disadvantaged by his negligent valuation[24].

1 For the meaning of 'valuer' see para 401 ante.

2 Eg the rental value of premises for the purpose of a rent review. See also *Campbell v Edwards* [1976] 1 All ER 785, [1976] 1 WLR 403, CA (surveyor appointed to determine the surrender value of a lease); and *Arenson v Casson Beckman Rutley & Co* [1977] AC 405, [1975] 3 All ER 901, HL (auditors instructed to value shares in a private company pursuant to an agreement for their sale at the price so determined).

3 See *Sutcliffe v Thackrah* [1974] AC 727 at 745, [1974] 1 All ER 859 at 870, HL, per Lord Morris of Borth-y-Gest and at 735 and at 862 per Lord Reid. 'The position of a valuer is very different from an arbitrator. If a valuer is negligent in making a valuation he may be sued by the party – vendor or purchaser – who is injured by his wrong valuation. But an arbitrator is different. In my opinion he cannot be sued by either party to the dispute': *Campbell v Edwards* [1976] 1 All ER 785 at 788, [1976] 1 WLR 403 at 408, CA, per Lord Denning MR. As to the meaning of 'arbitrator' see ARBITRATION vol 2 (Reissue) para 673 et seq. It has been argued that such an arbitrator, being appointed by one or more of the parties to the eventual dispute, does not exercise 'judicial functions' analogous to those of a judge or statutory arbitrator, whose appointment is in no way governed by parties to individual disputes which eventually come before him: see *Arenson v Casson Beckman Rutley & Co* [1977] AC 405 at 431–432, [1975] 3 All ER 901 at 918–919, HL, per Lord Kilbrandon (uncle gave shares to nephew (his employee); shares to be sold back to uncle if employment terminated at value determined by company's auditors; employment terminated and valuation and sale took place; subsequent valuation when company 'went public' disclosed apparent negligence in original (low) valuation; nephew sued uncle; held that auditor was liable if he made valuation negligently unless he could show that a formulated dispute between at least two parties had been submitted to him to resolve in such a manner that he was called upon to exercise a judicial function and the parties had agreed to accept his decision).

4 See the text and notes 6–10 infra.

5 See para 411 post.

6   Ie on a date to be appointed by order made by the Secretary of State: see the Arbitration Act 1996 s 109(1), (2). At the date at which this volume states the law, no such order had been made.

7   As to a valuer's negligence see paras 415, 419 et seq post.

8   See the Arbitration Act 1996 s 29(1) (not yet in force: see note 6 supra). This immunity is to apply to an employee or agent of an arbitrator as it applies to the arbitrator himself: see s 29(2) (not yet in force). The provisions of Pt I (ss 1–84) will apply only where the arbitration agreement is in writing, and any other agreement between the parties as to any matter is to be effective for the purposes of Pt I only if in writing: s 5(1) (not yet in force).

9   It has been doubted whether it is right to allow immunity to attach to arbitrators as a class when that class includes arbitrators whose role is primarily to use their professional expertise as a mutual valuer might do (see *Arenson v Casson Beckman Rutley & Co* [1977] AC 405 at 442, [1975] 3 All ER 901 at 927, HL, per Lord Fraser); and it has been questioned whether a valuer appointed as arbitrator under the Arbitration Acts who has a purely investigatory role, and who performs no function even remotely resembling the judicial function save that he finally decides a dispute or difference that has arisen between the parties, should enjoy a judicial immunity which so-called 'quasi-arbitrators' do not, albeit that the question has yet to be determined conclusively (see *Arenson v Casson Beckman Rutley & Co* supra at 440 and at 925 per Lord Salmon).

10   See eg *Turner v Goulden* (1873) LR 9 CP 57, and this view was supported obiter by a majority of the House of Lords in *Sutcliffe v Thackrah* [1974] AC 727, [1974] 1 All ER 859, HL. See also *Campbell v Edwards* [1976] 1 All ER 785 at 788, [1976] 1 WLR 403 at 408, CA, per Lord Denning MR; but see note 9 supra. The Supply of Goods and Services Act 1982 s 13, which implies a duty of reasonable care and skill into a contract for the supply of a service, does not apply to services rendered by an arbitrator: Supply of Services (Exclusion of Implied Terms) Order 1985, SI 1985/1, art 2.

11   As to the remission or setting aside of an arbitrator's award see ARBITRATION vol 2 (Reissue) para 690 et seq.

12   See *Arenson v Casson Beckman Rutley & Co* [1977] AC 405 at 441, [1975] 3 All ER 901 at 927, HL, per Lord Fraser.

13   '"Quasi-arbitrator" and "quasi-judicial functions" have been invoked but never defined. They cannot mean more than in much the same position as an arbitrator or judge': *Sutcliffe v Thackrah* [1974] AC 727 at 758, [1974] 1 All ER 859 at 882, HL, per Lord Salmon. 'There may be circumstances in which what is in effect an arbitration is not one that is within the provisions of the Arbitration Act. The expression quasi-arbitrator should only be used in that connection': *Sutcliffe v Thackrah* supra at 752–753 and at 876–877 per Lord Morris of Borth-y-Gest. See also, as to several possible meanings of 'quasi-arbitrator', *Arenson v Casson Beckman Rutley & Co* [1977] AC 405 at 422–423, [1975] 3 All ER 901 at 910–911, HL, per Lord Simon of Glaisdale. The expression appears subsequently to have acquired no settled meaning.

14   '...the mere word "umpire" is quite neutral, and does not cast any real light on the matter in dispute': *Safeway Food Stores Ltd v Banderway Ltd* [1983] 2 EGLR 116 at 118 per Goulding J.

15   The parties may arrange for the agent of one party to become an arbitrator as between them should a certain event occur, but this must be a definite arrangement: see *Sutcliffe v Thackrah* [1974] AC 727 at 745, [1974] 1 All ER 859 at 870, HL, obiter, per Lord Morris of Borth-y-Gest.

16   'You cannot make a valuer an arbitrator by calling him so or vice versa': *Taylor v Yielding* (1912) 56 Sol Jo 253 per Neville J.

17   *Taylor v Yielding* (1912) 56 Sol Jo 253 (agreement that value of shares would be determined by two valuers appointed by the parties or by an umpire appointed by the valuers was an agreement to arbitrate as to value and not a mere agreement to have a valuation); and see *Sutcliffe v Thackrah* [1974] AC 727, [1974] 1 All ER 859, HL; *Arenson v Casson Beckman Rutley & Co* [1977] AC 405, [1975] 3 All ER 901, HL.

18   See *Langham House Developments Ltd v Brompton Securities Ltd* [1980] 2 EGLR 117 (clause in lease concerning rent drafted so as to suggest intended valuation by nominated surveyor compared with adjacent clause concerning insurance which 'reeks of arbitration'; different intent inferred from obvious contrast); *Safeway Food Stores Ltd v Banderway Ltd* [1983] 2 EGLR 116 (meanings of contrasting clauses illuminated by comparison).

19   *North Eastern Co-operative Society Ltd v Newcastle-upon-Tyne City Council* [1987] 1 EGLR 142 (contrasting clauses in lease; 'independent surveyor or arbitrator' prescribed and instructed was not, in the event, an arbitrator, owing to circumstances of his appointment).

20   See *Sutcliffe v Thackrah* [1974] AC 727 at 738, [1974] 1 All ER 859 at 865, HL, per Lord Reid.

21   See *Sutcliffe v Thackrah* [1974] AC 727, [1974] 1 All ER 859, HL, especially at 745 and 870 per Lord Morris of Borth-y-Gest; *Arenson v Casson Beckman Rutley & Co* [1977] AC 405, [1975] 3 All ER 901, HL. See also *Palacath Ltd v Flanagan* [1985] 2 All ER 161, [1985] 1 EGLR 86 (surveyor determining rent under a rent review clause not acting as an arbitrator since he had been appointed as an expert and was entitled to rely on his own judgment and opinion and to reach a decision unfettered by the submissions of the parties).

22   *Arenson v Casson Beckman Rutley & Co* [1977] AC 405, [1975] 3 All ER 901, HL.

23 'The main difference between [a mutual valuer and an arbitrator] is that the latter, like the judge, has to decide a dispute that has already arisen, and he usually has rival contentions before him, while the mutual valuer is called in before a dispute has arisen, in order to avoid it': *Arenson v Casson Beckman Rutley & Co* [1977] AC 405 at 441, [1975] 3 All ER 901 at 927, HL, per Lord Fraser. 'In my view the essential prerequisite for [a valuer] to claim immunity is that, by the time the matter is submitted to him for decision, there should be a formulated dispute between at least two parties which his decision is required to resolve': *Arenson v Casson Beckman Rutley & Co* supra at 424 and 912 per Lord Simon of Glaisdale.

24 *Zubaida v Hargreaves* [1995] 1 EGLR 127 at 128, CA, per Hoffmann LJ (rent review; held on facts that RICS surveyor had not been negligent). See also *Campbell v Edwards* [1976] 1 All ER 785 at 788, [1976] 1 WLR 403 at 408, CA, per Lord Denning MR (rent review; agreed surveyor appointed to determine value of lease; report was 'non-speaking' report and had been prepared honestly and in good faith; held that landlord was bound by valuation); *Belvedere Motors Ltd v King* [1981] 2 EGLR 131 (independent surveyor acting as expert and not as arbitrator; action for alleged negligence nevertheless failed as duty of care performed); *Wallshire Ltd v Aarons* [1989] 1 EGLR 147 (independent surveyor acting as expert and not as arbitrator; no obligation on him in the circumstances to make inquiries of his own in relation to comparable properties other than those presented to him).

411. Judicial review of valuation. Where a valuer[1] acts as an arbitrator in making a valuation[2], an appeal from his valuation lies to the court[3] on a point of law[4].

Where a valuer acts as an independent expert in making a valuation[5], the extent to which his valuation is subject to review by the court depends upon the construction of the agreement under which he is appointed to act[6]. If, on its true construction, that agreement expressly or by implication confers upon the valuer the exclusive remit to determine a question, and provides for the parties to be bound by his determination, then the valuation is not open to review by the court if the valuer acted honestly and in good faith[7].

If the parties have agreed that the expert's decision should be final and conclusive, it remains so even where it is a 'speaking' valuation whose reasoning contains errors of law[8]. A 'non-speaking' valuation clearly cannot err in its reasoning if it contains no reasoning at all, and the relevant question is not whether defective reasoning can be found in a report that happens to be unusually voluble, but whether it is possible to say from all the evidence which is properly before the court what the valuer has done and why he has done it[9]. A valuation made by an independent expert may, however, be set aside where the agreement so provides[10], where the appointment of the expert is invalid[11], where there is fraud or collusion between the valuer and one of the parties[12], or where the expert has gone outside his remit by answering a different question from that which was remitted to him[13] or has failed to comply with any conditions imposed by the agreement[14].

1 For the meaning of 'valuer' see para 401 ante.

2 See para 410 ante.

3 Ie to the High Court under the Arbitration Act 1979 (see s 1; and ARBITRATION vol 2 (Reissue) para 706 et seq) or, as from a day to be appointed under the Arbitration Act 1996 s 109, to the High Court or a county court under the 1996 Act (see ss 69, 105 (not yet in force)).

4 See the Arbitration Act 1979 s 1(2); the Arbitration Act 1996 s 69(7) (not yet in force).

5 See para 410 ante.

6 The court has jurisdiction in advance of a valuation by an independent expert to determine a question as to the limits of the expert's remit or the conditions governing his valuation, but it will normally decline to do so where the question is merely hypothetical: *British Shipbuilders v VSEL Consortium plc* [1996] TLR 79 per Lightman J. See also *Norwich Union Life Insurance Society v P & O Property Holdings Ltd* [1993] 1 EGLR 164, CA; *Mercury Communications Ltd v Director General of Telecommunications* [1996] 1 All ER 575, [1996] 1 WLR 48, HL (contract between BT and Mercury provides for issue between them to be determined by Director General of Telecommunications; held that his actions could lead to disputes falling outside the realm of public law, and whether his determination may be challenged depends, inter alia, on terms of his remit in the contract).

7 *Campbell v Edwards* [1976] 1 All ER 785, [1976] 1 WLR 403, CA; *Baber v Kenwood Manufacturing Co* [1978] 1 Lloyd's Rep 175, CA; *Belchier v Reynolds* (1754) 3 Keny 87 at 91 per Strange MR.

8   *Jones v Sherwood Computer Services plc* [1992] 2 All ER 170, [1992] 1 WLR 277, CA (disapproving *Burgess v Purchase & Sons (Farms) Ltd* [1983] Ch 216, [1983] 2 All ER 4). 'If [the expert] has answered the right question in the wrong way, his decision will be binding. If he has answered the wrong question, his decision will be a nullity': *Nikko Hotels (UK) Ltd v MEPC plc* [1991] 2 EGLR 103 at 108 per Knox J. Earlier cases, which suggested that valuation could be impugned on the ground of mistake, now appear supportable only on the ground that the agreements under consideration did not confer exclusive jurisdiction on the valuers: see *Collier v Mason* (1858) 25 Beav 200 at 204 per Romilly MR; *Johnston v Chestergate Hat Manufacturing Co Ltd* [1915] 2 Ch 338; *Dean v Prince* [1954] Ch 409, [1954] 1 All ER 749, CA.

9   *Jones v Sherwood Computer Services plc* [1992] 2 All ER 170 at 177, [1992] 1 WLR 277 at 284, CA, per Dillon LJ.

10   *British Shipbuilders v VSEL Consortium plc* [1996] TLR 79.

11   Eg because it is made out of time: see *Darlington Borough Council v Waring & Gillow (Holdings) Ltd* [1988] 2 EGLR 159.

12   *Campbell v Edwards* [1976] 1 All ER 785 at 788, [1976] 1 WLR 403 at 407, CA, per Lord Denning MR.

13   Ie such as would occur if an independent expert appointed to value shares in a company valued the wrong number of shares or valued shares in the wrong company: *Jones v Sherwood Computer Services plc* [1992] 2 All ER 170 at 179, [1992] 1 WLR 277 at 287, CA, per Dillon LJ.

14   *Nikko Hotels (UK) Ltd v MEPC plc* [1991] 2 EGLR 103 at 108 per Knox J; *Pontsarn Investments Ltd v Kansallis-Osake-Pankki* [1992] 1 EGLR 148; *British Shipbuilders v VSEL Consortium plc* [1996] TLR 79.

3. VALUER AND CLIENT

412. Basis of relationship. The engagement or instruction of a valuer is normally a matter of contract between the valuer and the client[1]. Where the client engages a firm of valuers, the contract is made with the firm and not with the individual who may carry out the valuation[2], and the firm is responsible to the client for the due performance of its contractual obligations by its employees and probably for the performance of a person other than an employee to whom it delegates the task of valuation[3].

The relationship which is created between the valuer and the person who appoints him is not merely one of agent and principal, but of professional person and client[4], and documents which a valuer brings into existence in order to carry out the service which he is engaged to perform are therefore the property of the valuer and not of the client[5].

1   Such a contract is one for the supply of a service and is governed by the Supply of Goods and Services Act 1982 Pt II (ss 12–16). The contract need not be made in any particular form, but chartered surveyors and incorporated valuers are required by their rules of professional conduct to provide written confirmation of instructions: *RICS Appraisal and Valuation Manual* (1st Edn, 1995) Practice Statement 2.

2   The individual valuer may nevertheless be liable to the client in tort for negligence: see *Smith v Eric S Bush, Harris v Wyre Forest District Council* [1990] 1 AC 831 at 866, [1989] 2 All ER 514 at 537, HL, per Lord Griffiths; and see paras 415–416 post.

3   *Luxmoore-May v Messenger May Baverstock (a firm)* [1990] 1 All ER 1067, [1990] 1 WLR 1009, CA (auctioneers).

4   *Leicestershire County Council v Michael Faraday & Partners Ltd* [1941] 2 KB 205, [1941] 2 All ER 483, CA.

5   *Leicestershire County Council v Michael Faraday & Partners Ltd* [1941] 2 KB 205, [1941] 2 All ER 483, CA; *London School Board v Northcroft* (1889) 2 Hudson's BC (4th Edn) 147.

413. Remuneration of valuer. A valuer is entitled to charge the client for his professional services, in accordance with the contract under which he is engaged[1]. It was formerly common practice for valuers to charge by reference to a scale of fees published by the Royal Institution of Chartered Surveyors[2], but that institution has now abolished scale fees.

Where an authority acquires land compulsorily, or by agreement when the parties know that it could be acquired compulsorily[3], the surveyors' fees incurred by the former owner are calculated according to Ryde's Scale, which applies in its revised form as from 1 July 1996[4]. Expenditure such as the fees paid by the owner to a valuer or surveyor properly incurred in preparing the owner's claim for compensation and negotiating its settlement should be included in any compensation awarded against the acquiring authority[5]. Whether fees have been properly incurred for this purpose is a question of fact[6].

If the valuer and client do not expressly agree about how much the valuer is to be paid, or as to how that amount is to be determined, a term will be implied into the contract between them that the client will pay a reasonable charge[7]. What is a reasonable charge is a question of fact[8].

A valuer is not entitled to be paid for services which have been performed negligently, and are therefore useless to the client[9]. Payment made for such services may be reclaimed[10].

1   Where services are rendered in connection with litigation, an agreement under which fees are payable on a contingency basis is unenforceable on grounds of public policy, although this does not apply to fees payable to a surveyor for securing a reduction in the rateable value of a client's property, not least because a local valuation court is not a court of law: *Pickering v Sogex Services (UK) Ltd* [1982] 1 EGLR 42. Nor does this stricture apply to fees for obtaining planning permission, as, even if such an arrangement is in breach of the rules of the profession, such a breach is not necessarily contrary to law: *Picton Jones & Co v Arcadia Developments Ltd* [1989] 1 EGLR 43. This remains the case even if such services may require the surveyor to appear before a valuation tribunal or a public planning inquiry. The Courts and Legal Services Act 1990 s 58, which allows a solicitor to enter into a conditional fee agreement in certain limited circumstances, has not changed public policy because of its narrow scope: see *Aratra Potato Co Ltd v Taylor Joynson Garrett (a firm)* [1995] 4 All ER 695 at 707 per Garland J. See further SOLICITORS vol 44(1) (Reissue) paras 188–189.
2   As to the Royal Institution of Chartered Surveyors see para 402 ante.
3   As to valuations and surveys carried out in connection with the compulsory acquisition of land see para 404 ante.
4   Ryde's Scale was formerly published by the Royal Institution of Chartered Surveyors, and is now published by the Valuation Office. As to the Valuation Office see para 403 ante.
5   See *LCC v Tobin* [1959] 1 All ER 649, [1959] 1 WLR 354, CA; *Johns v Edmonton Corpn* (1958) 9 P & CR 366 at 370, Lands Tribunal.
6   *Beckett v Birmingham Corpn* (1956) 6 P & C R 352 at 354. As to the measure of compensation on compulsory acquisition generally see COMPULSORY ACQUISITION vol 8(1) (Reissue) paras 233 et seq, 295 et seq (compensation for disturbance). Surveyors' fees may be included in the compensation recoverable by a landowner from an acquiring authority on the withdrawal of a notice to treat: *Duke of Grafton v Secretary of State for Air* (1956) 6 P & CR 374, CA; *Merediths Ltd v LCC* (1957) 9 P & CR 128, Lands Tribunal. As to the recovery of such compensation generally see COMPULSORY ACQUISITION vol 8(1) (Reissue) para 120.
7   See the Supply of Goods and Services Act 1982 s 15(1); *Miller v Beal* (1879) 27 WR 403.
8   Supply of Goods and Services Act 1982 s 15(2). Where a surveyor appears as an expert witness on a client's behalf, a reasonable fee will normally be based upon the surveyor's time and trouble and not upon the value of the property concerned: *Upsdell v Stewart* (1793) Peake 255; *Debenham v King's College, Cambridge* (1884) 1 TLR 170; *Drew v Josolyne* (1888) 4 TLR 717; *Faraday v Tamworth Union* (1916) 86 LJ Ch 436. However, a surveyor may be entitled by a binding custom to a fee assessed on some other basis: *Wilkie v Scottish Aviation Ltd* 1956 SC 198 at 205 obiter per Lord Clyde.
9   *Moneypenny v Hartland* (1824) 1 C & P 352; *Whitty v Lord Dillon* (1860) 2 F & F 67; *Sincock v Bangs (Reading)* (1952) 160 Estates Gazette 134; *Hill v Debenham Tewson and Chinnocks* (1958) 171 EG 835; *Buckland v Watts* (1968) 208 Estates Gazette 969. Where the services, albeit negligently performed, nevertheless retain some value to the client, he cannot refuse to pay for them: see *Hutchinson v Harris* (1978) 10 BLR 19, CA.
10   *Chong v Scott Collins & Co* (1954) 164 Estates Gazette 662.

414. Valuer's liability to client. A valuer will be liable to his client for breach of contract if he fails to carry out the service which he has expressly undertaken to perform[1], or if he breaches an express term of the contract under which he is engaged[2]. In addition, a valuer other than one acting as an arbitrator[3] will be liable for breach of an implied term of his contract[4] if he does not carry out the agreed service with reasonable care and skill[5], or if he does not carry out that service within a reasonable time[6].

A valuer who fails to exhibit the requisite standard of professional skill and care may alternatively be liable to the client in negligence[7].

1   See *Moss v Heckingbottom* (1958) 172 Estates Gazette 207.

2   See generally CONTRACT.

3   As to acting as an arbitrator see para 410 ante.

4   A person who holds himself out as a valuer impliedly represents that he has the necessary skill, knowledge and competence so to act: *Jenkins v Betham* (1855) 15 CB 168; *Harmer v Cornelius* (1858) 5 CBNS 236.

5   Supply of Goods and Services Act 1982 s 13. As to what amounts to reasonable care and skill see paras 418–420 post.

6   Supply of Goods and Services Act 1982 s 14(1). This applies only where the contract does not itself fix either the time for performance or the means by which that time is to be determined: see s 14(1). What is a reasonable time is a question of fact: s 14(2).

7   *Henderson v Merrett Syndicates Ltd* [1995] 2 AC 145, [1994] 3 All ER 506, HL; *Arenson v Casson Beckman Rutley & Co* [1977] AC 405 at 430, [1975] 3 All ER 901 at 917, HL, per Lord Kilbrandon and at 434 and 920 per Lord Salmon; *Smith v Eric S Bush, Harris v Wyre Forest District Council* [1990] 1 AC 831 at 870, [1989] 2 All ER 514 at 540, HL, per Lord Jauncey; *South Australia Asset Management Corpn v York Montague Ltd* [1996] 3 All ER 365 at 369, [1996] 27 EG 125 at 126, HL, per Lord Hoffmann. This may benefit the client in terms of the limitation period applicable to his claim: see para 426 post.

4. VALUER AND THIRD PARTIES

415. Basis of valuer's liability to third parties. Where a valuer[1] knows[2] that his report will be shown to a third party who will act in reliance on it, he owes a duty of care in tort to that party[3], provided that there is a sufficiently proximate relationship between them[4]. A duty of care may also be owed by a valuer who ought to know, though he does not actually know, that a third party is likely to rely on his report[5], even if the third party is not actually shown the report[6], and at least where there is a high degree of probability of such reliance[7]. A valuer does not, however, owe a duty of care to a third party of whose likely reliance he neither knows nor ought to know[8], and a surveyor employed in relation to one property is not liable to the eventual purchaser of an adjacent property[9].

1   Ie other than one acting as an arbitrator: see para 410 ante. For the meaning of 'valuer' see para 401 ante.

2   Such knowledge may be actual or inferential: *Caparo Industries plc v Dickman* [1990] 2 AC 605 at 638, [1990] 1 All ER 568 at 589, HL, per Lord Oliver.

3   It is not necessary for the valuer to know the identity of the particular third party, so long as he is aware of him as a member of an identifiable class, such as prospective purchaser (*Shankie-Williams v Heavey* [1986] 2 EGLR 139, CA) or prospective mortgagee (*Corisand Investments Ltd v Druce & Co* [1978] 2 EGLR 86; *Assured Advances Ltd v Ashbee & Co* [1994] EGCS 169).

4   *Cann v Willson* (1888) 39 ChD 39, overruled by *Le Lievre v Gould* [1893] 1 QB 491, CA, but specifically approved in *Hedley Byrne & Co Ltd v Heller & Partners Ltd* [1964] AC 465, [1963] 2 All ER 575, HL; *Smith v Eric S Bush, Harris v Wyre Forest District Ccouncil* [1990] 1 AC 831 at 865, [1989] 2 All ER 514 at 536, HL, per Lord Griffiths. A sufficiently proximate relationship has been held to exist between a prospective purchaser and a surveyor engaged by the vendor (*Shankie-Williams v Heavey* [1986] 2 EGLR 139, CA; *Bourne v McEvoy Timber Preservation* [1976] 1 EGLR 100) and between a mortgagee, and the mortgagee's insurers, and a valuer engaged by a prospective borrower (*Banque Bruxelles Lambert SA v Eagle Star Insurance Co Ltd* [1995] 2 All ER 769 per Phillips J; revsd in part on other grounds [1995] QB 375, [1995] 2 All ER 769, CA). However, it has been held that a surveyor advising a mortgagee on the exercise of his power of sale, following repossession of the mortgaged property, owes no duty to the mortgagor to ensure that the property is not sold at an undervalue: *Huish v Ellis* [1995] NPC 3. Nor does a marine surveyor employed by a vessel's classification society owe a duty of care to the owner of cargo carried on the vessel: *Marc Rich & Co v Bishop Rock Marine Co Ltd* [1996] AC 211, [1995] 3 All ER 307, HL.

5   See *Bourne v McEvoy Timber Preservation* [1976] 1 EGLR 100; *UCB Bank plc v Dundas & Wilson* 1989 SLT 243; *Wolverhampton Ltd v Herring Son & Daw plc* [1996] EGCS 137 (letter from seller who had instructed the valuer agreed that the plaintiff, the prospective buyer, could rely on valuation as if the plaintiff were a person on whose instruction it had been made).

6   *Smith v Eric S Bush, Harris v Wyre Forest District Council* [1990] 1 AC 831, [1989] 2 All ER 514, HL;
     Beaumont v Humberts (a firm) [1990] 2 EGLR 166, CA.

7   'The necessary proximity arises from the surveyor's knowledge that the overwhelming probability is that
     the purchaser will rely on his valuation – the evidence was that the surveyors knew that approximately
     90% of purchasers did so – and the fact that the surveyor only obtains the work because the purchaser is
     willing to pay his fee ... I would certainly wish to stress that, in cases where the advice has not been given
     for the specific purpose of the recipient acting on it, it should only be in cases where the adviser knows
     that there is a high degree of probability that some other identifiable person will act on the advice that a
     duty of care should be imposed': *Smith v Eric S Bush, Harris v Wyre Forest District Council* [1990] 1 AC 831
     at 865, [1989] 2 All ER 514 at 536, HL, per Lord Griffiths.

8   *Le Lievre v Gould* [1893] 1 QB 491, CA, revsd on other grounds in *Hedley Byrne & Co Ltd v Heller &
     Partners Ltd* [1964] AC 465, [1963] 2 All ER 575, HL. See also *Beaumont v Humberts* [1990] 2 EGLR 166,
     CA.

9   *Shankie-Williams v Heavey* [1986] 2 EGLR 139 (adjacent flat).

416. Valuation for mortgage purposes. A valuer who reports on a property for a
prospective mortgagee, knowing that a prospective purchaser is likely to rely on his report
when deciding whether or not to buy the property, owes a duty of care to that purchaser[1].
The purchaser may rely on a valuer's report which is shown to him, and on a report
which is not shown to him where it is reasonable for him to assume from the offer of a
loan on mortgage that the property has been valued at no less than the amount of the
loan[2]. Where, however, the existing owner of a property wishes to raise money on the
security of a property (such as by a remortgage or further advance) a valuer who makes a
report to the prospective mortgagee cannot be liable to the owner for a negligent over-
valuation, since the owner does not suffer a loss merely by receiving the requested loan[3].

A mortgagee will be vicariously liable to the purchaser for the negligence of a valuer
who is the mortgagee's employee[4], but will not be so liable for the negligence of an
independent valuer whom the purchaser has engaged[5] unless the mortgagee is in breach
of the duty which he owes to the purchaser to take reasonable care to engage a reasonably
competent valuer[6], or he has adopted the valuer's report as his own[7].

1   *Smith v Eric S Bush, Harris v Wyre Forest District Council* [1990] 1 AC 831, [1989] 2 All ER 514, HL,
     approving *Yianni v Edwin Evans & Sons* [1982] QB 438, [1981] 3 All ER 592. A valuer has been held to
     be more likely to know of the purchaser's reliance where the property valued is comparatively cheap
     (*Smith v Eric S Bush, Harris v Wyre Forest District Council* supra at 872 and at 541 per Lord Jauncey of
     Tullichettle), but such reliance may be implied in relation to more expensive properties where the
     evidence and circumstances warrant (*Beaumont v Humberts* [1990] 2 EGLR 166, CA (reinstatement value
     of house bought for £110,000 in 1984)), or to the purchaser of a small shop (*Qureshi v Liassides* (22 April
     1994, unreported; revsd on another point 22 March 1996, unreported, CA)).

2   *Smith v Eric S Bush, Harris v Wyre Forest District Council* [1990] 1 AC 831, [1989] 2 All ER 514, HL; *Yianni
     v Edwin Evans & Sons* [1982] QB 438, [1981] 3 All ER 592. See also *Nash v Evens & Matta* [1988] 1 EGLR
     130 at 132 per Ewbank J (rusted wall-tie in late nineteenth century cavity-walled house only revealed by
     structural survey two years later; house, owing to age, appearance and absence of cracks had previously
     been imagined to have solid walls).

3   *Saddington v Colleys Professional Services* [1995] EGCS 109, CA.

4   *Smith v Eric S Bush, Harris v Wyre Forest District Council* [1990] 1 AC 831, [1989] 2 All ER 514, HL; *Beaton
     v Nationwide Building Society* [1991] 2 EGLR 145.

5   *Smith v Eric S Bush, Harris v Wyre Forest District Council* [1990] 1 AC 831 at 865, [1989] 2 All ER 514 at
     536, HL, per Lord Griffiths. See also *Halifax Building Society v Edell* [1992] Ch 436 at 454 per Morritt J.

6   *Smith v Eric S Bush, Harris v Wyre Forest District Council* [1990] 1 AC 831 at 865, [1989] 2 All ER 514 at
     536, HL, per Lord Griffiths. See also *Ward v McMaster* [1985] IR 29, Irish HC (careless valuation by valuer
     for the local authority which lent part of purchase price; house unsafe and recommended to be
     demolished).

7   See *Beresforde v Chesterfield Borough Council* [1989] 2 EGLR 149, CA.

5. EXTENT OF VALUER'S LIABILITY

(1) LIABILITY FOR FRAUDULENT VALUATION

417. Fraudulent valuation. A valuer who makes a valuation which is fraudulent, namely one which he knows to be false or which he makes recklessly without regard to whether it is true or false, with the intention that it should be acted upon, is liable to an action of deceit by any person who was intended to act upon that valuation and who acts upon it to his detriment[1]. A disclaimer attached to such a valuation will not be effective to exclude or restrict the valuer's liability for fraud[2]. Nor can the defence of contributory negligence be used in an action for deceit, even by one whose liability is purely vicarious and who is not personally guilty of fraud[3].

Special provisions apply in relation to the limitation period where an action against a valuer is based on fraud[4].

1   See *Derry v Peek* (1889) 14 App Cas 337, HL; and MISREPRESENTATION vol 31 para 1057 et seq. As to deceit generally see MISREPRESENTATION vol 31 para 1090 et seq.
2   See *S Pearson & Son Ltd v Dublin Corpn* [1907] AC 351, HL; and *Commercial Banking Co of Sydney Ltd v RH Brown & Co* [1972] 2 Lloyd's Rep 360 (Aust HC).
3   *Alliance & Leicester Building Society v Edgestop Ltd* [1994] 2 All ER 38, [1993] 1 WLR 1462.
4   See para 426 post.

(2) PROFESSIONAL STANDARDS

418. In general. The standard which a valuer or surveyor is required to achieve is that of the ordinary skilled person exercising the same skill as himself[1]. He is not liable for a mere error of judgment, unless the error was one that no reasonably well-informed and competent member of the profession could have made[2]. The required standard will normally be the same whether a claim is made in contract or tort[3], and whether it is made by a client or a third party[4].

Whether or not a valuer has exercised the required standard of skill and care is a question of fact[5] on which expert witnesses may be called to give evidence[6]. This question is to be answered in the light of knowledge which is current in the profession at the time of the valuation or survey, with care being taken to guard against hindsight[7]. A valuer will thus be adjudged negligent if he fails to take reasonable steps to keep his professional knowledge up to date[8]. However, failure to comply with guidance notes issued by the relevant professional bodies does not necessarily constitute negligence[9].

1   See *Bolam v Friern Hospital Management Committee* [1957] 2 All ER 118 at 121, [1957] 1 WLR 582 at 586 per McNair J. The standard will not be lower because a defendant has no professional qualifications (*Freeman v Marshall & Co* (1966) 200 Estates Gazette 777); nor because he lacks relevant experience (*Kenney v Hall, Pain & Foster* [1976] 2 EGLR 29; *Baxter v FW Gapp & Co Ltd* [1938] 4 All ER 457 at 459 per Goddard LJ; *Whalley v Roberts and Roberts* [1990] 1 EGLR 164).
2   *Saif Ali v Sydney Mitchell & Co* [1980] AC 198 at 220, [1978] 3 All ER 1033 at 1043, HL, per Lord Diplock; *Banque Bruxelles Lambert SA v Eagle Star Insurance Co Ltd* [1995] 2 All ER 769 at 821 per Phillips J (on appeal [1995] QB 375, [1995] 2 All ER 769, CA).
3   However, the contract under which the valuer is engaged may limit the service which is to be provided, and to which the standard of skill and care will therefore apply: see *Predeth v Castle Phillips Finance Co Ltd* [1986] 2 EGLR 144, CA (surveyor asked for a 'cash sale valuation' held to be under no duty to provide an open market valuation as well); *Sutcliffe v Sayer* [1987] 1 EGLR 155, CA (estate agent asked to advise potential purchaser on asking price held to be under no duty to warn that defects might render property

difficult to resell); *Tenenbaum v Garrod* [1988] 2 EGLR 178, CA. Cf *McIntyre v Herring Son & Daw* [1988] 1 EGLR 231. As to the possibility of excluding or restricting liability by contract see para 425 post.

4   The standard will not be lower merely because the valuer does not charge a fee for the service which he carries out (*Kenney v Hall, Pain & Foster* [1976] 2 EGLR 29 at 33 per Goff J) nor because he charges a standard fee, and therefore one which may be low for the work required in valuing some properties (*Roberts v J Hampson & Co* [1989] 2 All ER 504 at 510, [1990] 1 WLR 94 at 101 per Ian Kennedy J).

5   This issue will not as a general rule be suitable to be resolved on an application for summary judgment under RSC Ord 14: *European Partners In Capital (EPIC) Holdings BV v Goddard & Smith* [1992] 2 EGLR 155 at 157, CA, per Scott LJ.

6   As to the power of the court to appoint an expert under RSC Ord 40 see *Abbey National Mortgages plc v Key Surveyors Nationwide Ltd* [1996] 3 All ER 184, [1996] 33 EG 88, CA.

7   *Private Bank & Trust Co Ltd v S (UK) Ltd* [1993] 1 EGLR 144 at 146 per Rice J. See also *Hill v Debenham, Tewson and Chinnocks* (1958) 171 Estates Gazette 835.

8   See *Hooberman v Salter Rex* [1985] 1 EGLR 144; *Peach v Iain G Chalmers & Co* [1992] 2 EGLR 135, Ct of Sess; *Weedon v Hindwood, Clarke & Esplin* [1975] 1 EGLR 82; *Corisand Investments Ltd v Druce & Co* [1978] 2 EGLR 86.

9   *PK Finans International (UK) Ltd v Andrew Downs & Co Ltd* [1992] 1 EGLR 172 at 174 per Sir Michael Ogden QC. For members of the Royal Institution of Chartered Surveyors, the Incorporated Society of Valuers and Auctioneers and the Institute of Revenues, Rating and Valuation (see para 402 ante), the *RICS Appraisal and Valuation Manual* (1st Edn, 1995) containing both mandatory Practice Statements and non-mandatory Guidance Notes applies to all valuations carried out from 1 January 1996: see para 402 ante.

419. Valuer's standard of care and skill. A person who holds himself out or purports to act as a valuer represents himself as having the skill and knowledge which a reasonably competent member of his profession or calling would have[1], and it is his duty to take reasonable care to give a reliable and informed opinion on the open market value of the land in question at the date of valuation[2]. In the absence of special instructions it is not a valuer's duty to advise on future movements in property prices, whether nationally or locally; his concern is with current value only[3].

Valuation is not an exact science[4], but rather a matter of opinion on which competent valuers may reach different conclusions[5]. A valuer is accordingly not guilty of negligence merely because another valuer produces a different answer[6], nor because his valuation turns out to be wrong[7]. However, a valuation which falls outside a permissible margin of error[8] brings into question the valuer's competence and the care with which he carried out his task[9].

A valuer is not negligent merely because he adopts a method of valuation which is not the best[10], provided that it is one which is accepted by a responsible body of opinion among valuers[11]. A valuer will, however, be negligent if he gives an open market valuation without considering the implications of a recent sale of the property, unless he has been specifically instructed to disregard it[12].

1   *Jenkins v Betham* (1855) 15 CB 168; *Harmer v Cornelius* (1858) 5 CBNS 236. The knowledge which a competent valuer may be expected to possess includes an understanding of the general legal rules governing particular types of valuation (*Jenkins v Betham* (1855) 15 CB 168) and an awareness of the state of the property market in general, and, while he is not expected to foresee a general collapse in property prices, his valuation must not contain a substantial speculative element (*Corisand Investments Ltd v Druce & Co* [1978] 2 EGLR 86 at 92 per Gibson J; *Private Bank & Trust Co Ltd v S (UK) Ltd* [1993] 1 EGLR 144). A valuer is normally expected to be familiar with property values in the relevant locality: *Baxter v F W Gapp & Co Ltd* [1938] 4 All ER 457 at 459 per Goddard LJ; *Singer & Friedlander Ltd v John D Wood & Co* [1977] 2 EGLR 84 per Watkins J; cf *Abbey National Mortgages plc v Key Surveyors Nationwide Ltd* [1996] 3 All ER 184 at 190–191, CA, per Sir Thomas Bingham MR.

2   *Banque Bruxelles Lambert SA v Eagle Star Insurance Co Ltd* [1995] QB 375 at 403–404, [1995] 2 All ER 769 at 840, CA, per Sir Thomas Bingham MR.

3   *Banque Bruxelles Lambert SA v Eagle Star Insurance Co Ltd* [1995] QB 375 at 404, [1995] 2 All ER 769 at 840, CA, per Sir Thomas Bingham MR. However, where a belief among buyers and sellers as to future market movements has an effect on current prices, his valuation should reflect this: *Banque Bruxelles Lambert SA v Eagle Star Insurance Co Ltd* supra. In advising trustees as to property on the security of which

it is proposed to invest trust funds, a valuer must advise as to the amount which it is safe to advance on that property, as well as its actual value: *Shaw v Cates* [1909] 1 Ch 389 at 398; *Re Solomon, Nore v Meyer* [1912] 1 Ch 261 at 274.

4   *Zubaida v Hargreaves* [1995] 1 EGLR 127 at 128, CA, per Hoffmann LJ; *Craneheath Securities Ltd v York Montague Ltd* [1996] 07 EG 141, CA, per Balcombe LJ.

5   *Singer & Friedlander Ltd v John D Wood & Co* [1977] 2 EGLR 84 at 85 per Watkins J; *Banque Bruxelles Lambert SA v Eagle Star Insurance Co Ltd* [1995] 2 All ER 769 at 789 per Phillips J (on appeal [1995] QB 375, [1995] 2 All ER 769, CA).

6   *Zubaida v Hargreaves* [1995] 1 EGLR 127 at 128, CA, per Hoffmann LJ; *Campbell v Edwards* [1976] 1 All ER 785 at 789, [1976] 1 WLR 403 at 408, CA, per Geoffrey Lane LJ.

7   *Baxter v FW Gapp & Co Ltd* [1938] 4 All ER 457 at 459 per Goddard LJ.

8   This is normally 10% either side of a notional 'right' figure, but can be extended to 15% either way, or a little more, in exceptional circumstances: *Singer & Friedlander Ltd v John D Wood & Co* [1977] 2 EGLR 84 at 85 per Watkins J. See also *Banque Bruxelles Lambert SA v Eagle Star Insurance Co Ltd* [1995] 2 All ER 769 at 789 per Phillips J (20% 'bracket') (on appeal [1995] QB 375, [1995] 2 All ER 769); *Nykredit Mortgage Bank plc v Edward Erdman Group Ltd* [1996] 02 EG 110 at 111, CA, per Staughton LJ.

9   *Singer & Friedlander Ltd v John D Wood & Co* [1977] 2 EGLR 84 at 85 per Watkins J. Conversely, a plaintiff cannot recover merely because there have been errors at some stages of a valuation, unless the final valuation can also be shown to be wrong: *Craneheath Securities Ltd v York Montague Ltd* [1996] 07 EG 141 at 142, CA, per Balcombe LJ; *South Australia Asset Management Corpn v York Montague Ltd* [1996] 3 All ER 365 at 381, [1996] 27 EG 125 at 132, HL, per Lord Hoffmann.

10   *Love v Mack* (1905) 92 LT 345 at 349–350 per Kekewich J.

11   *Singer & Friedlander Ltd v John D Wood & Co* [1977] 2 EGLR 84 at 87–88 per Watkins J. As to valuation methods adopted for different types of property see *Singer & Friedlander Ltd v John D Wood & Co* supra (development sites); *Mount Banking Corpn Ltd v Brian Cooper & Co* [1992] 2 EGLR 142; *Nykredit Mortgage Bank plc v Edward Erdman Group Ltd* [1996] 02 EG 110, CA (residual valuations of development projects); *Corisand Investments Ltd v Druce & Co* [1978] 2 EGLR 86 (hotels); *Craneheath Securities Ltd v York Montague Ltd* [1994] 1 EGLR 159, CA (restaurants); *Beaumont v Humberts* [1990] 2 EGLR 166, CA (insurance); *McIntyre v Herring Son & Daw* [1988] 1 EGLR 231 (rating); and *Zubaida v Hargreaves* [1995] 1 EGLR 127, CA (rent reviews).

12   *Banque Bruxelles Lambert SA v Eagle Star Insurance Co Ltd* [1995] 2 All ER 769 at 789–791 per Phillips J (on appeal [1995] QB 375, [1995] 2 All ER 769, CA).

420. Surveyor's standard of care and skill.

A surveyor's duty is to survey the property to the standard of a reasonably competent surveyor exercising due skill, care and diligence and possessing the necessary knowledge and experience[1]. In the absence of contrary agreement, a surveyor is normally expected to inspect all parts of the property which are visible[2], but not to uncover or open up those parts which are not visible[3]. However, a surveyor whose inspection reveals grounds for suspecting the existence of defects must take reasonable steps to follow the trail of suspicion[4].

1   *Kerridge v James Abbott & Partners* [1992] 2 EGLR 162. The extent and depth of inspection which is expected will depend on the type of survey to be carried out, although a surveyor must show the same level of expertise even when carrying out a limited inspection: *Cross v David Martin & Mortimer* [1989] 1 EGLR 154 at 155 per Phillips J. As to the limited inspection which is required in carrying out a mortgage valuation see *Roberts v J Hampson & Co* [1989] 2 All ER 504, [1990] 1 WLR 94; *Lloyd v Butler* [1990] 2 EGLR 155 at 160 per Henry J.

2   See *Hill v Debenham, Tewson & Chinnocks* (1958) 171 Estates Gazette 835; *Stewart v HA Brechin & Co* 1959 SC 306, Ct of Sess.

3   *Roberts v J Hampson & Co* [1989] 2 All ER 504 at 510, [1990] 1 WLR 94 at 101 per Ian Kennedy J.

4   *Roberts v J Hampson & Co* [1989] 2 All ER 504, [1990] 1 WLR 94; *Lloyd v Butler* [1990] 2 EGLR 155; *Sneesby v Goldings* [1995] 2 EGLR 102, CA.

(3) DAMAGES

421. Damages for negligent valuation; in general.

In order to recover damages[1] in respect of a negligent valuation, a plaintiff must establish that he has suffered loss or damage which the valuer's negligence caused or to which it contributed[2]. In normal circumstances, proof of the necessary causal link will require evidence that the plaintiff acted in reliance on information provided by the valuer[3]. Where such reliance is established, the damages awarded for a negligent valuation are such as would fairly and reasonably be considered as resulting[4] from the failure of the valuer to report as he should have done, had he used due care[5]. In particular, the damages should not impose upon the valuer responsibility for losses which would have occurred even if the valuation had been correct[6].

Damages awarded in cases of negligent valuation will not extend to any part of the plaintiff's loss which the plaintiff ought reasonably to have avoided[7]. Damages may also be reduced where the plaintiff's loss is offset by benefit he has received[8].

Subject to rules of court, in proceedings (whenever instituted) before the High Court for the recovery of debt or damages there may be included in any sum for which judgment is given simple interest, at such rate as the court thinks fit or as rules of court may provide, on all or any part of the debt or damages in respect of which judgment is given, or payment is made before judgment, for all or any part of the period between the date when the cause of action arose and (1) in the case of any sum paid before judgment, the date of the payment; and (2) in the case of the sum for which judgment is given, the date of the judgment[9]. Where damages are awarded against a negligent valuer, the court will normally exercise its statutory discretion to order that the damages shall bear simple interest[10].

1 Other than nominal damages, which may be awarded in an action for breach of contract whether or not the breach has caused any loss: see further CONTRACT; DAMAGES.

2 *Thomas Miller & Co v Richard Saunders & Partners* [1989] 1 EGLR 267 at 272 per Rougier J (tenant's surveyor who negligently failed to put forward relevant evidence at a rent review arbitration was held not liable for his client's losses, since the court was satisfied that the evidence in question would not have altered the arbitrator's decision).

3 See *Rona v Pearce* (1953) 162 Estates Gazette 380; *Shankie-Williams v Heavey* [1986] 2 EGLR 139, CA (claims against surveyors failed for lack of such evidence). However, it is not necessary for the plaintiff to have relied exclusively upon information from the defendant, provided that it played a real and substantial part in inducing him to act as he did: *Kenney v Hall, Pain & Foster* [1976] 2 EGLR 29 at 35 per Goff J; *HIT Finance Ltd v Lewis & Tucker Ltd* [1993] 2 EGLR 231 at 234 per Wright J; *JEB Fasteners Ltd v Marks Bloom & Co* [1983] 1 All ER 583 at 589, CA, per Stephenson LJ. A purchaser who has agreed to pay more for property than the value placed on it by his surveyor may nevertheless be held to have relied upon the surveyor's report: *Oswald v Countrywide Surveyors Ltd* [1996] 37 EG 140, CA.

4 As to what losses may be said to have resulted from such failure see *Banque Bruxelles Lambert SA v Eagle Star Insurance Co Ltd* [1995] QB 375 at 405–431, [1995] 2 All ER 769 at 841–864, CA, per Sir Thomas Bingham MR; but cf *South Australia Asset Management Corpn v York Montague Ltd* [1996] 3 All ER 365 at 371–376, [1996] 27 EG 125 at 126–129, HL, per Lord Hoffmann; and see para 423 post.

5 *Philips v Ward* [1956] 1 All ER 874 at 878, [1956] 1 WLR 471 at 475, CA, per Morris LJ (the correct measure of damages is the difference between the value of the property as described in valuer's report and its value in its actual condition, even if the cost of repairs is greater than that difference). As to the kind of losses which a valuer might reasonably be expected to foresee, and which are therefore not too remote a consequence of his negligence, see *Morgan v Perry* (1973) 229 Estates Gazette 1737; *Banque Bruxelles Lambert SA v Eagle Star Insurance Co Ltd* [1995] QB 375 at 405, [1995] 2 All ER 769 at 840, CA, per Sir Thomas Bingham MR (but see note 4 supra); *Drinnan v CW Ingram & Sons* 1967 SLT 205; *Allen v Ellis & Co* [1990] 1 EGLR 170 (survey report failed to mention roof in poor condition; it leaked; owner investigated and fell through; valuer liable for plaintiff's injuries). As to the correct measure of damages for negligent advice on the value of property for insurance purposes see *Beaumont v Humberts* [1990] 2 EGLR 166, CA.

6 *South Australia Asset Management Corpn v York Montague Ltd* [1996] 3 All ER 365 at 371, [1996] 27 EG 125 at 127, HL, per Lord Hoffmann (a duty of care which imposed such responsibility would not be fair and reasonable and could not therefore be justified either as an implied term of a contract or as a tortious duty). As to earlier law see *Banque Bruxelles Lambert SA v Eagle Star Insurance Co Ltd* [1995] QB 375, [1995] 2 All ER 769, CA. The earlier distinction between 'no transaction' and 'successful transaction' cases was not based on any principle and should be abandoned: *South Australia Asset Management Corpn v York Montague Ltd* supra. However, a different result might be justified if the valuer were engaged, not merely to provide information, but to advise on the suitability of a proposed transaction, as he would then

be responsible not merely for all the foreseeable consequences of the information being wrong, but for all the foreseeable loss which is a consequence of that course of action having been taken: *South Australia Asset Management Corpn v York Montague Ltd* supra at 372–373 and at 127–128 per Lord Hoffman.

7   As to the doctrine of mitigation of damage see DAMAGES vol 12 para 1193 et seq. As to the operation of this principle in the context of negligent valuations see paras 422 note 11, 423 note 6 post.

8   Eg, a mortgage lender who claims damages from a negligent valuer must bring into account the amount realised by a sale of the mortgaged property, and also any repayments made by the borrower prior to default: see para 423 notes 4–6 post. However, the principle of 'res inter alios acta' means that a plaintiff need not bring into account the proceeds of an insurance policy: *Banque Bruxelles Lambert SA v Eagle Star Insurance Co Ltd* [1995] 2 All ER 769 per Phillips J (on appeal [1995] QB 375, [1995] 2 All ER 769, CA). Nor need he bring into account a discretionary statutory grant given by a local authority to enable the plaintiff to repair defective property. 'I am clearly of the view that the sum does not fall to be deducted. Firstly, because it is irrelevant to a claim where the difference in value is the measure of damage and, secondly, because, to use legal shorthand, it is a collateral benefit which does not have to be taken into account': *Treml v Ernest W Gibson and Partners* [1984] 2 EGLR 162 at 164 per Popplewell J.

9   Supreme Court Act 1981 s 35A(1) (added by the Administration of Justice Act 1982 s 15(1), Sch 1 Pt 1). Thus the court's discretion extends to both the rate of interest awarded and the period over which it is to be calculated.

10   The court has refused to interfere with a trial judge's decision to apply the rate of interest laid down under the Judgments Act 1838 for interest on judgment debts, even where it considers that it would have been preferable to apply a rate of interest reflecting the cost or value of money over the relevant period: *Watts v Morrow* [1991] 4 All ER 937 at 960, [1991] 1 WLR 1421 at 1446, CA, per Bingham LJ.

422. Measure of damages in action by purchaser or vendor.

The proper measure of damages is the difference between what the property would have been worth[1] had it been in the condition in which the valuer represented it[2] and its actual value[3], which should have been reported to the party who relied on the valuer's report[4]. This remains the case even where the purchaser, acting reasonably to cut his losses, sells the property for more than he paid before the valuer admits liability or is found liable[5]. If, despite the negligent valuation, the purchaser paid no more than the property was worth in its actual condition, only nominal damages will be awarded[6]. If the purchaser chose to pay more than the property would have been worth had it been in the condition in which the valuer represented it, the valuer or surveyor is not liable for that excess[7]. Damages are assessed according to the difference in 'as represented' and 'actual' values which obtained when the purchaser became legally committed to the purchase, and the damages bear interest from that date until the date of judgment[8].

The purchaser is not entitled to recover the cost of repairing defects which the valuer or surveyor has negligently overlooked[9], although the cost of such repairs may be relevant evidence when assessing what the property is actually worth in its defective condition[10].

If the purchaser decides to dispose of the defective property, he will also be entitled to recover damages in relation to certain incidental losses, such as legal fees and other costs, occasioned by both the purchase and the resale[11]. If he decides to retain the property and rectify its defects, he will probably be entitled to recover in respect of reasonable incidental expenses, such as fees incurred in investigating the defects and the cost of alternative accommodation while repairs are being carried out[12], but damages are not recoverable for the cost of the repair work itself[13].

The damages recoverable from a negligent surveyor or valuer by the purchaser of a dwelling may include a sum for physical inconvenience and discomfort caused by the breach of duty and for mental suffering directly related to that inconvenience and discomfort[14]. That sum will reflect the amount and duration of the discomfort[15], but it should in any event be modest and not excessive[16].

Where a vendor sells property at an undervalue in reliance on advice negligently given to him by a valuer, the vendor may recover the difference between the market value of the property and the price for which he sold it[17].

1   This, in most cases, is the price paid, at least where no point is taken that the plaintiff chose to pay above market value: see *Watts v Morrow* [1991] 4 All ER 937 at 945, [1991] 1 WLR 1421 at 1430, CA, per Ralph Gibson LJ.

2   The plaintiff's damages will be reduced if in fact he bought it for less than this figure, as he will have suffered a correspondingly smaller loss, and if he bought it for so much less that he turns out to have paid no more than the property's actual value, he will get nominal damages only: see the text and notes 4–6 infra.

3   This figure should be that which the court considers it most likely that a reasonable valuer, using the information available at the relevant date, would have put forward as the amount which the property was most likely to fetch if sold on the open market; it is not the highest possible valuation which would not have been negligent: *South Australia Asset Management Corpn v York Montague Ltd* [1996] 3 All ER 365 at 378, [1996] 27 EG 125 at 130, HL, per Lord Hoffman.

4   See *Philips v Ward* [1956] 1 All ER 874 at 876, [1956] 1 WLR 471 at 473, CA, per Denning LJ; *Ford v White & Co* [1964] 2 All ER 755 at 758–761, [1964] 1 WLR 885 at 888–892 per Pennycuick J (plaintiffs bought house and vacant plot, with building restriction against the plot, at actual value; solicitor negligently failed to tell plaintiffs of restriction; held that plaintiffs had suffered no loss as the difference between the price paid and the property's actual value was nil; they were therefore in the same position as if the defendants had fulfilled their duty and so were not entitled to damages; the plaintiffs' claim in the case arose in contract, and not in tort, and agreement between the parties as to the measure of damage in the event of the court so deciding precluded an award of nominal damages); *Perry v Sidney Phillips & Son (a firm)* [1982] 3 All ER 705, [1982] 1 WLR 1297, CA; *Watts v Morrow* [1991] 4 All ER 937 at 945–954, [1991] 1 WLR 1421 at 1429–1439, CA, per Ralph Gibson LJ.

5   *Perry v Sidney Phillips & Son (a firm)* [1982] 3 All ER 705, [1982] 1 WLR 1297, CA (house, though defective, was sold unrepaired for more than the plaintiff paid for it); and see the text and note 8 infra.

6   *Upstone v GDW Carnegie & Co* 1978 SLT (Sh Ct) 4.

7   *Hardy v Wamsley-Lewis* (1967) 203 Estates Gazette 1039; but see *Oswald v Countrywide Surveyors Ltd* [1996] 37 EG 140, CA (plaintiffs paid £225,000 for property valued at £215,000; surveyor advised caution on woodworm but failed to notice death watch beetle; plaintiffs said they would have paid £165,000 for the property in its actual condition; on appeal held that it was open for the judge to decide as a matter of fact that the price paid by the plaintiffs was the best evidence of its market value in the condition in which the surveyor represented it, and that one could have regard to the cost of repairs in calculating its actual market value; allowance was made for betterment resulting from repairs).

8   *Perry v Sidney Phillips & Son* [1982] 3 All ER 705, [1982] 1 WLR 1297, CA; and see para 421 text and notes 9–10 ante.

9   *Philips v Ward* [1956] 1 All ER 874, [1956] 1 WLR 471, CA; *Perry v Sidney Phillips & Son* [1982] 3 All ER 705, [1982] 1 WLR 1297, CA; *Watts v Morrow* [1991] 4 All ER 937, [1991] 1 WLR 1421, CA.

10 *Steward v Rapley* [1989] 1 EGLR 159, CA. As to the position where a purchaser of a lease subsequently discovers that it contains terms to his disadvantage about which he was not warned see *Simple Simon Catering Ltd v Binstock Miller & Co* (1973) 228 Estates Gazette 527 at 529, CA, per Lord Denning MR.

11 *Philips v Ward* [1956] 1 All ER 874 at 879, [1956] 1 WLR 471 at 478, CA, per Romer LJ; *Watts v Morrow* [1991] 4 All ER 937 at 950, [1991] 1 WLR 1421 at 1435, CA, per Ralph Gibson LJ and at 959 and 1445 per Bingham LJ; *Heatley v William H Brown Ltd* [1992] 1 EGLR 289 at 296 per Peter Bowsher J, QC.

12 See eg *Morgan v Perry* (1973) 229 Estates Gazette 1737; *Treml v Ernest W Gibson and Partners* [1984] 2 EGLR 162; *Cross v David Martin & Mortimer* [1989] 1 EGLR 154 at 159 per Phillips J.

13 See note 5 ante.

14 *Perry v Sidney Phillips & Son* [1982] 3 All ER 705, [1982] 1 WLR 1297 CA (inconvenience, distress and discomfort); *Watts v Morrow* [1991] 4 All ER 937, [1991] 1 WLR 1421, CA (damages awarded for distress caused by physical consequences of breach but not for mental distress not caused by physical discomfort or inconvenience resulting from the breach); *Ezekiel v McDade* [1995] 2 EGLR 107 at 110, CA, per Nourse LJ. Damages may be awarded for discomfort foreseeably suffered during the period when defects in the property are repaired even though the cost of repairs is not itself recoverable: *Watts v Morrow* [1991] 4 All ER 937 at 960, [1991] 1 WLR 1421 at 1445, CA, per Bingham LJ. In the absence of such physical discomfort, however, a surveyor or valuer is not liable for distress, frustration, anxiety, displeasure, vexation, tension or aggravation suffered by the purchaser: *Perry v Sidney Phillips & Son* [1982] 3 All ER 705 at 712, [1982] 1 WLR 1297 at 1307, CA, per Kerr LJ; *Watts v Morrow* [1991] 4 All ER 937 at 956–957, 959, [1991] 1 WLR 1421 at 1442, 1445, CA.

15 *Watts v Morrow* [1991] 4 All ER 937 at 958, [1991] 1 WLR 1421 at 1443, CA, per Ralph Gibson LJ. A purchaser may be precluded by the doctrine of mitigation from recovering damages for discomfort suffered after the time when he ought reasonably to have repaired defects in the property: *Cross v David Martin & Mortimer* [1989] 1 EGLR 154 at 159 per Phillips J. However, where the defendant persists in denying liability, a purchaser does not act unreasonably in failing to carry out repairs which he lacks the

means to pay for: *Perry v Sidney Phillips & Son* [1982] 3 All ER 705, [1982] 1 WLR 1297, CA, distinguishing *Liesbosch (Owners) v SS Edison (Owners)* [1933] AC 449, HL.
16   *Perry v Sidney Phillips & Son* [1982] 3 All ER 705 at 709, [1982] 1 WLR 1297 at 1303, CA, per Lord Denning MR. Awards under this head have, however, been reduced on appeal: see *Watts v Morrow* [1991] 4 All ER 937, [1991] 1 WLR 1421, CA; *Ezekiel v McDade* [1995] 2 EGLR 107, CA.
17   *Weedon v Hindwood, Clarke & Esplin* [1975] 1 EGLR 82 (valuer negligently agreed too low a figure with the district valuer for the compulsory acquisition of his client's property); *Kenney v Hall, Pain & Foster* [1976] 2 EGLR 29 (valuer negligently over-estimated potential sale price of property; intending vendor relied on over-estimation when taking on other financial commitments; valuer liable for losses arising out of those commitments).

423. Measure of damages in action by mortgage lender. Where a valuer negligently values a property and a lender consequently agrees to advance money on the security of that property, the lender will not be able to recover damages greater than the amount by which the property has been overvalued because, in the absence of fraud, the valuer is responsible only for the foreseeable consequences of the valuation being wrong, and not for all the consequences of the loan having been made[1]. Where the lender would not have lent if he had known the property's actual value, and suffers losses because the value of the property falls after the mortgage has been taken out, he cannot recover for those losses if they exceed the amount of the overvaluation[2].

Subject to the limitation described above, the basic measure of damages recoverable by the lender in a case where, had the valuation been accurate, he would not have lent at all will consist of the entire amount which has been lent[3], together with all costs reasonably incurred in repossessing and reselling the mortgaged property[4], less whatever is recovered on the resale and any repayments of capital or interest made by the borrower[5]. The basic measure of damages recoverable by the lender in a case where, had the valuation been accurate, he would have lent a smaller amount will consist of the difference between what has been lent and lost and the smaller amount which would have been lent and lost if the valuer had provided an accurate valuation of the property, less any repayments of capital or interest made by the borrower[6].

In addition to these capital sums, the lender is entitled to damages to compensate him for the interest which he could have earned on the money had it not been locked up in the mortgage loan[7], although such damages will not reflect the high contractual rate provided for in the actual mortgage unless the lender can show that, had he not lent to the borrower in question, the money would in fact have earned interest at a comparable rate on another loan[8]. A lender is not, however, entitled to damages based on the cost of repairing the property[9].

1   *South Australia Asset Management Corpn v York Montague Ltd* [1996] 3 All ER 365, [1996] 27 EG 125, HL. However, where a valuer is engaged not merely to provide information, but to advise a lender as to whether or not a loan should be made, the valuer's responsibility for negligent advice will extend to all the foreseeable loss which is a consequence of the loan being made, including that which results from a subsequent fall in the value of the property: *South Australia Asset Management Corpn v York Montague Ltd* supra at 372 and at 127 per Lord Hoffmann.
2   *South Australia Asset Management Corpn v York Montague Ltd* [1996] 3 All ER 365, [1996] 27 EG 125, HL, per Lord Hoffman (overruling *Banque Bruxelles Lambert SA v Eagle Star Insurance Co Ltd* [1995] QB 375, [1995] 2 All ER 769, CA; and rejecting for this purpose the distinction between 'no transaction' and 'successful transaction' cases).
3   *Baxter v FW Gapp & Co Ltd* [1938] 4 All ER 457; affd [1939] 2 KB 271, [1939] 2 All ER 752, CA. Damages should not be assessed at the date of breach and should not reflect the difference between the amount of the loan and the value of the lender's rights under the mortgage: *South Australia Asset Management Corpn v York Montague Ltd* [1996] 3 All ER 365, [1996] 27 EG 125, HL.
4   *Baxter v FW Gapp & Co Ltd* [1938] 4 All ER 457; affd [1939] 2 KB 271, [1939] 2 All ER 752, CA; *Swingcastle Ltd v Alastair Gibson* [1991] 2 AC 223, [1991] 2 All ER 353, HL.
5   *London and South of England Building Society v Stone* [1983] 3 All ER 105, [1983] 1 WLR 1242, CA; see also *Banque Bruxelles Lambert SA v Eagle Star Insurance Co Ltd* [1995] 2 All ER 769 at 818 per Phillips J (on appeal [1995] QB 375, [1995] 2 All ER 769, CA). However, the lender will not be required to give

credit for sums which could have been, but which have not been, received (either from sale of the property or by taking action against the borrower on his personal covenant to pay) unless the lender is guilty of failing to take reasonable steps to mitigate his loss: *London and South of England Building Society v Stone* supra (personal covenant not enforced in order to protect commercial reputation), overruling *Eagle Star Insurance Co Ltd v Gale and Power* (1955) 166 Estates Gazette 37; *Nyckeln Finance Co Ltd v Stumpbrook Continuation Ltd* [1994] 2 EGLR 143 (failure to accept an offer for the property).

6   *Corisand Investments Ltd v Druce & Co* [1978] 2 EGLR 86. In this situation the lender will not be entitled to recover the cost of costs repossessing and reselling the mortgaged property, since these would have been incurred in any event: *Corisand Investments Ltd v Druce & Co* supra at 101 per Gibson J.

7   *Swingcastle Ltd v Alastair Gibson* [1991] 2 AC 223, [1991] 2 All ER 353, HL (overruling on this point *Baxter v FW Gapp & Co Ltd* [1938] 4 All ER 457; affd [1939] 2 KB 271, [1939] 2 All ER 752, CA).

8   As to the appropriate rate of interest to be adopted in assessing damages see *Swingcastle Ltd v Alastair Gibson* [1991] 2 AC 223, [1991] 2 All ER 353, HL; *Corisand Investments Ltd v Druce & Co* [1978] 2 EGLR 86; *HIT Finance Ltd v Lewis & Tucker Ltd* [1993] 2 EGLR 231; *Banque Bruxelles Lambert SA v Eagle Star Insurance Co Ltd* [1995] QB 375, [1995] 2 All ER 769, CA.

9   *London & South of England Building Society v Stone* [1983] 3 All ER 105, [1983] 1 WLR 1242, CA.

424. Reduction of damages for contributory negligence. Where a person who claims damages in respect of an inaccurate valuation is contributorily negligent, the damages recoverable may be reduced to such extent as the court thinks just and equitable[1]. A person may be contributorily negligent for this purpose where it is unreasonable for him to place reliance on the valuation in question[2]. In addition, a person who relies on a negligent valuation in deciding to enter into a transaction may be contributorily negligent if his decision to enter into that transaction is unreasonable on other grounds[3].

1   See the Law Reform (Contributory Negligence) Act 1945 s 1(1). The 1945 Act applies to claims in tort for negligence, and also to claims for breach of a contractual duty of care (which is the same as a duty which would arise in tort irrespective of any contract): *Forsikringsaktieselskapet Vesta v Butcher* [1989] AC 852, [1988] 2 All ER 43, CA. However, it does not apply to an action for breach of a contractual provision which does not depend on negligence by the defendant (*Barclays Bank plc v Fairclough Building Ltd* [1995] QB 214, [1995] 1 All ER 289, CA) or to an action in deceit arising out of a fraudulent valuation: *Alliance & Leicester Building Society v Edgestop Ltd* [1994] 2 All ER 38, [1993] 1 WLR 1462. As to contributory negligence in valuation cases see also *United Bank of Kuwait plc v Prudential Property Services Ltd* [1995] EGCS 190, CA; and NEGLIGENCE vol 34 para 68 et seq.

2   *Banque Bruxelles Lambert SA v Eagle Star Insurance Co Ltd* [1995] 2 All ER 769 per Phillips J (on appeal [1995] QB 375, [1995] 2 All ER 769, CA); *Nyckeln Finance Co Ltd v Stumpbrook Continuation Ltd* [1994] 2 EGLR 143 (the damages awarded against a negligent valuer were reduced on proof that the plaintiff mortgage lender was aware of a substantial discrepancy between the valuation on which reliance was placed and the price at which the subject property had just been sold on the open market). See also *PK Finans International (UK) Ltd v Andrew Downs & Co Ltd* [1992] 1 EGLR 172 (had the plaintiff lenders succeeded in establishing negligence against the defendant valuers, the court would have in any event held the plaintiffs responsible for 80% of their losses). As to the difficulty in establishing that a house purchaser has acted unreasonably in relying on a valuation or survey see *Yianni v Edwin Evans & Sons* [1982] QB 438, [1981] 3 All ER 592; *Davies v Parry* [1988] 1 EGLR 147; *Allen v Ellis & Co* [1990] 1 EGLR 170 at 172 per Garland J.

3   Eg where a mortgage lender has substantial reason for doubting the honesty or financial stability of the proposed borrower (see *HIT Finance Ltd v Lewis & Tucker Ltd* [1993] 2 EGLR 231 at 235 obiter per Wright J; *United Bank of Kuwait plc v Prudential Property Services Ltd* [1995] EGCS 190, CA; *Kendall Wilson Securities Ltd v Barraclough* [1986] 1 NZLR 576, (NZCA)); or where the amount lent represents an unreasonably high proportion of the estimated value of the property (*Platform Home Loans Ltd v Oyston Shipways Ltd* [1996] EGCS 146).

(4) LIMITATIONS ON LIABILITY

425. Exclusion or restriction of liability. In principle, a valuer may (1) exclude or restrict his liability for negligently causing financial loss to his client by means of an appropriate term in the contract under which he is engaged[1]; and (2) exclude or restrict his liability for negligently causing financial loss to a third party by means of an appropriate notice or disclaimer[2].

In either case the exclusion or restriction of liability must be reasonable in the circumstances[3], since a disclaimer of liability by or on behalf of a valuer is a notice which purports to exclude liability for negligence within the meaning of the Unfair Contract Terms Act 1977[4]. As such it is unlikely to be effective against a purchaser of an ordinary house where the valuer is instructed by the building society[5], although it might be effective in relation to those unusual residential or industrial properties whose purchasers are not generally expected to behave as the purchaser of an ordinary house would behave[6].

1   As to exclusion clauses generally see CONTRACT vol 9 para 363 et seq.
2   *Hedley Byrne & Co Ltd v Heller & Partners Ltd* [1964] AC 465, [1963] 2 All ER 575, HL; *Hadden v City of Glasgow District Council* 1986 SLT 557, Ct of Sess. To be effective, such a notice must be brought to the attention of the third party before he acts in reliance on the valuation: *Martin v Bell-Ingram* 1986 SLT 575, Ct of Sess.
3   See the Unfair Contract Terms Act 1977 s 2; and CONTRACT. In the case of a contract term, it must be shown that the term was a fair and reasonable one to have been included, having regard to the circumstances which were, or ought reasonably to have been, known to or in the contemplation of the parties when the contract was made: s 11(1). In relation to a notice not having contractual effect, the requirement of reasonableness under the 1977 Act is that it should be fair and reasonable to allow reliance on it, having regard to all the circumstances obtaining when the liability arose or, but for the notice, would have arisen: s 11(3). In either case, it is for those claiming that a contract term or notice satisfies the requirement of reasonableness to show that it does: s 11(5).
4   See ibid s 2(2). Such a disclaimer is therefore ineffective by reason of s 2(2) unless it satisfies the test of reasonableness provided by s 11(3): see the text and note 3 supra. These provisions do not extend to Scotland: see s 32(2).
5   *Roberts v J Hampson & Co (a firm)* [1989] 2 All ER 504 at 510, [1990] 1 WLR 94 at 101 per Ian Kennedy J; *Smith v Eric S Bush, Harris v Wyre Forest District Council* [1990] 1 AC 831, [1989] 2 All ER 514, HL.
6   *Smith v Eric S Bush, Harris v Wyre Forest District Council* [1990] 1 AC 831 at 857, [1989] 2 All ER 514 at 531–532, HL; *Beaton v Nationwide Building Society* [1991] 2 EGLR 145; *Stevenson v Nationwide Building Society* [1984] 2 EGLR 165 at 170 per Wilmers J, QC (the purchaser of a relatively substantial commercial property was an estate agent who was familiar with disclaimers; held that it was reasonable for the mortgage valuer to disclaim liability for negligence).

426–500. Limitation periods applicable to claim against valuer.

An action against a valuer for breach of contract may not be brought after the expiration of six years from the date on which the cause of action accrued[1], that is, the date on which the breach of contract occurred[2]. An action against a valuer which is founded on tort[3] may not be brought after the expiration of six years from the date on which the cause of action accrued[4], that is, the date on which the plaintiff suffered loss or damage[5].

A special time limit applies to any action for damages for negligence[6] where certain facts are not known to the plaintiff, or any person in whom the cause of action was previously vested[7], at the date on which the cause of action accrues[8]. In such circumstances the action must be brought either within six years of the date on which the cause of action accrued[9] or, if this period would expire later, within three years of the date on which the plaintiff or any person in whom the cause of action was vested before him first had both the necessary knowledge[10] and the right to bring the action[11]. However, such an action may not be brought after the expiration of 15 years from the occurrence of the act or omission which is alleged to constitute negligence[12].

Subject to certain provisions[13], where, in the case of any action for which a period of limitation is prescribed by the Limitation Act 1980[14], either (1) the action is based upon the fraud of the defendant[15]; or (2) any fact relevant to the plaintiff's right of action has been deliberately concealed[16] from him by the defendant; or (3) the action is for relief from the consequences of a mistake, the period of limitation will not begin to run until the plaintiff has discovered the fraud, concealment or mistake (as the case may be) or could with reasonable diligence have discovered it[17]. For these purposes, deliberate commission of a breach of duty in circumstances in which it is unlikely to be discovered for some time amounts to deliberate concealment of the facts involved in that breach of duty[18].

1   Limitation Act 1980 s 5.

2   If the contract in question is made by deed, the limitation period is 12 years: see ibid s 8.

3   As to the special time limit applicable to actions in tort for negligence where certain facts relevant to the cause of action are not known at the date of accrual see the text and notes 6–12 infra.

4   Limitation Act 1980 s 2. As to when the limitation period will begin where fraud is concealed see *Sheldon v RHM Outhwaite (Underwriting Agencies) Ltd* [1996] AC 102, [1995] 2 All ER 558, HL; *Westlake v Bracknell District Council* [1987] 1 EGLR 161 (valuer deliberately concealed the fact that his earlier inspection of a property had been negligently carried out); and the text and notes 13–18 infra.

5   Identification of relevant loss or damage is a question of fact: *Kitney v Jones Lang Wootton* [1988] 1 EGLR 145; *Whitley (FG) & Sons Co Ltd v Thomas Bickerton* [1993] 1 EGLR 139. A purchaser or tenant who relies on a negligent valuation or survey generally suffers loss for this purpose on entering into a binding contract to acquire the property: *Secretary of State for the Environment v Essex, Goodman & Suggitt* [1986] 2 All ER 69, [1985] 2 EGLR 168; *Spencer-Ward v Humberts* [1995] 1 EGLR 123, CA. Where a mortgagee would not have lent money but for a negligent over-valuation of the mortgaged property, the mortgagee's loss is suffered at the moment when the value of the property no longer affords sufficient security for the amount owed: *First National Commercial Bank plc v Humberts* [1995] 2 All ER 673, [1995] 1 EGLR 142, CA.

6   Ie an action in tort: *Iron Trades Mutual Insurance Co Ltd v JK Buckenham Ltd* [1990] 1 All ER 808, [1989] 2 Lloyd's Rep 85; *Société Commerciale de Réassurance v ERAS (International) Ltd, Re ERAS EIL appeals* [1992] 2 All ER 82n, [1992] 1 Lloyd's Rep 570, CA.

7   See the Limitation Act 1980 s 14A(5) (s 14A added by the Latent Damage Act 1986 s 1).

8   See the Limitation Act 1980 s 14A (as added: see note 7 supra); and LIMITATION OF ACTIONS. As to the knowledge which is relevant for this purpose see s 14A(6)–(10) (as so added); note 10 infra; and LIMITATION OF ACTIONS.

9   See the text and notes 4–5 supra.

10   For these purposes, a person's knowledge includes knowledge which he might reasonably have been expected to acquire (1) from facts observable or ascertainable by him; or (2) from facts ascertainable by him with the help of appropriate expert advice which it is reasonable for him to seek; but a person is not to be taken by virtue of the Limitation Act 1980 s 14A(10) (as added: see note 7 supra) to have knowledge of a fact ascertainable only with the help of expert advice so long as he has taken all reasonable steps to obtain (and, where appropriate, to act on) that advice: s 14A(10) (as so added). As to the degree of knowledge required to 'trigger' the three-year period see *Spencer-Ward v Humberts* [1995] 1 EGLR 123, CA. It is irrelevant that the plaintiffs did not know the identity of the negligent valuer when a simple inquiry would have revealed it: *Heathcote v David Marks & Co* [1996] 03 EG 128. A negligent valuation or survey gives rise to a single cause of action, and the plaintiff's knowledge of one defect which has been negligently overlooked therefore causes the three-year period to run in respect of all defects, including those which are discovered subsequently: *Hamlin v Edwin Evans* [1996] 47 EG 141, CA.

11   See the Limitation Act 1980 s 14A(5) (as added: see note 7 supra); and LIMITATION OF ACTIONS.

12   See ibid s 14B (added by the Latent Damage Act 1986 s 1); and LIMITATION OF ACTIONS.

13   Ie the Limitation Act 1980 s 32(3), (4A) (s 32(4A) (time limits in relation to defective products and fatal accidents) added by the Consumer Protection Act 1987 s 6(6), Sch 1 para 5): see LIMITATION OF ACTIONS.

14   As to the Limitation Act 1980 generally see LIMITATION OF ACTIONS.

15   References in ibid s 32(1) (as amended) to the defendant include references to the defendant's agent and to any person through whom the defendant claims and his agent: s 32(1) (amended by the Consumer Protection Act 1987 Sch 1 para 5).

16   Deliberate concealment of facts relevant to a cause of action will postpone the running of time until the concealment is or should be discovered, regardless of whether it is concealed when the cause of action accrues or afterwards: *Sheldon v RHM Outhwaite (Underwriting Agencies) Ltd* [1996] AC 102, [1995] 2 All ER 558, HL.

17   Limitation Act 1980 s 32(1) (as amended: see note 6 supra).

18   Ibid s 32(2). Nothing in s 32 (as amended) enables any action (1) to recover, or recover the value of, any property; or (2) to enforce any charge against, or set aside any transaction affecting, any property, to be brought against the purchaser of the property or any person claiming through him in any case where the property has been purchased for valuable consideration by an innocent third party since the fraud or concealment or (as the case may be) the transaction in which the mistake was made took place: s 32(3). A purchaser is an innocent third party for the purposes of s 32 (as amended) (a) in the case of fraud or concealment of any fact relevant to the plaintiff's right of action, if he was not a party to the fraud or (as the case may be) to the concealment of that fact and did not at the time of the purchase know or have reason to believe that the fraud or concealment had taken place; and (b) in the case of mistake, if he did not at the time of the purchase know or have reason to believe that the mistake had been made: s 32(4).

VARIATION OF TRUSTS

See TRUSTS

VENDOR AND PURCHASER

See SALE OF GOODS; SALE OF LAND

WAR AND ARMED CONFLICT

For	acquisition of land for defence purposes........... *see*	ROYAL FORCES
	armed forces	CONSTITUTIONAL LAW AND HUMAN RIGHTS; ROYAL FORCES
	blockade	PRIZE
	Board of Trade	CONSTITUTIONAL LAW AND HUMAN RIGHTS; TRADE, INDUSTRY AND INDUSTRIAL RELATIONS
	British citizenship...	BRITISH NATIONALITY, IMMIGRATION AND RACE RELATIONS
	Commonwealth..	COMMONWEALTH
	compulsory acquisition of land generally	COMPULSORY ACQUISITION
	copyright	COPYRIGHT
	courts-martial...	ROYAL FORCES
	Defence Council..	CONSTITUTIONAL LAW AND HUMAN RIGHTS; ROYAL FORCES
	defence organisations	FOREIGN RELATIONS LAW; ROYAL FORCES
	disclaimer of lease due to war damage	LANDLORD AND TENANT
	enemy alien, as party to proceedings................	BARRISTERS
	export controls..	TRADE, INDUSTRY AND INDUSTRIAL RELATIONS
	genocide	CRIMINAL LAW; FOREIGN RELATIONS LAW
	home guard	ROYAL FORCES
	hot pursuit	FOREIGN RELATIONS LAW
	international headquarters	ROYAL FORCES
	limitation periods	LIMITATION OF ACTIONS
	nuclear installations	FUEL AND ENERGY
	patents and registered designs	PATENTS AND REGISTERED DESIGNS
	prize	PRIZE
	reprisals..	FOREIGN RELATIONS LAW
	requisitioned vehicles......................................	ROYAL FORCES
	royal prerogative	CONSTITUTIONAL LAW AND HUMAN RIGHTS
	state of war, judicial notice of.........................	EVIDENCE
	trade marks	TRADE MARKS
	treason	CRIMINAL LAW
	treaties	FOREIGN RELATIONS LAW
	United Nations Organisation	FOREIGN RELATIONS LAW
	war, as frustration to contract	CONTRACT
	war risks insurance	INSURANCE

1. LEGALITY AND THE USE OF FORCE

501. Use of force by states. Until modern times there was no prohibition on the use of force by states, and resort to war was not illegal[1]. The Covenant of the League of Nations[2] contained restrictions upon the right of states to use force. By the International Treaty for the Renunciation of War as an Instrument of National Policy[3] the state parties condemned recourse to war for the solution of international controversies, and renounced it as an instrument of national policy in their relations with each other[4]. Under the Charter of the United Nations, member states must refrain in their international relations from the threat or use of force against the territorial integrity or political independence of any state, or in any other manner inconsistent with the purposes of the United Nations[5]. There are exceptions to this general prohibition when force may be used, as where it is employed by the United Nations itself through the medium of action authorised by the Security Council[6], by regional institutions under regional arrangements[7], and by states acting in individual or collective self-defence[8]. In all these cases, however, the use of force is either undertaken by the United Nations or subject to its control.

1 In time of peace the use of force by way, eg, of reprisals or self-defence was subject to limitations or conditions: see paras 502–505 post.

2 Ie the Treaty of Peace with Germany ('The Treaty of Versailles') (Versailles, 28 June 1919; TS 4 (1919); Cmd 153), Pt I (arts 1–26).

3 Ie 'The Pact of Paris' or 'The Kellogg-Briand Pact' (Paris, 27 August 1928; TS 29 (1929); Cmd 3410).

4 Ibid art 1. The parties agreed that settlement or solution of all disputes should never be sought except by pacific means: art 2. The pact preserved the right of states to go to war in self-defence or against another state which violated the treaty. It did not restrict the competence of the League of Nations (and now the United Nations) to take enforcement action by the use of armed force. The pact, which is still in force (although superseded in practice by the Charter of the United Nations (San Francisco, 26 June 1945; TS 67 (1946); Cmd 7015), is part of customary international law.

5 Ibid art 2 para 4. Thus the prohibition is not only of war in its technical sense but of any aggressive use of force. Under the preamble the member states undertake to ensure that armed force is not used save in the common interest. There is an obligation to settle international disputes peacefully: see art 2 para 3. The General Assembly reiterated the principles of the charter in its resolution concerning Friendly Relations and Co-operation among States in accordance with the Charter: General Assembly Resolution 2625 (XXV), 24 October 1970. It adopted a definition of 'aggression' by General Assembly Resolution 3314 (XXIX), 14 December 1974. The Charter of the United Nations art 2 para 4 reflects customary international law: see *Military and Paramilitary Activities in and Against Nicaragua (Nicaragua v United States of America) (No 2)* [1986] ICJ Reports 14, (1986) Times, 28 June. See also Hargrove 'The Nicaragua Judgment and the Future of the Law of Force and Self-Defense' (1987) 81 AJIL 135.

6 Charter of the United Nations arts 24, 39–50, 106. Chapter VII (arts 39–51) sets out the Security Council's powers with respect to threats to the peace, breaches of the peace and acts of aggression: see further FOREIGN RELATIONS LAW vol 18 paras 1811–1813. See also the Security Council resolutions following the invasion of Kuwait by Iraq on 2 August 1990: UN Security Council Resolution 660 (2 August 1990) (which demanded 'that Iraq withdraw immediately and unconditionally all its forces to the positions in which they were located on 1 August 1990'); and UN Security Council Resolutions 661 (6 August 1990); 665 (25 August 1990); 674 (29 October 1990); 678 (29 November 1990) (which authorised member states of the United Nations co-operating with the Government of Kuwait, unless Iraq on or before 15 January 1991 fully implemented Resolution 660, to use all necessary means to uphold and implement Resolution 660 and all subsequent relevant resolutions and to restore international peace and security in the area). See also UN Security Council Resolution 686 (2 March 1991) in which the Security Council took note of the letters of the Foreign Minister of Iraq confirming Iraq's agreement to comply fully with all of the relevant resolutions. See also Weller 'The United Nations and the jus ad bellum' in Rowe (ed) *The Gulf War 1990–91 in International and English Law* (1993) ch 2.

7 See the Charter of the United Nations art 53.

8   See ibid arts 51, 107. As to self-defence see para 1855 et seq post.

502. Use of force short of war; reprisals. Reprisals[1] are a method of retaliation for a breach of international law by means of action which would in other circumstances be itself an unjustifiable breach of international law[2]. At customary international law, reprisals must be preceded by a demand for redress and be commensurate with the provocation and in proportion to the injury suffered by the state resorting to reprisals[3]. Reprisals do not justify the taking of measures against an innocent third party[4]. The right to take reprisals may be excluded by treaty[5]. Unless the reprisals are used in self-defence they appear to be contrary to the Charter of the United Nations[6]. The use of pacific blockades, that is, the blockading of the coast of a state against the shipping of that state, may now be regarded as obsolete[7], except where it is ordered by the Security Council of the United Nations[8].

1   'Reprisals' must be distinguished from 'retorsion', which is a method of retaliation for an unlawful act by an act or omission which is strictly lawful, although unfriendly.

2   Thus the blockade and bombardment by the British fleet of the Greek coast in 1850 in the Don Pacifico affair was unjustified since Greece had not then committed any breach of international law: 2 Oppenheim's International Law (7th Edn) pp 137–138.

3   *Responsibility of Germany for Damage caused in Portuguese Colonies* 2 UN Rep 1011 (1928). The reprisal need not, however, be an exact retaliation in kind.

4   *German Reparations Case (The Cysne)* 2 UN Rep 1035 (1930) (misconduct of a belligerent would not justify the adversary in sinking a neutral ship). As to the doctrine of reprisals as a method employed by a belligerent to attempt to induce the opponent to observe the laws of war see notes 5–6 infra; and PRIZE. The taking of the concessions of British Petroleum Ltd by the Libyan Government in 1971 for the avowed purpose of reprisals for the alleged failure of the United Kingdom government to prevent the seizure of islands in the Persian Gulf by Iran appears to have been unlawful for this reason: see FOREIGN RELATIONS LAW vol 18 para 1729 note 2.

     'United Kingdom' means Great Britain and Northern Ireland: Interpretation Act 1978 s 5, Sch 1. 'Great Britain' means England, Scotland and Wales: Union with Scotland Act 1706 preamble art I; Interpretation Act 1978 s 22(1), Sch 2 para 5(a). Neither the Channel Islands nor the Isle of Man is within the United Kingdom. See further CONSTITUTIONAL LAW AND HUMAN RIGHTS vol 8(2) (Reissue) para 3.

5   Eg the Geneva Red Cross Conventions (which are set out in the Schedules to the Geneva Conventions Act 1957) prohibit the taking of reprisals against the sick and wounded, prisoners of war and civilians during armed conflict: see para 521 et seq post. This has been extended to prohibit reprisals against civilian objects too: see para 552 post.

6   As to whether armed reprisals are permitted under international law since the International Treaty for the Renunciation of War as an Instrument of National Policy ('The Kellogg-Briand Pact') (see para 501 note 3 ante) and the Charter of the United Nations (see para 501 note 4 ante) see 2 Oppenheim's International Law (7th Edn) pp 143–144; and see Bowett 'Reprisals involving Recourse to Armed Force' 66 AJIL 1.

7   In 1903 the coast of Venezuela was blockaded by the naval forces of European states, including Great Britain, for the purpose of attempting to compel the blockaded state to honour its debts. There may, however, have been a state of war. The right of states to have recourse to armed force for the recovery of contract debts was restricted by the International Convention respecting the Limitation of the Employment of Force for the Recovery of Contract Debts (Hague Convention II ('The Porter Convention')) (The Hague, 18 October 1907; TS 7 (1910); Cd 5028). The measures taken by the United States against Soviet shipping bound for Cuba in 1962 were described by President Kennedy as 'quarantine', mainly, it seems, to avoid the action being characterised as 'pacific blockade'. For a discussion of this case see Greig's International Law (2nd Edn) pp 339–344. As to the Hague Conventions see para 518 post.

8   Ie acting under the powers set out in the Charter of the United Nations art 41. In 1966 the Security Council determined upon sanctions against what was then Southern Rhodesia, including an embargo on oil and petroleum products. The United Kingdom government was called upon to use force if necessary to prevent the arrival at Beira of vessels reasonably believed to be carrying oil destined for Rhodesia: see UN Security Council Resolutions 232 (16 December 1966); 235 (29 May 1968).

503. Self-defence in customary international law. In customary international law a state has a right of self-defence against a threat to its integrity[1]. Self-defence is a justification for what would otherwise be an illegal resort to force. In order to justify a particular use of force as self-defence there must be a necessity of self-defence, instant and overwhelming, leaving no choice of means and no moment for deliberation[2]. In so far as it is justified at all, the hot pursuit by a state's authorities of persons from its territory into the territory of another could be justified as self-defence[3].

1   This includes a threat to its territory. As to whether it also includes a threat to its nationals abroad see para 504 post. As to the seizure of vessels on the high seas in self-defence see *The Virginius Case* (1874) 76 Parliamentary Papers (Spain No 3) 85.

2   See Mr Webster (US Secretary of State) to HM Minister at Washington, 24 April 1841, on the case of *The Caroline* 29 BFSP 1126 (anticipatory self-defence). The general principle stated by Mr Webster was agreed to by HM Minister on 28 July 1842: see at 1137–1138; and 30 BFSP 193 at 195–196.

3   It is not established that hot pursuit on land is sanctioned at international law. Hot pursuit on land finds no analogy in hot pursuit at sea. In the case of hot pursuit at sea, which begins in the territorial sea of the contiguous zone of the state whose authorities conduct the pursuit, the pursuit must cease on entry of the ship pursued into the territorial sea of another state: see FOREIGN RELATIONS LAW vol 18 para 1484. It does not, therefore, violate the territorial sovereignty of any other state, but hot pursuit on land does so, precisely. See Bowett's Self-Defence in International Law pp 38–41, where examples are given of hot pursuit (mainly of native American tribes) into the territory of neighbouring states by the authorities of the United States of America.

504. Self-defence and the United Nations Charter.

According to the Charter of the United Nations[1], nothing in it impairs the inherent right of individual or collective self-defence if an armed attack[2] occurs against a member of the United Nations, until the Security Council has taken measures necessary to maintain international peace and security[3]. It is controversial whether the charter merely regulates the use of self-defence in the event of an armed attack actually taking place upon a state, or whether it has thus modified the right of self-defence as it existed at the time of the entry into force of the charter. According to the first view, force may be employed in self-defence, even though the state which resorts to it is merely threatened with armed force or even when there is no threat or use of armed force by another state, but where there is, for example, propaganda or economic warfare[4]. According to the latter view, self-defence is only permitted when a state is actually attacked by armed force[5]. It is also controversial, therefore, whether self-defence may be employed in case of attacks or threats upon nationals abroad[6].

1   As to the Charter of the United Nations see para 501 note 4 ante.

2   See *Military and Paramilitary Activities in and Against Nicaragua (Nicaragua v United States of America) (No 2)* [1986] ICJ Reports 14 at para 195, (1986) Times, 28 June.

3   See the Charter of the United Nations art 51. Measures taken by member states in the exercise of the right of self-defence must be reported immediately to the Security Council and do not in any way affect the authority and the responsibility of that organ under the charter to take at any time such action as it deems necessary in order to maintain or restore international peace and security: art 51. See UN Security Council Resolution 502 (3 April 1982) which demanded 'an immediate withdrawal of all Argentinian forces from the Falkland Islands (Islas Malvinas)'. The United Kingdom could still maintain its right to act in self-defence according to the Charter of the United Nations art 51. For the meaning of 'United Kingdom' see para 502 note 4 ante.

4   See eg Bowett's Self-Defence in International Law pp 182–199; and the Commentary of the United Kingdom government on the Charter of the United Nations (Cmd 6666) para 38. The United Kingdom government argued before the Security Council that taking retaliatory action to prevent the recurrence of attacks on shipping on the high seas is embraced in the principle of self-defence: British Practice in International Law 1964 (II) 268 (United States bombing of North Vietnam). The United Kingdom treated the searching by Iran of a United Kingdom registered merchant ship on the high seas during the Iran-Iraq war in 1986 as an exercise of the inherent right of self-defence to stop and search a merchant vessel on the high seas if there is reasonable grounds for suspecting the ship is taking arms to the other

side for use in the conflict: see 90 HC Official Report (6th series), 28 January 1986, written answers cols 426–427.

5   See Brownlie *International Law and the Use of Force by States* p 251 et seq.

6   The Lord Chancellor argued, in connection with the Anglo-French action at Suez in 1956, that it did: see 199 HL Official Report (5th series), 1 November 1956, cols 1348–1359; and Bowett's Self-Defence in International Law p 191. See also the justification by Israel for the attack at Entebbe airport on 3 July 1976 to rescue its citizens held hostage (see Akehurst (1977) 5 Int Rels 3) and by the United States for its invasion of Panama in 1989 (see (1990) 84 AJIL 494). The overwhelming majority of contemporary legal opinion comes down against the existence of a right of humanitarian intervention: see United Kingdom Foreign Office Policy Document No 148 para 11.22 (1986) 57 BYIL 614, 616.

505. Collective self-defence. The Charter of the United Nations stipulates that member states have the right of collective self-defence[1]. The United Kingdom[2] is a party to several defensive alliances with other states, such as the Brussels Treaty Organisation[3], from which developed the Western European Union[4] and the North Atlantic Treaty Organisation (NATO)[5].

1   Charter of the United Nations art 51. This should be distinguished from a regional arrangement within art 53. As to the Charter of the United Nations see para 501 note 4 ante. It has been argued that it only refers to a situation where two or more states are each defending their individual rights which are under attack, but act collectively in doing so. According to this view, collective security agreements, which aim at the maintenance of international peace and security and which usually stipulate that an attack against one party is deemed to be an attack upon all the parties, are not strictly speaking collective exercises of the right of self-defence. This view does not appear to be fully borne out by state practice: see eg the agreements referred to in the text and notes 2–5 infra. However, these have sometimes been justified as regional arrangements as envisaged by art 53. As to the action of the United States in Vietnam in the 1960s see, by way of argument that this was an exercise of the right of collective self-defence, Memorandum of the Legal Adviser of the US State Department, The Legality of United States Participation in the Defense of Vietnam, 4 March 1966, 60 AJIL 565; see also Falk *The Vietnam War and International Law* (vols I, II). There is no rule that a state may act in collective self-defence in the absence of a request from a state which regards itself as a victim of an alleged armed attack: see *Military and Paramilitary Activities in and Against Nicaragua (Nicaragua v United States of America) (No 2)* [1986] ICJ Reports 14 at para 199, Times, 28 June.

2   For the meaning of 'United Kingdom' see para 502 note 4 ante.

3   See the Treaty of Economic, Social and Cultural Collaboration and Collective Self-Defence (Brussels, 17 March 1948; TS 1 (1949); Cmd 7599).

4   See the Protocols to the Treaty signed at Brussels on 17 March 1948 (Paris, 23 October 1954; TS 39 (1955); Cmd 9498), supplemented by the Agreement in implementation of Article V of Protocol No 11 of the Brussels Treaty of 17 March 1948 as modified by the Protocols signed at Paris on 23 October 1954 (Paris, 14 December 1958; TS 37 (1962); Cmnd 1712).

5   See the North Atlantic Treaty (Washington, 4 April 1949; TS 56 (1949); Cmd 7789); and see further FOREIGN RELATIONS LAW vol 18 para 1835.

2. WAR AND NEUTRALITY

(1) DECLARATION AND TERMINATION OF WAR

506. Existence and non-existence of a state of war. At common law no state of war exists between the United Kingdom and a foreign state until there has been a formal declaration of war by the Crown or hostilities have been commenced by the authority of the Crown on the basis that those hostilities constitute a 'war'[1]. Similarly a war may be terminated only by the authority of the Crown, and this is usually effected by a treaty of peace and announced to the nation by proclamation or Order in Council[2]. A certificate of the Secretary of State for Foreign and Commonwealth Affairs to the effect that the Crown is still at war with a foreign state is conclusive evidence that the state of war is not at an end[3]. During the course of a war with a foreign state all commerce and intercourse between British subjects resident in British territory and the subjects of that state, or with persons residing there, is prohibited except under licence[4]. Judicial notice will be taken of the existence of a state of war between this country and any other, when that is the fact, even after the termination of hostilities[5].

Declaration of war by the Crown has not been common practice since 1945, despite the fact that the armed forces of the Crown have since that date been engaged in armed conflicts outside the United Kingdom[6]. This practice has largely resulted from the impact of international law, which recognises an 'armed conflict' as the condition precedent for the applicability of the 'laws of war' and as an alternative to a state of war[7]. Where there is no formal declaration of war, or no recognition by Her Majesty's government that a state of war exists, between the United Kingdom and a foreign state, provisions such as the Trading with the Enemy Act 1939[8] and other legislation dependent upon a formal state of war will not be applicable[9]. Specific prohibitions on trade and commerce are usually enacted by orders made under the Import, Export and Customs Powers (Defence) Act 1939[10], the United Nations Act 1946[11] and the Emergency Laws (Re-enactments and Repeals) Act 1964. In addition, the European Community may prohibit trade and commerce between its member states and a foreign state[13]. These orders will often have a similar effect as if a formal state of war existed between the United Kingdom and a foreign state and the relevant legislation had been brought into effect[14].

1   As to the Crown and war and peace generally see CONSTITUTIONAL LAW AND HUMAN RIGHTS vol 8(2) (Reissue) paras 809–819. See also para 508 post. A declaration of war by the Crown on the advice of United Kingdom ministers does not now bind independent members of the Commonwealth; but such a declaration binds all colonies and other dependent territories of the Crown provided the intention to bind them is clearly expressed: see COMMONWEALTH vol 6 (Reissue) para 988 et seq. In certain circumstances the courts may regard a state of war as being in existence despite the lack of any formal declaration of war, and even though diplomatic relations between the two states have not been formally broken off: *Kawasaki Kisen Kabushiki Kaisha of Kobe v Bantham SS Co Ltd (No 2)* [1938] 3 All ER 80; affd [1939] 2 KB 544, [1939] 1 All ER 819, CA. The term 'war' was construed 'in the sense in which an ordinary commercial man would use it, or … as the captain of a tramp steamer would interpret it': [1938] 3 All ER 80 at 83 per Goddard J. This statement should be regarded with caution due to the possibility of an armed conflict taking place involving the armed forces of the Crown in circumstances where Her Majesty's government does not recognise a state of war as being in existence. For the meaning of 'United Kingdom' see para 502 note 4 ante.

2   As to the Crown and treaties of peace see CONSTITUTIONAL LAW AND HUMAN RIGHTS vol 8(2) (Reissue) para 810. A state of war may also be terminated, without a treaty of peace or Order in Council, by a declaration of the Crown duly notified: see *Re Grotrian, Cox v Grotrian* [1955] Ch 501 at 506, [1955] 1 All ER 788 at 790. For an example of the implementation of a treaty of peace see the Japanese Treaty of Peace Act 1951, authorising the making of Orders in Council. For an example of an Order in Council consequent on a peace treaty see Order in Council dated 9 February 1920, SR & O 1920/264 (referred to in *Re Grotrian, Cox v Grotrian* supra at 506 and at 791), which terminated the formal state of war with Germany in connection with the 1914–18 war. As to the termination of the 1939–45 war see para 509 post.

3   *R v Bottrill, ex p Kuechenmeister* [1947] KB 41 at 50, [1946] 2 All ER 434 at 436, CA. In a letter not drafted by a lawyer the expression 'for the duration of the war' has been construed as meaning merely 'until the end of hostilities', and a reference to 'the signing of an armistice' has been similarly construed: *Martin v Scottish Transport and General Workers Union* [1952] 1 All ER 691 at 694, HL. In the construction of gifts by will, a state of war has been held to terminate with the cessation of hostilities: see *Re Cooper, Bendall v Cooper* [1946] Ch 109, [1946] 1 All ER 28; *Re Grotrian, Cox v Grotrian* [1955] Ch 501, [1955] 1 All ER 788.

4   As to trading with the enemy generally see para 634 et seq post. A declaration of war does not automatically lead to the frustration of a contract, except where the declaration of war would make the performance of the contract illegal because it would involve trading with the enemy: *Finelvet AG v Vinava Shipping Co Ltd, The 'Chrysalis'* [1983] 2 All ER 658, [1983] 1 WLR 1469; *International Sea Tankers Inc v Hemisphere Shipping Co Ltd, The 'Wenjiang' (No 2)* [1983] 1 Lloyd's Rep 400. The continued performance of a contract will, however, be frustrated by the outbreak of war if it would have involved intercourse with or benefit to the enemy or detriment to the interests of Great Britain: see CONTRACT

vol 9 para 453. This will be so even if some partial provision for the effects of war has been made by the contracting parties: *Fibrosa Spolka Akcyjna v Fairbairn Lawson Combe Barbour Ltd* [1943] AC 32, [1942] 2 All ER 122, HL. See also *Atlantic Maritime Co Inc v Gibbon* [1954] 1 QB 88, [1953] 2 All ER 1086, CA.

5   As to judicial notice of a state of war see EVIDENCE vol 17 para 106. As to war damage see generally para 625 et seq post. As to the disclaimer of leases by reason of war damage and requisitioning of land see LANDLORD AND TENANT vol 27(1) (Reissue) paras 538–541. As to the law of prize see PRIZE vol 37 para 1301 et seq. As to the occupation of territory, and the conventions binding the United Kingdom in the conduct of its relations with other states and with other alien enemies during or as a result of war, see paras 517, 521 et seq post.

6   In 1982 the United Kingdom government indicated formally that it was not in a state of war with Argentina. The Lord President of the Council stated, 'should Argentina formally declare war against the United Kingdom, an immediate statement would be made to the House': see (1982) 53 BYIL 519 at 520.

7   'The laws of war' refer to those treaties or conventions discussed in para 516 text and note 1 post, along with the relevant principles of customary international law.

8   As to the Trading with the Enemy Act 1939 see para 634 et seq post. The Board of Trade may by order direct that the provisions of that Act apply in relation to any area specified in the order as they apply in relation to enemy territory: see s 15(1A) (as added); and para 636 post. It is suggested that that provision could not be interpreted so as to make the 1939 Act applicable to foreign territory when there is no state of war existing between the United Kingdom and that other state. See also McNair and Watts *The Legal Effects of War* (4th Edn, 1966) p 364.

    As to the Board of Trade generally see CONSTITUTIONAL LAW AND HUMAN RIGHTS vol 8(2) (Reissue) para 505; TRADE, INDUSTRY AND INDUSTRIAL RELATIONS vol 47 (Reissue) para 2.

9   'The law knows nothing of an intermediate state which is neither one thing nor the other – neither peace nor war': *Janson v Driefontein Consolidated Mines Ltd* [1902] AC 484 at 497, HL, per Lord Macnaghten; and see *The Gleneam* [1941] P 51, [1941] 1 All ER 371. In addition, litigation between British and enemy subjects may continue: *Eastern Carrying Insurance Co v National Benefit Life and Property Assurance Co Ltd* (1919) 35 TLR 292.

10   See the Import, Export and Customs Powers (Defence) Act 1939 s 1 (as amended); and CUSTOMS AND EXCISE vol 12 paras 1061–1063.

11   See the United Nations Act 1946 s 1(1), which refers to the Charter of the United Nations art 41 (measures not involving the use of armed force). As to the Charter of the United Nations see para 501 note 4 ante.

12   See the Emergency Laws (Re-enactments and Repeals) Act 1964 s 2; and para 599 post.

13   See eg EC Commission Regulation 2340/90 (OJ L213, 9.8.90, p 1); EC Council Regulation 3155/90 (OJ L304, 1.11.90, p 1).

14   See eg the Import, Export and Customs Powers (Defence) Act 1939 s 1; and the Export of Goods (Control) (Iraq and Kuwait Sanctions) Order 1990, SI 1990/1640.

507. Levying of war by British subjects.

Any person owing allegiance to the Crown[1] will be guilty of treason if he levies war against the monarch within the realm or if he adheres to the monarch's enemies by giving them aid or comfort within the realm or elsewhere[2]. He may also be guilty of inciting, aiding or abetting an act of treason[3] or of misprision of treason[4].

1   As to allegiance see generally BRITISH NATIONALITY, IMMIGRATION AND RACE RELATIONS vol 4(2) (Reissue) para 1; CONSTITUTIONAL LAW AND HUMAN RIGHTS vol 8(2) (Reissue) paras 29–33. An alien resident within British territory owes allegiance to the Crown even though he is not a British subject, and the protection of the Crown does not cease merely because British forces, for strategic or other reasons, have been temporarily withdrawn so that the enemy for a time exercises the rights of an army in occupation: *De Jager v A-G of Natal* [1907] AC 326 at 328, PC. An alien resident in British territory who goes abroad with a British passport also owes a duty of allegiance: see *Joyce v DPP* [1946] AC 347, [1946] 1 All ER 186, HL.

2   As to treason generally see CRIMINAL LAW vol 11(1) (Reissue) paras 76–88.

3   See CRIMINAL LAW vol 11(1) (Reissue) para 82.

4   See CRIMINAL LAW vol 11(1) (Reissue) para 83.

508. Declaration of war.

In order to constitute a legal state of war between the United Kingdom and a foreign state there must be either a formal declaration of war by the Crown[1] or hostilities must have been commenced by the authority of the Crown[2]. Thus hostilities against a foreign state, even though the whole nation joins in, without the concurrence of the executive do not constitute a legal state of war or a legal breach of the peaceful relations existing between the two countries[3]. Such acts of hostility without the authority of the Crown are in certain cases punishable with fine and imprisonment[4].

1   See also para 506 ante. Declarations of war are usually transmitted through the ambassador of the foreign government and announced to the nation by means of a proclamation. To ascertain the date of war, the declaration transmitted through the British ambassador at the foreign court to the Foreign Office may be used in evidence (*Thelluson v Cosling* (1803) 4 Esp 266), or, it seems, the proclamation announcing the war might be used under the Evidence Act 1845 s 3 (as amended). The necessity for a declaration of war is laid down in the International Convention relative to the Opening of Hostilities (Hague Convention III) (The Hague, 18 October 1907; TS 8 (1910); Cd 5029), whereby hostilities must not commence without previous and explicit warning, in the form either of a reasoned declaration of war or an ultimatum with a conditional declaration of war: art 1. There is also a duty to notify the existence of a state of war to neutral countries without delay: art 2. As to the Hague Conventions see para 518 post. The relevance of a declaration of war irrespective of the outlawry of aggressive war by the International Treaty for the Renunciation of War as an Instrument of National Policy ('The Kellogg-Briand Pact') (see para 501 note 3 ante) was affirmed by the International Military Tribunal at Nuremberg in its judgment of 30 September 1946 (Cmd 6964) 36–37. See also the Charter of the United Nations art 2 para 4; and 2 Oppenheim's International Law (7th Edn) p 290. As to the Charter of the United Nations see para 501 note 4 ante.

2   A de facto state of war may exist between two countries even though there has been no formal declaration, provided hostilities have actually commenced: *The Teutonia* (1872) LR 4 PC 171. For the purposes of offences under the Foreign Enlistment Act 1870 s 8, a declaration of war by one of two foreign belligerents, or a declaration of neutrality by this country, is not necessary, provided hostilities have actually commenced: *United States of America v Pelly* [1899] WN 11. See also para 513 post. However, a seizure of goods belonging to an alien enemy by the government of a foreign state intending to embark upon war with the United Kingdom, but before the commencement of actual hostilities or a formal declaration of war, does not relieve an insurer of the goods in the United Kingdom of his liability under the contract of insurance: *Janson v Driefontein Consolidated Mines Ltd* [1902] AC 484, 4 BILC 682, HL; see also *Nigel Gold Mining Co Ltd v Hoade* [1901] 2 KB 849. Where the policy contained a warranty against 'capture, seizure and detention, and the consequences thereof', it was held otherwise: *Robinson Gold Mining Co v Alliance Insurance Co* [1904] AC 359, HL. As to the effect of such a warranty where a neutral ship was captured as prize and subsequently lost by wreck see *Andersen v Marten* [1908] AC 334, HL. For the meaning of 'United Kingdom' see para 502 note 4 ante.

3   4 Co Inst 152; 1 Bl Com (14th Edn) 252, 257. War is a contention between two or more states, through their armed forces, for the purpose of overpowering each other and imposing such conditions of peace as the victor pleases: 2 Oppenheim's International Law (7th Edn) p 202.

4   Under the Foreign Enlistment Act 1870 various offences relating to the fitting out of ships, expeditions etc to be used in the service of any state at war with any friendly state are made punishable: see para 512 et seq post. By the rules of international law, as generally received, no breach of neutrality is committed by the government of a state in permitting its subjects to fit out and sell ships of war, arms etc in good faith to a friendly state at war with another friendly state, such ships, arms etc being merely articles of commerce, and neutrals being permitted to carry on their commerce with belligerents subject to the risk of capture and confiscation, if contraband. Contracts, therefore, between subjects of a neutral state to export contraband goods to a belligerent (*Re Grazebrook, ex p Chavasse* (1865) 4 De GJ & Sm 655, LC), or relating to trade with a blockaded port (*The Helen* (1865) LR 1 A & E 1), are not illegal, and may be enforced in the country in which they are made. Private persons taken in actual acts of hostility against a friendly state may, it seems, be treated as mere pirates or robbers by the latter (1 Bl Com (14th Edn) 257), though they are sometimes handed over to their own government for punishment. For an example of such a case see *R v Jameson* [1896] 2 QB 425, 3 BILC 611, DC, where, however, the government in question was under British suzerainty.

509. Termination of the 1939–45 war. The 1939–45 war was never terminated by a peace treaty as regards Germany although the state of war was formally terminated at 4 pm on 9 July 1951[1]. The state of war with Italy, Romania, Bulgaria, Hungary and Finland was ended on 15 September 1947[2], with Austria on 16 September 1947[3], and with Japan on 8 September 1951[4], and powers to make Orders in Council for carrying out the peace treaties were conferred by statute[5].

1   See the declaration published in the supplement to the London Gazette dated 9 July 1951 at p 3739, and corrected in the London Gazette dated 2 October 1951 at p 5117. See also the declaration dated 5 June 1945 on the Unconditional Surrender of Germany (Cmd 6648). As to the termination of war generally see para 506 ante.

2   See the declaration in the London Gazette dated 16 September 1947 at p 4339.

3   See the declaration in the London Gazette dated 16 September 1947 at p 4340.

4   See the Treaty of Peace with Japan (San Francisco, 8 September 1951; TS 33 (1952); Cmd 8601).

5   Ie by the Treaties of Peace (Italy, Romania, Bulgaria, Hungary and Finland) Act 1947 (see the Treaty of Peace with Italy (Paris, 10 February 1947; TS 50 (1948) Cmd 7481); and the Treaties of Peace with Bulgaria, with Finland, with Hungary and with Romania (Paris, 10 February 1947; TS 52–55 (1948); Cmds 7483–7486)); the Japanese Treaty of Peace Act 1951 (see the Treaty of Peace with Japan); and the Austrian State Treaty Act 1955 (see the State Treaty for the Re-establishment of an Independent and Democratic Austria (Vienna, 15 May 1955; TS 58 (1957); Cmnd 214)). As to Parliamentary sanction to treaties see CONSTITUTIONAL LAW AND HUMAN RIGHTS vol 8(2) (Reissue) para 802.

(2) PREROGATIVE POWERS IN WARTIME

510. Blockade and angary. In time of war the Crown may promulgate blockades of ports or any portion of the coast belonging to an enemy[1]. The Crown has also, by right of its prerogative, a jus angariae, that is to say a right to appropriate the property of a neutral where necessity requires in time of war. This right of angary can only be exercised subject to the right of the neutral owner to receive compensation, which may be enforced by legal process[2].

1   As to the requirements of international law regarding the establishment of a blockade see the Declaration of Paris respecting Maritime Law (Paris, 16 April 1856; 46 BFSP 26); 2 Oppenheim's International Law (7th Edn) pp 767–797; and PRIZE vol 37 para 1314 et seq.

2   *Commercial and Estates Co of Egypt v Ball* (1920) 36 TLR 526; *Commercial and Estates Co of Egypt v Board of Trade* [1925] 1 KB 271, CA. The rules relating to the right of angary are well-established rules of international law which have been received as part of English municipal law, and will be applied as such by English municipal courts. By international law a belligerent power has the right to requisition vessels or goods in the custody of its prize court pending a decision of the question whether they should be condemned or released, but such right is subject to certain limitations: *The Zamora* [1916] 2 AC 77 at 106, PC. For the limitations on the right of angary see PRIZE vol 37 para 1312 et seq. See also CONSTITUTIONAL LAW AND HUMAN RIGHTS vol 8(2) (Reissue) para 814.

511. Requisition of British ships. In time of war or national emergency the Crown has a prerogative right to requisition British ships in territorial waters[1]. The requisition of ships and of anything on board ship[2] and the requisition of shipping space were effected during the 1939–45 war under defence regulations[3] and compensation was payable in accordance with statute[4], there being established a shipping claims tribunal for determining disputes as to the payment of compensation[5].

1   See CONSTITUTIONAL LAW AND HUMAN RIGHTS vol 8(2) (Reissue) para 813; and see the Prerogative Order in Council Requisition of Ships Order 1982 (4 April 1982) (relating to the Falkland Islands conflict).

2   A mere order to discharge a cargo is not necessarily a requisition of the cargo: see *Nicolaou v Minister of War Transport* [1944] 2 All ER 322.

3   See the Defence (General) Regulations 1939, SR & O 1939/927, regs 53, 54 (revoked).

4   See the Compensation (Defence) Act 1939 s 1(1)(b), s 4 (as amended), ss 5, 6; and para 600 et seq post.

5   See ibid s 8(1), (2); and para 606 post. As to insurance of ships against war risks see INSURANCE vol 25 (Reissue) para 155 et seq.

(3) NEUTRALITY AND ILLEGAL ACTIVITIES

512. Foreign enlistment. It is a statutory offence[1]:

(1) for any British subject[2], within or without Her Majesty's dominions, to accept, or agree to accept, without Her Majesty's licence[3], any commission or engagement in the military or naval service[4] of any foreign state[5] at war[6] with any friendly state (that is, a foreign state which is at peace with Her Majesty)[7];

(2) for anyone, whether a British subject or not, within Her Majesty's dominions to induce any other person to accept, or agree to accept, any such commission or engagement[8];

(3) for any British subject without Her Majesty's licence to quit, or go on board any ship[9] with a view of quitting, Her Majesty's dominions with intent to accept any such commission or engagement[10];

(4) for anyone, whether a British subject or not, within Her Majesty's dominions to induce any other person to quit, or to go on board any ship with a view of quitting, Her Majesty's dominions with the like intent[11];

(5) for anyone to induce any other person to quit Her Majesty's dominions or to embark on any ship within Her Majesty's dominions under a misrepresentation or false representation of the service in which that person is to be engaged with the intent or in order that that person may accept, or agree to accept, any such commission[12];

(6) for the master[13] or owner of any ship without Her Majesty's licence knowingly to take, or engage to take, or to have on board the ship within Her Majesty's dominions any illegally enlisted person[14].

A person guilty of any such offence is punishable by a fine or imprisonment for not more than two years, or both by a fine and by such imprisonment, at the discretion of the court[15]. In the case of an offence under head (6) above, the ship must be detained until the trial and conviction or acquittal of the master or owner, and until all penalties inflicted on him have been paid, or until he has given security for the payment of those penalties to the satisfaction of two justices of the peace[16].

---

1   Ie under the Foreign Enlistment Act 1870 ss 4–7: see heads (1)–(6) in the text. It has been said that it was a misdemeanour at common law to enter the service of any foreign state without the leave of the Sovereign: 1 East PC 81. Mercenary service abroad was very common before the passing of the Foreign Enlistment Act 1870. It is said to be unlawful for a British subject to receive a pension from a foreign king or state without the Sovereign's licence: 3 Co Inst 144.

2   For the meaning of 'British subject' see BRITISH NATIONALITY, IMMIGRATION AND RACE RELATIONS vol 4(2) (Reissue) paras 3, 52 et seq; and as to British citizenship generally see BRITISH NATIONALITY, IMMIGRATION AND RACE RELATIONS vol 4(2) (Reissue) para 12 et seq.

3   A licence is required to be under the sign manual or to be signified by Order in Council or by proclamation: Foreign Enlistment Act 1870 s 15.

4   For these purposes, 'military service' includes military telecommunications and any other employment whatever in or in connection with any military operation; and 'naval service', as respects a person, includes service as a marine, employment as a pilot in piloting or directing the course of a ship of war or other ship when that ship is being used in any military or naval operation, and any employment whatever on board a ship of war, transport, store ship, privateer or ship under letters of marque; and as respects a ship, includes any user of a ship as a transport, store ship, privateer or ship under letters of marque: see ibid s 30 (definition of 'military service' amended by the Telecommunications Act 1984 s 109(1), Sch 4 para 5). For the meaning of 'ship' see note 9 infra. It is uncertain whether military or naval service for these purposes includes service in an air force; but see generally *Dyke v Elliott, The Gauntlett* (1872) LR 4 PC 184 at 192 (the definitions in the Foreign Enlistment Act 1870 are not restrictive but inclusive).

5   'Foreign state' includes any foreign prince, colony, province or part of any province or people, or any person or persons exercising or assuming to exercise the powers of government in or over any foreign country, colony, province or part of any province or people: ibid s 30. See also *R v Carlin, The Salvador* (1870) LR 3 PC 218 (a decision under the Foreign Enlistment Act 1819 (repealed)). For a discussion of the difficulties of interpretation and the application of the Foreign Enlistment Act 1870 in the case of mercenaries see the *Report of the Committee of Privy Counsellors appointed to inquire into the Recruitment of Mercenaries* (1976) (Cmnd 6569).

6   It is uncertain whether 'war' for these purposes includes international police action.

7   Foreign Enlistment Act 1870 s 4. For decisions with reference to illegal enlistment etc under the Foreign Enlistment Act 1819 (repealed) see *R v Rumble* (1864) 4 F & F 175; *R v Jones and Highat* (1864) 4 F & F 25; *R v Corbett* (1865) 4 F & F 555; *Burton v Pinkerton* (1867) LR 2 Exch 340.

8   Foreign Enlistment Act 1870 s 4; and see note 7 supra. The penalty for such inducement is the same as the penalty for the principal offence: see the text and note 15 infra.

9   'Ship' includes any description of boat, vessel, floating battery or floating craft and also any description of boat, vessel or other craft or battery made to move either on the surface of or under water, or sometimes on the surface of and sometimes under water: ibid s 30.

10 Ibid s 5.

11 Ibid s 5. The penalty for such inducement is the same as the penalty for the principal offence: see the text and note 15 infra.

12 Ibid s 6.

13 'Master' includes any person having charge or command of a ship: ibid s 30.

14 Ibid s 7. On the discovery of such an offence, all illegally enlisted persons are to be taken on shore immediately and not be allowed to return to the ship: s 7. 'Illegally enlisted person' means (1) any person who, being a British subject within or without Her Majesty's dominions, has without Her Majesty's licence accepted or agreed to accept such a commission or engagement as is mentioned in head (1) in the text; or (2) any person, being a British subject, who without such a licence is about to quit Her Majesty's dominions with intent to accept any such commission or engagement; or (3) any person who has been induced to embark under a misrepresentation or false representation of the service in which he is to be engaged with the intent that he may accept or agree to accept any such commission or engagement: s 7.

15 Ibid ss 4–7, 13 (amended by virtue of the Criminal Justice Act 1948 s 1(2)). Any person who aids, abets, counsels or procures the commission of any such offence is liable to be tried and punished as a principal offender: Foreign Enlistment Act 1870 s 12. As to participation in crime generally see CRIMINAL LAW vol 11(1) (Reissue) paras 43–50.

16 Ibid s 7.

513. Illegal shipbuilding etc. It is a statutory offence[1] for any person within Her Majesty's dominions and without Her Majesty's licence[2]:

(1)   to build[3] or agree to build or cause to be built any ship with intent or knowledge or having reasonable cause to believe that it is to be, or will be, employed in the military or naval service[4] of any foreign state[5] at war[6] with any friendly state[7]; or

(2)   to issue any commission for, or equip[8] or dispatch or cause or allow to be dispatched, any ship with the like intent or knowledge[9]; or

(3)   by adding to the number of guns, or by changing those on board for other guns, or by the addition of any equipment for war, to increase or augment, or procure to be increased or augmented, the warlike force of any ship which, at the time of her being within Her Majesty's dominions, was in the military or naval service of any foreign state at war with a friendly state[10].

A person guilty of any of these offences is punishable by a fine or imprisonment for not more than two years, or both by a fine and by such imprisonment, at the discretion of the court[11]. In the case of any offence under head (1) or head (2) above, the ship in respect of which the offence is committed is forfeited, with her equipment[12], to the Crown[13]. A person building, causing to be built or equipping a ship in pursuance of a contract made before the commencement of the war is not, however, liable to any such penalties if, forthwith upon Her Majesty's proclamation of neutrality, that person:

(a)   gives notice to the Secretary of State that he is so building, causing to be built or equipping the ship, and furnishes such particulars of the contract and of any matters relating to, or done or to be done under, the contract as may be required by the Secretary of State; and

(b)   gives such security and takes and permits to be taken such other measures as the Secretary of State may prescribe for ensuring that the ship is not dispatched, delivered or removed without Her Majesty's licence until the termination of the war[14].

1   Ie under the Foreign Enlistment Act 1870 ss 8, 10: see heads (1)–(3) in the text; and see *R v Sandoval* (1887) 3 TLR 411; *R v Granatelli* (1849) 7 State Tr NS 979; *A-G v Sillem* (1864) 2 H & C 431; *R v Rumble* (1864) 4 F & F 175; *Re Grazebrook, ex p Chavasse* (1865) 4 De GJ & Sm 655 (decisions under the Foreign Enlistment Act 1819 (repealed)).
2   As to the form of the licence see para 512 note 3 ante.
3   'Building', in relation to a ship, includes doing any act towards or incidental to the construction of a ship, and all words having relation to building are to be construed accordingly: Foreign Enlistment Act 1870 s 30. For the meaning of 'ship' see para 512 note 9 ante.
4   For the meaning of 'military service' and 'naval service' see para 512 note 4 ante.
5   For the meaning of 'foreign state' see para 512 note 5 ante.
6   As to evidence of the outbreak of war see *United States of America v Pelly* (1899) 47 WR 332.
7   Foreign Enlistment Act 1870 s 7. Where any ship is built by order of, or on behalf of, any foreign state when at war with a friendly state, or is delivered to, or to the order of, such foreign state, or any person who to the knowledge of the person building is an agent of such foreign state, or is paid for by such foreign state or such agent, and is employed in the military or naval service of such foreign state, that ship is, until the contrary is proved, deemed to have been built with a view to being so employed, and the burden lies on the builder of the ship of proving that he did not know that it was intended to be so employed in the military or naval service of the foreign state: s 9. For the meaning of 'friendly state' see para 512 ante.
8   'Equipping', in relation to a ship, includes furnishing a ship with any tackle, apparel, furniture, provisions, arms, munitions, or stores, or any other thing which is used in or about a ship for the purpose of fitting or adapting her for the sea or for naval service, and all words relating to equipment are to be construed accordingly: ibid s 30.
9   Ibid s 8. To let a tug to one of the combatants for the purpose of towing a prize with a prize crew on board to home waters of the captor is the dispatching of a ship for the purpose of taking part in the naval service of that combatant: *Dyke v Elliott, The Gauntlet* (1872) LR 4 PC 184.
10   Foreign Enlistment Act 1870 s 10.
11   Ibid ss 8, 10, 13 (amended by virtue of the Criminal Justice Act 1948 s 1(2)). Accessories may be punished as principals: see the Foreign Enlistment Act 1870 s 12; and para 512 text and note 15 ante.
12   'Ship and equipment' includes a ship and everything in or belonging to a ship: ibid s 30. Provision is made for the restoration to their owners of prizes captured by ships illegally built etc: see s 14; and PRIZE vol 37 para 1308.
13   Ibid s 8.
14   See ibid s 8.

514. Illegal expeditions. If any person within Her Majesty's dominions and without Her Majesty's licence[1] prepares or fits out any naval or military expedition to proceed against the dominions of any friendly state[2], any person engaged in the preparation or fitting out or assisting in it, or employed in any capacity in that expedition, is guilty of an offence[3]. If the illegal expedition is to any extent prepared within Her Majesty's dominions, the participation in it by a British subject outside those dominions is also an offence[4].

A person guilty of such an offence is punishable by a fine or imprisonment for a term not exceeding two years, or both by a fine and by such imprisonment, at the discretion of the court[5]. All ships and their equipment[6] and all arms and munitions of war used in or forming part of the expedition are to be forfeited to Her Majesty[7].

1   As to the form of licence see para 512 note 3 ante.
2   For the meaning of 'friendly state' see para 512 ante.

3 Foreign Enlistment Act 1870 s 11. It is not necessary in order to constitute an offence under s 11 that the expedition should be completely fitted out in this country; any act of preparation is sufficient: *R v Sandoval* (1887) 56 LT 526; and see *R v Jameson* [1896] 2 QB 425, DC.

4 *R v Jameson* [1896] 2 QB 425, DC. The Secretary of State and certain public officers have powers of search, seizure and detention of suspected vessels: see para 515 post.

5 Foreign Enlistment Act 1870 ss 11, 13 (amended by virtue of the Criminal Justice Act 1948 s 1(2)). Any overt act of preparation for such an expedition, eg the purchase of guns in this country which are sent to a foreign port to be shipped there on the vessel in which the expedition is to be made, is an offence against the 1870 Act: *R v Sandoval* (1887) 56 LT 526. Accessories are punished as principal offenders: see the Foreign Enlistment Act 1870 s 12; and para 512 text and note 15 ante.

6 For the meaning of 'ship' see para 512 note 9 ante; and for the meaning of 'ship and equipment' see para 513 note 12 ante.

7 Foreign Enlistment Act 1870 s 11.

515. Powers to seize and detain ships. The following officers may seize or detain any ship[1] liable to be seized or detained in pursuance of the provisions relating to foreign enlistment[2], illegal shipbuilding[3] and illegal expeditions[4]:

(1) any officer of Customs and Excise in the United Kingdom[5], subject to any special or general instructions from the Commissioners of Customs and Excise, or any officer of the Board of Trade[6], subject to any special or general instructions from that board;

(2) any officer of customs or public officer in any British possession[7], subject to any special or general instructions from the governor[8] of that possession;

(3) any commissioned officer on full pay in the military service[9] of the Crown, subject to any special or general instructions from his commanding officer; and

(4) any commissioned officer on full pay in the naval service[10] of the Crown, subject to any special or general instructions from the Defence Council or his superior officer[11].

Any officer authorised to seize or detain any ship in respect of any offence under those provisions may, for the purpose of enforcing that seizure or detention, call to his aid certain specified persons[12] and may put on board one or more of such persons to take charge of the ship and to enforce the statutory prohibitions[13]. Any officer so seizing or detaining any ship may use force for the purpose, if necessary, and if any person is killed or maimed by reason of his resisting that officer in the execution of his duties, or any person acting under his orders, that officer or other person is freely and fully indemnified both against Her Majesty and against all persons so killed, maimed or hurt[14].

If the Secretary of State or the chief executive authority[15] is satisfied that there is a reasonable and probable cause for believing that a ship within Her Majesty's dominions has been or is being built, commissioned, or equipped[16] contrary to the statutory provisions, and is about to be taken beyond the limits of those dominions, or that a ship is about to be dispatched contrary to those provisions, he has power to issue a warrant stating that there is reasonable and probable cause for such belief, and the officers mentioned above have power upon that warrant to seize and search that ship, and to detain it until it has been either condemned or released by process of law[17]. The owner of the ship or his agent may apply to the court[18] for its release, and the court must as soon as possible put the matter of the seizure and detention in course of trial between the applicant and the Crown[19]. If the applicant establishes to the court's satisfaction that the ship was not and is not being so built, commissioned or equipped, or intended to be dispatched, the ship must be released and restored, but must otherwise be detained until released by order of the Secretary of State or chief executive authority[20]. In cases where no proceedings are pending for its condemnation, the court may release any ship so detained on the owner giving security to its satisfaction that the ship will not be employed contrary to the statutory provisions, notwithstanding that the applicant may have failed to establish to the court's satisfaction that the ship was not and is not being so built, commissioned or equipped, or intended to be dispatched, and the Secretary of State or the chief executive authority may likewise release any ship so detained, either with or without the owner giving security[21]. If the court is of the opinion that there was not reasonable and probable cause for the detention, and if no such cause appears in the course of the proceedings, the court has power to declare that the owner is to be indemnified by the payment of costs and damages in respect of the detention, the amount of which is to be assessed by the court, and any amount so assessed is payable by the Treasury out of any money legally applicable for that purpose[22]. Nothing in these provisions affects any proceedings instituted or to be instituted for the condemnation of any ship detained under them where the ship is liable to forfeiture, except that if that ship is restored all proceedings for its condemnation are to be stayed[23]; and nothing in them applies to any foreign non-commissioned ship dispatched from any part of Her Majesty's dominions after having come within them under stress of weather or in the course of a peaceful voyage, and upon which ship no fitting out or equipping of a warlike character has taken place in this country[24].

Where it is represented to any such officer as is mentioned in heads (1) to (4) above, and that officer believes, that there is a reasonable and probable cause for believing that a ship within Her Majesty's dominions has been or is being built, commissioned or equipped contrary to the statutory provisions, and is about to be taken beyond the limits of those dominions, or that a ship is about to be dispatched contrary to those provisions, it is his duty to detain the ship and forthwith to communicate the fact of that detention to the Secretary of State or chief executive authority[25]. Upon the receipt of that communication, the Secretary of State or chief executive authority may order the ship to be released if he thinks there is no cause for detaining her, but if satisfied that there is reasonable and probable cause for believing that it was so built, commissioned or equipped or intended to be dispatched, he must issue his warrant stating that there is reasonable and probable cause for the belief communicated to him, and upon that warrant being issued further proceedings are to be taken in the same way as in cases where the seizure or detention has taken place on a warrant issued by the Secretary of State without any such communication[26].

The Secretary of State or the chief executive authority may, by warrant, empower any person to enter any dockyard or other place within Her Majesty's dominions and inquire as to the destination of any ship which may appear to him to be intended to be employed in the naval or military service of any foreign state at war with a friendly state, and to search that ship[27]. Neither the Secretary of State nor the chief executive authority is responsible in any action or other legal proceedings whatsoever for any warrant issued by him in pursuance of these provisions, and he is not examinable as a witness except at his own request in any court of justice in respect of the circumstances which led to the issue of the warrant[28].

1   For the meaning of 'ship' see para 512 note 9 ante.
2   Ie the Foreign Enlistment Act 1870 ss 4–7: see para 512 ante.
3   Ie ibid ss 8–10: see para 513 ante.
4   Ie ibid s 11: see para 514 ante.
5   For the purposes of the Foreign Enlistment Act 1870 generally, 'United Kingdom' includes the Isle of Man, the Channel Islands and other adjacent islands: s 30. For these purposes, however, special provision is made in relation to the Isle of Man: see s 21 (amended by the Isle of Man (Transfer of Functions) Order 1980, SI 1980/399, art 2, Schedule para 1). For the meaning of 'United Kingdom' generally see para 502 note 4 ante.
6   As to the Board of Trade see CONSTITUTIONAL LAW AND HUMAN RIGHTS vol 8(2) (Reissue) para 505; TRADE, INDUSTRY AND INDUSTRIAL RELATIONS vol 47 (Reissue) para 2.

7   'British possession' means any territory, colony, or place being part of Her Majesty's dominions, and not part of the United Kingdom as defined in note 5 supra: see the Foreign Enlistment Act 1870 s 30. As to the remaining such territories etc see COMMONWEALTH vol 6 (Reissue) para 978 et seq.

8   'Governor', as respects a British possession which consists of several constituent colonies, means the Governor General of the whole possession or the governor of any of the constituent colonies, and as respects any other British possession means the officer for the time being administering the government of that possession; also any person acting for or in the capacity of a governor is included under the term: ibid s 30 (definition amended by the Government of India (Adaptation of Acts of Parliament) Order 1937, SR & O 1937/230, art 2, Schedule).

9   For the meaning of 'military service' see para 512 note 4 ante.

10   For the meaning of 'naval service' see para 512 note 4 ante.

11   Foreign Enlistment Act 1870 s 21 (amended by the Customs and Excise Management Act 1979 s 177(1), Sch 4 para 1; the Defence (Transfer of Functions) (No 1) Order 1964, SI 1964/488, art 2, Sch 1 Pt I; and the Isle of Man (Transfer of Functions) Order 1980 (see note 5 supra)). Nothing contained in the Foreign Enlistment Act 1870, however, derogates from the power of the Court of Admiralty (now the Admiralty Division of the High Court) to direct any ship to be seized or detained by any officer by whom that court has power under its ordinary jurisdiction to direct a ship to be seized or detained: see s 21. Subject to the provisions of that Act providing for the award of damages by the court in certain cases in respect of the seizure or detention of a ship, no damages are payable, and no such officer as is mentioned in heads (1)–(4) in the text is responsible, either civilly or criminally, in respect of the seizure or detention of any ship in pursuance thereof: s 28. Such officers are referred to in the statute as 'the local authority': see s 21.

12   Ie any constable or officers of police, or any officers of the army, navy or marines of the Crown, or any customs and excise officers, or any harbour master or dock master, or any officers having authority by law to make seizures of ships: see ibid s 22 (amended by the Customs and Excise Management Act 1979 Sch 4 para 1).

13   Foreign Enlistment Act 1870 s 22.

14   Ibid s 22. See also s 28 (cited in note 11 supra).

15   'The chief executive authority' means (1) in Jersey, the Lieutenant Governor; (2) in Guernsey, Alderney and Sark and the dependent islands, the Lieutenant Governor; (3) in the Isle of Man, the Governor in Council; and (4) in any British possession, the governor: see ibid s 26 (amended by the Northern Ireland (Modification of Enactments – No 1) Order 1973, SI 1973/2163, art 14(2), Sch 6; and the Isle of Man (Transfer of Functions) Order 1980 Schedule para 2).

16   As to the meaning of 'built' and 'equipped' see para 513 notes 3, 8 ante.

17   Foreign Enlistment Act 1870 s 23.

18   Ie the Admiralty Division of the High Court: see ADMIRALTY vol 1(1) (Reissue) para 348. As to the jurisdiction of that court under the Foreign Enlistment Act 1870 see ss 16–20; and see also CRIMINAL LAW vol 11(1) (Reissue) para 634. Nothing contained in that Act is to subject to forfeiture any commissioned ship of any foreign state, or to give to any British court over or in respect of any ship entitled to recognition as a commissioned ship of any foreign state any jurisdiction which it would not have had if the Act had not been passed: s 32. For the meaning of 'foreign state' see para 512 note 5 ante.

19   Ibid s 23.

20   Ibid s 23. There is a right of appeal against any decision of the court under these provisions: see s 27.

21   See ibid s 23.

22   Ibid s 23. The court also has power to make a like order for the indemnity of the owner, on his application, in a summary way, in cases where the ship is released by the order of the Secretary of State or the chief executive authority before any application is made by the owner or his agent to the court for such release: s 23.

23   Where the court declares that the owner is to be indemnified by the payment of costs and damages for the detainer, all costs, charges and expenses incurred by the owner in or about any proceedings for the condemnation of the ship must be added to the costs and damages payable to him in respect of the detention of the ship: ibid s 23.

24   Ibid s 23.

25   See ibid s 24.

26   See ibid s 24. Where the Secretary of State or chief executive authority orders the ship to be released on the receipt of such a communication without issuing his warrant, the owner of the ship must be indemnified by the payment of costs and damages in respect of the detention upon application to the court in a summary way in like manner as he is entitled to be indemnified where the Secretary of State has issued his warrant and releases the ship before any application is made by the owner or his agent to the court for such release: s 24.

27   Ibid s 25.

28   See ibid s 29.

3. INTERNATIONAL AGREEMENTS AND CONVENTIONS

(1) IN GENERAL

516. The laws of war. The laws of war[1] are the rules which govern the conduct of war or other armed conflict[2]. They are binding upon both belligerents and upon neutrals. They are binding not only upon states, but also upon individuals, and in particular upon members of armed forces[3]. The laws of war, as part of international law, consist partly of customary rules which have been evolved by practice and partly of written rules expressly agreed upon by states in international agreements[4].

1   The laws of war are also known as international humanitarian law, defined as 'international rules, established by treaties or custom, which are specifically intended to solve humanitarian problems directly arising from international or non-international armed conflicts and which, for humanitarian reasons, limit the right of parties to a conflict to use the methods and means of warfare of their choice or protect persons and property that are, or may be, affected by conflict': Commentary on the Additional Protocols of 10 June 1977 to the Geneva Conventions of 12 August 1949, International Committee of the Red Cross (Geneva, 1987) p xxvii.

2   These rules apply in cases of armed conflict whether the conflict is lawful or unlawful in its inception under the rules of international law.

3   The argument that the laws of war are binding upon states only and not upon individuals was emphatically rejected by the International Military Tribunal at Nuremberg in its judgment of 30 September 1946 upon the cases of German War Criminals (Cmd 6964) 41. All the war crimes trials conducted after the 1939–45 war proceeded upon the basis of individual responsibility. See also *The Prosecutor v Dusko Tadic* (2 October 1995, unreported), Former Yugoslavia International Tribunal, Appeals Chamber. As to the Former Yugoslavia International Tribunal see para 563 post.

4   See *Schiffahrt-Treuhand GmbH v HM Procurator-General* [1953] AC 232 at 261–262, [1953] 1 All ER 364 at 372, PC. As to international agreements see para 517 post. References to the customs of war may be found in the War Crimes Act 1991 s 1(1)(b); and in the Statute of the International Tribunal for the Prosecution of Persons Responsible for Serious Violations of International Humanitarian Law Committed in the Territory of Former Yugoslavia since 1991 art 3 (adopted by UN Security Council Resolution 827 (25 May 1993)) as set out in the United Nations (International Tribunal) (Former Yugoslavia) Order 1996, SI 1996/716.

517. International agreements and conventions. Since 1856 there have been many international agreements and conventions[1] to regulate the conduct of war and to lessen the sufferings both of those engaged in it and also of the populations of the countries in which it takes place.

The main agreements are the Hague Conventions and Declarations of 1899[2] and 1907[3], and the Geneva Conventions of 1864, 1906, 1929 and 1949, known as the 'Geneva Red Cross Conventions'[4]. Among others are the Declaration of Paris 1856[5], dealing with aspects of warfare at sea; the Declaration of St Petersburg 1868[6], renouncing the use in war of small explosive projectiles; the Geneva Protocol 1925[7], prohibiting the use in war of gases and bacteriological methods of warfare; the Hague Convention and Protocol of 1954 on the protection of cultural property[8]; the Genocide Convention[9]; the Environmental Modification Techniques Convention[10]; the Biological Weapons Convention[11]; the Conventional Weapons Convention[12]; and the Chemical Weapons Convention[13].

Conventions (or treaties) to which the United Kingdom is a party have no direct effect in the law of the United Kingdom unless incorporated by an Act of Parliament[14].

1   In this context 'conventions' means treaties and denotes written rules. As to whether treaties are a source of law as opposed to a source of obligations see FOREIGN RELATIONS LAW vol 18 para 1402.

2   Ie the International Convention with respect to the Laws and Customs of War by Land (The Hague, 29 July 1899; TS 11 (1901); Cd 800). See also para 518 post.

3   See para 518 post.

4   Ie the Convention for the Amelioration of the Condition of the Wounded and Sick in Armed Forces in the Field (Geneva, 22 August 1864; BFSP 43); the International Convention for the Amelioration of the Condition of the Wounded and Sick of Armies in the Field (Geneva, 6 July 1906; 99 BFSP 968; Cd 3502); the Convention for the Amelioration of the Condition of the Wounded and Sick in Armed Forces in the Field (Geneva, 27 July 1929; TS 36 (1931); Cmd 3940); the Geneva Convention for the Amelioration of the Condition of the Wounded and Sick in Armed Forces in the Field (see para 521 note 2 post); the Geneva Convention for the Amelioration of the Condition of the Wounded, Sick and Shipwrecked Members of the Armed Forces at Sea (see para 521 note 3 post); the Convention on the Treatment of Prisoners of War (Geneva, 27 July 1929; TS 37 (1931); Cmd 3941); the Geneva Convention relative to the Treatment of Prisoners of War (see para 521 note 4 post); and the Geneva Convention relative to the Protection of Civilian Persons in Time of War (see para 521 note 5 post). As to the Geneva Red Cross Conventions (which are set out in the Schedules to the Geneva Conventions Act 1957) see para 521 et seq post.

5   Ie the Declaration of Paris respecting Maritime Law (Paris, 16 April 1856; 46 BFSP 26).

6   Ie the Declaration renouncing the Use in Time of War of Explosive Projectiles under 400 Grammes Weight (St Petersburg, 29 November to 11 December 1868; 58 BFSP 16).

7   Ie the Protocol concerning the Prohibition of the Use in War of Asphyxiating, Poisonous or other Gases and of Bacteriological Methods of Warfare (Geneva, 17 June 1925; TS 24 (1930); Cmd 3604).

8   Ie the Final Act, Convention and Protocol on the Protection of Cultural Property in the Event of Armed Conflict (The Hague, 14 May 1954; Misc 6 (1956); Cmd 9837).

9   Ie the Convention on the Prevention and Punishment of the Crime of Genocide (Paris, 9 December 1948; TS 58 (1970); Cmnd 4421). See further FOREIGN RELATIONS LAW para 1544; and see also the Genocide Act 1969; and CRIMINAL LAW vol 11(1) (Reissue) para 424.

10 Ie the Convention on the Prohibition of Military or Any Other Hostile Use of Environmental Modification Techniques: see para 520 note 1 post.

11 Ie the Convention on the Prohibition of the Development, Production and Stockpiling of Bacteriological (Biological) and Toxin Weapons and on their Destruction: see paras 568–571 post.

12 Ie the Convention on Prohibitions or Restrictions on the Use of Certain Conventional Weapons Which May Be Deemed to Be Excessively Injurious or to Have Indiscriminate Effects: see para 519 note 1 post. The United Kingdom has signalled its intention to ratify this convention: see para 519 post. For the meaning of 'United Kingdom' see para 502 note 4 ante.

13 Ie the Convention on the Prohibition of the Development, Production, Stockpiling and the Use of Chemical Weapons and on their Destruction: see para 572 et seq post.

14 As to treaties generally see FOREIGN RELATIONS LAW vol 18 para 1769 et seq.

518. The Hague Conventions. At the Hague Conference in 1899, declarations prohibiting the use of asphyxiating gases[1] and expanding bullets[2] were signed, and at a further Hague conference in 1907 conventions were signed relating to (1) the peaceful settlement of international disputes[3]; (2) the limitation of the use of force to recover contract debts[4]; (3) the opening of hostilities[5]; (4) the laws and customs of war on land[6]; (5) the rights and duties of neutral powers and persons in war on land[7]; (6) the status of enemy merchant ships at the outbreak of hostilities[8]; (7) the conversion of merchant ships into warships[9]; (8) the laying of submarine mines[10]; (9) bombardment by naval forces in wartime[11]; (10) the adaptation to maritime war of the principles of the Geneva Convention of 1864[12]; (11) restrictions on the exercise of the right of capture in naval war[13]; (12) the creation of an international prize court[14]; (13) the rights and duties of neutral powers in naval war[15]; and (14) the prohibition of the discharge of projectiles from balloons[16].

1   Ie the Declaration respecting Asphyxiating Gases (The Hague, 29 July 1899; TS 32 (1907); Cd 3751).

2   Ie the Declaration respecting Expanding Bullets (The Hague, 29 July 1899; TS 32 (1907); Cd 3751).

3   Ie the Convention for the Pacific Settlement of International Disputes (Hague Convention I) (The Hague, 18 October 1907; TS 6 (1971); Cmnd 4575).

4   Ie the International Convention respecting the Limitation of the Employment of Force for the Recovery of Contract Debts (Hague Convention II; 'The Porter Convention') (The Hague, 18 October 1907; TS 7 (1910); Cd 5028).

5   Ie the International Convention relative to the Opening of Hostilities (Hague Convention III) (The Hague, 18 October 1907; TS 8 (1910); Cd 5029).

6   Ie the International Convention concerning the Laws and Customs of War on Land (Hague Convention IV) (The Hague, 18 October 1907; TS 9 (1910); Cd 5030). To this convention and to the corresponding convention of 1899 are annexed regulations known as the Hague Regulations 1907 (Cd 4175). See also *Dutch Machines Case* (1949) Ann Dig 390.

7   Ie the International Convention respecting the Rights and Duties of Neutral Powers and Persons in War on Land (Hague Convention V) (The Hague, 18 October 1907). This convention was not ratified by the United Kingdom.

8   Ie the International Convention relative to the Status of Enemy Merchant-Ships at the Outbreak of Hostilities (Hague Convention VI) (The Hague, 18 October 1907; TS 10 (1910); Cd 5031).

9   Ie the International Convention relative to the Conversion of Merchant-Ships into War-Ships (Hague Convention VII) (The Hague, 18 October 1907; TS 11 (1910); Cd 5115).

10 Ie the International Convention relative to the Laying of Automatic Submarine Contact Mines (Hague Convention VIII) (The Hague, 18 October 1907; TS 12 (1910); Cd 5116).

11 Ie the International Convention respecting Bombardments by Naval Forces in Time of War (Hague Convention IX) (The Hague, 18 October 1907; TS 13 (1910); Cd 5117).

12 Ie the International Convention for the Adaptation to Maritime Warfare of the Principles of the Geneva Convention of 1906 (Hague Convention X) (The Hague, 18 October 1907; 100 BFSP 415). The Geneva Convention referred to is now the Geneva Convention for the Amelioration of the Condition of the Wounded, Sick and Shipwrecked Members of the Armed Forces at Sea: see para 521 et seq post.

13 Ie the International Convention relative to Certain Restrictions on the Exercise of the Right of Capture in Maritime War (Hague Convention XI) (The Hague, 18 October 1907; TS 14 (1910); Cd 5118).

14 Ie the International Convention relative to the Establishment of an International Prize Court (Hague Convention XII) (The Hague, 18 October 1907). This convention was not ratified by the United Kingdom.

15 Ie the International Convention respecting the Rights and Duties of Neutral Powers in Maritime Law (Hague Convention XIII) (The Hague, 18 October 1907; 100 BFSP 448). This convention was not ratified by the United Kingdom.

16 Ie the International Declaration prohibiting the Discharge of Projectiles and Explosives from Balloons (Hague Convention XIV) (The Hague, 18 October 1907; TS 15 (1910); Cd 5119).

519. The Conventional Weapons Convention. The Conventional Weapons Convention[1], which the United Kingdom has ratified[2], contains three protocols. Protocol I prohibits the use of any weapon the primary effect of which is to injure by fragments which escape detection by X-rays in the human body[3]; Protocol II imposes certain restrictions on the use of mines, booby-traps and other devices[4]; and Protocol III prohibits or restricts the use of incendiary weapons[5].

The convention and its annexed protocols apply to (1) all cases of declared war or of any other armed conflict which may arise between two or more of the high contracting parties, even if the state of war is not recognised by one of them, and all cases of partial or total occupation of the territory of a high contracting party, even if the occupation meets with no armed resistance[6]; and (2) armed conflicts in which peoples are fighting against colonial domination and alien occupation and against racist regimes in the exercise of their right of self-determination, as enshrined in the Charter of the United Nations and the Declaration on Principles of International Law concerning Friendly Relations and Co-operation among States in accordance with the Charter of the United Nations[7].

The Conventional Weapons Convention provides for the establishment of a review conference to consider amendments to any of the protocols[8]. In 1996 a review conference amended the second protocol[9], which now applies, in addition to the situations mentioned in heads (1) and (2) above, to the case of armed conflict not of an international character occurring in the territory of one of the high contracting parties[10]. It also prohibits the use of anti-personnel mines[11] which are not detectable[12], imposes certain restrictions on the use of remotely-delivered mines[13], prohibits the use of booby-traps and other devices[14], prohibits the transfer of mines whose use is prohibited[15], and imposes an obligation to record minefields, mined areas, mines, booby-traps and other devices[16]. After the cessation of active hostilities all minefields, mined areas, mines, booby-traps and other devices are to be cleared, removed or destroyed[17]. Each high contracting party is also required to take such measures as are feasible to protect a United Nations peacekeeping, observation or similar force or mission from the effects of mines, booby-traps and other devices in the area it controls[18]. Each high contracting party is required to take all appropriate steps, including legislative and other measures, to prevent and suppress violations of this protocol by persons or on territory under its jurisdiction or control[19].

1   Ie the Convention on Prohibitions or Restrictions on the Use of Certain Conventional Weapons Which May Be Deemed to Be Excessively Injurious or Have Indiscriminate Effects (New York, 10 April 1981 to 10 April 1982; Misc 23 (1981); Cmnd 8370) (the 'Conventional Weapons Convention 1981').

2   The United Kingdom deposited its instrument of ratification as a high contracting party to this convention on 13 February 1995: 255 HC Official Report (6th series), 23 February 1995, written answers col *280*. The United Kingdom became bound by the convention six months after it had deposited the instrument of ratification: Conventional Weapons Convention 1981 art 5 para 2. For the meaning of 'United Kingdom' see para 502 note 4 ante.

3   See the Conventional Weapons Convention 1981 Protocol on Non-detectable Fragments (Conventional Weapons Convention 1981 Protocol I).

4   See the Conventional Weapons Convention 1981 Protocol on Prohibitions or Restrictions on the Use of Mines, Booby-traps and Other Devices (Conventional Weapons Convention 1981 Protocol II).

5   See the Conventional Weapons Convention 1981 Protocol on Prohibitions or Restrictions on the Use of Incendiary Weapons (Conventional Weapons Convention 1981 Protocol III).

6   Ie the situations described in the Geneva Conventions Act 1957 Sch 1 art 2, Sch 2 art 2, Sch 3 art 2, Sch 4 art 2: see the Conventional Weapons Convention 1981 art 1; and para 522 post. As to the Geneva Red Cross Conventions 1949 (which are set out in the Schedules to the Geneva Conventions Act 1957) see para 521 et seq post.

7   Ie the situation described in the Geneva Conventions 1949 Protocol I art 1 para 4: see the Conventional Weapons Convention 1981 art 1. As to the application and implementation of the Geneva Conventions 1949 Protocol I see paras 521–522 post. The declaration referred to is the Charter of the United Nations and the Declaration on Principles of International Law Concerning Friendly Relations and Co-operation among States (General Assembly Resolution 2625 (XXV), 24 October 1970).

8   See the Conventional Weapons Convention 1981 art 8.

9   See the Conventional Weapons Convention 1981 Amended Protocol on Prohibitions or Restrictions on the Use of Mines, Booby-Traps and Other Devices (CCW/Conf I/144, 1 May 1996).

10   Ie the situation referred to in the Geneva Conventions Act 1957 Sch 1 art 3, Sch 2 art 3, Sch 3 art 3, Sch 4 art 3: see the Conventional Weapons Convention 1981 Protocol II art 2. It does not, however, apply to situations of internal disturbances and tensions, such as riots, isolated and sporadic acts of violence and other acts of a similar nature, as not being armed conflicts: see art 2. The Conventional Weapons Convention 1981 Protocol II therefore extends the prohibitions or restrictions covered in the Geneva Conventions 1949 Protocol II: see para 523 post. As to the application and implementation of Protocol II see paras 521–522 post. As to the amendment of the Conventional Weapons Convention 1981 Protocol II see note 9 supra.

11   See ibid Protocol II arts 4, 5. As to the amendment of Protocol II see note 9 supra.

12   As to specifications on detectability see ibid Protocol II Technical Annex. As to the amendment of Protocol II see note 9 supra.

13   See ibid Protocol II art 6. As to the amendment of Protocol II see note 9 supra.

14   See ibid Protocol II art 7. As to the amendment of Protocol II see note 9 supra.

15   Ie prohibited by ibid Protocol II: see art 8. As to the amendment of Protocol II see note 9 supra.

16   See ibid Protocol II art 9. As to the amendment of Protocol II see note 9 supra.

17   See ibid Protocol II art 10. As to the amendment of Protocol II see note 9 supra.

18   See ibid Protocol II art 12. The obligations arise when the head of the force or mission requests such protection. Article 12 also applies to protect in a similar, although not identical, way any humanitarian or fact-finding mission of the United Nations system, missions of the International Committee of the Red Cross and other humanitarian missions and missions of enquiry. The exchange of technological information and equipment is provided for in Protocol II art 11. As to the amendment of Protocol II see note 9 supra.

19   See ibid Protocol II art 14. As to the amendment of Protocol II see note 9 supra. It is not anticipated that legislation will be required to enable the United Kingdom to comply with this requirement, since art 14

requires parties to ensure the imposition of penal sanctions against persons who, contrary to the provisions of this protocol, wilfully kill or cause serious injury to civilians. Within the United Kingdom the criminal law is adequate for this purpose. If the acts are committed abroad they will almost certainly be committed by members of the armed forces, who are subject to the criminal law of England and Wales wherever they are serving: see the Army Act 1955 s 70 (as amended); the Air Force Act 1955 s 70 (as amended); and the Naval Discipline Act 1957 s 42.

The high contracting parties undertake to consult and co-operate with each other on all issues relating to the operation of the Conventional Weapons Convention 1981 Protocol II: see Protocol II art 13.

520. The Convention on the Prohibition of Military or Any Other Hostile Use of Environmental Modification Techniques. States accepting the obligations within this convention[1] undertake not to engage in military or other hostile use of environmental modification techniques[2] having widespread, long-lasting or severe effects as the means of destruction, damage or injury to any other state party[3].

1   Ie the Convention on the Prohibition of Military or Any Other Hostile Use of Environmental Modification Techniques (Geneva, 18 May 1977; TS 24 (1979); Cmnd 7469). This convention was ratified by the United Kingdom on 16 May 1978. For the meaning of 'United Kingdom' see para 502 note 4 ante.
2   Ie any technique for changing, through the deliberate manipulation of natural processes, the dynamics, composition or structure of the Earth, including its biota, lithosphere, hydrosphere and atmosphere, or of outer space: ibid art II.
3   See further para 552 post.

(2) GENEVA RED CROSS CONVENTIONS

(i) In general

521. The Geneva Red Cross Conventions. The United Kingdom[1] is a party to the four Geneva Red Cross Conventions of 1949. These are (1) the Convention for the Amelioration of the Condition of the Wounded and Sick in Armed Forces in the Field[2]; (2) the Convention for the Amelioration of the Condition of the Wounded, Sick and Shipwrecked Members of Armed Forces at Sea[3]; (3) the Convention relative to the Treatment of Prisoners of War[4]; and (4) the Convention relative to the Protection of Civilian Persons in Time of War[5].

Conventions (or treaties) to which the United Kingdom is a party have no direct effect in the law of the United Kingdom unless incorporated by an Act of Parliament[6]. Certain parts of the Geneva Red Cross Conventions have been incorporated into the law of the United Kingdom by the Geneva Conventions Act 1957[7], while other provisions have been incorporated in the Army Act 1955, the Air Force Act 1955, the Naval Discipline Act 1957 and by Royal Warrant[8].

In 1977 two protocols were added to the Geneva Red Cross Conventions of 1949. The Geneva Conventions 1949 Protocol I applies to international armed conflict[9] and the Geneva Conventions 1949 Protocol II applies to non-international armed conflict[10]. The Geneva Conventions (Amendment) Act 1995 prospectively incorporates certain provisions of these protocols into the laws of the United Kingdom[11].

The conventions enter into force for a contracting state six months after the deposit of its instrument of ratification or notification of its accession[12]. They may be denounced with effect from one year after notification of denunciation, but no denunciation can take effect during a conflict before peace is concluded and until operations connected with release and repatriation of the persons protected by the conventions have been terminated[13]. An inquiry into alleged violations of the conventions must be instituted at the request of a party to a conflict[14].

1 For the meaning of 'United Kingdom' see para 502 note 4 ante.

2 The first convention was the Convention for the Amelioration of the Condition of the Wounded and Sick of Armed Forces in the Field (Geneva, 22 August 1864; 55 BFSP 43); revised in the form of the International Convention for the Amelioration of the Condition of the Wounded and Sick of Armies in the Field (Geneva, 6 July 1906; 99 BFSP 968; Cd 3502); and again in the form of the Convention for the Amelioration of the Condition of the Wounded and Sick in Armed Forces in the Field (Geneva, 27 July 1929; TS 36 (1931); Cmd 3940); and now as the Geneva Convention for the Amelioration of the Condition of the Wounded and Sick in Armed Forces in the Field (Geneva, 12 August 1949; TS 39 (1958); Cmnd 550).

3 Ie the Geneva Convention for the Amelioration of the Condition of the Wounded, Sick and Shipwrecked Members of the Armed Forces at Sea (Geneva, 12 August 1949; TS 39 (1958); Cmnd 550).

4 This was initially the Convention on the Treatment of Prisoners of War (Geneva, 27 July 1929; TS 37 (1931); Cmd 3941); and now the Geneva Convention relative to the Treatment of Prisoners of War (Geneva, 12 August 1949; TS 39 (1958); Cmnd 550).

5 Ie the Geneva Convention relative to the Protection of Civilian Persons in Time of War (Geneva, 12 August 1949, TS 39 (1958); Cmnd 550).

6 As to treaties generally see FOREIGN RELATIONS LAW vol 18 para 1769 et seq.

7 The four conventions are set out as Schs 1–4 to the Geneva Conventions Act 1957. See also note 11 infra.
   The title and preamble to the Geneva Conventions Act 1957 do not make the Geneva Conventions statute: *Cheney v Conn (Inspector of Taxes)* [1968] 1 All ER 779 at 782, [1968] 1 WLR 242 at 247 per Ungoed-Thomas J.
   The provisions of the Geneva Conventions Act 1957 may be extended by Order in Council, subject to exceptions, to the Channel Islands, the Isle of Man and any colony: s 8(2) (prospectively amended by the Geneva Conventions (Amendment) Act 1995 s 5(b)). The Geneva Conventions Act 1957, except ss 4, 8(2), was extended to the territories specified in the Order by the Geneva Conventions Act (Colonial Territories) Order in Council 1959, SI 1959/1301. It has also been extended, with modifications, to Guernsey (see the Geneva Conventions Act (Guernsey) Order 1966, SI 1966/948), Jersey (see the Geneva Conventions Act (Jersey) Order 1966, SI 1966/949) and the Isle of Man (see the Geneva Conventions Act (Isle of Man) Order 1970, SI 1970/1677). For the practical application of the Geneva Conventions Act 1957 see Rowe (ed) *The Gulf War 1990–91 in International and English Law* (1993) Appendix I.

8 See eg the Army Act 1955 s 30 (as amended); the Air Force Act 1955 s 30 (as amended); and the Naval Discipline Act 1957 s 5 (as substituted). See also the Royal Warrant Governing the Maintenance of Discipline among Prisoners of War dated 7 August 1958 (amended by the Royal Warrants dated 13 January 1965 and 2 December 1968), Schedule 1 of which sets out the Prisoner of War Determination of Status Regulations and Schedule 2 of which sets out the Prisoners of War (Discipline) Regulations.

9 Ie the Protocol, additional to the Geneva Conventions of 12 August 1949, relating to the Protection of Victims of International Armed Conflicts done on 10 June 1977 (Geneva, 12 December 1977; Misc 19 (1977); Cmnd 6927) (Geneva Conventions 1949 Protocol I): see the Geneva Conventions Act 1957 s 7(1) (prospectively amended by the Geneva Conventions (Amendment) Act 1995 s 4(1), (4)).
   In any armed conflict, the right of the parties to the conflict to choose methods or means of warfare is not unlimited: Geneva Conventions 1949 Protocol I art 35 para 1. Protocol I sets out the basic rules relating to the methods and means of warfare: see Protocol I arts 35–42. The term 'armed conflict' is not defined in any of the conventions. It is, however, considered to be 'a difference arising between two states and leading to the intervention of armed forces': Commentary on the Geneva Convention I of 12 August 1949 (Jean Pictet, editor) International Committee of the Red Cross (Geneva, 1952) p 32). An armed conflict exists whenever there is a resort to armed force between states: *The Prosecutor v Dusko Tadic* (2 October 1995, unreported), Former Yugoslavia International Tribunal, Appeals Chamber, per Cassese P at para 70. As to the Former Yugoslavia International Tribunal see para 563 post.

10 Ie the Protocol, additional to the Geneva Conventions of 12 August 1949, relating to the Protection of Victims of Non-International Armed Conflicts done on 10 June 1977 (Geneva, 12 December 1977; Misc 19 (1977); Cmnd 6927) (Geneva Conventions 1949 Protocol II): see the Geneva Conventions Act 1957 s 7(1) (prospectively amended by the Geneva Conventions (Amendment) Act 1995 s 4(1), (6)).

11 As from a day to be appointed, the Geneva Conventions 1949 Protocol I and Protocol II are set out as respectively Sch 5 and Sch 6 to the Geneva Conventions Act 1957: see Schs 5, 6 (prospectively added by the Geneva Conventions (Amendment) Act 1995 s 6, Schedule).
   If the ratification by the United Kingdom of the Geneva Conventions 1949 Protocol I or Protocol II is subject to any reservation or accompanied by a declaration, it may be certified by Order in Council

that such a reservation or declaration has been made and the protocol must for the purposes of the Geneva Conventions Act 1957 be construed subject to and in accordance with such a reservation or declaration: Geneva Conventions Act 1957 s 7(3) (prospectively added by the Geneva Conventions (Amendment) Act 1995 s 4(1), (7)). If such a reservation or declaration is withdrawn wholly or partially, an Order in Council under the Geneva Conventions Act 1957 s 7(3) (as prospectively added) may certify that fact and revoke or amend any Order in Council containing the terms of that reservation or declaration: s 7(4) (prospectively added by the Geneva Conventions (Amendment) Act 1995 s 4(1), (7)). If the Geneva Conventions 1949 Protocol I is further revised under Protocol I art 98, the Geneva Conventions Act 1957 Sch 5 (as prospectively added) may be amended by Order in Council so as to ensure that it sets out the text of the Geneva Conventions 1949 Protocol I as in force in relation to the United Kingdom: Geneva Conventions Act 1957 s 7(5) (prospectively added by the Geneva Conventions (Amendment) Act 1995 s 4(1), (7)).

12 Geneva Conventions Act 1957 s 7(1), Sch 1 art 58, Sch 2 art 57, Sch 3 art 138, Sch 4 art 153. As to ratification and accession see Sch 1 arts 57, 60–62, Sch 2 arts 56, 59–61, Sch 3 arts 137, 139–141, Sch 4 arts 152, 155–157. As to other matters relating to the execution of the conventions see Sch 1 arts 55, 56, 59, 64, Sch 2 arts 54, 55, 58, 63, Sch 3 arts 127–128, 133–136, 143, Sch 4 arts 144–145, 150–151, 159. As to the procedural matters relating to the Geneva Conventions 1949 Protocol I see Protocol I arts 80–102. As to matters relating to the execution of Protocol II see Protocol II arts 19–28.

13 Geneva Conventions Act 1957 Sch 1 art 63, Sch 2 art 62, Sch 3 art 142, Sch 4 art 158.

14 Ibid Sch 1 art 52, Sch 2 art 53, Sch 3 art 132, Sch 4 art 149.

522. Application of the conventions. The contracting states must respect and ensure respect for the Geneva Red Cross Conventions in all circumstances[1]. The conventions apply in all cases of declared war or other armed conflict[2], even if a state of war is not recognised by one[3] state[4]. The conventions also apply to all cases of partial and total occupation of the territory of a contracting state, even if there is no armed resistance, and some provisions apply in peacetime[5]. In addition, the Geneva Conventions 1949 Protocol I[6] applies to armed conflicts in which peoples are fighting against colonial domination and alien occupation and against racist regimes in the exercise of their right of self-determination, as enshrined in the Charter of the United Nations[7] and the Declaration on Principles of International Law concerning Friendly Relations and Co-operation among States in accordance with the Charter of the United Nations[8]. The Geneva Conventions 1949 Protocol II[9] applies to all other armed conflicts which take place in the territory of a high contracting party between its armed forces and dissident armed forces or other organised armed groups which, under responsible command, exercise such control over a part of its territory as to enable them to carry out sustained and concerted military operations and to implement the Geneva Conventions 1949 Protocol II[10]. However, Protocol II does not apply to situations of internal disturbances and tensions, such as riots, isolated and sporadic acts of violence and other acts of a similar nature, as not being armed conflicts[11]. The high contracting parties must also, in peacetime, endeavour to train qualified personnel to facilitate the application of the Geneva Red Cross Conventions and of the Geneva Conventions 1949 Protocol I, and in particular the activities of the protecting powers[12].

If one of the parties to the conflict is not a party to the conventions, the states who are parties remain bound by them in their mutual relations, and in relation to the party to the conflict which is not a party to the conventions, if the latter accepts and applies its provisions[13].

1 Geneva Conventions Act 1957 s 7(1), Sch 1 art 1, Sch 2 art 1, Sch 3 art 1, Sch 4 art 1. This obligation is a wide one since it includes a requirement on the United Kingdom to ensure respect for the Geneva Red Cross Conventions even in respect of armed conflicts in which it is not a participant. As to the Geneva Red Cross Conventions (which are set out in the Schedules to the Geneva Conventions Act 1957) see para 521 ante.

2 As to the meaning of 'armed conflict' see para 521 note 9 ante.

3 For the view that this should read 'by one or both' see 2 Oppenheim's International Law (7th Edn) p 369 n 6.

4   See the Geneva Conventions Act 1957 Sch 1 art 2, Sch 2 art 2, Sch 3 art 2, Sch 4 art 2. In 1982, despite the existence of an armed conflict, the United Kingdom government did not consider that a state of war existed between the United Kingdom and Argentina: see para 506 note 6 ante. For the meaning of 'United Kingdom' see para 502 note 4 ante.

As to the application of the conventions to forces on board ship, and to forces put ashore, see the Geneva Conventions Act 1957 Sch 2 art 4.

5   See ibid Sch 1 art 2, Sch 2 art 2, Sch 3 art 2, Sch 4 art 2.

6   As to the Geneva Conventions 1949 Protocol I see paras 521 ante, 524 et seq post. The conventions and Protocol I apply from the beginning of any situation referred to in Protocol I art 1 and the application of the conventions and Protocol I cease, in the territory of parties to the conflict, on the general close of military operations and, in the case of occupied territories, on the termination of the occupation, except, in either circumstance, for those persons whose final release, repatriation or re-establishment takes place thereafter. These persons continue to benefit from the relevant provisions of the conventions and Protocol I until their final release, repatriation or re-establishment: Protocol I art 3.

7   Ie the Charter of the United Nations: see para 501 note 4 ante.

8   Geneva Conventions 1949 Protocol I art 1 para 4. Protocol I supplements the Geneva Red Cross Conventions and applies in the situations referred to in the Geneva Conventions Act 1957 Sch 1 art 2, Sch 2 art 2, Sch 3 art 2, Sch 4 art 2: Geneva Conventions 1949 Protocol I art 1 para 3. The declaration referred to is the Charter of the United Nations and the Declaration on Principles of International Law Concerning Friendly Relations and Co-operation among States (General Assembly Resolution 2625 (XXV), 24 October 1970).

The high contracting parties undertake to respect and to ensure respect for Protocol I in all circumstances: Geneva Conventions 1949 Protocol I art 1 para 1. In cases not covered by Protocol I or by other international agreements, civilians and combatants remain under the protection and authority of the principles of international law derived from established custom, from the principles of humanity and from the dictates of public conscience: Protocol I art 1 para 2. The application of the conventions and Protocol I and the conclusion of special agreements does not affect the legal status of the parties to the conflict: Protocol I art 4.

9   As to the Geneva Conventions 1949 Protocol II see paras 521 ante, 523 post.

10 Ibid Protocol II art 1 para 1. An armed conflict, in this context, exists whenever 'there is protracted violence between governmental authorities and organized armed groups or between such groups within a state': *The Prosecutor v Dusko Tadic* (2 October 1995, unreported), Former Yugoslavia International Tribunal, Appeals Chamber, at para 70 per Cassese P. This illustrates the level of activity of the armed conflict and the degree of organisation that the dissident forces or other organised groups must establish before the Geneva Conventions 1949 Protocol II will come into operation. As to the Former Yugoslavia International Tribunal see para 563 post.

11 Ibid Protocol II art 1 para 2. Protocol II is not to be invoked for the purpose of affecting the sovereignty of a state or the responsibility of the government, by all legitimate means, to maintain or re-establish law and order in the state, or to defend the national unity and territorial integrity of the state: Protocol II art 3 para 1. Protocol II is not to be invoked as a justification for intervening, directly or indirectly, for any reason, in the armed conflict or in the internal or external affairs of the high contacting party in the territory of which that conflict occurs: Protocol II art 3 para 2.

12 Ibid Protocol I art 6 para 1. This is to be done with the assistance of the national Red Cross societies: see Protocol I art 6. As to meetings to consider general problems concerning the application of the conventions and of Protocol I see Protocol I art 7. For the meaning of 'protecting power' see para 537 post.

13 See the Geneva Conventions Act 1957 Sch 1 art 2, Sch 2 art 2, Sch 3 art 2, Sch 4 art 2.

523. Conflicts not of an international character. In the case of an armed conflict not of an international character (such as a civil war) each party to the conflict must treat humanely persons who take no active part in the hostilities, including members of the armed forces who have laid down their arms or are rendered unable to take part by reason of sickness, wounds, detention or other cause, without distinction founded on race, colour, religion or faith, sex, birth or wealth[1]. Violence to life and person, including murder, mutilation, cruel treatment or torture, the taking of hostages, outrages upon personal dignity and the passing of sentences and carrying out of executions without a proper trial upon non-combatants, is prohibited[2]. The wounded and sick must be cared for[3]; and an impartial humanitarian body may offer its services to the parties to the conflict[4].

The Geneva Conventions 1949 Protocol II[5] develops and supplements these provisions[6] without modifying their existing conditions of application[7]. It provides that all persons[8] who do not take a direct part or who have ceased to take a direct part in hostilities are entitled to respect for their person, honour and convictions and religious practices[9]. They are to be treated humanely in all circumstances[10]. Children are to be provided with the care and aid they require[11]. The wounded, sick and shipwrecked, whether or not they have taken part in the armed conflict, are to be respected and protected and treated humanely[12]. All measures must be taken to search for, and collect, the wounded, sick and shipwrecked[13]. Medical and religious personnel are to be respected and protected and granted all available help for the performance of their duties[14]. No one may be punished for having carried out medical activities compatible with medical ethics, regardless of the person benefitting[15]. Medical units and transports are to be respected and protected at all times and are not to be the object of attack[16], unless a warning that they have been used to commit hostile acts outside their humanitarian function has remained unheeded after a reasonable time limit[17]. Medical and religious personnel, medical units and transports may, under the direction of the competent authority, display the distinctive emblem of the red cross, red crescent or red lion and sun on a white ground[18].

The Geneva Conventions 1949 Protocol II contains obligations to protect the civilian population from the effects of an armed conflict. Civilians are protected against the dangers arising from military operations and must not be the object of attack unless they take a direct part in hostilities[19]. It is prohibited to attack, destroy, remove or render useless objects indispensable to the survival of the civilian population[20]. Protection is given to works and installations containing dangerous forces, which must not be attacked if such an attack would cause the release of dangerous forces and consequent severe losses amongst the civilian population[21]. Cultural objects and places of worship, which constitute the cultural or spiritual heritage of peoples, are not to be attacked[22]. There must be no forced movement of the civilian population unless the security of the civilians or imperative military reasons so demand[23]. A high contracting party may give permission for the operation of relief actions where the civilian population is suffering undue hardship owing to the lack of the supplies essential for its survival[24].

There is no concept of lawful combatant or prisoner of war in a non-international armed conflict. Individuals who take part in the armed conflict are, in consequence, subject to the law of the state in whose territory the conflict is taking place. They are therefore liable to prosecution for criminal acts related to the armed conflict[25]. Persons whose liberty has been restricted must be treated humanely and, if it is decided to release them, necessary measures to ensure their safety must be taken[26]. The Geneva Conventions 1949 Protocol II requires that a person may only be prosecuted and punished in relation to a criminal offence by a court offering the essential guarantees of independence and impartiality[27].

1   Geneva Conventions Act 1957 s 7(1), Sch 1 art 3(1), Sch 2 art 3(1), Sch 3 art 3(1), Sch 4 art 3(1).
2   Ibid Sch 1 art 3(1), Sch 2 art 3(1), Sch 3 art 3(1), Sch 4 art 3(1).
3   Ibid Sch 1 art 3(2), Sch 2 art 3(2), Sch 3 art 3(2), Sch 4 art 3(2).
4   Ibid Sch 1 art 3, Sch 2 art 3, Sch 3 art 3, Sch 4 art 3. The parties to such conflict should try to bring into force by means of special agreements all or part of the provisions of all four Geneva Red Cross Conventions (see para 521 ante); and the application of these articles does not affect the legal status of the parties to the conflict: see Sch 1 art 3, Sch 2 art 3, Sch 3 art 3, Sch 4 art 3. The conventions are set out in the Schedules to the Geneva Conventions Act 1957.

A special agreement was entered into by the various parties involved in the armed conflict in Bosnia on 22 May 1992. It was stated to be 'without prejudice to the legal status of the parties to the conflict or to the international law of armed conflict in force' (ie whether the conflict was of an international or non-international character). The break-up of the former Yugoslavia illustrates the difficulty, in certain armed conflicts, of determining whether the conflict is an international or a non-international one at any given time.

5   As to the application and implementation of the Geneva Conventions 1949 Protocol II see paras 521–522 ante.

6   Ie the Geneva Conventions Act 1957 Sch 1 art 3, Sch 2 art 3, Sch 3 art 3, Sch 4 art 3.

7   See the Geneva Conventions 1949 Protocol II art 1 para 1.

8   Ibid Protocol II applies without adverse distinction founded on race, colour, sex, language, religion or belief, political or other opinion, national or social origin, wealth, birth, status, or on any other similar criteria to all persons affected by an armed conflict: see Protocol II art 2 para 1.

9   See ibid Protocol II art 4 para 1.

10 See ibid Protocol II art 4 para 1. Acts, or the threat of acts, such as violence to life, health and physical or mental well-being, cruel treatment (including torture, mutilation or corporal punishment), collective punishments, taking of hostages, acts of terrorism, outrages upon personal dignity (in particular humiliating and degrading treatment, rape, enforced prostitution and any form of indecent assault), slavery and pillage are prohibited at any time: see Protocol II art 4 para 2.

11 See ibid Protocol II art 4 para 3. In particular (1) children must receive an education; (2) steps must be taken to reunite separated families; (3) children under the age of 15 are to be given special protection and are not to be recruited in the armed forces; (4) measures are to be taken to remove children temporarily from the area of hostilities: see Protocol II art 4 para 3.

12 See ibid Protocol II art 7. There must be no distinction among them founded on any grounds other than medical ones: see Protocol II art 7 para 2.

13 See ibid Protocol II art 8.

14 See ibid Protocol II art 9.

15 See ibid Protocol II art 10 para 1. Persons engaged in medical activities are protected from being penalised for refusing or failing to give information concerning the wounded and sick who are, or have been, in their care: see Protocol II art 10 para 4.

16 See ibid Protocol II art 11 para 1.

17 See ibid Protocol II art 11 para 2.

18 See ibid Protocol II art 12; and para 532 post.

19 See ibid Protocol II art 13.

20 See ibid Protocol II art 14. Such indispensable objects include foodstuffs, agricultural areas for the production of foodstuffs, crops, livestock, drinking water installations and supplies and irrigation works: see Protocol II art 14. Starvation of civilians is specifically prohibited: see Protocol II art 14.

21 See ibid Protocol II art 15. Dangerous forces include dams, dykes and nuclear generating stations: see Protocol II art 15. Article 15 assumes that such objects would be military objectives, as to which see the Geneva Conventions 1949 Protocol I art 52 para 2; and para 552 text and note 6 post. As to Protocol I generally see para 521 ante; and as to its application and implementation see paras 521–522 ante.

22 See ibid Protocol II art 16. See also the Hague Convention for the Protection of Cultural Property in the Event of Armed Conflict (The Hague, 14 May 1954; Misc 6 (1956); Cmd 9837). The United Kingdom has not ratified this treaty. For the meaning of 'United Kingdom' see para 502 note 4 ante.

23 See the Geneva Conventions 1949 Protocol II art 17.

24 See ibid Protocol II art 18 para 2. Relief societies located in the territory of a high contracting party may offer their services: see Protocol II art 18 para 1.

25 See generally CRIMINAL LAW.

26 See the Geneva Conventions 1949 Protocol II art 5. Persons whose liberty has been restricted must (1) be treated and cared for in accordance with Protocol II art 7 (see text and note 12 supra) if they are wounded or sick; (2) be provided, to the same extent as the civilian population, with food and drinking water; (3) be allowed individual or collective relief; (4) be allowed to practise their religion; and (5) if made to work, have the benefit of working conditions similar to those enjoyed by the local civilian population: see Protocol II art 5 para 1.

27 See ibid Protocol II art 6 para 2. These guarantees include (1) informing the accused of the particulars of the offence without delay; (2) individual penal responsibility; (3) no one being guilty on account of any act or omission which was not a criminal offence at the time of commission; (4) innocence until guilt proven; (5) the right of the accused to be tried in his presence; (6) the right of the accused not to be compelled to testify against himself or to confess guilt: see Protocol II art 6 para 2. Protocol II art 6 is sufficiently widely drawn as to give authority for dissident armed forces or organised groups, as envisaged by Protocol II art 1 para 1, to hold courts, which themselves must offer the essential guarantees of independence and impartiality.

524. Grave breaches and abuse of the conventions. Any person, whatever his nationality, who, whether in or outside the United Kingdom[1], commits or aids, abets or procures the commission by any other person of any grave breach of the Geneva Red Cross Conventions or the Geneva Conventions 1949 Protocol I[2] is guilty of an offence, and on conviction on indictment, where the grave breach involved the wilful killing of a person protected by the convention or protocol in question, must be sentenced to imprisonment for life, and in the case of any other grave breach is liable to imprisonment for a term not exceeding 14 years[3].

Grave breaches of the Geneva Red Cross Conventions are those involving any of the following acts, if committed against persons or property protected by the relevant convention: wilful killing, torture or inhuman treatment, including biological experiments, wilfully causing great suffering or serious injury to body or health[4], extensive destruction and appropriation of property not justified by military necessity and carried out unlawfully and wantonly[5], compelling a prisoner of war or civilian[6] to serve in the forces of a hostile power or wilfully depriving him of the rights of fair and regular trial[7], and unlawful deportation or transfer or unlawful confinement of a civilian and taking of hostages[8].

The grave breaches in the Geneva Conventions 1949 Protocol I include the subjection of a person, who is in the power of a state other than the one on which he depends, to such acts as physical mutilations, medical or scientific experiments, removal of tissue organs for transplantation[9] or medical procedures inconsistent with generally accepted medical standards[10]. It is also a grave breach of the protocol, wilfully, in violation of the relevant provisions of the protocol, and causing death or serious injury to body or health: (1) to make civilians the object of an attack[11]; (2) to launch an indiscriminate attack against the civilian population or civilian objects[12]; (3) to launch an attack against works or installations containing dangerous forces[13]; (4) to make non-defended localities and de-militarised zones the object of attack[14]; (5) to make a person the object of an attack in the knowledge that he is hors de combat[15]; and (6) to use the distinctive emblems perfidiously[16].

When committed wilfully, and in violation of the conventions or the protocol, the following are regarded as grave breaches of the protocol: (a) the transfer by the occupying power of parts of its own civilian population into the territory it occupies, or the deportation or transfer of the population of the occupied territory within or outside this territory[17]; (b) an unjustifiable delay in the repatriation of prisoners of war or civilians[18]; (c) practices of apartheid or other inhuman and degrading practices based on racial discrimination[19]; (d) in certain circumstances making the cultural or spiritual heritage of peoples the object of attack[20]; (e) depriving a protected person of the rights of fair and regular trial[21]. All grave breaches of the Geneva Red Cross Conventions or of the Geneva Conventions 1949 Protocol I are regarded as war crimes[22].

---

1   In the extension of the Geneva Conventions Act 1957 to a territory etc by the orders cited in para 521 note 7 ante, a reference to the territory etc is to be substituted for 'United Kingdom': see those orders. For the meaning of 'United Kingdom' see para 502 note 4 ante.

2   There are no grave breach provisions in the Geneva Conventions 1949 Protocol II. As to the application and implementation of the Geneva Conventions 1949 Protocols I and II see paras 521–522 ante; and as to the Geneva Red Cross Conventions (which are set out in the Schedules to the Geneva Conventions Act 1957) see para 521 ante.

    If in proceedings for an offence under the Geneva Conventions Act 1957 s 1 (as prospectively amended) any question arises under Sch 1 art 2, Sch 2 art 2, Sch 3 art 2, Sch 4 art 2 or the Geneva Conventions 1949 Protocol I art 1 or art 3 (which relate to the circumstances in which the conventions and protocol apply: see para 522 ante), that question must be determined by the Secretary of State; and a certificate purporting to set out any such determination and to be signed by or on behalf of the Secretary of State must be received in evidence and be deemed to be so signed without further proof, unless the contrary is shown: Geneva Conventions Act 1957 ss 1(4), 7(1) (s 1(4) prospectively amended by the Geneva Conventions (Amendment) Act 1995 s 1(1), (5)).

3   Geneva Conventions Act 1957 ss 1(1), 7(1) (prospectively amended by the Geneva Conventions (Amendment) Act 1995 ss 1(1), (2), 4(1), (4)). As to the legal representation of persons brought up for trial see para 542 post.
     As to the obligations of high contracting parties with respect to grave breaches of, and acts contrary to, the Geneva Red Cross Conventions see the Geneva Conventions Act 1957 Sch 1 arts 49, 51, Sch 2 arts 50, 52, Sch 3 arts 129, 131, Sch 4 arts 146,148.

4   Ibid s 1(1A) (prospectively added by the Geneva Conventions (Amendment) Act 1995 s 1(3)); Geneva Conventions Act 1957 Sch 1 art 50, Sch 2 art 51, Sch 3 art 130, Sch 4 art 147.

5   Ibid s 1(1A) (as prospectively added: see note 4 supra), Sch 1 art 50, Sch 2 art 51, Sch 4 art 147.

6   Ie a protected person within ibid Sch 4 art 4: see para 545 post.

7   Ibid s 1(1A) (as prospectively added: see note 4 supra), Sch 3 art 130, Sch 4 art 147.

8   Ibid s 1(1A) (as prospectively added: see note 4 supra), Sch 4 art 147.

9   Ie other than in accordance with the Geneva Conventions 1949 Protocol I art 11 paras 1, 3.

10   Geneva Conventions Act 1957 s 1(1A) (as prospectively added: see note 4 supra); Geneva Conventions 1949 Protocol I art 11 paras 2–4.

11   Ie contrary to ibid Protocol I art 51: Geneva Conventions Act 1957 s 1(1A) (as prospectively added: see note 4 supra); Geneva Conventions 1949 Protocol I art 85 para 3(a).

12   Ie contrary to ibid Protocol I art 57 para 2(a)(iii): Geneva Conventions Act 1957 s 1(1A) (as prospectively added: see note 4 supra); Geneva Conventions 1949 Protocol I art 85 para 3(b).

13   Ie contrary to ibid Protocol I arts 56, 57 para 2(a)(iii): Geneva Conventions Act 1957 s 1(1A) (as prospectively added: see note 4 supra); Geneva Conventions 1949 Protocol I art 85 para 3(c).

14   Ie contrary to ibid Protocol I arts 59, 60: Geneva Conventions Act 1957 s 1(1A) (as prospectively added: see note 4 supra); Geneva Conventions 1949 Protocol I art 85 para 3(d).

15   Ie contrary to ibid Protocol I art 41: Geneva Conventions Act 1957 s 1(1A) (as prospectively added: see note 4 supra); Geneva Conventions 1949 Protocol I art 85 para 3(e).

16   Ie contrary to ibid Protocol I art 37: Geneva Conventions Act 1957 s 1(1A) (as prospectively added: see note 4 supra); Geneva Conventions 1949 Protocol I art 85 para 3(f). As to the distinctive emblems see para 532 post.

17   Ie contrary to the Geneva Conventions Act 1957 Sch 4 art 49: s 1(1A) (as prospectively added: see note 4 supra); Geneva Conventions 1949 Protocol I art 85 para 4(a).

18   Geneva Conventions Act 1957 s 1(1A) (as prospectively added: see note 4 supra); Geneva Conventions 1949 Protocol I art 85 para 4(b).

19   Geneva Conventions Act 1957 s 1(1A) (as prospectively added: see note 4 supra); Geneva Conventions 1949 Protocol I art 85 para 4(c).

20   Geneva Conventions Act 1957 s 1(1A) (as prospectively added: see note 4 supra); Geneva Conventions 1949 Protocol I art 85 para 4(d). See also Protocol I art 53; and para 552 post.

21   Geneva Conventions Act 1957 s 1(1A) (as prospectively added: see note 4 supra); Geneva Conventions 1949 Protocol I art 85 para 4(e). As to protected persons see Protocol I arts 44, 45, 73, 85 para 2; and paras 526, 533, 545 post.

22   Ibid Protocol I art 85 para 5. As to war crimes generally see para 563 et seq post.
     Proceedings for offences under the Geneva Conventions Act 1957 s 1 (as prospectively amended) must not be instituted in England except by or on behalf of the Director of Public Prosecutions: Geneva Conventions Act 1957 s 1(3) (amended by the Courts Act 1971 s 56(4), Sch 11 Pt IV; and prospectively amended by the Geneva Conventions (Amendment) Act 1995 s 1(4)). As to the representation of the accused see para 542 post. The enactments relating to the trial by courts-martial of persons who commit civil offences are to have effect for the purposes of the jurisdiction of courts-martial convened in the United Kingdom as if the Geneva Conventions Act 1957 s 1 had not been passed: s 1(5). As to the jurisdiction of courts-martial see ROYAL FORCES.

(ii) The Wounded, Sick and Shipwrecked

525. In general. The first two Geneva Red Cross Conventions are the Convention for the Amelioration of the Condition of the Wounded and Sick in Armed Forces in the Field[1], and the Convention for the Amelioration of the Condition of the Wounded, Sick and Shipwrecked Members of Armed Forces at Sea[2]. They are basically similar in their character and provisions. Neutral powers[3] must apply the provisions of the conventions by analogy to persons protected by these conventions who are received into or interned in their territory[4].

1   See para 521 note 2 ante. The convention is set out in the Geneva Conventions Act 1957 s 7(1), Sch 1. See generally para 521 ante. As to the execution of the convention see Sch 1 arts 45–48.
2   See para 521 note 3 ante. The convention is set out in ibid Sch 2. See generally para 521 ante. As to the execution of the convention see Sch 2 arts 46–49.
3   As to medical assistance from neutral countries or vessels see also ibid Sch 1 arts 27, 32, Sch 2 arts 17, 21.
4   Ibid Sch 1 art 4, Sch 2 art 5. See also the Geneva Conventions 1949 Protocol I art 19. As to the application and implementation of Protocol I see paras 521–522 ante. For the categories of protected persons see para 526 post.

526. Protected persons. The Geneva Convention for the Amelioration of the Condition of the Wounded and Sick in Armed Forces in the Field[1] and the Geneva Convention for the Amelioration of the Condition of the Wounded, Sick and Shipwrecked Members of the Armed Forces at Sea[2] apply to the wounded and sick, or shipwrecked at sea as the case may be, belonging to the following categories[3]:

(1)   members of the armed forces of a party to the conflict, as well as members of militias or volunteer corps forming part of such armed forces[4];

(2)   members of other militias and members of other volunteer corps, including those of organised resistance movements, belonging to a party to the conflict and operating in or outside their own territory, even if this territory is occupied, provided that such militias or volunteer corps or organised resistance movements fulfil the following conditions: (a) that of being commanded by a person responsible for his subordinates[5]; (b) that of having a fixed distinctive sign recognisable at a distance[6]; (c) that of carrying arms openly[7]; (d) that of conducting their operations in accordance with the laws and customs of war[8];

(3)   members of regular armed forces who profess allegiance to a government or an authority not recognised by the detaining power[9];

(4)   persons who accompany the armed forces without actually being members of them, such as civil members of military aircraft crews, war correspondents, supply contractors, members of labour units or of services responsible for the welfare of the armed forces, provided that they have received authorisation from the armed forces which they accompany[10];

(5)   members of crews including masters, pilots and apprentices, of the merchant marine and the crews of civil aircraft of the parties to the conflict, who do not benefit by more favourable treatment under any other provisions in international law[11];

(6)   inhabitants of a non-occupied territory who on the approach of the enemy spontaneously take up arms to resist the invading forces, without having had time to form themselves into regular armed units, provided they carry arms openly and respect the laws and customs of war[12].

1   See para 521 note 2 ante. The convention is set out in the Geneva Conventions Act 1957 s 7(1), Sch 1. See generally para 521 ante. This convention applies to protected persons who fall into the hands of the enemy until their final repatriation: see Sch 1 art 5.
2   See para 521 note 3 ante. The convention is set out in ibid Sch 2. See generally para 521 ante.
3   The Geneva Conventions 1949 Protocol I extends the categories of protected persons so that in addition to the categories of persons mentioned in the Geneva Conventions Act 1957 Sch 1 art 13, Sch 2 art 13 (see text and notes 4–12 infra) all members of the armed forces of a party to the conflict (see the Geneva Conventions 1949 Protocol I art 43) are entitled to protection if they are wounded or sick or shipwrecked at sea or in other waters: Protocol I art 44 para 8. As to the application and implementation of Protocol I see paras 521–522 ante.
4   Geneva Conventions Act 1957 Sch 1 art 13(1), Sch 2 art 13(1).
5   Ibid Sch 1 art 13(2)(a), Sch 2 art 13(2)(a).
6   Ibid Sch 1 art 13(2)(b), Sch 2 art 13(2)(b).
7   Ibid Sch 1 art 13(2)(c), Sch 2 art 13(1)(c).
8   Ibid Sch 1 art 13(2)(d), Sch 2 art 13(1)(d).

9   Ibid Sch 1 art 13(3), Sch 2 art 13(3). As to the detaining power see para 539 post.
10   Ibid Sch 1 art 13(4), Sch 2 art 13(4).
11   Ibid Sch 1 art 13(5), Sch 2 art 13(5).
12   Ibid Sch 1 art 13(6), Sch 2 art 13(6).

527. General protection. At all times, and particularly after an engagement, parties to a conflict must take measures to search for and collect the wounded, sick and shipwrecked, protect them from pillage and ensure their adequate care; and the dead must be searched for and their spoliation prevented[1]. Armistices or suspensions of fire must if possible be arranged to allow for the removal, exchange and transport of wounded persons from the battlefield[2]. At all times the wounded, sick and shipwrecked must be treated humanely without any adverse distinction founded on race, colour, religion or faith, sex, birth or wealth or any similar criteria[3].

1   Geneva Conventions Act 1957 s 7(1), Sch 1 arts 15, 18, Sch 2 art 18. See also the Geneva Conventions
     1949 Protocol I art 33 para 4. As to the application and implementation of Protocol I see paras 521–522
     ante. As to the categories of protected persons see para 526 ante.
2   Geneva Conventions Act 1957 Sch 1 art 15.
3   Ibid Sch 1 art 12, Sch 2 art 12. Subject to these provisions, the wounded, sick and shipwrecked of a
     belligerent who fall into enemy hands are prisoners of war: Sch 1 art 14, Sch 2 art 16. If wounded, sick
     or shipwrecked persons are taken on board a neutral aircraft or warship, it must be ensured, where
     international law requires, that they take no further part in the armed conflict: Sch 2 art 15.
        See also the Geneva Conventions 1949 Protocol I arts 10, 17. Reprisals against persons and objects
     protected in Protocol I Pt II (arts 8–34) are prohibited: Protocol I art 20. For the purposes of Protocol I
     'wounded' and 'sick' means persons, whether military or civilian, who, because of trauma, disease or
     other physical or mental disorder or disability, are in need of medical assistance or care and who refrain
     from any act of hostility. These terms also cover maternity cases, newborn babies and other persons who
     may be in need of immediate medical assistance or care, such as the infirm or expectant mothers, and who
     refrain from any act of hostility: Protocol I art 8(a). 'Shipwrecked' means persons, whether military or
     civilian, who are in peril at sea or in other waters as a result of misfortune affecting them or the vessel or
     aircraft carrying them and who refrain from any act of hostility; and these persons, provided that they
     continue to refrain from any act of hostility, continue to be considered shipwrecked during their rescue
     until they acquire another status under the conventions or Protocol I: Protocol I art 8(b).

528. Variation of rights. The parties to the conventions[1] may conclude special agreements on particular matters, but these must not adversely affect the situation of the wounded, sick or shipwrecked, or medical personnel or chaplains, nor restrict the rights conferred on them by the conventions[2]. Such persons may in no circumstances renounce in part or whole the rights secured to them under the conventions or under any such special agreements which may have been made[3].

1   Ie the Geneva Convention for the Amelioration of the Condition of the Wounded and Sick in Armed
     Forces in the Field (see para 521 note 2 ante), which is set out in the Geneva Conventions Act 1957 s 7(1),
     Sch 1; and the Geneva Convention for the Amelioration of the Condition of the Wounded, Sick and
     Shipwrecked Members of the Armed Forces at Sea (see para 521 note 3 ante), which is set out in the Geneva
     Conventions Act 1957 Sch 2. See generally para 521 ante.
2   See ibid Sch 1 art 6, Sch 2 art 6. The protecting power may assist in settling disagreements between
     conflicting parties as to the interpretation of the conventions: Sch 1 art 11, Sch 2 art 11. As to the
     protecting power see para 530 post.
3   See ibid Sch 1 art 7, Sch 2 art 7.

529. Information as to the wounded, sick or shipwrecked. Particulars of shipwrecked, wounded, sick or dead persons must be forwarded to the information bureau for prisoners of war[1].

1   See the Geneva Conventions Act 1957 s 7(1), Sch 1 art 16, Sch 2 art 19. As to the information bureau
     see para 536 post. Burial or cremation must be preceded by a careful examination to confirm death and
     establish identity: Sch 1 art 17, Sch 2 art 20.

530. The protecting power. The conventions[1] must be applied with the co-operation and under the scrutiny of the protecting powers, whose duty it is to safeguard the interests of the parties to the conflict and the protecting powers may appoint delegates for this purpose[2]. The high contracting parties may at any time entrust the duties of the protecting powers to an impartial organisation[3]. If protection cannot be arranged, the detaining power must request or accept the offer of the services of a humanitarian organisation such as the International Committee of the Red Cross to assume the humanitarian functions of the protecting power[4].

1   Ie the Geneva Convention for the Amelioration of the Condition of the Wounded and Sick in Armed Forces in the Field (see para 521 note 2 ante), which is set out in the Geneva Conventions Act 1957 s 7(1), Sch 1; and the Geneva Convention for the Amelioration of the Condition of the Wounded, Sick and Shipwrecked Members of the Armed Forces at Sea (see para 521 note 3 ante), which is set out in the Geneva Conventions Act 1957 Sch 2. See generally para 521 ante.

2   See ibid Sch 1 art 8, Sch 2 art 8. Delegates are to be appointed from amongst the protecting power's own nationals or the nationals of other neutral powers: Sch 1 art 8, Sch 2 art 8. As to the meaning of 'protecting power' see also para 537 post.

3   See ibid Sch 1 art 10, Sch 2 art 10.

4   See ibid Sch 1 art 10, Sch 2 art 10. The provisions of the conventions constitute no obstacle to the humanitarian activities which the International Committee of the Red Cross may, subject to the consent of the parties to the conflict, undertake for the protection and relief of the wounded, sick and shipwrecked, and medical personnel and chaplains: Sch 1 art 9, Sch 2 art 9. See also the Geneva Conventions 1949 Protocol I art 5, which deals with the methods by which a protecting power or substitute (such as the International Committee of the Red Cross) may be appointed. For the purposes of Protocol I, 'substitute' means an organisation acting in place of a protecting power in accordance with Protocol I art 5: Protocol I art 2(d). As to the application and implementation of Protocol I see paras 521–522 ante. As to the detaining power see para 539 post.

531. Medical units and transports. Medical units[1], medical transport[2] and hospital ships[3] are in no circumstances[4] to be attacked but must be respected and protected at all times[5]. Hospital ships are subject to control and search by the conflicting parties[6] and must give assistance without distinction of nationality[7]. Medical personnel and chaplains[8] are to be respected and protected[9], and, if captured, are to be retained only if the medical or spiritual needs of the prisoners of war so require[10].

1   See the Geneva Conventions Act 1957 s 7(1), Sch 1 art 19. As to medical units, including civilian medical units, see also the Geneva Conventions 1949 Protocol I arts 12–14. For the purposes of Protocol I 'medical units' (which may be permanent or temporary: see Protocol I art 8(k)) means establishments and other units, whether military or civilian, organised for medical purposes, namely the search for, collection, transportation, diagnosis or treatment (including first-aid treatment) of the wounded, sick and shipwrecked, or for the prevention of disease; and medical units may be fixed or mobile, permanent or temporary: Protocol I art 8(e). As to the application and implementation of Protocol I see paras 521–522 ante.

     As to hospital zones see the Geneva Conventions Act 1957 Sch 1 art 23. As to material and property of medical units, medical establishments and aid societies see Sch 1 arts 33, 34.

2   Medical aircraft must not be attacked while flying at agreed heights and times and on agreed routes; they must be clearly marked with the distinctive emblem (see para 532 post) and obey every summons to land: ibid Sch 1 art 36, Sch 2 art 39. Subject to any conditions or restrictions imposed by those powers, medical aircraft may fly over and, in case of necessity, land on the territory of neutral powers: Sch 1 art 37, Sch 2 art 40.

     As to ships chartered to transport medical equipment see Sch 2 art 38.

     As to medical vehicles see also the Geneva Conventions 1949 Protocol I art 21; and as to medical aircraft see also Protocol I arts 24–31. For the purposes of Protocol I, 'medical transportation' means the conveyance by land, water or air of the wounded, sick, shipwrecked, medical personnel, religious personnel, medical equipment or medical supplies protected by the conventions and Protocol I (Protocol I art 8(f)); and 'medical transports' (which may be permanent or temporary: see Protocol I art 8(k)) means any means of transportation, whether military or civilian, permanent or temporary, assigned exclusively to medical transportation and under the control of a competent authority of a party to the conflict: Protocol I art 8(g). For the purposes of Protocol I, 'medical vehicles' means any medical transports by land (Protocol I art 8(h)); and 'medical aircraft' means any medical transports by air (Protocol I art 8(j)).

3   See the Geneva Conventions Act 1957 Sch 1 art 20, Sch 2 arts 22–35. Small craft employed for coastal rescue operations are also to be respected and protected (Sch 2 art 27); so too are sick-bays, if fighting occurs on board a warship (Sch 2 art 28). Merchant vessels which have been transformed into hospital ships cannot be put to any other use during hostilities: Sch 2 art 33. See also the Geneva Conventions 1949 Protocol I arts 22–23. For the purposes of Protocol I, 'medical ships and craft' means any medical transports by water: Protocol I art 8(i).

4   Protection may, however, cease if they are used to commit, outside their humanitarian duties, acts harmful to the enemy: Geneva Conventions Act 1957 Sch 1 art 21, Sch 2 art 34. A warning must be given and remain unheeded after a reasonable time-limit before protection may cease: Sch 1 art 21, Sch 2 art 34. Certain conditions (eg the fact that they may be armed) are not to be considered as depriving them of protection: Sch 1 art 22, Sch 2 art 35. For an instance in which a hospital ship was held to be deprived of protection by being used as a signalling ship see *The Ophelia* [1916] 2 AC 206, PC.

5   See the Geneva Conventions Act 1957 Sch 1 arts 19, 20, 35, Sch 2 arts 22–26.

6   Ibid Sch 2 art 31. A hospital ship in a port which falls to the enemy is to be authorised to leave the port: Sch 2 art 29. As to the surrendering of the wounded, sick or shipwrecked on board hospital ships see Sch 2 art 14.

7   Ibid Sch 2 art 30.

8   These include the staff of national Red Cross and other voluntary aid societies (ibid Sch 1 art 26) and the religious, medical and hospital personnel of hospital ships and their crews (Sch 2 art 36). Members of the armed forces specially trained as hospital orderlies, nurses or auxiliary stretcher-bearers, if carrying out those duties when they fall into enemy hands, are also protected, though they become prisoners of war: Sch 1 arts 25, 29. As to prisoners of war generally see paras 533–544 post.

    As to protection of civilian medical personnel see also the Geneva Conventions 1949 Protocol I art 15 paras 1–4. For the purposes of Protocol I, 'medical personnel' (who may be permanent or temporary: see Protocol I art 8(k)) means those persons assigned, by a party to the conflict, exclusively to the medical purposes enumerated in the definition of 'medical units' in note 1 supra or to the administration of medical units or to the operation or administration of medical transports: Protocol I art 8(c). As to the protection of civilian religious personnel see Protocol I art 15 para 5. For the purposes of Protocol I, 'religious personnel' (who may be permanent or temporary: see Protocol I art 8(k)) means military or civilian persons, such as chaplains, who are exclusively engaged in the work of their ministry and attached (1) to the armed forces of a party to the conflict; (2) to medical units or medical transports of a party to the conflict; (3) to medical units or medical transports (other than hospital ships) (see Protocol I art 9 para 2); or (4) to civil defence organisations of a party to the conflict: Protocol I art 8(d).

9   Geneva Conventions Act 1957 Sch 1 arts 24–26, Sch 2 art 36. See also the Geneva Conventions 1949 Protocol I art 16.

10   Geneva Conventions Act 1957 Sch 1 art 28, Sch 2 art 37. Personnel whose retention is not indispensable are to be returned as soon as practicable, and pending return are not to be deemed prisoners of war: Sch 1 art 30, Sch 2 art 37. See also Sch 1 art 31.

532. The distinctive emblems. The heraldic emblem of the red cross on a white ground, which is the emblem and distinctive sign of the medical service of armed forces[1], must be displayed on the flags[2], armlets and all equipment employed in the medical service[3], and armlets must be worn on the left arm of medical personnel[4]. Hospital ships[5] must have all their exterior surfaces white and one or more dark red crosses must be painted on each side of the hull and on horizontal surfaces; a white flag with a red cross must be flown at the mainmast[6]. Subject to specified exceptions[7], the red cross emblem and the words 'Red Cross' and 'Geneva Cross' must not be employed, either in time of peace or war, except to indicate or to protect medical units and establishments, their personnel and material[8]. Similar restrictions apply to the distinguishing signs used to indicate hospital ships[9].

    It is not lawful for any person, without the authority of the Secretary of State, to use for any purpose whatsoever any of the following:

(1) a red cross with vertical and horizontal arms of the same length on, and completely surrounded by, a white ground, or the designation Red Cross or Geneva Cross or any design or wording so nearly resembling it as to be capable of being mistaken for, or understood as referring to it[10];

(2) a red crescent moon on, and completely surrounded by, a white ground, or the designation Red Crescent or any design or wording so nearly resembling it as to be capable of being mistaken for, or understood as referring to it[11];

(3) a lion passing from right to left of, and with its face turned towards, the observer, holding erect in its raised right forepaw a scimitar, with, appearing above the lion's back, the upper half of the sun shooting forth rays, or the designation Red Lion and Sun, in red on, and completely surrounded by, a white ground, or any design or wording so nearly resembling it as to be capable of being mistaken for, or understood as referring to it[12];

(4) an equilateral blue triangle on, and completely surrounded by, an orange ground (being the international distinctive sign of civil defence) or any design so nearly resembling that sign as to be capable of being mistaken for it[13];

(5) any of the specified distinctive signals[14] (being the signals of identification for medical units and transports) or any signal so nearly resembling any of those signals as to be capable of being mistaken for one of those signals[15];

(6) a white or silver cross with vertical and horizontal arms of the same length on, and completely surrounded by, a red ground, being the heraldic emblem of the Swiss Confederation, or any other design so nearly resembling that design as to be capable of being mistaken for that heraldic emblem[16].

These provisions extend to the use in or outside the United Kingdom of any such emblem, designation, design, wording, sign or signal on (a) any British ship; (b) any British-controlled aircraft or hovercraft[17].

If any one contravenes these provisions he is guilty of an offence and is liable on summary conviction to a fine not exceeding level 5 on the standard scale and to forfeit any goods or other article upon or in connection with which the emblem, designation, sign, signal, design or wording was used[18].

The Secretary of State may make regulations[19] (i) granting the authority (which may be subject to limitations and conditions) of the Secretary of State[20] to persons of any description prescribed in the regulations for the use of any emblem, designation, sign, signal, design or wording[21]; and (ii) making such provision as he may think appropriate for regulating the use for the purposes of the Geneva Red Cross Conventions, or the Geneva Conventions 1949 Protocol I or Protocol II[22] of any emblem, designation, sign or signal[23].

1 Geneva Conventions Act 1957 s 7(1), Sch 1 art 38. This reversal of the Swiss federal colours is a compliment to Switzerland: Sch 1 art 38. In the case, however, of countries already using those emblems, in place of the red cross, the red crescent or the red lion and sun on a white ground are also recognised: Sch 1 art 38. The latter is no longer used in practice.

2 The distinctive flag must be hoisted only over medical units and establishments entitled to be respected: ibid Sch 1 art 42. In certain circumstances it may be accompanied by the national flag of the belligerent or of the neutral power lending medical services: Sch 1 arts 42, 43.

3 Ibid Sch 1 art 39, Sch 2 art 41.

4 Ibid Sch 1 art 40, Sch 2 art 42. Members of the armed forces specially trained as hospital orderlies, nurses or auxiliary stretcher-bearers must, but only while carrying out medical duties, wear a white armlet bearing the distinctive sign in miniature: Sch 1 art 41.

Each party to the conflict is required to ensure that medical and religious personnel and medical units and transports are identifiable by means of the distinctive emblem and distinctive signals: see the Geneva Conventions 1949 Protocol I art 18, Annex I. As to the application and implementation of Protocol I see paras 521–522 ante.

5   This applies also to small craft employed for coastal rescue operations: Geneva Conventions Act 1957 Sch 2 arts 27, 43.

6   Ibid Sch 2 art 43. See also Sch 2 arts 44, 45.

7   Exceptions are made in favour of national Red Cross societies, the international Red Cross organisations and their authorised personnel and ambulances and aid stations used in time of peace for giving free treatment: ibid Sch 1 art 44.

8   Ibid Sch 1 art 44. See also the Geneva Conventions 1949 Protocol I art 38. The use of these emblems by companies, firms or individuals is prohibited by the Geneva Conventions Act 1957 Sch 1 art 53. See also Sch 1 art 54.

It is also prohibited to misuse deliberately in an armed conflict other emblems, eg the emblems of neutral states or adverse parties (see the Geneva Conventions 1949 Protocol I art 39) or the international distinctive sign for civil defence (see Protocol I art 66 para 8, Annex I).

9   Geneva Conventions Act 1957 Sch 2 art 44.

10 Ibid s 6(1)(a), (2)(b).

11 Ibid s 6(1)(b), (2)(b). As to trade marks see s 6(4), (4A) (prospectively added by the Geneva Conventions (Amendment) Act 1995 s 2(5)).

12 Geneva Conventions Act 1957 s 6(1)(c), (2)(b). See note 11 supra.

13 Ibid s 6(1)(d), (2)(c) (prospectively added by the Geneva Conventions (Amendment) Act 1995 ss 2(2), (3), 5(a)(i)).

14 Ie specified in the Geneva Conventions 1949 Protocol I Annex I Ch III.

15 Geneva Conventions Act 1957 s 6(1)(e), (2)(d) (prospectively added by the Geneva Conventions (Amendment) Act 1995 ss 2(2), (3), 5(a)(i)).

16 Geneva Conventions Act 1957 s 6(2)(a).

17 See ibid s 6(6) (prospectively amended by the Geneva Conventions (Amendment) Act 1995 s 2(1), (6)). For these purposes, 'British ship' means a British ship within the meaning of the Merchant Shipping Act 1995; 'British-controlled aircraft' means a British-controlled aircraft within the meaning of the Civil Aviation Act 1982 s 92; and 'British-controlled hovercraft' means a British-controlled hovercraft within the meaning of s 92 as applied to hovercraft by virtue of provision made under the Hovercraft Act 1968: see the Geneva Conventions Act 1957 s 6(6) (as so amended); the Interpretation Act 1978 s 17(2)(a).

18 Geneva Conventions Act 1957 s 6(3) (amended by the Geneva Conventions (Amendment) Act 1995 s 2(4)). 'Standard scale' means the standard scale of maximum fines for summary offences as set out in the Criminal Justice Act 1982 s 37(2) (as substituted): Interpretation Act 1978 s 5, Sch 1 (amended by the Criminal Justice Act 1988 s 170(1), Sch 15 para 58(a)). See CRIMINAL LAW vol 11(2) (Reissue) para 808; and MAGISTRATES. At the date at which this volume states the law, the standard scale is as follows: level 1, £200; level 2, £500; level 3, £1,000; level 4, £2,500; level 5, £5,000: Criminal Justice Act 1982 s 37(2) (substituted by the Criminal Justice Act 1991 s 17(1)). As to the determination of the amount of the fine actually imposed, as distinct from the level on the standard scale which it may not exceed, see the Criminal Justice Act 1991 s 18 (substituted by the Criminal Justice Act 1993 s 65); and MAGISTRATES.

Where an offence under the Geneva Conventions Act 1957 s 6 (as prospectively amended) committed by a body corporate is proved to have been committed with the consent or connivance of any director, manager, secretary or other officer of the body corporate, or any person purporting to act in any such capacity, he, as well as the body corporate, is deemed to be guilty of the offence and is liable to be proceeded against and punished accordingly: s 6(5). 'Director', in relation to any body corporate established by or under any enactment for the purpose of carrying on under national ownership any industry or part of an industry or undertaking, being a body corporate whose affairs are managed by the members thereof, means a member of that body: s 6(5).

Proceedings for an offence under s 6 (as prospectively amended) may not be instituted in England except by or on behalf of the Director of Public Prosecutions: s 6(7) (prospectively amended by the Geneva Conventions (Amendment) Act 1995 s 2(7)).

19 The power to make regulations is exercisable by statutory instrument which is subject to annulment in pursuance of a resolution of either House of Parliament: Geneva Conventions Act 1957 s 6A(3) (s 6A added by the Geneva Conventions (Amendment) Act 1995 s 3).

20 Ie for the purposes of the Geneva Conventions Act 1957 s 6(1), (2).

21 Ibid s 6A(1)(a) (as added: see note 19 supra). This is without prejudice to the Secretary of State's power to give his authority under s 6(1) or (2) otherwise than by regulations under s 6A (as so added): s 6A(2) (as so added).

22 Ie the Geneva Conventions 1949 Protocol II. As to Protocol II see paras 521, 523 ante; and as to its application and implementation see paras 521–522 ante. As to the Geneva Red Cross Conventions (which are set out in the Schedules to the Geneva Conventions Act 1957) see para 521 et seq ante.

23 Geneva Conventions Act 1957 s 6A(1)(b) (as added: see note 19 supra).

(iii) Prisoners of War

533. Protected persons. The persons to whom the provisions of the third Geneva Red Cross Convention[1] apply, known as protected persons under the convention, are as follows:

(1) prisoners of war, who may be (a) members of the armed forces of a party to the conflict, as well as members of militias or volunteer corps forming part of them[2]; (b) members of other militias and volunteer groups, including organised resistance movements belonging to a party to the conflict and operating inside or outside their own territory, even if this territory is occupied, provided they are commanded by a person responsible for his subordinates, have a fixed distinctive sign recognisable at a distance[3], carry arms openly and conduct their operations in accordance with the laws and customs of war[4]; (c) members of regular armed forces professing allegiance to a government or an authority not recognised by the detaining power[5]; (d) certain persons who accompany the armed forces if they have authorisation from these armed forces and are provided with identity cards[6]; (e) members of crews of the merchant marine[7] and civil aircraft[8]; (f) inhabitants of a non-occupied territory who spontaneously take up arms on the approach of the enemy[9], provided they carry arms openly and respect the laws and customs of war[10];

(2) persons[11] to be treated as if they were prisoners of war, that is (a) those who belong or have belonged to the armed forces of a country who are interned by the occupying power[12]; and (b) persons within categories (1)(a) to (f) above who are interned in compliance with the requirements of international law by a neutral or non-belligerent power[13].

The convention applies to these persons from the time they fall into the power of the enemy and until their final release and repatriation[14].

1   Ie the Geneva Convention relative to the Treatment of Prisoners of War: see para 521 note 4 ante. The convention is set out in the Geneva Conventions Act 1957 s 7(1), Sch 3: see generally para 521 ante. It does not protect nationals of the detaining power nor persons who owe a duty of allegiance to that power: *Public Prosecutor v Oie Hee Koi* [1968] AC 829, [1968] 1 All ER 419, PC. As to the detaining power see para 539 post.

2   Geneva Conventions Act 1957 Sch 3 art 4 para A(1).

3   A soldier in civilian clothes is not protected: *Osman Bin Haji Mohamed Ali v Public Prosecutor* [1969] 1 AC 430, [1968] 3 All ER 488, PC. The Geneva Conventions 1949 Protocol I art 44 para 3 provides that combatants are obliged to distinguish themselves from the civilian population. As to the application and implementation of Protocol I see paras 521–522 ante.

4   Geneva Conventions Act 1957 Sch 3 art 4 para A(2).

5   Ibid Sch 3 art 4 para A(3).

6   Ibid Sch 3 art 4 para A(4). These include civil members of military aircraft crews, war correspondents, supply contractors and members of labour units or services responsible for the welfare of the armed forces: Sch 3 art 4 para A(4); see also Sch 1 art 13(4), Sch 2 art 13(4). The identity cards must conform to a prescribed form: Sch 3 art 4 para A(4), Annex.

7   These include masters, pilots and apprentices: ibid Sch 3 art 4 para A(5).

8   Ibid Sch 3 art 4 para A(5).

9   This is known as 'levée en masse'.

10 Geneva Conventions Act 1957 Sch 3 art 4 para A(6). The categories of persons in head (1) in the text are the same as those protected under Sch 1 art 13, and Sch 2 art 13 (which relate to sick, wounded and shipwrecked members of the armed forces: see para 526 ante).

11 These categories of persons are not protected persons under ibid Sch 1 art 13, Sch 2 art 13.

12 Ibid Sch 3 art 4 para B(1). The provisions of Sch 3 art 4 in no way affect the status of medical personnel and chaplains as provided for in Sch 3 art 33 (see para 540 text and note 16 post): Sch 3 art 4 para C.

13 Ibid Sch 3 art 4 para B(2). For the meaning of 'protected prisoner of war' see para 537 note 1 post.

The definitions of 'prisoner of war' and 'combatant' have been extended by the Geneva Conventions 1949 Protocol I (which is expressed to be without prejudice to the Geneva Convention relative to the Treatment of Prisoners of War art 4: see the Geneva Conventions 1949 Protocol I art 44 para 6). Any combatant (defined in Protocol I as members of the armed forces of a party to a conflict other than medical personnel and chaplains: see Protocol I art 43 para 2) who falls into the power of an adverse party is a prisoner of war: Protocol I art 44 para 1. The armed forces of a party to a conflict consist of all organised armed forces, groups and units which are under a command responsible to that party for the conduct of its subordinates, even if that party is represented by a government or authority not recognised by an adverse party: see Protocol I art 43 para 1. Protocol I art 43 refers to a 'party to the conflict' since peoples fighting against colonial domination etc (see para 522 ante) are parties to the conflict although they may not, under international law, be a state. A person who takes part in hostilities and falls into the power of an adverse party is presumed to be a prisoner of war and therefore is protected by the Geneva Convention relative to the Treatment of Prisoners of War if he claims, or if he appears to be entitled to, prisoner of war status: see the Geneva Conventions 1949 Protocol I art 45 para 1. In such a case, his status is to be determined by a competent tribunal: see the Royal Warrant Governing the Maintenance of Discipline Among Prisoners of War dated 7 August 1958 (amended by the Royal Warrants dated 13 January 1965 and 2 December 1968 Sch 1). This was activated in 1991: see Risius 'Prisoners of War in the United Kingdom' in Rowe (ed) *The Gulf War 1990–91 in International and English Law* (1993) ch 14. A person who has taken part in hostilities and is not entitled to prisoner of war status is still entitled to the fundamental guarantees in the Geneva Conventions 1949 Protocol I art 75: see Protocol I art 45 para 3.

Combatants must distinguish themselves from civilians (defined in Protocol I as any person who does not belong to the categories in heads 1(a), (b), (c), (f) in the text or Protocol I art 43: see Protocol I art 50): see Protocol I art 44 para 3. Protocol I recognises that there are situations in armed conflicts where, owing to the nature of the hostilities an armed combatant cannot so distinguish himself, but an armed combatant will retain his status as a combatant provided that, in such situations, he carries his arms openly during each military engagement, and during such time as he is visible to the adversary while he is engaged in a military deployment: see Protocol I art 44 para 3. The United Kingdom government declared that it had signed Protocol I on the basis that in relation to Protocol I art 44 para 3 such a situation can exist only in occupied territory or in armed conflicts covered by Protocol I art 1 para 4 (see para 522 ante); and the government of the United Kingdom will interpret the word 'deployment' as meaning 'any movement towards a place from which an attack is to be launched': Roberts and Guelff (eds) *Documents on the Laws of War* (2nd Edn) pp 459–468. For the meaning of 'United Kingdom' see para 502 note 4 ante. As to the prohibition of feigning non-combatant status see the Geneva Conventions 1949 Protocol I art 37. Protocol I art 44 is not intended to change the practice of states regarding the wearing of uniforms by combatants assigned to regular uniformed armed units of a party to a conflict: see Protocol I art 44 para 7.

A combatant who fails to comply with the minimum requirement in Protocol I art 44 para 3 will forfeit his right to be treated as a prisoner of war, but is to be given, nevertheless, protections equivalent in all respects to those accorded to prisoners of war in the Geneva Convention relative to the Treatment of Prisoners of War and the Geneva Conventions 1949 Protocol I: see Protocol I art 44 paras 2, 4. He will not, however, be immune from national law in respect of his acts committed, even though they may otherwise be consistent with the laws of war.

A member of the armed forces of a party to an armed conflict who falls into the power of an adverse party while engaging in espionage will forfeit his right to be treated as a prisoner of war and may be treated as a spy: see Protocol I art 46; and the Hague Regulations 1907 regs 29, 30. As to the Hague Regulations 1907 see para 518 note 6. Quaere whether a non-United Kingdom citizen could be tried by a court established under the law of the United Kingdom for espionage committed against British forces abroad.

A mercenary (defined in the Geneva Conventions 1949 Protocol I art 47 para 2) has neither the right to be a combatant nor a prisoner of war: see Protocol I art 47. However, both spies and mercenaries are still entitled to the fundamental guarantees: see Protocol I art 75.

14   See the Geneva Conventions Act 1957 Sch 3 art 5.

534. General protection. Prisoners of war must at all times be treated humanely, and not be subjected to unlawful acts causing death or seriously endangering health, in particular mutilation or medical or scientific experiments[1]. They must be protected against acts of violence or intimidation or insults and public curiosity[2]. Reprisals against prisoners of war are prohibited[3]. They are entitled to respect for their persons and honour[4]. All prisoners of war must be treated generally alike without adverse distinction founded on race, nationality, religious belief or political opinions, or other similar criteria[5].

1   Geneva Conventions Act 1957 s 7(1), Sch 3 art 13. The detaining power is bound to provide for the medical attention of prisoners of war: see Sch 3 art 15. As to the detaining power see para 539 post.
2   Ibid Sch 3 art 13.
3   Ibid Sch 3 art 13.
4   Ibid Sch 3 art 14. Women are entitled to be treated as favourably as men, with due regard for their sex: Sch 3 art 14. Specific provisions are made for the treatment of women: see Sch 3 arts 25, 29, 49, 88, 97, 108.
5   Ibid Sch 3 art 16. This is subject to any privileged treatment which may be given due to the prisoner's state of health, age or professional qualification. The provisions of the Geneva Convention relative to the Treatment of Prisoners of War (see para 521 note 4 ante) relating to rank (see eg para 540 note 17 post) and sex (see note 4 supra) must be taken into consideration: Geneva Conventions Act 1957 Sch 3 art 16. The convention is set out in the Geneva Conventions Act 1957 Sch 3. See generally para 521 ante.

535. Variation of rights.

The parties to the Convention relative to the Treatment of Prisoners of War[1] may conclude special agreements on particular matters, but these do not adversely affect the situation of protected persons, medical personnel or chaplains, nor restrict the rights conferred on them by the convention[2]. Protected persons may in no circumstances renounce in part or in whole the rights secured to them under the convention or under any such special agreements that may have been made[3].

1   See para 521 note 4 ante. The convention is set out in the Geneva Conventions Act 1957 s 7(1), Sch 3: see generally para 521 ante.
2   Ibid Sch 3 art 6. The protecting power may assist in settling disagreements between conflicting parties as to the interpretation of the convention: Sch 3 art 11. As to the meaning of 'protecting power' see para 537 ante.
3   Ibid Sch 3 art 7. As to the categories of protected persons see para 533 ante.

536. Information as to prisoners of war.

On the outbreak of conflict and in all cases of occupation of territory each party to the convention[1] which is a party to the conflict must institute an official information bureau for prisoners of war who are within its power[2], and a central prisoners of war information agency must be created in a neutral country[3].

1   Ie the Geneva Convention relative to the Treatment of Prisoners of War (see para 521 note 4 ante). The convention is set out in the Geneva Conventions Act 1957 s 7(1), Sch 3: see generally para 521 ante.
2   See ibid Sch 3 arts 122, 124, where further obligations and rights as to the bureau are set out.
3   See ibid Sch 3 arts 123, 124, where the functions and rights of the agency are set out.

537. The protecting power.

In relation to a protected prisoner of war or protected internee[1] the protecting power is the power or organisation which is carrying out, in the interests of the power of which the protected person is a national, or of whose forces he is or was at any material time a member, the duties assigned to protecting powers under the Convention relative to the Treatment of Prisoners of War or the Convention relative to the Protection of Civilian Persons in Time of War or the Geneva Conventions 1949 Protocol I[2]. The convention must be applied with the co-operation and under the scrutiny of the protecting powers whose duty it is to safeguard the interests of the parties to the conflict and the protecting powers may appoint delegates for this purpose[3]. The high contracting parties may at any time agree to entrust the duties of the protecting powers to an impartial organisation[4]. If protection cannot be arranged, the detaining power must request or accept the offer of the services of a humanitarian organisation, such as the International Committee of the Red Cross, to assume the humanitarian functions of the protecting power[5].

The representatives or delegates of the protecting powers have permission to go to all places where prisoners of war may be[6]. They have full liberty to select the places they wish to visit, and the duration and frequency of such visits must not be limited[7]. Visits may only be prohibited exceptionally and temporarily for reasons of imperative military necessity[8].

1 'Protected prisoner of war' means a person protected by the Geneva Convention relative to the Treatment of Prisoners of War (see para 521 note 4 ante) (which is set out in the Geneva Conventions Act 1957 s 7(1), Sch 3) including a person protected as a prisoner of war under the Geneva Conventions 1949 Protocol I or a person entitled under Protocol I to the same protection as a prisoner of war (see para 533 ante): Geneva Conventions Act 1957 s 7(1) (prospectively amended by the Geneva Conventions (Amendment) Act 1995 s 4(1), (3)). 'Protected internee' means a person protected by the Geneva Convention relative to the Protection of Civilian Persons in Time of War (see para 521 note 5 ante) (which is set out in the Geneva Conventions Act 1957 Sch 4) including a person so protected by virtue of the Geneva Conventions 1949 Protocol I, and who is interned in the United Kingdom (see para 545 post): Geneva Conventions Act 1957 s 7(1) (prospectively amended by the Geneva Conventions (Amendment) Act 1995 s 4(1), (2)). This ensures that the terms 'protected prisoner of war' and 'protected internee' are extended so as to cover persons of such a category protected also by the Geneva Conventions 1949 Protocol I. As to the categories of protected persons see para 533 ante. As to the application and implementation of Protocol I see paras 521–522 ante.

For the purposes of Protocol I, 'protecting power' means a neutral or other state not a party to the conflict which has been designated by a party to the conflict and accepted by the adverse party and has agreed to carry out the functions assigned to a protecting power under the Geneva Red Cross Conventions and the protocol: Geneva Conventions 1949 Protocol I art 2(c). As to the Geneva Red Cross Conventions (which are set out in the Schedules to the Geneva Conventions Act 1957) see para 521 et seq ante.

In the extension of the Geneva Conventions Act 1957 to a territory etc by the orders cited in para 521 ante, a reference to the territory etc is to be substituted for the words 'United Kingdom': see the Geneva Conventions Act (Colonial Territories) Order in Council 1959, SI 1959/1301, art 2, Sch 2 para 1(1); the Geneva Conventions Act (Guernsey) Order 1966, SI 1966/948, art 1, Schedule para 1; the Geneva Conventions Act (Jersey) Order 1966, SI 1966/949, art 1, Schedule; and the Geneva Conventions Act (Isle of Man) Order 1970, SI 1970/1677, art 2, Schedule para 1. For the meaning of 'United Kingdom' see para 502 note 4 ante.

2 Ibid s 7(1) (prospectively amended by the Geneva Conventions (Amendment) Act 1995 s 4(1), (5)). During the Falklands War 1982 neither the United Kingdom nor Argentina formally appointed protecting powers under the Geneva Red Cross Conventions. Such an appointment rarely occurs in modern armed conflicts, although the United Kingdom asked Switzerland to represent it and Argentina requested similar assistance from Brazil. It is usually the International Committee of the Red Cross which performs many of the functions of a protecting power: see Junod 'Protection of the Victims of Armed Conflicts – Falkland-Malvinas Islands (1982)' Int Comm Red Cross (1984) p 20.

3 Geneva Conventions Act 1957 Sch 3 art 8. Delegates are to be appointed from amongst the protecting power's own nationals or the nationals of other neutral powers: Sch 3 art 8.

4 See ibid Sch 3 art 10.

5 Ibid Sch 3 art 10. The provisions of the convention constitute no obstacle to the humanitarian activities which the International Committee of the Red Cross may, subject to the consent of the parties to the conflict, undertake for the protection of prisoners of war and for their relief: Sch 3 art 9. See also the Geneva Conventions 1949 Protocol I art 5 which deals with the methods by which a protecting power or substitute (such as the International Committee of the Red Cross) may be appointed. For the meaning of 'substitute' in Protocol I see para 530 note 4 ante. As to the detaining power see para 539 post.

6 Geneva Conventions Act 1957 Sch 3 art 126.

7 Ibid Sch 3 art 126.

8 Ibid Sch 3 art 126.

538. International Committee of the Red Cross. Delegates of the International Committee of the Red Cross have the same prerogatives, in respect of visits to places where protected persons may be, as representatives and delegates of the protecting power[1]. Necessary facilities must be afforded to representatives of religious organisations and relief societies for visiting prisoners and distributing relief supplies and material intended for religious, educational or recreational purposes[2].

1　Geneva Conventions Act 1957 s 7(1), Sch 3 art 126. As to the protecting power and the right of its representatives to make visits see Sch 3 para 126; and para 537 ante. As to the categories of protected persons see para 533 ante.

2　Ibid Sch 3 art 125. This right is subject to the detaining power's essential security measures: Sch 3 art 125. In practice this is more significant than the powers of a protecting power, since a protecting power is rarely appointed in modern armed conflicts. As to the detaining power see para 539 post.

539. The detaining power. Prisoners of war are in the hands of the enemy state or 'detaining power', and not of the individuals or military units who have captured them[1]. The detaining power is responsible for their treatment, irrespective of the responsibilities of individuals for breaches of the Convention relative to the Treatment of Prisoners of War[2]. The detaining power may only transfer prisoners of war to a state which is a party to the convention and after it has satisfied itself of the willingness and ability of that state to apply the convention[3]. In such circumstances, responsibility for the application of the convention lies with the power to which they are transferred while they are in its custody[4].

When prisoners of war do not benefit from the activities of the protecting power[5], or of an organisation entrusted with the duties incumbent on the protecting power, the detaining power must request a neutral state, or an organisation which offers all guarantees of impartiality and efficacy, to undertake the protecting power's functions[6]. If such protection cannot be arranged the detaining power must request or accept the offer of services of a humanitarian organisation, such as the International Committee of the Red Cross[7].

1　Geneva Conventions Act 1957 s 7(1), Sch 3 art 12.

2　Ibid Sch 3 art 12. The Geneva Convention relative to the Treatment of Prisoners of War (see para 521 note 4 ante) is set out in the Geneva Conventions Act 1957 Sch 3: see generally para 521 ante.

3　Ibid Sch 3 art 12.

4　Ibid Sch 3 art 12. If the power to which they are transferred fails to carry out the provisions of the Geneva Convention relative to the Treatment of Prisoners of War, the transferring power must take effective measures to correct the situation or request the return of the prisoners of war: Geneva Conventions Act 1957 Sch 3 art 12.

5　As to the meaning of 'protecting power' see para 537 ante.

6　See the Geneva Conventions Act 1957 Sch 3 art 10; and para 537 ante.

7　Ibid Sch 3 art 10. See also the Geneva Conventions 1949 Protocol I art 5. As to the application and implementation of Protocol I see paras 521–522 ante.

540. Captivity. The text of the Geneva Convention relative to the Treatment of Prisoners of War[1] and its annexes and the contents of any special agreement must be posted in the prisoners' own language at places where all may read them[2].

When questioned, a prisoner of war is bound to give only his surname, first names and rank, date of birth, and army, regimental, personal or serial number, or equivalent information, and no form of coercion may be inflicted to secure information of any kind[3].

Prisoners of war may retain effects and articles of personal use[4], and must be moved humanely to camps out of danger as soon as possible[5]. They may be interned and released on parole or promise[6]. Internment must be on land in places affording every guarantee of hygiene and healthfulness, away from the fire of the combat zone[7]. Quarters must be as favourable as those of the forces of the detaining power[8], and rations[9] and clothing must be sufficient[10]. All sanitary measures must be taken which are necessary to ensure the cleanliness and healthfulness of camps and to prevent epidemics[11]. Each camp must have an infirmary[12], and there must be monthly medical inspections[13]. Prisoners of war are entitled to complete latitude in the exercise of their religious duties[14]; and intellectual, educational and recreational pursuits, and sports and games, must be encouraged[15]. Medical personnel and chaplains retained to assist prisoners of war are not considered as prisoners of war while retained, but are entitled to at least as favourable treatment as prisoners of war[16].

The detaining power is entitled to utilise the labour of prisoners of war who are physically fit[17], but they may only be compelled to do work of particular classes[18]; and fair working pay must be paid[19]. Money taken from prisoners of war on capture must be placed to their separate accounts[20], and monthly advances of pay must be made[21].

The sending and receiving of letters, and the receiving of parcels, by prisoners of war must be allowed[22], and facilities for the execution and transmission of documents, especially for powers of attorney or wills, must be provided[23]. Relief shipments for prisoners of war are exempt from import, customs and other dues[24].

Every prisoner of war camp must be put under the immediate authority of a responsible commissioned officer belonging to the regular armed force of the detaining power[25].

1   Ie the Geneva Convention relative to the Treatment of Prisoners of War: see para 521 note 4 ante. The convention is set out in the Geneva Conventions Act 1957 s 7(1), Sch 3: see generally para 521 ante.
2   Ibid Sch 3 art 41. Immediately upon prisoners of war falling into its power, the detaining power must inform them and the powers on which they depend, through the protecting power (see para 537 ante), of the measures taken to carry out the provisions of the convention: Sch 3 art 69. As to special agreements see para 535 ante. As to the detaining power see para 539 ante.
3   Ibid Sch 3 art 17.
4   Ibid Sch 3 art 18.
5   Ibid Sch 3 arts 19, 20. Wounded or sick may be kept back temporarily, if they would run greater risks by being moved: Sch 3 art 19.
6   Ibid Sch 3 art 21. Treatment should be with due regard to rank and age: Sch 3 arts 43, 44, 45.
7   Ibid Sch 3 arts 22, 23. As to transit camps see Sch 3 art 24; and as to transfer between camps see Sch 3 arts 46–48.
8   See ibid Sch 3 art 25.
9   See ibid Sch 3 art 26. There must be canteens in all camps: Sch 3 art 28.
10 See ibid Sch 3 art 27.
11 See ibid Sch 3 art 29. Prisoners of war having medical qualifications, though not attached to the forces' medical service, may be required by a detaining power to exercise their medical functions, and will then be excepted from other labour: Sch 3 art 32.
12 See ibid Sch 3 art 30.
13 Ibid Sch 3 art 31. As to medical examination for fitness to work see Sch 3 art 55.
14 Ibid Sch 3 art 34. If there is no retained chaplain or prisoner of war minister, a minister or qualified layman must be appointed if the prisoners so request: Sch 3 art 37.
15 Ibid Sch 3 art 38.
16 Ibid Sch 3 art 33. They are to continue to exercise their medical and spiritual functions: Sch 3 art 33. See further Sch 3 arts 35, 36.
17 Ibid Sch 3 art 49. Age, sex, rank and physical aptitude must be taken into account: Sch 3 art 49. Non-commissioned officers may only be required to do supervisory work; officers in no circumstances may be compelled to work: Sch 3 art 49. Working conditions must be suitable, and national safety regulations applied: Sch 3 art 51. As to the organisation and administration of labour detachments see Sch 3 art 56.
18 In addition to camp administration, installation or maintenance, the classes of work are: (1) agriculture; (2) industries connected with the production or extraction of raw materials, manufacturing industries (with the exception of metallurgical, machinery and chemical industries), public works and building operations which have no military character or purpose; (3) transport and handling of stores which are not military in character or purpose; (4) commercial business and arts and crafts; (5) domestic service; and (6) public utility services having no military character or purpose: ibid Sch 3 art 50.
19 Ibid Sch 3 arts 54, 61, 62. The duration of daily labour, including the time of any journey, must not be excessive or exceed that permitted for civilian workers in the district: Sch 3 art 53. Prisoners of war may not be assigned labour of an unhealthy, dangerous or humiliating nature: Sch 3 art 52. Prisoners of war who are injured as a consequence of their work must receive all necessary care: Sch 3 art 54. As to

compensation claims for injury see Sch 3 art 68. As to the treatment of prisoners of war working for private persons see Sch 3 art 57.

20   Ibid Sch 3 art 59. A detaining power may determine on the outbreak of hostilities the maximum amount of cash a prisoner of war may have in his possession: Sch 3 art 58. As to the obligations as to accounting see Sch 3 arts 64–66.

21   Ibid Sch 3 arts 60, 67. Prisoners of war are entitled to receive remittances of money: Sch 3 art 63.

22   Ibid Sch 3 arts 71, 72. The number may normally be limited to not less than two letters and four cards sent by each prisoner of war monthly: see Sch 3 art 71. Immediately on capture, or within the week after arrival at camp, and also in case of sickness or transfer, the prisoner of war must be enabled to write direct to his family, and to the central prisoners of war agency (see para 536 ante), a card similar to that prescribed by the convention: Sch 3 art 70. Censoring must be done quickly: Sch 3 art 76.

23   Ibid Sch 3 art 77. Should military operations prevent the powers concerned from fulfilling their obligation to assure the transport of the shipments referred to in Sch 3 arts 70, 71, 72, 77, alternative arrangements must be made: Sch 3 art 75.

24   Ibid Sch 3 arts 73, 74.

25   Ibid Sch 3 art 39. As to the saluting of officers and the wearing of badges of rank see Sch 3 arts 39, 40.

541. Complaints and discipline. Prisoners of war have a right to make known to the military authorities in whose power they are their requests regarding the conditions of captivity to which they are subjected, and they have an unrestricted right to apply through their prisoners' representative[1] or direct to the representative of the protecting power[2].

A prisoner of war is subject to the laws and regulations in force in the armed forces of the detaining power[3], but no punishment[4] contrary to the Convention relative to the Treatment of Prisoners of War is allowed[5]. No prisoner of war may be punished more than once for the same offence[6] or may be sentenced to any penalty except those provided in respect of members of the armed forces of the detaining power who have committed the same acts[7]. Repeated escapes or attempts to escape are not to be treated as an aggravating factor in proceedings for an offence committed during an escape or attempt to escape[8].

No prisoner of war may be tried or sentenced[9] for an act which is not forbidden by the law of the detaining power or by international law[10]. Judicial investigations must be conducted as rapidly as possible so that the trial may take place as soon as possible[11]. The detaining power must notify the protecting power of a decision to institute proceedings[12]. The prisoner of war is entitled to call witnesses, and to assistance from one of his prisoner comrades, an advocate of his own choice and, if necessary, an interpreter; and representatives of the protecting power may attend the trial, unless it is held in camera in the interests of state security[13]. Judgment must be reported immediately to the protecting power[14], and the prisoner of war must have a right of appeal in the same way as a member of the armed forces of the detaining power[15].

1   In officers' or mixed camps, the senior officer is the representative; in other camps representatives are elected by secret ballot: Geneva Conventions Act 1957 s 7(1), Sch 3 art 79. As to the duties and privileges of the prisoners' representatives see Sch 3 arts 80, 81.

2   Ibid Sch 3 art 78. As to the meaning of 'protecting power' see para 537 ante.

3   As to the detaining power see para 539 ante.

4   The punishments are fines, discontinuance of privileges above the treatment provided by the Geneva Convention relative to the Treatment of Prisoners of War (see para 521 note 4 ante), fatigue duties up to two hours daily (except for officers), or confinement: Geneva Conventions Act 1957 Sch 3 art 89. The duration of punishment must not exceed 30 days: Sch 3 art 90. While undergoing confinement as a disciplinary punishment, a prisoner of war continues to enjoy the benefits of the convention except in so far as they are necessarily rendered inapplicable by the mere fact of confinement: Sch 3 art 98. The convention is set out in Sch 3: see generally para 521 ante.

5   Ibid Sch 3 art 82. Proceedings will be either judicial or disciplinary (Sch 3 art 82); in deciding which to adopt, leniency is to be shown and wherever possible disciplinary rather than judicial proceedings should be taken (Sch 3 art 83). A prisoner must normally be tried only by a military court (Sch 3 art 84), and

retains the benefit of the convention even if convicted for acts committed prior to capture (Sch 3 art 85). Acts which constitute offences against discipline must be investigated immediately (Sch 3 art 96), and a prisoner is not to be kept in confinement pending the hearing unless a member of the armed forces of the detaining power would be so kept if accused of a similar offence, or unless it is essential in the interests of camp discipline (Sch 3 art 95).

6   Ibid Sch 3 art 86.

7   Ibid Sch 3 art 87. The treatment under judicial or disciplinary punishment may not be more severe than that applied to members of the detaining power's own forces of equivalent rank (Sch 3 art 88), and prisoners of war are not to be transferred to prisons for disciplinary punishment (Sch 3 art 97).

8   Ibid Sch 3 art 93. The use of weapons against prisoners of war, especially against those who are escaping or attempting to escape, is an extreme measure which must always be preceded by appropriate warnings: Sch 3 art 42. Escaped prisoners, if recaptured in a subsequent operation, are not liable to punishment for escaping (Sch 3 art 91), and if the prisoner is recaptured before completing his escape, he is liable only to disciplinary punishment (Sch 3 art 92). A prisoner of war who is recaptured must be handed over without delay to the competent military authority: Sch 3 art 92. If a prisoner of war is recaptured, the power on which he depends must be notified in accordance with Sch 3 art 122 provided notification of his escape has been made: Sch 3 art 94.

9   A prisoner of war can be sentenced only if the sentence has been pronounced by the same courts according to the same procedure as in the case of members of the armed forces of the detaining power, and the provisions of the convention have been observed: ibid Sch 3 art 102. Sentences must be served in the same establishments and under the same conditions as in the case of members of the armed forces of the detaining power, and these conditions must conform to the requirements of health and humanity: Sch 3 art 108. As to death sentences see Sch 3 arts 100, 101.

10 Ibid Sch 3 art 99.

11 Ibid Sch 3 art 103.

12 Ibid Sch 3 art 104.

13 Ibid Sch 3 art 105.

14 Ibid Sch 3 art 107.

15 Ibid Sch 3 art 106.

542. English law relating to trial. United Kingdom[1] municipal law includes particular provisions[2] regarding protected prisoners of war[3], and protected internees[4], and certain of these provisions[5] also apply to persons brought up for trial for grave breaches of the Geneva Red Cross Conventions of 1949 as set out in the Geneva Conventions Act 1957[6].

No court[7] before which a protected prisoner of war is brought up for trial for any offence, or a protected internee is brought up for trial for an offence for which he may be sentenced to death or to imprisonment for two years or more, may proceed with the trial until it is proved to the court's satisfaction that a notice[8] has been served not less than three weeks previously on the protecting power and, if the accused is a protected prisoner of war, on the accused and the prisoners' representative[9]. The notice must contain certain specified particulars, so far as they are known to the prosecutor, of the accused person's name and description, his place of detention, internment or residence, the offence with which he is charged, the court before which the trial is to take place and the time and place appointed for the trial[10].

The court before which a protected prisoner of war[11] is brought up for trial for any offence must not proceed with the trial unless the accused is represented[12] by counsel[13] and it is proved to the court's satisfaction that not less than 14 days have elapsed since instructions for the accused's representation at the trial were first given to the solicitor by whom that counsel was instructed[14].

If the court adjourns the trial to enable the above requirements[15] to be complied with[16], it may remand the accused for the period of the adjournment[17]. Where a protected prisoner of war or protected internee is sentenced to death[18] or to imprisonment for a term of two years or more, the time within which he must give notice of appeal or apply for leave to appeal to the Court of Appeal is the period from the date of his conviction or, in the case of an appeal against sentence, of his sentence, to the expiration of 28 days after the receipt by him of a notice[19] that the protecting power has been notified[20] of the conviction and sentence[21]. The Secretary of State may direct that any period during which a protected person[22] is in custody in connection with an offence for which he is subsequently imprisoned is to be deducted from the term of his imprisonment[23].

1   For the meaning of 'United Kingdom' see para 502 note 4 ante.
2   See the Geneva Conventions Act 1957 ss 2–5 (ss 4, 5 as amended).
3   For the meaning of 'protected prisoner of war' see para 537 note 1 ante.
4   For the meaning of 'protected internee' see para 537 note 1 ante.
5   See the Geneva Conventions Act 1957 s 3.
6   As to grave breaches of the Geneva Red Cross Conventions see para 524 ante. As to the Geneva Red Cross Conventions (which are set out in the Schedules to the Geneva Conventions Act 1957) see para 521 et seq ante.
7   'Court' does not include a court-martial: ibid s 7(1).
8   Unless the contrary is shown, a document purporting to be signed on behalf of the protecting power (see para 537 ante), or by the prisoners' representative (see note 9 infra), or by the person accused, or purporting to be an acknowledgment of the receipt of such a document by that power, representative or person, is sufficient evidence that the notice required by ibid s 2(1) was served on that power, representative or person on that day: s 2(3).
9   Ibid s 2(1). 'Prisoners' representative' means the person by whom the functions of prisoners' representative within the meaning of s 7(1), Sch 3 art 79 (see para 541 ante), were exercisable in relation to that prisoner at the camp or place at which he was last detained as a protected prisoner of war: s 2(4).
10 Ibid s 2(2).
11 Ibid s 3(1), (3)–(5) also applies to a person brought up for trial for an offence under s 1 (see para 524 ante): see s 3(1)(a).
12 If the accused is a protected prisoner of war, in the absence of counsel accepted by him, counsel instructed on behalf of the protecting power is to be regarded as representing him: ibid s 3(2).
13 In relation to proceedings at which a solicitor has a right of audience, references in ibid s 3(1)–(3) to counsel are to be construed, with any necessary modifications, as references to counsel or a solicitor: s 3(4). Any reference to solicitor is modified to include references to bodies recognised under the Administration of Justice Act 1985 s 9 (as amended): see the Solicitors Incorporated Practices Order 1991, SI 1991/2684; and SOLICITORS vol 44(1) (Reissue) para 383.
14 Geneva Conventions Act 1957 s 3(1)(b).
15 See the text to notes 11–14 supra.
16 If the court adjourns because the accused is not represented by counsel etc (see note 13 supra) it must direct that a solicitor and counsel (or, if satisfied that the nature of the charge and the interests of justice do not require representation by counsel, a solicitor only) be assigned to watch over the interests of the accused: Geneva Conventions Act 1957 s 3(3), (4). The manner of assignment is to be such as may be prescribed by Order in Council, and any solicitor or counsel so assigned is entitled to such fees and disbursements out of money provided by Parliament as may be prescribed by regulations made by the Secretary of State: s 3(5). At the date at which this volume states the law, no such Order in Council or regulations had been made.
17 Ibid ss 2(5), 3(1).
18 Under English law, the death penalty is no longer available for murder and may only be passed in very restricted circumstances: see CRIMINAL LAW vols 11(1), 11(2) (Reissue) paras 432, 1199. It is not available for grave breaches of the Geneva Red Cross Conventions or the Geneva Conventions 1949 Protocol I: see the Geneva Conventions Act 1957 s 1 (as prospectively amended); and para 524 ante. As to the application and implementation of the Geneva Conventions 1949 Protocol I see paras 521–522 ante.
19 In the case of a protected prisoner of war, the notice must be given by an officer of Her Majesty's forces, and in the case of a protected internee it must be given by or on behalf of the governor of the prison in which he is confined: see the Geneva Conventions Act 1957 s 4(1) substituted by the Criminal Appeal Act 1968 s 52(1), Sch 5 Pt I).
20 An obligation to notify the protecting power is imposed in the case of prisoners of war by the Geneva Conventions Act 1957 Sch 3 art 107 (see para 541 ante); and in the case of protected internees by Sch 4 arts 74, 126 (see para 561 post).
21 Ibid s 4(1) (as substituted: see note 19 supra). This provision applies notwithstanding anything in the enactments relating to those appeals: s 4(1) (as so substituted). As to appeals to the Court of Appeal see CRIMINAL LAW vol 11(2) (Reissue) para 1352 et seq. The period for applying to the Court of Appeal or to the House of Lords for leave to appeal to the House of Lords is 14 days from when the applicant receives notice that the protecting power has been notified of the decision of that court or the court's

refusal of leave, as the case may be: s 4(1A) (added by the Criminal Appeal Act 1968 Sch 5 Pt I); and see the Administration of Justice Act 1960 s 2(1); and CRIMINAL LAW vol 11(2) (Reissue) para 1437. In a case in which the Geneva Conventions Act 1957 s 4(1) (as substituted) applies, a reference to the period there mentioned is to be substituted for any reference to the period of 28 days after the date of conviction in the Criminal Appeal Act 1968 s 30(1)(a) (as substituted) (see CRIMINAL LAW vol 11(2) (Reissue) para 1362), which relates to the revesting and restitution of property on conviction: Geneva Conventions Act 1957 s 4(1) (as so substituted). As to appeals to the Courts-Martial Appeal Court see the Courts-Martial (Appeals) Act 1968 s 56, Sch 3; and ROYAL FORCES.

22 Ie a protected prisoner of war or protected internee.

23 See the Geneva Conventions Act 1957 s 5(1) (amended by the Northern Ireland (Modification of Enactments – No 1) Order 1973, SI 1973/2163). A protected prisoner of war who has been in custody for an offence for not less than three months must be transferred, if the Secretary of State so directs, into military custody: see the Geneva Conventions Act 1957 s 5(2) (as so amended).

543. Repatriation and release of prisoners of war. On the outbreak of hostilities, mixed medical commissions are to be appointed to examine sick and wounded prisoners of war with a view to repatriation[1]. Subject to the rule that no sick or injured prisoner may be repatriated against his will, seriously wounded and seriously sick prisoners of war must be repatriated when fit to travel[2]. Sentence to disciplinary punishment is not a ground for keeping back a prisoner from repatriation[3]. No repatriated person may be employed on active military service[4]. After the cessation of hostilities prisoners must be repatriated without delay[5].

1 Geneva Conventions Act 1957 s 7(1), Sch 3 art 112. Certain categories of wounded and sick have the right to present themselves for medical examination: Sch 3 art 113.

2 Ibid Sch 3 art 109. This requirement extends to prisoners who meet with accidents, not being self-inflicted: Sch 3 art 114. Certain categories of wounded and sick must be repatriated direct, and certain others may be accommodated in a neutral country: Sch 3 art 110. The detaining power, the power on which the prisoners of war depend and the neutral power are to endeavour to conclude agreements for this purpose: Sch 3 art 111. Costs of transporting prisoners from the frontiers of the detaining power are borne by the power on which the prisoners of war depend: Sch 3 art 116. As to the detaining power see para 539 ante.

3 Ibid Sch 3 art 115.

4 Ibid Sch 3 art 117.

5 Ibid Sch 3 art 118. The conditions for repatriation are similar to those for transfer between camps (see Sch 3 arts 46, 47, 48): Sch 3 art 119. For a practical application see Rowe 'Prisoners of War in the Gulf Area' in Rowe (ed) *The Gulf War 1990–91 in International and English Law* (1993) pp 202–204.

544. Death of prisoners of war. The death or serious injury of a prisoner of war caused or suspected to have been caused by a sentry, another prisoner of war or any other person, or due to an unknown cause, is to be the subject of an official inquiry by the detaining power[1]. Prisoners of war must be honourably buried after death; wills must be transmitted to the protecting power, and death certificates must be forwarded to the prisoners of war information bureau[2].

1 Geneva Conventions Act 1957 s 7(1), Sch 3 art 121. The statements of witnesses etc must be forwarded to the protecting power, and if the inquiry indicates guilt, the detaining power must take action against those responsible: Sch 3 art 121. As to the meaning of 'protecting power' see para 537 ante; and as to the detaining power see para 539 ante. See also Junod, 'Protection of the Victims of Armed Conflict – Falklands-Malvinas Islands' (1982) Int Comm Red Cross (1984) p 32.

2 Geneva Conventions Act 1957 Sch 3 art 120. A certified copy of a will must also be sent to the central prisoners of war information agency, and the detaining power must establish a grave registration service: Sch 3 art 120. As to the establishment of a central agency and an information bureau see para 536 ante.

(iv) Civilians

A. IN GENERAL

545. Protected persons. The fourth Geneva Red Cross Convention is the Convention relative to the Protection of Civilian Persons in Time of War[1]. The persons protected by this convention are those who at any given moment and in any manner whatsoever find themselves, during a conflict or occupation, in the hands of a party to the conflict or occupying power of which they are not nationals[2].

Nationals of a state which is not bound by the convention are not within its protection; and nationals of a neutral state who find themselves in the territory of a belligerent, as well as nationals of a co-belligerent state, are not protected persons so long as the state whose nationals they are has normal diplomatic relations with the state in whose hands they are[3]. Persons who are protected under the three conventions dealing with the sick, wounded and shipwrecked, and with prisoners of war[4], are not protected persons within the meaning of the fourth convention[5].

1   Ie the Geneva Convention relative to the Protection of Civilian Persons in Time of War: see para 521 note 5 ante. The convention is set out in the Geneva Conventions Act 1957 s 7(1), Sch 4: see generally para 521 ante.
2   Ibid Sch 4 art 4. The Geneva Conventions 1949 Protocol I art 73 provides that the category of protected persons includes persons who, before the beginning of hostilities, were considered as stateless persons or refugees under the relevant international instruments accepted by the parties concerned or under national legislation. See also the Convention relating to the Status of Refugees (28 July 1951; TS 39 (1954); Cmd 9171); and the Protocol relating to the Status of Refugees (31 Jan 1967; TS 15 (1969); Cmnd 3906). As to the application and implementation of the Geneva Conventions 1949 Protocol I see paras 521–522 ante.
3   Geneva Conventions Act 1957 Sch 4 art 4.
4   Ie the Geneva Convention for the Amelioration of the Condition of the Wounded and Sick in Armed Forces in the Field (see para 521 note 2 ante); the Geneva Convention for the Amelioration of the Condition of the Wounded, Sick and Shipwrecked Members of the Armed Forces at Sea (see para 521 note 3 ante); and the Geneva Convention relative to the Treatment of Prisoners of War (see para 521 note 4 ante). These conventions are set out in the Geneva Conventions Act 1957 Schs 1, 2, 3 respectively: see para 521 et seq ante. As to the categories of protected persons under these conventions see Sch 1 art 13, Sch 2 art 13, Sch 3 art 4; and paras 526, 533 ante.
5   Ibid Sch 4 art 4.

546. Persons not entitled to benefit. Two classes of persons are excluded from the protection of the Convention relative to the Protection of Civilian Persons in Time of War[1]: (1) where a party to the conflict is satisfied that an individual protected person is definitely suspected of or engaged in activities hostile to its security and within its territory, that person is not entitled to such rights and privileges under the convention as would, if exercised in his favour, be prejudicial to the security of the state; and (2) in occupied territory, where a protected person is detained as a spy or saboteur or as a person under definite suspicion of activity hostile to the security of the occupying power, and if absolute military security so requires, that person may be deemed to have forfeited the right of communication[2] provided for in the convention[3]. In either case, however, such persons are to be treated with humanity, and, if tried, must have the benefit of the rights of fair and regular trial[4]. At the earliest possible date such persons must be granted the full rights and privileges of a protected person[5].

1   See para 521 note 5 ante. The convention is set out in the Geneva Conventions Act 1957 s 7(1), Sch 4: see generally para 521 ante. As to the categories of protected persons see para 545 ante.
2   As to the right of communication see ibid Sch 4 arts 106–116; and para 562 post.

3 Ibid Sch 4 art 5. See also the Geneva Conventions 1949 Protocol I art 45 para 3. As to the application and implementation of Protocol I see paras 521–522 ante.

4 For the rights of fair trial see the Geneva Conventions Act 1957 Sch 4 arts 71–75; and para 561 post. The Geneva Conventions 1949 Protocol I provides for certain fundamental guarantees: see Protocol I art 75.

5 Geneva Conventions Act 1957 Sch 4 art 5.

547. Information as to civilians. The provisions of the Convention relative to the Protection of Civilian Persons in Time of War[1] are supplementary to the relevant sections of the Hague Regulations[2]. Upon the outbreak of a conflict and in all cases of occupation of territory, each of the parties to the convention who is a party to the conflict must establish an official information bureau responsible for receiving and transmitting information respecting protected persons in its power[3]. A central information agency for protected persons, in particular for internees, must be created in a neutral country[4].

1 See para 521 note 5 ante. The convention is set out in the Geneva Conventions Act 1957 s 7(1), Sch 4: see generally para 521 ante.

2 Ibid Sch 4 art 154. The Hague Regulations 1907 are annexed to the International Convention concerning the Laws and Customs of War on Land (Hague Convention IV): see para 518 note 6 ante. See especially regs 42–56. The regulations provide certain rules for the protection of civilians in territories under belligerent occupation, but do not regulate the treatment of civilians in the domestic territory of an occupied state. As to the Hague Conventions generally see para 518 ante.

3 Geneva Conventions Act 1957 Sch 4 art 136. See also Sch 4 arts 137–139, where the functions and duties of the information bureau are set out. As to the categories of protected persons see para 545 ante.

4 Ibid Sch 4 art 140. The information bureau and the agency enjoy certain exemptions from customs, postal and telegraph charges: see Sch 4 art 141.

548. Duration of application of convention. The provisions of the Convention relative to the Protection of Civilian Persons in Time of War[1] apply from the outset of any conflict[2] or occupation[3]. In the territory of parties to the conflict their application ceases on the general close of military operations, and in the case of occupied territory they cease to apply one year after the general close of military operations, apart from some provisions[4] which continue to apply during the occupation to the extent that the occupying power exercises the functions of government[5]. Protected persons whose release, repatriation or re-establishment takes place after such date must, in the meantime, benefit from the convention[6].

1 See para 521 note 5 ante. The convention is set out in the Geneva Conventions Act 1957 s 7(1), Sch 4: see generally para 521 ante.

2 'Conflicts' includes all cases of declared war or other armed conflict between two high contracting parties, even if the state of war is not recognised by one of them: ibid Sch 4 art 2.

3 Ibid Sch 4 art 6. 'Occupation' may be total or partial and includes cases where the occupation meets with no armed resistance: Sch 4 art 2.

4 Ie the provisions of ibid Sch 4 arts 1–12, 27, 29–34, 47, 49, 51–53, 59, 61–77, 143: Sch 4 art 6. See also para 522 note 6 ante.

5 Ibid Sch 4 art 6.

6 Ibid Sch 4 art 6. As to the categories of protected persons see para 545 ante.

549. The protecting powers. The Convention relative to the Protection of Civilian Persons in Time of War[1] must be applied with the co-operation and under the scrutiny of the protecting powers whose duty it is to safeguard the interests of the parties to the conflict and the protecting powers may appoint delegates for this purpose[2]. The high contracting parties may at any time agree to entrust the duties of the protecting powers to an impartial organisation[3]. If protection cannot be arranged, the detaining power must request or accept the offer of the services of a humanitarian organisation, such as the

International Committee of the Red Cross, to assume the humanitarian function of the protecting powers[4].

The representatives or delegates of the protecting powers have permission to go to all places where protected persons[5] are, and to all places where they may be[6]. They have full liberty to select the places they wish to visit, and the duration and frequency of such visits must not be limited[7]. Visits may only be prohibited exceptionally and temporarily for reasons of imperative military necessity[8].

1   See para 521 note 5 ante. The convention is set out in the Geneva Conventions Act 1957 s 7(1), Sch 4: see generally para 521 ante.
2   Ibid Sch 4 art 9. As to the meaning of 'protecting power' see para 537 ante. The delegates are to be appointed from amongst the protecting power's own nationals or the nationals of other neutral powers: Sch 4 art 9.
3   Ibid Sch 4 art 11.
4   Ibid Sch 4 art 11. The provisions of the convention constitute no obstacle to the humanitarian activities which the International Committee of the Red Cross may, subject to the consent of the parties to the conflict, undertake for the protection of civilian persons and for their relief: Sch 4 art 10. See also the Geneva Conventions 1949 Protocol I art 5, which deals with the methods by which a protecting power or substitute (such as the International Committee of the Red Cross) may be appointed. As to the meaning of 'substitute' in Protocol I see para 530 note 4 ante. As to the application and implementation of Protocol I see paras 521–522 ante. The convention refers to the 'detaining power' in relation to aliens in the territory of a party to the conflict and internees, and to the 'occupying power' in relation to protected persons in occupied territory.
5   As to the categories of protected persons see para 545 ante.
6   Geneva Conventions Act 1957 Sch 4 art 143.
7   Ibid Sch 4 art 143.
8   Ibid Sch 4 art 143.

550. Red Cross and relief organisations. Delegates of the International Committee of the Red Cross have the same prerogatives, in respect of visits to places where protected persons may be, as representatives of the protecting power[1]. Necessary facilities must be afforded to representatives of religious organisations and relief societies for visiting protected persons and distributing relief supplies and material intended for religious, educational or recreational purpose[2].

1   Geneva Conventions Act 1957 s 7(1), Sch 4 art 143. As to the categories of protected persons see para 545 ante. As to the meaning of 'protecting power' see para 537 ante. See also para 549 ante.
2   Ibid Sch 4 art 142. This right is subject to the detaining power̃s essential security measures: Sch 4 art 142. As to the detaining power see para 549 note 4 ante.

551. General protection of populations against certain consequences of war. The provisions of the Convention relative to the Protection of Civilian Persons in Time of War[1] which deal with general protection of populations against certain consequences of war[2] apply to the whole of the populations of the countries in conflict without any adverse distinction based, in particular, on race, nationality, religion or political opinion; and these provisions are intended to alleviate the sufferings caused by war[3].

To this end, hospital and safety zones may be established for the protection of the wounded, sick and aged, children[4] and mothers[5]; and neutralised zones[6] may be established in regions where fighting is taking place for the wounded and sick, and for civilians who take no part in hostilities and perform no work of a military character[7]. Civilian hospitals must in no circumstances be attacked[8], and hospital staff[9] and hospital trains[10] must be respected and protected. Free passage is to be allowed to consignments of medical and hospital stores and objects necessary for religious worship if intended only for civilians[11]. Correspondence of a strictly personal nature between members of families must be allowed[12], and inquiries for relatives by members of families dispersed owing to the war must be facilitated[13].

1 See para 521 note 5 ante. The convention is set out in the Geneva Conventions Act 1957 s 7(1), Sch 4: see generally para 521 ante.

2 Ie ibid Sch 4 Pt II (arts 13–26). These provisions govern the relations between a state and its own nationals and those of neutral states and co-belligerents in an armed conflict. See also the Geneva Conventions 1949 Protocol I Pt IV (arts 48–79), which sets out provisions relating to the general protection of the civilian population against effects of hostilities: see paras 552–553 post. As to the application and implementation of Protocol I see paras 521–522 ante.

3 Geneva Conventions Act 1957 Sch 4 art 13.

4 Measures for the maintenance and education of children who are orphaned or separated from their families must be taken: ibid Sch 4 art 24.

5 Ibid Sch 4 art 14. The wounded, sick and infirm, and expectant mothers, must be the object of particular protection (Sch 4 art 16); and local agreements for the removal of the wounded, sick, infirm and aged, and children and maternity cases, from besieged or encircled areas should be concluded (Sch 4 art 17).

6 As to the protection of declared non-dependent localities, and of agreed demilitarised zones, see the Geneva Conventions 1949 Protocol I arts 59, 60.

7 Geneva Conventions Act 1957 Sch 4 art 15.

8 Ibid Sch 4 art 18. They may be marked by the distinctive emblem (see para 532 ante) if authorised by the state: Sch 4 art 18. The protection of civilian hospitals is not to cease unless they are used, outside their humanitarian duties, to commit acts harmful to the enemy: Sch 4 art 19.

9 Ibid Sch 4 art 20.

10 Ibid Sch 4 art 21. Protection is also given to convoys of vehicles and vessels on sea carrying wounded and sick civilians, the infirm and maternity cases (Sch 4 art 21), and to aircraft exclusively employed for the removal of those persons (Sch 4 art 22).

11 Ibid Sch 4 art 23. The Geneva Conventions 1949 Protocol I provides for relief in favour of the civilian population: see Protocol I arts 68–71. The parties to an armed conflict may agree to relief actions where the civilian population is not adequately provided with food, medical supplies, clothing, bedding, shelter, other supplies essential to the survival of the civilian population and objects necessary for religious worship: Protocol I arts 69, 70. The parties to the conflict and all states party to Protocol I must allow and facilitate rapid and unimpeded passage of relief consignments, equipment and personnel: Protocol I art 70 para 2.

12 Geneva Conventions Act 1957 Sch 4 art 25.

13 Ibid Sch 4 art 26. The reunion of families dispersed as a result of armed conflicts is to be facilitated in every possible way: Geneva Conventions 1949 Protocol I art 74.

552. Protection of the civilian population against the effects of hostilities. In addition to the provisions concerning humanitarian protection contained in the Geneva Convention relative to the Protection of Civilian Persons in Time of War[1] and in other international agreements binding on the high contracting parties, and other rules of international law, the Geneva Conventions 1949 Protocol I[2] provides for the general protection of the civilian population[3] against the effects of hostilities[4]. In order to ensure respect for, and protection of, the civilian population and civilian objects, the parties to the conflict must at all times distinguish between the civilian population and combatants[5] and between civilian objects and military objectives[6]; and are to direct their operations only against military objectives[7].

The civilian population and individual civilians must enjoy general protection against dangers arising from military operations and must not be made the object of attack[8]. Acts or threats of violence the primary purpose of which is to spread terror among the civilian population are prohibited[9], as are indiscriminate attacks[10]. Reprisals against the civilian population are prohibited[11]. Acts of hostility against cultural objects[12] and places of worship which constitute the cultural or spiritual heritage of peoples[13], objects indispensable to the survival of the civilian population[14], the natural environment[15], and works and installations containing dangerous forces[16] are prohibited. In the conduct of military operations constant care must be taken to spare the civilian population, civilians and civilian objects[17]. Those who plan or decide upon an attack must take precautionary measures[18].

The parties to the conflict must, to the maximum extent feasible: (1) endeavour to remove the civilian population, individual civilians and civilian objects under their control from the vicinity of military objectives[19]; (2) avoid locating military objectives within or near densely populated areas; (3) take the other necessary precautions to protect the civilian population, individual civilians and civilian objects under their control against the dangers resulting from military operations[20].

1   See para 521 note 5 ante. The convention is set out in the Geneva Conventions Act 1957 s 7(1), Sch 4: see generally para 521 ante. As to the provisions concerning humanitarian protection see Sch 4 Pt II (arts 13–26); and para 551 ante.

2   As to the application and implementation of the Geneva Conventions 1949 Protocol I see paras 521–522 ante.

3   For the meaning of 'civilian' in ibid Protocol I see para 533 note 13 ante. A civilian is only protected until such time as he or she takes a direct part in hostilities: Protocol I art 51 para 3.

4   Ibid Protocol I art 49 para 4.

5   For the meaning of 'combatant' in ibid Protocol I see para 533 note 13 ante.

6   All objects other than military objectives are civilian objects: ibid Protocol I art 52 para 1. 'Military objectives' are limited to those objects which by their nature, location, purpose or use make an effective contribution to military action and whose total or partial destruction, capture or neutralisation, in the circumstances ruling at the time, offers a definite military advantage: Protocol I art 52 para 2. A presumption exists that an object which is normally dedicated to civilian purposes, such as a place of worship, a house or other dwelling or school, is not being used to make an effective contribution to military action: Protocol I art 52 para 3.

7   Ibid Protocol I art 48. This explains the need for a combatant to distinguish himself from a civilian in the circumstances referred to in Protocol I art 44 para 3: see para 533 ante.

8   Ibid Protocol I art 51 paras 1, 2. ôAttackō means acts of violence against the adversary whether in offence or defence: see Protocol I art 49 para 1. Protocol I applies to all attacks in whatever territory conducted, including the national territory of a party to the conflict but under the control of an adverse party: see Protocol I art 49 paras 2, 3.

9   Ibid Protocol I art 51 para 2.

10   Ibid Protocol I art 51 para 4. Indiscriminate attacks are attacks which (1) are not directed at a specific military objective; (2) employ a method or means of combat which cannot be directed at a specific military objective; or (3) employ a method or means of combat the effects of which cannot be limited as required by Protocol I and consequently are of a nature to strike military objectives and civilians or civilian objects without distinction: Protocol I art 51 para 4. (It is submitted that head (2) supra could include a missile which is intrinsically inaccurate.) In addition, an attack by bombardment by any method which treats as a single military objective a number of clearly separated and distinct military objectives located in a city, town or village or other area containing a similar concentration of civilian objects is an indiscriminate attack: Protocol I art 51 para 5(a). An attack which may be expected to cause incidental loss of civilian life, injury to civilians, damage to civilian objects or a combination of these, which would be excessive in relation to the concrete and direct military advantage anticipated, is also an indiscriminate attack: Protocol I art 51 para 5(b). This prohibition on causing excessive 'collateral damage' will often govern the choice of other methods or means of warfare. Thus, in the Gulf War 1990–91, laser-guided bombs rather than free-fall bombs dropped by aircraft were employed to attack military objectives. See further Hampson 'Means and Methods of Warfare in the Conflict in the Gulf' in Rowe (ed) *The Gulf War 1990–91 in International and English Law* (1993) ch 5.

11   See the Geneva Conventions 1949 Protocol I art 51 para 6. As to the prohibition of other reprisals see Protocol I art 52 para 1, art 53 para (c), art 54 para 4, art 55 para 2, art 56 para 4.

12   See the Hague Convention for the Protection of Cultural Property in the Event of Armed Conflict (see para 523 note 22 ante). See also the Hague Regulations 1907 reg 27. As to the Hague Regulations 1907 see para 518 note 6 ante.

13   See the Geneva Conventions 1949 Protocol I art 53. It is submitted that a church would not normally be a military objective unless it was used to make an effective contribution to military action.

14   See ibid Protocol I art 54. Such objects include foodstuffs, agricultural areas for the production of foodstuffs, crops, livestock, drinking water installations and supplies and irrigation works: see Protocol I art 54 para 2. Starvation of civilians is specifically prohibited: Protocol I art 54 para 1. As to the exceptions see Protocol I art 54 paras 3, 5.

15 See ibid Protocol I art 55. It is prohibited to employ methods or means of warfare which are intended, or may be expected, to cause widespread, long-term and severe damage to the natural environment: Protocol I art 35 para 3.

16 See ibid Protocol I art 56. Dangerous forces are dams, dykes and nuclear electrical generating stations: see Protocol I art 56. As to the exceptions see Protocol I art 56 para 2.

17 See ibid Protocol I art 57 para 1.

18 The precautions are:

(1) those who plan or decide upon an attack must (a) do everything feasible to verify that the objectives to be attacked are neither civilians nor civilian objects and are not subject to special protection but are military objectives and that it is not prohibited by the provisions of ibid Protocol I to attack them; (b) take all feasible precautions in the choice of means and methods of attack with a view to avoiding, and in any event minimising, incidental loss of civilian life, injury to civilians and damage to civilian objects; (c) refrain from deciding to launch any attack which may be expected to cause incidental loss of civilian life, injury to civilians, damage to civilian objects, or a combination thereof, which would be excessive in relation to the concrete and direct military advantage anticipated (Protocol I art 57 para 2(a));

(2) an attack must be cancelled or suspended if it becomes apparent that the objective is not a military one or is subject to special protection or that the attack may be expected to cause incidental loss of civilian life, injury to civilians, damage to civilian objects, or a combination thereof, which would be excessive in relation to the concrete and direct military advantage anticipated (Protocol I art 57 para 2(b));

(3) effective advance warning must be given of attacks which may affect the civilian population, unless circumstances do not permit (Protocol I art 57 para 2(c)).

See also the Hague Regulations 1907 reg 26.

19 This is without prejudice to the Geneva Conventions Act 1957 Sch 4 art 49: see para 557 post.

20 See the Geneva Conventions 1949 Protocol I art 58.

553. Civil defence. Civil defence is the performance of certain humanitarian tasks intended to protect the civilian[1] population against the dangers, and to help it to recover from the immediate effects, of hostilities or disasters and also to provide the conditions necessary for its survival[2]. Civilian defence organisations[3] and their personnel[4] must be respected and protected and they must be entitled to perform their civil defence tasks except in case of imperative military necessity[5]. Such protection ceases only if the civil defence organisations, their personnel, buildings, shelters and *matériel*[6] are used to commit, outside their proper tasks, acts harmful to the enemy[7]. In occupied territories, civilian civil defence organisations must receive the facilities necessary for the performance of their tasks from the authorities[8]. Civil defence personnel and property are to be marked with the international distinctive sign of civil defence[9].

1 For the meaning of 'civilian' in the Geneva Conventions 1949 Protocol I see para 533 note 13 ante. As to the application and implementation of Protocol I see paras 521–522 ante.

2 Ibid Protocol I art 61(a). The tasks are: (1) warning; (2) evacuation; (3) management of shelters; (4) management of blackout measures; (5) rescue; (6) medical services, including first aid, and religious assistance; (7) fire-fighting; (8) detection and marking of danger areas; (9) decontamination and similar protective measures; (10) provision of emergency accommodation and supplies; (11) emergency assistance in the restoration and maintenance of order in distressed areas; (12) emergency repair of indispensable public utilities; (13) emergency disposal of the dead; (14) assistance in the preservation of objects essential for survival; (15) complementary activities necessary to carry out any of the tasks mentioned above, including, but not limited to, planning and organisation: Protocol I art 61(a)(i)–(xv).

3 In ibid Protocol I, 'civil defence organisations' means those establishments and other units which are organised or authorised by the competent authorities of a party to the conflict to perform any of the tasks mentioned in note 2 supra and which are assigned and devoted exclusively to such tasks: Protocol I art 61(b).

4 In ibid Protocol I, 'personnel' of civil defence organisations means those persons assigned by a party to the conflict exclusively to the performance of the tasks mentioned in note 2 supra, including personnel assigned by the competent authority of that party exclusively to the administration of those organisations: Protocol I art 61(c).

5 Ibid Protocol I art 62 para 1. This provision also applies to civilians who, although not members of civilian civil defence organisations, respond to an appeal from the competent authorities and perform civil defence

tasks under their control: Protocol I art 62 para 2. Objects used for civil defence purposes may not be destroyed except by the party to which they belong: Protocol I art 62 para 3.

Protocol I arts 62, 63, 65 and 66 also apply to the civilian civil defence organisations of neutral or other states not parties to the conflict which perform civil defence tasks mentioned in note 2 supra in the territory of a party to the conflict, with the consent and under the control of that party: Protocol I art 64 para 1.

Members of the armed forces and military units assigned to civil defence organisations must also be respected and protected: Protocol I art 67 para 1.

6   In ibid Protocol I, '*matériel*' of civil defence organisations means equipment, supplies and transports used by those organisations for the performance of the tasks mentioned in note 2 supra: Protocol I art 61(d).

7   Ibid Protocol I art 65 para 1. Protection will only cease after a warning has been given which has remained unheeded: see Protocol I art 65 para 1. Certain acts are not considered harmful to the enemy: see Protocol I art 65 paras 2, 3.

8   Ibid Protocol I art 63 para 1.

9   See ibid Protocol I art 66, Annex I. As to the use and abuse of distinctive emblems and signs see para 532 ante.

B. STATUS AND TREATMENT OF PROTECTED PERSONS

554. In general. The rights of protected persons[1] include respect for their persons, honour, family rights, religious convictions and practices and their manners and customs[2]; and freedom to make applications to the protecting powers[3] and International Committee of the Red Cross organisations[4]. Their presence must not be used to render certain points or areas immune from military operation[5]. Physical and moral coercion[6], pillage and punishment for offences not personally committed are prohibited[7]. The party in whose hands protected persons may be is responsible for their treatment, irrespective of individual responsibility[8].

1   As to the categories of protected persons under the Geneva Convention relative to the Protection of Civilian Persons in Time of War (see para 521 note 5 ante) see para 545 ante. The convention is set out in the Geneva Conventions Act 1957 s 7(1), Sch 4: see generally para 521 ante.

2   Ibid Sch 4 art 27.

3   As to the meaning of 'protecting power' see para 537 ante.

4   Geneva Conventions Act 1957 Sch 4 art 30.

5   Ibid Sch 4 art 28.

6   Ibid Sch 4 art 31. Measures of a character which may cause physical suffering or extermination are prohibited: Sch 4 art 32.

7   Ibid Sch 4 art 33. The taking of hostages is specifically prohibited by Sch 4 art 34.

8   Ibid Sch 4 art 29.

555. Aliens in the territory of a party to the conflict. Protected persons[1] in the territory of a party to the conflict are entitled to leave[2]. If they remain, they may be compelled to work only to the same extent as that party's own nationals[3]. They may be interned only if the state's security makes it absolutely necessary[4]. Restrictive measures affecting them are to be cancelled as soon as possible after the close of hostilities[5]. In applying any measures of control the detaining power must not treat as enemy aliens, on the basis of their de jure nationality of an enemy state, persons who do not, in fact, enjoy the protection of any government[6]. Protected persons must not be transferred to a power which is not a party to the convention[7].

1   As to the categories of protected persons under the Geneva Convention relative to the Protection of Civilian Persons in Time of War (see para 521 note 5 ante) see para 545 ante. The convention is set out in the Geneva Conventions Act 1957 s 7(1), Sch 4: see generally para 521 ante.

2   Ibid Sch 4 art 35. This is subject to their departure not being contrary to the interests of the state: Sch 4 art 35. Conditions of their departure must be satisfactory: Sch 4 art 36. There is no provision dealing with

expulsion of aliens. Protected persons who are confined pending proceedings or serving a sentence involving loss of liberty must be treated humanely during their confinement: Sch 4 art 37.

3   Ibid Sch 4 art 40. If as a result of war they have lost gainful employment, they must be given the opportunity to find other gainful employment: Sch 4 art 39.

4   Ibid Sch 4 arts 41–43.

5   Ibid Sch 4 art 46.

6   Ibid Sch 4 art 44. Apart from certain special measures (see Sch 4 arts 27, 41), the situation of protected persons continues to be regulated, in principle, by the provisions concerning aliens in time of peace: Sch 4 art 38. As to the detaining power see para 549 note 4 ante.

7   Ibid Sch 4 art 45. The provisions concerning the transfer of protected persons to other powers are similar to the prisoner of war provisions: see Sch 3 art 12; and para 539 ante.

556. Variation of rights. The parties to the Convention relative to the Protection of Civilian Persons in Time of War[1] may conclude special agreements on particular matters, but they must not adversely affect the situation of protected persons[2], medical personnel or chaplains, nor restrict the rights conferred on them by the convention[3]. Protected persons may in no circumstances renounce in part or in whole the rights secured to them under the convention or under any such special agreements that have been made[4].

1   See para 521 note 5 ante. The convention is set out in the Geneva Conventions Act 1957 s 7(1), Sch 4: see generally para 521 ante.

2   As to the categories of protected person see para 545 ante.

3   Geneva Conventions Act 1957 Sch 4 art 7. The protecting power may assist in settling disagreements between conflicting parties as to the interpretation of the convention: Sch 4 art 12. As to the meaning of 'protecting power' see para 537 ante.

4   Ibid Sch 4 art 8.

557. Persons in occupied territories. Protected persons[1], other than those who are nationals of the state whose territory is occupied, are entitled to leave[2]. In relation to such persons, deprivation of rights, by changes in the institutions of government of the occupied territory, or by any agreement between the authorities of the territory and the occupying power or by any annexation by the occupying power of the whole or part of the occupied territory, are prohibited[3]. Also prohibited are forcible transfers[4] and conscriptions into the occupying power's armed forces[5]. Duties are imposed on the occupying power with respect to institutions for the care and education of children[6], food and medical supplies[7], hospitals and public health[8], relief schemes[9], relief consignments[10] and civil defence[11].

1   As to the categories of protected persons under the Geneva Convention relative to the Protection of Civilian Persons in Time of War (see para 521 note 5 ante) see para 545 ante. The convention is set out in the Geneva Conventions Act 1957 s 7(1), Sch 4: see generally para 521 ante.

2   Ibid Sch 4 art 48. This is subject to their departure not being contrary to the national interests of the state: see Sch 4 art 5.

3   Ibid Sch 4 art 47.

4   Ibid Sch 4 art 49.

5   Ibid Sch 4 art 51. Measures aimed at creating unemployment in order to induce workers in occupied territory to work for the occupying power are prohibited: Sch 4 art 52.

6   Ibid Sch 4 art 50.

7   Ibid Sch 4 art 55. See also the Geneva Conventions 1949 Protocol I arts 68–71. The occupying power is required to ensure the provision of clothing, bedding, means of shelter, other supplies essential to the survival of the civilian population and objects necessary for religious worship: Protocol I art 69. As to the application and implementation of Protocol I see paras 521–522 ante.

8   Geneva Conventions Act 1957 Sch 4 art 56. As to requisitioning of civilian hospitals see Sch 4 art 57.

9   Ibid Sch 4 art 59. The Red Cross and other relief societies must be permitted to continue their humanitarian activities: see Sch 4 art 63.

10   Ibid Sch 4 arts 60–62. As to provisions concerned with religious needs see Sch 4 art 58.

11   See the Geneva Conventions 1949 Protocol I arts 61–67; and para 553 ante.

558. Public and private property. Any destruction by the occupying power of real or personal property belonging individually or collectively to private persons or to the state, or to other public authorities, is prohibited except where such destruction is rendered absolutely necessary by military operations[1].

1   Geneva Conventions Act 1957 s 7(1), Sch 4 art 53.

559. Judges and public officials. The occupying power must preserve the status of judges and public officials in the occupied territories[1]. Sanctions or measures of coercion or discrimination must not be taken against them, if they abstain from fulfilling their functions for conscientious reasons, although the occupying power may remove them from their posts[2].

1   Geneva Conventions Act 1957 s 7(1), Sch 4 art 54.
2   Ibid Sch 4 art 54.

560. Penal laws. The ordinary penal laws and tribunals of the occupied territory remain in force except where they constitute a threat to the occupying power's security or an obstacle to the application of the Convention relative to the Protection of Civilian Persons in Time of War[1]. The occupying power may subject the population to new provisions essential for it to carry out its obligations under the convention, to maintain orderly government in the territory, and to ensure the security of the occupying forces and the administration[2]. No penal law enacted by the occupying power comes into force until it is published and brought to the notice of the inhabitants of the occupied territory in their own language, and such penal law must not be retroactive in operation[3]. Offences against this penal law may be tried by non-political military courts sitting in the occupied territory[4], but such courts may only apply those laws applicable before the offence was committed and which are in accordance with general principles of law; and the penalty must be proportionate to the offence[5].

1   Geneva Conventions Act 1957 s 7(1), Sch 4 art 64. The convention referred to is the Geneva Convention relative to the Protection of Civilian Persons in Time of War: see para 521 note 5 ante. The convention is set out in the Geneva Conventions Act 1957 s 7(1), Sch 4: see generally para 521 ante.
2   Ibid Sch 4 art 64.
3   Ibid Sch 4 art 65. The Geneva Conventions 1949 Protocol I provides for certain fundamental guarantees including a provision which states that no sentence may be passed and no penalty may be executed on a person found guilty of a penal offence related to the armed conflict except pursuant to a conviction pronounced by an impartial and regularly constituted court respecting certain generally recognised principles of regular judicial procedure: Protocol I art 75. These include a prohibition of the retroactive operation of penal laws: see Protocol I art 75 para 4(c). As to the application and implementation of Protocol I see paras 521–522 ante.
4   Geneva Conventions Act 1957 Sch 4 art 66.
5   Ibid Sch 4 art 67. See also the Geneva Conventions 1949 Protocol I art 75 para 4(c).

561. Trial and punishment of offenders. The Convention relative to the Protection of Civilian Persons in Time of War[1] regulates the trial and punishment of offenders by the courts of the occupying power. It includes the restriction of the right of an occupying power to try offences committed before the occupation, with the exception of breaches of the laws and customs of war[2]. No sentence may be passed except after a regular trial[3]. Also regulated are the right to present evidence[4], to appeal[5] and, if condemned to death, to petition for pardon or reprieve[6]. Representatives of the protecting power have the right to attend the trial unless the proceedings are to be held in camera[7]. The protecting power must be informed of proceedings involving the death penalty or imprisonment for two years or more[8]. Pre-trial detention is also regulated[9]. Protected persons who have been accused of offences or convicted by the courts in the occupied territory must be handed over at the close of occupation to the liberated territory's authorities[10].

1   See para 521 note 5 ante. The convention is set out in the Geneva Conventions Act 1957 s 7(1), Sch 4: see generally para 521 ante.
2   Ibid Sch 4 art 70. The Geneva Conventions 1949 Protocol I sets out specific provision for the prosecution and trial of persons accused of war crimes or crimes against humanity: see Protocol I art 75 para 7. As to war crimes generally see paras 563–567 post. As to the application and implementation of Protocol I see paras 521–522 ante.
3   Geneva Conventions Act 1957 Sch 4 art 71. See also the Geneva Conventions 1949 Protocol I art 75 para 4, which refers to an 'impartial and regularly constituted court'. Anyone charged with an offence is presumed innocent until proved guilty (Protocol I art 75 para 4(d)) and is entitled to be tried in his presence (Protocol I art 75 para 4(e)). No one may be prosecuted or punished by the same party for an offence in respect of which a final judgment acquitting or convicting that person has been previously pronounced under the same law and judicial procedure: Protocol I art 75 para 4(h). Judgment is to be pronounced publicly: Protocol I art 75 para 4(i).
4   Geneva Conventions Act 1957 Sch 4 art 72. No one is to be compelled to testify against himself or to confess his guilt: Geneva Conventions 1949 Protocol I art 75 para 4(f). Anyone charged with an offence has the right to examine witnesses: Protocol I art 75 para 4(g).
5   Geneva Conventions Act 1957 Sch 4 art 73. A convicted person is to be advised of his judicial and other remedies and of the time limits within which they may be exercised: Geneva Conventions 1949 Protocol I art 75 para 4(j).
6   Geneva Conventions Act 1957 Sch 4 art 75. See also the Geneva Conventions 1949 Protocol I art 75 para 4(j); and note 5 supra.
7   Geneva Conventions Act 1957 Sch 4 art 74. As to the meaning of 'protecting power' see para 537 ante.
8   Ibid Sch 4 art 74. As to the death penalty under English law see para 542 note 18 ante.
9   Ibid Sch 4 art 76. The duration of the period during which a protected person accused of an offence is under arrest or awaiting trial must be deducted from any period of imprisonment awarded: Sch 4 art 69. See also the Geneva Conventions 1949 Protocol I art 75 para 3. The accused must be informed of the particulars of the alleged offence without delay: Protocol I art 75 para 4(a). No one may be convicted of an offence except on the basis of individual penal responsibility: Protocol I art 75 para 4(b). As to the categories of protected persons see para 545 ante.
10 Geneva Conventions Act 1957 Sch 4 art 77. As to safety measures concerning protected persons see Sch 4 art 78.

562. Treatment of internees. Protected persons under the Convention relative to the Protection of Civilian Persons in Time of War[1] are to be interned only if the security of the detaining power makes it absolutely necessary[2], and internees are to retain their full civil capacity[3].

Places of internment must be put under the authority of a responsible officer[4] and are not to be situated in areas which are unhealthy[5] or particularly exposed to war dangers[6], and are to be provided with canteens[7] and infirmaries[8]. Internees are to be accommodated separately from prisoners of war and other prisoners[9]. Internees are to have at their disposal premises suitable for religious services[10]. The detaining power must encourage intellectual, educational and recreational pursuits, and sports and games, amongst internees[11]. Daily food rations are to be sufficient in quantity, quality and variety, and sufficient clothing is to be provided free of charge for internees unable to procure it[12]. At each place of internment an internee committee, chosen by secret ballot, is to represent the internees[13] and to further their well-being[14]. They are to be allowed to receive letters[15], parcels[16] and visitors[17] and, within limits, to manage their property[18]. An internee who is a party to court proceedings must not be prejudiced by reason of his internment[19].

In general, the existing laws of the detaining country are to continue to apply to internees[20], and acts which are made offences only when committed by internees are to entail disciplinary punishments only[21]. Repeated escapes or attempts to escape are not to be treated as an aggravating factor in proceedings for an offence committed during an escape or attempt to escape[22]. Internees must not be transferred to prison to undergo disciplinary punishment there[23].

Transfers of internees are to be effected humanely, generally by rail or other means of transport, and are to be notified in time for the internees to pack their luggage and inform their next of kin[24].

Internees who die during internment are to be honourably buried and their graves are to be properly maintained[25]. A certified copy of the official record of death[26] must be transmitted to the protecting power and the central information agency[27]. An official inquiry must be held into every death or serious injury of an internee caused or suspected to have been caused by any other person and every death from an unknown cause[28].

An internee must be released as soon as the reasons which necessitated his internment no longer exist[29], and all internment must cease as soon as possible after the close of hostilities[30]. Persons who are arrested, detained or interned for reasons related to the armed conflict enjoy the protection of the fundamental guarantees[31] until their final release, repatriation or re-establishment, even after the end of the armed conflict[32]. The detaining authority must, at its own expense, endeavour to ensure the return or repatriation of all internees[33]. The wounded, sick and shipwrecked, who are received or interned in the territory of a neutral state or of a state not party to the armed conflict, are to be afforded the same protections under Protocol I as in the territory of a state or a party involved in the armed conflict[34].

1   See para 521 note 5 ante. The convention is set out in the Geneva Conventions Act 1957 s 7(1), Sch 4: see generally para 521 ante. As to the categories of protected persons see para 545 ante.

2   Ibid Sch 4 arts 42, 79. Protected persons may, however, be interned for certain offences: Sch 4 arts 68, 79. Internees are entitled to have their cases reconsidered by a court or administrative body: Sch 4 art 43. See also Sch 4 arts 41, 78. As to the detaining power see para 549 note 4 ante.

3   Ibid Sch 4 art 80. They must be permitted to retain articles of personal use: Sch 4 art 97. Internees must not be employed as workers unless they so desire (Sch 4 art 95) and all labour detachments remain part of the place of internment (Sch 4 art 96). Medical attention must be provided (Sch 4 art 81) and the internees must, as far as possible, be accommodated according to their nationality, language and customs (Sch 4 art 82).

4   Ibid Sch 4 art 99. The disciplinary regime must be consistent with humanitarian principles and must not include regulations imposing on internees any physical exertion dangerous to health or involving physical or moral victimisation: Sch 4 art 100.

5   Ibid Sch 4 art 85.

6   Ibid Sch 4 art 83. Air raid shelters are to be provided where necessary: Sch 4 art 88.

7   Ibid Sch 4 art 87. They are to receive regular allowances sufficient for purchases of tobacco, toilet requisites etc: Sch 4 art 98.

8   Ibid Sch 4 art 91. There are to be monthly medical inspections: Sch 4 art 92. The Geneva Conventions 1949 Protocol I makes special provision in favour of women and children in relation to the treatment of persons in the power of a party to the conflict. As to the application and implementation of Protocol I see paras 521–522 ante.

9   Geneva Conventions Act 1957 Sch 4 art 84. Women are to be held in quarters separated from men's quarters (see the Geneva Conventions 1949 Protocol I art 75 para 5); and they are to be the object of special respect and must be protected against rape, forced prostitution and any other form of indecent assault (Protocol I art 76 para 1). Children too are to be the object of special respect and must be protected against any form of indecent assault (Protocol I art 77 para 1); and they are to be held in quarters separate from adults (see Protocol I art 77 para 4). As to the evacuation of children see Protocol I art 78.

10   Geneva Conventions Act 1957 Sch 4 art 86. Internees are to enjoy complete latitude in the exercise of their religious duties: Sch 4 art 93.

11   Ibid Sch 4 art 94.

12   Ibid Sch 4 arts 89, 90.

13   Ibid Sch 4 art 102. Internees are to have the right to petition the proper authorities with regard to their conditions of internment; they also have the right to apply through the internee committee or, if

considered necessary, may apply direct to the representatives of the protecting power: Sch 4 art 101. As to the meaning of 'protecting power' see para 537 ante.

14 Ibid Sch 4 art 103. Members of internee committees are not to be required to perform any other work if their duties are thereby rendered more difficult: Sch 4 art 104.

15 Ibid Sch 4 arts 106, 107. The censoring of correspondence is to be done as quickly as possible: Sch 4 art 112.

16 Ibid Sch 4 art 108. All relief shipments for internees are to be exempt from customs and other dues: Sch 4 art 110. As to relief shipments see further Sch 4 arts 109, 111.

17 Ibid Sch 4 art 116.

18 Ibid Sch 4 art 114. All reasonable facilities are to be provided for the transmission of wills, powers of attorney and other documents: Sch 4 art 113. Wills must be received for safe keeping by the responsible authorities, and in the event of death must be transmitted to the person designated: Sch 4 art 129.

19 Ibid Sch 4 art 115. Immediately on interning protected persons, the detaining power must inform them, the power to which they owe allegiance and their protecting power of the measures taken for executing these provisions (ie Sch 4 arts 105–116): Sch 4 art 105.

20 Ibid Sch 4 art 117. The courts or authorities must in passing sentence take into account the fact that the defendant is not a national of the detaining power: Sch 4 art 118. Schedule 4 arts 71–76 (see para 561 ante) apply by analogy to proceedings against internees in the detaining power's national territory: Sch 4 art 126. As to notice of trial, appeals and reduction from a term of imprisonment because of a period of previous custody see ss 2, 4, 5 (ss 4, 5 as amended); and para 542 ante.

21 Ibid Sch 4 art 117. Disciplinary punishments are (1) a fine; (2) discontinuance of privileges above the treatment provided for by the convention; (3) fatigue duties; and (4) confinement: Sch 4 art 119. The duration of punishment must not exceed 30 days: Sch 4 art 119. Acts which constitute offences against discipline must be investigated immediately: Sch 4 art 122. Disciplinary punishment may be ordered only by the commandant of the place of internment or other responsible officer, and before any punishment is awarded the accused has the right to be heard in his defence: Sch 4 art 123. Internees awarded disciplinary punishment must be allowed to exercise and to stay in the open air at least two hours daily: Sch 4 art 125.

22 Ibid Sch 4 arts 120, 121.

23 Ibid Sch 4 art 124.

24 Ibid Sch 4 arts 127, 128.

25 Ibid Sch 4 art 130. See also the Geneva Conventions 1949 Protocol I arts 32, 34.

26 Every death is to be certified by a doctor and a death certificate made out showing the cause of death: Geneva Conventions Act 1957 Sch 4 art 129.

27 Ibid Sch 4 art 129. As to the central information agency see para 547 ante.

28 Ibid Sch 4 art 131. The evidence of witnesses and a report are to be forwarded to the protecting power; if the inquiry indicates guilt, the detaining power must take action against those responsible: Sch 4 art 131.

29 Ibid Sch 4 art 132.

30 Ibid Sch 4 art 133.

31 Ie the Geneva Conventions 1949 Protocol I art 75.

32 Ibid Protocol I art 75 para 6. See also Protocol I art 3(b); and para 522 note 6 ante.

33 Geneva Conventions Act 1957 Sch 4 arts 134, 135.

34 See the Geneva Conventions 1949 Protocol I art 19; and para 525 ante.

(3) WAR CRIMES

563. War crimes under international law. International law recognises universal jurisdiction in respect of war crimes, which include violations of the laws or customs of war and crimes against humanity[1]. This gives all states the right to try war criminals, irrespective of where the offence was committed or the nationality of the perpetrators and victims.

As an alternative to the trial of alleged war criminals by a state, the international community may establish an international court for the trial of such persons. This may be established by treaty[2] or by the Security Council of the United Nations[3]. The International Tribunal for the Prosecution of Persons Responsible for Serious Violations of International Humanitarian Law Committed in the Territory of the Former Yugoslavia since 1991 is a tribunal established by the Security Council of the United Nations in 1993[4], as is the International Tribunal for the Prosecution of Persons

Responsible for Genocide and Other Serious Violations of International Humanitarian Law Committed in the Territory of Rwanda of 1994[5]. Like all members of the United Nations, the United Kingdom has agreed to accept and carry out the decisions of the Security Council[6]. This obligation must be implemented into the law of the United Kingdom to have any effect there[7]. Assistance within the United Kingdom to the Former Yugoslavia and the Rwanda International Tribunals, by, for example, the arrest and delivery of persons to the respective tribunals and provision for the discontinuance of proceedings of courts within the United Kingdom, is made possible by statutory instrument[8].

1   See *The Trial of German Major War Criminals: Proceedings of the International Military Tribunal Sitting at Nuremberg, Germany* HMSO London, 1950; *A-G of the Government of Israel v Eichmann* (1961) 36 ILR 5 (on appeal sub nom *Eichmann v A-G of Israel* (1962) 36 ILR 277). The United Kingdom established military courts for the trial and punishment of violations of the laws and usages of war committed during any war after 2 September 1939 by Royal Warrant, dated 14 June 1945, AO 81/1945. Offenders in territory occupied by British forces in the former German Reich were tried: see Rogers 'War Crimes Trials under the Royal Warrant: British Practice, 1945–1949' (1990) 39 ICLQ 780. For the meaning of 'United Kingdom' see para 502 note 4 ante.

2   See the *Agreement by the Government of the United Kingdom of Great Britain and Northern Ireland, the Government of the United States of America, the Provisional Government of the French Republic and the Government of the Union of Soviet Socialist Republics for the Prosecution and Punishment of the Major War Criminals of the European Axis* (London, 8 August 1945; Misc 10 (1945); Cmd 6668).

3   Ie under the Charter of the United Nations Ch VII. As to the United Nations generally see FOREIGN RELATIONS LAW vol 18 para 1811 et seq; and as to the Charter of the United Nations see para 501 note 4 ante.

4   See UN Security Council Resolutions 808 (22 February 1993) and 827 (25 May 1993).

5   UN Security Council Resolution 955 (8 November 1994).

6   See the Charter of the United Nations art 25.

7   As to the implementation of treaty obligations into the law of the United Kingdom see para 517 ante; and FOREIGN RELATIONS LAW vol 18 para 1405.

8   See the United Nations (International Tribunal) (Former Yugoslavia) Order 1996, SI 1996/716; and the United Nations (International Tribunal) (Rwanda) Order 1996, SI 1996/1296.

564. Liability for war crimes under English law. A number of treaties give national courts jurisdiction over the trial of alleged war criminals. The most important of these treaties are the four Geneva Red Cross Conventions[1], each of which contains provisions requiring states to enact legislation necessary to provide effective penal sanctions for persons committing, or ordering to be committed, any grave breach of the convention[2]. The conventions set out the acts or omissions which may constitute grave breaches and the Geneva Conventions Act 1957 sets out the penal sanctions for these offences under English law[3].

1   As to the Geneva Red Cross Conventions (which are set out in the Schedules to the Geneva Conventions Act 1957) see generally para 521 et seq ante. See also the Geneva Conventions 1949 Protocol I. As to the application and implementation of Protocol I see paras 521–522 ante.

2   See the Geneva Conventions Act 1957 s 7(1), Sch 1 art 49, Sch 2 art 50, Sch 3 art 129, Sch 4 art 146. As to grave breaches and abuse of the conventions see para 524 ante.

3   See ibid s 1 (as prospectively amended); and para 524 ante. Section 1 (as prospectively amended) illustrates the principle that international law permits states to exercise jurisdiction over alleged war criminals, whatever their nationality or the locus of the crime. However, an international war crimes tribunal (see para 563 ante) may request that a national court should defer to the competence of the international tribunal by discontinuing proceedings to which the request relates: see the United Nations (International Tribunal) (Rwanda) Order 1996, SI 1996/1296; and the United Nations (International Tribunal) (Former Yugoslavia) Order 1996, SI 1996/716.

     Penalties are also available under English law for the offence of genocide: see the Genocide Act 1969; and CRIMINAL LAW vol 11(1) (Reissue) para 424.

565. War crimes committed between 1 September 1939 and 5 June 1945.
In respect of alleged war crimes committed before the Geneva Conventions Act 1957
came into force, there was no legislation enabling a person to be tried within the United
Kingdom, until the passing of the War Crimes Act 1991[1]. This Act enables proceedings
to be brought in the United Kingdom against a person for murder, manslaughter or
culpable homicide, irrespective of his nationality at the time of the alleged offence,
provided that the offence (1) was committed during the period beginning with 1
September 1939 and ending with 5 June 1945 in a place which at the time was part of
Germany or under German occupation; and (2) constituted a violation of the laws and
customs of war[2]. No proceedings may be brought against any person unless he was on 8
March 1990, or has subsequently become, a British citizen or resident in the United
Kingdom, the Isle of Man or any of the Channel Islands[3]. No proceedings may be
brought in England and Wales without the consent of the Attorney General[4].

1   The War Crimes Act 1991 came into force on 9 May 1991 with the exception of s 1(4), Schedule which
     are currently not in force: see s 3(4); and note 4 infra. For the meaning of 'United Kingdom' see para 502
     note 4 ante.
2   See ibid s 1(1). As to the laws and customs of war see para 516 ante. See also the Charter of the
     International Military Tribunal (held at Nuremberg) art 6(b), annexed to the Agreement for the
     Prosecution and Punishment of the Major War Criminals of the European Axis; and The Manual of
     Military Law Part III (1958) at para 626.
3   War Crimes Act 1991 s 1(2). As to British citizenship generally see BRITISH NATIONALITY,
     IMMIGRATION AND RACE RELATIONS vol 4(2) (Reissue) para 12 et seq.
4   Ibid s 1(3). Proceedings in Northern Ireland require the consent of the Attorney General of Northern
     Ireland: s 1(3). Expenses are paid out of money provided by Parliament: see s 2.
        The War Crimes Act 1991, as originally enacted, contained a special procedure in lieu of committal
     where the Attorney General or the Director of Public Prosecutions was of the opinion that the evidence
     revealed a case of such complexity that it was appropriate that the case should without delay be taken over
     by the Crown court: see s 1(4), Schedule. However, this special procedure is not now being implemented
     and s 1(4) and the Schedule are respectively amended and repealed: see the Criminal Justice and Public
     Order Act 1994 ss 44(3), 168(3), Sch 4 Pt II para 72(b), Sch 11; and the Criminal Procedure and
     Investigations Act 1996 ss 44, 46, 79, 80, Schs 4, 5.

566. War crimes committed by members of the armed forces of the Crown.
Members of the Royal Navy, the Army and the Royal Air Force who commit an offence
against the criminal law of England and Wales may be dealt with under the respective
service discipline Act wherever the offence was committed[1]. Thus an individual may be
charged before a court-martial convened under the appropriate service discipline Act
with an offence, for example, of murder[2] in killing a prisoner of war or a civilian. In
addition, or in the alternative, a member of the armed forces of the Crown may be
charged before a court-martial or by a court in the United Kingdom with a grave breach
of the Geneva Red Cross Conventions[3].

1   See the Naval Discipline Act 1957 s 42 (as amended); the Army Act 1955 s 70 (as amended); the Air Force
     Act 1955 s 70 (as amended); and ROYAL FORCES vol 41 para 407 et seq.
2   If the offence was one of murder the courts in England and Wales would also have jurisdiction. Where
     the offence charged is one in which the courts in any part of the United Kingdom do not possess
     jurisdiction, a member of the armed forces may only be tried under the relevant service discipline Act (eg
     causing grievous bodily harm to a prisoner of war or to a civilian). For the meaning of 'United Kingdom'
     see para 502 note 4 ante.
3   As to the Geneva Red Cross Conventions (which are set out in the Schedules to the Geneva Conventions
     Act 1949) see para 521 et seq ante. As to grave breaches of the conventions see para 524 ante.

567. War crimes committed by enemy prisoners of war. Prisoners of war held by the armed forces of the Crown may be tried by a prisoner of war court-martial convened in any place for an offence of having committed, aided or abetted or procured the commission by any other person of a grave breach of the Geneva Red Cross Conventions[1]. Where the prisoner of war is held in the United Kingdom, the national courts would also have jurisdiction to try a prisoner of war in respect of a grave breach of those conventions[2].

1   See the Prisoners of War (Discipline) Regulations, Royal Warrant Governing the Maintenance of Discipline Among Prisoners of War (7 August 1958) art 7. As to the Geneva Red Cross Conventions (which are set out in the Schedules to the Geneva Conventions Act 1957) see para 521 et seq ante. As to grave breaches of the conventions see para 524 ante.
2   See the Geneva Conventions Act 1957 s 1 (as prospectively amended); and para 524 ante. For the meaning of 'United Kingdom' see para 502 note 4 ante.

(4) BIOLOGICAL, CHEMICAL AND NUCLEAR WEAPONS

(i) Biological Weapons

568. Introduction. The Biological Weapons Act 1974[1] was enacted in order to comply with the Convention on the Prohibition of the Development, Production and Stockpiling of Bacteriological (Biological) and Toxin Weapons and on their Destruction[2].

1   The Biological Weapons Act 1974 extends to Northern Ireland: ss 6(1), 7. It has been further extended with such exceptions, adaptations or modifications as specified by Her Majesty by Order in Council (see s 6(2), (3)) to Guernsey (Biological Weapons Act 1974 (Guernsey) Order 1974, SI 1974/1110); the Isle of Man (Biological Weapons Act 1974 (Isle of Man) Order 1974, SI 1974/1111); Jersey (Biological Weapons Act 1974 (Jersey) Order 1974, SI 1974/1112); and certain overseas territories (Biological Weapons Act 1974 (Overseas Territories) Order 1975, SI 1975/240).
2   Ie the Convention on the Prohibition of the Development, Production and Stockpiling of Bacteriological (Biological) and Toxin Weapons and on their Destruction (London, Moscow and Washington, 10 April 1972; TS 11 (1976); Cmnd 6397).

569. Offence relating to biological weapons. No person may develop, produce, stockpile, acquire or retain any biological agent[1] or toxin[2] of a type and in a quantity that has no justification for prophylactic, protective or other peaceful purposes; or any weapon, equipment or means of delivery designed to use biological agents or toxins for hostile purposes or in armed conflict[3]. Contravention of this provision is an offence, punishable on conviction on indictment by life imprisonment[4].

1   'Biological agent' means any microbial or other biological agent: Biological Weapons Act 1974 s 1(2).
2   'Toxin' means any toxin, whatever its origin or method of production: ibid s 1(2).
3   Ibid s 1(1).
4   Ibid s 1(3). Proceedings may not be instituted in England or Wales, except by or with the consent of the Attorney General; or in Northern Ireland, except by or with the consent of the Attorney General for Northern Ireland: s 2(1). The offence may not be tried by courts-martial under the Army Act 1955, the Air Force Act 1955 or the Naval Discipline Act 1957: see the Biological Weapons Act 1974 s 5.

570. Offence committed by bodies corporate. Where an offence[1] which is committed by a body corporate is proved to have been committed with the consent and connivance of, or to be attributable to any negligence on the part of, any director, manager, secretary or other similar officer of the body corporate, or any person who was purporting to act in any such capacity, he as well as the body corporate is guilty of that offence and is liable to be proceeded against and punished accordingly[2].

1   Ie an offence under the Biological Weapons Act 1974 s 1: see para 569 ante.
2   Ibid s 3.

571. Powers to search and obtain evidence. If a justice of the peace is satisfied by information on oath that there is reasonable ground for suspecting that an offence[1] has been, or is about to be, committed, he may grant a search warrant[2] authorising a constable (1) to enter, at any time within one month from the date of the warrant, any premises or place named in the warrant, if necessary by force, and to search the premises or place and every person found there; (2) to inspect any document found in the premises or place or in the possession of any person found there, and to take copies of, or seize or detain any such document; (3) to inspect, seize and detain any equipment so found; and (4) to inspect, sample, seize and detain any substance so found[3].

1   Ie an offence under the Biological Weapons Act 1974 s 1: see para 569 ante.
2   A warrant so issued may also authorise any person named in the warrant to accompany the constable and assist him in taking any of the steps mentioned in heads (1)–(4) in the text: ibid s 4(2).
3   Ibid s 4(1) (amended by the Police and Criminal Evidence Act 1984 s 119(2), Sch 7 Pt I).

(ii) Chemical Weapons

572. Introduction. The Chemical Weapons Act 1996[1] was enacted in order to comply with the Convention on the Prohibition of the Development, Production, Stockpiling and the Use of Chemical Weapons and on their Destruction[2].

1   See the Chemical Weapons Act 1996 ss 37, 39(4). The Act came into force on 16 September 1996: s 39(1); Chemical Weapons Act 1996 (Commencement) Order 1996, SI 1996/2054. The Chemical Weapons Act 1996 extends to Northern Ireland (s 39(2)), and may be extended with such exceptions, adaptations or modifications as may be specified by Order in Council to any of the Channel Islands, the Isle of Man or any colony (s 39(3)).
2   Ie the Convention on the Prohibition of the Development, Production, Stockpiling and the Use of Chemical Weapons and on their Destruction (Paris, 13 January 1993; Misc 21 (1993); Cm 2331) (the Chemical Weapons Convention).

573. Meaning of 'chemical weapons'. Chemical weapons are:
   (1)   toxic chemicals[1] and their precursors[2];
   (2)   munitions and other devices designed to cause death or harm through the toxic properties of toxic chemicals released by them; and
   (3)   equipment designed for use in connection with munitions and devices falling within head (2) above[3].

However, an object[4] is not a chemical weapon if the use or intended use is only for permitted purposes[5]. Permitted purposes are (a) peaceful purposes; (b) purposes related to protection against toxic chemicals; (c) legitimate military purposes[6]; and (d) purposes of enforcing the law[7].

1   A 'toxic chemical' is a chemical which through its chemical action on life processes can cause death, permanent harm or temporary incapacity to humans or animals; and the origin, method of production and place of production are immaterial: Chemical Weapons Act 1996 s 1(5).
2   A 'precursor' is a chemical reactant which takes part at any stage in the production (by whatever method) of a toxic chemical: ibid s 1(6).
3   Ibid s 1(1).
4   References to an object include references to a substance: ibid s 1(7).
5   See ibid ss 1(2), 2(2), (3), 10(1), 11(2).

6   'Legitimate military purposes' are all military purposes except those which depend on the use of the toxic properties of chemicals as a method of warfare in circumstances where the main object is to cause death, permanent harm or temporary incapacity to humans or animals: ibid s 1(4).

7   Ibid s 1(3).

574. Use, development, possession and transfer etc of chemical weapons.

No person may:

(1)   use a chemical weapon[1];

(2)   develop or produce a chemical weapon;

(3)   have a chemical weapon in his possession;

(4)   participate in the transfer[2] of a chemical weapon; or

(5)   engage in military preparations, or in preparations of a military nature, intending to use a chemical weapon[3].

In relation to the use of a chemical weapon, an object[4] is not a chemical weapon if the person uses the object only for permitted purposes[5]; and, in deciding whether permitted purposes are intended, the types and quantities of objects must be taken into account[6]. In relation to the offences mentioned in heads (2) to (4) above, an object is not a chemical weapon if the person does the act mentioned with the intention that the object will be used only for permitted purposes; and, in deciding whether permitted purposes are intended, the types and quantities of objects must be taken into account[7].

In proceedings for an offence under heads (1), (3) or (4) above relating to an object, it is a defence for the accused to prove that he neither knew nor suspected nor had reason to suspect that the object was a chemical weapon; or that he knew or suspected it to be a chemical weapon and as soon as reasonably practicable after he first so knew or suspected he took all reasonable steps to inform the Secretary of State or a constable of his knowledge or suspicion[8].

A person contravening this provision[9] is guilty of an offence[10]. The offence applies to acts done in the United Kingdom or elsewhere[11], and so far as it applies to acts done outside the United Kingdom, it applies to United Kingdom nationals[12], Scottish partnerships, and bodies incorporated under the law of any part of the United Kingdom[13]. Proceedings for an offence committed outside the United Kingdom may be taken, and the offence may for incidental purposes be treated as having been committed, in any place in the United Kingdom[14]. Her Majesty may by Order in Council extend the application of the provision, so far as it applies to acts done outside the United Kingdom, to bodies incorporated under the law of the Channel Islands, the Isle of Man or any colony[15].

1   For the meaning of 'chemical weapon' see para 573 ante.

2   A person participates in the transfer of an object if (1) he acquires or disposes of the object or enters into a contract to acquire or dispose of it; or (2) he makes arrangements under which another person acquires or disposes of the object or another person enters into a contract to acquire or dispose of it: Chemical Weapons Act 1996 s 2(4). To acquire an object is to buy it, hire it, borrow it or accept it as a gift: s 2(5)(a). To dispose of an object is to sell it, let it on hire, lend it or give it: s 2(5)(b).

3   Ibid s 2(1).

4   As to the meaning of 'object' see para 573 note 4 ante.

5   For the meaning of 'permitted purposes' see para 573 ante.

6   Chemical Weapons Act 1996 s 2(2).

7   Ibid s 2(3).

8   Ibid s 2(6). However, this does not prejudice any defence which it is open to a person charged with an offence under s 2 to raise apart from s 2(6): s 2(7).

9   Ie ibid s 2.

10   Ibid s 2(8). A person guilty of such an offence is liable on conviction on indictment to imprisonment for life: s 2(8). Proceedings for an offence under s 2 may not be instituted (1) in England and Wales, except by or with the consent of the Attorney General; (2) in Northern Ireland, except by or with the consent of the Attorney General for Northern Ireland: s 31(1).

11   Ibid s 3(1). For the meaning of 'United Kingdom' see para 502 note 4 ante.

12   A United Kingdom national is an individual who is (1) a British citizen, a British Dependent Territories citizen, a British National (Overseas) or a British Overseas citizen; (2) a person who under the British Nationality Act 1981 is a British subject; or (3) a British protected person within the meaning of that Act: Chemical Weapons Act 1996 s 3(4). As to the various categories of British nationality see further BRITISH NATIONALITY, IMMIGRATION AND RACE RELATIONS vol 4(2) (Reissue) para 1 et seq.

13   Ibid s 3(2).

14   Ibid s 3(5).

15   Ibid s 3(3).

575. Suspicious objects. If the Secretary of State has grounds to suspect that an object[1] is a chemical weapon[2] and there is at least one person who either appears to the Secretary of State to have the object in his possession, or who appears to the Secretary of State to have an interest which the Secretary of State believes is materially affected by the notice, he may serve on such a person a copy of a notice[3] which:

(1)   describes the object and states its location[4];

(2)   states that the Secretary of State suspects that the object is a chemical weapon and gives reasons for his suspicion[5];

(3)   states that he is considering whether to secure its destruction[6];

(4)   states that any person may make representations that the object is not a chemical weapon[7];

(5)   states that a person on whom the notice is served and who has the object in his possession must not relinquish possession before a date specified in the notice[8].

If a copy of such a notice is served on a person and the notice relates to an object in his possession at the time the copy is served, and he relinquishes possession before the date specified and he has no reasonable excuse for so relinquishing possession, he is guilty of an offence[9]. A person who knowingly makes a false or misleading statement in response to a copy of a notice is guilty of an offence[10].

1   As to the meaning of 'object' see para 573 note 4 ante.

2   For the meaning of 'chemical weapon' see para 573 ante. If an object is in the possession of a person who intends that it will be used only for permitted purposes, it is not a chemical weapon for the purposes of the Chemical Weapons Act 1996 s 4(1), (3); and in deciding whether permitted purposes are intended, the types and quantities of objects must be taken into account: s 10(1). As to permitted purposes see para 573 ante.

3   Ibid s 4(1). A notice, or a copy of a notice, under any provision of the Chemical Weapons Act 1996 may be served on a person (1) by delivering it to him in person; (2) by sending it by post to him at his usual or last-known residence or place of business in the United Kingdom; or (3) in the case of a body corporate, by delivering it to the secretary or clerk of the body corporate at its registered or principal office or sending it by post to the secretary or clerk of that body corporate at that office: s 34. For the meaning of 'United Kingdom' see para 502 note 4 ante.

4   Ibid s 4(3)(a).

5   Ibid s 4(3)(b).

6   Ie destruction under ibid ss 5–7 (see paras 576–578 post): s 4(3)(c). For the purposes of ss 4–9, to the extent that an object consists of a toxic chemical (see para 573 note 1 ante) or precursor (see para 573 note 2 ante), it is destroyed if it is permanently prevented from being used other than for permitted purposes: s 10(2)(a). To the extent that an object consists of a munition or other device designed to cause death or harm through toxic chemicals released by it, it is destroyed if it is permanently prevented from doing so: s 10(2)(b). To the extent that an object consists of equipment designed for use in connection with a munition or other device, it is destroyed if it is permanently prevented from being used: s 10(2)(c).

7   Ibid s 4(3)(d)

8   Ibid s 4(3)(e). Nothing in s 4 affects any power arising otherwise than by virtue of that section (such as the power to dispose of property in police possession in connection with the investigation of a suspected offence): s 10(4).

9   Ibid s 9(1). A person guilty of such an offence is liable on summary conviction to a fine of an amount not exceeding the statutory maximum and on conviction on indictment to a fine: s 9(4). Proceedings for an offence under this provision may not be instituted except by or with the consent of the Secretary of State: s 31(2). The 'statutory maximum' is the prescribed sum within the meaning of the Magistrates' Courts

Act 1980 s 32 (as amended) and, as from 1 October 1992, is £5,000: s 32(9) (amended by the Criminal Justice Act 1991 s 17(2)).

10   Chemical Weapons Act 1996 s 9(5). A person guilty of such an offence is liable on summary conviction to fine of an amount not exceeding the statutory maximum and on conviction on indictment to imprisonment for a term not exceeding two years or a fine, or to both: s 9(5). Proceedings for an offence under this provision may not be instituted except by or with the consent of the Secretary of State: s 31(2).

576. Power to remove or immobilise objects.

If the Secretary of State has reasonable cause to believe that (1) an object[1] is on premises[2] to which the public has access or which are occupied by a person who consents to action being taken; and (2) the object is a chemical weapon[3], the Secretary of State may authorise a person to enter the premises and to search them[4]. If a justice of the peace is satisfied on information on oath that there is reasonable cause to believe that an object is on premises (of whatever nature) and that it is a chemical weapon, he may issue a warrant in writing authorising a person acting under the authority of the Secretary of State to enter the premises, if necessary by force, at any time within one month from the time of the issue of the warrant and to search them[5].

A person who acts under an authorisation given under these provisions may take with him such other persons and such equipment as appear to him to be necessary[6]. If a person enters premises under such an authorisation and the object is found there, he may make the object safe[7] and he may seize and remove it, if it is reasonably practicable to do so, or he may, in any other case, affix a warning to the object, or to something in a conspicuous position near the object, stating that the object is not to be moved or interfered with before a date specified in the warning[8].

These powers conferred on an authorised person are only exercisable in the presence of a constable, if the authorisation or the warrant so provides[9]. A person who wilfully obstructs a person in (a) entering or searching premises under the authorisation[10]; or (b) making an object safe, seizing or removing an object, or affixing a warning[11]; or (c) attempting to do anything mentioned in heads (a) and (b) above, is guilty of an offence[12].

1   As to the meaning of 'object' see para 573 note 4 ante.

2   In the Chemical Weapons Act 1996 ss 5–9 'premises' includes land (including buildings), movable structures, vehicles, vessels, aircraft and hovercraft: s 10(3).

3   For the meaning of 'chemical weapon' see para 573 ante. If an object is in the possession of a person who intends that it will be used only for permitted purposes, it is not a chemical weapon for the purposes of ibid s 5(1), (2); and in deciding whether permitted purposes are intended the types and quantities of objects must be taken into account: s 10(1). As to permitted purposes see para 573 ante.

4   Ibid s 5(1).

5   Ibid s 5(2).

6   Ibid s 5(3).

7   An object is made safe if, without being destroyed, it is prevented from being an immediate danger (as where a fuse is neutralised or the object is smothered in foam): ibid s 5(4). As to the manner of destruction see para 575 note 6 ante.

8   Ibid s 5(4). If a warning is affixed and a person interferes with the warning, or moves or interferes with the object before the date specified in the warning, and he has no reasonable excuse for doing so, he is guilty of an offence: s 9(3). A person guilty of such an offence is liable on summary conviction to a fine of an amount not exceeding the statutory maximum and on conviction on indictment to a fine: s 9(4). Proceedings for this offence may not be instituted except by or with the consent of the Secretary of State: s 31(2). Nothing in s 5 affects any power arising otherwise than by virtue of that section (such as a power to dispose of property in police possession in connection with the investigation of a suspected offence): s 10(4). As to the statutory maximum see para 575 note 9 ante.

9   Ibid s 5(6). Section 5 applies whether or not any copy of a notice has been served under s 4 (see para 575 ante): s 5(7).

10   Ie under ibid s 5(1) or 5(2).

11   Ie under ibid s 5(4).

12 See ibid s 9(2)(a), (b), (d). A person guilty of such an offence is liable on summary conviction to a fine of
    an amount not exceeding the statutory maximum and on conviction on indictment to a fine: s 9(4).
    Proceedings for an offence under this provision may not be instituted except by or with the consent of
    the Secretary of State: s 31(2).

577. Power to destroy objects removed from premises. If the object[1] is removed
from the premises[2], and if at any time in the second six-month period[3] the Secretary of
State decides that the object should be destroyed[4], he may authorise a person to destroy
it[5]. If the object is removed and if at any time in the first six-month period any person
appears to the Secretary of State to have had the object in his possession immediately
before its removal, or any other person appears to the Secretary of State to have an interest
which the Secretary of State believes would be materially affected by the object's
destruction, the Secretary of State must serve on that person a copy of a notice[6] which:

(1) describes the object and states its location[7];
(2) states that the Secretary of State proposes to secure its destruction and gives the
     reasons for his proposal[8];
(3) states that the person on whom the copy of the notice is served may object to the
     Secretary of State's proposal[9]; and
(4) states that an objection (if made) must be made in writing to the Secretary of State
     before such date as is specified in the notice and must state why the object should
     not be destroyed[10].

A person who knowingly makes a false or misleading statement in response to a copy
of a notice is guilty of an offence[11].

Before the Secretary of State reaches a decision as to the object's proposed destruction,
he must allow any person on whom a copy of the notice has been served time to respond,
and he must take into account any objections to the object's proposed destruction
(whether made in response to a notice or otherwise)[12]. If an object is removed from the
premises and destroyed, the Secretary of State may recover any costs reasonably incurred
by him in connection with that removal and destruction from a responsible person[13].

If an object is removed from premises and at the end of the second six-month period
the Secretary of State has not authorised the destruction of the object and a person had
possession of the object immediately before its removal, the Secretary of State must return
the object to that person, or, if there is more than one, to such of them as the Secretary
of State thinks appropriate[14].

1   As to the meaning of 'object' see para 573 note 4 ante.
2   Ie under the Chemical Weapons Act 1996 s 5: see para 576 ante. For the meaning of 'premises' see para
    576 note 2 ante.
3   The first six-month period is the period of six months beginning with the day after the removal of the
    object: ibid s 6(1)(a). The second six-month period is the period of six months beginning with the day
    after the first six-month period: s 6(1)(b).
4   As to the manner of destruction see para 575 note 6 ante.
5   Chemical Weapons Act 1996 s 6(2). If a person wilfully obstructs a person in destroying an object under
    an authorisation given under s 6(2) or in attempting to do so, he is guilty of an offence and is liable on
    summary conviction to a fine of an amount not exceeding the statutory maximum and on conviction on
    indictment to a fine: s 9(2)(c), (d), (4). Proceedings for an offence under this provision may not be
    instituted except by or with the consent of the Secretary of State: s 31(2). As to the statutory maximum
    see para 575 note 9 ante.
6   Ibid s 6(3). As to the service of notices see para 575 note 3 ante.
7   Ibid s 6(4)(a).
8   Ibid s 6(4)(b).
9   Ibid s 6(4)(c).
10 Ibid s 6(4)(d). Nothing in s 6 affects any power arising otherwise than by virtue of that section (such as a
    power to dispose of property in police possession in connection with the investigation of a suspected
    offence): s 10(4).

11 Ibid s 9(5). A person guilty of such an offence is liable on summary conviction to a fine of an amount not exceeding the statutory maximum and on conviction on indictment to imprisonment for a term not exceeding two years or a fine, or to both: s 9(5). Proceedings for an offence under this provision may not be instituted except by or with the consent of the Secretary of State: s 31(2).

12 Ibid s 6(5).

13 Ibid s 6(6). A responsible person is any person who had possession of the object immediately before its removal: see s 6(6).

14 Ibid s 6(7).

578. Power to enter premises and destroy objects. Where a warning has been affixed to the object or to something in a conspicuous position near the object[1], if at any time in the second six-month period[2] the Secretary of State decides that the object should be destroyed[3] it may be destroyed in accordance with the statutory provisions[4]. If at any time in the second six-month period the Secretary of State does decide that the object should be destroyed, and the object is on premises[5] to which the public has access or which are occupied by a person who consents to action being taken, the Secretary of State may authorise a person to enter premises and to destroy the object if it is found there[6]. If (whatever the nature of the premises concerned) a justice of the peace is satisfied on information on oath that a warning has been affixed[7] and that the Secretary of State has decided at any time in the second six-month period that the object should be destroyed, he may issue a warrant in writing authorising a person acting under the Secretary of State's authority to enter the premises, if necessary by force, at any time within one month from the time of the issue of the warrant and to destroy the object if it is found there[8]. A person acting under such authorisation may take with him such other persons and such equipment as appear to him to be necessary[9]. These powers conferred on an authorised person are only exercisable in the presence of a constable, if the authorisation or warrant so provides[10].

A person is guilty of an offence if he wilfully obstructs a person:

(1) in entering or searching premises under an authorisation[11]; or

(2) in destroying an object under an authorisation[12]; or

(3) in attempting to do anything mentioned in heads (1) and (2) above[13].

If at any time in the first six-month period[14] any person appears to the Secretary of State to have had the object in his possession immediately before the warning was affixed, or any other person appears to the Secretary of State to have an interest which the Secretary of State believes would be materially affected by the object's destruction, the Secretary of State must serve on that person a copy of a notice[15] which:

(a) describes the object and states its location[16];

(b) states that the Secretary of State proposes to secure its destruction and gives the reasons for his proposal[17];

(c) states that the person on whom the copy of the notice is served may object to the Secretary of State's proposal[18]; and

(d) states that an objection (if made) must be made in writing to the Secretary of State before such date as is specified in the notice and must state why the object should not be destroyed[19].

A person who knowingly makes a false or misleading statement in response to a copy of a notice is guilty of an offence[20].

Before he reaches a decision as to the object's destruction, the Secretary of State must allow any person on whom a copy of a notice has been served time to respond, and take into account any objections to the object's proposed destruction (whether made in response to a notice or otherwise)[21].

Where an object is destroyed under these provisions, the Secretary of State may recover any costs reasonably incurred by him in connection with that destruction from a responsible person[22].

1   Ie under the Chemical Weapons Act 1996 s 5 (see para 576 ante): see s 7(1). As to the meaning of 'object' see para 573 note 4 ante.
2   The first six-month period is the period of six months beginning with the day after the warning was affixed: ibid s 7(1)(a). The second six-month period is the period of six months beginning with the day after the first six-month period ends: s 7(1)(b).
3   As to the manner of destruction see para 575 note 3 ante.
4   Chemical Weapons Act 1996 s 7(2).
5   For the meaning of 'premises' see para 576 note 2 ante.
6   Chemical Weapons Act 1996 s 7(6).
7   Ie under ibid s 5: see s 7(7).
8   Ibid s 7(7).
9   Ibid s 7(8).
10 Ibid s 7(9).
11 Ie authorisation given under ibid s 7(6) or (7): see s 9(2)(a).
12 Ie under ibid s 7(6) or (7): see s 9(2)(c).
13 See ibid s 9(2)(a), (c), (d). A person guilty of such an offence is liable on summary conviction to a fine of an amount not exceeding the statutory maximum and on conviction on indictment to a fine: s 9(4). Proceedings for an offence under this provision may not be instituted except by or with the consent of the Secretary of State: s 31(2). As to the statutory maximum see para 575 note 9 ante.
14 See note 2 supra.
15 Chemical Weapons Act 1996 s 7(3). As to the service of notices see para 575 note 3 ante.
16 Ibid s 7(4)(a).
17 Ibid s 7(4)(b).
18 Ibid s 7(4)(c).
19 Ibid s 7(4)(d). Nothing in s 7 affects any power arising otherwise than by virtue of that section (such as a power to dispose of property in police possession in connection with the investigation of a suspected offence): s 10(4).
20 Ibid s 9(5). A person guilty of such an offence is liable on summary conviction to a fine of an amount not exceeding the statutory maximum and on conviction on indictment to imprisonment for a term not exceeding two years or a fine, or to both: s 9(5). Proceedings for an offence under this provision may not be instituted except by or with the consent of the Secretary of State: s 31(2).
21 Ibid s 7(5).
22 Ibid s 7(10). A responsible person is any person who had possession of the object immediately before the warning was affixed under s 5: s 7(10).

579. Compensation for destruction of object. If a person claims that an object[1] has been destroyed[2] and that he had an interest which was materially affected by the destruction and he sustained loss as a result, and that no copy of a notice[3] was served on him, he may make an application for compensation[4]. If he makes an application for compensation to the High Court and the court finds that his claim is justified, the court may order the Secretary of State to pay to the applicant such amount (if any) by way of compensation as the court considers just[5]. If the court believes that the object would have been destroyed even if a copy of a notice had been served on the applicant, it must not order compensation to be paid under this provision[6].

1   As to the meaning of 'object' see para 573 note 4 ante.
2   Ie destroyed under the Chemical Weapons Act 1996 ss 6 or 7: see s 8(1)(a). As to the manner of destruction see para 575 note 6 ante.
3   Ie a notice under the section concerned: see ibid s 8(1)(c). As to the service of notices see para 575 note 3 ante.
4   See ibid s 8(1).
5   Ibid s 8(2).
6   Ibid s 8(3).

580. Premises for producing chemical weapons. No person may:

(1) construct premises he intends to be used to produce chemical weapons[1];

(2) alter premises in circumstances where he intends that they will be used to produce chemical weapons[2];

(3) install or construct equipment he intends to be used to produce chemical weapons[3];

(4) alter equipment in circumstances where he intends that it will be used to produce chemical weapons[4];

(5) permit the construction on land he occupies of premises he intends to be used to produce chemical weapons[5];

(6) permit premises on land he occupies to be altered in circumstances where he intends that they will be used to produce chemical weapons[6];

(7) permit the installation or construction on land he occupies of equipment he intends to be used to produce chemical weapons[7];

(8) permit equipment on land he occupies to be altered in circumstances where he intends that it will be used to produce chemical weapons[8].

A person contravening these provisions is guilty of an offence[9].

1   Chemical Weapons Act 1996 s 11(1)(a). For the meaning of 'chemical weapons' see para 573 ante. For the purposes of s 11(1), an object is not a chemical weapon if the person intends that the object will be used only for permitted purposes; and in deciding whether permitted purposes are intended the types and quantities of objects shall be taken into account: s 11(2). As to the meaning of 'object' see para 573 note 4 ante. As to permitted purposes see para 573 ante.

2   Ibid s 11(1)(b).

3   Ibid s 11(1)(c).

4   Ibid s 11(1)(d).

5   Ibid s 11(1)(e).

6   Ibid s 11(1)(f).

7   Ibid s 11(1)(g).

8   Ibid s 11(1)(h).

9   Ibid s 11(3). A person guilty of such an offence is liable on conviction on indictment to imprisonment for life: s 11(3). Proceedings for an offence under s 11 may not be instituted (1) in England and Wales, except by or with the consent of the Attorney General; (2) in Northern Ireland, except by or with the consent of the Attorney General for Northern Ireland: s 31(1).

581. Suspicion of existence of chemical weapons facilities. If the Secretary of State has grounds to suspect that any equipment or building is a chemical weapons production facility[1], and there is at least one person who falls within the relevant provision[2], the Secretary of State may serve on any person falling within that provision a copy of a notice[3] which:

(1) describes the equipment or building and states its location[4];

(2) states that the Secretary of State suspects that the equipment or building is a chemical weapons production facility and gives the reasons for his suspicion[5];

(3) states that he is considering whether to require the equipment or building to be destroyed[6] or altered[7]; and

(4) states that any person may make representations that the equipment or building is not a chemical weapons production facility[8].

A person who knowingly makes a false or misleading statement in response to such a notice is guilty of an offence[9].

If the notice relates to equipment it must state that the person on whom the notice is served and who has the equipment in his possession must not relinquish possession of, or alter or use, the equipment before a date specified in the notice[10]. If a person is served with a copy of a notice[11], relating to equipment in his possession at the time the copy is served, and he relinquishes possession of, or alters or uses, the equipment before the date specified[12] without reasonable excuse for doing so, he is guilty of an offence[13].

1   In the Chemical Weapons Act 1996 ss 12–15, 'chemical weapons production facility' has the meaning given by the definition of that expression in the Chemical Weapons Convention (see para 572 note 2 ante): see the Chemical Weapons Act 1996 ss 1(8), 18(1). For the meaning of 'chemical weapons' see para 573 ante.
2   Ie ibid s 12(2). The persons falling within s 12(2) are:
    (1)   any person who appears to the Secretary of State to occupy the land on which the equipment or building is situated (s 12(2)(a));
    (2)   if the Secretary of State's suspicion relates to equipment, any person not falling within head (1) supra and who appears to the Secretary of State to have the equipment in his possession (s 12(2)(b)); and
    (3)   any person not falling within heads (1) or (2) supra and who appears to the Secretary of State to have an interest which the Secretary of State believes is materially affected by the notice (s 12(2)(c)).
3   Ibid s 12(1). As to the service of notices see para 575 note 3 ante.
4   Ibid s 12(3)(a).
5   Ibid s 12(3)(b).
6   For the purposes of ibid ss 12–16, 'destroyed' and 'destruction' in relation to a building mean demolished and demolition: s 18(2).
7   Ibid s 12(3)(c).
8   Ibid s 12(3)(d).
9   Ibid s 17(5). A person guilty of such an offence is liable on summary conviction to a fine of an amount not exceeding the statutory maximum and on conviction on indictment to imprisonment for a term not exceeding two years or a fine, or to both: s 17(5). Proceedings for an offence under this provision may not be instituted except by or with the consent of the Secretary of State: s 31(2). As to the statutory maximum see para 575 note 9 ante.
10 Ibid s 12(4). Nothing in s 12 affects any power arising otherwise than by virtue of that section (such as the power to dispose of property in police possession in connection with the investigation of a suspected offence): s 18(3).
11 Ie under ibid s 12: see s 17(1)(a).
12 Ie under ibid s 12(4): s 17(1)(c).
13 Ibid s 17(1). A person guilty of such an offence is liable on summary conviction to a fine of an amount not exceeding the statutory maximum and on conviction on indictment to a fine: s 17(4). Proceedings for an offence under this provision may not be instituted except by or with the consent of the Secretary of State: s 31(2).

582. Notice requiring destruction or alteration of equipment or chemical weapons production facility. Irrespective of whether or not a copy of a notice has been served[1] relating to suspicious equipment or buildings[2], if the Secretary of State has reasonable cause to believe that any equipment or building is a chemical weapons production facility[3], and at least one person falls within the relevant provision[4], the Secretary of State may serve on each person falling within that provision a copy of a notice[5] which:

(1)   describes the equipment or building and states its location[6];
(2)   states that the Secretary of State believes the equipment or building is a chemical weapons production facility[7]; and
(3)   requires the equipment or building to be destroyed[8] or altered (as the case may be) in a manner, and before a date, specified in the notice[9].

If such a notice requires any equipment or building to be altered, a further notice may revoke the first notice, and require the equipment or building to be destroyed[10].

If a person is served with a copy of a notice[11], relating to equipment in his possession at the time the copy is served or to a building situated on land he occupies at that time, and any requirement set out in the notice is not fulfilled, he is guilty of an offence, unless he has a reasonable excuse for the requirement not being fulfilled[12].

If a justice of the peace is satisfied on information on oath that the qualifying condition is fulfilled[13], he may issue a warrant in writing authorising a person acting under the authority of the Secretary of State to take remedial action[14]. A person so authorised may (a) enter the land on which the equipment or building is situated, if necessary by force[15]; (b) do whatever is required to secure that the equipment or building is destroyed or altered in a manner specified in the notice[16]; (c) take with him such other persons and such equipment as appear to him to be necessary to help him to exercise the powers mentioned in heads (a) and (b) above[17]. These powers are only exercisable in the presence of a constable, if the warrant so provides[18]. If anything is done in exercise of these powers[19], the Secretary of State may recover any costs reasonably so incurred by him from a responsible person[20].

A person is guilty of an offence if he wilfully obstructs a person exercising, or attempting to exercise, the powers mentioned in heads (a) or (b) above or any other person taken with him as mentioned in head (c) above and helping him, or attempting to help him, to exercise those powers[21].

1   As to the service of notices see para 575 note 3 ante.
2   Ie under the Chemical Weapons Act 1996 s 12 (see para 581 ante): s 13(5).
3   As to the meaning of 'chemical weapons production facility' see para 581 note 1 ante. For the meaning of 'chemical weapons' see para 573 ante.
4   Ie the Chemical Weapons Act 1996 s 13(2). The persons falling within s 13(2) are:
     (1)   any person who appears to the Secretary of State to occupy the land on which the equipment or building is situated (s 13(2)(a));
     (2)   if the Secretary of State's belief relates to equipment, any person not falling within head (1) supra and who appears to the Secretary of State to have the equipment in his possession (s 13(2)(b)); and
     (3)   any person not falling within heads (1) or (2) supra and who appears to the Secretary of State to have an interest which the Secretary of State believes would be materially affected by the destruction or alteration of the equipment or building (s 13(2)(c)).
5   Ibid s 13(1).
6   Ibid s 13(3)(a).
7   Ibid s 13(3)(b).
8   For the meaning of 'destroyed' see para 581 note 6 ante.
9   Chemical Weapons Act 1996 s 13(3)(c).
10   Ibid s 13(4). In this case s 13(1)–(3) applies to the further notice accordingly: s 13(4). Nothing in s 13 affects any power arising otherwise than by virtue of that section (such as the power to dispose of property in police possession in connection with the investigation of a suspected offence): s 18(3).
11   Ie under ibid s 13: see s 17(2)(a).
12   Ibid s 17(2). A person guilty of such an offence is liable on summary conviction to a fine of an amount not exceeding the statutory maximum and on conviction on indictment to a fine: s 17(4). Proceedings for an offence under this provision may not be instituted except by or with the consent of the Secretary of State: s 31(2). As to the statutory maximum see para 575 note 9 ante.
13   Ie (1) that a notice has been prepared under ibid s 13 (see s 14(1)(a)); (2) that s 13(1)–(3) has been complied with (see s 14(1)(b)); (3) that the notice has not been revoked (s 14(1)(c)); and (4) that any requirement set out in the notice has not been complied with (s 14(1)(d)).
14   Ibid s 14(2).
15   Ibid s 14(3)(a).
16   Ibid s 14(3)(b).
17   Ibid s 14(3)(c).
18   Ibid s 14(4).
19   Ie the powers mentioned in ibid s 14: see s 14(5).
20   Ibid s 14(5). A responsible person is (1) in the case of equipment, any person in possession of the equipment at the time the land is entered; (2) in the case of a building, any person occupying the land at the time it is entered: s 14(5). Nothing in s 14 affects any power arising otherwise than by virtue of that section (such as the power to dispose of property in police possession in connection with the investigation of a suspected offence): s 18(3).
21   Ibid s 17(3). A person guilty of such an offence is liable on summary conviction to a fine of an amount not exceeding the statutory maximum and on conviction on indictment to a fine: s 17(4). Proceedings for an offence under this provision may not be instituted except by or with the consent of the Secretary of State: s 31(2).

583. Position where no notice can be served. If a justice of the peace is satisfied on information on oath that the qualifying condition is fulfilled[1], he may issue a warrant in writing authorising a person acting under the authority of the Secretary of State to take remedial action[2].

If a person is authorised by a warrant to take such remedial action he may (1) enter the land on which the equipment or building is situated, if necessary by force[3]; (2) do whatever is required to secure that the equipment or building is destroyed or altered in a manner specified in the proposals drawn up by the Secretary of State[4]; (3) take with him such other persons and such equipment as appear to him to be necessary to help him to exercise the powers mentioned in heads (1) and (2) above[5]. These powers conferred on an authorised person are only exercisable in the presence of a constable, if the warrant so provides[6]. If anything is done in exercise of these powers, the Secretary of State may recover any costs reasonably incurred by him in connection with their exercise from a responsible person[7].

A person is guilty of an offence if he wilfully obstructs a person exercising, or attempting to exercise, the powers mentioned in head (1) or (2) above, or any other person taken with him as mentioned in head (3) above and helping him, or attempting to help him, to exercise those powers[8].

1   Ie that (1) the Secretary of State has reasonable cause to believe that any equipment or building is a chemical weapons production facility (Chemical Weapons Act 1996 s 15(1)(a)); (2) in the period of six months beginning with the day after he formed his belief it has not been possible to serve a copy of a notice under ibid s 13 (see para 582 ante) because of certain circumstances (s 15(1)(b)); and (3) the Secretary of State has drawn up proposals for the destruction (see para 581 note 6 ante) or alteration of the equipment or building in a manner specified in the proposals (s 15(1)(c)). As to the meaning of 'chemical weapons production facility' see para 581 note 1 ante. For the meaning of 'chemical weapons' see para 573 ante. As to the service of notices see para 575 note 3 ante.

    The circumstances referred to in head (2) supra are that:
    (1) no person appeared to the Secretary of State to occupy the land on which the equipment or building is situated (ibid s 15(2)(a));
    (2) if the Secretary of State's belief relates to equipment, no person appeared to the Secretary of State to have the equipment in his possession (s 15(2)(b)); and
    (3) no person appeared to the Secretary of State to have an interest which the Secretary of State believed would be materially affected by the destruction or alteration of the equipment or building (s 15(2)(c)).

2   Ibid s 15(3).
3   Ibid s 15(4)(a).
4   Ibid s 15(4)(b).
5   Ibid s 15(4)(c).
6   Ibid s 15(5).
7   Ibid s 15(6). A responsible person is (1) in the case of equipment, any person in possession of the equipment at the time the land is entered; (2) in the case of a building, any person occupying the land at the time it is entered: s 15(6)(a), (b). Nothing in s 15 affects any power arising otherwise than by virtue of that section (such as the power to dispose of property in police possession in connection with the investigation of a suspected offence): s 18(3).
8   Ibid s 17(3). A person guilty of such an offence is liable on summary conviction to a fine of an amount not exceeding the statutory maximum and on conviction on indictment to a fine: s 17(4). Proceedings for an offence under this provision may not be instituted except by or with the consent of the Secretary of State: s 31(2). As to the statutory maximum see para 575 note 9 ante.

584. Compensation for destruction or alteration. An application for compensation may be made where a person claims that:
    (1) any equipment or building has been destroyed[1] or altered in compliance with a notice[2] or has been destroyed or altered as a result of such a notice not being complied with[3];

(2) he had an interest which was materially affected by the destruction or alteration and he sustained loss as a result[4]; and

(3) no copy of a notice was served[5].

An application may also be made where a person claims that (a) any equipment or building has been destroyed or altered because no notice could be served[6]; and (b) he had an interest which was materially affected by the destruction or alteration and he sustained loss as a result[7].

If the person concerned makes an application under this provision to the High Court and the court finds that his claim is justified, the court may order the Secretary of State to pay to the applicant such amount (if any) by way of compensation as the court considers just[8]. If the court believes that the equipment or building would have been destroyed or altered even if a copy of a notice had been served on the applicant[9], it must not order compensation to be paid under this provision[10].

1 For the meaning of 'destroyed' see para 581 note 6 ante.
2 Ie in compliance with a notice falling within the Chemical Weapons Act 1996 s 13(3): see s 16(1)(a). As to the service of notices see para 575 note 3 ante.
3 Ie under ibid s 14 (see para 312 ante): see s 16(1)(a).
4 Ibid s 16(1)(b).
5 Ie a notice served on him under ibid s 13 (see para 582 ante): see s 16(1)(c).
6 Ie under ibid s 15 (see para 583 ante): see s 16(2)(a).
7 See ibid s 16(2)(b).
8 Ibid s 16(3).
9 Ie under ibid s 13: see s 16(4).
10 Ibid s 16(4).

585. Restrictions on the use of certain chemicals for permitted purposes.

No person may (1) use a Schedule 1 toxic chemical or precursor[1] for a permitted purpose[2]; or (2) produce or have in his possession a Schedule 1 toxic chemical or precursor with the intention that it will be used for a permitted purpose[3]. A person contravening this provision is guilty of an offence[4]. However, this provision does not apply to anything done in accordance with the terms of a licence granted by the Secretary of State and having effect at the time it is done[5]. The Secretary of State may grant a licence in such circumstances and on such terms as he thinks fit, and may vary or revoke a licence by serving a notice to that effect on the person to whom the licence was granted[6]. A variation or revocation takes effect at such reasonable time as is specified in the notice[7]. The Secretary of State may by order make provision with respect to appealing against a refusal to grant, renew or vary a licence or against a variation or revocation of a licence[8].

A person who knowingly makes a false or misleading statement for the purpose of obtaining a licence or a renewal or variation of a licence, or of opposing a variation or revocation of a licence, is guilty of an offence[9].

1 A Schedule 1 toxic chemical or precursor is a toxic chemical or precursor listed in Schedule 1 to the annex on chemicals to the Chemical Weapons Convention (see para 572 note 2 ante); and is set out in the Schedule to the Chemical Weapons Act 1996: s 19(2), Schedule. For the meaning of 'toxic chemical' and 'precursor' see para 573 notes 1–2 ante.
2 As to permitted purposes see para 573 ante.
3 Chemical Weapons Act 1996 s 19(1).
4 Ibid s 19(3). A person guilty of such an offence is liable on summary conviction to a fine of an amount not exceeding the statutory maximum and on conviction on indictment to a fine: s 19(3). Proceedings for an offence under this provision may not be instituted except by or with the consent of the Secretary of State: s 31(2). As to the statutory maximum see para 575 note 9 ante.
5 Ibid s 20(1).
6 Ibid s 20(2).
7 Ibid s 20(3).

8   Ibid s 20(4). An order under s 20(4) must be made by statutory instrument subject to annulment in pursuance of a resolution of either House of Parliament: s 20(5).
9   Ibid s 20(6). A person guilty of such an offence is liable on summary conviction to a fine of an amount not exceeding the statutory maximum and on conviction on indictment to imprisonment for a term not exceeding two years or a fine, or to both: s 20(6). Proceedings for an offence under this provision may not be instituted except by or with the consent of the Secretary of State: s 31(2).

586. Information required for statutory purposes. If the Secretary of State has grounds to suspect that a person is committing or has committed an offence under the Chemical Weapons Act 1996, the Secretary of State may by notice served on the person require him to give certain information[1]. The information required must be information which the Secretary of State has reasonable cause to believe will help to establish whether the person is committing or has committed an offence[2]. A person who without reasonable excuse fails to comply with a notice served on him is guilty of an offence[3]; and a person on whom a notice is served, and who knowingly makes a false or misleading statement in response to it, is also guilty of an offence[4].

1   The information required must be specified in the notice: see the Chemical Weapons Act 1996 s 21(1). As to the service of notices see para 575 note 3 ante. The information must be given in such form, and within such reasonable period, as is specified in the notice: see s 21(1).
2   See ibid s 21(1).
3   Ibid s 21(2). A person guilty of such an offence is liable on summary conviction to a fine of an amount not exceeding the statutory maximum and on conviction on indictment to a fine: s 21(2). Proceedings for an offence under this provision may not be instituted except by or with the consent of the Secretary of State: s 31(2). As to the statutory maximum see para 575 note 9 ante.
4   Ibid s 21(3). A person guilty of such an offence is liable on summary conviction to a fine of an amount not exceeding the statutory maximum and on conviction on indictment to imprisonment for a term not exceeding two years or a fine, or to both: s 21(3). Proceedings for an offence under this provision may not be instituted except by or with the consent of the Secretary of State: s 31(2).

587. Information and records for the purposes of the Chemical Weapons Convention. The Secretary of State may by notice[1] served on any person[2] require him to give certain information[3]. The information required must be information which the Secretary of State has reasonable cause to believe is or will be needed in connection with anything to be done for the purposes of the Chemical Weapons Convention[4]; and the information may relate to a state of affairs subsisting before the coming into force of the Chemical Weapons Act 1996 or of the convention[5]. A person on whom such a notice is served, and who knowingly makes a false or misleading statement in response to it, is guilty of an offence[6].

The Secretary of State may by notice served on any person require him to keep such records as are specified in the notice; and the records must be records which the Secretary of State has reasonable cause to believe will facilitate the giving of required[7] information[8].

A person who without reasonable excuse fails to comply with a notice served on him under these provisions is guilty of an offence[9].

1   As to the service of notices see para 575 note 3 ante.
2   The Secretary of State may make regulations (which must be made by statutory instrument subject to annulment in pursuance of a resolution of either House of Parliament: Chemical Weapons Act 1996 s 23(6)) requiring persons of any description specified in the regulations to inform him that they are of such a description: s 23(1). Any such description must be so framed that persons within it are persons on whom the Secretary of State is likely to want to serve a notice under s 22: s 23(2). The Secretary of State must arrange for a statement of the fact that such regulations have been made to be published in such manner as is likely to bring them to the attention of persons affected by them: s 23(3); and see the London Gazette, 31 October 1996. In the exercise of these powers the Secretary of State has made the Chemical Weapons (Notification) Regulations 1996, SI 1996/2503 (amended

by SI 1996/2669) which describe certain persons who have to identify themselves to the Secretary of State as being persons on whom it is likely he will want to serve a notice under the Chemical Weapons Act 1996 s 22.

A person who without reasonable excuse fails to comply with a requirement imposed by the regulations is guilty of an offence and liable on summary conviction to a fine of an amount not exceeding the statutory maximum and on conviction on indictment to a fine: s 23(4). A person who knowingly makes a false or misleading statement in response to a requirement imposed by the regulations is guilty of an offence, and is liable on summary conviction to a fine of an amount not exceeding the statutory maximum and on conviction on indictment to imprisonment for a term not exceeding two years or a fine, or to both: s 23(5). Proceedings for offences under these provisions may not be instituted except by or with the consent of the Secretary of State: s 31(2). As to the statutory maximum see para 575 note 9 ante.

3   The information required must be specified in the notice; and must be given in such form, and within such reasonable period, as is specified in the notice: see ibid s 22(1).

4   Ie the Convention on the Prohibition of the Development, Production, Stockpiling and the Use of Chemical Weapons and on their Destruction: see para 572 note 2 ante.

5   Chemical Weapons Act 1996 s 22(1).

6   Ibid s 22(4). A person guilty of such an offence is liable on summary conviction to a fine of an amount not exceeding the statutory maximum and on conviction on indictment to imprisonment for a term not exceeding two years or a fine, or to both: s 22(4). Proceedings for an offence under this provision may not be instituted except by or with the consent of the Secretary of State: s 31(2).

7   Ie under ibid s 22(1).

8   Ibid s 22(2).

9   Ibid s 22(3). A person guilty of such an offence is liable on summary conviction to a fine of an amount not exceeding the statutory maximum and on conviction on indictment to a fine: s 22(3). Proceedings for an offence under this provision may not be instituted except by or with the consent of the Secretary of State: s 31(2).

588. Inspection authorisations. If it is proposed to conduct a routine inspection[1], a challenge inspection[2] or an assistance inspection[3] in the United Kingdom, the Secretary of State may issue an authorisation[4]. An authorisation must:

(1)   contain a description of the area (the specified area[5]) in which the inspection is to be conducted[6];

(2)   specify the type of inspection concerned[7];

(3)   state the names of the members of the inspection team by whom the inspection is to be carried out[9]; and

(4)   in the case of a challenge inspection, state the name of any observer[10] who may accompany the team[11].

Such an authorisation has the effect of authorising the inspection team to exercise within the specified area such rights of access, entry and unobstructed inspection as are conferred on them by the verification annex[12], and to do such other things within that area in connection with the inspection as they are entitled to do by virtue of the verification annex (including things concerning the maintenance, replacement or adjustment of any instrument or other object)[13]. The Secretary of State may reimburse any person in respect of expenditure incurred in connection with a routine inspection, a challenge inspection or an assistance inspection[14].

An authorisation has, in addition, the effect of authorising an in-country escort[15] to accompany the inspection team in accordance with the provisions of the verification annex[16], and authorising any constable to give such assistance as the in-country escort may request for the purpose of facilitating the conduct of the inspection in accordance with the verification annex[17]. In the case of a challenge inspection, an authorisation also has the effect of authorising the observer to exercise within the specified area such rights of access and entry as are conferred on him by the verification annex[18].

The occupier of any premises in relation to which it is proposed to exercise a right of entry in reliance on an authorisation, or on which an inspection is being carried out in reliance on such an authorisation, or a person acting on behalf of the occupier of any such premises, is entitled to require a copy of the authorisation to be shown to him by a member of the in–country escort[19].

The validity of any authorisation purporting to be issued under this provision in respect of any inspection may not be called in question in any court of law at any time before the conclusion of that inspection[20]. Accordingly, where an authorisation purports to be issued under this provision in respect of any inspection, no proceedings (of whatever nature) may be brought at any time before the conclusion of the inspection if they would, if successful, have the effect of preventing, delaying or otherwise affecting the carrying out of the inspection[21].

If, in any proceedings, any question arises whether a person at any time was or was not, in relation to any routine, challenge or assistance inspection, a member of the inspection team or a member of the in–country escort or the observer, a certificate issued by or under the authority of the Secretary of State stating any fact relating to that question is conclusive evidence of that fact[22].

1   A 'routine inspection' is an inspection conducted pursuant to Pts II–IX of the verification annex on implementation and verification to the Chemical Weapons Convention (see para 572 note 2 ante): Chemical Weapons Act 1996 s 24(a), (b).

2   A 'challenge inspection' is an inspection conducted pursuant to Pts II and X of the verification annex to the convention (see note 1 supra): Chemical Weapons Act 1996 s 24(c).

3   An 'assistance inspection' is an inspection conducted pursuant to Pts II and XI of the verification annex to the convention (see note 1 supra): Chemical Weapons Act 1996 s 24(d).

4   Ibid s 25(1). For the meaning of 'United Kingdom' see para 502 note 4 ante.

5   If an authorisation is issued under ibid s 25, the Secretary of State may issue an amendment varying the specified area; and (1) from the time when the amendment is expressed to take effect s 25 applies as if the specified area were the area as varied (s 25(11)(a)); (2) the validity of the amendment may not be called into question in any court of law at any time before the conclusion of the inspection (see s 25(8), (11)(b)); and (3) the Secretary of State may issue further amendments varying the specified area and in such a case heads (1)–(2) supra apply (s 25(11)(c)).

6   Ibid s 25(2)(a).

7   Ibid s 25(2)(b).

8   'Inspection team' has the meaning given in Pt I of the verification annex to the convention (see note 1 supra): Chemical Weapons Act 1996 s 24(e).

9   Ibid s 25(2)(c).

10   'Observer' has the meaning given in Pt I of the verification annex to the convention (see note 1 supra): Chemical Weapons Act 1996 s 24(e).

11   Ibid s 25(2)(d).

12   Ibid s 25(3)(a).

13   Ibid s 25(3)(b). As to the meaning of 'object' see para 573 note 4 ante.

14   Ibid s 28.

15   'In–country escort' has the meaning given in Pt I of the verification annex to the convention (see note 1 supra): Chemical Weapons Act 1996 s 24(e).

16   Ibid s 25(4)(a).

17   Ibid s 25(4)(b). The name of the person in charge of the in–country escort must be stated in the authorisation: s 25(4). Any constable giving assistance in accordance with s 25(4)(b) may use such reasonable force as he considers necessary for the purpose mentioned in that provision: s 25(6).

18   Ibid s 25(5).

19   Ibid s 25(7).

20   Ibid s 25(8).

21   Ibid s 25(9).

22   Ibid s 25(10).

589. Offences in connection with inspections. If an authorisation has been issued in respect of any inspection[1], a person is guilty of an offence[2] if he:

(1)   refuses without reasonable excuse to comply with any request made by any constable or a member of the in–country escort[3] for the purpose of facilitating the conduct of that inspection in accordance with the verification annex[4];

(2) interferes without reasonable excuse with any container, instrument or other object installed in the course of that inspection in accordance with the verification annex[5]; or

(3) wilfully obstructs any member of the inspection team[6] or of the in-country escort, or the observer, in the conduct of that inspection in accordance with the verification annex[7].

1   Ie under the Chemical Weapons Act 1996 s 25 (see para 588 ante): see s 26(1).
2   A person guilty of an offence under ibid s 26 is liable on summary conviction to a fine of an amount not exceeding the statutory maximum and on conviction on indictment to a fine: s 26(3). Proceedings for an offence under this provision may not be instituted except by or with the consent of the Secretary of State: s 31(2). As to the statutory maximum see para 575 note 9 ante.
3   As to the meaning of 'in-country escort' see para 588 note 15 ante.
4   Chemical Weapons Act 1996 s 26(1)(a). As to the verification annex see para 588 note 1 ante.
5   Ibid s 26(1)(b). This applies to interference which occurs at any time while the container, instrument or other object is retained in accordance with the verification annex: s 26(2).
6   As to the meaning of 'inspection team' see para 588 note 8 ante.
7   Chemical Weapons Act 1996 s 26(1)(c).

590. Privileges and immunities in connection with inspections.

Members of inspection teams[1] and observers[2] enjoy the same privileges and immunities as are enjoyed by diplomatic agents[3]. Samples and approved equipment[4] carried by members of an inspection team are inviolable and exempt from customs duties[5]. The privileges and immunities accorded to members of inspection teams and observers are enjoyed by them at any time when they are in the United Kingdom in connection with the carrying out there of a routine inspection[6], a challenge inspection[7] or an assistance inspection[8], or while in transit to or from the territory of another party to the Chemical Weapons Convention[9] in connection with the carrying out of such an inspection there[10]. If the immunity of a member of an inspection team is waived[11], and a notice made by the Secretary of State and informing the member of the waiver is delivered to him in person, then, from the time the notice is so delivered, these provisions do not have effect to confer immunity on that member[12].

If, in any proceedings, any question arises whether a person is or is not entitled to any privilege or immunity, a certificate issued by or under the authority of the Secretary of State stating any fact relating to that question is conclusive evidence of that fact[13].

1   As to the meaning of 'inspection team' see para 588 note 8 ante.
2   As to the meaning of 'observer' see para 588 note 10 ante.
3   Chemical Weapons Act 1996 s 27(1). The privileges and immunities are those in accordance with the Diplomatic Privileges Act 1964 s 2(1), Sch 1 arts 29, art 30 paras 1, 2, art 31 paras 1, 2, 3, art 34: see the Chemical Weapons Act 1996 s 27(1), (7). The Diplomatic Privileges Act 1964 Sch 1 sets out articles of the Vienna Convention on Diplomatic Relations (Vienna, 2 March to 14 April 1961; Misc 6 (1961); Cmnd 1368) having force of law in United Kingdom. For the meaning of 'United Kingdom' see para 502 note 4 ante.
     Such persons, in addition, enjoy the same privileges as are enjoyed by diplomatic agents in accordance with the Diplomatic Privileges Act 1964 Sch 1 art 36 para 1(b), except in relation to articles the importing or exporting of which is prohibited by law or controlled by the enactments relating to quarantine: Chemical Weapons Act 1996 s 27(2). 'Enactment' includes an enactment comprised in subordinate legislation (within the meaning of the Interpretation Act 1978: see STATUTES vol 44(1) (Reissue) para 1232): Chemical Weapons Act 1996 s 27(7).
4   'Approved equipment' and 'samples' are construed in accordance with the verification annex: ibid s 27(7). As to the verification annex see para 318 note 1 ante.
5   Ibid s 27(3). As to customs duties generally see CUSTOMS AND EXCISE.
6   For the meaning of 'routine inspection' see para 588 note 1 ante.
7   For the meaning of 'challenge inspection' see para 588 note 2 ante.
8   For the meaning of 'assistance inspection' see para 588 note 3 ante.

9   As to the Chemical Weapons Convention see para 572 note 2 ante.
10 Chemical Weapons Act 1996 s 27(4).
11 Ie in accordance with the verification annex: see ibid s 27(5).
12 Ibid s 27(5).
13 Ibid s 27(6).

591. Power to search and obtain evidence. If a justice of the peace is satisfied on information on oath that there is reasonable ground for suspecting that an offence under the Chemical Weapons Act 1996 is being, has been or is about to be committed on any premises or that evidence of the commission of such an offence is to be found there, he may issue a warrant in writing authorising a person acting under the authority of the Secretary of State to enter the premises, if necessary by force, at any time within one month from the time of the issue of the warrant and to search them[1].

A person who enters the premises under the authority of the warrant may:

(1)   take with him such other persons and such equipment as appear to him to be necessary[2];

(2)   inspect any document found on the premises which he has reasonable cause to believe may be required as evidence for the purposes of proceedings in respect of an offence under the Chemical Weapons Act 1996[3];

(3)   take copies of, or seize and remove, any such document[4];

(4)   inspect, seize and remove any device or equipment found on the premises which he has reasonable cause to believe may be required as such evidence[5];

(5)   inspect, sample, seize and remove any substance found on the premises which he has reasonable cause to believe may be required as such evidence[6];

(6)   search or cause to be searched any person found on the premises whom he has reasonable cause to believe to be in possession of any document, device, equipment or substance[7];

but no woman or girl may be searched except by a woman[8]. The powers conferred by a warrant are only exercisable in the presence of a constable, if the warrant so provides[9].

1   Chemical Weapons Act 1996 s 29(1).
2   Ibid s 29(2)(a).
3   Ibid s 29(2)(b).
4   Ibid s 29(2)(c).
5   Ibid s 29(2)(d).
6   Ibid s 29(2)(e).
7   Ibid s 29(2)(f).
8   See ibid s 29(2).
9   Ibid s 29(3).

592. Forfeiture in case of conviction. The court by or before which a person is convicted of an offence under the Chemical Weapons Act 1996 may order that anything shown to the court's satisfaction to relate to the offence must be forfeited, and either destroyed or otherwise dealt with in such manner as the court may order[1]. In particular, the court may order the thing to be dealt with as the Secretary of State may see fit; and in such a case the Secretary of State may direct that it be destroyed or otherwise dealt with[2]. Where the court proposes to order anything to be forfeited under these provisions and a person claiming to have an interest in it applies to be heard by the court, the court may not order that thing to be forfeited unless that person has been given an opportunity to show cause why the order should not be made[3].

1   Chemical Weapons Act 1996 s 30(1).
2   Ibid s 30(2).
3   Ibid s 30(3).

593. Offences committed by bodies corporate. Where an offence under the Chemical Weapons Act 1996 is committed by a body corporate and is proved to have been committed with the consent or connivance of, or to be attributable to any neglect on the part of, a director[1], manager, secretary or other similar officer of the body corporate, or any person who was purporting to act in any such capacity, he as well as the body corporate is guilty of that offence and is liable to be proceeded against and punished accordingly[2].

1   'Director', in relation to a body corporate whose affairs are managed by its members, means a member of the body corporate: Chemical Weapons Act 1996 s 31(4).
2   Ibid s 31(3).

594. Disclosure of information. Where information is obtained under, or in connection with anything done under, the Chemical Weapons Act 1996 or the Chemical Weapons Convention[1], and it relates to a particular business or other activity carried on by any person, so long as the business or activity continues to be carried on that information must not be disclosed except:

(1)   with the consent of the person for the time being carrying on the business or activity;

(2)   in connection with anything done for the purposes of the convention;

(3)   in connection with anything done for the purposes of the Chemical Weapons Act 1996[2];

(4)   in connection with the investigation of any criminal offence or for the purposes of any criminal proceedings;

(5)   in connection with the enforcement of any restriction on imports or exports;

(6)   in dealing with an emergency involving danger to the public;

(7)   with a view to ensuring the security of the United Kingdom; or

(8)   to the International Court of Justice for the purpose of enabling that court to deal with any dispute referred to it under the convention[3].

A person who discloses information in contravention of these provisions is guilty of an offence[4]. Where, however, a person proposes to disclose information in circumstances where the disclosure would not, by virtue of heads (2) to (8) above, contravene these provisions, he may disclose the information notwithstanding any obligation not to disclose it that would otherwise apply[5].

1   As to the Chemical Weapons Convention see para 572 note 2 ante.
2   The reference to the Chemical Weapons Act 1996 in s 32(2)(c) does not include a reference to s 33 (see para 595 post): s 32(3).
3   Ibid s 32(1), (2). For the meaning of 'United Kingdom' see para 502 note 4 ante.
4   Ibid s 32(4). A person guilty of such an offence is liable on summary conviction to a fine of an amount not exceeding the statutory maximum and on conviction on indictment to imprisonment for a term not exceeding two years or a fine, or to both: s 32(4). Proceedings for such an offence may not be instituted except by or with the consent of the Secretary of State: s 31(2). As to the statutory maximum see para 575 note 9 ante.
5   Ibid s 32(5).

595. Miscellaneous powers and duties of the Secretary of State. In each calendar year the Secretary of State must prepare a report on the operation of the

Chemical Weapons Act 1996, and lay a copy of the report before each House of Parliament[1]. Any expenses of the Secretary of State incurred in consequence of the Chemical Weapons Act 1996 must be paid out of money provided by Parliament[2]; and any sums received by the Secretary of State in consequence of that Act must be paid into the Consolidated Fund[3].

The Secretary of State may by order[4] make such additions to, omissions from or other modifications to the 1996 Act as he considers necessary or desirable to give effect to any amendment of the Chemical Weapons Convention[5].

1   Chemical Weapons Act 1996 s 33.
2   Ibid s 38(1).
3   Ibid s 38(2). As to the Consolidated Fund see CONSTITUTIONAL LAW AND HUMAN RIGHTS vol 8(2) (Reissue) para 711 et seq.
4   The power to make an order under ibid s 36 is, if the order solely modifies s 19(2), Schedule, exercisable by statutory instrument subject to annulment in pursuance of a resolution of either House of Parliament: s 36(2). The power to make any other order under s 36 is exercisable by statutory instrument, and no such order may be made unless a draft of it has been laid before and approved by resolution of each House of Parliament: s 36(3).
5   Chemical Weapons Act 1996 s 36(1). As to the Chemical Weapons Convention see para 572 note 2 ante.

(iii) Nuclear Weapons

596. In general. The testing, development and use of nuclear weapons are covered by a number of international treaties[1].

Since 1973 the Secretary of State has had the responsibility for explosive nuclear devices[2] and since 1991 he has had the power to make arrangements with respect to the Atomic Weapons Establishment concerning the activities connected with the development, production or maintenance of nuclear devices or with research into such devices or their effects[3].

1   See (1) the Treaty banning Nuclear Weapon Tests in the Atmosphere, in Outer Space and under Water (Moscow, 5 August 1963; TS 3 (1963); Cmnd 2245) which was ratified by the United Kingdom (and came into force) on 10 October 1963 but not incorporated into English law; (2) the Treaty on Principles Governing the Activities of States in Exploration and Use of Outer Space, including the Moon and Other Celestial Bodies (London, Moscow and Washington, 27 January 1967; TS 10 (1968); Cmnd 3519) which was ratified by the United Kingdom (and came into force) on 10 October 1963 but not incorporated into English law; (3) the Treaty on the Non-proliferation of Nuclear Weapons (London, Moscow and Washington, 1 July 1968; TS 88 (1970); Cmnd 4474) which was ratified by the United Kingdom on 27 and 29 November 1969 and entered into force on 5 March 1970 but was not incorporated into English law; (4) the Agreement for the Application of Safeguards in the United Kingdom in connection with the Treaty on the Non-proliferation of Nuclear Weapons (with Protocol) ('the Safeguards Agreement') (Vienna, 6 September 1976; Misc 2 (1977); Cmnd 6730) which was given effect in English law by the Nuclear Safeguards and Electricity (Finance) Act 1978; (5) the Treaty on the Prohibition of the Emplacement of Nuclear Weapons and Other Weapons of Mass Destruction on the Sea Bed and the Ocean Floor and the Subsoil thereof (London, Moscow and Washington, 11 February 1971; TS 13 (1973); Cmnd 5266) which was ratified by the United Kingdom (and came into force) on 18 May 1972 but was not incorporated into English law. As to the use or threat of use of nuclear weapons see *Legality of the Threat or Use of Nuclear Weapons (Request for Advisory Opinion by the General Assembly of the United Nations)* (1996) Times, 18 July, ICJ. See further FUEL AND ENERGY vol 19(2) (Reissue) para 1103.
2   See FUEL AND ENERGY vol 19(2) (Reissue) para 1126.
3   See FUEL AND ENERGY vol 19(2) (Reissue) para 1127.

4. WARTIME EMERGENCY LEGISLATION

(1) IN GENERAL

597. Primary and subordinate legislation. In anticipation of the outbreak of war in 1939 it was found necessary to augment the emergency powers vested in the Crown by virtue of the prerogative created and limited by the common law or by the exercise of the statutory power to issue proclamations of emergency and by Order in Council to make emergency regulations[1]. This augmentation was effected by the passing on 24 August 1939 of the Emergency Powers (Defence) Act 1939 (since repealed)[2]. That Act, which was originally limited to remain in force for one year from its passing[3] but which was continued in force throughout the 1939–45 war and for some time after hostilities had ceased[4], empowered the Crown by Order in Council to make defence regulations for the purpose of securing the public safety, the defence of the realm, the maintenance of public order, the efficient prosecution of any war in which the Crown might be engaged and the maintenance of essential supplies and services, and authorised the recovery of charges in connection with any scheme of control under such regulations. In the absence of contrary intention defence regulations had certain limited extra-territorial force[5], while the Emergency Powers (Defence) Act 1939 itself could be extended by Order in Council to the Channel Islands, the Isle of Man and certain overseas territories[6].

Pursuant to that Act, a considerable body of defence regulations having the force of statute[7] was made. Many of those regulations authorised the making by specified ministers, authorities or other persons of orders, directions, licences or other instruments. If duly signed by or on behalf of the relevant minister, authority or person all such instruments[8] were receivable in evidence and until the contrary was proved were deemed to be made or issued by that minister, authority or person, and prima facie evidence of the instrument might be given by production of a certified copy[9].

It is not open to the court to investigate the necessity or expediency of any defence regulation[10], and it is bound to assume that an order made under a defence regulation was necessary[11]. Neither can the court interfere with the decision of a minister admittedly made in good faith within the authority delegated to him by defence regulations[12]. No act done for the purpose of safeguarding national security will be rendered unlawful by the provisions[13] prohibiting discrimination in certain fields enacted by the Race Relations Act 1976[14]. However, the court will not hesitate to declare a defence regulation ultra vires if such is the case[15], and will investigate whether a person to whom a competent authority has properly delegated powers under defence regulations has acted in excess of the powers delegated or of the powers contained in the regulation[16].

1   As to prerogative powers in wartime see paras 510–511 ante. As to the royal prerogative generally see CONSTITUTIONAL LAW AND HUMAN RIGHTS vol 8(2) (Reissue) paras 367 et seq; 809–819 (war and peace); 820–822 (executive powers in emergencies).

2   The Emergency Powers (Defence) Act 1939 (repealed) fell into the class of statutes which, having been passed for the defence of the realm, will not, it has been said, be construed with the scrupulous nicety of eg a taxing Act: see *Norman v Mathews* (1916) 32 TLR 303 at 304, DC; affd 32 TLR 369, CA.

3   See the Emergency Powers (Defence) Act 1939 s 11(1) (repealed), as originally enacted. The duration of the Act was extended to two years by the Emergency Powers (Defence) Act 1940 s 1(3) (repealed).

4   On an address by both Houses of Parliament praying that the Emergency Powers (Defence) Act 1939 should be continued in force, the Crown was empowered to extend its operation by Order in Council for yearly periods: see s 11(1) proviso (as originally enacted). By means of such orders the Act was continued in force until 23 August 1945. However, before that date was reached, provision was made for the Act to continue

in force for a further period of six months commencing with 24 August 1945 and to expire at the end of that period: see s 11(1) (substituted by the Emergency Powers (Defence) Act 1945 s 1 (repealed)). Although the Emergency Powers (Defence) Act 1939 s 11(1) (as so substituted), contained a proviso, as formerly, giving power to continue the Act by Order in Council for further yearly periods, the power was never exercised and consequently the Act expired on 24 February 1946, and on the expiry of the Act the power to make defence regulations also ceased. The Emergency Powers (Defence) Act 1939 was formally repealed by the Emergency Laws (Repeal) Act 1959 s 10(3)(a), Sch 4 Pt I (repealed).

5   See the Emergency Powers (Defence) Act 1939 s 3 (repealed), which was replaced (with modifications) by the Emergency Laws (Repeal) Act 1959 Sch 3 paras 2, 3 (repealed). Provision was also made for the extra-territorial operation of the defence legislation of certain Commonwealth countries: see the Emergency Powers (Defence) Act 1939 s 5 (repealed).

6   See ibid s 4 (repealed).

7   See *Ernest v Metropolitan Police Comr* (1919) 89 LJKB 42, DC, where it was held that regulations under the Defence of the Realm Consolidation Act 1914 (repealed) might take away a statutory privilege or impose a statutory duty. Certain defence regulations effected temporary amendments to statutes, and in many cases the amendments have been made permanent by subsequent legislation.

8   See eg *Carlish v East Ham Corpn and Edwards* [1948] 2 KB 380, [1948] 2 All ER 550; *Lewisham Metropolitan Borough and Town Clerk v Roberts* [1949] 2 KB 608, [1949] 1 All ER 815, CA.

9   See the Emergency Powers (Defence) Act 1939 s 7 (repealed), which was replaced in almost identical terms by the Emergency Laws (Repeal) Act 1959 s 2, Sch 3 para 4 (repealed). As to the admissibility of certified copies of public documents see EVIDENCE vol 17 para 148.

10   *R v Comptroller-General of Patents, ex p Bayer Products Ltd* [1941] 2 KB 306, [1941] 2 All ER 677, CA. See also *Ex p Norman* (1915) 85 LJKB 203, DC.

11   *Progressive Supply Co Ltd v Dalton* [1943] Ch 54, [1942] 2 All ER 646.

12   *Point of Ayr Collieries Ltd v Lloyd-George* [1943] 2 All ER 546, CA. See also ADMINISTRATIVE LAW vol 1(1) (Reissue) paras 31, 74.

13   Ie the provisions of the Race Relations Act 1976 Pts II–IV (ss 4–16, 17–27, 28–33).

14   Ibid s 42.

15   *EH Jones (Machine Tools) Ltd v Farrell and Muirsmith* [1940] 3 All ER 608; cf *Chester v Bateson* [1920] 1 KB 829, DC. See CONSTITUTIONAL LAW AND HUMAN RIGHTS vol 8(2) (Reissue) para 6.

16   *John Fowler & Co (Leeds) Ltd v Duncan* [1941] Ch 450, [1941] 2 All ER 577. An authority to delegate powers may imply power to delegate the performance of any condition necessary for the exercise of the power: *Mungoni v A-G of Northern Rhodesia* [1960] AC 336, [1960] 1 All ER 446, PC.

598. Scope of defence regulations. Defence regulations gave far-reaching powers of control over the freedom of the individual and over trade and industry generally. The Defence (General) Regulations 1939[1] included provisions[2] for the security of the state, the maintenance of public safety and order, the control of employment, industry, commerce, supplies and internal trading, and conferred extensive powers of taking possession of land and other property.

In addition to the general regulations, separate codes of defence regulations (most of which have expired, lapsed or been revoked)[3] controlled specific matters such as agriculture[4], building societies[5], companies[6], exports[7], financial dealings[8], patents, designs and trade marks[9] and trading with the enemy[10].

1   Ie the Defence (General) Regulations 1939, SR & O 1939/927 (spent). These regulations were amended by numerous subsequent orders. Information regarding amendments to the defence regulations may be obtained from successive editions of the official volume of defence regulations, prepared in the Office of the Parliamentary Counsel to the Treasury, and published from time to time; the last edition (the 23rd) was published by HMSO in February 1957.

2   For a complete list of regulations which have at any time been included in the Defence (General) Regulations 1939 see 22 Halsbury's Statutory Instruments (1996 issue) 160 et seq.

3   See note 2 supra.

4   See the Defence (Agriculture and Fisheries) Regulations 1939, SR & O 1939/1303 (expired).

5   See the Defence (Building Societies) Regulations 1940, SR & O 1940/1137 (expired).

6   See the Defence (Companies) Regulations 1940, SR & O 1940/1213 (expired).

7   See the Defence (Encouragement of Exports) Regulations 1940, SR & O 1940/1210 (revoked).

8   See the Defence (Finance) Regulations 1939 which were originally contained in the Order in Council dated 25 August 1939, SR & O 1939/950 (revoked), but were subsequently set out in amended form in

the Defence (Finance) Regulations Amendment (No 2) Order 1939, SR & O 1939/1620 (spent). See also MONEY vol 32 paras 206, 273.

9   See the Defence (Patents, Trade Marks, etc) Regulations 1941, SR & O 1941/1780 (revoked).

10 Ie the Defence (Trading with the Enemy) Regulations 1940, SR & O 1940/1092 (revoked), which were given permanent effect by the Emergency Laws (Miscellaneous Provisions) Act 1953 s 2 (as amended), Sch 2 (as amended). As to trading with the enemy see para 634 et seq post.

599. Continuance in force of defence regulations. On the expiration of the power to make defence regulations under the Emergency Powers (Defence) Act 1939[1], all defence regulations made under that Act would have expired automatically if provision had not been made for the continuance in force of such of them as it was thought necessary to retain. This was effected by the Supplies and Services (Transitional Powers) Act 1945 (since repealed) and the Emergency Laws (Transitional Provisions) Act 1946. The great majority of the remaining defence regulations were repealed by the Emergency Laws (Re-enactments and Repeals) Act 1964[2], although certain powers conferred by regulations have been enacted permanently and others are continued temporarily.

It is clear that fresh emergency powers may be created by Parliament at any time as may be deemed necessary[3]. However, regulations which are in any case permanent cover the employment of the armed forces on civilian work of national importance[4], the power to control the prices of goods and services[5], and the power to control certain transactions ordered by governments or persons abroad in relation to currency, gold and securities[6].

1   The power to make defence regulations under the Emergency Powers (Defence) Act 1939 expired on 24 February 1946: see para 597 note 4 ante.

2   See the Emergency Laws (Re-enactments and Repeals) Act 1964 s 22(2), Sch 2 (repealed).

3   As to the sovereignty of Parliament see CONSTITUTIONAL LAW AND HUMAN RIGHTS vol 8(2) (Reissue) para 232 et seq.

4   See the Emergency Powers Act 1964 s 2.

5   See the Emergency Laws (Re-enactments and Repeals) Act 1964 s 1 (as amended), s 4 (repealed), s 6 (repealed), s 22(3) (repealed); Consumer Credit Act 1974 s 192(3)(a), Sch 4 (repealed in part); and also the National Health Service Act 1977 s 57.

6   See the Emergency Laws (Re-enactments and Repeals) Act 1964 s 2. Directions have been made in the Control of Gold, Securities, Payments and Credits (Kuwait) Directions 1990, SI 1990/1591; the Control of Gold, Securities, Payments and Credits (Republic of Iraq) Directions 1990, SI 1990/1616; the Control of Gold, Securities, Payments and Credits (Kuwait) (Revocation) Directions 1991, SI 1991/629; the Control of Gold, Securities, Payments and Credits (Serbia and Montenegro) Directions 1992, SI 1992/1265; and the Control of Gold, Securities, Payments and Credits (Serbia and Montenegro) (Revocation) Directions 1992, SI 1992/1381.

(2) COMPENSATION FOR REQUISITION ETC

(i) The Compensation (Defence) Act 1939

600. In general. The 1939–45 war legislation giving rights to compensation for the exercise of emergency powers[1] during the period of the emergency[2] dealt separately with compensation (1) for the requisition[3] of land[4]; (2) in respect of the doing of work on land[5]; (3) in respect of the requisition or acquisition of vessels, vehicles and aircraft[6]; (4) in respect of the taking of space or accommodation in ships and aircraft[7]; and (5) in respect of the requisition or acquisition of other goods[8]. These provisions remain unrepealed. They were applicable to acts done in exercise of emergency powers, but the relevant powers conferred by defence regulations have now all either expired or been revoked[9]. However, there are certain provisions still in force concerning compensation in relation to property other than land arising under emergency legislation, but they are limited to compensation in respect of acts done under the prerogative[10] and under statutory powers concerned with the control of aviation[11] and of telegraphic transmission of messages[12].

Whenever it appears to the Secretary of State that the public interest so requires he may bring into operation in the United Kingdom[13] provisions giving a general or field officer commanding any part of the regular forces the power to (a) issue a billeting requisition to any chief officer of police; and (b) requisition such vehicles as may be specified in the requisitioning order[14]. Payment is to be made for requisitioned billets and vehicles[15]. In time of war, whether actual or imminent, or of great national emergency, the Secretary of State may provide for the taking of possession of any aircraft, aerodrome, machinery, plant or material or require that the whole or any part of the undertaking of any British air transport business be placed at his disposal[16].

1　'Emergency powers' means any power conferred by the Air Navigation Act 1920 s 7 (as amended) or any power exercisable by virtue of the prerogative of the Crown: Compensation (Defence) Act 1939 s 17(1) (amended by the Statute Law (Repeals) Act 1973 s 1, Sch 1 Pt IX; and by the Statute Law (Repeals) Act 1976 s 1, Sch 1 Pt XX). 'Exercise' includes purported exercise: Compensation (Defence) Act 1939 s 17(1).

2　The period began on 24 August 1939 and continues until the emergency is declared by Order in Council to be at an end: ibid s 1(1). At the date at which this volume states the law, no such Order in Council had been made.

3　'Requisition' means, in relation to any property, taking possession of the property or requiring the property to be placed at the disposal of the requisitioning authority: ibid s 17(1).

4　See ibid ss 1(1)(a), 2 (as amended); and para 601 post. 'Land' includes (without prejudice to any of the provisions of the Interpretation Act 1978 s 22(1), Sch 2 Pt I para 5(b): see STATUTES vol 44(1) (Reissue) para 1383) land covered with water, and parts of houses or buildings: Compensation (Defence) Act 1939 s 17(1); Interpretation Act 1978 s 17(2)(a).

5　See the Compensation (Defence) Act 1939 s 3; and para 602 post.

6　See ibid s 4 (as amended); and para 603 post.

7　See ibid s 5; and para 604 post.

8　See ibid s 6; and para 605 post.

9　As to defence regulations generally see para 597 et seq ante.

10　As to prerogative powers in wartime see paras 510–511 ante; and CONSTITUTIONAL LAW AND HUMAN RIGHTS vol 8(2) (Reissue) para 811.

11　See the Compensation (Defence) Act 1939 s 17(1) (as amended: see note 1 supra). See also AVIATION vol 2 (Reissue) para 1657 et seq.

12　See ibid s 17(1) (as amended: see note 1 supra); and TELECOMMUNICATIONS.

13　For the meaning of 'United Kingdom' see para 502 note 4 ante.

14　See the Army Act 1955 ss 154, 165, 174. As to the requisitioning of aircraft see the Air Force Act 1955 s 172. See ROYAL FORCES vol 41 para 118 et seq.

15　See the Army Act 1955 s 158 (as amended), s 168, Sch 4 (as amended); and ROYAL FORCES vol 41 para 125.

16　See the Civil Aviation Act 1982 ss 62(1)(b), 63(1)(b); para 629 post; and AVIATION vol 2 (Reissue) para 1063 et seq.

601. Compensation in respect of taking possession of land; rental compensation.

The compensation payable in respect of the taking possession of any land[1] is the aggregate of the following sums:

(1)　a sum equal to the rent which might reasonably be expected to be payable by a tenant in occupation of the land, during the period for which possession of the land is retained in the exercise of emergency powers[2], under a lease granted immediately before the beginning of that period, whereby the tenant undertook to pay all usual tenant's rates and taxes and to bear the cost of the repairs and insurance and the other expenses, if any, necessary to maintain the land in a state to command that rent[3]; and

(2)　a sum equal to the cost of making good any damage to the land which may have occurred during the period for which possession is so retained (except in so far as the damage has been made good during that period by a person acting on behalf of the Crown), no account being taken of fair wear and tear[4] or of damage caused by war operations[5]; and,

(3)   in a case where the land is agricultural land[6], a sum equal to the amount (if any) which might reasonably have been expected to be payable in addition to rent by an incoming tenant, in respect of things previously done for the purpose of the cultivation of the land, and in respect of seeds, tillages, growing crops and other similar matters, under a lease of the land granted immediately before possession was taken of it in the exercise of emergency powers[7]; and

(4)   a sum equal to the amount of any expenses reasonably incurred otherwise than on behalf of the Crown, for the purpose of compliance with any directions given on behalf of the Crown in connection with the taking possession of the land[8].

In relation to rental compensation[9] in respect of the taking possession of land[10], the above provisions[11] have effect, as respects any period after 19 February 1948[12], subject to certain conditions[13]. Rental compensation must not in any case exceed the maximum applicable in that case[14]; and where the taking possession of land which gives rise to rental compensation occurred before 1 July 1948[15], the rental compensation must be assessed on the assumption that at all material times the land was subject to a permanent restriction[16] of development[17].

Where the requisitioned land[18] consists only of rent-restricted land[19], the rental compensation must not exceed the permissible rent[20].

Where the requisitioned land includes no rent-restricted land, the rental compensation must not exceed 160 per cent of what would be the amount, calculated by reference to the level of rental values obtaining in respect of comparable land at 31 March 1939, instead of by reference to the level obtaining immediately before possession of the land was taken, but otherwise in accordance with the Compensation (Defence) Act 1939 as originally enacted[21].

Where the requisitioned land consists partly of rent-restricted land and as to the remainder of other land, the amount (a) which would be the limit of rental compensation[22] if the requisitioned land consisted only of the rent-restricted land; and (b) which would be the limit of rental compensation for the whole of the requisitioned land if none of it were rent-restricted land, must be ascertained; and the rental compensation must not exceed the aggregate of the amount ascertained under head (a) above and so much of the amount ascertained under head (b) above as is properly apportionable to that part of the requisitioned land which is not rent-restricted land[23].

1   As to the meaning of 'land' see para 600 note 4 ante.
2   For the meaning of 'emergency powers' see para 600 note 1 ante.
3   Compensation (Defence) Act 1939 s 2(1)(a). Any compensation under head (1) in the text is considered as accruing due from day to day during the period for which the possession of the land is taken in the exercise of emergency powers, and is apportionable in respect of time accordingly, and must be paid to the person who for the time being would be entitled to occupy the land but for the fact that possession of it is retained in the exercise of such powers; but payments are not required to be made at intervals of less than three months: see s 2(2).

     For the purposes of the enactments relating to income tax any compensation under head (1) in the text is deemed to be rent payable for the land, the Crown is deemed to pay it as tenant occupier, and the person receiving it is deemed to receive it as landlord: s 2(2) (amended by the Finance Act 1963 s 73(7), (8), Sch 13 Pt I, Sch 14 Pt VI).
4   'Fair wear and tear', in relation to any property possession of which is taken on behalf of the Crown or which is requisitioned on behalf of the Crown, means such fair wear and tear as might have been expected to occur but for the fact that possession of the property was so taken or that the property was so requisitioned, as the case may be: Compensation (Defence) Act 1939 s 17(1).
5   Ibid s 2(1)(b). 'War operations' means action taken by an enemy, or action taken in combating an enemy or in repelling an imagined attack by an enemy: s 17(1). Any compensation under head (2) in the text accrues due at the end of the period for which possession of the land is retained in the exercise of emergency powers, and must be paid to the person who is then the owner of the land: s 2(3). 'Owner'

means (1) in relation to land, the person who is receiving the rackrent of the land, whether on his own account or as agent or trustee for any other person, or who would so receive the rackrent of the land if it were let at a rackrent; or (2) in relation to any property other than land, the person entitled to sell the property, it being assumed not to be subject to any mortgage, pledge, lien or other similar obligation; and in this definition the expression 'rackrent' in relation to any property means a rent which is not less than two-thirds of the rent at which the property might reasonably be expected to be let from year to year, free from all usual tenant's rates and taxes, and deducting the probable average annual cost of the repairs, insurance and other expenses (if any) necessary to maintain the same in a state to command such rent: Public Health Act 1936 s 343 (amended by the Statute Law (Repeals) Act 1993 s 1(1), Sch 1 Pt XIV; and applied by the Compensation (Defence) Act 1939 s 17(1)).

Where the damage in respect of which a sum is payable under s 2(1)(b) consists wholly or in part of the removal of fixed machinery or plant, such reduction, if any, in that compensation must be made as may appear to the Lands Tribunal to be just having regard to the way in which the machinery or plant has been dealt with, the likelihood of the machinery or plant being in fact replaced on the land and the reasonableness of replacing it, and any other circumstances which may appear to the tribunal to be relevant; provided that this does not authorise the making of any reduction if it would be inconsistent with any provision of any agreement (see s 15; and para 607 post): Requisitioned Land and War Works Act 1945 s 47. This provision originally referred to the General Claims Tribunal, but that tribunal was abolished and its jurisdiction transferred to the Lands Tribunal by the Land Powers (Defence) Act 1958 s 22. As to the Lands Tribunal see COMPULSORY ACQUISITION OF LAND vol 8(1) (Reissue) para 202 et seq.

The compulsory purchase price of land in the state in which it was when compensation accrued due under the Compensation (Defence) Act 1939 s 2(1)(b) must be calculated without regard to (a) war damage occurring during the period for which possession of the land was retained; or (b) any work done during that period in respect of which on such a compulsory acquisition the Requisitioned Land and War Works Act 1945 s 41(2), (3) (repealed) would apply: Requisitioned Land and War Works Act 1948 s 10(3)(a), (b). However, notwithstanding anything in the Requisitioned Land and War Works Act 1945 s 41 (repealed) regard must be had in calculating the price to all other damage occurring or work done on the land during that period: Requisitioned Land and War Works Act 1948 s 10(3).

Where, during the period for which possession of the land was retained, damage other than war damage occurred to any such work as is mentioned in head (b) supra, the amount to which the compensation is limited by virtue of s 10(1) (repealed) must be increased so as to take account of that damage to such extent as may be just having regard to any such expense, agreement or payment as is mentioned in the Requisitioned Land and War Works Act 1945 s 41(2), (3): Requisitioned Land and War Works Act 1948 s 10(4).

6 'Agricultural land' means any land used as arable, meadow or pasture land, land used for a plantation or a wood or for the growth of saleable underwood, or land used for the purpose of poultry farming, market gardens, nursery grounds, orchards or allotments, including allotment gardens within the meaning of the Allotments Act 1922: Compensation (Defence) Act 1939 s 17(1).

7 Ibid s 2(1)(c). Any compensation under head (3) in the text accrues due at the time when possession of the land is taken in the exercise of emergency powers, and must be paid to the person who, immediately before that time, was the occupier of the land: s 2(4).

8 Ibid s 2(1)(d). Any compensation under head (4) in the text accrues due at the time when the expenses in respect of which the compensation is payable are incurred, and must be paid to the person by whom or on whose behalf those expenses were incurred: s 2(5).

9 Ie compensation calculated in accordance with ibid s 2(1)(a) by reference to the rent which might reasonably be expected to be payable by a tenant in occupation of the land: see the Requisitioned Land and War Works Act 1948 s 7(1).

10 Where possession of any land is or has been retained in exercise of the right conferred by the Requisitioned Land and War Works Act 1945 s 28(2) (repealed) on the determination of some other right not conferred by emergency powers, the Requisitioned Land and War Works Act 1948 ss 7, 8, 10 apply as if possession had been taken on the determination of that other right: s 7(3). The Requisitioned Land and War Works Act 1945 s 28(2) (repealed) provided that any minister might retain or authorise the retention of any land in his possession or in that of any person who was occupying or using it under his authority, notwithstanding the determination of any other right to it.

'Emergency powers' means emergency powers for the purposes of the Compensation (Defence) Act 1939 (see para 600 note 1 ante), exercised during the war period or, in the case of powers conferred by the Requisitioned Land and War Works Act 1945, during any period during which those powers are exercisable; and the 'war period' means the period during which the Emergency Powers (Defence) Act 1939 (repealed) was in force: Requisitioned Land and War Works Act 1945 s 59(1). The Emergency Powers (Defence) Act 1939 (repealed) came into operation on 24 August 1939 and expired on 24 February 1946. For certain provisions the war period was extended, but the relevant date now for the end of the war period for the purposes of the 1945 Act (except for any purposes for which that period had come to an end before 7 July 1958) is 31 December 1958: Land Powers (Defence) Act 1958 s 1(2).

11   Ie the Compensation (Defence) Act 1939 s 2. As to whether any appreciation of value due to the emergency should be taken into consideration see s 2(1)(i) proviso (repealed); and the Requisitioned Land and War Works Act 1948 s 7(2).

12   Ie the commencement of the Requisitioned Land and War Works Act 1948.

13   Ie the provisions of ibid s 7: s 7(1).

14   Ie under ibid s 8: see the text and notes 18–23 infra.

15   Ie the appointed day for the purposes of the Town and Country Planning Act 1947 (repealed). See now the Town and Country Planning Act 1990 s 55(6), Sch 3; the Interpretation Act 1978 s 17(2)(a). See also TOWN AND COUNTRY PLANNING vol 46 (Reissue) para 703 et seq.

16   Ie such a restriction as is specified in the Town and Country Planning Act 1947 s 55(3) (repealed). See note 15 supra.

17   Requisitioned Land and War Works Act 1948 s 7(2).

18   'Requisitioned land' means the aggregate of the land in respect of which, in any case, rental compensation falls to be assessed: ibid s 8(4).

19   'Rent-restricted land' means land consisting of one or more rent-restricted properties or parts thereof and of no other land: ibid s 8(4). 'Rent-restricted property' means a property, whether or not the subject of a tenancy, in the case of which the following conditions are fulfilled: (1) that immediately before the time when possession was taken of the whole or part of the property in question the property or part was being used for residential purposes, or if it was not then being used that it had been used for residential purposes when last used before that time; and (2) that if an unfurnished tenancy of the property had been granted immediately before that time, the amount of the rent recoverable under the tenancy would have been restricted by the Rent and Mortgage Interest Restrictions Acts 1920 to 1939 (consolidated by the Rent Act 1968: see now the Rent Act 1977; the Interpretation Act 1978 s 17(2)(a); and LANDLORD AND TENANT): Requisitioned Land and War Works Act 1948 s 8(4). 'Unfurnished tenancy' means a tenancy under which a property is let for residential purposes, not being a tenancy where the application of the Rent and Mortgage Interest Restrictions Acts 1920 to 1939 (see supra) is excluded by reason of the property being let at a rent including payments in respect of board, attendance or use of furniture: Requisitioned Land and War Works Act 1948 s 8(4).

20   Ibid s 8(1). 'Permissible rent' means (1) in relation to a rent-restricted property, the maximum rent which would in accordance with the Rent and Mortgage Interest Restrictions Acts 1920 to 1939 (see note 19 supra) have been recoverable under the tenancy referred to in head (2) of the definition of rent-restricted property in note 19 supra, on the assumption that the tenant undertook to pay all usual tenant's rates and taxes and to bear the cost of the repairs and insurance and the other expenses if any, necessary to maintain the property in a state to command that rent; (2) in relation to part of a rent-restricted property, so much of the maximum rent as is properly apportionable to it: Requisitioned Land and War Works Act 1948 s 8(4).

21   Ibid s 8(2).

22   Ie under ibid s 8(1).

23   Ibid s 8(3).

602. Compensation in respect of doing work on land.

Compensation[1] under the Compensation (Defence) Act 1939 in respect of the doing of any work on any land[2] is payable only if the annual value of the land is diminished by reason of the doing of the work[3]. If, at any time after such compensation has become payable by reason of the doing of any work on any land, a person acting on behalf of the Crown (1) causes the land to be restored, so far as practicable, to the condition in which it would be but for the doing of the work; or (2) serves on the person for the time being entitled to occupy the land a written notice[4] of intention to discharge the liability for the compensation by making, not earlier than a date specified in the notice, payment of a lump sum in accordance with the statutory provisions[5], the period in respect of which compensation is payable by reason of the doing of the work ends with the date immediately preceding the date on which the restoration is completed or, as the case may be, the date specified in the notice[6]. However, no compensation, in relation to any land, is payable under these provisions in respect of any period for which possession of that land is taken on behalf of the Crown in the exercise of emergency powers[7].

The doing on any land of work to which these provisions apply is treated as a single operation with the doing of any other such work, whether before or after, except (a) work done before in respect of which any person has[8] become entitled to receive from the Crown a lump sum by way of compensation; and (b) work done before consisting of the construction of works in respect of which an amount has been paid to the minister[9]; and, on the doing of the later work, any award by the Lands Tribunal[10] of compensation in respect of the earlier work may, except as respects compensation accruing before the doing of the later work, be varied accordingly on the application of the Crown or of any other interested person[11].

1   The compensation so payable is, in the first instance, a sum calculated by reference to the diminution of the annual value of the land ascribable to the doing of the work, and must be paid in instalments, quarterly in arrears, to the person who for the time being is entitled to occupy the land: Compensation (Defence) Act 1939 s 3(2). Any compensation under this provision is considered as accruing due from day to day, and is apportionable in respect of time accordingly: s 3(2). 'Annual value' means, in relation to any land, the rent at which the land might reasonably be expected to be let from year to year, if the tenant undertook to pay all usual tenant's rates and taxes and to bear the costs of the repairs and insurance and other expenses, if any, necessary to maintain the land in a state to command that rent; and 'diminution of the annual value' means, in relation to the doing of any work on any land, the amount by which the annual value of the land is less than it would be if the work had not been done: s 3(9). In determining whether the annual value of any land is diminished by reason of the doing of any work on it, and in assessing any compensation under s 3 in respect of the doing of any work on any land, it must be assumed that the land cannot be restored to the condition in which it would be but for the doing of the work: s 3(6). This does not apply to compensation under s 3(4) (see note 6 infra): Requisitioned Land and War Works Act 1945 s 49. For the purposes of the Compensation (Defence) Act 1939 s 3, no account must be taken of any diminution or depreciation in value ascribable only to loss of pleasure or amenity: s 3(7).

     Nothing in s 3 applies to damage to land occurring while possession of the land is retained: Requisitioned Land and War Works Act 1948 s 11(2).

2   For the purposes of the Compensation (Defence) Act 1939 and the Requisitioned Land and War Works Act 1945, the 'doing of work on land' means the doing of any work on, over or below the surface of the land, and, in particular, includes the making of any erection or excavation, the placing of any thing, and the maintenance, removal, demolition, pulling down, destruction or rendering useless of any thing, on, over or below that surface: Compensation (Defence) Act 1939 s 17(2) (substituted by the Requisitioned Land and War Works Act 1945 s 50); Requisitioned Land and War Works Act 1945 s 59(2). As to the meaning of 'land' see para 600 note 4 ante.

3   Compensation (Defence) Act 1939 s 3(1).

4   Any notice which is required or authorised to be served by the Compensation (Defence) Act 1939 on any person may be served by post: s 16.

5   Ie the provisions contained in ibid s 3(4)

6   Ibid s 3(3). Where, by virtue of the operation of s 3(3) in relation to any work done on any land, the period in respect of which compensation under s 3(1) is payable by reason of the doing of the work comes to an end, then if, at the expiration of that period, the value of any estate or interest which a person then has in the land is less than it would be but for the doing of the work, there must be paid to him, by way of compensation, a sum equal to the amount of the depreciation in the value of the estate or interest; and that compensation is taken to accrue due at the expiration of that period: s 3(4).

     Where under s 3(4) any payment was made before 19 February 1948 in respect of a government oil pipeline or accessory works, the payment must be treated as a payment in respect of the estate or interest in question on account of the share attributable to that estate or interest of any compensation under the Requisitioned Land and War Works Act 1948 s 13(2), and interest under s 13(4) must be reduced accordingly; and after 19 February 1948 no payment under the Compensation (Defence) Act 1939 s 3(4) may be made in respect of a government oil pipeline or accessory works, whether it accrued due before or after 19 February 1948: Requisitioned Land and War Works Act 1948 s 13(5). As to government oil pipelines see para 620 post.

     However, in the case of a payment under the Compensation (Defence) Act 1939 s 3(4) which accrued due to any person before 19 February 1948 but has not been made before that date, that person is entitled to interest on the payment in accordance with the provisions of that Act as from the date when the payment accrued due until 19 February 1948: Requisitioned Land and War Works Act 1948 s 13(5) proviso.

As soon as may be after effecting any restoration or serving any notice in pursuance of the Compensation (Defence) Act 1939 s 3(3), the person by whom the restoration was effected or the notice was served must cause the fact of the restoration or the contents of the notice, as the case may be, to be published in such manner as he thinks best adapted for informing persons affected: s 3(5).

7   Ibid s 3(8).

8   Ie by virtue of ibid s 3(3) or by virtue of any agreement: see the Requisitioned Land and War Works Act 1945 s 48(1).

9   Ie under ibid Pt II (ss 4–14) (repealed) in pursuance of a report of the War Works Commission. The War Works Commission was established under s 1(1), and later dissolved by the War Works Commission (Dissolution) Order 1964, SI 1964/1578.

'Minister' means a minister of the Crown and includes the Commissioners of Works, the Board of Trade and the Board of Education, but does not include a minister of Northern Ireland: Requisitioned Land and War Works Act 1945 s 59(1) (amended by the Defence (Transfer of Functions) (No 1) Order 1964, SI 1964/488, art 2, Sch 1 Pt II). The functions and property of the Commissioners of Works under the 1945 Act are now vested in the Secretary of State: see the Secretary of State for the Environment Order 1970, SI 1970/1681 (partly revoked). As to the Board of Trade generally see CONSTITUTIONAL LAW AND HUMAN RIGHTS vol 8(2) (Reissue) para 505; TRADE, INDUSTRY AND INDUSTRIAL RELATIONS vol 47 (Reissue) para 2. The functions and property of the Board of Education are now vested in the Secretary of State for Education and Employment: see the Education Act 1944 s 2(1); the Secretary of State for Education and Science Order 1964, SI 1964/490; the Transfer of Functions (Science) Order 1992, SI 1992/1296; and the Transfer of Functions (Education and Employment) Order 1995, SI 1995/2986.

10   As to the jurisdiction of the Lands Tribunal see para 601 note 5 ante. As to the Lands Tribunal generally see COMPULSORY ACQUISITION OF LAND vol 8(1) (Reissue) para 202 et seq.

11   Requisitioned Land and War Works Act 1945 s 48(1). However, the power to vary awards conferred by s 48(1) does not apply to any award made before the passing of the Requisitioned Land and War Works Act 1945 in respect of any land, unless further work to which the Compensation (Defence) Act 1939 s 3 applies has been done on that land since the doing of the latest work to which the award relates: Requisitioned Land and War Works Act 1945 s 48(1) proviso.

Where, during the war period, any works have been constructed or other thing has been placed in, on or over any land by or by arrangement with a minister otherwise than in the exercise of emergency powers, then, unless it has been expressly agreed that the Crown is to have no interest in the works or the thing so constructed or placed, or the works or thing have or has been so constructed or placed in the exercise of powers conferred by any statute, s 48(1) has effect as if the construction or placing were work done on the land in the exercise of emergency powers: s 48(2). For the meaning of the 'war period' and 'emergency powers' see para 601 note 10 ante.

603. Transports and certain machinery. The compensation payable under the Compensation (Defence) Act 1939 for the requisition[1] in the exercise[2] of emergency powers[3] of any vessel[4], vehicle or aircraft[5] or excavator, crane or agricultural implement or agricultural, mining or quarrying machinery is the aggregate of five sums or such of them as are applicable in the circumstances[6]. These are:

(1)   a sum equal to the charge which might reasonably be expected to have been payable by a person during the period of the requisition under a charter or contract of hiring for the requisition period on the terms that he should be responsible for insurance, maintenance and running costs[7];

(2)   if an agreement was made by the Crown for the running of the vessel etc by the person who, but for the requisition, would have been entitled to possession or who is the owner[8], a sum equal to any maintenance and running expenses reasonably incurred by him during the requisition period and not taken into account under head (1) above[9];

(3)   a sum equal to the cost of making good any damage[10] (other than fair wear and tear[11]) not resulting in total loss occurring during the requisition period and not made good by the Crown[12];

(4)   in the case of total loss occurring during the requisition period, a sum equal to the value of the requisitioned property immediately prior to the damage causing the loss[13]; and

(5) a sum equal to any reasonable expenses incurred, otherwise than on behalf of the Crown, in complying with directions given on behalf of the Crown in connection with the requisition[14].

Any compensation payable under head (1) above is deemed to accrue from day to day during the period of requisition and is apportionable in respect of time accordingly, and is payable to the person who, at the time when it accrues, is the owner of the requisitioned property[15], who is, however, deemed to receive it as trustee for any person who by virtue of a subsisting charter or hiring contract would have been entitled to possession or use of the property but for the requisition[16].

So much of the compensation as amounts to the refund of expenses[17] accrues when the expenses in question are incurred, and is payable to the person by or on behalf of whom those expenses were incurred[18]. Compensation for damage or total loss[19] accrues at the end of the requisition period, and is payable to the owner of the property damaged or destroyed[20].

For these purposes 'total loss' has the same meaning as in insurance law and accordingly includes 'constructive total loss'[21], and upon payment of compensation for total loss[22] the Crown has rights similar to those of an insurer who has paid under a contract of insurance[23].

The compensation payable for the acquisition of property[24] of the kinds described is a sum equal to the value of that property immediately before the acquisition, no account being taken either of any appreciation due to emergency or of any compensation under head (1) or head (3) above which may have become payable in respect of the requisition of the property, and is payable to the person who is then the owner[25].

1   For the meaning of 'requisition' see para 600 note 3 ante.
2   As to the meaning of 'exercise' see para 600 note 1 ante.
3   For the meaning of 'emergency powers' see para 600 note 1 ante.
4   'Vessel' and 'ship' have the same meaning as 'ship' in the Merchant Shipping Act 1995: Compensation (Defence) Act 1939 s 17(1) (amended by the Merchant Shipping Act 1995 s 314(2), Sch 13 para 18). As to compensation for the requisition of vessels under repealed legislation see *Re Mersey Docks and Harbour Board and Admiralty Comrs* [1920] 3 KB 223, DC; *Brooke v R* [1921] 2 KB 110; *Elliott Steam Tug Co Ltd v Shipping Controllers* [1922] 1 KB 127, CA; *Federated Coal and Shipping Co Ltd v R* [1922] 2 KB 42; *A-G v Royal Mail Steam Packet Co* [1922] 2 AC 279, HL; *Moss SS Co v Board of Trade* [1924] AC 133, HL. As to the prerogative power to requisition ships see para 511 ante.
5   'Aircraft' means any flying machine, glider or airship or any balloon, whether fixed or free: Compensation (Defence) Act 1939 s 17(1).
6   Ibid s 4(1). The references in s 4 to 'excavator, crane or agricultural implement or agricultural, mining or quarrying machinery' were added by the Defence (General) Regulations 1939, SR & O 1939/927, reg 79C (added by SR & O 1941/1153 and amended by SR & O 1942/1279). Although the Defence (General) Regulations 1939 reg 79C was revoked by the Defence Regulations (No 3) Order 1950, SI 1950/182, it would appear that by virtue of the Interpretation Act 1978 s 16(1), Sch 2 para 3 (as applied by the Defence (General) Regulations 1939 reg 99B (now lapsed)) the revocation did not affect the amendments made by the Defence (General) Regulations 1939 reg 79C.
7   Compensation (Defence) Act 1939 s 4(1)(a). Compensation under this head is commonly referred to as 'the bareboat element': see *Port Line Ltd v Ben Line Steamers Ltd* [1958] 2 QB 146, [1958] 1 All ER 787. In computing what would be reasonable hiring charges, no account is to be taken of any appreciation in value due to the emergency: Compensation (Defence) Act 1939 s 4(1) proviso (i).
8   For the meaning of 'owner' see para 601 note 5 ante.
9   Compensation (Defence) Act 1939 s 4(1)(b).
10   No compensation will be payable in respect of any loss of or damage to any vehicle or aircraft arising in consequence of war operations unless it is shown that, at the time when the loss or damage occurred, the risk of the vehicle or aircraft being lost or damaged in consequence of war operations was materially increased by reason of their requisition in the exercise of emergency powers: ibid s 4(1) proviso (ii). For the meaning of 'war operations' see para 601 note 5 ante. No compensation will by virtue of head (3) in the text be payable in respect of any damage, if compensation in respect of expenses incurred for the purpose of making good that damage has accrued due by virtue of head (2) in the text: s 4(1) proviso (iii).

11 For the meaning of 'fair wear and tear' see para 601 note 4 ante. For the comparable position under the Army Act 1955 see s 168(1)(b).
12 Compensation (Defence) Act 1939 s 4(1)(c).
13 Ibid s 4(1)(d).
14 Ibid s 4(1)(e).
15 Ibid s 4(2). Payments under this provision are not to be required at intervals of less than one month: s 4(2).
16 Ibid s 4(3). See also *Port Line Ltd v Ben Line Steamers Ltd* [1958] 2 QB 146, [1958] 1 All ER 787. As to the apportionment of compensation in cases where the property is subject to a hire purchase agreement see HIRE PURCHASE AND CONSUMER CREDIT vol 22 paras 19, 257.
17 Ie compensation under heads (2), (5) in the text.
18 Compensation (Defence) Act 1939 s 4(4). Payments under this provision are not to be required at intervals of less than one month: s 4(4).
19 Ie compensation under heads (3)–(4) in the text.
20 Compensation (Defence) Act 1939 s 4(5).
21 As to total loss and constructive total loss see INSURANCE vol 25 (Reissue) para 282 et seq.
22 Ie compensation under head (4) in the text.
23 See the Compensation (Defence) Act 1939 s 4(6). These rights are to take over any interest in whatever remains of the property and all such rights and remedies in and in respect of the property as the Crown would have had if the payment had been made by the Crown as insurer under a contract of insurance against loss: see s 4(6).
24 As to the date treated as the date of acquisition or sale for the purposes of compensation and as to notice of sale see ibid s 4(8), (9).
25 Ibid s 4(7).

604. Taking space or accommodation in ships and aircraft. The compensation payable for taking space or accommodation in a ship or aircraft[1] is the aggregate of the following sums:

(1) a sum equal to the amount which might reasonably be expected to be payable for the use of that space or accommodation during the period for which it is taken, no account being taken of any appreciation in value due to the emergency[2]; and

(2) a sum equal to the amount of any expenses reasonably incurred, otherwise than on behalf of the Crown, in complying with directions given on behalf of the Crown in connection with the taking of the space or accommodation[3].

Any part of the compensation payable under head (1) is deemed to accrue from day to day during the period for which the space or accommodation is taken and is apportionable in respect of time accordingly[4]. This part of the compensation is payable to the person who is the owner[5] of the ship or aircraft at the time when the compensation accrues[6], but no payment can be required before the end of the above mentioned period[7]. Any part of the compensation which is payable under head (2) accrues at the time when the expenses in respect of which the compensation is payable are incurred and is payable to the person by or on behalf of whom they were incurred[8].

1 For the purposes of the Compensation (Defence) Act 1939 s 1, the taking of such space or accommodation is deemed to be a requisition of property: see s 1(2). For the meaning of 'requisition' see para 600 note 3 ante. As to the meaning of 'ship' see para 603 note 4 ante. For the meaning of 'aircraft' see para 603 note 5 ante. As to compensation generally see para 600 note ante.
2 Ibid s 5(1)(a). As to the period of the emergency see para 600 note 2 ante.
3 Ibid s 5(1)(b). Disputes as to the payment of compensation for the taking of space or accommodation in vessels are referred to the Shipping Claims Tribunal: see para 606 note 1 post; and SHIPPING.
4 Ibid s 5(2).
5 For the meaning of 'owner' see para 601 note 5 ante.
6 Where a person other than the owner is entitled to possession of, or to use, the ship or aircraft under a subsisting charter or hiring agreement or is, by virtue of a subsisting contract, the person who would have been entitled to use the space or accommodation if it had not been taken on behalf of the Crown, the owner receives the part of the compensation payable under head (1) as trustee for that person: Compensation (Defence) Act 1939 s 5(3).
7 Ibid s 5(2).
8 Ibid s 5(4).

605. Goods other than transports and certain machinery. The compensation payable in respect of the requisition[1] or acquisition of goods[2] other than vessels[3], vehicles, aircraft[4] and certain specified types of plant and machinery[5] is a sum equal to their market price[6], having regard to their condition at the time but no account being taken of any appreciation in value due to the emergency[7]. In the case of requisition or acquisition from an owner[8] who had produced the goods[9] with a view to sale, the compensation is not to exceed the reasonable cost of production and the profit which he might reasonably have been expected to make on a sale immediately before the requisition or acquisition, and, in the case of requisition or acquisition from an owner who bought the goods with a view to resale, the compensation is not to exceed the price which it was reasonable for him to pay and the profit which he might reasonably have been expected to make on a resale immediately before the requisition[10]. Except in these two cases no account is to be taken of any profit which might have been made on a sale of the goods[11]. Where at the date of requisition or acquisition the price or maximum price at which the goods might be sold was fixed by law, the compensation is limited to a sum not exceeding that price or maximum price[12].

The compensation payable includes a sum equal to the amount of any expenses reasonably incurred, otherwise than on behalf of the Crown, in complying with any directions given by or on behalf of the Crown in connection with the requisition or acquisition[13].

1 For the meaning of 'requisition' see para 600 note 3 ante.
2 'Goods' means chattels other than vessels, vehicles and aircraft: Compensation (Defence) Act 1939 s 17(1).
3 As to the meaning of 'vessel' see para 603 note 4 ante.
4 For the meaning of 'aircraft' see para 603 note 5 ante. As to the requisitioning of aircraft see para 600 note 14 ante.
5 Ie goods other than those in respect of which compensation is assessed under the Compensation (Defence) Act 1939 s 4 (see para 603 ante).
6 Ie the sum which the owner might reasonably have been expected to obtain upon a sale of the goods immediately before the requisition or acquisition: see ibid s 6(1).
7 Ibid s 6(1). Compensation accrues at the time of requisition or acquisition and, subject to certain statutory provisions, is payable to the then owner of the goods: see s 6(4). As to the situation where such goods are deemed free of mortgage, pledge or lien see s 14; and para 608 note 8 post. As to the determination of disputes as to the payment of compensation see para 606 note 1 post.
8 For the meaning of 'owner' see para 601 note 5 ante.
9 This includes the personal representative or successor in business of the actual producer: see the Compensation (Defence) Act 1939 s 6(2).
10 Ibid s 6(2)(a), (b).
11 See ibid s 6(2).
12 See ibid s 6(2) proviso.
13 Ibid s 6(3). Compensation under s 6(3) accrues at the time when the expenses are incurred and is payable to the person by or on behalf of whom they were incurred: s 6(5).

606. Tribunals for determining disputes. Any dispute as to whether any compensation is payable under the Compensation (Defence) Act 1939, or as to the amount of any compensation so payable, must, in default of agreement, be referred to, and determined by, the appropriate tribunal[1] whose decision is final; provided that at any stage in proceedings before it the tribunal may, and, if so directed by the High Court[2], must, state in the form of a special case for the opinion of that court any question of law arising in the course of the proceedings[3].

Each of the tribunals constituted under the Compensation (Defence) Act 1939 has the following powers:

(1) to make, with the concurrence of the Lord Chancellor, rules prescribing the procedure for notifying, presenting and hearing claims and all incidental matters[4];

(2) to order persons to attend and give evidence, and to produce and give discovery and inspection of documents, in like manner as in proceedings in the High Court[5];

(3) to award and assess, or direct the assessment of, such sums by way of costs as the tribunal in its discretion thinks just, and in particular to award costs to an unsuccessful claimant where such an award appears to the tribunal to be justified on the merits of the case[6];

(4) to call in the aid of one or more assessors specially qualified, and hear any claim wholly or partly with their assistance[7];

(5) to appoint an expert or experts to report on any matter material to the hearing of any claim[8];

(6) to determine, subject to the approval of the Treasury, the remuneration, if any, of such assessors and experts[9].

1   Disputes as to the payment of compensation for the requisition or acquisition of vessels or the taking of space or accommodation in vessels are referred to the Shipping Claims Tribunal: see the Compensation (Defence) Act 1939 s 8(1), (2). The remuneration and expenses of this tribunal are defrayed out of moneys provided by Parliament: see s 8(5). In the case of aircraft and property other than vessels, disputes are now referred to the Lands Tribunal: see s 8(3), (4) (repealed); and para 601 note 5 ante. As to the meaning of 'vessel' see para 603 note 4 ante. As to the Lands Tribunal generally see COMPULSORY ACQUISITION OF LAND vol 8(1) (Reissue) para 202 et seq.
2   The 'High Court' means the High Court of Justice in England: ibid s 17(1).
3   Ibid s 7.
4   Ibid s 9(1)(a). Rules made under head (1) in the text may contain provisions authorising a tribunal to take into consideration any matter which the tribunal considers relevant to the subject of the inquiry before it, notwithstanding that the matter is not admissible in evidence under the law relating to evidence: s 9(2). See further EVIDENCE.
5   Ibid s 9(1)(b). The High Court has, for the purposes of, and in relation to, any proceedings under the Compensation (Defence) Act 1939, the same power of making orders in respect of any of the matters specified in head (2) in the text as it has for the purpose of and in relation to an action or matter in that court: s 9(3).
6   Ibid s 9(1)(c).
7   Ibid s 9(1)(d).
8   Ibid s 9(1)(e).
9   Ibid s 9(1)(f).

607. Compensation payable. Any compensation under the Compensation (Defence) Act 1939 carries interest, as from the date on which it accrues due until payment, at such rate not exceeding five per cent per annum as the Treasury may from time to time by order prescribe[1]. All forms of compensation may be made the subject of an agreement in lieu of being ascertained under the statutory provisions[2].

No claim for any compensation may be entertained unless notice[3] of the claim has been given to the prescribed[4] authority within the requisite period[5]. No person is entitled to compensation in respect of the acquisition on behalf of the Crown of any currency, gold or securities, or in respect of the taking control on behalf of the Crown of any railway undertaking or any undertaking carried on by any person by whom a railway undertaking is carried on, or of any part of such an undertaking[6]. No compensation is payable to any person in respect of any loss of, or damage to, property, if and so far as (1) he has become entitled[7], to recover any sum by way of damages or indemnity; or (2) he is, at the time of the loss or damage, required under any contract with the Crown to be insured for such loss or damage[8].

1   Compensation (Defence) Act 1939 s 10. See eg the Interest on Compensation (Defence) Order 1940, SR & O 1940/107 (prescribing a rate of 2%). As to the basis of assessment of compensation see generally COMPULSORY ACQUISITION OF LAND vol 8(1) (Reissue) para 233 et seq.

2   See the Compensation (Defence) Act 1939 s 15.

3   As to the service of notices see para 602 note 4 ante.

4   Ie prescribed by rules made by the Treasury: Compensation (Defence) Act 1939 s 17(1).

5   See ibid s 11.

6   Ibid s 12(1).

7   Ie apart from the provisions of the Compensation (Defence) Act 1939.

8   Ibid s 12(2).

608. Property subject to hire-purchase agreements, mortgages or pledges. In a case where any property, in respect of the requisition[1] or acquisition of which compensation is required to be paid to the person who is the owner of the property immediately before the requisition or acquisition, is then in the possession of some other person by virtue of a hire-purchase agreement[2] or a conditional sale agreement[3], that person may[4], in relation to the making of any claim for compensation by the owner, make a claim to have the compensation apportioned[5]. In default of agreement between the parties, the latter claim must be referred to the tribunal[6] which has jurisdiction in the matter of any such claim by the owner, and that tribunal may apportion the compensation between the two parties[7].

Where any sum by way of compensation is paid in accordance with any provisions requiring compensation to be paid to the owner of any property, then, if at the time when the compensation accrues due, the property is subject to any mortgage, pledge, lien or other similar obligation, the sum so paid is deemed to be comprised in that mortgage, pledge, lien or other obligation[8].

1   For the meaning of 'requisition' see para 600 note 3 ante.

2   'Hire-purchase agreement' means an agreement which is a consumer credit agreement within the meaning of the Consumer Credit Act 1974, other than a conditional sale agreement, under which (1) goods are bailed or (in Scotland) hired in return for periodical payments by the person to whom they are bailed or hired; and (2) the property in the goods will pass to that person if the terms of the agreement are complied with and one or more of the following occurs: (a) the exercise of an option to purchase by that person; (b) the doing of any other specified act by any party to the agreement; (c) the happening of any other specified event: Compensation (Defence) Act 1939 s 17(1) (amended by the Consumer Credit Act 1974 s 192(3), Sch 4 para 8).

3   'Conditional sale agreement' means an agreement for the sale of goods which is a consumer credit agreement within the meaning of the Consumer Credit Act 1974 under which the purchase price or part of it is payable by instalments, and the property in the goods is to remain in the seller (notwithstanding that the buyer is to be in possession of the goods) until such conditions as to the payment of instalments or otherwise as may be specified in the agreement are fulfilled: Compensation (Defence) Act 1939 s 17(1) (as amended: see note 2 supra).

4   Ie by a notice given in the prescribed form and manner to the prescribed authority, within the requisite period: see ibid s 13. 'Prescribed' means prescribed by rules made by the Treasury: s 17(1). As to the service of notices see para 602 note 4 ante.

5   Ibid s 13.

6   As to tribunals for determining disputes as to compensation see para 606 ante.

7   Compensation (Defence) Act 1939 s 13.

8   Ibid s 14(1) (renumbered by the Statute Law (Repeals) Act 1989 s 1(2), Sch 2 para 10). Where any goods have been requisitioned in such circumstances as to give a right to compensation assessed under the Compensation (Defence) Act 1939 s 6 (see para 605 ante), the ownership of the goods is deemed to have vested in the Crown as from the time of requisition free from any mortgage, pledge, lien or similar obligation: s 14(2) (added by the Statute Law (Repeals) Act 1989 Sch 2 para 10). As to mortgages generally see MORTGAGES; as to pledges see PLEDGES AND PAWNS; and as to liens see LIEN.

(ii)   The Defence of the Realm (Acquisition of Land) Acts 1916 and 1920

609.   In general. Most of the powers conferred on government departments and the Crown relating to the treatment of requisitioned land[1] and war works in connection with the 1914–18 war have long since expired. However, certain provisions remain in force which relate to (1) the power to grant or demise land to a government department[2] in consideration of a fee farm or other rent[3]; (2) the use of land acquired under the power of acquisition[4]; (3) the disposition of land so acquired and the right of pre-emption of former owners[5]; (4) the maintenance of works laid on highways and the stopping up of highways[6]; and (5) the application of building laws to land occupied or acquired[7].

1   For the purposes of the Defence of the Realm (Acquisition of Land) Act 1916, and of the provisions of the Lands Clauses Acts incorporated with that Act, 'land' includes any building or part of a building, any pier, jetty, or other structure on the shore or bed of the sea or any river, and any easement or right over or in relation to land: Defence of the Realm (Acquisition of Land) Act 1916 s 12(1). For the purposes of the 1916 Act, except where the context otherwise requires, 'building' includes machinery and plant fixed or attached to the building: s 12(3) (amended by the Statute Law (Repeals) Act 1953 (repealed)). Power to acquire land on behalf of the Crown was conferred by the Defence of the Realm (Acquisition of Land) Act 1916 s 3(1)–(6) (repealed). As to the Lands Clauses Acts see COMPULSORY ACQUISITION OF LAND vol 8(1) (Reissue) para 11 et seq.

2   For these purposes a competent naval or military authority acting under the Acts relating to the defence of the realm is deemed to be a government department: Defence of the Realm (Acquisition of Land) Act 1916 s 12(5).

3   See ibid s 3(7); and para 610 post. As to fee farm rents see REAL PROPERTY vol 39 para 309; RENTCHARGES vol 39 para 1206.

4   See ibid s 4; and para 611 post.

5   See ibid s 5; and para 612 post.

6   See ibid s 6; and para 613 post.

7   See ibid s 11; and para 614 post.

610.   Grant or demise of land to a government department. Any person having power, whether subject to any consent or conditions or not, to sell land[1] authorised to be acquired by any government department[2] may, subject to the like consent and conditions, grant or demise the land in perpetuity or for any term of years to the government department at such fee farm or other rent[3], secured by such conditions of re-entry or otherwise as may be agreed, and with or without a right of renewal, or grant to the government department an option to acquire the land[4]. However, where the power to sell arises under the enactments relating to settled land[5], these powers must be exercised only with the consent of the trustees of the settlement for the purposes of those Acts, or with the sanction of the court[6].

Where possession has been taken of any land[7] under any agreement authorising the retention of the land for any period specified in the agreement, nothing in the Defence of the Realm (Acquisition of Land) Act 1916 authorises the retention of possession after the expiration of that period without the consent of the person with whom the agreement was made or the persons deriving title under him[8].

1   As to the meaning of 'land' see para 609 note 1 ante.

2   As to the meaning of 'government department' see para 609 note 2 ante. Power to acquire land on behalf of the Crown was conferred by the Defence of the Realm (Acquisition of Land) Act 1916 s 3(1)–(6) (repealed).

3   As to fee farm rents see REAL PROPERTY vol 39 para 309; RENTCHARGES vol 39 para 1206.

4   Defence of the Realm (Acquisition of Land) Act 1916 s 3(7).

5   Ie the Settled Lands Acts 1882 to 1890 (repealed and replaced by the Settled Land Act 1925): see SETTLEMENTS vol 42 para 675.

6   Defence of the Realm (Acquisition of Land) Act 1916 s 3(7) proviso.

7   For these purposes, the exercise or enjoyment of any easement or right over or in relation to land is deemed to be possession of that easement or right: see the Defence of the Realm (Acquisition of Land) Act 1920 s 6 (as amended).

8   Defence of the Realm (Acquisition of Land) Act 1916 s 13(3).

611. Use of land acquired under power of acquisition. Any land[1] which, or an interest in which, was acquired under the Defence of the Realm (Acquisition of Land) Act 1916 may be used by any government department[2] for the purpose for which it was used during the war or for any other purpose for which it could have been used had the land been acquired under the Defence Acts 1842 to 1873[3] or the Military Lands Acts 1892 to 1903[4], notwithstanding that such user could, but for the Defence of the Realm (Acquisition of Land) Act 1916, have been restrained as being in contravention of any covenant or for any other reason[5]. No one interested in any adjoining or neighbouring land or entitled to any riparian rights is entitled to restrain such user; but if any such person would otherwise[6] have been entitled to restrain such user, then, if application is made within three years after the date of the acquisition of the land or after the commencement of the user causing the depreciation, whichever is the later, he is entitled (1) if the land is used for a purpose for which it could have been used had the land been acquired under the Defence Acts 1842 to 1873, or the Military Lands Acts 1892 to 1903, to compensation[7] in respect of any breach of a restrictive covenant or damage caused by the pollution, abstraction, or diversion of water, or by the emission of noxious fumes[8]; and (2) if the land is used for any other purpose, to compensation in respect of any damage occasioned by such user[9].

However, where such compensation is claimed in respect of any land, the department may, at any time before the claim is determined, and on payment of all costs properly incurred by the claimant in respect of his claim, require the claimant to sell the land or his interest in it at such price as would have been proper if the value of the land had not been so depreciated[10]. These provisions do not deprive any one of the right to recover damages in respect of any injury to property caused by accident due to such user[11].

1   As to the meaning of 'land' see para 609 note 1 ante. Power to acquire land on behalf of the Crown was conferred by the Defence of the Realm (Acquisition of Land) Act 1916 s 3(1)–(6) (repealed).

2   As to the meaning of 'government department' see para 609 note 2 ante.

3   As to the Defence Acts 1842 to 1873 see ROYAL FORCES vol 41 para 117.

4   As to the Military Lands Acts 1892 to 1903 see ROYAL FORCES vol 41 para 111.

5   Defence of the Realm (Acquisition of Land) Act 1916 s 4.

6   Ie apart from the Defence of the Realm (Acquisition of Land) Act 1916.

7   In default of agreement, the compensation is to be determined by the Lands Tribunal: see ibid ss 4(i), (ii), 8 (repealed); the Railway and Canal Commission (Abolition) Act 1949 s 3(1); and the Lands Tribunal Act 1949 s 1(3)(a)(i). As to the Lands Tribunal see COMPULSORY ACQUISITION OF LAND vol 8(1) (Reissue) para 202 et seq.

8   Defence of the Realm (Acquisition of Land) Act 1916 s 4(i).

9   Ibid s 4(ii).

10 Ibid s 4(a).

11 Ibid s 4(b).

612. Disposition of land acquired and right of pre-emption. Where any land[1], or any interest in land, has been acquired by any government department[2], the department may at any time thereafter sell, lease, or otherwise dispose of the land or interest[3].

Where any such land is disposed of, then on the execution and delivery to the purchaser by the government department concerned of the necessary or proper assurance of the land disposed of, the purchaser, notwithstanding any defect in the title of the government department, stands possessed of such estate or interest as may be expressed or intended to be assured to him, freed and absolutely discharged from all prior interests; provided that if, at any time after such disposition, any such prior interest is established, compensation must be paid[4] with respect to interests in lands which by mistake have been omitted to be purchased[5].

Before any government department sells any such land it must, unless it is land on which permanent buildings[6] have been erected wholly or partly at the expense of the state or by arrangement with any government department or it is land used in connection with such buildings, first offer to sell[7] it to the person then entitled to the lands, if any, from which it was originally severed[8].

If any such person wishes to purchase such lands, then within six weeks after the offer he must notify the government department concerned; if he declines the offer, or if for six weeks he fails to notify the department of his intent to purchase the lands, his right of pre-emption ceases[9].

These provisions[10] apply in the case of a lease of land for a term exceeding 21 years in the same way as they apply to a sale of land, except where the land is leased for the purpose of its development in connection with any factory, building, camp, or other premises erected or established on land retained by the government[11].

Where land, or an interest in land[12], acquired under the Defence of the Realm (Acquisition of Land) Act 1916, was immediately before its acquisition subject to a restrictive covenant which before 4 November 1920 had lawfully been contravened, and the land or interest is disposed of in pursuance of the powers conferred by that Act[13], it may be disposed of free from the restriction imposed by the covenant[14]. Where, however, the covenant is one entered into for the protection and maintenance of any building scheme, or for the preservation of the amenities of any dwelling-house in the occupation of a person entitled to enforce the covenant, this provision does not apply unless the court[15] otherwise directs, on the application of the occupying department[16], and having regard to all the circumstance of the case[17].

Where any such land or interest is disposed of free from such restriction, no one has the right of enforcing the covenant against the person to whom the land or interest is disposed of or his successors in title; but if at any time after such disposition any person who would have had to enforce the covenant establishes such a right, compensation must be paid to him, and on payment of compensation the right is absolutely discharged as against him and all persons deriving title through him[18].

Where the land from which land acquired under the Defence of the Realm (Acquisition of Land) Act 1916 was severed is settled land[19], the tenant for life, or person having the powers of a tenant for life with respect to that land, is deemed[20] to be, and always to have been, the person entitled to the settled land[21].

The person by whom the right of pre-emption is or would for the time being be exercisable in respect of any land if a government department were offering that land for sale has power at any time to release that right so as to discharge in perpetuity the land, or any part of it to which the release relates, from all such right of pre-emption[22].

---

1   As to the meaning of 'land' see para 609 note 1 ante.

2   As to the meaning of 'government department' see para 609 note 2 ante. Power to acquire land on behalf of the Crown was conferred by the Defence of the Realm (Acquisition of Land) Act 1916 s 3(1)–(6) (repealed).

3   Ibid s 5(1).

4   Ie in accordance with the Lands Clauses Acts. As to the Lands Clauses Acts see COMPULSORY ACQUISITION OF LAND vol 8(1) (Reissue) para 11 et seq.

5   Defence of the Realm (Acquisition of Land) Act 1916 s 5(2).

6   As to the meaning of 'building' see para 609 note 1 ante.

7   If any person entitled to such pre-emption wishes to purchase any such lands, then, in the absence of agreement, the price or other consideration is to be determined in accordance with the Defence of the Realm (Acquisition of Land) Act 1916: see ss 5(5), 8 (repealed).

8   Ibid s 5(3) (amended by the Defence of the Realm (Acquisition of Land) Act 1920 s 2(1)).

9   Defence of the Realm (Acquisition of Land) Act 1916 s 5(4).

10   Ie ibid s 5(3) (as amended: see note 8 supra), s 5(4), (5).

11   Ibid s 5(6).

12   For these purposes the exercise or enjoyment of any easement or right over or in relation to land is deemed to be possession of that easement or right: Defence of the Realm (Acquisition of Land) Act 1920 s 6 (amended by the Statute Law Revision Act 1927).

13   Ie the Defence of the Realm (Acquisition of Land) Act 1916 s 5: see text and notes 1–11 supra.

14   Defence of the Realm (Acquisition of Land) Act 1920 s 1(1).

15   Ibid s 1(1) refers to the Railway and Canal Commission, but the commission was abolished and its functions are now exercised and performed by the High Court: see the Railway and Canal Commission (Abolition) Act 1949 s 1(1)(a).

16   'Government in possession' and 'occupying department' mean, and are deemed always to have meant, the government department for the time being in possession of land, notwithstanding that the department in possession is not the department by which or on whose behalf possession was originally taken, but is in possession by virtue of a transfer from that department or from some other department to which possession has subsequently been transferred: Defence of the Realm (Acquisition of Land) Act 1920 s 3(1)(b).

Where the occupying department has created or purported to create any tenancy or other interest in the land of which it is in possession in favour of some other person, or has allowed any other person to use or occupy that land, the occupying department is deemed to have continued in possession of the land, notwithstanding the interest of, or the use or occupation by, that other person: s 3(1)(c).

Possession by an occupying department is not deemed to have been affected or prejudiced by reason of the land or any part of it at any time ceasing or having ceased to be used for the purpose for which possession was originally taken, or otherwise being or having been used for any other purpose: s 3(1)(d).

17   Ibid s 1(1) proviso.

18   Ibid s 1(2). Compensation must be paid in accordance with the Lands Clauses Act with respect to interests in lands which have been omitted to be purchased: see the Defence of the Realm (Acquisition of Land) Act 1920 s 1(2). In assessing the compensation, the official arbitrator must take into consideration any compensation which may have been paid or be payable in respect of the covenant (ie under the Defence of the Realm (Acquisition of Land) Act 1916 s 4: see para 611 ante); and any compensation payable under these provisions is paid out of moneys provided by Parliament, but the sum to be expended must not exceed £50,000: Defence of the Realm (Acquisition of Land) Act 1920 s 1(2) proviso. The official arbitrator is now the Lands Tribunal: see the Land Compensation Act 1961 s 1. As to the Lands Tribunal see COMPULSORY ACQUISITION OF LAND vol 8(1) (Reissue) para 202 et seq.

19   Ie within the meaning of the Settled Lands Acts 1882 to 1890 (repealed and replaced by the Settled Land Act 1925): see SETTLEMENTS vol 42 para 675.

20   Ie for the purposes of the Defence of the Realm (Acquisition of Land) Act 1916 s 5 and the Defence of the Realm (Acquisition of Land) Act 1920 s 2.

21   Ibid s 2(2).

22   Ibid s 2(3).

613. Maintenance of works and stopping up of highways. Where, in the exercise or purported exercise of any prerogative right[1] of the Crown or any powers conferred by or under any enactment relating to the defence of the realm, or by agreement, or otherwise, for purposes connected with the 1914–18 war, any railway, tramway, cable line or pipes have been laid along, across, over, or under any public highway[2], it is lawful after the termination of the war for the railway etc to continue to be used and maintained along, across, over or under the highway, subject to such conditions as the Secretary of State[3], in the case of railways and tramways, and in other cases as the court[4] may by order prescribe, after giving the local authority[5] and the authority or person responsible for the maintenance of the highway or of any other railway or tramway laid on it an opportunity of being heard, and any such authority or person may apply to the Secretary of State or the court to make such an order[6]. However, where any such railway or tramway crosses the roadway on the level it is not lawful to use the crossing without the consent of the local authority[7].

In the event of the use of any such railway or tramway being discontinued, the government department[8] by which it was laid down or used must take up and remove the rails and restore the highway on which they are laid to the satisfaction of the authority or person responsible for the maintenance of that highway[9].

Where in exercise of any such right or powers any public highway was closed, it may be kept closed but only if the consent of the court is obtained[10]. Before giving such consent the court must give to the local authority and the authority or person responsible for the maintenance of the highway an opportunity of being heard, and may require as a condition of its consent the provision of another highway in the place of the highway closed; and any person interested in any land[11] adjoining any highway so closed who suffers loss or damage in consequence of its closing is entitled to such compensation as, in default of agreement, may be determined in accordance with the Defence of the Realm (Acquisition of Land) Act 1916 to be the amount of the loss or damage[12].

Where any such railway etc has been laid along, across, over, or under any public highway, or a public highway has been closed, in pursuance of an agreement with, or subject to any undertaking given to, the authority or person responsible for the maintenance of the highway, nothing in these provisions authorises the continuance of the user of the railway etc or the continuance of the closing of the highway beyond the time specified in the agreement or undertaking without the consent of the responsible authority or person[13].

1 As to the royal prerogative in time of war see paras 510–511 ante; and CONSTITUTIONAL LAW AND HUMAN RIGHTS vol 8(2) (Reissue) para 811. The powers conferred by the Defence of the Realm (Acquisition of Land) Act 1916 are in addition to and not in derogation of any other right or power of the Crown: s 14.

2 As to public highways generally see HIGHWAYS.

3 The Defence of the Realm (Acquisition of Land) Act 1916 s 6(1) refers to the Board of Trade, but the powers of the board under these provisions were transferred to the Minister of Transport, and then subsequently to the Secretary of State: see the Secretary of State for the Environment Order 1970, SI 1970/1681 (partly revoked). As to the Board of Trade generally see CONSTITUTIONAL LAW AND HUMAN RIGHTS vol 8(2) (Reissue) para 505; TRADE, INDUSTRY AND INDUSTRIAL RELATIONS vol 47 (Reissue) para 2.

4 The Defence of the Realm (Acquisition of Land) Act 1916 s 6(1) refers to the Railway and Canal Commission, but the commission was abolished and its functions are now exercised and performed by the High Court: see the Railway and Canal Commission (Abolition) Act 1949 s 1(1)(a).

5 'Local authority' means, in the case of a borough or urban district, the council of the borough or urban district, and elsewhere the county council: Defence of the Realm (Acquisition of Land) Act 1916 s 6(4).

6 Ibid s 6(1).

7 Ibid s 6(1) proviso. Such consent has been required since the expiration of two years from the termination of the 1914–18 war: see s 6(1) proviso. If any person considers that the consent of a local authority under this proviso has been unreasonably withheld, he may appeal to the Secretary of State (see note 3 supra) whose decision is final and has effect as if it were a decision of the authority; provided that the Secretary of State may, before considering any such appeal, require the appellant to deposit a specified sum to cover the costs of appeal: see the Defence of the Realm (Acquisition of Land) Act 1920 s 4(2).

8 As to the meaning of 'government department' see para 609 note 2 ante.

9 Defence of the Realm (Acquisition of Land) Act 1916 s 6(2).

10 See ibid s 6(3). Such consent has been required since the expiration of two years from the termination of the 1914–18 war: see s 6(3).

11 As to the meaning of 'land' see para 609 note 1 ante.

12 Defence of the Realm (Acquisition of Land) Act 1916 s 6(3).

13 Ibid s 6(5). See also *Secretary of State for War v Middlesex County Council* (1923) 39 TLR 357, where the court refused to close a public footpath over land which had been acquired.

614. Application of building laws. Any street, building[1], or work which has been formed, erected, or constructed otherwise than in accordance with statutory provisions or byelaws or regulations made under them on any land[2] which has been acquired permanently[3] must, unless the authority by which such provisions are enforced consents to their continuance, either be altered so as to comply with such provisions or be discontinued or removed within such reasonable time, not being less than two years, after that land or building has ceased to be occupied by a government department as that authority may order[4]. The owner has power to enter and carry out any works without the consent of any other person, and if he fails to comply with such order the authority may remove any such building or work and recover the expense incurred from the owner[5].

If any person feels aggrieved by the neglect or refusal of the authority to give its consent, or by the conditions on which the consent is given, or as to the time within which such discontinuance or removal is ordered, he may appeal to the Secretary of State for Health[6], whose decision is final and has effect as if it were a decision of the authority[7].

1   As to the meaning of 'building' see para 609 note 1 ante.
2   As to the meaning of 'land' see para 609 note 1 ante.
3   Ie under the Defence of the Realm (Acquisition of Land) Act 1916 s 3: see para 610 ante.
4   Ibid s 11(1). As to the meaning of 'government department' see para 609 note 2 ante.
5   Ibid s 11(1).
6   Ibid s 11(2) refers to the Local Government Board, but the powers of the board are now exercised by the Secretary of State for Health: see the Transfer of Functions (Health and Social Security) Order 1988, SI 1988/1843.
7   Defence of the Realm (Acquisition of Land) Act 1916 s 11(2). Before considering any such appeal, the Secretary of State may require the appellant to deposit a specified sum to cover the costs of appeal: see s 11(2).

615. Compensation. All compensation and purchase money payable by a government department[1] under the Defence of the Realm (Acquisition of Land) Act 1916, and all other expenses incurred by any government department under that Act, are to be defrayed out of money provided by Parliament[2].

Where consideration has been given or an advance made by the state for the erection, construction, or making of any building[3], work, or improvement on over or under any land[4] for purposes connected with the 1914–18 war, or where any money which would otherwise have been payable to the state has with the consent of a government department been applied towards the erection, construction, or making of any such building, work, or improvement, then that building, work, or improvement is deemed to have been erected, constructed, or made wholly or partly, as the case may be, at the expense of the state[5].

1   As to the meaning of 'government department' see para 609 note 2 ante.
2   Defence of the Realm (Acquisition of Land) Act 1916 s 9.
3   As to the meaning of 'building' see para 609 note 1 ante.
4   As to the meaning of 'land' see para 609 note 1 ante.
5   Defence of the Realm (Acquisition of Land) Act 1916 s 12(2).

616. Government department certificate. A certificate by any government department[1] (1) that possession has been taken of any land[2] for purposes connected with the 1914–18 war; or (2) that the department is in possession of such land or is the occupying department[3]; or (3) that a railway or tramway has been laid along, across, over, or under a public highway[4], or that a public highway has been closed, in the exercise of any prerogative right[5] of the Crown, or any powers conferred by or under any enactment relating to the defence of the realm for purposes connected with the 1914–18 war, is prima facie evidence of the facts stated[6].

1   As to the meaning of 'government department' see para 609 note 2 ante.
2   As to the meaning of 'land' see para 609 note 1 ante. For these purposes the exercise or enjoyment of any easement or right over or in relation to land is deemed to be possession of that easement or right: see the Defence of the Realm (Acquisition of Land) Act 1920 s 6 (as amended).
3   For the meaning of 'occupying department' see para 612 note 16 ante.
4   As to public highways generally see HIGHWAYS.
5   As to the royal prerogative in time of war see paras 510–511 ante; and CONSTITUTIONAL LAW AND HUMAN RIGHTS vol 8(2) (Reissue) para 811. The powers conferred by the Defence of the Realm (Acquisition of Land) Act 1916 are in addition to and not in derogation of any other right or power of the Crown: s 14.
6   Ibid s 10.

(iii) The Requisitioned Land and War Works Acts 1945 and 1948

617. In general. Most of the powers conferred on government departments and the Crown relating to the treatment of requisitioned land and war works in connection with the 1939–45 war have long since expired[1]. However, certain provisions[2] directed to empowering the acquisition of easements[3] and restrictive rights under the Defence Acts[4] and to the acquisition under those Acts of the surface of land without underlying strata or the acquisition of reversionary interests were made permanent[5], and may be applied for the purpose of the acquisition of land for oil installations[6]. Other subsisting provisions of the legislation confer power to defray the cost of the rehabilitation of land in certain cases[7], and confer power on a minister[8] to acquire any land by agreement under the Defence Acts with a view to the exchange of that land for other land to be acquired under those Acts[9].

The powers conferred by the Requisitioned Land and War Works Act 1945 are in addition to, and not in derogation of, any powers exercisable by virtue of any other Act or at common law[10].

1   See eg the Requisitioned Land and War Works Act 1945 Pt I (ss 1–3) (repealed), Pt II (ss 4–14) repealed; and the Requisitioned Land and War Works Act 1948 (partly repealed and extensively amended).
2   Ie the Requisitioned Land and War Works Act 1945 ss 33, 34 (both as amended): see para 622 post.
3   As to the meaning of 'easement' see para 622 note 5 post.
4   The 'Defence Acts' means any of the provisions of the Defence Acts 1842 to 1935, as amended, extended or applied by or under any enactment, including the Requisitioned Land and War Works Act 1945, and includes the provisions of the Lands Clauses Consolidation Acts Amendment Act 1860 s 7, and of the Militia (Lands and Buildings) Act 1873 s 7: Requisitioned Land and War Works Act 1945 s 59(1) (amended by the Defence (Transfer of Functions) (No 1) Order 1964, SI 1964/488, art 2, Sch 1 Pt II). As to the Defence Acts 1842 to 1935, and as to acquisition of land for defence purposes, see also ROYAL FORCES vol 41 para 117.
5   See the Requisitioned Land and War Works Act 1948 s 1(3) (repealed), which made permanent the Requisitioned Land and War Works Act 1945 ss 33, 34 (both as amended). As to provisions consequential on ss 33, 34 (both as amended) see ss 36–39; and para 622 post.
6   See the Land Powers (Defence) Act 1958 s 13, Sch 2 Pt II paras 12, 13(h) (amended by the Post Office Act 1969 s 137(1), Sch 8 Pt II); and para 621 post.
7   See the Requisitioned Land and War Works Act 1945 s 52 and the Requisitioned Land and War Works Act 1948 s 6, Schedule para 10 (both repealed by the Housing and Planning Act 1986 ss 48(1)(a), 49(2), Sch 12 Pt III in relation to undertakings given after 7 January 1987); and the Transfer of Functions (Minister of Health and Minister of Local Government and Planning) (No 2) Order 1951, SI 1951/753 (amended by SI 1951/1900).
8   For the meaning of 'minister' see para 602 note 9 ante.
9   Where a minister proposes to acquire any land under the Defence Acts, he may acquire any land by agreement with a view to its exchange for all or any of the first-mentioned land; provided that, where the first-mentioned land consists of or includes the whole or any part of any common to which the public have rights of access or of any open space, this power is extended so as to authorise the purchase of land with a view to its being substituted for the first-mentioned land otherwise than by way of exchange: Requisitioned Land and War Works Act 1945 s 53(1). 'Common' includes any land subject to be inclosed under the Inclosure Acts 1845 to 1882, and any town or village green; and 'open space' means any land

laid out as a public garden or used for the purposes of public recreation, or land being a disused burial ground: Requisitioned Land and War Works Act 1945 s 59(1).

Where a minister provides land in substitution for land acquired by him under the Defence Acts which is or forms part of a common, open space or fuel or field garden allotment, he may by order provide for vesting the first-mentioned land in the persons in whom the second-mentioned land was vested, subject to the same rights, trusts and incidents as attached to the second-mentioned land; provided that where the land is provided otherwise than by way of exchange, the persons in whom the land is to be vested must be such as may be specified in the order and the rights, trusts and incidents to which the land is to be subject must be such as may be so specified, being rights, trusts and incidents which in the opinion of the minister are as nearly as may be the same, so far as regards the rights of the public, as those which attached to the land acquired: Requisitioned Land and War Works Act 1945 s 53(2). 'Fuel or field garden allotment' means any allotment set out as a fuel allotment, or a field garden allotment, under an Inclosure Act: Requisitioned Land and War Works Act 1945 s 59(1).

See also ROYAL FORCES vol 41 para 117; and COMMONS vol 6 (Reissue) para 610.

10 Ibid s 59(8).

618. Provisions affecting highways and railways. Where any highway[1] has been stopped up or diverted in the exercise of emergency powers[2], the Secretary of State[3] may, if he is satisfied that in the public interest it is necessary or expedient to do so, by order authorise the permanent stopping up or diversion of the highway[4]. Such an order may provide for all or any of the following:

(1) for requiring, as a substitute for any highway stopped up under the order, the provision or improvement of another highway or other highways[5];

(2) for directing that any highway to be provided or improved, or any highway provided or improved before the making of the order, as a substitute for any highway stopped up under the order, is repairable by the inhabitants at large, and for specifying the authority which is to be the relevant highway authority[6];

(3) for directing that any highway to be provided or improved, or any highway provided or improved before the making of the order, as a substitute for a trunk road stopped up under the order is itself a trunk road for all or any of the purposes of the Highways Act 1980[7];

(4) for the retention or removal of any cables, wires, mains or pipes placed along, across, over or under the stopped up or diverted highway, and for the extinction, modification or preservation of any rights as to the use or maintenance of those cables etc[8];

(5) if any highway other than the original highway is to be or has been provided or improved, or if the original highway is to be permanently diverted, for authorising or requiring the provision of cables, wires, mains or pipes laid along, across, over or under that other highway, or, as the case may be, the highway as diverted, in lieu of any cables etc removed from the original highway, and for conferring rights as to the use or maintenance of cables etc so provided[9];

(6) for requiring out of moneys provided by Parliament or by specified authorities or persons (a) the payment of, or the making of contributions in respect of, the cost of doing any work required to be done by the order or any increased expenditure to be incurred which is ascribable to the doing of any such work or to the provision or improvement, before the making of the order, of any highway as a substitute for any highway stopped up under the order[10]; or (b) the repayment of, or the making of contributions in respect of, any compensation paid by the highway authority in respect of restrictions[11] as respects any highway stopped up or diverted under the order[12].

An order may contain such consequential, incidental and supplemental provisions as appear to the Secretary of State to be necessary or expedient for the purposes of the order, including provisions authorising the compulsory acquisition of land[13].

Where, in the exercise of emergency powers or, for war purposes[14], by agreement or otherwise, any railway or tramway or any cable, wire, main or pipe has been placed along, across, over or under any highway, the Secretary of State may, if he is satisfied that in the public interest it is necessary or expedient to do so, by order authorise the railway etc to be used and maintained along, across, over or under the highway, unless and until other provision is made by or under any Act, subject, however, to such conditions and limitations, if any, as may be specified in the order[15].

Any such order may contain such consequential, incidental and supplemental provisions as appear to the Secretary of State to be necessary or expedient for the purposes of the order[16].

1 As to highways generally see HIGHWAYS.
2 For the meaning of 'emergency powers' see para 601 note 10 ante.
3 The Requisitioned Land and War Works Act 1945 refers to the Minister of War Transport, but his functions are now exercised by the Secretary of State: see the Secretary of State for the Environment Order 1970, SI 1970/1681 (partly revoked).
4 Requisitioned Land and War Works Act 1945 s 15(1). The powers conferred by ss 15, 16 are limited (see s 20(1)) to expire two years after the end of the war period, but this limit does not apply to any varying or revoking order made under these provisions by virtue of the Land Powers (Defence) Act 1958 s 9(1): see s 9; and HIGHWAYS vol 21 (Reissue) para 174. For the meaning of the 'war period' see para 601 note 10 ante.
   See also the Requisitioned Land and War Works Act 1948 s 3(1).
5 Requisitioned Land and War Works Act 1945 s 15(2)(a).
6 Ibid s 15(2)(b).
7 Ibid s 15(2)(c).
8 Ibid s 15(2)(d).
9 Ibid s 15(2)(e).
10 Ibid s 15(2)(f)(i).
11 Ie imposed under the Restriction of Ribbon Development Act 1935 ss 1, 2 (both repealed).
12 Requisitioned Land and War Works Act 1945 s 15(2)(f)(ii).
13 Ibid s 15(3).
14 'War purposes' means any purposes connected with any war in which the Crown is engaged during the war period, whether or not at the relevant time that war had begun: ibid s 59(1).
15 Ibid s 16(1).
16 Ibid s 16(2).

619. Procedure and orders relating to highways. Before making an order[1] the Secretary of State[2] must publish his proposals by causing notice:

(1) to be advertised in two or more newspapers circulating in the locality in which the highways[3] to which the proposals relate are or will be situated[4]; and

(2) to be sent to every local authority[5] in whose area any such highway is or will be situated and to any water, sewerage, gas[6] or electricity undertakers having any cables, wires, mains or pipes laid along, across, over or under any such highway[7]; and

(3) to be sent to the Environment Agency where that agency has any mains or pipes laid along, across, over or under any such highways[8]; and

(4) to be displayed in a prominent position at the ends of so much of any highway as is proposed to be stopped up or diverted under the order[9]; and

(5) in the case of an order authorising the compulsory acquisition of land, to be served on every owner, lessee or occupier (except tenants for a period of a month or less) of any of the land proposed to be compulsorily acquired[10].

The notice must specify the place where copies of a draft of the proposed order may be obtained, and must state that the order will be made unless, within such period (not being less than three months from the date of the publication) as may be specified in the notice, written notice of objection to the order is given by any person to the Secretary of

State[11]. Such an order may not, however, be questioned in any legal proceedings and becomes operative on the date on which the notice is last published[12]. The order must comply with the published proposals[13].

No order authorising the permanent stopping up or diversion of a highway may be made after the highway has ceased to be temporarily stopped up or diverted and no order authorising the permanent use and maintenance along, across, over or under a highway of a railway, tramway, cable, wire, main or pipe may be made after the railway etc has been abandoned[14].

After making the order the Secretary of State must publish a notice that the order has been made and that copies of it may be obtained from a place specified in the notice on payment of a specified sum[15].

If any one wishes to question the validity of the order, or of any provision contained in it, on the ground that it is not within the statutory powers or that the statutory requirements have not been complied with in relation to the order, he may, within six weeks from the date on which the notice is last published in a newspaper, make an application to the High Court[16].

1   Ie under the Requisitioned Land and War Works Act 1945 Pt III (ss 15–22).
2   As to the transfer of functions to the Secretary of State see para 618 note 3 ante.
3   As to highways generally see HIGHWAYS.
4   Requisitioned Land and War Works Act 1945 s 17(1)(a).
5   'Local authority' means the council of a county, borough or district, or the Common Council of the City of London: ibid s 59(1) (amended by the Statute Law (Repeals) Act 1976 s 1(1), Sch 1 Pt XII); and for the purposes of the Requisitioned Land and War Works Act 1945 s 17(1) 'local authority' includes a parish council and the parish meeting of a rural parish not having a separate parish council: s 17(1).
6   The reference to a public gas supplier has effect as if it were a reference to public gas transporter: see the Gas Act 1995 ss 16(1), 17(5), Sch 4 para 2(2)(a), Sch 6; and see FUEL AND ENERGY.
7   Requisitioned Land and War Works Act 1945 s 17(1)(b) (amended by the Water Act 1989 s 190(1), Sch 25 para 8).
8   Requisitioned Land and War Works Act 1945 s 17(1)(bb) (added by the Water Act 1989 Sch 25 para 8). The Environment Agency replaced the National Rivers Authority: see the Environment Act 1995 ss 1–3; and WATER.
9   Requisitioned Land and War Works Act 1945 s 17(1)(c).
10   Ibid s 17(1)(d). Any notice required to be served under s 17(1)(d) may be served either:
     (1) by delivering it to the person on whom it is to be served (s 17(3)(a)); or
     (2) by leaving it at the usual or last known place of abode of that person (s 17(3)(b)); or
     (3) by sending it in a prepaid registered letter addressed to that person at his usual or last known place of abode (s 17(3)(c)); or
     (4) in the case of an incorporated company or body, by delivering it to the secretary or clerk of the company or body at their registered or principal office or sending it in a prepaid registered letter addressed to the secretary or clerk of the company or body at that office (s 17(3)(d)); or
     (5) if it is not practicable after reasonable inquiry to ascertain the name or address of the person on whom it should be served, by addressing it to him by the description of 'owner' or 'lessee' or 'occupier' of the land (describing it) to which it relates and by delivering it to some person on the land, or, if there is no person on the land to whom it can be delivered, by displaying it in a prominent position on the land (s 17(3)(e)).
11   Ibid s 17(2).
12   Ibid s 19(3).
13   See ibid s 20(1).
14   Ibid s 20(2).
15   Ibid s 19(1) (amended by the Decimal Currency Act 1969 s 10(1)). The sum must not exceed a specified amount: see the Requisitioned Land and War Works Act 1945 s 19(1).
16   Ibid s 19(2). On any such application the court (1) may by an interim order suspend the operation of the order or any provision contained in it, either generally or in so far as it affects any property of the applicant, until the final determination of the proceedings (s 19(2)(a)); and (2) if satisfied that the order or any provision contained in it is not within these statutory powers or that the interests of the applicant have been substantially prejudiced by any requirement of these provisions not having been complied with, may quash the order or any provision contained in it, either generally or in so far as it affects any property of the applicant (s 19(2)(b)).

620. Maintenance and use of works and continuance in possession; government oil pipelines.

Where government war works[1] have been constructed on any land[2], any minister may maintain and use, or authorise the maintenance and use of, those works for the purposes of the public service or for any purpose for which they were maintained or used in the exercise of emergency powers[3]. In connection with the use of any works or land under this provision any person having the use of the works or land may continue to exercise and enjoy all such rights and advantages as, immediately before the use began, were, by agreement or otherwise, being exercised or enjoyed in connection with the use of the works or land for war purposes by the person then having the use of it, including rights and advantages as to the taking of water, whether for the purposes of a water undertaking[4] or for other purposes[5]. In relation to government oil pipelines[6] and accessory works these provisions[7] have permanent effect, subject to certain provisions[8].

The powers conferred[9] include power to maintain and use any line or accessory works, or authorise the use of them for any purpose for which they are suitable[10].

A minister may remove any main or pipe or part of a main or pipe, being a government oil pipeline, or any accessory works, and may replace anything previously removed; and these provisions[11] apply to any replacement as if it had been the original thing removed[12]. If, in pursuance of an agreement with a minister, a government oil pipeline is diverted or any accessory works are moved to a new site, the provisions apply to the line as diverted, or to the works on the new site, as the case may be, as if it or they had been the original line or works[13].

If, without the consent of a minister, any building or structure is erected over a government oil pipeline or accessory works or the site of such a line or works, or so near to them as to obstruct the use of the line or works or access to them or to the site, a minister may cause the building or structure to be removed and may recover the cost of the removal from the person by whom the building or structure was erected[14]. Where, however, rights are for the time being exercisable by a minister[15] with respect to any oil pipeline or accessory works[16], there are restrictions on the activities that may be carried out in the vicinity of the pipeline or works without the consent of that minister[17]; and when these restrictions take effect as respects any land the above provisions[18] cease to apply to that land[19]. The restrictions are not effective unless registered in the appropriate local land charges register[20]. If, in consequence of the restrictions, the value of any subsisting interest in land is depreciated, then compensation equal to the amount of the depreciation is payable by the minister concerned[21].

Any person who without lawful authority tampers with, alters or removes a government oil pipeline or accessory works is liable on summary conviction to a fine not exceeding level 1 on the standard scale[22].

In respect of the exercise of these powers[23] compensation is payable by the Secretary of State[24]. Where the value of any land is diminished[25], compensation for the diminution is payable in the form of a lump sum of such amount as may be agreed between the Secretary of State and the persons interested in the land[26] or, in default of agreement, as may be determined by arbitration in the prescribed manner; and this compensation is divisible among those persons in such shares as they may agree, or, in default of agreement, as may be determined by arbitration[27]. Where in exercise of any power of use, maintenance, removal or replacement of a government oil pipeline or accessory works[28] a person suffers loss by reason of damage to crops or other growing things, stock, chattels or any land or buildings or works on, under or over land, he is entitled to compensation in respect of the damage of such amount as may be agreed between the Secretary of State and the person in question or, in default of agreement, as may be determined by arbitration[29].

The Treasury may by regulations[30] require, as a condition of the payment of compensation[31], (1) that except in such circumstances as may be prescribed a claim must be made in the prescribed form and manner and within such period as may be determined by or under the regulations[32]; and (2) that the prescribed documents of title to interests in land must be indorsed in the prescribed manner and that the prescribed evidence must be produced of the indorsement; and the registration requirement[33] does not apply where evidence of an indorsement has been produced in accordance with the regulations[34].

Where a pipeline is diverted, or works are moved[35], the registration requirement[36] does not apply to the line as diverted or to the works on the new site, but the rights conferred by the above provisions[37], as respects the land on which the line as diverted and any such works are constructed, are a local land charge; and for the purposes of the Local Land Charges Act 1975 the minister maintaining and using, or authorising the maintenance and use of, the line or works is to be treated as the originating authority as respects that charge[38]. Such rights registered in a local land charges register are a local land charge, but certain provisions of the Local Land Charges Act 1975[39] do not apply; and a certificate setting out the result of an official search of the appropriate local land charges register is, as respects any pipeline or accessory works, conclusive of the question whether, at the time of the issue of the certificate, registrable[40] rights were registered[41].

Any person authorised by a minister may enter upon any land of which the minister is not in possession, for the purpose of exercising any of these powers[42] or of restoring land where a government oil pipeline or accessory works are abandoned or of inspecting any such land or works[43]. Except in a case of emergency or for the purpose of inspection by a person producing, if required, written evidence of his authority to do so, entry upon any land may not be demanded as of right unless reasonable notice of the intended entry has been served on the occupier of the land in the required manner[44]; and where any land has been entered upon, for a purpose other than inspection only, without notice being served on the occupier of the land, the minister must cause notice of the entry to be served on the occupier in the required manner[45].

The Treasury may make regulations (a) for the protection of persons affected by the maintenance and use of government oil pipelines and accessory works, and in particular for requiring the minister or other person entitled to use them to keep any such line and works in good repair, to take such steps as may be prescribed for restoring land where the line or works are abandoned, and to indemnify persons against loss or damage caused by any failure to keep the line or works in good repair, and for relieving statutory undertakers and other persons of liabilities or obligations arising in consequence of any such failure or any exercise of the powers[46]; (b) for requiring notice to be given where a government oil pipeline or accessory works are abandoned, and for discontinuing the operation of the above provisions[47] where such a notice is given[48]; (c) for applying in relation to government oil pipelines passing under highways the provisions relating to the breaking-up of highways for the purposes of repairing pipes[49] and for excluding in relation to government oil pipelines the provisions[50] relating to retention of, inter alia, pipes on highways[51].

1   'Government war work' means work done during the war period for war purposes by or by arrangement with a minister, or under emergency powers (Requisitioned Land and War Works Act 1945 s 59(1)) and 'government war works' includes, and is deemed always to have included, any oil pipeline or accessory works which is completed before the end of 1958 and which is laid, installed or constructed by or under the authority of a minister in pursuance of the Defence (General) Regulations 1939, SR & O 1939/927, reg 50 (revoked) or in pursuance of an agreement in such circumstances that if the agreement had not been made the like pipeline or works could have been laid, installed or constructed in pursuance of that regulation: Land Powers (Defence) Act 1958 s 12(1). 'Works' includes buildings, structures and improvements (and, in particular, underground works and telegraphic lines), and references to the construction of works are construed accordingly: Requisitioned Land and War Works Act 1945 s 59(1).

For the meaning of 'war period' see para 601 note 10 ante; for the meaning of 'war purposes' see para 618 note 14 ante; and for the meaning of 'minister' see para 602 note 9 ante.

2 For the meaning of the 'doing of work on land' see para 602 note 2 ante.

3 Requisitioned Land and War Works Act 1945 s 28(1). For the meaning of 'emergency powers' see para 601 note 10 ante.

4 As to water undertakings see WATER.

5 Requisitioned Land and War Works Act 1945 s 28(3)(a).

6 'Government oil pipeline' means any government war works being the whole or part of a main or pipe installed for the transmission of petroleum: Requisitioned Land and War Works Act 1948 s 12(3). See also note 1 supra.

7 Ie the Requisitioned Land and War Works Act 1945 s 28(1), (3)(a). In general s 28 ceased to have effect at the end of 1960 by virtue of s 30 (repealed).

8 Requisitioned Land and War Works Act 1948 s 12(1). Section 12 does not apply after 31 December 1960 to any pipeline, or accessory works, unless the rights conferred by s 12(1) have been registered in the appropriate local land charges register; and on any application being made for that purpose to the authority keeping that register that authority must register the rights accordingly: s 14(1) (amended by the Land Powers (Defence) Act 1958 s 12(2); and by the Local Land Charges Act 1975 ss 12(2), 17(2), 19(1), Schs 1, 2). See also LAND CHARGES vol 26 para 774; SALE OF LAND vol 42 para 14.

In relation to works in exercise of the powers conferred by the Requisitioned Land and War Works Act 1948 s 12, certain provisions of the New Roads and Street Works Act 1991 are modified with regard to plans and to avoid an unacceptable diversion or change of a government oil pipeline: see the Land Powers (Defence) Act 1958 s 18A (added by the New Roads and Street Works Act 1991 s 168(1), Sch 8 Pt IV para 100). As to street works generally see HIGHWAYS.

9 Ie by the Requisitioned Land and War Works Act 1945 s 28.

10 Requisitioned Land and War Works Act 1948 s 12(2).

11 Ie the Requisitioned Land and War Works Act 1945 s 28; and the Requisitioned Land and War Works Act 1948.

12 Ibid s 12(4).

13 Ibid s 12(5).

14 Ibid s 12(6).

15 For the purposes of the Land Powers (Defence) Act 1958 generally, 'minister', except where the reference is to a particular minister, means any minister of the Crown: s 25(1) (amended by the Defence (Transfer of Functions) (No 1) Order 1964, SI 1964/488, art 2, Sch 1 Pt II).

16 Ie under the Requisitioned Land and War Works Act 1948 s 12(1) or under a wayleave order. As to wayleave orders see para 621 post. For the meaning of 'oil pipeline' for the purposes of the Land Powers (Defence) Act 1958 see para 621 note 5 post. As to acquisition of land and compensation see also ROYAL FORCES vol 41 para 117.

17 See the Land Powers (Defence) Act 1958 s 16(1). The minister may, if he thinks fit, direct that anything done in contravention of the restrictions is to be deemed to have been done with his consent: see s 16(4). The minister may take remedial action if the restrictions are contravened (see s 16(2)); and any expenses so incurred are recoverable from the occupier of the land on which the contravention was committed (see s 16(3)). 'Occupier', in relation to any land which is not occupied, means the person for the time being entitled to possession of that land: s 25(1).

18 Ie the Requisitioned Land and War Works Act 1948 s 12(6).

19 Land Powers (Defence) Act 1958 s 16(6). For the purposes of the 1958 Act 'land' includes land covered by water: s 25(1).

20 The restrictions do not take effect until notice of the restrictions is registered in the appropriate local land charges register; and, in relation to an owner, lessee or occupier of that land at the time when the application for registration is made, they do not take effect unless notice has been served on him: see the Land Powers (Defence) Act 1958 s 17(2) (amended by the Local Land Charges Act 1975 Sch 1). 'Owner' means a person, other than a mortgagee not in possession, who is for the time being entitled to dispose of the fee simple of the land, whether in possession or reversion, and includes also a person holding or entitled to the rents and profits of the land under a lease or agreement the unexpired term of which exceeds three years: Land Powers (Defence) Act 1958 s 25(1). As to registration of restrictions generally see s 17 (amended by the Local Land Charges Act 1975 Schs 1, 2; and the Local Government Act 1972 s 272(1), Sch 30). As to the service of notice see the Land Powers (Defence) Act 1958 s 23.

21 See ibid s 18(2). However, compensation is not payable under s 18(2) if compensation in respect of that land has been paid under the Requisitioned Land and War Works Act 1948 s 13 and it is shown that the whole or part of that compensation is attributable to the provisions of s 12(6) of that Act: Land Powers (Defence) Act 1958 s 18(2) proviso. The Treasury may by regulations require, as a condition of the payment of compensation under s 18, that a claim must be made in a prescribed form and manner and within a certain period: see s 18(4). The power to make regulations is exercisable by statutory instrument,

which is subject to annulment in pursuance of a resolution of either House of Parliament: s 24(1). See the Government Oil Pipe-lines (No 2) Regulations 1959, SI 1959/724. Any dispute as to a right of compensation under the Land Powers (Defence) Act 1958 s 18, or as to the amount of compensation, must be determined by the Lands Tribunal: s 18(5). As to the Lands Tribunal see COMPULSORY ACQUISITION OF LAND vol 8(1) (Reissue) para 202 et seq.

22 Requisitioned Land and War Works Act 1948 s 12(7) (amended by the Criminal Law Act 1977 s 31(6); and by the Criminal Justice Act 1982 s 46). As to the standard scale see para 532 note 18 ante.

23 Ie the powers conferred by the Requisitioned Land and War Works Act 1948 s 12.

24 Ie in accordance with the provisions of ibid s 13: s 13(1). The Secretary of State was substituted for the original reference to the Minister of Public Buildings and Works by the Secretary of State for the Environment Order 1970, SI 1970/1681 (partly revoked).

25 Ie by the coming into operation of the Requisitioned Land and War Works Act 1948 s 12.

26 References in ibid s 13(2) to persons interested in land do not include persons who fail to make a claim required by regulations: see s 13(7). As to the regulations see the text and notes 30–32 infra.

27 Ibid s 13(2). In assessing this compensation regard must be had to the rights to compensation conferred by s 13(6), and to ss 14–20 and to the provisions of regulations made under the 1948 Act: s 13(3). Disputes under s 13(2) or (6) are to be determined by the Lands Tribunal: s 17(1) (see note 30 infra); and see the Government Oil Pipe-lines Regulations 1959, SI 1959/715, reg 7. As to the Lands Tribunal see COMPULSORY ACQUISITION OF LAND vol 8(1) (Reissue) para 202 et seq.

The right to compensation conferred by the Requisitioned Land and War Works Act 1948 s 13(2) is, as respects any period after 19 February 1948, in substitution for any right to compensation under the Compensation (Defence) Act 1939 s 3(2) (see para 602 ante); and interest on any share of compensation under the Requisitioned Land and War Works Act 1948 s 13(2), at the like rate as is for the time being payable on compensation under the 1939 Act, runs as from 19 February 1948 and is payable at the time when the share is paid: Requisitioned Land and War Works Act 1948 s 13(4).

Where, at 7 July 1958, rights conferred by s 12(1) have not been registered (see note 8 supra) and no evidence of indorsement of documents of title has been produced (see text and note 34 infra), the date when rights to compensation under the 1948 Act are substituted for rights under the 1939 Act is 7 July 1958 or the date of the completion of the pipeline or works in question, whichever is the later: see the Land Powers (Defence) Act 1958 s 12(3).

Where under any agreement made before 7 July 1958 payments (whether referred to as compensation, rent or otherwise) are to be made in respect of a pipeline or works to which s 12(3) applies, and any such payments become payable in respect of a period after that date, the right to those payments must be taken to be in substitution for the right to any corresponding payment of compensation in respect of that period under the Requisitioned Land and War Works Act 1948 s 13: Land Powers (Defence) Act 1958 s 12(4).

28 Ie conferred by the Requisitioned Land and War Works Act 1948 s 13(5).

29 Ibid s 13(6) (amended by the Secretary of State for the Environment Order 1970). The Railway Clauses Consolidation Act 1845 ss 78–85 (as originally enacted) (which restrict the working of minerals, subject to compensation) apply in relation to any government oil pipeline or accessory works with the substitution (1) for references to the railway of references to the pipeline or works; (2) for references to the company of references to the minister or other person entitled to use the pipeline or works; and (3) for references to the special Act of references to the Requisitioned Land and War Works Act 1945 s 28: Requisitioned Land and War Works Act 1948 s 15(3). As to determination in default of agreement see note 27 supra.

30 The Treasury may by regulations prescribe anything authorised or required by the Requisitioned Land and War Works Act 1948 to be prescribed: s 17(1). Any such power to make regulations is exercisable by statutory instrument, which is subject to annulment by resolution of either House of Parliament: s 17(2), (3).

31 Ie payment of compensation under ibid s 13(2).

32 Ibid s 13(7).

33 See note 8 supra.

34 Requisitioned Land and War Works Act 1948 s 14(2).

35 See ibid s 12(5).

36 See note 8 supra.

37 Ie the Requisitioned Land and War Works Act 1948 s 12.

38 Ibid s 14(3) (amended by the Local Land Charges Act 1975 Sch 1).

39 Ie the Local Land Charges Act 1975 ss 5(2), 10 (as amended).

40 Ie registrable under the Requisitioned Land and War Works Act 1948 s 14(1).

41 Ibid s 14(4) (substituted by the Local Land Charges Act 1975 Sch 1).

42 Ie powers conferred by the Requisitioned Land and War Works Act 1948 s 12.

43 Ibid s 15(1). Section 13(6), (7) applies in relation to powers conferred by s 15(1) as it applies to the powers mentioned in s 13(6): s 15(2).

44 Ibid s 15(1)(i).
45 Ibid s 15(1)(ii).
46 Ie the powers conferred by ibid s 12 or s 15: see s 15(4)(a).
47 Ie ibid s 12 or s 15, and regulations made under s 15(4).
48 See ibid s 15(4)(b).
49 Ie the Water Industry Act 1991 s 158 (as amended): see WATER.
50 Ie the Requisitioned Land and War Works Act 1945 s 16.
51 See the Requisitioned Land and War Works Act 1948 s 15(4)(c) (amended by the Water Consolidation (Consequential Provisions) Act 1991 s 2(1), Sch 1 para 5).

621. Acquisition of land for oil installations; wayleave orders for oil pipelines and accessory works. The Secretary of State[1] may acquire by agreement, or may by order[2] provide[3] that the provisions of the Land Powers (Defence) Act 1958 relating to the acquisition of land[4] are to have effect for the purpose of the acquisition by him of (1) any land required for the construction of oil installations[5] which in his opinion are essential for the defence of the realm[6]; (2) any land on or under which there are oil installations which were government war works[7] immediately before 7 July 1958[8]; (3) any easement over or right restrictive of the user of any other land, being an easement or right which in his opinion is essential to the full enjoyment of any land on or under which an oil installation falling within heads (1) or (2) is to be or has been constructed[9].

A minister[10] may for any specified[11] purpose by order (a wayleave order[12]), and without further assurance, vest in himself with respect to any land specified in the order the right (a) to carry out (i) the laying of an oil pipeline; and (ii) the installation or construction of such minor works accessory to an oil pipeline[13], whether laid under that wayleave order or otherwise, as may be specified in the order, and from time to time maintain or remove any pipelines or works so laid, installed or constructed[14]; (b) to use any such pipeline or works for any purpose appearing to that minister to be expedient and not to be inconsistent with the purposes for which the order was made[15].

For the purpose of exercising any rights under a wayleave order, or restoring land where a pipeline or works laid, installed or constructed under an order is or are removed or abandoned, or inspecting any land, pipeline or works to which the order relates, any person authorised by the minister by whom the order was made may enter on any land not in the possession of that minister[16]; provided that notice of the entry must generally be given to the occupier of the land[17].

The Treasury may make regulations[18] for requiring notice to be given where a pipeline or works laid, installed or constructed under a wayleave order is or are removed or abandoned[19]; and generally for the protection of persons affected by the laying, installation, construction, maintenance or use under a wayleave order of pipelines or accessory works[20].

Where rights are for the time being exercisable by a minister with respect to any oil pipeline or accessory works[21], there are restrictions on the activities that may be carried out in the vicinity of the pipeline or works without the consent of that minister[22]. A wayleave order is a local land charge[23]. If, by virtue of a wayleave order, the value of any subsisting interest in land is depreciated, then compensation equal to the amount of the depreciation is payable by the minister concerned[24].

Any person who, in consequence of the exercise of the rights conferred by a wayleave order, suffers loss by reason of damage to any land or chattels, or is disturbed in the enjoyment of them, is entitled to compensation in respect of that damage or disturbance from the minister by whom the order was made[25].

1   The functions of the Minister of Power were transferred to the Minister of Technology (see the Minister of Technology Order 1969, SI 1969/1498) and then to the Secretary of State (see the Secretary of State

for Trade and Industry Order 1970, SI 1970/1537). These functions are now exercised by the Secretary of State for Trade and Industry: see the Secretary of State (New Departments) Order 1974, SI 1974/692; and the Transfer of Functions (Energy) Order 1992, SI 1992/1314. As to acquisition of land and compensation see also ROYAL FORCES vol 41 para 117.

2   Any power under any provision of the Land Powers (Defence) Act 1958 to make orders includes power to vary or revoke any previous order made under that provision: s 24(2).

3   Ie subject to the provisions concerning the procedure for making orders set out in ibid s 13, Sch 2 Pt I.

4   Ie ibid Sch 2 Pt II. As to the meaning of 'land' see para 620 note 19 ante.

5   'Oil installations' means any works for the storage or transmission of oil (including oil pipelines and works accessory to oil pipelines) and any works for giving access to, or otherwise required in connection with, any such works: ibid s 25(1). 'Oil pipeline' means any main or pipe for the transmission of oil, or for the transmission of water or any other substance in connection with the storage or transmission of oil, or any part of such a main or pipe: s 25(1). References to the maintenance of an oil pipeline or of accessory works must be construed as including references to the replacing of them, and the provisions of the Land Powers (Defence) Act 1958 apply to anything laid, installed or constructed by way of replacement as they previously applied to the thing replaced: s 25(4).

6   Ibid s 13(a).

7   Ie for the purposes of the Requisitioned Land and War Works Act 1945 Pt II (ss 4–14) (repealed). As to the meaning of 'government war works' see para 620 note 1 ante.

8   Land Powers (Defence) Act 1958 s 13(b).

9   Ibid s 13(c).

10   Ie (1) a Secretary of State, for defence purposes; (2) the Secretary of State (see note 1 supra), for the purpose of the provision and maintenance of facilities which in his opinion are essential for the defence of the realm; (3) any of those ministers, for the purpose of any diversion appearing to that minister to be necessary or expedient of an oil pipeline which is vested in or under the control of that minister and either is a government oil pipeline or was laid under a wayleave order made by that minister: Land Powers (Defence) Act 1958 s 14(3) (amended by the Defence (Transfer of Functions) (No 1) Order 1964, SI 1964/488, art 2, Sch 1 Pt II). For the meaning of 'minister' generally see para 620 note 15 ante; and for the meaning of 'government oil pipeline' see para 620 note 6 ante.
     'Defence purposes' includes any purpose of the naval, military or air forces of the Crown, the service of any visiting force within the meaning of the Visiting Forces Act 1952 Pt I (ss 1–12), and any purpose of the Secretary of State for Transport connected with the service of any of those forces: Land Powers (Defence) Act 1958 s 25(1). The Secretary of State for Transport now exercises the civil aviation functions of the former Minister of Supply: see the Transfer of Functions (Trade and Industry) Order 1983, SI 1983/1127.

11   See note 10 supra.

12   'Wayleave order' means an order made under the Land Powers (Defence) Act 1958 s 14(1): see s 25(1). As to the procedure for making orders see s 14, Sch 2 Pt I. In relation to works in exercise of the powers under a wayleave order certain provisions of the New Roads and Street Works Act 1991 are modified with regard to plans and to avoid an unacceptable diversion or change of a government oil pipeline: see the Land Powers (Defence) Act 1958 s 18A (added by the New Roads and Street Works Act 1991 s 168(1), Sch 8 Pt IV para 100). As to street works generally see HIGHWAYS.

13   'Minor works accessory to an oil pipeline' includes (1) manholes, inspection pits and similar works; (2) electrical apparatus for the operation or maintenance of an oil pipeline, and electric lines (within the meaning of the Electricity Act 1989 s 64(1): see FUEL AND ENERGY vol 19(2) (Reissue) para 870) provided mainly for the purpose of supplying electricity to such apparatus; (3) markers for indicating the position of an oil pipeline or of any such apparatus or electric line in so far as the pipeline, apparatus or electric line is placed below the surface of the land; (4) stiles, bridges, gates or other works for affording access to an oil pipeline: Land Powers (Defence) Act 1958 s 14(2) (amended by the Electricity Act 1989 s 112(1), Sch 16 para 9).

14   Land Powers (Defence) Act 1958 s 14(1)(a). These operations may be carried out in such positions (subject to any minor deviations found to be necessary or expedient) under or above the surface of that land, or partly under and partly above the surface of it, as may be specified in the order: s 14(1)(a).

15   Ibid s 14(1)(b). The working of minerals is restricted, subject to the payment of compensation: see s 15(2).

16   Ibid s 15(1). Any person who wilfully obstructs a person acting in the exercise of these powers is liable on summary conviction to a fine not exceeding level 1 on the standard scale: s 15(1), Sch 4 para 2. As to the standard scale see para 532 note 18 ante. Any person who in consequence of the exercise of these powers suffers loss by reason of damage to any land or chattels or is disturbed in the enjoyment of them is entitled to compensation, and any dispute as to a right of compensation or as to the amount of compensation must be determined by the Lands Tribunal: see Sch 4 para 3. As to the Lands Tribunal see COMPULSORY ACQUISITION OF LAND vol 8(1) (Reissue) para 202 et seq.

17 See ibid s 15(1) proviso. As to service of the notice see s 23. As to the meaning of 'occupier' see para 620 note 17 ante.

18 The power to make regulations is exercisable by statutory instrument, which is subject to annulment in pursuance of a resolution of either House of Parliament: ibid s 24(1). As to the regulations so made see the Government Oil Pipe-Lines (No 2) Regulations 1959, SI 1959/724.

19 Land Powers (Defence) Act 1958 s 15(3)(b).

20 Ibid s 15(3)(a).

21 Ie under the Requisitioned Land and War Works Act 1948 s 12(1) or under a wayleave order. As to the rights under s 12 see para 620 ante. As to acquisition of land and compensation see also ROYAL FORCES vol 41 para 117.

22 See the Land Powers (Defence) Act 1958 s 16(1). The minister may, if he thinks fit, direct that anything done in contravention of the restrictions is to be deemed to have been done with his consent: see s 16(4). The minister may take remedial action if the restrictions are contravened (see s 16(2), Sch 4 paras 1, 2); and any expenses so incurred are recoverable from the occupier of the land on which the contravention was committed (see s 16(3)).

23 Ibid s 17(1) (substituted by the Local Land Charges Act 1975 s 17(2), Sch 1). As to registration of wayleave orders see the Land Powers (Defence) Act 1958 s 17 (amended by the Local Land Charges Act 1975 Sch 1; the Local Land Charges Act 1975 s 19(1), Sch 2; and the Local Government Act 1972 s 272(1), Sch 30).

24 See the Land Powers (Defence) Act 1958 s 18(1). The Treasury may by regulations require, as a condition of the payment of compensation under s 18, that a claim must be made in a prescribed form and manner and within a certain period: see s 18(4). The power to make regulations is exercisable by statutory instrument, which is subject to annulment in pursuance of a resolution of either House of Parliament: s 24(1). See the Government Oil Pipe-Lines (No 2) Regulations 1959. Any dispute as to a right of compensation under the Land Powers (Defence) Act 1958 s 18, or as to the amount of compensation, must be determined by the Lands Tribunal: s 18(5). As to the Lands Tribunal see COMPULSORY ACQUISITION OF LAND vol 8(1) (Reissue) para 202 et seq.

25 Land Powers (Defence) Act 1958 s 18(3). See also note 24 supra.

622. Acquisition or extinction of easements; acquisition of levels of land or reversionary interests.

The power of any minister[1] to acquire land[2] under the Defence Acts for any purpose[3] is extended[4] so as to enable him to acquire any such easements[5] over or rights restrictive of the user[6] of any land as he requires for that purpose[7]. Surface land and minerals or lower strata may be acquired separately under the Defence Acts[8]; and, where the minister or any person on his behalf is in possession under a lease or tenancy, any interest reversionary on it may be acquired under those Acts[9]. Compensation is payable in respect of the diminution in the value of the interest in land of any person by the acquisition of the easement or restrictive right[10].

Procedure for the acquisition of an easement or restrictive right under these provisions is by notice to treat[11]. If the minister is of the opinion that he will be unable, or unable without undue delay, to acquire such an easement or restrictive right by agreement, he may, at any time within two months from the service of the notice to treat, execute a deed poll which is deemed[12] to be a deed of grant or covenant entered into with him by all necessary parties[13].

An easement or restrictive right may be released by a minister, wholly or in part, and with or without consideration[14], but the statutory provision for the discharge or modification of restrictive covenants[15] is inapplicable[16].

Where a minister having power to acquire land under the Defence Acts has so acquired or proposes to acquire any land which is subject to an easement, he may, by notice served on the persons and in the manner on whom and in which under those Acts a notice to treat would be required to be served for the compulsory acquisition of the dominant tenement, extinguish the easement or modify it in such manner and to such extent as may be specified in the notice[17].

1 For the meaning of 'minister' see para 602 note 9 ante. The power of a minister to acquire land under the Defence Acts is unaffected by the fact that his office may be temporary or that he can obtain or has obtained possession apart from those Acts: Requisitioned Land and War Works Act 1945 s 33(2). As to

the Defence Acts see para 617 note 4 ante.

2   Where a minister has acquired or has power to acquire any land under the Defence Acts or would have power to acquire any land if he did not already own it, and that land contains part of a continuous main or pipe or the whole or part of works used in connection with it, any rights necessary for or incidental to the maintenance or use of any part of the main or pipe which is in, over or under land not owned or acquired by the minister may, subject to and in accordance with the provisions of the Requisitioned Land and War Works Act 1945 relating to the acquisition of easements, be acquired by him as easements for the benefit of such of the first-mentioned land as he owns or acquires; and, if so acquired by him, such rights are deemed for all purposes to be such easements: s 59(4). In relation to the acquisition of any such rights, reference to easements which are in the opinion of the minister essential to the full enjoyment of the land must be construed as reference to easements which are essential in his opinion to the full enjoyment of the main or pipe: s 59(4) proviso.

3   Powers under the Requisitioned Land and War Works Act 1945 Pt VII (ss 32–39) (s 35 repealed), may be exercisable for the purposes of any visiting force: see the Visiting Forces Act 1952 s 8(1); the Visiting Forces and International Headquarters (Application of Law) Order 1965, SI 1965/1536, art 5(1); the International Headquarters and Defence Organisations Act 1964 s 1(2), Schedule para 7; and ROYAL FORCES vol 41 para 111.

4   This extension, which as originally enacted was temporary, has been made permanent: see para 617 ante.

5   'Easement' includes a right to support for any land or for any buildings or works, and a right to withdraw that support, and any such right obtained under the Defence Acts is deemed an easement: Requisitioned Land and War Works Act 1945 s 59(3). The power conferred to acquire easements includes power in the like manner and subject to the like provisions to acquire rights, as against all persons affected or to be affected, to take water from a watercourse for the benefit of any land, whether contiguous or not, for the like purposes and to the like extent as water could be taken by virtue of ownership of land contiguous to the watercourse at the place where it is proposed to take the water: Requisitioned Land and War Works Act 1948 s 6, Schedule para 9.

6   A covenant to limit the growth of trees or other vegetation on any land is deemed to confer a right restrictive of the user of that land, and references to rights restrictive of the user of land are construed accordingly: Requisitioned Land and War Works Act 1945 s 59(5).

     Where (1) a right restrictive of the user of any land has been acquired by a minister under the Defence Acts, whether by the execution of a deed poll or otherwise; and (2) between the date of the notice to treat and the acquisition of that right, any works have been constructed on, over or below the surface of the land adversely affected by the right; and (3) the construction of the works would have been an infringement of the right if it had taken place after the acquisition, the minister is entitled to remove the works and to recover the costs reasonably incurred in doing so from the person by whom the works were constructed: Requisitioned Land and War Works Act 1945 s 38(1).

7   Ibid s 33(1) (amended by the Statute Law (Repeals) Act 1973 s 1(1), Sch 1 Pt IX). Any power of any persons under the Defence Acts to sell or convey land is deemed to include power to create by grant to, or covenant with, a minister any easement or right which that minister has power to acquire under those Acts: Requisitioned Land and War Works Act 1945 s 36(2).

8   See ibid s 34(1) (amended by the Statute Law Repeals Act 1973 s 1(1), Sch 1 Pt IX; and by the Coal Industry Act 1994 s 67(1), Sch 9 para 2). As to the making permanent of the Requisitioned Land and War Works Act 1945 s 34 (as so amended) see para 617 ante. The acquisition of the minerals or lower strata without the surface is subject to the Coal Industry Act 1994 s 10(3): Requisitioned Land and War Works Act 1945 s 34(1) (as so amended). See also MINES vol 31 para 726.

9   See ibid s 34(2) (amended by the Statute Law (Repeals) Act 1973 Sch 1 Pt IX).

10   See the Requisitioned Land and War Works Act 1945 s 39. Questions of disputed compensation are referable to the Lands Tribunal: see the Land Compensation Act 1961 s 1. As to compensation generally and the Lands Tribunal see COMPULSORY ACQUISITION OF LAND vol 8(1) (Reissue) para 197 et seq.

11   Where, under the Defence Acts, a minister has power to acquire an easement over or right restrictive of the user of any land, he may, with a view to the creation by grant to him, or covenant with him, of the easement or right, serve a notice to treat for the acquisition of the easement or right on the persons who would, under those Acts or otherwise, be entitled to sell the land to be adversely affected by the easement or right, or otherwise have any interest in the land: Requisitioned Land and War Works Act 1945 s 36(1). Constructive service of a notice to treat is deemed service: s 59(7). A notice to treat for the acquisition of an easement relating to water may be addressed generally to all persons interested in any land which will be adversely affected, and, if so addressed, is deemed to be duly served by publication in the London Gazette and in such other manner as is best adapted, in the minister's opinion, for informing persons affected: s 36(3). See also note 13 infra.

12   Ie for the purposes of the Land Registration Act 1925 and the Land Charges Act 1972.

13   See the Requisitioned Land and War Works Act 1945 s 37(1), (2). Where the minister executes a deed poll under s 37, he must give notice of its effect in such manner as is in his opinion best adapted for

informing persons affected: s 37(5). A statement in the deed poll that the requirements of s 36(3) have been complied with is conclusive except for the purposes of proceedings begun within two years after the execution of the deed: s 37(4).

   Registration under the Land Registration Act 1925 and entry of notice of the easement or restrictive right may be effected without the production of the land certificate: see the Requisitioned Land and War Works Act 1945 s 37(3).

14   Ibid s 38(2).
15   Ie the Law of Property Act 1925 s 84 (as amended): see EQUITY vol 16 (Reissue) para 814.
16   Requisitioned Land and War Works Act 1945 s 38(3) (amended by the Law of Property Act 1969 s 28(10)).
17   Requisitioned Land and War Works Act 1948 s 4(2) (amended by the Statute Law (Repeals) Act 1973 Sch 1 Pt IX). Where an interest in a dominant tenement is vested in a person carrying on a statutory undertaking, the provisions of the Town and Country Planning Act 1990 ss 271–282 (see also the New Towns Act 1981 ss 26–30 (s 26 as amended), Sch 4 (as amended), Schs 7, 8) apply with adaptations as respects the interest of the person carrying on the statutory undertaking in lieu of any corresponding provisions of the Requisitioned Land and War Works Act 1948 s 4(2): see s 4(3); and the Extinguishment or Modification of Easements Regulations 1948, SI 1948/1582, reg 4. If there is a public inquiry into compensation, the minister must give reasons for his decision if requested: see the Tribunals and Inquiries Act 1992 s 10; and the Tribunals and Inquiries (Discretionary Inquiries) Order 1975, SI 1975/1379, arts 3, 4, Schedule Pt I para 53.

623. Minister's certificate. A certificate by any minister[1] as to (1) what government war work[2] has been done on any land[3]; (2) what government war use[4] had been made of any land; (3) what damage has occurred on any land owing to government war use of it; (4) the periods for which any land was in his possession or in that of any other minister or in the possession of any person occupying or using it under his authority or that of any other minister; and (5) whether any specified works were constructed on, over or below the surface of any land wholly or partly at the expense of the Crown or by arrangement with any minister, is evidence of the facts stated[5].

   Every document purporting to be such a certificate and to be signed by or on behalf of a minister or other person must be received in evidence and must, until the contrary is proved, be deemed to be such a certificate of that minister or person, and in any legal proceedings, including arbitrations, the production of a document purporting to be certified by or on behalf of the minister or person having power to give any such certificate to be a true copy of such a certificate is, unless the contrary is proved, sufficient evidence of the certificate[6].

1   For the meaning of 'minister' see para 602 note 9 ante.
2   For the meaning of 'government war work' see para 620 note 1 ante.
3   The 'doing of work on land' means the doing of any work on, over or below the surface of the land, and, in particular, includes the making of any erection or excavation, the placing of any thing, and the maintenance, removal, demolition, pulling down, destruction or rendering useless of any thing, on, over or below that surface: Requisitioned Land and War Works Act 1945 s 59(2). See also para 602 note 2 ante.
4   'Government war use' means, in relation to land, any use to which that land is put during the war period by or by arrangement with a minister, or under emergency powers: ibid s 59(1). For the meaning of the 'war period', and for the meaning of 'emergency powers', see para 601 note 10 ante.
5   Ibid s 58(1).
6   Ibid s 58(2).

624. Expenses. Any expenses incurred or compensation payable under or by virtue of the Requisitioned Land and War Works Act 1945 by any minister[1], and any increase attributable to that Act in any compensation payable by the Crown under any other Act, are defrayed out of moneys provided by Parliament[2]. Any sum paid[3] to any minister is to be paid into the Exchequer of the United Kingdom[4].

   Any increase in consequence of the provisions of the Requisitioned Land and War Works Act 1948 in the sums payable[5] under the Compensation (Defence) Act 1939 or the Requisitioned Land and War Works Act 1945, must be defrayed out of moneys provided by Parliament[6]. Any other expenses of a minister incurred under the provisions relating to easements over land acquired or proposed to be acquired under the Defence Acts[7], or relating to government oil pipelines[8], must also be defrayed out of moneys provided by Parliament[9].

Any expenditure attributable to the provisions of the Land Powers (Defence) Act 1958 incurred by any minister of the Crown in the United Kingdom is to be defrayed out of moneys provided by Parliament[10].

1 For the meaning of 'minister' see para 602 note 9 ante.
2 Requisitioned Land and War Works Act 1945 s 57(1) (amended by the Miscellaneous Financial Provisions Act 1955 s 4(4), Sch 2 Pt II (repealed)).
3 Ie under the Requisitioned Land and War Works Act 1945 or the Land Powers (Defence) Act 1958.
4 Requisitioned Land and War Works Act 1945 s 57(2); Land Powers (Defence) Act 1958 s 26(2). For the meaning of 'United Kingdom' see para 502 note 4 ante.
5 Ie out of moneys provided by Parliament.
6 Requisitioned Land and War Works Act 1948 s 16(a).
7 See para 622 ante. As to the Defence Acts see para 617 note 4 ante.
8 See para 620 ante. For the meaning of 'government oil pipelines' see para 620 note 6 ante.
9 Requisitioned Land and War Works Act 1948 s 16(b).
10 Land Powers (Defence) Act 1958 s 26(1)(a) (amended by the Defence (Transfer of Functions) (No 1) Order 1964, SI 1964/488, art 2, Sch 1 Pt II).

(3) WAR DAMAGE

625. War damage legislation. Legislation which was chiefly contained in the War Damage Act 1943[1] formerly existed by which payments were made in respect of war damage[2] to land occurring during the period from 3 September 1939 to 1 October 1964[3]. Such payments were initially made by the War Damage Commission[4] and later by the Commissioners of Inland Revenue. The legislation also required persons interested in the land to make contributions towards the expense of making such payments[5]. Claims for payments under the War Damage Act 1943 had to be made by 30 September 1968, and the right to receive such payments finally terminated on 30 September 1974[6]. The War Damage Acts 1943 to 1964 are now wholly repealed[7] together with various other enactments[8] relating to war damage and to war risks insurance. Legislation enabling local authorities to take possession of, or do work on, war damaged sites has now been repealed[9].

The right of a person at common law to obtain compensation from the Crown in respect of war damage has been abolished[10].

1 The War Damage Act 1943 was wholly repealed by the Statute Law (Repeals) Act 1981 s 1(1), Sch 1 Pt XI.
2 For the meaning of 'war damage' see para 626 post.
3 As to this period, referred to as 'the risk period' see the War Damage Act 1943 s 1(1)(a) (repealed) (amended by the War Damage Act 1964 s 1(3) (repealed)).
4 The War Damage Commission was constituted under the War Damage Act 1943 s 3 (repealed). By the War Damage Act 1964 s 2, the commission was dissolved and its functions were, with certain exceptions, transferred to the Commissioners of Inland Revenue.
5 See the War Damage Act 1943 s 1(1)(b) (repealed).
6 See the War Damage Act 1964 ss 1(1), (5), 7 (repealed).
7 By virtue of ibid s 14(2), the following Acts could be cited by the collective title of the War Damage Acts 1943 to 1964: the War Damage Act 1943, the War Damage (Public Utility Undertakings, etc) Act 1949, the War Damage (Clearance Payments) Act 1960 and the War Damage Act 1964. All these Acts were repealed by the Statute Law (Repeals) Act 1981 Sch 1 Pt XI.
8 The following other enactments relating to war damage were repealed by the Statute Law (Repeals) Act 1981 Sch 1 Pt XI: the Trustee (War Damage Insurance) Act 1941, and the Licensing Act 1964 s 118(3). The following enactments relating to war risks insurance were also repealed by the Statute Law (Repeals) Act 1981: the War Risks Insurance Act 1939, the Restriction of Advertisement (War Risks Insurance) Act 1939

s 1(2)(a), the War Damage Act 1941, the War Damage (Amendment) Act 1942, the Insurance Contracts (War Settlement) Act 1952 and the Marine and Aviation Insurance (War Risks) Act 1952 ss 5(1)(a)(ii), (iii), (b)(ii), 10(4).

9   The War Damaged Sites Act 1949 was repealed by the Statute Law (Repeals) Act 1986 s 1, Sch 1 Pt VII.

10   War Damage Act 1965 s 1(1). Where any proceedings to recover at common law compensation in respect of such damage or destruction were instituted before 2 June 1965, the court must, on the application of any party set aside or dismiss the proceedings, subject only to the determination of any question arising as to costs or expenses: s 1(2).

626. Meaning of 'war damage'. For the purposes of the War Damage Act 1943[1], 'war damage' meant (1) damage occurring, whether accidentally or not, as the direct result of action taken by the enemy[2], or action taken in combating the enemy or in repelling an imagined attack by the enemy[3]; (2) damage occurring, whether accidentally or not, as the direct result of measures taken under proper authority to avoid the spreading of, or otherwise to mitigate, the consequences of that damage[4]; and (3) accidental damage occurring as the direct result (a) of any precautionary or preparatory measures taken under proper authority with a view to preventing or hindering the carrying out of any attack by the enemy[5]; or (b) of precautionary or preparatory measures involving the doing of work on land and taken under proper authority in any way in anticipation of enemy action[6], being in either case measures involving a substantial degree of risk to property[7]. With Treasury consent the War Damage Commission[8] might treat as damage of the kind mentioned in head (2) above any physical change in land (whether or not it caused depreciation in the value of the land) which was the direct result of measures taken under proper authority to meet the circumstances created by damage occurring as mentioned in head (1) above[9].

1   As to the repeal of the War Damage Act 1943 see para 625 note 1 ante.

2   As to damage resulting from direct action by the enemy see *Re 36, 38, 40 and 42 Jamaica Street, Stepney* [1947] Ch 409, [1947] 1 All ER 754, CA; *Re 34, Bruton Street, Westminster* [1957] Ch 543, [1957] 2 All ER 539, CA.

3   War Damage Act 1943 s 2(1)(a) (repealed). In this context action against the enemy in relation to any ship or aircraft so engaged was deemed to continue until the ship or aircraft returned to its base, and the expression included naval, military or air reconnaissances and patrols: s 2(3) (repealed).

4   Ibid s 2(1)(b) (repealed).

5   Ibid s 2(1)(c)(i) (repealed).

6   Ibid s 2(1)(c)(ii) (repealed).

7   Ibid s 2(1) (repealed). The measures taken in head (3) in the text did not include the imposing of restrictions on the display of lights or measures taken for training purposes: s 2(1) proviso (repealed). References in the War Damage Act 1943 to the occurrence of war damage were to be construed as references to the taking of the action or measures specified in s 2 from which that damage resulted: s 2(4) (repealed).

8   As to the War Damage Commission see para 625 note 4 ante.

9   War Damage Act 1943 s 2(2) (repealed). No compensation was thus payable for depreciation so treated by the War Damage Commission or later by the Commissioners of Inland Revenue: s 109(2) (repealed).

(4) OTHER EMERGENCY CONTROL OF TRANSPORT AND ENERGY

627. Control of railways in time of hostilities, severe international tension or great national emergency. In time of hostilities, whether actual or imminent, severe international tension or great national emergency[1], the Secretary of State[2] may give directions[3] to such of the following persons as he may consider appropriate:

(1)   the Rail Regulator[4];

(2)   the Director of Passenger Rail Franchising[5];

(3)   any person who is the owner[6] or operator[7] of a relevant asset[8];

(4)   any person who provides railway services[9].

The power to give such directions to a person who is the owner or operator of a relevant asset or who provides railway services includes power:

(a)   in the case of a person who is the owner of a relevant asset, to direct that person to permit the use of, or to exercise his rights over, the relevant asset in such manner or for such purposes as may be specified in the direction;

(b)   in the case of a person who is the operator of a relevant asset, to direct that person to exercise his powers of management over the relevant asset in such manner or for such purposes as may be so specified; and

(c)   in the case of a person who provides railway services, to direct that person to do so in such manner or for such purposes as may be so specified[10].

The Secretary of State may also give directions at any time to any of those persons whom he may consider appropriate, requiring that person to participate in the planning of steps that might be taken in time of actual or imminent hostilities, severe international tension or great national emergency[11].

The regulator and the franchising director are each under a duty to comply with a direction so given to him, notwithstanding the requirements of any other enactment or instrument relating to him[12]; and a person who is the owner or operator of a relevant asset or who provides railway services is under a duty to comply with a direction so given to him, notwithstanding the requirements of any other enactment or instrument relating to him or to the use of, or the exercise of rights over, the relevant asset, the management of the relevant asset, or the railway services, and notwithstanding any other duty or obligation to which he may be subject[13].

Any person who, without reasonable excuse, contravenes or fails to comply with a direction so given to him is guilty of an offence and liable on summary conviction to a fine not exceeding the statutory maximum, or on conviction on indictment to a fine or imprisonment for a term not exceeding two years, or to both[14]. No proceedings may be instituted in England and Wales in respect of such an offence except by or with the consent of the Secretary of State or the Director of Public Prosecutions[15].

Any person (other than the regulator and the franchising director) who suffers direct injury or loss arising from compliance with a such direction given in time of actual or imminent hostilities, severe international tension or great national emergency is entitled to receive compensation from the Secretary of State of such amount as may be agreed by that person and the Secretary of State or, in default of agreement, of such amount as may be determined by an arbitrator appointed by the President for the time being of the Royal Institution of Chartered Surveyors[16]. Any sums required by the Secretary of State for paying such compensation must be paid out of money provided by Parliament[17].

1   'Great national emergency' means any natural disaster or other emergency which, in the opinion of the Secretary of State, is or may be likely to give rise to such disruption of the means of transport that the population, or a substantial part of the population, of Great Britain is or may be likely to be deprived of essential goods or services: Railways Act 1993 s 118(11).

2   The Secretary of State here concerned is the Secretary of State for Transport.

3   The power to give such directions to the regulator or the franchising director (see notes 4–5 infra) includes power to direct him to carry out his functions in such manner or for such purposes as may be specified in the direction: Railways Act 1993 s 118(3).

4   Ibid ss 1(1)(a), 118(1)(a). As to the regulator see further RAILWAYS.

5   Ibid ss 1(1)(b), 118(1)(b). As to the franchising director see further RAILWAYS.

6   'Owner', in relation to a relevant asset, means any person who is the owner of, or who has any right over or interest in, the relevant asset and whose consent is needed to the use of the relevant asset by any other person; and 'relevant asset' means a network, a station, a light maintenance depot or any track or rolling stock within the meaning of the Railways Act 1993 Pts I, II (ss 1–116) (see s 83(1); and RAILWAYS): s 118(11).

7   'Operator', in relation to a relevant asset, means the person having the management of the relevant asset for the time being: ibid s 118(11).

8   Ibid s 118(1)(c).

9   Ibid s 118(1)(d). For the meaning of 'railways services' see s 82(1); and RAILWAYS.

10 Ibid s 118(4).

11 Ibid s 118(2).

12 Ibid s 118(5).

13 Ibid s 118(6).

14 Ibid s 118(7). As to the statutory maximum see para 575 note 9 ante.

15 Ibid s 118(8).

16 Ibid s 118(9). As to the Royal Institution of Chartered Surveyors see VALUERS AND SURVEYORS para 402 ante.

17 Ibid s 118(10).

628. Shipping convoys. In times of war it has been the custom for cargo vessels to sail in convoy, to lessen the effect of enemy action[1]. As a result, a master of a ship may be placed under a contractual duty to sail in convoy by a term of the contract of carriage[2], expressed or implied, to that effect[3]. In time of war, ships may become subject to orders of the Defence Council, issued with legislative authority, in respect of their movements and navigation generally[4]; and these orders may enjoin obedience to routing instructions issued by the Defence Council or by a convoy commander[5]. It is the duty of the master or other person for the time being in command of any vessel comprised in a convoy under the command of an officer of Her Majesty's naval forces, or of any person duly appointed in that behalf, to obey, in all matters relating to the navigation or security of the convoy, any directions which may be given (1) where the convoy is escorted by any of Her Majesty's ships or vessels, by the commanding officer of any such ship or vessel; (2) in any case, by the officer or other person in command of the convoy, and to take such precautions for avoiding the enemy as may be required by any such directions[6]. If any such directions are not obeyed, any such commanding officer, or the officer or other person in command of the convoy, may compel obedience by force of arms[7]. Further, if the master or other person having command of any ship of any of Her Majesty's subjects in convoy with any of Her Majesty's ships of war[8] wilfully disobeys any lawful signal, instruction or command of the convoy commander or without leave deserts the convoy, he is liable upon conviction to a fine at the discretion of the court or to imprisonment for not more than one year[9].

During the 1939–45 war, the duty of obedience to convoy orders overrode contrary obligations under the regulations for preventing collisions at sea[10], and the master of a vessel was not therefore negligent in not complying with those regulations if he was executing convoy orders[11]. Otherwise, masters of vessels remained bound by the duty of good seamanship and, so far as the circumstances permitted, the duty to take the action prescribed by those regulations to avoid collision[12]. Where the master of a vessel accepts and undertakes the duties of a convoy commander, the owners of his vessel are not liable for damage by consequent collision caused by an act of negligence on the part of the master in the course of performing his duties as convoy commander[13].

1   As to the meaning of 'sailing in convoy' see *Hibbert v Pigou* (1783) 3 Doug KB 224. As to extent and condition of sailing in convoy see further *Jefferies v Legendra* (1691) Carth 216; *Lethulier's Case* (1692) 2 Salk 443; *Gordon v Morley, Campell v Bordieu* (1747) 2 Stra 1265; *Lilly v Ewer* (1779) 1 Doug KB 72; *Smith v Readshaw* (1781) 2 Park's Marine Insurances (8th Edn) 708; *Manning v Gist* (1782) 3 Doug KB 74; *D'Eguino v Bewicke* (1795) 2 Hy Bl 551; *De Garey v Clagget* (1795) 2 Park's Marine Insurances (8th Edn) 708; *Webb v Thomson* (1797) 1 Bos & P 5; *Audley v Duff* (1800) 2 Bos & P 111; *Anderson v Pitcher* (1800) 2 Bos & P 164. As to sailing in or without convoy in relation to marine insurance see *Harrington v Halkeld* (1778) 2 Park's Marine Insurances (8th Edn) 639; and INSURANCE vol 25 (Reissue) para 222.

2　As to contracts of carriage see generally SHIPPING.

3　See *Phillips v Baillie* (1784) 3 Doug KB 374; *Runquist v Ditchell* (1799) 3 Esp 64; *Magalhaens v Busher* (1814) 4 Camp 54.

4　During the 1939–45 war, the Admiralty had power to make navigation orders and a master of a vessel contravening or not complying with such an order was guilty of an offence: see the Defence (General) Regulations 1939, SR & O 1939/927, reg 43 (revoked).

5　For an example of such a navigation order see *The Vernon City* [1942] P 9; affd [1942] P 61, 72 Ll L Rep 223, CA.

6　Naval Discipline Act 1957 s 131(1) (amended by the Defence (Transfer of Functions) (No 1) Order 1964, SI 1964/488, art 2, Sch 1 Pt I).

7　Naval Discipline Act 1957 s 131(2). Neither the person using such force nor any person acting under his orders is liable for any injury, loss of life or damage to or loss of property resulting therefrom: s 131(2).

8　'Any of Her Majesty's ships of war' includes any hired armed ship or vessel in Her Majesty's service: Naval Prize Act 1864 s 2.

9　Ibid s 46 (amended by the Courts Act 1971 s 56(4), Sch 11 Pt IV; and by virtue of the Criminal Law Act 1977 s 32(1)).

10　As to the current regulations see SHIPPING.

11　*The Vernon City* [1942] P 9; affd [1942] P 61, 72 Ll L Rep 223, CA. See also *Larchbank (Owners) v British Petrol (Owners), The Larchbank* [1943] AC 299 at 305, 74 Ll L Rep 135 at 138, HL, per Lord Wright.

12　*The Scottish Musician* [1942] P 128, 72 Ll L Rep 284; *The FJ Wolfe* [1946] P 91, [1946] 1 All ER 359, CA. See also *The Emlyn* [1918] P 67.

13　*The Glaucus and City of Florence* [1948] P 95, 81 Ll L Rep 131. As to the duty of the commander of a naval escort in respect of the navigation of a convoy and the question of his liability for negligence in carrying out that duty see *The Sobieski* [1949] P 313, [1949] 1 All ER 701, CA, where a failure to take reasonable care made the escort commander personally liable, but this was not a fault in the navigation of his vessel, hence no contribution was ordered.

629. Control of aviation. In time of war, whether actual or imminent, or of great national emergency, the Secretary of State[1] has power to control aviation, British air transport and the Civil Aviation Authority[2].

All these provisions are discussed elsewhere in this work[3].

1　The Secretary of State here concerned is the Secretary of State for Transport.

2　See the Civil Aviation Act 1982 ss 62–63; and AVIATION vol 2 (Reissue) paras 1063–1065.

3　See note 2 supra.

630. Fuel and energy control. General and reserve powers exist under the Energy Act 1976 to control the supply and use of fuel and energy in times of actual or threatened emergency[1]. Road traffic and transport law may also be relaxed under those powers[2]. The Secretary of State[3] has additional powers to give directions for preserving the security of electricity supplies[4].

All these provisions are discussed elsewhere in this work[5].

1　See the Energy Act 1976 ss 1–6, 17–20 (as amended); and FUEL AND ENERGY vol 19(1) (Reissue) para 502 et seq.

2　See ibid s 4(2), Sch 1 (as amended); and ROAD TRAFFIC vol 40 para 706.

3　The Secretary of State here concerned is the Secretary of State for Trade and Industry.

4　See the Electricity Act 1989 s 96; and FUEL AND ENERGY vol 19(2) (Reissue) para 978.

5　See notes 1–2, 4 supra.

5. ALIEN ENEMIES, TRADE AND PROPERTY

(1) ALIEN ENEMIES

631. Occupation of territory. The temporary occupation of a friendly country by an enemy force does not automatically convert the territory into hostile territory, and a merchant residing in such a country does not necessarily become an alien enemy[1]. It is only when the occupation amounts to subjugation, and the territory is held under the enemy's dominion and effective control for a period sufficient to give the occupation a settled and relatively permanent character, that the territory acquires the character of enemy territory[2]. The subjugated territory may merely be part of a larger territory which, so far as unoccupied, retains its national character[3]. When a revolutionary war has taken place the courts will only recognise the existence or status of a new government after either de facto or de jure recognition by the Crown[4].

When forces of the Crown are in occupation of foreign territory, the Crown has certain rights over that territory[5].

1 *The Gerasimo* (1857) 11 Moo PCC 88, 2 BILC 544; see also *De Jager v A-G of Natal* [1907] AC 326, 5 BILC 74, PC. The subject of occupation of enemy territory is dealt with in the Hague Regulations 1907 (see para 518 note 6 ante) arts 42–56; and in the Geneva Convention relative to the Protection of Civilian Persons in Time of War (see para 521 note 5) arts 27–34, 477–478. The convention is set out in the Geneva Conventions Act 1957 s 7(1), Sch 4: see para 545 et seq ante. The convention and the Geneva Conventions 1949 Protocol I supplement the Hague Regulations 1907, without abrogating them, and deal primarily with the treatment of persons in the occupied territory, whereas the Hague Regulations 1907 are primarily concerned with property there. As to the application and implementation of the Geneva Conventions 1949 Protocol I see paras 521–522 ante.

2 *Sovfracht (V/O) v Van Udens Scheepvaart en Agentuur Maatschappij (NV Gebr)* [1943] AC 203 at 211, 220, [1943] 1 All ER 76 at 79, 84, HL; *Re Anglo-International Bank Ltd* [1943] Ch 233, [1943] 2 All ER 88, CA.

3 *Sovfracht (V/O) v Van Udens Scheepvaart en Agentuur Maatschappij (NV Gebr)* [1943] AC 203 at 229, [1943] 1 All ER 76 at 88, HL; *The Foltina* (1814) 1 Dods 450 at 457, 2 BILC 442; and see *SA Belge des Mines d'Aljustrel (Portugal) v Anglo Belgian Agency Ltd* [1915] 2 Ch 409, CA.

4 See *Bank of Ethiopia v National Bank of Egypt and Liguori* [1937] 1 Ch 513, [1937] 3 All ER 8; *Haile Selassie v Cable and Wireless Ltd (No 2)* [1939] Ch 182, [1938] 3 All ER 677, CA; *United States of America v McRae* (1869) LR 8 Eq 69, 2 BILC 259; *Spain v The Arantzazu Mendi* [1939] AC 256, [1939] 1 All ER 719, HL; and EVIDENCE vol 17 para 105.

5 See eg as to the position of the former Control Commission for Germany, and the validity of its legislation, *Grahame v DPP* (1947) Control Commission Criminal Appeal Reports 168. As to the Crown's powers in relation to emergencies and in particular under martial law see generally CONSTITUTIONAL LAW AND HUMAN RIGHTS vol 8(2) (Reissue) para 820 et seq.

632. Meaning of 'alien enemy'. The primary meaning of 'alien enemy' is one whose sovereign or state is at war with the Sovereign of England[1]. However, in reference to civil rights, 'alien enemy' is used by the United Kingdom[2] courts in a different sense and means one who is voluntarily[3] resident or who carries on business[4] in an enemy or enemy-subjugated country[5], even though he is a natural-born British subject[6] or a naturalised British subject[7], or the subject of a neutral state[8]. A subject of an enemy state who is neither residing nor carrying on business in an enemy or enemy-subjugated country is not an alien enemy with reference to civil rights, and so may maintain an action in this country[9].

By residing and trading in an allied or neutral state, a subject of an enemy state may acquire a friendly or neutral commercial domicile[10], which will protect his goods, if captured at sea, from condemnation[11]. A British born wife of an alien enemy separated from her husband and residing in a neutral or friendly country is not an alien enemy[12].

To prove that a person is an alien enemy at the time of the commencement of an action, it is not enough to show that he was some time before domiciled in territory which has become hostile[13].

1   *Sylvester's Case* (1703) 7 Mod Rep 150. This has been described as the 'natural' meaning of alien enemy: *Porter v Freudenberg, Kreglinger v S Samuel and Rosenfeld, Re Merten's Patents* [1915] 1 KB 857 at 867, CA. As to aliens generally see BRITISH NATIONALITY, IMMIGRATION AND RACE RELATIONS vol 4(2) (Reissue) para 66. The monarch's enemies are foreign states in actual hostility against her: see *Case of the Marshall of the King's Bench* (1455) YB 33, Hen VI fo 1, pl 3; and CRIMINAL LAW vol 11(1) (Reissue) para 428. A change of nationality by decree of an enemy state purporting to change any of its subjects to a stateless person or a subject of a neutral state will not be recognised by the courts: *R v Home Secretary, ex p L* [1945] KB 7, DC. See also *Lowenthal v A-G* [1948] 1 All ER 295. An alien enemy does not lose his enemy character merely by taking the oath of allegiance to a neutral sovereign; to do so he must completely abandon his previous national character: *The Johann Christoph* (1854) 2 Ecc & Ad 2. Nor does he lose his enemy character merely by being a party to purely formal documents: *The Soglasie* (1854) 2 Ecc & Ad 101.

2   For the meaning of 'United Kingdom' see para 502 note 4 ante.

3   'Residence' for the purpose of the statutory definition of 'enemy' (see the Trading with the Enemy Act 1939 s 2(1)(b); and para 635 post), however, means de facto residence and is not restricted to voluntary residence: see *Vamvakas v Custodian of Enemy Property* [1952] 2 QB 183 at 195, [1952] 1 All ER 629 at 631–632.

4   *M'Connell v Hector* (1802) 3 Bos & P 113. The disability of a person who so carries on business may be cured by a licence from the Crown: *Ex p Baglehole* (1812) 18 Ves 525; *Sovfracht (V/O) v Van Udens Scheepvaart en Agentuur Maatschappij (NV Gebr)* [1943] AC 203 at 218, [1943] 1 All ER 76 at 78, HL.

5   *Porter v Freudenberg, Kreglinger v s Samuel and Rosenfeld, Re Merten's Patents* [1915] 1 KB 857 at 867, 868, CA; *Sovfracht (V/O) v Van Udens Scheepvaart en Agentuur Maatschappij (NV Gebr)* [1943] AC 203 at 209, [1943] 1 All ER 76 at 78, HL. In time of war a person is normally considered as belonging to the country where he is resident and carries on trade: *The Abo* (1854) 1 Ecc & Ad 347; *The Aina* (1854) 1 Ecc & Ad 313. See also *The Antwerpen* [1919] P 252n.

6   *Scotland v South African Territories Ltd* (1917) 33 TLR 255. In this case, although a British subject was interned and thereafter no longer voluntarily residing in an enemy country, his internment was the outcome of his choosing to remain in enemy territory. Cf *Roberts v Hardy* (1815) 3 M & S 533, where it was held that mere residence of a British subject in an enemy country at the outbreak of war, and his remaining there subsequently, was insufficient to affect him with the disabilities attaching to an enemy, and it was said that he must be either trading in the enemy country or adhering to the enemy.

7   *R v Kupfer* [1915] 2 KB 321, CCA. As to British nationality and citizenship see generally BRITISH NATIONALITY, IMMIGRATION AND RACE RELATIONS vol 4(2) (Reissue) para 12 et seq.

8   *The Baltica* (1857) 11 Moo PCC 141 (neutral residing in enemy country as consul and also trading there); *Porter v Freudenberg, Kreglinger v S Samuel and Rosenfeld, Re Merten's Patents* [1915] 1 KB 857 at 869, CA. See also *The Anglo-Mexican (Part Cargo ex)* [1918] AC 422, PC; *The Lutzow* [1918] AC 435, PC.

9   *Re Duchess of Sutherland, Bechoff David & Co v Bubna* (1915) 31 TLR 248.

10   As to commercial domicile see CONFLICT OF LAWS vol 8(1) (Reissue) para 987; PRIZE vol 37 para 1332.

11   *The Flamenco, The Orduna* (1915) 32 TLR 53; *The Clan Grant (Part Cargo ex)* (1915) 31 TLR 321; *The Eumaeus* (1915) 85 LJP 130; *The Hypatia* [1917] P 36. See also para 633 note 4 post; and PRIZE vol 37 para 1332.

12   *Re Grimthorpe's Settlement, Lord Islington v Countess Czernin, Re Grimthorpe's Settlement, Beckett v Countess Czernin* [1918] WN 16.

13   *Harman v Kingston* (1811) 3 Camp 150 at 152.

633. Companies. A company incorporated in the United Kingdom[1] does not become an alien enemy merely because its shares are held by alien enemies; but it becomes an alien enemy if its agents or the persons in de facto control are alien enemies or if it carries on business in an enemy or enemy-subjugated country[2]. The same applies to a company incorporated in an allied state[3]. A company incorporated in an enemy country is an alien enemy regardless of how its shares are held[4].

1   For the meaning of 'United Kingdom' see para 502 note 4 ante.

2   *Daimler Co Ltd v Continental Tyre and Rubber Co (Great Britain) Ltd* [1916] 2 AC 307, HL; *Amorduct Manufacturing Co v Defries & Co* (1914) 84 LJKB 586; *The Poona* (1915) 84 LJP 150; *Re Hilckes, ex p Muhesa*

Rubber Plantations Ltd [1917] 1 KB 48, CA; *The Antwerpen* [1919] P 252n. See also COMPANIES vol 7(1) (1996 Reissue) para 94; CORPORATIONS vol 9 para 1225.

3   *Central India Mining Co Ltd v Société Coloniale Anversoise* [1920] 1 KB 753, CA. However, a company which thus acquires an enemy character does not cease to be an English company subject to English law and, in particular, to the common law prohibition against trading with the enemy: *Kuenigl v Donnersmarck* [1955] 1 QB 515, [1955] 1 All ER 46.

4   *The Roumanian* [1915] P 26 (affd [1916] 1 AC 124, PC); *Sovfracht (V/O) v Van Udens Scheepvaart en Agentuur Maatschappij (NV Gebr)* [1943] AC 203, [1943] 1 All ER 76, HL. However, enemy character may be avoided, in a case where the company carries on buying in an enemy-subjugated country, by transferring the commercial domicile to a country which is not an enemy country or enemy-subjugated: *Lubrafol (Owners) v SS Pamia (Owners), The Pamia* [1943] 1 All ER 269. See also *Isaacs v Barclays Bank Ltd and Barclays Bank (France) Ltd* [1943] 2 All ER 682; and cf para 632 text and note 11 ante.

(2) TRADING WITH THE ENEMY

634. Legislation prohibiting trading with the enemy. The permanent legislation concerned with the offence of trading with the enemy[1] came into operation on 3 September 1939[2], with a protection from liability for previous acts not unlawful at common law[3] and without prejudice to the exercise of any right or prerogative of the Crown[4]. The administration of the legislation is assigned to the Secretary of State[5], save that discretion over consenting to assignments of choses in action and transfers of negotiable instruments is entrusted to the Treasury[6]. The legislation[7] has been extended, subject to certain exceptions, adaptations and modifications, by Order in Council to the Isle of Man[8] and the Channel Islands[9] and may be so extended to any dependent territory[10], or a foreign country or territory[11] in which the Crown has jurisdiction[12].

Amendments to the Trading with the Enemy Act 1939 and provisions relating to the custodianship of enemy property[13], which were made temporarily during the 1939–45 war by defence regulations, have been permanently enacted[14].

1   Ie the Trading with the Enemy Act 1939. As to the power to require proof that goods exported have not reached an enemy or enemy territory see TRADE, INDUSTRY AND INDUSTRIAL RELATIONS vol 47 (Reissue) para 608. For the meaning of 'enemy' see para 635 post. For the meaning of 'trading with the enemy' see para 637 post.

2   Order in Council dated 8 September 1939, SR & O 1939/1195, made under the Trading with the Enemy Act 1939 s 17(2) (repealed).

3   Ibid s 17(2) proviso (repealed). Enactments relating to trading with the enemy which had been passed during the 1914–18 war were repealed by the Trading with the Enemy Act 1939 s 17(3), Schedule (repealed).

4   Ibid s 16. As to prerogative powers in wartime see paras 510–511 ante; and CONSTITUTIONAL LAW AND HUMAN RIGHTS vol 8(2) (Reissue) para 811.

5   See ibid ss 2(2), 3, 5, 7 (ss 3, 5, 7 as amended). The administration was formerly carried out by the Board of Trade whose functions were transferred to the Secretary of State by the Secretary of State for Trade and Industry Order 1970, SI 1970/1537. Expenses are defrayed by money provided by Parliament: Trading with the Enemy Act 1939 s 11(1). For a statement of the principles of administration of former trading with the enemy legislation see *Holt v AEG Electric Co Ltd* [1918] 1 Ch 320. As to the Board of Trade generally see CONSTITUTIONAL LAW AND HUMAN RIGHTS vol 8(2) (Reissue) para 505; TRADE, INDUSTRY AND INDUSTRIAL RELATIONS vol 47 (Reissue) para 2.

6   Trading with the Enemy Act 1939 s 4(1). See also paras 641–642 post.

7   Ie the provisions of the Trading with the Enemy Act 1939 other than s 14 (as amended). Any document stating that any authority or sanction is given under any of the provisions of the Trading with the Enemy Act 1939 by a Secretary of State or the Treasury, and purporting to be signed on behalf of the Secretary of State or the Treasury, or by a person who is empowered by the Act to do anything which may be done thereunder by the Secretary of State, is evidence of the facts stated in the document: s 12.

8   See the Trading with the Enemy (Isle of Man) Order in Council 1940, SR & O 1940/88.

9   See the Trading with the Enemy (Channel Islands) Order in Council 1940, SR & O 1940/87.

10   See the Trading with the Enemy Act 1939 s 14(d); and the Mandated and Trust Territories Act 1947 s 1(1) (as amended).

11 See the Trading with the Enemy (China Custodian) Order in Council 1944, SR & O 1944/100, providing for the administration of property held by the Custodian of Enemy Property for China.

12 Trading with the Enemy Act 1939 s 14 (amended by the Newfoundland (Consequential Provisions) Act 1950 s 1, Schedule). Any power conferred by the Trading with the Enemy Act 1939 to make an Order in Council or an order includes a power to vary or revoke the Order in Council or order: s 15(5).

13 See paras 643–644 post.

14 See the Emergency Laws (Miscellaneous Provisions) Act 1953 s 2 (as amended), Sch 2.

635. Meaning of 'enemy'. 'Enemy'[1] means (1) any state, or sovereign of a state, at war with the Crown[2]; (2) any individual resident in enemy territory[3]; (3) any body of persons, corporate or unincorporate, carrying on business[4] in any place, if and as long as the body is controlled by a person who is an enemy[5]; (4) any body of persons constituted or incorporated in, or under the laws of, a state at war with the Crown[6]; and (5) as respects any business carried on in enemy territory, any individual or body of persons, corporate or unincorporate, carrying on that business[7]. The Secretary of State[8] may by order direct that any specified person is to be deemed[9] to be an enemy[10].

1 Ie for the purposes of the Trading with the Enemy Act 1939: see infra and para 636 et seq post.

2 Ibid s 2(1)(a). See also note 7 infra.

3 Ibid s 2(1)(b). See also note 7 infra. For the meaning of 'enemy territory' see para 636 post.

4 As to the meaning of 'carrying on business' see *Central India Mining Co Ltd v Société Coloniale Anversoise* [1920] 1 KB 753, CA.

5 Trading with the Enemy Act 1939 s 2(1)(c) (amended by the Emergency Laws (Miscellaneous Provisions) Act 1953 s 2, Sch 2 para 3(a)). See also note 7 infra.

6 Trading with the Enemy Act 1939 s 2(1)(d) (as amended: see note 5 supra). See also note 7 infra.

7 Ibid s 2(1)(e) (as amended: see note 5 supra). 'Enemy' does not include any individual by reason only that he is an enemy subject: s 2(1) (amended by the Emergency Laws (Miscellaneous Provisions) Act 1953 Sch 2 para 3(b)). See also *Re Grimthorpe's Settlement, Beckett v Countess Czernin* [1918] WN 16, where an English wife was separated from her alien husband and was resident in a neutral territory but was held not to be an alien enemy under 1914–18 war legislation; and para 636 note 4 post. 'Resident' means de facto resident, irrespective of whether the residence is voluntary: *Re Hatch, Public Trustee v Hatch* [1948] Ch 592, [1948] 2 All ER 288; *Vamvakas v Custodian of Enemy Property* [1952] 2 QB 183, [1952] 1 All ER 629. However, a prisoner of war in enemy territory is not an 'enemy': *Vandyke v Adams* [1942] Ch 155, [1942] 1 All ER 139. See also *SA Belge des Mines d'Aljustrel (Portugal) v Anglo-Belgian Agency Ltd* [1915] 2 Ch 409, CA, where, during the 1914–18 war, a company incorporated in Belgium was held not to be an enemy within the trading with the enemy legislation and proclamations then in force, even though a large portion of the country was effectively in military occupation of the enemy, since the country as a whole was not territory in hostile occupation: *Salti et Fils v Procurator-General* [1919] AC 968, PC (meaning of 'enemy' in the proclamations issued during the 1914–18 war); *Re Anglo-International Bank Ltd* [1943] Ch 233, [1943] 2 All ER 88, CA (communication with enemy shareholders prohibited); *Adrema Werke Maschinenbau GmbH v Custodian of Enemy Property and Administrator of German Enemy Property* [1957] RPC 49, CA, where it was held that goodwill is property, and can therefore be enemy property.

8 As to the Secretary of State see para 634 note 5 ante.

9 Ie for the purposes of the Trading with the Enemy Act 1939.

10 Ibid s 2(2). All such existing orders were revoked by the Trading with the Enemy (Specified Persons) (Revocation) Order 1946, SR & O 1946/1041.

636. Meaning of 'enemy subject' and 'enemy territory'. 'Enemy subject' means[1] an individual who, not being either a British citizen or a citizen of British dependent territories[2], possesses the nationality of a state at war with the Crown[3], or a body of persons constituted in or incorporated under the laws of any such state[4]. 'Enemy territory' means any area which is under the sovereignty of, or in the occupation of, a power with whom the Crown is at war, not being an area in the occupation of the Crown or an allied power[5].

1   Ie for the purposes of the Trading with the Enemy Act 1939.

2   As to British citizens and citizens of British dependent territories see the British Nationality Act 1981; and BRITISH NATIONALITY, IMMIGRATION AND RACE RELATIONS vol 4(2) (Reissue) para 12 et seq.

3   Trading with the Enemy Act 1939 s 15(1)(a).

4   Ibid s 15(1)(b). In considering whether a person has been an enemy or an enemy subject, no account may be taken of any state of affairs before 3 September 1939: s 15(3). For the meaning of 'enemy' see para 635 ante.

5   Trading with the Enemy Act 1939 s 15(1). A certificate of a Secretary of State as to the sovereignty or occupation in any area, and the relevant dates of that sovereignty or occupation, is conclusive evidence of the facts stated: s 15(2). The Secretary of State (as to whom see para 634 note 5 ante) may by order direct that the provisions of the Trading with the Enemy Act 1939 are to apply in relation to a specified area as they apply in relation to enemy territory: s 15(1A) (added by the Emergency Laws (Miscellaneous Provisions) Act 1953 Sch 2 para 8). On the revocation or variation of any such order the area must still be treated for certain purposes (cf para 641 note 2 post) as enemy territory until the Secretary of State otherwise specifies: see the Emergency Laws (Miscellaneous Provisions) Act 1953 Sch 2 para 9(1)–(3). As to the suspension of limitation periods where a party to an action is in enemy territory see LIMITATION OF ACTIONS vol 28 para 925 et seq.

637. Meaning of 'trading with the enemy'. A person is deemed to have traded with the enemy[1] if he has any commercial, financial or other intercourse or dealings with or for the benefit[2] of an enemy[3], and in particular if he has supplied any goods to or for the benefit of an enemy, or obtained any goods[4] from an enemy, or traded in, or carried, any goods consigned to or from an enemy or destined for or coming from enemy territory[5], or has paid or transmitted any money, negotiable instrument or security for money to or for the benefit of an enemy or to a place in enemy territory[6], or has performed any obligation to, or discharged any obligation[7] of, an enemy[8], or if he has done certain[9] other things[10].

A person is not deemed to have traded with the enemy by reason only that he has done something under an authority given generally or specially by, or by any person authorised in that behalf by, the Secretary of State or the Treasury[11], or has received payment from an enemy of a sum of money due in respect of a transaction under which all obligations on the part of the payee had already been performed when the payment was received and had been performed at the time when the payer was not an enemy[12].

1   For the meaning of 'enemy' see para 635 ante. As to the offence of trading with the enemy and penalties see para 638 et seq post. The term 'enemy', in connection with penalties for trading with the enemy under the Trading with the Enemy Act 1939 s 1, includes a person acting on behalf of an enemy: s 1(3).

2   'For the benefit' are words of the widest possible character: see *Stockholms Enskilda Bank Aktiebalag v Schering Ltd* [1941] 1 KB 424, [1941] 1 All ER 257, CA, where payment by a surety releasing an enemy from liability was held to be illegal; *Re Anglo-International Bank Ltd* [1943] Ch 233, [1943] 2 All ER 88, CA, where communications with enemy shareholders were prohibited.

3   Trading with the Enemy Act 1939 s 1(2)(a).

4   See *R v Oppenheimer and Colbeck* [1915] 2 KB 755, CCA (meaning of obtaining goods, wares or merchandise for purpose of 1914–18 war proclamation).

5   Trading with the Enemy Act 1939 s 1(2)(a)(i).

6   Ibid s 1(2)(a)(ii).

7   'Discharged any obligation' means a complete discharge, and not a mere transfer of the obligation: *R and A Kohnstamm Ltd v Ludwig Krumm (London) Ltd* [1940] 2 KB 359, [1940] 3 All ER 84. See also *Stockholms Enskilda Bank Aktiebolag v Schering Ltd* [1941] 1 KB 424 at 440, [1941] 1 All ER 257 at 267, CA.

8   Trading with the Enemy Act 1939 s 1(2)(a)(iii).

9   Ie has done anything which under the provisions of the Trading with the Enemy Act 1939 subsequent to s 1(2) is to be treated as trading with the enemy: s 1(2)(b). For such provisions see ss 3A(7), 4(3), 6(1); and para 640 et seq post.

10   Ibid s 1(2)(b). References in the Trading with the Enemy Act 1939 to an attempt to trade with the enemy are to be construed accordingly: s 1(2) (amended by the Emergency Laws (Miscellaneous Provisions) Act 1953 s 2, Sch 2 para 2(1)).

11   See the Trading with the Enemy Act 1939 s 1(2) proviso (i). As to the transfer of functions to the Secretary of State see para 634 note 5 ante.

12 Ibid s 1(2) proviso (ii) (amended by the Emergency Laws (Miscellaneous Provisions) Act 1953 Sch 2 para 2(2)). See also *R and A Kohnstamm Ltd v Ludwig Krumm (London) Ltd* [1940] 2 KB 359, [1940] 3 All ER 84.

638. Offences, penalties and proceedings. It is an offence to trade or attempt to trade with the enemy[1]. The punishment on conviction on indictment is imprisonment for a term not exceeding seven years or a fine, or both[2], and, on summary conviction, imprisonment for a term not exceeding 12 months or a fine of an amount not exceeding the prescribed sum, or both[3]; and the court may order forfeiture of the goods[4] or money in respect of which the offence has been committed[5]. Proceedings[6] may be taken before the appropriate court in the United Kingdom[7] having jurisdiction in the place where the offender is for the time being[8]. Any person who, for the purpose of obtaining any authority or sanction[9] under the Trading with the Enemy Act 1939, or in giving any information for the purposes of the Act or any order under it, knowingly[10] or recklessly[11] makes a statement which is false in a material particular is liable on summary conviction to imprisonment for a term not exceeding six months or a fine not exceeding level 3 on the standard scale[12], or both[13].

Where an offence[14] committed by a body corporate is proved to have been committed with the consent or connivance of, or to have been attributable to any neglect on the part of, a director[15], manager, secretary or other officer of the body corporate, he as well as the body corporate is deemed to be guilty of the offence and is liable to be proceeded against and punished accordingly[16].

1 Trading with the Enemy Act 1939 s 1(1) (amended by the Emergency Laws (Miscellaneous Provisions) Act 1953 s 2, Sch 2 para 2(1)). For the meaning of 'enemy' see para 635 ante; and for the meaning of 'trading with the enemy' see para 637 ante.

2 Trading with the Enemy Act 1939 s 1(1)(a).

3 Ibid s 1(1)(b) (amended by the Magistrates' Courts Act 1980 s 32(2)). The 'prescribed sum' means £5,000 or such sum as is for the time being substituted in this definition by order under the Magistrates' Courts Act 1980 s 143(1) (substituted by the Criminal Justice Act 1982 s 48(1)(a)): Magistrates' Courts Act 1980 s 32(9) (amended by the Criminal Justice Act 1991 s 17(2)(c)). This provision has been extended to Guernsey: see the Criminal Justice (Guernsey) Order 1992, SI 1992/3202.

4 As to the forfeiture of prohibited goods and penalties for untrue declarations as to ultimate destination see the Import, Export and Customs Powers (Defence) Act 1939 ss 3, 7, 8; and TRADE, INDUSTRY AND INDUSTRIAL RELATIONS vol 47 (Reissue) para 606 et seq.

5 Trading with the Enemy Act 1939 s 1(1).

6 A prosecution may not be instituted except by or with the consent of the Director of Public Prosecutions: ibid s 1(4) (amended by the Criminal Jurisdiction Act 1975 s 14(5), Sch 6 Pt I)). Consent will in certain circumstances be presumed: *R v Metz* (1915) 84 LJKB 1462, CCA, decided on the similar provisions of the Trading with the Enemy Act 1914 s 1(4) (repealed). The fact that a document has been dispatched addressed to a person in enemy territory is, unless the contrary is proved, evidence, as against any person who was a party to the dispatch of the document, that the person to whom the document was dispatched was an enemy: Trading with the Enemy Act 1939 s 1(3A) (added by the Emergency Laws (Miscellaneous Provisions) Act 1953 Sch 2 para 2(4)).

7 For the meaning of 'United Kingdom' see para 502 note 4 ante.

8 Emergency Laws (Miscellaneous Provisions) Act 1953 Sch 2 para 2(3).

9 As to the authorities and sanctions see paras 637 ante, 641 post.

10 For the construction of the word 'knowingly' see *R v McVitie* [1960] 2 QB 483, [1960] 2 All ER 498, CCA (omission of the word 'knowingly' from particulars of offence charged).

11 A statement is reckless when it is made without caring whether it is true or false: *Derry v Peek* (1889) 14 App Cas 337, HL. As to the tests to be applied in determining whether a statement is reckless: cf *R v Bates* [1952] 2 All ER 842 (on appeal sub nom *R v Russell* [1953] 1 WLR 77, CCA); *R v MacKinnon* [1959] 1 QB 150, [1958] 2 All ER 657; and *R v Grunwald* [1963] 1 QB 935, [1960] 3 All ER 380, CCA.

12 As to the standard scale see para 532 note 18 ante.

13 Trading with the Enemy Act 1939 s 9(1) (amended by the Criminal Justice Act 1982 ss 38(1), (6), (8), 46(1), (4)). A person who wilfully obstructs another in the exercise of powers conferred on him by or under the Trading with the Enemy Act 1939 is liable on summary conviction to a fine not exceeding level 3 on the standard scale: Trading with the Enemy Act 1939 s 9(2) (as so amended).

14 Ie an offence under the Trading with the Enemy Act 1939.

15   For the purposes of the Trading with the Enemy Act 1939, a person is deemed to be a director if he occupies the position of a director, by whatever name called (s 15(4)), and for the purposes of s 10, a person is deemed to be a director of a body corporate if he is a person in accordance with whose directions or instructions the directors of that body act (s 15(4)), although a person is not, by reason only that the directors act on his advice given in a professional capacity, to be taken to be such a person (s 15(4) proviso).

16   Ibid s 10.

639. Inspection and supervision of businesses.

If the Secretary of State[1] thinks it expedient for securing compliance with the provisions[2] prohibiting trading with the enemy[3], he may by written order authorise an inspector to inspect books and documents belonging to or under the control of a named person, and to require him and any other person to give information as to the business carried on[4] by the named person, and to enter any premises used for that business[5]. On the inspector's report the Secretary of State, if it appears expedient for the above purpose to ensure that the business should be subject to supervision, may appoint a supervisor of the business with such powers as the Secretary of State may determine[6]. A person who, without reasonable cause, fails to produce for inspection or to furnish to an inspector or a supervisor any document or information duly requested is liable on summary conviction to a fine not exceeding level 3 on the standard scale[7] or imprisonment for a term not exceeding six months, or to both[8].

1   As to the Secretary of State see para 634 note 5 ante.
2   Ie provisions of the Trading With the Enemy Act 1939 s 1: see para 638 ante.
3   For the meaning of 'enemy' see para 635 ante.
4   As to the meaning of 'carrying on business' see para 635 note 4 ante.
5   Trading with the Enemy Act 1939 s 3(1).
6   Ibid s 3(2).
7   As to the standard scale see para 532 note 18 ante.
8   Trading with the Enemy Act 1939 s 3(3) (amended by virtue of the Criminal Justice Act 1982 ss 38(1), (6), (8), 46(1), (4)). A person, who, with intent to evade the provisions of the Trading with the Enemy Act 1939 s 3 (as amended), destroys, mutilates or defaces any book or other document which an inspector or supervisor is or may be authorised to inspect is liable, on conviction on indictment, to imprisonment for a term not exceeding five years or a fine, or to both (s 3(4)(a)), or, on summary conviction, to imprisonment for a term not exceeding 12 months or a fine not exceeding the prescribed sum, or to both (s 3(4)(b) (amended by virtue of the Magistrates' Courts Act 1980 s 32(2)). As to the prescribed sum see para 638 note 3 ante.

640. Power to control and wind up businesses.

Where a business is being carried on in the United Kingdom[1] by or on behalf of, or under the direction of, persons all or any of whom are enemies[2] or enemy subjects or appear to the Secretary of State[3] to be associated with enemies, the Secretary of State may either make a restriction order, being an order prohibiting the carrying on of the business either absolutely or except for such purposes and subject to such conditions as may be specified in the order, or make a winding-up order[4]. Contravention of an order is an offence of trading with the enemy[5]. By the order or by a subsequent order, the Secretary of State may appoint a controller[6] to supervise the carrying out of the order, and, in the case of a winding-up order, to conduct the winding up, with the powers of a liquidator in a voluntary winding up[7], and such other powers[8] as may be necessary or convenient to give full effect to the order[9].

Distribution of the assets[10] of the business while an order is in force is subject to the rules as to preferential payments which apply in the winding up of a company[11], and as regards unsecured debts[12] non-enemy creditors are to be given priority[13]; any balance after the discharge of all liabilities is to be distributed among persons interested in the business in such manner as the Secretary of State may direct[14]. An order is a bar to the presentation of a bankruptcy petition or petition for sequestration or summary sequestration against individuals or the presentation of a winding-up petition[15] or passing of a resolution for winding up in the case of a company, and to the taking of steps for enforcement of the rights of creditors, without the consent of the Secretary of State, but the Secretary of State may present a petition for winding up by the court and the order constitutes a ground on which a company may be so wound up[16].

1 For the meaning of 'United Kingdom' see para 502 note 4 ante.
2 For the meaning of 'enemy' see para 635 ante.
3 As to the Secretary of State see para 634 note 5 ante.
4 Trading with the Enemy Act 1939 s 3A(1) (s 3A added by the Emergency Laws (Miscellaneous Provisions) Act 1953 s 2, Sch 2 para 4). The making of a restriction order does not prejudice the making of a winding-up order at a subsequent date: Trading with the Enemy Act 1939 s 3A(1) (as so added).
5 Ibid s 3A(7) (as added: see note 4 supra). As to the effect of an area ceasing to be enemy territory see para 641 note 2 post.
6 The remuneration of the controller and the expenses incurred in carrying out the order to an amount certified by the Secretary of State are to be defrayed out of the business: ibid s 3A(9) (as added: see note 4 supra). The Secretary of State, on an application by a controller and after considering objections by interested persons, may by order grant him a release, and the order (which is subject to revocation on proof of fraud or concealment of any material fact) discharges him from all liability in respect of any act or default as controller: s 3A(6) (as so added).
7 This includes power in the name of the person carrying on the business or in the controller's name, and by deed or otherwise, to convey or transfer any property, and power to apply to the court to determine any question arising in the carrying out of the order: ibid s 3A(2) (as added: see note 4 supra). As to the powers of a liquidator in a voluntary winding up see COMPANIES vol 7(3) (1996 Reissue) para 2709 et seq.
8 See *Re Th Goldschmidt Ltd* [1917] 2 Ch 194; *Continho Caro & Co v Vermont & Co* [1917] 2 KB 587; *Re Fr Meyers Sohn Ltd* [1918] 1 Ch 169, CA.
9 Trading with the Enemy Act 1939 s 3A(2) (as added: see note 4 supra). The winding up is under the sole jurisdiction of the Secretary of State except so far as he may refer questions to the court (see note 7 supra), and the controller is his agent: *Re Banca Commerciale Italiana* [1943] 1 All ER 480.
10 Where any business for which a controller has been appointed has assets in enemy territory, the controller must first, if practicable, cause an estimate to be prepared of (1) the value of those assets; (2) the amount of any liabilities of the business to creditors, whether secured or unsecured, who are enemies; (3) the amount of the claims of persons who are enemies to participate, otherwise than as creditors of the business, in any distribution of assets of the business made while an order is in force; and where such an estimate is made, those liabilities and claims are deemed to have been satisfied out of the assets of the business in enemy territory, or to have been satisfied so far as those assets will go, and only the balance (if any) ranks for satisfaction out of the other assets of the business: Trading with the Enemy Act 1939 s 3A(4) (as added: see note 4 supra).
   Where an estimate has been prepared, a certificate of the controller as to the value or amount of any assets, claims or liabilities to which the estimate relates is conclusive for the purpose of determining the amount of the assets of the business available for discharging the other liabilities of the business and for distribution amongst other persons claiming to be interested in the business: s 3A(5) (as so added). However, this does not affect the rights of creditors of, and other persons interested in, the business against the assets of the business in enemy territory: s 3A(5) proviso (as so added). As to the meaning of 'assets' see *Re Vulcaan Coal Co, Harrison v Harbottle* [1922] 2 Ch 60; *Dresdner Bank v Russo-Asiatic Bank* [1923] 1 Ch 209.
11 As to winding up generally see COMPANIES vol 7(3) (1996 Reissue) para 2190 et seq.
12 For the meaning of 'debts' and 'creditors' and the relevant date for determining the enemy character of a creditor see *Re Banca Commerciale Italiana* [1942] Ch 406 at 412, 413, [1942] 2 All ER 208 at 211.
13 See the Trading with the Enemy Act 1939 s 3A(3) (as added: see note 4 supra). These provisions, however, in their application to the distribution of money which would in accordance with them fall to be paid to an enemy have effect subject to the provisions of s 7 (see para 643 post), and any order made under s 7: s 3A(3) proviso (as so added).
14 Ibid s 3A(3) (as added: see note 4 supra). See further *Re British Incandescent Mantle Works Ltd* (1923) 129 LT 126 (sale of business by controller).
15 See *Re Dieckmann* [1918] 1 Ch 331 (distinction between winding up and bankruptcy); *Re Cedes Electric Traction Ltd* [1918] 1 Ch 18.
16 Trading with the Enemy Act 1939 s 3A(8) (as added: see note 4 supra).

641. Transfer of choses in action and negotiable instruments. Except with Treasury sanction, no assignment[1] of a chose in action made by or on behalf of an enemy[2] is effective so as to confer on any person any rights or remedies in respect of the chose in action[3]. This applies also in relation to any transfer of any coupon or other security transferable by delivery, not being a negotiable instrument[4]. Except with Treasury sanction, neither a transfer of a negotiable instrument by or on behalf of an enemy, nor any subsequent transfer of it, is effective so as to confer any rights or remedies against any party to the instrument[5].

Any person who, by payment or otherwise, purports to discharge any liability from which he is accordingly relieved[6], knowing the facts by which he is so relieved, is deemed to have thereby traded with the enemy[7]. It is, however, a defence for the defendant to prove that at the time when he purported to discharge the liability he had reasonable grounds for believing that the liability was enforceable against him by order of a competent court, not being either a court having jurisdiction in the United Kingdom[8] or a court having jurisdiction in enemy territory, and would be enforced against him by such an order[9].

1   A vesting order by the court in respect of patents vested in an enemy as bare trustee for a British subject is not an assignment in this context: *Re IG Farbenindustrie Akt's Agreement* [1941] Ch 147, [1940] 4 All ER 486; revsd on other grounds [1944] Ch 41, [1943] 2 All ER 525, CA. See also *Novello & Co Ltd v Hinrichsen Edition Ltd* [1951] Ch 595, [1951] 1 All ER 779 (affd on appeal on another point [1951] Ch 1026, [1951] 2 All ER 457, CA); and CHOSES IN ACTION vol 6 (Reissue) para 80.

2   Where any area ceases to be enemy territory (see para 636 ante), it must, for the purposes of the Trading with the Enemy Act 1939 s 3A (as added) (see para 640 ante), ss 4, 5 (see infra; and para 642 post) and s 7 (see para 643 post), be treated as if there had been no such cessation, until such time as the Secretary of State may by order specify: Emergency Laws (Miscellaneous Provisions) Act 1953 s 2, Sch 2 para 9(1), (2). The area must be likewise treated for the purposes of any order made under the Trading with the Enemy Act 1939 s 7 (see para 643 post), save as expressly provided by any such order: Emergency Laws (Miscellaneous Provisions) Act 1953 Sch 2 para 9(1). For the meaning of 'enemy' see para 635 ante. As to the Secretary of State see para 634 note 5 ante.

3   Trading with the Enemy Act 1939 s 4(1). Section 4 does not apply to securities to which s 5 applies: s 4(5). See also para 642 post. As to dealings in enemy-owned patents, designs, copyright and trade marks see para 645 post.

4   Ibid s 4(2).

5   Ibid s 4(1).

6   Ie relieved by the Trading with the Enemy Act 1939: see the text and notes 3–4 supra.

7   Ibid s 4(3). For the meaning of 'trading with the enemy' see para 637 ante. As to penalties see para 638 ante.

8   For the meaning of 'United Kingdom' see para 502 note 4 ante.

9   Trading with the Enemy Act 1939 s 4(3) proviso (amended by the Emergency Laws (Miscellaneous Provisions) Act 1953 Sch 2 para 5). A person who has reasonable cause to believe that if he satisfied a claim in respect of a negotiable instrument or chose in action he would be committing an offence of trading with the enemy may, as a good discharge, pay the sum due into the High Court, to be dealt with according to an order of the court: Trading with the Enemy Act 1939 s 4(4).

642. Transfer and allotment of securities; purchase of enemy currency. If any securities[1] are transferred by or on behalf of an enemy[2], or if any securities issued by a company[3] are allotted or transferred to or for the benefit of an enemy subject[4] without the consent of the Secretary of State[5], then, except with the sanction of the Secretary of State, the transferee or allottee does not by virtue of the transfer or allotment acquire any rights or remedies in respect of the securities[6]. A body corporate issuing or managing the securities must not take cognisance of or otherwise act upon such a transfer except under the authority of the Secretary of State[6]. No share warrants, stock certificates or bonds, being warrants, certificates or bonds payable to bearer[7], may be issued in respect of securities registered or inscribed in the name of an enemy or a person acting on his behalf or for his benefit[8].

The purchase of enemy currency[9] is to be treated as trading with the enemy[10].

1   'Securities' means annuities, stock, shares, bonds, debentures or debenture stock registered or inscribed in any register, branch register or other book kept in the United Kingdom: Trading with the Enemy Act 1939 s 5(4). For the meaning of 'United Kingdom' see para 502 note 4 ante. As to payments of money to and vesting of property in the custodian of enemy property see paras 643–644 post. As to securities generally see COMPANIES; STOCK EXCHANGE.

2   For the meaning of 'enemy' see para 635 ante. As to the effect of territory ceasing to be enemy territory see para 641 note 2 ante; and as to enemy territory see para 636 ante.

3   Ie a company within the meaning of the Companies Act 1985 (see generally COMPANIES), or any corresponding enactment in force in Northern Ireland: Trading with the Enemy Act 1939 s 5(1)(b); Interpretation Act 1978 s 17(2)(a).

4   For the meaning of 'enemy subject' see para 636 ante.

5   As to the Secretary of State see para 634 note 5 ante.

6   Trading with the Enemy Act 1939 s 5(1).

7   Share warrants etc payable to bearer are negotiable instruments: see BILLS OF EXCHANGE vol 4(1) (Reissue) para 508 et seq.

8   Trading with the Enemy Act 1939 s 5(2). The penalty on summary conviction for a contravention of s 5 (as amended) is imprisonment for a term not exceeding six months or a fine not exceeding level 3 on the standard scale, or both: s 5(3) (amended by virtue of the Criminal Justice Act 1982 ss 38(1), (6), (8), 46(1), (4)). As to the standard scale see para 532 note 18 ante.

9   'Enemy currency' means any notes or coins circulating as currency in the area under the sovereignty of a power with whom the Crown is at war, not being an area occupied by the Crown or an allied power, or any other notes or coins declared by Treasury order to be enemy currency: Trading with the Enemy Act 1939 s 6(2).

10 Ibid s 6(1).

643. Custodianship of enemy property.

With a view to preventing the payment of money to enemies and of preserving enemy property[1] in contemplation of arrangements to be made at the conclusion of peace[2], the Secretary of State[3] may appoint custodians[4] of enemy property for England, Scotland and Northern Ireland respectively, and by order[5] (1) require payment of money[6] to be made to the prescribed[7] custodian[8]; (2) vest[9] property[10] and the right of transfer[11] in the prescribed custodian[12]; (3) confer and impose on the custodians and on any other person such rights, powers, duties and liabilities[13] as may be prescribed as respects enemy property[14] or money[15]; (4) require the payment of fees[16]; and (5) require the furnishing of returns and accounts and other information and the production of documents[17]; and (6) make incidental and supplementary provisions[18].

A person who pays a debt or deals with property contrary to the order[19] which applies to it is liable on summary conviction to imprisonment for a term not exceeding six months or a fine not exceeding level 3 on the standard scale[20], or to both; and the payment or dealing is void[21].

1   'Enemy property' means property belonging to or held or managed on behalf of an enemy or an enemy subject: Trading with the Enemy Act 1939 s 7(8)(a). For the meaning of 'enemy' and 'enemy subject' see paras 635–636 ante. 'Property' means real or personal property, and includes any estate or interest in real or personal property, any negotiable instrument, debt or other chose in action and any other right or interest whether in possession or not: s 7(8)(b). Certain rights of action in tort may not be property: *Maerkle v British and Continental Fur Co Ltd* [1954] 3 All ER 50 at 53, [1954] 1 WLR 1242 at 1247, CA. Goodwill is property: *Adrema Werke Maschinenbau GmbH v Custodian of Enemy Property and Administrator of German Enemy Property* [1957] RPC 49, CA. As to the effect of the operation of the Trading with the Enemy Act 1939 s 7 on a territory ceasing to be enemy territory see para 641 note 2 ante.

2   The effect of the words 'with a view to ... conclusion of peace' was considered in *RJ Reuter Co Ltd v Ferd Mulhens* [1954] Ch 50, [1953] 2 All ER 1160, CA.

3   As to the Secretary of State see para 634 note 5 ante.

4   A custodian is a Crown servant of a most unusual kind: see *Bank Voor Handel en Scheepvaart NV v Administrator of Hungarian Property* [1954] AC 584 at 609, 618, [1954] 1 All ER 969 at 978, 983, HL. As to the immunity from income tax in respect of income received by the custodian from property vested in him see *Bank Voor Handel en Scheepvaart NV v Administrator of Hungarian Property* supra at 609, 618 and at 978, 983.

5   Such an order has effect notwithstanding anything in any Act passed before the Trading with the Enemy Act 1939 (ie 5 September 1939): s 7(4).

6 Ie money which would, but for the existence of a state of war, be payable to or for the benefit of a person who is an enemy, or which would, but for the provisions of s 4 or s 5 (see paras 641–642 ante), be payable to any other person: s 7(1)(a). As to the requirement see para 644 post.

7 'Prescribed' means prescribed by an order under ibid s 7: s 7(8)(c).

8 Ibid s 7(1)(a).

9 The order may vest the property or provide for and regulate its vesting: ibid s 7(1)(b). The effect of vesting is to restrict the rights of the former owner to participation in any distribution under arrangements made on the conclusion of peace: *Maerkle v British and Continental Fur Co Ltd* [1954] 3 All ER 50, [1954] 1 WLR 1242, CA. Numerous vesting orders have been made, and the following are published in the SR & O and SI series: the Trading with the Enemy (Custodian) Order 1939, SR & O 1939/1198 (amended by SR & O 1940/94; SR & O 1940/734; SR & O 1940/883; SR & O 1941/765; SR & O 1942/342; SR & O 1944/914; SR & O 1945/1414; and modified by SR & O 1940/1113; SR & O 1945/850; SR & O 1945/1359; SR & O 1946/1061); the Trading with the Enemy (Insolvency) Order 1940, SR & O 1940/1419; the Trading with the Enemy (Foreign Currency Accounts) Order 1944, SR & O 1944/915; the Trading with the Enemy (Custodian) Order 1945, SR & O 1945/43 (amended by SI 1948/1047); the Trading with the Enemy (Custodian) (No 2) Order 1945, SR & O 1945/887; the Trading with the Enemy (Custodian) Order 1946, SR & O 1946/1039 (amended by SI 1948/1047); the Trading with the Enemy (Custodian) (Specified Persons) Order 1946, SR & O 1946/1040; the Trading with the Enemy (Custodian) (No 2) Order 1946, SR & O 1946/2141 (amended by SI 1948/1047); and the following statutory instruments having the title of Trading with the Enemy (Custodian) Order, namely SI 1949/1083; SI 1950/494; SI 1951/153, SI 1951/779, SI 1951/780, SI 1951/1625, SI 1951/1626. As to the vesting of claims in bankruptcy see para 644 post.

10 Ie such enemy property as may be prescribed: Trading with the Enemy Act 1939 s 7(1)(b).

11 Ie the right to transfer such other enemy property as may be prescribed, being enemy property which has not been, and is not required by the order to be, vested in the custodian: ibid s 7(1)(c). The Secretary of State has power to direct a custodian to sell securities to a person who is not the highest bidder or to any specified person without seeking other offers: see the Emergency Laws (Miscellaneous Provisions) Act 1953 s 2, Sch 2 para 6(6). In exercising a power to transfer or sell securities a custodian is not bound by any restriction as to transfer or condition as to price or purchasers in the articles of association, byelaws or other rules of the body corporate: see Sch 2 para 6(7). See also *Re Parana Plantations Ltd* [1948] 1 All ER 742; and *Nordisk Insulinlaboratorium v C L Bencard* (1934) Ltd [1953] Ch 430, [1953] 1 All ER 986, CA.

12 Trading with the Enemy Act 1939 s 7(1)(b), (c). See also para 644 post. Where a custodian dies or for any other reason ceases to hold office, the Secretary of State may by order vest in his successor any property or right vested in the former custodian: Emergency Laws (Miscellaneous Provisions) Act 1953 Sch 2 para 6(2).

13 These include, where it appears to the Secretary of State to be expedient that any business should be carried on or continue to be carried on in or from the United Kingdom, such rights, powers, duties and liabilities as respects the enemy property or money (see the text and notes 14–15 infra) as are necessary or expedient to enable the business to be carried on: ibid Sch 2 para 6(1). For the meaning of 'United Kingdom' see para 502 note 4 ante.

14 Ie property which has been or is required to be vested in the custodian by or under the order, property of which the right of transfer has been or is required to be so vested, and any other enemy property: see the Trading with the Enemy Act 1939 s 7(1)(d)(i)–(iii).

15 Ibid s 7(1)(d)(iv). 'Money' in this context means money which has been or is required to be paid to the custodian: s 7(1)(d)(iv).

16 Ibid s 7(1)(e). A custodian may be empowered by the order to remit or reduce fees: Emergency Laws (Miscellaneous Provisions) Act 1953 Sch 2 para 6(5). All fees received must be paid into the Exchequer: Trading with the Enemy Act 1939 s 7(7). See also para 644 post.

17 Ibid s 7(1)(f).

18 Ibid s 7(1). It seems that s 7 (as amended) does not enable the custodian to be given power to consent where consent to an advancement is required by a settlement: *Re Forster's Settlement, Forster v Custodian of Enemy Property for England* [1942] Ch 199 at 206, 207, [1942] 1 All ER 180 at 187. Grant of administration has been made to the Public Trustee on behalf of the custodian in respect of the estates of enemy nationals: see EXECUTORS vol 17 paras 718, 950. Where a requirement or direction with respect to money or property is addressed to a person by the custodian with his certificate that the money or property is within the order, the certificate is evidence of the facts stated, and the person is not liable in an action or other legal proceeding by reason only of compliance with the requirement or direction: Trading with the Enemy Act 1939 s 7(2). Payments, the vesting of property or the right to transfer property and directions in pursuance of an order under s 7 (as amended) are not invalidated by reason only that at the material time the person interested in the property had died or ceased to be, or although believed to be was in fact not, an enemy or enemy subject: s 7(3).

19 Ie the order under ibid s 7 (as amended).

20 As to the standard scale see para 532 note 18 ante.

21 Trading with the Enemy Act 1939 s 7(5) (amended by the Criminal Justice Act 1982 ss 38(1), (6), (8), 46(1), (4)). A person who, without reasonable cause, fails to produce or furnish any document or information required under an order is liable on summary conviction to a continuing daily penalty: see the Trading with the Enemy Act 1939 s 7(6).

644. Powers and duties of custodians and other persons. Money[1] payable to or for the benefit of an enemy[2], or deemed to be so payable, must be paid[3] to the custodian[4] who is empowered to sue for it[5]. The Secretary of State[6] may make vesting orders vesting enemy property[7] and rights of transfer in the custodian, and prescribing his powers[8]. Debts and claims provable by an enemy in bankruptcy or on a winding up are vested in the custodian, who may prove, agree and compromise accounts and appeal, and take other necessary proceedings[9].

Subject to directions of the Secretary of State[10], the custodian must hold[11] the money and property or right of transfer vested in him until the termination of the war[12]. Such money and property is free from liability to attachment or execution[13]. The receipt of the custodian is a good discharge to a payer[14]. The custodian may invest money in Treasury bills or other government securities[15]. He is authorised to charge fees calculated on the amount of the money or value of the property vested in him, but they may be remitted or reduced[16].

1 'Money' includes dividends, bonus or interest in respect of shares and other securities, capital repayments of securities, interest on loans or deposits, profits of businesses, debts on deposit or current account, insurance money, rents, payments under trust, wills or settlements and money arising under the Trading with the Enemy Act 1939 s 4 or s 5 (see paras 641–642 ante): Trading with the Enemy (Custodian) Order 1939, SR & O 1939/1198, art 1(ii), (iii).

2 For the meaning of 'enemy' see, by virtue of ibid art 9(ii), para 635 ante.

3 Payment must normally be within 14 days after the person concerned becomes an enemy or the money becomes payable and be made in English currency: see ibid art 1(iv) (amended by SR & O 1940/94).

4 Ibid art 1(i). The Trading with the Enemy (Custodian) Order 1939 (amended by SR & O 1940/94; SR & O 1940/734; SR & O 1940/883; SR & O 1940/1113; SR & O 1941/765; SR & O 1942/342; SR & O 1944/914; SR & O 1945/1414) contains provisions as to the powers and duties of custodians and of other persons. References to 'the custodian' are to be construed as references to such custodian of enemy property for any part of the United Kingdom as is prescribed by the Trading with the Enemy (Custodian) Order 1939: art 9(ii). For the meaning of 'United Kingdom' see para 502 note 4 ante.

5 Ibid art 1(vii), (viii) (added by SR & O 1941/765). The custodian is entitled to notice of payments due and to particulars of accounts and production of documents: art 1(vi) (added by SR & O 1941/765). Income directed to be held on protective trusts has been held payable to the custodian: see *Re Wittke, Reynolds and Gorst v King Edward's Hospital Fund for London and Custodian of Enemy Property* [1944] Ch 166, [1944] 1 All ER 383. Cf *Re Gourju's Will Trusts, Starling v Custodian of Enemy Property* [1943] Ch 24, [1942] 2 All ER 605. See also *Re Pozot's Settlement Trusts, Westminster Bank Ltd v Guerbois* [1952] Ch 427, [1952] 1 All ER 1107, CA, overruling *Fraenkel v Whitty* [1948] Ch 55, [1947] 2 All ER 646. The beneficial interest in property held by the custodian is in statutory suspense: *Bank Voor Handel en Scheepvaart NV v Slatford* [1953] 1 QB 248 at 288, [1952] 2 All ER 956 at 967, CA, per Evershed MR; revsd sub nom *Bank Voor Handel en Scheepvaart NV v Administrator of Hungarian Property* [1954] AC 584 at 608, [1954] 1 All ER 969 at 977, HL.

6 As to the Secretary of State see para 634 note 5 ante.

7 For the meaning of 'enemy property' see, by virtue of the Trading with the Enemy (Custodian) Order 1939 art 9(ii), para 643 note 1 ante.

8 Ibid art 2(i)–(iii). As to patents see art 2(iv); and para 645 note 3 post. Applications for vesting orders must be made to the Secretary of State: *Re De Barbe, Ellissen v Griffith* [1941] WN 218. As regards specified persons, rights to transfer securities (see the Trading with the Enemy (Custodian) Order 1946, SR & O 1946/1039 (amended by SI 1948/1047)) and debts (see the Trading with the Enemy (Custodian) (Specified Persons) Order 1946, SR & O 1946/1040) were vested in the custodian.

9 Trading with the Enemy (Insolvency) Order 1940, SR & O 1940/1419, arts 1, 2. The custodian must be notified by the debtor, liquidator or trustee as the case may be: see arts 3, 4. See also BANKRUPTCY vol 3(2) (Reissue) para 514.

10   Under a direction of the Secretary of State, the custodian may pay over any particular money or transfer any particular property to or for the benefit of the person who would but for the Trading with the Enemy Act 1939, or any order made under it, be entitled to it: Trading with the Enemy (Custodian) Order 1939 art 3(ii).

11   A custodian must, however, if the Treasury so directs, pay or transfer to persons specified in the direction (1) any money paid to him as being money which, but for the existence of a state of war, would have been payable to a person resident or carrying on business in enemy territory not under the sovereignty of a power with whom the Crown is at war or in any area in relation to which the Trading with the Enemy Act 1939 applies as it applies in relation to enemy territory; and (2) any property or transfer right vested in him as being property belonging to any such person: see the Emergency Laws (Miscellaneous Provisions) Act 1953 s 2, Sch 2 para 6(3)(a), (b).

     Where the right to transfer any securities registered or inscribed in a register, branch register or other book kept in the United Kingdom has been vested in a custodian of enemy property on the grounds that the securities belonged to, or were held or managed on behalf of (a) an individual resident in any enemy territory which is not under the sovereignty of a power with whom the Crown is at war, or in any area in relation to which the Trading with the Enemy Act 1939 applies as it applies in relation to enemy territory; (b) an individual or body of persons (whether corporate or unincorporate) carrying on business in any such territory or area; or (c) any body of persons (whether corporate or unincorporate) carrying on business in any place and controlled by any such individual or body of persons as is mentioned in heads (a) or (b) supra, and the right to transfer the securities has been exercised so as to vest the securities in the custodian or any person acting under his directions, the Secretary of State may by order direct that this provision applies to the securities: Emergency Laws (Miscellaneous Provisions) Act 1953 Sch 2 para 7(1). The Secretary of State must then give notice of the making of such an order to the company or other body in whose book the securities in question are registered or inscribed, and thereupon the securities vest in the person who would have been entitled to them but for the vesting in the custodian of the right to transfer the securities: Sch 2 para 7(2)(a). The company or other body must cause the securities to be registered or inscribed in the name of the person in whose name they were registered or inscribed immediately before the exercise by the custodian of his right to transfer the securities: Sch 2 para 7(2)(b). Notwithstanding anything in Sch 2 para 7(2)(b), where the person mentioned therein is not the same as the person in whom the securities are vested, and before the securities have been registered or inscribed (in pursuance of Sch 2 para 7(2)(b)) the person in whom they are vested has submitted to the company or body proof to their satisfaction of his title, the company or body may cause the securities to be registered or inscribed in his name: Sch 2 para 7(2)(c). The vesting, registration or inscription of any securities must be without prejudice to any lien or charge to which they were subject immediately before the time at which the order in question was revoked, and does not affect anything done before that time: Sch 2 para 7(3). 'Securities' means annuities, stock, shares, bonds, debentures or debenture stock: Sch 2 para 7(4).

     Further, a custodian may be required to pay or transfer money and property to the person acting as custodian of enemy property in any of Her Majesty's dominions or in any territory of an allied power or power at war with any power with which the Crown is at war: see Sch 2 para 6(4).

12   Trading with the Enemy (Custodian) Order 1939 art 3(i). As to the effect on the operation of orders made under the Trading with the Enemy Act 1939 s 7 (as amended) of a territory ceasing to be enemy territory see para 641 note 2 ante.

13   Trading with the Enemy (Custodian) Order 1939 art 3(iii).

14   Ibid art 3(iv). No person may, without the consent of the Secretary of State, deal with enemy property, save as directed by art 4. Persons holding or managing enemy property, enemy subjects, companies and partners must, within a certain time, furnish the custodian with certain information: see art 5. Where the custodian sells shares, stock or securities of a company, the company may, with the consent of the Secretary of State, purchase and reissue them: art 6(i). This transfer must be registered in the name of the custodian or that of the transferee, but subject to any lien of the company or other body, or to any other lien or charge of which the custodian has notice: art 6(ii). As to the particular custodian to receive payment, and transfers between custodians, see art 8.

15   Trading with the Enemy Investment Order 1940, SR & O 1940/1113, art 1. Any income received by a custodian of enemy property appointed under the Trading with the Enemy Act 1939 s 7 (as amended) from the investment of moneys coming into his hands in his capacity as custodian, being income received by way of discount on the purchase by him of Treasury bills or by way of interest on other loans made by him to the Treasury or on moneys placed by him in his name on deposit or current account at a bank, belongs to the Crown and must be paid into the Exchequer: Enemy Property Act 1953 s 4(1) (amended by the Statute Law (Repeals) Act 1976). This is deemed to have had effect as from the coming into operation of the Trading with the Enemy (Custodian) Order 1939, so that it is not construed as authorising or requiring the repayment of any sums paid by a custodian before 29 October 1953 otherwise than into the Exchequer: Enemy Property Act 1953 s 4(2).

16   See the Trading with the Enemy (Custodian) Order 1939 art 7 (amended by SR & O 1940/734; SR & O 1942/342). As to fees generally see para 643 note 16 ante.

(3) ENEMY INDUSTRIAL PROPERTY

645. Enemy-owned industrial property. The Patents, Designs, Copyright and Trade Marks (Emergency) Act 1939[1], which was passed shortly after the outbreak of the 1939–45 war to enable certain dealings in enemy-owned patents[2], registered designs, copyright and trade marks to be carried out without being rendered illegal by the law against trading with the enemy, is permanent legislation, although only operative when there are persons who fulfil the description of enemy or enemy subject[3].

A licence granted in favour of a United Kingdom[4] resident or a person resident in the Isle of Man in respect of a patent, registered design[5], copyright or design right[6], and any contract relating to such a licence, is not invalid under the law against trading with the enemy[7] by reason only that the proprietor or owner or any person otherwise interested in the patent, design, copyright or design right, or any party to the contract, is an enemy[8]. The comptroller[9] is empowered on application[10] by order[11] to revoke any such licence, to revoke or vary any conditions subject to which the licence has effect, or to revoke or vary any of the provisions of a contract relating to the licence in so far as they relate to the licence[12]. The comptroller may grant licences under enemy-owned patents, designs, copyrights and design rights[13] and may suspend the trade mark rights of an enemy or enemy subject[14].

A patent may be granted to, or a design or trade mark may be registered on the application of, an enemy alone or jointly with another person[15]. An Order in Council declaring a country to be a convention country[16] remains in force notwithstanding the outbreak of war with that country[17], and an Order in Council extending copyright protection to foreign works remains in force in the same circumstances unless revoked[18]. The comptroller has a discretion to refuse to take, or to suspend the taking of, any proceedings on or in relation to any application by an enemy for a patent or for the registration of a design or trade mark[19]. He also has discretion to extend the time limits in view of war circumstances[20].

1   The Patents, Designs, Copyright and Trade Marks (Emergency) Act 1939 is dealt with principally in PATENTS AND REGISTERED DESIGNS; COPYRIGHT vol 9 paras 824–825; TRADE MARKS vol 48 (Reissue) para 98. The Secretary of State (see para 634 note 5 ante) is empowered to make rules for regulating the practice under the Patents, Designs, Copyright and Trade Marks (Emergency) Act 1939 (see s 9(1)), and, with Treasury consent, to prescribe fees for applications and other matters (see s 9(2)). The Patents, Designs, Copyright and Trade Marks (Emergency) Rules 1939, SR & O 1939/1375 (amended by SR & O 1940/693), which are now spent, prescribed fees (see r 3, Sch 1) and forms (see rr 4, 7, 10, Sch 2) on applications and oppositions, and dealt with the leaving and service of documents (see r 5), agency (see r 6), evidence and statement of applicant's request (see r 8), copies to accompany application (see r 9 (as so amended)) and opposition (see r 10); and the relevant matters noted in note 9 infra.

2   'Patent' has the same meaning as in the Patents Act 1977: Patents, Designs, Copyright and Trade Marks (Emergency) Act 1939 s 10(1) (amended by the Copyright, Designs and Patents Act 1988 s 303(1), Sch 7 para 3(1), (5)).

3   As to patents legislation generally see PATENTS AND REGISTERED DESIGNS. In the Patents, Designs, Copyright and Trade Marks (Emergency) Act 1939 'enemy' and 'enemy subject' are defined by s 10(1) as having the same meaning as in the Trading with the Enemy Act 1939: see ss 2, 15(1); and paras 635–636 ante. For the purposes of the Patents, Designs, Copyright and Trade Marks (Emergency) Act 1939, entries in the registers kept at the Patents, Designs and Trade Marks Office relating to residence and nationality are prima facie evidence of a person's residence or nationality: s 7(1) (amended by the Trade Marks Act 1994 s 106(1), Sch 4 para 3(3)(c)).

4   For the meaning of 'United Kingdom' see para 502 note 4 ante.

5 'Design' has the same meaning in reference to a registered design as in the Registered Designs Act 1949: Patents, Designs, Copyright and Trade Marks (Emergency) Act 1939 s 10(1) (amended by the Copyright, Designs and Patents Act 1988 Sch 7 para 3(1), (5)).

6 'Design' has the same meaning in reference to design right as in the Copyright, Designs and Patents Act 1988 Pt III (ss 213–264): Patents, Designs, Copyright and Trade Marks (Emergency) Act 1939 s 10(1) (as amended: see note 5 supra).

7 Ie the Trading with the Enemy Act 1939 s 1 (as amended) (see para 637 ante), or any rule of law relating to intercourse or dealings with or for the benefit of enemies.

8 Patents, Designs, Copyright and Trade Marks (Emergency) Act 1939 s 1(1) (amended by the Copyright, Designs and Patents Act 1988 Sch 7 para 3(2), (3)). However, the Patents, Designs, Copyright and Trade Marks (Emergency) Act 1939 s 1 (as amended) does not render valid a grant or assignment of any such licence or any contract relating to any such licence if that grant, assignment or contract was made during a state of war and was unlawful under the law against trading with the enemy: s 1(1) proviso (a). Nor does s 1 (as amended) authorise the performance of a contract in a manner inconsistent with the law against trading with the enemy or with any enactment relating to the property, rights or capacity of enemies: s 1(1) proviso (b). See also COPYRIGHT vol 9 para 824; PATENTS AND REGISTERED DESIGNS vol 35 (Reissue) para 419.

9 'The comptroller' means the Comptroller-General of Patents, Designs and Trade Marks, and, in relation to trade marks, means the Comptroller-General in his capacity as the registrar within the meaning of the Trade Marks Act 1994: Patents, Designs, Copyright and Trade Marks (Emergency) Act 1939 s 10(1) (amended by the Trade Marks Act 1994 Sch 4 para 3(1), (3)(d)). Any act or thing directed to be done by or to the comptroller may be done by or to an assistant comptroller of the Patent Office: Patents, Designs, Copyright and Trade Marks (Emergency) Rules 1939 r 12.

10 Ie on application by the licensee or any other person interested.

11 Before deciding as to the making of an order under the Patents, Designs, Copyright and Trade Marks (Emergency) Act 1939, the comptroller must, unless it is inexpedient or impossible to do so, give to any person appearing to be interested an opportunity of being heard: s 8. No order is to be held invalid because a decision made for the purposes of the order that a particular person is an enemy or an enemy subject is wrong: s 7(2).

12 Ibid s 1(2) (amended by the Copyright, Designs and Patents Act 1988 Sch 7 para 3(2), (3)). An order for a variation may be revoked or varied by a subsequent order: Patents, Designs, Copyright and Trade Marks (Emergency) Act 1939 s 1(2) (as so amended).

13 See ibid s 2 (amended by the Copyright, Designs and Patents Act 1988 Sch 7 para 3(1), (3)); COPYRIGHT vol 9 para 824; PATENTS AND REGISTERED DESIGNS vol 35 (Reissue) para 427, 834.

14 See the Patents, Designs, Copyright and Trade Marks (Emergency) Act 1939 s 3 (substituted by the Trade Marks Act 1994 Sch 4 para 3(1), (2)).

15 See the Patents, Designs, Copyright and Trade Marks (Emergency) Act 1939 s 4(1) (amended by the Trade Marks Act 1994 Sch 4 para 3(3)), (4), (5); and PATENTS AND REGISTERED DESIGNS vol 35 (Reissue) para 555.

16 Ie an order under the Copyright, Designs and Patents Act 1988 s 159 or s 256: see the Patents, Designs, Copyright and Trade Marks (Emergency) Act 1939 s 5(1) (as amended).

17 As to the effect of war on licences by agreement see PATENTS AND REGISTERED DESIGNS vol 35 (Reissue) para 419.

18 See the Patents, Designs, Copyright and Trade Marks (Emergency) Act 1939 s 5(1) (amended by the Copyright, Designs and Patents Act 1988 Sch 7 para 3(1), (4)); and COPYRIGHT vol 9 para 824. Copyright or design right subsisting by virtue of such an Order in Council continues to subsist even though the owner becomes an enemy: see the Patents, Designs, Copyright and Trade Marks (Emergency) Act 1939 s 5(2) (as so amended); and COPYRIGHT vol 9 para 825.

19 See ibid s 4(3); and PATENTS AND REGISTERED DESIGNS vol 35 (Reissue) para 678.

20 The comptroller has discretion to extend the time limited by or under the Patents and Designs Act 1907, the Trade Marks Act 1994 or the Patents, Designs, Copyright and Trade Marks (Emergency) Act 1939 for doing any act, where he is satisfied (1) that the act was not done within the time limit because that a person was on active service or by reason of any other circumstances arising from the existence of a state of war which, in the opinion of the comptroller, justify an extension of the time limit; or (2) that, by reason of circumstances arising from the existence of a state of war, the doing of the act within the time limit would have been or would be injurious to the rights or interests of the person by or on whose behalf the act is or was to be done or to the public interest: s 6(1) (amended by the Patents and Designs Act 1946 s 6(2) (continued in force by the Statute Law (Repeals) Act 1986 Sch 2 para 3); and by the Trade Marks Act 1994 Sch 4 para 3(1), (3)(b)). Such an extension of the time for doing any act may be for any period that the comptroller thinks fit, notwithstanding that power is conferred to extend the time for doing that act for a specified period only: Patents, Designs, Copyright and Trade Marks (Emergency) Act 1939 s 6(2)(a). The extension may also be granted notwithstanding

that that time expired before any application or request for extension was made, or that, by reason of that act not having been done within that time, the relevant application, patent, registration or proceeding has ceased or expired, or become void or invalid or been treated as abandoned: s 6(2)(c). These powers may be exercised notwithstanding that their exercise benefits an enemy or an enemy subject, whether directly or indirectly: s 6(3).

646. Use of technical information by Crown contractors. For the purposes of any contract or order for the production[1] of defence materials[2], any person authorised by a competent authority[3] may make use of any technical information[4] of certain kinds[5] and supply articles produced with the aid of such information discharged from any restrictions[6] imposed by, or obligation to make payments under, agreements with third persons whenever made[7].

An authorisation for these purposes[8] must be in writing, and must specify the defence materials to which it relates and the restrictions and obligations relieved by it[9].

These provisions[10] do not affect any restriction or obligation imposed by an agreement to which a government department is party[11], and neither they nor any authorisation under them authorise the disclosure to a competent authority or any other person of any technical information to which they apply in contravention of any agreement[12].

1   'Production' includes repair, maintenance, testing and development: Defence Contracts Act 1958 s 8(1). The Defence Contracts Act 1958 was passed on 7 July 1958 and came into force at the expiration of the period of one month beginning with that date: s 8(1), (3). It extends to the Isle of Man and to Northern Ireland: s 8(4).

2   'Defence materials' means (1) articles required for the armed forces of the Crown or for such supply to foreign governments or to the United Nations as is authorised by certain enactments, being articles designed or adapted for the use of armed forces or components of such articles; (2) articles required for civil defence purposes, being articles designed or adapted for use for those purposes or components of such articles; and (3) articles required by the Secretary of State for Defence for the production of any such articles: ibid s 6(1) (amended by the Ministry of Aviation (Dissolution) Order 1971, SI 1971/719, art 3(2), Schedule para 4(2)).

3   'Competent authority' means a Secretary of State: Defence Contracts Act 1958 s 6(1) (amended by the Ministry of Aviation (Dissolution) Order 1971, Schedule para 4(2)).

4   The use of technical information includes the production and reproduction of drawings, models, plans or documents: Defence Contracts Act 1958 s 2(7).

5   Ie any specification or design for articles and any process or technique used in the production of articles (not being in any case a patented invention or registered design), and any drawing, model, plan, document or other information relating to the application or operation of any such specification, design, process or technique: ibid s 2(7). 'Article' includes any substance or material, and any plant, machinery or apparatus, whether affixed to land or not: ibid s 6(1).

6   The Defence Contracts Act 1958 applies in relation to restrictions subsisting by reason of the existence of copyright in any work as it applies in relation to restrictions imposed by agreement: s 6(2). 'Agreement' includes a licence, assignment or assignation: s 6(1).

7   Ibid s 2(1). Where, by an authorisation, any person is discharged from the obligation to make payments in respect of the use of any technical information or the supply of any articles, so much of any agreement as provides for the making by any other person of payments in respect of the use of the information or the supply of articles of that description is of no effect in relation to any use or supply in respect of which the first person is so discharged: s 2(4).

8   Ie for the purposes of ibid s 2(1): see s 2(2).

9   Ibid s 2(2). So much of an agreement as restricts the disclosure of the terms of that or any other agreement is ineffective in relation to the disclosure to the competent authority of information required by that authority to identify the restrictions and obligations relieved by it: s 2(2). An authorisation may be retrospective: s 2(3).

10 Ie ibid s 2.

11 Ibid s 2(5).

12 Ibid s 2(6).

647. Authorisation procedure and compensation. Except where disclosure of the production[1] or supply of the defence materials[2] in question would be prejudicial to the safety of the state[3], a competent authority must, before giving an authorisation in respect of any restriction or obligation to any person, serve on him written notice requesting him to treat with the party entitled to enforce the restriction or obligation for the waiver or the modification of such restriction or obligation, and must allow time[4] for an agreement[5] embodying such waiver or modification to be concluded[6]; and, where an authorisation is given, the competent authority must give notice of it to all persons affected or who, on making such inquiries as are reasonably practicable in the circumstances, appear to be affected by the authorisation[7].

Provision is made for the compensation out of public funds[8] of persons prejudicially affected by an authorisation, the amount of the compensation being determined by agreement made between those persons and the competent authority with Treasury approval or in default of agreement determined by the court[9], which is to have regard to certain specified factors and other relevant circumstances[10]. The court has a general jurisdiction[11] to determine any disputes[12] arising out of the power to grant authorisations[13].

1   As to the meaning of 'production' see para 646 note 1 ante.
2   For the meaning of 'defence materials' see para 646 note 2 ante.
3   See the Defence Contracts Act 1958 s 3(3). In any such case, the competent authority is not required to give notice of the authorisation (see s 3(2); and the text to note 7 infra) unless and until it is satisfied that the disclosure would no longer be prejudicial; and unless and until the competent authority otherwise directs, the person to whom the authorisation is given is discharged from any obligation to which he would otherwise be subject by virtue of any agreement to give information to any other person in respect of the use of the information or the supply of articles to which the authorisation relates: s 3(3). For the meaning of 'competent authority' see para 646 note 3 ante.
4   The time is such period, not being less than three months from the date of service of the notice, as may be specified in the notice, unless the person on whom the notice is served notifies the competent authority in writing that no agreement is likely to be concluded within that period: ibid s 3(1).
5   As to the meaning of 'agreement' see para 646 note 6 ante.
6   Defence Contracts Act 1958 s 3(1).
7   Ibid s 3(2).
8   See ibid s 5.
9   'The court', as respects England and Wales, means the High Court or any patents county court having jurisdiction by virtue of an order under the Copyright, Designs and Patents Act 1988 s 287: see the Defence Contracts Act 1958 s 4(4) (amended by the Patents Act 1977 s 132(6), Sch 5 para 4); and the Patents Act 1977 s 130(1) (amended by the Copyright, Designs and Patents Act 1988 ss 295, 303(1), Sch 5 para 5, Sch 7 para 23).
10   Defence Contracts Act 1958 s 4(1). Regard must be had to the following: (1) the extent of the use made in pursuance of the authorisation (s 4(1)(a)); (2) the value of any services performed by that person in connection with the conception, development, improvement or adaptation of any specification, design, process or technique used in pursuance of the authorisation (s 4(1)(b)); (3) any benefit or compensation which that person or any person from whom he derives title may have received, or may be entitled to receive, directly or indirectly from any government department in respect of the technical information so used (s 4(1)(c)); and (4) any other relevant circumstances (s 4(1)(d)).
11   Either party to the dispute may refer it to the court in such manner as may be prescribed by rules of court: see ibid s 4(2). The reference to the court must be begun by originating motion: see RSC Ord 104, r 21(1)(a)(iii); and PRACTICE AND PROCEDURE vol 37 para 137.
12   Ie any dispute between a competent authority and any other person as to the exercise of powers conferred by the Defence Contracts Act 1958 s 2 (see para 646 ante), or as to the making or amount of a payment under s 4.
13   Ibid s 4(2). The court is empowered to exclude the public from proceedings and to prohibit the publication of technical information disclosed in proceedings to the extent that it appears to the court to be necessary or expedient in the public interest or in the interests of any parties to the proceedings: see s 4(3).

648. Powers of supply. The Secretary of State[1] has various powers including the power to buy, sell and manufacture any articles[2] required by government departments for the discharge of their functions and also articles which are, in his opinion, essential to the needs of the community in the event of war[3].

1   Ie one of Her Majesty's Principal Secretaries of State for the time being: see the Interpretation Act 1978 s 5, Sch 1; and CONSTITUTIONAL LAW AND HUMAN RIGHTS vol 8(2) (Reissue) para 355 et seq.

2   'Articles' includes substances: Supply Powers Act 1975 s 7. However see also 'articles required for the public service' (defined in s 7); and TRADE, INDUSTRY AND INDUSTRIAL RELATIONS vol 47 (Reissue) para 602.

3   See generally ibid ss 1–5; and TRADE, INDUSTRY AND INDUSTRIAL RELATIONS vol 47 (Reissue) para 601 et seq.

(4) DISTRIBUTION OF ENEMY PROPERTY

649. Collection, realisation and distribution of German enemy property. In the absence of a peace treaty with Germany[1], the collection and realisation of German enemy property[2] and the distribution of the proceeds to persons who establish claims in respect of German enemy debts[3] are provided for by Order in Council[4].

By Order in Council[5] an administrator[6] was appointed by the Board of Trade[7], to whom German enemy property was to be transferred[8]. Also by Order in Council the manner of making claims[9] was prescribed, certain claims were excluded[10], the fees chargeable to persons making claims in respect of German enemy property were prescribed[11] and provision was made for the establishment of priorities[12], the determination and payment of claims[13] and the distribution of proceeds of the realisation of the property[14].

1   See para 509 ante.

2   'German enemy property' means property which, on 23 October 1950 (see the Distribution of German Enemy Property Act 1949 s 1; and the Distribution of German Enemy Property (No 1) Order 1950, SI 1950/1642, art 11), is, or at any time thereafter becomes, subject to control under the Trading with the Enemy Act 1939 s 7 (as amended) (see para 643 ante), being property, or the proceeds or income of property, which on or at any time after 3 September 1939, belonged to or was held or managed on behalf of (1) the German state; (2) any individual who, on or after 3 September 1939, was a German national resident in Germany or in any territory under the sovereignty of a state which on or at any time after 3 September 1939 was at war with the Crown; (3) any individual who was a German national on or after 3 September 1939 and (a) was included among the persons specified in any order made under the Trading with the Enemy Act 1939 s 2(2) (see para 635 ante); or (b) was a person whose property became subject to control under s 7 at a time when he was not an enemy; (4) any body of persons (whether corporate or unincorporate) which on or at any time after 3 September 1939 was a body incorporated or constituted in, or under the laws of, Germany; and (5) any body of persons (whether corporate on unincorporate) which on or at any time after 3 September 1939 was controlled by an individual or body mentioned in heads (2), (3) or (4) supra: Distribution of German Enemy Property Act 1949 s 8(1).

'Property' means real or personal property, and includes any estate or interest in real or personal property, any money, any negotiable instrument, debt or other chose in action, and any other right or interest whether in possession or not: s 8(1). Property which, or the right to transfer which, is vested in any custodian of enemy property (see the Trading with the Enemy Act 1939 s 7; and para 643 ante), and property which cannot be dealt with without the consent of the Secretary of State, is deemed to be subject to control under s 7: Distribution of German Enemy Property Act 1949 s 8(3), (4). For what is included in property rights and interests belonging to Hungarian nationals under the Treaty of Peace (Hungary) Order 1948, SI 1948/116, see *Bank Voor Handel en Scheepvaart v Slatford* [1953] 1 QB 248, [1951] 2 All ER 779.

'German national' does not include any person who acquired German nationality by reason of the inclusion in the German state after 1 March 1938 of any territory not comprised therein on that day: Distribution of German Enemy Property Act 1949 s 8(1). A person who at any time was resident in

Germany is deemed to have been a German national at that time unless it is proved to the satisfaction of the administrator, within such time and in such manner as may be prescribed by Order in Council, that he was not a German national at that time: s 8(2). 'Germany' means territory comprised in the German state on 1 March 1938: s 8(1).

3   'German enemy debt' means any sum due at 16 December 1949 (ie the passing of the Distribution of German Enemy Property Act 1949) in respect of an obligation incurred before 3 September 1939, which on that day was an obligation of any of the following persons: (1) the German state; (2) any individual who on that day was a German national resident in Germany; (3) any body of persons (whether corporate or unincorporate) which on that day was a body incorporated or constituted in or under the laws of Germany; and which was an obligation to any of the following persons:

    (a)   the government in the United Kingdom;

    (b)   any British subject or British protected person resident or carrying on business on that day in the United Kingdom;

    (c)   any body of persons (whether corporate or unincorporate) which on that day was a body incorporated or constituted under the laws in force in the United Kingdom;

except that where any person or body of persons specified in heads (b) and (c) supra carried on business on 3 September 1939 both in and outside the United Kingdom, any sum attributable to the business carried on outside the United Kingdom must be excluded: s 8(1)(a). References in the Distribution of German Enemy Property Act 1949 to the United Kingdom, except where the reference is to the government in the United Kingdom, include references to the Isle of Man and the Channel Islands: s 11(2). For the meaning of 'United Kingdom' generally see para 502 note 4 ante.

    'German enemy debt' also means any sum, not included in s 8(1)(a) being (i) a sum due at 16 December 1949, in respect of any bond of the German External Loan 1924, or the German Government International 5.5% Loan 1930, being a bond enfaced in accordance with the Supplementary Agreement for the execution of the Anglo-German Transfer Agreement, 1 July 1938, art 2; (ii) a sum due on 7 May 1945, in respect of any bond of the Austrian Government International Loan 1930, or the Austrian Government Credit Anstalt Bonds 1936; (iii) a sum due on 7 May 1945 in respect of any bond of the Austrian Government International Guaranteed Loan 1933–53, or the Austrian Government Guaranteed Conversion Loan 1934–59, which was in the beneficial ownership of a British holder (within the meaning of the Anglo-German Transfer Agreement art 4) on 1 July 1938; or (iv) a sum due at 16 December 1949 in respect of any bond of the Konversionskasse 4% Sterling Bonds: Distribution of German Enemy Property Act 1949 s 8(1)(b). These sums also include any sum due at 16 December 1949 in respect of any bond of the City of Saarbruecken 6% Sterling Loan of 1928, being a bond enfaced in accordance with the Supplementary Agreement for the execution of the Anglo-German Transfer Agreement art 2; and any sum due in respect of the following: the Potash Syndicate of Germany 25 year Sinking Fund Gold Loan; City of Berlin 6% Sterling Loan, 1927; City of Cologne 6% Sterling Loan, 1928; City of Dresden 5.5% Sterling Loan, 1927; City of Munich 6% Sterling Bonds; State of Hamburg 6% Sterling Loan of 1926; Hamburg Waterworks 6% Sterling Loan; The Free State of Saxony 6% 25 year Sterling Bonds of 1927; Province of Westphalia 7% Sterling Loan of 1926; Prussian Electric Company 6% 25 year Sterling Bonds: Distribution of German Enemy Property Act 1952 s 1, Schedule.

    A claim for unliquidated damages is not a debt: *Re Collbran* [1956] Ch 250, [1956] 1 All ER 310.

4   Distribution of German Enemy Property Act 1949 s 1(1). The Orders in Council made under this power are the Distribution of German Enemy Property (No 1) Order 1950, SI 1950/1642; and the Distribution of German Enemy Property (No 2) Order 1951, SI 1951/1899 (amended by SI 1952/633; SI 1961/2030). The power to make Orders in Council or orders under the Distribution of German Enemy Property Act 1949 includes the power to revoke or vary the same: s 5(1). All Orders in Council so made are subject to annulment by a resolution of either House of Parliament: s 5(2).

5   See the Distribution of German Enemy Property (No 1) Order 1950 art 3.

6   The administrator is a corporation sole under the name of the Administrator of German Enemy Property (Distribution of German Enemy Property Act 1949 s 1(3); Distribution of German Enemy Property (No 1) Order 1950 art 3) and may sue and be sued in that name: art 5.

7   References to the Board of Trade include reference to the Secretary of State: see the Secretary of State for Trade and Industry Order 1970, SI 1970/1537, arts 2(1), 7(4). The Secretary of State now concerned is the Secretary of State for Trade and Industry: see the Secretary of State (New Departments) Order 1974, SI 1974/692; and the Transfer of Functions (Trade and Industry) Order 1983, SI 1983/1127. The expenses of the Board of Trade under the Distribution of German Enemy Property Act 1949 are defrayed out of moneys provided by Parliament: s 7(1). As to the Board of Trade generally see CONSTITUTIONAL LAW AND HUMAN RIGHTS vol 8(2) (Reissue) para 505; TRADE, INDUSTRY AND INDUSTRIAL RELATIONS vol 47 (Reissue) para 2.

8   See the Distribution of German Enemy Property Act 1949 s 1(2)(a), (b). See also *Maerkle v British and Continental Fur Co Ltd* [1954] 3 All ER 50, [1954] 1 WLR 1242, CA; *Adrema Werke Maschinenbau GmbH v Custodian of Enemy Property and German Enemy Property Administrator* [1957] RPC 49, CA; *RJ Reuter Co*

Ltd v Ferd Mulhens [1954] Ch 50, [1953] 2 All ER 1160, CA; *Fischler v Roumanian Property Administrator* [1960] 3 All ER 433, [1960] 1 WLR 917, HL (revival of ownership of, or beneficial title to, money controlled by debts clearing office after treaty of peace). The Distribution of German Enemy Property (No 1) Order 1950 art 12 enabled the administrator to require a custodian to transfer to him any German enemy property in his control or in which he has the right of transfer. Money representing German enemy property in any colony, protectorate or trust territory placed at the disposal of the Crown was to be paid to the administrator and dealt with as other German enemy property: Distribution of German Enemy Property Act 1949 s 4(1). After the 1914–18 war the peace treaties were followed by the Treaty of Peace Act 1919, under which the Treaty of Peace Order 1919, SR & O 1919/1517, and various amending orders were made, and the Treaties of Peace (Austria and Bulgaria) Act 1920 (repealed), the Treaty of Peace (Hungary) Act 1921 (repealed), and the Treaty of Peace (Turkey) Act 1924 (repealed), under all of which further orders were made. For cases dealing with the effects of the treaties, Acts and orders, and particularly with what property was subject to charge under the Acts and the orders made under them see *The Marie Gartz* [1920] P 172; *Clearing Office Controller v Edwards & Co (Bread Street) Ltd* [1923] WN 245; *Re Levinstein, Levinstein v Levinstein* [1921] 2 Ch 251; *Re Biedermann, Best v Wertheim* [1922] 2 Ch 771, CA; *Favorke v Steinkopff* [1922] 1 Ch 174; *Re Neuburger's Settlement, Foreshew v Public Trustee* [1923] 1 Ch 508; *Luxardo v Public Trustee* [1924] 2 Ch 147, CA; *Hartmann v Konig* (1933) 50 TLR 114, HL; *New York Life Insurance Co v Public Trustee* [1924] 2 Ch 101, CA; *Fried v German Property Administrator* [1925] Ch 757; *Sutherland v German Property Administrator* [1934] 1 KB 423, CA; *Meyer & Co v Faber* [1921] 2 Ch 226; *Re Nierhaus* [1921] 1 Ch 269. See also *Clearing Office Controller v Weir & Co* (1925) 95 LJKB 88, CA (affd (1926) 135 LT 705, HL) (effect of joint decisions of clearing offices); *Groebel v Hungarian Property Administrator* (1925) 70 Sol Jo 345 (whether Attorney General a necessary party to an action against an administrator); *German Property Administrator v Knoop* [1933] Ch 439 (whether German government is trustee or agent for German nationals); *Holland v German Property Administrator* [1937] 2 All ER 807, CA (liability of trustees for payment of income to a German national).

9   See the Distribution of German Enemy Property Act 1949 s 1(2)(c), (5); and the Distribution of German Enemy Property (No 2) Order 1951, SI 1951/1899, art 4 (amended by SI 1952/633).

10 See the Distribution of German Enemy Property Act 1949 s 1(4)(a); and the Distribution of German Enemy Property (No 2) Order 1951 art 3 (amended by SI 1952/633).

11 See the Distribution of German Enemy Property Act 1949 s 1(2)(f); and the Distribution of German Enemy Property (No 2) Order 1951 art 11; and the London Gazette, 10 March 1953, p 1378. Fees recovered under the Distribution of German Enemy Property Act 1949 were to be paid into the Exchequer: s 7(2).

12 See ibid s 1(4)(b). The amount for which claims were to be permitted to rank was governed by the Distribution of German Enemy Property (No 2) Order 1951 Pt IV (arts 5, 6).

13 See the Distribution of German Enemy Property Act 1949 s 1(2)(d), (g), (6); and the Distribution of German Enemy Property (No 2) Order 1951 Pt V (arts 7–11) (amended by SI 1961/2030). The determination of the administrator in relation to a claim was final, subject to a right of appeal to the High Court on a point of law: see art 7(2).

14 See the Distribution of German Enemy Property Act 1949 s 1(2)(e), (4)(c).

650. German enemy property controlled by a United Kingdom company.

Where any German enemy property[1], on or at any time after 3 September 1939, belonged to, or was held or managed on behalf of, a German company[2], and it appears to the Board of Trade[3] that the company was on that day controlled, directly or indirectly, by a United Kingdom company[4], the Board may treat that property[5], to such extent as the Board thinks fit having regard to the extent of the interest of the United Kingdom company in German company, as property to which the United Kingdom company would have been entitled but for the operation of the Trading with the Enemy Act 1939, or any order made under that Act[6].

1   For the meaning of 'German enemy property' and 'property' see para 649 note 2 ante.
2   'German company' means a body incorporated in, or under the laws of, Germany: Distribution of German Enemy Property Act 1949 s 1(7).
3   As to the Board of Trade see para 649 note 7 ante.
4   'United Kingdom company' means a body incorporated in, or under the laws of, the United Kingdom: Distribution of German Enemy Property Act 1949 s 1(7). As to the meaning of 'United Kingdom' see para 649 note 3 ante.
5   Ie for the purposes of ibid s 1(6) (see para 649 ante).
6   Ibid s 1(7).

651. Offences relating to the distribution of German enemy property. If any person who (1) is prohibited[1] from dealing with any German enemy property[2] otherwise than with the consent of the administrator[3]; or (2) is required[4] to transfer such property to the administrator or otherwise to deal with it in accordance with the administrator's directions[5], contravenes or fails to comply with the prohibition or requirement, he is guilty of an offence[6]. Any person who, without reasonable excuse, fails to comply with any requirement[7] to furnish information or to produce books or documents[8], or who, in giving such information, knowingly or recklessly makes a statement which is false in a material particular[9], is guilty of an offence[10] and liable on summary conviction to a fine not exceeding the prescribed sum[11] or imprisonment for a term not exceeding three months, or to both[12], or on conviction on indictment to a fine or imprisonment for a term not exceeding two years, or to both[13].

1   Ie by or under an Order in Council made under the Distribution of German Enemy Property Act 1949 s 1.
2   For the meaning of 'German enemy property' see para 649 note 2 ante.
3   Distribution of German Enemy Property Act 1949 s 2(1)(a).
4   Ie by or under an Order in Council made under ibid s 1.
5   Ibid s 2(1)(b).
6   Ibid s 2(1).
7   Ie any requirement made by or under an Order in Council made under ibid s 1.
8   Ibid s 2(2)(a).
9   Ibid s 2(2)(b).
10   Ibid s 2(2).
11   As to the prescribed sum see para 638 note 3 ante.
12   Distribution of German Enemy Property Act 1949 s 2(3)(a) (amended by virtue of the Magistrates' Courts Act 1980 s 32(2)).
13   Distribution of German Enemy Property Act 1949 s 2(3)(b) (amended by virtue of the Criminal Law Act 1977 s 32(1)). The fine may be of any amount: see s 32(1). Where the offence is committed by a body corporate, every person who was at the time of the offence a director, general manager, secretary or other similar officer of the body corporate is deemed to be guilty of the offence unless he proves that the offence was committed without his consent or connivance and that he used due diligence to prevent its commission: see the Distribution of German Enemy Property Act 1949 s 2(4). 'Director' in relation to any body corporate established by or under any enactment for the purpose of carrying on under national ownership any industry or part of an industry or undertaking, being a body corporate whose affairs are managed by the members thereof, means a member of that body corporate: s 2(4). As to corporate liability generally see CRIMINAL LAW vol 11(1) (Reissue) para 35. Where an indemnity Act has been passed (see eg the Indemnity Act 1920 (repealed)), acts, other than malicious acts, will be protected: see CONSTITUTIONAL LAW AND HUMAN RIGHTS vol 8(2) (Reissue) para 821. See also *Marshal Shipping Co v Board of Trade* [1923] 2 KB 343, CA; *Bristol Channel Steamers Ltd v R* (1924) 131 LT 608; *Brocklebank Ltd v R* [1925] 1 KB 52, CA; *Marshal Shipping Co (in liquidation) v R* (1925) 41 TLR 285 (all cases on the Indemnity Act 1920 (repealed)).

652. Resolution of conflicting claims. Where arrangements have been made by or on behalf of the government in the United Kingdom[1] with the government of any country outside the United Kingdom or any person acting on its behalf for the resolution of conflicting claims to German enemy property[2] and corresponding property under the control of the government of that country, the Treasury may, for the purpose of giving effect to those arrangements, direct the administrator to transfer to a specified person such German enemy property or proceeds as may be specified, and the administrator must comply with any such direction[3]. Any property transferred in pursuance of those arrangements to any person acting on behalf of the government in the United Kingdom must be transferred to the administrator and dealt with in a like manner as German enemy property[4].

1   As to the meaning of 'United Kingdom' see para 649 note 3 ante.
2   For the meaning of 'German enemy property' see para 649 note 2 ante.
3   Distribution of German Enemy Property Act 1949 s 3(a).
4   Ibid s 3(b).

6. CIVIL DEFENCE

653. Legislation. Acts of Parliament passed in anticipation of the 1939–45 war, and placing on local authorities and on owners and occupiers of factories and commercial and other premises, and upon public utility undertakers, the duty to make schemes for the protection of persons and property from injury or damage in the event of hostile attack, have now been mostly repealed[1]. The remaining old legislation relates to certain powers to appropriate land and buildings[2] and the enforcement of measures to secure the functioning of undertakings in the event of hostile attack[3].

The Civil Defence Act 1948 makes further provision[4] and, in particular, imposes on the appropriate ministers the duty of arranging for the organisation and training of civil defence forces and services[5], the instruction of the public, and the provision of structures and other works for civil defence purposes[6].

The Civil Defence (Armed Forces) Act 1954 provides for the training in civil defence[7] matters of members of the armed forces[8].

The Civil Protection in Peacetime Act 1986 enables a local authority to use any of its civil defence resources[9] in taking action to avert, alleviate or eradicate the effects of an emergency or disaster, even if the event is unconnected with hostile foreign attack[10].

The legislation described above does not generally apply to Northern Ireland[11].

1   See especially the Air-Raid Precautions Act 1937 (repealed) and the Civil Defence Act 1939 (partly repealed).
2   See para 659 post.
3   See para 658 post.
4   The provisions of the Civil Defence Act 1948 are in addition to, and not in derogation of, the provisions of earlier enactments (ie the Civil Defence Act 1939): Civil Defence Act 1948 s 6(1) (amended by the Statute Law (Repeals) Act 1986 s 1(1), Sch 1 Pt XIII). The designated minister may by regulations bring into force suspended or spent provisions, and amend or repeal them: see the Civil Defence Act 1948 s 6(2). For the meaning of 'designated minister' see para 654 note 10 post; and as to the making of regulations see para 654 note 18 post. As to the suspension and revival of an Act see STATUTES vol 44(1) (Reissue) paras 1315–1316.
5   For the purposes of the Civil Defence Act 1948, 'civil defence' includes any measures not amounting to actual combat for affording defence against any form of hostile attack by a foreign power or for depriving any form of hostile attack by a foreign power of the whole or part of its effect, whether the measures are taken before, at or after the time of the attack; but it does not include the provision or maintenance of a shelter which is used or intended to be used wholly or mainly by naval, military or air forces: s 9(1). 'Civil defence forces' and 'civil defence services' mean respectively forces and services formed wholly or mainly to meet the needs of civil defence: s 9(1).
6   See paras 654–656 post.
7   For the purposes of the Civil Defence (Armed Forces) Act 1954, 'civil defence' includes any measures not amounting to actual combat for affording defence against any form of hostile attack by a foreign power or for depriving any form of hostile attack by a foreign power of the whole or part of its effect, whether the measures are taken before, at or after the time of the attack: s 3(2).
8   See paras 654, 656 post.
9   For the meaning of 'civil defence resources' see para 657 note 3 post.
10   See para 657 post.
11   See the Civil Defence Act 1939 s 92(1); the Civil Defence Act 1948 s 10(1) (amended by the Northern Ireland Constitution Act 1973 s 41(1), Sch 6 Pt I)); and the Civil Protection in Peacetime Act 1986 s 3(3).

654. Ministers and departments. Originally the central authority for air-raid precautions was the Secretary of State[1], but subsequently provision was made for the distribution of civil defence functions[2] by Order in Council among other ministers[3]. Changes in the departmental structure of the central government during and since the 1939–45 war, and the corresponding alterations in the designations and functions of ministers, had effect on the distribution of civil defence functions among them[4]. A number of orders were made designating certain ministers under the Civil Defence Act 1948[5], but these orders have now nearly all been revoked[6] with the result that the Secretary of State is still the principal central authority for civil defence[7], but other ministers and departments may have related functions in their respective spheres[8].

By Order in Council a minister may be designated for certain purposes of civil defence, and different ministers may be designated for different purposes[9]. A designated minister[10] may arrange for the exercise of his functions by another minister[11]. A designated minister must take such steps as appear to him to be necessary or expedient for civil defence purposes, and particularly in connection with (1) the organisation, formation, maintenance, equipment and training of civil defence forces and services[12];(2) the organisation, equipment and training for civil defence purposes of police forces[13], fire brigades[14] and employees of local[15] or police authorities employed primarily for other purposes; (3) the instruction of members of the public in civil defence and their equipment for the purposes of civil defence; (4) the provision, storage and maintenance of commodities and things required for civil defence; (5) the provision, construction, maintenance or alteration of premises, structures or excavations required for civil defence and the doing of any other work required for civil defence[16]. A designated minister is also responsible for the training in civil defence of members of the armed forces[17], and he may by regulations prescribe the civil defence functions of local and police authorities[18].

1   Schemes for air-raid precautions had to be submitted to the Secretary of State: see the Air-Raid Precautions Act 1937 (repealed).
2   For the purposes of the Civil Defence Act 1939, 'civil defence functions' means any functions conferred or imposed by or under that Act: s 90(1) (amended by the Statute Law (Repeals) Act 1976 s 1(1), Sch 1 Pt V)). As to the meaning of 'civil defence' in the Civil Defence Act 1948 see para 653 note 5 ante.
3   See the Civil Defence Act 1939 s 1 (repealed); and the Civil Defence Act 1948 ss 1, 9(2).
4   As to the transfer of ministerial functions generally see CONSTITUTIONAL LAW AND HUMAN RIGHTS vol 8(2) (Reissue) para 363.
5   Ie under the Civil Defence Act 1948 s 9(2).
6   See the Civil Defence (Designation Orders) (Revocation and Amendment) Order 1973, SI 1973/1759.
7   Civil Defence Act 1948 s 9(2) proviso.
8   In practice, the Home Secretary is the minister responsible for civil defence functions. As to the vesting in the Minister of Works (now the Secretary of State for the Environment: see the Minister of Works (Change of Style and Title) Order 1962, SI 1962/1549; and the Secretary of State for the Environment Order 1970, SI 1970/1681 (as amended)) of certain land and underground works constructed as air-raid shelters in London see the Underground Works (London) Act 1956.
9   See the Civil Defence Act 1948 s 9(2).
10 'Designated minister' means such minister as may be designated by Order in Council, and different ministers may be designated for different purposes or different provisions of the Civil Defence Act 1948; and if there is no provision made by Order in Council, 'designated minister' means the Secretary of State: s 9(2). Any such Order in Council may be revoked or varied by a subsequent Order in Council: s 9(2).
11 Ibid s 1(2).
12 For the meaning of 'civil defence forces' and 'civil defence services' see para 653 note 5 ante.
13 Any reference to the organisation, equipment or training for civil defence purposes of police forces includes a reference to the organisation, equipment and training of persons who are special constables for the police area in question: Civil Defence Act 1948 s 9(3).
14 'Fire brigade' means a fire brigade maintained in pursuance of the Fire Services Act 1947: Civil Defence Act 1948 s 9(1).
15 For the meaning of 'local authority' see para 655 note 1 post.
16 Civil Defence Act 1948 s 1(1).
17 See the Civil Defence (Armed Forces) Act 1954 s 1(1), (2).
18 See the Civil Defence Act 1948 s 2(1), (2) (amended by the Local Government Act 1972 s 27(1), Sch 30). Regulations made under the Civil Defence Act 1948 may make different provision for different cases or classes of case, authorities or undertakers, and may contain consequential and incidental provisions: s 8(1). The regulations are to be made by statutory instrument (s 8(2)); and must be approved in draft form by resolution of each House of Parliament (s 8(3)). As to the regulations made

see the Civil Defence (Police) Regulations 1954, SI 1954/252; and POLICE vol 36 para 239; and the Civil Defence (General Local Authority Functions) Regulations 1993, SI 1993/1812 (as amended); and para 656 post.

655. Local authorities. Every local authority[1] and police authority has certain civil defence[2] functions, which are prescribed by regulations made by the designated minister[3]. In exercising any of these functions a local authority must comply with any directions given by the designated minister[4].

Functions concerning civil defence plans and staff training are imposed upon county councils, metropolitan district councils, London borough councils and the Common Council of the City of London[5]. In each non-metropolitan county, every district council in the county must assist the county council in its civil defence functions[6]. For each metropolitan county[7], and for London, a fire and civil defence authority has been established[8] consisting of members of the constituent councils[9] appointed by them to be members of the authority[10]. These fire and civil defence authorities must assist any council in their areas in civil defence functions[11].

Local authorities can use their civil defence resources[12] in peacetime emergencies and disasters[13]; and they also have certain powers in connection with compulsory acquisition and appropriation of land[14] and entry onto land[15].

1 'Local authority' means (1) a billing authority or a precepting authority (see the Local Government Finance Act 1992 s 69); (2) a combined fire authority (see the Local Government Finance Act 1988 s 144(5)); (3) a levying body (see the Local Government Finance Act 1988 s 74 (as amended)); and (4) a body as regards which the provisions concerning special levies apply (see the Local Government Finance Act 1988 s 75 (as amended)): Civil Defence Act 1948 s 9(1) (amended by the Local Government Finance Act 1992 s 117(1), Sch 13 para 8; the Police and Magistrates' Courts Act 1994 s 93, Sch 9 Pt I; and the Local Government Finance (Repeals, Savings and Consequential Amendments) Order 1990, SI 1990/776, art 8, Sch 3 Pt I para 4). As to the general power of local authorities to delegate functions see the Local Government Act 1972 s 101(1); and LOCAL GOVERNMENT vol 28 para 1143; and as to billing and precepting authorities and levying bodies see LOCAL GOVERNMENT; RATING.

2 As to the meaning of 'civil defence' see para 653 note 5 ante.

3 Civil Defence Act 1948 s 2(1). As to the making of regulations see para 654 note 18 ante. As to the functions prescribed see the Civil Defence (General Local Authority Functions) Regulations 1993, SI 1993/1812 (as amended); and para 656 post. For the meaning of 'designated minister' see para 654 note 10 ante.

4 Ibid reg 8.

5 See ibid regs 2, 4, 6; and para 656 post. As to the areas and authorities in England see LOCAL GOVERNMENT vol 28 para 1030 et seq. As to the London area and emergencies and civil defence generally see LONDON GOVERNMENT vol 29 para 107.

6 See ibid reg 5.

7 Metropolitan counties were established under the Local Government Act 1972; their county councils were abolished by the Local Government Act 1985 s 1(1) but the counties themselves remained in existence, subject to any changes made by orders under the Local Government Act 1992 s 17 (as amended): see generally LOCAL GOVERNMENT.

8 See the Local Government Act 1985 ss 26(1), (2), 27(1).

9 The constituent councils in relation to a metropolitan county fire and civil defence authority are the councils of the metropolitan districts comprised in that county; and the constituent councils in relation to the London Fire and Civil Defence Authority are the London borough councils and the Common Council of the City of London: ibid ss 26(4), 27(3). As to the number of members to be appointed by each constituent council see s 29, Sch 10 (s 29 amended by the Police and Magistrates' Courts Act 1994 s 93, Sch 9 Pt I); and as to joint authorities generally see LOCAL GOVERNMENT; LONDON GOVERNMENT.

10 Local Government Act 1985 ss 26(3), 27(2).

11 See the Civil Defence (General Local Authority Functions) Regulations 1993 reg 7.

12 For the meaning of 'civil defence resources' see para 657 note 3 post.

13 See para 657 post.

14 See para 659 post.

15 See para 661 post.

656. Planning and public protection. The civil defence[1] functions of local authorities[2] are prescribed in the Civil Defence (General Local Authority Functions) Regulations 1993[3], which require each non-metropolitan county council, metropolitan district council, London borough council and the Common Council of the City of London[4] to make, keep under review and revise plans for its area and to carry out exercises based on those plans[5]. Each of these councils must also arrange for the training of an appropriate number of suitable members of its own staff, and of such other persons as it considers necessary, for the purposes of carrying out these plans and discharging other civil defence functions[6]. These councils must also, at the request of the designated minister[7], or where the council considers it appropriate (1) take such preparatory steps as may be necessary to ensure that the plans can be carried out; and (2) carry out any of those plans[8]. When making or revising plans councils are required to consult with any other council whose area may be affected by the plans[9]. Metropolitan district councils, London borough councils and the Common Council of the City of London must also consult with the relevant fire and civil defence authority[10]; and each of these councils may enter into an arrangement with the relevant fire and civil defence authority for the carrying out of all or any of its functions under these provisions[11]. Where a combination scheme has been made[12] with respect to a combined area which includes the area of a county council affected by a structural or boundary change[13], that council must also consult with the fire authority constituted by that scheme for that combined area[14]; and the council may enter into an arrangement with that authority for the carrying out of all or any of its functions under these provisions[15].

In non-metropolitan counties every district council must (a) at the request of the county council, furnish such information as may be requested of it[16]; (b) at the request of the designated minister, or of the county council, assist the county council in making and revising plans, taking preparatory steps to ensure that the plans can be carried out and in carrying out any of those plans[17]; (c) arrange for the training of an appropriate number of suitable members of its staff and make staff available to the county council for training[18].

The relevant fire and civil defence authority in metropolitan counties, and the London Fire and Civil Defence Authority, are each required to carry out, on behalf of any council in its area, the civil defence arrangements made with the council[19] and to assist the council in its civil defence functions[20].

Members of police forces[21] and fire brigades[22], and, if ministerial regulations so provide, employees of local authorities or police authorities employed primarily for purposes other than civil defence, are under a duty to comply with requirements as to training and taking part in civil defence[23]. The duties which members of the armed forces may be called upon to undertake as members of those forces include civil defence and training in civil defence[24].

1   As to the meaning of 'civil defence' see para 653 note 5 ante.
2   For the meaning of 'local authority' see para 655 note 1 ante.
3   Ie the Civil Defence (General Local Authority Functions) Regulations 1993, SI 1993/1812 (as amended: see note 13 infra).
4   For these purposes a reference to a council, in relation to the City of London, is a reference to the Common Council of the City of London: Civil Defence (General Local Authority Functions) Regulations 1993 reg 2.
5   Ibid regs 4(1)(a), 6(1)(a).
6   Ibid regs 4(1)(b), 6(1)(b). County councils must also arrange for the training of the staff of every district council in the county: reg 4(1)(b)(i).
7   For the meaning of 'designated minister' see para 654 note 10 ante.
8   Civil Defence (General Local Authority Functions) Regulations 1993 regs 4(1)(c), 6(1)(c).
9   Ibid regs 4(2), 6(2).
10   Ibid reg 6(2). The 'relevant fire and civil defence authority', in relation to a metropolitan district council, means the metropolitan county fire and civil defence authority for the area in which the area of the district

council is situated and, in relation to the council of a London borough or the City of London, means the London Fire and Civil Defence Authority: reg 6(4). As to the establishment of those authorities see para 655 ante.

11 Ibid reg 6(3).

12 Ie under the Fire Services Act 1947: see FIRE SERVICES.

13 As to the meaning of 'structural change' and 'boundary change' see the Local Government Act 1992 s 14(1)(a), (b); and LOCAL GOVERNMENT. Where, by virtue of a structural change, a district council has the functions of a county council in relation to its district, the Civil Defence (General Local Authority Functions) Regulations 1993 apply as if any reference to a county council were a reference to a district council, and reg 5 does not apply in relation to that district: reg 4(4) (added by SI 1996/330).

14 Ibid reg 4(3)(a) (as added: see note 13 supra).

15 Ibid reg 4(3)(b) (as added: see note 13 supra).

16 Ibid reg 5(a).

17 Ibid reg 5(b).

18 Ibid reg 5(c).

19 Ie arrangements made under ibid reg 6(3): see reg 7(a).

20 See ibid reg 7(b).

21 As to the meaning of 'police forces' see para 654 note 13 ante.

22 For the meaning of 'fire brigade' see para 654 note 14 ante. See also the provisions concerning fire authorities, and fire and civil defence authorities, discussed in the text and notes 10–20 supra.

23 See the Civil Defence Act 1948 s 5.

24 See the Civil Defence (Armed Forces) Act 1954 s 2.

657. Peacetime emergencies and disasters. Where an emergency or disaster involving destruction of, or danger to, life or property occurs or is imminent or there is reasonable ground for apprehending such an emergency or disaster, and a local authority[1] is of the opinion that the emergency or disaster is likely[2] to affect the whole or part of its area or all or some of the area's inhabitants, the authority may use any of its civil defence resources[3] in taking action[4] which is calculated to avert, alleviate or eradicate the effects or potential effects of the event in its area or among the area's inhabitants[5]. The emergency or disaster may be unconnected with any form of hostile attack by a foreign power[6].

Where a local authority's civil defence functions include the function of making, keeping under review and revising plans for any matter[7], the authority may perform that function so as to allow for the possible occurrence of such an emergency or disaster and may facilitate the use of all or any of its civil defence resources in connection with any such emergency or disaster that may occur or become imminent or which there are reasonable grounds for apprehending[8].

Any expenses incurred by a local authority in or in connection with the discharge of the functions conferred by the Civil Defence Act 1948[9] are not prevented from qualifying for grants[10] by the fact that they were incurred in circumstances resulting from the exercise of any power conferred by the Civil Protection in Peacetime Act 1986[11].

Any increase attributable to these provisions in the sums payable out of money provided by Parliament under any other Act is to be paid out of money so provided[12].

1 The Civil Protection in Peacetime Act 1986 applies to local authorities within the meaning of the Civil Defence Act 1948 (see para 655 note 1 ante) on whom civil defence functions are for the time being conferred under s 2 (as amended) (see paras 655–656 ante): Civil Protection in Peacetime Act 1986 s 1(1). 'Civil defence' has the same meaning as in the Civil Defence Act 1948 s 9(1) (see para 653 note 5 ante); and 'civil defence functions', in relation to a local authority, means all such functions as are for the time being conferred on the authority under s 2 (as amended) (see paras 655–656 ante): Civil Protection in Peacetime Act 1986 s 1(2).

2 'Likely' has been construed to mean that there is a reasonable prospect of a thing happening: *Dunning v Board of Governors of the United Liverpool Hospitals* [1973] 2 All ER 454 at 460, sub nom *Dunning v United Liverpool Hospitals' Board of Governors* [1973] 1 WLR 586 at 594, CA; overruled on another point by *McIvor v Southern Health and Social Services Board* [1978] 2 All ER 625, [1978] 1 WLR 757, HL. Cf *R v*

Sheppard [1981] AC 394 at 405, [1980] 3 All ER 899 at 904, HL, per Lord Diplock; and *R v Wills* [1990] Crim LR 714, CA.

3   'Civil defence resources', in relation to a local authority, means all the resources maintained, provided, used or held by the authority for civil defence purposes, including personnel (whether employees or volunteers), premises, equipment, services and facilities: Civil Protection in Peacetime Act 1986 s 1(2).

4   The local authority may take action either alone or jointly with any other person or body, and either in its area or elsewhere in or outside the United Kingdom: ibid s 2(1). For the meaning of 'United Kingdom' see para 502 note 4 ante.

5   Ibid s 2(1).

6   Ibid s 2(1).

7   See para 656 ante.

8   Civil Protection in Peacetime Act 1986 s 2(2).

9   Ie conferred by the Civil Defence Act 1948 s 2 (as amended): see paras 655–656 ante. These functions do not include any power conferred by the Civil Protection in Peacetime Act 1986 s 2(1) or (2): s 2(3).

10 Ie under the Civil Defence Act 1948 s 3 (as amended): see para 660 post.

11 Civil Protection in Peacetime Act 1986 s 2(3).

12 Ibid s 2(4).

658. Functioning of undertakings. The appropriate department[1] may serve a notice in writing[2] on any public utility undertakers[3] requiring them to make either or both of the following: (1) a written report stating what measures they have taken or are proposing to take to provide air-raid shelter[4] for the persons employed by them; and (2) a written report stating what measures they have taken or are taking or proposing to take to secure the functioning of their undertaking in the event of hostile attack[5]. It is the duty of the undertakers on receipt of such a notice to comply with its requirements[6].

The appropriate department may serve on any public utility undertakers a notice requiring them within a specified time to take such measures as may be specified in the notice, being measures concerned with the provision of air-raid shelter or measures to secure the functioning of their undertaking in the event of hostile attack[7].

These provisions were suspended in their application by the Civil Defence (Suspension of Powers) Act 1945[8], but have to some extent been revived or repealed and replaced by regulations made under the Civil Defence Act 1948[9].

1   'Appropriate department' means (1) in relation to any railway, canal, inland navigation, dock or harbour undertaking, the Secretary of State for Transport; (2) in relation to any gas undertaking, the Board of Trade (in practice, the Secretary of State for Trade and Industry); (3) in relation to any electricity undertaking, the Secretary of State (ie the Secretary of State for Trade and Industry); and (4) in relation to any water undertaking, the Secretary of State (ie the Secretary of State for the Environment: but see note 3 infra): Civil Defence Act 1939 s 90(1) (amended by the Electricity Act 1989 s 112(1), Sch 16 para 4; and by virtue of numerous orders transferring ministerial functions, including (a) in relation to transport, the Secretary of State for the Environment Order 1970, SI 1970/1681 (as amended); the Secretary of State for Transport Order 1976, SI 1976/1775 (as amended); the Minister of Transport Order 1979, SI 1979/571; and the Transfer of Functions (Transport) Order 1981, SI 1981/238); (b) in relation to the functions of the Board of Trade, the Secretary of State (New Departments) Order 1974, SI 1974/692; and the Transfer of Functions (Trade and Industry) Order 1983, SI 1983/1127; and see further CONSTITUTIONAL LAW AND HUMAN RIGHTS vol 8(2) (Reissue) para 505; TRADE, INDUSTRY AND INDUSTRIAL RELATIONS vol 47 (Reissue) para 2; and (c) in relation to water, the Transfer of Functions (Minister of Health and Minister of Local Government and Planning) (No 2) Order 1951, SI 1951/753; and the Secretary of State for the Environment Order 1970 (as amended)). In relation to the Post Office, the appropriate department is the Secretary of State (ie the Secretary of State for Trade and Industry): Post Office Act 1969 ss 6(1), 76, Sch 4 para 36(2) (amended by the British Telecommunications Act 1981 s 89, Sch 6 Pt I; and by virtue of the Ministry of Posts and Telecommunications (Dissolution) Order 1974, SI 1974/691, arts 2, 3(3)). In relation to the Civil Aviation Authority, the appropriate department is the Secretary of State (ie the Secretary of State for Transport): Civil Aviation Act 1982 s 19(2), Sch 2 para 2.

2   Any document which is required or authorised by or under the Civil Defence Act 1939 to be given to or served on any person may be given or served either (1) by delivering it to that person (s 80(a)); or (2) by leaving it at or sending it in a prepaid letter addressed to him at his last known residence or his last known business address (s 80(b)); or (3) in the case of a document to be given to or served on the occupier

of any premises, by addressing it to the person concerned by the description of 'occupier' and delivering it to someone on the premises, or, if there is no one there to whom it can be delivered, by affixing it or a copy of it to some conspicuous part of the premises (s 80(c)). 'Occupier', in relation to any unoccupied land, premises, building or part of a building, means the person entitled to the possession of it: s 90(1).

3   'Public utility undertakers' means any persons authorised by any enactment or order to construct, work or carry on any railway, canal, inland navigation, dock, harbour, or water undertaking, and also includes persons who, though not authorised by any enactment or order (other than the Public Health Act 1875 or the Public Health Act 1936) to do so, are engaged in supplying water to the public, and for that purpose make use of pipes or mains laid in any highway; and 'public utility undertaking' is to be construed accordingly: Civil Defence Act 1939 s 90(1) (amended by the Gas Act 1986 s 67(4), Sch 9 Pt I; and by the Electricity Act 1989 s 112(4), Sch 18). For these purposes, references to public utility undertakers include references to (1) the Post Office, and references to a public utility undertaking include its undertaking (see the Post Office Act 1969 Sch 4 para 36(1)); (2) the Civil Aviation Authority, and references to a public utility undertaking include its undertaking (see the Civil Aviation Act 1982 Sch 2 para 2); (3) a person who is carrying on activities which he is authorised by a licence or exemption under the Electricity Act 1989 to carry on, and references to an electricity undertaking are to be construed as references to the undertaking carried on by any such person (see s 112(1), Sch 16 para 1(3)); and (4) a public gas transporter (see the Gas Act 1995 s 16(1), Sch 4 para 2(5)). They do not, however, include references to the Environment Agency or to any water undertaker or sewerage undertaker and, accordingly, references to a public utility undertaking do not include references to the undertaking of the agency or of such an undertaker: Water Act 1989 s 190(1), Sch 25 para 1(4) (amended by virtue of the Environment Act 1995 ss 2, 3). Any premises occupied, or persons employed, by public utility undertakers who carry on a railway undertaking are deemed for the purposes of the Civil Defence Act 1939 to be occupied or employed for the purposes of their railway undertaking, unless the occupation or employment is wholly or mainly for the purposes of some harbour, dock or canal undertaking carried on by those undertakers: s 90(2). As to the Environment Agency, and water and sewerage undertakers, see WATER.

4   'Air-raid shelter' means protection, otherwise than by war-like means or by any article of apparel, from hostile attack from the air, and 'an air-raid shelter' means any premises, structure or excavation used or intended to be used to provide air-raid shelter: ibid s 90(1).

5   Ibid s 36(2) (amended by the Statute Law (Repeals) Act 1976 s 1(1), Sch 1 Pt V; and by the Statute Law (Repeals) Act 1993 s 1(1), Sch 1 Pt XVI). The form of reports may be prescribed by rules: see the Civil Defence Act 1939 s 76. At the date at which this volume states the law, no such rules had been made.

6   Ibid s 36(2) (as amended: see note 5 supra). As to penalties for failure to comply see para 661 post.

7   See ibid s 37(1). As to grants towards the expenses incurred see para 660 post. As to penalties for failure to comply see para 661 post.

8   Ie the Civil Defence (Suspension of Powers) Act 1945 s 2(1), Schedule para 4 (repealed).

9   Ie the Civil Defence Act 1948 s 6(2) (see para 653 note 4 ante).

     The Civil Defence Act 1939 ss 36, 37 (as amended) were revived to the extent that the Post Office is required to report on, and to take, measures to secure the functioning of its undertaking in the event of hostile attack: see the Civil Defence (Posts and Telecommunications) Regulations 1971, SI 1971/221, arts 1–6 (amended by virtue of the Ministry of Posts and Telecommunications (Dissolution) Order 1974).

     The Civil Defence Act 1939 s 36(2)(b) (see head (2) in the text), s 37 (in so far as it relates to measures to secure the functioning of an undertaking in the event of hostile attack) were repealed and replaced in relation to gas and electricity undertakings: see the Civil Defence (Gas Undertakers) Regulations 1954, SI 1954/269 (as amended); and FUEL AND ENERGY vol 19(1) (Reissue) para 568; the Civil Defence (Electricity Undertakings) Regulations 1954, SI 1954/377 (as amended); and FUEL AND ENERGY vol 19(2) (Reissue) para 978.

     The Civil Defence Act 1939 ss 36, 37 (as amended) (except in so far as they relate to the provision of air-raid shelters) were repealed and replaced in relation to railway, canal, inland navigation, dock and harbour undertakers: see the Civil Defence (Transport) Regulations 1954, SI 1954/274 (as amended); and RAILWAYS vol 38 para 739.

659. Powers in relation to land. Any local authority having any civil defence functions[1], or any public utility undertakers[2] upon whom civil defence obligations have been imposed[3], may, without formal appropriation, use for the purpose of discharging those functions or obligations any land or buildings in their ownership or control or leased to them[4]; and local authorities[5] having such land or buildings may permit other local authorities having civil defence functions to use the lands or buildings for those functions[6]. These provisions have effect notwithstanding anything contained in any Act, trust, covenant or restriction affecting the use of the land or buildings[7]; but the powers are exercisable only with the approval of the minister[8], who may give directions concerning the cessation of the use and the restoration of the premises to their former condition[9].

The designated minister[10] and certain local authorities[11] may be authorised to purchase compulsorily any land required by them for discharging their civil defence functions[12]; and the designated minister may also purchase any land required by any other minister or by any local or police authority for civil defence functions[13].

Where the designated minister or any local[14] or police authority[15] does any work for the purpose of providing or maintaining a civil defence shelter[16] he or it may, if it appears expedient, do that work and provide or maintain the shelter wholly or partly in, under or over any highway[17], subject to any restrictions and to any provisions as to compensation which may be prescribed by regulations[18], and provided that the designated minister or local authority, as the case may be, is satisfied that the shelter will not obstruct the highway so as to substantially diminish the utility of the highway to the public[19].

1   For the meaning of 'civil defence functions' for the purposes of the Civil Defence Act 1939 generally see para 654 note 2 ante. For the purposes of s 62(1), 'civil defence functions' includes functions prescribed in relation to a local authority by regulations made under the Civil Defence Act 1948 s 2 (see paras 655–656 ante): Civil Defence (Appropriation of Lands and Buildings) Regulations 1952, SI 1952/1913, reg 1.

2   For the meaning of 'public utility undertakers' see para 658 note 3 ante. The Civil Defence Act 1939 s 62(1)–(3) is applied in relation to notices, reports or other action by regulations relating to gas, transport and electricity undertakings respectively: see the Civil Defence (Gas Undertakers) Regulations 1954, SI 1954/269, reg 4(2) (as amended); the Civil Defence (Transport) Regulations 1954, SI 1954/274, reg 5(2) (as amended); and the Civil Defence (Electricity Undertakings) Regulations 1954, SI 1954/377, reg 3(2) (as amended).

3   Ie under the Civil Defence Act 1939 Pt V (ss 36–39) (as amended): see para 658 ante.

4   Ibid s 62(1)(a). 'Land', in any provision of the 1939 Act relating to the acquisition of land, includes any interest in land and any easement or right in, to, or over land: s 90(1).

5   'Local authority' as used here includes any billing authority or precepting authority (see the Local Government Finance Act 1992 s 69; and RATING) and metropolitan county passenger transport authority and any combination or joint committee of such authorities: Civil Defence Act 1939 s 62(1A)(a) (added by the Statute Law (Repeals) Act 1976 s 1(2), Sch 2 Pt II; substituted by the Local Government Finance (Miscellaneous Amendments and Repeal) Order 1990, SI 1990/1285, art 2, Schedule para 3; amended by the Local Government Finance Act 1992 s 117(1), Sch 13 para 6).

6   Civil Defence Act 1939 s 62(1)(b) (amended by the Statute Law (Repeals) Act 1976 Sch 1 Pt V).

7   Civil Defence Act 1939 s 62(1) (as amended: see note 6 supra).

8   Ibid s 62(2). The minister may impose conditions in relation to any particular exercise of these powers: s 62(2). 'Minister' was defined by s 1(2) (repealed) as meaning the minister specified in an order made under s 1(1) (repealed) or, if no order was in force, the Secretary of State.

9   See ibid s 62(3). 'Use', in relation to land owned by or leased to a local authority, includes the erection of buildings and other structures, the making of excavations, and the alteration and maintenance of any such buildings, structures or excavations; and, in relation to buildings owned by or leased to an authority, includes the alteration and maintenance of those buildings: s 62(4).

10   For the meaning of 'designated minister' see para 654 note 10 ante.

11   As to the local authorities who may be authorised to purchase land compulsorily see now the Acquisition of Land Act 1981 s 7(1) (as amended); and COMPULSORY ACQUISITION OF LAND vol 8(1) (Reissue) para 34.

12   Ie any of the functions exercisable by them under the Civil Defence Act 1948 ss 1, 2 (as amended) (see paras 654–655 ante), presumably including functions conferred by regulations under s 2 (as amended) (see para 656 ante): see s 4(1)(a). As to the meaning of 'civil defence' see para 653 note 5 ante. As to powers of entry on land see para 661 post.

13   Ibid s 4(1)(a), (b). The provisions of the Acquisition of Land Act 1981 apply to compulsory purchase under these provisions: see the Civil Defence Act 1948 s 4(1); and see generally COMPULSORY ACQUISITION OF LAND. The powers conferred by s 4 are in addition to and not in derogation of any powers which would otherwise be available in relation to any of the functions exercisable under the Civil Defence Act 1948: s 4(5).

14   For the meaning of 'local authority' for these purposes see para 655 note 1 ante.

15   As to police authorities see POLICE vol 36 para 225 et seq.

16 'Civil defence shelter' means any shelter other than a shelter which is used or intended to be used wholly or mainly by naval, military or air forces; and 'shelter' means any premises, structure or excavation used or intended to be used to provide shelter from any form of hostile attack by a foreign power: Civil Defence Act 1948 s 9(1).

17 Ibid s 4(2). As to highways generally see HIGHWAYS.

18 Ie prescribed by regulations made by the designated minister: ibid s 4(2) proviso (a). As to the making of regulations see para 654 note 18 ante. At the date at which this volume states the law, no such regulations had been made.

19 Ibid s 4(2) proviso (b).

660. Financial provision. Grants may be paid out of moneys provided by Parliament towards approved expenses[1] of public utility undertakers[2] in taking measures to secure the due functioning of their undertakings in the event of hostile attack[3]. Any expenses incurred by any minister in discharging his civil defence functions[4], including any sums required for paying grants or compensation, are to be paid out of money provided by Parliament[5].

Regulations made by the designated minister with the consent of the Treasury may authorise or require the payment by him of such grants towards expenses incurred by local[6] and police[7] authorities in or in connection with the discharge of civil defence functions[8] as may be prescribed by the regulations[9]. These grants may also be paid where the civil defence expenditure is incurred in circumstances resulting from the exercise of peacetime emergency or disaster powers[10].

The Secretary of State[11] must make regulations[12] for the payment by a local authority[13] or a police authority of compensation to civil defence employees for loss of employment or loss or diminution of emoluments[14]. The compensation is payable out of the same fund as civil defence expenditure[15], and grants may be made to cover expenses incurred in paying compensation[16].

1 'Approved expenses' means such expenses of a capital nature, incurred on measures to secure the due functioning of an undertaking in the event of hostile attack, as the appropriate department acting in accordance with general directions of the Treasury may approve for these purposes: Civil Defence Act 1939 s 39(2). For the meaning of 'appropriate department' see para 658 note 1 ante.

2 For the meaning of 'public utility undertakers' see para 658 note 3 ante. The Civil Defence Act 1939 s 39 does not apply to any railway undertaking: s 39(3) (amended by the Civil Defence (Electricity Undertakings) Act 1954 s 1 (repealed); and by the Statute Law (Repeals) Act 1993 s 1(1), Sch 1 Pt XVI).

3 Civil Defence Act 1939 s 39(1) (amended by the Statute Law (Repeals) Act 1993 Sch 1 Pt XVI). The grants must not exceed one-half of those expenses: Civil Defence Act 1939 s 39(1) (as so amended). All grants payable out of moneys provided by Parliament must be paid at such times and in such manner and subject to such conditions as to accounts, certificates and audit as the minister may with the approval of the Treasury determine: s 83(3) (amended by the Statute Law (Repeals) Act 1986 s 1(1), Sch 1 Pt XIII). As to the meaning of 'minister' see para 659 note 8 ante. Any grant may be made subject to any other conditions determined by the minister with Treasury approval: see the Civil Defence Act 1939 s 83(4) (as amended).

Section 39 was suspended in its application by the Civil Defence (Suspension of Powers) Act 1945 s 2(1), Schedule para 8 (repealed), but its provisions may be revived or repealed and replaced by regulations under the Civil Defence Act 1948 s 6(2): see para 653 note 4 ante. As to the regulations reviving the Civil Defence Act 1939 s 39 (as amended) see the Civil Defence (Posts and Telecommunications) Regulations 1971, SI 1971/221 (as amended) (in relation to the Post Office); and the Civil Defence (Electricity Undertakings) Regulations 1954, SI 1954/377 (as amended) (in relation to persons licensed to transmit, generate or supply electricity). The Civil Defence Act 1939 s 39 was repealed and replaced in relation to persons licensed under the Gas Act 1986 (see the Civil Defence (Gas Undertakers) Regulations 1954, SI 1954/269 (as amended)); and (except in so far as it relates to the provision of air-raid shelters) in relation to canal, inland navigation, dock and harbour undertakers (see the Civil Defence (Transport) Regulations 1954, SI 1954/274 (as amended)). See further para 658 note 9 ante.

4 Ie functions exercisable by him under or by virtue of the Civil Defence Act 1948: see paras 653–654, 659 ante, 661 post.

5   Ibid s 7(1). Any sums received under or by virtue of the 1948 Act by any minister must be paid into the Exchequer: s 7(1). Any increase resulting from any of the provisions of this Act in the sums which are to be paid to local authorities out of money provided by Parliament (ie under the Local Government Act 1948 Pt I (ss 1–16) (repealed) (exchequer grants): see now the Local Government Finance Act 1988 Pt V (ss 76–88B (as amended) (revenue support grants); and LOCAL GOVERNMENT) is to be paid out of money so provided: Civil Defence Act 1948 s 7(2). Any increase attributable to the Civil Defence (Armed Forces) Act 1954 in the sums payable out of money provided by Parliament under the Civil Defence Act 1948 s 7 is to be paid out of money so provided: Civil Defence (Armed Forces) Act 1954 s 1(4). Arrangements for the provision of training in civil defence (see s 1(1); and para 654 ante) may provide for the reimbursement by the designated minister, out of money so provided by Parliament, of such amounts as the Treasury may determine in respect of the pay of, and other expenses incurred on account of, members of the naval, military or air forces receiving training under those arrangements, being amounts which would otherwise fall to be met out of money provided by Parliament for navy, army or air force services: s 1(4). 'Designated minister' has the same meaning as in the Civil Defence Act 1948 s 9(2) (see para 654 note 10 ante): Civil Defence (Armed Forces) Act 1954 s 3(2).
6   For the meaning of 'local authority' see para 655 note 1 ante.
7   As to police authorities see POLICE vol 36 para 225 et seq.
8   Ie functions conferred under the Civil Defence Act 1948 s 2 (as amended) (see paras 655–656 ante).
9   Ibid s 3(1) (amended by the Water (Consequential Amendments) Regulations 1989, SI 1989/1968, reg 2, Sch 1). As to the making of regulations see para 654 note 18 ante. As to the regulations made see the Civil Defence (Grant) Regulations 1953, SI 1953/1777 (as amended). Grants may, in the case of certain expenses prescribed by the regulations, be grants which amount to complete reimbursement of the whole amount of the expenses, but in other cases must be grants of not more than three-quarters of the expenses: Civil Defence Act 1948 s 3(2). As to government specific grants generally see LOCAL GOVERNMENT vol 28 para 1274. Any grants towards expenses incurred by a police authority in England or Wales must be paid into the police fund: s 3(3) (amended by the Police Act 1964 s 64(3), Sch 10 Pt I). As to the police fund see POLICE vol 36 para 233.
10 See the Civil Protection in Peacetime Act 1986 s 2(3); and para 657 ante.
11 The Secretary of State here concerned is the Home Secretary.
12 Regulations must be made by statutory instrument, which is subject to annulment in pursuance of a resolution of either House of Parliament: Public Expenditure and Receipts Act 1968 s 4(5). As to the making of regulations see also s 4(3), (4). As to the regulations made see the Civil Defence (Compensation) (General) Regulations 1968, SI 1968/1344.
13 For these purposes 'local authority' has the same meaning as in the Civil Defence Act 1948 s 2 (as amended) (see para 655 note 1 ante): Public Expenditure and Receipts Act 1968 s 4(6).
14 Ibid s 4(1). The loss or diminution must be attributable to the revocation or amendment of any regulations made under the Civil Defence Act 1948 s 2 (as amended) (see paras 655–656 ante): Public Expenditure and Receipts Act 1968 s 4(1).
15 Ie under the Civil Defence Act 1948 s 2 (as amended): Public Expenditure and Receipts Act 1968 s 4(2).
16 The Civil Defence Act 1948 s 3 (as amended: see note 9 supra) is applied in relation to expenses incurred in paying compensation as if they were expenses incurred by virtue of s 2: Public Expenditure and Receipts Act 1968 s 4(2).

661. Enforcement and penalties. Directors and other officers of bodies corporate and members and officers of local authorities are liable, as well as the body or authority, if they consent to or connive at any offence punishable under the Civil Defence Act 1939 committed by that body or authority[1].

If any undertakers fail to make a report which they are required to make[2], they are liable on summary conviction to a fine not exceeding level 3 on the standard scale, and if the failure in respect of which they were convicted continues after the conviction they are liable on summary conviction to a fine for each day on which the failure continues[3]. Any person who makes in a report any statement which he knows to be false is liable on summary conviction to a fine not exceeding level 3 on the standard scale or imprisonment for a period not exceeding three months, or to both[4].

If any undertakers fail to comply with a notice requiring measures to be taken[5] they are liable on summary conviction to a fine not exceeding level 3 on the standard scale, and, if the failure in respect of which they were convicted continues after the conviction, they are liable on summary conviction to a fine not exceeding £50 for each day on which the failure continues[6]. However, the court by which any undertakers are convicted may fix a reasonable period from the date of conviction for compliance by the undertakers with the requirements of the notice, and, where a court has fixed such a period, the daily penalty is not recoverable in respect of any day before the expiration of that period[7].

Any authorised[8] person has a right, on producing some authenticated document showing his authority, to enter any premises at all reasonable hours for the purpose of enforcing the provisions of the Civil Defence Act 1939 and facilitating the performance of civil defence functions[9]. Any person who wilfully obstructs an authorised person in the exercise of this right is liable on summary conviction to a fine not exceeding level 1 on the standard scale[10].

Any person authorised by the designated minister[11], or any local or police authority[12] by whom functions are exercisable under the Civil Defence Act 1948[13], has the right to enter any land at all reasonable hours for the purpose of inspecting that or any other land with a view to ascertaining whether or not anything ought to be constructed or done there or any use made of it for civil defence purposes[14]. Before this right is exercised the authorised person must, if required, produce some duly authenticated document showing his authority[15], and he may not demand admission as of right to occupied land unless 24 hours' previous notice has been given to the occupier[16].

If any person (1) who is admitted in compliance with these provisions into a factory or workplace, discloses, otherwise than in the performance of his duty, to any person any information obtained by him in the factory or workplace with regard to any manufacturing process or trade secret; or (2) to whom, by reason of his official position, such information is disclosed, discloses it to any other person otherwise than in the performance of his duty, he is liable on summary conviction to a fine not exceeding level 3 on the standard scale or to imprisonment for a term not exceeding three months, or to both[17].

1 See the Civil Defence Act 1939 s 78.
2 Ie under ibid s 36(2) (as amended): see para 658 ante.
3 See ibid s 36(3) (amended by virtue of the Criminal Justice Act 1982 ss 38, 46). As to the standard scale see para 532 note 18 ante.
4 Civil Defence Act 1939 s 77 (amended by virtue of the Criminal Justice Act 1982 ss 38, 46; and by the Statute Law (Repeals) Act 1993 Sch 1 Pt XVI).
5 Ie under the Civil Defence Act 1939 s 37(1): see para 658 ante.
6 Ibid s 37(2) (amended by virtue of the Criminal Justice Act 1982 ss 38, 46).
7 Civil Defence Act 1939 s 37(2) proviso.
8 Ie authorised by the minister, the appropriate department or a local authority having any civil defence functions: see ibid s 79(1) (as amended: see note 9 infra). As to the meaning of 'minister' see para 659 note 8 ante. For the meaning of 'appropriate department' see para 658 note 1 ante; and for the meaning of 'civil defence functions' see para 654 note 2.
9 See the Civil Defence Act 1939 s 79(1), (2) (amended by the Statute Law (Repeals) Act 1993 s 1(1), Sch 1 Pt XVI). The Civil Defence Act 1939 s 79 was suspended in its application by the Civil Defence (Suspension of Powers) Act 1945 s 2(1), Schedule para 8 (repealed), but its provisions may be revived by regulations under the Civil Defence Act 1948 s 6(2): see para 653 note 4 ante. As to the regulations reviving the Civil Defence Act 1939 s 79 see the Civil Defence (Electricity Undertakings) Regulations 1954, SI 1954/377 (as amended); the Civil Defence (Gas Undertakers) Regulations 1954, SI 1954/269 (as amended); the Civil Defence (Transport) Regulations 1954, SI 1954/274 (as amended); and the Civil Defence (Posts and Telecommunications) Regulations 1971, SI 1971/221 (as amended). See further para 658 note 9 ante.
10 Civil Defence Act 1939 s 79(3) (amended by virtue of the Criminal Justice Act 1982 ss 38, 46; and see note 9 supra).
11 For the meaning of 'designated minister' see para 654 note 10 ante.
12 As to local and police authorities see para 655 et seq ante. For the meaning of 'local authority' see para 655 note 1 ante.
13 Ie under the Civil Defence Act 1948 ss 1, 2, 4(1), (2): see paras 654–656, 659 ante.
14 Ibid s 4(3). The powers are in addition to and not in derogation of any other available powers: see s 4(5). As to the meaning of 'civil defence' see para 653 note 5 ante.
15 Ibid s 4(3) proviso (a).

16 Ibid s 4(3) proviso (b).
17 Ibid s 4(4) (amended by virtue of the Criminal Justice Act 1982 ss 38, 46).

7. WAR PENSIONS

(1) WAR PENSIONS FOR MEMBERS OF THE ARMED FORCES AND THEIR DEPENDANTS

662. Form of pensions instruments for the armed forces. Any power of Her Majesty, whether under an enactment or otherwise, to make provision about pensions or other benefits for or in respect of persons who have been disabled or have died in consequence of service as members of the armed forces of the Crown is exercisable by Order in Council[1] and also continues to be exercisable in any manner in which it may otherwise be exercisable[2]. Such an order may, however, vary or revoke any instrument made otherwise than by Order in Council under these provisions in so far as the instrument relates to such pensions or other benefits[3]. In addition, Her Majesty may by Order in Council make such modifications as she considers appropriate[4] in:

(1)   any enactment relating to such pensions or other benefits as are mentioned above;

(2)   any enactment by virtue of which and any instrument by which provisions relating to such pensions or other benefits may be or are applied to service otherwise than in the armed forces; and

(3)   any other enactment or instrument which refers to, or to an instrument relating to, such pensions or other benefits[5].

Pensions, grants and allowances in respect of death or disability which is due to service as a member of the naval[6], military[7] or air forces[8] of the Crown are now payable in accordance with the provisions of the Naval, Military and Air Forces etc (Disablement and Death) Service Pensions Order 1983 which was made by virtue of the above provisions[9]. The service pensions order does not, therefore, apply exclusively to death or disability resulting from service in time of war and its detailed provisions are set out elsewhere in this work[10].

Where a claim is made in respect of disablement[11], or where death occurs, not later than seven years after the termination of service[12], it will be accepted that the disablement or death is due to service if (a) the disablement is due to an injury which is attributable to service or existed before or arose during service and has been, and remains, aggravated thereby[13]; or (b) the death was due to, or hastened by, an injury which was attributable to service or the aggravation by service of an injury which existed before or arose during service[14]. Where the claim is made in respect of disablement, or where death occurs, more than seven years after the termination of service, the disablement or death will be accepted as due to service if (i) the disablement is due to an injury which is attributable to service before the commencement of the 1914–18 war or after 30 September 1921 or existed before or arose during such service and has been and remains aggravated thereby[15]; or (ii) the death was due to, or substantially hastened by, an injury which was attributable to service or the aggravation by service of an injury which existed before or arose during service[16]. 'Injury' for these purposes includes wound or disease but excludes (A) any injury due to the effects of tobacco; and (B) any injury due to the use of tobacco or the consumption of alcohol, except where the person concerned suffers from a mental condition attributable to service, the degree of disablement in respect of that condition has been assessed at 50 per cent or more and he started or continued to use tobacco or to consume or continue to consume alcohol due to that condition[17].

In considering the term 'due to service' issues of causation arise[18], along with the burden of proof[19]. Where the claim is made not later than seven years after the termination of service there is no onus on the claimant to prove that the disablement or death is due to service[20] and where the claim is made more than seven years after the termination of service the benefit of any reasonable doubt as to whether the disablement or death was due to service is to be given to the claimant[21].

1   Social Security (Miscellaneous Provisions) Act 1977 s 12(1). Such an order must be made by statutory instrument and laid before Parliament after being made: s 12(1).
2   Ibid s 12(1). For other powers to make provision for war pensions see para 664 et seq post.
3   Ibid s 12(3).
4   Ie appropriate in consequence of the passing of ibid s 12(1) or the making of an order in pursuance thereof: s 12(2).
5   Ibid s 12(2). See the Naval, Military and Air Forces etc (Modifications of Enactments and other Instruments) Order 1978, SI 1978/1526; and paras 679, 681, 683–684 post.
6   'Member of the naval forces' means, in relation to service (1) before or during the 1914–18 war (see note 15 infra), a person defined for that purpose as an officer or rating; and (2) after 30 September 1921, an officer or rating of the Royal Navy or the Royal Marines, within the meaning of the principal Naval Regulations, excluding certain specified persons: see the Naval, Military and Air Forces etc (Disablement and Death) Service Pensions Order 1983, SI 1983/883, art 1(2), Sch 4 Pt II item 33 (amended by SI 1996/1638). 'Member of the armed forces' means a member of the naval forces, the military forces, or, as the case may be, the air forces, and any provision of the service pensions order relating to a member of the armed forces is to be construed as relating also to a woman member or member whose service has ended, and 'member' is to be construed accordingly: Sch 4 Pt II item 31. As to service before or during the 1914–18 war see paras 664–665 post.
7   'Member of the military forces' means, in relation to service (1) before or during the 1914–18 war (see note 15 infra), a person defined for that purpose as an officer or soldier; and (2) after 30 September 1921, an officer holding a commission in, or a soldier of, the army, whose unit is based in the United Kingdom or the Isle of Man, excluding certain specified persons: see ibid Sch 4 Pt II item 32 (amended by SI 1996/1638). See also note 6 supra. For the meaning of 'United Kingdom' see para 502 note 4 ante.
8   'Member of the air forces' means, in relation to service (1) before or during the 1914–18 war (see note 15 infra), a person defined for that purpose as an officer or airman; and (2) after 30 September 1921, an officer holding a commission in, or an airman of, the Royal Air Force, excluding certain specified persons: see ibid Sch 4 Pt II item 30 (amended by SI 1996/1638). See also note 6 supra.
9   See the Naval, Military and Air Forces etc (Disablement and Death) Service Pensions Order 1983 ('the service pensions order') (amended by SI 1983/1116; SI 1983/1521; SI 1984/1154; SI 1984/1687; SI 1985/1201; SI 1986/592; SI 1987/165; SI 1988/248; SI 1988/2248; SI 1989/156; SI 1990/250; SI 1990/1308; SI 1991/766; SI 1992/710; SI 1992/3208; SI 1993/598; SI 1994/772; SI 1994/1906; SI 1995/766; SI 1996/732; and SI 1996/1638). Payment was formerly made in accordance with Orders in Council made under the Naval and Marine Pay and Pensions Act 1865 (for naval forces), under Royal Warrants (for military forces), and in accordance with orders by Her Majesty under the Air Force (Constitution) Act 1917 (for air forces).
10 See ROYAL FORCES vol 41 para 333 et seq. As to the normal service pensions to which all members of the armed forces may become entitled see ROYAL FORCES vol 41 para 322 et seq.
11 'Disablement' means physical or mental injury or damage, or loss of physical or mental capacity, and 'disabled' is to be construed accordingly: Naval, Military and Air Forces etc (Disablement and Death) Service Pensions Order 1983 Sch 4 Pt II item 22. As to determination of the degree of disablement see art 9 (amended by SI 1992/3208; SI 1996/1638). A disablement award may not be made in respect of noise-induced sensorineural hearing loss, or a related condition or symptom if it is accompanied by noise-induced sensorineural hearing loss, unless the degree of disablement from that loss alone is assessed as being at least 20%: art 8(2A) (added by SI 1992/3208). 'Noise-induced sensorineural hearing loss' means damage to the cochlear hair cells of the inner ear which is caused by the exposure of the cochlea to noise, and a condition or symptom is to be treated as related to such hearing loss if it is another condition, or a symptom, which is the consequence of damage to the cochlear hair cells of the inner ear caused by the exposure of the cochlea to noise: art 8(2B) (as so added). An award in respect of the disablement of a member of the armed forces may not be made to take effect before the termination of his service or, in the case of an officer, while he is an officer on the Active List: see art 8(2).
12 For these purposes, 'service' means service as a member of the armed forces before the commencement of the 1914–18 war (see note 15 infra) or after 30 September 1921: ibid art 4(6) (amended by SI 1996/1638).

13 Ibid art 4(1)(a).
14 Ibid art 4(1)(b).
15 Ibid art 5(1)(a) (amended by SI 1996/1638). Note that the legislation uses the term 'the 1914 World War' rather than 'the 1914–18 war'.
16 Ibid art 5(1)(b).
17 Ibid Sch 4 Pt II item 27 (substituted by SI 1994/772).
18 See paras 667, 672 note 6, 690 note 4 post.
19 As to the burden of proof in relation to civilian injuries see para 672 post.
20 See the Naval, Military and Air Forces etc (Disablement and Death) Service Pensions Order 1983 art 4(2).
21 See ibid art 5(4).

663. Legal right to pensions and method of payment. The service pensions order[1] provides that, subject to the fulfilment of the relevant conditions, an award of a pension, grant or allowance may be made[2]. A claim for an award of any pension or allowance under the service pensions order must state the pension or allowance being claimed and must be made to the Secretary of State[3] either in a form approved by him for that purpose or in such other manner, whether in writing or otherwise, as he may accept as sufficient in any case[4]. However, the service pensions order does not impose any obligation on the Secretary of State to carry out its provisions beyond the duty he owes to the Crown, and it seems that no action will lie against him at the suit of an applicant in respect of his administration of that order or against decisions he makes in the course of carrying it out[5]. Where the Secretary of State has made an award under any Royal Warrant, Order in Council, order or scheme administered by him[6] in respect of the incapacity for work, disablement or death of any person, the person to whom the award has been made has a right to receive the sums payable thereunder[7].

Payment of a pension may be made provisionally or upon any other basis[8]. Pension awarded in terms of a weekly amount may be paid weekly in advance and pension not awarded in such terms may be paid quarterly or monthly in arrears[9]. Pension must be paid by such means as appear to the Secretary of State to be appropriate in the circumstances of the case or class of case[10]. Where, by reason of any provision in any instrument which amends a provision of the service pensions order, a change falls to be made in the rate of any pension which is payable weekly, and the date on which that change would otherwise fall to be made ('the prescribed date') is not the day of the week on which payment of pension is normally made ('the weekly pay day'), that change has effect only as from the first weekly pay day immediately following the prescribed date[11].

The Secretary of State may direct in relation to any particular case or class of case that a pension is to be paid by way of automated or other direct credit transfer into a bank or other account in the name of the person entitled to the pension or a person acting on his behalf, or in the joint names of the person entitled to the pension and his spouse, or the person entitled to the pension and a person acting on his behalf[12]. Pension so paid must be paid for periods of four weeks, or for such other periods as the Secretary of State may in any particular case or class of case determine[13]. It must be paid within seven days of the last day of each successive period so determined, and may be paid in advance, or in arrears, or partly in advance and partly in arrears, as the Secretary of State may in any particular case or class of case determine[14]. Payment of pension in this way may be terminated by the Secretary of State if the arrangement seems to him to be no longer appropriate to the particular case or class of case[15].

In determining whether a pension is payable to a person as a widow under the service pensions order in respect of any period beginning on or after 19 July 1995, no account may be taken of the fact that the widow has married another if, before the beginning of that period, the marriage has been terminated or the parties have been judicially separated[16].

1   Ie the Naval, Military and Air Forces etc (Disablement and Death) Service Pensions Order 1983, SI 1983/883 (as amended): see para 662 ante.
2   See ibid art 3(1) (substituted by SI 1986/592).
3   As to the Secretary of State see para 692 post.
4   Naval, Military and Air Forces etc (Disablement and Death) Service Pensions Order 1983 art 3(2) (as substituted: see note 2 supra).
5   See *Griffin v Lord Advocate* 1950 SC 448 at 450 per Lord Sorn, approved in *Jennings v Minister of Pensions* (2 February 1953, unreported), where, in dismissing a claim for a declaration that the plaintiff was entitled to a disability pension, Parker J said that it was plain that, apart from statute, no claim could be brought against any persons or person administering a Royal Warrant. Quaere, however, if an Order in Council is made not in the exercise of the prerogative but under a power delegated to the Crown by Parliament: see *Griffin v Lord Advocate* supra at 451 per Lord Sorn. See also the Personal Injuries (Civilians) Scheme 1983, SI 1983/686 (as amended), which was (and amendments to which continue to be) made under powers granted by the Personal Injuries (Emergency Provisions) Act 1939 ss 1, 2; and para 668 et seq post.
6   Ie any such Royal Warrant, Order in Council, order or scheme as is referred to in the Pensions Appeal Tribunals Act 1943 ss 1–3 (as amended): see para 691 post.
7   Ibid s 11. This provision does not, however, affect any condition to which the award or any payment thereunder is subject, or any power of the Secretary of State to vary or revoke the award, or to withhold, reduce or apply any payment thereunder, in accordance with any provision of the Royal Warrant, Order in Council, order or scheme: s 11 proviso. See also the War Pensions (Administrative Provisions) Act 1919 s 7 (as amended); the War Pensions Act 1920 s 8 (as amended); and para 664 post.
8   Naval, Military and Air Forces etc (Disablement and Death) Service Pensions Order 1983 art 66(1A) (added by SI 1988/2248).
9   Ibid art 66(1B) (as added: see note 8 supra). The Secretary of State may in any particular case or class of case determine that pension is to be paid in advance or in arrears or partly in advance and partly in arrears, and for a period different from that so specified: art 66(1C) (as so added).
10 Ibid art 66(1D) (as added: see note 8 supra).
11 Ibid art 66(2) (added by SI 1984/1154; amended by SI 1988/2248).
12 Ibid art 65A(1) (added by SI 1988/2248).
13 Ibid art 65A(2)(a) (as added: see note 12 supra).
14 Ibid art 65A(2)(b), (c) (as added: see note 12 supra). Where pension is so payable, the Secretary of State may make a particular payment by credit transfer otherwise than as provided by art 65A(2) (as added) if it appears to him to be appropriate to do so for the purpose of paying any arrears of pension or making a payment of pension at the termination of an award: art 65A(3) (as so added).
15 Ibid art 65A(4) (as added: see note 12 supra).
16 Pensions Act 1995 s 168(1), (3)(a). For these purposes, the reference to the termination of a marriage is to the termination of the marriage by death, dissolution or annulment, and the reference to judicial separation includes any legal separation obtained in a country or territory outside the British Islands and recognised in the United Kingdom; and a divorce, annulment or legal separation obtained in a country or territory outside the British Islands must, if the Secretary of State so determines, be treated as recognised in the United Kingdom even though no declaration as to its validity has been made by any court in the United Kingdom: s 168(2). The 'British Islands' means the United Kingdom, the Channel Islands and the Isle of Man: Interpretation Act 1978 s 5, Sch 1. For the meaning of 'United Kingdom' see para 502 note 4 ante.

664. Applications and awards in respect of service in the 1914–18 war.
Every officer[1] or man suffering from a disability attributable to, or aggravated by, naval, military or air force service during the 1914–18 war[2] and not due to his serious negligence or misconduct is entitled to receive such pension, gratuity or allowance as may be awarded by the Secretary of State[3] under any warrant or Order in Council in respect of such disability, and for the payment of which money has been provided by Parliament[4]. The widow or dependant of a deceased officer or man is also entitled to receive such pension, gratuity or allowance as is awarded by the Secretary of State under any warrant or Order in Council for the time being in force in respect of that officer or man and for the payment of which money has been provided by Parliament[5].

An application for a pension in respect of service in the 1914–18 war had to be made within seven years of the termination of active service or, at latest, by 31 August 1928[6]. Strictly speaking, all applications now made are therefore out of time except where death has occurred or a fresh disability has arisen as the direct result of a disability which has already been accepted, or where there is deterioration of an accepted disability. However, applications which would otherwise be out of time are accepted under powers conferred by the provisions of dispensing instruments[7] in pursuance of an undertaking given by the then Minister of Pensions in the House of Commons in 1929[8]. Pensions, grants and allowances in respect of death or disability which is due to such service are now payable under the provisions of the Naval, Military and Air Forces etc (Disablement and Death) Service Pensions Order 1983[9].

1   The entitlement to a disability pension also extends to nurses: see the War Pensions (Administrative Provisions) Act 1919 s 9.

2   The statutory expression used is 'this present war' which is defined as 'any war carried on by His Majesty at any time during the period from the fourth day of August 1914 to the thirtieth day after the date fixed under the Termination of the Present War (Definition) Act 1918 (repealed) as the date of the termination of that war, both inclusive': see the War Pensions Act 1920 s 2. References in the War Pensions Acts to pensions, grants and allowances, and to deceased or disabled officers or men, are respectively to be construed as references to pensions, grants and allowances granted, made or awarded in respect of wounds, disablements or other matters suffered, incurred or happening during that period, whether the officers or men to or in respect of whom the pensions, grants or allowances are granted, made or awarded, retired or were discharged from the service, or died before the expiration of that period, or whether they retired or were discharged or died after the expiration of that period, and to officers and men who died or were disabled through causes arising out of their service during that period, whether they retired or were discharged from the service or died before the expiration of that period, or whether they so retired, or were discharged, or died after the expiration of that period: see the War Pensions Act 1920 s 2. The date of termination of the war was declared to be 31 August 1921: see the Termination of the Present War (Definition) Act 1918 s 1 (repealed); and the Order in Council declaring the Date of the Termination of the War dated 10 August 1921, SR & O 1921/1276. 'The War Pensions Acts' means the Naval and Military War Pensions etc Act 1915 (which makes provision for the care of disabled officers and men after they have left the service); the Naval and Military War Pensions etc Act 1916 (Expenses) Act 1916 (repealed); in so far as it relates to the statutory committee (now dissolved), the Ministry of Pensions Act 1916; the Naval and Military War Pensions etc (Administrative Expenses) Act 1917 (which makes provision for the application of certain voluntary funds); the Naval and Military War Pensions etc (Transfer of Powers) Act 1917 (repealed); the Naval and Military War Pensions etc (Committees) Act 1917 (repealed); the War Pensions (Administrative Provisions) Act 1918 (war orphans: see para 693 post); the War Pensions (Administrative Provisions) Act 1919 (see the text and notes 3–4 infra); the War Pensions Act 1920; and the War Pensions Act 1921 (see the text and note 6 infra): see s 10(1).

3   As to the Secretary of State see para 692 post.

4   War Pensions (Administrative Provisions) Act 1919 s 7 (amended by virtue of the Secretary of State for Social Services Order 1968, SI 1968/1699, art 5(4)(a)).

5   War Pensions Act 1920 s 8(1) (amended by virtue of the Secretary of State for Social Services Order 1968, SI 1968/1699, art 5(4)(a)). In either case, the award of any such pension, gratuity or allowance is subject to the conditions contained in the warrant or order: see the War Pensions (Administrative Provisions) Act 1919 s 7; the War Pensions Act 1920 s 8(1). In the case of a widow or dependant, entitlement arose if the member of the armed forces in respect of whom the claim is made was killed while in the performance of military, naval or air force duty during the 1914–18 war, or died as the result of wounds or injuries received in the performance of that duty within seven years of receiving the wounds or injuries; or if he died of a disease certified as contracted or commencing while on active service during the war or as having been aggravated by that service, within seven years of his removal from duty on account of the disease; provided his death was not caused by his serious negligence or misconduct: see the Order in Council dated 11 June 1920, SR & O 1920/1021 (seamen and marines); the Order in Council dated 9 March 1921, SR & O 1921/360 (officers and nurses); the Order in Council dated 9 March 1921, SR & O 1921/361 (warrant officers); Royal Warrants dated 6 December 1919 (Cmd 457), 2 July 1920 (Cmd 811), 30 May 1949 (Cmd 7712), 28 June 1962 (Cmnd 1776); HC Paper (1920) No 120; HC Paper (1948–49) No 250 (amended by Cmnd 1774 (1962)). Entitlement also arose where the deceased was in receipt of a pension at the date of death and either the death was wholly due to the pensionable disability, or the pension was assessed at not less than 40% disability and in the opinion of the Secretary of State the circumstances of his death justified an award: Royal Warrant dated 6 December 1919 (Cmd 457) arts 17A, 17B (added by Royal Warrant dated 14 January 1924 (Cmd 2030)); Royal Warrant dated 2 July 1920 (Cmd 811) arts 16A, 16B (added by Royal Warrant dated 2 September 1924 (Cmd 2251)). As to entitlement to awards generally see now the Naval,

Military and Air Forces etc (Disablement and Death) Service Pensions Order 1983 Pt II arts 3–7 (as substituted); as to awards in respect of disablement see Pt III (arts 8–26A) (as amended); as to awards in respect of death see Pt IV (arts 27–42) (as amended); and see generally para 662 ante; and ROYAL FORCES vol 41 para 332 et seq.

6   See the War Pensions Act 1921 ss 5, 10(2) (amended by virtue of the Secretary of State for Social Services Order 1968, SI 1968/1699, art 5(4)(a)); and see also note 2 supra.

7   See Order in Council dated 19 December 1881; Royal Warrant dated 27 October 1884; Order by His Majesty dated 14 January 1922.

8   See 232 HC Official Report (5th series), 18 November 1929, cols 23–26.

9   Ie the Naval, Military and Air Forces etc (Disablement and Death) Service Pensions Order 1983 (as amended): see note 5 supra; and para 662 ante.

665. Awards in respect of service in earlier wars. Owing to the lapse of time, questions relating to pensions or grants awarded in respect of wounds, disabilities or other matters in any war which occurred before 4 August 1914 have virtually ceased to arise[1]. The persons to whom they applied and the conditions under which they were granted were contained in Royal Warrants in the case of soldiers[2] and in Orders in Council[3] in the case of seamen and marines[4]. From 29 July 1996, the definition of 'service' in the Naval, Military and Air Forces etc (Disablement and Death) Service Pensions Order 1983[5] has been extended to include service before the commencement of the 1914–18 war or after 30 September 1921 and not merely after 2 September 1939, as previously[6], and any such pensions are thus payable under the provisions of that order[7].

1   The principle of paying pensions or making equivalent grants in land, as compensation for war disablement, goes back to the reign of King Alfred, and for centuries took the form of voluntary payments at the goodwill of the pensioner's former commander. In the sixteenth century statutory provision was first made for payments to be made from the proceeds of rates levied on the locality in which the man enlisted: see eg 35 Eliz I c 4 (Disabled Soldiers) (1592–3) (repealed); 39 Eliz I c 21 (Disabled Soldiers) (1597–8) (repealed); and 43 Eliz I c 3 (Disabled Soldiers) (1601) (repealed). The Royal Chelsea Hospital for soldiers was opened in 1690, and the Greenwich Hospital for sailors in 1705: see further ROYAL FORCES vol 41 paras 158, 330. In 1854 the Patriotic Fund (later the Royal Patriotic Fund) was established by public subscription, from which small pensions for widows were paid and provision was made for the care and education of orphans: see ROYAL FORCES vol 41 para 357. At the outbreak of the 1914–18 war, pensions were administered by four authorities, namely the War Office, the Admiralty, the Chelsea Commissioners and the Royal Patriotic Fund Corporation. As to the transfer of these functions to the Minister of Pensions and thence to the Secretary of State see para 692 post.

2   See eg the Royal Warrant dated 1 November 1920 (Cmd 1034).

3   See eg the Order in Council dated 27 May 1921, SR & O 1921/967.

4   The provisions regarding officers and nurses disabled in consequence of former wars were contained in Royal Warrants dated 1 December 1914, 1 August 1917, 19 December 1919, 8 September 1923 (army); and in the Order in Council, dated 13 August 1920, SR & O 1920/1669; the Order in Council dated 13 October 1920, SR & O 1920/2088; the Order in Council dated 27 March 1923, SR & O 1923/407; and the Order in Council dated 11 October 1923, SR & O 1923/1239 (navy and marines). Generally, the effect of these warrants and orders was to increase pensions in respect of disablement in former wars to the level of pensions in respect of disablement in the 1914–18 war.

5   Ie the Naval, Military and Air Forces etc (Disablement and Death) Service Pensions Order 1983, SI 1983/883 (as amended): see para 662 ante.

6   See ibid arts 4, 5, 9–11, 21, 67, Schs 1, 2, 4 (amended for these purposes by SI 1996/1638).

7   See note 6 supra; and para 662 ante. This change was made in consequence of a transfer of responsibilities for such pensions from the Ministry of Defence to the Department of Social Security. Note that the legislation uses the term 'the 1914 World War' rather than 'the 1914–18 war'.

(2) OTHER WAR PENSIONS

(i) In general

666. Pensions instruments for persons other than members of the armed forces. The provisions of the service pensions order[1] have been applied with modifications by schemes made under the Pensions (Navy, Army, Air Force and Mercantile Marine) Act 1939, as amended by the Pensions (Mercantile Marine) Act 1942[2], to members of the merchant navy and the sea fishing service[3], and to naval auxiliary personnel[4], in cases where death or disablement is directly attributable[5] to a qualifying injury[6] or to detention[7]; another such scheme provides benefits for coastguards[8]. A scheme with provisions substantially similar to those of the service pensions order concerning pensions for members of the military forces has been made under the Polish Resettlement Act 1947 for members of the former Polish forces[9]; and provision for civilians who suffered war injuries[10], or, being civil defence volunteers, war service injuries[11], has been made by a scheme[12] under the Personal Injuries (Emergency Provisions) Act 1939. Pensions and other benefits under these instruments are all administered by the Secretary of State for Social Security[13].

1   Ie the Naval, Military and Air Forces etc (Disablement and Death) Service Pensions Order 1983, SI 1983/883 (as amended): see para 662 ante.

2   See para 676 et seq post.

3   See the War Pensions (Mercantile Marine) Scheme 1964, SI 1964/2058 (amended by SI 1972/1434; SI 1978/1526; SI 1988/639; SI 1989/540; SI 1993/692; modified by SI 1978/1526); and paras 679–680 post.

4   See the War Pensions (Naval Auxiliary Personnel) Scheme 1964, SI 1964/1985 (amended by SI 1972/1436; SI 1989/540; SI 1993/692; modified by SI 1978/1526); and para 681 post.

5   As to the meaning of 'attributable' see ROYAL FORCES vol 41 para 338.

6   Ie a war injury or a war risk injury: see para 667 post.

7   See the War Pensions (Naval Auxiliary Personnel) Scheme 1964 art 4; the War Pensions (Mercantile Marine) Scheme 1964 art 4; and para 679 et seq post. For the meaning of 'detention' see para 676 note 4 post. The War Pensions (Indian Seamen etc) Scheme 1944, SR & O 1944/1083, and the War Pensions (Chinese Seamen etc) Scheme 1944, SR & O 1944/1186, which formerly provided for a lower rate of war pension to be payable to certain non-British seamen, have been revoked.

8   See the War Pensions (Coastguards) Scheme 1944, SR & O 1944/500 (amended SI 1989/540; SI 1993/692; modified by SI 1978/1526); and para 681 post.

9   See the Pensions (Polish Forces) Scheme 1964, SI 1964/2007 (amended by SI 1967/293; SI 1972/1435; SI 1974/1045; modified by SI 1978/1526); and para 684 post.

10   For the meaning of 'war injury' see para 667 post.

11   For the meaning of 'war service injury' see para 668 note 5 post.

12   Ie the Personal Injuries (Civilians) Scheme 1983, SI 1983/686 (amended by SI 1983/1164; SI 1983/1540; SI 1984/1289; SI 1985/1313; SI 1986/628; SI 1987/191; SI 1988/367; SI 1988/2260; SI 1989/415; SI 1990/535; SI 1990/1300; SI 1991/708; SI 1992/702; SI 1992/3226; SI 1993/480; SI 1994/715; SI 1994/2021; SI 1995/445; SI 1996/502): see para 668 et seq post. Any assignment of, or charge on, an award under the scheme is void and an award does not pass to any trustee in bankruptcy: see the Personal Injuries (Emergency Provisions) Act 1939 s 7; and see generally CHOSES IN ACTION vol 6 para 79 et seq.

13   As to the devolution of functions on the Secretary of State see para 692 post.

667. War injuries, war risk injuries and war damage. 'War injuries' means physical injuries (1) caused by the discharge of any missile (including liquids and gas), by the use of any weapon, explosive or other noxious thing or by the doing of any other injurious act either by the enemy or in combating the enemy or in repelling an imagined attack by the enemy; or (2) caused by the impact on any person or property of any enemy aircraft or any aircraft belonging to or held by any person on behalf of, or for the benefit of, the Crown or any allied power, or any part of or anything dropped from such aircraft[1].

'War damage', for the purposes of the scheme providing compensation for war damage to certain seamen's effects[2], means loss of or damage to a person's effects caused as described in head (1) or head (2) above[3].

'War risk injury' means a physical injury sustained on or after 3 September 1939 at sea or in any other tidal water or in the waters of any harbour and attributable to:

(a) the taking of measures[4] to avoid, prevent or hinder enemy action against ships; or

(b) the absence by reason of war of any aid to the navigation of ships; or

(c) the carriage by reason of war of any cargo in a manner which would be abnormal in peacetime as involving danger to the ship; or

(d) the existence on board ship of any other conditions arising out of war which would be abnormal in peacetime[5],

provided that risk of the peril which caused the injury is substantially increased thereby[6].

A physical injury for the purposes of a war injury or a war risk injury includes tuberculosis and any other organic disease, and the aggravation of that disease[7]. It is not necessary to prove a traumatic cause, but an injury which is purely mental is not a physical injury for these purposes[8]. However, where mental disablement results from a physical injury, an award may be made in respect of the mental disablement[9]. Combating the enemy must be interpreted in a restricted sense and does not include the enforcement of a blackout[10] and there cannot be a qualifying injury on board ship in the absence of conditions arising out of the war which would be abnormal in time of peace[11].

Issues of causation have arisen in a number of reported cases. The 'discharge of any missile,' for example, need only be 'a' cause of the injury[12]. Thus, the tampering by a child with an incendiary bomb did not prevent the dropping of the bomb by the enemy from being a cause of the claimant's injuries[13].

1 Pensions (Navy, Army, Air Force and Mercantile Marine) Act 1939 s 10; Personal Injuries (Emergency Provisions) Act 1939 s 8(1); and see the War Pensions (Coastguards) Scheme 1944, SR & O 1944/500, art 1(14); the War Pensions (Naval Auxiliary Personnel) Scheme 1964, SI 1964/1985, art 2(14), Sch 1 para 1; the War Pensions (Mercantile Marine) Scheme 1964, SI 1964/2058, art 2(35), Sch 1 para 1; the Personal Injuries (Civilians) Scheme 1983, SI 1983/686, art 2(23) (amended by SI 1985/1313). Injuries which are not war injuries within the statutory definition may still attract compensation: see heads (a)–(d) in the text; and the Pensions (Mercantile Marine) Act 1942 s 1(2); and para 676 note 7 post.

2 Ie the Merchant Shipping (Compensation to Seamen – War Damage to Effects) Scheme 1982, SI 1982/1023: see paras 681, 695 post.

3 See ibid art 2; and see also the Pensions (Navy, Army, Air Force and Mercantile Marine) Act 1939 s 10; the Pensions (Navy, Army, Air Force and Mercantile Marine) Act 1939 s 1(2).

4 'Measures' does not include the prohibition or restriction of lights in the waters of a harbour other than navigational lights: see the War Pensions (Naval Auxiliary Personnel) Scheme 1964 Sch 1 para 2 proviso (i); the War Pensions (Mercantile Marine) Scheme 1964 Sch 1 para 2 proviso (i). See also *Bodman v Minister of Pensions* (1946) 1 WPAR 259; cf *Constable v Minister of Pensions* (1946) 1 WPAR 275.

5 War Pensions (Naval Auxiliary Personnel) Scheme 1964 Sch 1 para 2; War Pensions (Mercantile Marine) Scheme 1964 Sch 1 para 2. Cf the War Pensions (Coastguards) Scheme 1944 art 2(15) (applying the Pensions (Mercantile Marine) Act 1942 s 1(2)); and see para 681 post.

6 War Pensions (Naval Auxiliary Personnel) Scheme 1964 Sch 1 para 3; War Pensions (Mercantile Marine) Scheme 1964 Sch 1 para 3. See *Makin v Masson* [1948] LJR 325, CA (where carriage of an apparatus known as a torpedo defence boom was held to constitute a substantial increase of the risk of peril); and *Morris v Minister of Pensions* (1947) 1 WPAR 595.

7 Pensions (Mercantile Marine) Act 1942 s 5; War Pensions (Naval Auxiliary Personnel) Scheme 1964 Sch 1 para 4(c); War Pensions (Mercantile Marine) Scheme 1964 Sch 1 para 4(b); Personal Injuries (Civilians) Scheme 1983 art 2(18). See also *Goodman v Minister of Pensions* (1951) 5 WPAR 13; *Baird v Minister of Pensions* (1946) 1 WPAR 169 (psychoneurosis).

8 *Ex p Haines* [1945] KB 183, [1945] 1 All ER 349.

9 *Clarke v Minister of Pensions* (1946) 1 WPAR 233.

10 *Re Kemp* [1945] 1 All ER 571, 1 WPAR 55; *Bodman v Minister of Pensions* (1946) 1 WPAR 259. See also *Cameron v Minister of Pensions* (1944) 2 WPAR 415; *Minister of Pensions v Ffrench* [1946] KB 260, [1946] 1 All ER 272.

11 *Minister of Pensions v Jones* (1947) 1 WPAR 649.
12 It is not necessary that the discharge of the missile or other event should be 'the' cause of the injury in the sense either of the sole cause or of the effective and predominant cause: *Minister of Pensions v Chennell* [1947] KB 250 at 252, [1946] 2 All ER 719 at 720 per Denning J.
13 *Minister of Pensions v Chennell* [1947] KB 250, [1946] 2 All ER 719; see also *Minister of Pensions v Williams (OL)* [1947] KB 875, [1947] 2 All ER 93. As to the effect of serious negligence or misconduct see para 690 note 4 post.

(ii) Civilian Injuries

668. Power to make a scheme in respect of civilian injuries. The former Minister of Pensions was given power which has now been transferred to the Secretary of State[1] to make a scheme with the approval of the Treasury providing for the making of payments in respect of the following injuries sustained during the period of the 1939–46 emergency[2]: (1) war injuries[3] sustained by gainfully occupied persons[4], with such exceptions, if any, as might or may be specified in the scheme and by persons of such other classes as might or may be so specified; and (2) war service injuries[5] sustained by civil defence volunteers[6]. In respect of any such injury, a scheme may authorise the Secretary of State to make the following payments, in such circumstances and subject to such conditions as may be specified in it, to or in respect of the person injured:

(a) payments by way of allowance ('injury allowance') which are to be payable only so long as the person injured is incapacitated for work by the injury and has not received any such payments as are mentioned below[7]; and

(b) payments by way of pension or grant, which are to be payable only where the injury causes serious and prolonged disablement or death[8].

Any decision of the Secretary of State as to the making, refusal or amount, or as to the continuance or discontinuance, of a payment under a scheme may be varied by a subsequent decision of his, but save in so far as it is so varied it is final and conclusive[9], subject to certain limited rights of appeal[10].

1 As to the devolution of these powers on the Secretary of State see para 692 post.
2 The statutory expression used is 'the period of the present emergency' which means the period beginning with the commencement of the Personal Injuries (Emergency Provisions) Act 1939 (ie 3 September 1939) and ending with such date as His Majesty might by Order in Council declare to be the date on which the emergency that was the occasion of the passing of that Act came to an end: s 8(1). That date was 19 March 1946: see the Personal Injuries (Emergency Provisions) Act (End of Emergency) Order 1946, SR & O 1946/379. As respects war service injuries sustained by members of the National Fire Service, however, the period continued until 1 April 1948, except that the Personal Injuries (Emergency Provisions) Act 1939 s 3 (repealed) did not apply after 19 March 1946: see the Emergency Laws (Transitional Provisions) Act 1946 s 4(2) (repealed); the Fire Services Act 1947 s 39(3), Sch 5 para 2 (spent). See also the Personal Injuries (Civilians) Scheme 1983 art 2(17); and *Willcock v Muckle* [1951] 2 KB 844, [1951] 2 All ER 367 (to bring any of the emergency Acts to an end there must be an Order in Council dealing with that particular Act).
3 For the meaning of 'war injuries' see para 667 ante.
4 'Gainfully occupied person' means a person who is engaged in any trade, business, profession, office, employment or vocation and is wholly or substantially dependent thereon for a livelihood, or a person who, though temporarily unemployed, is normally so engaged and dependent: Personal Injuries (Emergency Provisions) Act 1939 s 8(1). See also the Personal Injuries (Civilians) Scheme 1983, SI 1983/686, art 2(12). This definition must be satisfied at the time when the qualifying injury is sustained: see arts 2(12), (14). 'Qualifying injury' means a war injury or war risk injury (see para 667 ante): art 2(20).
5 'War service injury', in relation to any civil defence volunteer, means a physical injury which the Secretary of State certifies to have been shown to his satisfaction to have arisen out of and in the course of the performance by the volunteer of his duties as a member of the civil defence organisation to which he belonged when the injury was sustained, and (except in the case of a war injury) not to have arisen out of and in the course of his employment in any other capacity: Personal Injuries (Emergency Provisions) Act 1939 s 8(1). See also the Personal Injuries (Civilians) Scheme 1983 art 2(24). 'Civil defence organisation' means any organisation established for civil defence purposes which is declared by

a scheme made under the 1939 Act to be a civil defence organisation for the purpose of that Act and the scheme; and 'civil defence volunteer', in relation to an injury, means a person certified by a responsible officer of a civil defence organisation to have been a member of that organisation at the time when the injury was sustained: Personal Injuries (Emergency Provisions) Act 1939 s 8(1); and see the Personal Injuries (Civilians) Scheme 1983 arts 2(5), (6), 4, Sch 1. No certificate may be given by the Secretary of State in relation to the definition of 'war service injury' for these purposes unless he has been furnished with a report about the injury in question by a responsible officer of the civil defence organisation of which the volunteer concerned was a member at the time when the injury was sustained; and any such certificate may be revoked by the Secretary of State at any time on new facts being brought to his notice: Personal Injuries (Emergency Provisions) Act 1939 s 8(2).

6 Ibid s 1(1). See the Personal Injuries (Civilians) Scheme 1983, SI 1983/686 (as amended); and paras 666 note 12 ante, 669 et seq post. A scheme may provide that it is to come into operation, or is to be deemed to have come into operation, on such date as may be specified in it; and may be amended or revoked by a subsequent scheme or by an order made by the Secretary of State with the consent of the Treasury: Personal Injuries (Emergency Provisions) Act 1939 s 2(1), (2). Every scheme, and every order so made, must be laid before both Houses of Parliament as soon as may be after it is made, and if either House, within the period of 40 days beginning with the day on which a scheme or such an order is laid before it, resolves that the scheme or order be annulled, it becomes void, but without prejudice to the validity of anything previously done under it, or to the making of a new scheme or order: s 2(3).

7 Ibid s 1(2)(a). In practice it is unlikely, in view of the passage of time, that any payments under s 1(2)(a) are now being made.

8 Ibid s 1(2)(b). A scheme may empower the Secretary of State to make regulations for giving effect to the purposes of the scheme: s 1(3). All expenses incurred by him in giving effect to a scheme must be defrayed out of money provided by Parliament: s 1(5).

9 Ibid s 1(4).

10 See the Pensions Appeal Tribunals Act 1943 s 3; and para 691 post.

669. Applications by civilians. As a general rule[1], applications for pensions under the civilian injuries scheme[2] had to be made within a period of three months from the date on which the qualifying injury[3] causing the disablement was sustained[4], or the relevant death occurred[5], but the Secretary of State[6] may direct otherwise with respect to any particular case or class of case[7]. An application must state the pension, allowance or benefit being claimed and must be made to the Secretary of State either in a form approved by him for that purpose or in such other manner, whether in writing or otherwise, as he may accept as sufficient in any case[8].

1 Where the application is in respect of disablement caused by a war injury to a person not gainfully occupied and under the age of 15, the three-month period runs from the fifteenth birthday, and where the disabled person was, on the material date, a whole-time serving member of the armed forces of the Crown, from the date on which he ceased to give such whole-time service: Personal Injuries (Civilians) Scheme 1983, SI 1983/686, art 54(2)(b), (c). For the meaning of 'gainfully occupied person' see para 668 note 4 ante.

2 Ie the Personal Injuries (Civilians) Scheme 1983, SI 1983/686 (as amended): see paras 666 note 12, 668 ante, 670 et seq post.

3 For the meaning of 'qualifying injury' see para 668 note 4 ante.

4 See the Personal Injuries (Civilians) Scheme 1983 art 54(2)(a).

5 See ibid art 54(3) (amended by SI 1987/191).

6 As to the Secretary of State see para 692 post.

7 See the Personal Injuries (Civilians) Scheme 1983 art 54(1) (amended by SI 1986/628).

8 Ibid art 54(1A) (added by SI 1986/628).

670. Entitlement to awards. Under the civilian injuries scheme[1], awards may be made in respect of war injuries[2] sustained by gainfully occupied persons[3], war injuries sustained by persons not gainfully occupied[4] and war service injuries[5] sustained by civil defence volunteers[6] which, in each case, were so sustained in the period of the emergency[7]. Subject to certain exceptions[8], an award may not be made in respect of a qualifying injury[9] sustained outside the United Kingdom by a person ordinarily resident outside the United Kingdom or by a person ordinarily resident there while he was absent for personal, domestic or pleasure purposes[10]. Where the qualifying injury or death in respect of which a claim for an award is or has been made was caused or contributed to by the serious negligence or misconduct of the person concerned, the Secretary of State[11] may withhold, cancel or reduce any such award[12]. Moreover, where a person who has sustained a qualifying injury or to whom an award in respect of another person has been made is or becomes ordinarily resident outside the United Kingdom, the Secretary of State may withhold or cancel any award of a pension to or in respect of that person or may, if he thinks fit having regard to the circumstances of the case, including the standard of living in the place where that person is or has become ordinarily resident, reduce the amount of the award[13]. The scheme does not apply to injuries sustained by members of visiting and allied forces[14].

If the person suffering a war injury, as distinct from a war service injury, was not gainfully occupied and was under the age of 15 or, being over that age, was a student or apprentice[15], he is treated for the purposes of the scheme as if he were gainfully occupied unless immediately before the injury was sustained he was suffering from a physical or mental disability to such an extent as to preclude the likelihood of his ever being able to earn his living[16], but no disablement award[17] may be made to such a person in respect of any period before he attained the age of 15 and then only if the conditions governing the making of an award are then satisfied[18].

1   Ie the Personal Injuries (Civilians) Scheme 1983, SI 1983/686 (as amended): see paras 666 et seq ante, 671 et seq post.
2   For the meaning of 'war injury' see para 667 ante.
3   Personal Injuries (Civilians) Scheme 1983 art 5(1)(a). For the meaning of 'gainfully occupied person' see para 668 note 4 ante. As to awards in respect of the disablement of such persons see Pt III (arts 8–25B) (as amended); and as to awards in respect of their death see Pt IV (arts 26–37) (as amended).
4   Ibid art 5(1)(b). As to awards in respect of such persons see ibid Pt V (arts 41–51) (as amended).
5   For the meaning of 'war service injury' see para 668 note 5 ante.
6   Personal Injuries (Civilians) Scheme 1983 art 5(1)(c). For the meaning of 'civil defence volunteer' see para 668 note 5 ante.
7   Ibid art 5(1). As to the period of the emergency see para 668 note 2 ante.
8   Nothing in this provision precludes the making of an award in respect of a war service injury sustained by a civil defence volunteer or a war injury sustained (1) by a person ordinarily resident in the United Kingdom while travelling by sea or by air from or to any place therein to or from any other such place or any place in the Irish Republic or the Isle of Man; (2) outside the United Kingdom and the Isle of Man by an overseas volunteer in the course of a journey which he made for the purpose of undertaking a war occupation or in the course of a journey which he made for the purpose of leaving any place to which he had made any such journey, or for the purpose of leaving any country in which he had carried on a war occupation, being a journey made at the expense of public funds; (3) by an overseas volunteer ordinarily resident in the Irish Republic in the course of a journey which he made from or to that Republic to or from the United Kingdom if he made the journey while he was on leave or holiday from a war occupation in which he was engaged, or the journey was the first journey to the Republic that he had made since he was last engaged in a war occupation; (4) in enemy territory or in territory which was, at the material date (ie the date of the injury: see art 2(14)), occupied by the enemy (a) by a British subject who was born in the United Kingdom or by the wife of such a subject or by a woman who was born in the United Kingdom and would have been such a subject but for her marriage to a person not of British nationality; (b) by a person whose death occurred as the direct result of the injury, if the claimant is either his widow who was born in the United Kingdom and is a British subject or but for her marriage to the deceased person would be a British subject or, where that widow has also died, is his dependent child, but an award under this head is discretionary and may not be made unless the person to whom or for whose benefit it may be made is residing in the United Kingdom: art 60(3). 'Overseas volunteer' means a person ordinarily resident outside the United Kingdom who had, in accordance with arrangements made by or on behalf of the government in the United Kingdom, volunteered or been required to undertake a war occupation; and 'war occupation', in relation to such a person, means service as a member of the armed forces of the Crown raised or established in the United Kingdom, work which might be selected for that volunteer by or on behalf of the government, or any other work which the Secretary of State considers it was in the national interest for the volunteer to perform during the period of the emergency: art 60(4). For the meaning of 'United Kingdom' see para 502 note 4 ante.

10 See ibid art 60(1), (2).

11 As to the Secretary of State see para 692 post.

12 See the Personal Injuries (Civilians) Scheme 1983 art 6.

13 Ibid art 61.

14 See ibid art 59; and ROYAL FORCES vol 41 para 127 et seq.

15 For these purposes, 'student' means a person who is receiving full-time instruction at a university, college, secondary school or technical school, or at any other establishment which, in the opinion of the Secretary of State, is a comparable educational establishment; and a person may continue to be a student for such period, not exceeding 13 weeks, after he ceases to receive full-time instruction and before he attains the age of 19 as the Secretary of State may in any particular case determine: ibid art 2(21). 'Apprentice' means a person undergoing full-time training for any trade, business, profession, office, employment or vocation, and receiving not more than nominal wages: art 2(4).

16 See ibid art 7(1), (2).

17 Ie under ibid Pt III (as amended): see para 673 post.

18 See ibid art 7(3).

671. Relief from liability to pay damages etc. Where, during the period of the emergency[1], any person sustained a war injury[2] or a civil defence volunteer sustained a war service injury[3], his right to damages or compensation in respect of that injury, whether by virtue of any statute or contract or at common law, was removed[4] and the only recompense available to him was that now conferred by the civilian injuries scheme[5]. The broad effect was that, in the case of war injuries, all rights to sue in tort or for breach of contract or to claim under any other enactment were taken away where the injury in question was a war injury and the cause of action was based on some negligence, nuisance or breach of duty[6]. Having regard to this, 'war injury' and 'war service injury' were narrowly interpreted by the courts so that the fundamental right of the subject of coming to the Queen's courts for redress of wrongs was not treated as taken away except by quite clear language[7]. Thus, where a local authority had taken over an underground station for use as an air-raid shelter and damage was caused by reason of the steps being defective, the plaintiff was entitled to recover damages in negligence[8].

The civilian injuries scheme makes provision for the prevention of double payments where any compensation has been granted in respect of a war injury under certain other enactments[9].

1 As to the period of the emergency see para 668 note 2 ante.

2 For the meaning of 'war injury' see para 667 ante.

3 For the meaning of 'war service injury' see para 668 note 5 ante.

4 See the Personal Injuries (Emergency Provisions) Act 1939 s 3 (repealed).

5 Ie the Personal Injuries (Civilians) Scheme 1983, SI 1983/686 (as amended), which superseded earlier schemes made under the like power: see paras 666 et seq ante, 672 et seq post.

6 *Billings v Reed* [1945] KB 11 at 15, [1944] 2 All ER 415 at 418, CA.

7 *Adams v Naylor* [1944] KB 750 at 759, [1944] 2 All ER 21 at 27, CA, per Scott LJ dissenting; on appeal [1946] AC 543, [1946] 2 All ER 241, HL.

8 *Baker v Bethnal Green Corpn* [1945] 1 All ER 135, CA.

9 See the Personal Injuries (Civilians) Scheme 1983 art 62.

672. Burden of proof. A claim in respect of disablement had to be made within three months of the date on which the qualifying injury[1] which caused it was sustained or the date on which the claimant subsequently became entitled to an award by reason of attaining the age of 15 or ceasing to give whole-time service as a member of the armed forces, whichever was the latest[2]. In any such claim there is no onus on the claimant to prove that disablement was caused by the qualifying injury[3]. A similar dispensation with regard to the burden of proof existed with regard to claims made in respect of a death[4] which occurred within seven years of the date on which the qualifying injury was sustained[5]. However, where death occurs more than seven years after the date of the qualifying injury, the onus of proving that it was the direct result of that injury is not removed, but the claimant must still be given the benefit of any reasonable doubt[6].

1   For the meaning of 'qualifying injury' see para 668 note 4 ante.
2   See the Personal Injuries (Civilians) Scheme 1983, SI 1983/686, art 54(1), (2) (amended by SI 1986/628).
3   Ibid art 5(2).
4   Claims in respect of death must be made within three months of the date of death: see ibid art 54(3) (amended by SI 1987/191).
5   Ibid art 5(2).
6   See ibid art 5(3). The onus is on the claimant to show that reasonable doubt exists whether his disablement was caused by the qualifying injury, and the benefit of that doubt must, by art 5(3), be given to the claimant: *Cadney v Minister of Pensions and National Insurance* [1965] 3 All ER 809, [1966] 1 WLR 80 per Edmund Davies J, following *Dickinson v Minister of Pensions* [1953] 1 QB 228, [1952] 2 All ER 1031 per Ormerod J.

673. Awards in respect of disablement. Awards may be made in respect of disablement provided that the disablement is serious and prolonged[1]. However, no pension may be awarded unless the resulting degree of disablement is 20 per cent or more[2], but, where it is less than 20 per cent and the Secretary of State[3] is satisfied, having regard to the nature of the disablement, that the payment of a lump sum would be appropriate, such a sum as the Secretary of State deems fit may be awarded[4]. 'Disablement' for this purpose means physical or mental injury or damage, or loss of physical or mental capacity, caused by that injury[5].

An assessment for the purposes of the Personal Injuries (Civilians) Scheme 1983 must be made in the same way as an assessment of the degree of disablement of a member of the armed forces for the purpose of the service pensions order[6].

The basic rates of pension payable under the civilian injuries scheme may be altered from time to time[7]. In addition to the basic rate, the following allowances may be payable if the appropriate conditions are satisfied: a constant attendance allowance[8]; an exceptionally severe disablement allowance[9]; a severe disablement occupational allowance[10]; an allowance for wear and tear of clothing where an artificial limb is worn[11]; an unemployability allowance[12]; an invalidity allowance[13]; a comforts allowance[14]; an allowance for lowered standard of occupation[15]; an age allowance where the injured person is aged 65 or more[16]; treatment allowances[17]; an allowance in respect of prolonged abstention from work[18]; an allowance for part-time treatment[19]; a mobility supplement[20]; and payment of medical expenses, including rehabilitative treatment[21].

1   See the Personal Injuries (Civilians) Scheme 1983, SI 1983/686, arts 8(1) proviso, 41(1) proviso.
2   See ibid arts 9(1), 41(3). An award may be made provisionally or upon any other basis: see art 9(1). Neither noise-induced sensorineural hearing loss nor a related condition or symptom may be taken into account in determining a person's degree of disablement if that loss alone is less than 20%: art 10(2B) (added by SI 1992/3226). 'Noise-induced sensorineural hearing loss' means damage to the cochlear hair cells of the inner ear which is caused by the exposure of the cochlea to noise, and a condition or symptom is to be treated as related to such hearing loss if it is another condition, or a symptom, which is the consequence of damage to the cochlear hair cells of the inner ear which is caused by the exposure of the cochlea to noise: art 2(14A) (as so added).
3   As to the Secretary of State see para 692 post.
4   See the Personal Injuries (Civilians) Scheme 1983 art 72 (amended by SI 1992/3226). No such sum is, however, payable in relation to noise-induced sensorineural hearing loss or a related condition or symptom if it is accompanied by noise-induced sensorineural hearing loss: art 72A (added by SI 1992/3226).
5   See ibid arts 8(2), 41(4). 'Physical injury' includes tuberculosis and any other organic disease, and the aggravation thereof: art 2(18).
6   See ibid art 10 (amended by SI 1992/3226), art 42, Sch 2. As to the service pensions order see para 662 et seq ante.
7   See ibid art 11, Sch 3 (substituted by SI 1996/502).
8   See ibid arts 14, 43.
9   See ibid arts 15, 44.

10   See ibid art 16 (amended by SI 1984/1675). There is, however, no such provision in respect of persons not gainfully occupied. For the meaning of 'gainfully occupied person' see para 668 note 4 ante.

11   See ibid arts 17, 46.

12   See ibid art 18 (amended by SI 1985/1313; SI 1992/702; SI 1995/502). There is, however, no such provision in respect of persons not gainfully occupied.

13   See ibid art 19. There is, however, no such provision in respect of persons not gainfully occupied.

14   See ibid arts 20, 45.

15   See ibid art 21 (amended by SI 1985/1313). There is, however, no such provision in respect of persons not gainfully occupied.

16   See ibid arts 22, 47.

17   See ibid art 23 (amended by SI 1986/628; SI 1992/702; SI 1993/480); art 48 (amended by SI 1986/628). As to the refusal of treatment see para 690 post.

18   See ibid art 24 (amended by SI 1993/480). There is, however, no such provision in respect of persons not gainfully occupied.

19   See ibid art 25 (amended by SI 1993/480). There is, however, no such provision in respect of persons not gainfully occupied.

20   See ibid art 25A (added by SI 1983/1164; amended by SI 1983/1540; SI 1986/628; SI 1990/1300; SI 1991/708; SI 1992/702; SI 1995/445); art 48A (added by SI 1984/1289).

21   See ibid art 25B (added by SI 1984/1289; amended by SI 1993/480); art 48B (added by SI 1984/1289).

674. Awards in respect of death. An award in respect of death may be made under the civilian injuries scheme[1] where the death is the direct result of a war injury[2] or, in the case of a civil defence volunteer[3], a war service injury[4].

Awards in respect of the death of gainfully occupied persons[5] or civil defence volunteers may be made as follows: widows' pensions[6]; rent allowances to surviving spouses[7] with children[8]; allowances to elderly surviving spouses[9]; pensions to unmarried dependants who lived as spouses[10]; temporary allowances to widows and unmarried dependants who lived as wives of severely disabled persons[11]; pensions to dependent widowers[12]; allowances in respect of children under the age of 15[13]; pensions to motherless or fatherless children under that age[14]; awards to or in respect of children over the age of 15[15]; and awards to or in respect of ineligible children of unemployable pensioners[16].

In the case of the death of a person who was not gainfully occupied, a pension based on pecuniary need may be awarded to a widow, a dependent widower or, where there is no widow or dependent widower, a dependent child[17] or, if there is no dependent child and, in the exceptional circumstances of any case, the Secretary of State[18] so directs, to a parent of the deceased to whose support the deceased had regularly contributed throughout the six-month period[19] expiring on the date of his death[20]. However, no such pension may be awarded unless the claimant is in pecuniary need because, by reason of the deceased's death, a pension, superannuation allowance, annuity or other income of which he was previously in receipt is no longer available to support the claimant[21]. Allowances to elderly surviving spouses[22] and temporary allowances to widows of severely disabled persons[23] are also payable.

In determining whether a pension is payable to a person as a widow under the scheme in respect of any period beginning on or after 19 July 1995, no account may be taken of the fact that the widow has married another if, before the beginning of that period, the marriage has been terminated or the parties have been judicially separated[24].

1   Ie the Personal Injuries (Civilians) Scheme 1983, SI 1983/686 (as amended): see paras 668 et seq ante, 675 post.

2   For the meaning of 'war injury' see para 667 ante.

3   For the meaning of 'civil defence volunteer' see para 668 note 5 ante.

4   See the Personal Injuries (Civilians) Scheme 1983 arts 26, 49. For the meaning of 'war service injury' see para 668 note 5 ante.

5   For the meaning of 'gainfully occupied person' see para 668 note 4 ante.

6   See the Personal Injuries (Civilians) Scheme 1983 art 27 (amended by SI 1994/2021).

7　'Surviving spouse' means the widow or, as the case may be, the dependent widower of a person referred to in ibid art 5(1)(a)–(c) (see para 670 ante): art 2(21A) (added by SI 1984/1289). 'Dependent widower', in relation to a deceased female person who sustained a qualifying injury, means a person who was married to the injured person at the date of her death and whose marriage to the injured person took place not later than the date of the injury, and who is incapable of self-support and in need: art 2(9), (14). For the meaning of 'qualifying injury' see para 668 note 4 ante.

8　See ibid art 28 (amended by SI 1984/1289; SI 1989/415; and SI 1993/480).

9　See ibid art 29 (substituted by SI 1984/1289).

10　See ibid art 30 (amended by SI 1984/1289). In relation to a person who has sustained a qualifying injury, 'unmarried dependant who lived as a spouse' means, where the injured person is dead, a person of the opposite sex who was wholly or substantially maintained by the injured person on a permanent bona fide domestic basis continuously throughout the period beginning six months before the material date (ie the date of the injury: see art 2(14)) and ending with the date of the injured person's death: see art 2(21B)(b) (added by SI 1984/1289).

11　See ibid art 31 (amended by SI 1983/1540). 'Unmarried dependant who lived as a wife' means, where the injured person is dead, a female person who was wholly or substantially maintained by him on a permanent bona fide domestic basis continuously throughout the period beginning six months before the material date and ending with the date of his death: see art 2(22)(b).

12　See ibid art 32.

13　See ibid art 33.

14　See ibid art 34.

15　See ibid art 35.

16　See ibid art 37 (substituted by SI 1984/1289).

17　'Dependent child', in relation to a deceased person who has sustained a qualifying injury, means his or her (1) legitimate or legitimated child; (2) stepchild; (3) adopted child; (4) illegitimate child who was not legitimated upon the marriage of the injured person to the child's mother or father; (5) illegitimate child whose other parent was, at the date of his marriage to the injured person or of his death, an unmarried person living as a spouse of that person; (6) illegitimate child not falling within heads (4) or (5) supra who either was dependent on the injured person at the date of his death or was born after his death; (7) foster-child who was being brought up and wholly maintained by the injured person as his child at the date of his death: see art 2(7) (amended by SI 1984/1289).

18　As to the Secretary of State see para 692 post.

19　Ie or such other period as the Secretary of State may determine: Personal Injuries (Civilians) Scheme 1983 art 49(1)(c).

20　Ibid art 49(1).

21　See ibid art 49(2).

22　See ibid art 50 (substituted by SI 1984/1289).

23　See ibid art 51.

24　Pensions Act 1995 s 168(1), (3)(b). For the meaning of 'termination of a marriage' and 'judicial separation' for these purposes see para 663 note 16 ante.

675. Payment of pensions. Payment of a pension under the Personal Injuries (Civilians) Scheme 1983[1] may be made provisionally or upon any other basis[2]. Pension may be paid weekly in advance[3] but the Secretary of State[4] may in any particular case or class of case determine that pension is to be paid in advance or in arrears or partly in advance and partly in arrears, and for a period different from that specified[5] by the scheme[6].

Pension is to be paid by such means as appear to the Secretary of State to be appropriate in the circumstances of the case or class of case[7]. He may direct in relation to any particular case or class of case that a pension is to be paid by way of automated or other direct credit transfer into a bank or other account in the name of a person entitled to the pension or a person acting on his behalf, or in the joint names of the person entitled to the pension and his spouse, or the person entitled to the pension and a person acting on his behalf[8]. Pension so paid must be paid for periods of four weeks, or for such other periods as the Secretary of State may in any particular case or class of case determine and within seven days of the last day of each successive period so determined[9]. It may be paid in advance, or in arrears, or partly in advance and partly in arrears, as the Secretary of State may in any particular case or class of case determine[10]. Payment of pension by direct credit transfer may be terminated by the Secretary of State if the arrangements seem to him to be no longer appropriate to that case or class of case[11].

1 Ie the Personal Injuries (Civilians) Scheme 1983, SI 1983/686 (as amended): see para 668 et seq ante.
2 Ibid art 75(1A) (added by SI 1988/2260).
3 Ibid art 75(1B) (as added: see note 2 supra).
4 As to the Secretary of State see para 692 post.
5 Ie specified in the Personal Injuries (Civilians) Scheme 1983 art 75(1B) (as added): see the text and note 3 supra.
6 Ibid art 75(1C) (as added: see note 2 supra).
7 Ibid art 75(1D) (as added: see note 2 supra). Amounts of pension including a fraction of a pence must be rounded up and other allowances and benefits rounded to the nearest pence: see art 75(2). Where, by reason of any provision in any instrument amending a provision of the scheme, a change falls to be made in the rate of any pension which is payable weekly, and the date on which that change would otherwise fall (the 'prescribed date') is not the day of the week on which payment of pension is normally made (the 'weekly pay day'), the change has effect only as from the first weekly pay day immediately following the prescribed date: art 75(3) (added by SI 1984/1289; amended by SI 1988/2260).
8 Ibid art 74A(1) (added by SI 1988/2260).
9 Ibid art 74A(2)(a), (b) (as added: see note 8 supra).
10 Ibid art 74A(2)(c) (as added: see note 8 supra). Where pension is payable in accordance with art 74A (as so added), the Secretary of State may make a particular payment by credit transfer otherwise than as provided by art 74A(2) (as so added) if it appears to him to be appropriate to do so for the purpose of paying any arrears of pension, or making a payment of pension at the termination of an award: art 74A(3) (as so added).
11 Ibid art 74A(4) (as added: see note 8 supra).

(iii) Schemes for the Mercantile Marine and Other Seafarers

676. Power to make awards to mariners in respect of war injuries and detention.
The Secretary of State[1] may, with the consent of the Treasury, make a scheme for:

(1) applying the provisions of any Naval War Pensions Order[2] to persons in cases where their death or disablement is directly attributable to their having sustained war injuries[3], or suffered detention[4], by reason of their service as mariners in British ships[5];

(2) the payment of allowances to or for the benefit of persons who have suffered such detention or to or for the benefit of their dependants[6].

The cases in which a person who has sustained an injury[7], or suffered detention, is to be treated as having done so by reason of his service in a British ship as a mariner are where the injury, or the capture on which his detention was consequent, as the case may be, occurred:

(a) while he was in the service of a British ship as a mariner;

(b) in the case of a person normally employed as a mariner, while he was in the service of a seagoing British ship in the British Islands[8] in which he was employed as a master or a member of its crew, notwithstanding that he was not employed in seagoing service in the ship;

(c) while he was at a place[9] outside the British Islands on leave from a British ship in which he was employed as a mariner and which was at a port[10] outside those islands;

(d) while he was at a place outside the British Islands in accordance with approved arrangements[11] for having persons available for employment as mariners;

(e) while he was at any place, except on land in the British Islands, in the course of proceeding to employment in a British ship as a mariner, or to a place to which he was going in accordance with such approved arrangements;

(f)   while he was at any place, except as mentioned above, in the course of returning to any part of the British Islands, to the country to which he belonged, or to any other approved country[12] from employment in a British ship as a mariner or from a place at which he had been in accordance with such approved arrangements, and before he first arrived on land in that part of the British Islands or, as the case may be, in that country; or

(g)   while he was waiting at any place outside the British Islands to proceed or return as mentioned above, whether the delay was due to sickness or to any other cause outside his control[13].

If it appears to the Secretary of State that the awards that could be authorised by the provisions of a scheme made by virtue of head (1) above would, in the case of mariners of any particular class, be inappropriate to the conditions of their employment or engagement, he may, with the consent of the Treasury and in lieu of making provision for the application in their case of a Naval War Pensions Order, make a scheme authorising in their case awards on account of the like matters as if the scheme were made under those provisions, but of such amount and character as may be determined by or under the scheme[14].

A scheme may also be made for compensating the persons to whom these provisions apply for war damage[15] to their effects[16].

A scheme made under these provisions may contain any such provisions as appear to the Secretary of State to be necessary or expedient for giving effect to its purpose, and in particular may make provision for the determination of questions with respect to its effect or operation and for empowering him to make regulations for giving effect to the purposes of the scheme[17]. It may be amended or revoked by a subsequent scheme or by an order made by the Secretary of State[18]. A scheme applying the provisions of a Naval War Pensions Order to mariners or other persons may apply the order subject to such additions and modifications as appear appropriate, having regard to the differences in the conditions of service of mariners and other persons and of officers and men of the naval forces of the Crown respectively or to other services, and subject to such conditions, limitations and exceptions as appear to the Secretary of State to be expedient[19].

All sums to be paid in respect of a pension or other payment awarded by virtue of a scheme must be paid out of money provided by Parliament[20].

1   As to the Secretary of State see para 692 post.
2   'Naval War Pensions Order' means an Order in Council whereby provision is made as respects officers and men of the naval forces of the Crown for the award of pensions or other payments on account of death or disablement attributable to service in those forces during war: Pensions (Navy, Army, Air Force and Mercantile Marine) Act 1939 s 10. The power to make such Orders in Council is now exercisable under the Social Security (Miscellaneous Provisions) Act 1977 s 12: see para 662 et seq ante; and ROYAL FORCES vol 41 para 333 et seq.
3   For the meaning of 'war injury' see para 667 ante.
4   'Detention', in relation to a mariner or other person, means detention consequent on the capture of the mariner or other person or of his ship effected by reason of the existence of a state of war: Pensions (Navy, Army, Air Force and Mercantile Marine) Act 1939 s 10. 'Capture' includes seizure, arrest or other restraint; and 'mariner', in relation to a ship, means the master or a member of the crew of the ship, being a person employed or engaged in seagoing service in that ship, and not being a member of the naval forces of the Crown or a person to whom the provisions of ss 4, 5 (as amended) (see paras 677–678 post) apply: s 10 (definition of 'mariner' amended by the Pensions (Mercantile Marine) Act 1942 s 6, Schedule). 'Ship' has the same meaning as in the Merchant Shipping Act 1995: Pensions (Navy, Army, Air Force and Mercantile Marine) Act 1939 s 10 (definition added by the Pensions (Mercantile Marine) Act 1942 Schedule; amended by the Merchant Shipping Act 1995 s 314(2), Sch 13 para 19(b)).
5   'British ship' does not include a ship forming part of the Royal Navy, but includes a ship not forming part of that navy which belongs to the Crown or is held by any person on behalf of or for the benefit of the Crown: see the Pensions (Navy, Army, Air Force and Mercantile Marine) Act 1939 s 10 (definition amended by the Pensions (Mercantile Marine) Act 1942 Schedule; and by the Armed Forces

Act 1981 s 28(2), Sch 5 Pt I). References in the Pensions (Navy, Army, Air Force and Mercantile Marine) Act 1939 s 3 (as amended), s 6(1)(a) (as amended) (see head (1) in the text; and the text and notes 6–16 infra) to British ships are to be construed, in relation to injuries, detention, loss or damage sustained or suffered by British subjects and British protected persons, as including references to other ships chartered on behalf of the Crown; and a scheme thereunder may make provision, as respects such cases as may be specified by or under the scheme, for treating the service or employment of British subjects and British protected persons as mariners in ships which are not British ships or such other ships as mentioned above as if it were service or employment in British ships: Pensions (Mercantile Marine) Act 1942 s 10(3). As to British subjects and British protected persons see BRITISH NATIONALITY, IMMIGRATION AND RACE RELATIONS vol 4(2) (Reissue) paras 3, 52 et seq, 58 et seq; and as to British citizenship generally see BRITISH NATIONALITY, IMMIGRATION AND RACE RELATIONS vol 4(2) (Reissue) para 12 et seq.

6 Pensions (Navy, Army, Air Force and Mercantile Marine) Act 1939 s 3(1) (s 3(1), (2) substituted by the Pensions (Mercantile Marine) Act 1942 s 2(1); amended by virtue of the Secretary of State for Social Services Order 1968, SI 1968/1699, art 5(4)(a)). See the War Pensions (Mercantile Marine) Scheme 1964, SI 1964/2058 (as amended); and para 679 et seq post.

7 In addition to war injuries within the statutory definition (see para 667 ante), these provisions also apply in relation to physical injuries sustained on or after 3 September 1939, at sea or in any other tidal water or in the waters of any harbour and attributable to (1) the taking of measures with a view to avoiding, preventing or hindering enemy action against ships, or as a precaution in anticipation of enemy action against ships, or for rescue or salvage purposes in consequence of enemy action against ships; (2) the absence, by reason of circumstances connected with any war in which the Crown may be engaged, of any aid to navigation for ships, or of any warning of danger to ships, being an aid or warning which would be normal in time of peace; (3) the carriage, by reason of circumstances connected with any such war, of any cargo in a manner which would be abnormal in time of peace and involves danger to the ship in which the cargo is carried or to her crew; or (4) the existence on board ship of any other conditions arising out of any such war which would be abnormal in time of peace: see the Pensions (Mercantile Marine) Act 1942 s 1(1), (2)(a)–(d). These injuries are referred to as 'war risk injuries' in the appropriate pension schemes: see para 667 heads (a)–(d) ante. In relation to injuries sustained in the waters of a harbour, the measures specified in head (1) supra do not include the prohibition or restriction of lights other than navigational lights; and an injury is treated as being attributable to the matters specified in heads (1)–(4) supra if, but only if, they substantially increased the risk of the peril occurring which caused the injury, loss or damage: s 1(2), (3). For these purposes, 'navigational light' means a light displayed, whether on a ship or otherwise, as an aid to navigation for ships or as a warning of danger to ships: s 1(4). 'Physical injury' includes tuberculosis and any other organic disease and the aggravation thereof: s 5. 'Harbour' means any harbour, whether natural or artificial, and any port, dock, haven, estuary, tidal or other river, canal or inland navigation to which seagoing ships have access; and 'tidal water' means any part of the sea, and any part of a river within the ebb and flow of the tide at ordinary spring tides, not being a harbour: s 10(2). For the meaning of 'salvage' see para 677 note 8 post.

8 For these purposes, 'British Islands' means Great Britain, Northern Ireland, the Channel Islands and the Isle of Man: Pensions (Navy, Army, Air Force and Mercantile Marine) Act 1939 s 10.

9 'Place' includes any point on land, in the air, or on or in the water: ibid s 10 (definition added by the Pensions (Mercantile Marine) Act 1942 Schedule).

10 'Port' includes any dock, harbour, pier, quay, wharf, mooring, anchorage or similar place: Pensions (Navy, Army, Air Force and Mercantile Marine) Act 1939 s 10 (definition substituted by the Pensions (Mercantile Marine) Act 1942 Schedule).

11 Ie arrangements made or approved by or on behalf of the then Minister of War Transport or (now) by the Secretary of State: see the Pensions (Navy, Army, Air Force and Mercantile Marine) Act 1939 s 3(2)(d) (as substituted: see note 13 infra). As to the dissolution of the Ministry of War Transport see the Ministry of War Transport (Dissolution) Order 1946, SR & O 1946/375.

12 Ie approved by or on behalf of the then Minister of War Transport or (now) by the Secretary of State: see the Pensions (Navy, Army, Air Force and Mercantile Marine) Act 1939 s 3(2)(f) (as substituted: see note 13 infra).

13 Ibid s 3(2) (substituted by the Pensions (Mercantile Marine) Act 1942 s 2(1)).

14 Pensions (Navy, Army, Air Force and Mercantile Marine) Act 1939 s 3(3) (amended by the Pensions (Mercantile Marine) Act 1942 Schedule; and by virtue of the Secretary of State for Social Services Order 1968 (see note 6 supra)).

15 For the meaning of 'war damage' see para 667 ante.

16 See the Pensions (Navy, Army, Air Force and Mercantile Marine) Act 1939 s 6(1)(a) (substituted by the Pensions (Mercantile Marine) Act 1942 s 2(2); extended by s 1(1)). 'Effects', in relation to any person, means any property carried on his person or in the ship in which he is serving or in the ship or other conveyance in which he is travelling, or otherwise accompanying him, at the time when the war damage

in question occurs: Pensions (Navy, Army, Air Force and Mercantile Marine) Act 1939 s 6(4). A scheme so made may fix the maximum amount payable under it in different circumstances specified in the scheme: s 6(2). See the Merchant Shipping (Compensation to Seamen – War Damage to Effects) Scheme 1982, SI 1982/1023; and paras 681, 695 post.

17 Pensions (Navy, Army, Air Force and Mercantile Marine) Act 1939 s 7(1) (amended by virtue of the Secretary of State for Social Services Order 1968: see note 6 supra). A scheme may provide that it is to come into operation, or is to be deemed to have come into operation, on such date as may be specified in it, whether before or after the commencement of the Pensions (Navy, Army, Air Force and Mercantile Marine) Act 1939: s 7(2); and see the Pensions (Mercantile Marine) Act 1942 s 8.

18 Pensions (Navy, Army, Air Force and Mercantile Marine) Act 1939 s 7(3) (as amended: see note 17 supra).

19 Ibid s 7(5) (as amended: see note 17 supra; further amended by the Pensions (Mercantile Marine) Act 1942 Schedule).

20 Pensions (Navy, Army, Air Force and Mercantile Marine) Act 1939 s 7(6); and see the Pensions (Mercantile Marine) Act 1942 s 9.

677. Power to make awards to pilots etc. The Secretary of State[1] may, with the consent of the Treasury, make a scheme for applying the provisions of any Naval War Pensions Order[2] to:

(1) pilots and apprentice pilots[3];

(2) masters and members of the crew of pilot boats[4], lightships[5], lighthouse tenders[6] and lightship tenders[7]; and

(3) any person other than a member of the naval forces of the Crown who, not being the master or a member of the crew of a ship, is regularly employed in salvage[8] operations in or from the British Islands,

in cases where their death or disablement is directly attributable to their having sustained war injuries[9], or suffered detention[10], by reason of their service[11]. He may also make a scheme, with the like consent, for the payment of allowances to or for the benefit of any such persons who have suffered such detention or to or for the benefit of their dependants[12].

For these purposes, a person is deemed to have sustained a war injury, or to have been detained, by reason of his service, if he sustained the injury, or if the capture[13] in consequence of which the detention occurs is effected:

(a) in the case of a master or member of the crew of a pilot boat, lighthouse tender or lightship tender, while he is in the service of the boat or tender or is at any place[14], except on land in the British Islands, in the course of proceeding to the boat or tender for the purpose of being in its service, or of returning from the boat or tender after being in its service[15];

(b) in the case of a pilot or apprentice pilot, at any time during a period while he was on a seagoing ship, if during some part of that period he was acting or was due to act as pilot or apprentice pilot, or while he was on board a pilot boat, or while he was at any place, except on land in the British Islands, while proceeding to or returning from a seagoing ship in which he was due to act, or had acted, as pilot or apprentice pilot, or to or from a pilot boat[16];

(c) in the case of a master or member of the crew of a lightship, while he is in the service of the lightship or is at any place, except on land in the British Islands, in the course of proceeding to the lightship for the purpose of being in its service or of returning from the lightship after being in its service[17];

(d) in the case of a salvage worker, while he was engaged in salvage operations taking place either at sea or in any tidal water or harbour[18] outside the British Islands, or while he was on leave at a place outside those islands during the carrying on of such salvage operations in which he was engaged, or while he was at any place, except on land in those islands, in the course of proceeding to or returning from engagement in such salvage operations or while he was waiting at any place outside those islands to proceed or return to or from such engagement (whether the delay was due to sickness or to any other cause outside his control)[19].

A scheme may also be made for compensating the persons to whom these provisions apply for war damage[20] to their effects[21].

A scheme made under these provisions may contain any such provisions as appear to the Secretary of State to be necessary or expedient for giving effect to its purpose, and in particular may make provision for the determination of questions with respect to its effect or operation and for empowering him to make regulations for giving effect to the purposes of the scheme[22]. It may be amended or revoked by a subsequent scheme or by an order made by the Secretary of State[23].

1 As to the Secretary of State see para 692 post.

2 See para 676 note 2 ante.

3 The persons to whom these provisions apply as being pilots and apprentice pilots are any pilot, and any person, whether an apprentice or not, training as a pilot, whose normal occupation as such is carried on in or from the British Islands and is that of acting as pilot or apprentice pilot in ships at sea or ships proceeding to or from sea from or to ports or pilotage districts in those islands which are at sea at some time while he is so acting; and 'apprentice pilot' includes any person training as a pilot: Pensions (Mercantile Marine) Act 1942 s 3(1). For the meaning of 'British Islands' see para 676 note 8 ante.

4 For these purposes, 'pilot boat' has the meaning assigned to it by the Pilotage Act 1987 s 6, except that it includes any vessel which for the time being is being used in the pilotage service of any pilotage district in the British Islands: Pensions (Navy, Army, Air Force and Mercantile Marine) Act 1939 s 4(4) (definition amended by the Pensions (Mercantile Marine) Act 1942 s 6, Schedule; and by the Pilotage Act 1987 s 32(4), Sch 2 para 1).

5 'Lightship' means a lightship belonging to a local or general lighthouse authority within the meaning of the Merchant Shipping Act 1995: Pensions (Navy, Army, Air Force and Mercantile Marine) Act 1939 s 4(4) (definition amended by the Merchant Shipping Act 1995 s 314(2), Sch 13 para 19(a)).

6 'Lighthouse tender' means a tender belong to any such authority as is mentioned in note 5 supra: Pensions (Navy, Army, Air Force and Mercantile Marine) Act 1939 s 4(4).

7 'Lightship tender' means a tender to a lightship: ibid s 4(4).

8 'Salvage' means the preservation or recovery of vessels wrecked, stranded or in distress, or their cargo or apparel, or the recovery of any other property from the water; and includes the removal of wrecks; and 'salvage operations' and 'salvage purposes' are to be construed accordingly: Pensions (Mercantile Marine) Act 1942 s 10(2).

9 For the meaning of 'war injury' see para 667 ante.

10 For the meaning of 'detention' see para 676 note 4 ante.

11 Pensions (Navy, Army, Air Force and Mercantile Marine) Act 1939 s 4(1)(a), (2) (amended by virtue of the Secretary of State for Social Services Order 1968, SI 1968/1699, art 5(4)(a)); Pensions (Mercantile Marine) Act 1942 s 4(1), (2). In relation to such a salvage worker as is mentioned in head (3) in the text, or to the master or a member of the crew of a ship regularly employed, or chartered for the purpose of being employed, in salvage operations, the reference in s 1(2)(a) (see para 676 note 7 head (1) ante) to measures taken for salvage purposes does not apply: s 4(4).

12 Pensions (Navy, Army, Air Force and Mercantile Marine) Act 1939 s 4(1)(b), (2); Pensions (Mercantile Marine) Act 1942 s 4(1), (2). See the War Pensions (Mercantile Marine) Scheme 1964, SI 1964/2058 (as amended); and para 679 et seq post.

13 For the meaning of 'capture' see para 676 note 4 ante.

14 For the meaning of 'place' see para 676 note 9 ante.

15 Pensions (Navy, Army, Air Force and Mercantile Marine) Act 1939 s 4(3)(b) (amended by the Pensions (Mercantile Marine) Act 1942 Schedule).

16 Pensions (Mercantile Marine) Act 1942 s 3(2).

17 Pensions (Navy, Army, Air Force and Mercantile Marine) Act 1939 s 4(3)(c) (as amended: see note 15 supra).

18 For the meaning of 'tidal water' and 'harbour' see para 676 note 7 ante.

19 Pensions (Mercantile Marine) Act 1942 s 4(1)(a)–(d).

20 For the meaning of 'war damage' see para 667 ante.

21 See the Pensions (Navy, Army, Air Force and Mercantile Marine) Act 1939 s 6(1)(b); the Pensions (Mercantile Marine) Act 1942 ss 3(3), 4(3). For the meaning of 'effects' see para 676 note 16 ante. At the date at which this volume states the law, no such scheme was in force for these purposes.

22 Pensions (Navy, Army, Air Force and Mercantile Marine) Act 1939 s 7(1) (amended by virtue of the Secretary of State for Social Services Order 1968: see note 11 supra).

23 Pensions (Navy, Army, Air Force and Mercantile Marine) Act 1939 s 7(3) (as amended: see note 22 supra). See further s 7(2), (5) (as amended); the Pensions (Mercantile Marine) Act 1942 s 8; and para 676 ante.

678. Power to make awards to certain persons serving on naval ships. The Secretary of State[1] may, with the consent of the Treasury, make a scheme for:

(1) applying the provisions of any Naval War Pensions Order[2] to persons employed or engaged on ships[3] forming part of the Royal Navy, being persons to whom the provisions of the order would not otherwise apply, in cases where their death or disablement is directly attributable to war injuries[4] sustained in such circumstances as may be specified in the scheme, or to detention[5] caused by reason of their service in such ships[6]; and

(2) the payment of allowances to or for the benefit of any such persons so detained, or to or for the benefit of their dependants[7].

If it appears to the Secretary of State that the awards that could be authorised by the provisions of a scheme made by virtue of head (1) above would, in the case of any such persons of any particular class, be inappropriate to the conditions of their employment or engagement, he may, with the consent of the Treasury and in lieu of making provision for the application in their case of a Naval War Pensions Order, make a scheme authorising in their case awards on account of the like matters as if the scheme were made under those provisions, but of such amount and character as may be determined by or under the scheme[8].

A scheme may also be made for compensating the persons to whom these provisions apply for war damage[9] to their effects[10].

A scheme made under these provisions may contain any such provisions as appear to the Secretary of State to be necessary or expedient for giving effect to its purpose, and in particular may make provision for the determination of questions with respect to its effect or operation and for empowering him to make regulations for giving effect to the purposes of the scheme[11]. It may be amended or revoked by a subsequent scheme or by an order made by the Secretary of State[12].

1   As to the Secretary of State see para 692 post.
2   See para 676 note 2 ante.
3   For the meaning of 'ship' see para 676 note 4 ante.
4   For the meaning of 'war injury' see para 667 ante.
5   For the meaning of 'detention' see para 676 note 4 ante.
6   Pensions (Navy, Army, Air Force and Mercantile Marine) Act 1939 s 5(1)(a) (amended by the Armed Forces Act 1981 s 20(1), Sch 3 Pt II para 7; and by virtue of the Secretary of State for Social Services Order 1968, SI 1968/1699, art 5(4)(a)).
7   Pensions (Navy, Army, Air Force and Mercantile Marine) Act 1939 s 5(1)(b). See the War Pensions (Coastguards) Scheme 1944, SR & O 1944/500 (as amended); the War Pensions (Naval Auxiliary Personnel) Scheme 1964, SI 1964/1985 (as amended); and para 681 post.
8   Pensions (Navy, Army, Air Force and Mercantile Marine) Act 1939 s 5(2) (amended by the Pensions (Mercantile Marine) Act 1942 s 6, Schedule; and by virtue of the Secretary of State for Social Services Order 1968: see note 6 supra).
9   For the meaning of 'war damage' see para 667 ante.
10 See the Pensions (Navy, Army, Air Force and Mercantile Marine) Act 1939 s 6(1)(c). At the date at which this volume states the law, no such scheme was in force for these purposes.
11 Pensions (Navy, Army, Air Force and Mercantile Marine) Act 1939 s 7(1) (amended by virtue of the Secretary of State for Social Services Order 1968: see note 6 supra).
12 Pensions (Navy, Army, Air Force and Mercantile Marine) Act 1939 s 7(3) (as amended: see note 11 supra). See further s 7(2), (5) (as amended); the Pensions (Mercantile Marine) Act 1942 s 8; and para 676 ante.

679. The mercantile marine scheme. The War Pensions (Mercantile Marine) Scheme 1964[1] applies the service pensions order[2] with specified modifications[3] to any person within one of the following descriptions whose disablement or death is directly attributable to a qualifying injury[4] sustained, or to detention[5] suffered, by reason of his service, that is to say, a member of the merchant navy or the sea fishing service[6], the pilotage service or the light vessel service[7] or a salvage worker[8]. All such persons are included in any references in the scheme to a 'mariner'[9].

1　Ie the War Pensions (Mercantile Marine) Scheme 1964, SI 1964/2058 (amended by SI 1972/1434; SI 1978/1526; SI 1987/585; SI 1988/639; SI 1989/540; and SI 1993/692). The scheme was made under the Pensions (Navy, Army, Air Force and Mercantile Marine) Act 1939 ss 3, 4, 7 (as amended): see paras 676–677 ante.

2　Ie the Naval, Military and Air Forces etc (Disablement and Death) Service Pensions Order 1983, SI 1983/883 (as amended): see para 662 et seq ante; and ROYAL FORCES vol 41 para 333 et seq.

3　See the War Pensions (Mercantile Marine) Scheme 1964 art 17, Sch 6; the Naval, Military and Air Forces etc (Modification of Enactments and other Instruments) Order 1978, SI 1978/1526, art 2, Schedule Pt II; the Interpretation Act 1978 s 17(2).

4　'Qualifying injury' means a war injury or a war risk injury: War Pensions (Mercantile Marine) Scheme 1964 art 2(27). See also para 667 ante. As to the qualifying injuries covered by the scheme see Sch 2.

5　'Detention', in relation to any person, means detention which is consequent on the capture of that person or of his ship effected by reason of the existence of a state of war: ibid art 2(6). As to the detention covered by the scheme see Sch 2.

6　See ibid arts 2(13), (16), (18), 4.

7　See ibid arts 2(15), (17), 5.

8　See ibid arts 2(31), 6.

9　See the War Pensions (Mercantile Marine) (Amendment) Scheme 1988, SI 1988/639, art 5.

680. General effect of the mercantile marine scheme. The war pension rights are very much less favourable for members of the merchant navy than for those of the armed forces[1]. In the first place, members of the merchant navy and other persons covered by the scheme are not entitled to a pension unless their disablement or death is directly attributable to a qualifying injury[2] sustained or detention[3] suffered which fulfils the required criteria[4], whereas members of the armed forces have only to show that disablement or death is due to service[5]. There is thus no presumption, as there is for the purposes of the service pensions order[6], that an injury which has led to a member's discharge or death during service which was not noted in a medical report on the commencement of his service must be accepted as due to service unless the contrary is proved[7]. In no case, however, is there an onus on a claimant under the mercantile marine scheme to prove that disablement or death is directly attributable to a qualifying injury or detention if the claim is made within seven years[8], and where, upon reliable evidence, a reasonable doubt exists on that question, the benefit of the doubt must be given to the claimant irrespective of when the claim is made[9]. Where there has been a previous disablement in respect of which a pension or grant is in payment out of public funds, otherwise than under the scheme, the assessment for the purposes of the scheme must be determined having regard to the previous disablement[10].

In determining whether a pension is payable to a person as a widow under the scheme in respect of any period beginning on or after 19 July 1995, no account may be taken of the fact that the widow has married another if, before the beginning of that period, the marriage has been terminated or the parties have been judicially separated[11]. This provision is in identical terms to that made for the purposes of the service pensions order[12].

Where during the period of the emergency[13] a member of the merchant navy suffered a war injury or a war risk injury, any right to damages or compensation in respect of that injury, whether by virtue of any statute or contract or at common law, was removed[14]; and the only recompense available to him was that now conferred by the War Pensions

(Mercantile Marine) Scheme 1964[15]. Thus a seaman who was injured while dismantling a guy from an apparatus which increased the risk and which had been negligently fitted was not entitled to recover damages for the negligence[16].

1 For a comparison of their respective rights see *Morris v Minister of Pensions* (1947) 1 WPAR 595 at 598 per Denning J.
2 For the meaning of 'qualifying injury' see para 679 note 4 ante.
3 For the meaning of 'detention' see para 679 note 5 ante.
4 See the War Pensions (Mercantile Marine) Scheme 1964, SI 1964/2058, arts 4–6, Sch 2.
5 See the Naval, Military and Air Forces etc (Disablement and Death) Service Pensions Order 1983, SI 1983/883, art 3 (as substituted); and para 663 ante. An injury will be 'due to service' if it is attributable to service: see *Horsfall v Minister of Pensions* (1944) 1 WPAR 7 (where an RAF officer collapsed and died after playing squash for his amusement, the death was not attributable to service; the nominated judge, Tucker J, stated: 'The words used are 'attributable to' and I think they have a different significance from 'in the course of'. See also *Standen v Minister of Pensions* (1947) 1 WPAR 905; *Giles v Minister of Pensions and National Insurance* (1955) 5 WPAR 445 (both involving injuries sustained during leave); *Richards v Minister of Pensions and National Insurance* (1956) 5 WPAR 631 (fight in barracks); *Miers v Minister of Pensions and National Insurance* (1964) 5 WPAR 673 (suicide); *Freeman v Minister of Pensions and National Insurance* [1966] 2 All ER 40 at 43, [1966] 1 WLR 456 at 461 per Edmund Davies J ('It is not necessary for the applicant to show ... that service conditions were the sole cause of the suicide; it is sufficient if they played a part in bringing it about').
6 See the Naval, Military and Air Forces etc (Disablement and Death) Service Pensions Order 1983 art 4(3).
7 See *Morris v Minister of Pensions* (1947) 1 WPAR 595 at 598 per Denning J.
8 War Pensions (Mercantile Marine) Scheme 1964 art 3(4).
9 See ibid art 3(4), (5).
10 See ibid art 18.
11 Pensions Act 1995 s 168(1), (3)(c). For the meaning of 'termination of a marriage' and 'judicial separation' for these purposes see para 663 note 16 ante.
12 See ibid s 168(1), (3)(a); and para 663 ante.
13 Ie 3 September 1939 to 19 March 1946: see para 668 note 2 ante.
14 See the Personal Injuries (Emergency Provisions) Act 1939 s 3, as extended by the Pensions (Mercantile Marine) Act 1942 s 7 (both repealed).
15 Restriction on the right to damages applied also to persons covered by the various schemes relating to particular classes of seafarers: see para 681 post. The War Pensions (Mercantile Marine) Scheme 1964 now makes provision to avoid double payments: see art 21 (amended by SI 1988/639).
16 *Makin v Masson* [1948] LJR 325, CA.

681. Other schemes for seafarers. In addition to the War Pensions (Mercantile Marine) Scheme 1964[1], a scheme compensating certain mariners[2] for war damage[3] to their effects[4] has been made[5]. There are also two other pension schemes concerning persons connected with the sea, the War Pensions (Naval Auxiliary Personnel) Scheme 1964[6] and the War Pensions (Coastguards) Scheme 1944[7]. The scheme concerning naval auxiliary personnel provides that the service pensions order[8] has effect with specified modifications[9] in relation to the persons covered by the scheme who are disabled or die, if their disablement or death is directly attributable to a qualifying injury[10] or detention[11]. Equivalent provision is made by the scheme concerning coastguards[12].

The War Pensions (Naval Auxiliary Personnel) Scheme 1964 covers persons subject to the Naval Discipline Act 1957[13] (by virtue of the application of that Act to civilians[14]) and who, in pursuance of a naval engagement, are employed in seagoing service in a ship forming part of the Royal Navy or in a depot ship pending becoming so employed or pending termination of such employment[15]. It also covers certain other persons engaged in ships forming part of the Royal Navy whose terms of enlistment provided that the scheme should apply to them[16].

The War Pensions (Coastguards) Scheme 1944 covers certain officers and men of HM Coastguard and of the Auxiliary Coastguard[17].

1   Ie the War Pensions (Mercantile Marine) Scheme 1964, SI 1964/2058 (as amended): see paras 679–680 ante.

2   Ie persons for whom the Secretary of State is authorised to provide compensation by a scheme made under the Pensions (Navy, Army, Air Force and Mercantile Marine) Act 1939 s 6(1)(a) (as substituted) (see para 676 ante): Merchant Shipping (Compensation to Seamen – War Damage to Effects) Scheme 1982, SI 1982/1023, art 2. Such compensation is restricted to mariners in the service of British registered ships in the circumstances arising out of the unlawful occupation of the Falkland Islands and their dependencies by the Argentine Republic in 1982: art 2. As to the Secretary of State see para 692 post.

3   For the meaning of 'war damage' see para 667 ante.

4   Compensation may be claimed in respect of personal effects, uniforms, and tools, instruments and technical books required in connection with shipboard duties: see the Merchant Shipping (Compensation to Seamen – War Damage to Effects) Scheme 1982 art 3.

5   See the Merchant Shipping (Compensation to Seamen – War Damage to Effects) Scheme 1982; and the text and notes 2–4 supra. Every claim for compensation under the scheme was to be made in such form and manner as might be approved by the Secretary of State; and except with his leave, no claim could be entertained unless made within a period of six months from the time when the war damage was sustained: see art 6. The time for making such claims has thus long since expired. In the event of the death of a person who, if he had survived, could have made such a claim, the claim could be made by his personal representatives: see art 4. As to the maximum amounts of compensation see art 3; and as to determining the amount to be paid to any person see art 5.

6   Ie the War Pensions (Naval Auxiliary Personnel) Scheme 1964, SI 1964/1985 (amended by SI 1972/1436; SI 1978/1526; SI 1989/540; SI 1993/692).

7   Ie the War Pensions (Coastguards) Scheme 1944, SR & O 1944/500 (amended by SI 1978/1526; SI 1989/540; SI 1993/692).

8   Ie the Naval, Military and Air Forces etc (Disablement and Death) Service Pensions Order 1983, SI 1983/883 (as amended): see paras 662–665 ante.

9   See the War Pensions (Naval Auxiliary Personnel) Scheme 1964 arts 2(8), 3(2), Sch 3; the Naval, Military and Air Forces etc (Modification of Enactments and other Instruments) Order 1978, SI 1978/1526, art 2, Table Pt II; the Interpretation Act 1978 s 17(2).

10 'Qualifying injury' means a war injury or a war risk injury, being in either case an injury sustained by the naval auxiliary member by reason of his service: War Pensions (Naval Auxiliary Personnel) Scheme 1964 art 2(10). For the meaning of 'war injury' and 'war risk injury' see para 667 ante.

11 See ibid arts 4(1), 6, 8. 'Detention', in relation to a naval auxiliary member, means detention which is consequent on the capture, seizure, arrest or other restraint of the naval auxiliary member or of his ship effected by reason of the existence of a state of war, and which is suffered by reason of his service: art 2(2).

12 See the War Pensions (Coastguards) Scheme 1944 arts 3, 5, 9; the Naval, Military and Air Forces etc (Modification of Enactments and other Instruments) Order 1978, SI 1978/1526, art 2, Table Pt II; the Interpretation Act 1978 s 17(2).

13 The Naval Discipline Act 1957 repeals and replaces the Naval Discipline Act 1866 which is referred to in the scheme. See generally ROYAL FORCES vol 41 para 12.

14 See the Naval Discipline Act 1957 s 118 (as amended); and ROYAL FORCES vol 41 para 20.

15 See the War Pensions (Naval Auxiliary Personnel) Scheme 1964 arts 2(6), 4(1); the Interpretation Act 1978 s 17(2).

16 See the War Pensions (Naval Auxiliary Personnel) Scheme 1964 art 4(2).

17 The persons concerned are those subject to what is now the Naval Discipline Act 1957 by virtue of the Coastguard Act 1925 s 2 (as amended) and the orders made under it, or by virtue of instructions issued by the Admiralty pursuant to the Defence (Auxiliary Coastguard) Regulations 1941, SR & O 1941/2059 (revoked): see the War Pensions (Coastguards) Scheme 1944 art 3.

682. Seamen and other persons employed abroad in the 1914–18 war.

The Injuries in War (Compensation) Acts 1914[1] conferred power to frame schemes as to pensions, allowances and other grants to be paid to persons, not being officers or men of any of the forces of the Crown, in respect of injuries or disablement suffered by them whilst employed afloat[2], or ashore outside the United Kingdom[3], in connection with warlike operations, and in the case of their death to their widows and other dependants[4]. A scheme in respect of injuries suffered by persons afloat was to be made by Order in Council[5] and may include persons not in the direct employment of the former Admiralty, Army or Air Council (now the Secretary of State for Defence), and persons employed on commissioned ships, notwithstanding that by reason of such employment they are subject[6] to naval discipline[7]. A scheme in respect of disablement suffered by persons ashore may also include persons not in such direct employment[8].

A separate scheme for merchant seamen was made after agreement between the government and an association of shipowners and mariners[9]. There must be paid out of money provided by Parliament or, if that money is insufficient, there must be charged on and paid out of the Consolidated Fund of the United Kingdom, such sums as are required for the purpose of fulfilling any obligations incurred before 15 August 1919 by the government of His late Majesty King George V in connection with the 1914–18 war relating to payments for compensation in respect of persons killed or injured on any merchant ship or fishing vessel[10].

1   See the Injuries in War (Compensation) Act 1914 (4 & 5 Geo 5 c 30); the Injuries in War (Compensation) Act 1914 (sess 2) (5 & 6 Geo 5 c 18).
2   A scheme in respect of persons employed afloat under the Admiralty, Army Council or Air Council was approved by Order in Council dated 27 May 1915, SR & O 1915/555 (amended by SR & O 1916/395; SR & O 1920/570; SR & O 1920/1307; SR & O 1920/2352; SR & O 1921/1690; SR & O 1924/1285; SI 1949/599; SI 1958/1266.
3   See the Injuries in War (Shore Employments) Compensation Scheme 1914, effective from 3 August 1914 (amended by schemes effective from 1 December 1917 and 1 January 1920 respectively; and by SI 1949/2285; SI 1953/699; SI 1955/1974; SI 1958/1003; SI 1961/1246; SI 1973/1635; SI 1974/1104; SI 1980/1731; SI 1981/1475; SI 1983/756; SI 1983/1713; SI 1985/299; SI 1985/1566; SI 1986/1095; SI 1987/529; SI 1988/624; SI 1989/420; SI 1990/946; SI 1991/911; SI 1993/807; SI 1993/1192; SI 1994/1012; SI 1995/979; SI 1996/573). For the meaning of 'United Kingdom' see para 502 note 4 ante.
4   See the Injuries in War (Compensation) Act 1914 s 1 (amended by the Defence (Transfer of Functions) (No 1) Order 1964, SI 1964/488, art 2, Sch 1 Pt I); the Injuries in War Compensation Act 1914 (sess 2) s 1(1) (as so amended), s 2; and the Air Force (Application of Enactments) (No 2) Order 1918, SR & O 1918/548.
5   Injuries in War (Compensation) Act 1914 s 1(1) (as amended: see note 4 supra).
6   Ie by virtue of what is now the Naval Discipline Act 1957 s 118 (as amended): see ROYAL FORCES.
7   See the Injuries in War (Compensation) Act 1914 s 1(2) (as amended: see note 4 supra).
8   See the Injuries in War (Compensation) Act 1914 (sess 2) s 1(2) (as amended: see note 4 supra).
9   See the Seamen's War Risks Compensation Scheme. The original authority for this was an agreement made on 14 October 1915 between the government and an association of shipowners and mariners known as the War Risks Association, and a similar agreement made with respect to the fishing industry in October 1916. These are now administered by the Secretary of State: see the Transfer of Functions (War Risks Compensation) Order 1953, SI 1953/1674. As to the Secretary of State see para 692 post.
10   Statute Law Revision Act 1958 s 4(1). As to the Consolidated Fund see CONSTITUTIONAL LAW AND HUMAN RIGHTS vol 8(2) (Reissue) para 711.

(iv) Miscellaneous Schemes

683. The Home Guard. There are two categories of Home Guard[1] for the purposes of pensions in respect of disablement or death. The first category comprises persons who served between 21 May 1940 and 31 December 1944, and for those persons pensions are provided under the Royal Warrant dated 21 December 1964[2], which applies the provisions of the service pensions order[3] with modifications[4]. The second category consists of male and female persons who, after 27 April 1952, were or are enrolled or re-engaged to serve in the Home Guard[5]. For them the service pensions order is also applied with modifications[6] by the Order by Her Majesty dated 22 December 1964, made under powers conferred by the Home Guard Act 1951[7].

Under both schemes, where a claim in respect of disablement or death is made, the disablement or death is accepted as due to service provided that (1) the disablement is due to an injury which is attributable to service or existed before or arose during service and has been and remains aggravated thereby; or (2) the death was due to or hastened by an injury which was attributable to service or the aggravation by service of an injury which existed before or arose during service[8]. Where the claim in respect of disablement was made not later than seven years after the termination of service as a member of the Home Guard, or the death occurred within that time and a claim is made at any time in respect of that death, there is no onus on the claimant to prove these conditions[9] and in all cases the benefit of any reasonable doubt as to their fulfilment must be given to the claimant[10]. 'Injury' for these purposes includes wound or disease but excludes (a) any injury due to the effects of tobacco; and (b) any injury due to the use of tobacco or the consumption of alcohol, except where the person concerned suffers from a mental condition attributable to service, the degree of disablement in respect of that condition has been assessed at 50 per cent or more and he started or continued to use tobacco or to consume or continue to consume alcohol due to that condition[11].

1 As to the Home Guard generally see ROYAL FORCES vol 41 paras 311–312.
2 See the Royal Warrant dated 21 December 1964 concerning Pensions and other Grants in respect of Disablement or Death due to service in the Home Guard (Cmnd 2563); (amended by Cmnd 5118; and by SI 1989/1335; SI 1993/597; SI 1994/771).
3 Ie the Naval, Military and Air Forces etc (Disablement and Death) Service Pensions Order 1983, SI 1983/883 (as amended): see para 662 et seq ante.
4 See the Royal Warrant dated 21 December 1964 arts 1(1), 2–5, Schedule; and the Naval, Military and Air Forces etc (Modification of Enactments and other Instruments) Order 1978, SI 1978/1526, art 2, Schedule Pt II; the Interpretation Act 1978 s 17(2).
5 See the Order by Her Majesty dated 22 December 1964 (Cmnd 2564); (amended by Cmnd 5119; and by SI 1989/1335; SI 1993/597; SI 1994/771). The Home Guard was stood down on 31 July 1957 and since then its activities have been suspended: see ROYAL FORCES vol 41 para 311.
6 For modifications see ibid arts 1(1), 3(1), Schedule; the Naval, Military and Air Forces etc (Modification of Enactments and other Instruments) Order 1978 Schedule Pt II; the Interpretation Act 1978 s 17(2).
7 See the Home Guard Act 1951 s 1(4) (as amended); and ROYAL FORCES para 311.
8 See the Royal Warrant dated 21 December 1964 arts 4(1), 5(1); the Order by Her Majesty dated 22 December 1964 arts 4(1), 5(1).
9 See the Royal Warrant dated 21 December 1964 art 4(2); the Order by Her Majesty dated 22 December 1964 art 4(2).
10 See the Royal Warrant dated 21 December 1964 arts 4(1), 5(4); the Order by Her Majesty dated 22 December 1964 arts 4(2), 5(4).
11 See the Royal Warrant dated 21 December 1964 art 1(3); the Order by Her Majesty dated 22 December 1964 art 1(3) (both substituted by SI 1994/771). For the meaning of 'war injury' generally see para 667 ante.

684. Polish forces. Power was conferred on the then Minister of Pensions (now the Secretary of State)[1] to make a scheme, with the consent of the Treasury, for applying the provisions of the service pensions order[2] to certain members of the former Polish forces[3] in relation to their disablement or death in consequence of service under British command[4]. The Pensions (Polish Forces) Scheme 1964[5] applies the service pensions order for those purposes with certain modifications[6]. No award or continued payment under an existing award may be made to or in respect of a member of the Polish forces in whose case the Secretary of State is satisfied that he is, or since the termination of his service has been or has become, resident in Poland[7] and the scheme is limited to payments which fall due for payment before 27 March 1997[8], but this period may be extended beyond that date by orders made by the Secretary of State with the consent of the Treasury[9].

In determining whether a pension is payable to a person as a widow under the scheme in respect of any period beginning on or after 19 July 1995, no account may be taken of the fact that the widow has married another if, before the beginning of that period, the marriage has been terminated or the parties have been judicially separated[10].

1   As to the Secretary of State see para 692 post.
2   Ie the Naval, Military and Air Forces etc (Disablement and Death) Service Pensions Order 1983, SI 1983/883 (as amended): see para 662 et seq ante.
3   Ie to members of the Polish naval detachment mentioned in the agreement between the United Kingdom government and the government of Poland on 18 November 1939, members of the Polish armed forces organised and employed under British command in pursuance of the agreement made between those governments on 5 August 1940, and members of the Polish resettlement forces: Polish Resettlement Act 1947 s 1(1); and see the Pensions (Polish Forces) Scheme 1964, SI 1964/2007, art 2(5). The 'Polish resettlement forces' means the Polish Resettlement Corps, the Polish Resettlement Corps (Royal Air Force) and the Polish Resettlement Sections of the Auxiliary Territorial Service and the Women's Auxiliary Air Force: see the Polish Resettlement Act 1947 s 10(1); the Pensions (Polish Forces) Scheme 1964 art 2(8).
4   See the Polish Resettlement Act 1947 ss 1(1), 10(2); the Naval, Military and Air Forces etc (Modification of Enactments and other Instruments) Order 1978, SI 1978/1526, art 2, Schedule Pt II; and the Interpretation Act 1978 s 17(2).
5   Ie the Pensions (Polish Forces) Scheme 1964, SI 1964/2007 (amended by SI 1972/95; SI 1972/1435; SI 1974/1045; SI 1978/1526; SI 1981/1876; SI 1992/317).
6   See ibid arts 2(9), 6, Sch 2; the Naval, Military and Air Forces etc (Modification of Enactments and other Instruments) Order 1978 Schedule Pt II; and the Interpretation Act 1978 s 17(2).
7   See the Pensions (Polish Forces) Scheme 1964 art 11. An allowance for a dependant not resident in Poland is not precluded by reason of residence there at some time since the termination of the member's service: see art 11 proviso.
8   See ibid art 14(1) (amended by SI 1972/95; SI 1981/1876; SI 1992/317). The original period for which a scheme might be made was five years but power was conferred to extend that period: see the Polish Resettlement Act 1947 s 1(1) proviso.
9   See ibid s 1(1) proviso.
10   Pensions Act 1995 s 168(1), (3)(c). For the meaning of references to the termination of a marriage and to judicial separation for these purposes see para 663 note 16 ante.

(3) WAR PENSIONS COMMITTEES

685. Establishment and membership of war pensions committees.

War pensions committees were originally constituted to deal with matters respecting pensions arising out of service in the 1914–18 war[1]. The Social Security Act 1989 repealed the relevant parts of the War Pensions Act 1921 dealing with war pensions committees and provided for the establishment and functions of these committees[2].

The Secretary of State[3] may by regulations[4] establish committees, known as war pensions committees, for such areas as may be specified by the regulations[5]. The regulations may, in particular, include provisions with respect to the membership of the committees, the manner in which the members are to be appointed and the period for which, and the terms on which, they are to hold office and the manner in which they may be removed[6].

Each of the specified areas[7] must have a war pensions committee, appropriately named[8]. Each committee, other than that for Northern Ireland, consists of 30 members appointed by the Secretary of State[9]. So far as practicable, the members so appointed must include:

(1)   12 members representative of war disablement pensioners[10];
(2)   three members representative of war widows[11];
(3)   five members representative of voluntary organisations engaged wholly or partly in the care of ex-servicemen or ex-servicewomen or the families of ex-servicemen or ex-servicewomen in the committee's area;
(4)   four members each of whom has been nominated by a local authority[12] exercising functions in any part of the area for which the committee is appointed[13].

Before appointing the members of such a committee, the Secretary of State must consult such bodies or organisations in the area which represent any of the interests referred to in heads (1) to (3) above as he thinks fit[14].

1   See the War Pensions Act 1921 ss 1, 2 (repealed).
2   See the Social Security Act 1989 s 25(6)(a).
3   As to the Secretary of State see para 692 post.
4   The power to make such regulations is exercisable by statutory instrument, subject to annulment in pursuance of a resolution of either House of Parliament: see the Social Security Act 1989 s 29(1), (3); the Social Security Contributions and Benefits Act 1992 s 175(2).
5   Social Security Act 1989 s 25(1). In exercise of the power so conferred, the Secretary of State has made the War Pensions Committees Regulations 1990, SI 1990/1349 (amended by SI 1995/3119; SI 1996/1790), which came into force on 1 January 1991: reg 1(1).
6   Social Security Act 1989 s 25(1)(a), (c).
7   Ie the areas specified in the War Pensions Committees Regulations 1990 regs 1(2), 2(1), Sch 1 col 2 (substituted by SI 1995/3119; amended by SI 1996/1790).
8   See ibid reg 2(1), (2), Sch 1 col 1 (as substituted: see note 7 supra).
9   Ibid reg 3(1). As to the committee for Northern Ireland see reg 4.
10 'War disablement pensioner' means a person in receipt of a war pension in respect of his disablement: ibid reg 1(2). 'War pension' means (1) any pension or other benefit, payable otherwise than under an enactment, for or in respect of a person who has died or been disabled in consequence of service as a member of the armed forces of the Crown; (2) any pension or benefit awarded under the Personal Injuries (Emergency Provisions) Act 1939 (see para 668 et seq ante); the Pensions (Navy, Army, Air Force and Mercantile Marine) Act 1939 (see para 676 et seq ante); or the Polish Resettlement Act 1947 (see para 684 ante); (3) any pension or other payment which constitutes such an obligation as is mentioned in the Statute Law Revision Act 1958 s 4(1) (see para 682 ante); (4) any other pension or benefit which is specified in an order made by the Secretary of State for these purposes; but does not include any pension administered by the Defence Council, the Minister of the Crown with responsibility for defence or the Commissioners for the Royal Hospital for Soldiers at Chelsea: Social Security Act 1989 s 25(4).
11 'War widow' means a widow who receives a war pension in respect of the death of her husband: War Pensions Committees Regulations 1990 reg 1(2).
12 'Local authority' means, in relation to a war pensions committee, (1) in England, the council of a county, district or London borough, the Council of the Isles of Scilly, the Common Council of the City of London, or a shadow authority, within the meaning of the Local Government Changes for England Regulations 1994, SI 1994/867 (see LOCAL GOVERNMENT), but excludes a council listed in the War Pensions Committees Regulations 1990 reg 1(2), Sch 1A (added by SI 1995/3119) (excepted authorities); (2) in Wales, a new principal council within the meaning of the Local Government Act 1972 s 21 (substituted by the Local Government (Wales) Act 1994 s 2): War Pensions Committees Regulations 1990 reg 1(2) (definition added by SI 1995/3119).
13 Ibid reg 3(3) (amended by SI 1995/3119).
14 Ibid reg 3(2).

686. Constitution and proceedings of committees. A member of a war pensions committee[1] holds office for a period not exceeding five years in any one term of appointment and may be reappointed[2]. He may resign by notice in writing sent to the Secretary of State[3] and may be removed by the Secretary of State on certain grounds[4]. A casual vacancy may be filled by the Secretary of State as may be necessary[5].

Each committee must appoint from among its members a chairman and vice-chairman[6]. The appointment must be by resolution specifying the period of appointment, which is not to extend beyond the appointee's term of appointment to the committee[7]. The first chairmen and vice-chairmen of the committees were appointed by the Secretary of State to hold office for the year commencing 1 January 1991 only[8].

The chairman or, in his absence, the vice-chairman, presides over committee meetings and where both are absent the members present must elect one of their number to act as chairman for that meeting[9].

The committee decides the time and place of its meetings[10]. Six members may requisition a meeting by giving notice in writing to the chairman who must call the meeting within four weeks of receiving the notice[11]. The quorum is one-quarter of the committee's members, disregarding any fractions[12], and decisions must be made by a simple majority of members present and voting[13].

A member may neither discuss nor vote on any matter concerning his relative, employer or employee[14].

A committee determines whether persons other than members may attend any of its meetings, but the Chief Welfare Officer or his deputy may attend any meeting of a committee or sub-committee[15]. Sub-committees may be appointed to carry out certain functions[16] of the committee[17]. A sub-committee which considers a complaint made to the committee by a person receiving or claiming war pension[18] must, as soon as reasonably practicable, submit to the committee a report about any hearing the sub-committee had of the complaint and any representations made by it to the Secretary of State[19].

Minutes of a meeting must be recorded in a minute book, and must include the names of members present at the meeting, be signed by the person presiding over the meeting at which they are approved as correct and be open to inspection by the Secretary of State[20].

1   As to the establishment and membership of war pensions committees see para 685 ante.
2   War Pensions Committees Regulations 1990, SI 1990/1349, reg 5, Sch 2 para 1.
3   Ibid Sch 2 para 4. As to the Secretary of State see para 692 post.
4   See ibid Sch 2 para 2. The Secretary of State may remove a member from office if he is satisfied that the member (1) is habitually absent from meetings of the committee or has been absent from three or more consecutive meetings, unless the absence is due to illness or due to a reason approved by the Secretary of State; (2) has become bankrupt or made an arrangement with his creditors; (3) is convicted of a crime and is sentenced to imprisonment or receives a suspended sentence; or (4) is otherwise unable or unfit to discharge the functions of a member: Sch 2 para 2(a)–(d).
5   Ibid Sch 2 para 3.
6   Ibid Sch 2 para 5(1). Where either office falls vacant, a replacement must be appointed at the next meeting: Sch 2 para 5(3).
7   Ibid Sch 2 para 5(2).
8   See ibid Sch 2 para 5(4).
9   Ibid Sch 2 para 6.
10   Ibid Sch 2 para 7(1). The Secretary of State decides the time and place of the first meeting after appointing or reappointing the members of a committee, apart from an appointment to fill a casual vacancy: Sch 2 para 7(2).
11   Ibid Sch 2 para 8.
12   Ibid Sch 2 para 9.
13   Ibid Sch 2 para 10. The person presiding over the meeting has a casting vote: Sch 2 para 10.
14   Ibid Sch 2 para 11.
15   Ibid Sch 2 para 12(1), (2). 'Chief Welfare Officer' means an officer of the Secretary of State who manages the War Pensioners' Welfare Service: reg 1(2).
16   Ie functions (1) under ibid reg 6(b)–(d) (see para 687 post); or (2) with the Secretary of State's approval, under reg 6(a) (see para 687 post): Sch 2 paras 14, 15(1). In the case of head (1) supra, up to four-fifths of the members of a committee may be appointed to a sub-committee: Sch 2 para 14. In the case of head (2) supra, the sub-committee must consist of at least three and not more than seven members, of whom at least half are members of the committee and any remainder are voluntary workers: Sch 2 para 15(3)(a). The sub-committee must make decisions by a simple majority and act in accordance with any directions of the committee: Sch 2 para 15(3)(b), (c). A committee must appoint as chairman of such a sub-committee a member of the committee who is also a member of the sub-committee, and he has a casting vote: see Sch 2 para 15(2), (3)(b).
17   See ibid Sch 2 paras 14, 15(1).
18   For the meaning of 'war pension' see para 685 note 10 ante.
19   War Pensions Committees Regulations 1990 Sch 2 para 16.
20   Ibid Sch 2 para 13.

687. Functions of committees. War pensions committees[1] have such functions relating to war pensions[2] and war pensioners[3] as may be conferred upon them by the regulations[4]; and the regulations may, in particular, provide that it is a committee's function to:

(1) consider any matter connected with war pensions or affecting war pensioners in its area[5] and, where appropriate, make recommendations to the Secretary of State[6] about that matter[7];

(2) consider complaints made to the committee by persons receiving or claiming war pensions, and, if the committee thinks fit, make representations about those complaints to the Secretary of State[8];

(3) consider any matter referred to the committee by the Secretary of State and report to him on those matters with such recommendations as the committee thinks fit[9]; and

(4) assist the War Pensioners' Welfare Service in looking after the welfare of war pensioners in its area[10].

The regulations may also include provisions with respect to the manner in which the committees are to discharge the functions conferred on them and they must exercise their functions subject to, and in accordance with, any such provisions[11].

A war pensions committee must consider the complaints and other matters referred to above, including any reports by the Secretary of State about the work of the War Pensioners' Welfare Service in its area[12] and must assist that welfare service as mentioned in head (4) above[13]. Any recommendations or representations which a committee makes to the Secretary of State must be by way of a resolution submitted to the Chief Welfare Officer[14].

A committee may request the Secretary of State to supply it with reports relevant to any matter which it is considering and must make any such request through the Chief Welfare Officer[15]. After consulting that officer, it may appoint voluntary workers to assist either the committee or a sub-committee to carry out its functions in relation to complaints by persons receiving or claiming war pension and assisting the War Pensioners' Welfare Service[16].

A committee or sub-committee in receipt of funds from charitable or other sources for the purpose of assisting the War Pensioners' Welfare Service must safeguard those funds and keep proper written accounts of all receipts and disbursements[17]. The accounts must be open to inspection by the Secretary of State[18].

1   As to the establishment and membership of war pensions committees see para 685 ante; and as to their constitution and proceedings see para 686 ante.
2   For the meaning of 'war pension' see para 685 note 10 ante.
3   'War pensioner' means a person in receipt of a war pension, in his capacity as such a pensioner: Social Security Act 1989 s 25(4).
4   Ibid s 25(2).
5   As to a committee's area see para 685 ante.
6   As to the Secretary of State see para 692 post.
7   Social Security Act 1989 s 25(2)(a); and see the War Pensions Committees Regulations 1990, SI 1990/1349, reg 6(d).
8   Social Security Act 1989 s 25(2)(b); and see the War Pensions Committees Regulations 1990 reg 6(a).
9   Social Security Act 1989 s 25(2)(c); and see the War Pensions Committees Regulations 1990 reg 6(b).
10 Social Security Act 1989 s 25(2)(d); and see the War Pensions Committees Regulations 1990 reg 6(c).
11 Social Security Act 1989 s 25(3).
12 See the War Pensions Committees Regulations 1990 reg 6(a), (b), (d), (e).
13 See ibid reg 6(c).
14 Ibid reg 7. For the meaning of 'Chief Welfare Officer' see para 686 note 15 ante.
15 Ibid reg 8.
16 Ibid reg 9.

17   Ibid reg 10(1). As to charities for ex-servicemen see ROYAL FORCES vol 41 para 357 et seq.
18   Ibid reg 10(2).

688. The central advisory committee. There must be a central advisory committee constituted, consisting of officers of the Department of Social Security[1], both local and central, ex-servicemen, and representatives of any war pensions committees[2] for the time being in existence, to consider such matters as may be put before that committee by the Secretary of State[3] for its advice[4]. The Secretary of State must ensure that the central advisory committee includes the chairmen of not less than 12 of the war pensions committees and includes at least one war disabled pensioner, and must cause that central advisory committee to be convened at least once in every year[5].

1   The statutory wording is 'Ministry', referring to the then Ministry of Pensions; but see para 692 post.
2   Ie any committees constituted under the Social Security Act 1989 s 25: see para 685 et seq ante.
3   As to the Secretary of State see para 692 post.
4   War Pensions Act 1921 s 3 (amended by the Social Security Act 1989 s 25(6)(b)).
5   Chronically Sick and Disabled Persons Act 1970 s 9(1) (amended by the Social Security Act 1989 s 25(5)).

(4) REVIEWS, DISQUALIFICATION AND FORFEITURE

689. Review of decisions, assessments and awards. Any decision accepting or rejecting a claim for pension, any assessment of the degree of disablement of a member of the armed forces or of a person to whom the civilian injuries scheme[1] applies or any final decision that there is no disablement or that the disablement has come to an end, in the case of a member of the armed forces, or that it is not or is no longer serious, in the case of a person to whom the civilian injuries scheme applies, may be reviewed by the Secretary of State[2] at any time on any ground[3].

Any award under the service pensions order[4] or the civilian injuries scheme may be reviewed by the Secretary of State at any time if he is satisfied that:

(1)   it was made in consequence of ignorance of, or a mistake as to, a material fact, or of a mistake as to the law;

(2)   there has been any relevant change of circumstances since the award was made; or

(3)   it was based on any decision or assessment such as is mentioned above, and that decision or assessment has been revised[5].

On such a review the Secretary of State may maintain, or continue, vary or cancel the decision, assessment or award and any revised decision, assessment or award must be such as may be appropriate having regard to the provisions of the relevant order or scheme[6].

1   Ie the Personal Injuries (Civilians) Scheme 1983, SI 1983/686 (as amended): see para 668 et seq ante.
2   As to the Secretary of State see para 692 post.
3   See the Naval, Military and Air Forces etc (Disablement and Death) Service Pensions Order 1983, SI 1983/883, art 67(1) (amended by SI 1994/772); the Personal Injuries (Civilians) Scheme 1983 art 76(1).
4   Ie the Naval, Military and Air Forces etc (Disablement and Death) Service Pensions Order 1983 (as amended): see para 662 et seq ante.
5   See ibid art 67(2) (amended by SI 1985/1201; SI 1994/772); the Personal Injuries (Civilians) Scheme 1983 art 76(2) (amended by SI 1985/1313).
6   See the Naval, Military and Air Forces etc (Disablement and Death) Service Pensions Order 1983 art 67(5); the Personal Injuries (Civilians) Scheme 1983 art 76(5). An award may only be revised to the detriment of a person in limited circumstances: see the Naval, Military and Air Forces etc (Disablement and Death) Service Pensions Order 1983 art 67(3), (4) (amended by SI 1984/1154); the Personal Injuries (Civilians) Scheme 1983 art 76(3), (4) (amended by SI 1984/1289). Special provision is made for the review of decisions, assessments and awards relating to the death or disablement of a member of the armed forces

which is due to service before or during the 1914–18 war: see the Naval, Military and Air Forces etc (Disablement and Death) Service Pensions Order 1983 art 67(8)–(11) (amended by SI 1996/1638).

690. Disqualification and forfeiture. The Secretary of State[1] may withhold, cancel or reduce any award which might otherwise be payable[2] where the injury[3] giving rise to the disablement or death in respect of which the claim is made was caused or contributed to by the serious negligence or misconduct[4] of the person concerned[5]. Where a person to or in respect of whom a pension or gratuity may be or has been awarded is, or was at the date of his death:

(1) imprisoned or detained in pursuance of a sentence or order of the court upon his being found guilty of an offence[6]; or

(2) deported from, required to leave or prohibited from entering the United Kingdom[7]; or

(3) in the case of a person to whom the civilian injuries scheme applies, an enemy alien and, as such, interned, detained or expelled from the United Kingdom[8],

the Secretary of State may withhold the award of the pension or gratuity or, if it has been awarded, direct that it is to be forfeited[9]. He may, however, subsequently restore it in whole or in part on such terms and from such date as he thinks fit[10].

A widow's or other adult dependant's pension (other than any pension awarded to a parent) ceases to be payable if the widow or dependant cohabits with another person as a spouse, but may be restored on cessation of the cohabitation where the Secretary of State sees fit[11]. Widows' pensions which ceased on remarriage are now restored where the subsequent marriage is terminated or where the parties to it become judicially separated[12].

Where the Secretary of State is satisfied that a person who has sustained an injury should, in his own interests, receive medical, surgical or rehabilitative treatment for his disablement but he unreasonably[13] refuses or neglects to undergo the treatment, the Secretary of State may withhold, cancel or reduce the award in the case of a person to whom the civilian injuries scheme applies[14] and may reduce any disablement pension by not more than half in the case of a member of the armed forces[15].

Where the Secretary of State is satisfied that a sum is due to the Crown or to a Secretary of State, a minister or government department from a person to or in respect of whom a pension or gratuity may be or has been awarded, or that an overpayment has been made to him by the Crown, the Secretary of State may deduct such amounts at such times as he thinks fit from the pension or other payment and apply the amounts so deducted in or towards the sum so due or the overpayment[16].

Where a person fails to draw his pension for a continuous period of not less than 12 months, the award may be cancelled and payment of any arrears may be withheld[17].

1 As to the Secretary of State see para 692 post. As to appeals from his decisions see para 691 post; and ROYAL FORCES vol 41 para 352 et seq.

2 Ie under the Naval, Military and Air Forces etc (Disablement and Death) Service Pensions Order 1983, SI 1983/883 (as amended) ('the service pensions order') (see para 662 et seq ante); or the Personal Injuries (Civilians) Scheme 1983, SI 1983/686 (as amended) ('the civilian injuries scheme') (see para 668 et seq ante). As to the other schemes applying the service pensions order with modifications see para 679 et seq ante.

3 For the meaning of 'injury' see para 662 ante (service pensions order), para 683 ante (Home Guard scheme); and for the meaning of 'qualifying injury' for the purposes of the civilian injuries scheme see para 668 note 4 ante.

4 The word 'serious' qualifies both negligence and misconduct: *Robertson v Minister of Pensions* (1952) 5 WPAR 245 at 266 per Ormerod J. In considering a motoring accident it may be taken into account whether the driving was of such a quality as would call for some criminal action in civil life: *Robertson v Minister of Pensions* supra at 266 per Ormerod J. However, Ormerod J explained that this statement was made only in argument in that case. It was not a prerequisite: see *Minister of Pensions and National Insurance v Griseti* (1955) 5 WPAR 457 (where unauthorised interference with enemy ammunition was

held to constitute serious negligence or misconduct, even though the man's conduct would not in civilian life have rendered him liable to prosecution). See also *Williams (H) v Minister of Pensions* [1947] 2 All ER 564, (1947) 1 WPAR 755, where a claimant had shot himself in the foot while cleaning his rifle. Cf where the chain of causation is broken by serious negligence or misconduct: see *Smith v Davey Paxman & Co (Colchester) Ltd* [1943] 1 All ER 286, CA, distinguished in *Minister of Pensions v Williams (OL)* [1947] KB 875, [1947] 2 All ER 93.

5   See the Naval, Military and Air Forces etc (Disablement and Death) Service Pensions Order 1983 art 6; the Personal Injuries (Civilians) Scheme 1983 art 6.

6   See the Naval, Military and Air Forces etc (Disablement and Death) Service Pensions Order 1983 art 62(1)(a); the Personal Injuries (Civilians) Scheme 1983 art 68(1)(a) (both amended by virtue of the Criminal Justice Act 1988 s 123(6), Sch 8 paras 1–3 to include references to detention in a young offenders institution).

7   This extends, in the case of a person to whom the service pensions order applies, to the Isle of Man, or, in the case of a person to whom the civilian injuries scheme applies, to Great Britain or Northern Ireland: see the Naval, Military and Air Forces etc (Disablement and Death) Service Pensions Order 1983 art 62(1)(b); the Personal Injuries (Civilians) Scheme 1983 art 68(1)(c). This also applies where such a person has had his certificate of naturalisation revoked: see the Naval, Military and Air Forces etc (Disablement and Death) Service Pensions Order 1983 art 62(1)(b); the Personal Injuries (Civilians) Scheme 1983 art 68(1)(c). For the meaning of 'United Kingdom' see para 502 note 4 ante.

8   Personal Injuries (Civilians) Scheme 1983 art 68(1)(b).

9   See the Naval, Military and Air Forces etc (Disablement and Death) Service Pensions Order 1983 art 62(1); the Personal Injuries (Civilians) Scheme 1983 art 68(1).

10   See the Naval, Military and Air Forces etc (Disablement and Death) Service Pensions Order 1983 art 62(2); the Personal Injuries (Civilians) Scheme 1983 art 68(2).

11   See the Naval, Military and Air Forces etc (Disablement and Death) Service Pensions Order 1983 art 42 (amended by SI 1984/1154; SI 1993/598; SI 1996/732); the Personal Injuries (Civilians) Scheme 1983 art 71 (amended by SI 1984/1289; SI 1993/480).

12   See the Pensions Act 1995 s 168; and paras 663, 674, 680, 684 ante.

13   Ie unreasonably in the opinion of the Secretary of State: see the Naval, Military and Air Forces etc (Disablement and Death) Service Pensions Order 1983 art 63(1); the Personal Injuries (Civilians) Scheme 1983 art 69(1). Misconduct on the part of a person which renders it necessary, in the opinion of the Secretary of State, for that person's treatment to be discontinued may be regarded as a refusal to receive treatment: Naval, Military and Air Forces etc (Disablement and Death) Service Pensions Order 1983 art 63(2); Personal Injuries (Civilians) Scheme 1983 art 69(2).

14   See ibid art 69(1).

15   See the Naval, Military and Air Forces etc (Disablement and Death) Service Pensions Order 1983 art 63(1).

16   See ibid art 60(1); and the Personal Injuries (Civilians) Scheme 1983 s 66(1) (amended by SI 1987/191).

17   See the Naval, Military and Air Forces etc (Disablement and Death) Service Pensions Order 1983 art 64(1); the Personal Injuries (Civilians) Scheme 1983 art 73(1).

(5) APPEALS

691. Rights of appeal. An appeal lies to a pensions appeal tribunal[1] against the following decisions by the Secretary of State[2]:

(1)   the rejection of any claim under the service pensions order[3] in respect of the disablement of any person on the ground that the injury[4] on which the claim is based is not attributable to any relevant service[5] and does not fulfil the required conditions[6];

(2)   the rejection of any claim under that order in respect of the death of any person on the ground that the necessary conditions are not fulfilled[7];

(3)   the rejection of any claim in respect of the disablement or death of any person made under the mercantile marine scheme[8] or the scheme for coastguards[9] on the grounds that the disablement or death of that person is not directly attributable to a war injury[10], war risk injury[11] or detention[12] or that the case is not one in which the specified conditions[13] are fulfilled[14];

(4)   the rejection of any claim in respect of the incapacity for work, disablement or death of any person made under the civilian injuries scheme[15] on the ground that the incapacity or disablement was not caused by, or the death was not the direct

result of, a war injury or, in the case of a civil defence volunteer[16], a war service injury[17];

 (5) the withholding or reduction of any award mentioned in heads (1) to (4) above on the ground that the injury or detention on which the claim is based was caused or contributed to by the serious negligence or misconduct of the person in question or, as the case may be, that his death was so caused or contributed to[18];

(6) the interim assessment of the degree of disablement of any person in the case of any such claim as is referred to in heads (1) to (4) above[19];

(7) the final assessment of the degree or nature of such disablement or a decision that there is no disablement, or that the disablement has come to an end or is not, or is no longer, serious or prolonged[20].

Notice of appeal must be given in the prescribed manner[21] and within the prescribed time limits[22].

Payment of a pension or gratuity may be suspended in whole or in part pending the determination of any such appeal[23].

1 As to the constitution and procedure of pensions appeal tribunals see ROYAL FORCES vol 41 para 355 et seq.

2 As to the Secretary of State see para 692 post.

3 Ie under the Naval, Military and Air Forces etc (Disablement and Death) Service Pensions Order 1983, SI 1983/883 (as amended) (see para 662 et seq ante) or under any such Royal Warrant, Order in Council or Order of His late Majesty or of Her Majesty as is administered by the Secretary of State: see the Pensions Appeal Tribunals Act 1943 s 1(1). As to such warrants and orders see eg the scheme for the Home Guard discussed in para 683 ante.

4 'Injury' includes wound or disease: Pensions Appeal Tribunals Act 1943 s 12(1). See also para 662 ante.

5 'Relevant service' means any service which, under the Royal Warrant, Order in Council or other order in question, is relevant for the purposes of that claim: ibid s 12(1) (definition substituted by the Pensions Appeal Tribunals Act 1949 s 1(1)).

6 See the Pensions Appeal Tribunals Act 1943 s 1(1), (2) (as amended); and ROYAL FORCES vol 41 para 352.

7 See ibid s 1(3) (as amended); s 1(3A) (as added); and ROYAL FORCES vol 41 para 352.

8 Ie under the War Pensions (Mercantile Marine) Scheme 1964, SI 1964/2058 (as amended): see para 679 et seq ante.

9 Ie under the War Pensions (Coastguards) Scheme 1944, SR & O 1944/500 (as amended): see para 681 ante.

10 For the meaning of 'war injury' see para 667 ante (definition applied by the Pensions Appeal Tribunals Act 1943 s 12(1)).

11 'War risk injury' means an injury falling within the Pensions (Mercantile Marine) Act 1942 s 1 (as amended) (see para 676 note 7 ante), except that, in relation to the persons referred to in s 4(4) (certain salvage workers: see para 677 note 11 ante), it means an injury falling within s 1 (as amended) as amended by s 4(4): Pensions Appeal Tribunals Act 1943 s 12(1).

12 For the meaning of 'detention' see para 676 note 4 ante (definition applied by ibid s 12(1)).

13 Ie that the case is not one in which (1) the person in question is to be treated for the purpose of the Pensions (Navy, Army, Air Force and Mercantile Marine) Act 1939 s 3 (as amended) (see para 676 ante) as having sustained the injury or suffered the detention by reason of his service as a mariner in a British ship; or (2) that person is to be treated for the purpose of s 4 (as amended) as having sustained the injury or suffered the detention by reason of his service; or (3) the injury was sustained in the circumstances specified in a scheme made under s 5 (as amended) (see para 678 ante) or the detention was caused by reason of his service in a ship forming part of the navy: see the Pensions Appeal Tribunals Act 1943 s 2(1)(a)–(d).

14 See ibid s 2(1). Where the Secretary of State rejects any such claim on one of the specified grounds and an appeal is brought from his decision, he must notify the appellant before the hearing that he also rejects the claim on the other specified ground, and thereupon the tribunal must treat the appeal as an appeal on the issue whether the claim was rightly rejected on both those grounds, and unless he does so, he is not entitled, if the appeal is allowed, subsequently to reject the claim on the other ground: s 2(2).

15 Ie under the Personal Injuries (Civilians) Scheme 1983, SI 1983/686 (as amended): see para 668 et seq ante.

16 For the meaning of 'civil defence volunteer' see para 668 note 5 ante (definition applied by the Pensions Appeal Tribunals Act 1943 s 12(1)).

17 See ibid s 3(1). For the meaning of 'war service injury' see para 668 note 5 ante (definition applied by s 12(1)). The Secretary of State must notify the claimant of his decision, specifying that it is made on that ground: s 3(1). Where an appeal is so brought in any case where the Secretary of State has refused to certify an injury sustained by a civil defence volunteer as a war service injury or has revoked such a certificate, the tribunal must consider whether it is a physical injury which arose out of and in the course of the performance by the volunteer of his duties as a member of the civil defence organisation to which he belonged at the time when the injury was sustained, and, except in the case of a war injury, did not arise out of and in the course of his employment in any other capacity, and if the tribunal decides that question in the affirmative, the injury is deemed to have been certified by the Secretary of State as a war service injury: s 3(2). As to the meaning of 'physical injury' see para 667 ante (definition applied by s 3(2)).

18 See ibid s 4(1), (2); and ROYAL FORCES vol 41 para 352.

19 See ibid s 5(1) (as amended); and ROYAL FORCES vol 41 para 353.

20 See ibid s 5(2) (as amended); and ROYAL FORCES vol 41 para 353.

21 See ROYAL FORCES vol 41 para 354.

22 See the Pensions Appeal Tribunals Act 1943 s 8 (as amended); and ROYAL FORCES vol 41 para 354.

23 See the Naval, Military and Air Forces etc (Disablement and Death) Service Pensions Order 1983 art 67A (added by SI 1994/772); the Personal Injuries (Civilians) Scheme 1983 art 76A (added by SI 1994/715).

(6) THE SECRETARY OF STATE

692. Devolution of pensions powers on the Secretary of State for Social Security. The Ministry of Pensions was established by the Ministry of Pensions Act 1916, under which the powers and duties of the Admiralty, the Commissioners of the Royal Hospital for Soldiers at Chelsea and of the Army Council and the Secretary of State for War with regard to pensions, other than purely service pensions, were transferred to the Minister of Pensions[1]. Similar powers in relation to the air force were conferred on the minister by the Air Force (Constitution) Act 1917[2]. The minister also took over the functions of the statutory committee of the Royal Patriotic Fund[3] under powers conferred on him by the Naval and Military War Pensions etc (Transfer of Powers) Act 1917[4]. By the War Pensions Act 1920[5] the minister was divested of the responsibility of administering pensions in respect of service after 30 September 1921[6], but responsibility for disability pensions in respect of service in the armed forces after 2 September 1939 was conferred on him by the Pensions (Navy, Army, Air Force and Mercantile Marine) Act 1939[7], and for civilians suffering war injuries or, being civil defence volunteers, war service injuries by the Personal Injuries (Emergency Provisions) Act 1939[8].

The Ministry of Pensions was dissolved on 31 August 1953, and the functions of the minister in relation to pensions[9] were transferred to the Minister of National Insurance, who was re-styled the Minister of Pensions and National Insurance[10]. The Ministry of Pensions and National Insurance was dissolved in 1966 and the functions of the Minister of Pensions and National Insurance were transferred to the Minister of Social Security[11], whose functions were transferred in 1968 to the Secretary of State for Social Services[12]. Those functions were further transferred in 1988 to the Secretary of State for Social Security[13] who is now responsible for the administration of war pensions schemes[14].

1 See the Ministry of Pensions Act 1916 s 2 (repealed).

2 Air Force (Constitution) Act 1917 s 2(3) proviso (as originally enacted).

3 See the Naval and Military War Pensions etc Act 1915 s 3 (as originally enacted). As to the Royal Patriotic Fund see ROYAL FORCES vol 41 para 357.

4 See the Naval and Military War Pensions etc (Transfer of Powers) Act 1917 s 1 (repealed).

5 See the War Pensions Act 1920 s 1 (as originally enacted).

6 Ie 30 days after the date fixed for the termination of the 1914–18 war: see the Termination of the Present War (Definition) Act 1918 s 1 (repealed); the War Pensions Act 1920 ss 1(1), 2 (as originally enacted); and the Order in Council dated 10 August 1921, SR & O 1921/1276.

7 See the Pensions (Navy, Army, Air Force and Mercantile Marine) Act 1939 s 1 (repealed).

8   See the Personal Injuries (Emergency Provisions) Act 1939 s 1; and para 668 ante. It follows that the minister was responsible for administering all pensions resulting from injuries suffered in service except service between 1 October 1921 and 2 September 1939, and service otherwise than in war before August 1914.

9   The functions of the Minister of Pensions so far as they related to medical and surgical treatment (including the supply and repair of artificial limbs and other appliances) and the provision of vehicles in England and Wales were transferred to the Minister of Health: Transfer of Functions (Ministry of Pensions) Order 1953, SI 1953/1198, arts 1 (3), 2(1)(a).

10 Ibid arts 2(1)(c), 3(1), made under the Ministers of the Crown (Transfer of Functions) Act 1946 (repealed).

11 See the Supplementary Benefit Act 1966 s 2(1)(a) (repealed). That Act was formerly called the Ministry of Social Security Act 1966: see the Social Security Act 1973 s 99(18) (repealed).

12 See the Secretary of State for Social Services Order 1968, SI 1968/1699, arts 2, 3.

13 See the Transfer of Functions (Health and Social Security) Order 1988, SI 1988/1843. As to the Secretary of State for Social Security see CONSTITUTIONAL LAW AND HUMAN RIGHTS vol 8(2) (Reissue) para 503.

14 See eg the Naval, Military and Air Forces etc (Disablement and Death) Service Pensions Order 1983, SI 1983/883, art 70; the Personal Injuries (Civilians) Scheme 1983, SI 1983/686, art 80. Payment of war pensions is undertaken by the War Pensions Agency (or Social Security War Pensions Agency), an executive agency within the Department of Social Security: see CONSTITUTIONAL LAW AND HUMAN RIGHTS vol 8(2) (Reissue) para 504.

693. Care of war orphans and neglected children. The Secretary of State[1] must make provision for the care of any children (including illegitimate children) of members of the armed forces who have died from causes arising out of their service in the 1914–18 war if those children are suffering from neglect or want of proper care[2]; and for neglected children in the United Kingdom[3] or the Isle of Man to or in respect of whom any pension is being paid on account of the death of a parent since 3 September 1939 under the service pensions order[4] or any of the schemes[5] providing similar benefits[6].

1   As to the Secretary of State see para 692 ante.

2   See the War Pensions (Administrative Provisions) Act 1918 s 9(1) (amended by virtue of the Secretary of State for Social Services Order 1968, SI 1968/1699, art 5(4)(a)). In practice no such cases are now likely to arise.

3   For the meaning of 'United Kingdom' see para 502 note 4 ante.

4   Ie under the Naval, Military and Air Forces etc (Disablement and Death) Service Pensions Order 1983, SI 1983/883 (as amended): see para 662 et seq ante.

5   As to pensions instruments for persons other than members of the armed forces see para 666 et seq ante.

6   See the War Orphans Act 1942 s 1(1), (4) (amended by the Armed Forces Act 1981 s 28(2), Sch 5 Pt I; and by virtue of the Secretary of State for Social Services Order 1968). See also ROYAL FORCES vol 41 para 360.

694. Miscellaneous duties of the Secretary of State. The Secretary of State[1] may administer any pension awarded to or in respect of any person if that person:

(1)   has not attained the age of 18; or

(2)   is, in the opinion of the Secretary of State, incapable of managing his affairs by reason of mental infirmity; or

(3)   is being maintained in a hospital or other institution[2]; or

(4)   is a person in whose case the award can be forfeited or has been restored[3];

or if, in any other case, the Secretary of State considers that it is in that person's interests that it should be so administered[4]. A pension which is so being administered may, as to the whole of it or such part as the Secretary of State thinks fit and at such times as he thinks fit, be applied for the benefit of the person to or in respect of whom it has been awarded or be paid to any person whom the Secretary of State considers a fit and proper person so to apply it[5].

The Secretary of State is charged with the duty of administering pensions and other sums payable under the law of the United States of America to certain persons resident in the United Kingdom[6] in pursuance of arrangements entered into between him and the Administrator of Veterans' Affairs appointed under the law of the United States of America[7].

1   As to the Secretary of State see para 692 ante.
2   Ie an institution to which the Naval, Military and Air Forces etc (Disablement and Death) Service Pensions Order 1983, SI 1983/883, art 56 applies (see art 61(1)(c)); or to which the Personal Injuries (Civilians) Scheme 1983, SI 1983/686, art 64 applies (see art 67(1)(c)).
3   Ie under the Naval, Military and Air Forces etc (Disablement and Death) Service Pensions Order 1983 art 62 (as amended) or the Personal Injuries (Civilians) Scheme 1983 art 68 (as amended): see para 690 ante.
4   See the Naval, Military and Air Forces etc (Disablement and Death) Service Pensions Order 1983 art 61(1); the Personal Injuries (Civilians) Scheme 1983 art 67(1) (amended by SI 1987/191).
5   See the Naval, Military and Air Forces etc (Disablement and Death) Service Pensions Order 1983 art 61(2); the Personal Injuries (Civilians) Scheme 1983 art 67(2) (amended by SI 1987/191).
6   For the meaning of 'United Kingdom' see para 502 note 4 ante.
7   See the USA Veterans' Pensions (Administration) Act 1949 s 1 (amended by the Mental Health Act 1983 s 148(1), Sch 4 para 9; and by the Administration of Estates (Small Payments) (Increase of Limit) Order 1984, SI 1984/539).

695. Exercise of powers to compensate for war damage to seamen's effects. The compensation scheme for war damage to seamen's effects[1] is the responsibility of the Secretary of State for Trade and Industry, who exercises the statutory powers conferred on the Board of Trade[2].

1   Ie the Merchant Shipping (Compensation to Seamen – War Damage to Effects) Scheme 1982, SI 1982/1023: see para 681 ante.
2   See the Pensions (Navy, Army, Air Force and Mercantile Marine) Act 1939 s 6 (as amended); the Secretary of State for Trade and Industry Order 1970, SI 1970/1537; para 676 ante; and TRADE, INDUSTRY AND INDUSTRIAL RELATIONS vol 47 (Reissue) para 2.

696. Duties of the Secretary of State for Education and Employment. When selecting persons for sheltered employment facilities under the Disabled Persons (Employment) Act 1944[1], the Secretary of State for Education and Employment[2] must give preference to persons who have served whole-time in the armed forces of the Crown or in the merchant navy or the mercantile marine and whose disability is due to that service[3].

1   Ie facilities under the Disabled Persons (Employment) Act 1944 s 15 (as amended): see EMPLOYMENT vol 16 (Reissue) para 241.
2   See the Minister of Labour Order 1959, SI 1959/1769; the Secretary of State for Employment and Productivity Order 1968, SI 1968/729; the Secretary of State for Trade and Industry Order 1970, SI 1970/1537, art 3(1); the Transfer of Functions (Education and Employment) Order 1995, SI 1995/2986.
3   See the Disabled Persons (Employment) Act 1944 s 16(1) (amended by the Employment and Training Act 1973 s 14(2), Sch 3 para 2, Sch 4; the Armed Forces Act 1981 s 28(2), Sch 5 Pt I; prospectively renumbered and amended by the Disability Discrimination Act 1995 s 61(6)). A disabled person's disability is to be treated as due to service of a particular kind only in such circumstances as may be prescribed: Disabled Persons (Employment) Act 1944 s 16(2) (added by the Disability Discrimination Act 1995 s 61(6)).

INDEX

Value Added Tax

CHARITY—*continued*
  VAT—*continued*
    exports, 176
    importation of charitable goods, relief, 116
    relevant goods, 173n7
    zero-rated supplies, 173
CHILD
  clothing and footwear, zero-rating, 174
CLOTHING
  zero-rating, 174
CLUB
  business activities for VAT purposes, 18
  VAT registration, 69
COLLECTORS' ITEM
  meaning, 22n9
  VAT—
    disallowance of input tax, 205
    repossessed items, disposal of, 22
COLLEGE
  VAT exemption, 150
COMMAND PAPERS
  Cm 1934 (Maastricht Treaty), 2n2
  Cmnd—
    4621 (VAT Green Paper), 1n1
    4929 (VAT White Paper), 1n1
    5179 (EC Treaty), 2n1
COMMISSIONERS OF CUSTOMS AND
  EXCISE
  information, power to require, 223, 224
  information notices as to VAT, 7
  trade bodies, VAT agreements with, 7
  value added tax administered by, 7
COMMODITY
  terminal markets, VAT, 197
COMPULSORY ACQUISITION
  tax point, 35
CONDITION PRECEDENT
  VAT appeal, as to, 297
CONFECTIONERY
  meaning, 159n16
  VAT, 159
CONSTRUCTION INDUSTRY
  developer's self-supply charge, 28
  VAT—
    change of use subsequent to zero-rating, 164
    disallowance of input tax in certain cases, 207
    incorrect certificates, civil penalty, 274
    place of supply, 47
    protected buildings, 165
    time of supply, 33
    zero-rated supplies, 163
CONSULTANT
  VAT—
    place of supply of services, 49
    reverse charge, 27
CO-OWNER
  VAT registration, 68
COSTS
  VAT and duties tribunal, 317
COUNCIL ON TRIBUNALS
  VAT and duties tribunal, supervision of, 293

COURT OF APPEAL
  VAT appeals, 321
CRASH HELMET
  zero-rating, 174
CREDIT
  VAT exemption of services, 149
CREMATION
  VAT exemption, 152
CRIMINAL PROCEEDINGS
  VAT offences, as to, 267
CROWN
  VAT liability, 194
DEBT
  bad debt relief, VAT, 260
DEFENCE (PLEADING)
  VAT appeals, 302, 303
DENTIST
  VAT—
    exempt supplies, 151
    relevant practitioners, 151n3
DEVELOPMENT
  developer's VAT self-supply charge, 28
DIRECTOR OF COMPANY
  VAT evasion, liability, 273
DISABLED PERSON
  aids for—
    VAT retail schemes, 187
    zero-rated supplies, 162, 170
DISCOVERY OF DOCUMENTS
  VAT and duties tribunal, 308
DISTRESS FOR TAXES
  VAT—
    breach of walking possession agreement, 281
    recovery of, 256
DRUG
  VAT retail scheme, 187
  zero-rating, 170
DWELLING
  construction of, zero-rated supplies, 163
  VAT refunds in certain cases, 259
EDUCATION
  VAT—
    eligible body: meaning, 150n2
    exempt supplies, 150
ELECTION (CHOICE)
  VAT, as to. *See under* VALUE ADDED TAX
EMPLOYER
  valuation of goods or services supplied by, 93
EMPLOYMENT AGENCY OR BUSINESS
  VAT—
    place of supply, 49
    reverse charge, 27
ENTERTAINMENT
  business, disallowance of input tax, 206
ENTRY ON LAND AND PREMISES
  VAT, powers as to, 285
EUROPEAN COURT OF JUSTICE
  VAT references to, 3n8, 322
EVIDENCE
  VAT appeal hearing, 316
EXTENSION OF TIME
  VAT appeal, 300n10

References are to paragraph numbers; superior figures refer to notes

References are to paragraph numbers; superior figures refer to notes

References are to paragraph numbers; superior figures refer to notes

References are to paragraph numbers; superior figures refer to notes

References are to paragraph numbers; superior figures refer to notes

References are to paragraph numbers; superior figures refer to notes

References are to paragraph numbers; superior figures refer to notes

Valuers and Surveyors

References are to paragraph numbers; superior figures refer to notes

War and Armed Conflict

References are to paragraph numbers; superior figures refer to notes

References are to paragraph numbers; superior figures refer to notes

References are to paragraph numbers; superior figures refer to notes

References are to paragraph numbers; superior figures refer to notes

WAR—*continued*
　emergency powers—*continued*
　　1945 and 1948 Acts, under—*continued*
　　　maintenance and use of war works, 620
　　　minister's certificate, 623
　　　notice requirements, 619
　　　oil installations, acquisition of land for, 621
　　　principles generally, 617
　　　procedure and orders relating to highways, 619
　　　provisions still in force, 617
　　　railways, 618
　　　reversionary interests, 622
　　　wayleave orders for pipelines etc, 621
　enemy. *See* ALIEN ENEMY; ENEMY; ENEMY PROPERTY
　Environmental Modification Techniques Convention, 520
　exceptions to general prohibition on use of force, 501
　existence of—
　　certificate of Foreign Secretary, 506
　　common law, 506
　　de facto, effect of, 508n[2]
　　judicial notice, 506
　foreign enlistment, 512
　friendly or neutral commercial domicile, acquisition of, 632
　Geneva Conventions. *See* GENEVA CONVENTIONS
　Hague Conventions—
　　generally, 517
　　list of, 518
　hot pursuit, 503n[3]
　illegal expeditions, 514
　illegal shipbuilding etc, 513
　international agreements and conventions—
　　Biological Weapons Convention, 568
　　Chemical Weapons Convention, 572
　　Conventional Weapons Convention 1981 . . 519
　　Environmental Modification Techniques Convention, 520
　　Geneva Conventions. *See* GENEVA CONVENTIONS
　　Hague Conventions, 517, 518
　　laws of war, 516
　　list of, 517
　　nuclear weapons, 596n[1]
　　war crimes. *See* WAR CRIMES
　international humanitarian law, 516
　judicial notice of existence of, 506
　Kellogg-Briand Pact, 501n[3], 502n[6]
　laws of war, 506n[7], 516
　legality—
　　force short of war, 502
　　hot pursuit, 503n[3]
　　laws of war, 516
　　pacific blockades, 502
　　reprisals, 502
　　self-defence—
　　　collective, 505

WAR—*continued*
　legality—*continued*
　　self-defence—*continued*
　　　international law, 503
　　　United Nations Charter, 504, 505
　　　use of force by states, 501
　levying by British subjects, 507
　mercenaries, recruitment of, 512n[5]
　NATO, 505
　neutrality and illegal activities, 513, 514
　nuclear weapons, 596
　occupation of territory, 631
　pension. *See* WAR PENSION
　Porter Convention, 518n[4]
　prerogative powers—
　　angary, 510
　　blockade, 510
　　declaration and termination of war, 506
　　requisition of British ships, 511
　requisition—
　　compensation. *See* compensation *above*
　　ships, powers, 511
　See also emergency powers *above*
　seizure and detention of ships, 515
　self-defence—
　　collective, 505
　　customary international law, 503
　　nationals abroad, 504n[6]
　　United Nations Charter, 504
　ship—
　　illegal activities, 513, 514
　　requisition powers, 511
　　seizure and detention, 515
　shipping convoys, 628
　termination—
　　Crown declaration, by, 506n[2]
　　Crown prerogative, 506
　　1939–45 war, 509
　trade restrictions—
　　armed conflict, during, 506
　　declaration of war, on, 506
　　EU, imposed by, 506n[13]
　trading with enemy. *See under* ENEMY
　Treaty of Versailles, 501n[2]
　United Nations Charter—
　　self-defence, 504
　　use of force, 501
　Western European Union, 505
WAR CRIMES
　breaches of Geneva Conventions, 524n[22]
　British armed forces, by, 566
　English law, liability under, 564
　establishment of tribunals, 563
　enemy prisoners of war, by, 567
　Geneva Conventions, 564
　international law, 563
　proceedings in UK in respect of 1939–45 war, 565
　1939–45 war, 565
WAR DAMAGE
　meaning, 626
　compensation, 625

References are to paragraph numbers; superior figures refer to notes

Words and Phrases

Words in parentheses indicate the context in which the word or phrase is used

References are to paragraph numbers; superior figures refer to notes

chemical weapon, 573
chemical weapons production facility, 581n[1]
chief executive authority, 515n[15]
child, dependent (civilian injuries scheme), 674n[17]
civil defence, 553, 653n[5,7]
civil defence functions, 654n[2]
civil defence organisations, 553n[3], 668n[5]
civil defence personnel, 553n[4]
civil defence resources, 657n[3]
civil defence shelter, 659n[16]
civil defence volunteer, 668n[5]
civilian, 533n[13]
collector (VAT), 256n[5]
collectors' items (VAT), 22n[9]
combatant, 533n[13]
common (requisition), 617n[9]
Community goods, 127n[4]
Community transport, 43n[1]
company—
    German, 650n[2]
    United Kingdom, 650n[4]
competent authority (defence contracts), 646n[3]
comptroller (Patents Etc), 656n[9]
conditional sale agreement (requisitioned goods), 608n[3]
confectionery, 159n[16]
conflict (Geneva Conventions), 548n[2]
connected (VAT), 201n[11]
connected person (fiscal warehousing), 133n[12]
consideration (VAT), 86
container (freight), 179n[1]
control (group), 66n[3]
controller (VAT), 226
conventions—
    (war), 517n[1]
    scheduled (Geneva Conventions), 524n[2]
costs (VAT and duties tribunal), 298n[5]
court—
    (enemy intellectual property), 647n[9]
    (Geneva Conventions), 542n[6]
credit, VAT, 202
credit transfer, 233n[7]
Crown interest (protected building), 165n[8]
currency, enemy, 642n[9]
current accounting year (VAT), 233n[3]
custodian (enemy property), 644n[4]
Customs and Excise Acts 1979 . . 105n[2]
damage, war, 626, 667
dangerous forces, works and installations containing, 552n[16]
datapost packet, 105n[6]
date of notification (VAT and duties tribunal), 300n[13]
de minimis rules (VAT), 213n[14]
defence, civil, 553, 653n[5,7]
Defence Acts, 617n[4]
defence materials, 646n[2]
defence purposes, 621n[10]
dependent—
    child, 674n[17]
    widower, 674n[7]

design (enemy-owned), 645n[5,6]
designated—
    activities (farmers etc), 79n[3], 80
    minister (civil defence), 654n[10]
    travel service, 31n[19]
designed solely for use by a handicapped person (appliance), 170n[12]
detention—
    (mariner), 676n[4], 679n[5]
    (naval auxiliary member), 681n[11]
developer (self-supply charge), 28n[3]
director (body corporate), 201n[10], 532n[18]
disability living allowance, 170n[24]
disablement (war pension), 662n[11]
dishonesty (VAT), 272n[2]
disputed decision (VAT), 293n[8]
distinctive emblem, 532
distinctive signal, 532
document (VAT), 11n[8]
doing of work on land (emergency powers), 602n[2], 623n[3]
Duchy interest (protected building), 165n[8]
dutiable goods, 89n[7]
duty point, 89n[9]
easement (emergency powers), 622n[5]
EC sales statement, 277n[1]
economic activity (VAT), 17n[1]
effects (mariner's), 676n[16]
eligible body—
    (charities: zero-rating), 173n[8]
    (cultural services), 157n[3]
    (VAT), 150n[2]
eligible goods (fiscal warehousing), 21n[5], 132n[3], 134n[1]
emergency powers, 600n[1], 601n[10]
enemy—
    (trade), 635
    alien, 632
    trading with, 637
enemy currency, 642n[9]
enemy debt, German, 649n[3]
enemy property—
    (custodianship), 643n[1]
    German, 649n[2]
enemy subject, 636
enemy territory, 636
entertain (VAT appeal), 297n[2]
equipping (ship), 513n[8]
escort, in-country, 588n[15]
evasion penalty appeal (VAT), 302n[3]
event (trade promotion), 113n[7]
exempt—
    acquisition (VAT), 13n[12], 141
    input tax, 209n[4]
    supply (VAT), 141
exercise (emergency powers), 600n[1]
expenses, approved (civil defence), 660n[1]
export house (VAT), 178n[1]
facilities, 18n[3]
fair wear and tear (requisitioned property), 601n[4]
finance agreement, 22n[11]

References are to paragraph numbers; superior figures refer to notes

References are to paragraph numbers; superior figures refer to notes

References are to paragraph numbers; superior figures refer to notes

THE

PUBLIC GENERAL ACTS

1989

[IN FOUR PARTS]

PART III

(Chapters 40—46)

with

Lists of the Public General Acts

HMSO publications are available from:

HMSO Publications Centre
(Mail and telephone orders only)
PO Box 276, London SW8 5DT
Telephone orders 071-873 9090
General enquiries 071-873 0011
(queuing system in operation for both numbers)

HMSO Bookshops
49 High Holborn, London WC1V 6HB   071-873 0011 (Counter service only)
258 Broad Street, Birmingham B1 2HE   021-643 3740
Southey House, 33 Wine Street, Bristol BS1 2BQ   (0272) 264306
9-21 Princess Street, Manchester M60 8AS   061-834 7201
80 Chichester Street, Belfast BT1 4JY   (0232) 238451
71 Lothian Road, Edinburgh EH3 9AZ   031-228 4181

HMSO's Accredited Agents
(see Yellow Pages)

And through good booksellers

d

PRINTED IN THE UNITED KINGDOM BY PAUL FREEMAN
Controller and Chief Executive of HMSO and
Queen's Printer of Acts of Parliament

e

CONTENTS

PART I

PART II

PART III

PART IV

TABLE I

Alphabetical List of

the Public General Acts of 1989

Alphabetical List (contd.)

TABLE II
Chronological List of the
Public General Acts of 1989

*Consolidation Act

TABLE III
Alphabetical List of
the Local and Personal Acts of 1989

TABLE IV

Chronological List of

the General Synod Measures of 1989

There were no measures passed by the General Synod of the Church of England during the year 1989.

Companies Act 1989

1989 CHAPTER 40

An Act to amend the law relating to company accounts; to make new provision with respect to the persons eligible for appointment as company auditors; to amend the Companies Act 1985 and certain other enactments with respect to investigations and powers to obtain information and to confer new powers exercisable to assist overseas regulatory authorities; to make new provision with respect to the registration of company charges and otherwise to amend the law relating to companies; to amend the Fair Trading Act 1973; to enable provision to be made for the payment of fees in connection with the exercise by the Secretary of State, the Director General of Fair Trading and the Monopolies and Mergers Commission of their functions under Part V of that Act; to make provision for safeguarding the operation of certain financial markets; to amend the Financial Services Act 1986; to enable provision to be made for the recording and transfer of title to securities without a written instrument; to amend the Company Directors Disqualification Act 1986, the Company Securities (Insider Dealing) Act 1985, the Policyholders Protection Act 1975 and the law relating to building societies; and for connected purposes.

[16th November 1989]

BE IT ENACTED by the Queen's most Excellent Majesty, by and with the advice and consent of the Lords Spiritual and Temporal, and Commons, in this present Parliament assembled, and by the authority of the same, as follows:—

A

PART I

COMPANY ACCOUNTS

Introduction

1. The provisions of this Part amend Part VII of the Companies Act 1985 (accounts and audit) by—

(a) inserting new provisions in place of sections 221 to 262 of that Act, and

(b) amending or replacing Schedules 4 to 10 to that Act and inserting new Schedules.

Provisions applying to companies generally

2. The following sections are inserted in Part VII of the Companies Act 1985 at the beginning of Chapter I (provisions applying to companies generally)—

"Accounting records

221.—(1) Every company shall keep accounting records which are sufficient to show and explain the company's transactions and are such as to—

(a) disclose with reasonable accuracy, at any time, the financial position of the company at that time, and

(b) enable the directors to ensure that any balance sheet and profit and loss account prepared under this Part complies with the requirements of this Act.

(2) The accounting records shall in particular contain—

(a) entries from day to day of all sums of money received and expended by the company, and the matters in respect of which the receipt and expenditure takes place, and

(b) a record of the assets and liabilities of the company.

(3) If the company's business involves dealing in goods, the accounting records shall contain—

(a) statements of stock held by the company at the end of each financial year of the company,

(b) all statements of stocktakings from which any such statement of stock as is mentioned in paragraph (a) has been or is to be prepared, and

(c) except in the case of goods sold by way of ordinary retail trade, statements of all goods sold and purchased, showing the goods and the buyers and sellers in sufficient detail to enable all these to be identified.

(4) A parent company which has a subsidiary undertaking in relation to which the above requirements do not apply shall take reasonable steps to secure that the undertaking keeps such accounting records as to enable the directors of the parent company to ensure that any balance sheet and profit and loss account prepared under this Part complies with the requirements of this Act.

(5) If a company fails to comply with any provision of this section, every officer of the company who is in default is guilty of an offence unless he shows that he acted honestly and that in the circumstances in which the company's business was carried on the default was excusable.

(6) A person guilty of an offence under this section is liable to imprisonment or a fine, or both.

Where and for how long records to be kept.

222.—(1) A company's accounting records shall be kept at its registered office or such other place as the directors think fit, and shall at all times be open to inspection by the company's officers.

(2) If accounting records are kept at a place outside Great Britain, accounts and returns with respect to the business dealt with in the accounting records so kept shall be sent to, and kept at, a place in Great Britain, and shall at all times be open to such inspection.

(3) The accounts and returns to be sent to Great Britain shall be such as to—

(a) disclose with reasonable accuracy the financial position of the business in question at intervals of not more than six months, and

(b) enable the directors to ensure that the company's balance sheet and profit and loss account comply with the requirements of this Act.

(4) If a company fails to comply with any provision of subsections (1) to (3), every officer of the company who is in default is guilty of an offence, and liable to imprisonment or a fine or both, unless he shows that he acted honestly and that in the circumstances in which the company's business was carried on the default was excusable.

(5) Accounting records which a company is required by section 221 to keep shall be preserved by it—

(a) in the case of a private company, for three years from the date on which they are made, and

(b) in the case of a public company, for six years from the date on which they are made.

This is subject to any provision contained in rules made under section 411 of the Insolvency Act 1986 (company insolvency rules).

(6) An officer of a company is guilty of an offence, and liable to imprisonment or a fine or both, if he fails to take all reasonable steps for securing compliance by the company with subsection (5) or intentionally causes any default by the company under that subsection.".

A company's financial year and accounting reference periods.

1985 c. 6.

3. The following sections are inserted in Part VII of the Companies Act 1985—

"A company's financial year and accounting reference periods

A company's financial year.

223.—(1) A company's "financial year" is determined as follows.

(2) Its first financial year begins with the first day of its first accounting reference period and ends with the last day of that period or such other date, not more than seven days before or after the end of that period, as the directors may determine.

(3) Subsequent financial years begin with the day immediately following the end of the company's previous financial year and end with the last day of its next accounting reference period or such other date, not more than seven days before or after the end of that period, as the directors may determine.

(4) In relation to an undertaking which is not a company, references in this Act to its financial year are to any period in respect of which a profit and loss account of the undertaking is required to be made up (by its constitution or by the law under which it is established), whether that period is a year or not.

(5) The directors of a parent company shall secure that, except where in their opinion there are good reasons against it, the financial year of each of its subsidiary undertakings coincides with the company's own financial year.

Accounting reference periods and accounting reference date.

224.—(1) A company's accounting reference periods are determined according to its accounting reference date.

(2) A company may, at any time before the end of the period of nine months beginning with the date of its incorporation, by notice in the prescribed form given to the registrar specify its accounting reference date, that is, the date on which its accounting reference period ends in each calendar year.

(3) Failing such notice, a company's accounting reference date is—

(a) in the case of a company incorporated before the commencement of section 3 of the Companies Act 1989, 31st March;

(b) in the case of a company incorporated after the commencement of that section, the last day of the month in which the anniversary of its incorporation falls.

(4) A company's first accounting reference period is the period of more than six months, but not more than 18 months, beginning with the date of its incorporation and ending with its accounting reference date.

(5) Its subsequent accounting reference periods are successive periods of twelve months beginning immediately after the end of the previous accounting reference period and ending with its accounting reference date.

(6) This section has effect subject to the provisions of section 225 relating to the alteration of accounting reference dates and the consequences of such alteration.

Alteration of accounting reference date.

225.—(1) A company may by notice in the prescribed form given to the registrar specify a new accounting reference date having effect in relation to the company's current accounting reference period and subsequent periods.

(2) A company may by notice in the prescribed form given to the registrar specify a new accounting reference date having effect in relation to the company's previous accounting reference period and subsequent periods if—

    (a) the company is a subsidiary undertaking or parent undertaking of another company and the new accounting reference date coincides with the accounting reference date of that other company, or

    (b) an administration order under Part II of the Insolvency Act 1986 is in force.

A company's "previous accounting reference period" means that immediately preceding its current accounting reference period.

(3) The notice shall state whether the current or previous accounting reference period—

    (a) is to be shortened, so as to come to an end on the first occasion on which the new accounting reference date falls or fell after the beginning of the period, or

    (b) is to be extended, so as to come to an end on the second occasion on which that date falls or fell after the beginning of the period.

(4) A notice under subsection (1) stating that the current accounting reference period is to be extended is ineffective, except as mentioned below, if given less than five years after the end of an earlier accounting reference period of the company which was extended by virtue of this section.

This subsection does not apply—

    (a) to a notice given by a company which is a subsidiary undertaking or parent undertaking of another company and the new accounting reference date coincides with that of the other company, or

    (b) where an administration order is in force under Part II of the Insolvency Act 1986,

or where the Secretary of State directs that it should not apply, which he may do with respect to a notice which has been given or which may be given.

(5) A notice under subsection (2)(a) may not be given if the period allowed for laying and delivering accounts and reports in relation to the previous accounting reference period has already expired.

(6) An accounting reference period may not in any case, unless an administration order is in force under Part II of the Insolvency Act 1986, be extended so as to exceed 18 months and a notice under this section is ineffective if the current or previous accounting reference period as extended in accordance with the notice would exceed that limit.".

Individual company accounts.
1985 c. 6.

4.—(1) The following section is inserted in Part VII of the Companies Act 1985—

"Annual accounts

Duty to prepare individual company accounts.

226.—(1) The directors of every company shall prepare for each financial year of the company—

    (a) a balance sheet as at the last day of the year, and

    (b) a profit and loss account.

Those accounts are referred to in this Part as the company's 'individual accounts'.

(2) The balance sheet shall give a true and fair view of the state of affairs of the company as at the end of the financial year; and the profit and loss account shall give a true and fair view of the profit or loss of the company for the financial year.

(3) A company's individual accounts shall comply with the provisions of Schedule 4 as to the form and content of the balance sheet and profit and loss account and additional information to be provided by way of notes to the accounts.

(4) Where compliance with the provisions of that Schedule, and the other provisions of this Act as to the matters to be included in a company's individual accounts or in notes to those accounts, would not be sufficient to give a true and fair view, the necessary additional information shall be given in the accounts or in a note to them.

(5) If in special circumstances compliance with any of those provisions is inconsistent with the requirement to give a true and fair view, the directors shall depart from that provision to the extent necessary to give a true and fair view.

Particulars of any such departure, the reasons for it and its effect shall be given in a note to the accounts.".

(2) Schedule 4 to the Companies Act 1985 (form and content of company accounts) is amended in accordance with Schedule 1 to this Act.

1985 c. 6.

5.—(1) The following section is inserted in Part VII of the Companies Act 1985—

Group accounts.

"Duty to prepare group accounts.

227.—(1) If at the end of a financial year a company is a parent company the directors shall, as well as preparing individual accounts for the year, prepare group accounts.

(2) Group accounts shall be consolidated accounts comprising—

   (a) a consolidated balance sheet dealing with the state of affairs of the parent company and its subsidiary undertakings, and

   (b) a consolidated profit and loss account dealing with the profit or loss of the parent company and its subsidiary undertakings.

(3) The accounts shall give a true and fair view of the state of affairs as at the end of the financial year, and the profit or loss for the financial year, of the undertakings included in the consolidation as a whole, so far as concerns members of the company.

(4) A company's group accounts shall comply with the provisions of Schedule 4A as to the form and content of the consolidated balance sheet and consolidated profit and loss account and additional information to be provided by way of notes to the accounts.

(5) Where compliance with the provisions of that Schedule, and the other provisions of this Act, as to the matters to be included in a company's group accounts or in notes to those accounts, would not be sufficient to give a true and fair view, the necessary additional information shall be given in the accounts or in a note to them.

(6) If in special circumstances compliance with any of those provisions is inconsistent with the requirement to give a true and fair view, the directors shall depart from that provision to the extent necessary to give a true and fair view.

Particulars of any such departure, the reasons for it and its effect shall be given in a note to the accounts.".

(2) Schedule 2 to this Act (form and content of group accounts) is inserted after Schedule 4 to the Companies Act 1985, as Schedule 4A.

(3) The following sections are inserted in Part VII of the Companies Act 1985—

"Exemption for parent companies included in accounts of larger group.

228.—(1) A company is exempt from the requirement to prepare group accounts if it is itself a subsidiary undertaking and its immediate parent undertaking is established under the law of a member State of the European Economic Community, in the following cases—

    (a) where the company is a wholly-owned subsidiary of that parent undertaking;

    (b) where that parent undertaking holds more than 50 per cent. of the shares in the company and notice requesting the preparation of group accounts has not been served on the company by shareholders holding in aggregate—

        (i) more than half of the remaining shares in the company, or

        (ii) 5 per cent. of the total shares in the company.

Such notice must be served not later than six months after the end of the financial year before that to which it relates.

(2) Exemption is conditional upon compliance with all of the following conditions—

    (a) that the company is included in consolidated accounts for a larger group drawn up to the same date, or to an earlier date in the same financial year, by a parent undertaking established under the law of a member State of the European Economic Community;

    (b) that those accounts are drawn up and audited, and that parent undertaking's annual report is drawn up, according to that law, in accordance with the provisions of the Seventh Directive (83/349/EEC);

    (c) that the company discloses in its individual accounts that it is exempt from the obligation to prepare and deliver group accounts;

    (d) that the company states in its individual accounts the name of the parent undertaking which draws up the group accounts referred to above and—

        (i) if it is incorporated outside Great Britain, the country in which it is incorporated,

        (ii) if it is incorporated in Great Britain, whether it is registered in England and Wales or in Scotland, and

        (iii) if it is unincorporated, the address of its principal place of business;

(e) that the company delivers to the registrar, within the period allowed for delivering its individual accounts, copies of those group accounts and of the parent undertaking's annual report, together with the auditors' report on them; and

(f) that if any document comprised in accounts and reports delivered in accordance with paragraph (e) is in a language other than English, there is annexed to the copy of that document delivered a translation of it into English, certified in the prescribed manner to be a correct translation.

(3) The exemption does not apply to a company any of whose securities are listed on a stock exchange in any member State of the European Economic Community.

(4) Shares held by directors of a company for the purpose of complying with any share qualification requirement shall be disregarded in determining for the purposes of subsection (1)(a) whether the company is a wholly-owned subsidiary.

(5) For the purposes of subsection (1)(b) shares held by a wholly-owned subsidiary of the parent undertaking, or held on behalf of the parent undertaking or a wholly-owned subsidiary, shall be attributed to the parent undertaking.

(6) In subsection (3) "securities" includes—

(a) shares and stock,

(b) debentures, including debenture stock, loan stock, bonds, certificates of deposit and other instruments creating or acknowledging indebtedness,

(c) warrants or other instruments entitling the holder to subscribe for securities falling within paragraph (a) or (b), and

(d) certificates or other instruments which confer—

(i) property rights in respect of a security falling within paragraph (a), (b) or (c),

(ii) any right to acquire, dispose of, underwrite or convert a security, being a right to which the holder would be entitled if he held any such security to which the certificate or other instrument relates, or

(iii) a contractual right (other than an option) to acquire any such security otherwise than by subscription.

Subsidiary undertakings included in the consolidation. 229.—(1) Subject to the exceptions authorised or required by this section, all the subsidiary undertakings of the parent company shall be included in the consolidation.

(2) A subsidiary undertaking may be excluded from consolidation if its inclusion is not material for the purpose of giving a true and fair view; but two or more undertakings may be excluded only if they are not material taken together.

(3) In addition, a subsidiary undertaking may be excluded from consolidation where—

(a) severe long-term restrictions substantially hinder the exercise of the rights of the parent company over the assets or management of that undertaking, or

(b) the information necessary for the preparation of group accounts cannot be obtained without disproportionate expense or undue delay, or

(c) the interest of the parent company is held exclusively with a view to subsequent resale and the undertaking has not previously been included in consolidated group accounts prepared by the parent company.

The reference in paragraph (a) to the rights of the parent company and the reference in paragraph (c) to the interest of the parent company are, respectively, to rights and interests held by or attributed to the company for the purposes of section 258 (definition of "parent undertaking") in the absence of which it would not be the parent company.

(4) Where the activities of one or more subsidiary undertakings are so different from those of other undertakings to be included in the consolidation that their inclusion would be incompatible with the obligation to give a true and fair view, those undertakings shall be excluded from consolidation.

This subsection does not apply merely because some of the undertakings are industrial, some commercial and some provide services, or because they carry on industrial or commercial activities involving different products or provide different services.

(5) Where all the subsidiary undertakings of a parent company fall within the above exclusions, no group accounts are required.".

1985 c. 6.

(4) The following section is inserted in Part VII of the Companies Act 1985—

"Treatment of individual profit and loss account where group accounts prepared.

230.—(1) The following provisions apply with respect to the individual profit and loss account of a parent company where—

(a) the company is required to prepare and does prepare group accounts in accordance with this Act, and

PART I

(b) the notes to the company's individual balance sheet show the company's profit or loss for the financial year determined in accordance with this Act.

(2) The profit and loss account need not contain the information specified in paragraphs 52 to 57 of Schedule 4 (information supplementing the profit and loss account).

(3) The profit and loss account must be approved in accordance with section 233(1) (approval by board of directors) but may be omitted from the company's annual accounts for the purposes of the other provisions below in this Chapter.

(4) The exemption conferred by this section is conditional upon its being disclosed in the company's annual accounts that the exemption applies.".

6.—(1) The following section is inserted in Part VII of the Companies Act 1985—

Additional disclosure required in notes to accounts. 1985 c. 6.

"Disclosure required in notes to accounts: related undertakings.

231.—(1) The information specified in Schedule 5 shall be given in notes to a company's annual accounts.

(2) Where the company is not required to prepare group accounts, the information specified in Part I of that Schedule shall be given; and where the company is required to prepare group accounts, the information specified in Part II of that Schedule shall be given.

(3) The information required by Schedule 5 need not be disclosed with respect to an undertaking which—

(a) is established under the law of a country outside the United Kingdom, or

(b) carries on business outside the United Kingdom,

if in the opinion of the directors of the company the disclosure would be seriously prejudicial to the business of that undertaking, or to the business of the company or any of its subsidiary undertakings, and the Secretary of State agrees that the information need not be disclosed.

This subsection does not apply in relation to the information required under paragraph 5(2), 6 or 20 of that Schedule.

(4) Where advantage is taken of subsection (3), that fact shall be stated in a note to the company's annual accounts.

(5) If the directors of the company are of the opinion that the number of undertakings in respect of which the company is required to disclose information under any provision of Schedule 5 to this Act is such that compliance with that provision would result in information of excessive length being given, the information need only be given in respect of—

(a) the undertakings whose results or financial position, in the opinion of the directors, principally affected the figures shown in the company's annual accounts, and

(b) undertakings excluded from consolidation under section 229(3) or (4).

This subsection does not apply in relation to the information required under paragraph 10 or 29 of that Schedule.

(6) If advantage is taken of subsection (5)—

(a) there shall be included in the notes to the company's annual accounts a statement that the information is given only with respect to such undertakings as are mentioned in that subsection, and

(b) the full information (both that which is disclosed in the notes to the accounts and that which is not) shall be annexed to the company's next annual return.

For this purpose the "next annual return" means that next delivered to the registrar after the accounts in question have been approved under section 233.

(7) If a company fails to comply with subsection (6)(b), the company and every officer of it who is in default is liable to a fine and, for continued contravention, to a daily default fine.".

(2) Schedule 3 to this Act (disclosure of information: related undertakings) is substituted for Schedule 5 to the Companies Act 1985.

1985 c. 6.

(3) The following section is inserted in Part VII of the Companies Act 1985—

"Disclosure required in notes to accounts: emoluments and other benefits of directors and others.

232.—(1) The information specified in Schedule 6 shall be given in notes to a company's annual accounts.

(2) In that Schedule—

Part I relates to the emoluments of directors (including emoluments waived), pensions of directors and past directors, compensation for loss of office to directors and past directors and sums paid to third parties in respect of directors' services,

Part II relates to loans, quasi-loans and other dealings in favour of directors and connected persons, and

Part III relates to transactions, arrangements and agreements made by the company or a subsidiary undertaking for officers of the company other than directors.

(3) It is the duty of any director of a company, and any person who is or has at any time in the preceding five years been an officer of the company, to give notice to the company of such matters relating to himself as may be necessary for the purposes of Part I of Schedule 6.

(4) A person who makes default in complying with subsection (3) commits an offence and is liable to a fine.".

(4) Schedule 6 to the Companies Act 1985 is amended in accordance with Schedule 4 to this Act.

1985 c. 6.

7. The following section is inserted in Part VII of the Companies Act 1985—

Approval and signing of accounts.

"Approval and signing of accounts

Approval and signing of accounts.

233.—(1) A company's annual accounts shall be approved by the board of directors and signed on behalf of the board by a director of the company.

(2) The signature shall be on the company's balance sheet.

(3) Every copy of the balance sheet which is laid before the company in general meeting, or which is otherwise circulated, published or issued, shall state the name of the person who signed the balance sheet on behalf of the board.

(4) The copy of the company's balance sheet which is delivered to the registrar shall be signed on behalf of the board by a director of the company.

(5) If annual accounts are approved which do not comply with the requirements of this Act, every director of the company who is party to their approval and who knows that they do not comply or is reckless as to whether they comply is guilty of an offence and liable to a fine.

For this purpose every director of the company at the time the accounts are approved shall be taken to be a party to their approval unless he shows that he took all reasonable steps to prevent their being approved.

(6) If a copy of the balance sheet—

   (a) is laid before the company, or otherwise circulated, published or issued, without the balance sheet having been signed as required by this section or without the required statement of the signatory's name being included, or

   (b) is delivered to the registrar without being signed as required by this section,

the company and every officer of it who is in default is guilty of an offence and liable to a fine.".

8.—(1) The following sections are inserted in Part VII of the Companies Act 1985—

"Directors' report

Duty to prepare directors' report.

234.—(1) The directors of a company shall for each financial year prepare a report—

   (a) containing a fair review of the development of the business of the company and its subsidiary undertakings during the financial year and of their position at the end of it, and

   (b) stating the amount (if any) which they recommend should be paid as dividend and the amount (if any) which they propose to carry to reserves.

(2) The report shall state the names of the persons who, at any time during the financial year, were directors of the company, and the principal activities of the company and its subsidiary undertakings in the course of the year and any significant change in those activities in the year.

(3) The report shall also comply with Schedule 7 as regards the disclosure of the matters mentioned there.

(4) In Schedule 7—

   Part I relates to matters of a general nature, including changes in asset values, directors' shareholdings and other interests and contributions for political and charitable purposes,

   Part II relates to the acquisition by a company of its own shares or a charge on them,

   Part III relates to the employment, training and advancement of disabled persons,

   Part IV relates to the health, safety and welfare at work of the company's employees, and

   Part V relates to the involvement of employees in the affairs, policy and performance of the company.

(5) In the case of any failure to comply with the provisions of this Part as to the preparation of a directors' report and the contents of the report, every person who was a director of the company immediately before the end of the period for laying and delivering accounts and reports for the financial year in question is guilty of an offence and liable to a fine.

(6) In proceedings against a person for an offence under this section it is a defence for him to prove that he took all reasonable steps for securing compliance with the requirements in question.

Approval and signing of directors' report.

234A.—(1) The directors' report shall be approved by the board of directors and signed on behalf of the board by a director or the secretary of the company.

(2) Every copy of the directors' report which is laid before the company in general meeting, or which is otherwise circulated, published or issued, shall state the name of the person who signed it on behalf of the board.

(3) The copy of the directors' report which is delivered to the registrar shall be signed on behalf of the board by a director or the secretary of the company.

(4) If a copy of the directors' report—

    (a) is laid before the company, or otherwise circulated, published or issued, without the report having been signed as required by this section or without the required statement of the signatory's name being included, or

    (b) is delivered to the registrar without being signed as required by this section,

the company and every officer of it who is in default is guilty of an offence and liable to a fine.''.

(2) Schedule 7 to the Companies Act 1985 (matters to be included in directors' report) is amended in accordance with Schedule 5 to this Act.   1985 c. 6.

9. The following sections are inserted in Part VII of the Companies Act 1985—   Auditors' report.

''Auditors' report

Auditors' report.   **235.**—(1) A company's auditors shall make a report to the company's members on all annual accounts of the company of which copies are to be laid before the company in general meeting during their tenure of office.

(2) The auditors' report shall state whether in the auditors' opinion the annual accounts have been properly prepared in accordance with this Act, and in particular whether a true and fair view is given—

    (a) in the case of an individual balance sheet, of the state of affairs of the company as at the end of the financial year,

    (b) in the case of an individual profit and loss account, of the profit or loss of the company for the financial year,

    (c) in the case of group accounts, of the state of affairs as at the end of the financial year, and the profit or loss for the financial year, of the undertakings included in the consolidation as a whole, so far as concerns members of the company.

(3) The auditors shall consider whether the information given in the directors' report for the financial year for which the annual accounts are prepared is consistent with those accounts; and if they are of opinion that it is not they shall state that fact in their report.

Signature of
auditors' report.

236.—(1) The auditors' report shall state the names of the auditors and be signed by them.

(2) Every copy of the auditors' report which is laid before the company in general meeting, or which is otherwise circulated, published or issued, shall state the names of the auditors.

(3) The copy of the auditors' report which is delivered to the registrar shall state the names of the auditors and be signed by them.

(4) If a copy of the auditors' report—

    (a) is laid before the company, or otherwise circulated, published or issued, without the required statement of the auditors' names, or

    (b) is delivered to the registrar without the required statement of the auditors' names or without being signed as required by this section,

the company and every officer of it who is in default is guilty of an offence and liable to a fine.

(5) References in this section to signature by the auditors are, where the office of auditor is held by a body corporate or partnership, to signature in the name of the body corporate or partnership by a person authorised to sign on its behalf.

Duties of
auditors.

237.—(1) A company's auditors shall, in preparing their report, carry out such investigations as will enable them to form an opinion as to—

    (a) whether proper accounting records have been kept by the company and proper returns adequate for their audit have been received from branches not visited by them, and

    (b) whether the company's individual accounts are in agreement with the accounting records and returns.

(2) If the auditors are of opinion that proper accounting records have not been kept, or that proper returns adequate for their audit have not been received from branches not visited by them, or if the company's individual accounts are not in agreement with the accounting records and returns, the auditors shall state that fact in their report.

(3) If the auditors fail to obtain all the information and explanations which, to the best of their knowledge and belief, are necessary for the purposes of their audit, they shall state that fact in their report.

(4) If the requirements of Schedule 6 (disclosure of information: emoluments and other benefits of directors and others) are not complied with in the annual accounts, the auditors shall include in their report, so far as they are reasonably able to do so, a statement giving the required particulars.".

PART I
Publication of
accounts and
reports.
1985 c. 6.

10. The following sections are inserted in Part VII of the Companies Act 1985—

"Publication of accounts and reports

Persons entitled to receive copies of accounts and reports.

238.—(1) A copy of the company's annual accounts, together with a copy of the directors' report for that financial year and of the auditors' report on those accounts, shall be sent to—

(a) every member of the company,

(b) every holder of the company's debentures, and

(c) every person who is entitled to receive notice of general meetings,

not less than 21 days before the date of the meeting at which copies of those documents are to be laid in accordance with section 241.

(2) Copies need not be sent—

(a) to a person who is not entitled to receive notices of general meetings and of whose address the company is unaware, or

(b) to more than one of the joint holders of shares or debentures none of whom is entitled to receive such notices, or

(c) in the case of joint holders of shares or debentures some of whom are, and some not, entitled to receive such notices, to those who are not so entitled.

(3) In the case of a company not having a share capital, copies need not be sent to anyone who is not entitled to receive notices of general meetings of the company.

(4) If copies are sent less than 21 days before the date of the meeting, they shall, notwithstanding that fact, be deemed to have been duly sent if it is so agreed by all the members entitled to attend and vote at the meeting.

(5) If default is made in complying with this section, the company and every officer of it who is in default is guilty of an offence and liable to a fine.

(6) Where copies are sent out under this section over a period of days, references elsewhere in this Act to the day on which copies are sent out shall be construed as references to the last day of that period.

Right to demand copies of accounts and reports.

239.—(1) Any member of a company and any holder of a company's debentures is entitled to be furnished, on demand and without charge, with a copy of the company's last annual accounts and directors' report and a copy of the auditors' report on those accounts.

(2) The entitlement under this section is to a single copy of those documents, but that is in addition to any copy to which a person may be entitled under section 238.

(3) If a demand under this section is not complied with within seven days, the company and every officer of it who is in default is guilty of an offence and liable to a fine and, for continued contravention, to a daily default fine.

(4) If in proceedings for such an offence the issue arises whether a person had already been furnished with a copy of the relevant document under this section, it is for the defendant to prove that he had.

Requirements in connection with publication of accounts.

240.—(1) If a company publishes any of its statutory accounts, they must be accompanied by the relevant auditors' report under section 235.

(2) A company which is required to prepare group accounts for a financial year shall not publish its statutory individual accounts for that year without also publishing with them its statutory group accounts.

(3) If a company publishes non-statutory accounts, it shall publish with them a statement indicating—

(a) that they are not the company's statutory accounts,

(b) whether statutory accounts dealing with any financial year with which the non-statutory accounts purport to deal have been delivered to the registrar,

(c) whether the company's auditors have made a report under section 235 on the statutory accounts for any such financial year, and

(d) whether any report so made was qualified or contained a statement under section 237(2) or (3) (accounting records or returns inadequate, accounts not agreeing with records and returns or failure to obtain necessary information and explanations);

and it shall not publish with the non-statutory accounts any auditors' report under section 235.

(4) For the purposes of this section a company shall be regarded as publishing a document if it publishes, issues or circulates it or otherwise makes it available for public inspection in a manner calculated to invite members of the public generally, or any class of members of the public, to read it.

(5) References in this section to a company's statutory accounts are to its individual or group accounts for a financial year as required to be delivered to the registrar under section 242; and references to the publication by a company of "non-statutory accounts" are to the publication of—

(a) any balance sheet or profit and loss account relating to, or purporting to deal with, a financial year of the company, or

(b) an account in any form purporting to be a balance sheet or profit and loss account for the group consisting of the company and its subsidiary undertakings relating to, or purporting to deal with, a financial year of the company,

otherwise than as part of the company's statutory accounts.

(6) A company which contravenes any provision of this section, and any officer of it who is in default, is guilty of an offence and liable to a fine.".

11. The following sections are inserted in Part VII of the Companies Act 1985—

"Laying and delivering of accounts and reports

Accounts and reports to be laid before company in general meeting.

241.—(1) The directors of a company shall in respect of each financial year lay before the company in general meeting copies of the company's annual accounts, the directors' report and the auditors' report on those accounts.

(2) If the requirements of subsection (1) are not complied with before the end of the period allowed for laying and delivering accounts and reports, every person who immediately before the end of that period was a director of the company is guilty of an offence and liable to a fine and, for continued contravention, to a daily default fine.

(3) It is a defence for a person charged with such an offence to prove that he took all reasonable steps for securing that those requirements would be complied with before the end of that period.

(4) It is not a defence to prove that the documents in question were not in fact prepared as required by this Part.

Accounts and reports to be delivered to the registrar.

242.—(1) The directors of a company shall in respect of each financial year deliver to the registrar a copy of the company's annual accounts together with a copy of the directors' report for that year and a copy of the auditors' report on those accounts.

If any document comprised in those accounts or reports is in a language other than English, the directors shall annex to the copy of that document delivered a translation of it into English, certified in the prescribed manner to be a correct translation.

(2) If the requirements of subsection (1) are not complied with before the end of the period allowed for laying and delivering accounts and reports, every person who immediately before the end of that period was a director of the company is guilty of an offence and liable to a fine and, for continued contravention, to a daily default fine.

(3) Further, if the directors of the company fail to make good the default within 14 days after the service of a notice on them requiring compliance, the court may on the application of any member or creditor of the company or of the registrar, make an order directing the directors (or any of them) to make good the default within such time as may be specified in the order.

The court's order may provide that all costs of and incidental to the application shall be borne by the directors.

(4) It is a defence for a person charged with an offence under this section to prove that he took all reasonable steps for securing that the requirements of subsection (1) would be complied with before the end of the period allowed for laying and delivering accounts and reports.

(5) It is not a defence in any proceedings under this section to prove that the documents in question were not in fact prepared as required by this Part.

Civil penalty for failure to deliver accounts.

242A.—(1) Where the requirements of section 242(1) are not complied with before the end of the period allowed for laying and delivering accounts and reports, the company is liable to a civil penalty.

This is in addition to any liability of the directors under section 242.

(2) The amount of the penalty is determined by reference to the length of the period between the end of the period allowed for laying and delivering accounts and reports and the day on which the requirements are complied with, and whether the company is a public or private company, as follows:—

Length of period	*Public company*	*Private company*
Not more than 3 months.	£500	£100
More than 3 months but not more than 6 months.	£1,000	£250
More than 6 months but not more than 12 months.	£2,000	£500
More than 12 months.	£5,000	£1,000

(3) The penalty may be recovered by the registrar and shall be paid by him into the Consolidated Fund.

(4) It is not a defence in proceedings under this section to prove that the documents in question were not in fact prepared as required by this Part.

Accounts of subsidiary undertakings to be appended in certain cases.

243.—(1) The following provisions apply where at the end of the financial year a parent company has as a subsidiary undertaking—

(a) a body corporate incorporated outside Great Britain which does not have an established place of business in Great Britain, or

(b) an unincorporated undertaking,

which is excluded from consolidation in accordance with section 229(4) (undertaking with activities different from the undertakings included in the consolidation).

(2) There shall be appended to the copy of the company's annual accounts delivered to the registrar in accordance with section 242 a copy of the undertaking's latest individual accounts and, if it is a parent undertaking, its latest group accounts.

If the accounts appended are required by law to be audited, a copy of the auditors' report shall also be appended.

(3) The accounts must be for a period ending not more than twelve months before the end of the financial year for which the parent company's accounts are made up.

(4) If any document required to be appended is in a language other than English, the directors shall annex to the copy of that document delivered a translation of it into English, certified in the prescribed manner to be a correct translation.

(5) The above requirements are subject to the following qualifications—

> (a) an undertaking is not required to prepare for the purposes of this section accounts which would not otherwise be prepared, and if no accounts satisfying the above requirements are prepared none need be appended;

> (b) a document need not be appended if it would not otherwise be required to be published, or made available for public inspection, anywhere in the world, but in that case the reason for not appending it shall be stated in a note to the company's accounts;

> (c) where an undertaking and all its subsidiary undertakings are excluded from consolidation in accordance with section 229(4), the accounts of such of the subsidiary undertakings of that undertaking as are included in its consolidated group accounts need not be appended.

(6) Subsections (2) to (4) of section 242 (penalties, &c. in case of default) apply in relation to the requirements of this section as they apply in relation to the requirements of subsection (1) of that section.

Period allowed for laying and delivering accounts and reports.

244.—(1) The period allowed for laying and delivering accounts and reports is—

> (a) for a private company, 10 months after the end of the relevant accounting reference period, and

> (b) for a public company, 7 months after the end of that period.

This is subject to the following provisions of this section.

(2) If the relevant accounting reference period is the company's first and is a period of more than 12 months, the period allowed is—

    (a) 10 months or 7 months, as the case may be, from the first anniversary of the incorporation of the company, or

    (b) 3 months from the end of the accounting reference period,

whichever last expires.

(3) Where a company carries on business, or has interests, outside the United Kingdom, the Channel Islands and the Isle of Man, the directors may, in respect of any financial year, give to the registrar before the end of the period allowed by subsection (1) or (2) a notice in the prescribed form—

    (a) stating that the company so carries on business or has such interests, and

    (b) claiming a 3 month extension of the period allowed for laying and delivering accounts and reports;

and upon such a notice being given the period is extended accordingly.

(4) If the relevant accounting period is treated as shortened by virtue of a notice given by the company under section 225 (alteration of accounting reference date), the period allowed for laying and delivering accounts is that applicable in accordance with the above provisions or 3 months from the date of the notice under that section, whichever last expires.

(5) If for any special reason the Secretary of State thinks fit he may, on an application made before the expiry of the period otherwise allowed, by notice in writing to a company extend that period by such further period as may be specified in the notice.

(6) In this section "the relevant accounting reference period" means the accounting reference period by reference to which the financial year for the accounts in question was determined.".

Remedies for failure to comply with accounting requirements. 1985 c. 6.

12. The following sections are inserted in Part VII of the Companies Act 1985—

"Revision of defective accounts and reports

Voluntary revision of annual accounts or directors' report.

245.—(1) If it appears to the directors of a company that any annual accounts of the company, or any directors' report, did not comply with the requirements of this Act, they may prepare revised accounts or a revised report.

(2) Where copies of the previous accounts or report
have been laid before the company in general meeting or
delivered to the registrar, the revisions shall be confined
to—

(a) the correction of those respects in which the
previous accounts or report did not comply with
the requirements of this Act, and

(b) the making of any necessary consequential
alterations.

(3) The Secretary of State may make provision by
regulations as to the application of the provisions of this
Act in relation to revised annual accounts or a revised
directors' report.

(4) The regulations may, in particular—

(a) make different provision according to whether
the previous accounts or report are replaced or
are supplemented by a document indicating the
corrections to be made;

(b) make provision with respect to the functions of
the company's auditors in relation to the revised
accounts or report;

(c) require the directors to take such steps as may be
specified in the regulations where the previous
accounts or report have been—

(i) sent out to members and others under
section 238(1),

(ii) laid before the company in general
meeting, or

(iii) delivered to the registrar,

or where a summary financial statement based
on the previous accounts or report has been sent
to members under section 251;

(d) apply the provisions of this Act (including those
creating criminal offences) subject to such
additions, exceptions and modifications as are
specified in the regulations.

(5) Regulations under this section shall be made by
statutory instrument which shall be subject to annulment
in pursuance of a resolution of either House of
Parliament.

Secretary of   245A.—(1) Where copies of a company's annual
State's notice in   accounts have been sent out under section 238, or a copy
respect of annual   of a company's annual accounts has been laid before the
accounts.   company in general meeting or delivered to the registrar,
and it appears to the Secretary of State that there is, or
may be, a question whether the accounts comply with the
requirements of this Act, he may give notice to the
directors of the company indicating the respects in which
it appears to him that such a question arises, or may arise.

(2) The notice shall specify a period of not less than one month for the directors to give him an explanation of the accounts or prepare revised accounts.

(3) If at the end of the specified period, or such longer period as he may allow, it appears to the Secretary of State that no satisfactory explanation of the accounts has been given and that the accounts have not been revised so as to comply with the requirements of this Act, he may if he thinks fit apply to the court.

(4) The provisions of this section apply equally to revised annual accounts, in which case the references to revised accounts shall be read as references to further revised accounts.

Application to court in respect of defective accounts.

245B.—(1) An application may be made to the court—

    (a) by the Secretary of State, after having complied with section 245A, or

    (b) by a person authorised by the Secretary of State for the purposes of this section,

for a declaration or declarator that the annual accounts of a company do not comply with the requirements of this Act and for an order requiring the directors of the company to prepare revised accounts.

(2) Notice of the application, together with a general statement of the matters at issue in the proceedings, shall be given by the applicant to the registrar for registration.

(3) If the court orders the preparation of revised accounts, it may give directions with respect to—

    (a) the auditing of the accounts,

    (b) the revision of any directors' report or summary financial statement, and

    (c) the taking of steps by the directors to bring the making of the order to the notice of persons likely to rely on the previous accounts,

and such other matters as the court thinks fit.

(4) If the court finds that the accounts did not comply with the requirements of this Act it may order that all or part of—

    (a) the costs (or in Scotland expenses) of and incidental to the application, and

    (b) any reasonable expenses incurred by the company in connection with or in consequence of the preparation of revised accounts,

shall be borne by such of the directors as were party to the approval of the defective accounts.

For this purpose every director of the company at the time the accounts were approved shall be taken to have been a party to their approval unless he shows that he took all reasonable steps to prevent their being approved.

(5) Where the court makes an order under subsection (4) it shall have regard to whether the directors party to the approval of the defective accounts knew or ought to have known that the accounts did not comply with the requirements of this Act, and it may exclude one or more directors from the order or order the payment of different amounts by different directors.

(6) On the conclusion of proceedings on an application under this section, the applicant shall give to the registrar for registration an office copy of the court order or, as the case may be, notice that the application has failed or been withdrawn.

(7) The provisions of this section apply equally to revised annual accounts, in which case the references to revised accounts shall be read as references to further revised accounts.

Other persons authorised to apply to court.

245C. (1) The Secretary of State may authorise for the purposes of section 245B any person appearing to him—

(a) to have an interest in, and to have satisfactory procedures directed to securing, compliance by companies with the accounting requirements of this Act,

(b) to have satisfactory procedures for receiving and investigating complaints about the annual accounts of companies, and

(c) otherwise to be a fit and proper person to be authorised.

(2) A person may be authorised generally or in respect of particular classes of case, and different persons may be authorised in respect of different classes of case.

(3) The Secretary of State may refuse to authorise a person if he considers that his authorisation is unnecessary having regard to the fact that there are one or more other persons who have been or are likely to be authorised.

(4) Authorisation shall be by order made by statutory instrument which shall be subject to annulment in pursuance of a resolution of either House of Parliament.

(5) Where authorisation is revoked, the revoking order may make such provision as the Secretary of State thinks fit with respect to pending proceedings.

(6) Neither a person authorised under this section, nor any officer, servant or member of the governing body of such a person, shall be liable in damages for anything done or purporting to be done for the purposes of or in connection with—

(a) the taking of steps to discover whether there are grounds for an application to the court,

(b) the determination whether or not to make such an application, or

(c) the publication of its reasons for any such decision,

unless the act or omission is shown to have been in bad faith.".

Exemptions and special provisions

Small and medium-sized companies and groups.
1985 c. 6.

13.—(1) The following sections are inserted in Part VII of the Companies Act 1985, as the beginning of a Chapter II—

"CHAPTER II

EXEMPTIONS, EXCEPTIONS AND SPECIAL PROVISIONS

Small and medium-sized companies and groups

Exemptions for small and medium-sized companies.

246.—(1) A company which qualifies as a small or medium-sized company in relation to a financial year—

(a) is exempt from the requirements of paragraph 36A of Schedule 4 (disclosure with respect to compliance with accounting standards), and

(b) is entitled to the exemptions provided by Schedule 8 with respect to the delivery to the registrar under section 242 of individual accounts and other documents for that financial year.

(2) In that Schedule—

Part I relates to small companies,

Part II relates to medium-sized companies, and

Part III contains supplementary provisions.

(3) A company is not entitled to the exemptions mentioned in subsection (1) if it is, or was at any time within the financial year to which the accounts relate—

(a) a public company,

(b) a banking or insurance company, or

(c) an authorised person under the Financial Services Act 1986,

or if it is or was at any time during that year a member of an ineligible group.

(4) A group is ineligible if any of its members is—

(a) a public company or a body corporate which (not being a company) has power under its constitution to offer its shares or debentures to the public and may lawfully exercise that power,

(b) an authorised institution under the Banking Act 1987,

(c) an insurance company to which Part II of the Insurance Companies Act 1982 applies, or

(d) an authorised person under the Financial Services Act 1986.

(5) A parent company shall not be treated as qualifying as a small company in relation to a financial year unless the group headed by it qualifies as a small group, and shall not be treated as qualifying as a medium-sized company in relation to a financial year unless that group qualifies as a medium-sized group (see section 249).

Qualification of company as small or medium-sized.

247.—(1) A company qualifies as small or medium-sized in relation to a financial year if the qualifying conditions are met—

(a) in the case of the company's first financial year, in that year, and

(b) in the case of any subsequent financial year, in that year and the preceding year.

(2) A company shall be treated as qualifying as small or medium-sized in relation to a financial year—

(a) if it so qualified in relation to the previous financial year under subsection (1); or

(b) if it was treated as so qualifying in relation to the previous year by virtue of paragraph (a) and the qualifying conditions are met in the year in question.

(3) The qualifying conditions are met by a company in a year in which it satisfies two or more of the following requirements—

Small company

1. Turnover	Not more than £2 million
2. Balance sheet total	Not more than £975,000
3. Number of employees	Not more than 50

Medium-sized company

1. Turnover	Not more than £8 million
2. Balance sheet total	Not more than £3.9 million
3. Number of employees	Not more than 250.

(4) For a period which is a company's financial year but not in fact a year the maximum figures for turnover shall be proportionately adjusted.

(5) The balance sheet total means—

(a) where in the company's accounts Format 1 of the balance sheet formats set out in Part I of Schedule 4 is adopted, the aggregate of the amounts shown in the balance sheet under the headings corresponding to items A to D in that Format, and

(b) where Format 2 is adopted, the aggregate of the amounts shown under the general heading "Assets".

(6) The number of employees means the average number of persons employed by the company in the year (determined on a weekly basis).

That number shall be determined by applying the method of calculation prescribed by paragraph 56(2) and (3) of Schedule 4 for determining the corresponding number required to be stated in a note to the company's accounts.".

1985 c. 6.

(2) Schedule 6 to this Act is substituted for Schedule 8 to the Companies Act 1985.

(3) The following sections are inserted in Part VII of the Companies Act 1985—

"Exemption for small and medium-sized groups.

248.—(1) A parent company need not prepare group accounts for a financial year in relation to which the group headed by that company qualifies as a small or medium-sized group and is not an ineligible group.

(2) A group is ineligible if any of its members is—

(a) a public company or a body corporate which (not being a company) has power under its constitution to offer its shares or debentures to the public and may lawfully exercise that power,

(b) an authorised institution under the Banking Act 1987,

(c) an insurance company to which Part II of the Insurance Companies Act 1982 applies, or

(d) an authorised person under the Financial Services Act 1986.

(3) If the directors of a company propose to take advantage of the exemption conferred by this section, it is the auditors' duty to provide them with a report stating whether in their opinion the company is entitled to the exemption.

(4) The exemption does not apply unless—

(a) the auditors' report states that in their opinion the company is so entitled, and

(b) that report is attached to the individual accounts of the company.

Qualification of group as small or medium-sized.

249.—(1) A group qualifies as small or medium-sized in relation to a financial year if the qualifying conditions are met—

(a) in the case of the parent company's first financial year, in that year, and

(b) in the case of any subsequent financial year, in that year and the preceding year.

(2) A group shall be treated as qualifying as small or medium-sized in relation to a financial year—

(a) if it so qualified in relation to the previous financial year under subsection (1); or

(b) if it was treated as so qualifying in relation to the
    previous year by virtue of paragraph (a) and the
    qualifying conditions are met in the year in
    question.

(3) The qualifying conditions are met by a group in a year in which it satisfies two or more of the following requirements—

Small group

1. Aggregate turnover	Not more than £2 million net (or £2.4 million gross)
2. Aggregate balance sheet total	Not more than £1 million net (or £1.2 million gross)
3. Aggregate number of employees	Not more than 50

Medium-sized group

1. Aggregate turnover	Not more than £8 million net (or £9.6 million gross)
2. Aggregate balance sheet total	Not more than £3.9 million net (or £4.7 million gross)
3. Aggregate number of employees	Not more than 250.

(4) The aggregate figures shall be ascertained by aggregating the relevant figures determined in accordance with section 247 for each member of the group.

In relation to the aggregate figures for turnover and balance sheet total, "net" means with the set-offs and other adjustments required by Schedule 4A in the case of group accounts and "gross" means without those set-offs and other adjustments; and a company may satisfy the relevant requirement on the basis of either the net or the gross figure.

(5) The figures for each subsidiary undertaking shall be those included in its accounts for the relevant financial year, that is—

(a) if its financial year ends with that of the parent company, that financial year, and

(b) if not, its financial year ending last before the end of the financial year of the parent company.

(6) If those figures cannot be obtained without disproportionate expense or undue delay, the latest available figures shall be taken.".

14. The following section is inserted in Part VII of the Companies Act 1985—

"Dormant companies

Resolution not
to appoint
auditors.

250.—(1) A company may by special resolution make itself exempt from the provisions of this Part relating to the audit of accounts in the following cases—

(a) if the company has been dormant from the time of its formation, by a special resolution passed before the first general meeting of the company at which annual accounts are laid;

(b) if the company has been dormant since the end of the previous financial year and—

(i) is entitled in respect of its individual accounts for that year to the exemptions conferred by section 246 on a small company, or would be so entitled but for being a member of an ineligible group, and

(ii) is not required to prepare group accounts for that year,

by a special resolution passed at a general meeting of the company at which the annual accounts for that year are laid.

(2) A company may not pass such a resolution if it is—

(a) a public company,

(b) a banking or insurance company, or

(c) an authorised person under the Financial Services Act 1986.

(3) A company is "dormant" during a period in which no significant accounting transaction occurs, that is, no transaction which is required by section 221 to be entered in the company's accounting records; and a company ceases to be dormant on the occurrence of such a transaction.

For this purpose there shall be disregarded any transaction arising from the taking of shares in the company by a subscriber to the memorandum in pursuance of an undertaking of his in the memorandum.

(4) Where a company is, at the end of a financial year, exempt by virtue of this section from the provisions of this Part relating to the audit of accounts—

(a) sections 238 and 239 (right to receive or demand copies of accounts and reports) have effect with the omission of references to the auditors' report;

(b) no copies of an auditors' report need be laid before the company in general meeting;

(c) no copy of an auditors' report need be delivered to the registrar, and if none is delivered, the copy of the balance sheet so delivered shall contain a statement by the directors, in a position immediately above the signature required by section 233(4), that the company was dormant throughout the financial year; and

(d) the company shall be treated as entitled in respect of its individual accounts for that year to the exemptions conferred by section 246 on a small company notwithstanding that it is a member of an ineligible group.

(5) Where a company which is exempt by virtue of this section from the provisions of this Part relating to the audit of accounts—

(a) ceases to be dormant, or

(b) would no longer qualify (for any other reason) to make itself exempt by passing a resolution under this section,

it shall thereupon cease to be so exempt.".

15. The following section is inserted in Part VII of the Companies Act 1985—

Public listed companies: provision of summary financial statement.
1985 c. 6.

"Listed public companies

Provision of summary financial statement to shareholders.

251.—(1) A public company whose shares, or any class of whose shares, are listed need not, in such cases as may be specified by regulations made by the Secretary of State, and provided any conditions so specified are complied with, send copies of the documents referred to in section 238(1) to members of the company, but may instead send them a summary financial statement.

In this subsection "listed" means admitted to the Official List of The International Stock Exchange of the United Kingdom and the Republic of Ireland Limited.

(2) Copies of the documents referred to in section 238(1) shall, however, be sent to any member of the company who wishes to receive them; and the Secretary of State may by regulations make provision as to the manner in which it is to be ascertained whether a member of the company wishes to receive them.

(3) The summary financial statement shall be derived from the company's annual accounts and the directors' report and shall be in such form and contain such information as may be specified by regulations made by the Secretary of State.

(4) Every summary financial statement shall—

(a) state that it is only a summary of information in the company's annual accounts and the directors' report;

(b) contain a statement by the company's auditors of their opinion as to whether the summary financial statement is consistent with those accounts and that report and complies with the requirements of this section and regulations made under it;

(c) state whether the auditors' report on the annual accounts was unqualified or qualified, and if it was qualified set out the report in full together with any further material needed to understand the qualification;

(d) state whether the auditors' report on the annual accounts contained a statement under—

　　(i) section 237(2) (accounting records or returns inadequate or accounts not agreeing with records and returns), or

　　(ii) section 237(3) (failure to obtain necessary information and explanations),

and if so, set out the statement in full.

(5) Regulations under this section shall be made by statutory instrument which shall be subject to annulment in pursuance of a resolution of either House of Parliament.

(6) If default is made in complying with this section or regulations made under it, the company and every officer of it who is in default is guilty of an offence and liable to a fine.

(7) Section 240 (requirements in connection with publication of accounts) does not apply in relation to the provision to members of a company of a summary financial statement in accordance with this section.".

Private companies: election to dispense with laying of accounts and reports before general meeting.
1985 c. 6.

16. The following sections are inserted in Part VII of the Companies Act 1985—

"Private companies

Election to dispense with laying of accounts and reports before general meeting.

252.—(1) A private company may elect (by elective resolution in accordance with section 379A) to dispense with the laying of accounts and reports before the company in general meeting.

(2) An election has effect in relation to the accounts and reports in respect of the financial year in which the election is made and subsequent financial years.

(3) Whilst an election is in force, the references in the following provisions of this Act to the laying of accounts before the company in general meeting shall be read as references to the sending of copies of the accounts to members and others under section 238(1)—

(a) section 235(1) (accounts on which auditors are to report),

(b) section 270(3) and (4) (accounts by reference to which distributions are justified), and

(c) section 320(2) (accounts relevant for determining company's net assets for purposes of ascertaining whether approval required for certain transactions);

and the requirement in section 271(4) that the auditors' statement under that provision be laid before the company in general meeting shall be read as a requirement that it be sent to members and others along with the copies of the accounts sent to them under section 238(1).

(4) If an election under this section ceases to have effect, section 241 applies in relation to the accounts and reports in respect of the financial year in which the election ceases to have effect and subsequent financial years.

Right of shareholder to require laying of accounts.

253.—(1) Where an election under section 252 is in force, the copies of the accounts and reports sent out in accordance with section 238(1)—

(a) shall be sent not less than 28 days before the end of the period allowed for laying and delivering accounts and reports, and

(b) shall be accompanied, in the case of a member of the company, by a notice informing him of his right to require the laying of the accounts and reports before a general meeting;

and section 238(5) (penalty for default) applies in relation to the above requirements as to the requirements contained in that section.

(2) Before the end of the period of 28 days beginning with the day on which the accounts and reports are sent out in accordance with section 238(1), any member or auditor of the company may by notice in writing deposited at the registered office of the company require that a general meeting be held for the purpose of laying the accounts and reports before the company.

(3) If the directors do not within 21 days from the date of the deposit of such a notice proceed duly to convene a meeting, the person who deposited the notice may do so himself.

(4) A meeting so convened shall not be held more than three months from that date and shall be convened in the same manner, as nearly as possible, as that in which meetings are to be convened by directors.

(5) Where the directors do not duly convene a meeting, any reasonable expenses incurred by reason of that failure by the person who deposited the notice shall be made good to him by the company, and shall be recouped by the company out of any fees, or other remuneration in respect of their services, due or to become due to such of the directors as were in default.

(6) The directors shall be deemed not to have duly convened a meeting if they convene a meeting for a date more than 28 days after the date of the notice convening it.".

Unlimited companies: exemption from requirement to deliver accounts and reports.
1985 c. 6.

17. The following section is inserted in Part VII of the Companies Act 1985—

"Unlimited companies

Exemption from requirement to deliver accounts and reports.

254.—(1) The directors of an unlimited company are not required to deliver accounts and reports to the registrar in respect of a financial year if the following conditions are met.

(2) The conditions are that at no time during the relevant accounting reference period—

(a) has the company been, to its knowledge, a subsidiary undertaking of an undertaking which was then limited, or

(b) have there been, to its knowledge, exercisable by or on behalf of two or more undertakings which were then limited, rights which if exercisable by one of them would have made the company a subsidiary undertaking of it, or

(c) has the company been a parent company of an undertaking which was then limited.

The references above to an undertaking being limited at a particular time are to an undertaking (under whatever law established) the liability of whose members is at that time limited.

(3) The exemption conferred by this section does not apply if at any time during the relevant accounting period the company carried on business as the promoter of a trading stamp scheme within the Trading Stamps Act 1964.

(4) Where a company is exempt by virtue of this section from the obligation to deliver accounts, section 240 (requirements in connection with publication of accounts) has effect with the following modifications—

(a) in subsection (3)(b) for the words from 'whether statutory accounts' to 'have been delivered to the registrar' substitute 'that the company is exempt from the requirement to deliver statutory accounts', and

(b) in subsection (5) for 'as required to be delivered to the registrar under section 242' substitute 'as prepared in accordance with this Part and approved by the board of directors'.".

18.—(1) The following sections are inserted in Part VII of the Companies Act 1985—

"Banking and insurance companies and groups

Special provisions for banking and insurance companies.

255.—(1) A banking or insurance company may prepare its individual accounts in accordance with Part I of Schedule 9 rather than Schedule 4.

(2) Accounts so prepared shall contain a statement that they are prepared in accordance with the special provisions of this Part relating to banking companies or insurance companies, as the case may be.

(3) In relation to the preparation of individual accounts in accordance with the special provisions of this Part relating to banking or insurance companies, the references to the provisions of Schedule 4 in section 226(4) and (5) (relationship between specific requirements and duty to give true and fair view) shall be read as references to the provisions of Part I of Schedule 9.

(4) The Secretary of State may, on the application or with the consent of the directors of a company which prepares individual accounts in accordance with the special provisions of this Part relating to banking or insurance companies, modify in relation to the company any of the requirements of this Part for the purpose of adapting them to the circumstances of the company.

This does not affect the duty to give a true and fair view.

Special provisions for banking and insurance groups.

255A.—(1) The parent company of a banking or insurance group may prepare group accounts in accordance with the provisions of this Part as modified by Part II of Schedule 9.

(2) Accounts so prepared shall contain a statement that they are prepared in accordance with the special provisions of this Part relating to banking groups or insurance groups, as the case may be.

(3) References in this Part to a banking group are to a group where—

(a) the parent company is a banking company, or

(b) at least one of the undertakings in the group is an authorised institution under the Banking Act 1987 and the predominant activities of the group are such as to make it inappropriate to prepare group accounts in accordance with the formats in Part I of Schedule 4.

(4) References in this Part to an insurance group are to a group where—

(a) the parent company is an insurance company, or

(b) the predominant activity of the group is insurance business and activities which are a direct extension of or ancillary to insurance business.

(5) In relation to the preparation of group accounts in accordance with the special provisions of this Part relating to banking or insurance groups, the references to the provisions of Schedule 4A in section 227(5) and (6) (relationship between specific requirements and duty to give true and fair view) shall be read as references to those provisions as modified by Part II of Schedule 9.

(6) The Secretary of State may, on the application or with the consent of the directors of a company which prepares group accounts in accordance with the special provisions of this Part relating to banking or insurance groups, modify in relation to the company any of the requirements of this Part for the purpose of adapting them to the circumstances of the company.

Modification of disclosure requirements in relation to banking company or group.

255B.—(1) In relation to a company which prepares accounts in accordance with the special provisions of this Part relating to banking companies or groups, the provisions of Schedule 5 (additional disclosure: related undertakings) have effect subject to Part III of Schedule 9.

(2) In relation to a banking company, or the parent company of a banking company, the provisions of Schedule 6 (disclosure: emoluments and other benefits of directors and others) have effect subject to Part IV of Schedule 9.

Directors' report where accounts prepared in accordance with special provisions.

255C.—(1) The following provisions apply in relation to the directors' report of a company for a financial year in respect of which it prepares accounts in accordance with the special provisions of this Part relating to banking or insurance companies or groups.

(2) The information required to be given by paragraph 6, 8 or 13 of Part I of Schedule 9 (which is allowed to be given in a statement or report annexed to the accounts), may be given in the directors' report instead.

Information so given shall be treated for the purposes of audit as forming part of the accounts.

(3) The reference in section 234(1)(b) to the amount proposed to be carried to reserves shall be construed as a reference to the amount proposed to be carried to reserves within the meaning of Part I of Schedule 9.

(4) If the company takes advantage, in relation to its individual or group accounts, of the exemptions conferred by paragraph 27 or 28 of Part I of Schedule 9, paragraph 1 of Schedule 7 (disclosure of asset values) does not apply.

(5) The directors' report shall, in addition to complying with Schedule 7, also comply with Schedule 10 (which specifies additional matters to be disclosed).''.

(2) The following section is inserted in Part VII of the Companies Act 1985—

"Power to apply provisions to banking partnerships.

255D.—(1) The Secretary of State may by regulations apply to banking partnerships, subject to such exceptions, adaptations and modifications as he considers appropriate, the provisions of this Part applying to banking companies.

(2) A "banking partnership" means a partnership which is an authorised institution under the Banking Act 1987.

(3) Regulations under this section shall be made by statutory instrument.

(4) No regulations under this section shall be made unless a draft of the instrument containing the regulations has been laid before Parliament and approved by a resolution of each House.".

(3) Schedule 9 to the Companies Act 1985 (form and content of special category accounts) is amended in accordance with Schedule 7 to this Act.

1985 c. 6.

(4) In that Schedule—

Part I contains amendments relating to the form and content of accounts of banking and insurance companies and groups,

Part II contains provisions with respect to the group accounts of banking and insurance groups,

Part III contains provisions adapting the requirements of Schedule 5 to the Companies Act 1985 (additional disclosure: related undertakings), and

Part IV contains provisions relating to the requirements of Schedule 6 to that Act (additional disclosure: emoluments and other benefits of directors and others).

(5) Schedule 8 to this Act (directors' report where accounts prepared in accordance with special provisions for banking and insurance companies and groups) is substituted for Schedule 10 to the Companies Act 1985.

Supplementary provisions

19. The following section is inserted in Part VII of the Companies Act 1985, as the beginning of a Chapter III—

Accounting standards.

"CHAPTER III

SUPPLEMENTARY PROVISIONS

Accounting standards

Accounting standards.

256.—(1) In this Part "accounting standards" means statements of standard accounting practice issued by such body or bodies as may be prescribed by regulations.

(2) References in this Part to accounting standards applicable to a company's annual accounts are to such standards as are, in accordance with their terms, relevant to the company's circumstances and to the accounts.

(3) The Secretary of State may make grants to or for the purposes of bodies concerned with—

(a) issuing accounting standards,

(b) overseeing and directing the issuing of such standards, or

(c) investigating departures from such standards or from the accounting requirements of this Act and taking steps to secure compliance with them.

(4) Regulations under this section may contain such transitional and other supplementary and incidental provisions as appear to the Secretary of State to be appropriate.".

Power to alter accounting requirements. 1985 c. 6.

20. The following section is inserted in Part VII of the Companies Act 1985—

"Power to alter accounting requirements

Power of Secretary of State to alter accounting requirements.

257.—(1) The Secretary of State may by regulations made by statutory instrument modify the provisions of this Part.

(2) Regulations which—

(a) add to the classes of documents required to be prepared, laid before the company in general meeting or delivered to the registrar,

(b) restrict the classes of company which have the benefit of any exemption, exception or special provision,

(c) require additional matter to be included in a document of any class, or

(d) otherwise render the requirements of this Part more onerous,

shall not be made unless a draft of the instrument containing the regulations has been laid before Parliament and approved by a resolution of each House.

(3) Otherwise, a statutory instrument containing regulations under this section shall be subject to annulment in pursuance of a resolution of either House of Parliament.

(4) Regulations under this section may—

(a) make different provision for different cases or classes of case,

(b) repeal and re-enact provisions with modifications of form or arrangement, whether or not they are modified in substance,

(c) make consequential amendments or repeals in other provisions of this Act, or in other enactments, and

    (d) contain such transitional and other incidental and supplementary provisions as the Secretary of State thinks fit.

(5) Any modification by regulations under this section of section 258 or Schedule 10A (parent and subsidiary undertakings) does not apply for the purposes of enactments outside the Companies Acts unless the regulations so provide.".

21.—(1) The following section is inserted in Part VII of the Companies Act 1985—

"Parent and subsidiary undertakings

Parent and subsidiary undertakings.

    258.—(1) The expressions "parent undertaking" and "subsidiary undertaking" in this Part shall be construed as follows; and a "parent company" means a parent undertaking which is a company.

    (2) An undertaking is a parent undertaking in relation to another undertaking, a subsidiary undertaking, if—

        (a) it holds a majority of the voting rights in the undertaking, or

        (b) it is a member of the undertaking and has the right to appoint or remove a majority of its board of directors, or

        (c) it has the right to exercise a dominant influence over the undertaking—

            (i) by virtue of provisions contained in the undertaking's memorandum or articles, or

            (ii) by virtue of a control contract, or

        (d) it is a member of the undertaking and controls alone, pursuant to an agreement with other shareholders or members, a majority of the voting rights in the undertaking.

    (3) For the purposes of subsection (2) an undertaking shall be treated as a member of another undertaking—

        (a) if any of its subsidiary undertakings is a member of that undertaking, or

        (b) if any shares in that other undertaking are held by a person acting on behalf of the undertaking or any of its subsidiary undertakings.

    (4) An undertaking is also a parent undertaking in relation to another undertaking, a subsidiary undertaking, if it has a participating interest in the undertaking and—

        (a) it actually exercises a dominant influence over it, or

        (b) it and the subsidiary undertaking are managed on a unified basis.

(5) A parent undertaking shall be treated as the parent undertaking of undertakings in relation to which any of its subsidiary undertakings are, or are to be treated as, parent undertakings; and references to its subsidiary undertakings shall be construed accordingly.

(6) Schedule 10A contains provisions explaining expressions used in this section and otherwise supplementing this section.".

1985 c. 6.

(2) Schedule 9 to this Act (parent and subsidiary undertakings: supplementary provisions) is inserted after Schedule 10 to the Companies Act 1985, as Schedule 10A.

Other interpretation provisions.

22. The following sections are inserted in Part VII of the Companies Act 1985—

"Other interpretation provisions

Meaning of "undertaking" and related expressions.

259.—(1) In this Part "undertaking" means—

(a) a body corporate or partnership, or

(b) an unincorporated association carrying on a trade or business, with or without a view to profit.

(2) In this Part references to shares—

(a) in relation to an undertaking with a share capital, are to allotted shares;

(b) in relation to an undertaking with capital but no share capital, are to rights to share in the capital of the undertaking; and

(c) in relation to an undertaking without capital, are to interests—

(i) conferring any right to share in the profits or liability to contribute to the losses of the undertaking, or

(ii) giving rise to an obligation to contribute to the debts or expenses of the undertaking in the event of a winding up.

(3) Other expressions appropriate to companies shall be construed, in relation to an undertaking which is not a company, as references to the corresponding persons, officers, documents or organs, as the case may be, appropriate to undertakings of that description.

This is subject to provision in any specific context providing for the translation of such expressions.

(4) References in this Part to "fellow subsidiary undertakings" are to undertakings which are subsidiary undertakings of the same parent undertaking but are not parent undertakings or subsidiary undertakings of each other.

(5) In this Part "group undertaking", in relation to an undertaking, means an undertaking which is—

    (a) a parent undertaking or subsidiary undertaking of that undertaking, or

    (b) a subsidiary undertaking of any parent undertaking of that undertaking.

Participating interests.

260.—(1) In this Part a "participating interest" means an interest held by an undertaking in the shares of another undertaking which it holds on a long-term basis for the purpose of securing a contribution to its activities by the exercise of control or influence arising from or related to that interest.

(2) A holding of 20 per cent. or more of the shares of an undertaking shall be presumed to be a participating interest unless the contrary is shown.

(3) The reference in subsection (1) to an interest in shares includes—

    (a) an interest which is convertible into an interest in shares, and

    (b) an option to acquire shares or any such interest;

and an interest or option falls within paragraph (a) or (b) notwithstanding that the shares to which it relates are, until the conversion or the exercise of the option, unissued.

(4) For the purposes of this section an interest held on behalf of an undertaking shall be treated as held by it.

(5) For the purposes of this section as it applies in relation to the expression "participating interest" in section 258(4) (definition of "subsidiary undertaking")—

    (a) there shall be attributed to an undertaking any interests held by any of its subsidiary undertakings, and

    (b) the references in subsection (1) to the purpose and activities of an undertaking include the purposes and activities of any of its subsidiary undertakings and of the group as a whole.

(6) In the balance sheet and profit and loss formats set out in Part I of Schedule 4, "participating interest" does not include an interest in a group undertaking.

(7) For the purposes of this section as it applies in relation to the expression "participating interest"—

    (a) in those formats as they apply in relation to group accounts, and

(b) in paragraph 20 of Schedule 4A (group accounts: undertakings to be accounted for as associated undertakings),

the references in subsections (1) to (4) to the interest held by, and the purposes and activities of, the undertaking concerned shall be construed as references to the interest held by, and the purposes and activities of, the group (within the meaning of paragraph 1 of that Schedule).

Notes to the accounts.

261.—(1) Information required by this Part to be given in notes to a company's annual accounts may be contained in the accounts or in a separate document annexed to the accounts.

(2) References in this Part to a company's annual accounts, or to a balance sheet or profit and loss account, include notes to the accounts giving information which is required by any provision of this Act, and required or allowed by any such provision to be given in a note to company accounts.

Minor definitions.

262.—(1) In this Part—

"annual accounts" means—

(a) the individual accounts required by section 226, and

(b) any group accounts required by section 227,

(but see also section 230 (treatment of individual profit and loss account where group accounts prepared));

"annual report", in relation to a company, means the directors' report required by section 234;

"balance sheet date" means the date as at which the balance sheet was made up;

"capitalisation", in relation to work or costs, means treating that work or those costs as a fixed asset;

"credit institution" means an undertaking carrying on a deposit-taking business within the meaning of the Banking Act 1987;

"fixed assets" means assets of a company which are intended for use on a continuing basis in the company's activities, and "current assets" means assets not intended for such use;

"group" means a parent undertaking and its subsidiary undertakings;

"included in the consolidation", in relation to group accounts, or "included in consolidated group accounts", means that the undertaking is included in the accounts by the method of full (and not proportional) consolidation, and references to an undertaking excluded from consolidation shall be construed accordingly;

"purchase price", in relation to an asset of a company or any raw materials or consumables used in the production of such an asset, includes any consideration (whether in cash or otherwise) given by the company in respect of that asset or those materials or consumables, as the case may be;

"qualified", in relation to an auditors' report, means that the report does not state the auditors' unqualified opinion that the accounts have been properly prepared in accordance with this Act or, in the case of an undertaking not required to prepare accounts in accordance with this Act, under any corresponding legislation under which it is required to prepare accounts;

"true and fair view" refers—

(a) in the case of individual accounts, to the requirement of section 226(2), and

(b) in the case of group accounts, to the requirement of section 227(3);

"turnover", in relation to a company, means the amounts derived from the provision of goods and services falling within the company's ordinary activities, after deduction of—

(i) trade discounts,

(ii) value added tax, and

(iii) any other taxes based on the amounts so derived.

(2) In the case of an undertaking not trading for profit, any reference in this Part to a profit and loss account is to an income and expenditure account; and references to profit and loss and, in relation to group accounts, to a consolidated profit and loss account shall be construed accordingly.

(3) References in this Part to "realised profits" and "realised losses", in relation to a company's accounts, are to such profits or losses of the company as fall to be treated as realised in accordance with principles generally accepted, at the time when the accounts are prepared, with respect to the determination for accounting purposes of realised profits or losses.

This is without prejudice to—

(a) the construction of any other expression (where appropriate) by reference to accepted accounting principles or practice, or

(b) any specific provision for the treatment of profits or losses of any description as realised.

Index of defined expressions.

262A. The following Table shows the provisions of this Part defining or otherwise explaining expressions used in this Part (other than expressions used only in the same section or paragraph)—

PART I

accounting reference date and accounting reference period	section 224
accounting standards and applicable accounting standards	section 256
annual accounts	
(generally)	section 262(1)
(includes notes to the accounts)	section 261(2)
annual report	section 262(1)
associated undertaking (in Schedule 4A)	paragraph 20 of that Schedule
balance sheet (includes notes)	section 261(2)
balance sheet date	section 262(1)
banking group	section 255A(3)
capitalisation (in relation to work or costs)	section 262(1)
credit institution	section 262(1)
current assets	section 262(1)
fellow subsidiary undertaking	section 259(4)
financial year	section 223
fixed assets	section 262(1)
group	section 262(1)
group undertaking	section 259(5)
historical cost accounting rules (in Schedule 4)	paragraph 29 of that Schedule
included in the consolidation and related expressions	section 262(1)
individual accounts	section 262(1)
insurance group	section 255A(4)
land of freehold tenure and land of leasehold tenure (in relation to Scotland)	
—in Schedule 4	paragraph 93 of that Schedule
—in Schedule 9	paragraph 36 of that Schedule
lease, long lease and short lease	
—in Schedule 4	paragraph 83 of that Schedule
—in Schedule 9	paragraph 34 of that Schedule
listed investment	
—in Schedule 4	paragraph 84 of that Schedule
—in Schedule 9	paragraph 33 of that Schedule
notes to the accounts	section 261(1)
parent undertaking (and parent company)	section 258 and Schedule 10A
participating interest	section 260
pension costs (in Schedule 4)	paragraph 94(2) and (3) of that Schedule
period allowed for laying and delivering accounts and reports	section 244
profit and loss account	
(includes notes)	section 261(2)
(in relation to a company not trading for profit)	section 262(2)
provision	
—in Schedule 4	paragraphs 88 and 89 of that Schedule
—in Schedule 9	paragraph 32 of that Schedule
purchase price	section 262(1)

qualified	section 262(1)	
realised losses and realised profits	section 262(3)	
reserve (in Schedule 9)	paragraph 32 of that Schedule	
shares	section 259(2)	
social security costs (in Schedule 4)	paragraph 94(1) and (3) of that Schedule	
special provisions for banking and insurance companies and groups	sections 255 and 255A	
subsidiary undertaking	section 258 and Schedule 10A	
true and fair view	section 262(1)	
turnover	section 262(1)	
undertaking and related expressions	section 259(1) to (3)".	

Consequential amendments

23. The enactments specified in Schedule 10 have effect with the amendments specified there, which are consequential on the amendments made by the preceding provisions of this Part.

Consequential amendments.

PART II

ELIGIBILITY FOR APPOINTMENT AS COMPANY AUDITOR

Introduction

24.—(1) The main purposes of this Part are to secure that only persons who are properly supervised and appropriately qualified are appointed company auditors, and that audits by persons so appointed are carried out properly and with integrity and with a proper degree of independence.

Introduction.

(2) A "company auditor" means a person appointed as auditor under Chapter V of Part XI of the Companies Act 1985; and the expressions "company audit" and "company audit work" shall be construed accordingly.

1985 c. 6.

Eligibility for appointment

25.—(1) A person is eligible for appointment as a company auditor only if he—

Eligibility for appointment.

   (a) is a member of a recognised supervisory body, and

   (b) is eligible for the appointment under the rules of that body.

(2) An individual or a firm may be appointed a company auditor.

(3) In the cases to which section 34 applies (individuals retaining only 1967 Act authorisation) a person's eligibility for appointment as a company auditor is restricted as mentioned in that section.

26.—(1) The following provisions apply to the appointment as company auditor of a partnership constituted under the law of England and Wales or Northern Ireland, or under the law of any other country or territory in which a partnership is not a legal person.

Effect of appointment of partnership.

(2) The appointment is (unless a contrary intention appears) an appointment of the partnership as such and not of the partners.

(3) Where the partnership ceases, the appointment shall be treated as extending to—

    (a) any partnership which succeeds to the practice of that partnership and is eligible for the appointment, and

    (b) any person who succeeds to that practice having previously carried it on in partnership and is eligible for the appointment.

(4) For this purpose a partnership shall be regarded as succeeding to the practice of another partnership only if the members of the successor partnership are substantially the same as those of the former partnership; and a partnership or other person shall be regarded as succeeding to the practice of a partnership only if it or he succeeds to the whole or substantially the whole of the business of the former partnership.

(5) Where the partnership ceases and no person succeeds to the appointment under subsection (3), the appointment may with the consent of the company be treated as extending to a partnership or other person eligible for the appointment who succeeds to the business of the former partnership or to such part of it as is agreed by the company shall be treated as comprising the appointment.

Ineligibility on ground of lack of independence.

27.—(1) A person is ineligible for appointment as company auditor of a company if he is—

    (a) an officer or employee of the company, or

    (b) a partner or employee of such a person, or a partnership of which such a person is a partner,

or if he is ineligible by virtue of paragraph (a) or (b) for appointment as company auditor of any associated undertaking of the company.

For this purpose an auditor of a company shall not be regarded as an officer or employee of the company.

(2) A person is also ineligible for appointment as company auditor of a company if there exists between him or any associate of his and the company or any associated undertaking a connection of any such description as may be specified by regulations made by the Secretary of State.

The regulations may make different provisions for different cases.

(3) In this section "associated undertaking", in relation to a company, means—

    (a) a parent undertaking or subsidiary undertaking of the company, or

    (b) a subsidiary undertaking of any parent undertaking of the company.

(4) Regulations under this section shall be made by statutory instrument which shall be subject to annulment in pursuance of a resolution of either House of Parliament.

Effect of ineligibility.

28.—(1) No person shall act as a company auditor if he is ineligible for appointment to the office.

(2) If during his term of office a company auditor becomes ineligible for appointment to the office, he shall thereupon vacate office and shall forthwith give notice in writing to the company concerned that he has vacated it by reason of ineligibility.

(3) A person who acts as company auditor in contravention of subsection (1), or fails to give notice of vacating his office as required by subsection (2), is guilty of an offence and liable—

   (a) on conviction on indictment, to a fine, and

   (b) on summary conviction, to a fine not exceeding the statutory maximum.

(4) In the case of continued contravention he is liable on a second or subsequent summary conviction (instead of the fine mentioned in subsection (3)(b)) to a fine not exceeding one-tenth of the statutory maximum in respect of each day on which the contravention is continued.

(5) In proceedings against a person for an offence under this section it is a defence for him to show that he did not know and had no reason to believe that he was, or had become, ineligible for appointment.

29.—(1) Where a person appointed company auditor was, for any part of the period during which the audit was conducted, ineligible for appointment to that office, the Secretary of State may direct the company concerned to retain a person eligible for appointment as auditor of the company—

   (a) to audit the relevant accounts again, or

   (b) to review the first audit and to report (giving his reasons) whether a second audit is needed;

and the company shall comply with such a direction within 21 days of its being given.

Power of Secretary of State to require second audit.

(2) If a second audit is recommended the company shall forthwith take such steps as are necessary to comply with the recommendation.

(3) Where a direction is given under this section, the Secretary of State shall send a copy of the direction to the registrar of companies; and the company shall within 21 days of receiving any report under subsection (1)(b) send a copy of it to the registrar of companies.

The provisions of the Companies Act 1985 relating to the delivery of documents to the registrar apply for the purposes of this subsection.

1985 c. 6.

(4) Any statutory or other provisions applying in relation to the first audit shall apply, so far as practicable, in relation to a second audit under this section.

(5) If a company fails to comply with the requirements of this section, it is guilty of an offence and liable on summary conviction to a fine not exceeding the statutory maximum; and in the case of continued contravention it is liable on a second or subsequent summary conviction (instead of the fine mentioned above) to a fine not exceeding one-tenth of the statutory maximum in respect of each day on which the contravention is continued.

1988 c. 36.

(6) A direction under this section is, on the application of the Secretary of State, enforceable by injunction or, in Scotland, by an order under section 45 of the Court of Session Act 1988.

(7) If a person accepts an appointment, or continues to act, as company auditor at a time when he knows he is ineligible, the company concerned may recover from him any costs incurred by it in complying with the requirements of this section.

Recognition of supervisory bodies and professional qualifications

Supervisory bodies.

30.—(1) In this Part a "supervisory body" means a body established in the United Kingdom (whether a body corporate or an unincorporated association) which maintains and enforces rules as to—

(a) the eligibility of persons to seek appointment as company auditors, and

(b) the conduct of company audit work,

which are binding on persons seeking appointment or acting as company auditors either because they are members of that body or because they are otherwise subject to its control.

(2) In this Part references to the members of a supervisory body are to the persons who, whether or not members of the body, are subject to its rules in seeking appointment or acting as company auditors.

(3) In this Part references to the rules of a supervisory body are to the rules (whether or not laid down by the body itself) which the body has power to enforce and which are relevant for the purposes of this Part.

This includes rules relating to the admission and expulsion of members of the body, so far as relevant for the purposes of this Part.

(4) In this Part references to guidance issued by a supervisory body are to guidance issued or any recommendation made by it to all or any class of its members or persons seeking to become members which would, if it were a rule, fall within subsection (3).

(5) The provisions of Parts I and II of Schedule 11 have effect with respect to the recognition of supervisory bodies for the purposes of this Part.

Meaning of "appropriate qualification".

1985 c. 6.

31.—(1) A person holds an appropriate qualification for the purposes of this Part if—

(a) he was, by virtue of membership of a body recognised for the purposes of section 389(1)(a) of the Companies Act 1985, qualified for appointment as auditor of a company under that section immediately before 1st January 1990 and immediately before the commencement of section 25 above,

(b) he holds a recognised professional qualification obtained in the United Kingdom, or

(c) he holds an approved overseas qualification and satisfies any additional educational requirements applicable in accordance with section 33(4).

(2) A person who, immediately before 1st January 1990 and immediately before the commencement of section 25 above, was qualified for appointment as auditor of a company under section 389 of the Companies Act 1985 otherwise than by virtue of membership of a body recognised for the purposes of section 389(1)(a)—

> (a) shall be treated as holding an appropriate qualification for twelve months from the day on which section 25 comes into force, and
>
> (b) shall continue to be so treated if within that period he notifies the Secretary of State that he wishes to retain the benefit of his qualification.

The notice shall be in writing and shall contain such information as the Secretary of State may require.

(3) If a person fails to give such notice within the time allowed he may apply to the Secretary of State, giving such information as would have been required in connection with a notice, and the Secretary of State may, if he is satisfied—

> (a) that there was good reason why the applicant did not give notice in time, and
>
> (b) that the applicant genuinely intends to practise as an auditor in Great Britain,

direct that he shall be treated as holding an appropriate qualification for the purposes of this Part.

(4) A person who—

> (a) began before 1st January 1990 a course of study or practical training leading to a professional qualification in accountancy offered by a body established in the United Kingdom, and
>
> (b) obtained that qualification on or after that date and before 1st January 1996,

shall be treated as holding an appropriate qualification if the qualification is approved by the Secretary of State for the purposes of this subsection.

(5) Approval shall not be given unless the Secretary of State is satisfied that the body concerned has or, as the case may be, had at the relevant time adequate arrangements to ensure that the qualification is, or was, awarded only to persons educated and trained to a standard equivalent to that required in the case of a recognised professional qualification.

(6) A person shall not be regarded as holding an appropriate qualification for the purposes of this Part except in the above cases.

32.—(1) In this Part a "qualifying body" means a body established in the United Kingdom (whether a body corporate or an unincorporated association) which offers a professional qualification in accountancy.

Qualifying bodies and recognised professional qualifications.

(2) In this Part references to the rules of a qualifying body are to the rules (whether or not laid down by the body itself) which the body has power to enforce and which are relevant for the purposes of this Part.

This includes rules relating to—

> (a) admission to or expulsion from a course of study leading to a qualification,
>
> (b) the award or deprivation of a qualification, or

(c) the approval of a person for the purposes of giving practical training or the withdrawal of such approval,

so far as relevant for the purposes of this Part.

(3) In this Part references to guidance issued by any such body are to any guidance which the body issues, or any recommendation it makes to all or any class of persons holding or seeking to hold a qualification, or approved or seeking to be approved by the body for the purpose of giving practical training, which would, if it were a rule, fall within subsection (2).

(4) The provisions of Parts I and II of Schedule 12 have effect with respect to the recognition for the purposes of this Part of a professional qualification offered by a qualifying body.

33.—(1) The Secretary of State may declare that persons who—

(a) are qualified to audit accounts under the law of a specified country or territory outside the United Kingdom, or

(b) hold a specified professional qualification in accountancy recognised under the law of a country or territory outside the United Kingdom,

shall be regarded for the purposes of this Part as holding an approved overseas qualification.

(2) A qualification shall not be so approved by the Secretary of State unless he is satisfied that it affords an assurance of professional competence equivalent to that afforded by a recognised professional qualification.

(3) In exercising the power conferred by subsection (1) the Secretary of State may have regard to the extent to which persons—

(a) eligible under this Part for appointment as a company auditor, or

(b) holding a professional qualification recognised under this Part,

are recognised by the law of the country or territory in question as qualified to audit accounts there.

(4) The Secretary of State may direct that a person holding an approved overseas qualification shall not be treated as holding an appropriate qualification for the purposes of this Part unless he holds such additional educational qualifications as the Secretary of State may specify for the purpose of ensuring that such persons have an adequate knowledge of the law and practice in the United Kingdom relevant to the audit of accounts.

(5) Different directions may be given in relation to different qualifications.

(6) The Secretary of State may if he thinks fit, having regard to the considerations mentioned in subsections (2) and (3), withdraw his approval of an overseas qualification in relation to persons becoming qualified as mentioned in subsection (1)(a), or obtaining such a qualification as is mentioned in subsection (1)(b), after such date as he may specify.

34.—(1) A person whose only appropriate qualification is that he retains an authorisation granted by the Board of Trade or the Secretary of State under section 13(1) of the Companies Act 1967 is eligible only for appointment as auditor of an unquoted company.

Eligibility of individuals retaining only 1967 Act authorisation.
1967 c. 81.

(2) A company is "unquoted" if, at the time of the person's appointment, no shares or debentures of the company, or of a parent undertaking of which it is a subsidiary undertaking, have been quoted on a stock exchange (in Great Britain or elsewhere) or offered (whether in Great Britain or elsewhere) to the public for subscription or purchase.

(3) This section does not authorise the appointment of such a person as auditor of a company that carries on business as the promoter of a trading stamp scheme within the meaning of the Trading Stamps Act 1964.

1964 c. 71.

(4) References to a person eligible for appointment as company auditor under section 25 in enactments relating to eligibility for appointment as auditor of a body other than a company do not include a person to whom this section applies.

Duties of recognised bodies

35.—(1) The Secretary of State shall make regulations requiring the keeping of a register of—

The register of auditors.

  (a) the individuals and firms eligible for appointment as company auditor, and

  (b) the individuals holding an appropriate qualification who are responsible for company audit work on behalf of such firms.

(2) The regulations shall provide that each person's entry in the register shall give—

  (a) his name and address, and

  (b) in the case of a person eligible as mentioned in subsection (1)(a), the name of the relevant supervisory body,

together with such other information as may be specified by the regulations.

(3) The regulations may impose such obligations as the Secretary of State thinks fit—

  (a) on recognised supervisory bodies,

  (b) on persons eligible for appointment as company auditor, and

  (c) on any person with whom arrangements are made by one or more recognised supervisory bodies with respect to the keeping of the register.

(4) The regulations may include provision—

  (a) requiring the register to be open to inspection at such times and places as may be specified in the regulations or determined in accordance with them,

  (b) enabling a person to require a certified copy of an entry in the register, and

(c) authorising the charging of fees for inspection, or the provision of copies, of such reasonable amount as may be specified in the regulations or determined in accordance with them;

and may contain such other supplementary and incidental provisions as the Secretary of State thinks fit.

(5) Regulations under this section shall be made by statutory instrument which shall be subject to annulment in pursuance of a resolution of either House of Parliament.

(6) The obligations imposed by regulations under this section on such persons as are mentioned in subsection (3)(a) or (c) are enforceable on the application of the Secretary of State by injunction or, in Scotland, by an order under section 45 of the Court of Session Act 1988.

36.—(1) The Secretary of State shall make regulations requiring recognised supervisory bodies to keep and make available to the public the following information with respect to the firms eligible under their rules for appointment as a company auditor—

(a) in relation to a body corporate, the name and address of each person who is a director of the body or holds any shares in it,

(b) in relation to a partnership, the name and address of each partner,

and such other information as may be specified in the regulations.

(2) The regulations may impose such obligations as the Secretary of State thinks fit—

(a) on recognised supervisory bodies,

(b) on persons eligible for appointment as company auditor, and

(c) on any person with whom arrangements are made by one or more recognised supervisory bodies with respect to the keeping of the information.

(3) The regulations may include provision—

(a) requiring that the information be open to inspection at such times and places as may be specified in the regulations or determined in accordance with them,

(b) enabling a person to require a certified copy of the information or any part of it, and

(c) authorising the charging of fees for inspection, or the provision of copies, of such reasonable amount as may be specified in the regulations or determined in accordance with them;

and may contain such other supplementary and incidental provisions as the Secretary of State thinks fit.

(4) The regulations may make different provision in relation to different descriptions of information and may contain such other supplementary and incidental provisions as the Secretary of State thinks fit.

(5) Regulations under this section shall be made by statutory instrument which shall be subject to annulment in pursuance of a resolution of either House of Parliament.

(6) The obligations imposed by regulations under this section on such persons as are mentioned in subsection (2)(a) or (c) are enforceable on the application of the Secretary of State by injunction or, in Scotland, by an order under section 45 of the Court of Session Act 1988.

1988 c. 36.

37.—(1) The Secretary of State may require a recognised supervisory or qualifying body—

    (a) to notify him forthwith of the occurrence of such events as he may specify in writing and to give him such information in respect of those events as is so specified;

    (b) to give him, at such times or in respect of such periods as he may specify in writing, such information as is so specified.

Matters to be notified to the Secretary of State.

(2) The notices and information required to be given shall be such as the Secretary of State may reasonably require for the exercise of his functions under this Part.

(3) The Secretary of State may require information given under this section to be given in a specified form or verified in a specified manner.

(4) Any notice or information required to be given under this section shall be given in writing unless the Secretary of State specifies or approves some other manner.

38.—(1) The Secretary of State may by notice in writing require a recognised supervisory or qualifying body to give him such information as he may reasonably require for the exercise of his functions under this Part.

Power to call for information.

(2) The Secretary of State may require that any information which he requires under this section shall be given within such reasonable time and verified in such manner as he may specify.

39.—(1) If at any time it appears to the Secretary of State—

    (a) in the case of a recognised supervisory body, that any requirement of Schedule 11 is not satisfied,

    (b) in the case of a recognised professional qualification, that any requirement of Schedule 12 is not satisfied, or

    (c) that a recognised supervisory or qualifying body has failed to comply with an obligation to which it is subject by virtue of this Part,

Compliance orders.

he may, instead of revoking the relevant recognition order, make an application to the court under this section.

(2) If on such application the court decides that the subsection or requirement in question is not satisfied or, as the case may be, that the body has failed to comply with the obligation in question it may order the supervisory or qualifying body in question to take such steps as the court directs for securing that the subsection or requirement is satisfied or that the obligation is complied with.

(3) The jurisdiction conferred by this section is exercisable by the High Court and the Court of Session.

Directions to
comply with
international
obligations.

40.—(1) If it appears to the Secretary of State—

   (a) that any action proposed to be taken by a recognised supervisory or qualifying body, or a body established by order under section 46, would be incompatible with Community obligations or any other international obligations of the United Kingdom, or

   (b) that any action which that body has power to take is required for the purpose of implementing any such obligations,

he may direct the body not to take or, as the case may be, to take the action in question.

(2) A direction may include such supplementary or incidental requirements as the Secretary of State thinks necessary or expedient.

1988 c. 36.

(3) A direction under this section is enforceable on the application of the Secretary of State by injunction or, in Scotland, by an order under section 45 of the Court of Session Act 1988.

Offences

False and
misleading
statements.

41.—(1) A person commits an offence if—

   (a) for the purposes of or in connection with any application under this Part, or

   (b) in purported compliance with any requirement imposed on him by or under this Part,

he furnishes information which he knows to be false or misleading in a material particular or recklessly furnishes information which is false or misleading in a material particular.

(2) It is an offence for a person whose name does not appear on the register of auditors kept under regulations under section 35 to describe himself as a registered auditor or so to hold himself out as to indicate, or be reasonably understood to indicate, that he is a registered auditor.

(3) It is an offence for a body which is not a recognised supervisory or qualifying body to describe itself as so recognised or so to describe itself or hold itself out as to indicate, or be reasonably understood to indicate, that it is so recognised.

(4) A person guilty of an offence under subsection (1) is liable—

   (a) on conviction on indictment, to imprisonment for a term not exceeding two years or to a fine or both;

   (b) on summary conviction, to imprisonment for a term not exceeding six months or to a fine not exceeding the statutory maximum or both.

(5) A person guilty of an offence under subsection (2) or (3) is liable on summary conviction to imprisonment for a term not exceeding six months or to a fine not exceeding level 5 on the standard scale or both.

Where a contravention of subsection (2) or (3) involves a public display of the offending description, the maximum fine that may be imposed is (in place of that mentioned above) an amount equal to level 5 on the standard scale multiplied by the number of days for which the display has continued.

(6) It is a defence for a person charged with an offence under subsection (2) or (3) to show that he took all reasonable precautions and exercised all due diligence to avoid the commission of the offence.

42.—(1) Where an offence under this Part committed by a body corporate is proved to have been committed with the consent or connivance of, or to be attributable to any neglect on the part of, a director, manager, secretary or other similar officer of the body, or a person purporting to act in any such capacity, he as well as the body corporate is guilty of the offence and liable to be proceeded against and punished accordingly.

(2) Where the affairs of a body corporate are managed by its members, subsection (1) applies in relation to the acts and defaults of a member in connection with his functions of management as to a director of a body corporate.

(3) Where an offence under this Part committed by a partnership is proved to have been committed with the consent or connivance of, or to be attributable to any neglect on the part of, a partner, he as well as the partnership is guilty of the offence and liable to be proceeded against and punished accordingly.

(4) Where an offence under this Part committed by an unincorporated association (other than a partnership) is proved to have been committed with the consent or connivance of, or to be attributable to any neglect on the part of, any officer of the association or any member of its governing body, he as well as the association is guilty of the offence and liable to be proceeded against and punished accordingly.

43.—(1) An information relating to an offence under this Part which is triable by a magistrates' court in England and Wales may be so tried on an information laid at any time within twelve months after the date on which evidence sufficient in the opinion of the Director of Public Prosecutions or the Secretary of State to justify the proceedings comes to his knowledge.

(2) Proceedings in Scotland for an offence under this Part may be commenced at any time within twelve months after the date on which evidence sufficient in the Lord Advocate's opinion to justify the proceedings came to his knowledge or, where such evidence was reported to him by the Secretary of State, within twelve months after the date on which it came to the knowledge of the latter.

For the purposes of this subsection proceedings shall be deemed to be commenced on the date on which a warrant to apprehend or to cite the accused is granted, if the warrant is executed without undue delay.

(3) Subsection (1) does not authorise the trial of an information laid, and subsection (2) does not authorise the commencement of proceedings, more than three years after the commission of the offence.

(4) For the purposes of this section a certificate of the Director of Public Prosecutions, the Lord Advocate or the Secretary of State as to the date on which such evidence as is referred to above came to his knowledge is conclusive evidence.

(5) Nothing in this section affects proceedings within the time limits prescribed by section 127(1) of the Magistrates' Courts Act 1980 or section 331 of the Criminal Procedure (Scotland) Act 1975 (the usual time limits for criminal proceedings).

44.—(1) Summary proceedings for an offence under this Part may, without prejudice to any jurisdiction exercisable apart from this section, be taken against a body corporate or unincorporated association at any place at which it has a place of business and against an individual at any place where he is for the time being.

(2) Proceedings for an offence alleged to have been committed under this Part by an unincorporated association shall be brought in the name of the association (and not in that of any of its members), and for the purposes of any such proceedings any rules of court relating to the service of documents apply as in relation to a body corporate.

(3) Section 33 of the Criminal Justice Act 1925 and Schedule 3 to the Magistrates' Courts Act 1980 (procedure on charge of offence against a corporation) apply in a case in which an unincorporated association is charged in England and Wales with an offence under this Part as they apply in the case of a corporation.

(4) In relation to proceedings on indictment in Scotland for an offence alleged to have been committed under this Part by an unincorporated association, section 74 of the Criminal Procedure (Scotland) Act 1975 (proceedings on indictment against bodies corporate) applies as if the association were a body corporate.

(5) A fine imposed on an unincorporated association on its conviction of such an offence shall be paid out of the funds of the association.

Supplementary provisions

45.—(1) An applicant for a recognition order under this Part shall pay such fee in respect of his application as may be prescribed; and no application shall be regarded as duly made unless this subsection is complied with.

(2) Every recognised supervisory or qualifying body shall pay such periodical fees to the Secretary of State as may be prescribed.

(3) In this section "prescribed" means prescribed by regulations made by the Secretary of State, which may make different provision for different cases or classes of case.

(4) Regulations under this section shall be made by statutory instrument which shall be subject to annulment in pursuance of a resolution of either House of Parliament.

(5) Fees received by the Secretary of State by virtue of this Part shall be paid into the Consolidated Fund.

46.—(1) The Secretary of State may by order (a "delegation order") establish a body corporate to exercise his functions under this Part.

(2) A delegation order has the effect of transferring to the body established by it, subject to such exceptions and reservations as may be specified in the order, all the functions of the Secretary of State under this Part except—

(a) such functions under Part I of Schedule 14 (prevention of restrictive practices) as are excepted by regulations under section 47, and

(b) his functions in relation to the body itself;

and the order may also confer on the body such other functions supplementary or incidental to those transferred as appear to the Secretary of State to be appropriate.

(3) Any transfer of the functions under the following provisions shall be subject to the reservation that they remain exercisable concurrently by the Secretary of State—

(a) section 38 (power to call for information), and

(b) section 40 (directions to comply with international obligations);

and any transfer of the function of refusing to approve an overseas qualification, or withdrawing such approval, on the grounds referred to in section 33(3) (lack of reciprocity) shall be subject to the reservation that the function is exercisable only with the consent of the Secretary of State.

(4) A delegation order may be amended or, if it appears to the Secretary of State that it is no longer in the public interest that the order should remain in force, revoked by a further order under this section.

(5) Where functions are transferred or resumed, the Secretary of State may by order confer or, as the case may be, take away such other functions supplementary or incidental to those transferred or resumed as appear to him to be appropriate.

(6) The provisions of Schedule 13 have effect with respect to the status, constitution and proceedings of a body established by a delegation order, the exercise by it of certain functions transferred to it and other supplementary matters.

(7) An order under this section shall be made by statutory instrument.

(8) An order which has the effect of transferring or resuming any functions shall not be made unless a draft of it has been laid before and approved by resolution of each House of Parliament; and any other description of order shall be subject to annulment in pursuance of a resolution of either House of Parliament.

47.—(1) The provisions of Schedule 14 have effect with respect to certain matters relating to restrictive practices and competition law.

Restrictive practices.

(2) The Secretary of State may make provision by regulations as to the discharge of the functions under paragraphs 1 to 7 of that Schedule when a delegation order is in force.

(3) The regulations may—

(a) except any function from the effect of the delegation order,

(b) modify any of the provisions mentioned in subsection (2), and

(c) impose such duties on the body established by the delegation order, the Secretary of State and Director General of Fair Trading as appear to the Secretary of State to be appropriate.

(4) The regulations shall contain such provision as appears to the Secretary of State to be necessary or expedient for reserving to him the decision—

(a) to refuse recognition on the ground mentioned in paragraph 1(3) of that Schedule, or

(b) to exercise the powers conferred by paragraph 6 of that Schedule.

(5) For that purpose the regulations may—

(a) prohibit the body from granting a recognition order without the leave of the Secretary of State, and

(b) empower the Secretary of State to direct the body to exercise its powers in such manner as may be specified in the direction.

(6) Regulations under this section shall be made by statutory instrument which shall be subject to annulment in pursuance of a resolution of either House of Parliament.

Exemption from liability for damages.

48.—(1) Neither a recognised supervisory body, nor any of its officers or employees or members of its governing body, shall be liable in damages for anything done or omitted in the discharge or purported discharge of functions to which this subsection applies, unless the act or omission is shown to have been in bad faith.

(2) Subsection (1) applies to the functions of the body so far as relating to, or to matters arising out of—

(a) such rules, practices, powers and arrangements of the body to which the requirements of Part II of Schedule 11 apply, or

(b) the obligations with which paragraph 16 of that Schedule requires the body to comply,

(c) any guidance issued by the body, or

(d) the obligations to which the body is subject by virtue of this Part.

(3) Neither a body established by a delegation order, nor any of its members, officers or employees, shall be liable in damages for anything done or omitted in the discharge or purported discharge of the functions exercisable by virtue of an order under section 46, unless the act or omission is shown to have been in bad faith.

Service of notices.

49.—(1) This section has effect in relation to any notice, direction or other document required or authorised by or under this Part to be given to or served on any person other than the Secretary of State.

(2) Any such document may be given to or served on the person in question—

(a) by delivering it to him,

(b) by leaving it at his proper address, or

(c) by sending it by post to him at that address.

(3) Any such document may—

(a) in the case of a body corporate, be given to or served on the secretary or clerk of that body;

(b) in the case of a partnership, be given to or served on any partner;

(c) in the case of an unincorporated association other than a partnership, be given to or served on any member of the governing body of the association.

(4) For the purposes of this section and section 7 of the Interpretation
Act 1978 (service of documents by post) in its application to this section,
the proper address of any person is his last known address (whether of his
residence or of a place where he carries on business or is employed) and
also—

  (a) in the case of a person who is eligible under the rules of a
      recognised supervisory body for appointment as company
      auditor and who does not have a place of business in the United
      Kingdom, the address of that body;

  (b) in the case of a body corporate, its secretary or its clerk, the
      address of its registered or principal office in the United
      Kingdom;

  (c) in the case of an unincorporated association (other than a
      partnership) or a member of its governing body, its principal
      office in the United Kingdom.

50.—(1) The Secretary of State may by regulations make such
amendments of enactments as appear to him to be necessary or expedient
in consequence of the provisions of this Part having effect in place of
section 389 of the Companies Act 1985.

(2) That power extends to making such amendments as appear to the
Secretary of State necessary or expedient of—

  (a) enactments referring by name to the bodies of accountants
      recognised for the purposes of section 389(1)(a) of the
      Companies Act 1985, and

  (b) enactments making with respect to other statutory auditors
      provision as to the matters dealt with in relation to company
      auditors by section 389 of the Companies Act 1985.

(3) The provision which may be made with respect to other statutory
auditors includes provision as to—

  (a) eligibility for the appointment,

  (b) the effect of appointing a partnership which is not a legal person
      and the manner of exercise of the auditor's rights in such a case,
      and

  (c) ineligibility on the ground of lack of independence or any other
      ground.

(4) The regulations may contain such supplementary, incidental and
transitional provision as appears to the Secretary of State to be necessary
or expedient.

(5) The Secretary of State shall not make regulations under this section
with respect to any statutory auditors without the consent of—

  (a) the Minister responsible for their appointment or responsible for
      the body or person by, or in relation to whom, they are
      appointed, or

  (b) if there is no such Minister, the person by whom they are
      appointed.

(6) In this section a "statutory auditor" means a person appointed
auditor in pursuance of any enactment authorising or requiring the
appointment of an auditor or auditors.

PART II
1978 c. 30.

Power to make
consequential
amendments.
1985 c. 6.

(7) Regulations under this section shall be made by statutory instrument which shall be subject to annulment in pursuance of a resolution of either House of Parliament.

Power to make provision in consequence of changes affecting accountancy bodies.

51.—(1) The Secretary of State may by regulations make such amendments of enactments as appear to him to be necessary or expedient in consequence of any change of name, merger or transfer of engagements affecting—

(a) a recognised supervisory or qualifying body under this Part, or

(b) a body of accountants referred to in, or approved, authorised or otherwise recognised for the purposes of, any other enactment.

(2) Regulations under this section shall be made by statutory instrument which shall be subject to annulment in pursuance of a resolution of either House of Parliament.

Meaning of "associate".

52.—(1) In this Part "associate", in relation to a person, shall be construed as follows.

(2) In relation to an individual "associate" means—

(a) that individual's spouse or minor child or step-child,

(b) any body corporate of which that individual is a director, and

(c) any employee or partner of that individual.

(3) In relation to a body corporate "associate" means—

(a) any body corporate of which that body is a director,

(b) any body corporate in the same group as that body, and

(c) any employee or partner of that body or of any body corporate in the same group.

(4) In relation to a Scottish firm, or a partnership constituted under the law of any other country or territory in which a partnership is a legal person, "associate" means—

(a) any body corporate of which the firm is a director,

(b) any employee of or partner in the firm, and

(c) any person who is an associate of a partner in the firm.

(5) In relation to a partnership constituted under the law of England and Wales or Northern Ireland, or the law of any other country or territory in which a partnership is not a legal person, "associate" means any person who is an associate of any of the partners.

Minor definitions.

53.—(1) In this Part—

"address" means—

(a) in relation to an individual, his usual residential or business address, and

(b) in relation to a firm, its registered or principal office in Great Britain;

1985 c. 6.

"company" means any company or other body to which section 384 of the Companies Act 1985 (duty to appoint auditors) applies;

"director", in relation to a body corporate, includes any person occupying in relation to it the position of a director (by whatever name called) and any person in accordance with

whose directions or instructions (not being advice given in a
professional capacity) the directors of the body are accustomed
to act;

"enactment" includes an enactment contained in subordinate
legislation within the meaning of the Interpretation Act 1978; 1978 c. 30.

"firm" means a body corporate or a partnership;

"group", in relation to a body corporate, means the body corporate,
any other body corporate which is its holding company or
subsidiary and any other body corporate which is a subsidiary
of that holding company; and

"holding company" and "subsidiary" have the meaning given by
section 736 of the Companies Act 1985; 1985 c. 6.

"parent undertaking" and "subsidiary undertaking" have the same
meaning as in Part VII of the Companies Act 1985.

(2) For the purposes of this Part a body shall be regarded as
"established in the United Kingdom" if and only if—

(a) it is incorporated or formed under the law of the United Kingdom
or a part of the United Kingdom, or

(b) its central management and control is exercised in the United
Kingdom;

and any reference to a qualification "obtained in the United Kingdom" is
to a qualification obtained from such a body.

54. The following Table shows provisions defining or otherwise Index of defined
explaining expressions used in this Part (other than provisions defining or expressions.
explaining an expression used only in the same section)—

address	section 53(1)
appropriate qualification	section 31
associate	section 52
company	section 53(1)
company auditor, company audit and company audit work	section 24(2)
delegation order	section 46
director (of a body corporate)	section 53(1)
Director (in Schedule 14)	paragraph 1(1) of that Schedule
enactment	section 53(1)
established in the United Kingdom	section 53(2)
firm	section 53(1)
group (in relation to a body corporate)	section 53(1)
guidance	
-of a qualifying body	section 32(3)
-of a supervisory body	section 30(4)
holding company	section 53(1)
member (of a supervisory body)	section 30(2)
obtained in the United Kingdom	section 53(2)
parent undertaking	section 53(1)
purposes of this Part	section 24(1)
qualifying body	section 32(1)
recognised	
-in relation to a professional qualification	section 32(4) and Schedule 12
-in relation to a qualifying body	paragraph 2(1) of Schedule 12
-in relation to a supervisory body	section 30(5) and

Schedule 11

rules
   -of a qualifying body   section 32(2)
   -of a supervisory body   section 30(3)
subsidiary and subsidiary   section 53(1)
   undertaking
supervisory body   section 30(1)

PART III

INVESTIGATIONS AND POWERS TO OBTAIN INFORMATION

Amendments of the Companies Act 1985

Investigations by inspectors not leading to published report.

1985 c. 6.

55. In section 432 of the Companies Act 1985 (appointment of inspectors by Secretary of State), after subsection (2) (investigation of circumstances suggesting misconduct) insert—

"(2A) Inspectors may be appointed under subsection (2) on terms that any report they may make is not for publication; and in such a case, the provisions of section 437(3) (availability and publication of inspectors' reports) do not apply.".

Production of documents and evidence to inspectors.

56.—(1) Section 434 of the Companies Act 1985 (production of documents and evidence to inspectors) is amended as follows.

(2) In subsection (1) (duty of officers to assist inspectors), for "books and documents" substitute "documents".

(3) For subsection (2) (power to require production of documents, attendance or other assistance) substitute—

"(2) If the inspectors consider that an officer or agent of the company or other body corporate, or any other person, is or may be in possession of information relating to a matter which they believe to be relevant to the investigation, they may require him—

    (a) to produce to them any documents in his custody or power relating to that matter,

    (b) to attend before them, and

    (c) otherwise to give them all assistance in connection with the investigation which he is reasonably able to give;

and it is that person's duty to comply with the requirement.".

(4) For subsection (3) (power to examine on oath) substitute—

"(3) An inspector may for the purposes of the investigation examine any person on oath, and may administer an oath accordingly.".

(5) After subsection (5) insert—

"(6) In this section "documents" includes information recorded in any form; and, in relation to information recorded otherwise than in legible form, the power to require its production includes power to require the production of a copy of the information in legible form.".

(6) In section 436 of the Companies Act 1985 (obstruction of inspectors treated as contempt of court), for subsections (1) and (2) substitute—

"(1) If any person—

(a) fails to comply with section 434(1)(a) or (c),

(b) refuses to comply with a requirement under section 434(1)(b) or (2), or

(c) refuses to answer any question put to him by the inspectors for the purposes of the investigation,

the inspectors may certify that fact in writing to the court.".

57. In section 437 of the Companies Act 1985 (inspectors' reports), after subsection (1A) insert—

Duty of inspectors to report.

"(1B) If it appears to the Secretary of State that matters have come to light in the course of the inspectors' investigation which suggest that a criminal offence has been committed, and those matters have been referred to the appropriate prosecuting authority, he may direct the inspectors to take no further steps in the investigation or to take only such further steps as are specified in the direction.

(1C) Where an investigation is the subject of a direction under subsection (1B), the inspectors shall make a final report to the Secretary of State only where—

(a) they were appointed under section 432(1) (appointment in pursuance of an order of the court), or

(b) the Secretary of State directs them to do so.".

58. In section 438 of the Companies Act 1985 (power to bring civil proceedings on the company's behalf), for the opening words of subsection (1) down to "it appears to the Secretary of State" substitute "If from any report made or information obtained under this Part it appears to the Secretary of State".

Power to bring civil proceedings on the company's behalf.

59.—(1) Section 439 of the Companies Act 1985 (expenses of investigating a company's affairs) is amended as follows.

Expenses of investigating a company's affairs.

(2) For subsection (1) substitute—

"(1) The expenses of an investigation under any of the powers conferred by this Part shall be defrayed in the first instance by the Secretary of State, but he may recover those expenses from the persons liable in accordance with this section.

There shall be treated as expenses of the investigation, in particular, such reasonable sums as the Secretary of State may determine in respect of general staff costs and overheads.".

(3) In subsection (4) for "the inspectors' report" substitute "an inspectors' report".

(4) For subsection (5) substitute—

"(5) Where inspectors were appointed—

(a) under section 431, or

(b) on an application under section 442(3),

the applicant or applicants for the investigation is or are liable to such extent (if any) as the Secretary of State may direct.".

Power of Secretary of State to present winding-up petition.

1985 c. 6.
1986 c. 45.

60.—(1) Section 440 of the Companies Act 1985 (power of Secretary of State to present winding-up petition) is repealed; but the following amendments have the effect of re-enacting that provision, with modifications.

(2) In section 124(4) of the Insolvency Act 1986 (application by Secretary of State for company to be wound up by the court), for paragraph (b) substitute—

"(b) in a case falling within section 124A below.".

(3) After that section insert—

"Petition for winding up on grounds of public interest.

124A.—(1) Where it appears to the Secretary of State from—

(a) any report made or information obtained under Part XIV of the Companies Act 1985 (company investigations, &c.),

(b) any report made under section 94 or 177 of the Financial Services Act 1986 or any information obtained under section 105 of that Act,

(c) any information obtained under section 2 of the Criminal Justice Act 1987 or section 52 of the Criminal Justice (Scotland) Act 1987 (fraud investigations), or

(d) any information obtained under section 83 of the Companies Act 1989 (powers exercisable for purpose of assisting overseas regulatory authorities),

that it is expedient in the public interest that a company should be wound up, he may present a petition for it to be wound up if the court thinks it just and equitable for it to be so.

(2) This section does not apply if the company is already being wound up by the court.".

Inspectors' reports as evidence.

61. In section 441 of the Companies Act 1985 (inspectors' reports to be evidence), in subsection (1) for "sections 431 or 432" substitute "this Part".

Investigation of company ownership.

62. In section 442 of the Companies Act 1985 (power to investigate company ownership), for subsection (3) (investigation on application by members of company) substitute—

"(3) If an application for investigation under this section with respect to particular shares or debentures of a company is made to the Secretary of State by members of the company, and the number of applicants or the amount of shares held by them is not less than that required for an application for the appointment of inspectors under section 431(2)(a) or (b), then, subject to the following provisions, the Secretary of State shall appoint inspectors to conduct the investigation applied for.

(3A) The Secretary of State shall not appoint inspectors if he is satisfied that the application is vexatious; and where inspectors are appointed their terms of appointment shall exclude any matter in so far as the Secretary of State is satisfied that it is unreasonable for it to be investigated.

(3B) The Secretary of State may, before appointing inspectors, require the applicant or applicants to give security, to an amount not exceeding £5,000, or such other sum as he may by order specify, for payment of the costs of the investigation.

An order under this subsection shall be made by statutory instrument which shall be subject to annulment in pursuance of a resolution of either House of Parliament.

(3C) If on an application under subsection (3) it appears to the Secretary of State that the powers conferred by section 444 are sufficient for the purposes of investigating the matters which inspectors would be appointed to investigate, he may instead conduct the investigation under that section.".

63.—(1) Section 447 of the Companies Act 1985 (power of Secretary of State to require production of documents) is amended as follows.

(2) Omit subsection (1) (bodies in relation to which powers exercisable), and—

   (a) in subsections (2) and (3) for "any such body" substitute "a company",

   (b) in subsections (4) and (5) for "any body" and "a body" substitute "a company", and

   (c) in subsections (5) and (6) for "the body" substitute "the company".

(3) For "books or papers", wherever occurring, substitute "documents".

(4) In subsection (3) (power to authorise officer to require production of documents) after "an officer of his" insert "or any other competent person", after "the officer" in the first place where it occurs insert "or other person" and for "the officer" in the second place where it occurs substitute "he (the officer or other person)".

(5) In subsection (4) (power to require production of documents in possession of third party) after "an officer of his" and after "the officer" (twice) insert "or other person".

(6) In subsection (6), for the second sentence substitute—

   "Sections 732 (restriction on prosecutions), 733 (liability of individuals for corporate default) and 734 (criminal proceedings against unincorporated bodies) apply to this offence.".

(7) After subsection (8) insert—

"(9) In this section "documents" includes information recorded in any form; and, in relation to information recorded otherwise than in legible form, the power to require its production includes power to require the production of a copy of it in legible form.".

(8) In Schedule 24 to the Companies Act 1985 (punishment of offences), in the entry relating to section 447(6), for "books and papers" substitute "documents".

64.—(1) For section 448 of the Companies Act 1985 (entry and search of premises) substitute—

"Entry and search of premises.

448.—(1) A justice of the peace may issue a warrant under this section if satisfied on information on oath given by or on behalf of the Secretary of State, or by a person appointed or authorised to exercise powers under this Part, that there are reasonable grounds for believing that there are on any premises documents whose production has been required under this Part and which have not been produced in compliance with the requirement.

(2) A justice of the peace may also issue a warrant under this section if satisfied on information on oath given by or on behalf of the Secretary of State, or by a person appointed or authorised to exercise powers under this Part—

(a) that there are reasonable grounds for believing that an offence has been committed for which the penalty on conviction on indictment is imprisonment for a term of not less than two years and that there are on any premises documents relating to whether the offence has been committed,

(b) that the Secretary of State, or the person so appointed or authorised, has power to require the production of the documents under this Part, and

(c) that there are reasonable grounds for believing that if production was so required the documents would not be produced but would be removed from the premises, hidden, tampered with or destroyed.

(3) A warrant under this section shall authorise a constable, together with any other person named in it and any other constables—

(a) to enter the premises specified in the information, using such force as is reasonably necessary for the purpose;

(b) to search the premises and take possession of any documents appearing to be such documents as are mentioned in subsection (1) or (2), as the case may be, or to take, in relation to any such documents, any other steps which may appear to be necessary for preserving them or preventing interference with them;

(c) to take copies of any such documents; and

(d) to require any person named in the warrant to provide an explanation of them or to state where they may be found.

(4) If in the case of a warrant under subsection (2) the justice of the peace is satisfied on information on oath that there are reasonable grounds for believing that there are also on the premises other documents relevant to the investigation, the warrant shall also authorise the actions mentioned in subsection (3) to be taken in relation to such documents.

(5) A warrant under this section shall continue in force until the end of the period of one month beginning with the day on which it is issued.

(6) Any documents of which possession is taken under this section may be retained—

(a) for a period of three months; or

(b) if within that period proceedings to which the documents are relevant are commenced against any person for any criminal offence, until the conclusion of those proceedings.

(7) Any person who intentionally obstructs the exercise of any rights conferred by a warrant issued under this section or fails without reasonable excuse to comply with any requirement imposed in accordance with subsection (3)(d) is guilty of an offence and liable to a fine.

Sections 732 (restriction on prosecutions), 733 (liability of individuals for corporate default) and 734 (criminal proceedings against unincorporated bodies) apply to this offence.

(8) For the purposes of sections 449 and 451A (provision for security of information) documents obtained under this section shall be treated as if they had been obtained under the provision of this Part under which their production was or, as the case may be, could have been required.

(9) In the application of this section to Scotland for the references to a justice of the peace substitute references to a justice of the peace or a sheriff, and for the references to information on oath substitute references to evidence on oath.

(10) In this section "document" includes information recorded in any form.".

(2) In Schedule 24 to the Companies Act 1985 (punishment of offences), in the entry relating to section 448(5)— 1985 c. 6.

(a) in the first column for "448(5)" substitute "448(7)", and

(b) for the entry in the second column substitute—

> "Obstructing the exercise of any rights conferred by a warrant or failing to comply with a requirement imposed under subsection (3)(d).".

65.—(1) Section 449 of the Companies Act 1985 (provision for security of information obtained) is amended as follows.

(2) In subsection (1) (purposes for which disclosure permitted)—

(a) in the opening words for "body" (twice) substitute "company";

(b) for paragraph (c) substitute—

> "(c) for the purposes of enabling or assisting any inspector appointed under this Part, or under section 94 or 177 of the Financial Services Act 1986, to discharge his functions;";

(c) after that paragraph insert —

> "(cc) for the purpose of enabling or assisting any person authorised to exercise powers under section 44 of the Insurance Companies Act 1982, section 447 of this Act, section 106 of the Financial Services Act 1986 or section 84 of the Companies Act 1989 to discharge his functions;";

(d) in paragraph (d) for "or the Financial Services Act 1986" substitute ", the Financial Services Act 1986 or Part II, III or VII of the Companies Act 1989,";

(e) omit paragraph (e);

(f) in paragraph (h) for "(n) or (p)" substitute "or (n)";

(g) after that paragraph insert—

> "(hh) for the purpose of enabling or assisting a body established by order under section 46 of the Companies Act 1989 to discharge its functions under Part II of that Act, or of enabling or assisting a recognised supervisory or qualifying body within the meaning of that Part to discharge its functions as such;";

(h) after paragraph (l) insert—

> "(ll) with a view to the institution of, or otherwise for the purposes of, any disciplinary proceedings relating to the discharge by a public servant of his duties;";

(i) for paragraph (m) substitute—

> "(m) for the purpose of enabling or assisting an overseas regulatory authority to exercise its regulatory functions.".

(3) For subsection (1A) substitute—

> "(1A) In subsection (1)—
>
> (a) in paragraph (ll) "public servant" means an officer or servant of the Crown or of any public or other authority for the time being designated for the purposes of that paragraph by the Secretary of State by order made by statutory instrument; and
>
> (b) in paragraph (m) "overseas regulatory authority" and "regulatory functions" have the same meaning as in section 82 of the Companies Act 1989.".

(4) In subsection (1B) (disclosure to designated public authorities) for "designated for the purposes of this section" substitute "designated for the purposes of this subsection".

(5) In subsection (2), for the second sentence substitute—

"Sections 732 (restriction on prosecutions), 733 (liability of individuals for corporate default) and 734 (criminal proceedings against unincorporated bodies) apply to this offence.".

(6) For subsection (3) substitute—

"(3) For the purposes of this section each of the following is a competent authority—

(a) the Secretary of State,

(b) an inspector appointed under this Part or under section 94 or 177 of the Financial Services Act 1986,

(c) any person authorised to exercise powers under section 44 of the Insurance Companies Act 1982, section 447 of this Act, section 106 of the Financial Services Act 1986 or section 84 of the Companies Act 1989,

(d) the Department of Economic Development in Northern Ireland,

(e) the Treasury,

(f) the Bank of England,

(g) the Lord Advocate,

(h) the Director of Public Prosecutions, and the Director of Public Prosecutions for Northern Ireland,

(i) any designated agency or transferee body within the meaning of the Financial Services Act 1986, and any body administering a scheme under section 54 of or paragraph 18 of Schedule 11 to that Act (schemes for compensation of investors),

(j) the Chief Registrar of friendly societies and the Registrar of Friendly Societies for Northern Ireland,

(k) the Industrial Assurance Commissioner and the Industrial Assurance Commissioner for Northern Ireland,

(l) any constable,

(m) any procurator fiscal.

(3A) Any information which may by virtue of this section be disclosed to a competent authority may be disclosed to any officer or servant of the authority.".

(7) In subsection (4) (orders) for "subsection (1B)" substitute "subsection (1A)(a) or (1B)".

66.—(1) Section 450 of the Companies Act 1985 (punishment for destroying, mutilating, &c. company documents) is amended as follows.

(2) In subsection (1) for the opening words down to "insurance company" substitute "An officer of a company, or of an insurance company", for "body's" substitute "company's" and for "the body" substitute "the company".

Punishment for destroying, mutilating, &c. company documents.
1985 c. 6.

(3) For subsection (4) substitute—

"(4) Sections 732 (restriction on prosecutions), 733 (liability of individuals for corporate default) and 734 (criminal proceedings against unincorporated bodies) apply to an offence under this section.".

(4) After that subsection insert—

"(5) In this section "document" includes information recorded in any form.".

Punishment for furnishing false information.

1985 c. 6.

67. In section 451 of the Companies Act 1985 (punishment for furnishing false information), for the second sentence substitute—

"Sections 732 (restriction on prosecutions), 733 (liability of individuals for corporate default) and 734 (criminal proceedings against unincorporated bodies) apply to this offence.".

Disclosure of information by Secretary of State or inspector.

68. For section 451A of the Companies Act 1985 (disclosure of information by the Secretary of State) substitute—

"Disclosure of information by Secretary of State or inspector.

451A.—(1) This section applies to information obtained under sections 434 to 446.

(2) The Secretary of State may, if he thinks fit—

(a) disclose any information to which this section applies to any person to whom, or for any purpose for which, disclosure is permitted under section 449, or

(b) authorise or require an inspector appointed under this Part to disclose such information to any such person or for any such purpose.

(3) Information to which this section applies may also be disclosed by an inspector appointed under this Part to—

(a) another inspector appointed under this Part or an inspector appointed under section 94 or 177 of the Financial Services Act 1986, or

(b) a person authorised to exercise powers under section 44 of the Insurance Companies Act 1982, section 447 of this Act, section 106 of the Financial Services Act 1986 or section 84 of the Companies Act 1989.

(4) Any information which may by virtue of subsection (3) be disclosed to any person may be disclosed to any officer or servant of that person.

(5) The Secretary of State may, if he thinks fit, disclose any information obtained under section 444 to—

(a) the company whose ownership was the subject of the investigation,

(b) any member of the company,

(c) any person whose conduct was investigated in the course of the investigation,

(d) the auditors of the company, or

(e) any person whose financial interests appear to the Secretary of State to be affected by matters covered by the investigation.".

69.—(1) Section 452 of the Companies Act 1985 (privileged information) is amended as follows.

(2) In subsection (1), omit paragraph (b) (disclosure by bankers of information relating to their customers).

(3) After that subsection insert—

"(1A) Nothing in section 434, 443 or 446 requires a person (except as mentioned in subsection (1B) below) to disclose information or produce documents in respect of which he owes an obligation of confidence by virtue of carrying on the business of banking unless—

(a) the person to whom the obligation of confidence is owed is the company or other body corporate under investigation,

(b) the person to whom the obligation of confidence is owed consents to the disclosure or production, or

(c) the making of the requirement is authorised by the Secretary of State.

(1B) Subsection (1A) does not apply where the person owing the obligation of confidence is the company or other body corporate under investigation under section 431, 432 or 433.".

(4) In subsection (3) after "officer of his" insert "or other person".

70. In section 453 of the Companies Act 1985 (investigation of oversea companies), for subsection (1) substitute—

"(1) The provisions of this Part apply to bodies corporate incorporated outside Great Britain which are carrying on business in Great Britain, or have at any time carried on business there, as they apply to companies under this Act; but subject to the following exceptions, adaptations and modifications.

(1A) The following provisions do not apply to such bodies—

(a) section 431 (investigation on application of company or its members),

(b) section 438 (power to bring civil proceedings on the company's behalf),

(c) sections 442 to 445 (investigation of company ownership and power to obtain information as to those interested in shares, &c.), and

(d) section 446 (investigation of share dealings).

(1B) The other provisions of this Part apply to such bodies subject to such adaptations and modifications as may be specified by regulations made by the Secretary of State.".

71. In Schedule 22 to the Companies Act 1985 (provisions applying to unregistered companies), for the entry relating to Part XIV substitute—

"Part XIV   Investigation of companies and their   —".
(except section   affairs; requisition of documents.
446)

Amendments of the Financial Services Act 1986

Investigations
into collective
investment
schemes.
1986 c. 60.

72.—(1) Section 94 of the Financial Services Act 1986 (investigations into collective investment schemes) is amended as follows.

(2) For subsection (7) (privilege on grounds of banker's duty of confidentiality) substitute—

"(7) Nothing in this section requires a person (except as mentioned in subsection (7A) below) to disclose any information or produce any document in respect of which he owes an obligation of confidence by virtue of carrying on the business of banking unless—

(a) the person to whom the obligation of confidence is owed consents to the disclosure or production, or

(b) the making of the requirement was authorised by the Secretary of State.

(7A) Subsection (7) does not apply where the person owing the obligation of confidence or the person to whom it is owed is—

(a) the manager, operator or trustee of the scheme under investigation, or

(b) a manager, operator or trustee whose own affairs are under investigation.".

(3) After subsection (8) (duty of inspectors to report) insert—

"(8A) If it appears to the Secretary of State that matters have come to light in the course of the inspectors' investigation which suggest that a criminal offence has been committed, and those matters have been referred to the appropriate prosecuting authority, he may direct the inspectors to take no further steps in the investigation or to take only such further steps as are specified in the direction.

(8B) Where an investigation is the subject of a direction under subsection (8A), the inspectors shall make a final report to the Secretary of State only where the Secretary of State directs them to do so.".

(4) After subsection (9) add—

"(10) A person who is convicted on a prosecution instituted as a result of an investigation under this section may in the same proceedings be ordered to pay the expenses of the investigation to such extent as may be specified in the order.

There shall be treated as expenses of the investigation, in particular, such reasonable sums as the Secretary of State may determine in respect of general staff costs and overheads.".

Investigations
into affairs of
persons carrying
on investment
business.

73.—(1) Section 105 of the Financial Services Act 1986 (investigation into affairs of person carrying on investment business) is amended as follows.

(2) Omit subsection (7) (privilege on grounds of banker's duty of confidentiality).

(3) In subsection (9) (interpretation), in the definition of "documents", for "references to its production include references to producing" substitute "the power to require its production includes power to require the production of".

(4) After subsection (10) add—

"(11) A person who is convicted on a prosecution instituted as a result of an investigation under this section may in the same proceedings be ordered to pay the expenses of the investigation to such extent as may be specified in the order.

There shall be treated as expenses of the investigation, in particular, such reasonable sums as the Secretary of State may determine in respect of general staff costs and overheads.".

(5) In section 106 of the Financial Services Act 1986 (exercise of investigation powers by officer, &c.), after subsection (2) insert— 1986 c. 60.

"(2A) A person shall not by virtue of an authority under this section be required to disclose any information or produce any documents in respect of which he owes an obligation of confidence by virtue of carrying on the business of banking unless—

(a) he is the person under investigation or a related company,

(b) the person to whom the obligation of confidence is owed is the person under investigation or a related company,

(c) the person to whom the obligation of confidence is owed consents to the disclosure or production, or

(d) the imposing on him of a requirement with respect to such information or documents has been specifically authorised by the Secretary of State.

In this subsection "documents", "person under investigation" and "related company" have the same meaning as in section 105.".

74.—(1) Section 177 of the Financial Services Act 1986 (investigations into insider dealing) is amended as follows. Investigations into insider dealing.

(2) After subsection (2) (power to limit period or scope of investigation) insert—

"(2A) At any time during the investigation the Secretary of State may vary the appointment by limiting or extending the period during which the inspector is to continue his investigation or by confining the investigation to particular matters.".

(3) After subsection (5) (duty of inspectors to report) insert—

"(5A) If the Secretary of State thinks fit, he may direct the inspector to take no further steps in the investigation or to take only such further steps as are specified in the direction; and where an investigation is the subject of such a direction, the inspectors shall make a final report to the Secretary of State only where the Secretary of State directs them to do so.".

(4) For subsection (8) (privilege on grounds of banker's duty of confidentiality) substitute—

"(8) A person shall not under this section be required to disclose any information or produce any document in respect of which he owes an obligation of confidence by virtue of carrying on the business of banking unless—

> (a) the person to whom the obligation of confidence is owed consents to the disclosure or production, or

> (b) the making of the requirement was authorised by the Secretary of State.".

(5) In subsection (10) (definition of "documents") for "references to its production include references to producing" substitute "the power to require its production includes power to require the production of".

(6) After subsection (10) add—

"(11) A person who is convicted on a prosecution instituted as a result of an investigation under this section may in the same proceedings be ordered to pay the expenses of the investigation to such extent as may be specified in the order.

There shall be treated as expenses of the investigation, in particular, such reasonable sums as the Secretary of State may determine in respect of general staff costs and overheads.".

75.—(1) In section 179(3) of the Financial Services Act 1986 (persons who are "primary recipients" for purposes of provisions restricting disclosure of information)—

> (a) omit the word "and" preceding paragraph (i);

> (b) in that paragraph, after "any such person" insert "as is mentioned in paragraphs (a) to (h) above";

> (c) after that paragraph insert—

> > "(j) any constable or other person named in a warrant issued under this Act.".

(2) Section 180 of the Financial Services Act 1986 (exceptions from restrictions on disclosure) is amended as follows.

(3) In subsection (1) (purposes for which disclosure permitted)—

> (a) in paragraph (c), after "insolvency" insert "or by Part II, III or VII of the Companies Act 1989";

> (b) for paragraph (e) substitute—

> > "(e) for the purpose—

> > > (i) of enabling or assisting a designated agency to discharge its functions under this Act or Part VII of the Companies Act 1989,

> > > (ii) of enabling or assisting a transferee body or the competent authority to discharge its functions under this Act, or

> > > (iii) of enabling or assisting the body administering a scheme under section 54 above to discharge its functions under the scheme;";

> (c) after paragraph (h) insert—

"(hh) for the purpose of enabling or assisting a body established by order under section 46 of the Companies Act 1989 to discharge its functions under Part II of that Act, or of enabling or assisting a recognised supervisory or qualifying body within the meaning of that Part to discharge its functions as such;";

  (d) after paragraph (o) insert—

"(oo) with a view to the institution of, or otherwise for the purposes of, any disciplinary proceedings relating to the discharge by a public servant of his duties;";

  (e) in paragraph (p), after "under" insert "section 44 of the Insurance Companies Act 1982, section 447 of the Companies Act 1985," and after "above" insert "or section 84 of the Companies Act 1989";

  (f) after paragraph (q) insert—

"(qq) for the purpose of enabling or assisting an overseas regulatory authority to exercise its regulatory functions;".

 (4) After that subsection insert—

"(1A) In subsection (1)—

  (a) in paragraph (oo) "public servant" means an officer or servant of the Crown or of any public or other authority for the time being designated for the purposes of that paragraph by order of the Secretary of State; and

  (b) in paragraph (qq) "overseas regulatory authority" and "regulatory functions" have the same meaning as in section 82 of the Companies Act 1989.".

 (5) In subsection (3) (disclosure to designated public authorities) for "designated for the purposes of this section" substitute "designated for the purposes of this subsection".

 (6) Omit subsection (6) (disclosure to certain overseas authorities).

 (7) In subsection (9) (orders) for "subsection (3) or (8)" substitute "subsection (1A)(a), (3) or (8).

76.—(1) Section 199 of the Financial Services Act 1986 (powers of entry) is amended as follows.

Entry and search of premises.
1986 c. 60.

 (2) For subsections (1) and (2) substitute—

"(1) A justice of the peace may issue a warrant under this section if satisfied on information on oath given by or on behalf of the Secretary of State that there are reasonable grounds for believing that an offence has been committed—

  (a) under section 4, 47, 57, 130, 133 or 171(2) or (3) above, or

  (b) section 1, 2, 4 or 5 of the Company Securities (Insider Dealing) Act 1985,

and that there are on any premises documents relevant to the question whether that offence has been committed.

(2) A justice of the peace may also issue a warrant under this section if satisfied on information on oath given by or on behalf of the Secretary of State, or by a person appointed or authorised to exercise powers under section 94, 106 or 177 above, that there are reasonable grounds for believing that there are on any premises documents whose production has been required under section 94, 105 or 177 above and which have not been produced in compliance with the requirement.".

(3) In subsection (3)(b) for "subsection (1)(a) or (b)" substitute "subsection (1)".

(4) In subsection (5) (period for which documents may be retained), for paragraph (b) substitute—

"(b) if within that period proceedings to which the documents are relevant are commenced against any person for any criminal offence, until the conclusion of those proceedings.".

(5) In subsection (6) (offences) after "Any person who" insert "intentionally".

(6) In subsection (7) for "subsection (1)(a) above" substitute "subsection (1) above".

(7) For subsection (8) substitute—

"(8) In the application of this section to Scotland for the references to a justice of the peace substitute references to a justice of the peace or a sheriff, and for the references to information on oath substitute references to evidence on oath.".

(8) In subsection (9) (definition of "documents"), omit the words from "and, in relation" to the end.

Amendments of other enactments

Amendments of the Insurance Companies Act 1982.
1982 c. 50.

77.—(1) Part II of the Insurance Companies Act 1982 is amended as follows.

(2) In section 44 (power to obtain information and require production of documents), for "books or papers" (wherever occurring) substitute "documents", and for subsection (6) substitute—

"(6) In this section "document" includes information recorded in any form; and, in relation to information recorded otherwise than in legible form, the power to require its production includes power to require the production of a copy of the information in legible form.".

(3) After that section insert—

"Entry and search of premises.

44A.—(1) A justice of the peace may issue a warrant under this section if satisfied on information on oath given by or on behalf of the Secretary of State, or by a person authorised to exercise powers under section 44 above, that there are reasonable grounds for believing that there are on any premises documents whose production has been required under section 44(2) to (4) above and which have not been produced in compliance with the requirement.

(2) A justice of the peace may also issue a warrant under this section if satisfied on information on oath given by or on behalf of the Secretary of State, or by a person authorised to exercise powers under section 44 above—

    (a) that there are reasonable grounds for believing that an offence has been committed for which the penalty on conviction on indictment is imprisonment for a term of not less than two years and that there are on any premises documents relating to whether the offence has been committed,

    (b) that the Secretary of State or, as the case may be, the authorised person has power to require the production of the documents under section 44(2) to (4) above, and

    (c) that there are reasonable grounds for believing that if production was so required the documents would not be produced but would be removed from the premises, hidden, tampered with or destroyed.

(3) A warrant under this section shall authorise a constable, together with any other person named in it and any other constables—

    (a) to enter the premises specified in the information, using such force as is reasonably necessary for the purpose;

    (b) to search the premises and take possession of any documents appearing to be such documents as are mentioned in subsection (1) or (2), as the case may be, or to take, in relation to any such documents, any other steps which may appear to be necessary for preserving them or preventing interference with them;

    (c) to take copies of any such documents; and

    (d) to require any person named in the warrant to provide an explanation of them or to state where they may be found.

(4) If in the case of a warrant under subsection (2) the justice of the peace is satisfied on information on oath that there are reasonable grounds for believing that there are also on the premises other documents relevant to the investigation, the warrant shall also authorise the actions mentioned in subsection (3) to be taken in relation to such documents.

(5) A warrant under this section shall continue in force until the end of the period of one month beginning with the day on which it is issued.

(6) Any documents of which possession is taken under this section may be retained—

    (a) for a period of three months; or

(b) if within that period proceedings to which the documents are relevant are commenced against any person for any criminal offence, until the conclusion of those proceedings.

(7) In the application of this section to Scotland for the references to a justice of the peace substitute references to a justice of the peace or a sheriff, and for the references to information on oath substitute references to evidence on oath.

(8) In this section "document" includes information recorded in any form.".

(4) In section 47A(1) (restriction on disclosure of information), after "section 44(2) to (4)" insert "or 44A".

(5) In section 71 (offences and penalties), after subsection (2) insert—

"(2A) A person who intentionally obstructs the exercise of any rights conferred by a warrant issued under section 44A above or fails without reasonable excuse to comply with any requirement imposed in accordance with subsection (3)(d) of that section is guilty of an offence and liable—

(a) on conviction on indictment, to a fine, and

(b) on summary conviction, to a fine not exceeding the statutory maximum.".

(6) In section 71(6) (defence to failure to comply with requirement to produce books or papers) for "books or papers" substitute "documents".

Amendment of the Insolvency Act 1986.
1986 c. 45.

78. In section 218(5) of the Insolvency Act 1986 (investigation by Secretary of State on report by liquidator), for paragraph (a) substitute—

"(a) shall thereupon investigate the matter reported to him and such other matters relating to the affairs of the company as appear to him to require investigation, and".

Amendment of the Company Directors Disqualification Act 1986.
1986 c. 46.

79. In section 8 of the Company Directors Disqualification Act 1986 (disqualification after investigation of company), after "section 52 of the Criminal Justice (Scotland) Act 1987" insert "or section 83 of the Companies Act 1989".

Amendment of the Building Societies Act 1986.
1986 c. 53.

80. In section 53 of the Building Societies Act 1986 (confidentiality of information obtained by the Building Societies Commission), in subsection (7)(b) (functions of Secretary of State for purposes of which disclosure may be made) after sub-paragraph (ii) insert—

", or

(iii) Part II, III or VII of the Companies Act 1989;".

Amendments of the Banking Act 1987.
1987 c. 22.

81.—(1) In section 84(1) of the Banking Act 1987 (disclosure of information obtained under that Act), the Table showing the authorities to which, and functions for the purposes of which, disclosure may be made is amended as follows.

(2) In the entry relating to the Secretary of State, in column 2, for "or the Financial Services Act 1986" substitute ", the Financial Services Act 1986 or Part II, III or VII of the Companies Act 1989".

(3) For the entry relating to inspectors appointed by the Secretary of State substitute—

"An inspector appointed under Part XIV of the Companies Act 1985 or section 94 or 177 of the Financial Services Act 1986.

Functions under that Part or that section.".

(4) For the entry beginning "A person authorised by the Secretary of State" substitute—

"A person authorised to exercise powers under section 44 of the Insurance Companies Act 1982, section 447 of the Companies Act 1985, section 106 of the Financial Services Act 1986 or section 84 of the Companies Act 1989.

Functions under that section.".

(5) For the entry relating to a designated agency or transferee body or the competent authority (within the meaning of the Financial Services Act 1986) substitute—

1986 c. 60.

"A designated agency (within the meaning of the Financial Services Act 1986).

Functions under the Financial Services Act 1986 or Part VII of the Companies Act 1989.

A transferee body or the competent authority (within the meaning of the Financial Services Act 1986).

Functions under the Financial Services Act 1986.".

Powers exercisable to assist overseas regulatory authorities

82.—(1) The powers conferred by section 83 are exercisable by the Secretary of State for the purpose of assisting an overseas regulatory authority which has requested his assistance in connection with inquiries being carried out by it or on its behalf.

Request for assistance by overseas regulatory authority.

(2) An "overseas regulatory authority" means an authority which in a country or territory outside the United Kingdom exercises—

(a) any function corresponding to—

(i) a function under the Financial Services Act 1986 of a designated agency, transferee body or competent authority (within the meaning of that Act),

(ii) a function of the Secretary of State under the Insurance Companies Act 1982, the Companies Act 1985 or the Financial Services Act 1986, or

1982 c. 50.
1985 c. 6.

(iii) a function of the Bank of England under the Banking Act 1987, or

1987 c. 22.

(b) any function in connection with the investigation of, or the enforcement of rules (whether or not having the force of law) relating to, conduct of the kind prohibited by the Company Securities (Insider Dealing) Act 1985, or

1985 c. 9.

(c) any function prescribed for the purposes of this subsection by order of the Secretary of State, being a function which in the opinion of the Secretary of State relates to companies or financial services.

An order under paragraph (c) shall be made by statutory instrument which shall be subject to annulment in pursuance of a resolution of either House of Parliament.

(3) The Secretary of State shall not exercise the powers conferred by section 83 unless he is satisfied that the assistance requested by the overseas regulatory authority is for the purposes of its regulatory functions.

An authority's "regulatory functions" means any functions falling within subsection (2) and any other functions relating to companies or financial services.

(4) In deciding whether to exercise those powers the Secretary of State may take into account, in particular—

(a) whether corresponding assistance would be given in that country or territory to an authority exercising regulatory functions in the United Kingdom;

(b) whether the inquiries relate to the possible breach of a law, or other requirement, which has no close parallel in the United Kingdom or involves the assertion of a jurisdiction not recognised by the United Kingdom;

(c) the seriousness of the matter to which the inquiries relate, the importance to the inquiries of the information sought in the United Kingdom and whether the assistance could be obtained by other means;

(d) whether it is otherwise appropriate in the public interest to give the assistance sought.

(5) Before deciding whether to exercise those powers in a case where the overseas regulatory authority is a banking supervisor, the Secretary of State shall consult the Bank of England.

A "banking supervisor" means an overseas regulatory authority with respect to which the Bank of England has notified the Secretary of State, for the purposes of this subsection, that it exercises functions corresponding to those of the Bank under the Banking Act 1987.

1987 c. 22.

(6) The Secretary of State may decline to exercise those powers unless the overseas regulatory authority undertakes to make such contribution towards the costs of their exercise as the Secretary of State considers appropriate.

(7) References in this section to financial services include, in particular, investment business, insurance and banking.

Power to require information, documents or other assistance.

83.—(1) The following powers may be exercised in accordance with section 82, if the Secretary of State considers there is good reason for their exercise.

(2) The Secretary of State may require any person—

(a) to attend before him at a specified time and place and answer questions or otherwise furnish information with respect to any matter relevant to the inquiries,

(b) to produce at a specified time and place any specified documents which appear to the Secretary of State to relate to any matter relevant to the inquiries, and

(c) otherwise to give him such assistance in connection with the inquiries as he is reasonably able to give.

(3) The Secretary of State may examine a person on oath and may administer an oath accordingly.

(4) Where documents are produced the Secretary of State may take copies or extracts from them.

(5) A person shall not under this section be required to disclose information or produce a document which he would be entitled to refuse to disclose or produce on grounds of legal professional privilege in proceedings in the High Court or on grounds of confidentiality as between client and professional legal adviser in proceedings in the Court of Session, except that a lawyer may be required to furnish the name and address of his client.

(6) A statement by a person in compliance with a requirement imposed under this section may be used in evidence against him.

(7) Where a person claims a lien on a document, its production under this section is without prejudice to his lien.

(8) In this section "documents" includes information recorded in any form; and, in relation to information recorded otherwise than in legible form, the power to require its production includes power to require the production of a copy of it in legible form.

84.—(1) The Secretary of State may authorise an officer of his or any other competent person to exercise on his behalf all or any of the powers conferred by section 83.

(2) No such authority shall be granted except for the purpose of investigating—

    (a) the affairs, or any aspects of the affairs, of a person specified in the authority, or

    (b) a subject-matter so specified,

being a person who, or subject-matter which, is the subject of the inquiries being carried out by or on behalf of the overseas regulatory authority.

(3) No person shall be bound to comply with a requirement imposed by a person exercising powers by virtue of an authority granted under this section unless he has, if required, produced evidence of his authority.

(4) A person shall not by virtue of an authority under this section be required to disclose any information or produce any documents in respect of which he owes an obligation of confidence by virtue of carrying on the business of banking unless—

    (a) the imposing on him of a requirement with respect to such information or documents has been specifically authorised by the Secretary of State, or

    (b) the person to whom the obligation of confidence is owed consents to the disclosure or production.

In this subsection "documents" has the same meaning as in section 83.

(5) Where the Secretary of State authorises a person other than one of his officers to exercise any powers by virtue of this section, that person shall make a report to the Secretary of State in such manner as he may require on the exercise of those powers and the results of exercising them.

Penalty for
failure to comply
with
requirement, &c.

85.—(1) A person who without reasonable excuse fails to comply with a requirement imposed on him under section 83 commits an offence and is liable on summary conviction to imprisonment for a term not exceeding six months or to a fine not exceeding level 5 on the standard scale, or both.

(2) A person who in purported compliance with any such requirement furnishes information which he knows to be false or misleading in a material particular, or recklessly furnishes information which is false or misleading in a material particular, commits an offence and is liable—

    (a) on conviction on indictment, to imprisonment for a term not exceeding two years or to a fine, or both;

    (b) on summary conviction, to imprisonment for a term not exceeding six months or to a fine not exceeding the statutory maximum, or both.

Restrictions on
disclosure of
information.

86.—(1) This section applies to information relating to the business or other affairs of a person which—

    (a) is supplied by an overseas regulatory authority in connection with a request for assistance, or

    (b) is obtained by virtue of the powers conferred by section 83, whether or not any requirement to supply it is made under that section.

(2) Except as permitted by section 87 below, such information shall not be disclosed for any purpose—

    (a) by the primary recipient, or

    (b) by any person obtaining the information directly or indirectly from him,

without the consent of the person from whom the primary recipient obtained the information and, if different, the person to whom it relates.

(3) The "primary recipient" means, as the case may be—

    (a) the Secretary of State,

    (b) any person authorised under section 84 to exercise powers on his behalf, and

    (c) any officer or servant of any such person.

(4) Information shall not be treated as information to which this section applies if it has been made available to the public by virtue of being disclosed in any circumstances in which, or for any purpose for which, disclosure is not precluded by this section.

(5) A person who contravenes this section commits an offence and is liable—

    (a) on conviction on indictment, to imprisonment for a term not exceeding two years or to a fine, or both;

    (b) on summary conviction, to imprisonment for a term not exceeding three months or to a fine not exceeding the statutory maximum, or both.

87.—(1) Information to which section 86 applies may be disclosed—

    (a) to any person with a view to the institution of, or otherwise for the purposes of, relevant proceedings,

    (b) for the purpose of enabling or assisting a relevant authority to discharge any relevant function (including functions in relation to proceedings),

    (c) to the Treasury, if the disclosure is made in the interests of investors or in the public interest,

    (d) if the information is or has been available to the public from other sources,

    (e) in a summary or collection of information framed in such a way as not to enable the identity of any person to whom the information relates to be ascertained, or

    (f) in pursuance of any Community obligation.

(2) The relevant proceedings referred to in subsection (1)(a) are—

    (a) any criminal proceedings,

    (b) civil proceedings arising under or by virtue of the Financial Services Act 1986 and proceedings before the Financial Services Tribunal, and

1986 c. 60.

    (c) disciplinary proceedings relating to—

        (i) the exercise by a solicitor, auditor, accountant, valuer or actuary of his professional duties, or

        (ii) the discharge by a public servant of his duties.

(3) In subsection (2)(c)(ii) "public servant" means an officer or servant of the Crown or of any public or other authority for the time being designated for the purposes of that provision by order of the Secretary of State.

(4) The relevant authorities referred to in subsection (1)(b), and the relevant functions in relation to each such authority, are as follows—

Authority	*Functions*	
The Secretary of State.	Functions under the enactments relating to companies, insurance companies or insolvency, or under the Financial Services Act 1986 or Part II, this Part or Part VII of this Act.	
An inspector appointed under Part XIV of the Companies Act 1985 or section 94 or 177 of the Financial Services Act 1986.	Functions under that Part or that section.	1985 c. 6.
A person authorised to exercise powers under section 44 of the Insurance Companies Act 1982, section 447 of the Companies Act 1985, section 106 of the Financial Services Act 1986 or section 84 of this Act.	Functions under that section.	1982 c. 50.
An overseas regulatory authority.	Its regulatory functions (within the meaning of section 82 of this Act).	

PART III	*Authority*	*Functions*
	The Department of Economic Development in Northern Ireland or a person appointed or authorised by that Department.	Functions conferred on it or him by the enactments relating to companies or insolvency.
1986 c. 60.	A designated agency within the meaning of the Financial Services Act 1986.	Functions under that Act or Part VII of this Act.
	A transferee body or the competent authority within the meaning of the Financial Services Act 1986.	Functions under that Act.
	The body administering a scheme under section 54 of the Financial Services Act 1986.	Functions under the scheme.
	A recognised self-regulating organisation, recognised professional body, recognised investment exchange, recognised clearing house or recognised self-regulating organisation for friendly societies (within the meaning of the Financial Services Act 1986).	Functions in its capacity as an organisation, body, exchange or clearing house recognised under that Act.
	The Chief Registrar of friendly societies, the Registrar of Friendly Societies for Northern Ireland and the Assistant Registrar of Friendly Societies for Scotland.	Functions under the Financial Services Act 1986 or the enactments relating to friendly societies or building societies.
1987 c. 22.	The Bank of England.	Functions under the Banking Act 1987 and any other functions.
	The Deposit Protection Board.	Functions under the Banking Act 1987.
	A body established by order under section 46 of this Act.	Functions under Part II of this Act.
	A recognised supervisory or qualifying body within the meaning of Part II of this Act.	Functions as such a body.
	The Industrial Assurance Commissioner and the Industrial Assurance Commissioner for Northern Ireland.	Functions under the enactments relating to industrial assurance.
1977 c. 46.	The Insurance Brokers Registration Council.	Functions under the Insurance Brokers (Registration) Act 1977.
	The Official Receiver or, in Northern Ireland, the Official Assignee for company liquidations or for bankruptcy.	Functions under the enactments relating to insolvency.
1986 c. 45.	A recognised professional body (within the meaning of section 391 of the Insolvency Act 1986).	Functions in its capacity as such a body under the Insolvency Act 1986.
1986 c. 53.	The Building Societies Commission.	Functions under the Building Societies Act 1986.
	The Director General of Fair Trading.	Functions under the Financial Services Act 1986.

(5) The Secretary of State may by order amend the Table in subsection (4) so as to—

   (a) add any public or other authority to the Table and specify the relevant functions of that authority,

   (b) remove any authority from the Table, or

   (c) add functions to, or remove functions from, those which are relevant functions in relation to an authority specified in the Table;

and the order may impose conditions subject to which, or otherwise restrict the circumstances in which, disclosure is permitted.

(6) An order under this section shall be made by statutory instrument which shall be subject to annulment in pursuance of a resolution of either House of Parliament.

88.—(1) The following provisions apply where it appears to the Secretary of State that a request for assistance by an overseas regulatory authority may involve the powers conferred by section 83 being exercised in Northern Ireland in relation to matters which are transferred matters within the meaning of the Northern Ireland Constitution Act 1973. Exercise of powers in relation to Northern Ireland.

1973 c. 36.

(2) The Secretary of State shall before deciding whether to accede to the request consult the Department of Economic Development in Northern Ireland, and if he decides to accede to the request and it appears to him—

   (a) that the powers should be exercised in Northern Ireland, and

   (b) that the purposes for which they should be so exercised relate wholly or primarily to transferred matters,

he shall by instrument in writing authorise the Department to exercise in Northern Ireland his powers under section 83.

(3) The following provisions have effect in relation to the exercise of powers by virtue of such an authority with the substitution for references to the Secretary of State of references to the Department of Economic Development in Northern Ireland—

   (a) section 84 (exercise of powers by officer, &c.),

   (b) section 449 of the Companies Act 1985, section 53 or 54 of the Building Societies Act 1986, sections 179 and 180 of the Financial Services Act 1986, section 84 of the Banking Act 1987 and sections 86 and 87 above (restrictions on disclosure of information), and 1985 c. 6.
1986 c. 53.
1986 c. 60.
1987 c. 22.

   (c) section 89 (authority for institution of criminal proceedings);

and references to the Secretary of State in other enactments which proceed by reference to those provisions shall be construed accordingly as being or including references to the Department.

(4) The Secretary of State may after consultation with the Department of Economic Development in Northern Ireland revoke an authority given to the Department under this section.

(5) In that case nothing in the provisions referred to in subsection (3)(b) shall apply so as to prevent the Department from giving the Secretary of State any information obtained by virtue of the authority; and (without prejudice to their application in relation to disclosure by the Department) those provisions shall apply to the disclosure of such information by the Secretary of State as if it had been obtained by him in the first place.

(6) Nothing in this section affects the exercise by the Secretary of State of any powers in Northern Ireland—

    (a) in a case where at the time of acceding to the request it did not appear to him that the circumstances were such as to require him to authorise the Department of Economic Development in Northern Ireland to exercise those powers, or

    (b) after the revocation by him of any such authority;

and no objection shall be taken to anything done by or in relation to the Secretary of State or the Department on the ground that it should have been done by or in relation to the other.

Prosecutions.

89. Proceedings for an offence under section 85 or 86 shall not be instituted—

    (a) in England and Wales, except by or with the consent of the Secretary of State or the Director of Public Prosecutions;

    (b) in Northern Ireland, except by or with the consent of the Secretary of State or the Director of Public Prosecutions for Northern Ireland.

Offences by bodies corporate, partnerships and unincorporated associations.

90.—(1) Where an offence under section 85 or 86 committed by a body corporate is proved to have been committed with the consent or connivance of, or to be attributable to any neglect on the part of, a director, manager, secretary or other similar officer of the body, or a person purporting to act in any such capacity, he as well as the body corporate is guilty of the offence and liable to be proceeded against and punished accordingly.

(2) Where the affairs of a body corporate are managed by its members, subsection (1) applies in relation to the acts and defaults of a member in connection with his functions of management as to a director of a body corporate.

(3) Where an offence under section 85 or 86 committed by a partnership is proved to have been committed with the consent or connivance of, or to be attributable to any neglect on the part of, a partner, he as well as the partnership is guilty of the offence and liable to be proceeded against and punished accordingly.

(4) Where an offence under section 85 or 86 committed by an unincorporated association (other than a partnership) is proved to have been committed with the consent or connivance of, or to be attributable to any neglect on the part of, any officer of the association or any member of its governing body, he as well as the association is guilty of the offence and liable to be proceeded against and punished accordingly.

Jurisdiction and procedure in respect of offences.

91.—(1) Summary proceedings for an offence under section 85 may, without prejudice to any jurisdiction exercisable apart from this section, be taken against a body corporate or unincorporated association at any place at which it has a place of business and against an individual at any place where he is for the time being.

(2) Proceedings for an offence alleged to have been committed under section 85 or 86 by an unincorporated association shall be brought in the name of the association (and not in that of any of its members), and for the purposes of any such proceedings any rules of court relating to the service of documents apply as in relation to a body corporate.

PART III
1925 c. 86.
1980 c. 43.

(3) Section 33 of the Criminal Justice Act 1925 and Schedule 3 to the Magistrates' Courts Act 1980 (procedure on charge of offence against a corporation) apply in a case in which an unincorporated association is charged in England and Wales with an offence under section 85 or 86 as they apply in the case of a corporation.

(4) In relation to proceedings on indictment in Scotland for an offence alleged to have been committed under section 85 or 86 by an unincorporated association, section 74 of the Criminal Procedure (Scotland) Act 1975 (proceedings on indictment against bodies corporate) applies as if the association were a body corporate. 1975 c. 21.

(5) Section 18 of the Criminal Justice Act (Northern Ireland) 1945 and Schedule 4 to the Magistrates' Courts (Northern Ireland) Order 1981 (procedure on charge of offence against a corporation) apply in a case in which an unincorporated association is charged in Northern Ireland with an offence under section 85 or 86 as they apply in the case of a corporation. 1945 c. 15 (N.I.)
S.I. 1981/1675
(N.I.26).

(6) A fine imposed on an unincorporated association on its conviction of such an offence shall be paid out of the funds of the association.

PART IV

REGISTRATION OF COMPANY CHARGES

Introduction

92. The provisions of this Part amend the provisions of the Companies Act 1985 relating to the registration of company charges— Introduction.
1985 c. 6.

   (a) by inserting in Part XII of that Act (in place of sections 395 to 408 and 410 to 423) new provisions with respect to companies registered in Great Britain, and

   (b) by inserting as Chapter III of Part XXIII of that Act (in place of sections 409 and 424) new provisions with respect to oversea companies.

Registration in the companies charges register

93. The following sections are inserted in Part XII of the Companies Act 1985— Charges requiring registration.

"Registration in the company charges register

Introductory provisions.

   395.—(1) The purpose of this Part is to secure the registration of charges on a company's property.

   (2) In this Part—

     "charge" means any form of security interest (fixed or floating) over property, other than an interest arising by operation of law; and

     "property", in the context of what is the subject of a charge, includes future property.

   (3) It is immaterial for the purposes of this Part where the property subject to a charge is situated.

(4) References in this Part to "the registrar" are—

    (a) in relation to a company registered in England and Wales, to the registrar of companies for England and Wales, and

    (b) in relation to a company registered in Scotland, to the registrar of companies for Scotland;

and references to registration, in relation to a charge, are to registration in the register kept by him under this Part.

Charges requiring registration.

396.—(1) The charges requiring registration under this Part are—

    (a) a charge on land or any interest in land, other than—

        (i) in England and Wales, a charge for rent or any other periodical sum issuing out of the land,

        (ii) in Scotland, a charge for any rent, ground annual or other periodical sum payable in respect of the land;

    (b) a charge on goods or any interest in goods, other than a charge under which the chargee is entitled to possession either of the goods or of a document of title to them;

    (c) a charge on intangible movable property (in Scotland, incorporeal moveable property) of any of the following descriptions—

        (i) goodwill,

        (ii) intellectual property,

        (iii) book debts (whether book debts of the company or assigned to the company),

        (iv) uncalled share capital of the company or calls made but not paid;

    (d) a charge for securing an issue of debentures; or

    (e) a floating charge on the whole or part of the company's property.

(2) The descriptions of charge mentioned in subsection (1) shall be construed as follows—

    (a) a charge on a debenture forming part of an issue or series shall not be treated as falling within paragraph (a) or (b) by reason of the fact that the debenture is secured by a charge on land or goods (or on an interest in land or goods);

    (b) in paragraph (b) "goods" means any tangible movable property (in Scotland, corporeal moveable property) other than money;

    (c) a charge is not excluded from paragraph (b) because the chargee is entitled to take possession in case of default or on the occurrence of some other event;

(d) in paragraph (c)(ii) "intellectual property" means—

>> (i) any patent, trade mark, service mark, registered design, copyright or design right, or

>> (ii) any licence under or in respect of any such right;

(e) a debenture which is part of an issue or series shall not be treated as a book debt for the purposes of paragraph (c)(iii);

(f) the deposit by way of security of a negotiable instrument given to secure the payment of book debts shall not be treated for the purposes of paragraph (c)(iii) as a charge on book debts;

(g) a shipowner's lien on subfreights shall not be treated as a charge on book debts for the purposes of paragraph (c)(iii) or as a floating charge for the purposes of paragraph (e).

(3) Whether a charge is one requiring registration under this Part shall be determined—

(a) in the case of a charge created by a company, as at the date the charge is created, and

(b) in the case of a charge over property acquired by a company, as at the date of the acquisition.

(4) The Secretary of State may by regulations amend subsections (1) and (2) so as to add any description of charge to, or remove any description of charge from, the charges requiring registration under this Part.

(5) Regulations under this section shall be made by statutory instrument which shall be subject to annulment in pursuance of a resolution of either House of Parliament.

(6) In the following provisions of this Part references to a charge are, unless the context otherwise requires, to a charge requiring registration under this Part.

Where a charge not otherwise requiring registration relates to property by virtue of which it requires to be registered and to other property, the references are to the charge so far as it relates to property of the former description.".

94. The following section is inserted in Part XII of the Companies Act 1985—

The companies charges register.

1985 c. 6.

"The companies charges register.

397.—(1) The registrar shall keep for each company a register, in such form as he thinks fit, of charges on property of the company.

(2) The register shall consist of a file containing with respect to each charge the particulars and other information delivered to the registrar under the provisions of this Part.

(3) Any person may require the registrar to provide a certificate stating the date on which any specified particulars of, or other information relating to, a charge were delivered to him.

(4) The certificate shall be signed by the registrar or authenticated by his official seal.

(5) The certificate shall be conclusive evidence that the specified particulars or other information were delivered to the registrar no later than the date stated in the certificate; and it shall be presumed unless the contrary is proved that they were not delivered earlier than that date.".

Delivery of
particulars for
registration.

1985 c. 6.

95. The following sections are inserted in Part XII of the Companies Act 1985—

"Company's
duty to deliver
particulars of
charge for
registration.

398.—(1) It is the duty of a company which creates a charge, or acquires property subject to a charge—

(a) to deliver the prescribed particulars of the charge, in the prescribed form, to the registrar for registration, and

(b) to do so within 21 days after the date of the charge's creation or, as the case may be, the date of the acquisition;

but particulars of a charge may be delivered for registration by any person interested in the charge.

(2) Where the particulars are delivered for registration by a person other than the company concerned, that person is entitled to recover from the company the amount of any fees paid by him to the registrar in connection with the registration.

(3) If a company fails to comply with subsection (1), then, unless particulars of the charge have been delivered for registration by another person, the company and every officer of it who is in default is liable to a fine.

(4) Where prescribed particulars in the prescribed form are delivered to the registrar for registration, he shall file the particulars in the register and shall note, in such form as he thinks fit, the date on which they were delivered to him.

(5) The registrar shall send to the company and any person appearing from the particulars to be the chargee, and if the particulars were delivered by another person interested in the charge to that person, a copy of the particulars filed by him and of the note made by him as to the date on which they were delivered.

Effect of failure
to deliver
particulars for
registration.

399.—(1) Where a charge is created by a company and no prescribed particulars in the prescribed form are delivered for registration within the period of 21 days after the date of the charge's creation, the charge is void against—

(a) an administrator or liquidator of the company, and

(b) any person who for value acquires an interest in or right over property subject to the charge,

where the relevant event occurs after the creation of the charge, whether before or after the end of the 21 day period.

This is subject to section 400 (late delivery of particulars).

(2) In this Part "the relevant event" means—

(a) in relation to the voidness of a charge as against an administrator or liquidator, the beginning of the insolvency proceedings, and

(b) in relation to the voidness of a charge as against a person acquiring an interest in or right over property subject to a charge, the acquisition of that interest or right;

and references to "a relevant event" shall be construed accordingly.

(3) Where a relevant event occurs on the same day as the charge is created, it shall be presumed to have occurred after the charge is created unless the contrary is proved.

Late delivery of particulars.

400.—(1) Where prescribed particulars of a charge created by a company, in the prescribed form, are delivered for registration more than 21 days after the date of the charge's creation, section 399(1) does not apply in relation to relevant events occurring after the particulars are delivered.

(2) However, where in such a case—

(a) the company is at the date of delivery of the particulars unable to pay its debts, or subsequently becomes unable to pay its debts in consequence of the transaction under which the charge is created, and

(b) insolvency proceedings begin before the end of the relevant period beginning with the date of delivery of the particulars,

the charge is void as against the administrator or liquidator.

(3) For this purpose—

(a) the company is "unable to pay its debts" in the circumstances specified in section 123 of the Insolvency Act 1986; and

(b) the "relevant period" is—

(i) two years in the case of a floating charge created in favour of a person connected with the company (within the meaning of section 249 of that Act),

(ii) one year in the case of a floating charge created in favour of a person not so connected, and

(iii) six months in any other case.

(4) Where a relevant event occurs on the same day as the particulars are delivered, it shall be presumed to have occurred before the particulars are delivered unless the contrary is proved.".

Delivery of
further particulars.

1985 c. 6.

96. The following section is inserted in Part XII of the Companies Act 1985—

"Delivery of
further
particulars.

401.—(1) Further particulars of a charge, supplementing or varying the registered particulars, may be delivered to the registrar for registration at any time.

(2) Further particulars must be in the prescribed form signed by or on behalf of both the company and the chargee.

(3) Where further particulars are delivered to the registrar for registration and appear to him to be duly signed, he shall file the particulars in the register and shall note, in such form as he thinks fit, the date on which they were delivered to him.

(4) The registrar shall send to the company and any person appearing from the particulars to be the chargee, and if the particulars were delivered by another person interested in the charge to that other person, a copy of the further particulars filed by him and of the note made by him as to the date on which they were delivered.".

Effect of
omissions and
errors in
registered
particulars.

97. The following section is inserted in Part XII of the Companies Act 1985—

"Effect of
omissions and
errors in
registered
particulars.

402.—(1) Where the registered particulars of a charge created by a company are not complete and accurate, the charge is void, as mentioned below, to the extent that rights are not disclosed by the registered particulars which would be disclosed if they were complete and accurate.

(2) The charge is void to that extent, unless the court on the application of the chargee orders otherwise, as against—

(a) an administrator or liquidator of the company, and

(b) any person who for value acquires an interest in or right over property subject to the charge,

where the relevant event occurs at a time when the particulars are incomplete or inaccurate in a relevant respect.

(3) Where a relevant event occurs on the same day as particulars or further particulars are delivered, it shall be presumed to have occurred before those particulars are delivered unless the contrary is proved.

(4) The court may order that the charge is effective as against an administrator or liquidator of the company if it is satisfied—

    (a) that the omission or error is not likely to have misled materially to his prejudice any unsecured creditor of the company, or

    (b) that no person became an unsecured creditor of the company at a time when the registered particulars of the charge were incomplete or inaccurate in a relevant respect.

(5) The court may order that the charge is effective as against a person acquiring an interest in or right over property subject to the charge if it is satisfied that he did not rely, in connection with the acquisition, on registered particulars which were incomplete or inaccurate in a relevant respect.

(6) For the purposes of this section an omission or inaccuracy with respect to the name of the chargee shall not be regarded as a failure to disclose the rights of the chargee.".

98. The following section is inserted in Part XII of the Companies Act 1985—

Memorandum of charge ceasing to affect company's property.
1985 c. 6.

"Memorandum of charge ceasing to affect company's property.

    403.—(1) Where a charge of which particulars have been delivered ceases to affect the company's property, a memorandum to that effect may be delivered to the registrar for registration.

    (2) The memorandum must be in the prescribed form signed by or on behalf of both the company and the chargee.

    (3) Where a memorandum is delivered to the registrar for registration and appears to him to be duly signed, he shall file it in the register, and shall note, in such form as he thinks fit, the date on which it was delivered to him.

    (4) The registrar shall send to the company and any person appearing from the memorandum to be the chargee, and if the memorandum was delivered by another person interested in the charge to that person, a copy of the memorandum filed by him and of the note made by him as to the date on which it was delivered.

    (5) If a duly signed memorandum is delivered in a case where the charge in fact continues to affect the company's property, the charge is void as against—

    (a) an administrator or liquidator of the company, and

    (b) any person who for value acquires an interest in or right over property subject to the charge,

where the relevant event occurs after the delivery of the memorandum.

(6) Where a relevant event occurs on the same day as the memorandum is delivered, it shall be presumed to have occurred before the memorandum is delivered unless the contrary is proved.".

Further provisions with respect to voidness of charges.

1985 c. 6.

99. The following sections are inserted in Part XII of the Companies Act 1985—

"Further provisions with respect to voidness of charges

Exclusion of voidness as against unregistered charges.

404.—(1) A charge is not void by virtue of this Part as against a subsequent charge unless some or all of the relevant particulars of that charge are duly delivered for registration—

    (a) within 21 days after the date of its creation, or

    (b) before complete and accurate relevant particulars of the earlier charge are duly delivered for registration.

(2) Where relevant particulars of the subsequent charge so delivered are incomplete or inaccurate, the earlier charge is void as against that charge only to the extent that rights are disclosed by registered particulars of the subsequent charge duly delivered for registration before the corresponding relevant particulars of the earlier charge.

(3) The relevant particulars of a charge for the purposes of this section are those prescribed particulars relating to rights inconsistent with those conferred by or in relation to the other charge.

Restrictions on voidness by virtue of this Part.

405.—(1) A charge is not void by virtue of this Part as against a person acquiring an interest in or right over property where the acquisition is expressly subject to the charge.

(2) Nor is a charge void by virtue of this Part in relation to any property by reason of a relevant event occurring after the company which created the charge has disposed of the whole of its interest in that property.

Effect of exercise of power of sale.

406.—(1) A chargee exercising a power of sale may dispose of property to a purchaser freed from any interest or right arising from the charge having become void to any extent by virtue of this Part—

    (a) against an administrator or liquidator of the company, or

    (b) against a person acquiring a security interest over property subject to the charge;

and a purchaser is not concerned to see or inquire whether the charge has become so void.

(2) The proceeds of the sale shall be held by the chargee in trust to be applied—

> First, in discharge of any sum effectively secured by prior incumbrances to which the sale is not made subject;

> Second, in payment of all costs, charges and expenses properly incurred by him in connection with the sale, or any previous attempted sale, of the property;

> Third, in discharge of any sum effectively secured by the charge and incumbrances ranking *pari passu* with the charge;

> Fourth, in discharge of any sum effectively secured by incumbrances ranking after the charge;

and any residue is payable to the company or to a person authorised to give a receipt for the proceeds of the sale of the property.

(3) For the purposes of subsection (2)—

> (a) prior incumbrances include any incumbrance to the extent that the charge is void as against it by virtue of this Part; and

> (b) no sum is effectively secured by a charge to the extent that it is void as against an administrator or liquidator of the company.

(4) In this section—

> (a) references to things done by a chargee include things done by a receiver appointed by him, whether or not the receiver acts as his agent;

> (b) "power of sale" includes any power to dispose of, or grant an interest out of, property for the purpose of enforcing a charge (but in relation to Scotland does not include the power to grant a lease), and references to "sale" shall be construed accordingly; and

> (c) "purchaser" means a person who in good faith and for valuable consideration acquires an interest in property.

(5) The provisions of this section as to the order of application of the proceeds of sale have effect subject to any other statutory provision (in Scotland, any other statutory provision or rule of law) applicable in any case.

(6) Where a chargee exercising a power of sale purports to dispose of property freed from any such interest or right as is mentioned in subsection (1) to a person other than a purchaser, the above provisions apply, with any necessary modifications, in relation to a disposition to a purchaser by that person or any successor in title of his.

(7) In Scotland, subsections (2) and (7) of section 27 of the Conveyancing and Feudal Reform (Scotland) Act 1970 apply to a chargee unable to obtain a discharge for any payment which he is required to make under subsection (2) above as they apply to a creditor in the circumstances mentioned in those subsections.

Effect of voidness on obligation secured.

407.—(1) Where a charge becomes void to any extent by virtue of this Part, the whole of the sum secured by the charge is payable forthwith on demand; and this applies notwithstanding that the sum secured by the charge is also the subject of other security.

(2) Where the charge is to secure the repayment of money, the references in subsection (1) to the sum secured include any interest payable.".

Additional information to be registered.

1985 c. 6.

100. The following sections are inserted in Part XII of the Companies Act 1985—

"Additional information to be registered

Particulars of taking up of issue of debentures.

408.—(1) Where particulars of a charge for securing an issue of debentures have been delivered for registration, it is the duty of the company—

(a) to deliver to the registrar for registration particulars in the prescribed form of the date on which any debentures of the issue are taken up, and of the amount taken up, and

(b) to do so before the end of the period of 21 days after the date on which they are taken up.

(2) Where particulars in the prescribed form are delivered to the registrar for registration under this section, he shall file them in the register.

(3) If a company fails to comply with subsection (1), the company and every officer of it who is in default is liable to a fine.

Notice of appointment of receiver or manager, &c.

409.—(1) If a person obtains an order for the appointment of a receiver or manager of a company's property, or appoints such a receiver or manager under powers contained in an instrument, he shall within seven days of the order or of the appointment under those powers, give notice of that fact in the prescribed form to the registrar for registration.

(2) Where a person appointed receiver or manager of a company's property under powers contained in an instrument ceases to act as such receiver or manager, he shall, on so ceasing, give notice of that fact in the prescribed form to the registrar for registration.

(3) Where a notice under this section in the prescribed form is delivered to the registrar for registration, he shall file it in the register.

(4) If a person makes default in complying with the requirements of subsection (1) or (2), he is liable to a fine.

(5) This section does not apply in relation to companies registered in Scotland (for which corresponding provision is made by sections 53, 54 and 62 of the Insolvency Act 1986).

Notice of crystallisation of floating charge, &c.

410.—(1) The Secretary of State may by regulations require notice in the prescribed form to be given to the registrar of—

    (a) the occurrence of such events as may be prescribed affecting the nature of the security under a floating charge of which particulars have been delivered for registration, and

    (b) the taking of such action in exercise of powers conferred by a fixed or floating charge of which particulars have been delivered for registration, or conferred in relation to such a charge by an order of the court, as may be prescribed.

(2) The regulations may make provision as to—

    (a) the persons by whom notice is required to be, or may be, given, and the period within which notice is required to be given;

    (b) the filing in the register of the particulars contained in the notice and the noting of the date on which the notice was given; and

    (c) the consequences of failure to give notice.

(3) As regards the consequences of failure to give notice of an event causing a floating charge to crystallise, the regulations may include provision to the effect that the crystallisation—

    (a) shall be treated as ineffective until the prescribed particulars are delivered, and

    (b) if the prescribed particulars are delivered after the expiry of the prescribed period, shall continue to be ineffective against such persons as may be prescribed,

subject to the exercise of such powers as may be conferred by the regulations on the court.

(4) The regulations may provide that if there is a failure to comply with such of the requirements of the regulations as may be prescribed, such persons as may be prescribed are liable to a fine.

(5) Regulations under this section shall be made by statutory instrument which shall be subject to annulment in pursuance of a resolution of either House of Parliament.

(6) Regulations under this section shall not apply in relation to a floating charge created under the law of Scotland by a company registered in Scotland.".

PART IV

Copies of instruments and register to be kept by company

Copies of
instruments and
register to be kept
by company.

1985 c. 6.

101. The following sections are inserted in Part XII of the Companies Act 1985—

"Copies of instruments and register to be kept by company

Duty to keep
copies of
instruments and
register.

411.—(1) Every company shall keep at its registered office a copy of every instrument creating or evidencing a charge over the company's property.

In the case of a series of uniform debentures, a copy of one debenture of the series is sufficient.

(2) Every company shall also keep at its registered office a register of all such charges, containing entries for each charge giving a short description of the property charged, the amount of the charge and (except in the case of securities to bearer) the names of the persons entitled to it.

(3) This section applies to any charge, whether or not particulars are required to be delivered to the registrar for registration.

(4) If a company fails to comply with any requirement of this section, the company and every officer of it who is in default is liable to a fine.

Inspection of
copies and
register.

412.—(1) The copies and the register referred to in section 411 shall be open to the inspection of any creditor or member of the company without fee; and to the inspection of any other person on payment of such fee as may be prescribed.

(2) Any person may request the company to provide him with a copy of—

    (a) any instrument creating or evidencing a charge over the company's property, or

    (b) any entry in the register of charges kept by the company, on payment of such fee as may be prescribed.

This subsection applies to any charge, whether or not particulars are required to be delivered to the registrar for registration.

(3) The company shall send the copy to him not later than ten days after the day on which the request is received or, if later, on which payment is received.

(4) If inspection of the copies or register is refused, or a copy requested is not sent within the time specified above—

    (a) the company and every officer of it who is in default is liable to a fine, and

    (b) the court may by order compel an immediate inspection of the copies or register or, as the case may be, direct that the copy be sent immediately.".

Supplementary provisions

102. The following section is inserted in Part XII of the Companies Act 1985—

"Supplementary provisions

Power to make further provision by regulations.

413.—(1) The Secretary of State may by regulations make further provision as to the application of the provisions of this Part in relation to charges of any description specified in the regulations.

Nothing in the following provisions shall be construed as restricting the generality of that power.

(2) The regulations may require that where the charge is contained in or evidenced or varied by a written instrument there shall be delivered to the registrar for registration, instead of particulars or further particulars of the charge, the instrument itself or a certified copy of it together with such particulars as may be prescribed.

(3) The regulations may provide that a memorandum of a charge ceasing to affect property of the company shall not be accepted by the registrar unless supported by such evidence as may be prescribed, and that a memorandum not so supported shall be treated as not having been delivered.

(4) The regulations may also provide that where the instrument creating the charge is delivered to the registrar in support of such a memorandum, the registrar may mark the instrument as cancelled before returning it and shall send copies of the instrument cancelled to such persons as may be prescribed.

(5) The regulations may exclude or modify, in such circumstances and to such extent as may be prescribed, the operation of the provisions of this Part relating to the voidness of a charge.

(6) The regulations may require, in connection with the delivery of particulars, further particulars or a memorandum of the charge's ceasing to affect property of the company, the delivery of such supplementary information as may be prescribed, and may—

(a) apply in relation to such supplementary information any provisions of this Part relating to particulars, further particulars or such a memorandum, and

(b) provide that the particulars, further particulars or memorandum shall be treated as not having been delivered until the required supplementary information is delivered.

(7) Regulations under this section shall be made by statutory instrument which shall be subject to annulment in pursuance of a resolution of either House of Parliament.".

103. The following sections are inserted in Part XII of the Companies Act 1985—

"Date of
creation of
charge.

414.—(1) References in this Part to the date of creation of a charge by a company shall be construed as follows.

(2) A charge created under the law of England and Wales shall be taken to be created—

 (a) in the case of a charge created by an instrument in writing, when the instrument is executed by the company or, if its execution by the company is conditional, upon the conditions being fulfilled, and

 (b) in any other case, when an enforceable agreement is entered into by the company conferring a security interest intended to take effect forthwith or upon the company acquiring an interest in property subject to the charge.

(3) A charge created under the law of Scotland shall be taken to be created—

 (a) in the case of a floating charge, when the instrument creating the floating charge is executed by the company, and

 (b) in any other case, when the right of the person entitled to the benefit of the charge is constituted as a real right.

(4) Where a charge is created in the United Kingdom but comprises property outside the United Kingdom, any further proceedings necessary to make the charge valid or effectual under the law of the country where the property is situated shall be disregarded in ascertaining the date on which the charge is to be taken to be created.

Prescribed
particulars and
related
expressions.

415.—(1) References in this Part to the prescribed particulars of a charge are to such particulars of, or relating to, the charge as may be prescribed.

(2) The prescribed particulars may, without prejudice to the generality of subsection (1), include—

 (a) whether the company has undertaken not to create other charges ranking in priority to or *pari passu* with the charge, and

 (b) whether the charge is a market charge within the meaning of Part VII of the Companies Act 1989 or a charge to which the provisions of that Part apply as they apply to a market charge.

(3) References in this Part to the registered particulars of a charge at any time are to such particulars and further particulars of the charge as have at that time been duly delivered for registration.

(4) References in this Part to the registered particulars of a charge being complete and accurate at any time are to their including all the prescribed particulars which would be required to be delivered if the charge were then newly created.

Notice of matters disclosed on register.

416.—(1) A person taking a charge over a company's property shall be taken to have notice of any matter requiring registration and disclosed on the register at the time the charge is created.

(2) Otherwise, a person shall not be taken to have notice of any matter by reason of its being disclosed on the register or by reason of his having failed to search the register in the course of making such inquiries as ought reasonably to be made.

(3) The above provisions have effect subject to any other statutory provision as to whether a person is to be taken to have notice of any matter disclosed on the register.

Power of court to dispense with signature.

417.—(1) Where it is proposed to deliver further particulars of a charge, or to deliver a memorandum of a charge ceasing to affect the company's property, and—

    (a) the chargee refuses to sign or authorise a person to sign on his behalf, or cannot be found, or

    (b) the company refuses to authorise a person to sign on its behalf,

the court may on the application of the company or the chargee, or of any other person having a sufficient interest in the matter, authorise the delivery of the particulars or memorandum without that signature.

(2) The order may be made on such terms as appear to the court to be appropriate.

(3) Where particulars or a memorandum are delivered to the registrar for registration in reliance on an order under this section, they must be accompanied by an office copy of the order.

In such a case the references in sections 401 and 403 to the particulars or memorandum being duly signed are to their being otherwise duly signed.

(4) The registrar shall file the office copy of the court order along with the particulars or memorandum.".

104. The following sections are inserted in Part XII of the Companies Act 1985—

Interpretation, &c.
1985 c. 6.

"Regulations.

418. Regulations under any provision of this Part, or prescribing anything for the purposes of any such provision—

    (a) may make different provision for different cases, and

(b) may contain such supplementary, incidental and transitional provisions as appear to the Secretary of State to be appropriate.

Minor definitions.

419.—(1) In this Part—

"chargee" means the person for the time being entitled to exercise the security rights conferred by the charge;

"issue of debentures" means a group of debentures, or an amount of debenture stock, secured by the same charge; and

"series of debentures" means a group of debentures each containing or giving by reference to another instrument a charge to the benefit of which the holders of debentures of the series are entitled *pari passu*.

(2) References in this Part to the creation of a charge include the variation of a charge which is not registrable so as to include property by virtue of which it becomes registrable.

The provisions of section 414 (construction of references to date of creation of charge) apply in such a case with any necessary modifications.

(3) References in this Part to the date of acquisition of property by a company are—

(a) in England and Wales, to the date on which the acquisition is completed, and

(b) in Scotland, to the date on which the transaction is settled.

(4) In the application of this Part to a floating charge created under the law of Scotland, references to crystallisation shall be construed as references to the attachment of the charge.

(5) References in this Part to the beginning of insolvency proceedings are to—

(a) the presentation of a petition on which an administration order or winding-up order is made, or

(b) the passing of a resolution for voluntary winding up.

Index of defined expressions.

420. The following Table shows the provisions of this Part defining or otherwise explaining expressions used in this Part (other than expressions used only in the same section)—

charge	sections 395(2) and 396(6)	PART IV
charge requiring registration	section 396	
chargee	section 419(1)	
complete and accurate (in relation to registered particulars)	section 415(4)	
creation of charge	section 419(2)	
crystallisation (in relation to Scottish floating charge)	section 419(4)	
date of acquisition (of property by a company)	section 419(3)	
date of creation of charge	section 414	
further particulars	section 401	
insolvency proceedings, beginning of	section 419(5)	
issue of debentures	section 419(1)	
memorandum of charge ceasing to affect company's property	section 403	
prescribed particulars	section 415(1) and (2)	
property	section 395(2)	
registered particulars	section 415(3)	
registrar and registration in relation to a charge	section 395(4)	
relevant event	section 399(2)	
series of debentures	section 419(1).".	

105. The provisions set out in Schedule 15 are inserted in Part XXIII of the Companies Act 1985 (oversea companies), as a Chapter III (registration of charges).

Charges on property of oversea company.
1985 c. 6.

106. In Schedule 22 to the Companies Act 1985 (provisions applying to unregistered companies), at the appropriate place insert—

Application of provisions to unregistered companies.

"Part XII	Registration of company charges; copies of instruments and register to be kept by company.	Subject to section 718(3).".

107. The enactments specified in Schedule 16 have effect with the amendments specified there, which are consequential on the amendments made by the preceding provisions of this Part.

Consequential amendments.

PART V

OTHER AMENDMENTS OF COMPANY LAW

A company's capacity and related matters

108.—(1) In Chapter III of Part I of the Companies Act 1985 (a company's capacity; formalities of carrying on business), for section 35 substitute—

A company's capacity and the power of the directors to bind it.

PART V

"A company's capacity not limited by its memorandum.

35.—(1) The validity of an act done by a company shall not be called into question on the ground of lack of capacity by reason of anything in the company's memorandum.

(2) A member of a company may bring proceedings to restrain the doing of an act which but for subsection (1) would be beyond the company's capacity; but no such proceedings shall lie in respect of an act to be done in fulfilment of a legal obligation arising from a previous act of the company.

(3) It remains the duty of the directors to observe any limitations on their powers flowing from the company's memorandum; and action by the directors which but for subsection (1) would be beyond the company's capacity may only be ratified by the company by special resolution.

A resolution ratifying such action shall not affect any liability incurred by the directors or any other person; relief from any such liability must be agreed to separately by special resolution.

(4) The operation of this section is restricted by section 30B(1) of the Charities Act 1960 and section 112(3) of the Companies Act 1989 in relation to companies which are charities; and section 322A below (invalidity of certain transactions to which directors or their associates are parties) has effect notwithstanding this section.

Power of directors to bind the company.

35A.—(1) In favour of a person dealing with a company in good faith, the power of the board of directors to bind the company, or authorise others to do so, shall be deemed to be free of any limitation under the company's constitution.

(2) For this purpose—

(a) a person "deals with" a company if he is a party to any transaction or other act to which the company is a party;

(b) a person shall not be regarded as acting in bad faith by reason only of his knowing that an act is beyond the powers of the directors under the company's constitution; and

(c) a person shall be presumed to have acted in good faith unless the contrary is proved.

(3) The references above to limitations on the directors' powers under the company's constitution include limitations deriving—

(a) from a resolution of the company in general meeting or a meeting of any class of shareholders, or

(b) from any agreement between the members of the company or of any class of shareholders.

(4) Subsection (1) does not affect any right of a member of the company to bring proceedings to restrain the doing of an act which is beyond the powers of the directors; but no such proceedings shall lie in respect of an act to be done in fulfilment of a legal obligation arising from a previous act of the company.

(5) Nor does that subsection affect any liability incurred by the directors, or any other person, by reason of the directors' exceeding their powers.

(6) The operation of this section is restricted by section 30B(1) of the Charities Act 1960 and section 112(3) of the Companies Act 1989 in relation to companies which are charities; and section 322A below (invalidity of certain transactions to which directors or their associates are parties)has effect notwithstanding this section.

No duty to enquire as to capacity of company or authority of directors.

35B. A party to a transaction with a company is not bound to enquire as to whether it is permitted by the company's memorandum or as to any limitation on the powers of the board of directors to bind the company or authorise others to do so.".

(2) In Schedule 21 to the Companies Act 1985 (effect of registration of companies not formed under that Act), in paragraph 6 (general application of provisions of Act), after sub-paragraph (5) insert—   1985 c. 6.

"(6) Where by virtue of sub-paragraph (4) or (5) a company does not have power to alter a provision, it does not have power to ratify acts of the directors in contravention of the provision.".

(3) In Schedule 22 to the Companies Act 1985 (provisions applying to unregistered companies), in the entries relating to Part I, in the first column for "section 35" substitute "sections 35 to 35B".

109.—(1) In Part X of the Companies Act 1985 (enforcement of fair dealing by directors), after section 322 insert—

Invalidity of certain transactions involving directors.

"Invalidity of certain transactions involving directors, etc.

322A.—(1) This section applies where a company enters into a transaction to which the parties include—

(a) a director of the company or of its holding company, or

(b) a person connected with such a director or a company with whom such a director is associated,

and the board of directors, in connection with the transaction, exceed any limitation on their powers under the company's constitution.

(2) The transaction is voidable at the instance of the company.

(3) Whether or not it is avoided, any such party to the transaction as is mentioned in subsection (1)(a) or (b), and any director of the company who authorised the transaction, is liable—

(a) to account to the company for any gain which he has made directly or indirectly by the transaction, and

(b) to indemnify the company for any loss or damage resulting from the transaction.

(4) Nothing in the above provisions shall be construed as excluding the operation of any other enactment or rule of law by virtue of which the transaction may be called in question or any liability to the company may arise.

(5) The transaction ceases to be voidable if—

(a) restitution of any money or other asset which was the subject-matter of the transaction is no longer possible, or

(b) the company is indemnified for any loss or damage resulting from the transaction, or

(c) rights acquired bona fide for value and without actual notice of the directors' exceeding their powers by a person who is not party to the transaction would be affected by the avoidance, or

(d) the transaction is ratified by the company in general meeting, by ordinary or special resolution or otherwise as the case may require.

(6) A person other than a director of the company is not liable under subsection (3) if he shows that at the time the transaction was entered into he did not know that the directors were exceeding their powers.

(7) This section does not affect the operation of section 35A in relation to any party to the transaction not within subsection (1)(a) or (b).

But where a transaction is voidable by virtue of this section and valid by virtue of that section in favour of such a person, the court may, on the application of that person or of the company, make such order affirming, severing or setting aside the transaction, on such terms, as appear to the court to be just.

(8) In this section "transaction" includes any act; and the reference in subsection (1) to limitations under the company's constitution includes limitations deriving—

(a) from a resolution of the company in general meeting or a meeting of any class of shareholders, or

(b) from any agreement between the members of the company or of any class of shareholders.".

1985 c. 6.   (2) In Schedule 22 to the Companies Act 1985 (provisions applying to unregistered companies), in the entries relating to Part X, insert—

| "section 322A | Invalidity of certain transactions involving directors, etc. | Subject to section 718(3)." |

110. In Chapter I of Part I of the Companies Act 1985 (company formation), after section 3 (forms of memorandum) insert—

PART V
Statement of company's objects.
1985 c. 6.

"Statement of company's objects: general commercial company.

    3A. Where the company's memorandum states that the object of the company is to carry on business as a general commercial company—

    (a) the object of the company is to carry on any trade or business whatsoever, and

    (b) the company has power to do all such things as are incidental or conducive to the carrying on of any trade or business by it.".

(2) In the same Chapter, for section 4 (resolution to alter objects) substitute—

"Resolution to alter objects.

    4.—(1) A company may by special resolution alter its memorandum with respect to the statement of the company's objects.

    (2) If an application is made under the following section, an alteration does not have effect except in so far as it is confirmed by the court.".

111.—(1) In the Charities Act 1960, for section 30 (charitable companies) substitute—

Charitable companies.
1960 c. 58.

"Charitable companies: winding up.

    30. Where a charity may be wound up by the High Court under the Insolvency Act 1986, a petition for it to be wound up under that Act by any court in England or Wales having jurisdiction may be presented by the Attorney General, as well as by any person authorised by that Act.

Charitable companies: alteration of objects clause.

    30A.—(1) Where a charity is a company or other body corporate having power to alter the instruments establishing or regulating it as a body corporate, no exercise of that power which has the effect of the body ceasing to be a charity shall be valid so as to affect the application of—

    (a) any property acquired under any disposition or agreement previously made otherwise than for full consideration in money or money's worth, or any property representing property so acquired,

    (b) any property representing income which has accrued before the alteration is made, or

    (c) the income from any such property as aforesaid.

    (2) Where a charity is a company, any alteration by it of the objects clause in its memorandum of association is ineffective without the prior written consent of the Commissioners; and it shall deliver a copy of that consent to the registrar of companies under section 6(1)(a) or (b) of the Companies Act 1985 along with the printed copy of the memorandum as altered.

(3) Section 6(3) of that Act (offences) applies in relation to a default in complying with subsection (2) as regards the delivery of a copy of the Commissioners' consent.

Charitable companies: invalidity of certain transactions.

30B.—(1) Sections 35 and 35A of the Companies Act 1985 (capacity of company not limited by its memorandum; power of directors to bind company) do not apply to the acts of a company which is a charity except in favour of a person who—

(a) gives full consideration in money or money's worth in relation to the act in question, and

(b) does not know that the act is not permitted by the company's memorandum or, as the case may be, is beyond the powers of the directors,

or who does not know at the time the act is done that the company is a charity.

(2) However, where such a company purports to transfer or grant an interest in property, the fact that the act was not permitted by the company's memorandum or, as the case may be, that the directors in connection with the act exceeded any limitation on their powers under the company's constitution, does not affect the title of a person who subsequently acquires the property or any interest in it for full consideration without actual notice of any such circumstances affecting the validity of the company's act.

(3) In any proceedings arising out of subsection (1) the burden of proving—

(a) that a person knew that an act was not permitted by the company's memorandum or was beyond the powers of the directors, or

(b) that a person knew that the company was a charity,

lies on the person making that allegation.

(4) Where a company is a charity, the ratification of an act under section 35(3) of the Companies Act 1985, or the ratification of a transaction to which section 322A of that Act applies (invalidity of certain transactions to which directors or their associates are parties), is ineffective without the prior written consent of the Commissioners.

Charitable companies: status to appear on correspondence, etc.

30C.—(1) Where a company is a charity and its name does not include the word "charity" or the word "charitable", the fact that the company is a charity shall be stated in English in legible characters—

(a) in all business letters of the company,

(b) in all its notices and other official publications,

(c) in all bills of exchange, promissory notes, endorsements, cheques and orders for money or goods purporting to be signed by or on behalf of the company,

(d) in all conveyances purporting to be executed by the company, and

(e) in all its bills of parcels, invoices, receipts and letters of credit.

(2) In subsection (1)(d) "conveyance" means any instrument creating, transferring, varying or extinguishing an interest in land.

(3) Section 349(2) to (4) of the Companies Act 1985 (offences in connection with failure to include required particulars in business letters, &c.) apply in relation to a contravention of subsection (1) above.".

(2) In section 46 of the Charities Act 1960 (definitions), at the appropriate place insert—

" 'company' means a company formed and registered under the Companies Act 1985, or to which the provisions of that Act apply as they apply to such a company;".

112.—(1) In the following provisions (which extend to Scotland only)—

(a) "company" means a company formed and registered under the Companies Act 1985, or to which the provisions of that Act apply as they apply to such a company; and

(b) "charity" means a body established for charitable purposes only (that expression having the same meaning as in the Income Tax Acts).

(2) Where a charity is a company or other body corporate having power to alter the instruments establishing or regulating it as a body corporate, no exercise of that power which has the effect of the body ceasing to be a charity shall be valid so as to affect the application of—

(a) any property acquired by virtue of any transfer, contract or obligation previously effected otherwise than for full consideration in money or money's worth, or any property representing property so acquired,

(b) any property representing income which has accrued before the alteration is made, or

(c) the income from any such property as aforesaid.

(3) Sections 35 and 35A of the Companies Act 1985 (capacity of company not limited by its memorandum; power of directors to bind company) do not apply to the acts of a company which is a charity except in favour of a person who—

(a) gives full consideration in money or money's worth in relation to the act in question, and

(b) does not know that the act is not permitted by the company's memorandum or, as the case may be, is beyond the powers of the directors,

or who does not know at the time the act is done that the company is a charity.

(4) However, where such a company purports to transfer or grant an interest in property, the fact that the act was not permitted by the company's memorandum or, as the case may be, that the directors in connection with the act exceeded any limitation on their powers under the company's constitution, does not affect the title of a person who subsequently acquires the property or any interest in it for full consideration without actual notice of any such circumstances affecting the validity of the company's act.

(5) In any proceedings arising out of subsection (3) the burden of proving—

(a) that a person knew that an act was not permitted by the company's memorandum or was beyond the powers of the directors, or

(b) that a person knew that the company was a charity,

lies on the person making that allegation.

(6) Where a company is a charity and its name does not include the word "charity" or the word "charitable", the fact that the company is a charity shall be stated in English in legible characters—

(a) in all business letters of the company,

(b) in all its notices and other official publications,

(c) in all bills of exchange, promissory notes, endorsements, cheques and orders for money or goods purporting to be signed by or on behalf of the company,

(d) in all conveyances purporting to be executed by the company, and

(e) in all its bills of parcels, invoices, receipts and letters of credit.

(7) In subsection (6)(d) "conveyance" means any document for the creation, transfer, variation or extinction of an interest in land.

1985 c. 6.

(8) Section 349(2) to (4) of the Companies Act 1985 (offences in connection with failure to include required particulars in business letters, &c.) apply in relation to a contravention of subsection (6) above.

De-regulation of private companies

Written resolutions of private companies.

113.—(1) Chapter IV of Part XI of the Companies Act 1985 (meetings and resolutions) is amended as follows.

(2) After section 381 insert—

"Written resolutions of private companies

Written resolutions of private companies.

381A.—(1) Anything which in the case of a private company may be done—

(a) by resolution of the company in general meeting, or

(b) by resolution of a meeting of any class of members of the company,

may be done, without a meeting and without any previous notice being required, by resolution in writing signed by or on behalf of all the members of the company who at the date of the resolution would be entitled to attend and vote at such meeting.

(2) The signatures need not be on a single document provided each is on a document which accurately states the terms of the resolution.

(3) The date of the resolution means when the resolution is signed by or on behalf of the last member to sign.

(4) A resolution agreed to in accordance with this section has effect as if passed—

    (a) by the company in general meeting, or

    (b) by a meeting of the relevant class of members of the company,

as the case may be; and any reference in any enactment to a meeting at which a resolution is passed or to members voting in favour of a resolution shall be construed accordingly.

(5) Any reference in any enactment to the date of passing of a resolution is, in relation to a resolution agreed to in accordance with this section, a reference to the date of the resolution, unless section 381B(4) applies in which case it shall be construed as a reference to the date from which the resolution has effect.

(6) A resolution may be agreed to in accordance with this section which would otherwise be required to be passed as a special, extraordinary or elective resolution; and any reference in any enactment to a special, extraordinary or elective resolution includes such a resolution.

(7) This section has effect subject to the exceptions specified in Part I of Schedule 15A; and in relation to certain descriptions of resolution under this section the procedural requirements of this Act have effect with the adaptations specified in Part II of that Schedule.

Rights of auditors in relation to written resolution.

381B.—(1) A copy of any written resolution proposed to be agreed to in accordance with section 381A shall be sent to the company's auditors.

(2) If the resolution concerns the auditors as auditors, they may within seven days from the day on which they receive the copy give notice to the company stating their opinion that the resolution should be considered by the company in general meeting or, as the case may be, by a meeting of the relevant class of members of the company.

(3) A written resolution shall not have effect unless—

    (a) the auditors notify the company that in their opinion the resolution—

        (i) does not concern them as auditors, or

        (ii) does so concern them but need not be considered by the company in general meeting or, as the case may be, by a meeting of the relevant class of members of the company, or

(b) the period for giving a notice under subsection (2) expires without any notice having been given in accordance with that subsection.

(4) A written resolution previously agreed to in accordance with section 381A shall not have effect until that notification is given or, as the case may be, that period expires.

Written resolutions: supplementary provisions.

381C.—(1) Sections 381A and 381B have effect notwithstanding any provision of the company's memorandum or articles.

(2) Nothing in those sections affects any enactment or rule of law as to—

(a) things done otherwise than by passing a resolution, or

(b) cases in which a resolution is treated as having been passed, or a person is precluded from alleging that a resolution has not been duly passed.".

(3) After section 382 insert—

"Recording of written resolutions.

382A.—(1) Where a written resolution is agreed to in accordance with section 381A which has effect as if agreed by the company in general meeting, the company shall cause a record of the resolution (and of the signatures) to be entered in a book in the same way as minutes of proceedings of a general meeting of the company.

(2) Any such record, if purporting to be signed by a director of the company or by the company secretary, is evidence of the proceedings in agreeing to the resolution; and where a record is made in accordance with this section, then, until the contrary is proved, the requirements of this Act with respect to those proceedings shall be deemed to be complied with.

(3) Section 382(5) (penalties) applies in relation to a failure to comply with subsection (1) above as it applies in relation to a failure to comply with subsection (1) of that section; and section 383 (inspection of minute books) applies in relation to a record made in accordance with this section as it applies in relation to the minutes of a general meeting.".

Written resolutions: supplementary provisions.

1985 c. 6.

114.—(1) In the Companies Act 1985 the following Schedule is inserted after Schedule 15—

"SCHEDULE 15A

WRITTEN RESOLUTIONS OF PRIVATE COMPANIES

PART I

EXCEPTIONS

1. Section 381A does not apply to—

(a) a resolution under section 303 removing a director before the expiration of his period of office, or

(b) a resolution under section 391 removing an auditor before
the expiration of his term of office.

PART II

ADAPTATION OF PROCEDURAL REQUIREMENTS

Introductory

2.—(1) In this Part of this Schedule (which adapts certain requirements of this Act in relation to proceedings under section 381A)—

    (a) a "written resolution" means a resolution agreed to, or proposed to be agreed to, in accordance with that section, and

    (b) a "relevant member" means a member by whom, or on whose behalf, the resolution is required to be signed in accordance with that section.

(2) A written resolution is not effective if any of the requirements of this Part of this Schedule is not complied with.

Section 95 (disapplication of pre-emption rights)

3.—(1) The following adaptations have effect in relation to a written resolution under section 95(2) (disapplication of pre-emption rights), or renewing a resolution under that provision.

(2) So much of section 95(5) as requires the circulation of a written statement by the directors with a notice of meeting does not apply, but such a statement must be supplied to each relevant member at or before the time at which the resolution is supplied to him for signature.

(3) Section 95(6) (offences) applies in relation to the inclusion in any such statement of matter which is misleading, false or deceptive in a material particular.

Section 155 (financial assistance for purchase of company's own shares or those of holding company)

4. In relation to a written resolution giving approval under section 155(4) or (5) (financial assistance for purchase of company's own shares or those of holding company), section 157(4)(a) (documents to be available at meeting) does not apply, but the documents referred to in that provision must be supplied to each relevant member at or before the time at which the resolution is supplied to him for signature.

Sections 164, 165 and 167 (authority for off-market purchase or contingent purchase contract of company's own shares)

5.—(1) The following adaptations have effect in relation to a written resolution—

    (a) conferring authority to make an off-market purchase of the company's own shares under section 164(2),

    (b) conferring authority to vary a contract for an off-market purchase of the company's own shares under section 164(7), or

    (c) varying, revoking or renewing any such authority under section 164(3).

(2) Section 164(5) (resolution ineffective if passed by exercise of voting rights by member holding shares to which the resolution relates) does not apply; but for the purposes of section 381A(1) a member holding shares to which the resolution relates shall not be regarded as a member who would be entitled to attend and vote.

(3) Section 164(6) (documents to be available at company's registered office and at meeting) does not apply, but the documents referred to in that provision and, where that provision applies by virtue of section 164(7), the further documents referred to in that provision must be supplied to each relevant member at or before the time at which the resolution is supplied to him for signature.

(4) The above adaptations also have effect in relation to a written resolution in relation to which the provisions of section 164(3) to (7) apply by virtue of—

    (a) section 165(2) (authority for contingent purchase contract), or

    (b) section 167(2) (approval of release of rights under contract approved under section 164 or 165).

Section 173 (approval for payment out of capital)

6.—(1) The following adaptations have effect in relation to a written resolution giving approval under section 173(2) (redemption or purchase of company's own shares out of capital).

(2) Section 174(2) (resolution ineffective if passed by exercise of voting rights by member holding shares to which the resolution relates) does not apply; but for the purposes of section 381A(1) a member holding shares to which the resolution relates shall not be regarded as a member who would be entitled to attend and vote.

(3) Section 174(4) (documents to be available at meeting) does not apply, but the documents referred to in that provision must be supplied to each relevant member at or before the time at which the resolution is supplied to him for signature.

Section 319 (approval of director's service contract)

7. In relation to a written resolution approving any such term as is mentioned in section 319(1) (director's contract of employment for more than five years), section 319(5) (documents to be available at company's registered office and at meeting) does not apply, but the documents referred to in that provision must be supplied to each relevant member at or before the time at which the resolution is supplied to him for signature.

Section 337 (funding of director's expenditure in performing his duties)

8. In relation to a written resolution giving approval under section 337(3)(a) (funding a director's expenditure in performing his duties), the requirement of that provision that certain matters be disclosed at the meeting at which the resolution is passed does not apply, but those matters must be disclosed to each relevant member at or before the time at which the resolution is supplied to him for signature.".

(2) The Schedule inserted after Schedule 15 to the Companies Act 1985 by the Companies (Mergers and Divisions) Regulations 1987 is renumbered "15B"; and accordingly, in section 427A of that Act (also inserted by those regulations), in subsections (1) and (8) for "15A" substitute "15B".

1985 c. 6.
S.I. 1987/1991

115.—(1) In Part IV of the Companies Act 1985 (allotment of shares and debentures), in section 80(1) (authority of company required for certain allotments) after "this section" insert "or section 80A"; and after that section insert—

Election by private company to dispense with certain requirements.

"Election by private company as to duration of authority.

80A.—(1) A private company may elect (by elective resolution in accordance with section 379A) that the provisions of this section shall apply, instead of the provisions of section 80(4) and (5), in relation to the giving or renewal, after the election, of an authority under that section.

(2) The authority must state the maximum amount of relevant securities that may be allotted under it and may be given—

(a) for an indefinite period, or

(b) for a fixed period, in which case it must state the date on which it will expire.

(3) In either case an authority (including an authority contained in the articles) may be revoked or varied by the company in general meeting.

(4) An authority given for a fixed period may be renewed or further renewed by the company in general meeting.

(5) A resolution renewing an authority—

(a) must state, or re-state, the amount of relevant securities which may be allotted under the authority or, as the case may be, the amount remaining to be allotted under it, and

(b) must state whether the authority is renewed for an indefinite period or for a fixed period, in which case it must state the date on which the renewed authority will expire.

(6) The references in this section to the maximum amount of relevant securities that may be allotted shall be construed in accordance with section 80(6).

(7) If an election under this section ceases to have effect, an authority then in force which was given for an indefinite period or for a fixed period of more than five years—

    (a) if given five years or more before the election ceases to have effect, shall expire forthwith, and

    (b) otherwise, shall have effect as if it had been given for a fixed period of five years.".

1985 c. 6.

(2) In Chapter IV of Part XI of the Companies Act 1985 (meetings and resolutions), after section 366 (annual general meeting) insert—

"Election by private company to dispense with annual general meetings.

366A.—(1) A private company may elect (by elective resolution in accordance with section 379A) to dispense with the holding of annual general meetings.

(2) An election has effect for the year in which it is made and subsequent years, but does not affect any liability already incurred by reason of default in holding an annual general meeting.

(3) In any year in which an annual general meeting would be required to be held but for the election, and in which no such meeting has been held, any member of the company may, by notice to the company not later than three months before the end of the year, require the holding of an annual general meeting in that year.

(4) If such a notice is given, the provisions of section 366(1) and (4) apply with respect to the calling of the meeting and the consequences of default.

(5) If the election ceases to have effect, the company is not obliged under section 366 to hold an annual general meeting in that year if, when the election ceases to have effect, less than three months of the year remains.

This does not affect any obligation of the company to hold an annual general meeting in that year in pursuance of a notice given under subsection (3).".

(3) In the same Chapter, in sections 369(4) and 378(3) (majority required to sanction short notice of meeting) insert—

"A private company may elect (by elective resolution in accordance with section 379A) that the above provisions shall have effect in relation to the company as if for the references to 95 per cent. there were substituted references to such lesser percentage, but not less than 90 per cent., as may be specified in the resolution or subsequently determined by the company in general meeting.".

Elective resolution of private company.

116.—(1) Chapter IV of Part XI of the Companies Act 1985 (meetings and resolutions) is amended as follows.

(2) After section 379 insert—

"Elective resolution of private company.

379A.—(1) An election by a private company for the purposes of—

    (a) section 80A (election as to duration of authority to allot shares),

(b) section 252 (election to dispense with laying of accounts and reports before general meeting),

(c) section 366A (election to dispense with holding of annual general meeting),

(d) section 369(4) or 378(3) (election as to majority required to authorise short notice of meeting), or

(e) section 386 (election to dispense with appointment of auditors annually),

shall be made by resolution of the company in general meeting in accordance with this section.

Such a resolution is referred to in this Act as an "elective resolution".

(2) An elective resolution is not effective unless—

(a) at least 21 days' notice in writing is given of the meeting, stating that an elective resolution is to be proposed and stating the terms of the resolution, and

(b) the resolution is agreed to at the meeting, in person or by proxy, by all the members entitled to attend and vote at the meeting.

(3) The company may revoke an elective resolution by passing an ordinary resolution to that effect.

(4) An elective resolution shall cease to have effect if the company is re-registered as a public company.

(5) An elective resolution may be passed or revoked in accordance with this section, and the provisions referred to in subsection (1) have effect, notwithstanding any contrary provision in the company's articles of association.".

(3) In section 380 (registration of resolutions), in subsection (4) (resolutions to which the section applies), after paragraph (b) insert—

"(bb) an elective resolution or a resolution revoking such a resolution;".

117.—(1) The Secretary of State may by regulations make provision enabling private companies to elect, by elective resolution in accordance with section 379A of the Companies Act 1985, to dispense with compliance with such requirements of that Act as may be specified in the regulations, being requirements which appear to the Secretary of State to relate primarily to the internal administration and procedure of companies.

Power to make further provision by regulations. 1985 c. 6.

(2) The regulations may add to, amend or repeal provisions of that Act; and may provide for any such provision to have effect, where an election is made, subject to such adaptations and modifications as appear to the Secretary of State to be appropriate.

(3) The regulations may make different provision for different cases and may contain such supplementary, incidental and transitional provisions as appear to the Secretary of State to be appropriate.

(4) Regulations under this section shall be made by statutory instrument.

(5) No regulations under this section shall be made unless a draft of the instrument containing the regulations has been laid before Parliament and approved by a resolution of each House.

Appointment and removal of auditors and related matters

Introduction.
1985 c. 6.

118.—(1) The following sections amend the provisions of the Companies Act 1985 relating to auditors by inserting new provisions in Chapter V of Part XI of that Act.

(2) The new provisions, together with the amendment made by section 124, replace the present provisions of that Chapter except section 389 (qualification for appointment as auditor) which is replaced by provisions in Part II of this Act.

Appointment of
auditors.

119.—(1) The following sections are inserted in Chapter V of Part XI of the Companies Act 1985 (auditors)—

"Appointment of auditors

Duty to appoint
auditors.

384.—(1) Every company shall appoint an auditor or auditors in accordance with this Chapter.

This is subject to section 388A (dormant company exempt from obligation to appoint auditors).

(2) Auditors shall be appointed in accordance with section 385 (appointment at general meeting at which accounts are laid), except in the case of a private company which has elected to dispense with the laying of accounts in which case the appointment shall be made in accordance with section 385A.

(3) References in this Chapter to the end of the time for appointing auditors are to the end of the time within which an appointment must be made under section 385(2) or 385A(2), according to whichever of those sections applies.

(4) Sections 385 and 385A have effect subject to section 386 under which a private company may elect to dispense with the obligation to appoint auditors annually.

Appointment at
general meeting
at which
accounts laid.

385.—(1) This section applies to every public company and to a private company which has not elected to dispense with the laying of accounts.

(2) The company shall, at each general meeting at which accounts are laid, appoint an auditor or auditors to hold office from the conclusion of that meeting until the conclusion of the next general meeting at which accounts are laid.

(3) The first auditors of the company may be appointed by the directors at any time before the first general meeting of the company at which accounts are laid; and auditors so appointed shall hold office until the conclusion of that meeting.

(4) If the directors fail to exercise their powers under subsection (3), the powers may be exercised by the company in general meeting.

Appointment by private company which is not obliged to lay accounts.

385A.—(1) This section applies to a private company which has elected in accordance with section 252 to dispense with the laying of accounts before the company in general meeting.

(2) Auditors shall be appointed by the company in general meeting before the end of the period of 28 days beginning with the day on which copies of the company's annual accounts for the previous financial year are sent to members under section 238 or, if notice is given under section 253(2) requiring the laying of the accounts before the company in general meeting, the conclusion of that meeting.

Auditors so appointed shall hold office from the end of that period or, as the case may be, the conclusion of that meeting until the end of the time for appointing auditors for the next financial year.

(3) The first auditors of the company may be appointed by the directors at any time before—

   (a) the end of the period of 28 days beginning with the day on which copies of the company's first annual accounts are sent to members under section 238, or

   (b) if notice is given under section 253(2) requiring the laying of the accounts before the company in general meeting, the beginning of that meeting;

and auditors so appointed shall hold office until the end of that period or, as the case may be, the conclusion of that meeting.

(4) If the directors fail to exercise their powers under subsection (3), the powers may be exercised by the company in general meeting.

(5) Auditors holding office when the election is made shall, unless the company in general meeting determines otherwise, continue to hold office until the end of the time for appointing auditors for the next financial year; and auditors holding office when an election ceases to have effect shall continue to hold office until the conclusion of the next general meeting of the company at which accounts are laid.

Election by private company to dispense with annual appointment.

386.—(1) A private company may elect (by elective resolution in accordance with section 379A) to dispense with the obligation to appoint auditors annually.

(2) When such an election is in force the company's auditors shall be deemed to be re-appointed for each succeeding financial year on the expiry of the time for appointing auditors for that year, unless—

(a) a resolution has been passed under section 250 by virtue of which the company is exempt from the obligation to appoint auditors, or

(b) a resolution has been passed under section 393 to the effect that their appointment should be brought to an end.

(3) If the election ceases to be in force, the auditors then holding office shall continue to hold office—

(a) where section 385 then applies, until the conclusion of the next general meeting of the company at which accounts are laid;

(b) where section 385A then applies, until the end of the time for appointing auditors for the next financial year under that section.

(4) No account shall be taken of any loss of the opportunity of further deemed re-appointment under this section in ascertaining the amount of any compensation or damages payable to an auditor on his ceasing to hold office for any reason.

Appointment by Secretary of State in default of appointment by company.

387.—(1) If in any case no auditors are appointed, re-appointed or deemed to be re-appointed before the end of the time for appointing auditors, the Secretary of State may appoint a person to fill the vacancy.

(2) In such a case the company shall within one week of the end of the time for appointing auditors give notice to the Secretary of State of his power having become exercisable.

If a company fails to give the notice required by this subsection, the company and every officer of it who is in default is guilty of an offence and liable to a fine and, for continued contravention, to a daily default fine.

Filling of casual vacancies.

388.—(1) The directors, or the company in general meeting, may fill a casual vacancy in the office of auditor.

(2) While such a vacancy continues, any surviving or continuing auditor or auditors may continue to act.

(3) Special notice is required for a resolution at a general meeting of a company—

(a) filling a casual vacancy in the office of auditor, or

(b) re-appointing as auditor a retiring auditor who was appointed by the directors to fill a casual vacancy.

(4) On receipt of notice of such an intended resolution the company shall forthwith send a copy of it—

(a) to the person proposed to be appointed, and

(b) if the casual vacancy was caused by the resignation of an auditor, to the auditor who resigned.

Dormant company exempt from obligation to appoint auditors.

388A.—(1) A company which by virtue of section 250 (dormant companies: exemption from provisions as to audit of accounts) is exempt from the provisions of Part VII relating to the audit of accounts is also exempt from the obligation to appoint auditors.

(2) The following provisions apply if the exemption ceases.

(3) Where section 385 applies (appointment at general meeting at which accounts are laid), the directors may appoint auditors at any time before the next meeting of the company at which accounts are to be laid; and auditors so appointed shall hold office until the conclusion of that meeting.

(4) Where section 385A applies (appointment by private company not obliged to lay accounts), the directors may appoint auditors at any time before—

    (a) the end of the period of 28 days beginning with the day on which copies of the company's annual accounts are next sent to members under section 238, or

    (b) if notice is given under section 253(2) requiring the laying of the accounts before the company in general meeting, the beginning of that meeting;

and auditors so appointed shall hold office until the end of that period or, as the case may be, the conclusion of that meeting.

(5) If the directors fail to exercise their powers under subsection (3) or (4), the powers may be exercised by the company in general meeting.".

(2) In Schedule 24 to the Companies Act 1985 (punishment of offences), at the appropriate place insert—

1985 c. 6.

| "387(2) Company failing to give Secretary of State notice of non-appointment of auditors. | Summary. | One-fifth of the statutory maximum. | One-fiftieth of the statutory maximum.". |

(3) In section 46(2) of the Banking Act 1987 (duty of auditor of authorised institution to give notice to Bank of England of certain matters) for "appointed under section 384" substitute "appointed under Chapter V of Part XI"; and in section 46(4) (adaptation of references in relation to Northern Ireland) for "sections 384," substitute "Chapter V of Part XI and sections".

1987 c. 22.

120.—(1) The following sections are inserted in Chapter V of Part XI of the Companies Act 1985 (auditors)—

Rights of auditors.

"Rights of auditors

Rights to information.

389A.—(1) The auditors of a company have a right of access at all times to the company's books, accounts and vouchers, and are entitled to require from the company's officers such information and explanations as they think necessary for the performance of their duties as auditors.

(2) An officer of a company commits an offence if he knowingly or recklessly makes to the company's auditors a statement (whether written or oral) which—

(a) conveys or purports to convey any information or explanations which the auditors require, or are entitled to require, as auditors of the company, and

(b) is misleading, false or deceptive in a material particular.

A person guilty of an offence under this subsection is liable to imprisonment or a fine, or both.

(3) A subsidiary undertaking which is a body corporate incorporated in Great Britain, and the auditors of such an undertaking, shall give to the auditors of any parent company of the undertaking such information and explanations as they may reasonably require for the purposes of their duties as auditors of that company.

If a subsidiary undertaking fails to comply with this subsection, the undertaking and every officer of it who is in default is guilty of an offence and liable to a fine; and if an auditor fails without reasonable excuse to comply with this subsection he is guilty of an offence and liable to a fine.

(4) A parent company having a subsidiary undertaking which is not a body corporate incorporated in Great Britain shall, if required by its auditors to do so, take all such steps as are reasonably open to it to obtain from the subsidiary undertaking such information and explanations as they may reasonably require for the purposes of their duties as auditors of that company.

If a parent company fails to comply with this subsection, the company and every officer of it who is in default is guilty of an offence and liable to a fine.

(5) Section 734 (criminal proceedings against unincorporated bodies) applies to an offence under subsection (3).

Right to attend company meetings, &c.

390.—(1) A company's auditors are entitled—

(a) to receive all notices of, and other communications relating to, any general meeting which a member of the company is entitled to receive;

(b) to attend any general meeting of the company; and

(c) to be heard at any general meeting which they attend on any part of the business of the meeting which concerns them as auditors.

(2) In relation to a written resolution proposed to be agreed to by a private company in accordance with section 381A, the company's auditors are entitled—

(a) to receive all such communications relating to the resolution as, by virtue of any provision of Schedule 15A, are required to be supplied to a member of the company,

(b) to give notice in accordance with section 381B of their opinion that the resolution concerns them as auditors and should be considered by the company in general meeting or, as the case may be, by a meeting of the relevant class of members of the company,

(c) to attend any such meeting, and

(d) to be heard at any such meeting which they attend on any part of the business of the meeting which concerns them as auditors.

(3) The right to attend or be heard at a meeting is exercisable in the case of a body corporate or partnership by an individual authorised by it in writing to act as its representative at the meeting.".

(2) In section 734 of the Companies Act 1985 (criminal proceedings against unincorporated bodies), in subsection (1) (offences in relation to which the provisions apply), after "under" insert "section 389A(3) or". *1985 c. 6.*

(3) In Schedule 24 to the Companies Act 1985 (punishment of offences) at the appropriate place insert—

"389A(2)	Officer of company making false, misleading or deceptive statement to auditors.	1. On indictment. 2. Summary.	2 years or a fine; or both. 6 months or the statutory maximum; or both.
389A(3)	Subsidiary undertaking or its auditor failing to give information to auditors of parent company.	Summary.	One-fifth of the statutory maximum.
389A(4)	Parent company failing to obtain from subsidiary undertaking information for purposes of audit.	Summary.	One-fifth of the statutory maximum.".

(4) In Schedule 4 to the Iron and Steel Act 1982 (constitution and proceedings of publicly-owned companies that are private companies), in paragraph 3(6) (entitlement of auditors to attend and be heard at general meetings, &c.) for "387(1)" substitute "390(1)". *1982 c. 25.*

121. The following sections are inserted in Chapter V of Part XI of the Companies Act 1985 (auditors)— *Remuneration of auditors.*

"Remuneration of auditors

Remuneration of auditors. 390A.—(1) The remuneration of auditors appointed by the company in general meeting shall be fixed by the company in general meeting or in such manner as the company in general meeting may determine.

(2) The remuneration of auditors appointed by the directors or the Secretary of State shall be fixed by the directors or the Secretary of State, as the case may be.

(3) There shall be stated in a note to the company's annual accounts the amount of the remuneration of the company's auditors in their capacity as such.

(4) For the purposes of this section "remuneration" includes sums paid in respect of expenses.

(5) This section applies in relation to benefits in kind as to payments in cash, and in relation to any such benefit references to its amount are to its estimated money value.

The nature of any such benefit shall also be disclosed.

Remuneration of auditors or their associates for non-audit work.

390B.—(1) The Secretary of State may make provision by regulations for securing the disclosure of the amount of any remuneration received or receivable by a company's auditors or their associates in respect of services other than those of auditors in their capacity as such.

(2) The regulations may—

(a) provide that "remuneration" includes sums paid in respect of expenses,

(b) apply in relation to benefits in kind as to payments in cash, and in relation to any such benefit require disclosure of its nature and its estimated money value,

(c) define "associate" in relation to an auditor,

(d) require the disclosure of remuneration in respect of services rendered to associated undertakings of the company, and

(e) define "associated undertaking" for that purpose.

(3) The regulations may require the auditors to disclose the relevant information in their report or require the relevant information to be disclosed in a note to the company's accounts and require the auditors to supply the directors of the company with such information as is necessary to enable that disclosure to be made.

(4) The regulations may make different provision for different cases.

(5) Regulations under this section shall be made by statutory instrument which shall be subject to annulment in pursuance of a resolution of either House of Parliament.".

Removal, resignation, &c. of auditors.

1985 c. 6.

122.—(1) The following sections are inserted in Chapter V of Part XI of the Companies Act 1985 (auditors)—

"Removal, resignation, &c. of auditors

Removal of auditors.

391.—(1) A company may by ordinary resolution at any time remove an auditor from office, notwithstanding anything in any agreement between it and him.

(2) Where a resolution removing an auditor is passed at a general meeting of a company, the company shall within 14 days give notice of that fact in the prescribed form to the registrar.

If a company fails to give the notice required by this subsection, the company and every officer of it who is in default is guilty of an offence and liable to a fine and, for continued contravention, to a daily default fine.

(3) Nothing in this section shall be taken as depriving a person removed under it of compensation or damages payable to him in respect of the termination of his appointment as auditor or of any appointment terminating with that as auditor.

(4) An auditor of a company who has been removed has, notwithstanding his removal, the rights conferred by section 390 in relation to any general meeting of the company—

(a) at which his term of office would otherwise have expired, or

(b) at which it is proposed to fill the vacancy caused by his removal.

In such a case the references in that section to matters concerning the auditors as auditors shall be construed as references to matters concerning him as a former auditor.

Rights of auditors who are removed or not re-appointed.

391A.—(1) Special notice is required for a resolution at a general meeting of a company—

(a) removing an auditor before the expiration of his term of office, or

(b) appointing as auditor a person other than a retiring auditor.

(2) On receipt of notice of such an intended resolution the company shall forthwith send a copy of it to the person proposed to be removed or, as the case may be, to the person proposed to be appointed and to the retiring auditor.

(3) The auditor proposed to be removed or (as the case may be) the retiring auditor may make with respect to the intended resolution representations in writing to the company (not exceeding a reasonable length) and request their notification to members of the company.

(4) The company shall (unless the representations are received by it too late for it to do so)—

(a) in any notice of the resolution given to members of the company, state the fact of the representations having been made, and

(b) send a copy of the representations to every member of the company to whom notice of the meeting is or has been sent.

(5) If a copy of any such representations is not sent out as required because received too late or because of the company's default, the auditor may (without prejudice to his right to be heard orally) require that the representations be read out at the meeting.

(6) Copies of the representations need not be sent out and the representations need not be read at the meeting if, on the application either of the company or of any other person claiming to be aggrieved, the court is satisfied that the rights conferred by this section are being abused to secure needless publicity for defamatory matter; and the court may order the company's costs on the application to be paid in whole or in part by the auditor, notwithstanding that he is not a party to the application.

Resignation of auditors.

392.—(1) An auditor of a company may resign his office by depositing a notice in writing to that effect at the company's registered office.

The notice is not effective unless it is accompanied by the statement required by section 394.

(2) An effective notice of resignation operates to bring the auditor's term of office to an end as of the date on which the notice is deposited or on such later date as may be specified in it.

(3) The company shall within 14 days of the deposit of a notice of resignation send a copy of the notice to the registrar of companies.

If default is made in complying with this subsection, the company and every officer of it who is in default is guilty of an offence and liable to a fine and, for continued contravention, a daily default fine.

Rights of resigning auditors.

392A.—(1) This section applies where an auditor's notice of resignation is accompanied by a statement of circumstances which he considers should be brought to the attention of members or creditors of the company.

(2) He may deposit with the notice a signed requisition calling on the directors of the company forthwith duly to convene an extraordinary general meeting of the company for the purpose of receiving and considering such explanation of the circumstances connected with his resignation as he may wish to place before the meeting.

(3) He may request the company to circulate to its members—

    (a) before the meeting convened on his requisition, or

    (b) before any general meeting at which his term of office would otherwise have expired or at which it is proposed to fill the vacancy caused by his resignation,

a statement in writing (not exceeding a reasonable length) of the circumstances connected with his resignation.

(4) The company shall (unless the statement is received too late for it to comply)—

    (a) in any notice of the meeting given to members of the company, state the fact of the statement having been made, and

(b) send a copy of the statement to every member of the company to whom notice of the meeting is or has been sent.

(5) If the directors do not within 21 days from the date of the deposit of a requisition under this section proceed duly to convene a meeting for a day not more than 28 days after the date on which the notice convening the meeting is given, every director who failed to take all reasonable steps to secure that a meeting was convened as mentioned above is guilty of an offence and liable to a fine.

(6) If a copy of the statement mentioned above is not sent out as required because received too late or because of the company's default, the auditor may (without prejudice to his right to be heard orally) require that the statement be read out at the meeting.

(7) Copies of a statement need not be sent out and the statement need not be read out at the meeting if, on the application either of the company or of any other person who claims to be aggrieved, the court is satisfied that the rights conferred by this section are being abused to secure needless publicity for defamatory matter; and the court may order the company's costs on such an application to be paid in whole or in part by the auditor, notwithstanding that he is not a party to the application.

(8) An auditor who has resigned has, notwithstanding his resignation, the rights conferred by section 390 in relation to any such general meeting of the company as is mentioned in subsection (3)(a) or (b).

In such a case the references in that section to matters concerning the auditors as auditors shall be construed as references to matters concerning him as a former auditor.

Termination of appointment of auditors not appointed annually.

393.—(1) When an election is in force under section 386 (election by private company to dispense with annual appointment), any member of the company may deposit notice in writing at the company's registered office proposing that the appointment of the company's auditors be brought to an end.

No member may deposit more than one such notice in any financial year of the company.

(2) If such a notice is deposited it is the duty of the directors—

(a) to convene a general meeting of the company for a date not more than 28 days after the date on which the notice was given, and

(b) to propose at the meeting a resolution in a form enabling the company to decide whether the appointment of the company's auditors should be brought to an end.

PART V

(3) If the decision of the company at the meeting is that the appointment of the auditors should be brought to an end, the auditors shall not be deemed to be re-appointed when next they would be and, if the notice was deposited within the period immediately following the distribution of accounts, any deemed re-appointment for the financial year following that to which those accounts relate which has already occurred shall cease to have effect.

The period immediately following the distribution of accounts means the period beginning with the day on which copies of the company's annual accounts are sent to members of the company under section 238 and ending 14 days after that day.

(4) If the directors do not within 14 days from the date of the deposit of the notice proceed duly to convene a meeting, the member who deposited the notice (or, if there was more than one, any of them) may himself convene the meeting; but any meeting so convened shall not be held after the expiration of three months from that date.

(5) A meeting convened under this section by a member shall be convened in the same manner, as nearly as possible, as that in which meetings are to be convened by directors.

(6) Any reasonable expenses incurred by a member by reason of the failure of the directors duly to convene a meeting shall be made good to him by the company; and any such sums shall be recouped by the company from such of the directors as were in default out of any sums payable, or to become payable, by the company by way of fees or other remuneration in respect of their services.

(7) This section has effect notwithstanding anything in any agreement between the company and its auditors; and no compensation or damages shall be payable by reason of the auditors' appointment being terminated under this section.".

1985 c. 6.

(2) In Schedule 24 to the Companies Act 1985 (punishment of offences), at the appropriate place insert—

"391(2)	Failing to give notice to registrar of removal of auditor.	Summary.	One-fifth of the statutory maximum.	One-fiftieth of the statutory maximum.
392(3)	Company failing to forward notice of auditor's resignation to registrar.	1. On indictment.	A fine.	
		2. Summary.	The statutory maximum.	One-tenth of the statutory maximum.
392A(5)	Directors failing to convene meeting requisitioned by resigning auditor.	1. On indictment.	A fine.	
		2. Summary.	The statutory maximum.".	

Statement by person ceasing to hold office as auditor.

123.—(1) The following section is inserted in Chapter V of Part XI of the Companies Act 1985 (auditors)—

"Statement by person ceasing to hold office as auditor.

394.—(1) Where an auditor ceases for any reason to hold office, he shall deposit at the company's registered office a statement of any circumstances connected with his ceasing to hold office which he considers should be brought to the attention of the members or creditors of the company or, if he considers that there are no such circumstances, a statement that there are none.

(2) In the case of resignation, the statement shall be deposited along with the notice of resignation; in the case of failure to seek re-appointment, the statement shall be deposited not less than 14 days before the end of the time allowed for next appointing auditors; in any other case, the statement shall be deposited not later than the end of the period of 14 days beginning with the date on which he ceases to hold office.

(3) If the statement is of circumstances which the auditor considers should be brought to the attention of the members or creditors of the company, the company shall within 14 days of the deposit of the statement either—

    (a) send a copy of it to every person who under section 238 is entitled to be sent copies of the accounts, or

    (b) apply to the court.

(4) The company shall if it applies to the court notify the auditor of the application.

(5) Unless the auditor receives notice of such an application before the end of the period of 21 days beginning with the day on which he deposited the statement, he shall within a further seven days send a copy of the statement to the registrar.

(6) If the court is satisfied that the auditor is using the statement to secure needless publicity for defamatory matter—

    (a) it shall direct that copies of the statement need not be sent out, and

    (b) it may further order the company's costs on the application to be paid in whole or in part by the auditor, notwithstanding that he is not a party to the application;

and the company shall within 14 days of the court's decision send to the persons mentioned in subsection (3)(a) a statement setting out the effect of the order.

(7) If the court is not so satisfied, the company shall within 14 days of the court's decision—

    (a) send copies of the statement to the persons mentioned in subsection (3)(a), and

    (b) notify the auditor of the court's decision;

and the auditor shall within seven days of receiving such notice send a copy of the statement to the registrar.

E

PART V

Offences of
failing to comply
with s.394.

394A.—(1) If a person ceasing to hold office as auditor fails to comply with section 394 he is guilty of an offence and liable to a fine.

(2) In proceedings for an offence under subsection (1) it is a defence for the person charged to show that he took all reasonable steps and exercised all due diligence to avoid the commission of the offence.

(3) Sections 733 (liability of individuals for corporate default) and 734 (criminal proceedings against unincorporated bodies) apply to an offence under subsection (1).

(4) If a company makes default in complying with section 394, the company and every officer of it who is in default is guilty of an offence and liable to a fine and, for continued contravention, to a daily default fine.''.

1985 c. 6.

(2) In Schedule 24 to the Companies Act 1985 (punishment of offences), at the appropriate place insert—

''394A(1)	Person ceasing to hold office as auditor failing to deposit statement as to circumstances.	1. On indictment. 2. Summary.	A fine. The statutory maximum.	
394A(4)	Company failing to comply with requirements as to statement of person ceasing to hold office as auditor.	1. On indictment. 2. Summary.	A fine. The statutory maximum.	One-tenth of the statutory maximum.''.

(3) In section 733 of the Companies Act 1985 (liability of individuals for corporate default), in subsection (1) (offences in relation to which provisions apply) after "216(3)" insert ", 394A(1)".

(4) In section 734 of the Companies Act 1985 (criminal proceedings against unincorporated bodies), in subsection (1) (offences in relation to which the provisions apply), after "under" insert "section 394A(1) or".

(5) In Schedule 22 to the Companies Act 1985 (unregistered companies), in the entry for sections 384 to 393, for "393" substitute "394A".

Auditors of trade
unions and
employers'
associations.

1974 c. 52.

124. In section 11 of the Trade Union and Labour Relations Act 1974 (duties of trade unions and employers' associations as to auditors, &c.), after subsection (8) insert—

"(9) Where a trade union or employers' association to which this section applies is a company within the meaning of the Companies Act 1985—

(a) subsection (3) above, and the provisions of paragraphs 6 to 15 of Schedule 2 to this Act, do not apply, and

(b) the rights and powers conferred, and duties imposed, by paragraphs 16 to 21 of that Schedule belong to the auditors of the company appointed under Chapter V of Part XI of that Act.".

Company records and related matters   PART V

125.—(1) For section 706 of the Companies Act 1985 (size, durability, &c. of documents delivered to the registrar) substitute—

Delivery of documents to the registrar.

1985 c. 6.

"Delivery to the registrar of documents in legible form.

706.—(1) This section applies to the delivery to the registrar under any provision of the Companies Acts of documents in legible form.

(2) The document must—

(a) state in a prominent position the registered number of the company to which it relates,

(b) satisfy any requirements prescribed by regulations for the purposes of this section, and

(c) conform to such requirements as the registrar may specify for the purpose of enabling him to copy the document.

(3) If a document is delivered to the registrar which does not comply with the requirements of this section, he may serve on the person by whom the document was delivered (or, if there are two or more such persons, on any of them) a notice indicating the respect in which the document does not comply.

(4) Where the registrar serves such a notice, then, unless a replacement document—

(a) is delivered to him within 14 days after the service of the notice, and

(b) complies with the requirements of this section (or section 707) or is not rejected by him for failure to comply with those requirements,

the original document shall be deemed not to have been delivered to him.

But for the purposes of any enactment imposing a penalty for failure to deliver, so far as it imposes a penalty for continued contravention, no account shall be taken of the period between the delivery of the original document and the end of the period of 14 days after service of the registrar's notice.

(5) Regulations made for the purposes of this section may make different provision with respect to different descriptions of document.".

(2) For section 707 of the Companies Act 1985 (power of registrar to accept information on microfilm, &c.) substitute—

"Delivery to the registrar of documents otherwise than in legible form.

707.—(1) This section applies to the delivery to the registrar under any provision of the Companies Acts of documents otherwise than in legible form.

(2) Any requirement to deliver a document to the registrar, or to deliver a document in the prescribed form, is satisfied by the communication to the registrar of the requisite information in any non-legible form prescribed for the purposes of this section by regulations or approved by the registrar.

(3) Where the document is required to be signed or sealed, it shall instead be authenticated in such manner as may be prescribed by regulations or approved by the registrar.

(4) The document must—

   (a) contain in a prominent position the registered number of the company to which it relates,

   (b) satisfy any requirements prescribed by regulations for the purposes of this section, and

   (c) be furnished in such manner, and conform to such requirements, as the registrar may specify for the purpose of enabling him to read and copy the document.

(5) If a document is delivered to the registrar which does not comply with the requirements of this section, he may serve on the person by whom the document was delivered (or, if there are two or more such persons, on any of them) a notice indicating the respect in which the document does not comply.

(6) Where the registrar serves such a notice, then, unless a replacement document—

   (a) is delivered to him within 14 days after the service of the notice, and

   (b) complies with the requirements of this section (or section 706) or is not rejected by him for failure to comply with those requirements,

the original document shall be deemed not to have been delivered to him.

But for the purposes of any enactment imposing a penalty for failure to deliver, so far as it imposes a penalty for continued contravention, no account shall be taken of the period between the delivery of the original document and the end of the period of 14 days after service of the registrar's notice.

(7) The Secretary of State may by regulations make further provision with respect to the application of this section in relation to instantaneous forms of communication.

(8) Regulations made for the purposes of this section may make different provision with respect to different descriptions of document and different forms of communication, and as respects delivery to the registrar for England and Wales and delivery to the registrar for Scotland.".

Keeping and inspection of company records.
1985 c. 6.

126.—(1) In Part XXIV of the Companies Act 1985 (the registrar of companies, his functions and offices), after the sections inserted by section 125 above, insert—

"The keeping of company records by the registrar.

707A.—(1) The information contained in a document delivered to the registrar under the Companies Acts may be recorded and kept by him in any form he thinks fit, provided it is possible to inspect the information and to produce a copy of it in legible form.

This is sufficient compliance with any duty of his to keep, file or register the document.

(2) The originals of documents delivered to the registrar in legible form shall be kept by him for ten years, after which they may be destroyed.

(3) Where a company has been dissolved, the registrar may, at any time after the expiration of two years from the date of the dissolution, direct that any records in his custody relating to the company may be removed to the Public Record Office; and records in respect of which such a direction is given shall be disposed of in accordance with the enactments relating to that Office and the rules made under them.

This subsection does not extend to Scotland.

(4) In subsection (3) "company" includes a company provisionally or completely registered under the Joint Stock Companies Act 1844.".

(2) For sections 709 and 710 of the Companies Act 1985 (inspection of documents kept by the registrar) substitute—   1985 c. 6.

"Inspection, &c. of records kept by the registrar.   709.—(1) Any person may inspect any records kept by the registrar for the purposes of the Companies Acts and may require—

    (a) a copy, in such form as the registrar considers appropriate, of any information contained in those records, or

    (b) a certified copy of, or extract from, any such record.

(2) The right of inspection extends to the originals of documents delivered to the registrar in legible form only where the record kept by the registrar of the contents of the document is illegible or unavailable.

(3) A copy of or extract from a record kept at any of the offices for the registration of companies in England and Wales or Scotland, certified in writing by the registrar (whose official position it is unnecessary to prove) to be an accurate record of the contents of any document delivered to him under the Companies Acts, is in all legal proceedings admissible in evidence as of equal validity with the original document and as evidence of any fact stated therein of which direct oral evidence would be admissible.

In England and Wales this is subject to compliance with any applicable rules of court under section 5 of the Civil Evidence Act 1968 or section 69(2) of the Police and Criminal Evidence Act 1984 (which relate to evidence from computer records).

(4) Copies of or extracts from records furnished by the registrar may, instead of being certified by him in writing to be an accurate record, be sealed with his official seal.

(5) No process for compelling the production of a record kept by the registrar shall issue from any court except with the leave of the court; and any such process shall bear on it a statement that it is issued with the leave of the court.

Certificate of incorporation.

710. Any person may require a certificate of the incorporation of a company, signed by the registrar or authenticated by his official seal.

Provision and authentication by registrar of documents in non-legible form.

710A.—(1) Any requirement of the Companies Acts as to the supply by the registrar of a document may, if the registrar thinks fit, be satisfied by the communication by the registrar of the requisite information in any non-legible form prescribed for the purposes of this section by regulations or approved by him.

(2) Where the document is required to be signed by him or sealed with his official seal, it shall instead be authenticated in such manner as may be prescribed by regulations or approved by the registrar.".

Supplementary provisions as to company records and related matters.

1985 c. 6.

127.—(1) In Part XXIV of the Companies Act 1985 (the registrar of companies, his functions and offices), after section 715 insert—

"Interpretation.

715A.—(1) In this Part—

"document" includes information recorded in any form; and

"legible", in the context of documents in legible or non-legible form, means capable of being read with the naked eye.

(2) References in this Part to delivering a document include sending, forwarding, producing or (in the case of a notice) giving it.".

(2) In section 708(1) of the Companies Act 1985 (fees)—

(a) in paragraph (a) for the words from "any notice or other document" to the end substitute "any document which under those Acts is required to be delivered to him", and

(b) in paragraph (b) omit "or other material".

(3) Omit sections 712 and 715 of the Companies Act 1985 (removal and destruction of old records).

(4) In section 713(1) (enforcement of duty to make returns, &c.), for the words from "file with" to "or other document" substitute "deliver a document to the registrar of companies".

1986 c. 45.
1986 c. 46.

(5) In section 735A(2) of the Companies Act 1985 (provisions applying to Insolvency Act 1986 and Company Directors Disqualification Act 1986 as to the Companies Acts)—

(a) after "707(1)," insert "707A(1),",

(b) after "708(1)(a) and (4)," insert "709(1) and (3),", and

(c) for "710(5)" substitute "710A".

(6) After section 735A of the Companies Act 1985 insert—

"Relationship of this Act to Parts IV and V of the Financial Services Act 1986.

735B. In sections 704(5), 706(1), 707(1), 707A(1), 708(1)(a) and (4), 709(1) and (3), 710A and 713(1) references to the Companies Acts include Parts IV and V of the Financial Services Act 1986.".

(7) In Schedule 22 to the Companies Act 1985 (unregistered companies), in the entry for Part XXIV for "sections 706, 708 to 710, 712 and 713" substitute "sections 706 to 710A, 713 and 715A".

Miscellaneous

128. In Chapter I of Part I of the Companies Act 1985 (company formation), after section 8 (Tables A, C, D and E) insert—

Form of articles for partnership company.

"Table G.

8A.—(1) The Secretary of State may by regulations prescribe a Table G containing articles of association appropriate for a partnership company, that is, a company limited by shares whose shares are intended to be held to a substantial extent by or on behalf of its employees.

(2) A company limited by shares may for its articles adopt the whole or any part of that Table.

(3) If in consequence of regulations under this section Table G is altered, the alteration does not affect a company registered before the alteration takes effect, or repeal as respects that company any portion of the Table.

(4) Regulations under this section shall be made by statutory instrument which shall be subject to annulment in pursuance of a resolution of either House of Parliament.".

129.—(1) In Chapter I of Part I of the Companies Act 1985 (company formation), for section 23 (membership of holding company) substitute—

Membership of holding company.

"Membership of holding company.

23.—(1) Except as mentioned in this section, a body corporate cannot be a member of a company which is its holding company and any allotment or transfer of shares in a company to its subsidiary is void.

(2) The prohibition does not apply where the subsidiary is concerned only as personal representative or trustee unless, in the latter case, the holding company or a subsidiary of it is beneficially interested under the trust.

For the purpose of ascertaining whether the holding company or a subsidiary is so interested, there shall be disregarded—

(a) any interest held only by way of security for the purposes of a transaction entered into by the holding company or subsidiary in the ordinary course of a business which includes the lending of money;

(b) any such interest as is mentioned in Part I of Schedule 2.

(3) The prohibition does not apply where the subsidiary is concerned only as a market maker.

For this purpose a person is a market maker if—

(a) he holds himself out at all normal times in compliance with the rules of a recognised investment exchange other than an overseas investment exchange (within the meaning of the Financial Services Act 1986) as willing to buy and sell securities at prices specified by him, and

(b) he is recognised as so doing by that investment exchange.

(4) Where a body corporate became a holder of shares in a company—

(a) before 1st July 1948, or

(b) on or after that date and before the commencement of section 129 of the Companies Act 1989, in circumstances in which this section as it then had effect did not apply,

but at any time after the commencement of that section falls within the prohibition in subsection (1) above in respect of those shares, it may continue to be a member of that company; but for so long as that prohibition would apply, apart from this subsection, it has no right to vote in respect of those shares at meetings of the company or of any class of its members.

(5) Where a body corporate becomes a holder of shares in a company after the commencement of that section in circumstances in which the prohibition in subsection (1) does not apply, but subsequently falls within that prohibition in respect of those shares, it may continue to be a member of that company; but for so long as that prohibition would apply, apart from this subsection, it has no right to vote in respect of those shares at meetings of the company or of any class of its members.

(6) Where a body corporate is permitted to continue as a member of a company by virtue of subsection (4) or (5), an allotment to it of fully paid shares in the company may be validly made by way of capitalisation of reserves of the company; but for so long as the prohibition in subsection (1) would apply, apart from subsection (4) or (5), it has no right to vote in respect of those shares at meetings of the company or of any class of its members.

(7) The provisions of this section apply to a nominee acting on behalf of a subsidiary as to the subsidiary itself.

(8) In relation to a company other than a company limited by shares, the references in this section to shares shall be construed as references to the interest of its members as such, whatever the form of that interest.".

PART V
1985 c. 6.

Company
contracts and
execution of
documents by
companies.

(2) In Schedule 2 to the Companies Act 1985 (interpretation of references to "beneficial interest"), in paragraphs 1(1), 3(1) and 4(2) for "as respects section 23(4)" substitute "as this paragraph applies for the purposes of section 23(2)".

130.—(1) In Chapter III of Part I of the Companies Act 1985 (a company's capacity; the formalities of carrying on business), for section 36 (form of company contracts) substitute—

"Company contracts: England and Wales.

36. Under the law of England and Wales a contract may be made—

(a) by a company, by writing under its common seal, or

(b) on behalf of a company, by any person acting under its authority, express or implied;

and any formalities required by law in the case of a contract made by an individual also apply, unless a contrary intention appears, to a contract made by or on behalf of a company.".

(2) After that section insert—

"Execution of documents: England and Wales.

36A.—(1) Under the law of England and Wales the following provisions have effect with respect to the execution of documents by a company.

(2) A document is executed by a company by the affixing of its common seal.

(3) A company need not have a common seal, however, and the following subsections apply whether it does or not.

(4) A document signed by a director and the secretary of a company, or by two directors of a company, and expressed (in whatever form of words) to be executed by the company has the same effect as if executed under the common seal of the company.

(5) A document executed by a company which makes it clear on its face that it is intended by the person or persons making it to be a deed has effect, upon delivery, as a deed; and it shall be presumed, unless a contrary intention is proved, to be delivered upon its being so executed.

(6) In favour of a purchaser a document shall be deemed to have been duly executed by a company if it purports to be signed by a director and the secretary of the company, or by two directors of the company, and, where it makes it clear on its face that it is intended by the person or persons making it to be a deed, to have been delivered upon its being executed.

A "purchaser" means a purchaser in good faith for valuable consideration and includes a lessee, mortgagee or other person who for valuable consideration acquires an interest in property.".

(3) After the section inserted by subsection (2) insert—

"Execution of
documents:
Scotland.

36B.—(1) Under the law of Scotland the following provisions have effect with respect to the execution of documents by a company.

(2) A document—

 (a) is signed by a company if it is signed on its behalf by a director, or by the secretary, of the company or by a person authorised to sign the document on its behalf, and

 (b) is subscribed by a company if it is subscribed on its behalf by being signed in accordance with the provisions of paragraph (a) at the end of the last page.

(3) A document shall be presumed, unless the contrary is shown, to have been subscribed by a company in accordance with subsection (2) if—

 (a) it bears to have been subscribed on behalf of the company by a director, or by the secretary, of the company or by a person bearing to have been authorised to subscribe the document on its behalf; and

 (b) it bears—

  (i) to have been signed by a person as a witness of the subscription of the director, secretary or other person subscribing on behalf of the company; or

  (ii) (if the subscription is not so witnessed) to have been sealed with the common seal of the company.

(4) A presumption under subsection (3) as to subscription of a document does not include a presumption—

 (a) that a person bearing to subscribe the document as a director or the secretary of the company was such director or secretary; or

 (b) that a person subscribing the document on behalf of the company bearing to have been authorised to do so was authorised to do so.

(5) Notwithstanding subsection (3)(b)(ii), a company need not have a common seal.

(6) Any reference in any enactment (including an enactment contained in a subordinate instrument) to a probative document shall, in relation to a document executed by a company after the commencement of section 130 of the Companies Act 1989, be construed as a reference to a document which is presumed under subsection (3) above to be subscribed by the company.

(7) Subsections (1) to (4) above do not apply where an enactment (including an enactment contained in a subordinate instrument) provides otherwise.".

(4) After the section inserted by subsection (3) insert—

"Pre-
incorporation
contracts, deeds
and obligations.

36C.—(1) A contract which purports to be made by or on behalf of a company at a time when the company has not been formed has effect, subject to any agreement to the contrary, as one made with the person purporting to act for the company or as agent for it, and he is personally liable on the contract accordingly.

(2) Subsection (1) applies—

(a) to the making of a deed under the law of England and Wales, and

(b) to the undertaking of an obligation under the law of Scotland,

as it applies to the making of a contract.".

(5) In Schedule 22 of the Companies Act 1985 (provisions applying to unregistered companies), at the appropriate place insert—   1985 c. 6.

"Section 36	Company contracts.	Subject to section 718(3).
Sections 36A and 36B	Execution of documents.	Subject to section 718(3).
Section 36C	Pre-incorporation contracts, deeds and obligations.	Subject to section 718(3).".

(6) The Secretary of State may make provision by regulations applying sections 36 to 36C of the Companies Act 1985 (company contracts; execution of documents; pre-incorporation contracts, deeds and obligations) to companies incorporated outside Great Britain, subject to such exceptions, adaptations or modifications as may be specified in the regulations.

Regulations under this subsection shall be made by statutory instrument which shall be subject to annulment in pursuance of a resolution of either House of Parliament.

(7) Schedule 17 contains further minor and consequential amendments relating to company contracts, the execution of documents by companies and related matters.

131.—(1) In Part IV of the Companies Act 1985 (allotment of shares and debentures), before section 112 and after the heading *"Other matters arising out of allotment &c."*, insert—   Members' rights to damages, &c.

"Right to
damages, &c.
not affected.

111A. A person is not debarred from obtaining damages or other compensation from a company by reason only of his holding or having held shares in the company or any right to apply or subscribe for shares or to be included in the company's register in respect of shares.".

(2) In section 116 of the Companies Act 1985 (extended operation of certain provisions applying to public companies) for "and 110 to 115" substitute ", 110, 111 and 112 to 115".

132. In Chapter VI of Part V of the Companies Act 1985 (financial assistance by company for purchase of its own shares), in section 153 (transactions not prohibited), for subsection (4)(b) (provision of money in accordance with employees' share scheme) substitute—   Financial assistance for purposes of employees' share scheme.

"(b) the provision by a company, in good faith in the interests of the company, of financial assistance for the purposes of an employees' share scheme,".

133.—(1) In Part V of the Companies Act 1985 (share capital, its increase, maintenance and reduction), Chapter III (redeemable shares, purchase by a company of its own shares) is amended as follows.

(2) After section 159 (power to issue redeemable shares) insert—

"Terms and
manner of
redemption.

159A.—(1) Redeemable shares may not be issued unless the following conditions are satisfied as regards the terms and manner of redemption.

(2) The date on or by which, or dates between which, the shares are to be or may be redeemed must be specified in the company's articles or, if the articles so provide, fixed by the directors, and in the latter case the date or dates must be fixed before the shares are issued.

(3) Any other circumstances in which the shares are to be or may be redeemed must be specified in the company's articles.

(4) The amount payable on redemption must be specified in, or determined in accordance with, the company's articles, and in the latter case the articles must not provide for the amount to be determined by reference to any person's discretion or opinion.

(5) Any other terms and conditions of redemption shall be specified in the company's articles.

(6) Nothing in this section shall be construed as requiring a company to provide in its articles for any matter for which provision is made by this Act.".

(3) In section 160 (financing, &c. of redemption)—

(a) omit subsection (3) (which is superseded by the new section 159A), and

(b) in subsection (4) (cancellation of shares on redemption) for "redeemed under this section" substitute "redeemed under this Chapter".

(4) In section 162 (power of company to purchase own shares), for subsection (2) (application of provisions relating to redeemable shares) substitute—

"(2) Sections 159, 160 and 161 apply to the purchase by a company under this section of its own shares as they apply to the redemption of redeemable shares.".

134.—(1) Part VI of the Companies Act 1985 (disclosure of interests in shares) is amended as follows.

(2) In section 199(2) (notifiable interests), for the words from "the percentage" to the end substitute "3 per cent. of the nominal value of that share capital".

The order bringing the above amendment into force may make such provision as appears to the Secretary of State appropriate as to the obligations of a person whose interest in a company's shares becomes notifiable by virtue of the amendment coming into force.

(3) In sections 202(1) and (4) and 206(8) (which require notification of certain matters within a specified period) for "5 days" substitute "2 days".

(4) In section 202 (particulars to be contained in notification), for subsection (3) substitute—

"(3) A notification (other than one stating that a person no longer has a notifiable interest) shall include the following particulars, so far as known to the person making the notification at the date when it is made—

(a) the identity of each registered holder of shares to which the notification relates and the number of such shares held by each of them, and

(b) the number of such shares in which the interest of the person giving the notification is such an interest as is mentioned in section 208(5).".

(5) After section 210 insert—

"Power to make further provision by regulations.

210A.—(1) The Secretary of State may by regulations amend—

(a) the definition of "relevant share capital" (section 198(2)),

(b) the percentage giving rise to a "notifiable interest" (section 199(2)),

(c) the periods within which an obligation of disclosure must be fulfilled or a notice must be given (sections 202(1) and (4) and 206(8)),

(d) the provisions as to what is taken to be an interest in shares (section 208) and what interests are to be disregarded (section 209), and

(e) the provisions as to company investigations (section 212);

and the regulations may amend, replace or repeal the provisions referred to above and make such other consequential amendments or repeals of provisions of this Part as appear to the Secretary of State to be appropriate.

(2) The regulations may in any case make different provision for different descriptions of company; and regulations under subsection (1)(b), (c) or (d) may make different provision for different descriptions of person, interest or share capital.

(3) The regulations may contain such transitional and other supplementary and incidental provisions as appear to the Secretary of State to be appropriate, and may in particular make provision as to the obligations of a person whose interest in a company's shares becomes or ceases to be notifiable by virtue of the regulations.

(4) Regulations under this section shall be made by statutory instrument.

(5) No regulations shall be made under this section unless a draft of the regulations has been laid before and approved by a resolution of each House of Parliament.".

(6) Any regulations made under section 209(1)(j) which are in force immediately before the repeal of that paragraph by this Act shall have effect as if made under section 210A(1)(d) as inserted by subsection (5) above.

135.—(1) The Secretary of State may by regulations made by statutory instrument make such amendments of the provisions of the Companies Act 1985 relating to orders imposing restrictions on shares as appear to him necessary or expedient—

(a) for enabling orders to be made in a form protecting the rights of third parties;

(b) with respect to the circumstances in which restrictions may be relaxed or removed;

(c) with respect to the making of interim orders by a court.

(2) The provisions referred to in subsection (1) are section 210(5), section 216(1) and (2), section 445 and Part XV of the Companies Act 1985.

(3) The regulations may make different provision for different cases and may contain such transitional and other supplementary and incidental provisions as appear to the Secretary of State to be appropriate.

(4) Regulations under this section shall not be made unless a draft of the regulations has been laid before Parliament and approved by resolution of each House of Parliament.

136. For section 287 of the Companies Act 1985 (registered office) substitute—

287.—(1) A company shall at all times have a registered office to which all communications and notices may be addressed.

(2) On incorporation the situation of the company's registered office is that specified in the statement sent to the registrar under section 10.

(3) The company may change the situation of its registered office from time to time by giving notice in the prescribed form to the registrar.

(4) The change takes effect upon the notice being registered by the registrar, but until the end of the period of 14 days beginning with the date on which it is registered a person may validly serve any document on the company at its previous registered office.

(5) For the purposes of any duty of a company—

(a) to keep at its registered office, or make available for public inspection there, any register, index or other document, or

(b) to mention the address of its registered office in any document,

a company which has given notice to the registrar of a change in the situation of its registered office may act on the change as from such date, not more than 14 days after the notice is given, as it may determine.

(6) Where a company unavoidably ceases to perform at its registered office any such duty as is mentioned in subsection (5)(a) in circumstances in which it was not practicable to give prior notice to the registrar of a change in the situation of its registered office, but—

(a) resumes performance of that duty at other premises as soon as practicable, and

(b) gives notice accordingly to the registrar of a change in the situation of its registered office within 14 days of doing so,

it shall not be treated as having failed to comply with that duty.

(7) In proceedings for an offence of failing to comply with any such duty as is mentioned in subsection (5), it is for the person charged to show that by reason of the matters referred to in that subsection or subsection (6) no offence was committed.".

137.—(1) In section 310 of the Companies Act 1985 (provisions exempting officers and auditors from liability), for subsection (3) (permitted provisions) substitute—

Effecting of insurance for officers and auditors of company.
1985 c. 6.

"(3) This section does not prevent a company—

(a) from purchasing and maintaining for any such officer or auditor insurance against any such liability, or

(b) from indemnifying any such officer or auditor against any liability incurred by him—

(i) in defending any proceedings (whether civil or criminal) in which judgment is given in his favour or he is acquitted, or

(ii) in connection with any application under section 144(3) or (4) (acquisition of shares by innocent nominee) or section 727 (general power to grant relief in case of honest and reasonable conduct) in which relief is granted to him by the court.".

(2) In Part I of Schedule 7 to the Companies Act 1985 (general matters to be dealt with in directors' report), after paragraph 5 insert—

"Insurance effected for officers or auditors

5A. Where in the financial year the company has purchased or maintained any such insurance as is mentioned in section 310(3)(a) (insurance of officers or auditors against liabilities in relation to the company), that fact shall be stated in the report."

138. Part X of the Companies Act 1985 (enforcement of fair dealing by directors) is amended as follows—

    (a) in section 332(1)(b) (short-term quasi-loans) for "£1,000" substitute "£5,000";

    (b) in section 334 (loans of small amounts) for "£2,500" substitute "£5,000";

    (c) in section 338(4) and (6) (loans or quasi-loans by money-lending company) for "£50,000" substitute "£100,000".

139.—(1) In Part XI of the Companies Act 1985 (company administration and procedure), for Chapter III (annual return) substitute—

"CHAPTER III

ANNUAL RETURN

363.—(1) Every company shall deliver to the registrar successive annual returns each of which is made up to a date not later than the date which is from time to time the company's "return date", that is—

    (a) the anniversary of the company's incorporation, or

    (b) if the company's last return delivered in accordance with this Chapter was made up to a different date, the anniversary of that date.

(2) Each return shall—

    (a) be in the prescribed form,

    (b) contain the information required by or under the following provisions of this Chapter, and

    (c) be signed by a director or the secretary of the company;

and it shall be delivered to the registrar within 28 days after the date to which it is made up.

(3) If a company fails to deliver an annual return in accordance with this Chapter before the end of the period of 28 days after a return date, the company is guilty of an offence and liable to a fine and, in the case of continued contravention, to a daily default fine.

The contravention continues until such time as an annual return made up to that return date and complying with the requirements of subsection (2) (except as to date of delivery) is delivered by the company to the registrar.

(4) Where a company is guilty of an offence under subsection (3), every director or secretary of the company is similarly liable unless he shows that he took all reasonable steps to avoid the commission or continuation of the offence.

(5) The references in this section to a return being delivered "in accordance with this Chapter" are—

(a) in relation to a return made after the commencement of section 139 of the Companies Act 1989, to a return with respect to which all the requirements of subsection (2) are complied with;

(b) in relation to a return made before that commencement, to a return with respect to which the formal and substantive requirements of this Chapter as it then had effect were complied with, whether or not the return was delivered in time.

Contents of annual return: general.

364.—(1) Every annual return shall state the date to which it is made up and shall contain the following information—

(a) the address of the company's registered office;

(b) the type of company it is and its principal business activities;

(c) the name and address of the company secretary;

(d) the name and address of every director of the company;

(e) in the case of each individual director—

(i) his nationality, date of birth and business occupation, and

(ii) such particulars of other directorships and former names as are required to be contained in the company's register of directors;

(f) in the case of any corporate director, such particulars of other directorships as would be required to be contained in that register in the case of an individual;

(g) if the register of members is not kept at the company's registered office, the address of the place where it is kept;

(h) if any register of debenture holders (or a duplicate of any such register or a part of it) is not kept at the company's registered office, the address of the place where it is kept;

(i) if the company has elected—

(i) to dispense under section 252 with the laying of accounts and reports before the company in general meeting, or

(ii) to dispense under section 366A with the holding of annual general meetings,

a statement to that effect.

(2) The information as to the company's type shall be given by reference to the classification scheme prescribed for the purposes of this section.

(3) The information as to the company's principal business activities may be given by reference to one or more categories of any prescribed system of classifying business activities.

(4) A person's "name" and "address" mean, respectively—

> (a) in the case of an individual, his Christian name (or other forename) and surname and his usual residential address;

> (b) in the case of a corporation or Scottish firm, its corporate or firm name and its registered or principal office.

(5) In the case of a peer, or an individual usually known by a title, the title may be stated instead of his Christian name (or other forename) and surname or in addition to either or both of them.

(6) Where all the partners in a firm are joint secretaries, the name and principal office of the firm may be stated instead of the names and addresses of the partners.

Contents of annual return: particulars of share capital and shareholders.

364A.—(1) The annual return of a company having a share capital shall contain the following information with respect to its share capital and members.

(2) The return shall state the total number of issued shares of the company at the date to which the return is made up and the aggregate nominal value of those shares.

(3) The return shall state with respect to each class of shares in the company—

> (a) the nature of the class, and

> (b) the total number and aggregate nominal value of issued shares of that class at the date to which the return is made up.

(4) The return shall contain a list of the names and addresses of every person who—

> (a) is a member of the company on the date to which the return is made up, or

> (b) has ceased to be a member of the company since the date to which the last return was made up (or, in the case of the first return, since the incorporation of the company);

and if the names are not arranged in alphabetical order the return shall have annexed to it an index sufficient to enable the name of any person in the list to be easily found.

(5) The return shall also state—

    (a) the number of shares of each class held by each member of the company at the date to which the return is made up, and

    (b) the number of shares of each class transferred since the date to which the last return was made up (or, in the case of the first return, since the incorporation of the company) by each member or person who has ceased to be a member, and the dates of registration of the transfers.

(6) The return may, if either of the two immediately preceding returns has given the full particulars required by subsections (4) and (5), give only such particulars as relate to persons ceasing to be or becoming members since the date of the last return and to shares transferred since that date.

(7) Subsections (4) and (5) do not require the inclusion of particulars entered in an overseas branch register if copies of those entries have not been received at the company's registered office by the date to which the return is made up.

Those particulars shall be included in the company's next annual return after they are received.

(8) Where the company has converted any of its shares into stock, the return shall give the corresponding information in relation to that stock, stating the amount of stock instead of the number or nominal value of shares.

Supplementary provisions: regulations and interpretation.

365.—(1) The Secretary of State may by regulations make further provision as to the information to be given in a company's annual return, which may amend or repeal the provisions of sections 364 and 364A.

(2) Regulations under this section shall be made by statutory instrument which shall be subject to annulment in pursuance of a resolution of either House of Parliament.

(3) For the purposes of this Chapter, except section 363(2)(c) (signature of annual return), a shadow director shall be deemed to be a director.".

(2) Where a company was, immediately before the commencement of this section, in default with respect to the delivery of one or more annual returns, this section does not affect its obligation to make such a return (in accordance with Chapter III of Part XI of the Companies Act 1985 as it then had effect) or any liability arising from failure to do so.   1985 c. 6.

(3) In Schedule 24 to the Companies Act 1985 (punishment of offences) in the entry relating to section 363(7), in the first column for "363(7)" substitute "363(3)".

(4) In Schedule 1 to the Company Directors Disqualification Act 1986 (matters relevant to determining unfitness of directors), in paragraph 4 (failure of company to comply with certain provisions), for sub-paragraphs (f) and (g) substitute—

"(f) section 363 (duty of company to make annual returns);".

(5) In section 565(6) of the Income and Corporation Taxes Act 1988 (conditions for exemption from provisions relating to sub-contractors in construction industry: compliance with requirements of Companies Act 1985), in paragraph (d) for "sections 363, 364 and 365" substitute "sections 363 to 365".

140.—(1) In section 463 of the Companies Act 1985 (effect of floating charge on winding up), in subsection (1) for the words "On the commencement of the winding up of a company," there shall be substituted the words "Where a company goes into liquidation within the meaning of section 247(2) of the Insolvency Act 1986,".

(2) Section 464 of the Companies Act 1985 (ranking of floating charges) is amended as follows.

(3) In subsection (1)(b) at the beginning there shall be inserted the words "with the consent of the holder of any subsisting floating charge or fixed security which would be adversely affected,".

(4) After subsection (1) there shall be inserted the following subsection—

"(1A) Where an instrument creating a floating charge contains any such provision as is mentioned in subsection (1)(a), that provision shall be effective to confer priority on the floating charge over any fixed security or floating charge created after the date of the instrument.".

(5) For subsection (3) there shall be substituted—

"(3) The order of ranking of the floating charge with any other subsisting or future floating charges or fixed securities over all or any part of the company's property is determined in accordance with the provisions of subsections (4) and (5) except where it is determined in accordance with any provision such as is mentioned in paragraph (a) or (b) of subsection (1).".

(6) In subsection (5) at the end there shall be added the following paragraph—

"; and

(e) (in the case of a floating charge to secure a contingent liability other than a liability arising under any further advances made from time to time) the maximum sum to which that contingent liability is capable of amounting whether or not it is contractually limited.".

(7) In subsection (6) after the words "subject to" there shall be inserted the words "Part XII and to".

(8) In section 466 of the Companies Act 1985 (alteration of floating charges), subsections (4) and (5) and in subsection (6) the words "falling under subsection (4) of this section" shall cease to have effect.

141.—(1) Section 651 of the Companies Act 1985 (power of court to declare dissolution of company void) is amended as follows.

(2) In subsection (1) omit the words "at any time within 2 years of the date of the dissolution".

(3) After subsection (3) add—

"(4) Subject to the following provisions, an application under this section may not be made after the end of the period of two years from the date of the dissolution of the company.

(5) An application for the purpose of bringing proceedings against the company—

(a) for damages in respect of personal injuries (including any sum claimed by virtue of section 1(2)(c) of the Law Reform (Miscellaneous Provisions) Act 1934 (funeral expenses)), or

(b) for damages under the Fatal Accidents Act 1976 or the Damages (Scotland) Act 1976,

may be made at any time; but no order shall be made on such an application if it appears to the court that the proceedings would fail by virtue of any enactment as to the time within which proceedings must be brought.

(6) Nothing in subsection (5) affects the power of the court on making an order under this section to direct that the period between the dissolution of the company and the making of the order shall not count for the purposes of any such enactment.

(7) In subsection (5)(a) "personal injuries" includes any disease and any impairment of a person's physical or mental condition.".

(4) An application may be made under section 651(5) of the Companies Act 1985 as inserted by subsection (3) above (proceedings for damages for personal injury, &c.) in relation to a company dissolved before the commencement of this section notwithstanding that the time within which the dissolution might formerly have been declared void under that section had expired before commencement.

But no such application shall be made in relation to a company dissolved more than twenty years before the commencement of this section.

(5) Except as provided by subsection (4), the amendments made by this section do not apply in relation to a company which was dissolved more than two years before the commencement of this section.

142.—(1) In Part XXIV of the Companies Act 1985 (the registrar of companies, his functions and offices), after section 711 insert—

"Exclusion of deemed notice.   711A.—(1) A person shall not be taken to have notice of any matter merely because of its being disclosed in any document kept by the registrar of companies (and thus available for inspection) or made available by the company for inspection.

(2) This does not affect the question whether a person is affected by notice of any matter by reason of a failure to make such inquiries as ought reasonably to be made.

PART V
Application to declare dissolution of company void.
1985 c. 6.

Abolition of doctrine of deemed notice.

(3) In this section 'document' includes any material which contains information.

(4) Nothing in this section affects the operation of—

(a) section 416 of this Act (under which a person taking a charge over a company's property is deemed to have notice of matters disclosed on the companies charges register), or

(b) section 198 of the Law of Property Act 1925 as it applies by virtue of section 3(7) of the Land Charges Act 1972 (under which the registration of certain land charges under Part XII, or Chapter III of Part XXIII, of this Act is deemed to constitute actual notice for all purposes connected with the land affected).".

1985 c. 6.

(2) In Schedule 22 to the Companies Act 1985 (unregistered companies), in the entry for Part XXIV at the appropriate place insert—

"Section 711A   Abolition of doctrine of   Subject to section 718(3).".
                 deemed notice.

Rights of inspection and related matters.

143.—(1) In Part XXV of the Companies Act 1985 (miscellaneous and supplementary provisions), after section 723 insert—

"Obligations of company as to inspection of registers, &c.

723A.—(1) The Secretary of State may make provision by regulations as to the obligations of a company which is required by any provision of this Act—

(a) to make available for inspection any register, index or document, or

(b) to provide copies of any such register, index or document, or part of it;

and a company which fails to comply with the regulations shall be deemed to have refused inspection or, as the case may be, to have failed to provide a copy.

(2) The regulations may make provision as to the time, duration and manner of inspection, including the circumstances in which and extent to which the copying of information is permitted in the course of inspection.

(3) The regulations may define what may be required of the company as regards the nature, extent and manner of extracting or presenting any information for the purposes of inspection or the provision of copies.

(4) Where there is power to charge a fee, the regulations may make provision as to the amount of the fee and the basis of its calculation.

(5) Regulations under this section may make different provision for different classes of case.

(6) Nothing in any provision of this Act or in the regulations shall be construed as preventing a company from affording more extensive facilities than are required by the regulations or, where a fee may be charged, from charging a lesser fee than that prescribed or no fee at all.

(7) Regulations under this section shall be made by
statutory instrument which shall be subject to annulment
in pursuance of a resolution of either House of
Parliament.".

(2) In section 169(5) of the Companies Act 1985 (contract for purchase
by company of its own shares), omit the words from ", during business
hours" to "for inspection)".

(3) In section 175(6) of the Companies Act 1985 (statutory declaration
and auditors' report relating to payment out of capital), in paragraph (b)
omit the words from "during business hours" to "period".

(4) In section 191 of the Companies Act 1985 (register of debenture
holders)—

  (a) in subsection (1), omit the words from "(but" to "for
      inspection)" and for the words from "a fee of 5 pence" to the
      end substitute "such fee as may be prescribed";

  (b) in subsection (2) for the words from "10 pence" to the end
      substitute "such fee as may be prescribed"; and

  (c) in subsection (3), after "on payment" insert "of such fee as may
      be prescribed" and omit paragraphs (a) and (b).

(5) In section 219 of the Companies Act 1985 (register of interests in
shares, &c.)—

  (a) in subsection (1), omit the words from "during" to "for
      inspection)"; and

  (b) in subsection (2) for the words from "10 pence" to "required to
      be copied" substitute "such fee as may be prescribed".

(6) In section 288 of the Companies Act 1985 (register of directors and
secretaries), in subsection (3), omit the words from "during" to "for
inspection)" and for the words from "5 pence" to the end substitute "such
fee as may be prescribed".

(7) In section 318 of the Companies Act 1985 (directors' service
contracts), in subsection (7) omit the words from ", during business
hours" to "for inspection)".

(8) In section 356 of the Companies Act 1985 (register and index of
members' names)—

  (a) in subsection (1), omit "during business hours" and for "the
      appropriate charge" substitute "such fee as may be prescribed";

  (b) omit subsection (2);

  (c) in subsection (3) for "the appropriate charge" substitute "such
      fee as may be prescribed"; and

  (d) omit subsection (4).

(9) In section 383 of the Companies Act 1985 (minutes of proceedings
of general meetings)—

  (a) in subsection (1), omit "during business hours";

  (b) omit subsection (2); and

  (c) in subsection (3), after "entitled" insert "on payment of such fee
      as may be prescribed" and omit the words from "at a charge"
      to the end.

(10) In Part IV of Schedule 13 to the Companies Act 1985 (register of directors' interests)—

(a) in paragraph 25, omit the words from "during" to "for inspection)" and for the words from "5 pence" to the end substitute "such fee as may be prescribed"; and

(b) in paragraph 26(1), for the words from "10 pence" to the end substitute "such fee as may be prescribed".

(11) In Schedule 22 to the Companies Act 1985 (provisions applying to unregistered companies), in the entry relating to Part XXV at the appropriate place insert—

| "Section 723A | Rights of inspection and related matters. | To apply only so far as this provision has effect in relation to provisions applying by virtue of the foregoing provisions of this Schedule.". |

"Subsidiary", "holding company" and "wholly-owned subsidiary".

144.—(1) In Part XXVI of the Companies Act 1985 (general interpretation provisions), for section 736 substitute—

""Subsidiary", holding company" and "wholly-owned subsidiary".

736.—(1) A company is a "subsidiary" of another company, its "holding company", if that other company—

(a) holds a majority of the voting rights in it, or

(b) is a member of it and has the right to appoint or remove a majority of its board of directors, or

(c) is a member of it and controls alone, pursuant to an agreement with other shareholders or members, a majority of the voting rights in it,

or if it is a subsidiary of a company which is itself a subsidiary of that other company.

(2) A company is a "wholly-owned subsidiary" of another company if it has no members except that other and that other's wholly-owned subsidiaries or persons acting on behalf of that other or its wholly-owned subsidiaries.

(3) In this section "company" includes any body corporate.

Provisions supplementing s. 736.

736A.—(1) The provisions of this section explain expressions used in section 736 and otherwise supplement that section.

(2) In section 736(1)(a) and (c) the references to the voting rights in a company are to the rights conferred on shareholders in respect of their shares or, in the case of a company not having a share capital, on members, to vote at general meetings of the company on all, or substantially all, matters.

(3) In section 736(1)(b) the reference to the right to appoint or remove a majority of the board of directors is to the right to appoint or remove directors holding a majority of the voting rights at meetings of the board on all, or substantially all, matters; and for the purposes of that provision—

    (a) a company shall be treated as having the right to appoint to a directorship if—

        (i) a person's appointment to it follows necessarily from his appointment as director of the company, or

        (ii) the directorship is held by the company itself; and

    (b) a right to appoint or remove which is exercisable only with the consent or concurrence of another person shall be left out of account unless no other person has a right to appoint or, as the case may be, remove in relation to that directorship.

(4) Rights which are exercisable only in certain circumstances shall be taken into account only—

    (a) when the circumstances have arisen, and for so long as they continue to obtain, or

    (b) when the circumstances are within the control of the person having the rights;

and rights which are normally exercisable but are temporarily incapable of exercise shall continue to be taken into account.

(5) Rights held by a person in a fiduciary capacity shall be treated as not held by him.

(6) Rights held by a person as nominee for another shall be treated as held by the other; and rights shall be regarded as held as nominee for another if they are exercisable only on his instructions or with his consent or concurrence.

(7) Rights attached to shares held by way of security shall be treated as held by the person providing the security—

    (a) where apart from the right to exercise them for the purpose of preserving the value of the security, or of realising it, the rights are exercisable only in accordance with his instructions;

    (b) where the shares are held in connection with the granting of loans as part of normal business activities and apart from the right to exercise them for the purpose of preserving the value of the security, or of realising it, the rights are exercisable only in his interests.

(8) Rights shall be treated as held by a company if they are held by any of its subsidiaries; and nothing in subsection (6) or (7) shall be construed as requiring rights held by a company to be treated as held by any of its subsidiaries.

(9) For the purposes of subsection (7) rights shall be treated as being exercisable in accordance with the instructions or in the interests of a company if they are exercisable in accordance with the instructions of or, as the case may be, in the interests of—

> (a) any subsidiary or holding company of that company, or

> (b) any subsidiary of a holding company of that company.

(10) The voting rights in a company shall be reduced by any rights held by the company itself.

(11) References in any provision of subsections (5) to (10) to rights held by a person include rights falling to be treated as held by him by virtue of any other provision of those subsections but not rights which by virtue of any such provision are to be treated as not held by him.

(12) In this section "company" includes any body corporate.".

(2) Any reference in any enactment (including any enactment contained in subordinate legislation within the meaning of the Interpretation Act 1978) to a "subsidiary" or "holding company" within the meaning of section 736 of the Companies Act 1985 shall, subject to any express amendment or saving made by or under this Act, be read as referring to a subsidiary or holding company as defined in section 736 as substituted by subsection (1) above.

1978 c. 30.
1985 c. 6.

This applies whether the reference is specific or general, or express or implied.

(3) In Part XXVI of the Companies Act 1985 (general interpretation provisions), after section 736A insert—

"Power to amend ss. 736 and 736A.   736B.—(1) The Secretary of State may by regulations amend sections 736 and 736A so as to alter the meaning of the expressions "holding company", "subsidiary" or "wholly-owned subsidiary".

(2) The regulations may make different provision for different cases or classes of case and may contain such incidental and supplementary provisions as the Secretary of State thinks fit.

(3) Regulations under this section shall be made by statutory instrument which shall be subject to annulment in pursuance of a resolution of either House of Parliament.

(4) Any amendment made by regulations under this section does not apply for the purposes of enactments outside the Companies Acts unless the regulations so provide.

(5) So much of section 23(3) of the Interpretation Act 1978 as applies section 17(2)(a) of that Act (effect of repeal and re-enactment) to deeds, instruments and documents other than enactments shall not apply in relation to any repeal and re-enactment effected by regulations made under this section.".

(4) Schedule 18 contains amendments and savings consequential on the amendments made by this section; and the Secretary of State may by regulations make such further amendments or savings as appear to him to be necessary or expedient.

(5) Regulations under this section shall be made by statutory instrument which shall be subject to annulment in pursuance of a resolution of either House of Parliament.

(6) So much of section 23(3) of the Interpretation Act 1978 as applies section 17(2)(a) of that Act (presumption as to meaning of references to enactments repealed and re-enacted) to deeds or other instruments or documents does not apply in relation to the repeal and re-enactment by this section of section 736 of the Companies Act 1985.

1978 c. 30.

1985 c. 6.

145. The Companies Act 1985 has effect with the further amendments specified in Schedule 19.

Minor amendments.

PART VI

MERGERS AND RELATED MATTERS

146. After section 75 of the Fair Trading Act 1973 there is inserted—

Restriction on references where prior notice given. 1973 c. 41.

"Restriction on power to make merger reference where prior notice has been given

General rule where notice given by acquirer and no reference made within period for considering notice.

75A.—(1) Notice may be given to the Director by a person authorised by regulations to do so of proposed arrangements which might result in the creation of a merger situation qualifying for investigation.

(2) The notice must be in the prescribed form and state that the existence of the proposal has been made public.

(3) If the period for considering the notice expires without any reference being made to the Commission with respect to the notified arrangements, no reference may be made under this Part of this Act to the Commission with respect to those arrangements or to the creation or possible creation of any merger situation qualifying for investigation which is created in consequence of carrying those arrangements into effect.

(4) Subsection (3) of this section is subject to sections 75B(5) and 75C of this Act.

(5) A notice under subsection (1) of this section is referred to in sections 75B to 75F of this Act as a "merger notice".

The role of the Director.

75B.—(1) The Director shall, when the period for considering any merger notice begins, take such action as he considers appropriate to bring the existence of the proposal, the fact that the merger notice has been given and the date on which the period for considering the notice may expire to the attention of those who in his opinion would be affected if the arrangements were carried into effect.

(2) The period for considering a merger notice is the period of twenty days, determined in accordance with subsection (9) of this section, beginning with the first day after—

    (a) the notice has been received by the Director, and

    (b) any fee payable to the Director in respect of the notice has been paid.

(3) The Director may, and shall if required to do so by the Secretary of State, by notice to the person who gave the merger notice—

    (a) extend the period mentioned in subsection (2) of this section by a further ten days, and

    (b) extend that period as extended under paragraph (a) of this subsection by a further fifteen days.

(4) The Director may by notice to the person who gave the merger notice request him to provide the Director within such period as may be specified in the notice with such information as may be so specified.

(5) If the Director gives to the person who gave the merger notice (in this subsection referred to as "the relevant person") a notice stating that the Secretary of State is seeking undertakings under section 75G of this Act, section 75A(3) of this Act does not prevent a reference being made to the Commission unless—

    (a) after the Director has given that notice, the relevant person has given a notice to the Director stating that he does not intend to give such undertakings, and

    (b) the period of ten days beginning with the first day after the notice under paragraph (a) of this subsection was received by the Director has expired.

(6) A notice by the Director under subsection (3), (4) or (5) of this section must either be given to the person who gave the merger notice before the period for considering the merger notice expires or be sent in a properly addressed and pre-paid letter posted to him at such time that, in the ordinary course of post, it would be delivered to him before that period expires.

(7) The Director may, at any time before the period for considering any merger notice expires, reject the notice if—

    (a) he suspects that any information given in respect of the notified arrangements, whether in the merger notice or otherwise, by the person who gave the notice or any connected person is in any material respect false or misleading,

(b) he suspects that it is not proposed to carry the notified arrangements into effect, or

(c) any prescribed information is not given in the merger notice or any information requested by notice under subsection (4) of this section is not provided within the period specified in the notice.

(8) If—

(a) under subsection (3)(b) of this section the period for considering a merger notice has been extended by a further fifteen days, but

(b) the Director has not made any recommendation to the Secretary of State under section 76(b) of this Act as to whether or not it would in the Director's opinion be expedient for the Secretary of State to make a reference to the Commission with respect to the notified arrangements,

then, during the last five of those fifteen days, the power of the Secretary of State to make a reference to the Commission with respect to the notified arrangements is not affected by the absence of any such recommendation.

(9) In determining any period for the purposes of subsections (2), (3) and (5) of this section no account shall be taken of—

(a) Saturday, Sunday, Good Friday and Christmas Day, and

(b) any day which is a bank holiday in England and Wales.

Cases where power to refer unaffected.

75C.—(1) Section 75A(3) of this Act does not prevent any reference being made to the Commission if—

(a) before the end of the period for considering the merger notice, it is rejected by the Director under section 75B(7) of this Act,

(b) before the end of that period, any of the enterprises to which the notified arrangements relate cease to be distinct from each other,

(c) any information (whether prescribed information or not) that—

(i) is, or ought to be, known to the person who gave the merger notice or any connected person, and

(ii) is material to the notified arrangements;

is not disclosed to the Secretary of State or the Director by such time before the end of that period as may be specified in regulations,

(d) at any time after the merger notice is given but before the enterprises to which the notified arrangements relate cease to be distinct from each other, any of those enterprises ceases to be distinct from any enterprise other than an enterprise to which those arrangements relate,

(e) the six months beginning with the end of the period for considering the merger notice expires without the enterprises to which the notified arrangements relate ceasing to be distinct from each other,

(f) the merger notice is withdrawn, or

(g) any information given in respect of the notified arrangements, whether in the merger notice or otherwise, by the person who gave the notice or any connected person is in any material respect false or misleading.

(2) Where—

(a) two or more transactions which have occurred or, if any arrangements are carried into effect, will occur may be treated for the purposes of a merger reference as having occurred simultaneously on a particular date, and

(b) subsection (3) of section 75A of this Act does not prevent such a reference with respect to the last of those transactions,

that subsection does not prevent such a reference with respect to any of those transactions which actually occurred less than six months before—

(i) that date, or

(ii) the actual occurrence of another of those transactions with respect to which such a reference may be made (whether or not by virtue of this subsection).

(3) In determining for the purposes of subsection (2) of this section the time at which any transaction actually occurred, no account shall be taken of any option or other conditional right until the option is exercised or the condition is satisfied.

Regulations.

75D.—(1) The Secretary of State may make regulations for the purposes of sections 75A to 75C of this Act.

(2) The regulations may, in particular—

(a) provide for section 75B(2) or (3) or section 75C(1)(e) of this Act to apply as if any reference to a period of days or months were a reference to a period specified in the regulations for the purposes of the provision in question,

(b) provide for the manner in which any merger notice is authorised or required to be given, rejected or withdrawn, and the time at which any merger notice is to be treated as received or rejected,

(c) provide for the manner in which any information requested by the Director or any other material information is authorised or required to be provided or disclosed, and the time at which such information is to be treated as provided or disclosed,

(d) provide for the manner in which any notice under section 75B of this Act is authorised or required to be given,

(e) provide for the time at which any notice under section 75B(5)(a) of this Act is to be treated as received,

(f) provide for the address which is to be treated for the purposes of section 75B(6) of this Act and of the regulations as a person's proper address,

(g) provide for the time at which any fee is to be treated as paid, and

(h) provide that a person is, or is not, to be treated, in such circumstances as may be specified in the regulations, as acting on behalf of a person authorised by regulations to give a merger notice or a person who has given such a notice.

(3) The regulations may make different provision for different cases.

(4) Regulations under this section shall be made by statutory instrument.

Interpretation of sections 75A to 75D.

75E. In this section and sections 75A to 75D of this Act—

"connected person", in relation to the person who gave a merger notice, means—

(a) any person who, for the purposes of section 77 of this Act, is associated with him, or

(b) any subsidiary of the person who gave the merger notice or of any person so associated with him,

"merger notice" is to be interpreted in accordance with section 75A(5) of this Act,

"notified arrangements" means the arrangements mentioned in the merger notice or arrangements not differing from them in any material respect,

"prescribed" means prescribed by the Director by notice having effect for the time being and published in the London, Edinburgh and Belfast Gazettes,

"regulations" means regulations under section 75D of this Act, and "subsidiary" has the meaning given by section 75(4K) of this Act,

and references to the enterprises to which the notified arrangements relate are references to those enterprises that would have ceased to be distinct from one another if the arrangements mentioned in the merger notice in question had been carried into effect at the time when the notice was given.

Power to amend sections 75B to 75D.

75F.—(1) The Secretary of State may, for the purpose of determining the effect of giving a merger notice and the steps which may be or are to be taken by any person in connection with such a notice, by regulations made by statutory instrument amend sections 75B to 75D of this Act.

(2) The regulations may make different provision for different cases and may contain such incidental and supplementary provisions as the Secretary of State thinks fit.

(3) No regulations shall be made under this section unless a draft of the regulations has been laid before and approved by resolution of each House of Parliament.".

Undertakings as alternative to merger reference. 1973 c. 41.

147. In Part V of the Fair Trading Act 1973 after the sections inserted by section 146 of this Act there is inserted—

"Undertakings as alternative to merger reference

Acceptance of undertakings.

75G.—(1) Where—

(a) the Secretary of State has power to make a merger reference to the Commission under section 64 or 75 of this Act,

(b) the Director has made a recommendation to the Secretary of State under section 76 of this Act that such a reference should be made, and

(c) the Director has (in making that recommendation or subsequently) given advice to the Secretary of State specifying particular effects adverse to the public interest which in his opinion the creation of the merger situation qualifying for investigation may have or might be expected to have,

the Secretary of State may, instead of making a merger reference to the Commission, accept from such of the parties concerned as he considers appropriate undertakings complying with subsections (2) and (3) of this section to take specified action which the Secretary of State considers appropriate to remedy or prevent the effects adverse to the public interest specified in the advice.

(2) The undertakings must provide for one or more of the following—

    (a) the division of a business by the sale of any part of the undertaking or assets or otherwise (for which purpose all the activities carried on by way of business by any one person or by any two or more interconnected bodies corporate may be treated as a single business),

    (b) the division of a group of interconnected bodies corporate, and

    (c) the separation, by the sale of any part of the undertaking or assets concerned or other means, of enterprises which are under common control otherwise than by reason of their being enterprises of interconnected bodies corporate.

(3) The undertakings may also contain provision—

    (a) preventing or restricting the doing of things which might prevent or impede the division or separation,

    (b) as to the carrying on of any activities or the safeguarding of any assets until the division or separation is effected,

    (c) for any matters necessary to effect or take account of the division or separation, and

    (d) for enabling the Secretary of State to ascertain whether the undertakings are being fulfilled.

(4) If the Secretary of State has accepted one or more undertakings under this section, no reference may be made to the Commission with respect to the creation or possible creation of the merger situation qualifying for investigation by reference to which the undertakings were accepted, except in a case falling within subsection (5) of this section.

(5) Subsection (4) of this section does not prevent a reference being made to the Commission if material facts about the arrangements or transactions, or proposed arrangements or transactions, in consequence of which the enterprises concerned ceased or may cease to be distinct enterprises were not—

    (a) notified to the Secretary of State or the Director, or

    (b) made public,

before the undertakings were accepted.

(6) In subsection (5) of this section "made public" has the same meaning as in section 64 of this Act.

Publication of undertakings.

75H.—(1) The Secretary of State shall arrange for—

    (a) any undertaking accepted by him under section 75G of this Act,

F

(b) the advice given by the Director for the purposes of subsection (1)(c) of that section in any case where such an undertaking has been accepted, and

(c) any variation or release of such an undertaking,

to be published in such manner as he may consider appropriate.

(2) In giving advice for the purposes of section 75G(1)(c) of this Act the Director shall have regard to the need for excluding, so far as practicable, any matter to which subsection (4) of this section applies.

(3) The Secretary of State shall exclude from any such advice as published under this section—

(a) any matter to which subsection (4) of this section applies and in relation to which he is satisfied that its publication in the advice would not be in the public interest, and

(b) any other matter in relation to which he is satisfied that its publication in the advice would be against the public interest.

(4) This subsection applies to—

(a) any matter which relates to the private affairs of an individual, where publication of that matter would or might, in the opinion of the Director or the Secretary of State, as the case may be, seriously and prejudicially affect the interests of that individual, and

(b) any matter which relates specifically to the affairs of a particular body of persons, whether corporate or unincorporate, where publication of that matter would or might, in the opinion of the Director or the Secretary of State, as the case may be, seriously and prejudicially affect the interests of that body, unless in his opinion the inclusion of that matter relating specifically to that body is necessary for the purposes of the advice.

(5) For the purposes of the law relating to defamation, absolute privilege shall attach to any advice given by the Director for the purposes of section 75G(1)(c) of this Act.

Review of undertakings.

75J. Where an undertaking has been accepted by the Secretary of State under section 75G of this Act, it shall be the duty of the Director—

(a) to keep under review the carrying out of that undertaking, and from time to time consider whether, by reason of any change of circumstances, the undertaking is no longer appropriate and either—

(i) one or more of the parties to it can be released from it, or

(ii) it needs to be varied or to be superseded by a new undertaking, and

(b) if it appears to him that the undertaking has not been or is not being fulfilled, that any person can be so released or that the undertaking needs to be varied or superseded, to give such advice to the Secretary of State as he may think proper in the circumstances.

Order of Secretary of State where undertaking not fulfilled.

75K.—(1) The provisions of this section shall have effect where it appears to the Secretary of State that an undertaking accepted by him under section 75G of this Act has not been, is not being or will not be fulfilled.

(2) The Secretary of State may by order made by statutory instrument exercise such one or more of the powers specified in paragraphs 9A and 12 to 12C and Part II of Schedule 8 to this Act as he may consider it requisite to exercise for the purpose of remedying or preventing the adverse effects specified in the advice given by the Director for the purposes of section 75G(1)(c) of this Act; and those powers may be so exercised to such extent and in such manner as the Secretary of State considers requisite for that purpose.

(3) In determining whether, or to what extent or in what manner, to exercise any of those powers, the Secretary of State shall take into account any advice given by the Director under section 75J(b) of this Act.

(4) The provision contained in an order under this section may be different from that contained in the undertaking.

(5) On the making of an order under this section, the undertaking and any other undertaking accepted under section 75G of this Act by reference to the same merger situation qualifying for investigation are released by virtue of this section.".

148. After section 93 of the Fair Trading Act 1973 there is inserted—

Enforcement of undertakings.
1973 c. 41.

"Enforcement of undertakings.

93A.—(1) This section applies where a person (in this section referred to as "the responsible person") has given an undertaking which—

(a) has been accepted by the Secretary of State under section 75G of this Act,

(b) has been accepted by the appropriate Minister or Ministers under section 88 of this Act after the commencement of this section, or

(c) has been accepted by the Director under section 4 or 9 of the Competition Act 1980 after that time.

(2) Any person may bring civil proceedings in respect of any failure, or apprehended failure, of the responsible person to fulfil the undertaking, as if the obligations imposed by the undertaking on the responsible person had been imposed by an order to which section 90 of this Act applies.".

Temporary restrictions on share dealings.

1973 c. 41.

149.—(1) In section 75 of the Fair Trading Act 1973 (reference in anticipation of merger), after subsection (4) there is inserted—

"(4A) Where a merger reference is made under this section, it shall be unlawful, except with the consent of the Secretary of State under subsection (4C) of this section—

(a) for any person carrying on any enterprise to which the reference relates or having control of any such enterprise or for any subsidiary of his, or

(b) for any person associated with him or for any subsidiary of such a person,

directly or indirectly to acquire, at any time during the period mentioned in subsection (4B) of this section, an interest in shares in a company if any enterprise to which the reference relates is carried on by or under the control of that company.

(4B) The period referred to in subsection (4A) of this section is the period beginning with the announcement by the Secretary of State of the making of the merger reference concerned and ending—

(a) where the reference is laid aside at any time, at that time,

(b) where the time (including any further period) allowed to the Commission for making a report on the reference expires without their having made such a report, on the expiration of that time,

(c) where a report of the Commission on the reference not including such conclusions as are referred to in section 73(1)(b) of this Act is laid before Parliament, at the end of the day on which the report is so laid,

(d) where a report of the Commission on the reference including such conclusions is laid before Parliament, at the end of the period of forty days beginning with the day on which the report is so laid,

and where such a report is laid before each House on different days, it is to be treated for the purposes of this subsection as laid on the earlier day.

(4C) The consent of the Secretary of State—

(a) may be either general or special,

(b) may be revoked by the Secretary of State, and

(c) shall be published in such way as, in the opinion of the Secretary of State, to give any person entitled to the benefit of it an adequate opportunity of getting to know of it, unless in the Secretary of State's opinion publication is not necessary for that purpose.

(4D) Section 93 of this Act applies to any contravention or apprehended contravention of subsection (4A) of this section as it applies to a contravention or apprehended contravention of an order to which section 90 of this Act applies.

(4E) Subsections (4F) to (4K) of this section apply for the interpretation of subsection (4A).

(4F) The circumstances in which a person acquires an interest in shares include those where—

(a) he enters into a contract to acquire the shares (whether or not for cash),

(b) not being the registered holder, he acquires a right to exercise, or to control the exercise of, any right conferred by the holding of the shares, or

(c) he acquires a right to call for delivery of the shares to himself or to his order or to acquire an interest in the shares or assumes an obligation to acquire such an interest,

but does not include those where he acquires an interest in pursuance of an obligation assumed before the announcement by the Secretary of State of the making of the merger reference concerned.

(4G) The circumstances in which a person acquires a right mentioned in subsection (4F) of this section—

(a) include those where he acquires a right or assumes an obligation the exercise or fulfilment of which would give him that right, but

(b) does not include those where he is appointed as proxy to vote at a specified meeting of a company or of any class of its members or at any adjournment of the meeting or he is appointed by a corporation to act as its representative at any meeting of the company or of any class of its members,

and references to rights and obligations in this subsection and subsection (4F) of this section include conditional rights and conditional obligations.

(4H) Any reference to a person carrying on or having control of any enterprise includes a group of persons carrying on or having control of an enterprise and any member of such a group.

(4J) Sections 65(2) to (4) and 77(1) and (4) to (6) of this Act apply to determine whether any person or group of persons has control of any enterprise and whether persons are associated as they apply for the purposes of section 65 of this Act to determine whether enterprises are brought under common control.

(4K) "Subsidiary" has the meaning given by section 736 of the Companies Act 1985, but that section and section 736A of that Act also apply to determine whether a company is a subsidiary of an individual or of a group of persons as they apply to determine whether it is a subsidiary of a company and references to a subsidiary in subsections (8) and (9) of section 736A as so applied are to be read accordingly.

(4L) In this section—

"company" includes any body corporate, and

"share" means share in the capital of a company, and includes stock.

(4M) Nothing in subsection (4A) of this section makes anything done by a person outside the United Kingdom unlawful unless he is—

(a) a British citizen, a British Dependent Territories citizen, a British Overseas citizen or a British National (Overseas),

(b) a body corporate incorporated under the law of the United Kingdom or of a part of the United Kingdom, or

(c) a person carrying on business in the United Kingdom, either alone or in partnership with one or more other persons.".

(2) This section does not apply in relation to any merger reference made before the passing of this Act.

Obtaining control by stages.
1973 c. 41.

150.—(1) After section 66 of the Fair Trading Act 1973 there is inserted—

"Obtaining control by stages.

66A.—(1) Where an enterprise is brought under the control of a person or group of persons in the course of two or more transactions (referred to in this section as a "series of transactions") falling within subsection (2) of this section, those transactions may, if the Secretary of State or, as the case may be, the Commission thinks fit, be treated for the purposes of a merger reference as having occurred simultaneously on the date on which the latest of them occurred.

(2) The transactions falling within this subsection are—

(a) any transaction which—

       (i) enables that person or group of persons directly or indirectly to control or materially to influence the policy of any person carrying on the enterprise,

       (ii) enables that person or group of persons to do so to a greater degree, or

       (iii) is a step (whether direct or indirect) towards enabling that person or group of persons to do so, and

    (b) any transaction whereby that person or group of persons acquires a controlling interest in the enterprise or, where the enterprise is carried on by a body corporate, in that body corporate.

(3) Where a series of transactions includes a transaction falling within subsection (2)(b) of this section, any transaction occurring after the occurrence of that transaction is to be disregarded for the purposes of subsection (1) of this section.

(4) Where the period within which a series of transactions occurs exceeds two years, the transactions that may be treated as mentioned in subsection (1) of this section are any of those transactions that occur within a period of two years.

(5) Sections 65(2) to (4) and 77(1) and (4) to (6) of this Act apply for the purposes of this section to determine whether an enterprise is brought under the control of a person or group of persons and whether a transaction falls within subsection (2) of this section as they apply for the purposes of section 65 of this Act to determine whether enterprises are brought under common control.

(6) In determining for the purposes of this section the time at which any transaction occurs, no account shall be taken of any option or other conditional right until the option is exercised or the condition is satisfied.".

(2) This section does not apply in relation to any merger reference made before the passing of this Act.

151. At the end of Part VIII of the Fair Trading Act 1973 there is inserted—

False or misleading information.
1973 c. 41.

"False or misleading information.

    93B.—(1) If a person furnishes any information—

    (a) to the Secretary of State, the Director or the Commission in connection with any of their functions under Parts IV, V, VI or this Part of this Act or under the Competition Act 1980, or

(b) to the Commission in connection with the functions of the Commission under the Telecommunications Act 1984 or the Airports Act 1986,

and either he knows the information to be false or misleading in a material particular, or he furnishes the information recklessly and it is false or misleading in a material particular, he is guilty of an offence.

(2) A person who—

   (a) furnishes any information to another which he knows to be false or misleading in a material particular, or

   (b) recklessly furnishes any information to another which is false or misleading in a material particular,

knowing that the information is to be used for the purpose of furnishing information as mentioned in subsection (1)(a) or (b) of this section, is guilty of an offence.

(3) A person guilty of an offence under subsection (1) or (2) of this section is liable—

   (a) on summary conviction, to a fine not exceeding the statutory maximum, and

   (b) on conviction on indictment, to imprisonment for a term not exceeding two years or to a fine or to both.

(4) Section 129(1) of this Act does not apply to an offence under this section.".

Fees.

152.—(1) The Secretary of State may by regulations made by statutory instrument require the payment to him or to the Director of such fees as may be prescribed by the regulations in connection with the exercise by the Secretary of State, the Director and the Commission of their functions under Part V of the Fair Trading Act 1973.

1973 c. 41.

(2) The regulations may provide for fees to be payable—

   (a) in respect of—

      (i) an application for the consent of the Secretary of State under section 58(1) of the Fair Trading Act 1973 to the transfer of a newspaper or of newspaper assets, and

      (ii) a notice under section 75A(1) of that Act, and

   (b) on the occurrence of any event specified in the regulations.

(3) The events that may be specified in the regulations by virtue of subsection (2)(b) above include—

   (a) the making by the Secretary of State of a merger reference to the Commission under section 64 or 75 of the Fair Trading Act 1973,

   (b) the announcement by the Secretary of State of his decision not to make a merger reference in any case where, at the time the announcement is made, he would under one of those sections have power to make a such a reference.

(4) The regulations may also contain provision—

  (a) for ascertaining the persons by whom fees are payable,

  (b) specifying whether any fee is payable to the Secretary of State or to the Director,

  (c) for the amount of any fee to be calculated by reference to matters which may include—

    (i) in a case involving functions of the Secretary of State under sections 57 to 61 of the Fair Trading Act 1973, the number of newspapers concerned, the number of separate editions (determined in accordance with the regulations) of each newspaper and the average circulation per day of publication (within the meaning of Part V of that Act) of each newspaper, and

1973 c. 41.

    (ii) in any other case, the value (determined in accordance with the regulations) of any assets concerned,

  (d) as to the time when any fee is to be paid, and

  (e) for the repayment by the Secretary of State or the Director of the whole or part of any fee in specified circumstances.

(5) The regulations may make different provision for different cases.

(6) Subsections (2) to (5) above do not prejudice the generality of subsection (1) above.

(7) In determining the amount of any fees to be prescribed by the regulations, the Secretary of State may take into account all costs incurred by him and by the Director in respect of the exercise by him, by the Commission and by the Director of their respective functions—

  (a) under Part V of the Fair Trading Act 1973, and

  (b) under Parts I, VII and VIII of that Act in relation to merger references or other matters arising under Part V.

(8) A statutory instrument containing regulations under this section shall be subject to annulment in pursuance of a resolution of either House of Parliament.

(9) Fees paid to the Secretary of State or the Director under this section shall be paid into the Consolidated Fund.

(10) In this section—

  "the Commission",

  "the Director", and

  "merger reference",

have the same meaning as in the Fair Trading Act 1973, and "newspaper" has the same meaning as in Part V of that Act.

(11) References in this section to Part V of the Fair Trading Act 1973 and to merger references under section 64 or 75 of that Act or under that Part include sections 29 and 30 of the Water Act 1989 and any reference under section 29 of that Act.

1989 c. 15.

PART VI
Other
amendments
about mergers
and related
matters.

153. Schedule 20 to this Act has effect.

PART VII

FINANCIAL MARKETS AND INSOLVENCY

Introduction

Introduction.

154. This Part has effect for the purposes of safeguarding the operation of certain financial markets by provisions with respect to—

(a) the insolvency, winding up or default of a person party to transactions in the market (sections 155 to 172),

(b) the effectiveness or enforcement of certain charges given to secure obligations in connection with such transactions (sections 173 to 176), and

(c) rights and remedies in relation to certain property provided as cover for margin in relation to such transactions or subject to such a charge (sections 177 to 181).

Recognised investment exchanges and clearing houses

Market
contracts.

155.—(1) This Part applies to the following descriptions of contract connected with a recognised investment exchange or recognised clearing house.

The contracts are referred to in this Part as "market contracts".

(2) In relation to a recognised investment exchange, this Part applies to—

(a) contracts entered into by a member or designated non-member of the exchange which are made on or otherwise subject to the rules of the exchange; and

(b) contracts subject to the rules of the exchange entered into by the exchange for the purposes of or in connection with the provision of clearing services.

A "designated non-member" means a person in respect of whom action may be taken under the default rules of the exchange but who is not a member of the exchange.

(3) In relation to a recognised clearing house, this Part applies to contracts subject to the rules of the clearing house entered into by the clearing house for the purposes of or in connection with the provision of clearing services for a recognised investment exchange.

(4) The Secretary of State may by regulations make further provision as to the contracts to be treated as "market contracts", for the purposes of this Part, in relation to a recognised investment exchange or recognised clearing house.

(5) The regulations may add to, amend or repeal the provisions of subsections (2) and (3) above.

156.—(1) The Financial Services Act 1986 shall have effect as if the requirements set out in Schedule 21 to this Act (the "additional requirements") were among those specified in that Act for recognition of an investment exchange or clearing house.

(2) In particular, that Act shall have effect—

    (a) as if the requirements set out in Part I of that Schedule were among those specified in Schedule 4 to that Act (requirements for recognition of UK investment exchange),

    (b) as if the requirements set out in Part II of that Schedule were among those specified in section 39(4) of that Act (requirements for recognition of UK clearing house), and

    (c) as if the requirement set out in Part III of that Schedule was among those specified in section 40(2) of that Act (requirements for recognition of overseas investment exchange or clearing house).

(3) The additional requirements do not affect the status of an investment exchange or clearing house recognised before the commencement of this section, but if the Secretary of State is of the opinion that any of those requirements is not met in the case of such a body, he shall within one month of commencement give notice to the body stating his opinion.

(4) Where the Secretary of State gives such a notice, he shall not—

    (a) take action to revoke the recognition of such a body on the ground that any of the additional requirements is not met, unless he considers it essential to do so in the interests of investors, or

    (b) apply on any such ground for a compliance order under section 12 of the Financial Services Act 1986,

until after the end of the period of six months beginning with the date on which the notice was given.

(5) The Secretary of State may extend, or further extend, that period if he considers there is good reason to do so.

157.—(1) A recognised UK investment exchange or recognised UK clearing house shall give the Secretary of State at least 14 days' notice of any proposal to amend, revoke or add to its default rules; and the Secretary of State may within 14 days from receipt of the notice direct the exchange or clearing house not to proceed with the proposal, in whole or in part.

(2) A direction under this section may be varied or revoked.

(3) Any amendment or revocation of, or addition to, the default rules of an exchange or clearing house in breach of a direction under this section is ineffective.

158.—(1) The general law of insolvency has effect in relation to market contracts, and action taken under the rules of a recognised investment exchange or recognised clearing house with respect to such contracts, subject to the provisions of sections 159 to 165.

(margin notes:)

PART VII
Additional requirements for recognition: default rules, &c.
1986 c. 60.

Change in default rules.

Modifications of the law of insolvency.

(2) So far as those provisions relate to insolvency proceedings in respect of a person other than a defaulter, they apply in relation to—

(a) proceedings in respect of a member or designated non-member of a recognised investment exchange or a member of a recognised clearing house, and

(b) proceedings in respect of a party to a market contract begun after a recognised investment exchange or recognised clearing house has taken action under its default rules in relation to a person party to the contract as principal,

but not in relation to any other insolvency proceedings, notwithstanding that rights or liabilities arising from market contracts fall to be dealt with in the proceedings.

(3) The reference in subsection (2)(b) to the beginning of insolvency proceedings is to—

(a) the presentation of a bankruptcy petition or a petition for sequestration of a person's estate, or

(b) the presentation of a petition for an administration order or a winding-up petition or the passing of a resolution for voluntary winding up, or

(c) the appointment of an administrative receiver.

(4) The Secretary of State may make further provision by regulations modifying the law of insolvency in relation to the matters mentioned in subsection (1).

(5) The regulations may add to, amend or repeal the provisions mentioned in subsection (1), and any other provision of this Part as it applies for the purposes of those provisions, or provide that those provisions have effect subject to such additions, exceptions or adaptations as are specified in the regulations.

Proceedings of exchange or clearing house take precedence over insolvency procedures.

159.—(1) None of the following shall be regarded as to any extent invalid at law on the ground of inconsistency with the law relating to the distribution of the assets of a person on bankruptcy, winding up or sequestration, or in the administration of an insolvent estate—

(a) a market contract,

(b) the default rules of a recognised investment exchange or recognised clearing house,

(c) the rules of a recognised investment exchange or recognised clearing house as to the settlement of market contracts not dealt with under its default rules.

1986 c. 45.
1985 c. 66.

(2) The powers of a relevant office-holder in his capacity as such, and the powers of the court under the Insolvency Act 1986 or the Bankruptcy (Scotland) Act 1985 shall not be exercised in such a way as to prevent or interfere with—

(a) the settlement in accordance with the rules of a recognised investment exchange or recognised clearing house of a market contract not dealt with under its default rules, or

(b) any action taken under the default rules of such an exchange or clearing house.

This does not prevent a relevant office-holder from afterwards seeking to recover any amount under section 163(4) or 164(4) or prevent the court from afterwards making any such order or decree as is mentioned in section 165(1) or (2) (but subject to subsections (3) and (4) of that section).

(3) Nothing in the following provisions of this Part shall be construed as affecting the generality of the above provisions.

(4) A debt or other liability arising out of a market contract which is the subject of default proceedings may not be proved in a winding up or bankruptcy, or in Scotland claimed in a winding up or sequestration, until the completion of the default proceedings.

A debt or other liability which by virtue of this subsection may not be proved or claimed shall not be taken into account for the purposes of any set-off until the completion of the default proceedings.

(5) For the purposes of subsection (4) the default proceedings shall be taken to be completed in relation to a person when a report is made under section 162 stating the sum (if any) certified to be due to or from him.

160.—(1) It is the duty of—

    (a) any person who has or had control of any assets of a defaulter, and

    (b) any person who has or had control of any documents of or relating to a defaulter,

to give a recognised investment exchange or recognised clearing house such assistance as it may reasonably require for the purposes of its default proceedings.

This applies notwithstanding any duty of that person under the enactments relating to insolvency.

(2) A person shall not under this section be required to provide any information or produce any document which he would be entitled to refuse to provide or produce on grounds of legal professional privilege in proceedings in the High Court or on grounds of confidentiality as between client and professional legal adviser in proceedings in the Court of Session.

(3) Where original documents are supplied in pursuance of this section, the exchange or clearing house shall return them forthwith after the completion of the relevant default proceedings, and shall in the meantime allow reasonable access to them to the person by whom they were supplied and to any person who would be entitled to have access to them if they were still in the control of the person by whom they were supplied.

(4) The expenses of a relevant office-holder in giving assistance under this section are recoverable as part of the expenses incurred by him in the discharge of his duties; and he shall not be required under this section to take any action which involves expenses which cannot be so recovered, unless the exchange or clearing house undertakes to meet them.

There shall be treated as expenses of his such reasonable sums as he may determine in respect of time spent in giving the assistance.

Duty to give assistance for purposes of default proceedings.

(5) The Secretary of State may by regulations make further provision as to the duties of persons to give assistance to a recognised investment exchange or recognised clearing house for the purposes of its default proceedings, and the duties of the exchange or clearing house with respect to information supplied to it.

The regulations may add to, amend or repeal the provisions of subsections (1) to (4) above.

(6) In this section "document" includes information recorded in any form.

Supplementary provisions as to default proceedings.

161.—(1) If the court is satisfied on an application by a relevant office-holder that a party to a market contract with a defaulter intends to dissipate or apply his assets so as to prevent the office-holder recovering such sums as may become due upon the completion of the default proceedings, the court may grant such interlocutory relief (in Scotland, such interim order) as it thinks fit.

(2) A liquidator or trustee of a defaulter or, in Scotland, a permanent trustee on the sequestrated estate of the defaulter shall not—

(a) declare or pay any dividend to the creditors, or

(b) return any capital to contributories,

unless he has retained what he reasonably considers to be an adequate reserve in respect of any claims arising as a result of the default proceedings of the exchange or clearing house concerned.

(3) The court may on an application by a relevant office-holder make such order as it thinks fit altering or dispensing from compliance with such of the duties of his office as are affected by the fact that default proceedings are pending or could be taken, or have been or could have been taken.

1986 c. 45.

1985 c. 66.
1987 c. 18.

(4) Nothing in section 10(1)(c), 11(3), 126, 128, 130, 185 or 285 of the Insolvency Act 1986 (which restrict the taking of certain legal proceedings and other steps), and nothing in any rule of law in Scotland to the like effect as the said section 285, in the Bankruptcy (Scotland) Act 1985 or in the Debtors (Scotland) Act 1987 as to the effect of sequestration, shall affect any action taken by an exchange or clearing house for the purpose of its default proceedings.

Duty to report on completion of default proceedings.

162.—(1) A recognised investment exchange or recognised clearing house shall, on the completion of proceedings under its default rules, report to the Secretary of State on its proceedings stating in respect of each creditor or debtor the sum certified by them to be payable from or to the defaulter or, as the case may be, the fact that no sum is payable.

(2) The exchange or clearing house may make a single report or may make reports from time to time as proceedings are completed with respect to the transactions affecting particular persons.

(3) The exchange or clearing house shall supply a copy of every report under this section to the defaulter and to any relevant office-holder acting in relation to him or his estate.

(4) When a report under this section is received by the Secretary of State, he shall publish notice of that fact in such manner as he thinks appropriate for bringing it to the attention of creditors and debtors of the defaulter.

(5) An exchange or clearing house shall make available for inspection by a creditor or debtor of the defaulter so much of any report by it under this section as relates to the sum (if any) certified to be due to or from him or to the method by which that sum was determined.

(6) Any such person may require the exchange or clearing house, on payment of such reasonable fee as the exchange or clearing house may determine, to provide him with a copy of any part of a report which he is entitled to inspect.

163.—(1) The following provisions apply with respect to the net sum certified by a recognised investment exchange or recognised clearing house, upon proceedings under its default rules being duly completed in accordance with this Part, to be payable by or to a defaulter.

Net sum payable on completion of default proceedings.

(2) If, in England and Wales, a bankruptcy or winding-up order has been made, or a resolution for voluntary winding up has been passed, the debt—

(a) is provable in the bankruptcy or winding up or, as the case may be, is payable to the relevant office-holder, and

(b) shall be taken into account, where appropriate, under section 323 of the Insolvency Act 1986 (mutual dealings and set-off) or the corresponding provision applicable in the case of winding up,

1986 c. 45.

in the same way as a debt due before the commencement of the bankruptcy, the date on which the body corporate goes into liquidation (within the meaning of section 247 of the Insolvency Act 1986) or, in the case of a partnership, the date of the winding-up order.

(3) If, in Scotland, an award of sequestration or a winding-up order has been made, or a resolution for voluntary winding up has been passed, the debt—

(a) may be claimed in the sequestration or winding up or, as the case may be, is payable to the relevant office-holder, and

(b) shall be taken into account for the purposes of any rule of law relating to set-off applicable in sequestration or winding up,

in the same way as a debt due before the date of sequestration (within the meaning of section 73(1) of the Bankruptcy (Scotland) Act 1985) or the commencement of the winding up (within the meaning of section 129 of the Insolvency Act 1986).

1985 c. 66.

(4) However, where (or to the extent that) a sum is taken into account by virtue of subsection (2)(b) or (3)(b) which arises from a contract entered into at a time when the creditor had notice—

(a) that a bankruptcy petition or, in Scotland, a petition for sequestration was pending, or

(b) that a meeting of creditors had been summoned under section 98 of the Insolvency Act 1986 or that a winding-up petition was pending,

the value of any profit to him arising from the sum being so taken into account (or being so taken into account to that extent) is recoverable from him by the relevant office-holder unless the court directs otherwise.

(5) Subsection (4) does not apply in relation to a sum arising from a contract effected under the default rules of a recognised investment exchange or recognised clearing house.

(6) Any sum recoverable by virtue of subsection (4) ranks for priority, in the event of the insolvency of the person from whom it is due, immediately before preferential or, in Scotland, preferred debts.

Disclaimer of property, rescission of contracts, &c.

164.—(1) Sections 178, 186, 315 and 345 of the Insolvency Act 1986 (power to disclaim onerous property and court's power to order rescission of contracts, &c.) do not apply in relation to—

   (a) a market contract, or

   (b) a contract effected by the exchange or clearing house for the purpose of realising property provided as margin in relation to market contracts.

In the application of this subsection in Scotland, the reference to sections 178, 315 and 345 shall be construed as a reference to any rule of law having the like effect as those sections.

(2) In Scotland, a permanent trustee on the sequestrated estate of a defaulter or a liquidator is bound by any market contract to which that defaulter is a party and by any contract as is mentioned in subsection (1)(b) above notwithstanding section 42 of the Bankruptcy (Scotland) Act 1985 or any rule of law to the like effect applying in liquidations.

1985 c. 66.

(3) Sections 127 and 284 of the Insolvency Act 1986 (avoidance of property dispositions effected after commencement of winding up or presentation of bankruptcy petition), and section 32(8) of the Bankruptcy (Scotland) Act 1985 (effect of dealing with debtor relating to estate vested in permanent trustee), do not apply to—

   (a) a market contract, or any disposition of property in pursuance of such a contract,

   (b) the provision of margin in relation to market contracts,

   (c) a contract effected by the exchange or clearing house for the purpose of realising property provided as margin in relation to a market contract, or any disposition of property in pursuance of such a contract, or

   (d) any disposition of property in accordance with the rules of the exchange or clearing house as to the application of property provided as margin.

(4) However, where—

   (a) a market contract is entered into by a person who has notice that a petition has been presented for the winding up or bankruptcy or sequestration of the estate of the other party to the contract, or

(b) margin in relation to a market contract is accepted by a person who has notice that such a petition has been presented in relation to the person by whom or on whose behalf the margin is provided,

the value of any profit to him arising from the contract or, as the case may be, the amount or value of the margin is recoverable from him by the relevant office-holder unless the court directs otherwise.

(5) Subsection (4)(a) does not apply where the person entering into the contract is a recognised investment exchange or recognised clearing house acting in accordance with its rules, or where the contract is effected under the default rules of such an exchange or clearing house; but subsection (4)(b) applies in relation to the provision of margin in relation to such a contract.

(6) Any sum recoverable by virtue of subsection (4) ranks for priority, in the event of the insolvency of the person from whom it is due, immediately before preferential or, in Scotland, preferred debts.

165.—(1) No order shall be made in relation to a transaction to which this section applies under—

Adjustment of prior transactions.

(a) section 238 or 339 of the Insolvency Act 1986 (transactions at an under-value),

1986 c. 45.

(b) section 239 or 340 of that Act (preferences), or

(c) section 423 of that Act (transactions defrauding creditors).

(2) As respects Scotland, no decree shall be granted in relation to any such transaction—

(a) under section 34 or 36 of the Bankruptcy (Scotland) Act 1985 or section 242 or 243 of the Insolvency Act 1986 (gratuitous alienations and unfair preferences), or

1985 c. 66.

(b) at common law on grounds of gratuitous alienations or fraudulent preferences.

(3) This section applies to—

(a) a market contract to which a recognised investment exchange or recognised clearing house is a party or which is entered into under its default rules, and

(b) a disposition of property in pursuance of such a market contract.

(4) Where margin is provided in relation to a market contract and (by virtue of subsection (3)(a) or otherwise) no such order or decree as is mentioned in subsection (1) or (2) has been, or could be, made in relation to that contract, this section applies to—

(a) the provision of the margin,

(b) any contract effected by the exchange or clearing house in question for the purpose of realising the property provided as margin, and

(c) any disposition of property in accordance with the rules of the exchange or clearing house as to the application of property provided as margin.

166.—(1) The powers conferred by this section are exercisable in relation to a recognised UK investment exchange or recognised UK clearing house.

Powers of Secretary of State to give directions.

(2) Where in any case an exchange or clearing house has not taken action under its default rules—

> (a) if it appears to the Secretary of State that it could take action, he may direct it to do so, and
>
> (b) if it appears to the Secretary of State that it is proposing to take or may take action, he may direct it not to do so.

(3) Before giving such a direction the Secretary of State shall consult the exchange or clearing house in question; and he shall not give a direction unless he is satisfied, in the light of that consultation—

> (a) in the case of a direction to take action, that failure to take action would involve undue risk to investors or other participants in the market, or
>
> (b) in the case of a direction not to take action, that the taking of action would be premature or otherwise undesirable in the interests of investors or other participants in the market.

(4) A direction shall specify the grounds on which it is given.

(5) A direction not to take action may be expressed to have effect until the giving of a further direction (which may be a direction to take action or simply revoking the earlier direction).

(6) No direction shall be given not to take action if, in relation to the person in question—

> (a) a bankruptcy order or an award of sequestration of his estate has been made, or an interim receiver or interim trustee has been appointed, or
>
> (b) a winding up order has been made, a resolution for voluntary winding up has been passed or an administrator, administrative receiver or provisional liquidator has been appointed;

and any previous direction not to take action shall cease to have effect on the making or passing of any such order, award or appointment.

(7) Where an exchange or clearing house has taken or been directed to take action under its default rules, the Secretary of State may direct it to do or not to do such things (being things which it has power to do under its default rules) as are specified in the direction.

The Secretary of State shall not give such a direction unless he is satisfied that it will not impede or frustrate the proper and efficient conduct of the default proceedings.

(8) A direction under this section is enforceable, on the application of the Secretary of State, by injunction or, in Scotland, by an order under section 45 of the Court of Session Act 1988; and where an exchange or clearing house has not complied with a direction, the court may make such order as it thinks fit for restoring the position to what it would have been if the direction had been complied with.

1988 c. 36.

Application to determine whether default proceedings to be taken.

167.—(1) Where there has been made or passed in relation to a member or designated non-member of a recognised investment exchange or a member of a recognised clearing house—

> (a) a bankruptcy order or an award of sequestration of his estate, or an order appointing an interim receiver of his property, or

(b) an administration or winding up order, a resolution for voluntary winding up or an order appointing a provisional liquidator,

and the exchange or clearing house has not taken action under its default rules in consequence of the order, award or resolution or the matters giving rise to it, a relevant office-holder appointed by, or in consequence of or in connection with, the order, award or resolution may apply to the Secretary of State.

(2) The application shall specify the exchange or clearing house concerned and the grounds on which it is made.

(3) On receipt of the application the Secretary of State shall notify the exchange or clearing house, and unless within three business days after the day on which the notice is received the exchange or clearing house—

(a) takes action under its default rules, or

(b) notifies the Secretary of State that it proposes to do so forthwith,

then, subject as follows, the provisions of sections 158 to 165 above do not apply in relation to market contracts to which the member or designated non-member in question is a party or to anything done by the exchange or clearing house for the purposes of, or in connection with, the settlement of any such contract.

For this purpose a "business day" means any day which is not a Saturday or Sunday, Christmas Day, Good Friday or a bank holiday in any part of the United Kingdom under the Banking and Financial Dealings Act 1971.

(4) The provisions of sections 158 to 165 are not disapplied if before the end of the period mentioned in subsection (3) the Secretary of State gives the exchange or clearing house a direction under section 166(2)(a) (direction to take action under default rules).

No such direction may be given after the end of that period.

(5) If the exchange or clearing house notifies the Secretary of State that it proposes to take action under its default rules forthwith, it shall do so; and that duty is enforceable, on the application of the Secretary of State, by injunction or, in Scotland, by an order under section 45 of the Court of Session Act 1988.

168.—(1) Section 114 of the Financial Services Act 1986 (power to transfer functions to designated agency) applies to the functions of the Secretary of State under this Part in relation to a UK investment exchange or clearing house, with the exception of his functions with respect to the making of orders and regulations.

(2) If immediately before the commencement of this section—

(a) a designated agency is exercising all functions in relation to such bodies which are capable of being transferred under that section, and

(b) no draft order is lying before Parliament resuming any of those functions,

the order bringing this section into force shall have effect as a delegation order made under that section transferring to that agency all the functions which may be transferred by virtue of this section.

(3) The Secretary of State may—

(a) in the circumstances mentioned in subsection (3), (4) or (5) of section 115 of the Financial Services Act 1986, or

(b) if it appears to him that a designated agency is unable or unwilling to discharge all or any of the functions under this Part which have been transferred to it,

make an order under that section resuming all functions under this Part which have been transferred to the agency.

This does not affect his power to make an order under subsection (1) or (2) of that section with respect to such functions.

Supplementary provisions.

169.—(1) Section 61 of the Financial Services Act 1986 (injunctions and restitution orders) applies in relation to a contravention of any provision of the rules of a recognised investment exchange or recognised clearing house relating to the matters mentioned in Schedule 21 to this Act as it applies in relation to a contravention of any provision of such rules relating to the carrying on of investment business.

(2) The following provisions of the Financial Services Act 1986—

section 12 (compliance orders), as it applies by virtue of section 37(8) or 39(8),

section 37(7)(b) (revocation of recognition of UK investment exchange), and

section 39(7)(b) (revocation of recognition of UK clearing house),

apply in relation to a failure by a recognised investment exchange or recognised clearing house to comply with an obligation under this Part as to a failure to comply with an obligation under that Act.

(3) Where the recognition of an investment exchange or clearing house is revoked under the Financial Services Act 1986, the Secretary of State may, before or after the revocation order, give such directions as he thinks fit with respect to the continued application of the provisions of this Part, with such exceptions, additions and adaptations as may be specified in the direction, in relation to cases where a relevant event of any description specified in the directions occurred before the revocation order takes effect.

(4) The references in sections 119 and 121 of the Financial Services Act 1986 (competition) to what is necessary for the protection of investors shall be construed as including references to what is necessary for the purposes of this Part.

(5) Section 204 of the Financial Services Act 1986 (service of notices) applies in relation to a notice, direction or other document required or authorised by or under this Part to be given to or served on any person other than the Secretary of State.

Other exchanges and clearing houses

Certain overseas exchanges and clearing houses.

170.—(1) The Secretary of State may by regulations provide that this Part applies in relation to contracts connected with an overseas investment exchange or clearing house which is approved by him in accordance with such procedures as may be specified in the regulations, as satisfying such requirements as may be so specified, as it applies in relation to contracts connected with a recognised investment exchange or clearing house.

(2) The Secretary of State shall not approve an overseas investment exchange or clearing house unless he is satisfied—

  (a) that the rules and practices of the body, together with the law of the country in which the body's head office is situated, provide adequate procedures for dealing with the default of persons party to contracts connected with the body, and

  (b) that it is otherwise appropriate to approve the body.

(3) The reference in subsection (2)(a) to default is to a person being unable to meet his obligations.

(4) The regulations may apply in relation to the approval of a body under this section such of the provisions of the Financial Services Act 1986 as the Secretary of State considers appropriate.

1986 c. 60.

(5) The Secretary of State may make regulations which, in relation to a body which is so approved—

  (a) apply such of the provisions of the Financial Services Act 1986 as the Secretary of State considers appropriate, and

  (b) provide that the provisions of this Part apply with such exceptions, additions and adaptations as appear to the Secretary of State to be necessary or expedient;

and different provision may be made with respect to different bodies or descriptions of body.

(6) Where the regulations apply any provisions of the Financial Services Act 1986, they may provide that those provisions apply with such exceptions, additions and adaptations as appear to the Secretary of State to be necessary or expedient.

171.—(1) The Secretary of State may by regulations provide that this Part applies to contracts of any specified description in relation to which settlement arrangements are provided by a person for the time being included in a list maintained by the Bank of England for the purposes of this section, as it applies to contracts connected with a recognised investment exchange or recognised clearing house.

Certain money market institutions.

(2) The Secretary of State shall not make any such regulations unless he is satisfied, having regard to the extent to which the contracts in question—

  (a) involve, or are likely to involve, investments falling within paragraph 2 of Schedule 5 to the Financial Services Act 1986 (money market investments), or

641 C19

  (b) are otherwise of a kind dealt in by persons supervised by the Bank of England,

that it is appropriate that the arrangements should be subject to the supervision of the Bank of England.

(3) The approval of the Treasury is required for—

  (a) the conditions imposed by the Bank of England for admission to the list maintained by it for the purposes of this section, and

(b) the arrangements for a person's admission to and removal from the list;

and any regulations made under this section shall cease to have effect if the approval of the Treasury is withdrawn, but without prejudice to their having effect again if approval is given for fresh conditions or arrangements.

(4) The Bank of England shall publish the list as for the time being in force and provide a certified copy of it at the request of any person wishing to refer to it in legal proceedings.

A certified copy shall be evidence (in Scotland, sufficient evidence) of the contents of the list; and a copy purporting to be certified by or on behalf of the Bank shall be deemed to have been duly certified unless the contrary is shown.

(5) Regulations under this section may, in relation to a person included in the list—

1986 c. 60.

(a) apply, with such exceptions, additions and adaptations as appear to the Secretary of State to be necessary or expedient, such of the provisions of the Financial Services Act 1986 as he considers appropriate, and

(b) provide that the provisions of this Part apply with such exceptions, additions and adaptations as appear to the Secretary of State to be necessary or expedient.

(6) Before making any regulations under this section, the Secretary of State shall consult the Treasury and the Bank of England.

1987 c. 22.

(7) In section 84(1) of the Banking Act 1987 (disclosure of information obtained under that Act), in the Table showing the authorities to which, and functions for the purposes of which, disclosure may be made, at the end add—

"A person included in the list maintained by the Bank for the purposes of section 171 of the Companies Act 1989.	Functions under settlement arrangements to which regulations under that section relate.".

Settlement arrangements provided by the Bank of England.

172.—(1) The Secretary of State may by regulations provide that this Part applies to contracts of any specified description in relation to which settlement arrangements are provided by the Bank of England, as it applies to contracts connected with a recognised investment exchange or recognised clearing house.

(2) Regulations under this section may provide that the provisions of this Part apply with such exceptions, additions and adaptations as appear to the Secretary of State to be necessary or expedient.

(3) Before making any regulations under this section, the Secretary of State shall consult the Treasury and the Bank of England.

Market charges

Market charges.

173.—(1) In this Part "market charge" means a charge, whether fixed or floating, granted—

(a) in favour of a recognised investment exchange, for the purpose of securing debts or liabilities arising in connection with the settlement of market contracts,

(b) in favour of a recognised clearing house, for the purpose of securing debts or liabilities arising in connection with their ensuring the performance of market contracts, or

(c) in favour of a person who agrees to make payments as a result of the transfer of specified securities made through the medium of a computer-based system established by the Bank of England and The Stock Exchange, for the purpose of securing debts or liabilities of the transferee arising in connection therewith.

(2) Where a charge is granted partly for purposes specified in subsection (1)(a), (b) or (c) and partly for other purposes, it is a "market charge" so far as it has effect for the specified purposes.

(3) In subsection (1)(c)—

"specified securities" means securities for the time being specified in the list in Schedule 1 to the Stock Transfer Act 1982, and includes any right to such securities; and   1982 c. 41.

"transfer", in relation to any such securities or right, means a transfer of the beneficial interest.

(4) The Secretary of State may by regulations make further provision as to the charges granted in favour of any such person as is mentioned in subsection (1)(a), (b) or (c) which are to be treated as "market charges" for the purposes of this Part; and the regulations may add to, amend or repeal the provisions of subsections (1) to (3) above.

(5) The regulations may provide that a charge shall or shall not be treated as a market charge if or to the extent that it secures obligations of a specified description, is a charge over property of a specified description or contains provisions of a specified description.

(6) Before making regulations under this section in relation to charges granted in favour of a person within subsection (1)(c), the Secretary of State shall consult the Treasury and the Bank of England.

174.—(1) The general law of insolvency has effect in relation to market charges and action taken in enforcing them subject to the provisions of section 175.   Modifications of the law of insolvency.

(2) The Secretary of State may by regulations make further provision modifying the law of insolvency in relation to the matters mentioned in subsection (1).

(3) The regulations may add to, amend or repeal the provisions mentioned in subsection (1), and any other provision of this Part as it applies for the purposes of those provisions, or provide that those provisions have effect with such exceptions, additions or adaptations as are specified in the regulations.

(4) The regulations may make different provision for cases defined by reference to the nature of the charge, the nature of the property subject to it, the circumstances, nature or extent of the obligations secured by it or any other relevant factor.

(5) Before making regulations under this section in relation to charges granted in favour of a person within section 173(1)(c), the Secretary of State shall consult the Treasury and the Bank of England.

175.—(1) The following provisions of the Insolvency Act 1986 (which relate to administration orders and administrators) do not apply in relation to a market charge—

(a) sections 10(1)(b) and 11(3)(c) (restriction on enforcement of security while petition for administration order pending or order in force), and

(b) section 15(1) and (2) (power of administrator to deal with charged property);

and section 11(2) of that Act (receiver to vacate office when so required by administrator) does not apply to a receiver appointed under a market charge.

(2) However, where a market charge falls to be enforced after an administration order has been made or a petition for an administration order has been presented, and there exists another charge over some or all of the same property ranking in priority to or *pari passu* with the market charge, the court may order that there shall be taken after enforcement of the market charge such steps as the court may direct for the purpose of ensuring that the chargee under the other charge is not prejudiced by the enforcement of the market charge.

(3) The following provisions of the Insolvency Act 1986 (which relate to the powers of receivers) do not apply in relation to a market charge—

(a) section 43 (power of administrative receiver to dispose of charged property), and

(b) section 61 (power of receiver in Scotland to dispose of an interest in property).

(4) Sections 127 and 284 of the Insolvency Act 1986 (avoidance of property dispositions effected after commencement of winding up or presentation of bankruptcy petition), and section 32(8) of the Bankruptcy (Scotland) Act 1985 (effect of dealing with debtor relating to estate vested in permanent trustee), do not apply to a disposition of property as a result of which the property becomes subject to a market charge or any transaction pursuant to which that disposition is made.

(5) However, if a person (other than the chargee under the market charge) who is party to a disposition mentioned in subsection (4) has notice at the time of the disposition that a petition has been presented for the winding up or bankruptcy or sequestration of the estate of the party making the disposition, the value of any profit to him arising from the disposition is recoverable from him by the relevant office-holder unless the court directs otherwise.

(6) Any sum recoverable by virtue of subsection (5) ranks for priority, in the event of the insolvency of the person from whom it is due, immediately before preferential or, in Scotland, preferred debts.

(7) In a case falling within both subsection (4) above (as a disposition of property as a result of which the property becomes subject to a market charge) and section 164(3) (as the provision of margin in relation to a market contract), section 164(4) applies with respect to the recovery of the amount or value of the margin and subsection (5) above does not apply.

176.—(1) The Secretary of State may by regulations provide that the general law of insolvency has effect in relation to charges of such descriptions as may be specified in the regulations, and action taken in enforcing them, subject to such provisions as may be specified in the regulations.

(2) The regulations may specify any description of charge granted in favour of—

(a) a body approved under section 170 (certain overseas exchanges and clearing houses),

(b) a person included in the list maintained by the Bank of England for the purposes of section 171 (certain money market institutions),

(c) the Bank of England,

(d) an authorised person within the meaning of the Financial Services Act 1986, or

(e) an international securities self-regulating organisation within the meaning of that Act,

for the purpose of securing debts or liabilities arising in connection with or as a result of the settlement of contracts or the transfer of assets, rights or interests on a financial market.

(3) The regulations may specify any description of charge granted for that purpose in favour of any other person in connection with exchange facilities or clearing services provided by a recognised investment exchange or recognised clearing house or by any such body, person, authority or organisation as is mentioned in subsection (2).

(4) Where a charge is granted partly for the purpose specified in subsection (2) and partly for other purposes, the power conferred by this section is exercisable in relation to the charge so far as it has effect for that purpose.

(5) The regulations may—

(a) make the same or similar provision in relation to the charges to which they apply as is made by or under sections 174 and 175 in relation to market charges, or

(b) apply any of those provisions with such exceptions, additions or adaptations as are specified in the regulations.

(6) Before making regulations under this section relating to a description of charges defined by reference to their being granted—

(a) in favour of a person included in the list maintained by the Bank of England for the purposes of section 171, or in connection with exchange facilities or clearing services provided by a person included in that list, or

(b) in favour of the Bank of England, or in connection with settlement arrangements provided by the Bank,

the Secretary of State shall consult the Treasury and the Bank of England.

(7) Regulations under this section may provide that they apply or do not apply to a charge if or to the extent that it secures obligations of a specified description, is a charge over property of a specified description or contains provisions of a specified description.

Market property

Application of
margin not
affected by certain
other interests.

177.—(1) The following provisions have effect with respect to the application by a recognised investment exchange or recognised clearing house of property (other than land) held by the exchange or clearing house as margin in relation to a market contract.

(2) So far as necessary to enable the property to be applied in accordance with the rules of the exchange or clearing house, it may be so applied notwithstanding any prior equitable interest or right, or any right or remedy arising from a breach of fiduciary duty, unless the exchange or clearing house had notice of the interest, right or breach of duty at the time the property was provided as margin.

(3) No right or remedy arising subsequently to the property being provided as margin may be enforced so as to prevent or interfere with the application of the property by the exchange or clearing house in accordance with its rules.

(4) Where an exchange or clearing house has power by virtue of the above provisions to apply property notwithstanding an interest, right or remedy, a person to whom the exchange or clearing house disposes of the property in accordance with its rules takes free from that interest, right or remedy.

Priority of floating
market charge
over subsequent
charges.

178.—(1) The Secretary of State may by regulations provide that a market charge which is a floating charge has priority over a charge subsequently created or arising, including a fixed charge.

(2) The regulations may make different provision for cases defined, as regards the market charge or the subsequent charge, by reference to the description of charge, its terms, the circumstances in which it is created or arises, the nature of the charge, the person in favour of whom it is granted or arises or any other relevant factor.

Priority of market
charge over
unpaid vendor's
lien.

179. Where property subject to an unpaid vendor's lien becomes subject to a market charge, the charge has priority over the lien unless the chargee had actual notice of the lien at the time the property became subject to the charge.

Proceedings
against market
property by
unsecured
creditors.

180.—(1) Where property (other than land) is held by a recognised investment exchange or recognised clearing house as margin in relation to market contracts or is subject to a market charge, no execution or other legal process for the enforcement of a judgment or order may be commenced or continued, and no distress may be levied, against the property by a person not seeking to enforce any interest in or security over the property, except with the consent of—

   (a) in the case of property provided as cover for margin, the investment exchange or clearing house in question, or

   (b) in the case of property subject to a market charge, the person in whose favour the charge was granted.

1986 c. 45.
1985 c. 66.

(2) Where consent is given the proceedings may be commenced or continued notwithstanding any provision of the Insolvency Act 1986 or the Bankruptcy (Scotland) Act 1985.

(3) Where by virtue of this section a person would not be entitled to enforce a judgment or order against any property, any injunction or other remedy granted with a view to facilitating the enforcement of any such judgment or order shall not extend to that property.

(4) In the application of this section to Scotland, the reference to execution being commenced or continued includes a reference to diligence being carried out or continued, and the reference to distress being levied shall be omitted.

181.—(1) The power of the Secretary of State to make provision by regulations under—

    (a) section 170, 171 or 172 (power to extend provisions relating to market contracts), or

    (b) section 176 (power to extend provisions relating to market charges),

includes power to apply sections 177 to 180 to any description of property provided as cover for margin in relation to contracts in relation to which the power is exercised or, as the case may be, property subject to charges in relation to which the power is exercised.

(2) The regulations may provide that those sections apply with such exceptions, additions and adaptations as may be specified in the regulations.

Supplementary provisions

182.—(1) The powers conferred by this section are exercisable by the court where insolvency proceedings in respect of—

    (a) a member of a recognised investment exchange or a recognised clearing house, or

    (b) a person by whom a market charge has been granted,

are begun on or after 22nd December 1988 and before the commencement of this section.

That person is referred to in this section as "the relevant person".

(2) For the purposes of this section "insolvency proceedings" means proceedings under Part II, IV, V or IX of the Insolvency Act 1986 (administration, winding up and bankruptcy) or under the Bankruptcy (Scotland) Act 1985; and references in this section to the beginning of such proceedings are to—

    (a) the presentation of a petition on which an administration order, winding-up order, bankruptcy order or award of sequestration is made, or

    (b) the passing of a resolution for voluntary winding up.

(3) This section applies in relation to—

    (a) in England and Wales, the administration of the insolvent estate of a deceased person, and

    (b) in Scotland, the administration by a judicial factor appointed under section 11A of the Judicial Factors (Scotland) Act 1889 of the insolvent estate of a deceased person,

as it applies in relation to insolvency proceedings.

In such a case references to the beginning of the proceedings shall be construed as references to the death of the relevant person.

(4) The court may on an application made, within three months after the commencement of this section, by—

　(a) a recognised investment exchange or recognised clearing house, or

　(b) a person in whose favour a market charge has been granted,

make such order as it thinks fit for achieving, except so far as assets of the relevant person have been distributed before the making of the application, the same result as if the provisions of Schedule 22 had come into force on 22nd December 1988.

(5) The provisions of that Schedule ("the relevant provisions") reproduce the effect of certain provisions of this Part as they appeared in the Bill for this Act as introduced into the House of Lords and published on that date.

(6) The court may in particular—

　(a) require the relevant person or a relevant office-holder—

　　　(i) to return property provided as cover for margin or which was subject to a market charge, or to pay to the applicant or any other person the proceeds of realisation of such property, or

　　　(ii) to pay to the applicant or any other person such amount as the court estimates would have been payable to that person if the relevant provisions had come into force on 22nd December 1988 and market contracts had been settled in accordance with the rules of the recognised investment exchange or recognised clearing house, or a proportion of that amount if the property of the relevant person or relevant office-holder is not sufficient to meet the amount in full;

　(b) provide that contracts, rules and dispositions shall be treated as not having been void;

　(c) modify the functions of a relevant office-holder, or the duties of the applicant or any other person, in relation to the insolvency proceedings, or indemnify any such person in respect of acts or omissions which would have been proper if the relevant provisions had been in force;

　(d) provide that conduct which constituted an offence be treated as not having done so;

　(e) dismiss proceedings which could not have been brought if the relevant provisions had come into force on 22nd December 1988, and reverse the effect of any order of a court which could not, or would not, have been made if those provisions had come into force on that date.

(7) An order under this section shall not be made against a relevant office-holder if the effect would be that his remuneration, costs and expenses could not be met.

183.—(1) The references to insolvency law in section 426 of the Insolvency Act 1986 (co-operation with courts exercising insolvency jurisdiction in other jurisdictions) include, in relation to a part of the United Kingdom, the provisions made by or under this Part and, in relation to a relevant country or territory within the meaning of that section, so much of the law of that country or territory as corresponds to any provisions made by or under this Part.

PART VII
Insolvency
proceedings in
other jurisdictions.
1986 c. 45.

(2) A court shall not, in pursuance of that section or any other enactment or rule of law, recognise or give effect to—

    (a) any order of a court exercising jurisdiction in relation to insolvency law in a country or territory outside the United Kingdom, or

    (b) any act of a person appointed in such a country or territory to discharge any functions under insolvency law,

in so far as the making of the order or the doing of the act would be prohibited in the case of a court in the United Kingdom or a relevant office-holder by provisions made by or under this Part.

(3) Subsection (2) does not affect the recognition or enforcement of a judgment required to be recognised or enforced under or by virtue of the Civil Jurisdiction and Judgments Act 1982.

1982 c. 27.

184.—(1) Where a relevant office-holder takes any action in relation to property of a defaulter which is liable to be dealt with in accordance with the default rules of a recognised investment exchange or recognised clearing house, and believes and has reasonable grounds for believing that he is entitled to take that action, he is not liable to any person in respect of any loss or damage resulting from his action except in so far as the loss or damage is caused by the office-holder's own negligence.

Indemnity for
certain acts, &c.

(2) Any failure by a recognised investment exchange or recognised clearing house to comply with its own rules in respect of any matter shall not prevent that matter being treated for the purposes of this Part as done in accordance with those rules so long as the failure does not substantially affect the rights of any person entitled to require compliance with the rules.

(3) No recognised investment exchange or recognised clearing house, nor any officer or servant or member of the governing body of a recognised investment exchange or recognised clearing house, shall be liable in damages for anything done or omitted in the discharge or purported discharge of any functions to which this subsection applies unless the act or omission is shown to have been in bad faith.

(4) The functions to which subsection (3) applies are the functions of the exchange or clearing house so far as relating to, or to matters arising out of—

    (a) its default rules, or

    (b) any obligations to which it is subject by virtue of this Part.

(5) No person exercising any functions by virtue of arrangements made pursuant to paragraph 5 or 12 of Schedule 21 (delegation of functions in connection with default procedures), nor any officer or servant of such a person, shall be liable in damages for anything done or omitted in the discharge or purported discharge of those functions unless the act or omission is shown to have been in bad faith.

PART VII
Power to make
further provision
by regulations.

185.—(1) The Secretary of State may by regulations make such further provision as appears to him necessary or expedient for the purposes of this Part.

(2) Provision may, in particular, be made—

(a) for integrating the provisions of this Part with the general law of insolvency, and

(b) for adapting the provisions of this Part in their application to overseas investment exchanges and clearing houses.

(3) Regulations under this section may add to, amend or repeal any of the provisions of this Part or provide that those provisions have effect subject to such additions, exceptions or adaptations as are specified in the regulations.

Supplementary
provisions as to
regulations.

186.—(1) Regulations under this Part may make different provision for different cases and may contain such incidental, transitional and other supplementary provisions as appear to the Secretary of State to be necessary or expedient.

(2) Regulations under this Part shall be made by statutory instrument which shall be subject to annulment in pursuance of a resolution of either House of Parliament.

Construction of
references to
parties to market
contracts.

187.—(1) Where a person enters into market contracts in more than one capacity, the provisions of this Part apply (subject as follows) as if the contracts entered into in each different capacity were entered into by different persons.

(2) References in this Part to a market contract to which a person is a party include (subject as follows, and unless the context otherwise requires) contracts to which he is party as agent.

(3) The Secretary of State may by regulations—

(a) modify or exclude the operation of subsections (1) and (2), and

(b) make provision as to the circumstances in which a person is to be regarded for the purposes of those provisions as acting in different capacities.

Meaning of
"default rules"
and related
expressions.

188.—(1) In this Part "default rules" means rules of a recognised investment exchange or recognised clearing house which provide for the taking of action in the event of a person appearing to be unable, or likely to become unable, to meet his obligations in respect of one or more market contracts connected with the exchange or clearing house.

(2) References in this Part to a "defaulter" are to a person in respect of whom action has been taken by a recognised investment exchange or recognised clearing house under its default rules, whether by declaring him to be a defaulter or otherwise; and references in this Part to "default" shall be construed accordingly.

(3) In this Part "default proceedings" means proceedings taken by a recognised investment exchange or recognised clearing house under its default rules.

(4) If an exchange or clearing house takes action under its default rules in respect of a person, all subsequent proceedings under its rules for the purposes of or in connection with the settlement of market contracts to which the defaulter is a party shall be treated as done under its default rules.

189.—(1) The following are relevant office-holders for the purposes of this Part—

(a) the official receiver,

(b) any person acting in relation to a company as its liquidator, provisional liquidator, administrator or administrative receiver,

(c) any person acting in relation to an individual (or, in Scotland, any debtor within the meaning of the Bankruptcy (Scotland) Act 1985) as his trustee in bankruptcy or interim receiver of his property or as permanent or interim trustee in the sequestration of his estate,

(d) any person acting as administrator of an insolvent estate of a deceased person.

(2) In subsection (1)(b) "company" means any company, society, association, partnership or other body which may be wound up under the Insolvency Act 1986.

190.—(1) In this Part—

"administrative receiver" has the meaning given by section 251 of the Insolvency Act 1986;

"charge" means any form of security, including a mortgage and, in Scotland, a heritable security;

"clearing house" has the same meaning as in the Financial Services Act 1986;

"interim trustee" and "permanent trustee" have the same meaning as in the Bankruptcy (Scotland) Act 1985;

"investment" and "investment exchange" have the same meaning as in the Financial Services Act 1986;

"overseas", in relation to an investment exchange or clearing house, means having its head office outside the United Kingdom;

"recognised" means recognised under the Financial Services Act 1986;

"set-off", in relation to Scotland, includes compensation;

"The Stock Exchange" means The International Stock Exchange of the United Kingdom and the Republic of Ireland Limited;

"UK", in relation to an investment exchange or clearing house, means having its head office in the United Kingdom.

(2) References in this Part to settlement in relation to a market contract are to the discharge of the rights and liabilities of the parties to the contract, whether by performance, compromise or otherwise.

(3) In this Part the expressions "margin" and "cover for margin" have the same meaning.

(4) References in this Part to ensuring the performance of a transaction have the same meaning as in the Financial Services Act 1986.

(5) For the purposes of this Part a person shall be taken to have notice of a matter if he deliberately failed to make enquiries as to that matter in circumstances in which a reasonable and honest person would have done so.

This does not apply for the purposes of a provision requiring "actual notice".

(6) References in this Part to the law of insolvency include references to every provision made by or under the Insolvency Act 1986 or the Bankruptcy (Scotland) Act 1985; and in relation to a building society references to insolvency law or to any provision of the Insolvency Act 1986 are to that law or provision as modified by the Building Societies Act 1986.

(7) In relation to Scotland, references in this Part—

(a) to sequestration include references to the administration by a judicial factor of the insolvent estate of a deceased person, and

(b) to an interim or permanent trustee include references to a judicial factor on the insolvent estate of a deceased person,

unless the context otherwise requires.

191. The following Table shows provisions defining or otherwise explaining expressions used in this Part (other than provisions defining or explaining an expression used only in the same section or paragraph)—

administrative receiver	section 190(1)
charge	section 190(1)
clearing house	section 190(1)
cover for margin	section 190(3)
default rules (and related expressions)	section 188
designated non-member	section 155(2)
ensuring the performance of a transaction	section 190(4)
insolvency law (and similar expressions)	section 190(6)
interim trustee	section 190(1) and (7)(b)
investment	section 190(1)
investment exchange	section 190(1)
margin	section 190(3)
market charge	section 173
market contract	section 155
notice	section 190(5)
overseas (in relation to an investment exchange or clearing house)	section 190(1)
party (in relation to a market contract)	section 187
permanent trustee	section 190(1) and (7)(b)
recognised	section 190(1)
relevant office-holder	section 189
sequestration	section 190(7)(a)
set off (in relation to Scotland)	section 190(1)
settlement and related expressions (in relation to a market contract)	section 190(2)
The Stock Exchange	section 190(1)
trustee, interim or permanent (in relation to Scotland)	section 190(7)(b)

UK (in relation to an investment exchange   section 190(1).
    or clearing house)

PART VIII

AMENDMENTS OF THE FINANCIAL SERVICES ACT 1986

192. In Chapter V of Part I of the Financial Services Act 1986 (conduct of investment business), after section 47 insert—

Statements of
principle.
1986 c. 60.

"Statements of
principle.

47A.—(1) The Secretary of State may issue statements of principle with respect to the conduct and financial standing expected of persons authorised to carry on investment business.

(2) The conduct expected may include compliance with a code or standard issued by another person, as for the time being in force, and may allow for the exercise of discretion by any person pursuant to any such code or standard.

(3) Failure to comply with a statement of principle under this section is a ground for the taking of disciplinary action or the exercise of powers of intervention, but it does not of itself give rise to any right of action by investors or other persons affected or affect the validity of any transaction.

(4) The disciplinary action which may be taken by virtue of subsection (3) is—

(a) the withdrawal or suspension of authorisation under section 28 or the termination or suspension of authorisation under section 33,

(b) the giving of a disqualification direction under section 59,

(c) the making of a public statement under section 60, or

(d) the application by the Secretary of State for an injunction, interdict or other order under section 61(1);

and the reference in that subsection to powers of intervention is to the powers conferred by Chapter VI of this Part.

(5) Where a statement of principle relates to compliance with a code or standard issued by another person, the statement of principle may provide—

(a) that failure to comply with the code or standard shall be a ground for the taking of disciplinary action, or the exercise of powers of intervention, only in such cases and to such extent as may be specified; and

(b) that no such action shall be taken, or any such power exercised, except at the request of the person by whom the code or standard in question was issued.

(6) The Secretary of State shall exercise his powers in such manner as appears to him appropriate to secure compliance with statements of principle under this section.

Modification or waiver of statements of principle in particular cases.

47B.—(1) The relevant regulatory authority may on the application of any person—

(a) modify a statement of principle issued under section 47A so as to adapt it to his circumstances or to any particular kind of business carried on by him, or

(b) dispense him from compliance with any such statement of principle, generally or in relation to any particular kind of business carried on by him.

(2) The powers conferred by this section shall not be exercised unless it appears to the relevant regulatory authority—

(a) that compliance with the statement of principle in question would be unduly burdensome for the applicant having regard to the benefit which compliance would confer on investors, and

(b) that the exercise of those powers will not result in any undue risk to investors.

(3) The powers conferred by this section may be exercised unconditionally or subject to conditions; and section 47A(3) applies in the case of failure to comply with a condition as in the case of failure to comply with a statement of principle.

(4) The relevant regulatory authority for the purposes of this section is—

(a) in the case of a member of a recognised self-regulating organisation or professional body, in relation to investment business in the carrying on of which he is subject to the rules of the organisation or body, that organisation or body;

(b) in any other case, or in relation to other investment business, the Secretary of State.

(5) The references in paragraph 4(1) of Schedule 2 and paragraph 4(2) of Schedule 3 (requirements for recognition of self-regulating organisations and professional bodies) to monitoring and enforcement of compliance with statements of principle include monitoring and enforcement of compliance with conditions imposed by the organisation or body under this section.".

Restriction of right to bring action for contravention of rules, regulations, &c.

1986 c. 60.

193.—(1) In Chapter V of Part I of the Financial Services Act 1986 (conduct of investment business), after section 62 (actions for damages) insert—

"Restriction of right of action.

62A.—(1) No action in respect of a contravention to

which section 62 above applies shall lie at the suit of a person other than a private investor, except in such circumstances as may be specified by regulations made by the Secretary of State.

(2) The meaning of the expression "private investor" for the purposes of subsection (1) shall be defined by regulations made by the Secretary of State.

(3) Regulations under subsection (1) may make different provision with respect to different cases.

(4) The Secretary of State shall, before making any regulations affecting the right to bring an action in respect of a contravention of any rules or regulations made by a person other than himself, consult that person.".

(2) In section 114(5) of the Financial Services Act 1986 (transfer of functions to designated agency: excluded functions), after paragraph (d) insert—

1986 c. 60.

    "(dd) section 62A;".

(3) In Schedule 11 to the Financial Services Act 1986 (friendly societies), after paragraph 22 insert—

    "22A.—(1) No action in respect of a contravention to which paragraph 22(4) above applies shall lie at the suit of a person other than a private investor, except in such circumstances as may be specified by regulations made by the Registrar.

    (2) The meaning of the expression "private investor" for the purposes of sub-paragraph (1) shall be defined by regulations made by the Registrar.

    (3) Regulations under sub-paragraph (1) may make different provision with respect to different cases.

    (4) The Registrar shall, before making any regulations affecting the right to bring an action in respect of a contravention of any rules or regulations made by a person other than himself, consult that person.".

(4) In paragraph 28(5) of Schedule 11 to the Financial Services Act 1986 (transfer of Registrar's functions to transferee body), after "paragraphs 2 to 25" insert "(except paragraph 22A)".

194. In Chapter V of Part I of the Financial Services Act 1986 (conduct of investment business), after section 63 insert—

Application of designated rules and regulations to members of self-regulating organisations.

"Application of designated rules and regulations to members of self-regulating organisations.

    63A.—(1) The Secretary of State may in rules and regulations under—

        (a) section 48 (conduct of business rules),

        (b) section 49 (financial resources rules),

        (c) section 55 (clients' money regulations), or

(d) section 56 (regulations as to unsolicited calls),

designate provisions which apply, to such extent as may be specified, to a member of a recognised self-regulating organisation in respect of investment business in the carrying on of which he is subject to the rules of the organisation.

(2) It may be provided that the designated rules or regulations have effect, generally or to such extent as may be specified, subject to the rules of the organisation.

(3) A member of a recognised self-regulating organisation who contravenes a rule or regulation applying to him by virtue of this section shall be treated as having contravened the rules of the organisation.

(4) It may be provided that, to such extent as may be specified, the designated rules or regulations may not be modified or waived (under section 63B below or section 50) in relation to a member of a recognised self-regulating organisation.

Where such provision is made any modification or waiver previously granted shall cease to have effect, subject to any transitional provision or saving contained in the rules or regulations.

(5) Except as mentioned in subsection (1), the rules and regulations referred to in that subsection do not apply to a member of a recognised self-regulating organisation in respect of investment business in the carrying on of which he is subject to the rules of the organisation.

Modification or waiver of designated rules and regulations.

63B.—(1) A recognised self-regulating organisation may on the application of a member of the organisation—

(a) modify a rule or regulation designated under section 63A so as to adapt it to his circumstances or to any particular kind of business carried on by him, or

(b) dispense him from compliance with any such rule or regulation, generally or in relation to any particular kind of business carried on by him.

(2) The powers conferred by this section shall not be exercised unless it appears to the organisation—

(a) that compliance with the rule or regulation in question would be unduly burdensome for the applicant having regard to the benefit which compliance would confer on investors, and

(b) that the exercise of those powers will not result in any undue risk to investors.

(3) The powers conferred by this section may be exercised unconditionally or subject to conditions; and section 63A(3) applies in the case of a contravention of a condition as in the case of contravention of a designated rule or regulation.

(4) The reference in paragraph 4(1) of Schedule 2 (requirements for recognition of self-regulating organisations) to monitoring and enforcement of compliance with rules and regulations includes monitoring and enforcement of compliance with conditions imposed by the organisation under this section.".

195. In Chapter V of Part I of the Financial Services Act 1986 (conduct of investment business), after the sections inserted by section 194 above, insert—

"Codes of
practice.

63C.—(1) The Secretary of State may issue codes of practice with respect to any matters dealt with by statements of principle issued under section 47A or by rules or regulations made under any provision of this Chapter.

(2) In determining whether a person has failed to comply with a statement of principle—

(a) a failure by him to comply with any relevant provision of a code of practice may be relied on as tending to establish failure to comply with the statement of principle, and

(b) compliance by him with the relevant provisions of a code of practice may be relied on as tending to negative any such failure.

(3) A contravention of a code of practice with respect to a matter dealt with by rules or regulations shall not of itself give rise to any liability or invalidate any transaction; but in determining whether a person's conduct amounts to contravention of a rule or regulation—

(a) contravention by him of any relevant provision of a code of practice may be relied on as tending to establish liability, and

(b) compliance by him with the relevant provisions of a code of practice may be relied on as tending to negative liability.

(4) Where by virtue of section 63A (application of designated rules and regulations to members of self-regulating organisations) rules or regulations—

(a) do not apply, to any extent, to a member of a recognised self-regulating organisation, or

(b) apply, to any extent, subject to the rules of the organisation,

a code of practice with respect to a matter dealt with by the rules or regulations may contain provision limiting its application to a corresponding extent.".

196. In Part I of the Financial Services Act 1986 (regulation of investment business), after section 128 insert—

"CHAPTER XV

RELATIONS WITH OTHER REGULATORY AUTHORITIES

Relevance of other controls.

128A. In determining—

(a) in relation to a self-regulating organisation, whether the requirements of Schedule 2 are met, or

(b) in relation to a professional body, whether the requirements of Schedule 3 are met,

the Secretary of State shall take into account the effect of any other controls to which members of the organisation or body are subject.

Relevance of information given and action taken by other regulatory authorities.

128B.—(1) The following provisions apply in the case of—

(a) a person whose principal place of business is in a country or territory outside the United Kingdom, or

(b) a person whose principal business is other than investment business;

and in relation to such a person "the relevant regulatory authority" means the appropriate regulatory authority in that country or territory or, as the case may be, in relation to his principal business.

(2) The Secretary of State may regard himself as satisfied with respect to any matter relevant for the purposes of this Part if—

(a) the relevant regulatory authority informs him that it is satisfied with respect to that matter, and

(b) he is satisfied as to the nature and scope of the supervision exercised by that authority.

(3) In making any decision with respect to the exercise of his powers under this Part in relation to any such person, the Secretary of State may take into account whether the relevant regulatory authority has exercised, or proposes to exercise, its powers in relation to that person.

(4) The Secretary of State may enter into such arrangements with other regulatory authorities as he thinks fit for the purposes of this section.

(5) Where any functions under this Part have been transferred to a designated agency, nothing in this section shall be construed as affecting the responsibility of the Secretary of State for the discharge of Community obligations or other international obligations of the United Kingdom.

Enforcement in support of overseas regulatory authority.

128C.—(1) The Secretary of State may exercise his disciplinary powers or powers of intervention at the request of, or for the purpose of assisting, an overseas regulatory authority.

(2) The disciplinary powers of the Secretary of State means his powers—

    (a) to withdraw or suspend authorisation under section 28 or to terminate or suspend authorisation under section 33,

    (b) to give a disqualification direction under section 59,

    (c) to make a public statement under section 60, or

    (d) to apply for an injunction, interdict or other order under section 61(1);

and the reference to his powers of intervention is to the powers conferred by Chapter VI of this Part.

(3) An "overseas regulatory authority" means an authority in a country or territory outside the United Kingdom which exercises—

    (a) any function corresponding to—

        (i) a function of the Secretary of State under this Act, the Insurance Companies Act 1982 or the Companies Act 1985,

        (ii) a function under this Act of a designated agency, transferee body or competent authority, or

        (iii) a function of the Bank of England under the Banking Act 1987, or

    (b) any functions in connection with the investigation of, or the enforcement of rules (whether or not having the force of law) relating to, conduct of the kind prohibited by the Company Securities (Insider Dealing) Act 1985, or

    (c) any function prescribed for the purposes of this subsection, being a function which in the opinion of the Secretary of State relates to companies or financial services.

(4) In deciding whether to exercise those powers the Secretary of State may take into account, in particular—

    (a) whether corresponding assistance would be given in that country or territory to an authority exercising regulatory functions in the United Kingdom;

    (b) whether the case concerns the breach of a law, or other requirement, which has no close parallel in the United Kingdom or involves the assertion of a jurisdiction not recognised by the United Kingdom;

    (c) the seriousness of the case and its importance to persons in the United Kingdom;

    (d) whether it is otherwise appropriate in the public interest to give the assistance sought.

(5) The Secretary of State may decline to exercise those powers unless the overseas regulatory authority undertakes to make such contribution towards the cost of their exercise as the Secretary of State considers appropriate.

(6) The reference in subsection (3)(c) to financial services includes, in particular, investment business, insurance and banking.".

Construction of references to incurring civil liability.

1986 c. 60.

197.—(1) In section 150(6) of the Financial Services Act 1986 (exclusion of liability in respect of false or misleading listing particulars), at the end insert—

"The reference above to a person incurring liability includes a reference to any other person being entitled as against that person to be granted any civil remedy or to rescind or repudiate any agreement.".

(2) In section 154(5) of the Financial Services Act 1986 (exclusion of civil liability in respect of advertisements or other information in connection with listing application), at the end insert—

"The reference above to a person incurring civil liability includes a reference to any other person being entitled as against that person to be granted any civil remedy or to rescind or repudiate any agreement.".

Offers of unlisted securities.

198.—(1) In Part V of the Financial Services Act 1986 (offers of unlisted securities), after section 160 insert—

"Exemptions.

160A.—(1) The Secretary of State may by order exempt from sections 159 and 160 when issued in such circumstances as may be specified in the order—

(a) advertisements appearing to him to have a private character, whether by reason of a connection between the person issuing them and those to whom they are addressed or otherwise;

(b) advertisements appearing to him to deal with investments only incidentally;

(c) advertisements issued to persons appearing to him to be sufficiently expert to understand any risks involved;

(d) such other classes of advertisements as he thinks fit.

(2) The Secretary of State may by order exempt from sections 159 and 160 an advertisement issued in whatever circumstances which relates to securities appearing to him to be of a kind that can be expected normally to be bought or dealt in only by persons sufficiently expert to understand any risks involved.

(3) An order under subsection (1) or (2) may require a person who by virtue of the order is authorised to issue an advertisement to comply with such requirements as are specified in the order.

(4) An order made by virtue of subsection (1)(a), (b) or (c) or subsection (2) shall be subject to annulment in pursuance of a resolution of either House of Parliament; and no order shall be made by virtue of subsection (1)(d) unless a draft of it has been laid before and approved by a resolution of each House of Parliament.".

(2) The following amendments of the Financial Services Act 1986 are consequential on that above.

1986 c. 60.

(3) In section 159, in subsection (1) omit the words from the beginning to "section 161 below," and after subsection (2) insert—

"(3) Subsection (1) above has effect subject to section 160A (exemptions) and section 161 (exceptions).".

(4) In section 160, in subsection (1) omit the words from the beginning to "section 161 below," and for subsections (6) to (9) substitute—

"(6) Subsection (1) above has effect subject to section 160A (exemptions) and section 161 (exceptions).".

(5) In section 171, in subsection (1)(b) and subsection (3) for "section 160(6) or (7)" substitute "section 160A".

199. In Part V of the Financial Services Act 1986 (offers of unlisted securities), in section 170 (advertisements by private companies and old public companies), for subsections (2) to (4) substitute—

Offers of securities by private companies and old public companies.

"(2) The Secretary of State may by order exempt from subsection (1) when issued in such circumstances as may be specified in the order—

    (a) advertisements appearing to him to have a private character, whether by reason of a connection between the person issuing them and those to whom they are addressed or otherwise;

    (b) advertisements appearing to him to deal with investments only incidentally;

    (c) advertisements issued to persons appearing to him to be sufficiently expert to understand any risks involved;

    (d) such other classes of advertisements as he thinks fit.

(3) The Secretary of State may by order exempt from subsection (1) an advertisement issued in whatever circumstances which relates to securities appearing to him to be of a kind that can be expected normally to be bought or dealt in only by persons sufficiently expert to understand any risks involved.

(4) An order under subsection (2) or (3) may require a person who by virtue of the order is authorised to issue an advertisement to comply with such requirements as are specified in the order.

(4A) An order made by virtue of subsection (2)(a), (b) or (c) or subsection (3) shall be subject to annulment in pursuance of a resolution of either House of Parliament; and no order shall be made by virtue of subsection (2)(d) unless a draft of it has been laid before and approved by a resolution of each House of Parliament.".

PART VIII
Jurisdiction of
High Court and
Court of Session.

1986 c. 60.

200.—(1) In the Financial Services Act 1986, for section 188 (jurisdiction as respects actions concerning designated agency, &c.), substitute—

"Jurisdiction of High Court and Court of Session.

188.—(1) Proceedings arising out of any act or omission (or proposed act or omission) of—

    (a) a recognised self-regulating organisation,

    (b) a designated agency,

    (c) a transferee body, or

    (d) the competent authority,

in the discharge or purported discharge of any of its functions under this Act may be brought in the High Court or the Court of Session.

(2) The jurisdiction conferred by subsection (1) is in addition to any other jurisdiction exercisable by those courts.".

1982 c. 27.

(2) In Schedule 5 to the Civil Jurisdiction and Judgments Act 1982 (proceedings excluded from general provisions as to allocation of jurisdiction within the United Kingdom), for paragraph 10 substitute—

"*Financial Services Act 1986*

10. Proceedings such as are mentioned in section 188 of the Financial Services Act 1986.".

Directions to
secure
compliance with
international
obligations.

201. In the Financial Services Act 1986, for section 192 (international obligations) substitute—

"International obligations.

192.—(1) If it appears to the Secretary of State—

    (a) that any action proposed to be taken by an authority or body to which this section applies would be incompatible with Community obligations or any other international obligations of the United Kingdom, or

    (b) that any action which that authority or body has power to take is required for the purpose of implementing any such obligation,

he may direct the authority or body not to take or, as the case may be, to take the action in question.

(2) The authorities and bodies to which this section applies are the following—

    (a) a recognised self-regulating organisation,

    (b) a recognised investment exchange (other than an overseas investment exchange),

    (c) a recognised clearing house (other than an overseas clearing house),

    (d) a designated agency,

    (e) a transferee body,

    (f) a competent authority.

(3) This section also applies to an approved exchange within the meaning of Part V of this Act in respect of any action which it proposes to take or has power to take in respect of rules applying to a prospectus by virtue of a direction under section 162(3) above.

(4) A direction under this section may include such supplementary or incidental requirements as the Secretary of State thinks necessary or expedient.

(5) Where the function of making or revoking a recognition order in respect of an authority or body to which this section applies is exercisable by a designated agency, any direction in respect of that authority or body shall be a direction requiring the agency to give the authority or body such a direction as is specified in the direction given by the Secretary of State.

(6) A direction under this section is enforceable, on the application of the person who gave it, by injunction or, in Scotland, by an order under section 45 of the Court of Session Act 1988.".

202. In section 195 of the Financial Services Act 1986 (circumstances in which certain offers of debentures not treated as offers to the public), for "repaid within less than one year of the date of issue" substitute "repaid within five years of the date of issue".

Offers of short-dated debentures.

1986 c. 60.

203.—(1) In Schedule 2 to the Financial Services Act 1986 (requirements for recognition of self-regulating organisations), in paragraph 3 (safeguards for investors) for sub-paragraphs (1) and (2) substitute—

Standard of protection for investors.

"(1) The organisation must have rules governing the carrying on of investment business by its members which, together with the statements of principle, rules, regulations and codes of practice to which its members are subject under Chapter V of Part I of this Act, are such as to afford an adequate level of protection for investors.

(2) In determining in any case whether an adequate level of protection is afforded for investors of any description, regard shall be had to the nature of the investment business carried on by members of the organisation, the kinds of investors involved and the effectiveness of the organisation's arrangements for enforcing compliance.".

(2) In Schedule 3 to the Financial Services Act 1986 (requirements for recognition of professional bodies), for paragraph 3 (safeguards for investors) substitute—

"3.—(1) The body must have rules regulating the carrying on of investment business by persons certified by it which, together with the statements of principle, rules, regulations and codes of practice to which those persons are subject under Chapter V of Part I of this Act, afford an adequate level of protection for investors.

(2) In determining in any case whether an adequate level of protection is afforded for investors of any description, regard shall be had to the nature of the investment business carried on by persons certified by the body, the kinds of investors involved and the effectiveness of the body's arrangements for enforcing compliance.".

(3) The order bringing this section into force may provide that, for a transitional period, a self-regulating organisation or professional body may elect whether to comply with the new requirement having effect by virtue of subsection (1) or (2) above or with the requirement which it replaces.

The Secretary of State may by order specify when the transitional period is to end.

Costs of
compliance.
1986 c. 60.

204.—(1) In Schedule 2 to the Financial Services Act 1986 (requirements for recognition of self-regulating organisations), after paragraph 3 insert—

"Taking account of costs of compliance

3A. The organisation must have satisfactory arrangements for taking account, in framing its rules, of the cost to those to whom the rules would apply of complying with those rules and any other controls to which they are subject.";

and in Schedule 3 to that Act (requirements for recognition of professional body), after paragraph 3 insert—

"Taking account of costs of compliance

3A. The body must have satisfactory arrangements for taking account, in framing its rules, of the cost to those to whom the rules would apply of complying with those rules and any other controls to which they are subject.".

(2) The additional requirements having effect by virtue of subsection (1) do not affect the status of a self-regulating organisation or professional body recognised before the commencement of that subsection; but if the Secretary of State is of the opinion that any of those requirements is not met in the case of such an organisation or body, he shall within one month of commencement give notice to the organisation or body stating his opinion.

(3) Where the Secretary of State gives such a notice, he shall not—

(a) take action to revoke the recognition of such an organisation or body on the ground that any of the additional requirements is not met, unless he considers it essential to do so in the interests of investors, or

(b) apply on any such ground for a compliance order under section 12 of the Financial Services Act 1986,

until after the end of the period of six months beginning with the date on which the notice was given.

(4) In Schedule 7 to the Financial Services Act 1986 (qualifications of designated agency), after paragraph 2 insert—

"Taking account of costs of compliance

2A.—(1) The agency must have satisfactory arrangements for taking account, in framing any provisions which it proposes to make in the exercise of its legislative functions, of the cost to those to whom the provisions would apply of complying with those provisions and any other controls to which they are subject.

(2) In this paragraph "legislative functions" means the functions of issuing or making statements of principle, rules, regulations or codes of practice.".

(5) The additional requirement having effect by virtue of subsection (4) above does not affect the status of a designated agency to which functions have been transferred before the commencement of that subsection; but if the Secretary of State is of the opinion the requirement is not met in the case of such an agency, he shall within one month of commencement give notice to the agency stating his opinion.

(6) Where the Secretary of State gives such a notice, he shall not take action under section 115(2) of the Financial Services Act 1986 to resume 1986 c. 60. any functions exercisable by such an agency on the ground that the additional requirement is not met until after the end of the period of six months beginning with the date on which the notice was given.

(7) References in this section to a recognised self-regulating organisation include a recognised self-regulating organisation for friendly societies and references to a designated agency include a transferee body (within the meaning of that Act).

In relation to such an organisation or body—

(a) references to the Secretary of State shall be construed as references to the Registrar (within the meaning of Schedule 11 to the Financial Services Act 1986), and

(b) the reference to section 12 of that Act shall be construed as a reference to paragraph 6 of that Schedule.

205.—(1) In Schedule 4 to the Financial Services Act 1986 (requirements for recognition of investment exchange), after paragraph 5 insert—

Requirements for recognition of investment exchange.

"Supplementary

6.—(1) The provisions of this Schedule relate to an exchange only so far as it provides facilities for the carrying on of investment business; and nothing in this Schedule shall be construed as requiring an exchange to limit dealings on the exchange to dealings in investments.

(2) The references in this Schedule, and elsewhere in this Act, to ensuring the performance of transactions on an exchange are to providing satisfactory procedures (including default procedures) for the settlement of transactions on the exchange.".

(2) The above amendment shall be deemed always to have had effect.

(3) In section 207(1) of the Financial Services Act 1986 (interpretation), at the appropriate place insert—

> " "ensure" and "ensuring", in relation to the performance of transactions on an investment exchange, have the meaning given in paragraph 6 of Schedule 4 to this Act;".

Consequential amendments and delegation of functions on commencement.

206.—(1) The Financial Services Act 1986 has effect with the amendments specified in Schedule 23 which are consequential on the amendments made by sections 192, 194 and 195.

(2) If immediately before the commencement of any provision of this Part which amends Part I of the Financial Services Act 1986—

> (a) a designated agency is exercising by virtue of a delegation order under section 114 of that Act any functions of the Secretary of State under that Part, and

> (b) no draft order is lying before Parliament resuming any of those functions,

the order bringing that provision into force may make, in relation to any functions conferred on the Secretary of State by the amendment, any such provision as may be made by an order under that section.

(3) If immediately before the commencement of any provision of Schedule 23 which amends Part III of the Financial Services Act 1986—

> (a) a transferee body (within the meaning of that Act) is exercising by virtue of a transfer order under paragraph 28 of Schedule 11 to that Act any functions of the Registrar under that Part, and

> (b) no draft order is lying before Parliament resuming any of those functions,

the order bringing that provision into force may make, in relation to any functions conferred on the Registrar by the amendment, any such provision as may be made by an order under that paragraph.

(4) References in the Financial Services Act 1986 to a delegation order made under section 114 of that Act or to a transfer order made under paragraph 28 of Schedule 11 to that Act include an order made containing any such provision as is authorised by subsection (2) or (3).

PART IX

TRANSFER OF SECURITIES

Transfer of securities.

207.—(1) The Secretary of State may make provision by regulations for enabling title to securities to be evidenced and transferred without a written instrument.

In this section—

> (a) "securities" means shares, stock, debentures, debenture stock, loan stock, bonds, units of a collective investment scheme within the meaning of the Financial Services Act 1986 and other securities of any description;

> (b) references to title to securities include any legal or equitable interest in securities; and

> (c) references to a transfer of title include a transfer by way of security.

(2) The regulations may make provision—

    (a) for procedures for recording and transferring title to securities, and

    (b) for the regulation of those procedures and the persons responsible for or involved in their operation.

(3) The regulations shall contain such safeguards as appear to the Secretary of State appropriate for the protection of investors and for ensuring that competition is not restricted, distorted or prevented.

(4) The regulations may for the purpose of enabling or facilitating the operation of the new procedures make provision with respect to the rights and obligations of persons in relation to securities dealt with under the procedures.

But the regulations shall be framed so as to secure that the rights and obligations in relation to securities dealt with under the new procedures correspond, so far as practicable, with those which would arise apart from any regulations under this section.

(5) The regulations may include such supplementary, incidental and transitional provisions as appear to the Secretary of State to be necessary or expedient.

In particular, provision may be made for the purpose of giving effect to—

    (a) the transmission of title to securities by operation of law;

    (b) any restriction on the transfer of title to securities arising by virtue of the provisions of any enactment or instrument, court order or agreement;

    (c) any power conferred by any such provision on a person to deal with securities on behalf of the person entitled.

(6) The regulations may make provision with respect to the persons responsible for the operation of the new procedures—

    (a) as to the consequences of their insolvency or incapacity, or

    (b) as to the transfer from them to other persons of their functions in relation to the new procedures.

(7) The regulations may for the purposes mentioned above—

    (a) modify or exclude any provision of any enactment or instrument, or any rule of law;

    (b) apply, with such modifications as may be appropriate, the provisions of any enactment or instrument (including provisions creating criminal offences);

    (c) require the payment of fees, or enable persons to require the payment of fees, of such amounts as may be specified in the regulations or determined in accordance with them;

    (d) empower the Secretary of State to delegate to any person willing and able to discharge them any functions of his under the regulations.

(8) The regulations may make different provision for different cases.

(9) Regulations under this section shall be made by statutory instrument; and no such regulations shall be made unless a draft of the instrument has been laid before and approved by resolution of each House of Parliament.

PART X

MISCELLANEOUS AND GENERAL PROVISIONS

Miscellaneous

Summary proceedings in Scotland for offences in connection with disqualification of directors.
1986 c. 46.
1986 c. 45.

208. In section 21 of the Company Directors Disqualification Act 1986 (application of provisions of the Insolvency Act 1986), after subsection (3) add—

"(4) For the purposes of summary proceedings in Scotland, section 431 of that Act applies to summary proceedings for an offence under section 11 or 13 of this Act as it applies to summary proceedings for an offence under Parts I to VII of that Act.".

Prosecutions in connection with insider dealing.
1985 c. 8.

209. In section 8 of the Company Securities (Insider Dealing) Act 1985 (punishment of contraventions), in subsection (2) (institution of proceedings in England and Wales), for "by the Secretary of State or by, or with the consent of, the Director of Public Prosecutions" substitute "by, or with the consent of, the Secretary of State or the Director of Public Prosecutions".

Restriction of duty to supply statements of premium income.
1975 c. 75.

210.—(1) Schedule 3 to the Policyholders Protection Act 1975 (provisions with respect to levies on authorised insurance companies) is amended as follows.

(2) For paragraph 4 (statements of premium income to be sent to Secretary of State) substitute—

"4.—(1) The Secretary of State may by notice in writing require an authorised insurance company to send him a statement of—

(a) any income of the company for the year preceding that in which the notice is received by the company which is income liable to the general business levy, and

(b) any income of the company for that year which is income liable to the long term business levy.

(2) An authorised insurance company which receives a notice under this paragraph shall send the statement required by the notice to the Secretary of State within three months of receiving the notice.

(3) Where an authorised insurance company is required under this paragraph to send a statement to the Secretary of State in respect of income of both descriptions mentioned in sub-paragraph (1)(a) and (b) above it shall send a separate statement in respect of income of each description.".

1982 c. 50.

(3) In paragraph 5(3) (application of provisions of the Insurance Companies Act 1982 to failure to meet obligation imposed by paragraph 4) for "the obligation imposed on an insurance company by paragraph 4" substitute "an obligation imposed on an insurance company under paragraph 4".

(4) In paragraph 6 (declaration and enforcement of levies) omit sub-paragraph (4) (provision about notices).

(5) After paragraph 7 insert—

"Notices under paragraphs 4 and 6

8. A notice under paragraph 4 or 6 above may be sent by post, and a letter containing such a notice shall be deemed to be properly addressed if it is addressed to the insurance company to which it is sent at its last known place of business in the United Kingdom.".

211.—(1) In section 104 of the Building Societies Act 1986 (power to assimilate law relating to building societies and law relating to companies), in subsection (2) (relevant provisions of that Act), omit the word "and" before paragraph (d) and after that paragraph add—

> "; and

> (e) section 110 (provisions exempting officers and auditors from liability).".

Building societies: miscellaneous amendments.
1986 c. 53.

(2) In Schedule 15 to the Building Societies Act 1986 (application of companies winding-up legislation)—

(a) in paragraph 1(a) (provisions of Insolvency Act 1986 applied) for "and XII" substitute ", XII and XIII";

1986 c. 45.

(b) in paragraph 3(2)(b) (adaptations: references to be omitted), omit ", a shadow director".

(3) In the Company Directors Disqualification Act 1986, after section 22 insert—

1986 c. 46.

"Application of Act to building societies.

22A.—(1) This Act applies to building societies as it applies to companies.

(2) References in this Act to a company, or to a director or an officer of a company include, respectively, references to a building society within the meaning of the Building Societies Act 1986 or to a director or officer, within the meaning of that Act, of a building society.

(3) In relation to a building society the definition of "shadow director" in section 22(5) applies with the substitution of "building society" for "company".

(4) In the application of Schedule 1 to the directors of a building society, references to provisions of the Insolvency Act or the Companies Act include references to the corresponding provisions of the Building Societies Act 1986.".

General

212. The enactments mentioned in Schedule 24 are repealed to the extent specified there.

Repeals.

213.—(1) The provisions of this Act extend to Northern Ireland so far as they amend, or provide for the amendment of, an enactment which so extends.

Provisions extending to Northern Ireland.

(2) So far as any provision of this Act amends the Companies Act 1985 or the Insolvency Act 1986, its application to companies registered or incorporated in Northern Ireland is subject to section 745(1) of the Companies Act 1985 or section 441(2) of the Insolvency Act 1986, as the case may be.

(3) In Part III (investigations and powers to obtain information), sections 82 to 91, (powers exercisable to assist overseas regulatory authorities) extend to Northern Ireland.

(4) Part VI (mergers and related matters) extends to Northern Ireland.

(5) In Part VII (financial markets and insolvency) the following provisions extend to Northern Ireland—

   (a) sections 154 and 155 (introductory provisions and definition of "market contract"),

   (b) section 156 and Schedule 21 (additional requirements for recognition of investment exchange or clearing house),

   (c) sections 157, 160, 162, and 166 to 169 (provisions relating to recognised investment exchanges and clearing houses),

   (d) sections 170 to 172 (power to extend provisions to other financial markets),

   (e) section 184 (indemnity for certain acts), and

   (f) sections 185 to 191 (supplementary provisions).

1986 c. 60.

(6) Part VIII (amendments of Financial Services Act 1986) extends to Northern Ireland.

(7) Part IX (transfer of securities) extends to Northern Ireland.

1973 c. 36.

Subject to any Order made after the passing of this Act by virtue of section 3(1)(a) of the Northern Ireland Constitution Act 1973, the transfer of securities shall not be a transferred matter for the purposes of that Act but shall for the purposes of section 3(2) be treated as specified in Schedule 3 to that Act.

(8) In Part X (miscellaneous and general provisions), this section and sections 214 to 216 (general provisions) extend to Northern Ireland.

(9) Except as mentioned above, the provisions of this Act do not extend to Northern Ireland.

Making of corresponding provision for Northern Ireland.
1974 c. 28.
729

214.—(1) An Order in Council under paragraph 1(1)(b) of Schedule 1 to the Northern Ireland Act 1974 (legislation for Northern Ireland in the interim period) which contains a statement that it is only made for purposes corresponding to the purposes of provisions of this Act to which this section applies—

   (a) shall not be subject to paragraph 1(4) and (5) of that Schedule (affirmative resolution of both Houses of Parliament), but

   (b) shall be subject to annulment in pursuance of a resolution of either House of Parliament.

(2) The provisions of this Act to which this section applies are—

   (a) Parts I to V, and

   (b) Part VII, except sections 156, 157, 169 and Schedule 21.

215.—(1) The following provisions of this Act come into force on Royal Assent—

PART X

Commencement and transitional provisions.

   (a) in Part V (amendments of company law), section 141 (application to declare dissolution of company void);

   (b) in Part VI (mergers)—

      (i) sections 147 to 150, and

      (ii) paragraphs 2 to 12, 14 to 16, 18 to 20, 22 to 25 of Schedule 20, and section 153 so far as relating to those paragraphs;

   (c) in Part VIII (amendments of the Financial Services Act 1986), section 202 (offers of short-dated debentures);

1986 c. 60.

   (d) in Part X (miscellaneous and general provisions), the repeals made by Schedule 24 in sections 71, 74, 88 and 89 of, and Schedule 9 to, the Fair Trading Act 1973, and section 212 so far as relating to those repeals.

1973 c. 41.

(2) The other provisions of this Act come into force on such day as the Secretary of State may appoint by order made by statutory instrument; and different days may be appointed for different provisions and different purposes.

(3) An order bringing into force any provision may contain such transitional provisions and savings as appear to the Secretary of State to be necessary or expedient.

(4) The Secretary of State may also by order under this section amend any enactment which refers to the commencement of a provision brought into force by the order so as to substitute a reference to the actual date on which it comes into force.

216. This Act may be cited as the Companies Act 1989.

Short title.

SCHEDULES

Section 4(2).

SCHEDULE 1

Form and Content of Company Accounts

1985 c. 6.

1. Schedule 4 to the Companies Act 1985 (form and content of company accounts) is amended as follows.

Group undertakings

2.—(1) For "group companies", wherever occurring, substitute "group undertakings".

(2) That expression occurs—

(a) in Balance Sheet Format 1, in Items B.III.1 and 2, C.II.2, C.III.1, E.6 and H.6;

(b) in Balance Sheet Format 2—

(i) under the heading "ASSETS", in Items B.III.1 and 2, C.II.2 and C.III.1;

(ii) under the heading "LIABILITIES", in Item C.6;

(c) in the Profit and Loss Accounts Formats—

(i) in Format 1, Item 7;

(ii) in Format 2, Item 9;

(iii) in Format 3, Item B.3;

(iv) in Format 4, Item B.5;

(d) in Notes (15) and (16) to the profit and loss account formats; and

(e) in the second sentence of paragraph 53(2) (exclusion from requirement to state separately certain loans).

Participating interests

3.—(1) For "shares in related companies", wherever occurring, substitute "participating interests".

(2) That expression occurs—

(a) in Balance Sheet Format 1, Item B.III.3;

(b) in Balance Sheet Format 2, under the heading "ASSETS", in Item B.III.3;

(c) in the Profit and Loss Accounts Formats—

(i) in Format 1, Item 8;

(ii) in Format 2, Item 10;

(iii) in Format 3, Item B.4;

(iv) in Format 4, Item B.6.

4.—(1) For "related companies", wherever occurring in any other context, substitute "undertakings in which the company has a participating interest".

(2) Those contexts are—

(a) in Balance Sheet Format 1, in Items B.III.4, C.II.3, E.7 and H.7;

(b) in Balance Sheet Format 2—

(i) under the heading "ASSETS", in Items B.III.4 and C.II.3;

(ii) under the heading "LIABILITIES", in Item C.7.

Consistency of accounting policies

5. For paragraph 11 (consistency of accounting policy from one year to the next) substitute—

"11. Accounting policies shall be applied consistently within the same accounts and from one financial year to the next.".

Revaluation reserve

6. In paragraph 34 (revaluation reserve), for sub-paragraph (3) (circumstances in which reduction of reserve required or permitted) substitute—

"(3) An amount may be transferred from the revaluation reserve—

(a) to the profit and loss account, if the amount was previously charged to that account or represents realised profit, or

(b) on capitalisation;

and the revaluation reserve shall be reduced to the extent that the amounts transferred to it are no longer necessary for the purposes of the valuation method used.

(3A) In sub-paragraph (3)(b) "capitalisation", in relation to an amount standing to the credit of the revaluation reserve, means applying it in wholly or partly paying up unissued shares in the company to be allotted to members of the company as fully or partly paid shares.

(3B) The revaluation reserve shall not be reduced except as mentioned in this paragraph.".

Compliance with accounting standards

7. After paragraph 36 (disclosure of accounting policies) insert—

"36A. It shall be stated whether the accounts have been prepared in accordance with applicable accounting standards and particulars of any material departure from those standards and the reasons for it shall be given.".

Provision for taxation

8. For paragraph 47 (provision for taxation) substitute—

"47. The amount of any provision for deferred taxation shall be stated separately from the amount of any provision for other taxation.".

Loans in connection with assistance for purchase of company's own shares

9. In paragraph 51(2) (disclosure of outstanding loans in connection with certain cases of financial assistance for purchase of company's own shares), after "153(4)(b)" insert ", (bb)".

Obligation to show corresponding amounts for previous financial year

10. In paragraph 58(3) (exceptions from obligation to show corresponding amount for previous financial year), for paragraphs (a) to (c) substitute—

"(a) paragraph 13 of Schedule 4A (details of accounting treatment of acquisitions),

(b) paragraphs 2, 8(3), 16, 21(1)(d), 22(4) and (5), 24(3) and (4) and 27(3) and (4) of Schedule 5 (shareholdings in other undertakings),

(c) Parts II and III of Schedule 6 (loans and other dealings in favour of directors and others), and

(d) paragraphs 42 and 46 above (fixed assets and reserves and provisions).".

Special provisions where company is parent company or subsidiary undertaking

11.—(1) For the heading to Part IV (special provisions where the company is a holding or subsidiary company) substitute—

"Part IV

Special Provisions Where Company is a Parent Company or Subsidiary Undertaking".

(2) In that Part for paragraph 59 substitute—

"Dealings with or interests in group undertakings

59. Where a company is a parent company or a subsidiary undertaking and any item required by Part I of this Schedule to be shown in the company's balance sheet in relation to group undertakings includes—

(a) amounts attributable to dealings with or interests in any parent undertaking or fellow subsidiary undertaking, or

(b) amounts attributable to dealings with or interests in any subsidiary undertaking of the company,

the aggregate amounts within paragraphs (a) and (b) respectively shall be shown as separate items, either by way of subdivision of the relevant item in the balance sheet or in a note to the company's accounts.".

(3) After that paragraph insert—

"Guarantees and other financial commitments in favour of group undertakings

59A. Commitments within any of sub-paragraphs (1) to (5) of paragraph 50 (guarantees and other financial commitments) which are undertaken on behalf of or for the benefit of—

(a) any parent undertaking or fellow subsidiary undertaking, or

(b) any subsidiary undertaking of the company,

shall be stated separately from the other commitments within that sub-paragraph, and commitments within paragraph (a) shall also be stated separately from those within paragraph (b).".

SCHEDULE 2

[Schedule 4A to the Companies Act 1985]

Form and Content of Group Accounts

General rules

1.—(1) Group accounts shall comply so far as practicable with the provisions of Schedule 4 as if the undertakings included in the consolidation ("the group") were a single company.

(2) In particular, for the purposes of paragraph 59 of that Schedule (dealings with or interests in group undertakings) as it applies to group accounts—

(a) any subsidiary undertakings of the parent company not included in the consolidation shall be treated as subsidiary undertakings of the group, and

(b) if the parent company is itself a subsidiary undertaking, the group shall be treated as a subsidiary undertaking of any parent undertaking of that company, and the reference to fellow-subsidiary undertakings shall be construed accordingly.

(3) Where the parent company is treated as an investment company for the purposes of Part V of that Schedule (special provisions for investment companies) the group shall be similarly treated.

2.—(1) The consolidated balance sheet and profit and loss account shall incorporate in full the information contained in the individual accounts of the undertakings included in the consolidation, subject to the adjustments authorised or required by the following provisions of this Schedule and to such other adjustments (if any) as may be appropriate in accordance with generally accepted accounting principles or practice.

(2) If the financial year of a subsidiary undertaking included in the consolidation differs from that of the parent company, the group accounts shall be made up—

  (a) from the accounts of the subsidiary undertaking for its financial year last ending before the end of the parent company's financial year, provided that year ended no more than three months before that of the parent company, or

  (b) from interim accounts prepared by the subsidiary undertaking as at the end of the parent company's financial year.

3.—(1) Where assets and liabilities to be included in the group accounts have been valued or otherwise determined by undertakings according to accounting rules differing from those used for the group accounts, the values or amounts shall be adjusted so as to accord with the rules used for the group accounts.

(2) If it appears to the directors of the parent company that there are special reasons for departing from sub-paragraph (1) they may do so, but particulars of any such departure, the reasons for it and its effect shall be given in a note to the accounts.

(3) The adjustments referred to in this paragraph need not be made if they are not material for the purpose of giving a true and fair view.

4. Any differences of accounting rules as between a parent company's individual accounts for a financial year and its group accounts shall be disclosed in a note to the latter accounts and the reasons for the difference given.

5. Amounts which in the particular context of any provision of this Schedule are not material may be disregarded for the purposes of that provision.

Elimination of group transactions

6.—(1) Debts and claims between undertakings included in the consolidation, and income and expenditure relating to transactions between such undertakings, shall be eliminated in preparing the group accounts.

(2) Where profits and losses resulting from transactions between undertakings included in the consolidation are included in the book value of assets, they shall be eliminated in preparing the group accounts.

(3) The elimination required by sub-paragraph (2) may be effected in proportion to the group's interest in the shares of the undertakings.

(4) Sub-paragraphs (1) and (2) need not be complied with if the amounts concerned are not material for the purpose of giving a true and fair view.

Acquisition and merger accounting

7.—(1) The following provisions apply where an undertaking becomes a subsidiary undertaking of the parent company.

(2) That event is referred to in those provisions as an "acquisition", and references to the "undertaking acquired" shall be construed accordingly.

8. An acquisition shall be accounted for by the acquisition method of accounting unless the conditions for accounting for it as a merger are met and the merger method of accounting is adopted.

9.—(1) The acquisition method of accounting is as follows.

(2) The identifiable assets and liabilities of the undertaking acquired shall be included in the consolidated balance sheet at their fair values as at the date of acquisition.

In this paragraph the "identifiable" assets or liabilities of the undertaking acquired means the assets or liabilities which are capable of being disposed of or discharged separately, without disposing of a business of the undertaking.

(3) The income and expenditure of the undertaking acquired shall be brought into the group accounts only as from the date of the acquisition.

(4) There shall be set off against the acquisition cost of the interest in the shares of the undertaking held by the parent company and its subsidiary undertakings the interest of the parent company and its subsidiary undertakings in the adjusted capital and reserves of the undertaking acquired.

For this purpose—

"the acquisition cost" means the amount of any cash consideration and the fair value of any other consideration, together with such amount (if any) in respect of fees and other expenses of the acquisition as the company may determine, and

"the adjusted capital and reserves" of the undertaking acquired means its capital and reserves at the date of the acquisition after adjusting the identifiable assets and liabilities of the undertaking to fair values as at that date.

(5) The resulting amount if positive shall be treated as goodwill, and if negative as a negative consolidation difference.

10.—(1) The conditions for accounting for an acquisition as a merger are—

(a) that at least 90 per cent. of the nominal value of the relevant shares in the undertaking acquired is held by or on behalf of the parent company and its subsidiary undertakings,

(b) that the proportion referred to in paragraph (a) was attained pursuant to an arrangement providing for the issue of equity shares by the parent company or one or more of its subsidiary undertakings,

(c) that the fair value of any consideration other than the issue of equity shares given pursuant to the arrangement by the parent company and its subsidiary undertakings did not exceed 10 per cent. of the nominal value of the equity shares issued, and

(d) that adoption of the merger method of accounting accords with generally accepted accounting principles or practice.

(2) The reference in sub-paragraph (1)(a) to the "relevant shares" in an undertaking acquired is to those carrying unrestricted rights to participate both in distributions and in the assets of the undertaking upon liquidation.

11.—(1) The merger method of accounting is as follows.

(2) The assets and liabilities of the undertaking acquired shall be brought into the group accounts at the figures at which they stand in the undertaking's accounts, subject to any adjustment authorised or required by this Schedule.

(3) The income and expenditure of the undertaking acquired shall be included in the group accounts for the entire financial year, including the period before the acquisition.

(4) The group accounts shall show corresponding amounts relating to the previous financial year as if the undertaking acquired had been included in the consolidation throughout that year.

(5) There shall be set off against the aggregate of—

(a) the appropriate amount in respect of qualifying shares issued by the parent company or its subsidiary undertakings in consideration for the acquisition of shares in the undertaking acquired, and

(b) the fair value of any other consideration for the acquisition of shares in the undertaking acquired, determined as at the date when those shares were acquired,

the nominal value of the issued share capital of the undertaking acquired held by the parent company and its subsidiary undertakings.

(6) The resulting amount shall be shown as an adjustment to the consolidated reserves.

(7) In sub-paragraph (5)(a) "qualifying shares" means—

(a) shares in relation to which section 131 (merger relief) applies, in respect of which the appropriate amount is the nominal value; or

(b) shares in relation to which section 132 (relief in respect of group reconstructions) applies, in respect of which the appropriate amount is the nominal value together with any minimum premium value within the meaning of that section.

12.—(1) Where a group is acquired, paragraphs 9 to 11 apply with the following adaptations.

(2) References to shares of the undertaking acquired shall be construed as references to shares of the parent undertaking of the group.

(3) Other references to the undertaking acquired shall be construed as references to the group; and references to the assets and liabilities, income and expenditure and capital and reserves of the undertaking acquired shall be construed as references to the assets and liabilities, income and expenditure and capital and reserves of the group after making the set-offs and other adjustments required by this Schedule in the case of group accounts.

13.—(1) The following information with respect to acquisitions taking place in the financial year shall be given in a note to the accounts.

(2) There shall be stated—

(a) the name of the undertaking acquired or, where a group was acquired, the name of the parent undertaking of that group, and

(b) whether the acquisition has been accounted for by the acquisition or the merger method of accounting;

and in relation to an acquisition which significantly affects the figures shown in the group accounts, the following further information shall be given.

(3) The composition and fair value of the consideration for the acquisition given by the parent company and its subsidiary undertakings shall be stated.

(4) The profit or loss of the undertaking or group acquired shall be stated—

(a) for the period from the beginning of the financial year of the undertaking or, as the case may be, of the parent undertaking of the group, up to the date of the acquisition, and

(b) for the previous financial year of that undertaking or parent undertaking;

and there shall also be stated the date on which the financial year referred to in paragraph (a) began.

SCH. 2   (5) Where the acquisition method of accounting has been adopted, the book values immediately prior to the acquisition, and the fair values at the date of acquisition, of each class of assets and liabilities of the undertaking or group acquired shall be stated in tabular form, including a statement of the amount of any goodwill or negative consolidation difference arising on the acquisition, together with an explanation of any significant adjustments made.

(6) Where the merger method of accounting has been adopted, an explanation shall be given of any significant adjustments made in relation to the amounts of the assets and liabilities of the undertaking or group acquired, together with a statement of any resulting adjustment to the consolidated reserves (including the re-statement of opening consolidated reserves).

(7) In ascertaining for the purposes of sub-paragraph (4), (5) or (6) the profit or loss of a group, the book values and fair values of assets and liabilities of a group or the amount of the assets and liabilities of a group, the set-offs and other adjustments required by this Schedule in the case of group accounts shall be made.

14.—(1) There shall also be stated in a note to the accounts the cumulative amount of goodwill resulting from acquisitions in that and earlier financial years which has been written off.

(2) That figure shall be shown net of any goodwill attributable to subsidiary undertakings or businesses disposed of prior to the balance sheet date.

15. Where during the financial year there has been a disposal of an undertaking or group which significantly affects the figures shown in the group accounts, there shall be stated in a note to the accounts—

(a) the name of that undertaking or, as the case may be, of the parent undertaking of that group, and

(b) the extent to which the profit or loss shown in the group accounts is attributable to profit or loss of that undertaking or group.

16. The information required by paragraph 13, 14 or 15 above need not be disclosed with respect to an undertaking which—

(a) is established under the law of a country outside the United Kingdom, or

(b) carries on business outside the United Kingdom,

if in the opinion of the directors of the parent company the disclosure would be seriously prejudicial to the business of that undertaking or to the business of the parent company or any of its subsidiary undertakings and the Secretary of State agrees that the information should not be disclosed.

Minority interests

17.—(1) The formats set out in Schedule 4 have effect in relation to group accounts with the following additions.

(2) In the Balance Sheet Formats a further item headed "Minority interests" shall be added—

(a) in Format 1, either after item J or at the end (after item K), and

(b) in Format 2, under the general heading "LIABILITIES", between items A and B;

and under that item shall be shown the amount of capital and reserves attributable to shares in subsidiary undertakings included in the consolidation held by or on behalf of persons other than the parent company and its subsidiary undertakings.

(3) In the Profit and Loss Account Formats a further item headed "Minority interests" shall be added—

(a) in Format 1, between items 14 and 15,

(b) in Format 2, between items 16 and 17,

(c) in Format 3, between items 7 and 8 in both sections A and B, and

(d) in Format 4, between items 9 and 10 in both sections A and B;

and under that item shall be shown the amount of any profit or loss on ordinary activities attributable to shares in subsidiary undertakings included in the consolidation held by or on behalf of persons other than the parent company and its subsidiary undertakings.

(4) In the Profit and Loss Account Formats a further item headed "Minority interests" shall be added—

(a) in Format 1, between items 18 and 19,

(b) in Format 2, between items 20 and 21,

(c) in Format 3, between items 9 and 10 in section A and between items 8 and 9 in section B, and

(d) in Format 4, between items 11 and 12 in section A and between items 10 and 11 in section B;

and under that item shall be shown the amount of any profit or loss on extraordinary activities attributable to shares in subsidiary undertakings included in the consolidation held by or on behalf of persons other than the parent company and its subsidiary undertakings.

(5) For the purposes of paragraph 3(3) and (4) of Schedule 4 (power to adapt or combine items)—

(a) the additional item required by sub-paragraph (2) above shall be treated as one to which a letter is assigned, and

(b) the additional items required by sub-paragraphs (3) and (4) above shall be treated as ones to which an Arabic number is assigned.

Interests in subsidiary undertakings excluded from consolidation

18. The interest of the group in subsidiary undertakings excluded from consolidation under section 229(4) (undertakings with activities different from those of undertakings included in the consolidation), and the amount of profit or loss attributable to such an interest, shall be shown in the consolidated balance sheet or, as the case may be, in the consolidated profit and loss account by the equity method of accounting (including dealing with any goodwill arising in accordance with paragraphs 17 to 19 and 21 of Schedule 4).

Joint ventures

19.—(1) Where an undertaking included in the consolidation manages another undertaking jointly with one or more undertakings not included in the consolidation, that other undertaking ("the joint venture") may, if it is not—

(a) a body corporate, or

(b) a subsidiary undertaking of the parent company,

be dealt with in the group accounts by the method of proportional consolidation.

(2) The provisions of this Part relating to the preparation of consolidated accounts apply, with any necessary modifications, to proportional consolidation under this paragraph.

Associated undertakings

20.—(1) An "associated undertaking" means an undertaking in which an undertaking included in the consolidation has a participating interest and over whose operating and financial policy it exercises a significant influence, and which is not—

(a) a subsidiary undertaking of the parent company, or

(b) a joint venture dealt with in accordance with paragraph 19.

(2) Where an undertaking holds 20 per cent. or more of the voting rights in another undertaking, it shall be presumed to exercise such an influence over it unless the contrary is shown.

(3) The voting rights in an undertaking means the rights conferred on shareholders in respect of their shares or, in the case of an undertaking not having a share capital, on members, to vote at general meetings of the undertaking on all, or substantially all, matters.

(4) The provisions of paragraphs 5 to 11 of Schedule 10A (rights to be taken into account and attribution of rights) apply in determining for the purposes of this paragraph whether an undertaking holds 20 per cent. or more of the voting rights in another undertaking.

21.—(1) The formats set out in Schedule 4 have effect in relation to group accounts with the following modifications.

(2) In the Balance Sheet Formats the items headed "Participating interests", that is—

(a) in Format 1, item B.III.3, and

(b) In Format 2, item B.III.3 under the heading "ASSETS",

shall be replaced by two items, "Interests in associated undertakings" and "Other participating interests".

(3) In the Profit and Loss Account Formats, the items headed "Income from participating interests", that is—

(a) in Format 1, item 8,

(b) in Format 2, item 10,

(c) in Format 3, item B.4, and

(d) in Format 4, item B.6,

shall be replaced by two items, "Income from interests in associated undertakings" and "Income from other participating interests".

22.—(1) The interest of an undertaking in an associated undertaking, and the amount of profit or loss attributable to such an interest, shall be shown by the equity method of accounting (including dealing with any goodwill arising in accordance with paragraphs 17 to 19 and 21 of Schedule 4).

(2) Where the associated undertaking is itself a parent undertaking, the net assets and profits or losses to be taken into account are those of the parent and its subsidiary undertakings (after making any consolidation adjustments).

(3) The equity method of accounting need not be applied if the amounts in question are not material for the purpose of giving a true and fair view.

SCHEDULE 3

[SCHEDULE 5 TO THE COMPANIES ACT 1985]

DISCLOSURE OF INFORMATION: RELATED UNDERTAKINGS

PART I

COMPANIES NOT REQUIRED TO PREPARE GROUP ACCOUNTS

Subsidiary undertakings

1.—(1) The following information shall be given where at the end of the financial year the company has subsidiary undertakings.

(2) The name of each subsidiary undertaking shall be stated.

(3) There shall be stated with respect to each subsidiary undertaking—

(a) if it is incorporated outside Great Britain, the country in which it is incorporated;

(b) if it is incorporated in Great Britain, whether it is registered in England and Wales or in Scotland;

(c) if it is unincorporated, the address of its principal place of business.

(4) The reason why the company is not required to prepare group accounts shall be stated.

(5) If the reason is that all the subsidiary undertakings of the company fall within the exclusions provided for in section 229, it shall be stated with respect to each subsidiary undertaking which of those exclusions applies.

Holdings in subsidiary undertakings

2.—(1) There shall be stated in relation to shares of each class held by the company in a subsidiary undertaking—

(a) the identity of the class, and

(b) the proportion of the nominal value of the shares of that class represented by those shares.

(2) The shares held by or on behalf of the company itself shall be distinguished from those attributed to the company which are held by or on behalf of a subsidiary undertaking.

Financial information about subsidiary undertakings

3.—(1) There shall be disclosed with respect to each subsidiary undertaking—

(a) the aggregate amount of its capital and reserves as at the end of its relevant financial year, and

(b) its profit or loss for that year.

(2) That information need not be given if the company is exempt by virtue of section 228 from the requirement to prepare group accounts (parent company included in accounts of larger group).

(3) That information need not be given if—

(a) the subsidiary undertaking is not required by any provision of this Act to deliver a copy of its balance sheet for its relevant financial year and does not otherwise publish that balance sheet in Great Britain or elsewhere, and

(b) the company's holding is less than 50 per cent. of the nominal value of the shares in the undertaking.

(4) Information otherwise required by this paragraph need not be given if it is not material.

(5) For the purposes of this paragraph the "relevant financial year" of a subsidiary undertaking is—

    (a) if its financial year ends with that of the company, that year, and

    (b) if not, its financial year ending last before the end of the company's financial year.

Financial years of subsidiary undertakings

4. Where the financial year of one or more subsidiary undertakings did not end with that of the company, there shall be stated in relation to each such undertaking—

    (a) the reasons why the company's directors consider that its financial year should not end with that of the company, and

    (b) the date on which its last financial year ended (last before the end of the company's financial year).

Instead of the dates required by paragraph (b) being given for each subsidiary undertaking the earliest and latest of those dates may be given.

Further information about subsidiary undertakings

5.—(1) There shall be disclosed—

    (a) any qualifications contained in the auditors' reports on the accounts of subsidiary undertakings for financial years ending with or during the financial year of the company, and

    (b) any note or saving contained in such accounts to call attention to a matter which, apart from the note or saving, would properly have been referred to in such a qualification,

in so far as the matter which is the subject of the qualification or note is not covered by the company's own accounts and is material from the point of view of its members.

(2) The aggregate amount of the total investment of the company in the shares of subsidiary undertakings shall be stated by way of the equity method of valuation, unless—

    (a) the company is exempt from the requirement to prepare group accounts by virtue of section 228 (parent company included in accounts of larger group), and

    (b) the directors state their opinion that the aggregate value of the assets of the company consisting of shares in, or amounts owing (whether on account of a loan or otherwise) from, the company's subsidiary undertakings is not less than the aggregate of the amounts at which those assets are stated or included in the company's balance sheet.

(3) In so far as information required by this paragraph is not obtainable, a statement to that effect shall be given instead.

Shares and debentures of company held by subsidiary undertakings

6.—(1) The number, description and amount of the shares in and debentures of the company held by or on behalf of its subsidiary undertakings shall be disclosed.

(2) Sub-paragraph (1) does not apply in relation to shares or debentures in the case of which the subsidiary undertaking is concerned as personal representative or, subject as follows, as trustee.

(3) The exception for shares or debentures in relation to which the subsidiary undertaking is concerned as trustee does not apply if the company, or any subsidiary undertaking of the company, is beneficially interested under the trust, otherwise than by way of security only for the purposes of a transaction entered into by it in the ordinary course of a business which includes the lending of money.

(4) Schedule 2 to this Act has effect for the interpretation of the reference in sub-paragraph (3) to a beneficial interest under a trust.

Significant holdings in undertakings other than subsidiary undertakings

7.—(1) The information required by paragraphs 8 and 9 shall be given where at the end of the financial year the company has a significant holding in an undertaking which is not a subsidiary undertaking of the company.

(2) A holding is significant for this purpose if—

(a) it amounts to 10 per cent. or more of the nominal value of any class of shares in the undertaking, or

(b) the amount of the holding (as stated or included in the company's accounts) exceeds one-tenth of the amount (as so stated) of the company's assets.

8.—(1) The name of the undertaking shall be stated.

(2) There shall be stated—

(a) if the undertaking is incorporated outside Great Britain, the country in which it is incorporated;

(b) if it is incorporated in Great Britain, whether it is registered in England and Wales or in Scotland;

(c) if it is unincorporated, the address of its principal place of business.

(3) There shall also be stated—

(a) the identity of each class of shares in the undertaking held by the company, and

(b) the proportion of the nominal value of the shares of that class represented by those shares.

9.—(1) Where the company has a significant holding in an undertaking amounting to 20 per cent. or more of the nominal value of the shares in the undertaking, there shall also be stated—

(a) the aggregate amount of the capital and reserves of the undertaking as at the end of its relevant financial year, and

(b) its profit or loss for that year.

(2) That information need not be given if—

(a) the company is exempt by virtue of section 228 from the requirement to prepare group accounts (parent company included in accounts of larger group), and

(b) the investment of the company in all undertakings in which it has such a holding as is mentioned in sub-paragraph (1) is shown, in aggregate, in the notes to the accounts by way of the equity method of valuation.

(3) That information need not be given in respect of an undertaking if—

(a) the undertaking is not required by any provision of this Act to deliver a copy of its balance sheet for its relevant financial year and does not otherwise publish that balance sheet in Great Britain or elsewhere, and

(b) the company's holding is less than 50 per cent. of the nominal value of the shares in the undertaking.

(4) Information otherwise required by this paragraph need not be given if it is not material.

(5) For the purposes of this paragraph the "relevant financial year" of an undertaking is—

(a) if its financial year ends with that of the company, that year, and

(b) if not, its financial year ending last before the end of the company's financial year.

Arrangements attracting merger relief

10.—(1) This paragraph applies to arrangements attracting merger relief, that is, where a company allots shares in consideration for the issue, transfer or cancellation of shares in another body corporate ("the other company") in circumstances such that section 130 of this Act (share premium account) does not, by virtue of section 131(2) (merger relief), apply to the premiums on the shares.

(2) If the company makes such an arrangement during the financial year, the following information shall be given—

(a) the name of the other company,

(b) the number, nominal value and class of shares allotted,

(c) the number, nominal value and class of shares in the other company issued, transferred or cancelled, and

(d) particulars of the accounting treatment adopted in the company's accounts in respect of the issue, transfer or cancellation.

(3) Where the company made such an arrangement during the financial year, or during either of the two preceding financial years, and there is included in the company's profit and loss account—

(a) any profit or loss realised during the financial year by the company on the disposal of—

(i) any shares in the other company, or

(ii) any assets which were fixed assets of the other company or any of its subsidiary undertakings at the time of the arrangement, or

(b) any part of any profit or loss realised during the financial year by the company on the disposal of any shares (other than shares in the other company) which was attributable to the fact that there were at the time of the disposal amongst the assets of the company which issued the shares, or any of its subsidiary undertakings, such shares or assets as are described in paragraph (a) above,

then, the net amount of that profit or loss or, as the case may be, the part so attributable shall be shown, together with an explanation of the transactions to which the information relates.

(4) For the purposes of this paragraph the time of the arrangement shall be taken to be—

(a) where as a result of the arrangement the other company becomes a subsidiary undertaking of the company, the date on which it does so or, if the arrangement in question becomes binding only on the fulfilment of a condition, the date on which that condition is fulfilled;

(b) if the other company is already a subsidiary undertaking of the company, the date on which the shares are allotted or, if they are allotted on different days, the first day.

Parent undertaking drawing up accounts for larger group

11.—(1) Where the company is a subsidiary undertaking, the following information shall be given with respect to the parent undertaking of—

(a) the largest group of undertakings for which group accounts are drawn up and of which the company is a member, and

(b) the smallest such group of undertakings.

(2) The name of the parent undertaking shall be stated.

(3) There shall be stated—

(a) if the undertaking is incorporated outside Great Britain, the country in which it is incorporated;

(b) if it is incorporated in Great Britain, whether it is registered in England and Wales or in Scotland;

(c) if it is unincorporated, the address of its principal place of business.

(4) If copies of the group accounts referred to in sub-paragraph (1) are available to the public, there shall also be stated the addresses from which copies of the accounts can be obtained.

Identification of ultimate parent company

12.—(1) Where the company is a subsidiary undertaking, the following information shall be given with respect to the company (if any) regarded by the directors as being the company's ultimate parent company.

(2) The name of that company shall be stated.

(3) If known to the directors, there shall be stated—

(a) if that company is incorporated outside Great Britain, the country in which it is incorporated;

(b) if it is incorporated in Great Britain, whether it is registered in England and Wales or in Scotland.

(4) In this paragraph "company" includes any body corporate.

Constructions of references to shares held by company

13.—(1) References in this Part of this Schedule to shares held by a company shall be construed as follows.

(2) For the purposes of paragraphs 2 to 5 (information about subsidiary undertakings)—

(a) there shall be attributed to the company any shares held by a subsidiary undertaking, or by a person acting on behalf of the company or a subsidiary undertaking; but

(b) there shall be treated as not held by the company any shares held on behalf of a person other than the company or a subsidiary undertaking.

(3) For the purposes of paragraphs 7 to 9 (information about undertakings other than subsidiary undertakings)—

(a) there shall be attributed to the company shares held on its behalf by any person; but

(b) there shall be treated as not held by a company shares held on behalf of a person other than the company.

(4) For the purposes of any of those provisions, shares held by way of security shall be treated as held by the person providing the security—

  (a) where apart from the right to exercise them for the purpose of preserving the value of the security, or of realising it, the rights attached to the shares are exercisable only in accordance with his instructions, and

  (b) where the shares are held in connection with the granting of loans as part of normal business activities and apart from the right to exercise them for the purpose of preserving the value of the security, or of realising it, the rights attached to the shares are exercisable only in his interests.

PART II

COMPANIES REQUIRED TO PREPARE GROUP ACCOUNTS

Introductory

14. In this Part of this Schedule "the group" means the group consisting of the parent company and its subsidiary undertakings.

Subsidiary undertakings

15.—(1) The following information shall be given with respect to the undertakings which are subsidiary undertakings of the parent company at the end of the financial year.

(2) The name of each undertaking shall be stated.

(3) There shall be stated—

  (a) if the undertaking is incorporated outside Great Britain, the country in which it is incorporated;

  (b) if it is incorporated in Great Britain, whether it is registered in England and Wales or in Scotland;

  (c) if it is unincorporated, the address of its principal place of business.

(4) It shall also be stated whether the subsidiary undertaking is included in the consolidation and, if it is not, the reasons for excluding it from consolidation shall be given.

(5) It shall be stated with respect to each subsidiary undertaking by virtue of which of the conditions specified in section 258(2) or (4) it is a subsidiary undertaking of its immediate parent undertaking.

That information need not be given if the relevant condition is that specified in subsection (2)(a) of that section (holding of a majority of the voting rights) and the immediate parent undertaking holds the same proportion of the shares in the undertaking as it holds voting rights.

Holdings in subsidiary undertakings

16.—(1) The following information shall be given with respect to the shares of a subsidiary undertaking held—

  (a) by the parent company, and

  (b) by the group;

and the information under paragraphs (a) and (b) shall (if different) be shown separately.

(2) There shall be stated—

  (a) the identity of each class of shares held, and

  (b) the proportion of the nominal value of the shares of that class represented by those shares.

Financial information about subsidiary undertakings not included in the consolidation

17.—(1) There shall be shown with respect to each subsidiary undertaking not included in the consolidation—

(a) the aggregate amount of its capital and reserves as at the end of its relevant financial year, and

(b) its profit or loss for that year.

(2) That information need not be given if the group's investment in the undertaking is included in the accounts by way of the equity method of valuation or if—

(a) the undertaking is not required by any provision of this Act to deliver a copy of its balance sheet for its relevant financial year and does not otherwise publish that balance sheet in Great Britain or elsewhere, and

(b) the holding of the group is less than 50 per cent. of the nominal value of the shares in the undertaking.

(3) Information otherwise required by this paragraph need not be given if it is not material.

(4) For the purposes of this paragraph the "relevant financial year" of a subsidiary undertaking is—

(a) if its financial year ends with that of the company, that year, and

(b) if not, its financial year ending last before the end of the company's financial year.

Further information about subsidiary undertakings excluded from consolidation

18.—(1) The following information shall be given with respect to subsidiary undertakings excluded from consolidation.

(2) There shall be disclosed—

(a) any qualifications contained in the auditors' reports on the accounts of the undertaking for financial years ending with or during the financial year of the company, and

(b) any note or saving contained in such accounts to call attention to a matter which, apart from the note or saving, would properly have been referred to in such a qualification,

in so far as the matter which is the subject of the qualification or note is not covered by the consolidated accounts and is material from the point of view of the members of the parent company.

(3) In so far as information required by this paragraph is not obtainable, a statement to that effect shall be given instead.

Financial years of subsidiary undertakings

19. Where the financial year of one or more subsidiary undertakings did not end with that of the company, there shall be stated in relation to each such undertaking—

(a) the reasons why the company's directors consider that its financial year should not end with that of the company, and

(b) the date on which its last financial year ended (last before the end of the company's financial year).

Instead of the dates required by paragraph (b) being given for each subsidiary undertaking the earliest and latest of those dates may be given.

Shares and debentures of company held by subsidiary undertakings

20.—(1) The number, description and amount of the shares in and debentures of the company held by or on behalf of its subsidiary undertakings shall be disclosed.

(2) Sub-paragraph (1) does not apply in relation to shares or debentures in the case of which the subsidiary undertaking is concerned as personal representative or, subject as follows, as trustee.

(3) The exception for shares or debentures in relation to which the subsidiary undertaking is concerned as trustee does not apply if the company or any of its subsidiary undertakings is beneficially interested under the trust, otherwise than by way of security only for the purposes of a transaction entered into by it in the ordinary course of a business which includes the lending of money.

(4) Schedule 2 to this Act has effect for the interpretation of the reference in sub-paragraph (3) to a beneficial interest under a trust.

Joint ventures

21.—(1) The following information shall be given where an undertaking is dealt with in the consolidated accounts by the method of proportional consolidation in accordance with paragraph 19 of Schedule 4A (joint ventures)—

(a) the name of the undertaking;

(b) the address of the principal place of business of the undertaking;

(c) the factors on which joint management of the undertaking is based; and

(d) the proportion of the capital of the undertaking held by undertakings included in the consolidation.

(2) Where the financial year of the undertaking did not end with that of the company, there shall be stated the date on which a financial year of the undertaking last ended before that date.

Associated undertakings

22.—(1) The following information shall be given where an undertaking included in the consolidation has an interest in an associated undertaking.

(2) The name of the associated undertaking shall be stated.

(3) There shall be stated—

(a) if the undertaking is incorporated outside Great Britain, the country in which it is incorporated;

(b) if it is incorporated in Great Britain, whether it is registered in England and Wales or in Scotland;

(c) if it is unincorporated, the address of its principal place of business.

(4) The following information shall be given with respect to the shares of the undertaking held—

(a) by the parent company, and

(b) by the group;

and the information under paragraphs (a) and (b) shall be shown separately.

(5) There shall be stated—

(a) the identity of each class of shares held, and

(b) the proportion of the nominal value of the shares of that class represented by those shares.

(6) In this paragraph "associated undertaking" has the meaning given by paragraph 20 of Schedule 4A; and the information required by this paragraph shall be given notwithstanding that paragraph 22(3) of that Schedule (materiality) applies in relation to the accounts themselves.

Other significant holdings of parent company or group

23.—(1) The information required by paragraphs 24 and 25 shall be given where at the end of the financial year the parent company has a significant holding in an undertaking which is not one of its subsidiary undertakings and does not fall within paragraph 21 (joint ventures) or paragraph 22 (associated undertakings).

(2) A holding is significant for this purpose if—

    (a) it amounts to 10 per cent. or more of the nominal value of any class of shares in the undertaking, or

    (b) the amount of the holding (as stated or included in the company's individual accounts) exceeds one-tenth of the amount of its assets (as so stated).

24.—(1) The name of the undertaking shall be stated.

(2) There shall be stated—

    (a) if the undertaking is incorporated outside Great Britain, the country in which it is incorporated;

    (b) if it is incorporated in Great Britain, whether it is registered in England and Wales or in Scotland;

    (c) if it is unincorporated, the address of its principal place of business.

(3) The following information shall be given with respect to the shares of the undertaking held by the parent company.

(4) There shall be stated—

    (a) the identity of each class of shares held, and

    (b) the proportion of the nominal value of the shares of that class represented by those shares.

25.—(1) Where the company has a significant holding in an undertaking amounting to 20 per cent. or more of the nominal value of the shares in the undertaking, there shall also be stated—

    (a) the aggregate amount of the capital and reserves of the undertaking as at the end of its relevant financial year, and

    (b) its profit or loss for that year.

(2) That information need not be given in respect of an undertaking if—

    (a) the undertaking is not required by any provision of this Act to deliver a copy of its balance sheet for its relevant financial year and does not otherwise publish that balance sheet in Great Britain or elsewhere, and

    (b) the company's holding is less than 50 per cent. of the nominal value of the shares in the undertaking.

(3) Information otherwise required by this paragraph need not be given if it is not material.

(4) For the purposes of this paragraph the "relevant financial year" of an undertaking is—

    (a) if its financial year ends with that of the company, that year, and

    (b) if not, its financial year ending last before the end of the company's financial year.

26.—(1) The information required by paragraphs 27 and 28 shall be given where at the end of the financial year the group has a significant holding in an undertaking which is not a subsidiary undertaking of the parent company and does not fall within paragraph 21 (joint ventures) or paragraph 22 (associated undertakings).

(2) A holding is significant for this purpose if—

(a) it amounts to 10 per cent. or more of the nominal value of any class of shares in the undertaking, or

(b) the amount of the holding (as stated or included in the group accounts) exceeds one-tenth of the amount of the group's assets (as so stated).

27.—(1) The name of the undertaking shall be stated.

(2) There shall be stated—

(a) if the undertaking is incorporated outside Great Britain, the country in which it is incorporated;

(b) if it is incorporated in Great Britain, whether it is registered in England and Wales or in Scotland;

(c) if it is unincorporated, the address of its principal place of business.

(3) The following information shall be given with respect to the shares of the undertaking held by the group.

(4) There shall be stated—

(a) the identity of each class of shares held, and

(b) the proportion of the nominal value of the shares of that class represented by those shares.

28.—(1) Where the holding of the group amounts to 20 per cent. or more of the nominal value of the shares in the undertaking, there shall also be stated—

(a) the aggregate amount of the capital and reserves of the undertaking as at the end of its relevant financial year, and

(b) its profit or loss for that year.

(2) That information need not be given if—

(a) the undertaking is not required by any provision of this Act to deliver a copy of its balance sheet for its relevant financial year and does not otherwise publish that balance sheet in Great Britain or elsewhere, and

(b) the holding of the group is less than 50 per cent. of the nominal value of the shares in the undertaking.

(3) Information otherwise required by this paragraph need not be given if it is not material.

(4) For the purposes of this paragraph the "relevant financial year" of an outside undertaking is—

(a) if its financial year ends with that of the parent company, that year, and

(b) if not, its financial year ending last before the end of the parent company's financial year.

Arrangements attracting merger relief

29.—(1) This paragraph applies to arrangements attracting merger relief, that is, where a company allots shares in consideration for the issue, transfer or cancellation of shares in another body corporate ("the other company") in circumstances such that section 130 of this Act (share premium account) does not, by virtue of section 131(2) (merger relief), apply to the premiums on the shares.

(2) If the parent company made such an arrangement during the financial year, the following information shall be given—

(a) the name of the other company,

(b) the number, nominal value and class of shares allotted,

(c) the number, nominal value and class of shares in the other company issued, transferred or cancelled, and

(d) particulars of the accounting treatment adopted in the parent company's individual and group accounts in respect of the issue, transfer or cancellation, and

(e) particulars of the extent to which and manner in which the profit or loss for the financial year shown in the group accounts is affected by any profit or loss of the other company, or any of its subsidiary undertakings, which arose before the time of the arrangement.

(3) Where the parent company made such an arrangement during the financial year, or during either of the two preceding financial years, and there is included in the consolidated profit and loss account—

(a) any profit or loss realised during the financial year on the disposal of—

(i) any shares in the other company, or

(ii) any assets which were fixed assets of the other company or any of its subsidiary undertakings at the time of the arrangement, or

(b) any part of any profit or loss realised during the financial year on the disposal of any shares (other than shares in the other company) which was attributable to the fact that there were at the time of the disposal amongst the assets of the company which issued the shares, or any of its subsidiary undertakings, such shares or assets as are described in paragraph (a) above,

then, the net amount of that profit or loss or, as the case may be, the part so attributable shall be shown, together with an explanation of the transactions to which the information relates.

(4) For the purposes of this paragraph the time of the arrangement shall be taken to be—

(a) where as a result of the arrangement the other company becomes a subsidiary undertaking of the company in question, the date on which it does so or, if the arrangement in question becomes binding only on the fulfilment of a condition, the date on which that condition is fulfilled;

(b) if the other company is already a subsidiary undertaking of that company, the date on which the shares are allotted or, if they are allotted on different days, the first day.

Parent undertaking drawing up accounts for larger group

30.—(1) Where the parent company is itself a subsidiary undertaking, the following information shall be given with respect to that parent undertaking of the company which heads—

(a) the largest group of undertakings for which group accounts are drawn up and of which that company is a member, and

(b) the smallest such group of undertakings.

(2) The name of the parent undertaking shall be stated.

(3) There shall be stated—

(a) if the undertaking is incorporated outside Great Britain, the country in which it is incorporated;

SCH. 3

(b) if it is incorporated in Great Britain, whether it is registered in England and Wales or in Scotland;

(c) if it is unincorporated, the address of its principal place of business.

(4) If copies of the group accounts referred to in sub-paragraph (1) are available to the public, there shall also be stated the addresses from which copies of the accounts can be obtained.

Identification of ultimate parent company

31.—(1) Where the parent company is itself a subsidiary undertaking, the following information shall be given with respect to the company (if any) regarded by the directors as being that company's ultimate parent company.

(2) The name of that company shall be stated.

(3) If known to the directors, there shall be stated—

(a) if that company is incorporated outside Great Britain, the country in which it is incorporated;

(b) if it is incorporated in Great Britain, whether it is registered in England and Wales or in Scotland.

(4) In this paragraph "company" includes any body corporate.

Construction of references to shares held by parent company or group

32.—(1) References in this Part of this Schedule to shares held by the parent company or the group shall be construed as follows.

(2) For the purposes of paragraphs 16, 22(4) and (5) and 23 to 25 (information about holdings in subsidiary and other undertakings)—

(a) there shall be attributed to the parent company shares held on its behalf by any person; but

(b) there shall be treated as not held by the parent company shares held on behalf of a person other than the company.

(3) References to shares held by the group are to any shares held by or on behalf of the parent company or any of its subsidiary undertakings; but there shall be treated as not held by the group any shares held on behalf of a person other than the parent company or any of its subsidiary undertakings.

(4) Shares held by way of security shall be treated as held by the person providing the security—

(a) where apart from the right to exercise them for the purpose of preserving the value of the security, or of realising it, the rights attached to the shares are exercisable only in accordance with his instructions, and

(b) where the shares are held in connection with the granting of loans as part of normal business activities and apart from the right to exercise them for the purpose of preserving the value of the security, or of realising it, the rights attached to the shares are exercisable only in his interests.

Section 6(4).

SCHEDULE 4

DISCLOSURE OF INFORMATION: EMOLUMENTS AND OTHER BENEFITS OF DIRECTORS AND OTHERS

1985 c. 6.

1. Schedule 6 to the Companies Act 1985 is amended as follows.

2. For the heading substitute—

"DISCLOSURE OF INFORMATION: EMOLUMENTS AND OTHER BENEFITS OF
DIRECTORS AND OTHERS".

3. Insert the following provisions (which reproduce, with amendments, the former Part V of Schedule 5 to that Act) as Part I—

"PART I

CHAIRMAN'S AND DIRECTORS' EMOLUMENTS, PENSIONS AND
COMPENSATION FOR LOSS OF OFFICE

Aggregate amount of directors' emoluments

1.—(1) The aggregate amount of directors' emoluments shall be shown.

(2) This means the emoluments paid to or receivable by any person in respect of—

    (a) his services as a director of the company, or

    (b) his services while director of the company—

        (i) as director of any of its subsidiary undertakings, or

        (ii) otherwise in connection with the management of the affairs of the company or any of its subsidiary undertakings.

(3) There shall also be shown, separately, the aggregate amount within sub-paragraph (2)(a) and (b)(i) and the aggregate amount within sub-paragraph (2)(b)(ii).

(4) For the purposes of this paragraph the "emoluments" of a person include—

    (a) fees and percentages,

    (b) sums paid by way of expenses allowance (so far as those sums are chargeable to United Kingdom income tax),

    (c) contributions paid in respect of him under any pension scheme, and

    (d) the estimated money value of any other benefits received by him otherwise than in cash,

and emoluments in respect of a person's accepting office as director shall be treated as emoluments in respect of his services as director.

Details of chairman's and directors' emoluments

2. Where the company is a parent company or a subsidiary undertaking, or where the amount shown in compliance with paragraph 1(1) is £60,000 or more, the information required by paragraphs 3 to 6 shall be given with respect to the emoluments of the chairman and directors, and emoluments waived.

3.—(1) The emoluments of the chairman shall be shown.

(2) The "chairman" means the person elected by the directors to be chairman of their meetings, and includes a person who, though not so elected, holds an office (however designated) which in accordance with the company's constitution carries with it functions substantially similar to those discharged by a person so elected.

(3) Where there has been more than one chairman during the year, the emoluments of each shall be stated so far as attributable to the period during which he was chairman.

(4) The emoluments of a person need not be shown if his duties as chairman were wholly or mainly discharged outside the United Kingdom.

4.—(1) The following information shall be given with respect to the emoluments of directors.

(2) There shall be shown the number of directors whose emoluments fell within each of the following bands—

not more than £5,000,

more than £5,000 but not more than £10,000,

more than £10,000 but not more than £15,000,

and so on.

(3) If the emoluments of any of the directors exceeded that of the chairman, there shall be shown the greatest amount of emoluments of any director.

(4) Where more than one person has been chairman during the year, the reference in sub-paragraph (3) to the emoluments of the chairman is to the aggregate of the emoluments of each person who has been chairman, so far as attributable to the period during which he was chairman.

(5) The information required by sub-paragraph (2) need not be given in respect of a director who discharged his duties as such wholly or mainly outside the United Kingdom; and any such director shall be left out of account for the purposes of sub-paragraph (3).

5. In paragraphs 3 and 4 "emoluments" has the same meaning as in paragraph 1, except that it does not include contributions paid in respect of a person under a pension scheme.

Emoluments waived

6.—(1) There shall be shown—

(a) the number of directors who have waived rights to receive emoluments which, but for the waiver, would have fallen to be included in the amount shown under paragraph 1(1), and

(b) the aggregate amount of those emoluments.

(2) For the purposes of this paragraph it shall be assumed that a sum not receivable in respect of a period would have been paid at the time at which it was due, and if such a sum was payable only on demand, it shall be deemed to have been due at the time of the waiver.

Pensions of directors and past directors

7.—(1) There shall be shown the aggregate amount of directors' or past directors' pensions.

(2) This amount does not include any pension paid or receivable under a pension scheme if the scheme is such that the contributions under it are substantially adequate for the maintenance of the scheme; but, subject to this, it includes any pension paid or receivable in respect of any such services of a director or past director as are mentioned in paragraph 1(2), whether to or by him or, on his nomination or by virtue of dependence on or other connection with him, to or by any other person.

(3) The amount shown shall distinguish between pensions in respect of services as director, whether of the company or any of its subsidiary undertakings, and other pensions.

(4) References to pensions include benefits otherwise than in cash and in relation to so much of a pension as consists of such a benefit references to its amount are to the estimated money value of the benefit.

The nature of any such benefit shall also be disclosed.

Compensation to directors for loss of office

8.—(1) There shall be shown the aggregate amount of any compensation to directors or past directors in respect of loss of office.

(2) This amount includes compensation received or receivable by a director or past director for—

  (a) loss of office as director of the company, or

  (b) loss, while director of the company or on or in connection with his ceasing to be a director of it, of—

        (i) any other office in connection with the management of the company's affairs, or

        (ii) any office as director or otherwise in connection with the management of the affairs of any subsidiary undertaking of the company;

and shall distinguish between compensation in respect of the office of director, whether of the company or any of its subsidiary undertakings, and compensation in respect of other offices.

(3) References to compensation include benefits otherwise than in cash; and in relation to such compensation references to its amount are to the estimated money value of the benefit.

The nature of any such compensation shall be disclosed.

(4) References to compensation for loss of office include compensation in consideration for, or in connection with, a person's retirement from office.

Sums paid to third parties in respect of directors' services

9.—(1) There shall be shown the aggregate amount of any consideration paid to or receivable by third parties for making available the services of any person—

  (a) as a director of the company, or

  (b) while director of the company—

        (i) as director of any of its subsidiary undertakings, or

        (ii) otherwise in connection with the management of the affairs of the company or any of its subsidiary undertakings.

(2) The reference to consideration includes benefits otherwise than in cash; and in relation to such consideration the reference to its amount is to the estimated money value of the benefit.

The nature of any such consideration shall be disclosed.

(3) The reference to third parties is to persons other than—

  (a) the director himself or a person connected with him or body corporate controlled by him, and

  (b) the company or any of its subsidiary undertakings.

Supplementary

10.—(1) The following applies with respect to the amounts to be shown under paragraphs 1, 7, 8 and 9.

(2) The amount in each case includes all relevant sums paid by or receivable from—

  (a) the company; and

  (b) the company's subsidiary undertakings; and

(c) any other person,

except sums to be accounted for to the company or any of its subsidiary undertakings or, by virtue of sections 314 and 315 of this Act (duty of directors to make disclosure on company takeover; consequence of non-compliance), to past or present members of the company or any of its subsidiaries or any class of those members.

(3) The amount to be shown under paragraph 8 shall distinguish between the sums respectively paid by or receivable from the company, the company's subsidiary undertakings and persons other than the company and its subsidiary undertakings.

(4) References to amounts paid to or receivable by a person include amounts paid to or receivable by a person connected with him or a body corporate controlled by him (but not so as to require an amount to be counted twice).

11.—(1) The amounts to be shown for any financial year under paragraphs 1, 7, 8 and 9 are the sums receivable in respect of that year (whenever paid) or, in the case of sums not receivable in respect of a period, the sums paid during that year.

(2) But where—

(a) any sums are not shown in a note to the accounts for the relevant financial year on the ground that the person receiving them is liable to account for them as mentioned in paragraph 10(2), but the liability is thereafter wholly or partly released or is not enforced within a period of 2 years; or

(b) any sums paid by way of expenses allowance are charged to United Kingdom income tax after the end of the relevant financial year,

those sums shall, to the extent to which the liability is released or not enforced or they are charged as mentioned above (as the case may be), be shown in a note to the first accounts in which it is practicable to show them and shall be distinguished from the amounts to be shown apart from this provision.

12. Where it is necessary to do so for the purpose of making any distinction required by the preceding paragraphs in an amount to be shown in compliance with this Part of this Schedule, the directors may apportion any payments between the matters in respect of which these have been paid or are receivable in such manner as they think appropriate.

Interpretation

13.—(1) The following applies for the interpretation of this Part of this Schedule.

(2) A reference to a subsidiary undertaking of the company—

(a) in relation to a person who is or was, while a director of the company, a director also, by virtue of the company's nomination (direct or indirect) of any other undertaking, includes (subject to the following sub-paragraph) that undertaking, whether or not it is or was in fact a subsidiary undertaking of the company, and

(b) for the purposes of paragraphs 1 to 7 (including any provision of this Part of this Schedule referring to paragraph 1) is to an undertaking which is a subsidiary undertaking at the time the services were rendered, and for the purposes of paragraph 8 to a subsidiary undertaking immediately before the loss of office as director.

(3) The following definitions apply—

    (a) "pension" includes any superannuation allowance, superannuation gratuity or similar payment,

    (b) "pension scheme" means a scheme for the provision of pensions in respect of services as director or otherwise which is maintained in whole or in part by means of contributions, and

    (c) "contribution", in relation to a pension scheme, means any payment (including an insurance premium) paid for the purposes of the scheme by or in respect of persons rendering services in respect of which pensions will or may become payable under the scheme except that it does not include any payment in respect of two or more persons if the amount paid in respect of each of them is not ascertainable.

(4) References in this Part of this Schedule to a person being "connected" with a director, and to a director "controlling" a body corporate, shall be construed in accordance with section 346.

Supplementary

14. This Part of this Schedule requires information to be given only so far as it is contained in the company's books and papers or the company has the right to obtain it from the persons concerned.".

4.—(1) For the heading to the present Part I substitute—

"PART II

LOANS, QUASI-LOANS AND OTHER DEALINGS IN FAVOUR OF DIRECTORS"

(2) Paragraphs 1 to 3 and 5 to 14 of that Part shall be renumbered 15 to 27, and internal cross-references in that Part shall be renumbered accordingly.

(3) Paragraph 4 is omitted.

(4) In paragraph 1 (renumbered 15) for "Group accounts" substitute "The group accounts of a holding company, or if it is not required to prepare group accounts its individual accounts,".

(5) For the heading before paragraph 11 (renumbered 24) substitute—

"Excluded transactions"

5. In paragraph 14 (renumbered 27), make the existing provision sub-paragraph (1) and after it insert—

    "(2) In this Part of this Schedule "director" includes a shadow director.".

6.—(1) For the heading to the present Part II substitute—

"PART III

OTHER TRANSACTIONS, ARRANGEMENTS AND AGREEMENTS"

(2) Paragraphs 15 to 17 of that Part shall be renumbered 28 to 30, and internal cross-references in that Part shall be renumbered accordingly.

(3) In paragraph 16 (renumbered 29), for "made as mentioned in section 233(1)" substitute "made by the company or a subsidiary of it for persons who at any time during the financial year were officers of the company (but not directors or shadow directors)".

7. Omit the present Part III (disclosure required in case of banking companies), the substance of which is reproduced in Part IV of Schedule 7 to this Act.

SCHEDULE 5

MATTERS TO BE INCLUDED IN DIRECTORS' REPORT

1. Schedule 7 to the Companies Act 1985 (matters to be included in directors' report) is amended as follows.

Subsidiary undertakings

2.—(1) In paragraph 1(1) (significant changes in fixed assets) for "subsidiaries" substitute "subsidiary undertakings".

(2) In paragraph 6 (general information), for "subsidiaries" in each place where it occurs (three times) substitute "subsidiary undertakings".

Directors' interests

3. For paragraph 2 (directors' interests) substitute—

"2.—(1) The information required by paragraphs 2A and 2B shall be given in the directors' report, or by way of notes to the company's annual accounts, with respect to each person who at the end of the financial year was a director of the company.

(2) In those paragraphs—

    (a) "the register" means the register of directors' interests kept by the company under section 325; and

    (b) references to a body corporate being in the same group as the company are to its being a subsidiary or holding company, or another subsidiary of a holding company, of the company.

2A.—(1) It shall be stated with respect to each director whether, according to the register, he was at the end of the financial year interested in shares in or debentures of the company or any other body corporate in the same group.

(2) If he was so interested, there shall be stated the number of shares in and amount of debentures of each body (specifying it) in which, according to the register, he was then interested.

(3) If a director was interested at the end of the financial year in shares in or debentures of the company or any other body corporate in the same group—

    (a) it shall also be stated whether, according to the register, he was at the beginning of the financial year (or, if he was not then a director, when he became one) interested in shares in or debentures of the company or any other body corporate in the same group, and

    (b) if he was so interested, there shall be stated the number of shares in and amount of debentures of each body (specifying it) in which, according to the register, he was then interested.

(4) In this paragraph references to an interest in shares or debentures have the same meaning as in section 324; and references to the interest of a director include any interest falling to be treated as his for the purposes of that section.

(5) The reference above to the time when a person became a director is, in the case of a person who became a director on more than one occasion, to the time when he first became a director.

SCH. 5

2B.—(1) It shall be stated with respect to each director whether, according to the register, any right to subscribe for shares in or debentures of the company or another body corporate in the same group was during the financial year granted to, or exercised by, the director or a member of his immediate family.

(2) If any such right was granted to, or exercised by, any such person during the financial year, there shall be stated the number of shares in and amount of debentures of each body (specifying it) in respect of which, according to the register, the right was granted or exercised.

(3) A director's "immediate family" means his or her spouse and infant children; and for this purpose "children" includes step-children, and "infant", in relation to Scotland, means pupil or minor.

(4) The reference above to a member of the director's immediate family does not include a person who is himself or herself a director of the company.".

SCHEDULE 6

Section 13(2).

[SCHEDULE 8 TO THE COMPANIES ACT 1985]

EXEMPTIONS FOR SMALL AND MEDIUM-SIZED COMPANIES

PART I

SMALL COMPANIES

Balance sheet

1.—(1) The company may deliver a copy of an abbreviated version of the full balance sheet, showing only those items to which a letter or Roman number is assigned in the balance sheet format adopted under Part I of Schedule 4, but in other respects corresponding to the full balance sheet.

(2) If a copy of an abbreviated balance sheet is delivered, there shall be disclosed in it or in a note to the company's accounts delivered—

  (a) the aggregate of the amounts required by note (5) of the notes on the balance sheet formats set out in Part I of Schedule 4 to be shown separately for each item included under debtors (amounts falling due after one year), and

  (b) the aggregate of the amounts required by note (13) of those notes to be shown separately for each item included under creditors in Format 2 (amounts falling due within one year or after more than one year).

(3) The provisions of section 233 as to the signing of the copy of the balance sheet delivered to the registrar apply to a copy of an abbreviated balance sheet delivered in accordance with this paragraph.

Profit and loss account

2. A copy of the company's profit and loss account need not be delivered.

Disclosure of information in notes to accounts

3.—(1) Of the information required by Part III of Schedule 4 (information to be given in notes to accounts if not given in the accounts themselves) only the information required by the following provisions need be given—

  paragraph 36 (accounting policies),

  paragraph 38 (share capital),

  paragraph 39 (particulars of allotments),

  paragraph 42 (fixed assets), so far as it relates to those items to which a letter or Roman number is assigned in the balance sheet format adopted, paragraph 48(1) and (4) (particulars of debts),

paragraph 58(1) (basis of conversion of foreign currency amounts into sterling),

paragraph 58(2) (corresponding amounts for previous financial year), so far as it relates to amounts stated in a note to the company's accounts by virtue of a requirement of Schedule 4 or under any other provision of this Act.

(2) Of the information required by Schedule 5 to be given in notes to the accounts, the information required by the following provisions need not be given—

paragraph 4 (financial years of subsidiary undertakings),

paragraph 5 (additional information about subsidiary undertakings),

paragraph 6 (shares and debentures of company held by subsidiary undertakings),

paragraph 10 (arrangements attracting merger relief).

(3) Of the information required by Schedule 6 to be given in notes to the accounts, the information required by Part I (directors' and chairman's emoluments, pensions and compensation for loss of office) need not be given.

Directors' report

4. A copy of the directors' report need not be delivered.

PART II

MEDIUM-SIZED COMPANIES

Profit and loss account

5. The company may deliver a profit and loss account in which the following items listed in the profit and loss account formats set out in Part I of Schedule 4 are combined as one item under the heading "gross profit or loss"—

Items 1, 2, 3 and 6 in Format 1;

Items 1 to 5 in Format 2;

Items A.1, B.1 and B.2 in Format 3;

Items A.1, A.2 and B.1 to B.4 in Format 4.

Disclosure of information in notes to accounts

6. The information required by paragraph 55 of Schedule 4 (particulars of turnover) need not be given.

PART III

SUPPLEMENTARY PROVISIONS

Statement that advantage taken of exemptions

7.—(1) Where the directors of a company take advantage of the exemptions conferred by Part I or Part II of this Schedule, the company's balance sheet shall contain—

(a) a statement that advantage is taken of the exemptions conferred by Part I or, as the case may be, Part II of this Schedule, and

(b) a statement of the grounds on which, in the directors' opinion, the company is entitled to those exemptions.

(2) The statements shall appear in the balance sheet immediately above the signature required by section 233.

Special auditors' report

8.—(1) If the directors of a company propose to take advantage of the exemptions conferred by Part I or II of this Schedule, it is the auditors' duty to provide them with a report stating whether in their opinion the company is entitled to those exemptions and whether the documents to be proposed to be delivered in accordance with this Schedule are properly prepared.

(2) The accounts delivered shall be accompanied by a special report of the auditors stating that in their opinion—

    (a) the company is entitled to the exemptions claimed in the directors' statement, and

    (b) the accounts to be delivered are properly prepared in accordance with this Schedule.

(3) In such a case a copy of the auditors' report under section 235 need not be delivered separately, but the full text of it shall be reproduced in the special report; and if the report under section 235 is qualified there shall be included in the special report any further material necessary to understand the qualification.

(4) Section 236 (signature of auditors' report) applies to a special report under this paragraph as it applies to a report under section 235.

Dormant companies

9. Paragraphs 7 and 8 above do not apply where the company is exempt by virtue of section 250 (dormant companies) from the obligation to appoint auditors.

Requirements in connection with publication of accounts

10.—(1) Where advantage is taken of the exemptions conferred by Part I or II of this Schedule, section 240 (requirements in connection with publication of accounts) has effect with the following adaptations.

(2) Accounts delivered in accordance with this Schedule and accounts in the form in which they would be required to be delivered apart from this Schedule are both "statutory accounts" for the purposes of that section.

(3) References in that section to the auditors' report under section 235 shall be read, in relation to accounts delivered in accordance with this Schedule, as references to the special report under paragraph 8 above.

SCHEDULE 7

Sᴘᴇᴄɪᴀʟ Pʀᴏᴠɪsɪᴏɴs ғᴏʀ Bᴀɴᴋɪɴɢ ᴀɴᴅ Iɴsᴜʀᴀɴᴄᴇ Cᴏᴍᴘᴀɴɪᴇs ᴀɴᴅ Gʀᴏᴜᴘs

Preliminary

Section 18(3) and (4).

Schedule 9 to the Companies Act 1985 is amended in accordance with this Schedule, as follows—   1985 c. 6.

    (a) for the heading of the Schedule substitute "Sᴘᴇᴄɪᴀʟ Pʀᴏᴠɪsɪᴏɴs ғᴏʀ Bᴀɴᴋɪɴɢ ᴀɴᴅ Iɴsᴜʀᴀɴᴄᴇ Cᴏᴍᴘᴀɴɪᴇs ᴀɴᴅ Gʀᴏᴜᴘs";

    (b) omit the introductory paragraph preceding Part I, together with its heading;

    (c) make the present provisions of Parts I to V of the Schedule (as amended by Part I of this Schedule) Part I of the Schedule, and accordingly—

        (i) for the descriptive Part heading before paragraph 2 substitute "Fᴏʀᴍ ᴀɴᴅ Cᴏɴᴛᴇɴᴛ ᴏғ Aᴄᴄᴏᴜɴᴛs", and

        (ii) omit the Part headings before paragraphs 19, 27, 31 and 32;

    (d) the provisions of Parts II, III and IV of this Schedule have effect as Parts II, III and IV of Schedule 9 to the Companies Act 1985.

PART I

FORM AND CONTENT OF ACCOUNTS

1. In paragraph 10(1)(c) of Schedule 9 to the Companies Act 1985 (disclosure of outstanding loans in connection with certain cases of financial assistance for purchase of company's own shares), after "153(4)(b)" insert ", (bb)".

2. In paragraph 13 of that Schedule (information supplementing balance sheet), omit sub-paragraph (3) (information as to acquisition of, or creation of lien or charge over, company's own shares).

3. In paragraph 17(5) of that Schedule (statement of turnover: companies exempt from requirement) for "neither a holding company nor a subsidiary of another body corporate" substitute "neither a parent company nor a subsidiary undertaking".

4. After paragraph 18 of that Schedule insert—

"Supplementary provisions

18A.—(1) Accounting policies shall be applied consistently within the same accounts and from one financial year to the next.

(2) If it appears to the directors of a company that there are special reasons for departing from the principle stated in sub-paragraph (1) in preparing the company's accounts in respect of any financial year, they may do so; but particulars of the departure, the reasons for it and its effect shall be given in a note to the accounts.

18B. It shall be stated whether the accounts have been prepared in accordance with applicable accounting standards, and particulars of any material departure from those standards and the reasons for it shall be given.

18C.—(1) In respect of every item shown in the balance sheet or profit and loss account, or stated in a note to the accounts, there shall be shown or stated the corresponding amount for the financial year immediately preceding that to which the accounts relate, subject to sub-paragraph (3).

(2) Where the corresponding amount is not comparable, it shall be adjusted and particulars of the adjustment and the reasons for it shall be given in a note to the accounts.

(3) Sub-paragraph (1) does not apply in relation to an amount shown—

    (a) as an amount the source or application of which is required by paragraph 8 above (reserves and provisions),

    (b) in pursuance of paragraph 13(10) above (acquisitions and disposals of fixed assets),

    (c) by virtue of paragraph 13 of Schedule 4A (details of accounting treatment of acquisitions),

    (d) by virtue of paragraph 2, 8(3), 16, 21(1)(d), 22(4) or (5), 24(3) or (4) or 27(3) or (4) of Schedule 5 (shareholdings in other undertakings), or

    (e) by virtue of Part II or III of Schedule 6 (loans and other dealings in favour of directors and others).".

5.—(1) Before paragraph 19 of that Schedule insert the heading *"Provisions where company is parent company or subsidiary undertaking"*; and that paragraph is amended as follows.

(2) In sub-paragraph (1) for the words from "is a holding company" onwards substitute "is a parent company".

(3) In sub-paragraph (2)—

    (a) for "subsidiaries" (four times) substitute "subsidiary undertakings", and

    (b) in paragraph (a), for "Part I" substitute "paragraphs 5, 6, 10, 13 and 14".

(4) Omit sub-paragraphs (3) to (7).

6. For paragraph 20 of that Schedule substitute—

    "20.—(1) This paragraph applies where the company is a subsidiary undertaking.

    (2) The balance sheet of the company shall show—

        (a) the aggregate amount of its indebtedness to undertakings of which it is a subsidiary undertaking or which are fellow subsidiary undertakings, and

        (b) the aggregate amount of the indebtedness of all such undertakings to it,

distinguishing in each case between indebtedness in respect of debentures and otherwise.

    (3) The balance sheet shall also show the aggregate amount of assets consisting of shares in fellow subsidiary undertakings.".

7. Omit paragraphs 21 to 26 of that Schedule.

8.—(1) Before paragraph 27 of that Schedule insert the heading *"Exceptions for certain companies"*; and that paragraph is amended as follows.

(2) In sub-paragraph (2)—

    (a) for "Part I of this Schedule" substitute "paragraphs 2 to 18 of this Schedule", and

    (b) in paragraph (b) for the words from "paragraphs 15" to the end substitute "and paragraph 15".

(3) In sub-paragraph (4), omit "of the said Part I".

9. In paragraph 28 of that Schedule, in sub-paragraph (1) (twice) and in sub-paragraph (2) for "Part I" substitute "paragraphs 2 to 18".

10. After that paragraph insert—

    "28A. Where a company is entitled to, and has availed itself of, any of the provisions of paragraph 27 or 28 of this Schedule, section 235(2) only requires the auditors to state whether in their opinion the accounts have been properly prepared in accordance with this Act.".

11. Omit paragraphs 29 to 31 of that Schedule.

12. Before paragraph 32 of that Schedule insert the heading *"Interpretation"*; and in sub-paragraphs (1) and (2) of that paragraph for "this Schedule" substitute "this Part of this Schedule".

13. In paragraph 36 of that Schedule for "this Schedule" substitute "this Part of this Schedule".

PART II

[PART II OF SCHEDULE 9 TO THE COMPANIES ACT 1985]

ACCOUNTS OF BANKING OR INSURANCE GROUP

Undertakings to be included in consolidation

1. The following descriptions of undertaking shall not be excluded from consolidation under section 229(4) (exclusion of undertakings whose activities are different from those of the undertakings consolidated)—

(a) in the case of a banking group, an undertaking (other than a credit institution) whose activities are a direct extension of or ancillary to banking business;

(b) in the case of an insurance group, an undertaking (other than one carrying on insurance business) whose activities are a direct extension of or ancillary to insurance business.

For the purposes of paragraph (a) "banking" means the carrying on of a deposit-taking business within the meaning of the Banking Act 1987.

General application of provisions applicable to individual accounts

2.—(1) In paragraph 1 of Schedule 4A (application to group accounts of provisions applicable to individual accounts), the reference in sub-paragraph (1) to the provisions of Schedule 4 shall be construed as a reference to the provisions of Part I of this Schedule; and accordingly—

(a) the reference in sub-paragraph (2) to paragraph 59 of Schedule 4 shall be construed as a reference to paragraphs 19(2) and 20 of Part I of this Schedule; and

(b) sub-paragraph (3) shall be omitted.

(2) The general application of the provisions of Part I of this Schedule in place of those of Schedule 4 is subject to the following provisions.

Treatment of goodwill

3.—(1) The rules in paragraph 21 of Schedule 4 relating to the treatment of goodwill, and the rules in paragraphs 17 to 19 of that Schedule (valuation of fixed assets) so far as they relate to goodwill, apply for the purpose of dealing with any goodwill arising on consolidation.

(2) Goodwill shall be shown as a separate item in the balance sheet under an appropriate heading; and this applies notwithstanding anything in paragraph 10(1)(b) or (2) of Part I of this Schedule (under which goodwill, patents and trade marks may be stated in the company's individual accounts as a single item).

Minority interests and associated undertakings

4. The information required by paragraphs 17 and 20 to 22 of Schedule 4A (minority interests and associated undertakings) to be shown under separate items in the formats set out in Part I of Schedule 4 shall be shown separately in the balance sheet and profit and loss account under appropriate headings.

Companies entitled to benefit of exemptions

5.—(1) Where a banking or insurance company is entitled to the exemptions conferred by paragraph 27 or 28 of Part I of this Schedule, a group headed by that company is similarly entitled.

(2) Paragraphs 27(4), 28(2) and 28A (accounts not to be taken to be other than true and fair; duty of auditors) apply accordingly where advantage is taken of those exemptions in relation to group accounts.

Information as to undertaking in which shares held as result of financial assistance operation

6.—(1) The following provisions apply where the parent company of a banking group has a subsidiary undertaking which—

(a) is a credit institution of which shares are held as a result of a financial assistance operation with a view to its reorganisation or rescue, and

(b) is excluded from consolidation under section 229(3)(c) (interest held with a view to resale).

(2) Information as to the nature and terms of the operation shall be given in a
note to the group accounts and there shall be appended to the copy of the group
accounts delivered to the registrar in accordance with section 242 a copy of the
undertaking's latest individual accounts and, if it is a parent undertaking, its
latest group accounts.

If the accounts appended are required by law to be audited, a copy of the
auditors' report shall also be appended.

(3) If any document required to be appended is in a language other than
English, the directors shall annex to the copy of that document delivered a
translation of it into English, certified in the prescribed manner to be a correct
translation.

(4) The above requirements are subject to the following qualifications—

    (a) an undertaking is not required to prepare for the purposes of this
        paragraph accounts which would not otherwise be prepared, and if no
        accounts satisfying the above requirements are prepared none need be
        appended;

    (b) the accounts of an undertaking need not be appended if they would not
        otherwise be required to be published, or made available for public
        inspection, anywhere in the world, but in that case the reason for not
        appending the accounts shall be stated in a note to the consolidated
        accounts.

(5) Where a copy of an undertaking's accounts is required to be appended to
the copy of the group accounts delivered to the registrar, that fact shall be stated
in a note to the group accounts.

(6) Subsections (2) to (4) of section 242 (penalties, &c. in case of default) apply
in relation to the requirements of this paragraph as regards the delivery of
documents to the registrar as they apply in relation to the requirements of
subsection (1) of that section.

Part III

[Part III of Schedule 9 to the Companies Act 1985]

Additional Disclosure: Related Undertakings

1. Where accounts are prepared in accordance with the special provisions of
this Part relating to banking companies or groups, there shall be disregarded for
the purposes of—

    (a) paragraphs 7(2)(a), 23(2)(a) and 26(2)(a) of Schedule 5 (information
        about significant holdings in undertakings other than subsidiary
        undertakings: definition of 10 per cent. holding), and

    (b) paragraphs 9(1), 25(1) and 28(1) of that Schedule (additional
        information in case of 20 per cent. holding),

any holding of shares not comprised in the equity share capital of the
undertaking in question.

Part IV

[Part IV of Schedule 9 to the Companies Act 1985]

Additional Disclosure: Emoluments and Other Benefits of Directors and Others

1. The provisions of this Part of this Schedule have effect with respect to the
application of Schedule 6 (additional disclosure: emoluments and other benefits
of directors and others) to a banking company or the holding company of such
a company.

Loans, quasi-loans and other dealings

2. Part II of Schedule 6 (loans, quasi-loans and other dealings) does not apply for the purposes of accounts prepared by a banking company, or a company which is the holding company of a banking company, in relation to a transaction or arrangement of a kind mentioned in section 330, or an agreement to enter into such a transaction or arrangement, to which that banking company is a party.

Other transactions, arrangements and agreements

3.—(1) Part III of Schedule 6 (other transactions, arrangements and agreements) applies for the purposes of accounts prepared by a banking company, or a company which is the holding company of a banking company, only in relation to a transaction, arrangement or agreement made by that banking company for—

    (a) a person who was a director of the company preparing the accounts, or who was connected with such a director, or

1987 c. 22.   (b) a person who was a chief executive or manager (within the meaning of the Banking Act 1987) of that company or its holding company.

(2) References in that Part to officers of the company shall be construed accordingly as including references to such persons.

(3) In this paragraph "director" includes a shadow director.

(4) For the purposes of that Part as it applies by virtue of this paragraph, a company which a person does not control shall not be treated as connected with him.

(5) Section 346 of this Act applies for the purposes of this paragraph as regards the interpretation of references to a person being connected with a director or controlling a company.

Section 18(5).   SCHEDULE 8

[SCHEDULE 10 TO THE COMPANIES ACT 1985]

DIRECTORS' REPORT WHERE ACCOUNTS PREPARED IN ACCORDANCE WITH SPECIAL PROVISIONS FOR BANKING OR INSURANCE COMPANIES OR GROUPS

Recent issues

1.—(1) This paragraph applies where a company prepares individual accounts in accordance with the special provisions of this Part relating to banking or insurance companies.

(2) If in the financial year to which the accounts relate the company has issued any shares or debentures, the directors' report shall state the reason for making the issue, the classes of shares or debentures issued and, as respects each class, the number of shares or amount of debentures issued and the consideration received by the company for the issue.

Turnover and profitability

2.—(1) This paragraph applies where a company prepares group accounts in accordance with the special provisions of this Part relating to banking or insurance groups.

(2) If in the course of the financial year to which the accounts relate the group carried on business of two or more classes (other than banking or discounting or a class prescribed for the purposes of paragraph 17(2) of Part I of Schedule 9) that in the opinion of the directors differ substantially from each other, there shall be contained in the directors' report a statement of—

(a) the proportions in which the turnover for the financial year (so far as stated in the consolidated accounts) is divided amongst those classes (describing them), and

(b) as regards business of each class, the extent or approximate extent (expressed in money terms) to which, in the opinion of the directors, the carrying on of business of that class contributed to or restricted the profit or loss of the group for that year (before taxation).

(3) In sub-paragraph (2) "the group" means the undertakings included in the consolidation.

(4) For the purposes of this paragraph classes of business which in the opinion of the directors do not differ substantially from each other shall be treated as one class.

Labour force and wages paid

3.—(1) This paragraph applies where a company prepares individual or group accounts in accordance with the special provisions of this Part relating to banking or insurance companies or groups.

(2) There shall be stated in the directors' report—

(a) the average number of persons employed by the company or, if the company prepares group accounts, by the company and its subsidiary undertakings, and

(b) the aggregate amount of the remuneration paid or payable to persons so employed.

(3) The average number of persons employed shall be determined by adding together the number of persons employed (whether throughout the week or not) in each week of the financial year and dividing that total by the number of weeks in the financial year.

(4) The aggregate amount of the remuneration paid or payable means the total amount of remuneration paid or payable in respect of the financial year; and for this purpose remuneration means gross remuneration and includes bonuses, whether payable under contract or not.

(5) The information required by this paragraph need not be given if the average number of persons employed is less than 100.

(6) No account shall be taken for the purposes of this paragraph of persons who worked wholly or mainly outside the United Kingdom.

(7) This paragraph does not apply to a company which is a wholly-owned subsidiary of a company incorporated in Great Britain.

SCHEDULE 9

Section 21(2).

[SCHEDULE 10A TO THE COMPANIES ACT 1985]

PARENT AND SUBSIDIARY UNDERTAKINGS: SUPPLEMENTARY PROVISIONS

Introduction

1. The provisions of this Schedule explain expressions used in section 258 (parent and subsidiary undertakings) and otherwise supplement that section.

Voting rights in an undertaking

2.—(1) In section 258(2)(a) and (d) the references to the voting rights in an undertaking are to the rights conferred on shareholders in respect of their shares or, in the case of an undertaking not having a share capital, on members, to vote at general meetings of the undertaking on all, or substantially all, matters.

(2) In relation to an undertaking which does not have general meetings at which matters are decided by the exercise of voting rights, the references to holding a majority of the voting rights in the undertaking shall be construed as references to having the right under the constitution of the undertaking to direct the overall policy of the undertaking or to alter the terms of its constitution.

Right to appoint or remove a majority of the directors

3.—(1) In section 258(2)(b) the reference to the right to appoint or remove a majority of the board of directors is to the right to appoint or remove directors holding a majority of the voting rights at meetings of the board on all, or substantially all, matters.

(2) An undertaking shall be treated as having the right to appoint to a directorship if—

(a) a person's appointment to it follows necessarily from his appointment as director of the undertaking, or

(b) the directorship is held by the undertaking itself.

(3) A right to appoint or remove which is exercisable only with the consent or concurrence of another person shall be left out of account unless no other person has a right to appoint or, as the case may be, remove in relation to that directorship.

Right to exercise dominant influence

4.—(1) For the purposes of section 258(2)(c) an undertaking shall not be regarded as having the right to exercise a dominant influence over another undertaking unless it has a right to give directions with respect to the operating and financial policies of that other undertaking which its directors are obliged to comply with whether or not they are for the benefit of that other undertaking.

(2) A "control contract" means a contract in writing conferring such a right which—

(a) is of a kind authorised by the memorandum or articles of the undertaking in relation to which the right is exercisable, and

(b) is permitted by the law under which that undertaking is established.

(3) This paragraph shall not be read as affecting the construction of the expression "actually exercises a dominant influence" in section 258(4)(a).

Rights exercisable only in certain circumstances or temporarily incapable of exercise

5.—(1) Rights which are exercisable only in certain circumstances shall be taken into account only—

(a) when the circumstances have arisen, and for so long as they continue to obtain, or

(b) when the circumstances are within the control of the person having the rights.

(2) Rights which are normally exercisable but are temporarily incapable of exercise shall continue to be taken into account.

Rights held by one person on behalf of another

6. Rights held by a person in a fiduciary capacity shall be treated as not held by him.

7.—(1) Rights held by a person as nominee for another shall be treated as held by the other.

(2) Rights shall be regarded as held as nominee for another if they are exercisable only on his instructions or with his consent or concurrence.

Rights attached to shares held by way of security

8. Rights attached to shares held by way of security shall be treated as held by the person providing the security—

(a) where apart from the right to exercise them for the purpose of preserving the value of the security, or of realising it, the rights are exercisable only in accordance with his instructions, and

(b) where the shares are held in connection with the granting of loans as part of normal business activities and apart from the right to exercise them for the purpose of preserving the value of the security, or of realising it, the rights are exercisable only in his interests.

Rights attributed to parent undertaking

9.—(1) Rights shall be treated as held by a parent undertaking if they are held by any of its subsidiary undertakings.

(2) Nothing in paragraph 7 or 8 shall be construed as requiring rights held by a parent undertaking to be treated as held by any of its subsidiary undertakings.

(3) For the purposes of paragraph 8 rights shall be treated as being exercisable in accordance with the instructions or in the interests of an undertaking if they are exercisable in accordance with the instructions of or, as the case may be, in the interests of any group undertaking.

Disregard of certain rights

10. The voting rights in an undertaking shall be reduced by any rights held by the undertaking itself.

Supplementary

11. References in any provision of paragraphs 6 to 10 to rights held by a person include rights falling to be treated as held by him by virtue of any other provision of those paragraphs but not rights which by virtue of any such provision are to be treated as not held by him.

SCHEDULE 10

AMENDMENTS CONSEQUENTIAL ON PART I

PART I

AMENDMENTS OF THE COMPANIES ACT 1985

1. In section 46 (meaning of "unqualified" auditors' report in section 43(3)), for subsections (2) to (6) substitute—

"(2) If the balance sheet was prepared for a financial year of the company, the reference is to an auditors' report stating without material qualification the auditors' opinion that the balance sheet has been properly prepared in accordance with this Act.

(3) If the balance sheet was not prepared for a financial year of the company, the reference is to an auditors' report stating without material qualification the auditors' opinion that the balance sheet has been properly prepared in accordance with the provisions of this Act which would have applied if it had been so prepared.

For the purposes of an auditors' report under this subsection the provisions of this Act shall be deemed to apply with such modifications as are necessary by reason of the fact that the balance sheet is not prepared for a financial year of the company.

(4) A qualification shall be regarded as material unless the auditors state in their report that the matter giving rise to the qualification is not material for the purpose of determining (by reference to the company's balance sheet) whether at the balance sheet date the amount of the company's net assets was not less than the aggregate of its called up share capital and undistributable reserves.

In this subsection "net assets" and "undistributable reserves" have the meaning given by section 264(2) and (3).".

2. In section 209(5)(a)(i) for "an authorised institution" substitute "a banking company".

3. In sections 211(9) and 215(4) for "paragraph 3 or 10 of Schedule 5" substitute "section 231(3)".

4. In section 271(3), for "section 236" substitute "section 235".

5. In section 272(3)—

(a) for "section 228" substitute "section 226", and

(b) for "section 238" substitute "section 233".

6. In sections 272(5) and 273(7) for "section 241(3)(b)" substitute "the second sentence of section 242(1)".

7. In section 276(b) for "34(4)(b)" substitute "34(3)(a)".

8. For section 279 substitute—

"Distributions by banking or insurance companies.   279. Where a company's accounts relevant for the purposes of this Part are prepared in accordance with the special provisions of Part VII relating to banking or insurance companies, sections 264 to 275 apply with the modifications shown in Schedule 11.".

9. In section 289(4) for "section 252(5)" substitute "section 250(3)".

10. In sections 338(4), 339(4), 343(1)(a) and 344(2) for "an authorised institution", wherever occurring, substitute "a banking company".

11. In section 343(2) and (4) for "paragraph 4 of Schedule 6, be required by section 232" substitute "paragraph 2 of Part IV of Schedule 9, be required".

12. In section 699(3) for "section 241(3)" substitute "section 242(1)".

13. In Part XXIII (oversea companies), for Chapter II (delivery of accounts) substitute—

"CHAPTER II

DELIVERY OF ACCOUNTS AND REPORTS

Preparation of accounts and reports by oversea companies.   700.—(1) Every oversea company shall in respect of each financial year of the company prepare the like accounts and directors' report, and cause to be prepared such an auditors' report, as would be required if the company were formed and registered under this Act.

(2) The Secretary of State may by order—

(a) modify the requirements referred to in subsection (1) for the purpose of their application to oversea companies;

(b) exempt an oversea company from those requirements or from such of them as may be specified in the order.

(3) An order may make different provision for different cases or classes of case and may contain such incidental and supplementary provisions as the Secretary of State thinks fit.

(4) An order under this section shall be made by statutory instrument which shall be subject to annulment in pursuance of a resolution of either House of Parliament.

Oversea company's financial year and accounting reference periods.

701.—(1) Sections 223 to 225 (financial year and accounting reference periods) apply to an oversea company, subject to the following modifications.

(2) For the references to the incorporation of the company substitute references to the company establishing a place of business in Great Britain.

(3) Omit section 225(4) (restriction on frequency with which current accounting reference period may be extended).

Delivery to registrar of accounts and reports of oversea company.

702.—(1) An oversea company shall in respect of each financial year of the company deliver to the registrar copies of the accounts and reports prepared in accordance with section 700.

If any document comprised in those accounts or reports is in a language other than English, the directors shall annex to the copy delivered a translation of it into English, certified in the prescribed manner to be a correct translation.

(2) In relation to an oversea company the period allowed for delivering accounts and reports is 13 months after the end of the relevant accounting reference period.

This is subject to the following provisions of this section.

(3) If the relevant accounting reference period is the company's first and is a period of more than 12 months, the period allowed is 13 months from the first anniversary of the company's establishing a place of business in Great Britain.

(4) If the relevant accounting period is treated as shortened by virtue of a notice given by the company under section 225 (alteration of accounting reference date), the period allowed is that applicable in accordance with the above provisions or three months from the date of the notice under that section, whichever last expires.

(5) If for any special reason the Secretary of State thinks fit he may, on an application made before the expiry of the period otherwise allowed, by notice in writing to an oversea company extend that period by such further period as may be specified in the notice.

(6) In this section "the relevant accounting reference period" means the accounting reference period by reference to which the financial year for the accounts in question was determined.

Penalty for non-compliance.

703.—(1) If the requirements of section 702(1) are not complied with before the end of the period allowed for delivering accounts and reports, or if the accounts and reports delivered do not comply with the requirements of this Act, the company and every person who immediately before the end of that period was a director of the company is guilty of an offence and liable to a fine and, for continued contravention, to a daily default fine.

(2) It is a defence for a person charged with such an offence to prove that he took all reasonable steps for securing that the requirements in question would be complied with.

(3) It is not a defence in relation to a failure to deliver copies to the registrar to prove that the documents in question were not in fact prepared as required by this Act.".

14. In section 711(1)(k) for "section 241 (annual accounts)" substitute "section 242(1) (accounts and reports)".

15. For section 742 (expressions used in connection with accounts) substitute—

"Expressions used in connection with accounts.

742.—(1) In this Act, unless a contrary intention appears, the following expressions have the same meaning as in Part VII (accounts)—

"annual accounts",

"accounting reference date" and "accounting reference period",

"balance sheet" and "balance sheet date",

"current assets",

"financial year", in relation to a company,

"fixed assets",

"parent company" and "parent undertaking",

"profit and loss account", and

"subsidiary undertaking".

(2) References in this Act to "realised profits" and "realised losses", in relation to a company's accounts, shall be construed in accordance with section 262(3).".

16. In section 744 (interpretation), omit the definition of "authorised institution" and at the appropriate place insert—

"'banking company' means a company which is authorised under the Banking Act 1987;".

17. In Schedule 1, in paragraph 2(2)(a) for "section 252(5)" substitute "section 250(3)".

18.—(1) Schedule 2 (interpretation of references to "beneficial interest") is amended as follows.

(2) After the heading at the beginning of the Schedule, and before the cross-heading preceding paragraph 1, insert the following heading—

"PART I

REFERENCES IN SECTIONS 23, 145, 146 AND 148".

(3) In paragraph 1—

(a) in sub-paragraph (1) omit "paragraph 60(2) of Schedule 4, or paragraph 19(3) of Schedule 9"; and

(b) omit sub-paragraph (5).

(4) In paragraph 3—

(a) in sub-paragraph (1) omit ", paragraph 60(2) of Schedule 4 or paragraph 19(3) of Schedule 9"; and

(b) omit sub-paragraph (3).

(5) In paragraph 4—

    (a) in sub-paragraph (1) omit "(whether as personal representative or otherwise)", and

    (b) in sub-paragraph (2) omit ", paragraph 60(2) of Schedule 4 and paragraph 19(3) of Schedule 9";

and at the end add—

    "(3) As respects sections 145, 146 and 148, sub-paragraph (1) above applies where a company is a personal representative as it applies where a company is a trustee.".

(6) In paragraph 5(1) for "this Schedule" substitute "this Part of this Schedule".

(7) After paragraph 5 insert the following—

"Part II

References in Schedule 5

Residual interests under pension and employees' share schemes

6.—(1) Where shares in an undertaking are held on trust for the purposes of a pension scheme or an employees' share scheme, there shall be disregarded any residual interest which has not vested in possession, being an interest of the undertaking or any of its subsidiary undertakings.

(2) In this paragraph a "residual interest" means a right of the undertaking in question (the "residual beneficiary") to receive any of the trust property in the event of—

    (a) all the liabilities arising under the scheme having been satisfied or provided for, or

    (b) the residual beneficiary ceasing to participate in the scheme, or

    (c) the trust property at any time exceeding what is necessary for satisfying the liabilities arising or expected to arise under the scheme.

(3) In sub-paragraph (2) references to a right include a right dependent on the exercise of a discretion vested by the scheme in the trustee or any other person; and references to liabilities arising under a scheme include liabilities that have resulted or may result from the exercise of any such discretion.

(4) For the purposes of this paragraph a residual interest vests in possession—

    (a) in a case within sub-paragraph (2)(a), on the occurrence of the event there mentioned, whether or not the amount of the property receivable pursuant to the right mentioned in that sub-paragraph is then ascertained;

    (b) in a case within sub-paragraph (2)(b) or (c), when the residual beneficiary becomes entitled to require the trustee to transfer to that beneficiary any of the property receivable pursuant to that right.

Employer's charges and other rights of recovery

7.—(1) Where shares in an undertaking are held on trust, there shall be disregarded—

    (a) if the trust is for the purposes of a pension scheme, any such rights as are mentioned in sub-paragraph (2) below;

(b) if the trust is for the purposes of an employees' share scheme, any such rights as are mentioned in paragraph (a) of that sub-paragraph,

being rights of the undertaking or any of its subsidiary undertakings.

(2) The rights referred to are—

(a) any charge or lien on, or set-off against, any benefit or other right or interest under the scheme for the purpose of enabling the employer or former employer of a member of the scheme to obtain the discharge of a monetary obligation due to him from the member, and

(b) any right to receive from the trustee of the scheme, or as trustee of the scheme to retain, an amount that can be recovered or retained under section 47 of the Social Security Pensions Act 1975 (deduction of premium from refund of pension contributions) or otherwise as reimbursement or partial reimbursement for any state scheme premium paid in connection with the scheme under Part III of that Act.

Trustee's right to expenses, remuneration, indemnity, &c.

8. Where an undertaking is a trustee, there shall be disregarded any rights which the undertaking has in its capacity as trustee including, in particular, any right to recover its expenses or be remunerated out of the trust property and any right to be indemnified out of that property for any liability incurred by reason of any act or omission of the undertaking in the performance of its duties as trustee.

Supplementary

9.—(1) The following applies for the interpretation of this Part of this Schedule.

(2) "Undertaking", and "shares" in relation to an undertaking, have the same meaning as in Part VII.

(3) This Part of this Schedule applies in relation to debentures as it applies in relation to shares.

(4) "Pension scheme" means any scheme for the provision of benefits consisting of or including relevant benefits for or in respect of employees or former employees; and "relevant benefits" means any pension, lump sum, gratuity or other like benefit given or to be given on retirement or on death or in anticipation of retirement or, in connection with past service, after retirement or death.

(5) In sub-paragraph (4) of this paragraph and in paragraph 7(2) "employee" and "employer" shall be read as if a director of an undertaking were employed by it.".

19.—(1) Part II of Schedule 3 (prospectuses: auditors' and accountants' reports to be set out) is amended as follows.

(2) In paragraph 16 (auditors' reports), in sub-paragraph (2) for "subsidiaries" substitute "subsidiary undertakings" and for sub-paragraph (3) substitute—

"(3) If the company has subsidiary undertakings, the report shall—

(a) deal separately with the company's profits or losses as provided by sub-paragraph (2), and in addition deal either—

(i) as a whole with the combined profits or losses of its subsidiary undertakings, so far as they concern members of the company, or

(ii) individually with the profits or losses of each of its subsidiary undertakings, so far as they concern members of the company,

or, instead of dealing separately with the company's profits or losses, deal as a whole with the profits or losses of the company and (so far as they concern members of the company) with the combined profits and losses of its subsidiary undertakings; and

(b) deal separately with the company's assets and liabilities as provided by sub-paragraph (2), and in addition deal either—

(i) as a whole with the combined assets and liabilities of its subsidiary undertakings, with or without the company's assets and liabilities, or

(ii) individually with the assets and liabilities of each of its subsidiary undertakings,

indicating, as respects the assets and liabilities of its subsidiary undertakings, the allowance to be made for persons other than members of the company.".

(3) For paragraph 18 (accountants' reports) substitute—

"18.—(1) The following provisions apply if—

(a) the proceeds of the issue are to be applied directly or indirectly in any manner resulting in the acquisition by the company of shares in any other undertaking, or any part of the proceeds is to be so applied, and

(b) by reason of that acquisition or anything to be done in consequence of or in connection with it, that undertaking will become a subsidiary undertaking of the company.

(2) There shall be set out in the prospectus a report made by accountants upon—

(a) the profits or losses of the other undertaking in respect of each of the five financial years immediately preceding the issue of the prospectus, and

(b) the assets and liabilities of the other undertaking at the last date to which its accounts were made up.

(3) The report shall—

(a) indicate how the profits or losses of the other undertaking would in respect of the shares to be acquired have concerned members of the company and what allowance would have fallen to be made, in relation to assets and liabilities so dealt with, for holders of other shares, if the company had at all material times held the shares to be acquired, and

(b) where the other undertaking is a parent undertaking, deal with the profits or losses and the assets and liabilities of the undertaking and its subsidiary undertakings in the manner provided by paragraph 16(3) above in relation to the company and its subsidiary undertakings.

(4) In this paragraph "undertaking" and "shares", in relation to an undertaking, have the same meaning as in Part VII.".

(4) In paragraph 22 (eligibility of accountants to make reports), for sub-paragraph (2) substitute—

"(2) Such a report shall not be made by an accountant who is an officer or servant, or a partner of or in the employment of an officer or servant, of—

(a) the company or any of its subsidiary undertakings,

(b) a parent undertaking of the company or any subsidiary undertaking of such an undertaking.".

20. In paragraph 12(b) of Schedule 4, for "section 238" substitute "section 233".

21.—(1) Schedule 11 is amended as follows.

(2) For the heading substitute "Modifications of Part VIII Where Company's Accounts Prepared in Accordance with Special Provisions for Banking or Insurance Companies".

(3) In paragraphs 1 and 2(a) for "Schedule 9" substitute "Part I of Schedule 9".

(4) In paragraph 4—

(a) in sub-paragraph (a) for "Schedule 9" substitute "Part I of Schedule 9", and

(b) omit sub-paragraphs (b) and (c).

(5) In paragraph 5—

(a) in sub-paragraph (a) for "Part III of Schedule 9" substitute "paragraph 27 or 28 of Schedule 9", and

(b) omit sub-paragraph (b).

(6) In paragraph 6—

(a) in sub-paragraph (a), for "section 228" substitute "section 226" and for "section 258 and Schedule 9" substitute "section 255 and Part I of Schedule 9", and

(b) in sub-paragraph (b), for "Part III of Schedule 9" substitute "paragraph 27 or 28 of Schedule 9".

(7) In paragraph 7(a) for "Schedule 9" substitute "Part I of Schedule 9".

22.—(1) In Schedule 15A (renumbered 15B) (provisions applicable to mergers and divisions of public companies), paragraph 6 (documents to be made available for inspection) is amended as follows.

(2) In sub-paragraph (1)(b) (directors' report on merger or division), after "directors' report" insert "referred to in paragraph 4 above".

(3) For sub-paragraph (1)(d) and (e) substitute—

"(d) the company's annual accounts, together with the relevant directors' report and auditors' report, for the last three financial years ending on or before the relevant date; and

(e) if the last of those financial years ended more than six months before the relevant date, an accounting statement in the form described in the following provisions.".

(4) In sub-paragraph (1), after the paragraphs add—

"In paragraphs (d) and (e) "the relevant date" means one month before the first meeting of the company summoned under section 425(1) or for the purposes of paragraph 1.".

(5) For sub-paragraphs (2) to (5) substitute—

"(2) The accounting statement shall consist of—

(a) a balance sheet dealing with the state of the affairs of the company as at a date not more than three months before the draft terms were adopted by the directors, and

(b) where the company would be required to prepare group accounts if that date were the last day of a financial year, a consolidated balance sheet dealing with the state of affairs of the company and its subsidiary undertakings as at that date.

(3) The requirements of this Act as to balance sheets forming part of a company's annual accounts, and the matters to be included in notes thereto, apply to any balance sheet required for the accounting statement, with such modifications as are necessary by reason of its being prepared otherwise than as at the last day of a financial year.

(4) Any balance sheet required for the accounting statement shall be approved by the board of directors and signed on behalf of the board by a director of the company.

(5) In relation to a company within the meaning of Article 3 of the Companies (Northern Ireland) Order 1986, the references in this paragraph to the requirements of this Act shall be construed as reference to the corresponding requirements of that Order.".

23. In Schedule 22 (provisions applying to unregistered companies), in the entry relating to Part VII, in column 1, for "Schedule 10" substitute "Schedules 10 and 10A".

24.—(1) Schedule 24 (punishment of offences) is amended as follows.

(2) The existing entries for provisions in Part VII are amended as follows, and shall be re-ordered according to the new order of the sections in that Part:

Provision of Part VII	*Amendment*
223(1)	In column 1, for "223(1)" substitute "221(5) or 222(4)".
223(2)	In column 1, for "223(2)" substitute "222(6). In column 2, for "222(4)" substitute "222(5)".
231(3)	In column 1, for "231(3)" substitute "231(6)".
231(4)	In column 1, for "231(4)" substitute "232(4)". In column 2, for "Schedule 5, Part V" substitute "Schedule 6, Part I".
235(7)	In column 1, for "235(7)" substitute "234(5)". In column 2, for "the section" substitute "Part VII".
238(2)	In column 1, for "238(2)" substitute "233(6)".
240(5)	In column 1, for "240(5)" substitute "238(5)". In column 2, for "company balance sheet" substitute "company's annual accounts".
243(1)	In column 1, for "243(1)" substitute "241(2) or 242(2)". In column 2, for "company accounts" substitute "company's annual accounts, directors' report and auditors' report".
245(1)	Omit the entry.
245(2)	Omit the entry.
246(2)	In column 1, for "246(2)" substitute "239(3)". In column 2, after "accounts" insert "and reports".
254(6)	In column 1, for "254(6)" substitute "240(6)". In column 2, for the present words substitute "Failure to comply with requirements in connection with publication of accounts".
255(5)	Omit the entry.

260(3)   Omit the entry.

(3) At the appropriate places insert the following new entries—

"233(5)	Approving defective accounts.	1. On indictment.	A fine
		2. Summary.	The statutory maximum.
234A(4)	Laying, circulating or delivering directors' report without required signature.	Summary.	One-fifth of the statutory maximum.
236(4)	Laying, circulating or delivering auditors' report without required signature.	Summary.	One-fifth of the statutory maximum.
251(6)	Failure to comply with requirements in relation to summary financial statements.	Summary.	One-fifth of the statutory maximum.".

(4) In the entry for section 703(1) (failure by oversea company to comply with requirements as to accounts and reports), in column 2 for the words from "s.700" to the end substitute "requirements as to accounts and reports".

Part II

Amendments of Other Enactments

Betting, Gaming and Lotteries Act 1963 (c.2)

25. In Schedule 2 to the Betting, Gaming and Lotteries Act 1963 (registered pool promoters), in paragraph 24(2) (duties with respect to delivery of accounts and audit) for the words from "and the following provisions" to "their report)" substitute "and sections 235(2) and 237(1) and (3) of the Companies Act 1985 (matters to be stated in auditors' report and responsibility of auditors in preparing their report)".

Harbours Act 1964 (c.40)

26.—(1) Section 42 of the Harbours Act 1964 (accounts and reports of statutory harbour undertakers) is amended as follows.

(2) For subsection (2) substitute—

"(2) Where a statutory harbour undertaker is a parent undertaking with subsidiary undertakings which carry on harbour activities or any associated activities, then, it shall be the duty of the company also to prepare group accounts relating to the harbour activities and associated activities carried on by it and its subsidiary undertakings."

1985 c. 6.

(3) In subsection (6) (application of provisions of the Companies Act 1985)—

(a) in paragraph (a) for "company accounts" substitute "individual company accounts";

(b) in paragraph (c) omit the words "required to be attached to a company's balance sheet".

(4) In subsection (9), for the definition of "holding company" and "subsidiary" substitute—

"'parent undertaking' and 'subsidiary undertaking' have the same meaning as in Part VII of the Companies Act 1985;".

Coal Industry Act 1971 (c.16)

27.—(1) Section 8 of the Coal Industry Act 1971 (further provisions as to accounts of British Coal Corporation) is amended as follows.

(2) In subsections (1) and (2) for "subsidiaries" (three times) substitute "subsidiary undertakings".

(3) After subsection (2) insert—

"(3) In this section 'subsidiary undertaking' has the same meaning as in Part VII of the Companies Act 1985.".

Aircraft and Shipbuilding Industries Act 1977 (c.3)

28.—(1) Section 17 of the Aircraft and Shipbuilding Industries Act 1977 (British Shipbuilders: accounts and audit) is amended as follows.

(2) In subsection (1)(c) (duty to prepare consolidated accounts) for "subsidiaries" substitute "subsidiary undertakings".

(3) In subsection (9) (copies of accounts to be sent to the Secretary of State) for "subsidiaries" substitute "subsidiary undertakings" and for "subsidiary" substitute "subsidiary undertaking".

(4) After subsection (9) add—

"(10) In this section "subsidiary undertaking" has the same meaning as in Part VII of the Companies Act 1985.".

Crown Agents Act 1979 (c.43)

29. In section 22 of the Crown Agents Act 1979 (accounts and audit), in subsection (2) (duty to prepare consolidated accounts) for "subsidiaries" (three times) substitute "subsidiary undertakings", and at the end of that subsection add—

"In this subsection "subsidiary undertaking" has the same meaning as in Part VII of the Companies Act 1985.".

British Telecommunications Act 1981 (c.38)

30. In section 75 of the British Telecommunications Act 1981 (accounts of the Post Office), in subsection (1)(c)(i) for "subsidiaries" substitute "subsidiary undertakings within the meaning of Part VII of the Companies Act 1985".

Transport Act 1981 (c.56)

31. In section 11(4) of the Transport Act 1981, for "section 235" substitute "section 234".

Iron and Steel Act 1982 (c.25)

32. In section 24(5) of the Iron and Steel Act 1982 (meaning of "directors' report") for the words from "which, under section 235" to the end substitute "which is required to be prepared under section 234 of the Companies Act 1985".

Oil and Pipelines Act 1985 (c.62)

33. In Schedule 3 to the Oil and Pipelines Act 1985 (Oil and Pipelines Agency: financial and other provisions), in paragraph 9(2) (duty to prepare consolidated accounts) for "subsidiaries" (three times) substitute "subsidiary undertakings", and at the end of that sub-paragraph add—

"In this sub-paragraph "subsidiary undertaking" has the same meaning as in Part VII of the Companies Act 1985.".

Patents, Designs and Marks Act 1986 (c.39)

34. In Schedule 2 to the Patents, Designs and Marks Act 1986 (service marks), in paragraph 1(2) (provisions in which reference to trade mark includes service mark) for sub-paragraph (ii) substitute—

"(ii) Part I of Schedule 4 and paragraphs 5(2)(d) and 10(1)(b) and (2) of Schedule 9 (form of company balance sheets); and".

Company Directors Disqualification Act 1986 (c.46)

35.—(1) The Company Directors Disqualification Act 1986 is amended as follows.

(2) In section 3(3)(b) (default orders)—

(a) in sub-paragraph (i) for "section 244" substitute "section 242(4)", and

(b) after that sub-paragraph insert—

"(ia) section 245B of that Act (order requiring preparation of revised accounts),".

(3) In Schedule 1, for paragraph 5 substitute—

"5. The extent of the director's responsibility for any failure by the directors of the company to comply with—

(a) section 226 or 227 of the Companies Act (duty to prepare annual accounts), or

(b) section 233 of that Act (approval and signature of accounts).".

Financial Services Act 1986 (c.60)

36.—(1) The Financial Services Act 1986 is amended as follows.

(2) In section 117(4) and (5), for "section 227" substitute "section 226".

(3) In Schedule 1, for paragraph 30 substitute—

"30.—(1) For the purposes of this Schedule a group shall be treated as including any body corporate in which a member of the group holds a qualifying capital interest.

(2) A qualifying capital interest means an interest in relevant shares of the body corporate which the member holds on a long-term basis for the purpose of securing a contribution to its own activities by the exercise of control or influence arising from that interest.

(3) Relevant shares means shares comprised in the equity share capital of the body corporate of a class carrying rights to vote in all circumstances at general meetings of the body.

(4) A holding of 20 per cent. or more of the nominal value of the relevant shares of a body corporate shall be presumed to be a qualifying capital interest unless the contrary is shown.

(5) In this paragraph "equity share capital" has the same meaning as in the Companies Act 1985 and the Companies (Northern Ireland) Order 1986.".

Banking Act 1987 (c.22)

37.—(1) The Banking Act 1987 is amended as follows.

(2) In section 46(2) (duties of auditor of authorised institution), in paragraph (c) for "section 236" substitute "section 235(2)" and for "section 237" substitute "section 235(3) or section 237"; and in section 46(4) (adaptation of references for Northern Ireland) for "236 and 237" substitute "235(2) and 235(3) and 237".

(3) After section 105 insert—

"Meaning of "related company".   105A.—(1) In this Act a "related company", in relation to an institution or the holding company of an institution, means a body corporate (other than a subsidiary) in which the institution or holding company holds a qualifying capital interest.

(2) A qualifying capital interest means an interest in relevant shares of the body corporate which the institution or holding company holds on a long-term basis for the purpose of securing a contribution to its own activities by the exercise of control or influence arising from that interest.

(3) Relevant shares means shares comprised in the equity share capital of the body corporate of a class carrying rights to vote in all circumstances at general meetings of the body.

(4) A holding of 20 per cent. or more of the nominal value of the relevant shares of a body corporate shall be presumed to be a qualifying capital interest unless the contrary is shown.

(5) In this paragraph "equity share capital" has the same meaning as in the Companies Act 1985 and the Companies (Northern Ireland) Order 1986.".

(4) In section 106(1) (interpretation), for the definition of "related company" substitute—

" "related company" has the meaning given by section 105A above;".

Income and Corporation Taxes Act 1988 (c.1)

38.—(1) The Income and Corporation Taxes Act 1988 is amended as follows.

(2) In section 180 (annual return of registered profit-related pay scheme), in subsection (3) for "section 242(3)" substitute "section 244(3)".

(3) In section 565(6) (conditions for exemption from provisions relating to sub-contractors in construction industry: compliance with requirements of Companies Act 1985), in paragraph (a) for "section 227 and 241" substitute "sections 226, 241 and 242". 1985 c. 6.

Dartford–Thurrock Crossing Act 1988 (c.20)

39. In section 33 of the Dartford–Thurrock Crossing Act 1988 (duty to lay before Parliament copies of accounts of persons appointed to levy tolls), for subsection (2) substitute—

"(2) In relation to a company "accounts" in subsection (1) means the company's annual accounts for a financial year, together with the relevant directors' report and the auditors' report on those accounts.

Expressions used in this subsection have the same meaning as in Part VII of the Companies Act 1985.".

SCHEDULE 11   Section 30(5).

RECOGNITION OF SUPERVISORY BODY

PART I

GRANT AND REVOCATION OF RECOGNITION

Application for recognition of supervisory body

1.—(1) A supervisory body may apply to the Secretary of State for an order declaring it to be a recognised supervisory body for the purposes of this Part of this Act.

(2) Any such application—

(a) shall be made in such manner as the Secretary of State may direct, and

(b) shall be accompanied by such information as the Secretary of State may reasonably require for the purpose of determining the application.

SCH. 11

(3) At any time after receiving an application and before determining it the Secretary of State may require the applicant to furnish additional information.

(4) The directions and requirements given or imposed under sub-paragraphs (2) and (3) may differ as between different applications.

(5) Any information to be furnished to the Secretary of State under this paragraph shall, if he so requires, be in such form or verified in such manner as he may specify.

(6) Every application shall be accompanied by a copy of the applicant's rules and of any guidance issued by the applicant which is intended to have continuing effect and is issued in writing or other legible form.

Grant and refusal of recognition

2.—(1) The Secretary of State may, on an application duly made in accordance with paragraph 1 and after being furnished with all such information as he may require under that paragraph, make or refuse to make an order (a "recognition order") declaring the applicant to be a recognised supervisory body for the purposes of this Part of this Act.

(2) The Secretary of State shall not make a recognition order unless it appears to him, from the information furnished by the body and having regard to any other information in his possession, that the requirements of Part II of this Schedule are satisfied as respects that body.

(3) The Secretary of State may refuse to make a recognition order in respect of a body if he considers that its recognition is unnecessary having regard to the existence of one or more other bodies which maintain and enforce rules as to the appointment and conduct of company auditors and which have been or are likely to be recognised.

(4) Where the Secretary of State refuses an application for a recognition order he shall give the applicant a written notice to that effect specifying which requirements in the opinion of the Secretary of State are not satisfied or stating that the application is refused on the ground mentioned in sub-paragraph (3).

(5) A recognition order shall state the date on which it takes effect.

Revocation of recognition

3.—(1) A recognition order may be revoked by a further order made by the Secretary of State if at any time it appears to him—

(a) that any requirement of Part II of this Schedule is not satisfied in the case of the body to which the recognition order relates ("the recognised body"),

(b) that the recognised body has failed to comply with any obligation to which it is subject by virtue of this Part of this Act, or

(c) that the continued recognition of the body is undesirable having regard to the existence of one or more other bodies which have been or are to be recognised.

(2) An order revoking a recognition order shall state the date on which it takes effect and that date shall not be earlier than three months after the day on which the revocation order is made.

(3) Before revoking a recognition order the Secretary of State shall give written notice of his intention to do so to the recognised body, take such steps as he considers reasonably practicable for bringing the notice to the attention of members of the body and publish it in such manner as he thinks appropriate for bringing it to the attention of any other persons who are in his opinion likely to be affected.

(4) A notice under sub-paragraph (3) shall state the reasons for which the Secretary of State proposes to act and give particulars of the rights conferred by sub-paragraph (5).

(5) A body on which a notice is served under sub-paragraph (3), any member of the body and any other person who appears to the Secretary of State to be affected may within three months after the date of service or publication, or within such longer time as the Secretary of State may allow, make written representations to the Secretary of State and, if desired, oral representations to a person appointed for that purpose by the Secretary of State; and the Secretary of State shall have regard to any representations made in accordance with this sub-paragraph in determining whether to revoke the recognition order.

(6) If in any case the Secretary of State considers it essential to do so in the public interest he may revoke a recognition order without regard to the restriction imposed by sub-paragraph (2) and notwithstanding that no notice has been given or published under sub-paragraph (3) or that the time for making representations in pursuance of such a notice has not expired.

(7) An order revoking a recognition order may contain such transitional provisions as the Secretary of State thinks necessary or expedient.

(8) A recognition order may be revoked at the request or with the consent of the recognised body and any such revocation shall not be subject to the restrictions imposed by sub-paragraphs (1) and (2) or the requirements of sub-paragraphs (3) to (5).

(9) On making an order revoking a recognition order the Secretary of State shall give the body written notice of the making of the order, take such steps as he considers reasonably practicable for bringing the making of the order to the attention of members of the body and publish a notice of the making of the order in such manner as he thinks appropriate for bringing it to the attention of any other persons who are in his opinion likely to be affected.

PART II

REQUIREMENTS FOR RECOGNITION

Holding of appropriate qualification

4.—(1) The body must have rules to the effect that a person is not eligible for appointment as a company auditor unless—

(a) in the case of an individual, he holds an appropriate qualification;

(b) in the case of a firm—

(i) the individuals responsible for company audit work on behalf of the firm hold an appropriate qualification, and

(ii) the firm is controlled by qualified persons (see paragraph 5 below).

(2) This does not prevent the body from imposing more stringent requirements.

(3) A firm which has ceased to comply with the conditions mentioned in sub-paragraph (1)(b) may be permitted to remain eligible for appointment as a company auditor for a period of not more than three months.

5.—(1) The following provisions explain what is meant in paragraph 4(1)(b)(ii) by a firm being "controlled by qualified persons".

(2) For this purpose references to a person being qualified are, in relation to an individual, to his holding an appropriate qualification, and in relation to a firm, to its being eligible for appointment as a company auditor.

(3) A firm shall be treated as controlled by qualified persons if, and only if—

(a) a majority of the members of the firm are qualified persons, and

(b) where the firm's affairs are managed by a board of directors, committee or other management body, a majority of the members of that body are qualified persons or, if the body consists of two persons only, at least one of them is a qualified person.

(4) A majority of the members of a firm means—

(a) where under the firm's constitution matters are decided upon by the exercise of voting rights, members holding a majority of the rights to vote on all, or substantially all, matters;

(b) in any other case, members having such rights under the constitution of the firm as enable them to direct its overall policy or alter its constitution.

(5) A majority of the members of the management body of a firm means—

(a) where matters are decided at meetings of the management body by the exercise of voting rights, members holding a majority of the rights to vote on all, or substantially all, matters at such meetings;

(b) in any other case, members having such rights under the constitution of the firm as enable them to direct its overall policy or alter its constitution.

1985 c. 6.
(6) The provisions of paragraphs 5 to 11 of Schedule 10A to the Companies Act 1985 (rights to be taken into account and attribution of rights) apply for the purposes of this paragraph.

Auditors to be fit and proper persons

6.—(1) The body must have adequate rules and practices designed to ensure that the persons eligible under its rules for appointment as a company auditor are fit and proper persons to be so appointed.

(2) The matters which the body may take into account for this purpose in relation to a person must include—

(a) any matter relating to any person who is or will be employed by or associated with him for the purposes of or in connection with company audit work; and

(b) in the case of a body corporate, any matter relating to any director or controller of the body, to any other body corporate in the same group or to any director or controller of any such other body; and

(c) in the case of a partnership, any matter relating to any of the partners, any director or controller of any of the partners, any body corporate in the same group as any of the partners and any director or controller of any such other body.

(3) In sub-paragraph (2)(b) and (c) "controller", in relation to a body corporate, means a person who either alone or with any associate or associates is entitled to exercise or control the exercise of 15 per cent. or more of the rights to vote on all, or substantially all, matters at general meetings of the body or another body corporate of which it is a subsidiary.

Professional integrity and independence

7.—(1) The body must have adequate rules and practices designed to ensure—

(a) that company audit work is conducted properly and with integrity, and

(b) that persons are not appointed company auditor in circumstances in which they have any interest likely to conflict with the proper conduct of the audit.

(2) The body must also have adequate rules and practices designed to ensure that no firm is eligible under its rules for appointment as a company auditor unless the firm has arrangements to prevent—

    (a) individuals who do not hold an appropriate qualification, and

    (b) persons who are not members of the firm,

from being able to exert any influence over the way in which an audit is conducted in circumstances in which that influence would be likely to affect the independence or integrity of the audit.

Technical standards

8. The body must have rules and practices as to the technical standards to be applied in company audit work and as to the manner in which those standards are to be applied in practice.

Procedures for maintaining competence

9. The body must have rules and practices designed to ensure that persons eligible under its rules for appointment as a company auditor continue to maintain an appropriate level of competence in the conduct of company audits.

Monitoring and enforcement

10.—(1) The body must have adequate arrangements and resources for the effective monitoring and enforcement of compliance with its rules.

(2) The arrangements for monitoring may make provision for that function to be performed on behalf of the body (and without affecting its responsibility) by any other body or person who is able and willing to perform it.

Membership, eligibility and discipline

11. The rules and practices of the body relating to—

    (a) the admission and expulsion of members,

    (b) the grant and withdrawal of eligibility for appointment as a company auditor, and

    (c) the discipline it exercises over its members,

must be fair and reasonable and include adequate provision for appeals.

Investigation of complaints

12.—(1) The body must have effective arrangements for the investigation of complaints—

    (a) against persons who are eligible under its rules to be appointed company auditor, or

    (b) against the body in respect of matters arising out of its functions as a supervisory body.

(2) The arrangements may make provision for the whole or part of that function to be performed by and to be the responsibility of a body or person independent of the body itself.

Meeting of claims arising out of audit work

13.—(1) The body must have adequate rules or arrangements designed to ensure that persons eligible under its rules for appointment as a company auditor take such steps as may reasonably be expected of them to secure that they are able to meet claims against them arising out of company audit work.

(2) This may be achieved by professional indemnity insurance or other appropriate arrangements.

Register of auditors and other information to be made available

14. The body must have rules requiring persons eligible under its rules for appointment as a company auditor to comply with any obligations imposed on them by regulations under section 35 or 36.

Taking account of costs of compliance

15. The body must have satisfactory arrangements for taking account, in framing its rules, of the cost to those to whom the rules would apply of complying with those rules and any other controls to which they are subject.

Promotion and maintenance of standards

16. The body must be able and willing to promote and maintain high standards of integrity in the conduct of company audit work and to co-operate, by the sharing of information and otherwise, with the Secretary of State and any other authority, body or person having responsibility in the United Kingdom for the qualification, supervision or regulation of auditors.

Section 32(4).

SCHEDULE 12

RECOGNITION OF PROFESSIONAL QUALIFICATION

PART I

GRANT AND REVOCATION OF RECOGNITION

Application for recognition of professional qualification

1.—(1) A qualifying body may apply to the Secretary of State for an order declaring a qualification offered by it to be a recognised professional qualification for the purposes of this Part of this Act.

(2) Any such application—

(a) shall be made in such manner as the Secretary of State may direct, and

(b) shall be accompanied by such information as the Secretary of State may reasonably require for the purpose of determining the application.

(3) At any time after receiving an application and before determining it the Secretary of State may require the applicant to furnish additional information.

(4) The directions and requirements given or imposed under sub-paragraphs (2) and (3) may differ as between different applications.

(5) Any information to be furnished to the Secretary of State under this section shall, if he so requires, be in such form or verified in such manner as he may specify.

In the case of examination standards, the verification required may include independent moderation of the examinations over such period as the Secretary of State considers necessary.

(6) Every application shall be accompanied by a copy of the applicant's rules and of any guidance issued by it which is intended to have continuing effect and is issued in writing or other legible form.

Grant and refusal of recognition

2.—(1) The Secretary of State may, on an application duly made in accordance with paragraph 1 and after being furnished with all such information as he may require under that paragraph, make or refuse to make an order (a "recognition order") declaring the qualification in respect of which the application was made to be a recognised professional qualification for the purposes of this Part of this Act.

In this Part of this Act a "recognised qualifying body" means a qualifying body offering a recognised professional qualification.

(2) The Secretary of State shall not make a recognition order unless it appears to him, from the information furnished by the applicant and having regard to any other information in his possession, that the requirements of Part II of this Schedule are satisfied as respects the qualification.

(3) Where the Secretary of State refuses an application for a recognition order he shall give the applicant a written notice to that effect specifying which requirements, in his opinion, are not satisfied.

(4) A recognition order shall state the date on which it takes effect.

Revocation of recognition

3.—(1) A recognition order may be revoked by a further order made by the Secretary of State if at any time it appears to him—

(a) that any requirement of Part II of this Schedule is not satisfied in relation to the qualification to which the recognition order relates, or

(b) that the qualifying body has failed to comply with any obligation to which it is subject by virtue of this Part of this Act.

(2) An order revoking a recognition order shall state the date on which it takes effect and that date shall not be earlier than three months after the day on which the revocation order is made.

(3) Before revoking a recognition order the Secretary of State shall give written notice of his intention to do so to the qualifying body, take such steps as he considers reasonably practicable for bringing the notice to the attention of persons holding the qualification or in the course of studying for it and publish it in such manner as he thinks appropriate for bringing it to the attention of any other persons who are in his opinion likely to be affected.

(4) A notice under sub-paragraph (3) shall state the reasons for which the Secretary of State proposes to act and give particulars of the rights conferred by sub-paragraph (5).

(5) A body on which a notice is served under sub-paragraph (3), any person holding the qualification or in the course of studying for it and any other person who appears to the Secretary of State to be affected may within three months after the date of service or publication, or within such longer time as the Secretary of State may allow, make written representations to the Secretary of State and, if desired, oral representations to a person appointed for that purpose by the Secretary of State; and the Secretary of State shall have regard to any representations made in accordance with this subsection in determining whether to revoke the recognition order.

(6) If in any case the Secretary of State considers it essential to do so in the public interest he may revoke a recognition order without regard to the restriction imposed by sub-paragraph (2) and notwithstanding that no notice has been given or published under sub-paragraph (3) or that the time for making representations in pursuance of such a notice has not expired.

(7) An order revoking a recognition order may contain such transitional provisions as the Secretary of State thinks necessary or expedient.

(8) A recognition order may be revoked at the request or with the consent of the qualifying body and any such revocation shall not be subject to the restrictions imposed by sub-paragraphs (1) and (2) or the requirements of sub-paragraphs (3) to (5).

(9) On making an order revoking a recognition order the Secretary of State shall give the qualifying body written notice of the making of the order, take such steps as he considers reasonably practicable for bringing the making of the order to the attention of persons holding the qualification or in the course of studying for it and publish a notice of the making of the order in such manner as he thinks appropriate for bringing it to the attention of any other persons who are in his opinion likely to be affected.

PART II

REQUIREMENTS FOR RECOGNITION

Entry requirements

4.—(1) The qualification must only be open to persons who have attained university entrance level or have a sufficient period of professional experience.

(2) In relation to a person who has not been admitted to a university or other similar establishment in the United Kingdom, attaining university entrance level means—

  (a) being educated to such a standard as would entitle him to be considered for such admission on the basis of—

      (i) academic or professional qualifications obtained in the United Kingdom and recognised by the Secretary of State to be of an appropriate standard, or

      (ii) academic or professional qualifications obtained outside the United Kingdom which the Secretary of State considers to be of an equivalent standard; or

  (b) being assessed on the basis of written tests of a kind appearing to the Secretary of State to be adequate for the purpose, with or without oral examination, as of such a standard of ability as would entitle him to be considered for such admission.

(3) The assessment, tests and oral examination referred to in sub-paragraph (2)(b) may be conducted by the qualifying body or by some other body approved by the Secretary of State.

Course of theoretical instruction

5. The qualification must be restricted to persons who have completed a course of theoretical instruction in the subjects prescribed for the purposes of paragraph 7 or have a sufficient period of professional experience.

Sufficient period of professional experience

6.—(1) The references in paragraphs 4 and 5 to a sufficient period of professional experience are to not less than seven years' experience in a professional capacity in the fields of finance, law and accountancy.

(2) Periods of theoretical instruction in the fields of finance, law and accountancy may be deducted from the required period of professional experience, provided the instruction—

  (a) lasted at least one year, and

  (b) is attested by an examination recognised by the Secretary of State for the purposes of this paragraph;

but the period of professional experience may not be so reduced by more than four years.

(3) The period of professional experience together with the practical training required in the case of persons satisfying the requirement in paragraph 5 by virtue of having a sufficient period of professional experience must not be shorter than the course of theoretical instruction referred to in that paragraph and the practical training required in the case of persons satisfying the requirement of that paragraph by virtue of having completed such a course.

Examination

7.—(1) The qualification must be restricted to persons who have passed an examination (at least part of which is in writing) testing—

(a) theoretical knowledge of the subjects prescribed for the purposes of this paragraph by regulations made by the Secretary of State, and

(b) ability to apply that knowledge in practice,

and requiring a standard of attainment at least equivalent to that required to obtain a degree from a university or similar establishment in the United Kingdom.

(2) The qualification may be awarded to a person without his theoretical knowledge of a subject being tested by examination if he has passed a university or other examination of equivalent standard in that subject or holds a university degree or equivalent qualification in it.

(3) The qualification may be awarded to a person without his ability to apply his theoretical knowledge of a subject in practice being tested by examination if he has received practical training in that subject which is attested by an examination or diploma recognised by the Secretary of State for the purposes of this paragraph.

(4) Regulations under this paragraph shall be made by statutory instrument which shall be subject to annulment in pursuance of a resolution of either House of Parliament.

Practical training

8.—(1) The qualification must be restricted to persons who have completed at least three years' practical training of which—

(a) part was spent being trained in company audit work, and

(b) a substantial part was spent being trained in company audit work or other audit work of a description approved by the Secretary of State as being similar to company audit work.

For this purpose "company audit work" includes the work of a person appointed as auditor under the Companies (Northern Ireland) Order 1986 or under the law of a country or territory outside the United Kingdom where it appears to the Secretary of State that the law and practice with respect to the audit of company accounts is similar to that in the United Kingdom. S.I. 1986/1032 (N.I. 6).

(2) The training must be given by persons approved by the body offering the qualification as persons as to whom the body is satisfied, in the light of undertakings given by them and the supervision to which they are subject (whether by the body itself or some other body or organisation), that they will provide adequate training.

(3) At least two-thirds of the training must be given by a fully-qualified auditor, that is, a person—

(a) eligible in accordance with this Part of this Act to be appointed as a company auditor, or

(b) satisfying the corresponding requirements of the law of Northern Ireland or another member State of the European Economic Community.

The body offering the qualification

9.—(1) The body offering the qualification must have—

(a) rules and arrangements adequate to ensure compliance with the requirements of paragraphs 4 to 8, and

(b) adequate arrangements for the effective monitoring of its continued compliance with those requirements.

(2) The arrangements must include arrangements for monitoring the standard of its examinations and the adequacy of the practical training given by the persons approved by it for that purpose.

Section 46(6).

SCHEDULE 13

SUPPLEMENTARY PROVISIONS WITH RESPECT TO DELEGATION ORDER

Introductory

1. The following provisions have effect in relation to a body established by a delegation order under section 46; and any power to make provision by order is to make provision by order under that section.

Status

2. The body shall not be regarded as acting on behalf of the Crown and its members, officers and employees shall not be regarded as Crown servants.

Name, members and chairman

3.—(1) The body shall be known by such name as may be specified in the delegation order.

(2) The body shall consist of such persons (not being less than eight) as the Secretary of State may appoint after such consultation as he thinks appropriate; and the chairman of the body shall be such person as the Secretary of State may appoint from amongst its members.

(3) The Secretary of State may make provision by order as to the terms on which the members of the body are to hold and vacate office and as to the terms on which a person appointed as chairman is to hold and vacate the office of chairman.

Financial provisions

4.—(1) The body shall pay to its chairman and members such remuneration, and such allowances in respect of expenses properly incurred by them in the performance of their duties, as the Secretary of State may determine.

(2) As regards any chairman or member in whose case the Secretary of State so determines, the body shall pay or make provision for the payment of—

(a) such pension, allowance or gratuity to or in respect of that person on his retirement or death, or

(b) such contributions or other payment towards the provision of such a pension, allowance or gratuity,

as the Secretary of State may determine.

(3) Where a person ceases to be a member of the body otherwise than on the expiry of his term of office and it appears to the Secretary of State that there are special circumstances which make it right for him to receive compensation, the body shall make a payment to him by way of compensation of such amount as the Secretary of State may determine.

Proceedings

5.—(1) The delegation order may contain such provision as the Secretary of State considers appropriate with respect to the proceedings of the body.

(2) The order may, in particular—

    (a) authorise the body to discharge any functions by means of committees consisting wholly or partly of members of the body;

    (b) provide that the validity of proceedings of the body, or of any such committee, is not affected by any vacancy among the members or any defect in the appointment of any member.

Fees

6.—(1) The body may retain fees payable to it.

(2) The fees shall be applied for meeting the expenses of the body in discharging its functions and for any purposes incidental to those functions.

(3) Those expenses include any expenses incurred by the body on such staff, accommodation, services and other facilities as appear to it to be necessary or expedient for the proper performance of its functions.

(4) In prescribing the amount of fees in the exercise of the functions transferred to it the body shall prescribe such fees as appear to it sufficient to defray those expenses, taking one year with another.

(5) Any exercise by the body of the power to prescribe fees requires the approval of the Secretary of State; and the Secretary of State may, after consultation with the body, by order vary or revoke any regulations made by it prescribing fees.

Legislative functions

7.—(1) Regulations made by the body in the exercise of the functions transferred to it shall be made by instrument in writing, but not by statutory instrument.

(2) The instrument shall specify the provision of this Part of this Act under which it is made.

(3) The Secretary of State may by order impose such requirements as he thinks necessary or expedient as to the circumstances and manner in which the body must consult on any regulations it proposes to make.

8.—(1) Immediately after an instrument is made it shall be printed and made available to the public with or without payment.

(2) A person shall not be taken to have contravened any regulation if he shows that at the time of the alleged contravention the instrument containing the regulation had not been made available as required by this paragraph.

9.—(1) The production of a printed copy of an instrument purporting to be made by the body on which is endorsed a certificate signed by an officer of the body authorised by it for the purpose and stating—

    (a) that the instrument was made by the body,

    (b) that the copy is a true copy of the instrument, and

    (c) that on a specified date the instrument was made available to the public as required by paragraph 8,

is prima facie evidence or, in Scotland, sufficient evidence of the facts stated in the certificate.

(2) A certificate purporting to be signed as mentioned in sub-paragraph (1) shall be deemed to have been duly signed unless the contrary is shown.

(3) Any person wishing in any legal proceedings to cite an instrument made by the body may require the body to cause a copy of it to be endorsed with such a certificate as is mentioned in this paragraph.

Report and accounts

10.—(1) The body shall at least once in each year for which the delegation order is in force make a report to the Secretary of State on the discharge of the functions transferred to it and on such other matters as the Secretary of State may by order require.

(2) The Secretary of State shall lay before Parliament copies of each report received by him under this paragraph.

(3) The Secretary of State may, with the consent of the Treasury, give directions to the body with respect to its accounts and the audit of its accounts and it is the duty of the body to comply with the directions.

(4) A person shall not be appointed auditor of the body unless he is eligible for appointment as a company auditor under section 25.

Other supplementary provisions

11.—(1) The transfer of a function to a body established by a delegation order does not affect anything previously done in the exercise of the function transferred; and the resumption of a function so transferred does not affect anything previously done in exercise of the function resumed.

(2) The Secretary of State may by order make such transitional and other supplementary provision as he thinks necessary or expedient in relation to the transfer or resumption of a function.

(3) The provision that may be made in connection with the transfer of a function includes, in particular, provision—

    (a) for modifying or excluding any provision of this Part of this Act in its application to the function transferred;

    (b) for applying to the body established by the delegation order, in connection with the function transferred, any provision applying to the Secretary of State which is contained in or made under any other enactment;

    (c) for the transfer of any property, rights or liabilities from the Secretary of State to that body;

    (d) for the carrying on and completion by that body of anything in process of being done by the Secretary of State when the order takes effect;

    (e) for the substitution of that body for the Secretary of State in any instrument, contract or legal proceedings.

(4) The provision that may be made in connection with the resumption of a function includes, in particular, provision—

    (a) for the transfer of any property, rights or liabilities from that body to the Secretary of State;

    (b) for the carrying on and completion by the Secretary of State of anything in process of being done by that body when the order takes effect;

    (c) for the substitution of the Secretary of State for that body in any instrument, contract or legal proceedings.

12. Where a delegation order is revoked, the Secretary of State may by order make provision—

(a) for the payment of compensation to persons ceasing to be employed by the body established by the delegation order; and

(b) as to the winding up and dissolution of the body.

SCHEDULE 14

Section 47(1).

SUPERVISORY AND QUALIFYING BODIES: RESTRICTIVE PRACTICES

PART I

PREVENTION OF RESTRICTIVE PRACTICES

Refusal of recognition on grounds related to competition

1.—(1) The Secretary of State shall before deciding whether to make a recognition order in respect of a supervisory body or professional qualification send to the Director General of Fair Trading (in this Schedule referred to as "the Director") a copy of the rules and of any guidance which the Secretary of State is required to consider in making that decision together with such other information as the Secretary of State considers will assist the Director.

(2) The Director shall consider whether the rules or guidance have, or are intended or likely to have, to any significant extent the effect of restricting, distorting or preventing competition, and shall report to the Secretary of State; and the Secretary of State shall have regard to his report in deciding whether to make a recognition order.

(3) The Secretary of State shall not make a recognition order if it appears to him that the rules and any guidance of which copies are furnished with the application have, or are intended or likely to have, to any significant extent the effect of restricting, distorting or preventing competition, unless it appears to him that the effect is reasonably justifiable having regard to the purposes of this Part of this Act.

Notification of changes to rules or guidance

2.—(1) Where a recognised supervisory or qualifying body amends, revokes or adds to its rules or guidance in a manner which may reasonably be regarded as likely—

(a) to restrict, distort or prevent competition to any significant extent, or

(b) otherwise to affect the question whether the recognition order granted to the body should continue in force,

it shall within seven days give the Secretary of State written notice of the amendment, revocation or addition.

(2) Notice need not be given under sub-paragraph (1) of the revocation of guidance not intended to have continuing effect or issued otherwise than in writing or other legible form, or of any amendment or addition to guidance which does not result in or consist of guidance which is intended to have continuing effect and is issued in writing or other legible form.

Continuing scrutiny by the Director General of Fair Trading

3.—(1) The Director shall keep under review the rules made or guidance issued by a recognised supervisory or qualifying body, and if he is of the opinion that any rules or guidance of such a body have, or are intended or likely to have, to any significant extent the effect of restricting, distorting or preventing competition, he shall report his opinion to the Secretary of State, stating what in his opinion the effect is or is likely to be.

(2) The Secretary of State shall send to the Director copies of any notice received by him under paragraph 2, together with such other information as he considers will assist the Director.

(3) The Director may report to the Secretary of State his opinion that any matter mentioned in such a notice does not have, and is not intended or likely to have, to any significant extent the effect of restricting, distorting or preventing competition.

(4) The Director may from time to time consider whether—

(a) any practices of a recognised supervisory or qualifying body in its capacity as such, or

(b) any relevant practices required or contemplated by the rules or guidance of such a body or otherwise attributable to its conduct in its capacity as such,

have, or are intended or likely to have, to any significant extent the effect of restricting, distorting or preventing competition and, if so, what that effect is or is likely to be; and if he is of that opinion he shall make a report to the Secretary of State stating his opinion and what the effect is or is likely to be.

(5) The practices relevant for the purposes of sub-paragraph (4)(b) in the case of a recognised supervisory body are practices engaged in for the purposes of, or in connection with, appointment as a company auditor or the conduct of company audit work by persons who—

(a) are eligible under its rules for appointment as a company auditor, or

(b) hold an appropriate qualification and are directors or other officers of bodies corporate which are so eligible or partners in, or employees of, partnerships which are so eligible.

(6) The practices relevant for the purposes of sub-paragraph (4)(b) in the case of a recognised qualifying body are—

(a) practices engaged in by persons in the course of seeking to obtain a recognised professional qualification from that body, and

(b) practices engaged in by persons approved by the body for the purposes of giving practical training to persons seeking such a qualification and which relate to such training.

Investigatory powers of the Director

4.—(1) The following powers are exercisable by the Director for the purpose of investigating any matter in connection with his functions under paragraph 1 or 3.

(2) The Director may by a notice in writing require any person to produce, at a time and place specified in the notice, to the Director or to any person appointed by him for the purpose, any documents which are specified or described in the notice and which are documents in his custody or under his control and relating to any matter relevant to the investigation.

(3) The Director may by a notice in writing require any person to furnish to the Director such information as may be specified or described in the notice, and specify the time within which and the manner and form in which any such information is to be furnished.

(4) A person shall not under this paragraph be required to produce any document or disclose any information which he would be entitled to refuse to produce or disclose on grounds of legal professional privilege in proceedings in the High Court or on the grounds of confidentiality as between client and professional legal adviser in proceedings in the Court of Session.

(5) Subsections (6) to (8) of section 85 of the Fair Trading Act 1973 (enforcement provisions) apply in relation to a notice under this paragraph as they apply in relation to a notice under subsection (1) of that section but as if, in subsection (7) of that section, for the words from "any one" to "the Commission" there were substituted "the Director".

SCH. 14
1973 c. 41.

Publication of Director's reports

5.—(1) The Director may, if he thinks fit, publish any report made by him under paragraph 1 or 3.

(2) He shall exclude from a published report, so far as practicable, any matter which relates to the affairs of a particular person (other than the supervisory or qualifying body concerned) the publication of which would or might in his opinion seriously and prejudicially affect the interests of that person.

Powers exercisable by the Secretary of State in consequence of report

6.—(1) The powers conferred by this section are exercisable by the Secretary of State if, having received and considered a report from the Director under paragraph 3(1) or (4), it appears to him that—

  (a) any rules made or guidance issued by a recognised supervisory or qualifying body, or

  (b) any such practices as are mentioned in paragraph 3(4),

have, or are intended or likely to have, to any significant extent the effect of restricting, distorting or preventing competition and that that effect is greater than is reasonably justifiable having regard to the purposes of this Part of this Act.

(2) The powers are—

  (a) to revoke the recognition order granted to the body concerned,

  (b) to direct it to take specified steps for the purpose of securing that the rules, guidance or practices in question do not have the effect mentioned in sub-paragraph (1), and

  (c) to make alterations in the rules of the body for that purpose.

(3) The provisions of paragraph 3(2) to (5), (7) and (9) of Schedule 11 or, as the case may be, Schedule 12 have effect in relation to the revocation of a recognition order under sub-paragraph (2)(a) above as they have effect in relation to the revocation of such an order under that Schedule.

(4) Before the Secretary of State exercises the power conferred by sub-paragraph (2)(b) or (c) above he shall—

  (a) give written notice of his intention to do so to the body concerned and take such steps (whether by publication or otherwise) as he thinks appropriate for bringing the notice to the attention of any other person who in his opinion is likely to be affected by the exercise of the power, and

  (b) have regard to any representation made within such time as he considers reasonable by the body or any such other person.

(5) A notice under sub-paragraph (4) shall give particulars of the manner in which the Secretary of State proposes to exercise the power in question and state the reasons for which he proposes to act; and the statement of reasons may include matters contained in any report received by him under paragraph 4.

Supplementary provisions

7.—(1) A direction under paragraph 6 is, on the application of the Secretary of State, enforceable by injunction or, in Scotland, by an order under section 45 of the Court of Session Act 1988.

1988 c. 36.

(2) The fact that any rules made by a recognised supervisory or qualifying body have been altered by the Secretary of State, or pursuant to a direction of the Secretary of State, under paragraph 6 does not preclude their subsequent alteration or revocation by that body.

(3) In determining for the purposes of this Part of this Schedule whether any guidance has, or is likely to have, any particular effect the Secretary of State and the Director may assume that the persons to whom it is addressed will act in conformity with it.

PART II

CONSEQUENTIAL EXEMPTIONS FROM COMPETITION LAW

Fair Trading Act 1973 (c. 41)

8.—(1) For the purpose of determining whether a monopoly situation within the meaning of the Fair Trading Act 1973 exists by reason of the circumstances mentioned in section 7(1)(c) of that Act (supply of services by or for group of two or more persons), no account shall be taken of—

(a) the rules of or guidance issued by a recognised supervisory or qualifying body, or

(b) conduct constituting such a practice as is mentioned in paragraph 3(4) above.

(2) Where a recognition order is revoked there shall be disregarded for the purpose mentioned in sub-paragraph (1) any such conduct as is mentioned in that sub-paragraph which occurred while the order was in force.

(3) Where on a monopoly reference under section 50 or 51 of the Fair Trading Act 1973 falling within section 49 of that Act (monopoly reference not limited to the facts) the Monopolies and Mergers Commission find that a monopoly situation within the meaning of that Act exists and—

(a) that the person (or, if more than one, any of the persons) in whose favour it exists is—

(i) a recognised supervisory or qualifying body, or

(ii) a person of a description mentioned in paragraph 3(5) or (6) above, or

(b) that any such person's conduct in doing anything to which the rules of such a body relate is subject to guidance issued by the body,

the Commission in making their report on that reference shall exclude from their consideration the question whether the rules or guidance of the body concerned, or the acts or omissions of that body in its capacity as such, operate or may be expected to operate against the public interest.

Restrictive Trade Practices Act 1976 (c. 34)

9.—(1) The Restrictive Trade Practices Act 1976 does not apply to an agreement for the constitution of a recognised supervisory or qualifying body in so far as it relates to rules of or guidance issued by the body, and incidental matters connected therewith, including any term deemed to be contained in it by virtue of section 8(2) or 16(3) of that Act.

(2) Nor does that Act apply to an agreement the parties to which consist of or include—

(a) a recognised supervisory or qualifying body, or

(b) any such person as is mentioned in paragraph 3(5) or (6) above,

by reason that it includes any terms the inclusion of which is required or contemplated by the rules or guidance of that body.

(3) Where an agreement ceases by virtue of this paragraph to be subject to registration—

(a) the Director shall remove from the register maintained by him under the Act of 1976 any particulars which are entered or filed in that register in respect of the agreement, and

(b) any proceedings in respect of the agreement which are pending before the Restrictive Practices Court shall be discontinued.

(4) Where a recognition order is revoked, sub-paragraphs (1) and (2) above shall continue to apply for a period of six months beginning with the day on which the revocation takes effect, as if the order were still in force.

(5) Where an agreement which has been exempt from registration by virtue of this paragraph ceases to be exempt in consequence of the revocation of a recognition order, the time within which particulars of the agreement are to be furnished in accordance with section 24 of and Schedule 2 to the Act of 1976 shall be the period of one month beginning with the day on which the agreement ceased to be exempt from registration.

(6) Where in the case of an agreement registered under the 1976 Act a term ceases to fall within sub-paragraph (2) above in consequence of the revocation of a recognition order and particulars of that terms have not previously been furnished to the Director under section 24 of that Act, those particulars shall be furnished to him within the period of one month beginning with the day on which the term ceased to fall within that sub-paragraph.

Competition Act 1980 (c. 21)

10.—(1) No course of conduct constituting any such practice as is mentioned in paragraph 3(4) above shall constitute an anti-competitive practice for the purposes of the Competition Act 1980.

(2) Where a recognition order is revoked there shall not be treated as an anti-competitive practice for the purposes of that Act any such course of conduct as is mentioned in sub-paragraph (1) which occurred while the order was in force.

SCHEDULE 15

CHARGES ON PROPERTY OF OVERSEA COMPANIES

The following provisions are inserted in Part XXIII of the Companies Act 1985—

"CHAPTER III

REGISTRATION OF CHARGES

Introductory provisions.

703A.—(1) The provisions of this Chapter have effect for securing the registration in Great Britain of charges on the property of a registered oversea company.

(2) Section 395(2) and (3) (meaning of "charge" and "property") have effect for the purposes of this Chapter.

(3) A "registered oversea company", in relation to England and Wales or Scotland, means an oversea company which has duly delivered documents to the registrar for that part of Great Britain under section 691 and has not subsequently given notice to him under section 696(4) that it has ceased to have an established place of business in that part.

(4) References in this Chapter to the registrar shall be construed in accordance with section 703E below and references to registration, in relation to a charge, are to registration in the register kept by him under this Chapter.

Charges requiring registration.

703B.—(1) The charges requiring registration under this Chapter are those which if created by a company registered in Great Britain would require registration under Part XII of this Act.

(2) Whether a charge is one requiring registration under this Chapter shall be determined—

(a) in the case of a charge over property of a company at the date it delivers documents for registration under section 691, as at that date,

(b) in the case of a charge created by a registered oversea company, as at the date the charge is created, and

(c) in the case of a charge over property acquired by a registered oversea company, as at the date of the acquisition.

(3) In the following provisions of this Chapter references to a charge are, unless the context otherwise requires, to a charge requiring registration under this Chapter.

Where a charge not otherwise requiring registration relates to property by virtue of which it requires to be registered and to other property, the references are to the charge so far as it relates to property of the former description.

The register.

703C.—(1) The registrar shall keep for each registered oversea company a register, in such form as he thinks fit, of charges on property of the company.

(2) The register shall consist of a file containing with respect to each such charge the particulars and other information delivered to the registrar under or by virtue of the following provisions of this Chapter.

(3) Section 397(3) to (5) (registrar's certificate as to date of delivery of particulars) applies in relation to the delivery of any particulars or other information under this Chapter.

Company's duty to deliver particulars of charges for registration.

703D.—(1) If when an oversea company delivers documents for registration under section 691 any of its property is situated in Great Britain and subject to a charge, it is the company's duty at the same time to deliver the prescribed particulars of the charge, in the prescribed form, to the registrar for registration.

(2) Where a registered oversea company—

(a) creates a charge on property situated in Great Britain, or

(b) acquires property which is situated in Great Britain and subject to a charge,

it is the company's duty to deliver the prescribed particulars of the charge, in the prescribed form, to the registrar for registration within 21 days after the date of the charge's creation or, as the case may be, the date of the acquisition.

This subsection does not apply if the property subject to the charge is at the end of that period no longer situated in Great Britain.

(3) Where the preceding subsections do not apply and property of a registered oversea company is for a continuous period of four months situated in Great Britain and subject to a charge, it is the company's duty before the end of that period to deliver the prescribed particulars of the charge, in the prescribed form, to the registrar for registration.

(4) Particulars of a charge required to be delivered under subsections (1), (2) or (3) may be delivered for registration by any person interested in the charge.

(5) If a company fails to comply with subsection (1), (2) or (3), then, unless particulars of the charge have been delivered for registration by another person, the company and every officer of it who is in default is liable to a fine.

(6) Section 398(2), (4) and (5) (recovery of fees paid in connection with registration, filing of particulars in register and sending of copy of particulars filed and note as to date) apply in relation to particulars delivered under this Chapter.

Registrar to whom particulars, &c. to be delivered.

703E.—(1) The particulars required to be delivered by section 703D(1) (charges over property of oversea company becoming registered in a part of Great Britain) shall be delivered to the registrar to whom the documents are delivered under section 691.

(2) The particulars required to be delivered by section 703D(2) or (3) (charges over property of registered oversea company) shall be delivered—

(a) if the company is registered in one part of Great Britain and not in the other, to the registrar for the part in which it is registered, and

(b) if the company is registered in both parts of Great Britain but the property subject to the charge is situated in one part of Great Britain only, to the registrar for that part;

and in any other case the particulars shall be delivered to the registrars for both parts of Great Britain.

(3) Other documents required or authorised by virtue of this Chapter to be delivered to the registrar shall be delivered to the registrar or registrars to whom particulars of the charge to which they relate have been, or ought to have been, delivered.

(4) If a company gives notice under section 696(4) that it has ceased to have an established place of business in either part of Great Britain, charges over property of the company shall cease to be subject to the provisions of this Chapter, as regards registration in that part of Great Britain, as from the date on which notice is so given.

This is without prejudice to rights arising by reason of events occurring before that date.

Effect of failure to deliver particulars, late delivery and effect of errors and omissions.

703F.—(1) The following provisions of Part XII—

(a) section 399 (effect of failure to deliver particulars),

(b) section 400 (late delivery of particulars), and

(c) section 402 (effect of errors and omissions in particulars delivered),

apply, with the following modifications, in relation to a charge created by a registered oversea company of which particulars are required to be delivered under this Chapter.

(2) Those provisions do not apply to a charge of which particulars are required to be delivered under section 703D(1) (charges existing when company delivers documents under section 691).

(3) In relation to a charge of which particulars are required to be delivered under section 703D(3) (charges registrable by virtue of property being within Great Britain for requisite period), the references to the period of 21 days after the charge's creation shall be construed as references to the period of four months referred to in that subsection.

Delivery of further particulars or memorandum.

703G. Sections 401 and 403 (delivery of further particulars and memorandum of charge ceasing to affect company's property) apply in relation to a charge of which particulars have been delivered under this Chapter.

Further provisions with respect to voidness of charges.

703H.—(1) The following provisions of Part XII apply in relation to the voidness of a charge by virtue of this Chapter—

(a) section 404 (exclusion of voidness as against unregistered charges),

(b) section 405 (restrictions on cases in which charge is void),

(c) section 406 (effect of exercise of power of sale), and

(d) section 407 (effect of voidness on obligation secured).

(2) In relation to a charge of which particulars are required to be delivered under section 703D(3) (charges registrable by virtue of property being within Great Britain for requisite period), the reference in section 404 to the period of 21 days after the charge's creation shall be construed as a reference to the period of four months referred to in that subsection.

Additional information to be registered.

703I.—(1) Section 408 (particulars of taking up of issue of debentures) applies in relation to a charge of which particulars have been delivered under this Chapter.

(2) Section 409 (notice of appointment of receiver or manager) applies in relation to the appointment of a receiver or manager of property of a registered oversea company.

(3) Regulations under section 410 (notice of crystallisation of floating charge, &c.) may apply in relation to a charge of which particulars have been delivered under this Chapter; but subject to such exceptions, adaptations and modifications as may be specified in the regulations.

Copies of instruments and register to be kept by company.

703J.—(1) Sections 411 and 412 (copies of instruments and register to be kept by company) apply in relation to a registered oversea company and any charge over property of the company situated in Great Britain.

(2) They apply to any charge, whether or not particulars are required to be delivered to the registrar.

(3) In relation to such a company the references to the company's registered office shall be construed as references to its principal place of business in Great Britain.

Power to make further provision by regulations.

703K.—(1) The Secretary of State may by regulations make further provision as to the application of the provisions of this Chapter, or the provisions of Part XII applied by this Chapter, in relation to charges of any description specified in the regulations.

(2) The regulations may apply any provisions of regulations made under section 413 (power to make further provision with respect to application of Part XII) or make any provision which may be made under that section with respect to the application of provisions of Part XII.

Provisions as to situation of property.

703L.—(1) The following provisions apply for determining for the purposes of this Chapter whether a vehicle which is the property of an oversea company is situated in Great Britain—

(a) a ship, aircraft or hovercraft shall be regarded as situated in Great Britain if, and only if, it is registered in Great Britain;

(b) any other description of vehicle shall be regarded as situated in Great Britain on a day if, and only if, at any time on that day the management of the vehicle is directed from a place of business of the company in Great Britain;

and for the purposes of this Chapter a vehicle shall not be regarded as situated in one part of Great Britain only.

(2) For the purposes of this Chapter as it applies to a charge on future property, the subject-matter of the charge shall be treated as situated in Great Britain unless it relates exclusively to property of a kind which cannot, after being acquired or coming into existence, be situated in Great Britain; and references to property situated in a part of Great Britain shall be similarly construed.

Other supplementary provisions.

703M. The following provisions of Part XII apply for the purposes of this Chapter—

(a) section 414 (construction of references to date of creation of charge),

(b) section 415 (prescribed particulars and related expressions),

(c) section 416 (notice of matters disclosed on the register),

(d) section 417 (power of court to dispense with signature),

(e) section 418 (regulations) and

(f) section 419 (minor definitions).

Index of defined expressions.

703N. The following Table shows the provisions of this Chapter and Part XII defining or otherwise explaining expressions used in this Chapter (other than expressions used only in the same section)—

charge	sections 703A(2), 703B(3) and 395(2)
charge requiring registration	sections 703B(1) and 396
creation of charge	sections 703M(f) and 419(2)
date of acquisition (of property by a company)	sections 703M(f) and 419(3)
date of creation of charge	sections 703M(a) and 414
property	sections 703A(2) and 395(2)
registered oversea company	section 703A(3)
registrar and registration in relation to a charge	sections 703A(4) and 703E
situated in Great Britain	
in relation to vehicles	section 703L(1)
in relation to future property	section 703L(2)".

Section 107.

SCHEDULE 16

AMENDMENTS CONSEQUENTIAL ON PART IV

Land Charges Act 1972 (c. 61)

1.—(1) Section 3 of the Land Charges Act 1972 (registration of land charges) is amended as follows.

(2) In subsection (7) (registration in companies charges register to have same effect as registration under that Act), for "any of the enactments mentioned in subsection (8) below" substitute "Part XII, or Chapter III of Part XXIII, of the Companies Act 1985 (or corresponding earlier enactments)".

(3) In subsection (8) for "The enactments" substitute "The corresponding earlier enactments" and at the end insert "as originally enacted".

Companies Act 1985 (c. 6)

2.—(1) Schedule 24 to the Companies Act 1985 (punishment of offences) is amended as follows.

(2) For the entries relating to sections 399(3) to 423(3) (offences under Part XII: registration of charges) substitute—

"398(3)	Company failing to deliver particulars of charge to registrar.	1. On indictment. 2. Summary.	A fine. The statutory maximum.
408(3)	Company failing to deliver particulars of taking up of issue of debentures.	Summary.	One-fifth of the statutory maximum.
409(4)	Failure to give notice to registrar of appointment of receiver or manager, or of his ceasing to act.	Summary.	One-fifth of the statutory maximum.
410(4)	Failure to comply with requirements of regulations under s.410.	Summary.	One-fifth of the statutory maximum.
411(4)	Failure to keep copies of charging instruments or register at registered office.	1. On indictment. 2. Summary.	A fine. The statutory maximum.

412(4)	Refusing inspection of charging instrument or register or failing to supply copies.	Summary.	One-fifth of the statutory maximum.".	SCH. 16

(3) After the entry relating to section 703(1) insert—

"703D(5)	Oversea company failing to deliver particulars of charge to registrar.	1. On indictment. 2. Summary.	A fine. The statutory maximum.".

Insolvency Act 1986 (c. 45)

3.—(1) The Insolvency Act 1986 is amended as follows.

(2) In section 9(3) (restrictions on making administration order where administrative receiver has been appointed), in paragraph (b) (exceptions) insert—

> "(i) be void against the administrator to any extent by virtue of the provisions of Part XII of the Companies Act 1985 (registration of company charges),";

and renumber the existing sub-paragraphs as (ii) to (iv).

(3) In sections 45(5), 53(2), 54(3) and 62(5) (offences of failing to deliver documents relating to appointment or cessation of appointment of receiver) omit the words "and, for continued contravention, to a daily default fine".

Company Directors Disqualification Act 1986 (c. 46)

4. In Schedule 1 to the Company Directors Disqualification Act 1986 (matters relevant to determining unfitness of directors), in paragraph 4 (failure of company to comply with certain provisions), for sub-paragraph (h) substitute—

> "(h) sections 398 and 703D (duty of company to deliver particulars of charges on its property).".

SCHEDULE 17

COMPANY CONTRACTS, SEALS, &C.: FURTHER PROVISIONS

Execution of deeds abroad

1.—(1) Section 38 of the Companies Act 1985 (execution of deeds abroad) is amended as follows.

(2) In subsection (1) (appointment of attorney to execute deeds), after "A company may" insert "under the law of England and Wales".

(3) For subsection (2) (effect of deed executed by attorney) substitute—

> "(2) A deed executed by such an attorney on behalf of the company has the same effect as if it were executed under the company's common seal.".

Official seal for use abroad

2.—(1) Section 39 of the Companies Act 1985 (power to have official seal for use abroad) is amended as follows.

(2) In subsection (1), after "A company" insert "which has a common seal" and for "the common seal of the company" substitute "its common seal".

(3) For subsection (2) (effect of sealing with official seal) substitute—

"(2) The official seal when duly affixed to a document has the same effect as the company's common seal.".

(4) In subsection (3) (instrument authorising person to affix official seal), after "by writing under its common seal" insert "or, in the case of a company registered in Scotland, subscribed in accordance with section 36B,".

Official seal for share certificates, &c.

1985 c. 6.

3.—(1) Section 40 of the Companies Act 1985 (official seal for share certificates, &c.) is amended as follows.

(2) After "A company" insert "which has a common seal" and for "the company's common seal" substitute "its common seal".

(3) At the end add—

" The official seal when duly affixed to a document has the same effect as the company's common seal.".

Authentication of documents

4. In section 41 of the Companies Act 1985 (authentication of documents), for the words from "may be signed" to the end substitute "is sufficiently authenticated for the purposes of the law of England and Wales by the signature of a director, secretary or other authorised officer of the company.".

Share certificate as evidence of title

5. For section 186 of the Companies Act 1985 (certificate to be evidence of title) substitute—

"Certificate to be evidence of title.

186.—(1) A certificate under the common seal of the company (or, in the case of a company registered in Scotland, subscribed in accordance with section 36B) specifying any shares held by a member is—

(a) in England and Wales, prima facie evidence, and

(b) in Scotland, sufficient evidence unless the contrary is shown,

of his title to the shares.".

Share warrants to bearer

6. For section 188 of the Companies Act 1985 (issue and effect of share warrant to bearer) substitute—

"Issue and effect of share warrant to bearer.

188.—(1) A company limited by shares may, if so authorised by its articles, issue with respect to any fully paid shares a warrant (a "share warrant") stating that the bearer of the warrant is entitled to the shares specified in it.

(2) A share warrant issued under the company's common seal (or, in the case of a company registered in Scotland, subscribed in accordance with section 36B) entitles the bearer to the shares specified in it; and the shares may be transferred by delivery of the warrant.

(3) A company which issues a share warrant may, if so authorised by its articles, provide (by coupons or otherwise) for the payment of the future dividends on the shares included in the warrant.".

Identification of company on common seal   SCH. 17

7. In section 350 of the Companies Act 1985 (identification of company on 1985 c. 6. company seal), for subsection (1) substitute—

> "(1) A company which has a common seal shall have its name engraved in legible characters on the seal; and if it fails to comply with this subsection it is liable to a fine.".

Floating charges under Scots law

8. In section 462 of the Companies Act 1985 (power of company to create floating charge), for subsections (2) and (3) substitute—

> "(2) In the case of a company which the Court of Session has jurisdiction to wind up, a floating charge may be created only by a written instrument which is presumed under section 36B to be subscribed by the company.".

9. In section 466(2) of the Companies Act 1985 (execution of instrument altering floating charge)—

(a) at the beginning of the subsection insert "Without prejudice to any enactment or rule of law regarding the execution of documents,";

(b) omit paragraph (a);

(c) at the end of paragraph (b) insert "; or", and

(d) omit paragraph (d) and the word "or" preceding it.

10. In section 53(3) of the Insolvency Act 1986 (execution of instrument 1986 c. 45. appointing receiver), in paragraph (a) for "in accordance with the provisions of section 36 of the Companies Act as if it were a contract" substitute "in accordance with section 36B of the Companies Act 1985".

SCHEDULE 18   Section 144(4).

"SUBSIDIARY" AND RELATED EXPRESSIONS: CONSEQUENTIAL AMENDMENTS
AND SAVINGS

Coal Industry Nationalisation Act 1946 (c. 59)

1. In Schedule 2A to the Coal Industry Nationalisation Act 1946 (eligibility for superannuation benefits), in the definition of "subsidiary" in paragraph 5 of the Table, for "section 154 of the Companies Act 1948" substitute "section 736 of the Companies Act 1985".

Electricity Act 1947 (c. 54)

2. In section 67 of the Electricity Act 1947 (interpretation)—

(a) in the definition of "holding company" for "the definition contained in the Companies Act 1947" substitute "section 736 of the Companies Act 1985", and

(b) in the definition of "subsidiary company" for "the Companies Act 1947" substitute "section 736 of the Companies Act 1985".

Landlord and Tenant Act 1954 (c. 56)

3. In section 42 of the Landlord and Tenant Act 1954 (groups of companies), in subsection (1) for "the same meaning as is assigned to it for the purposes of the Companies Act 1985 by section 736 of that Act" substitute "the meaning given by section 736 of the Companies Act 1985".

Transport Act 1962 (c. 46)

4. In the Transport Act 1946, in the definition of "subsidiary" in section 92(1) (interpretation) omit the words "(taking references in that section to a company as being references to a body corporate)".

Harbours Act 1964 (c. 40)

5. In section 57(1) of the Harbours Act 1964 (interpretation), in the definition of "marine work" for "section 154 of the Companies Act 1948" substitute "section 736 of the Companies Act 1985".

General Rate Act 1967 (c. 9)

6. In section 32A of the General Rate Act 1967 (rateable premises of Transport Boards), in the definition of "subsidiary" in subsection (6) omit the words "(taking references in that section to a company as being references to a body corporate)".

Transport Act 1968 (c. 73)

7. For the purposes of Part V of the Transport Act 1968 (licensing of road haulage operators) as it applies in relation to licences granted before the commencement of section 144(1), the expression "subsidiary" has the meaning given by section 736 of the Companies Act 1985 as originally enacted.

1985 c. 6.

Post Office Act 1969 (c. 48)

8. In section 86 of the Post Office Act 1969 (interpretation), in subsection (2) for "736(5)(b)" substitute "736".

Industry Act 1972 (c. 63)

9. In section 10 of the Industry Act 1972 (construction credits), in subsection (9) for "for the purposes of the Companies Act 1985 by section 736 of that Act" substitute "by section 736 of the Companies Act 1985".

Coal Industry Act 1973 (c. 8)

10. In section 12(1) of the Coal Industry Act 1973 (interpretation) for the definition of "subsidiary" and "wholly-owned subsidiary" substitute—

"'subsidiary' and 'wholly-owned subsidiary' have the meanings given by section 736 of the Companies Act 1985;".

Industry Act 1975 (c. 68)

11. In section 37(1) of the Industry Act 1975 (interpretation), in the definition of "wholly-owned subsidiary" for "section 736(5)(b)" substitute "section 736".

Scottish Development Agency Act 1975 (c. 69)

12. In section 25(1) of the Scottish Development Agency Act 1975 (interpretation), in the definition of "wholly-owned subsidiary" for "section 736(5)(b)" substitute "section 736".

Welsh Development Agency Act 1975 (c. 70)

13. In section 27(1) of the Welsh Development Agency Act 1975 (interpretation), in the definition of "wholly-owned subsidiary" for "section 736(5)(b)" substitute "section 736".

Restrictive Trade Practices Act 1976 (c. 41)

14.—(1) This paragraph applies to agreements (within the meaning of the Restrictive Trade Practices Act 1976) made before the commencement of section 144(1); and "registrable" means subject to registration under that Act.

(2) An agreement which was not registrable before the commencement of section 144(1) shall not be treated as registrable afterwards by reason only of that provision having come into force; and an agreement which was registrable before the commencement of that provision shall not cease to be registrable by reason of that provision coming into force.

Industrial Common Ownership Act 1976 (c. 78)

15. In section 2(5) of the Industrial Common Ownership Act 1976 (common ownership and co-operative enterprises) for "for the purposes of the Companies Act 1985" substitute "as defined by section 736 of the Companies Act 1985 or for the purposes of".

Aircraft and Shipbuilding Industries Act 1977 (c. 3)

16. In section 56(1) of the Aircraft and Shipbuilding Industries Act 1977 (interpretation), in the definition of "subsidiary" for "the same meaning as in" substitute "the meaning given by section 736 of".

Nuclear Industry (Finance) Act 1977 (c. 7)

17. In section 3 of the Nuclear Industry (Finance) Act 1977 (expenditure on acquisition of shares in National Nuclear Corporation Ltd and subsidiaries), after "within the meaning of" insert "section 736 of".

Coal Industry Act 1977 (c. 39)

18. In section 14(1) of the Coal Industry Act 1977 (interpretation), in the definition of "wholly-owned subsidiary" for "section 736(5)(b)" substitute "section 736".

Shipbuilding (Redundancy Payments) Act 1978 (c. 11)

19. In section 1(4) of the Shipbuilding (Redundancy Payments) Act 1978 (schemes for payments to redundant workers), for the definitions of "subsidiary" and "wholly-owned subsidiary" substitute—

"'subsidiary' and 'wholly-owned subsidiary' have the meanings given by section 736 of the Companies Act 1985;".

Capital Gains Tax Act 1979 (c. 14)

20. In section 149 of the Capital Gains Tax Act 1979 (employee trusts), in subsection (7) for "the same meaning as in" substitute "the meaning given by section 736 of".

Crown Agents Act 1979 (c. 43)

21. In section 31(1) of the Crown Agents Act 1979 (interpretation), in the definition of "wholly-owned subsidiary" for "section 736(5)(b)" substitute "section 736(2)".

Competition Act 1980 (c. 21)

22. In sections 11(3)(f) and 12 of the Competition Act 1980 (references relating to public bodies, &c.), after "within the meaning of" insert "section 736 of".

British Aerospace Act 1980 (c. 26)

23. In section 14(1) of the British Aerospace Act 1980 (interpretation)—

    (a) in the definition of "subsidiary" for "the same meaning as in", and

    (b) in the definition of "wholly-owned subsidiary" for "the same meaning as it has for the purposes of section 150 of the Companies Act 1948",

substitute "the meaning given by section 736 of the Companies Act 1985".

Local Government, Planning and Land Act 1980 (c. 65)

24. In sections 100(1), 141(7) and 170(1)(d) and (2) of the Local Government, Planning and Land Act 1980 (which refer to wholly-owned subsidiaries) for "within the meaning of section 736(5)(b)" substitute "as defined by section 736".

British Telecommunications Act 1981 (c. 38)

25. In section 85 of the British Telecommunications Act 1981 (interpretation), for subsection (2) substitute—

    "(2) Any reference in this Act to a subsidiary or wholly-owned subsidiary shall be construed in accordance with section 736 of the Companies Act 1985.".

Transport Act 1981 (c. 56)

26. In section 4(2) of the Transport Act 1981 (interpretation of provisions relating to activities of British Railways Board), for "section 154 of the Companies Act 1985" substitute "section 736 of the Companies Act 1985".

Value Added Tax Act 1983 (c. 55)

27. In section 29 of the Value Added Tax Act 1983 (groups of companies), in subsection (8) after "within the meaning of" insert "section 736 of".

Telecommunications Act 1984 (c. 12)

28. In section 73(1) of the Telecommunications Act 1984 (interpretation of Part V), for "the same meaning as in" substitute "the meaning given by section 736 of".

London Regional Transport Act 1984 (c. 32)

29. In section 68 of the London Regional Transport Act 1984 (interpretation), for the definition of "subsidiary" substitute—

    ""subsidiary" (subject to section 62 of this Act) has the meaning given by section 736 of the Companies Act 1985;".

Inheritance Tax Act 1984 (c. 51)

30.—(1) The Inheritance Tax Act 1984 is amended as follows.

(2) In section 13 (dispositions by close companies for benefit of employees), in the definition of "subsidiary" in subsection (5) for "the same meaning as in" substitute "the meaning given by section 736 of".

(3) In section 103 (introductory provisions relating to relief for business property), in subsection (2) for "the same meanings as in" substitute "the meanings given by section 736 of".

(4) In section 234 (interest on instalments) in subsection (3) for "within the meaning of" substitute "as defined in section 736 of".

31. In section 14 of the Ordnance Factories and Military Services Act 1984 (interpretation), for the definitions of "subsidiary" and "wholly-owned subsidiary" substitute—

""subsidiary" and "wholly-owned subsidiary" have the meanings given by section 736 of the Companies Act 1985.".

Companies Act 1985 (c. 6)

32.—(1) The following provisions have effect with respect to the operation of section 23 of the Companies Act 1985 (prohibition on subsidiary being a member of its holding company).

(2) In relation to times, circumstances and purposes before the commencement of section 144(1) of this Act, the references in section 23 to a subsidiary or holding company shall be construed in accordance with section 736 of the Companies Act 1985 as originally enacted.

(3) Where a body corporate becomes or ceases to be a subsidiary of a holding company by reason of section 144(1) coming into force, the prohibition in section 23 of the Companies Act 1985 shall apply (in the absence of exempting circumstances), or cease to apply, accordingly.

33.—(1) Section 153 of the Companies Act 1985 (transactions excepted from prohibition on company giving financial assistance for acquisition of its own shares) is amended as follows.

(2) In subsection (4)(bb) (employees' share schemes) for "a company connected with it" substitute "a company in the same group".

(3) For subsection (5) substitute—

"(5) For the purposes of subsection (4)(bb) a company is in the same group as another company if it is a holding company or subsidiary of that company, or a subsidiary of a holding company of that company.".

34. Section 293 of the Companies Act 1985 (age limit for directors) does not apply in relation to a director of a company if—

(a) he had attained the age of 70 before the commencement of section 144(1) of this Act, and

(b) the company became a subsidiary of a public company by reason only of the commencement of that subsection.

35. Nothing in section 144(1) affects the operation of Part XIIIA of the Companies Act 1985 (takeover offers) in relation to a takeover offer made before the commencement of that subsection.

36. For the purposes of section 719 of the Companies Act 1985 (power to provide for employees on transfer or cessation of business), a company which immediately before the commencement of section 144(1) was a subsidiary of another company shall not be treated as ceasing to be such a subsidiary by reason of that subsection coming into force.

37. For the purposes of section 743 of the Companies Act 1985 (meaning of "employees' share scheme"), a company which immediately before the commencement of section 144(1) was a subsidiary of another company shall not be treated as ceasing to be such a subsidiary by reason of that subsection coming into force.

38. In Schedule 25 to the Companies Act 1985 "subsidiary" has the meaning given by section 736 of that Act as originally enacted.

Transport Act 1985 (c. 67)

39. In section 137(1) of the Transport Act 1985 (interpretation), in the definition of "subsidiary" for the words from "as defined" to the end substitute "within the meaning of section 736 of the Companies Act 1985 as originally enacted (and not as substituted by section 144(1) of the Companies Act 1989);".

Housing Act 1985 (c. 68)

40. In section 622 of the Housing Act 1985 (minor definitions: general), in the definition of "subsidiary" for "the same meaning as in" substitute "the meaning given by section 736 of".

Housing Associations Act 1985 (c. 69)

41. In section 101 of the Housing Associations Act 1985 (minor definitions: Part II), in the definition of "subsidiary" for "the same meaning as in" substitute "the meaning given by section 736 of".

Atomic Energy Authority Act 1986 (c. 3)

42. In section 9 of the Atomic Energy Authority Act 1986 (interpretation), in the definition of "subsidiary" and "wholly-owned subsidiary" for "have the same meaning as in" substitute "have the meaning given by section 736 of".

Airports Act 1986 (c. 31)

43. In section 82 of the Airports Act 1986 (general interpretation), in the definition of "subsidiary" for "has the same meaning as in" substitute "has the meaning given by section 736 of".

Gas Act 1986 (c. 44)

44. In the Gas Act 1986—

    (a) in section 48(1) (interpretation of Part I), in the definitions of "holding company" and "subsidiary", and

    (b) in section 61(1) (interpretation of Part II), in the definition of "subsidiary",

for "has the same meaning as in" substitute "has the meaning given by section 736 of".

Building Societies Act 1986 (c. 53)

45. In section 119 of the Building Societies Act 1986 (interpretation), in the definition of "subsidiary" for "has the same meaning as in" substitute "has the meaning given by section 736 of".

Income and Corporation Taxes Act 1988 (c. 1)

46. In section 141 of the Income and Corporation Taxes Act 1988 (benefits in kind: non-cash vouchers), in the definition of "subsidiary" in subsection (7) for "section 736(5)(b)" substitute "section 736".

British Steel Act 1988 (c. 35)

47. In section 15(1) of the British Steel Act 1988 (interpretation), in the definition of "subsidiary" for "has the same meaning as in" substitute "has the meaning given by section 736 of".

SCHEDULE 19

MINOR AMENDMENTS OF THE COMPANIES ACT 1985

Correction of cross-reference

1. In section 131(1) of the Companies Act 1985 (merger relief) for "section 132(4)" substitute "section 132(8)".

This amendment shall be deemed always to have had effect.

Particulars to be given of directors and secretaries

2.—(1) Section 289 of the Companies Act 1985 (particulars of directors required to be entered in register) is amended as follows.

(2) In subsection (1)(a) (particulars of individual directors)—

(a) in sub-paragraph (i) for "Christian name and surname" and in sub-paragraph (ii) for "Christian name or surname" substitute "name", and

(b) for sub-paragraph (vii) substitute—

"(vii) the date of his birth;".

(3) In subsection (1)(b) (particulars of other directors) after "corporation" insert "or Scottish firm" and after "corporate" insert "or firm".

(4) For subsection (2) substitute—

"(2) In subsection (1)(a)—

(a) "name" means a person's Christian name (or other forename) and surname, except that in the case of a peer, or an individual usually known by a title, the title may be stated instead of his Christian name (or other forename) and surname, or in addition to either or both of them; and

(b) the reference to a former name does not include—

(i) in the case of a peer, or an individual normally known by a British title, the name by which he was known previous to the adoption of or succession to the title, or

(ii) in the case of any person, a former name which was changed or disused before he attained the age of 18 years or which has been changed or disused for 20 years or more, or

(iii) in the case of a married woman, the name by which she was known previous to the marriage.".

3.—(1) Section 290 of the Companies Act 1985 (particulars of secretaries to be entered in register) is amended as follows.

(2) In subsection (1)(a) (particulars of individuals) for "Christian name and surname" and "Christian name or surname" substitute "name".

(3) For subsection (3) substitute—

"(3) Section 289(2)(a) and (b) apply for the purposes of the obligation under subsection (1)(a) of this section to state the name or former name of an individual.".

4.—(1) Section 305 of the Companies Act 1985 (directors' names on company correspondence, &c.) is amended as follows.

(2) In subsection (1) for the words from "the Christian name" onwards substitute "the name of every director of the company".

(3) For subsection (4) substitute—

"(4) For the purposes of the obligation under subsection (1) to state the name of every director of the company, a person's "name" means—

> (a) in the case of an individual, his Christian name (or other forename) and surname; and

> (b) in the case of a corporation or Scottish firm, its corporate or firm name.

(5) The initial or a recognised abbreviation of a person's Christian name or other forename may be stated instead of the full Christian name or other forename.

(6) In the case of a peer, or an individual usually known by a title, the title may be stated instead of his Christian name (or other forename) and surname or in addition to either or both of them.

(7) In this section "director" includes a shadow director and the reference in subsection (3) to an "officer" shall be construed accordingly.".

5.—(1) Section 686 of the Companies Act 1985 (documents to be delivered to registrar on registration of company not formed under companies legislation) is amended as follows.

(2) In subsection (1) (particulars to be delivered to registrar), for paragraph (b) (particulars of directors and managers) substitute—

> "(b) a list showing with respect to each director or manager of the company—

>> (i) in the case of an individual, his name, address, occupation and date of birth,

>> (ii) in the case of a corporation or Scottish firm, its corporate or firm name and registered or principal office,".

(3) After that subsection insert—

> "(1A) For the purposes of subsection (1)(b)(i) a person's 'name' means his Christian name (or other forename) and surname, except that in the case of a peer, or an individual usually known by a title, the title may be stated instead of his Christian name (or other forename) and surname or in addition to either or both of them.".

6. In section 691 of the Companies Act 1985 (documents to be delivered to registrar on registration of oversea company), for subsection (2) (particulars of directors and secretary) substitute—

> "(2) The list referred to in subsection (1)(b)(i) shall contain the following particulars with respect to each director—

>> (a) in the case of an individual—

>>> (i) his name,

>>> (ii) any former name,

>>> (iii) his usual residential address,

>>> (iv) his nationality,

>>> (v) his business occupation (if any),

>>> (vi) if he has no business occupation but holds other directorships, particulars of them, and

>>> (vii) his date of birth;

>> (b) in the case of a corporation or Scottish firm, its corporate or firm name and registered or principal office.

(3) The list referred to in subsection (1)(b)(i) shall contain the following particulars with respect to the secretary (or, where there are joint secretaries, with respect to each of them)—

(a) in the case of an individual, his name, any former name and his usual residential address;

(b) in the case of a corporation or Scottish firm, its corporate or firm name and registered or principal office.

Where all the partners in a firm are joint secretaries of the company, the name and principal office of the firm may be stated instead of the particulars required by paragraph (a).

(4) In subsections (2)(a) and (3)(a) above—

(a) "name" means a person's Christian name (or other forename) and surname, except that in the case of a peer, or an individual usually known by a title, the title may be stated instead of his Christian name (or other forename) and surname, or in addition to either or both of them; and

(b) the reference to a former name does not include—

(i) in the case of a peer, or an individual normally known by a British title, the name by which he was known previous to the adoption of or succession to the title, or

(ii) in the case of any person, a former name which was changed or disused before he attained the age of 18 years or which has been changed or disused for 20 years or more, or

(iii) in the case of a married woman, the name by which she was known previous to the marriage.".

7.—(1) Schedule 1 to the Companies Act 1985 (particulars of directors and secretaries to be sent to registrar) is amended as follows. 1985 c. 6.

(2) In paragraph 1(a) (particulars of individual directors)—

(a) for "Christian name and surname" and "Christian name or surname" substitute "name"; and

(b) for the words from "and, in the case" to the end substitute "and his date of birth".

(3) In paragraph 1(b) (particulars of other directors) after "corporation" insert "or Scottish firm" and after "corporate" insert "or firm".

(4) In paragraph 3(1)(a) (particulars of individual secretaries) for "Christian name and surname" (twice) substitute "name".

(5) For paragraph 4 substitute—

"4. In paragraphs 1(a) and 3(1)(a) above—

(a) "name" means a person's Christian name (or other forename) and surname, except that in the case of a peer, or an individual usually known by a title, the title may be stated instead of his Christian name (or other forename) and surname or in addition to either or both of them; and

(b) the reference to a former name does not include—

(i) in the case of a peer, or an individual normally known by a British title, the name by which he was known previous to the adoption of or succession to the title, or

(ii) in the case of any person, a former name which was changed or disused before he attained the age of 18 years or which has been changed or disused for 20 years or more, or

(iii) in the case of a married woman, the name by which she was known previous to the marriage.".

Transactions with directors not requiring authorisation

8. In section 321 of the Companies Act 1985 (exceptions from provisions requiring authorisation for substantial property transactions with directors, &c.), after subsection (3) insert—

"(4) Section 320(1) does not apply to a transaction on a recognised investment exchange which is effected by a director, or a person connected with him, through the agency of a person who in relation to the transaction acts as an independent broker.

For this purpose an "independent broker" means—

(a) in relation to a transaction on behalf of a director, a person who independently of the director selects the person with whom the transaction is to be effected, and

(b) in relation to a transaction on behalf of a person connected with a director, a person who independently of that person or the director selects the person with whom the transaction is to be effected;

and "recognised", in relation to an investment exchange, means recognised under the Financial Services Act 1986.".

Time limit for holding extraordinary general meeting convened on members' requisition

9. In section 368 of the Companies Act 1985 (extraordinary general meeting on members' requisition), after subsection (7) add—

"(8) The directors are deemed not to have duly convened a meeting if they convene a meeting for a date more than 28 days after the date of the notice convening the meeting.".

Removal of restriction on transfer of shares

10.—(1) In section 456(3) of the Companies Act 1985 (removal of restrictions by order of court), in paragraph (b) (order where shares to be sold)—

(a) for "sold" substitute "transferred for valuable consideration", and

(b) for "sale" substitute "transfer".

(2) In section 454(2) and (3) (which refer to section 456(3)(b)) for "sell" and "sale" substitute "transfer".

Protection of company's members against unfair prejudice

11. In Part XVII of the Companies Act 1985 (protection of company's members against unfair prejudice)—

(a) in section 459(1) (application by company member), and

(b) in section 460(1)(b) (application by Secretary of State),

for "unfairly prejudicial to the interests of some part of the members" substitute "unfairly prejudicial to the interests of its members generally or of some part of its members".

Requirements for registration by joint stock companies

12. In section 684(1) of the Companies Act 1985 (requirements for registration by joint stock companies: documents to be delivered to registrar), in paragraph (b) (list of members on specified day) for "(not more than 6 clear days before the day of registration)" substitute "(not more than 28 clear days before the day of registration)".

Delivery of documents by oversea companies

13. In Chapter I of Part XXIII of the Companies Act 1985 (oversea companies: 1985 c. 6. registration, &c.), for section 696 (office where documents to be filed) substitute—

"Registrar to whom documents to be delivered.

696.—(1) References to the registrar in relation to an oversea company (except references in Chapter III of this Part (registration of charges): see section 703E), shall be construed in accordance with the following provisions.

(2) The documents which an oversea company is required to deliver to the registrar shall be delivered—

(a) to the registrar for England and Wales if the company has established a place of business in England and Wales, and

(b) to the registrar for Scotland if the company has established a place of business in Scotland;

and if the company has an established place of business in both parts of Great Britain, the documents shall be delivered to both registrars.

(3) If a company ceases to have a place of business in either part of Great Britain, it shall forthwith give notice of that fact to the registrar for that part; and from the date on which notice is so given it is no longer obliged to deliver documents to that registrar.".

Companies' registered numbers

14. For section 705 of the Companies Act 1985 (companies' registered numbers) substitute—

"Companies' registered numbers.

705.—(1) The registrar shall allocate to every company a number, which shall be known as the company's registered number.

(2) Companies' registered numbers shall be in such form, consisting of one or more sequences of figures or letters, as the registrar may from time to time determine.

(3) The registrar may upon adopting a new form of registered number make such changes of existing registered numbers as appear to him necessary.

(4) A change of a company's registered number has effect from the date on which the company is notified by the registrar of the change; but for a period of three years beginning with the date on which that notification is sent by the registrar the requirement of section 351(1)(a) as to the use of the company's registered number on business letters and order forms is satisfied by the use of either the old number or the new.

(5) In this section "company" includes—

(a) any oversea company which has complied with section 691 (delivery of statutes to registrar, &c.), other than a company which appears to the registrar not to have a place of business in Great Britain; and

(b) any body to which any provision of this Act applies by virtue of section 718 (unregistered companies).".

Exemptions from limit of 20 on members of partnership

1985 c. 6.   15.—(1) Section 716 of the Companies Act 1985 (prohibition of formation of company, association or partnership with more than 20 members unless registered as company, &c.) is amended as follows.

(2) In subsection (2) (exemptions), after paragraph (c) insert—

"(d) for any purpose prescribed by regulations (which may include a purpose mentioned above), of a partnership of a description so prescribed.";

1986 c. 60.   and omit the words inserted by paragraph 22 of Schedule 16 to the Financial Services Act 1986.

(3) For subsections (3) and (4) substitute—

"(3) In subsection (2)(a) "solicitor"—

(a) in relation to England and Wales, means solicitor of the Supreme Court, and

(b) in relation to Scotland, means a person enrolled or deemed enrolled as a solicitor in pursuance of the Solicitors (Scotland) Act 1980.

(4) In subsection (2)(c) "recognised stock exchange" means—

(a) The International Stock Exchange of the United Kingdom and the Republic of Ireland Limited, and

(b) any other stock exchange for the time being recognised for the purposes of this section by the Secretary of State by order made by statutory instrument.".

16.—(1) Section 717 of the Companies Act 1985 (limited partnerships: limit on number of members) is amended as follows.

1907 c. 24.   (2) In subsection (1) (exemptions from limit of 20 members under section 4(2) of Limited Partnerships Act 1907), after paragraph (c) insert—

"(d) to a partnership carrying on business of any description prescribed by regulations (which may include a business of any description mentioned above), of a partnership of a description so prescribed.";

and omit the words inserted by paragraph 22 of Schedule 16 to the Financial Services Act 1986.

(3) For subsections (2) and (3) substitute—

"(2) In subsection (1)(a) "solicitor"—

(a) in relation to England and Wales, means solicitor of the Supreme Court, and

(b) in relation to Scotland, means a person enrolled or deemed enrolled as a solicitor in pursuance of the Solicitors (Scotland) Act 1980.

(3) In subsection (1)(c) "recognised stock exchange" means—

(a) The International Stock Exchange of the United Kingdom and the Republic of Ireland Limited, and

(b) any other stock exchange for the time being recognised for the purposes of this section by the Secretary of State by order made by statutory instrument.".

Meaning of "officer who is in default"

17. In section 730 of the Companies Act 1985 (punishment of offences), in subsection (5) (meaning of "officer who is in default"), after "company" (twice) insert "or other body".   1985 c. 6.

Offences committed by partnerships and other unincorporated bodies

18. In section 734 of the Companies Act 1985 (criminal proceedings against unincorporated bodies), at the end add—

"(5) Where such an offence committed by a partnership is proved to have been committed with the consent or connivance of, or to be attributable to any neglect on the part of, a partner, he as well as the partnership is guilty of the offence and liable to be proceeded against and punished accordingly.

(6) Where such an offence committed by an unincorporated body (other than a partnership) is proved to have been committed with the consent or connivance of, or to be attributable to any neglect on the part of, any officer of the body or any member of its governing body, he as well as the body is guilty of the offence and liable to be proceeded against and punished accordingly.".

Meaning of "office copy" in Scotland

19. In Part XXVI of the Companies Act 1985 (interpretation), after section 743 insert—

"Meaning of "office copy" in Scotland.   743A. References in this Act to an office copy of a court order shall be construed, as respects Scotland, as references to a certified copy interlocutor.".

Index of defined expressions

20. In Part XXVI of the Companies Act 1985 (interpretation), after section 744 insert—

"Index of defined expressions.   744A. The following Table shows provisions defining or otherwise explaining expressions for the purposes of this Act generally—

accounting reference date, accounting reference period	sections 224 and 742(1)
acquisition (in relation to a non-cash asset)	section 739(2)
agent	section 744
allotment (and related expressions)	section 738
annual accounts	sections 261(2), 262(1) and 742(1)
annual general meeting	section 366
annual return	section 363
articles	section 744
authorised minimum	section 118
balance sheet and balance sheet date	sections 261(2), 262(1) and 742(1)
bank holiday	section 744
banking company	section 744
body corporate	section 740
books and papers, books or papers	section 744

called-up share capital	section 737(1)
capital redemption reserve	section 170(1)
the Companies Acts	section 744
companies charges register	section 397
company	section 735(1)
the Consequential Provisions Act	section 744
corporation	section 740
the court (in relation to a company)	section 744
current assets	sections 262(1) and 742(1)
debenture	section 744
director	section 741(1)
document	section 744
elective resolution	section 379A
employees' share scheme	section 743
equity share capital	section 744
existing company	section 735(1)
extraordinary general meeting	section 368
extraordinary resolution	section 378(1)
financial year (of a company)	sections 223 and 742(1)
fixed assets	sections 262(1) and 742(1)
floating charge (in Scotland)	section 462
the former Companies Acts	section 735(1)
the Gazette	section 744
hire-purchase agreement	section 744
holding company	section 736
the Insider Dealing Act	section 744
the Insolvency Act	section 735A(1)
insurance company	section 744
the Joint Stock Companies Acts	section 735(3)
limited company	section 1(2)
member (of a company)	section 22
memorandum (in relation to a company)	section 744
non-cash asset	section 739(1)
number (in relation to shares)	section 744
office copy (in relation to a court order in Scotland)	section 743A
officer (in relation to a body corporate)	section 744
official seal (in relation to the registrar of companies)	section 744
oversea company	section 744
overseas branch register	section 362
paid up (and related expressions)	section 738
parent company and parent undertaking	sections 258 and 742(1)
place of business	section 744

prescribed	section 744
private company	section 1(3)
profit and loss account	sections 261(2), 262(1) and 742(1)
prospectus	section 744
public company	section 1(3)
realised profits or losses	sections 262(3) and 742(2)
registered number (of a company)	section 705(1)
registered office (of a company)	section 287
registrar and registrar of companies	section 744
resolution for reducing share capital	section 135(3)
shadow director	section 741(2) and (3)
share	section 744
share premium account	section 130(1)
share warrant	section 188
special notice (in relation to a resolution)	section 379
special resolution	section 378(2)
subsidiary	section 736
subsidiary undertaking	sections 258 and 742(1)
transfer (in relation to a non-cash asset)	section 739(2)
uncalled share capital	section 737(2)
undistributable reserves	section 264(3)
unlimited company	section 1(2)
unregistered company	section 718
wholly-owned subsidiary	section 736(2)".

Fraudulent trading by unregistered companies

21. In Schedule 22 to the Companies Act 1985 (provisions applying to unregistered companies), at the appropriate place insert—

"Part XVI   Fraudulent trading   —".
                   by a company.

SCHEDULE 20

AMENDMENTS ABOUT MERGERS AND RELATED MATTERS

Fair Trading Act 1973 (c. 41)

1. In section 46 of the Fair Trading Act 1973, subsection (3) is omitted.

2.—(1) In section 60 of that Act—

(a) in subsection (1) for "the period of three months beginning with the date of the" there is substituted "such period (not being longer than three months beginning with the date of the reference) as may be specified in the",

(b) in subsection (2) for "original period of three months" there is substituted "period specified in the newspaper merger reference", and

(c) in subsection (3) for "subsection (1)" there is substituted "the newspaper merger reference".

(2) This paragraph does not apply in relation to any newspaper merger reference made before the passing of this Act.

3. In section 63(1) of that Act, for "to 75 of this Act shall have effect in relation to merger references other than" there is substituted "to 75K of this Act shall not have effect in relation to".

4. In section 66 of that Act—

    (a) in subsections (1) and (3), after "the Secretary of State" there is inserted "or the Commission", and

    (b) in subsection (4), after "this section" there is inserted "and to section 66A of this Act".

5.—(1) In section 67 of that Act, in subsection (2)(a), for the words from "any enterprise" to the end there is substituted—

    "(i) any enterprise which remains under the same ownership and control, or

    (ii) if none of the enterprises remains under the same ownership and control, the enterprise having the assets with the highest value, and".

(2) In subsection (4) of that section—

    (a) after "section 66" there is inserted "or subsection (1) of section 66A", and

    (b) for "that subsection" there is substituted "either of those subsections".

6. In section 68(4) of that Act, after "the Secretary of State" there is inserted "or, as the case may be, the Commission".

7. In section 71 of that Act—

    (a) in subsection (1) the words "made under section 69(4) of this Act", and

    (b) subsection (2),

are omitted.

8. In section 74(1) of that Act—

    (a) the words "and does not impose on the Commission a limitation under section 69(4) of this Act" are omitted, and

    (b) in paragraph (d), for "paragraph 12" there is substituted "paragraphs 12 and 12A".

9. In section 75(4) of that Act—

    (a) after "sections 66" there is inserted "66A", and

    (b) for paragraphs (a) and (b) there is substituted—

        "(a) section 66 shall apply, where an event by which any enterprises cease as between themselves to be distinct enterprises will occur if the arrangements are carried into effect, as if the event had occurred immediately before the date of the reference;

        (aa) section 66A shall apply, where a transaction falling within subsection (2) of that section will occur if the arrangements are carried into effect, as if the transaction had occurred immediately before the date of the reference;

        (b) in section 67(4) the references to subsection (1) of section 66 and subsection (1) of section 66A shall be construed as references to those subsections as modified in accordance with paragraph (a) or (aa) of this subsection;".

10. Paragraphs 4 to 9 (and the repeals in Schedule 24 corresponding to paragraphs 7 and 8(a)) do not apply in relation to any merger reference made before the passing of this Act.

11. At the end of section 76 of that Act there is added—

"(2) In exercising his duty under this section the Director shall take into consideration any representations made to him by persons appearing to him to have a substantial interest in any such arrangements or transactions or by bodies appearing to him to represent substantial numbers of persons who have such an interest.".

12.—(1) In section 83 of that Act, after subsection (3) there is inserted—

"(3A) Without prejudice to subsection (3) above, if the Minister or Ministers to whom any such report is made consider that it would not be in the public interest to disclose—

(a) any matter contained in the report relating to the private affairs of an individual whose interests would, in the opinion of the Minister or Ministers, be seriously and prejudicially affected by the publication of that matter, or

(b) any matter contained in the report relating specifically to the affairs of a particular person whose interests would, in the opinion of the Minister or Ministers, be seriously and prejudicially affected by the publication of that matter,

the Minister or Ministers shall exclude that matter from the copies of the report as laid before Parliament and from the report as published under this section.".

(2) This paragraph does not apply in relation to any report made before the passing of this Act.

13.—(1) In section 85 of that Act, for subsection (7) there is substituted—

"(7) If any person (referred to in subsection (7A) of this section as 'the defaulter') refuses or otherwise fails to comply with any notice under subsection (1) of this section, any one of those who, in relation to the investigation in question, are performing the functions of the Commission may certify that fact in writing to the court and the court may enquire into the case.

(7A) If, after hearing any witness who may be produced against or on behalf of the defaulter and any statement which may be offered in defence, the court is satisfied that the defaulter did without reasonable excuse refuse or otherwise fail to comply with the notice, the court may punish the defaulter (and, in the case of a body corporate, any director or officer) in like manner as if the defaulter had been guilty of contempt of court.".

(2) Subsections (5) and (6)(b) of that section are omitted.

14.—(1) In section 88 of that Act, in subsection (1) for the words from "if requested" to "the relevant parties" there is substituted "to comply with any request of the appropriate Minister or Ministers to consult with any persons mentioned in the request (referred to below in this section as 'the relevant parties')".

(2) After subsection (2) of that section there is inserted—

"(2A) Where—

(a) an undertaking is given under this section after the commencement of this subsection, or

(b) an undertaking given under this section is varied or released after that time,

the Minister to whom the undertaking is or was given shall cause the undertaking or, as the case may be, the variation or release to be published in such manner as the Minister may consider appropriate.".

(3) In subsection (4) of that section—

(a) in paragraph (a) for "it" there is substituted "the undertaking is no longer appropriate and either the relevant parties (or any of them) can be released from the undertaking or the undertaking", and

(b) in paragraph (b) for "that it" there is substituted "that any person can be so released or that an undertaking",

and in subsection (5), after "varied" (in both places) there is inserted "or revoked".

(4) In subsection (6) of that section the words from "'the relevant parties'" to the "and" immediately following paragraph (c) are omitted.

(5) Sub-paragraphs (1) and (4) (and the repeal in Schedule 24 corresponding to sub-paragraph (4)) do not apply in relation to any report made before the passing of this Act.

15.—(1) In section 89 of that Act, in subsection (1), for paragraphs (a) and (b) there is substituted—

"(a) in the circumstances specified in subsection (1) of any of the following sections—

(i) sections 56, 73 and 75K of this Act, and

(ii) section 10 of the Competition Act 1980,

the Secretary of State makes, has made, or has under consideration the making of, an order under the section in question exercising any of the powers specified in Schedule 8 to this Act, or

(b) in the circumstances specified in subsection (1) of section 12 of the Competition Act 1980 the Secretary of State makes, has made, or has under consideration the making of, an order under subsection (5) of that section exercising any of those powers.".

(2) In subsection (2) of that section, "Part II of" is omitted.

(3) In subsection (3) of that section, after paragraph (b) there is inserted—

"(bb) require any person to furnish any such information to the Director as may be specified or described in the order;".

1973 c. 41.   (4) The amendments made by sub-paragraphs (1) to (3) have effect in relation to the making of any order under section 89 of the Fair Trading Act 1973 after the passing of this Act, whether the principal order (within the meaning of that section) was made before or after that time.

16.—(1) Section 90 of that Act is amended as follows.

(2) In subsection (1) after "section 74" there is inserted ", section 75K".

(3) For subsection (5) there is substituted—

"(5) Nothing in any order to which this section applies shall have effect so as to—

(a) cancel or modify conditions in licences granted—

(i) under a patent granted under the Patents Act 1949 or the Patents Act 1977 or a European patent (UK) (within the meaning of the Patents Act 1977), or

(ii) in respect of a design registered under the Registered Designs Act 1949,

by the proprietor of the patent or design, or

(b) require an entry to be made in the register of patents or the register of designs to the effect that licences under such a patent or such a design are to be available as of right.".

17. In section 132(1) of that Act, after "85(6)" there is inserted "section 93B".

18.—(1) In Schedule 3 to that Act, in paragraph 16(2) for "75" there is substituted "73".

(2) This paragraph does not apply in relation to any report made before the passing of this Act.

19.—(1) Schedule 8 to that Act is amended as follows.

(2) After paragraph 9 there is inserted—

"9A.—(1) An order may require a person supplying goods or services to publish—

(a) any such accounting information in relation to the supply of the goods or services, and

(b) any such information in relation to—

(i) the quantities of goods or services supplied, or

(ii) the geographical areas in which they are supplied,

as may be specified or described in the order.

(2) In this paragraph "accounting information", in relation to a supply of goods or services, means information as to—

(a) the costs of the supply, including fixed costs and overheads,

(b) the manner in which fixed costs and overheads are calculated and apportioned for accounting purposes of the supplier, and

(c) the income attributable to the supply.".

(3) After paragraph 12 there is inserted—

"12A. An order may require any person to furnish any such information to the Director as may be specified or described in the order.

12B. An order may require any activities to be carried on separately from any other activities.

12C. An order may prohibit or restrict the exercise of any right to vote exercisable by virtue of the holding of any shares, stock or securities.".

20.—(1) In Schedule 9 to that Act, in paragraph 4 the words from "either" to the end are omitted.

(2) This paragraph has effect in relation to the laying of any draft order under paragraph 4 of Schedule 9 to the Fair Trading Act 1973 after the passing of this Act, whether the notice under that Schedule was published before or after that time.

1973 c. 41.

Competition Act 1980 (c. 21)

21. In section 3(8) of the Competition Act 1980—

(a) for "(5)" there is substituted "(6)", and

(b) at the end there is inserted "but as if, in subsection (7) of that section, for the words from 'any one' to 'the Commission' there were substituted 'the Director'".

22. In section 4(4) of that Act for paragraph (a) there is substituted—

"(a) to arrange for—

(i) any undertaking accepted by him under this section, and

(ii) any variation or release of such an undertaking after the passing of the Companies Act 1989,

to be published in such manner as appears to him to be appropriate,".

23. In section 9(4) of that Act—

(a) in paragraph (a), after "undertaking" there is inserted "and of any variation of it after the passing of the Companies Act 1989", and

(b) in paragraph (b), after "undertaking" there is inserted "and any variation or release of it after that time".

24. In section 29(1)(a) of that Act after "section" there is inserted "75G or".

Telecommunications Act 1984 (c. 12)

25.—(1) In section 13(9) of the Telecommunications Act 1984, after "Commission)" there is inserted "together with section 24 of the Competition Act 1980 (modification of provisions about performance of Commission's functions)".

S.I. 1989/122.

(2) The Monopolies and Mergers Commission (Performance of Functions) Order 1989 shall have effect as if sub-paragraph (1) above had come into force immediately before the making of the Order.

Financial Services Act 1986 (c. 60)

26. In section 123(3) of the Financial Services Act 1986—

(a) for "(5)" there is substituted "(6)", and

(b) at the end there is inserted "but as if, in subsection (7) of that section, for the words from 'any one' to 'the Commission' there were substituted 'the Director'".

Section 156(1).

SCHEDULE 21

ADDITIONAL REQUIREMENTS FOR RECOGNITION

PART I

U.K. INVESTMENT EXCHANGES

Default rules

1.—(1) The exchange must have default rules which, in the event of a member of the exchange appearing to be unable to meet his obligations in respect of one or more market contracts, enable action to be taken in respect of unsettled market contracts to which he is party.

(2) The rules may authorise the taking of the same or similar action in relation to a member who appears to be likely to become unable to meet his obligations in respect of one or more market contracts.

(3) The rules must enable action to be taken in respect of all unsettled market contracts, other than those entered into by a recognised clearing house for the purposes of or in connection with the provision of clearing services for the exchange.

(4) As regards contracts entered into by the exchange for the purposes of or in connection with the provision of its own clearing services, the rules must contain provision corresponding to that required by paragraphs 9 to 11 below in the case of a UK clearing house.

(5) As regards other contracts the rules must contain provision complying with paragraphs 2 and 3 below.

Content of rules

2.—(1) The rules must provide for all rights and liabilities between those party as principal to unsettled market contracts to which the defaulter is party as principal to be discharged and for there to be paid by one party to the other such sum of money (if any) as may be determined in accordance with the rules.

(2) The rules must further provide—

    (a) for the sums so payable in respect of different contracts between the same parties to be aggregated or set off so as to produce a net sum, and

    (b) for the certification by or on behalf of the exchange of the net sum payable or, as the case may be, of the fact that no sum is payable.

(3) The rules may make special provision with respect to, or exclude from the provisions required by sub-paragraphs (1) and (2), contracts of any description prescribed for the purposes of this sub-paragraph by regulations made by the Secretary of State.

Notification to other parties affected

3. The exchange must have adequate arrangements for securing that—

    (a) parties to unsettled market contracts with a defaulter acting as principal are notified as soon as reasonably practicable of the default and of any decision taken under the rules in relation to contracts to which they are a party; and

    (b) parties to unsettled market contracts with a defaulter acting as agent and the defaulter's principals are notified as soon as reasonably practicable of the default and of the identity of the other party to the contract.

Application of default rules to designated non-members

4.—(1) The rules may make the same or similar provision in relation to designated non-members as in relation to members of the exchange.

(2) If such provision is made, the exchange must have adequate procedures—

    (a) for designating the persons, or descriptions of person, in respect of whom action may be taken,

    (b) for keeping under review the question which persons or descriptions of person should be or remain so designated, and

    (c) for withdrawing such designation.

(3) The procedures shall be designed to secure that a person is not or does not remain designated if failure by him to meet his obligations in respect of one or more market contracts would be unlikely adversely to affect the operation of the market, and that a description of persons is not or does not remain designated if failure by a person of that description to meet his obligations in respect of one or more market contracts would be unlikely adversely to affect the operation of the market.

(4) The exchange must have adequate arrangements—

    (a) for bringing a designation or withdrawal of designation to the attention of the person or description of persons concerned, and

    (b) where a description of persons is designated, or the designation of a description of persons is withdrawn, for ascertaining which persons fall within that description.

Delegation of functions in connection with default procedures

5. The rules may make provision for the whole or part of the functions mentioned in paragraphs 1 to 4 to be performed by another body or person on behalf of the exchange.

Co-operation with other authorities

6. The exchange must be able and willing to co-operate, by the sharing of information and otherwise, with the Secretary of State, any relevant office-holder and any other authority or body having responsibility for any matter arising out of, or connected with, the default of a member of the exchange or any designated non-member.

Margin

7. Where the exchange provides its own clearing arrangements and margined transactions are effected, paragraph 14 below applies as it applies in relation to a clearing house.

PART II

U.K. CLEARING HOUSES

Default rules

8.—(1) The clearing house must have default rules which, in the event of a member of the clearing house appearing to be unable to meet his obligations in respect of one or more market contracts, enable action to be taken to close out his position in relation to all unsettled market contracts to which he is a party.

(2) The rules may authorise the taking of the same or similar action where a member appears to be likely to become unable to meet his obligations in respect of one or more market contracts.

Content of rules

9.—(1) The rules must provide for all rights and liabilities of the defaulter under or in respect of unsettled market contracts to be discharged and for there to be paid by or to the defaulter such sum of money (if any) as may be determined in accordance with the rules.

(2) The rules must further provide—

(a) for the sums so payable by or to the defaulter in respect of different contracts to be aggregated or set off so as to produce a net sum;

(b) for that sum—

(i) if payable by the defaulter to the clearing house, to be set off against any property provided by or on behalf of the defaulter as cover for margin (or the proceeds of realisation of such property) so as to produce a further net sum, and

(ii) if payable by the clearing house to the defaulter to be aggregated with any property provided by or on behalf of the defaulter as cover for margin (or the proceeds of realisation of such property); and

(c) for the certification by or on behalf of the clearing house of the sum finally payable or, as the case may be, of the fact that no sum is payable.

10.—(1) The reference in paragraph 9 to the rights and liabilities of a defaulter under or in respect of an unsettled market contract includes (without prejudice to the generality of that provision) rights and liabilities arising in consequence of action taken under provisions of the rules authorising—

(a) the effecting by the clearing house of corresponding contracts in relation to unsettled market contracts to which the defaulter is a party;

(b) the transfer of the defaulter's position under an unsettled market contract to another member of the clearing house;

(c) the exercise by the clearing house of any option granted by an unsettled market contract.

(2) A "corresponding contract" means a contract on the same terms (except as to price or premium) as the market contract, but under which the person who is the buyer under the market contract agrees to sell and the person who is the seller under the market contract agrees to buy.

This sub-paragraph applies with any necessary modifications in relation to a market contract which is not an agreement to sell.

(3) The reference in paragraph 9 to the rights and liabilities of a defaulter under or in respect of an unsettled market contract does not include, where he acts as agent, rights or liabilities of his arising out of the relationship of principal and agent.

Notification to other parties affected

11. The clearing house must have adequate arrangements for securing that parties to unsettled market contracts with a defaulter are notified as soon as reasonably practicable of the default and of any decision taken under the rules in relation to contracts to which they are a party.

Delegation of functions in connection with default procedures

12. The rules may make provision for the whole or part of the functions mentioned in paragraphs 8 to 11 to be performed by another body or person on behalf of the clearing house.

Co-operation with other authorities

13. The clearing house must be able and willing to co-operate, by the sharing of information and otherwise, with the Secretary of State, any relevant office-holder and any other authority or body having responsibility for any matter arising out of, or connected with, the default of a member of the clearing house.

Margin

14.—(1) The rules of the clearing house must provide that, in the event of a default, margin provided by the defaulter for his own account is not to be applied to meet a shortfall on a client account.

(2) This is without prejudice to the requirements of any relevant regulations under section 55 of the Financial Services Act 1986 (clients' money).

Part III

Overseas investment exchanges and clearing houses

15.—(1) The rules and practices of the body, together with the law of the country in which the body's head office is situated, must be such as to provide adequate procedures for dealing with the default of persons party to market contracts connected with the body.

(2) The reference in sub-paragraph (1) to default is to a person being unable to meet his obligations.

SCHEDULE 22

Financial Markets and Insolvency: Provisions Applying to Pre-commencement Cases

Introductory

1. The provisions of this Schedule have effect for the purpose of safeguarding the operation of certain financial markets—

    (a) in the event of the insolvency, winding up or default of a person party to transactions in the market (paragraphs 2 to 8), and

    (b) as regards the effectiveness or enforcement of certain charges given to secure obligations in connection with such transactions (paragraphs 9 to 12).

Recognised investment exchanges and clearing houses

2.—(1) This Schedule applies to the following descriptions of contract connected with a recognised investment exchange or recognised clearing house.

The contracts are referred to in this Schedule as "market contracts".

(2) In relation to a recognised investment exchange, this Schedule applies to—

    (a) contracts entered into by a member or designated non-member of the exchange which are—

        (i) made on or otherwise subject to the rules of the exchange,

        (ii) on terms expressed to be as traded on the exchange, or

        (iii) on the same terms as those on which an equivalent contract would be made on the exchange; and

    (b) contracts subject to the rules of the exchange entered into by the exchange for the purposes of or in connection with the provision of clearing services.

A "designated non-member" means a person in respect of whom action may be taken under the default rules of the exchange but who is not a member of the exchange.

(3) In relation to a recognised clearing house, this Schedule applies to contracts subject to the rules of the clearing house entered into by the clearing house for the purposes of or in connection with the provision of clearing services for a recognised investment exchange.

This includes contracts effected under or in consequence of action taken by the clearing house under its default rules.

3. The general law of insolvency has effect in relation to market contracts, and action taken under the rules of a recognised investment exchange or recognised clearing house with respect to such contracts, subject to the following provisions of this Schedule.

4.—(1) None of the following shall be regarded as to any extent invalid at law on the ground of inconsistency with the law relating to the distribution of the assets of a person on bankruptcy, winding up or sequestration, or in the administration of an insolvent estate—

    (a) a market contract,

    (b) the rules of a recognised investment exchange or recognised clearing house as to the settlement of market contracts,

    (c) the default rules of a recognised investment exchange or recognised clearing house.

SCH. 22
1986 c. 45.
1985 c. 66.

(2) The powers of a relevant office-holder in his capacity as such, and the powers of the court under the Insolvency Act 1986 or the Bankruptcy (Scotland) Act 1985, shall not be exercised in such a way as to prevent or interfere with—

    (a) the settlement of a market contract in accordance with the rules of a recognised investment exchange or recognised clearing house,

    (b) any action taken under the default rules of such an exchange or clearing house.

(3) Nothing in the following provisions of this Schedule shall be construed as affecting the generality of sub-paragraph (2).

(4) A debt or other liability arising out of a market contract which is the subject of default proceedings may not be proved in a winding up or bankruptcy, or in Scotland claimed in a winding up or sequestration, until the completion of the default proceedings.

A debt or other liability which by virtue of this sub-paragraph may not be proved or claimed shall not be taken into account for the purposes of any set-off until the completion of the default proceedings.

5.—(1) A liquidator or trustee of a defaulter shall not—

    (a) declare or pay any dividend to the creditors, or

    (b) return any capital to contributories,

unless he has retained what he reasonably considers to be an adequate reserve in respect of any claims arising as a result of the default proceedings of the exchange or clearing house concerned.

(2) Nothing in section 11(3), 130 or 285 of the Insolvency Act 1986 (which restrict the taking of certain legal proceedings and other steps), and nothing in the Bankruptcy (Scotland) Act 1985, shall affect any action taken by an exchange or clearing house for the purpose of its default proceedings.

6.—(1) The following provisions apply with respect to the net sum certified by a recognised investment exchange or recognised clearing house, upon the completion of proceedings under its default rules, to be payable by or to a defaulter.

(2) If, in England and Wales, a bankruptcy or winding up order has been made, or a resolution for voluntary winding up has been passed, the debt—

    (a) is provable in the bankruptcy or winding up or, as the case may be, is payable to the relevant office-holder, and

    (b) shall be taken into account, where appropriate, under section 323 of the Insolvency Act 1986 (mutual dealings and set-off) or the corresponding provision applicable in the case of a winding up,

in the same way as a debt due before the commencement of the bankruptcy or winding up.

(3) If, in Scotland, an award of sequestration or a winding-up order has been made, or a resolution for voluntary winding up has been passed, the debt—

    (a) may be claimed in the sequestration or winding up or, as the case may be, is payable to the relevant office-holder, and

    (b) shall be taken into account for the purposes of any rule of law relating to compensation or set-off applicable in sequestration or winding up,

in the same way as a debt due before the date of sequestration (within the meaning of section 73(1) of the Bankruptcy (Scotland) Act 1985) or the commencement of the winding up.

7.—(1) Sections 178, 186, 315 and 345 of the Insolvency Act 1986 (power to disclaim onerous property and court's power to order rescission of contracts, &c.) do not apply in relation to—

    (a) a market contract, or

(b) a contract effected by the exchange or clearing house for the purpose of realising property provided as margin in relation to market contracts.

In the application of this sub-paragraph in Scotland, the reference to sections 178 and 315 shall be construed as a reference to any rule of law having the like effect as those sections.

(2) Sections 127 and 284 of the Insolvency Act 1986 (avoidance of property dispositions effected after commencement of winding up or presentation of bankruptcy petition) do not apply to—

(a) a market contract, or any disposition of property in pursuance of such a contract,

(b) the provision of margin in relation to market contracts,

(c) a contract effected by the exchange or clearing house for the purpose of realising property provided as margin in relation to a market contract, or any disposition of property in pursuance of such a contract, or

(d) any disposition of property in accordance with the rules of the exchange or clearing house as to the application of property provided as margin.

(3) However, if a person enters into a market contract knowing that a petition has been presented for the winding up or bankruptcy of the other party to the contract, the value of any profit or benefit to him arising from the contract is recoverable from him by the relevant office-holder unless the court directs otherwise.

(4) Any sum recoverable by virtue of sub-paragraph (3) has the same priority, in the event of the insolvency of the person from whom it is due, as if it were secured by a fixed charge.

8.—(1) No order shall be made in relation to a market contract under—

(a) section 238 or 339 of the Insolvency Act 1986 (transactions at an under-value),

(b) section 239 or 340 of that Act (preferences), or

(c) section 423 of that Act (transactions defrauding creditors),

unless the court is satisfied that the person in favour of whom the contract was made knew at the time he entered into it that it was at an under-value (within the meaning of the relevant provision) or, as the case may be, that a preference was being given.

(2) As respects Scotland, no decree shall be granted in relation to a market contract—

(a) under section 34 or 36 of the Bankruptcy (Scotland) Act 1985 or section 242 or 243 of the Insolvency Act 1986 (gratuitous alienations and unfair preferences), or

(b) at common law,

unless the court is satisfied that the person with whom the contract was made knew at the time he entered into it that it was challengeable under any of the provisions mentioned in paragraph (a) or at common law.

(3) Sub-paragraphs (1) and (2) apply in relation to—

(a) a disposition of property in pursuance of a market contract,

(b) the provision of margin in relation to market contracts,

(c) a contract effected by a recognised investment exchange or recognised clearing house for the purpose of realising property provided as margin, or

(d) a disposition of property in accordance with the rules of the exchange or clearing house as to the application of property provided as margin,

as they apply in relation to the making of a market contract.

Market charges

9.—(1) The charges to which paragraphs 10 to 12 apply are charges, whether fixed or floating, granted—

    (a) in favour of a recognised investment exchange, for the purpose of securing debts or liabilities arising in connection with the settlement of market contracts,

    (b) in favour of a recognised clearing house, for the purpose of securing debts or liabilities arising in connection with their ensuring the performance of market contracts, or

    (c) in favour of a person who agrees to make payments as a result of the transfer of specified securities made through the medium of a computer-based system established by the Bank of England and The Stock Exchange, for the purpose of securing debts or liabilities of the transferee arising in connection with the payments.

Those charges are referred to in this Schedule as "market charges".

(2) Where a charge is granted partly for purposes specified in sub-paragraph (1)(a), (b) or (c) and partly for other purposes, paragraphs 10 to 12 apply to it so far as it has effect for the specified purposes; and the expression "market charge" shall be construed accordingly.

(3) In this paragraph and paragraphs 10 to 12—

    "charge" means any form of security, including a mortgage and, in Scotland, a heritable security; and

    "specified securities" means securities for the time being specified in the list in Schedule 1 to the Stock Transfer Act 1982, and includes any right to such securities.

1982 c. 41.

10. The general law of insolvency has effect in relation to market charges and action taken in enforcing them subject to the following provisions of this Schedule.

11.—(1) Sections 10(1)(b) and 11(3)(c) of the Insolvency Act 1986 (no enforcement of security while petition for administration order pending or order in force) do not apply to a market charge.

1986 c. 45.

(2) Section 11(2) of that Act (receiver to vacate office when so required by administrator) does not apply to a receiver appointed under a market charge.

(3) Section 15(1) and (2) of that Act (administrator's power to deal with charged property) do not apply to a market charge.

(4) Sections 127 and 284 of that Act (avoidance of property dispositions effected after commencement of winding up or presentation of bankruptcy petition) do not apply to—

    (a) a disposition of property as a result of which the property becomes subject to a market charge, or any transaction pursuant to which that disposition is made, or

    (b) any disposition of property made in enforcing a market charge.

(5) However, if a person (other than the chargee under the market charge) who is a party to a disposition mentioned in sub-paragraph (4)(a) knows at the time of the disposition that a petition has been presented for the winding up or bankruptcy of the party making the disposition, the value of any profit or benefit to him arising from the disposition is recoverable from him by the relevant office-holder unless the court directs otherwise.

(6) Any sum recoverable by virtue of sub-paragraph (5) has the same priority, in the event of the insolvency of the person from whom it is due, as if it were secured by a fixed charge.

12.—(1) No legal proceedings, execution or other legal process may be commenced or continued, and no distress may be levied against property which is, or becomes, subject to a market charge except with the consent of the person in whose favour the charge was granted or the leave of the court.

(2 The court may give leave subject to such terms as it thinks fit.

(3) Sub-paragraph (1) does not apply to proceedings to enforce any security over, or any equitable interest in, the property.

(4) Sections 10(1)(c), 11(3)(d), 130(3) and 285(3) of the Insolvency Act 1986 (which restrict the taking of certain legal proceedings and other steps) have effect accordingly.

(5) In the application of this paragraph to Scotland, the reference to execution being commenced or continued includes a reference to diligence being carried out or continued, and the reference to distress being levied shall be omitted.

Supplementary provisions

13.—(1) In this Schedule "default rules" means—

(a) in relation to a recognised investment exchange, rules which provide in the event of a member or designated non-member of the exchange appearing to be unable, or likely to become unable, to meet his obligations in respect of one or more market contracts, for the settlement forthwith of all unsettled market contracts to which he is a party as principal, other than those whose performance is ensured by a recognised clearing house;

(b) in relation to a recognised clearing house, rules which provide in the event of a member of the clearing house appearing to be unable, or likely to become unable, to meet his obligations in respect of any market contract, for the closing out of his position in relation to all market contracts to which he is a party.

(2) References in this Schedule to a "defaulter" are to a person in respect of whom action has been taken by a recognised investment exchange or recognised clearing house under its default rules, whether by declaring him to be a defaulter or otherwise; and references in this Schedule to "default" shall be construed accordingly.

(3) In this Schedule "default proceedings" means proceedings taken by a recognised investment exchange or recognised clearing house under its default rules.

14.—(1) The following are relevant office-holders for the purposes of this Schedule—

(a) the official receiver,

(b) any person acting in relation to a company as its liquidator, provisional liquidator, administrator or administrative receiver,

(c) any person acting in relation to an individual (or, in Scotland, a deceased debtor) as his trustee in bankruptcy or interim receiver of his property or as permanent or interim trustee in the sequestration of his estate,

(d) any person acting as administrator (or, in Scotland, as judicial factor) of an insolvent estate of a deceased person.

(2) Sub-paragraph (1)(c) applies in relation to a partnership, and any debtor within the meaning of the Bankruptcy (Scotland) Act 1985, as it applies in relation to an individual.

(3) In this paragraph—

"administrative receiver" has the meaning given by section 251 of the Insolvency Act 1986;

"company" means a company within the meaning of section 735(1) of the Companies Act 1985 or a company which may be wound up under Part V of the Insolvency Act 1986 (unregistered companies); and

Sᴄʜ. 22
1985 c. 6.
1986 c. 45

"interim trustee" and "permanent trustee" have the same meaning as in the Bankruptcy (Scotland) Act 1985.

1985 c.66.

15.—(1) In this Schedule—

"clearing house" has the same meaning as in the Financial Services Act 1986;

1986 c. 60.

"investment" and "investment exchange" have the same meaning as in the Financial Services Act 1986;

"recognised" means recognised under the Financial Services Act 1986;

"The Stock Exchange" means The International Stock Exchange of the United Kingdom and the Republic of Ireland Limited.

(2) References in this Schedule to ensuring the performance of a transaction have the same meaning as in the Financial Services Act 1986.

(3) References in this Schedule to a market contract to which a person is a party include, unless the contrary intention appears, contracts to which he is party as agent.

SCHEDULE 23

Section 206(1).

Consequential Amendments of the Financial Services Act 1986

Part I

General Amendments

1.—(1) Section 13 of the Financial Services Act 1986 (power to direct alteration of rules of recognised self-regulating organisation) is amended as follows.

(2) Omit subsection (1).

(3) For subsection (2) substitute—

"(2) If at any time it appears to the Secretary of State that—

(a) a recognised self-regulating organisation is concerned with two or more kinds of investment business, and

(b) the requirement in paragraph 3(1) of Schedule 2 to this Act is not satisfied in respect of investment business of one or more but not all of those kinds,

he may, instead of revoking the recognition order or making an application under section 12 above, direct the organisation to alter, or himself alter, its rules so that they preclude a member from carrying on investment business of a kind in respect of which that requirement is not satisfied, unless he is an authorised person otherwise than by virtue of membership of the organisation or is an exempted person in respect of that business.".

(4) For subsection (3) substitute—

"(3) A direction under this section is enforceable on the application of the Secretary of State by injunction or, in Scotland, by an order under section 45 of the Court of Session Act 1988.".

(5) Omit subsections (4) to (6).

2.—(1) Section 48 of the Financial Services Act 1986 (conduct of business rules) is amended as follows.

(2) In subsection (1) omit the words "members of a recognised self-regulating organisation or" and "organisation or".

(3) After subsection (10) insert—

"(11) Section 63A below (application of designated rules) has effect as regards the application of rules under this section to members of recognised self-regulating organisations in respect of investment business in the carrying on of which they are subject to the rules of the organisation.".

3.—(1) Section 49 of the Financial Services Act 1986 (financial resources rules) is amended as follows.

(2) For subsection (1) substitute—

"(1) The Secretary of State may make rules requiring—

(a) a person authorised to carry on investment business by virtue of section 25 or 31 above, or

(b) a member of a recognised self-regulating organisation carrying on investment business in the carrying on of which he is subject to the rules of the organisation,

to have and maintain in respect of that business such financial resources as are required by the rules.".

(3) After subsection (2) insert—

"(3) Section 63A below (application of designated rules) has effect as regards the application of rules under this section to members of recognised self-regulating organisations in respect of investment business in the carrying on of which they are subject to the rules of the organisation.".

4. In section 50 of the Financial Services Act 1986 (power of Secretary of State to modify conduct of business and financial resources rules for particular cases), after subsection (3) insert—

"(4) The powers conferred by subsection (1) above shall not be exercised in a case where the powers conferred by section 63B below are exercisable (powers of recognised self-regulating organisation in relation to designated rules).".

5. In section 52 of the Financial Services Act 1986 (notification regulations), in subsection (3) (application to member of recognised self-regulating organisation or professional body), for "subject to any of the rules made under section 48 above" substitute "not subject to the rules of that organisation or body".

6.—(1) Section 55 of the Financial Services Act 1986 (clients' money) is amended as follows.

(2) In subsection (2)(b) and (e) omit the words "a member of a recognised self-regulating organisation or" and "organisation or".

(3) In subsection (3) omit the words "organisation or".

(4) After subsection (5) insert—

"(6) Section 63A below (application of designated regulations) has effect as regards the application of regulations under this section to members of recognised self-regulating organisations in respect of investment business in the carrying on of which they are subject to the rules of the organisation.".

7. In section 56 of the Financial Services Act 1986 (unsolicited calls), for subsection (7) substitute—

"(7) Section 63A below (application of designated regulations) has effect as regards the application of regulations under this section to members of recognised self-regulating organisations in respect of investment business in the carrying on of which they are subject to the rules of the organisation.

As it applies to such persons in respect of such business the reference in subsection (1) above to conduct permitted by regulations made by the Secretary of State shall be construed—

(a) where or to the extent that the regulations do not apply, as a reference to conduct permitted by the rules of the organisation; and

(b) where or to the extent that the regulations do apply but are expressed to have effect subject to the rules of the organisation, as a reference to conduct permitted by the regulations together with the rules of the organisation.

(7A) In the application of this section to anything done by a person certified by a recognised professional body in carrying on investment business in the carrying on of which he is subject to the rules of the body, the reference in subsection (1) above to conduct permitted by regulations made by the Secretary of State shall be construed as a reference to conduct permitted by the rules of the body.".

8. In section 86 of the Financial Services Act 1986 (collective investment schemes constituted in other member States), in subsection (7) (restriction on application of conduct of business rules), at the end add—

"This subsection also applies to statements of principle under section 47A and codes of practice under section 63A so far as they relate to matters falling within the rule-making power in section 48.".

9. In section 95 of the Financial Services Act 1986 (collective investment schemes: contraventions), after subsection (2) add—

"(3) The disciplinary action which may be taken by virtue of section 47A(3) (failure to comply with statement of principle) includes—

(a) the giving of a direction under section 91(2), and

(b) the application by the Secretary of State for an order under section 93;

and subsection (6) of section 47A (duty of the Secretary of State as to exercise of powers) has effect accordingly.".

10.—(1) Section 107 of the Financial Services Act 1986 (appointment of auditors) is amended as follows.

(2) For subsection (1) (power to make rules) substitute—

"(1) The Secretary of State may make rules requiring—

(a) a person authorised to carry on investment business by virtue of section 25 or 31 above, or

(b) a member of a recognised self-regulating organisation carrying on investment business in the carrying on of which he is subject to the rules of the organisation,

and who, apart from the rules, is not required by or under any enactment to appoint an auditor, to appoint as an auditor a person satisfying such conditions as to qualifications and otherwise as may be specified in or imposed under the rules.".

(3) After subsection (3) add—

"(4) In its application to members of recognised self-regulating organisations, this section has effect subject to section 107A below.".

11. After section 107 of the Financial Services Act 1986 insert—

"Application of audit rules to members of self-regulating organisations.

107A.—(1) The Secretary of State may in rules under section 107 designate provisions which apply, to such extent as may be specified, to a member of a recognised self-regulating organisation in respect of investment business in the carrying on of which he is subject to the rules of the organisation.

SCH. 23

1986 c. 60.

(2) It may be provided that the designated rules have effect, generally or to such extent as may be specified, subject to the rules of the organisation.

(3) A member of a recognised self-regulating organisation who contravenes a rule applying to him by virtue of that section shall be treated as having contravened the rules of the organisation.

(4) Except as mentioned above, rules made under section 107 do not apply to members of recognised self-regulating organisations in respect of investment business in the carrying on of which they are subject to the rules of the organisation.

(5) A recognised self-regulating organisation may on the application of a member of the organisation—

    (a) modify a rule designated under this section so as to adapt it to his circumstances or to any particular kind of business carried on by him, or

    (b) dispense him from compliance with any such rule, generally or in relation to any particular kind of business carried on by him.

(6) The powers conferred by subsection (5) shall not be exercised unless it appears to the organisation—

    (a) that compliance with the rule in question would be unduly burdensome for the applicant having regard to the benefit which compliance would confer on investors, and

    (b) that the exercise of those powers will not result in any undue risk to investors.

(7) The powers conferred by subsection (5) may be exercised unconditionally or subject to conditions; and subsection (3) applies in the case of a contravention of a condition as in the case of contravention of a designated rule.

(8) The reference in paragraph 4(1) of Schedule 2 (requirements for recognition of self-regulating organisations) to monitoring and enforcement of compliance with rules includes monitoring and enforcement of compliance with conditions imposed by the organisation under subsection (7).".

1986 c. 60.

12.—(1) Section 114 of the Financial Services Act 1986 (power to transfer functions to designated agency) is amended as follows.

(2) For subsection (9) substitute—

"(9) The Secretary of State shall not make a delegation order transferring any legislative functions unless—

    (a) the agency has furnished him with a copy of the instruments it proposes to issue or make in the exercise of those functions, and

    (b) he is satisfied that those instruments will afford investors an adequate level of protection and, in the case of such provisions as are mentioned in Schedule 8 to this Act, comply with the principles set out in that Schedule.

In this subsection "legislative functions" means the functions of issuing or making statements of principle, rules, regulations or codes of practice.".

(3) In subsection (12) for "rules or regulations made" substitute "statements of principle, rules, regulations or codes of practice issued or made".

13.—(1) Section 115 of the Financial Services Act 1986 (resumption of transferred functions) is amended as follows.

SCH. 23
1986 c. 60.

(2) For subsection (5) substitute—

"(5) Where the transferred functions consist of or include any legislative functions, an order may be made under subsection (2) above if at any time it appears to the Secretary of State that the instruments issued or made by the agency do not satisfy the requirements of section 114(9)(b) above.".

(3) In subsection (7)—

(a) in the opening words, for "subsection (2)(b) above" substitute "this section", and

(b) in paragraph (a) for "functions of making rules or regulations" substitute "functions of issuing or making statements of principle, rules, regulations or codes of practice".

14.—(1) Section 119 of the Financial Services Act 1986 (competition scrutiny: recognition orders) is amended as follows.

(2) In subsection (1) (considerations relevant to making of recognition order), for paragraphs (a) and (b) substitute—

"(a) in the case of a self-regulating organisation, the rules and any guidance of which copies are furnished with the application for the order, together with any statements of principle, rules, regulations or codes of practice to which members of the organisation would be subject by virtue of Chapter V of this Part,

(b) in the case of an investment exchange, the rules and any guidance of which copies are furnished with the application for the order, together with any arrangements of which particulars are furnished with the application,

(c) in the case of a clearing house, the rules and any guidance of which copies are furnished with the application for the order,".

(3) In subsection (2) (circumstances in which powers are exercisable in relation to recognised body), for paragraphs (a) to (c) substitute—

"(a) in the case of a self-regulating organisation—

(i) any rules made or guidance issued by the organisation,

(ii) any practices of the organisation, or

(iii) any practices of persons who are members of, or otherwise subject to the rules made by, the organisation,

together with any statements of principle, rules, regulations or codes of practice to which members of the organisation are subject by virtue of Chapter V of this Part,

(b) in the case of a recognised investment exchange—

(i) any rules made or guidance issued by the exchange,

(ii) any practices of the exchange, or

(iii) any practices of persons who are members of, or otherwise subject to the rules made by, the exchange,

(c) in the case of a recognised clearing house—

(i) any rules made or guidance issued by the clearing house,

(ii) any practices of the clearing house, or

(iii) any practices of persons who are members of, or otherwise subject to the rules made by, the clearing house,

or any clearing arrangements made by the clearing house,".

SCH. 23

(4) In subsection (3) (powers exercisable in relation to recognised body)—

(a) in paragraph (b) for "the rules" substitute "its rules, or the", and

(b) in paragraph (c) for "the rules" substitute "its rules".

(5) In subsection (5) (construction of references to practices)—

(a) for "paragraph (b)" substitute "paragraph (a)(ii), (b)(ii) and (c)(ii)", and

(b) omit the words from "and the practices referred to in paragraph (c)" to the end.

(6) After that subsection insert—

"(6) The practices referred to in paragraph (a)(iii), (b)(iii) and (c)(iii) of subsection (2) above are—

(a) in relation to a recognised self-regulating organisation, practices in relation to business in respect of which the persons in question are subject to—

(i) the rules of the organisation, or

(ii) statements of principle, rules, regulations or codes of practice to which its members are subject by virtue of Chapter V of this Part,

and which are required or contemplated by the rules of the organisation or by those statements, rules, regulations or codes, or by guidance issued by the organisation,

(b) in relation to a recognised investment exchange or clearing house, practices in relation to business in respect of which the persons in question are subject to the rules of the exchange or clearing house, and which are required or contemplated by its rules or guidance,

or which are otherwise attributable to the conduct of the organisation, exchange or clearing house as such.".

1986 c. 60.

15.—(1) Section 121 of the Financial Services Act 1986 (competition scrutiny: designated agencies) is amended as follows.

(2) In subsection (1) for "rules, regulations" substitute "statements of principle, rules, regulations, codes of practice".

(3) In subsection (2)(a) and (c) for "rules or regulations made" substitute "statements of principle, rules, regulations or codes of practice issued or made".

(4) In subsection (3)(b) for "rules, regulations" substitute "statements of principle, rules, regulations, codes of practice".

(5) In subsection (4) for "rules or regulations" (twice) substitute "statements of principle, rules, regulations or codes of practice".

16.—(1) Section 122 of the Financial Services Act 1986 (reports by Director General of Fair Trading) is amended as follows.

(2) In subsection (1) for "and regulations" substitute ", statements of principle, regulations and codes of practice".

(3) In subsection (2) for "regulations," substitute "statements of principle, regulations, codes of practice,".

(4) In subsection (4)—

(a) in paragraph (a) for "rules, guidance, arrangements and regulations" substitute "rules, statements of principle, regulations, codes of practice, guidance and arrangements", and

(b) in the words following the paragraphs, for "rules, guidance, arrangements, regulations" substitute "rules, statements of principle, regulations, codes of practice, guidance, arrangements", and for

"rules, guidance, arrangements or regulations" substitute "rules,
statements of principle, regulations, codes of practice, guidance or
arrangements".

17.—(1) Section 124 of the Financial Services Act 1986 (matters to be left out
of account for certain purposes in connection with competition scrutiny) is
amended as follows.

(2) In subsection (1) (matters to be left out of account in determining whether
monopoly situation exists), in paragraph (c) for "rules or regulations made or
guidance issued" substitute "statements of principle, rules, regulations, codes of
practice or guidance issued or made".

(3) In subsection (3) (matters to be excluded from consideration where
monopoly situation exists)—

(a) in paragraph (a), for "rules or regulations made" substitute "statements
of principle, rules, regulations or codes of practice issued or made",

(b) in paragraph (b), for "rules or regulations" substitute "statements of
principle, rules, regulations or codes of practice", and

(c) in the closing words, for "rules, regulations" substitute "statements of
principle, rules, regulations, codes of practice".

18. For section 205 of the Financial Services Act 1986 (regulations, rules and
orders) substitute—

"General power   205. The Secretary of State may make regulations prescribing
to make   anything which by this Act is authorised or required to be
regulations.   prescribed.

Supplementary   205A.—(1) The following provisions apply to any power of
provisions with   the Secretary of State under this Act—
respect to
subordinate   (a) to issue statements of principle,
legislation.
                         (b) to make rules or regulations,

                         (c) to make orders (other than such orders as are excepted
                             by subsection (4) below), or

                         (d) to issue codes of practice.

(2) Any such power is exercisable by statutory instrument
and includes power to make different provision for different
cases.

(3) Except as otherwise provided, a statutory instrument
containing statements of principle, rules or regulations shall be
subject to annulment in pursuance of a resolution of either
House of Parliament.

(4) The above provisions do not apply to a recognition order,
an order declaring a collective investment scheme to be an
authorised unit trust scheme or a recognised scheme or to an
order revoking any such order.".

19. In section 206(1) of the Financial Services Act 1986 (publication of
information and advice)—

(a) in paragraph (a), for "rules and regulations made" substitute
"statements of principle, rules, regulations and codes of practice issued
or made", and

(b) in paragraph (b) for "rules or regulations" substitute "statements of
principle, rules, regulations or codes of practice".

20. In Schedule 2 to the Financial Services Act 1986 (requirements for
recognition of self-regulating organisations), in paragraph 4(1) (monitoring and
enforcement) for "rules or regulations" substitute "statements of principle, rules,
regulations or codes of practice".

21. In Schedule 3 to the Financial Services Act 1986 (requirements for recognition of professional bodies), in paragraph 4(2) (monitoring and enforcement) for "rules or regulations" substitute "statements of principle, rules, regulations or codes of practice".

22. In Schedule 7 to the Financial Services Act 1986 (qualifications of designated agency), in paragraph 2(2) (arrangements for discharge of functions: matters to be decided upon by the governing body) for "rules or regulations must be made" substitute "statements of principle, rules, regulations and codes of practice must be issued or made".

23.—(1) Schedule 8 to the Financial Services Act 1986 (principles applicable to designated agency's rules and regulations) is amended as follows.

(2) In the heading for "Rules and Regulations" substitute "Legislative Provisions".

(3) For paragraph 1, and the cross-heading preceding it, substitute—

"Introduction

1.—(1) In this Schedule "legislative provisions" means the provisions of statements of principle, rules, regulations and codes of practice issued or made under Part I of this Act.

(2) References in this Schedule to "conduct of business provisions" are to rules made under section 48 of this Act and statements of principle and codes of practice so far as they relate to matters falling within that rule-making power.

(3) References in this Schedule to provisions made for the purposes of a specified section or Chapter are to rules or regulations made under that section or Chapter and statements of principle and codes of practice so far as they relate to matters falling within that power to make rules or regulations.

Standards

1A. The conduct of business provisions and the other legislative provisions must promote high standards of integrity and fair dealing in the conduct of investment business.".

(4) In paragraphs 2 to 7, 9, 11 and 12 for "conduct of business rules" substitute "conduct of business provisions".

(5) In paragraph 7 for "those rules and rules under" substitute "those provisions and provisions made for the purposes of".

(6) In paragraph 8 for "Rules made under" substitute "Provisions made for the purposes of".

(7) In paragraph 9 for "regulations made under" substitute "provisions made for the purposes of".

(8) In paragraph 10 for "Rules made under" substitute "Provisions made for the purposes of" and for "under those sections" substitute "for the purposes of those sections".

(9) In paragraph 12 for "rules and regulations made under" substitute "provisions made for the purposes of".

24.—(1) Schedule 9 to the Financial Services Act 1986 (designated agency: exercise of transferred functions) is amended as follows.

(2) In paragraph 4(1) (copies of instruments to be sent to Secretary of State), for "any rules or regulations made" substitute "any statements of principle, rules, regulations or codes of practice issued or made".

(3) For paragraphs 5 and 6 substitute—

"5. Paragraphs 6 to 9 below have effect instead of section 205A of this Act in relation to statements of principle, rules, regulations and codes of practice issued or made by a designated agency in the exercise of powers transferred to it by a delegation order.

6. Any such power is exercisable by instrument in writing and includes power to make different provision for different cases.".

(4) In paragraph 8 (instruments to be printed and made available to public)—

(a) in sub-paragraph (1) for "is made" substitute "is issued or made", and

(b) in sub-paragraph (2) for "rule or regulation" (twice) substitute "statement of principle, rule, regulation or code of practice".

(5) In paragraph 9 (proof of instruments), for "made by the agency" (twice) substitute "made or issued by the agency".

(6) For paragraph 12 (consultation) substitute—

"12.—(1) Where a designated agency proposes, in the exercise of powers transferred to it by a delegation order, to issue or make any statements of principle, rules, regulations or codes of practice, it shall publish the proposed instrument in such manner as appears to it best calculated to bring the proposals to the attention of the public, together with a statement that representations about the proposals (and, in particular, representations as to the cost of complying with the proposed provisions) can be made to the agency within a specified time.

(2) Before issuing or making the instrument the agency shall have regard to any representations duly made in accordance with that statement.

(3) The above requirements do not apply—

(a) where the agency considers that the delay involved in complying with them would be prejudicial to the interests of investors;

(b) to the issuing or making of an instrument in the same, or substantially the same, terms as a proposed instrument which was furnished by the agency to the Secretary of State for the purposes of section 114(9) of this Act.".

25.—(1) Schedule 10 to the Financial Services Act 1986 (application of investment business provisions to regulated insurance companies) is amended as follows.

(2) In paragraph 4 (modification of conduct of business rules), after sub-paragraph (2) insert—

"(2A) Sub-paragraphs (1) and (2) also apply to statements of principle under section 47A and codes of practice under section 63A so far as they relate to matters falling within the rule-making power in section 48.".

(3) In paragraph 7 (withdrawal of authorisation) after sub-paragraph (2) insert—

"(3) The disciplinary action which may be taken by virtue of section 47A(3) of this Act (failure to comply with statement of principle) includes—

(a) the withdrawal of authorisation under section 11(2)(a) of the Insurance Companies Act 1982, and

(b) the giving of a direction under section 13(2A) of that Act;

and subsection (6) of section 47A (duty of the Secretary of State as to exercise of powers) has effect accordingly.".

K

Part II

Amendments Relating to Friendly Societies

26. Schedule 11 to the Financial Services Act 1986 (friendly societies) is amended as follows.

27. In paragraph 3(2) (competition scrutiny: recognition of self-regulating organisation for friendly societies), after "sent to him under this sub-paragraph" insert ", together with any statements of principle, rules, regulations or codes of practice to which members of the organisation would be subject by virtue of this Schedule,".

28.—(1) Paragraph 4 (requirements for recognition of self-regulating organisation for friendly societies) is amended as follows.

(2) In sub-paragraph (4)—

(a) in paragraph (a) for "22" substitute "22D", and

(b) omit paragraph (b).

(3) In sub-paragraph (5) for "22" substitute "22D".

29. Omit paragraph 7.

30.—(1) Paragraph 10 (competition scrutiny: circumstances in which powers are exercisable in relation to recognised self-regulating organisation for friendly societies) is amended as follows.

(2) In sub-paragraph (1), after paragraph (c) insert "together with any statements of principle, rules, regulations or codes of practice to which members of the organisation are subject by virtue of this Schedule,".

(3) In sub-paragraph (2)—

(a) in paragraph (b), for "the rules" substitute "its rules, or the", and

(c) in paragraph (c), for "the rules" substitute "its rules".

(4) In sub-paragraph (3) (construction of references to practices), omit the words from "and the practices referred to in paragraph (c)" to the end; and after that sub-paragraph insert—

"(3A) The practices referred to in paragraph (c) of sub-paragraph (1) above are practices in relation to business in respect of which the persons in question are subject to—

(a) the rules of the organisation, or

(b) statements of principle, rules, regulations or codes of practice to which its members are subject by virtue of this Schedule,

and which are required or contemplated by the rules of the organisation or by those statements, rules, regulations or codes, or by guidance issued by the organisation, or which are otherwise attributable to the conduct of the organisation as such.".

31. In paragraph 13, for "Paragraphs 14 to 25" substitute "Paragraphs 13A to 25".

32. Before paragraph 14 and after the heading "*Conduct of investment business*", insert—

"13A.—(1) The Registrar may issue statements of principle with respect to the conduct expected of regulated friendly societies.

(2) The conduct expected may include compliance with a code or standard issued by another person, as for the time being in force, and may allow for the exercise of discretion by any person pursuant to any such code or standard.

(3) Failure to comply with a statement of principle under this paragraph is a ground for the taking of disciplinary action or the exercise of powers of intervention, but it does not give rise to any right of action by investors or other persons affected or affect the validity of any transaction.

(4) The disciplinary action which may be taken by virtue of sub-paragraph (3) is—

(a) the making of a public statement under paragraph 21, or

(b) the application by the Registrar for an injunction, interdict or other order under paragraph 22(1), or

(c) any action under paragraph 26 or 27 of this Schedule;

and the reference in that sub-paragraph to powers of intervention is to the powers conferred by Chapter VI of Part I of this Act.

(5) Where a statement of principle relates to compliance with a code or standard issued by another person, the statement of principle may provide—

(a) that failure to comply with the code or standard shall be a ground for the taking of disciplinary action, or the exercise of powers of intervention, only in such cases and to such extent as may be specified; and

(b) that no such action shall be taken, or any such power exercised, except at the request of the person by whom the code or standard in question was issued.

(6) The Registrar shall exercise his powers in such manner as appears to him appropriate to secure compliance with statements of principle under this paragraph.

13B.—(1) The relevant regulatory authority may on the application of a regulated friendly society—

(a) modify a statement of principle issued under paragraph 13A so as to adapt it to the circumstances of the society or to any particular kind of business carried on by it, or

(b) dispense the society from compliance with any such statement of principle, generally or in relation to any particular kind of business carried on by it.

(2) The powers conferred by this paragraph shall not be exercised unless it appears to the relevant regulatory authority—

(a) that compliance with the statement of principle in question would be unduly burdensome for the applicant having regard to the benefit which compliance would confer on investors, and

(b) that the exercise of those powers will not result in any undue risk to investors.

(3) The powers conferred by this paragraph may be exercised unconditionally or subject to conditions; and paragraph 13A(3) applies in the case of failure to comply with a condition as in the case of failure to comply with a statement of principle.

(4) The relevant regulatory authority for the purposes of this paragraph is—

(a) in the case of a member society of a recognised self-regulating organisation for friendly societies, in relation to investment business in the carrying on of which it is subject to the rules of the organisation, that organisation;

(b) in any other case, or in relation to other investment business, the Registrar.

(5) The reference in paragraph 4(1) of Schedule 2 as applied by paragraph 4 above (requirements for recognition of self-regulating organisation for friendly societies) to monitoring and enforcement of compliance with statements of principle includes monitoring and enforcement of compliance with conditions imposed by the organisation under this paragraph.".

33.—(1) Paragraph 14 (conduct of business rules) is amended as follows.

(2) In sub-paragraph (1), omit the words "other than a member society".

(3) After sub-paragraph (2) insert—

"(2A) Paragraph 22B below has effect as regards the application of rules under this paragraph to member societies in respect of investment business in the carrying on of which they are subject to the rules of a recognised self-regulating organisation for friendly societies.".

(4) In sub-paragraph (3), omit the word "and" after paragraph (a); and after paragraph (b) insert—

"; and

(c) for the references in subsection (4) to section 63B and a recognised self-regulating organisation there shall be substituted references to paragraph 13B and a recognised self-regulating organisation for friendly societies.".

34.—(1) Paragraph 19 (clients' money regulations) is amended as follows.

(2) In sub-paragraph (2) for the words from "(but with the substitution" to the end substitute "(but with the substitution for the reference in paragraph (e) of subsection (2) to the Secretary of State of a reference to the Registrar)".

(3) After that sub-paragraph insert—

"(3) Paragraph 22B below has effect as regards the application of regulations under this paragraph to member societies in respect of investment business in the carrying on of which they are subject to the rules of a recognised self-regulating organisation for friendly societies.".

35. For paragraph 20 (unsolicited calls) substitute—

"20.—(1) Regulations under section 56(1) of this Act shall not permit anything to be done by a regulated friendly society but that section shall not apply to anything done by such a society in the course of or in consequence of an unsolicited call which, as respects the society, constitutes the carrying on of regulated business, if it is permitted to be done by the society by regulations made by the Registrar with the consent of the Secretary of State.

(2) Paragraph 22B below has effect as regards the application of regulations under this paragraph to member societies in respect of investment business in the carrying on of which they are subject to the rules of a recognised self-regulating organisation for friendly societies.

(3) As it applies to such persons in respect of such business, the reference in sub-paragraph (1) above to conduct permitted by regulations made by the Registrar with the consent of the Secretary of State shall be construed—

(a) where or to the extent that the regulations do not apply, as a reference to conduct permitted by the rules of the organisation; and

(b) where or to the extent that the regulations do apply but are expressed to have effect subject to the rules of the organisation, as a reference to conduct permitted by the regulations together with the rules of the organisation.".

36. After paragraph 22 (and after the paragraph inserted by section 193(3))
insert—

"22B.—(1) The Registrar may in rules and regulations under—

    (a) paragraph 14 (conduct of business rules),

    (b) paragraph 19 (clients' money regulations), or

    (c) paragraph 20 (regulations as to unsolicited calls),

designate provisions which apply, to such extent as may be specified, to a member society in respect of investment business in the carrying on of which it is subject to the rules of a recognised self-regulating organisation for friendly societies.

(2) It may be provided that the designated rules or regulations have effect, generally or to such extent as may be specified, subject to the rules of the organisation.

(3) A member society which contravenes a rule or regulation applying to it by virtue of this paragraph shall be treated as having contravened the rules of the relevant recognised self-regulating organisation for friendly societies.

(4) It may be provided that, to such extent as may be specified, the designated rules or regulations may not be modified or waived (under paragraph 22C below or section 50) in relation to a member society.

Where such provision is made any modification or waiver previously granted shall cease to have effect, subject to any transitional provision or saving contained in the rules or regulations.

(5) Except as mentioned in sub-paragraph (1), the rules and regulations referred to in that sub-paragraph do not apply to a member society in respect of investment business in the carrying on of which it is subject to the rules of a recognised self-regulating organisation for friendly societies.

22C.—(1) A recognised self-regulating organisation for friendly societies may on the application of a society which is a member of the organisation—

    (a) modify a rule or regulation designated under paragraph 22B so as to adapt it to the circumstances of the society or to any particular kind of business carried on by it, or

    (b) dispense the society from compliance with any such rule or regulation, generally or in relation to any particular kind of business carried on by it.

(2) The powers conferred by this paragraph shall not be exercised unless it appears to the organisation—

    (a) that compliance with the rule or regulation in question would be unduly burdensome for the applicant having regard to the benefit which compliance would confer on investors, and

    (b) that the exercise of those powers will not result in any undue risk to investors.

(3) The powers conferred by this paragraph may be exercised unconditionally or subject to conditions; and paragraph 22B(3) applies in the case of a contravention of a condition as in the case of contravention of a designated rule or regulation.

(4) The reference in paragraph 4(1) of Schedule 2 as applied by paragraph 4 above (requirements for recognition of self-regulating organisation for friendly societies) to monitoring and enforcement of compliance with rules and regulations includes monitoring and enforcement of compliance with conditions imposed by the organisation under this paragraph.

22D.—(1) The Registrar may issue codes of practice with respect to any matters dealt with by statements of principle issued under paragraph 13A or by rules or regulations made under any provision of this Schedule.

(2) In determining whether a society has failed to comply with a statement of principle—

(a) a failure by it to comply with any relevant provision of a code of practice may be relied on as tending to establish failure to comply with the statement of principle, and

(b) compliance by it with the relevant provisions of a code of practice may be relied on as tending to negative any such failure.

(3) A contravention of a code of practice with respect to a matter dealt with by rules or regulations shall not of itself give rise to any liability or invalidate any transaction; but in determining whether a society's conduct amounts to contravention of a rule or regulation—

(a) contravention by it of any relevant provision of a code of practice may be relied on as tending to establish liability, and

(b) compliance by it with the relevant provisions of a code of practice may be relied on as tending to negative liability.

(4) Where by virtue of paragraph 22B (application of designated rules and regulations to member societies) rules or regulations—

(a) do not apply, to any extent, to a member society of a recognised self-regulating organisation for friendly societies, or

(b) apply, to any extent, subject to the rules of the organisation,

a code of practice with respect to a matter dealt with by the rules or regulations may contain provision limiting its application to a corresponding extent.".

37. For paragraph 29 (transfer of functions of making rules or regulations) substitute—

"29.—(1) The Registrar shall not make a transfer order transferring any legislative functions to a transferee body unless—

(a) the body has furnished him and the Secretary of State with a copy of the instruments it proposes to issue or make in the exercise of those functions, and

(b) they are both satisfied that those instruments will—

(i) afford investors an adequate level of protection,

(ii) in the case of provisions corresponding to those mentioned in Schedule 8 to this Act, comply with the principles set out in that Schedule, and

(iii) take proper account of the supervision of friendly societies by the Registrar under the enactments relating to friendly societies.

(2) In this paragraph "legislative functions" means the functions of issuing or making statements of principle, rules, regulations or codes of practice.".

38. In paragraph 30(2), for "rules or regulations made" substitute "statements of principle, rules, regulations or codes of practice issued or made".

39. In paragraph 31(6)(c), for "as if the reference to section 205(2) were a reference to paragraph 45(1) below" substitute "as if the reference to section 205A were a reference to paragraph 45(1) and (3) below".

40. For paragraph 34 substitute—

"34.—(1) A transferee body to which the Registrar has transferred any legislative functions may exercise those functions without the consent of the Secretary of State.

(2) In this paragraph "legislative functions" means the functions of issuing or making statements of principle, rules, regulations or codes of practice.".

41. In paragraph 36 (competition scrutiny: transferee bodies) in sub-paragraphs (1) and (3)(b) for "rules, regulations" substitute "statements of principle, rules, regulations, codes of practice".

42. In paragraph 38(1) (publication of information and advice)—

(a) in paragraph (a), for "rules and regulations made" substitute "statements of principle, rules, regulations and codes of practice issued or made", and

(b) in paragraph (b) for "rules or regulations" substitute "statements of principle, rules, regulations or codes of practice".

43. In paragraph 45—

(a) in sub-paragraph (1) for "make regulations, rules or orders" substitute "issue or make statements of principle, rules, regulations, orders or codes of practice", and

(b) in sub-paragraph (3) for "regulations, rules or orders" substitute "statements of principle, rules, regulations, orders or codes of practice.".

SCHEDULE 24

REPEALS

Chapter	Short title	Extent of repeal
1964 c. 40.	Harbours Act 1964.	In section 42(6), the words "required to be attached to a company's balance sheet".
1973 c. 41.	Fair Trading Act 1973.	Section 46(3). In section 71, in subsection (1) the words "made under section 69(4) of this Act" and subsection (2). In section 74(1), the words from "and does not" to "section 69(4) of this Act". In section 85, subsection (5) and, in subsection (6), paragraph (b) and the word "or" preceding it. In section 88(6), the words from "the relevant parties" to the "and" immediately following paragraph (c). In section 89(2), the words "Part II of". In Schedule 9, in paragraph 4 the words from "either" to the end.
1985 c. 6.	Companies Act 1985.	Section 160(3).

Chapter	Short title	Extent of repeal
1985 c. 6—*cont.*	Companies Act 1985—*cont.*	In section 169(5), the words from ", during business hours" to "for inspection)". In section 175(6)(b), the words from "during business hours" to "period". In section 191— (a) in subsection (1), the words from "(but" to "for inspection)"; (b) in subsection (3), paragraphs (a) and (b). Section 201. In section 202(1), the words "(except where section 201(3) applies)". Section 209(1)(j). In section 219(1), the words from "during" to "for inspection)". In section 288(3), the words from "during" to "for inspection)". In section 318(7), the words from "during" to "for inspection)". In section 356— (a) in subsection (1), the words "during business hours"; (b) subsections (2) and (4). In section 383— (a) in subsection (1), the words "during business hours"; (b) subsection (2); (c) in subsection (3), the words from "at a charge" to the end. Section 389. Section 435. Section 440. Section 443(4). In section 446— (a) in subsection (3), paragraph (b) and the word "and" preceding it; (b) subsection (7). Section 447(1). In section 449(1)— (a) the words "or 448"; (b) paragraph (e). Section 452(1)(b). In section 460(1), the words "(inspection of company's books and papers)" and "under section 440".

Chapter	Short title	Extent of repeal
1985 c. 6—*cont.*	Companies Act 1985—*cont.*	In section 464(5), at the end of paragraph (c), the word "and". In section 466— (a) in subsection (2), paragraph (a) and (d) and the word "or" preceding the latter; (b) subsections (4) and (5); (c) in subsection (6), the words "falling under subsection (4) of this section". In section 651(1), the words "at any time within 2 years of the date of the dissolution". In section 708(1)(b), the words "or other material". Sections 712 and 715. In section 716(2), the words following paragraph (c). In section 717(1), the words following paragraph (c). In section 733(3), the words from "then" to "216(3)". In section 735A(1), the words "440, 449(1)(a) and (d)". In section 744, the definitions of "annual return", "authorised institution", "authorised minimum", "expert", "floating charge", "joint stock company" and "undistributable reserves". In section 746, the words "Except as provided by section 243(6),". In Schedule 2— (a) in paragraph 1(1), the words "paragraph 60(2) of Schedule 4 or paragraph 19(3) of Schedule 9"; (b) paragraph 1(5); (c) in paragraph 2(1), the word "23,"; (d) paragraph 2(2); (e) in paragraph 3(1), the words "paragraph 60(2) of Schedule 4 or paragraph 19(3) of Schedule 9"; (f) paragraph 3(3);

SCH. 24

Chapter	Short title	Extent of repeal
1985 c. 6—*cont.*	Companies Act 1985—*cont.*	(g) in paragraph 4(1), the words "(whether as personal representative or otherwise)"; (h) in paragraph 4(2), the words "paragraph 60(2) of Schedule 4 or paragraph 19(3) of Schedule 9". In Schedule 4, paragraphs 50(6), 53(7), 60 to 70, 74, 75, 77 to 81, 87, 90 to 92 and 95. In Schedule 9— (a) paragraphs 1, 13(3) and (18), 16, 18(5), 19(3) to (7) and 21 to 26; (b) in paragraph 27(4), the words "of the said Part I"; (c) in paragraph 28, in sub-paragraph (1) the words "to which Part II of the Insurance Companies Act 1982 applies" and in sub-paragraph (2) the words "of Part I of this Schedule"; (d) paragraphs 29 to 31. In Schedule 11— (a) paragraph 4(b) and (c); (b) paragraph 5(b). In Schedule 13, in paragraph 25, the words from "during" to "for inspection)". Schedule 15. In Schedule 22— (a) the entry relating to section 36(4); (b) in the entry relating to sections 363 to 365, the words "(with Schedule 15)"; (c) in the entry relating to sections 384 to 393, in column 2, the word "qualifications". In Schedule 24, the entries relating to sections 245(1), 245(2), 255(5), 260(3), 287(3), 365(3), 384(5), 386(2), 389(10), 390(7), 391(4), 392(2) and 393.
1985 c. 65.	Insolvency Act 1985.	In Schedule 6, paragraphs 7(3), 23 and 45.
1986 c. 45.	Insolvency Act 1986.	In sections 45(5), 53(2), 54(3) and 62(5), the words "and, for continued contravention, to a daily default fine".

Chapter	Short title	Extent of repeal
1986 c. 45—*cont.*	Insolvency Act 1986—*cont.*	In Schedule 10, the entries in column 5 relating to sections 45(5), 53(2), 54(3) and 62(5). In Part I of Schedule 13, the entries relating to sections 222(4), 225 and 733(3).
1986 c. 46.	Company Directors Disqualification Act 1986.	In section 21(2), the words "and section 431 (summary proceedings)".
1986 c. 53.	Building Societies Act 1986.	In Schedule 15, in paragraph 3(2)(b), the words ", a shadow director". In Schedule 18, paragraphs 16 and 17.
1986 c. 60.	Financial Services Act 1986.	In section 13— (a) subsection (1); (b) subsections (4) to (6). In section 48(1), the words "members of a recognised self-regulating organisation or" and "organisation or". In section 55— (a) in subsection (2)(b) and (e), the words "a member of a recognised self-regulating organisation or" and "organisation or"; (b) in subsection (3), the words "organisation or". In section 94— (a) in subsection (3), the words "except section 435(1)(a) and (b) and (2)"; (b) in subsection (4), the words "or its affairs", "and the affairs mentioned in subsection (1) or (2) above" and "or director". Section 105(7). In section 119(5), the words from "and the practices referred to in paragraph (c)" to the end. In sections 159(1) and 160(1), the words from the beginning to "section 161 below". In section 179(3), the word "and" preceding paragraph (i). Section 180(6). Section 196(3). Section 198(1).

Chapter	Short title	Extent of repeal
1986 c. 60—*cont.*	Financial Services Act 1986—*cont.*	In section 199(9), the words from "and, in relation" to the end. In Schedule 11— (a) paragraph 4(4)(b); (b) paragraph 7; (c) in paragraph 10(3), the words from "and the practices referred to in paragraph (c)" to the end; (d) in paragraph 14(1), the words "other than a member society"; (e) in paragraph 14(3), the word "and" after paragraph (a). In Schedule 16, paragraph 22.
1987 c. 22.	Banking Act 1987.	In the Table in section 84(1), the entry relating to persons appointed under section 94, 106 or 177 of the Financial Services Act 1986. Section 90(1). In Schedule 6— (a) paragraph 18(1) to (6); (b) in paragraph 18(7), the words "and (1A)"; (c) paragraph 18(8) and (9); (d) in paragraph 27(3), the words "and (6)".
1987 c. 41.	Criminal Justice (Scotland) Act 1987.	Section 55(a).
1988 c. 1.	Income and Corporation Taxes Act 1988.	Section 565(6)(b).
1988 c. 33.	Criminal Justice Act 1988.	Section 145(a).
1988 c. 48.	Copyright, Designs and Patents Act 1988.	In Schedule 7, paragraph 31.

Children Act 1989

1989 CHAPTER 41

An Act to reform the law relating to children; to provide for local authority services for children in need and others; to amend the law with respect to children's homes, community homes, voluntary homes and voluntary organisations; to make provision with respect to fostering, child minding and day care for young children and adoption; and for connected purposes.

[16th November 1989]

BE IT ENACTED by the Queen's most Excellent Majesty, by and with the advice and consent of the Lords Spiritual and Temporal, and Commons, in this present Parliament assembled, and by the authority of the same, as follows:—

PART I

INTRODUCTORY

1.—(1) When a court determines any question with respect to— *Welfare of the child.*

    (a) the upbringing of a child; or

    (b) the administration of a child's property or the application of any income arising from it,

the child's welfare shall be the court's paramount consideration.

(2) In any proceedings in which any question with respect to the upbringing of a child arises, the court shall have regard to the general principle that any delay in determining the question is likely to prejudice the welfare of the child.

(3) In the circumstances mentioned in subsection (4), a court shall have regard in particular to—

    (a) the ascertainable wishes and feelings of the child concerned (considered in the light of his age and understanding);

    (b) his physical, emotional and educational needs;

    (c) the likely effect on him of any change in his circumstances;

(d) his age, sex, background and any characteristics of his which the court considers relevant;

(e) any harm which he has suffered or is at risk of suffering;

(f) how capable each of his parents, and any other person in relation to whom the court considers the question to be relevant, is of meeting his needs;

(g) the range of powers available to the court under this Act in the proceedings in question.

(4) The circumstances are that—

(a) the court is considering whether to make, vary or discharge a section 8 order, and the making, variation or discharge of the order is opposed by any party to the proceedings; or

(b) the court is considering whether to make, vary or discharge an order under Part IV.

(5) Where a court is considering whether or not to make one or more orders under this Act with respect to a child, it shall not make the order or any of the orders unless it considers that doing so would be better for the child than making no order at all.

Parental responsibility for children.

2.—(1) Where a child's father and mother were married to each other at the time of his birth, they shall each have parental responsibility for the child.

(2) Where a child's father and mother were not married to each other at the time of his birth—

(a) the mother shall have parental responsibility for the child;

(b) the father shall not have parental responsibility for the child, unless he acquires it in accordance with the provisions of this Act.

1987 c. 42.

(3) References in this Act to a child whose father and mother were, or (as the case may be) were not, married to each other at the time of his birth must be read with section 1 of the Family Law Reform Act 1987 (which extends their meaning).

(4) The rule of law that a father is the natural guardian of his legitimate child is abolished.

(5) More than one person may have parental responsibility for the same child at the same time.

(6) A person who has parental responsibility for a child at any time shall not cease to have that responsibility solely because some other person subsequently acquires parental responsibility for the child.

(7) Where more than one person has parental responsibility for a child, each of them may act alone and without the other (or others) in meeting that responsibility; but nothing in this Part shall be taken to affect the operation of any enactment which requires the consent of more than one person in a matter affecting the child.

(8) The fact that a person has parental responsibility for a child shall not entitle him to act in any way which would be incompatible with any order made with respect to the child under this Act.

(9) A person who has parental responsibility for a child may not surrender or transfer any part of that responsibility to another but may arrange for some or all of it to be met by one or more persons acting on his behalf.

(10) The person with whom any such arrangement is made may himself be a person who already has parental responsibility for the child concerned.

(11) The making of any such arrangement shall not affect any liability of the person making it which may arise from any failure to meet any part of his parental responsibility for the child concerned.

3.—(1) In this Act "parental responsibility" means all the rights, duties, powers, responsibilities and authority which by law a parent of a child has in relation to the child and his property.

Meaning of "parental responsibility".

(2) It also includes the rights, powers and duties which a guardian of the child's estate (appointed, before the commencement of section 5, to act generally) would have had in relation to the child and his property.

(3) The rights referred to in subsection (2) include, in particular, the right of the guardian to receive or recover in his own name, for the benefit of the child, property of whatever description and wherever situated which the child is entitled to receive or recover.

(4) The fact that a person has, or does not have, parental responsibility for a child shall not affect—

    (a) any obligation which he may have in relation to the child (such as a statutory duty to maintain the child); or

    (b) any rights which, in the event of the child's death, he (or any other person) may have in relation to the child's property.

(5) A person who—

    (a) does not have parental responsibility for a particular child; but

    (b) has care of the child,

may (subject to the provisions of this Act) do what is reasonable in all the circumstances of the case for the purpose of safeguarding or promoting the child's welfare.

4.—(1) Where a child's father and mother were not married to each other at the time of his birth—

Acquisition of parental responsibility by father.

    (a) the court may, on the application of the father, order that he shall have parental responsibility for the child; or

    (b) the father and mother may by agreement ("a parental responsibility agreement") provide for the father to have parental responsibility for the child.

(2) No parental responsibility agreement shall have effect for the purposes of this Act unless—

    (a) it is made in the form prescribed by regulations made by the Lord Chancellor; and

    (b) where regulations are made by the Lord Chancellor prescribing the manner in which such agreements must be recorded, it is recorded in the prescribed manner.

(3) Subject to section 12(4), an order under subsection (1)(a), or a parental responsibility agreement, may only be brought to an end by an order of the court made on the application—

(a) of any person who has parental responsibility for the child; or

(b) with leave of the court, of the child himself.

(4) The court may only grant leave under subsection (3)(b) if it is satisfied that the child has sufficient understanding to make the proposed application.

Appointment of guardians.

5.—(1) Where an application with respect to a child is made to the court by any individual, the court may by order appoint that individual to be the child's guardian if—

(a) the child has no parent with parental responsibility for him; or

(b) a residence order has been made with respect to the child in favour of a parent or guardian of his who has died while the order was in force.

(2) The power conferred by subsection (1) may also be exercised in any family proceedings if the court considers that the order should be made even though no application has been made for it.

(3) A parent who has parental responsibility for his child may appoint another individual to be the child's guardian in the event of his death.

(4) A guardian of a child may appoint another individual to take his place as the child's guardian in the event of his death.

(5) An appointment under subsection (3) or (4) shall not have effect unless it is made in writing, is dated and is signed by the person making the appointment or—

(a) in the case of an appointment made by a will which is not signed by the testator, is signed at the direction of the testator in accordance with the requirements of section 9 of the Wills Act 1837; or

1837 c. 26.

(b) in any other case, is signed at the direction of the person making the appointment, in his presence and in the presence of two witnesses who each attest the signature.

(6) A person appointed as a child's guardian under this section shall have parental responsibility for the child concerned.

(7) Where—

(a) on the death of any person making an appointment under subsection (3) or (4), the child concerned has no parent with parental responsibility for him; or

(b) immediately before the death of any person making such an appointment, a residence order in his favour was in force with respect to the child,

the appointment shall take effect on the death of that person.

(8) Where, on the death of any person making an appointment under subsection (3) or (4)—

(a) the child concerned has a parent with parental responsibility for him; and

   (b) subsection (7)(b) does not apply,

the appointment shall take effect when the child no longer has a parent who has parental responsibility for him.

   (9) Subsections (1) and (7) do not apply if the residence order referred to in paragraph (b) of those subsections was also made in favour of a surviving parent of the child.

   (10) Nothing in this section shall be taken to prevent an appointment under subsection (3) or (4) being made by two or more persons acting jointly.

   (11) Subject to any provision made by rules of court, no court shall exercise the High Court's inherent jurisdiction to appoint a guardian of the estate of any child.

   (12) Where rules of court are made under subsection (11) they may prescribe the circumstances in which, and conditions subject to which, an appointment of such a guardian may be made.

   (13) A guardian of a child may only be appointed in accordance with the provisions of this section.

   6.—(1) An appointment under section 5(3) or (4) revokes an earlier such appointment (including one made in an unrevoked will or codicil) made by the same person in respect of the same child, unless it is clear (whether as the result of an express provision in the later appointment or by any necessary implication) that the purpose of the later appointment is to appoint an additional guardian.

Guardians: revocation and disclaimer.

   (2) An appointment under section 5(3) or (4) (including one made in an unrevoked will or codicil) is revoked if the person who made the appointment revokes it by a written and dated instrument which is signed—

     (a) by him; or

     (b) at his direction, in his presence and in the presence of two witnesses who each attest the signature.

   (3) An appointment under section 5(3) or (4) (other than one made in a will or codicil) is revoked if, with the intention of revoking the appointment, the person who made it—

     (a) destroys the instrument by which it was made; or

     (b) has some other person destroy that instrument in his presence.

   (4) For the avoidance of doubt, an appointment under section 5(3) or (4) made in a will or codicil is revoked if the will or codicil is revoked.

   (5) A person who is appointed as a guardian under section 5(3) or (4) may disclaim his appointment by an instrument in writing signed by him and made within a reasonable time of his first knowing that the appointment has taken effect.

   (6) Where regulations are made by the Lord Chancellor prescribing the manner in which such disclaimers must be recorded, no such disclaimer shall have effect unless it is recorded in the prescribed manner.

(7) Any appointment of a guardian under section 5 may be brought to an end at any time by order of the court—

(a) on the application of any person who has parental responsibility for the child;

(b) on the application of the child concerned, with leave of the court; or

(c) in any family proceedings, if the court considers that it should be brought to an end even though no application has been made.

Welfare reports.

7.—(1) A court considering any question with respect to a child under this Act may—

(a) ask a probation officer; or

(b) ask a local authority to arrange for—

(i) an officer of the authority; or

(ii) such other person (other than a probation officer) as the authority considers appropriate,

to report to the court on such matters relating to the welfare of that child as are required to be dealt with in the report.

(2) The Lord Chancellor may make regulations specifying matters which, unless the court orders otherwise, must be dealt with in any report under this section.

(3) The report may be made in writing, or orally, as the court requires.

(4) Regardless of any enactment or rule of law which would otherwise prevent it from doing so, the court may take account of—

(a) any statement contained in the report; and

(b) any evidence given in respect of the matters referred to in the report,

in so far as the statement or evidence is, in the opinion of the court, relevant to the question which it is considering.

(5) It shall be the duty of the authority or probation officer to comply with any request for a report under this section.

Part II

Orders With Respect To Children In Family Proceedings

General

Residence, contact and other orders with respect to children.

8.—(1) In this Act —

"a contact order" means an order requiring the person with whom a child lives, or is to live, to allow the child to visit or stay with the person named in the order, or for that person and the child otherwise to have contact with each other;

"a prohibited steps order" means an order that no step which could be taken by a parent in meeting his parental responsibility for a child, and which is of a kind specified in the order, shall be taken by any person without the consent of the court;

"a residence order" means an order settling the arrangements to be made as to the person with whom a child is to live; and "a specific issue order" means an order giving directions for the purpose of determining a specific question which has arisen, or which may arise, in connection with any aspect of parental responsibility for a child.

(2) In this Act "a section 8 order" means any of the orders mentioned in subsection (1) and any order varying or discharging such an order.

(3) For the purposes of this Act "family proceedings" means any proceedings—

(a) under the inherent jurisdiction of the High Court in relation to children; and

(b) under the enactments mentioned in subsection (4),

but does not include proceedings on an application for leave under section 100(3).

(4) The enactments are—

(a) Parts I, II and IV of this Act;

(b) the Matrimonial Causes Act 1973;   1973 c. 18.

(c) the Domestic Violence and Matrimonial Proceedings Act 1976;   1976 c. 50.

(d) the Adoption Act 1976;   1976 c. 36.

(e) the Domestic Proceedings and Magistrates' Courts Act 1978;   1978 c. 22.

(f) sections 1 and 9 of the Matrimonial Homes Act 1983;   1983 c. 19.

(g) Part III of the Matrimonial and Family Proceedings Act 1984.   1984 c. 42.

9.—(1) No court shall make any section 8 order, other than a residence order, with respect to a child who is in the care of a local authority.

Restrictions on making section 8 orders.

(2) No application may be made by a local authority for a residence order or contact order and no court shall make such an order in favour of a local authority.

(3) A person who is, or was at any time within the last six months, a local authority foster parent of a child may not apply for leave to apply for a section 8 order with respect to the child unless—

(a) he has the consent of the authority;

(b) he is a relative of the child; or

(c) the child has lived with him for at least three years preceding the application.

(4) The period of three years mentioned in subsection (3)(c) need not be continuous but must have begun not more than five years before the making of the application.

(5) No court shall exercise its powers to make a specific issue order or prohibited steps order—

(a) with a view to achieving a result which could be achieved by making a residence or contact order; or

(b) in any way which is denied to the High Court (by section 100(2)) in the exercise of its inherent jurisdiction with respect to children.

(6) No court shall make any section 8 order which is to have effect for a period which will end after the child has reached the age of sixteen unless it is satisfied that the circumstances of the case are exceptional.

(7) No court shall make any section 8 order, other than one varying or discharging such an order, with respect to a child who has reached the age of sixteen unless it is satisfied that the circumstances of the case are exceptional.

Power of court
to make section
8 orders.

10.—(1) In any family proceedings in which a question arises with respect to the welfare of any child, the court may make a section 8 order with respect to the child if—

(a) an application for the order has been made by a person who—

(i) is entitled to apply for a section 8 order with respect to the child; or

(ii) has obtained the leave of the court to make the application; or

(b) the court considers that the order should be made even though no such application has been made.

(2) The court may also make a section 8 order with respect to any child on the application of a person who—

(a) is entitled to apply for a section 8 order with respect to the child; or

(b) has obtained the leave of the court to make the application.

(3) This section is subject to the restrictions imposed by section 9.

(4) The following persons are entitled to apply to the court for any section 8 order with respect to a child—

(a) any parent or guardian of the child;

(b) any person in whose favour a residence order is in force with respect to the child.

(5) The following persons are entitled to apply for a residence or contact order with respect to a child—

(a) any party to a marriage (whether or not subsisting) in relation to whom the child is a child of the family;

(b) any person with whom the child has lived for a period of at least three years;

(c) any person who—

(i) in any case where a residence order is in force with respect to the child, has the consent of each of the persons in whose favour the order was made;

(ii) in any case where the child is in the care of a local authority, has the consent of that authority; or

(iii) in any other case, has the consent of each of those (if any) who have parental responsibility for the child.

(6) A person who would not otherwise be entitled (under the previous provisions of this section) to apply for the variation or discharge of a section 8 order shall be entitled to do so if—

(a) the order was made on his application; or

(b) in the case of a contact order, he is named in the order.

(7) Any person who falls within a category of person prescribed by rules of court is entitled to apply for any such section 8 order as may be prescribed in relation to that category of person.

(8) Where the person applying for leave to make an application for a section 8 order is the child concerned, the court may only grant leave if it is satisfied that he has sufficient understanding to make the proposed application for the section 8 order.

(9) Where the person applying for leave to make an application for a section 8 order is not the child concerned, the court shall, in deciding whether or not to grant leave, have particular regard to—

    (a) the nature of the proposed application for the section 8 order;

    (b) the applicant's connection with the child;

    (c) any risk there might be of that proposed application disrupting the child's life to such an extent that he would be harmed by it; and

    (d) where the child is being looked after by a local authority—

        (i) the authority's plans for the child's future; and

        (ii) the wishes and feelings of the child's parents.

(10) The period of three years mentioned in subsection (5)(b) need not be continuous but must not have begun more than five years before, or ended more than three months before, the making of the application.

11.—(1) In proceedings in which any question of making a section 8 order, or any other question with respect to such an order, arises, the court shall (in the light of any rules made by virtue of subsection (2))—

    (a) draw up a timetable with a view to determining the question without delay; and

    (b) give such directions as it considers appropriate for the purpose of ensuring, so far as is reasonably practicable, that that timetable is adhered to.

(2) Rules of court may—

    (a) specify periods within which specified steps must be taken in relation to proceedings in which such questions arise; and

    (b) make other provision with respect to such proceedings for the purpose of ensuring, so far as is reasonably practicable, that such questions are determined without delay.

(3) Where a court has power to make a section 8 order, it may do so at any time during the course of the proceedings in question even though it is not in a position to dispose finally of those proceedings.

(4) Where a residence order is made in favour of two or more persons who do not themselves all live together, the order may specify the periods during which the child is to live in the different households concerned.

(5) Where—

    (a) a residence order has been made with respect to a child; and

    (b) as a result of the order the child lives, or is to live, with one of two parents who each have parental responsibility for him,

the residence order shall cease to have effect if the parents live together for a continuous period of more than six months.

General principles and supplementary provisions.

(6) A contact order which requires the parent with whom a child lives to allow the child to visit, or otherwise have contact with, his other parent shall cease to have effect if the parents live together for a continuous period of more than six months.

(7) A section 8 order may—

    (a) contain directions about how it is to be carried into effect;

    (b) impose conditions which must be complied with by any person—

        (i) in whose favour the order is made;

        (ii) who is a parent of the child concerned;

        (iii) who is not a parent of his but who has parental responsibility for him; or

        (iv) with whom the child is living,

    and to whom the conditions are expressed to apply;

    (c) be made to have effect for a specified period, or contain provisions which are to have effect for a specified period;

    (d) make such incidental, supplemental or consequential provision as the court thinks fit.

Residence orders and parental responsibility.

12.—(1) Where the court makes a residence order in favour of the father of a child it shall, if the father would not otherwise have parental responsibility for the child, also make an order under section 4 giving him that responsibility.

(2) Where the court makes a residence order in favour of any person who is not the parent or guardian of the child concerned that person shall have parental responsibility for the child while the residence order remains in force.

(3) Where a person has parental responsibility for a child as a result of subsection (2), he shall not have the right—

1976 c. 36.

    (a) to consent, or refuse to consent, to the making of an application with respect to the child under section 18 of the Adoption Act 1976;

    (b) to agree, or refuse to agree, to the making of an adoption order, or an order under section 55 of the Act of 1976, with respect to the child; or

    (c) to appoint a guardian for the child.

(4) Where subsection (1) requires the court to make an order under section 4 in respect of the father of a child, the court shall not bring that order to an end at any time while the residence order concerned remains in force.

Change of child's name or removal from jurisdiction.

13.—(1) Where a residence order is in force with respect to a child, no person may—

    (a) cause the child to be known by a new surname; or

    (b) remove him from the United Kingdom;

without either the written consent of every person who has parental responsibility for the child or the leave of the court.

(2) Subsection (1)(b) does not prevent the removal of a child, for a period of less than one month, by the person in whose favour the residence order is made.

(3) In making a residence order with respect to a child the court may grant the leave required by subsection (1)(b), either generally or for specified purposes.

14.—(1) Where—

Enforcement of residence orders.

    (a) a residence order is in force with respect to a child in favour of any person; and

    (b) any other person (including one in whose favour the order is also in force) is in breach of the arrangements settled by that order,

the person mentioned in paragraph (a) may, as soon as the requirement in subsection (2) is complied with, enforce the order under section 63(3) of the Magistrates' Courts Act 1980 as if it were an order requiring the other person to produce the child to him.

1980 c. 43.

(2) The requirement is that a copy of the residence order has been served on the other person.

(3) Subsection (1) is without prejudice to any other remedy open to the person in whose favour the residence order is in force.

Financial relief

15.—(1) Schedule 1 (which consists primarily of the re-enactment, with consequential amendments and minor modifications, of provisions of the Guardianship of Minors Acts 1971 and 1973, the Children Act 1975 and of sections 15 and 16 of the Family Law Reform Act 1987) makes provision in relation to financial relief for children.

Orders for financial relief with respect to children.
1975 c. 72.
1987 c. 42.

(2) The powers of a magistrates' court under section 60 of the Magistrates' Courts Act 1980 to revoke, revive or vary an order for the periodical payment of money shall not apply in relation to an order made under Schedule 1.

Family assistance orders

16.—(1) Where, in any family proceedings, the court has power to make an order under this Part with respect to any child, it may (whether or not it makes such an order) make an order requiring—

Family assistance orders.

    (a) a probation officer to be made available; or

    (b) a local authority to make an officer of the authority available,

to advise, assist and (where appropriate) befriend any person named in the order.

(2) The persons who may be named in an order under this section ("a family assistance order") are—

    (a) any parent or guardian of the child;

    (b) any person with whom the child is living or in whose favour a contact order is in force with respect to the child;

    (c) the child himself.

(3) No court may make a family assistance order unless—

    (a) it is satisfied that the circumstances of the case are exceptional; and

(b) it has obtained the consent of every person to be named in the order other than the child.

(4) A family assistance order may direct—

(a) the person named in the order; or

(b) such of the persons named in the order as may be specified in the order,

to take such steps as may be so specified with a view to enabling the officer concerned to be kept informed of the address of any person named in the order and to be allowed to visit any such person.

(5) Unless it specifies a shorter period, a family assistance order shall have effect for a period of six months beginning with the day on which it is made.

(6) Where—

(a) a family assistance order is in force with respect to a child; and

(b) a section 8 order is also in force with respect to the child,

the officer concerned may refer to the court the question whether the section 8 order should be varied or discharged.

(7) A family assistance order shall not be made so as to require a local authority to make an officer of theirs available unless—

(a) the authority agree; or

(b) the child concerned lives or will live within their area.

(8) Where a family assistance order requires a probation officer to be made available, the officer shall be selected in accordance with arrangements made by the probation committee for the area in which the child lives or will live.

(9) If the selected probation officer is unable to carry out his duties, or dies, another probation officer shall be selected in the same manner.

PART III

LOCAL AUTHORITY SUPPORT FOR CHILDREN AND FAMILIES

Provision of services for children and their families

Provision of services for children in need, their families and others.

17.—(1) It shall be the general duty of every local authority (in addition to the other duties imposed on them by this Part)—

(a) to safeguard and promote the welfare of children within their area who are in need; and

(b) so far as is consistent with that duty, to promote the upbringing of such children by their families,

by providing a range and level of services appropriate to those children's needs.

(2) For the purpose principally of facilitating the discharge of their general duty under this section, every local authority shall have the specific duties and powers set out in Part 1 of Schedule 2.

(3) Any service provided by an authority in the exercise of functions conferred on them by this section may be provided for the family of a particular child in need or for any member of his family, if it is provided with a view to safeguarding or promoting the child's welfare.

(4) The Secretary of State may by order amend any provision of Part I of Schedule 2 or add any further duty or power to those for the time being mentioned there.

(5) Every local authority—

(a) shall facilitate the provision by others (including in particular voluntary organisations) of services which the authority have power to provide by virtue of this section, or section 18, 20, 23 or 24; and

(b) may make such arrangements as they see fit for any person to act on their behalf in the provision of any such service.

(6) The services provided by a local authority in the exercise of functions conferred on them by this section may include giving assistance in kind or, in exceptional circumstances, in cash.

(7) Assistance may be unconditional or subject to conditions as to the repayment of the assistance or of its value (in whole or in part).

(8) Before giving any assistance or imposing any conditions, a local authority shall have regard to the means of the child concerned and of each of his parents.

(9) No person shall be liable to make any repayment of assistance or of its value at any time when he is in receipt of income support or family credit under the Social Security Act 1986.

1986 c. 50.

(10) For the purposes of this Part a child shall be taken to be in need if—

(a) he is unlikely to achieve or maintain, or to have the opportunity of achieving or maintaining, a reasonable standard of health or development without the provision for him of services by a local authority under this Part;

(b) his health or development is likely to be significantly impaired, or further impaired, without the provision for him of such services; or

(c) he is disabled,

and "family", in relation to such a child, includes any person who has parental responsibility for the child and any other person with whom he has been living.

(11) For the purposes of this Part, a child is disabled if he is blind, deaf or dumb or suffers from mental disorder of any kind or is substantially and permanently handicapped by illness, injury or congenital deformity or such other disability as may be prescribed; and in this Part—

"development" means physical, intellectual, emotional, social or behavioural development; and

"health" means physical or mental health.

18.—(1) Every local authority shall provide such day care for children in need within their area who are—

Day care for pre-school and other children.

(a) aged five or under; and

(b) not yet attending schools,

as is appropriate.

(2) A local authority may provide day care for children within their area who satisfy the conditions mentioned in subsection (1)(a) and (b) even though they are not in need.

(3) A local authority may provide facilities (including training, advice, guidance and counselling) for those—

(a) caring for children in day care; or

(b) who at any time accompany such children while they are in day care.

(4) In this section "day care" means any form of care or supervised activity provided for children during the day (whether or not it is provided on a regular basis).

(5) Every local authority shall provide for children in need within their area who are attending any school such care or supervised activities as is appropriate—

(a) outside school hours; or

(b) during school holidays.

(6) A local authority may provide such care or supervised activities for children within their area who are attending any school even though those children are not in need.

(7) In this section "supervised activity" means an activity supervised by a responsible person.

Review of provision for day care, child minding etc.

19.—(1) Every local authority in England and Wales shall review—

(a) the provision which they make under section 18;

(b) the extent to which the services of child minders are available within their area with respect to children under the age of eight; and

(c) the provision for day care within their area made for children under the age of eight by persons other, than the authority, required to register under section 71(1)(b).

(2) A review under subsection (1) shall be conducted—

(a) together with the appropriate local education authority; and

(b) at least once in every review period.

(3) Every local authority in Scotland shall, at least once in every review period, review—

(a) the provision for day care within their area made for children under the age of eight by the local authority and by persons required to register under section 71(1)(b); and

(b) the extent to which the services of child minders are available within their area with respect to children under the age of eight.

(4) In conducting any such review, the two authorities or, in Scotland, the authority shall have regard to the provision made with respect to children under the age of eight in relevant establishments within their area.

(5) In this section—

"relevant establishment" means any establishment which is mentioned in paragraphs 3 and 4 of Schedule 9 (hospitals, schools and other establishments exempt from the registration requirements which apply in relation to the provision of day care); and

"review period" means the period of one year beginning with the commencement of this section and each subsequent period of three years beginning with an anniversary of that commencement.

(6) Where a local authority have conducted a review under this section they shall publish the result of the review—

(a) as soon as is reasonably practicable;

(b) in such form as they consider appropriate; and

(c) together with any proposals they may have with respect to the matters reviewed.

(7) The authorities conducting any review under this section shall have regard to—

(a) any representations made to any one of them by any relevant health authority or health board; and

(b) any other representations which they consider to be relevant.

(8) In the application of this section to Scotland, "day care" has the same meaning as in section 79 and "health board" has the same meaning as in the National Health Service (Scotland) Act 1978.

1978 c. 29.

Provision of accommodation for children

20.—(1) Every local authority shall provide accommodation for any child in need within their area who appears to them to require accommodation as a result of—

Provision of accommodation for children: general.

(a) there being no person who has parental responsibility for him;

(b) his being lost or having been abandoned; or

(c) the person who has been caring for him being prevented (whether or not permanently, and for whatever reason) from providing him with suitable accommodation or care.

(2) Where a local authority provide accommodation under subsection (1) for a child who is ordinarily resident in the area of another local authority, that other local authority may take over the provision of accommodation for the child within—

(a) three months of being notified in writing that the child is being provided with accommodation; or

(b) such other longer period as may be prescribed.

(3) Every local authority shall provide accommodation for any child in need within their area who has reached the age of sixteen and whose welfare the authority consider is likely to be seriously prejudiced if they do not provide him with accommodation.

(4) A local authority may provide accommodation for any child within their area (even though a person who has parental responsibility for him is able to provide him with accommodation) if they consider that to do so would safeguard or promote the child's welfare.

(5) A local authority may provide accommodation for any person who has reached the age of sixteen but is under twenty-one in any community home which takes children who have reached the age of sixteen if they consider that to do so would safeguard or promote his welfare.

(6) Before providing accommodation under this section, a local authority shall, so far as is reasonably practicable and consistent with the child's welfare—

(a) ascertain the child's wishes regarding the provision of accommodation; and

(b) give due consideration (having regard to his age and understanding) to such wishes of the child as they have been able to ascertain.

(7) A local authority may not provide accommodation under this section for any child if any person who—

(a) has parental responsibility for him; and

(b) is willing and able to—

(i) provide accommodation for him; or

(ii) arrange for accommodation to be provided for him,

objects.

(8) Any person who has parental responsibility for a child may at any time remove the child from accommodation provided by or on behalf of the local authority under this section.

(9) Subsections (7) and (8) do not apply while any person—

(a) in whose favour a residence order is in force with respect to the child; or

(b) who has care of the child by virtue of an order made in the exercise of the High Court's inherent jurisdiction with respect to children,

agrees to the child being looked after in accommodation provided by or on behalf of the local authority.

(10) Where there is more than one such person as is mentioned in subsection (9), all of them must agree.

(11) Subsections (7) and (8) do not apply where a child who has reached the age of sixteen agrees to being provided with accommodation under this section.

21.—(1) Every local authority shall make provision for the reception and accommodation of children who are removed or kept away from home under Part V.

(2) Every local authority shall receive, and provide accommodation for, children—

    (a) in police protection whom they are requested to receive under section 46(3)(f);

    (b) whom they are requested to receive under section 38(6) of the Police and Criminal Evidence Act 1984;

    (c) who are—

        (i) on remand under section 23(1) of the Children and Young Persons Act 1969; or

        (ii) the subject of a supervision order imposing a residence requirement under section 12AA of that Act,

    and with respect to whom they are the designated authority.

(3) Where a child has been—

    (a) removed under Part V; or

    (b) detained under section 38 of the Police and Criminal Evidence Act 1984,

and he is not being provided with accommodation by a local authority or in a hospital vested in the Secretary of State, any reasonable expenses of accommodating him shall be recoverable from the local authority in whose area he is ordinarily resident.

Duties of local authorities in relation to children looked after by them

22.—(1) In this Act, any reference to a child who is looked after by a local authority is a reference to a child who is—

    (a) in their care; or

    (b) provided with accommodation by the authority in the exercise of any functions (in particular those under this Act) which stand referred to their social services committee under the Local Authority Social Services Act 1970.

(2) In subsection (1) "accommodation" means accommodation which is provided for a continuous period of more than 24 hours.

(3) It shall be the duty of a local authority looking after any child—

    (a) to safeguard and promote his welfare; and

    (b) to make such use of services available for children cared for by their own parents as appears to the authority reasonable in his case.

(4) Before making any decision with respect to a child whom they are looking after, or proposing to look after, a local authority shall, so far as is reasonably practicable, ascertain the wishes and feelings of—

    (a) the child;

    (b) his parents;

    (c) any person who is not a parent of his but who has parental responsibility for him; and

Marginal notes:

PART III

Provision of accommodation for children in police protection or detention or on remand, etc.

1984 c. 60.

1969 c. 54.

General duty of local authority in relation to children looked after by them.

1970 c. 42.

(d) any other person whose wishes and feelings the authority consider to be relevant,

regarding the matter to be decided.

(5) In making any such decision a local authority shall give due consideration—

(a) having regard to his age and understanding, to such wishes and feelings of the child as they have been able to ascertain;

(b) to such wishes and feelings of any person mentioned in subsection (4)(b) to (d) as they have been able to ascertain; and

(c) to the child's religious persuasion, racial origin and cultural and linguistic background.

(6) If it appears to a local authority that it is necessary, for the purpose of protecting members of the public from serious injury, to exercise their powers with respect to a child whom they are looking after in a manner which may not be consistent with their duties under this section, they may do so.

(7) If the Secretary of State considers it necessary, for the purpose of protecting members of the public from serious injury, to give directions to a local authority with respect to the exercise of their powers with respect to a child whom they are looking after, he may give such directions to the authority.

(8) Where any such directions are given to an authority they shall comply with them even though doing so is inconsistent with their duties under this section.

Provision of accommodation and maintenance by local authority for children whom they are looking after.

23.—(1) It shall be the duty of any local authority looking after a child—

(a) when he is in their care, to provide accommodation for him; and

(b) to maintain him in other respects apart from providing accommodation for him.

(2) A local authority shall provide accommodation and maintenance for any child whom they are looking after by—

(a) placing him (subject to subsection (5) and any regulations made by the Secretary of State) with—

(i) a family;

(ii) a relative of his; or

(iii) any other suitable person,

on such terms as to payment by the authority and otherwise as the authority may determine;

(b) maintaining him in a community home;

(c) maintaining him in a voluntary home;

(d) maintaining him in a registered children's home;

(e) maintaining him in a home provided by the Secretary of State under section 82(5) on such terms as the Secretary of State may from time to time determine; or

(f) making such other arrangements as—

(i) seem appropriate to them; and

(ii) comply with any regulations made by the Secretary of State.

(3) Any person with whom a child has been placed under subsection (2)(a) is referred to in this Act as a local authority foster parent unless he falls within subsection (4).

(4) A person falls within this subsection if he is—

(a) a parent of the child;

(b) a person who is not a parent of the child but who has parental responsibility for him; or

(c) where the child is in care and there was a residence order in force with respect to him immediately before the care order was made, a person in whose favour the residence order was made.

(5) Where a child is in the care of a local authority, the authority may only allow him to live with a person who falls within subsection (4) in accordance with regulations made by the Secretary of State.

(6) Subject to any regulations made by the Secretary of State for the purposes of this subsection, any local authority looking after a child shall make arrangements to enable him to live with—

(a) a person falling within subsection (4); or

(b) a relative, friend or other person connected with him,

unless that would not be reasonably practicable or consistent with his welfare.

(7) Where a local authority provide accommodation for a child whom they are looking after, they shall, subject to the provisions of this Part and so far as is reasonably practicable and consistent with his welfare, secure that—

(a) the accommodation is near his home; and

(b) where the authority are also providing accommodation for a sibling of his, they are accommodated together.

(8) Where a local authority provide accommodation for a child whom they are looking after and who is disabled, they shall, so far as is reasonably practicable, secure that the accommodation is not unsuitable to his particular needs.

(9) Part II of Schedule 2 shall have effect for the purposes of making further provision as to children looked after by local authorities and in particular as to the regulations that may be made under subsections (2)(a) and (f) and (5).

Advice and assistance for certain children

24.—(1) Where a child is being looked after by a local authority, it shall be the duty of the authority to advise, assist and befriend him with a view to promoting his welfare when he ceases to be looked after by them.

Advice and assistance for certain children.

(2) In this Part "a person qualifying for advice and assistance" means a person within the area of the authority who is under twenty-one and who was, at any time after reaching the age of sixteen but while still a child—

(a) looked after by a local authority;

(b) accommodated by or on behalf of a voluntary organisation;

(c) accommodated in a registered children's home;

(d) accommodated—

    (i) by any health authority or local education authority; or

    (ii) in any residential care home, nursing home or mental nursing home,

for a consecutive period of at least three months; or

(e) privately fostered,

but who is no longer so looked after, accommodated or fostered.

(3) Subsection (2)(d) applies even if the period of three months mentioned there began before the child reached the age of sixteen.

(4) Where—

(a) a local authority know that there is within their area a person qualifying for advice and assistance;

(b) the conditions in subsection (5) are satisfied; and

(c) that person has asked them for help of a kind which they can give under this section,

they shall (if he was being looked after by a local authority or was accommodated by or on behalf of a voluntary organisation) and may (in any other case) advise and befriend him.

(5) The conditions are that—

(a) it appears to the authority that the person concerned is in need of advice and being befriended;

(b) where that person was not being looked after by the authority, they are satisfied that the person by whom he was being looked after does not have the necessary facilities for advising or befriending him.

(6) Where as a result of this section a local authority are under a duty, or are empowered, to advise and befriend a person, they may also give him assistance.

(7) Assistance given under subsections (1) to (6) may be in kind or, in exceptional circumstances, in cash.

(8) A local authority may give assistance to any person who qualifies for advice and assistance by virtue of subsection (2)(a) by—

(a) contributing to expenses incurred by him in living near the place where he is, or will be—

    (i) employed or seeking employment; or

    (ii) receiving education or training; or

(b) making a grant to enable him to meet expenses connected with his education or training.

(9) Where a local authority are assisting the person under subsection (8) by making a contribution or grant with respect to a course of education or training, they may—

(a) continue to do so even though he reaches the age of twenty-one before completing the course; and

(b) disregard any interruption in his attendance on the course if he resumes it as soon as is reasonably practicable.

(10) Subsections (7) to (9) of section 17 shall apply in relation to assistance given under this section (otherwise than under subsection (8)) as they apply in relation to assistance given under that section.

(11) Where it appears to a local authority that a person whom they have been advising and befriending under this section, as a person qualifying for advice and assistance, proposes to live, or is living, in the area of another local authority, they shall inform that other local authority.

(12) Where a child who is accommodated—

(a) by a voluntary organisation or in a registered children's home;

(b) by any health authority or local education authority; or

(c) in any residential care home, nursing home or mental nursing home,

ceases to be so accommodated, after reaching the age of sixteen, the organisation, authority or (as the case may be) person carrying on the home shall inform the local authority within whose area the child proposes to live.

(13) Subsection (12) only applies, by virtue of paragraph (b) or (c), if the accommodation has been provided for a consecutive period of at least three months.

Secure accommodation

25.—(1) Subject to the following provisions of this section, a child who is being looked after by a local authority may not be placed, and, if placed, may not be kept, in accommodation provided for the purpose of restricting liberty ("secure accommodation") unless it appears—

Use of accommodation for restricting liberty.

(a) that—

(i) he has a history of absconding and is likely to abscond from any other description of accommodation; and

(ii) if he absconds, he is likely to suffer significant harm; or

(b) that if he is kept in any other description of accommodation he is likely to injure himself or other persons.

(2) The Secretary of State may by regulations—

(a) specify a maximum period—

(i) beyond which a child may not be kept in secure accommodation without the authority of the court; and

(ii) for which the court may authorise a child to be kept in secure accommodation;

(b) empower the court from time to time to authorise a child to be kept in secure accommodation for such further period as the regulations may specify; and

(c) provide that applications to the court under this section shall be made only by local authorities.

PART III

(3) It shall be the duty of a court hearing an application under this section to determine whether any relevant criteria for keeping a child in secure accommodation are satisfied in his case.

(4) If a court determines that any such criteria are satisfied, it shall make an order authorising the child to be kept in secure accommodation and specifying the maximum period for which he may be so kept.

(5) On any adjournment of the hearing of an application under this section, a court may make an interim order permitting the child to be kept during the period of the adjournment in secure accommodation.

(6) No court shall exercise the powers conferred by this section in respect of a child who is not legally represented in that court unless, having been informed of his right to apply for legal aid and having had the opportunity to do so, he refused or failed to apply.

(7) The Secretary of State may by regulations provide that—

    (a) this section shall or shall not apply to any description of children specified in the regulations;

    (b) this section shall have effect in relation to children of a description specified in the regulations subject to such modifications as may be so specified;

    (c) such other provisions as may be so specified shall have effect for the purpose of determining whether a child of a description specified in the regulations may be placed or kept in secure accommodation.

(8) The giving of an authorisation under this section shall not prejudice any power of any court in England and Wales or Scotland to give directions relating to the child to whom the authorisation relates.

(9) This section is subject to section 20(8).

Supplemental

Review of cases and inquiries into representations.

26.—(1) The Secretary of State may make regulations requiring the case of each child who is being looked after by a local authority to be reviewed in accordance with the provisions of the regulations.

(2) The regulations may, in particular, make provision—

    (a) as to the manner in which each case is to be reviewed;

    (b) as to the considerations to which the local authority are to have regard in reviewing each case;

    (c) as to the time when each case is first to be reviewed and the frequency of subsequent reviews;

    (d) requiring the authority, before conducting any review, to seek the views of—

        (i) the child;

        (ii) his parents;

        (iii) any person who is not a parent of his but who has parental responsibility for him; and

(iv) any other person whose views the authority consider to be relevant,

including, in particular, the views of those persons in relation to any particular matter which is to be considered in the course of the review;

(e) requiring the authority to consider, in the case of a child who is in their care, whether an application should be made to discharge the care order;

(f) requiring the authority to consider, in the case of a child in accommodation provided by the authority, whether the accommodation accords with the requirements of this Part;

(g) requiring the authority to inform the child, so far as is reasonably practicable, of any steps he may take under this Act;

(h) requiring the authority to make arrangements, including arrangements with such other bodies providing services as it considers appropriate, to implement any decision which they propose to make in the course, or as a result, of the review;

(i) requiring the authority to notify details of the result of the review and of any decision taken by them in consequence of the review to—

(i) the child;

(ii) his parents;

(iii) any person who is not a parent of his but who has parental responsibility for him; and

(iv) any other person whom they consider ought to be notified;

(j) requiring the authority to monitor the arrangements which they have made with a view to ensuring that they comply with the regulations.

(3) Every local authority shall establish a procedure for considering any representations (including any complaint) made to them by—

(a) any child who is being looked after by them or who is not being looked after by them but is in need;

(b) a parent of his;

(c) any person who is not a parent of his but who has parental responsibility for him;

(d) any local authority foster parent;

(e) such other person as the authority consider has a sufficient interest in the child's welfare to warrant his representations being considered by them,

about the discharge by the authority of any of their functions under this Part in relation to the child.

(4) The procedure shall ensure that at least one person who is not a member or officer of the authority takes part in—

(a) the consideration; and

(b) any discussions which are held by the authority about the action (if any) to be taken in relation to the child in the light of the consideration.

(5) In carrying out any consideration of representations under this section a local authority shall comply with any regulations made by the Secretary of State for the purpose of regulating the procedure to be followed.

(6) The Secretary of State may make regulations requiring local authorities to monitor the arrangements that they have made with a view to ensuring that they comply with any regulations made for the purposes of subsection (5).

(7) Where any representation has been considered under the procedure established by a local authority under this section, the authority shall—

(a) have due regard to the findings of those considering the representation; and

(b) take such steps as are reasonably practicable to notify (in writing)—

(i) the person making the representation;

(ii) the child (if the authority consider that he has sufficient understanding); and

(iii) such other persons (if any) as appear to the authority to be likely to be affected,

of the authority's decision in the matter and their reasons for taking that decision and of any action which they have taken, or propose to take.

(8) Every local authority shall give such publicity to their procedure for considering representations under this section as they consider appropriate.

Co-operation between authorities.

27.—(1) Where it appears to a local authority that any authority or other person mentioned in subsection (3) could, by taking any specified action, help in the exercise of any of their functions under this Part, they may request the help of that other authority or person, specifying the action in question.

(2) An authority whose help is so requested shall comply with the request if it is compatible with their own statutory or other duties and obligations and does not unduly prejudice the discharge of any of their functions.

(3) The persons are—

(a) any local authority;

(b) any local education authority;

(c) any local housing authority;

(d) any health authority; and

(e) any person authorised by the Secretary of State for the purposes of this section.

(4) Every local authority shall assist any local education authority with the provision of services for any child within the local authority's area who has special educational needs.

28.—(1) Where—

(a) a child is being looked after by a local authority; and

(b) the authority propose to provide accommodation for him in an establishment at which education is provided for children who are accommodated there,

they shall, so far as is reasonably practicable, consult the appropriate local education authority before doing so.

(2) Where any such proposal is carried out, the local authority shall, as soon as is reasonably practicable, inform the appropriate local education authority of the arrangements that have been made for the child's accommodation.

(3) Where the child ceases to be accommodated as mentioned in subsection (1)(b), the local authority shall inform the appropriate local education authority.

(4) In this section "the appropriate local education authority" means—

(a) the local education authority within whose area the local authority's area falls; or,

(b) where the child has special educational needs and a statement of his needs is maintained under the Education Act 1981, the local education authority who maintain the statement.

1981 c. 60.

29.—(1) Where a local authority provide any service under section 17 or 18, other than advice, guidance or counselling, they may recover from a person specified in subsection (4) such charge for the service as they consider reasonable.

Recoupment of cost of providing services etc.

(2) Where the authority are satisfied that that person's means are insufficient for it to be reasonably practicable for him to pay the charge, they shall not require him to pay more than he can reasonably be expected to pay.

(3) No person shall be liable to pay any charge under subsection (1) at any time when he is in receipt of income support or family credit under the Social Security Act 1986.

1986 c. 50.

(4) The persons are—

(a) where the service is provided for a child under sixteen, each of his parents;

(b) where it is provided for a child who has reached the age of sixteen, the child himself; and

(c) where it is provided for a member of the child's family, that member.

(5) Any charge under subsection (1) may, without prejudice to any other method of recovery, be recovered summarily as a civil debt.

(6) Part III of Schedule 2 makes provision in connection with contributions towards the maintenance of children who are being looked after by local authorities and consists of the re-enactment with modifications of provisions in Part V of the Child Care Act 1980.

1980 c. 5.

(7) Where a local authority provide any accommodation under section 20(1) for a child who was (immediately before they began to look after him) ordinarily resident within the area of another local authority, they may recover from that other authority any reasonable expenses incurred by them in providing the accommodation and maintaining him.

(8) Where a local authority provide accommodation under section 21(1) or (2)(a) or (b) for a child who is ordinarily resident within the area of another local authority and they are not maintaining him in—

(a) a community home provided by them;

(b) a controlled community home; or

(c) a hospital vested in the Secretary of State,

they may recover from that other authority any reasonable expenses incurred by them in providing the accommodation and maintaining him.

(9) Where a local authority comply with any request under section 27(2) in relation to a child or other person who is not ordinarily resident within their area, they may recover from the local authority in whose area the child or person is ordinarily resident any expenses reasonably incurred by them in respect of that person.

Miscellaneous.

30.—(1) Nothing in this Part shall affect any duty imposed on a local authority by or under any other enactment.

(2) Any question arising under section 20(2), 21(3) or 29(7) to (9) as to the ordinary residence of a child shall be determined by agreement between the local authorities concerned or, in default of agreement, by the Secretary of State.

(3) Where the functions conferred on a local authority by this Part and the functions of a local education authority are concurrent, the Secretary of State may by regulations provide by which authority the functions are to be exercised.

(4) The Secretary of State may make regulations for determining, as respects any local education authority functions specified in the regulations, whether a child who is being looked after by a local authority is to be treated, for purposes so specified, as a child of parents of sufficient resources or as a child of parents without resources.

PART IV

CARE AND SUPERVISION

General

Care and supervision orders.

31.—(1) On the application of any local authority or authorised person, the court may make an order—

(a) placing the child with respect to whom the application is made in the care of a designated local authority; or

(b) putting him under the supervision of a designated local authority or of a probation officer.

(2) A court may only make a care order or supervision order if it is satisfied—

(a) that the child concerned is suffering, or is likely to suffer, significant harm; and

(b) that the harm, or likelihood of harm, is attributable to—

> (i) the care given to the child, or likely to be given to him if the order were not made, not being what it would be reasonable to expect a parent to give to him; or
>
> (ii) the child's being beyond parental control.

(3) No care order or supervision order may be made with respect to a child who has reached the age of seventeen (or sixteen, in the case of a child who is married).

(4) An application under this section may be made on its own or in any other family proceedings.

(5) The court may—

> (a) on an application for a care order, make a supervision order;
>
> (b) on an application for a supervision order, make a care order.

(6) Where an authorised person proposes to make an application under this section he shall—

> (a) if it is reasonably practicable to do so; and
>
> (b) before making the application,

consult the local authority appearing to him to be the authority in whose area the child concerned is ordinarily resident.

(7) An application made by an authorised person shall not be entertained by the court if, at the time when it is made, the child concerned is—

> (a) the subject of an earlier application for a care order, or supervision order, which has not been disposed of; or
>
> (b) subject to—
>
>> (i) a care order or supervision order;
>>
>> (ii) an order under section 7(7)(b) of the Children and Young Persons Act 1969; or
>>
>> (iii) a supervision requirement within the meaning of the Social Work (Scotland) Act 1968.

1969 c. 54.

1968 c. 49.

(8) The local authority designated in a care order must be—

> (a) the authority within whose area the child is ordinarily resident; or
>
> (b) where the child does not reside in the area of a local authority, the authority within whose area any circumstances arose in consequence of which the order is being made.

(9) In this section—

> "authorised person" means—
>
>> (a) the National Society for the Prevention of Cruelty to Children and any of its officers; and
>>
>> (b) any person authorised by order of the Secretary of State to bring proceedings under this section and any officer of a body which is so authorised;
>
> "harm" means ill-treatment or the impairment of health or development;

"development" means physical, intellectual, emotional, social or behavioural development;

"health" means physical or mental health; and

"ill-treatment" includes sexual abuse and forms of ill-treatment which are not physical.

(10) Where the question of whether harm suffered by a child is significant turns on the child's health or development, his health or development shall be compared with that which could reasonably be expected of a similar child.

(11) In this Act—

"a care order" means (subject to section 105(1)) an order under subsection (1)(a) and (except where express provision to the contrary is made) includes an interim care order made under section 38; and

"a supervision order" means an order under subsection (1)(b) and (except where express provision to the contrary is made) includes an interim supervision order made under section 38.

Period within which application for order under this Part must be disposed of.

32.—(1) A court hearing an application for an order under this Part shall (in the light of any rules made by virtue of subsection (2))—

(a) draw up a timetable with a view to disposing of the application without delay; and

(b) give such directions as it considers appropriate for the purpose of ensuring, so far as is reasonably practicable, that that timetable is adhered to.

(2) Rules of court may—

(a) specify periods within which specified steps must be taken in relation to such proceedings; and

(b) make other provision with respect to such proceedings for the purpose of ensuring, so far as is reasonably practicable, that they are disposed of without delay.

Care orders

Effect of care order.

33.—(1) Where a care order is made with respect to a child it shall be the duty of the local authority designated by the order to receive the child into their care and to keep him in their care while the order remains in force.

(2) Where—

(a) a care order has been made with respect to a child on the application of an authorised person; but

(b) the local authority designated by the order was not informed that that person proposed to make the application,

the child may be kept in the care of that person until received into the care of the authority.

(3) While a care order is in force with respect to a child, the local authority designated by the order shall—

(a) have parental responsibility for the child; and

(b) have the power (subject to the following provisions of this section) to determine the extent to which a parent or guardian of the child may meet his parental responsibility for him.

(4) The authority may not exercise the power in subsection (3)(b) unless they are satisfied that it is necessary to do so in order to safeguard or promote the child's welfare.

(5) Nothing in subsection (3)(b) shall prevent a parent or guardian of the child who has care of him from doing what is reasonable in all the circumstances of the case for the purpose of safeguarding or promoting his welfare.

(6) While a care order is in force with respect to a child, the local authority designated by the order shall not—

(a) cause the child to be brought up in any religious persuasion other than that in which he would have been brought up if the order had not been made; or

(b) have the right—

(i) to consent or refuse to consent to the making of an application with respect to the child under section 18 of the Adoption Act 1976;

1976 c. 36.

(ii) to agree or refuse to agree to the making of an adoption order, or an order under section 55 of the Act of 1976, with respect to the child; or

(iii) to appoint a guardian for the child.

(7) While a care order is in force with respect to a child, no person may—

(a) cause the child to be known by a new surname; or

(b) remove him from the United Kingdom,

without either the written consent of every person who has parental responsibility for the child or the leave of the court.

(8) Subsection (7)(b) does not—

(a) prevent the removal of such a child, for a period of less than one month, by the authority in whose care he is; or

(b) apply to arrangements for such a child to live outside England and Wales (which are governed by paragraph 19 of Schedule 2).

(9) The power in subsection (3)(b) is subject (in addition to being subject to the provisions of this section) to any right, duty, power, responsibility or authority which a parent or guardian of the child has in relation to the child and his property by virtue of any other enactment.

34.—(1) Where a child is in the care of a local authority, the authority shall (subject to the provisions of this section) allow the child reasonable contact with—

Parental contact etc. with children in care.

(a) his parents;

(b) any guardian of his;

(c) where there was a residence order in force with respect to the child immediately before the care order was made, the person in whose favour the order was made; and

(d) where, immediately before the care order was made, a person had care of the child by virtue of an order made in the exercise of the High Court's inherent jurisdiction with respect to children, that person.

(2) On an application made by the authority or the child, the court may make such order as it considers appropriate with respect to the contact which is to be allowed between the child and any named person.

(3) On an application made by—

(a) any person mentioned in paragraphs (a) to (d) of subsection (1); or

(b) any person who has obtained the leave of the court to make the application,

the court may make such order as it considers appropriate with respect to the contact which is to be allowed between the child and that person.

(4) On an application made by the authority or the child, the court may make an order authorising the authority to refuse to allow contact between the child and any person who is mentioned in paragraphs (a) to (d) of subsection (1) and named in the order.

(5) When making a care order with respect to a child, or in any family proceedings in connection with a child who is in the care of a local authority, the court may make an order under this section, even though no application for such an order has been made with respect to the child, if it considers that the order should be made.

(6) An authority may refuse to allow the contact that would otherwise be required by virtue of subsection (1) or an order under this section if—

(a) they are satisfied that it is necessary to do so in order to safeguard or promote the child's welfare; and

(b) the refusal—

(i) is decided upon as a matter of urgency; and

(ii) does not last for more than seven days.

(7) An order under this section may impose such conditions as the court considers appropriate.

(8) The Secretary of State may by regulations make provision as to—

(a) the steps to be taken by a local authority who have exercised their powers under subsection (6);

(b) the circumstances in which, and conditions subject to which, the terms of any order under this section may be departed from by agreement between the local authority and the person in relation to whom the order is made;

(c) notification by a local authority of any variation or suspension of arrangements made (otherwise than under an order under this section) with a view to affording any person contact with a child to whom this section applies.

(9) The court may vary or discharge any order made under this section on the application of the authority, the child concerned or the person named in the order.

(10) An order under this section may be made either at the same time as the care order itself or later.

(11) Before making a care order with respect to any child the court shall—

    (a) consider the arrangements which the authority have made, or propose to make, for affording any person contact with a child to whom this section applies; and

    (b) invite the parties to the proceedings to comment on those arrangements.

Supervision orders

35.—(1) While a supervision order is in force it shall be the duty of the supervisor—

    (a) to advise, assist and befriend the supervised child;

    (b) to take such steps as are reasonably necessary to give effect to the order; and

    (c) where—

        (i) the order is not wholly complied with; or

        (ii) the supervisor considers that the order may no longer be necessary,

    to consider whether or not to apply to the court for its variation or discharge.

Supervision orders.

(2) Parts I and II of Schedule 3 make further provision with respect to supervision orders.

36.—(1) On the application of any local education authority, the court may make an order putting the child with respect to whom the application is made under the supervision of a designated local education authority.

Education supervision orders.

(2) In this Act "an education supervision order" means an order under subsection (1).

(3) A court may only make an education supervision order if it is satisfied that the child concerned is of compulsory school age and is not being properly educated.

(4) For the purposes of this section, a child is being properly educated only if he is receiving efficient full-time education suitable to his age, ability and aptitude and any special educational needs he may have.

(5) Where a child is—

    (a) the subject of a school attendance order which is in force under section 37 of the Education Act 1944 and which has not been complied with; or

    (b) a registered pupil at a school which he is not attending regularly within the meaning of section 39 of that Act,

then, unless it is proved that he is being properly educated, it shall be assumed that he is not.

(6) An education supervision order may not be made with respect to a child who is in the care of a local authority.

(7) The local education authority designated in an education supervision order must be—

    (a) the authority within whose area the child concerned is living or will live; or

    (b) where—

        (i) the child is a registered pupil at a school; and

        (ii) the authority mentioned in paragraph (a) and the authority within whose area the school is situated agree,

the latter authority.

(8) Where a local education authority propose to make an application for an education supervision order they shall, before making the application, consult the social services committee (within the meaning of the Local Authority Social Services Act 1970) of the appropriate local authority.

(9) The appropriate local authority is—

    (a) in the case of a child who is being provided with accommodation by, or on behalf of, a local authority, that authority; and

    (b) in any other case, the local authority within whose area the child concerned lives, or will live.

(10) Part III of Schedule 3 makes further provision with respect to education supervision orders.

Powers of court

37.—(1) Where, in any family proceedings in which a question arises with respect to the welfare of any child, it appears to the court that it may be appropriate for a care or supervision order to be made with respect to him, the court may direct the appropriate authority to undertake an investigation of the child's circumstances.

(2) Where the court gives a direction under this section the local authority concerned shall, when undertaking the investigation, consider whether they should—

    (a) apply for a care order or for a supervision order with respect to the child;

    (b) provide services or assistance for the child or his family; or

    (c) take any other action with respect to the child.

(3) Where a local authority undertake an investigation under this section, and decide not to apply for a care order or supervision order with respect to the child concerned, they shall inform the court of—

    (a) their reasons for so deciding;

    (b) any service or assistance which they have provided, or intend to provide, for the child and his family; and

    (c) any other action which they have taken, or propose to take, with respect to the child.

(4) The information shall be given to the court before the end of the period of eight weeks beginning with the date of the direction, unless the court otherwise directs.

(5) The local authority named in a direction under subsection (1) must be—

    (a) the authority in whose area the child is ordinarily resident; or

(b) where the child does not reside in the area of a local authority, the authority within whose area any circumstances arose in consequence of which the direction is being given.

(6) If, on the conclusion of any investigation or review under this section, the authority decide not to apply for a care order or supervision order with respect to the child—

    (a) they shall consider whether it would be appropriate to review the case at a later date; and

    (b) if they decide that it would be, they shall determine the date on which that review is to begin.

38.—(1) Where—

    (a) in any proceedings on an application for a care order or supervision order, the proceedings are adjourned; or

    (b) the court gives a direction under section 37(1),

the court may make an interim care order or an interim supervision order with respect to the child concerned.

(2) A court shall not make an interim care order or interim supervision order under this section unless it is satisfied that there are reasonable grounds for believing that the circumstances with respect to the child are as mentioned in section 31(2).

(3) Where, in any proceedings on an application for a care order or supervision order, a court makes a residence order with respect to the child concerned, it shall also make an interim supervision order with respect to him unless satisfied that his welfare will be satisfactorily safeguarded without an interim order being made.

(4) An interim order made under or by virtue of this section shall have effect for such period as may be specified in the order, but shall in any event cease to have effect on whichever of the following events first occurs—

    (a) the expiry of the period of eight weeks beginning with the date on which the order is made;

    (b) if the order is the second or subsequent such order made with respect to the same child in the same proceedings, the expiry of the relevant period;

    (c) in a case which falls within subsection (1)(a), the disposal of the application;

    (d) in a case which falls within subsection (1)(b), the disposal of an application for a care order or supervision order made by the authority with respect to the child;

    (e) in a case which falls within subsection (1)(b) and in which—

        (i) the court has given a direction under section 37(4), but

        (ii) no application for a care order or supervision order has been made with respect to the child,

    the expiry of the period fixed by that direction.

(5) In subsection (4)(b) "the relevant period" means—

    (a) the period of four weeks beginning with the date on which the order in question is made; or

(b) the period of eight weeks beginning with the date on which the first order was made if that period ends later than the period mentioned in paragraph (a).

(6) Where the court makes an interim care order, or interim supervision order, it may give such directions (if any) as it considers appropriate with regard to the medical or psychiatric examination or other assessment of the child; but if the child is of sufficient understanding to make an informed decision he may refuse to submit to the examination or other assessment.

(7) A direction under subsection (6) may be to the effect that there is to be—

(a) no such examination or assessment; or

(b) no such examination or assessment unless the court directs otherwise.

(8) A direction under subsection (6) may be—

(a) given when the interim order is made or at any time while it is in force; and

(b) varied at any time on the application of any person falling within any class of person prescribed by rules of court for the purposes of this subsection.

(9) Paragraphs 4 and 5 of Schedule 3 shall not apply in relation to an interim supervision order.

(10) Where a court makes an order under or by virtue of this section it shall, in determining the period for which the order is to be in force, consider whether any party who was, or might have been, opposed to the making of the order was in a position to argue his case against the order in full.

Discharge and variation etc. of care orders and supervision orders.

39.—(1) A care order may be discharged by the court on the application of—

(a) any person who has parental responsibility for the child;

(b) the child himself; or

(c) the local authority designated by the order.

(2) A supervision order may be varied or discharged by the court on the application of—

(a) any person who has parental responsibility for the child;

(b) the child himself; or

(c) the supervisor.

(3) On the application of a person who is not entitled to apply for the order to be discharged, but who is a person with whom the child is living, a supervision order may be varied by the court in so far as it imposes a requirement which affects that person.

(4) Where a care order is in force with respect to a child the court may, on the application of any person entitled to apply for the order to be discharged, substitute a supervision order for the care order.

(5) When a court is considering whether to substitute one order for another under subsection (4) any provision of this Act which would otherwise require section 31(2) to be satisfied at the time when the proposed order is substituted or made shall be disregarded.

40.—(1) Where—

(a) a court dismisses an application for a care order; and

(b) at the time when the court dismisses the application, the child concerned is the subject of an interim care order,

the court may make a care order with respect to the child to have effect subject to such directions (if any) as the court may see fit to include in the order.

(2) Where—

(a) a court dismisses an application for a care order, or an application for a supervision order; and

(b) at the time when the court dismisses the application, the child concerned is the subject of an interim supervision order,

the court may make a supervision order with respect to the child to have effect subject to such directions (if any) as the court may see fit to include in the order.

(3) Where a court grants an application to discharge a care order or supervision order, it may order that—

(a) its decision is not to have effect; or

(b) the care order, or supervision order, is to continue to have effect but subject to such directions as the court sees fit to include in the order.

(4) An order made under this section shall only have effect for such period, not exceeding the appeal period, as may be specified in the order.

(5) Where—

(a) an appeal is made against any decision of a court under this section; or

(b) any application is made to the appellate court in connection with a proposed appeal against that decision,

the appellate court may extend the period for which the order in question is to have effect, but not so as to extend it beyond the end of the appeal period.

(6) In this section "the appeal period" means—

(a) where an appeal is made against the decision in question, the period between the making of that decision and the determination of the appeal; and

(b) otherwise, the period during which an appeal may be made against the decision.

Guardians ad litem

41.—(1) For the purpose of any specified proceedings, the court shall appoint a guardian ad litem for the child concerned unless satisfied that it is not necessary to do so in order to safeguard his interests.

(2) The guardian ad litem shall—

    (a) be appointed in accordance with rules of court; and

    (b) be under a duty to safeguard the interests of the child in the manner prescribed by such rules.

(3) Where—

    (a) the child concerned is not represented by a solicitor; and

    (b) any of the conditions mentioned in subsection (4) is satisfied,

the court may appoint a solicitor to represent him.

(4) The conditions are that—

    (a) no guardian ad litem has been appointed for the child;

    (b) the child has sufficient understanding to instruct a solicitor and wishes to do so;

    (c) it appears to the court that it would be in the child's best interests for him to be represented by a solicitor.

(5) Any solicitor appointed under or by virtue of this section shall be appointed, and shall represent the child, in accordance with rules of court.

(6) In this section "specified proceedings" means any proceedings—

    (a) on an application for a care order or supervision order;

    (b) in which the court has given a direction under section 37(1) and has made, or is considering whether to make, an interim care order;

    (c) on an application for the discharge of a care order or the variation or discharge of a supervision order;

    (d) on an application under section 39(4);

    (e) in which the court is considering whether to make a residence order with respect to a child who is the subject of a care order;

    (f) with respect to contact between a child who is the subject of a care order and any other person;

    (g) under Part V;

    (h) on an appeal against—

        (i) the making of, or refusal to make, a care order, supervision order or any order under section 34;

        (ii) the making of, or refusal to make, a residence order with respect to a child who is the subject of a care order; or

        (iii) the variation or discharge, or refusal of an application to vary or discharge, an order of a kind mentioned in sub-paragraph (i) or (ii);

        (iv) the refusal of an application under section 39(4); or

        (v) the making of, or refusal to make, an order under Part V; or

    (i) which are specified for the time being, for the purposes of this section, by rules of court.

(7) The Secretary of State may by regulations provide for the establishment of panels of persons from whom guardians ad litem appointed under this section must be selected.

(8) Subsection (7) shall not be taken to prejudice the power of the Lord Chancellor to confer or impose duties on the Official Solicitor under section 90(3) of the Supreme Court Act 1981.

(9) The regulations may, in particular, make provision—

(a) as to the constitution, administration and procedures of panels;

(b) requiring two or more specified local authorities to make arrangements for the joint management of a panel;

(c) for the defrayment by local authorities of expenses incurred by members of panels;

(d) for the payment by local authorities of fees and allowances for members of panels;

(e) as to the qualifications for membership of a panel;

(f) as to the training to be given to members of panels;

(g) as to the co-operation required of specified local authorities in the provision of panels in specified areas; and

(h) for monitoring the work of guardians ad litem.

(10) Rules of court may make provision as to—

(a) the assistance which any guardian ad litem may be required by the court to give to it;

(b) the consideration to be given by any guardian ad litem, where an order of a specified kind has been made in the proceedings in question, as to whether to apply for the variation or discharge of the order;

(c) the participation of guardians ad litem in reviews, of a kind specified in the rules, which are conducted by the court.

(11) Regardless of any enactment or rule of law which would otherwise prevent it from doing so, the court may take account of—

(a) any statement contained in a report made by a guardian ad litem who is appointed under this section for the purpose of the proceedings in question; and

(b) any evidence given in respect of the matters referred to in the report,

in so far as the statement or evidence is, in the opinion of the court, relevant to the question which the court is considering.

42.—(1) Where a person has been appointed as a guardian ad litem under this Act he shall have the right at all reasonable times to examine and take copies of—

(a) any records of, or held by, a local authority which were compiled in connection with the making, or proposed making, by any person of any application under this Act with respect to the child concerned; or

(b) any other records of, or held by, a local authority which were compiled in connection with any functions which stand referred to their social services committee under the Local Authority Social Services Act 1970, so far as those records relate to that child.

PART IV

(2) Where a guardian ad litem takes a copy of any record which he is entitled to examine under this section, that copy or any part of it shall be admissible as evidence of any matter referred to in any—

(a) report which he makes to the court in the proceedings in question; or

(b) evidence which he gives in those proceedings.

(3) Subsection (2) has effect regardless of any enactment or rule of law which would otherwise prevent the record in question being admissible in evidence.

PART V

PROTECTION OF CHILDREN

Child assessment orders.

43.—(1) On the application of a local authority or authorised person for an order to be made under this section with respect to a child, the court may make the order if, but only if, it is satisfied that—

(a) the applicant has reasonable cause to suspect that the child is suffering, or is likely to suffer, significant harm;

(b) an assessment of the state of the child's health or development, or of the way in which he has been treated, is required to enable the applicant to determine whether or not the child is suffering, or is likely to suffer, significant harm; and

(c) it is unlikely that such an assessment will be made, or be satisfactory, in the absence of an order under this section.

(2) In this Act "a child assessment order" means an order under this section.

(3) A court may treat an application under this section as an application for an emergency protection order.

(4) No court shall make a child assessment order if it is satisfied—

(a) that there are grounds for making an emergency protection order with respect to the child; and

(b) that it ought to make such an order rather than a child assessment order.

(5) A child assessment order shall—

(a) specify the date by which the assessment is to begin; and

(b) have effect for such period, not exceeding 7 days beginning with that date, as may be specified in the order.

(6) Where a child assessment order is in force with respect to a child it shall be the duty of any person who is in a position to produce the child—

(a) to produce him to such person as may be named in the order; and

(b) to comply with such directions relating to the assessment of the child as the court thinks fit to specify in the order.

(7) A child assessment order authorises any person carrying out the assessment, or any part of the assessment, to do so in accordance with the terms of the order.

(8) Regardless of subsection (7), if the child is of sufficient understanding to make an informed decision he may refuse to submit to a medical or psychiatric examination or other assessment.

(9) The child may only be kept away from home—

    (a) in accordance with directions specified in the order;

    (b) if it is necessary for the purposes of the assessment; and

    (c) for such period or periods as may be specified in the order.

(10) Where the child is to be kept away from home, the order shall contain such directions as the court thinks fit with regard to the contact that he must be allowed to have with other persons while away from home.

(11) Any person making an application for a child assessment order shall take such steps as are reasonably practicable to ensure that notice of the application is given to—

    (a) the child's parents;

    (b) any person who is not a parent of his but who has parental responsibility for him;

    (c) any other person caring for the child;

    (d) any person in whose favour a contact order is in force with respect to the child;

    (e) any person who is allowed to have contact with the child by virtue of an order under section 34; and

    (f) the child,

before the hearing of the application.

(12) Rules of court may make provision as to the circumstances in which—

    (a) any of the persons mentioned in subsection (11); or

    (b) such other person as may be specified in the rules,

may apply to the court for a child assessment order to be varied or discharged.

(13) In this section "authorised person" means a person who is an authorised person for the purposes of section 31.

44.—(1) Where any person ("the applicant") applies to the court for an order to be made under this section with respect to a child, the court may make the order if, but only if, it is satisfied that—

    (a) there is reasonable cause to believe that the child is likely to suffer significant harm if—

        (i) he is not removed to accommodation provided by or on behalf of the applicant; or

        (ii) he does not remain in the place in which he is then being accommodated;

    (b) in the case of an application made by a local authority—

        (i) enquiries are being made with respect to the child under section 47(1)(b); and

Orders for emergency protection of children.

(ii) those enquiries are being frustrated by access to the child being unreasonably refused to a person authorised to seek access and that the applicant has reasonable cause to believe that access to the child is required as a matter of urgency; or

(c) in the case of an application made by an authorised person—

(i) the applicant has reasonable cause to suspect that a child is suffering, or is likely to suffer, significant harm;

(ii) the applicant is making enquiries with respect to the child's welfare; and

(iii) those enquiries are being frustrated by access to the child being unreasonably refused to a person authorised to seek access and the applicant has reasonable cause to believe that access to the child is required as a matter of urgency.

(2) In this section—

(a) "authorised person" means a person who is an authorised person for the purposes of section 31; and

(b) "a person authorised to seek access" means—

(i) in the case of an application by a local authority, an officer of the local authority or a person authorised by the authority to act on their behalf in connection with the enquiries; or

(ii) in the case of an application by an authorised person, that person.

(3) Any person—

(a) seeking access to a child in connection with enquiries of a kind mentioned in subsection (1); and

(b) purporting to be a person authorised to do so,

shall, on being asked to do so, produce some duly authenticated document as evidence that he is such a person.

(4) While an order under this section ("an emergency protection order") is in force it—

(a) operates as a direction to any person who is in a position to do so to comply with any request to produce the child to the applicant;

(b) authorises—

(i) the removal of the child at any time to accommodation provided by or on behalf of the applicant and his being kept there; or

(ii) the prevention of the child's removal from any hospital, or other place, in which he was being accommodated immediately before the making of the order; and

(c) gives the applicant parental responsibility for the child.

(5) Where an emergency protection order is in force with respect to a child, the applicant—

(a) shall only exercise the power given by virtue of subsection (4)(b) in order to safeguard the welfare of the child;

(b) shall take, and shall only take, such action in meeting his parental responsibility for the child as is reasonably required to safeguard or promote the welfare of the child (having regard in particular to the duration of the order); and

(c) shall comply with the requirements of any regulations made by the Secretary of State for the purposes of this subsection.

(6) Where the court makes an emergency protection order, it may give such directions (if any) as it considers appropriate with respect to—

(a) the contact which is, or is not, to be allowed between the child and any named person;

(b) the medical or psychiatric examination or other assessment of the child.

(7) Where any direction is given under subsection (6)(b), the child may, if he is of sufficient understanding to make an informed decision, refuse to submit to the examination or other assessment.

(8) A direction under subsection (6)(a) may impose conditions and one under subsection (6)(b) may be to the effect that there is to be—

(a) no such examination or assessment; or

(b) no such examination or assessment unless the court directs otherwise.

(9) A direction under subsection (6) may be—

(a) given when the emergency protection order is made or at any time while it is in force; and

(b) varied at any time on the application of any person falling within any class of person prescribed by rules of court for the purposes of this subsection.

(10) Where an emergency protection order is in force with respect to a child and—

(a) the applicant has exercised the power given by subsection (4)(b)(i) but it appears to him that it is safe for the child to be returned; or

(b) the applicant has exercised the power given by subsection (4)(b)(ii) but it appears to him that it is safe for the child to be allowed to be removed from the place in question,

he shall return the child or (as the case may be) allow him to be removed.

(11) Where he is required by subsection (10) to return the child the applicant shall—

(a) return him to the care of the person from whose care he was removed; or

(b) if that is not reasonably practicable, return him to the care of—

(i) a parent of his;

(ii) any person who is not a parent of his but who has parental responsibility for him; or

(iii) such other person as the applicant (with the agreement of the court) considers appropriate.

(12) Where the applicant has been required by subsection (10) to return the child, or to allow him to be removed, he may again exercise his powers with respect to the child (at any time while the emergency protection order remains in force) if it appears to him that a change in the circumstances of the case makes it necessary for him to do so.

(13) Where an emergency protection order has been made with respect to a child, the applicant shall, subject to any direction given under subsection (6), allow the child reasonable contact with—

(a) his parents;

(b) any person who is not a parent of his but who has parental responsibility for him;

(c) any person with whom he was living immediately before the making of the order;

(d) any person in whose favour a contact order is in force with respect to him;

(e) any person who is allowed to have contact with the child by virtue of an order under section 34; and

(f) any person acting on behalf of any of those persons.

(14) Wherever it is reasonably practicable to do so, an emergency protection order shall name the child; and where it does not name him it shall describe him as clearly as possible.

(15) A person shall be guilty of an offence if he intentionally obstructs any person exercising the power under subsection (4)(b) to remove, or prevent the removal of, a child.

(16) A person guilty of an offence under subsection (15) shall be liable on summary conviction to a fine not exceeding level 3 on the standard scale.

Duration of emergency protection orders and other supplemental provisions.

45.—(1) An emergency protection order shall have effect for such period, not exceeding eight days, as may be specified in the order.

(2) Where—

(a) the court making an emergency protection order would, but for this subsection, specify a period of eight days as the period for which the order is to have effect; but

(b) the last of those eight days is a public holiday (that is to say, Christmas Day, Good Friday, a bank holiday or a Sunday),

the court may specify a period which ends at noon on the first later day which is not such a holiday.

(3) Where an emergency protection order is made on an application under section 46(7), the period of eight days mentioned in subsection (1) shall begin with the first day on which the child was taken into police protection under section 46.

(4) Any person who—

(a) has parental responsibility for a child as the result of an emergency protection order; and

(b) is entitled to apply for a care order with respect to the child,

may apply to the court for the period during which the emergency protection order is to have effect to be extended.

(5) On an application under subsection (4) the court may extend the period during which the order is to have effect by such period, not exceeding seven days, as it thinks fit, but may do so only if it has reasonable cause to believe that the child concerned is likely to suffer significant harm if the order is not extended.

(6) An emergency protection order may only be extended once.

(7) Regardless of any enactment or rule of law which would otherwise prevent it from doing so, a court hearing an application for, or with respect to, an emergency protection order may take account of—

(a) any statement contained in any report made to the court in the course of, or in connection with, the hearing; or

(b) any evidence given during the hearing,

which is, in the opinion of the court, relevant to the application.

(8) Any of the following may apply to the court for an emergency protection order to be discharged—

(a) the child;

(b) a parent of his;

(c) any person who is not a parent of his but who has parental responsibility for him; or

(d) any person with whom he was living immediately before the making of the order.

(9) No application for the discharge of an emergency protection order shall be heard by the court before the expiry of the period of 72 hours beginning with the making of the order.

(10) No appeal may be made against the making of, or refusal to make, an emergency protection order or against any direction given by the court in connection with such an order.

(11) Subsection (8) does not apply—

(a) where the person who would otherwise be entitled to apply for the emergency protection order to be discharged—

(i) was given notice (in accordance with rules of court) of the hearing at which the order was made; and

(ii) was present at that hearing; or

(b) to any emergency protection order the effective period of which has been extended under subsection (5).

(12) A court making an emergency protection order may direct that the applicant may, in exercising any powers which he has by virtue of the order, be accompanied by a registered medical practitioner, registered nurse or registered health visitor, if he so chooses.

46.—(1) Where a constable has reasonable cause to believe that a child would otherwise be likely to suffer significant harm, he may—

(a) remove the child to suitable accommodation and keep him there; or

(b) take such steps as are reasonable to ensure that the child's removal from any hospital, or other place, in which he is then being accommodated is prevented.

Removal and accommodation of children by police in cases of emergency.

(2) For the purposes of this Act, a child with respect to whom a constable has exercised his powers under this section is referred to as having been taken into police protection.

(3) As soon as is reasonably practicable after taking a child into police protection, the constable concerned shall—

   (a) inform the local authority within whose area the child was found of the steps that have been, and are proposed to be, taken with respect to the child under this section and the reasons for taking them;

   (b) give details to the authority within whose area the child is ordinarily resident ("the appropriate authority") of the place at which the child is being accommodated;

   (c) inform the child (if he appears capable of understanding)—

      (i) of the steps that have been taken with respect to him under this section and of the reasons for taking them; and

      (ii) of the further steps that may be taken with respect to him under this section;

   (d) take such steps as are reasonably practicable to discover the wishes and feelings of the child;

   (e) secure that the case is inquired into by an officer designated for the purposes of this section by the chief officer of the police area concerned; and

   (f) where the child was taken into police protection by being removed to accommodation which is not provided—

      (i) by or on behalf of a local authority; or

      (ii) as a refuge, in compliance with the requirements of section 51,

   secure that he is moved to accommodation which is so provided.

(4) As soon as is reasonably practicable after taking a child into police protection, the constable concerned shall take such steps as are reasonably practicable to inform—

   (a) the child's parents;

   (b) every person who is not a parent of his but who has parental responsibility for him; and

   (c) any other person with whom the child was living immediately before being taken into police protection,

of the steps that he has taken under this section with respect to the child, the reasons for taking them and the further steps that may be taken with respect to him under this section.

(5) On completing any inquiry under subsection (3)(e), the officer conducting it shall release the child from police protection unless he considers that there is still reasonable cause for believing that the child would be likely to suffer significant harm if released.

(6) No child may be kept in police protection for more than 72 hours.

(7) While a child is being kept in police protection, the designated officer may apply on behalf of the appropriate authority for an emergency protection order to be made under section 44 with respect to the child.

(8) An application may be made under subsection (7) whether or not the authority know of it or agree to its being made.

(9) While a child is being kept in police protection—

(a) neither the constable concerned nor the designated officer shall have parental responsibility for him; but

(b) the designated officer shall do what is reasonable in all the circumstances of the case for the purpose of safeguarding or promoting the child's welfare (having regard in particular to the length of the period during which the child will be so protected).

(10) Where a child has been taken into police protection, the designated officer shall allow—

(a) the child's parents;

(b) any person who is not a parent of the child but who has parental responsibility for him;

(c) any peison with whom the child was living immediately before he was taken into police protection;

(d) any person in whose favour a contact order is in force with respect to the child;

(e) any person who is allowed to have contact with the child by virtue of an order under section 34; and

(f) any person acting on behalf of any of those persons,

to have such contact (if any) with the child as, in the opinion of the designated officer, is both reasonable and in the child's best interests.

(11) Where a child who has been taken into police protection is in accommodation provided by, or on behalf of, the appropriate authority, subsection (10) shall have effect as if it referred to the authority rather than to the designated officer.

47.—(1) Where a local authority—

  Local authority's duty to investigate.

(a) are informed that a child who lives, or is found, in their area—

(i) is the subject of an emergency protection order; or

(ii) is in police protection; or

(b) have reasonable cause to suspect that a child who lives, or is found, in their area is suffering, or is likely to suffer, significant harm,

the authority shall make, or cause to be made, such enquiries as they consider necessary to enable them to decide whether they should take any action to safeguard or promote the child's welfare.

(2) Where a local authority have obtained an emergency protection order with respect to a child, they shall make, or cause to be made, such enquiries as they consider necessary to enable them to decide what action they should take to safeguard or promote the child's welfare.

(3) The enquiries shall, in particular, be directed towards establishing—

(a) whether the authority should make any application to the court, or exercise any of their other powers under this Act, with respect to the child;

(b) whether, in the case of a child—

(i) with respect to whom an emergency protection order has been made; and

(ii) who is not in accommodation provided by or on behalf of the authority,

it would be in the child's best interests (while an emergency protection order remains in force) for him to be in such accommodation; and

(c) whether, in the case of a child who has been taken into police protection, it would be in the child's best interests for the authority to ask for an application to be made under section 46(7).

(4) Where enquiries are being made under subsection (1) with respect to a child, the local authority concerned shall (with a view to enabling them to determine what action, if any, to take with respect to him) take such steps as are reasonably practicable—

(a) to obtain access to him; or

(b) to ensure that access to him is obtained, on their behalf, by a person authorised by them for the purpose,

unless they are satisfied that they already have sufficient information with respect to him.

(5) Where, as a result of any such enquiries, it appears to the authority that there are matters connected with the child's education which should be investigated, they shall consult the relevant local education authority.

(6) Where, in the course of enquiries made under this section—

(a) any officer of the local authority concerned; or

(b) any person authorised by the authority to act on their behalf in connection with those enquiries—

(i) is refused access to the child concerned; or

(ii) is denied information as to his whereabouts,

the authority shall apply for an emergency protection order, a child assessment order, a care order or a supervision order with respect to the child unless they are satisfied that his welfare can be satisfactorily safeguarded without their doing so.

(7) If, on the conclusion of any enquiries or review made under this section, the authority decide not to apply for an emergency protection order, a child assessment order, a care order or a supervision order they shall—

(a) consider whether it would be appropriate to review the case at a later date; and

(b) if they decide that it would be, determine the date on which that review is to begin.

(8) Where, as a result of complying with this section, a local authority conclude that they should take action to safeguard or promote the child's welfare they shall take that action (so far as it is both within their power and reasonably practicable for them to do so).

(9) Where a local authority are conducting enquiries under this section, it shall be the duty of any person mentioned in subsection (11) to assist them with those enquiries (in particular by providing relevant information and advice) if called upon by the authority to do so.

(10) Subsection (9) does not oblige any person to assist a local authority where doing so would be unreasonable in all the circumstances of the case.

(11) The persons are—

(a) any local authority;

(b) any local education authority;

(c) any local housing authority;

(d) any health authority; and

(e) any person authorised by the Secretary of State for the purposes of this section.

(12) Where a local authority are making enquiries under this section with respect to a child who appears to them to be ordinarily resident within the area of another authority, they shall consult that other authority, who may undertake the necessary enquiries in their place.

48.—(1) Where it appears to a court making an emergency protection order that adequate information as to the child's whereabouts—

Powers to assist in discovery of children who may be in need of emergency protection.

(a) is not available to the applicant for the order; but

(b) is available to another person,

it may include in the order a provision requiring that other person to disclose, if asked to do so by the applicant, any information that he may have as to the child's whereabouts.

(2) No person shall be excused from complying with such a requirement on the ground that complying might incriminate him or his spouse of an offence; but a statement or admission made in complying shall not be admissible in evidence against either of them in proceedings for any offence other than perjury.

(3) An emergency protection order may authorise the applicant to enter premises specified by the order and search for the child with respect to whom the order is made.

(4) Where the court is satisfied that there is reasonable cause to believe that there may be another child on those premises with respect to whom an emergency protection order ought to be made, it may make an order authorising the applicant to search for that other child on those premises.

(5) Where—

(a) an order has been made under subsection (4);

(b) the child concerned has been found on the premises; and

(c) the applicant is satisfied that the grounds for making an emergency protection order exist with respect to him,

the order shall have effect as if it were an emergency protection order.

(6) Where an order has been made under subsection (4), the applicant shall notify the court of its effect.

(7) A person shall be guilty of an offence if he intentionally obstructs any person exercising the power of entry and search under subsection (3) or (4).

(8) A person guilty of an offence under subsection (7) shall be liable on summary conviction to a fine not exceeding level 3 on the standard scale.

(9) Where, on an application made by any person for a warrant under this section, it appears to the court—

    (a) that a person attempting to exercise powers under an emergency protection order has been prevented from doing so by being refused entry to the premises concerned or access to the child concerned; or

    (b) that any such person is likely to be so prevented from exercising any such powers,

it may issue a warrant authorising any constable to assist the person mentioned in paragraph (a) or (b) in the exercise of those powers, using reasonable force if necessary.

(10) Every warrant issued under this section shall be addressed to, and executed by, a constable who shall be accompanied by the person applying for the warrant if—

    (a) that person so desires; and

    (b) the court by whom the warrant is issued does not direct otherwise.

(11) A court granting an application for a warrant under this section may direct that the constable concerned may, in executing the warrant, be accompanied by a registered medical practitioner, registered nurse or registered health visitor if he so chooses.

(12) An application for a warrant under this section shall be made in the manner and form prescribed by rules of court.

(13) Wherever it is reasonably practicable to do so, an order under subsection (4), an application for a warrant under this section and any such warrant shall name the child; and where it does not name him it shall describe him as clearly as possible.

Abduction of children in care etc.

49.—(1) A person shall be guilty of an offence if, knowingly and without lawful authority or reasonable excuse, he—

    (a) takes a child to whom this section applies away from the responsible person;

    (b) keeps such a child away from the responsible person; or

    (c) induces, assists or incites such a child to run away or stay away from the responsible person.

(2) This section applies in relation to a child who is—

    (a) in care;

    (b) the subject of an emergency protection order; or

    (c) in police protection,

and in this section "the responsible person" means any person who for the time being has care of him by virtue of the care order, the emergency protection order, or section 46, as the case may be.

(3) A person guilty of an offence under this section shall be liable on summary conviction to imprisonment for a term not exceeding six months, or to a fine not exceeding level 5 on the standard scale, or to both.

50.—(1) Where it appears to the court that there is reason to believe that a child to whom this section applies—

    (a) has been unlawfully taken away or is being unlawfully kept away from the responsible person;

    (b) has run away or is staying away from the responsible person; or

    (c) is missing,

the court may make an order under this section ("a recovery order").

PART V

Recovery of abducted children etc.

(2) This section applies to the same children to whom section 49 applies and in this section "the responsible person" has the same meaning as in section 49.

(3) A recovery order—

    (a) operates as a direction to any person who is in a position to do so to produce the child on request to any authorised person;

    (b) authorises the removal of the child by any authorised person;

    (c) requires any person who has information as to the child's whereabouts to disclose that information, if asked to do so, to a constable or an officer of the court;

    (d) authorises a constable to enter any premises specified in the order and search for the child, using reasonable force if necessary.

(4) The court may make a recovery order only on the application of—

    (a) any person who has parental responsibility for the child by virtue of a care order or emergency protection order; or

    (b) where the child is in police protection, the designated officer.

(5) A recovery order shall name the child and—

    (a) any person who has parental responsibility for the child by virtue of a care order or emergency protection order; or

    (b) where the child is in police protection, the designated officer.

(6) Premises may only be specified under subsection (3)(d) if it appears to the court that there are reasonable grounds for believing the child to be on them.

(7) In this section—

"an authorised person" means—

        (a) any person specified by the court;

        (b) any constable;

        (c) any person who is authorised—

            (i) after the recovery order is made; and

            (ii) by a person who has parental responsibility for the child by virtue of a care order or an emergency protection order,

        to exercise any power under a recovery order; and

"the designated officer" means the officer designated for the purposes of section 46.

(8) Where a person is authorised as mentioned in subsection (7)(c)—

    (a) the authorisation shall identify the recovery order; and

PART V

(b) any person claiming to be so authorised shall, if asked to do so, produce some duly authenticated document showing that he is so authorised.

(9) A person shall be guilty of an offence if he intentionally obstructs an authorised person exercising the power under subsection (3)(b) to remove a child.

(10) A person guilty of an offence under this section shall be liable on summary conviction to a fine not exceeding level 3 on the standard scale.

(11) No person shall be excused from complying with any request made under subsection (3)(c) on the ground that complying with it might incriminate him or his spouse of an offence; but a statement or admission made in complying shall not be admissible in evidence against either of them in proceedings for an offence other than perjury.

(12) Where a child is made the subject of a recovery order whilst being looked after by a local authority, any reasonable expenses incurred by an authorised person in giving effect to the order shall be recoverable from the authority.

(13) A recovery order shall have effect in Scotland as if it had been made by the Court of Session and as if that court had had jurisdiction to make it.

S.I. 1981/1675 (N.I. 26).

(14) In this section "the court", in relation to Northern Ireland, means a magistrates' court within the meaning of the Magistrates' Courts (Northern Ireland) Order 1981.

Refuges for children at risk.

51.—(1) Where it is proposed to use a voluntary home or registered children's home to provide a refuge for children who appear to be at risk of harm, the Secretary of State may issue a certificate under this section with respect to that home.

(2) Where a local authority or voluntary organisation arrange for a foster parent to provide such a refuge, the Secretary of State may issue a certificate under this section with respect to that foster parent.

(3) In subsection (2) "foster parent" means a person who is, or who from time to time is, a local authority foster parent or a foster parent with whom children are placed by a voluntary organisation.

(4) The Secretary of State may by regulations—

(a) make provision as to the manner in which certificates may be issued;

(b) impose requirements which must be complied with while any certificate is in force; and

(c) provide for the withdrawal of certificates in prescribed circumstances.

(5) Where a certificate is in force with respect to a home, none of the provisions mentioned in subsection (7) shall apply in relation to any person providing a refuge for any child in that home.

(6) Where a certificate is in force with respect to a foster parent, none of those provisions shall apply in relation to the provision by him of a refuge for any child in accordance with arrangements made by the local authority or voluntary organisation.

(7) The provisions are—

    (a) section 49;

    (b) section 71 of the Social Work (Scotland) Act 1968 (harbouring children who have absconded from residential establishments etc.), so far as it applies in relation to anything done in England and Wales; 1968 c. 49.

    (c) section 32(3) of the Children and Young Persons Act 1969 (compelling, persuading, inciting or assisting any person to be absent from detention, etc.), so far as it applies in relation to anything done in England and Wales; 1969 c. 54.

    (d) section 2 of the Child Abduction Act 1984. 1984 c. 37.

52.—(1) Without prejudice to section 93 or any other power to make such rules, rules of court may be made with respect to the procedure to be followed in connection with proceedings under this Part. Rules and regulations.

(2) The rules may, in particular make provision—

    (a) as to the form in which any application is to be made or direction is to be given;

    (b) prescribing the persons who are to be notified of—

        (i) the making, or extension, of an emergency protection order; or

        (ii) the making of an application under section 45(4) or (8) or 46(7); and

    (c) as to the content of any such notification and the manner in which, and person by whom, it is to be given.

(3) The Secretary of State may by regulations provide that, where—

    (a) an emergency protection order has been made with respect to a child;

    (b) the applicant for the order was not the local authority within whose area the child is ordinarily resident; and

    (c) that local authority are of the opinion that it would be in the child's best interests for the applicant's responsibilities under the order to be transferred to them,

that authority shall (subject to their having complied with any requirements imposed by the regulations) be treated, for the purposes of this Act, as though they and not the original applicant had applied for, and been granted, the order.

(4) Regulations made under subsection (3) may, in particular, make provision as to—

    (a) the considerations to which the local authority shall have regard in forming an opinion as mentioned in subsection (3)(c); and

(b) the time at which responsibility under any emergency protection order is to be treated as having been transferred to a local authority.

Part VI

Community Homes

Provision of
community
homes by local
authorities.

53.—(1) Every local authority shall make such arrangements as they consider appropriate for securing that homes ("community homes") are available—

(a) for the care and accommodation of children looked after by them; and

(b) for purposes connected with the welfare of children (whether or not looked after by them),

and may do so jointly with one or more other local authorities.

(2) In making such arrangements, a local authority shall have regard to the need for ensuring the availability of accommodation—

(a) of different descriptions; and

(b) which is suitable for different purposes and the requirements of different descriptions of children.

(3) A community home may be a home—

(a) provided, managed, equipped and maintained by a local authority; or

(b) provided by a voluntary organisation but in respect of which a local authority and the organisation—

(i) propose that, in accordance with an instrument of management, the management, equipment and maintenance of the home shall be the responsibility of the local authority; or

(ii) so propose that the management, equipment and maintenance of the home shall be the responsibility of the voluntary organisation.

(4) Where a local authority are to be responsible for the management of a community home provided by a voluntary organisation, the authority shall designate the home as a controlled community home.

(5) Where a voluntary organisation are to be responsible for the management of a community home provided by the organisation, the local authority shall designate the home as an assisted community home.

(6) Schedule 4 shall have effect for the purpose of supplementing the provisions of this Part.

Directions that
premises be no
longer used for
community
home.

54.—(1) Where it appears to the Secretary of State that—

(a) any premises used for the purposes of a community home are unsuitable for those purposes; or

(b) the conduct of a community home—

(i) is not in accordance with regulations made by him under paragraph 4 of Schedule 4; or

    (ii) is otherwise unsatisfactory,

he may, by notice in writing served on the responsible body, direct that as from such date as may be specified in the notice the premises shall not be used for the purposes of a community home.

    (2) Where—

        (a) the Secretary of State has given a direction under subsection (1); and

        (b) the direction has not been revoked,

he may at any time by order revoke the instrument of management for the home concerned.

    (3) For the purposes of subsection (1), the responsible body—

        (a) in relation to a community home provided by a local authority, is that local authority;

        (b) in relation to a controlled community home, is the local authority specified in the home's instrument of management; and

        (c) in relation to an assisted community home, is the voluntary organisation by which the home is provided.

    55.—(1) Where any dispute relating to a controlled community home arises between the local authority specified in the home's instrument of management and—

        (a) the voluntary organisation by which the home is provided; or

        (b) any other local authority who have placed, or desire or are required to place, in the home a child who is looked after by them,

the dispute may be referred by either party to the Secretary of State for his determination.

    (2) Where any dispute relating to an assisted community home arises between the voluntary organisation by which the home is provided and any local authority who have placed, or desire to place, in the home a child who is looked after by them, the dispute may be referred by either party to the Secretary of State for his determination.

    (3) Where a dispute is referred to the Secretary of State under this section he may, in order to give effect to his determination of the dispute, give such directions as he thinks fit to the local authority or voluntary organisation concerned.

    (4) This section applies even though the matter in dispute may be one which, under or by virtue of Part II of Schedule 4, is reserved for the decision, or is the responsibility, of—

        (a) the local authority specified in the home's instrument of management; or

        (b) (as the case may be) the voluntary organisation by which the home is provided.

Determination of disputes relating to controlled and assisted community homes.

M

(5) Where any trust deed relating to a controlled or assisted community home contains provision whereby a bishop or any other ecclesiastical or denominational authority has power to decide questions relating to religious instruction given in the home, no dispute which is capable of being dealt with in accordance with that provision shall be referred to the Secretary of State under this section.

(6) In this Part "trust deed", in relation to a voluntary home, means any instrument (other than an instrument of management) regulating—

(a) the maintenance, management or conduct of the home; or

(b) the constitution of a body of managers or trustees of the home.

56.—(1) The voluntary organisation by which a controlled or assisted community home is provided shall not cease to provide the home except after giving to the Secretary of State and the local authority specified in the home's instrument of management not less than two years' notice in writing of their intention to do so.

(2) A notice under subsection (1) shall specify the date from which the voluntary organisation intend to cease to provide the home as a community home.

(3) Where such a notice is given and is not withdrawn before the date specified in it, the home's instrument of management shall cease to have effect on that date and the home shall then cease to be a controlled or assisted community home.

(4) Where a notice is given under subsection (1) and the home's managers give notice in writing to the Secretary of State that they are unable or unwilling to continue as its managers until the date specified in the subsection (1) notice, the Secretary of State may by order—

(a) revoke the home's instrument of management; and

(b) require the local authority who were specified in that instrument to conduct the home until—

(i) the date specified in the subsection (1) notice; or

(ii) such earlier date (if any) as may be specified for the purposes of this paragraph in the order,

as if it were a community home provided by the local authority.

(5) Where the Secretary of State imposes a requirement under subsection (4)(b)—

(a) nothing in the trust deed for the home shall affect the conduct of the home by the local authority;

(b) the Secretary of State may by order direct that for the purposes of any provision specified in the direction and made by or under any enactment relating to community homes (other than this section) the home shall, until the date or earlier date specified as mentioned in subsection (4)(b), be treated as a controlled or assisted community home;

(c) except in so far as the Secretary of State so directs, the home shall until that date be treated for the purposes of any such enactment as a community home provided by the local authority; and

(d) on the date or earlier date specified as mentioned in subsection (4)(b) the home shall cease to be a community home.

57.—(1) The local authority specified in the instrument of management for a controlled or assisted community home may give—

    (a) the Secretary of State; and

    (b) the voluntary organisation by which the home is provided,

not less than two years' notice in writing of their intention to withdraw their designation of the home as a controlled or assisted community home.

PART VI

Closure by local authority of controlled or assisted community home.

(2) A notice under subsection (1) shall specify the date ("the specified date") on which the designation is to be withdrawn.

(3) Where—

    (a) a notice is given under subsection (1) in respect of a controlled or assisted community home;

    (b) the home's managers give notice in writing to the Secretary of State that they are unable or unwilling to continue as managers until the specified date; and

    (c) the managers' notice is not withdrawn,

the Secretary of State may by order revoke the home's instrument of management from such date earlier than the specified date as may be specified in the order.

(4) Before making an order under subsection (3), the Secretary of State shall consult the local authority and the voluntary organisation.

(5) Where a notice has been given under subsection (1) and is not withdrawn, the home's instrument of management shall cease to have effect on—

    (a) the specified date; or

    (b) where an earlier date has been specified under subsection (3), that earlier date,

and the home shall then cease to be a community home.

58.—(1) Where—

    (a) the instrument of management for a controlled or assisted community home is revoked or otherwise ceases to have effect under section 54(2), 56(3) or (4)(a) or 57(3) or (5); or

    (b) any premises used for the purposes of such a home are (at any time after 13th January 1987) disposed of, or put to use otherwise than for those purposes,

the proprietor shall become liable to pay compensation ("the appropriate compensation") in accordance with this section.

Financial provisions applicable on cessation of controlled or assisted community home or disposal etc. of premises.

(2) Where the instrument of management in force at the relevant time relates—

    (a) to a controlled community home; or

    (b) to an assisted community home which, at any time before the instrument came into force, was a controlled community home,

the appropriate compensation is a sum equal to that part of the value of any premises which is attributable to expenditure incurred in relation to the premises, while the home was a controlled community home, by the authority who were then the responsible authority.

(3) Where the instrument of management in force at the relevant time relates—

    (a) to an assisted community home; or

    (b) to a controlled community home which, at any time before the instrument came into force, was an assisted community home,

the appropriate compensation is a sum equal to that part of the value of the premises which is attributable to the expenditure of money provided by way of grant under section 82, section 65 of the Children and Young Persons Act 1969 or section 82 of the Child Care Act 1980.

1969 c. 54.
1980 c. 5.

(4) Where the home is, at the relevant time, conducted in premises which formerly were used as an approved school or were an approved probation hostel or home, the appropriate compensation is a sum equal to that part of the value of the premises which is attributable to the expenditure—

1933 c. 12.

    (a) of sums paid towards the expenses of the managers of an approved school under section 104 of the Children and Young Persons Act 1933; or

1973 c. 62.

    (b) of sums paid under section 51(3)(c) of the Powers of Criminal Courts Act 1973 in relation to expenditure on approved probation hostels or homes.

(5) The appropriate compensation shall be paid—

    (a) in the case of compensation payable under subsection (2), to the authority who were the responsible authority at the relevant time; and

    (b) in any other case, to the Secretary of State.

(6) In this section—

"disposal" includes the grant of a tenancy and any other conveyance, assignment, transfer, grant, variation or extinguishment of an interest in or right over land, whether made by instrument or otherwise;

"premises" means any premises or part of premises (including land) used for the purposes of the home and belonging to the proprietor;

"the proprietor" means—

    (a) the voluntary organisation by which the home is, at the relevant time, provided; or

    (b) if the premises are not, at the relevant time, vested in that organisation, the persons in whom they are vested;

"the relevant time" means the time immediately before the liability to pay arises under subsection (1); and

"the responsible authority" means the local authority specified in the instrument of management in question.

(7) For the purposes of this section an event of a kind mentioned in subsection (1)(b) shall be taken to have occurred—

    (a) in the case of a disposal, on the date on which the disposal was completed or, in the case of a disposal which is effected by a series of transactions, the date on which the last of those transactions was completed;

(b) in the case of premises which are put to different use, on the date on which they first begin to be put to their new use.

(8) The amount of any sum payable under this section shall be determined in accordance with such arrangements—

    (a) as may be agreed between the voluntary organisation by which the home is, at the relevant time, provided and the responsible authority or (as the case may be) the Secretary of State; or

    (b) in default of agreement, as may be determined by the Secretary of State.

(9) With the agreement of the responsible authority or (as the case may be) the Secretary of State, the liability to pay any sum under this section may be discharged, in whole or in part, by the transfer of any premises.

(10) This section has effect regardless of—

    (a) anything in any trust deed for a controlled or assisted community home;

    (b) the provisions of any enactment or instrument governing the disposition of the property of a voluntary organisation.

Part VII

Voluntary Homes and Voluntary Organisations

59.—(1) Where a voluntary organisation provide accommodation for a child, they shall do so by—

    (a) placing him (subject to subsection (2)) with—

        (i) a family;

        (ii) a relative of his; or

        (iii) any other suitable person,

    on such terms as to payment by the organisation and otherwise as the organisation may determine;

    (b) maintaining him in a voluntary home;

    (c) maintaining him in a community home;

    (d) maintaining him in a registered children's home;

    (e) maintaining him in a home provided by the Secretary of State under section 82(5) on such terms as the Secretary of State may from time to time determine; or

    (f) making such other arrangements (subject to subsection (3)) as seem appropriate to them.

Provision of accommodation by voluntary organisations.

(2) The Secretary of State may make regulations as to the placing of children with foster parents by voluntary organisations and the regulations may, in particular, make provision which (with any necessary modifications) is similar to the provision that may be made under section 23(2)(a).

(3) The Secretary of State may make regulations as to the arrangements which may be made under subsection (1)(f) and the regulations may in particular make provision which (with any necessary modifications) is similar to the provision that may be made under section 23(2)(f).

(4) The Secretary of State may make regulations requiring any voluntary organisation who are providing accommodation for a child—

    (a) to review his case; and

    (b) to consider any representations (including any complaint) made to them by any person falling within a prescribed class of person,

in accordance with the provisions of the regulations.

(5) Regulations under subsection (4) may in particular make provision which (with any necessary modifications) is similar to the provision that may be made under section 26.

(6) Regulations under subsections (2) to (4) may provide that any person who, without reasonable excuse, contravenes or fails to comply with a regulation shall be guilty of an offence and liable on summary conviction to a fine not exceeding level 4 on the standard scale.

Registration and regulation of voluntary homes.

60.—(1) No voluntary home shall be carried on unless it is registered in a register to be kept for the purposes of this section by the Secretary of State.

(2) The register may be kept by means of a computer.

(3) In this Act "voluntary home" means any home or other institution providing care and accommodation for children which is carried on by a voluntary organisation but does not include—

    (a) a nursing home, mental nursing home or residential care home;

    (b) a school;

    (c) any health service hospital;

    (d) any community home;

    (e) any home or other institution provided, equipped and maintained by the Secretary of State; or

    (f) any home which is exempted by regulations made for the purposes of this section by the Secretary of State.

(4) Schedule 5 shall have effect for the purpose of supplementing the provisions of this Part.

Duties of voluntary organisations.

61.—(1) Where a child is accommodated by or on behalf of a voluntary organisation, it shall be the duty of the organisation—

    (a) to safeguard and promote his welfare;

    (b) to make such use of the services and facilities available for children cared for by their own parents as appears to the organisation reasonable in his case; and

    (c) to advise, assist and befriend him with a view to promoting his welfare when he ceases to be so accommodated.

(2) Before making any decision with respect to any such child the organisation shall, so far as is reasonably practicable, ascertain the wishes and feelings of—

    (a) the child;

    (b) his parents;

(c) any person who is not a parent of his but who has parental responsibility for him; and

(d) any other person whose wishes and feelings the organisation consider to be relevant,

regarding the matter to be decided.

(3) In making any such decision the organisation shall give due consideration—

(a) having regard to the child's age and understanding, to such wishes and feelings of his as they have been able to ascertain;

(b) to such other wishes and feelings mentioned in subsection (2) as they have been able to ascertain; and

(c) to the child's religious persuasion, racial origin and cultural and linguistic background.

62.—(1) Every local authority shall satisfy themselves that any voluntary organisation providing accommodation— Duties of local authorities.

(a) within the authority's area for any child; or

(b) outside that area for any child on behalf of the authority,

are satisfactorily safeguarding and promoting the welfare of the children so provided with accommodation.

(2) Every local authority shall arrange for children who are accommodated within their area by or on behalf of voluntary organisations to be visited, from time to time, in the interests of their welfare.

(3) The Secretary of State may make regulations—

(a) requiring every child who is accommodated within a local authority's area, by or on behalf of a voluntary organisation, to be visited by an officer of the authority—

(i) in prescribed circumstances; and

(ii) on specified occasions or within specified periods; and

(b) imposing requirements which must be met by any local authority, or officer of a local authority, carrying out functions under this section.

(4) Subsection (2) does not apply in relation to community homes.

(5) Where a local authority are not satisfied that the welfare of any child who is accommodated by or on behalf of a voluntary organisation is being satisfactorily safeguarded or promoted they shall—

(a) unless they consider that it would not be in the best interests of the child, take such steps as are reasonably practicable to secure that the care and accommodation of the child is undertaken by—

(i) a parent of his;

(ii) any person who is not a parent of his but who has parental responsibility for him; or

(iii) a relative of his; and

(b) consider the extent to which (if at all) they should exercise any of their functions with respect to the child.

(6) Any person authorised by a local authority may, for the purpose of enabling the authority to discharge their duties under this section—

(a) enter, at any reasonable time, and inspect any premises in which children are being accommodated as mentioned in subsection (1) or (2);

(b) inspect any children there;

(c) require any person to furnish him with such records of a kind required to be kept by regulations made under paragraph 7 of Schedule 5 (in whatever form they are held), or allow him to inspect such records, as he may at any time direct.

(7) Any person exercising the power conferred by subsection (6) shall, if asked to do so, produce some duly authenticated document showing his authority to do so.

(8) Any person authorised to exercise the power to inspect records conferred by subsection (6)—

(a) shall be entitled at any reasonable time to have access to, and inspect and check the operation of, any computer and any associated apparatus or material which is or has been in use in connection with the records in question; and

(b) may require—

(i) the person by whom or on whose behalf the computer is or has been so used; or

(ii) any person having charge of, or otherwise concerned with the operation of, the computer, apparatus or material,

to afford him such assistance as he may reasonably require.

(9) Any person who intentionally obstructs another in the exercise of any power conferred by subsection (6) or (8) shall be guilty of an offence and liable on summary conviction to a fine not exceeding level 3 on the standard scale.

Part VIII

Registered Children's Homes

Children not to be cared for and accommodated in unregistered children's homes.

63.—(1) No child shall be cared for and provided with accommodation in a children's home unless the home is registered under this Part.

(2) The register may be kept by means of a computer.

(3) For the purposes of this Part, "a children's home"—

(a) means a home which provides (or usually provides or is intended to provide) care and accommodation wholly or mainly for more than three children at any one time; but

(b) does not include a home which is exempted by or under any of the following provisions of this section or by regulations made for the purposes of this subsection by the Secretary of State.

(4) A child is not cared for and accommodated in a children's home when he is cared for and accommodated by—

(a) a parent of his;

(b) a person who is not a parent of his but who has parental responsibility for him; or

(c) any relative of his.

(5) A home is not a children's home for the purposes of this Part if it is—

(a) a community home;

(b) a voluntary home;

(c) a residential care home, nursing home or mental nursing home;

(d) a health service hospital;

(e) a home provided, equipped and maintained by the Secretary of State; or

(f) a school (but subject to subsection (6)).

(6) An independent school is a children's home if—

(a) it provides accommodation for not more than fifty children; and

(b) it is not approved by the Secretary of State under section 11(3)(a) of the Education Act 1981.

1981 c. 60.

(7) A child shall not be treated as cared for and accommodated in a children's home when—

(a) any person mentioned in subsection (4)(a) or (b) is living at the home; or

(b) the person caring for him is doing so in his personal capacity and not in the course of carrying out his duties in relation to the home.

(8) In this Act "a registered children's home" means a children's home registered under this Part.

(9) In this section "home" includes any institution.

(10) Where any child is at any time cared for and accommodated in a children's home which is not a registered children's home, the person carrying on the home shall be—

(a) guilty of an offence; and

(b) liable to a fine not exceeding level 5 on the standard scale,

unless he has a reasonable excuse.

(11) Schedule 6 shall have effect with respect to children's homes.

(12) Schedule 7 shall have effect for the purpose of setting out the circumstances in which a person may foster more than three children without being treated as carrying on a children's home.

64.—(1) Where a child is accommodated in a children's home, it shall be the duty of the person carrying on the home to—

(a) safeguard and promote the child's welfare;

(b) make such use of the services and facilities available for children cared for by their own parents as appears to that person reasonable in the case of the child; and

(c) advise, assist and befriend him with a view to promoting his welfare when he ceases to be so accommodated.

(2) Before making any decision with respect to any such child the person carrying on the home shall, so far as is reasonably practicable, ascertain the wishes and feelings of—

(a) the child;

(b) his parents;

(c) any other person who is not a parent of his but who has parental responsibility for him; and

(d) any person whose wishes and feelings the person carrying on the home considers to be relevant,

regarding the matter to be decided.

(3) In making any such decision the person concerned shall give due consideration—

(a) having regard to the child's age and understanding, to such wishes and feelings of his as he has been able to ascertain;

(b) to such other wishes and feelings mentioned in subsection (2) as he has been able to ascertain; and

(c) to the child's religious persuasion, racial origin and cultural and linguistic background.

(4) Section 62, except subsection (4), shall apply in relation to any person who is carrying on a children's home as it applies in relation to any voluntary organisation.

Persons disqualified from carrying on, or being employed in, children's homes.

65.—(1) A person who is disqualified (under section 68) from fostering a child privately shall not carry on, or be otherwise concerned in the management of, or have any financial interest in, a children's home unless he has—

(a) disclosed to the responsible authority the fact that he is so disqualified; and

(b) obtained their written consent.

(2) No person shall employ a person who is so disqualified in a children's home unless he has—

(a) disclosed to the responsible authority the fact that that person is so disqualified; and

(b) obtained their written consent.

(3) Where an authority refuse to give their consent under this section, they shall inform the applicant by a written notice which states—

(a) the reason for the refusal;

(b) the applicant's right to appeal against the refusal to a Registered Homes Tribunal under paragraph 8 of Schedule 6; and

(c) the time within which he may do so.

(4) Any person who contravenes subsection (1) or (2) shall be guilty of an offence and liable on summary conviction to imprisonment for a term not exceeding six months or to a fine not exceeding level 5 on the standard scale or to both.

(5) Where a person contravenes subsection (2) he shall not be guilty of an offence if he proves that he did not know, and had no reasonable grounds for believing, that the person whom he was employing was disqualified under section 68.

PART IX

PRIVATE ARRANGEMENTS FOR FOSTERING CHILDREN

66.—(1) In this Part—

(a) "a privately fostered child" means a child who is under the age of sixteen and who is cared for, and provided with accommodation by, someone other than—

(i) a parent of his;

(ii) a person who is not a parent of his but who has parental responsibility for him; or

(iii) a relative of his; and

(b) "to foster a child privately" means to look after the child in circumstances in which he is a privately fostered child as defined by this section.

(2) A child is not a privately fostered child if the person caring for and accommodating him—

(a) has done so for a period of less than 28 days; and

(b) does not intend to do so for any longer period.

(3) Subsection (1) is subject to—

(a) the provisions of section 63; and

(b) the exceptions made by paragraphs 1 to 5 of Schedule 8.

(4) In the case of a child who is disabled, subsection (1)(a) shall have effect as if for "sixteen" there were substituted "eighteen".

(5) Schedule 8 shall have effect for the purposes of supplementing the provision made by this Part.

Privately fostered children.

67.—(1) It shall be the duty of every local authority to satisfy themselves that the welfare of children who are privately fostered within their area is being satisfactorily safeguarded and promoted and to secure that such advice is given to those caring for them as appears to the authority to be needed.

Welfare of privately fostered children.

(2) The Secretary of State may make regulations—

(a) requiring every child who is privately fostered within a local authority's area to be visited by an officer of the authority—

(i) in prescribed circumstances; and

(ii) on specified occasions or within specified periods; and

(b) imposing requirements which are to be met by any local authority, or officer of a local authority, in carrying out functions under this section.

(3) Where any person who is authorised by a local authority to visit privately fostered children has reasonable cause to believe that—

(a) any privately fostered child is being accommodated in premises within the authority's area; or

   (b) it is proposed to accommodate any such child in any such premises,

he may at any reasonable time inspect those premises and any children there.

(4) Any person exercising the power under subsection (3) shall, if so required, produce some duly authenticated document showing his authority to do so.

(5) Where a local authority are not satisfied that the welfare of any child who is privately fostered within their area is being satisfactorily safeguarded or promoted they shall—

   (a) unless they consider that it would not be in the best interests of the child, take such steps as are reasonably practicable to secure that the care and accommodation of the child is undertaken by—

        (i) a parent of his;

        (ii) any person who is not a parent of his but who has parental responsibility for him; or

        (iii) a relative of his; and

   (b) consider the extent to which (if at all) they should exercise any of their functions under this Act with respect to the child.

Persons disqualified from being private foster parents.

68.—(1) Unless he has disclosed the fact to the appropriate local authority and obtained their written consent, a person shall not foster a child privately if he is disqualified from doing so by regulations made by the Secretary of State for the purposes of this section.

(2) The regulations may, in particular, provide for a person to be so disqualified where—

   (a) an order of a kind specified in the regulations has been made at any time with respect to him;

   (b) an order of a kind so specified has been made at any time with respect to any child who has been in his care;

   (c) a requirement of a kind so specified has been imposed at any time with respect to any such child, under or by virtue of any enactment;

   (d) he has been convicted of any offence of a kind so specified, or has been placed on probation or discharged absolutely or conditionally for any such offence;

   (e) a prohibition has been imposed on him at any time under section 69 or under any other specified enactment;

   (f) his rights and powers with respect to a child have at any time been vested in a specified authority under a specified enactment.

(3) Unless he has disclosed the fact to the appropriate local authority and obtained their written consent, a person shall not foster a child privately if—

   (a) he lives in the same household as a person who is himself prevented from fostering a child by subsection (1); or

   (b) he lives in a household at which any such person is employed.

(4) Where an authority refuse to give their consent under this section, they shall inform the applicant by a written notice which states—

- (a) the reason for the refusal;
- (b) the applicant's right under paragraph 8 of Schedule 8 to appeal against the refusal; and
- (c) the time within which he may do so.

(5) In this section—

"the appropriate authority" means the local authority within whose area it is proposed to foster the child in question; and

"enactment" means any enactment having effect, at any time, in any part of the United Kingdom.

69.—(1) This section applies where a person—

Power to prohibit private fostering.

- (a) proposes to foster a child privately; or
- (b) is fostering a child privately.

(2) Where the local authority for the area within which the child is proposed to be, or is being, fostered are of the opinion that—

- (a) he is not a suitable person to foster a child;
- (b) the premises in which the child will be, or is being, accommodated are not suitable; or
- (c) it would be prejudicial to the welfare of the child for him to be, or continue to be, accommodated by that person in those premises,

the authority may impose a prohibition on him under subsection (3).

(3) A prohibition imposed on any person under this subsection may prohibit him from fostering privately—

- (a) any child in any premises within the area of the local authority; or
- (b) any child in premises specified in the prohibition;
- (c) a child identified in the prohibition, in premises specified in the prohibition.

(4) A local authority who have imposed a prohibition on any person under subsection (3) may, if they think fit, cancel the prohibition—

- (a) of their own motion; or
- (b) on an application made by that person,

if they are satisfied that the prohibition is no longer justified.

(5) Where a local authority impose a requirement on any person under paragraph 6 of Schedule 8, they may also impose a prohibition on him under subsection (3).

(6) Any prohibition imposed by virtue of subsection (5) shall not have effect unless—

- (a) the time specified for compliance with the requirement has expired; and
- (b) the requirement has not been complied with.

(7) A prohibition imposed under this section shall be imposed by notice in writing addressed to the person on whom it is imposed and informing him of—

    (a) the reason for imposing the prohibition;

    (b) his right under paragraph 8 of Schedule 8 to appeal against the prohibition; and

    (c) the time within which he may do so.

Offences.

70.—(1) A person shall be guilty of an offence if—

    (a) being required, under any provision made by or under this Part, to give any notice or information—

        (i) he fails without reasonable excuse to give the notice within the time specified in that provision; or

        (ii) he fails without reasonable excuse to give the information within a reasonable time; or

        (iii) he makes, or causes or procures another person to make, any statement in the notice or information which he knows to be false or misleading in a material particular;

    (b) he refuses to allow a privately fostered child to be visited by a duly authorised officer of a local authority;

    (c) he intentionally obstructs another in the exercise of the power conferred by section 67(3);

    (d) he contravenes section 68;

    (e) he fails without reasonable excuse to comply with any requirement imposed by a local authority under this Part;

    (f) he accommodates a privately fostered child in any premises in contravention of a prohibition imposed by a local authority under this Part;

    (g) he knowingly causes to be published, or publishes, an advertisement which he knows contravenes paragraph 10 of Schedule 8.

(2) Where a person contravenes section 68(3), he shall not be guilty of an offence under this section if he proves that he did not know, and had no reasonable ground for believing, that any person to whom section 68(1) applied was living or employed in the premises in question.

(3) A person guilty of an offence under subsection (1)(a) shall be liable on summary conviction to a fine not exceeding level 5 on the standard scale.

(4) A person guilty of an offence under subsection (1)(b), (c) or (g) shall be liable on summary conviction to a fine not exceeding level 3 on the standard scale.

(5) A person guilty of an offence under subsection (1)(d) or (f) shall be liable on summary conviction to imprisonment for a term not exceeding six months, or to a fine not exceeding level 5 on the standard scale, or to both.

(6) A person guilty of an offence under subsection (1)(e) shall be liable on summary conviction to a fine not exceeding level 4 on the standard scale.

(7) If any person who is required, under any provision of this Part, to give a notice fails to give the notice within the time specified in that provision, proceedings for the offence may be brought at any time within six months from the date when evidence of the offence came to the knowledge of the local authority.

(8) Subsection (7) is not affected by anything in section 127(1) of the Magistrates' Courts Act 1980 (time limit for proceedings).   1980 c. 43.

Part X

Child Minding and Day Care for Young Children

71.—(1) Every local authority shall keep a register of—   Registration.

    (a) persons who act as child minders on domestic premises within the authority's area; and

    (b) persons who provide day care for children under the age of eight on premises (other than domestic premises) within that area.

(2) For the purposes of this Part—

    (a) a person acts as a child minder if—

        (i) he looks after one or more children under the age of eight, for reward; and

        (ii) the period, or the total of the periods, which he spends so looking after children in any day exceeds two hours; and

    (b) a person does not provide day care for children unless the period, or the total of the periods, during which children are looked after exceeds two hours in any day.

(3) Where a person provides day care for children under the age of eight on different premises situated within the area of the same local authority, that person shall be separately registered with respect to each of those premises.

(4) A person who—

    (a) is the parent, or a relative, of a child;

    (b) has parental responsibility for a child; or

    (c) is a foster parent of a child,

does not act as a child minder for the purposes of this Part when looking after that child.

(5) Where a person is employed as a nanny for a child, she does not act as a child minder when looking after that child wholly or mainly in the home of the person so employing her.

(6) Where a person is so employed by two different employers, she does not act as a child minder when looking after any of the children concerned wholly or mainly in the home of either of her employers.

(7) A local authority may refuse to register an applicant for registration under subsection (1)(a) if they are satisfied that—

    (a) the applicant; or

(b) any person looking after, or likely to be looking after, any children on any premises on which the applicant is, or is likely to be, child minding,

is not fit to look after children under the age of eight.

(8) A local authority may refuse to register an applicant for registration under subsection (1)(a) if they are satisfied that—

   (a) any person living, or likely to be living, at any premises on which the applicant is, or is likely to be, child minding; or

   (b) any person employed, or likely to be employed, on those premises,

is not fit to be in the proximity of children under the age of eight.

(9) A local authority may refuse to register an applicant for registration under subsection (1)(b) if they are satisfied that any person looking after, or likely to be looking after, any children on the premises to which the application relates is not fit to look after children under the age of eight.

(10) A local authority may refuse to register an applicant for registration under subsection (1)(b) if they are satisfied that—

   (a) any person living, or likely to be living, at the premises to which the application relates; or

   (b) any person employed, or likely to be employed, on those premises,

is not fit to be in the proximity of children under the age of eight.

(11) A local authority may refuse to register an applicant for registration under this section if they are satisfied—

   (a) in the case of an application under subsection (1)(a), that any premises on which the applicant is, or is likely to be, child minding; or

   (b) in the case of an application under subsection (1)(b), that the premises to which the application relates,

are not fit to be used for looking after children under the age of eight, whether because of their condition or the condition of any equipment used on the premises or for any reason connected with their situation, construction or size.

(12) In this section—

   "domestic premises" means any premises which are wholly or mainly used as a private dwelling;

   "premises" includes any vehicle.

(13) For the purposes of this Part a person acts as a nanny for a child if she is employed to look after the child by—

   (a) a parent of the child;

   (b) a person who is not a parent of the child but who has parental responsibility for him; or

   (c) a person who is a relative of the child and who has assumed responsibility for his care.

(14) For the purposes of this section, a person fosters a child if—

   (a) he is a local authority foster parent in relation to the child;

(b) he is a foster parent with whom the child has been placed by a voluntary organisation; or

(c) he fosters the child privately.

(15) Any register kept under this section—

(a) shall be open to inspection by members of the public at all reasonable times; and

(b) may be kept by means of a computer.

(16) Schedule 9 shall have effect for the purpose of making further provision with respect to registration under this section including, in particular, further provision for exemption from the requirement to be registered and provision for disqualification.

72.—(1) Where a local authority register a person under section 71(1)(a), they shall impose such reasonable requirements on him as they consider appropriate in his case.

(2) In imposing requirements on him, the authority shall—

(a) specify the maximum number of children, or the maximum number of children within specified age groups, whom he may look after when acting as a child minder;

(b) require him to secure that any premises on which he so looks after any child, and the equipment used in those premises, are adequately maintained and kept safe;

(c) require him to keep a record of the name and address of—

(i) any child so looked after by him on any premises within the authority's area;

(ii) any person who assists in looking after any such child; and

(iii) any person living, or likely at any time to be living, at those premises;

(d) require him to notify the authority in writing of any change in the persons mentioned in paragraph (c)(ii) and (iii).

(3) The Secretary of State may by regulations make provision as to—

(a) requirements which must be imposed by local authorities under this section in prescribed circumstances;

(b) requirements of such descriptions as may be prescribed which must not be imposed by local authorities under this section.

(4) In determining the maximum number of children to be specified under subsection (2)(a), the authority shall take account of the number of other children who may at any time be on any premises on which the person concerned acts, or is likely to act, as a child minder.

(5) Where, in addition to the requirements mentioned in subsection (2), a local authority impose other requirements, those other requirements must not be incompatible with any of the subsection (2) requirements.

(6) A local authority may at any time vary any requirement imposed under this section, impose any additional requirement or remove any requirement.

PART X

Requirements to be complied with by persons providing day care for young children.

73.—(1) Where a local authority register a person under section 71(1)(b) they shall impose such reasonable requirements on him as they consider appropriate in his case.

(2) Where a person is registered under section 71(1)(b) with respect to different premises within the area of the same authority, this section applies separately in relation to each registration.

(3) In imposing requirements on him, the authority shall—

   (a) specify the maximum number of children, or the maximum number of children within specified age groups, who may be looked after on the premises;

   (b) require him to secure that the premises, and the equipment used in them, are adequately maintained and kept safe;

   (c) require him to notify the authority of any change in the facilities which he provides or in the period during which he provides them;

   (d) specify the number of persons required to assist in looking after children on the premises;

   (e) require him to keep a record of the name and address of—

      (i) any child looked after on the registered premises;

      (ii) any person who assists in looking after any such child; and

      (iii) any person who lives, or is likely at any time to be living, at those premises;

   (f) require him to notify the authority of any change in the persons mentioned in paragraph (e)(ii) and (iii).

(4) The Secretary of State may by regulations make provision as to—

   (a) requirements which must be imposed by local authorities under this section in prescribed circumstances;

   (b) requirements of such descriptions as may be prescribed which must not be imposed by local authorities under this section.

(5) In subsection (3), references to children looked after are to children looked after in accordance with the provision of day care made by the registered person.

(6) In determining the maximum number of children to be specified under subsection (3)(a), the authority shall take account of the number of other children who may at any time be on the premises.

(7) Where, in addition to the requirements mentioned in subsection (3), a local authority impose other requirements, those other requirements must not be incompatible with any of the subsection (3) requirements.

(8) A local authority may at any time vary any requirement imposed under this section, impose any additional requirement or remove any requirement.

74.—(1) A local authority may at any time cancel the registration of any person under section 71(1)(a) if—

    (a) it appears to them that the circumstances of the case are such that they would be justified in refusing to register that person as a child minder;

    (b) the care provided by that person when looking after any child as a child minder is, in the opinion of the authority, seriously inadequate having regard to the needs of that child; or

    (c) that person has—

        (i) contravened, or failed to comply with, any requirement imposed on him under section 72; or

        (ii) failed to pay any annual fee under paragraph 7 of Schedule 9 within the prescribed time.

(2) A local authority may at any time cancel the registration of any person under section 71(1)(b) with respect to particular premises if—

    (a) it appears to them that the circumstances of the case are such that they would be justified in refusing to register that person with respect to those premises;

    (b) the day care provided by that person on those premises is, in the opinion of the authority, seriously inadequate having regard to the needs of the children concerned; or

    (c) that person has—

        (i) contravened, or failed to comply with, any requirement imposed on him under section 73; or

        (ii) failed to pay any annual fee under paragraph 7 of Schedule 9 within the prescribed time.

(3) A local authority may at any time cancel all registrations of any person under section 71(1)(b) if it appears to them that the circumstances of the case are such that they would be justified in refusing to register that person with respect to any premises.

(4) Where a requirement to carry out repairs or make alterations or additions has been imposed on a registered person under section 72 or 73, his registration shall not be cancelled on the ground that the premises are not fit to be used for looking after children if—

    (a) the time set for complying with the requirements has not expired, and

    (b) it is shown that the condition of the premises is due to the repairs not having been carried out or the alterations or additions not having been made.

(5) Any cancellation under this section must be in writing.

(6) In considering the needs of any child for the purposes of subsection (1)(b) or (2)(b), a local authority shall, in particular, have regard to the child's religious persuasion, racial origin and cultural and linguistic background.

75.—(1) If—

    (a) a local authority apply to the court for an order—

        (i) cancelling a registered person's registration;

(ii) varying any requirement imposed on a registered person under section 72 or 73; or

(iii) removing a requirement or imposing an additional requirement on such a person; and

(b) it appears to the court that a child who is being, or may be, looked after by that person, or (as the case may be) in accordance with the provision for day care made by that person, is suffering, or is likely to suffer, significant harm,

the court may make the order.

(2) Any such cancellation, variation, removal or imposition shall have effect from the date on which the order is made.

(3) An application under subsection (1) may be made *ex parte* and shall be supported by a written statement of the authority's reasons for making it.

(4) Where an order is made under this section, the authority shall serve on the registered person, as soon as is reasonably practicable after the making of the order—

(a) notice of the order and of its terms; and

(b) a copy of the statement of the authority's reasons which supported their application for the order.

(5) Where the court imposes or varies any requirement under subsection (1), the requirement, or the requirement as varied, shall be treated for all purposes, other than those of section 77, as if it had been imposed under section 72 or (as the case may be) 73 by the authority concerned.

Inspection.

76.—(1) Any person authorised to do so by a local authority may at any reasonable time enter—

(a) any domestic premises within the authority's area on which child minding is at any time carried on; or

(b) any premises within their area on which day care for children under the age of eight is at any time provided.

(2) Where a local authority have reasonable cause to believe that a child is being looked after on any premises within their area in contravention of this Part, any person authorised to do so by the authority may enter those premises at any reasonable time.

(3) Any person entering premises under this section may inspect—

(a) the premises;

(b) any children being looked after on the premises;

(c) the arrangements made for their welfare; and

(d) any records relating to them which are kept as a result of this Part.

(4) Every local authority shall exercise their power to inspect the premises mentioned in subsection (1) at least once every year.

(5) Any person inspecting any records under this section—

(a) shall be entitled at any reasonable time to have access to, and inspect and check the operation of, any computer and any associated apparatus or material which is, or has been, in use in connection with the records in question; and

(b) may require—

(i) the person by whom or on whose behalf the computer is or has been so used; or

(ii) any person having charge of, or otherwise concerned with the operation of, the computer, apparatus or material,

to afford him such reasonable assistance as he may require.

(6) A person exercising any power conferred by this section shall, if so required, produce some duly authenticated document showing his authority to do so.

(7) Any person who intentionally obstructs another in the exercise of any such power shall be guilty of an offence and liable on summary conviction to a fine not exceeding level 3 on the standard scale.

77.—(1) Not less than 14 days before— Appeals.

(a) refusing an application for registration under section 71;

(b) cancelling any such registration;

(c) refusing consent under paragraph 2 of Schedule 9;

(d) imposing, removing or varying any requirement under section 72 or 73; or

(e) refusing to grant any application for the variation or removal of any such requirement,

the authority concerned shall send to the applicant, or (as the case may be) registered person, notice in writing of their intention to take the step in question ("the step").

(2) Every such notice shall—

(a) give the authority's reasons for proposing to take the step; and

(b) inform the person concerned of his rights under this section.

(3) Where the recipient of such a notice informs the authority in writing of his desire to object to the step being taken, the authority shall afford him an opportunity to do so.

(4) Any objection made under subsection (3) may be made in person or by a representative.

(5) If the authority, after giving the person concerned an opportunity to object to the step being taken, decide nevertheless to take it they shall send him written notice of their decision.

(6) A person aggrieved by the taking of any step mentioned in subsection (1) may appeal against it to the court.

(7) Where the court imposes or varies any requirement under subsection (8) or (9) the requirement, or the requirement as varied, shall be treated for all purposes (other than this section) as if it had been imposed by the authority concerned.

(8) Where the court allows an appeal against the refusal or cancellation of any registration under section 71 it may impose requirements under section 72 or (as the case may be) 73.

(9) Where the court allows an appeal against such a requirement it may, instead of cancelling the requirement, vary it.

(10) In Scotland, an appeal under subsection (6) shall be by summary application to the sheriff and shall be brought within 21 days from the date of the step to which the appeal relates.

(11) A step of a kind mentioned in subsection (1)(b) or (d) shall not take effect until the expiry of the time within which an appeal may be brought under this section or, where such an appeal is brought, before its determination.

Offences.

78.—(1) No person shall provide day care for children under the age of eight on any premises within the area of a local authority unless he is registered by the authority under section 71(1)(b) with respect to those premises.

(2) If any person contravenes subsection (1) without reasonable excuse, he shall be guilty of an offence.

(3) No person shall act as a child minder on domestic premises within the area of a local authority unless he is registered by the authority under section 71(1)(a).

(4) Where it appears to a local authority that a person has contravened subsection (3), they may serve a notice ("an enforcement notice") on him.

(5) An enforcement notice shall have effect for a period of one year beginning with the date on which it is served.

(6) If a person with respect to whom an enforcement notice is in force contravenes subsection (3) without reasonable excuse he shall be guilty of an offence.

(7) Subsection (6) applies whether or not the subsequent contravention occurs within the area of the authority who served the enforcement notice.

(8) Any person who without reasonable excuse contravenes, or otherwise fails to comply with, any requirement imposed on him under section 72 or 73 shall be guilty of an offence.

(9) If any person—

(a) acts as a child minder on domestic premises at any time when he is disqualified by regulations made under paragraph 2 of Schedule 9; or

(b) contravenes any of sub-paragraphs (3) to (5) of paragraph 2,

he shall be guilty of an offence.

(10) Where a person contravenes sub-paragraph (3) of paragraph 2 he shall not be guilty of an offence under this section if he proves that he did not know, and had no reasonable grounds for believing, that the person in question was living or employed in the household.

(11) Where a person contravenes sub-paragraph (5) of paragraph 2 he shall not be guilty of an offence under this section if he proves that he did not know, and had no reasonable grounds for believing, that the person whom he was employing was disqualified.

(12) A person guilty of an offence under this section shall be liable on summary conviction—

(a) in the case of an offence under subsection (8), to a fine not exceeding level 4 on the standard scale;

(b) in the case of an offence under subsection (9), to imprisonment for a term not exceeding six months, or to a fine not exceeding level 5 on the standard scale, or to both; and

(c) in the case of any other offence, to a fine not exceeding level 5 on the standard scale.

79. In the application to Scotland of this Part—

Application of this Part to Scotland.

(a) "the court" means the sheriff;

(b) "day care" means any form of care or of activity supervised by a responsible person provided for children during the day (whether or not it is provided on a regular basis);

(c) "education authority" has the same meaning as in the Education (Scotland) Act 1980;

1980 c. 44.

(d) "local authority foster parent" means a foster parent with whom a child is placed by a local authority;

(e) for references to a person having parental responsibility for a child there shall be substituted references to a person in whom parental rights and duties relating to the child are vested; and

(f) for references to fostering a child privately there shall be substituted references to maintaining a foster child within the meaning of the Foster Children (Scotland) Act 1984.

1984 c. 56.

PART XI

SECRETARY OF STATE'S SUPERVISORY FUNCTIONS AND RESPONSIBILITIES

80.—(1) The Secretary of State may cause to be inspected from time to time any—

Inspection of children's homes etc. by persons authorised by Secretary of State.

(a) children's home;

(b) premises in which a child who is being looked after by a local authority is living;

(c) premises in which a child who is being accommodated by or on behalf of a local education authority or voluntary organisation is living;

(d) premises in which a child who is being accommodated by or on behalf of a health authority is living;

(e) premises in which a child is living with a person with whom he has been placed by an adoption agency;

(f) premises in which a child who is a protected child is, or will be, living;

(g) premises in which a privately fostered child, or child who is treated as a foster child by virtue of paragraph 9 of Schedule 8, is living or in which it is proposed that he will live;

(h) premises on which any person is acting as a child minder;

(i) premises with respect to which a person is registered under section 71(1)(b);

(j) residential care home, nursing home or mental nursing home required to be registered under the Registered Homes Act 1984 and used to accommodate children;

1984 c. 23.

(k) premises which are provided by a local authority and in which any service is provided by that authority under Part III;

(l) independent school providing accommodation for any child;

(2) An inspection under this section shall be conducted by a person authorised to do so by the Secretary of State.

(3) An officer of a local authority shall not be so authorised except with the consent of that authority.

(4) The Secretary of State may require any person of a kind mentioned in subsection (5) to furnish him with such information, or allow him to inspect such records (in whatever form they are held), relating to—

(a) any premises to which subsection (1) or, in relation to Scotland, subsection (1)(h) or (i) applies;

(b) any child who is living in any such premises;

(c) the discharge by the Secretary of State of any of his functions under this Act; or

(d) the discharge by any local authority of any of their functions under this Act,

as the Secretary of State may at any time direct.

(5) The persons are any—

(a) local authority;

(b) voluntary organisation;

(c) person carrying on a children's home;

(d) proprietor of an independent school;

(e) person fostering any privately fostered child or providing accommodation for a child on behalf of a local authority, local education authority, health authority or voluntary organisation;

(f) local education authority providing accommodation for any child;

(g) person employed in a teaching or administrative capacity at any educational establishment (whether or not maintained by a local education authority) at which a child is accommodated on behalf of a local authority or local education authority;

(h) person who is the occupier of any premises in which any person acts as a child minder (within the meaning of Part X) or provides day care for young children (within the meaning of that Part);

(i) person carrying on any home of a kind mentioned in subsection (1)(j).

(6) Any person inspecting any home or other premises under this section may—

(a) inspect the children there; and

(b) make such examination into the state and management of the home or premises and the treatment of the children there as he thinks fit.

(7) Any person authorised by the Secretary of State to exercise the power to inspect records conferred by subsection (4)—

    (a) shall be entitled at any reasonable time to have access to, and inspect and check the operation of, any computer and any associated apparatus or material which is or has been in use in connection with the records in question; and

    (b) may require—

        (i) the person by whom or on whose behalf the computer is or has been so used; or

        (ii) any person having charge of, or otherwise concerned with the operation of, the computer, apparatus or material,

    to afford him such reasonable assistance as he may require.

(8) A person authorised to inspect any premises under this section shall have a right to enter the premises for that purpose, and for any purpose specified in subsection (4), at any reasonable time.

(9) Any person exercising that power shall, if so required, produce some duly authenticated document showing his authority to do so.

(10) Any person who intentionally obstructs another in the exercise of that power shall be guilty of an offence and liable on summary conviction to a fine not exceeding level 3 on the standard scale.

(11) The Secretary of State may by order provide for subsections (1), (4) and (6) not to apply in relation to such homes, or other premises, as may be specified in the order.

(12) Without prejudice to section 104, any such order may make different provision with respect to each of those subsections.

81.—(1) The Secretary of State may cause an inquiry to be held into any matter connected with— *Inquiries.*

    (a) the functions of the social services committee of a local authority, in so far as those functions relate to children;

    (b) the functions of an adoption agency;

    (c) the functions of a voluntary organisation, in so far as those functions relate to children;

    (d) a registered children's home or voluntary home;

    (e) a residential care home, nursing home or mental nursing home, so far as it provides accommodation for children;

    (f) a home provided by the Secretary of State under section 82(5);

    (g) the detention of a child under section 53 of the Children and Young Persons Act 1933. *1933 c. 12.*

(2) Before an inquiry is begun, the Secretary of State may direct that it shall be held in private.

(3) Where no direction has been given, the person holding the inquiry may if he thinks fit hold it, or any part of it, in private.

(4) Subsections (2) to (5) of section 250 of the Local Government Act 1972 (powers in relation to local inquiries) shall apply in relation to an inquiry under this section as they apply in relation to a local inquiry under that section. *1972 c. 70.*

(5) In this section "functions" includes powers and duties which a person has otherwise than by virtue of any enactment.

82.—(1) The Secretary of State may (with the consent of the Treasury) defray or contribute towards—

    (a) any fees or expenses incurred by any person undergoing approved child care training;

    (b) any fees charged, or expenses incurred, by any person providing approved child care training or preparing material for use in connection with such training; or

    (c) the cost of maintaining any person undergoing such training.

(2) The Secretary of State may make grants to local authorities in respect of expenditure incurred by them in providing secure accommodation in community homes other than assisted community homes.

(3) Where—

    (a) a grant has been made under subsection (2) with respect to any secure accommodation; but

    (b) the grant is not used for the purpose for which it was made or the accommodation is not used as, or ceases to be used as, secure accommodation,

the Secretary of State may (with the consent of the Treasury) require the authority concerned to repay the grant, in whole or in part.

(4) The Secretary of State may make grants to voluntary organisations towards—

    (a) expenditure incurred by them in connection with the establishment, maintenance or improvement of voluntary homes which, at the time when the expenditure was incurred—

        (i) were assisted community homes; or

        (ii) were designated as such; or

    (b) expenses incurred in respect of the borrowing of money to defray any such expenditure.

(5) The Secretary of State may arrange for the provision, equipment and maintenance of homes for the accommodation of children who are in need of particular facilities and services which—

    (a) are or will be provided in those homes; and

    (b) in the opinion of the Secretary of State, are unlikely to be readily available in community homes.

(6) In this Part—

    "child care training" means training undergone by any person with a view to, or in the course of—

        (a) his employment for the purposes of any of the functions mentioned in section 83(9) or in connection with the adoption of children or with the accommodation of children in a residential care home, nursing home or mental nursing home; or

        (b) his employment by a voluntary organisation for similar purposes;

"approved child care training" means child care training which is approved by the Secretary of State; and

"secure accommodation" means accommodation provided for the purpose of restricting the liberty of children.

(7) Any grant made under this section shall be of such amount, and shall be subject to such conditions, as the Secretary of State may (with the consent of the Treasury) determine.

83.—(1) The Secretary of State may conduct, or assist other persons in conducting, research into any matter connected with—

Research and returns of information.

(a) his functions, or the functions of local authorities, under the enactments mentioned in subsection (9);

(b) the adoption of children; or

(c) the accommodation of children in a residential care home, nursing home or mental nursing home.

(2) Any local authority may conduct, or assist other persons in conducting, research into any matter connected with—

(a) their functions under the enactments mentioned in subsection (9);

(b) the adoption of children; or

(c) the accommodation of children in a residential care home, nursing home or mental nursing home.

(3) Every local authority shall, at such times and in such form as the Secretary of State may direct, transmit to him such particulars as he may require with respect to—

(a) the performance by the local authority of all or any of their functions—

(i) under the enactments mentioned in subsection (9); or

(ii) in connection with the accommodation of children in a residential care home, nursing home or mental nursing home; and

(b) the children in relation to whom the authority have exercised those functions.

(4) Every voluntary organisation shall, at such times and in such form as the Secretary of State may direct, transmit to him such particulars as he may require with respect to children accommodated by them or on their behalf.

(5) The Secretary of State may direct the clerk of each magistrates' court to which the direction is expressed to relate to transmit—

(a) to such person as may be specified in the direction; and

(b) at such times and in such form as he may direct,

such particulars as he may require with respect to proceedings of the court which relate to children.

(6) The Secretary of State shall in each year lay before Parliament a consolidated and classified abstract of the information transmitted to him under subsections (3) to (5).

PART XI

(7) The Secretary of State may institute research designed to provide information on which requests for information under this section may be based.

(8) The Secretary of State shall keep under review the adequacy of the provision of child care training and for that purpose shall receive and consider any information from or representations made by—

(a) the Central Council for Education and Training in Social Work;

(b) such representatives of local authorities as appear to him to be appropriate; or

(c) such other persons or organisations as appear to him to be appropriate,

concerning the provision of such training.

(9) The enactments are—

(a) this Act;

(b) the Children and Young Persons Acts 1933 to 1969;

1983 c. 20.

(c) section 116 of the Mental Health Act 1983 (so far as it relates to children looked after by local authorities);

1984 c. 36.

(d) section 10 of the Mental Health (Scotland) Act 1984 (so far as it relates to children for whom local authorities have responsibility).

Local authority failure to comply with statutory duty: default power of Secretary of State.

84.—(1) If the Secretary of State is satisfied that any local authority has failed, without reasonable excuse, to comply with any of the duties imposed on them by or under this Act he may make an order declaring that authority to be in default with respect to that duty.

(2) An order under subsection (1) shall give the Secretary of State's reasons for making it.

(3) An order under subsection (1) may contain such directions for the purpose of ensuring that the duty is complied with, within such period as may be specified in the order, as appear to the Secretary of State to be necessary.

(4) Any such direction shall, on the application of the Secretary of State, be enforceable by mandamus.

PART XII

MISCELLANEOUS AND GENERAL

Notification of children accommodated in certain establishments

Children accommodated by health authorities and local education authorities.

85.—(1) Where a child is provided with accommodation by any health authority or local education authority ("the accommodating authority")—

(a) for a consecutive period of at least three months; or

(b) with the intention, on the part of that authority, of accommodating him for such a period,

the accommodating authority shall notify the responsible authority.

(2) Where subsection (1) applies with respect to a child, the accommodating authority shall also notify the responsible authority when they cease to accommodate the child.

(3) In this section "the responsible authority" means—

(a) the local authority appearing to the accommodating authority to be the authority within whose area the child was ordinarily resident immediately before being accommodated; or

(b) where it appears to the accommodating authority that a child was not ordinarily resident within the area of any local authority, the local authority within whose area the accommodation is situated.

(4) Where a local authority have been notified under this section, they shall—

(a) take such steps as are reasonably practicable to enable them to determine whether the child's welfare is adequately safeguarded and promoted while he is accommodated by the accommodating authority; and

(b) consider the extent to which (if at all) they should exercise any of their functions under this Act with respect to the child.

86.—(1) Where a child is provided with accommodation in any residential care home, nursing home or mental nursing home—

(a) for a consecutive period of at least three months; or

(b) with the intention, on the part of the person taking the decision to accommodate him, of accommodating him for such period,

the person carrying on the home shall notify the local authority within whose area the home is carried on.

Children accommodated in residential care, nursing or mental nursing homes.

(2) Where subsection (1) applies with respect to a child, the person carrying on the home shall also notify that authority when he ceases to accommodate the child in the home.

(3) Where a local authority have been notified under this section, they shall—

(a) take such steps as are reasonably practicable to enable them to determine whether the child's welfare is adequately safeguarded and promoted while he is accommodated in the home; and

(b) consider the extent to which (if at all) they should exercise any of their functions under this Act with respect to the child.

(4) If the person carrying on any home fails, without reasonable excuse, to comply with this section he shall be guilty of an offence.

(5) A person authorised by a local authority may enter any residential care home, nursing home or mental nursing home within the authority's area for the purpose of establishing whether the requirements of this section have been complied with.

(6) Any person who intentionally obstructs another in the exercise of the power of entry shall be guilty of an offence.

(7) Any person exercising the power of entry shall, if so required, produce some duly authenticated document showing his authority to do so.

(8) Any person committing an offence under this section shall be liable on summary conviction to a fine not exceeding level 3 on the standard scale.

Welfare of children accommodated in independent schools.

87.—(1) It shall be the duty of—

(a) the proprietor of any independent school which provides accommodation for any child; and

(b) any person who is not the proprietor of such a school but who is responsible for conducting it,

to safeguard and promote the child's welfare.

(2) Subsection (1) does not apply in relation to a school which is a children's home or a residential care home.

(3) Where accommodation is provided for a child by an independent school within the area of a local authority, the authority shall take such steps as are reasonably practicable to enable them to determine whether the child's welfare is adequately safeguarded and promoted while he is accommodated by the school.

(4) Where a local authority are of the opinion that there has been a failure to comply with subsection (1) in relation to a child provided with accommodation by a school within their area, they shall notify the Secretary of State.

(5) Any person authorised by a local authority may, for the purpose of enabling the authority to discharge their duty under this section, enter at any reasonable time any independent school within their area which provides accommodation for any child.

(6) Any person entering an independent school in exercise of the power conferred by subsection (5) may carry out such inspection of premises, children and records as is prescribed by regulations made by the Secretary of State for the purposes of this section.

(7) Any person exercising that power shall, if asked to do so, produce some duly authenticated document showing his authority to do so.

(8) Any person authorised by the regulations to inspect records—

(a) shall be entitled at any reasonable time to have access to, and inspect and check the operation of, any computer and any associated apparatus or material which is or has been in use in connection with the records in question; and

(b) may require—

(i) the person by whom or on whose behalf the computer is or has been so used; or

(ii) any person having charge of, or otherwise concerned with the operation of, the computer, apparatus or material,

to afford him such assistance as he may reasonably require.

(9) Any person who intentionally obstructs another in the exercise of any power conferred by this section or the regulations shall be guilty of an offence and liable on summary conviction to a fine not exceeding level 3 on the standard scale.

(10) In this section "proprietor" has the same meaning as in the Education Act 1944.

1944 c. 31.

Adoption

PART XII

Amendments of
adoption
legislation.
1976 c. 36.
1978 c. 28.

88.—(1) The Adoption Act 1976 shall have effect subject to the amendments made by Part I of Schedule 10.

(2) The Adoption (Scotland) Act 1978 shall have effect subject to the amendments made by Part II of Schedule 10.

Paternity tests

89. In section 20 of the Family Law Reform Act 1969 (power of court to require use of tests to determine paternity), the following subsections shall be inserted after subsection (1)—

Tests to establish
paternity.
1969 c. 46.

"(1A) Where—

(a) an application is made for a direction under this section; and

(b) the person whose paternity is in issue is under the age of eighteen when the application is made,

the application shall specify who is to carry out the tests.

(1B) In the case of a direction made on an application to which subsection (1A) applies the court shall—

(a) specify, as the person who is to carry out the tests, the person specified in the application; or

(b) where the court considers that it would be inappropriate to specify that person (whether because to specify him would be incompatible with any provision made by or under regulations made under section 22 of this Act or for any other reason), decline to give the direction applied for."

Criminal care and supervision orders

90.—(1) The power of a court to make an order under subsection (2) of section 1 of the Children and Young Persons Act 1969 (care proceedings in juvenile courts) where it is of the opinion that the condition mentioned in paragraph (f) of that subsection ("the offence condition") is satisfied is hereby abolished.

Care and
supervision
orders in criminal
proceedings.
1969 c. 54.

(2) The powers of the court to make care orders—

(a) under section 7(7)(a) of the Children and Young Persons Act 1969 (alteration in treatment of young offenders etc.); and

(b) under section 15(1) of that Act, on discharging a supervision order made under section 7(7)(b) of that Act,

are hereby abolished.

(3) The powers given by that Act to include requirements in supervision orders shall have effect subject to amendments made by Schedule 12.

Effect and duration of orders etc.

91.—(1) The making of a residence order with respect to a child who is the subject of a care order discharges the care order.

Effect and
duration of orders
etc.

(2) The making of a care order with respect to a child who is the subject of any section 8 order discharges that order.

(3) The making of a care order with respect to a child who is the subject of a supervision order discharges that other order.

(4) The making of a care order with respect to a child who is a ward of court brings that wardship to an end.

(5) The making of a care order with respect to a child who is the subject of a school attendance order made under section 37 of the Education Act 1944 discharges the school attendance order.

(6) Where an emergency protection order is made with respect to a child who is in care, the care order shall have effect subject to the emergency protection order.

(7) Any order made under section 4(1) or 5(1) shall continue in force until the child reaches the age of eighteen, unless it is brought to an end earlier.

(8) Any—

(a) agreement under section 4; or

(b) appointment under section 5(3) or (4),

shall continue in force until the child reaches the age of eighteen, unless it is brought to an end earlier.

(9) An order under Schedule 1 has effect as specified in that Schedule.

(10) A section 8 order shall, if it would otherwise still be in force, cease to have effect when the child reaches the age of sixteen, unless it is to have effect beyond that age by virtue of section 9(6).

(11) Where a section 8 order has effect with respect to a child who has reached the age of sixteen, it shall, if it would otherwise still be in force, cease to have effect when he reaches the age of eighteen.

(12) Any care order, other than an interim care order, shall continue in force until the child reaches the age of eighteen, unless it is brought to an end earlier.

(13) Any order made under any other provision of this Act in relation to a child shall, if it would otherwise still be in force, cease to have effect when he reaches the age of eighteen.

(14) On disposing of any application for an order under this Act, the court may (whether or not it makes any other order in response to the application) order that no application for an order under this Act of any specified kind may be made with respect to the child concerned by any person named in the order without leave of the court.

(15) Where an application ("the previous application") has been made for—

(a) the discharge of a care order;

(b) the discharge of a supervision order;

(c) the discharge of an education supervision order;

(d) the substitution of a supervision order for a care order; or

(e) a child assessment order,

no further application of a kind mentioned in paragraphs (a) to (e) may be made with respect to the child concerned, without leave of the court, unless the period between the disposal of the previous application and the making of the further application exceeds six months.

(16) Subsection (15) does not apply to applications made in relation to interim orders.

(17) Where—

    (a) a person has made an application for an order under section 34;

    (b) the application has been refused; and

    (c) a period of less than six months has elapsed since the refusal,

that person may not make a further application for such an order with respect to the same child, unless he has obtained the leave of the court.

Jurisdiction and procedure etc.

92.—(1) The name "domestic proceedings", given to certain proceedings in magistrates' courts, is hereby changed to "family proceedings" and the names "domestic court" and "domestic court panel" are hereby changed to "family proceedings court" and "family panel", respectively.

Jurisdiction of courts.

(2) Proceedings under this Act shall be treated as family proceedings in relation to magistrates' courts.

(3) Subsection (2) is subject to the provisions of section 65(1) and (2) of the Magistrates' Courts Act 1980 (proceedings which may be treated as not being family proceedings), as amended by this Act.

1980 c. 43.

(4) A magistrates' court shall not be competent to entertain any application, or make any order, involving the administration or application of—

    (a) any property belonging to or held in trust for a child; or

    (b) the income of any such property.

(5) The powers of a magistrates' court under section 63(2) of the Act of 1980 to suspend or rescind orders shall not apply in relation to any order made under this Act.

(6) Part I of Schedule 11 makes provision, including provision for the Lord Chancellor to make orders, with respect to the jurisdiction of courts and justices of the peace in relation to—

    (a) proceedings under this Act; and

    (b) proceedings under certain other enactments.

(7) For the purposes of this Act "the court" means the High Court, a county court or a magistrates' court.

(8) Subsection (7) is subject to the provision made by or under Part I of Schedule 11 and to any express provision as to the jurisdiction of any court made by any other provision of this Act.

(9) The Lord Chancellor may by order make provision for the principal registry of the Family Division of the High Court to be treated as if it were a county court for such purposes of this Act, or of any provision made under this Act, as may be specified in the order.

(10) Any order under subsection (9) may make such provision as the Lord Chancellor thinks expedient for the purpose of applying (with or without modifications) provisions which apply in relation to the procedure in county courts to the principal registry when it acts as if it were a county court.

(11) Part II of Schedule 11 makes amendments consequential on this section.

93.—(1) An authority having power to make rules of court may make such provision for giving effect to—

 (a) this Act;

 (b) the provisions of any statutory instrument made under this Act; or

 (c) any amendment made by this Act in any other enactment,

as appears to that authority to be necessary or expedient.

(2) The rules may, in particular, make provision—

 (a) with respect to the procedure to be followed in any relevant proceedings (including the manner in which any application is to be made or other proceedings commenced);

 (b) as to the persons entitled to participate in any relevant proceedings, whether as parties to the proceedings or by being given the opportunity to make representations to the court;

 (c) with respect to the documents and information to be furnished, and notices to be given, in connection with any relevant proceedings;

 (d) applying (with or without modification) enactments which govern the procedure to be followed with respect to proceedings brought on a complaint made to a magistrates' court to relevant proceedings in such a court brought otherwise than on a complaint;

 (e) with respect to preliminary hearings;

 (f) for the service outside the United Kingdom, in such circumstances and in such manner as may be prescribed, of any notice of proceedings in a magistrates' court;

 (g) for the exercise by magistrates' courts, in such circumstances as may be prescribed, of such powers as may be prescribed (even though a party to the proceedings in question is outside England and Wales);

 (h) enabling the court, in such circumstances as may be prescribed, to proceed on any application even though the respondent has not been given notice of the proceedings;

 (i) authorising a single justice to discharge the functions of a magistrates' court with respect to such relevant proceedings as may be prescribed;

 (j) authorising a magistrates' court to order any of the parties to such relevant proceedings as may be prescribed, in such circumstances as may be prescribed, to pay the whole or part of the costs of all or any of the other parties.

(3) In subsection (2)—

"notice of proceedings" means a summons or such other notice of proceedings as is required; and "given", in relation to a summons, means "served";

"prescribed" means prescribed by the rules; and

"relevant proceedings" means any application made, or proceedings brought, under any of the provisions mentioned in paragraphs (a) to (c) of subsection (1) and any part of such proceedings.

(4) This section and any other power in this Act to make rules of court are not to be taken as in any way limiting any other power of the authority in question to make rules of court.

(5) When making any rules under this section an authority shall be subject to the same requirements as to consultation (if any) as apply when the authority makes rules under its general rule making power.

94.—(1) An appeal shall lie to the High Court against—

(a) the making by a magistrates' court of any order under this Act; or

(b) any refusal by a magistrates' court to make such an order.

(2) Where a magistrates' court has power, in relation to any proceedings under this Act, to decline jurisdiction because it considers that the case can more conveniently be dealt with by another court, no appeal shall lie against any exercise by that magistrates' court of that power.

(3) Subsection (1) does not apply in relation to an interim order for periodical payments made under Schedule 1.

(4) On an appeal under this section, the High Court may make such orders as may be necessary to give effect to its determination of the appeal.

(5) Where an order is made under subsection (4) the High Court may also make such incidental or consequential orders as appear to it to be just.

(6) Where an appeal from a magistrates' court relates to an order for the making of periodical payments, the High Court may order that its determination of the appeal shall have effect from such date as it thinks fit to specify in the order.

(7) The date so specified must not be earlier than the earliest date allowed in accordance with rules of court made for the purposes of this section.

(8) Where, on an appeal under this section in respect of an order requiring a person to make periodical payments, the High Court reduces the amount of those payments or discharges the order—

(a) it may order the person entitled to the payments to pay to the person making them such sum in respect of payments already made as the High Court thinks fit; and

(b) if any arrears are due under the order for periodical payments, it may remit payment of the whole, or part, of those arrears.

(9) Any order of the High Court made on an appeal under this section (other than one directing that an application be re-heard by a magistrates' court) shall, for the purposes—

(a) of the enforcement of the order; and

(b) of any power to vary, revive or discharge orders,

be treated as if it were an order of the magistrates' court from which the appeal was brought and not an order of the High Court.

(10) The Lord Chancellor may by order make provision as to the circumstances in which appeals may be made against decisions taken by courts on questions arising in connection with the transfer, or proposed transfer, of proceedings by virtue of any order under paragraph 2 of Schedule 11.

(11) Except to the extent provided for in any order made under subsection (10), no appeal may be made against any decision of a kind mentioned in that subsection.

Attendance of child at hearing under Part IV or V.

95.—(1) In any proceedings in which a court is hearing an application for an order under Part IV or V, or is considering whether to make any such order, the court may order the child concerned to attend such stage or stages of the proceedings as may be specified in the order.

(2) The power conferred by subsection (1) shall be exercised in accordance with rules of court.

(3) Subsections (4) to (6) apply where—

(a) an order under subsection (1) has not been complied with; or

(b) the court has reasonable cause to believe that it will not be complied with.

(4) The court may make an order authorising a constable, or such person as may be specified in the order—

(a) to take charge of the child and to bring him to the court; and

(b) to enter and search any premises specified in the order if he has reasonable cause to believe that the child may be found on the premises.

(5) The court may order any person who is in a position to do so to bring the child to the court.

(6) Where the court has reason to believe that a person has information about the whereabouts of the child it may order him to disclose it to the court.

Evidence given by, or with respect to, children.

96.—(1) Subsection (2) applies where a child who is called as a witness in any civil proceedings does not, in the opinion of the court, understand the nature of an oath.

(2) The child's evidence may be heard by the court if, in its opinion—

(a) he understands that it is his duty to speak the truth; and

(b) he has sufficient understanding to justify his evidence being heard.

(3) The Lord Chancellor may by order make provision for the admissibility of evidence which would otherwise be inadmissible under any rule of law relating to hearsay.

(4) An order under subsection (3) may only be made with respect to—

(a) civil proceedings in general or such civil proceedings, or class of civil proceedings, as may be prescribed; and

(b) evidence in connection with the upbringing, maintenance or welfare of a child.

(5) An order under subsection (3)—

    (a) may, in particular, provide for the admissibility of statements which are made orally or in a prescribed form or which are recorded by any prescribed method of recording;

    (b) may make different provision for different purposes and in relation to different descriptions of court; and

    (c) may make such amendments and repeals in any enactment relating to evidence (other than in this Act) as the Lord Chancellor considers necessary or expedient in consequence of the provision made by the order.

(6) Subsection (5)(b) is without prejudice to section 104(4).

(7) In this section—

    "civil proceedings" and "court" have the same meaning as they have in the Civil Evidence Act 1968 by virtue of section 18 of that Act; 1968 c. 64. and

    "prescribed" means prescribed by an order under subsection (3).

97.—(1) Rules made under section 144 of the Magistrates' Courts Act 1980 may make provision for a magistrates' court to sit in private in proceedings in which any powers under this Act may be exercised by the court with respect to any child. *Privacy for children involved in certain proceedings. 1980 c. 43.*

(2) No person shall publish any material which is intended, or likely, to identify—

    (a) any child as being involved in any proceedings before a magistrates' court in which any power under this Act may be exercised by the court with respect to that or any other child; or

    (b) an address or school as being that of a child involved in any such proceedings.

(3) In any proceedings for an offence under this section it shall be a defence for the accused to prove that he did not know, and had no reason to suspect, that the published material was intended, or likely, to identify the child.

(4) The court or the Secretary of State may, if satisfied that the welfare of the child requires it, by order dispense with the requirements of subsection (2) to such extent as may be specified in the order.

(5) For the purposes of this section—

    "publish" includes—

        (a) broadcast by radio, television or cable television; or

        (b) cause to be published; and

    "material" includes any picture or representation.

(6) Any person who contravenes this section shall be guilty of an offence and liable, on summary conviction, to a fine not exceeding level 4 on the standard scale.

(7) Subsection (1) is without prejudice to—

    (a) the generality of the rule making power in section 144 of the Act of 1980; or

    (b) any other power of a magistrates' court to sit in private.

PART XII   (8) Section 71 of the Act of 1980 (newspaper reports of certain proceedings) shall apply in relation to any proceedings to which this section applies subject to the provisions of this section.

Self-incrimination.   **98.**—(1) In any proceedings in which a court is hearing an application for an order under Part IV or V, no person shall be excused from—

    (a) giving evidence on any matter; or

    (b) answering any question put to him in the course of his giving evidence,

on the ground that doing so might incriminate him or his spouse of an offence.

(2) A statement or admission made in such proceedings shall not be admissible in evidence against the person making it or his spouse in proceedings for an offence other than perjury.

Legal aid.   **99.**—(1) The Legal Aid Act 1988 is amended as mentioned in
1988 c. 34.   subsections (2) to (4).

(2) In section 15 (availability of, and payment for, representation under provisions relating to civil legal aid), for the words "and (3)" in subsection (1) there shall be substituted "to (3B)"; and the following subsections shall be inserted after subsection (3)—

"(3A) Representation under this Part shall not be available—

    (a) to any local authority; or

    (b) to any other body which falls within a prescribed description,

for the purposes of any proceedings under the Children Act 1989.

(3B) Regardless of subsection (2) or (3), representation under this Part must be granted where a child who is brought before a court under section 25 of the 1989 Act (use of accommodation for restricting liberty) is not, but wishes to be, legally represented before the court."

(3) In section 19(5) (scope of provisions about criminal legal aid), at the end of the definition of "criminal proceedings" there shall be added "and also includes proceedings under section 15 of the Children and Young
1969 c. 54.   Persons Act 1969 (variation and discharge of supervision orders) and section 16(8) of that Act (appeals in such proceedings)".

(4) Sections 27, 28 and 30(1) and (2) (provisions about legal aid in care, and other, proceedings in relation to children) shall cease to have effect.

(5) The Lord Chancellor may by order make such further amendments in the Legal Aid Act 1988 as he considers necessary or expedient in consequence of any provision made by or under this Act.

100.—(1) Section 7 of the Family Law Reform Act 1969 (which gives the High Court power to place a ward of court in the care, or under the supervision, of a local authority) shall cease to have effect.

(2) No court shall exercise the High Court's inherent jurisdiction with respect to children—

    (a) so as to require a child to be placed in the care, or put under the supervision, of a local authority;

    (b) so as to require a child to be accommodated by or on behalf of a local authority;

    (c) so as to make a child who is the subject of a care order a ward of court; or

    (d) for the purpose of conferring on any local authority power to determine any question which has arisen, or which may arise, in connection with any aspect of parental responsibility for a child.

(3) No application for any exercise of the court's inherent jurisdiction with respect to children may be made by a local authority unless the authority have obtained the leave of the court.

(4) The court may only grant leave if it is satisfied that—

    (a) the result which the authority wish to achieve could not be achieved through the making of any order of a kind to which subsection (5) applies; and

    (b) there is reasonable cause to believe that if the court's inherent jurisdiction is not exercised with respect to the child he is likely to suffer significant harm.

(5) This subsection applies to any order—

    (a) made otherwise than in the exercise of the court's inherent jurisdiction; and

    (b) which the local authority is entitled to apply for (assuming, in the case of any application which may only be made with leave, that leave is granted).

101.—(1) The Secretary of State may make regulations providing—

    (a) for prescribed orders which—

        (i) are made by a court in Northern Ireland; and

        (ii) appear to the Secretary of State to correspond in their effect to orders which may be made under any provision of this Act,

    to have effect in prescribed circumstances, for prescribed purposes of this Act, as if they were orders of a prescribed kind made under this Act;

    (b) for prescribed orders which—

        (i) are made by a court in England and Wales; and

(ii) appear to the Secretary of State to correspond in their effect to orders which may be made under any provision in force in Northern Ireland,

to have effect in prescribed circumstances, for prescribed purposes of the law of Northern Ireland, as if they were orders of a prescribed kind made in Northern Ireland.

(2) Regulations under subsection (1) may provide for the order concerned to cease to have effect for the purposes of the law of Northern Ireland, or (as the case may be) the law of England and Wales, if prescribed conditions are satisfied.

(3) The Secretary of State may make regulations providing for prescribed orders which—

(a) are made by a court in the Isle of Man or in any of the Channel Islands; and

(b) appear to the Secretary of State to correspond in their effect to orders which may be made under this Act,

to have effect in prescribed circumstances for prescribed purposes of this Act, as if they were orders of a prescribed kind made under this Act.

(4) Where a child who is in the care of a local authority is lawfully taken to live in Northern Ireland, the Isle of Man or any of the Channel Islands, the care order in question shall cease to have effect if the conditions prescribed in regulations made by the Secretary of State are satisfied.

(5) Any regulations made under this section may—

(a) make such consequential amendments (including repeals) in—

1969 c. 54.

(i) section 25 of the Children and Young Persons Act 1969 (transfers between England and Wales and Northern Ireland); or

(ii) section 26 (transfers between England and Wales and Channel Islands or Isle of Man) of that Act,

as the Secretary of State considers necessary or expedient; and

(b) modify any provision of this Act, in its application (by virtue of the regulations) in relation to an order made otherwise than in England and Wales.

Search warrants

Power of constable to assist in exercise of certain powers to search for children or inspect premises.

102.—(1) Where, on an application made by any person for a warrant under this section, it appears to the court—

(a) that a person attempting to exercise powers under any enactment mentioned in subsection (6) has been prevented from doing so by being refused entry to the premises concerned or refused access to the child concerned; or

(b) that any such person is likely to be so prevented from exercising any such powers,

it may issue a warrant authorising any constable to assist that person in the exercise of those powers, using reasonable force if necessary.

(2) Every warrant issued under this section shall be addressed to, and executed by, a constable who shall be accompanied by the person applying for the warrant if—

(a) that person so desires; and

(b) the court by whom the warrant is issued does not direct otherwise.

(3) A court granting an application for a warrant under this section may direct that the constable concerned may, in executing the warrant, be accompanied by a registered medical practitioner, registered nurse or registered health visitor if he so chooses.

(4) An application for a warrant under this section shall be made in the manner and form prescribed by rules of court.

(5) Where—

(a) an application for a warrant under this section relates to a particular child; and

(b) it is reasonably practicable to do so,

the application and any warrant granted on the application shall name the child; and where it does not name him it shall describe him as clearly as possible.

(6) The enactments are—

(a) sections 62, 64, 67, 76, 80, 86 and 87;

(b) paragraph 8(1)(b) and (2)(b) of Schedule 3;

(c) section 33 of the Adoption Act 1976 (duty of local authority to secure that protected children are visited from time to time). 1976 c. 36.

General

103.—(1) This section applies where any offence under this Act is committed by a body corporate. *Offences by bodies corporate.*

(2) If the offence is proved to have been committed with the consent or connivance of or to be attributable to any neglect on the part of any director, manager, secretary or other similar officer of the body corporate, or any person who was purporting to act in any such capacity, he (as well as the body corporate) shall be guilty of the offence and shall be liable to be proceeded against and punished accordingly.

104.—(1) Any power of the Lord Chancellor or the Secretary of State under this Act to make an order, regulations, or rules, except an order under section 54(2), 56(4)(a), 57(3), 84 or 97(4) or paragraph 1(1) of Schedule 4, shall be exercisable by statutory instrument. *Regulations and orders.*

(2) Any such statutory instrument, except one made under section 17(4), 107 or 108(2), shall be subject to annulment in pursuance of a resolution of either House of Parliament.

(3) An order under section 17(4) shall not be made unless a draft of it has been laid before, and approved by a resolution of, each House of Parliament.

(4) Any statutory instrument made under this Act may—

(a) make different provision for different cases;

(b) provide for exemptions from any of its provisions; and

(c) contain such incidental, supplemental and transitional provisions as the person making it considers expedient.

105.—(1) In this Act—

"adoption agency" means a body which may be referred to as an adoption agency by virtue of section 1 of the Adoption Act 1976;

"bank holiday" means a day which is a bank holiday under the Banking and Financial Dealings Act 1971;

"care order" has the meaning given by section 31(11) and also includes any order which by or under any enactment has the effect of, or is deemed to be, a care order for the purposes of this Act; and any reference to a child who is in the care of an authority is a reference to a child who is in their care by virtue of a care order;

"child" means, subject to paragraph 16 of Schedule 1, a person under the age of eighteen;

"child assessment order" has the meaning given by section 43(2);

"child minder" has the meaning given by section 71;

"child of the family", in relation to the parties to a marriage, means—

(a) a child of both of those parties;

(b) any other child, not being a child who is placed with those parties as foster parents by a local authority or voluntary organisation, who has been treated by both of those parties as a child of their family;

"children's home" has the same meaning as in section 63;

"community home" has the meaning given by section 53;

"contact order" has the meaning given by section 8(1);

"day care" has the same meaning as in section 18;

"disabled", in relation to a child, has the same meaning as in section 17(11);

"district health authority" has the same meaning as in the National Health Service Act 1977;

"domestic premises" has the meaning given by section 71(12);

"education supervision order" has the meaning given in section 36;

"emergency protection order" means an order under section 44;

"family assistance order" has the meaning given in section 16(2);

"family proceedings" has the meaning given by section 8(3);

"functions" includes powers and duties;

"guardian of a child" means a guardian (other than a guardian of the estate of a child) appointed in accordance with the provisions of section 5;

"harm" has the same meaning as in section 31(9) and the question of whether harm is significant shall be determined in accordance with section 31(10);

"health authority" means any district health authority and any special health authority established under the National Health Service Act 1977;

"health service hospital" has the same meaning as in the National Health Service Act 1977;

PART XII
1977 c. 49.

"hospital" has the same meaning as in the Mental Health Act 1983, except that it does not include a special hospital within the meaning of that Act;

1983 c. 20.

"ill-treatment" has the same meaning as in section 31(9);

"independent school" has the same meaning as in the Education Act 1944;

1944 c. 31.

"local authority" means, in relation to England and Wales, the council of a county, a metropolitan district, a London Borough or the Common Council of the City of London and, in relation to Scotland, a local authority within the meaning of section 1(2) of the Social Work (Scotland) Act 1968;

1968 c. 49.

"local authority foster parent" has the same meaning as in section 23(3);

"local education authority" has the same meaning as in the Education Act 1944;

"local housing authority" has the same meaning as in the Housing Act 1985;

1985 c. 68.

"mental nursing home" has the same meaning as in the Registered Homes Act 1984;

1984 c. 23.

"nursing home" has the same meaning as in the Act of 1984;

"parental responsibility" has the meaning given in section 3;

"parental responsibility agreement" has the meaning given in section 4(1);

"prescribed" means prescribed by regulations made under this Act;

"privately fostered child" and "to foster a child privately" have the same meaning as in section 66;

"prohibited steps order" has the meaning given by section 8(1);

"protected child" has the same meaning as in Part III of the Adoption Act 1976;

1976 c. 36.

"registered children's home" has the same meaning as in section 63;

"registered pupil" has the same meaning as in the Education Act 1944;

"relative", in relation to a child, means a grandparent, brother, sister, uncle or aunt (whether of the full blood or half blood or by affinity) or step-parent;

"residence order" has the meaning given by section 8(1);

"residential care home" has the same meaning as in the Registered Homes Act 1984;

"responsible person", in relation to a child who is the subject of a supervision order, has the meaning given in paragraph 1 of Schedule 3;

"school" has the same meaning as in the Education Act 1944 or, in relation to Scotland, in the Education (Scotland) Act 1980;

1980 c. 44.

"service", in relation to any provision made under Part III, includes any facility;

"signed", in relation to any person, includes the making by that person of his mark;

"special educational needs" has the same meaning as in the Education Act 1981;

"special health authority" has the same meaning as in the National Health Service Act 1977;

"specific issue order" has the meaning given by section 8(1);

"supervision order" has the meaning given by section 31(11);

"supervised child" and "supervisor", in relation to a supervision order or an education supervision order, mean respectively the child who is (or is to be) under supervision and the person under whose supervision he is (or is to be) by virtue of the order;

"upbringing", in relation to any child, includes the care of the child but not his maintenance;

"voluntary home" has the meaning given by section 60;

"voluntary organisation" means a body (other than a public or local authority) whose activities are not carried on for profit.

(2) References in this Act to a child whose father and mother were, or (as the case may be) were not, married to each other at the time of his birth must be read with section 1 of the Family Law Reform Act 1987 (which extends the meaning of such references).

(3) References in this Act to—

(a) a person with whom a child lives, or is to live, as the result of a residence order; or

(b) a person in whose favour a residence order is in force,

shall be construed as references to the person named in the order as the person with whom the child is to live.

(4) References in this Act to a child who is looked after by a local authority have the same meaning as they have (by virtue of section 22) in Part III.

(5) References in this Act to accommodation provided by or on behalf of a local authority are references to accommodation so provided in the exercise of functions which stand referred to the social services committee of that or any other local authority under the Local Authority Social Services Act 1970.

(6) In determining the "ordinary residence" of a child for any purpose of this Act, there shall be disregarded any period in which he lives in any place—

(a) which is a school or other institution;

(b) in accordance with the requirements of a supervision order under this Act or an order under section 7(7)(b) of the Children and Young Persons Act 1969; or

(c) while he is being provided with accommodation by or on behalf of a local authority.

(7) References in this Act to children who are in need shall be construed in accordance with section 17.

(8) Any notice or other document required under this Act to be served on any person may be served on him by being delivered personally to him, or being sent by post to him in a registered letter or by the recorded delivery service at his proper address.

(9) Any such notice or other document required to be served on a body corporate or a firm shall be duly served if it is served on the secretary or clerk of that body or a partner of that firm.

(10) For the purposes of this section, and of section 7 of the Interpretation Act 1978 in its application to this section, the proper address of a person—

1978 c. 30.

(a) in the case of a secretary or clerk of a body corporate, shall be that of the registered or principal office of that body;

(b) in the case of a partner of a firm, shall be that of the principal office of the firm; and

(c) in any other case, shall be the last known address of the person to be served.

106.—(1) Any—

Financial provisions.

(a) grants made by the Secretary of State under this Act; and

(b) any other expenses incurred by the Secretary of State under this Act,

shall be payable out of money provided by Parliament.

(2) Any sums received by the Secretary of State under section 58, or by way of the repayment of any grant made under section 82(2) or (4) shall be paid into the Consolidated Fund.

107. Her Majesty may by Order in Council direct that any of the provisions of this Act shall extend to any of the Channel Islands with such exceptions and modifications as may be specified in the Order.

Application to Channel Islands.

108.—(1) This Act may be cited as the Children Act 1989.

Short title, commencement extent etc.

(2) Sections 89 and 96(3) to (7), and paragraph 35 of Schedule 12, shall come into force on the passing of this Act and paragraph 36 of Schedule 12 shall come into force at the end of the period of two months beginning with the day on which this Act is passed but otherwise this Act shall come into force on such date as may be appointed by order made by the Lord Chancellor or the Secretary of State, or by both acting jointly.

(3) Different dates may be appointed for different provisions of this Act and in relation to different cases.

(4) The minor amendments set out in Schedule 12 shall have effect.

(5) The consequential amendments set out in Schedule 13 shall have effect.

(6) The transitional provisions and savings set out in Schedule 14 shall have effect.

(7) The repeals set out in Schedule 15 shall have effect.

(8) An order under subsection (2) may make such transitional provisions or savings as appear to the person making the order to be necessary or expedient in connection with the provisions brought into force by the order, including—

    (a) provisions adding to or modifying the provisions of Schedule 14; and

    (b) such adaptations—

        (i) of the provisions brought into force by the order; and

        (ii) of any provisions of this Act then in force,

as appear to him necessary or expedient in consequence of the partial operation of this Act.

(9) The Lord Chancellor may by order make such amendments or repeals, in such enactments as may be specified in the order, as appear to him to be necessary or expedient in consequence of any provision of this Act.

(10) This Act shall, in its application to the Isles of Scilly, have effect subject to such exceptions, adaptations and modifications as the Secretary of State may by order prescribe.

(11) The following provisions of this Act extend to Scotland—

    section 19;

    section 25(8);

    section 50(13);

    Part X;

    section 80(1)(h) and (i), (2) to (4), (5)(a), (b) and (h) and (6) to (12);

    section 88;

    section 104 (so far as necessary);

    section 105 (so far as necessary);

    subsections (1) to (3), (8) and (9) and this subsection;

    in Schedule 2, paragraph 24;

    in Schedule 12, paragraphs 1, 7 to 10, 18, 27, 30(a) and 41 to 44;

    in Schedule 13, paragraphs 18 to 23, 32, 46, 47, 50, 57, 62, 63, 68(a) and (b) and 71;

    in Schedule 14, paragraphs 1, 33 and 34;

    in Schedule 15, the entries relating to—

        (a) the Custody of Children Act 1891;

        (b) the Nurseries and Child Minders Regulation Act 1948;

        (c) section 53(3) of the Children and Young Persons Act 1963;

        (d) section 60 of the Health Services and Public Health Act 1968;

        (e) the Social Work (Scotland) Act 1968;

        (f) the Adoption (Scotland) Act 1978;

        (g) the Child Care Act 1980;

Margin notes:

1891 c. 3.

1948 c. 53.

1963 c. 37.

1968 c. 46.

1968 c. 49.

1978 c. 28.

1980 c. 5.

(h) the Foster Children (Scotland) Act 1984;

(i) the Child Abduction and Custody Act 1985; and

(j) the Family Law Act 1986.

(12) The following provisions of this Act extend to Northern Ireland—

section 50;

section 101(1)(b), (2) and (5)(a)(i);

subsections (1) to (3), (8) and (9) and this subsection;

in Schedule 2, paragraph 24;

in Schedule 12, paragraphs 7 to 10, 18 and 27;

in Schedule 13, paragraphs 21, 22, 46, 47, 57, 62, 63, 68(c) to (e) and 69 to 71;

in Schedule 14, paragraphs 18, 28 to 30 and 38(a); and

in Schedule 15, the entries relating to the Guardianship of Minors Act 1971, the Children Act 1975, the Child Care Act 1980, and the Family Law Act 1986.

SCHEDULES

Section 15(1).

SCHEDULE 1

FINANCIAL PROVISION FOR CHILDREN

Orders for financial relief against parents

1.—(1) On an application made by a parent or guardian of a child, or by any person in whose favour a residence order is in force with respect to a child, the court may—

    (a) in the case of an application to the High Court or a county court, make one or more of the orders mentioned in sub-paragraph (2);

    (b) in the case of an application to a magistrates' court, make one or both of the orders mentioned in paragraphs (a) and (c) of that sub-paragraph.

(2) The orders referred to in sub-paragraph (1) are—

    (a) an order requiring either or both parents of a child—

        (i) to make to the applicant for the benefit of the child; or

        (ii) to make to the child himself,

such periodical payments, for such term, as may be specified in the order;

    (b) an order requiring either or both parents of a child—

        (i) to secure to the applicant for the benefit of the child; or

        (ii) to secure to the child himself,

such periodical payments, for such term, as may be so specified;

    (c) an order requiring either or both parents of a child—

        (i) to pay to the applicant for the benefit of the child; or

        (ii) to pay to the child himself,

such lump sum as may be so specified;

    (d) an order requiring a settlement to be made for the benefit of the child, and to the satisfaction of the court, of property—

        (i) to which either parent is entitled (either in possession or in reversion); and

        (ii) which is specified in the order;

    (e) an order requiring either or both parents of a child—

        (i) to transfer to the applicant, for the benefit of the child; or

        (ii) to transfer to the child himself,

such property to which the parent is, or the parents are, entitled (either in possession or in reversion) as may be specified in the order.

(3) The powers conferred by this paragraph may be exercised at any time.

(4) An order under sub-paragraph (2)(a) or (b) may be varied or discharged by a subsequent order made on the application of any person by or to whom payments were required to be made under the previous order.

(5) Where a court makes an order under this paragraph—

    (a) it may at any time make a further such order under sub-paragraph (2)(a), (b) or (c) with respect to the child concerned if he has not reached the age of eighteen;

    (b) it may not make more than one order under sub-paragraph (2)(d) or (e) against the same person in respect of the same child.

(6) On making, varying or discharging a residence order the court may exercise any of its powers under this Schedule even though no application has been made to it under this Schedule.

Orders for financial relief for persons over eighteen

2.—(1) If, on an application by a person who has reached the age of eighteen, it appears to the court—

(a) that the applicant is, will be or (if an order were made under this paragraph) would be receiving instruction at an educational establishment or undergoing training for a trade, profession or vocation, whether or not while in gainful employment; or

(b) that there are special circumstances which justify the making of an order under this paragraph,

the court may make one or both of the orders mentioned in sub-paragraph (2).

(2) The orders are—

(a) an order requiring either or both of the applicant's parents to pay to the applicant such periodical payments, for such term, as may be specified in the order;

(b) an order requiring either or both of the applicant's parents to pay to the applicant such lump sum as may be so specified.

(3) An application may not be made under this paragraph by any person if, immediately before he reached the age of sixteen, a periodical payments order was in force with respect to him.

(4) No order shall be made under this paragraph at a time when the parents of the applicant are living with each other in the same household.

(5) An order under sub-paragraph (2)(a) may be varied or discharged by a subsequent order made on the application of any person by or to whom payments were required to be made under the previous order.

(6) In sub-paragraph (3) "periodical payments order" means an order made under—

(a) this Schedule;

(b) section 6(3) of the Family Law Reform Act 1969; 1969 c. 46.

(c) section 23 or 27 of the Matrimonial Causes Act 1973; 1973 c. 18.

(d) Part I of the Domestic Proceedings and Magistrates' Courts Act 1978, 1978 c. 22.

for the making or securing of periodical payments.

(7) The powers conferred by this paragraph shall be exercisable at any time.

(8) Where the court makes an order under this paragraph it may from time to time while that order remains in force make a further such order.

Duration of orders for financial relief

3.—(1) The term to be specified in an order for periodical payments made under paragraph 1(2)(a) or (b) in favour of a child may begin with the date of the making of an application for the order in question or any later date but—

(a) shall not in the first instance extend beyond the child's seventeenth birthday unless the court thinks it right in the circumstances of the case to specify a later date; and

(b) shall not in any event extend beyond the child's eighteenth birthday.

(2) Paragraph (b) of sub-paragraph (1) shall not apply in the case of a child if it appears to the court that—

(a) the child is, or will be or (if an order were made without complying with that paragraph) would be receiving instruction at an educational establishment or undergoing training for a trade, profession or vocation, whether or not while in gainful employment; or

(b) there are special circumstances which justify the making of an order without complying with that paragraph.

(3) An order for periodical payments made under paragraph 1(2)(a) or 2(2)(a) shall, notwithstanding anything in the order, cease to have effect on the death of the person liable to make payments under the order.

(4) Where an order is made under paragraph 1(2)(a) or (b) requiring periodical payments to be made or secured to the parent of a child, the order shall cease to have effect if —

(a) any parent making or securing the payments; and

(b) any parent to whom the payments are made or secured,

live together for a period of more than six months.

Matters to which court is to have regard in making orders for financial relief

4.—(1) In deciding whether to exercise its powers under paragraph 1 or 2, and if so in what manner, the court shall have regard to all the circumstances including—

(a) the income, earning capacity, property and other financial resources which each person mentioned in sub-paragraph (4) has or is likely to have in the foreseeable future;

(b) the financial needs, obligations and responsibilities which each person mentioned in sub-paragraph (4) has or is likely to have in the foreseeable future;

(c) the financial needs of the child;

(d) the income, earning capacity (if any), property and other financial resources of the child;

(e) any physical or mental disability of the child;

(f) the manner in which the child was being, or was expected to be, educated or trained.

(2) In deciding whether to exercise its powers under paragraph 1 against a person who is not the mother or father of the child, and if so in what manner, the court shall in addition have regard to—

(a) whether that person had assumed responsibility for the maintenance of the child and, if so, the extent to which and basis on which he assumed that responsibility and the length of the period during which he met that responsibility;

(b) whether he did so knowing that the child was not his child;

(c) the liability of any other person to maintain the child.

(3) Where the court makes an order under paragraph 1 against a person who is not the father of the child, it shall record in the order that the order is made on the basis that the person against whom the order is made is not the child's father.

(4) The persons mentioned in sub-paragraph (1) are—

(a) in relation to a decision whether to exercise its powers under paragraph 1, any parent of the child;

(b) in relation to a decision whether to exercise its powers under paragraph 2, the mother and father of the child;

(c) the applicant for the order;

(d) any other person in whose favour the court proposes to make the order.

Provisions relating to lump sums

5.—(1) Without prejudice to the generality of paragraph 1, an order under that paragraph for the payment of a lump sum may be made for the purpose of enabling any liabilities or expenses—

  (a) incurred in connection with the birth of the child or in maintaining the child; and

  (b) reasonably incurred before the making of the order,

to be met.

(2) The amount of any lump sum required to be paid by an order made by a magistrates' court under paragraph 1 or 2 shall not exceed £1000 or such larger amount as the Secretary of State may from time to time by order fix for the purposes of this sub-paragraph.

(3) The power of the court under paragraph 1 or 2 to vary or discharge an order for the making or securing of periodical payments by a parent shall include power to make an order under that provision for the payment of a lump sum by that parent.

(4) The amount of any lump sum which a parent may be required to pay by virtue of sub-paragraph (3) shall not, in the case of an order made by a magistrates' court, exceed the maximum amount that may at the time of the making of the order be required to be paid under sub-paragraph (2), but a magistrates' court may make an order for the payment of a lump sum not exceeding that amount even though the parent was required to pay a lump sum by a previous order under this Act.

(5) An order made under paragraph 1 or 2 for the payment of a lump sum may provide for the payment of that sum by instalments.

(6) Where the court provides for the payment of a lump sum by instalments the court, on an application made either by the person liable to pay or the person entitled to receive that sum, shall have power to vary that order by varying—

  (a) the number of instalments payable;

  (b) the amount of any instalment payable;

  (c) the date on which any instalment becomes payable.

Variation etc. of orders for periodical payments

6.—(1) In exercising its powers under paragraph 1 or 2 to vary or discharge an order for the making or securing of periodical payments the court shall have regard to all the circumstances of the case, including any change in any of the matters to which the court was required to have regard when making the order.

(2) The power of the court under paragraph 1 or 2 to vary an order for the making or securing of periodical payments shall include power to suspend any provision of the order temporarily and to revive any provision so suspended.

(3) Where on an application under paragraph 1 or 2 for the variation or discharge of an order for the making or securing of periodical payments the court varies the payments required to be made under that order, the court may provide that the payments as so varied shall be made from such date as the court may specify, not being earlier than the date of the making of the application.

(4) An application for the variation of an order made under paragraph 1 for the making or securing of periodical payments to or for the benefit of a child may, if the child has reached the age of sixteen, be made by the child himself.

(5) Where an order for the making or securing of periodical payments made under paragraph 1 ceases to have effect on the date on which the child reaches the age of sixteen, or at any time after that date but before or on the date on which he reaches the age of eighteen, the child may apply to the court which made the order for an order for its revival.

(6) If on such an application it appears to the court that—

(a) the child is, will be or (if an order were made under this sub-paragraph) would be receiving instruction at an educational establishment or undergoing training for a trade, profession or vocation, whether or not while in gainful employment; or

(b) there are special circumstances which justify the making of an order under this paragraph,

the court shall have power by order to revive the order from such date as the court may specify, not being earlier than the date of the making of the application.

(7) Any order which is revived by an order under sub-paragraph (5) may be varied or discharged under that provision, on the application of any person by whom or to whom payments are required to be made under the revived order.

(8) An order for the making or securing of periodical payments made under paragraph 1 may be varied or discharged, after the death of either parent, on the application of a guardian of the child concerned.

Variation of orders for secured periodical payments after death of parent

7.—(1) Where the parent liable to make payments under a secured periodical payments order has died, the persons who may apply for the variation or discharge of the order shall include the personal representatives of the deceased parent.

(2) No application for the variation of the order shall, except with the permission of the court, be made after the end of the period of six months from the date on which representation in regard to the estate of that parent is first taken out.

(3) The personal representatives of a deceased person against whom a secured periodical payments order was made shall not be liable for having distributed any part of the estate of the deceased after the end of the period of six months referred to in sub-paragraph (2) on the ground that they ought to have taken into account the possibility that the court might permit an application for variation to be made after that period by the person entitled to payments under the order.

(4) Sub-paragraph (3) shall not prejudice any power to recover any part of the estate so distributed arising by virtue of the variation of an order in accordance with this paragraph.

(5) Where an application to vary a secured periodical payments order is made after the death of the parent liable to make payments under the order, the circumstances to which the court is required to have regard under paragraph 6(1) shall include the changed circumstances resulting from the death of the parent.

(6) In considering for the purposes of sub-paragraph (2) the question when representation was first taken out, a grant limited to settled land or to trust property shall be left out of account and a grant limited to real estate or to personal estate shall be left out of account unless a grant limited to the remainder of the estate has previously been made or is made at the same time.

(7) In this paragraph "secured periodical payments order" means an order for secured periodical payments under paragraph 1(2)(b).

Financial relief under other enactments

8.—(1) This paragraph applies where a residence order is made with respect to a child at a time when there is in force an order ("the financial relief order") made under any enactment other than this Act and requiring a person to contribute to the child's maintenance.

(2) Where this paragraph applies, the court may, on the application of—

    (a) any person required by the financial relief order to contribute to the child's maintenance; or

    (b) any person in whose favour a residence order with respect to the child is in force,

make an order revoking the financial relief order, or varying it by altering the amount of any sum payable under that order or by substituting the applicant for the person to whom any such sum is otherwise payable under that order.

Interim orders

9.—(1) Where an application is made under paragraph 1 or 2 the court may, at any time before it disposes of the application, make an interim order—

    (a) requiring either or both parents to make such periodical payments, at such times and for such term as the court thinks fit; and

    (b) giving any direction which the court thinks fit.

(2) An interim order made under this paragraph may provide for payments to be made from such date as the court may specify, not being earlier than the date of the making of the application under paragraph 1 or 2.

(3) An interim order made under this paragraph shall cease to have effect when the application is disposed of or, if earlier, on the date specified for the purposes of this paragraph in the interim order.

(4) An interim order in which a date has been specified for the purposes of sub-paragraph (3) may be varied by substituting a later date.

Alteration of maintenance agreements

10.—(1) In this paragraph and in paragraph 11 "maintenance agreement" means any agreement in writing made with respect to a child, whether before or after the commencement of this paragraph, which—

    (a) is or was made between the father and mother of the child; and

    (b) contains provision with respect to the making or securing of payments, or the disposition or use of any property, for the maintenance or education of the child,

and any such provisions are in this paragraph, and paragraph 11, referred to as "financial arrangements".

(2) Where a maintenance agreement is for the time being subsisting and each of the parties to the agreement is for the time being either domiciled or resident in England and Wales, then, either party may apply to the court for an order under this paragraph.

(3) If the court to which the application is made is satisfied either—

    (a) that, by reason of a change in the circumstances in the light of which any financial arrangements contained in the agreement were made (including a change foreseen by the parties when making the agreement), the agreement should be altered so as to make different financial arrangements; or

    (b) that the agreement does not contain proper financial arrangements with respect to the child,

then that court may by order make such alterations in the agreement by varying or revoking any financial arrangements contained in it as may appear to it to be just having regard to all the circumstances.

(4) If the maintenance agreement is altered by an order under this paragraph, the agreement shall have effect thereafter as if the alteration had been made by agreement between the parties and for valuable consideration.

SCH. 1

(5) Where a court decides to make an order under this paragraph altering the maintenance agreement—

(a) by inserting provision for the making or securing by one of the parties to the agreement of periodical payments for the maintenance of the child; or

(b) by increasing the rate of periodical payments required to be made or secured by one of the parties for the maintenance of the child,

then, in deciding the term for which under the agreement as altered by the order the payments or (as the case may be) the additional payments attributable to the increase are to be made or secured for the benefit of the child, the court shall apply the provisions of sub-paragraphs (1) and (2) of paragraph 3 as if the order were an order under paragraph 1(2)(a) or (b).

(6) A magistrates' court shall not entertain an application under sub-paragraph (2) unless both the parties to the agreement are resident in England and Wales and at least one of the parties is resident in the commission area (within the meaning of the Justices of the Peace Act 1979) for which the court is appointed, and shall not have power to make any order on such an application except—

1979 c. 55.

(a) in a case where the agreement contains no provision for periodical payments by either of the parties, an order inserting provision for the making by one of the parties of periodical payments for the maintenance of the child;

(b) in a case where the agreement includes provision for the making by one of the parties of periodical payments, an order increasing or reducing the rate of, or terminating, any of those payments.

(7) For the avoidance of doubt it is hereby declared that nothing in this paragraph affects any power of a court before which any proceedings between the parties to a maintenance agreement are brought under any other enactment to make an order containing financial arrangements or any right of either party to apply for such an order in such proceedings.

11.—(1) Where a maintenance agreement provides for the continuation, after the death of one of the parties, of payments for the maintenance of a child and that party dies domiciled in England and Wales, the surviving party or the personal representatives of the deceased party may apply to the High Court or a county court for an order under paragraph 10.

(2) If a maintenance agreement is altered by a court on an application under this paragraph, the agreement shall have effect thereafter as if the alteration had been made, immediately before the death, by agreement between the parties and for valuable consideration.

(3) An application under this paragraph shall not, except with leave of the High Court or a county court, be made after the end of the period of six months beginning with the day on which representation in regard to the estate of the deceased is first taken out.

(4) In considering for the purposes of sub-paragraph (3) the question when representation was first taken out, a grant limited to settled land or to trust property shall be left out of account and a grant limited to real estate or to personal estate shall be left out of account unless a grant limited to the remainder of the estate has previously been made or is made at the same time.

(5) A county court shall not entertain an application under this paragraph, or an application for leave to make an application under this paragraph, unless it would have jurisdiction to hear and determine proceedings for an order under section 2 of the Inheritance (Provision for Family and Dependants) Act 1975 in relation to the deceased's estate by virtue of section 25 of the County Courts Act 1984 (jurisdiction under the Act of 1975).

1975 c. 63.
1984 c. 28.

(6) The provisions of this paragraph shall not render the personal representatives of the deceased liable for having distributed any part of the estate of the deceased after the expiry of the period of six months referred to in sub-paragraph (3) on the ground that they ought to have taken into account the possibility that a court might grant leave for an application by virtue of this paragraph to be made by the surviving party after that period.

(7) Sub-paragraph (6) shall not prejudice any power to recover any part of the estate so distributed arising by virtue of the making of an order in pursuance of this paragraph.

Enforcement of orders for maintenance

12.—(1) Any person for the time being under an obligation to make payments in pursuance of any order for the payment of money made by a magistrates' court under this Act shall give notice of any change of address to such person (if any) as may be specified in the order.

(2) Any person failing without reasonable excuse to give such a notice shall be guilty of an offence and liable on summary conviction to a fine not exceeding level 2 on the standard scale.

(3) An order for the payment of money made by a magistrates' court under this Act shall be enforceable as a magistrates' court maintenance order within the meaning of section 150(1) of the Magistrates' Courts Act 1980.

Direction for settlement of instrument by conveyancing counsel

13. Where the High Court or a county court decides to make an order under this Act for the securing of periodical payments or for the transfer or settlement of property, it may direct that the matter be referred to one of the conveyancing counsel of the court to settle a proper instrument to be executed by all necessary parties.

Financial provision for child resident in country outside England and Wales

14.—(1) Where one parent of a child lives in England and Wales and the child lives outside England and Wales with—

(a) another parent of his;

(b) a guardian of his; or

(c) a person in whose favour a residence order is in force with respect to the child,

the court shall have power, on an application made by any of the persons mentioned in paragraphs (a) to (c), to make one or both of the orders mentioned in paragraph 1(2)(a) and (b) against the parent living in England and Wales.

(2) Any reference in this Act to the powers of the court under paragraph 1(2) or to an order made under paragraph 1(2) shall include a reference to the powers which the court has by virtue of sub-paragraph (1) or (as the case may be) to an order made by virtue of sub-paragraph (1).

Local authority contribution to child's maintenance

15.—(1) Where a child lives, or is to live, with a person as the result of a residence order, a local authority may make contributions to that person towards the cost of the accommodation and maintenance of the child.

(2) Sub-paragraph (1) does not apply where the person with whom the child lives, or is to live, is a parent of the child or the husband or wife of a parent of the child.

Interpretation

16.—(1) In this Schedule "child" includes, in any case where an application is made under paragraph 2 or 6 in relation to a person who has reached the age of eighteen, that person.

(2) In this Schedule, except paragraphs 2 and 15, "parent" includes any party to a marriage (whether or not subsisting) in relation to whom the child concerned is a child of the family; and for this purpose any reference to either parent or both parents shall be construed as references to any parent of his and to all of his parents.

Sections 17, 23
and 29.

SCHEDULE 2

LOCAL AUTHORITY SUPPORT FOR CHILDREN AND FAMILIES

PART I

PROVISION OF SERVICES FOR FAMILIES

Identification of children in need and provision of information

1.—(1) Every local authority shall take reasonable steps to identify the extent to which there are children in need within their area.

(2) Every local authority shall—

(a) publish information—

(i) about services provided by them under sections 17, 18, 20 and 24; and

(ii) where they consider it appropriate, about the provision by others (including, in particular, voluntary organisations) of services which the authority have power to provide under those sections; and

(b) take such steps as are reasonably practicable to ensure that those who might benefit from the services receive the information relevant to them.

Maintenance of a register of disabled children

2.—(1) Every local authority shall open and maintain a register of disabled children within their area.

(2) The register may be kept by means of a computer.

Assessment of children's needs

3. Where it appears to a local authority that a child within their area is in need, the authority may assess his needs for the purposes of this Act at the same time as any assessment of his needs is made under—

1970 c. 44.

(a) the Chronically Sick and Disabled Persons Act 1970;

1981 c. 60.

(b) the Education Act 1981;

1986 c. 33.

(c) the Disabled Persons (Services, Consultation and Representation) Act 1986; or

(d) any other enactment.

Prevention of neglect and abuse

4.—(1) Every local authority shall take reasonable steps, through the provision of services under Part III of this Act, to prevent children within their area suffering ill-treatment or neglect.

(2) Where a local authority believe that a child who is at any time within their area—

(a) is likely to suffer harm; but

(b) lives or proposes to live in the area of another local authority

they shall inform that other local authority.

(3) When informing that other local authority they shall specify—

(a) the harm that they believe he is likely to suffer; and

(b) (if they can) where the child lives or proposes to live.

Provision of accommodation in order to protect child

5.—(1) Where—

(a) it appears to a local authority that a child who is living on particular premises is suffering, or is likely to suffer, ill treatment at the hands of another person who is living on those premises; and

(b) that other person proposes to move from the premises,

the authority may assist that other person to obtain alternative accommodation.

(2) Assistance given under this paragraph may be in cash.

(3) Subsections (7) to (9) of section 17 shall apply in relation to assistance given under this paragraph as they apply in relation to assistance given under that section.

Provision for disabled children

6. Every local authority shall provide services designed—

(a) to minimise the effect on disabled children within their area of their disabilities; and

(b) to give such children the opportunity to lead lives which are as normal as possible.

Provision to reduce need for care proceedings etc.

7. Every local authority shall take reasonable steps designed—

(a) to reduce the need to bring—

(i) proceedings for care or supervision orders with respect to children within their area;

(ii) criminal proceedings against such children;

(iii) any family or other proceedings with respect to such children which might lead to them being placed in the authority's care; or

(iv) proceedings under the inherent jurisdiction of the High Court with respect to children;

(b) to encourage children within their area not to commit criminal offences; and

(c) to avoid the need for children within their area to be placed in secure accommodation.

Provision for children living with their families

8. Every local authority shall make such provision as they consider appropriate for the following services to be available with respect to children in need within their area while they are living with their families—

(a) advice, guidance and counselling;

(b) occupational, social, cultural or recreational activities;

(c) home help (which may include laundry facilities);

(d) facilities for, or assistance with, travelling to and from home for the purpose of taking advantage of any other service provided under this Act or of any similar service;

(e) assistance to enable the child concerned and his family to have a holiday.

Family centres

9.—(1) Every local authority shall provide such family centres as they consider appropriate in relation to children within their area.

(2) "Family centre" means a centre at which any of the persons mentioned in sub-paragraph (3) may—

(a) attend for occupational, social, cultural or recreational activities;

(b) attend for advice, guidance or counselling; or

(c) be provided with accommodation while he is receiving advice, guidance or counselling.

(3) The persons are—

(a) a child;

(b) his parents;

(c) any person who is not a parent of his but who has parental responsibility for him;

(d) any other person who is looking after him.

Maintenance of the family home

10. Every local authority shall take such steps as are reasonably practicable, where any child within their area who is in need and whom they are not looking after is living apart from his family—

(a) to enable him to live with his family; or

(b) to promote contact between him and his family,

if, in their opinion, it is necessary to do so in order to safeguard or promote his welfare.

Duty to consider racial groups to which children in need belong

11. Every local authority shall, in making any arrangements—

(a) for the provision of day care within their area; or

(b) designed to encourage persons to act as local authority foster parents,

have regard to the different racial groups to which children within their area who are in need belong.

PART II

CHILDREN LOOKED AFTER BY LOCAL AUTHORITIES

Regulations as to placing of children with local authority foster parents

12. Regulations under section 23(2)(a) may, in particular, make provision—

(a) with regard to the welfare of children placed with local authority foster parents;

(b) as to the arrangements to be made by local authorities in connection with the health and education of such children;

(c) as to the records to be kept by local authorities;

(d) for securing that a child is not placed with a local authority foster parent unless that person is for the time being approved as a local authority foster parent by such local authority as may be prescribed;

(e) for securing that where possible the local authority foster parent with whom a child is to be placed is—

    (i) of the same religious persuasion as the child; or

    (ii) gives an undertaking that the child will be brought up in that religious persuasion;

(f) for securing that children placed with local authority foster parents, and the premises in which they are accommodated, will be supervised and inspected by a local authority and that the children will be removed from those premises if their welfare appears to require it;

(g) as to the circumstances in which local authorities may make arrangements for duties imposed on them by the regulations to be discharged, on their behalf.

Regulations as to arrangements under section 23(2)(f)

13. Regulations under section 23(2)(f) may, in particular, make provision as to—

(a) the persons to be notified of any proposed arrangements;

(b) the opportunities such persons are to have to make representations in relation to the arrangements proposed;

(c) the persons to be notified of any proposed changes in arrangements;

(d) the records to be kept by local authorities;

(e) the supervision by local authorities of any arrangements made.

Regulations as to conditions under which child in care is allowed to live with parent, etc.

14. Regulations under section 23(5) may, in particular, impose requirements on a local authority as to—

(a) the making of any decision by a local authority to allow a child to live with any person falling within section 23(4) (including requirements as to those who must be consulted before the decision is made, and those who must be notified when it has been made);

(b) the supervision or medical examination of the child concerned;

(c) the removal of the child, in such circumstances as may be prescribed, from the care of the person with whom he has been allowed to live.

Promotion and maintenance of contact between child and family

15. —(1) Where a child is being looked after by a local authority, the authority shall, unless it is not reasonably practicable or consistent with his welfare, endeavour to promote contact between the child and—

(a) his parents;

(b) any person who is not a parent of his but who has parental responsibility for him; and

(c) any relative, friend or other person connected with him.

(2) Where a child is being looked after by a local authority—

(a) the authority shall take such steps as are reasonably practicable to secure that—

    (i) his parents; and

    (ii) any person who is not a parent of his but who has parental responsibility for him,

are kept informed of where he is being accommodated; and

(b) every such person shall secure that the authority are kept informed of his or her address.

(3) Where a local authority ("the receiving authority") take over the provision of accommodation for a child from another local authority ("the transferring authority") under section 20(2)—

    (a) the receiving authority shall (where reasonably practicable) inform—

        (i) the child's parents; and

        (ii) any person who is not a parent of his but who has parental responsibility for him;

    (b) sub-paragraph (2)(a) shall apply to the transferring authority, as well as the receiving authority, until at least one such person has been informed of the change; and

    (c) sub-paragraph (2)(b) shall not require any person to inform the receiving authority of his address until he has been so informed.

(4) Nothing in this paragraph requires a local authority to inform any person of the whereabouts of a child if—

    (a) the child is in the care of the authority; and

    (b) the authority has reasonable cause to believe that informing the person would prejudice the child's welfare.

(5) Any person who fails (without reasonable excuse) to comply with sub-paragraph (2)(b) shall be guilty of an offence and liable on summary conviction to a fine not exceeding level 2 on the standard scale.

(6) It shall be a defence in any proceedings under sub-paragraph (5) to prove that the defendant was residing at the same address as another person who was the child's parent or had parental responsibility for the child and had reasonable cause to believe that the other person had informed the appropriate authority that both of them were residing at that address.

Visits to or by children: expenses

16.—(1) This paragraph applies where—

    (a) a child is being looked after by a local authority; and

    (b) the conditions mentioned in sub-paragraph (3) are satisfied.

(2) The authority may—

    (a) make payments to—

        (i) a parent of the child;

        (ii) any person who is not a parent of his but who has parental responsibility for him; or

        (iii) any relative, friend or other person connected with him,

    in respect of travelling, subsistence or other expenses incurred by that person in visiting the child; or

    (b) make payments to the child, or to any person on his behalf, in respect of travelling, subsistence or other expenses incurred by or on behalf of the child in his visiting—

        (i) a parent of his;

        (ii) any person who is not a parent of his but who has parental responsibility for him; or

        (iii) any relative, friend or other person connected with him.

(3) The conditions are that—

(a) it appears to the authority that the visit in question could not otherwise be made without undue financial hardship; and

(b) the circumstances warrant the making of the payments.

Appointment of visitor for child who is not being visited

17.—(1) Where it appears to a local authority in relation to any child that they are looking after that—

(a) communication between the child and—

(i) a parent of his, or

(ii) any person who is not a parent of his but who has parental responsibility for him,

has been infrequent; or

(b) he has not visited or been visited by (or lived with) any such person during the preceding twelve months,

and that it would be in the child's best interests for an independent person to be appointed to be his visitor for the purposes of this paragraph, they shall appoint such a visitor.

(2) A person so appointed shall—

(a) have the duty of visiting, advising and befriending the child; and

(b) be entitled to recover from the authority who appointed him any reasonable expenses incurred by him for the purposes of his functions under this paragraph.

(3) A person's appointment as a visitor in pursuance of this paragraph shall be determined if—

(a) he gives notice in writing to the authority who appointed him that he resigns the appointment; or

(b) the authority give him notice in writing that they have terminated it.

(4) The determination of such an appointment shall not prejudice any duty under this paragraph to make a further appointment.

(5) Where a local authority propose to appoint a visitor for a child under this paragraph, the appointment shall not be made if—

(a) the child objects to it; and

(b) the authority are satisfied that he has sufficient understanding to make an informed decision.

(6) Where a visitor has been appointed for a child under this paragraph, the local authority shall determine the appointment if—

(a) the child objects to its continuing; and

(b) the authority are satisfied that he has sufficient understanding to make an informed decision.

(7) The Secretary of State may make regulations as to the circumstances in which a person appointed as a visitor under this paragraph is to be regarded as independent of the local authority appointing him.

Power to guarantee apprenticeship deeds etc.

18.—(1) While a child is being looked after by a local authority, or is a person qualifying for advice and assistance, the authority may undertake any obligation by way of guarantee under any deed of apprenticeship or articles of clerkship which he enters into.

SCH. 2   (2) Where a local authority have undertaken any such obligation under any deed or articles they may at any time (whether or not they are still looking after the person concerned) undertake the like obligation under any supplemental deed or articles.

Arrangements to assist children to live abroad

19.—(1) A local authority may only arrange for, or assist in arranging for, any child in their care to live outside England and Wales with the approval of the court.

(2) A local authority may, with the approval of every person who has parental responsibility for the child arrange for, or assist in arranging for, any other child looked after by them to live outside England and Wales.

(3) The court shall not give its approval under sub-paragraph (1) unless it is satisfied that—

(a) living outside England and Wales would be in the child's best interests;

(b) suitable arrangements have been, or will be, made for his reception and welfare in the country in which he will live;

(c) the child has consented to living in that country; and

(d) every person who has parental responsibility for the child has consented to his living in that country.

(4) Where the court is satisfied that the child does not have sufficient understanding to give or withhold his consent, it may disregard sub-paragraph (3)(c) and give its approval if the child is to live in the country concerned with a parent, guardian, or other suitable person.

(5) Where a person whose consent is required by sub-paragraph (3)(d) fails to give his consent, the court may disregard that provision and give its approval if it is satisfied that that person—

(a) cannot be found;

(b) is incapable of consenting; or

(c) is withholding his consent unreasonably.

1976 c. 36.   (6) Section 56 of the Adoption Act 1976 (which requires authority for the taking or sending abroad for adoption of a child who is a British subject) shall not apply in the case of any child who is to live outside England and Wales with the approval of the court given under this paragraph.

(7) Where a court decides to give its approval under this paragraph it may order that its decision is not to have effect during the appeal period.

(8) In sub-paragraph (7) "the appeal period" means—

(a) where an appeal is made against the decision, the period between the making of the decision and the determination of the appeal; and

(b) otherwise, the period during which an appeal may be made against the decision.

Death of children being looked after by local authorities

20.—(1) If a child who is being looked after by a local authority dies, the authority—

(a) shall notify the Secretary of State;

(b) shall, so far as is reasonably practicable, notify the child's parents and every person who is not a parent of his but who has parental responsibility for him;

(c) may, with the consent (so far as it is reasonably practicable to obtain it) of every person who has parental responsibility for the child, arrange for the child's body to be buried or cremated; and

(d) may, if the conditions mentioned in sub-paragraph (2) are satisfied, make payments to any person who has parental responsibility for the child, or any relative, friend or other person connected with the child, in respect of travelling, subsistence or other expenses incurred by that person in attending the child's funeral.

(2) The conditions are that—

(a) it appears to the authority that the person concerned could not otherwise attend the child's funeral without undue financial hardship; and

(b) that the circumstances warrant the making of the payments.

(3) Sub-paragraph (1) does not authorise cremation where it does not accord with the practice of the child's religious persuasion.

(4) Where a local authority have exercised their power under sub-paragraph (1)(c) with respect to a child who was under sixteen when he died, they may recover from any parent of the child any expenses incurred by them.

(5) Any sums so recoverable shall, without prejudice to any other method of recovery, be recoverable summarily as a civil debt.

(6) Nothing in this paragraph affects any enactment regulating or authorising the burial, cremation or anatomical examination of the body of a deceased person.

Part III

Contributions Towards Maintenance of Children Looked After by Local Authorities

Liability to contribute

21.—(1) Where a local authority are looking after a child (other than in the cases mentioned in sub-paragraph (7)) they shall consider whether they should recover contributions towards the child's maintenance from any person liable to contribute ("a contributor").

(2) An authority may only recover contributions from a contributor if they consider it reasonable to do so.

(3) The persons liable to contribute are—

(a) where the child is under sixteen, each of his parents;

(b) where he has reached the age of sixteen, the child himself.

(4) A parent is not liable to contribute during any period when he is in receipt of income support or family credit under the Social Security Act 1986.

1986 c. 50.

(5) A person is not liable to contribute towards the maintenance of a child in the care of a local authority in respect of any period during which the child is allowed by the authority (under section 23(5)) to live with a parent of his.

(6) A contributor is not obliged to make any contribution towards a child's maintenance except as agreed or determined in accordance with this Part of this Schedule.

(7) The cases are where the child is looked after by a local authority under—

(a) section 21;

(b) an interim care order;

(c) section 53 of the Children and Young Persons Act 1933.

1933 c. 12.

Agreed contributions

22.—(1) Contributions towards a child's maintenance may only be recovered if the local authority have served a notice ("a contribution notice") on the contributor specifying—

    (a) the weekly sum which they consider that he should contribute; and

    (b) arrangements for payment.

(2) The contribution notice must be in writing and dated.

(3) Arrangements for payment shall, in particular, include—

    (a) the date on which liability to contribute begins (which must not be earlier than the date of the notice);

    (b) the date on which liability under the notice will end (if the child has not before that date ceased to be looked after by the authority); and

    (c) the date on which the first payment is to be made.

(4) The authority may specify in a contribution notice a weekly sum which is a standard contribution determined by them for all children looked after by them.

(5) The authority may not specify in a contribution notice a weekly sum greater than that which they consider—

    (a) they would normally be prepared to pay if they had placed a similar child with local authority foster parents; and

    (b) it is reasonably practicable for the contributor to pay (having regard to his means).

(6) An authority may at any time withdraw a contribution notice (without prejudice to their power to serve another).

(7) Where the authority and the contributor agree—

    (a) the sum which the contributor is to contribute; and

    (b) arrangements for payment,

(whether as specified in the contribution notice or otherwise) and the contributor notifies the authority in writing that he so agrees, the authority may recover summarily as a civil debt any contribution which is overdue and unpaid.

(8) A contributor may, by serving a notice in writing on the authority, withdraw his agreement in relation to any period of liability falling after the date of service of the notice.

(9) Sub-paragraph (7) is without prejudice to any other method of recovery.

Contribution orders

23.—(1) Where a contributor has been served with a contribution notice and has—

    (a) failed to reach any agreement with the local authority as mentioned in paragraph 22(7) within the period of one month beginning with the day on which the contribution notice was served; or

    (b) served a notice under paragraph 22(8) withdrawing his agreement,

the authority may apply to the court for an order under this paragraph.

(2) On such an application the court may make an order ("a contribution order") requiring the contributor to contribute a weekly sum towards the child's maintenance in accordance with arrangements for payment specified by the court.

(3) A contribution order—

  (a) shall not specify a weekly sum greater than that specified in the contribution notice; and

  (b) shall be made with due regard to the contributor's means.

(4) A contribution order shall not—

  (a) take effect before the date specified in the contribution notice; or

  (b) have effect while the contributor is not liable to contribute (by virtue of paragraph 21); or

  (c) remain in force after the child has ceased to be looked after by the authority who obtained the order.

(5) An authority may not apply to the court under sub-paragraph (1) in relation to a contribution notice which they have withdrawn.

(6) Where—

  (a) a contribution order is in force;

  (b) the authority serve another contribution notice; and

  (c) the contributor and the authority reach an agreement under paragraph 22(7) in respect of that other contribution notice,

the effect of the agreement shall be to discharge the order from the date on which it is agreed that the agreement shall take effect.

(7) Where an agreement is reached under sub-paragraph (6) the authority shall notify the court—

  (a) of the agreement; and

  (b) of the date on which it took effect.

(8) A contribution order may be varied or revoked on the application of the contributor or the authority.

(9) In proceedings for the variation of a contribution order, the authority shall specify—

  (a) the weekly sum which, having regard to paragraph 22, they propose that the contributor should contribute under the order as varied; and

  (b) the proposed arrangements for payment.

(10) Where a contribution order is varied, the order—

  (a) shall not specify a weekly sum greater than that specified by the authority in the proceedings for variation; and

  (b) shall be made with due regard to the contributor's means.

(11) An appeal shall lie in accordance with rules of court from any order made under this paragraph.

Enforcement of contribution orders etc.

24.—(1) A contribution order made by a magistrates' court shall be enforceable as a magistrates' court maintenance order (within the meaning of section 150(1) of the Magistrates' Courts Act 1980).

1980 c. 43.

(2) Where a contributor has agreed, or has been ordered, to make contributions to a local authority, any other local authority within whose area the contributor is for the time being living may—

  (a) at the request of the local authority who served the contribution notice; and

(b) subject to agreement as to any sum to be deducted in respect of services rendered,

collect from the contributor any contributions due on behalf of the authority who served the notice.

(3) In sub-paragraph (2) the reference to any other local authority includes a reference to—

(a) a local authority within the meaning of section 1(2) of the Social Work (Scotland) Act 1968; and

(b) a Health and Social Services Board established under Article 16 of the Health and Personal Social Services (Northern Ireland) Order 1972.

(4) The power to collect sums under sub-paragraph (2) includes the power to—

(a) receive and give a discharge for any contributions due; and

(b) (if necessary) enforce payment of any contributions,

even though those contributions may have fallen due at a time when the contributor was living elsewhere.

(5) Any contribution collected under sub-paragraph (2) shall be paid (subject to any agreed deduction) to the local authority who served the contribution notice.

(6) In any proceedings under this paragraph, a document which purports to be—

(a) a copy of an order made by a court under or by virtue of paragraph 23; and

(b) certified as a true copy by the clerk of the court,

shall be evidence of the order.

(7) In any proceedings under this paragraph, a certificate which—

(a) purports to be signed by the clerk or some other duly authorised officer of the local authority who obtained the contribution order; and

(b) states that any sum due to the authority under the order is overdue and unpaid,

shall be evidence that the sum is overdue and unpaid.

Regulations

25. The Secretary of State may make regulations—

(a) as to the considerations which a local authority must take into account in deciding—

(i) whether it is reasonable to recover contributions; and

(ii) what the arrangements for payment should be;

(b) as to the procedures they must follow in reaching agreements with—

(i) contributors (under paragraphs 22 and 23); and

(ii) any other local authority (under paragraph 23).

SCHEDULE 3

SUPERVISION ORDERS

PART I

GENERAL

Meaning of "responsible person"

1. In this Schedule, "the responsible person", in relation to a supervised child, means—

    (a) any person who has parental responsibility for the child; and

    (b) any other person with whom the child is living.

Power of supervisor to give directions to supervised child

2.—(1) A supervision order may require the supervised child to comply with any directions given from time to time by the supervisor which require him to do all or any of the following things—

    (a) to live at a place or places specified in the directions for a period or periods so specified;

    (b) to present himself to a person or persons specified in the directions at a place or places and on a day or days so specified;

    (c) to participate in activities specified in the directions on a day or days so specified.

(2) It shall be for the supervisor to decide whether, and to what extent, he exercises his power to give directions and to decide the form of any directions which he gives.

(3) Sub-paragraph (1) does not confer on a supervisor power to give directions in respect of any medical or psychiatric examination or treatment (which are matters dealt with in paragraphs 4 and 5).

Imposition of obligations on responsible person

3.—(1) With the consent of any responsible person, a supervision order may include a requirement—

    (a) that he take all reasonable steps to ensure that the supervised child complies with any direction given by the supervisor under paragraph 2;

    (b) that he take all reasonable steps to ensure that the supervised child complies with any requirement included in the order under paragraph 4 or 5;

    (c) that he comply with any directions given by the supervisor requiring him to attend at a place specified in the directions for the purpose of taking part in activities so specified.

(2) A direction given under sub-paragraph (1)(c) may specify the time at which the responsible person is to attend and whether or not the supervised child is required to attend with him.

(3) A supervision order may require any person who is a responsible person in relation to the supervised child to keep the supervisor informed of his address, if it differs from the child's.

Psychiatric and medical examinations

4.—(1) A supervision order may require the supervised child—

    (a) to submit to a medical or psychiatric examination; or

    (b) to submit to any such examination from time to time as directed by the supervisor.

(2) Any such examination shall be required to be conducted—

  (a) by, or under the direction of, such registered medical practitioner as may be specified in the order;

  (b) at a place specified in the order and at which the supervised child is to attend as a non-resident patient; or

  (c) at—

      (i) a health service hospital; or

      (ii) in the case of a psychiatric examination, a hospital or mental nursing home,

  at which the supervised child is, or is to attend as, a resident patient.

(3) A requirement of a kind mentioned in sub-paragraph (2)(c) shall not be included unless the court is satisfied, on the evidence of a registered medical practitioner, that—

  (a) the child may be suffering from a physical or mental condition that requires, and may be susceptible to, treatment; and

  (b) a period as a resident patient is necessary if the examination is to be carried out properly.

(4) No court shall include a requirement under this paragraph in a supervision order unless it is satisfied that—

  (a) where the child has sufficient understanding to make an informed decision, he consents to its inclusion; and

  (b) satisfactory arrangements have been, or can be, made for the examination.

Psychiatric and medical treatment

1983 c. 20.

5.—(1) Where a court which proposes to make or vary a supervision order is satisfied, on the evidence of a registered medical practitioner approved for the purposes of section 12 of the Mental Health Act 1983, that the mental condition of the supervised child—

  (a) is such as requires, and may be susceptible to, treatment; but

  (b) is not such as to warrant his detention in pursuance of a hospital order under Part III of that Act,

the court may include in the order a requirement that the supervised child shall, for a period specified in the order, submit to such treatment as is so specified.

(2) The treatment specified in accordance with sub-paragraph (1) must be—

  (a) by, or under the direction of, such registered medical practitioner as may be specified in the order;

  (b) as a non-resident patient at such a place as may be so specified; or

  (c) as a resident patient in a hospital or mental nursing home.

(3) Where a court which proposes to make or vary a supervision order is satisfied, on the evidence of a registered medical practitioner, that the physical condition of the supervised child is such as requires, and may be susceptible to, treatment, the court may include in the order a requirement that the supervised child shall, for a period specified in the order, submit to such treatment as is so specified.

(4) The treatment specified in accordance with sub-paragraph (3) must be—

  (a) by, or under the direction of, such registered medical practitioner as may be specified in the order;

  (b) as a non-resident patient at such place as may be so specified; or

  (c) as a resident patient in a health service hospital.

(5) No court shall include a requirement under this paragraph in a supervision order unless it is satisfied—

(a) where the child has sufficient understanding to make an informed decision, that he consents to its inclusion; and

(b) that satisfactory arrangements have been, or can be, made for the treatment.

(6) If a medical practitioner by whom or under whose direction a supervised person is being treated in pursuance of a requirement included in a supervision order by virtue of this paragraph is unwilling to continue to treat or direct the treatment of the supervised child or is of the opinion that—

(a) the treatment should be continued beyond the period specified in the order;

(b) the supervised child needs different treatment;

(c) he is not susceptible to treatment; or

(d) he does not require further treatment,

the practitioner shall make a report in writing to that effect to the supervisor.

(7) On receiving a report under this paragraph the supervisor shall refer it to the court, and on such a reference the court may make an order cancelling or varying the requirement.

PART II

MISCELLANEOUS

Life of supervision order

6.—(1) Subject to sub-paragraph (2) and section 91, a supervision order shall cease to have effect at the end of the period of one year beginning with the date on which it was made.

(2) A supervision order shall also cease to have effect if an event mentioned in section 25(1)(a) or (b) of the Child Abduction and Custody Act 1985 (termination of existing orders) occurs with respect to the child. 1985 c. 60.

(3) Where the supervisor applies to the court to extend, or further extend, a supervision order the court may extend the order for such period as it may specify.

(4) A supervision order may not be extended so as to run beyond the end of the period of three years beginning with the date on which it was made.

Limited life of directions

7.—(1) The total number of days in respect of which a supervised child or (as the case may be) responsible person may be required to comply with directions given under paragraph 2 or 3 shall not exceed 90 or such lesser number (if any) as the supervision order may specify.

(2) For the purpose of calculating that total number of days, the supervisor may disregard any day in respect of which directions previously given in pursuance of the order were not complied with.

Information to be given to supervisor etc.

8.—(1) A supervision order may require the supervised child—

(a) to keep the supervisor informed of any change in his address; and

(b) to allow the supervisor to visit him at the place where he is living.

SCH. 3

(2) The responsible person in relation to any child with respect to whom a supervision order is made shall—

    (a) if asked by the supervisor, inform him of the child's address (if it is known to him); and

    (b) if he is living with the child, allow the supervisor reasonable contact with the child.

Selection of supervisor

9.—(1) A supervision order shall not designate a local authority as the supervisor unless—

    (a) the authority agree; or

    (b) the supervised child lives or will live within their area.

(2) A court shall not place a child under the supervision of a probation officer unless—

    (a) the appropriate authority so request; and

    (b) a probation officer is already exercising or has exercised, in relation to another member of the household to which the child belongs, duties imposed on probation officers—

1973 c. 62.

        (i) by paragraph 8 of Schedule 3 to the Powers of Criminal Courts Act 1973; or

        (ii) by rules under paragraph 18(1)(b) of that Schedule.

(3) In sub-paragraph (2) "the appropriate authority" means the local authority appearing to the court to be the authority in whose area the supervised child lives or will live.

(4) Where a supervision order places a person under the supervision of a probation officer, the officer shall be selected in accordance with arrangements made by the probation committee for the area in question.

(5) If the selected probation officer is unable to carry out his duties, or dies, another probation officer shall be selected in the same manner.

Effect of supervision order on earlier orders

10. The making of a supervision order with respect to any child brings to an end any earlier care or supervision order which—

    (a) was made with respect to that child; and

    (b) would otherwise continue in force.

Local authority functions and expenditure

11.—(1) The Secretary of State may make regulations with respect to the exercise by a local authority of their functions where a child has been placed under their supervision by a supervision order.

(2) Where a supervision order requires compliance with directions given by virtue of this section, any expenditure incurred by the supervisor for the purposes of the directions shall be defrayed by the local authority designated in the order.

PART III

EDUCATION SUPERVISION ORDERS

Effect of orders

12.—(1) Where an education supervision order is in force with respect to a child, it shall be the duty of the supervisor—

    (a) to advise, assist and befriend, and give directions to—

(i) the supervised child; and

(ii) his parents,

in such a way as will, in the opinion of the supervisor, secure that he is properly educated;

(b) where any such directions given to—

(i) the supervised child; or

(ii) a parent of his,

have not been complied with, to consider what further steps to take in the exercise of the supervisor's powers under this Act.

(2) Before giving any directions under sub-paragraph (1) the supervisor shall, so far as is reasonably practicable, ascertain the wishes and feelings of—

(a) the child; and

(b) his parents,

including, in particular, their wishes as to the place at which the child should be educated.

(3) When settling the terms of any such directions, the supervisor shall give due consideration—

(a) having regard to the child's age and understanding, to such wishes and feelings of his as the supervisor has been able to ascertain; and

(b) to such wishes and feelings of the child's parents as he has been able to ascertain.

(4) Directions may be given under this paragraph at any time while the education supervision order is in force.

13.—(1) Where an education supervision order is in force with respect to a child, the duties of the child's parents under sections 36 and 39 of the Education Act 1944 (duty to secure education of children and to secure regular attendance of registered pupils) shall be superseded by their duty to comply with any directions in force under the education supervision order. 1944 c. 31.

(2) Where an education supervision order is made with respect to a child—

(a) any school attendance order—

(i) made under section 37 of the Act of 1944 with respect to the child; and

(ii) in force immediately before the making of the education supervision order,

shall cease to have effect; and

(b) while the education supervision order remains in force, the following provisions shall not apply with respect to the child—

(i) section 37 of that Act (school attendance orders);

(ii) section 76 of that Act (pupils to be educated in accordance with wishes of their parents);

(iii) sections 6 and 7 of the Education Act 1980 (parental preference and appeals against admission decisions); 1980 c. 20.

(c) a supervision order made with respect to the child in criminal proceedings, while the education supervision order is in force, may not include an education requirement of the kind which could otherwise be included under section 12C of the Children and Young Persons Act 1969; 1969 c. 54.

(d) any education requirement of a kind mentioned in paragraph (c), which was in force with respect to the child immediately before the making of the education supervision order, shall cease to have effect.

Effect where child also subject to supervision order

14.—(1) This paragraph applies where an education supervision order and a supervision order, or order under section 7(7)(b) of the Children and Young Persons Act 1969, are in force at the same time with respect to the same child.

(2) Any failure to comply with a direction given by the supervisor under the education supervision order shall be disregarded if it would not have been reasonably practicable to comply with it without failing to comply with a direction given under the other order.

Duration of orders

15.—(1) An education supervision order shall have effect for a period of one year, beginning with the date on which it is made.

(2) An education supervision order shall not expire if, before it would otherwise have expired, the court has (on the application of the authority in whose favour the order was made) extended the period during which it is in force.

(3) Such an application may not be made earlier than three months before the date on which the order would otherwise expire.

(4) The period during which an education supervision order is in force may be extended under sub-paragraph (2) on more than one occasion.

(5) No one extension may be for a period of more than three years.

(6) An education supervision order shall cease to have effect on—

(a) the child's ceasing to be of compulsory school age; or

(b) the making of a care order with respect to the child;

and sub-paragraphs (1) to (4) are subject to this sub-paragraph.

Information to be given to supervisor etc.

16.—(1) An education supervision order may require the child—

(a) to keep the supervisor informed of any change in his address; and

(b) to allow the supervisor to visit him at the place where he is living.

(2) A person who is the parent of a child with respect to whom an education supervision order has been made shall—

(a) if asked by the supervisor, inform him of the child's address (if it is known to him); and

(b) if he is living with the child, allow the supervisor reasonable contact with the child.

Discharge of orders

17.—(1) The court may discharge any education supervision order on the application of—

(a) the child concerned;

(b) a parent of his; or

(c) the local education authority concerned.

(2) On discharging an education supervision order, the court may direct the local authority within whose area the child lives, or will live, to investigate the circumstances of the child.

Offences

18.—(1) If a parent of a child with respect to whom an education supervision order is in force persistently fails to comply with a direction given under the order he shall be guilty of an offence.

(2) It shall be a defence for any person charged with such an offence to prove that—

> (a) he took all reasonable steps to ensure that the direction was complied with;

> (b) the direction was unreasonable; or

> (c) he had complied with—

>> (i) a requirement included in a supervision order made with respect to the child; or

>> (ii) directions given under such a requirement,

> and that it was not reasonably practicable to comply both with the direction and with the requirement or directions mentioned in this paragraph.

(3) A person guilty of an offence under this paragraph shall be liable on summary conviction to a fine not exceeding level 3 on the standard scale.

Persistent failure of child to comply with directions

19.—(1) Where a child with respect to whom an education supervision order is in force persistently fails to comply with any direction given under the order, the local education authority concerned shall notify the appropriate local authority.

(2) Where a local authority have been notified under sub-paragraph (1) they shall investigate the circumstances of the child.

(3) In this paragraph "the appropriate local authority" has the same meaning as in section 36.

Miscellaneous

20. The Secretary of State may by regulations make provision modifying, or displacing, the provisions of any enactment about education in relation to any child with respect to whom an education supervision order is in force to such extent as appears to the Secretary of State to be necessary or expedient in consequence of the provision made by this Act with respect to such orders.

Interpretation

21. In this Part of this Schedule "parent" has the same meaning as in the Education Act 1944 (as amended by Schedule 13).

1944 c. 31.

SCHEDULE 4

Section 53(6).

Management and Conduct of Community Homes

Part I

Instruments of Management

Instruments of management for controlled and assisted community homes

1.—(1) The Secretary of State may by order make an instrument of management providing for the constitution of a body of managers for any voluntary home which is designated as a controlled or assisted community home.

(2) Sub-paragraph (3) applies where two or more voluntary homes are designated as controlled community homes or as assisted community homes.

Sch. 4

(3) If—

     (a) those homes are, or are to be, provided by the same voluntary organisation; and

     (b) the same local authority is to be represented on the body of managers for those homes,

a single instrument of management may be made by the Secretary of State under this paragraph constituting one body of managers for those homes or for any two or more of them.

(4) The number of persons who, in accordance with an instrument of management, constitute the body of managers for a voluntary home shall be such number (which must be a multiple of three) as may be specified in the instrument.

(5) The instrument shall provide that the local authority specified in the instrument shall appoint—

     (a) in the case of a voluntary home which is designated as a controlled community home, two-thirds of the managers; and

     (b) in the case of a voluntary home which is designated as an assisted community home, one-third of them.

(6) An instrument of management shall provide that the foundation managers shall be appointed, in such manner and by such persons as may be specified in the instrument—

     (a) so as to represent the interests of the voluntary organisation by which the home is, or is to be, provided; and

     (b) for the purpose of securing that—

         (i) so far as is practicable, the character of the home as a voluntary home will be preserved; and

         (ii) subject to paragraph 2(3), the terms of any trust deed relating to the home are observed.

(7) An instrument of management shall come into force on such date as it may specify.

(8) If an instrument of management is in force in relation to a voluntary home the home shall be (and be known as) a controlled community home or an assisted community home, according to its designation.

(9) In this paragraph—

"foundation managers", in relation to a voluntary home, means those of the managers of the home who are not appointed by a local authority in accordance with sub-paragraph (5); and

"designated" means designated in accordance with section 53.

2.—(1) An instrument of management shall contain such provisions as the Secretary of State considers appropriate.

(2) Nothing in the instrument of management shall affect the purposes for which the premises comprising the home are held.

(3) Without prejudice to the generality of sub-paragraph (1), an instrument of management may contain provisions—

     (a) specifying the nature and purpose of the home (or each of the homes) to which it relates;

     (b) requiring a specified number or proportion of the places in that home (or those homes) to be made available to local authorities and to any other body specified in the instrument; and

(c) relating to the management of that home (or those homes) and the charging of fees with respect to—

    (i) children placed there; or

    (ii) places made available to any local authority or other body.

(4) Subject to sub-paragraphs (1) and (2), in the event of any inconsistency between the provisions of any trust deed and an instrument of management, the instrument of management shall prevail over the provisions of the trust deed in so far as they relate to the home concerned.

(5) After consultation with the voluntary organisation concerned and with the local authority specified in its instrument of management, the Secretary of State may by order vary or revoke any provisions of the instrument.

PART II

MANAGEMENT OF CONTROLLED AND ASSISTED COMMUNITY HOMES

3.—(1) The management, equipment and maintenance of a controlled community home shall be the responsibility of the local authority specified in its instrument of management.

(2) The management, equipment and maintenance of an assisted community home shall be the responsibility of the voluntary organisation by which the home is provided.

(3) In this paragraph—

"home" means a controlled community home or (as the case may be) assisted community home; and

"the managers", in relation to a home, means the managers constituted by its instrument of management; and

"the responsible body", in relation to a home, means the local authority or (as the case may be) voluntary organisation responsible for its management, equipment and maintenance.

(4) The functions of a home's responsible body shall be exercised through the managers.

(5) Anything done, liability incurred or property acquired by a home's managers shall be done, incurred or acquired by them as agents of the responsible body.

(6) In so far as any matter is reserved for the decision of a home's responsible body by—

    (a) sub-paragraph (8);

    (b) the instrument of management;

    (c) the service by the body on the managers, or any of them, of a notice reserving any matter,

that matter shall be dealt with by the body and not by the managers.

(7) In dealing with any matter so reserved, the responsible body shall have regard to any representations made to the body by the managers.

(8) The employment of persons at a home shall be a matter reserved for the decision of the responsible body.

(9) Where the instrument of management of a controlled community home so provides, the responsible body may enter into arrangements with the voluntary organisation by which that home is provided whereby, in accordance with such terms as may be agreed between them and the voluntary organisation, persons who are not in the employment of the responsible body shall undertake duties at that home.

(10) Subject to sub-paragraph (11)—

    (a) where the responsible body for an assisted community home proposes to engage any person to work at that home or to terminate without notice the employment of any person at that home, it shall consult the local authority specified in the instrument of management and, if that authority so direct, the responsible body shall not carry out its proposal without their consent; and

    (b) that local authority may, after consultation with the responsible body, require that body to terminate the employment of any person at that home.

(11) Paragraphs (a) and (b) of sub-paragraph (10) shall not apply—

    (a) in such cases or circumstances as may be specified by notice in writing given by the local authority to the responsible body; and

    (b) in relation to the employment of any persons or class of persons specified in the home's instrument of management.

(12) The accounting year of the managers of a home shall be such as may be specified by the responsible body.

(13) Before such date in each accounting year as may be so specified, the managers of a home shall submit to the responsible body estimates, in such form as the body may require, of expenditure and receipts in respect of the next accounting year.

(14) Any expenses incurred by the managers of a home with the approval of the responsible body shall be defrayed by that body.

(15) The managers of a home shall keep—

    (a) proper accounts with respect to the home; and

    (b) proper records in relation to the accounts.

(16) Where an instrument of management relates to more than one home, one set of accounts and records may be kept in respect of all the homes to which it relates.

PART III

REGULATIONS

4.—(1) The Secretary of State may make regulations—

    (a) as to the placing of children in community homes;

    (b) as to the conduct of such homes; and

    (c) for securing the welfare of children in such homes.

(2) The regulations may, in particular—

    (a) prescribe standards to which the premises used for such homes are to conform;

    (b) impose requirements as to the accommodation, staff and equipment to be provided in such homes, and as to the arrangements to be made for protecting the health of children in such homes;

    (c) provide for the control and discipline of children in such homes;

    (d) impose requirements as to the keeping of records and giving of notices in respect of children in such homes;

    (e) impose requirements as to the facilities which are to be provided for giving religious instruction to children in such homes;

    (f) authorise the Secretary of State to give and revoke directions requiring—

    (i) the local authority by whom a home is provided or who are specified in the instrument of management for a controlled community home, or

    (ii) the voluntary organisation by which an assisted community home is provided,

to accommodate in the home a child looked after by a local authority for whom no places are made available in that home or to take such action in relation to a child accommodated in the home as may be specified in the directions;

(g) provide for consultation with the Secretary of State as to applicants for appointment to the charge of a home;

(h) empower the Secretary of State to prohibit the appointment of any particular applicant except in the cases (if any) in which the regulations dispense with such consultation by reason that the person to be appointed possesses such qualifications as may be prescribed;

(i) require the approval of the Secretary of State for the provision and use of accommodation for the purpose of restricting the liberty of children in such homes and impose other requirements (in addition to those imposed by section 25) as to the placing of a child in accommodation provided for that purpose, including a requirement to obtain the permission of any local authority who are looking after the child;

(j) provide that, to such extent as may be provided for in the regulations, the Secretary of State may direct that any provision of regulations under this paragraph which is specified in the direction and makes any such provision as is referred to in paragraph (a) or (b) shall not apply in relation to a particular home or the premises used for it, and may provide for the variation or revocation of any such direction by the Secretary of State.

(3) Without prejudice to the power to make regulations under this paragraph conferring functions on—

(a) the local authority or voluntary organisation by which a community home is provided; or

(b) the managers of a controlled or assisted community home,

regulations under this paragraph may confer functions in relation to a controlled or assisted community home on the local authority named in the instrument of management for the home.

SCHEDULE 5

Voluntary Homes and Voluntary Organisations

Part I

Registration of Voluntary Homes

General

1.—(1) An application for registration under this paragraph shall—

(a) be made by the persons intending to carry on the home to which the application relates; and

(b) be made in such manner, and be accompanied by such particulars, as the Secretary of State may prescribe.

(2) On an application duly made under sub-paragraph (1) the Secretary of State may—

(a) grant or refuse the application, as he thinks fit; or

(b) grant the application subject to such conditions as he considers appropriate.

(3) The Secretary of State may from time to time—

   (a) vary any condition for the time being in force with respect to a voluntary home by virtue of this paragraph; or

   (b) impose an additional condition,

either on the application of the person carrying on the home or without such an application.

(4) Where at any time it appears to the Secretary of State that the conduct of any voluntary home—

   (a) is not in accordance with regulations made under paragraph 7; or

   (b) is otherwise unsatisfactory,

he may cancel the registration of the home and remove it from the register.

(5) Any person who, without reasonable excuse, carries on a voluntary home in contravention of—

   (a) section 60; or

   (b) a condition to which the registration of the home is for the time being subject by virtue of this Part,

shall be guilty of an offence.

(6) Any person guilty of such an offence shall be liable on summary conviction to a fine not exceeding—

   (a) level 5 on the standard scale, if his offence is under sub-paragraph (5)(a); or

   (b) level 4, if it is under sub-paragraph (5)(b).

(7) Where the Secretary of State registers a home under this paragraph, or cancels the registration of a home, he shall notify the local authority within whose area the home is situated.

Procedure

2.—(1) Where—

   (a) a person applies for registration of a voluntary home; and

   (b) the Secretary of State proposes to grant his application,

the Secretary of State shall give him written notice of his proposal and of the conditions subject to which he proposes to grant the application.

(2) The Secretary of State need not give notice if he proposes to grant the application subject only to conditions which—

   (a) the applicant specified in the application; or

   (b) the Secretary of State and the applicant have subsequently agreed.

(3) Where the Secretary of State proposes to refuse such an application he shall give notice of his proposal to the applicant.

(4) The Secretary of State shall give any person carrying on a voluntary home notice of a proposal to—

   (a) cancel the registration of the home;

   (b) vary any condition for the time being in force with respect to the home by virtue of paragraph 1; or

   (c) impose any additional condition.

(5) A notice under this paragraph shall give the Secretary of State's reasons for his proposal.

Right to make representations

3.—(1) A notice under paragraph 2 shall state that within 14 days of service of the notice any person on whom it is served may (in writing) require the Secretary of State to give him an opportunity to make representations to the Secretary of State concerning the matter.

(2) Where a notice has been served under paragraph 2, the Secretary of State shall not determine the matter until either—

   (a) any person on whom the notice was served has made representations to him concerning the matter; or

   (b) the period during which any such person could have required the Secretary of State to give him an opportunity to make representations has elapsed without the Secretary of State being required to give such an opportunity; or

   (c) the conditions specified in sub-paragraph (3) are satisfied.

(3) The conditions are that—

   (a) a person on whom the notice was served has required the Secretary of State to give him an opportunity to make representations to the Secretary of State;

   (b) the Secretary of State has allowed him a reasonable period to make his representations; and

   (c) he has failed to make them within that period.

(4) The representations may be made, at the option of the person making them, either in writing or orally.

(5) If he informs the Secretary of State that he desires to make oral representations, the Secretary of State shall give him an opportunity of appearing before, and of being heard by, a person appointed by the Secretary of State.

Decision of Secretary of State

4.—(1) If the Secretary of State decides to adopt the proposal, he shall serve notice in writing of his decision on any person on whom he was required to serve notice of his proposal.

(2) A notice under this paragraph shall be accompanied by a notice explaining the right of appeal conferred by paragraph 5.

(3) A decision of the Secretary of State, other than a decision to grant an application for registration subject only to such conditions as are mentioned in paragraph 2(2) or to refuse an application for registration, shall not take effect—

   (a) if no appeal is brought, until the end of the period of 28 days referred to in paragraph 5(3); and

   (b) if an appeal is brought, until it is determined or abandoned.

Appeals

5.—(1) An appeal against a decision of the Secretary of State under Part VII shall lie to a Registered Homes Tribunal.

(2) An appeal shall be brought by notice in writing given to the Secretary of State.

(3) No appeal may be brought by a person more than 28 days after service on him of notice of the decision.

(4) On an appeal, the Tribunal may confirm the Secretary of State's decision or direct that it shall not have effect.

(5) A Tribunal shall also have power on an appeal to—

    (a) vary any condition for the time being in force by virtue of Part VII with respect to the home to which the appeal relates;

    (b) direct that any such condition shall cease to have effect; or

    (c) direct that any such condition as it thinks fit shall have effect with respect to the home.

Notification of particulars with respect to voluntary homes

6.—(1) It shall be the duty of the person in charge of any voluntary home established after the commencement of this Act to send to the Secretary of State within three months from the establishment of the home such particulars with respect to the home as the Secretary of State may prescribe.

(2) It shall be the duty of the person in charge of any voluntary home (whether established before or after the commencement of this Act) to send to the Secretary of State such particulars with respect to the home as may be prescribed.

(3) The particulars must be sent—

    (a) in the case of a home established before the commencement of this Act, in every year, or

    (b) in the case of a home established after the commencement of this Act, in every year subsequent to the year in which particulars are sent under sub-paragraph (1),

by such date as the Secretary of State may prescribe.

(4) Where the Secretary of State by regulations varies the particulars which are to be sent to him under sub-paragraph (1) or (2) by the person in charge of a voluntary home—

    (a) that person shall send to the Secretary of State the prescribed particulars within three months from the date of the making of the regulations;

    (b) where any such home was established before, but not more than three months before, the making of the regulations, compliance with paragraph (a) shall be sufficient compliance with the requirement of sub-paragraph (1) to send the prescribed particulars within three months from the establishment of the home;

    (c) in the year in which the particulars are varied, compliance with paragraph (a) by the person in charge of any voluntary home shall be sufficient compliance with the requirement of sub-paragraph (2) to send the prescribed particulars before the prescribed date in that year.

(5) If the person in charge of a voluntary home fails, without reasonable excuse, to comply with any of the requirements of this paragraph he shall be guilty of an offence.

(6) Any person guilty of such an offence shall be liable on summary conviction to a fine not exceeding level 2 on the standard scale.

Part II

Regulations as to Voluntary Homes

Regulations as to conduct of voluntary homes

7.—(1) The Secretary of State may make regulations—

    (a) as to the placing of children in voluntary homes;

    (b) as to the conduct of such homes; and

    (c) for securing the welfare of children in such homes.

(2) The regulations may, in particular—

(a) prescribe standards to which the premises used for such homes are to conform;

(b) impose requirements as to the accommodation, staff and equipment to be provided in such homes, and as to the arrangements to be made for protecting the health of children in such homes;

(c) provide for the control and discipline of children in such homes;

(d) require the furnishing to the Secretary of State of information as to the facilities provided for—

(i) the parents of children in the homes; and

(ii) persons who are not parents of such children but who have parental responsibility for them; and

(iii) other persons connected with such children,

to visit and communicate with the children;

(e) authorise the Secretary of State to limit the number of children who may be accommodated in any particular voluntary home;

(f) prohibit the use of accommodation for the purpose of restricting the liberty of children in such homes;

(g) impose requirements as to the keeping of records and giving of notices with respect to children in such homes;

(h) impose requirements as to the facilities which are to be provided for giving religious instruction to children in such homes;

(i) require notice to be given to the Secretary of State of any change of the person carrying on or in charge of a voluntary home or of the premises used by such a home.

(3) The regulations may provide that a contravention of, or failure to comply with, any specified provision of the regulations without reasonable excuse shall be an offence against the regulations.

(4) Any person guilty of such an offence shall be liable to a fine not exceeding level 4 on the standard scale.

Disqualification

8. The Secretary of State may by regulation make provision with respect to the disqualification of persons in relation to voluntary homes of a kind similar to that made in relation to children's homes by section 65.

SCHEDULE 6

Section 63(11).

Registered Children's Homes

Part I

Registration

Application for registration

1.—(1) An application for the registration of a children's home shall be made—

(a) by the person carrying on, or intending to carry on, the home; and

(b) to the local authority for the area in which the home is, or is to be, situated.

(2) The application shall be made in the prescribed manner and shall be accompanied by—

(a) such particulars as may be prescribed; and

(b) such reasonable fee as the local authority may determine.

(3) In this Schedule "prescribed" means prescribed by regulations made by the Secretary of State.

(4) If a local authority are satisfied that a children's home with respect to which an application has been made in accordance with this Schedule complies or (as the case may be) will comply—

    (a) with such requirements as may be prescribed, and

    (b) with such other requirements (if any) as appear to them to be appropriate,

they shall grant the application, either unconditionally or subject to conditions imposed under paragraph 2.

(5) Before deciding whether or not to grant an application a local authority shall comply with any prescribed requirements.

(6) Regulations made for the purposes of sub-paragraph (5) may, in particular, make provision as to the inspection of the home in question.

(7) Where an application is granted, the authority shall notify the applicant that the home has been registered under this Act as from such date as may be specified in the notice.

(8) If the authority are not satisfied as mentioned in sub-paragraph (4), they shall refuse the application.

(9) For the purposes of this Act, an application which has not been granted or refused within the period of twelve months beginning with the date when it is served on the authority shall be deemed to have been refused by them, and the applicant shall be deemed to have been notified of their refusal at the end of that period.

(10) Where a school to which section 63(1) applies is registered it shall not cease to be a registered children's home by reason only of a subsequent change in the number of children for whom it provides accommodation.

Conditions imposed on registration

2.—(1) A local authority may grant an application for registration subject to such conditions relating to the conduct of the home as they think fit.

(2) A local authority may from time to time—

    (a) vary any condition for the time being in force with respect to a home by virtue of this paragraph; or

    (b) impose an additional condition,

either on the application of the person carrying on the home or without such an application.

(3) If any condition imposed or varied under this paragraph is not complied with, the person carrying on the home shall, if he has no reasonable excuse, be guilty of an offence and liable on summary conviction to a fine not exceeding level 4 on the standard scale.

Annual review of registration

3.—(1) In this Part "the responsible authority", in relation to a registered children's home means the local authority who registered it.

(2) The responsible authority for a registered children's home shall, at the end of the period of twelve months beginning with the date of registration, and annually thereafter, review its registration for the purpose of determining whether the registration should continue in force or be cancelled under paragraph 4(3).

(3) If on any such annual review the responsible authority are satisfied that the home is being carried on in accordance with the relevant requirements they shall determine that, subject to sub-paragraph (4), the registration should continue in force.

(4) The responsible authority shall give to the person carrying on the home notice of their determination under sub-paragraph (3) and the notice shall require him to pay to the authority with respect to the review such reasonable fee as the authority may determine.

(5) It shall be a condition of the home's continued registration that the fee is so paid before the expiry of the period of twenty-eight days beginning with the date on which the notice is received by the person carrying on the home.

(6) In this Schedule "the relevant requirements" means any requirements of Part VIII and of any regulations made under paragraph 10, and any conditions imposed under paragraph 2.

Cancellation of registration

4.—(1) The person carrying on a registered children's home may at any time make an application, in such manner and including such particulars as may be prescribed, for the cancellation by the responsible authority of the registration of the home.

(2) If the authority are satisfied, in the case of a school registered by virtue of section 63(6), that it is no longer a school to which that provision applies, the authority shall give to the person carrying on the home notice that the registration of the home has been cancelled as from the date of the notice.

(3) If on any annual review under paragraph 3, or at any other time, it appears to the responsible authority that a registered home is being carried on otherwise than in accordance with the relevant requirements, they may determine that the registration of the home should be cancelled.

(4) The responsible authority may at any time determine that the registration of a home should be cancelled on the ground—

(a) that the person carrying on the home has been convicted of an offence under this Part or any regulations made under paragraph 10; or

(b) that any other person has been convicted of such an offence in relation to the home.

Procedure

5.—(1) Where—

(a) a person applies for the registration of a children's home; and

(b) the local authority propose to grant his application,

they shall give him written notice of their proposal and of the conditions (if any) subject to which they propose to grant his application.

(2) The authority need not give notice if they propose to grant the application subject only to conditions which—

(a) the applicant specified in the application; or

(b) the authority and the applicant have subsequently agreed.

(3) The authority shall give an applicant notice of a proposal to refuse his application.

(4) The authority shall give any person carrying on a registered children's home notice of a proposal—

(a) to cancel the registration;

(b) to vary any condition for the time being in force with respect to the home by virtue of Part VIII; or

(c) to impose any additional condition.

(5) A notice under this paragraph shall give the local authority's reasons for their proposal.

Right to make representations

6.—(1) A notice under paragraph 5 shall state that within 14 days of service of the notice any person on whom it is served may in writing require the local authority to give him an opportunity to make representations to them concerning the matter.

(2) Where a notice has been served under paragraph 5, the local authority shall not determine the matter until—

(a) any person on whom the notice was served has made representations to them concerning the matter;

(b) the period during which any such person could have required the local authority to give him an opportunity to make representations has elapsed without their being required to give such an opportunity; or

(c) the conditions specified in sub-paragraph (3) below are satisfied.

(3) The conditions are—

(a) that a person on whom the notice was served has required the local authority to give him an opportunity to make representations to them concerning the matter;

(b) that the authority have allowed him a reasonable period to make his representations; and

(c) that he has failed to make them within that period.

(4) The representations may be made, at the option of the person making them, either in writing or orally.

(5) If he informs the local authority that he desires to make oral representations, the authority shall give him an opportunity of appearing before and of being heard by a committee or sub-committee of theirs.

Decision of local authority

7.—(1) If the local authority decide to adopt a proposal of theirs to grant an application, they shall serve notice in writing of their decision on any person on whom they were required to serve notice of their proposal.

(2) A notice under this paragraph shall be accompanied by an explanation of the right of appeal conferred by paragraph 8.

(3) A decision of a local authority, other than a decision to grant an application for registration subject only to such conditions as are mentioned in paragraph 5(2) or to refuse an application for registration, shall not take effect—

(a) if no appeal is brought, until the end of the period of 28 days referred to in paragraph 8(3); and

(b) if an appeal is brought, until it is determined or abandoned.

Appeals

8.—(1) An appeal against a decision of a local authority under Part VIII shall lie to a Registered Homes Tribunal.

(2) An appeal shall be brought by notice in writing given to the local authority.

(3) No appeal shall be brought by a person more than 28 days after service on him of notice of the decision.

(4) On an appeal the Tribunal may confirm the local authority's decision or direct that it shall not have effect.

(5) A Tribunal shall also have power on an appeal—

(a) to vary any condition in force with respect to the home to which the appeal relates by virtue of paragraph 2;

(b) to direct that any such condition shall cease to have effect; or

(c) to direct that any such condition as it thinks fit shall have effect with respect to the home.

(6) A local authority shall comply with any direction given by a Tribunal under this paragraph.

Prohibition on further applications

9.—(1) Where an application for the registration of a home is refused, no further application may be made within the period of six months beginning with the date when the applicant is notified of the refusal.

(2) Sub-paragraph (1) shall have effect, where an appeal against the refusal of an application is determined or abandoned, as if the reference to the date when the applicant is notified of the refusal were a reference to the date on which the appeal is determined or abandoned.

(3) Where the registration of a home is cancelled, no application for the registration of the home shall be made within the period of six months beginning with the date of cancellation.

(4) Sub-paragraph (3) shall have effect, where an appeal against the cancellation of the registration of a home is determined or abandoned, as if the reference to the date of cancellation were a reference to the date on which the appeal is determined or abandoned.

Part II

Regulations

10.—(1) The Secretary of State may make regulations—

(a) as to the placing of children in registered children's homes;

(b) as to the conduct of such homes; and

(c) for securing the welfare of the children in such homes.

(2) The regulations may in particular—

(a) prescribe standards to which the premises used for such homes are to conform;

(b) impose requirements as to the accommodation, staff and equipment to be provided in such homes;

(c) impose requirements as to the arrangements to be made for protecting the health of children in such homes;

(d) provide for the control and discipline of children in such homes;

(e) require the furnishing to the responsible authority of information as to the facilities provided for—

(i) the parents of children in such homes;

(ii) persons who are not parents of such children but who have parental responsibility for them; and

(iii) other persons connected with such children,
to visit and communicate with the children;

SCH. 6

(f) impose requirements as to the keeping of records and giving of notices with respect to children in such homes;

(g) impose requirements as to the facilities which are to be provided for giving religious instruction to children in such homes;

(h) make provision as to the carrying out of annual reviews under paragraph 3;

(i) authorise the responsible authority to limit the number of children who may be accommodated in any particular registered home;

(j) prohibit the use of accommodation for the purpose of restricting the liberty of children in such homes;

(k) require notice to be given to the responsible authority of any change of the person carrying on or in charge of a registered home or of the premises used by such a home;

(l) make provision similar to that made by regulations under section 26.

(3) The regulations may provide that a contravention of or failure to comply with any specified provision of the regulations, without reasonable excuse, shall be an offence against the regulations.

(4) Any person guilty of such an offence shall be liable on summary conviction to a fine not exceeding level 4 on the standard scale.

Section 63(12).

SCHEDULE 7

FOSTER PARENTS: LIMITS ON NUMBER OF FOSTER CHILDREN

Interpretation

1. For the purposes of this Schedule, a person fosters a child if—

(a) he is a local authority foster parent in relation to the child;

(b) he is a foster parent with whom the child has been placed by a voluntary organisation; or

(c) he fosters the child privately.

The usual fostering limit

2. Subject to what follows, a person may not foster more than three children ("the usual fostering limit").

Siblings

3. A person may exceed the usual fostering limit if the children concerned are all siblings with respect to each other.

Exemption by local authority

4.—(1) A person may exceed the usual fostering limit if he is exempted from it by the local authority within whose area he lives.

(2) In considering whether to exempt a person, a local authority shall have regard, in particular, to—

(a) the number of children whom the person proposes to foster;

(b) the arrangements which the person proposes for the care and accommodation of the fostered children;

(c) the intended and likely relationship between the person and the fostered children;

(d) the period of time for which he proposes to foster the children; and

(e) whether the welfare of the fostered children (and of any other children
who are or will be living in the accommodation) will be safeguarded
and promoted.

(3) Where a local authority exempt a person, they shall inform him by notice
in writing—

(a) that he is so exempted;

(b) of the children, described by name, whom he may foster; and

(c) of any condition to which the exemption is subject.

(4) A local authority may at any time by notice in writing—

(a) vary or cancel an exemption; or

(b) impose, vary or cancel a condition to which the exemption is subject,
and, in considering whether to do so, they shall have regard in particular to the
considerations mentioned in sub-paragraph (2).

(5) The Secretary of State may make regulations amplifying or modifying the
provisions of this paragraph in order to provide for cases where children need to
be placed with foster parents as a matter of urgency.

Effect of exceeding fostering limit

5.—(1) A person shall cease to be treated as fostering and shall be treated as
carrying on a children's home if—

(a) he exceeds the usual fostering limit; or

(b) where he is exempted under paragraph 4,—

(i) he fosters any child not named in the exemption; and

(ii) in so doing, he exceeds the usual fostering limit.

(2) Sub-paragraph (1) does not apply if the children concerned are all siblings
in respect of each other.

Complaints etc.

6.—(1) Every local authority shall establish a procedure for considering any
representations (including any complaint) made to them about the discharge of
their functions under paragraph 4 by a person exempted or seeking to be
exempted under that paragraph.

(2) In carrying out any consideration of representations under sub-paragraph
(1), a local authority shall comply with any regulations made by the Secretary of
State for the purposes of this paragraph.

SCHEDULE 8
PRIVATELY FOSTERED CHILDREN
Exemptions

1. A child is not a privately fostered child while he is being looked after by a
local authority.

2.—(1) A child is not a privately fostered child while he is in the care of any
person—

(a) in premises in which any—

(i) parent of his;

(ii) person who is not a parent of his but who has parental
responsibility for him; or

(iii) person who is a relative of his and who has assumed

responsibility for his care,

is for the time being living;

(b) in any children's home;

(c) in accommodation provided by or on behalf of any voluntary organisation;

(d) in any school in which he is receiving full-time education;

(e) in any health service hospital;

(f) in any residential care home, nursing home or mental nursing home; or

(g) in any home or institution not specified in this paragraph but provided, equipped and maintained by the Secretary of State.

(2) Sub-paragraph (1)(b) to (g) does not apply where the person caring for the child is doing so in his personal capacity and not in the course of carrying out his duties in relation to the establishment mentioned in the paragraph in question.

3. A child is not a privately fostered child while he is in the care of any person in compliance with—

1969 c. 54.

(a) an order under section 7(7)(b) of the Children and Young Persons Act 1969; or

1968 c. 49.

(b) a supervision requirement within the meaning of the Social Work (Scotland) Act 1968.

4. A child is not a privately fostered child while he is liable to be detained, or 1983 c. 20. subject to guardianship, under the Mental Health Act 1983.

5. A child is not a privately fostered child while—

(a) he is placed in the care of a person who proposes to adopt him under arrangements made by an adoption agency within the meaning of—

1976 c. 36.

(i) section 1 of the Adoption Act 1976;

1978 c. 28.

(ii) section 1 of the Adoption (Scotland) Act 1978; or

S.I. 1987/2203 (N.I. 22).

(iii) Article 3 of the Adoption (Northern Ireland) Order 1987; or

(b) he is a protected child.

Power of local authority to impose requirements

6.—(1) Where a person is fostering any child privately, or proposes to foster any child privately, the appropriate local authority may impose on him requirements as to—

(a) the number, age and sex of the children who may be privately fostered by him;

(b) the standard of the accommodation and equipment to be provided for them;

(c) the arrangements to be made with respect to their health and safety; and

(d) particular arrangements which must be made with respect to the provision of care for them,

and it shall be his duty to comply with any such requirement before the end of such period as the authority may specify unless, in the case of a proposal, the proposal is not carried out.

(2) A requirement may be limited to a particular child, or class of child.

(3) A requirement (other than one imposed under sub-paragraph (1)(a)) may be limited by the authority so as to apply only when the number of children fostered by the person exceeds a specified number.

(4) A requirement shall be imposed by notice in writing addressed to the person on whom it is imposed and informing him of—

(a) the reason for imposing the requirement;

(b) his right under paragraph 8 to appeal against it; and

(c) the time within which he may do so.

(5) A local authority may at any time vary any requirement, impose any additional requirement or remove any requirement.

(6) In this Schedule—

(a) "the appropriate local authority" means—

(i) the local authority within whose area the child is being fostered; or

(ii) in the case of a proposal to foster a child, the local authority within whose area it is proposed that he will be fostered; and

(b) "requirement", in relation to any person, means a requirement imposed on him under this paragraph.

Regulations requiring notification of fostering etc.

7.—(1) The Secretary of State may by regulations make provision as to—

(a) the circumstances in which notification is required to be given in connection with children who are, have been or are proposed to be fostered privately; and

(b) the manner and form in which such notification is to be given.

(2) The regulations may, in particular—

(a) require any person who is, or proposes to be, involved (whether or not directly) in arranging for a child to be fostered privately to notify the appropriate authority;

(b) require any person who is—

(i) a parent of a child; or

(ii) a person who is not a parent of his but who has parental responsibility for a child,

and who knows that it is proposed that the child should be fostered privately, to notify the appropriate authority;

(c) require any parent of a privately fostered child, or person who is not a parent of such a child but who has parental responsibility for him, to notify the appropriate authority of any change in his address;

(d) require any person who proposes to foster a child privately, to notify the appropriate authority of his proposal;

(e) require any person who is fostering a child privately, or proposes to do so, to notify the appropriate authority of—

(i) any offence of which he has been convicted;

(ii) any disqualification imposed on him under section 68; or

(iii) any prohibition imposed on him under section 69;

(f) require any person who is fostering a child privately, to notify the appropriate authority of any change in his address;

(g) require any person who is fostering a child privately to notify the appropriate authority in writing of any person who begins, or ceases, to be part of his household;

(h) require any person who has been fostering a child privately, but has ceased to do so, to notify the appropriate authority (indicating, where the child has died, that that is the reason).

Appeals

8.—(1) A person aggrieved by—

    (a) a requirement imposed under paragraph 6;

    (b) a refusal of consent under section 68;

    (c) a prohibition imposed under section 69;

    (d) a refusal to cancel such a prohibition;

    (e) a refusal to make an exemption under paragraph 4 of Schedule 7;

    (f) a condition imposed in such an exemption; or

    (g) a variation or cancellation of such an exemption,

may appeal to the court.

(2) The appeal must be made within fourteen days from the date on which the person appealing is notified of the requirement, refusal, prohibition, condition, variation or cancellation.

(3) Where the appeal is against—

    (a) a requirement imposed under paragraph 6;

    (b) a condition of an exemption imposed under paragraph 4 of Schedule 7; or

    (c) a variation or cancellation of such an exemption,

the requirement, condition, variation or cancellation shall not have effect while the appeal is pending.

(4) Where it allows an appeal against a requirement or prohibition, the court may, instead of cancelling the requirement or prohibition—

    (a) vary the requirement, or allow more time for compliance with it; or

    (b) if an absolute prohibition has been imposed, substitute for it a prohibition on using the premises after such time as the court may specify unless such specified requirements as the local authority had power to impose under paragraph 6 are complied with.

(5) Any requirement or prohibition specified or substituted by a court under this paragraph shall be deemed for the purposes of Part IX (other than this paragraph) to have been imposed by the local authority under paragraph 6 or (as the case may be) section 69.

(6) Where it allows an appeal against a refusal to make an exemption, a condition imposed in such an exemption or a variation or cancellation of such an exemption, the court may—

    (a) make an exemption;

    (b) impose a condition; or

    (c) vary the exemption.

(7) Any exemption made or varied under sub-paragraph (6), or any condition imposed under that sub-paragraph, shall be deemed for the purposes of Schedule 7 (but not for the purposes of this paragraph) to have been made, varied or imposed under that Schedule.

(8) Nothing in sub-paragraph (1)(e) to (g) confers any right of appeal on—

    (a) a person who is, or would be if exempted under Schedule 7, a local authority foster parent; or

    (b) a person who is, or would be if so exempted, a person with whom a child is placed by a voluntary organisation.

Extension of Part IX to certain school children during holidays

9.—(1) Where a child under sixteen who is a pupil at a school which is not maintained by a local education authority lives at the school during school holidays for a period of more than two weeks, Part IX shall apply in relation to the child as if—

(a) while living at the school, he were a privately fostered child; and

(b) paragraphs 2(1)(d) and 6 were omitted.

(2) Sub-paragraph (3) applies to any person who proposes to care for and accommodate one or more children at a school in circumstances in which some or all of them will be treated as private foster children by virtue of this paragraph.

(3) That person shall, not less than two weeks before the first of those children is treated as a private foster child by virtue of this paragraph during the holiday in question, give written notice of his proposal to the local authority within whose area the child is ordinarily resident ("the appropriate authority"), stating the estimated number of the children.

(4) A local authority may exempt any person from the duty of giving notice under sub-paragraph (3).

(5) Any such exemption may be granted for a special period or indefinitely and may be revoked at any time by notice in writing given to the person exempted.

(6) Where a child who is treated as a private foster child by virtue of this paragraph dies, the person caring for him at the school shall, not later than 48 hours after the death, give written notice of it—

(a) to the appropriate local authority; and

(b) where reasonably practicable, to each parent of the child and to every person who is not a parent of his but who has parental responsibility for him.

(7) Where a child who is treated as a foster child by virtue of this paragraph ceases for any other reason to be such a child, the person caring for him at the school shall give written notice of the fact to the appropriate local authority.

Prohibition of advertisements relating to fostering

10. No advertisement indicating that a person will undertake, or will arrange for, a child to be privately fostered shall be published, unless it states that person's name and address.

Avoidance of insurances on lives of privately fostered children

11. A person who fosters a child privately and for reward shall be deemed for the purposes of the Life Assurance Act 1774 to have no interest in the life of the child. 1774 c. 48.

SCHEDULE 9 Section 71(16).

Child Minding and Day Care for Young Children

Applications for registration

1.—(1) An application for registration under section 71 shall be of no effect unless it contains—

(a) a statement with respect to the applicant which complies with the requirements of regulations made for the purposes of this paragraph by the Secretary of State; and

(b) a statement with respect to any person assisting or likely to be assisting in looking after children on the premises in question, or living or likely to be living there, which complies with the requirements of such regulations.

(2) Where a person provides, or proposes to provide, day care for children under the age of eight on different premises situated within the area of the same local authority, he shall make a separate application with respect to each of those premises.

(3) An application under section 71 shall be accompanied by such fee as may be prescribed.

(4) On receipt of an application for registration under section 71 from any person who is acting, or proposes to act, in any way which requires him to be registered under that section, a local authority shall register him if the application is properly made and they are not otherwise entitled to refuse to do so.

Disqualification from registration

2.—(1) A person may not be registered under section 71 if he is disqualified by regulations made by the Secretary of State for the purposes of this paragraph.

(2) The regulations may, in particular, provide for a person to be disqualified where—

(a) an order of a prescribed kind has been made at any time with respect to him;

(b) an order of a prescribed kind has been made at any time with respect to any child who has been in his care;

(c) a requirement of a prescribed kind has been imposed at any time with respect to such a child, under or by virtue of any enactment;

(d) he has at any time been refused registration under Part X or any other prescribed enactment or had any such registration cancelled;

(e) he has been convicted of any offence of a prescribed kind, or has been placed on probation or discharged absolutely or conditionally for any such offence;

(f) he has at any time been disqualified from fostering a child privately;

1984 c. 56.

(g) a prohibition has been imposed on him at any time under section 61, section 10 of the Foster Children (Scotland) Act 1984 or any other prescribed enactment;

(h) his rights and powers with respect to a child have at any time been vested in a prescribed authority under a prescribed enactment.

(3) A person who lives—

(a) in the same household as a person who is himself disqualified by the regulations; or

(b) in a household at which any such person is employed,

shall be disqualified unless he has disclosed the fact to the appropriate local authority and obtained their written consent.

(4) A person who is disqualified shall not provide day care, or be concerned in the management of, or have any financial interest in, any provision of day care unless he has—

(a) disclosed the fact to the appropriate local authority; and

(b) obtained their written consent.

(5) No person shall employ, in connection with the provision of day care, a person who is disqualified, unless he has—

(a) disclosed to the appropriate local authority the fact that that person is so disqualified; and

(b) obtained their written consent.

(6) In this paragraph "enactment" means any enactment having effect, at any time, in any part of the United Kingdom.

Exemption of certain schools

3.—(1) Section 71 does not apply in relation to any child looked after in any—

(a) school maintained or assisted by a local education authority;

(b) school under the management of an education authority;

(c) school in respect of which payments are made by the Secretary of State under section 100 of the Education Act 1944;

1944 c. 31.

(d) independent school;

(e) grant-aided school;

(f) grant maintained school;

(g) self-governing school;

(h) play centre maintained or assisted by a local education authority under section 53 of the Act of 1944, or by an education authority under section 6 of the Education (Scotland) Act 1980.

1980 c. 44.

(2) The exemption provided by sub-paragraph (1) only applies where the child concerned is being looked after in accordance with provision for day care made by—

(a) the person carrying on the establishment in question as part of the establishment's activities; or

(b) a person employed to work at that establishment and authorised to make that provision as part of the establishment's activities.

(3) In sub-paragraph (1)—

"assisted" and "maintained" have the same meanings as in the Education Act 1944;

"grant maintained" has the same meaning as in section 52(3) of the Education Reform Act 1988; and

1988 c. 40.

"grant-aided school", "self-governing school" and (in relation to Scotland) "independent school" have the same meaning as in the Education (Scotland) Act 1980.

Exemption for other establishments

4.—(1) Section 71(1)(b) does not apply in relation to any child looked after in—

(a) a registered children's home;

(b) a voluntary home;

(c) a community home;

(d) a residential care home, nursing home or mental nursing home required to be registered under the Registered Homes Act 1984;

1984 c. 23.

(e) a health service hospital;

(f) a home provided, equipped and maintained by the Secretary of State; or

(g) an establishment which is required to be registered under section 61 of the Social Work (Scotland) Act 1968.

1968 c. 49.

(2) The exemption provided by sub-paragraph (1) only applies where the child concerned is being looked after in accordance with provision for day care made by—

    (a) the department, authority or other person carrying on the establishment in question as part of the establishment's activities; or

    (b) a person employed to work at that establishment and authorised to make that provision as part of the establishment's activities.

(3) In this paragraph "a health service hospital" includes a health service hospital within the meaning of the National Health Service (Scotland) Act 1978.

Exemption for occasional facilities

5.—(1) Where day care for children under the age of eight is provided in particular premises on less than six days in any year, that provision shall be disregarded for the purposes of section 71 if the person making it has notified the appropriate local authority in writing before the first occasion on which the premises concerned are so used in that year.

(2) In sub-paragraph (1) "year" means the year beginning with the day on which the day care in question is (after the commencement of this paragraph) first provided in the premises concerned and any subsequent year.

Certificates of registration

6.—(1) Where a local authority register a person under section 71 they shall issue him with a certificate of registration.

(2) The certificate shall specify—

    (a) the registered person's name and address;

    (b) in a case falling within section 71(1)(b), the address or situation of the premises concerned; and

    (c) any requirements imposed under section 72 or 73.

(3) Where, due to a change of circumstances, any part of the certificate requires to be amended, the authority shall issue an amended certificate.

(4) Where the authority are satisfied that the certificate has been lost or destroyed, they shall issue a copy, on payment by the registered person of such fee as may be prescribed.

Fees for annual inspection of premises

7.—(1) Where—

    (a) a person is registered under section 71, and

    (b) the local authority concerned make an annual inspection of the premises in question under section 76,

they shall serve on that person a notice informing him that the inspection is to be carried out and requiring him to pay to them such fee as may be prescribed.

(2) It shall be a condition of the continued registration of that person under section 71 that the fee is so paid before the expiry of the period of twenty-eight days beginning with the date on which the inspection is carried out.

Co-operation between authorities

8.—(1) Where it appears to a local authority that any local education authority or, in Scotland, education authority could, by taking any specified action, help in the exercise of any of their functions under Part X, they may request the help of that local education authority, or education authority, specifying the action in question.

(2) An authority whose help is so requested shall comply with the request if it is compatible with their own statutory or other duties and obligations and does not unduly prejudice the discharge of any of their functions.

Sᴄʜ. 9

SCHEDULE 10

Section 88.

Aᴍᴇɴᴅᴍᴇɴᴛѕ ᴏꜰ Aᴅᴏᴘᴛɪᴏɴ Lᴇɢɪѕʟᴀᴛɪᴏɴ

Pᴀʀᴛ I

Aᴍᴇɴᴅᴍᴇɴᴛѕ ᴏꜰ Aᴅᴏᴘᴛɪᴏɴ Aᴄᴛ 1976 (ᴄ. 36)

1. In section 2 (local authorities' social services) for the words from "relating to" to the end there shall be substituted—

> "(a) under the Children Act 1989, relating to family assistance orders, local authority support for children and families, care and supervision and emergency protection of children, community homes, voluntary homes and organisations, registered children's homes, private arrangements for fostering children, child minding and day care for young children and children accommodated by health authorities and local education authorities or in residential care, nursing or mental nursing homes or in independent schools; and

> (b) under the National Health Service Act 1977, relating to the provision of care for expectant and nursing mothers."

1977 c. 49.

2. In section 11 (restrictions on arranging adoptions and placing of children) for subsection (2) there shall be substituted—

> "(2) An adoption society which is—

> (a) approved as respects Scotland under section 3 of the Adoption (Scotland) Act 1978; or

1978 c. 28.

> (b) registered as respects Northern Ireland under Article 4 of the Adoption (Northern Ireland) Order 1987,

S.I. 1987/2203 (N.I. 22).

> but which is not approved under section 3 of this Act, shall not act as an adoption society in England and Wales except to the extent that the society considers it necessary to do so in the interests of a person mentioned in section 1 of the Act of 1978 or Article 3 of the Order of 1987."

3.—(1) In section 12 (adoption orders), in subsection (1) for the words "vesting the parental rights and duties relating to a child in" there shall be substituted "giving parental responsibility for a child to".

(2) In subsection (2) of that section for the words "the parental rights and duties so far as they relate" there shall be substituted "parental responsibility so far as it relates".

(3) In subsection (3) of that section for paragraph (a) there shall be substituted—

> "(a) the parental responsibility which any person has for the child immediately before the making of the order;

> (aa) any order under the Children Act 1989";

and in paragraph (b) for the words from "for any period" to the end there shall be substituted "or upbringing for any period after the making of the order."

4. For section 14(1) (adoption by married couple) there shall be substituted—

> "(1) An adoption order shall not be made on the application of more than one person except in the circumstances specified in subsections (1A) and (1B).

SCH. 10

(1A) An adoption order may be made on the application of a married couple where both the husband and the wife have attained the age of 21 years.

(1B) An adoption order may be made on the application of a married couple where—

    (a) the husband or the wife—

        (i) is the father or mother of the child; and

        (ii) has attained the age of 18 years:

    and

    (b) his or her spouse has attained the age of 21 years."

5.—(1) In section 16 (parental agreement), in subsection (1) for the words from "in England" to "Scotland)" there shall be substituted—

        "(i) in England and Wales, under section 18;

1978 c. 28.

        (ii) in Scotland, under section 18 of the Adoption (Scotland) Act 1978; or

        (iii) in Northern Ireland, under Article 17(1) or 18(1) of the Adoption (Northern Ireland) Order 1987."

S.I. 1987/2203
(N.I. 22).

(2) In subsection (2)(c) of that section for the words "the parental duties in relation to" there shall be substituted "his parental responsibility for".

6.—(1) In section 18 (freeing child for adoption), after subsection (2) there shall be inserted—

    "(2A) For the purposes of subsection (2) a child is in the care of an adoption agency if the adoption agency is a local authority and he is in their care."

(2) In subsection (5) of that section, for the words from "the parental rights" to "vest in" there shall be substituted "parental responsibility for the child is given to", and for the words "and (3)" there shall be substituted "to (4)".

(3) For subsections (7) and (8) of that section there shall be substituted–

    "(7) Before making an order under this section in the case of a child whose father does not have parental responsibility for him, the court shall satisfy itself in relation to any person claiming to be the father that—

        (a) he has no intention of applying for–

            (i) an order under section 4(1) of the Children Act 1989, or

            (ii) a residence order under section 10 of that Act, or

        (b) if he did make any such application, it would be likely to be refused.

    (8) Subsections (5) and (7) of section 12 apply in relation to the making of an order under this section as they apply in relation to the making of an order under that section."

7. In section 19(2) (progress reports to former parents) for the words "in which the parental rights and duties were vested" there shall be substituted "to which parental responsibility was given".

8.—(1) In section 20 (revocation of section 18 order), in subsections (1) and (2) for the words "the parental rights and duties", in both places where they occur, there shall be substituted "parental responsibility".

(2) For subsection (3) of that section there shall be substituted—

    "(3) The revocation of an order under section 18 ("a section 18 order") operates—

        (a) to extinguish the parental responsibility given to the adoption agency under the section 18 order;

(b) to give parental responsibility for the child to—

(i) the child's mother; and

(ii) where the child's father and mother were married to each other at the time of his birth, the father; and

(c) to revive—

(i) any parental responsibility agreement,

(ii) any order under section 4(1) of the Children Act 1989, and

(iii) any appointment of a guardian in respect of the child (whether made by a court or otherwise),

extinguished by the making of the section 18 order.

(3A) Subject to subsection (3)(c), the revocation does not–

(a) operate to revive—

(i) any order under the Children Act 1989, or

(ii) any duty referred to in section 12(3)(b),

extinguished by the making of the section 18 order; or

(b) affect any person's parental responsibility so far as it relates to the period between the making of the section 18 order and the date of revocation of that order."

9. For section 21 (transfer of parental rights and duties between adoption agencies) there shall be substituted—

"Variation of section 18 order so as to substitute one adoption agency for another.

21.—(1) On an application to which this section applies, an authorised court may vary an order under section 18 so as to give parental responsibility for the child to another adoption agency ('the substitute agency') in place of the agency for the time being having parental responsibility for the child under the order ('the existing agency').

(2) This section applies to any application made jointly by—

(a) the existing agency; and

(b) the would-be substitute agency.

(3) Where an order under section 18 is varied under this section, section 19 shall apply as if the substitute agency had been given responsibility for the child on the making of the order."

10.—(1) In section 22 (notification to local authority of adoption application), after subsection (1) there shall be inserted the following subsections—

"(1A) An application for such an adoption order shall not be made unless the person wishing to make the application has, within the period of two years preceding the making of the application, given notice as mentioned in subsection (1).

(1B) In subsections (1) and (1A) the references to the area in which the applicant or person has his home are references to the area in which he has his home at the time of giving the notice."

(2) In subsection (4) of that section for the word "receives" there shall be substituted "receive" and for the words "in the care of" there shall be substituted "looked after by".

11. In section 25(1) (interim orders) for the words "vesting the legal custody of the child in" there shall be substituted "giving parental responsibility for the child to".

12. In—

(a) section 27(1) and (2) (restrictions on removal where adoption agreed or application made under section 18); and

(b) section 28(1) and (2) (restrictions on removal where applicant has provided home for 5 years),

for the words "actual custody", in each place where they occur, there shall be substituted "home".

13. After section 27(2) there shall be inserted—

"(2A) For the purposes of subsection (2) a child is in the care of an adoption agency if the adoption agency is a local authority and he is in their care."

14.—(1) After section 28(2) there shall be inserted—

"(2A) The reference in subsections (1) and (2) to any enactment does not include a reference to section 20(8) of the Children Act 1989".

(2) For subsection (3) of that section there shall be substituted—

"(3) In any case where subsection (1) or (2) applies and—

(a) the child was being looked after by a local authority before he began to have his home with the applicant or, as the case may be, the prospective adopter, and

(b) the child is still being looked after by a local authority,

the authority which are looking after the child shall not remove him from the home of the applicant or the prospective adopter except in accordance with section 30 or 31 or with the leave of a court."

(3) In subsection (5) of that section—

(a) for the word "receives" there shall be substituted "receive"; and

(b) for the words "in the care of another local authority or of a voluntary organisation" there shall be substituted "looked after by another local authority".

15. In section 29 (return of child taken away in breach of section 27 or 28) for subsections (1) and (2) there shall be substituted—

"(1) An authorised court may, on the application of a person from whose home a child has been removed in breach of—

(a) section 27 or 28,

(b) section 27 or 28 of the Adoption (Scotland) Act 1978, or

(c) Article 28 or 29 of the Adoption (Northern Ireland) Order 1987,

order the person who has so removed the child to return the child to the applicant.

(2) An authorised court may, on the application of a person who has reasonable grounds for believing that another person is intending to remove a child from his home in breach of—

(a) section 27 or 28,

(b) section 27 or 28 of the Adoption (Scotland) Act 1978, or

(c) Article 28 or 29 of the Adoption (Northern Ireland) Order 1987,

by order direct that other person not to remove the child from the applicant's home in breach of any of those provisions."

16.—(1) In section 30 (return of children placed for adoption by adoption agencies), in subsection (1) there shall be substituted—

(a) for the words "delivered into the actual custody of" the words "placed with";

(b) in paragraph (a) for the words "retain the actual custody of the child" the words "give the child a home"; and

(c) in paragraph (b) for the words "actual custody" the word "home".

(2) In subsection (3) of that section for the words "in his actual custody" there shall be substituted "with him".

17.—(1) In section 31 (application of section 30 where child not placed for adoption), in subsection (1) for the words from "child", where it first occurs, to "except" there shall be substituted "child—

(a) who is (when the notice is given) being looked after by a local authority; but

(b) who was placed with that person otherwise than in pursuance of such arrangements as are mentioned in section 30(1),

that section shall apply as if the child had been placed in pursuance of such arrangements".

(2) In subsection (2) of that section for the words "for the time being in the care of" there shall be substituted "(when the notice is given) being looked after by".

(3) In subsection (3) of that section—

(a) for the words "remains in the actual custody of" there shall be substituted "has his home with"; and

(b) for the words "section 45 of the Child Care Act 1980" there shall be substituted "Part III of Schedule 2 to the Children Act 1989".

(4) At the end of that section there shall be added—

"(4) Nothing in this section affects the right of any person who has parental responsibility for a child to remove him under section 20(8) of the Children Act 1989".

18.—(1) In section 32 (meaning of "protected child"), in subsection (2) for the words "section 37 of the Adoption Act 1958" there shall be substituted-

"(a) section 32 of the Adoption (Scotland) Act 1978; or

(b) Article 33 of the Adoption (Northern Ireland) Order 1987."

(2) In subsection (3) of that section for paragraph (a) there shall be substituted—

"(a) he is in the care of any person-

(i) in any community home, voluntary home or registered children's home;

(ii) in any school in which he is receiving full-time education;

(iii) in any health service hospital";

and at the end of that subsection there shall be added—

"(d) he is in the care of any person in any home or institution not specified in this subsection but provided, equipped and maintained by the Secretary of State."

(3) After that subsection there shall be inserted—

"(3A) In subsection (3) 'community home', 'voluntary home', 'registered children's home', 'school' and 'health service hospital' have the same meaning as in the Children Act 1989."

(4) For subsection (4) of that section there shall be substituted—

"(4) A protected child ceases to be a protected child—

(a) on the grant or refusal of the application for an adoption order;

(b) on the notification to the local authority for the area where the child has his home that the application for an adoption order has been withdrawn;

(c) in a case where no application is made for an adoption order, on the expiry of the period of two years from the giving of the notice;

(d) on the making of a residence order, a care order or a supervision order under the Children Act 1989 in respect of the child;

(e) on the appointment of a guardian for him under that Act;

(f) on his attaining the age of 18 years; or

(g) on his marriage,

whichever first occurs.

(5) In subsection (4)(d) the references to a care order and a supervision order do not include references to an interim care order or interim supervision order."

19.—(1) In section 35 (notices and information to be given to local authorities), in subsection (1) for the words "who has a protected child in his actual custody" there shall be substituted "with whom a protected child has his home".

(2) In subsection (2) of that section for the words "in whose actual custody he was" there shall be substituted "with whom he had his home".

20.—(1) In section 51 (disclosure of birth records of adopted children), in subsection (1) for the words "subsections (4) and (6)" there shall be substituted "what follows".

(2) For subsections (3) to (7) of that section there shall be substituted—

"(3) Before supplying any information to an applicant under subsection (1), the Registrar General shall inform the applicant that counselling services are available to him—

(a) if he is in England and Wales—

(i) at the General Register Office;

(ii) from the local authority in whose area he is living;

(iii) where the adoption order relating to him was made in England and Wales, from the local authority in whose area the court which made the order sat; or

(iv) from any other local authority;

(b) if he is in Scotland—

(i) from the regional or islands council in whose area he is living;

(ii) where the adoption order relating to him was made in Scotland, from the council in whose area the court which made the order sat; or

(iii) from any other regional or islands council;

(c) if he is in Northern Ireland—

(i) from the Board in whose area he is living;

(ii) where the adoption order relating to him was made in Northern Ireland, from the Board in whose area the court which made the order sat; or

(iii) from any other Board;

(d) if he is in the United Kingdom and his adoption was arranged by an adoption society—

(i) approved under section 3,

(ii) approved under section 3 of the Adoption (Scotland) Act 1978,

(iii) registered under Article 4 of the Adoption (Northern Ireland) Order 1987,

from that society.

SCH. 10
1978 c. 28.
S.I. 1987/2203
(N.I. 22).

(4) Where an adopted person who is in England and Wales—

(a) applies for information under —

(i) subsection (1), or

(ii) Article 54 of the Adoption (Northern Ireland) Order 1987, or

(b) is supplied with information under section 45 of the Adoption (Scotland) Act 1978,

it shall be the duty of the persons and bodies mentioned in subsection (5) to provide counselling for him if asked by him to do so.

(5) The persons and bodies are—

(a) the Registrar General;

(b) any local authority falling within subsection (3)(a)(ii) to (iv);

(c) any adoption society falling within subsection (3)(d) in so far as it is acting as an adoption society in England and Wales.

(6) If the applicant chooses to receive counselling from a person or body falling within subsection (3), the Registrar General shall send to the person or body the information to which the applicant is entitled under subsection (1).

(7) Where a person—

(a) was adopted before 12th November 1975, and

(b) applies for information under subsection (1),

the Registrar General shall not supply the information to him unless he has attended an interview with a counsellor arranged by a person or body from whom counselling services are available as mentioned in subsection (3).

(8) Where the Registrar General is prevented by subsection (7) from supplying information to a person who is not living in the United Kingdom, he may supply the information to any body which—

(a) the Registrar General is satisfied is suitable to provide counselling to that person, and

(b) has notified the Registrar General that it is prepared to provide such counselling.

(9) In this section—

"a Board" means a Health and Social Services Board established under Article 16 of the Health and Personal Social Services (Northern Ireland) Order 1972; and

S.I. 1972/1265
(N.I. 14).

"prescribed" means prescribed by regulations made by the Registrar General."

21. After section 51 there shall be inserted—

"Adoption Contact Register.

51A.—(1) The Registrar General shall maintain at the General Register Office a register to be called the Adoption Contact Register.

(2) The register shall be in two parts—

(a) Part I: Adopted Persons; and

(b) Part II: Relatives.

(3) The Registrar General shall, on payment of such fee as may be prescribed, enter in Part I of the register the name and address of any adopted person who fulfils the conditions in subsection (4) and who gives notice that he wishes to contact any relative of his.

(4) The conditions are that—

(a) a record of the adopted person's birth is kept by the Registrar General; and

(b) the adopted person has attained the age of 18 years and—

(i) has been supplied by the Registrar General with information under section 51; or

(ii) has satisfied the Registrar General that he has such information as is necessary to enable him to obtain a certified copy of the record of his birth.

(5) The Registrar General shall, on payment of such fee as may be prescribed, enter in Part II of the register the name and address of any person who fulfils the conditions in subsection (6) and who gives notice that he wishes to contact an adopted person.

(6) The conditions are that—

(a) a record of the adopted person's birth is kept by the Registrar General; and

(b) the person giving notice under subsection (5) has attained the age of 18 years and has satisfied the Registrar General that—

(i) he is a relative of the adopted person; and

(ii) he has such information as is necessary to enable him to obtain a certified copy of the record of the adopted person's birth.

(7) The Registrar General shall, on receiving notice from any person named in an entry in the register that he wishes the entry to be cancelled, cancel the entry.

(8) Any notice given under this section must be in such form as may be determined by the Registrar General.

(9) The Registrar General shall transmit to an adopted person whose name is entered in Part I of the register the name and address of any relative in respect of whom there is an entry in Part II of the register.

(10) Any entry cancelled under subsection (7) ceases from the time of cancellation to be an entry for the purposes of subsection (9).

(11) The register shall not be open to public inspection or search and the Registrar General shall not supply any person with information entered in the register (whether in an uncancelled or a cancelled entry) except in accordance with this section.

(12) The register may be kept by means of a computer.

(13) In this section—

(a) "relative" means any person (other than an adoptive relative) who is related to the adopted person by blood (including half-blood) or marriage;

(b) "address" includes any address at or through which the person concerned may be contacted; and

(c) "prescribed" means prescribed by the Secretary of State."

22.—(1) In section 55 (adoption of children abroad), in subsection (1) after the word "Scotland" there shall be inserted "or Northern Ireland" and for the words "vesting in him the parental rights and duties relating to the child" there shall be substituted "giving him parental responsibility for the child".

(2) In subsection (3) of that section for the words "word '(Scotland)'" there shall be substituted "words '(Scotland)' or '(Northern Ireland)'."

23.—(1) In section 56 (restriction on removal of children for adoption outside Great Britain),—

(a) in subsections (1) and (3) for the words "transferring the actual custody of a child to", in both places where they occur, there shall be substituted "placing a child with"; and

(b) in subsection (3)(a) for the words "in the actual custody of" there shall be substituted "with".

(2) In subsection (1) of that section—

(a) for the words from "or under" to "abroad)" there shall be substituted "section 49 of the Adoption (Scotland) Act 1978 or Article 57 of the Adoption (Northern Ireland) Order 1987"; and

(b) for the words "British Islands" there shall be substituted "United Kingdom, the Channel Islands and the Isle of Man".

1978 c. 28.
S.I. 1987/2203
(N.I. 22).

24.—(1) In section 57 (prohibition on certain payments) in subsection (1)(c), for the words "transfer by that person of the actual custody of a child" there shall be substituted "handing over of a child by that person".

(2) In subsection (3A)(b) of that section, for the words "in the actual custody of" there shall be substituted "with".

25. After section 57 there shall be inserted—

"Permitted allowances.

57A.—(1) The Secretary of State may make regulations for the purpose of enabling adoption agencies to pay allowances to persons who have adopted, or intend to adopt, children in pursuance of arrangements made by the agencies.

(2) Section 57(1) shall not apply to any payment made by an adoption agency in accordance with the regulations.

(3) The regulations may, in particular, make provision as to—

(a) the procedure to be followed by any agency in determining whether a person should be paid an allowance;

(b) the circumstances in which an allowance may be paid;

(c) the factors to be taken into account in determining the amount of an allowance;

(d) the procedure for review, variation and termination of allowances; and

(e) the information about allowances to be supplied by any agency to any person who is intending to adopt a child.

(4) Any scheme approved under section 57(4) shall be revoked as from the coming into force of this section.

(5) Section 57(1) shall not apply in relation to any payment made—

(a) in accordance with a scheme revoked under subsection (4) or section 57(5)(b); and

(b) to a person to whom such payments were made before the revocation of the scheme.

(6) Subsection (5) shall not apply where any person to whom any payments may lawfully be made by virtue of subsection (5) agrees to receive (instead of such payments) payments complying with regulations made under this section."

26.—(1) In section 59 (effect of determination and orders made in Scotland and overseas in adoption proceedings), in subsection (1) for the words "Great Britain" there shall be substituted "the United Kingdom".

(2) For subsection (2) of that section there shall be substituted—

"(2) Subsections (2) to (4) of section 12 shall apply in relation to an order freeing a child for adoption (other than an order under section 18) as if it were an adoption order; and, on the revocation in Scotland or Northern Ireland of an order freeing a child for adoption, subsections (3) and (3A) of section 20 shall apply as if the order had been revoked under that section."

27. In section 60 (evidence of adoption in Scotland and Northern Ireland), in paragraph (a) for the words "section 22(2) of the Adoption Act 1958" there shall be substituted "section 45(2) of the Adoption (Scotland) Act 1978" and in paragraph (b) for the words from "section 23(4)" to "in force" there shall be substituted "Article 63(1) of the Adoption (Northern Ireland) Order 1987".

28. In section 62(5)(b) (courts), for the words from "section 8" to "child)" there shall be substituted—

"(i) section 12 or 18 of the Adoption (Scotland) Act 1978; or

(ii) Article 12, 17 or 18 of the Adoption (Northern Ireland) Order 1987".

29. After section 65 (guardians ad litem and reporting officers) there shall be inserted—

"Panels for selection of guardians ad litem and reporting officers.

65A.—(1) The Secretary of State may by regulations provide for the establishment of panels of persons from whom guardians ad litem and reporting officers appointed under rules made under section 65 must be selected.

(2) The regulations may, in particular, make provision—

(a) as to the constitution, administration and procedures of panels;

(b) requiring two or more specified local authorities to make arrangements for the joint management of a panel;

(c) for the defrayment by local authorities of expenses incurred by members of panels;

(d) for the payment by local authorities of fees and allowances for members of panels;

(e) as to the qualifications for membership of a panel;

(f) as to the training to be given to members of panels;

(g) as to the co-operation required of specified local authorities in the provision of panels in specified areas; and

(h) for monitoring the work of guardians ad litem and reporting officers.

SCH. 10

(3) Rules of court may make provision as to the assistance which any guardian ad litem or reporting officer may be required by the court to give to it."

30.—(1) Section 72(1) (interpretation) shall be amended as follows.

(2) In the definition of "adoption agency" for the words from "section 1" to the end there shall be substituted "—

(a) section 1 of the Adoption (Scotland) Act 1978; and

(b) Article 3 of the Adoption (Northern Ireland) Order 1987."

1978 c. 28.

S.I. 1987/2203 (N.I. 22).

(3) For the definition of "adoption order" there shall be substituted—

"'adoption order'—

(a) means an order under section 12(1); and

(b) in sections 12(3) and (4), 18 to 20, 27, 28 and 30 to 32 and in the definition of 'British adoption order' in this subsection includes an order under section 12 of the Adoption (Scotland) Act 1978 and Article 12 of the Adoption (Northern Ireland) Order 1987 (adoption orders in Scotland and Northern Ireland respectively); and

(c) in sections 27, 28 and 30 to 32 includes an order under section 55, section 49 of the Adoption (Scotland) Act 1978 and Article 57 of the Adoption (Northern Ireland) Order 1987 (orders in relation to children being adopted abroad)."

(4) For the definition of "British adoption order" there shall be substituted—

"'British adoption order' means—

(a) an adoption order as defined in this subsection, and

(b) an order under any provision for the adoption of a child effected under the law of any British territory outside the United Kingdom."

(5) For the definition of "guardian" there shall be substituted—

"'guardian' has the same meaning as in the Children Act 1989."

(6) In the definition of "order freeing a child for adoption" for the words from "section 27(2)" to the end there shall be substituted "sections 27(2) and 59 includes an order under—

(a) section 18 of the Adoption (Scotland) Act 1978; and

(b) Article 17 or 18 of the Adoption (Northern Ireland) Order 1987".

(7) After the definition of "overseas adoption" there shall be inserted—

"'parent' means, in relation to a child, any parent who has parental responsibility for the child under the Children Act 1989;

'parental responsibility' and 'parental responsibility agreement' have the same meaning as in the Children Act 1989."

(8) After the definition of "United Kingdom national" there shall be inserted—

"'upbringing' has the same meaning as in the Children Act 1989."

(9) For section 72(1A) there shall be substituted the following subsections—

"(1A) In this Act, in determining with what person, or where, a child has his home, any absence of the child at a hospital or boarding school and any other temporary absence shall be disregarded.

(1B) In this Act, references to a child who is in the care of or looked after by a local authority have the same meaning as in the Children Act 1989."

31. For section 74(3) and (4) (extent) there shall be substituted—

"(3) This Act extends to England and Wales only."

PART II

AMENDMENTS OF ADOPTION (SCOTLAND) ACT 1978 (C. 28)

32. In section 11 (restrictions on arranging of adoptions and placing of children) for subsection (2) there shall be substituted—

"(2) An adoption society which is—

1976 c. 36.

(a) approved as respects England and Wales under section 3 of the Adoption Act 1976; or

S.I. 1987/2203
(N.I. 22).

(b) registered as respects Northern Ireland under Article 4 of the Adoption (Northern Ireland) Order 1987,

but which is not approved under section 3 of this Act, shall not act as an adoption society in Scotland except to the extent that the society considers it necessary to do so in the interests of a person mentioned in section 1 of that Act or, as the case may be, Article 3 of that Order."

33. For section 14(1) (adoption by married couple) there shall be substituted—

1975 c. 72.

"(1) Subject to section 53(1) of the Children Act 1975 (which provides for the making of a custody order instead of an adoption order in certain cases), an adoption order shall not be made on the application of more than one person except in the circumstances specified in subsections (1A) and (1B).

(1A) An adoption order may be made on the application of a married couple where both the husband and the wife have attained the age of 21 years.

(1B) An adoption order may be made on the application of a married couple where—

(a) the husband or the wife—

(i) is the father or mother of the child; and

(ii) has attained the age of 18 years; and

(b) his or her spouse has attained the age of 21 years."

34. In section 16(1)(a) (parental agreement) for the words from "in England" to "revoked", in the second place where it occurs, there shall be substituted—

"(i) in Scotland under section 18;

(ii) in England and Wales under section 18 of the Adoption Act 1976; or

(iii) in Northern Ireland under Article 17(1) or 18(1) of the Adoption (Northern Ireland) Order 1987,

and not revoked".

35. In section 18(5) (effect of order freeing child for adoption) for the words "and (3)" there shall be substituted "to (4)".

36. In section 20(3)(c) (revocation of section 18 order) the words "section 12(3)(b) of the Adoption Act 1976 or of" shall cease to have effect.

37. For section 21 (transfer of parental rights and duties between adoption agencies) there shall be substituted—

"Variation of section 18 order so as to substitute one adoption agency for another.

21.—(1) On an application to which this section applies an authorised court may vary an order under section 18 so as to transfer the parental rights and duties relating to the child from the adoption agency in which they are vested under the order ('the existing agency') to another adoption agency ('the substitute agency').

(2) This section applies to any application made jointly by the existing agency and the would-be substitute agency.

(3) Where an order under section 18 is varied under this section, section 19 shall apply as if the parental rights and duties relating to the child had vested in the substitute agency on the making of the order."

38. In section 22(4) (notification to local authority of adoption application) for the word "receives" there shall be substituted "receive".

39. In section 29 (return of child taken away in breach of section 27 or 28) after the word "1976" in each place where it occurs there shall be inserted "or Article 28 or 29 of the Adoption (Northern Ireland) Order 1987".

S.I. 1987/2203 (N.I. 22).

40. In section 32 (meaning of "protected child"), at the end of subsection (2) there shall be added "or Article 33 of the Adoption (Northern Ireland) Order 1987".

41. In section 45 (adopted children register)—

(a) for the words from "or an approved" in subsection (5) to the end of subsection (6) there shall be substituted—

"Board or adoption society falling within subsection (6) which is providing counselling for that adopted person.

(6) Where the Registrar General for Scotland furnishes an adopted person with information under subsection (5), he shall advise that person that counselling services are available—

(a) if the person is in Scotland—

(i) from the local authority in whose area he is living;

(ii) where the adoption order relating to him was made in Scotland, from the local authority in whose area the court which made the order sat; or

(iii) from any other local authority in Scotland;

(b) if the person is in England and Wales—

(i) from the local authority in whose area he is living;

(ii) where the adoption order relating to him was made in England and Wales, from the local authority in whose area the court which made the order sat; or

(iii) from any other local authority in England and Wales;

(c) if the person is in Northern Ireland—

(i) from the Board in whose area he is living;

(ii) where the adoption order relating to him was made in Northern Ireland, from the Board in whose area the court which made the order sat; or

(iii) from any other Board;

(d) if the person is in the United Kingdom and his adoption was arranged by an adoption society—

(i) approved under section 3;

(ii) approved under section 3 of the Adoption Act 1976; or 1976 c. 36.

(iii) registered under Article 4 of the Adoption (Northern Ireland) Order 1987,

from that society.

(6A) Where an adopted person who is in Scotland—

(a) is furnished with information under subsection (5); or

(b) applies for information under—

(i) section 51(1) of the Adoption Act 1976; or

(ii) Article 54 of the Adoption (Northern Ireland) Order 1987,

any body mentioned in subsection (6B) to which the adopted person applies for counselling shall have a duty to provide counselling for him.

(6B) The bodies referred to in subsection (6A) are—

(a) any local authority falling within subsection (6)(a); and

(b) any adoption society falling within subsection (6)(d) so far as it is acting as an adoption society in Scotland.";

(b) in subsection (7)—

(i) for the word "under" there shall be substituted "from a local authority, Board or adoption society falling within";

(ii) for the words "or adoption society which is providing that counselling" there shall be substituted ", Board or adoption society"; and

(iii) after the word "authority" where it second occurs there shall be inserted ", Board"; and

(c) after subsection (9) there shall be inserted the following subsection—

"(10) In this section—

"Board" means a Health and Social Services Board established under Article 16 of the Health and Personal Social Services (Northern Ireland) Order 1972; and

"local authority", in relation to England and Wales, means the council of a county (other than a metropolitan county), a metropolitan district, a London borough or the Common Council of the City of London."

S.I. 1972/1265
(N.I. 14).

42. In section 49 (adoption of children abroad)—

(a) in subsection (1) after the word "Scotland" there shall be inserted "or Northern Ireland"; and

(b) in subsection (3) for the words "word 'England'" there shall be substituted "words '(England)' or '(Northern Ireland)' ".

43. In section 50(1) (restriction on removal of children for adoption outside Great Britain) after the word "1976" there shall be inserted "or Article 57 of the Adoption (Northern Ireland) Order 1987".

44. In section 53(1) (effect of determination and orders made in England and Wales and overseas in adoption proceedings)—

(a) in subsection (1) for the words "Great Britain" there shall be substituted "the United Kingdom"; and

(b) for subsection (2) there shall be substituted—

"(2) Subsections (2) to (4) of section 12 shall apply in relation to an order freeing a child for adoption (other than an order under section 18) as if it were an adoption order; and on the revocation in England and Wales or Northern Ireland of an order freeing a child for adoption subsection (3) of section 20 shall apply as if the order had been revoked under that section."

45. In section 54(b) (evidence of adoption in Northern Ireland) for the words from "section 23(4)" to "in force" there shall be substituted "Article 63(1) of the Adoption (Northern Ireland) Order 1987".

46. In section 65(1) (interpretation)—

(a) in the definition of "adoption agency", at the end there shall be added "and an adoption agency within the meaning of Article 3 of the Adoption (Northern Ireland) Order 1987 (adoption agencies in Northern Ireland)";

(b) for the definition of "adoption order" there shall be substituted—

"'adoption order'—

(a) means an order under section 12(1); and

(b) in sections 12(3) and (4), 18 to 20, 27, 28 and 30 to 32 and in the definition of "British adoption order" in this subsection includes an order under section 12 of the Adoption Act 1976 and Article 12 of the Adoption (Northern Ireland) Order 1987 (adoption orders in England and Wales and Northern Ireland respectively); and

1976 c. 36.

(c) in sections 27, 28 and 30 to 32 includes an order under section 49, section 55 of the Adoption Act 1976 and Article 57 of the Adoption (Northern Ireland) Order 1987 (orders in relation to children being adopted abroad);";

S.I. 1987/2203 (N.I. 22).

(c) for the definition of "British adoption order" there shall be substituted—

"'British adoption order' means—

(a) an adoption order as defined in this subsection; and

(b) an order under any provision for the adoption of a child effected under the law of any British territory outside the United Kingdom;";

(d) in the definition of "order freeing a child for adoption" for the words from "section 27(2)" to the end there shall be substituted "sections 27(2) and 53 includes an order under—

(a) section 18 of the Adoption Act 1976; and

(b) Article 17 or 18 of the Adoption (Northern Ireland) Order 1987;".

SCHEDULE 11

Section 92.

JURISDICTION

PART I

GENERAL

Commencement of proceedings

1.—(1) The Lord Chancellor may by order specify proceedings under this Act or the Adoption Act 1976 which may only be commenced in—

(a) a specified level of court;

(b) a court which falls within a specified class of court; or

(c) a particular court determined in accordance with, or specified in, the order.

(2) The Lord Chancellor may by order specify circumstances in which specified proceedings under this Act or the Adoption Act 1976 (which might otherwise be commenced elsewhere) may only be commenced in—

(a) a specified level of court;

(b) a court which falls within a specified class of court; or

(c) a particular court determined in accordance with, or specified in, the order.

(3) The Lord Chancellor may by order make provision by virtue of which, where specified proceedings with respect to a child under—

(a) this Act;

(b) the Adoption Act 1976; or

(c) the High Court's inherent jurisdiction with respect to children,

have been commenced in or transferred to any court (whether or not by virtue of an order under this Schedule), any other specified family proceedings which may affect, or are otherwise connected with, the child may, in specified circumstances, only be commenced in that court.

(4) A class of court specified in an order under this Schedule may be described by reference to a description of proceedings and may include different levels of court.

Transfer of proceedings

2.—(1) The Lord Chancellor may by order provide that in specified circumstances the whole, or any specified part of, specified proceedings to which this paragraph applies shall be transferred to—

(a) a specified level of court;

(b) a court which falls within a specified class of court; or

(c) a particular court determined in accordance with, or specified in, the order.

(2) Any order under this paragraph may provide for the transfer to be made at any stage, or specified stage, of the proceedings and whether or not the proceedings, or any part of them, have already been transferred.

(3) The proceedings to which this paragraph applies are—

(a) any proceedings under this Act;

(b) any proceedings under the Adoption Act 1976;

(c) any other proceedings which—

   (i) are family proceedings for the purposes of this Act, other than proceedings under the inherent jurisdiction of the High Court; and

   (ii) may affect, or are otherwise connected with, the child concerned.

(4) Proceedings to which this paragraph applies by virtue of sub-paragraph (3)(c) may only be transferred in accordance with the provisions of an order made under this paragraph for the purpose of consolidating them with proceedings under—

(a) this Act;

(b) the Adoption Act 1976; or

(c) the High Court's inherent jurisdiction with respect to children.

(5) An order under this paragraph may make such provision as the Lord Chancellor thinks appropriate for excluding proceedings to which this paragraph applies from the operation of any enactment which would otherwise govern the transfer of those proceedings, or any part of them.

Hearings by single justice

3.—(1) In such circumstances as the Lord Chancellor may by order specify—

(a) the jurisdiction of a magistrates' court to make an emergency protection order;

(b) any specified question with respect to the transfer of specified proceedings to or from a magistrates' court in accordance with the provisions of an order under paragraph 2,

may be exercised by a single justice.

(2) Any provision made under this paragraph shall be without prejudice to any other enactment or rule of law relating to the functions which may be performed by a single justice of the peace.

General

4.—(1) For the purposes of this Schedule—

(a) the commencement of proceedings under this Act includes the making of any application under this Act in the course of proceedings (whether or not those proceedings are proceedings under this Act); and

(b) there are three levels of court, that is to say the High Court, any county court and any magistrates' court.

(2) In this Schedule "specified" means specified by an order made under this Schedule.

(3) Any order under paragraph 1 may make provision as to the effect of commencing proceedings in contravention of any of the provisions of the order.

(4) An order under paragraph 2 may make provision as to the effect of a failure to comply with any of the provisions of the order.

(5) An order under this Schedule may—

(a) make such consequential, incidental or transitional provision as the Lord Chancellor considers expedient, including provision amending any other enactment so far as it concerns the jurisdiction of any court or justice of the peace;

(b) make provision for treating proceedings which are—

(i) in part proceedings of a kind mentioned in paragraph (a) or (b) of paragraph 2(3); and

(ii) in part proceedings of a kind mentioned in paragraph (c) of paragraph 2(3),

as consisting entirely of proceedings of one or other of those kinds, for the purposes of the application of any order made under paragraph 2.

Part II

Consequential Amendments

The Administration of Justice Act 1964 (c. 42)

5. In section 38 of the Administration of Justice Act 1964 (interpretation), the definition of "domestic court", which is spent, shall be omitted.

The Domestic Proceedings and Magistrates' Courts Act 1978 (c. 22)

6. In the Domestic Proceedings and Magistrates' Courts Act 1978—

(a) for the words "domestic proceedings", wherever they occur in sections 16(5)(c) and 88(1), there shall be substituted "family proceedings";

(b) for the words "domestic court panel", wherever they occur in section 16(5)(b), there shall be substituted "family panel".

The Justices of the Peace Act 1979 (c. 55)

7. In the Justices of the Peace Act 1979—

(a) for the words "domestic proceedings", wherever they occur in section 16(5), there shall be substituted "family proceedings";

(b) for the words "domestic court", wherever they occur in section 17(3), there shall be substituted "family proceedings court";

(c) for the words "domestic courts", wherever they occur in sections 38(2) and 58(1) and (5), there shall be substituted "family proceedings courts".

The Magistrates' Courts Act 1980 (c. 43)

8. In the Magistrates' Courts Act 1980—

   (a) in section 65(1) (meaning of family proceedings), the following paragraph shall be inserted after paragraph (m)—

      "(n) the Children Act 1989";

   (b) in section 65(2)(a) for the words "and (m)" there shall be substituted "(m) and (n)";

   (c) for the words "domestic proceedings", wherever they occur in sections 65(1), (2) and (3), 66(1) and (2), 67(1), (2) and (7), 69(1), (2), (3) and (4), 70(2) and (3), 71(1) and (2), 72(1), 73, 74(1), 121(8) and 150(1), there shall be substituted "family proceedings";

   (d) for the words "domestic court panel", wherever they occur in sections 66(2), 67(2), (4), (5), (7) and (8) and 68(1), (2) and (3), there shall be substituted "family panel";

   (e) for the words "domestic court panels", wherever they occur in section 67(3), (4), (5) and (6), there shall be substituted "family panels";

   (f) for the words "domestic courts", wherever they occur in sections 67(1) and (3) and 68(1), there shall be substituted "family proceedings courts";

   (g) for the words "domestic court", wherever they occur in section 67(2) and (5), there shall be substituted "family proceedings court".

The Supreme Court Act 1981 (c. 54)

9. In paragraph 3 of Schedule 1 to the Supreme Court Act 1981 (distribution of business to the Family Division of the High Court), the following sub-paragraph shall be added at the end—

   "(e) proceedings under the Children Act 1989".

The Matrimonial and Family Proceedings Act 1984 (c. 42)

10. In section 44 of the Matrimonial and Family Proceedings Act 1984 (domestic proceedings in magistrates' courts to include applications to alter maintenance agreements) for the words "domestic proceedings", wherever they occur, there shall be substituted "family proceedings".

The Insolvency Act 1986 (c. 45)

11.—(1) In section 281(5)(b) of the Insolvency Act 1986 (discharge not to release bankrupt from bankruptcy debt arising under any order made in family proceedings or in domestic proceedings), the words "or in domestic proceedings" shall be omitted.

(2) In section 281(8) of that Act (interpretation), for the definitions of "domestic proceedings" and "family proceedings" there shall be substituted—

   "family proceedings" means—

      (a) family proceedings within the meaning of the Magistrates' Courts Act 1980 and any proceedings which would be such proceedings but for section 65(1)(ii) of that Act (proceedings for variation of order for periodical payments); and

      (b) family proceedings within the meaning of Part V of the Matrimonial and Family Proceedings Act 1984."

SCHEDULE 12

MINOR AMENDMENTS

The Custody of Children Act 1891 (c. 3)

1. The Custody of Children Act 1891 (which contains miscellaneous obsolete provisions with respect to the custody of children) shall cease to have effect.

The Children and Young Persons Act 1933 (c. 12)

2. In section 1(2)(a) of the Children and Young Persons Act 1933 (cruelty to persons under sixteen), after the words "young person" there shall be inserted ", or the legal guardian of a child or young person,".

3. Section 40 of that Act shall cease to have effect.

The Education Act 1944 (c. 31)

4. In section 40(1) of the Education Act 1944 (enforcement of school attendance), the words from "or to imprisonment" to the end shall cease to have effect.

The Marriage Act 1949 (c. 76)

5.—(1) In section 3 of the Marriage Act 1949 (consent required to the marriage of a child by common licence or superintendent registrar's certificate), in subsection (1) for the words "the Second Schedule to this Act" there shall be substituted "subsection (1A) of this section".

(2) After that subsection there shall be inserted—

"(1A) The consents are—

(a) subject to paragraphs (b) to (d) of this subsection, the consent of—
    (i) each parent (if any) of the child who has parental responsibility for him; and
    (ii) each guardian (if any) of the child;

(b) where a residence order is in force with respect to the child, the consent of the person or persons with whom he lives, or is to live, as a result of the order (in substitution for the consents mentioned in paragraph (a) of this subsection);

(c) where a care order is in force with respect to the child, the consent of the local authority designated in the order (in addition to the consents mentioned in paragraph (a) of this subsection);

(d) where neither paragraph (b) nor (c) of this subsection applies but a residence order was in force with respect to the child immediately before he reached the age of sixteen, the consent of the person or persons with whom he lived, or was to live, as a result of the order (in substitution for the consents mentioned in paragraph (a) of this subsection).

(1B) In this section 'guardian of a child', 'parental responsibility', 'residence order' and 'care order' have the same meaning as in the Children Act 1989."

The Births and Deaths Registration Act 1953 (c. 20)

6.—(1) Sections 10 and 10A of the Births and Deaths Registration Act 1953 (registration of father, and re-registration, where parents not married) shall be amended as follows.

(2) In sections 10(1) and 10A(1) for paragraph (d) there shall be substituted—

"(d) at the request of the mother or that person on production of—

(i) a copy of a parental responsibility agreement made between them in relation to the child; and

(ii) a declaration in the prescribed form by the person making the request stating that the agreement was made in compliance with section 4 of the Children Act 1989 and has not been brought to an end by an order of a court; or

(e) at the request of the mother or that person on production of—

(i) a certified copy of an order under section 4 of the Children Act 1989 giving that person parental responsibility for the child; and

(ii) a declaration in the prescribed form by the person making the request stating that the order has not been brought to an end by an order of a court; or

(f) at the request of the mother or that person on production of—

(i) a certified copy of an order under paragraph 1 of Schedule 1 to the Children Act 1989 which requires that person to make any financial provision for the child and which is not an order falling within paragraph 4(3) of that Schedule; and

(ii) a declaration in the prescribed form by the person making the request stating that the order has not been discharged by an order of a court; or

(g) at the request of the mother or that person on production of—

(i) a certified copy of any of the orders which are mentioned in subsection (1A) of this section which has been made in relation to the child; and

(ii) a declaration in the prescribed form by the person making the request stating that the order has not been brought to an end or discharged by an order of a court."

(3) After sections 10(1) and 10A(1) there shall be inserted—

"(1A) The orders are—

(a) an order under section 4 of the Family Law Reform Act 1987 that that person shall have all the parental rights and duties with respect to the child;

(b) an order that that person shall have custody or care and control or legal custody of the child made under section 9 of the Guardianship of Minors Act 1971 at a time when such an order could only be made in favour of a parent;

(c) an order under section 9 or 11B of that Act which requires that person to make any financial provision in relation to the child;

(d) an order under section 4 of the Affiliation Proceedings Act 1957 naming that person as putative father of the child."

(4) In section 10(2) for the words "or (d)" there shall be substituted "to (g)".

(5) In section 10(3) for the words from " 'relevant order' " to the end there shall be substituted " 'parental responsibility agreement' has the same meaning as in the Children Act 1989".

(6) In section 10A(2) in paragraphs (b) and (c) for the words "paragraph (d)" in both places where they occur there shall be substituted "any of paragraphs (d) to (g)".

The Army Act 1955 (c. 18)

7. In section 151 of the Army Act 1955 (deductions from pay for maintenance of wife or child), in subsection (1A)(a) for the words "in the care of a local authority in England or Wales" there shall be substituted "being looked after by a local authority in England or Wales (within the meaning of the Children Act 1989)".

8.—(1) Schedule 5A to that Act (powers of court on trial of civilian) shall be amended as follows.

(2) For paragraphs 7(3) and (4) there shall be substituted—

"(3) While an authorisation under a reception order is in force the order shall (subject to sub-paragraph (4) below) be deemed to be a care order for the purposes of the Children Act 1989, and the authorised authority shall be deemed to be the authority designated in that deemed care order.

(3A) In sub-paragraph (3) above "care order" means a care order which is not an interim care order under section 38 of the Children Act 1989.

(4) The Children Act 1989 shall apply to a reception order which is deemed to be a care order by virtue of sub-paragraph (3) above as if sections 31(8) (designated local authority), 91 (duration of care order etc.) and 101 (effect of orders as between different jurisdictions) were omitted."

(3) In sub-paragraph (5)(c) for the words from "attains" to the end there shall be substituted "attains 18 years of age".

(4) In paragraph 8(1) for the words "Children and Young Persons Act 1969" there shall be substituted "Children Act 1989".

The Air Force Act 1955 (c. 19)

9. Section 151(1A) of the Air Force Act 1955 (deductions from pay for maintenance of wife or child) shall have effect subject to the amendment that is set out in paragraph 7 in relation to section 151(1A) of the Army Act 1955.

10. Schedule 5A to that Act (powers of court on trial of civilian) shall have effect subject to the amendments that are set out in paragraph 8(2) to (4) in relation to Schedule 5A to the Army Act 1955.

The Sexual Offences Act 1956 (c. 69)

11. In section 19(3) of the Sexual Offences Act 1956 (abduction of unmarried girl under eighteen from parent or guardian) for the words "the lawful care or charge of" there shall be substituted "parental responsibility for or care of".

12. In section 20(2) of that Act (abduction of unmarried girl under sixteen from parent or guardian) for the words "the lawful care or charge of" there shall be substituted "parental responsibility for or care of".

13. In section 21(3) of that Act (abduction of defective from parent or guardian) for the words "the lawful care or charge of" there shall be substituted "parental responsibility for or care of".

14. In section 28 of that Act (causing or encouraging prostitution of, intercourse with, or indecent assault on, girl under sixteen) for subsections (3) and (4) there shall be substituted—

"(3) The persons who are to be treated for the purposes of this section as responsible for a girl are (subject to subsection (4) of this section)—

(a) her parents;

(b) any person who is not a parent of hers but who has parental responsibility for her; and

(c) any person who has care of her.

(4) An individual falling within subsection (3)(a) or (b) of this section is not to be treated as responsible for a girl if—

    (a) a residence order under the Children Act 1989 is in force with respect to her and he is not named in the order as the person with whom she is to live; or

    (b) a care order under that Act is in force with respect to her."

15. Section 38 of that Act (power of court to divest person of authority over girl or boy in case of incest) shall cease to have effect.

16.—(1) In section 43 of that Act (power to search for and recover woman detained for immoral purposes), in subsection (5) for the words "the lawful care or charge of" there shall be substituted "parental responsibility for or care of".

(2) In subsection (6) of that section, for the words "section forty of the Children and Young Persons Act 1933" there shall be substituted "Part V of the Children Act 1989".

17. After section 46 of that Act there shall be inserted—

"Meaning of 'parental responsibility'.   46A. In this Act 'parental responsibility' has the same meaning as in the Children Act 1989."

The Naval Discipline Act 1957 (c. 53)

18. Schedule 4A to the Naval Discipline Act 1957 (powers of court on trial of civilian) shall have effect subject to the amendments that are set out in paragraph 8(2) to (4) in relation to Schedule 5A to the Army Act 1955.

The Children and Young Persons Act 1963 (c. 37)

19. Section 3 of the Children and Young Persons Act 1963 (children and young persons beyond control) shall cease to have effect.

The Children and Young Persons Act 1969 (c. 54)

20. In section 5 of the Children and Young Persons Act 1969 (restrictions on criminal proceedings for offences by young persons), in subsection (2), for the words "section 1 of this Act" there shall be substituted " Part IV of the Children Act 1989".

21. After section 7(7) of that Act (alteration in treatment of young offenders, etc.) there shall be inserted—

"(7B) An order under subsection (7)(c) of this section shall not require a person to enter into a recognisance—

    (a) for an amount exceeding £1,000; or

    (b) for a period exceeding—

        (i) three years; or

        (ii) where the young person concerned will attain the age of eighteen in a period shorter than three years, that shorter period.

(7C) Section 120 of the Magistrates' Courts Act 1980 shall apply to a recognisance entered into in pursuance of an order under subsection (7)(c) of this section as it applies to a recognisance to keep the peace."

22. In section 12A of that Act (young offenders) for subsections (1) and (2) there shall be substituted—

"(1) This subsection applies to any supervision order made under section 7(7) of this Act unless it requires the supervised person to comply with directions given by the supervisor under section 12(2) of this Act."

23. After that section there shall be inserted—

"Requirement for young offender to live in local authority accommodation.

12AA.—(1) Where the conditions mentioned in subsection (6) of this section are satisfied, a supervision order may impose a requirement ('a residence requirement') that a child or young person shall live for a specified period in local authority accommodation.

(2) A residence requirement shall designate the local authority who are to receive the child or young person and that authority shall be the authority in whose area the child or young person resides.

(3) The court shall not impose a residence requirement without first consulting the designated authority.

(4) A residence requirement may stipulate that the child or young person shall not live with a named person.

(5) The maximum period which may be specified in a residence requirement is six months.

(6) The conditions are that—

(a) a supervision order has previously been made in respect of the child or young person;

(b) that order imposed—

(i) a requirement under section 12A(3) of this Act; or

(ii) a residence requirement;

(c) he is found guilty of an offence which—

(i) was committed while that order was in force;

(ii) if it had been committed by a person over the age of twenty-one, would have been punishable with imprisonment; and

(iii) in the opinion of the court is serious; and

(d) the court is satisfied that the behaviour which constituted the offence was due, to a significant extent, to the circumstances in which he was living,

except that the condition in paragraph (d) of this subsection does not apply where the condition in paragraph (b)(ii) is satisfied.

(7) For the purposes of satisfying itself as mentioned in subsection (6)(d) of this section, the court shall obtain a social inquiry report which makes particular reference to the circumstances in which the child or young person was living.

(8) Subsection (7) of this section does not apply if the court already has before it a social inquiry report which contains sufficient information about the circumstances in which the child or young person was living.

(9) A court shall not include a residence requirement in respect of a child or young person who is not legally represented at the relevant time in that court unless—

(a) he has applied for legal aid for the purposes of the proceedings and the application was refused on the ground that it did not appear that his resources were such that he required assistance; or

(b) he has been informed of his right to apply for legal aid for the purposes of the proceedings and has had the opportunity to do so, but nevertheless refused or failed to apply.

(10) In subsection (9) of this section—

(a) 'the relevant time' means the time when the court is considering whether or not to impose the requirement; and

(b) 'the proceedings' means—

(i) the whole proceedings; or

(ii) the part of the proceedings relating to the imposition of the requirement.

(11) A supervision order imposing a residence requirement may also impose any of the requirements mentioned in sections 12, 12A, 12B or 12C of this Act.

(12) In this section 'social inquiry report' has the same meaning as in section 2 of the Criminal Justice Act 1982.''

1982 c. 48.

24.—(1) In section 15 of that Act (variation and discharge of supervision orders), in subsections (1)(a), (2A), (3)(e) and (4) after the word "12A", in each place where it occurs, there shall be inserted "12AA".

(2) In subsection (4) of that section for the words "(not being a juvenile court)" there shall be substituted "other than a juvenile court".

25.—(1) In section 16 of that Act (provisions supplementary to section 15), in subsection (3) for the words "either direct" to the end there shall be substituted—

"(i) direct that he be released forthwith; or

(ii) remand him."

(2) In subsection (4) of that section—

(a) in paragraph (a) for the words "an interim order made by virtue of" there shall be substituted "a remand under";

(b) in paragraph (b) for the words "makes an interim order in respect of" there shall be substituted "remands", and

(c) for the words "make an interim order in respect of" there shall be substituted "remand".

(3) In subsections (5)(b) and (c) and (6)(a) after the word "12A", in each place where it occurs, there shall be inserted "12AA".

26. For section 23 of that Act (remand to care of local authorities etc.) there shall be substituted—

"Remand to local authority accommodation, committal of young persons of unruly character, etc.

23.—(1) Where a court—

(a) remands or commits for trial a child charged with homicide or remands a child convicted of homicide; or

(b) remands a young person charged with or convicted of one or more offences or commits him for trial or sentence,

and he is not released on bail, then, unless he is a young person who is certified by the court to be of unruly character, the court shall remand him to local authority accommodation.

(2) A court remanding a person to local authority accommodation shall designate the authority who are to receive him and that authority shall be the authority in whose area it appears to the court that—

(a) he resides; or

(b) the offence or one of the offences was committed.

(3) Where a person is remanded to local authority accommodation, it shall be lawful for any person acting on behalf of the designated authority to detain him.

(4) The court shall not certify a young person as being of unruly character unless—

(a) he cannot safely be remanded to local authority accommodation; and

(b) the conditions prescribed by order made by the Secretary of State under this subsection are satisfied in relation to him.

(5) Where the court certifies that a young person is of unruly character, it shall commit him—

(a) to a remand centre, if it has been notified that such a centre is available for the reception from the court of such persons; and

(b) to a prison, if it has not been so notified.

(6) Where a young person is remanded to local authority accommodation, a court may, on the application of the designated authority, certify him to be of unruly character in accordance with subsection (4) of this section (and on so doing he shall cease to be remanded to local authority accommodation and subsection (5) of this section shall apply).

(7) For the purposes of subsection (6) of this section, "a court" means—

(a) the court which remanded the young person; or

(b) any magistrates' court having jurisdiction in the place where that person is for the time being,

and in this section "court" and "magistrates' court" include a justice.

(8) This section has effect subject to—

(a) section 37 of the Magistrates' Courts Act 1980 (committal to the Crown Court with a view to a sentence of detention in a young offender institution); and

(b) section 128(7) of that Act (remands to the custody of a constable for periods of not more than three days),

but section 128(7) shall have effect in relation to a child or young person as if for the reference to three clear days there were substituted a reference to twenty-four hours."

27.—(1) In section 32 of that Act (detention of absentees), for subsection (1A) there shall be substituted the following subsections—

"(1A) If a child or young person is absent, without the consent of the responsible person—

(a) from a place of safety to which he has been taken under section 16(3) of this Act; or

(b) from local authority accommodation—

(i) in which he is required to live under section 12AA of this Act; or

(ii) to which he has been remanded under section 23(1) of this Act,

he may be arrested by a constable anywhere in the United Kingdom or Channel Islands without a warrant.

(1B) A person so arrested shall be conducted to—

(a) the place of safety;

(b) the local authority accommodation; or

(c) such other place as the responsible person may direct,

at the responsible person's expense.

(1C) In this section 'the responsible person' means the person who made the arrangements under section 16(3) of this Act or, as the case may be, the authority designated under section 12AA or 23 of this Act."

(2) In subsection (2B) of that section for the words "person referred to in subsection (1A)(a) or (b) (as the case may be) of this section" there shall be substituted "responsible person".

28. In section 34(1) of that Act (transitional modifications of Part I for persons of specified ages)—

(a) in paragraph (a), for the words "13(2) or 28(4) or (5)" there shall be substituted "or 13(2)"; and

(b) in paragraph (e), for the words "section 23(2) or (3)" there shall be substituted "section 23(4) to (6)".

29. In section 70(1) of that Act (interpretation)—

(a) after the definition of "local authority" there shall be inserted—

"'local authority accommodation' means accommodation provided by or on behalf of a local authority (within the meaning of the Children Act 1989)"; and

(b) in the definition of "reside" for "12(4) and (5)" there shall be substituted "12B(1) and (2)".

30. In section 73 of that Act (extent, etc.)—

(a) in subsection (4)(a) for "32(1), (3) and (4)" there shall be substituted "32(1) to (1C) and (2A) to (4)"; and

(b) in subsection (6) for "32(1), (1A)" there shall be substituted "32(1) to (1C)".

The Matrimonial Causes Act 1973 (c. 18)

31. For section 41 of the Matrimonial Causes Act 1973 (restrictions on decrees for dissolution, annulment or separation affecting children) there shall be substituted—

"Restrictions on decrees for dissolution, annulment or separation affecting children.

41.—(1) In any proceedings for a decree of divorce or nullity of marriage, or a decree of judicial separation, the court shall consider—

(a) whether there are any children of the family to whom this section applies; and

(b) where there are any such children, whether (in the light of the arrangements which have been, or are proposed to be, made for their upbringing and welfare) it should exercise any of its powers under the Children Act 1989 with respect to any of them.

(2) Where, in any case to which this section applies, it appears to the court that—

(a) the circumstances of the case require it, or are likely to require it, to exercise any of its powers under the Act of 1989 with respect to any such child;

(b) it is not in a position to exercise that power or (as the case may be) those powers without giving further consideration to the case; and

(c) there are exceptional circumstances which make it desirable in the interests of the child that the court should give a direction under this section,

it may direct that the decree of divorce or nullity is not to be made absolute, or that the decree of judicial separation is not to be granted, until the court orders otherwise.

(3) This section applies to—

(a) any child of the family who has not reached the age of sixteen at the date when the court considers the case in accordance with the requirements of this section; and

(b) any child of the family who has reached that age at that date and in relation to whom the court directs that this section shall apply."

32. In section 42 of that Act, subsection (3) (declaration by court that party to marriage unfit to have custody of children of family) shall cease to have effect.

33. In section 52(1) of that Act (interpretation), in the definition of "child of the family", for the words "has been boarded-out with those parties" there shall be substituted "is placed with those parties as foster parents".

The National Health Service Act 1977 (c. 49)

34. In Schedule 8 to the National Health Service Act 1977 (functions of local social services authorities), the following sub-paragraph shall be added at the end of paragraph 2—

"(4A) This paragraph does not apply in relation to persons under the age of 18."

The Child Care Act 1980 (c. 5)

35. Until the repeal of the Child Care Act 1980 by this Act takes effect, the definition of "parent" in section 87 of that Act shall have effect as if it applied only in relation to Part I and sections 13, 24, 64 and 65 of that Act (provisions excluded by section 2(1)(f) of the Family Law Reform Act 1987 from the application of the general rule in that Act governing the meaning of references to relationships between persons). 1987 c. 42.

The Education Act 1981 (c. 60)

36. The following section shall be inserted in the Education Act 1981, after section 3—

"Provision outside England and Wales for certain children.

3A.—(1) A local authority may make such arrangements as they think fit to enable any child in respect of whom they maintain a statement under section 7 to attend an establishment outside England and Wales which specialises in providing for children with special needs.

(2) In subsection (1) above "children with special needs" means children who have particular needs which would be special educational needs if those children were in England and Wales.

(3) Where an authority make arrangements under this section with respect to a child, those arrangements may, in particular, include contributing to or paying—

(a) fees charged by the establishment;

(b) expenses reasonably incurred in maintaining him while he is at the establishment or travelling to or from it;

(c) those travelling expenses;

(d) expenses reasonably incurred by any person accompanying him while he is travelling or staying at the establishment.

(4) This section is not to be taken as in any way limiting any other powers of a local education authority."

The Child Abduction Act 1984 (c. 37)

37.—(1) Section 1 of the Child Abduction Act 1984 (offence of abduction by parent, etc.) shall be amended as follows.

(2) For subsections (2) to (4) there shall be substituted—

"(2) A person is connected with a child for the purposes of this section if—

(a) he is a parent of the child; or

(b) in the case of a child whose parents were not married to each other at the time of his birth, there are reasonable grounds for believing that he is the father of the child; or

(c) he is a guardian of the child; or

(d) he is a person in whose favour a residence order is in force with respect to the child; or

(e) he has custody of the child.

(3) In this section 'the appropriate consent', in relation to a child, means—

(a) the consent of each of the following—

(i) the child's mother;

(ii) the child's father, if he has parental responsibility for him;

(iii) any guardian of the child;

(iv) any person in whose favour a residence order is in force with respect to the child;

(v) any person who has custody of the child; or

(b) the leave of the court granted under or by virtue of any provision of Part II of the Children Act 1989; or

(c) if any person has custody of the child, the leave of the court which awarded custody to him.

(4) A person does not commit an offence under this section by taking or sending a child out of the United Kingdom without obtaining the appropriate consent if—

(a) he is a person in whose favour there is a residence order in force with respect to the child, and

(b) he takes or sends him out of the United Kingdom for a period of less than one month.

(4A) Subsection (4) above does not apply if the person taking or sending the child out of the United Kingdom does so in breach of an order under Part II of the Children Act 1989."

(3) In subsection (5) for the words from "but" to the end there shall be substituted—

"(5A) Subsection (5)(c) above does not apply if—

(a) the person who refused to consent is a person—

(i) in whose favour there is a residence order in force with respect to the child; or

(ii) who has custody of the child; or

(b) the person taking or sending the child out of the United Kingdom is, by so acting, in breach of an order made by a court in the United Kingdom."

(4) For subsection (7) there shall be substituted—

"(7) For the purposes of this section—

(a) 'guardian of a child', 'residence order' and 'parental responsibility' have the same meaning as in the Children Act 1989; and

(b) a person shall be treated as having custody of a child if there is in force an order of a court in the United Kingdom awarding him (whether solely or jointly with another person) custody, legal custody or care and control of the child."

(5) In subsection (8) for the words from "or voluntary organisation" to "custodianship proceedings or" there shall be substituted "detained in a place of safety, remanded to a local authority accommodation or the subject of".

38.—(1) In section 2 of that Act (offence of abduction of child by other persons), in subsection (1) for the words from "Subject" to "above" there shall be substituted "Subject to subsection (3) below, a person, other than one mentioned in subsection (2) below."

(2) For subsection (2) of that section there shall be substituted—

"(2) The persons are—

(a) where the father and mother of the child in question were married to each other at the time of his birth, the child's father and mother;

(b) where the father and mother of the child in question were not married to each other at the time of his birth, the child's mother; and

(c) any other person mentioned in section 1(2)(c) to (e) above.

SCH. 12

(3) In proceedings against any person for an offence under this section, it shall be a defence for that person to prove—

    (a) where the father and mother of the child in question were not married to each other at the time of his birth—

        (i) that he is the child's father; or

        (ii) that, at the time of the alleged offence, he believed, on reasonable grounds, that he was the child's father; or

    (b) that, at the time of the alleged offence, he believed that the child had attained the age of sixteen."

39. At the end of section 3 of that Act (construction of references to taking, sending and detaining) there shall be added "and

    (d) references to a child's parents and to a child whose parents were (or were not) married to each other at the time of his birth shall be construed in accordance with section 1 of the Family Law Reform Act 1987 (which extends their meaning)."

40.—(1) The Schedule to that Act (modifications of section 1 for children in certain cases) shall be amended as follows.

(2) In paragraph 1(1) for the words "or voluntary organisation" there shall be substituted "within the meaning of the Children Act 1989".

(3) For paragraph 2(1) there shall be substituted—

    "(1) This paragraph applies in the case of a child who is—

    (a) detained in a place of safety under section 16(3) of the Children and Young Persons Act 1969; or

    (b) remanded to local authority accommodation under section 23 of that Act."

(4) In paragraph 3(1)—

    (a) in paragraph (a) for the words "section 14 of the Children Act 1975" there shall be substituted "section 18 of the Adoption Act 1976"; and

    (b) in paragraph (d) for the words "section 25 of the Children Act 1975 or section 53 of the Adoption Act 1958" there shall be substituted "section 55 of the Adoption Act 1976".

(5) In paragraph 3(2)(a)—

    (a) in sub-paragraph (i), for the words from "order or," to "Children Act 1975" there shall be substituted "section 18 order or, if the section 18 order has been varied under section 21 of that Act so as to give parental responsibility to another agency", and

    (b) in sub-paragraph (ii), for the words "(c) or (e)" there shall be substituted "or (c)".

(6) At the end of paragraph 3 there shall be added—

    "(3) Sub-paragraph (2) above shall be construed as if the references to the court included, in any case where the court is a magistrates' court, a reference to any magistrates' court acting for the same area as that court".

(7) For paragraph 5 there shall be substituted—

    "5. In this Schedule—

    (a) 'adoption agency' and 'adoption order' have the same meaning as in the Adoption Act 1976; and

    (b) 'area', in relation to a magistrates' court, means the petty sessions area (within the meaning of the Justices of the Peace Act 1979) for which the court is appointed."

The Foster Children (Scotland) Act 1984 (c. 56)

41. In section 1 of the Foster Children (Scotland) Act 1984 (definition of foster child)—

(a) for the words "he is— (a)" there shall be substituted "(a) he is"; and

(b) the words "for a period of more than 6 days" and the words from "The period" to the end shall cease to have effect.

42. In section 2(2) of that Act (exceptions to section 1), for paragraph (f) there shall be substituted—

"(f) if he has been in that person's care for a period of less than 28 days and that person does not intend to undertake his care for any longer period."

43. In section 7(1) of that Act (persons disqualified from keeping foster children)—

(a) the word "or" at the end of paragraph (e) shall be omitted; and

(b) after paragraph (f) there shall be inserted "or

(g) he is disqualified from fostering a child privately (within the meaning of the Children Act 1989) by regulations made under section 68 of that Act,".

The Disabled Persons (Services, Consultation and Representation) Act 1986 (c. 33)

44. In section 2(5) of the Disabled Persons (Services, Consultation and Representation) Act 1986 (circumstances in which authorised representative has right to visit etc. disabled person), after paragraph (d) there shall be inserted—

"(dd) in accommodation provided by any educational establishment."

The Legal Aid Act 1988 (c. 34)

45. In paragraph 2 of Part I of Schedule 2 to the Legal Aid Act 1988 (proceedings in magistrates' courts to which the civil legal aid provisions of Part IV of the Act apply), the following sub-paragraph shall be added at the end—

"(g) proceedings under the Children Act 1989."

SCHEDULE 13

Consequential Amendments

The Wills Act 1837 (c. 26)

1. In section 1 of the Wills Act 1837 (interpretation), in the definition of "will", for the words "and also to a disposition by will and testament or devise of the custody and tuition of any child" there shall be substituted "and also to an appointment by will of a guardian of a child".

The Children and Young Persons Act 1933 (c. 12)

2. In section 1(1) of the Children and Young Persons Act 1933 (cruelty to persons under sixteen) for the words "has the custody, charge or care of" there shall be substituted "has responsibility for".

3. In the following sections of that Act—

(a) 3(1) (allowing persons under sixteen to be in brothels);

(b) 4(1) and (2) (causing or allowing persons under sixteen to be used for begging);

(c) 11 (exposing children under twelve to risk of burning); and

    (d) 25(1) (restrictions on persons under eighteen going abroad for the purpose of performing for profit),

for the words "the custody, charge or care of" there shall, in each case, be substituted "responsibility for".

4. In section 10(1A) of that Act (vagrants preventing children from receiving education), for the words from "to bring the child" to the end there shall be substituted "to make an application in respect of the child or young person for an education supervision order under section 36 of the Children Act 1989".

5. For section 17 of that Act (interpretation of Part I) there shall be substituted the following section—

"Interpretation of Part I.

    17.—(1) For the purposes of this Part of this Act, the following shall be presumed to have responsibility for a child or young person—

    (a) any person who—

        (i) has parental responsibility for him (within the meaning of the Children Act 1989); or

        (ii) is otherwise legally liable to maintain him; and

    (b) any person who has care of him.

    (2) A person who is presumed to be responsible for a child or young person by virtue of subsection (1)(a) shall not be taken to have ceased to be responsible for him by reason only that he does not have care of him."

6.—(1) In section 34 of that Act (attendance at court of parent of child or young person charged with an offence etc.), in subsection (1) after the word "offence" there shall be inserted "is the subject of an application for a care or supervision order under Part IV of the Children Act 1989".

(2) In subsection (7) of that section after the words "Children and Young Persons Act 1969" there shall be inserted "or Part IV of the Children Act 1989".

(3) After subsection (7) of that section there shall be inserted—

    "(7A) If it appears that at the time of his arrest the child or young person is being provided with accommodation by or on behalf of a local authority under section 20 of the Children Act 1989, the local authority shall also be informed as described in subsection (3) above as soon as it is reasonably practicable to do so."

7. In section 107(1) of that Act (interpretation)—

    (a) in the definition of "guardian", for the words "charge of or control over" there shall be substituted "care of";

    (b) for the definition of legal guardian there shall be substituted—

    "'legal guardian', in relation to a child or young person, means a guardian of a child as defined in the Children Act 1989".

The Education Act 1944 (c. 31)

8.—(1) Section 40 of the Education Act 1944 (enforcement of school attendance) shall be amended as follows.

(2) For subsection (2) there shall be substituted—

    "(2) Proceedings for such offences shall not be instituted except by a local education authority.

(2A) Before instituting such proceedings the local education authority shall consider whether it would be appropriate, instead of or as well as instituting the proceedings, to apply for an education supervision order with respect to the child."

(3) For subsections (3) and (4) there shall be substituted—

"(3) The court—

(a) by which a person is convicted of an offence against section 37 of this Act; or

(b) before which a person is charged with an offence under section 39 of this Act,

may direct the local education authority instituting the proceedings to apply for an education supervision order with respect to the child unless the authority, having consulted the appropriate local authority, decide that the child's welfare will be satisfactorily safeguarded even though no education supervision order is made.

(3A) Where, following such a direction, a local education authority decide not to apply for an education supervision order they shall inform the court of the reasons for their decision.

(3B) Unless the court has directed otherwise, the information required under subsection (3A) shall be given to the court before the end of the period of eight weeks beginning with the date on which the direction was given.

(4) Where—

(a) a local education authority apply for an education supervision order with respect to a child who is the subject of a school attendance order; and

(b) the court decides that section 36(3) of the Children Act 1989 prevents it from making the order;

the court may direct that the school attendance order shall cease to be in force."

(4) After subsection (4) there shall be inserted—

"(5) In this section—

'appropriate local authority' has the same meaning as in section 36(9) of the Children Act 1989; and

'education supervision order' means an education supervision order under that Act."

9. In section 71 of that Act (complaints with respect to independent schools), the following paragraph shall be added after paragraph (d), in subsection (1)—

"(e) there has been a failure, in relation to a child provided with accommodation by the school, to comply with the duty imposed by section 87 of the Children Act 1989 (welfare of children accommodated in independent schools);".

10. After section 114(1C) of that Act (interpretation) there shall be inserted the following subsections—

"(1D) In this Act, unless the context otherwise requires, 'parent', in relation to a child or young person, includes any person—

(a) who is not a parent of his but who has parental responsibility for him, or

(b) who has care of him,

except for the purposes of the enactments mentioned in subsection (1E) of this section, where it only includes such a person if he is an individual.

(1E) The enactments are—

(a) sections 5(4), 15(2) and (6), 31 and 65(1) of, and paragraph 7(6) of Schedule 2 to, the Education (No. 2) Act 1986; and

(b) sections 53(8), 54(2), 58(5)(k), 60 and 61 of the Education Reform Act 1988.

(1F) For the purposes of subsection (1D) of this section—

(a) 'parental responsibility' has the same meaning as in the Children Act 1989; and

(b) in determining whether an individual has care of a child or young person any absence of the child or young person at a hospital or boarding school and any other temporary absence shall be disregarded."

The National Assistance Act 1948 (c. 29)

11.—(1) In section 21(1)(a) of the National Assistance Act 1948 (persons for whom local authority is to provide residential accommodation) after the word "persons" there shall be inserted "aged eighteen or over".

(2) In section 29(1) of that Act (welfare arrangements for blind, deaf, dumb and crippled persons) after the words "that is to say persons" and after the words "and other persons" there shall, in each case, be inserted "aged eighteen or over".

The Reserve and Auxiliary Forces (Protection of Civil Interests) Act 1951 (c. 65)

12. For section 2(1)(d) of the Reserve and Auxiliary Forces (Protection of Civil Interests) Act 1951 (cases in which leave of the appropriate court is required before enforcing certain orders for the payment of money), there shall be substituted—

"(d) an order for alimony, maintenance or other payment made under sections 21 to 33 of the Matrimonial Causes Act 1973 or made, or having effect as if made, under Schedule 1 to the Children Act 1989."

The Mines and Quarries Act 1954 (c. 70)

13. In section 182(1) of the Mines and Quarries Act 1954 (interpretation), in the definition of "parent", for the words from "or guardian" to first "young person" there shall be substituted "of a young person or any person who is not a parent of his but who has parental responsibility for him (within the meaning of the Children Act 1989)".

The Administration of Justice Act 1960 (c. 65)

14. In section 12 of the Administration of Justice Act 1960 (publication of information relating to proceedings in private), in subsection (1) for paragraph (a) there shall be substituted—

"(a) where the proceedings—

(i) relate to the exercise of the inherent jurisdiction of the High Court with respect to minors;

(ii) are brought under the Children Act 1989; or

(iii) otherwise relate wholly or mainly to the maintenance or upbringing of a minor;".

The Factories Act 1961 (c. 34)

15. In section 176(1) of the Factories Act 1961 (interpretation), in the definition of "parent", for the words from "or guardian" to first "young person" there shall be substituted "of a child or young person or any person who is not a parent of his but who has parental responsibility for him (within the meaning of the Children Act 1989)".

The Criminal Justice Act 1967 (c. 80)

16. In section 67(1A)(c) of the Criminal Justice Act 1967 (computation of sentences of imprisonment passed in England and Wales) for the words "in the care of a local authority" there shall be substituted "remanded to local authority accommodation."

The Health Services and Public Health Act 1968 (c. 46)

17.—(1) In section 64(3)(a) of the Health Services and Public Health Act 1968 (meaning of "relevant enactments" in relation to power of Minister of Health or Secretary of State to provide financial assistance), for sub-paragraph (xix) inserted by paragraph 19 of Schedule 5 to the Child Care Act 1980 there shall be substituted—

1980 c. 5.

"(xx) the Children Act 1989."

(2) In section 65(3)(b) of that Act (meaning of "relevant enactments" in relation to power of local authority to provide financial and other assistance), for sub-paragraph (xx) inserted by paragraph 20 of Schedule 5 to the Child Care Act 1980 there shall be substituted—

"(xxi) the Children Act 1989."

The Social Work (Scotland) Act 1968 (c. 49)

18. In section 2(2) of the Social Work (Scotland) Act 1968 (matters referred to social work committee) after paragraph (j) there shall be inserted—

"(k) section 19 and Part X of the Children Act 1989,".

19. In section 5(2)(c) of that Act (power of Secretary of State to make regulations) for the words "and (j)" there shall be substituted "to (k)".

20. In section 21(3) of that Act (mode of provision of accommodation and maintenance) for the words "section 21 of the Child Care Act 1980" there shall be substituted "section 23 of the Children Act 1989".

21. In section 74(6) of that Act (parent of child in residential establishment moving to England or Wales) for the words from "Children and Young Persons Act 1969" to the end there shall be substituted "Children Act 1989, but as if section 31(8) were omitted".

22. In section 75(2) of that Act (parent of child subject to care order etc. moving to Scotland), for the words "Children and Young Persons Act 1969" there shall be substituted "Children Act 1989".

23. In section 86(3) of that Act (meaning of ordinary residence for purpose of adjustments between authority providing accommodation and authority of area of residence), the words "the Child Care Act 1980 or" shall be omitted and after the words "education authority" there shall be inserted "or placed with local authority foster parents under the Children Act 1989".

Q

The Civil Evidence Act 1968 (c. 64)

24. In section 12(5)(b) of the Civil Evidence Act 1968 (findings of paternity etc. as evidence in civil proceedings - meaning of "relevant proceedings") for sub-paragraph (iv) there shall be substituted—

"(iv) paragraph 23 of Schedule 2 to the Children Act 1989."

The Administration of Justice Act 1970 (c. 31)

25. In Schedule 8 to the Administration of Justice Act 1970 (maintenance orders for purposes of Maintenance Orders Act 1958 and the 1970 Act), in paragraph 6 for the words "section 47 or 51 of the Child Care Act 1980" there shall be substituted "paragraph 23 of Schedule 2 to the Children Act 1989".

The Local Authority Social Services Act 1970 (c. 42)

26.—(1) In Schedule 1 to the Local Authority Social Services Act 1970 (enactments conferring functions assigned to social service committee)—

(a) in the entry relating to the Mental Health Act 1959, for the words "sections 8 and 9" there shall be substituted "section 8"; and

(b) in the entry relating to the Children and Young Persons Act 1969, for the words "sections 1, 2 and 9" there shall be substituted "section 9".

(2) At the end of that Schedule there shall be added—

"Children Act 1989. The whole Act, in so far as it confers functions on a local authority within the meaning of that Act.	Welfare reports. Consent to application for residence order in respect of child in care. Family assistance orders. Functions under Part III of the Act (local authority support for children and families). Care and supervision. Protection of children. Functions in relation to community homes, voluntary homes and voluntary organisations, registered children's homes, private arrangements for fostering children, child minding and day care for young children. Inspection of children's homes on behalf of Secretary of State. Research and returns of information. Functions in relation to children accommodated by health authorities and local education authorities or in residential care, nursing or mental nursing homes or in independent schools."

The Chronically Sick and Disabled Persons Act 1970 (c. 44)

27. After section 28 of the Chronically Sick and Disabled Persons Act 1970 there shall be inserted—

"Application of Act to authorities having functions under the Children Act 1989.   28A. This Act applies with respect to disabled children in relation to whom a local authority have functions under Part III of the Children Act 1989 as it applies in relation to persons to whom section 29 of the National Assistance Act 1948 applies."

The Courts Act 1971 (c. 23)

28. In Part I of Schedule 9 to the Courts Act 1971 (substitution of references to Crown Court), in the entry relating to the Children and Young Persons Act 1969, for the words "Sections 2(12), 3(8), 16(8), 21(4)(5)" there shall be substituted "Section 16(8).".

The Attachment of Earnings Act 1971 (c. 32)

29. In Schedule 1 to the Attachment of Earnings Act 1971 (maintenance orders to which that Act applies), in paragraph 7, for the words "section 47 or 51 of the Child Care Act 1980" there shall be substituted "paragraph 23 of Schedule 2 to the Children Act 1989".

The Tribunals and Inquiries Act 1971 (c. 62)

30. In Schedule 1 to the Tribunals and Inquiries Act 1971 (tribunals under direct supervision of the Council on Tribunals) for paragraph 4 there shall be substituted—

"Registration of voluntary homes and children's homes under the Children Act 1989. | 4. Registered Homes Tribunals constituted under Part III of the Registered Homes Act 1984."

The Local Government Act 1972 (c. 70)

31.—(1) In section 102(1) of the Local Government Act 1972 (appointment of committees) for the words "section 31 of the Child Care Act 1980" there shall be substituted "section 53 of the Children Act 1989".

(2) In Schedule 12A to that Act (access to information: exempt information), in Part III (interpretation), in paragraph 1(1)(b) for the words "section 20 of the Children and Young Persons Act 1969" there shall be substituted "section 31 of the Children Act 1989".

The Employment of Children Act 1973 (c. 24)

32.—(1) In section 2 of the Employment of Children Act 1973 (supervision by education authorities), in subsection (2)(a) for the words "guardian or a person who has actual custody of" there shall be substituted "any person responsible for".

(2) After that subsection there shall be inserted—

"(2A) For the purposes of subsection (2)(a) above a person is responsible for a child—

(a) in England and Wales, if he has parental responsibility for the child or care of him; and

(b) in Scotland, if he is his guardian or has actual custody of him.".

The Domicile and Matrimonial Proceedings Act 1973 (c. 45)

33.—(1) In Schedule 1 to the Domicile and Matrimonial Proceedings Act 1973 (proceedings in divorce etc. stayed by reference to proceedings in other jurisdiction), paragraph 11(1) shall be amended as follows—

(a) at the end of the definition of "lump sum" there shall be added "or an order made in equivalent circumstances under Schedule 1 to the Children Act 1989 and of a kind mentioned in paragraph 1(2)(c) of that Schedule";

(b) in the definition of "relevant order", at the end of paragraph (b), there shall be added "or an order made in equivalent circumstances under Schedule 1 to the Children Act 1989 and of a kind mentioned in paragraph 1(2)(a) or (b) of that Schedule";

(c) in paragraph (c) of that definition, after the word "children)" there shall be inserted "or a section 8 order under the Children Act 1989"; and

(d) in paragraph (d) of that definition for the words "the custody, care or control" there shall be substituted "care".

(2) In paragraph 11(3) of that Schedule—

(a) the word "four" shall be omitted; and

(b) for the words "the custody of a child and the education of a child" there shall be substituted "or any provision which could be made by a section 8 order under the Children Act 1989".

The Powers of Criminal Courts Act 1973 (c. 62)

34. In Schedule 3 to the Powers of Criminal Courts Act 1973 (the probation and after-care service and its functions), in paragraph 3(2A) after paragraph (b) there shall be inserted—

"and

(c) directions given under paragraph 2 or 3 of Schedule 3 to the Children Act 1989".

The Rehabilitation of Offenders Act 1974 (c. 53)

35.—(1) Section 7(2) of the Rehabilitation of Offenders Act 1974 (limitations on rehabilitation under the Act) shall be amended as follows.

(2) For paragraph (c) there shall be substituted—

"(c) in any proceedings relating to adoption, the marriage of any minor, the exercise of the inherent jurisdiction of the High Court with respect to minors or the provision by any person of accommodation, care or schooling for minors;

(cc) in any proceedings brought under the Children Act 1989;"

(3) For paragraph (d) there shall be substituted—

"(d) in any proceedings relating to the variation or discharge of a supervision order under the Children and Young Persons Act 1969, or on appeal from any such proceedings".

The Domestic Proceedings and Magistrates' Courts Act 1978 (c. 22)

36. For section 8 of the Domestic Proceedings and Magistrates' Courts Act 1978 (orders for the custody of children) there shall be substituted—

"Restrictions on making of orders under this Act: welfare of children.
    8. Where an application is made by a party to a marriage for an order under section 2, 6 or 7 of this Act, then, if there is a child of the family who is under the age of eighteen, the court shall not dismiss or make a final order on the application until it has decided whether to exercise any of its powers under the Children Act 1989 with respect to the child."

37. In section 19(3A)(b) (interim orders) for the words "subsections (2) and" there shall be substituted "subsection".

38. For section 20(12) of that Act (variation and revocation of orders for periodical payments) there shall be substituted—

"(12) An application under this section may be made—

(a) where it is for the variation or revocation of an order under section 2, 6, 7 or 19 of this Act for periodical payments, by either party to the marriage in question; and

(b) where it is for the variation of an order under section 2(1)(c), 6 or 7 of this Act for periodical payments to or in respect of a child, also by the child himself, if he has attained the age of sixteen."

39.—(1) For section 20A of that Act (revival of orders for periodical payments) there shall be substituted—

"Revival of orders for periodical payments.

20A.—(1) Where an order made by a magistrates' court under this Part of this Act for the making of periodical payments to or in respect of a child (other than an interim maintenance order) ceases to have effect—

(a) on the date on which the child attains the age of sixteen, or

(b) at any time after that date but before or on the date on which he attains the age of eighteen,

the child may apply to the court which made the order for an order for its revival.

(2) If on such an application it appears to the court that—

(a) the child is, will be or (if an order were made under this subsection) would be receiving instruction at an educational establishment or undergoing training for a trade, profession or vocation, whether or not while in gainful employment, or

(b) there are special circumstances which justify the making of an order under this subsection,

the court shall have power by order to revive the order from such date as the court may specify, not being earlier than the date of the making of the application.

(3) Any order revived under this section may be varied or revoked under section 20 in the same way as it could have been varied or revoked had it continued in being."

40. In section 23(1) of that Act (supplementary provisions with respect to the variation and revocation of orders) for the words "14(3), 20 or 21" there shall be substituted "20" and for the words "section 20 of this Act" there shall be substituted "that section".

41.—(1) In section 25 of that Act (effect on certain orders of parties living together), in subsection (1)(a) for the words "6 or 11(2)" there shall be substituted "or 6".

(2) In subsection (2) of that section—

(a) in paragraph (a) for the words "6 or 11(2)" there shall be substituted "or 6"; and

(b) after paragraph (a) there shall be inserted "or".

42. In section 29(5) of that Act (appeals) for the words "sections 14(3), 20 and 21" there shall be substituted "section 20".

43. In section 88(1) of that Act (interpretation)—

(a) in the definition of "child", for the words from "an illegitimate" to the end there shall be substituted "a child whose father and mother were not married to each other at the time of his birth"; and

(b) in the definition of "child of the family", for the words "being boarded-out with those parties" there shall be substituted "placed with those parties as foster parents".

The Magistrates' Courts Act 1980 (c. 43)

44.—(1) In section 59(2) of the Magistrates' Courts Act 1980 (periodical payments through justices' clerk) for the words "the Guardianship of Minors Acts 1971 and 1973" there shall be substituted "(or having effect as if made under) Schedule 1 to the Children Act 1989".

(2) For section 62(5) of that Act (payments to children) there shall be substituted—

"(5) In this section references to the person with whom a child has his home—

(a) in the case of any child who is being looked after by a local authority (within the meaning of section 22 of the Children Act 1989), are references to that local authority; and

(b) in any other case, are references to the person who, disregarding any absence of the child at a hospital or boarding school and any other temporary absence, has care of the child.".

The Supreme Court Act 1981 (c. 54)

45.—(1) In section 18 of the Supreme Court Act 1981 (restrictions on appeals to Court of Appeal)—

(a) in subsection (1)(h)(i), for the word "custody" there shall be substituted "residence"; and

(b) in subsection (1)(h)(ii) for the words "access to", in both places, there shall be substituted "contact with".

(2) In section 41 of that Act (wards of court), the following subsection shall be inserted after subsection (2)—

"(2A) Subsection (2) does not apply with respect to a child who is the subject of a care order (as defined by section 105 of the Children Act 1989)."

(3) In Schedule 1 to that Act (distribution of business in High Court), for paragraph 3(b)(ii) there shall be substituted—

"(ii) the exercise of the inherent jurisdiction of the High Court with respect to minors, the maintenance of minors and any proceedings under the Children Act 1989, except proceedings solely for the appointment of a guardian of a minor's estate;".

The Armed Forces Act 1981 (c. 55)

46. In section 14 of the Armed Forces Act 1981 (temporary removal to, and detention in, place of safety abroad or in the United Kingdom of service children in need of care and control), in subsection (9A) for the words "the Children and Young Persons Act 1933, the Children and Young Persons Act 1969" there shall be substituted "the Children Act 1989".

The Civil Jurisdiction and Judgments Act 1982 (c. 27)

47. In paragraph 5(a) of Schedule 5 to the Civil Jurisdiction and Judgments Act 1982 (maintenance and similar payments excluded from Schedule 4 to that Act) for the words "section 47 or 51 of the Child Care Act 1980" there shall be substituted "paragraph 23 of Schedule 2 to the Children Act 1989".

The Mental Health Act 1983 (c. 20)

48.—(1) For section 27 of the Mental Health Act 1983 (children and young persons in care of local authority) there shall be substituted the following section—

"Children and young persons in care.

27. Where—

(a) a patient who is a child or young person is in the care of a local authority by virtue of a care order within the meaning of the Children Act 1989; or

(b) the rights and powers of a parent of a patient who is a child or young person are vested in a local authority by virtue of section 16 of the Social Work (Scotland) Act 1968,

the authority shall be deemed to be the nearest relative of the patient in preference to any person except the patient's husband or wife (if any)."

(2) Section 28 of that Act (nearest relative of minor under guardianship, etc.) is amended as mentioned in sub-paragraphs (3) and (4).

(3) For subsection (1) there shall be substituted—

"(1) Where—

(a) a guardian has been appointed for a person who has not attained the age of eighteen years; or

(b) a residence order (as defined by section 8 of the Children Act 1989) is in force with respect to such a person,

the guardian (or guardians, where there is more than one) or the person named in the residence order shall, to the exclusion of any other person, be deemed to be his nearest relative."

(4) For subsection (3) there shall be substituted—

"(3) In this section "guardian" does not include a guardian under this Part of this Act."

(5) In section 131(2) of that Act (informal admission of patients aged sixteen or over) for the words from "notwithstanding" to the end there shall be substituted "even though there are one or more persons who have parental responsibility for him (within the meaning of the Children Act 1989)".

The Registered Homes Act 1984 (c. 23)

49.—(1) In section 1(5) of the Registered Homes Act 1984 (requirement of registration) for paragraphs (d) and (e) there shall be substituted—

"(d) any community home, voluntary home or children's home within the meaning of the Children Act 1989."

(2) In section 39 of that Act (preliminary) for paragraphs (a) and (b) there shall be substituted—

"(a) the Children Act 1989."

The Mental Health (Scotland) Act 1984 (c. 36)

50. For section 54 of the Mental Health (Scotland) Act 1984 (children and young persons in care of local authority) there shall be substituted the following section—

"Children and young persons in care of local authority.

54. Where—

(a) the rights and powers of a parent of a patient who is a child or young person are vested in a local authority by virtue of section 16 of the Social Work (Scotland) Act 1968; or

(b) a patient who is a child or young person is in the care of a local authority by virtue of a care order made under the Children Act 1989,

the authority shall be deemed to be the nearest relative of the patient in preference to any person except the patient's husband or wife (if any)."

The Matrimonial and Family Proceedings Act 1984 (c. 42)

51. In section 38(2)(b) of the Matrimonial and Family Proceedings Act 1984 (transfer of family proceedings from High Court to county court) after the words "a ward of court" there shall be inserted "or any other proceedings which relate to the exercise of the inherent jurisdiction of the High Court with respect to minors".

The Police and Criminal Evidence Act 1984 (c. 60)

52. In section 37(14) of the Police and Criminal Evidence Act 1984 (duties of custody officer before charge) after the words "Children and Young Persons Act 1969" there shall be inserted "or in Part IV of the Children Act 1989".

53.—(1) In section 38 of that Act (duties of custody officer after charge), in subsection (6) for the words from "make arrangements" to the end there shall be substituted "secure that the arrested juvenile is moved to local authority accommodation".

(2) After that subsection there shall be inserted—

"(6A) In this section 'local authority accommodation' means accommodation provided by or on behalf of a local authority (within the meaning of the Children Act 1989).

(6B) Where an arrested juvenile is moved to local authority accommodation under subsection (6) above, it shall be lawful for any person acting on behalf of the authority to detain him.".

(3) In subsection (8) of that section for the words "Children and Young Persons Act 1969" there shall be substituted "Children Act 1989".

54. In section 39(4) of that Act (responsibilities in relation to persons detained) for the words "transferred to the care of a local authority in pursuance of arrangements made" there shall be substituted "moved to local authority accommodation".

55. In Schedule 2 to that Act (preserved powers of arrest) in the entry relating to the Children and Young Persons Act 1969 for the words "Sections 28(2) and" there shall be substituted "Section".

The Surrogacy Arrangements Act 1985 (c. 49)

56. In section 1(2)(b) of the Surrogacy Arrangements Act 1985 (meaning of "surrogate mother", etc.) for the words "the parental rights being exercised" there shall be substituted "parental responsibility being met".

The Child Abduction and Custody Act 1985 (c. 60)

57.—(1) In section 9(a) and 20(2)(a) of the Child Abduction and Custody Act 1985 (orders with respect to which court's powers suspended), for the words "any other order under section 1(2) of the Children and Young Persons Act 1969" there shall be substituted "a supervision order under section 31 of the Children Act 1989".

(2) At the end of section 27 of that Act (interpretation), there shall be added—

"(4) In this Act a decision relating to rights of access in England and Wales means a decision as to the contact which a child may, or may not, have with any person."

(3) In Part I of Schedule 3 to that Act (orders in England and Wales which are custody orders for the purposes of the Act), for paragraph 1 there shall be substituted—

"1. The following are the orders referred to in section 27(1) of this Act—

(a) a care order under the Children Act 1989 (as defined by section 31(11) of that Act, read with section 105(1) and Schedule 14);

(b) a residence order (as defined by section 8 of the Act of 1989); and

(c) any order made by a court in England and Wales under any of the following enactments—

(i) section 9(1), 10(1)(a) or 11(a) of the Guardianship of Minors Act 1971;

(ii) section 42(1) or (2) or 43(1) of the Matrimonial Causes Act 1973;

(iii) section 2(2)(b), 4(b) or (5) of the Guardianship Act 1973 as applied by section 34(5) of the Children Act 1975;

(iv) section 8(2)(a), 10(1) or 19(1)(ii) of the Domestic Proceedings and Magistrates Courts Act 1978;

(v) section 26(1)(b) of the Adoption Act 1976."

The Disabled Persons (Services, Consultation and Representation) Act 1986 (c. 33)

58. In section 1(3) of the Disabled Persons (Services, Consultation and Representation) Act 1986 (circumstances in which regulations may provide for the appointment of authorised representatives of disabled persons)—

(a) in paragraph (a), for the words "parent or guardian of a disabled person under the age of sixteen" there shall be substituted—

"(i) the parent of a disabled person under the age of sixteen, or

(ii) any other person who is not a parent of his but who has parental responsibility for him"; and

(b) in paragraph (b), for the words "in the care of" there shall be substituted "looked after by".

59.—(1) Section 2 of that Act (circumstances in which authorised representative has right to visit etc. disabled person) shall be amended as follows.

(2) In subsection (3)(a) for the words from second "the" to "by" there shall be substituted "for the words 'if so requested by the disabled person' there shall be substituted 'if so requested by any person mentioned in section 1(3)(a)(i) or (ii)'."

(3) In subsection (5) after paragraph (b) there shall be inserted—

"(bb) in accommodation provided by or on behalf of a local authority under Part III of the Children Act 1989, or".

(4) After paragraph (c) of subsection (5) there shall be inserted—

"(cc) in accommodation provided by a voluntary organisation in accordance with arrangements made by a local authority under section 17 of the Children Act 1989, or".

60. In section 5(7)(b) of that Act (disabled persons leaving special education) for the word "guardian" there shall be substituted "other person who is not a parent of his but who has parental responsibility for him".

61.—(1) In section 16 of that Act (interpretation) in the definition of "disabled person", in paragraph (a) for the words from "means" to "applies" there shall be substituted "means—

"(i) in the case of a person aged eighteen or over, a person to whom section 29 of the 1948 Act applies, and

(ii) in the case of a person under the age of eighteen, a person who is disabled within the meaning of Part III of the Children Act 1989".

(2) After the definition of "parent" in that section there shall be inserted—

" 'parental responsibility' has the same meaning as in the Children Act 1989."

(3) In the definition of "the welfare enactments" in that section, in paragraph (a) after the words "the 1977 Act" there shall be inserted "and Part III of the Children Act 1989".

(4) At the end of that section there shall be added—

"(2) In this Act any reference to a child who is looked after by a local authority has the same meaning as in the Children Act 1989."

The Family Law Act 1986 (c. 55)

62.—(1) The Family Law Act 1986 shall be amended as follows.

(2) Subject to paragraphs 63 to 71, in Part I—

(a) for the words "custody order", in each place where they occur, there shall be substituted "Part I order";

(b) for the words "proceedings with respect to the custody of", in each place where they occur, there shall be substituted "Part I proceedings with respect to"; and

(c) for the words "matters relating to the custody of", in each place where they occur, there shall be substituted "Part I matters relating to".

(3) For section 42(7) (general interpretation of Part I) there shall be substituted—

"(7) In this Part—

(a) references to Part I proceedings in respect of a child are references to any proceedings for a Part I order or an order corresponding to a Part I order and include, in relation to proceedings outside the United Kingdom, references to proceedings before a tribunal or other authority having power under the law having effect there to determine Part I matters; and

(b) references to Part I matters are references to matters that might be determined by a Part I order or an order corresponding to a Part I order."

63.—(1) In section 1 (orders to which Part I of the Act of 1986 applies), in subsection (1)—

(a) for paragraph (a) there shall be substituted—

"(a) a section 8 order made by a court in England and Wales under the Children Act 1989, other than an order varying or discharging such an order"; and

(b) for paragraph (d) there shall be substituted the following paragraphs—

"(d) an order made by a court in England and Wales in the exercise of the inherent jurisdiction of the High Court with respect to children—

(i) so far as it gives care of a child to any person or provides for contact with, or the education of, a child; but

(ii) excluding an order varying or revoking such an order;

(e) an order made by the High Court in Northern Ireland in the exercise of its jurisdiction relating to wardship—

(i) so far as it gives care and control of a child to any person or provides for the education of or access to a child; but

(ii) excluding an order relating to a child of whom care or care and control is (immediately after the making of the order) vested in the Department of Health and Social Services or a Health and Social Services Board."

(2) In subsection (2) of that section, in paragraph (c) for "(d)" there shall be substituted "(e)".

(3) For subsections (3) to (5) of that section there shall be substituted—

"(3) In this Part, 'Part I order'—

(a) includes any order which would have been a custody order by virtue of this section in any form in which it was in force at any time before its amendment by the Children Act 1989; and

(b) (subject to sections 32 and 40 of this Act) excludes any order which would have been excluded from being a custody order by virtue of this section in any such form."

64. For section 2 there shall be substituted the following sections—

"Jurisdiction: general.

2.—(1) A court in England and Wales shall not have jurisdiction to make a section 1(1)(a) order with respect to a child in or in connection with matrimonial proceedings in England and Wales unless the condition in section 2A of this Act is satisfied.

(2) A court in England and Wales shall not have jurisdiction to make a section 1(1)(a) order in a non-matrimonial case (that is to say, where the condition in section 2A of this Act is not satisfied) unless the condition in section 3 of this Act is satisfied.

(3) A court in England and Wales shall not have jurisdiction to make a section 1(1)(d) order unless—

(a) the condition in section 3 of this Act is satisfied, or

(b) the child concerned is present in England and Wales on the relevant date and the court considers that the immediate exercise of its powers is necessary for his protection.

Jurisdiction in or in connection with matrimonial proceedings.

2A.—(1) The condition referred to in section 2(1) of this Act is that the matrimonial proceedings are proceedings in respect of the marriage of the parents of the child concerned and—

(a) the proceedings—

(i) are proceedings for divorce or nullity of marriage, and

(ii) are continuing;

(b) the proceedings—

(i) are proceedings for judicial separation,

(ii) are continuing,

and the jurisdiction of the court is not excluded by subsection (2) below; or

(c) the proceedings have been dismissed after the beginning of the trial but—

    (i) the section 1(1)(a) order is being made forthwith, or

    (ii) the application for the order was made on or before the dismissal.

(2) For the purposes of subsection (1)(b) above, the jurisdiction of the court is excluded if, after the grant of a decree of judicial separation, on the relevant date, proceedings for divorce or nullity in respect of the marriage are continuing in Scotland or Northern Ireland.

(3) Subsection (2) above shall not apply if the court in which the other proceedings there referred to are continuing has made—

(a) an order under section 13(6) or 21(5) of this Act (not being an order made by virtue of section 13(6)(a)(i)), or

(b) an order under section 14(2) or 22(2) of this Act which is recorded as being made for the purpose of enabling Part I proceedings to be taken in England and Wales with respect to the child concerned.

(4) Where a court—

(a) has jurisdiction to make a section 1(1)(a) order in or in connection with matrimonial proceedings, but

(b) considers that it would be more appropriate for Part I matters relating to the child to be determined outside England and Wales,

the court may by order direct that, while the order under this subsection is in force, no section 1(1)(a) order shall be made by any court in or in connection with those proceedings."

65.—(1) In section 3 (habitual residence or presence of child concerned) in subsection (1) for "section 2" there shall be substituted "section 2(2)".

(2) In subsection (2) of that section for the words "proceedings for divorce, nullity or judicial separation" there shall be substituted "matrimonial proceedings".

66.—(1) In section 6 (duration and variation of Part I orders), for subsection (3) there shall be substituted the following subsections—

"(3) A court in England and Wales shall not have jurisdiction to vary a Part I order if, on the relevant date, matrimonial proceedings are continuing in Scotland or Northern Ireland in respect of the marriage of the parents of the child concerned.

(3A) Subsection (3) above shall not apply if—

(a) the Part I order was made in or in connection with proceedings for divorce or nullity in England and Wales in respect of the marriage of the parents of the child concerned; and

(b) those proceedings are continuing.

(3B) Subsection (3) above shall not apply if—

(a) the Part I order was made in or in connection with proceedings for judicial separation in England and Wales;

(b) those proceedings are continuing; and

(c) the decree of judicial separation has not yet been granted."

(2) In subsection (5) of that section for the words from "variation of" to "if the ward" there shall be substituted "variation of a section 1(1)(d) order if the child concerned".

(3) For subsections (6) and (7) of that section there shall be substituted the following subsections—

"(6) Subsection (7) below applies where a Part I order which is—

(a) a residence order (within the meaning of the Children Act 1989) in favour of a person with respect to a child,

(b) an order made in the exercise of the High Court's inherent jurisdiction with respect to children by virtue of which a person has care of a child, or

(c) an order—

(i) of a kind mentioned in section 1(3)(a) of this Act,

(ii) under which a person is entitled to the actual possession of a child,

ceases to have effect in relation to that person by virtue of subsection (1) above.

(7) Where this subsection applies, any family assistance order made under section 16 of the Children Act 1989 with respect to the child shall also cease to have effect.

(8) For the purposes of subsection (7) above the reference to a family assistance order under section 16 of the Children Act 1989 shall be deemed to include a reference to an order for the supervision of a child made under—

(a) section 7(4) of the Family Law Reform Act 1969,

(b) section 44 of the Matrimonial Causes Act 1973,

(c) section 2(2)(a) of the Guardianship Act 1973,

(d) section 34(5) or 36(3)(b) of the Children Act 1975, or

(e) section 9 of the Domestic Proceedings and Magistrates' Courts Act 1978;

but this subsection shall cease to have effect once all such orders for the supervision of children have ceased to have effect in accordance with Schedule 14 to the Children Act 1989."

67. For section 7 (interpretation of Chapter II) there shall be substituted—

"Interpretation of Chapter II.

7. In this Chapter—

(a) 'child' means a person who has not attained the age of eighteen;

(b) 'matrimonial proceedings' means proceedings for divorce, nullity of marriage or judicial separation;

(c) 'the relevant date' means, in relation to the making or variation of an order—

(i) where an application is made for an order to be made or varied, the date of the application (or first application, if two or more are determined together), and

(ii) where no such application is made, the date on which the court is considering whether to make or, as the case may be, vary the order; and

(d) 'section 1(1)(a) order' and 'section 1(1)(d) order' mean orders falling within section 1(1)(a) and (d) of this Act respectively."

68. In each of the following sections—

    (a) section 11(2)(a) (provisions supplementary to sections 9 and 10),

    (b) section 13(5)(a) (jurisdiction ancillary to matrimonial proceedings),

    (c) section 20(3)(a) (habitual residence or presence of child),

    (d) section 21(4)(a) (jurisdiction in divorce proceedings, etc.), and

    (e) section 23(4)(a) (duration and variation of custody orders),

for "4(5)" there shall be substituted "2A(4)".

69. In each of the following sections—

    (a) section 19(2) (jurisdiction in cases other than divorce, etc.),

    (b) section 20(6) (habitual residence or presence of child), and

    (c) section 23(5) (duration and variation of custody orders),

for "section 1(1)(d)" there shall be substituted "section 1(1)(e)".

70. In section 34(3) (power to order recovery of child) for paragraph (a) there shall be substituted—

    "(a) section 14 of the Children Act 1989".

71.—(1) In section 42 (general interpretation of Part I), in subsection (4)(a) for the words "has been boarded out with those parties" there shall be substituted "is placed with those parties as foster parents".

(2) In subsection (6) of that section, in paragraph (a) after the word "person" there shall be inserted "to be allowed contact with or".

The Local Government Act 1988 (c. 9)

72. In Schedule 1 to the Local Government Act 1988 (competition) at the end of paragraph 2(4) (cleaning of buildings: buildings to which competition provisions do not apply) for paragraph (c) there shall be substituted—

    "(c) section 53 of the Children Act 1989."

Amendments of local Acts

73.—(1) Section 16 of the Greater London Council (General Powers) Act 1981 (exemption from provisions of Part IV of the Act of certain premises) shall be amended as follows.

(2) After paragraph (g) there shall be inserted—

    "(gg) used as a children's home as defined in section 63 of the Children Act 1989".

(3) In paragraph (h)—

    (a) for the words "section 56 of the Child Care Act 1980" there shall be substituted "section 60 of the Children Act 1989";

    (b) for the words "section 57" there shall be substituted "section 60"; and

    (c) for the words "section 32" there shall be substituted "section 53".

(4) In paragraph (i), for the words "section 8 of the Foster Children Act 1980" there shall be substituted "section 67 of the Children Act 1989".

74.—(1) Section 10(2) of the Greater London Council (General Powers) Act 1984 (exemption from provisions of Part IV of the Act of certain premises) shall be amended as follows.

(2) In paragraph (d)—

    (a) for the words "section 56 of the Child Care Act 1980" there shall be substituted "section 60 of the Children Act 1989";

(b) for the words "section 57" there shall be substituted "section 60"; and

(c) for the words "section 31" there shall be substituted "section 53".

(3) In paragraph (e), for the words "section 8 of the Foster Children Act 1980" there shall be substituted "section 67 of the Children Act 1989".

(4) In paragraph (l) for the words "section 1 of the Children's Homes Act 1982" there shall be substituted "section 63 of the Children Act 1989".

SCHEDULE 14

Tʀᴀɴsɪᴛɪᴏɴᴀʟs ᴀɴᴅ Sᴀᴠɪɴɢs

Pending proceedings, etc.

Section 108(6).

1.—(1) Subject to sub-paragraph (4), nothing in any provision of this Act (other than the repeals mentioned in sub-paragraph (2)) shall affect any proceedings which are pending immediately before the commencement of that provision.

(2) The repeals are those of—

(a) section 42(3) of the Matrimonial Causes Act 1973 (declaration by court that party to marriage unfit to have custody of children of family); and

1973 c. 18.

(b) section 38 of the Sexual Offences Act 1956 (power of court to divest person of authority over girl or boy in cases of incest).

1956 c. 69.

(3) For the purposes of the following provisions of this Schedule, any reference to an order in force immediately before the commencement of a provision of this Act shall be construed as including a reference to an order made after that commencement in proceedings pending before that commencement.

(4) Sub-paragraph (3) is not to be read as making the order in question have effect from a date earlier than that on which it was made.

(5) An order under section 96(3) may make such provision with respect to the application of the order in relation to proceedings which are pending when the order comes into force as the Lord Chancellor considers appropriate.

2. Where, immediately before the day on which Part IV comes into force, there was in force an order under section 3(1) of the Children and Young Persons Act 1963 (order directing a local authority to bring a child or young person before a juvenile court under section 1 of the Children and Young Persons Act 1969), the order shall cease to have effect on that day.

1963 c. 37.

Cᴜsᴛᴏᴅʏ ᴏʀᴅᴇʀs, ᴇᴛᴄ.

Cessation of declarations of unfitness, etc.

3. Where, immediately before the day on which Parts I and II come into force, there was in force—

(a) a declaration under section 42(3) of the Matrimonial Causes Act 1973 (declaration by court that party to marriage unfit to have custody of children of family); or

(b) an order under section 38(1) of the Sexual Offences Act 1956 divesting a person of authority over a girl or boy in a case of incest;

the declaration or, as the case may be, the order shall cease to have effect on that day.

The Family Law Reform Act 1987 (c. 42)

Conversion of orders under section 4

4. Where, immediately before the day on which Parts I and II come into force, there was in force an order under section 4(1) of the Family Law Reform Act 1987 (order giving father parental rights and duties in relation to a child), then, on and after that day, the order shall be deemed to be an order under section 4 of this Act giving the father parental responsibility for the child.

Orders to which paragraphs 6 to 11 apply

5.—(1) In paragraphs 6 to 11 "an existing order" means any order which—

(a) is in force immediately before the commencement of Parts I and II;

(b) was made under any enactment mentioned in sub-paragraph (2);

(c) determines all or any of the following—

(i) who is to have custody of a child;

(ii) who is to have care and control of a child;

(iii) who is to have access to a child;

(iv) any matter with respect to a child's education or upbringing; and

(d) is not an order of a kind mentioned in paragraph 15(1).

(2) The enactments are—

1978 c. 22.   (a) the Domestic Proceedings and Magistrates' Courts Act 1978;

1975 c. 72.   (b) the Children Act 1975;

1973 c. 18.   (c) the Matrimonial Causes Act 1973;

(d) the Guardianship of Minors Acts 1971 and 1973;

1965 c. 72.   (e) the Matrimonial Causes Act 1965;

1960 c. 48.   (f) the Matrimonial Proceedings (Magistrates' Courts) Act 1960.

(3) For the purposes of this paragraph and paragraphs 6 to 11 "custody" includes legal custody and joint as well as sole custody but does not include access.

Parental responsibility of parents

6.—(1) Where—

(a) a child's father and mother were married to each other at the time of his birth; and

(b) there is an existing order with respect to the child,

each parent shall have parental responsibility for the child in accordance with section 2 as modified by sub-paragraph (3).

(2) Where—

(a) a child's father and mother were not married to each other at the time of his birth; and

(b) there is an existing order with respect to the child,

section 2 shall apply as modified by sub-paragraphs (3) and (4).

(3) The modification is that for section 2(8) there shall be substituted—

"(8) The fact that a person has parental responsibility for a child does not entitle him to act in a way which would be incompatible with any existing order or any order made under this Act with respect to the child".

(4) The modifications are that—

(a) for the purposes of section 2(2), where the father has custody or care and control of the child by virtue of any existing order, the court shall be deemed to have made (at the commencement of that section) an order under section 4(1) giving him parental responsibility for the child; and

(b) where by virtue of paragraph (a) a court is deemed to have made an order under section 4(1) in favour of a father who has care and control of a child by virtue of an existing order, the court shall not bring the order under section 4(1) to an end at any time while he has care and control of the child by virtue of the order.

Persons who are not parents but who have custody or care and control

7.—(1) Where a person who is not the parent or guardian of a child has custody or care and control of him by virtue of an existing order, that person shall have parental responsibility for him so long as he continues to have that custody or care and control by virtue of the order.

(2) Where sub-paragraph (1) applies, Parts I and II shall have effect as modified by this paragraph.

(3) The modifications are that—

(a) for section 2(8) there shall be substituted—

"(8) The fact that a person has parental responsibility for a child does not entitle him to act in a way which would be incompatible with any existing order or with any order made under this Act with respect to the child";

(b) at the end of section 10(4) there shall be inserted—

"(c) any person who has custody or care and control of a child by virtue of any existing order"; and

(c) at the end of section 34(1)(c) there shall be inserted—

"(cc) where immediately before the care order was made there was an existing order by virtue of which a person had custody or care and control of the child, that person."

Persons who have care and control

8.—(1) Sub-paragraphs (2) to (6) apply where a person has care and control of a child by virtue of an existing order, but they shall cease to apply when that order ceases to have effect.

(2) Section 5 shall have effect as if—

(a) for any reference to a residence order in favour of a parent or guardian there were substituted a reference to any existing order by virtue of which the parent or guardian has care and control of the child; and

(b) for subsection (9) there were substituted—

"(9) Subsections (1) and (7) do not apply if the existing order referred to in paragraph (b) of those subsections was one by virtue of which a surviving parent of the child also had care and control of him."

(3) Section 10 shall have effect as if for subsection (5)(c)(i) there were substituted—

"(i) in any case where by virtue of an existing order any person or persons has or have care and control of the child, has the consent of that person or each of those persons".

(4) Section 20 shall have effect as if for subsection (9)(a) there were substituted "who has care and control of the child by virtue of an existing order."

(5) Section 23 shall have effect as if for subsection (4)(c) there were substituted—

"(c) where the child is in care and immediately before the care order was made there was an existing order by virtue of which a person had care and control of the child, that person."

(6) In Schedule 1, paragraphs 1(1) and 14(1) shall have effect as if for the words "in whose favour a residence order is in force with respect to the child" there were substituted "who has been given care and control of the child by virtue of an existing order".

Persons who have access

9.—(1) Sub-paragraphs (2) to (4) apply where a person has access by virtue of an existing order.

(2) Section 10 shall have effect as if after subsection (5) there were inserted—

"(5A) Any person who has access to a child by virtue of an existing order is entitled to apply for a contact order."

(3) Section 16(2) shall have effect as if after paragraph (b) there were inserted—

"(bb) any person who has access to the child by virtue of an existing order."

(4) Sections 43(11), 44(13) and 46(10), shall have effect as if in each case after paragraph (d) there were inserted—

"(dd) any person who has been given access to him by virtue of an existing order."

Enforcement of certain existing orders

10.—(1) Sub-paragraph (2) applies in relation to any existing order which, but for the repeal by this Act of—

1971 c. 3.   (a) section 13(1) of the Guardianship of Minors Act 1971;

1975 c. 72.   (b) section 43(1) of the Children Act 1975; or

1978 c. 22.   (c) section 33 of the Domestic Proceedings and Magistrates' Courts Act 1978,

(provisions concerning the enforcement of custody orders) might have been enforced as if it were an order requiring a person to give up a child to another person.

(2) Where this sub-paragraph applies, the existing order may, after the repeal of the enactments mentioned in sub-paragraph (1)(a) to (c), be enforced under section 14 as if—

(a) any reference to a residence order were a reference to the existing order; and

(b) any reference to a person in whose favour the residence order is in force were a reference to a person to whom actual custody of the child is given by an existing order which is in force.

(3) In sub-paragraph (2) "actual custody", in relation to a child, means the actual possession of his person.

Discharge of existing orders

11.—(1) The making of a residence order or a care order with respect to a child who is the subject of an existing order discharges the existing order.

(2) Where the court makes any section 8 order (other than a residence order) with respect to a child with respect to whom any existing order is in force, the existing order shall have effect subject to the section 8 order.

(3) The court may discharge an existing order which is in force with respect to a child—

    (a) in any family proceedings relating to the child or in which any question arises with respect to the child's welfare; or

    (b) on the application of—

        (i) any parent or guardian of the child;

        (ii) the child himself; or

        (iii) any person named in the order.

(4) A child may not apply for the discharge of an existing order except with the leave of the court.

(5) The power in sub-paragraph (3) to discharge an existing order includes the power to discharge any part of the order.

(6) In considering whether to discharge an order under the power conferred by sub-paragraph (3) the court shall, if the discharge of the order is opposed by any party to the proceedings, have regard in particular to the matters mentioned in section 1(3).

GUARDIANS

Existing guardians to be guardians under this Act

12.—(1) Any appointment of a person as guardian of a child which—

    (a) was made—

        (i) under sections 3 to 5 of the Guardianship of Minors Act 1971;   1971 c. 3.

        (ii) under section 38(3) of the Sexual Offences Act 1956; or   1956 c. 69.

        (iii) under the High Court's inherent jurisdiction with respect to children; and

    (b) has taken effect before the commencement of section 5,

shall (subject to sub-paragraph (2)) be deemed, on and after the commencement of section 5, to be an appointment made and having effect under that section.

(2) Where an appointment of a person as guardian of a child has effect under section 5 by virtue of sub-paragraph (1)(a)(ii), the appointment shall not have effect for a period which is longer than any period specified in the order.

Appointment of guardian not yet in effect

13. Any appointment of a person to be a guardian of a child—

    (a) which was made as mentioned in paragraph 12(1)(a)(i); but

    (b) which, immediately before the commencement of section 5, had not taken effect,

shall take effect in accordance with section 5 (as modified, where it applies, by paragraph 8(2)).

Persons deemed to be appointed as guardians under existing wills

14. For the purposes of the Wills Act 1837 and of this Act any disposition by   1837 c. 26. will and testament or devise of the custody and tuition of any child, made before the commencement of section 5 and paragraph 1 of Schedule 13, shall be deemed to be an appointment by will of a guardian of the child.

SCH. 14

CHILDREN IN CARE

Children in compulsory care

15.—(1) Sub-paragraph (2) applies where, immediately before the day on which Part IV comes into force, a person was—

(a) in care by virtue of—

1969 c. 54.   (i) a care order under section 1 of the Children and Young Persons Act 1969;

(ii) a care order under section 15 of that Act, on discharging a supervision order made under section 1 of that Act; or

(iii) an order or authorisation under section 25 or 26 of that Act;

(b) deemed, by virtue of—

1955 c. 18.   (i) paragraph 7(3) of Schedule 5A to the Army Act 1955;

1955 c. 19.   (ii) paragraph 7(3) of Schedule 5A to the Air Force Act 1955; or

1957 c. 53.   (iii) paragraph 7(3) of Schedule 4A to the Naval Discipline Act 1957,

to be the subject of a care order under the Children and Young Persons Act 1969;

(c) in care—

1980 c. 5.   (i) under section 2 of the Child Care Act 1980; or

(ii) by virtue of paragraph 1 of Schedule 4 to that Act (which extends the meaning of a child in care under section 2 to include children in care under section 1 of the Children Act 1948),

1948 c. 43.

and a child in respect of whom a resolution under section 3 of the Act of 1980 or section 2 of the Act of 1948 was in force;

(d) a child in respect of whom a resolution had been passed under section 65 of the Child Care Act 1980;

(e) in care by virtue of an order under—

1960 c. 48.   (i) section 2(1)(e) of the Matrimonial Proceedings (Magistrates' Courts) Act 1960;

1969 c. 46.   (ii) section 7(2) of the Family Law Reform Act 1969;

1973 c. 18.   (iii) section 43(1) of the Matrimonial Causes Act 1973; or

1973 c. 29.   (iv) section 2(2)(b) of the Guardianship Act 1973;

1978 c. 22.   (v) section 10 of the Domestic Proceedings and Magistrates' Courts Act 1978,

(orders having effect for certain purposes as if the child had been received into care under section 2 of the Child Care Act 1980);

(f) in care by virtue of an order made, on the revocation of a custodianship order, under section 36 of the Children Act 1975; or

1975 c. 72.

(g) in care by virtue of an order made, on the refusal of an adoption order, under section 26 of the Adoption Act 1976 or any order having effect (by virtue of paragraph 1 of Schedule 2 to that Act) as if made under that section.

1976 c. 36.

(2) Where this sub-paragraph applies, then, on and after the day on which Part IV commences—

(a) the order or resolution in question shall be deemed to be a care order;

(b) the authority in whose care the person was immediately before that commencement shall be deemed to be the authority designated in that deemed care order; and

(c) any reference to a child in the care of a local authority shall include a reference to a person who is the subject of such a deemed care order,

and the provisions of this Act shall apply accordingly, subject to paragraph 16.

Modifications

16.—(1) Sub-paragraph (2) only applies where a person who is the subject of a care order by virtue of paragraph 15(2) is a person falling within sub-paragraph (1)(a) or (b) of that paragraph.

(2) Where the person would otherwise have remained in care until reaching the age of nineteen, by virtue of—

    (a) section 20(3)(a) or 21(1) of the Children and Young Persons Act 1969; or   1969 c. 54.

    (b) paragraph 7(5)(c)(i) of—

        (i) Schedule 5A to the Army Act 1955;   1955 c. 18.

        (ii) Schedule 5A to the Air Force Act 1955; or   1955 c. 19.

        (iii) Schedule 4A to the Naval Discipline Act 1957,   1957 c. 53.

this Act applies as if in section 91(12) for the word "eighteen" there were substituted "nineteen".

(3) Where a person who is the subject of a care order by virtue of paragraph 15(2) is a person falling within sub-paragraph (1)(b) of that paragraph, this Act applies as if section 101 were omitted.

(4) Sub-paragraph (5) only applies where a child who is the subject of a care order by virtue of paragraph 15(2) is a person falling within sub-paragraph (1)(e) to (g) of that paragraph.

(5) Where a court, on making the order, or at any time thereafter, gave directions under—

    (a) section 4(4)(a) of the Guardianship Act 1973; or   1973 c. 29.

    (b) section 43(5)(a) of the Matrimonial Causes Act 1973,   1973 c. 18.

as to the exercise by the authority of any powers, those directions shall continue to have effect (regardless of any conflicting provision in this Act) until varied or discharged by a court under this sub-paragraph.

Children placed with parent etc. while in compulsory care

17.—(1) This paragraph applies where a child is deemed by paragraph 15 to be in the care of a local authority under an order or resolution which is deemed by that paragraph to be a care order.

(2) If, immediately before the day on which Part III comes into force, the child was allowed to be under the charge and control of—

    (a) a parent or guardian under section 21(2) of the Child Care Act 1980; or   1980 c. 5.

    (b) a person who, before the child was in the authority's care, had care and control of the child by virtue of an order falling within paragraph 5,

on and after that day the provision made by and under section 23(5) shall apply as if the child had been placed with the person in question in accordance with that provision.

Orders for access to children in compulsory care

18.—(1) This paragraph applies to any access order—

    (a) made under section 12C of the Child Care Act 1980 (access orders with respect to children in care of local authorities); and

    (b) in force immediately before the commencement of Part IV.

(2) On and after the commencement of Part IV, the access order shall have effect as an order made under section 34 in favour of the person named in the order.

19.—(1) This paragraph applies where, immediately before the commencement of Part IV, an access order made under section 12C of the Act of 1980 was suspended by virtue of an order made under section 12E of that Act (suspension of access orders in emergencies).

(2) The suspending order shall continue to have effect as if this Act had not been passed.

(3) If—

(a) before the commencement of Part IV; and

(b) during the period for which the operation of the access order is suspended,

the local authority concerned made an application for its variation or discharge to an appropriate juvenile court, its operation shall be suspended until the date on which the application to vary or discharge it is determined or abandoned.

Children in voluntary care

20.—(1) This paragraph applies where, immediately before the day on which Part III comes into force—

(a) a child was in the care of a local authority—

1980 c. 5.
(i) under section 2(1) of the Child Care Act 1980; or

(ii) by virtue of paragraph 1 of Schedule 4 to that Act (which extends the meaning of references to children in care under section 2 to include references to children in care under section 1 of the 1948 c. 43. Children Act 1948); and

(b) he was not a person in respect of whom a resolution under section 3 of the Act of 1980 or section 2 of the Act of 1948 was in force.

(2) Where this paragraph applies, the child shall, on and after the day mentioned in sub-paragraph (1), be treated for the purposes of this Act as a child who is provided with accommodation by the local authority under Part III, but he shall cease to be so treated once he ceases to be so accommodated in accordance with the provisions of Part III.

(3) Where—

(a) this paragraph applies; and

(b) the child, immediately before the day mentioned in sub-paragraph (1), was (by virtue of section 21(2) of the Act of 1980) under the charge and control of a person falling within paragraph 17(2)(a) or (b),

the child shall not be treated for the purposes of this Act as if he were being looked after by the authority concerned.

Boarded out children

21.—(1) Where, immediately before the day on which Part III comes into force, a child in the care of a local authority—

(a) was—

(i) boarded out with a person under section 21(1)(a) of the Child Care Act 1980; or

(ii) placed under the charge and control of a person, under section 21(2) of that Act; and

(b) the person with whom he was boarded out, or (as the case may be) placed, was not a person falling within paragraph 17(2)(a) or (b),

on and after that day, he shall be treated (subject to sub-paragraph (2)) as having been placed with a local authority foster parent and shall cease to be so treated when he ceases to be placed with that person in accordance with the provisions of this Act.

(2) Regulations made under section 23(2)(a) shall not apply in relation to a person who is a local authority foster parent by virtue of sub-paragraph (1) before the end of the period of twelve months beginning with the day on which Part III comes into force and accordingly that person shall for that period be subject—

    (a) in a case falling within sub-paragraph (1)(a)(i), to terms and regulations mentioned in section 21(1)(a) of the Act of 1980; and

    (b) in a case falling within sub-paragraph (1)(a)(ii), to terms fixed under section 21(2) of that Act and regulations made under section 22A of that Act,

as if that Act had not been repealed by this Act.

Children in care to qualify for advice and assistance

22. Any reference in Part III to a person qualifying for advice and assistance shall be construed as including a reference to a person within the area of the local authority in question who is under twenty-one and who was, at any time after reaching the age of sixteen but while still a child—

    (a) a person falling within—

        (i) any of paragraphs (a) to (g) of paragraph 15(1); or

        (ii) paragraph 20(1); or

    (b) the subject of a criminal care order (within the meaning of paragraph 34).

Emigration of children in care

23. Where—

    (a) the Secretary of State has received a request in writing from a local authority that he give his consent under section 24 of the Child Care Act 1980 to the emigration of a child in their care; but

    1980 c. 5.

    (b) immediately before the repeal of the Act of 1980 by this Act, he has not determined whether or not to give his consent,

section 24 of the Act of 1980 shall continue to apply (regardless of that repeal) until the Secretary of State has determined whether or not to give his consent to the request.

Contributions for maintenance of children in care

24.—(1) Where, immediately before the day on which Part III of Schedule 2 comes into force, there was in force an order made (or having effect as if made) under any of the enactments mentioned in sub-paragraph (2), then, on and after that day—

    (a) the order shall have effect as if made under paragraph 23(2) of Schedule 2 against a person liable to contribute; and

    (b) Part III of Schedule 2 shall apply to the order, subject to the modifications in sub-paragraph (3).

(2) The enactments are—

    (a) section 11(4) of the Domestic Proceedings and Magistrates' Courts Act 1978;   1978 c. 22.

    (b) section 26(2) of the Adoption Act 1976;   1976 c. 36.

    (c) section 36(5) of the Children Act 1975;   1975 c. 72.

    (d) section 2(3) of the Guardianship Act 1973;   1973 c. 29.

SCH. 14
1960 c. 48.

(e) section 2(1)(h) of the Matrimonial Proceedings (Magistrates' Courts) Act 1960,

(provisions empowering the court to make an order requiring a person to make periodical payments to a local authority in respect of a child in care).

(3) The modifications are that, in paragraph 23 of Schedule 2—

(a) in sub-paragraph (4), paragraph (a) shall be omitted;

(b) for sub-paragraph (6) there shall be substituted—

"(6) Where—

(a) a contribution order is in force;

(b) the authority serve a contribution notice under paragraph 22; and

(c) the contributor and the authority reach an agreement under paragraph 22(7) in respect of the contribution notice,

the effect of the agreement shall be to discharge the order from the date on which it is agreed that the agreement shall take effect"; and

(c) at the end of sub-paragraph (10) there shall be inserted—

"and

(c) where the order is against a person who is not a parent of the child, shall be made with due regard to—

(i) whether that person had assumed responsibility for the maintenance of the child, and, if so, the extent to which and basis on which he assumed that responsibility and the length of the period during which he met that responsibility;

(ii) whether he did so knowing that the child was not his child;

(iii) the liability of any other person to maintain the child."

SUPERVISION ORDERS

Orders under section 1(3)(b) or 21(2) of the 1969 Act

25.—(1) This paragraph applies to any supervision order—

(a) made—

1969 c. 54.

(i) under section 1(3)(b) of the Children and Young Persons Act 1969; or

(ii) under section 21(2) of that Act on the discharge of a care order made under section 1(3)(c) of that Act; and

(b) in force immediately before the commencement of Part IV.

(2) On and after the commencement of Part IV, the order shall be deemed to be a supervision order made under section 31 and—

(a) any requirement of the order that the child reside with a named individual shall continue to have effect while the order remains in force, unless the court otherwise directs;

(b) any other requirement imposed by the court, or directions given by the supervisor, shall be deemed to have been imposed or given under the appropriate provisions of Schedule 3.

(3) Where, immediately before the commencement of Part IV, the order had been in force for a period of more than six months, it shall cease to have effect at the end of the period of six months beginning with the day on which Part IV comes into force unless—

(a) the court directs that it shall cease to have effect at the end of a different period (which shall not exceed three years);

(b) it ceases to have effect earlier in accordance with section 91; or

(c) it would have ceased to have had effect earlier had this Act not been passed.

(4) Where sub-paragraph (3) applies, paragraph 6 of Schedule 3 shall not apply.

(5) Where, immediately before the commencement of Part IV, the order had been in force for less than six months it shall cease to have effect in accordance with section 91 and paragraph 6 of Schedule 3 unless—

(a) the court directs that it shall cease to have effect at the end of a different period (which shall not exceed three years); or

(b) it would have ceased to have had effect earlier had this Act not been passed.

Other supervision orders

26.—(1) This paragraph applies to any order for the supervision of a child which was in force immediately before the commencement of Part IV and was made under—

(a) section 2(1)(f) of the Matrimonial Proceedings (Magistrates Courts) Act 1960;   *1960 c. 48.*

(b) section 7(4) of the Family Law Reform Act 1969;   *1969 c. 46.*

(c) section 44 of the Matrimonial Causes Act 1973;   *1973 c. 18.*

(d) section 2(2)(a) of the Guardianship Act 1973;   *1973 c. 29.*

(e) section 34(5) or 36(3)(b) of the Children Act 1975;   *1975 c. 72.*

(f) section 26(1)(a) of the Adoption Act 1976; or   *1976 c. 36.*

(g) section 9 of the Domestic Proceedings and Magistrates Courts Act 1978.   *1978 c. 22.*

(2) The order shall not be deemed to be a supervision order made under any provision of this Act but shall nevertheless continue in force for a period of one year beginning with the day on which Part IV comes into force unless—

(a) the court directs that it shall cease to have effect at the end of a lesser period; or

(b) it would have ceased to have had effect earlier had this Act not been passed.

PLACE OF SAFETY ORDERS

27.—(1) This paragraph applies to—

(a) any order or warrant authorising the removal of a child to a place of safety which—

(i) was made, or issued, under any of the enactments mentioned in sub-paragraph (2); and

(ii) was in force immediately before the commencement of Part IV; and

(b) any interim order made under section 23(5) of the Children and Young Persons Act 1963 or section 28(6) of the Children and Young Persons Act 1969.   *1963 c. 37.*   *1969 c. 54.*

(2) The enactments are—

(a) section 40 of the Children and Young Persons Act 1933 (warrant to search for or remove child);   *1933 c. 12.*

SCH. 14
1969 c. 54.

    (b) section 28(1) of the Children and Young Persons Act 1969 (detention of child in place of safety);

1976 c. 36.

    (c) section 34(1) of the Adoption Act 1976 (removal of protected children from unsuitable surroundings);

1980 c. 6.

    (d) section 12(1) of the Foster Children Act 1980 (removal of foster children kept in unsuitable surroundings).

(3) The order or warrant shall continue to have effect as if this Act had not been passed.

(4) Any enactment repealed by this Act shall continue to have effect in relation to the order or warrant so far as is necessary for the purposes of securing that the effect of the order is what it would have been had this Act not been passed.

1963 c. 37.

(5) Sub-paragraph (4) does not apply to the power to make an interim order or further interim order given by section 23(5) of the Children and Young Persons Act 1963 or section 28(6) of the Children and Young Persons Act 1969.

(6) Where, immediately before section 28 of the Children and Young Persons Act 1969 is repealed by this Act, a child is being detained under the powers granted by that section, he may continue to be detained in accordance with that section but subsection (6) shall not apply.

RECOVERY OF CHILDREN

1980 c. 5.

28. The repeal by this Act of subsection (1) of section 16 of the Child Care Act 1980 (arrest of child absent from compulsory care) shall not affect the operation of that section in relation to any child arrested before the coming into force of the repeal.

29.—(1) This paragraph applies where—

    (a) a summons has been issued under section 15 or 16 of the Child Care Act 1980 (recovery of children in voluntary or compulsory care); and

    (b) the child concerned is not produced in accordance with the summons before the repeal of that section by this Act comes into force.

(2) The summons, any warrant issued in connection with it and section 15 or (as the case may be) section 16, shall continue to have effect as if this Act had not been passed.

30. The amendment by paragraph 27 of Schedule 12 of section 32 of the Children and Young Persons Act 1969 (detention of absentees) shall not affect the operation of that section in relation to—

    (a) any child arrested; or

    (b) any summons or warrant issued,

under that section before the coming into force of that paragraph.

VOLUNTARY ORGANISATIONS: PARENTAL RIGHTS RESOLUTIONS

31.—(1) This paragraph applies to a resolution—

    (a) made under section 64 of the Child Care Act 1980 (transfer of parental rights and duties to voluntary organisations); and

    (b) in force immediately before the commencement of Part IV.

(2) The resolution shall continue to have effect until the end of the period of six months beginning with the day on which Part IV comes into force unless it is brought to an end earlier in accordance with the provisions of the Act of 1980 preserved by this paragraph.

(3) While the resolution remains in force, any relevant provisions of, or made under, the Act of 1980 shall continue to have effect with respect to it.

(4) Sub-paragraph (3) does not apply to—

(a) section 62 of the Act of 1980 and any regulations made under that section (arrangements by voluntary organisations for emigration of children); or

(b) section 65 of the Act of 1980 (duty of local authority to assume parental rights and duties).

(5) Section 5(2) of the Act of 1980 (which is applied to resolutions under Part VI of that Act by section 64(7) of that Act) shall have effect with respect to the resolution as if the reference in paragraph (c) to an appointment of a guardian under section 5 of the Guardianship of Minors Act 1971 were a reference to an appointment of a guardian under section 5 of this Act.

1971 c. 3.

FOSTER CHILDREN

32.—(1) This paragraph applies where—

(a) immediately before the commencement of Part VIII, a child was a foster child within the meaning of the Foster Children Act 1980; and

1980 c. 6.

(b) the circumstances of the case are such that, had Parts VIII and IX then been in force, he would have been treated for the purposes of this Act as a child who was being provided with accommodation in a children's home and not as a child who was being privately fostered.

(2) If the child continues to be cared for and provided with accommodation as before, section 63(1) and (10) shall not apply in relation to him if—

(a) an application for registration of the home in question is made under section 63 before the end of the period of three months beginning with the day on which Part VIII comes into force; and

(b) the application has not been refused or, if it has been refused—

(i) the period for an appeal against the decision has not expired; or

(ii) an appeal against the refusal has been made but has not been determined or abandoned.

(3) While section 63(1) and (10) does not apply, the child shall be treated as a privately fostered child for the purposes of Part IX.

NURSERIES AND CHILD MINDING

33.—(1) Sub-paragraph (2) applies where, immediately before the commencement of Part X, any premises are registered under section 1(1)(a) of the Nurseries and Child-Minders Regulation Act 1948 (registration of premises, other than premises wholly or mainly used as private dwellings, where children are received to be looked after).

1948 c. 53.

(2) During the transitional period, the provisions of the Act of 1948 shall continue to have effect with respect to those premises to the exclusion of Part X.

(3) Nothing in sub-paragraph (2) shall prevent the local authority concerned from registering any person under section 71(1)(b) with respect to the premises.

(4) In this paragraph "the transitional period" means the period ending with—

(a) the first anniversary of the commencement of Part X; or

(b) if earlier, the date on which the local authority concerned registers any person under section 71(1)(b) with respect to the premises.

34.—(1) Sub-paragraph (2) applies where, immediately before the commencement of Part X—

(a) a person is registered under section 1(1)(b) of the Act of 1948 (registration of persons who for reward receive into their homes children under the age of five to be looked after); and

(b) all the children looked after by him as mentioned in section 1(1)(b) of that Act are under the age of five.

(2) During the transitional period, the provisions of the Act of 1948 shall continue to have effect with respect to that person to the exclusion of Part X.

(3) Nothing in sub-paragraph (2) shall prevent the local authority concerned from registering that person under section 71(1)(a).

(4) In this paragraph "the transitional period" means the period ending with—

(a) the first anniversary of the commencement of Part X; or

(b) if earlier, the date on which the local authority concerned registers that person under section 71(1)(a).

CHILDREN ACCOMMODATED IN CERTAIN ESTABLISHMENTS

35. In calculating, for the purposes of section 85(1)(a) or 86(1)(a), the period of time for which a child has been accommodated any part of that period which fell before the day on which that section came into force shall be disregarded.

CRIMINAL CARE ORDERS

36.—(1) This paragraph applies where, immediately before the commencement of section 90(2) there was in force an order ("a criminal care order") made—

1969 c. 54.

(a) under section 7(7)(a) of the Children and Young Persons Act 1969 (alteration in treatment of young offenders etc.); or

(b) under section 15(1) of that Act, on discharging a supervision order made under section 7(7)(b) of that Act.

(2) The criminal care order shall continue to have effect until the end of the period of six months beginning with the day on which section 90(2) comes into force unless it is brought to an end earlier in accordance with—

(a) the provisions of the Act of 1969 preserved by sub-paragraph (3)(a); or

(b) this paragraph.

(3) While the criminal care order remains in force, any relevant provisions—

(a) of the Act of 1969; and

1980 c. 5.

(b) of the Child Care Act 1980,

shall continue to have effect with respect to it.

(4) While the criminal care order remains in force, a court may, on the application of the appropriate person, make—

(a) a residence order;

(b) a care order or a supervision order under section 31;

(c) an education supervision order under section 36 (regardless of subsection (6) of that section); or

(d) an order falling within sub-paragraph (5),

and shall, on making any of those orders, discharge the criminal care order.

(5) The order mentioned in sub-paragraph (4)(d) is an order having effect as if it were a supervision order of a kind mentioned in section 12AA of the Act of 1969 (as inserted by paragraph 23 of Schedule 12), that is to say, a supervision order—

(a) imposing a requirement that the child shall live for a specified period in local authority accommodation; but

(b) in relation to which the conditions mentioned in subsection (4) of section 12AA are not required to be satisfied.

(6) The maximum period which may be specified in an order made under sub-paragraph (4)(d) is six months and such an order may stipulate that the child shall not live with a named person.

(7) Where this paragraph applies, section 5 of the Rehabilitation of Offenders Act 1974 (rehabilitation periods for particular sentences) shall have effect regardless of the repeals in it made by this Act.

(8) In sub-paragraph (4) "appropriate person" means—

(a) in the case of an application for a residence order, any person (other than a local authority) who has the leave of the court;

(b) in the case of an application for an education supervision order, a local education authority; and

(c) in any other case, the local authority to whose care the child was committed by the order.

MISCELLANEOUS

Consents under the Marriage Act 1949 (c. 76)

37.—(1) In the circumstances mentioned in sub-paragraph (2), section 3 of and Schedule 2 to the Marriage Act 1949 (consents to marry) shall continue to have effect regardless of the amendment of that Act by paragraph 5 of Schedule 12.

(2) The circumstances are that—

(a) immediately before the day on which paragraph 5 of Schedule 12 comes into force, there is in force—

(i) an existing order, as defined in paragraph 5(1); or

(ii) an order of a kind mentioned in paragraph 16(1); and

(b) section 3 of and Schedule 2 to the Act of 1949 would, but for this Act, have applied to the marriage of the child who is the subject of the order.

The Children Act 1975 (c. 72)

38. The amendments of other enactments made by the following provisions of the Children Act 1975 shall continue to have effect regardless of the repeal of the Act of 1975 by this Act—

(a) section 68(4), (5) and (7) (amendments of section 32 of the Children and Young Persons Act 1969); and

(b) in Schedule 3—

(i) paragraph 13 (amendments of Births and Deaths Registration Act 1953);

(ii) paragraph 43 (amendment of Perpetuities and Accumulations Act 1964);

(iii) paragraphs 46 and 47 (amendments of Health Services and Public Health Act 1968); and

(iv) paragraph 77 (amendment of Parliamentary and Other Pensions Act 1972).

The Child Care Act 1980 (c. 5)

39. The amendment made to section 106(2)(a) of the Children and Young Persons Act 1963 by paragraph 26 of Schedule 5 to the Child Care Act 1980 shall continue to have effect regardless of the repeal of the Act of 1980 by this Act.

Sch. 14

1988 c. 34.

Legal aid

40. The Lord Chancellor may by order make such transitional and saving provisions as appear to him to be necessary or expedient, in consequence of any provision made by or under this Act, in connection with the operation of any provisions of the Legal Aid Act 1988 (including any provision of that Act which is amended or repealed by this Act).

Section 108(7).

SCHEDULE 15

Repeals

Chapter	Short title	Extent of repeal
1891 c. 3.	The Custody of Children Act 1891.	The whole Act.
1933 c. 12.	The Children and Young Persons Act 1933.	In section 14(2), the words from "may also" to "together, and". In section 34(8), "(a)" and the words from "and (b)" to the end. Section 40. In section 107(1), the definitions of "care order" and "interim order".
1944 c. 31.	The Education Act 1944.	In section 40(1), the words from "or to imprisonment" to the end. In section 114(1), the definition of parent.
1948 c. 53.	The Nurseries and Child-Minders Regulation Act 1948.	The whole Act.
1949 c. 76.	The Marriage Act 1949.	In section 3(1), the words "unless the child is subject to a custodianship order, when the consent of the custodian and, where the custodian is the husband or wife of a parent of the child of that parent shall be required". Section 78(1A). Schedule 2.
1956 c. 69.	The Sexual Offences Act 1956.	Section 38.
1959 c. 72.	The Mental Health Act 1959.	Section 9.
1963 c. 37.	The Children and Young Persons Act 1963.	Section 3. Section 23. In section 29(1), the words "under section 1 of the Children and Young Persons Act 1969 or". Section 53(3). In Schedule 3, paragraph 11.

Chapter	Short title	Extent of repeal
1964 c. 42.	The Administration of Justice Act 1964.	In section 38, the definition of "domestic court".
1968 c. 46.	The Health Services and Public Health Act 1968.	Section 60. In section 64(3)(a), sub-paragraphs (vi), (vii), (ix) and (xv). In section 65(3)(b), paragraphs (vii), (viii) and (x).
1968 c. 49.	The Social Work (Scotland) Act 1968.	Section 1(4)(a). Section 5(2)(d). In section 86(3), the words "the Child Care Act 1980 or". In Schedule 8, paragraph 20.
1969 c. 46.	The Family Law Reform Act 1969.	Section 7.
1969 c. 54.	The Children and Young Persons Act 1969.	Sections 1 to 3. In section 7, in subsection (7) the words "to subsection (7A) of this section and", paragraph (a) and the words from "and subsection (13) of section 2 of this Act" to the end; and subsection (7A). Section 7A. In section 8(3), the words from "and as if the reference to acquittal" to the end. In section 9(1), the words "proceedings under section 1 of this Act or". Section 11A. Section 14A. In section 15, in subsection (1) the words "and may on discharging the supervision order make a care order (other than an interim order) in respect of the supervised person"; in subsection (2) the words "and the supervision order was not made by virtue of section 1 of this Act or on the occasion of the discharge of a care order"; in subsection (2A), the words "or made by a court on discharging a care order made under that subsection"; and in subsection (4), the words "or made by a court on discharging a care order made under that section".

Chapter	Short title	Extent of repeal
		In section 16, in subsection (6)(a), the words "a care order or"; and in subsection (8) the words "or, in a case where a parent or guardian of his was a party to the proceedings on an application under the preceding section by virtue of an order under section 32A of this Act, the parent or guardian". In section 17, paragraphs (b) and (c). Sections 20 to 22. Section 27(4). Section 28. Sections 32A to 32C. In section 34(2) the words "under section 1 of this Act or", the words "2(3) or" and the words "and accordingly in the case of such a person the reference in section 1(1) of this Act to the said section 2(3) shall be construed as including a reference to this subsection". In section 70, in subsection (1), the definitions of "care order" and "interim order"; and in subsection (2) the words "21(2), 22(4) or (6) or 28(5)" and the words "care order or warrant". In Schedule 5, paragraphs 12(1), 37, 47 and 48.
1970 c. 34.	The Marriage (Registrar General's Licence) Act 1970.	In section 3(b), the words from "as amended" to "1969".
1970 c. 42.	The Local Authority Social Services Act 1970.	In Schedule 1, in the entry relating to the Children and Young Persons Act 1969, the words "welfare, etc. of foster children"; the entries relating to the Matrimonial Causes Act 1973, section 44, the Domestic Proceedings and Magistrates' Courts Act 1978, section 9, the Child Care Act 1980 and the Foster Children Act 1980.
1971 c. 3.	The Guardianship of Minors Act 1971.	The whole Act.

Chapter	Short title	Extent of repeal
1971 c. 23.	The Courts Act 1971.	In Schedule 8, paragraph 59(1).
1972 c. 18.	The Maintenance Orders (Reciprocal Enforcement) Act 1972.	Section 41.
1972 c. 70.	The Local Government Act 1972.	In Schedule 23, paragraphs 4 and 9(3).
1972 c. 71.	The Criminal Justice Act 1972.	Section 51(1).
1973 c. 18.	The Matrimonial Causes Act 1973.	Sections 42 to 44. In section 52(1), the definition of "custody". In Schedule 2, paragraph 11.
1973 c. 29.	The Guardianship Act 1973.	The whole Act.
1973 c. 45.	The Domicile and Matrimonial Proceedings Act 1973.	In Schedule 1, in paragraph 11(1) the definitions of "custody" and "education" and in paragraph 11(3) the word "four".
1973 c. 62.	The Powers of Criminal Courts Act 1973.	In section 13(1), the words "and the purposes of section 1(2)(bb) of the Children and Young Persons Act 1969". In Schedule 3, in paragraph 3(2A), the word "and" immediately preceding paragraph (b).
1974 c. 53.	The Rehabilitation of Offenders Act 1974.	In section 1(4)(b) the words "or in care proceedings under section 1 of the Children and Young Persons Act 1969". In section 5, in subsection 5(e), the words "a care order or"; and in subsection (10) the words "care order or".
1975 c. 72.	The Children Act 1975.	The whole Act.
1976 c. 36.	The Adoption Act 1976.	Section 11(5). Section 14(3). In section 15, in subsection (1), the words from "subject" to "cases)" and subsection (4). Section 26. In section 28(5), the words "or the organisation". Section 34. Section 36(1)(c). Section 37(1), (3) and (4). Section 55(4). In section 57, in subsection (2), the words from "and the court" to the end and subsections (4) to (10).

R

Chapter	Short title	Extent of repeal
		In section 72(1), the definition of "place of safety", in the definition of "local authority" the words from " and" to the end and, in the definition of "specified order", the words "Northern Ireland or".
		In Schedule 3, paragraphs 8, 11, 19, 21, and 22.
1977 c. 45.	The Criminal Law Act 1977.	Section 58(3).
1977 c. 49.	The National Health Service Act 1977.	In section 21, in subsection (1)(a) the words "and young children".
		In Schedule 8, in paragraph 1(1), the words from "and of children" to the end; in paragraph 2(2) the words from "or (b) to persons who" to "arrangements"; and in paragraph 3(1) "(a)" and the words from "or (b) a child" to "school age".
		In Schedule 15, paragraphs 10 and 25.
1978 c. 22.	The Domestic Proceedings and Magistrates' Courts Act 1978.	Sections 9 to 15.
		In section 19, in subsection (1) the words "following powers, that is to say" and sub-paragraph (ii), subsections (2) and (4), in subsection (7) the words "and one interim custody order" and in subsection (9) the words "or 21".
		In section 20, subsection (4) and in subsection (9) the words "subject to the provisions of section 11(8) of this Act".
		Section 21.
		In section 24, the words "or 21" in both places where they occur.
		In section 25, in subsection (1) paragraph (b) and the word "or" immediately preceding it and in subsection (2) paragraphs (c) and (d).
		Section 29(4).
		Sections 33 and 34.
		Sections 36 to 53.
		Sections 64 to 72.
		Sections 73(1) and 74(1) and (3).

Chapter	Short title	Extent of repeal
		In section 88(1), the definition of "actual custody".
		In Schedule 2, paragraphs 22, 23, 27, 29, 31, 36, 41 to 43, 46 to 50.
1978 c. 28.	The Adoption (Scotland) Act 1978.	In section 20(3)(c), the words "section 12(3)(b) of the Adoption Act 1976 or of".
		In section 45(5), the word "approved".
		Section 49(4).
		In section 65(1), in the definition of "local authority", the words from "and" to the end and, in the definition of "specified order", the words "Northern Ireland or".
1978 c. 30.	The Interpretation Act 1978.	In Schedule 1, the entry with respect to the construction of certain expressions relating to children.
1980 c. 5.	The Child Care Act 1980.	The whole Act.
1980 c. 6.	The Foster Children Act 1980.	The whole Act.
1980 c. 43.	The Magistrates' Courts Act 1980.	In section 65(1), paragraphs (e) and (g) and the paragraph (m) inserted in section 65 by paragraph 82 of Schedule 2 to the Family Law Reform Act 1987.
		In section 81(8), in the definition of "guardian" the words "by deed or will" and in the definition of "sums adjudged to be paid by a conviction" the words from "as applied" to the end.
		In section 143(2), paragraph (i).
		In Schedule 7, paragraphs 78, 83, 91, 92, 110, 116, 117, 138, 157, 158, 165, 166 and 199 to 201.
1981 c. 60.	The Education Act 1981.	In Schedule 3, paragraph 9.
1982 c. 20.	The Children's Homes Act 1982.	The whole Act.
1982 c. 48.	The Criminal Justice Act 1982.	Sections 22 to 25.
		Section 27.
		In Schedule 14, paragraphs 45 and 46.

Chapter	Short title	Extent of repeal
1983 c. 20.	The Mental Health Act 1983.	In section 26(5), paragraph (d) and the word "or" immediately preceding it. In section 28(1), the words "(including an order under section 38 of the Sexual Offences Act 1956)". In Schedule 4, paragraphs 12, 26(a), (b) and (c), 35, 44, 50 and 51.
1983 c. 41.	The Health and Social Services and Social Security Adjudications Act 1983.	Section 4(1). Sections 5 and 6. In section 11, in subsection (2) the words "the Child Care Act 1980 and the Children's Homes Act 1982". In section 19, subsections (1) to (5). Schedule 1. In Schedule 2, paragraphs 3, 9 to 14, 20 to 24, 27, 28, 34, 37 and 46 to 62. In Schedule 4, paragraphs 38 to 48. In Schedule 9, paragraphs 5, 16 and 17.
1984 c. 23.	The Registered Homes Act 1984.	In Schedule 1, in paragraph 5, sub-paragraph (a) and paragraphs 6, 7 and 8.
1984 c. 28.	The County Courts Act 1984.	In Schedule 2, paragraph 56.
1984 c. 37.	The Child Abduction Act 1984.	In section 3, the word "and" immediately preceding paragraph (c). In the Schedule, in paragraph 1(2) the words "or voluntary organisation" and paragraph 3(1)(e).
1984 c. 42.	The Matrimonial and Family Proceedings Act 1984.	In Schedule 1, paragraphs 19 and 23.
1984 c. 56.	The Foster Children (Scotland) Act 1984.	In section 1, the words "for a period of more than 6 days" and the words from "The period" to the end. In section 7(1), the word "or" at the end of paragraph (e). In Schedule 2, paragraphs 1 to 3 and 8.
1984 c. 60.	The Police and Criminal Evidence Act 1984.	In section 37(15), the words "and is not excluded from this Part of this Act by section 52 below". Section 39(5). Section 52.

Chapter	Short title	Extent of repeal
		In section 118(1), in the definition of parent or guardian, paragraph (b) and the word "and" immediately preceding it. In Schedule 2, the entry relating to section 16 of the Child Care Act 1980. In Schedule 6, paragraphs 19(a) and 22.
1985 c. 23.	The Prosecution of Offences Act 1985.	Section 27.
1985 c. 60.	The Child Abduction and Custody Act 1985.	Section 9(c). Section 20(2)(b) and (c). Section 25(3) and (5). In Schedule 3, paragraph 1(2).
1986 c. 28.	The Children and Young Persons (Amendment) Act 1986.	The whole Act.
1986 c. 33.	The Disabled Persons (Services, Consultation and Representation) Act 1986.	In section 16, in the definition of "guardian", paragraph (a).
1986 c. 45.	The Insolvency Act 1986.	In section 281(5)(b), the words "in domestic proceedings".
1986 c. 50.	The Social Security Act 1986.	In Schedule 10, paragraph 51.
1986 c. 55.	The Family Law Act 1986.	In section 1(2), in paragraph (a) the words "(a) or" and paragraph (b). Section 3(4) to (6). Section 4. Section 35(1). In section 42(6), in paragraph (b) the words "section 42(6) of the Matrimonial Causes Act 1973 or", in paragraph (c) the words "section 42(7) of that Act or" and in paragraph (d) the words "section 19(6) of the Domestic Proceedings and Magistrates' Courts Act 1978 or". In Schedule 1, paragraphs 10, 11, 13, 16, 17, 20 and 23.
1987 c. 42.	The Family Law Reform Act 1987.	Section 3. Sections 4 to 7. Sections 9 to 16. In Schedule 2, paragraphs 11, 14, 51, 67, 68, 94 and 95. In Schedule 3, paragraphs 11 and 12.
1988 c. 34.	The Legal Aid Act 1988.	Section 3(4)(c).

Chapter	Short title	Extent of repeal
		Section 27. Section 28. In section 30, subsections (1) and (2). In Part I of Schedule 2, paragraph 2(a) and (e).

Local Government and Housing Act 1989

1989 CHAPTER 42

An Act to make provision with respect to the members, officers and other staff and the procedure of local authorities; to amend Part III of the Local Government Act 1974 and Part II of the Local Government (Scotland) Act 1975 and to provide for a national code of local government conduct; to make further provision about the finances and expenditure of local authorities (including provision with respect to housing subsidies) and about companies in which local authorities have interests; to make provision for and in connection with renewal areas, grants towards the cost of improvement and repair of housing accommodation and the carrying out of works of maintenance, repair and improvement; to amend the Housing Act 1985 and Part III of the Local Government Finance Act 1982; to make amendments of and consequential upon Parts I, II and IV of the Housing Act 1988; to amend the Local Government Finance Act 1988 and the Abolition of Domestic Rates Etc. (Scotland) Act 1987 and certain enactments relating, as respects Scotland, to rating and valuation, and to provide for the making of grants; to make provision with respect to the imposition of charges by local authorities; to make further provision about certain existing grants and about financial assistance to and planning by local authorities in respect of emergencies; to amend sections 102 and 211 of the Local Government (Scotland) Act 1973; to amend the Local Land Charges Act 1975; to enable local authorities in Wales to be known solely by Welsh language names; to provide for the transfer of new town housing stock; to amend certain of the provisions of the Housing (Scotland) Act 1987 relating to a secure tenant's right to purchase his house; to amend section 47 of the Race Relations Act 1976; to confer certain powers on the Housing Corporation, Housing for Wales and Scottish Homes;

to make provision about security of tenure for certain tenants under long tenancies; to provide for the making of grants and giving of guarantees in respect of certain activities carried on in relation to the construction industry; to provide for the repeal of certain enactments relating to improvement notices, town development and education support grants; to make, as respects Scotland, further provision in relation to the phasing of progression to registered rent for houses let by housing associations or Scottish Homes and in relation to the circumstances in which rent increases under assured tenancies may be secured; and for connected purposes.

[16th November 1989]

BE IT ENACTED by the Queen's most Excellent Majesty, by and with the advice and consent of the Lords Spiritual and Temporal, and Commons, in this present Parliament assembled, and by the authority of the same, as follows:—

PART I

LOCAL AUTHORITY MEMBERS, OFFICERS, STAFF AND COMMITTEES ETC.

Political restriction of officers and staff

Disqualification and political restriction of certain officers and staff.

1.—(1) A person shall be disqualified from becoming (whether by election or otherwise) or remaining a member of a local authority if he holds a politically restricted post under that local authority or any other local authority in Great Britain.

1975 c. 24.

(2) In the House of Commons Disqualification Act 1975, in Part III of Schedule 1 (other disqualifying offices) there shall be inserted at the appropriate place—

"Person holding a politically restricted post, within the meaning of Part I of the Local Government and Housing Act 1989, under a local authority, within the meaning of that Part."

1972 c. 70.

(3) In section 80 of the Local Government Act 1972 (disqualification for election and holding office as member of local authority)—

    (a) in subsection (1)(a) (paid office holders and employees), the words "joint board, joint authority or" shall be omitted; and

    (b) in subsection (6) (extension of meaning of "local authority"), after the word "includes" there shall be inserted "a joint board and".

1973 c. 65.

(4) In section 31 of the Local Government (Scotland) Act 1973 (which makes corresponding provision for Scotland)—

    (a) in subsection (1)(a)(ii), the words "or joint board" shall be omitted; and

    (b) after subsection (1) there shall be inserted the following subsection—

"(1A) A person is disqualified for being a member of a joint board if he or a partner of his holds any paid office or employment (other than the office of chairman or vice-chairman of the board) or other place of profit in the gift or disposal of the board."

(5) The terms of appointment or conditions of employment of every person holding a politically restricted post under a local authority (including persons appointed to such posts before the coming into force of this section) shall be deemed to incorporate such requirements for restricting his political activities as may be prescribed for the purposes of this subsection by regulations made by the Secretary of State.

(6) Regulations under subsection (5) above may contain such incidental provision and such supplemental, consequential and transitional provision in connection with their other provisions as the Secretary of State considers appropriate and, without prejudice to section 190(1) below, may contain such exceptions for persons appointed in pursuance of section 9 below as he thinks fit.

(7) So far as it has effect in relation to disqualification for election, this section has effect with respect to any election occurring not less than two months after the coming into force of this section and, so far as it relates to becoming in any other way a member of a local authority, this section has effect with respect to any action which, apart from this section, would result in a person becoming a member of the authority not less than two months after the coming into force of this section.

(8) If, immediately before the expiry of the period of two months referred to in subsection (7) above, a person who is a member of a local authority holds a politically restricted post under that or any other local authority, nothing in this section shall apply to him until the expiry of the period for which he was elected or for which he otherwise became a member of the authority.

2.—(1) The following persons are to be regarded for the purposes of this Part as holding politically restricted posts under a local authority—

   (a) the person designated under section 4 below as the head of the authority's paid service;

   (b) the statutory chief officers;

   (c) a non-statutory chief officer;

   (d) a deputy chief officer;

   (e) the monitoring officer designated under section 5 below;

   (f) any person holding a post to which he was appointed in pursuance of section 9 below; and

   (g) any person not falling within paragraphs (a) to (f) above whose post is for the time being specified by the authority in a list maintained in accordance with subsection (2) below and any directions under section 3 below or with section 100G(2) of the Local Government Act 1972 or section 50G(2) of the Local Government (Scotland) Act 1973 (list of officers to whom powers are delegated).

(2) It shall be the duty of every local authority to prepare and maintain a list of such of the following posts under the authority, namely—

(a) the full time posts the annual rate of remuneration in respect of which is or exceeds £19,500 or such higher amount as may be specified in or determined under regulations made by the Secretary of State;

(b) the part time posts the annual rate of remuneration in respect of which would be or exceed that amount if they were full time posts in respect of which remuneration were paid at the same rate as for the part time post; and

(c) posts not falling within paragraph (a) or (b) above the duties of which appear to the authority to fall within subsection (3) below,

1972 c. 70.
1973 c. 65.
as are not posts for the time being exempted under section 3 below, posts for the time being listed under section 100G(2) of the Local Government Act 1972 or section 50G(2) of the Local Government (Scotland) Act 1973 or posts of a description specified in regulations made by the Secretary of State for the purposes of this subsection.

(3) The duties of a post under a local authority fall within this subsection if they consist in or involve one or both of the following, that is to say—

(a) giving advice on a regular basis to the authority themselves, to any committee or sub-committee of the authority or to any joint committee on which the authority are represented;

(b) speaking on behalf of the authority on a regular basis to journalists or broadcasters.

(4) It shall be the duty of every local authority to deposit the first list prepared under subsection (2) above with their proper officer before the expiry of the period of two months beginning with the coming into force of this section; and it shall also be their duty, on subsequently making any modifications of that list, to deposit a revised list with that officer.

(5) It shall be the duty of every local authority in performing their duties under this section to have regard to such general advice as may be given by virtue of subsection (1)(b) of section 3 below by a person appointed under that subsection.

(6) In this section "the statutory chief officers" means—

1944 c. 31.
1980 c. 44.
(a) the chief education officer or director of education appointed under section 88 of the Education Act 1944 or section 78 of the Education (Scotland) Act 1980;

1947 c. 41.
(b) the chief officer of a fire brigade maintained under the Fire Services Act 1947 and appointed under regulations made under section 18(1)(a) of that Act;

1970 c. 42.
1968 c. 49.
(c) the director of social services or director of social work appointed under section 6 of the Local Authority Social Services Act 1970 or section 3 of the Social Work (Scotland) Act 1968; and

1985 c. 51.
1988 c. 41.
(d) the officer having responsibility, for the purposes of section 151 of the Local Government Act 1972, section 73 of the Local Government Act 1985, section 112 of the Local Government

Finance Act 1988 or section 6 below or for the purposes of section 95 of the Local Government (Scotland) Act 1973, for the administration of the authority's financial affairs.

(7) In this section "non-statutory chief officer" means, subject to the following provisions of this section—

(a) a person for whom the head of the authority's paid service is directly responsible;

(b) a person who, as respects all or most of the duties of his post, is required to report directly or is directly accountable to the head of the authority's paid service; and

(c) any person who, as respects all or most of the duties of his post, is required to report directly or is directly accountable to the local authority themselves or any committee or sub-committee of the authority.

(8) In this section "deputy chief officer" means, subject to the following provisions of this section, a person who, as respects all or most of the duties of his post, is required to report directly or is directly accountable to one or more of the statutory or non-statutory chief officers.

(9) A person whose duties are solely secretarial or clerical or are otherwise in the nature of support services shall not be regarded as a non-statutory chief officer or a deputy chief officer for the purposes of this Part.

(10) Nothing in this section shall have the effect of requiring any person to be regarded as holding a politically restricted post by reason of his holding—

(a) the post of head teacher or principal of a school, college or other educational institution or establishment which, in England and Wales, is maintained or assisted by a local education authority or, in Scotland, is under the management of or is assisted by an education authority; or

(b) any other post as a teacher or lecturer in any such school, college, institution or establishment,

or of requiring any such post to be included in any list prepared and maintained under this section.

(11) Regulations under this section may contain such incidental provision and such supplemental, consequential and transitional provision in connection with their other provisions as the Secretary of State considers appropriate.

3.—(1) It shall be the duty of the Secretary of State to appoint a person—

Grant and supervision of exemptions from political restriction.

(a) to carry out the functions in relation to political restriction which are conferred by subsections (2) to (7) below; and

(b) to give such general advice with respect to the determination of questions arising by virtue of section 2(3) above as that person considers appropriate after consulting such representatives of local government and such organisations appearing to him to represent employees in local government as he considers appropriate.

(2) A person appointed under subsection (1) above—

    (a) shall consider any application for exemption from political restriction which is made to him, in respect of any post under a local authority, by the holder for the time being of that post; and

    (b) may, on the application of any person or otherwise, give directions to a local authority requiring it to include a post in the list maintained by the authority under section 2(2) above.

(3) An application shall not be made by virtue of subsection (2)(a) above in respect of a post under a local authority except where—

    (a) the authority have specified or are proposing to specify the post in the list maintained by the authority under subsection (2) of section 2 above; and

    (b) in the case of a post falling within paragraph (a) or (b) of that subsection, the authority have certified whether or not, in their opinion, the duties of the post fall within subsection (3) of that section;

and it shall be the duty of a local authority to give a certificate for the purposes of paragraph (b) above in relation to any post if they are requested to do so by the holder of that post.

(4) If, on an application made by virtue of subsection (2)(a) above in respect of any post under a local authority, the person to whom the application is made is satisfied that the duties of the post do not fall within section 2(3) above, that person shall direct—

    (a) that, for so long as the direction has effect in accordance with its terms, the post is not to be regarded as a politically restricted post; and

    (b) that, accordingly, the post is not to be specified in the list maintained by that authority under section 2(2) above or, as the case may be, is to be removed from that list.

(5) A person appointed under subsection (1) above shall not give a direction under subsection (2)(b) above in respect of any post under a local authority except where he is satisfied that the post—

    (a) is a post the duties of which fall within section 2(3) above; and

    (b) is neither included in any list maintained by the authority in accordance with section 2(2) above, section 100G(2) of the Local Government Act 1972 or section 50G(2) of the Local Government (Scotland) Act 1973 nor of a description specified in any regulations under section 2(2) above.

1972 c. 70.
1973 c. 65.

(6) It shall be the duty of a local authority—

    (a) to give a person appointed under subsection (1) above all such information as that person may reasonably require for the purpose of carrying out his functions under this section;

    (b) to comply with any direction under this section with respect to the list maintained by the authority; and

    (c) on being given a direction by virtue of subsection (2)(b) above, to notify the terms of the direction to the holder for the time being of the post to which the direction relates.

(7) It shall be the duty of a person appointed under subsection (1) above, in carrying out his functions under this section, to give priority, according to the time available before the election, to any application made by virtue of subsection (2)(a) above by a person who certifies that it is made for the purpose of enabling him to be a candidate in a forthcoming election.

(8) The Secretary of State may—

    (a) appoint different persons under subsection (1) above for England and for Wales;

    (b) provide for the appointment of such numbers of staff to assist any person appointed under that subsection, and to act on that person's behalf, as the Secretary of State may with the consent of the Treasury determine;

    (c) pay to or in respect of a person appointed under that subsection and members of such a person's staff such remuneration and such other sums by way of, or towards, the payment of pensions, allowances and gratuities as the Secretary of State may so determine; and

    (d) provide for a person appointed under that subsection and such a person's staff to hold office on such other terms as the Secretary of State may so determine.

Duties of particular officers

4.—(1) It shall be the duty of every relevant authority—

    (a) to designate one of their officers as the head of their paid service; and

    (b) to provide that officer with such staff, accommodation and other resources as are, in his opinion, sufficient to allow his duties under this section to be performed.

Designation and reports of head of paid service.

(2) It shall be the duty of the head of a relevant authority's paid service, where he considers it appropriate to do so in respect of any proposals of his with respect to any of the matters specified in subsection (3) below, to prepare a report to the authority setting out his proposals.

(3) Those matters are—

    (a) the manner in which the discharge by the authority of their different functions is co-ordinated;

    (b) the number and grades of staff required by the authority for the discharge of their functions;

    (c) the organisation of the authority's staff; and

    (d) the appointment and proper management of the authority's staff.

(4) It shall be the duty of the head of a relevant authority's paid service, as soon as practicable after he has prepared a report under this section, to arrange for a copy of it to be sent to each member of the authority.

(5) It shall be the duty of a relevant authority to consider any report under this section by the head of their paid service at a meeting held not more than three months after copies of the report are first sent to members of the authority; and nothing in section 101 of the Local Government Act   1972 c. 70.

1972 or in section 56 of, or Schedule 10 or 20 to, the Local Government (Scotland) Act 1973 (delegation) shall apply to the duty imposed by virtue of this subsection.

(6) In this section "relevant authority"—

    (a) in relation to England and Wales, means a local authority of any of the descriptions specified in paragraphs (a) to (e) of section 21(1) below; and

    (b) in relation to Scotland, means a regional, islands or district council.

(7) This section shall come into force at the expiry of the period of two months beginning on the day this Act is passed.

Designation and reports of monitoring officer.
5.—(1) It shall be the duty of every relevant authority—

    (a) to designate one of their officers (to be known as "the monitoring officer") as the officer responsible for performing the duties imposed by this section; and

    (b) to provide that officer with such staff, accommodation and other resources as are, in his opinion, sufficient to allow those duties to be performed;

and the officer so designated may be the head of the authority's paid service but shall not be their chief finance officer.

(2) It shall be the duty of a relevant authority's monitoring officer, if it at any time appears to him that any proposal, decision or omission by the authority, by any committee, sub-committee or officer of the authority or by any joint committee on which the authority are represented constitutes, has given rise to or is likely to or would give rise to—

    (a) a contravention by the authority, by any committee, sub-committee or officer of the authority or by any such joint committee of any enactment or rule of law or of any code of practice made or approved by or under any enactment; or

1974 c. 7.
1975 c. 30.
    (b) any such maladministration or injustice as is mentioned in Part III of the Local Government Act 1974 (Local Commissioners) or Part II of the Local Government (Scotland) Act 1975 (which makes corresponding provision for Scotland),

to prepare a report to the authority with respect to that proposal, decision or omission.

(3) It shall be the duty of a relevant authority's monitoring officer—

    (a) in preparing a report under this section to consult so far as practicable with the head of the authority's paid service and with their chief finance officer; and

    (b) as soon as practicable after such a report has been prepared by him or his deputy, to arrange for a copy of it to be sent to each member of the authority.

(4) The references in subsection (2) above, in relation to a relevant authority in England and Wales, to a committee or sub-committee of the authority and to a joint committee on which they are represented shall be taken to include references to any of the following, that is to say—

    (a) any police committee the members of which include persons appointed by the authority;

(b) any local fisheries committee the members of which include persons so appointed;

(c) any National Parks Committee the members of which include persons so appointed; and

(d) any sub-committee appointed by a committee falling within paragraphs (a) to (c) above;

but in relation to any such committee or sub-committee the reference in subsection (3)(b) above to each member of the authority shall have effect as a reference to each member of the committee or, as the case may be, of the committee which appointed the sub-committee.

(5) It shall be the duty of a relevant authority and of any such committee as is mentioned in subsection (4) above—

(a) to consider any report under this section by a monitoring officer or his deputy at a meeting held not more than twenty-one days after copies of the report are first sent to members of the authority or committee; and

(b) without prejudice to any duty imposed by virtue of section 115 of the Local Government Finance Act 1988 (duties in respect of conduct involving contraventions of financial obligations) or otherwise, to ensure that no step is taken for giving effect to any proposal or decision to which such a report relates at any time while the implementation of the proposal or decision is suspended in consequence of the report;

1988 c. 41.

and nothing in section 101 of the Local Government Act 1972 or in section 56 of, or Schedule 10 or 20 to, the Local Government (Scotland) Act 1973 (delegation) shall apply to the duty imposed by virtue of paragraph (a) above.

1972 c. 70.
1973 c. 65.

(6) For the purposes of paragraph (b) of subsection (5) above the implementation of a proposal or decision to which a report under this section relates shall be suspended in consequence of the report until the end of the first business day after the day on which consideration of that report under paragraph (a) of that subsection is concluded.

(7) The duties of a relevant authority's monitoring officer under this section shall be performed by him personally or, where he is unable to act owing to absence or illness, personally by such member of his staff as he has for the time being nominated as his deputy for the purposes of this section.

(8) In this section—

"business day", in relation to a relevant authority, means any day which is not a Saturday or Sunday, Christmas Day, Good Friday or any day which is a bank holiday under the Banking and Financial Dealings Act 1971 in the part of Great Britain where the area of the authority is situated;

1971 c. 80.

"chief finance officer", in relation to a relevant authority, means the officer having responsibility, for the purposes of section 151 of the Local Government Act 1972, section 73 of the Local Government Act 1985, section 112 of the Local Government Finance Act 1988 or section 6 below or for the purposes of section 95 of the Local Government (Scotland) Act 1973, for the administration of the authority's financial affairs; and

1985 c. 51.

"relevant authority"—

(a) in relation to England and Wales, means a local authority of any of the descriptions specified in paragraphs (a) to (j) of section 21(1) below; and

(b) in relation to Scotland, means a local authority.

(9) This section shall come into force at the expiry of the period of two months beginning on the day this Act is passed.

Officer responsible for financial administration of certain authorities.

6.—(1) On and after the commencement day the Common Council shall—

(a) make arrangements for the proper administration of such of its financial affairs as relate to it in its capacity as a local authority, police authority or port health authority, and

(b) secure that one of its officers has responsibility for the administration of those affairs.

1897 c. cxxxiii.

(2) Section 17 of the City of London Sewers Act 1897 (functions of the chamberlain of the City of London as regards financial affairs) shall cease to have effect on the commencement day.

(3) On and after the commencement day the person having responsibility for the administration of certain of the financial affairs of the Common Council under subsection (1) above shall—

(a) be a member of one or more of the bodies specified in subsection (5) below; or

(b) be the person who immediately before that day was the chamberlain of the City of London; or

1988 c. 41.

(c) be a person who qualifies by virtue of section 113(2)(b) of the Local Government Finance Act 1988 (existing office holders) as a person who may be given responsibility for the financial affairs of an authority mentioned in section 111(2)(a) to (k) of that Act; or

(d) fulfil two or more of those conditions.

1985 c. 51.

(4) On and after the commencement day the person having responsibility for the administration of the financial affairs of a new successor body under section 73 of the Local Government Act 1985 shall—

(a) be a member of one or more of the bodies specified in subsection (5) below; or

(b) be the person who immediately before that day had responsibility for the administration of the financial affairs of the body concerned under the said section 73; or

(c) be a person who qualifies by virtue of section 113(2)(b) of the Local Government Finance Act 1988 (existing office holders) as a person who may be given responsibility for the financial affairs of an authority mentioned in section 111(2)(a) to (k) of that Act; or

(d) fulfil two or more of those conditions.

(5) The bodies referred to in subsections (3)(a) and (4)(a) above are—

(a) the Institute of Chartered Accountants in England and Wales;

(b) the Institute of Chartered Accountants of Scotland;

    (c) the Chartered Association of Certified Accountants;

    (d) the Chartered Institute of Public Finance and Accountancy;

    (e) the Institute of Chartered Accountants in Ireland;

    (f) the Chartered Institute of Management Accountants;

    (g) any other body of accountants established in the United Kingdom and for the time being approved by the Secretary of State for the purposes of this section.

    (6) The Secretary of State may make regulations containing, as regards the Common Council and any new successor body to which section 73 of the Local Government Act 1985 applies, provisions equivalent to sections 114 to 116 of the Local Government Finance Act 1988 (reports etc.) subject to— *1985 c. 51.* *1988 c. 41.*

    (a) modifications to confine the provisions to the Common Council in its capacity as a local authority, police authority or port health authority; and

    (b) any other modifications the Secretary of State thinks fit;

and any such regulations may contain such incidental provision and such supplemental, consequential and transitional provision in connection with their other provisions as the Secretary of State considers appropriate.

    (7) In this section—

    "the commencement day" means the day on which this section comes into force;

    "the Common Council" means the Common Council of the City of London;

    "new successor body" means a body corporate established at any time by an order under section 67(3) of the Local Government Act 1985 (new body succeeding to residuary body's functions).

    (8) This section shall come into force at the expiry of the period of two months beginning on the day this Act is passed.

Appointment and management etc. of staff

    7.—(1) Every appointment of a person to a paid office or employment under— *All staff to be appointed on merit.*

    (a) a local authority or parish or community council in England and Wales, or

    (b) a local authority in Scotland,

shall be made on merit.

    (2) Subsection (1) above applies to all appointments made by, or by any committee of, a local authority or parish or community council, whether made under section 112 of the Local Government Act 1972 or section 64 of the Local Government (Scotland) Act 1973 (appointment of staff) or otherwise, but has effect subject to— *1972 c. 70.* *1973 c. 65.*

    (a) sections 9 and 12 of the Disabled Persons (Employment) Act 1944 (quotas and reserved employment); *1944 c. 10.*

    (b) section 18 of the Fire Services Act 1947 (regulations as to appointment etc. of chief officers and fire brigades); *1947 c. 41.*

(c) section 7 of the Sex Discrimination Act 1975 (discrimination permitted in relation to employment where sex of employee is a genuine occupational qualification);

(d) section 5 of the Race Relations Act 1976 (discrimination permitted in relation to employment where being of a particular racial group is a genuine occupational qualification); and

(e) section 113 of the Local Government Finance Act 1988 and section 6 above (qualifications of officers responsible for administration of financial affairs of certain authorities).

(3) This section shall come into force at the expiry of the period of two months beginning on the day this Act is passed.

Duty to adopt standing orders with respect to staff.

8.—(1) The Secretary of State may by regulations require relevant authorities, subject to such variations as may be authorised by the regulations—

(a) to incorporate such provision as may be prescribed by the regulations in standing orders relating to their staff; and

(b) to make or refrain from making such other modifications of any such standing orders as may be so prescribed.

(2) For the purposes of this section standing orders relate to the staff of a relevant authority if they make provision for regulating—

(a) the appointment of persons to paid office or employment under the authority; or

(b) the dismissal of persons holding such office or employment and the taking of other disciplinary action against such persons.

(3) Without prejudice to the generality of subsection (1) above, regulations under this section may require a relevant authority's standing orders—

(a) so to restrict the manner of exercising the power to take steps for or towards the selection of candidates for interview, or for appointment, as to make it exercisable only by the authority themselves, by a committee or sub-committee of the authority or by particular officers of the authority;

(b) to restrict the power of the authority or any of their committees or sub-committees—

(i) to give directions to persons making appointments on their behalf as to the identity of the individuals to be appointed; or

(ii) otherwise to interfere with the making of appointments by such persons;

(c) to require the monitoring officer of the authority to prepare a report to the authority in respect of every proposed appointment of a person to a politically restricted post;

(d) to require every such report to state whether, in the opinion of the monitoring officer, the proposed appointment can be made—

(i) without any contravention of any provision made by or under this Part; and

      (ii) without any matter being taken into account which could not properly be taken into account;

   and, if in his opinion it cannot be so made, his reasons; and

  (e) to prohibit the authority or any committee, sub-committee or other person acting on their behalf from dismissing or taking other disciplinary action against a person holding office or employment under the authority except in accordance with recommendations contained in a report made to the authority by an independent person of such a description as is prescribed by the regulations.

(4) Regulations under this section may contain such incidental provision and such supplemental, consequential and transitional provision in connection with their other provisions as the Secretary of State considers appropriate; and that provision may include—

  (a) provision which, for the purposes of any such restriction as is mentioned in subsection (3) above, makes modifications of any enactment with respect to the delegation of a relevant authority's functions;

  (b) provision which (with or without modifications) applies provisions of section 5 above in relation to any report prepared in consequence of regulations made by virtue of subsection (3)(c) above;

  (c) provision specifying the consequences—

      (i) in relation to any appointment or contract of employment;

      (ii) in relation to any proceedings on a complaint to an industrial tribunal; and

      (iii) in relation to any expenditure incurred by the authority,

   of any contravention of standing orders made in pursuance of the regulations; and

  (d) without prejudice to section 190(1) below, special provision in relation to the appointment of persons in pursuance of section 9 below and in relation to the appointment of persons for the purposes of functions exercised by joint committees on which relevant authorities are represented.

(5) In this section "relevant authority"—

  (a) in relation to England and Wales, means a local authority of any of the descriptions specified in paragraphs (a) to (e) of section 21(1) below; and

  (b) in relation to Scotland, means a regional, islands or district council.

  9.—(1) Nothing in section 7(1) above or in any enactment, standing order or rule of law by virtue of which it is unlawful for a relevant authority or any committee or sub-committee of such an authority to have regard to any person's political activities or affiliations in determining whether he should be appointed to any paid office or employment under the authority shall apply to the appointment of a person in pursuance of this section. *Assistants for political groups.*

(2) An appointment is an appointment in pursuance of this section if—

    (a) the appointment is made for the purpose of providing assistance, in the discharge of any of their functions as members of a relevant authority, to the members of any political group to which members of the authority belong;

    (b) the terms of the appointment comply with subsection (3) below;

    (c) the appointment is to one of not more than three posts which a relevant authority have decided to create for the purposes of this section; and

    (d) each of those posts falls, under the standing orders of the authority, to be filled from time to time in accordance with the wishes of a political group to which the post has been allocated under those standing orders.

(3) The terms on which any person is appointed to or holds any appointment in pursuance of this section must be such as secure that the annual rate of remuneration for the post is less than the relevant amount and that the appointment terminates at or before the end of—

    (a) in the case of a post under an authority in England and Wales, the day in the appropriate year on which the authority hold the meeting which they are required to hold in pursuance of paragraph 1 of Part I of Schedule 12 to the Local Government Act 1972 (annual meeting of principal councils); and

1972 c. 70.

    (b) in the case of a post under an authority in Scotland, the first day after the appointment on which a meeting is held in pursuance of the requirement under paragraph 1 of Schedule 7 to the Local Government (Scotland) Act 1973 that a meeting is held within twenty-one days from the date of an election.

1973 c. 65.

(4) For the purposes of subsection (3) above the annual rate of remuneration for a post under a relevant authority is less than the relevant amount if the annual rate of remuneration in respect of the post—

    (a) is less than £13,500 or such higher amount as the Secretary of State may by order made by statutory instrument specify; and

    (b) where that post is a part time post, would be less than that amount if it were a full time post and carried remuneration at the same rate;

and a statutory instrument containing an order under this subsection shall be subject to annulment in pursuance of a resolution of either House of Parliament.

(5) The standing orders of a relevant authority the members of which are divided into different political groups shall, for the purposes of subsection (2)(d) above—

    (a) prohibit the making of an appointment to any post allocated to a political group until the authority have allocated a post to each of the groups which qualify for one;

    (b) prohibit the allocation of a post to a political group which does not qualify for one; and

    (c) prohibit the allocation of more than one post to any one political group.

(6) Subject to subsection (7) below, where the members of a relevant authority are divided into different political groups, a group shall qualify for a post if—

  (a) the membership of that group comprises at least one-tenth of the membership of the authority;

  (b) the number of the other groups (if any) which are larger than that group does not exceed two; and

  (c) where the number of the other groups which are the same size as or larger than that group exceeds two, the authority have determined that that group should be a group to which a post is allocated;

and it shall be the duty of a relevant authority, before making any allocation for the purposes of this section in a case in which there are groups which would qualify for posts if paragraph (c) above were disregarded, to make such determinations under that paragraph as secure that there are no more nor less than three groups which do qualify for a post.

(7) Where the members of a relevant authority are divided into political groups only one of which has a membership that comprises one-tenth or more of the membership of the authority—

  (a) the groups qualifying for a post shall be that group and one other group; and

  (b) the other group shall be the one with the next largest membership or, in a case in which there is more than one group with the next largest membership, such one of those groups as may be determined by the authority;

and, in such a case, it shall be the duty of the authority to determine which of the groups with the next largest membership is to qualify for a post before making any allocation for the purposes of this section to the group with the largest membership.

(8) Neither a relevant authority nor any committee or sub-committee of a relevant authority shall exercise any power under—

  (a) section 101 of the Local Government Act 1972 (delegation); or 1972 c. 70.

  (b) section 56 of, or Schedule 10 or 20 to, the Local Government (Scotland) Act 1973 (which makes corresponding provision for Scotland), 1973 c. 65.

so as to arrange for the discharge of any of the authority's functions by any person who holds a post under the authority to which he was appointed in pursuance of this section.

(9) No person holding any office or employment under a relevant authority shall be required to work under the direction of a person holding a post to which he was appointed in pursuance of this section except for the purpose of providing that person, or the political group to which his post is allocated, with secretarial or clerical services.

(10) Without prejudice to section 8 above, the Secretary of State may, for the purposes of this section and any standing orders relating to appointments in pursuance of this section, by regulations make provision—

(a) as to the circumstances in which the members of a relevant authority are to be treated as divided into different political groups;

(b) as to the persons who are to be treated as members of such a group and as to when a person is to be treated as having ceased to be a member of such a group;

(c) requiring the question whether a person is or is not a member of a political group to be determined in such manner as may be provided for by or under the regulations;

(d) requiring a relevant authority from time to time to review allocations made for the purposes of this section;

(e) specifying the manner in which, and times at which, the wishes of a political group are to be expressed and the consequences of a failure by such a group to express its wishes;

and regulations under this section may contain such incidental provision and such supplemental, consequential and transitional provision in connection with their other provisions as the Secretary of State considers appropriate.

(11) In this section—

"appropriate year", in relation to a post held by any person under a relevant authority, means—

1972 c. 70.

(a) where the authority is one in relation to which provision for whole council elections has been made by virtue of section 7(4)(a) or 26(2)(a) of the Local Government Act 1972, the period of twelve months beginning with the first such election to be held after that person is appointed to that post; and

(b) in any other case, the period of twelve months beginning with the third anniversary of that person's appointment to that post;

"membership", in relation to a relevant authority, means the number of persons who are for the time being members of the authority;

"relevant authority"—

(a) in relation to England and Wales, means the council of any county, district or London borough; and

(b) in relation to Scotland, means a regional, islands or district council.

Limit on paid leave for local authority duties.
1978 c. 44.

10.—(1) Notwithstanding anything in subsection (4) of section 29 of the Employment Protection (Consolidation) Act 1978 (conditions of time off for public duties), where—

(a) a local authority permit an employee of theirs to take time off for the purpose of performing the duties of a member of a relevant council; and

(b) those duties do not include the duties of chairman of the council,

it shall be unlawful for the authority to make any payment of remuneration or other payment to that employee in respect of so much (if any) of any time off for that purpose as is in excess of two hundred and eight hours in any one financial year and is time off to which the employee would not be entitled apart from his membership of that council.

(2) In this section—

"chairman", in relation to a relevant council, includes any corresponding office the holder of which is referred to as mayor or Lord Mayor or by any other description;

"employee" has the same meaning as in the Employment Protection (Consolidation) Act 1978;   1978 c. 44.

"financial year" means the twelve months ending with 31st March; and

"relevant council" means the council of any county, district or London borough, the Common Council of the City of London, a parish or community council or any council in Scotland which is a local authority for the purposes of subsection (1) of section 29 of that Act (time off for public duties);

and subsection (3) of that section (meaning of duties of a member of a body) shall apply for the purposes of this section as it applies for the purposes of that section.

11.—(1) Nothing in section 17 of the Local Government Finance Act 1982 or section 79 of the Local Government Act 1985 (public inspection of accounts etc.) or in section 101 or 106 of the Local Government (Scotland) Act 1973 (which makes corresponding provision for Scotland) shall entitle any person—   Confidentiality of staff records. 1982 c. 32. 1985 c. 51. 1973 c. 65.

(a) to inspect so much of any document as contains personal information about a member of the relevant body's staff; or

(b) to require any such information to be disclosed in answer to any question.

(2) Information shall be regarded as personal information about a member of the relevant body's staff if it relates specifically to a particular individual and is available to that body for reasons connected with the fact—

(a) that that individual holds or has held any office or employment under that body; or

(b) that payments or other benefits in respect of any office or employment under any other person are or have been made or provided to that individual by that body.

(3) In this section—

"document" includes accounts, books, deeds, contracts, bills, vouchers and receipts; and "relevant body" in relation to accounts which are required to be audited in accordance with Part III of the said Act of 1982 or Part VII of the said Act of 1973, means the body whose accounts are required to be audited or, as the case may be, the Common Council of the City of London;

and references in this section to a payment made or benefit provided to an individual in respect of any office or employment include references to a payment made or benefit provided to him in respect of his ceasing to hold the office or employment.

(4) This section shall have effect only in relation to—

(a) the inspection of, or of documents relating to, accounts for periods beginning on or after 1st April 1990; and

(b) the disclosure of information in answer to questions about such accounts.

Conflict of interest in staff negotiations.

12.—(1) It shall be the duty of a local authority to secure that, so far as practicable, the interests of that authority in any negotiations with respect to the terms and conditions on which persons in local authority employment hold office or are employed are never represented, whether directly or indirectly by, or by persons who include—

(a) a person who is both a member of the authority and in such employment; or

(b) a person who is both a member of the authority and an official or employee of a trade union whose members include persons in local authority employment.

(2) In this section—

1988 c. 19.

"member", in relation to a trade union, includes any person who is a member of that union within the meaning of the Employment Act 1988; and

1974 c. 52.

"official" and "trade union" have the same meanings as in the Trade Union and Labour Relations Act 1974;

and a person shall be treated for the purposes of this section as in local authority employment if he holds any paid office or employment under a local authority or any such paid office or employment under any other person as, by virtue of section 80(1)(a) of the Local Government Act 1972 or section 31(1)(a) of the Local Government (Scotland) Act 1973, disqualifies him for membership of any authority.

1972 c. 70.
1973 c. 65.

(3) This section shall come into force at the expiry of the period of two months beginning on the day this Act is passed.

Voting rights of members of certain committees

Voting rights of members of certain committees: England and Wales.

13.—(1) Subject to the following provisions of this section, a person who—

(a) is a member of a committee appointed under a power to which this section applies by a relevant authority and is not a member of that authority;

(b) is a member of a joint committee appointed under such a power by two or more relevant authorities and is not a member of any of those authorities; or

(c) is a member of a sub-committee appointed under such a power by such a committee as is mentioned in paragraph (a) or (b) above and is not a member of the relevant authority, or one of the relevant authorities, which appointed that committee,

shall for all purposes be treated as a non-voting member of that committee, joint committee or, as the case may be, sub-committee.

(2) The powers to which this section applies are—

    (a) the powers conferred on any relevant authority by subsection (1) of section 102 of the Local Government Act 1972 (ordinary committees, joint committees and sub-committees); 1972 c. 70.

    (b) the powers exercisable by any relevant authority in accordance with any arrangements approved under paragraph 1 of Part II of Schedule 1 to the Education Act 1944, by virtue of any order under paragraph 3 of that Part of that Schedule or by virtue of paragraph 10 of that Part of that Schedule (education committees, joint education committees and education sub-committees); 1944 c. 31.

    (c) the powers exercisable by any relevant authority for the purposes of section 2 of the Local Authority Social Services Act 1970 (social services committees) or by virtue of section 4 of that Act (joint social services committees and sub-committees). 1970 c. 42.

(3) Nothing in subsection (1) above shall require a person to be treated as a non-voting member of a committee or sub-committee falling within subsection (4) below; but, except—

    (a) in the case of a sub-committee appointed by a committee falling within paragraph (e) of that subsection; and

    (b) in such cases as may be prescribed by regulations made by the Secretary of State,

a person who is a member of a sub-committee falling within that subsection shall for all purposes be treated as a non-voting member of that sub-committee unless he is a member of the committee which appointed the sub-committee.

(4) A committee or sub-committee falls within this subsection if it is—

    (a) a committee appointed for the purposes of section 2 or 3(4) of the Police Act 1964 (constitution of a committee of a relevant authority as a police authority); 1964 c. 48.

    (b) a local fisheries committee for any sea fisheries district;

    (c) a committee established in accordance with any regulations made by virtue of section 7 of the Superannuation Act 1972 (regulations making provision for the superannuation of persons employed in local government service etc.); 1972 c. 11.

    (d) a National Parks Committee;

    (e) a committee appointed under section 102(4) of the Local Government Act 1972 (appointment of advisory committees by local authorities);

    (f) a committee constituted in accordance with Part I of Schedule 2 to the Education Act 1980 (appeal committees for hearing school admissions appeals); 1980 c. 20.

(g) a committee established exclusively for the purpose of discharging such functions of a relevant authority as may be prescribed by regulations made by the Secretary of State;

(h) a sub-committee appointed by a committee falling within any of paragraphs (a) to (g) above or such a sub-committee as is so prescribed.

(5) Nothing in this section shall prevent—

(a) any arrangements for the purposes of paragraph 1 of Part II of Schedule 1 to the Education Act 1944 (education committees);

(b) any order under paragraph 3 of that Part (joint education committees and sub-committees of joint education committees); or

(c) any order under paragraph 10 of that Part (sub-committees of education committees),

from providing for a person who is not a member of a local education authority to be appointed as a voting member of an education committee or joint education committee, or of a sub-committee of such a committee or joint committee, in accordance with such provisions of the arrangements or order as are approved or made by the Secretary of State for the purpose of securing the representation on that committee, joint committee or sub-committee of persons who appoint foundation governors of voluntary schools in the area of the authority or, as the case may be, in the area of any of the authorities which have appointed the joint education committee.

(6) The Secretary of State may, if it appears to him appropriate to do so in consequence of the preceding provisions of this section, withdraw any approval given before the coming into force of this section in relation to any arrangements for the purposes of paragraph 1 of Part II of Schedule 1 to the said Act of 1944.

(7) Where a person is treated by virtue of this section as a non-voting member of any committee, joint committee or sub-committee, he shall not be entitled to vote at any meeting of the committee, joint committee or sub-committee on any question which falls to be decided at that meeting; and the reference in subsection (5) above to a voting member, in relation to any education committee or sub-committee of an education committee, is a reference to a person who is entitled to vote at any meeting of that committee or sub-committee on any question which falls to be decided at that meeting.

(8) In subsection (3) of section 102 of the Local Government Act 1972, the words from "but at least" onwards (which require at least two-thirds of certain committees to be members of the appointing authority or authorities) shall be omitted.

(9) In this section—

"foundation governors" has the same meaning as in the Education Act 1944; and

"relevant authority" means a local authority of any of the descriptions specified in paragraphs (a) to (j) of section 21(1) below or any parish or community council;

and references in this section to voting include references to making use of a casting vote.

PART I
Voting rights of
members of
certain
committees:
Scotland.
1973 c. 65.

14.—(1) Subject to the following provisions of this section, a person who—

(a) is a member of a committee appointed under subsection (1) of section 57 of the Local Government (Scotland) Act 1973 by a relevant authority and is not a member of that authority;

(b) is a member of a joint committee appointed under that subsection by two or more relevant authorities and is not a member of any of those authorities; or

(c) is a member of a sub-committee appointed under that subsection by such a committee as is mentioned in paragraph (a) or (b) above and is not a member of the relevant authority, or one of the relevant authorities, which appointed that committee,

shall for all purposes be treated as a non-voting member of that committee, joint committee or, as the case may be, sub-committee.

(2) Subject to the following provisions of this section, a person who—

(a) is a member of an education committee appointed under section 124 of the Local Government (Scotland) Act 1973 by an education authority and is not a member of that authority;

(b) is a member of a joint committee appointed under paragraph 7 of Schedule 10 to that Act by two or more education authorities and is not a member of any of these authorities; or

(c) is a member of a sub-committee appointed under paragraph 8 of that Schedule by an education committee or such a joint committee and is not a member of the education committee or, as the case may be, one of the education authorities which appointed the joint committee,

shall for all purposes be treated as a non-voting member of that committee, joint committee or, as the case may be, sub-committee.

(3) Subject to the following provisions of this section, a person who—

1968 c. 49.

(a) is a member of a social work committee appointed under section 2 of the Social Work (Scotland) Act 1968 by a local authority for the purposes of that Act and is not a member of that authority;

(b) is a member of a joint committee appointed under paragraph 6 of Schedule 20 to the Local Government (Scotland) Act 1973 by two or more such authorities and is not a member of any of those authorities; or

(c) is a member of a sub-committee appointed under paragraph 7 of that Schedule by a social work committee or such a joint committee and is not a member of the social work committee or, as the case may be, one of the local authorities which appointed the joint committee,

shall for all purposes be treated as a non-voting member of that committee, joint committee or, as the case may be, sub-committee.

(4) Nothing in subsections (1) to (3) above shall require a person to be treated as a non-voting member of a committee or sub-committee falling within subsection (5) below; but, except—

(a) in the case of a sub-committee appointed by a committee falling within paragraph (b) of that subsection; and

(b) in such cases as may be prescribed by regulations made by the Secretary of State,

a person who is a member of a sub-committee falling within that subsection shall for all purposes be treated as a non-voting member of that sub-committee unless he is a member of the committee which appointed the sub-committee.

(5) A committee or sub-committee falls within this subsection if it is—

(a) a committee established in accordance with any regulations made by virtue of section 7 of the Superannuation Act 1972 (regulations making provision for the superannuation of persons employed in local government service etc.);

(b) a committee appointed under section 57(4) of the Local Government (Scotland) Act 1973 (appointment of advisory committees by local authorities);

(c) a committee constituted in accordance with Schedule A1 to the Education (Scotland) Act 1980 (appeal committees for hearing placing and other appeals);

(d) a Children's Panel Advisory Committee formed under paragraph 3 of Schedule 3 to the Social Work (Scotland) Act 1968;

(e) a committee established exclusively for the purpose of discharging such functions of a relevant authority as may be prescribed by regulations made by the Secretary of State;

(f) a sub-committee appointed by a committee falling within any of paragraphs (a) to (e) above or such a sub-committee as is so prescribed.

(6) Nothing in this section shall prevent the appointment as a voting member of—

(a) an education committee; or

(b) a joint committee appointed under paragraph 7 of Schedule 10 to the Local Government (Scotland) Act 1973; or

(c) a sub-committee appointed under paragraph 8 of that Schedule,

of a person appointed to the education committee under paragraph (a) of subsection (3) of section 124 of that Act (appointment of certain persons to education committees).

(7) Where a person is treated by virtue of this section as a non-voting member of any committee, joint committee or sub-committee, he shall not be entitled to vote at any meeting of the committee, joint committee or sub-committee on any question which falls to be decided at that meeting; and the reference in subsection (6) above to a voting member, in relation to any such committee, joint committee or sub-committee as is mentioned in that subsection, is a reference to a person who is entitled to vote at any meeting of that committee, joint committee or sub-committee on any question which falls to be decided at that meeting.

(8) In the Local Government (Scotland) Act 1973—

(a) in section 57(3), the words from "but at least" onwards (which require at least two-thirds of certain committees to be members of the appointing authority or authorities);

(b) in section 161(6), the words from "but at least" onwards (which make corresponding provision in relation to a social work committee);

(c) in Schedule 10, paragraph 11 (which requires at least half of a joint education committee to be members of the appointing authorities);

(d) in Schedule 20, paragraph 10 (which requires at least two-thirds of a joint social work committee to be members of the appointing authorities),

shall be omitted.

(9) In this section "relevant authority" means a regional, islands or district council; and references in this section to voting include references to making use of a casting vote.

Political balance on committees etc.

15.—(1) It shall be the duty of a relevant authority having power from time to time to make appointments to a body to which this section applies to review the representation of different political groups on that body—

Duty to allocate seats to political groups.

(a) where the members of the authority are divided into different political groups at the time when this section comes into force, as soon as practicable after that time;

(b) where the authority hold annual meetings in pursuance of paragraph 1 of Part I of Schedule 12 to the Local Government Act 1972 (annual meeting of principal councils) and the members of the authority are divided into different political groups at the time of any such meeting, at or as soon as practicable after the meeting;

1972 c. 70.

(c) where, at the time of the meeting required by paragraph 1 of Schedule 7 to the Local Government (Scotland) Act 1973 to be held in an election year within twenty-one days of the election, the members of the authority are divided into different political groups, at or as soon as practicable after the meeting;

1973 c. 65.

(d) as soon as practicable after any such division as is mentioned in paragraphs (a) to (c) above occurs; and

(e) at such other times as may be prescribed by regulations made by the Secretary of State.

(2) Except in such cases as may be prescribed by regulations made by the Secretary of State, it shall be the duty of every committee of a relevant authority which is a committee having power from time to time to make appointments to a body to which this section applies to review the representation of different political groups on that body—

(a) where the members of the authority are divided into different political groups at the time when this section comes into force, as soon as practicable after that time; and

(b) as soon as practicable after any occasion on which the members of the committee are changed in consequence of a determination under this section.

(3) Where at any time the representation of different political groups on a body to which this section applies falls to be reviewed under this section by any relevant authority or committee of a relevant authority, it shall be the duty of that authority or committee, as soon as practicable after the review, to determine the allocation to the different political groups into which the members of the authority are divided of all the seats which fall to be filled by appointments made from time to time by that authority or committee.

(4) Subject to subsection (6) below, it shall be the duty of a relevant authority or committee of a relevant authority—

(a) in performing their duty under subsection (3) above; and

(b) in exercising their power, at times not mentioned in subsection (3) above, to determine the allocation to different political groups of seats on a body to which this section applies,

to make only such determinations as give effect, so far as reasonably practicable, to the principles specified in subsection (5) below.

(5) The principles mentioned in subsection (4) above, in relation to the seats on any body which fall to be filled by appointments made by any relevant authority or committee of a relevant authority, are—

(a) that not all the seats on the body are allocated to the same political group;

(b) that the majority of the seats on the body is allocated to a particular political group if the number of persons belonging to that group is a majority of the authority's membership;

(c) subject to paragraphs (a) and (b) above, that the number of seats on the ordinary committees of a relevant authority which are allocated to each political group bears the same proportion to the total of all the seats on the ordinary committees of that authority as is borne by the number of members of that group to the membership of the authority; and

(d) subject to paragraphs (a) to (c) above, that the number of the seats on the body which are allocated to each political group bears the same proportion to the number of all the seats on that body as is borne by the number of members of that group to the membership of the authority.

(6) Where any relevant authority or committee of a relevant authority are required, in determining the allocation to different political groups of seats on a body to which this section applies, to give effect to the principles specified in subsection (5) above—

(a) any seats which, in accordance—

(i) with provision made by virtue of subsection (5) of section 13 above; or

(ii) with subsection (6) of section 14 above,

are to be or may be filled by the appointment of persons who are not members of the authority shall be taken into account for the purpose of determining how many seats constitute a majority of the seats on a body mentioned in either of those subsections; but

(b) that authority or committee shall, in making that determination, disregard for all other purposes any seats which, in accordance with any such provision, the said subsection (6) or otherwise, are to be or may be so filled;

and for the purposes of this subsection a seat on an advisory committee of a relevant authority or on a sub-committee appointed by such an advisory committee shall not be treated as one which may be so filled unless the authority have determined that it must be so filled.

(7) Schedule 1 to this Act shall have effect for determining the bodies to which this section applies and for the construction of this section and sections 16 and 17 below.

16.—(1) Where any relevant authority or any committee of a relevant authority have determined the allocation to different political groups of the seats on a body to which section 15 above applies, it shall be the duty of that authority or committee so to exercise their power to make appointments to that body as to give effect—

Duty to give effect to allocations.

(a) as soon as practicable after the determination; and

(b) if a vacancy subsequently occurs on that body, as soon as practicable after the occurrence of the vacancy,

to such wishes about who is to be appointed to the seats on that body which are allocated to a particular political group as are expressed by that group.

(2) Where—

(a) any person has been appointed, otherwise than for a fixed term, to a body to which section 15 above applies; and

(b) that appointment was made, in pursuance of subsection (1) above, in accordance with the wishes of a political group,

then, so long as that person's seat continues to be allocated to that group, the authority or committee which made the appointment shall act in accordance with the wishes of that group in determining whether and when to terminate the appointment.

(3) The proceedings of a body to which section 15 above applies shall not be invalidated by any defect by virtue of this section or that section in the appointment of any person to that body.

(4) This section applies in relation to an allocation of seats to different political groups whether or not that allocation is made in pursuance of any duty under section 15 above.

17.—(1) Subject to subsection (2) below, sections 15 and 16 above shall not apply in relation to appointments by a relevant authority or committee of a relevant authority to any body in so far as different provision is made by arrangements approved by the authority or committee—

Exceptions to and extensions of political balance requirements.

(a) in such manner as may be prescribed by regulations made by the Secretary of State; and

(b) without any member of the authority or committee voting against them.

(2) Arrangements approved under subsection (1) above in relation to any body shall not affect any duty imposed by virtue of section 15(1)(c), (d) or (e) or (2) above on a relevant authority or committee to review the representation of different political groups on that body; and, accordingly, such arrangements shall cease to have effect when any such duty arises.

(3) The Secretary of State may, for the purpose of securing what appears to him to be the appropriate representation of different political groups on any sub-committee falling within subsection (4) below, by regulations make such provision as he thinks fit.

(4) The sub-committees that fall within this subsection are those to which appointments may be made by bodies to which section 15 above applies but which are not themselves such bodies.

(5) Without prejudice to the generality of subsection (3) above, regulations under that subsection may contain provision applying, with or without modifications, any provision made by or under section 15 or 16 above, subsections (1) and (2) above or Schedule 1 to this Act.

Allowances

Schemes for basic, attendance and special responsibility allowances for local authority members.

18.—(1) The Secretary of State may by regulations authorise or require any such relevant authority as may be specified or described in the regulations to make a scheme providing for the payment of—

    (a) a basic allowance for every member of the authority who is a councillor;

    (b) an attendance allowance in relation to the carrying out by any such member of such duties as may be specified in or determined under the regulations; and

    (c) a special responsibility allowance for any such member who has such special responsibilities in relation to the authority as may be so specified or determined.

(2) Regulations under this section may also authorise or require a scheme made by a relevant authority under the regulations to include provision for the payment to appointed members of allowances in respect of such losses of earnings and expenses as—

    (a) are necessarily sustained or incurred in the carrying out, in connection with their membership of the authority or any committee or sub-committee of the authority, of duties specified in or determined under the regulations; and

    (b) are not of a description in respect of which provision is made for an allowance under any of sections 174 to 176 of the Local Government Act 1972 or sections 46 to 48 of the Local Government (Scotland) Act 1973.

1972 c. 70.
1973 c. 65.

(3) Without prejudice to the generality of the powers conferred by subsections (1) and (2) above, regulations under this section may contain such provision as the Secretary of State considers appropriate for requiring a scheme made by a relevant authority under the regulations—

    (a) to make it a condition of any payment by way of allowance that, in the financial year to which the payment would relate, the aggregate amount which the authority has paid out or is already liable to pay out under the scheme does not exceed such maximum amount as may be specified in or determined under the regulations;

(b) to make provision for different maximum amounts to be applicable, for the purposes of any such condition, in relation to different allowances or in relation to different members or members of different groups;

(c) to make provision in relation to claims which cannot be paid by virtue of any such condition and provision for the payment to members of the authority who are councillors of an amount by way of supplement to the basic allowance where, in any financial year, the aggregate paid out or owing under the scheme is less than an amount specified in or determined under the regulations;

(d) to provide that the amount authorised by virtue of subsection (2) above to be paid by way of allowance in any case shall not exceed such amount as may be so specified or determined;

(e) to contain such provision as may be so specified or determined with respect to the general administration of the scheme, with respect to the manner in which, time within which and forms on which claims for any allowance are to be made and with respect to the information to be provided in support of any such claim;

(f) to contain such provision as may be so specified or determined for avoiding the duplication of payments or of allowances, for determining the bodies by which payments of allowances are to be made and for the apportionment of payments between different bodies.

(4) Regulations under this section may—

(a) prohibit the payment, otherwise than in accordance with sections 174 to 176 of the Local Government Act 1972 or sections 46 to 48 of the Local Government (Scotland) Act 1973 or in such other cases as may be specified in the regulations, of any allowance to a member of a relevant authority who is a councillor or to any appointed member of a relevant authority; 1972 c. 70.
1973 c. 65.

(b) impose requirements on a relevant authority with respect to the publication, in the minutes of that authority or otherwise, of the details of amounts paid in pursuance of a scheme made under the regulations; and

(c) contain such incidental provision and such supplemental, consequential and transitional provision in connection with the other provisions of the regulations as the Secretary of State considers appropriate.

(5) In this section "relevant authority" means—

(a) a local authority of any of the descriptions specified in any of the paragraphs of section 21(1) below, other than paragraphs (d) and (j), or in section 21(2) below;

(b) any body on which a body which is a relevant authority by virtue of paragraph (a) above is represented and which is designated as a relevant authority for the purposes of this section by regulations made by the Secretary of State; or

(c) any appeal committee so designated which is constituted in accordance with paragraph 2 or 3 of Schedule 2 to the Education Act 1980;

and references in this section to an appointed member, in relation to a relevant authority, are references to any person who is a member of the authority without being a councillor or who is a member of one or more of the authority's committees or sub-committees without being a member of the authority.

(6) In this section any reference to a councillor includes a reference to a member of the authority concerned who, in accordance with regulations under this section, is to be treated as if he were a councillor.

Members' interests

Members' interests.

19.—(1) The Secretary of State may by regulations require each member of a local authority—

(a) to give a general notice to the proper officer of the authority setting out such information about the member's direct and indirect pecuniary interests as may be prescribed by the regulations, or stating that he has no such interests; and

(b) from time to time to give to that officer such further notices as may be so prescribed for the purpose of enabling that officer to keep the information provided under the regulations up to date.

(2) Any member of a local authority who—

(a) without reasonable excuse fails to comply with the requirements of any regulations under this section; or

(b) in giving a notice in compliance with any such requirement, provides information which he knows to be false or misleading in a material particular or recklessly provides information which is false or misleading in a material particular,

shall be guilty of an offence and liable, on summary conviction, to a fine not exceeding level 4 on the standard scale.

(3) Proceedings for an offence under subsection (2) above shall not be instituted in England and Wales except by or with the consent of the Director of Public Prosecutions.

1972 c. 70.
1973 c. 65.

(4) Neither section 96 of the Local Government Act 1972 (general notice of pecuniary interests) nor section 40 of the Local Government (Scotland) Act 1973 (corresponding provision for Scotland) shall apply in relation to any notice given in pursuance of any regulations under this section; but such regulations may provide—

(a) that the giving of a notice in pursuance of any such regulations shall be deemed to be sufficient disclosure for the purposes of section 94 of the said Act of 1972 (disability of members of authorities for voting on account of interest in contracts etc.) or for the purposes of section 38 of the said Act of 1973; and

(b) that the proper officer of a local authority is to maintain such records of the information contained in notices given to him as may be prescribed by the regulations and is to keep those records open to inspection by members of the public.

(5) A local authority shall not be entitled (whether by means of making it a condition of any appointment or by any other means whatever) to impose any obligations on their members to disclose any interests other than those that they are required to disclose by virtue of section 94 of the Local Government Act 1972, section 38 of the Local Government (Scotland) Act 1973 or any regulations under this section.

1972 c. 70.
1973 c. 65.

(6) Regulations under this section may contain such incidental provision and such supplemental, consequential and transitional provision in connection with their other provisions as the Secretary of State considers appropriate.

(7) References in this section to the indirect pecuniary interests of a member of a local authority shall include references to any such interests as, by virtue of any connection between that member or his spouse and any other person, would fall to be disclosed—

(a) in the case of a local authority in England and Wales, under section 94 of the Local Government Act 1972; or

(b) in the case of a local authority in Scotland, under section 38 of the Local Government (Scotland) Act 1973,

if the authority were proposing to enter into a contract with that other person.

Duty to adopt certain procedural standing orders

20.—(1) The Secretary of State may by regulations require relevant authorities, subject to such variations as may be authorised by the regulations—

Duty to adopt certain procedural standing orders.

(a) to incorporate such provision as may be prescribed by the regulations in standing orders for regulating their proceedings and business; and

(b) to make or refrain from making such other modifications of any such standing orders as may be so prescribed.

(2) Without prejudice to the generality of subsection (1) above, regulations under this section may require such standing orders as are mentioned in that subsection to contain provision which, notwithstanding any enactment or the decision of any relevant authority or committee or sub-committee of a relevant authority, authorises persons who are members of such an authority, committee or sub-committee—

(a) to requisition meetings of the authority or of any of their committees or sub-committees;

(b) to require a decision of a committee or sub-committee of the authority to be referred to and reviewed by the authority themselves or by a committee of the authority;

(c) to require that a vote with respect to a matter falling to be decided by the authority or by any of their committees or sub-committees is to be taken in a particular manner.

(3) Regulations under this section may contain such incidental provision and such supplemental, consequential and transitional provision in connection with their other provisions as the Secretary of State considers appropriate.

(4) In this section "relevant authority"—

    (a) in relation to England and Wales, means a local authority of any of the descriptions specified in paragraphs (a) to (j) of section 21(1) below or any parish or community council; and

    (b) in relation to Scotland, means a local authority.

Interpretation of Part I

Interpretation of Part I.

21.—(1) Any reference in this Part to a local authority is, in relation to England and Wales, a reference to a body of one of the following descriptions—

    (a) a county council;

    (b) a district council;

    (c) a London borough council;

    (d) the Common Council of the City of London in its capacity as a local authority, police authority or port health authority;

    (e) the Council of the Isles of Scilly;

1947 c. 41.
    (f) a fire authority constituted by a combination scheme under the Fire Services Act 1947;

1964 c. 48.
    (g) a combined police authority established by an amalgamation scheme under the Police Act 1964;

1985 c. 51.
    (h) an authority established under section 10 of the Local Government Act 1985 (waste disposal authorities);

    (i) a joint authority established by Part IV of that Act (police, fire services, civil defence and transport);

    (j) any body established pursuant to an order under section 67 of that Act (successors to residuary bodies);

    (k) the Broads Authority;

    (l) any joint board the constituent members of which consist of any of the bodies specified above; and

    (m) a joint or special planning board constituted for a National Park by an order under paragraph 1 or paragraph 3 of Schedule 17 to the Local Government Act 1972.

1972 c. 70.

(2) Any reference in this Part to a local authority is, in relation to Scotland, a reference to a regional, islands or district council or a joint board within the meaning of section 235(1) of the Local Government (Scotland) Act 1973.

1973 c. 65.

(3) In this Part—

"contravention" includes a failure to comply;

"modifications" includes additions, alterations and omissions;

"proper officer"—

    (a) in relation to a local authority in England and Wales, has the same meaning as in the Local Government Act 1972; and

    (b) in relation to a local authority in Scotland, has the same meaning as in the Local Government (Scotland) Act 1973; and

"subordinate legislation" has the same meaning as in the Interpretation Act 1978.

1978 c. 30.

(4) References in this Part to an officer of a local authority or to a paid office under a local authority do not include references to, or to the office of, the chairman or vice-chairman of the authority (whether referred to as such, as mayor, Lord Mayor, deputy mayor, as Lord Provost or otherwise).

PART II

LOCAL GOVERNMENT ADMINISTRATION

22.—(1) Section 23 of the Local Government Act 1974 (constitution and functions of Commissions for Local Administration) shall have effect with the amendments specified in subsections (2) to (4) below.

Advisory
Commissioners.
1974 c. 7.

(2) In subsection (1), at the end, there shall be added the words "but each of the Commissions may include persons appointed to act as advisers, not exceeding the number appointed to conduct investigations."

(3) In subsection (3), after the words "Parliamentary Commissioner" there shall be inserted the words "or an advisory member".

(4) In subsections (4), (5) and (6) the word "Local" shall be omitted.

(5) In Schedule 4 to the said Act, in paragraph 3 (remuneration), at the end there shall be inserted the following sub-paragraph—

"(3) Sub-paragraphs (1) and (2) above apply in relation to Commissioners who are advisory members of the Commission as they apply in relation to Local Commissioners."

23.—(1) In section 23 of the Local Government Act 1974 (appointment and functions of Commissions for Local Administration) there shall be inserted, after subsection (12), the following subsections—

Advice and
guidance by
Commissions for
Local
Administration
and Scottish
Commissioner.

"(12A) Each of the Commissions may, after consultation with the representative persons and authorities concerned, provide to the authorities or any of the authorities to which this Part of this Act applies such advice and guidance about good administrative practice as appears to the Commission to be appropriate and may arrange for it to be published for the information of the public.

(12B) The representative persons and authorities concerned are—

(a) for the purposes of subsection (12) above, such persons appearing to the Commission to represent authorities in England or, as the case may be, authorities in Wales to which this Part of this Act applies, and in the case of such authorities as are not so represented, those authorities; and

(b) for the purposes of subsection (12A) above, such of those persons and authorities as the Commission think appropriate."

(2) In section 21 of the Local Government (Scotland) Act 1975 (appointment and functions of Commissioner for Local Administration in Scotland) there shall be inserted, after subsection (4), the following subsection—

1975 c. 30.

"(4A) The Commissioner may, after consultation with such associations of local authorities as appear to him to be appropriate, provide to the authorities to which this Part of this Act applies such advice and guidance about good administrative practice as appears to him to be appropriate and may arrange for it to be published for the information of the public."

Expenses of
Commissions for
Local
Administration.
1974 c. 7.

24.—(1) The following provisions shall be substituted for paragraphs 6 to 11 of Schedule 4 to the Local Government Act 1974—

"Expenses of the Commissions

6.—(1) Each of the Commissions shall be treated as if they were a specified body for the purposes of sections 78 and 79 (revenue support grant) of the Local Government Finance Act 1988 ("the 1988 Act"), and those sections shall accordingly have effect with the following modifications.

(2) Before making a determination under section 78 of the 1988 Act, the Secretary of State shall, except in the case mentioned in paragraph 8 below, take into account estimates of the expenses of each Commission together with any observations thereon made and submitted to him in accordance with paragraph 7 below.

(3) The Secretary of State may also take into account any other information available to him as to the expenses of the Commissions, whatever its source.

(4) A determination under section 78 of the 1988 Act shall not be invalid merely because the requirements of paragraph 7 below were not complied with.

(5) For the purposes of section 78(7) of the 1988 Act, each Commission shall be treated as if they were also a notifiable authority.

7.—(1) Each Commission shall prepare an estimate of the expenses which they will incur in the forthcoming financial year with a view to submitting it to the Secretary of State.

(2) Each Commission shall send copies of the estimate to such representatives of local government as the Secretary of State directs for consideration by those representatives.

(3) Any observations by those representatives shall be submitted to the Commission within one month of the receipt of the Commission's estimate, and it shall be the duty of the Commission to take any such observations into consideration before submitting their estimate of their expenses to the Secretary of State.

(4) Each Commission shall, not later than such date in any year as the Secretary of State specifies in writing to the Commission, submit their estimate of their expenses for the forthcoming financial year to the Secretary of State together with copies of all observations made under this paragraph by the representatives of local government or, if none were made, together with a statement of that fact.

8. Where a Commission fail to submit an estimate of their expenses for the forthcoming financial year under paragraph 7 above, the Secretary of State may, for the purposes of a determination under section 78 of the 1988 Act, assume those expenses to be such as he sees fit."

(2) Anything done before the passing of this Act which corresponds to a thing authorised or required to be done by any provision of the paragraphs 6(2) and (3), 7 and 8 substituted by subsection (1) above and done for the purposes of sections 78 and 79 of the Local Government Finance Act 1988 shall be treated as validly done under that provision and those sections shall have effect accordingly.

1988 c. 41.

(3) The foregoing provisions shall have effect for the financial years beginning on or after 1st April 1990.

25.—(1) The representative body for England and the representative body for Wales designated under section 24 of the Local Government Act 1974 are hereby dissolved and accordingly that section shall cease to have effect.

Annual reports of Commissions: new provisions.

1974 c. 7.

(2) After section 23 of that Act there shall be inserted the following section—

"Annual reports for representatives etc.

23A.—(1) For the financial year ending in 1990 and for each subsequent financial year, each of the Commissions shall prepare a general report on the discharge of their functions and shall submit it—

(a) to such persons as appear to the Commission to represent authorities in England or, as the case may be, authorities in Wales to which this Part of this Act applies, and

(b) in the case of such authorities as are not so represented, to those authorities.

(2) The report shall be submitted as soon as may be after the Commission have received the reports for the year from Local Commissioners under section 23(11) above, and each Commission shall submit copies of those reports, together with their own report.

(3) Each Commission shall arrange for the publication of the report submitted by them under subsection (1) above and of the reports of which copies are submitted by them under subsection (2) above.

(4) Before arranging for the publication of a report under subsection (3) above the Commission concerned shall give a reasonable opportunity for the representative persons and authorities to whom the report was submitted to comment on it.

(5) Without prejudice to the generality of subsection (4) above, comments made by the representative persons and authorities by virtue of that subsection may relate to particular classes of authorities to which this Part of this Act applies.

(6) Where the Commission for Local Administration in Wales consist of only one Local Commissioner, section 23(11) above and subsection (2) above shall have effect with the necessary modifications."

Implementation of recommendations of Commissioners for Local Administration in England and Wales.
1974 c. 7.

26.—(1) In section 31 of the Local Government Act 1974 (action to be taken in relation to adverse reports), the following subsections shall be substituted for subsections (1) to (2A)—

"(1) This section applies where a Local Commissioner reports that injustice has been caused to a person aggrieved in consequence of maladministration.

(2) The report shall be laid before the authority concerned and it shall be the duty of that authority to consider the report and, within the period of three months beginning with the date on which they received the report, or such longer period as the Local Commissioner may agree in writing, to notify the Local Commissioner of the action which the authority have taken or propose to take.

(2A) If the Local Commissioner—

(a) does not receive the notification required by subsection (2) above within the period allowed by or under that subsection, or

(b) is not satisfied with the action which the authority concerned have taken or propose to take, or

(c) does not within a period of three months beginning with the end of the period so allowed, or such longer period as the Local Commissioner may agree in writing, receive confirmation from the authority concerned that they have taken action, as proposed, to the satisfaction of the Local Commissioner,

he shall make a further report setting out those facts and making recommendations.

(2B) Those recommendations are such recommendations as the Local Commissioner thinks fit to make with respect to action which, in his opinion, the authority concerned should take to remedy the injustice to the person aggrieved and to prevent similar injustice being caused in the future.

(2C) Section 30 above, with any necessary modifications, and subsection (2) above shall apply to a report under subsection (2A) above as they apply to a report under that section.

(2D) If the Local Commissioner—

(a) does not receive the notification required by subsection (2) above as applied by subsection (2C) above within the period allowed by or under that subsection or is satisfied before the period allowed by that subsection has expired that the authority concerned have decided to take no action, or

(b) is not satisfied with the action which the authority concerned have taken or propose to take, or

(c) does not within a period of three months beginning with the end of the period allowed by or under subsection (2) above as applied by subsection (2C) above, or such longer period as the Local Commissioner may agree in writing, receive confirmation from the authority concerned that they have taken action, as proposed, to the satisfaction of the Local Commissioner,

he may, by notice to the authority, require them to arrange for a statement to be published in accordance with subsections (2E) and (2F) below.

(2E) The statement referred to in subsection (2D) above is a statement, in such form as the authority concerned and the Local Commissioner may agree, consisting of—

(a) details of any action recommended by the Local Commissioner in his further report which the authority have not taken;

(b) such supporting material as the Local Commissioner may require; and

(c) if the authority so require, a statement of the reasons for their having taken no action on, or not the action recommended in, the report.

(2F) The requirements for the publication of the statement are that—

(a) publication shall be in any two editions within a fortnight of a newspaper circulating in the area of the authority agreed with the Local Commissioner or, in default of agreement, nominated by him; and

(b) publication in the first such edition shall be arranged for the earliest practicable date.

(2G) If the authority concerned—

(a) fail to arrange for the publication of the statement in accordance with subsections (2E) and (2F) above, or

(b) are unable, within the period of one month beginning with the date on which they received the notice under subsection (2D) above, or such longer period as the Local Commissioner may agree in writing, to agree with the Local Commissioner the form of the statement to be published,

the Local Commissioner shall arrange for such a statement as is mentioned in subsection (2E) above to be published in any two editions within a fortnight of a newspaper circulating within the authority's area.

(2H) The authority concerned shall reimburse the Commission on demand any reasonable expenses incurred by the Local Commissioner in performing his duty under subsection (2G) above."

(2) This section shall not have effect in relation to a report made before the coming into force of this section.

PART II
Implementation of
recommendations
of Commissioner
for Local
Administration in
Scotland.
1975 c. 30.

27.—(1) In section 29 of the Local Government (Scotland) Act 1975 (action to be taken in relation to adverse reports), the following subsections shall be substituted for subsections (1) to (2A)—

"(1) This section applies where the Commissioner reports that injustice has been caused to a person aggrieved in consequence of maladministration.

(2) The report shall be laid before the authority concerned and it shall be the duty of that authority to consider the report and, within the period of three months beginning with the date on which they received the report, or such longer period as the Commissioner may agree in writing, to notify the Commissioner of the action which the authority have taken or propose to take.

(2A) If the Commissioner—

(a) does not receive the notification required by subsection (2) abqve within the period allowed by or under that subsection, or

(b) is not satisfied with the action which the authority concerned have taken or propose to take, or

(c) does not within a period of three months beginning with the end of the period so allowed, or such longer period as the Commissioner may agree in writing, receive confirmation from the authority concerned that they have taken action, as proposed, to the satisfaction of the Commissioner,

he shall make a further report setting out those facts and making recommendations.

(2B) Those recommendations are such recommendations as the Commissioner thinks fit to make with respect to the action which, in his opinion, the authority concerned should take to remedy the injustice to the person aggrieved and to prevent similar injustice being caused in the future.

(2C) Section 28 of this Act, with any necessary modifications, and subsection (2) above shall apply to a report under subsection (2A) above as they apply to a report under that section.

(2D) If the Commissioner—

(a) does not receive the notification required by subsection (2) above as applied by subsection (2C) above within the period allowed by or under that subsection or is satisfied before the period allowed by that subsection has expired that the authority concerned have decided to take no action; or

(b) is not satisfied with the action which the authority concerned have taken or propose to take; or

(c) does not within a period of three months beginning with the end of the period allowed by or under subsection (2) above as applied by subsection (2C) above, or such longer period as the Commissioner may agree in writing, receive confirmation from the authority concerned that they have taken action, as proposed, to the satisfaction of the Commissioner,

he may, by notice to the authority, require them to arrange for a statement to be published in accordance with subsections (2E) and (2F) below.

(2E) The statement referred to in subsection (2D) above is a statement, in such form as the authority concerned and the Commissioner may agree, consisting of—

    (a) details of any action recommended by the Commissioner in his further report which the authority have not taken;

    (b) such supporting material as the Commissioner may require; and

    (c) if the authority so require, a statement of the reasons for their having taken no action on, or not the action recommended in, the report.

(2F) The requirements for the publication of the statement are that—

    (a) publication shall be in any two editions within a fortnight of a newspaper circulating in the area of the authority agreed with the Commissioner or, in default of agreement, nominated by him; and

    (b) publication in the first such edition shall be arranged for the earliest practicable date.

(2G) If the authority concerned—

    (a) fail to arrange for the publication of the statement in accordance with subsections (2E) and (2F) above, or

    (b) are unable, within the period of one month beginning with the date on which they received the notice under subsection (2D) above, or such longer period as the Commissioner may agree in writing, to agree with the Commissioner the form of the statement to be published,

the Commissioner shall arrange for such a statement as is mentioned in subsection (2E) above to be published in any two editions within a fortnight of a newspaper circulating within the authority's area.

(2H) The authority concerned shall reimburse the Commissioner on demand any reasonable expenses incurred by the Commissioner in performing his duty under subsection (2G) above."

(2) In section 32 of the Local Government (Scotland) Act 1975 (interpretation of provisions about investigations by the Commissioner) the following subsection shall be inserted after subsection (2)—   1975 c. 30.

"(2A) Except in the case of a joint board or joint committee, references in this Part of this Act to the authority concerned are, in relation to action taken by or on behalf of an authority to whom this Part of this Act applies (whether by virtue of subsection (1) or (2) of section 23 of this Act), references to that authority."

(3) This section shall not have effect in relation to a report made before the coming into force of this section.

PART II
Consideration of
adverse reports:
England and
Wales.
1974 c. 7.

28.—(1) The following section shall be inserted after section 31 of the Local Government Act 1974—

"Consideration
of adverse
reports.

31A.—(1) Subject to subsection (3) below, any power of an authority to have their functions discharged by any person or body of persons acting for the authority shall, as respects the consideration of a further report of the Local Commissioner under section 31(2A) above, be subject to the restriction that, if it is proposed that the authority should take no action on, or not the action recommended in, the report, consideration of the report shall be referred to the authority.

(2) Consideration of a further report of the Local Commissioner under section 31(2A) above by any such committee of a local authority as is referred to in an enactment specified in section 101(9) of the Local Government Act 1972 or by any appeal committee constituted in accordance with paragraph 1 of Schedule 2 to. the Education Act 1980 shall be subject to a corresponding restriction.

(3) The restriction imposed by subsections (1) and (2) above does not apply where the report recommends action to be taken by—

(a) a joint committee established under the said section 101, or

(b) any committee referred to in an enactment specified in paragraph (c), (d) or (h) of the said section 101(9).

(4) If an authority considering a further report of the Local Commissioner under section 31(2A) above take into consideration a report by a person or body with an interest in the Local Commissioner's report, they shall not conclude their consideration of the Local Commissioner's report without also having taken into consideration a report by a person or body with no interest in the Local Commissioner's report.

(5) No member of an authority to which this Part of this Act applies or of a committee mentioned in subsection (2) or (3) above shall vote on any question with respect to a report or further report under this Part of this Act in which he is named and criticised by a Local Commissioner.

(6) Section 25(4) and (5) above do not apply to this section."

(2) This section shall not have effect in relation to a report made before the coming into force of section 26 above.

29.—(1) The following section shall be inserted after section 29 of the Local Government (Scotland) Act 1975—

"Consideration
of adverse
reports.

29A.—(1) Subject to subsection (3) below, any power of an authority to have their functions discharged by any person or body of persons acting for the authority shall, as respects the consideration of a further report of the Commissioner under section 29(2A) of this Act, be subject to the restriction that, if it is proposed to take no action on, or not the action recommended in, the report, consideration of the report shall be referred to the authority.

(2) Consideration of a further report of the Commissioner under section 29(2A) of this Act by—

    (a) any such committee as is mentioned in section 23(2) of this Act; or

    (b) an education committee appointed under section 124 of the Act of 1973;

shall be subject to a corresponding restriction.

(3) The restriction imposed by subsections (1) and (2) above does not apply where the report recommends action to be taken by a joint committee—

    (a) established under section 56 of the Act of 1973 or under paragraph 7 of Schedule 10 or paragraph 6 of Schedule 20 to that Act (local authority, education and social work joint committees); or

    (b) referred to in paragraph (a), (b), or (e) of section 23(2) of this Act (fire, police and local government and teachers' superannuation joint committees).

(4) If an authority considering a further report of the Commissioner under section 29(2A) of this Act take into consideration a report by a person or body with an interest in the Commissioner's report, they shall not conclude their consideration of the Commissioner's report without also having taken into consideration a report by a person or body with no interest in the Commissioner's report.

(5) No member of an authority to which this Part of this Act applies or of a committee mentioned in subsection (2) or (3) above shall vote on any question with respect to a report or further report under this Part of this Act in which he is named and criticised by the Commissioner."

(2) This section shall not have effect in relation to a report made before the coming into force of section 27 above.

30.—(1) Before section 34 of the Local Government (Scotland) Act 1973 there shall be inserted the following section—

"Acceptance of Office

33A.—(1) A person elected to office as a councillor of a local authority shall not, unless—

    (a) he has made a declaration of acceptance of office in a form prescribed by an order made by the Secretary of State; and

Declaration of acceptance of office of councillor etc.
1973 c. 65.

Declaration of acceptance of office of councillor.

(b) the declaration has within two months from the day of the election been delivered to the proper officer of the local authority,

act in the office except for the purpose of taking such a declaration.

(2) If such a declaration is not made and delivered to the proper officer within the appointed time, the office of the person elected shall at the expiration of that time become vacant.

(3) The declaration shall be made before either—

(a) two members of the local authority to which the declarant is elected; or

(b) the proper officer of the local authority; or

(c) the sheriff; or

(d) a justice of the peace.

(4) Any person before whom a declaration is authorised to be made under this section may take the declaration."

1972 c. 70.

(2) In section 83 of the Local Government Act 1972 (declaration of acceptance of office) in subsection (1) and subsection (4), for the words "rules under section 42 above" there shall be substituted the words "an order made by the Secretary of State".

National Code of Local Government Conduct.

31.—(1) The Secretary of State, for the guidance of members of local authorities, may issue a code of recommended practice as regards the conduct of members of such authorities to be known as the National Code of Local Government Conduct.

(2) The Secretary of State may revise or withdraw a code issued under this section.

(3) The Secretary of State, before issuing, revising or withdrawing a code, shall consult—

(a) as respects England and Wales, such representatives of local government, and

(b) as respects Scotland, such associations of local authorities,

as appear to him to be appropriate.

(4) A code shall not be issued unless a draft of it has been laid before and approved by a resolution of each House of Parliament.

(5) Where the Secretary of State proposes to revise a code, he shall lay a draft of the proposed alterations before each House of Parliament and—

(a) he shall not make the revision until after the expiration of the period of 40 days beginning with the day on which the draft is laid (or, if copies are laid before each House of Parliament on different days, with the later of those days); and

(b) if within that period either House resolves that the alterations be withdrawn, he shall not proceed with the proposed alterations (but without prejudice to the laying of a further draft).

(6) In reckoning any period of 40 days for the purposes of subsection (5) above no account shall be taken of any time during which Parliament is dissolved or prorogued or during which both Houses are adjourned for more than four days.

(7) The form of declaration of acceptance of office under section 83 of the Local Government Act 1972 or section 33A of the Local Government (Scotland) Act 1973 may include an undertaking by the declarant to be guided by the National Code of Local Government Conduct in the performance of his functions.

1972 c. 70.
1973 c. 65.

(8) In this section—

"local authority" means—

(a) as respects England and Wales, a county council, a district council, a London borough council, a parish council, a community council, the Common Council of the City of London or the Council of the Isles of Scilly;

(b) as respects Scotland, a regional, islands or district council or a joint board or joint committee within the meaning of section 235(1) of the Local Government (Scotland) Act 1973; and

"member", in relation to a local authority, includes any person who, whether or not a member of the authority, is a member of a committee or sub-committee of the authority or of any joint committee of theirs.

32.—(1) In section 30 of the Local Government Act 1974 (reports on investigations by Local Commissioners)—

Anonymity in reports on investigations.
1974 c. 7.

(a) in subsection (3) (report only to identify a person if the Local Commissioner thinks it necessary), after the words "shall not" there shall be inserted the words ", except where subsection (3A) below applies,"; and

(b) the following subsection shall be inserted after subsection (3)—

"(3A) Where the Local Commissioner is of the opinion—

(a) that action constituting maladministration was taken which involved a member of the authority concerned, and

(b) that the member's conduct constituted a breach of the National Code of Local Government Conduct,

then, unless the Local Commissioner is satisfied that it would be unjust to do so, the report shall name the member and give particulars of the breach."

(2) In section 28 of the Local Government (Scotland) Act 1975 (reports on investigations by Commissioner)—

1975 c. 30.

(a) in subsection (3) (report only to identify a person if the Commissioner thinks it necessary), after the words "shall not" there shall be inserted the words ", except where subsection (3A) below applies,"; and

(b) the following subsection shall be inserted after subsection (3)—

"(3A) Where the Commissioner is of the opinion—

(a) that action constituting maladministration was taken which involved a member of the authority concerned, and

(b) that the member's conduct constituted a breach of the National Code of Local Government Conduct,

then, unless the Commissioner is satisfied that it would be unjust to do so, the report shall name the member and give particulars of the breach."

PART III

ECONOMIC DEVELOPMENT AND DISCRETIONARY EXPENDITURE BY LOCAL AUTHORITIES

Promotion of economic development.

33.—(1) Subject to sections 34 and 35 below, the functions of every relevant authority shall include the taking of such steps as they may from time to time consider appropriate for promoting the economic development of their area.

(2) Subject to those sections and without prejudice to any other provision made by or under this Act, those steps may include participation in and the encouragement of, and provision of financial and other assistance for—

    (a) the setting up or expansion of any commercial, industrial or public undertaking—

        (i) which is to be or is situated in the authority's area; or

        (ii) the setting up or expansion of which appears likely to increase the opportunities for employment of persons living in that area;

    and

    (b) the creation or protection of opportunities for employment with any such undertaking or with any commercial, industrial or public undertaking opportunities for employment with which have been or appear likely to be made available to persons living in that area.

(3) For the purposes of this section a relevant authority shall be treated as providing financial assistance to any person if they do or agree to do any of the following, that is to say—

    (a) make a grant to that person;

    (b) make a loan to that person or provide him with any other form of credit;

    (c) guarantee the performance of any of that person's obligations;

    (d) indemnify that person in respect of any liability, loss or damage;

    (e) invest in that person's undertaking, in the case of a body corporate, by acquiring share or loan capital in that body or otherwise;

    (f) provide that person with any property, services or other financial benefit (including the remission in whole or in part of any liability or obligation) for no consideration or for a consideration which does not satisfy such conditions as may be specified in regulations made by the Secretary of State;

    (g) join with any other person in doing anything falling within paragraphs (a) to (f) above;

(h) enter into such other transaction, in the nature of anything falling within paragraphs (a) to (g) above, as may be specified in regulations made by the Secretary of State.

(4) Regulations under this section may contain such incidental provision and such supplemental, consequential and transitional provision in connection with their other provisions as the Secretary of State considers appropriate.

(5) In this section and sections 34 and 35 below—

"financial year" means the twelve months ending with 31st March;

"relevant authority" means the council of any county, district or London borough, the Common Council of the City of London in its capacity as a local authority or the Council of the Isles of Scilly.

34.—(1) The powers of a relevant authority by virtue of section 33 above, and their powers by virtue of other enactments, shall not include power, for the promotion of the economic development of their area, to take any such steps as may be specified or described for the purposes of this section in regulations made by the Secretary of State.

Restrictions on promotion of economic development.

(2) Without prejudice to the generality of subsection (1) above, the Secretary of State may by regulations impose such conditions, and such other restrictions, as may be specified in or determined under the regulations on the exercise, for the purpose of promoting the economic development of their area, of any power of a relevant authority by virtue of section 33 above or any other enactment to provide financial assistance to any person.

(3) The Secretary of State may by order made by statutory instrument impose such a financial limit as may be specified in or determined under the order on the following expenditure, that is to say, such expenditure as—

(a) is or is of a description so specified or determined; and

(b) by virtue of section 33 above or any other enactment is incurred in any financial year for the purpose of promoting the economic development of their area by a relevant authority so specified or determined.

(4) A statutory instrument containing an order under subsection (3) above shall be subject to annulment in pursuance of a resolution of either House of Parliament.

(5) Regulations under this section may contain such incidental provision and such supplemental, consequential and transitional provision in connection with their other provisions as the Secretary of State considers appropriate.

35.—(1) It shall be the duty of a relevant authority, in determining whether and in what manner to incur any expenditure for the purpose of promoting the economic development of their area, to have regard to such guidance with respect to expenditure for that purpose as may have been given by the Secretary of State to that authority, to relevant authorities of a description applicable to that authority or to relevant authorities generally.

Guidance and consultation about promotion of economic development.

(2) It shall be the duty of a relevant authority, before the beginning of each financial year, to determine whether they will take any steps in that year for the promotion of the economic development of their area.

(3) Where under subsection (2) above a relevant authority make a determination in relation to any financial year that they will take steps in that year for the promotion of the economic development of their area, it shall be the duty of that authority, before the beginning of that year—

(a) to prepare a document setting out their proposals as to the steps to be taken and setting out the other matters mentioned in subsection (4) below;

(b) to make that document available—

(i) to such bodies as are representative of commercial or industrial undertakings in their area;

(ii) to such of the persons carrying on commercial, industrial and public undertakings in their area as they consider appropriate; and

(iii) to such other persons as they think it desirable to consult about the proposals contained in it; and

(c) to consult the persons to whom the document is made available about the proposals contained in it.

(4) The other matters which are required to be set out in the document relating to a relevant authority's proposals as to the taking of any steps are—

(a) the authority's proposals as to the expenditure to be incurred by them in taking those steps and as to the extent to which that expenditure is to be capital or revenue expenditure and is to be attributable to different proposals;

(b) the authority's estimate of any income likely to accrue from the implementation of their proposals; and

(c) what the authority intend the implementation of their proposals to achieve.

Amendments of existing power to incur discretionary expenditure.
1972 c. 70.

36.—(1) Section 137 of the Local Government Act 1972 (power of local authorities to incur expenditure for certain purposes not otherwise authorised) shall be amended in accordance with subsections (2) to (8) below and, accordingly, after the coming into force of this section, shall have effect as set out in Schedule 2 to this Act.

(2) In subsection (1), after the words "in the interests of" there shall be inserted "and will bring direct benefit to"; after the words "incur any expenditure" there shall be inserted "(a)" and at the end there shall be added the words "nor

(b) unless the direct benefit accruing to their area or any part of it or to all or some of the inhabitants of their area will be commensurate with the expenditure to be incurred".

(3) After subsection (1) there shall be inserted the following subsection—

"(1A) In any case where—

(a) by virtue of paragraph (a) of subsection (1) above, a local authority are prohibited from incurring expenditure for a particular purpose, and

(b) the power or duty of the authority to incur expenditure for that purpose is in any respect limited or conditional (whether by being restricted to a particular group of persons or in any other way),

the prohibition in that paragraph shall extend to all expenditure to which that power or duty would apply if it were not subject to any limitation or condition."

(4) Subsections (2A) and (2B) (which relate to the giving of financial assistance to persons carrying on commercial or industrial undertakings) shall cease to have effect and, in subsection (2C), paragraph (a) (which relates to publicity on the promotion of the economic development of the authority's area) shall also cease to have effect.

(5) In subsection (3) (contributions permitted to charitable and public service funds etc.),—

(a) for the words "as aforesaid" there shall be substituted "to the following provisions of this section";

(b) in paragraph (b) after the words "public service" there shall be inserted "(whether to the public at large or to any section of it)"; and

(c) at the end of paragraph (c) there shall be added "or by such a person or body as is referred to in section 83(3)(c) of the Local Government (Scotland) Act 1973".

(6) In subsection (4) (expenditure not to exceed the product of a 2p rate) for the words following "not exceed" there shall be substituted "the amount produced by multiplying—

(a) such sum as is for the time being appropriate to the authority under subsection (4AA) below, by

(b) the relevant population of the authority's area";

and subsection (8) (which relates to the computation of a 2p rate) shall cease to have effect.

(7) After subsection (4) there shall be inserted the following subsections—

"(4AA) For the purposes of subsection (4)(a) above, except in so far as the Secretary of State by order specifies a different sum in relation to an authority of a particular description,—

(a) the sum appropriate to a county council or the council of a non-metropolitan district is £2.50;

(b) the sum appropriate to a metropolitan district council, a London borough council or the Common Council is £5.00; and

(c) the sum appropriate to a parish or community council is £3.50.

(4AB) For the purposes of subsection (4)(b) above the relevant population of a local authority's area shall be determined in accordance with regulations made by the Secretary of State; and a statutory instrument containing such regulations shall be subject to annulment in pursuance of a resolution of the House of Commons."

(8) In subsection (4B) (amounts deductible in determining expenditure under the section) for paragraph (a) there shall be substituted the following paragraph—

"(a) the amount of any expenditure which forms part of the authority's gross expenditure for that year under this section and in respect of which any grant has been or is to be paid under any enactment by a Minister of the Crown, within the meaning of the Ministers of the Crown Act 1975 (whether or not the grant covers the whole of the expenditure)".

1973 c. 65.

(9) In section 83(3) of the Local Government (Scotland) Act 1973 (contributions permitted to charitable and public service funds etc.), at the end of paragraph (c) there shall be added "or by such a person or body as is referred to in section 137(3)(c) of the Local Government Act 1972".

Conditions of provision of financial assistance.
1972 c. 70.

37. After section 137 of the Local Government Act 1972 there shall be inserted the following section—

"Financial assistance to be conditional on provision of information.

137A.—(1) If in any financial year a local authority provides financial assistance—

(a) to a voluntary organisation, as defined in subsection (2D) of section 137 above, or

(b) to a body or fund falling within subsection (3) of that section,

and the total amount so provided to that organisation, body or fund in that year equals or exceeds the relevant minimum, then, as a condition of the assistance, the authority shall require the organisation, body or fund, within the period of twelve months beginning on the date when the assistance is provided, to furnish to the authority a statement in writing of the use to which that amount has been put.

(2) In this section "financial assistance" means assistance by way of grant or loan or by entering into a guarantee to secure any money borrowed and, in relation to any financial assistance,—

(a) any reference to the amount of the assistance is a reference to the amount of money granted or lent by the local authority or borrowed in reliance on the local authority's guarantee; and

(b) any reference to the date when the assistance is provided is a reference to the date on which the grant or loan is made or, as the case may be, on which the guarantee is entered into.

(3) The relevant minimum referred to in subsection (1) above is £2,000 or such higher sum as the Secretary of State may by order specify.

(4) It shall be a sufficient compliance with a requirement imposed by virtue of subsection (1) above that there is furnished to the local authority concerned an annual report or accounts which contain the information required to be in the statement.

(5) A statement (or any report or accounts) provided to a local authority in pursuance of such a requirement shall be deposited with the proper officer of the authority.

(6) In this section "local authority" includes the Common Council."

38.—(1) Section 142 of the Local Government Act 1972 (provision of information, etc.) shall be amended as follows.

(2) There shall be inserted after subsection (2)—

"(2A) A local authority may assist voluntary organisations to provide for individuals—

(a) information and advice concerning those individuals' rights and obligations; and

(b) assistance, either by the making or receiving of communications or by providing representation to or before any person or body, in asserting those rights or fulfilling those obligations."

PART IV

REVENUE ACCOUNTS AND CAPITAL FINANCE OF LOCAL AUTHORITIES

Introductory

39.—(1) For financial years beginning on or after 1st April 1990, this Part has effect with respect to the finances of the following authorities (in this Part referred to as "local authorities")—

(a) a county council;

(b) a district council;

(c) a London borough council;

(d) the Common Council of the City of London;

(e) the Council of the Isles of Scilly;

(f) an authority established under section 10 of the Local Government Act 1985 (waste disposal authorities);

(g) a joint authority established by Part IV of that Act (police, fire services, civil defence and transport);

(h) a joint or special planning board constituted for a National Park by an order under paragraph 1 or paragraph 3 of Schedule 17 to the Local Government Act 1972;

(i) the Broads Authority;

(j) a combined police authority established by an amalgamation scheme under the Police Act 1964; and

(k) any other body prescribed by regulations under subsection (3) below.

(2) The reference in subsection (1)(d) above to the Common Council of the City of London is a reference to that Council in their capacity as a local authority, a police authority or a port health authority.

(3) The Secretary of State may by regulations prescribe for the purposes of subsection (1)(k) above any body which is (or any class of bodies each of which is)—

    (a) a levying body, within the meaning of section 74 of the Local Government Finance Act 1988;

    (b) a body to which section 75 of that Act applies (bodies having power to issue special levies);

    (c) a body to which section 118 of that Act applies; or

    (d) a precepting authority, as defined in section 144(2) of that Act.

(4) Regulations under subsection (3) above may provide that, in relation to a body prescribed by the regulations, the following provisions of this Part shall have effect subject to such modifications as may be specified in the regulations.

(5) For the purposes of the application of this Part, the Secretary of State may by order make provision for treating things done by or to—

    (a) a company which, in accordance with Part V of this Act, is under the control of a local authority, or

    (b) a company which, in accordance with that Part, is for the time being subject to the influence of an authority, or

    (c) a trust to which, by virtue of an order under section 72 below, the provisions of section 69 below are applicable, or

    (d) a Passenger Transport Executive and any company which, in accordance with that Part, is either under the control or for the time being subject to the influence of such an Executive,

in such cases and to such extent as may be provided in the order as if they were done by or to the local authority specified or determined in accordance with the order; and, where an order so provides in relation to a local authority, that authority together with any companies and Executive concerned are in subsection (6) below referred to as members of a local authority group.

(6) Without prejudice to the generality of subsection (5) above, an order under that subsection—

    (a) may provide for the application of the provisions of this Part to the members of a local authority group subject to such modifications as may be specified in the order;

    (b) may make provision as to the way in which dealings between members of a local authority group and changes in the capitalisation or capital structure of any company in a local authority group are to be brought into account for the purposes of this Part; and

    (c) may contain such incidental, supplementary and transitional provisions as the Secretary of State considers appropriate.

(7) The power to make an order under subsection (5) above—

    (a) shall be exercisable by statutory instrument subject to annulment in pursuance of a resolution of either House of Parliament; and

    (b) may make different provision in relation to different cases or descriptions of case.

(8) This Part has effect in place of the provisions of Part VIII of the Local Government, Planning and Land Act 1980.

40.—(1) References in this Part to expenditure for capital purposes shall be construed in accordance with this section.

(2) Subject to subsections (5) and (6) below, the following expenditure (relating to tangible assets) is expenditure for capital purposes, namely, expenditure on—

   (a) the acquisition, reclamation, enhancement or laying out of land, exclusive of roads, buildings and other structures;

   (b) the acquisition, construction, preparation, enhancement or replacement of roads, buildings and other structures; and

   (c) the acquisition, installation or replacement of movable or immovable plant, machinery and apparatus and vehicles and vessels.

(3) For the purposes of subsection (2) above, "enhancement", in relation to any asset, means the carrying out of works which are intended—

   (a) to lengthen substantially the useful life of the asset; or

   (b) to increase substantially the open market value of the asset; or

   (c) to increase substantially the extent to which the asset can or will be used for the purposes of or in connection with the functions of the local authority concerned;

but expenditure on the enhancement of an asset shall not be regarded as expenditure for capital purposes unless it should be so regarded in accordance with proper practices.

(4) Subject to subsection (5) below, the following expenditure, in so far as it is not expenditure on approved investments, is expenditure for capital purposes, namely, expenditure on—

   (a) the making of advances, grants or other financial assistance to any person towards expenditure incurred or to be incurred by him on the matters mentioned in paragraphs (a) to (c) of subsection (2) above or on the acquisition of investments; and

   (b) the acquisition of share capital or loan capital in any body corporate.

(5) The Secretary of State may by regulations provide—

   (a) that expenditure which, apart from the provision made by the regulations, would not be expenditure for capital purposes shall be such expenditure; or

   (b) that expenditure which, apart from the provision made by the regulations, would be expenditure for capital purposes shall not be such expenditure.

(6) Notwithstanding anything in the preceding provisions of this section, if the Secretary of State so directs, expenditure which—

   (a) is of a description or for a purpose specified in the direction, and

   (b) has been or is to be incurred by a particular local authority, and

   (c) does not exceed such amount as is specified in the direction, and

(d) was or will be incurred during a period specified in the direction,

may be treated by the authority concerned as expenditure for capital purposes.

Charge of expenditure to revenue accounts

Expenditure to be charged to revenue account.

41.—(1) All expenditure incurred by a local authority, other than expenditure excluded by section 42 below, must be charged to a revenue account of the authority and unless, in accordance with proper practices (exclusive of this subsection), it is appropriate to charge some or all of any particular item of expenditure to a revenue account for an earlier or a later financial year, the expenditure shall be charged to a revenue account of the authority for the year in which it is incurred.

(2) In relation to a local authority, any reference to a revenue account is a reference to one of the following accounts for a financial year of the authority, namely—

(a) a revenue account which the authority are required to keep by virtue of any enactment;

(b) a revenue account which the authority are required to keep in order to comply with proper practices; or

(c) any other revenue account which the authority decide to keep in accordance with proper practices.

(3) The reference in subsection (1) above to expenditure incurred by a local authority in any financial year includes the following (whether or not giving rise to actual payments)—

(a) any amount which does not form part of the authority's capital receipts and which is set aside for the year by the authority as provision to meet credit liabilities, otherwise than by virtue of any of subsections (2) to (4) of section 63 below; and

(b) any other amount which is set aside for the year by the authority as reasonably necessary for the purpose of providing for any liability or loss which is likely or certain to be incurred but is uncertain as to the amount or the date on which it will arise (or both);

and the reference in subsection (5) below to expenditure incurred by a local authority shall be construed in accordance with this subsection.

(4) Subsection (2) above has effect not only for the purposes of this Act but also for the purposes of—

(a) any enactment passed after or in the same Session as this Act; and

(b) any earlier enactment which is amended by this Act or by any such enactment as is referred to in paragraph (a) above.

(5) Nothing in this section or the following provisions of this Part shall permit an authority to charge to a revenue account which they are required to keep by virtue of Part VI of this Act or any other enactment any expenditure incurred by a local authority which could not otherwise be so charged.

42.—(1) Expenditure falling within subsection (2) below is excluded from the obligation in section 41(1) above but, if it is consistent with proper practices and the authority so wish, any such expenditure may be charged to a revenue account of the authority for the financial year in which it is incurred or an earlier or later financial year.

(2) Subject to subsection (4) below, the expenditure referred to in subsection (1) above is as follows—

    (a) expenditure arising from the discharge of any liability of the authority under a credit arrangement, other than an arrangement excluded by regulations under paragraph 11 of Schedule 3 to this Act;

    (b) expenditure arising from the discharge of any liability of the authority in respect of money borrowed by the authority, other than a liability in respect of interest;

    (c) expenditure which, in reliance on a credit approval, the authority have determined under section 56(1)(a) below is not to be chargeable to a revenue account of the authority;

    (d) expenditure on making approved investments;

    (e) expenditure consisting of the application or payment of capital receipts as mentioned in subsections (7) to (9) of section 59 below;

    (f) expenditure which is met out of the usable part of capital receipts, in accordance with section 60(2) below;

    (g) expenditure for capital purposes which the authority determine is, or is to be, reimbursed or met out of money provided, or to be provided, by any other person, excluding grants from a Community institution;

    (h) expenditure in respect of payments out of a superannuation fund which the authority are required to keep by virtue of the Superannuation Act 1972; and

    (i) expenditure in respect of payments out of a trust fund which is held for charitable purposes and of which the authority are a trustee.

(3) A determination under subsection (2)(g) above may not be made later than 30th September in the financial year following that in which the expenditure in question is incurred.

(4) Regulations made by the Secretary of State may amend subsection (2) above—

    (a) by adding a description of expenditure specified in the regulations to the expenditure falling within that subsection; or

    (b) by removing a description of expenditure specified in the regulations from the expenditure falling within that subsection (whether the expenditure so specified was within that subsection as originally enacted or was added by virtue of this subsection).

(5) Where, by virtue of subsection (1) above, expenditure of any description is excluded from the obligation in section 41(1) above, it shall also be excluded from any requirement arising under any enactment (including an enactment in Part VI of this Act) under which the expenditure is required to be charged to a revenue account or any particular revenue account; but if—

(a) an authority decide that expenditure of that description should be charged to a revenue account as mentioned in subsection (1) above, and

(b) under any such requirement that expenditure (apart from this subsection) would have to be charged to a particular revenue account,

that expenditure may be charged only to that revenue account.

Borrowing

Borrowing powers.

43.—(1) Subject to the following provisions of this Part, as part of the proper management of their affairs, a local authority may borrow money for any purpose relevant to their functions under any enactment.

(2) Except with the approval of the Secretary of State given with the consent of the Treasury, a local authority may not borrow money in any manner other than—

(a) by overdraft or short term from the Bank of England or from a body or partnership which, at the time the borrowing is undertaken, is an authorised institution within the meaning of the Banking Act 1987; or

1987 c. 22.

(b) from the National Debt Commissioners or from the Public Works Loan Commissioners; or

(c) by means of a loan instrument;

and in paragraph (a) above borrowing "short term" shall be construed in accordance with section 45(6) below.

(3) In the exercise of the powers conferred by paragraphs (a) to (c) of subsection (2) above, a local authority may not, without the consent of the Treasury, borrow from a lender outside the United Kingdom or otherwise than in sterling.

(4) Subject to any provision made by regulations under subsection (5) below, for the purposes of this Part, a loan instrument is any document which, directly or by reference to any other document,—

(a) contains an acknowledgment (by the borrower, the lender or both) that a loan has been made to the local authority concerned or that, in connection with the provision of funds to the authority, a payment or repayment is due from the authority; and

(b) states the dates on which the authority are to make payments or repayments; and

(c) states the amount of each of those payments or repayments or the method by which that amount is to be calculated; and

(d) specifies the means, if any, by which the rights or obligations under the instrument are transferable; and

(e) except in the case of an instrument which is transferable by delivery, specifies the name or description of the person to whom payments or repayments are due; and

(f) in the case of an instrument issued by two or more local authorities acting jointly, states what proportion of the payments or repayments due are the responsibility of each of the authorities concerned.

(5) With the consent of the Treasury, the Secretary of State may make regulations—

(a) regulating the terms of loan instruments and the manner of their issue, transfer or redemption;

(b) restricting the issue of instruments which are transferable by delivery;

(c) regulating the manner in which any payments or repayments are to be made to the holder of the instrument; and

(d) making provision for the custody and, where appropriate, eventual destruction of documents relating to loan instruments;

and any document which, at the time it comes into being, does not comply with any provision then made under paragraphs (a) to (c) above is not a loan instrument for the purposes of this Part.

(6) Any approval given by the Secretary of State under subsection (2) above and any consent given by the Treasury under subsection (3) above may be given generally or in a particular case or to authorities of a particular description or by reference to borrowing or securities of a particular description and may be given subject to conditions.

(7) In so far as any local authority have power under any private or local Act to borrow money (whether for general or specific purposes), any such power shall cease to have effect for financial years beginning on or after 1st April 1990.

(8) Subject to subsection (7) above, subsections (2) to (6) above apply to all borrowing powers for the time being available to a local authority under any enactment, whenever passed.

44.—(1) A local authority may not at any time borrow an amount which would cause the total of—

Borrowing limits etc.

(a) the amount outstanding at that time by way of principal of money borrowed by the authority, and

(b) the aggregate cost (as determined below) at that time of the credit arrangements entered into by the authority, other than arrangements excluded by regulations under paragraph 11 of Schedule 3 to this Act,

to exceed the aggregate credit limit for the time being applicable to the authority by virtue of section 62 below.

(2) The Secretary of State may by regulations make provision, in the interests of prudent financial management, regulating borrowing by local authorities; and a local authority may not borrow to any extent or in any manner which would contravene any provision of the regulations.

(3) A local authority may not borrow any amount which would cause any limit for the time being determined by the authority under section 45 below to be exceeded.

(4) References in this section and sections 45 to 47 below to borrowing by an authority are references to borrowing not only under section 43 above but also under any other power for the time being available to the authority under any enactment, whenever passed.

(5) For the purposes of subsection (1) above, the temporary use by a local authority for a purpose other than that of the fund in question of money forming part of such a superannuation fund or trust fund as is referred to in paragraph (h) or paragraph (i) of subsection (2) of section 42 above shall be treated as borrowing.

(6) A person lending money to a local authority shall not be bound to enquire whether the authority have power to borrow the money and shall not be prejudiced by the absence of any such power.

The authority's own limits.

45.—(1) For the purposes of this Part, for each financial year every local authority shall determine—

(a) an amount of money (in this Part referred to as "the overall borrowing limit") which is for the time being the maximum amount which the authority may have outstanding by way of borrowing;

(b) an amount of money (in this Part referred to as "the short-term borrowing limit"), being a part of the overall borrowing limit, which is for the time being the maximum amount which the authority may have outstanding by way of short term borrowing; and

(c) a limit on the proportion of the total amount of interest payable by the authority which is at a rate or rates which can be varied by the person to whom it is payable or which vary by reference to any external factors.

(2) Subject to subsection (3) below, the duty to determine the limits referred to in subsection (1) above shall be performed before the beginning of the financial year to which the limits are to relate.

(3) Where a local authority have determined a limit for a financial year under subsection (1) above, the authority may at any time (whether before or after the beginning of that year) vary that limit by making a new determination thereof.

1972 c. 70.

(4) Section 101 of the Local Government Act 1972 (arrangements for discharge of functions of local authorities by committees, officers etc.) shall not apply to the duty to make a determination under subsection (1) above of any limit or to the power to vary a limit under subsection (3) above.

(5) Without prejudice to subsection (4) above, in section 101(6) of the Local Government Act 1972 (which provides that certain functions, including borrowing, shall be discharged only by the authority) the words "or borrowing money" shall be omitted.

(6) For the purposes of subsection (1)(b) above, a local authority borrow money short term if the sum borrowed is repayable—

(a) without notice; or

(b) at less than twelve months notice; or

(c) within twelve months of the date of the borrowing.

46.—(1) Every local authority shall maintain a register giving particulars of all the loans in respect of which loan instruments are issued by or to the authority on or after 1st April 1990 and, if they think it appropriate, a local authority may appoint as a registrar for some or all of the purposes of such a register a person who is neither an officer nor any other employee of the authority.

(2) In the register required to be maintained by a local authority under this section, the authority shall, not later than 30th September 1990, enter particulars of all outstanding loans in respect of which any payment or repayment falls to be made by the authority (whether or not any loan instruments have been issued), other than those resulting from borrowing as mentioned in paragraph (a) or paragraph (b) of subsection (2) of section 43 above; and, for this purpose, an "outstanding loan" is one which was made before 1st April 1990 and in respect of which any payment or repayment falls to be made on or after that date.

(3) Subject to the following provisions of this section, a register required to be maintained under this section shall be in such form as the authority concerned consider appropriate; but that form must be such that the register is, or is capable of being reproduced, in legible form.

(4) A register maintained under this section shall contain, with respect to each loan of which particulars are required to be registered,—

(a) except in the case of a loan in respect of which there has been issued an instrument (whether or not being a loan instrument) transferable by delivery, the name or description, and the address, of the person to whom payments or repayments are due;

(b) the dates on which the payments or repayments are to be made; and

(c) the amount of each of those payments or repayments or the method by which that amount is to be calculated.

(5) A local authority may remove from a register maintained under this section particulars of any loan in respect of which no more payments or repayments fall to be made.

(6) With the consent of the Treasury, the Secretary of State may make regulations—

(a) generally with respect to the keeping of a register required to be maintained under this section;

(b) modifying all or any of the particulars specified in paragraphs (a) to (c) of subsection (4) above; and

(c) specifying additional particulars which are to be entered in a register maintained under this section.

(7) A copy of an entry in a register maintained under this section which is certified by a registrar of the register and purports to show particulars entered pursuant to subsection (4) or subsection (6) above shall be prima facie evidence of the matters specified in the entry.

(8) A certification by a registrar of a register maintained under this section of any instrument of transfer of a loan instrument is to be taken as a representation by him to any person acting on the faith of the certification that there have been produced to the registrar such documents as on their face show a prima facie title to the loan instrument

PART IV

in the transferor named in the instrument of transfer; but such a certification shall not be taken as a representation that the transferor has any title to the loan instrument.

(9) If—

  (a) the name of any person is, without sufficient cause, entered in or omitted from a register maintained under this section, or

  (b) default is made or unnecessary delay takes place in making any entry required to be made in such a register,

the person aggrieved may apply to the High Court or a county court for rectification of the register.

(10) Where an application is made under subsection (9) above, the court—

  (a) may refuse the application or order rectification of the register;

  (b) may decide any question relating to the title of a person who is a party to the application to have his name entered in or omitted from the register; and

  (c) generally may decide any question necessary or expedient to be decided for rectification of the register.

Security for money borrowed etc.

47.—(1) All money borrowed by a local authority (whether before or after the coming into force of this section), together with any interest thereon, shall be charged indifferently on all the revenues of the authority.

(2) Subject to subsection (3) below, all securities created by a local authority shall rank equally without any priority.

(3) Subsection (2) above does not affect any priority existing at, or any right to priority conferred by a security created before, 1st June 1934.

(4) If at any time any principal or interest due in respect of any borrowing by a local authority remains unpaid for a period of two months after demand in writing, then, subject to subsection (5) below, the person entitled to the sum due may, without prejudice to any other remedy, apply to any court having jurisdiction in respect of a claim for that sum for the appointment of a receiver; and, if it thinks fit, the court may appoint a receiver on such terms and with such powers as the court thinks fit.

(5) No application may be made under subsection (4) above unless the sum due in respect of the borrowing concerned amounts to not less than £5,000 or such other amount as may from time to time be prescribed for the purposes of this subsection by regulations made by the Secretary of State.

(6) The court to whom an application is made under subsection (4) above may confer upon the receiver any such powers of collecting, receiving and recovering the revenues of the local authority and of issuing levies and precepts and setting, collecting and recovering community charges as are possessed by the local authority.

(7) Except as provided by subsection (1) above, a local authority may not mortgage or charge any of their property as security for money borrowed or otherwise owing by them; and any security purporting to be given in contravention of this subsection shall be unenforceable.

Credit arrangements

48.—(1) Subject to the following provisions of this section, a local Credit
authority shall be taken for the purposes of this Part to have entered into arrangements.
a credit arrangement—

(a) in any case where they become the lessees of any property
(whether land or goods); and

(b) in any case (not falling within paragraph (a) above) where, under
a single contract or two or more contracts taken together, it is
estimated by the authority that the value of the consideration
which the authority have still to give at the end of a relevant
financial year for or in connection with the provision to the
authority of any land, goods or services or any other kind of
benefit is greater than the value of the consideration (if any)
which the authority were still to receive immediately before the
beginning of that financial year; and

(c) in any case where the authority enter into a transaction of a
description for the time being prescribed for the purposes of this
section by regulations made by the Secretary of State;

and, in any such case, the "credit arrangement" is the lease, the single
contract or, as the case may be, the two or more contracts taken together.

(2) The estimate required to be made under paragraph (b) of
subsection (1) above shall be made at the time the contract or, as the case
may be, the later or last of the contracts constituting the credit
arrangement is entered into; and the reference in that paragraph to a
relevant financial year is a reference to a financial year which begins after
the contract or, as the case may be, the first of the contracts constituting
the arrangement was entered into.

(3) Subject to section 52 below, references in this Part, other than this
section, to a credit arrangement do not apply to a credit arrangement
which comes into being before 1st April 1990; and for the purpose of this
Part a credit arrangement comes into being—

(a) where subsection (1)(a) above applies, at the time the local
authority become the lessees;

(b) where subsection (1)(b) above applies, at the time the contract
or, as the case may be, the later or latest of the contracts
constituting the arrangement is entered into; and

(c) where subsection (1)(c) above applies, at the time the authority
enter into the transaction concerned or such other time as may
be specified in the regulations concerned.

(4) Where a contract constitutes, or two or more contracts taken
together constitute, a credit arrangement, no account shall be taken under
this section of any later contract which has the effect of varying the effect
of the contract or, as the case may be, of the two or more contracts taken
together.

(5) A contract is not a credit arrangement to the extent that it is a
contract under which a local authority borrows money; and a lease or
contract which is excluded from this section by regulations made by the
Secretary of State is not a credit arrangement.

(6) It is immaterial for the purposes of this section whether the consideration given or received by a local authority under any contract is given to or received from the person by whom the land, goods, services or other benefit are in fact provided to the authority; and for the purposes of this section, and any of the following provisions of this Part relating to credit arrangements, in any case where the consideration under a contract consists, in whole or in part,—

(a) of an undertaking to do or to refrain from doing something at a future time (whether specified or not), or

(b) of a right to do or to refrain from doing something at such a future time,

that consideration shall be regarded as neither given nor received until the undertaking is performed or, as the case may be, the right is exercised.

(7) Where the consideration under a contract consists, in whole or in part, of an option, the estimate required to be made under subsection (1)(b) above shall be made—

(a) on the assumption that the option will be exercised or, if the option could be exercised in different ways, on the assumption that it will be exercised in each of those ways, and

(b) on the assumption that the option will not be exercised,

and if, on any of those assumptions, the contract would on those estimates constitute, alone or together with one or more other contracts, a credit arrangement, it shall be regarded as doing so regardless of whether the option is or is not in fact exercised; and in this subsection "option" includes any right which is exercisable or not at the discretion of a party to the contract.

(8) If an existing contract is varied and the variation does not in law itself constitute a contract, it shall be regarded as such for the purposes of this section and, accordingly, subject to subsection (4) above, the existing contract and the variation shall be regarded as two contracts to be taken together.

Initial and subsequent cost of credit arrangements.

49.—(1) Subject to subsection (3) and section 52 below, for the purposes of this Part the initial cost of a credit arrangement is the amount which, at the time the arrangement comes into being, the local authority estimate will be the aggregate of—

(a) any consideration which falls to be given by the authority under the arrangement in the financial year in which it comes into being; and

(b) the value of the consideration falling to be given by the authority under the arrangement in any subsequent financial year, determined in accordance with subsection (2) below.

(2) For each subsequent financial year referred to in subsection (1)(b) above, the value of the consideration falling to be given in that year shall be determined by the formula—

$$\frac{x}{\left(1 + \frac{r}{100}\right)^n}$$

where—

"x" is the amount of the consideration which the authority estimate will be given by them under the arrangement in that financial year;

"r" is the percentage rate of discount prescribed for the financial year in which the arrangement came into being by regulations made by the Secretary of State for the purposes of this section; and

"n" is the financial year in which the consideration falls to be given expressed as a year subsequent to the financial year in which the arrangement came into being (so that the first of the subsequent financial years is 1, the next financial year is 2, and so on).

(3) Subsection (2) above does not apply to a credit arrangement of a description excluded from that subsection by regulations made by the Secretary of State; and, in relation to a credit arrangement which is so excluded, regulations so made shall make provision for the method of calculating the initial cost and the cost of the arrangement at any time.

(4) Subject to subsection (3) above and sections 51 and 52 below, the cost of a credit arrangement at any time after it has come into being shall be determined in accordance with subsections (1) and (2) above (in like manner as the determination of the initial cost) but on the basis of an estimate made at the time in question and leaving out of account any consideration which has been given by the authority under the arrangement before that time.

(5) In the application of this section to a credit arrangement which consists, in whole or in part, of a contract, the consideration under which falls within subsection (7) of section 48 above,—

(a) if the credit arrangement exists only on the basis of one of the assumptions in that subsection, the local authority shall make that assumption for the purposes of this section; and

(b) if the credit arrangement would exist on the basis of any two or more of those assumptions, the authority shall for the purposes of this section make whichever of those assumptions seems to them most likely.

50.—(1) A local authority may not enter into a credit arrangement for any purpose unless, if they incurred expenditure for that purpose, it would be expenditure for capital purposes, and any reference in the following provisions of this Part to "capital purposes", in relation to a credit arrangement, shall be construed accordingly.

Limits on powers to enter into credit arrangements.

(2) A local authority may not enter into a credit arrangement unless, at the time the arrangement comes into being, there is available to the authority an amount of credit cover equal to the initial cost of the arrangement.

(3) For the purposes of this section, each of the following amounts constitutes, in relation to a credit arrangement, an amount of credit cover available to a local authority,—

(a) an amount for the time being authorised by a credit approval issued to the authority;

(b) an amount of the usable part of capital receipts which, in accordance with a determination under section 60(2) below referring to the arrangement, is applied by the authority as provision to meet credit liabilities; and

(c) an amount which, in accordance with a determination of the authority referring to the arrangement, is set aside from a revenue account by the authority as provision to meet credit liabilities (being an amount over and above what they are required so to set aside by virtue of any other provision of this Part).

(4) A local authority may not enter into a credit arrangement at any time if to do so would at that time cause the total referred to in section 44(1) above to exceed the aggregate credit limit for the time being applicable to the authority by virtue of section 62 below.

(5) A determination under subsection (3)(c) above may not be made later than 30th September in the financial year following that in which falls the time when there comes into being the credit arrangement for which the credit cover is made available.

(6) Except in so far as they are applied by section 52 below, the preceding provisions of this section do not apply in relation to a transitional credit arrangement.

Variation of credit arrangements.

51.—(1) This section (other than subsection (10) below) applies where the terms of a credit arrangement entered into by a local authority are varied (whether by the making of a new contract or otherwise) in such a way that, if the effect of the variation had been part of the arrangement at the time it came into being, the initial cost would have been greater than it was.

(2) If, in the case of a credit arrangement falling within subsection (5) of section 49 above,—

(a) the option in question is exercised in a way different from that which was assumed for the purposes of that section, or

(b) it was assumed for the purposes of that section that the option in question would not be exercised but it is in fact exercised,

the exercise of the option shall be regarded for the purposes of this section as a variation of the terms of the credit arrangement; and if, in such a case, it was assumed for the purposes of section 49 above that the option would be exercised (or would be exercised in a particular way) and it subsequently appears to the local authority that it will not in fact be exercised, the option shall be assumed to have been abandoned and that abandonment shall be regarded for the purposes of this section as a variation of the terms of the credit arrangement.

(3) A local authority may not at any time agree to such a variation as is mentioned in subsection (1) above if to do so would mean that, immediately after the variation, the total referred to in section 44(1) above would exceed the aggregate credit limit for the time being applicable to the authority by virtue of section 62 below.

(4) Where a credit arrangement is varied as mentioned in subsection (1) above, the local authority shall secure that there is available to it an amount of credit cover equal to whichever is the less of—

(a) the difference between the total amount of consideration paid and payable under the arrangement, disregarding the variation and the total amount of the consideration paid and payable under the arrangement as varied; and

(b) the difference between the adjusted cost of the arrangement and the credit cover already made available in connection with the arrangement in accordance with section 50 above;

and subsections (3) and (5) of section 50 above apply for the purposes of this section as they apply for the purposes of that section, except that, in subsection (5), the reference to the time when the arrangement comes into being shall be construed as a reference to the time when it is varied.

(5) Subject to subsection (7) below, the adjusted cost of the arrangement referred to in subsection (4)(b) above is the aggregate of—

(a) the consideration which, in the financial year in which the arrangement is varied and in any earlier financial year, has been or falls to be given by the local authority; and

(b) the amount which, at the time of the variation, the authority estimate will be the cost of the arrangement, as varied, in each subsequent financial year determined as follows.

(6) Subject to subsection (7) below, for any subsequent financial year the cost of the arrangement as varied shall be determined by the formula in section 49(2) above but, for this purpose,—

"x" is the amount of the consideration which the authority estimate will be given by them in that financial year under the arrangement as varied;

"r" is the percentage rate of discount for the financial year in which the arrangement is varied, as prescribed by regulations made by the Secretary of State for the purposes of section 49 above;

"n" is the financial year in which the consideration falls to be given, expressed as a year subsequent to the financial year in which the arrangement is varied (so that the first of the subsequent financial years is 1, the next is 2, and so on).

(7) Subsections (5) and (6) above do not apply in relation to a credit arrangement as to which the method of calculating the initial cost and the cost at any time is provided for by regulations under section 49(3) above; and any adjusted cost or cost which would otherwise fall to be determined in accordance with those subsections shall be determined in accordance with provisions made by the regulations.

(8) Where a credit arrangement is varied as mentioned in subsection (1) above, the cost of the arrangement at any time after the variation shall be determined in accordance with subsections (5) and (6) above (in like manner as the determination of the adjusted cost) but on the basis of an estimate made at the time in question and leaving out of account any consideration which has been given by the authority under the arrangement before that time.

(9) If, at any time after the terms of a credit arrangement have been varied as mentioned in subsection (1) above, the terms of the arrangement are again varied, the preceding provisions of this section shall have effect with any necessary modifications and, in particular, as if,—

(a) the reference in subsection (1) above to the time the arrangement came into being were a reference to the time at which the arrangement was varied (or, as the case may be, last varied) as mentioned in that subsection;

(b) the reference in that subsection to the initial cost were a reference to the adjusted cost of the arrangement as so varied (or last varied); and

(c) the reference in paragraph (b) of subsection (4) above to the credit cover already made available in accordance with section 50 above included a reference to any additional credit cover made available under that subsection at the time of an earlier variation.

(10) If at any time the terms of a credit arrangement are varied otherwise than as mentioned in subsection (1) above, then, so far as the variation affects the consideration falling to be paid by the local authority in any year, account shall be taken of the variation in determining the cost of the arrangement at any subsequent time (under subsection (8) above or subsection (3) or subsection (4) of section 49 above) but for other purposes the variation shall be disregarded.

Transitional credit arrangements.

52.—(1) Subject to the following provisions of this section, a local authority shall be taken to have entered into a transitional credit arrangement if, applying the rules in section 48(3) above, the arrangement came into being on or after 7th July 1988 and before 1st April 1990; and, except in so far as any provision of this Part otherwise provides, any reference in this Part to a credit arrangement includes a reference to a transitional credit arrangement.

(2) Notwithstanding that a credit arrangement came into being as mentioned in subsection (1) above it is not a transitional credit arrangement if—

(a) under the arrangement the local authority concerned became the lessees of any property (whether land or goods) and the arrangement was a credit arrangement by reason only of section 48(1)(a) above; or

(b) by virtue of subsection (11) or subsection (12) of section 80 of the Local Government, Planning and Land Act 1980 (valuation etc.) the amount of prescribed expenditure which the authority is to be taken as having paid on entering into the arrangement was nil; or

1980 c. 65.

(c) by virtue of regulations under paragraph 4 of Schedule 12 to that Act, any expenditure of the authority under the arrangement was not prescribed expenditure; or

(d) the arrangement related only to works which, in whole or in part, were carried out before 1st April 1990 and in relation to which, by reason only of regulations under subsection (7) of section 80A of that Act (payment for works), subsection (1) of that section did not apply or, to the extent that the works were carried out on or after that date, would not have applied if they had been carried out before that date.

(3) For the purpose of the application of sections 49 and 51 above in relation to a transitional credit arrangement—

   (a) such an arrangement shall be taken to have come into being (in the form in which it was on 1st April 1990) on that date (and, accordingly, any consideration given under the arrangement before that date shall be disregarded); and

   (b) the local authority shall be taken to have made available in connection with the arrangement (and in accordance with section 50 above) an amount of credit cover equal to the cost of the arrangement on 1st April 1990.

Credit approvals

53.—(1) Before the beginning of each financial year, the Secretary of State shall issue to each local authority, in the form of a notice in writing, a credit approval with respect to the authority's credit arrangements and expenditure for capital purposes during that year.

(2) A credit approval issued under this section (in this Part referred to as a "basic credit approval") may be nil but, subject to that, shall be expressed as an amount of money.

(3) A basic credit approval shall have effect only for the financial year in respect of which it is issued and may be limited by excluding from the purposes for which the approval may be used capital purposes of a description specified in the approval.

(4) Where regulations made by the Secretary of State so require, a basic credit approval shall specify, directly or by reference to tables or other documents specified in the approval, a period (in this Part referred to as the "amortisation period") during which the authority to whom the approval is issued are required to set aside, from a revenue account, as provision to meet credit liabilities, amounts determined in accordance with the regulations.

(5) Under subsection (4) above, if the regulations so provide, a basic credit approval may specify different amortisation periods in relation to the use of the approval in respect of credit arrangements and expenditure for capital purposes of different descriptions.

54.—(1) Any Minister of the Crown may at any time issue to a local authority, in the form of a notice in writing, a credit approval (in this Part referred to as a "supplementary credit approval").

(2) A supplementary credit approval shall be expressed as an amount of money and shall be limited to credit arrangements and expenditure for capital purposes of a description specified in the approval (but, if the Minister concerned considers appropriate, all capital purposes may be so specified).

(3) A supplementary credit approval shall have effect for such period as is specified in the approval; and where such an approval is issued not more than six months after the end of a financial year, it may specify a period which begins or begins and ends at any time during that financial year.

(4) Subject to subsection (5) below, subsections (4) and (5) of section 53 above apply in relation to a supplementary credit approval as they apply in relation to a basic credit approval.

Basic credit approvals.

Supplementary credit approvals.

(5) In the case of a supplementary credit approval issued in respect of expenditure which is treated by the authority concerned as expenditure for capital purposes by virtue only of directions under section 40(6) above, the approval must specify an amortisation period and the maximum amortisation period which may be specified shall be seven years.

Criteria for issuing credit approvals.

55.—(1) In determining the amount of a basic credit approval or a supplementary credit approval to be issued to a local authority, the Secretary of State or other Minister may have regard, subject to the following provisions of this section, to such factors as appear to him to be appropriate.

(2) Without prejudice to the generality of subsection (1) above, the Secretary of State or other Minister may, in particular, have regard—

   (a) to the amount of any grants or contributions which it appears to him that the authority concerned have received and are likely to receive from any person in respect of expenditure incurred by the authority or to be incurred by them before the expiry of the period for which the credit approval is to have effect; and

   (b) subject to subsection (3) below, to the amount of capital receipts which it appears to him that the authority have received, might reasonably be expected to have received or to receive or are likely to receive before the expiry of the period for which the credit approval is to have effect.

(3) In determining the amount of a credit approval, the Secretary of State or other Minister shall not take account of capital receipts—

   (a) to the extent that the authority concerned are required to set aside the receipts as provision for credit liabilities; or

   (b) to the extent that they are applied or paid as mentioned in subsections (7) to (9) of section 59 below.

(4) In determining the amount of the basic credit approval or of a supplementary credit approval to be issued to a particular local authority in any financial year, the Secretary of State or other Minister shall not take account of the extent to which it appears to him that the local authority are or are likely to be in a position to finance expenditure for capital purposes from a revenue account.

1980 c. 65.

(5) In this section "capital receipts" includes sums which constituted capital receipts for the purposes of Part VIII of the Local Government, Planning and Land Act 1980, whether or not they fall to be treated as capital receipts under section 58 below.

Use of credit approvals by local authorities.

56.—(1) Subject to Part I of Schedule 3 to this Act, where a local authority have received a basic credit approval or a supplementary credit approval, then, if they so determine, the approval may be treated wholly or partly—

   (a) as authority not to charge to a revenue account an amount of expenditure which is defrayed during the period for which the approval has effect and which is for capital purposes to which the approval applies; or

(b) as authority, within the period for which the approval has effect, to enter into or agree to a variation of a credit arrangement for purposes to which the approval applies.

(2) Where a local authority have received a basic credit approval or a supplementary credit approval and that approval is not extinguished under section 57 below or Part I of Schedule 3 to this Act, then, if or to the extent that they have not made a determination with respect to it under subsection (1) above, the authority may, if they so determine, transfer the approval, reduced where appropriate under that section or Part, to another local authority, either in whole or in part; and, where such a transfer is made,—

(a) the transfer of the approval (or part) shall not be regarded for the purposes of this Part as its use by the transferor authority; and

(b) this Part (including this section) shall have effect as if the approval (subject to any reduction as mentioned above) had been issued, in whole or as to the part transferred, directly to the transferee authority.

(3) To the extent that and at the time when, in reliance on a credit approval,—

(a) an amount of expenditure which is not charged to a revenue account of the authority concerned is defrayed, or

(b) the authority concerned enter into or agree to a variation of a credit arrangement,

the credit approval shall be regarded as used and, accordingly, shall not be available on any subsequent occasion or for any other purpose.

(4) Subsection (3) above applies whether or not the determination under subsection (1) above precedes the date on which the expenditure is defrayed or, as the case may be, the credit arrangement is entered into or varied.

(5) A determination by a local authority under subsection (1) above that a credit approval is to be treated as mentioned in paragraph (a) or paragraph (b) of that subsection may not be made later than 30th September in the financial year following that in which the authority defray the expenditure or, as the case may be, enter into or vary the credit arrangement in question.

57.—(1) In this section "specified capital grants" means grants, contributions and subsidies—

(a) which are paid to local authorities in aid of their expenditure for capital purposes;

(b) which are neither commuted payments falling within subsection (2) of section 63 below nor single or other payments falling within subsection (3) of that section; and

(c) which are, or to the extent that they are, specified for the purposes of this section by regulations made by the Secretary of State.

(2) If at any time a local authority receive a specified capital grant, such, if any, of the authority's credit approvals as are relevant to that grant shall, in accordance with the following provisions of this section, be reduced or, as the case may be, extinguished by deducting therefrom an amount equal to the grant.

(3) For the purposes of this section, a credit approval is relevant to a specified capital grant if—

> (a) the approval has effect at the time the grant is received or at any time thereafter; and
>
> (b) the purposes for which the approval may be used are or include the purposes towards expenditure on which the grant is made.

(4) Subject to subsections (5) and (6) below, where, by virtue of subsection (2) above, a deduction is required in respect of a specified capital grant,—

> (a) the deduction shall be applied to the credit approvals which are relevant to the grant in the order in which those approvals were received;
>
> (b) subject to paragraph (d) below, the reduction or extinguishment of any such approval shall be regarded as taking place when the grant is received;
>
> (c) if the amount of the deduction exceeds the total of the credit approvals which are relevant to the grant and were received before the grant, the excess shall be applied in reduction (or extinguishment) of credit approvals which are so relevant and are received later; and
>
> (d) any such reduction or extinguishment of a later credit approval as is referred to in paragraph (c) above shall be regarded as taking place when the approval is received.

(5) Notwithstanding anything in subsection (4) above, any reduction or extinguishment of a credit approval which is required to be made under Part I of Schedule 3 to this Act shall be applied before any reduction or extinguishment under this section.

(6) In any case where—

> (a) before the time when a specified capital grant is received by a local authority, the authority have made a determination under subsection (1) of section 56 above with respect to a credit approval which is relevant to that grant, and
>
> (b) by virtue of subsection (3) of that section, that credit approval is to any extent to be regarded as having been used before that time,

the credit approval shall not, to that extent, be taken into account under subsections (2) and (4) above; but, subject to that, the making of a determination under section 56(1) above with respect to a credit approval shall not affect the operation of those subsections in relation to it.

Capital receipts

Capital receipts.

58.—(1) For the purposes of this Part, the capital receipts of a local authority are, subject to the following provisions of this section, those sums received by the authority in respect of—

> (a) the disposal of any interest in an asset if, at the time of disposal, expenditure on the acquisition of the asset would be expenditure for capital purposes;
>
> (b) the disposal of any investment other than an investment which, at the time of disposal, is an approved investment;

(c) the repayment of, or a payment in respect of, any grants or other financial assistance of such a description that, if the expenditure on the grant or assistance had been incurred at the time of the repayment or payment, it would have constituted expenditure for capital purposes; or

(d) the repayment of the principal of an advance (not being an approved investment) made by the authority for such a purpose that, if the advance had been made at the time of the repayment, expenditure incurred on it would have constituted expenditure for capital purposes;

and those sums become capital receipts at the time they are in fact received.

(2) The following sums are not capital receipts for the purposes of this Part, namely, sums received by an authority in respect of—

(a) the disposal of an interest in an asset which, at the time of the disposal, is an asset of a superannuation fund which the authority are required to keep by virtue of the Superannuation Act 1972; or

(b) the disposal of an investment held for the purposes of such a superannuation fund; or

(c) any repayment or payment such as is mentioned in paragraph (c) or paragraph (d) of subsection (1) above which is made to such a superannuation fund.

1972 c. 11.

(3) Subsection (1) above applies to sums received on or after 1st April 1990 but regardless of when the disposal or advance was made or the grant or other financial assistance was given and, in particular, whether or not it was made or given on or after that date but, in the case of a disposal made before that date, the reference in paragraph (a) or, as the case may be, paragraph (b) of subsection (1) above to the time of the disposal shall be construed as a reference to 1st April 1990.

(4) Subject to subsection (6) below, to the extent that any sums which were received by a local authority before 1st April 1990 and either—

(a) constituted capital receipts for the purposes of Part VIII of the Local Government, Planning and Land Act 1980, or

1980 c. 65.

(b) did not constitute such receipts by virtue of regulations under section 75(5) of that Act but are specified for the purposes of this subsection by regulations made by the Secretary of State,

are represented in the authority's accounts for the financial year ending immediately before that date either by amounts shown as capital receipts which are unapplied as at the end of that year or by amounts included in the balance as at the end of that year of any fund established by the authority under paragraph 16 of Schedule 13 to the Local Government Act 1972, those sums shall be treated for the purposes of this Part as capital receipts received by the authority on that date; and any reference in this Part to "1980 Act receipts" is a reference to sums which are capital receipts by virtue of this subsection.

1972 c. 70.

(5) So far as may be necessary for the purposes of this Part, a local authority shall identify which (if any) sums falling within paragraphs (a) and (b) of subsection (4) above are represented by amounts included as mentioned in that subsection in the balance of a fund established as so mentioned.

(6) Subsection (4) above does not apply to a sum in respect of which an amount shown as an unapplied capital receipt or included in a balance as mentioned in that subsection is, on 1st April 1990, held in an investment which is not on that date an approved investment; and, so far as may be necessary for the purposes of this Part, where on that date a local authority hold investments which are not then approved investments, the authority shall identify which (if any) of the amounts so shown or included are to be treated as held in such investments.

(7) Where an asset or investment falling within paragraph (a) or paragraph (b) of subsection (1) above is disposed of and the whole or part of the purchase price is not received by the authority at the time of the disposal, then, subject to subsection (9) below, any interest payable to the authority in respect of the whole or any part of the price shall not be regarded as a capital receipt.

(8) Subject to subsection (9) below, in the case of a disposal of an asset which consists of the grant, assignment or surrender of a leasehold interest in any land or the lease of any other asset, only the following are capital receipts, —

(a) any premium paid on the grant or assignment;

(b) any consideration received in respect of the surrender;

(c) any sum paid by way of rent more than three months before the beginning of the rental period to which it relates;

(d) any sum paid by way of rent in respect of a rental period which exceeds one year; and

(e) so much of any other sum paid by way of rent as, in accordance with directions given by the Secretary of State, falls to be treated as a capital receipt.

(9) If the Secretary of State by regulations so provides,—

(a) the whole or such part as may be determined under the regulations of a sum received by a local authority and which, apart from this subsection, would not be a capital receipt shall be such a receipt; and

(b) the whole or such part as may be so determined of a sum which, apart from this subsection, would be a capital receipt shall not be such a receipt.

(10) This section and sections 59 to 61 below have effect subject to Part II of Schedule 3 to this Act in relation to certain disposals, payments and repayments occurring before 1st April 1990.

The reserved part of capital receipts.

59.—(1) At the time when a local authority receive a capital receipt, a part of that receipt (in this Part referred to as "the reserved part") shall be set aside by the authority as provision to meet credit liabilities.

(2) Subject to the following provisions of this section, the reserved part of a capital receipt shall be—

1985 c. 68.

(a) in the case of a receipt in respect of the disposal of dwelling-houses held for the purposes of Part II of the Housing Act 1985 (provision of housing), 75 per cent; and

(b) in the case of any other receipt, 50 per cent.

(3) The Secretary of State may by regulations alter the percentage which (by virtue of subsection (2) above or the previous exercise of this power) is for the time being the reserved part of any capital receipt or provide that the amount which is the reserved part of any capital receipt shall be determined in accordance with the regulations; and any such regulations may make different provision in relation to—

(a) different descriptions of capital receipts; and

(b) different descriptions of local authority;

and where the regulations specify a percentage, it may be any percentage from nil to 100.

(4) If the Secretary of State by regulations so provides, capital receipts of a description specified in the regulations shall be treated for the purposes only of this section as reduced by an amount determined in accordance with the regulations.

(5) In the exercise of the power conferred by subsection (3) or subsection (4) above, capital receipts and local authorities may be differentiated in any manner which appears to the Secretary of State to be appropriate and, in particular,—

(a) capital receipts may be differentiated by reference to the source from which they are derived including, in the case of receipts derived from disposals, different descriptions of disposals; and

(b) local authorities may be differentiated by reference to their type, their credit ceilings and the nature of their statutory powers and duties.

(6) Without prejudice to subsection (3) above, in any case where—

(a) the consent of the Secretary of State is required for a disposal of a dwelling-house or any other property, and

(b) the Secretary of State gives a direction under this subsection with respect to a capital receipt in respect of that disposal,

subsection (2) above shall have effect in relation to that capital receipt as if it provided that the reserved part of the receipt were a percentage thereof specified in the direction or, according as the direction provides, an amount determined in accordance with the direction; but any direction under this subsection relating to a 1980 Act receipt shall be made before 1st April 1990.

(7) Subsection (1) above does not apply to a capital receipt received by an authority as trustee of a trust fund which is held for charitable purposes.

(8) Where a local authority receive a capital receipt in respect of an asset, investment, grant or other financial assistance which was originally acquired or made by the authority wholly or partly out of moneys provided by Parliament on terms which require, or enable a Minister of the Crown to require, the payment of any sum to such a Minister on or by reference to the disposal of the asset or investment or the repayment of the grant or assistance, the amount of the capital receipt shall be treated for the purposes of the preceding provisions of this section as reduced by the sum which appears to the authority to be so payable, including, in the case of a 1980 Act receipt, any sum which was payable, but was not in fact paid, before 1st April 1990.

(9) Where a local authority receive a capital receipt, not being a 1980 Act receipt, in respect of—

    (a) a disposal of land held for the purposes of Part II of the Housing Act 1985, or

    (b) any other disposal of land made by virtue of Part V (the right to buy) of that Act,

the amount of the capital receipt shall be treated for the purposes of the preceding provisions of this section as reduced by so much of the receipt as is applied by the authority in defraying the administrative costs of and incidental to any such disposal.

60.—(1) This section applies to the balance of any capital receipts received by a local authority after deducting—

    (a) the reserved part of each such receipt; and

    (b) any sum which, by virtue of subsection (8) or subsection (9) of section 59 above, falls to be deducted in determining the amount of any receipt for the purposes of the preceding provisions of that section;

but nothing in this section applies to a capital receipt which falls within section 59(7) above.

(2) The balance referred to in subsection (1) above (in this Part referred to as "the usable part" of the authority's capital receipts) shall be applied by the local authority, according as they determine, in one of the following ways, or partly in one way and partly in the other,—

    (a) to meet expenditure incurred for capital purposes; or

    (b) as provision to meet credit liabilities;

and, subject to subsection (3) below, may be so applied in the financial year in which the receipts are received or in any later financial year.

(3) A determination by a local authority under subsection (2) above as to the manner in which the usable part of their capital receipts are to be applied may not be made later than 30th September in the financial year following that in which, in accordance with the determination, the receipts are to be applied.

(4) For the purposes of this Part, to the extent that the usable part of an authority's capital receipts are applied as mentioned in subsection (2)(a) above, it shall be taken to be so applied at the time when the expenditure in question is defrayed.

(5) For the purposes of this Part, to the extent that the usable part of an authority's capital receipts are applied as mentioned in subsection (2)(b) above, it shall be taken to be so applied—

    (a) if it is used as an amount of credit cover as mentioned in section 50(3)(b) above, when the credit arrangement in question is entered into or varied; and

    (b) subject to subsection (6) below, in any other case, on the last day of the financial year in which (pursuant to the local authority's determination) it is so applied.

(6) In the case of a determination under subsection (2) above which—

    (a) relates to the application of the usable part of a 1980 Act receipt in the financial year beginning on 1st April 1990, and

(b) is made not later than 30th September 1990,

subsection (5)(b) above shall have effect with the substitution of a reference to 1st April 1990 for the reference to the last day of the financial year in which the usable part is so applied.

61.—(1) This section applies where—

> (a) the whole or part of the consideration received by a local authority on or after 1st April 1990 for a disposal falling within section 58(1) above either is not in money or consists of money which, at the request or with the agreement of the local authority concerned, is paid otherwise than to the authority; or
>
> (b) the right of a local authority to receive such a repayment or payment as is referred to in section 58(1) above is assigned or waived for a consideration which is received on or after 1st April 1990 and which, in whole or in part, is not in money or which, at the request or with the agreement of the local authority, is paid otherwise than to the authority; or
>
> (c) on a disposal falling within section 58(8) above, any consideration is received on or after 1st April 1990 and, if it had been in money paid to the authority, it would have been a capital receipt.

(2) Where this section applies in relation to any consideration, there shall be determined the amount which would have been the capital receipt if the consideration had been wholly in money paid to the local authority; and, subject to subsection (3) below, the amount so determined is in this section referred to as "the notional capital receipt".

(3) From the amount which, apart from this subsection, would be the notional capital receipt in relation to a disposal, repayment or payment there shall be deducted any amount of money that was paid or is payable to the local authority in respect of that disposal, repayment or payment and in respect of which section 59 above actually applies or will actually apply when the payment is received.

(4) Where consideration to which this section applies is received in respect of a disposal, repayment or payment, the local authority shall set aside, at the time of the disposal or the assignment or waiver of the repayment or payment, and as provision to meet credit liabilities, an amount which, except in so far as regulations made or directions given by the Secretary of State otherwise provide, shall be equal to that which, under section 59 above, would be the reserved part of the notional capital receipt.

(5) The amount falling to be set aside by a local authority under subsection (4) above shall be so set aside—

> (a) from the usable part of the authority's capital receipts; or
>
> (b) from a revenue account of the authority.

(6) If the Secretary of State by regulations so provides,—

> (a) consideration which is not in money, which is received by a local authority and which is of a description specified in the regulations, or

(b) consideration which is in money, which is paid otherwise than to the authority and which is of a description specified in the regulations,

shall be treated for the purposes of subsections (2), (4) and (5) above as consideration to which this section applies and, in relation to any such consideration, subsection (4) above shall apply with such modifications as are specified in the regulations.

Aggregate credit limit

62.—(1) For each local authority there shall be an aggregate credit limit which, subject to subsection (2) below, at any time shall be the total at that time of—

(a) the authority's temporary revenue borrowing limit;

(b) the authority's temporary capital borrowing limit;

(c) the authority's credit ceiling, as determined under Part III of Schedule 3 to this Act; and

(d) the excess of the authority's approved investments and cash over their usable capital receipts;

but the reference in paragraph (d) above to approved investments and cash does not include investments or cash held for the purposes of such a superannuation fund or trust fund as is referred to in paragraph (h) or paragraph (i) of subsection (2) of section 42 above.

(2) On an application made by a local authority, the Secretary of State may direct that, for any period specified in the direction, the amount which, apart from the direction, would be the authority's aggregate credit limit at any time during that period shall be increased by an amount specified in the direction with respect to that period; and any increase specified in a direction under this subsection may be expressed to have effect subject to compliance with such terms and conditions as may be so specified.

(3) Subject to subsection (4) below, an authority's temporary revenue borrowing limit at any time is whichever is the less of—

(a) the total sums which at that time remain to be received by the authority and which, as income, fall or will fall to be credited to a revenue account of the authority for the current financial year; and

(b) the aggregate of—

(i) the total sums which, up to and including that time (whether in the current or a previous financial year), the authority have disbursed in respect of expenditure which falls to be charged to a revenue account of the authority for the current financial year; and

(ii) any relevant arrears in respect of which provision has been or is to be charged to such a revenue account or which have been or are to be written off and charged to such a revenue account;

and for the purposes of paragraph (b)(ii) above "relevant arrears" are amounts in respect of income which remain to be received by the authority and which, as income, fall to be credited to a revenue account of the authority for the financial year beginning two years before the beginning of the current financial year.

(4) At any time in a financial year the amount which, apart from this subsection, would be an authority's temporary revenue borrowing limit shall be increased by the addition of an amount in respect of the immediately preceding financial year, being whichever is the less of—

    (a) the excess (if any) of the total sums which, up to and including that time, the authority have disbursed in respect of expenditure falling to be charged to a revenue account of the authority for that preceding year over the total sums which, up to and including that time, the authority have received in respect of income falling to be credited to such a revenue account; and

    (b) the total sums which at that time remain to be received by the authority and which, as income, fall or will fall to be credited to a revenue account of the authority for that preceding year.

(5) An authority's temporary capital borrowing limit at any time is so much of the expenditure defrayed by the authority for capital purposes in the eighteen months ending at that time as is due to be, but at that time has not yet been, re-imbursed by any other person, excluding expenditure which is to be re-imbursed or met out of grants from a Community institution; and for this purpose it is immaterial whether the re-imbursement is due as a result of an obligation arising by statute, contract or otherwise or is to take the form of a grant or other obligation voluntarily undertaken.

(6) If at any time an authority's usable capital receipts exceed their approved investments and cash referred to in paragraph (d) of subsection (1) above, the amount taken into account under that paragraph shall be a negative amount.

(7) Where an amount taken into account under paragraph (c) or paragraph (d) of subsection (1) above is a negative amount, it shall be a deduction in determining the total referred to in that subsection.

(8) Any reference in this section to an authority's usable capital receipts at any time is a reference to the usable part of the authority's capital receipts so far as they have not been applied before that time.

Amounts set aside to meet credit liabilities

63.—(1) Without prejudice to any other provision of this Part under which a local authority are required or authorised to set aside any amount as provision to meet credit liabilities, in each financial year a local authority shall, by virtue of this section, set aside, from such revenue account or accounts as the authority think fit, as provision to meet credit liabilities, an amount determined by the authority, being not less than the minimum revenue provision for that year referred to in Part IV of Schedule 3 to this Act.

Duty to set certain amounts aside as provision to meet credit liabilities.

(2) Where, by virtue of section 157 below, the Secretary of State makes to a local authority a commuted payment, within the meaning of that section, the authority shall, at the time the payment is received, set aside an amount equal to that payment as provision to meet credit liabilities.

(3) If, otherwise than by virtue of section 157 below, the Secretary of State or any other Minister of the Crown commutes into a single payment (or into a smaller number of payments than would otherwise be payable) sums which would otherwise have been paid to a local authority annually or by reference to any other period of time, the authority shall, at the time

that single payment or, as the case may be, each of that smaller number of payments is received, set aside an amount equal to the payment as provision to meet credit liabilities.

(4) Where a local authority receive any sum by way of grant from a Community institution towards the authority's expenditure on capital purposes, they shall at the time the sum is received, set aside an amount equal to that sum as provision to meet credit liabilities.

(5) A determination under subsection (1) above shall be made not later than 30th September in the financial year following that to which the determination relates.

Use of amounts set aside to meet credit liabilities.

64.—(1) Amounts for the time being set aside by a local authority (whether voluntarily or pursuant to a requirement under this Part) as provision to meet credit liabilities may, subject to subsection (2) below, be applied only for one or more of the following purposes—

    (a) to meet any liability of the authority in respect of money borrowed by the authority, other than a liability in respect of interest;

    (b) to meet any liability of the authority in respect of credit arrangements, other than those excluded by regulations under paragraph 11 of Schedule 3 to this Act; and

    (c) where a credit approval has been used as authority not to charge particular expenditure to a revenue account, to meet that expenditure.

(2) Subject to the following provisions of this section if, on the date which is the relevant date for any financial year, a local authority's credit ceiling, as determined under Part III of Schedule 3 to this Act, is a negative amount, any such amount as is referred to in subsection (1) above may in that financial year—

    (a) be applied for purposes specified by regulations made by the Secretary of State; or

    (b) be transferred to a body so specified.

(3) The aggregate of the amounts which may be applied by a local authority in accordance with subsection (2) above in any financial year shall not exceed the amount by which the authority's credit ceiling on the relevant date is less than nil.

(4) References in subsections (2) and (3) above to the relevant date shall be construed as follows—

    (a) for the financial year beginning on 1st April 1990, the relevant date is that date; and

    (b) for any subsequent financial year, the relevant date is the last day of the preceding financial year.

(5) Regulations under subsection (2) above may specify conditions with which a local authority must comply in applying or transferring any amount as mentioned in that subsection and with respect to any amount so applied or transferred; and an amount shall not be taken to be applied or transferred under that subsection unless any such conditions are complied with.

Supplementary

65.—(1) The Secretary of State may serve on a local authority a notice   Information. requiring the authority to supply to him such information as is specified in the notice and is required by him—

(a) for the purpose of deciding whether to exercise his powers, and how to perform his functions, under this Part; or

(b) for the purpose of ascertaining whether an authority have acted, or are likely to act, in accordance with this Part; or

(c) for the purpose of assisting the formulation of government economic policies;

but no information shall be required for the purpose specified in paragraph (c) above unless it relates to, or to plans or proposals about, the finances and expenditure of the authority or of any company in which the authority have an interest.

(2) If the information specified in a notice under this section is in the possession or under the control of the authority on whom the notice is served, the authority shall supply the information required in such form and manner, and at such time, as is specified in the notice and, if the notice so requires, the information shall be certified (according as is specified in the notice) in one or both of the following ways,—

(a) by the chief finance officer of the authority, within the meaning of section 5 above, or by such other person as may be specified in the notice; and

(b) under arrangements made by the Audit Commission for Local Authorities in England and Wales.

(3) If a local authority fail to comply with subsection (2) above, the Secretary of State may decide—

(a) whether to exercise his powers, and how to perform his functions, under this Part, or

(b) whether the authority have acted, or are likely to act, in accordance with this Part,

on the basis of such assumptions and estimates as he thinks fit.

(4) In deciding—

(a) whether to exercise his powers, and how to perform his functions, under this Part, or

(b) whether an authority have acted, or are likely to act, in accordance with this Part,

the Secretary of State may also take into account any other information available to him, whatever its source and whether or not obtained under a provision contained in or made under this or any other enactment.

66.—(1) In this Part—   Interpretation of Part IV.

(a) "approved investments" means investments approved for the purposes of this Part by regulations made by the Secretary of State;

(b) "financial year" means the period of twelve months beginning on 1st April;

(c) "Minister of the Crown" has the same meaning as in the Ministers of the Crown Act 1975; and

(d) "1980 Act receipt" has the meaning given by section 58(4) above.

(2) For the purposes of this Part, a local authority—

(a) incur a liability in respect of a payment at the time when they become unconditionally liable to make the payment; and

(b) discharge a liability in respect of a payment at the time when they make the actual payment, whether or not they have at that time become unconditionally liable to do so.

(3) In relation to a credit arrangement,—

(a) any reference in this Part to consideration given or to be given by the local authority under the arrangement does not include a reference to any consideration which is given before the time the arrangement comes into being (as defined in section 48(3) above); and

(b) any reference in this Part to a liability of the local authority under the arrangement does not include a reference to a liability which is met by the making of a payment before that time.

(4) In relation to a local authority, references in this Part to proper practices are references to those accounting practices—

(a) which the authority are required to follow by virtue of any enactment; or

(b) which, whether by reference to any generally recognised published code or otherwise, are regarded as proper accounting practices to be followed in the keeping of the accounts of local authorities, either generally or of the description concerned;

but, in the event of any conflict in any respect between the practices falling within paragraph (a) above and those falling within paragraph (b) above, only those falling within paragraph (a) above are to be regarded as proper practices.

(5) Subsection (4) above has effect not only for the purposes of this Act but also for the purposes of—

(a) any enactment passed after or in the same Session as this Act; and

(b) Part III of the Local Government Finance Act 1982 and the Local Government Finance Act 1988.

(6) If, under or by virtue of any enactment, all or any of the liabilities of an authority (in this subsection referred to as "the original authority") in respect of a loan to or borrowing (or money borrowed) by the authority have become liabilities of another local authority (in this subsection referred to as "the current authority") then, in so far as regulations made by the Secretary of State so provide,—

(a) in relation to the current authority, any reference in this Part to a loan to or borrowing (or money borrowed) by that authority includes a reference to the loan to or borrowing (or money borrowed) by the original authority; and

(b) if the original authority is a local authority for the purposes of this Part, any reference to a loan to or borrowing (or money borrowed) by that authority excludes a reference to the loan, borrowing (or money borrowed) in respect of which the liabilities have become those of the current authority.

(7) For the avoidance of doubt, except as provided by section 44(5) above, any reference in this Part to borrowing by a local authority does not include a reference to the temporary use by an authority of money forming part of a particular fund of the authority for a purpose other than that of the fund.

PART V

COMPANIES IN WHICH LOCAL AUTHORITIES HAVE INTERESTS

67.—(1) Any reference in this Part to a company is a reference to a body corporate of one of the following descriptions—

Application of, and orders under, Part V.

    (a) a company limited by shares;

    (b) a company limited by guarantee and not having a share capital;

    (c) a company limited by guarantee and having a share capital;

    (d) an unlimited company; and

    (e) a society registered or deemed to be registered under the Industrial and Provident Societies Act 1965 or under the Industrial and Provident Societies Act (Northern Ireland) 1969.

1965 c. 12.
1969 c. 24. (N.I.)

(2) Expressions used in paragraphs (a) to (d) of subsection (1) above have the same meaning as in Chapter I of Part I of the Companies Act 1985 or the corresponding enactment for the time being in force in Northern Ireland.

1985 c. 6.

(3) Any reference in this Part to a local authority is a reference to a body of one of the following descriptions—

    (a) a county council;

    (b) a district council;

    (c) a London borough council;

    (d) the Common Council of the City of London in its capacity as a local authority, police authority or port health authority;

    (e) the Council of the Isles of Scilly;

    (f) a parish council;

    (g) a community council;

    (h) a fire authority constituted by a combination scheme under the Fire Services Act 1947;

1947 c. 41.

    (i) a police authority constituted under section 2 of the Police Act 1964 or a combined police authority established by an amalgamation scheme under that Act;

1964 c. 48.

    (j) an authority established under section 10 of the Local Government Act 1985 (waste disposal authorities);

1985 c. 51.

    (k) a joint authority established by Part IV of that Act (police, fire services, civil defence and transport);

    (l) any body established pursuant to an order under section 67 of that Act (successors to residuary bodies);

(m) the Broads Authority;

(n) any joint board the constituent members of which consist of any of the bodies specified above;

(o) a joint or special planning board constituted for a National Park by an order under paragraph 1 or paragraph 3 of Schedule 17 to the Local Government Act 1972; and

1972 c. 70.

(p) a Passenger Transport Executive.

(4) Any power to make an order under this Part shall be exercisable by statutory instrument subject to annulment in pursuance of a resolution of either House of Parliament; and under any such power different provision may be made for different cases and different descriptions of cases (including different provision for different areas).

Companies controlled by local authorities and arm's length companies.
1985 c. 6.

68.—(1) For the purposes of this Part, unless the Secretary of State otherwise directs, a company is for the time being under the control of a local authority if—

(a) by virtue of section 736 of the Companies Act 1985 the company is at that time a subsidiary of the local authority for the purposes of that Act; or

(b) paragraph (a) above does not apply but the local authority have at that time power to control a majority of the votes at a general meeting of the company as mentioned in subsection (3) below; or

(c) paragraph (a) above does not apply but the local authority have at that time power to appoint or remove a majority of the board of directors of the company; or

(d) the company is under the control of another company which, by virtue of this subsection, is itself under the control of the local authority;

and, for the purposes of paragraph (d) above, any question whether one company is under the control of another shall be determined by applying the preceding provisions of this subsection, substituting a reference to the other company for any reference to the local authority.

(2) A direction under subsection (1) above—

(a) may be limited in time and may be made conditional upon such matters as appear to the Secretary of State to be appropriate; and

(b) may be made with respect to a particular company or a description of companies specified in the direction.

(3) The reference in subsection (1)(b) above to a power to control a majority of votes at a general meeting of the company is a reference to a power which is exercisable—

(a) in the case of a company limited by shares, through the holding of equity share capital in any one or more of the following ways, namely, by the local authority, by nominees of the local authority and by persons whose shareholding is under the control of the local authority; or

(b) in the case of any company, through the holding of votes at a general meeting of the company in any one or more of the following ways, namely, by the local authority, by a group of members of the company the composition of which is controlled by the local authority and by persons who have contractually bound themselves to vote in accordance with the instructions of the local authority; or

(c) partly in one of those ways and partly in the other.

(4) Subsection (3) of section 736A of the Companies Act 1985 (right to appoint or remove a majority of a company's board of directors) and the following provisions of that section as they have effect in relation to subsection (3) apply for the purposes of subsection (1)(c) above with the substitution for the word "right", wherever it occurs, of the word "power".

(5) For the purposes of subsection (3)(a) above, a person's shareholding is under the control of a local authority if—

(a) his right to hold the shares arose because of some action which the authority took, or refrained from taking, in order to enable him to have the right; and

(b) the local authority, alone or jointly with one or more other persons can require him to transfer his shareholding (or any part of it) to another person.

(6) Notwithstanding that, by virtue of the preceding provisions of this section, a company is for the time being under the control of a local authority, the company is for the purposes of this Part an "arm's length company", in relation to any financial year if, at a time before the beginning of that year, the authority resolved that the company should be an arm's length company and, at all times from the passing of that resolution up to the end of the financial year in question, the following conditions have applied while the company has been under the control of the local authority,—

(a) that each of the directors of the company was appointed for a fixed term of at least two years;

(b) that, subject to subsection (7) below, no director of the company has been removed by resolution under section 303 of the Companies Act 1985;

(c) that not more than one-fifth of the directors of the company have been members or officers of the authority;

(d) that the company has not occupied (as tenant or otherwise) any land in which the authority have an interest otherwise than for the best consideration reasonably obtainable;

(e) that the company has entered into an agreement with the authority that the company will use its best endeavours to produce a specified positive return on its assets;

(f) that, except for the purpose of enabling the company to acquire fixed assets or to provide it with working capital, the authority have not lent money to the company or guaranteed any sum borrowed by it or subscribed for any securities in the company;

(g) that the authority have not made any grant to the company except in pursuance of an agreement or undertaking entered into before the financial year (within the meaning of the Companies Act 1985) of the company in which the grant was made; and

(h) that the authority have not made any grant to the company the amount of which is in any way related to the financial results of the company in any period.

(7) If the Secretary of State so directs, the removal of a director shall be disregarded for the purposes of subsection (6)(b) above; but the Secretary of State shall not give such a direction if it appears to him that the director was removed with a view to influencing the management of the company for other than commercial reasons.

69.—(1) For the purposes of this Part, unless the Secretary of State otherwise directs, a company which is not at the time under the control of a local authority is for the time being subject to the influence of a local authority if it is not a banking or insurance company or a member of a banking or insurance group and at that time there is such a business relationship between the company and the authority as is referred to in subsection (3) below and either—

(a) at least 20 per cent. of the total voting rights of all the members having the right to vote at a general meeting of the company are held by persons who are associated with the authority as mentioned in subsection (5) below; or

(b) at least 20 per cent. of the directors of the company are persons who are so associated; or

(c) at least 20 per cent. of the total voting rights at a meeting of the directors of the company are held by persons who are so associated.

(2) A direction under subsection (1) above—

(a) may be limited in time and may be made conditional upon such matters as appear to the Secretary of State to be appropriate; and

(b) may be made with respect to a particular company or a description of companies specified in the direction.

(3) For the purposes of this section there is a business relationship between a company and a local authority at any time if the condition in any one or more of the following paragraphs is fulfilled—

(a) within a period of twelve months which includes that time the aggregate of the payments to the company by the authority or by another company which is under the control of the authority represents more than one-half of the company's turnover, as shown in its profit and loss account for the most recent financial year for which the company's auditors have made a report on the accounts or, if there is no such account, as estimated by the authority for the period of twelve months preceding the date of the estimate or for such part of that period as follows the formation of the company;

(b) more than one-half of the company's turnover referred to in paragraph (a) above is derived from the exploitation of assets of any description in which the local authority or a company under the control of the authority has an interest (disregarding an interest in land which is in reversion on a lease granted for more than 7 years);

(c) the aggregate of—

(i) grants made either by the authority and being expenditure for capital purposes or by a company under the control of the authority, and

(ii) the nominal value of shares or stock in the company which is owned by the authority or by a company under the control of the authority,

exceeds one-half of the net assets of the company;

(d) the aggregate of—

(i) grants falling within paragraph (c)(i) above,

(ii) loans or other advances made or guaranteed by the authority or by a company under the control of the authority, and

(iii) the nominal value referred to in paragraph (c)(ii) above,

exceeds one-half of the fixed and current assets of the company;

(e) the company at that time occupies land by virtue of an interest which it obtained from the local authority or a company under the control of the authority and which it so obtained at less than the best consideration reasonably obtainable; and

(f) the company intends at that time to enter into (or complete) a transaction and, when that is done, there will then be a business relationship between the company and the authority by virtue of any of paragraphs (a) to (e) above.

(4) In subsection (3) above—

(a) the reference in paragraph (c) to the net assets of the company shall be construed in accordance with section 152(2) of the Companies Act 1985; and

(b) the reference in paragraph (d) to the fixed and current assets of the company shall be construed in accordance with paragraph 77 of Schedule 4 to that Act;

and in either case, the reference is a reference to those assets as shown in the most recent balance sheet of the company on which, at the time in question, the auditors have made a report or, if there is no such balance sheet, as estimated by the local authority for the time in question.

(5) For the purposes of this section, a person is at any time associated with a local authority if—

(a) he is at that time a member of the authority;

(b) he is at that time an officer of the authority;

(c) he is at that time both an employee and either a director, manager, secretary or other similar officer of a company which is under the control of the authority; or

(d) at any time within the preceding four years he has been associated with the authority by virtue of paragraph (a) above.

(6) If and to the extent that the Secretary of State by order so provides, a person is at any time associated with a local authority if—

(a) at that time he is, or is employed by or by a subsidiary of, a person who for the time being has a contractual relationship with the authority to provide—

(i) advice with regard to the authority's interest in any company (whether existing or proposed to be formed), or

(ii) advice with regard to the management of an undertaking or the development of land by a company (whether existing or proposed to be formed) with which it is proposed that the authority should enter into any lease, licence or other contract or to which it is proposed that the authority should make any grant or loan, or

(iii) services which facilitate the exercise of the authority's rights in any company (whether by acting as the authority's representative at a meeting of the company or as a director appointed by the authority or otherwise);

(b) at any time within the preceding four years, he has been associated with the authority by virtue of paragraph (b) or paragraph (c) of subsection (5) above;

(c) he is at that time the spouse of, or carries on business in partnership with, a person who is associated with the authority by virtue of subsection (5)(a) above; or

(d) he holds a relevant office in a political association or other body which, in the nomination paper of a person who is an elected member of the authority, formed part of that person's description.

(7) For the purposes of subsection (6)(d) above, an office in a political association or body is relevant to a local authority in the following circumstances—

(a) if the association or body is active only in the area of the local authority, any office in it is relevant; and

(b) in any other case, an office is relevant only if it is in a branch or other part of the association or body which is active in the area of the local authority.

(8) In relation to a company which is an industrial and provident society, any reference in this section to the directors of the company is a reference to the members of the committee of management.

(9) Subject to subsections (4) and (8) and section 67 above, expressions used in this section have the same meaning as in the Companies Act 1985.

1985 c. 6.

Requirements for companies under control or subject to influence of local authorities.

70.—(1) In relation to companies under the control of local authorities and companies subject to the influence of local authorities, the Secretary of State may by order make provision regulating, forbidding or requiring the taking of certain actions or courses of action; and an order under this subsection may—

(a) make provision in relation to those companies which are arm's length companies different from that applicable to companies which are not; and

(b) make provision in relation to companies under the control of local authorities different from that applicable in relation to companies under the influence of local authorities.

(2) It shall be the duty of every local authority to ensure, so far as practicable, that any company under its control complies with the provisions for the time being made by order under subsection (1) above; and if a local authority fails to perform that duty in relation to any

company, any payment made by the authority to that company and any other expenditure incurred by the authority in contravention of any such provisions shall be deemed for the purposes of Part III of the Local Government Finance Act 1982 (accounts and audits) to be expenditure which is unlawful.

(3) In order to secure compliance, in relation to companies subject to the influence of local authorities, with provisions made by virtue of subsection (1) above, an order under that subsection may prescribe requirements to be complied with by any local authority in relation to conditions to be included in such leases, licences, contracts, gifts, grants or loans as may be so prescribed which are made with or to a company subject to the influence of the local authority.

(4) It shall be the duty of every local authority to comply with any requirements for the time being prescribed under subsection (3) above; and if a local authority fails to perform that duty, any expenditure which is incurred by the local authority under the lease, licence, contract, gift, grant or loan in question shall be deemed for the purposes of Part III of the Local Government Finance Act 1982 to be expenditure which is unlawful.

(5) Without prejudice to the generality of the power conferred by subsection (1) above, an order under that subsection may make provision requiring a company or local authority to obtain the consent of the Secretary of State, or of the Audit Commission for Local Authorities in England and Wales, before taking any particular action or course of action.

71.—(1) In relation to a local authority, subsection (2) below applies to any company other than—

(a) a company which is or, if the action referred to in that subsection is taken, will be under the control of the local authority; and

(b) a company of a description specified for the purposes of this section by an order made by the Secretary of State;

and in this section an "authorised company" means a company falling within paragraph (b) above.

(2) Except with the approval of the Secretary of State, in relation to a company to which this subsection applies, a local authority may not—

(a) subscribe for, or acquire, whether in their own name or in the name of a nominee, any shares or share warrants in the company;

(b) become or remain a member of the company if it is limited by guarantee;

(c) exercise any power, however arising, to nominate any person to become a member of the company;

(d) exercise any power to appoint directors of the company;

(e) permit any officer of the authority, in the course of his employment, to make any such nomination or appointment as is referred to in paragraph (c) or paragraph (d) above; or

(f) permit an officer of the authority, in the course of his employment, to become or remain a member or director of the company.

(3) Any approval of the Secretary of State under subsection (2) above may be general or relate to any specific matter or company.

(4) A local authority may not take any action, or refrain from exercising any right, which would have the result that a person who is disqualified from membership of the authority (otherwise than by being employed by that or any other local authority or by a company which is under the control of a local authority) becomes a member or director of an authorised company or is authorised, in accordance with section 375 of the Companies Act 1985, to act as the authority's representative at a general meeting of an authorised company (or at meetings of an authorised company which include a general meeting).

(5) In any case where,—

   (a) in accordance with section 375 of the Companies Act 1985, a local authority have authorised a member or officer of the authority to act as mentioned in subsection (4) above, or

   (b) a member or officer of a local authority has become a member or director of an authorised company as mentioned in subsection (7) below,

the authority shall make arrangements (whether by standing orders or otherwise) for enabling members of the authority, in the course of proceedings of the authority (or of any committee or sub-committee thereof), to put to the member or officer concerned questions about the activities of the company.

(6) Nothing in subsection (5) above shall require the member or officer referred to in that subsection to disclose any information about the company which has been communicated to him in confidence.

(7) Any member or officer of a local authority who has become a member or director of an authorised company by virtue of—

   (a) a nomination made by the authority, or

   (b) election at a meeting of the company at which voting rights were exercisable (whether or not exercised) by the authority or by a person bound to vote in accordance with the instructions of the authority, or

   (c) an appointment made by the directors of another company, the majority of whom became directors of that company by virtue of a nomination made by the authority or election at a meeting of the company at which voting rights were exercisable as mentioned in paragraph (b) above,

shall make a declaration to the authority, in such form as they may require, of any remuneration or re-imbursement of expenses which he receives from the company as a member or director or in respect of anything done on behalf of the company.

(8) Subject to section 67 above, expressions used in this section have the same meaning as in the Companies Act 1985.

Trusts influenced by local authorities.

72.—(1) The Secretary of State may by order made by statutory instrument adapt the provisions of section 69 above so as to make them applicable to trusts which are not charitable; and, subject to subsection (2) below, this Part shall apply in relation to trusts which are subject to local authority influence by virtue of that section as so adapted as it applies in relation to companies which are subject to local authority influence.

(2) In the exercise of the power conferred by section 70 above, as applied in relation to trusts by subsection (1) above, the Secretary of State may make different provision for trusts as compared with companies.

73.—(1) In any case where—

(a) apart from this section a company would not be under the control of any one local authority, but

(b) if the actions, powers and interests of two or more local authorities were treated as those of one authority alone, the company would be under the control of that one authority,

the company shall be treated for the purposes of this Part as under the control of each of the two or more local authorities mentioned in paragraph (b) above.

(2) In any case where, apart from this section, a company would not be treated as being subject to the influence of any one local authority, it shall be treated as being subject to the influence of each of a number of local authorities (in this section referred to as a "group") if the conditions in subsection (3) below are fulfilled with respect to the company and the group of authorities.

(3) The conditions referred to in subsection (2) above are—

(a) that at least one of the conditions in paragraphs (a) to (e) of subsection (3) of section 69 above would be fulfilled—

(i) if any reference therein to the company being under the control of a local authority were a reference to its being under the control of any one of the authorities in the group or of any two or more of them taken together; and

(ii) if any other reference therein to the local authority were a reference to any two or more of the authorities in the group taken together; and

(b) that at least one of the conditions in paragraphs (a) to (c) of subsection (1) of section 69 above would be fulfilled if any reference therein to the local authority were a reference to those local authorities who are taken into account under sub-paragraph (i) or sub-paragraph (ii) of paragraph (a) above taken together; and

(c) that if the condition (or one of the conditions) which would be fulfilled as mentioned in paragraph (b) above is that in subsection (1)(a) of section 69 above, then, so far as concerns each local authority in the group, at least one person who, in terms of subsection (5) of that section, is associated with that authority has the right to vote at a general meeting of the company; and

(d) that, if paragraph (c) above does not apply, then, so far as concerns each local authority in the group, a person who, in terms of section 69(5) above, is associated with the authority is a director of the company.

(4) For the purposes of this Part, anything done, and any power exercisable, by a committee or sub-committee of a local authority, or by any of the authority's officers, shall be treated as done or, as the case may be, exercisable by the authority.

(5) For the purposes of this Part, anything done, and any power exercisable, by a joint committee of two or more local authorities or by a sub-committee of such a joint committee shall be treated as done or, as the case may be, exercisable by each of the local authorities concerned.

PART VI

HOUSING FINANCE

Housing accounts

Duty to keep Housing Revenue Account.

74.—(1) A local housing authority shall keep, in accordance with proper practices, an account, called the "Housing Revenue Account", of sums falling to be credited or debited in respect of—

1985 c. 68.

(a) houses and other buildings which have been provided under Part II of the Housing Act 1985 (provision of housing);

(b) land which has been acquired or appropriated for the purposes of that Part;

(c) houses purchased under section 192 of that Act (purchase of house found on appeal against repair notice to be unfit and beyond repair at reasonable cost);

1926 c. 56.

(d) dwellings in respect of which a local authority have received assistance under section 1 or section 4(2A) of the Housing (Rural Workers) Act 1926;

(e) any property which—

(i) with the consent of the Secretary of State given under section 417(1) of the Housing Act 1985,

1958 c. 42.

(ii) with the consent of a Minister given under section 50(1)(e) of the Housing (Financial Provisions) Act 1958, or

(iii) by virtue of section 50(2) of that Act (houses vesting in local authority on default of another person),

was brought within the corresponding account kept under Part XIII of the Housing Act 1985 for years beginning before 1st April 1990; and

(f) such land, houses or other buildings not within the preceding paragraphs as the Secretary of State may direct.

(2) References in subsection (1) above and the other provisions of this Part to provisions of the Housing Act 1985 include, where the context so admits, references to the corresponding provisions of earlier enactments; and the reference in paragraph (b) of that subsection to land acquired for the purposes of Part II of that Act includes—

1957 c. 56.

(a) land which a local authority were deemed to have acquired under Part V of the Housing Act 1957 by virtue of section 57(6) of that Act (land acquired for re-development in pursuance of re-development plan) before the repeal of that section on 25th August 1969; and

(b) any structures on such land which were made available to a local authority under section 1 of the Housing (Temporary Accommodation) Act 1944 (prefabs). PART VI
1944 c. 36.

(3) Paragraphs (a) to (e) of subsection (1) above shall not apply to—

(a) land, houses or other buildings disposed of by the authority;

(b) land acquired by the authority for the purpose of disposing of houses provided, or to be provided, on the land, or of disposing of the land to a person who intends to provide housing accommodation on it;

(c) houses provided by the authority on land so acquired; or

(d) such land, houses or other buildings as the Secretary of State may direct;

and paragraph (a) of that subsection shall not apply to houses and other buildings provided on or before 6th February 1919.

(4) A local housing authority not possessing property to which subsection (1) above applies shall nevertheless keep a Housing Revenue Account unless the Secretary of State consents to their not doing so and they comply with such conditions (if any) as may be specified in the consent.

(5) In this Part—

(a) references to the houses or other property of an authority within the authority's Housing Revenue Account are references to the houses, dwellings or other property to which subsection (1) above for the time being applies; and

(b) references (however expressed) to a disposal are references to a conveyance of the freehold, or a grant or assignment of a lease (other than a shared ownership lease) which is a long tenancy within the meaning given by section 115 of the Housing Act 1985. 1985 c. 68.

(6) Sections 417 to 420 of, and Schedule 14 to, the Housing Act 1985 (which are superseded by this section, sections 75 to 78 below and Schedule 4 to this Act) shall cease to have effect.

75. Schedule 4 to this Act shall have effect with respect to the keeping of a local housing authority's Housing Revenue Account, as follows— The keeping of the Housing Revenue Account.

Part I - Credits to the account.

Part II - Debits to the account.

Part III - Special cases.

Part IV - Supplementary provisions.

76.—(1) This section applies where for any year ("the relevant year") a local housing authority who are required to keep a Housing Revenue Account possess any houses or other property within the account. Duty to prevent debit balance on Housing Revenue Account.

(2) The authority shall, during the months of January and February immediately preceding the relevant year, formulate proposals which satisfy the requirements of subsection (3) below and relate to—

(a) the income of the authority for the year from rents and other charges in respect of houses and other property within their Housing Revenue Account;

(b) the expenditure of the authority for the year in respect of the repair, maintenance, supervision and management of such property; and

(c) such other matters connected with the exercise of the authority's functions in relation to such property as the Secretary of State may direct.

(3) Proposals formulated by the authority under subsection (2) above satisfy the requirements of this subsection at any time if, on the assumption that the following will prove correct, namely—

(a) the best assumptions that they are able to make at that time as to all matters which may affect the amounts falling to be credited or debited to their Housing Revenue Account for the relevant year; and

(b) the best estimates that they are able to make at that time of the amounts which, on those assumptions, will fall to be so credited or debited,

implementation of the proposals will secure that the account for that year does not show a debit balance.

(4) No assumptions shall be made under subsection (3) above as to the exercise by the Secretary of State of any power except on the basis of information published by him or on his behalf or supplied by him to the authority.

(5) Subject to subsections (6) and (7) below, the authority shall implement the proposals formulated by them under subsection (2) above.

(6) The authority shall from time to time determine whether the proposals formulated under subsection (2) above satisfy the requirements of subsection (3) above; and—

(a) if they determine that question in the affirmative, they may make such revisions of the proposals as they think fit, so long as the proposals (as so revised) continue to satisfy those requirements;

(b) if they determine that question in the negative, they shall make such revisions of the proposals as are reasonably practicable towards securing that the proposals (as so revised) satisfy those requirements.

(7) Where the proposals formulated under subsection (2) above are revised under subsection (6) above, subsections (3) to (6) above shall apply in relation to the proposals as so revised as they applied in relation to the proposals as originally formulated.

(8) The authority shall, within one month of formulating their proposals under subsection (2) above, or of revising those proposals under subsection (6) above, prepare a statement setting out—

(a) those proposals as so formulated or so revised;

(b) the estimates made by them under subsection (3)(b) above on the basis of which those proposals were so formulated or so revised; and

(c) such other particulars relating to those proposals and estimates as the Secretary of State may direct;

and a direction under paragraph (c) above may specify the manner in which the particulars are to be set out in the statement.

(9) The authority shall, until the end of the year next following the relevant year, keep copies of the statement which is for the time being the latest statement prepared by them under subsection (8) above available for inspection by the public without charge at all reasonable hours at one or more of their offices; and any person shall be entitled to take copies of, or extracts from, that statement when so made available.

77.—(1) A local housing authority who are required to keep a Housing Revenue Account may also keep, in accordance with proper practices, an account called the "Housing Repairs Account". Power to keep Housing Repairs Account.

(2) An authority who keep a Housing Repairs Account shall carry to the credit of the account for any year—

    (a) sums transferred for the year from their Housing Revenue Account; and

    (b) sums receivable by the authority for the year in connection with the repair or maintenance of houses or other property within their Housing Revenue Account (either from their tenants or from the sale of scrapped or salvaged materials).

(3) The authority shall carry to the debit of the account for any year—

    (a) all expenditure incurred by them for the year in connection with the repair or maintenance of houses or other property within their Housing Revenue Account;

    (b) such expenditure incurred by them for the year in connection with the improvement or replacement of houses or other property within their Housing Revenue Account as may from time to time be determined by the Secretary of State; and

    (c) sums transferred for the year to the Housing Revenue Account in accordance with subsection (5) below.

(4) The authority shall secure that sufficient credits are carried to the account to secure that no debit balance is shown in the account for any year.

(5) The authority may carry some or all of any credit balance in the account for any year to the credit of their Housing Revenue Account.

(6) So much of any credit balance shown in an authority's Housing Repairs Account at the end of the year beginning 1st April 1989 as is not carried to the credit of their Housing Revenue Account for that year shall be carried forward and credited to some other revenue account of theirs for the year beginning 1st April 1990.

78. The Secretary of State may give directions as to the accounting practices (whether actual or prospective) which are to be followed by a local housing authority in the keeping of their Housing Revenue Account or Housing Repairs Account. Directions to secure proper accounting.

Housing subsidies

79.—(1) Housing Revenue Account subsidy shall be payable for each year to local housing authorities. Housing Revenue Account subsidy.

PART VI

(2) Housing Revenue Account subsidy shall be paid by the Secretary of State at such times, in such manner and subject to such conditions as to records, certificates, audit or otherwise as he may, with the agreement of the Treasury, determine.

1985 c. 68.

(3) Sections 421 to 427A of the Housing Act 1985 (which are superseded, in their application to local housing authorities, by this section and sections 80 and 86 below) shall cease to apply in relation to such authorities.

Calculation of Housing Revenue Account subsidy.

80.—(1) The amount of Housing Revenue Account subsidy (if any) payable to a local housing authority for a year shall be calculated in accordance with such formulae as the Secretary of State may from time to time determine; and for any year the first such determination shall be made before the 25th December immediately preceding that year.

(2) If the amount so calculated is a negative amount, the authority shall for that year carry the equivalent positive amount from their Housing Revenue Account to the credit of some other revenue account of theirs.

(3) In determining a formula for the purposes of this section for any year, the Secretary of State may include variables framed (in whatever way he considers appropriate) by reference to—

(a) any amounts which fall to be or were credited or debited to the authority's Housing Revenue Account for that year or any previous year;

(b) any amounts which, on such assumptions as the Secretary of State may determine (whether or not borne out or likely to be borne out by events), would fall to be or would have been so credited or debited; and

(c) such other matters relating to the authority, or to (or to tenants of) houses and other property which are or have been within the account, as he thinks fit;

and the Secretary of State may make any determination falling to be made for the purposes of a formula on the basis of information received by him on or before such date as he thinks fit.

(4) Without prejudice to the generality of subsection (3) above, a formula may require it to be assumed that the amount for any year of the rental income or housing expenditure of each authority (or each authority in England or in Wales) is to be determined—

(a) by taking the amount which the Secretary of State considers (having regard, amongst other things, to past and expected movements in incomes, costs and prices) should be or should have been the aggregate amount for that year of the rental incomes or, as the case may be, the housing expenditure of all of the authorities (or all of the authorities in England or Wales) taken together; and

(b) by apportioning that amount between them in such manner as the Secretary of State considers appropriate (which may involve, if he thinks fit, inferring the aggregate values of the houses and other property within their respective Housing Revenue Accounts from the average values of any of the houses and other property which they have disposed of);

and in this subsection "rental income" means income falling within item 1 of Part I of Schedule 4 to this Act and "housing expenditure" means expenditure falling within item 1 of Part II of that Schedule or falling to be debited to the authorities' Housing Repairs Accounts.

81.—(1) In subsection (2) of section 30 of the Social Security Act 1986 (housing benefit finance), for the words "total housing benefit" there shall be substituted the words "relevant benefit" and there shall be added at the end the words "and in this subsection 'relevant benefit' means total housing benefit excluding, in the case of a local authority in England and Wales, any Housing Revenue Account rebates granted by them".

(2) In subsection (5)(a) of that section, for sub-paragraphs (i) and (ii) there shall be substituted the words "for the credit of a revenue account of theirs which is not a Housing Revenue Account or Housing Repairs Account".

(3) For subsection (6) of that section there shall be substituted the following subsection—

"(6) Every local housing authority shall for each year carry to the credit of their Housing Revenue Account from some other revenue account of theirs which is not a Housing Repairs Account an amount equal to the aggregate of—

(a) so much of each Housing Revenue Account rebate granted by them during the year as was granted in the exercise of a discretion conferred by the housing benefit scheme or in pursuance of such modifications of that scheme as are mentioned in paragraph (b) of subsection (6) of section 28 above (general modifications); and

(b) unless the authority otherwise determine, so much of each such rebate as was granted in pursuance of such modifications of that scheme as are mentioned in paragraph (a) of that subsection (modifications for disregarding war disablement pensions or war widows' pensions)."

(4) In subsection (10) of that section, the words "rate fund" shall cease to have effect.

(5) In section 84(1) of that Act (general interpretation), in the definition of "Housing Revenue Account dwelling" for the words from "Part XIII of the Housing Act 1985)" to the end there shall be substituted the words "Part VI of the Local Government and Housing Act 1989)".

82.—(1) Where, in the case of any local housing authorities to whom no housing subsidy is payable for the year beginning 1st April 1989, houses or other property within their respective Housing Revenue Accounts—

(a) are disposed of in that year, or

U

(b) are in that year the subject of such other transactions as the Secretary of State may determine,

residual debt subsidy shall be payable for that year to those authorities in respect of costs relating to the houses or other property.

(2) Residual debt subsidy shall be paid by the Secretary of State at such times, in such manner and subject to such conditions as to records, certificates, audit or otherwise as he may, with the agreement of the Treasury, determine.

(3) Payment of residual debt subsidy shall be subject to the making of a claim for it in such form, and containing such particulars, as the Secretary of State may from time to time determine.

(4) Residual debt subsidy paid to a local housing authority shall be credited to the authority's Housing Revenue Account and, accordingly, for the year beginning 1st April 1989 the reference to housing subsidy in item 3 in Part I of Schedule 14 to the Housing Act 1985 shall be taken to include a reference to residual debt subsidy.

1985 c. 68.

Calculation of residual debt subsidy.

83.—(1) The amount of the residual debt subsidy (if any) payable to a local housing authority shall be calculated—

(a) in accordance with such formulae as the Secretary of State may from time to time determine; and

(b) by reference to such houses or other property as the Secretary of State may for the time being determine.

(2) A determination of the Secretary of State under this section may relate to disposals or other transactions which occur before the making of the determination.

Adjustment of housing subsidy for year 1989-90.

84.—(1) In any case where, apart from this subsection and subsection (2) below, the amount of housing subsidy payable to a local housing authority for the year beginning 1st April 1989 would be reduced or extinguished as a result of the transfer from the authority to a housing action trust of housing, land or other property as mentioned in section 74 of the Housing Act 1988, the Secretary of State, in the exercise of his power under section 423(2) of the Housing Act 1985, may adjust the authority's base amount for that year to take account of the effect of that transfer.

1988 c. 50.

(2) If, in accordance with subsection (1) above, the Secretary of State can make an adjustment of a local housing authority's base amount for the year beginning 1st April 1989 to take account of a transfer of housing, land or other property to a housing action trust, he may, instead of or as well as making such an adjustment, take account of the effect of the transfer in the making or varying of any determination for that year under section 424 (housing costs differential) or in the making of any determination under section 425 (local contribution differential) of the Housing Act 1985.

(3) Subsections (1) and (2) above shall be deemed to have been in force so as to be applicable for the year beginning 1st April 1989.

Supplementary

85.—(1) A local housing authority, and any officer or employee of a local housing authority concerned with their housing functions, shall supply the Secretary of State with such information as he may specify, either generally or in any particular case, for the purpose of enabling the Secretary of State to exercise his functions under section 80 or 83 above.

(2) A local housing authority shall supply the Secretary of State with such certificates supporting the information required by him as he may specify.

(3) If a local housing authority, or any officer or employee of a local housing authority concerned with their housing functions, fails to comply with subsection (1) or (2) above before the end of such period as the Secretary of State may specify, he may exercise his functions under section 80 or 83 above on the basis of such assumptions and estimates as he sees fit.

86.—(1) Where Housing Revenue Account subsidy or residual debt subsidy has been paid to a local housing authority and it appears to the Secretary of State that the case falls within rules published by him, he may recover from the authority the whole or such part of the payment as he may determine in accordance with the rules, with interest from such time and at such rates as he may so determine.

(2) Without prejudice to other methods of recovery, a sum recoverable under this section may be recovered by withholding or reducing subsidy.

87.—(1) A determination made or direction given by the Secretary of State under this Part—

(a) may make different provision for different cases or descriptions of cases, including different provision for different areas, for different local housing authorities or for different descriptions of local housing authorities;

(b) may be made before, during or after the end of the year to which it relates; and

(c) may be varied or revoked by a subsequent determination or direction.

(2) Before making a determination or giving a direction under this Part relating to all local housing authorities or any description of such authorities, the Secretary of State shall consult such representatives of local government and relevant professional bodies as appear to him to be appropriate; and, before making a determination or giving a direction relating to a particular local housing authority, he shall consult that authority.

(3) As soon as practicable after making a determination under this Part, the Secretary of State shall send a copy of the determination to the local housing authority or authorities to which it relates.

PART VI
Construction and
application of
Part VI.
1985 c. 68.

88.—(1) In this Part—

   (a) expressions which are used in Part XIII of the Housing Act 1985 (general financial provisions) have the same meaning as in that Part;

   (b) references to a local housing authority's Housing Revenue Account or Housing Repairs Account include, where the context so admits, references to the corresponding account kept by them under that Part;

   (c) references to a revenue account of a local housing authority other than their Housing Revenue Account do not include references to a Housing Repairs Account; and

   (d) references to proper practices shall be construed in accordance with section 66(4) above.

(2) Sections 82 to 84 above and, so far as relating to those sections or residual debt subsidy, this section and sections 85 to 87 above, have effect for the year beginning on 1st April 1989.

(3) Subject to subsection (2) above, this Part has effect for years beginning on or after 1st April 1990.

(4) If, before the passing of this Act, any statement was made by or on behalf of the Secretary of State—

   (a) that, if this Part were then in force, he would make, under section 83 above, such a determination as is set out in the statement, and

   (b) that, when this Act is passed, he is to be regarded as having made under that section the determination set out in the statement,

the determination set out in the statement shall have effect as if it had been validly made under section 83 above at the time of the statement.

(5) Any consultation undertaken—

   (a) before the passing of this Act, and

   (b) before the making of such a statement as is referred to in subsection (4) above, and

   (c) in connection with a determination proposed to be set out in the statement,

shall be as effective, in relation to that determination, as if this Part had been in force at the time the consultation was undertaken.

(6) Any consultation undertaken before the passing of this Act in connection with a determination proposed to be made under this Part shall be as effective, in relation to that determination, as if this Part had been in force at the time the consultation was undertaken.

PART VII

RENEWAL AREAS

Declaration of
renewal area.

89.—(1) Where a local housing authority, upon consideration of such a report as is mentioned in subsection (3) below and of any other matters which the authority consider relevant, are satisfied—

   (a) that the living conditions in an area within their district consisting primarily of housing accommodation are unsatisfactory, and

   (b) that those conditions can most effectively be dealt with by declaring the area to be a renewal area, P<small>ART</small> VII

then, subject to the following provisions of this Part, they may cause the area to be defined on a map and by resolution declare it to be a renewal area.

   (2) A renewal area may not include—

     (a) any land which lies within a designated area, within the meaning of Part III of the Housing Act 1988 (housing action trusts); or   1988 c. 50.

     (b) any parcel of land which is not contiguous with another parcel of land within the area.

   (3) The report referred to in subsection (1) above is one prepared, at the request of the local housing authority, by a person appearing to the authority to be suitably qualified (who may be an officer of the authority) and shall include particulars of the following matters—

     (a) the living conditions in the area concerned;

     (b) the ways in which those conditions may be improved (whether by the declaration of a renewal area or otherwise);

     (c) the powers available to the authority if the area is declared to be a renewal area;

     (d) the authority's detailed proposals for the exercise of those powers during the period that the area will be a renewal area (if so declared);

     (e) the cost of those proposals; and

     (f) the financial resources available, or likely to be available, to the authority (from whatever source) for implementing those proposals;

and the report shall contain a recommendation, with reasons, as to whether a renewal area should be declared.

   (4) In considering whether to declare an area to be a renewal area, a local housing authority shall have regard to such guidance as may from time to time be given by the Secretary of State.

   (5) Before exercising their power to declare an area to be a renewal area, a local housing authority shall take such steps as the Secretary of State may direct with respect to—

     (a) the publicity to be given to the proposed exercise of the power;

     (b) the persons from whom representations with respect to that proposed exercise are to be invited; and

     (c) the consideration of any such representations.

   (6) Subject to section 95 below, an area which is declared to be a renewal area shall be such an area for the period of ten years.

   (7) A resolution declaring an area to be a renewal area has effect from the day on which it is passed and is a local land charge.

90.—(1) An area may not be declared to be a renewal area unless,— Conditions for declaration of

     (a) the area contains not less than a specified minimum number of dwellings; renewal area.

PART VII

(b) of the dwellings in the area, not less than a specified proportion are privately owned;

(c) such conditions as may be specified with respect to the physical condition of the dwellings in the area and the financial circumstances of those living in the area are fulfilled; and

(d) such other conditions as may be specified are fulfilled;

and in this subsection "specified" means specified by directions made by the Secretary of State.

(2) For the purposes of subsection (1)(b) above, a dwelling is privately owned unless a freehold or a leasehold interest in it is held by—

(a) a local authority;

(b) a new town corporation;

(c) an urban development corporation;

(d) a housing action trust; or

(e) the Development Board for Rural Wales.

1985 c. 68.

(3) Expressions used in paragraphs (a) to (d) of subsection (2) above have the meaning assigned by section 4 of the Housing Act 1985.

(4) In this section "dwelling" includes a house in multiple occupation.

Steps to be taken after declaration of renewal area.

91.—(1) As soon as may be after declaring an area to be a renewal area a local housing authority shall—

(a) publish in two or more newspapers circulating in the locality (of which one at least shall, if practicable, be a local newspaper) a notice of the resolution identifying the area and naming a place where a copy of the resolution, the map on which the renewal area is defined and the report referred to in section 89 above may be inspected at all reasonable times;

(b) take such further steps as appear to the authority best designed to secure that the resolution is brought to the attention of persons residing or owning property in the area and that those persons are informed of the name and address of the person to whom should be addressed inquiries and representations concerning action to be taken with respect to the renewal area;

(c) provide, or secure the provision of, a service of information and advice to persons residing or owning property in the area who wish to carry out works to housing accommodation in the area; and

(d) send to the Secretary of State the documents specified in subsection (2) below.

(2) The documents mentioned in subsection (1)(d) above are—

(a) a copy of the resolution, the map on which the renewal area is defined and the report referred to in section 89 above; and

(b) a statement containing such information, relating to the declaration of the renewal area or the local housing authority's proposals for the area, as the Secretary of State may for the time being require, either generally or with respect to authorities in a particular area or in any particular case.

92.—(1) Where a local housing authority have declared an area to be a renewal area, they shall from time to time publish, in such manner as appears to them best designed to secure that the information is brought to the attention of persons residing or owning property in the area, information with respect to—

(a) the action they propose to take in relation to the area,

(b) the action they have taken in relation to the area, and

(c) the assistance available for the carrying out of works in the area,

being such information as appears to them best designed to further the purpose for which the area was declared a renewal area.

(2) In exercising their functions under subsection (1) above, a local housing authority shall comply with such directions (relating to any of the matters mentioned in that subsection) as may from time to time be given by the Secretary of State.

93.—(1) Where a local housing authority have declared an area to be a renewal area, the authority may exercise the powers conferred by this section.

(2) For the purpose of securing or assisting in securing all or any of the objectives mentioned in subsection (3) below, the authority may acquire by agreement, or be authorised by the Secretary of State to acquire compulsorily, any land in the area on which there are premises consisting of or including housing accommodation or which forms part of the curtilage of any such premises; and the authority may provide housing accommodation on land acquired under this subsection.

(3) The objectives referred to in subsection (2) above are—

(a) the improvement or repair of the premises, either by the authority or by a person to whom they propose to dispose of the premises;

(b) the proper and effective management and use of the housing accommodation, either by the authority or by a person to whom they propose to dispose of the premises comprising the accommodation; and

(c) the well-being of the persons for the time being residing in the area.

(4) For the purpose of effecting or assisting the improvement of the amenities in the area, the authority may acquire by agreement, or be authorised by the Secretary of State to acquire compulsorily, any land in the area (including land which the authority propose to dispose of to another person who intends to effect or assist the improvement of those amenities).

(5) The authority may—

(a) carry out works (including works of demolition) on land owned by the authority in the area (whether or not that land was acquired under subsection (2) or subsection (4) above); and

        (b) assist in the carrying out of works on any land in the area not owned by the authority, either by providing grants, loans or guarantees or by incurring expenditure for the benefit of the person assisted or by executing the works themselves or by providing materials for the carrying out of the works;

but assistance may not be given under paragraph (b) above in respect of works for which assistance is being or has been provided under Part VIII of this Act.

(6) The authority may enter into an agreement with a housing association or other person under which, in accordance with the terms of the agreement, all or any of the authority's functions under subsection (5) above are to be exercisable by that association or other person.

(7) If after—

        (a) the authority have entered into a contract for the acquisition of land under subsection (2) or subsection (4) above, or

        (b) a compulsory purchase order authorising the acquisition of land under either of those subsections has been confirmed,

the renewal area concerned ceases to be such an area or the land is excluded from the area, the provisions of the subsection in question shall continue to apply as if the land continued to be in a renewal area.

(8) The powers conferred by this section are without prejudice to any power which a local housing authority may have under or by virtue of any other enactment.

Power to apply for orders extinguishing right to use vehicles on highway.
1971 c. 78.

94.—(1) A local housing authority who have declared a renewal area may exercise the powers of a local planning authority under section 212 of the Town and Country Planning Act 1971 (extinguishment of right to use vehicles on certain highways) with respect to a highway in that area notwithstanding that they are not the local planning authority, but subject to the following provisions.

(2) The local housing authority shall not make an application under subsection (2) or subsection (8) of that section (application to Secretary of State to make or revoke order extinguishing right to use vehicles) except with the consent of the local planning authority.

(3) If the local housing authority are not also the highway authority, any such application made by them shall in the first place be sent to the highway authority who shall transmit it to the Secretary of State.

(4) Where an order under subsection (2) of that section (order extinguishing right to use vehicles) has been made on an application made by a local housing authority by virtue of this section, any compensation under subsection (5) of that section (compensation for loss of access to highway) is payable by them instead of by the local planning authority.

Exclusion of land from, or termination of, renewal area.

95.—(1) Subject to subsection (2) below, a local housing authority may by resolution—

        (a) exclude land from a renewal area; or

        (b) declare that an area shall cease to be a renewal area;

and as soon as may be after passing such a resolution the authority shall take the steps required by subsections (3) to (5) below.

(2) Before exercising any power under subsection (1) above, an authority shall take such steps as the Secretary of State may direct with respect to—

    (a) the publicity to be given to the proposed exercise of the power;

    (b) the persons from whom representations with respect to that proposed exercise are to be invited; and

    (c) the consideration of any such representations.

(3) The authority shall send to the Secretary of State—

    (a) a copy of the resolution; and

    (b) such other information with respect to the resolution as the Secretary of State may specify either generally or in any particular case.

(4) The authority shall publish in two or more newspapers circulating in the locality (of which one at least shall, if practicable, be a local newspaper) a notice of the resolution—

    (a) identifying the renewal area;

    (b) describing the effect of the resolution;

    (c) naming a place at which a copy of the resolution may be inspected at all reasonable times; and

    (d) in the case of a resolution excluding land, identifying the land excluded from the renewal area.

(5) The authority shall take such further steps as appear to them best designed to secure that the resolution is brought to the attention of persons residing or owning property in the renewal area.

(6) A resolution under subsection (1) above has effect from the day on which it is passed.

(7) A resolution under subsection (1) above does not affect the continued operation of the provisions of this Part, or any other enactment relating to renewal areas, in relation to works begun before the date on which the exclusion or cessation takes effect; but the resolution does have effect with respect to works which have not been begun before that date, notwithstanding that expenditure in respect of the works has been approved before that date.

96.—(1) The Secretary of State may pay contributions to local housing authorities towards such expenditure incurred by them under this Part as he may determine.

Contributions by the Secretary of State.

(2) The rate or rates of the contributions, the calculation of the expenditure to which they relate and the manner of their payment shall be such as may be determined by the Secretary of State with the consent of the Treasury; and any determination under this subsection or subsection (1) above may be made generally, or with respect to a particular local housing authority or description of authority, including a description framed by reference to authorities in a particular area.

(3) Contributions under this section shall be payable subject to such conditions as to records, certificates, audit or otherwise as the Secretary of State may, with the approval of the Treasury, impose.

(4) If, before the declaration of a renewal area, a local housing authority are satisfied that the rate of contributions which, in accordance with a determination under subsection (2) above, would otherwise be applicable to the authority will not be adequate, bearing in mind the action they propose to take with regard to the area, they may, before making the declaration, apply to the Secretary of State for contributions at a higher rate in respect of that area.

(5) An application under subsection (4) above shall be made in such form and shall contain such particulars as the Secretary of State may determine; and, if such an application is made, the authority shall not declare the area concerned to be a renewal area until the application is approved, refused or withdrawn.

(6) If an application under subsection (4) above is approved, the Secretary of State may pay contributions under subsection (1) above in respect of the area concerned at such higher rate as he may determine under subsection (2) above.

Powers of entry and penalty for obstruction.

97.—(1) A person authorised by the local housing authority or the Secretary of State may at any reasonable time, on giving not less than seven days' notice of his intention to the occupier, and to the owner if the owner is known, enter premises—

(a) for the purpose of survey and examination where it appears to the authority or the Secretary of State that survey or examination is necessary in order to determine whether any powers under this Part should be exercised; or

(b) for the purpose of survey or valuation where the authority are authorised by this Part to acquire the premises compulsorily.

(2) An authorisation for the purposes of this section—

(a) shall be in writing stating the particular purpose or purposes for which the entry is authorised; and

(b) shall, if so required, be produced for inspection by the occupier or anyone acting on his behalf.

(3) It is a summary offence intentionally to obstruct an officer of the local housing authority or of the Secretary of State, or a person authorised to enter premises under subsection (1) above, in the performance of anything which that officer, authority or person is by this Part required or authorised to do.

(4) A person who commits an offence under subsection (3) above is liable on conviction to a fine not exceeding level 3 on the standard scale.

(5) In this section "owner", in relation to premises,—

(a) means a person (other than a mortgagee not in possession) who is for the time being entitled to dispose of the fee simple in the premises, whether in possession or reversion, and

(b) includes also a person holding or entitled to the rents and profits of the premises under a lease of which the unexpired term exceeds three years.

98.—(1) The provisions of this Part have effect in place of Part VIII of the Housing Act 1985 (housing action areas and general improvement areas) and, accordingly, after the appointed day, a local housing authority shall no longer have power under that Part to declare an area a housing action area or a general improvement area.

(2) If, apart from this subsection, a general improvement area would remain in existence on the first anniversary of the appointed day, the area shall, by virtue of this section cease to be a general improvement area on that first anniversary.

(3) In any case where, immediately before the appointed day, the period for which a housing action area has effect exceeds two years, the duration of that area shall, by virtue of this section, be such that, subject to subsection (4) below, it ends on the first anniversary of the appointed day.

(4) Nothing in subsection (3) above affects the power of a local housing authority,—

(a) by resolution under section 250(1)(b) of the Housing Act 1985, to bring a housing action area to an end; or

(b) by resolution under section 251 of that Act, to extend, on one occasion only, the duration of a housing action area by a period of two years.

(5) In the application of section 245 of the Housing Act 1985 (contributions by Secretary of State towards expenditure of local housing authorities relating to environmental works in housing action areas) in relation to expenditure—

(a) which was incurred on or after 14th June 1989, and

(b) in respect of which no contribution under that section was paid before the appointed day,

for subsection (2) of that section there shall be substituted the following subsection—

"(2) In the case of any expenditure, the contribution—

(a) shall be equal to one-half of the amount of the expenditure; and

(b) shall be payable in one sum or by two or more instalments, according as the Secretary of State may determine."

(6) In the application of section 259 of the Housing Act 1985 (contributions by Secretary of State towards expenditure of local housing authorities relating to general improvement areas) in relation to expenditure—

(a) which was incurred on or after 14th June 1989, and

(b) in respect of which no contribution under that section was paid before the appointed day,

for subsection (2) of that section there shall be substituted the following subsection—

"(2) In the case of any expenditure, the contribution—

(a) shall be equal to one-half of the amount of the expenditure; and

PART VII

(b) shall be payable in one sum or by two or more instalments, according as the Secretary of State may determine."

(7) In the preceding provisions of this section "the appointed day" means the day appointed for the coming into force of this section.

Directions and guidance.

99. Any power under this Part to give directions or guidance may be so exercised as to make different provision for different cases, different descriptions of cases and different areas and, in particular, with respect to different local housing authorities or descriptions of authority (including a description framed by reference to authorities in a particular area).

Interpretation of Part VII.

100.—(1) In this Part, except where the context otherwise requires,—

"dwelling" means a building or part of a building occupied or intended to be occupied as a separate dwelling, together with any yard, garden, outhouses and appurtenances belonging to or usually enjoyed with it;

1985 c. 68.

"house in multiple occupation" has the same meaning as in Part XI of the Housing Act 1985, except that it does not include any part of such a house which is occupied as a separate dwelling by persons who do form a single household;

"housing accommodation" means dwellings, houses in multiple occupation and hostels;

"local housing authority" and any reference to the district of such an authority shall be construed in accordance with sections 1 and 2 of the Housing Act 1985.

(2) Part XVII of the Housing Act 1985 (compulsory purchase and land compensation) applies in relation to this Part as if it were contained in that Act.

PART VIII

GRANTS TOWARDS COST OF IMPROVEMENTS AND REPAIRS ETC.

Introductory

Grants for improvements and repairs.

101.—(1) In accordance with this Part, grants are payable by local housing authorities towards the cost of works required—

(a) for the improvement or repair of dwellings, houses in multiple occupation or the common parts of buildings containing one or more flats; and

(b) for the provision of dwellings or houses in multiple occupation by the conversion of a house or other building; and

(c) for the provision of facilities for disabled persons in dwellings and in the common parts of buildings containing one or more flats.

(2) In this Part—

(a) a grant relating to the improvement or repair of a dwelling or to the provision of dwellings by the conversion of a house or other building is referred to as a "renovation grant"; and

(b) a grant relating to the improvement or repair of the common parts of a building is referred to as a "common parts grant"; and

(c) a grant for the provision of facilities for a disabled person in a dwelling or in the common parts of a building containing one or more flats is referred to as a "disabled facilities grant"; and

(d) a grant for the improvement or repair of a house in multiple occupation or for the provision of a house in multiple occupation by the conversion of a house or other building is referred to as an "HMO grant";

and in the following provisions of this Part the expression "grant", without more, means any of these types of grant.

(3) No grant is payable under this Part if the person who would otherwise qualify as the applicant for the grant is—

(a) a local authority;

(b) a new town corporation;

(c) an urban development corporation;

(d) a housing action trust;

(e) the Development Board for Rural Wales;

(f) a joint authority established by Part IV of the Local Government Act 1985;

(g) a residuary body established by Part VII of that Act; or

(h) an authority established under section 10(1) of that Act (waste disposal).

1985 c. 51.

(4) Expressions used in paragraphs (a) to (d) of subsection (3) above have the meanings assigned by section 4 of the Housing Act 1985.

1985 c. 68.

(5) The provisions of this Part have effect in place of the provisions of Part XV of the Housing Act 1985 (grants for works of improvement, repair and conversion), other than section 523 thereof (assistance for provision of separate service pipe for water supply), and, without prejudice to the generality of subsection (3) of section 195 below,—

(a) any application made under section 461 of that Act which has not been approved by the local housing authority before the day appointed under section 195 below for the coming into force of this section shall be of no effect on and after that day; and

(b) any application under section 521 of that Act (schemes for grants for thermal insulation) in respect of which the applicant has not been notified before the day so appointed that he may proceed to execute works in accordance with a scheme under that section shall be of no effect on and after that day.

102.—(1) No grant shall be paid unless an application for it is made to the local housing authority concerned in accordance with the provisions of this Part and is approved by them.

Applications for grants.

(2) An application for a grant shall be in writing and shall specify the premises to which it relates and contain—

(a) particulars of the works in respect of which the grant is sought (in this Part referred to as "the relevant works");

(b) unless the local housing authority otherwise direct in any particular case, at least two estimates from different contractors of the cost of carrying out the relevant works;

(c) particulars of any preliminary or ancillary services and charges in respect of the cost of which the grant is also sought; and

(d) such other particulars as may be prescribed.

(3) In this Part "preliminary or ancillary services and charges", in relation to an application for a grant, means services and charges which—

(a) relate to the application and the preparation for and the carrying out of works; and

(b) are specified for the purposes of this subsection by the Secretary of State.

(4) The Secretary of State may by regulations prescribe a form of application for a grant and an application for a grant to which any such regulations apply shall not be validly made unless it is in the prescribed form.

Preliminary conditions

The age of the property.

103.—(1) A local housing authority may not entertain an application for a grant, other than a disabled facilities grant, unless they are satisfied that, at the date of the application, the dwelling, common parts or house or other building concerned was provided not less than the relevant period before that date.

(2) In subsection (1) above—

(a) "provided" means provided by construction or conversion; and

(b) "the relevant period" means ten years or such other period as the Secretary of State may by order provide.

The interest of the applicant in the property.

104.—(1) Subject to subsection (4) and section 136 below, a local housing authority may not entertain an application for a grant, other than a common parts grant, unless they are satisfied that—

(a) the applicant has, or proposes to acquire, an owner's interest in every parcel of land on which the relevant works are to be carried out; or

(b) in the case of an application for a renovation grant (other than an application in respect of works required for the provision of one or more dwellings by the conversion of a house or other building), the applicant is a tenant of the dwelling (alone or jointly with others) but does not have, or propose to acquire, an owner's interest in the dwelling; or

(c) in the case of an application for a disabled facilities grant in respect of works to a dwelling, the applicant is a tenant of the dwelling (alone or jointly with others) but does not have, or propose to acquire, an owner's interest in the dwelling; or

(d) in the case of an application for a disabled facilities grant in respect of works to the common parts of a building containing one or more flats, the applicant is a tenant of a flat in the building (alone or jointly with others) but does not have, or propose to acquire, such an owner's interest as is referred to in paragraph (a) above;

and references in this Part to an "owner's application" or a "tenant's application" shall be construed accordingly.

(2) In this Part "owner's interest" means an interest which—

    (a) is held by the applicant alone or jointly with others; and

    (b) is either an estate in fee simple absolute in possession or a term of years absolute of which not less than five years remain unexpired at the date of the application.

(3) Where a local housing authority entertain an owner's application made by a person who proposes to acquire the necessary interest, they shall not approve the application until they are satisfied that he has done so.

(4) In accordance with directions given by the Secretary of State, a local housing authority may treat the condition in subsection (1)(a) above as fulfilled by a person who has, or proposes to acquire, an owner's interest in only part of the land concerned; and directions under this subsection may make different provision with respect to different cases or descriptions of cases, including different provision for different areas.

(5) A local housing authority may not entertain a tenant's application unless—

    (a) the tenant is required by the terms of his tenancy to carry out the relevant works and his tenancy is not of a description excluded from this subsection by an order made by the Secretary of State; or

    (b) his tenancy is of a description specified for the purposes of this subsection by an order made by the Secretary of State; or

    (c) his application is for a disabled facilities grant.

105.—(1) A local housing authority may not entertain an application for a common parts grant unless they are satisfied—

    (a) that, at the date of the application, at least the required proportion of the flats in the building concerned is occupied by occupying tenants; and

    (b) that the application is either a landlord's common parts application or a tenants' common parts application.

Common parts grants: preliminary conditions.

(2) In this Part—

    (a) an "occupying tenant", in relation to a flat in a building, is a person—

        (i) who has (alone or jointly with others) such an interest in the flat as is mentioned in any of paragraphs (b) to (e) of subsection (4) below; and

        (ii) who occupies the flat as his only or main residence;

    (b) a "landlord's common parts application", in relation to works to the common parts of a building, is an application for a common parts grant made by a person who—

        (i) has (alone or jointly with others) such an interest in the building as is mentioned in paragraph (a) or paragraph (b) of subsection (4) below; and

        (ii) has a duty or power to carry out the relevant works; and

    (c) a "tenants' common parts application", in relation to works to the common parts of a building, is an application for a common parts grant made, subject to subsection (3) below, by at least three-quarters of the occupying tenants of the building who, under their tenancies, have a duty to carry out, or to make a contribution in respect of the carrying out of, some or all of the relevant works;

and in any case where a tenancy is held by two or more persons jointly, those persons shall be regarded as a single occupying tenant in deciding, for the purposes of paragraph (c) above, whether the application is made by at least three-quarters of the occupying tenants referred to in that paragraph.

(3) For the purposes of paragraph (c) of subsection (2) above, a tenant whose tenancy is of a description specified for the purpose of that paragraph by an order made by the Secretary of State shall be treated as an occupying tenant falling within that paragraph; and a person who falls within paragraph (b)(i) of that subsection and has a duty or power to carry out any of the relevant works may also join in a tenants' common parts application; and, where such a person does join in an application, he is in this Part referred to as a "participating landlord".

(4) The interests referred to in subsection (2) above are as follows—

    (a) an estate in fee simple absolute in possession;

    (b) a term of years absolute of which not less than five years remain unexpired at the date of the application;

1954 c. 56.

    (c) a tenancy to which section 1 of the Landlord and Tenant Act 1954 or Schedule 10 to this Act applies (long tenancies at low rents);

    (d) an assured tenancy, a protected tenancy, a secure tenancy, a protected occupancy or a statutory tenancy; and

    (e) a tenancy which satisfies such conditions as may be prescribed by order made by the Secretary of State.

(5) The required proportion mentioned in subsection (1) above is three-quarters or such other proportion as may be—

    (a) prescribed for the purposes of this section by an order made by the Secretary of State; or

    (b) approved by him, in relation to a particular case or description of case, on application made by the local housing authority concerned.

Certificate as to future occupation, etc.

106.—(1) Subject to sections 126 and 136 below, a local housing authority may not entertain an application for a renovation grant or a disabled facilities grant unless it is accompanied by a certificate falling within one of subsections (2) to (5) below in respect of the dwelling, building or flat to which the application relates.

(2) A certificate under this subsection (an "owner-occupation certificate") certifies—

    (a) that the applicant has, or proposes to acquire, an owner's interest in the dwelling or building; and

    (b) that he, or a member of his family, intends to live in the dwelling or, as the case may be, a flat in the building as his (or that member's) only or main residence for a period of not less than twelve months beginning on the certified date.

(3) A certificate under this subsection (a "tenant's certificate") certifies—

    (a) that the applicant is a tenant of the dwelling who falls within paragraph (a) or paragraph (b) of subsection (5) of section 104 above or that his application is a tenant's application for a disabled facilities grant; and

    (b) that he or a member of his family intends to live in the dwelling or, as the case may be, a flat in the building as his (or that member's) only or main residence.

(4) A certificate under this subsection (a "certificate of intended letting") certifies that the applicant has or proposes to acquire an owner's interest in the dwelling or building and intends to or already has let the dwelling or, as the case may be, one or more flats in the building as a residence—

    (a) to someone other than a member of his family; and

    (b) for a period of not less than five years beginning on the certified date; and

    (c) except where the application relates to a disabled facilities grant, on a tenancy which is not a long tenancy.

(5) A certificate under this subsection (a "special certificate") certifies that the applicant has, or proposes to acquire, an owner's interest in the dwelling or building and is an applicant of a class prescribed for the purposes of this section.

(6) A local housing authority may not entertain a tenant's application unless—

    (a) it is also accompanied by a certificate of intended letting made by the person who at the time of the application is the landlord under the tenancy; or

    (b) they consider it unreasonable in the circumstances to seek such a certificate.

(7) A local housing authority may not entertain an application for an HMO grant unless it is accompanied by a certificate that the applicant has or proposes to acquire an owner's interest in the house in question and intends—

    (a) to license the use of part of it as a residence as mentioned in paragraphs (a) to (c) of subsection (4) above, or

    (b) to let part of it as a residence as mentioned in those paragraphs,

or has already so licensed or let part of it.

(8) A local housing authority may not entertain an application for a common parts grant unless it is accompanied by a certificate signed by the applicant or, as the case may be, by each of the applicants which—

    (a) specifies the interest of the applicant or, as the case may be, each of the applicants in the building or in each flat in the building; and

    (b) certifies that the required proportion, within the meaning of section 105 above, of the flats in the building is occupied by occupying tenants.

Certain dwellings
and works
excluded from
grant aid.

1985 c. 68.

Restrictions on grant aid

107.—(1) In each of the cases in subsection (2) below, the local housing authority may not approve an application for a grant unless—

    (a) it is an application which they are required to approve by virtue of section 112 below and completion of the relevant works is necessary to comply with a notice under section 189 of the Housing Act 1985 (repair notice requiring works to render premises fit for human habitation); or

    (b) it is an application which they are required to approve by virtue of section 113 below.

(2) The cases referred to in subsection (1) above are as follows—

    (a) if, in the case of an application in respect of a dwelling or house which is not fit for human habitation, the local housing authority consider that the carrying out of the relevant works will not be sufficient to cause the dwelling or house to be fit for human habitation;

    (b) if or to the extent that the relevant works have been completed before the date of service of the notice of refusal under section 116(1) below;

    (c) if, within the period of three months beginning on the date of service of the notice of refusal, the authority intend to make a closing or demolition order relating to the dwelling, house or building under section 264 or section 265 of the Housing Act 1985;

    (d) if, within the period of twelve months beginning on the date of service of the notice of refusal, the authority intend to declare a clearance area under section 289 of the Housing Act 1985 for an area which includes the dwelling, house or building;

    (e) if the dwelling, house or building is or forms part of a building of a class designated under section 528 or section 559 of the Housing Act 1985 (defective dwellings), the applicant is eligible for assistance under Part XVI of that Act in respect of a defective dwelling which is or forms part of the dwelling, house or building concerned and the relevant works are, within the meaning of that Part, work required to re-instate that defective dwelling; and

    (f) if, in the case of an application for a common parts grant, the local housing authority consider that the carrying out of the relevant works will not be sufficient to cause the building to meet the requirements mentioned in paragraphs (a) to (e) of section 604(2) of the Housing Act 1985.

(3) Where a group repair scheme has been approved by the Secretary of State, a local housing authority may not approve an application for a grant in so far as it relates to works which will be carried out in pursuance of agreements entered into, or to be entered into, in pursuance of the scheme.

(4) A local housing authority may not approve an application for a grant so far as it relates to works which are of a description excluded from grant aid by directions made by the Secretary of State.

(5) Unless it is an application which they are required to approve by virtue of section 113 below, a local housing authority may not approve an application for an HMO grant so far as it relates to works—

    (a) which relate to means of escape from fire or other fire precautions; and

    (b) which are required to be carried out under or by virtue of any enactment (whenever passed).

(6) If directions made by the Secretary of State under subsection (4) above specify a description of works for which grant aid is not to be available without his consent, a local housing authority may not approve an application for a grant, so far as it relates to works of that description, unless the Secretary of State has given his consent with respect to those works.

(7) Directions under subsection (4) above may be made with respect to local housing authorities generally or to a particular local housing authority.

(8) The Secretary of State may give his consent for the purposes of subsection (6) above—

    (a) with respect to local housing authorities generally or to a particular local housing authority; or

    (b) with respect to applications generally or to a particular description of applications.

108.—(1) Subject to subsections (2) and (3) below, a local housing authority may not approve an application for a grant if the relevant works have been commenced before the application is approved and shall serve a notice of refusal to that effect on the applicant.

Restriction on grants for works already begun.

(2) Subsection (1) above does not apply to—

    (a) an application which the local housing authority are required to approve by virtue of section 112 below if completion of the relevant works is necessary to comply with a notice under section 189 of the Housing Act 1985 (repair notice requiring works to render premises fit for human habitation); or

1985 c. 68.

    (b) an application which the local housing authority are required to approve by virtue of section 113 below.

(3) Where the relevant works have not been completed, the authority concerned may approve the application for a grant if they are satisfied that there were good reasons for beginning the works before the application was approved.

(4) Where an authority decide to approve an application in accordance with subsection (3) above—

    (a) they may, with the consent of the applicant, treat the application as varied so that the relevant works are limited to those that remain to be completed at the date of the application; and

    (b) in determining for the purposes of sections 112, 114 and 115 below the physical condition of the dwelling, common parts or house or other building concerned, they shall consider the condition of the premises at the date of the application.

109.—(1) Where an application for a grant is accompanied by an owner-occupation certificate, a tenant's certificate or a special certificate, then, if the financial resources of the applicant exceed the applicable amount, the amount of any grant which may be paid shall be reduced from what it would otherwise have been in accordance with regulations made by the Secretary of State with the consent of the Treasury.

(2) For the purposes of this Part, the Secretary of State may by regulations made with the consent of the Treasury—

(a) make provision for the determination of the amount which is to be taken to be the financial resources of an applicant for a grant; and

(b) make provision for the determination of the applicable amount referred to in subsection (1) above.

(3) Without prejudice to the generality of subsection (2) above, regulations under this section—

(a) may make provision for account to be taken of the income, assets, needs and outgoings not only of the applicant himself but also of his spouse, any person living with him or intending to live with him and any person on whom he is dependent or who is dependent on him;

(b) may make provision for amounts specified in or determined under the regulations to be taken into account for particular purposes.

110.—(1) Subject to section 126 below, this section applies—

(a) where an application for a grant is accompanied by a certificate of intended letting with respect to a dwelling and is not a tenant's application; and

(b) where an application for an HMO grant is accompanied by a certificate under section 106(7) above; and

(c) where, by virtue of section 136 below, sections 104 and 106 above do not apply to an application for a grant; and

(d) where an application for a grant is a landlord's common parts application.

(2) Subject to the following provisions of this section and to section 116(5) below, the amount of the grant (if any) shall be such as may be determined by the local housing authority, having regard to—

(a) the cost of the relevant works;

(b) if the dwelling is currently let or subject to a statutory tenancy, the amount of the rent payable and of any increase which might reasonably be expected in that rent to take account of the relevant works, when completed;

(c) if paragraph (b) above does not apply, the amount of the rent which might reasonably be expected to be obtained on a letting of the dwelling on the open market under an assured tenancy (assuming that no premium is paid); and

(d) such other matters as the Secretary of State may direct.

(3) In considering the matters in paragraphs (b) and (c) of subsection (2) above, the local housing authority may seek and act upon the advice of rent officers; and, for this purpose, in section 121 of the Housing Act 1988 (additional functions of rent officers) at the end of subsection (1) there shall be added the words "and applications to which section 110 of the Local Government and Housing Act 1989 applies".

(4) Where the applicant is a charity or the application is in respect of glebe land, the local housing authority shall also have regard—

  (a) to any obligation or practice on the part of the applicant to let dwellings at a rent less than that which could be obtained on the open market;

  (b) to any financial resources available to the applicant in addition to the rent from the dwelling; and

  (c) generally to the circumstances of the applicant concerned.

(5) In the case of an application for an HMO grant, in subsections (2) and (4) above, any reference to rent shall be construed as a reference to the aggregate of the consideration under licences or lettings of the house in question and any reference to letting a dwelling shall be construed accordingly.

(6) Where the application is for a grant in respect of the residence house of an ecclesiastical benefice, paragraphs (b) and (c) of subsection (2) above shall not apply and the local housing authority shall also have regard—

  (a) to any financial resources available to the applicant; and

  (b) generally to the circumstances of the applicant.

(7) In a case where the application is a landlord's common parts application, each of the dwellings in the building concerned shall be taken into account under paragraph (b) or paragraph (c) of subsection (2) above so as to determine an aggregate rent for the purposes of that subsection.

111.—(1) This section applies where an application for a grant is a tenants' common parts application.

(2) The local housing authority shall decide how much of the cost of the relevant works is attributable to the applicants (in this section referred to as "the attributable cost"); and, for the purposes of this section, the attributable cost is an amount equal to the proportion, referred to in subsection (3) below, of the cost of the relevant works.

(3) The proportion mentioned in subsection (2) above is as follows—

  (a) where it can be ascertained, the proportion that the aggregate of each of the applicant's respective liabilities to carry out or contribute to the carrying out of the relevant works bears to the aggregate of all such liabilities on the part of all persons (including the applicants) so liable; or

(b) where the proportion mentioned in paragraph (a) above cannot be ascertained, the proportion that the number of applicants bears to the number of persons (including the applicants) liable to carry out or contribute to the carrying out of works to the building;

and in any case where the interest by virtue of which the liability referred to in paragraph (b) above arises is held jointly by two or more persons, those persons shall be regarded as a single person in deciding for the purposes of that paragraph the number of persons so liable.

(4) The local housing authority shall then apportion the attributable cost to each of the applicants—

(a) in a case where the attributable cost is calculated by reference to the proportion mentioned in paragraph (a) of subsection (3) above, according to the proportion that his liabilities to carry out or contribute to the carrying out of the relevant works bears to the aggregate of the applicants' liabilities mentioned in that paragraph; or

(b) in a case where the attributable cost is calculated by reference to the proportion mentioned in paragraph (b) of that subsection, equally;

and the amount of grant payable shall be the aggregate of the grants that would be payable to each of the applicants under section 109 above or, in the case of a participating landlord, section 110 above if each of the applicants was an individual applicant under section 109 above or, as the case may be, section 110 above in respect of his apportionment of the attributable cost under paragraph (a) or, as the case may be, paragraph (b) above.

Approvals, notification and payment

Duty to approve applications to render certain dwellings fit for human habitation.

112.—(1) Subject to the preceding provisions of this Part, on receipt of an application for a renovation grant (other than an application in respect of works required for the provision of one or more dwellings by the conversion of a house or other building), the local housing authority shall determine, with respect to the dwelling, whether the dwelling is fit for human habitation.

(2) In any case where the local housing authority—

(a) determine under subsection (1) above that a dwelling is not fit for human habitation, and

(b) consider that completion of the relevant works will cause the dwelling to be fit for human habitation, and

(c) are satisfied that completion of the relevant works is the most satisfactory course of action,

then, subject to subsections (4) and (5) below, they shall approve the application so far as it relates to that dwelling.

1985 c. 68.

(3) If, in the case of any application, the local housing authority consider that the relevant works include works for which assistance is available under Part XVI of the Housing Act 1985 (assistance for owners of defective housing), they shall treat the application as if the relevant works did not include those works.

(4) If, in the case of any application, other than one to which section 113 or section 115(6) below applies, the local housing authority consider that the relevant works include works in addition to those which will cause the dwelling to be fit for human habitation ("the additional works"), they shall treat the application—

(a) as an application under this section in so far as it relates to works other than the additional works; and

(b) as an application under section 115 below in so far as it relates to the additional works;

but, for the purposes of section 116 below and the subsequent provisions of this Part, the two applications shall be treated as one application.

(5) A local housing authority shall not be under a duty under this section to approve an application—

(a) which is accompanied by a certificate of intended letting and is not a tenant's application; or

(b) if they expect, within the period of twelve months beginning with the date of receipt of the application, to prepare a group repair scheme in respect of a building which includes or comprises the dwelling.

(6) Section 604 of the Housing Act 1985 (fitness for human habitation) applies for the purposes of this Part, as it applies for the purposes of that Act. 1985 c. 68.

(7) In deciding whether they are satisfied as mentioned in subsection (2)(c) above, the local housing authority shall have regard to any guidance given under section 604A of the Housing Act 1985 and, for that purpose, the authority shall treat any guidance given in respect of the serving of a repair notice under section 189(1) of that Act as guidance given in respect of the completion of the relevant works.

113.—(1) Subject to section 112(3) above and subsection (3) below, a local housing authority shall approve an application falling within section 110(1) above (in this section referred to as a "landlord's application") if completion of the relevant works is necessary to comply with a notice or notices under one or more of the following provisions— Duty to approve applications arising out of certain statutory notices.

(a) section 189 of the Housing Act 1985 (repair notice requiring works to render premises fit for human habitation);

(b) section 190 of that Act (repair notice in respect of premises in state of disrepair but not unfit); and

(c) section 352 of that Act (notice requiring works to render premises fit for number of occupants).

(2) Subject to section 112(3) above and subsection (3) below, a local housing authority shall approve an application for a grant which is accompanied by an owner-occupation certificate (in this section referred to as an "owner-occupier's application") if completion of the relevant works is necessary to comply with a notice under section 190 of the Housing Act 1985.

(3) If, in the case of a landlord's application or an owner-occupier's application, the local housing authority consider that the relevant works include works ("the additional works") in addition to those necessary to comply with a notice under section 189, section 190 or section 352 of the Housing Act 1985, they shall treat the application—

(a) as an application to which this section applies in so far as it relates to works other than the additional works; and

(b) as an application to which section 115 below applies in so far as it relates to the additional works.

Approval of applications to provide certain facilities for the disabled.

114.—(1) A local housing authority shall not approve an application for a disabled facilities grant unless they are satisfied—

(a) that the relevant works are necessary and appropriate to meet the needs of the disabled occupant; and

(b) that it is reasonable and practicable to carry out the relevant works, having regard to the age and condition of the dwelling or building;

and, in considering the matters specified in paragraph (a) above, the local housing authority shall consult the welfare authority.

(2) A local housing authority shall not approve an application for a disabled facilities grant in respect of works to the common parts of a building containing one or more flats unless they are satisfied that the applicant has a power or is under a duty to carry out the relevant works.

(3) Subject to the preceding provisions of this Part, a local housing authority shall approve an application for a disabled facilities grant if the relevant works are for any one or more of the following purposes—

(a) facilitating access by the disabled occupant to and from the dwelling or the building in which the dwelling or, as the case may be, flat is situated;

(b) facilitating access by the disabled occupant to a room used or usable as the principal family room;

(c) facilitating access by the disabled occupant to, or providing for the disabled occupant, a room used or usable for sleeping;

(d) facilitating access by the disabled occupant to, or providing for the disabled occupant, a room in which there is a lavatory, bath, shower or washhand basin or facilitating the use by the disabled occupant of such a facility;

(e) facilitating the preparation and cooking of food by the disabled occupant;

(f) improving any heating system in the dwelling to meet the needs of the disabled occupant or, if there is no existing heating system in the dwelling or any such system is unsuitable for use by the disabled occupant, providing a heating system suitable to meet his needs;

(g) facilitating the use by the disabled occupant of a source of power, light or heat by altering the position of one or more means of access to or control of that source or by providing additional means of control; and

(h) facilitating access and movement by the disabled occupant around the dwelling in order to enable him to care for a person who is normally resident in the dwelling and is in need of such care.

(4) Subject to the preceding provisions of this Part, a local housing authority may approve an application for a disabled facilities grant where the relevant works do not fall within subsection (3) above but are for the purpose of making the dwelling or building suitable for the accommodation, welfare or employment of the disabled occupant.

(5) In this section "the disabled occupant" means the disabled person for whose benefit it is proposed to carry out any of the relevant works.

(6) In this Part "disabled person" means—

    (a) a person who is registered in pursuance of arrangements made under section 29(1) of the National Assistance Act 1948 (handicapped persons' welfare); or

    (b) any other person for whose welfare arrangements have been made under that provision or, in the opinion of the welfare authority, might be made under it.

1948 c. 29.

(7) For the purposes of this section, "welfare authority" means the council which is the local authority for the purposes of the Local Authority Social Services Act 1970 for the area in which the dwelling is situated.

1970 c. 42.

115.—(1) Subject to the preceding provisions of this Part, a local housing authority may approve an application for a grant, other than a common parts grant, in any case where—

Discretionary approval of certain applications.

    (a) the relevant works go beyond or are other than those which will cause the dwelling to be fit for human habitation, but

    (b) the authority are satisfied that the relevant works are necessary for one or more of the purposes set out in subsection (3) below.

(2) Subject to the preceding provisions of this Part, a local housing authority may approve an application for a common parts grant if the authority are satisfied that the relevant works—

    (a) are necessary for one or more of the purposes set out in paragraphs (a) and (c) to (g) of subsection (3) below; or

    (b) will cause the building to meet the requirements mentioned in paragraphs (a) to (e) of section 604(2) of the Housing Act 1985.

1985 c. 68.

(3) The purposes referred to in subsection (1) above are—

    (a) to put the dwelling or building in reasonable repair;

    (b) to provide the dwelling by the conversion of a house or other building;

    (c) to provide adequate thermal insulation;

    (d) to provide adequate facilities for space heating;

    (e) to provide satisfactory internal arrangements;

    (f) to ensure that the dwelling or building complies with such requirements with respect to construction or physical condition as may for the time being be specified by the Secretary of State for the purposes of this section; and

    (g) to ensure that there is compliance with such requirements with respect to the provision or condition of services and amenities to or within the dwelling or building as may for the time being be so specified.

PART VIII

(4) In the case of an application for an HMO grant, any reference in subsections (1) and (3) above to the dwelling shall be construed as a reference to the house.

(5) In considering whether to approve an application for a grant in exercise of their discretion under subsection (1) or subsection (2) above, the local housing authority shall have regard to the expected life of the building (taking account, where appropriate, of the effect of carrying out the relevant works).

(6) Subject to the preceding provisions of this Part, a local housing authority may approve an application falling within section 110(1) above (in this section referred to as a "landlord's application") if—

> (a) the relevant works are for the purpose of rendering the dwelling or house to which the application relates fit for human habitation, or

> (b) in the case of an application for an HMO grant, the relevant works are for the purpose of enabling the house in question to meet one or more of the requirements in subsection (1A) of section 352 of the Housing Act 1985,

1985 c. 68.

and (in either case) the authority are satisfied that the relevant works are necessary for the purpose concerned.

(7) If in the opinion of the local housing authority the relevant works are more or less extensive than is necessary to achieve the result referred to in paragraph (b) of subsection (2) above or any of the purposes set out in subsection (3) above or, as the case may be, the purpose falling within subsection (6) above, the authority may, with the consent of the applicant, treat the application as varied so that the relevant works are limited to or, as the case may be, include such works as seem to the authority to be necessary for that purpose.

(8) In determining what is "reasonable repair", in relation to a dwelling or building for the purposes of subsection (3)(a) above, a local housing authority—

> (a) shall have regard to the age and character of the dwelling or building and the locality in which it is situated; and

> (b) shall disregard the state of internal decorative repair.

(9) In the exercise of the powers conferred by paragraphs (f) and (g) of subsection (3) above, the Secretary of State—

> (a) may specify requirements generally or for particular cases; and

> (b) may specify different requirements for different areas.

Approval and refusal of applications.

116.—(1) A local housing authority shall, by notice in writing, notify an applicant for a grant as soon as reasonably practicable, and, in any event, not later than six months after the date of the application concerned, whether the application is approved or refused.

(2) Where an authority decide to approve an application for a grant, they shall determine—

> (a) which of the relevant works, taking into account any variation of the application under section 108(4)(a) or section 115(7) above, are eligible for grant (in this Part referred to as "the eligible works");

    (b) the amount of the expenses which in their opinion are properly to be incurred in the execution of the eligible works;

    (c) the amount of the costs which in their opinion have been or are to be properly incurred with respect to preliminary or ancillary services and charges; and

    (d) the amount of grant they have decided to pay in respect of the eligible works, taking into account paragraphs (b) and (c) above, subsection (5) below and such of sections 109 to 115 above as may be applicable;

and shall specify in the notice under subsection (1) above the eligible works, the total of the amounts referred to in paragraphs (b) and (c) above (in this Part referred to as "the estimated expense") and the amount of the grant.

    (3) Where an application for a grant is approved, then, except—

    (a) with the consent of the Secretary of State, or

    (b) as provided by section 118(1) below,

the local housing authority may not impose any condition in relation to the approval or making of the grant, whether purporting to operate by way of a condition of the grant, a personal covenant or otherwise; and the consent of the Secretary of State under paragraph (a) above may be given either generally or in relation to any one or more specified authorities.

    (4) If, after an application for a grant has been approved, the authority are satisfied that, owing to circumstances beyond the control of the applicant, —

    (a) the eligible works cannot be, or could not have been, carried out on the basis of the amount of expenses referred to in subsection (2)(b) above, or

    (b) the eligible works cannot be, or could not have been, carried out without carrying out additional works which could not have been reasonably foreseen at the time the application was made,

the authority may re-determine the estimated expense and, subject to subsection (5) below, the amount of the grant.

    (5) The Secretary of State may, if he thinks fit, by order prescribe a maximum amount, or a formula for calculating a maximum amount, of grant which a local housing authority may pay in respect of an application for a grant; and an authority may not pay any grant in excess of that amount.

    117.—(1) Where the local housing authority have approved an application for a grant, they shall pay the grant, subject to subsection (3) below and to sections 133 and 134 below.   Payment of grants.

    (2) The grant may be paid—

    (a) in whole after the completion of the eligible works, or

    (b) in part by instalments as the works progress and the balance after completion of the works.

    (3) The payment of a grant, or part of a grant, is conditional upon—

    (a) the eligible works or the corresponding part of the works being executed to the satisfaction of the authority; and

    (b) the authority being provided with an acceptable invoice, demand or receipt for payment for the works and any preliminary or ancillary services and charges in respect of which the grant or part of the grant is to be paid.

(4) For the purposes of subsection (3) above an invoice, demand or receipt is acceptable if it satisfies the authority and is not given by the applicant or a member of his family.

(5) Where a grant is paid by instalments, the aggregate of the instalments paid before the completion of the eligible works shall not at any time exceed nine-tenths of the amount of the grant.

Conditions of grants and repayments

Conditions as to completion of works.

118.—(1) In approving an application for a grant, a local housing authority may require as a condition of the grant that the eligible works are carried out in accordance with such specification as they determine.

(2) Subject to subsection (3) below, it is a condition of the grant that the eligible works are carried out within twelve months from the date of approval of the application concerned.

(3) The authority may, if they think fit, extend the period of twelve months referred to in subsection (2) above and may, in particular, do so where they are satisfied that the eligible works cannot be, or could not have been, carried out without carrying out other works which could not have been reasonably foreseen at the time the application was made.

Condition as to availability for letting.

119.—(1) This section applies where an application for a renovation grant or a disabled facilities grant, other than an application for a disabled facilities grant in respect of works to the common parts of a building containing flats, has been approved by a local housing authority and the application for the grant was accompanied by a certificate of intended letting.

(2) It is a condition of the grant that throughout the initial period—

    (a) the dwelling will be let or available for letting as a residence, and not for a holiday, on a tenancy which is not a long tenancy by the owner for the time being of the dwelling to a person who is not connected with him, or

    (b) the dwelling will be occupied or available for occupation by a member of the agricultural population in pursuance of a contract of service and otherwise than as a tenant,

disregarding any part of that period in which neither of the above paragraphs applies but the dwelling is occupied by a person who is a protected occupier under the Rent (Agriculture) Act 1976 or is occupied under an assured agricultural occupancy, within the meaning of Part I of the Housing Act 1988.

1976 c. 80.

1988 c. 50.

(3) For the purposes of subsection (2) above, a person is connected with the owner for the time being of a dwelling if,—

    (a) in a case where personal representatives or trustees are the owner, he is a person who under the will or intestacy or, as the case may be, under the terms of the trust concerned is beneficially entitled to an interest in the dwelling or to the proceeds of sale of the dwelling; and

    (b) in any other case, he is a member of the family of the owner.

(4) It is also a condition of the grant—

    (a) that if, at any time within the initial period, the local housing authority by whom the grant was paid serve notice on the owner of the dwelling requiring him to do so, he will, within the period of twenty-one days beginning on the date on which the notice was served, furnish to the authority a statement showing how the condition in subsection (2) above is being fulfilled; and

    (b) that, if required to do so by the owner of the dwelling, any tenant of the dwelling will furnish the owner with such information as he may reasonably require to enable him to comply with a notice served under paragraph (a) above.

(5) A condition under subsection (2) or subsection (4) above is a local land charge and shall, subject to subsection (9) and section 125 below, remain in force with respect to the dwelling for a period of five years from the certified date.

(6) So long as a condition under subsection (2) or subsection (4) above remains in force with respect to a dwelling—

    (a) it is binding on any person, other than a local housing authority or registered housing association, who is for the time being the owner of the dwelling; and

    (b) it is enforceable against all other persons having an interest in the dwelling as if it were a condition of the terms of every tenancy of, or of property including, the dwelling.

(7) In the event of a breach of a condition under subsection (2) or subsection (4) above, the local housing authority may demand that the owner for the time being of the dwelling pay a sum equal to the amount of the grant less so much (if any) of it as has already been repaid under section 120 below, together with compound interest on that sum as from the certified date, calculated at such reasonable rate as the local housing authority may determine and with yearly rests.

(8) The local housing authority may determine not to make such a demand or may demand a lesser amount.

(9) On satisfaction of the liability arising from a demand under this section, the conditions under subsections (2) and (4) above and subsection (2) of section 120 below shall cease to be in force with respect to the dwelling in question.

120.—(1) This section applies where an application for a renovation grant (other than a tenant's application) has been approved by a local housing authority and the application for the grant was accompanied by a certificate of intended letting.

Condition requiring repayment of grant in case of certain disposals where certificate of intended letting given.

PART VIII   (2) It is a condition of the grant that—

> (a) where an owner makes a relevant disposal (other than an exempt disposal) of the dwelling with vacant possession within the initial period, he shall pay to the local housing authority on demand the amount of the grant; and
>
> (b) where an owner makes such a disposal otherwise than with vacant possession within the initial period, he shall pay to the authority on demand the amount of the grant, reduced by one-fifth for each complete year which has elapsed after the certified date and before the disposal.

(3) A condition under subsection (2) above is a local land charge and shall, subject to subsection (5) and section 125 below, remain in force with respect to the dwelling for a period of five years from the certified date.

(4) So long as a condition under subsection (2) above remains in force with respect to a dwelling it is binding on any person who is for the time being an owner of the dwelling.

(5) On satisfaction of the liability arising from a demand under this section, any condition under subsection (2) above shall cease to be in force with respect to the dwelling in question.

(6) The expressions "relevant disposal" and "exempt disposal" have the meanings assigned by section 124 below.

Condition requiring repayment of grant in case of certain disposals where owner-occupation certificate given.

121.—(1) This section applies where an application for a renovation grant has been approved by a local housing authority and the application for the grant was accompanied by an owner-occupation certificate.

(2) It is a condition of the grant that, where an owner makes a relevant disposal (other than an exempt disposal) of the dwelling within the period of three years beginning on the certified date, he shall pay to the authority on demand the amount of the grant, reduced by one-third for each complete year which has elapsed after the certified date and before the disposal.

(3) A condition under subsection (2) above is a local land charge and shall, subject to subsections (5) to (7) and section 125 below, remain in force with respect to the dwelling for a period of three years from the certified date.

(4) So long as a condition under subsection (2) above remains in force with respect to a dwelling it is binding on any person who is for the time being an owner of the dwelling.

(5) In any case where—

> (a) there is a relevant disposal of the dwelling concerned which is an exempt disposal; or
>
> (b) there is a relevant disposal of the dwelling concerned (not being an exempt disposal) for no consideration or for consideration of an amount less than that either prescribed, or calculated in accordance with a formula prescribed, by regulations made by the Secretary of State;

any condition under subsection (2) above shall cease to be in force with respect to the dwelling.

(6) On satisfaction of the liability arising from a demand under this section, any condition under subsection (2) above shall cease to be in force with respect to the dwelling in question.

(7) In any case where—

  (a) within the period referred to in subsection (2) above an owner makes a relevant disposal of the dwelling concerned (not being an exempt disposal), and

  (b) the authority having the right to demand payment from the owner as mentioned in that subsection are satisfied that he is elderly or infirm and is making the disposal with the intention of going to live in sheltered housing or a residential care home as his only or main residence,

the authority may determine not to make any demand under subsection (2) above and, on the making of such a determination, any condition under that subsection shall cease to be in force with respect to the dwelling.

(8) The expressions "relevant disposal" and "exempt disposal" have the meanings assigned by section 124 below.

122.—(1) This section applies where an application for an HMO grant has been approved by a local housing authority; and in the following provisions of this section "the house" means the house to which the eligible works relate.

Conditions relating to HMO grant.

(2) It is a condition of the grant that, throughout the initial period, the house will be residentially occupied or available for residential occupation, under tenancies or licences, by persons who are not connected with the owner for the time being of the house.

(3) The references in subsection (2) above to residential occupation do not include occupation for a holiday; and subsection (3) of section 119 above applies for the purposes of subsection (2) above, substituting a reference to a house for any reference to a dwelling.

(4) It is also a condition of the grant—

  (a) that if, at any time within the initial period, the local housing authority by whom the grant was paid serve notice on the owner of the house requiring him to do so, he will, within the period of twenty-one days beginning on the date on which the notice was served, furnish to the authority a statement showing how the condition in subsection (2) above is being fulfilled; and

  (b) that, if required to do so by the owner of the house, any tenant or licensee in residential occupation of the house will furnish the owner with such information as he may reasonably require to enable him to comply with a notice served under paragraph (a) above.

(5) In any case where—

  (a) there is, with respect to the house, a breach of a condition under subsection (2) or subsection (4) above, or

(b) at any time within the initial period the local housing authority have given a direction under section 354 of the Housing Act 1985 (power to limit number of occupants of house) with respect to the house and that direction has not been revoked or varied under section 357 of that Act,

the authority may demand that the owner for the time being of the house pay a sum equal to the amount of the grant, together with compound interest on that sum as from the certified date, calculated at such reasonable rate as the authority may determine and with yearly rests: but the authority may determine not to make such a demand or may demand a lesser amount.

(6) It is also a condition of the grant that, if an owner makes a relevant disposal of the house (other than an exempt disposal) within the initial period, he shall pay to the local housing authority on demand the amount of the grant.

(7) A condition under any of subsections (2), (4) and (6) above (in the following provisions of this section referred to as "an HMO condition") is a local land charge and, subject to subsection (9) and section 125 below, shall remain in force with respect to the house for a period of five years from the certified date.

(8) So long as an HMO condition remains in force with respect to a house it is binding on any person, other than a local housing authority or registered housing association, who is for the time being an owner of the house.

(9) On satisfaction of the liability arising from a demand under subsection (5) or subsection (6) above, any HMO condition shall cease to be in force with respect to the house.

(10) The expressions "relevant disposal" and "exempt disposal" have the meanings assigned by section 124 below.

Condition requiring repayment of grant on certain disposals in case of landlord's common parts application.

123.—(1) This section applies where a landlord's common parts application has been approved by a local housing authority.

(2) It is a condition of the grant that where the applicant makes a relevant disposal (other than an exempt disposal) of the building within the initial period, he shall pay to the local housing authority on demand the amount of the grant.

(3) A condition under subsection (2) above is a local land charge and shall, subject to subsection (5) and section 125 below, remain in force with respect to the building for a period of five years from the certified date.

(4) So long as a condition under subsection (2) above remains in force with respect to a building it is binding on any person who is for the time being a successor in title to that interest in the building by virtue of which, under section 105(2)(b) above, the applicant made his application.

(5) On satisfaction of the liability arising from a demand under this section, any condition under subsection (2) above shall cease to be in force with respect to the building in question.

(6) The expressions "relevant disposal" and "exempt disposal" have the meanings assigned by section 124 below.

124.—(1) A disposal, whether of the whole or part of the dwelling, is a relevant disposal for the purposes of sections 120 to 123 above if it is—

    (a) a conveyance of the freehold or an assignment of the lease, or

    (b) the grant of a lease (other than a mortgage term) for a term of more than 21 years otherwise than at a rack rent.

(2) For the purposes of subsection (1)(b) above it shall be assumed—

    (a) that any option to renew or extend a lease or sub-lease, whether or not forming part of a series of options, is exercised, and

    (b) that any option to terminate a lease or sub-lease is not exercised.

(3) A disposal is an exempt disposal for the purposes of sections 120 to 123 above if it is—

    (a) a disposal of the whole of the dwelling and a conveyance of the freehold or an assignment of the lease and the person or each of the persons to whom it is made is a qualifying person as defined in subsection (4) below;

    (b) a vesting of the whole of the dwelling in a person taking under a will or on an intestacy;

    (c) a disposal of the whole of the dwelling in pursuance of an order made under section 24 of the Matrimonial Causes Act 1973 (property adjustment orders in connection with matrimonial proceedings) or section 2 of the Inheritance (Provision for Family and Dependants) Act 1975 (orders as to financial provision to be made from estate);

    (d) a compulsory disposal as defined in section 161 of the Housing Act 1985 (meaning of compulsory disposal);

    (e) a disposal of property consisting of land included in the dwelling by virtue of section 184 of that Act (land let with or used for the purposes of the dwelling-house); or

    (f) a disposal under which the interest of a person entitled to assistance by way of repurchase under Part XVI of that Act (assistance for owners of defective housing) is acquired in accordance with Schedule 20 to that Act.

(4) A person is a qualifying person for the purposes of subsection (3)(a) above if—

    (a) in the case of an individual, he is—

        (i) the person, or one of the persons, by whom the disposal is made;

        (ii) the spouse, or former spouse, of that person or one of those persons; or

        (iii) a member of the family of that person or one of those persons; or

    (b) in the case of a company, it is an associated company of the company by whom the disposal is made;

and, for the purposes of paragraph (b) above, section 416 of the Income and Corporation Taxes Act 1988 (meaning of associated company) shall apply in determining whether a company is an associated company of another.

V

Margin notes:

PART VIII

Meaning of relevant disposal and exempt disposal for the purposes of sections 120 to 123.

1973 c. 18.

1975 c. 63.

1985 c. 68.

1988 c. 1.

PART VIII

(5) For the purposes of sections 120 to 123 above, the grant of an option enabling a person to call for a relevant disposal which is not an exempt disposal shall be treated as such a disposal made to him.

Repayment of grant.

125.—(1) Any reference in this section to a "grant condition" is a reference to a condition for the time being in force under subsection (2) or subsection (4) of section 119 above, subsection (2) of section 120 above, subsection (2) of section 121 above, any of subsections (2), (4) and (6) of section 122 above or subsection (2) of section 123 above.

(2) If at any time while a grant condition remains in force with respect to a dwelling, house or building.—

> (a) the owner of the dwelling, house or building to which the condition relates pays the amount of the grant to the local housing authority by whom the grant was made, or

> (b) a mortgagee of the interest of the owner in that dwelling, house or building being a mortgagee entitled to exercise a power of sale, makes such a payment,

the grant condition and any other grant conditions shall cease to be in force with respect to that dwelling, house or building.

(3) In the case of a grant condition imposed on a landlord's common parts application any reference in subsection (2) above to the owner of the building is a reference to the applicant or any such successor in title as is referred to in section 123(4) above.

(4) An amount paid by a mortgagee under subsection (2)(b) above shall be treated as part of the sums secured by the mortgage and may be discharged accordingly.

(5) The purposes authorised for the application of capital money by—

1925 c. 18.
> (a) section 73 of the Settled Land Act 1925,

1925 c. 20.
> (b) that section as applied by section 28 of the Law of Property Act 1925 in relation to trusts for sale, and

1925 c. 24.
> (c) section 26 of the Universities and College Estates Act 1925,

include the making of payments under subsection (2) above.

Renovation grants relating to two or more dwellings.

126.—(1) Subject to subsection (2) below, no application for a renovation grant may be made in respect of more than one dwelling.

(2) A single application may be made for a renovation grant towards the cost of works required for the provision of two or more dwellings by the conversion of a house or other building.

(3) In the case of such a single application as is referred to in subsection (2) above—

> (a) for the purposes of section 106 above, a separate certificate may be given in respect of each dwelling or in respect of any one or more of them;

> (b) if the application is accompanied by more than one certificate and at least one of them is an owner-occupation certificate or a special certificate the application shall be treated as falling within section 109 above and not within section 110 above;

> (c) each dwelling shall be treated separately for the purposes of sections 119 to 125 above; and

(d) the grant shall, for those purposes, be treated as apportioned equally between each of the dwellings, and any reference in those sections to the amount of the grant shall be construed accordingly.

Group repair schemes

127.—(1) In accordance with a scheme under this section prepared by a local housing authority and approved by the Secretary of State, the authority may, with the consent of the persons participating in the scheme, enter into agreements to secure the carrying out of such external works to qualifying buildings to which the scheme relates as will ensure that, on completion of the works, the exterior of those buildings will be in reasonable repair; and in this Part such a scheme is referred to as a "group repair scheme".

(2) The approval of the Secretary of State under subsection (1) above may be given either to a specific scheme or generally to schemes which fulfil such criteria as he may from time to time specify; and any such approval may be made conditional upon compliance with requirements specified by him.

(3) Every person who, at the date of the approval of the scheme, has an owner's interest in a dwelling or other premises comprised in a building to which a group repair scheme relates and who fulfils the conditions in subsection (5) below is eligible to participate in the scheme as an assisted participant unless that person is—

(a) the council of a county, district or London borough, the Common Council of the City of London or the Council of the Isles of Scilly;

(b) a development corporation or the Commission for the New Towns;

(c) the Development Board for Rural Wales;

(d) a housing action trust; or

(e) a registered housing association, within the meaning of the Housing Associations Act 1985.

(4) Any of the bodies specified in paragraphs (a) to (e) of subsection (3) above which has an owner's interest in a dwelling or other premises comprised in a building to which a group repair scheme relates is eligible to participate in the scheme as an unassisted participant.

(5) The conditions referred to in subsection (3) above are—

(a) that, as respects the dwelling or other premises in which he has an owner's interest, the person concerned either is able to give possession of any part of the building to which external works are proposed to be carried out or has the consent of the occupier of that part to the carrying out of those works; and

(b) that, if the owner's interest which he has is an interest in a dwelling and this paragraph is not excluded by subsection (6) below, he gives a certificate of future occupation which falls within subsection (2) or subsection (4) of section 106 above; and

PART VIII

   (c) that, if the owner's interest which the person concerned has is an interest in a house in multiple occupation and that person is not a charity or the trustee of a charity, he gives a certificate under section 106(7) above.

   (6) Paragraph (b) of subsection (5) above does not apply if—

   (a) the person concerned is a charity or the trustee of a charity; or

   (b) the dwelling is the residence house of an ecclesiastical benefice.

   (7) If the Secretary of State so directs in the case of any scheme or any description of scheme, such of the provisions of this section and sections 128 to 130 below as are specified in the direction shall not apply in relation to that scheme or, as the case may be, in relation to a scheme of that description.

   (8) Section 99 above applies to the power to give directions under subsection (7) above as it applies to a power to give directions under Part VII of this Act.

Qualifying buildings and external works, etc.

   128.—(1) A building is not a qualifying building in relation to a group repair scheme unless, at the time the scheme is prepared, the whole or some part of the exterior of the building is not in reasonable repair and that lack of reasonable repair affects at least 75 per cent. of the houses contained in the building.

   (2) Every group repair scheme shall relate to at least one qualifying building (in this section referred to as "the primary building") which was constructed so as to comprise not less than four separate houses and may also relate to one or more other qualifying buildings if the following conditions are fulfilled with respect to each of them—

   (a) the building was constructed so as to comprise at least one house and is contiguous or adjacent to the primary building; and

   (b) the exterior of the building is not in reasonable repair and is in need of works similar to those required to the exterior of the primary building; and

   (c) carrying out the works to the building and the primary building at the same time is the most effective way of securing the repair of each of them.

   (3) The question whether a building was constructed so as to comprise not less than four houses or at least one house shall be determined according to the configuration of the building at the date of its construction.

   (4) For the purposes of this section—

   (a) a terrace of houses shall be regarded as one building except that, if it appears appropriate to a local housing authority to do so, having regard in particular to the requirements of subsection (1) above, they may treat part only of the terrace as a building; and

   (b) if, apart from this paragraph, one building would be regarded as containing two or more purpose-built flats and one or more houses, the part of the building containing the purpose-built flats and the part or parts of the building containing the houses shall be regarded as separate buildings.

(5) In relation to a group repair scheme, "external works" are works to any part of the exterior of a building to which the scheme relates and, so far only as may be necessary to give satisfactory effect to such works, additional works to other parts of the building.

(6) For the purposes of this Part, the exterior of a building means—

(a) any part thereof which is exposed to the elements of wind and rain or otherwise faces into the open air (including, in particular, roofs, chimneys, walls, doors, windows, rainwater goods and external pipework); and

(b) the curtilage of the building, including any wall within the curtilage which is constructed as a retaining wall or otherwise to protect the structure of the building;

and, in relation to works to any part of the curtilage referred to in paragraph (b) above, the reference in subsection (5) above to additional works to other parts of the building includes a reference to additional works on land outside the curtilage.

(7) In this section—

(a) "house" means a dwelling which is not a flat (and, accordingly, does not include a house constructed as a house in multiple occupation); and

(b) a "purpose-built flat" means a part of a building which, at the date of the construction of the building, was constructed as a flat.

(8) For the purposes of this Part, unless the exterior of a building is substantially free from rising or penetrating damp, it shall not be regarded as in reasonable repair.

129.—(1) Those persons who are eligible to participate in a group repair scheme and who participate in the scheme by signifying consent (in this section referred to as "scheme consent"), in accordance with the terms of the scheme, to the proposals to carry out the external works specified in the scheme shall be liable, subject to subsection (2) below, to contribute to the cost, as notified to them under the scheme, of such of those works as relate to the house or other premises in which they have an interest at a rate determined in accordance with this section. Contributions by participants and limitations on works.

(2) For the purposes of subsection (1) above, "house" includes premises which were originally constructed as a house but which, by the time the group repair scheme is prepared, have been divided so as to form one or more flats, with or without other premises; and, in the case of a house which has been so divided, the cost of such of the external works as relate to the house shall be apportioned between the several parts into which the house has been divided in such way as may be agreed between the persons with owner's interests in those parts or, in default of agreement, equally.

(3) In the case of a person who participates in a scheme as an unassisted participant, the rate of contribution shall be 100 per cent.

(4) In the case of a person who participates in a scheme as an assisted participant but whose owner's interest in the part of the qualifying building in question is an interest in premises other than a house or flat, the rate of contribution, subject to subsection (5) below, shall be—

(a) 25 per cent. in a case where the qualifying building is in a renewal area; and

(b) 50 per cent. in any other case;

and in this subsection "house" includes a house in multiple occupation.

(5) The Secretary of State may by order amend paragraph (a) or paragraph (b) of subsection (4) above so as to specify a percentage different from that which applied before the coming into force of the order.

(6) In the case of any other person who participates in a scheme as an assisted participant, the rate of contribution shall be such percentage as may be determined by the local housing authority, being a percentage between nil and that which would be appropriate if subsection (4) above applied; and, in making their determination under this subsection in the case of any person, the authority shall have regard—

(a) to the way in which section 109 or section 110 above would apply in his case if he were an applicant for a renovation grant or, as the case may require, an HMO grant; and

(b) to any guidance given by the Secretary of State for the purposes of this section;

and section 99 above applies to the power to give guidance as mentioned in paragraph (b) above as it applies to any power to give guidance under Part VII of this Act.

(7) Except as provided by subsection (8) below, no external works shall be carried out to a part of a building which consists of a house, flat or other premises in respect of which no person eligible to participate has signified scheme consent.

(8) Subsection (7) above does not apply—

(a) to works carried out to a part of a building in respect of which there is no person (or no ascertainable person) eligible to participate in the scheme; or

(b) to works which—

(i) are carried out to a part of a building in respect of which the person eligible to participate consents to their being carried out but has not signified scheme consent (and, accordingly, is not liable to contribute); and

(ii) it is necessary to carry out in order satisfactorily to carry out any external works specified in the scheme to another part of the building in respect of which a person eligible to participate has signified scheme consent.

Payment of balance of costs in case of certain disposals.

130.—(1) When the external works specified in a group repair scheme are completed, the local housing authority shall, for the purposes of this section, send to each assisted participant a certificate specifying the date on which the works were completed to their satisfaction; and in subsection (2) below that date is referred to as "the completion date".

(2) It shall be a condition of participation in a group repair scheme as an assisted participant that if, before the expiry of the period of three years beginning with the completion date, the assisted participant makes a relevant disposal (other than an exempt disposal) of the dwelling or other premises in which he had an owner's interest at the date of the approval of the scheme, then, subject to subsection (6) below, he shall pay to the

local housing authority on demand the outstanding balance determined in accordance with subsections (3) and (4) below or such lesser amount, being not less than one-third of that outstanding balance, as the authority may specify in the demand.

(3) Subject to subsection (4) below, in the case of any assisted participant, the outstanding balance referred to in subsection (2) above is the difference between—

(a) the cost, as notified to him under the scheme, of such of the external works specified in the scheme as relate to the house or other premises in which his owner's interest subsisted; and

(b) the amount of the contribution in respect of that cost paid by him by virtue of section 129 above.

(4) If, in the case of any assisted participant, the cost of the external works relating to the house in which he had an owner's interest falls to be apportioned as mentioned in subsection (2) of section 129 above, the reference in subsection (3) above to the cost of the works relating to the house shall be construed as a reference to that part of the cost which is apportioned to the part of the house in which his owner's interest subsisted.

(5) Section 124 above applies for the purposes of this section as it applies for the purposes of sections 120 to 123 above, except that for any reference in that section to the dwelling there shall be substituted a reference to the house (or part of a house) or other premises in which the assisted participant had an owner's interest.

(6) The duty of an assisted participant under subsection (2) above shall cease to apply if he makes such a disposal as is mentioned in that subsection either for no consideration or for consideration of an amount less than that either prescribed, or calculated in accordance with a formula prescribed, by regulations made by the Secretary of State.

(7) In subsections (3) to (5) above "house" shall be construed in accordance with section 129(2) above.

Minor works

131.—(1) Subject to the provisions of regulations under subsection (3) below, on an application made to them for the purpose, a local housing authority may give assistance as mentioned in subsection (2) below—

(a) for the provision or improvement of thermal insulation in a dwelling;

(b) for the carrying out of works of repair to a dwelling which, at the time of the application, is included in a clearance area, within the meaning of section 289 of the Housing Act 1985, or which the authority intend to include in such an area within the period of twelve months beginning at the date of the application;

(c) to an elderly owner or tenant of a dwelling for the carrying out of works of repair, improvement or adaptation;

(d) for the carrying out of works to adapt a dwelling to enable an elderly person who is not an owner or tenant of the dwelling but who is or proposes to be resident in the dwelling to be cared for; or

Assistance for provision of minor works to dwellings.

1985 c. 68.

(e) for any other purpose specified by order made by the Secretary of State.

(2) Assistance under this section may be in the form of a grant or the provision of materials but—

(a) the total amount or value of the assistance given on any one application shall not exceed £1,000 or such other sum as may be determined for the purposes of this paragraph in accordance with regulations under subsection (3) below;

(b) the total amount or value of assistance given under this section in any period of three years in respect of any one dwelling shall not exceed £3,000 or such other sum as may be determined for the purposes of this paragraph in accordance with regulations under subsection (3) below; and

(c) no assistance may be given under this section in respect of works if they are or are included in the eligible works in relation to an application for a grant which has been approved under the preceding provisions of this Part.

(3) The Secretary of State may by regulations make provision for the determination of sums for the purposes of paragraphs (a) and (b) of subsection (2) above and, in addition, may for the purposes of this section specify—

(a) the manner in which an application for assistance is to be made and the content of such an application;

(b) the descriptions of dwellings and works in respect of which assistance may be given;

(c) the descriptions of persons to whom assistance may be given;

(d) the procedure for dealing with applications under subsection (1) above and for ensuring that works are carried out to any standard specified in the regulations; and

(e) the way in which the amount of assistance to be given on any application is to be calculated, taking account, in such manner and to such extent as may be determined under the regulations, of the financial circumstances of the applicant.

Supplementary provisions

Contributions by the Secretary of State.

132.—(1) The Secretary of State may pay contributions to local housing authorities towards such expenditure incurred by them under this Part as he may determine.

(2) The rate or rates of the contributions, the calculation of the expenditure to which they relate and the manner of their payment shall be such as may be determined by the Secretary of State with the consent of the Treasury.

(3) A determination under subsection (1) or subsection (2) above may be made—

(a) generally, or

(b) with respect to a particular local housing authority or description of authority, including a description framed by reference to authorities in a particular area,

and may make different provision in relation to different cases or descriptions of case.

(4) Subsections (3) to (6) of section 96 above shall apply in relation to this section, substituting a reference to subsection (1) or, as the case may be, subsection (2) above for any reference to the corresponding subsection of that section.

(5) In the application of section 516 of the Housing Act 1985 (contributions by Secretary of State towards expense of grants under Part XV of that Act) in relation to a case where—

1985 c. 68.

(a) an application under section 461 of that Act has been approved by the local housing authority after 14th June 1989, and

(b) the date which is the certified date, as defined in section 499(3) of that Act, in relation to the works to which that application relates falls on or after the day appointed under section 195 below for the coming into force of section 101 above,

for subsection (2) there shall be substituted the following subsection—

"(2) In the case of any grant, the contribution—

(a) shall be equal to a percentage of the amount of the grant determined under subsections (3) and (4) below; and

(b) shall be payable in one sum or by two or more instalments, according as the Secretary of State may determine."

133.—(1) In relation to a grant or an application for a grant, references in the preceding provisions of this Part, and in subsection (2) below, to the applicant shall be construed in relation to any time after his death as a reference to his personal representatives.

Persons entitled to grants.

(2) Where an application for a grant is approved but before the certified date the applicant ceases to be a person entitled to apply for a grant of that description—

(a) in the case of any grant, other than a common parts grant, no grant shall be paid or, as the case may be, no further instalments shall be paid, and

(b) in the case of a common parts grant, other than one made on a tenants' common parts application, the local housing authority may refuse to pay the grant or any further instalment,

and the authority may demand that any instalment of the grant which has been paid be repaid forthwith, together with interest from the date on which it was paid until repayment at such reasonable rate as the authority may determine.

(3) For the purposes of subsection (2) above an applicant ceases to be a person entitled to apply for a grant, other than a common parts grant,—

(a) if he ceases to have the owner's interest by virtue of which the condition in section 104(1)(a) above was (or was treated as) fulfilled, or

(b) if he ceases to be a tenant of the dwelling, or

(c) if he, or a member of his family, ceases to have the intention specified in a certificate under subsection (2), subsection (3) or subsection (4) (as the case may be) of section 106 above, or

(d) if, in the case of an applicant for an HMO grant, he ceases to have the intention specified in a certificate under section 106(7) above.

(4) For the purposes of subsection (2) above an applicant whose application is a landlord's common parts application ceases to be a person entitled to apply for a common parts grant—

(a) if he ceases to have a duty or power to carry out the relevant works; or

(b) if he ceases to have such an interest in the building as is referred to in paragraph (a) or paragraph (b) of section 105(4) above.

Cases in which grants may be re-calculated, withheld or repaid.

134.—(1) Where an application for a grant has been approved by the local housing authority, subsection (2) below applies in any case where—

(a) the eligible works are not completed to the satisfaction of the authority within the period specified under subsection (2) of section 118 above, or such extended period as they may allow under subsection (3) of that section; or

(b) the authority ascertain that the aggregate of the cost of completing the eligible works and the costs incurred with respect to preliminary or ancillary services and charges, is or is likely to be lower than the estimated expense; or

(c) the authority ascertain that without their knowledge the eligible works were started before the application was approved and the application was neither—

(i) one which they were required to approve by virtue of section 112 above in a case where completion of the relevant works was necessary to comply with a notice under section 189 of the Housing Act 1985 (repair notice requiring works to render premises fit for human habitation); nor

1985 c. 68.

(ii) one which they were required to approve by virtue of section 113 above.

(2) Where this subsection applies, the authority may—

(a) refuse to pay the grant or any further instalment of grant which remains to be paid; or

(b) make a reduction in the grant which, in a case falling within subsection (1)(b) above, is to be a reduction proportionate to the reduction in the estimated expense;

and may demand repayment by the applicant forthwith, in whole or part, of the grant or any instalment of the grant paid, together with interest at such reasonable rate as the authority may determine from the date of payment until repayment.

Power of local housing authority to carry out works which would attract grant.

135.—(1) A local housing authority may by agreement with a person having the requisite interest execute at his expense—

(a) any works towards the cost of which a grant under this Part is payable or might be paid on an application duly made and approved; and

(b) any further works which it is in their opinion necessary or desirable to execute together with the works mentioned in paragraph (a) above.

(2) Except in the case of a common parts grant, the "requisite interest" means an owner's interest in every parcel of land on which the works are to be carried out or, in a case where (if an application was made) section 104(4) above might apply, in part only of the land concerned.

(3) In the case of a common parts grant, the reference in subsection (1) above to a person having the requisite interest is a reference to the person who—

(a) has a power or duty to carry out the relevant works; and

(b) has such an interest in the building or in a flat in the building as is referred to in subsection (4) of section 105 above.

136. Sections 104 and 106 above do not apply to—

Parsonages, charities etc.

(a) an application for a grant in respect of glebe land or the residence house of an ecclesiastical benefice; and

(b) an application for a grant made by a charity or on behalf of a charity by the charity trustees of the charity.

137.—(1) Orders under this Part—

Orders and regulations.

(a) may make different provision with respect to different cases or descriptions of cases, including different provision for different areas; and

(b) shall be made by statutory instrument which shall be subject to annulment in pursuance of a resolution of either House of Parliament.

(2) Orders and regulations under this Part may contain such incidental, supplemental or transitional provisions as the Secretary of State considers appropriate.

138.—(1) In this Part, except where the context otherwise requires,—

Interpretation of Part VIII.

"agricultural population" means—

(a) persons whose employment or latest employment is or was employment in agriculture or in an industry mainly dependent on agriculture, and

(b) the dependents of those persons;

and for this purpose "agriculture" includes dairy-farming and poultry-farming and the use of land as grazing, meadow or pasture land, or orchard or osier land or woodland, or for market gardens or nursery grounds;

"certified date" means the date certified by the local housing authority as the date on which the execution of the eligible works is completed to their satisfaction;

"charity" does not include a registered housing association but, subject to that, has the same meaning as in the Charities Act 1960;

1960 c. 58.

"common parts", in relation to a building, includes the structure and exterior of the building and common facilities provided, whether in the building or elsewhere, for persons who include the occupiers of one or more flats in the building;

"disabled person" has the meaning assigned by section 114(6) above;

"dwelling" means a building or part of a building occupied or intended to be occupied as a separate dwelling, together with any yard, garden, outhouses and appurtenances belonging to it or usually enjoyed with it;

"the eligible works" shall be construed in accordance with section 116(2)(a) above;

"the estimated expense" shall be construed in accordance with section 116(2) above;

"flat", in relation to a building, means a dwelling which is a separate set of premises, whether or not on the same floor, divided horizontally from some other part of the building;

"group repair scheme" has the meaning assigned by section 127(1) above;

"house in multiple occupation" has the same meaning as in Part VII above;

"improvement" includes alteration and enlargement;

"initial period" means the period of five years beginning with the certified date;

"landlord's common parts application" has the meaning assigned by section 105(2)(b) above;

"local housing authority" has the same meaning as in the Housing Act 1985;

"long tenancy" has the meaning assigned by section 115 of that Act;

"occupying tenant" has the meaning assigned by section 105(2)(a) above;

"owner", in relation to a dwelling, means the person who—

(a) is for the time being entitled to receive from a lessee of the dwelling (or would be so entitled if the dwelling were let) a rent of not less than two-thirds of the net annual value of the dwelling; and

(b) is not himself liable as lessee of the dwelling, or of property which includes the dwelling, to pay such a rent to a superior landlord;

and, in relation to a house in multiple occupation, "owner" has the same meaning as in Part XI of the Housing Act 1985;

"owner's interest" has the meaning assigned by section 104(2) above;

"participating landlord" has the meaning assigned by section 105(3) above;

"preliminary or ancillary services and charges" has the meaning assigned by section 102(3) above;

"prescribed" means prescribed by regulations made by the Secretary of State;

"the relevant works" has the meaning assigned by section 102(2)(a) above;

"tenancy" includes a sub-tenancy and an agreement for a tenancy or sub-tenancy;

"tenant" includes a sub-tenant and any person deriving title under the original tenant or sub-tenant;

"tenants' common parts application" has the meaning assigned by section 105(2)(c) above.

(2) Section 113 of the Housing Act 1985 (meaning of "members of a person's family") shall apply in determining whether a person is a member of another's family for the purposes of this Part.

1985 c. 68.

PART IX

MISCELLANEOUS AND GENERAL

Local Government Finance Act 1988, local finance (Scotland) and block grants

139. Schedule 5 to this Act (which amends the Local Government Finance Act 1988) shall have effect.

Local Government Finance Act 1988: amendments.

1988 c. 41.

140.—(1) For section 3 of the Abolition of Domestic Rates Etc. (Scotland) Act 1987 (determination of non-domestic rates) there shall be substituted the following section—

Scottish non-domestic rates: interim provisions. 1987 c. 47.

"Non-domestic rates: interim provisions.

3A.—(1) The Secretary of State shall, in respect of each of the financial years specified in subsection (2) below, prescribe for each local authority a rate which shall be their non-domestic rate in respect of that year.

(2) The financial years referred to in subsection (1) above are those beginning with the financial year 1990-91 and ending with that immediately before the financial year in respect of which the non-domestic rate is first prescribed under section 3B of this Act.

(3) Non-domestic rates shall be levied in accordance with section 7 of the Local Government (Scotland) Act 1975 by each rating authority in respect of lands and heritages—

(a) which are subjects (other than part residential subjects) in respect of which there is an entry in the valuation roll, according to their rateable value or, where a rateable value has been prescribed or determined in respect of the lands and heritages under section 128 of the Local Government Finance Act 1988, according to that rateable value; or

(b) which are part residential subjects, according to that part of their rateable value which is shown in the apportionment note as relating to the non-residential use of those subjects or, where a rateable value has been prescribed or determined in respect of the lands and heritages under section 128 of the Local Government

Finance Act 1988, according to that part of that rateable value which is so shown in the apportionment note.

(4) The rates prescribed under subsection (1) above shall be known—

    (a) in the case of the regional council, as the non-domestic regional rate;

    (b) in the case of the district council, as the non-domestic district rate; and

    (c) in the case of the islands council, as the non-domestic islands rate."

(2) Accordingly—

    (a) references (however expressed) in any enactment to the non-domestic rate determined by a local authority under section 3 of the Abolition of Domestic Rates Etc. (Scotland) Act 1987 shall be construed as references to the non-domestic rate prescribed for the local authority under section 3A of that Act;

    (b) in section 109(2) of the Local Government (Scotland) Act 1973 for the words from "non-domestic district rate" onward there shall be substituted the words "information as may reasonably be required for the preparation of demand notes for the purposes of levying the non-domestic district rate";

    (c) section 110A(2) of the Local Government (Scotland) Act 1973 and section 128(2) of and paragraph 16 of Schedule 12 to the Local Government Finance Act 1988 shall cease to have effect.

1987 c. 47.

1973 c. 65.

1988 c. 41.

Scottish non-domestic rate.

141.—(1) For section 3A of the Abolition of Domestic Rates Etc. (Scotland) Act 1987 there shall be substituted the following section—

"Unified non-domestic rate.

    3B.—(1) The Secretary of State shall, in respect of each of the financial years specified in subsection (2) below, prescribe a rate which shall be the non-domestic rate to be levied throughout Scotland in respect of that financial year.

    (2) The financial years referred to in subsection (1) above are those beginning with the first financial year after the coming into force of section 141 of the Local Government and Housing Act 1989.

    (3) Subject to subsection (4) below, the non-domestic rate shall be levied in accordance with section 7 of the Local Government (Scotland) Act 1975 by each rating authority in respect of lands and heritages in their area being lands and heritages—

        (a) which are subjects (other than part residential subjects) in respect of which there is an entry in the valuation roll, according to their rateable value or, where a rateable value has been prescribed or determined in respect of the lands and heritages under section 128 of the Local Government Finance Act 1988, according to that rateable value; or

(b) which are part residential subjects, according to that part of their rateable value which is shown in the apportionment note as relating to the non-residential use of those subjects or, where a rateable value has been prescribed or determined in respect of the lands and heritages under section 128 of the Local Government Finance Act 1988, according to that part of that rateable value which is so shown in the apportionment note.

(4) In the application of section 7 of the Local Government (Scotland) Act 1975 to the levying of the non-domestic rate prescribed under this section, for the words "to which the rate relates" in each of subsections (1) and (2) of that section there shall be substituted the words "of the rating authority"."

(2) Accordingly—

(a) references (however expressed) in any enactment to the non-domestic rate determined by or prescribed in relation to a local authority under section 3 of the Abolition of Domestic Rates Etc. (Scotland) Act 1987 shall be construed as references to the non-domestic rate prescribed under section 3B of that Act;

(b) in section 109 of the Local Government (Scotland) Act 1973 (rating authorities)—

1973 c. 65

(i) for paragraphs (a) and (b) of subsection (1) there shall be substituted the following paragraph—

"(a) in the case of the non-domestic rate prescribed under section 3B of the Abolition of Domestic Rates Etc. (Scotland) Act 1987, the regional council and the islands council;"; and

(ii) in subsection (2) for the words from "non-domestic district rate" onward there shall be substituted the words "information as may reasonably be required for the preparation of demand notes for the purposes of levying the non-domestic rate".

(3) For section 110 of the Local Government (Scotland) Act 1973 (payments by regional councils to district councils in respect of district rates) there shall be substituted the following section—

"Division between regional and district councils of amount collected by way of non-domestic rate.

110. The Secretary of State may by regulations provide as to the division among the regional council and the councils of the districts within the area of the regional council of the amount collected by way of the non-domestic rate in that area in respect of a financial year."

(4) Section 111(1)(a), (b) and (d) of the Local Government (Scotland) Act 1973 (power to make regulations as to certain matters connected with non-domestic rates) shall cease to have effect.

142. In section 10 of the Abolition of Domestic Rates Etc. (Scotland) Act 1987 (liability for and calculation of standard community charge) for subsections (6) and (7) there shall be substituted the following subsections—

Powers to vary incidence of standard community charge: Scotland. 1987 c. 47.

"(6) The standard community charge due to a local authority in respect of any premises in respect of any financial year shall be the product of the personal community charge determined in respect of that year by the local authority and—

(a) where the premises are in a specified class, the standard community charge multiplier determined in respect of that class by the authority; or

(b) where the premises are not in a specified class, the standard community charge multiplier determined by the authority in relation to such premises,

in respect of that year.

(7) A specified class is one which has been prescribed under this subsection or determined under regulations made under subsection (7F) below.

(7A) A local authority shall determine their standard community charge multiplier or multipliers before such date in each year as is prescribed.

(7B) A standard community charge multiplier must be one of the following, 0, $\frac{1}{2}$, 1, $1\frac{1}{2}$, 2.

(7C) A local authority may resolve that different standard community charge multipliers shall apply in relation to different classes of premises prescribed under subsection (7) above.

(7D) A standard community charge multiplier relating to a class of premises prescribed under subsection (7) above shall not exceed such maximum multiplier as may be prescribed in relation to that class.

(7E) In prescribing classes under subsection (7) above, the Secretary of State may classify premises by reference to such factors as he thinks fit, including, without prejudice to that generality—

(a) the physical characteristics of premises or any part of them;

(b) the fact that premises are, or any part of them is, unoccupied;

(c) the fact that premises are, or any part of them is, occupied for prescribed purposes;

(d) the fact that premises are, or any part of them is, occupied by persons of prescribed descriptions;

(e) the circumstances of persons liable to pay the standard community charge.

(7F) The Secretary of State may, by regulations, make provision—

(a) enabling local authorities or local authorities of such class or classes as he may specify in the regulations—

(i) to determine, in relation to their areas, classes of premises additional to those prescribed under subsection (7) above;

(ii) to determine different such classes of premises in relation to different parts of their areas; and

(iii) to resolve that different standard community charge multipliers shall apply in relation to different classes of premises determined under the regulations, and

(b) requiring them, when determining a class or classes under the regulations, to classify premises only by reference to one or more prescribed factors being such factors as the Secretary of State thinks fit.

(7G) Regulations under subsection (7F) above may make provision enabling the district council to resolve that different standard community charge multipliers shall apply in relation to such different classes of premises as have, in relation to the district, been determined under the regulations by the council of the region in which the district is situated.

(7H) A regional council may resolve that different standard community charge multipliers shall apply in relation to the same specified class of premises in different districts within the region."

143.—The following section shall be inserted after section 9 of the Abolition of Domestic Rates Etc. (Scotland) Act 1987—

Reduced liability for personal community charges: Scotland.
1987 c. 47.

"Reduced liability for personal community charge.

9A.—(1) The Secretary of State may make regulations as regards any case where—

(a) a person is or was liable to pay, in respect of any time in such financial year as is prescribed, the personal community charge determined by a local authority in respect of that year; and

(b) prescribed conditions are fulfilled.

(2) Regulations under this section may provide that the amount of a person's liability in respect of personal community charge shall not be such amount as it would be apart from the regulations or, as the case may be, such amount as it was, but instead such smaller amount as is arrived at in accordance with prescribed rules.

(3) The conditions mentioned in subsection (1) above may be prescribed by reference to such factors as the Secretary of State sees fit; and in particular such factors may include all or any of the following—

(a) rates for a period before 1 April 1989;

(b) the circumstances of or other matters relating to the person concerned;

(c) an amount relating to the local authority concerned and specified, or to be specified, for the purposes of the regulations in a report laid, or to be laid, before the House of Commons;

(d) such other amounts as may be prescribed or arrived at in a prescribed manner;

(e) the making of an application by the person concerned.

(4) The rules mentioned in subsection (2) above may be prescribed by reference to such factors as the Secretary of State sees fit; and in particular such factors may include all or any of the factors mentioned in subsection (3)(a) to (d) above.

(5) Without prejudice to the generality of section 31(2) of this Act, regulations under this section may include—

(a) provision requiring the Secretary of State to specify in a report, for the purposes of the regulations, an amount in relation to each local authority;

(b) provision requiring him to lay the report before the House of Commons;

(c) provision for the review of any prescribed decision of a local authority relating to the application or operation of the regulations.

(6) To the extent that he would not have power to do so apart from this subsection, the Secretary of State may—

(a) include in regulations under this section such amendments of any social security instrument as he thinks expedient in consequence of the regulations under this section;

(b) include in any social security instrument such provision as he thinks expedient in consequence of regulations under this section.

and any such amendments or provision may be deemed by the regulations or, as the case may be, instrument to have come into effect prior to the date of coming into force of the regulations or instrument.

(7) In subsection (6) above "social security instrument" means an order or regulations made, or falling to be made, by the Secretary of State under the Social Security Act 1986."

Community
charge grants:
Scotland.
1987 c. 47.

144. The following section shall be inserted after section 23 of the Abolition of Domestic Rates Etc. (Scotland) Act 1987—

"PART IIIA

COMMUNITY CHARGE GRANTS

Community charge grants.

23A.—(1) If regulations under section 9A have effect in respect of a financial year, the Secretary of State may, with the consent of the Treasury, pay a grant to a local authority in respect of that year.

(2) The amount of the grant shall be such as the Secretary of State may, with the consent of the Treasury, determine.

(3) A grant under this section shall be paid at such time, or in instalments of such amounts and at such times, as the Secretary of State may, with the consent of the Treasury, determine.

(4) In making any payment of grant under this section the Secretary of State may impose such conditions as he may, with the consent of the Treasury, determine; and the conditions may relate to the repayment in specified circumstances of all or part of the amount paid, or otherwise.

(5) In deciding whether to pay a grant under this section, and in determining the amount of any such grant, the Secretary of State shall have regard to his estimate of the aggregate of—

(a) any amount which, in consequence of the regulations, the local authority might reasonably be expected to lose, or to have lost, by way of payments in respect of community charges in respect of the financial year concerned; and

(b) any administrative expenses the local authority might reasonably be expected to incur, or to have incurred, in respect of the financial year in giving effect to the regulations."

145. Schedule 6 to this Act (which amends the Abolition of Domestic Rates Etc. (Scotland) Act 1987 and other enactments) shall have effect.

Amendment of Abolition of Domestic Rates Etc. (Scotland) Act 1987 and other enactments: Scotland.
1987 c. 47.

146.—(1) The Secretary of State may, with the consent of the Treasury, pay a grant (in this section referred to as a "special grant") in accordance with this section to a charging authority.

Special grants.

(2) Before making any one or more special grants, the Secretary of State shall make a determination stating, with respect to the special grant or, as the case may be, each of the special grants,—

(a) to which authority it is to be paid,

(b) the purpose for which it is to be paid, and

(c) the amount of the grant,

and that determination shall be made with the consent of the Treasury and shall be specified in a report (to be called a special grant report) which shall contain such explanation as the Secretary of State considers desirable of the main features of the determination.

(3) A special grant report shall be laid before the House of Commons and, as soon as is reasonably practicable after the report has been so laid, the Secretary of State shall send a copy of it to any charging authority to whom a special grant is proposed to be paid in accordance with the determination in the report.

(4) No special grant shall be paid unless the special grant report containing the determination relating to the grant has been approved by a resolution of the House of Commons.

(5) A special grant report may specify conditions which the Secretary of State, with the consent of the Treasury, intends to impose on the payment of (or of any instalment of) any special grant to which the report relates; and the conditions may require the provision of returns or other information before a payment is made to the local authority concerned or relate to the use of the amount paid, or to the repayment in specified circumstances of all or part of the amount paid, or otherwise.

(6) Without prejudice to compliance with any conditions imposed as mentioned in subsection (5) above, a special grant shall be paid at such time or in instalments of such amounts and at such times as the Secretary of State may, with the consent of the Treasury, determine.

(7) For the purposes of this section each of the following is a charging authority—

    (a) a district council;

    (b) a London borough council;

    (c) the Common Council of the City of London; and

    (d) the Council of the Isles of Scilly.

Adjustment of block grant.

147.—(1) This section applies for any year in relation to which, immediately before the passing of this Act, the obligation imposed on the Secretary of State by the paragraph 5 pooling provisions to ascertain the actual amount of the increases and decreases of block grant to be made for the year in accordance with those provisions had not yet arisen.

(2) As soon as is reasonably practicable after the passing of this Act the Secretary of State shall ascertain, for a year for which this section applies, the amount of the increases and decreases of block grant which ought to be made in accordance with the paragraph 5 pooling provisions.

(3) Subsection (4), subsection (5) or subsection (6) below (as the case may be) applies where, for the purpose of so ascertaining, the Secretary of State needs to find the amount of a local authority's expenditure in relation to the year or the amount of any part of that expenditure.

(4) Where the year begins in 1987 or before, he shall find the amount concerned by reference to—

    (a) figures which relate to the authority's actual expenditure incurred for the year and which were received by him before the relevant date, or

(b) if no such figures were received by him before that date, any other information in his possession on that date about the expenditure incurred by the authority for the year.

(5) Where the year begins in 1988, he shall find the amount concerned by reference to any information in his possession on the relevant date about the expenditure incurred and likely to be incurred by the authority for the year.

(6) Where the year begins in 1989, he shall find the amount concerned by reference to any information in his possession on the relevant date about the expenditure likely to be incurred by the authority for the year.

(7) Where the year begins in 1988, and the amount concerned is the amount of the authority's relevant education expenditure for the year, he shall find the amount by reference to—

(a) audited accounts which relate to that expenditure, which are in such form as the Secretary of State may specify and which were received by him before the second relevant date; or

(b) if no such accounts were received by him before the second relevant date, any information in his possession on the relevant date about that expenditure;

and subsection (5) above shall have effect subject to the preceding provisions of this subsection.

(8) In making payments of block grant after the passing of this Act, the Secretary of State shall adjust amounts paid so as to take account, so far as practicable, of increases and decreases ascertained under subsection (2) above.

(9) As regards anything done after the passing of this Act for a year for which this section applies, the paragraph 5 pooling provisions shall have effect—

(a) with the omission of paragraph 5(2) of Schedule 10 to the 1980 Act, and

(b) with such other modifications as result from this section.

(10) In this section—

"local authority", in relation to any year, means any body which for that year is a local authority for the purposes of Part VI of the 1980 Act;

"the 1980 Act" means the Local Government, Planning and Land Act 1980; 1980 c. 65.

"the paragraph 5 pooling provisions" means paragraph 5 of Schedule 10 to the 1980 Act and regulations made under that paragraph (adjustment of block grant);

"the relevant date" means 1st February 1989 and "the second relevant date" means 1st October 1989;

"year" means a period of twelve months beginning with 1st April.

(11) For the purposes of this section an authority's relevant education expenditure for the year beginning in 1988 is its expenditure which—

(a) was incurred in the year, and

(b) was incurred by way of payments falling within regulation 3(3)(d) or (e) of the Block Grant (Education Adjustments) (England) Regulations 1987.

Rate support grant, 1985/86.

148. The Rate Support Grant Supplementary Report (England) (No. 4) 1985/86 (which was approved by a resolution of the House of Commons on 19th January 1989) shall have effect, and be deemed always to have had effect, as if, in Annex VI (principles for calculating grant-related poundages), for the formula set out in paragraph 4 (grant-related poundages for total expenditure at or above the threshold level) there were substituted—

$$\text{"GRP} = \text{GRP at GRE} + 0\cdot69\text{p} \times \text{threshold amount}$$

$$+ \ 0\cdot8625\text{p} \ \times \left(\frac{\text{total expenditure} - \text{GRE}}{\text{population}} - \text{threshold amount} \right)\text{".}$$

Statutory references to rating.

149.—(1) In the case of a provision which is made by or under any enactment and refers to a rate or a rateable value or any other factor connected with rating, the Secretary of State may make regulations—

(a) providing that the reference shall instead be to some other factor (whether or not connected with rating); or

(b) providing for the factor to be amended (whether by limiting its operation or in any other way);

1988 c. 41.

and this section shall have effect in place of section 119 of the Local Government Finance Act 1988.

(2) Regulations under this section—

(a) may make provision in such manner as the Secretary of State thinks fit (whether by amending provisions or otherwise);

(b) may provide for a factor expressed by reference to valuation, rent, a premium, the length of a lease, anything connected with rating, or any other matter whatever;

(c) may provide for a factor expressed by reference to a combination of matters (whether expressed in terms of a formula or otherwise);

(d) may provide for a factor which includes a method of adjustment (whether by reference to indexation or otherwise);

(e) may make provision with respect to the resolution of disputes (whether by a court or otherwise); and

(f) may contain such supplementary, incidental, consequential or transitional provisions as appear to the Secretary of State to be necessary or expedient.

(3) A factor expressed by reference to rent may be by reference to ground rent, rent of premises at a market rate, rent as limited by law, or otherwise.

1978 c. 30.

(4) Nothing in this section shall be construed as limiting the power conferred by section 14 of the Interpretation Act 1978 to revoke, amend or vary regulations previously made under this section.

(5) In this section "enactment" means an enactment contained in Schedule 10 to this Act, or in any other Act whether passed before or in the same Session as this Act; and for this purpose "Act" includes a private or local Act.

(6) Without prejudice to the generality of the powers conferred by this section, section 37 of the Landlord and Tenant Act 1954 (which provides for compensation by reference to rateable values) shall be amended in accordance with Schedule 7 to this Act.

1954 c. 56.

Charges by certain authorities

150.—(1) The Secretary of State may make regulations providing that a charge may be imposed in respect of anything—

Power to allow charges.

> (a) which is done by any relevant authority or by any relevant authority of a prescribed description,
>
> (b) which is prescribed or falls within a prescribed description,
>
> (c) in respect of which there is no power or duty to impose a charge apart from the regulations, and
>
> (d) which is not done in the course of exercising an excepted function.

(2) The regulations may include such provision as the Secretary of State sees fit as regards charges for which the regulations provide; and nothing in subsections (3) to (5) below or section 190(1) below is to prejudice this.

(3) The regulations—

> (a) may be made as regards services rendered, documents issued, or any other thing done by an authority (whether in pursuance of a power or a duty);
>
> (b) may provide that the amount of a charge (if imposed) is to be at the authority's discretion or to be at its discretion subject to a maximum.

(4) Where the regulations provide that a charge may not exceed a maximum amount they may—

> (a) provide for one amount, or a scale of amounts to cover different prescribed cases;
>
> (b) prescribe, as regards any amount, a sum or a method of calculating the amount.

(5) The regulations may include such supplementary, incidental, consequential or transitional provisions as appear to the Secretary of State to be necessary or expedient.

(6) No regulations may be made under this section unless a draft of them has been laid before and approved by a resolution of each House of Parliament.

151.—(1) Subject to subsection (4) below, this section applies in the case of an existing provision to the extent that the provision allows (as opposed to requires) a charge to be imposed in respect of anything which is done by relevant authorities (or any of them) and which is not done in the course of exercising an excepted function.

Power to amend provisions about charges.

(2) The Secretary of State may make regulations—

(a) repealing the provision concerned to the extent that it so provides,

(b) amending the provision to that extent, or

(c) repealing the provision to that extent and replacing it with new provisions;

and subsection (6) of section 150 above applies in relation to regulations under this section as it applies in relation to regulations under that section.

(3) For the purposes of subsection (1) above—

(a) the charge may be expressed in terms of making a charge, paying a fee, or otherwise;

(b) the charge may relate to services rendered, documents issued, or any other thing done by a relevant authority (whether in pursuance of a power or a duty).

(4) A charge does not fall within subsection (1) above if—

(a) it is one whose proceeds fall (or part of whose proceeds falls) to be paid into the Consolidated Fund;

(b) it is a charge amounting to local taxation; or

(c) it is one as respects which provision is made by section 49 of the Water (Scotland) Act 1980 (charges in respect of water supplied by meter).

1980 c. 45.

(5) Regulations under subsection (2) above may not require the imposition of a charge; and subsection (6) below shall have effect subject to this.

(6) The regulations may include such provision as the Secretary of State sees fit as regards charges; and nothing in subsections (7) to (9) below or section 190(1) below is to prejudice this.

(7) The regulations may provide that the amount of a charge (if imposed) is to be at the authority's discretion or to be at its discretion subject to a maximum.

(8) Where the regulations provide that a charge may not exceed a maximum amount they may—

(a) provide for one amount, or a scale of amounts to cover different prescribed cases;

(b) prescribe, as regards any amount, a sum or a method of calculating the amount.

(9) The regulations—

(a) may confer discretion as to the amount in a case where an existing provision confers none (or vice versa);

(b) may, in a case where an existing provision confers a discretion as to the amount, confer a different one; and

(c) may include such supplementary, incidental, consequential or transitional provisions as appear to the Secretary of State to be necessary or expedient.

(10) For the purposes of this section an existing provision is a provision of an Act passed before, or in the same Session as, this Act.

(11) In this section "Act" includes a private or local Act.   PART IX

152.—(1) For the purposes of sections 150 and 151 above the following are excepted functions—   Interpretation, consultation and commencement of ss. 150 and 151.

    (a) functions relating to education in schools;

    (b) functions relating to the provision of a public library service;

    (c) functions relating to fire fighting, that is to say, the extinction of fire and the protection of life and property in case of fire;

    (d) functions relating to the registration of electors;

    (e) functions relating to the conduct of elections;

    (f) all functions of the police except those relating to the removal, delivery, disposal, custody or immobilisation of vehicles.

(2) For the purposes of those sections in their application to England and Wales, each of the following is a relevant authority—

    (a) a county council;

    (b) a district council;

    (c) a London borough council;

    (d) the Common Council of the City of London;

    (e) the Council of the Isles of Scilly;

    (f) a fire authority constituted by a combination scheme under the Fire Services Act 1947;   1947 c. 41.

    (g) a combined police authority established by an amalgamation scheme under the Police Act 1964;   1964 c. 48.

    (h) an authority established under section 10 of the Local Government Act 1985 (waste disposal authorities);   1985 c. 51.

    (i) a joint authority established by Part IV of that Act (police, fire services, civil defence and transport);

    (j) an authority or board constituted a port health authority at any time by an order under section 2 of the Public Health (Control of Disease) Act 1984;   1984 c. 22.

    (k) a joint or special planning board constituted for a National Park by an order under paragraph 1 or paragraph 3 of Schedule 17 to the Local Government Act 1972; and   1972 c. 70.

    (l) the Broads Authority.

(3) For the purposes of those sections in their application to Scotland, each of the following is a relevant authority—

    (a) a regional council,

    (b) a district council,

    (c) an islands council,

    (d) a port local authority or joint port local authority constituted under section 172 of the Public Health (Scotland) Act 1897,   1897 c. 38.

    (e) a joint board or joint committee within the meaning of section 235(1) of the Local Government (Scotland) Act 1973, and   1973 c. 65.

    (f) a water development board within the meaning of section 109(1) of the Water (Scotland) Act 1980.   1980 c. 45.

(4) The Secretary of State may by order made by statutory instrument provide for any other body to be, or for a body to cease to be, a relevant authority for the purposes of those sections; and a statutory instrument containing an order under this subsection shall be subject to annulment in pursuance of a resolution of either House of Parliament.

(5) In those sections "prescribed" means prescribed by the regulations concerned.

(6) Before exercising any power to make regulations under section 150 or section 151 above, the Secretary of State shall consult—

> (a) as respects England and Wales, such representatives of local government, and

> (b) as respects Scotland, such associations of local authorities,

as appear to him to be appropriate.

(7) This section and sections 150 and 151 above shall come into force at the expiry of the period of two months beginning on the day this Act is passed.

Charges:
temporary traffic
signs.
1984 c.27

153.—(1) In section 65 of the Road Traffic Regulation Act 1984 (powers and duties of highways authorities and roads authorities as to placing of traffic signs) after subsection (3) there shall be inserted the following subsection—

> "(3A) No charge may be made—

>> (a) in England and Wales, by a highway authority which is the council of a county, metropolitan district or London borough or the Common Council of the City of London, or

>> (b) in Scotland, by a local roads authority,

> with respect to the exercise of their power under subsection (1) above to permit a traffic sign to be placed on or near any road in their area if—

>> (i) the sign conveys information of a temporary nature or is otherwise intended to be placed only temporarily; and

>> (ii) the sign is to be placed by a body which is prescribed for the purposes of this subsection as being a body appearing to the Secretary of State to be representative of the interests of road users or any class of road users."

(2) Subsection (1) above does not apply in any case where, before this section comes into force, the payment of a charge has been agreed.

Charges: library
services.
1964 c. 75.

154.—(1) For subsections (2) to (5) of section 8 of the Public Libraries and Museums Act 1964 (exceptions to restrictions on charging for library facilities) there shall be substituted the following subsections—

> "(2) Subject to subsections (3) and (4) below, the Minister may by regulations—

>> (a) authorise library authorities to make charges for such library facilities made available by them as may be specified in the regulations; and

(b) make such provision as regards charges by library authorities for library facilities, other than provision requiring the making of charges, as he thinks fit.

(3) Nothing in any regulations under this section shall authorise any charges to be made by a library authority for lending any written material to any person where—

(a) it is the duty of the authority under section 7(1) above to make facilities for borrowing available to that person;

(b) the material is lent in the course of providing such facilities to that person on any library premises;

(c) the material is lent in a form in which it is readable without the use of any electronic or other apparatus; and

(d) that person is not a person who has required any such apparatus to be used, or made available to him, for putting the material into such a form in order that he may borrow it;

but this subsection shall not prevent any regulations under this section from authorising the making of charges in respect of the use of any facility for the reservation of written materials or in respect of borrowed materials which are returned late or in a damaged condition.

(4) Nothing in any regulations under this section shall authorise any charges to be made by a library authority for making facilities available for any person to do any of the following on any library premises, that is to say—

(a) reading the whole or any part of any of the written materials for the time being held by the authority in a form in which they are readable without the use of any electronic or other apparatus or in microform;

(b) consulting (whether or not with the assistance of any such apparatus or of any person) such catalogues, indexes or similar articles as are maintained, in any form whatever, exclusively for the purposes of that authority's public library service.

(5) Without prejudice to the generality of subsection (2) above, the power to make regulations under this section shall include power—

(a) to confer a discretion as to the amount of any charge made under the regulations;

(b) to provide for such a discretion to be exercisable subject to such maximum amount or scale of maximum amounts as may be specified in or determined under the regulations;

(c) to require library authorities to take such steps as may be specified or described in the regulations for making the amounts of their charges for library facilities known to the public;

(d) to make such other incidental provision and such supplemental, consequential and transitional provision as the Minister thinks necessary or expedient; and

Part IX

(e) to make different provision for different cases, including different provision in relation to different persons, circumstances or localities.

(5A) The power to make regulations under this section shall be exercisable by statutory instrument; and no regulations may be made under this section unless a draft of them has been laid before and approved by a resolution of each House of Parliament."

(2) After subsection (6) of that section there shall be inserted the following subsection—

"(7) In this section—

'library premises' means—

(a) any premises which are occupied by a library authority and are premises where library facilities are made available by the authority, in the course of their provision of a public library service, to members of the public;

(b) any vehicle which is used by a library authority for the purpose of providing such a service and is a vehicle in which facilities are so made available;

'the Minister' means—

(a) in relation to library authorities whose areas are in England, the Lord President of the Council; and

(b) in relation to library authorities whose areas are in Wales, the Secretary of State;

and

'written material' means—

(a) any book, journal, pamphlet or other similar article; or

1988 c. 48.

(b) any reprographic copy (within the meaning of the Copyright, Designs and Patents Act 1988) of any article falling within paragraph (a) above or any other reproduction of such an article made by any means whatever."

(3) This section shall come into force on such day as the Lord President of the Council and the Secretary of State, acting jointly, may by order made by statutory instrument appoint; and different days may be so appointed for different provisions or for different purposes.

Miscellaneous local government provisions

Emergency financial assistance to local authorities.

155.—(1) In any case where—

(a) an emergency or disaster occurs involving destruction of or danger to life or property, and

(b) as a result, one or more local authorities incur expenditure on, or in connection with, the taking of immediate action (whether by the carrying out of works or otherwise) to safeguard life or property, or to prevent suffering or severe inconvenience, in their area or among its inhabitants,

the Secretary of State may establish a scheme under this section for the giving of financial assistance to those authorities in respect of that expenditure.

(2) Financial assistance given pursuant to a scheme under this section shall take the form of grants paid by the Secretary of State with the consent of the Treasury and, subject to that, the terms and conditions of a scheme shall be such as the Secretary of State considers appropriate to the circumstances of the particular emergency or disaster concerned.

(3) Without prejudice to the generality of subsection (2) above, a scheme under this section may—

(a) make the payment of grants conditional upon the making of claims of a description specified in the scheme;

(b) make provision with respect to the expenditure qualifying for grant and the rates and amounts of grants;

(c) make provision in certain specified circumstances for the repayment of any grant, in whole or in part; and

(d) make different provision for different local authorities or descriptions of authority and for different areas.

(4) In the application of this section to England and Wales, any reference to a local authority is a reference to—

(a) a county council;

(b) a district council;

(c) a London borough council;

(d) the Common Council of the City of London;

(e) the Council of the Isles of Scilly;

(f) the Receiver for the Metropolitan Police District; or

(g) a joint authority established by Part IV of the Local Government Act 1985, other than a metropolitan county passenger transport authority.

1985 c. 51.

(5) In the application of this section to Scotland, any reference to a local authority is a reference to—

(a) a regional council;

(b) a district council;

(c) an islands council; or

(d) a joint board or joint committee within the meaning of the Local Government (Scotland) Act 1973.

1973 c. 65.

(6) The reference in subsection (1)(b) above to expenditure incurred by a local authority includes, in the case of an authority in England and Wales, expenditure incurred in defraying, or contributing towards defraying, expenditure incurred by a parish or community council.

(7) This section shall come into force on 1st April 1990.

PART IX
Contingency
planning and co-
ordination in
respect of
emergencies or
disasters.
1972 c. 70.

156.—(1) In section 138 of the Local Government Act 1972 (powers of principal councils with respect to emergencies or disasters) after subsection (1) there shall be inserted the following subsection—

"(1A) If a principal council are of the opinion that it is appropriate to undertake contingency planning to deal with a possible emergency or disaster which, if it occurred,—

(a) would involve destruction of or danger to life or property, and

(b) would be likely to affect the whole or part of their area,

they may incur such expenditure as they consider necessary on that planning (whether relating to a specific kind of such possible emergency or disaster or generally in relation to possible emergencies or disasters falling within paragraphs (a) and (b) above)."

(2) In subsection (3) of that section—

(a) for the words from the beginning to "authorise" there shall be substituted "Nothing in this section authorises"; and

(b) for the words "the power conferred by that subsection is" there shall be substituted "the powers conferred by subsections (1) and (1A) above are".

(3) At the end of the section there shall be added the following subsections—

"(5) With the consent of the Secretary of State, a metropolitan county fire and civil defence authority and the London Fire and Civil Defence Authority may incur expenditure in co-ordinating planning by principal councils in connection with their functions under subsection (1) above.

(6) In this section "contingency planning" means the making, keeping under review and revising of plans and the carrying out of training associated with the plans."

157.—(1) In any case where, by virtue of any enactment, the Secretary of State has a power or duty to make to a local authority any annual or other periodic payments by way of contribution, grant or subsidy towards expenditure incurred or to be incurred by the local authority, the Secretary of State—

(a) may determine to commute any such payments which would otherwise fall due on or after 1st April 1990 either into a single payment or into such number of payments (being less than would otherwise be payable) as he considers appropriate; and

(b) may, if he thinks it appropriate, pay to the Public Works Loans Commissioners the whole or any part of any single or other payment determined under paragraph (a) above so as to reduce or extinguish such debt (whether then due or not) of the local authority to those Commissioners as the Secretary of State thinks fit.

(2) The amount required to reduce or extinguish a debt as mentioned in paragraph (b) of subsection (1) above shall be such as may be determined by the Public Works Loans Commissioners and where, by virtue of that paragraph, only part of a commuted payment is paid to those Commissioners, the balance shall be paid to the local authority concerned.

(3) Subsection (1) above applies whether the annual or other periodic payments began, or would otherwise begin, before, on or after the passing of this Act and applies notwithstanding anything in any enactment requiring the payments to be made over a period of twenty years or any other specified period.

(4) A single or other payment falling to be made by virtue of subsection (1) above is in this section referred to as a "commuted payment" and the calculation of the amount of any commuted payment shall be such as appears to the Secretary of State to be appropriate.

(5) In any case where the amount of any annual or other periodic payment such as is mentioned in subsection (1) above is, at the passing of this Act, calculated by reference to a rate of interest which varies from time to time, the Secretary of State may substitute a fixed rate of interest.

(6) In this section "local authority", as respects England and Wales, means any of the following—

    (a) a county council;

    (b) a district council;

    (c) a London borough council;

    (d) the Common Council of the City of London;

    (e) the Council of the Isles of Scilly;

    (f) the Receiver for the Metropolitan Police District;

    (g) a police authority constituted under section 2 of the Police Act 1964 or a combined police authority established by an amalgamation scheme under that Act;   1964 c. 48.

    (h) a joint authority established by Part IV of the Local Government Act 1985; and   1985 c. 51.

    (i) a residuary body established under Part VII of that Act;

and, as respects Scotland, means a regional, islands or district council or a joint board or joint committee within the meaning of section 235(1) of the Local Government (Scotland) Act 1973.   1973 c. 65.

(7) If, after a commuted payment has been made to a local authority or to the Public Works Loans Commissioners, it appears to the Secretary of State that the payment was smaller or greater than it should have been (whether by virtue of a miscalculation, the occurrence of any event, the failure to comply with any condition or otherwise) the Secretary of State may, as the case may require,—

    (a) make a further payment to the authority concerned or to those Commissioners; or

    (b) require the repayment or payment to him by that authority of such sum as he may direct.

PART IX

(8) Without prejudice to the operation of the preceding provisions of this section, with respect to—

    (a) any contribution in respect of an expense incurred on or after 1st April 1990; and

    (b) so much of any contribution in respect of an expense incurred before that date as has not been made before that date,

1985 c. 68.

section 569 of the Housing Act 1985 (contribution by Secretary of State to certain expenses incurred by local housing authorities) shall be amended as follows—

    (i) in subsection (2) (which relates to contributions as annual payments) for the words following "shall be" there shall be substituted the words "equal to the relevant percentage of the amount of the expense incurred"; and

    (ii) subsection (5) (which relates to annual loan charges) shall cease to have effect.

1972 c. 70.
1973 c. 65.

(9) Without prejudice to the generality of section 230 of the Local Government Act 1972 or section 235(1) of the Local Government (Scotland) Act 1973 (local authorities' duty to make reports and returns to the Secretary of State), every local authority and the Inner London Education Authority shall furnish to the Secretary of State such information as he may by notice in writing reasonably require for the purposes of this section and, if the notice so specifies, any such information shall be certified and audited in such manner and supplied not later than such date and in such form as may be so specified.

(10) Nothing in this section applies in relation to any payments to which, under Part IV of Schedule 15 to the Housing Act 1985 (superseded contributions etc.: town development subsidy), provision already exists for the commutation of payments.

Electronic transfer
of documents.
1975 c. 76.

158.—(1) In subsection (2) of section 9 of the Local Land Charges Act 1975, the words "A requisition under this section must be in writing, and" shall be omitted.

(2) In subsection (2) of section 14 of that Act after the word "include" there shall be inserted "(a)", and at the end of that subsection there shall be inserted the following paragraphs—

    "(b) power to make rules providing for the use of electronic means in the making of requisitions for, and in the issue of, official search certificates, notwithstanding subsection (3) of section 231 of the Local Government Act 1972 (service of documents on local authorities) provided that—

        (i) such rules shall not provide that a requisition is duly made by electronic means, except where the local authority to whom it is made consents to the use of those means, or that an official search certificate is duly issued by electronic means, except where the person requiring the search consents to the use of those means; and

        (ii) such consent may be given either generally or in relation to a specified document or description of documents, and either before or after the making of the requisition or the issue of the certificate; and

    (c) power to make rules modifying the application of sections 10 and 11 above in cases where—

(i) the rules provide for the making of a requisition for, or the issuing of, an official search certificate by electronic means, and

(ii) there has been any error or failure in those means."

159.—(1) Section 211 of the Local Government (Scotland) Act 1973 (provision for default of local authority) shall be amended in accordance with this section.

Prevention of continuance or recurrence of default of local authority: Scotland.

1973 c. 65.

(2) After subsection (2) there shall be inserted the following subsections—

"(2A) If the Secretary of State or appropriate Minister—

(a) is about to make an order under subsection (2) above; and

(b) is satisfied that the failure to which the order relates has continued or recurred,

he may, in that order and without any local inquiry, declare the authority to be in default in respect of the continuance or recurrence of the failure and direct them for the purpose of remedying the default to take such steps and within such time or times as may be specified in the order.

(2B) The Secretary of State or appropriate Minister may, in an order under subsection (2) above, notify the local authority that any continuance or recurrence of the failure in respect of which the authority have been declared to be in default happening after the date of the order may be made the subject of an application to the Court of Session under subsection (3A) below."

(3) After subsection (3) there shall be inserted the following subsection—

"(3A) If—

(a) a local authority have been notified under subsection (2B) above; and

(b) there has been any such continuance or recurrence as is mentioned in that subsection of the failure to which the notification relates,

the Court of Session may, on the application of the Lord Advocate on behalf of the Secretary of State or appropriate Minister, order specific performance of the functions in respect of which there has been such continuance or recurrence of the failure and do otherwise as to the court appears to be just."

160.—(1) For the purpose of enabling local authorities in Wales to be known solely by Welsh language names, the provisions of the Local Government Act 1972 specified in Schedule 8 to this Act shall be amended in accordance with that Schedule.

(2) Any reference in the provisions amended by Schedule 8 to this Act to a specially convened meeting of a council is a reference to a meeting of which notice is given as required by Schedule 12 to the Local Government Act 1972 but with the substitution for the words "three clear days" in paragraph 4(2) of that Schedule (principal councils) or, as the case may be, paragraph 26(2) (community councils) of "fourteen clear days".

PART IX

Miscellaneous housing provisions

Housing
authorities not
required to keep a
housing stock.
1985 c. 68.

161.—(1) At the end of section 9 of the Housing Act 1985 (provision of housing accommodation) there shall be added the following subsection—

"(5) Nothing in this Act shall be taken to require (or to have at any time required) a local housing authority itself to acquire or hold any houses or other land for the purposes of this Part."

1987 c. 26.

(2) At the end of section 2 of the Housing (Scotland) Act 1987 (powers of local authorities to provide housing accommodation) there shall be added the following subsection—

"(6) Nothing in this Act shall be taken to require (or to have at any time required) a local authority itself to acquire or hold any houses or other land for the purposes of this Part."

Determination of
rents.

162. In section 24 of the Housing Act 1985 (rents), there shall be added at the end the following subsections—

"(3) In exercising their functions under this section, a local housing authority shall have regard in particular to the principle that the rents of houses of any class or description should bear broadly the same proportion to private sector rents as the rents of houses of any other class or description.

(4) In subsection (3) "private sector rents", in relation to houses of any class or description, means the rents which would be recoverable if they were let on assured tenancies within the meaning of the Housing Act 1988 by a person other than the authority."

Exchanges
between secure
and assured
tenants.

163.—(1) Section 92 of the Housing Act 1985 (assignment of secure tenancies by way of exchange) shall be amended in accordance with subsections (2) and (3) below.

(2) At the end of subsection (1) there shall be added the words "or to an assured tenant who satisfies the conditions in subsection (2A)".

(3) After subsection (2) there shall be inserted the following subsection—

"(2A) The conditions to be satisfied with respect to an assured tenant are—

(a) that the landlord under his assured tenancy is either the Housing Corporation, Housing for Wales, a registered housing association or a housing trust which is a charity; and

(b) that he intends to assign his assured tenancy to the secure tenant referred to in subsection (1) or to another secure tenant who satisfies the condition in subsection (2)."

(4) In section 117 of the Housing Act 1985 (index of defined expressions for Part IV) before the entry relating to "cemetery" there shall be inserted—

"assured tenancy ... ... section 622".

Exception to the
right to buy in
case of certain
dwelling-houses
for persons of
pensionable age.

164.—(1) In Schedule 5 to the Housing Act 1985 (exceptions to the right to buy), for paragraph 11 (certain dwelling-houses for persons of pensionable age) there shall be substituted the following paragraph—

"11.—(1) The right to buy does not arise if the Secretary of State has determined, on the application of the landlord, that it is not to be capable of being exercised with respect to the dwelling-house.

(2) The Secretary of State shall so determine if, and only if, he is satisfied that the dwelling-house—

    (a) is particularly suitable, having regard to its location, size, design, heating system and other features, for occupation by persons of pensionable age, and

    (b) was let to the tenant or a predecessor in title of his for occupation by a person of pensionable age (whether the tenant or predecessor or another person).

(3) The Secretary of State shall for the purposes of this paragraph disregard the presence of any feature provided by the tenant or a predecessor in title of his.

(4) An application for a determination under this paragraph shall be made within the period for service of the landlord's notice under section 124 (notice admitting or denying right to buy).

(5) This paragraph does not apply unless the dwelling-house concerned was first let before 1st January 1990."

(2) Subsection (1) above does not apply in any case where the tenant's notice claiming to exercise the right to buy was served before the day on which this section comes into force.

(3) For the purposes of subsection (2) above, no account shall be taken of any steps taken under section 177 of the Housing Act 1985 (amendment or withdrawal and re-service of notice to correct mistakes).

1985 c. 68.

165.—(1) In the Housing Act 1985,—

Unfit housing etc.

    (a) Part VI (repair notices) shall be amended in accordance with Part I of Schedule 9 to this Act;

    (b) Part IX (slum clearance) shall be amended in accordance with Part II of that Schedule;

    (c) Part XI (houses in multiple occupation) shall be amended in accordance with Part III of that Schedule;

    (d) Part XVII (compulsory purchase and land compensation) shall be amended in accordance with Part IV of that Schedule; and

    (e) Part XVIII (miscellaneous and general) shall be amended in accordance with Part V of that Schedule.

(2) Part VII of the Housing Act 1985 (improvement notices) shall cease to have effect.

(3) For any financial year beginning after the day appointed for the coming into force of this subsection the following provisions of this section shall have effect in place of sections 312 to 314 of the Housing Act 1985 (slum clearance subsidy); and in those provisions "slum clearance functions" means any of the functions under the provisions of Part IX of that Act relating to—

    (a) the demolition, closing or purchase of unfit premises,

    (b) the demolition of obstructive buildings, and

(c) clearance areas,

but does not include functions under sections 308 to 311 of that Act (owner's redevelopment or improvement).

(4) On such conditions as he may determine the Secretary of State may pay slum clearance subsidy to a local housing authority in respect of any financial year for which, applying such method of calculation as may be determined by the Secretary of State, the authority have incurred a loss in connection with the exercise of their slum clearance functions; and the rate or rates of the subsidy and the manner in which it is paid shall be such as may be determined by him.

(5) If for any financial year, applying such method of calculation as is referred to in subsection (4) above, a local housing authority have incurred a surplus in connection with the exercise of their slum clearance functions, the Secretary of State may require the authority to pay to him such sum as he may determine in respect of that surplus, together with interest thereon from such time and at such rate or rates as he may determine.

(6) Any determination of the Secretary of State under subsection (4) or subsection (5) above—

(a) shall be made with the consent of the Treasury;

(b) may be made generally or with respect to a particular local housing authority or description of authority, including a description framed by reference to authorities in a particular area; and

(c) may make different provision for different cases or descriptions of case.

(7) If, before the declaration of a renewal area under Part VII of this Act, a local housing authority are satisfied that the rate of slum clearance subsidy which, in accordance with a determination under subsection (4) above, would otherwise be applicable to the authority will not be adequate, bearing in mind the action they propose to take with regard to the area, they may, before making the declaration, apply to the Secretary of State for a subsidy at a higher rate in respect of that area.

(8) An application under subsection (7) above shall be made in such form and contain such particulars as the Secretary of State may determine; and, if such an application is made, the authority shall not declare the area concerned to be a renewal area until the application is approved, refused or withdrawn.

(9) If an application under subsection (7) above is approved, the Secretary of State may pay slum clearance subsidy in respect of the area concerned at such higher rate as he may determine under subsection (4) above.

Amendments relating to defective housing.
1985 c. 68.
1987 c. 26.

166.—(1) Part XVI of the Housing Act 1985 (in this section referred to as "the 1985 Act") and Part XIV of the Housing (Scotland) Act 1987 (in this section referred to as "the 1987 Act") (assistance for owners of defective housing) shall each be amended in accordance with this section.

(2) In section 537 of the 1985 Act and section 265 of the 1987 Act (determination of form of assistance to which applicant is entitled) in subsection (1) after the word "determine" there shall be inserted "as soon as reasonably practicable".

(3) In section 539 of the 1985 Act and section 267 of the 1987 Act (meaning of "work required for reinstatement" etc.) after subsection (1) there shall be inserted the following subsection—

"(1A) In any case where—

(a) the most satisfactory way of dealing with the qualifying defect is substantially to demolish the building that consists of or includes the defective dwelling or a part of that building, and

(b) it is practicable to rebuild the building or part concerned on, or substantially on, its existing foundations and reconstruct the dwelling to the same, or substantially the same, plan,

the work required to carry out those operations shall be regarded for the purposes of this Part as work required to reinstate the defective dwelling."

(4) In section 561 of the 1985 Act and section 289 of the 1987 Act (Secretary of State's control over designation, variation or revocation)—

(a) in subsection (2) after the word "before" there shall be inserted "the cut-off date or if it is later" and after the words "two months" there shall be inserted "or such longer period as the Secretary of State may direct for the purposes of this subsection under subsection (2A) below";

(b) after that subsection there shall be inserted the subsection specified in subsection (5) below; and

(c) in subsection (3) for the words "within that period" there shall be substituted "before the cut-off date or, if it is later, the expiry of the period for the time being specified in or for the purposes of subsection (2) above".

(5) The subsection referred to in subsection (4)(b) above is as follows—

"(2A) If, within the period for the time being specified in or (by virtue of the previous operation of this subsection) for the purposes of subsection (2) above, the Secretary of State is satisfied that he does not have reasonably sufficient information to enable him to come to a decision with respect to the resolution concerned, he may direct for the purposes of that subsection that it shall have effect as if for the period so specified there were substituted such longer period as is specified in the direction."

(6) In section 567 of the 1985 Act (modifications of Part XVI in relation to shared ownership leases) for subsections (1) to (3) there shall be substituted the following subsections—

"(1) If it appears to a local housing authority that the interest of a person eligible for assistance in respect of a defective dwelling in their area is—

(a) a shared ownership lease, or

(b) the freehold acquired under the terms of a shared ownership lease,

the authority shall prepare and submit to the Secretary of State a scheme providing for the provisions of this Part to have effect, in their application to such a case, subject to such modifications as may be specified in the scheme.

(2) A scheme under subsection (1) above shall not have effect unless approved by the Secretary of State; and any such approval may be made conditional upon compliance with requirements specified by him."

(7) Any power of the Secretary of State to make regulations under subsection (4) of section 567 of the 1985 Act shall cease to have effect; and in paragraph (d) of that subsection after the word "class" there shall be inserted "or description".

Reports to tenants etc. on local housing authority functions.

167.—(1) In accordance with the provisions of this section, every local housing authority shall, for each year, furnish to each person who at the end of that year is one of their housing revenue account tenants a report containing such information as may be determined by the Secretary of State relating to the functions of the authority as a local housing authority during that year (including functions which in that year were exercised by any other person as agent of the authority).

(2) In this section "year" means a period of twelve months beginning on 1st April; and the report relating to any year shall be furnished as soon as practicable after the end of that year and, in any event, not later than six months after the end of that year.

(3) In this section "housing revenue account tenant", in relation to a local housing authority, means a person who, as tenant or licensee, occupies a house or other property within the authority's Housing Revenue Account; and, in the case of joint tenants or joint licensees, it shall be a sufficient compliance with the obligation under subsection (1) above to furnish each housing revenue account tenant with a report that a single copy of it is furnished to the tenants or licensees jointly.

(4) At the same time as they furnish a report under this section to their housing revenue account tenants, a local housing authority shall send a copy of the report to the Secretary of State.

(5) The power to make a determination under subsection (1) above may be so exercised as to make different provision for different cases or descriptions of cases, including different provision for different areas, for different local housing authorities or for different descriptions of local housing authorities.

(6) The reference in subsection (3) above to a house or other property within an authority's Housing Revenue Account shall be construed in accordance with section 74(5) above.

1985 c. 68.

(7) In this section "tenant" has the same meaning as in the Housing Act 1985.

(8) Before making a determination under this section, the Secretary of State shall consult such representatives of local government as appear to him to be appropriate.

Contributions towards costs of housing mobility arrangements.

168.—(1) The Secretary of State may with the consent of the Treasury make grants or loans towards the cost of arrangements for enabling or assisting persons to move and become,—

(a) in England and Wales, tenants or licensees of dwellings; and

(b) in Scotland, tenants of houses.

(2) The grants or loans may be made subject to such conditions as the Secretary of State may determine and may be made so as to be repayable or, as the case may be, repayable earlier if there is a breach of such a condition.

(3) In this section—

"dwelling" means a building or a part of a building occupied or intended to be occupied as a separate dwelling;

"house" has the same meaning as in the Housing (Scotland) Act 1987; and

"tenant" does not include a tenant under a long lease within the meaning of the Landlord and Tenant Act 1987 or, as respects Scotland, under a lease for a period exceeding 20 years.

1987 c. 26.

1987 c. 31.

(4) Section 107 of the Housing Act 1985 and section 80 of the Housing (Scotland) Act 1987 (which make provision similar to that made by the preceding provisions of this section, but limited to secure tenants) shall cease to have effect.

1985 c. 68.

169.—(1) A relevant authority shall have power to provide professional, technical and administrative services for owners or occupiers of dwellings in connection with their arranging or carrying out relevant works or to encourage or facilitate the carrying out of such works, whether or not on payment of such charges as the authority may determine.

Powers of local authorities and Secretary of State as respects services etc. for owners and occupiers of houses for work on them.

(2) Works are relevant works in relation to a dwelling or, as the case may be, a dwelling in any area, if they are works of any of the following descriptions, that is to say—

(a) works to cause the dwelling to be fit for human habitation,

(b) where the occupant is disabled, works for any of the purposes specified in section 114(3) or (4) above,

(c) works for any of the purposes specified in section 115(3) above, and

(d) works for any of the purposes specified in or under section 131(1) above.

(3) It shall be the duty of a relevant authority exercising any power conferred by subsection (1) above—

(a) to consider whether or not to make a charge for exercising it; and

(b) to take such measures as are reasonably available to them to secure contributions from other persons towards the cost of exercising it.

(4) A relevant authority shall have power to give financial assistance in any form to—

(a) any housing association,

(b) any charity, or

(c) any body, or body of any description, approved by the Secretary of State,

towards the cost of the provision by that association, charity or body of services of any description for owners or occupiers of dwellings in arranging works of maintenance, repair or improvement or the encouraging or facilitating the carrying out of such works.

PART IX

(5) It shall be the duty of a relevant authority—

(a) in deciding whether to exercise any power conferred by subsection (4) above in relation to any association, charity or body, to have regard to the existence and extent of any financial assistance available from other persons to that association, charity or body; and

(b) in exercising any power conferred by subsection (4) above in relation to any association, charity or body—

(i) to have regard to whether that association, charity or body has made or will make charges and their amount; and

(ii) to encourage the association, charity or body to take such measures as are reasonably available to them to secure contributions from other persons.

(6) The Secretary of State may, with the consent of the Treasury, give financial assistance in any form to any person in respect of expenditure incurred or to be incurred by that person in connection with the provision,whether or not by that person, of services of any description for owners or occupiers of dwellings in arranging or carrying out works of maintenance, repair or improvement, or in connection with the encouraging or facilitating, whether or not by that person, the carrying out of such works.

(7) The giving of financial assistance under subsection (6) above shall be on such terms (which may include terms as to repayment) as the Secretary of State, with the consent of the Treasury, considers appropriate.

(8) The person receiving assistance shall comply with the terms on which it is given and compliance may be enforced by the Secretary of State.

(9) In this section—

"charity" means any institution, corporate or not, which is established for charitable purposes and is subject to the control of the High Court in the exercise of the Court's jurisdiction with respect to charities;

1985 c. 69.

"housing association" means a housing association within the meaning of section 1(1) of the Housing Associations Act 1985, or a body established by such a housing association for the purpose of, or having among its purposes or objects, those mentioned in section 4(3)(e) of that Act (providing services of any description for owners or occupiers of houses in arranging or carrying out works of maintenance, repair or improvement, or encouraging or facilitating the carrying out of such works);

1985 c. 68.

"local housing authority" shall be construed in accordance with section 1 of the Housing Act 1985; and

"relevant authority" means a local housing authority or county council.

Powers of local authorities and Secretary of State as respects services, etc., for owners and occupiers of houses for work on them: Scotland.

170.—(1) A relevant authority shall have power to provide professional, technical and administrative services for owners or occupiers of houses in connection with their arranging or carrying out relevant works or to encourage or facilitate the carrying out of such works, whether or not on payment of such charges as the authority may determine.

(2) Relevant works are such works as may be specified in regulations made by the Secretary of State and such works may be so specified by reference to such factors (including factors relating to persons of such descriptions as may be so specified) as the Secretary of State thinks fit.

(3) It shall be the duty of a relevant authority exercising any power conferred by subsection (1) above—

    (a) to consider whether or not to make a charge for exercising it; and

    (b) to take such measures as are reasonably available to them to secure contributions from other persons towards the cost of exercising it.

(4) A relevant authority shall have power to give financial assistance in any form to—

    (a) any housing association,

    (b) any charity, or

    (c) any body, or body of any description, approved by the Secretary of State,

towards the cost of the provision by that association, charity or body of services of any description for owners or occupiers of houses in arranging works of maintenance, repair or improvement or the encouraging or facilitating the carrying out of such works.

(5) It shall be the duty of a relevant authority—

    (a) in deciding whether to exercise any power conferred by subsection (4) above in relation to any association, charity or body, to have regard to the existence and extent of any financial assistance available from other persons to that association, charity or body; and

    (b) in exercising any power conferred by subsection (4) above in relation to any association, charity or body—

        (i) to have regard to whether that association, charity or body has made or will make charges and their amount; and

        (ii) to encourage the association, charity or body to take such measures as are reasonably available to them to secure contributions from other persons.

(6) The Secretary of State may, with the consent of the Treasury, give financial assistance in any form to any person in respect of expenditure incurred or to be incurred by that person in connection with the provision, whether or not by that person, of services of any description for owners or occupiers of houses in arranging or carrying out works of maintenance, repair or improvement or in connection with the encouraging or facilitating, whether or not by that person, the carrying out of such works.

(7) The giving of financial assistance under subsection (6) above shall be on such terms (which may include terms as to repayment) as the Secretary of State, with the consent of the Treasury, considers appropriate.

(8) The person receiving assistance shall comply with the terms on which it is given and compliance may be enforced by the Secretary of State.

(9) In this section—

"charity" means any body, corporate or not, established for charitable purposes;

"charitable purposes" shall be construed in the same way as if it were contained in the Income Tax Acts;

1987 c. 26.

"house" has the meaning given by section 338 of the Housing (Scotland) Act 1987;

1985 c. 69.

"housing association" means a housing association within the meaning of section 1(1) of the Housing Associations Act 1985, or a body established by such a housing association for the purpose of, or having among its purposes or objects, those mentioned in section 4(3)(e) of that Act (providing services of any description for owners or occupiers of houses in arranging or carrying out works of maintenance, repair or improvement, or encouraging or facilitating the carrying out of such works);

"relevant authority" means a regional, islands or district council.

Winding up of home purchase assistance scheme.

171.—(1) The Secretary of State may by order make provision for the purpose of bringing to an end the scheme for assistance for first-time buyers which—

1985 c. 68.

(a) as respects England and Wales, is contained in sections 445 to 450 of the Housing Act 1985, and

(b) as respects Scotland, is contained in sections 222 to 227 of the Housing (Scotland) Act 1987,

and in the following provisions of this section, the enactments specified in paragraphs (a) and (b) above together with any orders and directions made under those enactments are referred to as "the assistance legislation".

(2) Without prejudice to the generality of the power conferred by subsection (1) above, an order under that subsection—

(a) may specify a date or dates with effect from which account will no longer be taken under the assistance legislation of matters specified in the order;

(b) may vary the terms of advances to lending institutions so as to commute what would otherwise be a number of payments or repayments to or by such an institution into a single payment or a smaller number of payments of such amount and payable at such time or times as may be determined in accordance with the order; and

(c) may provide for the amendment or repeal, in whole or in part, of the assistance legislation with effect from such date or dates and subject to such transitional provisions as may be specified in the order.

(3) The following powers, namely,—

(a) the powers conferred on the Secretary of State by subsection (3) of section 446 of the Housing Act 1985 and subsection (3) of section 223 of the Housing (Scotland) Act 1987 to relax or modify the conditions in subsection (2) of each of those sections respectively (conditions qualifying a purchaser for assistance), and

(b) any power to make an order under any provision of the assistance legislation,

may be so exercised as to make provision for the purpose referred to in subsection (1) above.

(4) The power to make an order under subsection (1) above shall be exercisable by statutory instrument which shall be subject to annulment in pursuance of a resolution of either House of Parliament.

172.—(1) Subject to the following provisions of this section, the Secretary of State may by regulations make provision for requiring and authorising each new town corporation to take such steps as may be prescribed for making and giving effect to proposals for disposing of their housing stock, either by transferring it as a whole to a prescribed person or by transferring different parts of it to different prescribed persons.

(2) Regulations under subsection (1) above shall not require a new town corporation to transfer any dwelling or associated property, rights, liabilities or obligations to any person other than—

    (a) the district council within whose district the dwelling is situated; or

    (b) a person approved for the purposes of, and in accordance with, the regulations by the Housing Corporation or Housing for Wales.

(3) Regulations under subsection (1) above shall not require a new town corporation to give effect to a proposal for the transfer of any dwelling if the dwelling is one in respect of which a notice has been served under section 122 of the Housing Act 1985 (notice of a claim to exercise the right to buy) before the prescribed time and such other conditions as may be prescribed are satisfied.

(4) A new town corporation shall not, in pursuance of any regulations under subsection (1) above, transfer any dwellings, or any associated property, rights, liabilities or obligations, to any person except with the consent of the Secretary of State; and the Secretary of State shall not give his consent to a proposed transfer unless he is satisfied—

    (a) that there has been compliance with all such requirements with respect to the publication of information about the proposal and matters connected with its implementation, and with respect to consultation about the proposal, as are prescribed;

    (b) that all such steps have been taken as are prescribed for the purpose of protecting the interests of the occupiers of the dwellings or the interests of the occupiers of any dwellings excluded from the proposal by virtue of subsection (3) above or any such consultation; and

    (c) that the terms on which the transfer is made—

        (i) require such price to be paid for the property transferred as appears to him to be the price which, on the prescribed assumptions, it would realise if sold on the open market by a willing vendor; and

        (ii) include all such other terms as are prescribed.

(5) Regulations under subsection (1) above may contain such incidental provision and such supplemental, consequential and transitional provision in connection with their other provisions as the Secretary of State considers appropriate, including, without prejudice to the generality of the foregoing, provision corresponding to sub-paragraphs (2) and (3) of paragraph 2 of Schedule 12 to the Housing Act 1988 (matters relating to registration of title).

(6) Subject to subsection (7) below, Part III of the New Towns Act 1981 (transfer of dwellings and associated property to district councils) shall cease to have effect.

(7) Nothing in subsection (6) above shall—

(a) affect the operation after the time when that subsection comes into force of so much of any transfer scheme made under Part III of the said Act of 1981 before that time as contains management arrangements with respect to land in which a new town corporation have an interest;

(b) affect the application after that time of section 50 of that Act (financial arrangements) in relation to any transfer scheme made under that Part before that time; or

(c) prevent the Secretary of State from exercising his power to make grants to a district council under section 51A of that Act (grants in respect of defects in transferred dwellings) where the grants are paid before the 1st April 1990 or such later date as the Secretary of State may by order made by statutory instrument appoint in relation to that council;

and a statutory instrument containing an order under this subsection shall be subject to annulment in pursuance of a resolution of either House of Parliament.

(8) In this section—

"dwelling" means any building or part of a building occupied, or erected or adapted for occupation, as a dwelling or as a hostel (including any land belonging to it or usually enjoyed with it);

"housing stock", in relation to a new town corporation, means—

(a) the dwellings (whether or not in the area of a particular new town) which are vested in that corporation and were erected, adapted or acquired for occupation as dwellings; and

(b) except so far as may be prescribed, any associated property, rights, liabilities and obligations of that corporation;

"liabilities and obligations", in relation to a new town corporation, includes liabilities and obligations which, apart from the regulations, would not be capable of being assigned or transferred by the corporation, including liabilities and obligations under Part V of the Housing Act 1985 (the right to buy);

"new town corporation" means the Commission for the New Towns, the Development Board for Rural Wales or a development corporation, within the meaning of the New Towns Act 1981; and

"prescribed" means prescribed by or determined under regulations under subsection (1) above.

(9) For the purposes of this section the following property, rights, liabilities and obligations of a new town corporation shall be treated as associated with any dwellings comprised in their housing stock, that is to say—

> (a) any interest of the corporation in any land occupied or set aside for occupation or use with the dwellings;

> (b) any interest of the corporation in land in the vicinity of the dwellings which is held by them for the benefit or use of the persons living in those dwellings (rather than the inhabitants of a new town as a whole) or for providing facilities for the persons living in those dwellings, and any other property and any rights of the corporation so held;

> (c) any property and rights held by the corporation—

>> (i) for the administration of an estate comprising the dwellings or any associated property;

>> (ii) for the maintenance or service of the dwellings or any associated property; or

>> (iii) otherwise in connection with any such property;

> (d) any rights, liabilities and obligations which the corporation have in connection with any of the dwellings or any associated property or in connection with any dwellings which were previously part of their housing stock;

> (e) any interest of the corporation in land set aside by them as an open space for the use or enjoyment of persons living in the dwellings (rather than for the use of the inhabitants of a new town as a whole).

173.—(1) Where a dwelling which is for the time being subject to a secure tenancy is transferred under section 172 above to a person approved as mentioned in subsection (2)(b) of that section (in this section referred to as an "approved person"), that person shall not dispose of it except—

> (a) with the consent of the Secretary of State, which may be given either unconditionally or subject to conditions; or

> (b) by an exempt disposal, as defined in section 81(8) of the Housing Act 1988;

and any reference in the following provisions of this section to an initial transfer is a reference to the transfer of a dwelling to an approved person under section 172 above.

Consent required for subsequent disposals.

1988 c. 50.

(2) Where an estate or interest in a dwelling of the approved person who acquired it on the initial transfer has been mortgaged or charged, the prohibition in subsection (1) above applies also to a disposal by the mortgagee or chargee in exercise of a power of sale or leasing, whether or not the disposal is in the name of the approved person; and in any case where—

> (a) by operation of law or by virtue of an order of a court, the dwelling which has been acquired on the initial transfer passes or is transferred from the approved person to another person, and

(b) that passing or transfer does not constitute a disposal for which consent is required under this section,

this section (including, where there is more than one such passing or transfer, this subsection) shall apply as if the other person to whom the dwelling passes or is transferred were the approved person.

(3) Where subsection (1) above applies—

    (a) the new town corporation by whom the initial transfer is made shall furnish to the approved person a copy of the consent of the Secretary of State under section 172(4) above; and

    (b) the instrument by which the initial transfer is effected shall contain a statement in a form approved by the Chief Land Registrar that the requirement of this section as to consent applies to a subsequent disposal of the dwelling by the approved person.

(4) For the purposes of this section the grant of an option to purchase the fee simple or any other interest in a dwelling is a disposal and a consent given to such a disposal extends to a disposal made in pursuance of the option.

(5) Before giving any consent required by virtue of this section, the Secretary of State—

    (a) shall satisfy himself that the person who is seeking the consent has taken appropriate steps to consult every tenant of any dwelling proposed to be disposed of; and

    (b) shall have regard to the responses of any such tenants to that consultation.

1985 c. 69.

(6) If, apart from subsection (7) below, the consent of the Housing Corporation or Housing for Wales would be required under section 9 of the Housing Associations Act 1985 (control of dispositions of land by housing associations) for a disposal in respect of which, by virtue of subsection (1) above, the consent of the Secretary of State is required, the Secretary of State shall consult that body before giving his consent for the purposes of this section.

(7) No consent shall be required under the said section 9 for any disposal in respect of which consent is given in accordance with subsection (6) above.

1925 c. 21.

(8) Where the title of the new town corporation to the dwelling which is transferred by the initial transfer is not registered, and the initial transfer is a conveyance, grant or assignment of a description mentioned in section 123 of the Land Registration Act 1925 (compulsory registration of title)—

    (a) that section applies in relation to the instrument by which the initial transfer is effected, whether or not the dwelling is in an area in which an Order in Council under section 120 of that Act (areas of compulsory registration) is in force;

    (b) the corporation shall give the approved person a certificate in a form approved by the Chief Land Registrar stating that the corporation is entitled to make the transfer subject only to such encumbrances, rights and interests as are stated in the instrument by which the initial transfer is effected or summarised in the certificate; and

(c) for the purpose of registration of title, the Chief Land Registrar shall accept such a certificate as evidence of the facts stated in it, but if as a result he has to meet a claim against him under the Land Registration Acts 1925 to 1986 the corporation by whom the initial transfer was made is liable to indemnify him.

(9) On an application being made for registration of a disposition of registered land or, as the case may be, of the title under a disposition of unregistered land, if the instrument by which the initial transfer is effected contains the statement required by subsection (3) above, the Chief Land Registrar shall enter in the register a restriction stating the requirement of this section as to consent to a subsequent disposal.

(10) In this section—

    (a) "dwelling" and "new town corporation" have the same meaning as in section 172 above; and

    (b) "secure tenancy" has the meaning assigned by section 79 of the Housing Act 1985.   1985 c. 68.

174.—(1) Part IV of the Housing Act 1988 (change of landlord: secure tenants) shall be amended in accordance with this section.   Payment of disposal cost by instalments. 1988 c. 50.

(2) At the end of section 99 (determination of purchase price) there shall be added the following subsections—

> "(7) In a notice under subsection (1) above or by a separate notice given to the applicant not later than seven days after the date of a determination under subsection (6) above, the landlord may notify the applicant that if there is a disposal cost which is such that, in accordance with regulations under section 104(2A) below, it may be paid by instalments, the landlord intends to pay that cost by instalments.

> (8) Where the landlord notifies the applicant as mentioned in subsection (7) above, he shall furnish to the applicant, in such form and certified in such manner as may be prescribed, such information as may be prescribed in order to enable the applicant to consider the application of the regulations to the disposal cost and to assess the likely effect of the payment by instalments."

(3) In section 103 (notice by applicant of intention to proceed), in subsection (4) at the end of paragraph (d) the word "and" shall be omitted and at the end of paragraph (e) there shall be added "and

    (f) if there is a disposal cost attributable to that property and the landlord has notified the applicant as mentioned in section 99(7) above of his intention to pay the disposal cost by instalments, either a statement of the basis on which, in accordance with regulations under section 104(2A) below, the disposal cost is to be paid by instalments or a statement that the disposal cost is not such that those regulations permit it to be paid by instalments".

(4) In section 104 (duty to complete and consequences of completion) after subsection (2) there shall be inserted the following subsection—

"(2A) In such cases as may be prescribed and where the applicant has been notified as mentioned in section 99(7) above, a disposal cost may be paid by instalments of such amounts (which may include interest) and payable at such times and over such period as may be prescribed."

Repeal of the Town Development Act 1952.
1952 c. 54.

175. No undertaking shall be given under section 2 or 4 of the Town Development Act 1952 (Government and local authority contributions for the purposes of town development), and no payment shall be made in pursuance of any such undertaking, at any time after 31st March 1990; and that Act shall cease to have effect except for the purposes of any town development (within the meaning of that Act) in relation to which any undertaking has been given before that date under section 2 of that Act.

Amendment of definition of occupation for purposes of purchase of house by secure tenant: Scotland.
1987 c. 26.

176.—(1) In section 61(10) of the Housing (Scotland) Act 1987 (definition of occupation of house for purposes of purchase by secure tenant)—

(a) in paragraph (a)(v) (occupation by member of tenant's family succeeding to tenancy may be treated, at discretion of landlord, as occupation for purposes of right to buy) the words "in the discretion of the landlord" shall be omitted; and

(b) in paragraph (b) (rules for determining period of occupation) there shall be added at the end— "and

(iii) there shall be added to the period of occupation of a house by a joint tenant any earlier period during which he was at least 16 years of age and occupied the house as a member of the family of the tenant or of one or more of the joint tenants of the house."

(2) This section does not apply in any case where the application to purchase the house under section 63(2) of that Act has been served before the coming into force of this section.

Sale to secure tenants of houses provided for persons of pensionable age: Scotland.

177. In section 69 of the Housing (Scotland) Act 1987 (Secretary of State's power to authorise refusal to sell certain houses provided for persons of pensionable age) after subsection (1) there shall be inserted the following subsection—

"(1A) This section applies only to houses first let on a secure tenancy before 1st January 1990."

Application of secure tenant's right to buy to cases where landlord is lessee: Scotland.

178.—(1) In section 76 of the Housing (Scotland) Act 1987 (duty of landlords to provide information to secure tenants)—

(a) in subsection (1)(a)—

(i) for the word "not" there shall be substituted the word "neither"; and

(ii) after the word "house" there shall be inserted the words "nor holds the interest of the landlord under a registered lease of the house or of land which includes it";

(b) in subsection (2) for the words "heritable proprietor of the house" there shall be substituted the words "either the heritable proprietor of the house or the holder of the interest of the landlord under a registered lease of the house or of land which includes it"; and

(c) in subsection (3)(b) at the end there shall be inserted the words "or a local authority is the holder of the interest of the landlord under a registered lease of the house or of land which includes it."

(2) After section 84 of that Act there shall be inserted the following section—

"Application of right to buy to cases where landlord is lessee.

84A.—(1) Sections 61 to 84 (but not 76 or 77) and 216 (the "right to buy" provisions) shall, with the modifications set out in this section, apply so as to provide for—

(a) the acquisition by the tenant of a house let on a secure tenancy of the landlord's interest in the house as lessee under a registered lease of the house or of land which includes it or as assignee of that interest; and

(b) the obtaining of a loan by the tenant in that connection,

as these sections apply for the purposes of the purchase of a house by the tenant from the landlord as heritable proprietor of it and the obtaining by the tenant of a loan in that connection.

(2) References in the right to buy provisions to the purchase or sale of a house shall be construed respectively as references to the acquisition or disposal of the landlord's interest in the house by way of a registered assignation of that interest and cognate expressions shall be construed accordingly.

(3) The reference in section 61(2)(b) to the landlord's being the heritable proprietor of the house shall be construed as a reference to the landlord's being the holder of the interest of the lessee under a registered lease of the house or of land which includes it.

(4) References in the right to buy provisions to the market value of or price to be paid for a house shall be construed respectively as references to the market value of the landlord's interest in the house and to the price to be paid for acquiring that interest.

(5) References in section 64(1) to the tenant's enjoyment and use of a house as owner shall be construed as references to his enjoyment and use of it as assignee of the landlord's interest in the house.

(6) The reference in subsection (4) of section 64 to an option being offered to the landlord or to any other person to purchase the house in advance of its sale to a third party shall be construed as a reference to an option being offered to have the interest acquired by the tenant

PART IX

re-assigned to the landlord or assigned to the other person in advance of its being disposed of to a third party; and the references in subsection (5) and (9) of that section to an option to purchase shall be construed accordingly.

(7) In this section and section 76—

"registered lease" means a lease—

(a) which is recorded in the general register of sasines; or

(b) in respect of which the interest of the lessee is registered in the Land Register of Scotland

under the Registration of Leases (Scotland) Act 1857; and

"registered assignation" means, in relation to such a lease, an assignation thereof which is so recorded or in respect of which the interest of the assignee has been so registered."

Amendment of powers of Scottish Homes to dispose of land.
1988 c. 43.

179. In section 2 of the Housing (Scotland) Act 1988 (which, amongst other things, enables Scottish Homes to dispose of land)—

(a) in subsection (2) (powers of Scottish Homes), after "(3)" there shall be inserted "and (3A)";

(b) in subsection (3)(b)—

(i) after "above" there shall be inserted the words ", other than the power under paragraph (h) to dispose of land,"; and

(ii) for the word "with" where secondly occurring there shall be substituted the words "between it and";

(c) after subsection (3) there shall be inserted the following subsection—

"(3A) The power conferred by subsection (2)(h) above upon Scottish Homes to dispose of land may be exercised only with the consent of the Secretary of State (which consent may be given in relation to particular cases or classes of case and may be made subject to conditions)."; and

(d) subsection (6) (certain land not to be disposed of, without consent, for less than best price) shall be omitted.

Race relations: codes of practice in housing field.
1976 c. 74.
1988 c. 50.

180. The amendments of section 47 of the Race Relations Act 1976 (codes of practice) made by subsections (2) and (3) of section 137 of the Housing Act 1988 (codes of practice in the field of rented housing) shall be varied as follows—

(a) in subsection (1)(c) of the said section 47 the words following "field of housing" shall be omitted; and

(b) the word "rented", where it occurs in subsections (1)(d) and (3A) of that section, shall be omitted.

Duty of landlord to inform secure tenant seeking to buy house about changes in law: Scotland.
1987 c. 26.

181. In section 76 of the Housing (Scotland) Act 1987 (duty of landlords to provide information to secure tenants) there shall be added at the end the following subsections—

"(4) Where—

(a) by way of any enactment (including an enactment made under this Act), any change is to be made in the law relating to the calculation of the price at which the tenant of a house is entitled under this Act to purchase it, being a change which does not come into force upon the passing or making of that enactment but which, when it does come into force will affect the price of the house, and

(b) the house is one in respect of which an application to purchase has, in the period ending with the coming into force of the change, been served under section 63(1) and not withdrawn but no contract of sale of the house has been constituted under section 66(2),

the landlord shall, upon the passing or making of that enactment or, if later, upon the service of the application to purchase, forthwith give written notice to the tenant stating the nature of the change and how it will affect the price and suggesting that the tenant should seek appropriate advice.

(5) For the purposes of subsection (4), a change in the law will affect the price of a house if, on the day it falls to be calculated under the law as changed, the price will be different from what it would have been that day had there been no such change."

Other provisions

182. In Part I of the Housing Associations Act 1985 (regulation of housing associations) after section 27 there shall be inserted the following section—

Power to monitor activities of registered housing associations. 1985 c. 69.

"Power of Corporation to monitor associations.

27A.—(1) If at any time required to do so by the Corporation,—

(a) a registered housing association shall produce to a person authorised in that behalf by the Corporation such books, accounts and other documents relating to the association's business as may be specified by the Corporation; and

(b) any officer, employee or member of the committee of the registered housing association shall provide an explanation of any such books, accounts and other documents.

(2) Where, by virtue of subsection (1), any books, accounts or other documents are produced to a person authorised in that behalf by the Corporation, he may take copies of or make extracts from them.

(3) In the application of this section to a registered housing association which is a charity,—

(a) the reference in subsection (1)(a) to the association's business shall be construed as a reference to its housing activities; and

(b) the reference to a member of the committee includes a reference to a trustee of the association."

PART IX
Extension of
powers of
Housing
Corporation and
Housing for
Wales to give
financial
assistance.
1985 c. 69.

183. For section 87 of the Housing Associations Act 1985 (grants towards expenses in promoting or assisting registered housing associations) there shall be substituted the following section—

"Financial assistance with respect to formation, management, etc. of certain housing associations.

87.—(1) The Corporation may give financial assistance to any person in respect of the following activities—

(a) promoting and giving advice on the formation of registered housing associations and co-operative housing associations (in this section referred to collectively as "relevant associations");

(b) managing, providing services for, and giving advice on the running of, relevant associations; and

(c) assisting tenants and licensees of a relevant association to take part in the management of the association or of some or all of the dwellings provided by the association.

(2) Assistance under this section may be in the form of grants, loans, guarantees or incurring expenditure for the benefit of the person assisted or in such other way as the Corporation considers appropriate, except that the Corporation may not, in giving any form of financial assistance, purchase loan or share capital in a company.

(3) With respect to financial assistance under this section, the following—

(a) the procedure to be followed in relation to applications for assistance,

(b) the circumstances in which assistance is or is not to be given,

(c) the method for calculating, and any limitations on, the amount of assistance, and

(d) the manner in which, and the time or times at which, assistance is to be given,

shall be such as may be specified by the Corporation, acting in accordance with such principles as it may from time to time determine.

(4) In giving assistance under this section, the Corporation may provide that the assistance is conditional upon compliance by the person to whom the assistance is given with such conditions as it may specify.

(5) Where assistance under this section is given in the form of a grant, subsections (1), (2) and (7) to (9) of section 52 of the Housing Act 1988 (recovery, etc. of grants) shall apply as they apply in relation to a grant to which that section applies, but with the substitution, for any reference in those subsections to the registered housing association to which the grant has been given, of a reference to the person to whom assistance is given under this section.

(6) Section 53 of the Housing Act 1988 (determinations under Part II) shall apply in relation to a determination under this section as it applies to a determination under sections 50 to 52 of that Act."

PART IX

184.—(1) In Part III of the Local Government Finance Act 1982 (the Audit Commission for Local Authorities in England and Wales) after section 28 there shall be inserted the following section—

Extension of functions of Audit Commission. 1982 c. 32.

"Functions of Commission in relation to national health service.

28A.—(1) At the request of the Secretary of State, the Commission may—

(a) promote or undertake studies designed to improve economy, efficiency and effectiveness in the management or operations of any of the bodies specified in section 98(1) of the National Health Service Act 1977 (accounts to be kept by Health Authorities, Family Practitioner Committees, special trustees and the Dental Practice Board);

(b) appoint an auditor to audit the accounts of any of those bodies for a financial year;

(c) make available officers of the Commission to assist with the studies referred to in paragraph (a) above;

(d) make available officers of the Commission to assist an auditor appointed by the Commission under paragraph (b) above or by the Secretary of State under the said section 98(1) in carrying out his audit of any of those bodies;

(e) provide advice to the Secretary of State on any proposal to transfer responsibility for the audit of the accounts of any of those bodies to the Commission; and

(f) provide training for persons in relation to the audit of the accounts of those bodies, including training for securing economy, efficiency and effectiveness in the provision of services by those bodies.

(2) Where a request is made to the Commission to appoint an auditor as mentioned in subsection (1)(b) above, section 13 above shall apply as it applies in relation to the appointment of an auditor to audit the accounts of any body whose accounts are required to be audited in accordance with this Part of this Act subject to the following modifications—

(a) subsections (3) and (4) shall be omitted; and

(b) in subsection (5) for the words "has such other qualifications as may be" there shall be substituted the words "is a person for the time being".

(3) Subject to subsection (2) above, references in the foregoing provisions of this Part of this Act to an audit carried out thereunder do not include an audit carried out pursuant to a request under subsection (1) above.

(4) Where any services are to be provided pursuant to a request under subsection (1) above, the Commission shall agree with the Secretary of State, and charge him, such fees as will cover the full cost of providing the services."

(2) In section 29 of that Act (miscellaneous functions of Commission) in subsection (1)—

(a) in paragraph (a) after the words "Minister of the Crown" there shall be inserted "or public authority";

(b) at the end of paragraph (c) there shall be inserted the words "or

(d) for certifying any return by the body which, by or under any enactment, is required or authorised to be certified by the body's auditor or under arrangements made by the Commission"; and

(c) at the end there shall be added the words "and in paragraph (a) above "public authority" means a body established by or under the Treaties or by or under any enactment".

1977 c. 49.

(3) In section 98(1) of the National Health Service Act 1977 after the words "audited by auditors appointed by the Secretary of State" there shall be inserted "or by the Audit Commission for Local Authorities in England and Wales at his request".

Publication of reports of Controller of Audit: Scotland.
1973 c. 65.

185. In section 102 of the Local Government (Scotland) Act 1973 (reports to Commission for Local Authority Accounts by Controller of Audit)—

(a) in subsections (1) and (2) there shall, in each case, be added at the end the words "and may send a copy of any report so made to any other person he thinks fit"; and

(b) after subsection (2) there shall be inserted the following subsection—

"(2A) A local authority shall, forthwith upon their receiving a copy of a report sent to them under subsection (1) or (2) above, supply a copy of that copy report to each member of the authority and make additional copies available for public inspection."

Security of tenure on ending of long residential tenancies.
1954 c. 56.

186.—(1) Schedule 10 to this Act shall have effect (in place of Part I of the Landlord and Tenant Act 1954) to confer security of tenure on certain tenants under long tenancies and, in particular, to establish assured periodic tenancies when such long tenancies come to an end.

(2) Schedule 10 to this Act applies, and section 1 of the Landlord and Tenant Act 1954 does not apply, to a tenancy of a dwelling-house—

(a) which is a long tenancy at a low rent, as defined in Schedule 10 to this Act; and

(b) which is entered into on or after the day appointed for the coming into force of this section, otherwise than in pursuance of a contract made before that day.

(3) If a tenancy—

    (a) is in existence on 15th January 1999, and

    (b) does not fall within subsection (2) above, and

    (c) immediately before that date was, or was deemed to be, a long tenancy at a low rent for the purposes of Part I of the Landlord and Tenant Act 1954,

then, on and after that date (and so far as concerns any notice specifying a date of termination on or after that date and any steps taken in consequence thereof), section 1 of that Act shall cease to apply to it and Schedule 10 to this Act shall apply to it unless, before that date, the landlord has served a notice under section 4 of that Act specifying a date of termination which is earlier than that date.

(4) The provisions of Schedule 10 to this Act have effect notwithstanding any agreement to the contrary, but nothing in this subsection or that Schedule shall be construed as preventing the surrender of a tenancy.

(5) Section 18 of the Landlord and Tenant Act 1954 (duty of tenants of residential property to give information to landlords or superior landlords) shall apply in relation to property comprised in a long tenancy at a low rent, within the meaning of Schedule 10 to this Act, as it applies to property comprised in a long tenancy at a low rent within the meaning of Part I of that Act, except that the reference in that section to subsection (1) of section 3 of that Act shall be construed as a reference to sub-paragraph (1) of paragraph 3 of Schedule 10 to this Act.

(6) Where, by virtue of subsection (3) above, Schedule 10 to this Act applies to a tenancy which is not a long tenancy at a low rent as defined in that Schedule, it shall be deemed to be such a tenancy for the purposes of that Schedule.

187.—(1) The Secretary of State may, for the purpose of promoting or facilitating the carrying on of any of the activities specified in subsection (2) below, do one or both of the following, that is to say—

    (a) make grants to any person who carries on any such activities;

    (b) guarantee the repayment of the principal of, the payment of interest on and the discharge of any other financial obligation in connection with sums borrowed temporarily by any such person.

(2) The activities mentioned in subsection (1) above are—

    (a) the assessment of, and of applications of, materials, products, systems and techniques used or proposed for use in the construction industry; and

    (b) the issue of certificates, promotion of common standards and publication of information with respect to any such materials, products, systems or techniques.

(3) The consent of the Treasury shall be required for the exercise by the Secretary of State of his power under this section to make a grant or give a guarantee; but, subject to that consent and to the following provisions of this section, that power shall be a power to make a grant or give a guarantee in such manner and on such conditions as he thinks fit.

(4) Immediately after a guarantee is given under this section, the Secretary of State shall lay a statement of the guarantee before each House of Parliament.

(5) Where any sums are paid out in fulfilment of a guarantee given under this section in respect of any person's borrowing, that person shall make to the Secretary of State, at such times and in such manner as the Secretary of State may, with the consent of the Treasury, from time to time direct—

    (a) payments, of such amounts as the Secretary of State may so direct, in or towards repayment of those sums; and

    (b) payments of interest, at such rate as the Secretary of State may so direct, on what is outstanding for the time being in respect of those sums.

(6) As soon as possible after the end of any financial year in which—

    (a) any sums are paid out in fulfilment of a guarantee given under this section, or

    (b) any liability in respect of the principal of sums so paid out, or in respect of interest on any such sums, is outstanding,

the Secretary of State shall lay before each House of Parliament a statement relating to the sums.

Repeal of s. 2 of the Education (Grants and Awards) Act 1984.
1984 c. 11.

188. Section 2 of the Education (Grants and Awards) Act 1984 (limit on expenditure approved for grant purposes) shall not apply in relation to any expenditure approved for the financial year beginning with 1st April 1990 or any subsequent financial year.

Grants by Secretary of State towards costs of magistrates' courts etc.
1979 c. 55.

189.—(1) Section 59 of the Justices of the Peace Act 1979 (grants by Secretary of State to responsible authorities) shall be amended in accordance with this section.

(2) In subsection (1), in paragraph (a) the words "or this Part" shall be omitted and at the end of the subsection there shall be added "and

    (c) of their functions under this Part of this Act or, in the case of the Receiver, his corresponding functions".

(3) In subsection (3) after the word "section" there shall be inserted "towards the net cost to a responsible authority in any year of the matters mentioned in paragraphs (a) and (b) of subsection (1) above" and for the words from "the expenditure" onwards there shall be substituted "that net cost".

(4) After subsection (4) there shall be inserted the following subsection—

"(4A) In determining the amount of the grant towards the net cost of the functions referred to in subsection (1)(c) above, the Secretary of State may disregard, in whole or in part, such items of expenditure as he thinks fit."

Supplementary

Regulations.

190.—(1) Under any power to make regulations conferred by any provision of this Act, different provision may be made for different cases and different descriptions of cases (including different provision for different areas).

(2) Any power to make regulations conferred by any provision of this Act shall be exercisable by statutory instrument which, except in the case of a statutory instrument containing regulations under section 150 or section 151 or Schedule 10, shall be subject to annulment in pursuance of a resolution of either House of Parliament.

191.—(1) Where any provision of this Act which extends to England and Wales confers (directly or by amendment of another Act) a power on the Secretary of State to make regulations, orders, rules or determinations or to give directions or specify any matter, the power may be exercised differently for England and Wales, whether or not it is exercised separately.

Separate provisions for Wales.

(2) This section is without prejudice to section 190(1) above and to any other provision of this Act or of any Act amended by this Act by virtue of which powers may be exercised differently in different cases or in any other circumstances.

192.—(1) There shall be paid out of money provided by Parliament—

Financial provisions.

(a) any sums required for the payment by the Secretary of State of grants, subsidies or contributions under this Act;

(b) any sums required by the Secretary of State for fulfilling any guarantees under this Act;

(c) any other expenses of the Secretary of State under this Act; and

(d) any increase attributable to this Act in the sums so payable under any other enactment.

(2) Any sums received by the Secretary of State under this Act shall be paid into the Consolidated Fund.

193.—(1) This Act applies to the Isles of Scilly subject to such exceptions, adaptations and modifications as the Secretary of State may by order direct.

Application to Isles of Scilly.

(2) The power to make an order under this section shall be exercisable by statutory instrument which shall be subject to annulment in pursuance of a resolution of either House of Parliament.

194.—(1) Schedule 11 to this Act, which contains minor amendments and amendments consequential on the provisions of this Act, shall have effect.

Amendments and repeals.

(2) The enactments specified in Part I of Schedule 12 to this Act, which relate to or are superseded by the provisions of Part IV of this Act, are hereby repealed to the extent specified in the third column of that Schedule; and the Secretary of State may by order made by statutory instrument make provision (in consequence of the said Part IV) amending, repealing or revoking (with or without savings) any provision of an Act passed before or in the same session as this Act, or of an instrument made under an Act before the passing of this Act.

(3) In subsection (2) above "Act" includes a private or local Act and a statutory instrument by which the power in that subsection is exercised shall be subject to annulment in pursuance of a resolution of either House of Parliament.

(4) The other enactments specified in Part II of Schedule 12 to this Act, which include some that are spent, are hereby repealed to the extent specified in the third column of that Schedule, but subject to any provision at the end of that Schedule.

Short title, commencement and extent.

195.—(1) This Act may be cited as the Local Government and Housing Act 1989.

(2) The provisions of sections 1 and 2, 9, 10, 13 to 20 above, Parts II to V (with the exception in Part II of section 24), VII and VIII and (in this Part) sections 140 to 145, 156, 159, 160, 162, 164, 165, 167 to 173, 175 to 180, 182 and 183, 185, 186 and 194, except in so far as it relates to paragraphs 104 to 106 of Schedule 11, shall come into force on such day as the Secretary of State may by order made by statutory instrument appoint, and different days may be so appointed for different provisions or for different purposes.

(3) An order under subsection (2) above may contain such transitional provisions and savings (whether or not involving the modification of any statutory provision) as appear to the Secretary of State necessary or expedient in connection with the provisions brought into force by the order.

(4) Subject to subsection (5) below, this Act, except Parts I and II and sections 36(9), 140 to 145, 150 to 152, 153, 155, 157, 159, 161, 166, 168, 170, 171, 176 to 182, 185, 190, 192, 194(1), 194(4) and this section, extends to England and Wales only.

(5) Notwithstanding anything in subsection (4) above, any provision of Schedule 11 or Part II of Schedule 12 to this Act which amends or repeals any provision of the following enactments does not extend to Scotland—

1892 c. 43.   (a) the Military Lands Act 1892;

1983 c. 52.   (b) the Local Authorities (Expenditure Powers) Act 1983.

(6) This Act does not extend to Northern Ireland.

SCHEDULES

SCHEDULE 1   Section 15.

POLITICAL BALANCE ON LOCAL AUTHORITY COMMITTEES ETC.

Bodies to which section 15 applies

1. Subject to such exceptions as may be prescribed by regulations made by the Secretary of State, section 15 of this Act applies, in relation to any relevant authority or committee of a relevant authority—

    (a) to any ordinary committee or ordinary sub-committee of the authority;

    (b) to any advisory committee of the authority and to any sub-committee appointed by such an advisory committee; and

    (c) to any such body falling within paragraph 2 below as is a body at least three seats on which fall from time to time to be filled by appointments made by the authority or committee.

2.—(1) For the purposes of paragraph 1 above, in its application in relation to relevant authorities in England and Wales or the committees of such authorities, a body falls within this paragraph if it is a body of any of the following descriptions, that is to say—

    (a) a relevant authority which is a local authority of any of the descriptions specified in paragraphs (f) to (j) of section 21(1) of this Act;

    (b) a local authority of any of the descriptions specified in paragraphs (k) and (m) of section 21(1) of this Act;

    (c) any police authority constituted under section 2 of the Police Act 1964 (county police forces);   1964 c. 48.

    (d) a local fisheries committee for any sea fisheries district;

    (e) a committee established in accordance with any regulations made by virtue of section 7 of the Superannuation Act 1972 (regulations making provision for the superannuation of persons employed in local government service etc.);   1972 c. 11.

    (f) a National Parks Committee;

    (g) a board or committee appointed by one or more relevant authorities in exercise of a power conferred by a local enactment, being a board or committee seats on which are required to be filled by the appointment of members of that authority or of those authorities;

    (h) a joint committee not falling within sub-paragraphs (a) to (g) above appointed by two or more relevant authorities under section 102(1)(b) of the Local Government Act 1972.   1972 c. 70.

(2) For the purposes of paragraph 1 above, in its application in relation to relevant authorities in Scotland or to the committees of such authorities, a body falls within this paragraph if it is—

    (a) a joint board within the meaning of section 235(1) of the Local Government (Scotland) Act 1973;   1973 c. 65.

    (b) a board or committee appointed by one or more relevant authorities in exercise of a power conferred by a local enactment, being a board or committee seats on which are required to be filled by the appointment of members of that authority or of those authorities;

    (c) a joint committee appointed by two or more relevant authorities under section 57(1)(b) of the Local Government (Scotland) Act 1973.

Construction of sections 15 to 17

3.—(1) The Secretary of State may, for the purposes of sections 15 and 16 of this Act, by regulations make provision—

    (a) as to the circumstances in which the members of a relevant authority are to be treated as divided into different political groups;

    (b) as to the persons who are to be treated as members of such a group and as to when a person is to be treated as having ceased to be a member of such a group;

    (c) requiring the question whether a person is or is not a member of a political group to be determined in such manner as may be provided for by or under the regulations;

    (d) specifying the manner in which, and times at which, the wishes of such a group are to be expressed and the consequences of a failure by such a group to express its wishes.

(2) Regulations under this paragraph may make provision modifying the provisions of sections 15 and 16 of this Act in relation to any case in which some of the members of a relevant authority fall to be treated as members of one or more political groups and the others do not.

4.—(1) In sections 15 to 17 of this Act and this Schedule—

"advisory committee", in relation to a relevant authority, means a committee appointed by the authority under section 102(4) of the Local Government Act 1972 or section 57(4) of the Local Government (Scotland) Act 1973 (advisory committees);

"education committee", in relation to a relevant authority in England and Wales, means any committee appointed by the authority in accordance with arrangements approved under Part II of Schedule 1 to the Education Act 1944;

"membership", in relation to a relevant authority, means the number of persons who are for the time being members of the authority, disregarding any person who is treated as continuing to be a member of the authority by virtue of section 3(3) of the Local Government Act 1972 (chairman to continue as a member until replaced);

"ordinary committee"—

    (a) in relation to any relevant authority in England and Wales, means the authority's education committee, their social services committee or any other committee of the authority appointed under section 102(1)(a) of the Local Government Act 1972, not being a body to which section 15 of this Act applies by virtue of paragraph 2 above; and

    (b) in relation to any relevant authority in Scotland, means the authority's education committee, their social work committee or any committee of the authority appointed under section 57(1)(a) of the Local Government (Scotland) Act 1973;

"relevant authority"—

    (a) in relation to England and Wales, means a local authority of any of the descriptions specified in paragraphs (a) to (c) or (f) to (j) of section 21(1) of this Act; and

    (b) in relation to Scotland, means a local authority;

    and

"seat", in relation to a body to which section 15 of this Act applies, means such a position as a member of that body as—

    (a) entitles the person holding the position to vote at meetings of the body on any question which falls to be decided at such a meeting; and

1972 c. 70.
1973 c. 65.

1944 c. 31.

SCH. 1

(b) in the case of a position as member of an advisory committee or of a sub-committee appointed by an advisory committee, is not a position which the authority or committee have determined must be filled by the appointment of a person who is not a member of the authority.

(2) In this Schedule—

"ordinary sub-committee"—

(a) in relation to any relevant authority in England and Wales, means any sub-committee of the authority's education committee or social services committee or any other sub-committee of that authority appointed under section 102(1)(c) of the Local Government Act 1972 by an ordinary committee of that authority; and

1972 c. 70.

(b) in relation to any relevant authority in Scotland, means any sub-committee of an ordinary committee;

"social services committee", in relation to any relevant authority in England and Wales, means any committee established by the authority under section 2 of the Local Authority Social Services Act 1970; and

1970 c. 42.

"social work committee", in relation to a relevant authority in Scotland, means any committee appointed by the authority under section 2 of the Social Work (Scotland) Act 1968.

1968 c. 49.

(3) References in this paragraph to voting include references to making use of a casting vote.

Supplemental regulation making power

5. Regulations under section 15 or 17 of this Act or under this Schedule may contain such incidental provision and such supplemental, consequential and transitional provision in connection with their other provisions as the Secretary of State considers appropriate.

SCHEDULE 2

Section 36.

LOCAL GOVERNMENT ACT 1972, SECTION 137, AS AMENDED

"Power of local authorities to incur expenditure for certain purposes not otherwise authorised.

137.—(1) A local authority may, subject to the provisions of this section, incur expenditure which in their opinion is in the interests of, and will bring direct benefit to, their area or any part of it or all or some of its inhabitants, but a local authority shall not, by virtue of this subsection, incur any expenditure—

(a) for a purpose for which they are, either unconditionally or subject to any limitation or to the satisfaction of any condition, authorised or required to make any payment by or by virtue of any other enactment; nor

(b) unless the direct benefit accruing to their area or any part of it or to all or some of the inhabitants of their area will be commensurate with the expenditure to be incurred.

(1A) In any case where—

(a) by virtue of paragraph (a) of subsection (1) above, a local authority are prohibited from incurring expenditure for a particular purpose, and

    (b) the power or duty of the authority to incur expenditure for that purpose is in any respect limited or conditional (whether by being restricted to a particular group of persons or in any other way),

the prohibition in that paragraph shall extend to all expenditure to which that power or duty would apply if it were not subject to any limitation or condition.

(2) It is hereby declared that the power of a local authority to incur expenditure under subsection (1) above includes power to do so by contributing towards the defraying of expenditure by another local authority in or in connection with the exercise of that other authority's functions.

(2C) A local authority may incur expenditure under subsection (1) above on publicity only by way of assistance to a public body or voluntary organisation where the publicity is incidental to the main purpose for which the assistance is given; but the following provisions of this section apply to expenditure incurred by a local authority under section 142 below on information as to the services provided by them under this section, or otherwise relating to their functions under this section, as they apply to expenditure incurred under this section.

(2D) In subsection (2C) above—

    "publicity" means any communication, in whatever form, addressed to the public at large or to a section of the public; and

    "voluntary organisation" means a body which is not a public body but whose activities are carried on otherwise than for profit.

(3) A local authority may, subject to the following provisions of this section, incur expenditure on contributions to any of the following funds, that is to say—

    (a) the funds of any charitable body in furtherance of its work in the United Kingdom; or

    (b) the funds of any body which provides any public service (whether to the public as a whole or to any section of it) in the United Kingdom otherwise than for the purposes of gain; or

    (c) any fund which is raised in connection with a particular event directly affecting persons resident in the United Kingdom on behalf of whom a public appeal for contributions has been made by the Lord Mayor of London or the chairman of a principal council or by a committee of which the Lord Mayor of London or the chairman of a principal council is a member or by such a person or body as is referred to in section 83(3)(c) of the Local Government (Scotland) Act 1973.

(4) The expenditure of a local authority under this section in any financial year shall not exceed the amount produced by multiplying—

    (a) such sum as is for the time being appropriate to the authority under subsection (4AA) below, by

    (b) the relevant population of the authority's area.

(4AA) For the purposes of subsection (4)(a) above, except in
so far as the Secretary of State by order specifies a different sum
in relation to an authority of a particular description,—

    (a) the sum appropriate to a county council or the council
        of a non-metropolitan district is £2.50;

    (b) the sum appropriate to a metropolitan district council,
        a London borough council or the Common Council is
        £5.00; and

    (c) the sum appropriate to a parish or community council
        is £3.50.

(4AB) For the purposes of subsection (4)(b) above the
relevant population of a local authority's area shall be
determined in accordance with regulations made by the
Secretary of State; and a statutory instrument containing such
regulations shall be subject to annulment in pursuance of a
resolution of the House of Commons.

(4A) For the purpose of determining whether a local
authority have exceeded the limit set out in subsection (4)
above, their expenditure in any financial year under this section
shall be taken to be the difference between their gross
expenditure under this section for that year and the aggregate
of the amounts specified in subsection (4B) below.

(4B) The amounts mentioned in subsection (4A) above
are—

    (a) the amount of any expenditure which forms part of the
        authority's gross expenditure for that year under this
        section and in respect of which any grant has been or
        is to be paid under any enactment by a Minister of the
        Crown, within the meaning of the Ministers of the
        Crown Act 1975 (whether or not the grant covers the
        whole of the expenditure);

    (b) the amount of any repayment in that year of the
        principal of a loan for the purpose of financing
        expenditure under this section in any year;

    (c) so much of any amount raised by public subscription
        as is spent in that year for a purpose for which the
        authority are authorised by this section to incur
        expenditure;

    (d) any grant received by the authority for that year out
        of the European Regional Development Fund or the
        Social Fund of the European Economic Community,
        in so far as the grant is in respect of an activity in
        relation to which the authority incurred expenditure
        in that year under this section;

    (e) the amount of any repayment in that year of a loan
        under this section made by the authority in any year;
        and

    (f) the amount of any expenditure—

            (i) which is incurred by the authority in that year
        in circumstances specified in an order made by the
        Secretary of State; or

            (ii) which is incurred by the authority in that
        year and is of a description so specified; or

(iii) which is defrayed by any grant or other payment to the authority which is made in or in respect of that year and is of a description so specified.

(5) A statutory instrument containing an order under this section may apply to all local authorities or may make different provision in relation to local authorities of different descriptions.

(6) Any such instrument shall be subject to annulment in pursuance of a resolution of either House of Parliament.

(7) The accounts of a local authority by whom expenditure is incurred under this section shall include a separate account of that expenditure, and section 24 of the Local Government Finance Act 1982 (rights of inspection) shall apply in relation to any such separate account of a local authority as it applies in relation to any statement of accounts prepared by them pursuant to regulations under section 23 of that Act.

(9) In this section "local authority" includes the Common Council."

SCHEDULE 3

PROVISIONS SUPPLEMENTING PART IV

PART I

EFFECT OF OVERSPEND IN 1989-90 ON CREDIT APPROVALS

1980 c. 65.

1.—(1) If Part VIII of the Local Government, Planning and Land Act 1980 (in this Part of this Schedule referred to as "the 1980 Act") applied to the prescribed expenditure of a local authority for the financial year 1989-90, it shall be determined whether—

(a) the total of the payment, made (or treated as made) in respect of that prescribed expenditure

   exceeded

(b) the aggregate of the amounts which, in relation to that authority, fell within paragraphs (a) to (e) of subsection (3) of section 72 of the 1980 Act for that financial year.

(2) If for any local authority there is such an excess as is referred to in sub-paragraph (1) above, it is in the following provisions of this Part of this Schedule referred to as the "1989-90 overspend" of the authority.

2.—(1) Where a local authority have a 1989-90 overspend, their basic credit approval for the financial year 1990-91 shall be taken to be reduced or, as the case may be, extinguished by deducting from the approval an amount equal to the overspend.

(2) Any reduction or extinguishment of an authority's basic credit approval under this paragraph shall be regarded as taking place immediately after the approval is received by the authority.

3.—(1) If a local authority's 1989-90 overspend exceeds their basic credit approval for the financial year 1990-91 (so that that approval is extinguished) the excess shall be applied in reduction (or extinguishment) of other basic credit approvals issued to the authority in the order in which they are received by the authority until the whole of the excess is so applied.

(2) Any reduction or extinguishment of an authority's basic credit approval under this paragraph shall be regarded as taking place immediately after the approval is received by the authority.

4. Not later than 30th September 1990, each local authority to the prescribed expenditure of which Part VIII of the 1980 Act applied for the financial year 1989-90 shall determine the amount of their 1989-90 overspend (if any).   SCH. 3

5. In this Part of this Schedule—

(a) "prescribed expenditure" has the same meaning as in Part VIII of the 1980 Act; and

(b) "the financial year 1989-90" means the financial year beginning on 1st April 1989 and "the financial year 1990-91" means that beginning on 1st April 1990.

PART II

NON-MONETARY CONSIDERATION RECEIVED BEFORE APRIL 1990

6. This Part of this Schedule applies in any case where—

(a) within the period beginning on 2nd February 1989 and ending on 31st March 1990 a local authority receive any consideration in respect of a disposal or the right to a repayment or payment; and

(b) the disposal occurs or the right to a repayment or payment arises on or after 2nd February 1989; and

(c) if the consideration were received on 1st April 1990, section 61 of this Act would apply in relation to it.

7.—(1) On the assumption that the consideration falling within paragraph 6 above was received by the local authority on 1st April 1990, there shall be determined, in accordance with section 61 of this Act, the amount of the notional capital receipt referable to the consideration and, from that, there shall be deducted so much (if any) of the consideration as is in money and is paid within the period referred to in paragraph 6(a) above.

(2) If the amount determined under sub-paragraph (1) above ("the non-monetary consideration") exceeds the payments (if any) in respect of prescribed expenditure which, in the case in question, the local authority are taken to make for the purposes of Part VIII of the Local Government, Planning and Land Act 1980, the local authority shall set aside, as provision to meet credit liabilities, the amount specified in sub-paragraph (3) below and that amount shall be so set aside on 1st April 1990 or, if it is later, at the time of the disposal or the assignment or waiver of the repayment or payment in question.   1980 c. 65.

(3) Except in so far as regulations made or directions given by the Secretary of State otherwise provide, the amount referred to in sub-paragraph (2) above is that which, under section 59 of this Act, would be the reserved part of a capital receipt which—

(a) is of an amount equal to the excess referred to in that sub-paragraph; and

(b) is received in respect of a disposal or a right to a repayment or payment of the description in question.

PART III

CREDIT CEILING

8.—(1) Subject to any prescribed modifications, the credit ceiling of a local authority at 1st April 1990 (in this Schedule referred to as the authority's "initial credit ceiling") is the amount by which the aggregate of—

(a) so much of any advances made before that date from a loans fund established by the authority under paragraph 15 of Schedule 13 to the Local Government Act 1972 as has not been repaid before that date, and   1972 c. 70.

X

(b) the total cost of the authority's transitional credit arrangements, as defined in section 52 of this Act, less such (if any) as may be excluded from this paragraph by regulations made by the Secretary of State,

exceeds the total of the receipts which the authority are required to bring into account under paragraph 9 below; and, if there is no such excess, the authority's initial credit ceiling shall be nil or, as the case may be, a negative amount.

(2) In sub-paragraph (1) above "prescribed" means prescribed by regulations made by the Secretary of State.

9.—(1) Subject to sub-paragraph (2) below, the receipts which a local authority are required to bring into account to determine their initial credit ceiling are the following 1980 Act receipts, namely,—

(a) those which on 1st April 1990 are required to be set aside as provision to meet credit liabilities; and

(b) those which, on or before 30th September 1990, the authority determine, in accordance with section 60(2) of this Act, to set aside as provision to meet credit liabilities.

(2) A local authority are not under sub-paragraph (1) above required to bring into account so much of any capital receipt as, in accordance with section 50(3) of this Act, is applied by the authority as provision to meet credit liabilities unless it is so applied in relation to a credit arrangement excluded by regulations under paragraph 11 below.

10.—(1) At any time on or after 1st April 1990, a local authority's credit ceiling shall be determined, subject to any prescribed modifications, in accordance with the following provisions of this Part of this Schedule.

(2) In sub-paragraph (1) above "prescribed" means prescribed by regulations made by the Secretary of State.

11.—(1) If, at any time on or after 1st April 1990, a credit approval is used by a local authority to any extent as mentioned in section 56(3) of this Act, then, subject to sub-paragraph (2) below, the authority's credit ceiling shall at that time be increased by an amount equal to the extent to which the credit approval is so used.

(2) If, in reliance on a credit approval, a local authority enter into or agree to the variation of a credit arrangement of a description excluded by regulations made by the Secretary of State under this paragraph, no account shall be taken under sub-paragraph (1) above of that use of the credit approval.

12.—(1) If, at any time on or after 1st April 1990, a local authority set aside an amount as provision to meet credit liabilities (whether or not pursuant to a requirement to do so) then, subject to sub-paragraph (2) below, the authority's credit ceiling shall at that time be reduced by an amount equal to the amount so set aside (and, by virtue of this paragraph, that ceiling may, accordingly, be a negative amount).

(2) This paragraph does not apply with respect to—

(a) an amount which, in relation to a credit arrangement, other than one excluded by regulations under paragraph 11 above, is applied or charged (as an amount of credit cover) as mentioned in paragraph (b) or paragraph (c) of subsection (3) of section 50 of this Act; or

(b) a 1980 Act receipt which, in accordance with paragraph 9 above, is brought into account to determine the authority's initial credit ceiling; or

(c) so much of an amount set aside under section 63 of this Act as provision to meet credit liabilities as (in accordance with Part IV of this Schedule) is referable to notional interest on credit arrangements.

(3) For the purposes of this paragraph, an amount set aside under subsection (1) of section 63 of this Act in respect of any financial year shall be treated as set aside on the last day of that year.

13. If, at any time on or after 1st April 1990 a local authority apply or transfer under subsection (2) of section 64 of this Act an amount set aside as mentioned in subsection (1) of that section, the authority's credit ceiling shall at that time be increased by an amount equal to the amount so applied or transferred.

14.—(1) If, at any time on or after 1st April 1990, any debt of a local authority is reduced or extinguished by virtue of such a payment as is referred to in section 157(1)(b) of this Act, the authority's credit ceiling shall at that time be reduced by an amount equal to the reduction in the debt or, as the case may be, to the amount of the extinguished debt (and, by virtue of this paragraph, the credit ceiling may, accordingly, be a negative amount).

(2) If, at any time on or after 1st April 1990, a local authority are required under section 157(7)(b) of this Act to repay or pay any sum to the Secretary of State, the authority's credit ceiling shall at the time that sum is repaid or paid be increased by an amount equal to that sum.

PART IV

MINIMUM REVENUE PROVISION

15.—(1) Subject to sub-paragraphs (2) and (3) below, for any financial year other than that beginning on 1st April 1990, a local authority's minimum revenue provision shall be the aggregate of—

    (a) an amount in respect of principal which, except in so far as regulations made by the Secretary of State otherwise provide, shall be the prescribed percentage of the authority's adjusted credit ceiling on the last day of the immediately preceding year; and

    (b) an amount in respect of notional interest on each credit arrangement entered into by the authority which came into being before the beginning of that year, other than an arrangement excluded by regulations under paragraph 11 above.

(2) If a local authority's credit ceiling on the last day of a financial year is nil or a negative amount, the authority's minimum revenue provision for the immediately following financial year shall be nil.

(3) In the case of a credit arrangement falling within section 49(3) of this Act, the Secretary of State may by regulations provide that the amount referred to in sub-paragraph (1)(b) above is nil.

16.—(1) Subject to sub-paragraphs (2) and (3) below, for the financial year beginning on 1st April 1990, a local authority's minimum revenue provision shall be the aggregate of—

    (a) an amount in respect of principal which, except in so far as regulations made by the Secretary of State otherwise provide, shall be the prescribed percentage of the authority's adjusted initial credit ceiling; and

    (b) an amount in respect of notional interest on each transitional credit arrangement entered into by the authority, other than an arrangement excluded by regulations under paragraph 11 above.

(2) If a local authority's initial credit ceiling is nil or a negative amount, the authority's minimum revenue provision for the financial year referred to in sub-paragraph (1) above shall be nil.

(3) In the case of a transitional credit arrangement falling within section 49(3) of this Act, the Secretary of State may by regulations provide that the amount referred to in sub-paragraph (1)(b) above is nil.

17. In paragraphs 15(1)(a) and 16(1)(a) above "the prescribed percentage" means such percentage, which may be any percentage from nil to 100, as may be prescribed by regulations made by the Secretary of State; and different percentages may be so prescribed in relation to different amounts taken into account in determining an authority's adjusted credit ceiling or initial credit ceiling.

18.—(1) Any reference in this Part of this Schedule to an authority's adjusted credit ceiling at any time or their adjusted initial credit ceiling is a reference to their credit ceiling or, as the case may be, initial credit ceiling, determined in accordance with Part III of this Schedule as modified, in such manner as the Secretary of State considers appropriate, by regulations made by him for the purposes of this Part of this Schedule.

(2) Without prejudice to the generality of sub-paragraph (1) above, for the purpose of determining an authority's adjusted credit ceiling or adjusted initial credit ceiling at any time, regulations under this paragraph may require amounts which are taken into account in determining the authority's credit ceiling or initial credit ceiling to be treated as having been repaid, in whole or in part, by reference to amounts set aside as provision for credit liabilities and also, in such cases as may be specified in the regulations, may require a local authority to determine which of the amounts so taken into account are to be treated as so repaid.

19.—(1) Subject to paragraphs 15(3) and 16(3) above, for any financial year, the amount referred to in paragraph 15(1)(b) or paragraph 16(1)(b) above in respect of notional interest on a credit arrangement is that determined by the formula—

$$\frac{a \times b}{100}$$

where, subject to sub-paragraphs (2) and (3) below,—

"a" is the cost of the arrangement on 1st April in that financial year; and

"b" is the percentage rate of discount prescribed under section 49(2) of this Act for the financial year in which the arrangement came into being or, in the case of a transitional credit arrangement, for the financial year beginning on 1st April 1990.

(2) In the case of a credit arrangement which has been varied as mentioned in section 51(1) of this Act, "b" in the formula in sub-paragraph (1) above is the percentage rate of discount prescribed under section 49(2) of this Act for the financial year in which the arrangement was so varied or, as the case may be, last varied.

(3) In the case of a credit arrangement falling within section 49(3) of this Act, the Secretary of State may by regulations provide that "b" in the formula in sub-paragraph (1) above shall be such figure as may be specified in, or determined under, the regulations.

20. Regulations under this Part of this Schedule—

(a) may make provision by reference to amounts determined by local authorities in respect of particular financial years; and

(b) may require such determinations to be made within such time limits as may be specified in the regulations.

SCHEDULE 4

THE KEEPING OF THE HOUSING REVENUE ACCOUNT

PART I

CREDITS TO THE ACCOUNT

For each year a local housing authority who are required to keep a Housing Revenue Account ("the account") shall carry to the credit of the account amounts equal to the items listed in this Part of this Schedule.

Item 1: rents

The income of the authority for the year from rents and charges in respect of houses and other property within the account.

This item includes rent remitted by way of rebate.

Item 2: charges for services and facilities

The income of the authority for the year in respect of services or facilities provided by them in connection with the provision by them of houses and other property within the account—

    (a) including income in respect of services or facilities provided under sections 10 and 11 of the Housing Act 1985 (power to provide furniture, board and laundry facilities); but   1985 c. 68.

    (b) not including payments for the purchase of furniture or hire-purchase instalments for furniture.

If the Secretary of State so directs, this item shall include, or not include, such income as may be determined by or under the direction.

Item 3: Housing Revenue Account subsidy

Housing Revenue Account subsidy payable to the authority for the year.

Item 4: contributions towards expenditure

Contributions of any description payable to the authority for the year towards expenditure falling to be debited to the account (for that or any other year).

If the Secretary of State so directs, this item shall not include so much of any such contributions as may be determined by or under the direction.

Item 5: housing benefit transfers

Sums transferred for the year from some other revenue account of the authority in accordance with section 30(6) of the Social Security Act 1986   1986 c. 50. (housing benefit transfers).

Item 6: transfers from the Housing Repairs Account

Sums transferred for the year from the authority's Housing Repairs Account in accordance with section 77(5) of this Act (credit balance for year).

Item 7: reduced provision for bad or doubtful debts

The following, namely—

    (a) any sums debited to the account for a previous year under paragraph (a) of item 7 of Part II of this Schedule which have been recovered by the authority during the year; and

(b) any amount by which, in the opinion of the authority, any provision debited to the account for a previous year under paragraph (b) of that item should be reduced.

If the Secretary of State so directs, no sums shall be credited under paragraph (a) above, and no amount shall be credited under paragraph (b) above, except (in either case) in such circumstances and to such extent as may be specified in the direction.

Item 8: sums calculated as determined by Secretary of State

Sums calculated for the year in accordance with such formulae as the Secretary of State may from time to time determine.

In determining any formula for the purposes of this item, the Secretary of State may include variables framed (in whatever way he considers appropriate) by reference to such matters relating to the authority, or to (or to tenants of) houses and other property which are or have been within the account, as he thinks fit.

Item 9: sums directed by Secretary of State

Any sums which for the year the Secretary of State directs the authority to carry to the credit of the account from some other revenue account of theirs.

Item 10: credit balance from previous year

Any credit balance shown in the account for the previous year.

This item does not include so much of any such balance so shown as is carried to the credit of some other revenue account of the authority in accordance with paragraph 1 or 2 of Part III of this Schedule.

PART II

DEBITS TO THE ACCOUNT

For each year a local housing authority who are required to keep a Housing Revenue Account ("the account") shall carry to the debit of the account amounts equal to the items listed in this Part of this Schedule.

Item 1: expenditure on repairs, maintenance and management

The expenditure of the authority for the year in respect of the repair, maintenance, supervision and management of houses and other property within the account, but not including expenditure properly debited to the authority's Housing Repairs Account.

If the Secretary of State so directs, this item shall include, or not include, such expenditure as may be determined by or under the direction.

Item 2: expenditure for capital purposes

Any expenditure of the authority in respect of houses and other property within the account which—

(a) is capital expenditure (other than excluded expenditure) for the year; or

(b) is excluded expenditure for the year, or any previous or subsequent year, which the authority decide should be charged to a revenue account for the year.

In this item "capital expenditure" means expenditure for capital purposes within the meaning of Part IV of this Act and "excluded expenditure" means expenditure excluded from the obligation in section 41(1) of this Act.

Item 3: rents, rates, taxes and other charges

The rents, rates, taxes and other charges which the authority are liable to pay for the year in respect of houses and other property within the account.

Item 4: rent rebates

The rent rebates granted for the year to tenants of houses and other property within the account.

Item 5: sums transferred under section 80(2)

Sums transferred for the year to some other revenue account of the authority in accordance with section 80(2) of this Act (Housing Revenue Account subsidy of a negative amount).

Item 6: contributions to Housing Repairs Account

Sums transferred for the year to the authority's Housing Repairs Account.

Item 7: provision for bad or doubtful debts

The following, namely—

    (a) any sums credited to the account for the year or any previous year under item 1 or 2 of Part I of this Schedule which, in the opinion of the authority, are bad debts which should be written off; and

    (b) any provision for doubtful debts which, in their opinion, should be made in respect of sums so credited.

If the Secretary of State so directs, no sums shall be debited under paragraph (a) above, and no provision shall be debited under paragraph (b) above, except (in either case) in such circumstances and to such extent as may be specified in the direction.

Item 8: sums calculated as determined by Secretary of State

Sums calculated for the year in accordance with such formulae as the Secretary of State may from time to time determine.

In determining any formula for the purposes of this item, the Secretary of State may include variables framed (in whatever way he considers appropriate) by reference to such matters relating to the authority, or to (or to tenants of) houses or other property which are or have been within the account, as he thinks fit.

Item 9: debit balance from previous year

Any debit balance shown in the account for the previous year.

This item does not include any such balance so shown which is carried to the debit of some other revenue account of the authority in accordance with paragraph 1 of Part III of this Schedule.

Part III

Special Cases

Balance for year 1989-90

1.—(1) The following, namely—

    (a) any debit balance shown in a local housing authority's Housing Revenue Account for the year beginning 1st April 1989;

(b) so much of any credit balance so shown as exceeds the limit mentioned in sub-paragraph (2) below,

shall be carried forward and debited or credited, as the case may require, not to their Housing Revenue Account for the year beginning 1st April 1990 but to some other revenue account of theirs for that year.

(2) The limit referred to in sub-paragraph (1) above is £150 multiplied by the number of dwellings in the authority's Housing Revenue Account on 31st March 1990 or £5 million, whichever is the lesser amount.

Credit balance where no HRA subsidy payable

2. A local housing authority to whom no Housing Revenue Account subsidy is payable for any year may carry the whole or part of any credit balance shown in their Housing Revenue Account for that year to the credit of some other revenue account of theirs.

Amenities shared by the whole community

3.—(1) Where benefits or amenities—

(a) arising from the exercise of a local housing authority's functions under Part II of the Housing Act 1985 (provision of housing); and

(b) provided for persons housed by the authority,

are shared by the community as a whole, the authority shall make such contributions to their Housing Revenue Account from some other revenue account of theirs as, having regard to the amounts of the contributions and the period over which they are made, will properly reflect the community's share of the benefits or amenities.

(2) The Secretary of State may give such directions as he considers appropriate as to the performance by local housing authorities of their duty under sub-paragraph (1) above.

(3) Where it appears to the Secretary of State that an authority have failed to comply with sub-paragraph (1) above or any directions under sub-paragraph (2) above, he may give them such directions as appear to him appropriate to ensure compliance.

(4) A direction under sub-paragraph (3) above may contain particulars as to the amounts of the contributions and the years for which they are to be made.

Land disposed of at less than market value

4. The Secretary of State in giving his consent under any enactment for the disposal at less than market value of land within their Housing Revenue Account may impose a condition requiring the authority to make a contribution to the account from some other revenue account of theirs for such years and of such amount, or of any amount calculated in such manner, as he may determine.

Adjustment of accounts on appropriation of land

5.—(1) Where land is appropriated by a local housing authority for the purposes of Part II of the Housing Act 1985 (provision of housing), or on the discontinuance of use for those purposes, such adjustment shall be made in the Housing Revenue Account, the Housing Repairs Account and other revenue accounts of the authority as the Secretary of State may direct.

(2) Except where sub-paragraph (1) above applies, any direction given under section 24 of the Town and Country Planning Act 1959 (adjustment of accounts on appropriation of land) concerning the Housing Revenue Account of a local housing authority shall apply in relation to the account to be kept under section 74 of this Act as it would have applied to the account to be kept under section 50 of the Housing (Financial Provisions) Act 1958.

SCH. 4
1959 c. 53.

1958 c. 42.

Transfers of housing stock between authorities in London

6.—(1) Where houses and other property within the Housing Revenue Account have been transferred from one authority to another under section 23(3) of the London Government Act 1963 (orders transferring land held by London borough council or Common Council of City of London), the Secretary of State may by order direct, for any of the purposes of this Part of this Act—

1963 c. 33.

(a) within whose Housing Revenue Account the transferred houses and property are to be treated as falling; and

(b) how relevant items are to be treated in the Housing Revenue Accounts of the authorities to whom the order applies.

(2) The order may be made to apply to a description of local housing authorities specified in the order or to a specified local housing authority, and may make different provision in respect of different years or for different purposes in relation to the same year.

(3) An order under this paragraph may amend an order made under section 23(3) of the London Government Act 1963 and may provide that one authority shall pay to another in respect of houses and property to which it relates such amounts calculated by such methods and in respect of such items and such years as appear to the Secretary of State to be appropriate.

(4) An order under this paragraph—

(a) shall be made by the Secretary of State with the concurrence of the Treasury, and

(b) shall be made by statutory instrument which shall be subject to annulment in pursuance of a resolution of either House of Parliament.

(5) Before making an order under this paragraph, the Secretary of State shall consult such representatives of local government as appear to him to be appropriate; and, before making an order applying to a particular local housing authority, he shall consult that authority.

Contributions in respect of land in certain areas

7. Where a contribution under—

(a) section 259 of the Housing Act 1985 (contributions by Secretary of State towards expenditure on general improvement area); or

1985 c. 68.

(b) section 96 of this Act (contributions by Secretary of State towards expenditure on renewal area),

has been paid towards expenditure incurred by a local housing authority in relation to land held by them for the purposes of Part II of that Act (provision of housing), neither the expenditure nor the contribution shall be carried to the Housing Revenue Account except with the consent of the Secretary of State.

Part IV

Supplementary Provisions

Duty to supply information

1.—(1) A local housing authority, and any officer or employee of a local housing authority concerned with their housing functions, shall supply the Secretary of State with such information as he may specify, either generally or in any particular case, for the purpose of enabling the Secretary of State to ascertain the state or likely state of the authority's Housing Revenue Account for any year.

(2) A local housing authority shall supply the Secretary of State with such certificates supporting the information required by him as he may specify.

Directions excluding or modifying statutory provisions

2.—(1) The Secretary of State may, as respects any houses or other property within the Housing Revenue Account, direct that all or any of the provisions of this Part of this Act relating to the account shall not apply, or shall apply subject to such modifications as may be specified in the direction.

(2) The Secretary of State may direct that the provisions of this Part of this Act relating to the Housing Revenue Account shall apply to a local housing authority subject to such modifications as are specified in the direction.

(3) A direction may be given for such period and subject to such conditions as may be specified in the direction.

Orders amending statutory provisions

3.—(1) The Secretary of State may by order provide that all or any of the preceding provisions of this Schedule shall have effect subject to such amendments as are specified in the order.

(2) An order under this paragraph shall be made by statutory instrument which shall be subject to annulment in pursuance of a resolution of either House of Parliament.

Section 139.

SCHEDULE 5

Local Government Finance Act 1988: Amendments

Introduction

1988 c. 41.

1. The Local Government Finance Act 1988 shall be amended as mentioned in the following provisions of this Schedule.

Community charges

2.—(1) Section 2 (persons subject to personal community charge) shall be amended as follows.

(2) The following subsection shall be inserted after subsection (1)—

"(1A) But a person cannot be subject to a charging authority's personal community charge on a day which falls before 1 December 1989."

(3) The following subsections shall be substituted for subsection (5) (residence of students)—

"(5) Subsection (5A) below applies in the case of a person if—

(a) he is undertaking a full-time course of education, and

(b) for at least some of the time while undertaking the course he is, or proposes to be, resident in England and Wales for the purpose of making attendances in term time in connection with the course.

(5A) On a day on which he is undertaking the course he shall be treated as having his sole or main residence in—

   (a) the place where he is resident at any time on the day for the purpose of making attendances in term time in connection with the course;

   (b) if he is not resident in a place for that purpose at any time on the day, the place where he was last resident for that purpose;

   (c) if he is not resident in a place for that purpose at any time on the day, and he has not been resident in a place for that purpose, the place where he would be taken to have his sole or main residence if this subsection did not apply to him."

3. In section 3 (persons subject to standard community charge) the following subsection shall be inserted after subsection (5)—

"(6) Notwithstanding anything in subsections (1) to (5) above, a person cannot be subject to a charging authority's standard community charge on a day which falls before 1 December 1989."

4. In section 5 (persons subject to collective community charge) the following subsection shall be inserted after subsection (1)—

"(1A) But a person cannot be subject to a charging authority's collective community charge on a day which falls before 1 December 1989."

5. The following section shall be inserted after section 13—

"Reduced liability.

13A.—(1) The Secretary of State may make regulations as regards any case where—

   (a) a person is liable to pay an amount to an authority in respect of a personal community charge as it has effect for any chargeable financial year which is prescribed, and

   (b) prescribed conditions are fulfilled.

(2) The regulations may provide that the amount he is liable to pay shall be an amount which—

   (a) is less than the amount it would be apart from the regulations, and

   (b) is found in accordance with prescribed rules.

(3) This section applies whether the liability to pay the amount mentioned in subsection (1) above arises under section 12 above or arises under that section read with section 13 above.

(4) The conditions mentioned in subsection (1) above may be prescribed by reference to such factors as the Secretary of State sees fit; and in particular such factors may include all or any of the following—

   (a) rates for a period before 1 April 1990;

   (b) the circumstances of, or other matters relating to, the person concerned;

   (c) an amount relating to the authority concerned and specified, or to be specified, for the purposes of the regulations in a report laid, or to be laid, before the House of Commons;

   (d) such other amounts as may be prescribed or arrived at in a prescribed manner;

   (e) the making of an application by the person concerned.

(5) The rules mentioned in subsection (2) above may be prescribed by reference to such factors as the Secretary of State sees fit; and in particular such factors may include all or any of the factors mentioned in subsection (4)(a) to (d) above.

(6) Without prejudice to the generality of section 143(2) below, regulations under this section may include—

    (a) provision requiring the Secretary of State to specify in a report, for the purposes of the regulations, an amount in relation to each charging authority;

    (b) provision requiring him to lay the report before the House of Commons;

    (c) provision for the review of any prescribed decision of a charging authority relating to the application or operation of the regulations;

    (d) provision that no appeal may be made to a valuation and community charge tribunal in respect of such a decision, notwithstanding section 23(2) below.

(7) To the extent that he would not have power to do so apart from this subsection, the Secretary of State may—

    (a) include in regulations under this section such amendments of any social security instrument as he thinks expedient in consequence of the regulations under this section;

    (b) include in any social security instrument such provision as he thinks expedient in consequence of regulations under this section.

(8) In subsection (7) above "social security instrument" means an order or regulations made, or falling to be made, by the Secretary of State under the Social Security Act 1986."

6. In section 16 (joint and several liability: spouses) in subsection (1)(b) for "(read with section 13 above, where it is appropriate)" there shall be substituted "(or that section read with section 13 or 13A above, or both)".

7. In subsection (3) of section 26 (community charges registration officer for the Common Council) for the word "chamberlain" there shall be substituted "person having responsibility for the administration of certain of the financial affairs of the Council under section 6(1) of the Local Government and Housing Act 1989".

8. The following section shall be inserted after section 26—

"Registration officer: information.

26A.—(1) Subsection (2) below applies where—

    (a) the Secretary of State serves a notice on a registration officer for a charging authority requiring him to supply to the Secretary of State information specified in the notice,

    (b) the information is required by the Secretary of State for a purpose other than that of carrying out his functions under this Act, and

    (c) the information is not personal information.

(2) The officer shall supply the information required, and shall do so in such form and manner and at such time as the Secretary of State specifies in the notice.

(3) Personal information is information which relates to an individual (living or dead) who can be identified from that information or from that and other information supplied to any person by the registration officer; and personal information includes any expression of opinion about the individual and any indication of the intentions of any person in respect of the individual."

9.—(1) Section 30 (students) shall be amended as follows.

(2) The following subsection shall be inserted after subsection (1)—

"(1A) For the purposes of this Part a person shall be treated as undertaking a qualifying course of education on a particular day if (and only if) he fulfils such conditions as may be prescribed by regulations made by the Secretary of State."

(3) In subsection (2)—

(a) for "The regulations" there shall be substituted "Regulations under this section", and

(b) after "(1)" there shall be inserted "or (1A)".

(4) In subsection (3) for "The regulations" there shall be substituted "Regulations under subsection (1) above".

(5) The following subsection shall be inserted after subsection (3)—

"(3A) Regulations under subsection (1A) above must be so framed that undertaking a course of higher education is not treated as undertaking a qualifying course of education for the purposes of this Part."

(6) In subsection (4) for "The regulations" there shall be substituted "Regulations under this section".

(7) The following subsection shall be inserted after subsection (5)—

"(6) A course of higher education is a course of any description mentioned in Schedule 6 to the Education Reform Act 1988."

10.—(1) Schedule 1 (exemption) shall be amended as follows.

(2) The following paragraph shall be substituted for paragraph 5 (children)—

"5. A person is an exempt individual on a particular day if the day falls within a week for which—

(a) a person is entitled to child benefit in respect of the individual, or

(b) a person would be entitled to child benefit in respect of the individual but for paragraph 1(c) of Schedule 1 to the Child Benefit Act 1975."

(3) The following paragraphs shall be substituted for paragraph 6 (students)—

"6. A person is an exempt individual on a particular day if—

(a) the day falls within a period in which he is undertaking a full-time course of education, and

(b) on the day he is resident in Scotland or Northern Ireland for the purpose of undertaking the course.

6A. A person is an exempt individual on a particular day if—

(a) he is aged under 20 on the day,

(b) the day falls within a period in which he is undertaking a qualifying course of education, and

(c) the course is not undertaken in consequence of an office or employment held by the person."

11.—(1) Schedule 2 (administration) shall be amended as follows.

(2) The following paragraphs shall be substituted for paragraph 2(2)(l)—

"(l) that a notice must be in a prescribed form,

(la) that a notice must contain prescribed matters,

(lb) that a notice must not contain other prescribed matters,

(lc) that where a notice is invalid because it does not comply with regulations under paragraph (l) or (la) above, and the circumstances are such as may be prescribed, a requirement contained in the notice by virtue of regulations under paragraph (f) or (k) above shall nevertheless have effect as if the notice were valid,

(ld) that where a notice is invalid because it does not comply with regulations under paragraph (l) above, and a requirement has effect by virtue of regulations under paragraph (lc) above, the authority must take prescribed steps to issue to the chargeable person a document in the form which the notice would have taken had it complied with regulations under paragraph (l) above,

(le) that where a notice is invalid because it does not comply with regulations under paragraph (la) above, and a requirement has effect by virtue of regulations under paragraph (lc) above, the authority must take prescribed steps to inform the chargeable person of such of the matters prescribed under paragraph (la) above as were not contained in the notice,".

(3) In paragraph 2(2)(m) the words from "and" to the end shall be omitted.

(4) For paragraph 5 (discounts) there shall be substituted the following paragraphs—

"5.—(1) Regulations under this Schedule may include provision empowering an authority, subject to such conditions as may be prescribed, to accept, in such cases as the authority may determine and in satisfaction of a person's sole liability to pay an amount (the chargeable amount) in respect of the authority's community charge as it has effect for a chargeable financial year or any shorter period, an amount which—

(a) is determined by the authority; and

(b) is payable in a single lump sum; and

(c) is less than the authority's estimate of the chargeable amount.

(2) The regulations may include provision empowering or requiring the authority to make such adjustments (whether by way of an additional sum due to the authority or by way of repayment or credit by the authority or otherwise) as may be prescribed where the chargeable amount is subsequently estimated to be or proves to be greater or less than the amount originally (or last) estimated.

(3) The regulations may include, as regards a case where persons are jointly and severally liable to pay the chargeable amount, provision equivalent to that included under sub-paragraphs (1) and (2) above subject to any modifications the Secretary of State sees fit.

(4) The regulations may include provision that, in a case where an authority have made provision by virtue of any of sub-paragraphs (1) to (3) above, any provision which is included in regulations under this Schedule by virtue of paragraph 2 or 3 above and is prescribed under this sub-paragraph shall not apply.

5A.—(1) Regulations under this Schedule may include provision that where—

    (a) a person has sole liability to pay a sum on account in respect of an authority's community charge,

    (b) a sum smaller than that sum is paid, and

    (c) such conditions as may be prescribed are fulfilled,

the authority may accept the smaller sum in satisfaction of the liability to pay the sum on account.

    (2) The regulations may include provision that—

    (a) for prescribed purposes the sum on account shall be treated as having been paid in full;

    (b) for other prescribed purposes the fact that only the smaller sum has been paid shall be taken into account.

    (3) The regulations may include, as regards a case where persons are jointly and severally liable to pay a sum on account in respect of an authority's community charge, provision equivalent to that included under sub-paragraphs (1) and (2) above subject to any modifications the Secretary of State sees fit."

(5) In paragraph 9 (information) in sub-paragraph (1) for "is mentioned in sub-paragraph (2)" there shall be substituted "falls within sub-paragraph (2) or (2A)".

(6) In paragraph 9, in sub-paragraph (2) after "The information" there shall be inserted "falling within this sub-paragraph".

(7) In paragraph 9, the following sub-paragraph shall be inserted after sub-paragraph (2)—

    "(2A) The information falling within this sub-paragraph is information whether, on any day specified in the request, any person so specified is undertaking a qualifying course of education."

(8) The following paragraph shall be inserted after paragraph 9—

    "9A.—(1) Regulations under this Schedule may include provision that—

    (a) a registrar of births and deaths shall supply to the registration officer for any appropriate charging authority which is prescribed such particulars of such deaths as may be prescribed;

    (b) the Registrar General for England and Wales shall supply to the registration officer for any charging authority which is prescribed such particulars of such deaths as may be prescribed.

    (2) The regulations may include provision as to the times at which and the manner in which the particulars are to be supplied.

    (3) In relation to a registrar of births and deaths, an appropriate charging authority is a charging authority whose area includes all or part of, or falls within, the registrar's sub-district."

(9) Paragraph 12 (information) shall be omitted.

(10) The following paragraph shall be inserted after paragraph 13—

    "13A.—(1) Regulations under this Schedule may include provision that a registration officer for a charging authority—

    (a) may supply relevant information to any person who requests it for a purpose not relating to this Part;

    (b) may charge a prescribed fee for supplying the information;

    (c) shall account for and pay any such fee to the charging authority for which he is the registration officer.

Sch. 5

(2) Information is relevant information if—

   (a) it was obtained by the officer for the purpose of carrying out his functions under this Part, and

   (b) it is not personal information.

(3) Personal information is information which relates to an individual (living or dead) who can be identified from that information or from that and other information supplied to any person by the registration officer; and personal information includes any expression of opinion about the individual and any indication of the intentions of any person in respect of the individual."

12.—(1) Schedule 3 (penalties) shall be amended as follows.

(2) In paragraph 1(2), (4) and (6) for "a second time" there shall be substituted "again".

(3) The following sub-paragraph shall be inserted after paragraph 1(7)—

"(7A) Sub-paragraphs (2), (4) and (6) above apply each time the authority repeats a request."

(4) In paragraph 2(4), (6) and (9) for "a second time" there shall be substituted "again".

(5) The following sub-paragraph shall be inserted after paragraph 2(11)—

"(11A) Sub-paragraphs (4), (6) and (9) above apply each time the officer repeats a request."

13.—(1) Schedule 4 (enforcement) shall be amended as follows.

(2) In paragraph 3 (liability orders) the following sub-paragraph shall be inserted after sub-paragraph (2)—

"(2A) The regulations may include provision that, where the sum payable is paid after the order has been applied for but before it is made, the magistrates' court shall nonetheless make the order in respect of a sum (of an amount determined in accordance with prescribed rules) in respect of the costs incurred in applying for it."

(3) In paragraph 4(2)(c) (information which a debtor under a liability order may be required to supply to a charging authority), at the end there shall be inserted "or is relevant to whether another person is jointly and severally liable with the debtor for the whole or any part of the amount in respect of which the liability order was made".

(4) At the end of paragraph 10(1) (winding up) there shall be added "or, as the case may be, section 221(5)(b) of that Act (winding up of unregistered companies)".

(5) In paragraph 15(4)(b) (restriction on other methods of enforcement where warrant of commitment issued or term of imprisonment fixed), for "or charging may be taken against that one" there shall be substituted "bankruptcy, winding up or charging may be taken against any of them".

Charges and multipliers

14.—(1) Section 32 (amount for personal community charges) shall be amended as follows.

(2) The following subsections shall be inserted after subsection (2)—

"(2A) No amount may be set before the earlier of the following—

   (a) 1 March in the financial year preceding that for which the amount is set;

(b) the date of the issue to the authority of the last precept capable of being issued to it for the financial year for which the amount is set.

(2B) No amount may be set unless the authority has calculated an amount in relation to the year under section 95(4) below.

(2C) A purported setting of an amount, if done in contravention of subsection (2A) or (2B) above, shall be treated as not having occurred."

(3) The following subsections shall be inserted after subsection (5)—

"(6) Where the authority is a relevant charging authority, for the purposes of subsection (2A) above no account shall be taken of any precept capable of being issued to it by a relevant precepting authority.

(7) For the purposes of subsection (6) above a district council, the Common Council and the Council of the Isles of Scilly are relevant charging authorities, and—

(a) in relation to a district council, a relevant precepting authority is any parish or community council, chairman of a parish meeting or charter trustees with power to issue a precept to the district council;

(b) in relation to the Common Council, a relevant precepting authority is the sub-treasurer of the Inner Temple or the under-treasurer of the Middle Temple;

(c) in relation to the Council of the Isles of Scilly, a relevant precepting authority is any parish council or chairman of a parish meeting with power to issue a precept to the Council."

15.—(1) Section 33 (setting of different amounts for personal community charges) shall be amended as follows.

(2) In subsection (4)(a) for "its expenses needed to meet a levy" there shall be substituted "the expenses of meeting a levy or special levy".

(3) In subsection (4) the word "and" at the end of paragraph (c) shall be omitted.

(4) In subsection (4) at the end of paragraph (d) there shall be inserted "; and

(e) provided a resolution of a charging authority to the following effect is in force, the expenses incurred by it in performing in a part of its area a function performed elsewhere in its area by a body with power to issue a levy or special levy to it are its special expenses or (if the resolution relates to some only of those expenses) those to which the resolution relates are its special expenses."

(5) The following subsection shall be inserted after subsection (4)—

"(4A) The following rules shall apply to the making of a resolution under subsection (4)(e) above by a charging authority—

(a) no such resolution may be made unless the body mentioned in subsection (4)(e) above is one in relation to which the charging authority has made under subsection (4)(a) above a resolution which is in force;

(b) the resolution under subsection (4)(e) above may not be made so as to be in force at any time when that under subsection (4)(a) above is not in force;

(c) the fact that the resolution under subsection (4)(a) above relates to all the expenses concerned does not mean that the resolution under subsection (4)(e) above must relate to all the expenses concerned;

(d) the fact that the resolution under subsection (4)(a) above relates to part of the expenses concerned does not mean that the resolution under subsection (4)(e) above must relate to part, or any particular part, of the expenses concerned."

16.—(1) Section 34 (power to set substituted amounts for personal community charges) shall be amended as follows.

(2) The following shall be substituted for subsection (2)—

"(2) Any amount set in substitution under this section—

(a) must be set in accordance with sections 32 and 33 above, ignoring section 32(2) for this purpose, and

(b) if set by a special authority as a result of its having set a multiplier in substitution under paragraph 10 of Schedule 7 below, must be set by reference to the multiplier set in substitution."

(3) At the end of subsection (4) there shall be inserted ", or if the amount is set by a special authority as a result of its having set a multiplier in substitution under paragraph 10 of Schedule 7 below."

17.—(1) Section 35 (duty to set substituted amounts for personal community charges) shall be amended as follows.

(2) In subsection (3) the following paragraph shall be inserted after paragraph (d)—

"(da) the amount must be set by reference to the estimates mentioned in section 32(4)(b) and (d) above and made by the authority when it set (or last set) an amount or amounts for the year under section 32 or 34 above;".

(3) In subsection (3)(e) for "(d)" there shall be substituted "(da)".

(4) In subsection (5) the following paragraph shall be inserted after paragraph (c)—

"(ca) the amount must be set by reference to the estimates mentioned in section 32(4)(b) and (d) above and made by the authority when it set (or last set) an amount or amounts for the year under section 32 or 34 above;".

(5) In subsection (5)(d) for "and (c)" there shall be substituted "to (ca)".

(6) Subsections (6) and (7) shall be omitted.

18.—(1) Section 40 (standard community charge multipliers) shall be amended as follows.

(2) In subsection (3) for "in regulations made by the Secretary of State" there shall be substituted "for the purposes of this section by the authority".

(3) In subsection (4) for "specified" there shall be substituted "prescribed" and for ", 1½ and 2" there shall be substituted "and 1½".

(4) The following subsections shall be substituted for subsection (11)—

"(11) A charging authority may specify a class for the purposes of this section by reference only to one or more of the following factors—

(a) the use to which properties are put or are intended to be put;

(b) whether properties are occupied;

(c) the period for which properties have been unoccupied;

(d) the circumstances, other than financial circumstances, of persons subject to standard community charges;

(e) the capacity in which persons are subject to standard community charges;

(f) whether properties fall within a class prescribed in regulations under this section.

(11A) The Secretary of State in regulations under this section may prescribe a class by reference to such factors as he sees fit."

(5) In subsection (12) for "(11)" there shall be substituted "(11A)" and for "specified" there shall be substituted "prescribed".

(6) The following subsections shall be inserted after subsection (12)—

"(13) An authority which has exercised the power to specify classes for the purposes of this section shall, before the end of 21 days beginning with the day of doing so, publish a notice giving details of the exercise of the power in at least one newspaper circulating in the authority's area.

(14) Failure to comply with subsection (13) above does not invalidate the exercise of the power.

(15) The power of a charging authority to specify classes for the purposes of this section includes power to amend or revoke a specification made in exercise of the power.

(16) The Secretary of State may by order amend subsection (11) above by the insertion of such additional factors as he thinks fit."

Non-domestic rating

19. In section 41 (local rating lists) the following subsections shall be inserted after subsection (6)—

"(6A) As soon as is reasonably practicable after compiling a list the valuation officer shall send a copy of it to the authority.

(6B) As soon as is reasonably practicable after receiving the copy the authority shall deposit it at its principal office."

20. In section 42 (contents of local lists) in subsection (4) for paragraphs (a) and (b) there shall be substituted "the rateable value of the hereditament".

21.—(1) Section 44 (occupied hereditaments: supplementary) shall be amended as follows.

(2) In subsection (2) the words from "or" to the end shall be omitted.

(3) Subsection (3) shall be omitted.

22. The following section shall be inserted after section 44—

"Partly occupied hereditaments.

44A.—(1) Where a hereditament is shown in a charging authority's local non-domestic rating list and it appears to the authority that part of the hereditament is unoccupied but will remain so for a short time only the authority may require the valuation officer for the authority to apportion the rateable value of the hereditament between the occupied and unoccupied parts of the hereditament and to certify the apportionment to the authority.

(2) The reference in subsection (1) above to the rateable value of the hereditament is a reference to the rateable value shown under section 42(4) above as regards the hereditament for the day on which the authority makes its requirement.

(3) For the purposes of this section an apportionment under subsection (1) above shall be treated as applicable for any day which—

(a) falls within the operative period in relation to the apportionment, and

(b) is a day for which the rateable value shown under section 42(4) above as regards the hereditament to which the apportionment relates is the same as that so shown for the day on which the authority requires the apportionment.

(4) References in this section to the operative period in relation to an apportionment are references to the period beginning—

(a) where requiring the apportionment does not have the effect of bringing to an end the operative period in relation to a previous apportionment under subsection (1) above, with the day on which the hereditament to which the apportionment relates became partly unoccupied, and

(b) where requiring the apportionment does have the effect of bringing to an end the operative period in relation to a previous apportionment under subsection (1) above, with the day immediately following the end of that period,

and ending with the first day on which one or more of the events listed below occurs.

(5) The events are—

(a) the occupation of any of the unoccupied part of the hereditament to which the apportionment relates;

(b) the ending of the rate period in which the authority requires the apportionment;

(c) the requiring of a further apportionment under subsection (1) above in relation to the hereditament to which the apportionment relates;

(d) the hereditament to which the apportionment relates becoming completely unoccupied.

(6) Subsection (7) below applies where—

(a) a charging authority requires an apportionment under subsection (1) above, and

(b) the hereditament to which the apportionment relates does not fall within a class prescribed under section 45(1)(d) below.

(7) In relation to any day for which the apportionment is applicable, section 43 above shall have effect as regards the hereditament as if the following subsections were substituted for section 44(2)—

"(2) A is such part of the rateable value shown for the day under section 42(4) above as regards the hereditament as is assigned by the relevant apportionment to the occupied part of the hereditament.

(2A) In subsection (2) above "the relevant apportionment" means the apportionment under section 44A(1) below which relates to the hereditament and is treated for the purposes of section 44A below as applicable for the day."

(8) Subsection (9) below applies where—

(a) a charging authority requires an apportionment under subsection (1) above, and

SCH. 5

(b) the hereditament to which the apportionment relates falls within a class prescribed under section 45(1)(d) below.

(9) In relation to any day for which the apportionment is applicable, section 43 above shall have effect as regards the hereditament as if the following subsections were substituted for section 44(2)—

"(2) A is the sum of—

(a) such part of the rateable value shown for the day under section 42(4) above as regards the hereditament as is assigned by the relevant apportionment to the occupied part of the hereditament, and

(b) one half of such part of that rateable value as is assigned by the relevant apportionment to the unoccupied part of the hereditament.

(2A) In subsection (2) above "the relevant apportionment" means the apportionment under section 44A(1) below which relates to the hereditament and is treated for the purposes of section 44A below as applicable for the day."

(10) References in subsections (1) to (5) above to the hereditament, in relation to a hereditament which is partly domestic property or partly exempt from local non-domestic rating, shall, except where the reference is to the rateable value of the hereditament, be construed as references to such part of the hereditament as is neither domestic property nor exempt from local non-domestic rating."

23.—(1) Section 45 (unoccupied hereditaments: liability) shall be amended as follows.

(2) In subsection (1)(d) for "description" there shall be substituted "class".

(3) The following subsections shall be inserted after subsection (8)—

"(9) For the purposes of subsection (1)(d) above a class may be prescribed by reference to such factors as the Secretary of State sees fit.

(10) Without prejudice to the generality of subsection (9) above, a class may be prescribed by reference to one or more of the following factors—

(a) the physical characteristics of hereditaments;

(b) the fact that hereditaments have been unoccupied at any time preceding the day mentioned in subsection (1) above;

(c) the fact that the owners of hereditaments fall within prescribed descriptions."

24. In section 46 (unoccupied hereditaments: supplementary) in subsection (2) the words from "or" to the end shall be omitted.

25. The following section shall be inserted after section 46—

"Unoccupied hereditaments: new buildings.
46A.—(1) Schedule 4A below (which makes provision with respect to the determination of a day as the completion day in relation to a new building) shall have effect.

(2) Where—

(a) a completion notice is served under Schedule 4A below, and

(b) the building to which the notice relates is not completed on or before the relevant day,

then for the purposes of section 42 above and Schedule 6 below the building shall be deemed to be completed on that day.

(3) For the purposes of subsection (2) above the relevant day in relation to a completion notice is—

(a) where an appeal against the notice is brought under paragraph 4 of Schedule 4A below, the day stated in the notice, and

(b) where no appeal against the notice is brought under that paragraph, the day determined under that Schedule as the completion day in relation to the building to which the notice relates.

(4) Where—

(a) a day is determined under Schedule 4A below as the completion day in relation to a new building, and

(b) the building is not occupied on that day,

it shall be deemed for the purposes of section 45 above to become unoccupied on that day.

(5) Where—

(a) a day is determined under Schedule 4A below as the completion day in relation to a new building, and

(b) the building is one produced by the structural alteration of an existing building,

the hereditament which comprised the existing building shall be deemed for the purposes of section 45 above to have ceased to exist, and to have been omitted from the list, on that day.

(6) In this section—

(a) "building" includes part of a building, and

(b) references to a new building include references to a building produced by the structural alteration of an existing building where the existing building is comprised in a hereditament which, by virtue of the alteration, becomes, or becomes part of, a different hereditament or different hereditaments."

26.—(1) Section 47 (discretionary relief) shall be amended as follows.

(2) In subsection (1)(b) for "regulations under section 57 below or regulations under section 58 below" there shall be substituted "regulations under section 58 below or any provision of or made under Schedule 7A below".

(3) In subsection (5) for "57 or 58 below" there shall be substituted "58 below and of any provision of or made under Schedule 7A below".

27. In section 49 (reduction or remission of liability) in subsection (3) for the words from "and the effect" to the end of the subsection there shall be substituted ", the effect of any regulations under section 58 below, and the effect of any provision of or made under Schedule 7A below."

28. In section 52 (central rating lists) the following subsections shall be inserted after subsection (6)—

"(6A) As soon as is reasonably practicable after compiling a list the central valuation officer shall send a copy of it to the Secretary of State.

(6B) As soon as is reasonably practicable after receiving the copy the Secretary of State shall deposit it at his principal office."

29.—(1) Section 53 (contents of central lists) shall be amended as follows.

(2) In subsection (1) for "a description" there shall be substituted "one or more descriptions".

(3) In subsection (2)(b) for "the" there shall be substituted "any".

(4) For subsection (4) there shall be substituted the following subsections—

"(4) Where regulations are for the time being in force under this section prescribing a description of non-domestic hereditament in relation to a person designated in the regulations ("the previously designated person"), amending regulations altering the designated person in relation to whom that description of hereditament is prescribed may have effect from a date earlier than that on which the amending regulations are made.

(4A) Where, by virtue of subsection (4) above, the designated person in relation to any description of non-domestic hereditament is changed from a date earlier than the making of the regulations,—

(a) any necessary alteration shall be made with effect from that date to a central non-domestic rating list on which any hereditament concerned is shown; and

(b) an order making the provision referred to in paragraph 3(2) of Schedule 6 below and specifying a description of hereditament by reference to the previously designated person shall be treated, with effect from that date, as referring to the person designated by the amending regulations."

30.—(1) Section 55 (alteration of lists) shall be amended as follows.

(2) In subsection (4) (content of regulations)—

(a) in paragraph (b) after "as to the" there shall be inserted "manner and" and at the end there shall be added "and the information to be included in a proposal";

(b) in paragraph (d) for "making" there shall be substituted "and subsequent to the making of"; and

(c) after paragraph (d) there shall be inserted—

"(dd) as to the circumstances within which and the conditions upon which a proposal may be withdrawn".

(3) In subsection (5) (regulations about appeals), for the words from "about" to "its alteration" there shall be substituted "between a valuation officer and another person making a proposal for the alteration of a list—

(a) about the validity of the proposal; or

(b) about the accuracy of the list".

(4) In subsection (7)(b) the words "at a prescribed rate" shall be omitted.

(5) The following subsection shall be inserted after subsection (7)—

"(7A) The regulations may include provision that—

(a) where a valuation officer for a charging authority has informed the authority of an alteration of a list a copy of which has been deposited by the authority under section 41(6B) above, the authority must alter the copy accordingly;

(b) where the central valuation officer has informed the Secretary of State of an alteration of a list a copy of which has been deposited under section 52(6B) above, the Secretary of State must alter the copy accordingly."

SCH. 5

31. The following section shall be substituted for section 57 (special provision for 1990-95)—

"Special provision for 1990-95.   57. Schedule 7A below (which contains special provision for 1990–95) shall have effect."

32. The following section shall be substituted for section 59—

"Contributions in aid.   59. Where a contribution in aid of non-domestic rating is made in respect of a Crown hereditament, the contribution shall be paid to the Secretary of State."

33. In section 64 (hereditaments) the following subsections shall be inserted after subsection (7)—

"(7A) The Secretary of State may by order provide that subsection (6) above shall also apply in relation to any hereditament of a prescribed class.

(7B) For the purposes of subsection (7A) above a class may be prescribed by reference to such factors as the Secretary of State sees fit.

(7C) Without prejudice to the generality of subsection (7B) above, a class may be prescribed by reference to one or more of the following factors—

(a) the physical characteristics of hereditaments;

(b) the fact that hereditaments are unoccupied or are occupied for prescribed purposes or by persons of prescribed descriptions.

(7D) A hereditament is a Crown hereditament if—

(a) it is occupied by or on behalf of the Crown for public purposes,

(b) though unoccupied, it appears that it will be occupied by or on behalf of the Crown for public purposes when next in occupation, or

(c) it is provided and maintained by an authority mentioned in subsection (7) above for purposes connected with the administration of justice, police purposes or other Crown purposes."

34. In section 65 (owners and occupiers) the following subsection shall be inserted after subsection (8)—

"(8A) In a case where—

(a) land consisting of a hereditament is used (permanently or temporarily) for the exhibition of advertisements or for the erection of a structure used for the exhibition of advertisements,

(b) section 64(2) above does not apply, and

(c) apart from this subsection, the hereditament is not occupied,

the hereditament shall be treated as occupied by the person permitting it to be so used or, if that person cannot be ascertained, its owner."

35.—(1) Section 67 (interpretation etc.) shall be amended as follows.

(2) In subsection (5) after "property on a particular day," there shall be inserted "or is a Crown hereditament on a particular day,".

(3) The following subsection shall be inserted after subsection (9) (power to show class of hereditament in central non-domestic rating list)—

"(9A) In subsection (9) above "class" means a class expressed by reference to whether hereditaments—

(a) are occupied or owned by a person designated under section 53(1) above, and

(b) fall within any description prescribed in relation to him under section 53(1)."

36. The following Schedule shall be inserted after Schedule 4—

"SCHEDULE 4A

NON-DOMESTIC RATING: NEW BUILDINGS (COMPLETION DAYS)

Completion notices

1.—(1) If it comes to the notice of a charging authority that the work remaining to be done on a new building in its area is such that the building can reasonably be expected to be completed within 3 months, the authority shall serve a notice under this paragraph on the owner of the building as soon as is reasonably practicable unless the valuation officer otherwise directs in writing.

(2) If it comes to the notice of a charging authority that a new building in its area has been completed, the authority may serve a notice under this paragraph on the owner of the building unless the valuation officer otherwise directs in writing.

(3) A charging authority may withdraw a notice under this paragraph by serving on the owner of the building to which the notice relates a subsequent notice under this paragraph.

(4) Where an appeal under paragraph 4 below has been brought against a notice under this paragraph, the power conferred by sub-paragraph (3) above shall only be exercisable with the consent in writing of the owner of the building to which the notice relates.

(5) The power conferred by sub-paragraph (3) above shall cease to be exercisable in relation to a notice under this paragraph once a day has been determined under this Schedule as the completion day in relation to the building to which the notice relates.

(6) In this Schedule "completion notice" means a notice under this paragraph.

2.—(1) A completion notice shall specify the building to which it relates and state the day which the authority proposes as the completion day in relation to the building.

(2) Where at the time a completion notice is served it appears to the authority that the building to which the notice relates is not completed, the authority shall propose as the completion day such day, not later than 3 months from and including the day on which the notice is served, as the authority considers is a day by which the building can reasonably be expected to be completed.

(3) Where at the time a completion notice is served it appears to the authority that the building to which the notice relates is completed, the authority shall propose as the completion day the day on which the notice is served.

Determination of completion day

3.—(1) If the person on whom a completion notice is served agrees in writing with the authority by whom the notice is served that a day specified by the agreement shall be the completion day in relation to the building, that day shall be the completion day in relation to it.

(2) Where such an agreement as is mentioned in sub-paragraph (1) above is made, the completion notice relating to the building shall be deemed to have been withdrawn.

4.—(1) A person on whom a completion notice is served may appeal to a valuation and community charge tribunal against the notice on the ground that the building to which the notice relates has not been or, as the case may be, cannot reasonably be expected to be completed by the day stated in the notice.

(2) Where a person appeals against a completion notice and the appeal is not withdrawn or dismissed, the completion day shall be such day as the tribunal shall determine.

5. Where a completion notice is not withdrawn and no appeal under paragraph 4 above is brought against the notice or any appeal under that paragraph is dismissed or withdrawn, the day stated in the notice shall be the completion day in relation to the building.

Position pending appeal

6.—(1) Where an appeal under paragraph 4 above is brought against a completion notice, then in relation to any day on which the appeal is pending section 45 above shall apply by virtue of section 46A(4) above as if the day stated in the notice had been determined under this Schedule as the completion day in relation to the building to which the notice relates.

(2) The Secretary of State may make regulations providing for the making of financial adjustments where sub-paragraph (1) applies but the day stated in the completion notice is not actually determined as the completion day in relation to the building to which the notice relates.

(3) Regulations under sub-paragraph (2) above may include—

(a) provision requiring payments to be made,

(b) provision requiring payments to be made together with payments of interest, and

(c) provision as to the recovery (by deduction or otherwise) of sums due.

(4) For the purpose of deciding, for the purposes of this paragraph, whether an appeal is pending on a particular day, the state of affairs existing immediately before the day ends shall be treated as having existed throughout the day.

Duty to inform valuation officer

7.—(1) A charging authority shall supply to the valuation officer a copy of any completion notice served by it.

(2) If a charging authority withdraws a completion notice, it shall inform the valuation officer of that fact.

(3) A charging authority shall supply the valuation officer with details of any agreement to which it is a party and by virtue of which a completion day is determined under this Schedule in relation to a building.

Supplementary

8. Without prejudice to any other mode of service, a completion notice may be served on a person—

(a) by sending it in a prepaid registered letter, or by the recorded delivery service, addressed to that person at his usual or last known place of abode or, in a case where an address for service has been given by that person, at that address;

(b) in the case of an incorporated company or body, by delivering it to the secretary or clerk of the company or body at their registered or principal office or sending it in a prepaid registered letter or by the recorded delivery service addressed to the secretary or clerk of the company or body at that office; or

(c) where the name or address of that person cannot be ascertained after reasonable inquiry, by addressing it to him by the description of "owner" of the building (describing it) to which the notice relates and by affixing it to some conspicuous part of the building.

9.—(1) This paragraph applies in the case of a building to which work remains to be done which is customarily done to a building of the type in question after the building has been substantially completed.

(2) It shall be assumed for the purposes of this Schedule that the building has been or can reasonably be expected to be completed at the end of such period beginning with the date of its completion apart from the work as is reasonably required for carrying out the work.

10.—(1) Section 46A(6) applies for the purposes of this Schedule.

(2) In this Schedule—

"completion notice" has the meaning given by paragraph 1(6) above;

"owner", in relation to a building, means the person entitled to possession of the building;

references to the valuation officer, in relation to a charging authority, are references to the valuation officer for the authority."

37.—(1) Schedule 5 (exemptions) shall be amended as follows.

(2) In paragraph 7 (agricultural buildings) in each of sub-paragraphs (1)(b) and (3), for "(together with the body)" there shall be substituted "or are together with the body".

(3) In paragraph 9 (exemption for fish farms) the following shall be inserted after sub-paragraph (4)—

"(4A) But an activity does not constitute fish farming if the fish or shellfish are or include fish or shellfish which—

(a) are purely ornamental, or

(b) are bred, reared or cultivated for exhibition."

(4) After paragraph 18 there shall be inserted—

"Road crossings over watercourses etc.

18A.—(1) A hereditament which is occupied (as mentioned in section 65 of this Act) is exempt to the extent that it consists of, or of any of the appurtenances of, a fixed road crossing over an estuary, river or other watercourse.

(2) For the purposes of this paragraph, a fixed road crossing means a bridge, viaduct, tunnel or other construction providing a means for road vehicles or pedestrians or both to cross the estuary, river or other watercourse concerned.

(3) For the purposes of sub-paragraph (2) above—

(a) a bridge may be a fixed road crossing notwithstanding that it is designed so that part of it can be swung, raised or otherwise moved in order to facilitate passage across, above or below it; but

(b) the expression "bridge" does not include a floating bridge, that is to say, a ferry operating between fixed chains.

(4) The reference in sub-paragraph (1) above to the appurtenances of a fixed road crossing is a reference to—

   (a) the carriageway and any footway thereof;

   (b) any building, other than office buildings, used in connection with the crossing; and

   (c) any machinery, apparatus or works used in connection with the crossing or with any of the items mentioned in paragraphs (a) and (b) above.''

38.—(1) Schedule 6 shall be amended as follows.

(2) In paragraph 1 the words '', and parts of them,'' shall be omitted.

(3) In paragraph 2, in sub-paragraph (1) after ''non-domestic hereditament'' there shall be inserted ''none of which consists of domestic property and none of which is exempt from local non-domestic rating''.

(4) In paragraph 2, the following sub-paragraphs shall be inserted after sub-paragraph (1)—

''(1A) The rateable value of a composite hereditament none of which is exempt from local non-domestic rating shall be taken to be an amount equal to the rent which, assuming such a letting of the hereditament as is required to be assumed for the purposes of sub-paragraph (1) above, would reasonably be attributable to the non-domestic use of property.

(1B) The rateable value of a non-domestic hereditament which is partially exempt from local non-domestic rating shall be taken to be an amount equal to the rent which, assuming such a letting of the hereditament as is required to be assumed for the purposes of sub-paragraph (1) above, would, as regards the part of the hereditament which is not exempt from local non-domestic rating, be reasonably attributable to the non-domestic use of property.''

(5) In paragraph 2, in sub-paragraph (6) for the words from ''day the alteration'' to the end there shall be substituted ''material day.''

(6) In paragraph 2, the following sub-paragraph shall be inserted after sub-paragraph (6)—

''(6A) For the purposes of sub-paragraph (6) above—

   (a) where the determination is occasioned by a proposal for an alteration disputing the accuracy of a previous alteration to the list, the material day is the day by reference to which the matters mentioned in sub-paragraph (7) below fell to be assessed when determining the rateable value with a view to making the disputed alteration;

   (b) where the determination is occasioned by any proposal for an alteration other than one disputing the accuracy of a previous alteration to the list, the material day is the day the proposal is made;

   (c) where the determination is occasioned otherwise than by a proposal for an alteration, the material day is the day the alteration is entered in the list.''

(7) In paragraph 2, in sub-paragraph (7) after paragraph (c) there shall be inserted—

''(cc) the quantity of refuse or waste material which is brought onto and permanently deposited on the hereditament,''.

(8) In paragraph 2, in sub-paragraph (8) for ''description'' there shall be substituted ''class''.

(9) In paragraph 2, in sub-paragraph (9) after ''(1)'' there shall be inserted '', (1A) or (1B)''.

(10) In paragraph 2, the following sub-paragraphs shall be inserted after sub-paragraph (10)—

"(11) For the purposes of sub-paragraph (8) above a class may be prescribed by reference to such factors as the Secretary of State sees fit.

(12) Without prejudice to the generality of sub-paragraph (11) above, a class may be prescribed by reference to one or more of the following factors—

(a) the physical characteristics of hereditaments;

(b) the fact that hereditaments are unoccupied or are occupied for prescribed purposes or by persons of prescribed descriptions.

(13) In this paragraph references to the non-domestic use of property are references to use otherwise than in such a manner as to constitute the property domestic property."

(11) The following paragraphs shall be inserted after paragraph 2—

"2A.—(1) This paragraph applies to any hereditament the whole or any part of which consists in buildings which are—

(a) used for the breeding and rearing of horses or ponies or for either of those purposes; and

(b) are occupied together with any agricultural land or agricultural building.

(2) The rateable value of any hereditament to which this paragraph applies shall be taken to be the amount determined under paragraph 2 above less whichever is the smaller of the following amounts—

(a) such amount as the Secretary of State may by order specify for the purposes of this paragraph; and

(b) the amount which but for this paragraph would be determined under paragraph 2 above in respect of so much of the hereditament as consists of buildings so used and occupied.

(3) In this paragraph—

"agricultural land" means any land of more than two hectares which is agricultural land within the meaning of paragraph 2 of Schedule 5 above and is not land used exclusively for the pasturing of horses or ponies; and

"agricultural building" shall be construed in accordance with paragraphs 3 to 7 of that Schedule.

2B.—(1) This paragraph applies where—

(a) the rateable value of a hereditament consisting of an area of a caravan site is determined with a view to making an alteration to a list which has been compiled (whether or not it is still in force),

(b) the area is treated as one hereditament by virtue of regulations under section 64(3)(b),

(c) immediately before the day the alteration is entered in the list or (if the alteration is made in pursuance of a proposal) the day the proposal is made, the list includes a hereditament consisting of an area of the caravan site treated as one hereditament by virtue of such regulations, and

(d) the area mentioned in paragraph (b) above and the area mentioned in paragraph (c) above are wholly or partly the same.

(2) In relation to a caravan pitch which is included both in the area mentioned in sub-paragraph (1)(b) above and in the area mentioned in sub-paragraph (1)(c) above, sub-paragraph (3) below rather than paragraph 2(6) above shall apply as respects the matters mentioned in sub-paragraph (4) below.

(3) The matters mentioned in sub-paragraph (4) below shall be taken to be as they were assumed to be for the purposes of determining the rateable value of the hereditament mentioned in sub-paragraph (1)(c) above when that rateable value was last determined.

(4) The matters are—

    (a) the nature of the caravan on the pitch, and

    (b) the physical state of that caravan.

(5) For the purposes of this paragraph—

    "caravan" has the same meaning as it has for the purposes of Part I of the Caravan Sites and Control of Development Act 1960, and

    "caravan site" means any land in respect of which a site licence is required under Part I of that Act, or would be so required if paragraph 4 and paragraph 11 of Schedule 1 to the Act (exemption of certain land occupied and supervised by organisations concerned with recreational activities and of land occupied by local authorities) were omitted."

(12) In paragraph 3(1)—

    (a) for "description" there shall be substituted "class", and

    (b) for "paragraph 2" there shall be substituted "paragraphs 2 to 2B".

(13) In paragraph 3(2) for "paragraph 2" there shall be substituted "paragraphs 2 to 2B".

(14) In paragraph 3, the following sub-paragraphs shall be inserted after sub-paragraph (2)—

    "(3) For the purposes of sub-paragraph (1) above a class may be prescribed by reference to such factors as the Secretary of State sees fit.

    (4) Without prejudice to the generality of sub-paragraph (3) above, a class may be prescribed by reference to one or more of the following factors—

        (a) the physical characteristics of hereditaments;

        (b) the fact that hereditaments are unoccupied or are occupied for prescribed purposes or by persons of prescribed descriptions."

(15) Paragraph 4 shall be omitted.

39.—(1) Schedule 7 (multipliers) shall be amended as follows.

(2) In paragraph 7(1) for the words from "Regulations" to "that" there shall be substituted "In relation to a relevant financial year the Secretary of State may make regulations providing that".

(3) In paragraph 8(3) for "section 57" there shall be substituted "paragraph 7".

(4) In paragraph 9(4) (certain orders ineffective unless in force before 1 January) for "January" there shall be substituted "March".

(5) In paragraph 10(1) (special authority's power to set multiplier in substitution) the words "because of a failure to fulfil paragraph 9(2) or (3) above" shall be omitted.

40. The following Schedule shall be inserted after Schedule 7—

"SCHEDULE 7A

Nᴏɴ-Dᴏᴍᴇsᴛɪᴄ Rᴀᴛɪɴɢ: 1990-95

Definitions

1.—(1) The transitional period is the period consisting of the financial years beginning in 1990, 1991, 1992, 1993 and 1994.

(2) A transitional day is a day falling in the transitional period.

2.—(1) As regards a transitional day a hereditament is a defined hereditament if the first and second conditions are fulfilled; but this is subject to sub-paragraphs (4) and (5) below.

(2) The first condition is that the hereditament is shown for 31 March 1990 in a valuation list maintained under Part V of the 1967 Act.

(3) The second condition is that the hereditament is shown in a local non-domestic rating list, and a rateable value is shown in the list for the hereditament, for—

(a) 1 April 1990,

(b) the transitional day (if different from 1 April 1990), and

(c) each day (if any) falling after 1 April 1990 and before the transitional day.

(4) If the hereditament is not a right falling within section 64(2) above, the hereditament is not a defined hereditament as regards the transitional day unless the rateable value shown for the hereditament in the local non-domestic rating list for 1 April 1990 is £500 or more.

(5) If the hereditament is one falling within sub-paragraph (8) below, the hereditament is not a defined hereditament as regards the transitional day unless a person who is a qualifying person in relation to the hereditament as regards that day is also a person to whom sub-paragraph (6) or (7) below applies.

(6) This sub-paragraph applies to a person if—

(a) he occupied all or part of the hereditament on 31 March 1990, and

(b) he has been a qualifying person in relation to the hereditament as regards each day (if any) falling after 31 March 1990 and before the transitional day.

(7) This sub-paragraph applies to a person if—

(a) he was the owner of the whole of the hereditament on 31 March 1990,

(b) none of the hereditament was occupied on 31 March 1990,

(c) he occupied all or part of the hereditament on at least one day in the period beginning with 1 April 1988 and ending with 30 March 1990, and

(d) he has been a qualifying person in relation to the hereditament as regards each day which falls before the transitional day and falls after the last (or only) day in the period mentioned in paragraph (c) above on which he occupied all or part of the hereditament.

(8) A hereditament falls within this sub-paragraph if, assuming it to be a defined hereditament as regards 1 April 1990, paragraph 9 below would apply to the hereditament for that day by virtue of paragraph 7 below.

(9) For the purposes of this paragraph a person is a qualifying person in relation to a hereditament as regards a day if—

(a) he occupies all or part of the hereditament on that day, or

(b) where none of the hereditament is occupied on that day, he is the owner of the whole of the hereditament on that day.

3.—(1) The notional chargeable amount for a hereditament for each day in a relevant year shall be found by applying the formula—

$$\frac{A \times B}{C}$$

(2) A is the rateable value shown for the hereditament for 1 April 1990 in the local non-domestic rating list.

(3) Subject to sub-paragraph (4) below, B is the non-domestic rating multiplier for the relevant year concerned.

(4) Where the hereditament is situated in the area of a special authority, B is the authority's non-domestic rating multiplier for the relevant year concerned.

(5) C is the number of days in the relevant year concerned.

(6) Relevant years are financial years falling in the transitional period.

4.—(1) The base liability for a hereditament for each day in the financial year beginning in 1990 shall be found by applying the formula—

$$\frac{A \times B}{C}$$

(2) A is the rateable value of the hereditament, as determined under paragraph 6 below.

(3) B is the general rate poundage effective for 31 March 1990 for the rating area (within the meaning of the 1967 Act) in which the hereditament is situated.

(4) C is the number of days in the financial year beginning in 1989.

(5) The base liability for a hereditament for each day in a relevant year (the year concerned) other than the financial year beginning in 1990 shall be found by applying the formula—

$$BL \times AF$$

(6) Relevant years are financial years falling in the transitional period.

(7) BL is the base liability for the hereditament for each day in the financial year immediately preceding the year concerned.

(8) AF is the appropriate fraction for the hereditament for each day in the financial year immediately preceding the year concerned.

5.—(1) Sub-paragraph (2) below applies in a case where the notional chargeable amount for a hereditament for each day in a relevant year exceeds the base liability for the hereditament for each day in the year.

(2) The appropriate fraction for the hereditament for each day in the year shall be found by applying the formula—

$$\frac{X}{100} \times \frac{RPI(1)}{RPI(2)}$$

(3) X is 120 if—

(a) the hereditament is situated in Greater London and the rateable value shown for it in the local non-domestic rating list for 1 April 1990 is £15,000 or more, or

(b) it is situated outside Greater London and the rateable value shown for it in the local non-domestic rating list for 1 April 1990 is £10,000 or more.

(4) X is 115 if—

   (a) the hereditament is situated in Greater London and the rateable value shown for it in the local non-domestic rating list for 1 April 1990 is less than £15,000, or

   (b) it is situated outside Greater London and the rateable value shown for it in the local non-domestic rating list for 1 April 1990 is less than £10,000.

(5) RPI(1) is the retail prices index for September of the financial year preceding the relevant year concerned.

(6) RPI(2) is the retail prices index for September of the financial year which precedes that preceding the relevant year concerned.

(7) Sub-paragraph (8) below applies in a case where the notional chargeable amount for a hereditament for each day in a relevant year does not exceed the base liability for the hereditament for each day in the year.

(8) The appropriate fraction for the hereditament for each day in the year shall be such as is—

   (a) specified for the case by order made by the Secretary of State, or

   (b) found in accordance with rules prescribed for the case by order so made.

(9) In making an order under this paragraph the Secretary of State shall have regard to the object of securing (so far as practicable) that the aggregate amount payable to him and all charging authorities by way of non-domestic rates as regards a relevant year is the same as it would in his opinion be likely to be apart from this Schedule.

(10) Relevant years are financial years falling in the transitional period.

6.—(1) This paragraph has effect to determine A in relation to a hereditament for the purposes of paragraph 4 above.

(2) In a case where a rateable value is shown for the hereditament for 15 February 1989 in the old valuation list, A is the value so shown; but this is subject to sub-paragraph (3) below.

(3) If—

   (a) a relevant proposal is (or relevant proposals are) made to alter the rateable value shown for the hereditament in that list, and

   (b) as a result of any such proposal a rateable value is shown for the hereditament in that list for a relevant day,

A is the rateable value shown in that list for the hereditament for the last (or only) relevant day for which a rateable value is shown as a result of any such proposal.

(4) For the purposes of sub-paragraph (3) above a relevant proposal is a proposal—

   (a) made by a valuation officer at any time, or

   (b) made by a person other than a valuation officer, and received by a valuation officer, before 15 February 1989.

(5) In a case where a rateable value is not shown for the hereditament for 15 February 1989 in the old valuation list, A is the rateable value shown in that list for the hereditament for the first relevant day for which a rateable value is shown; but this is subject to sub-paragraph (6) below.

(6) If—

    (a) a relevant proposal is (or relevant proposals are) made to alter the rateable value shown for the hereditament in that list, and

    (b) as a result of any such proposal a rateable value is shown for the hereditament in that list for a relevant day,

A is the rateable value shown in that list for the hereditament for the last (or only) relevant day for which a rateable value is shown as a result of any such proposal.

(7) For the purposes of sub-paragraph (6) above a relevant proposal is a proposal made by a valuation officer at any time.

(8) In the case of a hereditament—

    (a) occupied by or on behalf of the Crown for public purposes in the period beginning with 15 February 1989 and ending with 31 March 1990, and

    (b) in respect of which a contribution is made by the Crown in aid of rates for that period,

references in sub-paragraphs (2) to (6) above to rateable value are to value representing rateable value (which is required to be shown by section 37 of the 1967 Act).

(9) For the purposes of this paragraph a relevant day is a day falling after 15 February 1989 and before 1 April 1990.

(10) For the purposes of this paragraph the old valuation list is the valuation list, maintained under Part V of the 1967 Act, in which the hereditament is shown for 31 March 1990.

Chargeable amounts

7.—(1) Paragraph 9 below applies to a hereditament for a transitional day (the day concerned) if—

    (a) as regards the hereditament the day concerned is a chargeable day for which a chargeable amount falls to be determined under section 43 above,

    (b) as regards the day concerned the hereditament is a defined hereditament,

    (c) NCA exceeds BL,

    (d) NCA exceeds (BL x AF), and

    (e) in a case where the day concerned is not 1 April 1990, paragraph 9 below applies to the hereditament for each transitional day preceding the day concerned, and it does so by virtue of this paragraph.

(2) In a case where the hereditament is situated in the area of a special authority, the reference to (BL $\times$ AF) is a reference to it adjusted by finding the appropriate amount and—

    (a) if the appropriate amount is positive, adding it to (BL x AF), or

    (b) if the appropriate amount is negative, subtracting the equivalent positive amount from (BL $\times$ AF).

(3) For the purposes of sub-paragraph (2) above the appropriate amount is the amount found by applying the formula—

$$\frac{D \times (E - F)}{G}$$

(4) For the purposes of this paragraph—

(a) NCA is the notional chargeable amount for the hereditament for the day concerned,

(b) BL is the base liability for the hereditament for the day concerned,

(c) AF is the appropriate fraction for the hereditament for the day concerned,

(d) D is the rateable value shown for the hereditament in the local non-domestic rating list for 1 April 1990,

(e) E is the non-domestic rating multiplier of the special authority concerned for the financial year in which the day concerned falls,

(f) F is the non-domestic rating multiplier for the financial year in which the day concerned falls, and

(g) G is the number of days in the financial year in which the day concerned falls.

8.—(1) Paragraph 9 below applies to a hereditament for a transitional day (the day concerned) if—

(a) as regards the hereditament the day concerned is a chargeable day for which a chargeable amount falls to be determined under section 43 above,

(b) as regards the day concerned the hereditament is a defined hereditament,

(c) NCA is less than BL,

(d) NCA is less than (BL × AF), and

(e) in a case where the day concerned is not 1 April 1990, paragraph 9 below applies to the hereditament for each transitional day preceding the day concerned, and it does so by virtue of this paragraph.

(2) In a case where the hereditament is situated in the area of a special authority, the reference to (BL × AF) is a reference to it adjusted by finding the appropriate amount and—

(a) if the appropriate amount is positive, adding it to (BL × AF), or

(b) if the appropriate amount is negative, subtracting the equivalent positive amount from (BL × AF).

(3) For the purposes of sub-paragraph (2) above the appropriate amount is the amount found by applying the formula—

$$\frac{D \times (E - F)}{G}$$

(4) For the purposes of this paragraph—

(a) NCA is the notional chargeable amount for the hereditament for the day concerned,

(b) BL is the base liability for the hereditament for the day concerned,

(c) AF is the appropriate fraction for the hereditament for the day concerned,

(d) D is the rateable value shown for the hereditament in the local non-domestic rating list for 1 April 1990,

(e) E is the non-domestic rating multiplier of the special authority concerned for the financial year in which the day concerned falls,

(f) F is the non-domestic rating multiplier for the financial year in which the day concerned falls, and

(g) G is the number of days in the financial year in which the day concerned falls.

9.—(1) In a case where this paragraph applies, for the purpose of ascertaining the chargeable amount for the day concerned under section 43 above that section shall have effect subject to the following amendments.

(2) The following subsections shall be substituted for subsections (4) and (5)—

"(4) Subject to subsection (5) below, the chargeable amount for a chargeable day shall be calculated by finding the amount represented by (BL x AF).

(5) Where subsection (6) below applies the chargeable amount for a chargeable day shall be calculated by—

(a) finding the amount represented by (BL x AF), and

(b) dividing that amount by 5."

(3) The following subsections shall be inserted after subsection (6)—

"(6A) In a case where the hereditament is situated in the area of a special authority, a reference to (BL x AF) is a reference to it adjusted by finding the appropriate amount and—

(a) if the appropriate amount is positive, adding it to (BL x AF), or

(b) if the appropriate amount is negative, subtracting the equivalent positive amount from (BL x AF).

(6B) For the purposes of subsection (6A) above the appropriate amount is the amount found by applying the formula—

$$\frac{D \times (E - F)}{G},,$$

(4) For the purposes of section 43 above as amended by this paragraph BL, AF, D, E, F and G shall be construed in accordance with paragraphs 7 and 8 above.

Regulations

10.—(1) The Secretary of State may make regulations containing rules about the determination under section 45 or 54 above of a chargeable amount for a transitional day.

(2) The rules may make provision which he considers to be equivalent to that made by or under paragraphs 1 to 9 above, subject to any modifications he thinks fit.

11.—(1) The Secretary of State may make regulations containing rules supplementing or modifying or excluding, for any case he considers appropriate and to such extent as he considers appropriate, any relevant provision.

(2) For the purpose of the determination under section 43, 45 or 54 above of a chargeable amount for a transitional day, the Secretary of State may make regulations applying any relevant provision (subject to any modifications he thinks fit) to any case—

(a) where he considers it appropriate to do so, and

(b) where the relevant provision would not (whether by virtue of regulations under sub-paragraph (1) above or otherwise) apply apart from the regulations under this sub-paragraph.

(3) A relevant provision is a provision made by or under paragraphs 1 to 9 above or by regulations under paragraph 10 above.

12. Without prejudice to the generality of section 143(1) and (2) above and paragraphs 10 and 11 above, regulations under those paragraphs may include provision—

SCH. 5

> (a) imposing duties and conferring powers on valuation officers (whether as regards determinations, certificates or otherwise) in relation to the ascertainment of rateable values;
>
> (b) as to appeals relating to things done or not done by such officers."

41. In Schedule 8 (non-domestic rating: pooling) in Part I, in paragraph 2 (non-domestic rating accounts: credits and debits) in sub-paragraph (1)(b) for "regulations made under section 59(2)" there shall be substituted "section 59".

42.—(1) In Schedule 8 (non-domestic rating: pooling) Part II (non-domestic rating contributions) shall be amended as follows.

(2) In paragraph 5, at the end of sub-paragraph (1) there shall be added "and has effect subject to any provision made by virtue of paragraph 6(2A) below".

(3) In paragraph 6, after sub-paragraph (2) there shall be inserted the following sub-paragraphs—

> "(2A) Regulations under paragraph 4 above may incorporate in the rules provision for adjustments to be made in the calculation of the amount of an authority's non-domestic rating contribution under paragraph 5(2) or 5(6) above, being adjustments to take account of relevant changes affecting the amount of the authority's non-domestic rating contribution for an earlier year.
>
> (2B) For the purposes of sub-paragraph (2A) above, a change is a relevant change if it results from a decision, determination or other matter which (whether by reason of the time at which it was taken, made or occurred or otherwise) was not taken into account by the authority in the calculation under paragraph 5(6) above of the amount of its non-domestic rating contribution for the earlier year in question."

43.—(1) In Schedule 8 (non-domestic rating: pooling) Part III (distribution) shall be amended as follows.

(2) The following sub-paragraph shall be substituted for paragraph 9(6)—

> "(6) As regards a particular financial year the relevant population of a charging authority is the relevant population, calculated under paragraph 4 of Schedule 12A below, of the area of the authority for the year."

(3) Paragraph 9(7) shall be omitted.

(4) In paragraph 11(1) for the words from "As soon as" to "calculate how much of it" there shall be substituted "If the revenue support grant report for a chargeable financial year is approved by resolution of the House of Commons, as soon as is reasonably practicable after the report is approved the Secretary of State shall calculate how much of the distributable amount for the year".

(5) Paragraph 11(3) shall be omitted.

(6) In paragraph 12(1) for the words from "If the revenue" to "is approved" (in the second place where those words occur) there shall be substituted "As soon as is reasonably practicable after the county and district shares for a chargeable financial year have been calculated under paragraph 11 above".

(7) The following sub-paragraph shall be substituted for paragraph 12(5)—

> "(5) As regards a particular financial year the relevant population of a council is the relevant population, calculated under paragraph 4 of Schedule 12A below, of the area of the council for the year."

(8) Paragraph 12(6) shall be omitted.

44.—(1) In Schedule 9 (administration) paragraph 2 (collection and recovery) shall be amended as follows.

(2) The following paragraphs shall be substituted for sub-paragraph (2)(g)—

"(g) that a notice must be in a prescribed form,

(ga) that a notice must contain prescribed matters,

(gb) that a notice must not contain other prescribed matters,

(gc) that where a notice is invalid because it does not comply with regulations under paragraph (g) or (ga) above, and the circumstances are such as may be prescribed, a requirement contained in the notice by virtue of regulations under paragraph (e) or (f) above shall nevertheless have effect as if the notice were valid,

(gd) that where a notice is invalid because it does not comply with regulations under paragraph (g) above, and a requirement has effect by virtue of regulations under paragraph (gc) above, the payee must take prescribed steps to issue to the ratepayer a document in the form which the notice would have taken had it complied with regulations under paragraph (g) above,

(ge) that where a notice is invalid because it does not comply with regulations under paragraph (ga) above, and a requirement has effect by virtue of regulations under paragraph (gc) above, the payee must take prescribed steps to inform the ratepayer of such of the matters prescribed under paragraph (ga) above as were not contained in the notice,".

(3) In sub-paragraph (2)(h) the words from "and" to the end shall be omitted.

(4) The following sub-paragraph shall be inserted after sub-paragraph (2)—

"(2A) Regulations under this Schedule may include provision that where—

(a) an amount paid by the ratepayer in excess of his liability falls to be repaid or credited, and

(b) the circumstances are such as may be prescribed,

an additional amount by way of interest shall be paid or credited."

45. In Schedule 9 the following paragraph shall be inserted after paragraph 4—

"4A.—(1) Regulations under this Schedule may include provision that a charging authority and a person liable to pay it an amount under section 43 or 45 above may enter into an agreement that—

(a) any interest of his in the hereditament as regards which the liability arises shall be charged to secure payment of the amount, and

(b) in consideration of the charge the authority will take no steps for a period specified in the agreement to recover any payment in respect of the amount.

(2) The regulations may include—

(a) provision that the agreement may also extend to any further amount the person may become liable to pay to the authority under section 43 or 45 above as regards the hereditament;

(b) provision that the agreement may provide for the payment of interest on sums outstanding and for interest payable to be secured by the charge;

(c) provision restricting the period which may be specified as mentioned in sub-paragraph (1)(b) above."

46.—(1) Paragraph 5 of Schedule 9 (power to require information to be supplied to a valuation officer) shall be amended as follows.

(2) In sub-paragraph (1) for the words from "requiring" to the end there shall be substituted "requesting him to supply to the officer information—

(a) which is specified in the notice, and

(b) which the officer reasonably believes will assist him in carrying out functions conferred or imposed on him by or under this Part."

(3) After sub-paragraph (1) there shall be inserted—

"(1A) A notice under this paragraph must state that the officer believes the information requested will assist him in carrying out functions conferred or imposed on him by or under this Part."

(4) In sub-paragraph (2)—

(a) for "required" (in the first place where the word occurs) there shall be substituted "requested", and

(b) for "required" (in the second place where the word occurs) there shall be substituted "specified".

47.—(1) Paragraph 6 of Schedule 9 (authority's duty to supply information to valuation officer) shall be amended as follows.

(2) In sub-paragraph (1) for "relevant" there shall be substituted "charging", and in consequence sub-paragraph (2) shall be omitted.

(3) After sub-paragraph (1) there shall be inserted—

"(1A) The Secretary of State may make regulations containing provision that, at such times and in such manner as may be prescribed, a charging authority shall supply to the valuation officer for the authority information of such description as may be prescribed."

48. The following paragraphs shall be substituted for paragraph 8 of Schedule 9 (inspection)—

"8.—(1) A person may require a valuation officer to give him access to such information as will enable him to establish what is the state of a list, or has been its state at any time since it came into force, if—

(a) the officer is maintaining the list, and

(b) the list is in force or has been in force at any time in the preceding 5 years.

(2) A person may require a charging authority to give him access to such information as will enable him to establish what is the state of a copy of a list, or has been its state at any time since it was deposited, if—

(a) the authority has deposited the copy under section 41(6B) above, and

(b) the list is in force or has been in force at any time in the preceding 5 years.

(3) A person may require the Secretary of State to give him access to such information as will enable him to establish what is the state of a copy of a list, or has been its state at any time since it was deposited, if—

(a) the Secretary of State has deposited the copy under section 52(6B) above, and

(b) the list is in force or has been in force at any time in the preceding 5 years.

(4) A person may require a charging authority to give him access to such information as will enable him to establish what is the state of a copy of a proposed list if—

(a) the authority has deposited the copy under section 41(6) above, and

(b) the list itself is not yet in force.

(5) A person may require the Secretary of State to give him access to such information as will enable him to establish what is the state of a copy of a proposed list if—

(a) the Secretary of State has deposited the copy under section 52(6) above, and

(b) the list itself is not yet in force.

(6) A requirement under any of the preceding provisions of this paragraph must be complied with at a reasonable time and place and without payment being sought; but the information may be in documentary or other form, as the person or authority of whom the requirement is made thinks fit.

(7) Where access is given under this paragraph to information in documentary form the person to whom access is given may—

(a) make copies of (or of extracts from) the document;

(b) require a person having custody of the document to supply to him a photographic copy of (or of extracts from) the document.

(8) Where access is given under this paragraph to information in a form which is not documentary the person to whom access is given may—

(a) make transcripts of (or of extracts from) the information;

(b) require a person having control of access to the information to supply to him a copy in documentary form of (or of extracts from) the information.

(9) If a reasonable charge is required for a facility under sub-paragraph (7) or (8) above, the sub-paragraph concerned shall not apply unless the person seeking to avail himself of the facility pays the charge.

(10) If without reasonable excuse a person having custody of a document containing, or having control of access to, information access to which is sought under this paragraph—

(a) intentionally obstructs a person in exercising a right under sub-paragraph (1), (2), (3), (4), (5), (7)(a) or (8)(a) above, or

(b) refuses to comply with a requirement under sub-paragraph (7)(b) or (8)(b) above,

he shall be liable on summary conviction to a fine not exceeding level 1 on the standard scale.

9.—(1) A person may, at a reasonable time and without making payment, inspect any proposal made or notice of appeal given under regulations made under section 55 above, if made or given as regards a list which is in force when inspection is sought or has been in force at any time in the preceding 5 years.

(2) A person may—

(a) make copies of (or of extracts from) a document mentioned in sub-paragraph (1) above, or

(b) require a person having custody of such a document to supply to him a photographic copy of (or of extracts from) the document.

(3) If a reasonable charge is required for a facility under sub-paragraph (2) above, the sub-paragraph shall not apply unless the person seeking to avail himself of the facility pays the charge.

(4) If without reasonable excuse a person having custody of a document mentioned in sub-paragraph (1) above—

   (a) intentionally obstructs a person in exercising a right under sub-paragraph (1) or (2)(a) above, or

   (b) refuses to supply a copy to a person entitled to it under sub-paragraph (2)(b) above,

he shall be liable on summary conviction to a fine not exceeding level 1 on the standard scale."

Precepts and levies

49.—(1) Section 68 (precepts to be issued) shall be amended as follows.

(2) In subsection (2) (precepts to be issued before 11 March) for "11 March" there shall be substituted "1 March".

(3) For subsection (4) there shall be substituted the following subsections—

   "(4) The items are—

   (a) the expenditure the authority estimates it will incur in the year in performing its functions in the year and will charge to a revenue account for the year;

   (b) such allowance as the authority estimates will be appropriate for contingencies in relation to expenditure to be charged to a revenue account for the year;

   (c) the financial reserves which the authority estimates it will be appropriate to raise in the year for meeting the estimated expenditure referred to in subsection (4A) below; and

   (d) such financial reserves as are sufficient to meet so much of the amount estimated by the authority to be a revenue account deficit for any earlier financial year as has not already been provided for.

   (4A) The estimated expenditure referred to in subsection (4)(c) above is—

   (a) that which the authority estimates that, in the financial year following the year in question, it will incur, will charge to a revenue account and will have to defray before sums yielded by way of precepts are sufficiently available; and

   (b) that which the authority estimates it will incur in the financial year referred to in paragraph (a) above or any subsequent financial year in performing its functions and which will be charged to a revenue account for that or any other year.

   (4B) References in subsections (4) and (4A) above to expenditure incurred by the authority shall be construed in accordance with section 41(3) of the Local Government and Housing Act 1989."

50. In section 69 (precepted authorities) the following subsections shall be substituted for subsection (7)—

   "(7) As regards precepts for a particular financial year the relevant population of the area of an English charging authority is the relevant population, calculated under paragraph 4 of Schedule 12A below, of the area for the year.

   (7A) As regards precepts for a particular financial year the relevant population of the area of a Welsh charging authority is the relevant population, calculated under paragraph 5 of Schedule 12A below, of the area for the year.

(7B) As regards precepts for a particular financial year the relevant population of part of the area of a charging authority is the relevant population, calculated under paragraph 6 of Schedule 12A below, of the part for the year."

51. In section 70(2) (county council's general and special expenses) in paragraph (b) for "its expenses needed to meet" there shall be substituted "the expenses of meeting".

52.—(1) Section 73 (information) shall be amended as follows.

(2) In subsection (2) after "require" there shall be inserted "the Secretary of State or".

(3) The following subsections shall be inserted after subsection (2)—

"(2A) Where regulations under Schedule 2 or 9 below contain provision about the contents or form of a notice to be served by a charging authority, they may also require the Secretary of State or any appropriate precepting authority to supply the charging authority with prescribed information if the Secretary of State considers it to be information the charging authority needs to ensure that the provision is met.

(2B) Where any person other than the Secretary of State fails to supply information to a charging authority in accordance with regulations by virtue of subsection (2) or (2A) above he shall be liable to indemnify the authority against any loss or damage which the authority sustains in consequence of the failure."

(4) In subsection (3) after "(2)" there shall be inserted "or (2A)".

53. In section 74 (levies) in subsection (5)(a) after "72 above" there shall be inserted "or in Schedule 12A below or in regulations under section 73(1) above or in regulations under Schedule 12A below".

54. The following section shall be inserted after section 74—

"Levies: information.

74A.—(1) Where regulations under Schedule 2 or 9 below impose a duty on a charging authority to supply information to any person, they may also require any appropriate levying body to supply the charging authority with prescribed information if the Secretary of State considers it to be information the charging authority needs in order to fulfil its duty.

(2) For the purposes of subsection (1) above a body is an appropriate levying body in relation to a charging authority if—

(a) it has power to issue a levy to the charging authority, or

(b) it has power to issue a levy to a county council which has power to issue a precept to the charging authority."

55.—(1) Section 75 (special levies) shall be amended as follows.

(2) In subsection (2) for "Secretary of State" there shall be substituted "appropriate Minister".

(3) In subsection (7)(a)—

(a) after "72 above" there shall be inserted "or in Schedule 12A below or in regulations under section 73(1) above or in regulations under Schedule 12A below", and

(b) for "Secretary of State" there shall be substituted "appropriate Minister".

(4) At the end of that section there shall be added the following subsection—

"(8) In this section "the appropriate Minister" has the same meaning as in section 118 below."

SCH. 5

56. The following section shall be inserted after section 75—

"Special levies: information.

75A.—(1) Where regulations under Schedule 2 or 9 below impose a duty on a charging authority to supply information to any person, they may also require any appropriate levying body to supply the charging authority with prescribed information if the Secretary of State considers it to be information the charging authority needs in order to fulfil its duty.

(2) For the purposes of subsection (1) above a body is an appropriate levying body in relation to a charging authority if it has power to issue a special levy to the charging authority."

Grants

57.—(1) Section 77 (information) shall be omitted.

(2) This paragraph shall not affect the operation of section 77 as regards a case where a notice has been served under it before the coming into force of this paragraph.

58.—(1) Section 82 (calculation of revenue support grant payable) shall be amended as follows.

(2) At the end of subsection (3) there shall be inserted "; and he may decide different dates for different kinds of information."

(3) In subsection (4) after "date" there shall be inserted "(or the dates and kinds of information)".

59.—(1) Section 84 (special provision for transitional years) shall be amended as follows.

(2) In subsection (3) the following paragraphs shall be substituted for paragraphs (b) and (c)—

"(b) may contain provision for one transitional year, or for more than one, as the Secretary of State thinks fit;

(c) may make different provision for different authorities;

(d) if it contains provision for more than one transitional year, may make different provision for the different years."

(3) In subsection (5) after "transitional year" there shall be inserted "for which the report contains provision".

60. In section 88 (transport grants: supplementary), in subsections (4) and (6) for the words from "prescribed expenditure" onwards there shall, in each case, be substituted "expenditure for capital purposes within the meaning of Part IV of the Local Government and Housing Act 1989".

61. The following section shall be inserted after section 88—

"Community charge grants

Community charge grants.

88A.—(1) If regulations under section 13A above have effect as regards a chargeable financial year the Secretary of State may, with the consent of the Treasury, pay a grant to a charging authority as regards that financial year.

(2) The amount of the grant shall be such as the Secretary of State may with the consent of the Treasury determine.

(3) A grant under this section shall be paid at such time, or in instalments of such amounts and at such times, as the Secretary of State may with the consent of the Treasury determine.

(4) In making any payment of grant under this section the Secretary of State may impose such conditions as he may with the consent of the Treasury determine; and the conditions may relate to the repayment in specified circumstances of all or part of the amount paid, or otherwise.

(5) In deciding whether to pay a grant under this section, and in determining the amount of any such grant, the Secretary of State shall have regard to his estimate of the aggregate of—

(a) any amount which, in consequence of the regulations, the authority might reasonably be expected to lose, or to have lost, by way of payments in respect of community charges as they have effect for the financial year concerned, and

(b) any administrative expenses the authority might reasonably be expected to incur, or to have incurred, in giving effect to the regulations in their application to the financial year concerned."

Funds

62. In section 89(4) (use of sums paid into charging authority's collection fund) for "settlement" there shall be substituted "the making", and consequently in section 89(5) for "settling" there shall be substituted "making".

63.—(1) In section 95 (calculations to be made by authorities) for subsection (2) there shall be substituted the following subsections—

"(2) The authority must calculate the aggregate of—

(a) the expenditure the authority estimates it will incur in the year in performing its functions in the year and will charge to a revenue account for the year;

(b) such allowance as the authority estimates will be appropriate for contingencies in relation to expenditure to be charged to a revenue account for the year;

(c) the financial reserves which the authority estimates it will be appropriate to raise in the year for meeting the estimated expenditure referred to in subsection (2A) below;

(d) such financial reserves as are sufficient to meet so much of the amount estimated by the authority to be a revenue account deficit for any earlier financial year as has not already been provided for; and

(e) any amounts it estimates will be charged to a revenue account in respect of the authority's general fund or City fund, as the case may be, by virtue of a transfer,—

(i) pursuant to regulations under section 89(5) above, of such an additional sum as is referred to in subsection (3)(d) of section 98 below; or

(ii) pursuant to a direction under subsection (5) of that section, of such an amount as is referred to in that subsection.

(2A) The estimated expenditure referred to in subsection (2)(c) above is—

(a) that which the authority estimates that, in the financial year following the year in question, it will incur, will charge to a revenue account and will have to defray before sums to be transferred as regards that year from its collection fund to its general fund or to the City fund (as the case may be) become sufficiently available; and

(b) that which the authority estimates it will incur in the financial year referred to in paragraph (a) above or any subsequent financial year in performing its functions and which will be charged to a revenue account for that or any other year.

(2B) References in subsections (2) and (2A) above to expenditure incurred by the authority shall be construed in accordance with section 41(3) of the Local Government and Housing Act 1989."

(2) In subsection (3) of that section, for the words following "the aggregate of" there shall be substituted—

"(a) the sums which it estimates will be payable for the year into its general fund or into the City fund (as the case may be) and in respect of which amounts are to be credited to a revenue account for the year;

(b) the amounts which it estimates will be transferred from its collection fund to its general fund or the City fund (as the case may be) pursuant to a direction under section 98(4) below and credited to a revenue account for the year; and

(c) the amount of the financial reserves which the authority estimates that it will use in order to provide for the items mentioned in paragraphs (a), (b) and (e) of subsection (2) above."

(3) In subsection (7) of that section, after the word "which" there shall be inserted "in accordance with section 97 below".

64. In section 98 (transfers between funds) in subsection (3)(d) the words "and calculated in a prescribed manner" shall be omitted.

65. In section 99 (regulations) in subsection (2)(d) the words "at such rate as may be prescribed" shall be omitted.

Financial administration

66. The following subsection shall be inserted after subsection (3) of section 114 (functions of chief finance officer)—

"(3A) It shall be the duty of the chief finance officer of a relevant authority, in preparing a report in pursuance of subsection (2) above, to consult so far as practicable—

(a) with the person who is for the time being designated as the head of the authority's paid service under section 4 of the Local Government and Housing Act 1989; and

(b) with the person who is for the time being responsible for performing the duties of the authority's monitoring officer under section 5 of that Act."

Existing rates

67.—(1) In section 118 (power to abolish or modify existing rates), at the end of subsection (1) there shall be added "and, in the case of an internal drainage board, there shall be disregarded for the purposes of paragraph (b) above any agreement under section 81 of the Land Drainage Act 1976 under which the board have agreed that no drainage rate will be levied on occupiers or owners of certain rateable hereditaments".

(2) In subsections (2) and (4) of that section for the words "Secretary of State" there shall be substituted "appropriate Minister".

SCH. 5   (3) At the end of subsection (5) of that section there shall be added "and "the appropriate Minister" means—

(a) as respects any internal drainage board whose district is wholly within England, the Minister of Agriculture, Fisheries and Food;

(b) as respects any internal drainage board whose district is partly in England and partly in Wales, that Minister and the Secretary of State acting jointly; and

(c) as respects any other body, the Secretary of State."

Information

68. The following section shall be inserted after section 139—

"Information.   139A.—(1) Subsection (2) below applies where—

(a) the Secretary of State serves a notice on a relevant authority or relevant officer requiring it or him to supply to the Secretary of State information specified in the notice,

(b) the information is required by the Secretary of State for the purpose of deciding whether to exercise his powers, and how to perform his functions, under this Act, and

(c) the information is not personal information.

(2) The authority or officer shall supply the information required, and shall do so in such form and manner and at such time as the Secretary of State specifies in the notice.

(3) If an authority or officer fails to comply with subsection (2) above the Secretary of State may assume the information required to be such as he sees fit; and in such a case the Secretary of State may decide in accordance with the assumption whether to exercise his powers, and how to perform his functions, under this Act.

(4) In deciding whether to exercise his powers, and how to perform his functions, under this Act the Secretary of State may also take into account any other information available to him, whatever its source and whether or not obtained under a provision contained in or made under this or any other Act.

(5) Each of the following is a relevant authority—

(a) a charging authority;

(b) a precepting authority.

(6) The community charges registration officer for a charging authority is a relevant officer.

(7) Personal information is information which relates to an individual (living or dead) who can be identified from that information or from that and other information supplied to any person by the authority or officer concerned; and personal information includes any expression of opinion about the individual and any indication of the intentions of any person in respect of the individual.

(8) This section shall have effect before 1 April 1990 as if after paragraph (b) of subsection (5) above there were inserted—

"(c) the Inner London Education Authority." "

England and Wales: separate administration

69.—(1) Section 140 (separate administration in England and Wales) shall be amended as follows.

(2) In subsection (1) after "VII" there shall be inserted ", and paragraphs 1 to 4 of Schedule 12A below,".

(3) In subsection (2) the word "and" at the end of paragraph (e) shall be omitted, and after paragraph (f) there shall be inserted "and

(g) separate reports under Schedule 12A below shall be made."

(4) In subsection (3) after "VII" there shall be inserted ", and paragraphs 1 to 4 of Schedule 12A below,".

Payments

70. The following subsection shall be inserted at the end of section 141 (payments to and from authorities)—

"(9) In the application of this section to England, the second relevant provisions also include section 81 of the Education Reform Act 1988 (recovery from local funds of sums in respect of maintenance grant)".

71. The following sections shall be inserted after section 141—

"Payments: further provisions.

141A.—(1) The Secretary of State may make regulations in relation to any case where—

(a) he is liable to pay to an English charging authority at any time an amount or amounts under one or more of the first relevant provisions, and

(b) a precepting authority which has power to issue a precept to the charging authority is liable to pay to him at the same time an amount under the second relevant provision.

(2) The regulations may provide that if the total of the amount or amounts mentioned in subsection (1)(a) above exceeds the charging authority's relevant amount the Secretary of State may set off an amount equal to that amount in paying that total.

(3) The regulations may provide that if the total of the amount or amounts mentioned in subsection (1)(a) above is equal to or less than the charging authority's relevant amount no payment need be made in respect of that total.

(4) The regulations may provide that where the Secretary of State sets off or refrains from paying an amount under any provision included under subsection (2) or (3) above—

(a) the Secretary of State's liability to the charging authority shall be treated as discharged to the extent of an amount equal to that amount,

(b) what the precepting authority is liable to pay to the Secretary of State shall be treated as reduced by an amount equal to that amount, and

(c) an amount equal to that amount shall be due from the precepting authority to the charging authority.

(5) The regulations may provide that an amount due from the precepting authority to the charging authority by virtue of provision included under subsection (4)(c) above shall be recoverable by such method as may be prescribed (whether by making a deduction from an amount payable in respect of a precept or otherwise).

(6) The regulations may provide that—

(a) where an amount due from the precepting authority to the charging authority by virtue of provision included under subsection (4)(c) above is recovered by payment to the charging authority, that authority shall pay into its collection fund an amount equal to the amount paid to it;

(b) where an amount due from the precepting authority to the charging authority by virtue of provision included under subsection (4)(c) above is recovered by making a deduction from an amount payable in respect of a precept, the charging authority shall retain in its collection fund an amount equal to the amount deducted.

(7) Without prejudice to section 143(2) below, the regulations may include provision—

(a) requiring prescribed provisions of this Act (such as sections 79(2) and 86(2)) to be read subject to the regulations;

(b) requiring prescribed provisions of this Act (such as paragraph 2 of Schedule 8) to be read as if references to payments made were to payments which would have been made apart from the regulations.

(8) Where the Secretary of State is liable to pay to the charging authority at any time an amount or amounts under one or more of the first relevant provisions, for the purposes of this section and regulations under it—

(a) the amount or amounts shall be treated as reduced by anything he may set off, by virtue of regulations under section 141 above, in paying the amount or amounts;

(b) he shall be treated as not liable to pay any such amount or amounts if, by virtue of regulations under that section, no payment need be made in respect of the amount or amounts.

Section 141A: interpretation.

141B.—(1) This section applies for the purposes of section 141A above.

(2) The charging authority's relevant amount shall be determined by applying the formula—

$$\frac{A \times B}{C}$$

(3) A is the amount mentioned in section 141A(1)(b) above.

(4) B is the relevant population (calculated by reference to the time mentioned in section 141A(1) above) of the charging authority.

(5) C is the aggregate of the relevant populations (calculated by reference to the time mentioned in section 141A(1) above) of all charging authorities which fulfil the following conditions—

(a) they are authorities to which the precepting authority has power to raise a precept, and

(b) they are authorities to which the Secretary of State is liable to pay at the time mentioned in section 141A(1) above an amount or amounts under one or more of the first relevant provisions.

(6) As regards any particular time the relevant population of a charging authority is the relevant population, calculated under paragraph 4 of Schedule 12A below, of the area of the authority for the financial year in which the time falls.

(7) The first relevant provisions are sections 83 and 86 above, paragraph 5(10) of Schedule 8 below, regulations made under paragraph 6(5) of that Schedule, and paragraph 9 of that Schedule.

(8) The second relevant provision is section 81 of the Education Reform Act 1988 (recovery from local funds of sums in respect of maintenance grant)."

Orders and regulations

72.—(1) Section 143 (orders and regulations) shall be amended as follows.

(2) In subsection (2) after "Secretary of State" there shall be inserted "the Minister of Agriculture, Fisheries and Food".

(3) In subsection (3) for "(9)" there shall be substituted "(9B)".

(4) In subsection (4) the words "57 or" shall be omitted.

(5) In subsection (5) after "118 above" there shall be inserted "other than regulations relating to an internal drainage board".

(6) The following subsections shall be inserted after subsection (9)—

"(9A) The power to make an order under paragraph 5 of Schedule 7A below shall be exercisable by statutory instrument, and no such order shall be made unless a draft of it has been laid before and approved by resolution of each House of Parliament.

(9B) The power to make regulations under paragraph 5 or 6 of Schedule 12A below shall be exercisable by statutory instrument subject to annulment in pursuance of a resolution of the House of Commons."

(7) In subsection (10) after "118 above" there shall be inserted "other than regulations relating to an internal drainage board".

Relevant population

73. The following section shall be inserted after section 145—

"Interpretation: relevant population.

145A. Schedule 12A below (which contains provisions about relevant population) shall have effect."

74. The following Schedule shall be inserted after Schedule 12—

"SCHEDULE 12A

RELEVANT POPULATION

Population of area

1.—(1) For the purposes of this paragraph and paragraphs 2 to 4 below each of the following is a relevant authority—

(a) an English charging authority;

(b) a Welsh district council;

(c) a Welsh county council.

(2) For the purposes of paragraphs 2 to 4 below each of the following is a notifiable authority—

(a) a charging authority,

(b) a county council,

(c) a metropolitan county police authority,

(d) the Northumbria Police Authority,

(e) a metropolitan county fire and civil defence authority,

(f) the London Fire and Civil Defence Authority, and

(g) the Receiver for the Metropolitan Police District.

2.—(1) The Secretary of State shall make a report containing rules for calculating the relevant population of the area of each relevant authority.

(2) Before making the report the Secretary of State shall notify to such representatives of local government as appear to him to be appropriate the general nature of its intended contents.

(3) The report shall be laid before the House of Commons.

(4) As soon as is reasonably practicable after the report is laid before the House of Commons the Secretary of State shall send a copy of it to each notifiable authority.

(5) After making the report the Secretary of State may make a further report or reports, and any such report—

(a) may replace any previous report under this paragraph, or

(b) may amend any previous report under this paragraph.

(6) A report under sub-paragraph (5)(a) above shall contain revised rules for calculating the relevant population of the area of each relevant authority.

(7) A report under sub-paragraph (5)(b) above shall contain amendments to the rules contained in the report which it amends.

(8) Sub-paragraphs (2) to (4) above shall apply to any report under sub-paragraph (5) above as they apply to one under sub-paragraph (1) above.

(9) A report under this paragraph shall state the day on which it is to come into force and the first financial year for which it is to operate.

3.—(1) This paragraph applies where in accordance with paragraph 2 above a report has been made and laid before the House of Commons.

(2) If the report is approved by resolution of the House of Commons it shall come into force on the day stated in the report.

(3) If the report is made under paragraph 2(1) or (5)(a), on and after the day it comes into force the rules it contains shall have effect for calculating the relevant population of the area of each relevant authority for all chargeable financial years

beginning with the first financial year for which it states it is to operate; but this is subject to the effect of any subsequent report under paragraph 2(5).

(4) If the report is made under paragraph 2(5)(b), on and after the day it comes into force the rules it amends read subject to the amendments shall have effect for calculating the relevant population of the area of each relevant authority for all chargeable financial years beginning with the first financial year for which it states it is to operate; but this is subject to the effect of any subsequent report under paragraph 2(5).

4.—(1) As soon as is reasonably practicable after a revenue support grant report for a financial year has been approved by resolution of the House of Commons, the Secretary of State shall calculate the relevant population of the area of each relevant authority for the year in accordance with the rules for the time being effective (as regards the year) under paragraph 3 above.

(2) If the Secretary of State decides that he will leave out of account information received by him after a particular date in making a calculation under sub-paragraph (1) above the calculation shall be made accordingly; and he may decide different dates for different kinds of information.

(3) Sub-paragraph (2) above applies only if the Secretary of State informs each notifiable authority in writing of his decision and of the date (or the dates and kinds of information) concerned; but he may do this at any time before the calculation is made under this paragraph.

(4) As soon as is reasonably practicable after making a calculation under sub-paragraph (1) above the Secretary of State shall—

    (a) inform each relevant authority of what he calculates as the relevant population of its area for the year;

    (b) where the relevant authority is an English charging authority, inform each appropriate precepting authority of what he calculates as the relevant population of the area of the charging authority for the year.

(5) For the purposes of sub-paragraph (4) above an appropriate precepting authority, in relation to a charging authority, is a precepting authority which is a notifiable authority and which has power to issue a precept to the charging authority.

5.—(1) The Secretary of State shall make regulations containing rules for calculating for chargeable financial years the relevant population of the area of each Welsh charging authority.

(2) A Welsh charging authority shall calculate the relevant population of its area for a chargeable financial year in accordance with the rules for the time being effective (as regards the year) under the regulations.

(3) The calculation shall be made as soon as is reasonably practicable after such date as is specified for the year in the regulations made under sub-paragraph (1) above.

(4) As soon as is reasonably practicable after making a calculation under sub-paragraph (2) above a Welsh charging authority shall inform each appropriate precepting authority of what the charging authority calculates as the relevant population of the area of the charging authority for the year.

(5) For the purposes of sub-paragraph (4) above an appropriate precepting authority, in relation to a charging authority, is a precepting authority which is a notifiable authority and which has power to issue a precept to the charging authority.

Population of part of area

6.—(1) This paragraph applies where the relevant population of part of a charging authority's area needs to be found for the purposes of section 69 above.

(2) The Secretary of State shall make regulations containing rules for calculating for chargeable financial years the relevant population of any such part.

(3) The charging authority shall calculate the relevant population of the part for a chargeable financial year in accordance with the rules for the time being effective (as regards the year) under the regulations.

(4) The calculation shall be made—

(a) where the authority is English, as soon as is reasonably practicable after a revenue support grant report for the year has been approved by resolution of the House of Commons;

(b) where the authority is Welsh, as soon as is reasonably practicable after such date as is specified for the year in the regulations made under sub-paragraph (2) above."

Information

75. In section 146 (interpretation) the following subsection shall be inserted after subsection (5)—

"(5A) Unless the context otherwise requires, "information" includes accounts, estimates and returns."

Tribunals

76.—(1) Schedule 11 (tribunals) shall be amended as follows.

(2) In paragraph 2 (jurisdiction) the following paragraph shall be inserted at the end—

"(c) paragraph 4 of Schedule 4A above."

(3) In paragraph 8(4)(f) (orders of tribunals) after "responsible individual" there shall be inserted "or as a certification officer".

General

77.—(1) This paragraph applies to each of the following amendments made by this Schedule—

(a) the amendment of paragraph 1(2) of Schedule 3 to the 1988 Act (read with paragraph 1(7A) of that Schedule),

(b) the amendment of paragraph 1(4) of that Schedule (read with paragraph 1(7A)), and

(c) the amendment of paragraph 1(6) of that Schedule (read with paragraph 1(7A)).

(2) Subject to sub-paragraph (3) below, the amendment applies whether the request or the conduct of the person requested occurs before or on or after the relevant day.

(3) The amendment does not apply in the case of a request made before the relevant day if before it was made two or more requests were already made to supply the same information, allow inspection of the same records, or send a copy of the same records, under the same provision.

(4) Sub-paragraph (3) above does not prevent further requests being made on or after the relevant day or the amendment applying in the case of such requests.

(5) In this paragraph "the relevant day" means the day on which the relevant period ends; and the relevant period is the period of 2 months beginning on the day this Act is passed.

78.—(1) This paragraph applies to each of the following amendments made by this Schedule—

(a) the amendment of paragraph 2(4) of Schedule 3 to the 1988 Act (read with paragraph 2(11A) of that Schedule),

(b) the amendment of paragraph 2(6) of that Schedule (read with paragraph 2(11A)), and

(c) the amendment of paragraph 2(9) of that Schedule (read with paragraph 2(11A)).

(2) Subject to sub-paragraph (3) below, the amendment applies whether the request or the conduct of the person requested occurs before or on or after the relevant day.

(3) The amendment does not apply in the case of a request made before the relevant day if before it was made two or more requests were already made to allow inspection of the same records, send a copy of the same records, or supply the same information, under the same provision.

(4) Sub-paragraph (3) above does not prevent further requests being made on or after the relevant day or the amendment applying in the case of such requests.

(5) In this paragraph "the relevant day" means the day on which the relevant period ends; and the relevant period is the period of 2 months beginning on the day this Act is passed.

79.—(1) Paragraphs 7, 8, 52, 54, 56 and 66 above shall come into force at the expiry of the period of 2 months beginning on the day this Act is passed.

(2) Paragraphs 49(3), 60 and 63 above shall come into force on such day as the Secretary of State may by order made by statutory instrument appoint; and

(a) different days may be so appointed for different provisions or for different purposes;

(b) section 195(3) of this Act shall apply to an order under this sub-paragraph as it applies to an order under section 195(2).

(3) The 1988 Act shall be treated as having been enacted with the amendments made by this Schedule, except in so far as the amendments are made by paragraph 12, 57, or 68 above or any of the paragraphs mentioned in sub-paragraph (1) or (2) above.

80. In this Schedule "the 1988 Act" means the Local Government Finance Act 1988.

1988 c. 41.

SCHEDULE 6

AMENDMENT OF SCOTTISH ENACTMENTS

Valuation appeals to Lands Tribunal for Scotland

1949 c. 42.   1. In section 1 of the Lands Tribunal Act 1949 (which provides as to, amongst other things, the jurisdiction of the Lands Tribunal for Scotland) after subsection (3B) there shall be inserted the following subsection—

"(3BA) The Lands Tribunal for Scotland may also determine any appeal against the decision of a valuation appeal committee not to refer to the Tribunal any appeal or complaint made to the committee and, where the Tribunal upholds such an appeal, the appeal or complaint made to the committee shall, for the purposes of this section, be regarded as having been referred by the committee to the Tribunal for determination under subsection (3A) above."

1963 c. 12.   2. In section 15 of the Local Government (Financial Provisions) (Scotland) Act 1963—

(a) after subsection (2) there shall be inserted the following subsection—

"(2AA) A valuation appeal committee, on the joint application of the assessor and an appellant or complainer made within such period as may be prescribed by regulations made by the Secretary of State, shall refer the appeal or complaint to the Lands Tribunal for Scotland for determination under section 1(3A) of the Lands Tribunal Act 1949."; and

(b) in subsection (2A) (regulations about valuation appeals to the Lands Tribunal for Scotland)—

(i) for the word "governing" there shall be substituted the words "as to";

(ii) the word "and" between paragraphs (a) and (b) shall be omitted; and

(iii) at the end there shall be added the following paragraphs—

"(c) the giving by a valuation appeal committee of reasons for its decision not to refer to the Tribunal any appeal or complaint made to the committee; and

(d) the circumstances and manner in which an appeal may be made to the Tribunal for determination under subsection (3BA) of section 1 of the Lands Tribunal Act 1949 (jurisdiction of the Tribunal to determine appeal against decision of valuation appeal committee not to refer an appeal or complaint to the Tribunal)."

Rateable value of certain buildings used for breeding or rearing horses

1956 c. 60.   3. In subsection (1) of section 6 of the Valuation and Rating (Scotland) Act 1956 (ascertainment of annual and rateable values) for the words "the next following section" there shall be substituted the words "sections 7 to 7B".

4. In that Act the following section shall be inserted after section 7A—

"Rateable value of certain buildings used for breeding or rearing horses.

7B.—(1) This section applies to any lands and heritages the whole or any part of which consists of buildings which are—

(a) used for the breeding and rearing of horses or for either of those purposes; and

(b) occupied together with any agricultural land or agricultural building.

(2) The rateable value of any lands and heritages to which this section applies shall be taken to be the amount determined under section 6 of this Act less whichever is the smaller of the following amounts—

   (a) such amount as the Secretary of State may by order specify for the purposes of this section;

   (b) the amount which but for this section would be determined under that section in respect of so much of the lands and heritages as consists of buildings so used and occupied.

(3) An order under subsection (2) of this section shall be made by statutory instrument which shall be subject to annulment in pursuance of a resolution of either House of Parliament.

(4) In this section—

"agricultural land" means any land of more than two hectares which is agricultural lands and heritages within the meaning of subsection (2) of section 7 of this Act and is not land used exclusively for the pasturing of horses;

   "agricultural building" has the same meaning as in that subsection; and

   "horses" has the same meaning as in section 6(4) of the Riding Establishments Act 1964."

Application of regulations about determination of net annual value

5. In section 6 of the Valuation and Rating (Scotland) Act 1956, after subsection (8B) (further provision as to regulations relating to determination of net annual value) there shall be inserted the following subsections—   1956 c. 60.

   "(8C) For the purposes of subsection (8B) above, cases may be defined, described or classified by reference to such factors as the Secretary of State thinks fit.

   (8D) Without prejudice to the generality of subsection (8C) above, a case may be defined, described or classified by reference to one or more of the following factors—

   (a) the physical characteristics of lands and heritages;

   (b) the fact that lands and heritages are unoccupied or are occupied for purposes prescribed by the regulations or by persons of descriptions so prescribed."

Rateable value for purposes of levying rates after 1st April 1990

6. In section 7 of the Local Government (Scotland) Act 1975 (levying of rates) in subsection (1A) there shall be inserted at the end the words "; and references in this subsection to an apportioned value of part residential subjects are references to that part of that value which is shown in the apportionment note as relating to the non-residential use of the subjects,".   1975 c. 30.

7. In section 128 of the Local Government Finance Act 1988 (levying of rates after 1st April 1990)—   1988 c. 41.

   (a) in subsection (1)—

      (i) for the word "Every" there shall be inserted the words "The non-domestic"; and

      (ii) after the word "regards" there shall be inserted the words "different areas and";

   (b) after that subsection there shall be inserted the following subsections—

"(1A) The considerations referred to in paragraph (b) of subsection (1) above shall be such as the Secretary of State thinks fit and may, without prejudice to that generality, include considerations which otherwise would not relate to the determination of the rateable value of lands and heritages.

(1B) The classification of lands and heritages for the purposes of subsection (1) above shall be by reference to such factors as the Secretary of State thinks fit and may, without prejudice to that generality, include the circumstances of persons by whom rates are payable.

(1C) Regulations made under this section may, in relation to lands and heritages which are part residential subjects (within the meaning of the Abolition of Domestic Rates Etc. (Scotland) Act 1987), provide for the apportionment of the rateable value prescribed or determined under this section in respect of the subjects as between the residential and non-residential use of the subjects.

(1D) A rateable value prescribed or determined under this section in respect of any lands and heritages shall be the rateable value of the lands and heritages for the purpose of the levying of the non-domestic rate but not for any other purposes."; and

(c) subsection (3) shall cease to have effect.

Exemption of church premises from the non-domestic rate

1956 c. 60.   8.—(1) In section 22 of the Valuation and Rating (Scotland) Act 1956 (exemption of churches etc. from rates)—

(a) for subsection (1) there shall be substituted the following subsections—

"(1) No non-domestic rate shall be levied on any premises to the extent that they consist of—

(a) a building occupied by a religious body and used for the purpose of religious worship;

(b) a church hall, chapel hall or similar premises used in connection with a building such as is referred to in paragraph (a) above for the purposes of the religious body which occupies that building; or

(c) any premises occupied by a religious body and used by it for carrying out administrative or other activities relating to the organisation of the conduct of religious worship in a building such as is referred to in paragraph (a) above.

(1A) Subsection (1) above shall have effect with respect to the year 1990-91 and each subsequent year.

(1B) Subsection (1)(c) above shall have effect also with respect to the year 1989-90."; and

(b) subsection (4) shall be omitted.

1962 c. 9.   (2) In subsection (9) of section 4 of the Local Government (Financial Provisions etc.) (Scotland) Act 1962 (exception from relief under that section of premises exempt under said section 22), after "(b)" there shall be inserted "or (c)".

(3) The amendment made by sub-paragraph (1) above, to the extent necessary to give effect to subsection (1)(c) of the said section 22, and the amendment made by sub-paragraph (2) above shall be deemed to have come into force on 1st April 1989.

9. In the Local Government (Financial Provisions etc.) (Scotland) Act 1962—   1962 c. 9.

    (a) in section 4, subsections (3) and (4), and

    (b) the first Schedule,

shall be omitted.

Duty to notify registration officer about liability for collective community charge

10. In subsection (1) of section 18 of the Abolition of Domestic Rates Etc.   1987 c. 47.
(Scotland) Act 1987 (duty to notify registration officer of certain matters) for the
words "the personal or standard community charge" there shall be substituted
the words "any of the community charges".

Interest not payable on backdated liability for community charges where there is
reasonable excuse for non-registration

11.—(1) In subsection (3)(a) of section 18 of the Abolition of Domestic Rates
Etc. (Scotland) Act 1987 (interest of backdated liability for community charges)
after the words "together with" there shall be inserted the words ", unless he
satisfies the levying authority that he has a reasonable excuse for not having been
registered,".

(2) The amendment made by sub-paragraph (1) above shall be deemed to have
come into force at the same time as the said section 18.

Exemption from personal community charge

12. In paragraph 4 of Schedule 1A to the Abolition of Domestic Rates Etc.
(Scotland) Act 1987 (exemption of the severely mentally impaired) there shall be
added at the end the following sub-paragraphs—

    "(6) Regulations under sub-paragraph (5) above may provide that, in
the circumstances set out in the regulations, a certificate given for the
purposes of sub-paragraph (1)(c) above shall continue to have effect for the
purposes of this paragraph notwithstanding that the definition of severe
mental impairment upon which the certificate proceeds has been
substituted by the regulations.

    (7) Regulations under sub-paragraph (5) above made in respect of the
financial year 1989-90 may provide that a person—

        (a) who was not within the old definition of severely mentally impaired
but who, being within the new definition of that expression, is
exempt; and

        (b) in respect of whom such conditions as are prescribed are fulfilled

may be treated as having been exempt as from such date prior to the coming
into force of the regulations as may be provided for in the regulations.

    (8) In sub-paragraph (7) above, the "old" definition is the definition in
force immediately before the coming into force of regulations under sub-
paragraph (5) above and the "new" definition is the definition being
substituted for the old definition by regulations under that sub-
paragraph."

13. For paragraph 5 of Schedule 1A to the Abolition of Domestic Rates Etc.
(Scotland) Act 1987 (exemption of person in respect of whom another is entitled
to child benefit) there shall be substituted the following paragraph—

    "5. A person is exempt if—

        (a) another person is entitled to child benefit in respect of him; or

        (b) a person would be entitled to child benefit in respect of him but for
paragraph 1(b) or (c) of Schedule 1 to the Child Benefit Act
1975."

14. After paragraph 6 of Schedule 1A to the Abolition of Domestic Rates Etc. (Scotland) Act 1987 there shall be inserted the following paragraph—

"6A.—(1) A person is exempt if—

(a) he is aged under 20;

(b) he is undertaking a qualifying course of education; and

(c) the course is not undertaken in consequence of an office or employment held by the person.

(2) For the purposes of this paragraph, a person shall be treated as undertaking a qualifying course of education if (and only if) he fulfils such conditions as may be prescribed."

15. In paragraph 12(c) of Schedule 1A to the Abolition of Domestic Rates Etc. (Scotland) Act 1987 (exemption for persons residing in premises subject to non-domestic rates) there shall be added at the end "but are not part residential subjects".

Liability for non-domestic water rate

16.—(1) In section 40(3) of the Water (Scotland) Act 1980 (which provides as to who is liable for the non-domestic water rate) there shall be inserted at the end the words "or who would be liable to pay those non-domestic rates but for any enactment which exempts the lands and heritages from those rates or by or under which any relief or remission from liability for those rates is given".

(2) The amendment made by sub-paragraph (1) above shall be deemed to have come into force at the same time as paragraph 29 of Schedule 5 to the Abolition of Domestic Rates Etc. (Scotland) Act 1987.

Premises in respect of which non-domestic water rate is leviable

17.—(1) In section 41 of the Water (Scotland) Act 1980 (levy of non-domestic water rate on certain premises)—

(a) in the proviso to subsection (1) (rate to be levied on one half of rateable value or lower fraction resolved by water authority)—

(i) after the word "aforesaid" there shall be inserted the words "or to any class of such premises"; and

(ii) after the words "those premises" there shall be inserted the words "or, as the case may be, to premises in that class"; and

(b) in subsection (4) (premises subject to the rate) after the words "other premises" there shall be inserted the words "of whatsoever kind but".

(2) The amendments made by sub-paragraph (1) above shall be deemed always to have been in force.

Exemption of formula valued premises from non-domestic water rate

18. In section 6 of the Local Government (Scotland) Act 1975 (valuation by formula of certain lands and heritages) after subsection (1) there shall be inserted the following subsection—

"(1A) The Secretary of State may by order provide that the non-domestic water rate shall not be leviable in respect of formula valued lands and heritages or of such formula valued lands and heritages or of such class or description of formula valued lands and heritages as may be prescribed for the purposes of this subsection.

In this subsection, "formula valued lands and heritages" are lands and heritages which have, or lands and heritages of a class or description which has, been prescribed for the purposes of subsection (1) above."

19. In section 40 of the Water (Scotland) Act 1980 (non-domestic water rate)—

    (a) in subsection (1), after the word "Act" there shall be inserted the words "and section 6(1A) of the Local Government (Scotland) Act 1975 (exemption of formula valued premises from non-domestic water rate)";

    (b) subsection (7) shall be omitted.

Liability for non-domestic sewerage rate

20.—(1) In paragraph 20 of Schedule 5 to the Abolition of Domestic Rates Etc. (Scotland) Act 1987 (liability for non-domestic sewerage rate) there shall be added at the end the words "or who would be liable to pay the non-domestic rate but for any enactment which exempts those premises from that rate or by or under which relief or remission from liability for that rate is given."

(2) The amendment made by sub-paragraph (1) above shall be deemed to have come into force at the same time as the said paragraph 20.

Reduced liability for non-domestic sewerage rate in respect of certain church and charity premises

21.—(1) In Schedule 5 to the Abolition of Domestic Rates Etc. (Scotland) Act 1987—

    (a) in paragraph 19 (which provides as to, amongst other things, the levying of the non-domestic sewerage rate), for the word "paragraph" there shall be inserted the words "paragraphs 19A and"; and

    (b) after paragraph 19 there shall be inserted the following paragraph—

        "19A.—(1) Where, in respect of a financial year, the non-domestic sewerage rate is leviable under paragraph 19 above in respect of lands and heritages which are both—

        (a) church or charity premises; and

        (b) premises to which, by virtue of subsection (4) of section 41 of the Water (Scotland) Act 1980, that section applies, whether or not they are premises in respect of which the non-domestic water rate is leviable,

        the non-domestic sewerage rate shall be levied not according to the rateable value of those lands and heritages or that part thereof which is shown in the apportionment note as relating to their non-residential use but instead in accordance with sub-paragraph (2) below.

        (2) Where—

        (a) the water authority, in a resolution under subsection (1) of the said section 41, made with respect to the lands and heritages mentioned in sub-paragraph (1) above or to a class of premises which includes those lands and heritages, have specified for the purposes of that subsection in respect of that year a fraction of net annual value smaller than one half, then the non-domestic sewerage rate shall be levied according to that smaller fraction of the rateable value of those lands and heritages or, as the case may be, that part thereof; and

        (b) the water authority have not so specified a smaller fraction, then the non-domestic sewerage rate shall be levied according to one half of the rateable value of those lands and heritages or, as the case may be, that part thereof.

        (3) In sub-paragraph (1) above "church or charity premises" means—

SCH. 6
(a) premises, to the extent to which, under section 22(1) of the Valuation and Rating (Scotland) Act 1956 (exemption from non-domestic rates of church premises etc.), no non-domestic rate is leviable on them in respect of the financial year; or

(b) lands and heritages in respect of which relief in respect of the non-domestic rate is given in respect of the financial year under subsection (2) of section 4 of the Local Government (Financial Provisions etc.) (Scotland) Act 1962 (relief for premises occupied by charities); or

(c) lands and heritages in respect of which a reduction of or remission from the non-domestic rate has effect in respect of the financial year under subsection (5) of the said section 4."

(2) The amendments made by sub-paragraph (1) above shall be deemed to have come into force at the same time as the said paragraph 19.

Public inspection of community charges register

1987 c. 47.   22. In section 20(2)(a)(ii) of the Abolition of Domestic Rates Etc. (Scotland) Act 1987 after "premises", where secondly occurring, there shall be inserted "or the sex of that person".

Exclusion from voting disability of local authority members who are community charge payers

1973 c. 65.   23.—(1) In section 41(4) of the Local Government (Scotland) Act 1973 (exclusion from voting disability) after the word "as", where first occurring, there shall be inserted the words "a person who is liable to pay any of the community charges or community water charges imposed under the Abolition of Domestic Rates Etc. (Scotland) Act 1987 or who would be so liable but for any enactment or anything provided or done under any enactment or as".

(2) The amendment made by sub-paragraph (1) above shall be deemed to have come into force at the same time as sections 8 to 11 of the Abolition of Domestic Rates Etc. (Scotland) Act 1987.

Revocation of civil penalties imposed by registration officer

24.—(1) In section 17 of the Abolition of Domestic Rates Etc. (Scotland) Act 1987 (which provides for, amongst other things, the imposition of civil penalties) after subsection (11) there shall be inserted the following subsection—

"(11A) If, after the imposition of a civil penalty under subsection (10) or (11) above but before the making of any appeal under subsection (12) below against that imposition, the registration officer, in the light of information which he did not consider when imposing the penalty—

(a) is no longer satisfied as to the matter as to which he was satisfied under paragraph (a) or (b) of subsection (10) above or paragraph (c) of subsection (11) above before imposing the penalty; or

(b) is satisfied that the responsible person upon whom the penalty was imposed did have a reasonable excuse,

he may revoke the imposition of the penalty; and on such revocation any money paid to the regional or islands council by the responsible person by way of that penalty shall be repaid by them to him."

(2) The amendment made by sub-paragraph (1) above shall be deemed to have come into force at the same time as the said section 17.

Evidence in appeals under Abolition of Domestic Rates Etc. (Scotland) Act 1987

25. In section 29 of the Abolition of Domestic Rates Etc. (Scotland) Act 1987 (appeals) after subsection (1) there shall be inserted the following subsection— 1987 c. 47.

"(1A) The sheriff may, in considering an appeal under this Act, hear and receive evidence.

This subsection is without prejudice to—

(a) any other enactment, or

(b) any rule of law,

relating to the hearing or receiving of evidence in summary applications."

No liability for community water charges where water previously supplied free

26.—(1) In paragraph 8 of Schedule 5 to the Abolition of Domestic Rates Etc. (Scotland) Act 1987 (qualifying conditions for liability to pay community water charges) there shall be added at the end "and

(c) that the supply of water provided is not one which the water authority were, immediately before 16 May 1949, and continue to be under an obligation to provide free of charge."

(2) The amendment made by sub-paragraph (1) above shall be deemed to have come into force at the same time as the said paragraph 8.

Provision of information by registration officer

27. The following section shall be inserted after section 20B of the Abolition of Domestic Rates Etc. (Scotland) Act 1987—

"Registration officer: provision of information to Secretary of State.

20C.—(1) Subsection (2) below applies where—

(a) the Secretary of State serves a notice on the registration officer requiring him to supply to the Secretary of State information specified in the notice;

(b) the information is in the possession or control of the registration officer and was obtained by him for the purpose of carrying out his functions under this Act; and

(c) the information is not personal information.

(2) The registration officer shall supply the information required, and shall do so in such form and manner and at such time as the Secretary of State specifies in the notice.

(3) Regulations under this section may include provision that the registration officer may—

(a) supply relevant information to any person who requests it;

(b) charge a prescribed fee for supplying the information.

(4) Information is relevant information if—

(a) it was obtained by the registration officer for the purpose of carrying out his functions under this Act; and

(b) it is not personal information.

(5) Personal information is information which relates to an individual (living or dead) who can be identified from that information or from that and other information supplied to any person by the registration officer; and personal information

Sch. 6

includes any expression of opinion about the individual and any indication of the intentions of any person in respect of the individual."

Revenue support grants

1987 c. 47.

28. In section 23(2) of the Abolition of Domestic Rates Etc. (Scotland) Act 1987, for the words from "a" onward there shall be substituted the words "grants (to be known as "revenue support grants") to local authorities".

29. For paragraphs 1 to 3 of Schedule 4 to that Act (revenue support grants) there shall be substituted the following paragraphs—

"1.—(1) The local authorities to which revenue support grant is payable in respect of a financial year shall be such local authorities as are specified by order made by the Secretary of State.

(2) The amount of revenue support grant payable in respect of a financial year to a local authority so specified shall be such amount as is determined in relation to the local authority by order made by the Secretary of State.

(3) The Secretary of State may at any time by order amend or revoke any order made under this paragraph and any amount of revenue support grant which has been paid and which, in consequence of anything done under this paragraph, falls to be repaid may be recovered by the Secretary of State whenever and however he thinks fit.

2.—(1) An order under paragraph 1 above shall be made only with the consent of the Treasury.

(2) Before making an order under paragraph 1 above the Secretary of State shall consult such associations of local authorities as appear to him to be appropriate.

(3) An order under paragraph 1 above together with a report of the considerations which led to its provisions shall be laid before the Commons House of Parliament but shall have no effect until approved by a resolution of that House."

Section 149.

SCHEDULE 7

Compensation Provisions of Landlord and Tenant Act 1954, Part II

1954 c. 56.

1. Any reference in this Schedule to a section which is not otherwise identified is a reference to that section of the Landlord and Tenant Act 1954, Part II of which relates to security of tenure for business, professional and other tenants.

2.—(1) Subject to the following provisions of this Schedule, section 37 (compensation where order for new tenancy precluded on certain grounds) shall have effect with the amendments set out below.

(2) At the beginning of subsection (2) there shall be inserted the words "Subject to subsections (5A) to (5D) of this section".

(3) After subsection (5) there shall be inserted the following subsections—

"(5A) If part of the holding is domestic property, as defined in section 66 of the Local Government Finance Act 1988,—

(a) the domestic property shall be disregarded in determining the rateable value of the holding under subsection (5) of this section; and

(b) if, on the date specified in subsection (5)(a) of this section, the tenant occupied the whole or any part of the domestic property, the amount of compensation to which he is entitled under subsection (1) of this section shall be increased by the addition of a sum equal to his reasonable expenses in removing from the domestic property.

(5B) Any question as to the amount of the sum referred to in paragraph (b) of subsection (5A) of this section shall be determined by agreement between the landlord and the tenant or, in default of agreement, by the court.

(5C) If the whole of the holding is domestic property, as defined in section 66 of the Local Government Finance Act 1988, for the purposes of subsection (2) of this section the rateable value of the holding shall be taken to be an amount equal to the rent at which it is estimated the holding might reasonably be expected to let from year to year if the tenant undertook to pay all usual tenant's rates and taxes and to bear the cost of the repairs and insurance and the other expenses (if any) necessary to maintain the holding in a state to command that rent.

(5D) The following provisions shall have effect as regards a determination of an amount mentioned in subsection (5C) of this section—

    (a) the date by reference to which such a determination is to be made is the date on which the landlord's notice under section 25 or, as the case may be, subsection (6) of section 26 of this Act is given;

    (b) any dispute arising, whether in proceedings before the court or otherwise, as to such a determination shall be referred to the Commissioners of Inland Revenue for decision by a valuation officer;

    (c) an appeal shall lie to the Lands Tribunal from such a decision but, subject to that, such a decision shall be final."

(4) At the end of subsection (8) (definition of "the appropriate multiplier") there shall be added the words "and different multipliers may be so prescribed in relation to different cases".

3. The amendments made by paragraph 2 above do not have effect unless the date which, apart from paragraph 4 below, is relevant for determining the rateable value of the holding under subsection (5) of section 37 is on or after 1st April 1990.

4.—(1) Subject to paragraph 3 above and paragraph 5 below, in any case where—

    (a) the tenancy concerned was entered into before 1st April 1990 or was entered into on or after that date in pursuance of a contract made before that date, and

    (b) the landlord's notice under section 25 or, as the case may be, section 26(6) is given before 1st April 2000, and

    (c) within the period referred to in section 29(3) for the making of an application under section 24(1), the tenant gives notice to the landlord that he wants the special basis of compensation provided for by this paragraph,

the amendments made by paragraph 2 above shall not have effect and section 37 shall, instead, have effect with the modification specified in sub-paragraph (2) below.

(2) The modification referred to in sub-paragraph (1) above is that the date which is relevant for the purposes of determining the rateable value of the holding under subsection (5) of section 37 shall be 31st March 1990 instead of the date on which the landlord's notice is given.

5. In any case where—

    (a) paragraph 4(1)(a) above applies, and

(b) on 31st March 1990, the rateable value of the holding could be determined only in accordance with paragraph (c) of subsection (5) of section 37,

no notice may be given under paragraph 4(1)(b) above.

Section 160.

SCHEDULE 8

WELSH LANGUAGE NAMES FOR LOCAL AUTHORITIES

1972 c. 70.

1. Any reference in the following provisions of this Schedule to a section is a reference to that section of the Local Government Act 1972.

2.—(1) In section 21 (constitution of principal councils in Wales) in subsection (3) after the words "body corporate" there shall be inserted "and, subject to subsection (4) below, shall be known".

(2) After subsection (3) of that section there shall be inserted the following subsections—

"(4) If and so long as this subsection is in force in relation to a principal council, subsection (3) above shall have effect in relation to that council as if for the words "The County Council" there were substituted "Cyngor Sir" or, as the case may be, as if for the words "The District Council" there were substituted "Cyngor Dosbarth".

(5) Subsection (4) above shall come into force in relation to a principal council three months after the day on which, at a specially convened meeting of the council, it is resolved by a two-thirds majority of the members present and voting that the Welsh language form of the council's description shall be used; and that subsection shall cease to be in force in relation to a principal council three months after the day on which, at a specially convened meeting of the council, it is resolved by a similar majority that the Welsh language form of the council's description shall cease to be used."

3.—(1) In section 33 (constitution and powers of community council) in subsection (2) for the words "body corporate" there shall be inserted "and, subject to subsection (2A) below, shall be known".

(2) After subsection (2) of that section there shall be inserted the following subsections—

"(2A) If and so long as this subsection is in force in relation to a community council, subsection (2) above shall have effect in relation to that council as if for the words "The Community Council" there were substituted "Cyngor Cymuned".

(2B) Subsection (2A) above shall come into force in relation to a community council three months after the day on which, at a specially convened meeting of the council, it is resolved by a two-thirds majority of the members present and voting that the Welsh language form of the council's description shall be used; and that subsection shall cease to be in force in relation to a community council three months after the day on which, at a specially convened meeting of the council, it is resolved by a similar majority that the Welsh language form of the council's description shall cease to be used."

4. In section 74 (change of name of county, district etc.) in subsection (3) (notice of change of name) and in subsection (4) (change not to affect rights, liabilities etc.) after the words "this section", in each case, there shall be inserted "or by virtue of a resolution under section 21(5) above".

5. In section 76 (change of name of community) in subsection (2) (notice of change of name) and in subsection (3) (change not to affect rights, liabilities etc.) after the words "this section", in each case, there shall be inserted "or by virtue of a resolution under section 33(2B) above".

6. After section 245 (status of certain districts, parishes and communities) there shall be inserted the following section—

"Power for borough and town councils in Wales to adopt Welsh language form of their descriptions, etc.

245A.—(1) If and so long as this subsection is in force in relation to a district in Wales which, by virtue of section 245(1) above, has the status of a borough or for which, by virtue of section 245(4) above, the style of borough may be used—

    (a) the council shall bear the name "Cyngor Bwrdeistref" instead of "Council of the Borough" or "Borough Council";

    (b) the chairman of the council shall be entitled to the style "maer" instead of "mayor"; and

    (c) the vice-chairman of the council shall be entitled to the style "dirprwy faer" instead of "deputy mayor".

(2) Subject to subsection (3) below, subsection (1) above shall come into force in relation to a district which has the status of a borough, or for which the style of borough may be used, three months after the day on which, at a specially convened meeting of the council, it is resolved by a two-thirds majority of the members present and voting that the Welsh language form of the council's description shall be used.

(3) A resolution under subsection (2) above may be passed by the council of a district in Wales notwithstanding that, at the time it is passed, the council does not have the status of a borough; but, if a resolution is passed at such a time, subsection (1) above shall not come into force unless, nor earlier than, the status of a borough is conferred on the district by virtue of section 245(1) above.

(4) Subsection (1) above shall cease to be in force in relation to a district which has the status of a borough, or for which the style of borough may be used, three months after the day on which, at a specially convened meeting of the council, it is resolved by a two-thirds majority of the members present and voting that the Welsh language form of the council's description shall cease to be used.

(5) If and so long as this subsection is in force in relation to a community which, by virtue of section 245(6) above, has the status of a town—

    (a) the council shall bear the name "Cyngor Tref" instead of "council of the town" or "town council";

    (b) the chairman of the council shall be entitled to the style "maer y dref" instead of "town mayor"; and

    (c) the vice-chairman of the council shall be entitled to the style "dirprwy faer y dref" instead of "deputy town mayor".

(6) Subsection (5) above shall come into force in relation to a community which has the status of a town three months after the day on which, at a specially convened meeting of the council, it is resolved by a two-thirds majority of the members present and voting that the Welsh language form of the council's description shall be used.

(7) Subsection (5) above shall cease to be in force in relation to a community which has the status of a town three months after the day on which, at a specially convened meeting of the council, it is resolved by a two-thirds majority of the members present and voting that the Welsh language form of the council's description shall cease to be used.

(8) Subsection (10) of section 245 above has effect in relation to this section as it has effect in relation to the foregoing provisions of that section."

Section 165.

SCHEDULE 9

AMENDMENTS OF PARTS VI, IX, XI, XVII AND XVIII OF THE HOUSING ACT 1985

PART I

AMENDMENTS OF PART VI

1.—(1) In section 189 (repair notice in respect of unfit house), in subsection (1), after the words "dwelling-house", in the first two places where they occur, there shall be inserted "or house in multiple occupation" and for the words from "unless they are satisfied" onwards there shall be substituted "if they are satisfied, in accordance with section 604A, that serving a notice under this subsection is the most satisfactory course of action".

(2) In subsection (1A) of that section—

(a) for the words "a dwelling-house which is a flat" there shall be substituted "either a dwelling-house which is a flat or a flat in multiple occupation";

(b) for the words from "by reason" to "outside the flat" there shall be substituted "by virtue of section 604(2)"; and

(c) for the words from "that part of the building" onwards there shall be substituted "the part of the building in question if they are satisfied, in accordance with section 604A, that serving a notice under this subsection is the most satisfactory course of action".

(3) After subsection (1A) there shall be inserted the following subsection—

"(1B) In the case of a house in multiple occupation, a repair notice may be served on the person managing the house instead of on the person having control; and where a notice is so served, then, subject to section 191, the person managing the house shall be regarded as the person having control of it for the purposes of the provisions of this Part following that section."

(4) In subsection (2) of that section, in paragraph (a) after the words "works specified in the notice" there shall be inserted "(which may be works of repair or improvement or both)" and for the words "seventh day after the notice becomes operative" there shall be substituted "twenty-eighth day after the notice is served", and in paragraph (b) after the words "dwelling-house" there shall be inserted "or, as the case may be, house in multiple occupation".

(5) In subsection (3) of that section—

(a) after the words "serving the notice" there shall be inserted "(a)";

(b) after the words "building concerned" there shall be inserted "or

(b) on the person having control of or, as the case may be, on the person managing the house in multiple occupation which is concerned"; and

(c) in the words following paragraph (b), as set out above, for the words "or part of the building" there shall be substituted "part of the building or house".

(6) After subsection (5) there shall be added the following subsection—

"(6) This section has effect subject to the provisions of section 190A."

2.—(1) In section 190 (repair notice in respect of house in state of disrepair but not unfit)—

   (a) at the beginning of each of subsections (1) and (1A) there shall be inserted the words "Subject to subsection (1B)";

   (b) in subsection (1), after the words "dwelling-house", in each place where they occur, there shall be inserted "or house in multiple occupation" and at the end of paragraph (b) of that subsection there shall be added "or, in the case of a house in multiple occupation, the persons occupying it (whether as tenants or licensees)"; and

   (c) in subsection (1A) after the words "a flat" there shall be inserted "including a flat in multiple occupation" and at the end of paragraph (b) of that subsection there shall be added "or, in the case of a flat in multiple occupation, the persons occupying it (whether as tenants or licensees)".

(2) After subsections (1A) there shall be inserted the following subsections—

"(1B) The authority may not serve a notice under subsection (1) or subsection (1A) unless—

   (a) there is an occupying tenant of the dwelling-house or flat concerned; or

   (b) the dwelling-house or building concerned falls within a renewal area within the meaning of Part VII of the Local Government and Housing Act 1989.

(1C) In the case of a house in multiple occupation, a notice under subsection (1) or subsection (1A) may be served on the person managing the house instead of on the person having control of it; and where a notice is so served, then, subject to section 191, the person managing the house shall be regarded as the person having control of it for the purposes of the provisions of this Part following that section."

(3) In subsection (2)(a) of that section for the words "seventh day after the notice becomes operative" there shall be substituted "twenty-eighth day after the notice is served".

(4) In subsection (3) of that section—

   (a) after the words "serving the notice" there shall be inserted "(a)";

   (b) after the words "building concerned" there shall be inserted "or

      (b) on the person having control of or, as the case may be, on the person managing the house in multiple occupation which is concerned"; and

   (c) in the words following paragraph (b), as set out above, for the words "or part of the building" there shall be substituted "part of the building or house".

3. After that section there shall be inserted the following section—

"Effect on section 189 of proposal to include premises in group repair scheme.

190A.—(1) A local housing authority shall not be under a duty to serve a repair notice under subsection (1) or, as the case may be, subsection (1A) of section 189 if, at the same time as they satisfy themselves as mentioned in the subsection in question, they determine—

     (a) that the premises concerned form part of a building which would be a qualifying building in relation to a group repair scheme; and

(b) that, within the period of twelve months beginning at that time, they expect to prepare a group repair scheme in respect of the qualifying building (in this section referred to as a "relevant scheme");

but where, having so determined, the authority do serve such a notice, they may do so with respect only to those works which, in their opinion, will not be carried out to the premises concerned in pursuance of the relevant scheme.

(2) Subject to subsection (3), subsection (1) shall apply in relation to the premises concerned from the time referred to in subsection (1) until the date on which the works specified in a relevant scheme are completed to the authority's satisfaction (as certified under section 130(1) of the Local Government and Housing Act 1989).

(3) Subsection (1) shall cease to have effect in relation to the premises concerned on the day when the first of the following events occurs, that is to say,—

(a) the local housing authority determine not to submit a relevant scheme to the Secretary of State for approval; or

(b) the expiry of the period referred to in subsection (1)(b) without either the approval of a relevant scheme within that period or the submission of a relevant scheme to the Secretary of State within that period; or

(c) the Secretary of State notifies the authority that he does not approve a relevant scheme; or

(d) the authority ascertain that a relevant scheme, as submitted or approved, will not, for whatever reason, involve the carrying out of any works to the premises concerned.

(4) In any case where, in accordance with subsection (1), the authority serve a repair notice under subsection (1) or, as the case may be, subsection (1A) of section 189 with respect only to certain of the works which would otherwise be specified in the notice, subsection (2)(b) of that section shall have effect with respect to the notice as if after the word "notice" there were inserted the words "when taken together with works proposed to be carried out under a group repair scheme".

(5) In this section and section 189 "group repair scheme" and "qualifying building" have the same meaning as in Part VIII of the Local Government and Housing Act 1989."

4.—(1) In section 191 (appeals against repair notices), in subsection (1A) after the words "dwelling-house" there shall be inserted "house in multiple occupation" and after that subsection there shall be inserted the following subsection—

"(1B) Without prejudice to the generality of subsection (1), it shall be a ground of appeal, in the case of a repair notice under section 189, that making a closing order under section 264 or a demolition order under section 265 is the most satisfactory course of action; and, where the grounds on which an appeal is brought are or include that specified in this subsection, the court, on the hearing of the appeal, shall have regard to any guidance given to the local housing authority under section 604A."

(2) In subsection (3) of that section the words "(repair notice in respect of unfit dwelling-house)" shall be omitted and for the words from "the judge shall" onwards there shall be substituted—

"and the reason or one of the reasons for allowing the appeal is that making a closing order under section 264 or a demolition order under section 265 is the most satisfactory course of action, the judge shall, if requested to do so by the appellant or the local housing authority, include in his judgement a finding to that effect".

(3) In subsection (3B) of that section after the words "dwelling-house", in both places where they occur, there shall be inserted "or house in multiple occupation".

5. After that section there shall inserted the following section—

"Execution of works by local housing authority by agreement
191A.—(1) The local housing authority may by agreement with the person having control of any premises execute at his expense any works which he is required to execute in respect of the premises in pursuance of a repair notice served under section 189 or section 190.

(2) For that purpose the authority shall have all such rights as that person would have against any occupying tenant of, and any other person having an interest in, the premises (or any part of the premises)."

6. Section 192 (power to purchase house found on appeal to be unfit and beyond repair at reasonable expense) shall cease to have effect.

7. In section 193 (power of local housing authority to execute works), in subsection (4) after the words "dwelling-house" there shall be inserted "house in multiple occupation" and for the words "in default of the person on whom the repair notice was served" there shall be substituted "in a case where the repair notice has not been complied with".

8.—(1) In section 197 (powers of entry), in subsection (1)—

(a) for the words "24 hours'" there shall be substituted "seven days'";

(b) at the end of paragraph (a) there shall be inserted "or"; and

(c) paragraph (c) and the word "or" immediately preceding it shall be omitted.

(2) At the end of subsection (2) of that section there shall be added the words "and shall, if so required, be produced for inspection by the occupier or anyone acting on his behalf".

9. In section 198 (penalty for obstruction), in subsection (1) after the word "offence" there shall be inserted "intentionally".

10. Section 205 (application of provisions to temporary or movable structures) shall cease to have effect.

11. Section 206 (repair at reasonable expense) shall cease to have effect.

12.—(1) In section 207 (minor definitions), in subsection (1) in the definition beginning "dwelling-house" after the word "flat", in the first place where it occurs, there shall be inserted "other than in the expression "flat in multiple occupation"" and after that definition there shall be inserted—

" "house in multiple occupation" and "flat in multiple occupation" have the same meaning as in Part XI".

(2) In that subsection for the definition beginning "occupying tenant" there shall be substituted—

" "occupying tenant", in relation to a dwelling-house, means a person (other than an owner-occupier) who—

(a) occupies or is entitled to occupy the dwelling-house as a lessee; or

(b) is a statutory tenant of the dwelling-house; or

SCH. 9

(c) occupies the dwelling-house as a residence under a restricted contract; or

(d) is a protected occupier, within the meaning of the Rent (Agriculture) Act 1976; or

(e) is a licensee under an assured agricultural occupancy;"

(3) In that subsection after the definition of "owner" there shall be inserted—

" "owner-occupier", in relation to a dwelling-house, means the person who, as owner or lessee under a long tenancy, within the meaning of Part I of the Leasehold Reform Act 1967, occupies or is entitled to occupy the dwelling-house;

"person managing" has the same meaning as in Part XI".

(4) In that subsection in the definition beginning "person having control" for the words "subject to section 191(3A)" there shall be substituted "subject to sections 189(1B), 190(1C) and 191" and in paragraph (a) after the words "dwelling-house" there shall be inserted "or house in multiple occupation".

(5) In that subsection in the definition beginning "premises" after the words "dwelling-house" there shall be inserted "house in multiple occupation".

(6) In subsection (2) of that section after the words "dwelling-house", in the first place where they occur, there shall be inserted "or house in multiple occupation".

13. In section 208 (index of defined expressions for Part VI)—

(a) the entries beginning "house" and "reasonable expense" shall be omitted;

(b) in the entry beginning "occupying tenant" for the words in the second column there shall be substituted "section 207"; and

(c) at the appropriate places in alphabetical order there shall be inserted the following entries—

"dwelling-house	sections 205 and 207"
"flat	section 207"
"house in multiple occupation (and flat in multiple occupation)	section 345"
"owner-occupier	section 207"
"person managing	section 398"
"premises	section 207"
"restricted contract	section 622"
"statutory tenant	section 622"

PART II

AMENDMENTS OF PART IX

14. For sections 264 (power to accept undertaking as to reconstruction or use of unfit house) and 265 (demolition or closing order to be made where no undertaking accepted or undertaking broken) there shall be substituted the following sections—

"Power to make closing order.

264.—(1) Where the local housing authority are satisfied that a dwelling-house or house in multiple occupation is unfit for human habitation and that, in accordance with section 604A, taking action under this subsection is the most satisfactory course of action, they shall make a closing order with respect to the dwelling-house or house in multiple occupation.

(2) Where the local housing authority are satisfied that, in a building containing one or more flats, some or all of the flats are unfit for human habitation and that, in accordance with section 604A, taking action under this subsection is the most satisfactory course of action, they shall make a closing order with respect to the whole or part of the building.

(3) In deciding for the purposes of subsection (2)—

    (a) whether to make a closing order with respect to the whole or part of the building; or

    (b) in respect of which part of the building to make a closing order;

the authority shall have regard to such guidance as may from time to time be given by the Secretary of State under section 604A.

(4) This section has effect subject to section 300(1) (power to purchase for temporary housing use houses liable to be demolished or closed).

Power to make demolition order.

265.—(1) Where the local housing authority are satisfied that—

    (a) a dwelling-house which is not a flat, or

    (b) a house in multiple occupation which is not a flat in multiple occupation,

is unfit for human habitation and that, in accordance with section 604A, taking action under this subsection is the most satisfactory course of action, they shall make a demolition order with respect to the dwelling-house or house concerned.

(2) Where the local housing authority are satisfied that, in a building containing one or more flats, some or all of the flats are unfit for human habitation and that, in accordance with section 604A, taking action under this subsection is the most satisfactory course of action, they shall make a demolition order with respect to the building.

(3) This section has effect subject to sections 300(1) (power to purchase for temporary housing use houses liable to be demolished or closed) and 304(1) (listed buildings and buildings protected by notice pending listing)."

15. Section 266 (power to make closing order as to part of building) shall cease to have effect.

16.—(1) In section 268 (service of notice of order), in subsection (1), paragraph (a) shall be omitted and in paragraph (b) the word "other" shall be omitted.

(2) After that subsection there shall be inserted the following subsection—

"(1A) Where the premises in respect of which a demolition or closing order is made is a building or part of a building containing flats, any reference in paragraphs (b) and (c) of subsection (1) to "the premises" includes a reference to the flats in the building or part of the building concerned."

17.—(1) In section 269 (right of appeal against order), in subsection (2) after the word "premises" there shall be inserted "or part of the premises".

(2) After that subsection there shall be inserted the following subsection—

"(2A) Without prejudice to the generality of subsection (1), it shall be a ground of appeal—

(a) in the case of a closing order, that serving a repair notice under section 189 or making a demolition order under section 265 is the most satisfactory course of action; and

(b) in the case of a demolition order, that serving a repair notice under section 189 or making a closing order under section 264 is the most satisfactory course of action;

and, where the grounds on which an appeal is brought are or include that specified in paragraph (a) or paragraph (b), the court, on hearing the appeal, shall have regard to any guidance given to the local housing authority under section 604A."

(3) In subsection (3) of that section, paragraph (b) and the word "and" immediately preceding it shall be omitted.

(4) After that subsection there shall be inserted the following subsection—

"(3A) Where an appeal is allowed against a closing or demolition order and the reason or one of the reasons for allowing the appeal is that specified in paragraph (a) or, as the case may be, paragraph (b) of subsection (2A), the judge shall, if requested to do so by the appellant or the local housing authority, include in his judgement a finding to that effect."

(5) Subsections (4) and (5) of that section shall cease to have effect.

18.—(1) In section 270 (demolition orders: recovery of possession of building to be demolished), in subsection (1)—

(a) after the word "operative" there shall be inserted "with respect to any premises";

(b) for the words from "the occupier" to "relates" there shall be substituted "any occupier of the premises or any part of the premises"; and

(c) in paragraphs (b) and (c) for the word "building" there shall be substituted "premises".

(2) In subsections (2), (3), (4) and (5) of that section—

(a) for the words "the building", in each place where they occur, there shall be substituted "the premises";

(b) for the word "it", in each place where it occurs, there shall be substituted "them"; and

(c) for the words "a building", in each place where they occur, there shall be substituted "any premises".

19. In section 273 (demolition orders: cleansing before demolition), in subsection (4) for the word "house" there shall be substituted "premises".

20.—(1) In section 274 (demolition orders: power to permit reconstruction of condemned house), in subsection (1) for the word "house", in each place where it occurs, there shall be substituted "premises".

(2) In subsection (2) of that section—

(a) for the word "houses" there shall be substituted "dwelling-houses or houses in multiple occupation";

(b) for the word "house" there shall be substituted "premises"; and

(c) for the word "it" there shall be substituted "them".

(3) In subsection (4) of that subsection—

(a) for the words "a house" there shall be substituted "any premises";

(b) for the word "it" there shall be substituted "them"; and

(c) for the words "the house" there shall be substituted "the premises or part of the premises".

21.—(1) In section 275 (demolition orders: substitution of closing order to permit use otherwise than for human habitation), in subsection (1)—

(a) for the words "a house" there shall be substituted "any premises"; and

(b) for the words "the house", in each place where they occur, there shall be substituted "the premises".

(2) In subsection (2) of that section, for the words following "on" there shall be substituted "every person on whom they would be required by section 268 to serve a copy of a closing order made under section 264".

22. In section 278 (closing orders: determination of order on premises being rendered fit), in subsection (1) for the words "premises", in the first place where they occur, there shall be substituted "dwelling-house, house in multiple occupation or, in the case of a building containing flats, the flats concerned".

23.—(1) In section 279 (closing orders: substitution of demolition order), in subsection (1) for the words "subsection (2)" there shall be substituted "subsections (2) and (2A)".

(2) In subsection (2) of that section the words "section 266 (parts of buildings and underground rooms)" shall be omitted.

(3) After that subsection there shall be inserted the following subsection—

"(2A) The power conferred by subsection (1) is not exercisable in relation to a closing order made under section 264(1) where the dwelling-house concerned is a flat or, as the case may be, where the house in multiple occupation is a flat in multiple occupation."

24. Sections 280, 281 and 282 (which relate to the closing etc. of underground rooms) shall cease to have effect.

25.—(1) In section 289 (declaration of clearance area), in subsection (2)—

(a) at the beginning there shall be inserted the words "Subject to subsections (2B) to (2F), (4) and (5B)";

(b) in paragraph (a) for the words "houses in the area" there shall be substituted "buildings in the area which are dwelling-houses or houses in multiple occupation or contain one or more flats (in this section referred to as "residential buildings")"; and

(c) in the words following paragraph (b) after the word "and" there shall be inserted "in accordance with subsection 604A" and for the words "method of dealing with the conditions in the area" there shall be substituted "course of action".

(2) After that subsection there shall be inserted the following subsections—

"(2A) A residential building containing one or more flats shall be treated for the purposes of this section as unfit for human habitation if some or all of the flats within it are unfit for human habitation.

(2B) Before declaring an area to be a clearance area, the authority shall—

(a) serve notice of their intention to include a building in the clearance area on every person who has an interest in the building (whether as freeholder, lessee or mortgagee) and also, in the case of a residential building, on every person who has such an interest in any flat in the building; and

(b) take reasonable steps to inform any occupiers of a residential building who do not have such an interest in the building or a flat in the building as is referred to in paragraph (a) of their intention to include the building in the clearance area; and

(c) publish in two or more newspapers circulating in the locality (of which one at least shall, if practicable, be a local newspaper) notice of their intention to declare the area to be a clearance area.

(2C) A notice served under paragraph (a) of subsection (2B) shall invite representations from the person on whom the notice was served within such reasonable period, being not less than twenty-eight days after the date on which the notice is served, as may be specified in the notice.

(2D) The authority shall, by the steps taken in relation to occupiers of a residential building as mentioned in paragraph (b) of subsection (2B), invite representations from those occupiers within such reasonable period, expiring not less than twenty-eight days after the date on which the steps are taken, as may be specified by the authority.

(2E) A notice published in accordance with paragraph (c) of subsection (2B) shall invite representations from any interested persons within such reasonable period, being not less than twenty-eight days after the date on which the notice is published, as may be specified in the notice.

(2F) The authority shall consider all representations made under subsections (2C), (2D) and (2E) and, in the light of the representations, shall take whichever of the following decisions they think appropriate, that is to say—

(a) they may decide to declare the area to be a clearance area; or

(b) they may decide to declare the area to be a clearance area but exclude such residential buildings which are unfit for human habitation as they think fit; or

(c) they may decide not to declare the area to be a clearance area."

(3) In subsection (3) of that section,—

(a) for the words "If the authority are so satisfied" there shall be substituted the words "Subject to subsection (5B), where the authority decide to declare an area to be a clearance area in accordance with paragraph (a) or paragraph (b) of subsection (2F)"; and

(b) in paragraph (a), for the words from "any building" onwards there shall be substituted—

"(i) any residential building which is not unfit for human habitation or dangerous or injurious to health;

(ii) any other building which is not dangerous or injurious to health; and

(iii) any residential buildings which, by virtue of subsection (2F)(b), they have decided to exclude from the area; and".

(4) After subsection (5) there shall be inserted the following subsections—

"(5A) Where a residential building which is unfit for human habitation is not included within a clearance area, whether by virtue of paragraph (b) or paragraph (c) of subsection (2F), the authority shall forthwith, in accordance with section 604A (disregarding guidance under that section in respect of this section), take action in respect of the building (and any flat contained within it) under whichever of sections 189, 264 and 265 it considers to be the most satisfactory course of action.

(5B) Subject to section 578A, a clearance area may not include any parcel of land which is not contiguous with another parcel of land within the area; and, where the effect of subsection (3) would otherwise be that a clearance area would comprise two or more separate and distinct areas, paragraph (b) of that subsection shall have effect as if for the words "pass a resolution declaring the area so defined" there were substituted "if the effect of paragraph (a) would otherwise be that the area would comprise two or more separate and distinct areas, pass a separate resolution in respect of each of those areas declaring each of them".

26. In section 291 (method of dealing with land acquired for clearance), in subsection (3) the words "Schedule 11 (rehabilitation orders)" shall be omitted.

27.—(1) In section 294 (extinguishment of public rights of way over land acquired), at the end of subsection (1) there shall be added the words "as from such date as the Secretary of State in approving the order may direct".

(2) In subsection (2) of that section for the words from "they may make" onwards there shall be substituted "an order made by the authority in advance of the purchase and approved by the Secretary of State (whether before or after the purchase) shall extinguish that right as from such date as the Secretary of State in approving the order may direct".

(3) In subsection (3) of that section—

(a) for the word "six" there shall be substituted "four"; and

(b) after the word "publication" there shall be inserted "then, subject to subsection (4)".

(4) After that subsection there shall be inserted the following subsection—

"(4) The Secretary of State may dispense with such an inquiry as is referred to in subsection (3) if he is satisfied that in the special circumstances of the case the holding of such an inquiry is unnecessary."

28. Section 299 and Schedule 11 (rehabilitation orders in respect of houses in clearance areas) shall cease to have effect.

29.—(1) In section 300 (purchase of houses liable to be demolished or closed), in subsection (1)—

(a) after the word "under" there shall be inserted "section 264 or";

(b) for the word "house", in the first place where it occurs, there shall be substituted "dwelling-house (not being a flat), a house in multiple occupation (not being a flat in multiple occupation) or the whole of a building"; and

(c) for the word "house", in the second place where it occurs, there shall be substituted "dwelling-house, house in multiple occupation or, as the case may be, building".

(2) In subsection (2) of that section—

(a) for the words "a house" there shall be substituted "any premises"; and

(b) in paragraph (b) for "269" there shall be substituted "269(1), (2), (3) and (6)".

(3) In subsection (3) of that section for the word "house" there shall be substituted "dwelling-house, house in multiple occupation or building".

30.—(1) In section 301 (retention of houses acquired for clearance), in subsection (1) for the word "houses", in each place where it occurs, there shall be substituted "residential buildings".

(2) In subsection (2) of that section for the word "house", in each place where it occurs, there shall be substituted "residential building".

(3) In subsection (3) of that section for the word "houses", in each place where it occurs, there shall be substituted "residential buildings".

(4) After that subsection there shall be inserted the following subsection—

"(4) In this section and section 302 "residential building" has the same meaning as it has in section 289."

31. In section 302 (management and repair of house acquired under s. 300 or retained under s. 301)—

(a) for the word "house", in each place where it occurs except in paragraph (c), there shall be substituted "residential building"; and

(b) in paragraph (c) for the word "house" there shall be substituted "residential building or any flat in the building".

32.—(1) In section 304 (closing order to be in respect of listed building), in subsection (1)—

(a) for the words from "(unfit" to "cost)" there shall be substituted "(power to make demolition order)"; and

(b) for the words "that section" there shall be substituted "section 264".

(2) In subsection (2) of that section—

(a) for the word "house", in each place where it occurs, there shall be substituted "dwelling-house, house in multiple occupation or building"; and

(b) for the words "section 265" there shall be substituted "section 264".

(3) In subsection (3) of that section for the word "house", in each place where it occurs, there shall be substituted "dwelling-house, house in multiple occupation or building".

33.—(1) In section 305 (building becoming listed when subject to compulsory purchase for clearance), in subsection (5)—

(a) for the word "building", in the first place where it occurs, there shall be substituted "residential building"; and

(b) for the words from "take whichever" onwards there shall be substituted the words " in accordance with section 604A (disregarding guidance under that section in respect of sections 265 and 289), take action under whichever of sections 189 and 264 it considers to be the most satisfactory course of action."

(2) In subsection (6) of that section for the word "house", in each place where it occurs, there shall be substituted "residential building".

(3) After subsection (7) of that section there shall be inserted the following subsection—

"(8) In this section "residential building" has the same meaning as in section 289; and subsection (2A) of that section shall apply in determining whether a residential building containing one or more flats is unfit for human habitation for the purposes of subsection (4) as it applies for the purposes of that section."

34. In section 306 (building becoming listed when acquired by agreement for clearance), in subsection (2), in paragraph (b) for the word "house" there shall be substituted "residential building (within the meaning of section 289)".

35. In section 309 (recovery of possession of premises for purposes of approved re-development), in subsection (2) for the word "house", in each place where it occurs, there shall be substituted "dwelling-house".

36.—(1) In section 310 (certificate of fitness resulting from owner's improvements or alterations), in subsection (1)—

(a) for the word "house", in the first place where it occurs, there shall be substituted "dwelling-house, house in multiple occupation or building containing one or more flats"; and

(b) for the word "house", in the second place where it occurs, there shall be substituted "dwelling-house, the house or the flat or flats in the building".

(2) In subsection (3) of that section for the words "house is" there shall be substituted "dwelling-house or house is or, as the case may be, the flat or flats in the building is or are".

(3) In subsection (4) of that section for the word "house", in each place where it occurs, there shall be substituted "dwelling-house, house in multiple occupation or building".

37. In section 315 (power of court to order occupier or owner to permit things to be done), in subsection (1)—

(a) in paragraph (a) the words "or person having control" shall be omitted; and

(b) in paragraph (b) for the words "owner or person having control" there shall be substituted "or owner".

38. In section 318 (power of court to authorise execution of works on unfit premises or for improvement), in subsection (1) for the word "houses" there shall be substituted "dwelling-houses or houses in multiple occupation or both".

39.—(1) In section 319 (powers of entry), in subsection (1) for the words "24 hours"" there shall be substituted "seven days"".

(2) At the end of subsection (2) of that section there shall be added the words "and shall, if so required, be produced for inspection by the occupier or anyone acting on his behalf".

40.—(1) In section 320 (penalty for obstruction), in subsection (1) after the word "offence" there shall be inserted "intentionally".

(2) In subsection (2) of that section for the words "level 2" there shall be substituted "level 3".

41. Section 321 (repair at reasonable expense) shall cease to have effect.

42. In section 322 (minor definitions)—

(a) for the definition of "house" there shall be substituted—

" dwelling-house" and "flat", except in the expression "flat in multiple occupation", shall be construed in accordance with subsection (2) and "the building", in relation to a flat, means the building containing the flat;

"house in multiple occupation" and "flat in multiple occupation" have the same meaning as in Part XI";

(b) the definition of "person having control" shall be omitted; and

(c) at the end there shall be added—

" "premises", in relation to a demolition or closing order, means the dwelling-house, house in multiple occupation, building or part of a building in respect of which the closing order or, as the case may be, demolition order is made.

(2) For the purposes of this Part, "dwelling-house" includes any yard, garden, outhouses and appurtenances belonging to it or usually enjoyed with it and section 183 shall have effect to determine whether a dwelling-house is a flat.

(3) Except where the context otherwise requires, any reference in this Part (other than this section) to a flat is a reference to a dwelling-house which is a flat or to a flat in multiple occupation."

43. In section 323 (index of defined expressions: Part IX)—

(a) the entries beginning "the full standard", "general improvement area", "house", "land liable to be cleared", "person having control", "slum clearance functions", "slum clearance subsidy" and "year" shall be omitted

(b) in the entries beginning "fit (or unfit) for human habitation" and "unfit (or fit) for human habitation" for the words in the second column there shall be substituted "section 604"; and

(c) at the appropriate places in alphabetical order there shall be inserted the following entries—

"dwelling-house	sections 266 and 322"
"flat	section 322"
"house in multiple occupation	section 322"
"premises	section 322".

PART III

AMENDMENTS OF PART XI

44. At the end of section 345 (meaning of "multiple occupation") there shall be added the following subsection—

"(2) For the purposes of this section "house", in the expression "house in multiple occupation", includes any part of a building which—

(a) apart from this subsection would not be regarded as a house; and

(b) was originally constructed or subsequently adapted for occupation by a single household;

and any reference in this Part to a flat in multiple occupation is a reference to a part of a building which, whether by virtue of this subsection or without regard to it, constitutes a house in multiple occupation."

45.—(1) In section 346 (registration schemes), in subsection (1), paragraph (b) and the word "and" immediately preceding it shall be omitted.

(2) In subsection (2) of that section the words "or building" shall be omitted and for the words "paragraphs (a) and (b)" there shall be substituted "paragraph (a)".

(3) In subsection (3) of that section the words "or building", in each place where they occur, shall be omitted.

(4) In subsection (6) of that section—

(a) at the beginning there shall be inserted "Subject to section 347(4)";

(b) for the words from "except in a case" to "level 2" there shall be substituted "level 3"; and

(c) at the end there shall be added the words "and, if the contravention or failure continues, he commits a further summary offence and is liable on conviction to a fine not exceeding one-tenth of the amount corresponding to that level for every day or part of a day during which the contravention or failure continues".

46. In section 347 (control provisions), in subsection (4)—

(a) for the words "A person" there shall be substituted "Where a person is"; and

(b) for the words from "is liable" to the end there shall be substituted "the said section 346(6) shall have effect as if for the words "level 3" there were substituted "level 4"."

47. In section 349 (steps required to inform public about scheme), in subsection (2), in paragraph (b) the words "and buildings" shall be omitted.

48.—(1) In section 350 (power to require information for purposes of scheme), in subsection (1) the words "or building", in each place where they occur, shall be omitted.

(2) In subsection (2) of that section after the word "exceeding" there shall be inserted "(a)" and at the end there shall be added "in the case of such a failure; or

(b) level 3 on the standard scale in the case of such a mis-statement".

49.—(1) In section 352 (power to require execution of works to render premises fit for number of occupants), in subsection (1) at the beginning there shall be inserted "Subject to section 365" and for the words from "the condition of a house" onwards there shall be substituted—

"in the opinion of the authority, a house in multiple occupation fails to meet one or more of the requirements in paragraphs (a) to (e) of subsection (1A) and, having regard to the number of individuals or households or both for the time being accommodated on the premises, by reason of that failure the premises are not reasonably suitable for occupation by those individuals or households.

(1A) The requirements in respect of a house in multiple occupation referred to in subsection (1) are the following, that is to say,—

(a) there are satisfactory facilities for the storage, preparation and cooking of food including an adequate number of sinks with a satisfactory supply of hot and cold water;

(b) it has an adequate number of suitably located water-closets for the exclusive use of the occupants;

(c) it has, for the exclusive use of the occupants, an adequate number of suitably located fixed baths or showers and wash-hand basins each of which is provided with a satisfactory supply of hot and cold water;

(d) subject to section 365, there are adequate means of escape from fire; and

(e) there are adequate other fire precautions."

(2) In subsection (2) of that section, at the beginning there shall be inserted "Subject to subsection (2A)", for the word "premises", in both places where it occurs, there shall be substituted "house" and at the end of that subsection there shall be added—

"but the notice shall not specify any works to any premises outside the house".

(3) After that subsection there shall be inserted the following subsection—

"(2A) Where the authority have exercised or propose to exercise their powers under section 368 to secure that part of the house is not used for human habitation, they may specify in the notice such work only as in their opinion is required to meet such of the requirements in subsection (1A) as may be applicable if that part is not so used."

(4) In subsection (3) of that section for paragraph (b) there shall be substituted—

"(b) on the person managing the house;";

and in the words following that paragraph after the word "lessee" there shall be inserted "occupier".

(5) After subsection (5) of that section there shall be inserted the following subsections—

"(5A) A notice served under this section is a local land charge.

(5B) Each local housing authority shall—

(a) maintain a register of notices served by the authority under subsection (1) after the coming into force of this subsection;

(b) ensure the register is open to inspection by the public free of charge at all reasonable hours; and

(c) on request, and on payment of any such reasonable fee as the authority may require, supply copies of entries in the register to any person."

(6) Subsection (6) of that section shall cease to have effect.

50. In each of the following provisions, that is to say—

(a) section 352, in subsection (4) (effect of notice), and

(b) section 372 (power to require execution of works to remedy neglect of management), in subsection (3) (effect of notice),

for the words from "within such period" onwards there shall be substituted the words "as follows, namely,—

(a) to begin those works not later than such reasonable date, being not earlier than the twenty-first day after the date of service of the notice, as is specified in the notice; and

(b) to complete those works within such reasonable period as is so specified."

51. In section 353 (appeal against notice under section 352), in subsection (2)—

(a) in paragraph (a) for the words "considerations set out in subsection (1)" there shall be substituted "requirements set out in subsection (1A)"; and

(b) after paragraph (d) there shall be inserted—

"(dd) that the date specified for the beginning of the works is not reasonable".

52. In section 354 (power to limit number of occupants of house), in subsection (1), in paragraph (a) for the words "considerations set out in subsection (1)" there shall be substituted "requirements set out in subsection (1A)".

53.—(1) In section 365 (means of escape from fire: general provisions as to exercise of powers) for subsections (1) and (2) there shall be substituted the following subsections—

"(1) In any case where—

(a) the local housing authority have the power to serve a notice under subsection (1) of section 352 in respect of a house in multiple occupation, and

(b) the reason, or one of the reasons, by virtue of which that power arises is a failure to meet the requirement in paragraph (d) of subsection (1A) of that section,

the authority shall in addition have the power for that reason to accept an undertaking or make a closing order under section 368 in respect of the house.

(2) Where by virtue of subsection (1) the local housing authority have powers in respect of a house in multiple occupation to serve a notice under section 352(1) for the reason mentioned in subsection (1)(b) and to accept an undertaking or make a closing order under section 368, they may exercise such of those powers as appear to them appropriate; and where the house is of such description or is occupied in such manner as the Secretary of State may specify by order for the purposes of this subsection, the authority shall be under a duty to so exercise those powers.

(2A) The local housing authority shall not serve a notice under section 352(1) for the reason mentioned in subsection (1)(b) or accept an undertaking or make a closing order under section 368 if the house is of such description or is occupied in such manner as the Secretary of State may specify by order for the purposes of this subsection."

(2) In subsection (3) of that section for "366" there shall be substituted "352 for the reason mentioned in subsection (1)(b)".

(3) In subsection (4) of that section after "(2)" there shall be inserted "or (2A)" and at the end of that subsection there shall be inserted the following subsection—

"(5) Nothing in this section affects the power of the local housing authority to serve a notice under subsection (1) of section 352 if the house also fails to meet one or more of the requirements in paragraphs (a) to (c) and (e) of subsection (1A) of that section."

54. Sections 366 and 367 (means of escape from fire: power by notice to require execution of works and appeals against notice) shall cease to have effect.

55.—(1) In section 368 (means of escape from fire: power to secure that part of house not used for human habitation), in subsection (1) at the beginning there shall be inserted "Subject to section 365".

(2) In subsection (3) of that section for "£5" there shall be substituted "one-tenth of the amount corresponding to that level".

(3) In subsection (5) of that section—

(a) for the words from "section 265" to "unfit for human habitation)" there shall be substituted "section 264";

(b) for the words "the modification that" there shall be substituted "with the following modifications—

(a) the reference in section 278(1) (premises rendered fit) to the house in multiple occupation shall be construed as a reference to the part of the house in respect of which the closing order under subsection (4) is made;

(b)"; and

(c) at the end there shall be added "and

(c) section 279 (substitution of demolition orders) shall be omitted".

56.—(1) In section 369 (the management code for houses in multiple occupation) at the beginning of subsection (2) there shall be inserted "Subject to subsection (2A)" and after the words "all means of water supply and drainage in the house" there shall be inserted—

"all means of escape from fire and all apparatus, systems and other things provided by way of fire precautions;";

and at the end of that subsection there shall be added the words "and to ensure that all means of escape from fire are kept clear of obstructions".

(2) After subsection (2) of that section there shall be inserted the following subsection—

"(2A) The person managing the house shall only be liable by virtue of the regulations under subsection (2) to ensure the repair, maintenance, cleansing and good order of any premises outside the house if and to the extent that he has power or is otherwise liable to ensure those matters in respect of any such premises."

(3) In subsection (3) of that section, paragraphs (b) and (f) and in paragraph (c) the words from "and in particular" onwards shall be omitted.

(4) In subsection (5) of that section the words "as applied under section 370 in relation to a house" shall be omitted.

57. Sections 370 and 371 (application of the management code to a house by order of the local housing authority and appeals relating to such orders) shall cease to have effect; and in section 381(4) of that Act "370" shall be omitted.

58. In section 372 (power of local housing authority to require execution of works to remedy neglect of management), in subsection (1)—

(a) the words from "to which" to "management code)" in the first place where they occur, and

(b) paragraph (b) and the word "or" immediately preceding it,

shall be omitted.

59. In section 373 (appeal against notice under section 372), in subsection (2), after paragraph (c) there shall be inserted—

"(cc) that the date specified for the beginning of the works is not reasonable".

60. Section 374 (application of code etc. to buildings other than houses) shall cease to have effect.

61. In section 375 (carrying out of works by local housing authority), for subsections (2) and (3) (compliance with notice and carrying out of works in default) there shall be substituted the following subsections—

"(2) Compliance with a notice means beginning and completing the works specified in the notice—

(a) if no appeal is brought against the notice, not later than such date and within such period as is specified in the notice;

(b) if an appeal is brought against the notice and is not withdrawn, not later than such date and within such period as may be fixed by the court determining the appeal; and

(c) if an appeal brought against the notice is withdrawn, not later than the twenty-first day after the date of withdrawal of the appeal and within such period (beginning on that twenty-first day) as is specified in the notice.

(3) If, before the expiry of the period which under subsection (2) is appropriate for completion of the works specified in the notice, it appears to the local housing authority that reasonable progress is not being made towards compliance with the notice, the authority may themselves do the work required to be done by the notice.

(3A) Not less than seven days before a local housing authority enter any house for the purpose of doing any works by virtue of subsection (1) or subsection (3), they shall serve notice of their intention to do so on the person on whom the notice referred to in subsection (1) was served and, if they think fit, also on any other owner of the house.

(3B) If, after a local housing authority have served notice under subsection (3A), the works are in fact carried out (otherwise than by the authority), any administrative and other expenses incurred by the authority with a view to doing the work themselves in accordance with subsection (1) or subsection (3) shall be treated for the purposes of subsection (4) (and Schedule 10) as expenses incurred by them under this section in carrying out the works in a case where the notice referred to in subsection (1) has not been complied with.

62. In section 376 (penalty for failure to execute works), in subsection (2) (further offence), for the words "that the period for compliance has expired" there shall be substituted "the expiry of the period which under section 375(2) is appropriate for completion of the works in question".

63. In section 377 (powers of court to facilitate execution of works etc.), in subsection (3) for "£20" there shall be substituted "one-tenth of the amount corresponding to that level".

64. In section 378 (provisions for protection of owners), in subsection (2) for paragraph (b) there shall be substituted—

"(b) to which regulations under section 369 (the management code) apply".

65. In section 379 (making of control order), in subsection (1) paragraph (c) except for the final "or" shall be omitted.

66. In section 387 (right of entry for inspection and carrying out of works), in subsection (5) for "£20" there shall be substituted "one-tenth of the amount corresponding to that level".

67. In section 395 (power of entry), at the end of subsection (3), there shall be added the words "and shall, if so required, be produced for inspection by the occupier or anyone acting on his behalf".

68.—(1) In section 396 (penalty for obstruction), in subsection (1) after the words "offence" there shall be inserted "intentionally".

(2) In subsection (2) of that section for the words "level 2" there shall be substituted "level 3".

69. In section 400 (index of defined expressions: Part XI), at the appropriate place in alphabetical order there shall be inserted the following entry—

"flat in multiple occupation   section 345".

70.—(1) In Schedule 10 (recovery of expenses incurred by local housing authority), in paragraph 1 (introductory) for the words "in default of the person on whom the notice was served" there shall be substituted "in a case where the notice has not been complied with".

(2) In paragraph 2 of that Schedule (recovery of expenses), in sub-paragraph (1)—

(a) in paragraph (a) after the words "dwelling-house" there shall be inserted "house in multiple occupation"; and

(b) for paragraph (b) there shall be substituted—

"(b) where the works were required by a notice under section 352 or 372 (notices relating to houses in multiple occupation), from the person having control of the house or the person managing the house, as the authority think fit;".

(3) Paragraph 5 of that Schedule (order for payment by instalments) shall cease to have effect and in paragraph 6 (appeals) after sub-paragraph (1A) there shall be inserted the following sub-paragraph—

"(1B) Where the demand for recovery of expenses relates to works carried out by virtue of subsection (3) of section 375, it shall be a ground of appeal that, at the time the local housing authority served notice under subsection (3A) of that section, reasonable progress was being made towards compliance with the notice in question."

(4) After paragraph 6 of that Schedule there shall be inserted the following paragraph—

Sch. 9   *"Expenses and interest recoverable from occupiers*

6A.—(1) Where a demand becomes operative by virtue of paragraph 3(3) or 6(3), the local housing authority may serve notice on any person—

(a) who occupies the premises concerned, or part of those premises, as the tenant or licensee of the person on whom the demand was served under paragraph 3(1), and

(b) who, by virtue of his tenancy or licence, pays rent or any sum in the nature of rent to the person on whom the demand was served,

stating the amount of expenses recoverable by the authority and requiring all future payments of rent or sums in the nature of rent, whether already accrued due or not, by such tenant or licensee to be made direct to the authority until the expenses recoverable by the authority, together with interest accrued due, have been duly paid.

(2) In the case of a demand which was served on any person as agent or trustee for another person (in this sub-paragraph referred to as "the principal or beneficiary") sub-paragraph (1) shall have effect as if the reference in each of paragraphs (a) and (b) to the person on whom the demand was served were a reference to that person or the principal or beneficiary.

(3) Subject to sub-paragraph (4), where a notice is served under sub-paragraph (1) then, unless the authority by further notice served on the tenant or licensee otherwise direct, it shall operate to transfer to the authority the right to recover, receive and give a discharge for the rent or sums in the nature of rent.

(4) The right of the authority to recover, receive and give a discharge for any rent or sums in the nature of rent by virtue of this paragraph shall be postponed to any right in respect of that rent or those sums which may at any time be vested in a superior landlord by virtue of a notice under section 6 of the Law of Distress Amendment Act 1908."

71. In Schedule 13 (further provision relating to control orders under Part XI of that Act) in sub-paragraph (4) of paragraph 21—

(a) in paragraph (a) the word "366" shall be omitted;

(b) at the end of paragraph (a) there shall be inserted "or";

(c) paragraph (c) and the word "or" immediately preceding it shall be omitted; and

(d) in the words following paragraph (c) the words "or order" shall be omitted.

Part IV

Amendments of Part XVII

72. After section 578 (general enactments relating to compulsory purchase etc. apply subject to this Part) there shall be inserted the following section—

"Modification of compulsory purchase order in case of acquisition of land for clearance.

578A.—(1) Subsection (2) applies where the local housing authority make a compulsory purchase order, within the meaning of the Acquisition of Land Act 1981, in respect of land they have determined to purchase under section 290 (acquisition of land comprised, surrounded by or adjoining a clearance area).

(2) Where this subsection applies, the Secretary of State may, in accordance with section 13 of the Acquisition of Land Act 1981 (confirmation of order), confirm the order with modifications notwithstanding that the effect of the modifications made by him in excluding any land or buildings

from the clearance area concerned is to sever the area into two or more separate and distinct areas; and, in such a case, the severance shall not prevent those areas from continuing to be treated as one clearance area for the purposes of the provisions of Part IX."

73. Sections 579 to 581 (special provision as regards acquisition of land for clearance, incorporation of enactments relating to mineral rights and acquisition of commons, open spaces etc.) shall cease to have effect.

74. In section 582 (restriction on recovery of possession after making compulsory purchase order), in subsection (1), in paragraph (a) the words from "section 192" to "beyond repair) or" shall be omitted.

75. After section 584 there shall be inserted the following sections—

"Compensation payable in case of closing and demolition orders.
584A.—(1) Subject to subsection (3), where a closing order under section 264 or a demolition order under section 265 is made in respect of any premises, the local housing authority shall pay to every owner of the premises an amount determined in accordance with subsection (2).

(2) The amount referred to in subsection (1) is the diminution in the compulsory purchase value of the owner's interest in the premises as a result of the making of the closing order or, as the case may be, the demolition order; and that amount—

(a) shall be determined as at the date of the making of the order in question; and

(b) shall be determined (in default of agreement) as if it were compensation payable in respect of the compulsory purchase of the interest in question and shall be dealt with accordingly.

(3) In any case where—

(a) a closing order has been made in respect of any premises, and

(b) by virtue of section 279 (closing orders: substitution of demolition order), the closing order is revoked and a demolition order is made in its place,

the amount payable to the owner under subsection (1) in connection with the demolition order shall be reduced by the amount (if any) paid to the owner or a previous owner under that subsection in connection with the closing order.

(4) For the purposes of this section—

"compulsory purchase value", in relation to an owner's interest in premises, means the compensation which would be payable in respect of the compulsory purchase of that interest if it fell to be assessed in accordance with the Land Compensation Act 1961; and

"premises" has the meaning assigned by section 322 (minor definitions for the purposes of Part IX).

Repayment on revocation of demolition or closing order.
584B.—(1) Where a payment in respect of any premises has been made by a local housing authority under section 584A(1) in connection with a demolition or closing order and—

      (a) the demolition order is revoked under section 274 (revocation of demolition order to permit reconstruction of premises), or

      (b) the closing order is determined under section 278 (determination of closing order on premises being rendered fit),

then, if at that time the person to whom the payment was made has the same interest in the premises as he had at the time the payment was made, he shall on demand repay to the authority the amount of the payment.

(2) In any case where—

      (a) a payment in respect of any premises has been made by a local housing authority under section 584A(1) in connection with a closing order, and

      (b) by virtue of section 278, the order is determined as respects part of the premises, and

      (c) the person to whom the payment was made (in this section referred to as "the recipient") had, at the time the payment was made, an owner's interest in the part of the premises concerned (whether or not he had such an interest in the rest of the premises),

then, if at the time of the determination of the closing order the recipient has the same interest in the premises as he had at the time the payment was made, he shall on demand pay to the authority an amount determined in accordance with subsections (3), (4) and (5).

(3) The amount referred to in subsection (2) is whichever is the less of—

      (a) the amount by which the value of the interest of the recipient in the premises increases as a result of the determination of the closing order; and

      (b) the amount paid to the recipient under section 584A(1) in respect of his interest in the premises;

and the amount referred to in paragraph (a) shall be determined as at the date of the determination of the closing order.

(4) For the purpose of assessing the amount referred to in subsection (3)(a), the rules set out in section 5 of the Land Compensation Act 1961 shall, so far as applicable and subject to any necessary modifications, have effect as they have effect for the purpose of assessing compensation for the compulsory acquisition of an interest in land.

(5) Any dispute as to the amount referred to in subsection (3)(a) shall be referred to and determined by the Lands Tribunal; and section 2 and subsections (1)(a) and (4) to (6) of section 4 of the Land Compensation Act 1961 shall, subject to any necessary modifications, apply for the purposes of this section as they apply for the purposes of that Act.

(6) In this section "premises" has the same meaning as in section 584A."

76. Sections 585 to 595 (which concern site value compensation for unfit houses and related matters and certain other land compensation matters) shall cease to have effect.

77. Section 598 (disregard of things done to obtain increased compensation) shall cease to have effect.

78. In section 599 (application of compensation due to another local authority) the words from "section 192" to "beyond repair"" shall be omitted.

79.—(1) In section 600 (powers of entry), in subsection (1) for the words "24 hours"" there shall be substituted "seven days"".

(2) At the end of subsection (2) of that section there shall be added the words "and shall, if so required, be produced for inspection by the occupier or anyone acting on his behalf".

80.—(1) In section 601 (penalty for obstruction), in subsection (1) after the word "offence" there shall be inserted "intentionally".

(2) In subsection (2) of that section for the words "level 2" there shall be substituted "level 3".

81. In section 602 (minor definitions)—

   (a) the definition of "house" shall be omitted; and

   (b) in paragraph (b) of the definition of "owner" after the word "premises" there shall be inserted "or part of the premises".

82. For section 603 (index of defined expressions: Part XVII) there shall be substituted the following section—

"Index of defined expressions: Part XVII.   603. The following Table shows provisions defining or otherwise explaining expressions used in this Part (other than provisions defining or otherwise explaining an expression used in the same section or paragraph):—

clearance area	section 289
closing order	section 264
demolition order	section 265
compulsory purchase value	section 584A
lease and lessee	section 621
local housing authority	section 1, 2(2)."

Part V

Amendments of Part XVIII

83. For section 604 there shall be substituted the following section—

"Fitness for human habitation.   604.—(1) Subject to subsection (2) below, a dwelling-house is fit for human habitation for the purposes of this Act unless, in the opinion of the local housing authority, it fails to meet one or more of the requirements in paragraphs (a) to (i) below and, by reason of that failure, is not reasonably suitable for occupation,—

   (a) it is structurally stable;

   (b) it is free from serious disrepair;

   (c) it is free from dampness prejudicial to the health of the occupants (if any);

   (d) it has adequate provision for lighting, heating and ventilation;

   (e) it has an adequate piped supply of wholesome water;

   (f) there are satisfactory facilities in the dwelling-house for the preparation and cooking of food, including a sink with a satisfactory supply of hot and cold water;

   (g) it has a suitably located water-closet for the exclusive use of the occupants (if any);

SCH. 9

(h) it has, for the exclusive use of the occupants (if any), a suitably located fixed bath or shower and wash-hand basin each of which is provided with a satisfactory supply of hot and cold water; and

(i) it has an effective system for the draining of foul, waste and surface water;

and any reference to a dwelling-house being unfit for human habitation shall be construed accordingly.

(2) Whether or not a dwelling-house which is a flat satisfies the requirements in subsection (1), it is unfit for human habitation for the purposes of this Act if, in the opinion of the local housing authority, the building or a part of the building outside the flat fails to meet one or more of the requirements in paragraphs (a) to (e) below and, by reason of that failure, the flat is not reasonably suitable for occupation,—

(a) the building or part is structurally stable;

(b) it is free from serious disrepair;

(c) it is free from dampness;

(d) it has adequate provision for ventilation; and

(e) it has an effective system for the draining of foul, waste and surface water.

(3) Subsection (1) applies in relation to a house in multiple occupation with the substitution of a reference to the house for any reference to a dwelling-house.

(4) Subsection (2) applies in relation to a flat in multiple occupation with the substitution for any reference to a dwelling-house which is a flat of a reference to the flat in multiple occupation.

(5) The Secretary of State may by order amend the provisions of subsection (1) or subsection (2) in such manner and to such extent as he considers appropriate; and any such order—

(a) may contain such transitional and supplementary provisions as the Secretary of State considers expedient; and

(b) shall be made by statutory instrument which shall be subject to annulment in pursuance of a resolution of either House of Parliament."

84. After that section there shall be inserted the following section—

"Authority to consider guidance given by Secretary of State in deciding whether to take action under section 189, section 264, section 265 or section 289.

604A.—(1) In deciding for the purposes of sections 189, 264, 265 and 289 whether the most satisfactory course of action, in respect of any dwelling-house, house in multiple occupation or building, is, if applicable,—

(a) serving notice under subsection (1) of section 189; or

(b) serving notice under subsection (1A) of that section; or

(c) making a closing order under subsection (1) of section 264; or

(d) making a closing order under subsection (2) of that section with respect to the whole or a part of the building concerned; or

(e) making a demolition order under subsection (1) of section 265; or

(f) making a demolition order subsection (2) of that section; or

(g) declaring the area in which the dwelling-house, house in multiple occupation or building is situated to be a clearance area in accordance with section 289;

the local housing authority shall have regard to such guidance as may from time to time be given by the Secretary of State.

(2) The Secretary of State may give guidance under subsection (1) to authorities generally or may give different guidance to different descriptions of authority or to authorities in different areas; and, without prejudice to the matters in respect of which the Secretary of State may give guidance, he may, in particular, give guidance in respect of financial and social considerations to be taken into account by authorities.

(3) Where the Secretary of State proposes to give guidance under subsection (1), or to revise guidance already given, he shall lay a draft of the proposed guidance or alterations before each House of Parliament and—

(a) he shall not give the guidance or revise the guidance until after the expiration of the period of forty days beginning with the day on which the draft is laid (or, if copies are laid before each House of Parliament on different days, with the later of those days); and

(b) if within that period either House resolves that the guidance or alterations be withdrawn he shall not proceed with the proposed alterations (but without prejudice to the laying of a further draft).

(4) In computing for the purposes of subsection (3) the period of forty days no account shall be taken of any time during which Parliament is dissolved or prorogued or during which both Houses are adjourned for more than four days."

85. For section 605 there shall be substituted the following section—

"Consideration by local housing authority of housing conditions in their district.   605.—(1) The local housing authority shall at least once in each year consider the housing conditions in their district with a view to determining what action to take in performance of their functions under—

(a) Part VI (repair notices);

(b) Part IX (slum clearance);

(c) Part XI (houses in multiple occupation);

(d) Part VII of the Local Government and Housing Act 1989 (renewal areas); and

(e) Part VIII of that Act (grants towards cost of improvements and repairs etc.).

(2) For the purposes of carrying out their duty under subsection (1), the authority and their officers shall comply with any directions the Secretary of State may give and shall keep such records and supply him with such information as he may specify."

86. In section 606 (reports on particular houses or areas), for the word "house", in each place where it occurs, there shall be substituted "dwelling-house or house in multiple occupation".

SCH. 9   87. In section 608 (acquisition of ancient monuments etc.), in paragraph (a) the words from "section 192" to "beyond repair) or" shall be omitted.

88. In section 610 (power of court to authorise conversion of houses into flats), in subsection (1)—

(a) for the words "a house" there shall be substituted "any premises";

(b) for the word "house", in each subsequent place where it occurs, there shall be substituted "premises"; and

(c) in paragraph (a) for the words "is situated, it" there shall be substituted "are situated, they" and for the words "tenement" and "tenements" there shall be substituted "dwelling-house" and "dwelling-houses" respectively.

89. In section 612 (exclusion of Rent Act protection) for the word "house" there shall be substituted "dwelling-house".

90.—(1) In section 623 (minor definitions: Part XVIII), for the definition of "house" there shall be substituted—

""dwelling-house" and "flat", except in the expression "flat in multiple occupation", shall be construed in accordance with subsection (2);

"house in multiple occupation" and "flat in multiple occupation" have the same meaning as in Part XI;".

(2) At the end of that section there shall be inserted the following subsection—

"(2) For the purposes of this Part, "dwelling-house" includes any yard, garden, outhouses and appurtenances belonging to it or usually enjoyed with it and section 183 shall have effect to determine whether a dwelling-house is a flat."

91. In section 624 (index of defined expressions: Part XVIII)—

(a) the entry beginning "house" shall be omitted; and

(b) at the appropriate places in alphabetical order there shall be inserted the following entries—

"dwelling-house	section 623"
"flat	section 623"
"flat in multiple occupation	section 623"
"house in multiple occupation	section 623"

Section 186.

SCHEDULE 10

SECURITY OF TENURE ON ENDING OF LONG RESIDENTIAL TENANCIES

Preliminary

1.—(1) This Schedule applies to a long tenancy of a dwelling-house at a low rent as respects which for the time being the following condition (in this Schedule referred to as "the qualifying condition") is fulfilled, that is to say, that the circumstances (as respects the property let under the tenancy, the use of that property and all other relevant matters) are such that, if the tenancy were not at a low rent, it would at that time be an assured tenancy within the meaning of Part I of the Housing Act 1988.

1988 c. 50.

(2) For the purpose only of determining whether the qualifying condition is fulfilled with respect to a tenancy, Schedule 1 to the Housing Act 1988 (tenancies which cannot be assured tenancies) shall have effect with the omission of paragraph 1 (which excludes tenancies entered into before, or pursuant to contracts made before, the coming into force of Part I of that Act).

(3) At any time within the period of twelve months ending on the day preceding the term date, application may be made to the court as respects any long tenancy of a dwelling-house at a low rent, not being at the time of the application a tenancy as respects which the qualifying condition is fulfilled, for an order declaring that the tenancy is not to be treated as a tenancy to which this Schedule applies.

(4) Where an application is made under sub-paragraph (3) above—

(a) the court, if satisfied that the tenancy is not likely immediately before the term date to be a tenancy to which this Schedule applies but not otherwise, shall make the order; and

(b) if the court makes the order, then, notwithstanding anything in sub-paragraph (1) above the tenancy shall not thereafter be treated as a tenancy to which this Schedule applies.

(5) A tenancy to which this Schedule applies is hereinafter referred to as a long residential tenancy.

(6) Anything authorised or required to be done under the following provisions of this Schedule in relation to a long residential tenancy shall, if done before the term date in relation to a long tenancy of a dwelling-house at a low rent, not be treated as invalid by reason only that at the time at which it was done the qualifying condition was not fulfilled as respects the tenancy.

(7) In determining for the purposes of any provision of this Schedule whether the property let under a tenancy was let as a separate dwelling, the nature of the property at the time of the creation of the tenancy shall be deemed to have been the same as its nature at the time in relation to which the question arises, and the purpose for which it was let under the tenancy shall be deemed to have been the same as the purpose for which it is or was used at the last-mentioned time.

2.—(1) This paragraph has effect for the interpretation of certain expressions used in this Schedule.

(2) Except where the context otherwise requires, expressions to which a meaning is assigned for the purposes of the 1988 Act or Part I of that Act have the same meaning in this Schedule.

(3) "Long tenancy" means a tenancy granted for a term of years certain exceeding 21 years, whether or not subsequently extended by act of the parties or by any enactment, but excluding any tenancy which is, or may become, terminable before the end of the term by notice given to the tenant.

(4) A tenancy is "at a low rent" if either no rent is payable under the tenancy or the maximum rent payable at any time is less than two-thirds of the rateable value for the time being of the dwelling-house under the tenancy.

(5) Paragraph 3(2) of Schedule 1 to the 1988 Act applies to determine whether the rent under a tenancy falls within sub-paragraph (4) above and Part II of that Schedule applies to determine the rateable value of a dwelling-house for the purposes of that sub-paragraph.

(6) "Long residential tenancy" and "qualifying condition" have the meaning assigned by paragraph 1 above and the following expressions shall be construed as follows—

"the 1954 Act" means the Landlord and Tenant Act 1954;   1954 c. 56.

"the 1988 Act" means the Housing Act 1988;   1988 c. 50.

"assured periodic tenancy" shall be construed in accordance with paragraph 9(4) below;

"the date of termination" has the meaning assigned by paragraph 4(4) below;

"disputed terms" shall be construed in accordance with paragraph 11(1)(a) below;

Sch. 10

"election by the tenant to retain possession" shall be construed in accordance with paragraph 4(7) below;

"former 1954 Act tenancy" means a tenancy to which, by virtue of section 186(3) of this Act, this Schedule applies on and after 15th January 1999;

"the implied terms" shall be construed in accordance with paragraph 4(5)(a) below;

"landlord" shall be construed in accordance with paragraph 19(1) below;

"landlord's notice" means a notice under sub-paragraph (1) of paragraph 4 below and such a notice is—

(a) a "landlord's notice proposing an assured tenancy" if it contains such proposals as are mentioned in sub-paragraph (5)(a) of that paragraph; and

(b) a "landlord's notice to resume possession" if it contains such proposals as are referred to in sub-paragraph (5)(b) of that paragraph;

"specified date of termination", in relation to a tenancy in respect of which a landlord's notice is served, means the date specified in the notice as mentioned in paragraph 4(1)(a) below;

"tenant's notice" shall be construed in accordance with paragraph 10(1)(a) below;

"term date", in relation to a tenancy granted for a term of years certain, means the date of expiry of that term;

"the terms of the tenancy specified in the landlord's notice" shall be construed in accordance with paragraph 4(6) below; and

"undisputed terms" shall be construed in accordance with paragraph 11(2) below.

Continuation of long residential tenancies

3.—(1) A tenancy which, immediately before the term date, is a long residential tenancy shall not come to an end on that date except by being terminated under the provisions of this Schedule, and, if not then so terminated, shall subject to those provisions continue until so terminated and, while continuing by virtue of this paragraph, shall be deemed to be a long residential tenancy (notwithstanding any change in circumstances).

(2) Sub-paragraph (1) above does not apply in the case of a former 1954 Act tenancy the term date of which falls before 15th January 1999 but if, in the case of such a tenancy,—

(a) the tenancy is continuing immediately before that date by virtue of section 3 of the 1954 Act, and

(b) on that date the qualifying condition (as defined in paragraph 1(1) above) is fulfilled,

then, subject to the provisions of this Schedule, the tenancy shall continue until terminated under those provisions and, while continuing by virtue of this paragraph, shall be deemed to be a long residential tenancy (notwithstanding any change in circumstances).

(3) Where by virtue of this paragraph a tenancy continues after the term date, the tenancy shall continue at the same rent and in other respects on the same terms as before the term date.

Termination of tenancy by the landlord

4.—(1) Subject to sub-paragraph (2) below and the provisions of this Schedule as to the annulment of notices in certain cases, the landlord may terminate a long residential tenancy by a notice in the prescribed form served on the tenant—

(a) specifying the date at which the tenancy is to come to an end, being either the term date or a later date; and

SCH. 10

(b) so served not more than twelve nor less than six months before the date so specified.

(2) In any case where—

(a) a landlord's notice has been served, and

(b) an application has been made to the court or a rent assessment committee under the following provisions of this Schedule other than paragraph 6, and

(c) apart from this paragraph, the effect of the notice would be to terminate the tenancy before the expiry of the period of three months beginning with the date on which the application is finally disposed of,

the effect of the notice shall be to terminate the tenancy at the expiry of the said period of three months and not at any other time.

(3) The reference in sub-paragraph (2)(c) above to the date on which the application is finally disposed of shall be construed as a reference to the earliest date by which the proceedings on the application (including any proceedings on or in consequence of an appeal) have been determined and any time for appealing or further appealing has expired, except that if the application is withdrawn or any appeal is abandoned the reference shall be construed as a reference to the date of withdrawal or abandonment.

(4) In this Schedule "the date of termination", in relation to a tenancy in respect of which a landlord's notice is served, means,—

(a) where the tenancy is continued as mentioned in sub-paragraph (2) above, the last day of the period of three months referred to in that sub-paragraph; and

(b) in any other case, the specified date of termination.

(5) A landlord's notice shall not have effect unless—

(a) it proposes an assured monthly periodic tenancy of the dwelling-house and a rent for that tenancy (such that it would not be a tenancy at a low rent) and, subject to sub-paragraph (6) below, states that the other terms of the tenancy shall be the same as those of the long residential tenancy immediately before it is terminated (in this Schedule referred to as "the implied terms"); or

(b) it gives notice that, if the tenant is not willing to give up possession at the date of termination of the property let under the tenancy, the landlord proposes to apply to the court, on one or more of the grounds specified in paragraph 5(1) below, for the possession of the property let under the tenancy and states the ground or grounds on which he proposes to apply.

(6) In the landlord's notice proposing an assured tenancy the landlord may propose terms of the tenancy referred to in sub-paragraph (5)(a) above different from the implied terms; and any reference in the following provisions of this Schedule to the terms of the tenancy specified in the landlord's notice is a reference to the implied terms or, if the implied terms are varied by virtue of this sub-paragraph, to the implied terms as so varied.

(7) A landlord's notice shall invite the tenant, within the period of two months beginning on the date on which the notice was served, to notify the landlord in writing whether,—

(a) in the case of a landlord's notice proposing an assured tenancy, the tenant wishes to remain in possession; and

(b) in the case of a landlord's notice to resume possession, the tenant is willing to give up possession as mentioned in sub-paragraph (5)(b) above;

and references in this Schedule to an election by the tenant to retain possession are references to his notifying the landlord under this sub-paragraph that he wishes to remain in possession or, as the case may be, that he is not willing to give up possession.

5.—(1) Subject to the following provisions of this paragraph, the grounds mentioned in paragraph 4(5)(b) above are—

(a) Ground 6 in, and those in Part II of, Schedule 2 to the 1988 Act, other than Ground 16;

(b) the ground that, for the purposes of redevelopment after the termination of the tenancy, the landlord proposes to demolish or reconstruct the whole or a substantial part of the premises; and

(c) the ground that the premises or part of them are reasonably required by the landlord for occupation as a residence for himself or any son or daughter of his over eighteen years of age or his or his spouse's father or mother and, if the landlord is not the immediate landlord, that he will be at the specified date of termination.

(2) Ground 6 in Schedule 2 to the 1988 Act may not be specified in a landlord's notice to resume possession if the tenancy is a former 1954 Act tenancy; and in the application of that Ground in accordance with sub-paragraph (1) above in any other case, paragraph (c) shall be omitted.

(3) In its application in accordance with sub-paragraph (1) above, Ground 10 in Schedule 2 to the 1988 Act shall have effect as if, in paragraph (b)—

(a) the words "except where subsection (1)(b) of section 8 of this Act applies" were omitted; and

(b) for the words "notice under that section relating to those proceedings" there were substituted "landlord's notice to resume possession (within the meaning of Schedule 10 to the Local Government and Housing Act 1989)".

(4) The ground mentioned in sub-paragraph (1)(b) above may not be specified in a landlord's notice to resume possession unless the landlord is a body to which section 28 of the Leasehold Reform Act 1967 applies and the premises are required for relevant development within the meaning of that section; and on any application by such a body under paragraph 13 below for possession on that ground, a certificate given by a Minister of the Crown as provided by subsection (1) of that section shall be conclusive evidence that the premises are so required.

(5) The ground mentioned in sub-paragraph (1)(c) above may not be specified in a landlord's notice to resume possession if the interest of the landlord, or an interest which is merged in that interest and but for the merger would be the interest of the landlord, was purchased or created after 18th February 1966.

Interim rent

6.—(1) On the date of service of a landlord's notice proposing an assured tenancy, or at any time between that date and the date of termination, the landlord may serve a notice on the tenant in the prescribed form proposing an interim monthly rent to take effect from a date specified in the notice, being not earlier than the specified date of termination, and to continue while the tenancy is continued by virtue of the preceding provisions of this Schedule.

(2) Where a notice has been served under sub-paragraph (1) above,—

(a) within the period of two months beginning on the date of service, the tenant may refer the interim monthly rent proposed in the notice to a rent assessment committee; and

(b) if the notice is not so referred, then, with effect from the date specified in the notice or, if it is later, the expiry of the period mentioned in paragraph (a) above, the interim monthly rent proposed in the notice shall be the rent under the tenancy.

(3) Where, under sub-paragraph (2) above, the rent specified in a landlord's notice is referred to a rent assessment committee, the committee shall determine the monthly rent at which, subject to sub-paragraph (4) below, the committee consider that the premises let under the tenancy might reasonably be expected to be let on the open market by a willing landlord under a monthly periodic tenancy—

(a) which begins on the day following the specified date of termination;

(b) under which the other terms are the same as those of the existing tenancy at the date on which was given the landlord's notice proposing an assured tenancy; and

(c) which affords the tenant security of tenure equivalent to that afforded by Chapter I of Part I of the 1988 Act in the case of an assured tenancy (other than an assured shorthold tenancy) in respect of which possession may not be recovered under any of Grounds 1 to 5 in Part I of Schedule 2 to that Act.

(4) Subsections (2), (4) and (5) of section 14 of the 1988 Act shall apply in relation to a determination of rent under sub-paragraph (3) above as they apply in relation to a determination under that section subject to the modifications in sub-paragraph (5) below; and in this paragraph "rent" shall be construed in accordance with subsection (4) of that section.

(5) The modifications of section 14 of the 1988 Act referred to in sub-paragraph (4) above are that in subsection (2), the reference in paragraph (b) to a relevant improvement being carried out shall be construed as a reference to an improvement being carried out during the long residential tenancy and the reference in paragraph (c) to a failure to comply with any term of the tenancy shall be construed as a reference to a failure to comply with any term of the long residential tenancy.

(6) Where a reference has been made to a rent assessment committee under sub-paragraph (2) above, then, the rent determined by the committee (subject, in a case where section 14(5) of the 1988 Act applies, to the addition of the appropriate amount in respect of rates) shall be the rent under the tenancy with effect from the date specified in the notice served under sub-paragraph (1) above or, if it is later, the expiry of the period mentioned in paragraph (a) of sub-paragraph (2) above.

7.—(1) Nothing in paragraph 6 above affects the right of the landlord and the tenant to agree the interim monthly rent which is to have effect while the tenancy is continued by virtue of the preceding provisions of this Schedule and the date from which that rent is to take effect; and, in such a case,—

(a) notwithstanding the provisions of paragraph 6 above, that rent shall be the rent under the tenancy with effect from that date; and

(b) no steps or, as the case may be, no further steps may be taken by the landlord or the tenant under the provisions of that paragraph.

(2) Nothing in paragraph 6 above requires a rent assessment committee to continue with a determination under sub-paragraph (3) of that paragraph—

(a) if the tenant gives notice in writing that he no longer requires such a determination; or

(b) if the long residential tenancy has come to an end on or before the specified date of termination.

SCH. 10   (3) Notwithstanding that a tenancy in respect of which an interim monthly rent has effect in accordance with paragraph 6 above or this paragraph is no longer at a low rent, it shall continue to be regarded as a tenancy at a low rent and, accordingly, shall continue to be a long residential tenancy.

Termination of tenancy by the tenant

8.—(1) A long residential tenancy may be brought to an end at the term date by not less than one month's notice in writing given by the tenant to his immediate landlord.

(2) A tenancy which is continuing after the term date by virtue of paragraph 3 above may be brought to an end at any time by not less than one month's notice in writing given by the tenant to his immediate landlord, whether the notice is given before or after the term date of the tenancy.

(3) The fact that the landlord has served a landlord's notice or that there has been an election by the tenant to retain possession shall not prevent the tenant from giving notice under this paragraph terminating the tenancy at a date earlier than the specified date of termination.

The assured periodic tenancy

9.—(1) Where a long residential tenancy (in this paragraph referred to as "the former tenancy") is terminated by a landlord's notice proposing an assured tenancy, then, subject to sub-paragraph (3) below, the tenant shall be entitled to remain in possession of the dwelling-house and his right to possession shall depend upon an assured periodic tenancy arising by virtue of this paragraph.

(2) The assured periodic tenancy referred to in sub-paragraph (1) above is one—

(a) taking effect in possession on the day following the date of termination;

(b) deemed to have been granted by the person who was the landlord under the former tenancy on the date of termination to the person who was then the tenant under that tenancy;

(c) under which the premises let are the dwelling-house;

(d) under which the periods of the tenancy, and the intervals at which rent is to be paid, are monthly beginning on the day following the date of termination;

(e) under which the rent is determined in accordance with paragraphs 10 to 12 below; and

(f) under which the other terms are determined in accordance with paragraphs 10 to 12 below.

(3) If, at the end of the period of two months beginning on the date of service of the landlord's notice, the qualifying condition was not fulfilled as respects the tenancy, the tenant shall not be entitled to remain in possession as mentioned in sub-paragraph (1) above unless there has been an election by the tenant to retain possession; and if, at the specified date of termination, the qualifying condition is not fulfilled as respects the tenancy, then, notwithstanding that there has been such an election, the tenant shall not be entitled to remain in possession as mentioned in that sub-paragraph.

(4) Any reference in the following provisions of this Schedule to an assured periodic tenancy is a reference to an assured periodic tenancy arising by virtue of this paragraph.

10.—(1) Where a landlord's notice proposing an assured tenancy has been served on the tenant,—

(a) within the period of two months beginning on the date of service of the notice, the tenant may serve on the landlord a notice in the prescribed form proposing either or both of the following, that is to say,—

(i) a rent for the assured periodic tenancy different from that proposed in the landlord's notice; and

(ii) terms of the tenancy different from those specified in the landlord's notice,

and such a notice is in this Schedule referred to as a "tenant's notice"; and

(b) if a tenant's notice is not so served, then, with effect from the date on which the assured periodic tenancy takes effect in possession,—

(i) the rent proposed in the landlord's notice shall be the rent under the tenancy; and

(ii) the terms of the tenancy specified in the landlord's notice shall be terms of the tenancy.

(2) Where a tenant's notice has been served on the landlord under sub-paragraph (1) above—

(a) within the period of two months beginning on the date of service of the notice, the landlord may by an application in the prescribed form refer the notice to a rent assessment committee; and

(b) if the notice is not so referred, then, with effect from the date on which the assured periodic tenancy takes effect in possession,—

(i) the rent (if any) proposed in the tenant's notice, or, if no rent is so proposed, the rent proposed in the landlord's notice, shall be the rent under the tenancy; and

(ii) the other terms of the tenancy (if any) proposed in the tenant's notice and, in so far as they do not conflict with the terms so proposed, the terms specified in the landlord's notice shall be terms of the tenancy.

11.—(1) Where, under sub-paragraph (2) of paragraph 10 above, a tenant's notice is referred to a rent assessment committee, the committee, having regard only to the contents of the landlord's notice and the tenant's notice, shall decide—

(a) whether there is any dispute as to the terms (other than those relating to the amount of the rent) of the assured periodic tenancy (in this Schedule referred to as "disputed terms") and, if so, what the disputed terms are; and

(b) whether there is any dispute as to rent under the tenancy;

and where the committee decide that there are disputed terms and that there is a dispute as to the rent under the tenancy, they shall make a determination under sub-paragraph (3) below before they make a determination under sub-paragraph (5) below.

(2) Where, under paragraph 10(2) above, a tenant's notice is referred to a rent assessment committee, any reference in this Schedule to the undisputed terms is a reference to those terms (if any) which—

(a) are proposed in the landlord's notice or the tenant's notice; and

(b) do not relate to the amount of the rent; and

(c) are not disputed terms.

2A

SCH. 10   (3) If the rent assessment committee decide that there are disputed terms, they shall determine whether the terms in the landlord's notice, the terms in the tenant's notice, or some other terms, dealing with the same subject matter as the disputed terms are such as, in the committee's opinion, might reasonably be expected to be found in an assured monthly periodic tenancy of the dwelling-house (not being an assured shorthold tenancy)—

(a) which begins on the day following the date of termination;

(b) which is granted by a willing landlord on terms which, except so far as they relate to the subject matter of the disputed terms, are the undisputed terms; and

(c) in respect of which possession may not be recovered under any of Grounds 1 to 5 in Part I of Schedule 2 to the 1988 Act;

and the committee shall, if they consider it appropriate, specify an adjustment of the undisputed terms to take account of the terms so determined and shall, if they consider it appropriate, specify an adjustment of the rent to take account of the terms so determined and, if applicable, so adjusted.

(4) In making a determination under sub-paragraph (3) above, or specifying an adjustment of the rent or undisputed terms under that sub-paragraph, there shall be disregarded any effect on the terms or the amount of rent attributable to the granting of a tenancy to a sitting tenant.

(5) If the rent assessment committee decide that there is a dispute as to the rent under the assured periodic tenancy, the committee shall determine the monthly rent at which, subject to sub-paragraph (6) below, the committee consider that the dwelling-house might reasonably be expected to be let in the open market by a willing landlord under an assured tenancy (not being an assured shorthold tenancy)—

(a) which is a monthly periodic tenancy;

(b) which begins on the day following the date of termination;

(c) in respect of which possession may not be recovered under any of Grounds 1 to 5 in Part I of Schedule 2 to the 1988 Act; and

(d) the terms of which (other than those relating to the amount of the rent) are the same as—

(i) the undisputed terms; or

(ii) if there has been a determination under sub-paragraph (3) above, the terms determined by the committee under that sub-paragraph and the undisputed terms (as adjusted, if at all, under that sub-paragraph).

(6) Subsections (2), (4) and (5) of section 14 of the 1988 Act shall apply in relation to a determination of rent under sub-paragraph (5) above as they apply in relation to a determination under that section subject to the modifications in sub-paragraph (7) below; and in this paragraph "rent" shall be construed in accordance with subsection (4) of that section.

(7) The modifications of section 14 of the 1988 Act referred to in sub-paragraph (6) above are that in subsection (2), the reference in paragraph (b) to a relevant improvement being carried out shall be construed as a reference to an improvement being carried out during the long residential tenancy and the reference in paragraph (c) to a failure to comply with any term of the tenancy shall be construed as a reference to a failure to comply with any term of the long residential tenancy.

(8) Where a reference has been made to a rent assessment committee under sub-paragraph (2) of paragraph 10 above, then,—

(a) if the committee decide that there are no disputed terms and that there is no dispute as to the rent, paragraph 10(2)(b) above shall apply as if the notice had not been so referred,

(b) where paragraph (a) above does not apply then, so far as concerns the amount of the rent under the tenancy, if there is a dispute as to the rent, the rent determined by the committee (subject, in a case where section 14(5) of the 1988 Act applies, to the addition of the appropriate amount in respect of rates) and, if there is no dispute as to the rent, the rent specified in the landlord's notice or, as the case may be, the tenant's notice (subject to any adjustment under sub-paragraph (3) above) shall be the rent under the tenancy, and

(c) where paragraph (a) above does not apply and there are disputed terms, then, so far as concerns the subject matter of those terms, the terms determined by the committee under sub-paragraph (3) above shall be terms of the tenancy and, so far as concerns any undisputed terms, those terms (subject to any adjustment under sub-paragraph (3) above) shall also be terms of the tenancy,

with effect from the date on which the assured periodic tenancy takes effect in possession.

(9) Nothing in this Schedule affects the right of the landlord and the tenant under the assured periodic tenancy to vary by agreement any term of the tenancy (including a term relating to rent).

12.—(1) Subsections (2) to (4) of section 41 of the 1988 Act (rent assessment committees: information powers) shall apply where there is a reference to a rent assessment committee under the preceding provisions of this Schedule as they apply where a matter is referred to such a committee under Chapter I or Chapter II of Part I of the 1988 Act.

(2) Nothing in paragraph 10 or paragraph 11 above affects the right of the landlord and the tenant to agree any terms of the assured periodic tenancy (including a term relating to the rent) before the tenancy takes effect in possession (in this sub-paragraph referred to as "the expressly agreed terms"); and, in such case,—

(a) the expressly agreed terms shall be terms of the tenancy in substitution for any terms dealing with the same subject matter which would otherwise, by virtue of paragraph 10 or paragraph 11 above, be terms of the tenancy; and

(b) where a reference has already been made to a rent assessment committee under sub-paragraph (2) of paragraph 10 above but there has been no determination by the committee under paragraph 11 above,—

(i) the committee shall have regard to the expressly agreed terms, as notified to them by the landlord and the tenant, in deciding, for the purposes of paragraph 11 above, what the disputed terms are and whether there is any dispute as to the rent; and

(ii) in making any determination under paragraph 11 above the committee shall not make any adjustment of the expressly agreed terms, as so notified.

(3) Nothing in paragraph 11 above requires a rent assessment committee to continue with a determination under that paragraph—

(a) if the long residential tenancy has come to an end; or

(b) if the landlord serves notice in writing on the committee that he no longer requires such a determination;

and, where the landlord serves notice as mentioned in paragraph (b) above, then, for the purposes of sub-paragraph (2) of paragraph 10 above, the landlord shall be treated as not having made a reference under paragraph (a) of that sub-paragraph and, accordingly, paragraph (b) of that sub-paragraph shall, subject to sub-paragraph (2) above, have effect for determining rent and other terms of the assured periodic tenancy.

Landlord's application for possession

13.—(1) Where a landlord's notice to resume possession has been served on the tenant and either—

(a) there is an election by the tenant to retain possession, or

(b) at the end of the period of two months beginning on the date of service of the notice, the qualifying condition is fulfilled as respects the tenancy,

the landlord may apply to the court for an order under this paragraph on such of the grounds mentioned in paragraph 5(1) above as may be specified in the notice.

(2) The court shall not entertain an application under sub-paragraph (1) above unless the application is made—

(a) within the period of two months beginning on the date of the election by the tenant to retain possession; or

(b) if there is no election by the tenant to retain possession, within the period of four months beginning on the date of service of the landlord's notice.

(3) Where the ground or one of the grounds for claiming possession specified in the landlord's notice is Ground 6 in Part I of Schedule 2 to the 1988 Act, then, if on an application made under sub-paragraph (1) above the court is satisfied that the landlord has established that ground, the court shall order that the tenant shall, on the date of termination, give up possession of the property then let under the tenancy.

(4) Subject to sub-paragraph (6) below, where the ground or one of the grounds for claiming possession specified in the landlord's notice is any of Grounds 9 to 15 in Part II of Schedule 2 to the 1988 Act or the ground mentioned in paragraph 5(1)(c) above, then, if on an application made under sub-paragraph (1) above the court is satisfied that the landlord has established that ground and that it is reasonable that the landlord should be granted possession, the court shall order that the tenant shall, on the date of termination, give up possession of the property then let under the tenancy.

(5) Part III of Schedule 2 to the 1988 Act shall have effect for supplementing Ground 9 in that Schedule (as that ground applies in relation to this Schedule) as it has effect for supplementing that ground for the purposes of that Act, subject to the modification that in paragraph 3(1), in the words following paragraph (b) the reference to the assured tenancy in question shall be construed as a reference to the long residential tenancy in question.

(6) Where the ground or one of the grounds for claiming possession specified in the landlord's notice is that mentioned in paragraph 5(1)(c) above, the court shall not make the order mentioned in sub-paragraph (4) above on that ground if it is satisfied that, having regard to all the circumstances of the case, including the question whether other accommodation is available for the landlord or the tenant, greater hardship would be caused by making the order than by refusing to make it.

(7) Where the ground or one of the grounds for claiming possession specified in the landlord's notice is that mentioned in paragraph 5(1)(b) above, then, if on an application made under sub-paragraph (1) above the court is satisfied that the landlord has established that ground and is further satisfied—

(a) that on that ground possession of those premises will be required by the landlord on the date of termination, and

(b) that the landlord has made such preparations (including the obtaining or, if that is not reasonably practicable in the circumstances, preparations relating to the obtaining of any requisite permission or consent, whether from any authority whose permission or consent is required under any enactment or from the owner of any interest in any property) for proceeding with the redevelopment as are reasonable in the circumstances,

the court shall order that the tenant shall, on the date of termination, give up possession of the property then let under the tenancy.

14.—(1) Where, in a case falling within sub-paragraph (7) of paragraph 13 above, the court is not satisfied as mentioned in that sub-paragraph but would be satisfied if the date of termination of the tenancy had been such date (in this paragraph referred to as "the postponed date") as the court may determine, being a date later, but not more than one year later, than the specified date of termination, the court shall, if the landlord so requires, make an order as mentioned in sub-paragraph (2) below.

(2) The order referred to in sub-paragraph (1) above is one by which the court specifies the postponed date and orders—

(a) that the tenancy shall not come to an end on the date of termination but shall continue thereafter, as respects the whole of the property let under the tenancy, at the same rent and in other respects on the same terms as before that date; and

(b) that, unless the tenancy comes to an end before the postponed date, the tenant shall on that date give up possession of the property then let under the tenancy.

(3) Notwithstanding the provisions of paragraph 13 above and the preceding provisions of this paragraph and notwithstanding that there has been an election by the tenant to retain possession, if the court is satisfied, at the date of the hearing, that the qualifying condition is not fulfilled as respects the tenancy, the court shall order that the tenant shall, on the date of termination, give up possession of the property then let under the tenancy.

(4) Nothing in paragraph 13 above or the preceding provisions of this paragraph shall prejudice any power of the tenant under paragraph 8 above to terminate the tenancy; and sub-paragraph (2) of that paragraph shall apply where the tenancy is continued by an order under sub-paragraph (2) above as it applies where the tenancy is continued by virtue of paragraph 3 above.

Provisions where tenant not ordered to give up possession

15.—(1) The provisions of this paragraph shall have effect where the landlord is entitled to make an application under sub-paragraph (1) of paragraph 13 above but does not obtain an order under that paragraph or paragraph 14 above.

(2) If at the expiration of the period within which an application under paragraph 13(1) above may be made the landlord has not made such an application, the landlord's notice to resume possession, and anything done in pursuance thereof, shall cease to have effect.

(3) If before the expiration of the period mentioned in sub-paragraph (2) above the landlord has made an application under paragraph 13(1) above but the result of the application, at the time when it is finally disposed of, is that no order is made, the landlord's notice to resume possession shall cease to have effect.

(4) In any case where sub-paragraph (3) above applies, then, if within the period of one month beginning on the date that the application to the court is finally disposed of the landlord serves on the tenant a landlord's notice proposing an assured tenancy, the earliest date which may be specified in the notice as the date of termination shall, notwithstanding anything in paragraph 4(1)(b) above, be the day following the last day of the period of four months beginning on the date of service of the subsequent notice.

(5) The reference in sub-paragraphs (3) and (4) above to the time at which an application is finally disposed of shall be construed as a reference to the earliest time at which the proceedings on the application (including any proceedings on or in consequence of an appeal) have been determined and any time for appealing or further appealing has expired, except that if the application is withdrawn or any appeal is abandoned the reference shall be construed as a reference to the time of withdrawal or abandonment.

(6) A landlord's notice to resume possession may be withdrawn at any time by notice in writing served on the tenant (without prejudice, however, to the power of the court to make an order as to costs if the notice is withdrawn after the landlord has made an application under paragraph 13(1) above).

(7) In any case where sub-paragraph (6) above applies, then, if within the period of one month beginning on the date of withdrawal of the landlord's notice to resume possession the landlord serves on the tenant a landlord's notice proposing an assured tenancy, the earliest date which may be specified in the notice as the date of termination shall, notwithstanding anything in paragraph 4(1)(b) above, be the day following the last day of the period of four months beginning on the date of service of the subsequent notice or the day following the last day of the period of six months beginning on the date of service of the withdrawn notice, whichever is the later.

Tenancies granted in continuation of long tenancies

16.—(1) Where on the coming to the end of a tenancy at a low rent the person who was the tenant immediately before the coming to an end thereof becomes (whether by grant or by implication of the law) the tenant under another tenancy at a low rent of a dwelling-house which consists of the whole or any part of the property let under the previous tenancy, then, if the previous tenancy was a long tenancy or is deemed by virtue of this paragraph to have been a long tenancy, the new tenancy shall be deemed for the purposes of this Schedule to be a long tenancy, irrespective of its terms.

(2) In relation to a tenancy from year to year or other tenancy not granted for a term of years certain, being a tenancy which by virtue of sub-paragraph (1) above is deemed for the purposes of this Schedule to be a long tenancy, the preceding provisions of this Schedule shall have effect subject to the modifications set out below.

(3) In sub-paragraph (6) of paragraph 2 above for the expression beginning "term date" there shall be substituted—

" "term date", in relation to any such tenancy as is mentioned in paragraph 16(2) below, means the first date after the coming into force of this Schedule on which, apart from this Schedule, the tenancy could have been brought to an end by notice to quit given by the landlord".

(4) Notwithstanding anything in sub-paragraph (3) of paragraph 3 above, where by virtue of that paragraph the tenancy is continued after the term date, the provisions of this Schedule as to the termination of a tenancy by notice shall have effect, subject to sub-paragraph (5) below, in substitution for and not in addition to any such provisions included in the terms on which the tenancy had effect before the term date.

(5) The minimum period of notice referred to in paragraph 8(1) above shall be one month or such longer period as the tenant would have been required to give to bring the tenancy to an end at the term date.

(6) Where the tenancy is not terminated under paragraph 4 or paragraph 8 above at the term date, then, whether or not it would have continued after that date apart from the provisions of this Schedule, it shall be treated for the purposes of those provisions as being continued by virtue of paragraph 3 above.

Agreements as to the grant of new tenancies

17. In any case where, prior to the date of termination of a long residential tenancy, the landlord and the tenant agree for the grant to the tenant of a future tenancy of the whole or part of the property let under the tenancy at a rent other than a low rent and on terms and from a date specified in the agreement, the tenancy shall continue until that date but no longer; and, in such a case, the provisions of this Schedule shall cease to apply in relation to the tenancy with effect from the date of the agreement.

Assumptions on which to determine future questions

18. Where under this Schedule any question falls to be determined by the court or a rent assessment committee by reference to circumstances at a future date, the court or committee shall have regard to all rights, interests and obligations under or relating to the tenancy as they subsist at the time of the determination and to all relevant circumstances as those then subsist and shall assume, except in so far as the contrary is shown, that those rights, interests, obligations and circumstances will continue to subsist unchanged until that future date.

Landlords and mortgagees in possession

19.—(1) Section 21 of the 1954 Act (meaning of "the landlord" and provisions as to mesne landlords) shall apply in relation to this Schedule as it applies in relation to Part I of that Act but subject to the following modifications—

    (a) any reference to Part I of that Act shall be construed as a reference to this Schedule; and

    (b) subsection (4) (which relates to statutory tenancies arising under that Part) shall be omitted.

(2) Section 67 of the 1954 Act (mortgagees in possession) applies for the purposes of this Schedule except that for the reference to that Act there shall be substituted a reference to this Schedule.

(3) In accordance with sub-paragraph (1) above, Schedule 5 to the 1954 Act shall also apply for the purpose of this Schedule but subject to the following modifications—

    (a) any reference to Part I of the 1954 Act shall be construed as a reference to the provisions of this Schedule (other than this sub-paragraph);

    (b) any reference to section 21 of the 1954 Act shall be construed as a reference to that section as it applies in relation to this Schedule;

    (c) any reference to subsection (1) of section 4 of that Act shall be construed as a reference to sub-paragraph (1) of paragraph 4 above;

    (d) any reference to the court includes a reference to a rent assessment committee;

    (e) paragraphs 6 to 8 and 11 shall be omitted;

    (f) any reference to a particular subsection of section 16 of the 1954 Act shall be construed as a reference to that subsection as it applies in relation to this Schedule;

    (g) any reference to a tenancy to which section 1 of the 1954 Act applies shall be construed as a reference to a long residential tenancy; and

    (h) expressions to which a meaning is assigned by any provision of this Schedule (other than this sub-paragraph) shall be given that meaning.

Application of other provisions of the 1954 Act

20.—(1) Section 16 of the 1954 Act (relief for tenant where landlord proceeding to enforce covenants) shall apply in relation to this Schedule as it applies in relation to Part I of that Act but subject to the following modifications—

(a) in subsection (1) the reference to a tenancy to which section 1 of the 1954 Act applies shall be construed as a reference to a long residential tenancy;

(b) in subsection (2) the reference to Part I of that Act shall be construed as a reference to this Schedule;

(c) subsection (3) shall have effect as if the words "(without prejudice to section ten of this Act)" were omitted; and

(d) in subsection (7) the reference to subsection (3) of section 2 of the 1954 Act shall be construed as a reference to paragraph 1(6) above.

(2) Section 55 of the 1954 Act (compensation for possession obtained by misrepresentation) shall apply in relation to this Schedule as it applies in relation to Part I of that Act.

1927 c. 36.

(3) Section 63 of the 1954 Act (jurisdiction of court for purposes of Parts I and II of the 1954 Act and of Part I of the Landlord and Tenant Act 1927) shall apply in relation to this Schedule and section 186 of this Act as it applies in relation to Part I of that Act.

(4) Section 65 of the 1954 Act (provisions as to reversions) applies for the purposes of this Schedule except that for any reference to that Act there shall be substituted a reference to this Schedule.

(5) Subsection (4) of section 66 of the 1954 Act (service of notices) shall apply in relation to this Schedule as it applies in relation to that Act.

21.—(1) Where this Schedule has effect in relation to a former 1954 Act tenancy the term date of which falls before 15th January 1999, any reference (however expressed) in the preceding provisions of this Schedule to the dwelling-house (or the property) let under the tenancy shall have effect as a reference to the premises qualifying for protection, within the meaning of the 1954 Act.

(2) Notwithstanding that at any time section 1 of the 1954 Act does not, and this Schedule does, apply to a former 1954 Act tenancy, any question of what are the premises qualifying for protection or (in that context) what is the tenancy shall be determined for the purposes of this Schedule in accordance with Part I of that Act.

Crown application

22.—(1) This Schedule shall apply where—

(a) there is an interest belonging to Her Majesty in right of the Crown and that interest is under the management of the Crown Estate Commissioners, or

(b) there is an interest belonging to Her Majesty in right of the Duchy of Lancaster or belonging to the Duchy of Cornwall,

as if it were an interest not so belonging.

(2) Where an interest belongs to Her Majesty in right of the Duchy of Lancaster, then, for the purposes of this Schedule, the Chancellor of the Duchy of Lancaster shall be deemed to be the owner of the interest.

(3) Where an interest belongs to the Duchy of Cornwall, then, for the purposes of this Schedule, such person as the Duke of Cornwall, or other possessor for the time being of the Duchy of Cornwall, appoints shall be deemed to be the owner of the interest.

SCHEDULE 11

Section 194.

Minor And Consequential Amendments

The Military Lands Act 1892

1. In section 8 of the Military Lands Act 1892 (provisions as to disbandment 1892 c. 43. of volunteer corps etc.) subsection (3) shall be omitted.

The Small Holdings and Allotments Act 1908

2. In section 52 of the Small Holdings and Allotments Act 1908 (borrowing 1908 c. 36. powers and expenses) subsection (3) shall be omitted.

The Prevention of Corruption Act 1916

3. In section 4 of the Prevention of Corruption Act 1916 (short title and 1916 c. 64. interpretation), at the end of subsection (2) (meaning of "public body") there shall be added "and companies which, in accordance with Part V of the Local Government and Housing Act 1989, are under the control of one or more local authorities".

The Education Act 1944

4. In Part II of Schedule 1 to the Education Act 1944 (education committees), 1944 c. 31. after paragraph 5 there shall be inserted the following paragraph—

"5A.—(1) The Secretary of State may by directions to local education authorities require every education committee, or education committee of a description specified in the direction, to include persons appointed, in accordance with the directions, for securing the representation on the committee of persons who appoint foundation governors of voluntary schools in the area for which the committee acts.

(2) The power of the Secretary of State to give directions under sub-paragraph (1) of this paragraph shall be exercisable in relation to sub-committees of education committees as it is exercisable in relation to the committees themselves.

(3) Arrangements approved under paragraph 1 above, orders made under paragraph 3 above and restrictions imposed under paragraph 10 below shall have effect (whether approved, made or imposed before or after the coming into force of this paragraph or the giving of the direction) subject to the requirements of any direction under this paragraph."

The Sexual Offences Act 1956

5. In Schedule 1 to the Sexual Offences Act 1956 (rights of landlord where 1956 c. 69. tenant convicted of permitting use of premises as a brothel) at the end of paragraph 5 there shall be added "Part I of the Housing Act 1988 and Schedule 10 to the Local Government and Housing Act 1989".

The Public Works Loans Act 1965

6. In section 2 of the Public Works Loans Act 1965 (new form of local loan and 1965 c. 63. automatic charge for securing it),—

    (a) in subsection (3) for the words "Part IX of the said Act of 1933" there shall be substituted "section 43 of the Local Government and Housing Act 1989 (borrowing powers)"; and

    (b) in subsection (5) for the words "section 197 of the Local Government Act 1933" there shall be substituted "section 47 of the Local Government and Housing Act 1989 (security for money borrowed)".

Sch. 11

1967 c. 61.

1967 c. 88.

The Public Works Loans Act 1967

7. In section 2 of the Public Works Loans Act 1967 (amendments as to local loans and automatic charges under s.2 of Act of 1965), in subsection (2) for the words "Part IX of the Local Government Act 1933" there shall be substituted "section 43 of the Local Government and Housing Act 1989 (borrowing powers)".

The Leasehold Reform Act 1967

8. In section 3 of the Leasehold Reform Act 1967 (meaning of "long tenancy"), in subsection (5) after "1954" there shall be inserted "under Schedule 10 to the Local Government and Housing Act 1989".

9. In section 9 of that Act (purchase price and costs of enfranchisement, and tenant's right to withdraw), in subsection (1A), in paragraph (b) after the word "premises" there shall be inserted—

"(i) if the tenancy is such a tenancy as is mentioned in subsection (2) or subsection (3) of section 186 of the Local Government and Housing Act 1989, or is a tenancy which is a long tenancy at a low rent for the purposes of Part I of the Landlord and Tenant Act 1954 in respect of which the landlord is not able to serve a notice under section 4 of that Act specifying a date of termination earlier than 15th January 1999, under the provisions of Schedule 10 to the Local Government and Housing Act 1989; and

(ii) in any other case".

10. In section 16 of that Act (exclusion of further rights after extension of lease) after subsection (1A) there shall be inserted the following subsection—

"(1B) A tenancy extended under section 14 above shall not be an assured tenancy or an assured agricultural occupancy, within the meaning of Part I of the Housing Act 1988, and Schedule 10 to the Local Government and Housing Act 1989 shall not apply to a tenancy so extended."

11. In section 22 of that Act (validity of tenants' notices, effect on the 1954 Act and on notices to quit etc. and procedure generally), in subsection (1) after paragraph (c) there shall be inserted the following paragraph—

"(cc) for adapting the procedure under Schedule 10 to the Local Government and Housing Act 1989, and for relating to one another proceedings under that Schedule and proceedings under this Part of this Act; and".

12. In section 37 of that Act (interpretation of Part I), in subsection (2)—

(a) after "1954" there shall be inserted "or paragraph 16(2) of Schedule 10 to the Local Government and Housing Act 1989";

(b) for the words "that Act", in the first place where they occur, there shall be substituted "the said Act of 1954 or, as the case may be, the said Schedule 10";

(c) for the words "that Act", in the second place where they occur, there shall be substituted "the said Act of 1954 or, as the case may be, the coming into force of the said Schedule 10"; and

(d) for the words "that Act", in the third place where they occur, there shall be substituted "the said Act of 1954 or, as the case may be, the said Schedule 10".

13.—(1) In Schedule 3 to that Act (validity of tenants' notices, effect on the 1954 Act etc. and procedure generally), in paragraph 1, in sub-paragraph (1) after "1954" there shall be inserted "or paragraph 17 of Schedule 10 to the Local Government and Housing Act 1989".

(2) In paragraph 2 of that Schedule—

    (a) in sub-paragraph (1) after "1954" there shall be inserted "or served under paragraph 4(1) of Schedule 10 to the Local Government and Housing Act 1989";

    (b) in sub-paragraph (2) after "1954" there shall be inserted "or under paragraph 4(1) of Schedule 10 to the Local Government and Housing Act 1989" and after the word "given" there shall be inserted "or served"; and

    (c) in sub-paragraph (3)—

        (i) after "1954" there shall be inserted "or served under paragraph 4(1) of Schedule 10 to the Local Government and Housing Act 1989";

        (ii) after the words "shall be" there shall be inserted—

            "(i) in the case of a notice given under the said Act of 1954"; and

        (iii) at the end there shall be added—

            "(ii) in the case of a notice served under the said Schedule 10, the date of termination specified in the previous notice or the expiration of the period of four months beginning on the date of service of the new notice, whichever is the later".

(3) In paragraph 3 of that Schedule, after sub-paragraph (2) there shall be inserted—

    "(3) The reference in sub-paragraph (2) above to section 16(2) of, and paragraph 9 of Schedule 5 to, the Landlord and Tenant Act 1954 includes a reference to those provisions as they apply in relation to Schedule 10 to the Local Government and Housing Act 1989."

(4) In paragraph 4 of that Schedule, after sub-paragraph (5) there shall be inserted—

    "(6) The references in this paragraph—

        (a) to section 16 of the Landlord and Tenant Act 1954 and subsection (2) of that section, and

        (b) paragraph 9 of Schedule 5 to that Act and sub-paragraph (2) of that paragraph,

    include references to those provisions as they apply in relation to Schedule 10 to the Local Government and Housing Act 1989."

(5) In paragraph 10 of that Schedule—

    (a) in sub-paragraph (1)—

        (i) after "1954" there shall be inserted "or under paragraph 4(1) of Schedule 10 to the Local Government and Housing Act 1989"; and

        (ii) in paragraph (a) for the words "either of those sections" there shall be substituted "any of those provisions"; and

    (b) in sub-paragraph (4) after "1954" there shall be inserted "or under paragraph 4(1) of Schedule 10 to the Local Government and Housing Act 1989".

The International Organisations Act 1968

14. In Schedule 1 to the International Organisations Act 1968 (privileges and immunities) after paragraph 9A there shall be inserted the following paragraph—   1968 c. 48.

"9B. The like exemption or relief from being subject to a community charge, or being liable to pay anything in respect of a community charge or anything by way of contribution in respect of a collective community charge, as is accorded to or in respect of the head of a diplomatic mission."

The Social Work (Scotland) Act 1968

1968 c. 49.

15. For paragraph 8 of Schedule 3 to the Social Work (Scotland) Act 1968 (expenses of children's panel members) there shall be substituted the following paragraph—

"8. A local authority may pay—

(a) to a member or possible member of the children's panel,

(b) to a member of the Children's Panel Advisory Committee,

such allowances as may be determined by the Secretary of State; and he may determine differently in relation to different cases or classes of case."

The Transport Act 1968

1968 c. 73.

16. In section 12 of the Transport Act 1968 (borrowing powers of Executive), in subsection (4) for the words from "and to borrow money for that purpose" onwards there shall be substituted "but only if the rate of interest payable by the Executive to the Authority in respect of the loan is not less than that which would be payable by the Authority if they were to borrow the same sum on equivalent terms (disregarding any terms as to interest) from another person".

The Local Authority Social Services Act 1970

1970 c. 42.

17. In section 4 of the Local Authority Social Services Act 1970, after subsection (1) there shall be inserted the following subsection—

"(1A) A local authority may establish sub-committees of their social services committee and may delegate to any such sub-committee any of the functions of the committee."

18. In section 5(4) of that Act for the words "section 4(2)" there shall be substituted "subsection (1A) or subsection (2) of section 4".

The Town and Country Planning Act 1971

1971 c. 78.

19. In section 130 of the Town and Country Planning Act 1971 (displacement of persons from land acquired or appropriated) in subsection (3) after the words "nothing in" there shall be inserted "Part I of the Housing Act 1988 or".

20. In section 192 of that Act (scope of planning blight provisions), in subsection (1) after paragraph (h) there shall be inserted the following paragraph—

"(ha) is land indicated by information published in pursuance of section 92 of the Local Government and Housing Act 1989 as land which a local authority propose to acquire in exercise of their powers under Part VII of that Act (renewal areas); or".

The Local Government Act 1972

1972 c. 70.

21. In section 80 of the Local Government Act 1972 (disqualifications for election and holding office as members of local authority), in subsection (1) after paragraph (a) there shall be inserted the following paragraph—

"(aa) holds any employment in a company which, in accordance with Part V of the Local Government and Housing Act 1989 other than section 73, is under the control of the local authority; or".

22. In section 94(5)(b) of that Act (allowances not to be treated as pecuniary interests), after the word "below" there shall be inserted the words "or under any scheme made by virtue of section 18 of the Local Government and Housing Act 1989".

23. In subsection (6) of section 97 of that Act (exclusion of disability from speaking and voting by reason of small shareholdings), for "£1,000" there shall be substituted "£5,000".

24. In section 100G of that Act (duty of principal councils to publish information), for paragraph (b) of subsection (1) there shall be substituted the following paragraph—

"(b) in respect of every committee or sub-committee of the council—

(i) the members of the council who are members of the committee or sub-committee or who are entitled, in accordance with any standing orders relating to the committee or sub-committee, to speak at its meetings or any of them;

(ii) the name and address of every other person who is a member of the committee or sub-committee or who is entitled, in accordance with any standing orders relating to the committee or sub-committee, to speak at its meetings or any of them otherwise than in the capacity of an officer of the council; and

(iii) the functions in relation to the committee or sub-committee of every person falling within sub-paragraph (i) above who is not a member of the committee or sub-committee and of every person falling within sub-paragraph (ii) above."

25. In section 102 of that Act (appointment of committees)—

(a) in paragraph (a) of subsection (1), after "may appoint a committee" there shall be inserted "or a sub-committee";

(b) in subsection (2), for "the appointing committee" there shall be substituted "the appointing authority or committee (as the case may be)"; and

(c) after subsection (4) there shall be inserted the following subsection—

"(4A) A local authority may appoint one or more sub-committees of a committee appointed by them under subsection (4) above to advise the committee with respect to any matter relating to the discharge of functions with respect to which the committee is appointed to advise."

26. Sections 173 and 173A of that Act (attendance allowance and financial loss allowance) shall be amended as follows—

(a) for the words "local authority", wherever they occur, there shall be substituted "parish or community council";

(b) in subsection (3) of each of those sections, for the word "authority" there shall be substituted "council"; and

(c) for the words "body to which this section applies" in subsection (4) of section 173 there shall be substituted "parish or community council".

27. In section 175 of that Act (allowances for conferences and meetings)—

(a) in subsection (1) (allowances payable), for the words from "allowances in the nature of" onwards there shall be substituted "allowances in the nature of an attendance allowance and an allowance for travelling and subsistence, as they think fit.

(1A) Payments made under subsection (1) above shall be of such reasonable amounts as the body in question may determine in a particular case or class of case but shall not exceed—

(a) in the case of payments of an allowance in the nature of an attendance allowance, such amounts as may be specified in or determined under regulations made by the Secretary of State; and

(b) in the case of payments of an allowance in the nature of an allowance for travel and subsistence in respect of a conference or meeting held in the United Kingdom, such amounts as may be specified under section 174 above for the corresponding allowance under that section;

and regulations made by the Secretary of State may make it a condition of any payment mentioned in paragraph (a) above that, in the financial year to which the payment would relate, the aggregate amount which the body in question has paid or is already liable to pay in respect of any prescribed allowance or allowances does not exceed such maximum amount as may be specified in or determined under the regulations.";

(b) in subsection (3B) (conferences to which section applies in relation to joint boards and committees), for the words "such body as is mentioned in section 177(1)(d) or (e) below" there shall be substituted the words "body which is a joint board, joint authority or other combined body all the members of which are representatives of local authorities".

28.—(1) Section 177 of that Act shall be amended as follows.

(2) For subsection (1) (bodies to which sections 173 to 175 apply) there shall be substituted the following subsection—

"(1) Subject to paragraph 4 of Schedule 2 to the Education Act 1980 (application of certain allowances to appeal committees), sections 174 and 175 above apply—

(a) to the bodies specified in section 21(1) of the Local Government and Housing Act 1989, except—

(i) the Common Council;

(ii) a body established pursuant to an order under section 67 of the Local Government Act 1985 (successors to residuary bodies); and

(iii) without prejudice to section 265 below, the Council of the Isles of Scilly;

(b) to any prescribed body on which a body to which those sections apply by virtue of paragraph (a) above is represented; and

(c) to any parish or community council."

(3) For subsection (2) (meaning of "approved duties") there shall be substituted the following subsection—

"(2) In sections 173 to 176 above "approved duty", in relation to a member of a body, means such duties as may be specified in or determined under regulations made by the Secretary of State."

(4) In subsection (4) (members not excluded from discussion of allowances), at the end there shall be inserted the words "or under any scheme made by virtue of section 18 of the Local Government and Housing Act 1989".

29. In section 178(2) of that Act (regulations with respect to allowances), for the words "177 or 177A" there shall be substituted "or 177".

30. In sub-paragraphs (1) and (2) of paragraph 41 of Schedule 12 to that Act (recording the minutes of meetings of local authorities), for the word "following" there shall be substituted "suitable"; and after sub-paragraph (3) of that paragraph there shall be inserted the following sub-paragraph—

"(4) For the purposes of sub-paragraphs (1) and (2) above the next suitable meeting of a local authority is their next following meeting or, where standing orders made by the authority in accordance with regulations under section 20 of the Local Government and Housing Act 1989 provide for another meeting of the authority to be regarded as suitable, either the next following meeting or that other meeting."

The Land Compensation Act 1973

31. In section 37 of the Land Compensation Act 1973 (disturbance payments for persons without compensatable interests), in subsection (2), in paragraph (c) for the words from "an owner-occupier's supplement" onwards there shall be substituted the words "a payment under section 584A(1) of the Housing Act 1985 (compensation payable in case of closing and demolition orders)". 1973 c. 26.

32.—(1) In section 42(6) of that Act, in the definition of "Housing Revenue Account dwelling", for the words from "Part XIII of the Housing Act 1985)" to the end there shall be substituted the words "Part VI of the Local Government and Housing Act 1989)". 1985 c. 68.

(2) This paragraph has effect for years beginning on or after 1st April 1990 and in this sub-paragraph "year" has the same meaning as in Part XIII of the Housing Act 1985 (general financial provisions).

The Local Government (Scotland) Act 1973

33. In section 38(4)(b) of the Local Government (Scotland) Act 1973 (allowances not to be treated as pecuniary interests) after the word "Act" there shall be inserted the words "or under any scheme made by virtue of section 18 of the Local Government and Housing Act 1989." 1973 c. 65.

34. In section 47 of that Act (allowances for conferences and meetings)—

(a) in subsection (1) (allowances payable), for the words from "allowances in the nature of" onwards there shall be substituted "allowances in the nature of an attendance allowance and an allowance for travel and subsistence, as they think fit.

(1A) payments made under subsection (1) above shall be of such reasonable amounts as the body in question may determine in a particular case or class of case but shall not exceed—

(a) in the case of payments of an allowance in the nature of an attendance allowance, such amounts as may be specified in or determined under regulations made by the Secretary of State; and

(b) in the case of payments of an allowance in the nature of an allowance for travel and subsistence in respect of a conference or meeting held in the United Kingdom, such amounts as may be specified under section 46 above for the corresponding allowance under that section;

and regulations made by the Secretary of State may make it a condition of any payment mentioned in paragraph (a) above that, in the financial year to which the payment would relate, the aggregate amount which the body in question has paid or is already liable to pay in respect of any prescribed allowance or allowances does not exceed such maximum amount as may be specified in or determined under the regulations.";

(b) in subsection (3A) (conferences to which section applies in relation to joint boards and committees), for the words "such body as is mentioned in section 49(1)(c) or (d) below" there shall be substituted the words "body which is a joint board, joint authority or other combined body all the members of which are representatives of local authorities".

35.—(1) Section 49 of that Act shall be amended as follows.

(2) For subsection (1) (bodies to which sections 46 and 47 apply) there shall be substituted the following subsection—

"(1) Sections 46 and 47 above apply—

(a) to the bodies specified in section 21(2) of the Local Government and Housing Act 1989; and

(b) to any prescribed body on which a body to which those sections apply by virtue of paragraph (a) above is represented."

(3) For subsection (2) (meaning of "approved duties") there shall be substituted the following subsection—

"(2) In sections 46 to 48 above "approved duty", in relation to a member of a body, means such duties as may be specified in or determined under regulations made by the Secretary of State."

(4) In subsection (4) (members not excluded from discussion of allowances), at the end there shall be inserted the words "or under any scheme made by virtue of section 18 of the Local Government and Housing Act 1989".

36. In sub-paragraph (1) of paragraph 7 of Schedule 7 to that Act (recording the minutes of meetings of local authorities) for the word "following" there shall be substituted the word "suitable"; and after sub-paragraph (2) of that paragraph there shall be inserted the following sub-paragraph—

"(3) For the purposes of sub-paragraph (1) above, the next suitable meeting of a local authority is their next following meeting or, where standing orders made by the authority in accordance with regulations under section 20 of the Local Government and Housing Act 1989 provide for another meeting of the authority to be regarded as suitable, either the next following meeting or that other meeting."

The Local Government Act 1974

37. In section 23(4) of the Local Government Act 1974 (consultation in appointing Local Commissioners), for the words "appropriate representative body," there shall be substituted the words "such persons as appear to the Secretary of State to represent authorities in England or, as the case may be, authorities in Wales to which this Part of this Act applies".

38. In section 23(12) of that Act (triennial reports to Part III authorities) the words "(through the appropriate representative body designated under section 24 below)" shall be omitted and at the end there shall be inserted the words "and shall send copies of those recommendations or conclusions to the representative persons and authorities concerned".

39.—(1) In section 31(3)(a) of that Act (further provisions about reports on investigations), for "(1) or (2A)" there shall be substituted "(2) or (2C)".

(2) This paragraph shall not have effect in relation to a report made before the coming into force of section 26 of this Act.

40. In section 32(1) of that Act (publications enjoying absolute privilege for the purposes of the law of defamation), the following paragraph shall be inserted at the end—

"(e) the publication of any matter by inclusion in a statement published in accordance with section 31(2D), (2E) and (2F) or (2G) above."

41. In Schedule 4 to that Act (further provisions about the Commissions)—

(a) in paragraph 6, after "Subject to" there shall be inserted "section 31(2H) above and"; and

(b) in paragraph 7, after "Subject to" there shall be inserted "section 31(2H) above and".

The Housing Act 1974

42. At the end of section 131(4) of the Housing Act 1974 (commencement orders, savings) there shall be added the words "and an order under subsection (3) above may be revoked or varied by a further order under that subsection which may itself contain such savings with respect to the effect of the revocation or variation as appear to the Secretary of State to be appropriate".

1974 c. 44.

The Local Government (Scotland) Act 1975

43. In section 4 of the Local Government (Scotland) Act 1975 (valuation appeal committees) after subsection (7) there shall be inserted the following subsection—

1975 c. 30.

"(7A) There shall be paid to members of a valuation appeal committee and to members of a local valuation panel such allowances as may be determined by the Secretary of State."

44.—(1) In section 29(3)(a) of that Act (further provisions about reports on investigations), for "(1) or (2A)" there shall be substituted "(2) or (2C)".

(2) This paragraph shall not have effect in relation to a report made before the coming into force of section 27 of this Act.

45. In section 30(1) of that Act (publications enjoying absolute privilege for the purposes of the law of defamation), the following paragraph shall be inserted at the end—

"(e) the publication of any matter by inclusion in a statement published in accordance with section 29(2D), (2E) and (2F) or (2G) of this Act."

46. In Schedule 4 to that Act (further provisions about the Commissioner) in paragraph 5, at the beginning, there shall be inserted "Subject to section 29(2H) of this Act,".

The Local Government (Miscellaneous Provisions) Act 1976

47. In section 33 of the Local Government (Miscellaneous Provisions) Act 1976 (restoration or continuation of supply of water, gas or electricity) in subsection (4) for the word "and", where it first occurs, there shall be substituted "the sum so recoverable, together with any interest accrued due, shall, until recovered, be a charge on the premises concerned and if" and at the end of that subsection there shall be inserted the following subsection—

1976 c. 57.

"(4A) A charge under subsection (4) above takes effect from the date when the council makes the payment referred to in that subsection and, for the purposes of enforcing a charge,—

(a) the council shall have the same powers and remedies, under the Law of Property Act 1925 and otherwise, as if it were a mortgagee by deed having powers of sale and lease, of accepting surrenders of leases and, subject to paragraph (b) below, of appointing a receiver; and

(b) the power to appoint a receiver shall be exercisable at any time after the expiry of one month from the date when the charge takes effect."

48. In section 40 of that Act (local authorities not affected by trusts attaching to certain securities issued by them), in subsection (1) after the word "officer" there shall be inserted "or other person".

SCH. 11

The Rent (Agriculture) Act 1976

1976 c. 80.

49. In section 33 of the Rent (Agriculture) Act 1976 (suspension of condition attached to planning permission), in subsection (2) after the words "let on or subject to" there shall be inserted "an assured agricultural occupancy, within the meaning of Chapter III of Part I of the Housing Act 1988, or".

50. In Schedule 2 to that Act (meaning of "relevant licence" and "relevant tenancy"), in paragraph 2 (meaning of "relevant tenancy") after "applies" there shall be inserted "a tenancy to which Schedule 10 to the Local Government and Housing Act 1989 applies".

The Rent Act 1977

1977 c. 42.

51. In section 74 of the Rent Act 1977 (regulations made by Secretary of State), in subsection (1), in paragraph (b) (procedure of rent officers and rent assessment committees) after "1988" there shall be inserted "or Schedule 10 to the Local Government and Housing Act 1989".

52.—(1) In section 116 of that Act (dwelling subject to statutory tenancy: works to which the tenant is unwilling to consent) in subsection (2) for the words from "paragraph (a)" to "paragraph (b)" there shall be substituted "any of paragraphs (a) to (c)".

(2) At the end of subsection (3) of that section there shall be added "or

(c) that the works were specified in an application for a renovation grant, a common parts grant, a disabled facilities grant or an HMO grant under Part VIII of the Local Government and Housing Act 1989 and the application has been approved."

(3) At the end of subsection (5) of that section there shall be added the words "or, as the case may be, with any condition under section 118(2) of the Local Government and Housing Act 1989".

53.—(1) In section 137 of that Act (effect on sub-tenancy of determination of superior tenancy), in subsection (5) after the words "a protected tenancy" there shall be inserted "or an assured tenancy, within the meaning of Part I of the Housing Act 1988".

(2) In subsection (6) of that section—

(a) in paragraph (a) after "1954" there shall be inserted "or, as the case may be, served under paragraph 4(1) of Schedule 10 to the Local Government and Housing Act 1989";

(b) in paragraph (b) for the words "that Act" there shall be substituted "the said Act of 1954 or, as the case may be, paragraph 3 of the said Schedule 10"; and

(c) in the words following paragraph (b) for the words "Part I of that Act" there shall be substituted "Part I of the said Act of 1954 or, as the case may be, the said Schedule 10".

The Protection from Eviction Act 1977

1977 c. 43.

54. In section 8 of the Protection from Eviction Act 1977 (interpretation), in subsection (1) (meaning of "statutorily protected tenancy") after paragraph (e) there shall be inserted—

"(f) a tenancy to which Schedule 10 to the Local Government and Housing Act 1989 applies".

The Education (Scotland) Act 1980

1980 c. 44.

55. In Schedule A1 to the Education (Scotland) Act 1980, for paragraph 9 there shall be substituted the following paragraph—

"9. There shall be paid to members of an appeal committee constituted in accordance with this Schedule such allowances as may be determined by the Secretary of State."

SCH. 11

The Local Government, Planning and Land Act 1980

56. In section 98 of the Local Government, Planning and Land Act 1980 (disposal of land at direction of Secretary of State), in subsection (8), at the end of paragraph (b) the word "or" shall be omitted and at the end of paragraph (c) there shall be added—

1980 c. 65.

"or

(d) in any case where the body to whom this Part of this Act applies is one of the bodies specified in subsection (8A) below, the other body is a company under the control or subject to the influence of that body within the meaning of Part V of the Local Government and Housing Act 1989 (companies in which local authorities have interests).

(8A) The bodies referred to in subsection (8)(d) above are—

(a) a county council;

(b) a district council;

(c) a London borough council;

(d) the Common Council of the City of London; and

(e) a joint authority established by Part IV of the Local Government Act 1985."

57. In section 100 of that Act (interpretation and extent of Part X) for subsection (1) there shall be substituted the following subsections—

"(1) Except where the context otherwise requires, in this Part of this Act, "subsidiary", in relation to a body to whom this Part of this Act applies, means—

(a) if that body is a county council, district council, London borough council, the Common Council of the City of London or a joint authority established by Part IV of the Local Government Act 1985, a company under the control, or subject to the influence, of that body within the meaning of Part V of the Local Government and Housing Act 1989 (companies in which local authorities have interests); and

(b) in the case of any other body, a wholly-owned subsidiary of that body.

(1A) In this Part of this Act, "wholly-owned subsidiary" has the meaning assigned to it by section 736 of the Companies Act 1985."

The New Towns Act 1981

58. In Schedule 9 to the New Towns Act 1981 (additional provisions as to the Commission for the New Towns), in paragraph 6 (sealing and execution of documents) after the word "member", in the first place where it occurs, there shall be inserted "or officer of the Commission".

1981 c. 64.

The Stock Transfer Act 1982

59. In section 1 of the Stock Transfer Act 1982 (transfer of certain securities through a computerised system), in subsection (3), in paragraph (b) for the words "paragraph 4 of Schedule 13 to the Local Government Act 1972" there shall be substituted "section 43 of the Local Government and Housing Act 1989 (borrowing powers)".

1982 c. 41.

SCH. 11

1984 c. 28.

The County Courts Act 1984

60. In section 77 of the County Courts Act 1984 (appeals: general provisions), in subsection (6) after paragraph (ee) there shall be inserted the following paragraph—

> "(ef) paragraph 13(4) of Schedule 10 to the Local Government and Housing Act 1989; or".

Rent (Scotland) Act 1984

1984 c. 58.

61. In section 58(7) of the Rent (Scotland) Act 1984 (power to vary sum of £104 specified in phasing formula under section 58(2)) for the words "the sum specified in" there shall be substituted the words "or repealing any of the provisions of".

The Housing Act 1985

1985 c. 68.

62. In section 8 of the Housing Act 1985 (periodical review of housing needs), in subsection (2) for the words from "inspections" onwards there shall be substituted "the consideration of the housing conditions in their district under section 605".

63. In each of sections 47(4) and 48(3A) of that Act (limitation of service charges etc.), after the words "Part XV" there shall be inserted "of this Act or Part VIII of the Local Government and Housing Act 1989".

64. In section 54 of that Act (powers of entry), at the end of subsection (2) there shall be added the words "and shall, if so required, be produced for inspection by the occupier or anyone acting on his behalf".

65.—(1) In section 55 of that Act (penalty for obstruction), in subsection (1) after the word "offence" there shall be inserted "intentionally".

(2) In subsection (2) of that section for the words "level 2" there shall be substituted "level 3".

66. In section 100 of that Act (power to reimburse cost of secure tenant's improvements), after subsection (2) there shall be inserted the following subsection—

> "(2A) In subsection (2)—
>
> > (a) the reference to an improvement grant under Part XV includes a reference to a renovation grant, disabled facilities grant or HMO grant under Part VIII of the Local Government and Housing Act 1989; and
> >
> > (b) the reference to a common parts grant under Part XV includes a reference to a common parts grant under the said Part VIII."

67. In section 101 of that Act (rent not to be increased on account of tenant's improvements), after subsection (1) there shall be inserted the following subsection—

> "(1A) In subsection (1)—
>
> > (a) the reference to an improvement grant under Part XV includes a reference to a renovation grant, disabled facilities grant or HMO grant under Part VIII of the Local Government and Housing Act 1989; and
> >
> > (b) the reference to a common parts grant under Part XV includes a reference to a common parts grant under the said Part VIII."

68. In section 244 of that Act (environmental works), in subsection (3) after the word "works" there shall be inserted "(a)", after the word "grant", in the last place where it occurs, there shall be inserted "under Part XV" and at the end there shall be added "or

SCH. 11

"(b) which are included in the external works specified in a group repair scheme, within the meaning of Part VIII of the Local Government and Housing Act 1989, in which the person concerned is eligible to participate.

(3A) In subsection (3)—

(a) the reference to an improvement grant under Part XV includes a reference to a renovation grant, disabled facilities grant or HMO grant under Part VIII of the Local Government and Housing Act 1989; and

(b) the reference to a common parts grant under Part XV includes a reference to a common parts grant under the said Part VIII."

69. In section 255 of that Act (general powers of local housing authority in general improvement areas) after subsection (2) there shall be inserted the following subsection—

"(3) In subsection (2)(b)—

(a) the reference to an improvement grant under Part XV includes a reference to a renovation grant, disabled facilities grant or HMO grant under Part VIII of the Local Government and Housing Act 1989; and

(b) the reference to a common parts grant under Part XV includes a reference to a common parts grant under the said Part VIII."

70. In section 289 of that Act (declaration of clearance area), subsection (6) shall cease to have effect.

71. In section 327 of that Act (penalty for occupier causing or permitting overcrowding), in subsection (3)—

(a) for the words "level 1" there shall be substituted "level 2"; and

(b) for "£2" there shall be substituted "one-tenth of the amount corresponding to that level".

72. In section 331 of that Act (penalty for landlord causing or permitting overcrowding), in subsection (3)—

(a) for the words "level 1" there shall be substituted "level 2", and

(b) for "£2" there shall be substituted "one-tenth of the amount corresponding to that level".

73. In section 340 of that Act (powers of entry), at the end of subsection (2) there shall be added the words "and shall, if so required, be produced for inspection by the occupier or anyone acting on his behalf".

74.—(1) In section 341 of that Act (penalty for obstruction), in subsection (1) after the word "offence" there shall be inserted "intentionally".

(2) In subsection (2) of that section for the words "level 2" there shall be substituted "level 3".

75. In section 408 of that Act (offences under Part XII), in subsection (2)—

(a) for the words "level 1" there shall be substituted "level 2", and

(b) for "£2" there shall be substituted "one-tenth of the amount corresponding to that level".

76.—(1) In section 412 of that Act (penalty for obstruction), in subsection (1) for the word "wilfully" there shall be substituted "intentionally".

(2) In subsection (2) of that section for the words "level 1" there shall be substituted "level 3".

77.—(1) In subsection (1) of section 421 of that Act (housing subsidy), for the words "housing authorities" there shall be substituted the words "new town corporations and the Development Board for Rural Wales".

(2) In subsection (2) of that section, for paragraphs (a) and (b) there shall be substituted the words "to the body's housing account".

(3) This paragraph and paragraphs 78 to 84 below have effect for years beginning on or after 1st April 1990 and in this sub-paragraph "year" has the same meaning as in Part XIII of that Act (general financial provisions).

78.—(1) In subsection (1) of section 422 of that Act (calculation of housing subsidy for local housing authorities), for the words "local housing authority" there shall be substituted the words "new town corporation" and for the word "authority's" there shall be substituted the word "corporation's".

(2) In subsection (2) of that section, for the word "authority" there shall be substituted the word "corporation".

79.—(1) In subsection (1) of section 423 of that Act (the base amount), for the words "local housing authority's" there shall be substituted the words "new town corporation's" and for the word "authority" there shall be substituted the word "corporation".

(2) In subsection (2) of that section, the words "any description of authority or" shall cease to have effect.

80.—(1) In subsection (1) of section 424 of that Act (the housing costs differential), for the words "local housing authority's" there shall be substituted the words "new town corporation's".

(2) In subsection (2) of that section, for the words "local housing authority's" there shall be substituted the words "new town corporation's", for the word "authority", in each place where it occurs, there shall be substituted the word "corporation" and for the words "the authority's Housing Revenue Account" there shall be substituted the words "the corporation's housing account".

(3) For subsection (3) of that section there shall be substituted the following subsection—

"(3) A determination may be made for all new town corporations or different determinations may be made for individual corporations; and a determination may be varied or revoked in relation to all or any of the corporations for which it was made."

(4) In subsection (4) of that section, for the words "local housing authorities", in both places where they occur, there shall be substituted the words "new town corporations".

81.—(1) In subsection (1) of section 425 of that Act (the local contribution differential), for the words "local housing authority's" there shall be substituted the words "new town corporation's".

(2) In subsection (2) of that section, for the words "An authority's" there shall be substituted the words "A corporation's", for the word "authority", in both places where it occurs, there shall be substituted the word "corporation", for the words "Housing Revenue Account" there shall be substituted the words "housing account" and for the words "general rate fund" there shall be substituted the words "general revenue account".

(3) For subsection (4) of that section there shall be substituted the following subsection—

"(4) A determination may be made for all new town corporations or different determinations may be made for different corporations or groups of corporations."

(4) In subsection (5) of that section, for the words "local housing authorities", in both places where they occur, there shall be substituted the words "new town corporations".

(5) In subsection (6) of that section, for the word "authorities" there shall be substituted the words "corporations".

82. For section 426 of that Act there shall be substituted the following section—

"Calculation of housing subsidy for Board.

426.—(1) Sections 422 to 425 (calculation of housing subsidy) apply in relation to the Development Board for Rural Wales as they apply in relation to new town corporations, but subject to subsections (2) and (3).

(2) Section 425(2)(a) (reckonable income to include contributions from corporation's general revenue account) has effect with the substitution for the reference to any contribution made by the corporation out of their general revenue account of a reference to any contribution made by the Board out of revenue.

(3) The consultation required by section 424(4) or 425(5) (consultation before making general determinations) shall be with the Board."

83. In section 427(1) of that Act (recoupment of subsidy in certain cases), for the words "local housing authority or other body" there shall be substituted the words "new town corporation or the Development Board for Rural Wales" and for the words "the authority or other body" there shall be substituted the words "that body".

84. In section 427A of that Act (entitlement to subsidy in case of land subject to a management agreement), for the words "local housing authority or other body" there shall be substituted the words "new town corporation or the Development Board for Rural Wales" and for the words "that authority or body's" there shall be substituted the words "that body's".

85. In section 582 of that Act (restriction on recovery of possession after making of compulsory purchase order), in subsection (1)(b) for the words "section 243(2) (land in housing action area" there shall be substituted "section 93(2) of the Local Government and Housing Act 1989 (land in renewal area".

86. In section 584 of that Act (power to enter and determine short tenancies of land acquired or appropriated), in subsection (1), the word "or", in the last place where it occurs, shall be omitted and after the words "the provisions of Part IX relating to clearance areas," there shall be inserted "or

Part VII of the Local Government and Housing Act 1989 (renewal areas)".

87. In Schedule 14 to that Act (the keeping of the Housing Revenue Account), in Part V (other supplementary provisions), in paragraph 8 (contributions in respect of land in general improvement area), after the words "section 259" there shall be inserted "of this Act", after the words "general improvement area)" there shall be inserted "or section 96 of the Local Government and Housing Act 1989 (contributions by Secretary of State towards expenditure on renewal area)" and after the words "Part II" there shall be inserted "of this Act".

88. In Schedule 16 to that Act (local authority mortgage interest rates), for paragraph 4 there shall be substituted the following paragraph—

"4.—(1) The rate declared under paragraph 3(a) or (b) shall be a rate calculated in such manner as the Secretary of State may determine.

(2) A determination under this paragraph—

(a) may make different provision for different cases or descriptions of cases, including different provision for different areas, for different local authorities or for different descriptions of local authorities; and

(b) may be varied or withdrawn by a subsequent determination.

(3) As soon as practicable after making a determination under this paragraph, the Secretary of State shall send a copy of the determination to the local authority or authorities to which it relates."

The Landlord and Tenant Act 1985

1985 c. 70.

89. In section 14 of the Landlord and Tenant Act 1985 (leases to which section 11—repairing obligations in short leases—applies: exceptions), in subsection (4) after the words "Rent Act 1977" there shall be inserted "or paragraph 8 of Schedule 1 to the Housing Act 1988".

90. In section 20A of that Act (service charges) after the words "Housing Act 1985" there shall be inserted "or Part VIII of the Local Government and Housing Act 1989" and at the end there shall be added the following subsection—

"(2) In any case where—

(a) relevant costs are incurred or to be incurred on the carrying out of works which are included in the external works specified in a group repair scheme, within the meaning of Part VIII of the Local Government and Housing Act 1989, and

(b) the landlord participated or is participating in that scheme as an assisted participant,

the amount which, in relation to the landlord, is the outstanding balance determined in accordance with subsections (3) and (4) of section 130 of that Act shall be deducted from the costs, and the amount of the service charge payable shall be reduced accordingly."

91.—(1) In section 21 of that Act (summary of relevant costs for the purposes of service charges), in subsection (5) after the words "Housing Act 1985" there shall be inserted "or Part VIII of the Local Government and Housing Act 1989".

(2) After subsection (5A) of that section there shall be inserted the following subsection—

"(5B) The summary shall state whether any of the costs relate to works which are included in the external works specified in a group repair scheme, within the meaning of Part VIII of the Local Government and Housing Act 1989, in which the landlord participated or is participating as an assisted participant."

The Education Act 1986

1986 c. 40.

92. In section 4(2)(a) of the Education Act 1986 (definition of "the pooling provisions" for the purposes of sections 2 and 3 of that Act) after "that Schedule" there shall be inserted "and section 147 of the Local Government and Housing Act 1989".

The Housing (Scotland) Act 1987

1987 c. 26.

93. In section 61(3) of the Housing (Scotland) Act 1987 (application of right to buy to tenants under secure tenancies granted after acquisition by landlord of defective dwelling) for "282(3)" there shall be substituted "282(2) or (3)".

94. In section 62(1) of that Act (price at which secure tenant entitled to buy house to be market value less discount) there shall be inserted after "fixed" the words "as at the date of service of the application to purchase".

95. In section 239A(1) of that Act (directions to prevent duplications of grant), at the end there shall be inserted the words "or are or are not to perform their duties under this Part".

The Local Government Act 1988

96. In section 25 of the Local Government Act 1988 (consent required for provision of financial assistance etc.) in subsection (1)(b) after the word "power" there shall be inserted "(whether conferred before or after the passing of this Act)".

1988 c. 9.

97. In section 33 of that Act (local authority companies), after subsection (2) there shall be inserted—

"(2A) In relation to England and Wales, a company is also associated with a local authority, or relevant public body, to which Part V of the Local Government and Housing Act 1989 applies (companies in which local authorities have interests) if the company is under the control or subject to the influence of the authority or body within the meaning of that Part or the authority or body has a minority interest in the company."

The Education Reform Act 1988

98. The following subsection shall be inserted after section 81(8) of the Education Reform Act 1988 (method of recovering from local funds sums in respect of maintenance)—

1988 c. 40.

"(8A) Where the authority mentioned in subsection (8) above is an English authority, that subsection shall have effect as if the reference in paragraph (b) to grant did not include a reference to revenue support grant or additional grant (as to deductions from which provision is made by sections 141 to 141B of the Local Government Finance Act 1988)."

The Housing (Scotland) Act 1988

99. In section 16 of the Housing (Scotland) Act 1988—

1988 c. 43.

(a) in paragraph (b) (ii) of subsection (1) (tenant under statutory assured tenancy not bound by certain original provisions for rent increases)—

(i) after the words "specified in" there shall be inserted the words "or fixed by reference to factors specified in"; and

(ii) after the words "there specified" there shall be inserted the words ", or fixed by reference to factors there specified,"; and

(b) after that subsection there shall be inserted the following subsection—

"(1A) The factors referred to in subsection (1) (b) (ii) above must be—

(a) factors which, once specified, are not wholly within the control of the landlord; and

(b) such as will enable the tenant at all material times to ascertain without undue difficulty any amount or percentage falling to be fixed by reference to them."

100. In section 24 of that Act—

(a) in subsection (1) (procedure for securing rent increase in assured tenancies)—

(i) for the word "an" there shall be substituted the words "a statutory"; and

Sch. 11

(ii) in each of paragraphs (a) and (b), after the word "was" there shall be inserted the words "at the time of service of the notice".

(b) in subsection (5) (saving, from rent increase procedure for assured tenancies, of operation of certain tenancy provisions for such increases)—

(i) for the words from "affects" to "tenancy", where first occurring, there shall be substituted the following—

"(a) extends to a statutory assured tenancy of which there is a term".

(ii) after the words "specified in" there shall be inserted the words ", or fixed by reference to factors specified in,";

(iii) after the words "there specified" there shall be inserted the words ", or fixed by reference to factors there specified,"; and

(iv) there shall be inserted at the end the words "or

(b) affects the operation of any term of a contractual tenancy which makes provision for an increase in rent (including provision whereby the rent for a particular period will or may be greater than that for an earlier period)"; and

(c) after that subsection there shall be inserted the following subsection—

"(6) The factors referred to in subsection (5) above must be—

(a) factors which, once specified, are not wholly within the control of the landlord; and

(b) such as will enable the tenant at all material times to ascertain without undue difficulty any amount or percentage falling to be fixed by reference to them."

The Housing Act 1988

1988 c. 50.

101. In section 7 of the Housing Act 1988 (orders for possession), in subsection (3) for the words "subsection (6)" there shall be substituted "subsections (5A) and (6)".

(2) In subsection (4) of that section for the words "subsection (6)" there shall be substituted "subsections (5A) and (6)".

(3) After subsection (5) of that section there shall be inserted the following subsection—

"(5A) The court shall not make an order for possession of a dwelling-house let on an assured periodic tenancy arising under Schedule 10 to the Local Government and Housing Act 1989 on any of the following grounds, that is to say,—

(a) Grounds 1, 2 and 5 in Part I of Schedule 2 to this Act;

(b) Ground 16 in Part II of that Schedule; and

(c) if the assured periodic tenancy arose on the termination of a former 1954 Act tenancy, within the meaning of the said Schedule 10, Ground 6 in Part I of Schedule 2 to this Act."

102. In section 15 of that Act (limited prohibition on assignment etc. without consent), in subsection (3) after the words "which is not a statutory periodic tenancy" there shall be inserted "or an assured periodic tenancy arising under Schedule 10 to the Local Government and Housing Act 1989".

103. In section 21 of that Act (recovery of possession on expiry or termination of assured shorthold tenancy), in subsection (1)(a) for the words "a statutory periodic tenancy" there shall be substituted "an assured shorthold periodic tenancy (whether statutory or not)".

104. In section 34 of that Act (new protected tenancies etc. restricted to special cases), in subsection (1) for paragraph (d) there shall be substituted the following paragraph—

> "(d) it is a tenancy under which the interest of the landlord was at the time the tenancy was granted held by a new town corporation, within the meaning of section 80 of the Housing Act 1985, and, before the date which has effect by virtue of paragraph (a) or paragraph (b) of subsection (4) of section 38 below, ceased to be so held by virtue of a disposal by the Commission for the New Towns made pursuant to a direction under section 37 of the New Towns Act 1981".

105.—(1) In section 35 of that Act (removal of special regimes for tenancies of housing associations etc.) in subsection (2) for paragraph (d) there shall be substituted the following paragraph—

> "(d) it is a tenancy under which the interest of the landlord was at the time the tenancy was granted held by a new town corporation, within the meaning of section 80 of the Housing Act 1985, and, before the date which has effect by virtue of paragraph (a) or paragraph (b) of subsection (4) of section 38 below, ceased to be so held by virtue of a disposal by the Commission for the New Towns made pursuant to a direction under section 37 of the New Towns Act 1981".

(2) At the beginning of subsection (4) of that section there shall be inserted the words "Subject to section 38 (4A) below".

106.—(1) In section 38 of that Act (transfer of existing tenancies from public to private sector) at the beginning of subsection (3) there shall be inserted "Subject to subsections (4) and (4A) below".

(2) In subsection (4) of that section (special provisions for tenancies held of a new town corporation) after the words "Housing Act 1985" there shall be inserted "and which subsequently ceases to be so held by virtue of a disposal by the Commission for the New Towns made pursuant to a direction under section 37 of the New Towns Act 1981".

(3) After subsection (4) of that section there shall be inserted the following subsection—

> "(4A) Where, by virtue of a disposal falling within subsection (4) above and made before the date which has effect by virtue of paragraph (a) or paragraph (b) of that subsection, the interest of the landlord under a tenancy passes to a registered housing association, then, notwithstanding anything in subsection (3) above, so long as the tenancy continues to be held by a body which would have been specified in subsection (1) of section 80 of the Housing Act 1985 if the repeal of provisions of that section effected by this Act had not been made, the tenancy shall continue to be a secure tenancy and to be capable of being a housing association tenancy."

107. In section 105 of that Act (consent required for subsequent disposals after change of landlords under Part IV),

(a) at the end of subsection (4) (consent may be subject to conditions) there shall be added the words "and, without prejudice to the generality of the conditions subject to which consent may be given, a condition may be imposed requiring a payment by the new landlord either to the public sector landlord from whom he or, where subsection (3) above applies, a predecessor of his acquired the property or to such other person as may be specified in the consent"; and

(b) in subsection (7) (exempt disposals) in paragraph (b) for the words from "having the right" onwards there shall be substituted "exercising the right to buy it under Part V of the 1985 Act".

108. In Schedule 2 to that Act (grounds for possession of dwelling-houses let on assured tenancies), in Part I (grounds on which court must order possession), in Ground 6 in the paragraph following paragraph (c)—

    (a) after the words "joint tenants", in the second place where they occur, there shall be inserted "of the dwelling-house concerned";

    (b) for the words "of the dwelling-house concerned" there shall be substituted "or, as the case may be, under a tenancy to which Schedule 10 to the Local Government and Housing Act 1989 applied"; and

    (c) after the words "earlier assured tenancy", in the second place where they occur, there shall be inserted "or, as the case may be, to the grant of the tenancy to which the said Schedule 10 applied".

109. In Schedule 2 to that Act (grounds for possession of dwelling-houses let on assured tenancies) at the end of Ground 6 (landlord intending to demolish or reconstruct) there shall be added the following paragraph—

"For the purposes of this ground, every acquisition under Part IV of this Act shall be taken to be an acquisition for money or money's worth; and in any case where—

    (i) the tenancy (in this paragraph referred to as "the current tenancy") was granted to a person (alone or jointly with others) who, immediately before it was granted, was a tenant under a tenancy of a different dwelling-house (in this paragraph referred to as "the earlier tenancy"), and

    (ii) the landlord under the current tenancy is the person who, immediately before that tenancy was granted, was the landlord under the earlier tenancy, and

    (iii) the condition in paragraph (b) above could not have been fulfilled with respect to the earlier tenancy by virtue of an acquisition under Part IV of this Act (including one taken to be such an acquisition by virtue of the previous operation of this paragraph),

the acquisition of the landlord's interest under the current tenancy shall be taken to have been under that Part and the landlord shall be taken to have acquired that interest after the grant of the current tenancy."

110. In Schedule 5 to that Act (Housing for Wales), in paragraph 5 (remuneration and allowances), in sub-paragraph (1)—

    (a) for the words "Secretary of State" there shall be substituted "Corporation"; and

    (b) for the word "he" there shall be substituted "Secretary of State".

1985 c. 69.
111. In Schedule 6 to that Act, in paragraph 9 (amendments of section 15 of Housing Associations Act 1985), in sub-paragraph (2) for "(3)" there shall be substituted "(2A)".

1985 c. 68.
112. In Schedule 18 to that Act (enactments repealed) at the end of paragraph 4 at the end of that Schedule (scope of repeals of section 80 of the Housing Act 1985) there shall be added "and

    (c) do not have effect in relation to a tenancy while it is a housing association tenancy."

The Social Security Act 1989

1989 c. 24.
113. In paragraph 2(6) of Schedule 8 to the Social Security Act 1989 (interpretation of provisions relating to incapacity for work), for paragraphs (a) and (b) of the definition of "councillor's allowance" there shall be substituted the following paragraphs—

"(a) section 173 or 177 of the Local Government Act 1972 or a scheme
made by virtue of section 18 of the Local Government and
Housing Act 1989, other than such an allowance as is mentioned
in section 173(4) of that Act of 1972 or in section 18(2) of that Act
of 1989; or

(b) section 49 of the Local Government (Scotland) Act 1973 or a
scheme made by virtue of section 18 of the Local Government
and Housing Act 1989, other than such an allowance as is
mentioned in section 18(2) of that Act of 1989".

Section 194.

SCHEDULE 12

ENACTMENTS REPEALED

PART I

LOCAL AUTHORITY FINANCE

Chapter	Short title	Extent of repeal
38 and 39 Vict. c. 83.	The Local Loans Act 1875.	The whole Act.
45 and 46 Vict. c. 50.	The Municipal Corporations Act 1882.	In Part I of Schedule 9, the entry relating to the Local Loans Act 1875.
48 and 49 Vict. c. 30.	The Local Loans Sinking Funds Act 1885.	The whole Act.
51 & 52 Vict. c. 25.	The Railway and Canal Traffic Act 1888.	In section 54, subsections (3) and (4). In section 55, the words from "The term "conservancy authority"" onwards.
55 & 56 Vict. c. 43.	The Military Lands Act 1892.	Section 8(3).
8 Edw. 7 c. 36.	The Small Holdings and Allotments Act 1908.	Section 52(3).
9 and 10 Geo. 6 c. 58.	The Borrowing (Control and Guarantees) Act 1946.	In section 1, in the proviso to subsection (1) the words "(other than a local authority)".
11 & 12 Geo. 6 c. 26.	The Local Government Act 1948.	In section 125(2)(d), the words from "section thirty" to "Act) or".
7 and 8 Eliz. 2 c. 53.	The Town and Country Planning Act 1959.	Section 27.
1964 c. 9.	The Public Works Loans Act 1964.	In section 6, in subsection (1) the words from "section 216(1)" to "London Government Act 1939 and".
1964 c. 48.	The Police Act 1964.	In section 8, subsection (2).
1968 c. 73.	The Transport Act 1968.	In section 12, subsection (6) and in subsection (7), in paragraph (b), the words "section 203 of the Local Government Act 1933 and".
1969 c. 19.	The Decimal Currency Act 1969.	In Schedule 2, paragraph 14.
1971 c. 78.	The Town and Country Planning Act 1971.	In section 123, subsection (8).
1972 c. 70.	The Local Government Act 1972.	In section 68, subsections (6) and (7). Section 123(6). Section 153.

Chapter	Short title	Extent of repeal
		In section 172, the words from the beginning to "their funds, and". In Schedule 13, paragraphs 1 to 22 and paragraph 26.
1974 c. 7.	The Local Government Act 1974.	In Schedule 7, paragraph 12.
1976 c. 57.	The Local Government (Miscellaneous Provisions) Act 1976.	Section 28.
1980 c. 65.	The Local Government, Planning and Land Act 1980.	Sections 71 to 80B. Sections 82 to 85. Schedule 12.
1982 c. 32.	The Local Government Finance Act 1982.	In section 5, subsection (1). In Schedule 5, paragraph 8(3).
1982 c. 41.	The Stock Transfer Act 1982.	In section 5, subsection (1).
1985 c. 51.	The Local Government Act 1985.	Sections 70 and 71. In section 74(5), the words from "(including" to "1875)". Sections 75 and 76. In section 77, in subsection (1), paragraph (a) and in subsection (3), paragraph (c) and the word "and" immediately preceding it. In Schedule 14, paragraph 17 and in paragraph 59(1), paragraphs (c) and (d).
1985 c. 67.	The Transport Act 1985.	In Schedule 3, paragraph 29.
1985 c. 68.	The Housing Act 1985.	In section 34, subsection (4B). In section 43, subsection (4B). Section 430.
1986 c. 10.	The Local Government Act 1986.	Section 8.
1986 c. 31.	The Airports Act 1986.	In section 21, subsections (1) to (3) and in subsection (4) the words from the beginning to "1980; and". In section 22, subsections (1) to (4). Section 71.
1987 c. 6.	The Local Government Finance Act 1987.	In Schedule 1, paragraphs 7 and 8.
1987 c. 44.	The Local Government Act 1987.	Section 1. The Schedule.
1988 c. 4.	The Norfolk and Suffolk Broads Act 1988.	In section 14(14), the words from "section 34" to "1875 and". In Schedule 6, paragraph 21.

Chapter	Short title	Extent of repeal
1988 c. 40.	The Education Reform Act 1988.	In section 177, subsection (4). In section 190, in subsection (5), paragraph (b) and the word "and" immediately preceding it. In section 201, in subsection (5), paragraph (b) and the word "and" immediately preceding it. In Schedule 12, paragraphs 47 and 48.
1988 c. 41.	The Local Government Finance Act 1988.	Sections 130 to 132.
1988 c. 50.	The Housing Act 1988.	Section 129(5)(a). In section 132, subsections (4) and (5). Section 136.

PART II

OTHER REPEALS

Chapter	Short title	Extent of repeal
1897 c. cxxxiii.	The City of London Sewers Act 1897.	Section 17.
15 & 16 Geo 6 & 1 Eliz. 2. c. 54.	The Town Development Act 1952.	The whole Act.
4 and 5 Eliz. 2. c. 60.	The Valuation and Rating (Scotland) Act 1956.	Section 22(4).
9 & 10 Eliz. 2. c. 33.	The Land Compensation Act 1961.	Section 10. Schedule 2.
10 & 11 Eliz. 2. c. 9.	The Local Government (Financial Provisions etc.) (Scotland) Act 1962.	In section 4, subsections (3) and (4). The first Schedule.
10 & 11 Eliz. 2. c. 38.	The Town and Country Planning Act 1962.	In Schedule 12, the entry relating to the Town Development Act 1952.
1968 c. 72.	The Town and Country Planning Act 1968.	Section 99.
1971 c. 78.	The Town and Country Planning Act 1971.	In Schedule 23, the entry relating to the Town Development Act 1952.
1972 c. 70.	The Local Government Act 1972.	In section 80, in subsection (1)(a), the words "joint board, joint authority or". In section 101, in subsection (6), the words "or borrowing money".

Chapter	Short title	Extent of repeal
		In section 102(3), the words from "but at least" onwards.
		Section 110.
		In section 137, subsections (2A), (2B), (2C)(a) and (8).
		In section 177, subsection (2A) and in subsection (3), the words "(but not for the purposes of subsection (2A) above)", and subsection (5).
		Section 177A.
		In section 178, in subsection (1), the words "and 177A".
		Section 185.
		Section 265A(1)(g).
		Schedule 18.
1973 c. 26.	The Land Compensation Act 1973.	In section 29, in subsection (1), in paragraph (b), the words from "or the service" onwards and in subsection (7), in paragraph (c), the words "211, 264 or" and the words from "(undertaking" onwards.
		In section 37, in subsection (1), in paragraph (b), the words from "or the service" onwards and in subsection (2), paragraph (b)(ii).
		Section 39(1)(d).
		In section 73, subsections (4) and (5).
1973 c. 37.	The Water Act 1973.	In Schedule 8, paragraphs 64 and 65.
1973 c. 65.	The Local Government (Scotland) Act 1973.	In section 31(1)(a)(ii), the words "or joint board".
		Sections 45 and 45A.
		Section 49(1A).
		Section 49A.
		In section 57(3), the words from "but at least" onwards.
		Section 110A(2).
		In section 111(1), paragraphs (a), (b) and (d).
		In section 161(6), the words from "but at least" onwards.
		In Schedule 10, paragraph 11.

Chapter	Short title	Extent of repeal
1974 c. 7.	The Local Government Act 1974.	In Schedule 20, paragraph 10.
		In section 23, in subsections (4), (5) and (6) the word "Local" and in subsection (12), the words "(through the appropriate representative body designated under section 24 below)".
		Section 24.
		In section 25(4)(b), the words from "or section 110" to "authorities)".
		In section 34(1), the definition of "representative body".
1974 c. 44.	The Housing Act 1974.	In Schedule 13, paragraphs 38(1)(a) and 39(1)(a) and in paragraph 40(1) the words from "and at the end of that paragraph" onwards.
1975 c. 30.	The Local Government (Scotland) Act 1975.	In Schedule 6, in Part II, paragraph 46.
1975 c. 76.	The Local Land Charges Act 1975.	In section 9, in subsection (2), the words from the beginning to "in writing, and".
1976 c. 74.	The Race Relations Act 1976.	In section 47, in subsection (1)(c), the words following "field of housing", and in subsections (1)(d) and (3A), the word "rented".
1979 c. 55.	The Justices of the Peace Act 1979.	In section 59, in subsection (1)(a) the words "or this Part".
1980 c. 20.	The Education Act 1980.	In Schedule 2, in paragraph 4, the words "173(4) and".
1980 c. 45.	The Water (Scotland) Act 1980.	Section 40(7).
1980 c. 65.	The Local Government, Planning and Land Act 1980.	Section 26(1) to (3).
1981 c. 64.	The New Towns Act 1981.	Part III.
		In section 72(1), paragraph (b) and the word "or" immediately preceding it.
		In Schedule 9, in sub-paragraph (2) of paragraph 3, the words from "but" onwards.
1981 c. 67.	The Acquisition of Land Act 1981.	In the Table in paragraph 1 of Schedule 4, the entry relating to the Town Development Act 1952.

Chapter	Short title	Extent of repeal
1983 c. 52.	The Local Authorities (Expenditure Powers) Act 1983.	The whole Act.
1984 c. 11.	The Education (Grants and Awards) Act 1984.	In section 1, in subsection (6) the words "or section 2 below" and in subsection (7), the words "or section 2 below" and "in those sections". Section 2.
1985 c. 5.	The New Towns and Urban Development Corporations Act 1985.	Sections 3 and 4. In Schedule 2, paragraph 2. In Schedule 3, paragraph 7.
1985 c. 51.	The Local Government Act 1985.	Section 33. In Schedule 8, paragraphs 8 and 9(2). In Schedule 14, paragraphs 19 and 20.
1985 c. 68.	The Housing Act 1985.	Section 107. In section 191(3) the words "(repair notice in respect of unfit dwelling-house)". Section 192. In section 197, in subsection (1), paragraph (c) and the word "or" immediately preceding it. Sections 205 and 206. In section 208, the entries beginning "house" and "reasonable expense". Sections 209 to 238. Section 266. In section 268, in subsection (1), paragraph (a) and, in paragraph (b), the word "other". In section 269, in subsection (3), paragraph (b) and the word "and" immediately preceding it; and subsections (4) and (5). In section 279(2) the words "section 266 (parts of buildings and underground rooms)". Sections 280 to 282. Section 289(6). In section 291(3) the words "Schedule 11 (rehabilitation orders)". Section 299. In section 300, subsection (4). Sections 312 to 314. In section 315(1)(a) the words "or person having control".

Chapter	Short title	Extent of repeal
		Section 321.
		In section 322 the definition of "person having control".
		In section 323, the entries beginning "the full standard", "general improvement area", "house", "land liable to be cleared", "person having control", "slum clearance functions", "slum clearance subsidy" and "year".
		In section 346, in subsection (1) paragraph (b) and the word "and" immediately preceding it and in subsections (2) and (3) the words "or building" in each place where they occur.
		In section 349, in subsection (2)(b) the words "and buildings".
		In section 350, in subsection (1) the words "or building" in each place where they occur.
		Section 352(6).
		Sections 366 and 367.
		In section 369, in subsection (3), paragraph (b), in paragraph (c) the words from "and in particular" onwards and paragraph (f); in subsection (5) the words from "as applied" to "a house".
		Sections 370 and 371.
		In section 372(1) the words from "to which" to "management code)", the word "or" at the end of paragraph (a) and paragraph (b).
		Section 374.
		In section 375, in subsection (1) the word "366".
		In section 376, in subsection (1) the word "366", in subsection (3) the words "and to the period for compliance" and subsection (4).
		In section 377, in subsection (1)(a) the word "366".
		In section 378, in subsection (2)(a) the word "366".
		Section 379(1)(c), except the word "or".

Chapter	Short title	Extent of repeal
		In section 381, in subsection (4) the words "366, 370".
		In section 392, in subsection (5)(a) the word "366".
		Sections 417 to 420.
		In section 423(2), the words "any description of authority or".
		In section 434, the entries beginning "general rate fund", "hostel", "houses or other property within the account", "Housing Repairs Account", "Housing Revenue Account" and "loan charges".
		In section 459, the entry beginning "Housing Revenue Account".
		Sections 460 to 522.
		Sections 524 to 526.
		In section 567, in subsection (4), paragraph (c) except for the final "or", in subsection (5), the words "regulations under subsection (4)(c) or" and subsection (6).
		In section 569, subsection (5).
		Sections 579 to 581.
		In section 582, the words from "section 192" to "beyond repair) or".
		Sections 585 to 595.
		Section 598.
		In section 599, the words from "section 192" to "beyond repair)".
		In section 602, the definition of "house".
		In section 608, the words from "section 192" to "beyond repair) or".
		In section 624 the entry beginning "house".
		In Schedule 10, in paragraph 1, the words "section 214 or 215 (improvement notices)" and the word "366", in paragraph 2(2)(b) the word "366", paragraph 5 and in paragraph 6, in sub-paragraph (1) the words from "or by an order" to "such expenses" and the words "or of the order"

Chapter	Short title	Extent of repeal
		and in sub-paragraphs (2) and (3) the words "or order"; and in paragraph 8(1) the word "366". Schedule 11. Schedule 12. In Schedule 13, in paragraph 21(4), the word "366" in paragraph (a), the word "or" at the end of paragraph (b), paragraph (c) and the words "or order". Schedule 14. Schedules 22 to 24.
1985 c. 71.	The Housing (Consequential Provisions) Act 1985.	In Schedule 2, paragraph 4, in paragraph 24, sub-paragraphs (2)(a), (3)(a), (3)(c) and (4)(a) and paragraphs (c) to (f) of sub-paragraph (8) and paragraph 49.
1986 c. 1.	The Education (Amendment) Act 1986.	Sections 1 and 3.
1986 c. 10.	The Local Government Act 1986.	Section 11.
1986 c. 50.	The Social Security Act 1986.	In section 30(10), the words "rate fund".
1986 c. 63	The Housing and Planning Act 1986.	Section 1. Section 15. Section 20. Section 42(1)(d). Schedule 3. In Schedule 5, sub-paragraphs (1) and (5) of paragraph 10.
1987 c. 26.	The Housing (Scotland) Act 1987.	In section 61(10)(a)(v), the words "in the discretion of the landlord". Section 80.
1987 c. 47.	The Abolition of Domestic Rates Etc. (Scotland) Act 1987.	In Schedule 1, paragraph 28(a)(ii) and (iii).
1988 c. 4.	The Norfolk and Suffolk Broads Act 1988.	In Schedule 6, in paragraph 10, sub-paragraphs (6) and (7).
1988 c. 9.	The Local Government Act 1988.	In section 25, in subsection (2), in paragraph (d) the words "an improvement notice" and in paragraph (e) the words "of an improvement notice under Part VII of the said Act of 1985 or" and the

Chapter	Short title	Extent of repeal
		words "or the acceptance of an undertaking under the said Part VII". In Schedule 3, paragraphs 7(2) and (3) and 15(a).
1988 c. 41.	The Local Government Finance Act 1988.	In section 33(4) the word "and" at the end of paragraph (c). In section 35, in subsections (3)(c) and (5)(c) the words "or under subsection (6) below", and subsections (6) and (7). In section 44, in subsection (2), the words from "or" to the end and subsection (3). In section 46(2), the words from "or" to the end. In section 55(7)(b) the words "at a prescribed rate". Section 77. In section 98(3)(d) the words "and calculated in a prescribed manner". In section 99(2)(d) the words "at such rate as may be prescribed". Section 119. Section 128(2). In section 140(2) the word "and" at the end of paragraph (e). In section 143(4) the words "57 or". In Schedule 2, in paragraph 2(2)(m), the words from "and" to the end; paragraph 12. In Schedule 6, in paragraph 1 the words ", and parts of them," and paragraph 4. In Schedule 7, in paragraph 10(1) the words "because of a failure to fulfil paragraph 9(2) or (3) above". In Schedule 8, paragraphs 9(7), 11(3) and 12(6). In Schedule 9, in paragraph 2(2)(h), the words from "and" to the end; paragraph 6(2). In Schedule 12, paragraphs 16 and 37.
1988 c. 43.	The Housing (Scotland) Act 1988.	Section 2(6).

SCH. 12

Chapter	Short title	Extent of repeal
1988 c. 50.	The Housing Act 1988.	In section 103, in subsection (4), at the end of paragraph (d) the word "and". Section 129(5)(b). Section 130(2). Section 131.
1989 c. 15.	The Water Act 1989.	In Schedule 25, paragraph 19 and in paragraph 80(2), the words from "to", in the first place where it occurs, to "his power", in the first place where they occur.

1. The repeal in the City of London Sewers Act 1897 shall have effect on the commencement day, within the meaning of section 6 of this Act.

2. The repeals in Parts XIII and XIV of the Housing Act 1985, section 30 of the Social Security Act 1986 and section 129 of the Housing Act 1988 shall have effect for years beginning on or after 1st April 1990.

3. The repeals in Schedule 3 to the Local Government Act 1988 shall have effect in relation to reports made after the coming into force of, in the case of paragraph 7(2) and (3), section 26 and, in the case of paragraph 15(a), section 27 of this Act.

4. The repeals in the Local Government Finance Act 1988 shall have effect in accordance with Schedule 5 to this Act.

Statute Law (Repeals) Act 1989

1989 CHAPTER 43

An Act to promote the reform of the statute law by the repeal, in accordance with recommendations of the Law Commission and the Scottish Law Commission, of certain enactments which (except in so far as their effect is preserved) are no longer of practical utility, and to make other provision in connection with the repeal of those enactments.   [16th November 1989]

A.D. 1989.

BE IT ENACTED by the Queen's most Excellent Majesty, by and with the advice and consent of the Lords Spiritual and Temporal, and Commons, in this present Parliament assembled, and by the authority of the same, as follows:—

1.—(1) The enactments mentioned in Schedule 1 to this Act are hereby repealed to the extent specified in the third column of that Schedule.

Repeals and associated provisions.

(2) Schedule 2 to this Act shall have effect.

2.—(1) This Act extends to Northern Ireland.

Extent.

(2) Any repeal by this Act of an enactment which extends to the Isle of Man shall also extend there.

(3) Subject to subsection (2) above, this Act does not repeal any enactment so far as the enactment forms part of the law of a country outside the United Kingdom; but Her Majesty may by Order in Council provide that the repeal by this Act of any enactment specified in the Order shall on a date so specified extend to any of the Channel Islands or any colony.

3.—(1) This Act may be cited as the Statute Law (Repeals) Act 1989.

Short title and commencement.

(2) The repeal by this Act of—

    (a) section 3 of the Federation of Malaya Independence Act 1957, and

1957 c. 60.

     (b) section 5 of the Malaysia Act 1963,

shall come into force on such day as the Lord Chancellor may by order made by statutory instrument appoint.

SCHEDULES

SCHEDULE 1   Section 1(1).

REPEALS

PART I

ADMINISTRATION OF JUSTICE

Chapter	Short title	Extent of repeal
Group 1 - Bankruptcy Acts 1883, 1890 and 1913		
12 & 13 Vict. c.xciv.	City of London Municipal Elections Act 1849.	In section 9, the words "shall declare himself or shall be declared bankrupt or insolvent, or".
46 & 47 Vict. c.52.	Bankruptcy Act 1883.	The whole Act.
53 & 54 Vict. c.71.	Bankruptcy Act 1890.	The whole Act.
3 & 4 Geo. 5. c.34.	Bankruptcy and Deeds of Arrangement Act 1913.	The whole Act.
1985 c.66.	Bankruptcy (Scotland) Act 1985.	In Schedule 7, paragraph 2.
Group 2 - Police Acts		
2 & 3 Vict. c.47.	Metropolitan Police Act 1839.	Sections 13 and 29. Section 61 from "and the owner" onwards. Sections 62, 69, 73 and 77. Section 78 from "and all" onwards.
2 & 3 Vict. c.xciv.	City of London Police Act 1839.	Sections 18, 20, 21, 23, 26 and 27. In section 28, the proviso. Section 29. In section 31, the words "take into custody" and "and every person so found". Section 34. In section 35 — (a) paragraph 9 from "during" to "service, and"; (b) paragraph 10 from "or wilfully break" onwards; (c) in paragraph 12, the words "indecent or obscene", where first occurring, and from "or write" to "representation"; (d) paragraph 14 from "(except" to "duty)"; (e) the words from "And it shall be lawful" onwards. Sections 38 and 39.

Sch. 1

Chapter	Short title	Extent of repeal
2 & 3 Vict. c.xciv.—*cont.*	City of London Police Act 1839.—*cont.*	Section 42 from "and the owner" onwards. Sections 43 to 48. Sections 50 to 54. Sections 97 to 103.
10 & 11 Vict. c.89.	Town Police Clauses Act 1847.	The following provisions as they apply to England and Wales— Sections 15 and 30. In section 36, the words "take into custody" and "and every person so found". In sections 61 and 65, the words from "and in default" onwards. Section 75.
49 & 50 Vict. c.22.	Metropolitan Police Act 1886.	Section 1 from "This Act and" onwards. Schedule 1.
60 & 61 Vict. c.30.	Police (Property) Act 1897.	Section 1(1) from "or under section sixty-six" to "London". Section 1(3).
62 & 63 Vict. c.26.	Metropolitan Police Act 1899.	Section 1(2) from "either" to "Parliament, or" and from "or apportioned" to the end of the subsection.
4 & 5 Geo. 5. c.34.	Police Reservists (Allowances) Act 1914.	The whole Act.
5 & 6 Geo. 5. c.32.	Irish Police (Naval and Military Service) Act 1915.	Section 1(1).
1964 c.48.	Police Act 1964.	In Schedule 9, the entries relating to the Metropolitan Police Act 1839, the City of London Police Act 1839, the Town Police Clauses Act 1847, the National Insurance (Industrial Injuries) Act 1946, the Homicide Act 1957 and the Road Traffic and Roads Improvement Act 1960.
1976 c.63.	Bail Act 1976.	In Schedule 2, paragraph 2.

Group 3 - Scottish Courts, &c.

6 Geo. 4. c.86.	Courts of Justice (Scotland) Act 1825.	The whole Act.
9 Geo. 4. c.29.	Circuit Courts (Scotland) Act 1828.	Sections 6 and 16. Schedules A and C.
11 Geo. 4 & 1 Will. 4. c.37.	Criminal Law (Scotland) Act 1830.	Sections 9, 11 and 14.

Chapter	Short title	Extent of repeal
11 & 12 Vict. c.79.	Justiciary (Scotland) Act 1848.	The whole Act.
31 & 32 Vict. c.95.	Justiciary Court (Scotland) Act 1868.	The whole Act.
50 & 51 Vict. c.35.	Criminal Procedure (Scotland) Act 1887.	Section 46.
55 & 56 Vict. c.21.	High Court of Justiciary (Scotland) Act 1892.	The whole Act.
7 Edw. 7. c.51.	Sheriff Courts (Scotland) Act 1907.	Section 3(m).
17 & 18 Geo. 5. c.35.	Sheriff Courts and Legal Officers (Scotland) Act 1927.	Section 7.
3 & 4 Geo. 6. c.15.	Solicitors (Emergency Provisions) Act 1940.	The whole Act.
12, 13 & 14 Geo. 6. c.63.	Legal Aid and Solicitors (Scotland) Act 1949.	The whole Act.
2 & 3 Eliz. 2. c.48.	Summary Jurisdiction (Scotland) Act 1954.	Section 74.
1972 c.11.	Superannuation Act 1972.	In Schedule 6, paragraph 11.
1976 c.6.	Solicitors (Scotland) Act 1976.	The whole Act.
1976 c.14.	Fatal Accidents and Sudden Deaths Inquiry (Scotland) Act 1976.	Section 10(2), (3) and (5).
1980 c.55.	Law Reform (Miscellaneous Provisions) (Scotland) Act 1980.	Section 11(1) from "and accordingly" onwards; and section 11(2). Section 28(2). Schedule 3.

Group 4 - Vagrancy Law

Chapter	Short title	Extent of repeal
5 Geo. 4. c.83.	Vagrancy Act 1824.	The following provisions as they apply to England and Wales— Section 3 from the beginning to "manner; and". Section 4 from "every person pretending" to "subjects;" Section 5 from the beginning to "by virtue of this Act;" and from "and every person apprehended" to "so apprehended". In section 10, the words "in the house of correction". In section 22, the words "Provided also, that" and from "nor to alter" (where first occurring) onwards.
6 Geo. 4. c.97.	Universities Act 1825.	Section 3.

Chapter	Short title	Extent of repeal
34 & 35 Vict. c.96.	Pedlars Act 1871.	Section 13 as it applies to England and Wales.
57 & 58 Vict. c.lx.	Cambridge University and Corporation Act 1894.	Section 6.
Group 5 - General Repeals		
11 Geo. 2. c.19.	Distress for Rent Act 1737.	Section 14.
60 Geo. 3 & 1 Geo. 4. c.1.	Unlawful Drilling Act 1819.	Section 4.
1 & 2 Will. 4. c.32.	Game Act 1831.	In sections 3, 4, 12, 23, 24, 25, 27, 28, 30, 31 and 32, as they apply to England and Wales or Northern Ireland, the words "together with the costs of the conviction". Section 38.
8 & 9 Vict. c.124.	Leases Act 1845.	The whole Act, but without prejudice to any existing lease.
11 & 12 Vict. c.42.	Indictable Offences Act 1848.	Section 32 from the beginning to "Act, but".
14 & 15 Vict. c.19.	Prevention of Offences Act 1851.	The whole Act.
24 & 25 Vict. c.100.	Offences against the Person Act 1861.	Sections 39, 40 and 76, as they apply to England and Wales.
25 & 26 Vict. c.14.	Crown Suits (Isle of Man) Act 1862.	The whole Act.
27 & 28 Vict. c.24.	Naval Agency and Distribution Act 1864.	In section 2, the definition of "the High Court of Admiralty".
31 & 32 Vict. c.37.	Documentary Evidence Act 1868.	In the Schedule, the entry relating to the Poor Law Board.
32 & 33 Vict. c.62.	Debtors Act 1869.	Sections 18 and 23.
38 & 39 Vict. c.86.	Conspiracy and Protection of Property Act 1875.	Sections 10, 11, 13, 19 and 20.
46 & 47 Vict. c.3.	Explosive Substances Act 1883.	Section 7(4).
46 & 47 Vict. c.38.	Trial of Lunatics Act 1883.	Section 4.
50 & 51 Vict. c.53.	Escheat (Procedure) Act 1887.	The whole Act.
9 & 10 Geo. 5. c.71.	Sex Disqualification (Removal) Act 1919.	Section 1 from "Provided that" onwards. Section 2 as it applies to Scotland.
13 & 14 Geo. 5. c.9. (N.I.)	Criminal Evidence Act (Northern Ireland) 1923.	Section 5(1) from "except" onwards.

Chapter	Short title	Extent of repeal
15 & 16 Geo. 5. c.28.	Administration of Justice Act 1925.	Section 22(3). Section 22(4) from the beginning to "section, and" and the word "other" wherever occurring.
25 & 26 Geo. 5. c.25.	Counterfeit Currency (Convention) Act 1935.	The whole Act.
12, 13 & 14 Geo. 6. c.101.	Justices of the Peace Act 1949.	Sections 41, 43 and 45. Section 46(3) from "except" onwards. Schedule 7.
14 & 15 Geo. 6. c.65.	Reserve and Auxiliary Forces (Protection of Civil Interests) Act 1951.	The following provisions except as they extend to Northern Ireland— In section 27(1), the proviso from "or if" onwards. Section 38(6)(b) and the preceding "or". Section 46(4). Section 53. In Part I of Schedule 2— (a) in paragraph 6, the words "other than the metropolitan police court area" and "such"; (b) paragraphs 18 and 19. In Part II of Schedule 2— (a) in paragraph 3, the words "a standing joint committee or" and in column 2 the words "committee or"; (b) paragraphs 4(a), 5(a) and 6(a).
6 & 7 Eliz. 2. c.51.	Public Records Act 1958.	In Schedule 2, the entries relating to the Import Duties Act 1932, the Defence (General) Regulations 1939 and the Legal Aid and Solicitors (Scotland) Act 1949.
7 & 8 Eliz. 2. c.57.	Street Offences Act 1959.	Section 1(5).
7 & 8 Eliz. 2. c.65.	Fatal Accidents Act 1959.	The whole Act.
8 & 9 Eliz. 2. c.9.	Judicial Pensions Act 1959.	Section 3.
1968 c.69.	Justices of the Peace Act 1968.	In Schedule 3, paragraphs 1 and 6.
1970 c.31.	Administration of Justice Act 1970.	Section 30. In Schedule 4, paragraph 2.
1971 c.32.	Attachment of Earnings Act 1971.	In Schedule 2, paragraph 2.
1973 c.15.	Administration of Justice Act 1973.	Sections 19 and 20. Schedule 5.

SCH. 1

Chapter	Short title	Extent of repeal
1974 c.47.	Solicitors Act 1974.	Section 75(a).
1980 c.43.	Magistrates' Courts Act 1980.	In Schedule 1, paragraphs 15, 21 and 24.
1981 c.54.	Supreme Court Act 1981.	Section 11(10). Section 89(5), (6) and (7). In Schedule 6, paragraphs 1, 2(2), 3 and 6.
1982 c.53.	Administration of Justice Act 1982.	Section 60.
1984 c.28.	County Courts Act 1984.	In Schedule 3, paragraphs 1 to 3, 4(2) and 10.

PART II
FINANCE

Chapter	Short title	Extent of repeal
Group 1 - Land Tax		
27 Geo. 3. c.34.	Duchy of Lancaster Act 1787.	In section 2, the words "after deducting the land tax chargeable thereon".
38 Geo. 3. c.5.	Land Tax Act 1797.	The whole Act.
42 Geo. 3. c.116.	Land Tax Redemption Act 1802.	The whole Act.
50 Geo. 3. c.58.	Land Tax Redemption Act 1810.	The whole Act.
53 Geo. 3. c.123.	Land Tax Redemption Act 1813.	The whole Act.
57 Geo. 3. c.100.	Land Tax Redemption Act 1817.	The whole Act.
26 & 27 Vict. c.49.	Duchy of Cornwall Management Act 1863.	Section 8 from "or in the redemption" to "for that purpose."
59 & 60 Vict. c.28.	Finance Act 1896.	Part VI.
12, 13 & 14 Geo. 6. c.47.	Finance Act 1949.	Part V. Section 52(6). Schedule 9. In Schedule 11, Part VI.
1963 c.25.	Finance Act 1963.	Section 68. In Schedule 14, Parts V and VI.
Group 2 - Other Repeals		
14 Geo. 3. c.21.	Bank of Ayr Act 1774.	The whole Act.
7 Geo. 4. c.6.	Bank Notes Act 1826.	The whole Act.
19 & 20 Vict. c.43.	Hereditary Revenues Act 1856.	The whole Act.
43 & 44 Vict. c.8.	Isle of Man Loans Act 1880.	The whole Act.

Chapter	Short title	Extent of repeal
44 & 45 Vict. c.38.	Public Works Loans Act 1881.	The whole Act.
55 & 56 Vict. c.35.	Colonial Stock Act 1892.	Section 3.
1 Edw. 7. c.7.	Finance Act 1901.	Section 10(3) from "in the case of a customs duty" to "excise duty"; and section 10(4).
9 Edw. 7. c.47.	Development and Road Improvement Funds Act 1909.	The whole Act.
4 & 5 Geo. 5. c.30.	Injuries in War (Compensation) Act 1914.	In section 1(3), the words "or to any compensation under the Workmen's Compensation Act 1906", "the Employers' Liability Act 1880 or" and from "or to any gratuity" to "1909".
5 & 6 Geo. 5. c.18.	Injuries in War (Compensation) Act 1914 (Session 2).	Section 1(3) from "or to any gratuity" to "1914".
5 & 6 Geo. 5. c.93.	War Loan (Supplemental Provisions) Act 1915.	The whole Act.
7 & 8 Geo. 5. c.54.	Naval and Military War Pensions, &c. (Committees) Act 1917.	The whole Act as it applies to the Isle of Man.
11 & 12 Geo. 5. c.39.	Admiralty Pensions Act 1921.	In section 2(3)(a), the words "and the Injuries in War (Compensation) Act 1915; or".
14 & 15 Geo. 5. c.21.	Finance Act 1924.	Sections 35 and 37.
14 & 15 Geo. 5. c.19 (N.I.)	Finance Act (Northern Ireland) 1924.	Section 8.
17 & 18 Geo. 5. c.15.	Workmen's Compensation (Transfer of Funds) Act 1927.	The whole Act.
25 & 26 Geo. 5. c.23.	Superannuation Act 1935.	The whole Act.
2 & 3 Geo. 6. c.11.	Czecho-Slovakia (Restrictions on Banking Accounts, &c.) Act 1939.	The whole Act.
6 & 7 Geo. 6. c.6.	Workmen's Compensation Act 1943.	The whole Act.
14 Geo. 6. c.12.	Foreign Compensation Act 1950.	The preamble and section 2. Section 4(4). Section 6(3) from "beginning" to "period".
11 & 12 Eliz. 2. c.4.	Foreign Compensation Act 1962.	The preamble and sections 1 and 2.

SCH. 1

Chapter	Short title	Extent of repeal
1963 c.25.	Finance Act 1963.	Section 5. Section 62(5). In Schedule 14, Part I.
1964 c.60.	Emergency Laws (Re-enactments and Repeals) Act 1964.	Section 6.
1965 c.10.	Superannuation (Amendment) Act 1965.	The whole Act.
1965 c.62.	Redundancy Payments Act 1965.	The whole Act.
1966 c.18.	Finance Act 1966.	Section 53(5).
1967 c.53.	Prices and Incomes Act 1967.	The whole Act.
1968 c.13.	National Loans Act 1968.	Section 3(7) to (10). Schedule 3.
1968 c.32.	Industrial Expansion Act 1968.	The whole Act.
1969 c.19.	Decimal Currency Act 1969.	Section 3(3)(f).
1969 c.20.	Foreign Compensation Act 1969.	The preamble and section 1. Section 2(2). Section 3(11) and (12). Section 4(1).
1971 c.24.	Coinage Act 1971.	In Schedule 2, the entry relating to section 42 of the Customs Consolidation Act 1876.
1972 c.74.	Counter-Inflation (Temporary Provisions) Act 1972.	The whole Act.
1973 c.7.	Concorde Aircraft Act 1973.	The whole Act.
1974 c.24.	Prices Act 1974.	Sections 1, 6 and 8(2). In the Schedule— (a) paragraphs 1, 2 and 4; (b) paragraph 3 except as it has effect for the purposes of paragraph 9.
1975 c.18.	Social Security (Consequential Provisions) Act 1975.	In Schedule 3, paragraphs 23 and 34.
1975 c.32.	Prices Act 1975.	Section 1.
1975 c.55.	Statutory Corporations (Financial Provisions) Act 1975.	Sections 1 and 2. Schedule 1.
1975 c.57.	Remuneration, Charges and Grants Act 1975.	The whole Act.
1977 c.33.	Price Commission Act 1977.	Section 17.
1978 c.36.	House of Commons (Administration) Act 1978.	In Schedule 2, paragraph 4.

Chapter	Short title	Extent of repeal
1978 c.44.	Employment Protection (Consolidation) Act 1978.	In Schedule 15, paragraphs 6, 7, 9, 11, 13, 16 and 19. In Schedule 16, paragraph 1.
1980 c.21.	Competition Act 1980.	Section 1. Schedule 1.
1981 c.35.	Finance Act 1981.	In section 135(1), the words "and capital transfer tax".
1982 c.16.	Civil Aviation Act 1982.	In Schedule 15, paragraph 7.
1983 c.29.	Miscellaneous Financial Provisions Act 1983.	Section 3.
1985 c.54.	Finance Act 1985.	In Schedule 25, paragraph 10.

Part III

Ireland

Chapter	Short title	Extent of repeal
12 & 13 Geo. 5. c.4.	Irish Free State (Agreement) Act 1922.	The whole Act.
13 Geo. 5. Sess. 2. c.1.	Irish Free State Constitution Act 1922 (Session 2).	The whole Act.
13 Geo. 5. Sess. 2. c.2.	Irish Free State (Consequential Provisions) Act 1922 (Session 2).	Section 1(1) except the words "the First Schedule to this Act shall" and "have effect". Section 2. Section 5 except as it applies to estate duty and stamp duties. Section 6(1) (b) and (c). Schedule 2.
15 & 16 Geo. 5. c.77.	Ireland (Confirmation of Agreement) Act 1925.	The whole Act.
20 & 21 Geo. 5. c.4.	Irish Free State (Confirmation of Agreement) Act 1929.	The whole Act.

Part IV

Local Government

Chapter	Short title	Extent of repeal
8 & 9 Will. 3. c.37 (1696).	An Act for explaining and enforcing the Act [2 Will. & Mar. Sess. 2. c.8] and for widening the street at the south end of London Bridge.	The whole Act.

Chapter	Short title	Extent of repeal
2 & 3 Vict. c.xciv.	City of London Police Act 1839.	The preamble and section 1. In section 2, the definitions of "house" and "rate". In section 3, the words "not less than eight hundred pounds". Sections 7 and 10. Sections 58 to 69, 71 to 86, 88 to 91, 93 to 96, 104 and 105. The following words, wherever occurring— "and liberties", "and the liberties thereof", "or the liberties thereof".
10 & 11 Vict. c.89.	Town Police Clauses Act 1847.	Sections 77 and 78 as they apply to England and Wales.
27 & 28 Vict. c.55.	Metropolitan Police Act 1864.	The whole Act.
29 & 30 Vict. c.79.	Local Government Supplemental Act 1866 (No. 2).	The whole Act.
38 & 39 Vict. c.55.	Public Health Act 1875.	Section 3. In section 4— (a) the definitions from that of "Borough" to that of "Guardians" and from that of "Sewer" onwards; (b) in the definition of "Street", the words "(not being a county bridge)". Sections 313 and 317. Schedule 4. In Part III of Schedule 5, the paragraphs relating to the Act 35 & 36 Vict. c.79.
39 & 40 Vict. c.56.	Commons Act 1876.	In section 37, the definitions of "municipal borough", "improvement Act district" and "local government district".
45 & 46 Vict. c.50.	Municipal Corporations Act 1882.	Sections 2, 220 and 260. In Part I of Schedule 9, the entries relating to the Town Gardens Protection Act 1863, the Dogs Act 1871, the Public Health Act 1875 and the Commons Act 1876.
53 & 54 Vict. c.59.	Public Health Acts Amendment Act 1890.	Section 1.
56 & 57 Vict. c.73.	Local Government Act 1894.	Section 27(1)(a) and (2).

Chapter	Short title	Extent of repeal
7 Edw. 7. c.53.	Public Health Acts Amendment Act 1907.	Section 1. In section 13, as it applies to England and Wales, the definitions of "the commencement of this Part" and "the commencement of this section".
9 & 10 Geo. 5. c.lxxiii.	City of London Police Act 1919.	The whole Act.
10 & 11 Geo. 5. c.xxvii.	City of London (Various Powers) Act 1920.	Section 14.
15 & 16 Geo. 5. c.71.	Public Health Act 1925.	Section 1(5). In Schedule 4, the words from "(except" to "section")".
19 & 20 Geo. 5. c.17.	Local Government Act 1929.	Sections 121 to 126. In section 134, the definitions of "Registration officer", "Road officer" and "Transferred officer". Schedule 8.
23 & 24 Geo. 5. c.43.	Local Government and other Officers Superannuation (Temporary Provisions) Act 1933.	The whole Act.
26 Geo. 5 & 1 Edw. 8. c.49.	Public Health Act 1936.	Section 287(6). In section 343(1), the definitions of "bridge authority", "county district", "emoluments", "highway authority" and "hospital". Section 345. Section 346(1)(d) and (2).
11 & 12 Geo. 6. c.26.	Local Government Act 1948.	Sections 105, 125 and 138.
14 & 15 Geo. 6. c.65.	Reserve and Auxiliary Forces (Protection of Civil Interests) Act 1951.	Section 50(2), as it applies to Great Britain.
9 & 10 Eliz. 2. c.64.	Public Health Act 1961.	Section 52(1) from "and section three" onwards. Section 53(2) from "and sections three" onwards; and section 53(5). Section 54(6) from "and sections three" onwards.
1964 c.18.	Rating (Interim Relief) Act 1964.	The whole Act.
1966 c.42.	Local Government Act 1966.	Section 15. In section 40(1), the words "regulations or rules".

SCH. 1

Chapter	Short title	Extent of repeal
1966 c.42. —*cont.*	Local Government Act 1966.—*cont.*	In section 40(2), the words "other than section 2 or 3". In section 40(3), the words "regulations or rules under this Act or" and "32". In section 41(1), the definitions of "the appropriate Minister", "dwelling-house", "hereditament", "joint board", "land", "rate", "rate period", "rate support grant order", "rating authority" and "year". Section 41(2) and (3).
1972 c.70.	Local Government Act 1972.	Sections 17 and 36. Section 217(7). Section 250(2) from "or may instead" to "affirmation".
1973 c.65.	Local Government (Scotland) Act 1973.	In Schedule 25, paragraph 24.
1974 c.7.	Local Government Act 1974.	In Schedule 6, paragraph 5.
1979 c.55.	Justices of the Peace Act 1979.	In Schedule 2, paragraph 19.
1980 c.53.	Health Services Act 1980.	In Schedule 1, paragraph 15.
1980 c.65.	Local Government, Planning and Land Act 1980.	Sections 182, 187, 188, 189 and 190.
1985 c.72.	Weights and Measures Act 1985.	Section 69(6).

PART V

MEDICINE

Chapter	Short title	Extent of repeal
55 Geo. 3. c.194.	Apothecaries Act 1815.	The whole Act.
14 & 15 Vict. c.99.	Evidence Act 1851.	Section 8.
37 & 38 Vict. c.34.	Apothecaries Act Amendment Act 1874.	The whole Act.
7 Edw. 7. c.xxii.	Apothecaries Act 1907.	The whole Act.
2 & 3 Eliz. 2. c.61.	Pharmacy Act 1954.	Section 4(2)(b).
1977 c.49.	National Health Service Act 1977.	In Schedule 14, paragraph 7(2).

PART VI

OVERSEAS JURISDICTION

Chapter	Short title	Extent of repeal
13 & 14 Vict. c.70.	Canterbury Settlements Lands Act 1850.	The whole Act.
14 & 15 Vict. c.84.	Canterbury Association Act 1851.	The whole Act.
15 & 16 Vict. c.72.	New Zealand Constitution Act 1852.	The whole Act.
28 & 29 Vict. c.63.	Colonial Laws Validity Act 1865.	Section 7.
39 & 40 Vict. c.59.	Appellate Jurisdiction Act 1876.	Section 23.
56 & 57 Vict. c.72.	Colonial Acts Confirmation Act 1894.	The whole Act.
58 & 59 Vict. c.34.	Colonial Boundaries Act 1895.	Section 1(2) and (3). The Schedule.
1 Edw. 7. c.29.	Colonial Acts Confirmation Act 1901.	The whole Act.
7 Edw. 7. c.7.	Australian States Constitution Act 1907.	The whole Act.
24 & 25 Geo. 5. c.49.	Whaling Industry (Regulation) Act 1934.	In section 1, the words "or associated state" and "or associated states". Section 11 from "or British protectorate" onwards. Section 12(b) and the preceding "or". In section 13(1), the word "Newfoundland"; and section 13(2). Section 15.
11 & 12 Geo. 6. c.3.	Burma Independence Act 1947.	The whole Act.
11 & 12 Geo. 6. c.4.	New Zealand Constitution (Amendment) Act 1947.	The whole Act.
5 & 6 Eliz. 2. c.60.	Federation of Malaya Independence Act 1957.	Section 3.
10 & 11 Eliz. 2. c.19.	West Indies Act 1962.	Sections 1 and 2. Section 4(5) and (6).
10 & 11 Eliz. 2. c.23.	South Africa Act 1962.	In Schedule 2, paragraph 6. In Schedule 3, paragraphs 7 and 10.
1963 c.35.	Malaysia Act 1963.	Section 5.
1966 c.14.	Guyana Independence Act 1966.	Section 6. Section 8(1) and (3).
1971 c.19.	Carriage of Goods by Sea Act 1971.	Section 5(1)(d).

Chapter	Short title	Extent of repeal
1979 c.60.	Zimbabwe Act 1979.	In Schedule 2, paragraph 4 as it applies to Great Britain.

PART VII

PLANNING AND LAND

Chapter	Short title	Extent of repeal
Group 1 - General Repeals		
22 Vict. c.12.	Defence Act 1859.	Section 2 from "but this enactment" onwards.
31 & 32 Vict. c.89.	Inclosure, &c. Expenses Act 1868.	In section 1, the proviso. Section 3.
33 & 34 Vict. c.13.	Survey Act 1870.	The whole Act.
1 & 2 Geo. 5. c.49.	Small Landholders (Scotland) Act 1911.	In section 4(14), the words "any powers or duties under the Survey Act 1870, or".
25 & 26 Geo. 5. c.47.	Restriction of Ribbon Development Act 1935.	The whole Act.
6 & 7 Geo. 6. c.5.	Minister of Town and Country Planning Act 1943.	The whole Act.
6 & 7 Geo. 6. c.43.	Town and Country Planning (Interim Development) (Scotland) Act 1943.	The whole Act.
8 & 9 Geo. 6 c.43.	Requisitioned Land and War Works Act 1945.	Sections 17(4), 18 and 22(2). In section 59(1), the definitions of "Defence Regulation", "dwelling-house" and "local planning authority"; and section 59(6). Section 60(3) from "for any reference to a justices' licence" onwards; and section 60(12) from "and for" to "1947". Section 61(9) and (11).
9 & 10 Geo. 6. c.35.	Building Restrictions (War-Time Contraventions) Act 1946.	The whole Act as it relates to building laws, that is— Section 1(1); and in section 1(2), the words "with a building law or", "building law or" and "as the case may be."

Chapter	Short title	Extent of repeal
9 & 10 Geo. 6. c.35.—*cont.*	Building Restrictions (War-Time Contraventions) Act 1946.—*cont.*	In sections 2, 3(1), 4(1) and 7(6), the words "building law or", "building laws or", and "law or", wherever occurring. Section 3(2) to (6). In section 5(1), the words "building law or" and "with a building law or". In section 7(1), the definitions of "building law" and "local Act"; and section 7(2) and (4). Section 8(5)(a). Section 9(5)(c) and 9(6).
10 & 11 Geo. 6. c.51.	Town and Country Planning Act 1947.	Section 119. In Schedule 8, the entries relating to the Roads Improvement Act 1925, the Trunk Roads Act 1936, the Requisitioned Land and War Works Act 1945 and the Trunk Roads Act 1946.
10 & 11 Geo. 6. c.53.	Town and Country Planning (Scotland) Act 1947.	In Schedule 8, the entries relating to section 60(12) of the Requisitioned Land and War Works Act 1945 and the Trunk Roads Act 1936.
11 & 12 Geo. 6. c.17.	Requisitioned Land and War Works Act 1948.	In the Schedule, paragraph 1.
12, 13 & 14 Geo. 6. c.42.	Lands Tribunal Act 1949.	Section 1(3)(d) and (8)(b).
2 & 3 Eliz. 2. c.72.	Town and Country Planning Act 1954.	Section 69(1) and (2). Section 72(2) and (3).
2 & 3 Eliz. 2. c.73.	Town and Country Planning (Scotland) Act 1954.	Section 69(1), (2), (3), (4), (6), (7) and (8). Section 71(2).
7 & 8 Eliz. 2. c.24.	Building (Scotland) Act 1959.	Section 6(8) from "section seventeen" to "1935". In Schedule 9, paragraph 4.
7 & 8 Eliz. 2. c.53.	Town and Country Planning Act 1959.	Sections 14 to 16. In section 57(1), the definition of "highway". Section 57(10) and (11).
7 & 8 Eliz. 2. c.70.	Town and Country Planning (Scotland) Act 1959.	Sections 14 to 16.
9 & 10 Eliz. 2. c.33.	Land Compensation Act 1961.	Section 13. Section 40(5). Section 41 from "or served" to "1945".

Chapter	Short title	Extent of repeal
10 & 11 Eliz. 2. c.36.	Local Authorities (Historic Buildings) Act 1962.	In section 1(1)(b), as it applies to Scotland, the words "with the consent of the Secretary of State,".
10 & 11 Eliz. 2. c.38.	Town and Country Planning Act 1962.	Section 224. In Schedule 12, the entry relating to the Highways Act 1959.
1963 c.33.	London Government Act 1963.	Section 62(1)(d). In Schedule 17, paragraph 20(b).
1963 c.51.	Land Compensation (Scotland) Act 1963.	Section 21. Section 48 from "or served" to "1945".
1967 c.69.	Civic Amenities Act 1967.	In section 5(a), the words "and the Minister of Housing and Local Government" and "and the Secretary of State".
1968 c.72.	Town and Country Planning Act 1968.	Sections 27, 58, 103, 104, 105, 107 and 109(3). Schedule 10.
1969 c.30.	Town and Country Planning (Scotland) Act 1969.	Sections 58 and 102. In section 103(1), the definition of "the Act of 1959"; and section 103(2) and (4). Section 104.
1972 c.11.	Superannuation Act 1972.	Section 19.
1973 c.65.	Local Government (Scotland) Act 1973.	In Schedule 15, paragraph 25. In Schedule 25, paragraph 15.
1981 c.69.	Wildlife and Countryside Act 1981.	Section 72(1).
1984 c.12.	Telecommunications Act 1984.	In Schedule 4, paragraph 20.
1984 c.54.	Roads (Scotland) Act 1984.	In Schedule 9, paragraph 29.
1984 c.55.	Building Act 1984.	In Schedule 6, paragraph 1.
	Group 2 - Architects' Registration	
21 & 22 Geo. 5. c.33.	Architects (Registration) Act 1931.	Section 3(3) from "within" to "thereafter" except the word "to"; and section 3(4) from "not later" to "thereafter" except the word "annually". Section 6(1)(b). In Schedule 1— (a) paragraph 1 from "Provided that" onwards; (b) paragraph 4. In Schedule 2, the proviso to paragraph 1. In Schedule 3, the proviso.

SCH. 1

Chapter	Short title	Extent of repeal
1 & 2 Geo. 6. c.54.	Architects Registration Act 1938.	Section 1(1) from "and where" onwards; and section 1(2). Section 2. In section 3(c)(i), the words "or this Act".
1969 c.42.	Architects Registration (Amendment) Act 1969.	Section 2.

Group 3 - Duchy of Lancaster

Chapter	Short title	Extent of repeal
19 Geo. 3. c.45.	Duchy of Lancaster Act 1779.	Sections 4 and 6. Section 7 from "and also" to "for ever". Sections 8, 9 and 11. Section 12 so far as it relates to assurances for enfranchisement. Section 13 from "or by the enfranchisement" to "hereditaments".
27 Geo. 3. c.34.	Duchy of Lancaster Act 1787.	Section 3.
48 Geo. 3. c.73.	Duchy of Lancaster Act 1808.	Section 10 from "and of ground" to "county or district" where secondly occurring. In section 12, the words "enfranchisements of copyholds and" and "respectively". In section 17, the words "enfranchisements of copyholds, and". In section 18, the words "for the enfranchisement of any copyhold or". Section 31.

PART VIII
RELIGIOUS DISABILITIES

Chapter	Short title	Extent of repeal
31 Hen. 8. c.13.	Suppression of Religious Houses Act 1539.	Section 19.
34 & 35 Hen. 8. c.19.	Religious Houses Act 1542.	The whole Act.
37 Hen. 8. c.20.	Religious Houses Act 1545.	The whole Act.
1 Eliz. 1. c.24.	Religious Houses Act 1558.	The whole Act.
13 Anne c.13.	Presentation of Benefices Act 1713.	Sections 9 and 11.
2 & 3 Will. 4. c.115.	Roman Catholic Charities Act 1832.	The whole Act.

Chapter	Short title	Extent of repeal
9 & 10 Vict. c.59.	Religious Disabilities Act 1846.	The whole Act.
18 & 19 Vict. c.86.	Liberty of Religious Worship Act 1855.	The whole Act.
30 & 31 Vict. c.62.	Test Abolition Act 1867.	The whole Act.
16 & 17 Geo. 5. c.55.	Roman Catholic Relief Act 1926.	The whole Act.

PART IX

SOUTH YORKSHIRE

Chapter or Number	Short title	Extent of repeal
	Group 1 - Barnsley	
3 Geo. 4. c.xxv.	Barnsley Improvement Act 1822.	The whole Act.
16 Vict. c.24.	Public Health Supplemental Act 1853 (No. 1).	Section 5. In the Schedule, the order relating to Barnsley.
16 & 17 Vict. c.cvii.	Barnsley Waterworks Act 1853.	The whole Act except sections 1, 44, 45, 60, 61, 64 and 66.
23 & 24 Vict. c.44.	Local Government Supplemental Act 1860.	In the Schedule, the order relating to Barnsley.
25 & 26 Vict. c.xxxii.	Barnsley Local Board Act 1862.	The whole Act except sections 1, 13 and 20.
29 & 30 Vict. c.xcviii.	Barnsley Local Board Amendment Act 1866.	The whole Act.
38 & 39 Vict. c.ccxi.	Local Government Board's Provisional Orders Confirmation (Abingdon, Barnsley &c.) Act 1875.	In the Schedule, the order relating to Barnsley.
42 & 43 Vict. c.cxxiv.	Wombwell Local Board Gas Act 1879.	The whole Act except sections 1 and 14 and Schedule 1.
43 & 44 Vict. c.lxxxiii.	Local Government Board's Provisional Orders Confirmation (Alnwick Union &c.) Act 1880.	In the Schedule, both the orders relating to Barnsley.
47 & 48 Vict. c.ccxiv.	Local Government Board's Provisional Orders Confirmation (No. 7) Act 1884.	In the Schedule, the order relating to Barnsley.
53 & 54 Vict. c.clxxxix.	Electric Lighting Orders Confirmation (No. 4) Act 1890.	In the Schedule, the Barnsley Electric Lighting Order except Articles 1, 2, 15 and 16.

Chapter or Number	Short title	Extent of repeal
55 & 56 Vict. c.lxix.	Local Government Board's Provisional Orders Confirmation (No. 2) Act 1892.	Section 2. In the Schedule, the order relating to Barnsley.
56 & 57 Vict. c.cxv.	Local Government Board's Provisional Orders Confirmation (No. 4) Act 1893.	In the Schedule, the order relating to Barnsley.
58 & 59 Vict. c.xli.	Local Government Board's Provisional Orders Confirmation (No. 2) Act 1895.	In the Schedule, the Hemsworth Rural (Hemsworth) Order.
59 & 60 Vict. c.lii.	Barnsley Corporation (Water) Act 1896.	Sections 2 and 4 to 6. Section 7(2) and (3). Sections 8, 9 and 15 to 18. Section 19(1); and section 19(2) from "and the Corporation" onwards. Section 21. Section 23 from "and Thickwoods Brook" to "catchwater (No. 1)". Sections 24 to 32, 35, 36, 39, 40, 42, 43, 46 to 59 and 61 to 67. Schedules 1 and 2.
63 & 64 Vict. c.clv.	Barnsley Corporation (Water) Act 1900.	The whole Act except sections 1, 7, 13 and 15.
2 Edw. 7. c.lxxxi.	Local Government Board's Provisional Orders Confirmation (No. 5) Act 1902.	In the Schedule, the Barnsley Order 1902.
3 Edw. 7. c.lxv.	Local Government Board's Provisional Orders Confirmation (Gas) Act 1903.	In the Schedule, the Cudworth Gas Order 1903.
7 Edw. 7. c.cli.	Local Government Board's Provisional Orders Confirmation (No. 1) Act 1907.	In the Schedule, the Barnsley Order 1907.
1 & 2 Geo. 5. c.cli.	Local Government Board's Provisional Orders Confirmation (Gas) Act 1911.	In the Schedule, the Cudworth Gas Order 1911 except Articles 1, 2 and 7(2).
2 & 3 Geo. 5. c.cxiv.	Electric Lighting Orders Confirmation (No. 1) Act 1912.	In the Schedule, the Hoyland Nether Electric Lighting Order 1912.
2 & 3 Geo. 5. c.cxxxviii.	Local Government Board's Provisional Orders Confirmation (No. 12) Act 1912.	The whole Act.

Chapter or Number	Short title	Extent of repeal
3 & 4 Geo. 5. c.cxxxi.	Local Government Board's Provisional Orders Confirmation (No. 7) Act 1913.	In the Schedule, the Wombwell Order 1913 except Article 1 and Schedule A.
4 & 5 Geo. 5. c.xli.	Barnsley Corporation Act 1914.	The whole Act.
5 & 6 Geo. 5. c.lxxxv.	Electric Lighting Orders Confirmation (No. 5) Act 1915.	The whole Act.
5 & 6 Geo. 5. c.xciii.	Local Government Board's Provisional Orders Confirmation (No. 8) Act 1915.	In the Schedule, the Wombwell Order 1915 except Article 14; and in that Article paragraph (1) from "or in case" to "Article", paragraph (3) from "the amount" onwards and paragraph (6).
11 & 12 Geo. 5. c.cii.	Ministry of Health Provisional Order Confirmation (Barnsley Extension) Act 1921.	The whole Act.
13 & 14 Geo. 5. c.lxxxix.	Barnsley Corporation Act 1923.	The whole Act except sections 1, 2, 4, 5, 11, 12(5) to (9), 13(5) to (9), 16, 18 to 22, 24 and 112.
16 & 17 Geo. 5. c.xix.	Ministry of Health Provisional Orders Confirmation (No. 1) Act 1926.	In the Schedule, the Barnsley Order 1926.
17 & 18 Geo. 5. c.xxi.	Barnsley Corporation (Water) Act 1927.	The whole Act except— (a) sections 1, 3, 4, 16 to 21, 23, 24(5), 25, 26 and 36; (b) section 10 as it extends and applies section 45 of the Barnsley Corporation (Water) Act 1896.
17 & 18 Geo. 5. c.xxxiv.	Ministry of Health Provisional Orders Confirmation (No. 5) Act 1927.	In the Schedule, the Barnsley Order 1927.
S.R. & O. 1929 No. 961.	Wombwell Gas (Charges) Order 1929.	The whole Order.
20 & 21 Geo. 5. c.lxxiii.	Barnsley and District Light Railways (Abandonment) Act 1930.	The whole Act.
S.R. & O. 1931 No. 646.	Wombwell Gas Order 1931.	The whole Order except Articles 1 and 10.
23 & 24 Geo. 5. c.xlvi.	Dearne District Traction Act 1933.	The whole Act.
S.R. & O. 1935 No. 588.	Borough of Barnsley (Scale of Water Charges) Order 1935.	The whole Order.

Chapter or Number	Short title	Extent of repeal
1 Edw. 8 and 1 Geo. 6. c.xxxviii.	Barnsley Corporation Act 1937.	The whole Act except sections 1, 2, 4(1)(a) and (2), 5, 6, 10(1), 18 and 19 as they apply to the Council's market undertaking.
12 & 13 Geo. 6. c.li.	Barnsley Corporation Act 1949.	The whole Act except sections 1, 3, 6 and 106.
S.I. 1952 No. 531.	Barnsley Water Order 1952.	Articles 3, 8 and 12. Schedule 2.
4 & 5 Eliz. 2. c.lxxxv.	Barnsley Corporation Act 1956.	The whole Act except sections 1, 2, 3(b), 4, 5, 7, 9, 13, 16 to 18, 29, 80 and 85.
S.I. 1960 No. 641.	Barnsley Corporation (Water Charges) Order 1960.	The whole Order.
S.I. 1960 No. 1195.	Barnsley Water Order 1960.	The whole Order.
S.I. 1961 No. 1877.	Barnsley Water Order 1961.	The whole Order.
S.I. 1961 No. 2057.	Barnsley Water (Cranberry Holes) Order 1961.	Articles 3 and 6. The Schedule.
S.I. 1962 No. 2873.	Barnsley Water (Penistone Boreholes) Order 1962.	Articles 3 and 6. The Schedule.
S.I. 1964 No. 1866.	Barnsley Corporation (Reduction of Compensation Water) Order 1964.	The whole Order.
S.I. 1965 No. 419.	Barnsley (Water Charges) Order 1965.	The whole Order.
S.I. 1965 No. 1728.	Barnsley Water Order 1965.	The whole Order.
S.I. 1968 No. 1660.	Barnsley Water Order 1968.	Articles 4 and 5. Schedule 2.
S.I. 1970 No. 1575.	Barnsley Corporation (Reduction of Compensation Water) Order 1970.	The whole Order.

Group 2 - Doncaster

Chapter or Number	Short title	Extent of repeal
43 Geo. 3. c.cxlvii.	Doncaster Improvement Act 1803.	The whole Act.
14 & 15 Vict. c.98.	Public Health Supplemental Act 1851 No. 2.	In the Schedule, the order relating to Doncaster.
36 & 37 Vict. c.cxxix.	Doncaster Corporation Waterworks Act 1873.	Sections 2, 3, 37 and 39 to 42. The Schedule.
43 & 44 Vict. c.xxix.	Doncaster Corporation Waterworks Act 1880.	Sections 2 and 4.
45 & 46 Vict. c.xxxiv.	Local Government Board's Provisional Orders Confirmation (Poor Law) Act 1882.	In the Schedule, the order relating to Doncaster Union.

Chapter or Number	Short title	Extent of repeal
58 & 59 Vict. c.xci.	Local Government Board's Provisional Orders Confirmation (No. 12) Act 1895.	In the Schedule, the Counties of Nottingham and West Riding of Yorkshire (Auckley and Wallingwells) Order 1895.
61 & 62 Vict. c.xl.	Electric Lighting Orders Confirmation (No. 4) Act 1898.	In the Schedule, the Doncaster Corporation Electric Lighting Order 1898 except Articles 1, 2, 15 and 16.
62 & 63 Vict. c.xxxiv.	Electric Lighting Orders Confirmation (No. 1) Act 1899.	In the Schedule, the Mexborough Electric Lighting Order 1899 except Articles 1, 2, 15 and 16.
63 & 64 Vict. c.clxxx.	Local Government Board's Provisional Orders Confirmation (No. 11) Act 1900.	In the Schedule, the Doncaster and Mexborough Joint Hospital Order 1900.
1900 Cd. 59.	Doncaster Corporation Light Railways Order 1899.	The whole Order except Articles 1, 29, 30 and 31.
1 Edw. 7. c.cl.	Local Government Board's Provisional Orders Confirmation (No.9) Act 1901.	In the Schedule, the Doncaster Rural Order 1900.
1902 Cd. 1250.	Doncaster Corporation Light Railways (Deviation &c.) Order 1902.	The whole Order.
1903 Cd. 1572.	Doncaster Corporation Light Railways (Extensions) Order 1903.	The whole Order.
4 Edw. 7. c.ciii.	Doncaster Corporation Act 1904.	The whole Act except sections 1, 15, 33, 55(1) and 199 and Schedule 2.
8 Edw. 7. c.lviii.	Doncaster Corporation Act 1908.	The whole Act except sections 1, 9 to 11 and 42.
10 Edw. 7. c.xx.	Thorne and District Water Act 1910.	Sections 46 and 49(3).
1911 Cd. 5801.	Doncaster Corporation Light Railways (Extension) Order 1911.	The whole Order.
2 & 3 Geo. 5. c.cxv.	Electric Lighting Orders Confirmation (No. 2) Act 1912.	In the Schedule, the Doncaster Corporation Electric Lighting (Extension) Order 1912.
3 & 4 Geo. 5. c.cxxix.	Local Government Board's Provisional Orders Confirmation (No. 5) Act 1913.	In the Schedule, the Doncaster Order 1913.

Chapter or Number	Short title	Extent of repeal
3 & 4 Geo. 5. c.cl.	Electric Lighting Orders Confirmation (No. 2) Act 1913.	Section 5. In the Schedule, the Doncaster Corporation Electric Lighting (Extension) Order 1913.
4 & 5 Geo. 5. c.clxxx.	Local Government Board's Provisional Orders Confirmation (No. 20) Act 1914.	The whole Act.
1914 Cd. 7406.	Doncaster Corporation Light Railways (Extensions) Order 1914.	The whole Order.
5 & 6 Geo. 5. c.xv.	Doncaster Corporation Act 1915.	The whole Act except sections 1, 39 and 142 and Schedule 2.
11 & 12 Geo. 5. c.lxx.	Ministry of Health Provisional Orders Confirmation (No. 7) Act 1921.	In the Schedule, Article 10(6) and (7) of the Doncaster Order 1921.
12 & 13 Geo. 5. c.lxxii.	Doncaster Corporation Act 1922.	The whole Act except sections 1, 34, 64 and 109.
S.R. & O. 1922 No. 449.	Doncaster Corporation Light Railways (Extension) Order 1922.	The whole Order.
14 & 15 Geo. 5. c.lxxxi.	Ministry of Health Provisional Orders Confirmation (No. 9) Act 1924.	In the Schedule, the Doncaster Order 1924.
15 & 16 Geo. 5. c.lxxxiv.	Ministry of Health Provisional Orders Confirmation (No. 8) Act 1925.	In the Schedule, the Adwick-le-Street Order 1925.
16 & 17 Geo. 5. c.xxvii.	Doncaster Corporation Act 1926.	The whole Act.
16 & 17 Geo. 5. c.lviii.	Ministry of Health Provisional Orders Confirmation (No. 9) Act 1926.	In the Schedule, Article 25 of the Thorne and District Water Order 1926.
19 & 20 Geo. 5. c.xxvi.	Doncaster Corporation (Trolley Vehicles) Order Confirmation Act 1929.	The whole Act.
20 & 21 Geo. 5. c.cxlv.	Ministry of Health Provisional Orders Confirmation (Doncaster, Saint Ives (Cornwall) and Scarborough) Act 1930.	In the Schedule, the Doncaster Order 1930.
21 & 22 Geo. 5. c.lvii.	Doncaster Corporation Act 1931.	The whole Act except sections 1, 5, 8, 10, 33, 41 and 146.
26 Geo. 5 & 1 Edw. 8. c.xlvii.	Doncaster Corporation (Trolley Vehicles) Order Confirmation Act 1936.	The whole Act.

Chapter or Number	Short title	Extent of repeal
9 Geo. 6. c.iii.	Ministry of Health Provisional Order Confirmation (Doncaster) Act 1945.	In the Schedule, Article 2 of the Doncaster Order 1945.
14 Geo. 6. c.xl.	Doncaster Corporation Act 1950.	The whole Act except sections 1, 62, 137 and 144.
S.I. 1953 No. 1348.	Doncaster Corporation Trolley Vehicles (Increase of Charges) Order 1953.	The whole Order.
4 Eliz. 2. c.vi.	Doncaster Corporation (Trolley Vehicles) Order Confirmation Act 1955.	The whole Act.
5 & 6 Eliz. 2. c.xxvi.	Doncaster Corporation (Trolley Vehicles) Order Confirmation Act 1957.	The whole Act.
S.I. 1960 No. 624.	Don Valley Water Board Order 1960.	The whole Order except Article 13 as it applies to the water undertaking of the former Isle of Axholme Rural District Council.
10 & 11 Eliz. 2. c.xxiv.	Ministry of Housing and Local Government Provisional Order Confirmation (Doncaster) Act 1962.	The whole Act.
S.I. 1962 No. 1924.	Doncaster and District Joint Water Board Order 1962.	Articles 3 and 27. In Schedule 1, Part I. Schedule 2.
S.I. 1963 No. 599.	Doncaster and District Joint Water Board Order 1963.	The whole Order.
S.I. 1963 No. 1736.	Doncaster and District Joint Water Board (No. 2) Order 1963.	The whole Order.
1970 c.viii.	Doncaster Corporation Act 1970.	The whole Act.
	Group 3 - Rotherham	
41 Geo. 3. c.lxvi.	Rotherham Market and Improvement Act 1801.	The whole Act.
9 & 10 Vict. c.ccxcv.	Wath-upon-Dearne Improvement Act 1846.	The whole Act.
15 & 16 Vict. c.42.	First Public Health Supplemental Act 1852.	Sections 2, 3 and 9. In the Schedule, the order relating to Rotherham and Kimberworth.
18 & 19 Vict. c.xxxii.	Rotherham Gaslight Act 1855.	The whole Act.

Chapter or Number	Short title	Extent of repeal
26 & 27 Vict. c.cxvii.	Rotherham and Kimberworth Local Board of Health Act 1863.	The whole Act except— (a) sections 1, 2 and 13 to 20; (b) section 88 from "The Board" to "such markets and fairs"; (c) sections 89, 110 and 112.
33 & 34 Vict. c.cxxxiv.	Rotherham and Kimberworth Local Board of Health Act 1870.	The whole Act.
38 & 39 Vict. c.lxx.	Rotherham Corporation Act 1875.	The whole Act.
40 & 41 Vict. c.xxiv.	Rotherham Corporation Act 1877.	The whole Act.
42 & 43 Vict. c.li.	Rawmarsh Local Board Act 1879.	The whole Act except sections 1, 9 and 14 and the Schedule.
42 & 43 Vict. c.cxci.	Rotherham Borough Extension and Sewerage Act 1879.	Sections 2 to 4, 6 to 18, 21 to 27, 29 to 35, 37 to 41, 43 to 49, 53, 56, 57, 66 to 75, 77 to 80 and 82 to 145. Schedules 1 to 4.
43 & 44 Vict. c.clxxviii.	Local Government Board's Provisional Orders Confirmation (Bethesda &c.) Act 1880.	In the Schedule, the order relating to Rotherham.
44 & 45 Vict. c.lxi.	Local Government Board's Provisional Orders Confirmation (Berwick-upon-Tweed &c.) Act 1881.	In the Schedule, the order relating to Swinton.
44 & 45 Vict. c.cxlv.	Rotherham, Parkgate and Rawmarsh Tramways Act 1881.	The whole Act.
44 & 45 Vict. c.clxii.	Local Government Board's Provisional Orders Confirmation (Acton &c.) Act 1881.	Section 3. In the Schedule, the order relating to Wath-upon-Dearne.
45 & 46 Vict. c.ccxxxvii.	Rotherham Corporation Act 1882.	The whole Act.
48 & 49 Vict. c.cxxviii.	Local Government Board's Provisional Orders Confirmation (No. 6) Act 1885.	In the Schedule, the order relating to Swinton.
51 & 52 Vict. c.lxii.	Local Government Board's Provisional Orders Confirmation (No. 4) Act 1888.	Section 2. In the Schedule, Article 2 of the order relating to Rawmarsh.
53 & 54 Vict. c.lxxxiv.	Local Government Board's Provisional Orders Confirmation (No. 5) Act 1890.	In the Schedule, the Rotherham Order 1890.

Chapter or Number	Short title	Extent of repeal
55 & 56 Vict. c.cc.	Local Government Board's Provisional Orders Confirmation (No. 9) Act 1892.	In the Schedule, the order relating to Rawmarsh.
59 & 60 Vict. c.xxvi.	Rotherham Corporation Act 1896.	The whole Act except sections 1, 4, 6, 13 and 14 and Schedule 1.
61 & 62 Vict. c.xxxviii.	Electric Lighting Orders Confirmation (No. 2) Act 1898.	In the Schedule, the Rawmarsh Electric Lighting Order 1898 except Articles 1, 2, 15 and 16, and the Rotherham Corporation Electric Lighting Order 1898 except Articles 1, 2, 15 and 16.
62 & 63 Vict. c.xxxv.	Electric Lighting Orders Confirmation (No. 2) Act 1899.	In the Schedule, the Wath-upon-Dearne Electric Lighting Order 1899 except Articles 1, 2, 15 and 16.
62 & 63 Vict. c.cix.	Local Government Board's Provisional Orders Confirmation (No. 3) Act 1899.	In the Schedule, the Rotherham Rural Order 1899.
62 & 63 Vict. c.cx.	Local Government Board's Provisional Orders Confirmation (No. 5) Act 1899.	In the Schedule, the Rotherham Order 1899.
62 & 63 Vict. c.cxxxv.	Electric Lighting Orders Confirmation (No. 10) Act 1899.	In the Schedule, the Swinton Electric Lighting Order 1899 except Articles 1, 2, 15 and 16.
63 & 64 Vict. c.cxxxv.	Rawmarsh Urban District Council (Tramways) Act 1900.	The whole Act except sections 1, 3, 26, 27 and section 49(6), (8) to (11) and (14).
63 & 64 Vict. c.cliii.	Rotherham Corporation Act 1900.	The whole Act except sections 1, 2, 4, 61 and 62 and Schedule 4.
63 & 64 Vict. c.clxxii.	Gas Orders Confirmation (No. 3) Act 1900.	The whole Act.
2 Edw. 7. c.lxx.	Local Government Board's Provisional Orders Confirmation (No. 1) Act 1902.	In the Schedule, the Rotherham Order 1902.
2 Edw. 7 c.ccx.	Local Government Board's Provisional Orders Confirmation (No. 12) Act 1902.	In the Schedule, the Borough of Rotherham Order (No. 2).
3 Edw. 7. c.cxxxii.	Gas Orders Confirmation (No. 1) Act 1903.	In the Schedule, the Conisbrough Gas Order 1903.

Chapter or Number	Short title	Extent of repeal
4 Edw. 7. c.ccxxxii.	Rotherham Corporation Act 1904.	The whole Act except sections 1, 154 and 197.
5 Edw. 7. c.lxx.	Local Government Board's Provisional Orders Confirmation (No. 3) Act 1905.	In the Schedule, the Swinton Order 1905.
8 Edw. 7. c.lx.	Swinton and Mexborough Gas Act 1908.	The whole Act.
8 Edw. 7. c.xciii.	Wath and Bolton Gas Board Act 1908.	The whole Act except sections 1, 3 and 34 and Schedule 3.
9 Edw. 7. c.lxvi.	Swinton and Mexborough Gas Board Act 1909.	The whole Act.
10 Edw. 7 & 1 Geo. 5. c.lxxxiv.	Local Government Board's Provisional Orders Confirmation (No. 7) Act 1910.	In the Schedule, the Rotherham Order 1910 and the Rotherham Order (No. 2) 1910.
1 & 2 Geo. 5. c.cxvi.	Rotherham Corporation Act 1911.	The whole Act except sections 1, 4, 46, 52, 94 and 100.
2 & 3 Geo. 5. c.clii.	Gas Orders Confirmation (No. 1) Act 1912.	In the Schedule, the Conisbrough Gas Order 1912.
3 & 4 Geo. 5. c.xxiii.	Local Government Board's Provisional Orders Confirmation (No. 1) Act 1913.	In the Schedule, the Kiveton Park Rural Order 1913.
4 & 5 Geo. 5. c.lxv.	Tramways Order Confirmation Act 1914.	The whole Act.
4 & 5 Geo. 5. c.cxxxi.	Local Government Board's Provisional Orders Confirmation (No. 10) Act 1914.	In the Schedule, the Rotherham Order (No. 1) 1914.
5 & 6 Geo. 5. c.lii.	Rotherham Corporation Act 1915.	The whole Act.
6 & 7 Geo. 5. c.xxxvi.	Local Government Board's Provisional Orders Confirmation (No. 7) Act 1916.	In the Schedule, the Swinton and Mexborough Gas Order 1916.
8 & 9 Geo. 5. c.xxxvii.	Rotherham Corporation Act 1918.	The whole Act except sections 1, 4, 41 and 43.
9 & 10 Geo. 5. c.xlvii.	Rotherham Corporation Act 1919.	The whole Act.
9 & 10 Geo. 5. c.cxvi.	Swinton and Mexborough Gas Board Act 1919.	The whole Act except sections 1 and 13(5) and (7).
10 & 11 Geo. 5. c.cxi.	Ministry of Health Provisional Orders Confirmation (No. 4) Act 1920.	In the Schedule, the Rotherham Rural Order 1920.

SCH. 1

Chapter or Number	Short title	Extent of repeal
11 & 12 Geo. 5. c.lxiii.	Ministry of Health Provisional Orders Confirmation (No. 9) Act 1921.	In the Schedule, the Rotherham Rural Order 1921.
11 & 12 Geo. 5. c.lxxxvi.	Rotherham Corporation Act 1921.	The whole Act.
13 & 14 Geo. 5. c.xxvii.	Rawmarsh Urban District Council Act 1923.	The whole Act.
13 & 14 Geo. 5. c.xxxviii.	Ministry of Health Provisional Orders Confirmation (No. 5) Act 1923.	In the Schedule, the Rotherham Order 1923.
S.R. & O. 1923 No. 749.	Rotherham Gas (Charges) Order 1923.	The whole Order.
14 & 15 Geo. 5. c.lxix.	Rotherham Corporation Act 1924.	The whole Act except sections 1, 4, 32, 47 to 49 and 125.
16 & 17 Geo. 5. c.liii.	Ministry of Health Provisional Orders Confirmation (No. 4) Act 1926.	In the Schedule, the Rotherham Order 1926.
17 & 18 Geo. 5. c.liv.	Rotherham Corporation (Trolley Vehicles) Order Confirmation Act 1927.	The whole Act.
18 & 19 Geo. 5. c.cxi.	Rotherham Corporation Act 1928.	The whole Act except sections 1, 4, 34(1), 38, 56 and 130.
20 & 21 Geo. 5. c.clxxvi.	Rotherham Corporation Act 1930.	The whole Act except sections 1, 4, 18, 20, 77 and 103.
S.R. & O. 1930 No. 115.	Rawmarsh Gas Order 1930.	The whole Order.
S.R. & O. 1930 No. 170.	Rawmarsh Gas (Charges) Order 1930.	The whole Order.
21 & 22 Geo. 5. c.liii.	Rotherham Rural District Council Act 1931.	The whole Act.
21 & 22 Geo. 5. c.lxxii.	Public Works Facilities Scheme (Rotherham Corporation) Confirmation Act 1931.	The whole Act.
S.R. & O. 1932 No. 507.	Rotherham Gas Order 1932.	The whole Order.
S.R. & O. 1932 No. 958.	Rotherham Gas (No. 2) Order 1932.	The whole Order except Articles 1, 3, 10 and 14 and Schedule 4.
23 & 24 Geo. 5. c.lxiv.	Ministry of Health Provisional Order Confirmation (Wath, Swinton and District Joint Hospital District) Act 1933.	The whole Act.

Chapter or Number	Short title	Extent of repeal
24 & 25 Geo. 5. c.lxxi.	Rotherham Corporation (Trolley Vehicles) Order Confirmation Act 1934.	The whole Act.
1 Edw. 8 & 1 Geo. 6. c.lxxx.	Rotherham Corporation Act 1937.	The whole Act except sections 1, 4, 22, 28, 71 and 94 and Schedule 3.
1 & 2 Geo. 6. c.lxxvii.	Ministry of Health Provisional Order Confirmation (Rawmarsh) Act 1938.	The whole Act.
9 & 10 Geo. 6. c.liv.	Rotherham Corporation Act 1946.	The whole Act except sections 1, 4, 25 to 28 and 50 and Schedule 1.
S.I. 1954 No. 1450.	Rotherham (Repeal of Local Enactments) Order 1954.	The whole Order.
8 & 9 Eliz. 2. c.xxiv.	Mexborough and Swinton Traction Act 1960.	The whole Act except sections 1(1) and 5(1).
S.I. 1962 No. 485.	Rotherham Corporation Water Order 1962.	The whole Order.
1965 c.xviii.	Ministry of Housing and Local Government Provisional Order Confirmation (Rotherham) Act 1965.	The whole Act.

Group 4 - Sheffield

Chapter or Number	Short title	Extent of repeal
28 & 29 Vict. c.41.	Local Government Supplemental Act 1865 (No. 3).	In the Schedule, the order relating to Sheffield.
30 & 31 Vict. c.65.	Local Government Supplemental Act 1867 (No. 2).	In the Schedule, the order relating to Sheffield.
31 & 32 Vict. c.lxxxvi.	Local Government Supplemental Act 1868 (No. 5).	In the Schedule, the order relating to Sheffield.
57 & 58 Vict. c.xcvii.	Swinton Local Board Act 1894.	Section 6.
59 & 60 Vict. c.ci.	Local Government Board's Provisional Orders Confirmation (No. 6) Act 1896.	In the Schedule, the Stocksbridge Order 1896.
59 & 60 Vict. c.cxc.	Sheffield Corporation Water Act 1896.	The whole Act.
62 & 63 Vict. c.cclxix.	Derwent Valley Water Act 1899.	Sections 165 to 168 and 170 to 177.
1 Edw. 7. c.lxxx.	Derwent Valley Water Act 1901.	Section 30.
4 Edw. 7. c.cxcvi.	Derwent Valley Water Act 1904.	Section 42.
7 Edw. 7. c.xciii.	Sheffield Corporation Act 1907.	The whole Act.

Chapter or Number	Short title	Extent of repeal
9 Edw. 7. c.lxiii.	Derwent Valley Water Act 1909.	Section 20.
1 & 2 Geo. 5. c.xviii.	Swinton Urban District Council Act 1911.	Section 17.
4 & 5 Geo. 5. c.xliii.	Mexborough Urban District Council Act 1914.	The whole Act.
8 & 9 Geo. 5. c.lxi.	Sheffield Corporation (Consolidation) Act 1918.	Section 3. Section 5 as it applies to enactments concerning lands, railways, waterworks, electric lighting and town police. Sections 6 to 36, 38 to 40, 118 to 135, 138 to 156, 158 to 161, 164 to 173, 175 to 182, 184, 188, 190 to 197 and 199 to 211. Section 213 from "Provided that" to "Power Company:". Sections 214, 216 and 218 to 220. Section 225(1) and (2) as they apply to slaughterhouses and abattoirs, and section 225(3). Sections 226, 229 to 234, 238, 240 to 274, 277, 278, 279, 282, 284, 287 to 294, 297 to 300, 302 to 305, 307 to 311, 313, 318 to 320, 322 to 324, 326 to 336, 338, 339, 341 to 355, 357 to 361, 363, 365 to 372, 374 to 389, 391, 396 to 412, 414 to 416, 419 to 452, 454 to 476, 483, 484, 486 to 490, 492 to 500, 503, 505, 508 to 531, 533 and 534. Schedules 1 to 13.
9 & 10 Geo. 5. c.xlix.	Sheffield Corporation Act 1919.	The whole Act except sections 1, 2, 4 and 17 to 21.
10 & 11 Geo. 5. c.lxxiv.	Dearne Valley Water Act 1920.	Sections 25 and 29.
10 & 11 Geo. 5. c.xcii.	Sheffield Corporation Act 1920.	The whole Act.
11 & 12 Geo. 5. c.lxii.	Ministry of Health Provisional Orders Confirmation (No. 6) Act 1921.	In the Schedule, the Sheffield Order 1921.

Chapter or Number	Short title	Extent of repeal
11 & 12 Geo. 5. c.lxix.	Ministry of Health Provisional Orders Confirmation (Sheffield Extension) Act 1921.	The whole Act.
13 & 14 Geo. 5. c.lxiii.	Ministry of Health Provisional Orders Confirmation (No. 9) Act 1923.	In the Schedule, the Sheffield (Water &c.) Order 1923.
13 & 14 Geo. 5. c.xcix.	Chesterfield Corporation Act 1923.	Section 130(6).
14 & 15 Geo. 5. c.xvi.	Ministry of Health Provisional Orders Confirmation (No. 4) Act 1924.	In the Schedule, the Sheffield Order 1924.
14 & 15 Geo. 5. c.lxxxi.	Ministry of Health Provisional Orders Confirmation (No. 9) Act 1924.	In the Schedule, the Sheffield Order (No. 2) 1924.
15 & 16 Geo. 5. c.xxxvi.	Sheffield Corporation Act 1925.	The whole Act.
15 & 16 Geo. 5. c.lxxxi.	Ministry of Health Provisional Orders Confirmation (No. 5) Act 1925.	In the Schedule, the Sheffield (Compulsory Purchase of Lands) Order 1925.
15 & 16 Geo. 5. c.lxxxv.	Ministry of Health Provisional Orders Confirmation (No. 9) Act 1925.	In the Schedule, the Sheffield Order 1925.
16 & 17 Geo. 5. c.lv.	Ministry of Health Provisional Orders Confirmation (No. 6) Act 1926.	In the Schedule, the Sheffield Order 1926.
17 & 18 Geo. 5. c.xxxvii.	Ministry of Health Provisional Orders Confirmation (No. 8) Act 1927.	In the Schedule, the Sheffield Order 1927.
17 & 18 Geo. 5. c.xxxviii.	Ministry of Health Provisional Orders Confirmation (No. 9) Act 1927.	In the Schedule, the Sheffield (Acquisition of Lands) Order 1927.
17 & 18 Geo. 5. c.xliii.	Sheffield Corporation Tramways Order Confirmation Act 1927.	The whole Act.
18 & 19 Geo. 5. c.liii.	Ministry of Health Provisional Orders Confirmation (No. 5) Act 1928.	In the Schedule, the Mexborough Order 1928.
18 & 19 Geo. 5. c.lxxxvii.	Sheffield Corporation Act 1928.	The whole Act except sections 1, 2, 4, 38, 76, 92, 98, 121, 122 and 269.
22 & 23 Geo. 5. c.xv.	Sheffield Corporation Act 1932.	The whole Act.

SCH. 1

Chapter or Number	Short title	Extent of repeal
23 & 24 Geo. 5. c.xix.	Ministry of Health Provisional Order Confirmation (Sheffield) Act 1933.	The whole Act.
23 & 24 Geo. 5. c.lxx.	Sheffield Extension Act 1933.	The whole Act.
25 & 26 Geo. 5. c.xliv.	Sheffield Corporation Tramways Order Confirmation Act 1935.	The whole Act.
1 Edw. 8 & 1 Geo. 6. c.xxxi.	Sheffield Corporation Act 1937.	The whole Act except sections 1, 2, 4, 34 and 92.
1 & 2 Geo. 6. c.lxxiii.	Ministry of Health Provisional Order Confirmation (Wath-upon-Dearne) Act 1938.	The whole Act.
S.R. & O. 1938 No. 1596.	County of York, West Riding and County Borough of Sheffield (Alteration of Boundaries) Order 1938.	The whole Order.
2 & 3 Geo. 6. c.ciii.	Sheffield Corporation Act 1939.	Sections 3, 5 to 26, 32(1)(2)(4) and (5), 33(2) and (4), 42, 45, 47, 49, 66 to 71, 73 and 75 to 82. Schedules 1 and 2.
11 & 12 Geo. 6. c.xxxi.	Ministry of Health Provisional Order Confirmation (Sheffield) Act 1948.	The whole Act.
S.I. 1956 No. 1454.	Sheffield Water Order 1956.	The whole Order except Articles 1, 2 and 9.
S.I. 1956 No. 1455.	Sheffield Water (Charges etc.) Order 1956.	The whole Order.
S.I. 1957 No. 1153.	Dearne Valley Water Board Order 1957.	Article 6. Schedule 2.
S.I. 1958 No. 1383.	Sheffield Water Order 1958.	Articles 3, 4 and 6. Schedule 2.
S.I. 1961 No. 231.	Sheffield Water Order 1961.	Article 4. Article 14(2) to (5), and (14), as they apply to the British Railways Board. The Schedule.
S.I. 1962 No. 478.	Sheffield Water (Regrouping) Order 1962.	Articles 13 and 15(2). Schedules 1, 4 and 6.
S.I. 1962 No. 1249.	Sheffield (Amendment of Local Enactment) Order 1962.	The whole Order.
S.I. 1963 No. 572.	Sheffield Water (Dearne Valley) Order 1963.	Articles 12, 13(1) and 14(2). Schedule 1.

Chapter or Number	Short title	Extent of repeal
S.I. 1963 No. 660.	North Derbyshire Water Board Order 1962.	Articles 4 to 13, 15, 17 to 20, 21(1), (3) and (4), 22, 23, 26(2) and (3) and 27 to 47. In Schedule 1, Part II. Schedules 3, 5 and 6.
S.I. 1964 No. 670.	Sheffield Water Order 1964.	Article 4. Article 10(2) to (5), and (14), as they apply to the British Railways Board. The Schedule.
S.I. 1966 No. 133.	Sheffield Water Order 1966.	The whole Order.
S.I. 1966 No. 1116.	Sheffield Water (No. 2) Order 1966.	The whole Order.
S.I. 1967 No. 104.	Sheffield Order 1967.	The whole Order.
S.I. 1969 No. 489.	North Derbyshire Water Board (Charges) Order 1969.	The whole Order.
1971. c.iii.	Ministry of Housing and Local Government Provisional Orders Confirmation (Melton Mowbray and Sheffield) Act 1971.	In the Schedule, the Sheffield Order 1970.
S.I. 1971 No. 25.	Decimal Currency (Amendment of Local Enactments etc.) Order 1971.	Article 31.
S.I. 1974 No. 644.	Sheffield Water (Wentworth Estate) Order 1974.	Articles 5 and 7 to 15.
Group 5 - West Riding Enactments		
56 & 57 Vict. c.cxxxii.	Local Government Board's Provisional Orders Confirmation (No. 16) Act 1893.	In the Schedule, the order relating to Rivers of the West Riding of Yorkshire.
57 & 58 Vict. c.clxvi.	West Riding of Yorkshire Rivers Act 1894.	The whole Act.
1 Edw. 7. c.cxvi.	Yorkshire Electric Power Act 1901.	Sections 2, 3, 5 to 29, 31 to 42, 45, 47 to 49, 52 to 60 and 62 to 75. Schedule 2.
10 Edw. 7 & 1 Geo. 5. c.xxi.	Yorkshire Electric Power Act 1910.	The whole Act.
4 & 5 Geo. 5. c.lxxxv.	Yorkshire Electric Power Act 1914.	The whole Act.
8 & 9 Geo. 5. c.viii.	Yorkshire Electric Power Act 1918.	The whole Act.
12 & 13 Geo. 5. c.xxiii.	Yorkshire Electric Power Act 1922.	The whole Act.
17 & 18 Geo. 5. c.xxv.	Yorkshire Electric Power Act 1927.	The whole Act.

SCH. 1

Chapter or Number	Short title	Extent of repeal
26 Geo. 5 & 1 Edw. 8. c.xxxi.	Yorkshire Electric Power Act 1936.	The whole Act.
S.R. & O. 1936 No. 1127.	Doncaster, Rotherham and Wakefield Extension Order 1936.	The whole Order.
1 & 2 Geo. 6. c.c.	West Yorkshire Gas Distribution Act 1938.	The whole Act except sections 1, 4, 71 and 73 to 75.
9 & 10 Geo. 6. c.lvi.	West Yorkshire Gas Distribution Act 1946.	The whole Act except sections 1(1) and 6 and the Schedule.
11 & 12 Geo. 6. c.lii.	West Riding County Council (General Powers) Act 1948.	The whole Act.
14 & 15 Geo. 6. c.xliii.	West Riding County Council (General Powers) Act 1951.	The whole Act.
1964 c.xxxix.	West Riding County Council (General Powers) Act 1964.	The whole Act.
1970 c.xxv.	West Riding County Council Act 1970.	The whole Act.

PART X

TRANSPORT

Chapter	Short title	Extent of repeal
51 Geo. 3. c.ccv.	Eynesford Road Act 1811.	The whole Act.
1 & 2 Will. 4. c.22.	London Hackney Carriage Act 1831.	Section 4. In section 56, the words "any officer of stamp duties, or".
5 & 6 Will. 4. c.50.	Highway Act 1835.	Section 5, except the definition of "highways", and in that definition the words "(not being county bridges)". Section 22. Section 78 from the beginning to "accepted) or"; and from "in case such driver" onwards. Section 112.
6 & 7 Vict. c.86.	London Hackney Carriages Act 1843.	Section 2, except the definition of "proprietor".
30 & 31 Vict. c.127.	Railway Companies Act 1867.	Section 2 from "Except" to "provided". In section 3, the definitions of "share" and "Gazette".

Chapter	Short title	Extent of repeal
30 & 31 Vict. c.134.	Metropolitan Streets Act 1867.	In section 3, the definition of "Magistrate" and the words "and the liberties thereof", wherever occurring. Section 27 from the beginning to "Metropolitan Police".
31 & 32 Vict. c.119.	Regulation of Railways Act 1868.	Sections 27 and 28 as they apply to Great Britain. Schedule 1.
32 & 33 Vict. c.115.	Metropolitan Public Carriage Act 1869.	In sections 2 and 9, the words "and the liberties thereof". Section 13 from "in the manner" onwards.
36 & 37 Vict. c.48.	Regulation of Railways Act 1873.	In section 3, the definition of "mails".
36 & 37 Vict. c.76.	Railway Regulation Act (Returns of Signal Arrangements, Workings, &c.) 1873.	The whole Act.
38 & 39 Vict. c.cxc.	Channel Tunnel Company (Limited) Act 1875.	The whole Act.
40 & 41 Vict. c.60.	Canal Boats Act 1877.	The whole Act.
51 & 52 Vict. c.25.	Railway and Canal Traffic Act 1888.	Section 43(3). Section 49. Section 53.
59 & 60 Vict. c.48.	Light Railways Act 1896.	Section 26(1), (9) and (10). In Schedule 2— (a) in the entry relating to the Regulation of Railways Act 1868, the words "nineteen" and "twenty-seven, twenty-eight"; (b) the entry relating to the Railway Regulation Act (Returns of Signal Arrangements, Workings, &c.) 1873.
9 & 10 Geo. 5. c.38.	Merchant Shipping (Wireless Telegraphy) Act 1919.	The whole Act as it applies to the Isle of Man.
10 & 11 Geo. 5. c.72.	Roads Act 1920.	Section 4. Schedule 1.
22 & 23 Geo. 5. c.9.	Merchant Shipping (Safety and Load Line Conventions) Act 1932.	The following provisions as they apply to the Isle of Man— (a) Part I, except sections 12, 24, 27, 29 and 30; (b) Section 71.
24 & 25 Geo. 5. c.50.	Road Traffic Act 1934.	The whole Act.

SCH. 1

Chapter	Short title	Extent of repeal
1 Edw. 8 & 1 Geo. 6. c.5.	Trunk Roads Act 1936.	The whole Act.
9 & 10 Geo. 6. c.30.	Trunk Roads Act 1946.	The whole Act.
11 & 12 Geo. 6. c.44.	Merchant Shipping Act 1948.	Sections 1 to 4, as they apply to the Isle of Man.
12, 13 & 14 Geo. 6. c.32.	Special Roads Act 1949.	The whole Act.
12, 13 & 14 Geo. 6. c.91.	Air Corporations Act 1949.	The whole Act as it applies to the Isle of Man.
14 Geo. 6. c.24.	Highways (Provision of Cattle Grids) Act 1950.	The whole Act.
4 & 5 Eliz. 2. c.67.	Road Traffic Act 1956.	The whole Act.
8 & 9 Eliz. 2. c.63.	Road Traffic and Roads Improvement Act 1960.	The whole Act.
1963 c.33.	London Government Act 1963.	In section 9(6), the words "the Road Traffic and Roads Improvement Act 1960". Section 15. Schedule 5.
1965 c.36.	Gas Act 1965.	In Schedule 2, as it applies to Scotland, paragraphs 7(3)(c) and 12(1)(c).
1968 c.4.	Erskine Bridge Tolls Act 1968.	Section 12(1) from "Without prejudice" to "1949".
1968 c.73.	Transport Act 1968.	Section 143. Schedule 15.
1972 c.11.	Superannuation Act 1972.	In Schedule 4, the entry relating to the Channel Tunnel Planning Council.
1972 c.70.	Local Government Act 1972.	In Schedule 21, paragraph 96.
1980 c.66.	Highways Act 1980.	In sections 219(4)(i) and 329(4), the words from "the National Freight Corporation" to "this Act". In Schedule 23, paragraphs 15 and 24.
1984 c.27.	Road Traffic Regulation Act 1984.	In Schedule 10, paragraph 12.
1984 c.54.	Roads (Scotland) Act 1984.	In Schedule 11, the entry relating to the Gas Act 1965.
1985 c.67.	Transport Act 1985.	In Schedule 8, the entry relating to the Town Police Clauses Act 1847.

PART XI

MISCELLANEOUS

Chapter	Short title	Extent of repeal
1424 c.25 (Sc.).	Innkeepers Act 1424.	The whole Act.
1579 c.8 (Sc.).	Sunday Act 1579.	The whole Act.
1661 c.281 (Sc.).	Sunday Act 1661.	The whole Act.
35 Geo. 3. c.103.	Painshill Estate Act 1795.	The whole Act.
25 & 26 Vict. c.34.	Portsdown Fair Act 1862.	The whole Act.
44 & 45 Vict. c.59.	Statute Law Revision and Civil Procedure Act 1881.	The whole Act.
51 & 52 Vict. c.3.	Statute Law Revision Act 1888.	The whole Act.
51 & 52 Vict. c.57.	Statute Law Revision (No. 2) Act 1888.	The whole Act.
52 & 53 Vict. c.30.	Board of Agriculture Act 1889.	In Part II of Schedule 1, the headings "Tithe Rentcharge Acts" and "Copyhold Acts" and the entries under those headings.
6 Edw. 7. c.14.	Alkali, &c. Works Regulation Act 1906.	In section 27(1), as it applies to England and Wales, the definition of "the Public Health Act". Section 30.
10 Edw. 7 & 1 Geo. 5. c.23.	Companies (Converted Societies) Act 1910.	The whole Act.
15 & 16 Geo. 5 c.88.	Coastguard Act 1925.	Section 3(2).
16 & 17 Geo. 5. c.36.	Parks Regulation (Amendment) Act 1926.	In section 1, the proviso.
22 & 23 Geo. 5. c.51.	Sunday Entertainments Act 1932.	In section 4, the words "1625 to". In section 5, the definitions of "contravention" and "Sunday Observance Acts 1625 to 1780".
9 & 10 Geo. 6. c.26.	Emergency Laws (Transitional Provisions) Act 1946.	The whole Act.
10 & 11 Geo. 6. c.41.	Fire Services Act 1947.	Sections 27(6), 30(7), and 31(2) and (3). Section 39(3). Schedule 5.
11 & 12 Geo. 6. c.29.	National Assistance Act 1948.	Section 31 as it applies to Scotland.
10 & 11 Eliz. 2. c.24.	National Assistance Act 1948 (Amendment) Act 1962.	The whole Act.

SCH. 1

Chapter	Short title	Extent of repeal
1964 c.15.	Defence (Transfer of Functions) Act 1964.	Section 1(3)(c) and the preceding "or".
1968 c.46.	Health Services and Public Health Act 1968.	In Schedule 4, the entries relating to— (a) sections 31 and 33 of the National Assistance Act 1948; (b) the National Assistance Act 1948 (Amendment) Act 1962.
1970 c.40.	Agriculture Act 1970.	Section 113(3). Schedule 5.
1972 c.70.	Local Government Act 1972.	Section 112(4) from "to public analysts" to "1984 or".
1973 c.65.	Local Government (Scotland) Act 1973.	Section 64(5)(b).
1975 c.4.	Biological Standards Act 1975.	Section 3.
1980 c.28.	Iran (Temporary Powers) Act 1980.	The whole Act.
1983 c.2.	Representation of the People Act 1983.	In Schedule 7, paragraphs 3 and 6. In Schedule 8, paragraph 16.
1984 c.30.	Food Act 1984.	In Schedule 10, paragraph 22.
1985 c.50.	Representation of the People Act 1985.	Section 18(1). In Schedule 4, paragraph 90.
1986 c.61.	Education (No. 2) Act 1986.	In Schedule 4, paragraph 7.
1987 c.19.	Billiards (Abolition of Restrictions) Act 1987.	The whole Act.

Section 1(2).

SCHEDULE 2

CONSEQUENTIAL PROVISIONS

PART I

AMENDMENTS CONSEQUENTIAL ON THE REPEAL OF THE BANKRUPTCY ACTS 1883, 1890 AND 1913

City of London Municipal Elections Act 1849 (c.xciv)

1. After section 8A of the City of London Municipal Elections Act 1849 there shall be inserted the following section—

"Disqualification in case of bankruptcy.

8B.—(1) A person who is adjudged bankrupt shall be disqualified for being elected to or holding any of the following offices in the City of London, namely, Lord Mayor, alderman and common councilman.

(2) Where a person is disqualified under this section, the disqualification shall cease—

(a) on his discharge from bankruptcy; or

(b) if the bankruptcy order is previously annulled, on the date of its annulment.

(3) Where a person is adjudged bankrupt while holding any office mentioned in this section, his office shall immediately become vacant."

District Courts (Scotland) Act 1975 (c.20)

2. After section 13 of the District Courts (Scotland) Act 1975 there shall be inserted the following section—

"Disqualification in case of sequestration or bankruptcy.

13A.—(1) Subject to subsections (2) and (3) below, a person shall be disqualified for being appointed or acting as a justice of the peace if he is a person whose estate has been sequestrated in Scotland or who has been adjudged bankrupt elsewhere than in Scotland.

(2) Where a person is disqualified under this section by reason of his estate having been sequestrated, the disqualification shall cease if and when—

(a) the award of sequestration is recalled or reduced; or

(b) he is discharged under or by virtue of the Bankruptcy (Scotland) Act 1985.

1985 c. 66.

(3) Where a person is disqualified under this section by reason of having been adjudged bankrupt, the disqualification shall cease if and when—

(a) the adjudication of bankruptcy against him is annulled; or

(b) he is discharged.".

Justices of the Peace Act 1979 (c.55)

3. After section 63 of the Justices of the Peace Act 1979 there shall be inserted the following section—

"Disqualification in case of bankruptcy.

63A.—(1) A person who is adjudged bankrupt shall be disqualified for being appointed or acting as a justice of the peace.

(2) Where a person is disqualified under this section, the disqualification shall cease—

(a) on his discharge from bankruptcy; or

(b) if the bankruptcy order is previously annulled, on the date of its annulment."

Supreme Court Act 1981 (c.54)

4. After section 138 of the Supreme Court Act 1981 there shall be inserted the following sections—

"Sales under executions.

138A.—(1) Where any goods seized under a writ of execution issued from the High Court are to be sold for a sum exceeding £20 (including legal incidental expenses), the sale shall, unless the court otherwise orders, be made by public auction, and not by bill of sale or private contract, and shall be publicly advertised by the sheriff on, and during 3 days preceding, the day of sale.

(2) Where any goods are seized under a writ of execution issued from the High Court and the sheriff has notice of another execution or other executions, the court shall not consider an application for leave to sell privately until the prescribed notice has been given to the other execution creditor or creditors, who may appear before the court and be heard on the application.

SCH. 2

Protection of officer selling goods under execution.

138B.—(1) Where any goods in the possession of an execution debtor at the time of seizure by a sheriff or other officer charged with the enforcement of a writ of execution issued from the High Court are sold by the sheriff or other officer without any claims having been made to them—

(a) the purchaser of the goods so sold shall acquire a good title to those goods; and

(b) no person shall be entitled to recover against the sheriff or other officer, or anyone lawfully acting under his authority, for any sale of the goods or for paying over the proceeds prior to the receipt of a claim to the goods,

unless it is proved that the person from whom recovery is sought had notice, or might by making reasonable enquiry have ascertained, that the goods were not the property of the execution debtor.

(2) Nothing in this section shall affect the right of any lawful claimant (that is to say, any person who proves that at the time of sale he had a title to any goods so seized and sold) to any remedy to which he may be entitled against any person other than the sheriff or other officer.

1986 c. 45.

(3) The provisions of this section have effect subject to those of sections 183, 184 and 346 of the Insolvency Act 1986.''

PART II

OTHER PROVISIONS

Apothecaries Acts 1815, 1874 and 1907

1815 c. 194.
1874 c. 34.
1907 c. xxii.

5. The repeal by this Act of the Apothecaries Act 1815, the Apothecaries Act Amendment Act 1874 and the Apothecaries Act 1907 shall not affect the powers of the Master, Warden and Society of the Art and Mystery of Apothecaries in the City of London to make provision in connection with the grant and holding of licenciates in medicine and surgery and of other qualifications.

Capital Punishment Amendment Act 1868 (c.24)

1868 c. 95.

6. Section 13 of the Capital Punishment Amendment Act 1868 (which modifies that Act in its application to Scotland) shall continue to have effect with the amendment made by section 19 of the Justiciary Court (Scotland) Act 1868, that is, with the substitution of "section 5" for "the sixth section."

Metropolitan Public Carriage Act 1869 (c.115)

1934 c. 50.

7. Section 8 of the Metropolitan Public Carriage Act 1869 (which includes provision for the period of validity of cab drivers' licences in London) shall continue to have effect with the amendment made by section 39 of the Road Traffic Act 1934, that is, with the substitution of "three years" for "one year".

Irish Free State (Agreement) Act 1922 (c.4)

8. The repeal by this Act of the Irish Free State (Agreement) Act 1922 shall not affect the validity or otherwise of any Act of the Parliament of Northern Ireland passed before the 18th July 1973 (when that Parliament ceased to exist).

Irish Free State (Consequential Provisions) Act 1922 (Session 2) (c.2)

9. In section 5 of the Irish Free State (Consequential Provisions) Act 1922 (Session 2), for subsection (4) (application to Northern Ireland of provisions as to relief from double taxation) there shall be substituted—

> "(4) This section shall apply to Northern Ireland in like manner as it applies to Great Britain".

Compensation (Defence) Act 1939 (c.75)

10. Section 14 of the Compensation (Defence) Act 1939 shall be renumbered as subsection (1) of that section and after that subsection there shall be inserted the following subsection (which preserves the effect of section 16 of the Emergency Laws (Transitional Provisions) Act 1946)—

1946 c. 26.

> "(2) Where any goods have been requisitioned in such circumstances as to give a right to compensation assessed under section 6 of this Act, the ownership of the goods shall be deemed to have vested in the Crown as from the time of requisition free from any mortgage, pledge, lien or similar obligation".

Building Restrictions (War-Time Contraventions) Act 1946 (c.35)

11. In section 7(1) of the Building Restrictions (War-Time Contraventions) Act 1946, for the definition of "war period", there shall be substituted—

> "war period" means the period extending from the 3rd September 1939 to the 26th March 1946.

Foreign Compensation Act 1950 (c.12)

12.—(1) In section 3 of the Foreign Compensation Act 1950 (distribution of compensation payable by foreign governments) paragraph (c) shall be omitted and the following subsection shall be inserted, the existing section being renumbered as subsection (1)—

"(2) An Order in Council under this section may make provision—

> (a) for defining the persons who are to be qualified, in respect of nationality or status, to make applications to the Commission for the purpose of establishing claims under this section and for imposing any other conditions to be fulfilled before such claims can be entertained;

> (b) for prescribing the matters which have to be established to the satisfaction of the Commission by persons making such applications;

> (c) for requiring documents of title relating to property in respect of which claims are established to be surrendered to the Commission and for securing the abandonment or extinction of rights in respect of which claims are established."

(2) In section 4 of the Foreign Compensation Act 1950 (procedure of Commission), subsection (3) shall be amended—

> (a) by substituting for the words from "shall, in" to "Act" the word "may";

> (b) by omitting the words from "and the rules" onwards.

Development of Inventions Act 1967 (c.32)

13. Section 7(2) of the Development of Inventions Act 1967 (which provides for the limit on loans to the National Research Development Corporation) shall continue to have effect with the amendment made by section 11 of the Industrial Expansion Act 1968, that is, with the substitution of "£50 million" for "£25 million".

1968 c. 32.

SCH. 2

Highways Act 1980 (c.66)

1936 c. 5.
1946 c. 30.

14. After section 284 of the Highways Act 1980 there shall be inserted the following section (which preserves the residual effect of the Trunk Roads Acts 1936 and 1946)—

"Trunk roads: miscellaneous functions of Secretary of State.

1890 c. 59.

1925 c. 71.

284A. The persons who may exercise the functions conferred by—

(a) section 40 of the Public Health Acts Amendment Act 1890 (cabmen's shelters);

(b) section 42 of that Act (statues and monuments);

(c) section 14 of the Public Health Act 1925 (public drinking fountains, seats, etc.),

shall, in relation to any trunk road, include the Secretary of State."

Opticians Act 1989

1989 CHAPTER 44

An Act to consolidate certain enactments relating to opticians with amendments to give effect to recommendations of the Law Commission and the Scottish Law Commission.

[16th November 1989]

B E IT ENACTED by the Queen's most Excellent Majesty, by and with the advice and consent of the Lords Spiritual and Temporal, and Commons, in this present Parliament assembled, and by the authority of the same, as follows:—

PART I

THE GENERAL OPTICAL COUNCIL

The Council

1.—(1) There shall continue to be a body corporate known as the General Optical Council (in this Act referred to as "the Council").

Constitution and functions of the Council.

(2) The Council shall have the general function of promoting high standards of professional education and professional conduct among opticians and the additional functions assigned to the Council by or under this Act.

(3) There shall continue to be a registrar of the Council.

(4) The Council shall be constituted in accordance with Schedule 1 to this Act and the supplementary provisions relating to the Council and the registrar contained in that Schedule shall have effect.

The Council's Committees

2.—(1) There shall continue to be a committee of the Council known as the Education Committee, to whom the Council shall refer for advice on all matters relating to optical training and examinations.

The Education Committee.

(2) The Education Committee shall continue to be constituted in accordance with rules made by the Council, but the rules shall secure that the Committee includes—

(a) one person appearing to the Council to represent persons training student ophthalmic opticians;

(b) one person appearing to the Council to represent persons training student dispensing opticians; and

(c) one person nominated by the Secretary of State,

being in each case persons who are not members of the Council.

The Companies Committee.

3.—(1) There shall continue to be a committee of the Council known as the Companies Committee, to whom the Council shall refer for advice on all matters relating to bodies corporate carrying on business as ophthalmic or dispensing opticians, other than matters required by this Act to be referred to the Investigating Committee or the Disciplinary Committee.

(2) The Companies Committee shall continue to be constituted in accordance with rules made by the Council, but the rules shall secure that the Committee includes—

(a) at least one person appearing to the Council to represent the interests of bodies corporate carrying on business as ophthalmic opticians; and

(b) at least one person appearing to them to represent the interests of bodies corporate carrying on business as dispensing opticians,

being in each case persons who are not members of the Council.

(3) Before making rules under this section the Council shall consult organisations appearing to the Council to represent the interests of a substantial number of the bodies corporate carrying on business as ophthalmic opticians and as dispensing opticians respectively.

The Investigating Committee.

4.—(1) There shall continue to be a committee of the Council known as the Investigating Committee, for the preliminary investigation of cases in which it is alleged that an individual or body corporate is liable to have made against him or it a disciplinary order or a direction under section 19 below.

(2) Any such case is hereafter in this Act referred to as a "disciplinary case".

(3) It shall be the function of the Investigating Committee to decide whether a disciplinary case ought to be referred to the Disciplinary Committee to be dealt with by them in accordance with the following provisions of this Act.

(4) The Council shall make rules as to the constitution of the Investigating Committee, and any such rules shall include provision requiring the Investigating Committee, on the occasion of a disciplinary case involving an allegation against a body corporate or against a director or employee of a body corporate, to co-opt as a member of the Committee for that occasion a person selected by them from whichever of the following panels is appropriate—

(a) a panel of persons appointed by the Council as capable of representing the interests of bodies corporate carrying on business as ophthalmic opticians; and

(b) a panel of persons appointed by the Council as capable of representing the interests of bodies corporate carrying on business as dispensing opticians,

being, in either case, persons appointed after consultation with organisations appearing to the Council to represent the interests of a substantial number of the bodies concerned.

5.—(1) There shall continue to be a committee of the Council known as the Disciplinary Committee, for the consideration and determination—

(a) of disciplinary cases referred to them under section 4 above; and

(b) of any other cases of which they have cognizance under the following provisions of this Act.

(2) The Council shall make rules—

(a) as to the constitution of the Disciplinary Committee;

(b) as to the times and places of the meetings of the Committee; and

(c) as to the Committee's quorum; and the mode of summoning members of the Committee.

(3) Rules under this section shall secure that a person, other than the Chairman of the Council, who has acted in relation to any disciplinary case as a member of the Investigating Committee does not act in relation to that case as a member of the Disciplinary Committee.

6.—(1) The Council may set up a committee for any purpose (other than a purpose for which this Act requires that there shall be a committee of the Council) and may delegate to a committee set up under this section, with or without restrictions or conditions, as they think fit, any functions exercisable by them except the following—

(a) the power to make rules under this Act;

(b) any functions expressly conferred by this Act on some other committee; and

(c) subject to any express provision for delegation in the rules, any functions expressly conferred on the Council by rules under this Act.

(2) The number of members of a committee set up under this section and their term of office shall be fixed by the Council.

(3) A committee set up under this section may include persons who are not members of the Council, but at least two-thirds of the members of every such committee shall be members of the Council.

(4) Every member of a committee set up under this section who at the time of his appointment was a member of the Council shall, upon ceasing to be a member of the Council, also cease to be a member of the committee.

(5) For the purposes of this section a member of the Council shall not be deemed to have ceased by reason of retirement to be a member of it if he has again been nominated or elected a member of it not later than the date of his retirement.

PART II

REGISTRATION AND TRAINING OF OPTICIANS

The registers and lists

Registers of
opticians.

7. The Council shall continue to maintain—

(a) two registers of ophthalmic opticians, one for the registration of persons engaged or proposing to engage both in the testing of sight and in the fitting and supply of optical appliances and the other for the registration of persons engaged or proposing to engage in the testing of sight, but not in the fitting and supply of optical appliances; and

(b) a register of dispensing opticians,

each containing the names, addresses and qualifications, and such other particulars as may be prescribed, of all persons who are entitled under the provisions of this Act to be registered in it and who apply in the prescribed manner to be so registered.

Qualifications for
being registered.

8.—(1) Any person who satisfies the Council—

(a) that he holds a qualification as an ophthalmic optician or dispensing optician for the time being approved by them under section 12 below, being a qualification granted to him after receiving instruction from one or more of the institutions so approved; and

(b) that he has had adequate practical experience in the work of an ophthalmic or dispensing optician,

shall be entitled to be registered in the appropriate register.

(2) Any person who satisfies the Council—

(a) that he holds a qualification as an ophthalmic optician or dispensing optician for the time being recognised by them for the purposes of this subsection, being a qualification granted outside the United Kingdom; and

(b) that he has had adequate practical experience in the work of an ophthalmic or dispensing optician; and

(c) that he is of good character,

shall be entitled to be registered in the appropriate register.

(3) Any person who on 1st January 1959 was entitled to have his name included in one of the health service ophthalmic lists, and whose name had not at that time been removed from one of those lists by direction of a health service tribunal, shall be entitled to be registered in the appropriate register.

(4) Any person who on an application made not later than 1st June 1961 satisfied the Council—

(a) that on the date of his application he held a qualification as an ophthalmic optician or dispensing optician recognised by them for the purposes of this subsection; and

(b) that he had had adequate practical experience in the work of an ophthalmic or dispensing optician; and

(c) that he was of good character,

shall be entitled to be registered in the appropriate register.

(5) Any person who on an application made after lst June 1961 but before this Act came into force satisfied the Council—

(a) that on lst June 1961 he held a qualification such as is mentioned in paragraph (a) of subsection (4) above; and

(b) that he had had adequate practical experience in the work of an ophthalmic or dispensing optician; and

(c) that he was of good character,

shall be entitled to be registered in the appropriate register.

(6) Any person who on an application made after this Act comes into force satisfies the Council—

(a) that on lst June 1961 he held a qualification such as is mentioned in paragraph (a) of subsection (4) above; and

(b) that he has had adequate practical experience in the work of an ophthalmic or dispensing optician; and

(c) that he is of good character,

shall be entitled to be registered in the appropriate register.

(7) In the case of a person whose qualifications (including experience) are appropriate for an ophthalmic optician, both registers of ophthalmic opticians and the register of dispensing opticians are appropriate registers for the purposes of this section and, in the case of a person whose qualifications (including experience) are only appropriate for a dispensing optician, the register of dispensing opticians is appropriate for those purposes.

(8) A person shall not be registered at the same time in more than one register.

(9) Where the Council have refused to grant an application for registration under subsection (4), (5) or (6) above, the Privy Council, on representations being made to them, may if they think fit, after considering the representations and after communicating with the Council, order the Council to grant the application.

9.—(1) The Council shall continue to maintain—

(a) a list of bodies corporate carrying on business as ophthalmic opticians; and

(b) a list of bodies corporate carrying on business as dispensing opticians,

each containing the names, principal places of business and such other particulars as may be prescribed of the bodies which are entitled under the following provisions of this Act to be enrolled in it and apply in the prescribed manner to be so enrolled.

List of bodies corporate carrying on business as opticians.

PART II

(2) Subject to subsection (3) below, a body corporate shall be entitled to be enrolled in the appropriate list—

(a) if it satisfies the Council that a majority of its directors are registered opticians or, in the case of a body corporate having only one director, that he is a registered optician;

(b) if on 20th November 1957 its name or a name under which it carried on business was included in one of the health service ophthalmic lists or if it subsequently came into existence on the reconstruction of a body corporate entitled to be enrolled by virtue of this paragraph;

(c) if it satisfies the Council—

(i) that the greater part of its business consists of activities other than the testing of sight and the fitting and supply of optical appliances; and

(ii) that so much of its business as consists of the testing of sight is carried on under the management of a registered ophthalmic optician; and

(iii) that so much of its business as consists of the fitting and supply of optical appliances is carried on under the management of a registered optician; or

(d) if—

1965 c.12.
1969 c.24. (N.I.)

(i) it is a society registered under the Industrial and Provident Societies Act 1965 or the Industrial and Provident Societies Act (Northern Ireland) 1969; and

(ii) it satisfies the Council that so much of its business as consists of the testing of sight, or of the fitting and supply of optical applicances, as the case may be, is carried on under such management as is mentioned in paragraph (c)(ii) and (iii) above.

(3) A body corporate shall not be entitled to be enrolled by virtue of subsection (2)(b) above if its name, or the name of any body on whose reconstruction it came into existence, or a name under which it or any such body carried on business has at any time—

(a) been removed from one of the health service ophthalmic lists by direction of a health service tribunal; or

(b) been erased from the list maintained under subsection (1) above in consequence of an erasure order.

General provisions as to registers and lists.

10.—(1) The Council may make rules with respect to the form and keeping of the registers and lists and the making of entries and alterations in them and, in particular—

(a) regulating the making of applications for registration or enrolment or for transfer from one register or list to another, and providing for the evidence to be produced in support of any such application;

(b) providing for the notification to the Council of any change in the particulars entitling a person to be registered or a body corporate to be enrolled;

(c) prescribing a fee to be charged on the entry of a name in, or the restoration of a name to, the register or list;

(d) prescribing a fee to be charged in respect of the retention in the register or list of any name in any year subsequent to the year in which the name was first entered in the register or list;

(e) providing for the entry in the register of qualifications (whether or not approved under section 12(2) below) possessed by persons whose names are registered in it and for the removal of such qualifications from the register, and prescribing a fee to be charged in respect of the entry;

(f) authorising the registrar—

(i) to refuse to enter a name in, or restore it to, the register or list until a fee prescribed for the entry or restoration has been paid; and

(ii) to erase from the register or list the name of a person who or body corporate which, after the prescribed notices and warnings, fails to pay the fee prescribed in respect of the retention of that name in the register or list;

(g) prescribing anything required or authorised to be prescribed by the provisions of this Act relating to the registers or lists.

(2) On registering the death of an ophthalmic or dispensing optician a registrar shall send forthwith by post to the registrar of the Council a copy certified under his hand of the entry relating to the death in the register of deaths; and the cost of the certificate and of sending it by post shall be payable by the registrar of the Council to the registrar of births and deaths from whom it is received.

(3) Rules under this section which provide for the erasure of a name from the register or list on failure to pay a fee shall provide for its restoration to the register or list on the making of the prescribed application in that behalf and on payment of that fee and any additional fee prescribed in respect of the restoration.

(4) Rules under this section prescribing fees may provide for the charging of different fees in different classes of cases.

11.—(1) The Council shall cause the registers and lists to be printed and published as often as they think fit.

Publication of registers and lists.

(2) Where any of the registers or lists is not published in any year, the Council shall cause any alterations in the entries in that register or list which have been made since its last publication to be printed and published within that year.

(3) A copy of any of the registers or lists purporting to be printed and published by the Council shall, as altered by any alterations purporting to be printed and published by the Council, be evidence in all proceedings that the individuals specified in that register are registered in it or, as the case may be, that the bodies corporate specified in that list are enrolled in it, and the absence of the name of any individual or body corporate from any such copy of a register or list shall be evidence, until the contrary is shown, that he is not registered in that register or, as the case may be, that it is not enrolled in that list.

(4) In the case of an individual or body corporate whose name does not appear in any such copy of a register or list as altered, a certified copy, under the hand of the registrar, of the entry relating to that individual or body corporate in the register or list shall be evidence of the entry.

Training and Qualifications

Approval of
training
institutions and
qualifications.

12.—(1) The Council may approve for the purposes of this Act any institution (hereafter in this Act referred to as "an approved training institution") where the instruction given to persons training as opticians appears to the Council to be such as to secure to them adequate knowledge and skill for the practice of their profession.

(2) The Council may approve for the purposes of this Act any qualification (hereafter in this Act referred to as "an approved qualification") which appears to the Council to be granted to candidates who reach such a standard of proficiency at a qualifying examination as to secure to them adequate knowledge and skill for the practice of their profession.

(3) An institution may be approved under this section as suitable for the giving of all, or some part of, the instruction necessary for the training of ophthalmic opticians or of dispensing opticians, or of both, and a qualification may be so approved as suitable to be granted to ophthalmic opticians or to dispensing opticians.

(4) Where the Council have refused to approve an institution or qualification under this section as suitable for any purpose, the Privy Council, on representations being made to them within one month of the refusal, may, if they think fit, after considering the representations and after communicating with the Council, order the Council to approve the institution or qualification as suitable for that purpose.

(5) The Council shall from time to time publish a list of approved training institutions and approved qualifications, indicating the purpose for which the approval was granted.

Supervision of
training
institutions and
qualifying
examinations.

13.—(1) It shall be the duty of the Council to keep themselves informed of the nature of the instruction given by any approved training institution to persons training as opticians and of the examinations on the results of which approved qualifications are granted.

(2) For the purposes of their duty under subsection (1) above the Council may appoint persons to visit approved training institutions and to attend at the examinations held by the bodies which grant approved qualifications.

(3) No visitor shall interfere with the giving of any instruction or the holding of any examination.

(4) It shall be the duty of visitors to report to the Council—

  (a) as to the sufficiency of the instruction given by the institutions visited by them, or of the examinations attended by them; and

  (b) as to any other matters relating to such institutions or examinations which may be specified by the Council either generally or in any particular case.

(5) Where it appears to the Council (as a result of a report under subsection (4) above or otherwise)—

   (a) that—

      (i) the instruction given by any approved training institution to persons training as opticians; or

      (ii) the examinations taken by such persons,

     are not such as to secure the possession by them of adequate knowledge and skill for the practice of their profession; and

   (b) that for that reason the approval of the institution or qualification in question should be withdrawn,

the Council shall give notice in writing to the institution or body of their opinion, sending with the notice a copy of any report on which their opinion is based.

(6) On the receipt of the notice the institution or body may, within such period (not being less than one month) as the Council may have specified in the notice, make to the Council observations on the notice and any report sent with it or objections to the notice and report.

(7) As soon as may be after the expiration of the period specified under subsection (6) above the Council shall determine whether or not to withdraw their approval of the institution or qualification, taking into account any observations or objections duly made under that subsection.

(8) The Council shall give notice in writing of any decision under this section to withdraw approval of an institution or qualification to the institution or body concerned and the decision shall not take effect until the expiration of one month from the date of the giving of the notice or, if during that time that institution or body makes representations with respect to the decision to the Privy Council, until the representations are finally dealt with.

(9) Where an institution has been approved as suitable for more than one purpose, the Council, instead of entirely withdrawing approval of the institution, may withdraw approval in relation to one or some of the purposes only and references in this section to the withdrawal of approval shall be construed accordingly.

(10) Where the Council have decided to withdraw approval of an institution or a qualification (whether entirely or to a limited extent), the Privy Council, on representations being made to them within one month from the giving of notice of the decision may, if they think fit, after considering the representations and after communicating with the Council, order the Council to annul the withdrawal of approval or, in the case of an institution approved as suitable for more than one purpose, to withdraw approval in relation to one or some of the purposes only.

PART II   (11) The Council may pay to visitors appointed under this section such fees and such travelling and subsistence allowances, to be paid as part of the expenses of the Council, as the Council may with the approval of the Privy Council determine.

PART III

DISCIPLINARY PROCEEDINGS

Disciplinary orders.

14. In this Act—

"disciplinary order" means—

(a) an erasure order;

(b) a suspension order;

(c) a penalty order;

"erasure order" means—

(a) in relation to a registered optician, an order that his name shall be erased from the register; and

(b) in relation to an enrolled body corporate, an order that its name shall be erased from the list in which it is enrolled;

"suspension order" means—

(a) in relation to a registered optician, an order that his registration shall be suspended for a period specified in the order; and

(b) in relation to an enrolled body corporate, an order that its enrolment in the list in which it is enrolled shall be suspended for a period specified in the order; and

"penalty order" means an order that a registered optician or an enrolled body corporate shall pay to the Council a sum specified in the order.

Suspension orders.

15.—(1) The period specified in a suspension order shall not exceed twelve months.

(2) While the registration of a person in the register is suspended by virtue of a suspension order, he shall be treated as not being registered, notwithstanding that his name still appears in the register.

(3) While the enrolment of a body corporate is suspended by virtue of a suspension order, it shall be treated as not being enrolled, notwithstanding that its name still appears in the list.

(4) Where a suspension order is made against a person or body corporate, the registrar shall make in the register or list a note of that fact and of the period for which the registration or enrolment is to be suspended; and the registrar shall erase the note at such time as the order for any reason ceases to have effect.

Penalty orders.

16.—(1) A penalty order may specify any sum not exceeding the maximum penalty.

(2) In this section "the maximum penalty" means £1,000 or such sum as is for the time being substituted in this definition by an order in force under subsection (3) below.

(3) If it appears to the Privy Council that there has been a change in the value of money since the last occasion when the maximum penalty was fixed, whether by the coming into force of the original penalty provision or by order under this section, the Privy Council may by order substitute for the sum specified in subsection (2) above such other sum as appears to them justified by the change.

(4) An order under subsection (3) above shall not affect the punishment for an offence committed before the order comes into force.

(5) A penalty order shall specify a period within which the sum specified in it is to be paid.

(6) The Council may recover the sum specified in a penalty order from the person or body against whom the order was made if that person or body does not pay it within the period specified in the order.

(7) The Council shall pay a sum paid under a penalty order or recovered under subsection (6) above into the Consolidated Fund.

(8) In subsection (3) above "the original penalty provision" means section 10C of the Opticians Act 1958 (which was inserted in that Act by section 4 of the Health and Social Security Act 1984 and is replaced by this section).

1958 c.32.
1984 c.48.

17.—(1) If any registered optician—

Powers of Disciplinary Committee.

   (a) is convicted by any court in the United Kingdom of any criminal offence; or

   (b) is judged by the Disciplinary Committee to have been guilty of serious professional misconduct,

the Committee may make a disciplinary order against him.

(2) If—

   (a) an enrolled body corporate is convicted of an offence under this Act, or of aiding, abetting, counselling or procuring the commission of, or inciting another person to commit, such an offence; or

   (b) in the case of a body corporate which is for the time being enrolled by virtue of paragraph (a), (c) or (d) of section 9(2) above, the Disciplinary Committee is of opinion that the condition, or any of the conditions, for the enrolment of the body corporate under that subsection is no longer satisfied,

the Committee may make a disciplinary order against that body corporate.

(3) Where a registered optician dies while he is either a director of an enrolled body corporate or the manager of that part of the business of an enrolled body corporate which consists of the testing of sight or the fitting and supply of optical appliances, he shall be deemed, for the purposes of subsection (2) above, to have continued to be a director of that body or a manager of that part of its business, as the case may be, until the expiration of three months beginning with the date of his death or until a director or manager is appointed in his place, whichever occurs first.

(4) If it appears to the Disciplinary Committee that a registered optician or an enrolled body corporate—

    (a) has contravened or failed to comply with any rules made under section 30 below; or

    (b) has failed to pay the sum specified in a penalty order within the period there specified,

the Committee may make a disciplinary order against the optician or body corporate.

(5) If it appears to the Disciplinary Committee—

    (a) that a registered optician or enrolled body corporate is engaged in the fitting and supply of optical appliances; and

    (b) that the arrangements made by the optician or body corporate for carrying on his practice or his or its business are not such as to secure that the fitting and supply of optical appliances in the course of that practice or business are carried out by, or under the supervision of—

        (i) an ophthalmic optician registered in the register of ophthalmic opticians engaged or proposing to engage both in the testing of sight and in the fitting and supply of optical appliances; or

        (ii) a registered dispensing optician,

the Committee may make a disciplinary order against that optician or body corporate.

(6) Where—

    (a) a disciplinary order is made against a director of an enrolled body corporate; or

    (b) a responsible officer of an enrolled body corporate is convicted of an offence under this Act; or

    (c) a disciplinary order is made against a registered optician employed by an enrolled body corporate and the act or omission constituting the ground on which the order was made was instigated or connived at by a responsible officer of the body corporate, or, if the act or omission was a continuing act or omission, a responsible officer of the body corporate had or reasonably ought to have had knowledge of its continuance,

the Disciplinary Committee may make a disciplinary order against the body corporate.

(7) In a case—

    (a) where—

        (i) an enrolled body corporate is convicted of an offence under this Act; and

        (ii) the offence was instigated or connived at by a responsible officer of the body corporate, or, if the offence was a continuing offence, a responsible officer of the body corporate had or reasonably ought to have had knowledge of its continuance; or

(b) where—

    (i) a disciplinary order is made against an enrolled body corporate; and

    (ii) the act or omission constituting the ground on which the order was made was instigated or connived at by a responsible officer of the body corporate, or, if the act or omission was a continuing act or omission, a responsible officer of the body corporate had or reasonably ought to have had knowledge of its continuance,

the Disciplinary Committee may, if the responsible officer is a registered optician, make a disciplinary order against him.

(8) The Disciplinary Committee shall not take a case into consideration—

    (a) during any period within which proceedings by way of appeal may be brought which may result in subsection (6) or (7) above being rendered inapplicable in that case; or

    (b) while any such proceedings are pending.

(9) Where it appears to the Disciplinary Committee—

    (a) that a body corporate which carries on business as an ophthalmic or dispensing optician at more than one set of premises is liable to have a disciplinary order made against it; and

    (b) that the events giving rise to the liability were confined, or substantially confined, to a particular set of premises,

the Committee may, instead of making a disciplinary order against the body corporate, direct that the body corporate shall not use the title of optician, ophthalmic optician, dispensing optician, registered optician, enrolled optician or optometrist in connection with that set of premises; and if at any time thereafter it appears to the Committee that the body corporate has contravened a direction in force under this subsection, the Committee may make a disciplinary order against the body corporate.

(10) A direction under subsection (9) above shall remain in force until revoked, on an application made to them in that behalf, by the Disciplinary Committee.

(11) When the Disciplinary Committee—

    (a) make a disciplinary order against an individual or body corporate; or

    (b) direct that a body corporate shall not use any of the titles specified in subsection (9) above in connection with a set of premises,

the registrar shall serve on that individual or body a notification of the order or direction.

(12) Any power conferred by this section to make a disciplinary order is a power to make—

    (a) an erasure order;

    (b) a suspension order;

    (c) a penalty order; or

2D

PART III

(d) an erasure order or suspension order together with a penalty order.

(13) In this Act "responsible officer" means any director, manager, secretary or other similar officer of a body corporate, or of a branch or department of a body corporate, or any person purporting to act in any such capacity.

Restoration of names erased as result of disciplinary cases etc.

18.—(1) Where an erasure order has been made against an individual or body corporate, the name of that individual or body corporate shall not again be registered in any of the registers or lists unless the Disciplinary Committee on application made to them in that behalf otherwise direct.

(2) An application under subsection (1) above for the restoration of a name to the register or list from which it has been erased or for the entry of a name in one of the other registers or lists shall not be made to the Committee—

(a) within ten months of the date of erasure; or

(b) within ten months of the Committee's decision on a previous application under that subsection.

Erasure from register and list on grounds of fraud or error.

19.—(1) If it is proved to the satisfaction of the Disciplinary Committee that any entry in a register or list has been fraudulently or incorrectly made, the Committee may, if they think fit, direct that the entry shall be erased.

(2) An individual may be registered or a company enrolled in pursuance of any provision of this Act notwithstanding that his or its name has been erased under this section, but if it was so erased on the ground of fraud, that individual or company shall not be registered or enrolled except on an application in that behalf to the Disciplinary Committee, and on any such application the Committee may, if they think fit, direct that the individual or body corporate shall not be registered or enrolled, or shall not be registered or enrolled until the expiration of such period as may be specified in the direction.

(3) Where the Disciplinary Committee direct that the name of an individual or body corporate shall be erased from a register or list under this section, the registrar shall serve a notification of the direction on that individual or body.

Service of notifications.

20.—(1) A notification under section 17 or 19 above which is required to be served on a person may be served by being delivered personally, or being sent by post in a registered letter or by the recorded delivery service.

1978 c.30.

(2) For the purposes of this section, and of section 7 of the Interpretation Act 1978 (which defines "service by post") in its application to this section, a letter to a person other than a body corporate containing such a notification shall be deemed to be properly addressed if it is addressed to him at his address in the register or at his last known address if that address differs from his address in the register and it appears to the registrar that the notification is more likely to reach him at his last known address.

(3) A notification which is required to be served on a body corporate shall be duly served if it is served on the secretary or clerk of that body.

(4) For the purposes of this section, and of section 7 of the Interpretation Act 1978 in its application to this section, the proper address of a person, in the case of a body corporate or the secretary or clerk of a body corporate, shall be its address in the list or the address of its registered or principal office if that address differs from its address in the list and it appears to the registrar that the notification is more likely to reach the body corporate or its secretary or clerk there.

21.—(1) For the purposes of any proceedings under this Act before the Disciplinary Committee (whether relating to disciplinary cases or otherwise) in England and Wales or Northern Ireland—

(a) the Committee may administer oaths; and

(b) any party to the proceedings may sue out writs of subpoena ad testificandum and duces tecum;

but no person shall be compelled under any such writ to produce any document which he could not be compelled to produce on the trial of an action.

(2) Section 36 of the Supreme Court Act 1981 and section 67 of the Judicature (Northern Ireland) Act 1978 (subpoena issued in High Court to run throughout United Kingdom) shall apply in relation to any such proceedings in England and Wales and in Northern Ireland respectively as they apply in relation to causes or matters in the High Court.

(3) For the purposes of any such proceedings in Scotland, the Committee may administer oaths and the Court of Session shall on the application of any party to the proceedings have the like power as in any action in that court—

(a) to grant warrant for the citation of witnesses and havers to give evidence or to produce documents before the Committee, and for the issue of letters of second diligence against any witness or haver failing to appear after due citation;

(b) to grant warrant for the recovery of documents; and

(c) to grant commissions to persons to take the evidence of witnesses or to examine havers and receive their exhibits and productions.

(4) The Council shall make rules as to the procedure to be followed and the rules of evidence to be observed in proceedings before the Disciplinary Committee, and in particular—

(a) for securing that notice that the proceedings are to be brought shall be given, at such time and in such manner as may be specified in the rules, to the individual or body corporate alleged to be liable to have a disciplinary order or a direction under section 19 above made against him or it;

(b) for securing that any party to the proceedings shall, if he so requires, be entitled to be heard by the Committee;

(c) for enabling any party to the proceedings to be represented by counsel or solicitor or (if the rules so provide and the party so elects) by a person of such other description as may be specified in the rules;

(d) for requiring proceedings before the Committee to be held in public except in so far as may be provided by the rules;

(e) for requiring, in cases where it is alleged that a registered optician has been guilty of serious professional misconduct, that where the Committee judge that the allegation has not been proved they shall record a finding that the optician is not guilty of such conduct in respect of the matters to which the allegation relates;

(f) for requiring, in cases where it is alleged that a registered optician or enrolled body corporate is liable to have a disciplinary order made against him or it under section 17(4) or (5) above, that where the Committee judge that the allegation has not been proved they shall record a finding that the optician or body corporate is not guilty of the matters alleged.

(5) As respects proceedings for the restoration of names to the register or list, or for the revocation of a direction under section 17(9) above, the Council shall have power to make rules with respect to all or any of the matters specified in subsection (4) above, but shall not be required to do so, and separate rules under this section may be made as respects such proceedings.

(6) Before making rules under this section the Council shall consult such organisations representing the interests of opticians and bodies corporate carrying on business as opticians as appear to the Council requisite to be consulted.

Assessors to
Disciplinary
Committee.

22.—(1) For the purpose of advising the Disciplinary Committee on questions of law arising in proceedings before them there shall in all such proceedings be an assessor to the Committee who shall be a barrister, advocate or solicitor of not less than ten years' standing.

(2) The power of appointing assessors under this section shall be exercisable by the Council, but if no assessor appointed by them is available to act at any particular proceedings, the Disciplinary Committee may appoint an assessor under this section to act at those proceedings.

(3) The Lord Chancellor may make rules as to the functions of assessors appointed under this section, and in particular, rules under this subsection may contain—

(a) such provisions for securing—

(i) that where an assessor advises the Committee on any question of law as to evidence, procedure or any other matters specified in the rules, he shall do so in the presence of every party, or person representing a party, to the proceedings who appears at the proceedings or, if the advice is tendered after the Committee have begun to deliberate as to their findings, that every such party or person shall be informed what advice the assessor has tendered;

(ii) that every such party or person shall be informed if in any case the Committee do not accept the advice of the assessor on any such question; and

(b) such incidental and supplementary provisions,

as appear to the Lord Chancellor expedient.

(4) Subject to the provisions of this section, an assessor under this section may be appointed either generally or for any particular proceedings or class of proceedings, and shall hold and vacate office in accordance with the terms of the instrument under which he is appointed.

PART III

(5) Any remuneration paid by the Council to persons appointed to act as assessors shall be at such rates as the Privy Council may approve.

23.—(1) At any time within 28 days from the service of a notification in relation to an individual or body corporate under section 17 or 19 above, that individual or body corporate may, in accordance with such rules as Her Majesty in Council may by Order provide for the purposes of this section, appeal to Her Majesty in Council; and the Judicial Committee Act 1833 shall apply in relation to the Disciplinary Committee as it applies to such courts as are mentioned in section 3 of that Act.

Appeals in disciplinary and other cases.

1833 c.41.

(2) The Council may appear as respondent on any such appeal, and for the purpose of enabling directions to be given as to the costs of any such appeal the Council shall be deemed to be a party to the appeal, whether they appear on the hearing of the appeal or not.

(3) Where—

(a) no appeal is brought against—

(i) a disciplinary order; or

(ii) a direction under section 17(9) above; or

(iii) a direction under section 19 above; or

(b) such an appeal is brought but withdrawn or struck out for want of prosecution,

the order or direction shall take effect on the expiration of the time for appealing or, as the case may be, on the withdrawal or striking out of the appeal.

(4) Subject as aforesaid, where an appeal is brought against any such order or direction, it shall take effect if and when the appeal is dismissed and not otherwise.

PART IV

RESTRICTIONS ON TESTING OF SIGHT, FITTING

OF CONTACT LENSES, SALE AND SUPPLY OF OPTICAL

APPLIANCES AND USE OF TITLES AND DESCRIPTIONS

24.—(1) Subject to the following provisions of this section, a person who is not a registered medical practitioner or registered ophthalmic optician shall not test the sight of another person.

Testing of sight.

(2) Subsection (1) above shall not apply to the testing of sight by a person recognised by a medical authority as a medical student, if carried out as part of a course of instruction approved by that authority for medical students or as part of an examination so approved.

(3) The Council may by rules exempt from subsection (1) above the testing of sight by persons training as ophthalmic opticians, or any prescribed class of such persons, in such cases and subject to compliance with such conditions as may be prescribed by the rules.

PART IV

(4) Any person who contravenes subsection (1) above shall be liable on summary conviction to a fine of an amount not exceeding level 4 on the standard scale.

Fitting of contact lenses.

25.—(1) Subject to the following provisions of this section, a person who is not a registered medical practitioner or registered optician shall not fit contact lenses.

(2) Subsection (1) above shall not apply to the fitting of contact lenses by a person recognised by a medical authority as a medical student, if carried out as part of a course of instruction approved by that authority for medical students or as part of an examination so approved.

(3) The Council may by rules exempt from subsection (1) above the fitting of contact lenses by persons training as opticians, or any prescribed class of such persons, in such cases and subject to compliance with such conditions as may be prescribed by the rules.

(4) Any person who contravenes subsection (1) above shall be liable on summary conviction to a fine of an amount not exceeding level 4 on the standard scale.

Duties to be performed on sight testing.

26.—(1) The Secretary of State may by regulations provide that, subject to any exceptions specified in the regulations, when a registered medical practitioner or registered ophthalmic optician tests the sight of another person, it shall be his duty—

(a) to perform such examinations of the eye for the purpose of detecting injury, disease or abnormality in the eye or elsewhere as the regulations may require, and

(b) immediately following the test to give the person whose sight he has tested a written statement—

(i) that he has carried out the examinations that the regulations require, and

(ii) that he is or (as the case may be) is not referring him to a registered medical practitioner.

(2) Except in circumstances specified in regulations under subsection (3)(b) below, it shall also be his duty to give the person whose sight he has tested, immediately following the test, either a signed, written prescription for an optical appliance or a signed, written statement that he does not need to wear or use an optical appliance.

(3) The Secretary of State may by regulations specify—

(a) particulars to be included in a prescription or statement provided in fulfilment of the duty imposed by subsection (2) above; and

(b) circumstances in which that duty does not arise.

(4) A person shall not be required as a condition of having his sight tested—

(a) to undertake to purchase from a specified person any optical appliance the testing of his sight may show he requires to wear or use; or

(b) to pay a fee before the testing is carried out.

(5) A fee shall be payable in a case where a duty arises under this section only if that duty has been fulfilled.

(6) Any term of an agreement for a testing of sight which is inconsistent with this section shall be unenforceable, and any sum paid in respect of a fee otherwise than in pursuance of this section shall be recoverable.

(7) In this section "fee" means any payment in connection—

(a) with testing sight in accordance with regulations under this section;

(b) with fulfilling any duty imposed by this section; or

(c) with the supply of optical appliances.

(8) Any power to make regulations conferred by this section includes power to make different provision for different classes of case.

(9) In the application of this section to Northern Ireland for any reference to the Secretary of State there shall be substituted a reference to the Department of Health and Social Services for Northern Ireland.

27.—(1) Subject to the following provisions of this section, a person shall not sell any optical appliance unless the sale is effected by or under the supervision of a registered medical practitioner or registered optician.

Sale and supply of optical appliances.

(2) Subsection (1) above shall not apply to an excluded sale.

(3) In subsection (2) above "excluded sale" means a sale for a person not under the age of 16 of spectacles which have two single vision lenses of the same positive spherical power not exceeding 4 dioptres where the sale is wholly for the purpose of correcting, remedying or relieving the condition known as presbyopia; and for the purposes of this subsection lenses are to be taken to have the same positive spherical power if the difference between them is within the tolerances relating to the power of such lenses specified from time to time in the British Standard Specification.

(4) Subsection (1) above shall apply to the supply of an optical appliance in the course of the practice or business of an ophthalmic optician or dispensing optician, whether by the person carrying on the practice or business or by a person employed by him, if the supply was effected in pursuance of arrangements made—

(a) with a Minister of the Crown or Government department (including a Northern Ireland department); or

(b) with any body on whom functions are conferred by or by virtue of—

(i) the National Health Service Act 1977 ;

1977 c.49.

(ii) the National Health Service (Scotland) Act 1978 ; or

1978 c.29.

(iii) the Health and Personal Social Services (Northern Ireland) Order 1972 ,

S.I.1972/1265 (N.I.14).

as it applies to the sale of an optical appliance.

(5) Subsection (1) above shall not apply to the sale of an optical appliance—

(a) to a registered medical practitioner, registered optician or enrolled body corporate for the purposes of his practice or of his or its business;

(b) to a manufacturer of or dealer in optical appliances for the purposes of his business;

(c) to any authority or person carrying on a hospital, clinic, nursing home or other institution providing medical or surgical treatment;

(d) to a Minister of the Crown or Government department (including a Northern Ireland department);

(e) for the purpose of its export; or

(f) in accordance with an order under subsection (6) below.

(6) An order under this subsection is an order made by the Privy Council and specifying—

(a) optical appliances to which it applies; and

(b) conditions subject to which their sale is exempted from the requirements of subsection (1) above.

(7) Any such order relating to optical appliances consisting of or including one or more lenses shall specify, as a condition subject to which the sale of any such appliance is so exempted, the condition that the appliance must be in accordance with a written prescription which—

(a) has been given by a registered medical practitioner or registered ophthalmic optician following a testing of sight by him; and

(b) bears a date not more than such time as is specified in the order before the prescription is presented to the proposed seller of the appliance.

(8) An order under subsection (6) above may not specify as appliances to which it applies—

(a) contact lenses; or

(b) any optical appliance for a person under 16 years of age.

(9) On any prosecution for selling an optical appliance in contravention of subsection (1) above it shall be a defence for the defendant to prove—

(a) that he sold the appliance as an antique or secondhand article; and

(b) that he did not know, and had no reason to believe, that the appliance was bought for the purpose of being used for correcting, remedying or relieving a defect of sight.

(10) A person who contravenes subsection (1) above shall be liable on summary conviction to a fine of an amount not exceeding level 4 on the standard scale.

Penalty for pretending to be registered etc.

28.—(1) Any individual—

(a) who takes or uses the title of ophthalmic optician or the title of optometrist when he is not registered in either of the registers of ophthalmic opticians; or

(b) who takes or uses the title of dispensing optician when he is not registered in the register of dispensing opticians; or

(c) who takes or uses the title of registered optician or enrolled optician when he is not registered in any of the registers; or

(d) who takes or uses any name, title, addition or description falsely implying that he is registered in any of the registers; or

(e) who otherwise pretends that he is registered in any of the registers,

shall be liable on summary conviction to a fine of an amount not exceeding level 4 on the standard scale.

(2) On any prosecution for an offence under subsection (1)(d) or (e) above, the taking or use of the title of optician by a person to whom this subsection applies is to be taken to imply that he is registered in one of the registers, but the implication may be rebutted if the defendant proves that he took or, as the case may be, used the title in circumstances where it would have been unreasonable for people to believe, in consequence of his taking or, as the case may be, use of it, that he was in fact registered in one of the registers.

(3) Subject to subsection (4) below, subsection (2) above applies to a person who carries on the business—

(a) of selling optical appliances; or

(b) of supplying optical appliances in pursuance of arrangements made as mentioned in section 27(4) above.

(4) Subsection (2) above does not apply to a person who sells or supplies optical appliances only as mentioned in section 27(5)(a) to (e) above.

(5) Any body corporate—

(a) which takes or uses the title of ophthalmic optician or the title of optometrist when it is not enrolled in the list of bodies corporate carrying on business as ophthalmic opticians; or

(b) which takes or uses the title of dispensing optician when it is not enrolled in the list of bodies corporate carrying on business as dispensing opticians; or

(c) which takes or uses the title of registered optician or enrolled optician when it is not enrolled in either of the lists; or

(d) which takes or uses any name, title, addition or description falsely implying that it is enrolled in either of the lists; or

(e) which otherwise pretends that it is enrolled in either of the lists,

shall be liable on summary conviction to a fine of an amount not exceeding level 4 on the standard scale.

(6) On any prosecution for an offence under subsection (5)(d) or (e) above, the taking or use of the title of optician by a body corporate to which this subsection applies is to be taken to imply that it is enrolled in one of the lists, but the implication may be rebutted if the body corporate proves that it took or, as the case may be, used the title in circumstances where it would have been unreasonable for people to believe, in consequence of its taking or, as the case may be, use of it, that it was in fact enrolled in either of the lists.

(7) Subject to subsection (8) below, subsection (5) above applies to a body corporate which carries on the business—

(a) of selling optical appliances; or

(b) of supplying optical appliances in pursuance of arrangements made as mentioned in section 27(4) above.

(8) Subsection (5) above does not apply to a body corporate which sells or supplies optical appliances only as mentioned in section 27(5)(a) to (e) above.

(9) It is immaterial for the purposes of this section whether a title was used alone or in combination with any other words.

Provision as to death or bankruptcy of registered optician.

29.—(1) Where a registered optician dies at a time when he is carrying on business or is in practice as an optician, then during the three years beginning with his death or such longer period as the Council may in any particular case allow, section 28 above shall not operate to prevent—

(a) his executors or administrators;

(b) his widow;

(c) any of his children; or

(d) trustees on behalf of his widow or any of his children,

from taking or using in relation to that business or practice, but in conjunction with the name in which he carried it on, any title which he was entitled to take or use immediately before his death.

(2) Where a registered optician becomes bankrupt at a time when he is carrying on business or is in practice as an optician, then, during the three years beginning with the bankruptcy, section 28 above shall not operate to prevent his trustee in bankruptcy from taking or using in relation to that business or practice, but in conjunction with the name in which he carried it on, any title which he was entitled to take or use immediately before the bankruptcy.

(3) Where—

(a) a person by virtue of subsection (1) or (2) above takes or uses any title in relation to the business or practice—

(i) of a deceased optician; or

(ii) of an optician who has become bankrupt; and

(b) an offence under section 24, 25 or 27 above is committed in the course of that business or practice,

the Disciplinary Committee may, if they think fit, direct that subsection (1) or (2) above shall cease to apply in relation to that business or practice.

(4) This Act shall have effect in relation to any case in which it is alleged that there has been a conviction of any such offence and to any direction under subsection (3) above as it has effect in relation to a disciplinary case and a disciplinary order.

(5) In its application to Scotland subsection (2) above shall have effect as if—

(a) for the reference to a registered optician becoming bankrupt there were substituted a reference to the estate of a registered optician being sequestrated (cognate expressions being construed accordingly); and

(b) for the reference to a registered optician's trustee in bankruptcy there were substituted a reference to the permanent trustee on his sequestrated estate.

(6) In its application to Northern Ireland subsection (2) above shall have effect as if for a registered optician's trustee in bankruptcy there were substituted a reference to the assignee in bankruptcy.

30. Where an offence under this Act which has been committed by a body corporate is proved to have been committed with the consent or connivance of, or to be attributable to any neglect on the part of, any responsible officer of the body corporate, he, as well as the body corporate, shall be deemed to be guilty of that offence and shall be liable to be proceeded against and punished accordingly.

PART V

MISCELLANEOUS AND SUPPLEMENTARY

Miscellaneous

31.—(1) Subject to subsection (2) below, the Council may make rules prohibiting or regulating—

(a) the use by registered opticians and enrolled bodies corporate of any means of giving publicity, whether by advertisements or not, to their practice or business of ophthalmic or dispensing opticians;

(b) the carrying on of practice or business by registered opticians and enrolled bodies corporate under names other than those under which they are registered or enrolled;

(c) the administration of drugs by registered opticians, enrolled bodies corporate and their employees in the course of their practice or business of ophthalmic or dispensing opticians;

(d) the practice of orthoptics by registered opticians, enrolled bodies corporate and their employees;

(e) the prescription, supply and fitting by registered opticians, enrolled bodies corporate and their employees of contact lenses.

(2) The power of the Council to make rules by virtue of subsection (1)(a) above shall not include power to prohibit the display, for the purposes of the practice or business of a registered optician or enrolled body corporate, of optical appliances or parts of optical appliances on premises where the fitting and supply of optical appliances is being carried on as part of that business or practice or in any building comprising those premises.

(3) The Council may make rules specifying requirements which registered opticians, enrolled bodies corporate or employees of registered opticians or enrolled bodies corporate must meet if they are to prescribe, fit or supply contact lenses.

(4) The power conferred by subsection (3) above is a power—

(a) in relation to registered opticians or employees of registered opticians or of enrolled bodies corporate, to specify qualifications which they must have; and

(b) in relation to enrolled bodies corporate, to specify conditions which they must satisfy.

(5) The Council shall make and submit to the Privy Council rules providing that where it appears to a registered optician that a person consulting him is suffering from an injury or disease of the eye, the optician shall, except in an emergency or where that person is consulting him for the purpose of being given treatment in accordance with rules under subsection (1)(d) above or in such other cases as may be prescribed,

being cases in which it is, owing to special circumstances, impracticable or inexpedient to do so, take the prescribed steps to refer that person to a registered medical practitioner for advice and treatment.

(6) Rules under this section may make different provision for different classes of cases.

Expenses and accounts of the Council.

32.—(1) The Council may, after paying their expenses, allocate any money, other than a sum paid under a penalty order or recovered under section 16(6) above, received by them whether by way of fees or otherwise to purposes connected with optical education and research or any other public purposes connected with the profession of ophthalmic opticians or dispensing opticians in such manner as they may think fit.

(2) The Council shall keep accounts of all sums received or paid by them and the accounts for each financial year of the Council shall be audited by auditors to be appointed by them and shall as soon as may be after they have been audited be published and laid before Parliament.

(3) No person shall be qualified to be appointed auditor under subsection (2) above unless he is a member of one or more of the following bodies—

the Institute of Chartered Accountants in England and Wales;

the Institute of Chartered Accountants of Scotland;

the Chartered Association of Certified Accountants;

the Institute of Chartered Accountants in Ireland;

1985 c.6.

any other body of accountants established in the United Kingdom for the time being recognised for the purposes of section 389(l)(a) of the Companies Act 1985 by the Secretary of State.

Default powers of Privy Council.

33.—(1) If at any time it appears to the Privy Council that the Council have failed, but ought, to discharge a function of theirs to which this section applies, the Privy Council may notify their opinion to the Council and may direct them to discharge such of those functions, and in such manner and within such time or times, as may be specified in the direction.

(2) If the Council fail to comply with any directions of the Privy Council under subsection (1) above, the Privy Council may themselves discharge any function of the Council to which this section applies.

(3) This section applies to all functions of the Council under this Act except—

(a) their functions under sections 1, 8, 12, 13, 22 and 32(1) above; and

(b) their power to make rules under subsection (3) of section 21 above as respects such proceedings as are mentioned in subsection (4) of that section.

Subordinate legislation procedure.

34.—(1) Rules made by the Council under this Act and a scheme submitted by them under paragraph 3 of Schedule 1 to this Act shall not come into force until approved by order of the Privy Council.

(2) The Privy Council may approve rules under section 21(3) or 31(1)(a) above and any such scheme either as submitted to them or subject to such modifications as appear to them requisite.

(3) Where the Privy Council propose to approve any such rules or scheme subject to modifications, they shall notify to the Council the modifications they propose to make and consider any observations of the Council on them.

(4) The Privy Council, after consulting the Council, may by order vary or revoke any rules made under section 31(1)(a) above and previously approved by them (whether the approval was before or after the commencement of this subsection).

(5) The powers—

(a) of the Privy Council to make orders under this Act;

(b) of the Lord Chancellor to make rules under section 22 above; and

(c) of the Secretary of State to make regulations under section 26 above,

shall be exercisable by statutory instrument.

(6) Subject to subsection (7) below, a statutory instrument containing—

(a) an order of the Privy Council to which this subsection applies; or

(b) regulations made by the Secretary of State under section 26 above,

shall be subject to annulment in pursuance of a resolution of either House of Parliament.

(7) Subsection (6) above applies to the following orders of the Privy Council—

(a) an order approving rules under section 4, 5 or 31 above other than an order such as is mentioned in subsection (9)(a) below; and

(b) an order approving a scheme under paragraph 3 of Schedule 1 to this Act; and

(c) an order under section 16(3) or 27 above or under paragraph 13 of Schedule 1 to this Act.

(8) No order to which this subsection applies shall be made unless a draft of the order has been laid before and approved by resolution of each House of Parliament.

(9) Subsection (8) above applies to an order—

(a) which is made by virtue of subsection (2) above and approves rules under section 31(1)(a) above subject to modifications; or

(b) which is made by virtue of subsection (4) above,

unless it is contained in a statutory instrument that states that the Council have indicated their consent to the terms of the order either in the course of consultations under this section or in observations under subsection (3) above.

(10) The power of the Department of Health and Social Services for Northern Ireland to make regulations under section 26 above shall be exercisable by statutory rule for the purposes of the Statutory Rules (Northern Ireland) Order 1979; and any such regulations shall be subject to negative resolution within the meaning of the Interpretation Act (Northern Ireland) 1954.

S.I. 1979 No. 1573 (N.I. 12).

1954 c.33 (N.I.).

PART V
Privy Council
quorum and
documents.

35.—(1) For the purpose of exercising any powers conferred by this Act on the Privy Council (other than the power of hearing appeals against disciplinary orders or directions under section 19 above) the quorum of the Privy Council shall be two.

(2) Any document purporting to be—

(a) an instrument of appointment or approval made by the Privy Council under this Act or any other instrument so made; and

(b) signed by the Clerk of the Privy Council or by any other person authorised by the Privy Council in that behalf,

shall be evidence of the fact that the instrument was so made and of the terms of the instrument.

Supplementary

Interpretation.

36.—(1) In this Act, unless the context otherwise requires—

"approved training institution"' and "approved qualification" have the meanings respectively assigned to them by section 12 above;

"body corporate" includes a partnership in Scotland and, in relation to such a partnership, a reference to a director or other officer of a body corporate is a reference to a partner;

"the Council" means the General Optical Council;

"disciplinary case" has the meaning assigned to it by section 4 above;

"disciplinary order" has the meaning assigned to it by section 14 above;

"dispensing optician" means a person engaged or proposing to engage in the fitting and supply of optical appliances;

"enrolled" means enrolled in either of the lists and "enrolment" shall be construed accordingly;

"erasure order" has the meaning assigned to it by section 14 above;

"functions" includes powers and duties;

"health service ophthalmic lists" means the lists of ophthalmic opticians or dispensing opticians undertaking to provide general ophthalmic services or supplementary eye services which on 1st January 1959 were kept by virtue of the following—

1946 c.81.

(a) section 41 of the National Health Service Act 1946 ;

1947 c.27.

(b) section 42 of the National Health Service (Scotland) Act 1947; and

1948 c.3. (N.I.)

(c) section 21 of the Health Services Act (Northern Ireland) 1948;

"list" means the list of bodies corporate carrying on business as ophthalmic opticians or the list of bodies corporate carrying on business as dispensing opticians;

"medical authority" means one of the universities and other bodies who choose appointed members of the General Medical Council;

"ophthalmic optician" means a person engaged or proposing to engage in the testing of sight (otherwise than as a registered medical practitioner or a person recognised by a medical authority as a medical student), whether or not he is also engaged or proposing to engage in the fitting and supply of optical appliances;

"optical appliance" means an appliance designed to correct, remedy or relieve a defect of sight;

"penalty order" has the meaning assigned to it by section 14 above;

"prescribed" means prescribed by rules under this Act;

"register" means either of the registers of ophthalmic opticians or the register of dispensing opticians and, except where used in relation to medical practitioners, "registered" and "registration" have corresponding meanings;

"registered dispensing optician" means a person who is registered in the register of dispensing opticians;

"registered ophthalmic optician" means a person who is registered in either of the registers of ophthalmic opticians;

"registered optician" means a person who is registered in any of the registers;

"responsible officer" has the meaning assigned to it by section 17(13) above;

"suspension order" has the meaning assigned to it by section 14 above.

(2) References in this Act to testing sight are references to testing sight with the object of determining whether there is any and, if so, what defect of sight and of correcting, remedying or relieving any such defect of an anatomical or physiological nature by means of an optical appliance prescribed on the basis of the determination.

37.—(1) In the definition of "ophthalmic optician" in section 128(1) of the National Health Service Act 1977 and section 108(1) of the National Health Service (Scotland) Act 1978—

Consequential amendments and repeals.
1977 c.49.
1978 c.29.

(a) for "section 2 of the Opticians Act 1958" there shall be substituted "section 7 of the Opticians Act 1989"; and

(b) for "section 4" there shall be substituted "section 9".

(2) In paragraph 13(1)(b) of Schedule 14 to the National Health Service Act 1977, for "to" there shall be substituted, ", 82 and".

(3) In Schedule 6 to the Value Added Tax Act 1983, in paragraph (b) of Item 1 of Group 7—

1983 c.55.

(a) for "Opticians Act 1958" there shall be substituted "Opticians Act 1989"; and

(b) for "section 4" there shall be substituted "section 9".

(4) The enactments mentioned in Schedule 2 to this Act are repealed to the extent specified in the third column of that Schedule.

(5) Paragraphs 3 to 5 of Schedule 3 to the Criminal Justice (Northern Ireland) Order 1986 are revoked.

S.I. 1986 No. 1883 (N.I. 15).

38. This Act shall come into force at the end of the period of three months beginning with the day on which it is passed.

Commencement.

PART V
Short title and
extent.

39.—(1) This Act may be cited as the Opticians Act 1989.

(2) This Act extends to Northern Ireland.

SCHEDULES

SCHEDULE 1

CONSTITUTION ETC. OF COUNCIL

Membership etc.

1. The Council shall consist of—

   (a) six persons nominated by the Privy Council;

   (b) seven persons chosen to represent registered ophthalmic opticians;

   (c) three persons chosen to represent registered dispensing opticians;

   (d) six persons nominated by the examining bodies mentioned in this Schedule; and

   (e) six registered medical practitioners.

2.—(1) Subject to sub-paragraph (2) below, any person nominated by the Privy Council under paragraph 1(a) above shall not be—

   (a) a registered optician;

   (b) a registered medical practitioner; or

   (c) a director of a body corporate carrying on business as opticians.

(2) One of the persons so nominated by the Privy Council shall be a person appearing to them to be specially qualified to advise the Council on educational problems generally and may be a registered optician or registered medical practitioner so long as he is not in practice as an optician or medical practitioner.

3.—(1) The persons chosen to represent the registered ophthalmic or dispensing opticians on the Council shall be elected, subject to the provisions of this Schedule relating to casual vacancies, in accordance with the scheme under paragraph 3 of Schedule 1 to the Opticians Act 1958 approved by the Privy Council on 13th May 1974, as that scheme has effect at the commencement of this Act.

(2) The Council may at any time submit to the Privy Council a scheme for the variation or for the revocation and replacement of the scheme mentioned in sub-paragraph (1) above or any scheme varying or replacing that scheme.

4. Of the persons nominated by the examining bodies—

   (a) three shall be nominated by the British College of Optometrists;

   (b) two shall be nominated by the Association of British Dispensing Opticians; and

   (c) one, who shall be a person engaged in the education or examination of persons training as ophthalmic opticians, shall be nominated jointly by—

      (i) the City University;

      (ii) the University of Aston in Birmingham;

      (iii) the University of Bradford;

      (iv) the University of Manchester Institute of Science and Technology;

      (v) the University of Wales College of Cardiff; and

      (vi) the Glasgow College of Technology.

5. Of the six registered medical practitioners on the Council—

(a) four shall be ophthalmologists and shall be nominated by the College of Ophthalmologists and one of the four shall be a person appearing to the College to be a suitable person to represent ophthalmologists practising in Scotland;

(b) one shall be a medical practitioner engaged in the pre-clinical training of students and shall be nominated by the Privy Council after consultation with persons or bodies appearing to them to have special knowledge and experience of such training;

(c) one shall be a general medical practitioner nominated by the Privy Council after consultation with organisations appearing to the Privy Council to be representative of the medical profession.

6.—(1) On 1st January 1992, and at the end of each succeeding period of five years commencing on that date, the following members of the Council shall retire, that is to say—

(a) two of the members nominated by the Privy Council under paragraph 1(a) above, neither of them being the person appointed as specially qualified to advise on educational problems generally;

(b) those chosen to represent registered opticians; and

(c) the four ophthalmologists nominated by the College of Ophthalmologists.

(2) All the members who do not retire under sub-paragraph (1) above shall retire on 1st January 1994 and at the end of each succeeding period of five years commencing on that date.

(3) Elections or nominations required to fill any vacancy occurring at the end of any period shall, so far as is practicable, be held or made before the end of that period.

7.—(1) A member of the Council may at any time, by notice in writing addressed to the registrar, resign his office.

(2) Where a casual vacancy occurs among the members of the Council—

(a) if the member whose office has become vacant was chosen to represent registered opticians, the vacancy shall be filled by a person nominated by the Council as being a person having qualifications for membership similar to that member's;

(b) in any other case, the vacancy shall be filled by a person nominated by the like authority after the like consultation, if any, as in the case of the member whose office has become vacant.

(3) A person nominated to fill a casual vacancy shall hold office until the date upon which the member whose vacancy he has filled would have regularly retired.

8.—(1) The chairman of the Council shall be nominated by the Privy Council from among the members nominated by the Privy Council under paragraph 1(a) above.

(2) The chairman shall hold office until he next retires from membership of the Council.

9. A person ceasing to be chairman or member of the Council shall be eligible to be again nominated or elected chairman or member.

The registrar

10. The registrar shall be appointed by the Council and shall hold and vacate office in accordance with the terms of his appointment.

Powers of Council

11.—(1) Subject to the following provisions of this Schedule, the Council shall have power to do anything which in their opinion is calculated to facilitate the proper discharge of their functions.

(2) The Council shall, in particular, have power—

(a) to appoint, in addition to a registrar, such officers and servants as the Council may determine;

(b) to pay to the members of the Council or of the Council's committees such fees for attendance at meetings of the Council or committees and such travelling and subsistence allowances while attending such meetings or while on any other business of the Council as the Council may with the approval of the Privy Council determine;

(c) to pay to their officers and servants such remuneration as the Council may determine;

(d) as regards any officers or servants in whose case they may determine to do so, to pay to or in respect of them such pensions and gratuities, or provide and maintain for them such superannuation schemes (whether contributory or not), as the Council may determine.

(3) The powers of the Council and any of the Council's committees may be exercised notwithstanding any vacancy and no proceedings of the Council or a committee shall be invalidated by any defect in the nomination or election of a member.

12. The Council may make standing orders for regulating the proceedings (including quorum) of the Council and the proceedings of any of its committees except the Disciplinary Committee.

Power of Privy Council to alter membership of Council etc.

13.—(1) Subject to sub-paragraph (2) below, the Privy Council may by order, after consultation with the Council and any other body or person they think fit to consult, make such alterations in the membership of the Council as may be expedient in view of changes in circumstances, and may make consequential alterations in relation to the committees which this Act requires the Council to maintain and consequential amendments to this Schedule.

(2) In sub-paragraph (1) above "alterations in the membership of the Council" means alterations—

(a) as to the numbers of members;

(b) as to the qualifications which a person must have to be a member; and

(c) as to who may nominate members.

(3) An order under this paragraph shall not operate to reduce below seven the number of members chosen to represent registered opticians on the Council.

(4) An order under this paragraph may revoke any previous order made under this paragraph or paragraph 13 of Schedule 1 to the Opticians Act 1958 if it appears to the Privy Council, after such consultation as is mentioned in sub-paragraph (1) above, that the order ought to be revoked.   1958 c.32.

Section 37.

SCHEDULE 2

REPEALS

Chapter	Short title	Extent of repeal
6 & 7 Eliz.2 c.32.	Opticians Act 1958.	The whole Act.
1975 c.21.	Criminal Procedure (Scotland) Act 1975.	In Schedule 7A, paragraphs 11 to 13.
1977 c.45.	Criminal Law Act 1977.	In Schedule 1, paragraphs 14 to 16.
1977 c.49.	National Health Service Act 1977.	In Schedule 15, paragraphs 19 and 20.
1978 c.29	National Health Service (Scotland) Act 1978.	In Schedule 16, paragraph 11.
1981 c.54.	Supreme Court Act 1981.	In Schedule 5, the entry relating to the Opticians Act 1958.
1984 c.48.	Health and Social Security Act 1984.	Section 1(1) and (2). Sections 2 to 4. In section 26(6), the words "section 1(1) and (2);" and the words "sections 2 to 4 and Schedule 2;". Schedule 2.
1985 c.9.	Companies Consolidation (Consequential Provisions) Act 1985.	In Schedule 2, the entry relating to the Opticians Act 1958.
1988 c.49.	Health and Medicines Act 1988.	Section 13(6) and (7). Section 14. In section 26(2), the words "section 14". In section 27(3), the words "13(6) and (7), 14".

Prisons (Scotland) Act 1989

1989 CHAPTER 45

An Act to consolidate certain enactments relating to prisons and other institutions for offenders in Scotland and connected matters.   [16th November 1989]

BE IT ENACTED by the Queen's most Excellent Majesty, by and with the advice and consent of the Lords Spiritual and Temporal, and Commons, in this present Parliament assembled, and by the authority of the same, as follows:—

Central administration

1. All powers and jurisdiction in relation to prisons and prisoners which before the commencement of the Prisons (Scotland) Act 1877 were exercisable by any other authority shall, subject to the provisions of this Act, continue to be exercisable by the Secretary of State.

General control over prisons in Scotland.
1877 c. 53.

2.—(1) There shall be employed for the purposes of this Act such inspectors and other officers and servants as the Secretary of State, with the sanction of the Treasury as to number, may appoint.

Appointment of officers and servants for the purposes of this Act.

(2) There shall be paid out of moneys provided by Parliament to the inspectors and officers and servants appointed in pursuance of the foregoing subsection such salaries as the Secretary of State may, with the consent of the Treasury determine.

3.—(1) The general superintendence of prisons shall be vested in the Secretary of State, who shall appoint the governors and other officers of prisons including medical officers, being medical practitioners duly registered under the Medical Acts.

General superintendence of prisons.

(2) The Secretary of State shall appoint to each prison a chaplain being a minister or a licentiate of the Church of Scotland.

(3) The Secretary of State shall make contracts and do all other acts necessary for the maintenance of the prisons and prisoners therein.

(4) There shall be provided such office accommodation in connection with the general superintendence of prisons as the Secretary of State, with the consent of the Treasury, may determine.

General duties in relation to prisons.

4.—(1) Subject to any directions of the Secretary of State officers duly authorised by him shall visit and inspect all prisons and examine the state of the buildings, the conduct of officers, the treatment and conduct of the prisoners and all other matters concerning the management of prisons.

(2) The Secretary of State may, by himself or by any authorised officer, exercise in relation to any prison and the prisoners therein all powers and jurisdiction exercisable by the prison authority of a prison by virtue of any Act of Parliament or by any rules duly made thereunder.

Report to Parliament.

5.—(1) The Secretary of State shall, at such time or times as he may think fit, cause a report to be prepared of the condition of the prisons and prisoners, and shall lay such report before Parliament.

(2) A report prepared under subsection (1) above shall state the various manufacturing processes carried on in each prison with such particulars as to the kinds and quantities of, and the commercial value of the labour on, the manufactures, and as to the number of prisoners employed and otherwise as may in the opinion of the Secretary of State be best calculated to afford information to Parliament.

Annual return of punishments.

6. The Secretary of State shall make a yearly return to Parliament of all punishments inflicted within each prison and the offences for which they were inflicted.

Appointment and functions of Her Majesty's Chief Inspector of Prisons for Scotland.

7.—(1) Her Majesty may appoint a person to be Chief Inspector of Prisons for Scotland.

(2) It shall be the duty of the Chief Inspector to inspect or arrange for the inspection of prisons in Scotland and to report to the Secretary of State on them.

(3) The Chief Inspector shall in particular report to the Secretary of State on the treatment of prisoners and conditions in prisons.

(4) The Secretary of State may refer specific matters connected with prisons in Scotland and prisoners in them to the Chief Inspector and direct him to report on them.

(5) The Chief Inspector shall in each year submit to the Secretary of State a report in such form as the Secretary of State may direct, and the Secretary of State shall lay a copy of that report before Parliament.

(6) The Chief Inspector shall be paid such salary and allowances as the Secretary of State may with the consent of the Treasury determine.

(7) In this section, references to prisons include legalised police cells within the meaning of section 14(1) of this Act.

Visiting committees.

8.—(1) Rules made under section 39 of this Act shall provide for the constitution, for prisons, of visiting committees appointed, at such times, in such manner, for such periods and by such regional, island and district councils as may be prescribed by the rules.

(2) Rules made under section 39 of this Act shall prescribe the functions of visiting committees, and shall among other things require the members to pay frequent visits to the prison and hear any complaints which may be made by the prisoners and report to the Secretary of State

any matter which they consider it expedient to report; and any member of a visiting committee may at any time enter the prison and shall have free access to every part thereof and to every prisoner.

(3) The Secretary of State may pay—

(a) to the members of any visiting committee appointed under or in pursuance of this section such allowances in respect of loss of earnings or travelling or subsistence or other expenses necessarily suffered or incurred in the performance of their duties, and

(b) to the officers of any such committee such remuneration (whether by way of salary or fees) and such allowances in respect of travelling or subsistence expenses,

as the Secretary of State may with the consent of the Treasury determine.

9.—(1) Where in any prison the number of prisoners who belong to a religious denomination other than the Church of Scotland is such as in the opinion of the Secretary of State to require the appointment of a minister of that denomination, the Secretary of State may appoint such a minister to that prison. Appointment of prison ministers.

(2) The Secretary of State may pay a minister appointed under the foregoing subsection such remuneration as he thinks reasonable.

(3) The Secretary of State may allow a minister of any denomination other than the Church of Scotland to visit prisoners of his denomination in a prison to which no minister of that denomination has been appointed under this section.

(4) No prisoner shall be visited against his will by such a minister as is mentioned in the last foregoing subsection; but every prisoner not belonging to the Church of Scotland shall be allowed, in accordance with the arrangements in force in the prison in which he is confined, to attend chapel or to be visited by the chaplain.

(5) The governor of a prison shall on the reception of each prisoner record the religious denomination to which the prisoner declares himself to belong, and shall give to any minister who under this section is appointed to the prison or permitted to visit prisoners therein a list of the prisoners who have declared themselves to belong to his denomination; and the minister shall not be permitted to visit any other prisoners.

Confinement and treatment of prisoners

10. Prisoners shall be committed to such prison as may be appointed by rules under this Act, and a convicted criminal prisoner may be removed by the Secretary of State from any one prison to any other prison for the purpose of undergoing any part of his sentence. Place of confinement of prisoners.

11.—(1) Rules under section 39 of this Act may provide in what manner an appellant within the meaning of section 279 of the 1975 Act, when in custody, is to be taken to, kept in custody at, and brought back from, any place at which he is entitled to be present for the purposes of that Act, or any place to which the High Court of Justiciary or any judge thereof, may order him to be taken for the purposes of any proceedings of that court. Removal of prisoners for judicial and other purposes.

(2) The Secretary of State may, if he is satisfied that a person detained in Scotland in a prison requires medical or surgical treatment of any description, direct him to be taken to a hospital or other suitable place for the purpose of the treatment.

(3) Where any person is directed under the last foregoing subsection to be taken to any place he shall, unless the Secretary of State otherwise directs, be kept in custody while being so taken, while at that place, and while being taken back to the prison in which he is required in accordance with law to be detained.

(4) The governor or any officer of a prison may execute any warrant issued by the High Court of Justiciary for the removal of a prisoner in that prison to any other prison for the purpose of trial before that court.

(5) The Secretary of State may make regulations as to the mode in which and the officers by whom warrants issued under the last foregoing subsection shall be executed.

Photographing and measuring of prisoners.

12. The Secretary of State may make regulations as to the measuring and photographing of prisoners and such regulations may prescribe the time or times at which, and the manner and dress in which prisoners shall be measured and photographed, and the number of copies of the measurements and photographs of each prisoner which shall be made and the persons to whom they shall be sent.

Legal custody of prisoner.

13. A person shall be deemed to be in legal custody—

    (a) while he is confined in or being taken to or from any prison in which he may be lawfully confined; or

    (b) while he is working or is, for any other reason, outside the prison in the custody or under the control of an officer of the prison; or

    (c) while he is being taken to any place to which he is required or authorised by or under this Act to be taken; or

    (d) while he is kept in custody in pursuance of such requirement or authorisation.

Legalised police cells.

14.—(1) The Secretary of State, on the application of a police authority, may from time to time by rules under this Act declare that any police cells or other premises in the possession of the police authority shall be a legal prison for the detention of prisoners before, during or after trial for any period not exceeding 30 days. Any such police cells or other premises are hereinafter referred to as legalised police cells.

(2) Any person charged with or convicted of any crime or offence committed within any region or islands area who might have been lawfully confined in a prison situated therein may be lawfully confined in any legalised police cells situated in that region or islands area for such period as aforesaid.

(3) The maintenance of prisoners confined in any legalised police cells shall be deemed to be the maintenance of prisoners under this Act:

Provided that the police authority shall not be entitled to any payment for the use of the legalised police cells or for services rendered by any of their officers in connection with the detention or removal of the prisoners so confined.

(4) The police authority, notwithstanding anything in this section, shall at all times have a prior claim to the uninterrupted use of any legalised police cells in their area.

(5) For the purposes of this section the police authority of any region or islands area in which there are any legalised police cells and all persons in their employment shall be subject to the provisions of this Act and any rules made thereunder.

(6) It shall be the duty of the Secretary of State to make any arrangements required for the removal of any prisoners confined in legalised police cells in the islands area of Orkney or of Shetland.

(7) In this section the expression "police authority" means the council of a region or islands area, except that where there is an amalgamation scheme in force under the Police (Scotland) Act 1967 it means a joint police committee.

1967 c. 77.

(8) For the purposes of sections 8 and 39 of this Act, legalised police cells shall be deemed to be prisons.

15.—(1) A sheriff or justice of the peace may visit any prison within his jurisdiction or in which a prisoner is confined for any offence committed within his jurisdiction, and may examine the condition of the prison and of the prisoners therein and enter in the visitors book to be kept by the governor of the prison any observations on the condition of the prison or on any abuses therein.

Right of sheriff or justice to visit prison.

(2) Nothing in the foregoing subsection shall authorise a sheriff or justice of the peace to communicate with any prisoner except on the subject of his treatment in the prison nor to visit any prisoner under sentence of death.

(3) It shall be the duty of the governor of a prison to draw the attention of the visiting committee at their next visit to any entry in the visitors book made in pursuance of this section.

Discharge of prisoners

16.—(1) Where a prisoner would, but for this subsection, be discharged on a Saturday or Sunday, he shall be discharged on the preceding Friday.

Discharge of prisoners.

(2) A prisoner discharged from a prison situated outside the district or islands area in which he was convicted shall be entitled to be taken back to that district or islands area at the expense of the Secretary of State.

17.—(1) When a prisoner is discharged from prison the Secretary of State may provide him with the means of returning to his home by causing his fare to be paid or in any other convenient manner.

Allowances to prisoner on discharge.

(2) The Secretary of State may make such payments to or in respect of persons released or about to be released from prisons as he may, with the consent of the Treasury, determine.

18.—(1) For the purpose of exercising the functions conferred on it by this Act as respects Scotland there shall be a body to be known as the Parole Board for Scotland, consisting of a chairman and not less than four other members appointed by the Secretary of State.

Constitution and functions of Parole Board and local review committees.

(2) It shall be the duty of the Board to advise the Secretary of State with respect to—

  (a) the release on licence under section 22, 25 or 26 of this Act and the recall under section 25, 28, 31 or 32 of this Act of persons whose cases have been referred to the Board by the Secretary of State;

  (b) the conditions of such licences and the variation or cancellation of such conditions; and

  (c) any other matter so referred which is connected with the recall of persons to whom the said section 31 or 32 applies or the release on licence or recall of persons to whom the said section 22, 25 or 26 applies.

(3) The following provisions shall have effect with respect to the proceedings of the Board on any case referred to it, that is to say—

  (a) the Board shall deal with the case on consideration of any documents given to it by the Secretary of State and of any reports it has called for and any information whether oral or in writing that it has obtained; and

  (b) if in any particular case the Board thinks it necessary to interview the person to whom the case relates before reaching a decision, the Board may request one of its members to interview him and shall take into account the report of that interview by that member;

and, without prejudice to the foregoing, the Secretary of State may by rules make provision with respect to the proceedings of the Board on cases referred to it, including provision authorising such cases to be dealt with by a prescribed number of members of the Board.

(4) The documents to be given by the Secretary of State to the Board under the last foregoing subsection shall include—

  (a) where the case referred to the Board is one of release under section 22, 25 or 26 of this Act, any written representations made by the person to whom the case relates in connection with or since his last interview in accordance with rules under the next following subsection;

  (b) where the case so referred relates to a person recalled under section 25, 28, 31 or 32 of this Act, any written representations made under that section.

(5) The Secretary of State may by rules make provision—

  (a) for the establishment and constitution of local review committees having the duty of reviewing at such times or in such circumstances as may be prescribed by or determined under the rules the cases of persons who are or will become eligible for release under section 22, 25 or 26 of this Act, and reporting to the Secretary of State on their suitability for release on licence; and

  (b) for the interview of such persons by a member of any such committee (not being a prison officer);

and rules under this subsection may make different provision for different cases.

(6) The supplementary provisions contained in Schedule 1 to this Act shall have effect with respect to the Parole Board and local review committees.

.

Detention and transfer of young offenders

19.—(1) The Secretary of State may provide—

(a) remand centres, that is to say places for the detention of persons not less than 14 but under 21 years of age who are remanded or committed in custody for trial or sentence; and

(b) young offenders institutions, that is to say, places in which offenders sentenced to detention in a young offenders institution may be kept.

Remand centres and young offenders institutions.

(2) The Secretary of State shall provide in remand centres facilities for the observation and examination of any person detained therein on whose physical or mental condition a medical report may be desirable for the assistance of the court in determining the most suitable method of dealing with his case.

(3) The Secretary of State shall appoint for every remand centre and young offenders institution a visiting committee of which not less than two members shall be justices of the peace and not less than such number of members as may be prescribed by the rules shall be women.

(4) The following provisions, that is to say—

(a) sections 8(2) and (3), 11(2) and (3), 12 and 38 of this Act, and

(b) subject as hereinafter provided, sections 1 to 7, 9, 10, 11(1), (4) and (5), 13 to 17, 24, 33 to 37 and 41 of this Act,

shall apply to remand centres and young offenders institutions, to persons detained therein and to visiting committees appointed therefor under subsection (3) above in like manner as the said provisions apply to prisons, prisoners and visiting committees appointed for prisons under section 8(1) of this Act:

Provided that—

(i) section 11(4) and (5) of this Act shall not apply to young offenders institutions;

(ii) section 24 of this Act shall not apply to remand centres;

(iii) the provisions specified in paragraph (b) of this subsection, other than those mentioned in paragraphs (i) and (ii) of this proviso, shall apply as aforesaid subject to such adaptations and modifications as may be made by rules of the Secretary of State.

20. A person who is required to be taken to a young offenders institution or remand centre may, until arrangements can be made for taking him there, be temporarily detained elsewhere.

Temporary detention of persons liable to detention in young offenders institution or remand centre.

Transfer to prison of persons over 21, and maximum age for detention in young offenders institution.

21.—(1) Subject to the provisions of this section, where a person serving a sentence of detention in a young offenders institution has attained the age of 21 years, the Secretary of State shall have power to transfer him to prison.

(2) No person shall be detained in a young offenders institution after he has attained the age of 23 years, and accordingly any person so detained shall, not later than the day immediately preceding his twenty-third birthday, be transferred to prison.

(3) Where a person has been transferred to prison under this section, he shall be treated for the purpose of his serving the unexpired part of his sentence and of his supervision on release as if the sentence of detention passed upon him were a sentence of imprisonment for a like term, and the provisions of the 1975 Act and this Act relating to the treatment and supervision of prisoners shall apply to him accordingly:

Provided that section 212, or as the case may be section 421, of the 1975 Act (recall on reconviction) shall continue to apply to a person so transferred to prison.

Release on licence, etc.

Release on licence of persons serving determinate sentences.

22.—(1) The Secretary of State may, if recommended to do so by the Parole Board, release on licence a person, who is serving a sentence of imprisonment, other than imprisonment for life, or a sentence of detention in a young offender institution imposed in England and Wales, after he has served not less than one-third of his sentence or the specified period, whichever expires the later.

(2) In subsection (1) above, "the specified period" means 12 months or such period, not more than 12 months, as the Secretary of State may by order provide.

(3) An order under subsection (2) above may make such incidental or supplementary provision (including provision amending enactments) as the Secretary of State considers appropriate.

1977 c. 45.

(4) Where a sentence of imprisonment for an offence has been passed on a person with an order under subsection (1) of section 47 of the Criminal Law Act 1977 (sentences partly suspended in England and Wales)—

    (a) if the offender has not been released from prison since the sentence for the offence was passed, the only portion of that sentence that is to be taken into account for the purposes of subsection (1) of this section is any portion of it that he is required to serve in prison under subsection (1) or (3) of the said section 47; and

    (b) if he is released from prison but part of his sentence for the offence is subsequently restored under subsection (3) of that section, he shall be treated for the purpose of subsection (1) of this section as if his only sentence for the offence were the part of his sentence so restored.

(5) A person whose sentence falls to be reduced under section 67 of the Criminal Justice Act 1967 (sentences in England and Wales) shall, for the purpose of determining under subsection (1) above whether he has served one-third of his sentence, be treated as if any period spent in custody and taken into account under that section were included in his sentence and as if he had served that period as part of that sentence.

1967 c. 80.

(6) A person subject to a licence under this section shall comply with such conditions, if any, as may for the time being be specified in the licence.

(7) The Secretary of State shall consult the Parole Board before including on release, or subsequently inserting, a condition in a licence under this section or varying or cancelling any such condition; and for the purposes of this subsection the Secretary of State shall be treated as having consulted the Board about a proposal to include, insert, vary or cancel a condition in any case if he has consulted the Board about the implementation of proposals of that description generally or in that class of case.

(8) A licence granted to any person under this section shall, unless previously revoked under section 62 of the Criminal Justice Act 1967 or section 28 of this Act, remain in force until a date specified in the licence, being the date on which he could have been discharged from prison on remission of part of his sentence under rules made under section 39 of this Act if, after the date of his release on licence, he had not forfeited remission of any part of the sentence under the rules.

23. If, in any case falling within such class of cases as the Secretary of State may determine after consultation with the Parole Board, a local review committee recommends the release on licence of a person to whom subsection (1) of section 22 of this Act applies, the Secretary of State shall not be obliged to refer the case to the Board before releasing him under that subsection and, unless he nevertheless refers it to the Board, may so release him without any recommendation by the Board.

Release on licence without recommendation of Parole Board.

24. Rules made under section 39 of this Act may make provision whereby, in such circumstances as may be prescribed by the rules, a person serving a sentence of imprisonment for such a term as may be so prescribed, may be granted remission of such part of that sentence as may be so prescribed on the ground of his industry and good conduct; and on the discharge of a person from a prison in pursuance of any such remission as aforesaid his sentence shall expire.

Remission for good conduct.

25.—(1) Subject to subsection (2) below, the Secretary of State may release on licence, on such conditions as may for the time being be specified in the licence, a person detained under section 206 of the 1975 Act (detention of children convicted on indictment).

Release on licence of children convicted on indictment.

(2) Where a person has been sentenced under the said section 206 to be detained for a period exceeding 18 months, the Secretary of State—

(a) shall not release him on licence under subsection (1) above except on the recommendation of the Parole Board; and

(b) shall consult the Board with regard to the inclusion or subsequent insertion of any condition in the licence or the variation or cancellation of any such condition; but for the purposes of this paragraph the Secretary of State shall be treated as having consulted the Board about a proposal to include, insert, vary or cancel a condition in any case if he has consulted the Board about the implementation of proposals of that description generally or in that class of case.

(3) A licence granted under subsection (1) above shall, unless previously revoked under subsection (4) below, remain in force until the expiry of the period of—

    (a) detention specified by the court under the said section 206, or

    (b) 12 months from the date of release under the licence,

whichever is the later.

(4) The Secretary of State may—

    (a) on the recommendation of the Parole Board, or

    (b) at his own instance, where it appears to him to be in the public interest to do so before consultation with the Board is practicable,

revoke a licence granted under subsection (1) above and recall the person released under the licence to a place in which the Secretary of State directs that he should be detained; and on such revocation, the person shall be liable to be detained in pursuance of his sentence, and, if at large, shall be deemed to be unlawfully at large.

(5) The Secretary of State shall inform a person recalled under subsection (4) above of the reasons for his recall, so that the person may make representations in writing to the Parole Board with respect to his recall; and the Board may, on receipt of such representations, require the Secretary of State to release him on licence forthwith.

(6) Subject to subsection (5) above, a person detained in pursuance of subsection (4) above shall remain in detention until the expiry of the period of—

    (a) detention specified by the court under the said section 206; or

    (b) three months from the date of the commencement of his detention in pursuance of the said subsection (4),

whichever is the later:

Provided that the Secretary of State may, at any time before the expiry of the period referred to in paragraph (a) above, again release him on licence.

Release on licence of persons sentenced to imprisonment for life, etc.

26.—(1) The Secretary of State may, if recommended to do so by the Parole Board, release on licence a person serving a sentence of imprisonment for life, or a sentence of custody for life imposed in England and Wales, or a person detained under section 205(2) or (3) of the 1975 Act (persons under 21 convicted of murder); but shall not release on licence such a person except after consultation with the Lord Justice-General together with the trial judge, if available.

(2) Subsections (6) and (7) of section 22 of this Act shall apply in relation to a licence under this section as they apply in relation to a licence under that section.

27.—(1) If the Secretary of State is satisfied that by reason of the condition of a prisoner's health it is undesirable to detain him in prison, but that, such condition of health being due in whole or in part to the prisoner's own conduct in prison, it is desirable that his release should be temporary and conditional only, the Secretary of State may, if he thinks fit, having regard to all the circumstances of the case, by order authorise the temporary discharge of the prisoner for such period and subject to such conditions as may be stated in the order.

(2) Where an order of temporary discharge is made in the case of a prisoner not under sentence, the order shall contain conditions requiring the attendance of the prisoner at any further proceedings on his case at which his presence may be required.

(3) Any prisoner discharged under this section shall comply with any conditions stated in the order of temporary discharge, and shall return to prison at the expiration of the period stated in the order, or of such extended period as may be fixed by any subsequent order of the Secretary of State, and, if the prisoner fails so to comply or return, he may be arrested without warrant and taken back to prison.

(4) Where a prisoner under sentence is discharged in pursuance of an order of temporary discharge, the currency of the sentence shall be suspended from the day on which he is discharged from prison under the order to the day on which he is received back into prison, so that the former day shall be reckoned and the latter shall not be reckoned as part of the sentence.

(5) Nothing in this section shall affect the duties of the medical officer of a prison in respect of a prisoner whom the Secretary of State does not think fit to discharge under this section.

Power of Secretary of State to discharge prisoners temporarily on account of their health.

28.—(1) Where the Parole Board recommends the recall of any person who is subject to a licence under section 22 or 26 of this Act, the Secretary of State may revoke that person's licence and recall him to prison.

(2) The Secretary of State may revoke the licence of any such person and recall him as aforesaid without consulting the Board, where it appears to him that it is expedient in the public interest to recall that person before such consultation is practicable.

(3) A person recalled to prison under the foregoing provisions of this section may make representations in writing with respect to his recall and shall on his return to prison be informed of the reasons for his recall and of his right to make such representations.

(4) The Secretary of State shall refer to the Parole Board the case of a person recalled under subsection (1) above who makes representations under the last foregoing subsection and shall in any event so refer the case of a person returned to prison after being recalled under subsection (2) above.

(5) Where the Board recommends the immediate release on licence of a person whose case is referred to it under this section, the Secretary of State shall give effect to the recommendation, and where it is necessary for that purpose to release that person under subsection (1) of section 26 of this Act, the Secretary of State shall do so without the consultation required by that subsection.

Revocation of licences and conviction of prisoners on licence.

1967 c. 80.

(6) If a person subject to a licence under section 60 or 61 of the Criminal Justice Act 1967 or section 22 or 26 of this Act is convicted by the High Court of Justiciary, or by a sheriff, whether summarily or on indictment, of an offence punishable on indictment with imprisonment, the court by which he is convicted may, whether or not it passes any other sentence on him, revoke the licence.

(7) On the revocation of the licence of any person under this section, he shall be liable to be detained in pursuance of his sentence, and, if at large, shall be deemed to be unlawfully at large.

(8) If, in the case of a person subject to a licence under section 60 of the Criminal Justice Act 1967 (release on licence) or section 22 of this Act, a Crown Court or the High Court of Justiciary or a sheriff revokes that licence under section 62 of the Criminal Justice Act 1967 or, as the case may be, under this section, the Secretary of State shall not thereafter release him under subsection (1) of the said section 22 before the expiration of the specified period from the date of revocation or before the expiration of one-third of the period during which the licence would have remained in force, whichever is the later; but the foregoing provision shall not affect any power to release him otherwise than under that subsection.

(9) In subsection (8) above, "the specified period" has the same meaning as in section 22(2) above.

(10) This section shall have effect, in its application to a person sentenced in England and Wales to detention in a young offender institution or sentenced to be detained under section 205(2) of the 1975 Act (punishment of person under 18 for murder), as if for any reference to a prison there were substituted a reference to any place in which that person was detained immediately before he was released on licence.

(11) This section shall have effect, in its application to a person sentenced to be detained under section 205(3), 207 or 415 of the 1975 Act (detention of young offenders) as if for any reference to a prison there were substituted a reference to a young offenders institution.

Determination of age.

29. Without prejudice to section 43(7) of this Act, for the purposes of the provisions of this Act relating to licences or persons on licence, the age of any person at the time when sentence was passed on him shall be deemed to have been that which appears to the Secretary of State to have been his age at that time.

Supervision after release

Supervision of certain prisoners after release.

30.—(1) If it appears to the Secretary of State that a person serving a sentence of imprisonment is a person to whom this section applies, he shall, by notice given to such person in accordance with subsection (3) below, place him under supervision on his release from prison.

(2) Subject to the provisions of subsection (7) below, this section applies—

> (a) to any person serving a sentence of imprisonment for a term of three years or more;

(b) to any person serving a sentence of imprisonment for a term of not less than six months, but less than three years, who is under the age of 26 years at the commencement of the sentence;

but does not apply to a person serving a sentence of imprisonment for life.

(3) Before the release from prison of any person to whom this section applies, the Secretary of State shall cause to be given to him a notice ("a notice of supervision") giving the name and address of the person who is to be his supervising officer in the first instance, and specifying the requirements with which he has to comply while under supervision; and a notice given to any person under this subsection shall contain a statement that it is given to him as falling within a specified class of the persons to whom this section for the time being applies.

(4) Subject to this section and sections 214 and 423 of the 1975 Act, every person to whom this section applies shall, after his release from prison and until the expiry of the period of 12 months from the date of his release, be under supervision, and shall, while under that supervision, be required—

(a) to keep in touch with his supervising officer in accordance with such instructions as may from time to time be given by that officer; and

(b) to comply with the directions of his supervising officer as to conduct; and

(c) to comply with such other requirements as may be specified in his notice of supervision.

(5) At any time during the period referred to in subsection (4) above the Secretary of State may, by notice in writing given to a person under supervision as aforesaid,—

(a) discharge him from supervision, or

(b) replace as from a specified date his supervising officer by another supervising officer whose name and address shall be specified in that notice, or

(c) cancel or modify any other of the requirements specified in his notice of supervision.

(6) The Secretary of State may by order substitute a lower limit of three months instead of six months in paragraph (b) of subsection (2) above.

(7) This section shall not apply to persons serving a sentence of imprisonment commencing before such date as may be prescribed by order of the Secretary of State under this subsection; and any such order may prescribe different dates in respect of sentences described in paragraphs (a) and (b) respectively of subsection (2) above, and, in respect of sentences comprised in the said paragraph (b), either according to the length of the term of imprisonment under a sentence or to the age of the person on whom it is passed.

31.—(1) A child released after detention under section 206 of the 1975 Act who has not been released on licence during the period of detention may be required, by notice given by the Secretary of State on his release, to be under the supervision of such officer as may be specified in the notice, and to comply, while the notice is in force, with such conditions as may be specified.

Supervision of children after release.

2E

(2) Subject to subsection (5) below, the supervision requirement shall not continue after the expiry of the period of 12 months from the date of release.

(3) The Secretary of State may, on giving notice to the person concerned, at any time vary or cancel a requirement or condition specified under subsection (1) above.

(4) A period of supervision required under subsection (1) above shall not extend beyond the date on which the person under supervision attains the age of 23 years.

(5) Where, before a supervision requirement expires, the Secretary of State is satisfied that the person to whom it relates has failed to comply with its terms and either—

(a) the Parole Board so recommends, or

(b) it appears to him to be in the public interest to do so before consultation with the Board is practicable,

he may recall the person to detention for a period not exceeding three months; and a person at large after such recall shall be deemed to be unlawfully at large.

(6) The Secretary of State shall inform a person recalled under subsection (5) above of the reasons for his recall, so that the person may make representations in writing to the Parole Board with respect to his recall; and the Board may, on receipt of such representations, require the Secretary of State to release him forthwith.

(7) The Secretary of State may at any time release a person detained by virtue of subsection (5) above.

(8) The powers conferred by subsection (5) above may be exercised as often as it appears to the Secretary of State that the person concerned has failed to comply with the supervision requirement; but no person may be recalled to detention for periods totalling more than three months by virtue of that subsection.

(9) A recall under subsection (5) above may continue beyond the date of expiry of the supervision requirement unless the person to whom it relates is not in custody at that date.

(10) In this section, "child" has the same meaning as in section 462(1) (interpretation) of the 1975 Act.

Supervision of persons released from young offenders institution.

32.—(1) This section applies in relation to persons sentenced under section 207 or 415 of the 1975 Act (detention of young offenders).

(2) Subject to sections 212 and 421 of the 1975 Act (which relate to recall of young offenders on re-conviction) and to subsections (4) to (6) and (10) below, a person in relation to whom this section applies may, where he has been sentenced to a period of (or, as the case may be, periods totalling) six months or more, be required, by notice of the Secretary of State given to the person on his release from that detention, both to be under the supervision of such officer as may be specified in the notice and to comply, while under the supervision, with such conditions as may be so specified; and the supervision shall continue—

    (a) in a case where such release is on licence under section 60(1) or section 61 of the Criminal Justice Act 1967 or section 22(1) or 26 1967 c. 80. of this Act, until the expiry of the period of 12 months from the date of such release or until the expiry of the licence, whichever is the later;

    (b) in any other case—

        (i) where the term was less than 18 months, until the expiry of the period of six months from the date of such release; or

        (ii) where the term was 18 months or more, until the expiry of the period of 12 months from the date of such release.

(3) In a case such as is mentioned in paragraph (a) of subsection (2) above, the requirement and conditions specified by the Secretary of State under that subsection shall be in addition to any conditions specified in the licence mentioned in that paragraph.

(4) Without prejudice to subsection (7) below, a period of supervision required under subsection (2) above shall not extend beyond the date on which the person under supervision attains the age of 23 years.

(5) The Secretary of State may by order extend the provisions of subsection (2) above to persons in relation to whom this section applies whose detention is for less than six months but not less than three months.

(6) The Secretary of State may, on giving notice to the person concerned, at any time modify or cancel a requirement, or condition, which is specified under subsection (2) above.

(7) Subject to subsections (9) and (10) below, where, before the expiry of the period for which a person is required under this section to be under supervision, the Secretary of State is satisfied that the person has failed to conform to the requirement or has failed to comply with a condition for the time being specified in the notice given to him under subsection (2) above and either—

    (a) the Parole Board so recommends, or

    (b) it appears to him to be in the public interest to do so before consultation with the Board is practicable,

he may (except in a case such as is mentioned in paragraph (a) of subsection (2) above) recall the person to a young offenders institution; and thereupon the person shall be liable to be detained in that institution for a period not exceeding three months, and if at large shall be deemed to be unlawfully at large.

(8) The Secretary of State shall inform a person recalled under subsection (7) above of the reasons for his recall, so that the person may make representations in writing to the Parole Board with respect to his recall; and the Board may, on receipt of such representations, require the Secretary of State to release him forthwith.

(9) A recall under subsection (7) above shall cease to have effect at the expiry of the first period mentioned in that subsection unless the person to whom it relates is then in custody thereunder.

(10) The Secretary of State may at any time release a person who is, by virtue of subsection (7) above, detained; and the provisions of this section shall apply to a person released under subsection (8) above or this subsection as if, following the release mentioned in subsection (2) above, neither the recall under the said subsection (7) nor the subsequent release

under subsection (8) above or this subsection had taken place, except that the period of detention between the recall and the subsequent release shall be deducted from the period for which the person would otherwise be liable to be detained were he again to be recalled.

Miscellaneous

Duties of governor of prison.

33. The governor of a prison shall—

(a) as far as practicable, visit the whole of the prison and see every prisoner at least once in every 24 hours, and, in default of such daily visits, state in his journal the extent of and the reason for such default;

(b) as soon as practicable draw the attention of the medical officer to any prisoner whose state of mind or body appears to require attention and carry into effect the written directions of the medical officer as to alterations in the discipline or treatment of such prisoner;

(c) notify the medical officer without delay of the illness of any prisoner, and deliver to him daily a list of prisoners complaining of illness;

(d) deliver to the chaplain and to the medical officer lists of prisoners confined to their cells; and

(e) keep records regarding the commitment to and liberation from the prison of prisoners committed thereto in pursuance of criminal warrants and when so required exhibit such records to the sheriff within whose jurisdiction the prison is situated.

Notification of and inquiry into death of prisoner.

34. The governor of a prison shall, in the event of the death of a prisoner, give immediate notice thereof to the procurator fiscal within whose area the prison is situated, and to the visiting committee, and, where practicable, to the nearest relative of the prisoner.

Return of warrants for or sentences of imprisonment.

35. Where a warrant for imprisonment is granted or a sentence of imprisonment is pronounced by any court, a return thereof shall be made by the clerk of the court to the Secretary of State at such time and in such form as he may determine.

Legal estate in prison.

36. The legal estate in every prison and in all heritable or moveable property belonging to a prison shall be vested in the Secretary of State and may be disposed of in such manner as the Secretary of State, with the consent of the Treasury, may determine.

Discontinuance of prison.

37.—(1) The Secretary of State may by order discontinue any prison, and any prison so discontinued shall be sold or otherwise disposed of as the Secretary of State, with the consent of the Treasury, may direct.

(2) For the purposes of this section a prison shall not be deemed to be discontinued by reason only of its appropriation for use as a remand centre or young offenders institution.

38.—(1) The Secretary of State may purchase by agreement, or compulsorily, any land required for the alteration, enlargement or rebuilding of a prison or for building or establishing a new prison or for any other purpose connected with the management of a prison (including the provision of accommodation for officers or servants employed therein).

Acquisition of land for prisons.

(2) For the purpose of the compulsory purchase of land by the Secretary of State under the foregoing subsection, the Acquisition of Land (Authorisation Procedure) (Scotland) Act 1947 shall apply as if section 1(1)(d) (which refers to the compulsory purchase of land by the Secretary of State under the National Health Service (Scotland) Act 1972) included a reference to the foregoing subsection.

1947 c. 42.

1972 c. 58.

(3) In relation to the purchase of land by agreement under this section, the Lands Clauses Acts (except the provisions relating to the purchase of land otherwise than by agreement and the provisions relating to access to the special Act, and except sections 120 to 125 (sale of superfluous lands) of the Lands Clauses Consolidation (Scotland) Act 1845) shall be incorporated with this section, and in construing those Acts as so incorporated this section shall be deemed to be the special Act and references to the promoters of the undertaking shall be construed as references to the Secretary of State.

1845 c. 19.

39.—(1) The Secretary of State may make rules for the regulation and management of prisons, remand centres and young offenders institutions respectively, and for the classification, treatment, employment, discipline and control of persons required to be detained therein.

Rules for the management of prisons and other institutions.

(2) Rules made under this section shall make provision for ensuring that a person who is charged with any offence under the rules shall be given a proper opportunity of presenting his case.

(3) Rules made under this section may provide for the training of particular classes of persons and their allocation for that purpose to any prison or other institution in which they may lawfully be detained.

(4) Rules made under this section may provide for the appointment of a convenient prison or prisons—

(a) in which prisoners are to be confined before and during trial, or at either of such times;

(b) in which particular classes of prisoners may be confined;

(c) in which civil prisoners may be confined during the period of their imprisonment.

(5) Rules made under this section shall provide for the special treatment of the following persons whilst required to be detained in a prison, that is to say—

(a) any appellant within the meaning of section 279 of the 1975 Act pending the determination of his appeal;

(b) any other person detained in a prison, not being a person serving a sentence imposed on conviction of an offence.

(6) Rules made under this section may provide for the temporary release of persons serving a sentence of imprisonment or detention.

Persons
unlawfully at
large.

40.—(1) Any person who, having been sentenced to imprisonment or to detention in a young offenders institution, or having been committed to a prison or remand centre, is unlawfully at large may be arrested by a constable or prison officer without warrant and taken to the place in which he is required in accordance with law to be detained.

(2) Where any person sentenced to imprisonment or to detention in a young offenders institution is, at any time during the period for which he is liable to be detained in pursuance of the sentence, absent, otherwise than with lawful authority, from the prison or young offenders institution, as the case may be, then, unless the Secretary of State otherwise directs, no account shall be taken, in calculating the period for which he is liable to be so detained, of any time during which he is so absent:

Provided that this subsection shall not apply to any period during which any such person as aforesaid is detained in pursuance of an order of any court in the United Kingdom in a prison, young offenders institution or remand centre.

1967 c. 80.

(3) Without prejudice to section 69(2) of the Criminal Justice Act 1967, in subsection (2) above references to a prison shall be construed as including references to a place which is the subject of a direction of the Secretary of State under section 206 of the 1975 Act (detention of children convicted on indictment).

(4) For the purposes of this section, a person who, after being temporarily released in pursuance of rules made under section 39(6) of this Act, is at large at any time during the period for which he is liable to be detained in pursuance of his sentence shall be deemed to be unlawfully at large if the period for which he was temporarily released has expired or if an order recalling him has been made by the Secretary of State in pursuance of the rules.

Unlawful
introduction of
tobacco, etc.,
into prison.

41.—(1) Any person who brings, or introduces or attempts by any means to bring or introduce, into a prison any letter, tobacco, spirits or other article not allowed by rules made under section 39 of this Act shall be guilty of an offence and shall be liable on conviction by a court of summary jurisdiction to a fine not exceeding level 3 on the standard scale or to imprisonment for any period not exceeding 30 days.

(2) For the purposes of the foregoing subsection a person shall be deemed to introduce an article into a prison if he conveys it to a prisoner outside the prison or places it anywhere outside the prison with intent that it shall come into the possession of a prisoner.

(3) It shall be lawful for any officer of the prison to apprehend an offender against this section.

Exercise of
power to make
rules, etc.

42.—(1) Any power of the Secretary of State to make rules or regulations under this Act, and the power of the Secretary of State to make an order under section 22(2), 30(6) or (7), 32(5) or 37(1) of this Act, shall be exercisable by statutory instrument.

(2) Any statutory instrument containing regulations made under section 12 or an order made under section 37(1) of this Act and the draft of any statutory instrument containing rules made under section 39 of this Act shall be laid before Parliament.

(3) Any rule made under section 18(3) or (5) of this Act or any statutory instrument containing an order under section 30(6) or (7) or 32(5) of this Act shall be subject to annulment in pursuance of a resolution of either House of Parliament.

(4) An order shall not be made under section 22(2) of this Act unless a draft of the order has been laid before Parliament and approved by a resolution of each House of Parliament.

43.—(1) In this Act, unless the context otherwise requires, the following expressions have the meanings hereby respectively assigned to them— *Interpretation.*

"the 1975 Act" means the Criminal Procedure (Scotland) Act 1975;   *1975 c. 21.*

"court" does not include a court-martial;

"criminal prisoner" means a person committed to prison in respect of a charge or conviction of a criminal offence and "civil prisoner" includes any other prisoner;

"local review committee" has the same meaning as in section 18(5) of this Act;

"Parole Board" means the Parole Board for Scotland;

"prison" includes any prison other than a naval, military or air force prison;

"prisoner" means a person committed for trial, safe custody, punishment or otherwise; and

"sentence of imprisonment" does not include a committal in default of payment of any sum of money or for failure to do or abstain from doing anything required to be done or left undone.

(2) For the purposes of any reference, however expressed, in this Act (other than in section 25) to the term of imprisonment or other detention to which a person has been sentenced or which, or part of which, he has served, consecutive terms and terms which are wholly or partly concurrent shall be treated as a single term.

(3) Any reference in this Act, however expressed, to a previous conviction or sentence shall be construed as a reference to a previous conviction by a court in any part of Great Britain and to a previous sentence passed by any such court.

(4) Any reference in this Act to an offence punishable with imprisonment shall be construed, in relation to any offender, without regard to any prohibition or restriction imposed by or under any enactment on the imprisonment of offenders of his age.

(5) References, however expressed, in this Act (other than in section 30) to imprisonment shall, so far as those provisions apply to institutions provided under section 19 of this Act, be construed as including detention in those institutions.

(6) For the purpose of this Act the maintenance of a prisoner shall include all necessary expenses incurred in respect of the prisoner for food, clothing, custody and removal from one place to another from the period from the date of the order for his committal to prison until his death or discharge from prison.

(7) Where the age of any person at any time is material for the purposes of any provision of this Act regulating the powers of a court, his age at the material time shall be deemed to be or to have been that which appears to the court, after considering any available evidence, to be or to have been his age at that time.

Expenses.

44. All expenses incurred in the maintenance of prisons and prisoners and all other expenses of the Secretary of State under this Act shall be defrayed out of moneys provided by Parliament.

Amendments and repeals.

45.—(1) The enactments mentioned in Schedule 2 to this Act shall have effect subject to the amendments specified therein, being amendments consequential on the provisions of this Act.

(2) The enactments mentioned in Schedule 3 to this Act are hereby repealed to the extent specified in the third column of that Schedule.

Short title, commencement and extent.

46.—(1) This Act may be cited as the Prisons (Scotland) Act 1989.

(2) This Act shall come into force at the end of the period of three months beginning with the date on which it is passed.

(3) This Act shall extend to Scotland only.

SCHEDULES

SCHEDULE 1

Section 18.

PROVISIONS AS TO PAROLE BOARD AND LOCAL REVIEW COMMITTEES

The Parole Board

1. The Parole Board shall include among its members—

    (a) a person who holds or has held judicial office;

    (b) a registered medical practitioner who is a psychiatrist;

    (c) a person appearing to the Secretary of State to have knowledge and experience of the supervision or after-care of discharged prisoners; and

    (d) a person appearing to the Secretary of State to have made a study of the causes of delinquency or the treatment of offenders.

2. A person appointed to be a member of the Parole Board shall hold and vacate office under the terms of the instrument by which he is appointed, but may at any time resign his office; and a person who ceases to hold office as a member of the Parole Board shall be eligible for reappointment.

3. There shall be paid to the members of the Board such remuneration and allowances as the Secretary of State may with the consent of the Treasury determine.

4. The expenses of the Board under the last foregoing paragraph and any other expenses incurred by the Board in discharging its functions under section 18 of this Act shall be defrayed by the Secretary of State out of moneys provided by Parliament.

5. The Board shall as soon as practicable after the end of each year make to the Secretary of State a report on the performance of its functions during that year, and the Secretary of State shall lay a copy of each report so made before Parliament.

Local review committees

6. The Secretary of State may out of moneys provided by Parliament pay to members of local review committees, and to persons assisting in or concerned with the carrying out of the functions of any such committee, travelling or other allowances in accordance with such scales as may be determined by him with the consent of the Treasury, and may out of such moneys defray any other expenses of such committees to such amount as may be so determined.

SCHEDULE 2

Section 45(1).

AMENDMENT OF ENACTMENTS

Children and Young Persons (Scotland) Act 1937

1. In section 57(3) of the Children and Young Persons (Scotland) Act 1937, for the word "206" there shall be substituted the words "205 or 206", and after the word "1975" there shall be inserted the words "or section 25 of the Prisons (Scotland) Act 1989".   1937 c. 37.

2. In section 87(1) and (3) of that Act, after the words "Act 1975" there shall be inserted the words "and of the Prisons (Scotland) Act 1989".

Army Act 1955

3. In section 71AA(6B) of the Army Act 1955 and in paragraph 10(6B) of Schedule 5A to that Act, for the words "Section 12 of the Criminal Justice (Scotland) Act 1963" there shall be substituted the words "Section 32 of the Prisons (Scotland) Act 1989".

Air Force Act 1955

4. In section 71AA(6B) of the Air Force Act 1955 and in paragraph 10(6B) of Schedule 5A to that Act, for the words "Section 12 of the Criminal Justice (Scotland) Act 1963" there shall be substituted the words "Section 32 of the Prisons (Scotland) Act 1989".

Naval Discipline Act 1957

5. In section 43AA(6B) of the Naval Discipline Act 1957 and in paragraph 10(6B) of Schedule 4A to that Act, for the words "Section 12 of the Criminal Justice (Scotland) Act 1963" there shall be substituted the words "Section 32 of the Prisons (Scotland) Act 1989".

6. In section 88 of that Act, in subsection (3)(c), for the words from "thirty-five" to "1952" there shall be substituted the words "39 of the Prisons (Scotland) Act 1989", and, in subsection (4), for the words "37 of the Prisons (Scotland) Act 1952" there shall be substituted the words "40 of the Prisons (Scotland) Act 1989".

Criminal Justice Act 1961

7. In section 30(1)(b) of the Criminal Justice Act 1961, for the words "37 of the Prisons (Scotland) Act 1952" there shall be substituted the words "40 of the Prisons (Scotland) Act 1989".

Criminal Justice (Scotland) Act 1963

8. In Schedule 1 to the Criminal Justice (Scotland) Act 1963, in paragraph 13, for the words "paragraph 2 of this Schedule" there shall be substituted the words "section 30(3) of the Prisons (Scotland) Act 1989".

Criminal Justice Act 1967

9. In section 69(2) of the Criminal Justice Act 1967, for the words "37 of the Prisons (Scotland) Act 1952" there shall be substituted the words "40 of the Prisons (Scotland) Act 1989".

Courts-Martial (Appeals) Act 1968

10. In section 52 of the Courts-Martial (Appeals) Act 1968, for paragraph (e) there shall be substituted the following paragraph—

"(e) section 39 of the Prisons (Scotland) Act 1989; or".

Criminal Procedure (Scotland) Act 1975

11. In section 205A(1) of the Criminal Procedure (Scotland) Act 1975, for the words "61 of the Criminal Justice Act 1967" there shall be substituted the words "26 of the Prisons (Scotland) Act 1989".

12. For section 206(1) of that Act, there shall be substituted the following section—

"Detention of children convicted on indictment. 206. Subject to section 205 of this Act, where a child is convicted and the court is of the opinion that no other method of dealing with him is appropriate, it may sentence him to be detained for a period which it shall specify in the sentence; and the child shall during that period be liable to be detained in such place and on such conditions as the Secretary of State may direct."

13. In sections 207(11) and 415(11) of that Act, for the words from the beginning to "shall apply" there shall be substituted the words "Section 18 (functions of Parole Board), section 24 (remission for good conduct) and sections 22, 26, 28 and 29 (release on licence) of the Prisons (Scotland) Act 1989 shall apply".

14. In sections 212 and 421 of that Act, in subsection (1), after the word "1967" there shall be inserted the words "or section 22(1) or section 26 of the Prisons (Scotland) Act 1989", and, in subsection (2), for the words "12 of the Criminal Justice (Scotland) Act 1963" there shall be substituted the words "32 of the said Act of 1989".

15. In sections 214 and 423 of that Act—

(a) in subsection (1), for the words from "Schedule" to "1963" there shall be substituted the words "section 30 of the Prisons (Scotland) Act 1989";

(b) in subsection (2)(b), for the words from "paragraph" to "1963" there shall be substituted the words "section 30(4) of the said Act of 1989";

(c) in subsection (6), for the words from "Schedule" to "1963" there shall be substituted the words "section 30 of the said Act of 1989";

(d) in subsection (7), for the words "the said Schedule" (where those words first occur) there shall be substituted the words "section 30 of the said Act of 1989", and, in paragraph (a) thereof, for the words "paragraph 1 of the said Schedule" there shall be substituted the words "subsection (4) of the said section 30"; and

(e) in subsection (8), for the words "paragraph 3 of the said Schedule" there shall be substituted the words "subsection (5) of section 30 of the said Act of 1989", and for the words from "section 14" to "1963" there shall be substituted the words "the said section 30".

16. In section 462(1) of that Act, for the words "Prisons (Scotland) Act 1952", wherever these words occur, there shall be substituted the words "Prisons (Scotland) Act 1989".

Law Reform (Miscellaneous Provisions) (Scotland) Act 1980

17. In Schedule 1 to the Law Reform (Miscellaneous Provisions) (Scotland) Act 1980, in paragraph (v) of Group B of Part I, for the words "59(6) of the Criminal Justice Act 1967" there shall be substituted the words "18(5) of the Prisons (Scotland) Act 1989".

Contempt of Court Act 1981

18. In section 15(6) of the Contempt of Court Act 1981, for the words "60 of the Criminal Justice Act 1967" there shall be substituted the words "22 of the Prisons (Scotland) Act 1989".

Mental Health (Scotland) Act 1984

19. In section 74(8) of the Mental Health (Scotland) Act 1984, for the words "37 of the Prisons (Scotland) Act 1952" there shall be substituted the words "40 of the Prisons (Scotland) Act 1989".

SCHEDULE 3

REPEALS

Chapter	Short title	Extent of repeal
Edw. 8 & 1 Geo. 6. c. 37.	Children and Young Persons (Scotland) Act 1937.	In section 62(b), the words "subsection (2) of".
15 & 16 Geo. 6 & 1 Eliz. 2. c. 61.	Prisons (Scotland) Act 1952.	The whole Act.
9 & 10 Eliz. 2 c. 39.	Criminal Justice Act 1961.	Section 30(4).
1963 c. 39.	Criminal Justice (Scotland) Act 1963.	Section 10. Section 12. Section 14. Section 50. Section 51. Section 54. In Schedule 1, paragraphs 1 to 3 and, in paragraph 14, the words "Part I of this Schedule or". In Schedule 5, the entry relating to the Prisons (Scotland) Act 1952.
1967 c. 80.	Criminal Justice Act 1967.	Sections 59 to 62. Section 64. Section 100(2A). Schedule 2.
1972 c. 71.	Criminal Justice Act 1972.	Section 35.
1975 c. 21.	Criminal Procedure (Scotland) Act 1975.	In section 206, subsections (2) to (7). Section 206A. Section 213. Section 422. In Schedule 9, paragraphs 16, 31 to 35 and 41.
1977 c. 45.	Criminal Law Act 1977.	In Schedule 12, paragraph 7(4) to (6) of the entry relating to the Criminal Justice Act 1967.
1980 c. 62.	Criminal Justice (Scotland) Act 1980.	Section 44. Section 45(2). Schedule 5. In Schedule 7, paragraphs 1 to 6, 14, 15 and 17 to 20.
1982 c. 48.	Criminal Justice Act 1982.	Section 33(a) and (b). Section 57(2). In Schedule 14, paragraphs 18 to 21.
1985 c. 73.	Law Reform (Miscellaneous Provisions) (Scotland) Act 1985.	Section 42. Section 44. Section 45.

Chapter	Short title	Extent of repeal
1988 c. 33.	Criminal Justice Act 1988.	In Schedule 9, paragraph 1. In Schedule 15, paragraph 18.

SCH. 3

Consolidated Fund (No. 2) Act 1989

1989 CHAPTER 46

An Act to apply certain sums out of the Consolidated Fund to the service of the years ending on 31st March 1990 and 1991.

[21st December 1989]

Most Gracious Sovereign,

WE, Your Majesty's most dutiful and loyal subjects, the Commons of the United Kingdom in Parliament assembled, towards making good the supply which we have cheerfully granted to Your Majesty in this Session of Parliament, have resolved to grant unto Your Majesty the sums hereinafter mentioned; and do therefore most humbly beseech Your Majesty that it may be enacted and be it enacted by the Queen's most Excellent Majesty, by and with the advice and consent of the Lords Spiritual and Temporal, and Commons, in this present Parliament assembled, and by the authority of the same, as follows.—

1. The Treasury may issue out of the Consolidated Fund of the United Kingdom and apply towards making good the supply granted to Her Majesty for the service of the year ending on 31st March 1990 the sum of £2,881,928,000.

Issue out of the Consolidated Fund for the year ending 31st March 1990.

2. The Treasury may issue out of the Consolidated Fund of the United Kingdom and apply towards making good the supply granted to Her Majesty for the service of the year ending on 31st March 1991 the sum of £58,271,200,000.

Issue out of the Consolidated Fund for the year ending 31st March 1991.

3. This Act may be cited as the Consolidated Fund (No. 2) Act 1989.

Short title.

INDEX

TO THE

PUBLIC GENERAL ACTS 1989

A

Exploration and exploitation

§ 1 and Sch. General prohibition. I, pp. 603, 612.
   2.   Exception for prospecting activities I, p. 604.

Licensing of prospecting activities

   3.   Grant of licences. I, p 605.
   4.   Transfer, variation, suspension or termination of licences. I, p. 605.
   5.   Obligation of licensees to indemnify government against claims. I, p. 605.

Other controls

   6.   Power to make regulations. I, p. 606.
   7.   Power to give directions. I, p. 606.
   8.   Appointment of inspectors. I, p. 607.
   9.   Disclosure of information. I, p. 607.

Criminal and civil liability

  10.   Offences under Act. I, p. 607.
  11.   Application of criminal law to certain persons. I, p. 608.
  12.   Strict liability for certain loss or damage etc. I, p. 609.
  13.   Civil liability for breach of statutory duty. I, p. 609.

British Antarctic Territory

  14.   Jurisdiction with respect to proceedings under territorial law. I, p. 609.

Supplemental

  15.   Powers of arrest etc. I, p. 610.
  16.   Evidence. I, p, 610.
  17.   Status of Commission. I, p. 611.
  18.   Financial provisions. I, p. 611.
  19.   Index of defined expressions. I, p. 611.
  20.   Short title, commencement and extent. I, p. 611.
  Schedule—Strict liability for certain loss or damage etc. I, p. 612.
    Part I—Provisions of the Convention having effect of law. I, p. 612.
    Part II—Provision for construing the provisions set out in Part I. I, p. 613.

PART XII

MISCELLANEOUS AND GENERAL

Notification of children accommodated in certain establishments

Adoption

Paternity tests

Criminal care and supervision orders

Effect and duration of orders etc.

Jurisdiction and procedure etc.

Search warrants

General

D

E

PART I

INTRODUCTORY

General

PART II

RESTRICTIONS ON RETURN

PART III

PROCEDURE

General

F

Part I

The Fair Employment Commission, the Fair Employment Tribunal and the Functions of the Commission and the Tribunal

Part II

New Duties of Employers in Respect of Their Workforces

Chapter II

Value Added Tax

Zero-rating etc.

Other provisions

Chapter III

Miscellaneous

Part II

Income Tax, Corporation Tax and Capital Gains Tax

Chapter I

General

Income tax rates and allowances

Corporation tax rates etc.

Receipts basis etc.

Interest

Benefits in kind

Medical insurance

Charities

PART I

FOOTBALL MATCHES IN ENGLAND AND WALES

Preliminary

§ 1. Scope and interpretation of this Part, II, p. 1357.

National Membership Scheme

2. Offences relating to unauthorised attendance at designated football matches, II, p. 1359.
3. The football Membership Authority, II, p. 1359.
4. National membership scheme: making, approval, modification etc, II, p. 1360.
5. National membership scheme: contents and penalties, II, p. 1361.
6. Phased application of scheme, II, p. 1363.
7 and Sch. 1. Disqualification for membership of scheme, II, p. 1363, 1380.

Licences to admit spectators

8 and Sch. 2. The Football Licensing Authority, II, pp. 1365, 1381.
9. Offence of admitting spectators to unlicensed premises, II, p. 1365.
10. Licences to admit spectators: general, II, p. 1365.
11. Power of Secretary of State to require conditions in licences relating to seating, II, p. 1367.
12. Licences to admit spectators: revocation and suspension, II, p. 1368.
13. Licensing authority's powers in relation to safety at football grounds, II, p. 1369.

PART II

FOOTBALL MATCHES OUTSIDE ENGLAND AND WALES

Preliminary

14 and Sch. 1. Scope and interpretation of this Part, II, p. 1370.

Restriction orders

15. Restriction orders, II, p. 1371.
16. Effect of order, II, p. 1371.
17. Application to terminate restriction order, II, p. 1372.
18. Information, II, p. 1372.

Reporting

19. Functions of enforcing authority and local police, II, p. 1373.
20. Exemtions from requirement to report as respects a match, II, p. 1374.
21. Functions of enforcing authority: supplementary provisions, II, p. 1375.

Relevant offences outside England and Wales

22 and Sch. 1. Restriction orders arising out of offences outside England and Wales, II, pp. 1376, 1380.

PART III

GENERAL

23. Further provision about, and appeals against, declarations of relevance, II, p. 1377.
24. Offences by bodies corporate, II, p. 1378.
25. Service of document, II, p. 1378.

L

14.   Voting rights of members of certain committees: Scotland, III, p. 2085.

Political balance on committees etc.

15 and Sch. 1.   Duty to allocate seats to political groups, III, pp. 2087, 2245.
16.   Duty to give effect to allocations, III, p. 2089.
17.   Exceptions to and extensions of political balance requirements, III, p. 2089.

Allowances

18.   Schemes for basic, attendance and special responsibility allowances for local authority members, III, p. 2090.

Members' interests

19.   Members' interests, III, p. 2092.

Duty to adopt certain proceduaral standing orders

20.   Duty to adopt certain procedural standing orders, III, p. 2093.

Interpretation of Part I

21.   Interpretation of Part I, III, p. 2094.

PART II

LOCAL GOVERNMENT ADMINISTRATION

22.   Advisory Commissioners, III, p. 2095.
23.   Advice and guidance by Commissions for Local Administration and Scottish Commissioner, III, p. 2095.
24.   Expenses of Commissions for Local Administration, III, p. 2096.
25.   Annual reports of Commissions: new provisions, III, p. 2097.
26.   Implementation of recommendations of Commissioners for Local Administration in England and Wales, III, p. 2098.
27.   Implementation of recommendations of Commissioner for Local Administration in Scotland, III, p. 2100.
28.   Consideration of adverse reports: England and Wales, III, p. 2102.
29.   Consideration of adverse reports: Scotland, III, p. 2102.
30.   Declaration of acceptance of office of councillor etc., III, p. 2103.
31.   National Code of Local Government Conduct, III, p. 2104.
32.   Anonymity in reports on investigations, III, p. 2105.

PART III

ECONOMIC DEVELOPMENT AND DISCRETIONARY EXPENDITURE BY LOCAL AUTHORITIES

33.   Promotion of economic development, III, p. 2106.
34.   Restrictions on promotion of economic development, III, p. 2107.
35.   Guidance and consultation about promotion of economic development, III, p. 2107.
36 and Sch. 2. Amendments of existing power to incur discretionary expenditure, III, pp. 2108, 2247.
37.   Conditions of provision of financial assistance, III, p. 2110.
38.   Information etc. on individuals' rights, III, p. 2111.

PART IV

REVENUE ACCOUNTS AND CAPITAL FINANCE OF LOCAL AUTHORITIES

Introductory

39.   Application of Part IV, III, p. 2111.
40.   Capital purposes, III, p. 2113.

Charge of expenditure to revenue accounts

41.   Expenditure to be charged to revenue account, III, p. 2114.
42.   Expenditure excluded from section 41(1), III, p. 2115.

Borrowing

43.   Borrowing powers, III, p. 2116.
44.   Borrowing limits etc, III, p. 2117.
45.   The authority's own limits, III, p. 2118.
46.   Register of loan instruments and certain existing loans, III, p. 2119.
47.   Security for money borrowed etc., III, p. 2120.

Credit arrangements

48.   Credit arrangements, III, p. 2121.
49.   Initial and subsequent cost of credit arrangements, III, p. 2122.
50.   Limits on powers to enter into credit arrangements, III, p. 2123.
51.   Variation on credit arrangements, III, p. 2124.
52.   Transitional credit arrangements, III, p. 2126.

M

N

O

PART I

THE GENERAL OPTICAL COUNCIL

The Council

The Council's Committees

PART II

REGISTRATION AND TRAINING OF OPTICIANS

The registers and lists

Training and Qualifications

PART III

DISCIPLINARY PROCEEDINGS

R

Contributions

§ 1. Amendments relating to primary Class 1 contributions, I, p. 671.
2. Repayment of contributions where earnings become repayable, I, p. 673.
3. Abolition of Treasury supplement to contributions, I, p. 673.
4. Earnings factors, I, p. 673.

Liability to maintain children

5. Liability of parents to maintain children under the age of nineteen in respect of whom income support is paid, I, p. 675.

Benefits under the principal Act

6. Benefits for women widowed before 11th April 1988, I, p. 675.
7 and Sch. 1. Abolition of earnings rule etc., I, pp. 678, 700.
8. Mobility allowance: increase of age limit to 80 years, I, p. 678.
9. Extension to personal pensions of occupational pension provisions relating to the abatement of unemployment benefit and the meaning of "earnings", I, p. 679.
10. Unemployment benefit: requirement to seek employment actively, I, p. 679.
11. Requalification for unemployment benefit, I, p. 680.
12. Disqualification for unemployment benefit, I, p. 680.

Income-related benefits

13. Income support and unemployment, I, p. 682.
14. Housing benefit to take the form of payments or reductions, I, p. 683.
15. Housing benefit subsidy, I, p. 683.
16. Expenses of Secretary of State in making transitional payments relating to income support and housing benefit, I, p. 685.

Up-rating

17. Rectification of mistakes in up-rating orders, I, p. 686.
18. Effect of alteration in the component rates of income support, I, p. 687.

Information and adjudication

19 and Sch. 2. Unauthorised disclosure of information relating to particular persons, I, pp. 689, 705.
20. Disclosure of information by Inland Revenue for social security purposes, I, p. 691.
21 and Sch. 3. Miscellaneous amendments relating to adjudication, I, pp. 691, 706.

Recovery from damages etc. of sums equivalent to benefit

22 and Sch. 4. Recovery of sums equivalent to benefit from compensation payments in respect of accidents, injuries and diseases, I, pp. 692, 712.

Occupational and personal pensions etc.

23 and Sch. 5. Equal treatment for men and women, I, pp. 694, 724.
24 and Sch. 6. Miscellaneous amendments relating to pensions, I, pp. 694, 731.

War pensions committees

25. Establishment and functions of war pensions committees, I, p. 694.

General and supplementary provisions

26 and Sch. 7. Pre-consolidation amendments, I, pp. 696, 737.
27. Application to the Crown, I, p. 696.
28. Financial provisions, I, p. 696.
29. Regulations and orders: general provisions, I, p. 697.
30. Interpretation, I, p. 698.
31 and Schs. 8, 9. Minor and consequential amendments, repeals and transitional provisions, I, pp. 739, 749.
32. Corresponding provision for Northern Ireland, I, p. 698.
33. Short title, commencement and extent, I, p. 698.
Schedule 1—Abolition of Earnings Rule etc., I, p. 700.
Schedule 2—Persons Employed in Social Security Administration or Adjudication, I, p. 705.
Schedule 3—Adjudication, I, p.706.

T

W

PART I

PRELIMINARY

The National Rivers Authority and the advisory committees

The transfer of the water authorities' functions etc.

The Director General of Water Services and the customer service committees

General duties

PART II

WATER SUPPLY AND SEWERAGE SERVICES

CHAPTER I

APPOINTMENT AND REGULATION OF WATER AND SEWERAGE UNDERTAKERS

Making and conditions of appointments

Modification of appointment conditions

Enforcement orders

Special administration orders